OFFICIAL Major League BASEBALL FACT BOOK
2001 EDITION

D1450990

OFFICIAL Major League BASEBALL FACT BOOK

2001 EDITION

The Sporting News

Historical statistics from *Total Baseball,* the official encyclopedia of Major League Baseball.

Statistical assistance provided by STATS, Inc., Skokie, Ill.

Copyright ©2001 by The Sporting News, a division of Vulcan Print Media,
10176 Corporate Square Drive, Suite 200, St. Louis, MO 63132-2924. All rights reserved. Printed in the U.S.A.

No part of the *Official Major League Baseball Fact Book* may be reproduced or transmitted in any form or by any means, electronic or mechanical, including photocopy, recording or any information storage and retrieval system now known or to be invented, without permission in writing from the publisher, except by a reviewer who wishes to quote brief passages in connection with a review written for inclusion in a magazine, newspaper or broadcast.

THE SPORTING NEWS is a registered trademark of The Sporting News, a division of Vulcan Print Media.

ISBN: 0-89204-646-5

10 9 8 7 6 5 4 3 2 1

Contents

Contents

Introduction

Of baseball's many attractive qualities, the one that's perhaps most endearing to us is the game's timelessness.

The game is timeless in the very nature of the way it's played. There's no clock signalling a beginning or an end. A baseball game can go on forever, inning upon inning; you never know beforehand precisely when it might end.

The game is timeless over history. The game today is very much like the game that was played 100 years ago, before the modern era was ushered in. It likely will be roughly the same 100 years from now as well.

That sense of timelessness is a quality we want to bring you in this book, the Official Major League Baseball Fact Book. Whether you're picking up this book during spring training, during the All-Star break or during the World Series, you'll find timely—and timeless—information that you might need.

In a navigable and useful form, the Fact Book presents fans with the details, numbers and pictures of baseball's long and distinguished history. This all-inclusive book looks both to the season ahead and back at the seasons and players that have brought us to 2001.

There are images of the past: Mickey Mantle's 1956 Triple Crown season, Bucky Dent's unlikely homer in 1978, Pete Rose's all-time hits title. We offer a season-by-season review of each team and some of the great players who have played for them, including those players—like Nolan Ryan or Hank Aaron—who sit at the top of the statistical ladders. For a baseball historian, this is a must-have book.

We also offer an extended glimpse back at the 2000 season, including playoff stories and boxes, all the statistics a baseball fan could want and plenty of analysis that The Sporting News has been known for for over 100 years.

And finally, we'll prepare you for the 2001 season ahead and keep you informed throughout the season. We offer player information and projections, team directories, schedules, stadium diagrams, and ticket and broadcast information. Included as well are biographies of baseball's prominent faces and award winners, players who will be as fondly remembered 100 years from now as players of yesteryear are remembered today.

—The Sporting News

2001 Preview

Orioles third baseman Cal Ripken enters his 21st season with the same team, a remarkable achievement in today's game. Last season Ripken collected his 3,000th career hit.

Introduction

GIANT PROSPECTS FOR BONDS

He has won three Most Valuable Player awards, eight Gold Gloves, nine All-Star Game selections and recognition from The Sporting News as Player of the Decade for the 1990s. But the numbers that best define the ever-lengthening Hall of Fame credentials of Barry Bonds are 400 and 400—the career home run and stolen base plateaus he alone has reached.

Now Bonds is on the threshold of extending that distinction to an almost imperceptible level. He needs only six home runs to join the exclusive 500-home run club, an honor he figures to achieve early in the 2001 season. He needs only 29 steals to reach 500, a task that is reachable in 2001 but far from a lock at age 37. Only three other players in history have hit 300 home runs and stolen 300 bases. Bonds soon will tower over them at 500-500.

As if that's not enough, the San Francisco left fielder is a good bet to reach a third milestone in 2001—he needs only 95 RBIs for 1,500. He has averaged more than 108 over the last five seasons.

But the number Bonds would most like to achieve is much more modest. Four times he has played for teams that reached the National League Championship Series—and four times he has failed to reach the World Series. The Giants, whose 97 wins topped all major league teams in 2000, were knocked out in a disappointing Division Series loss to the New York Mets and Bonds would like nothing more than to lead his team to a championship.

Bonds will not be the only player with milestone possibilities. Ken Griffey Jr. needs a Mark McGwire-like 62 home runs to reach 500 and Sammy Sosa (14) and Albert Belle (19) both appear to be locks for 400 homers. Cal Ripken still has worlds to conquer as he nears the end of his career, as do Harold Baines and Rickey Henderson.

Ripken, who reached the 400-homer plateau in 1999 and got his 3,000th hit in 2000, needs only 14 doubles to reach 600 and four total bases (one measly home run) for 5,000. The ageless Henderson needs four doubles for 500 and Baines is only 145 hits away from 3,000, 13 doubles away from 500 and 16 homers away from 400.

One of the more interesting spotlights will shine on Boston shortstop Nomar Garciaparra, who won his second straight batting title in 2000 and became the first American League righthanded hitter to win consecutive titles since Joe DiMaggio in 1939 and '40. If Garciaparra can win again, he will become the only righthanded hitter in American League history to win three in a row. Honus Wagner and Rogers Hornsby are the only National League righthanders to accomplish the feat in the post-1900 era.

New York Mets lefthander John Franco still has an outside shot at overtaking all-time saves leader Lee Smith (478), but he pitched last season in a setup role and saved only four games, inching his career total to 420. New York Yankees righthander Roger Clemens appears to be running out of time as he works toward the 300-win plateau. Clemens, who will turn 39 during the 2001 season, is still 40 victories shy of his mark.

Hard-hitting San Francisco left fielder Barry Bonds is on target to become baseball's first 500-500 man in the 2001 season.

LOOKING AHEAD

Look for St. Louis first baseman Mark McGwire to resume his assault on the magical 600-home run plateau in 2001. Big Mac was sidelined for much of the 2000 season and hit only 32 homers, down significantly from his 1998 and '99 totals of 70 and 65. Still, he moved up to seventh place on the all-time list with 554, passing Jimmie Foxx, Mickey Mantle and Mike Schmidt. A modest 46 (for McGwire) in 2001 will vault him past Reggie Jackson (563), Harmon Killebrew (573) and Frank Robinson (586) and into the 600 company of Hank Aaron, Babe Ruth and Willie Mays. ... Chicago right fielder Sammy Sosa took advantage of McGwire's absence to win his first home run title in 2000 and became only the second player (McGwire was the other) to hit 50 or more homers in three straight seasons. Now he will try to beat McGwire head-to-head, an accomplishment that eluded him in 1998 and '99 when he hit 129 home runs. Sosa will be trying to match the record of four 50-plus homer seasons shared by McGwire and Ruth. ... The New York Yankees will be looking to extend their World Series championship record to 27—far ahead of the nine recorded by second-place St. Louis and the Athletics franchise. The Yanks have won four Series in the last five years, three in a row, and are hoping to inch closer to the all-time record of five straight Series titles from 1949-53. That feat, of course, was accomplished by the Yankees. ... The Atlanta Braves will be gunning for their 10th straight division championship. Five of those titles vaulted them to World Series appearances and one resulted in a championship (1995). ... Familiar names in unfamiliar places: Mike Hampton and Denny Neagle (Colorado), Alex Rodriguez (Texas), Mike Mussina (New York Yankees), Manny Ramirez (Boston). ... After playing their final games at County Stadium and Three Rivers Stadium, the Milwaukee Brewers and Pittsburgh Pirates will open new ballparks in 2001. After being delayed for a year because of a construction accident, Milwaukee's Miller Park will become the new home of the Brewers on April 6 and PNC Park will provide a new atmosphere for Pirates fans when it opens April 9.

—Ron Smith

MAJOR LEAGUE BASEBALL DIRECTORY

Commissioner Bud Selig

Address .... 245 Park Avenue, New York, NY 10167
Telephone .... 212-931-7800; 212-949-5654 (FAX)
Website .... www.mlb.com
Commissioner of Baseball .... Allan H. "Bud" Selig
President & chief operating officer .... Paul Beeston
Executive vice president., baseball operations .... Richard "Sandy" Alderson
Executive vice president, administration .... Robert A. DuPuy
Executive vice president, labor relations and human resources .... Robert D. Manfred, Jr.
Executive vice president, business .... Timothy J. Brosnan
Senior vice president, public relations .... Richard Levin
Senior vice president, security and facilities .... Kevin Hallinan
Senior vice president and general counsel .... Thomas J. Ostertag
Senior vice president, baseball operations .... Jimmie Lee Solomon
Senior vice president and chief financial officer .... Jeffrey White
Senior vice president, team services .... Mark Gorris
Vice president, club relations and scheduling .... Katy Feeney
Vice president, club relations .... Phyllis Merhige
Vice president, on field operations .... Frank Robinson
Vice president, umpiring .... Ralph Nelson
Vice president, international baseball operations and security liaison .... Louis Melendez
Vice president, marketing .... Kathleen Francis
Vice president., broadcasting .... Leslie Sullivan
Vice president, human resources and office services .... Wendy L. Lewis
Vice president and general counsel, Labor relations .... Frank Coonelly
Vice president and general counsel, legal business affairs .... Ethan G. Orlinsky
Vice president, accounting and treasurer .... Robert Clark
Vice president, international business operations .... Paul Archey
Vice president, licensing .... Howard Smith
Vice president, business affairs .... Christopher Tully
Vice president, special events .... Marla Miller
Vice president, programming and sales .... James Scott
Vice president and executive producer, productions .... Dave Gavant

President & COO Paul Beeston

LABOR RELATIONS COMMITTEE

Address .... 245 Park Avenue, New York, NY 10167
Telephone .... 212-931-7401, 212-949-5690 (FAX)
Executive V.P., labor and human resources .... Robert D. Manfred Jr.
Vice president and general labor counsel .... Francis X. Coonelly
Associate counsels .... Derek Jackson, Paul Mifsud
Deputy general counsel .... Jennifer Gefsky
System administration .... John Ricco

NATIONAL BASEBALL HALL OF FAME AND MUSEUM

Address .... P.O. Box 590, Cooperstown, NY 13326
Telephone .... 607-547-7200, 607-547-2044 (FAX)
Hall of Fame board of directors chairman .... Jane Forbes Clark
President .... Dale Petroskey
Vice president of business and administration .... Bill Haase
Vice president and chief curator .... William T. Spencer Jr.
Curator of collections .... Peter P. Clark
Executive director of retail marketing .... Barbara Shinn
Controller .... Frances L. Althiser
Librarian .... James L. Gates
Vice president of communications and education .... Jeff Idelson

NATIONAL ASSOCIATION OF PROFESSIONAL BASEBALL LEAGUES

Address .... P.O. Box A, St. Petersburg, FL 33731
Telephone .... 727-822-6937; 727-821-5819 (FAX)
President .... Mike Moore
Vice president/administration .... Pat O'Conner
Executive director of special operations .... Misann Ellmaker
General counsel .... Scott Poley
Director/licensing .... Brian Earle
Director/media relations .... Jim Ferguson
Director of baseball operations .... Tim Brunswick
Director of marketing .... Rod Meadows
Director of business/finance .... Eric Krupa
Director of Professional Baseball Umpire Corporation .... Mike Fitzpatrick
Director/Professional Baseball Employment Opportunities .... Ann Perkins

MAJOR LEAGUE BASEBALL PLAYERS ASSOCIATION

Address .... 12 E. 49th St., 24th Floor, New York, NY 10017
Telephone .... 212-826-0808, 212-752-3649 (FAX)
Executive director and general counsel .... Donald M. Fehr
Special assistants .... Tony Bernazard, Phil Bradley, Steve Rogers
Associate general counsel .... Eugene D. Orza
Assistant general counsel .... Doyle R. Pryor, Michael Weiner
Counsel .... Robert Leneghan
Director of licensing .... Judy Heeter
Director of communications .... Greg Bouris

MAJOR LEAGUE BASEBALL PLAYERS ALUMNI ASSOCIATION

Address .... 1631 Mesa Avenue, Suite C, Colorado Springs, Colo. 80906
Telephone .... 719-477-1870, 719-477-1875 (FAX)
President .... Brooks Robinson
Vice presidents .... Bob Boone, George Brett, Mike Hegan
Chuck Hinton, Al Kaline, Carl Erskine
Rusty Staub, Robin Yount
Vice chairman .... Fred Valentine

MAJOR LEAGUE SCOUTING BUREAU

Address .... 3500 Porsche Way, Suite 100, Ontario, CA 91764
Telephone .... 909-980-1881, 909-980-7794 (FAX)
Director .... Frank Marcos

BASEBALL ASSISTANCE TEAM INC.

Address .... 245 Park Avenue, New York, NY 10167
Telephone 212-931-7821
Chairman .... Ralph Branca
President .... Earl Wilson
President emeritus .... Joe Garagiola
Vice presidents .... Joe Black, Bob Gibson, Ed Stack, Frank Torre
Executive director .... James J. Martin
Secretary .... Tom Ostertag
Treasurer .... Jeff White

ASSOCIATION OF PROFESSIONAL BASEBALL PLAYERS OF AMERICA

Address .... 1820 W. Orangewood Ave., Suite 206, Orange, CA 92868
Telephone .... 714-935-9993, 714-935-0431 (FAX)
President .... John J. McHale
Vice presidents .... Roland Hemond, Robert Kennedy
Secretary/treasurer .... Dick Beverage

BASEBALL WRITERS' ASSOCIATION OF AMERICA

President .... Ian MacDonald, Montreal Gazette
Vice president .... Bill Center, San Diego Union Tribune
Secretary/treasurer .... Jack O'Connell, Hartford Courant

WORLD UMPIRES ASSOCIATION

Address .... P.O. Box 760, Cocoa, FL 32923-0760
Telephone .... 321-637-3471; 321-633-7018 (FAX)
President .... John Hirschbeck
Vice president .... Joe Brinkman
Secretary/treasurer .... Tim Welke
Labor counsel .... Joel Smith

ELIAS SPORTS BUREAU

Address .... 500 Fifth Ave., New York, NY 10110
Telephone .... 212-869-1530, 212-354-0980 (FAX)
General manager .... Seymour Siwoff

SPORTSTICKER ENTERPRISES, L.P.

Address .... Harborside Financial Center, 800 Plaza Two, Jersey City, NJ 07311
Boston office .... Boston Fish Pier, West Building No. 1, Suite 302, Boston, MA 02210
Telephone .... 201-309-1200; 201-860-9742 (FAX)
Boston office .... 617-951-0070; 617-737-9960 (FAX)
General manager .... Jim Morganthaler
Director, special projects .... Jay Virshbo
Director, minor league operations .... Jim Keller

Anaheim Angels

American League West Division

2001 SEASON

Angels 2001 SCHEDULE

Home games shaded; D—Day game (games starting before 5 p.m.)
*—All-Star Game at Safeco Field (Seattle)

APRIL

SUN	MON	TUE	WED	THU	FRI	SAT
1	2	3 D TEX	4 TEX	5 TEX	6 OAK	7 D OAK
8 D OAK	9	10 TEX	11 TEX	12 TEX	13 SEA	14 SEA
15 D SEA	16 OAK	17 OAK	18 OAK	19 SEA	20 SEA	21 D SEA
22 D SEA	23	24 CLE	25 CLE	26 CLE	27 TOR	28 D TOR
29 D TOR	30					

MAY

SUN	MON	TUE	WED	THU	FRI	SAT
		1 CWS	2 CWS	3 CWS	4 DET	5 DET
6 D DET	7	8 CWS	9 CWS	10 CWS	11 DET	12 D DET
13 D DET	14	15 TOR	16 TOR	17 TOR	18 CLE	19 CLE
20 CLE	21	22 BAL	23 D BAL	24	25 TB	26 D TB
27 D TB	28 D TB	29 MIN	30 MIN	31 MIN		

JUNE

SUN	MON	TUE	WED	THU	FRI	SAT
					1 KC	2 KC
3 D KC	4	5 OAK	6 OAK	7 OAK	8 LA	9 D LA
10 D LA	11	12 SF	13 SF	14 D SF	15 LA	16 LA
17 D LA	18	19 TEX	20 TEX	21 TEX	22 SEA	23 SEA
24 D SEA	25 TEX	26 TEX	27 TEX	28 TEX	29 SEA	30 D SEA

JULY

SUN	MON	TUE	WED	THU	FRI	SAT
1 SEA	2 OAK	3 OAK	4 D OAK	5 D OAK	6 COL	7 COL
8 D COL	9	10 *	11	12 ARI	13 ARI	14 ARI
15 SD	16 SD	17 D SD	18 TB	19 D TB	20 BAL	21 D BAL
22 D BAL	23 D BAL	24 TB	25 TB	26 TB	27 BAL	28 BAL
29 BAL	30	31 BOS				

AUGUST

SUN	MON	TUE	WED	THU	FRI	SAT
			1 BOS	2 BOS	3 NYY	4 D NYY
5 D NYY	6 D NYY	7 CWS	8 CWS	9 CWS	10 TOR	11 TOR
12 TOR	13	14 DET	15 DET	16 D DET	17 CLE	18 D CLE
19 D CLE	20 BOS	21 BOS	22 BOS	23 BOS	24 NYY	25 D NYY
26 NYY	27	28 KC	29 KC	30 KC	31 MIN	

SEPTEMBER

SUN	MON	TUE	WED	THU	FRI	SAT
						1 MIN
2 D MIN	3	4 KC	5 KC	6 KC	7 MIN	8 MIN
9 D MIN	10 SEA	11 SEA	12 SEA	13 OAK	14 OAK	15 D OAK
16 OAK	17	18 SEA	19 SEA	20 D SEA	21 TEX	22 TEX
23 D TEX	24	25 OAK	26 OAK	27 D OAK	28 TEX	29 TEX
30 D TEX						

FRONT-OFFICE DIRECTORY

Owner .... The Walt Disney Company
Chairman and chief executive officer, The Walt Disney Co. .... Michael Eisner
President .... Tony Tavares
Vice president and general manager .... Bill Stoneman
Vice president of finance/administration .... Andy Roundtree
Vice president, advertising sales and broadcasting .... John Covarrubias
Vice president, sales, marketing and operations .... Kevin Uhlich
Vice president, communications .... Tim Mead
Vice president, business and legal affairs .... Rick Schlesinger
Assistant general manager .... Ken Forsch
Special assistant to the general manager .... Preston Gomez
Legal counsel/contract negotiations .... Mark Rosenthal
Director, scouting .... Donny Rowland
Director, player development .... Darrell Miller
Manager, baseball operations .... Tony Reagins
Equipment manager .... Ken Higdon
Visiting clubhouse manager .... Brian Harkins
Senior video coordinator .... Diego Lopez
Manager, baseball information .... Larry Babcock
Manager, media services .... Nancy Mazmanian
Manager, publications .... Doug Ward
Manager, community relations .... Matt Bennett
Media services/travel coordinator .... Tom Taylor
Director, marketing .... Roberto Alvarado
Manager, ticket operations .... Sheila Brazelton

MINOR LEAGUE AFFILIATES

Class	Team	League	Manager
AAA	Salt Lake	Pacific Coast	Garry Templeton
AA	Arkansas	Texas	Mike Brumley
A	Cedar Rapids	Midwest	Tyrone Boykin
A	Rancho Cucamonga	California	Tim Wallach
Rookie	Mesa Angels	Arizona	Brian Harper
Rookie	Provo	Pioneer	Tom Kotchman

BROADCAST INFORMATION

Radio: KLAC-AM (570).
TV: KCAL-TV (Channel 9).
Cable TV: Fox Sports West.

SPRING TRAINING

Ballpark (city): Tempe Diablo Stadium (Tempe, Ariz.).
Ticket information: 602-254-3300, 800-326-0331.

ASSISTANCE STAFF

Medical director
Dr. Lewis Yocum

Team physician
Dr. Craig Milhouse

Head athletic trainer
Ned Bergert

International supervisor
Clay Daniel

Eastern supervisor
Guy Mader

Western supervisor
Tom Davis

Midwestern supervisor
Ron Marigny

National cross-checkers
Rick Ingalls, Hank Sargent

Major league scouts
Jay Hankins, Jon Niederer, Rich Schlenker, Moose Stubing, Dale Sutherland, Gary Sutherland, John Van Ornum

Scouts
Don Archer, Todd Blyleven, Brian Bridges, Jon Bunnell, John Burden, Tom Burns, Todd Claus, Tim Corcoran, Jeff Crane, David Crowson, Bobby Dejardin, Kevin Ham, Al Hammell, Tom Kotchman, Dan Lynch, Chris McAlpin, Mike Powers, Marc Russo, Jeff Scholzen, Jack Uhey

International scouts
Amador Arias, Arnold Cochrane, Luis Cuevas, Felipe Gutierrez, Mario Mendoza, Tak Kawamoto, Leo Perez, Carlos Porte, Takanori Takeuchi, Grant Weir

BALLPARK INFORMATION

Ballpark (capacity, surface)
Edison International Field of Anaheim (45,050, grass)

Address
2000 Gene Autry Way
Anaheim, CA 92806

Official website
www.angelsbaseball.com

Business phones
714-940-2000

Ticket information
714-634-2000

Ticket prices
$24 (terrace MVP)
$22 (club loge, field box)
$20 (terrace box)
$15 (lower view MVP)
$12 (lower view box)
$10 (view)
$8 (RF pavilion-adult)
$7 (LF pavilion-adult)
$6 (RF pavilion-child)
$4 (LF pavilion-child)

Field dimensions (from home plate)
To left field at foul line, 330 feet
To center field, 400 feet
To right field at foul line, 330 feet

First game played
April 19, 1966 (White Sox 3, Angels 1)

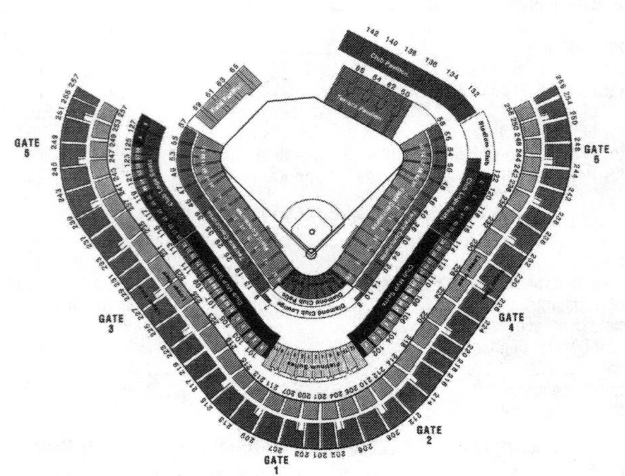

Follow the Angels all season at: www.sportingnews.com/baseball/teams/angels/

ANGELS SPRING ROSTER

No.	PITCHERS	B/T	Ht./Wt.	Born	2000 clubs	Projection
18	Alvarez, Juan	L/L	6-0/175	8-9-73	Edmonton, Anaheim	Lefthander could end up in bullpen this year.
45	Cooper, Brian	R/R	6-1/185	10-22-76	Edmonton, Ana., Lake Elsinore	Pitched in the majors last year, even though he wasn't ready.
47	Espina, Rendy	L/L	6-0/180	5-11-78	Tennessee	Posted a 2.11 ERA in 53 games in AA last season.
27	Fyhrie, Michael	R/R	6-2/203	12-9-69	Anaheim, Edmonton	Solid reliever who had a 2.39 ERA in 32 games with the Angels.
68	Green, Steve	R/R	6-2/195	1-26-78	Erie, Edmonton	He will need a full season at AAA. Did not win once in eight starts with Edmonton.
21	Hasegawa, Shigetoshi	R/R	5-11/178	8-1-68	Anaheim	Had 10 wins and nine saves out of the bullpen.
65	Holtz, Mike	L/L	5-9/188	10-10-72	Edmonton, Anaheim	Still having a rough go trying to pitch in the majors.
43	Levine, Al	R/R	6-3/198	5-22-68	Anaheim, Erie	Had a 3.87 ERA in 51 appearances. Can start if needed.
33	Lukasiewicz, Mark	L/L	6-7/240	3-8-73	Syracuse, Tennessee	Reliever from the minors looking to battle for a spot with the bullpen.
66	Miadich, Bart	R/R	6-4/205	2-3-76	Erie, Edmonton	Could be a long reliever to replace Mark Petkovsek.
59	Nina, Elvin	R/R	6-0/185	11-25-75	Erie, Edmonton	If he has a strong spring, he could be in the rotation.
36	Ortiz, Ramon	R/R	6-0/175	5-23-76	Ana., Lake Elsinore, Edmonton	Could be ready for a full year in the majors. He needs to stay healthy.
40	Percival, Troy	R/R	6-3/236	8-9-69	Anaheim, Lake Elsinore	You can count on him for another 30-save season.
58	Pote, Lou	R/R	6-3/208	8-27-71	Anaheim, Edmonton	Had success as a reliever with the Angels. Had 44 strikeouts while only walking 17.
34	Rapp, Pat	R/R	6-3/215	7-13-67	Baltimore	Should benefit from playing with a better team.
60	Schoeneweis, Scott	L/L	6-0/186	10-2-73	Ana., Lake Elsinore, Edmonton	Had seven wins, but needs to cut down on his ERA, which was 5.45.
62	Shields, Scot	R/R	6-1/175	7-22-75	Edmonton	Led the Pacific Coast League in strikeouts. Could be in the rotation.
54	Turnbow, Derrick	R/R	6-3/180	1-25-78	Anaheim	Wasn't used very much last season, but could see more action this season.
	Valdes, Ismael	R/R	6-4/225	8-21-73	Chicago N.L., Los Angeles	Looking to rebound from injury plagued season.
56	Washburn, Jarrod	L/L	6-1/198	8-13-74	Lake Elsinore, Edmonton, Ana.	Had only seven wins, in 14 starts. Needs to stay healthy for Angels to compete.
57	Weber, Ben	R/R	6-4/180	11-17-69	San Fran., Fresno, Erie, Ana.	Had success in 10 games at the end of the season.
32	Wise, Matt	R/R	6-4/190	11-18-75	Edmonton, Anaheim	He only needs major league experience to be a starter for the Angels.

No.	CATCHERS	B/T	Ht./Wt.	Born	2000 clubs	Projection
6	Fabregas, Jorge	L/R	6-3/215	3-13-70	Omaha, Kansas City	Hit .282 in 43 games with Royals last year.
1	Molina, Bengie	R/R	5-11/207	7-20-74	Anaheim	Had a breakout season as everyday catcher with the Angels.
44	Wooten, Shawn	R/R	5-10/205	7-24-72	Erie, Edmonton, Anaheim	If he has a strong spring, he could end up as the starter on opening day.

No.	INFIELDERS	B/T	Ht./Wt.	Born	2000 clubs	Projection
37	Barnes, Larry	L/L	6-1/195	7-23-74	Edmonton	Probably ticketed for AAA with Mo Vaughn still on the team.
38	Caceres, Wilmy	B/R	6-0/165	10-2-78	Chattanooga	Decent hitter who will likely be in AAA for a year.
9	DiSarcina, Gary	R/R	6-2/195	11-19-67	Anaheim	Injuries interrupted what could have been a good year.
22	Eckstein, David	R/R	5-8/165	1-20-75	Pawtucket, Edmonton	Could be a good utility player if he hits well.
10	Gil, Benji	R/R	6-2/190	10-6-72	Anaheim	Likely to be a utility player with DiSarcina back.
25	Glaus, Troy	R/R	6-5/229	8-3-76	Anaheim	Led the A.L. in home runs, should duplicate those numbers again.
2	Kennedy, Adam	L/R	6-1/180	1-10-76	Anaheim	Should improve upon last year's numbers now that he had a year in the majors.
23	Spiezio, Scott	B/R	6-2/225	9-21-72	Anaheim	Served as Angels DH last season, will have some competition for the job this year.
42	Vaughn, Mo	L/R	6-1/268	12-15-67	Anaheim	Should be everyday first baseman as long as his ankle holds up.

No.	OUTFIELDERS	B/T	Ht./Wt.	Born	2000 clubs	Projection
16	Anderson, Garret	L/L	6-3/220	6-30-72	Anaheim	Showed power numbers last year, could do the same this year.
46	Bartee, Kimera	R/R	6-0/200	7-21-72	Louisville, Cincinnati	Will be in Class AAA since it's unlikely he will break into the Angels outfield
17	Erstad, Darin	L/L	6-2/212	6-4-74	Anaheim	Last year, this guy did it all. This year, he should do it again.
48	Guzman, Elpidio	L/L	6-0/165	2-24-79	Lake Elsinore	Probably will end up in Class AAA, but definitely on the move in the system.
53	Haynes, Nathan	L/L	5-9/170	9-7-79	Erie	Speedy outfielder had 37 stolen bases last year.
3	Palmeiro, Orlando	L/L	5-11/175	1-19-69	Anaheim	Platooned in outfield. Doesn't have the power of Salmon, Erstad or Anderson.
15	Salmon, Tim	R/R	6-3/231	8-24-68	Anaheim	Was healthy for full season and he put up good numbers, 34 home runs, 97 RBIs.

THE COACHING STAFF

Mike Scioscia, manager: He accomplished what few thought was possible at the beginning of the season: he managed the Angels to an above-.500 record. A team that no one gave a chance to succeed finished 82-80. Scioscia did a remarkable job considering he didn't have a great pitching staff. This season should be a tougher challenge with every team in the A.L. West figuring to be improved.

Bud Black: He did a good job as pitching coach with the little he had to work with. His 15 years of major league experience will help with a relatively young staff.

Alfredo Griffin: Entering his second year as first base coach with the team.

Mickey Hatcher: Was a tremendous influence as hitting coach. Helped turn around an inconsistent offense.

Joe Maddon: Returns as bench coach for another season. Certainly a calming influence on the bench; now in his eighth season.

Bobby Ramos: Did a good job last year as bullpen coach. He will have to find a replacement for Mark Petkovsek.

Ron Roenicke: Returns for second season as third base coach.

THE TOP NEWCOMERS

Jorge Fabregas: Should help provide a veteran presence behind the plate, something that was missing from last year's team.

Pat Rapp: Had a decent year playing for Baltimore. He will benefit from having a veteran like Bud Black as a pitching coach and should post better numbers this season.

Ismael Valdes: Will help bolster a young pitching staff. Had a so-so season split between Cubs and Dodgers.

THE TOP PROSPECTS

Wilmy Caceres: Middle infielder who can steal bases. May still be a year away, but gives Anaheim an option at shortstop it didn't have before.

Shawn Wooten: He can hit for average and drive in runs. Will have a hard time cracking the lineup this season. But, he can play third base, first base and catcher.

BALTIMORE ORIOLES

AMERICAN LEAGUE EAST DIVISION

2001 SEASON

Orioles
2001 SCHEDULE
Home games shaded; D—Day game (games starting before 5 p.m.)
*—All-Star Game at Safeco Field (Seattle)

APRIL

SUN	MON	TUE	WED	THU	FRI	SAT
1	2 D BOS	3	4 BOS	5 BOS	6 CLE	7 D CLE
8 D CLE	9	10 BOS	11 BOS	12 BOS	13 TB	14 D TB
15 D TB	16 TB	17 CLE	18 CLE	19 D CLE	20 TB	21 D TB
22 D TB	23	24 DET	25 DET	26 D DET	27 MIN	28 MIN
29 D MIN	30 TB					

MAY

SUN	MON	TUE	WED	THU	FRI	SAT
		1 TB	2 TB	3 NYY	4 NYY	5 D NYY
6 D NYY	7	8 TB	9 TB	10 TB	11 NYY	12 D NYY
13 D NYY	14	15 DET	16 DET	17 DET	18 MIN	19 D MIN
20 D MIN	21	22 ANA	23 D ANA	24	25 TEX	26 D TEX
27 D TEX	28 TEX	29 SEA	30 SEA	31 SEA		

JUNE

SUN	MON	TUE	WED	THU	FRI	SAT
					1 OAK	2 D OAK
3 D OAK	4	5 NYY	6 NYY	7 NYY	8 MON	9 D MON
10 D MON	11	12 NYM	13 NYM	14 NYM	15 PHI	16 PHI
17 D PHI	18 TOR	19 TOR	20 TOR	21 CWS	22 CWS	23 D CWS
24 D CWS	25 TOR	26 TOR	27 TOR	28 D TOR	29 CWS	30 CWS

JULY

SUN	MON	TUE	WED	THU	FRI	SAT
1 D CWS	2	3 NYY	4 D NYY	5 NYY	6 PHI	7 D PHI
8 D PHI	9	10 *	11	12 ATL	13 ATL	14 ATL
15 D FLA	16 FLA	17 FLA	18 TEX	19 TEX	20 ANA	21 D ANA
22 D ANA	23 D ANA	24 TEX	25 TEX	26 TEX	27 ANA	28 ANA
29 ANA	30	31 TB				

AUGUST

SUN	MON	TUE	WED	THU	FRI	SAT
			1 TB	2 D TB	3 TOR	4 D TOR
5 D TOR	6 KC	7 KC	8 KC	9 KC	10 BOS	11 D BOS
12 D BOS	13	14 KC	15 KC	16 D KC	17 BOS	18 BOS
19 D BOS	20	21 TB	22 TB	23 TB	24 TOR	25 D TOR
26 D TOR	27	28 OAK	29 OAK	30 OAK	31 SEA	

SEPTEMBER

SUN	MON	TUE	WED	THU	FRI	SAT
						1 D SEA
2 D SEA	3 OAK	4 OAK	5 D OAK	6	7 SEA	8 SEA
9 D SEA	10	11 TOR	12 TOR	13 TOR	14 BOS	15 D BOS
16 D BOS	17	18 TOR	19 TOR	20 TOR	21 NYY	22 D NYY
23 D NYY	24 BOS	25 BOS	26 BOS	27 BOS	28 NYY	29 D NYY
30 D NYY						

FRONT-OFFICE DIRECTORY

Chairman/chief executive officer .... Peter Angelos
Vice chairman, chief operating officer .... Joe Foss
Executive vice president .... John Angelos
Vice president/chief financial officer .... Robert Ames
Vice president, baseball operations .... Syd Thrift
Director, minor league operations .... Don Buford
Director of scouting .... Tony DeMacio
Assistant dir., minor league operations .... Tripp Norton
Special assistants to the v.p., baseball operations .... Ed Kenney Jr., Bob Schaeffer, Danny Garcia
Traveling secretary .... Philip Itzoe
Director, public relations .... Bill Stetka
Manager, baseball information .... Kevin Behan
Director, ballpark operations .... Roger Hayden
Director, community relations .... Julie Wagner
Director, computer services .... James Kline
Director, publishing and advertising .... Jessica Fisher
Director, fan and ticket services .... Donald Grove
Director, sales .... Matthew Dryer

MINOR LEAGUE AFFILIATES

Class	Team	League	Manager
AAA	Rochester	International	Andy Etchebarren
AA	Bowie	Eastern	Dave Machemer
A	Frederick	Carolina	Dave Cash
A	Delmarva	South Atlantic	Joe Ferguson
Rookie	Bluefield	Appalachian	Joe Almaraz
Rookie	Gulf Coast Orioles	Gulf Coast	Jesus Alfaro

BROADCAST INFORMATION

Radio: WBAL-AM (1090).
TV: WJZ (Channel 13), WNUV (Channel 54), WFTY (Channel 50, Washington, D.C.).
Cable TV: Home Team Sports.

SPRING TRAINING

Ballpark (city): Fort Lauderdale Stadium (Fort Lauderdale, Fla.).
Ticket information: 954-523-3309, 305-358-5885.

ASSISTANCE STAFF

Head athletic trainer
Richard Bancells

Assistant athletic trainer
Brian Ebel

Strength and conditioning
Tim Bishop

Advance scout
Deacon Jones

Professional scouts
Danny Garcia, Curt Motton, Tim Thompson, Fred Uhlman Sr.

National cross-checkers
Mike Ledna, Shawn Pender

Regional cross-checkers
Dean Decillis, Deron Rombach, Logan White

Full-time scouts
Joe Almaraz, Dean Decillis, Ralph Garr Jr., John Gillette, Troy Hoerner, Jim Howard, Dave Jennings, Ray Kraczyk, Gil Kubski, Jeff Morris, Lamar North, Nick Presto, Harry Shelton, Ed Sprague, Marc Tramuta, Mike Tullier, Dominic Viola, Marc Ziegler

Director, Latin American scouting
Carlos Bernhardt

Caribbean & South American supervisor
Jesus Halabi

International scouts
Ubaldo Heredia, Salvator Ramirez, Arturo Sanchez, Brett Ward

BALLPARK INFORMATION

Ballpark (capacity, surface)
Oriole Park at Camden Yards (48,876, grass)
Address
333 W. Camden St.
Baltimore, MD 21201
Official website
www.theorioles.com
Business phone
410-685-9800
Ticket information
410-481-SEAT
Ticket prices
$35 (club box sec. 204-270)
$30 (field box sec. 20-54)
$27 (field box sec. 14-18, 56-58)
$23 (terrace box sec. 19-53)
$22 (LF club sec. 272-288; lower box sec. 6-12, 60-64)
$20 (terrace box sec. 1-17, 55-65)
$18 (LF lower box sec. 66-86; upper box sec. 306-372)
$16 (LF upper box sec. 374-388; lower reserve sec. 19-53)
$13 (upper reserve, sec. 306-372; lower reserve sec. 4, 7-17, 55-87)
$11 (LF upper reserve, sec. 374-388)
$9 (bleachers sec. 90-98)
$7 (standing room)
Field dimensions (from home plate)
To left field at foul line, 333 feet
To center field, 400 feet
To right field at foul line, 318 feet
First game played
April 6, 1992 (Orioles 2, Indians 0)

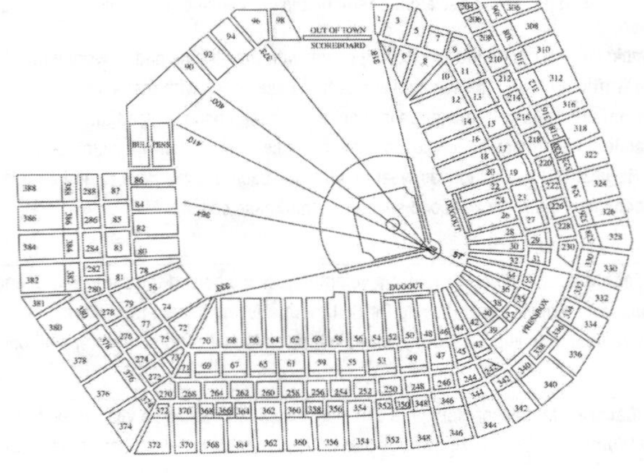

Follow the Orioles all season at: www.sportingnews.com/baseball/teams/orioles/

ORIOLES SPRING ROSTER

No.	PITCHERS	B/T	Ht./Wt.	Born	2000 clubs	Projection
	Bale, John	L/L	6-4/205	5-22-74	Syracuse, Toronto	Starting pitcher who is progressing well, but not likely to stick with squad to start.
	Douglass, Sean	R/R	6-6/200	4-28-79	Bowie	Solid starter still a couple years away from the pros.
19	Erickson, Scott	R/R	6-4/230	2-2-68	Frederick, Bowie, Baltimore	Injuries slowed him last season, but tough pitcher when healthy.
51	Falkenborg, Brian	R/R	6-6/195	1-18-78	DID NOT PLAY	Coming back from season long injury and may find spot in bullpen.
	Figueroa, Juan	R/R	6-3/150	6-24-79	Win.-Salem, Birmingham, Bowie	Hard throwing starter with potential, but likely to start in minors.
27	Groom, Buddy	L/L	6-2/207	7-10-65	Baltimore	Solid out of the bullpen and gives Orioles lots of games.
57	Guzman, Juan	R/R	6-2/184	3-4-78	Bowie, Frederick	Solid starter with potential to be in rotation, but not yet.
	Hamilton, Jimmy	L/L	6-3/190	8-1-75	Rochester, Bowie	Bullpen prospect still a year away.
	Hentgen, Pat	R/R	6-2/195	11-13-68	St. Louis	Durable starter who will give team six good innings almost every start.
41	Johnson, Jason	R/R	6-6/235	10-27-73	Rochester, Baltimore	Starter trying to break into rotation, but has struggled when given the chance.
50	Kohlmeier, Ryan	R/R	6-2/195	6-25-77	Rochester, Baltimore	Solid out of the bulllpen and closer of the future, if not this year.
47	McElroy, Chuck	L/L	6-0/205	10-1-67	Baltimore	Capable lefty specialist out of the bullpen who will pitch 40 games.
31	Mercedes, Jose	R/R	6-1/180	3-5-71	Baltimore	Solid finish last year gives him inside track for spot in rotation.
75	Mills, Alan	R/R	6-1/195	10-18-66	Los Angeles, Bal., Frederick	Durable relief pitcher tough on right handed batters.
	Nussbeck, Mark	R/L	6-4/180	5-25-74	Memphis, Rochester	Solid left handed starter still a year or two away from making impact.
53	Parrish, John	L/L	5-11/180	11-26-77	Bowie, Rochester, Baltimore	Will have to earn a spot in rotation this year.
43	Ponson, Sidney	R/R	6-1/225	11-2-76	Baltimore	Count on him to start 30 games as he has the past two seasons.
	Riley, Matt	L/L	6-1/201	8-2-79	Rochester, Bowie	Finished last year strong, but not ready for the big leagues yet.
60	Rivera, Luis	R/R	6-3/163	6-21-78	Atl., Rich., GC Braves, Roch., Bal.	Abilities to start or come out of bullpen might land him a spot on team.
52	Ryan, B.J.	L/L	6-6/230	12-28-75	Baltimore, Rochester	Had off year last year, but is a good lefty out of bullpen.
29	Spurgeon, Jay	R/R	6-6/210	7-5-76	Frederick, Bowie, Rochester, Bal.	Progressed all the way to majors in fourth season and could land spot in bullpen.
	Towers, Josh	R/R	6-1/165	2-26-77	Rochester	Solid starter with Rochester and most likely will start year there.
28	Trombley, Mike	R/R	6-2/204	4-14-67	Baltimore	Has pitched in more than 70 games three straight seasons.

No.	CATCHERS	B/T	Ht./Wt.	Born	2000 clubs	Projection
26	Fordyce, Brook	R/R	6-0/190	5-7-70	Charlotte, Chicago A.L., Bal.	Solid catcher who is starting to mature as a hitter.
51	Lunar, Fernando	R/R	6-1/190	5-25-77	Greenville, Atlanta, Bowie, Bal.	Trying to win spot as back up catcher. Solid catcher with decent bat.
37	Myers, Greg	L/R	6-2/225	4-14-66	Baltimore	Veteran in competition with Lunar for back up job.

No.	INFIELDERS	B/T	Ht./Wt.	Born	2000 clubs	Projection
14	Bordick, Mike	R/R	5-11/175	7-21-65	Baltimore, New York N.L.	Solid offensive shortstop who seemed to wear down late in season last year.
13	Coffie, Ivanon	L/R	6-1/192	5-16-77	Bowie, Baltimore, Rochester	Utiltiy player who could help Orioles off the bench.
18	Conine, Jeff	R/R	6-1/220	6-27-66	Baltimore	Production has tailed off, but still solid player who will DH and play first.
11	DeShields, Delino	L/R	6-1/175	1-15-69	Baltimore	Good contact hitter and lead off man who drove in 86 runs last year.
	Gibbons, Jay	L/L	6-0/200	3-2-77	Tennessee	Power hitter who could have first base job in near future.
15	Hairston, Jerry	R/R	5-10/175	5-29-76	Bal., Roch., GC Orioles, Fred.	Should be everyday second baseman since DeShields has moved to outfield.
39	Kinkade, Mike	R/R	6-1/210	5-6-73	Bing., N.Y. N.L., Bow., Roch., Bal.	Solid bench player who can play almost every position.
38	Richard, Chris	L/L	6-2/185	6-7-74	Memphis, St. Louis, Baltimore	Offensive talent who will see time at first and in the outfield.
8	Ripken, Cal	R/R	6-4/220	8-24-60	Baltimore	Still puts up numbers when healthy and can play solid defense at third.
	Segui, David	B/L	6-1/202	7-19-66	Texas, Cleveland	Solid defense at first and will give Orioles production in middle of line up.

No.	OUTFIELDERS	B/T	Ht./Wt.	Born	2000 clubs	Projection
9	Anderson, Brady	L/L	6-1/202	1-18-64	Baltimore	Production tailing off over the years, but still has good pop in bat.
88	Belle, Albert	R/R	6-2/225	8-25-66	Baltimore	Defense is shaky, but big run production should be expected.
40	Kingsale, Gene	B/R	6-3/194	8-20-76	GC Orioles, Fred., Bow., Roch., Bal.	Speedy outfielder and good contact hitter that could be valueable off bench.
32	Matos, Luis	R/R	6-0/179	10-30-78	Baltimore	Has speed and hits for decent average, but strikes out too much.
6	Mora, Melvin	R/R	5-10/180	2-2-72	New York N.L., Norfolk, Bal.	His starting spot to lose. Hits for average and can run well.

THE COACHING STAFF

Mike Hargrove, manager: After another disappointing season, Hargrove will be watched closely this year to see if his team progresses from last year. Hargrove enjoyed eight very successful seasons in Cleveland before landing the job in Baltimore last year.

Terry Crowley: Crowley returns for second year as hitting coach after spending eight years in that capacity with the Minnesota Twins.

Elrod Hendricks: Known for working with young pitchers and catchers, Hendricks begins his 24th season as bullpen coach.

Eddie Murray: Murray continues his stay in Baltimore as a coach after spending most of his successful career with the Orioles.

Sam Perlozzo: Perlozzo comes back for his fifth season coaching with the Orioles. This will be his 15th season overall working as a third base coach.

Tom Trebelhorn: Joins the Orioles staff after serving as manager of both the Chicago Cubs and Milwaukee Brewers.

Mark Wiley: Returns to Hargrove's staff as pitching coach after serving as his pitching coach in Cleveland.

THE TOP NEWCOMERS

Pat Hentgen: Durable starter who will give the Orioles a lot of innings and help mold young pitching staff.

David Segui: Orioles are hoping Segui gives them steady production in the middle of the line up after disappointing production out of the first base position last year. Segui's numbers show that he will give the Orioles the stability they are looking for.

THE TOP PROSPECTS

Juan Figueroa: Hard thrower acquired in Charles Johnson deal. Still a few years away from making an impact on the Oriole pitching staff.

Jerry Hairston: Solid hitter and sound defensive player who will get his share of playing time this year.

Mark Nussbeck: Crafty left hander that could be making an impact with the Orioles rotation in the next few season.

BOSTON RED SOX

AMERICAN LEAGUE EAST DIVISION

2001 SEASON

Red Sox 2001 SCHEDULE

Home games shaded; D—Day game (games starting before 5 p.m.)
*—All-Star Game at Safeco Field (Seattle)

APRIL

SUN	MON	TUE	WED	THU	FRI	SAT
1	2 D BAL	3	4 BAL	5 BAL	6 D TB	7 TB
8 D TB	9	10 BAL	11 BAL	12 BAL	13 NYY	14 D NYY
15 D NYY	16 D NYY	17 TB	18 TB	19 TB	20 NYY	21 D NYY
22 D NYY	23	24 MIN	25 MIN	26 MIN	27 KC	28 D KC
29 D KC	30					

MAY

SUN	MON	TUE	WED	THU	FRI	SAT
		1 SEA	2 SEA	3 SEA	4 OAK	5 D OAK
6 OAK	7	8 SEA	9 SEA	10 SEA	11 OAK	12 D OAK
13 D OAK	14	15 MIN	16 MIN	17 D MIN	18 KC	19 KC
20 D KC	21	22 NYY	23 NYY	24 D NYY	25 TOR	26 TOR
27 D TOR	28 NYY	29	30 NYY	31 TOR		

JUNE

SUN	MON	TUE	WED	THU	FRI	SAT
					1 TOR	2 D TOR
3 D TOR	4	5 DET	6 DET	7 DET	8 PHI	9 D PHI
10 D PHI	11	12 FLA	13 FLA	14 FLA	15 ATL	16 ATL
17 D ATL	18	19 TB	20 TB	21 TB	22 TOR	23 TOR
24 D TOR	25 TB	26 TB	27 TB	28 TB	29 TOR	30 TOR

JULY

SUN	MON	TUE	WED	THU	FRI	SAT
1 D TOR	2 D TOR	3 CLE	4 D CLE	5 CLE	6 ATL	7 ATL
8 D ATL	9	10 *	11	12 NYM	13 NYM	14 D NYM
15 D MON	16 MON	17 MON	18 TOR	19 TOR	20 CWS	21 D CWS
22 D CWS	23	24 TOR	25 TOR	26 TOR	27 CWS	28 CWS
29 D CWS	30	31 ANA				

AUGUST

SUN	MON	TUE	WED	THU	FRI	SAT
			1 ANA	2 ANA	3 TEX	4 D TEX
5 D TEX	6 TEX	7 OAK	8 OAK	9 D OAK	10 BAL	11 D BAL
12 D BAL	13	14 SEA	15 SEA	16 SEA	17 BAL	18 BAL
19 D BAL	20 ANA	21 ANA	22 ANA	23 ANA	24 TEX	25 TEX
26 TEX	27	28 CLE	29 CLE	30 CLE	31 NYY	

SEPTEMBER

SUN	MON	TUE	WED	THU	FRI	SAT
						1 D NYY
2 D NYY	3	4 CLE	5 CLE	6 CLE	7 NYY	8 D NYY
9 D NYY	10 NYY	11 TB	12 TB	13 TB	14 BAL	15 D BAL
16 D BAL	17	18 TB	19 TB	20 TB	21 DET	22 DET
23 D DET	24 BAL	25 BAL	26 BAL	27 BAL	28 DET	29 DET
30 D DET						

FRONT-OFFICE DIRECTORY

Chief executive officer .... John L. Harrington
Exec. v.p. and general manager .... Daniel F. Duquette
Executive vice president, administration .... John S. Buckley
V.p. and chief financial officer .... Robert C. Furbush
Vice president, baseball operations .... Michael D. Port
V.p., broadcasting and technology .... James P. Healey
Vice president, public affairs .... Richard L. Bresciani
Vice president, sales and marketing .... Lawrence C. Cancro
Vice president, stadium operations .... Joseph F. McDermott
Vice president, assistant g.m. and legal counsel .... Elaine W. Steward
Special assistants to the general manager .... Lee Thomas, Carlton E. Fisk
Dir. of communications and baseball information .... Kevin J. Shea
Dir. of human resources and office management .... Michele Julian
Vice president, scouting .... W. Wayne Britton
Executive director of int'l baseball operations .... R. Ray Poitevint
Director of player development .... Kent A. Qualls
Minor league field coordinator .... David P. Jauss
Coordinator of Florida operations .... Ryan Richeal
Traveling secretary .... John F. McCormick
Baseball administration coordinator .... Marci S. Blacker
Assistant scouting director .... Thomas L. Moore
Information technology manager .... Clay N. Rendon
Director of sales .... Michael D. Schetzel
Group sales manager .... Corey Bowdre
Season ticket manager .... Joseph F. Matthews
Telephone sales managers .... Sean Carragher, Marcell Saporita
Property maintenance manager .... John M. Caron
600 Club and suites manager .... Daniel E. Lyons
Baseball information coordinator .... Glenn Wilburn
Executive administrative assistant .... Lorraine Leong
Equipment manager and clubhouse operations .... J. Joseph Cochran
Controller .... Stanley H. Tran
Director of advertising and sponsorships .... Jeffrey E. Goldenberg
Director of facilities management .... Thomas L. Queenan Jr.
Director of 600 Club .... Patricia T. Flanagan
Director of ticket operations .... Joseph P. Helyar
Executive consultant, public affairs .... James "Lou" Gorman
Superintendent of grounds and maintenance .... Joseph P. Mooney
Ticket office manager .... Richard J. Beaton Jr.

MINOR LEAGUE AFFILIATES

Class	Team	League	Manager
AAA	Pawtucket	International	Gary Jones
AA	Trenton	Eastern	Billy Gardner Jr.
A	Augusta	South Atlantic	Mike Boulanger
A	Lowell	New York-Pennsylvania	Arnie Beyeler
A	Sarasota	Florida State	Ron Johnson
Rookie	Gulf Coast Red Sox	Gulf Coast	John Sanders

BALLPARK INFORMATION

Ballpark (capacity, surface)
Fenway Park (33,991, grass)
Address
4 Yawkey Way
Boston, MA 02215-3496
Official website
www.redsox.com
Business phone
617-267-9440
Ticket information
617-267-1700, 617-482-4769
Ticket prices
$55 (field box, loge box and infield roof)
$40 (reserved grandstand)
$30 (right-field boxes and right-field roof)
$25 (outfield grandstand)
$20 (lower bleachers)
$18 (upper bleachers)
Field dimensions (from home plate)
To left field at foul line, 310 feet
To center field, 420 feet
To right field at foul line, 302 feet
First game played
April 20, 1912 (Red Sox 7, New York Highlanders 6)

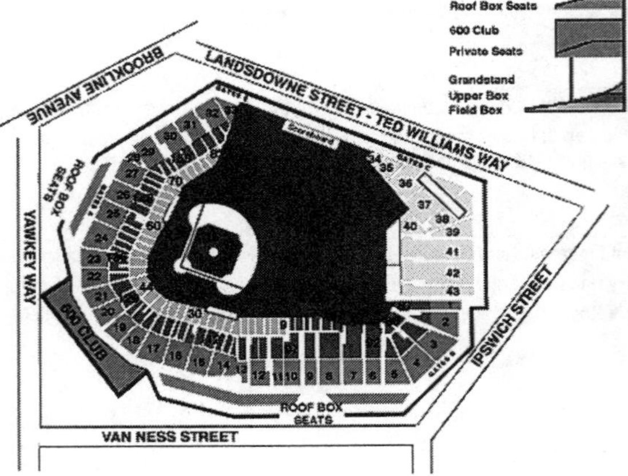

Follow the Red Sox all season at: www.sportingnews.com/baseball/teams/redsox/

ASSISTANCE STAFF

Head trainer
James W. Rowe Jr.
Assistant trainers
Christopher T. Correnti, Merle V. "B.J." Baker III
Medical director
Arthur M. Pappas, M.D.
Team physician
William J. Morgan, M.D.
Instructors
Theodore S. Williams, Carl M. Yastrzemski, Jim Rice, John M. Pesky, Edward J. Popowski, Charles T. Wagner
Major league scout
Frank J. Malzone
Major league special assignment scout
G. Edwin Haas
Director of Latin American scouting
Levy Ochoa
Scouts
Walter "Chet" Atkins, Raymond Boone, Buzz Bowers, Kevin Burrell, Ben Cherington, Edwin Correa, Ray Crone Jr., George Digby, Johnny DiPuglia, Danny Doyle, William Enos, Ray Fagnant, Steve Flores, Eddie Haas, Matt Haas, Ernie Jacobs, Wally Komatsubara, Chuck Koney, Kenneth "Jack" Lee, Don Lenhardt, Frank Malzone, Joe Mason, Steve McAllister, Tom Mooney, Gary Rajsich, Eddie Robinson, Jim Robinson, Ed Roebuck, Edward Scott, Mathew Sczesny, Harry Smith, Dick Sorkin, Jerry Stephenson, Joseph Stephenson, Lee Thomas, Fay Thompson, Charles T. Wagner, Jeffrey Zona, Mark Garcia, Jon Kodama, Ray Poitevint, Lee Sigman, Robinson Garcia, Sebastian Martinez, Jose Maza, Levy Ochoa, Carlos Ramirez, Michael Victoria

BROADCAST INFORMATION

Radio: WEEI-AM (680).
TV: WFXT (Fox 25).
Cable TV: New England Sports Network.

SPRING TRAINING

Ballpark (city): City of Palms Park (Fort Myers, Fla.).
Ticket information: 941-334-4700.

RED SOX SPRING ROSTER

No.	PITCHERS	B/T	Ht./Wt.	Born	2000 clubs	Projection
44	Arrojo, Rolando	R/R	6-4/220	7-18-68	Colorado, Boston	One-time Cuban ace is a former 14-game winner. Should win a spot in the rotation.
47	Beck, Rod	R/R	6-1/235	8-3-68	Pawtucket, Boston	Rebounded well from elbow surgery in '99 and will be the righthanded setup man.
	Castillo, Frank	R/R	6-1/200	4-1-69	Toronto	Had a solid season with Blue Jays last year and could be the No. 2 starter.
	Cho, Jin Ho	R/R	6-3/220	8-16-75	Sarasota, Trenton, Pawtucket	Boston thinks he can be a starter, but he will need more work at Class AA.
	Cone, David	L/R	6-1/200	1-2-63	New York A.L.	Looks to rebound from terrible 2000 season.
63	Crawford, Paxton	R/R	6-3/205	8-4-77	Trenton, Pawtucket, Boston	Youngster threw a no-hitter at Class AAA last season; has a shot at rotation spot.
55	Croushore, Rick	R/R	6-4/210	8-7-70	C.Spr., Colo., Pawtucket, Boston	Won't stick with a deep Red Sox bullpen unless his consistency improves.
39	Florie, Bryce	R/R	5-11/192	5-21-70	Boston, Sarasota, Trenton	Will attempt to battle back from a serious eye injury.
34	Garces, Richard	R/R	6-0/215	5-18-71	Boston	More of a situational guy, although he can be the setup man.
40	Lee, Sang	L/L	6-1/190	3-11-71	Pawtucket, Boston	After posting a 2.03 ERA at Pawtucket in 2000, he will be the top lefty in bullpen.
32	Lowe, Derek	R/R	6-6/200	6-1-73	Boston	Emerging sinkerballer has become one of the game's top closers.
45	Martinez, Pedro	R/R	5-11/170	10-25-71	Boston	His second consecutive Cy Young season was more impressive than last.
	Nomo, Hideo	R/R	6-2/230	8-31-68	Detroit	Although not as dominating, he still is serviceable enough for rotation.
53	Ohka, Tomo	R/R	6-1/179	3-18-76	Pawtucket, Boston	Japanese product dominated minors and should win the fifth spot in rotation.
38	Pena, Jesus	L/L	6-0/170	3-8-75	Char., Chi. A.L., Birm., Boston	Red Sox could use this lefty in middle relief, especially if Lee falters.
	Pena, Juan	R/R	6-5/215	6-27-77	DID NOT PLAY	Promising starter is coming off Tommy John surgery.
35	Pichardo, Hipolito	R/R	6-1/195	8-22-69	Pawtucket, Sarasota, Boston	Was very effective in relief, but his arm tired by September.
17	Saberhagen, Bret	R/R	6-1/200	4-11-64	Sarasota, Lowell, Pawt., Trenton	Career could be over because of arm injuries.
49	Wakefield, Tim	R/R	6-2/210	8-2-66	Boston	Versatile knuckleballer likely will bounce between the rotation and bullpen.

No.	CATCHERS	B/T	Ht./Wt.	Born	2000 clubs	Projection
10	Hatteberg, Scott	L/R	6-1/205	12-14-69	Boston	One of the game's best backups and a valuable lefthanded bat.
	Hillenbrand, Shea	R/R	6-1/200	7-27-75	Trenton	Bounced back well after an ACL injury at Class AA.
	Lomasney, Steve	R/R	6-0/195	8-29-77	Trenton, Gulf Coast Red Sox	One of Boston's top hitting prospects, but he needs more work in the minors.
33	Varitek, Jason	B/R	6-2/220	4-11-72	Boston	Excellent handler of the pitching staff; should rebound offensively after injury.

No.	INFIELDERS	B/T	Ht./Wt.	Born	2000 clubs	Projection
54	Burkhart, Morgan	B/L	5-11/225	1-29-72	Pawtucket, Boston	First baseman/DH impressed during 25 games in majors last season.
23	Daubach, Brian	L/R	6-1/201	2-11-72	Boston	Needs to put up bigger offensive numbers and be more consistent.
	Diaz, Juan	R/R	6-2/228	2-19-76	Sarasota, Trenton, Pawtucket	Shot from Class A to Class AAA last season before breaking his ankle in July.
5	Garciaparra, Nomar	R/R	6-0/180	7-23-73	Boston	Two-time batting champ is one of the game's best all-around players.
3	Lansing, Mike	R/R	6-0/195	4-3-68	Colorado, Boston	Second baseman struggled offensively in limited action late last season.
26	Merloni, Lou	R/R	5-10/195	4-6-71	Pawtucket, Boston	Boston cult hero can play all the infield positions and shined as a utilityman.
30	Offerman, Jose	B/R	6-0/190	11-8-68	Boston	Needs to bounce back from injuries and produce at the leadoff spot.
	Stenson, Dernell	L/L	6-1/230	6-17-78	Pawtucket	Will work on his defense at Class AAA Pawtucket.
	Stynes, Chris	R/R	5-10/185	1-19-73	Cincinnati	Youngster will battle for the third base job. Might win it because of his offense.
13	Valentin, John	R/R	6-0/185	2-18-67	Boston	Third baseman will return from knee injury.
	Veras, Wilton	R/R	6-2/198	1-19-78	Pawtucket, Boston	Failed in the majors last season and will get more seasoning at Pawtucket.

No.	OUTFIELDERS	B/T	Ht./Wt.	Born	2000 clubs	Projection
19	Bichette, Dante	R/R	6-2/235	11-18-63	Cincinnati, Boston	Slugger still has some pop in his bat and will handle the DH duties.
2	Everett, Carl	B/R	6-0/215	6-3-71	Boston	Huge offensive threat and a talented center fielder, but must improve attitude.
20	Lewis, Darren	R/R	6-0/190	8-28-67	Boston, Gulf Coast Red Sox	Excellent defensive player with a weak bat. Can play all three outfield positions.
7	Nixon, Trot	L/L	6-2/200	4-11-74	Boston, Gulf Coast Red Sox	Has 20-homer, 100-RBI potential, good arm and is poised for a breakout season.
25	O'Leary, Troy	L/L	6-0/200	8-4-69	Boston, Gulf Coast Red Sox	Probably will be dealt because of struggles last season and the arrival of Ramirez.
24	Ramirez, Manny	R/R	6-0/205	5-30-72	Cleveland, Akron, Buffalo	Baseball's best all-around run producer provides the big bat for Sox.

THE COACHING STAFF

Jimy Williams. manager: Williams is entering his fourth season as Red Sox manager, although many thought his days in Boston were over. After guiding the Red Sox to the wild card in 1998 and 1999, the team missed the playoffs last season. Williams, regarded as a "players' manager" butted heads with Everett and GM Dan Duquette in 2000 but survived to coach this season. Few coaches have done more with less (few offensive weapons, subpar starting pitching) the past few seasons, proof that players love playing for Williams.

Tommy Harper: Harper will be Boston's first base coach. He has almost 40 years of experience in professional baseball and has spent the majority of his coaching career in the Expos' organization.

John Cumberland: Cumberland returns for his third season as the team's bullpen coach. He also served as the pitching coach for Class AAA Pawtucket from 1996-98 and also briefly held that position with Boston in 1995. He has served in some coaching capacity with several organizations every year since 1982.

Joe Kerrigan: Going into his fifth season as the Red Sox pitching coach, Kerrigan still would like a legitimate No. 2 starter, but that won't be the case. Kerrigan guided Boston's pitching staff to the AL's best team ERA the past two seasons, which is an accomplishment considering the rotation basically is Pedro Martinez and four other lackluster starters. Boston's bullpen also has been very effective under Kerrigan.

Gene Lamont: Lamont takes over the third-base coaching duties from Wendell Kim, who was too aggressive and lost too many runners at home. Lamont has seven years of managerial experience on the major-league level, including the past four seasons with the Pirates.

Rick Down: This will be Down's first season as the team's hitting coach, after coming from the Dodgers, where he held that same position. Downs was a candidate for the LA managerial opening, and has had great success as the hitting coach with the Dodgers, Orioles and Yankees. He inherits the AL's second-worst team batting average and fourth-worst run-producing offense. But he does get Ramirez, too.

THE TOP NEWCOMERS

Frank Castillo: Boston will need a repeat of his 2000 performance with Toronto (10-5, 3.59 ERA). If he settles into the No. 2 spot, he could solidify the rotation — a huge key for the team.

David Cone: Struggled last year and went 4-14 with a 6.91 ERA. Red Sox are willing to take a chance that he can rebound to '99 form.

Hideo Nomo: Another in a long line of retreads signed by the team. Nomo still has good stuff and could thrive under pitching coach Joe Kerrigan. Has added a good slider to his arsenal.

Manny Ramirez: As one of baseball's best run-producers, he makes the heart of Boston's lineup deadly. No longer will the team finish near the bottom of the AL in hits, runs and homers.

Chris Stynes: Had career highs in homers and RBIs last season taking over third base for Reds. He is a gritty player with plenty of potential and could be the answer at third for the Sox.

THE TOP PROSPECTS

Juan Diaz: Played at the Class A, AA and AAA levels last season and will get a look in spring training. He has big-time power and is a good fielder. An ankle injury cost him a major-league call-up last season, but with first base somewhat unsettled, Diaz could stick around.

Steve Lomasney: A good catching prospect, but he struggled last season at Class AA Trenton. After a slow start, he battled injuries and inconsistency all season. His arm is strong, but he needs to work on his release. He is two years away from the majors —at least.

Dernell Stenson: The club's top hitting prospect has good bat speed and plenty of power. However, he doesn't hit for average and is a defensive liability (can you say DH?). He can play the outfield or first base, and could get a shot if Daubach struggles early. He'll start the season at Class AAA.

CHICAGO WHITE SOX

AMERICAN LEAGUE CENTRAL DIVISION

2001 SEASON

White Sox 2001 SCHEDULE

Home games shaded; D—Day game (games starting before 5 p.m.)
*—All-Star Game at Safeco Field (Seattle)

APRIL

SUN	MON	TUE	WED	THU	FRI	SAT
1	2 D CLE	3	4 CLE	5	6 D DET	7 D DET
8 D DET	9 CLE	10 CLE	11 D CLE	12	13 MIN	14 MIN
15 D MIN	16	17 DET	18 DET	19 DET	20 MIN	21 D MIN
22 D MIN	23	24 OAK	25 OAK	26 OAK	27 SEA	28 SEA
29 D SEA	30					

MAY

SUN	MON	TUE	WED	THU	FRI	SAT
		1 ANA	2 ANA	3 ANA	4 TEX	5 TEX
6 D TEX	7	8 ANA	9 ANA	10 ANA	11 TEX	12 TEX
13 D TEX	14	15 SEA	16 SEA	17 D SEA	18 OAK	19 D OAK
20 D OAK	21 D TOR	22	23 TOR	24 TOR	25 DET	26 DET
27 DET	28 TOR	29 TOR	30 TOR	31 DET		

JUNE

SUN	MON	TUE	WED	THU	FRI	SAT
					1 DET	2 DET
3 D DET	4	5 KC	6 KC	7 D KC	8 CUB	9 D CUB
10 D CUB	11	12 CIN	13 CIN	14 CIN	15 STL	16 D STL
17 D STL	18 KC	19 KC	20 D KC	21 BAL	22 BAL	23 D BAL
24 D BAL	25	26 MIN	27 MIN	28 D MIN	29 BAL	30 BAL

JULY

SUN	MON	TUE	WED	THU	FRI	SAT
1 D BAL	2 MIN	3 MIN	4 MIN	5 MIN	6 PIT	7 PIT
8 D PIT	9	10 *	11	12 D CUB	13 D CUB	14 D CUB
15 D MIL	16 MIL	17 D MIL	18 CLE	19 CLE	20 BOS	21 D BOS
22 D BOS	23 CLE	24 CLE	25 CLE	26 CLE	27 BOS	28 BOS
29 D BOS	30	31 KC				

AUGUST

SUN	MON	TUE	WED	THU	FRI	SAT
			1 KC	2 KC	3 TB	4 TB
5 D TB	6 D TB	7 ANA	8 ANA	9 ANA	10 SEA	11 SEA
12 D SEA	13	14 TEX	15 TEX	16 TEX	17 OAK	18 D OAK
19 D OAK	20 KC	21 KC	22 KC	23 KC	24 TB	25 D TB
26 D TB	27	28 DET	29 DET	30 DET	31 CLE	

SEPTEMBER

SUN	MON	TUE	WED	THU	FRI	SAT
						1 CLE
2 D CLE	3 CLE	4 DET	5 DET	6 D DET	7 CLE	8 D CLE
9 D CLE	10 CLE	11 NYY	12 NYY	13 NYY	14 MIN	15 D MIN
16 D MIN	17	18 NYY	19 NYY	20 NYY	21 KC	22 KC
23 D KC	24	25 MIN	26 MIN	27 D MIN	28 KC	29 KC
30 D KC						

FRONT-OFFICE DIRECTORY

Chairman ..... Jerry Reinsdorf
Vice chairman ..... Eddie Einhorn
Executive vice president ..... Howard Pizer
Senior vice president, general manager ..... Ken Williams
Senior vice president, marketing and broadcasting ..... Rob Gallas
Senior vice president, baseball ..... Jack Gould
Senior vice president and special advisor to Jerry Reinsdorf ..... Ron Schueler
Vice president, administration and finance ..... Tim Buzard
Vice president, stadium operations ..... Terry Savarise
Vice president, free agent and major league scouting ..... Larry Monroe
Special assistant to Jerry Reinsdorf ..... Dennis Gilbert
Special assistants to Ken Williams ..... George Bradley, Dave Yoakum
Executive advisor to Ken Williams ..... Roland Hemond
Special assignment ..... Bryan Little
Senior director of scouting ..... Duane Shaffer
Director of scouting ..... Doug Laumann
Director of player development ..... Bob Fontaine Jr.
Director of major league administration ..... Rick Hahn
Director of minor league administration ..... Grace Guerrero Zwit
Director of baseball operations systems ..... Dan Fabian
Director of minor league instruction ..... Jim Snyder
Manager of team travel ..... Ed Cassin
Assistant director of baseball operations systems ..... Andrew Pinter
Director of broadcasting and marketing ..... Bob Grim
Director of community relations ..... Christine Makowski
Director of sales ..... Jim Muno
Director of ticket operations ..... Bob DeVoy
Director of management information services ..... Don Brown
Director of human resources ..... Moira Foy
Controller ..... Bill Waters
Director of public relations ..... Scott Reifert

MINOR LEAGUE AFFILIATES

Class	Team	League	Manager
AAA	Charlotte	International	Nick Leyva
AA	Birmingham	Southern	Nick Capra
A	Kannapolis	South Atlantic	To be announced
A	Winston-Salem	Carolina	To be announced
Rookie	Bristol	Appalachian	R.J. Reynolds
Rookie	Tucson	Arizona	Jerry Hairston

BROADCAST INFORMATION

Radio: ESPN-AM (1000).
TV: WGN-TV (Channel 9).
Cable TV: Fox Sports Chicago.

SPRING TRAINING

Ballpark (city): Tucson Electric Park (Tucson, Ariz.).
Ticket information: 520-434-1111.

ASSISTANCE STAFF

Trainers
Herm Schneider
Brian Ball

Director of conditioning
Steve Odgers

Team physicians
Dr. James Boscardin, Dr. Hugo Cuadros, Dr. Bernard Feldman, Dr. David Orth, Dr. Scott Price, Dr. Lowell Scott Weil

Scouting national cross-checker
Ed Pebley

Scouting supervisors
Joe Butler, Ken Stauffer

Professional scouts
Larry Massie, Gary Pellant, Bill Young

Full-time scouts
Hernan Cortes, Nathan Durst, Denny Gonzalez, Matt Hattabaugh, Miguel Ibarra, John Kazanas, Paul Provas, Alex Slattery, Alex Cosmidis, Roberto Espinoza, Larry Grefer, Warren Hughes, George Kachigian, Jose Ortega, Mark Salas, John Tumminia

Part-time scouts
Tommy Butler, Curt Daniels, Mariano DeLeon, James Ellison, Jack Jolly, Dario Lodigiani, Glenn Murdock, Al Otto, Tony Rodriguez, Mike Shireley, Fermin Urbi, Javier Ceteno, Mike Davenport, John Doldoorian, Joe Ingalls, Robert Jones, Don Metzger, Paul Murphy, Wuarnner Rincones, Oswaldo Salazar, Keith Staab, Adam Virchis

BALLPARK INFORMATION

Ballpark (capacity, surface)
Comiskey Park (45,887, grass)
Address
333 W. 35th St.
Chicago, IL 60616
Official website
www.whitesox.com
Business phone
312-674-1000
Ticket information
312-674-1000
Ticket prices
$26 (lower deck box, club level)
$20 (lower deck reserved)
$18 (upper deck box, bleacher reserved)
$12 (upper deck reserved)
Field dimensions (from home plate)
To left field at foul line, 330 feet
To center field, 400 feet
To right field at foul line, 335 feet
First game played
April 18, 1991 (Tigers 16, White Sox 0)

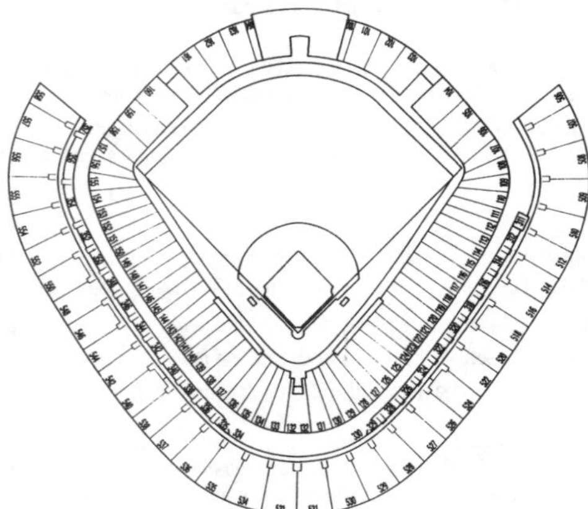

Follow the White Sox all season at: www.sportingnews.com/baseball/teams/whitesox/

WHITE SOX SPRING ROSTER

No.	PITCHERS	B/T	Ht./Wt.	Born	2000 clubs	Projection
37	Baldwin, James	R/R	6-3/210	7-15-71	Chicago A.L.	Continues to improve and that could mean more than 14 wins this year.
49	Barcelo, Lorenzo	R/R	6-4/220	8-10-77	Charlotte, Chicago A.L.	Did a good job out of bullpen and may have earned a spot there this year.
60	Biddle, Rocky	R/R	6-3/230	5-21-76	Birmingham, Chicago A.L.	Solid starter who is still a year or two away from majors.
56	Buehrle, Mark	L/L	6-2/200	3-23-79	Birmingham, Chicago A.L.	Lefthander who may get shot to start more games.
21	Eldred, Cal	R/R	6-4/237	11-24-67	Chicago A.L., Charlotte	Showed flashes of greatness last year, but injuries hurt him.
	Fogg, Josh	R/R	6-2/205	12-13-76	Birmingham	A top prospect who could see time in big leagues by end of season.
29	Foulke, Keith	R/R	6-0/200	10-19-72	Chicago A.L.	Hard-throwing closer who is only going to get better.
52	Garland, Jon	R/R	6-6/205	9-27-79	Charlotte, Chicago A.L., Birm.	White Sox high on this young pitcher who has chance to make rotation.
70	Ginter, Matt	R/R	6-1/215	12-24-77	Birmingham, Chicago A.L.	The White Sox top pick from two years ago has made great progress.
	Glover, Gary	R/R	6-5/205	12-3-76	Syracuse	Starter likely to begin the year in Charlotte.
46	Howry, Bobby	L/R	6-5/215	8-4-73	Chicago A.L.	One of the White Sox best relief pitchers.
50	Lowe, Sean	R/R	6-2/205	3-29-71	Chicago A.L., Charlotte	Versatile pitcher who can start or come out of bullpen.
40	Parque, Jim	L/L	5-11/165	2-8-76	Chicago A.L.	Had outstanding 2000 campaign and is getting better with more seasoning.
41	Simas, Bill	L/R	6-3/235	11-28-71	Chicago A.L.	Bullpen workhorse who has been consistent throughout his career.
	Vining, Ken	L/L	6-0/180	12-5-74	Birmingham	Lefty reliever not likely to make big league squad this year.
33	Wells, David	L/L	6-4/235	5-20-63	Toronto	Still one of the toughest starters, at 37, in the A.L.
32	Wells, Kip	R/R	6-3/196	4-21-77	Chicago A.L., Charlotte	Has shot to make rotation, but needs to improve from last season.
65	Wunsch, Kelly	L/L	6-5/220	7-12-72	Chicago A.L.	Lefty specialist who can come out of the bullpen or start.

No.	CATCHERS	B/T	Ht./Wt.	Born	2000 clubs	Projection
	Alomar, Sandy Jr.	R/R	6-5/220	6-18-66	Cleveland	Comes in to take over starter's job if healthy.
10	Johnson, Mark	L/R	6-0/185	9-12-75	Chicago A.L.	Chance to win starting job, but more likely to be backup.
15	Paul, Josh	R/R	6-1/185	5-19-75	Chicago A.L., Charlotte	Will have to be impressive to win a job behind the plate.

No.	INFIELDERS	B/T	Ht./Wt.	Born	2000 clubs	Projection
	Clayton, Royce	R/R	6-0/183	1-2-70	Texas	Solidifies the infield with his strong defense up the middle.
24	Crede, Joe	R/R	6-3/195	4-26-78	Birmingham, Chicago A.L.	After another MVP season in the minors, in line to take over third base job.
34	Dellaero, Jason	B/R	6-2/195	12-17-76	Birmingham	Struggled in minors last year and likely to stay there to start the season.
5	Durham, Ray	B/R	5-8/180	11-30-71	Chicago A.L.	As good offensively and defensively as any second baseman in the league.
	Garcia, Amaury	R/R	5-10/160	5-20-75	Calgary	Good offensive second baseman who might be valueable off the bench.
47	Graffanino, Tony	R/R	6-1/195	6-6-72	Tampa Bay, Durham, Chi. A.L.	Solid utilityman who can play several infield positions.
14	Konerko, Paul	R/R	6-3/211	3-5-76	Chicago A.L.	Starting to come around; expect better power numbers this year.
43	Perry, Herbert	R/R	6-2/220	9-15-69	Tampa Bay, Chicago A.L.	Will fill third base position until Crede takes over.
22	Valentin, Jose	L/R	5-10/190	10-12-69	Chicago A.L.	Coming off career year and most likely to be playing many positions this year.

No.	OUTFIELDERS	B/T	Ht./Wt.	Born	2000 clubs	Projection
26	Christensen, McKay	L/L	5-11/180	8-14-75	Chicago A.L., Charlotte	Defensive specialist off the bench who has good speed.
45	Lee, Carlos	R/R	6-2/220	6-20-76	Chicago A.L.	Turning into all-star outfielder after consecutive solid seasons.
39	Liefer, Jeff	L/R	6-3/195	8-17-74	Chicago A.L., Charlotte	Power-hitting prospect who has chance to come off the bench and DH.
30	Ordonez, Magglio	R/R	6-0/200	1-28-74	Chicago A.L.	Back-to-back 30 home run, 100 RBI and 100 runs scored seasons.
	Ramirez, Julio	R/R	5-11/170	8-10-77	Calgary	Speedy outfielder a few years away from the majors.
66	Rowand, Aaron	R/R	6-1/200	8-29-77	Birmingham	Power and speed have the White Sox high on this guy.
12	Singleton, Chris	L/L	6-2/195	8-15-72	Chicago A.L.	Solid all-around outfielder just starting to come into his own.

No.	DESIGNATED HITTERS	B/T	Ht./Wt.	Born	2000 clubs	Projection
35	Thomas, Frank	R/R	6-5/270	5-27-68	Chicago A.L.	Back in MVP form and surrounded by loads of talent.

THE COACHING STAFF

Jerry Manuel, manager: Took team to postseason last year and expectations are high again. This is a talented, young team.

Nardi Contreras: Enters his third full season as White Sox pitching coach and has coached with Manuel for five years.

Wallace Johnson: Returns as third base coach and also oversees the outfielders.

Von Joshua: Joshua, who has been in the White Sox organization since 1993, enters his third season as hitting coach.

Art Kusnyer: He has been White Sox bullpen coach on and off since 1980.

Mansoo Lee: Lee joins the coaching staff as bullpen catcher and has been coaching since 1998 where he was a hitting instructor in the Cleveland Indians organization.

Joe Nossek: Heading into his 11th season as bench coach and 31st year of baseball.

Gary Pettis: Takes over as first base coach; has been coaching since 1995 after enjoying a successful 11-year playing career.

THE TOP NEWCOMERS

Sandy Alomar Jr.: If he stays healthy, the White Sox won't miss Charles Johnson.

Royce Clayton: Gives the White Sox solid defense up the middle with Durham at second and Clayton at shortstop. Has a little pop in his bat and good speed, but not a great contact hitter.

David Wells: The White Sox finally get the number one starter they've been looking for. He will help the White Sox against a tougher A.L. Central this year.

THE TOP PROSPECTS

Rocky Biddle: Consistent starter who is starting to grow as a pitcher. Already has moved through minors quickly and could end up in majors by end of the season.

Jon Garland: Great numbers in minors, but struggled at times with White Sox. Still maturing as pitcher and could be a good one.

Matt Ginter: First-round pick two years ago is starting to show great progress. Could be in rotation by end of season.

Cleveland Indians

American League Central Division

2001 SEASON

Indians 2001 SCHEDULE

Home games shaded; D—Day game (games starting before 5 p.m.)
*—All-Star Game at Safeco Field (Seattle)

APRIL

SUN	MON	TUE	WED	THU	FRI	SAT
1	2 D CWS	3	4 CWS	5	6 BAL	7 D BAL
8 D BAL	9 CWS	10 CWS	11 D CWS	12 DET	13 DET	14 D DET
15 D DET	16	17 BAL	18 BAL	19 D BAL	20 DET	21 D DET
22 D DET	23	24 ANA	25 ANA	26 ANA	27 TEX	28 TEX
29 D TEX	30					

MAY

SUN	MON	TUE	WED	THU	FRI	SAT
		1 KC	2 KC	3 D KC	4 TB	5 D TB
6 D TB	7	8 KC	9 KC	10 KC	11 TB	12 TB
13 D TB	14	15 TEX	16 TEX	17 D TEX	18 ANA	19 ANA
20 ANA	21	22 DET	23 DET	24 DET	25 NYY	26 D NYY
27 D NYY	28 D DET	29 DET	30 DET	31		

JUNE

SUN	MON	TUE	WED	THU	FRI	SAT
					1 NYY	2 D NYY
3 D NYY	4 MIN	5 MIN	6 MIN	7 MIN	8 CIN	9 D CIN
10 D CIN	11	12 MIL	13 MIL	14 MIL	15 PIT	16 PIT
17 D PIT	18	19 MIN	20 MIN	21 MIN	22 KC	23 KC
24 D KC	25 NYY	26 NYY	27 D NYY	28	29 KC	30 KC

JULY

SUN	MON	TUE	WED	THU	FRI	SAT
1 D KC	2 KC	3 BOS	4 D BOS	5 BOS	6 STL	7 D STL
8 D STL	9	10 *	11	12 CIN	13 CIN	14 D CIN
15 D HOU	16 HOU	17 HOU	18 CWS	19 CWS	20 DET	21 D DET
22 D DET	23 CWS	24 CWS	25 CWS	26 CWS	27 DET	28 DET
29 D DET	30	31 OAK				

AUGUST

SUN	MON	TUE	WED	THU	FRI	SAT
			1 OAK	2 OAK	3 SEA	4 SEA
5 D SEA	6 SEA	7 MIN	8 MIN	9 D MIN	10 TEX	11 TEX
12 TEX	13	14 MIN	15 MIN	16 MIN	17 ANA	18 D ANA
19 D ANA	20 OAK	21 OAK	22 OAK	23 D OAK	24 SEA	25 D SEA
26 D SEA	27	28 BOS	29 BOS	30 BOS	31 CWS	

SEPTEMBER

SUN	MON	TUE	WED	THU	FRI	SAT
						1 CWS
2 D CWS	3 CWS	4 BOS	5 BOS	6 BOS	7 CWS	8 D CWS
9 D CWS	10 CWS	11 KC	12 KC	13 D KC	14 TOR	15 D TOR
16 D TOR	17	18 KC	19 KC	20 KC	21 MIN	22 MIN
23 D MIN	24 TOR	25 TOR	26 TOR	27	28 MIN	29 D MIN
30 D MIN						

FRONT-OFFICE DIRECTORY

President and chief executive officer .... Lawrence J. Dolan
Executive vice president, general manager .... John Hart
Executive vice president, business .... Dennis Lehman
Vice president, public relations .... Bob DiBiasio
Vice president and general counsel .... Paul J. Dolan
V.p., marketing and communications .... Jeff Overton
Vice president of baseball operations/asst. general manager .... Mark Shapiro
Vice president, finance .... Ken Stefanov
Director, team travel .... Mike Seghi
Director, player development .... Neal Huntington
Director, scouting .... John Mirabelli
Assistant director, scouting .... Brad Grant
Director, media relations .... Bart Swain
Manager, media relations, administration & credentials .... Susie Giuliano
Manager, media relations .... Curtis Danburg
Coordinator, media relations .... Jeff Sibel

MINOR LEAGUE AFFILIATES

Class	Team	League	Manager
AAA	Buffalo	International	Eric Wedge
AA	Akron	Eastern	Willie Upshaw
A	Kinston	Carolina	Brad Komminsk
A	Columbus	South Atlantic	Ted Kubiak
A	Mahoning Valley	New York-Pennsylvania	Chris Bando
Rookie	Burlington	Appalachian	Dave Turgeon

BROADCAST INFORMATION

Radio: WTAM (1100 AM).
TV: WUAB-TV (Channel 43).
Cable TV: Fox Sports Net Ohio.

SPRING TRAINING

Ballpark (city): Chain Of Lakes (Winter Haven, Fla.).
Ticket information: 813-287-8844.

ASSISTANCE STAFF

Head trainer
Paul Spicuzza

Assistant trainer
Jim Warfield

Clubhouse manager
Ted Walsh

Visiting clubhouse
Cy Buynak

Groundskeeper
Brandon Koehnke

Nat. cross-checker, West Coast supervisor
Jesse Flores

Nat. cross-checker, East Coast supervisor
Jerry Jordan

Midwest supervisor
Bob Mayer

Full-time scouts
Steve Abney
Keith Boeck
Paul Cogan
Dan Durst
Chris Jefts
Scott Meaney
Les Parari
Phil Rossi
Jason Smith
Doug Baker
Jim Bretz
Henry Cruz
Jim Gabella
Chad McDonald
Dave Miller
Chuck Ricci
Bill Schudlich
Shawn Whalen

BALLPARK INFORMATION

Ballpark (capacity, surface)
Jacobs Field (43,863, grass)
Address
2401 Ontario St.
Cleveland, OH 44115
Official website
www.indians.com
Business phone
216-420-4200
Ticket information
216-420-4200
Ticket prices
$40 (field box)
$27 (baseline box, IF lower box, view box)
$25 (lower box), $21 (IF upper box)
$20 (lower reserved, mezzanine, upper box)
$19 (field bleachers), $17 (bleachers)
$12 (upper reserved)
$7 (upper reserved general admission)
$6 (standing room)
Field dimensions (from home plate)
To left field at foul line, 325 feet
To center field, 405 feet
To right field at foul line, 325 feet
First game played
April 4, 1994 (Indians 4, Mariners 3, 11 innings)

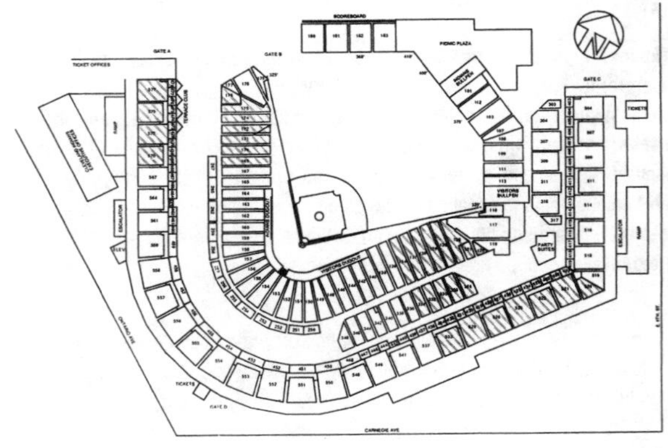

Follow the Indians all season at: www.sportingnews.com/baseball/teams/indians/

INDIANS SPRING ROSTER

No.	PITCHERS	B/T	Ht./Wt.	Born	2000 clubs	Projection
55	Baez, Danys	R/R	6-3/225	9-10-77	Kinston, Akron	Moved his way through minors last year and could find spot on roster.
	Vargas, Martin	R/R	6-0/155	2-22-78	Akron	Was a workhorse last season with 53 appearances and led the team in wins and saves.
64	Brammer, J.D.	R/R	6-4/235	1-30-75	Akron, Buffalo	Solid bullpen pitcher who could provide innings for the Tribe this year.
49	Brown, Jamie	R/R	6-2/205	3-31-77	Akron	Ate up innings as a starter at Akron and will most likely start the year in Class AAA.
34	Burba, Dave	R/R	6-4/240	7-7-66	Cleveland	Probably the Indians' most reliable starter last year. Expect much of the same.
	Cairncross, Cameron	L/L	6-0/195	5-11-72	Akron, Cleveland, Buffalo	Should provide the Indians with a solid lefthander out of the bullpen.
40	Colon, Bartolo	R/R	6-0/230	5-24-75	Cleveland, Buffalo	Can be one of the most dominating pitchers in the game when healthy.
	Day, Zach	R/R	6-4/185	6-15-78	Greensboro, Tampa, Akron	Pitched well in minors last year and could find spot in bullpen.
56	DePaula, Sean	R/R	6-4/215	11-7-73	Buffalo, Cleveland, Akron	Hard thrower with big upside who could help solidify Indians bullpen.
	Drese, Ryan	R/R	6-3/220	4-5-76	Kinston	Returning from injury that will prevent him from starting the year in Cleveland.
	Drew, Tim	R/R	6-1/195	8-31-78	Akron, Cleveland, Buffalo	Might find a spot in the bullpen, but a spot in the rotation is unlikely.
73	Rincon, Ricky	L/L	5-10/187	4-13-70	Cleveland	Solid lefthander out of the bullpen who will pitch well when healthy.
31	Finley, Chuck	L/L	6-6/225	11-26-62	Cleveland	The dominating lefthanded starter that the Indians were looking for.
20	Karsay, Steve	R/R	6-3/215	3-24-72	Cleveland	Takes over closer duties after finishing the year with 20 saves.
41	Nagy, Charles	L/R	6-3/200	5-5-67	Cleveland, Buffalo, Akron	Indians hope he can regain the form of old after battling injuries.
70	Padilla, Roy	L/L	6-5/227	8-4-75	Kinston, Akron	Trying to win spot in crowded and talented Indian bullpen.
39	Reed, Steve	R/R	6-2/212	3-11-66	Cleveland	Goes into the year as set-up man after filling that role nicely at end of 2000.
54	Riske, Dave	R/R	6-2/180	10-23-76	Buffalo, Akron	Could provide bullpen depth if he can stay healthy.
53	Shuey, Paul	R/R	6-3/215	9-16-70	Cleveland, Akron	Hard throwing reliever will try to steal closer role from Karsay.
46	Speier, Justin	R/R	6-4/205	11-6-73	Buffalo, Cleveland	Solid relief help that should provide Indians with more help out of the bullpen.
78	Westbrook, Jake	R/R	6-3/185	9-29-77	Columbus, New York A.L.	Going for a spot in the rotation, but probably still a couple of years away.
27	Wickman, Bob	R/R	6-1/234	2-6-69	Milwaukee, Cleveland	Provides the Indians with another closer after picking up 30 saves last season.
37	Woodard, Steve	L/R	6-4/217	5-15-75	Milwaukee, Cleveland	MIght find it hard to crack the rotation if all the starters remain heathy.
27	Wright, Jaret	R/R	6-2/230	12-29-75	Cleveland, Buffalo, Akron	Has dynamite stuff and could be ace of staff, but needs to rebound from injury.

No.	CATCHERS	B/T	Ht./Wt.	Born	2000 clubs	Projection
2	Diaz, Einar	R/R	5-10/185	12-28-72	Cleveland	With Sandy Alomar gone, the catching job is Diaz's to lose.
10	Taubensee, Eddie	L/R	6-3/230	10-31-68	Cincinnati	Solid catcher and good lefthanded bat off the Indians bench.

No.	INFIELDERS	B/T	Ht./Wt.	Born	2000 clubs	Projection
12	Alomar, Roberto	B/R	6-0/185	2-5-68	Cleveland	As good as it gets at second base; expect much of the same from the All-Star.
33	Branyan, Russell	L/R	6-3/195	12-19-75	Buffalo, Cleveland	Pure power-hitter will compete for at-bats off the bench.
6	Cabrera, Jolbert	R/R	6-0/177	12-8-72	Buffalo, Cleveland	Solid bench player who will give the Indians options.
12	Cordero, Wil	R/R	6-2/200	10-3-71	Pittsburgh, Cleveland	Expected to pick up some of the RBI slack left by Manny Ramirez.
17	Fryman, Travis	R/R	6-1/195	3-25-69	Cleveland	Another season like he had last year will make Ramirez's loss easier to swallow.
72	McDonald, John	R/R	5-11/175	9-24-74	Buff., Mah. Val., Cleve., Kinston	Injury plagued season last year will make it hard to find a spot in the majors.
25	Thome, Jim	L/R	6-4/240	8-27-70	Cleveland	Another big year is expected out of the power-hitting first baseman.
13	Vizquel, Omar	B/R	5-9/185	4-24-67	Cleveland	Arguably the best shortstop in the game, and his offense isn't too shabby, either.

No.	OUTFIELDERS	B/T	Ht./Wt.	Born	2000 clubs	Projection
23	Burks, Ellis	R/R	6-2/205	9-11-64	San Francisco	Could blossom in Cleveland by resting his knees at DH this year.
51	Cruz, Jacob	L/L	6-0/215	1-28-73	Cleveland	Hasn't been the player he was expected to be, but might get chance this year.
	Gonzalez, Juan	R/R	6-3/220	10-16-69	Detroit	Needs to prove he's still one of game's elite hitters after injury plagued season.
7	Lofton, Kenny	L/L	6-0/190	5-31-67	Cleveland	Proved last season that he's still one of most dangerous players in the game.
65	Peoples, Danny	R/R	6-1/207	1-20-75	Buffalo	Durable power hitter who will most likely start season in Buffalo.
10	Roberts, Dave	L/L	5-10/175	5-31-72	Buffalo, Cleveland	Trying to win a spot on the bench this year after a solid season in Buffalo.

THE COACHING STAFF

Charlie Manuel, manager: A lot of pressure is on Manuel as he heads into his second season at the helm. The Indians stayed with Manuel despite missing the playoffs for the first time in five years.

Luis Isaac: Returns as bullpen coach for eighth season; has been in the Indians organization since 1965.

Clarence Jones: Long-time Braves hitting coach returns for a third consecutive season with Cleveland.

Grady Little: Returns for a second season as team's bench coach and catching instructor.

Dick Pole: Pole is hoping the Indians pitching staff can return to heatlh as he heads into his second season as pitching coach.

Joel Skinner: Joins the Indians coaching staff this year after spending a successful career as a catcher for several teams including the Indians.

Ted Uhlaender: Returning for a second season as the team's baserunning and outfield coach.

Dan Williams: Williams has done a little of everything for the Indians the past six seasons: serving as catcher for the pitchers, throwing batting practice and hitting fungoes.

THE TOP NEWCOMERS

Ellis Burks: Will be looked upon to provide much of the production lost when Manny Ramirez left for Boston. While not the same player he once was, Burks can still provide a lot of offense if put in the right situation.

Juan Gonzalez: Will provide a dangerous bat if his back stays healthy.

Eddie Taubensee: Will platoon with Diaz behind the plate and provide some lefthanded pop off the bench.

THE TOP PROSPECTS

Russell Branyan: Showed great power in limited time with the Indians. Waiting in the wings for when Fryman vacates the third base position.

Danys Baez: Hard-throwing pitcher who defected from Cuba to sign with the Indians. Showed great progress in 2000 and could end up in the big leagues by the start of the 2001 season.

DETROIT TIGERS

AMERICAN LEAGUE CENTRAL DIVISION

2001 SEASON

Tigers 2001 SCHEDULE

Home games shaded; D—Day game (games starting before 5 p.m.)
*—All-Star Game at Safeco Field (Seattle)

APRIL

SUN	MON	TUE	WED	THU	FRI	SAT
1	2	3 D MIN	4	5 D MIN	6 D CWS	7 D CWS
8 D CWS	9 MIN	10 MIN	11 MIN	12 CLE	13 CLE	14 D CLE
15 D CLE	16	17 CWS	18 CWS	19 CWS	20 CLE	21 D CLE
22 D CLE	23	24 BAL	25 BAL	26 D BAL	27 TB	28 D TB
29 D TB	30					

MAY

SUN	MON	TUE	WED	THU	FRI	SAT
		1 TEX	2 TEX	3 D TEX	4 ANA	5 ANA
6 D ANA	7	8 TEX	9 TEX	10 D TEX	11 ANA	12 D ANA
13 D ANA	14	15 BAL	16 BAL	17 BAL	18 TB	19 D TB
20 D TB	21	22 CLE	23 CLE	24 CLE	25 CWS	26 CWS
27 CWS	28 D CLE	29 CLE	30 CLE	31 CWS		

JUNE

SUN	MON	TUE	WED	THU	FRI	SAT
					1 CWS	2 CWS
3 D CWS	4	5 BOS	6 BOS	7 BOS	8 MIL	9 MIL
10 D MIL	11	12 PIT	13 PIT	14 PIT	15 ARI	16 ARI
17 D ARI	18 NYY	19 NYY	20 NYY	21 NYY	22 MIN	23 MIN
24 D MIN	25 D MIN	26 KC	27 KC	28 D KC	29 MIN	30 MIN

JULY

SUN	MON	TUE	WED	THU	FRI	SAT
1 D MIN	2	3 KC	4 D KC	5 KC	6 CUB	7 CUB
8 D CUB	9	10 *	11	12 STL	13 STL	14 D STL
15 D CIN	16 CIN	17 CIN	18 NYY	19 NYY	20 CLE	21 D CLE
22 D CLE	23	24 NYY	25 NYY	26 D NYY	27 CLE	28 CLE
29 D CLE	30	31 SEA				

AUGUST

SUN	MON	TUE	WED	THU	FRI	SAT
			1 SEA	2 SEA	3 OAK	4 OAK
5 D OAK	6 D OAK	7 TEX	8 TEX	9 TEX	10 KC	11 KC
12 D KC	13	14 ANA	15 ANA	16 D ANA	17 KC	18 KC
19 D KC	20 SEA	21 SEA	22 SEA	23 D SEA	24 OAK	25 D OAK
26 D OAK	27	28 CWS	29 CWS	30 CWS	31 TOR	

SEPTEMBER

SUN	MON	TUE	WED	THU	FRI	SAT
						1 D TOR
2 D TOR	3	4 CWS	5 CWS	6 D CWS	7 TOR	8 TOR
9 D TOR	10 MIN	11 MIN	12 MIN	13 D MIN	14 KC	15 KC
16 D KC	17	18 MIN	19 MIN	20 D MIN	21 BOS	22 BOS
23 D BOS	24 KC	25 KC	26 KC	27 KC	28 BOS	29 BOS
30 D BOS						

FRONT-OFFICE DIRECTORY

Owner ....Michael Ilitch
President, chief executive officer ....John McHale Jr.
Vice president, baseball operations/general manager ....Randy Smith
Vice president, business operations....................David H. Glazier
Assistant general manager ....Steve Lubratich
Assistants to baseball operations....................Ricky Bennett, Hiroshi Yoshimura
Asst., bb operations, foreign affairs ....Ramon Pena
Special assistants to the general manager ....Al Hargesheimer, Randy Johnson
Director of scouting ....Greg Smith
Latin American liaison....................Luis Mayoral
Director minor league operations ....Dave Miller
Traveling secretary ....Bill Brown
Sr. dir., marketing and communications ....Tyler Barnes
Manager of public relations....................Jim Anderson
Manager, community relations ....Celia Bobrowsky
Coordinator, community relations ....Fred Feliciano
Coordinator, public relations ....Brian Britten
Coordinator, public relations....................Melanie Waters
Coordinator, community relations ....Masico Brown
Marketing manager ....Ellen Hill
Vice president, ballpark operations....................Tom Folk
Special assistant to the president ....Gary Vitto
Director of corporate sales ....Dan Sinagoga
Director of finance....................Jennifer Orow
Director of ticket services ....Ken Marchetti
Director of ticket sales ....Barry Gibson
Director of merchandise ....Kayla French

MINOR LEAGUE AFFILIATES

Class	Team	League	Manager
AAA	Toledo	International	Bruce Fields
AA	Erie	Southern	To be announced
A	Lakeland	Florida State	Skeeter Barnes
A	Oneonta	New York-Pennsylvania	Gary Green
A	West Michigan	Midwest	Kevin Bradshaw
Rookie	Gulf Coast Tigers	Gulf Coast	Howard Bushong

BROADCAST INFORMATION

Radio: WXYT-AM (1270).
TV: WKBD (Channel 50).
Cable TV: FOX Sports Detroit.

SPRING TRAINING

Ballpark (city): Marchant Stadium (Lakeland, Fla.).
Ticket information: 941-603-6278 or 941-603-6279.

ASSISTANCE STAFF

Manager, home clubhouse
Jim Schmakel

Assistant manager, visiting clubhouse
John Nelson

Team physicians
David J. Collon, M.D., Terry Lock, M.D., Louis Saco, M.D., Michael Workings, M.D.

Medical director/head trainer
Russ Miller

Assistant trainer
Steve Carter

Strength and conditioning coach
Dennie Taft

Scouts

Scott Bream	Bill Buck
Jerome Cochran	Tim Grieve
Rob Guzik	Jack Hays
Mike Herbert	Joe Hodges
Lou Laslo	Dennis Lieberthal
Jeff Malinoff	Mark Monahan
Pat Murtaugh	Steve Nichols
Frank Paine	Derrick Ross
Steve Taylor	Clyde Weir
Jeff Wetherby	Rob Wilfong
Ellis Williams	Steve Williams
Gary York	Harold Zonder

BALLPARK INFORMATION

Ballpark (capacity, surface)
Comerica Park (40,120)
Address
2100 Woodward
Detroit, MI 48201
Official website
www.detroittigers.com
Business phone
313-471-2000
Ticket information
313-471-BALL
Ticket prices
$60 (Tiger Den)
$35 (terrace, club)
$30 (infield box)
$25 & $15 (outfield box)
$20 (upper box)
$15 (mezzanine)
$14 (pavilion)
$12 (upper reserved)
$8 (bleachers)
Field dimensions (from home plate)
To left field at foul line, 345 feet
To center field, 420 feet
To right field at foul line, 330 feet
First game played
Scheduled for April 11, 2000 vs. Mariners

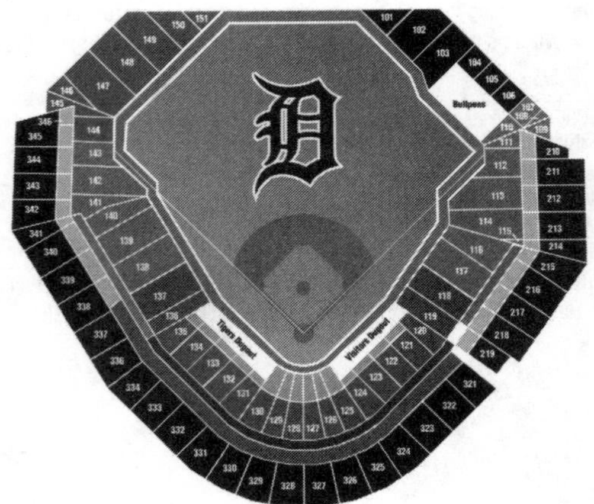

Follow the Tigers all season at: www.sportingnews.com/baseball/teams/tigers/

TIGERS SPRING ROSTER

No.	PITCHERS	B/T	Ht./Wt.	Born	2000 clubs	Projection
14	Anderson, Matt	R/R	6-4/200	8-17-76	Detroit	To be effective in set up role, he must control his blazing fastball.
	Borkowski, Dave	R/R	6-1/200	2-7-77	Toledo, Det., GC Tigers, Lakeland	Young right hander needs full season with big club to become effective starter.
50	Greisinger, Seth	R/R	6-3/200	7-29-75	DID NOT PLAY	Promising youngster must recover from elbow surgery.
	Heams, Shane	R/R	6-1/175	9-29-75	Jacksonville, Toledo	Hard-throwing Olympian needs to keep his head in the game.
	Holt, Chris	R/R	6-4/205	9-18-71	Houston	He will gobble up innings to take up some pressure off bullpen.
59	Jones, Todd	R/R	6-3/230	4-24-68	Detroit	No way he can repeat last year. Coming close will be good enough.
	Keller, Kris	R/R	6-2/225	3-1-78	Jacksonville	Only a matter of time before he brings heat to Detroit.
	Loux, Shane	R/R	6-2/205	8-13-79	Lakeland, Jacksonville	Led Class AA Jacksonville in wins.
	Maroth, Mike	L/L	6-0/180	8-17-77	Jacksonville	Could get a shot with Tigers if rotation falters.
	Miller, Matt	L/L	6-3/175	8-2-74	Jacksonville	Solid performance in Arizona Fall League put his name on 40-man roster.
30	Mlicki, Dave	R/R	6-4/205	6-8-68	Detroit, West Michigan, Toledo	Hopes for strong year after illness-plagued 2000.
38	Moehler, Brian	R/R	6-3/235	12-31-71	Detroit, West Michigan	Expect him to win—and lose—in the double digits every year.
27	Nitkowski, C.J.	L/L	6-3/205	3-9-73	Detroit	May have found his calling in demotion to bullpen.
28	Patterson, Danny	R/R	6-0/185	2-17-71	Detroit	Reliever acquired in Gonzalez deal put up solid numbers.
	Perisho, Matt	L/L	6-0/205	6-8-75	Texas	Team thinks lefty will fit in just fine at Comerica.
	Pettyjohn, Adam	L/R	6-3/190	6-11-77	Jacksonville, Toledo	Lefthanded starter is working his way up.
	Pineda, Luis	R/R	6-1/160	6-10-78	Lakeland	Not ready for majors after putting up decent ERA in 18 appearances in Class A.
37	Sparks, Steve	R/R	6-0/180	7-2-65	Toledo, Detroit	Tigers would love if he repeated 5-0 August of last year.
36	Weaver, Jeff	R/R	6-5/210	8-22-76	Toledo, Detroit	Hot-headed flame thrower could dominate in third pro season.

No.	CATCHERS	B/T	Ht./Wt.	Born	2000 clubs	
53	Cardona, Javier	R/R	6-1/185	9-15-75	Toledo, Detroit	Will make regular drives from Toledo to Detroit, and vice versa.
18	Fick, Robert	L/R	6-1/189	3-15-74	Detroit, Toledo	Team should find a place to play him so he can bat every day.
	Inge, Brandon	B/R	5-11/185	5-19-77	Jacksonville, Toledo	He's too far down on the list to see much time.
	Meluskey, Mitch	B/R	6-0/185	9-18-73	Houston	Meluskey brings good bat, questionable defense.
17	Munson, Eric	L/R	6-3/220	10-3-77	Jacksonville, Detroit	Heraled top prospect is still a year away from contributing.

No.	INFIELDERS	B/T	Ht./Wt.	Born	2000 clubs	
	Clark, Jermaine	L/R	5-10/175	9-29-76	New Haven	His solid bat could lead to a callup.
44	Clark, Tony	B/R	6-7/245	6-15-72	Detroit, Toledo	Slugging switch hitter needs to overcome slow start habit.
8	Cruz, Deivi	R/R	6-0/184	11-6-75	Detroit	Never strikes out, but never walks.
9	Easley, Damion	R/R	5-11/185	11-11-69	Detroit, Toledo	Sweet-fielding second baseman needs to get better at the plate.
17	Halter, Shane	R/R	6-0/180	11-8-69	Detroit	Versatility—he played all nine positions in one game—make him valuable.
33	Macias, Jose	B/R	5-10/173	1-25-74	Toledo, Detroit	Should contribute as utility man who can play the infield and outfield.
7	Palmer, Dean	R/R	6-1/210	12-27-68	Detroit	If strikeouts were software, he'd be Microsoft.
	Santana, Pedro	R/R	5-11/160	9-21-76	Jacksonville	He needs more seasoning before hitting the bigs.

No.	OUTFIELDERS	B/T	Ht./Wt.	Born	2000 clubs	
	Cedeno, Roger	B/R	6-1/205	8-16-74	Houston, New Orleans	First true leadoff hitter for Tigers since Tony Phillips.
34	Encarnacion, Juan	R/R	6-3/187	3-8-76	Detroit	Speedster needs to utilize his quickness on the basepaths.
4	Higginson, Bobby	L/R	5-11/195	8-18-70	Detroit	Rugged competitor has outstanding arm, solid bat.
29	Magee, Wendell	R/R	6-0/220	8-3-72	Detroit, Toledo	Ability to hit in clutch situations will keep him on the team.
43	McMillon, Billy	L/L	5-11/179	11-17-71	Toledo, Detroit	Pleased Garner with his bat in summer callup.
	Torres, Andres	B/R	5-10/175	1-26-78	Lakeland, Jacksonville	Weak stint at AA might have stalled his climb through the ranks.
	Wakeland, Chris	L/L	6-0/185	6-15-74	Toledo	Sweet hitting slugger still waiting for chance. Will it ever come?

THE COACHING STAFF

Phil Garner, manager: Players like Garner because he runs his team with common sense. He doesn't berate or embarrass players, but at the same time, he doesn't tolerate bad fundamentals. He's the kind of manager that inspires an undertalented team to overachieve.

Doug Mansolino: Third base coach moves into the dugout to be Garner's bench coach. He had coached third for three years for Garner.

Lance Parrish: Former Tigers catcher moves from bullpen coach to take over third base job. He'll have to be aggressive, as Tigers will need every run they can get.

Ed Ott: Ott, who hasn't coached in the majors since 1993, will be the bullpen coach. Ott and Garner go way back. Both were on the 1979 World Champion Pittsburgh Pirates, as was hitting coach Bill Madlock.

Bill Madlock: Returns for second year as hitting coach. He has the bats to work with, but he needs to make them more consistent. The team was shutout too many times last year.

Dan Warthen: The pitching coach has a chance to shine or fall flat on his face. Weaver and Anderson are talented works in progress. If they succeed, Warthen will look good.

Juan Samuel: He learned a thing or two about stealing bases during his playing career. As first base caoch, he needs to pass that knowledge on to Tigers' speedsters.

THE TOP NEWCOMERS

Chris Holt: Dependable starter will pitch 200-plus innings. Had an inflated ERA last year, which could be attributed to pitching at Enron Field.

Mitch Meluskey: Good hitting catcher will get plenty of playing time with Tigers. Will help tutor younger prospects.

THE TOP PROSPECTS

Eric Munson: Getting better every year. The team expects him to hit for power and average for years to come. He'll probably see some time in Detroit in 2001 and be a fixture in 2002. He was a first-round draft pick in 1999 and was up for a cup of coffee in 2000.

Chris Wakeland: Will turn 27 in June and is yet to get a call up. He should get his chance this year after hitting .270 with 28 homers and 76 RBIs for Class AAA Toledo.

Kansas City Royals

American League Central Division

2001 SEASON

Royals
2001 SCHEDULE
Home games shaded; D—Day game (games starting before 5 p.m.)
*—All-Star Game at Safeco Field (Seattle).

APRIL

SUN	MON	TUE	WED	THU	FRI	SAT
1	2 D NYY	3	4 NYY	5 D NYY	6 D MIN	7 D MIN
8 D MIN	9 NYY	10 NYY	11 D NYY	12 TOR	13 D TOR	14 D TOR
15 D TOR	16 MIN	17 MIN	18 D MIN	19	20 TOR	21 TOR
22 D TOR	23	24 TB	25 TB	26 D TB	27 BOS	28 D BOS
29 D BOS	30					

MAY

SUN	MON	TUE	WED	THU	FRI	SAT
		1 CLE	2 CLE	3 D CLE	4 MIN	5 MIN
6 D MIN	7	8 CLE	9 CLE	10 CLE	11 MIN	12 MIN
13 D MIN	14 MIN	15 TB	16 TB	17 TB	18 BOS	19 BOS
20 D BOS	21	22 OAK	23 OAK	24	25 SEA	26 SEA
27 D SEA	28 D SEA	29 TEX	30 TEX	31 D TEX		

JUNE

SUN	MON	TUE	WED	THU	FRI	SAT
					1 ANA	2 ANA
3 D ANA	4	5 CWS	6 CWS	7 D CWS	8 ARI	9 ARI
10 ARI	11	12 STL	13 STL	14 STL	15 MIL	16 MIL
17 D MIL	18 CWS	19 CWS	20 D CWS	21	22 CLE	23 CLE
24 D CLE	25	26 DET	27 DET	28 D DET	29 CLE	30 CLE

JULY

SUN	MON	TUE	WED	THU	FRI	SAT
1 D CLE	2 CLE	3 DET	4 D DET	5 DET	6 HOU	7 HOU
8 D HOU	9	10 *	11	12 PIT	13 PIT	14 D PIT
15 D CUB	16 CUB	17 D CUB	18 SEA	19 SEA	20 OAK	21 OAK
22 OAK	23 OAK	24 SEA	25 SEA	26 SEA	27 OAK	28 D OAK
29 D OAK	30	31 CWS				

AUGUST

SUN	MON	TUE	WED	THU	FRI	SAT
			1 CWS	2 CWS	3 MIN	4 MIN
5 D MIN	6 BAL	7 BAL	8 BAL	9 BAL	10 DET	11 DET
12 D DET	13	14 BAL	15 BAL	16 D BAL	17 DET	18 DET
19 D DET	20 CWS	21 CWS	22 CWS	23 CWS	24 MIN	25 MIN
26 D MIN	27	28 ANA	29 ANA	30 ANA	31 TEX	

SEPTEMBER

SUN	MON	TUE	WED	THU	FRI	SAT
						1 TEX
2 D TEX	3	4 ANA	5 ANA	6 ANA	7 TEX	8 TEX
9 D TEX	10	11 CLE	12 CLE	13 D CLE	14 DET	15 DET
16 D DET	17	18 CLE	19 CLE	20 CLE	21 CWS	22 CWS
23 D CWS	24 DET	25 DET	26 DET	27 DET	28 CWS	29 CWS
30 D CWS						

FRONT-OFFICE DIRECTORY

Board of directors....David Glass, Dan Glass, Ruth Glass, Don Glass, Dayna Glass, Julia Irene Kauffman, Herk Robinson
Chairman of the board & owner....David Glass
President....Dan Glass
Exec. v.p. and chief operating officer....Herk Robinson
Sr. v.p., business operations & administration....Art Chaudry
V.p. and general manager, baseball operations....Allard Baird
Vice president, baseball operations....George Brett
Vice president, operations....Jay Hinrichs
V.p., marketing and communications....Mike Levy
V.p., finance & information services....Dale Rohr
Asst. general manager, baseball operations....Muzzy Jackson
Senior advisor to the general manager....Art Stewart
Assistant to the general manager....Brian Murphy
Special assistant to the general manager....Pat Jones
Manager of major league operations....Karol Kyte
Senior director, scouting....Deric Ladnier
Senior director, minor league operations....Bob Hegman
Manager of team travel....Jeff Davenport
Director of community relations....Shani Tate
Director of human resources....Sylvia Patillo
Director of Lancer program....Rick Amos
Director, season ticket services....Joe Grigoli
Senior director/controller....John Luther
Director, payroll and benefits accounting....Tom Pfannenstiel
Senior director, information systems....Jim Edwards
Director, broadcast services & Royals alumni....Fred White
Senior director, media relations....David Witty
Director, corporate sponsorship sales....Kevin Battle
Director, group sales....Michele Kammerer
Director, marketing....Tonya Mangels
Director, event operations & revenue development....Chris Richardson
Director, groundskeeping & landscaping....Trevor Vance
Director, stadium operations....Rodney Lewallen
Director, ticket operations....Lance Buckley

MINOR LEAGUE AFFILIATES

Class	Team	League	Manager
AAA	Omaha	Pacific Coast	John Mizerock
AA	Wichita	Texas	Keith Bodie
A	Burlington	Midwest	Joe Szekely
A	Spokane	Northwest	Tom Poquette
A	Wilmington	Carolina	Jeff Garber
Rookie	Gulf Coast Royals	Gulf Coast	Lino Diaz

ASSISTANCE STAFF

Team physician
Dr. Steve Joyce

Athletic trainer
Nick Swartz

Assistant athletic trainer
Lee Kuntz

Strength and conditioning coordinator
Tim Maxey

Equipment manager
Mike Burkhalter

Visiting clubhouse manager
Chuck Hawke

Professional scouts
Rod Fridley, Louie Medina, Earl Winn

Special assignment scout
John Wathan

Regional cross-checkers
Jeff McKay, Dennis Woody

Latin American scouting coordinator
Albert Gonzalez

Dominican scouting coordinator
Luis Silverio

Territorial scouts
Bob Bishop, Mike Brown, Jason Bryans, Albert Gonzalez, Dave Herrera, Keith Hughes, Phil Huttman, Gary Johnson, Cliff Pastornicky, Johnny Ramos, Sean Rooney, Max Semler, Chet Sergo, Greg Smith, Gerald Turner, Brad Vaughn, Junior Vizcaino, Mark Willoughby

BROADCAST INFORMATION

Radio: KMBZ-AM (980).
TV: KMBC (Channel 9), KCWB (Channel 29).
Cable TV: Fox Sports Net.

SPRING TRAINING

Ballpark (city): Baseball City Stadium (Davenport, Fla.).
Ticket information: 941-424-2500.

BALLPARK INFORMATION

Ballpark (capacity, surface)
Kauffman Stadium (40,529, grass)

Address
P.O. Box 419969
Kansas City, MO 64141-6969

Official website
www.kcroyals.com

Business phone
816-921-8000

Ticket information
816-921-8000

Ticket prices
$19 (club box)
$17 (field box)
$15 (plaza reserved)
$12 (view upper box)
$11 (view upper reserved)
$7 (general admission)
$5.50 (Royal nights)

Field dimensions (from home plate)
To left field at foul line, 330 feet
To center field, 400 feet
To right field at foul line, 330 feet

First game played
April 10, 1973 (Royals 12, Rangers 1)

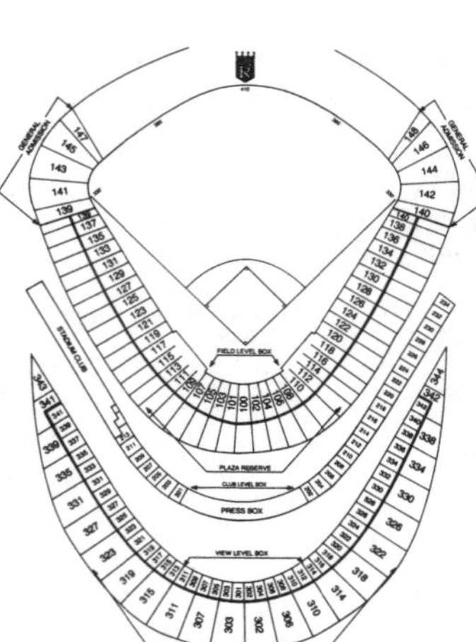

Follow the Royals all season at: www.sportingnews.com/baseball/teams/royals/

2001 PREVIEW

ROYALS SPRING ROSTER

No.	PITCHERS	B/T	Ht./Wt.	Born	2000 clubs	Projection
	Affeldt, Jeremy	L/L	6-4/185	6-5-79	Wilmington	Young and lefthanded, Affeldt will get more time in the minors after a spring look.
33	Durbin, Chad	R/R	6-2/200	12-3-77	Kansas City, Omaha	His strong, 23-year-old arm will attract plenty of attention during spring training.
49	Fussell, Chris	R/R	6-2/200	5-19-76	K.C., Omaha, G.C. Royals	An ability to both start and relieve bode well for his chances of making the team.
	Guerrero, Junior	R/R	6-2/175	8-21-79	Wichita	After a season at Class AA, Guerrero probably is not quite ready for prime time.
	Henry, Doug	R/R	6-4/205	12-10-63	Houston, San Francisco	Look for this former Giant to become the team's primary setup man.
	Hernandez, Roberto	R/R	6-4/250	11-11-64	Tampa Bay	The price was high, but the Royals now have their much-needed closer.
32	Laxton, Brett	L/R	6-1/210	10-5-73	Omaha, Kansas City	A mediocre season at Omaha and a tough 2000 trial make Laxton a longshot.
59	Meadows, Brian	R/R	6-4/220	11-21-75	San Diego, Kansas City	This rotation candidate might be a better fit in an undermanned bullpen.
45	Moreno, Orber	R/R	6-3/200	4-27-77	Did not play	Elbow surgery sidelined him in 2000 and now he has a lot to prove.
57	Mullen, Scott	R/L	6-2/190	1-17-75	Wichita, Omaha, Kansas City	A decent late-season showing earns him a look as a late-game lefty specialist.
36	Murray, Dan	R/R	6-1/195	11-21-73	Omaha, Kansas City	A bullpen candidate who has been vulnerable to the long ball.
41	Reichert, Dan	R/R	6-3/175	7-12-76	Kansas City	A valuable swing man who projects as a starter but could end up in the bullpen.
50	Rosado, Jose	L/L	6-0/185	11-9-74	Kansas City	The potential No. 1 starter if he's fully recovered from shoulder surgery.
46	Santiago, Jose	R/R	6-3/215	11-5-74	Kansas City, Omaha	After a difficult 2000 season, he will have to battle hard for a bullpen spot.
	Sonnier, Shawn	R/R	6-5/210	7-5-76	Wichita	This potential Kansas City closer needs at least another season in the minors.
34	Stein, Blake	R/R	6-7/240	8-3-73	Wilm'ton, Wichita, Omaha, K.C.	Finally healthy late in the season, he became the team's most dependable starter.
37	Suppan, Jeff	R/R	6-2/210	1-2-75	Kansas City	The team's most durable starter needs to show more consistency.
17	Suzuki, Mac	R/R	6-3/205	5-31-75	Kansas City	A pleasant surprise in 2000, Suzuki will take his place in the 2001 rotation.
51	Wilson, Kris	R/R	6-3/225	8-6-76	Kansas City	With the team's dire bullpen needs, this youngster will get a good spring look.

No.	CATCHERS	B/T	Ht./Wt.	Born	2000 clubs	Projection
22	Ortiz, Hector	R/R	6-0/205	5-15-74	Sacramento, Oakland	If the Royals can find him a magic bat, he could battle for the starting job.
22	Hinch, A.J.	R/R	6-1/207	10-14-69	Omaha, Kansas City	This career backup will need a good spring to make the regular-season roster.
	Phillips, Paul	R/R	5-11/180	4-15-77	Wichita	This good young prospect still might be a year away from the majors.
44	Zaun, Gregg	B/R	5-10/190	4-14-71	Kansas City, Omaha	A veteran presence for a young staff and a good bet to start at least part-time.

No.	INFIELDERS	B/T	Ht./Wt.	Born	2000 clubs	Projection
19	Delgado, Wilson	B/R	5-11/165	7-15-75	New York A.L., Kansas City	His value is his infield versatility. A potential backup at three positions.
3	Febles, Carlos	R/R	5-11/185	5-24-76	K.C., G. Coast, Wichita, Omaha	The injury-prone second baseman is a flashy fielder and dangerous with the bat.
8	Ordaz, Luis	R/R	5-11/170	8-12-75	Kansas City	He can provide valuable relief up the middle and start for short periods.
16	Randa, Joe	R/R	5-11/190	12-18-69	Kansas City	He has quietly developed into one of the game's most productive third basemen.
1	Sanchez, Rey	R/R	5-9/175	10-5-67	Kansas City	One of the most dependable shortstops in the game and he gets key hits.
29	Sweeney, Mike	R/R	6-3/225	7-22-73	American, Kansas City	His first base defense is catching up to his blazing bat.

No.	OUTFIELDERS	B/T	Ht./Wt.	Born	2000 clubs	Projection
15	Beltran, Carlos	B/R	6-1/190	4-24-77	K.C., G.Coast, Wilm'ton, Omaha	With Damon gone, center fielder Beltran will have to rediscover his 1999 form.
27	Brown, Dee	L/R	6-0/215	3-27-78	Omaha, Kansas City	A promising youngster who could challenge for time if an outfielder falters.
	Chavez, Endy	L/L	6-0/150	2-7-78	St. Lucie	This young speedster is a coming attraction, probably in 2002.
24	Dye, Jermaine	R/R	6-5/220	1-28-74	Kansas City	Offensively and defensively, he's one of the game's premier right fielders.
	Gomez, Alexis	L/L	6-2/160	8-6-80	Wilmington	An outfield prospect who needs more time in the minor leagues.
6	McCarty, Dave	R/L	6-5/215	11-23-69	Kansas City	He can back up at first and in the outfield and supply power off the bench.
14	Quinn, Mark	R/R	6-1/195	5-21-74	Kansas City, Omaha	Last year's Rookie of the Year candidate will open the season in left field.

THE COACHING STAFF

Tony Muser, manager: The low-key Muser has dragged the Royals out of the A.L. Central cellar and given the sucessful expansion franchise new life. The Royals will put a lot of runs on the board, play with enthusiasm and never quit, a reflection on Muser's professional ethics. Muser has been knocked for his use of the bullpen, which continually has lost leads over the last two seasons. But it will be interesting to see if he can change that perception with the addition of closer Roberto Hernandez and setup man Doug Henry.

Rich Dauer: The former Baltimore infielder has survived the transition from Boone to Muser and returns for another season as third base coach. Dauer has worked eight years in the Royals' system.

Tom Gamboa: The Royals new bullpen coach inherits a monster. But he should benefit greatly by the addition of Hernandez and Henry and several other new arms.

Lamar Johnson: He replaced Tom Poquette as hitting coach in 1999 after working in the same position for Milwaukee and has received rave reviews. The Royals rank among the A.L. leaders in most offensive categories and the young lineup will continue to benefit from his teaching.

Jamie Quirk: Another Boone-regime holdover, Quirk will continue as Muser's righthand man. Before joining Boone's staff in 1996, Quirk served two years as bullpen coach.

Brent Strom: He begins his second season as Royals pitching coach after replacing Mark Wiley. Strom spent the 1998 and 1999 seasons in the Montreal Expos organization, 1997 with the San Diego Padres and the previous seven seasons with the Houstons Astros organization.

Frank White: The distinguished former Royals star returns to his job as first base coach after joining Muser's staff in 1997. White, one of the most popular players in team history, is a Kansas City native.

THE TOP NEWCOMERS

Doug Henry: This experienced former Houston and San Francisco righthander will be expected to perform setup duty for new closer Roberto Hernandez.

Roberto Hernandez: He has been called the most valuable player in Tampa Bay's short major league history and he could be the answer to Kansas City's prayers. Hernandez is 36, but his fastball still reaches the plate at 98 mph and he still closes games consistently, something the Royals have not had since the prime years of Jeff Montgomery. He could be a difference maker.

A.J. Hinch: This former high-profile prospect now is a journeyman catcher trying to make a roster. If he can discover a batting stroke, he could get lots of playing time in K.C.

THE TOP PROSPECTS

Dee Brown: A young outfielder with plenty of offensive and defensive talent, Brown struggled during his late 2000 cameo with the Royals. With the trade of Damon, he will get a good, long look during spring training.

Minnesota Twins

American League Central Division

2001 SEASON

Twins 2001 SCHEDULE

Home games shaded; D—Day game (games starting before 5 p.m.)
*—All-Star Game at Safeco Field (Seattle)

APRIL

SUN	MON	TUE	WED	THU	FRI	SAT
1	2	3 D DET	4	5 D DET	6 D KC	7 D KC
8 D KC	9 DET	10 DET	11 DET	12	13 CWS	14 CWS
15 D CWS	16 KC	17 KC	18 D KC	19	20 CWS	21 D CWS
22 D CWS	23	24 BOS	25 BOS	26 BOS	27 BAL	28 BAL
29 D BAL	30 NYY					

MAY

SUN	MON	TUE	WED	THU	FRI	SAT
		1 NYY	2 NYY	3	4 KC	5 KC
6 D KC	7	8 NYY	9 NYY	10 NYY	11 KC	12 KC
13 D KC	14 KC	15 BOS	16 BOS	17 D BOS	18 BAL	19 D BAL
20 D BAL	21	22 SEA	23 D SEA	24	25 OAK	26 DH OAK
27 D OAK	28	29 ANA	30 ANA	31 ANA		

JUNE

SUN	MON	TUE	WED	THU	FRI	SAT
					1 TEX	2 TEX
3 D TEX	4 CLE	5 CLE	6 CLE	7 CLE	8 PIT	9 PIT
10 D PIT	11	12 HOU	13 HOU	14 HOU	15 D CUB	16 D CUB
17 D CUB	18	19 CLE	20 CLE	21 CLE	22 DET	23 DET
24 D DET	25 D DET	26 CWS	27 CWS	28 D CWS	29 DET	30 DET

JULY

SUN	MON	TUE	WED	THU	FRI	SAT
1 D DET	2 CWS	3 CWS	4 CWS	5 CWS	6 CIN	7 CIN
8 D CIN	9	10 *	11	12 MIL	13 MIL	14 MIL
15 D STL	16 STL	17 STL	18 OAK	19 OAK	20 SEA	21 SEA
22 D SEA	23 D SEA	24 OAK	25 OAK	26 D OAK	27 SEA	28 D SEA
29 D SEA	30	31 TOR				

AUGUST

SUN	MON	TUE	WED	THU	FRI	SAT
			1 TOR	2 D TOR	3 KC	4 KC
5 D KC	6	7 CLE	8 CLE	9 D CLE	10 TB	11 D TB
12 D TB	13 D TB	14 CLE	15 CLE	16 CLE	17 TB	18 TB
19 D TB	20 TOR	21 TOR	22 TOR	23 D TOR	24 KC	25 KC
26 D KC	27	28 TEX	29 TEX	30 TEX	31 ANA	

SEPTEMBER

SUN	MON	TUE	WED	THU	FRI	SAT
						1 ANA
2 D ANA	3	4 TEX	5 TEX	6 TEX	7 ANA	8 ANA
9 D ANA	10 DET	11 DET	12 DET	13 D DET	14 CWS	15 D CWS
16 D CWS	17	18 DET	19 DET	20 D DET	21 CLE	22 CLE
23 D CLE	24	25 CWS	26 CWS	27 D CWS	28 CLE	29 D CLE
30 D CLE						

FRONT-OFFICE DIRECTORY

Owner .... Carl R. Pohlad
President .... Jerry Bell
Chairman of executive committee .... Howard Fox
Directors .... Carl R. Pohlad, Eloise Pohlad, James O. Pohlad, Robert C. Pohlad, William M. Pohlad, T. Geron (Jerry) Bell, Kirby Puckett, Chris Clouser
Senior vice president, business affairs .... Dave St. Peter
Vice president, general manager .... Terry Ryan
Vice president, assistant general manager .... Bill Smith
Assistant general manager .... Wayne Krivsky
Executive vice president, baseball .... Kirby Puckett
Vice president, operations .... Matt Hoy
Director of minor leagues .... Jim Rantz
Director of scouting .... Mike Radcliff
Director of baseball operations .... Rob Antony
Traveling secretary .... Remzi Kiratli
Manager, media relations .... Sean Harlin

MINOR LEAGUE AFFILIATES

Class	Team	League	Manager
AAA	Edmonton	Pacific Coast	John Russell
AA	New Britain	Eastern	Stan Cliburn
A	Fort Myers	Florida State	Jose Marzan
A	Quad City	Midwest	Jeff Carter
Rookie	Elizabethton	Appalachian	Rudy Hernandez
Rookie	Gulf Coast Twins	Gulf Coast	Al Newman

BROADCAST INFORMATION

Radio: WCCO-AM (830).
TV: KMSP-TV (Channel 9).
Cable TV: Midwest SportsChannel.

SPRING TRAINING

Ballpark (city): Lee County Sports Complex (Fort Myers, Fla.).
Ticket information: 800-33-TWINS.

ASSISTANCE STAFF

Team physicians
Dr. Dan Buss
Dr. Tom Jetzer
Dr. VeeJay Eyunni
Dr. John Steubs

Scouts
Vern Followell (Pro Scouting Supervisor)
Deron Johnson (West Supervisor)
Earl Frishman (East Supervisor)
Mike Ruth (Midwest Supervisor)
Joel Lepel (Midwest Supervisor)
Kevin Bootay
Larry Corrigan
Marty Esposito
John Leavitt
Lee MacPhail
Gregg Miller
Tim O'Neil
Mark Quimuyog
Brad Weitzel
John Wilson
Ellsworth Brown
Cal Ermer
Bill Harford
Bill Lohr
Bill Mele
Bill Milos
Hector Otero
Ricky Taylor
Jay Weitzel
Mark Wilson

International scouts
David Kim
Jose Leon
Howard Norsetter
Yoshi Okamoto
Johnny Sierra

BALLPARK INFORMATION

Ballpark (capacity, surface)
Hubert H. Humphrey Metrodome
(48,678, artificial)
Address
34 Kirby Puckett Place
Minneapolis, MN 55415
Official website
www.twinsbaseball.com
Business phone
612-375-1366
Ticket information
1-800-33-TWINS
Ticket prices
$25 (lower deck club level)
$23 (Diamond View level)
$15 (lower deck reserved)
$10 (upper deck club level; g.a., lower LF)
$5 (g.a., upper deck)
Field dimensions (from home plate)
To left field at foul line, 343 feet
To center field, 408 feet
To right field at foul line, 327 feet
First game played
April 6, 1982 (Mariners 11, Twins 7)

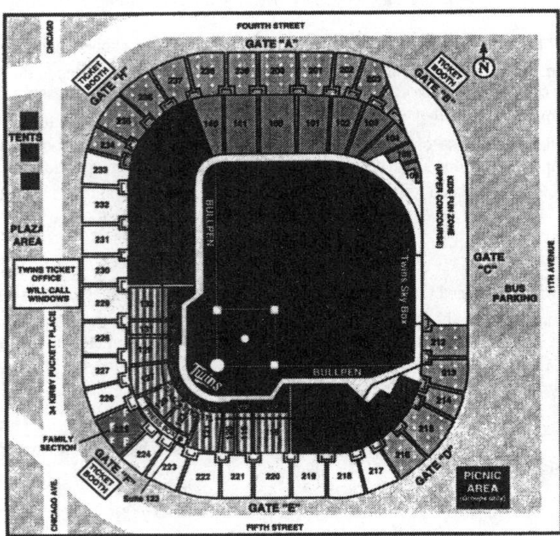

Follow the Twins all season at: www.sportingnews.com/baseball/teams/twins/

TWINS SPRING ROSTER

No.	PITCHERS	B/T	Ht./Wt.	Born	2000 clubs	Projection
	Balfour, Grant	R/R	6-2/170	12-30-77	Fort Myers	Can start or relieve, coaches like his arm and concentration.
59	Cressend, Jack	R/R	6-1/185	5-13-75	Salt Lake, Minnesota	Power pitcher struggled in 11 big-league innings, should be middle reliever.
18	Guardado, Eddie	R/L	6-0/194	10-2-70	Minnesota	Invaluable versatile lefty can close, set up or even spot start if needed.
32	Hawkins, LaTroy	R/R	6-5/204	12-21-72	Minnesota	Finally showing promise of years ago with team-high 14 saves, 3.39 ERA.
51	Kinney, Matt	R/R	6-5/220	12-16-76	New Britain, Salt Lake, Minn.	Has one of the best arms in the organization but still struggles with control.
	Knight, Brandon	L/R	6-0/170	10-1-75	Columbus	Team-high 10 wins for Yankees' Class AAA club; held hitters to .243 BA.
	Lohse, Kyle	R/R	6-2/190	10-4-78	New Britain	Was 3-18 in Class AA with a team-high 124 strikeouts.
	Martinez, Willie	R/R	6-2/180	1-4-78	Buffalo, Cleveland	Indians prospect couldn't crack starting rotation in Cleveland.
53	Mays, Joe	B/R	6-1/185	12-10-75	Minnesota, Salt Lake	Inconsistent, has shown signs of brilliance at times; needs confidence in stuff.
20	Miller, Travis	R/L	6-3/215	11-2-72	Minnesota	Another bullpen anchor; gives up too many hits but works out of jams (3.90 ERA).
	Mills, Ryan	L/R	6-5/205	7-21-77	Quad City, New Britain	Could be ace in waiting; has tremendous arm but has problems harnessing it.
21	Milton, Eric	L/L	6-3/220	8-4-75	Minnesota	Money says Radke is the ace; smart money says Milton is the future.
52	Mota, Danny	R/R	6-0/170	10-9-75	Ft. Myers, N. Brit., S. Lake, Minn.	Made jump from Class A to bigs last year; 82 IP and 97 Ks combined in minors.
22	Radke, Brad	R/R	6-2/188	10-27-72	Minnesota	Struggled to mediocre 12-16 mark; opponents hit at alarming .286 clip.
55	Redman, Mark	L/L	6-5/220	1-5-74	Minnesota	Rookie of Year candidate before faltering down stretch; could win 15-17 games.
	Rincon, Juan	R/R	5-11/190	1-23-79	Fort Myers, New Britain	Extremely raw, but durable pitcher; is at least two years away.
	Rivera, Saul	R/R	5-11/155	12-7-77	Fort Myers, New Britain	Great stuff, had 92 Ks in 75 innings between Class A and AA.
33	Romero, J.C.	B/L	5-11/195	6-4-76	Minnesota, Fort Myers, Salt Lake	Could contend for No. 5 starter's spot; more likely suited for bullpen role.
57	Santana, Johan	L/L	6-0/195	3-13-79	Minnesota	Yet another young lefty in the bullpen; allowed 158 hits and walks in 86 innings.
	Thomas, Brad	L/L	6-3/205	10-22-77	Fort Myers, New Britain	Aussie has live arm, lost his control after making jump from A to AA ball.
46	Wells, Bob	R/R	6-0/200	11-1-66	Minnesota	The other half of the closer tandem. Career is experiencing resurgence.

No.	CATCHERS	B/T	Ht./Wt.	Born	2000 clubs	Projection
12	Ardoin, Danny	R/R	6-0/218	7-8-74	Sac., Modesto, Salt Lake, Minn.	Has very strong arm and is good defensively, but hit just .125.
24	LeCroy, Matt	R/R	6-2/225	12-13-75	Minn., New Britain, Salt Lake	No. 1 catcher on opening day finished with .174 average; could also play first.
39	Moeller, Chad	R/R	6-3/210	2-18-75	Salt Lake, Minnesota	Another solid defensive backstop struggled at plate; is coming off knee surgery.
9	Pierzynski, A.J.	L/R	6-3/220	12-30-76	New Britain, Salt Lake, Minn.	Front-runner to be starter this year, at least in platoon system.

No.	INFIELDERS	B/T	Ht./Wt.	Born	2000 clubs	Projection
28	Blake, Casey	R/R	6-2/200	8-23-73	Syracuse, Salt Lake, Minnesota	Slugged .527 in PCL, is still at least a year away from big leagues.
1	Canizaro, Jay	R/R	5-9/178	7-4-73	Salt Lake, Minnesota	Solid, blue-collar second baseman has decent pop for middle infielder.
15	Guzman, Cristian	B/R	6-0/195	3-21-78	Minnesota	Could be an All-Star in N.L.; led majors with 20 triples.
7	Hocking, Denny	B/R	5-10/183	4-2-70	Minnesota	Versatile veteran hit .298 in a variety of roles.
47	Koskie, Corey	L/R	6-3/217	6-28-73	Minnesota	Came into his own at the plate, still hasn't realized power potential
25	Mientkiewicz, Doug	L/R	6-2/200	6-19-74	Salt Lake, Minnesota	Olympic hero can play first or DH; excellent hitter if out of Tom Kelly's doghouse.
27	Ortiz, David	L/L	6-4/230	11-18-75	Minnesota	Free swinger with tremendous power will see action at first and DH this year.
1	Rivas, Luis	R/R	5-11/175	8-30-79	New Britain, Salt Lake, Minn.	Hit .310 in 58 big-league at bats; good contact hitter with above-average speed.
	Sears, Todd	R/R	6-1/185	10-23-75	Carolina, New Britain, Salt Lake	Has hit well at every level but doesn't have much power.

No.	OUTFIELDERS	B/T	Ht./Wt.	Born	2000 clubs	Projection
31	Allen, Chad	R/R	6-1/195	2-6-75	Salt Lake, Minnesota	If he improved his plate discipline, he could be a great hitter.
40	Barnes, John	R/R	6-2/205	4-24-76	Salt Lake, Minnesota	Crushed pitchers to tune of .365 in AAA; hit .351 in 37 ABs with big club.
30	Buchanan, Brian	R/R	6-4/230	7-21-73	Salt Lake, Minnesota	Power-hitting RBI machine was overmatched in late-season callup.
48	Hunter, Torii	R/R	6-2/205	7-18-75	Minnesota	.280 BA is deceiving; could add 20 points if he wasn't free swinger.
11	Jones, Jacque	L/L	5-10/176	4-25-75	Minnesota	Led team with 19 HR, .463 SLG; covers serious ground in the outfield.
50	Lawton, Matt	L/R	5-10/186	11-3-71	Minnesota	The team's lone All-Star can do everything well.

THE COACHING STAFF

Tom Kelly. manager: Has been manager since September 1986; some question his rapport with younger players and whether he holds grudges.

Ron Gardenhire: Has been coaching or managing since 1988, was named third base coach in late 1998.

Paul Molitor: Future Hall of Famer is in his second year of coaching for his boyhood favorite team.

Rick Stelmaszek: Bullpen coach enters his 21st season as Twins coach, longest on the staff.

Dick Such: Twins pitching coach since 1985, will have abundance of youthful talent with which to work.

Scott Ullger: Began managerial career in minors in 1988, starts second season as hitting coach.

THE TOP PROSPECTS

Ryan Mills: Had a year to forget in Class AA (0-7, 9.28 ERA), but if he can harness his stuff, the big lefty can make the jump to the bigs. Look for a late-season callup.

Brian Buchanan: Didn't get much of a chance to play last year, but he's hit at every level and there's no reason to think that'll stop anytime soon.

John Barnes: Is as pure a hitter as they come; the Twins will have to find playing time somewhere for this guy.

Danny Mota: Might still be a year or two away from sticking with the big club, but there is no doubting his arm or his stuff.

NEW YORK YANKEES

AMERICAN LEAGUE EAST DIVISION

2001 SEASON

Yankees 2001 SCHEDULE

Home games shaded; D—Day game (games starting before 5 p.m.)
*—All-Star Game at Safeco Field (Seattle)

APRIL

SUN	MON	TUE	WED	THU	FRI	SAT
1	2 D KC	3	4 KC	5 D KC	6 TOR	7 D TOR
8 D TOR	9 KC	10 KC	11 D KC	12	13 BOS	14 D BOS
15 D BOS	16 D BOS	17 TOR	18 TOR	19 TOR	20 BOS	21 D BOS
22 D BOS	23	24 SEA	25 SEA	26 SEA	27 OAK	28 D OAK
29 D OAK	30 MIN					

MAY

SUN	MON	TUE	WED	THU	FRI	SAT
		1 MIN	2 MIN	3 BAL	4 BAL	5 D BAL
6 D BAL	7	8 MIN	9 MIN	10 MIN	11 BAL	12 D BAL
13 D BAL	14	15 OAK	16 OAK	17 D OAK	18 SEA	19 D SEA
20 D SEA	21	22 BOS	23 BOS	24 D BOS	25 CLE	26 D CLE
27 D CLE	28 BOS	29	30 BOS	31		

JUNE

SUN	MON	TUE	WED	THU	FRI	SAT
					1 CLE	2 D CLE
3 D CLE	4	5 BAL	6 BAL	7 BAL	8 ATL	9 D ATL
10 ATL	11	12 MON	13 MON	14 MON	15 NYM	16 D NYM
17 NYM	18 DET	19 DET	20 DET	21 DET	22 TB	23 D TB
24 D TB	25 CLE	26 CLE	27 D CLE	28	29 TB	30 D TB

JULY

SUN	MON	TUE	WED	THU	FRI	SAT
1 D TB	2 D TB	3 BAL	4 D BAL	5 BAL	6 NYM	7 D NYM
8 D NYM	9	10 *	11	12 FLA	13 FLA	14 D FLA
15 D PHI	16 PHI	17 PHI	18 DET	19 DET	20 TOR	21 D TOR
22 D TOR	23 TOR	24 DET	25 DET	26 D DET	27 TOR	28 D TOR
29 D TOR	30	31 TEX				

AUGUST

SUN	MON	TUE	WED	THU	FRI	SAT
			1 TEX	2 D TEX	3 ANA	4 D ANA
5 D ANA	6 D ANA	7 TB	8 TB	9 TB	10 OAK	11 D OAK
12 D OAK	13	14 TB	15 TB	16 D TB	17 SEA	18 D SEA
19 D SEA	20 TEX	21 TEX	22 TEX	23 TEX	24 ANA	25 D ANA
26 ANA	27	28 TOR	29 TOR	30 D TOR	31 BOS	

SEPTEMBER

SUN	MON	TUE	WED	THU	FRI	SAT
						1 D BOS
2 D BOS	3 D TOR	4 TOR	5 TOR	6	7 BOS	8 D BOS
9 D BOS	10 BOS	11 CWS	12 CWS	13 CWS	14 TB	15 D TB
16 D TB	17 TB	18 CWS	19 CWS	20 CWS	21 BAL	22 D BAL
23 D BAL	24	25 TB	26 TB	27	28 BAL	29 D BAL
30 D BAL						

FRONT-OFFICE DIRECTORY

Principal owner .... George M. Steinbrenner III
General partners .... Hal Z. Steinbrenner, Henry C. Steinbrenner, Steven W. Swindal
President .... Randy Levine
Chief operating officer .... Lonn A. Trost
Vice president, chief financial officer .... Martin Greenspun
Vice president, ticket operations .... Frank Swaine
Vice president .... Ed Weaver
Vice president, marketing .... Deborah A. Tymon
Vice president, administration .... Sonny Hight
Special advisors .... Yogi Berra, Reggie Jackson, Clyde King, Don Mattingly, Al Rosen, Dick Williams
Vice president, general manager .... Brian Cashman
Vice president, baseball operations .... Mark Newman
Assistant general manager .... Kim Ng
Vice president, major league scouting .... Gene Michael
Vice president, international and professional scouting .... Gordon Blakeley
Vice president, scouting .... Lin Garrett
Vice president, player personnel .... Billy Connors
Special assistant to the general manager .... Stump Merrill
Director of player development .... Rob Thomson
Director of player personnel .... Damon Oppenheimer
Director of baseball operations .... Dan Matheson
Assistant directors of baseball operations .... Rigo Garcia, Tommy Larsen
Traveling secretary .... David Szen
Equipment manager .... Rob Cucuzza
Visiting clubhouse manager .... Lou Cucuzza Jr.
Assistant, video operations .... Leo Astacio
Controller .... Robert Brown
Director of stadium operations .... Kirk Randazzo
Assistant director of stadium operations .... Doug Behar
Manager, information services .... Kris Zocco
Director of media relations & publicity .... Rick Cerrone
Assistant director of media relations & publicity .... Jason Zillo
Senior advisor .... Arthur Richman
Director of concessions & hospitality .... Joel White
Director of sponsorship services .... Michael Tustani
Sponsorship development manager .... Kristin Costello
Scoreboard & broadcasting manager .... Joe Pullia
Senior coordinator, sponsorship services .... Bill O'Sullivan

MINOR LEAGUE AFFILIATES

Class	Team	League	Manager
AAA	Columbus	International	Trey Hillman
AA	Norwich	Eastern	Dan Radison
A	Greensboro	South Atlantic	Stan Hough
A	Staten Island	New York-Pennsylvania	Joe Arnold
A	Tampa	Florida State	Tom Nieto
Rookie	Gulf Coast Yankees	Gulf Coast	Derek Shelton

ASSISTANCE STAFF

Team physician
Dr. Stuart Hershon

Head trainer
Gene Monahan

Assistant trainer
Steve Donohue

Strength and conditioning coach
Jeff Mangold

Stadium superintendent
Pete Pullara

Head groundskeeper
Dan Cunningham

Major league scouts
Ron Brand, Bob Didier, Ron Hansen, Wade Taylor

Pro scouts
John Cox, Joe Caro, Bill Emslie, Mick Kelleher, Carl "Stump" Merrill, Bob Miske

Regional cross-checkers
Joe Arnold, Tim Kelly, Greg Orr

Scouts
Mike Baker, Mark Batchko, Jim Benedict, Steve Boros, Dick Groch, David Jorn, Steve Lemke, Tim McIntosh, Jeff Patterson, Scott Pleis, Cesar Presbott, Gus Quattlebaum, Steve Swail, Leon Wurth

Foreign scouting
John Cox, Ricardo Finol, Dick Groch, Karl Heron, Ruddy Jabalera, Victor Mata, Jim Patterson, Jose "Tito" Quentero, Carlos Rios, Edgar Rodriguez, Arquimedes Rojas, Freddy Tiburcio

BROADCAST INFORMATION

Radio: WABC (770-AM).
TV: WNYW-TV (Channel 5).
Cable TV: Madison Square Garden Network.

SPRING TRAINING

Ballpark (city): Legends Field (Tampa, Fla.).
Ticket information: 813-879-2244, 813-287-8844.

BALLPARK INFORMATION

Ballpark (capacity, surface)
Yankee Stadium (57,530, grass)

Address
Yankee Stadium
E. 161 St. and River Ave., Bronx, NY 10451

Official website
www.yankees.com

Business phone
718-293-4300

Ticket information
212-307-1212, 718-293-6013

Ticket prices
$65 (Championship Seat, loge)
$55 (Championship Seat, main box)
$47 (main box MVP), $42 (field box & loge box MVP)
$37 (main reserved MVP), $37 (main & loge box)
$33 (tier box), $33 (main reserved),
$17 (tier reserved), $15 (tier reserved value)
$8 (bleachers)

Field dimensions (from home plate)
To left field at foul line, 318 feet
To center field, 408 feet
To right field at foul line, 314 feet

First game played
April 18, 1923 (Yankees 4, Red Sox 1)

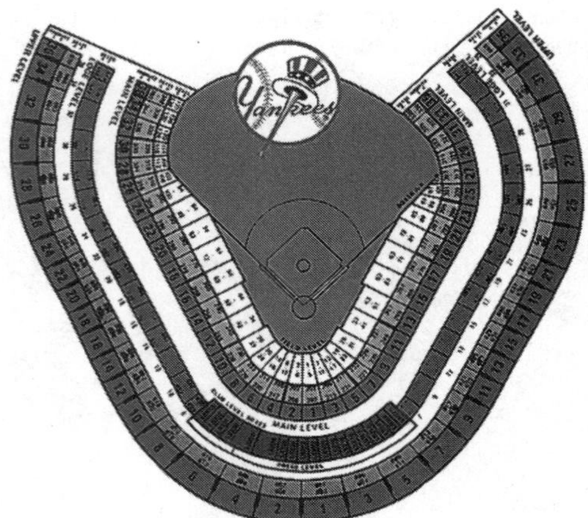

Follow the Yankees all season at: www.sportingnews.com/baseball/teams/yankees/

YANKEES SPRING ROSTER

No.	PITCHERS	B/T	Ht./Wt.	Born	2000 clubs	Projection
37	Boehringer, Brian	B/R	6-2/190	1-8-70	San Diego, Rancho Cucamonga	Established himself as a middle reliever in '96; now coming off elbow surgery.
	Bradley, Ryan	R/R	6-4/226	10-26-75	Columbus	Former first-round draft pick has stalled due to injury and ineffectiveness.
	Choate, Randy	L/L	6-3/180	9-5-75	Columbus, New York A.L.	Surprisingly effective as a situational lefty; has a good chance of joining bullpen.
22	Clemens, Roger	R/R	6-4/238	8-4-62	New York A.L.	Found old form as season wore on. Pitched better than 13-8.
64	De Los Santos, Luis	R/R	6-2/216	11-1-77	Gulf Coast Yankees	Was coming on until arm problems cost him the 2000 season.
76	Dingman, Craig	R/R	6-4/215	3-12-74	Columbus, New York A.L.	Showed early promise out of the bullpen, then struggled in September recall.
57	Einertson, Darrell	R/R	6-2/196	9-4-72	Columbus, New York A.L.	Brief but effective in relief (3.55 ERA) with Yankees in 2000.
26	Hernandez, Orlando	R/R	6-2/220	10-11-65	New York A.L., Tampa	Elbow problems limited his effectiveness, but still great in the clutch.
	Keisler, Randy	L/L	6-3/190	2-24-76	Norwich, Columbus, N.Y. A.L.	Went a combined 14-5 between classes AA and AAA last season.
	Lee, David	R/R	6-1/202	3-12-73	Colo., Colorado Springs	Reliever was acquired from the Rockies in January, will compete for roster spot.
	Lilly, Ted	L/L	6-0/185	1-4-76	Tampa, Columbus, New York A.L.	Was part of the Hideki Irabu trade with Montreal; decent minor league stats.
55	Mendoza, Ramiro	R/R	6-2/195	6-15-72	New York A.L., Tampa	Versatile righty likely will move into setup role.
35	Mussina, Mike	R/R	6-2/185	12-8-68	Baltimore	Former Orioles ace might finally get that 20-win season.
83	Noel, Ted	R/R	6-4/225	9-28-78	Tampa	Limited to four minor league appearances because of injury.
	Parker, Christian	R/R	6-1/200	7-3-75	Norwich	Righthander went 14-6 with a 3.13 ERA in AA last season.
46	Pettitte, Andy	L/L	6-5/225	6-15-72	New York A.L.	Rebounded with a 19-win season and a solid postseason.
42	Rivera, Mariano	R/R	6-2/185	11-29-69	New York A.L.	Showed he was human (five blown saves) last year but still an elite closer.
	Rogers, Brian	R/R	6-6/200	2-13-77	Norwich	Won 11 games in Class AA, but is looking at a season in Class AAA.
29	Stanton, Mike	L/L	6-1/215	6-2-67	New York A.L.	Setup man survived Steinbrenner's wrath and came up huge in postseason.
27	Watson, Allen	L/L	6-1/224	11-18-70	N.Y. A.L., Col., Tam., GC Yankees	Second southpaw in bullpen will try to overcome elbow and shoulder problems.

No.	CATCHERS	B/T	Ht./Wt.	Born	2000 clubs	Projection
9	Oliver, Joe	R/R	6-3/220	7-24-65	Seattle, Tacoma	Veteran backup is an upgrade over journeyman Chris Turner.
20	Posada, Jorge	B/R	6-2/200	8-17-71	New York A.L.	Developed into All-Star after becoming the Yankees' everyday catcher.

No.	INFIELDERS	B/T	Ht./Wt.	Born	2000 clubs	Projection
	Almonte, Erick	R/R	6-2/180	2-1-78	Norwich	Shortstop prospect hit well in Class AA; might need to learn another position.
15	Bellinger, Clay	R/R	6-3/215	11-18-68	New York A.L., Columbus	Valuable reserve is one of the savviest baserunners in the business.
18	Brosius, Scott	R/R	6-1/202	8-15-66	New York A.L., Tampa	Offensive numbers represent either a big decline or injuries taking toll.
2	Jeter, Derek	R/R	6-3/195	6-26-74	New York A.L., Tampa	A bargain at any price, but his production dipped a little last year.
68	Jimenez, D'Angelo	R/R	6-0/194	12-21-77	GC Yankees, Tampa, Columbus	Missed most of 2000 after automobile accident; might end up at second.
70	Johnson, Nick	L/L	6-3/224	9-19-78	DID NOT PLAY	First baseman sat out the season due to a wrist injury; still a top prospect.
11	Knoblauch, Chuck	R/R	5-9/175	7-7-68	New York A.L., Tampa	His dreadful defense has the team considering a shift to left field or DH.
24	Martinez, Tino	L/R	6-2/210	12-7-67	New York A.L.	His 94 RBIs represented his lowest total in six years.
	Seabol, Scott	R/R	6-4/200	5-17-75	Norwich	The nominal successor to Brosius at third base; hit 20 HRs in Class AA.
14	Sojo, Luis	R/R	5-11/185	1-3-66	Pittsburgh, New York A.L.	Bench player who made a big difference late, particularly in the postseason.
58	Soriano, Alfonso	R/R	6-1/160	1-7-78	New York A.L., Columbus	Talented but maddeningly inconsistent.

No.	OUTFIELDERS	B/T	Ht./Wt.	Born	2000 clubs	Projection
61	Frank, Mike	L/L	6-2/195	1-14-75	Louisville, Chatt., Columbus	Was part of Denny Neagle trade with Reds; organizational player at best.
31	Hill, Glenallen	R/R	6-3/230	3-22-65	Chicago N.L., New York A.L.	Caught fire after coming over in trade; hit 16 HRs in 40 games with Yanks.
28	Justice, David	L/L	6-3/200	4-14-66	Cleveland, New York A.L.	Another key mid-season addition; finished with 41 HRs and 118 RBIs overall.
84	McDonald, Donzell	B/R	5-11/180	2-20-75	Columbus, Norwich	Unlikely to make the varsity; struggled at two minor league levels in 2000.
21	O'Neill, Paul	L/L	6-4/215	2-25-63	New York A.L.	Back for one final go-round; quietly drove in 100 runs last year.
81	Pena, Wily	R/R	6-3/215	1-23-82	Greensboro, Staten Island	19-year-old prospect just reaching high Class A despite major league contract.
47	Spencer, Shane	R/R	5-11/225	2-20-72	New York A.L.	Was headed for a productive season until tearing up a knee.
51	Williams, Bernie	B/R	6-2/205	9-13-68	New York A.L.	Posted career highs in home runs and RBIs.

THE COACHING STAFF

Joe Torre, manager: Continued his successful stint as Yankees manager last season by leading team to fourth World Series title in last five years. He has won just under 500 games in five years on the job.

Willie Randolph: Turned down a chance to manage the Reds because the money wasn't right.

Lee Mazzilli: A candidate, along with Randolph, to succeed Torre as manager someday.

Mel Stottlemyre: Left the club in midseason to undergo cancer treatments; pitching staff respects him greatly.

Don Zimmer: Baseball lifer has become Torre's right-hand man; an unlikely close friend of Jeter.

Tony Cloninger: Former pitcher hit two grand slams in a game 35 years ago. Now he keeps the bullpen going strong.

Gary Denbo: The players' choice to succeed Chris Chambliss as hitting instructor.

Tom Nieto: Joins the staff as catching instructor after managing in the club's minor league system.

THE TOP NEWCOMERS

Brian Boehringer: Former Yankee returns to New York; can throw out of the bullpen or start a game. Will be looked on to fill the shoes of departed reliever Jeff Nelson.

Mike Mussina: His arrival gives the Yankees perhaps one of the best starting rotations in the history of baseball.

Joe Oliver: Brought in to back-up Posada at the catcher position after a solid season with the Mariners. Can still hit a little and plays solid defense.

THE TOP PROSPECTS

Erick Almonte: Solid shortstop prospect who can hit for power and average. The Yankees may think about moving Almonte to another position with Jeter likely locked into the shortstop position for years to come.

Randy Keisler: He is a solid starter with good control. May be used in the bullpen for a few seasons before finally cracking the rotation.

OAKLAND ATHLETICS

AMERICAN LEAGUE WEST DIVISION

2001 SEASON

Athletics
2001 SCHEDULE
Home games shaded; D—Day game (games starting before 5 p.m.)
*—All-Star Game at Safeco Field (Seattle)

APRIL

SUN	MON	TUE	WED	THU	FRI	SAT
1	2 SEA	3 SEA	4 D SEA	5	6 ANA	7 D ANA
8 D ANA	9	10 SEA	11 SEA	12 D SEA	13 TEX	14 D TEX
15 TEX	16 ANA	17 ANA	18 ANA	19 TEX	20 TEX	21 TEX
22 D TEX	23	24 CWS	25 CWS	26 CWS	27 NYY	28 D NYY
29 D NYY	30					

MAY

SUN	MON	TUE	WED	THU	FRI	SAT
		1 TOR	2 TOR	3 D TOR	4 BOS	5 D BOS
6 BOS	7	8 TOR	9 TOR	10 TOR	11 BOS	12 D BOS
13 D BOS	14	15 NYY	16 NYY	17 D NYY	18 CWS	19 D CWS
20 D CWS	21	22 KC	23 KC	24	25 MIN	26 DH MIN
27 D MIN	28	29 TB	30 D TB	31 D TB		

JUNE

SUN	MON	TUE	WED	THU	FRI	SAT
					1 BAL	2 D BAL
3 D BAL	4	5 ANA	6 ANA	7 ANA	8 SF	9 SF
10 D SF	11	12 SD	13 SD	14 D SD	15 SF	16 D SF
17 D SF	18 SEA	19 SEA	20 SEA	21 D SEA	22 TEX	23 D TEX
24 D TEX	25	26 SEA	27 SEA	28 D SEA	29 TEX	30 TEX

JULY

SUN	MON	TUE	WED	THU	FRI	SAT
1 TEX	2 ANA	3 ANA	4 D ANA	5 D ANA	6 ARI	7 ARI
8 D ARI	9	10 *	11	12 LA	13 LA	14 D LA
15 D COL	16 COL	17 D COL	18 MIN	19 MIN	20 KC	21 KC
22 KC	23 KC	24 MIN	25 MIN	26 D MIN	27 KC	28 D KC
29 D KC	30	31 CLE				

AUGUST

SUN	MON	TUE	WED	THU	FRI	SAT
			1 CLE	2 CLE	3 DET	4 DET
5 D DET	6 D DET	7 BOS	8 BOS	9 D BOS	10 NYY	11 D NYY
12 D NYY	13	14 TOR	15 TOR	16 D TOR	17 CWS	18 D CWS
19 D CWS	20 CLE	21 CLE	22 CLE	23 D CLE	24 DET	25 D DET
26 D DET	27	28 BAL	29 BAL	30 BAL	31 TB	

SEPTEMBER

SUN	MON	TUE	WED	THU	FRI	SAT
						1 D TB
2 D TB	3 BAL	4 BAL	5 D BAL	6	7 TB	8 D TB
9 D TB	10 TEX	11 TEX	12 D TEX	13 ANA	14 ANA	15 D ANA
16 ANA	17	18 TEX	19 TEX	20 TEX	21 SEA	22 D SEA
23 D SEA	24	25 ANA	26 ANA	27 D ANA	28 SEA	29 SEA
30 D SEA						

FRONT-OFFICE DIRECTORY

Owners .... Stephen C. Schott, Ken Hofmann
President .... Michael P. Crowley
Vice president and general manager .... Billy Beane
Assistant general manager .... Paul DePodesta
Special assistant to general manager .... Bill Rigney
Director of player development .... Keith Lieppman
Director of player personnel .... J.P. Ricciardi
Director of scouting .... Grady Fuson
Director of minor league operations .... Ted Polakowski
Director of baseball administration .... Pam Pitts
Traveling secretary .... Mickey Morabito
Scouting and player development coordinator .... Danny McCormack
Baseball operations assistant .... Dave Forst
Vice president, broadcasting and communications .... Ken Pries
Director of public relations .... Jim Young
Baseball information manager .... Mike Selleck
Broadcasting manager .... Robert Buan
Vice president, stadium operations .... David Rinetti
Vice president, sales and marketing .... David Alioto
Director of corporate sales .... Franklin Lowe
Director of promotions and special events .... Susan Weiglein
Director of ticket sales .... Steve Fanelli
Director of business services .... David Lozow
Executive assistant .... Carolyn Jones
Executive assistant, baseball operations .... Betty Shinoda

MINOR LEAGUE AFFILIATES

Class	Team	League	Manager
AAA	Sacramento	Pacific Coast	Bob Geren
AA	Midland	Texas	Tony DeFrancesco
A	Modesto	California	Greg Sparks
A	Vancouver	Northwest	Dave Joppie
A	Visalia	California	Juan Navarette
Rookie	Scotttsdale A's	Arizona	John Kuehl

BROADCAST INFORMATION

Radio: KABL-AM (960).
TV: KICU-TV (Channel 36).
Cable TV: Fox Sports Bay Area.

SPRING TRAINING

Ballpark (city): Phoenix Stadium (Phoenix, Ariz.).
Ticket information: 602-392-0074.

ASSISTANCE STAFF

Team physician
Dr. Allan Pont

Team orthopedist
Dr. Jerrald Goldman

Trainers
Larry Davis
Steven Sayles

Equipment manager
Steve Vucinich

Visiting clubhouse manager
Mike Thalblum

Special assignment scout
Dick Bogard

National cross-checkers
Ron Hopkins
Chris Pittaro

Major League advance scout
Bob Johnson

Supervisor of international scouting
Eric Kubota

Scouts
Steve Bowden
Tom Clark
Ruben Escalera
Kelly Heath
Tim Holt
John Kuehl
Rick Magnante
Gary McGraw
Kelsey Mucker
Billy Owens
John Poloni
Jim Pransky
Will Shock
Rich Sparks
Ron Vaughn

BALLPARK INFORMATION

Ballpark (capacity, surface)
Network Associates Coliseum (43,662, grass)

Address
Oakland Athletics
7677 Oakport St., Suite 200
Oakland, CA 94621

Official website
www.oaklandathletics.com

Business phone
510-638-4900

Ticket information
510-638-4627

Ticket prices
$30 (plaza club)
$25 (MVP infield)
$19 (field level-infield)
$18 (field level, plaza-infield)
$16 (plaza)
$8 (upper reserved)
$6 (bleachers)

Field dimensions (from home plate)
To left field at foul line, 330 feet
To center field, 400 feet
To right field at foul line, 330 feet

First game played
April 17, 1968 (Orioles 4, Athletics 1)

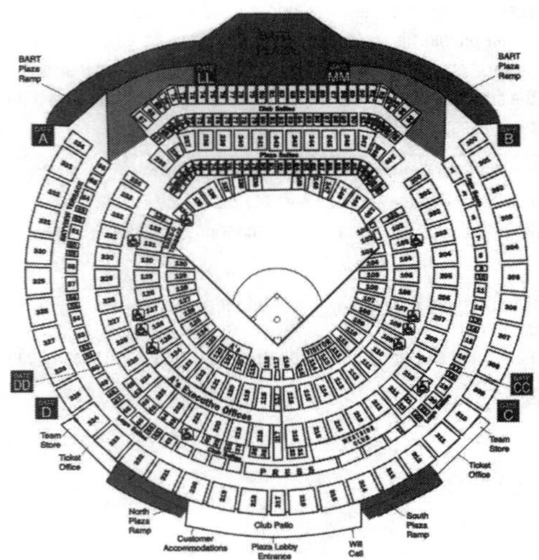

Follow the Athletics all season at: www.sportingnews.com/baseball/teams/athletics/

ATHLETICS SPRING ROSTER

No.	PITCHERS	B/T	Ht./Wt.	Born	2000 clubs	Projection
51	Vizcaino, Luis	R/R	5-11/169	6-1-77	Oakland, Sacramento	Headed for middle relief role or Class AAA.
36	Belitz, Todd	L/L	6-3/200	10-23-75	Durham, Sacramento, Oakland	Lefty might make squad as situational reliever.
	Bradford, Chad	R/R	6-5/205	9-14-74	Charlotte, Chicago A.L.	This sidearm thrower has a lot of potential and should gain a bullpen spot.
49	Enochs, Chris	R/R	6-3/225	10-11-75	Visalia	Has battled shoulder injuries the past few seasons.
	Guthrie, Mark	R/L	6-4/215	9-22-65	Chi. N.L., T.B., Tor.	He will battle for final spot in rotation, could pitch out of bullpen too.
32	Harville, Chad	R/R	5-9/180	9-16-76	Sacramento	Has tremendous velocity and may be the closer of the future.
31	Heredia, Gil	R/R	6-1/221	10-26-65	Oakland	Quiet, unassuming hurler again put up impressive numbers in 2000.
15	Hudson, Tim	R/R	6-0/160	7-14-75	Oakland	Nobody could have predicted his 20-win season from a sixth-round pick.
58	Ireland, Eric	R/R	6-1/170	3-11-77	Round Rock	Has a killer curveball, but suspect fastball has him stuck in the lower levels.
44	Isringhausen, Jason	R/R	6-3/210	9-7-72	Oakland	First full season as A's closer included his first ever All-Star appearance.
	Lidle, Cory	R/R	5-11/180	3-22-72	Durham, Tampa Bay	Impressed A's enough to trade for him. Will battle for spot in rotation.
52	Magnante, Mike	L/L	6-1/185	6-17-65	Oakland, Sacramento	This situational lefty struggled last season – hitters batted .311 against him.
33	Mathews, T.J.	R/R	6-1/214	1-19-70	Oakland, Sacramento	Chances of being a closer was shot last year by a 6.03 ERA.
45	Mecir, Jim	B/R	6-1/210	5-16-70	Tampa Bay, Oakland	After years of mediocrity, he has quietly become one of the best middle relievers.
59	Miller, Justin	R/R	6-2/195	8-27-77	Midland, Sacramento	This hard thrower will start at Class AAA and might be late season callup.
20	Mulder, Mark	L/L	6-6/200	8-5-77	Sacramento, Oakland	Was knocked around his rookie season, but always kept composure on the mound.
40	Olivares, Omar	R/R	6-1/205	7-6-67	Oakland, Modesto, Sacramento	Injuries and the arrival of youngsters were reasons for 6.75 ERA last season.
57	Pena, Juan	L/L	6-3/165	6-4-79	Modesto	At 21, this lefty has the pro scouts wringing their hands.
30	Prieto, Ariel	R/R	6-2/247	10-22-69	Sacramento, Oakland	He landed six emergency starts last season, but the team has more depth this year.
53	Snow, Bert	R/R	6-1/190	3-23-77	Sacramento, Midland	Had 101 strikeouts in 69-plus innings last season.
29	Tam, Jeff	R/R	6-1/202	8-19-70	Oakland	Solid bullpen contributor last season and will be again this season.
54	Vasquez, Leo	L/L	6-4/193	7-1-73	Midland	A big lefty with legitimate strikeout stuff. He'll spend the year at Class AAA.
75	Zito, Barry	L/L	6-4/205	5-13-78	Sacramento, Oakland	He has tremendous stuff, could hit some bumps in the road.

No.	CATCHERS	B/T	Ht./Wt.	Born	2000 clubs	Projection
13	Fasano, Sal	R/R	6-2/230	8-10-71	Oakland	The portly backstop is a solid backup for youngster Ramon Hernandez.
55	Hernandez, Ramon	R/R	6-0/227	5-20-76	Oakland	With A.J. Hinch now in Kansas City, the job is Hernandez's to lose.

No.	INFIELDERS	B/T	Ht./Wt.	Born	2000 clubs	Projection
49	Bellhorn, Mark	B/R	6-4/214	8-23-74	Sacramento, Oakland	Versatility and switch-hitting capabilities warrant a job, but that's all.
3	Chavez, Eric	L/R	6-0/204	12-7-77	Oakland	Streaky hitter's stats are slowly climbing year by year.
16	Giambi, Jason	L/R	6-3/235	1-8-71	Oakland	The ultimate team player. He's a great player and a super locker-room presence.
7	Giambi, Jeremy	L/L	6-0/200	9-30-74	Oakland, Sacramento	Jason's little bro will platoon in right.
37	Hart, Jason	R/R	6-3/225	9-5-77	Midland, Sacramento	This big first baseman has hit at every level, but is blocked by Jason Giambi.
11	Menechino, Frank	R/R	5-9/175	1-7-71	Oakland, Sacramento	Ortiz has the bead on the starting second base job, leaving him as a utility player.
2	Ortiz, Jose	R/R	5-9/177	6-13-77	Sacramento, Oakland	Oakland's top prospect has arrived. They have big plans for Ortiz.
5	Piatt, Adam	R/R	6-2/195	2-8-76	Sacramento, Oakland	Piatt has a big bat and will platoon in right field.
9	Saenz, Olmedo	R/R	6-0/185	10-8-70	Oakland, Sacramento	Versatile utilityman surprised team with a .313 average last year.
21	Salazar, Oscar	R/R	6-0/155	6-27-78	Sacramento, Midland	Can play all over the infield, but he'll only be an emergency call-up.
4	Tejada, Miguel	R/R	5-9/188	5-25-76	Oakland	This 5-9 shortstop jumped into the 30-homer club at age 24.
50	Valdez, Mario	L/R	6-1/210	11-19-74	Salt Lake, Sac., Visalia, Oak.	First baseman is playing for third organization in four years.

No.	OUTFIELDERS	B/T	Ht./Wt.	Born	2000 clubs	Projection
22	Byrnes, Eric	R/R	6-2/205	2-16-76	Midland, Sacramento, Oakland	Could be a legitimate .300 hitter in the majors, but has no place to play regularly.
28	Christenson, Ryan	R/R	6-0/210	3-28-74	Oakland	He hit .248 last season, doesn't have any power and can't steal bases.
	Damon, Johnny	L/L	6-2/190	11-5-73	Kansas City	A's traded for him to make a run at World Series.
24	Encarnacion, Mario	R/R	6-2/205	9-24-77	Sacramento, Modesto	Young Dominican has been slow to develop plate discipline and baseball skills.
12	Long, Terrence	L/L	6-1/190	2-29-76	Sacramento, Oakland	Showed enough power to be moved out of the leadoff spot.

No.	DESIGNATED HITTER	B/T	Ht./Wt.	Born	2000 clubs	Projection
5	Jaha, John	R/R	6-1/217	5-27-66	Oakland, Sacramento, Modesto	If healthy, will provide A's with much needed righthanded bat.

THE COACHING STAFF

Art Howe, manager: Led the A's to a division title last year and expectations are high this year with young talent and addition of Johnny Damon. Look for Howe to have this team ready to make a run at the World Series. But first they have to be ready for an ultra-competitive A.L. West.

Thad Bosley: Returns as the team's hitting coach for a third season.

Brad Fischer: Fischer enters his 23rd season in teh A's organization and fifth as bullpen coach.

Ken Macha: Hot managing prospect begins third season as Howe's bench coach.

Rick Peterson: Has talented group of young pitchers to work with in his fourth season as pitching coach.

Mike Quade: Begins second season as first base coach after spending 13 years as minor league manager.

Ron Washington: Continues to coach the infield and coach third base for a fifth season.

THE TOP NEWCOMERS

Johnny Damon: Provides the A's with solid defense in left or center field and the dynamic leadoff hitter that they have been searching for.

Mark Guthrie: He will be tried out as a starter, but he will have to win the job. If not a starter he can come out of the bullpen like he did last season.

Cory Lidle: Battling for number five spot in starting rotation. Hard thrower trying to make name for himself in Oakland after bouncing around several organizations.

THE TOP PROSPECTS

Mario Encarnacion: Talented outfielder still maturing into player, but has all the skills to be a good one.

Chad Harville: Hard thrower looking to take over closer role in the not to distant future.

SEATTLE MARINERS

AMERICAN LEAGUE WEST DIVISION

2001 SEASON

Mariners 2001 SCHEDULE

Home games shaded; D—Day game (games starting before 5 p.m.)
*—All-Star Game at Safeco Field (Seattle)

APRIL

SUN	MON	TUE	WED	THU	FRI	SAT
1	2 OAK	3 OAK	4 D OAK	5	6 TEX	7 TEX
8 D TEX	9	10 OAK	11 OAK	12 D OAK	13 ANA	14 ANA
15 D ANA	16 TEX	17 TEX	18 TEX	19 ANA	20 ANA	21 D ANA
22 D ANA	23	24 NYY	25 NYY	26 NYY	27 CWS	28 CWS
29 D CWS	30					

MAY

SUN	MON	TUE	WED	THU	FRI	SAT
		1 BOS	2 BOS	3 BOS	4 TOR	5 D TOR
6 D TOR	7	8 BOS	9 BOS	10 BOS	11 TOR	12 D TOR
13 D TOR	14	15 CWS	16 CWS	17 D CWS	18 NYY	19 D NYY
20 D NYY	21	22 MIN	23 D MIN	24	25 KC	26 KC
27 D KC	28 D KC	29 BAL	30 BAL	31 BAL		

JUNE

SUN	MON	TUE	WED	THU	FRI	SAT
					1 TB	2 TB
3 D TB	4 TEX	5 TEX	6 TEX	7	8 SD	9 SD
10 D SD	11	12 COL	13 COL	14 D COL	15 SD	16 SD
17 D SD	18 OAK	19 OAK	20 OAK	21 D OAK	22 ANA	23 ANA
24 D ANA	25	26 OAK	27 OAK	28 D OAK	29 ANA	30 D ANA

JULY

SUN	MON	TUE	WED	THU	FRI	SAT
1 ANA	2 TEX	3 TEX	4 TEX	5 TEX	6 LA	7 D LA
8 D LA	9	10 *	11	12 SF	13 SF	14 D SF
15 D ARI	16 ARI	17 D ARI	18 KC	19 KC	20 MIN	21 MIN
22 D MIN	23 D MIN	24 KC	25 KC	26 KC	27 MIN	28 D MIN
29 D MIN	30	31 DET				

AUGUST

SUN	MON	TUE	WED	THU	FRI	SAT
			1 DET	2 DET	3 CLE	4 CLE
5 D CLE	6 CLE	7 TOR	8 TOR	9 TOR	10 CWS	11 CWS
12 D CWS	13	14 BOS	15 BOS	16 BOS	17 NYY	18 D NYY
19 D NYY	20 DET	21 DET	22 DET	23 D DET	24 CLE	25 D CLE
26 D CLE	27	28 TB	29 TB	30 D TB	31 BAL	

SEPTEMBER

SUN	MON	TUE	WED	THU	FRI	SAT
						1 D BAL
2 D BAL	3 TB	4 TB	5 TB	6	7 BAL	8 BAL
9 D BAL	10 ANA	11 ANA	12 ANA	13 TEX	14 TEX	15 D TEX
16 D TEX	17	18 ANA	19 ANA	20 D ANA	21 OAK	22 D OAK
23 D OAK	24 TEX	25 TEX	26 TEX	27	28 OAK	29 OAK
30 D OAK						

FRONT-OFFICE DIRECTORY

Chairman and chief executive officer .... Howard Lincoln
Board of directors .... Howard Lincoln, chairman; John Ellis, chairman emeritus; Minoru Arakawa; Chris Larson; John McCaw; Frank Shrontz; Craig Watjen
President and chief operating officer .... Chuck Armstrong
Executive vice president, baseball operations .... Pat Gillick
Executive vice president, business operations .... Bob Aylward
Executive vice president, finance and ballpark ops. .... Kevin Mather
Vice president, baseball administration .... Lee Pelekoudas
Vice president, scouting and player development .... Roger Jongewaard
Vice president, communications .... Randy Adamack
Vice president, ballpark operations .... Neil Campbell
Controller .... Tim Kornegay
Supervisor, Pacific Rim scouting .... Ted Heid
Director, player development .... Benny Looper
Director, professional scouting .... Ken Compton
Director, scouting .... Frank Mattox
Director, team travel .... Ron Spellecy
Director, baseball information .... Tim Hevly
Director, public information .... Rebecca Hale
Special assignment .... Woody Woodward
Coordinator of baseball technical information .... Mike Kuharich
Coordinator of minor league instruction .... Mike Goff
Home clubhouse manager .... Scott Gilbert
Visiting clubhouse manager .... Henry Genzale

MINOR LEAGUE AFFILIATES

Class	Team	League	Manager
AAA	Tacoma	Pacific Coast	Dan Rohn
AA	San Antonio	Texas	Dave Brundage
A	Everett	Northwest	Terry Pollreisz
A	San Bernardino	California	To be announced
A	Wisconsin	Midwest	Gary Thurman
Rookie	Peoria Mariners	Arizona	Omer Munoz Jr.

BROADCAST INFORMATION

Radio: KIRO-AM (710).
TV: KIRO-TV (Channel 7).
Cable TV: Fox Sports Net Northwest.

SPRING TRAINING

Ballpark: Peoria Stadium (Peoria, Ariz.).
Ticket information: 602-784-4444.

ASSISTANCE STAFF

Medical director
Dr. Larry Pedegana
Trainers
Rick Griffin, Tom Newberg, Ken Roll
Team physicians
Dr. Mitchel Storey
Team dentist
Dr. Robert Hughes
Video coordinator
Carl Hamilton
Strength and conditioning coach
Allen Wirtala
Head groundskeeper
Bob Christopherson
Assistant groundskeeper
To be announced
Senior advisor
Bob Engle
Advance scout
Stan Williams
National cross-checker
Steve Jongewaard
Major league scouts
Bob Harrison, Bill Kearns, Steve Pope
Scouting supervisors
Curtis Dishman, Ken Madeja, John McMichen, Carroll Sembera.
Scouts
Dave Alexander, Pedro Avila, Craig Bell, Emilio Carrasquel, Rodney Davis, Sam Eldridge, Luis Fuenmayor, Phil Geisler, Pedro Grifol, Patrick Guerrero, Ron Hafner, Des Hamilton, Jae Lee, Stan Lewis, Mark Lummus, Ken Madejia, John Martin, Emiliano Martinez, David May, Mauro Mazzotti, John McMitchen, Julio Molina, Luis Molina, Joe Moreno, Omer Munoz Sr., Wayne Norton, Dana Papasedero, Myron Pines, Phil Pote, Carlos Ramirez, Steve Rath, Eric Robinson, Carroll Sembera, Scott Smith, Jamie Storvick, Harry Stricklett, Derek Valenzuela, Ray Vince, Curtis Wallace, Karl Williams

BALLPARK INFORMATION

Ballpark (capacity, surface)
Safeco Field (47,116, grass)
Address
1st Ave. S. & Atlantic
Seattle, WA 98104
Official website
www.seattlemariners.com
Business phone
206-346-4000
Ticket information
206-346-4001
Ticket prices
$37 (terrace club infield)
$32 (lower box)
$29 (terrace club outfield)
$27 (field)
$18 (view box, lower outfield reserved)
$14 (view reserved)
$9 (left field bleachers)
$5 (center field bleachers)
Field dimensions (from home plate)
To left field at foul line, 331 feet
To center field, 405 feet
To right field at foul line, 326 feet
First game played
July 15, 1999 (Padres 3, Mariners 2)

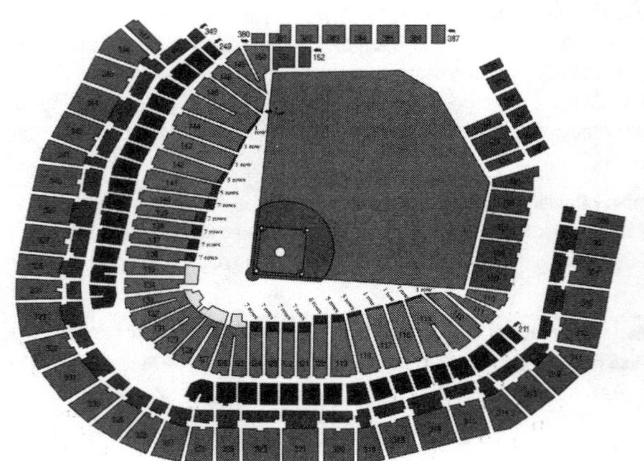

Follow the Mariners all season at: www.sportingnews.com/baseball/teams/mariners/

MARINERS SPRING ROSTER

No.	PITCHERS	B/T	Ht./Wt.	Born	2000 clubs	Projection
48	Abbott, Paul	R/R	6-3/195	9-15-67	Seattle	Solid starter who continues to improve and should be mainstay in rotation.
	Franklin, Ryan	R/R	6-3/165	3-5-73	Tacoma	Starter who could help out team in bullpen, but might start year in minors.
	Fuentes, Brian	L/L	6-4/220	8-9-75	New Haven	Hard thrower still developing skills and still a few years away from big leagues.
34	Garcia, Freddy	R/R	6-4/235	10-6-76	Seattle, Tacoma, Everett	Talented starter who could be ace of staff if he can stay injury free.
54	Halama, John	L/L	6-5/210	2-22-72	Seattle	Durable left handed starter who relies on control more than velocity.
58	Hodges, Kevin	R/R	6-4/200	6-24-73	Tacoma, Seattle	Valuleable pitcher to staff because he can start or come out of bullpen.
	Kaye, Justin	R/R	6-4/185	6-9-76	New Haven	Hard throwing closer of the future could land spot in bullpen.
55	Meche, Gil	R/R	6-3/200	9-8-78	Seattle, Tacoma, Wis., Everett	Promising starter who battled injuries last year. Should start season in rotation.
	Meyer, Jake	R/R	6-1/195	1-7-75	New Haven, AZL Mariners, Tac.	Relief pitcher coming off injury and most likely will start year in minors.
50	Moyer, Jamie	L/L	6-0/175	11-18-62	Seattle	Four consecutive seasons for Mariners with 10 wins or more.
43	Nelson, Jeff	R/R	6-8/235	11-17-66	New York A.L.	Valuable setup man who will pitch a lot of games.
36	Paniagua, Jose	R/R	6-2/190	8-20-73	Seattle	Solid relief pitcher can eat up a lot of innings.
38	Pineiro, Joel	R/R	6-1/180	9-25-78	New Haven, Tacoma, Seattle	Prospect who pitched in eight games with big club.
37	Ramsay, Robert	L/L	6-5/215	12-3-73	Tacoma, Seattle, Everett	Another key piece of the strong Mariners bullpen.
53	Rhodes, Arthur	L/L	6-2/205	10-24-69	Seattle	Left-handed reliever who threw in 72 games last year.
33	Rodriguez, Frankie	R/R	6-0/210	12-11-72	Seattle, Tacoma	Struggled at times with Mariners and trying to win spot in bullpen.
22	Sasaki, Kazuhiro	R/R	6-4/209	2-22-68	Seattle	Mariners hoping he can continue dominance of hitters in late innings.
30	Sele, Aaron	R/R	6-5/215	6-25-70	Seattle	Durable starter who has put up more than 15 wins in three straight seasons.
	Soriano, Rafael	R/R	6-1/175	12-19-79	Wisconsin	Young prospect waiting for spot in Mariner rotation to open up.
	Stark, Dennis	R/R	6-2/210	10-27-74	New Haven	Solid starter, but more likely to start season in Class AAA.
40	Tomko, Brett	R/R	6-4/215	4-7-73	Tacoma, Seattle	Highly touted pitcher who can start or relieve for Mariners.
	Watson, Mark	R/L	6-4/215	1-23-74	Buffalo, Cleveland, Tacoma	Pitcher who has bounced around and trying to win spot in bullpen.
	Wooten, Greg	R/R	6-7/210	3-30-74	New Haven	Ace of the New Haven staff could land spot; likely ticketed for Tacoma.
	Zimmerman, Jordan	R/L	6-0/200	4-28-75	AZL Mariners, Tacoma, Lanc.	Hard thrower looking for spot in bullpen.

No.	CATCHERS	B/T	Ht./Wt.	Born	2000 clubs	Projection
17	Lampkin, Tom	L/R	5-11/195	3-4-64	Tacoma, Seattle	Solid catcher and left-handed bat off bench.
16	Widger, Chris	R/R	6-2/215	5-21-71	Montreal, Seattle	Can hit with a little power, but might not land spot on team.
6	Wilson, Dan	R/R	6-3/202	3-25-69	Seattle, Everett, Tacoma	Defense continues to be solid, but offensive production has dropped off.

No.	INFIELDERS	B/T	Ht./Wt.	Born	2000 clubs	Projection
25	Bell, David	R/R	5-10/190	9-14-72	Seattle	Very good defensive third baseman and has decent bat.
	Boone, Bret	R/R	5-10/180	4-6-69	San Diego	Great glove at second and has some pop in his bat for a little guy.
	Grabowski, Jason	L/R	6-3/200	5-24-76	Tulsa	Third baseman can hit for average, but has some problems defensively.
8	Guillen, Carlos	B/R	6-1/180	9-30-75	Seattle, Tacoma	Shortstop job is his to lose with Alex Rodriguez gone.
4	McLemore, Mark	B/R	5-11/207	10-4-64	Seattle	With the addition of Boone, might see spot duty at DH and outfield.
5	Olerud, John	L/L	6-5/220	8-5-68	Seattle	Solid run producer and left handed bat in middle of line up. Also plays good defense.

No.	OUTFIELDERS	B/T	Ht./Wt.	Born	2000 clubs	Projection
19	Buhner, Jay	R/R	6-3/210	8-13-64	Seattle	Will spend some time at DH and in the outfield. Still can give team 20 home runs.
9	Cameron, Mike	R/R	6-6/190	1-8-73	Seattle	Has some speed and power. Good chance he will lead off this year.
1	Gipson, Charles	R/R	6-2/180	12-16-72	Seattle, Tacoma	Provides speed on the base paths and reliable defense in the outfield.
16	Javier, Stan	B/R	6-0/200	1-9-64	Seattle	Valuable outfielder off the bench who can still hit for average and run the bases.
18	Martin, Al	L/L	6-2/214	11-24-67	San Diego, Seattle	Solid all around outfielder who provides team with good left handed bat in line up.
	Sanders, Anthony	R/R	6-2/200	3-2-74	Tacoma, Seattle	Good outfielder who may be left off team because of log jam of players.
51	Suzuki, Ichiro	L/R	5-9/156	10-22-73	Orix	Big things are expected out of this first year player in the major leagues.

No.	DESIGNATED HITTER	B/T	Ht./Wt.	Born	2000 clubs	Projection
11	Martinez, Edgar	R/R	5-11/210	1-2-63	Seattle	Great offenisve bat who continues to drive in runs and hit for high average.

THE COACHING STAFF

Lou Pinella, manager: Continues to win games for the Mariners, but will have tough task this season with the loss of star player Alex Rodriguez. Pinella has guided the Mariners to three playoff appearances in eight seasons as manager.

John McLaren: McLaren begins his 15th season of coaching and his sixth as bench coach for Pinella.

John Moses: Joined the staff as first base and outfield coach last season after duties as advanced scout for the Mariners.

Dave Myers: Myers joins the Mariners staff and will be coaching third in his first season.

Gerald Perry: First season as Mariner hitting coach seemed to be a success last season as team belted 198 home runs and drove in 869 runs in a pitchers ball park. Perry coached in the Red Sox organization for three years before joining Seatte.

Bryan Price: Helped guide young Mariners pitching staff to solid season in his first year as pitching coach. Served as Mariners' minor league ptiching coordinator for three seasons before joining team last year.

Matt Sinatro: The former major league catcher enters his seventh season as bullpen coach.

THE TOP NEWCOMERS

Bret Boone: Solid defensively and provides good bat. Will be welcome addition for team looking to fill void of Alex Rodriguez.

Jeff Nelson: Gives the Mariners an even more dangerous bullpen. Will be a great set up man for Sasaki

Ichiro Suzuki: Line drive hitter that Mariners invested a lot of money. He racked up batting title after batting title in Japan Pacific League.

THE TOP PROSPECTS

Joel Pineiro: Starter who was 9-2 between New Haven and Tacoma in '00. Waiting for his chance to crack the starting rotation with the Mariners.

Rafael Soriano: Prospect gradually moving his way through system with Mariners anxiously awaiting his arrival. Posted 8-4 record with 2.87 ERA for Wisconsin last season.

Greg Wooten: Mariners are high on Wooten who compiled 17-3 record with 2.31 ERA in New Haven last year. Control pitcher who walked only 15 batters in 179 innnings pitched.

TAMPA BAY DEVIL RAYS

AMERICAN LEAGUE EAST DIVISION

2001 SEASON

Devil Rays 2001 SCHEDULE

Home games shaded; D—Day game (games starting before 5 p.m.)
*—All-Star Game at Safeco Field (Seattle)

APRIL

SUN	MON	TUE	WED	THU	FRI	SAT
1	2	3 TOR	4 TOR	5 D TOR	6 D BOS	7 BOS
8 D BOS	9 TOR	10 TOR	11 TOR	12	13 BAL	14 D BAL
15 D BAL	16 BAL	17 BOS	18 BOS	19 BOS	20 BAL	21 D BAL
22 D BAL	23	24 KC	25 KC	26 D KC	27 DET	28 D DET
29 D DET	30 BAL					

MAY

SUN	MON	TUE	WED	THU	FRI	SAT
		1 BAL	2 BAL	3	4 CLE	5 D CLE
6 D CLE	7	8 BAL	9 BAL	10 BAL	11 CLE	12 CLE
13 D CLE	14	15 KC	16 KC	17 KC	18 DET	19 D DET
20 D DET	21	22 TEX	23 TEX	24 TEX	25 ANA	26 D ANA
27 D ANA	28 D ANA	29 OAK	30 D OAK	31 D OAK		

JUNE

SUN	MON	TUE	WED	THU	FRI	SAT
					1 SEA	2 SEA
3 D SEA	4	5 TOR	6 TOR	7 D TOR	8 NYM	9 D NYM
10 D NYM	11	12 PHI	13 PHI	14 D PHI	15 FLA	16 FLA
17 D FLA	18	19 BOS	20 BOS	21 BOS	22 NYY	23 D NYY
24 D NYY	25 BOS	26 BOS	27 BOS	28 BOS	29 NYY	30 D NYY

JULY

SUN	MON	TUE	WED	THU	FRI	SAT
1 D NYY	2 D NYY	3 TOR	4 D TOR	5 TOR	6 FLA	7 D FLA
8 D FLA	9	10 *	11	12 MON	13 MON	14 D MON
15 D ATL	16 ATL	17 ATL	18 ANA	19 D ANA	20 TEX	21 D TEX
22 D TEX	23	24 ANA	25 ANA	26 ANA	27 TEX	28 TEX
29 TEX	30	31 BAL				

AUGUST

SUN	MON	TUE	WED	THU	FRI	SAT
			1 BAL	2 D BAL	3 CWS	4 CWS
5 D CWS	6 D CWS	7 NYY	8 NYY	9 NYY	10 MIN	11 D MIN
12 D MIN	13 D MIN	14 NYY	15 NYY	16 D NYY	17 MIN	18 MIN
19 D MIN	20	21 BAL	22 BAL	23 BAL	24 CWS	25 D CWS
26 D CWS	27	28 SEA	29 SEA	30 D SEA	31 OAK	

SEPTEMBER

SUN	MON	TUE	WED	THU	FRI	SAT
						1 D OAK
2 D OAK	3 SEA	4 SEA	5 SEA	6	7 OAK	8 D OAK
9 D OAK	10	11 BOS	12 BOS	13 BOS	14 NYY	15 D NYY
16 D NYY	17 NYY	18 BOS	19 BOS	20 BOS	21 TOR	22 TOR
23 D TOR	24	25 NYY	26 NYY	27 TOR	28 TOR	29 D TOR
30 D TOR						

FRONT-OFFICE DIRECTORY

Managing general partner/CEO ....Vincent J. Naimoli
Sr. v.p.baseball operations/general manager....Chuck LaMar
Sr. v.p.-admin. & general counsel ....John P. Higgins
Vice president of sales & marketing ....John Browne
Vice president of public relations....Rick Vaughn
Vice president of operations/facilities....Rick Nafe
Assistant general manager-baseball operations ....Bart Braun
Assistant general manager-administration ....Scott Proefrock
Special assistants to the general manager ....Eddie Bane, Bill Livesey
Director of scouting ....Dan Jennings
Senior advisor for baseball operations....Frank Howard
Field coordinator ....Tom Foley
Assistant to player development ....Mitch Lukevics
Traveling secretary ....Jeffrey Ziegler
Controller ....Patrick Smith
Director of human resources ....Louise "Jeep" Weber
Director of business administration....Bill Wiener Jr.
Senior director of corporate sales & broadcasting....Larry McCabe
Manager of broadcast operations....Joe Ciaravino
Managers of sponsorship coordination....Kelly Davis, Sean McHale, Lauren Miller
Manager of promotions & special events....Christopher Dean
Director of ticket operations....Robert Bennett
Assistant director of ticket operations....Ken Mallory
Assistant to the v.p. of public relations ....Carmen Molina
Director of publications....Matt Lorenz
Director of media relations ....Chris Costello
Assistant media relations manager ....Greg Landy
Manager of community relations ....Liz-Beth Lauck
Director of event productions & entertainment....John Franzone
Video producer....Jason Rundle
Video coordinator....Chris Fernandez

MINOR LEAGUE AFFILIATES

Class	Team	League	Manager
AAA	Durham	International	Bill Evers
AA	Orlando	Southern	Mike Ramsey
A	Bakersfield	California	To be announced
A	Charleston (S.C.)	South Atlantic	Buddy Biancalana
Rookie	Hudson Valley	New York-Pennsylvania	To be announced
Rookie	Princeton	Appalachian	Edwin Rodriguez

ASSISTANCE STAFF

Head trainer
Jamie Reed
Assistant head trainer
Ken Crenshaw
Strength & conditioning coordinator
To be announced
Medical team physician
Dr. Michael Reilly
Orthopaedic team physician
Dr. Koco Eaton
Head groundskeeper
Mike Williams
Clubhouse operations-home
Carlos Ledezma
Clubhouse operations-visitor
Guy Gallagher
Major League scouts
Jerry Gardner, Bart Johnson, Matt Keough, Al LaMacchia, Don Lindeberg, Don Williams
Crosscheckers
Jack Gillis, R.J. Harrison, Dave Roberts, Mac Seibert
Area scouts
Jonathan Bonifay, James Bonnici, Skip Bundy, Rickey Drexler, Kevin Elfering, Milt Hill, Hank King, Paul Kirsch, Benny Latino, Fred Repke, Joe Robinson Jr., Edwin Rodriguez, Scott Sealy, Dale Tilleman, Craig F. Weissmann, Doug Witt, Mike Zimmerman
Part-time scouts
Philip Elhage, Jose Perez, Juan Pringle, Junior Ramirez, Gustavo Rodriguez, Ron Stinnett, Freddy Torres, Mel Zitter

BROADCAST INFORMATION

Radio: WFLA-AM (970).
TV: MORE-TV (Channel 32); WTSP (Channel 10).
Cable TV: Fox Sports Net.

SPRING TRAINING

Ballpark (city): Florida Power Park Home of Al Lang Field (St. Petersburg, Fla.).
Ticket information: 727-825-3250.

BALLPARK INFORMATION

Ballpark (capacity, surface)
Tropicana Field (43,370, artificial)
Address
One Tropicana Drive, St. Petersburg, FL 33607
Official website
www.devilray.com
Business phone
727-825-3137
Ticket information
727-825-3250
Ticket prices
$195 (home plate box), $75 (field box)
$40 (lower club box), $35 (diamond club box, diamond club res.)
$30 (lower box), $23 (lower reserved, terrace box)
$19 (upper box), $14 (terrace reserved, outfield)
$10 (the beach, upper reserved), $8 (upper general admission)
Field dimensions (from home plate)
To left field at foul line, 315 feet
To center field, 404 feet
To right field at foul line, 322 feet
First game played
March 31, 1998 (Tigers 11, Devil Rays 6)

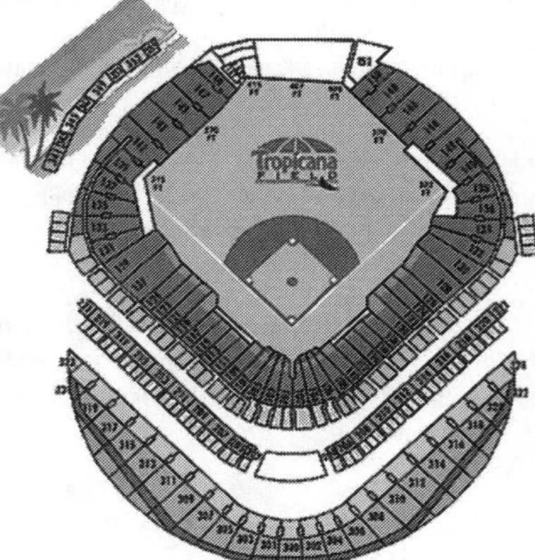

Follow the Devil Rays all season at: www.sportingnews.com/baseball/teams/devilrays/

DEVIL RAYS SPRING ROSTER

No.	PITCHERS	B/T	Ht./Wt.	Born	2000 clubs	Projection
40	Alvarez, Wilson	L/L	6-1/245	3-24-70	St. Petersburg	Can be the ace of the Devil Ray staff, but health is always a concern.
	Colome, Jesus	R/R	6-4/170	6-2-80	Midland, Orlando	Young starter needs a season of Class AAA.
38	Creek, Doug	L/L	6-0/200	3-1-69	Durham, Tampa Bay	Hard thrower out of the bullpen who will give Devil Rays a lot of games.
57	Guzman, Juan	R/R	5-11/195	10-28-66	T.B., St. Pete., Orlando, Durham	Tough starter when healthy. Missed most of last year with rotator cuff injury.
58	Harper, Travis	L/R	6-4/195	5-21-76	Orlando, Durham, Tampa Bay	On his way up through the organization and could help in rotation or bullpen.
	James, Delvin	R/R	6-4/222	1-3-78	St. Petersburg, Orlando	Solid starter moving his way up through the minors.
32	Lopez, Albie	R/R	6-2/240	8-18-71	Tampa Bay, Princeton	Valueable pitcher who can start or come out of bullpen.
	Phelps, Travis	R/R	6-2/195	7-25-77	Orlando, Durham	Starter with good velocity. Not likely to start the year with the Devil Rays.
35	Rekar, Bryan	R/R	6-3/220	6-3-72	Tampa Bay, Durham	Control pitcher who is maturing into solid starter.
24	Rupe, Ryan	R/R	6-5/230	3-31-75	Tampa Bay, Durham	Devil Rays hoping for breakthrough season in the rotation from young prospect.
	Seay, Bobby	L/L	6-2/221	6-20-78	Orlando	Good stuff, but still couple years away from making rotation.
	Standridge, Jason	R/R	6-4/217	11-9-78	St. Petersburg, Orlando	Moving his way up through organization for chance in starting rotation.
49	Sturtze, Tanyon	R/R	6-5/205	10-12-70	Chicago A.L., Tampa Bay	Valueable pitcher who will give team a lot of innings either as starter or reliever.
34	Wheeler, Dan	R/R	6-3/222	12-10-77	Tampa Bay, Durham	Durable starter not likely to make big league club yet.
	White, Matt	R/R	6-5/230	7-13-78	Orlando, Durham	Another young arm who may help in bullpen.
41	Wilson, Paul	R/R	6-5/235	3-28-73	St. Lucie, Norfolk, Tampa Bay	Devil Rays hoping former number one pick can stay healthy.
43	Yan, Esteban	R/R	6-4/230	6-22-74	Tampa Bay	Young, hard thrower who can come out of bullpen or start.

No.	CATCHERS	B/T	Ht./Wt.	Born	2000 clubs	Projection
8	Difelice, Mike	R/R	6-2/205	5-28-69	Tampa Bay	Solid defensive catcher who is good with young pitching staff.
6	Flaherty, John	R/R	6-1/200	10-21-67	Tampa Bay	Good hitting catcher who also does a nice job with throwing out base stealers.
81	Hall, Toby	R/R	6-3/205	10-21-75	Orlando, Durham, Tampa Bay	Catcher of the future who can hit for power and average.

No.	INFIELDERS	B/T	Ht./Wt.	Born	2000 clubs	Projection
	Abernathy, Brent	R/R	6-1/185	9-23-77	Syracuse, Durham	Infielder who can play several positions and help team off the bench.
	Brewer, Jace	R/R	6-0/170	8-6-79	Charleston, S.C.	2000 draft pick who Devil Rays want to get a good look at.
9	Castilla, Vinny	R/R	6-1/205	7-4-67	Tampa Bay, Durham	Devil Rays hoping he can regain form he had in Colorado.
28	Cox, Steve	L/L	6-4/222	10-31-74	Tampa Bay	Power hitter platooning in outfield.
21	Huff, Aubrey	L/R	6-4/221	12-20-76	Durham, Tampa Bay	If Castilla conitinues his struggles, Huff could see more time at third.
10	Johnson, Russ	R/R	5-10/180	2-22-73	Houston, Tampa Bay	Utility infielder with decent bat who will help team best coming off the bench.
16	Martinez, Felix	B/R	6-0/180	5-18-74	Durham, Tampa Bay	The starting shortstop position is his to lose. Decent bat, better glove.
29	McGriff, Fred	L/L	6-3/215	10-31-63	Tampa Bay	Continues to put up big power numbers, but nearing end of career.
71	Rolls, Damian	R/R	6-2/205	9-15-77	T.B., St. Petersburg, Orlando	Coming off injury plagued season and could help off the bench this year.
	Sandberg, Jared	R/R	6-3/212	3-2-78	Orlando, Durham	Solid defensive third baseman still a few years away from big leagues.
20	Smith, Bobby	R/R	6-3/190	5-10-74	Durham, Tampa Bay	Can hit for power and steal a base. Will help out team best off the bench this year.

No.	OUTFIELDERS	B/T	Ht./Wt.	Born	2000 clubs	Projection
	Grieve, Ben	L/R	6-4/230	5-4-76	Oakland	Gives Devil Rays right fielder and number three hitter in lineup.
30	Guillen, Jose	R/R	5-11/195	5-17-76	Durham, Tampa Bay	Has a chance to start this year after decent offensive season.
15	Kelly, Kenny	R/R	6-2/180	1-26-79	Orlando, Durham, Tampa Bay	Speedy outfielder still couple years away from making contribution to Devil Rays.
	Sanchez, Alex	L/L	5-10/180	8-26-76	Durham, Orlando	Very fast and can hit for average. Could be valuable off the bench.
14	Tyner, Jason	L/L	6-1/170	4-23-77	Norfolk, New York N.L., T.B.	Can hit for average and run. Might have chance to start with good training camp.
23	Vaughn, Greg	R/R	6-0/202	7-3-65	Tampa Bay	Injuries slowed him a bit last year, but still very dangerous power hitter.
4	Williams, Gerald	R/R	6-2/187	8-10-66	Tampa Bay	Durable leadoff hitter who did it all last year with 21 home runs and .274 average.
2	Winn, Randy	B/R	6-2/193	6-9-74	Durham, Tampa Bay	Very good hitter with some speed. Will be competing for time in the outfield.

THE COACHING STAFF

Larry Rothschild, manager: WIll be looked at closely this season after a disappointing year last season. The key for Rothschild will be getting his young pitching staff in order this year. Injuries hurt the team's powerful line-up last season

Wade Boggs: Joins the Devil Ray staff after hall of fame career that ended in Tampa Bay.

Jose Cardenal: Returns to coaching staff after coaching the first base position and outfielders last year. Cardenal had an 18 year major league career before turning to coaching where he has been on the coaching staff of three championship teams.

Terry Collins: Former manager of the Angels and Astros heads to the Devil Rays for his first season with the team.

Bill Fischer: Enjoyed 13 year major league career and helped guide the Red Sox pitching staff in the 1980's to one of the best staffs in the league. This is his first full season with the Devil Rays coaching staff.

Billy Hatcher: Enters his sixth season coaching in the Devil Rays organization. Hatcher played 12 seasons in the majors and will continue his duties as first base coach this season.

Hal McRae: Comes to the Devil Rays staff with managing experience after he managed the Kansas City Royals from 1991-94.

Darren Daulton: Former major league catcher who had his career cut short by injuries begins his first season as coach with the Devil Rays.

THE TOP NEWCOMERS

Ben Grieve: Solid left handed power hitter who will give Devil Rays good bat in middle of line up. His presence should help the numbers of Vaughn, McGriff and Castilla.

THE TOP PROSPECTS

Travis Harper: Pitched well in short stint with Devil Rays and showed he can help the team now. Knows how to pitch and could be in starting rotation by the end of the season.

Delvin James: Control pitcher is gradually working his way through the minors with impressive numbers. Atleast a year or two away.

Steve Cox: He will see playing time in outfield and DH this season. First base job is his after McGriff is gone.

Texas Rangers

American League West Division

2001 SEASON

Rangers 2001 SCHEDULE

Home games shaded; D—Day game (games starting before 5 p.m.)
*—All-Star Game at Safeco Field (Seattle) † Game played in San Juan, Puerto Rico.

APRIL

SUN	MON	TUE	WED	THU	FRI	SAT
1 † TOR	2	3 D ANA	4 ANA	5 ANA	6 SEA	7 SEA
8 D SEA	9	10 ANA	11 ANA	12 ANA	13 OAK	14 D OAK
15 OAK	16 SEA	17 SEA	18 SEA	19 OAK	20 OAK	21 OAK
22 D OAK	23	24 TOR	25 TOR	26	27 CLE	28 CLE
29 D CLE	30					

MAY

SUN	MON	TUE	WED	THU	FRI	SAT
		1 DET	2 DET	3 D DET	4 CWS	5 CWS
6 D CWS	7	8 DET	9 DET	10 D DET	11 CWS	12 CWS
13 D CWS	14	15 CLE	16 CLE	17 D CLE	18 TOR	19 TOR
20 D TOR	21	22 TB	23 TB	24 TB	25 BAL	26 D BAL
27 D BAL	28 BAL	29 KC	30 KC	31 D KC		

JUNE

SUN	MON	TUE	WED	THU	FRI	SAT
					1 MIN	2 MIN
3 D MIN	4 SEA	5 SEA	6 SEA	7	8 HOU	9 HOU
10 HOU	11 LA	12 LA	13 LA	14	15 HOU	16 D HOU
17 D HOU	18	19 ANA	20 ANA	21 ANA	22 OAK	23 D OAK
24 D OAK	25 ANA	26 ANA	27 ANA	28 ANA	29 OAK	30 OAK

JULY

SUN	MON	TUE	WED	THU	FRI	SAT
1 OAK	2 SEA	3 SEA	4 SEA	5 SEA	6 SD	7 D SD
8 D SD	9	10 *	11	12 COL	13 COL	14 COL
15 SF	16 SF	17 SF	18 BAL	19 BAL	20 TB	21 D TB
22 D TB	23	24 BAL	25 BAL	26 BAL	27 TB	28 TB
29 TB	30	31 NYY				

AUGUST

SUN	MON	TUE	WED	THU	FRI	SAT
			1 NYY	2 D NYY	3 BOS	4 D BOS
5 D BOS	6 BOS	7 DET	8 DET	9 DET	10 CLE	11 CLE
12 CLE	13	14 CWS	15 CWS	16 CWS	17 TOR	18 D TOR
19 D TOR	20 NYY	21 NYY	22 NYY	23 NYY	24 BOS	25 BOS
26 BOS	27	28 MIN	29 MIN	30 MIN	31 KC	

SEPTEMBER

SUN	MON	TUE	WED	THU	FRI	SAT
						1 KC
2 D KC	3	4 MIN	5 MIN	6 MIN	7 KC	8 KC
9 D KC	10 OAK	11 OAK	12 D OAK	13 SEA	14 SEA	15 D SEA
16 D SEA	17	18 OAK	19 OAK	20 OAK	21 ANA	22 ANA
23 D ANA	24 SEA	25 SEA	26 SEA	27	28 ANA	29 ANA
30 D ANA						

FRONT-OFFICE DIRECTORY

Chairman of the board .... Thomas O. Hicks
President .... James R. Lites
Executive vice president, general manager .... Doug Melvin
Executive vice president, business operations .... John F. McMichael
Executive vice president, broadcasting and sales .... Bill Strong
Executive vice president, marketing and communications .... Jeff Cogen
Senior vice president, communications .... John Blake
Sr. vice president, strategic planning .... Rick McLaughlin
Vice president, community development/relations .... Norm Lyons
Vice president, facilities and construction .... Billy Ray Johnson
Vice president, information technology .... Steve McNeill
Vice president, business operations .... Geoff Moore
Vice president, event operations .... Tim Murphy
Vice president, merchandising .... Steve Shilts
Vice president, corporate sales .... Charlie Seraphin
Vice president, advertising sales .... Tom Comerford
Director, human resources .... Terry Turner
Corporate counsel .... Casey Coffman
Assistant vice president, ticket sales .... Brian Byrnes
Assistant vice president, corporate services .... Jill Cogen
Assistant vice president, ticket operations .... Augie Manfredo
Assistant vice president, marketing .... Christy Martinez
Assistant vice president, suites & new media sales .... Brad Alberts
Assistant vice president, sponsorship sales .... Tom Fireoved
Controller .... Kellie Fischer
Assistant general manager .... Dan O'Brien
Director, Major League administration .... Judy Johns
Director, scouting .... Tim Hallgren
Assistant director, scouting .... Russ Ardolina
Director, player development .... Reid Nichols
Assistant director, player development .... John Lombardo
Assistant director, professional and international scouting .... Monty Clegg
Assistant to director of player development .... Debbie Bent
Director of travel .... Chris Lyngos
Director, community relations .... Taunee Paur Taylor
Director, community development .... Rhonda Houston
Assistant director, communications .... Dana Wilcox
Assistant director, media relations .... Amy Gunter
Media relations assistant .... Rich Rice
Senior director, events .... Lee Gleiser
Senior director, entertainment .... Chuck Morgan
Senior director, graphic design .... Rainer Uhlir

MINOR LEAGUE AFFILIATES

Class	Team	League	Manager
AAA	Oklahoma	Pacific Coast	DeMarlo Hale
AA	Tulsa	Texas	Paul Carey
A	Charlotte	Florida State	Darryl Kennedy
A	Savannah	South Atlantic	To be announced
Rookie	Gulf Coast Rangers	Gulf Coast	Carlos Subero
Rookie	Pulaski	Appalachian	Bruce Crabbe

ASSISTANCE STAFF

Director, medical services
Dr. John Conway

Head trainer
Danny Wheat

Visiting clubhouse manager
Kelly Terrell

Equipment & home clubhouse manager
Zack Minasian

National cross-checkers
Kip Fagg, Tim Hallgren
David Klipstein, Jeff Taylor

Latin coordinator
Manny Batista

Scouts
Dave Birecki, Ted Brzenk
Carl Cassell, Jim Cuthbert
Jay Eddings, Jim Fairey
Tim Fortugno, Mark Giegler
Joel Grampietro, Mike Grouse
Todd Guggiana, Doug Harris
Mark Harris, Zackary Hoyrst
Ray Jackson, Jim Lentine
Dennis Meeks, Gary Neibauer
Mike Paustian, Javier Rodriguez
Rick Schroeder, Randy Taylor
Aris Tirado, Ron Toenjes
Greg Whitworth, Jeff Wren

BROADCAST INFORMATION

Radio: KRLD-AM (1080); KESS (1270), Spanish.
TV: KDFI-TV (Channel 27).
Cable TV: Fox Sports Net.

SPRING TRAINING

Ballpark (city): Charlotte County Stadium (Port Charlotte, Fla.).
Ticket information: 941-625-9500.

BALLPARK INFORMATION

Ballpark (capacity, surface)
The Ballpark in Arlington (49,200, grass)
Address
1000 Ballpark Way, Arlington, TX 76011
Official website
www.texasrangers.com
Business phone
817-273-5222
Ticket information
817-273-5100
Ticket prices
$40 (lower box, club box), $32.50 (club reserved)
$28 (corner box), $22 (terrace club box)
$20 (left field, lower home run porch)
$16 (upper box), $13 (upper home run porch)
$12 (upper reserved, bleachers)
$6 (grandstand reserved), $5 (grandstand)
Field dimensions (from home plate)
To left field at foul line, 334 feet
To center field, 400 feet
To right field at foul line, 325 feet
First game played
April 11, 1994 (Brewers 4, Rangers 3)

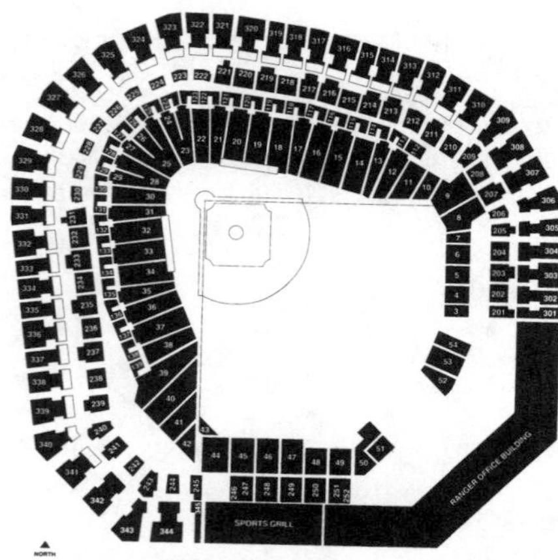

Follow the Rangers all season at: www.sportingnews.com/baseball/teams/rangers/

RANGERS SPRING ROSTER

No.	PITCHERS	B/T	Ht./Wt.	Born	2000 clubs	Projection
53	Benoit, Joaquin	R/R	6-3/205	7-26-79	Tulsa	Believed to have best raw stuff in Rangers' farm system, but he's a year away.
	Cedeno, Jovanny	R/R	6-0/160	10-25-79	Savannah	Sports an impressive arsenal, but 21-year-old is headed for Class AA.
30	Cordero, Francisco	R/R	6-2/200	8-11-77	Texas, Oklahoma	Closer of the future, and he should get more innings this season to prove it.
35	Crabtree, Tim	R/R	6-4/220	10-13-69	Texas	Will be a solid closer if John Wetteland doesn't return.
41	Cubillan, Darwin	R/R	6-2/170	11-15-74	Syracuse, Toronto, Okla., Texas	Compiled a 9.45 ERA in 20 appearances with Texas last season.
46	Davis, Doug	R/L	6-3/190	9-21-75	Texas, Oklahoma	Penciled in, for now, as the Rangers' No. 4 starter.
47	Elder, David	R/R	6-0/180	9-23-75	Tulsa	Struggles to throw strikes will keep him out of the bigs this season.
38	Glynn, Ryan	R/R	6-3/195	11-1-74	Oklahoma, Texas	Suspect stuff prevents him from being anything more than a fifth starter.
32	Helling, Rick	R/R	6-3/220	12-15-70	Texas	Won 11 games his first four seasons in the bigs, but 49 his last three years.
50	Johnson, Jonathan	R/R	6-0/180	7-16-74	Oklahoma, Texas	Didn't impress in 15 appearances in 2000. Thus, he'll start at Class AAA.
52	Kolb, Danny	R/R	6-4/215	3-29-75	Oklahoma, Texas	Middle reliever at best if he makes the team.
	Myette, Aaron	R/R	6-4/195	9-26-77	Birmingham, Charlotte, Chi. A.L.	Acquired in the Royce Clayton deal; will fight for a job in the rotation.
28	Oliver, Darren	R/L	6-2/210	10-6-70	Texas, Oklahoma, Tulsa	He's on a short leash in the rotation after going 2-9 with a 7.42 ERA last season.
45	Petkovsek, Mark	R/R	6-0/198	11-18-65	Anaheim, Lake Elsinore	Rubber-armed reliever who should tally 80-plus all-purpose innings again.
37	Rogers, Kenny	L/L	6-1/217	11-10-64	Texas	No. 2 starter should win 15-plus games with a mighty offense behind him.
49	Sikorski, Brian	R/R	6-1/190	7-27-74	Oklahoma, Texas	If everyone stays healthy, Sikorski is a Class AAA pitcher.
22	Thompson, Justin	L/L	6-4/215	3-8-73	Charlotte, Tulsa, Oklahoma	Has a lot to prove after missing all of 2000 recovering from shoulder surgery.
43	Venafro, Mike	L/L	5-10/180	8-2-73	Texas	Valuable lefty setup man led the team in appearances in 2000.
59	Zimmerman, Jeff	R/R	6-1/200	8-9-72	Texas	Dropped off considerably last year after a huge rookie year.

No.	CATCHERS	B/T	Ht./Wt.	Born	2000 clubs	Projection
33	Haselman, Bill	R/R	6-3/225	5-25-66	Texas	Valuable backup catcher, but won't see much time unless Pudge is hurt.
7	Rodriguez, Ivan	R/R	5-9/205	11-30-71	Texas	Arguably the best catcher ever is fully healed from a thumb injury.

No.	INFIELDERS	B/T	Ht./Wt.	Born	2000 clubs	Projection
11	Caminiti, Ken	B/R	6-0/200	4-21-63	Houston	Claims to be healthy and says he is looking forward to redeeming himself.
27	Catalanotto, Frank	L/R	6-0/195	4-27-74	Texas, Oklahoma	His inability to hit lefties limits him to part-time duty.
44	Dransfeldt, Kelly	R/R	6-2/195	4-16-75	Oklahoma, Texas	Headed to Class AAA. Has just 13 hits in 79 career at-bats (.165 average).
14	Galarraga, Andres	R/R	6-3/235	6-18-61	Atlanta	At 39, he's relegated to the DH role, but will occasionally spell Palmeiro.
	Hafner, Travis	L/L	6-3/215	6-3-77	Charlotte	This 31st-round draft pick is a longshot to make the bigs this season.
13	Lamb, Mike	L/R	6-1/195	8-9-75	Oklahoma, Texas	The Mike Lamb experiment at third base ended with the signing of Ken Caminiti.
25	Palmeiro, Rafael	L/L	6-0/190	9-24-64	Texas	Ageless wonder shows no signs of power reduction with 39 homers in '00.
	Pena, Carlos	L/L	6-2/210	5-17-78	Tulsa	Team's depth at first base keeps this 1998 first-round pick blocked from majors.
3	Rodriguez, Alex	R/R	6-3/210	7-27-75	Seattle	He has 252 million reasons to have a career year.
	Romano, Jason	R/R	6-0/185	6-24-79	Tulsa	Rangers are patient with this talented second baseman. He's headed for Class AAA.
4	Sheldon, Scott	R/R	6-3/215	11-20-68	Texas	He'll again fill the utility role with the club.
18	Velarde, Randy	R/R	6-0/200	11-24-62	Oakland, Midland, Sacramento	He'll hit in the No. 9 hole in a stacked lineup.
2	Young, Mike	R/R	6-0/185	10-19-76	Tennessee, Tulsa, Texas	He is a solid defensive player and has a good bat, but he'll peak at Class AAA.

No.	OUTFIELDERS	B/T	Ht./Wt.	Born	2000 clubs	Projection
9	Curtis, Chad	R/R	5-10/185	11-6-68	Texas	He was sent to the bench when Ricky Ledee arrived last season.
29	Greer, Rusty	L/L	6-0/195	1-21-69	Texas, Tulsa	Nagging leg injuries cut down his power numbers —and games—last season.
19	Kapler, Gabe	R/R	6-2/208	8-31-75	Texas, Oklahoma, Tulsa	At either right or center, this muscle-bound poster boy will be in lineup.
12	Ledee, Ricky	L/L	6-1/200	11-22-73	New York A.L., Cleveland, Texas	Still hasn't reached potential, and getting shuffled around last year didn't help.
21	Mateo, Ruben	R/R	6-0/185	2-10-78	Texas	After suffering broken leg last June, he may not be ready to start the season.
	Porter, Bo	R/R	6-2/195	7-5-72	Sacramento, Oakland	This speedster joins his third organization in as many seasons.

THE COACHING STAFF

Johnny Oates, manager: Oates returns for his seventh season in Texas, a sign of the loyalty the organization has for him and the stability he has brought to the dugout. He comes into this season with something to prove. After winning the A.L. West title three times in four years, the team stumbled to a last-place finish with a disappointing 71-91 mark last season. But a flurry of offseason veteran signings should work well with Oates' quiet, business-like approach and laid-back style.

Bucky Dent: This infield instructor's job got a whole lot easier with the signings of vets Alex Rodriguez and Randy Velarde. They are more sound defensively than the players they replaced: Royce Clayton and Luis Alicea.

Larry Hardy: A former pitcher and minor league manager, he enters his seventh season as the Rangers' bullpen coach.

Rudy Jaromillo: He's underrated as a hitting coach, but a glance at the Rangers' offensive numbers under his six-year tenure should prove his value.

Bobby Jones: Replaces Ed Napoleon (and his 30 years of coaching experience) as the first base coach.

NOTE: Pitching coach not hired yet

THE TOP NEWCOMERS

Ken Caminiti: After battling through nagging injuries over the last few years, Caminiti said he is feeling good again. After playing in just 137 games the last two seasons, we have our doubts.

Andres Galarraga: The veteran signing purge began with the "Big Cat," who made a solid comeback last season with Atlanta after missing the 1999 season with lymphoma. Galarraga will DH often and occasionally don the leather to replace Palmeiro.

Alex Rodriguez: Perhaps the best free agent in history heads to the ideal situation – he's in a devastating lineup at a home ballpark that favors his mighty righthanded swing. Rodriguez's 10-year, $252-million contract was the talk of the offseason, but Rangers owner Tom Hicks appeared ready and willing to shell out the big money to get him.

Randy Velarde: The Midland, Texas, native has headed closer to home. And he's a perfect fit for the Rangers—a solid defensive player, timely hitter and smart baserunner.

THE TOP PROSPECTS

Jovanny Cedeno: This 21-year-old Dominican is slight (6-0, 160), but throws in the low to mid-90s with an excellent changeup. Sound familiar? That's right, he's already drawing comparisons to Pedro Martinez. But he'll be stuck in the low minors until he hones his breaking ball and fills out a little bit.

Aaron Myette: His biggest enemy may be himself. He broke his pitching hand against a clubhouse wall last spring. But Myette had every reason to be frustrated—he was a talented hurler in an organization (the White Sox) loaded with young pitching talent. In Texas, the situation is much different. He should get serious consideration for a rotation spot.

Carlos Pena: Not only does the 22-year-old Pena have all the physical tools necessary to succeed in the majors, he's also one of the hardest working prospects in the Rangers' organization. The Rangers are moving him slowly up the ranks. He'll play for Class AAA Oklahoma this year but might join the team late in the season.

TORONTO BLUE JAYS

AMERICAN LEAGUE EAST DIVISION

2001 SEASON

Blue Jays 2001 SCHEDULE

Home games shaded; D—Day game (games starting before 5 p.m.)
*—All-Star Game at Safeco Field (Seattle) † Game played in San Juan, Puerto Rico.

APRIL

SUN	MON	TUE	WED	THU	FRI	SAT
1 † TEX	2	3 TB	4 TB	5 D TB	6 NYY	7 D NYY
8 D NYY	9 TB	10 TB	11 TB	12 KC	13 D KC	14 D KC
15 D KC	16	17 NYY	18 NYY	19 NYY	20 KC	21 KC
22 D KC	23	24 TEX	25 TEX	26	27 ANA	28 D ANA
29 D ANA	30					

MAY

SUN	MON	TUE	WED	THU	FRI	SAT
		1 OAK	2 OAK	3 D OAK	4 SEA	5 D SEA
6 D SEA	7	8 OAK	9 OAK	10 OAK	11 SEA	12 D SEA
13 D SEA	14	15 ANA	16 ANA	17 ANA	18 TEX	19 TEX
20 D TEX	21 D CWS	22	23 CWS	24 CWS	25 BOS	26 BOS
27 D BOS	28 CWS	29 CWS	30 CWS	31 BOS		

JUNE

SUN	MON	TUE	WED	THU	FRI	SAT
					1 BOS	2 D BOS
3 D BOS	4	5 TB	6 TB	7 D TB	8 FLA	9 D FLA
10 D FLA	11 ATL	12 ATL	13 ATL	14	15 MON	16 MON
17 D MON	18 BAL	19 BAL	20 BAL	21	22 BOS	23 BOS
24 D BOS	25 BAL	26 BAL	27 BAL	28 D BAL	29 BOS	30 BOS

JULY

SUN	MON	TUE	WED	THU	FRI	SAT
1 D BOS	2 D BOS	3 TB	4 D TB	5 TB	6 MON	7 D MON
8 D MON	9	10 *	11	12 PHI	13 PHI	14 D PHI
15 D NYM	16 NYM	17 NYM	18 BOS	19 BOS	20 NYY	21 D NYY
22 D NYY	23 NYY	24 BOS	25 BOS	26 BOS	27 NYY	28 D NYY
29 D NYY	30	31 MIN				

AUGUST

SUN	MON	TUE	WED	THU	FRI	SAT
			1 MIN	2 D MIN	3 BAL	4 D BAL
5 D BAL	6	7 SEA	8 SEA	9 SEA	10 ANA	11 ANA
12 ANA	13	14 OAK	15 OAK	16 D OAK	17 TEX	18 D TEX
19 D TEX	20 MIN	21 MIN	22 MIN	23 D MIN	24 BAL	25 D BAL
26 D BAL	27	28 NYY	29 NYY	30 D NYY	31 DET	

SEPTEMBER

SUN	MON	TUE	WED	THU	FRI	SAT
						1 D DET
2 D DET	3 D NYY	4 NYY	5 NYY	6	7 DET	8 DET
9 D DET	10	11 BAL	12 BAL	13 BAL	14 CLE	15 D CLE
16 D CLE	17	18 BAL	19 BAL	20 BAL	21 TB	22 TB
23 D TB	24 CLE	25 CLE	26 CLE	27 TB	28 TB	29 D TB
30 D TB						

FRONT-OFFICE DIRECTORY

President and chief executive officer....................Paul Godfrey
President, baseball & general manager....................Gord Ash
Senior vice president, finance and operations....................Stu Hutcheson
Senior vice president, sales and marketing....................Paul Allamby
Vice president, baseball....................Bob Mattick
Vice president, baseball....................Tim Wilken
V.p., baseball operations and assistant general manager....................Tim McCleary
Assistant general manager and director of player personnel....................Dave Stewart
Special assistant to pres., baseball and general manager....................Al Widmar
Special assistant to pres., baseball and g.m./dir. international scouting....................Wayne Morgan
Vice president, media relations....................Howard Starkman
Vice president, sales....................Greg McNamara
Vice president, finance and administration....................Susan Quigley
Vice president, corp. partnerships & bus. development....................Mark Lemmon
Director, scouting....................Chris Buckley
Assistant director, scouting....................Mark Snipp
Director, player development....................Jim Hoff
Director, minor leagues....................Bob Nelson
Director, Florida operations....................Ken Carson
Director, marketing....................Peter Cosentino
Director, operations....................Mario Coutinho
General manager, TBJ merchandising....................Michael Andrejak
Manager, team travel....................John Brioux

MINOR LEAGUE AFFILIATES

Class	Team	League	Manager
AAA	Syracuse	International	Omar Malave
AA	Tennessee	Southern	Rocket Wheeler
A	Auburn	New York-Penn.	To be announced
A	Charleston (WV)	South Atlantic	Rolando Pino
A	Dunedin	Florida State	Marty Pevey
Rookie	Medicine Hat	Pioneer	To be announced

BROADCAST INFORMATION

Radio: CHUM-AM (1050).
TV: CBC-TV.
Cable TV: The Sports Network, CTV SportsNet.

SPRING TRAINING

Ballpark (city): Dunedin Stadium at Grant Field (Dunedin, Fla.).
Ticket information: 800-707-8269; 727-733-0429.

ASSISTANCE STAFF

Trainers
George Poulis, Scott Shannon

Strength and conditioning coordinator
Jeff Krushell

Team physicians
Dr. Allan Gross, Dr. Steve Mirabello, Dr. Ron Taylor

Advance scout
Sal Butera

Special assignment scouts
Chris Bourjos, Duane Larson, Ted Lekas

Special assignment/nat. cross-checker
Mike Mangan

Southeast regional supervisor
Mike Cadahia

Northwest regional supervisor
Ron Tostenson

Dir., Canadian/Northeast reg. supervisor
Bill Byckowski

Scouts
Charles Aliano, Tony Arias, Jaymie Bayne, Andy Beene, Dave Blume, Rick Cerrone, Joey Davis, Ellis Dungan, Joe Ford, Tom Hinkle, Tim Huff, Jim Hughes, Edwin Lawrence, Marty Miller, Ty Nichols, Andy Pienovi, Demerius Pittman, Jorge Rivera, Jim Rooney, Joe Siers, Gerry Sobeck

BALLPARK INFORMATION

Ballpark (capacity, surface)
SkyDome (45,100, artificial)

Address
One Blue Jays Way
Suite 3200
Toronto, Ontario M5V 1J1

Official website
www.bluejays.com

Business phone
416-341-1000

Ticket information
416-341-1234 and 1-888-OK GO JAY

Ticket prices
$44 (premium dugout level)
$41 (field level-infield)
$35 (field level-bases)
$29 (field level-baselines)
$23 (100 & 200 level-outfield; SkyDeck-infield)
$16 (SkyDeck-bases)
$7 (Skydeck-baselines)

Field dimensions (from home plate)
To left field at foul line, 330 feet
To center field, 400 feet
To right field at foul line, 330 feet

First game played
June 5, 1989 (Brewers 5, Blue Jays 3)

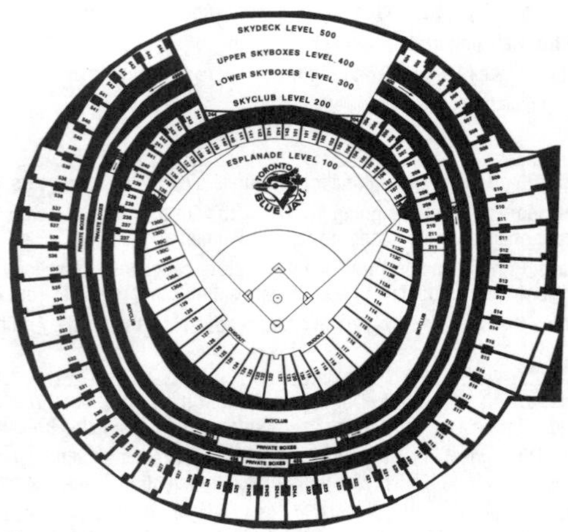

Follow the Blue Jays all season at: www.sportingnews.com/baseball/teams/bluejays/

BLUE JAYS SPRING ROSTER

No.	PITCHERS	B/T	Ht./Wt.	Born	2000 clubs	Projection
57	Beirne, Kevin	L/R	6-4/210	1-1-74	Charlotte, Chicago A.L.	Relief pitcher who will improve on last year's stats.
51	Borbon, Pedro	L/L	6-1/224	11-15-67	Toronto	Doesn't throw hard or accurately. Middle reliever may be out of baseball soon.
26	Carpenter, Chris	R/R	6-6/225	4-27-75	Toronto	Coming off disappointing season, will have to battle for spot in rotation.
38	Coco, Pasqual	R/R	6-1/185	9-24-77	Tennessee, Toronto	Strikeout pitcher could use another year in Class AAA.
45	Escobar, Kelvim	R/R	6-1/210	4-11-76	Toronto	Personal woes may have led to erratic control and bullpen, where he'll likely stay.
29	Eyre, Scott	L/L	6-1/200	5-30-72	Chicago A.L., Charlotte	Going from mediocre to worse. Maybe new venue will help.
36	File, Bob	R/R	6-4/210	1-28-77	Tennessee, Syracuse	Has good fastball, excellent control and fine shot at eventual setup role.
52	Frascatore, John	R/R	6-1/223	2-4-70	Toronto	Fiery middle reliever could be a setup man if he develops an off-speed pitch.
32	Halladay, Roy	R/R	6-6/230	5-14-77	Toronto, Syracuse	Couldn't find right mix of pitches last season, could be the same this year.
50	Hamilton, Joey	R/R	6-4/240	9-9-70	Syracuse, Toronto	Should be far enough removed from surgery to fill No. 3 or 4 starter job.
44	Koch, Billy	R/R	6-3/215	12-14-74	Toronto	Expect few walks, plenty of saves from Jays closer.
21	Loaiza, Esteban	R/R	6-3/205	12-31-71	Texas, Toronto	Went from Texas to Toronto with aplomb last year and should continue rise on field.
28	Painter, Lance	L/L	6-1/200	7-21-67	Toronto, Dunedin	Jays should have left well enough alone with unstartable middle reliever.
39	Parris, Steve	R/R	6-0/195	12-17-67	Cincinnati	Projected starter, but small A.L. parks don't bode well.
54	Perez, George	R/R	6-4/220	3-20-79	Queens	Overpowering in Class A, but still a year or two away.
19	Plesac, Dan	L/L	6-5/217	2-4-62	Arizona	Ex-closer's still tough against lefties and improving, at 39, against righties.
48	Quantrill, Paul	L/R	6-1/195	11-3-68	Toronto	On slow decline, now to middle relief, since breaking leg in 1999.
33	Sirotka, Mike	L/L	6-1/200	5-13-71	Chicago A.L.	White Sox most dependable starter the last three years; now Blue Jays best starter.
49	Woodards, Orlando	R/R	6-2/200	1-2-78	Dunedin	Was solid last year at Class A, striking out nearly one an inning.

No.	CATCHERS	B/T	Ht./Wt.	Born	2000 clubs	Projection
30	Castillo, Alberto	R/R	6-0/200	2-10-70	Toronto	Muffed opportunity last year with bat. Don't look for added ABs now.
9	Fletcher, Darrin	L/R	6-2/205	10-3-66	Toronto	Exhibits fine bat control and durability. Only RBI total is lagging.
6	Lawrence, Joe	R/R	6-2/190	2-13-77	Dunedin, Tennessee	Not a lot of power and must cut down on strikeouts.
17	Phelps, Josh	R/R	6-3/220	5-12-78	Tennessee, Toronto, Dunedin	Must gain more consistency with the bat. Will have another year to do it.
64	Werth, Jayson	R/R	6-5/190	5-20-79	Bowie, Frederick	All-around talent just needs time to develop.

No.	INFIELDERS	B/T	Ht./Wt.	Born	2000 clubs	Projection
7	Batista, Tony	R/R	6-0/205	12-9-73	Toronto	Starting third baseman suffers from lack of discipline at the plate.
18	Bush, Homer	R/R	5-10/208	11-12-72	Toronto	Second baseman hid injury last spring and saw batting average plummet from '99.
25	Delgado, Carlos	L/R	6-3/230	6-25-72	Toronto	First baseman and cleanup hitter challenged for Triple Crown last year.
3	Frye, Jeff	R/R	5-9/160	8-31-66	Boston, Colorado	Hard-nosed second baseman can steal bases, hit for average and field his position.
20	Fullmer, Brad	L/R	6-0/215	1-17-75	Toronto	First baseman and designated hitter, will face most lefties.
8	Gonzalez, Alex	R/R	6-0/195	4-8-73	Toronto, Syracuse	Slick-fielding shortstop who improved his power last year as average dropped.
3	Izturis, Cesar	B/R	5-9/175	2-10-80	Syracuse	Brilliant glove man handles bat half as well. Minors seem likely.
5	Woodward, Chris	R/R	6-0/185	6-27-76	Toronto, Syracuse	Utilityman has trouble with breaking pitch, which affects his fielding.

No.	OUTFIELDERS	B/T	Ht./Wt.	Born	2000 clubs	Projection
23	Cruz, Jose Jr.	B/R	6-0/200	4-19-74	Toronto	Struggling to live up to his potential. Has power but strikes out too often.
12	Freel, Ryan	R/R	5-10/185	3-8-76	Tennessee, Dunedin, Syracuse	He can play second, third and short and is fundamentally sound.
27	Greene, Todd	R/R	5-10/208	5-8-71	Syracuse, Toronto, Dunedin	Power will languish on the bench due to lingering effects of shoulder surgery.
43	Mondesi, Raul	R/R	5-11/230	3-12-71	Toronto	Had better attitude than expected after trade.
22	Mottola, Chad	R/R	6-3/225	10-15-71	Syracuse, Toronto	Solid power numbers at Class AAA, but must cut down on strikeouts.
27	Simmons, Brian	B/R	6-2/190	9-4-73	DID NOT PLAY	Likely to start in minors after missing all of 2000 season with injury.
24	Stewart, Shannon	R/R	6-1/205	2-25-74	Toronto, Dunedin	Left fielder has shown steady improvement, especially in power numbers.
15	Thompson, Andy	R/R	6-3/220	10-8-75	Syracuse, Toronto	Had lackluster year at Class AAA.
10	Wells, Vernon	R/R	6-1/215	12-8-78	Syracuse, Toronto	A five-tool player who will star in center for Jays, either now or later.
11	Wise, DeWayne	L/L	6-1/180	2-24-78	Toronto	Left fielder has excellent speed, needs more discipline at the plate.

THE COACHING STAFF

Buck Martinez, manager: A former Blue Jays catcher and long-time announcer with the team, the first-year manager makes a transition—from broadcast booth to bench—that others, such as Houston's Larry Dierker, have made with mixed results. Martinez is well liked, and as a man with 17 years of major league playing experience he certainly knows the ins and outs of the game. The question is, will he be able to persuade the Jays to manufacture runs instead of swinging for the fences every time, as he has vowed?

Terry Bevington: The Cubs' third-base coach is back for his third year with the team. He previously compiled a record of 222-214 as manager of the White Sox.

Gil Patterson: Comes to the Blue Jays to rejuvenate an erratic bullpen staff.

Cito Gaston: Despite winning two World Series as the Blue Jays' manager (1989-97), Gaston finds himself back for a second year and second tour of duty as the team's hitting coach. He knows the game but is sometimes short with young hitters.

Mark Connor: The highly regarded pitching coach spent many years as a coach with the Yankees before becoming the Diamondbacks' first pitching coach in 1998. Connor has worked under managers such as Billy Martin, Lou Piniella, Yogi Berra and Buck Showalter, in New York and Arizona. When Showalter was let go in Arizona, the Blue Jays benefited.

Cookie Rojas: He helped coach the Mets to the World Series last year, his fourth with the team. Now he joins a highly experienced Jays coaching crew. As infield coach for part of his stint in New York, Rojas has worked with the best.

Garth Iorg: The former infielder spent his entire nine-year playing career with the Blue Jays. Now he rejoins them as first-base coach. As a player he was a teammate of his new boss, Martinez.

THE TOP NEWCOMERS

Steve Parris: He was acquired from Cincinnati for a pair of top pitching prospects and will round out the Blue Jays rotation. The team expects to get 200 innings and at least 10 wins from him.

Dan Plesac: He is no longer the hard-throwing closer he once was, but Plesac can still pitch—mostly against lefthanders, though he made adjustments in his changeup and his position on the rubber last season that have helped him get righthanded batters out as well. Has a veteran's guile.

Mike Sirotka: Rounded into form last season and won 15 games. This control pitcher had an ERA under 4.00 and is younger than David Wells.

THE TOP PROSPECTS

Vernon Wells: The No. 5 pick in the 1997 draft is an excellent fielder and an all-around talent. He struggled last year in Class AAA after losing the battle for the starting center fielder's job in Toronto to

Shannon Stewart: Stewart established new highs in batting average, homers, RBIs, doubles and triples. Only drawback is a decline in his stolen bases. That all spells a possible move from the leadoff slot to the No. 3 or 5 spot in the order.

ARIZONA DIAMONDBACKS

NATIONAL LEAGUE WEST DIVISION

2001 SEASON

Diamondbacks 2001 SCHEDULE

Home games shaded; D—Day game (games starting before 5 p.m.)
*—All-Star Game at Safeco Field (Seattle)

APRIL

SUN	MON	TUE	WED	THU	FRI	SAT
1	2	3 LA	4 LA	5 LA	6 STL	7 D STL
8 D STL	9	10 LA	11 LA	12 LA	13 COL	14 D COL
15 D COL	16 STL	17 STL	18 STL	19	20 COL	21 COL
22 D COL	23 FLA	24 FLA	25 FLA	26 ATL	27 ATL	28 ATL
29 ATL	30					

MAY

SUN	MON	TUE	WED	THU	FRI	SAT
		1 MON	2 MON	3 MON	4 NYM	5 D NYM
6 D NYM	7 CIN	8 CIN	9 CIN	10	11 PHI	12 PHI
13 D PHI	14	15 CIN	16 CIN	17 D CIN	18 D CUB	19 D CUB
20 D CUB	21 SF	22 SF	23 SF	24 D SD	25 SD	26 SD
27 D SD	28 D SF	29 SF	30 SF	31		

JUNE

SUN	MON	TUE	WED	THU	FRI	SAT
					1 SD	2 SD
3 D SD	4 LA	5 LA	6 LA	7 D LA	8 KC	9 KC
10 KC	11	12 CUB	13 CUB	14 D CUB	15 DET	16 DET
17 D DET	18	19 LA	20 LA	21 COL	22 COL	23 D COL
24 D COL	25 HOU	26 HOU	27 HOU	28	29 COL	30 COL

JULY

SUN	MON	TUE	WED	THU	FRI	SAT
1 D COL	2	3 HOU	4 D HOU	5 HOU	6 OAK	7 OAK
8 D OAK	9	10 *	11	12 ANA	13 ANA	14 ANA
15 D SEA	16 SEA	17 D SEA	18 SD	19 D SD	20 SF	21 D SF
22 D SF	23 SD	24 SD	25 SD	26 SF	27 SF	28 SF
29 D SF	30	31 MON				

AUGUST

SUN	MON	TUE	WED	THU	FRI	SAT
			1 MON	2 D MON	3 NYM	4 D NYM
5 D NYM	6	7 FLA	8 FLA	9 D FLA	10 ATL	11 D ATL
12 D ATL	13 PIT	14 PIT	15 PIT	16	17 CUB	18 CUB
19 D CUB	20	21 PIT	22 PIT	23 PIT	24 PHI	25 D PHI
26 D PHI	27 PHI	28 SF	29 SF	30 SF	31 SD	

SEPTEMBER

SUN	MON	TUE	WED	THU	FRI	SAT
						1 SD
2 D SD	3	4 SF	5 SF	6 D SF	7 SD	8 D SD
9 D SD	10 SD	11 COL	12 COL	13 COL	14 MIL	15 MIL
16 D MIL	17 COL	18 COL	19 D COL	20 LA	21 LA	22 LA
23 D LA	24	25 MIL	26 MIL	27 MIL	28 LA	29 LA
30 D LA						

FRONT-OFFICE DIRECTORY

Managing general partner .... Jerry Colangelo
President .... Richard Dozer
Vice president and general manager .... Joe Garagiola Jr.
Senior vice president, sales and marketing .... Scott Brubaker
Vice president, finance .... Thomas Harris
Vice president, tickets and special services .... Dianne Aguilar
Vice president, sales .... Blake Edwards
Vice president, community affairs .... Mark Fernandez
Assistant general manager .... Sandy Johnson
Director of Hispanic marketing .... Richard Saenz
Director of Tucson operations .... Rich Tomey
Director of public relations .... Mike Swanson
Director of ballpark services .... Russ Amaral
Director of suite services .... Diney Mahoney
Director of team travel .... Roger Riley
Director of minor league operations .... Tommy Jones
Director of Pacific Rim operations .... Jim Marshall
Director of scouting .... Mike Rizzo
Assistant director of scouting .... Bob Miller

MINOR LEAGUE AFFILIATES

Class	Team	League	Manager
AAA	Tucson	Pacific Coast	Tom Spencer
AAA	El Paso	Texas	Al Pedrique
A	Lancaster	California	Scott Coolbaugh
A	South Bend	Midwest	Steve Scarsone
Rookie	Yakima	Northwest	Greg Lonigro
Rookie	Missoula	Pioneer	Chip Hale

BROADCAST INFORMATION

Radio: KTAR-AM (620).
TV: KTVK (Channel 3)
Cable TV: Fox Sports Net Arizona.

SPRING TRAINING

Ballpark (city): Tuscon Electric Park (Tucson, Ariz.).
Ticket information: 800-638-4253, 520-434-1111.

ASSISTANCE STAFF

Trainer
Paul Lessard

Assistant trainer
Dave Edwards

Club physician
Dr. Michael Lee

National scouting supervisor
Kendall Carter

Regional supervisors
Mark Baca, Ed Durkin
Kris Kline, Charles Scott

Scouting coordinators
Derek Bryant, Junior Noboa

Professional scouts
Bill Earnhart, Mike Piatnik

Major League and advance scouts
Mack Babitt, Jim Marshall
Phil Rizzo, Dick Scott

Special assignment scout
Bryan Lambe

Scouts
Ray Blanco, Ray Corbett
Mike Daughtry, Doug Gassaway
Jason Goligoski, Scott Jaster
Steve Kmetko, Hal Kurtzman
Greg Lonigro, Howard McCullough
Matt Merullo, Bob Steinkamp
Mike Valarezo, Luke Wren

BALLPARK INFORMATION

Ballpark (capacity, surface)
Bank One Ballpark (49,033)
Address
401 East Jefferson
Phoenix, AZ 85004
Official website
www.azdiamondbacks.com
Business phone
602-462-6500
Ticket information
602-514-8400
Ticket prices
$11 to $26 (lower level)
$1 to $17 (upper level)
$43 to $70 (lower level premium seats)
$29 and $36 (Infiniti Diamond level)
Field dimensions (from home plate)
To left field at foul line, 330 feet
To center field, 407 feet
To right field at foul line, 334 feet
First game played
March 31, 1998 (Rockies 9, Diamondbacks 2)

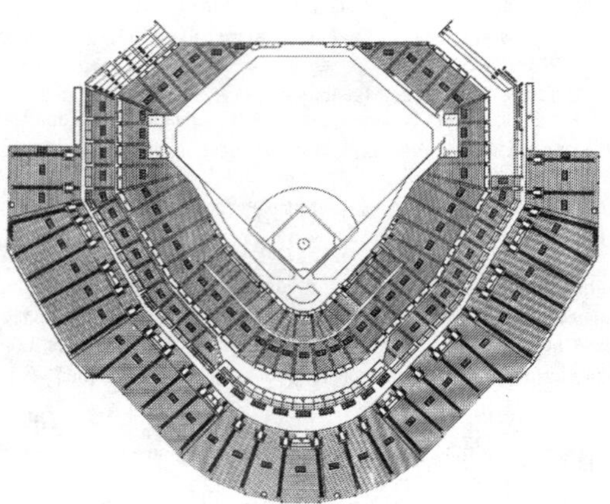

Follow the Diamondbacks all season at:
www.sportingnews.com/baseball/teams/diamondbacks/

DIAMONDBACKS SPRING ROSTER

No.	PITCHERS	B/T	Ht./Wt.	Born	2000 clubs	Projection
34	Anderson, Brian	B/L	6-1/183	4-26-72	Arizona	Has won 31 games in the last three seasons. Should win at least 10 this season.
43	Batista, Miguel	R/R	6-0/190	2-19-71	Montreal, Kansas City, Omaha	Will be battling for a spot in the bullpen.
47	Bierbroldt, Nick	L/L	6-5/185	5-16-78	Tucson, AZL D'backs, El Paso	Probably will end up in AAA. Maybe a year away from joining the rotation.
50	Guzman, Geraldo	R/R	6-2/180	11-28-73	Tucson, Arizona, El Paso	Went 5-4 in the majors last year. Might be the number five man in the rotation.
	Jacome, Jason	L/L	6-1/185	11-24-70	Yakult	Pitched in Japan last year. Will be battling for job.
51	Johnson, Randy	R/L	6-10/230	9-10-63	Arizona	Led league with 347 strikeouts. Should win at least 19 games this season.
49	Kim, Byung-Hyun	R/R	5-11/176	1-21-79	Arizona, Tucson	Has nasty stuff and can pitch long relief or close out games.
31	Mantei, Matt	R/R	6-1/190	7-7-73	Tucson, Arizona	Was a little inconsistent last year, needs to stay healthy to keep the closer job.
36	Morgan, Mike	R/R	6-2/220	10-8-59	Arizona	Journeyman reliever found a home in Diamondbacks bullpen.
24	Patterson, John	R/R	6-5/183	1-30-78	Tucson	Starter suffered injury plagued season in '00. Will be at AAA for a year at least.
65	Prinz, Bret	R/R	6-3/185	6-15-77	South Bend, El Paso	Converted to a reliever, he had nine wins and 26 saves last season.
27	Reynoso, Armando	R/R	6-0/204	5-1-66	Arizona	Wasn't as effective as past seasons, but still won 11 games.
66	Sanchez, Duaner	R/R	6-0/160	11-14-79	South Bend	Will be back in minor leagues after going 8-9 in 2000.
38	Schilling, Curt	R/R	6-4/231	11-14-66	Philadelphia, Arizona	Despite injury, he still tied for league lead in complete games.
36	Springer, Russ	R/R	6-4/205	11-7-68	Arizona	Reliever will have to cut down on his ERA (5.08) to stay with the club.
30	Stottlemyre, Todd	L/R	6-3/215	5-20-65	Arizona, AZL Diamondbacks	Won nine games, despite pitching with a partially torn rotator cuff.
22	Swindell, Greg	L/L	6-3/230	1-2-65	Arizona	Veteran lefthander had a decent season and allowed very few runs to score.

No.	CATCHERS	B/T	Ht./Wt.	Born	2000 clubs	Projection
48	Barajas, Rod	R/R	6-2/220	9-5-75	Tucson, Arizona	Will have to battle Huckaby for backup job.
45	Huckaby, Ken	R/R	6-1/205	1-27-71	Tucson	Will have full-time job at Tucson unless he hits better than Barajas in the spring.
26	Miller, Damian	R/R	6-2/212	10-13-69	Arizona	Number one catcher now that Stinnett is gone.

No.	INFIELDERS	B/T	Ht./Wt.	Born	2000 clubs	Projection
33	Bell, Jay	R/R	6-0/184	12-11-65	Arizona	Veteran second baseman had a sub-par season in '00.
44	Durazo, Erubiel	L/L	6-3/225	1-23-74	Arizona	Injuries limited him to 67 games last season. He might be third option at first.
64	Cintron, Alexander	B/R	6-1/170	12-17-78	El Paso	Shortstop prospect will get plenty of at-bats in Class AAA.
28	Colbrunn, Greg	R/R	6-0/205	7-26-69	Arizona	Proved he could be a valuable backup at first base.
4	Counsell, Craig	L/R	6-0/175	8-21-70	Tucson, Arizona	Is useful as a utility infielder. Hit .316 last season with Arizona.
2	Frias, Hanley	B/R	6-0/173	12-5-73	Arizona	Provides a switch hitter off the bench for the Diamondbacks.
17	Grace, Mark	L/L	6-2/200	6-28-64	Chicago N.L.	Veteran first baseman switches teams after 13 seasons with the Cubs.
7	Klassen, Danny	R/R	6-0/175	9-22-75	Tucson, Arizona	Needs to show he can hit major league pitching in order to stay in the majors.
63	Spivey, Junior	R/R	6-0/185	1-28-75	Tucson, El Paso	Hit well in injury plagued season. Could be in the majors with a good spring.
9	Williams, Matt	R/R	6-2/214	11-28-65	El Paso, Arizona, High Desert	Needs to stay healthy in order for this team to have a chance.
5	Womack, Tony	L/R	5-9/159	9-25-69	Arizona	He didn't get on base as much as he did in '99. But he did lead league in triples.

No.	OUTFIELDERS	B/T	Ht./Wt.	Born	2000 clubs	Projection
29	Bautista, Danny	R/R	5-11/170	5-24-72	Florida, Arizona	Hit .317 with Diamondbacks after trade from Florida.
6	Conti, Jason	L/R	5-11/180	1-27-75	Tucson, Arizona	With addition of Sanders, likely back to minors this season.
	Cummings, Midre	L/R	6-0/195	10-14-71	Minnesota, Boston	Will get a chance to earn a roster spot as lefthanded bat off the bench.
61	Cust, Jack	L/R	6-1/205	1-16-79	El Paso	Hit 20 home runs for AA El Paso in '00. Probably ticketed for Class AAA.
25	Dellucci, David	L/L	5-11/198	10-31-73	Ariz., Tuc., AZL D'backs, S. Bend	Couldn't crack the outfield rotation in '00, probably won't this season either.
12	Finley, Steve	L/L	6-2/180	3-12-65	Arizona	Improved his average over '99 season. Should put up similar numbers this season.
20	Gonzalez, Luis	L/R	6-2/190	9-2-67	Arizona	His average dipped some from '99, but you can count on him to hit at least .300.
8	Ryan, Rob	L/L	5-11/190	6-24-73	Tucson, Arizona	Will be ticketed for Class AAA.
	Sanders, Reggie	R/R	6-1/185	12-1-67	Atlanta	Looking to rebound from sub-par season with Atlanta.

THE COACHING STAFF

Bob Brenly, manager: Brenly is a former catcher with the Giants and had one All-Star season in the mid-80s. He was hired by the Diamondbacks out of the TV booth, where he had been an analyst for the club. He will probably be a player's manager as he replaces Buck Showalter, who was as strict and intense as they come. He inherits a good team, and should have success.

Bob Melvin: Melvin is a former teammate of Brenly's from San Francisco. In fact, the two shared catching duties. He was Tigers bench coach last season.

Eddie Rodriguez: Former Blue Jays third base coach will be Diamondbacks first base coach. He also coached the gold medal USA team in the 2000 Summer Olympics.

Chris Speier: Former minor league manager was hired to be the club's new third base coach. Brings 19 seasons of experience.

Dwayne Murphy: Former Gold-Glove winner serves as first base coach and outfield coach.

Glenn Sherlock: Helps to keep the bullpen in focus during the games. He will also help the young catchers learn the nuances of playing the position.

Bob Welch: Brought in by Diamondbacks to be pitching coach. Brings one Cy Young Award and 17 years of major league experience.

THE TOP NEWCOMERS

Mark Grace: He should have a career year batting in this lineup. He is a career .308 hitter and should provide the first baseman the Diamondbacks haven't had since the franchise started.

Reggie Sanders: If he hits like he did in September for the Braves, the Diamondbacks won't have to worry about a platoon for right field.

THE TOP PROSPECTS

Alexander Cintron: Has had two consecutive .300 plus seasons in the minors. Unfortunately, all he can do is hit for average. Will need to show something in AAA, or else he might end up as a utility player.

Junior Spivey: He can get on base and steal some bases too. Will probably be in AAA for a season and be groomed to take over for Jay Bell when the time comes.

ATLANTA BRAVES

NATIONAL LEAGUE EAST DIVISION

2001 SEASON

Braves 2001 SCHEDULE

Home games shaded; D—Day game (games starting before 5 p.m.)
*—All-Star Game at Safeco Field (Seattle)

APRIL

SUN	MON	TUE	WED	THU	FRI	SAT
1	2 D CIN	3 D NYM	4 NYM	5 NYM	6 FLA	7 FLA
8 D FLA	9 D NYM	10	11 NYM	12 NYM	13 PHI	14 PHI
15 D PHI	16 FLA	17 FLA	18 D FLA	19	20 PHI	21 PHI
22 D PHI	23 HOU	24 HOU	25 HOU	26 ARI	27 ARI	28 ARI
29 ARI	30					

MAY

SUN	MON	TUE	WED	THU	FRI	SAT
		1 MIL	2 MIL	3 MIL	4 STL	5 STL
6 D STL	7	8 SD	9 SD	10 D SD	11 LA	12 LA
13 D LA	14	15 COL	16 D COL	17 COL	18 SF	19 SF
20 D SF	21 FLA	22 FLA	23 FLA	24	25 PIT	26 PIT
27 D PIT	28 MON	29 MON	30 D MON	31		

JUNE

SUN	MON	TUE	WED	THU	FRI	SAT
					1 PIT	2 PIT
3 D PIT	4	5 MON	6 MON	7 MON	8 NYY	9 D NYY
10 NYY	11 TOR	12 TOR	13 TOR	14	15 BOS	16 BOS
17 D BOS	18 FLA	19 FLA	20 FLA	21 D FLA	22 NYM	23 D NYM
24 D NYM	25 PHI	26 PHI	27 D PHI	28 NYM	29 NYM	30 D NYM

JULY

SUN	MON	TUE	WED	THU	FRI	SAT
1 D NYM	2	3 PHI	4 PHI	5 PHI	6 BOS	7 BOS
8 D BOS	9	10 *	11	12 BAL	13 BAL	14 BAL
15 D TB	16 TB	17 TB	18 CIN	19 D CIN	20 MON	21 MON
22 D MON	23 CIN	24 CIN	25 D CIN	26 MON	27 MON	28 MON
29 D MON	30	31 STL				

AUGUST

SUN	MON	TUE	WED	THU	FRI	SAT
			1 STL	2 STL	3 MIL	4 D MIL
5 D MIL	6	7 HOU	8 HOU	9 HOU	10 ARI	11 D ARI
12 D ARI	13	14 COL	15 COL	16 COL	17 SF	18 D SF
19 D SF	20	21 SD	22 SD	23 SD	24 LA	25 LA
26 D LA	27 LA	28 MON	29 MON	30 MON	31 CUB	

SEPTEMBER

SUN	MON	TUE	WED	THU	FRI	SAT
						1 D CUB
2 D CUB	3 D MON	4 MON	5 MON	6	7 D CUB	8 D CUB
9 D CUB	10	11 PHI	12 D PHI	13 PHI	14 FLA	15 FLA
16 D FLA	17 PHI	18 PHI	19 PHI	20 PHI	21 NYM	22 NYM
23 D NYM	24 FLA	25 FLA	26 FLA	27	28 NYM	29 NYM
30 D NYM						

FRONT-OFFICE DIRECTORY

Owner ..... R.E. Turner III
Chairman of the board of directors ..... William C. Bartholomay
President ..... Stanley H. Kasten
Executive vice president and general manager ..... John Schuerholz
Senior vice president and assistant to the president ..... Henry L. Aaron
Senior vice president, administration ..... Bob Wolfe
Vice president, assistant general manager ..... Frank Wren
Vice president, director of marketing and broadcasting ..... Wayne Long
Vice president ..... Lee Douglas
Vice president of development ..... Janet Marie Smith
Vice president of human resources ..... Michelle Thomas
Special assistants to general manager ..... Jim Fregosi, Paul Snyder, Scott Nethery, Chuck McMichael
Special assistant to general manager/player development ..... Jose Martinez
Director of team travel and equipment manager ..... Bill Acree
Director of player development ..... Dick Balderson
Director of scouting ..... Roy Clark
Director of international and professional scouting ..... Dayton Moore
Senior director of promotions and civic affairs ..... Miles McRea
Vice president/controller ..... Chip Moore
Director of ticket sales ..... Paul Adams
Director of minor league business operations ..... Bruce Baldwin
Director of stadium operations and security ..... Larry Bowman
Field director ..... Ed Mangan
Director of ticket operations ..... Ed Newman
Team counsel ..... David Payne
Director of community relations ..... Cara Maglione
Director of audio video operations ..... Jennifer Berger
Director of corporate sales ..... Jim Allen
Director of public relations ..... Jim Schultz
Media relations manager ..... Glen Serra
Public relations assistants ..... Adam Lieberman, Meagan Swingle

MINOR LEAGUE AFFILIATES

Class	Team	League	Manager
AAA	Richmond	International	Carlos Tosca
AA	Greenville	Southern	Paul Runge
A	Myrtle Beach	Carolina	Brian Snitker
A	Macon	South Atlantic	Randy Ingle
A	Jamestown	New York-Penn	Jim Saul
Rookie	Danville	Appalachian	Ralph Henriquez
Rookie	Gulf Coast Braves	Gulf Coast	Rick Albert

BROADCAST INFORMATION

Radio: WSB-AM (750).
TV: TBS-TV (Channel 17).
Cable TV: FOX Sports Net, Turner South.

SPRING TRAINING

Ballpark (city): Disney's Wide World Sports Baseball Stadium (Kissimmee, Fla.).
Ticket information: 407-839-3900; 407-939-4263.

ASSISTANCE STAFF

Head trainer
Dave Pursley

Assistant trainer
Jeff Porter

Club physician
Dr. David T. Watson

Associate physicians
Dr. William Barber, Dr. John Cantwell
Dr. Norman Elliott

Major league scout
Bobby Wine

National supervisorss
Tim Conroy, John Flannery

Regional supervisors
Harold Cronin, Paul Faulk, Bob Wadsworth

Area supervisors
Mike Baker, Dan Bates, Tyrone Brooks, Stu Cann, Rob English, Ralph Garr, John Hagemann, "J" Harrison, Kurt Kemp, Marco Paddy, J.J. Picollo, Donnie Popllin, Willie Powell, John Ramey, John Stewart, Don Thomas, Terry Tripp

Scouts
Roberto Aquino, Nez Balelo, Neil Burke, Joe Caputo, Todd Cook, Matt Dodd, Edgar Fernandez, Jose Figueroa, Pedro Flores, Bill Froberg, Ruben Garcia, Diego Herrera, Luis Herrera, Nick Hostetler, Bob Isabelle, Rafael Josela, James Kane, Dewayne Kitts, Al Kubski, David Latham, Duk Jung Lee, Jose Leon, Robert Lucas, William Marcot, Giorgio Moretti, Jose Mota, Ernie Pedersen, Elvis Pineda, Ubaldo Salinas, Charlie Smith, Miguel Teren, Raymond Tew, Ted Thornton, Marv Throneberry, Carlos Torres, Bo Trumbo, Jerry Turner, Rip Tutor, Murray Zuk

International supervisors
Phil Dale, Rene Francisco, Julian Perez

International scouts
Amado Dinzey, Felix Francisco, Gil Garrido, Jason Lee, Andres Lopez, Hirouki Oya, Rolando Petit, Fernando Villescusa

BALLPARK INFORMATION

Ballpark (capacity, surface)
Turner Field (50,091, grass)
Address
P.O. Box 4064, Atlanta, GA 30302
Official website
www.atlantabraves.com
Business phone
404-522-7630
Ticket information
404-249-6400 or 800-326-4000
Ticket prices
$40 (dugout level), $32 (club level)
$27 (field level, terrace level)
$18 (field pavilion, terrace pavilion)
$12 (upper level), $5 (upper pavilion)
$1 (skyline)
Field dimensions (from home plate)
To left field at foul line, 335 feet
To center field, 401 feet
To right field at foul line, 330 feet
First game played
April 4, 1997 (Braves 5, Cubs 4)

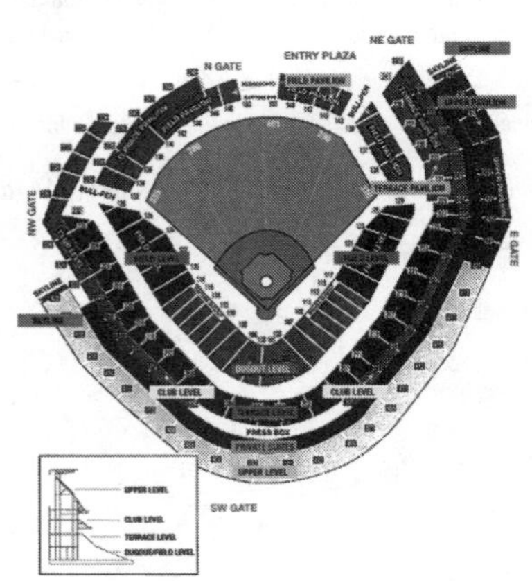

Follow the Braves all season at: www.sportingnews.com/baseball/teams/braves/

BRAVES SPRING ROSTER

No.	PITCHERS	B/T	Ht./Wt.	Born	2000 clubs	Projection
74	Abreu, Winston	R/R	6-2/155	4-5-77	Macon, Green., GC Braves, Rich.	Needs to stay healthy to ensure a future with the Braves.
19	Burkett, John	R/R	6-3/215	11-28-64	Atlanta	He'll see plenty of action as either a starter or long reliever.
47	Glavine, Tom	L/L	6-0/185	3-25-66	Atlanta	He'd be the ace anywhere else. Here, he'll win 20.
	Lewis, Derrick	R/R	6-5/215	5-7-76	Greenville	He'll get his chance to show he belongs, but not yet.
46	Ligtenberg, Kerry	R/R	6-2/215	5-11-71	Atlanta, Richmond	He'll do situational relief, and won't often pitch more than an inning.
31	Maddux, Greg	R/R	6-0/185	4-14-66	Atlanta	Hall of Famer-in waiting has impeccable control.
51	Marquis, Jason	L/R	6-1/185	8-21-78	Greenville, Atlanta, Richmond	He'll contribute as a fifth starter or long reliever.
30	McGlinchy, Kevin	R/R	6-5/220	6-28-77	Atl., Greenville, Rich., GC Braves	Any contribution would be a bonus, as club doesn't expect much.
34	Millwood, Kevin	R/R	6-4/220	12-24-74	Atlanta	Ten wins in 2000 were an aberration. He should win more.
	Moore, Trey	L/L	6-0/190	10-2-72	Ottawa, Montreal	He'll have a tough time cracking rotation.
61	Moss, Damian	R/L	6-0/187	11-24-76	Richmond	Could contribute to a vulnerable bullpen.
43	Perez, Odalis	L/L	6-0/150	6-7-78	DID NOT PLAY	Promising young lefty needs to overcome shoulder problems.
	Ramirez, Horacio	L/L	6-1/170	11-24-79	Myrtle Beach	Class A to pros is too big of a jump, especially for a team with solid rotation.
37	Remlinger, Mike	L/L	6-1/210	3-23-66	Atlanta	He is most valuable as a set up man, but could work middle relief.
49	Rocker, John	R/L	6-4/225	10-17-74	Atlanta, Richmond	Big, hard-throwing lefty is anchor of bullpen.
58	Seelbach, Chris	R/R	6-4/180	12-18-72	Richmond, Atlanta	Will get a chance if there's an injury or someone falters.
29	Smoltz, John	R/R	6-3/220	5-15-67	DID NOT PLAY	Strong return would almost guarantee playoff berth.
	Sobkowiak, Scott	R/R	6-5/230	10-26-77	Greenville	Tommy John surgery will slow ascent.
	Sylvester, Billy	R/R	6-5/220	10-1-76	Myrtle Beach	Outstanding reliever will eventually shore up weak area for Braves.
	Voyles, Brad	R/R	6-0/195	12-30-76	Myrtle Beach	Closer in the wings has John Rocker to overcome.

No.	CATCHERS	B/T	Ht./Wt.	Born	2000 clubs	Projection
9	Bako, Paul	L/R	6-2/205	6-20-72	Houston, Florida, Atlanta	May turn into specialist catching for Greg Maddux.
8	Lopez, Javy	R/R	6-3/200	11-5-70	Atlanta	Count on him for solid production, especially for a catcher.
12	Perez, Eddie	R/R	6-1/185	5-4-68	Atlanta	Backup catcher could be odd man out.

No.	INFIELDERS	B/T	Ht./Wt.	Born	2000 clubs	Projection
	Betemit, Wilson	B/R	6-2/155	7-28-80	Jamestown	No room up the middle for this prospect.
	Brogna, Rico	L/L	6-2/203	4-18-70	Philadelphia, Clearwater, Boston	He'll suffer by comparison to Galarraga.
2	DeRosa, Mark	R/R	6-1/195	2-2-75	Richmond, Atlanta	Utility guy likely back in Class AAA.
1	Furcal, Rafael	B/R	5-10/165	8-24-80	Greenville, Atlanta	Rookie of the Year too talented for sophomore slump.
	Garcia, Jesse	R/R	5-10/171	9-24-73	Baltimore, Rochester	Gives team added depth at short and second.
	Giles, Marcus	R/R	5-8/180	5-18-78	Greenville	His future may depend on what happens to Veras.
18	Helms, Wes	R/R	6-4/230	5-12-76	Richmond, Atlanta	Could see significant time if Chipper moves to right.
10	Jones, Chipper	B/R	6-4/210	4-24-72	Atlanta	Big contract, big bat, might move to outfield.
7	Lockhart, Keith	L/R	5-10/170	11-10-64	Atlanta	Solid pinch-hitter is effective as a starter, too.
4	Veras, Quilvio	B/R	5-10/183	4-3-71	Atlanta	Sitting out 2000 because of injury probably cost him his job in Atlanta.

No.	OUTFIELDERS	B/T	Ht./Wt.	Born	2000 clubs	Projection
	Aldridge, Cory	L/R	6-0/210	6-13-79	Myrtle Beach	Carolina League All-Star not likely to play in Atlanta.
25	Jones, Andruw	R/R	6-1/210	4-23-77	Atlanta	Confident, talented player needs to keep head in the game.
33	Jordan, Brian	R/R	6-1/205	3-29-67	Atlanta	Must rebound after disappointing 2000.
26	Lombard, George	L/R	6-0/202	9-14-75	Richmond, Atlanta	Backup outfielder needs to learn to hit the ball.
	Martinez, Dave	L/L	5-10/190	9-26-64	T.B., Chi. N.L., Texas, Toronto	Career .275 hitter will provide punch off the bench.
15	Surhoff, B.J.	L/R	6-1/200	8-4-64	Baltimore, Atlanta	Veteran presence should help out on team that got younger.

THE COACHING STAFF

Bobby Cox: The suggestion is that Cox had great players, but he never did anything with them. But that's not entirely fair. Cox did good work in getting the Braves to the postseason last year, especially considering John Smoltz missed the whole year. Cox showed his eye for talent by bringing up Rafael Furcal, the Rookie of the Year.

Pat Corrales: Corrales, the dugout coach, has been in baseball since before every player on the team was born. He's got plenty of managing experience, havng skippered three different teams.

Bobby Dews: For Dews, guiding the dugout won't be such a walk in the park this year. With Scott Kamieniecki and Terry Mulholland gone, the relief corps won't be as good as it was last year. Having John Rocker as the closer will help.

Leo Mazzone: If you want to say Mazzone has one of the easiest jobs in baseball because he coaches Greg Maddux, John Smoltz and Tom Glavine, that's fine. But remember that those guys wouldn't be where they are if it wasn't for Mazzone, who has worked with pitchers in the Braves organization since 1979.

Glenn Hubbard: Hubbard had an up-close view of infield action in his years as a second baseman-10 of them with the Braves. He will be in his third year coaching first for the Braves.

Ned Yost: The third base coach knows plenty about the Braves' tendencies. He coached Atlanta's Class A affiliate in Sumter before joining the major league staff in 1991. This will be his third season at third.

THE TOP NEWCOMERS

Rico Brogna: Has big shoes to fill in replacing Galarraga. Brogna, a career .270 hitter, could leave fans longing for the Big Cat. But, he's a great defensive first baseman.

THE TOP PROSPECTS

Wilson Betemit: Shortstop who plays great defense and hits for power and average. He's got a great arm. He's only 20 years old and has Rafael Furcal in front of him, but count on the Braves finding a place to put him.

Marcus Giles: If paired with Furcal, they could form a solid double play combination for many years to come.The younger brother of Pirate Brian Giles, Marcus Giles spent last year in Class AA.

CHICAGO CUBS

NATIONAL LEAGUE CENTRAL DIVISION

2001 SEASON

Cubs
2001 SCHEDULE
Home games shaded; D—Day game (games starting before 5 p.m.)
*—All-Star Game at Safeco Field (Seattle)

APRIL

SUN	MON	TUE	WED	THU	FRI	SAT
1	2 D MON	3	4 D MON	5 D MON	6 D PHI	7 D PHI
8 D PHI	9 MON	10 MON	11 MON	12	13 D PIT	14 D PIT
15 D PIT	16 PHI	17 D PHI	18 D PHI	19	20 PIT	21 D PIT
22 D PIT	23	24 COL	25 COL	26 D COL	27 SF	28 D SF
29 D SF	30					

MAY

SUN	MON	TUE	WED	THU	FRI	SAT
		1 SD	2 SD	3 D SD	4 D LA	5 D LA
6 D LA	7 MIL	8 MIL	9 MIL	10 D MIL	11 STL	12 D STL
13 D STL	14	15 HOU	16 HOU	17 D HOU	18 D ARI	19 D ARI
20 D ARI	21	22 CIN	23 D CIN	24 D CIN	25 D MIL	26 D MIL
27 D MIL	28 D CIN	29 CIN	30 CIN	31		

JUNE

SUN	MON	TUE	WED	THU	FRI	SAT
					1 MIL	2 MIL
3 D MIL	4	5 STL	6 D STL	7 D STL	8 CWS	9 D CWS
10 D CWS	11	12 ARI	13 ARI	14 D ARI	15 D MIN	16 D MIN
17 D MIN	18 STL	19 STL	20 STL	21 D STL	22 D MIL	23 D MIL
24 D MIL	25 NYM	26 D NYM	27 D NYM	28 CIN	29 CIN	30 D CIN

JULY

SUN	MON	TUE	WED	THU	FRI	SAT
1 D CIN	2	3 NYM	4 D NYM	5 NYM	6 DET	7 DET
8 D DET	9	10 *	11	12 D CWS	13 D CWS	14 D CWS
15 D KC	16 KC	17 D KC	18 PIT	19 PIT	20 HOU	21 HOU
22 D HOU	23 HOU	24 PIT	25 D PIT	26 D STL	27 D STL	28 D STL
29 STL	30	31 SD				

AUGUST

SUN	MON	TUE	WED	THU	FRI	SAT
			1 SD	2 D SD	3 LA	4 D LA
5 LA	6	7 COL	8 D COL	9 D COL	10 D SF	11 D SF
12 D SF	13 HOU	14 HOU	15 HOU	16	17 ARI	18 ARI
19 D ARI	20 MIL	21 D MIL	22 D MIL	23 D MIL	24 D STL	25 D STL
26 D STL	27	28 FLA	29 FLA	30 D FLA	31 ATL	

SEPTEMBER

SUN	MON	TUE	WED	THU	FRI	SAT
						1 D ATL
2 D ATL	3 D FLA	4 FLA	5 FLA	6	7 D ATL	8 D ATL
9 D ATL	10 CIN	11 CIN	12 D CIN	13 D CIN	14 D PIT	15 D PIT
16 D PIT	17	18 CIN	19 CIN	20 D CIN	21 HOU	22 HOU
23 D HOU	24 PIT	25 PIT	26 PIT	27 HOU	28 D HOU	29 D HOU
30 D HOU						

FRONT-OFFICE DIRECTORY

Board of directors ....Dennis FitzSimons, Andrew B. MacPhail, Andrew McKenna
President and chief executive officer ....Andrew B. MacPhail
Assistant general manager ....Jim Hendry
Director, baseball operations ....Scott Nelson
Special assistants to the general manageer ....Keith Champion, Larry Himes, Ken Kravec
Director of scouting ....John Stockstill
Director of player development ....Oneri Fleita
Major league advance scout ....Brad Mills
Traveling secretary ....Jimmy Bank
Executive v.p., business operations..................Mark McGuire
Manager, information systems ....Carl Rice
Senior legal counsel/corporate secretary ....Crane Kenney
Controller ....Jodi Norman
Director, human resources ....Jenifer Surma
Vice president, marketing and broadcasting ....John McDonough
Director, promotions and advertising ....Jay Blunk
Director, publications..................Lena McDonagh
Manager, publications ....Jim McArdle
Director, stadium operations ....Paul Rathje
Manager, event operations/security ....Mike Hill
Head groundskeeper..................Roger Baird
Director, ticket operations..................Frank Maloney
Director, media relations ....Sharon Pannozzo
Manager, media information ....Chuck Wasserstrom

MINOR LEAGUE AFFILIATES

Class	Team	League	Manager
AAA	Iowa	International	Bruce Kimm
AA	West Tenn	Southern	Dave Bialas
A	Boise	Northwest	Steve McFarland
A	Daytona	Florida State	Dave Trembley
A	Lansing	Midwest	Julio Garcia
Rookie	Mesa Cubs	Arizona	Carmelo Martinez

BROADCAST INFORMATION

Radio: WGN-AM (720).
TV: WGN-TV (Channel 9); WCIU-TV (Channel 26).
Cable TV: Fox Sports Net Chicago.

SPRING TRAINING

Ballpark (city): HoHoKam Park (Mesa, Ariz.).
Ticket information: 800-638-4253.

ASSISTANCE STAFF

Team physician
Michael Schafer, M.D.

Head athletic trainer
David Tumbas

Assistant athletic trainer
Sandy Krum

Strength and conditioning coordinator
Mark Wilbert

Home clubhouse manager, emeritus
Yosh Kawano

Home clubhouse manager
Tom Hellman

Visiting clubhouse manager
Dana Noeltner

Pacific Rim coordinator
Leon Lee

Regional scouting supervisors
Joe Housey, Brad Kelley, Jim Olander, Mike Soper

Scouts
Mark Adair, Billy Blitzer, Jim Crawford, Steve Fuller, Al Geddes, John Gracio, Bob Hale, Gene Handley, Bill Harford, Steve Hinton, Sam Hughes, Spider Jorgensen, Scott May, Brian Milner, Hector Ortega, Fred Peterson, Tad Powers, Steve Riha, Jose Serra, Mark Servais, Tom Shafer, Mike Soper, Billy Swoope, Jose Trujillo, Glen Van Proyen, Harry Von Suskil

BALLPARK INFORMATION

Ballpark (capacity, surface)
Wrigley Field (39,059, grass)

Address
1060 W. Addison St.
Chicago, IL 60613-4397

Official website
www.cubs.com

Business phone
773-404-2827

Ticket information
773-404-2827

Ticket prices
$30 (club box)
$28 (field box)
$23 (upper deck box, terrace box, family section)
$20 (bleachers)
$18 (terrace reserved)

Field dimensions (from home plate)
To left field at foul line, 355 feet
To center field, 400 feet
To right field at foul line, 353 feet

First game played
April 20, 1916 (Cubs 7, Reds 6)

Follow the Cubs all season at: www.sportingnews.com/baseball/teams/cubs/

CUBS SPRING ROSTER

No.	PITCHERS	B/T	Ht./Wt.	Born	2000 clubs	Projection
46	Bere, Jason	R/R	6-3/215	5-26-71	Milwaukee, Cleveland	Should be valuable and produce in the rotation.
	Chiasson, Scott	R/R	6-2/185	8-14-77	Visalia	Won 11 games in Class A ball, while averaging almost a strikeout an innning.
59	Duncan, Courtney	L/R	6-0/180	10-9-74	West Tenn	Won five games and had 26 saves in the Southern League.
44	Farnsworth, Kyle	R/R	6-4/215	4-14-76	Chicago N.L., Iowa	Will be battling for bullpen job, even though he had trouble with the job last season.
13	Fassero, Jeff	L/L	6-1/195	1-5-63	Boston	Won eight games and had sub 5.00 ERA for Boston last year.
31	Gissell, Chris	R/R	6-5/200	1-4-78	West Tenn	Finally had an above .500 season in the Southern League. Ticketed for AAA.
54	Gonzalez, Jeremi	R/R	6-2/215	1-8-75	Arizona Cubs, Lansing	Has been injured since July 1998. Cubs need him healthy.
45	Gordon, Tom	R/R	5-9/190	11-18-67	DID NOT PLAY	Former closer ready to make comeback after missing '00 season due to injury.
49	Heredia, Felix	L/L	6-0/180	6-18-76	Chicago N.L.	Durable and had seven wins out of the bullpen last year.
32	Lieber, Jon	L/R	6-3/225	4-2-70	Chicago N.L.	Cubs ace finally gets some help in the rotation this year.
33	McNichol, Brian	L/L	6-5/225	5-20-74	Iowa	Looks like he is finally being converted into a reliever.
43	Meyers, Mike	R/R	6-2/210	10-18-77	West Tenn, Iowa	Needs another season at Class AAA. Posted excellent numbers in Class AA.
52	Nation, Joey	L/L	6-2/205	9-28-78	West Tenn, Chicago N.L.	Former Braves prospect looks like he could make the rotation.
35	Ohman, Will	L/L	6-2/195	8-13-77	West Tenn, Chicago N.L.	Had success as reliever in Class AA, but will need a season of Class AAA.
48	Quevedo, Ruben	R/R	6-1/230	1-5-79	Iowa, Chicago N.L.	Good numbers at Class AAA, but got knocked around in 15 starts with big club.
36	Tapani, Kevin	R/R	6-1/190	2-18-64	Chicago N.L.	He won eight games, but had a 5.01 ERA. Tied his career high in strikeouts.
50	Tavarez, Julian	L/R	6-2/190	5-22-73	Colorado	Went 11-5 with Colorado. Pitched as a starter and out of the bullpen.
	Teut, Nathan	R/L	6-7/215	3-11-76	West Tenn	Tall lefthander won 11 games in Class AA. Could use a year of Class AAA though.
47	Van Poppel, Todd	R/R	6-5/235	12-9-71	Iowa, Chicago N.L.	Had a 3.75 ERA in 51 games out of the bullpen.
34	Wood, Kerry	R/R	6-5/230	6-16-77	Daytona, Iowa, Chicago N.L.	Returned from elbow surgery to go 8-7. Should be back to form this season.
	Yennaco, Jay	R/R	6-2/225	11-17-75	West Tenn	Quality reliever had five wins and 10 saves in Southern League.

No.	CATCHERS	B/T	Ht./Wt.	Born	2000 clubs	Projection
27	Girardi, Joe	R/R	5-11/200	10-14-64	Chicago N.L.	Provided veteran leadership behind the plate and posted decent offensive numbers.
	Hundley, Todd	B/R	5-11/199	5-27-69	Los Angeles, Albuquerque	Hit 24 home runs last year, should hit more playing home games at Wrigley.

No.	INFIELDERS	B/T	Ht./Wt.	Born	2000 clubs	Projection
	Coomer, Ron	R/R	5-11/206	11-18-66	Minnesota	Will help solidify each corner position this season.
56	Frese, Nate	R/R	6-3/200	7-10-77	Daytona	Shortstop only made 13 errors in 117 games.
	Gload, Ross	L/L	6-0/185	4-5-76	Portland, Iowa, Chicago N.L.	First baseman hit 30 home runs between Portland and Iowa.
12	Gutierrez, Ricky	R/R	6-1/195	5-23-70	Chicago N.L., Daytona	Had a good year at shortstop, batted .276 and made only seven errors.
	Hinske, Eric	L/R	6-2/225	8-5-77	West Tenn	Hit 20 home runs and had 14 stolen bases in Southern League.
20	Meyers, Chad	R/R	6-0/190	8-8-75	Chicago N.L., Iowa	Utility player might find a role on the bench, if not back to Class AAA.
33	Mueller, Bill	B/R	5-10/180	3-17-71	San Francisco	Switch hitting third baseman will provide leadership on the field.
11	Nieves, Jose	R/R	6-0/180	6-16-75	Chi. N.L., Day., W. Tenn, Iowa	Utility player saw action in 82 games.
57	Ojeda, Augie	B/R	5-9/170	12-20-74	Iowa, Chicago N.L.	Could be backup at shortstop if he hits in spring training.
	Smith, Jason	L/R	6-3/190	7-24-77	West Tenn	Shortstop prospect struck out 130 times in 481 at-bats.
7	Young, Eric	R/R	5-8/175	5-18-67	Chicago N.L.	Provided offense Cubs expected, 54 stolen bases, .297 average and 98 runs scored.
15	Zuleta, Julio	R/R	6-5/235	3-28-75	Chicago N.L., Iowa	Has chance to show he can hit in the majors now that Mark Grace is gone.

No.	OUTFIELDERS	B/T	Ht./Wt.	Born	2000 clubs	Projection
28	Brown, Roosevelt	L/R	5-11/195	8-3-75	Chicago N.L., Iowa	Could be part of the outfield of the future for the Cubs.
9	Buford, Damon	R/R	5-10/180	6-12-70	Chicago N.L.	Job could be in danger if Corey Patterson shows he's ready in spring.
51	Matthews, Gary	B/R	6-3/200	8-25-74	Iowa, Chicago N.L.	Probably will be a fourth outfielder or back in Class AAA.
20	Patterson, Corey	L/R	5-10/180	8-13-79	West Tenn, Chicago N.L.	If he has a good spring, he may end up as a starting outfielder.
	Randolph, Jaisen	B/R	6-0/180	1-19-79	West Tenn	Will end up in minors for the season, needs to work on batting average.
21	Sosa, Sammy	R/R	6-0/220	11-12-68	Chicago N.L.	Shouldn't be too hard for him to put up a fourth 50-homer season.
22	White, Rondell	R/R	6-1/210	2-23-72	Montreal, Chicago N.L.	Played in only 19 games with Cubs after trade from Montreal.

THE COACHING STAFF

Don Baylor, manager: Led the team through turmoil and trade rumors last year. Should have a better record this year now that he has a pitching staff to work with. Should be a competitive team in the N.L. Central.

Oscar Acosta: Coming into his second season as pitching coach. Will need to get some quality innings out of some youngsters in the bullpen.

Sandy Alomar, Sr.: Father of Roberto and Sandy Alomar Jr. is in second season as bullpen coach.

Gene Glynn: Did a good job with the infield defense last year. Also serves as third base coach.

Rene Lachemann: Brings 37 years of major league experience to the Cubs as bench coach.

Jeff Pentland: Has been the Cubs hitting coach since July 1997.

Billy Williams: In his 15th season with the Cubs as a coach. He is the first base coach and oversees outfield defense.

THE TOP NEWCOMERS

Jason Bere: Veteran starter was brought in to help fill in the rotation. Should be a good addition and a nice compliment to Lieber, Tapani, and Wood.

Julian Tavarez: Will see lots of action out of the bullpen. Probably will fill the long relief role.

Bill Mueller: His is a quality third baseman. While he won't put up flashy numbers, but he is solid and dependable.

THE TOP PROSPECTS

Ross Gload: HIt .404 with AAA Iowa in 28 games. With Zuleta at first, he will probably end up in Class AAA to learn to play the outfield.

Corey Patterson: This first-round pick from the draft of '98 will probably be given every opportunity to make the club this spring.

Julio Zuleta: If he can hit like he did in the minors, Cubs fans won't miss Mark Grace that much.

CINCINNATI REDS

NATIONAL LEAGUE CENTRAL DIVISION

2001 SEASON

Reds 2001 SCHEDULE

Home games shaded; D—Day game (games starting before 5 p.m.)
*—All-Star Game at Safeco Field (Seattle)

APRIL

SUN	MON	TUE	WED	THU	FRI	SAT
1	2 D ATL	3 PIT	4 PIT	5 D PIT	6 MIL	7 D MIL
8 D MIL	9 D PIT	10	11 PIT	12 PIT	13 NYM	14 D NYM
15 D NYM	16	17 MIL	18 MIL	19	20 NYM	21 D NYM
22 D NYM	23	24 SF	25 SF	26 D SF	27 COL	28 D COL
29 D COL	30					

MAY

SUN	MON	TUE	WED	THU	FRI	SAT
		1 LA	2 LA	3 LA	4 SD	5 D SD
6 D SD	7 ARI	8 ARI	9 ARI	10	11 HOU	12 HOU
13 HOU	14 HOU	15 ARI	16 ARI	17 D ARI	18 HOU	19 D HOU
20 D HOU	21	22 CUB	23 D CUB	24 D CUB	25 STL	26 STL
27 D STL	28 D CUB	29 CUB	30 CUB	31		

JUNE

SUN	MON	TUE	WED	THU	FRI	SAT
					1 STL	2 D STL
3 STL	4 STL	5 MIL	6 MIL	7	8 CLE	9 D CLE
10 D CLE	11	12 CWS	13 CWS	14 CWS	15 COL	16 COL
17 D COL	18 MIL	19 MIL	20 MIL	21 HOU	22 HOU	23 HOU
24 D HOU	25	26 STL	27 STL	28 CUB	29 CUB	30 D CUB

JULY

SUN	MON	TUE	WED	THU	FRI	SAT
1 D CUB	2 PIT	3 PIT	4 D PIT	5 D PIT	6 MIN	7 MIN
8 D MIN	9	10 *	11	12 CLE	13 CLE	14 D CLE
15 D DET	16 DET	17 DET	18 ATL	19 D ATL	20 FLA	21 FLA
22 D FLA	23 ATL	24 ATL	25 D ATL	26	27 FLA	28 FLA
29 D FLA	30	31 LA				

AUGUST

SUN	MON	TUE	WED	THU	FRI	SAT
			1 LA	2 LA	3 SD	4 SD
5 D SD	6	7 SF	8 SF	9 SF	10 COL	11 COL
12 D COL	13 STL	14 STL	15 STL	16 STL	17 MIL	18 MIL
19 D MIL	20 STL	21 STL	22 STL	23 D STL	24 MON	25 MON
26 D MON	27	28 HOU	29 HOU	30 D HOU	31 PIT	

SEPTEMBER

SUN	MON	TUE	WED	THU	FRI	SAT
						1 PIT
2 D PIT	3 D HOU	4 HOU	5 D HOU	6 PIT	7 PIT	8 PIT
9 D PIT	10 CUB	11 CUB	12 D CUB	13 D CUB	14 PHI	15 D PHI
16 D PHI	17	18 CUB	19 CUB	20 D CUB	21 MIL	22 MIL
23 D MIL	24	25 PHI	26 PHI	27 PHI	28 MON	29 D MON
30 D MON						

FRONT-OFFICE DIRECTORY

Chief executive officer .... Carl H. Lindner
Chief operating officer .... John Allen
General manager .... Jim Bowden
Assistant general manager .... Darrell "Doc" Rodgers
Director of player personnel .... Leland Maddox
Special assistant to the general manager/advance scout .... Gene Bennett
Special assistants to the general manager .... Larry Barton Jr., Johnny Bench, Al Goldis, Gary Hughes
Director of baseball administration .... Brad Kullman
Director of scouting .... Kasey McKeon
Assistant director of scouting .... Johnny Almaraz
Executive assistant to the general manager .... Lois Schneider
Senior advisor, player development .... Sheldon "Chief" Bender
Admin. assistant, player development .... Lois Hudson
Senior advisor, scouting .... Bob Zuk
Director of scouting administration .... Wilma Mann
Traveling secretary .... Gary Wahoff
Director of media relations .... Rob Butcher
Public relations assistant .... Larry Herms
Controller .... Anthony Ward
Director, stadium operations .... Dellan Mullin
Director, ticket department .... John O'Brien
Director of season/group sales .... Pat McCaffrey
Director of communications .... Mike Ringering
Assistant director of communications .... Ralph Mitchell
Director of new stadium development .... Jenny Gardner
Marketing consultant .... Cal Levy
Legal counsel .... Robert C. Martin
Director, group sales .... Brad Blettner
Assistant director, media relations .... Michael Vassallo
Exec. assistant to chief operating officer .... Joyce Pfarr
Business and broadcast administrator .... Ginny Kamp

MINOR LEAGUE AFFILIATES

Class	Team	League	Manager
AAA	Louisville	International	Dave Miley
AA	Chattanooga	Southern	Phil Wellman
A	Dayton	Midwest	Donnie Scott
A	Mudville	California	Len Dykstra
Rookie	Billings	Pioneer	To be announced
Rookie	Gulf Coast Reds	Gulf Coast	Edgar Caceres

BROADCAST INFORMATION

Radio: WLW-AM (700).
Cable TV: Fox Sports Net.

SPRING TRAINING

Ballpark (city): Ed Smith Stadium (Sarasota, Fla.).
Ticket information: 941-954-4101.

ASSISTANCE STAFF

Head trainer
Greg Lynn

Assistant trainer
Mark Mann

Conditioning coordinator
Lance Sewell

Field superintendent
Jeff Guilkey

Senior clubhouse & equipment manager
Bernie Stowe

Reds clubhouse & equipment manager
Rick Stowe

Visiting clubhouse & equipment manager
Mark Stowe

Major League scout/national cross-checker
Jeff Barton

Major League scout
De Jon Watson

Cross-checkers
Butch Baccala, John Castleberry, Alvin Rittman, Bill Scherrer

Director of international scouting
Jorge Oquendo

Scouting supervisors
Terry Abbott, Howard Bowens, John Brickley, Mark Corey, Rex De La Nuez, Robert Filotei, Jerry Flowers, Jimmy Gonzales, Robert Koontz, Craig Kornfeld, Steve Kring, Tom LeVasseur, Brian Mejia, Cotton Nye, Tom Severtson, Perry Smith, Brian Wilson, Greg Zunino

Scouts
Oswaldo Alvarez, John Bellino, George Blackburn, Fred Blair, Kevin Carcamo, Keith Chapman, Edwin Daub, Felix Delgado, Orlando Granda, Jim Grief, Don Gust, Frank Henderson, Don Hill, Thomas Herrera, Juan Linares, Victor Mateo, Denny Nagel, Rafael Nava, Everett Renteria, Glenn Serviente, Marlon Styles, Lee Toole, Ruben Vargas, Mike Wallace, John Walsh, Nathan Ware, Roger Weberg

BALLPARK INFORMATION

Ballpark (capacity, surface)
Cinergy Field (39,000, grass)
Address
100 Cinergy Field
Cincinnati, OH 45202
Official website
www.cincinnatireds.com
Business phone
513-421-4510
Ticket information
513-421-7337, 1-800-829-5353
Ticket prices
$28, $21 (blue level box seats)
$21, $16 (green level box seats)
$15 (yellow level box seats)
$14 (red level box seats)
$9 (red level reserved seats)
$5 ("top six" reserved seats)
Field dimensions (from home plate)
To left field at foul line, 330 feet
To center field, 404 feet
To right field at foul line, 330 feet
First game played
June 30, 1970 (Braves 8, Reds 2)

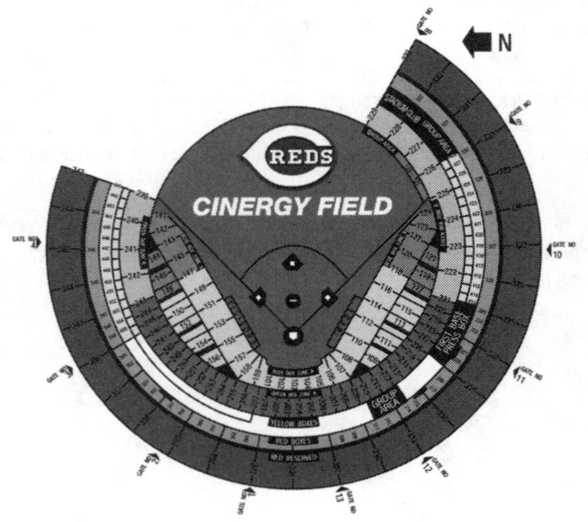

Follow the Reds all season at: www.sportingnews.com/baseball/teams/reds/

REDS SPRING ROSTER

No.	PITCHERS	B/T	Ht./Wt.	Born	2000 clubs	Projection
57	Andrews, Clayton	R/L	6-0/175	5-15-78	Syracuse, Toronto	Starter who most likely won't crack rotation, but may come out of bullpen.
61	Atchley, Justin	L/L	6-3/215	9-5-73	Louisville	Workhorse in minors who is still a couple years away from the big leagues.
29	Bell, Rob	R/R	6-5/225	1-17-77	Cincinnati, Louisville	Young starter with good stuff. Reds hoping for breakthrough season.
52	Brower, Jim	R/R	6-2/205	12-29-72	Buffalo, Cleveland	Starter with potential who could help out of the bullpen.
68	Estrella, Leo	R/R	6-1/185	2-20-75	Tennessee, Syracuse, Toronto	Worked his way through minors last year for a shot in the big leagues.
40	Etherton, Seth	R/R	6-1/200	10-17-76	Edmonton, Anaheim	Pitched well with Angels at times and could help out the Reds pitching staff.
43	Fernandez, Osvaldo	R/R	6-2/193	11-4-68	Chattanooga, Louis., Cincinnati	Great potential and could be surprise of the staff this season.
59	Glauber, Keith	R/R	6-2/190	1-18-72	Chattanooga, Louis., Cincinnati	Might have earned himself a spot in the bullpen last season.
32	Graves, Danny	R/R	5-11/185	8-7-73	Cincinnati	Did it all last year picking up 10 wins and racking up 30 saves.
38	Harnisch, Pete	R/R	6-0/228	9-23-66	Cincinnati, Louisville	Needs to get back to health to help shaky Reds starting rotation.
45	Dessens, Elmer	R/R	6-0/187	1-13-72	Louisville, Cincinnati	Valuable pitcher who can start or come out of the bullpen.
39	Mercado, Hector	L/L	6-3/235	4-29-74	Cincinnati, Louisville	Lefty who could help solidify Reds bullpen.
54	Reith, Brian	R/R	6-5/190	2-28-78	Tampa, Dayton, Chattanooga	Young starting pitcher with promise. Will have tough time cracking rotation.
53	Reitsma, Chris	R/R	6-5/214	12-31-77	Trenton, Sarasota	Another young starting pitcher who is probably still a few years away.
49	Reyes, Dennys	R/L	6-3/246	4-19-77	Cincinnati	Reliable out of the bullpen and can log a lot of games.
46	Riedling, John	R/R	5-11/190	8-29-75	Louisville, Cincinnati	Hard thrower who will be counted on out of bullpen.
56	Sullivan, Scott	R/R	6-3/210	3-13-71	Cincinnati	Valuable relief pitcher who can pitch in a lot of games and innings.
48	Williamson, Scott	R/R	6-0/185	2-17-76	Cincinnati	Strong out of bullpen and might see some time in the starting rotation.
51	Wohlers, Mark	R/R	6-4/207	1-23-70	Dayton, Louisville, Cincinnati	Earned a spot in bullpen with performance last season.
41	Yarnall, Ed	L/L	6-3/234	12-4-75	Louis., New York A.L., Columbus	Left hander that could find spot in bullpen or rotation.

No.	CATCHERS	B/T	Ht./Wt.	Born	2000 clubs	Projection
2	LaRue, Jason	R/R	5-11/200	3-19-74	Louisville, Cincinnati	Catching duties are for him to lose with Benito Santiago gone.
50	Sardinha, Dane	R/R	5-11/205	4-8-79	DID NOT PLAY	Very young catcher with potential. Probably a few years away from taking over.
	Stinnett, Kelly	R/R	5-11/225	2-4-70	Arizona	Brought in for backup to LaRue.

No.	INFIELDERS	B/T	Ht./Wt.	Born	2000 clubs	Projection
17	Boone, Aaron	R/R	6-2/200	3-9-73	Cincinnati	Missed part of last season with injury and still put up decent numbers.
21	Casey, Sean	L/R	6-4/225	7-2-74	Cincinnati	Solid first baseman with great bat and decent glove.
12	Castro, Juan	R/R	5-10/187	6-20-72	Louisville, Cincinnati	Could be valuable bench player who can fill several infield positions.
6	Dawkins, Gookie	R/R	6-1/180	5-12-79	Cincinnati, Chattanooga	Did not hit well last season, but has potential to be something special.
79	Espinosa, David	B/R	6-1/170	12-16-81	DID NOT PLAY	Larkin's eventual replacement at shortstop, but not for a few years.
11	Larkin, Barry	R/R	6-0/185	4-28-64	Cincinnati	Still one of the best shortstops in the game.
28	Larson, Brandon	R/R	6-0/210	5-24-76	Chattanooga, Louisville	Third baseman of the future. Most likely to start year in Louisville.
3	Reese, Pokey	R/R	5-11/180	6-10-73	Cincinnati	Good defensively and solid offensive player with speed.
16	Sadler, Donnie	R/R	5-6/175	6-17-75	Pawtucket, Boston	Can play almost every postition and help off the bench.

No.	OUTFIELDERS	B/T	Ht./Wt.	Born	2000 clubs	Projection
22	Clark, Brady	R/R	6-2/195	4-18-73	Louisville, Cincinnati	Solid season last year could help him make the big league club.
4	Coleman, Michael	R/R	5-11/215	8-16-75	Pawtucket	Bounced around minors for a few years and most likely will stay there.
77	Dunn, Adam	L/R	6-6/235	11-9-79	Dayton	Few years away from the majors, but has great offensive skills.
30	Griffey, Ken	L/L	6-3/205	11-21-69	Cincinnati	Expect better numbers out of him after year under his belt in Cinicinnati.
	Guerrero, Wilton	B/R	6-0/175	10-24-74	Montreal	Will get a chance to play every day if he hits consistently.
76	Melian, Jackson	R/R	6-2/190	1-7-80	Norwich, Chattanooga	Good outfielder with speed, but will start season in minors.
7	Ochoa, Alex	R/R	6-0/195	3-29-72	Cincinnati, Chattanooga	Coming off career year in first season with the Reds.
34	Tucker, Michael	L/R	6-2/185	6-25-71	Cincinnati	Production down a little and could split time in the outfield.
25	Young, Dmitri	B/R	6-2/235	10-11-73	Cincinnati	Defense is a question, but he can definitely hit.

THE COACHING STAFF

Bob Boone, manager: Boone gets another shot as manager after coaching the Royals from 1995 to 1997. Boone enjoyed a long Major League playing career for 19 seasons and will become just the sixth person to manage his son

Bill Doran: Doran has been in the Reds organization since 1995 after a 12 year playing career with the Astros, Reds and Brewers.

Tim Foli: Foli joins Boone's coaching staff for the second time in his career after coaching with him in Kansas City in 1996. Foli and Boone also played for the Angels together in 1982 and 1983.

Ken Griffey Sr.: After starring on Big Red Machine in the 70's, he now gets to see his son star on the Reds as a coach.

Don Gullett: Stays on as pitching coach for eighth consecutive season.

Tom Hume: Former Reds pitcher returns for sixth season on coaching staff.

Ron Oester: Oester was almost the next manager of the Reds, but remains on coaching staff for 25th season with Reds organization.

THE TOP NEWCOMERS

Kelly Stinnett: Picked up to backup LaRue and provide some pop off the bench. Good defensive catcher who will do a solid job backing up LaRue.

Wilton Guerrero: One of the best pinch hitters in the league the past few season and the Reds are looking forward to his bat off the bench this season. Can also start on a regular basis if needed.

THE TOP PROSPECTS

David Espinosa: The Red's shorstop of the future. Larkin still has a few years left and Espinosa should be ready to step in when Larkin vacates the position.

Dane Sardinha: Like Espinosa, Sardinha is a player who could take over a position in a few seasons. Sardinha was a highly touted catcher coming out of the draft last season.

Brandon Larson: Could be taking over the third base position by the end of the season or early next year. Can hit for power and average, health is the only question.

Colorado Rockies

National League West Division

2001 SEASON

Rockies 2001 SCHEDULE

Home games shaded; D—Day game (games starting before 5 p.m.)
*—All-Star Game at Safeco Field (Seattle)

APRIL

SUN	MON	TUE	WED	THU	FRI	SAT
1	2 D STL	3	4 STL	5 STL	6 SD	7 D SD
8 D SD	9 D STL	10	11 STL	12 D STL	13 ARI	14 D ARI
15 D ARI	16	17 SD	18 SD	19 D SD	20 ARI	21 ARI
22 D ARI	23	24 CUB	25 CUB	26 D CUB	27 CIN	28 D CIN
29 D CIN	30					

MAY

SUN	MON	TUE	WED	THU	FRI	SAT
		1 PHI	2 PHI	3 D PHI	4 PIT	5 PIT
6 D PIT	7 NYM	8 NYM	9 NYM	10 D NYM	11 MON	12 D MON
13 D MON	14	15 ATL	16 D ATL	17 ATL	18 FLA	19 FLA
20 D FLA	21 LA	22 LA	23 D LA	24 SF	25 SF	26 D SF
27 D SF	28 D LA	29 LA	30 LA	31		

JUNE

SUN	MON	TUE	WED	THU	FRI	SAT
					1 SF	2 D SF
3 D SF	4	5 HOU	6 HOU	7 HOU	8 STL	9 STL
10 D STL	11	12 SEA	13 SEA	14 D SEA	15 CIN	16 CIN
17 D CIN	18 HOU	19 HOU	20 HOU	21 ARI	22 ARI	23 D ARI
24 D ARI	25 SD	26 SD	27 SD	28	29 ARI	30 ARI

JULY

SUN	MON	TUE	WED	THU	FRI	SAT
1 D ARI	2	3 SD	4 SD	5 D SD	6 ANA	7 ANA
8 D ANA	9	10 *	11	12 TEX	13 TEX	14 TEX
15 D OAK	16 OAK	17 D OAK	18 SF	19 SF	20 LA	21 D LA
22 D LA	23 SF	24 SF	25 D SF	26 LA	27 LA	28 D LA
29 LA	30	31 PHI				

AUGUST

SUN	MON	TUE	WED	THU	FRI	SAT
			1 PHI	2 D PHI	3 PIT	4 PIT
5 D PIT	6	7 CUB	8 D CUB	9 D CUB	10 CIN	11 CIN
12 D CIN	13	14 ATL	15 ATL	16 ATL	17 FLA	18 FLA
19 D FLA	20	21 NYM	22 NYM	23 NYM	24 MIL	25 MIL
26 D MIL	27	28 LA	29 LA	30 LA	31 SF	

SEPTEMBER

SUN	MON	TUE	WED	THU	FRI	SAT
						1 D SF
2 D SF	3 D SF	4 LA	5 LA	6 LA	7 SF	8 D SF
9 D SF	10	11 ARI	12 ARI	13 ARI	14 SD	15 SD
16 D SD	17 ARI	18 ARI	19 D ARI	20 MON	21 MON	22 MON
23 D MON	24 SD	25 SD	26 SD	27 D SD	28 MIL	29 D MIL
30 D MIL						

FRONT-OFFICE DIRECTORY

Chairman, president and corporate executive officer....Jerry McMorris
Vice chairmen....Charles Monfort, Richard Monfort
Executive vice president, business operations....Keli McGregor
Executive vice president, general manager....Dan O'Dowd
Senior vice president, chief financial officer....Hal Roth
Vice president, finance....Michael Kent
Vice president, sales and marketing....Greg Feasel
Vice president, ticket operations and sales....Sue Ann McClaren
Senior director, public relations and communications....Jay Alves
Senior director, Coors Field operations....Kevin Kahn
Senior director, personnel and administration....Liz Stecklein
Senior director, corporate sales....Marcy English Glasser
Director of player personnel....Bill Geivett
Director of major league operations....Paul Egins
Director of scouting....Bill Schmidt
Manager of broadcasting....Jim Fairchild
Director, community affairs....Roger Kinney
Director, information systems....Bill Stephani
Director, merchandising....Jim Kellogg
Director, promotions and special events....Alan Bossart
Director, ticket sales....Jill Roberts
Director, ticket services & spring training business operations....Chuck Javernick

MINOR LEAGUE AFFILIATES

Class	Team	League	Manager
AAA	Colorado Springs	Pacific Coast	Chris Cron
AA	Carolina	Southern	Ron Gideon
A	Salem	Carolina	Dave Collins
A	Asheville	South Atlantic	Joe Mikulik
A	Tri-Cities	Northwest	Billy White
Rookie	Casper	Pioneer	P.J. Carey

BROADCAST INFORMATION

Radio: KOA-AM (850), KCUV-AM (1150).
TV: KWGN-TV (Channel 2).
Cable TV: Fox Sports Rocky Mountain.

SPRING TRAINING

Ballpark (city): Hi Corbett Field (Tucson, Ariz.).
Ticket information: 1-800-388-ROCK.

ASSISTANCE STAFF

Head groundskeeper
Mark Razum

Coordinator of instruction
Rick Mathews

Special assignment scout
Dave Holliday

Regional supervisors
Jay Darnell
Danny Montgomery

Major League scouts
Pat Daugherty
Dave Garcia
Jim Fregosi Jr.
Will George

Professional scouts
Joe McDonald
Steve Schryver
Art Pontarelli

Scouts
John Cedarburg
Dar Cox
Mike Ericson
Mike Garlatti
Bert Holt
Bill Hughes
Eric Johnson
Jay Matthews
Sean O'Connor
Tom Wheeler
Ty Coslow
Mike Day
Abe Flores
Orsino Hill
Greg Hopkins
Damon Iannelli
Bill Mackenzie
Lance Nichols
Ed Santa

International scouts
Phil Allen, Dario Arias, Kent Blasingame, Francisco Cartava, Cristobal A. Giron, Alexander Marquez, Brian McRobie, Atanacio Mendez, Jorge Moreno, Ramon Pena, Jorge Posada, Reed Spencer, Ron Steele

BALLPARK INFORMATION

Ballpark (capacity, surface)
Coors Field (50,445, grass)
Address
2001 Blake St., Denver, CO 80205-2000
Official website
www.coloradorockies.com
Business phone
303-292-0200
Ticket information
800-388-7625
Ticket prices
$32 (club level, infield)
$30 (club level, outfield
$27 (infield box)
$21.50 (outfield box)
$16/13 (lower reserved, infield/outfield)
$12 (upper reserved infield, RF box)
$11 (lower reserved corner)
$10 (RF mezzanine)
$9 (upper reserved, outfield; lower pavilion)
$8 (lower pavilion)
$7 (upper reserved corner)
$6/5 (lower/upper RF reserved)
$4/1 (rockpile)
Field dimensions (from home plate)
To left field at foul line, 347 feet
To center field, 415 feet
To right field at foul line, 350
First game played
April 26, 1995 (Rockies 11, Mets 9, 14 innings)

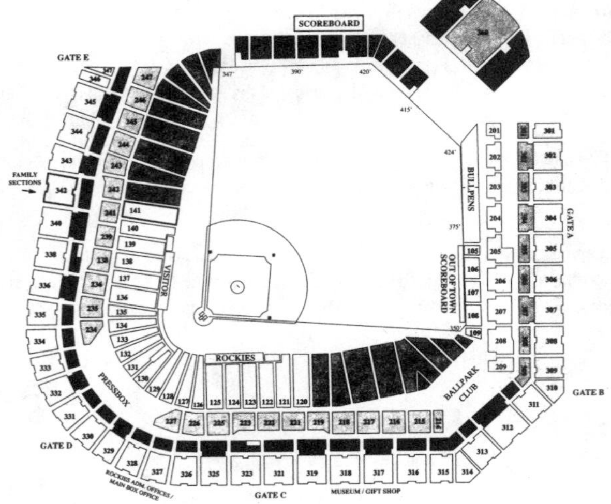

Follow the Rockies all season at: www.sportingnews.com/baseball/teams/rockies/

ROCKIES SPRING ROSTER

No.	PITCHERS	B/T	Ht./Wt.	Born	2000 clubs	Projection
34	Astacio, Pedro	R/R	6-2/210	11-28-69	Colorado	Will benefit from not having to be staff ace.
73	Averette, Robert	R/R	6-2/195	9-30-76	Chattanooga, Louisville, Carolina	Was in Class AAA briefly before trade to Rockies, needs full year in Class AAA.
41	Bohanon, Brian	L/L	6-2/240	8-1-68	Colorado	Had a sub-5.00 ERA in 34 games, will be solid number four starter.
56	Chacon, Shawn	R/R	6-3/212	12-23-77	Carolina	Led Southern League in shutouts and strikeouts. Led league in walks too.
43	Chouinard, Bobby	R/R	6-1/190	5-1-72	Colorado Springs, Colorado	Is effective in pitching one inning of relief work.
50	Christman, Tim	L/L	6-0/195	3-31-75	Carolina	Injury-prone reliever needs to stay healthy in order to reach the majors.
70	Cook, Aaron	R/R	6-3/175	2-8-79	Asheville, Salem	Tied for South Atlantic League lead in shutouts.
18	DeJean, Mike	R/R	6-2/212	9-28-70	Colorado Springs, Colorado	Another quality reliever in the bullpen for the Rockies.
45	Dipoto, Jerry	R/R	6-2/205	5-24-68	Colorado Springs, Colorado	Former closer will have similar set-up role again this season.
68	Dorame, Randey	L/L	6-2/205	1-23-79	V. Beach, San Antonio, Carolina	Solid starter acquired from Dodgers will need a season of Class AAA.
10	Hampton, Mike	R/L	5-10/180	9-9-72	New York N.L.	One of the best ground ball pitchers in the majors.
48	House, Craig	R/R	6-2/210	7-8-77	Salem, Carolina, C. Spr., Colo.	Skyrocketed through system to pitch in 16 games out of the bullpen with big club.
74	Hudson, Luke	R/R	6-3/195	5-2-77	Salem	Another good pitching prospect will end up in Class AA for most of the season.
49	Jimenez, Jose	R/R	6-3/228	7-7-73	Colorado	Had 5 wins and 24 saves in new role as Rockies closer.
60	Kalinowski, Josh	L/L	6-2/190	12-12-76	Carolina	Will have to bounce back from injury in order to stay in Rockies plans.
28	Myers, Mike	L/L	6-4/214	6-26-69	Colorado	Lefthanded situational pitcher is very effective. Had 1.99 ERA.
15	Neagle, Denny	L/L	6-3/225	9-13-68	Cincinnati, New York A.L.	Will help provide Rockies with a nasty one-two punch of starting pitchers.
40	Rose, Brian	R/R	6-3/215	2-13-76	Boston, Pawtucket, Colorado	Should be spot starter after trade from Red Sox.
52	Thomson, John	R/R	6-3/187	10-1-73	Arizona Rockies, Portland	Needs to stay healthy. He has been injured each of the last three years.
29	Villone, Ron	L/L	6-3/237	1-16-70	Cincinnati	Lefthanded starter who will improve the Rockies rotation over last year's group.
46	Wasdin, John	R/R	6-2/195	8-5-72	Boston, Pawtucket, Colorado	Will have to battle for a spot in the bullpen and for a spot in the rotation.
36	White, Gabe	L/L	6-2/200	11-20-71	Cincinnati, Colorado	11 wins, 82 strikeouts, 5 saves and a 2.17 ERA.
21	Yoshii, Masato	R/R	6-2/210	4-20-65	Colorado	Only won 6 games last year. Rockies will be looking for more production.

No.	CATCHERS	B/T	Ht./Wt.	Born	2000 clubs	Projection
8	Mayne, Brent	L/R	6-1/192	4-19-68	Colorado	Dependable catcher who can also hit. Has two straight .300 plus seasons.
15	Petrick, Ben	R/R	6-0/205	4-7-77	Colorado Springs, Colorado	Top catching prospect just needs major league experience.

No.	INFIELDERS	B/T	Ht./Wt.	Born	2000 clubs	Projection
2	Butler, Brent	R/R	6-0/180	2-11-78	Colorado Springs	Future second baseman batted .292 in Class AAA.
7	Cirillo, Jeff	R/R	6-1/195	9-23-69	Colorado	Had first season with 100 plus RBIs and 100 plus runs scored.
17	Helton, Todd	L/L	6-2/206	8-20-73	Colorado	Almost batted .400. As a consolation he led the league in hits, doubles and RBIs.
	Norton, Greg	B/R	6-1/205	7-6-72	Chicago A.L., Charlotte	Will help provide infield depth and a bat off the bench.
23	Pena, Elvis	B/R	5-11/155	9-15-76	Colorado, Carolina	Speedy middle infielder led Southern League in stolen bases.
5	Perez, Neifi	B/R	6-0/175	6-2-75	Colorado	Durable shortstop played in all 162 games. Is also a steady run producer.
22	Shumpert, Terry	R/R	6-0/200	8-16-66	Colorado	Utility player found action in 115 games.
	Sosa, Juan	R/R	6-1/175	8-19-75	Colorado Springs	Shortstop prospect is stuck in Class AAA behind Neifi Perez.
51	Uribe, Juan	R/R	5-11/175	7-22-80	Salem	Solid shortstop prospect could be a five tool player if things work out.
14	Walker, Todd	L/R	6-0/181	5-25-73	Minnesota, Salt Lake, Colorado	Minnesota cast-off may have found a home in Colorado.

No.	OUTFIELDERS	B/T	Ht./Wt.	Born	2000 clubs	Projection
	Gant, Ron	R/R	6-0/196	3-2-65	Philadelphia, Anaheim	Home run hitter should benefit from thin air of Denver.
27	Hollandsworth, Todd	L/L	6-2/215	4-20-73	Los Angeles, Colorado	Former Rookie of the Year took off after trade out of L.A.
9	Pierre, Juan	L/L	6-0/170	8-14-77	Carolina, C. Spr., Colorado	Sensational rookie needs to learn to hit more than singles.
33	Walker, Larry	L/R	6-3/237	12-1-66	Colorado	Needs to stay healthy all season to regain MVP form.

THE COACHING STAFF

Buddy Bell, manager: Had a great first season as manager. He will have a bigger challenge this year with trying to mold some newcomers into the rest of the team. As long as those players come close to reaching expectations, this should be a playoff team. He will have to keep everybody mentally ready for the game, especially when playing at home. The team went 82-80 last year and will need to win at least 15 more games for a playoff berth. Buddy Bell might be the man to take this club back to the postseason.

Rich Donnelly: Third base coach in a mainstay in Colorado. He followed Jim Leyland there and now is in his third season with the Rockies.

Toby Harrah: Has worked with Buddy Bell previously in Cincinnati and Detroit. He brings 16 years of experience to his job as bench coach.

Clint Hurdle: Has been hitting instructor since 1997 season. Who is going argue with the job he did last year?

Fred Kendall: Father of Jason Kendall, the starting catcher of the Pirates. He is in his second season as bullpen coach. Did a good job last year converting Jose Jimenez to a closer.

Marcel Lachemann: Might have the toughest job of allas pitching coach. Will have to help Hampton and Neagle adjust to the thin air while pitching at Coors Field.

Dallas Williams: In second year with Rockies as first base coach and baserunning coach. Helped to jumpstart Rockies running game last season, a trend that should continue this year.

THE TOP NEWCOMERS

Mike Hampton: Spurned offers from other teams to sign with Colorado. Will have to keep batters hitting the ball on the ground in order to be successful at Coors Field.

Denny Neagle: Was having a stellar year at Cincinnati, which turned into a so-so year after starting a few games for the Yankees. He should offer a good one-two punch with Hampton.

Ron Villone: The third lefthander should help to fill out the Rockies rotation. Won a combined 19 games in the last two seasons.

THE TOP PROSPECTS

Juan Pierre: Went through two levels of minor league ball to reach the majors last season. He needs to have more than 2 extra-base hits every 200 at-bats in order to stay in the majors.

Shawn Chacon: Rockies will keep a close eye on his development. He only won 10 games in 27 starts. A season in AAA will get him ready for 2002.

FLORIDA MARLINS

NATIONAL LEAGUE EAST DIVISION

2001 SEASON

Marlins 2001 SCHEDULE

Home games shaded; D—Day game (games starting before 5 p.m.)
*—All-Star Game at Safeco Field (Seattle)

APRIL

SUN	MON	TUE	WED	THU	FRI	SAT
1	2 D PHI	3 PHI	4 PHI	5	6 ATL	7 ATL
8 D ATL	9 PHI	10 PHI	11 PHI	12	13 MON	14 MON
15 D MON	16 ATL	17 ATL	18 D ATL	19 MON	20 MON	21 MON
22 D MON	23 ARI	24 ARI	25 ARI	26	27 HOU	28 D HOU
29 D HOU	30					

MAY

SUN	MON	TUE	WED	THU	FRI	SAT
		1 STL	2 STL	3 STL	4 MIL	5 MIL
6 D MIL	7 LA	8 LA	9 LA	10 LA	11 SD	12 SD
13 D SD	14	15 SF	16 SF	17 SF	18 COL	19 COL
20 D COL	21 ATL	22 ATL	23 ATL	24 NYM	25 NYM	26 D NYM
27 D NYM	28 PIT	29 PIT	30 PIT	31 NYM		

JUNE

SUN	MON	TUE	WED	THU	FRI	SAT
					1 NYM	2 NYM
3 D NYM	4	5 PIT	6 PIT	7 D PIT	8 TOR	9 D TOR
10 D TOR	11	12 BOS	13 BOS	14 BOS	15 TB	16 TB
17 D TB	18 ATL	19 ATL	20 ATL	21 D ATL	22 PHI	23 PHI
24 D PHI	25 MON	26 MON	27 MON	28 PHI	29 PHI	30 PHI

JULY

SUN	MON	TUE	WED	THU	FRI	SAT
1 D PHI	2	3 MON	4 MON	5 D MON	6 TB	7 D TB
8 D TB	9	10 *	11	12 NYY	13 NYY	14 D NYY
15 D BAL	16 BAL	17 BAL	18 NYM	19 D NYM	20 CIN	21 CIN
22 D CIN	23 NYM	24 NYM	25 NYM	26	27 CIN	28 CIN
29 D CIN	30	31 MIL				

AUGUST

SUN	MON	TUE	WED	THU	FRI	SAT
			1 MIL	2 D MIL	3 STL	4 STL
5 D STL	6	7 ARI	8 ARI	9 D ARI	10 HOU	11 HOU
12 D HOU	13	14 SF	15 SF	16 D SF	17 COL	18 COL
19 D COL	20	21 LA	22 LA	23 LA	24 SD	25 SD
26 D SD	27 SD	28 CUB	29 CUB	30 D CUB	31 NYM	

SEPTEMBER

SUN	MON	TUE	WED	THU	FRI	SAT
						1 NYM
2 D NYM	3 D CUB	4 CUB	5 CUB	6	7 NYM	8 NYM
9 D NYM	10	11 MON	12 MON	13 D MON	14 ATL	15 ATL
16 D ATL	17 MON	18 MON	19 MON	20	21 PHI	22 PHI
23 D PHI	24 ATL	25 ATL	26 ATL	27	28 PHI	29 PHI
30 D PHI						

FRONT-OFFICE DIRECTORY

Owner/chairman .... John W. Henry
Vice chairman .... David Ginsberg
President and general manager .... David Dombrowski
Vice president and assistant general manager .... Dave Littlefield
V.p. and assistant to the general manager .... Scott Reid
Vice president, baseball legal counsel .... John Westhoff
Exec. v.p., sales, marketing & communication .... Julio G. Rebull Jr.
V.p., communications & broadcasting .... Ron Colangelo
Vice president, scouting .... Al Avila
Vice president, finance .... Susan Jaison
Vice president, legal affairs/ballpark .... Lucinda Treat
Vice president, administration/corporate counsel .... Michael Whittle
Director of team travel .... Bill Beck
Sr. advisor & special assistant to general manager .... Whitey Lockman
Special assistants to the g.m. .... Andre Dawson, Orrin Freeman, Tony Perez
Director, Major League operations .... Dan Lunetta
Director, minor league operations .... Rick Williams
Manager, minor league operations .... Mike Parkinson
Manager, minor league administration .... Kim-Lee Carkeek Luchs
Manager, scouting administration .... Cheryl Evans
Director of media relations .... Steve Copses
Media relations coordinator .... Jonathan Jensen
Hispanic media coordinator .... Susu Rodriguez
Media information coordinator .... Andrew Feirstein
Manager, broadcasting .... Sandra van Meek
Manager, community affairs .... Israel Negron
Director, marketing .... Susan Budd
Manager, Marlins en Miami store .... Juan Martinez
Director, marketing partnerships .... Jim Frevola
Director, creative services & in-game .... Leslie Riguero
Director, season & group sales .... Pat McNamara
Manager, customer service .... Jeff Tanzer
Director, team security .... Dan Vaniman
Executive director, foundation .... Nancy Olson
Manager, baseball information systems .... David Kuan
MLB advanced media site editor .... Lindsay Reid

MINOR LEAGUE AFFILIATES

Class	Team	League	Manager
AAA	Calgary	Pacific Coast	Chris Chambliss
AA	Portland	Eastern	Rick Renteria
A	Brevard County	Florida State	Dave Huppert
A	Kane County	Midwest	Russ Morman
A	Utica	New York-Pennsylvania	Kevin Boles
Rookie	Gulf Coast Marlins	Gulf Coast	Jon Deeble

ASSISTANCE STAFF

Team physician
Dr. Dan Kanell

Head athletic trainer
Larry Starr

Strength and conditioning director
Rick Slate

Equipment manager
Mike Wallace

Visiting clubhouse manager
Matt Rosenthal

Coss-checkers
Murray Cook, David Chadd, Mike Russell, Tim Schmidt

Coordinator, Latin-American Scouting
Louie Eljaua

Director, Dominican Republic operations
Jesus Alou

Scouts
Ed Bockman, Kelvin Bowles, Al Diez, Lou Fitzgerald, Dr. Demi Mainieri, Charlie Silvera, John Booher, Ty Brown, Brad DelBarba, Jon Deeble, David Finley, Larry Keller, Bob Laurie, Steve Minor, Steve Mondile, Cucho Rodriguez, Doug Rogalski, Jim Rough, Dennis Sheehan, Keith Snider, Doug Strange, Mike Tosar, Stan Zielinski, Tom Evans, Fred Long, Dave McQueen, Dave Mumper, John Nilmeyer, Terry Sullivan, Dick Wilson, Pedro Cintron, Dick Smith, Pablo Lantigua, Cesar Santiago, Ramon Websterm, Alvaro Blanco, Hubert Silva, Miguel Angel Garcia, Ernesto Gomez, Jesus Laya, Jorge Rengel, German Robles, Oscar Sarmiento

BROADCAST INFORMATION

Radio: WQAM (560 AM); WQBA-AM (1140 AM, Spanish language).
TV: WAMI-TV (Channel 69).
Cable TV: Fox Sports Net.

SPRING TRAINING

Ballpark (city): Space Coast Stadium (Melbourne, Fla.).
Ticket information: 321-633-9200.

BALLPARK INFORMATION

Ballpark (capacity, surface)
Pro Player Stadium (36,331 grass)

Address
2267 N.W. 199th St., Miami, FL 33056

Official website
www.floridamarlins.com

Business phone
305-626-7400

Ticket information
305-350-5050

Ticket prices
$55 (founders club), $32 (club level section A)
$25 (infield box), $18 (power alley section C)
$15 (terrace box, mezzanine box), $12 (club level sections B & C-senior citizens)
$10 (outfield reserved, adult), $9 (mezzanine reserved, adult)
$5 (outfield reserved, children), $4 (fish tank-last three rows, adult)
$3 (mezzanine reserved, children), $2 (fish tank-last three rows, children)

Field dimensions (from home plate)
To left field at foul line, 330 feet
To center field, 434 feet
To right field at foul line, 345 feet

First game played
April 5, 1993 (Marlins 6, Dodgers 3)

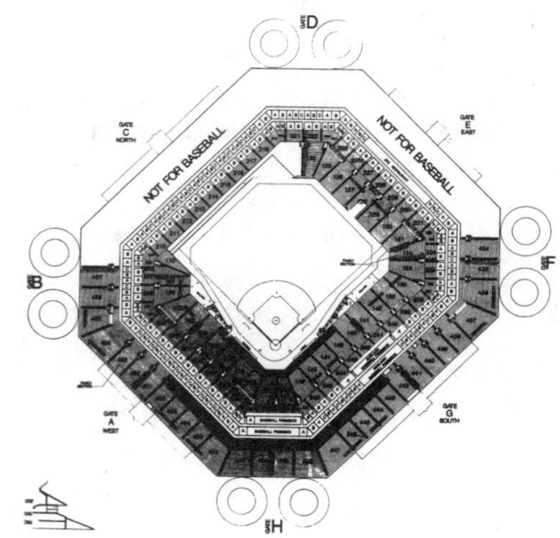

Follow the Marlins all season at: www.sportingnews.com/baseball/teams/marlins/

MARLINS SPRING ROSTER

No.	PITCHERS	B/T	Ht./Wt.	Born	2000 clubs	Projection
57	Alfonseca, Antonio	R/R	6-5/235	4-16-72	Florida	Gives Marlins stability after consecutive seasons with 20 or more saves.
55	Almanza, Armando	L/L	6-3/220	10-26-72	Florida	Hard throwing relief pitcher who is getting better with seasoning.
59	Almonte, Hector	R/R	6-2/190	10-17-75	Cal., Brev. Co., Port., GC Marlins	Moved through system last year, but still couple years away.
64	Anderson, Wes	R/R	6-4/175	9-10-79	Brevard County	Young prospect still learning, still a few years away.
27	Aybar, Manny	R/R	6-1/177	11-28-69	Colo., Cinc., Louisville, Florida	Live arm out of the bullpen who can eat up a lot of innnings.
61	Beckett, Josh	R/R	6-4/190	5-15-80	Kane County	Very young and talented starter who showed flashes of brillance at Kane County.
29	Bones, Ricky	R/R	6-0/202	4-7-69	Florida	Durable relief pitcher who can spot start if needed.
43	Burnett, A.J.	R/R	6-5/205	1-3-77	Florida, Brevard County, Calgary	Injury slowed talented starter at start of last year, but could be in for big season.
38	Cornelius, Reid	R/R	6-0/200	6-2-70	Calgary, Florida	Pitched well, but his job will be hard to keep with influx of young arms.
22	Darensbourg, Vic	L/L	5-10/165	11-13-70	Florida	Lefthanded specialist for Marlins out of bullpen. Can pitch over 50 games.
46	Dempster, Ryan	R/R	6-1/201	5-3-77	Florida	The hard throwing youngster had breakthrough season with 209 strikeouts.
32	Fernandez, Alex	R/R	6-1/225	8-13-69	Florida	Battled injuries again and can be tough pitcher if healthy, but don't count on it.
54	Goetz, Geoff	L/L	5-11/165	3-3-79	Brevard County, Portland	Young relief pitcher with good stuff who will be vying for a spot in bulllpen.
37	Grilli, Jason	R/R	6-4/185	11-11-76	Calgary, Florida	Injuries shortened season of prospect who has shot to make the club.
56	Knotts, Gary	R/R	6-4/200	2-12-77	Portland	Durable starter not ready to make jump to big leagues, but will in couple of years.
53	Lara, Nelson	R/R	6-4/185	7-15-78	Portland, Brevard County	Hard throwing reliever has not been able to find strike zone consistently.
41	Looper, Braden	R/R	6-5/225	10-28-74	Florida	Valueable relief pitcher who logged 145 games the past two seasons.
34	Miceli, Dan	R/R	6-0/225	9-9-70	Florida, GC Marlins, Brev. Co.	Consistent out of bullpen and solid set up man for Alfonseca.
53	Neal, Blaine	R/L	6-5/205	4-6-78	Brevard County	Solid fastball make him a closer of the future for Marlins, but not yet.
36	Nunez, Vladimir	R/R	6-4/224	3-15-75	Florida, Calgary	Began last year in rotation, but lost job with shaky start.
28	Penny, Brad	R/R	6-4/200	5-24-78	Florida, Brevard County, Calgary	Excelled as rookie in rotation last year and could be ace of staff by season's end.
21	Sanchez, Jesus	L/L	5-10/155	10-11-74	Florida	Left-handed pitcher who could help Marlins out of bullpen or as a starter.
45	Smith, Chuck	R/R	6-1/185	10-21-69	Oklahoma, Florida	Pitched very well in 19 starts and probably earned a spot.
47	Vargas, Claudio	R/R	6-3/210	5-19-79	Brevard County, Portland	Another young hard thrower, but still a couple years away.

No.	CATCHERS	B/T	Ht./Wt.	Born	2000 clubs	Projection
17	Castro, Ramon	R/R	6-3/225	3-1-76	Calgary, Florida	Solid defensive catcher will have to battle for spot.
23	Johnson, Charles	R/R	6-2/220	7-20-71	Baltimore, Chicago A.L.	Returns to Marlins after career offensive year.
52	Redmond, Mike	R/R	6-1/185	5-5-71	Florida	Hits for average and gives Marlins decent backup behind Johnson.

No.	INFIELDERS	B/T	Ht./Wt.	Born	2000 clubs	Projection
10	Berg, David	R/R	5-11/196	9-3-70	Brevard County, Florida	Solid utility man off the bench who can play several positions.
1	Castillo, Luis	B/R	5-11/196	9-12-75	Florida, Calgary	Hits for high average and led National League in stolen bases last year.
6	Fox, Andy	L/R	6-4/202	1-12-71	El Paso, Tucson, Arizona, Florida	Versatile player off the bench. Can play anywhere.
11	Gonzalez, Alex	R/R	6-0/170	2-15-77	Florida, Brevard County	Offensive production down last year, but still Marlins shortstop for years to come.
25	Lee, Derrek	R/R	6-5/242	9-6-75	Florida	Power hitter is starting to hit for average. Needs to cut down on strikeouts.
19	Lowell, Mike	R/R	6-4/205	2-24-74	Florida	Solid third baseman who provided nice offense for the Marlins last year.
15	Millar, Kevin	R/R	6-0/210	9-24-71	Florida	Quality back up can play all over the infield and provides good pop off bench.
3	Ozuna, Pablo	R/R	6-0/160	8-25-78	Portland, Florida	Continues to shine in minors, blocked by Castillo for now.
26	Rolison, Nate	L/R	6-6/240	3-27-77	Calgary, Florida	Young first baseman who can hit for power and average. Blocked by Lee.

No.	OUTFIELDERS	B/T	Ht./Wt.	Born	2000 clubs	Projection
18	Abbott, Jeff	R/L	6-2/200	8-17-72	Chicago A.L.	Valuable outfielder coming off the bench for the Marlins this year.
30	Floyd, Cliff	L/R	6-4/240	12-5-72	Florida	Consistent run producer and glove in the outfield.
7	Kotsay, Mark	L/L	6-0/201	12-2-75	Florida	Durable outfielder who is starting to blossom at the plate after batting .298 last year.
	Mottola, Chad	R/R	6-3/225	10-15-71	Syracuse, Toronto	Will compete for a spot in outfield after coming over from Blue Jays.
14	Nunez, Abraham	R/R	6-2/185	2-5-80	Portland, Brevard County	Young outfielder of the future with some unpolished skills as of now.
44	Wilson, Preston	R/R	6-2/208	7-19-74	Florida	Way too many strikeouts, but continues to put up big power numbers.

THE COACHING STAFF

John Boles, manager: Boles enters third season as manager after fairly successful campaign with very young team last year. With the addition of Johnson and the continued development of the young pitching staff, expectations may be higher for Boles this season.

Joe Breeden: He enters his second season as bench coach and eighth season with the Marlins' organizaiton.

Rick Dubee: Dubee continues to try to mold the young pitching staff as he continues his duties as pitching coach for a fourth season. This is Dubee's eighth season with the Marlins' organization.

Fredi Gonzalez: Gonzalez continues his duties as third base coach for a second season. Prior to coaching third, he was an eight year minor league manager and seven year member of the Marlins' organization.

Lynn Jones: Jones takes over as first base coach for the Marlins in his first season with the big league club. Jones spent the last eight seasons as a manager in the Marlins' organization.

Jack Maloof: Maloof stays on as hitting coach for a eighth consecutive season. He is a former minor league manager and hitting instructor.

Tony Taylor: Taylor enters his second season as coach of the infielder. He was previously a coach for the Phillies and a minor league manager before coaching in the Marlins' organization for the past six years.

THE TOP PROSPECTS

Josh Beckett: Second pick overall in 1999 draft, marching his way through Marlins organization. Posted 2-3 record and 2.12 ERA at Kane County.

Pablo Ozuna: Hits for very high average, can run the bases and plays solid defense at second. Marlins may leave him in Class AAA with Luis Castillo anchoring second.

Claudio Vargas: Young, hard thrower who went 10-5 with 3.28 ERA last year at Brevard County. Strikeout to walk ratio is very good for this young man.

THE TOP NEWCOMERS

Jeff Abbott: Helps solidfy the Marlins bench with a steady outfielder who can hit for average and has a little pop in his bat.

Charles Johnson: Gives the Marlins a veteran catcher to work with the young pitching staff. Johnson also provides some good offense at the bottom of line up.

HOUSTON ASTROS

NATIONAL LEAGUE CENTRAL DIVISION

2001 SEASON

Astros 2001 SCHEDULE

Home games shaded; D—Day game (games starting before 5 p.m.)
*—All-Star Game at Safeco Field (Seattle)

APRIL

SUN	MON	TUE	WED	THU	FRI	SAT
1	2	3 D MIL	4 MIL	5 MIL	6 PIT	7 D PIT
8 D PIT	9	10 MIL	11 MIL	12 D MIL	13 STL	14 D STL
15 D STL	16 PIT	17 PIT	18 PIT	19	20 STL	21 D STL
22 STL	23 ATL	24 ATL	25 ATL	26	27 FLA	28 D FLA
29 D FLA	30 NYM					

MAY

SUN	MON	TUE	WED	THU	FRI	SAT
		1 NYM	2 NYM	3	4 MON	5 MON
6 D MON	7 PHI	8 PHI	9 PHI	10	11 CIN	12 CIN
13 CIN	14 CIN	15 CUB	16 CUB	17 D CUB	18 CIN	19 D CIN
20 D CIN	21 SD	22 SD	23 D SD	24	25 LA	26 LA
27 D LA	28	29 SD	30 SD	31 D SD		

JUNE

SUN	MON	TUE	WED	THU	FRI	SAT
					1 LA	2 D LA
3 D LA	4	5 COL	6 COL	7 COL	8 TEX	9 TEX
10 TEX	11	12 MIN	13 MIN	14 MIN	15 TEX	16 D TEX
17 D TEX	18 COL	19 COL	20 COL	21 CIN	22 CIN	23 CIN
24 D CIN	25 ARI	26 ARI	27 ARI	28	29 MIL	30 MIL

JULY

SUN	MON	TUE	WED	THU	FRI	SAT
1 D MIL	2 MIL	3 ARI	4 D ARI	5 ARI	6 KC	7 KC
8 D KC	9	10 *	11	12 SD	13 SD	14 SD
15 D CLE	16 CLE	17 CLE	18 STL	19 D STL	20 CUB	21 CUB
22 D CUB	23 CUB	24 STL	25 D STL	26 PIT	27 PIT	28 PIT
29 D PIT	30	31 NYM				

AUGUST

SUN	MON	TUE	WED	THU	FRI	SAT
			1 NYM	2 NYM	3 MON	4 MON
5 D MON	6	7 ATL	8 ATL	9 ATL	10 FLA	11 FLA
12 D FLA	13 CUB	14 CUB	15 CUB	16 PIT	17 PIT	18 D PIT
19 D PIT	20	21 PHI	22 PHI	23 PHI	24 PIT	25 PIT
26 D PIT	27	28 CIN	29 CIN	30 D CIN	31 MIL	

SEPTEMBER

SUN	MON	TUE	WED	THU	FRI	SAT
						1 MIL
2 D MIL	3 D CIN	4 CIN	5 D CIN	6 MIL	7 MIL	8 MIL
9 D MIL	10	11 SF	12 SF	13 SF	14 STL	15 STL
16 D STL	17	18 SF	19 SF	20 D SF	21 CUB	22 CUB
23 D CUB	24 STL	25 STL	26 STL	27 CUB	28 D CUB	29 D CUB
30 D CUB						

FRONT-OFFICE DIRECTORY

Chairman and chief executive officer .... Drayton McLane Jr.
President, baseball operations .... Tal Smith
President, business operations .... Bob McClaren
General manager .... Gerry Hunsicker
Assistant general manager .... Tim Purpura
Director of baseball administration .... Barry Waters
Director of scouting .... David Lakey
Special asst. to the g.m. for international scouting and development .... Andres Reiner
Senior vice president, operations and communications .... Rob Matwick
Senior vice president, finance and administration .... Teresa Pelanne
Vice president, human resources .... Mike Anders
Vice president, security and traffic operations .... Don Collins
Vice president, community development .... Marian Harper
Vice president, market development .... Rosi Hernandez
Vice president, sales and broadcasting .... Jamie Hildreth
Vice president, engineering .... Bert Pope
Vice president, marketing .... Garry Sawka
Vice president, special events .... Kala Sorenson
Vice president, ticket sales and services .... John Sorrentino
Director of media relations .... Warren Miller
Assistant director of media relations .... Todd Fedewa

MINOR LEAGUE AFFILIATES

Class	Team	League	Manager
AAA	New Orleans	Pacific Coast	Tony Pena
AA	Round Rock	Texas	Jackie Moore
A	Lexington	South Atlantic	J.J. Cannon
A	Michigan	Midwest	John Massarelli
A	Pittsfield	New York-Pennsylvania	Ivan DeJesus
Rookie	Martinsville	Appalachian	Jorge Orta

BROADCAST INFORMATION

Radio: KTRH-AM (740); KXYZ-AM (1320, Spanish language).
TV: KNWS-TV (Channel 51).
Cable TV: Fox Sports Southwest.

SPRING TRAINING

Ballpark (city): Osceola County Stadium (Kissimmee, Fla.).
Ticket information: 407-839-3900.

ASSISTANCE STAFF

Professional scouts
Kimball Crossley, Gene DeBoer, Leo Labossiere, Joe Pittman, Tom Romenesko, Scipio Spinks

Major league scouts
Stan Benjamin, Bill Kelso, Jack Lind, Walt Matthews, Paul Weaver

Full-time scouts
Bob Blair
Ralph Bratton
Andrew Cotner
Doug Deutsch
David Henderson
Marc Johnson
Mike Maggart
Tom McCormack
Rusty Pendergrass
Joe Robinson
Frankie Thon
Nick Venuto
Gene Wellman
Joe Bogar
Chuck Carlson
Gerry Craft
James Farrar
Dan Huston
Brian Keegan
Jerry Marik
Mel Nelson
Bob Poole
Tad Slowik
Tim Tolman
Danny Watkins

Foreign scouts
Ricardo Aponte
Sergio A. Beltre
Arnold Elles
Mario Gonzalez
Rodney Linares
Carlos Maldonado
Oscar Padron
Rafael Ramirez
Anibal Reluz
Dr. Lester Storey
Pablo Torrealba
Mark Van Zanten
Jesus Aristimuno
Rafael Cariel
Orlando Fernandez
Julio Linares
Omar Lopez
Ramon Morales
Guillermo Ramirez
Wolfgang Ramos
Adriano Rodriguez
Alejandro Tavares
Calixto Vargas

BALLPARK INFORMATION

Ballpark (capacity, surface)
Enron Field (40,950, grass)
Address
P.O. Box 288
Houston, TX 77001-0288
Official website
www.astros.com
Business phone
713-259-8000
Ticket information
713-259-8500 or 800-ASTROS-2
Ticket prices
$29 (dugout)
$28 (club)
$25 (field box)
$24 (club)
$17 (Crawford box)
$15 (bullpen box)
$12 (mezzanine, terrace deck)
$10 (upper deck)
$5-$1 (outfield deck)
Field dimensions (from home plate)
To left field at foul line, 315 feet
To center field, 435 feet
To right field at foul line, 326 feet
First game played
April 7, 2000 (Phillies 4, Astros 1)

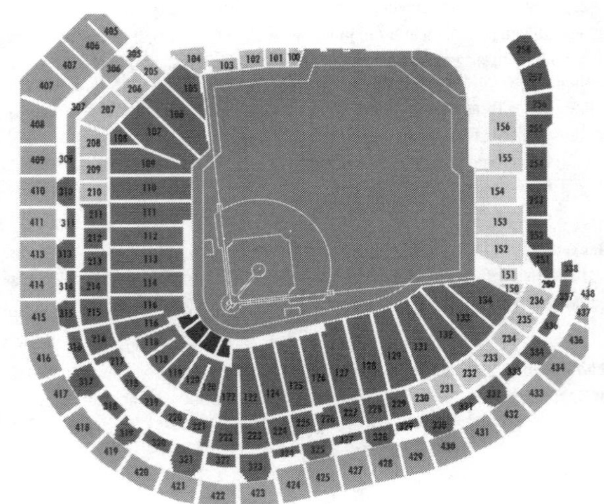

Follow the Astros all season at: www.sportingnews.com/baseball/teams/astros/

ASTROS SPRING ROSTER

No.	PITCHERS	B/T	Ht./Wt.	Born	2000 clubs	Projection
	Bottenfield, Kent	R/R	6-3/240	11-14-68	Anaheim, Philadelphia	Will eat up innings and be a dependable starter every fifth day.
	Brocail, Doug	L/R	6-5/235	5-16-67	Detroit	Valuable relief pitcher capable of throwing in a lot of games.
51	Cabrera, Jose	R/R	6-0/180	3-24-72	Houston, New Orleans	Durable relief pitcher likely to see a lot of games again this year.
	Cruz, Nelson	R/R	6-1/185	9-13-72	Toledo, Detroit	Will fight for a spot in the bullpen this year with his eyes set on the starting.
41	Dotel, Octavio	R/R	6-0/175	11-25-75	Houston	Hard thrower who can be dominating at times. Astros hope he breaks out this year.
50	Elarton, Scott	R/R	6-7/240	2-23-76	Hou., New Orleans, Round Rock	Emerged as ace of staff with 17 wins last season.
53	Franklin, Wayne	L/L	6-2/195	3-9-74	New Orleans, Houston	Fighting for spot in bullpen after up and down year with Astros.
	Hernandez, Carlos	L/L	5-10/145	4-22-80	Michigan	Starter who with potential. Still few years away from big leagues.
	Jackson, Mike	R/R	6-2/225	12-22-64	DID NOT PLAY	Out all last season. Astros hope he can regain form to solidfy bullpen.
	Kessel, Kyle	L/L	6-0/190	6-2-76	Kissimmee, Round Rock	Moved up in minors, but likely to stay there this year.
	Lidge, Brad	R/R	6-5/200	12-23-76	Kissimmee	Big, hard throwing starter trying to win spot on the team.
42	Lima, Jose	R/R	6-2/205	9-30-72	Houston	Will be tough for him to rebound form awful 2000 season.
36	Linebrink, Scott	R/R	6-3/185	8-4-76	Fresno, San Fran., Hou., N. Orl.	Could help out of bullpen, but will be tough for him to win job.
59	McKnight, Tony	R/R	6-5/205	6-29-77	Round Rock, New Orleans, Hou.	Moved his way through the minors and will try to crack rotation this year.
	Miller, Greg	L/L	6-5/215	9-30-79	Kissimmee, Round Rock	Solid starter likely to start season in minors.
52	Miller, Wade	R/R	6-2/185	9-13-76	New Orleans, Houston	Got a chance to start late last season and did fairly well.
	Oswalt, Roy	R/R	6-0/170	8-29-77	Kissimmee, Round Rock	Had outstanding year in minors and could be in rotation by end of year.
39	Powell, Jay	R/R	6-4/225	1-9-72	Hou., New Orleans, Round Rock	Disabled list slowed him down last year, but look for rebound season.
	Redding, Tim	R/R	6-0/180	2-12-78	Kissimmee, Round Rock	Future starter for Astros, but the future in not know.
37	Reynolds, Shane	R/R	6-3/210	3-26-68	Houston	All-star season cut short by injuries, but still a quality pitcher.
66	Rodriguez, Wilfredo	L/L	6-3/180	3-20-79	Round Rock, Kissimmee	Could start year in bullpen, but minors seem the likely choice.
13	Wagner, Billy	L/L	5-11/180	7-25-71	Houston	Dominant closer coming off injury. Should bounce back to form.

No.	CATCHERS	B/T	Ht./Wt.	Born	2000 clubs	Projection
	Ausmus, Brad	R/R	5-11/195	4-14-69	Detroit	Chance to take over starting job for Astros this season.
20	Eusebio, Tony	R/R	6-2/210	4-27-67	Houston	Good bat and will battle for starting job with Ausmus.
	Maldonado, Carlos	R/R	6-2/185	1-3-79	Round Rock	Catcher of the future for the Astros.

No.	INFIELDERS	B/T	Ht./Wt.	Born	2000 clubs	Projection
5	Bagwell, Jeff	R/R	6-0/195	5-27-68	Houston	If Astors contend, he might win MVP this year.
7	Biggio, Craig	R/R	5-11/180	12-14-65	Houston	Look for big year out of him after injury cost him last half of '00 season.
2	Ensberg, Morgan	R/R	6-2/210	8-26-75	Round Rock, Houston	Could be starting at third base in a few years.
3	Everett, Adam	R/R	6-0/156	2-2-77	New Orleans	Has a chance to start at shortstop, but may end up on bench this year.
1	Ginter, Keith	R/R	5-10/190	5-5-76	Round Rock, Houston	Might be valueable player off bench this year.
	Hayes, Charlie	R/R	6-0/215	5-29-65	Milwaukee	Given a shot to play third base, but might not make team.
4	Lugo, Julio	R/R	6-2/165	11-16-75	Houston	Versatile infielder who may start at shortstop.
62	McNeal, Aaron	R/R	6-3/230	4-28-78	Round Rock	Solid hitter and first baseman likely to spend another season in minors.
28	Spiers, Bill	L/R	6-2/190	6-5-66	Houston	Valueable bench player who can play any position. May start at third.
6	Truby, Chris	R/R	6-2/190	12-9-73	Houston, New Orleans	Third base job is his to lose.
	Vizcaino, Jose	B/R	6-1/180	3-26-68	Los Angeles, New York A.L.	Can play almost every postition and will help bench play.
31	Ward, Daryle	L/L	6-2/230	6-27-75	Houston	Good power hitter and could be starting in outfield.

No.	OUTFIELDERS	B/T	Ht./Wt.	Born	2000 clubs	Projection
18	Alou, Moises	R/R	6-3/195	7-3-66	Houston	Could put up even bigger numbers if healthy for a whole season at Enron Field.
29	Barker, Glen	R/R	5-10/180	5-10-71	Houston, New Orleans	Speedy outfielder who can hit for average. Likely to come off bench.
17	Berkman, Lance	B/L	6-1/205	2-10-76	New Orleans, Houston	Outfield job is his to lose after big year.
15	Hidalgo, Richard	R/R	6-3/190	7-2-75	Houston	Potential finally came through last year with monster year.

THE COACHING STAFF

Larry Dierker, manager: Dierker will be watched closely this year after a disappointing year. He has won three division titles and over 300 games, but that might not mean anything if the Astros falter again this year.

Jose Cruz: He is back for a fifth season as first base coach after spending most of a successful career with the Astros.

Mike Cubbage: Cubbage enters his 27th year of baseball and will be coaching third again this season.

Matt Galante: Galante enters is fourth season as bench coach after spending 1997 as a special assistant to the general manager.

Harry Spilman: Spent 12 seasons in the majors including the Astros. Spilman takes over as hitting coach this season.

Burt Hooten: Hooten becomes pitching coach after a 15 year playing career. He has been coaching since 1996.

John Tamargo: Tamargo goes into his 14th year of coaching as bullpen coach of the Astros.

THE TOP NEWCOMERS

Brad Ausmus: Comes back to the Astros with a shot at the starting catchers job. Has decent bat and is solid defensively.

Kent Bottenfield: He will benefit from not having to be the number one guy in a rotation. Should be comfortable pitching behind Elarton, Reynolds and Lima. He should win more than the eight he posted last season.

Doug Brocail: Relief pitcher who can eat up innings for Astros this season.

Charlie Hayes: Brought in for a chance to compete for third base job, but will likely end up as role player coming off the bench if he makes the team.

THE TOP PROSPECTS

Adam Everett: Shortstop of the future for the Astros. Has shot to make team this season before eventually becoming full time shortstop in a few years.

Brad Lidge: Good size and velocity make this pitcher one to watch in the future.

Roy Oswalt: Had tremendous season in the minors and could make the club this year in the bullpen before starting full time in the future.

Los Angeles Dodgers

National League West Division

2001 SEASON

Dodgers 2001 SCHEDULE

Home games shaded; D—Day game (games starting before 5 p.m.)
*—All-Star Game at Safeco Field (Seattle)

APRIL

SUN	MON	TUE	WED	THU	FRI	SAT
1	2 D MIL	3 ARI	4 ARI	5 ARI	6 SF	7 SF
8 SF	9	10 ARI	11 ARI	12 ARI	13 SD	14 SD
15 D SD	16	17 SF	18 SF	19 SF	20 SD	21 SD
22 D SD	23	24 PIT	25 PIT	26 PIT	27 PHI	28 PHI
29 D PHI	30					

MAY

SUN	MON	TUE	WED	THU	FRI	SAT
		1 CIN	2 CIN	3 CIN	4 D CUB	5 D CUB
6 D CUB	7 FLA	8 FLA	9 FLA	10 FLA	11 ATL	12 ATL
13 D ATL	14	15 MON	16 MON	17 MON	18 NYM	19 D NYM
20 D NYM	21 COL	22 COL	23 D COL	24	25 HOU	26 HOU
27 D HOU	28 D COL	29 COL	30 COL	31		

JUNE

SUN	MON	TUE	WED	THU	FRI	SAT
					1 HOU	2 D HOU
3 D HOU	4 ARI	5 ARI	6 ARI	7 D ARI	8 ANA	9 D ANA
10 D ANA	11 TEX	12 TEX	13 TEX	14	15 ANA	16 ANA
17 D ANA	18	19 ARI	20 ARI	21	22 SD	23 SD
24 D SD	25 SF	26 SF	27 D SF	28 SD	29 SD	30 SD

JULY

SUN	MON	TUE	WED	THU	FRI	SAT
1 D SD	2 SF	3 SF	4 SF	5 SF	6 SEA	7 D SEA
8 D SEA	9	10 *	11	12 OAK	13 OAK	14 D OAK
15 PIT	16 PIT	17 PIT	18 MIL	19 D MIL	20 COL	21 D COL
22 D COL	23 MIL	24 MIL	25 D MIL	26 COL	27 COL	28 D COL
29 COL	30	31 CIN				

AUGUST

SUN	MON	TUE	WED	THU	FRI	SAT
			1 CIN	2 CIN	3 CUB	4 D CUB
5 CUB	6	7 PIT	8 PIT	9 PIT	10 PHI	11 PHI
12 D PHI	13	14 MON	15 MON	16 D MON	17 NYM	18 NYM
19 D NYM	20	21 FLA	22 FLA	23 FLA	24 ATL	25 ATL
26 D ATL	27 ATL	28 COL	29 COL	30 COL	31 STL	

SEPTEMBER

SUN	MON	TUE	WED	THU	FRI	SAT
						1 STL
2 STL	3	4 COL	5 COL	6 COL	7 STL	8 D STL
9 D STL	10	11 SD	12 SD	13 D SD	14 SF	15 D SF
16 D SF	17 SD	18 SD	19 SD	20 ARI	21 ARI	22 ARI
23 D ARI	24 SF	25 SF	26 SF	27	28 ARI	29 ARI
30 D ARI						

FRONT-OFFICE DIRECTORY

President and CEO .... Bob Graziano
Board of directors .... Chase Carey, Peter Chernin, Peter O'Malley, Bob Graziano, Sam Fernandez
Executive vice president and general manager. .... Kevin Malone
Executive vice president and CMO .... Kris Rone
Senior vice president, communications .... Derrick Hall
Senior vice president .... Tommy Lasorda
Vice president, external affairs .... Tommy Hawkins
Traveling secretary .... Billy DeLury
Senior vice president and general counsel .... Santiago Fernandez
Vice president, spring training/minor league facilities .... Craig Callan
Director of player development .... Jerry Weinstein
Director, finance and CFO .... Christine Hurley
Dir. of management information services .... Mike Mularky
Director of sales and marketing .... Sergio Del Prado
Director, public relations .... John Olguin
Assistant director, team travel .... Shaun Rachau
Director, broadcasting and new media .... Brent Shyer
Director, community relations .... Don Newcombe
Vice president, stadium operations .... Doug Duennes
Director, ticket operations .... Billy Hunter
Assistant to the general manager, scouting .... Ed Creech
Director, scouting operations .... Matt Slater

MINOR LEAGUE AFFILIATES

Class	Team	League	Manager
AAA	Las Vegas	Pacific Coast	Rick Sofield
AA	Jacksonville	Southern	John Shoemaker
A	Vero Beach	Florida State	Dino Ebel
A	Wilmington	South Atlantic	To be announced
Rookie	Great Falls	Pioneer	Dave Silvestri
Rookie	Gulf Coast Dodgers	Gulf Coast	Juan Bustabad

BROADCAST INFORMATION

Radio: XTRA (1150); KWKW-AM (1330, Spanish language).
TV: KTLA-TV (Channel 5).
Cable TV: Fox Sports West 2.

SPRING TRAINING

Ballpark (city): Holman Stadium (Vero Beach, Fla.).
Ticket information: 561-569-6858.

ASSISTANCE STAFF

Head trainer
Stan Johnston

Assistant trainer
Matt Wilson

Physical therapist
Pat Screnar

Strength and conditioning
Todd Clausen

Club physicians
Dr. Herndon Harding Dr. Frank Jobe
Dr. Michael F. Mellman

Special assistant to general manager
Jeff Schugel

Senior scouting advisor
Don Welke

Pro scouts
Dan Freed, Carl Loewenstine, Vance Lovelace, Claude Osteen, Terry Reynolds, Ron Rizzi, Mark Weidemaier

Full-time scouts
John Barr, Gib Bodet, Mike Brito, Doug Carpenter, James Chapman, Bobby Darwin, Joseph Ferrone, Scott Groot, Michael Hankins, Clarence Johns, Hank Jones, Lon Joyce, Pat Kelly, John Kosciak, Marty Lamb, Jimmy Lester, Michael Leuzinger, James Merriweather, Camilio Pascual, Pablo Peguero, Bill Pleis, Scott Sharp, Mark Sheehy, Chris Smith, Bob Szymkowski, Thomas Thomas, Mitch Webster

BALLPARK INFORMATION

Ballpark (capacity, surface)
Dodger Stadium (56,000, grass)
Address
1000 Elysian Park Ave.
Los Angeles, CA 90012
Official website
www.dodgers.com
Business phone
323-224-1500
Ticket information
323-224-1448
Ticket prices
$17 (field box)
$15 (inner reserve)
$13 (loge box)
$10 (outer reserve)
$6 (top deck, left & right pavilion)
Field dimensions (from home plate)
To left field at foul line, 330 feet
To center field, 395 feet
To right field at foul line, 330 feet
First game played
April 10, 1962 (Reds 6, Dodgers 3)

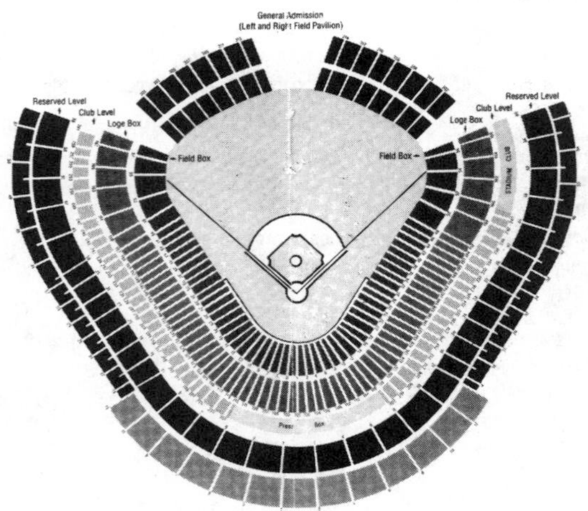

Follow the Dodgers all season at: www.sportingnews.com/baseball/teams/dodgers/

DODGERS SPRING ROSTER

No.	PITCHERS	B/T	Ht./Wt.	Born	2000 clubs	Projection
51	Adams, Terry	R/R	6-3/215	3-6-73	Los Angeles	Solid relief pitcher who will eat up innings out of the bullpen.
43	Ashby, Andy	R/R	6-1/202	7-11-67	Philadelphia, Atlanta	Will try to take some of the burden off of Brown's shoulder.
27	Brown, Kevin	R/R	6-4/200	3-14-65	Los Angeles	Hands down, one of the most dominating pitchers in the game.
60	Burnside, Adrian	R/L	6-3/168	3-15-77	San Antonio	One of the best pitchers in the organization, but likely to start year in minors.
37	Dreifort, Darren	R/R	6-2/211	5-3-72	Los Angeles	Signed huge deal in off season and will be looked upon to back it up.
56	Fetters, Mike	R/R	6-4/226	12-19-64	Los Angeles	Good set up man who will be counted on again this year after a strong season.
67	Foster, Kris	R/R	6-1/200	6-30-74	San Bernardino	Young, hard throwing relief pitcher who battled injuries last year.
48	Gagne, Eric	R/R	6-2/195	1-7-76	Albuquerque, Los Angeles	Talented starter who will be vying for a spot in the rotation.
49	Herges, Matt	L/R	6-0/200	4-1-70	Los Angeles	Workhorse out of the bullpen who can pitch in long or short relief.
60	Judd, Mike	R/R	6-1/217	6-30-75	Albuquerque, Los Angeles	Starter in the minors last year who will try to win spot in bullpen.
40	Masaoka, Onan	R/L	6-0/188	10-27-77	Los Angeles, Albuquerque	Solid out of the pen and will be looked upon for innings again this year.
	Nunez, Jose	L/L	6-2/175	3-14-79	Columbia	Lefty reliever fanned 112 in 95 $^{1}/_{3}$ innings at Class A Capital City.
30	Olson, Gregg	R/R	6-4/208	10-11-66	L.A., San Bern., Albuquerque	Will try to regain form of a few years ago to win a spot in Dodgers bullpen.
13	Osuna, Antonio	R/R	5-11/206	4-12-73	L.S., San Bern., Albuquerque	Another key piece of the Dodger bullpen who is a durable, hard thrower.
61	Park, Chan Ho	R/R	6-2/204	6-30-73	Los Angeles	Coming off 18 win season, helps one of better starting rotations in baseball.
33	Perez, Carlos	L/L	6-3/210	1-14-71	Los Angeles	After up and down season, will try to win a spot back in Dodger starting rotation.
	Prokopec, Luke	L/R	5-11/166	2-23-78	San Antonio, Los Angeles	Outstanding year in San Antonio may help his case for the Dodgers this season.
32	Reyes, Al	R/R	6-1/206	4-10-71	Rochester, Balt., Alb., L.A.	Spent little time in majors and that may be the case this year with bullpen loaded.
63	Ricketts, Chad	R/R	6-5/225	2-12-75	Albuquerque	Competing for spot in the bullpen after solid minor league campaign.
41	Shaw, Jeff	R/R	6-2/200	7-7-66	Los Angeles	Dodger closer looks to regain form of 34 save and 2.78 ERA from '99 season.
54	Williams, Jeff	R/L	6-0/185	6-6-72	Albuquerque, Los Angeles	Solid starter who will most likely open the season again in Alburquerque.

No.	CATCHERS	B/T	Ht./Wt.	Born	2000 clubs	Projection
21	Kreuter, Chad	B/R	6-2/200	8-26-64	Los Angeles	Goes into the season as the Dodgers every day catcher.
16	LoDuca, Paul	R/R	5-10/185	4-12-72	Albuquerque, Los Angeles	Looks to compete for starting catchers job after good season in Alburquerque.
36	Pena, Angel	R/R	5-10/228	2-16-75	Albuquerque	Solid catcher with some pop in his bat, will have trouble beating out incumbents.

No.	INFIELDERS	B/T	Ht./Wt.	Born	2000 clubs	Projection
	Allen, Luke	L/R	6-2/208	8-4-78	San Antonio	Good all-around player who will start the year in the minors.
29	Beltre, Adrian	R/R	5-11/170	4-7-79	Los Angeles	Has all-star ability, but hasn't shown it yet.
66	Bocachica, Hiram	R/R	5-11/165	3-4-76	Albuquerque, Los Angeles	Outstanding offensive talent who could provide some punch off bench.
3	Cora, Alex	L/R	6-0/180	10-18-75	Albuquerque, Los Angeles	The shortstop's job is his to lose as they head into the season.
3	Donnels, Chris	L/R	6-0/185	4-21-66	Albuquerque, Los Angeles	Had huge year in Albuquerque and Dodgers may use his bat off the bench.
8	Grudzielanek, Mark	R/R	6-1/185	6-30-70	Los Angeles	Dependable second baseman who the Dodgers can expect to play every day.
25	Hansen, Dave	L/R	6-0/195	11-24-68	Los Angeles	One of the top pinch hitters in the game.
23	Karros, Eric	R/R	6-4/226	11-4-67	Los Angeles	Big offensive numbers continue to pile up for Karros.

No.	OUTFIELDERS	B/T	Ht./Wt.	Born	2000 clubs	Projection
37	Aven, Bruce	R/R	5-9/180	3-4-72	Pittsburgh, Nashville, Alb., L.A.	Utility player who could spell some help in the outfield.
24	Goodwin, Tom	L/R	6-1/175	7-27-68	Colorado, Los Angeles	The leadoff man the Dodgers have been in search of the past few seasons.
15	Green, Shawn	L/L	6-4/200	11-10-72	Los Angeles	Played every day and put up decent numbers, but not what the team expected.
14	Santangelo, F.P.	B/R	5-10/190	10-24-67	Los Angeles, San Bernardino	Valuable man off the bench who struggled offensively last year.
10	Sheffield, Gary	R/R	5-11/205	11-18-68	Los Angeles	Had MVP type season last year with 43 home runs and 109 RBI's.
22	White, Devon	B/R	6-2/190	12-29-62	Los Angeles, San Bernardino	Will try to win a spot in the outfield, but most likely will be coming off bench.

THE COACHING STAFF

Jim Tracy, manager: After serving for two seasons as the Dodgers bench coach, Tracy takes over the head coaching duties of the Dodgers. Spent seven years as a minor league manager before coming to the Dodgers.

Jack Clark: Joins the Dodger coaching staff after successful 19 year playing career. Clark was one of the premier power hitters in the league in the 80's.

Jim Colburn: The former Brewer pitcher takes over as pitching coach for the Dodgers this season.

Glen Hoffman: Hoffman heads into his fourth season as coach for the Dodgers. He led the team to a 47-41 record in 1998 as manager.

Jim Lett: Started coaching in the minor leagues in 1977 and had first major league coaching experience with the Blue Jays in 1997.

Manny Mota: Mota begins his 32nd year with the Dodgers this season. He also spent 14 years as a player.

Jim Riggleman: Managed the Cubs for five seasons before heading to Cleveland as a bench coach last season.

John Shelby: Played on two championship teams as a player and spent seven years as a minor league manager. Shelby is in his second year with the Dodgers.

THE TOP NEWCOMERS

Andy Ashby: Picked up to help bolster the starting rotation. Ashby might give the Dodgers one of the best starting four in the league with Brown, Park and Dreifort rounding out the four.

THE TOP PROSPECTS

Hiram Bocachica: Second baseman of the future who has great power and the abilitly to hit for average.

Eric Gagne: May get chance to start in the rotation on every day basis this season. Has great stuff and knows how to pitch.

Angel Pena: Might not be taking over the catching duties for the Dodgers this season, but he isn't too far off with Hundley out of the way now. Hits for power and average.

MILWAUKEE BREWERS

NATIONAL LEAGUE CENTRAL DIVISION

2001 SEASON

Brewers 2001 SCHEDULE

Home games shaded; D—Day game (games starting before 5 p.m.)
*—All-Star Game at Safeco Field (Seattle)

APRIL

SUN	MON	TUE	WED	THU	FRI	SAT
1	2 D LA	3 D HOU	4 HOU	5 HOU	6 CIN	7 D CIN
8 D CIN	9	10 HOU	11 HOU	12 D HOU	13 SF	14 SF
15 D SF	16	17 CIN	18 CIN	19	20 SF	21 D SF
22 D SF	23	24 NYM	25 NYM	26 D NYM	27 MON	28 D MON
29 D MON	30					

MAY

SUN	MON	TUE	WED	THU	FRI	SAT
		1 ATL	2 ATL	3 ATL	4 FLA	5 FLA
6 D FLA	7 CUB	8 CUB	9 CUB	10 D CUB	11 PIT	12 PIT
13 D PIT	14 D PIT	15 PHI	16 PHI	17 PHI	18 PIT	19 PIT
20 D PIT	21	22 STL	23 STL	24 D STL	25 D CUB	26 D CUB
27 D CUB	28 D STL	29 STL	30 STL	31 STL		

JUNE

SUN	MON	TUE	WED	THU	FRI	SAT
					1 CUB	2 CUB
3 D CUB	4	5 CIN	6 CIN	7	8 DET	9 DET
10 D DET	11	12 CLE	13 CLE	14 CLE	15 KC	16 KC
17 D KC	18 CIN	19 CIN	20 CIN	21	22 D CUB	23 D CUB
24 D CUB	25 PIT	26 PIT	27 PIT	28 D PIT	29 HOU	30 HOU

JULY

SUN	MON	TUE	WED	THU	FRI	SAT
1 D HOU	2 HOU	3 D STL	4 STL	5 D STL	6 SF	7 D SF
8 D SF	9	10 *	11	12 MIN	13 MIN	14 MIN
15 D CWS	16 CWS	17 D CWS	18 LA	19 D LA	20 SD	21 SD
22 D SD	23 LA	24 LA	25 D LA	26	27 SD	28 SD
29 D SD	30	31 FLA				

AUGUST

SUN	MON	TUE	WED	THU	FRI	SAT
			1 FLA	2 D FLA	3 ATL	4 D ATL
5 D ATL	6	7 NYM	8 NYM	9 D NYM	10 MON	11 MON
12 D MON	13	14 PHI	15 PHI	16 D PHI	17 CIN	18 CIN
19 D CIN	20 CUB	21 D CUB	22 D CUB	23 D CUB	24 COL	25 COL
26 D COL	27 PIT	28 PIT	29 PIT	30	31 HOU	

SEPTEMBER

SUN	MON	TUE	WED	THU	FRI	SAT
						1 HOU
2 D HOU	3 PIT	4 PIT	5 PIT	6 HOU	7 HOU	8 HOU
9 D HOU	10 STL	11 STL	12 STL	13 D STL	14 ARI	15 ARI
16 D ARI	17 STL	18 STL	19 D STL	20	21 CIN	22 CIN
23 D CIN	24	25 ARI	26 ARI	27 ARI	28 COL	29 D COL
30 D COL						

FRONT-OFFICE DIRECTORY

President and chief executive officer .... Wendy Selig-Prieb
Senior vice president and general manager .... Dean Taylor
Vice president and general counsel .... Tom Gausden
Assistant general counsel .... Eugene "Pepi" Randolph
Special assistant to the president .... Sal Bando
Vice president, community and governmental affairs .... Lynn Sprangers
Vice president, corporate sales .... Dean Rennicke
Vice president, finance .... Paul Baniel
Vice president, marketing .... Laurel Prieb
Vice president, new ballpark development .... Michael Bucek
Vice president, player personnel .... David Wilder
Vice president, stadium operations .... Scott Jenkins
Vice president, ticket sales .... Bob Voight
Director, community relations .... Michael Downs
Director, event services .... Steve Ethier
Director, grounds .... Gary Vanden Berg
Director, media relations .... Jon Greenberg
Director, player development .... Greg Riddoch
Director, Brewers Gold Club & Baseball for Wisconsin .... Mike Harlan
Director, publications .... Mario Ziino
Director, ticket operations .... John Barnes
Director, scouting .... Jack Zduriencik
Director, clubhouse operations .... Tony Migliaccio
Traveling secretary .... Dan Larrea

MINOR LEAGUE AFFILIATES

Class	Team	League	Manager
AAA	Indianapolis	International	Wendell Kim
AA	Huntsville	Southern	Ed Romero
A	High Desert	California	Frank Kremblas
A	Beloit	Midwest	Don Money
Rookie	Maryvale	Arizona	Carlos Lezcano
Rookie	Ogden	Pioneer	Ed Sedar

BROADCAST INFORMATION

Radio: WTMJ-AM (620).
TV: WCGV-TV (Channel 24).
Cable TV: Midwest Sports Channel.

SPRING TRAINING

Ballpark (city): Maryvale Baseball Park (Phoenix, Ariz.).
Ticket information: 623-245-5500.

ASSISTANCE STAFF

Trainers
John Adam, Roger Caplinger

Strength and conditioning coach
Phil Falco

Team physician
Dr. Angelo Mattalino

National cross-checker
Larry Doughty

Southwest supervisor
Ric Wilson

Midwest supervisor
Tom Allison

International supervisor
Epy Guerrero

East Coast supervisor
Bobby Heck

Professional scouts
Hank Allen, Carl Blando, Dick Hager, Alan Regier, Daranka Shaheed

Major League scouts
Russ Bove, Ken Califano, Larry Haney, Bill Lajoie, Al Monchak, Chuck Tanner, Elanis Westbrooks, Dick Wiencek

Scouts
Larry Aaron, Fred Beane, Jeff Brookens, Felix Delgado, Edward Fastaia, Mike Farrell, Dick Foster, Mike Gibbons, Manolo Hernandez, Brian Johnson, Chris Knabenshue, Harvey Kuenn Jr., John Logan, Justin McCray, Tom McNamara, Brandon Newell, Larry Pardo, Douglas Reynolds, Corey Rodriguez, Bruce Seid, Jonathan Story, Tom Tanous, Andy Tomberlin, John Viney, Walter Youse

BALLPARK INFORMATION

Ballpark (capacity, surface)
Miller Park (To be announced, grass)

Address
One Brewers Way
Milwaukee, WI 53214-3652

Official website
www.milwaukeebrewers.com

Business phone
414-902-4400

Ticket information
414-902-4000, 1-800-993-7890

Ticket prices
$50 (field diamond box)
$32 (field IF box, club IF box)
$27 (field OF box, loge diamond box)
$24 (club OF box), $23 (loge IF box)
$20 (loge OF box), $16 (terrace IF box)
$14 (terrace OF box)
$10 (terrace reserved, field bleachers)
$6 (loge bleachers, club bleachers)
$5 (terrace bleachers)

Field dimensions (from home plate)
To left field at foul line, 342 feet
To center field, 400 feet
To right field at foul line, 345 feet

First game played
Scheduled for April 6, 2001 vs. Cincinnati

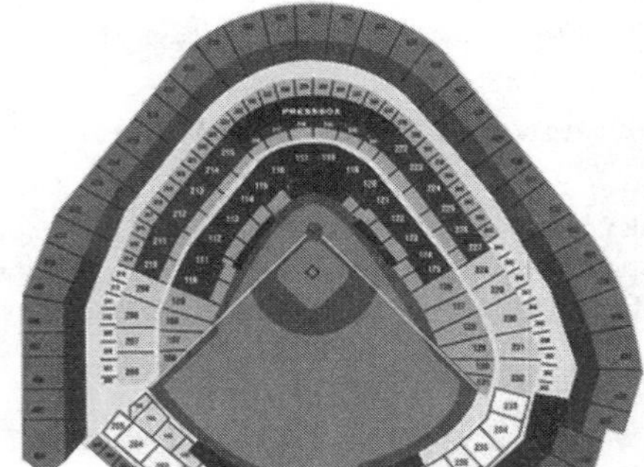

Follow the Brewers all season at: www.sportingnews.com/baseball/teams/brewers/

BREWERS SPRING ROSTER

No.	PITCHERS	B/T	Ht./Wt.	Born	2000 clubs	Projection
53	Acevedo, Juan	R/R	6-2/243	5-5-70	Milwaukee, Indianapolis	Hard-throwing reliever who can eat up lots of innings out of the bullpen.
65	Altman, Gene	R/R	6-7/235	9-1-78	Dayton, Beloit	Closer with live arm who may open season in minors to hone skills.
47	Buddie, Mike	R/R	6-3/219	12-12-70	Columbus, Indianapolis, Mil.	Relief pitcher who had good year in minors trying to earn spot in bullpen.
50	Chantres, Carlos	R/R	6-3/175	4-1-76	Charlotte	Young starter with chance to earn spot in rotation or come out of bullpen.
60	Childers, Matt	R/R	6-5/195	12-3-78	Beloit, Mudville	Promising starter throws hard, but he's still a few years from big leagues.
33	Cunnane, Will	R/R	6-2/200	4-24-74	San Diego, Las Vegas	Solid starter who hasn't been able to stick with major league club.
13	D'Amico, Jeff	R/R	6-7/250	12-27-75	Indianapolis, Milwaukee	Emerged as staff ace of last season. Brewers hope magic continues.
37	Davis, Kane	R/R	6-3/194	6-25-75	Akron, Buff., Cleveland, Mil., Ind.	Could be valuable for Brewers out of bullpen this season.
28	De Los Santos, Valerio	L/L	6-2/206	10-6-75	Milwaukee	Durable relief pitcher who can make an occasional start.
48	Estrada, Horacio	L/L	6-0/192	10-19-75	Indianapolis, Milwaukee	Solid minor league season and decent showing with Brewers last year.
40	Fox, Chad	R/R	6-3/190	9-3-70	DID NOT PLAY	Injury kept him out of baseball last year and could hurt chances to land spot.
56	Garcia, Jose	R/R	6-3/195	4-29-78	Huntsville	Starter on the rise, but not quite ready for the big leagues.
51	Haynes, Jimmy	R/R	6-4/214	9-5-72	Milwaukee	Durable starter who needs to be more consistent.
46	King, Ray	L/L	6-1/240	1-15-74	Iowa, Indianapolis, Milwaukee	Could be setup man for Brewers after great season out of bullpen in 2000.
38	Kolb, Brandon	R/R	6-1/190	11-20-73	Las Vegas, San Diego	Trying to win spot in bullpen and maybe even take closer role.
39	Leskanic, Curtis	R/R	6-0/196	4-2-68	Milwaukee	Outstanding out of bullpen last season and could be full-time closer in 2001.
55	Levrault, Allen	R/R	6-3/230	8-15-77	Indianapolis, Milwaukee	Solid starter who may be bigger help in bullpen this season.
	Mieses, Jose	R/R	6-1/165	10-14-79	Beloit, Mudville	The kid has a bright future, but he's a year or two away.
	Penney, Mike	R/R	6-1/190	3-29-77	Mudville, Huntsville, Ind.	Can start or relieve. Has chance to make team, but more likely to start in Class AAA.
26	Peterson, Kyle	L/R	6-3/220	4-9-76	Beloit, Huntsville	Had chance to be in rotation last year before injuries cut him down.
31	Rigdon, Paul	R/R	6-5/242	11-2-75	Buffalo, Cleveland, Milwaukee	Should have a job in starting rotation if everything goes well in spring training.
52	Roque, Rafael	L/L	6-4/201	10-27-73	Indianapolis, Milwaukee	Could help out in bullpen after strong season as starter in Indianapolis.
59	Snyder, John	R/R	6-3/206	8-16-74	Huntsville, Indianapolis, Mil.	His ERA needs to come down if he wants to continue to start for the Brewers.
41	Stull, Everett	R/R	6-3/206	8-24-71	Indianapolis, Milwaukee	Could be a valuable pitcher for Brewers as he can start or relieve.
49	Weathers, Dave	R/R	6-3/233	9-25-69	Milwaukee	Pitched in 60 games each of the last two years.
21	Wright, Jamey	R/R	6-5/236	12-24-74	Huntsville, Indianapolis, Mil.	Solid starter who is beginning to find his groove; could be a future staff ace.

No.	CATCHERS	B/T	Ht./Wt.	Born	2000 clubs	Projection
12	Blanco, Henry	R/R	5-11/224	8-29-71	Milwaukee, Indianapolis	Very good defensive catcher who can hit a little.
27	Brown, Kevin	R/R	6-2/224	4-21-73	Syracuse, Indianapolis, Mil.	Solid catcher who will be backup. But he does not have a very good bat.

No.	INFIELDERS	B/T	Ht./Wt.	Born	2000 clubs	Projection
22	Barker, Kevin	R/R	6-3/205	7-26-75	Milwaukee, Indianapolis	Struggled at the plate last year at Indianapolis and likely to stay there this season.
10	Belliard, Ron	R/R	5-8/190	7-4-76	Milwaukee	Durable second baseman who will hit for average and steal a few bases.
16	Collier, Lou	R/R	5-10/182	8-21-73	Indianapolis, Huntsville, Mil.	Could be a good utilityman for Brewers as he can play several positions.
18	Hernandez, Jose	R/R	6-1/186	7-14-69	Milwaukee, Indianapolis	Valuable player can start at shortstop and third. He's a solid hitter with some pop.
2	Houston, Tyler	L/R	6-1/218	1-17-71	Milwaukee	Likely to see time at third base and catcher. Can put up good power numbers.
1	Lopez, Luis	B/R	5-11/170	9-4-70	Milwaukee	Backup infielder who can play several positions. Better glove than bat.
8	Loretta, Mark	R/R	6-0/189	8-14-71	Milwaukee, Indianapolis	Injuries hampered him last season; has shortstop job if healthy.
11	Sexson, Richie	R/R	6-8/215	12-29-74	Cleveland, Milwaukee	Provided the righthanded power the Brewers needed in middle of their lineup.

No.	OUTFIELDERS	B/T	Ht./Wt.	Born	2000 clubs	Projection
20	Burnitz, Jeromy	L/R	6-0/213	4-15-69	Milwaukee	Average was down last year, but power numbers remained high.
39	Echevarria, Angel	R/R	6-3/230	5-25-71	Colo. Springs, Colorado, Mil.	Solid outfielder will try to win a spot on the bench.
9	Grissom, Marquis	R/R	5-11/190	4-17-67	Milwaukee	Good outfielder who still has offensive skills, but production has fallen off.
6	Hammonds, Jeffrey	R/R	6-0/200	3-5-71	Colorado	After a career year in Colorado, expected to bring some pop to the lineup.
5	Jenkins, Geoff	L/R	6-1/206	7-21-74	Milwaukee	Hits for average and power. Had big second half of season last year.

THE COACHING STAFF

Davey Lopes, manager: Had a decent first season as manager but expectations will be higher with addition of Hammonds and another year of experience for the young pitching staff.

Gary Allenson: Enters his second season as first base coach after managing Milwaukee's Class AAA team the previous two seasons.

Bob Apodaca: After serving 28 years in the Mets organization, Apodaca begins his second season as Brewers pitching coach.

Rod Carew: After successful eight-year run as Angels' hitting coach, enters his second season in same role with Brewers.

Bill Castro: Entering his 14th season in the Milwaukee organization and ninth as bullpen coach.

Jerry Royster: After a 16-year career as a major league player, Royster begins his second season as the team's bench coach. Before coaching in Milwaukee, he managed in the minors for the Padres and Dodgers.

Luis Salazar: After spending six seasons as a coach in the Brewers' minor leagues, Salazar takes over as first base coach in his first season with the big club.

THE TOP PROSPECTS

Jeffrey Hammonds: Expected to provide nice production for the Brewers toward the bottom of the lineup.

THE TOP NEWCOMERS

Gene Altman: The Brewers' closer of the future throws hard. Had 17 saves with a 2.15 ERA for Beloit last season.

Jason Childers: Hard-throwing prospect who had big year at Mudville (12-10 with 177 strikeouts while only walking 54). Most likely to see time with Brewers by end of season.

Jose Mieses: Went a combined 17-7 with 172 strikeouts in Beloit and Mudville. Still very young and has time to develop before the Brewers throw him into rotation.

MONTREAL EXPOS

NATIONAL LEAGUE EAST DIVISION

2001 SEASON

Expos 2001 SCHEDULE

Home games shaded; D—Day game (games starting before 5 p.m.)
*—All-Star Game at Safeco Field (Seattle)

APRIL

SUN	MON	TUE	WED	THU	FRI	SAT
1	2 D CUB	3	4 D CUB	5 D CUB	6 NYM	7 D NYM
8 D NYM	9 CUB	10 CUB	11 CUB	12	13 FLA	14 FLA
15 D FLA	16 NYM	17 NYM	18 D NYM	19 FLA	20 FLA	21 FLA
22 D FLA	23	24 STL	25 STL	26 D STL	27 MIL	28 D MIL
29 D MIL	30					

MAY

SUN	MON	TUE	WED	THU	FRI	SAT
		1 ARI	2 ARI	3 ARI	4 HOU	5 HOU
6 D HOU	7 SF	8 SF	9 SF	10 D SF	11 COL	12 D COL
13 D COL	14	15 LA	16 LA	17 LA	18 SD	19 SD
20 D SD	21 NYM	22 NYM	23 NYM	24	25 PHI	26 PHI
27 D PHI	28 ATL	29 ATL	30 D ATL	31 PHI		

JUNE

SUN	MON	TUE	WED	THU	FRI	SAT
					1 PHI	2 PHI
3 D PHI	4	5 ATL	6 ATL	7 ATL	8 BAL	9 D BAL
10 D BAL	11	12 NYY	13 NYY	14 NYY	15 TOR	16 TOR
17 D TOR	18 NYM	19 NYM	20 NYM	21 NYM	22 PIT	23 PIT
24 D PIT	25 FLA	26 FLA	27 FLA	28	29 PIT	30 PIT

JULY

SUN	MON	TUE	WED	THU	FRI	SAT
1 D PIT	2	3 FLA	4 FLA	5 D FLA	6 TOR	7 D TOR
8 D TOR	9	10 *	11	12 TB	13 TB	14 D TB
15 D BOS	16 BOS	17 BOS	18 PHI	19 D PHI	20 ATL	21 ATL
22 D ATL	23 PHI	24 PHI	25 D PHI	26 ATL	27 ATL	28 ATL
29 D ATL	30	31 ARI				

AUGUST

SUN	MON	TUE	WED	THU	FRI	SAT
			1 ARI	2 D ARI	3 HOU	4 HOU
5 D HOU	6	7 STL	8 STL	9 STL	10 MIL	11 MIL
12 D MIL	13	14 LA	15 LA	16 D LA	17 SD	18 SD
19 D SD	20	21 SF	22 SF	23 SF	24 CIN	25 CIN
26 D CIN	27	28 ATL	29 ATL	30 ATL	31 PHI	

SEPTEMBER

SUN	MON	TUE	WED	THU	FRI	SAT
						1 PHI
2 D PHI	3 D ATL	4 ATL	5 ATL	6 PHI	7 PHI	8 PHI
9 D PHI	10	11 FLA	12 FLA	13 D FLA	14 NYM	15 NYM
16 D NYM	17 FLA	18 FLA	19 FLA	20 COL	21 COL	22 COL
23 D COL	24	25 NYM	26 NYM	27 NYM	28 CIN	29 D CIN
30 D CIN						

FRONT-OFFICE DIRECTORY

Chairman, CEO & managing general partner .... Jeffrey H. Loria
Executive vice president .... David P. Samson
Vice president and general manager .... Jim Beattie
Vice president, director of international operations .... Fred Ferreira
Assistant general manager .... Larry Beinfest
Assistants to the general manager .... Mike Berger, Don Reynolds
Director, scouting .... Jim Fleming
Director, player development .... Tony LaCava
Assistant director, scouting .... Gregg Leonard
Assistant director, player development .... Adam Wogan
Assistant director, international scouting .... Randy Kierce
Coordinator, conditioning & team travel .... Sean Cunningham
Assistant, baseball operations .... Mike Wickham
Vice president & CFO .... Michel Bussiere
Vice president, stadium operations .... Claude Delorme
Director, media relations .... P.J. Loyello
Director, media services .... Monique Giroux
Director, advertising sales .... Hubert Richard
Director, broadcast activities & web site editor .... Marc Griffin
Director, promotions & special events .... Gina Hackl
Director, ticket sales .... John Di Terlizzi
Director, administration, sales & marketing .... Chantal Dalpe
Director, management information systems .... Yves Poulin

MINOR LEAGUE AFFILIATES

Class	Team	League	Manager
AAA	Ottawa	International	Stan Hough
AA	Harrisburg	Eastern	Luis Dorante
A	Clinton	Midwest	Steve Phillips
A	Jupiter	Florida State	Tim Leiper
A	Vermont	New York-Pennsylvania	Tony Barbone
Rookie	Gulf Coast Expos	Gulf Coast	Dave Dangler

ASSISTANCE STAFF

Team orthopedist
Dr. Larry Coughlin

Team physician
Dr. Mike Thomassin

Strength, conditioning & rehab coordinator
Paul Fournier

Major league scouts
Mike Berger, Bob Cluck, Joe Moeller, Donnie Reynolds, Tommy Thompson

Scouts
Alex Agostino, Matt Anderson, Carlos Berroa, Dennis Cardoza, Dave Dangler, Marc DelPiano, Scot Engler, Scott Goldby, John Hughes, Joe Jordan, Mark Leavitt, Joel Matthews, Stan Meek, Bob Oldis, Steve Payne, Pat Puccinelli, Joel Smith, Scott Stanley

BROADCAST INFORMATION

Radio: TTo be announced.
TV: To be announced.
Cable TV: TSN, RDS (French).

SPRING TRAINING

Ballpark (city): Roger Dean Stadium (Jupiter, Fla.).
Ticket information: 561-775-1818.

BALLPARK INFORMATION

Ballpark (capacity, surface)
Olympic Stadium (46,500, artificial)

Address
P.O. Box 500, Station M
Montreal, Que. H1V 3P2

Official website
www.montrealexpos.com

Business phone
514-253-3434

Ticket information
800-GO-EXPOS

Ticket prices
$36 (VIP box seats)
$26 (box seats)
$16 (terrace)
$8 (general admission)

Field dimensions (from home plate)
To left field at foul line, 325 feet
To center field, 404 feet
To right field at foul line, 325 feet

First game played
April 15, 1977 (Phillies 7, Expos 2)

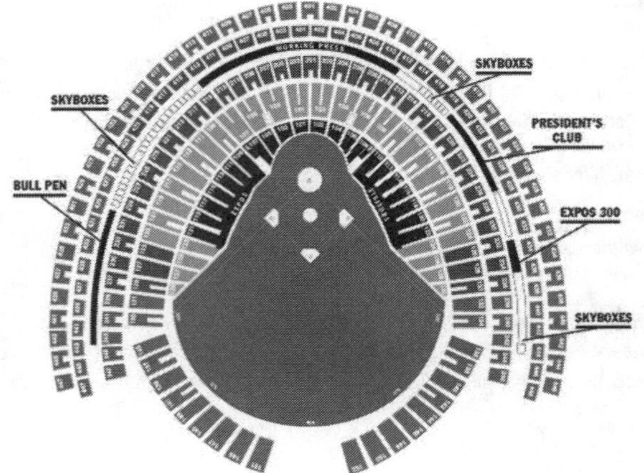

Follow the Expos all season at: www.sportingnews.com/baseball/teams/expos/

EXPOS SPRING ROSTER

No.	PITCHERS	B/T	Ht./Wt.	Born	2000 clubs	Projection
36	Armas, Tony	R/R	6-4/205	4-29-78	Jupiter, Ottawa, Montreal	Had 7 wins in only 17 starts.
48	Billingsley, Brent	L/L	6-2/200	4-19-75	Ottawa	Unless he shows improvement, will be back in Class AAA.
50	Blank, Matt	L/L	6-2/195	4-5-76	Montreal	Pitched in 13 games before injury cut his season short.
	Bridges, Donnie	R/R	6-4/195	12-10-78	Harrisburg, Jupiter	Had 16-12 combined record, should pitch in Class AAA for this season.
33	Burrows, Terry	L/L	6-1/185	11-28-68	Sacramento	Lefty who last pitched in majors in 1997.
48	Downs, Scott	L/L	6-2/190	3-17-76	Chicago N.L., Montreal	Only had one start in Montreal before injury cut his season short.
14	Irabu, Hideki	R/R	6-4/240	5-5-69	Montreal	Arm injury cut short what could have been a good year.
47	Johnson, Mike	L/R	6-2/170	10-3-75	Ottawa, Montreal	Pitched in long relief last year, probably will do same this season.
43	Lira, Felipe	R/R	6-0/170	4-26-72	Ottawa, Montreal	Expos have converted this starter to a long reliever.
37	Lloyd, Graeme	L/L	6-7/225	4-9-67	DID NOT PLAY	Could have helped the Expos young bullpen last season.
	Mattes, Troy	R/R	6-7/185	8-26-75	Harrisburg	Might make Expos rotation out of necessity, but could use season in Class AAA.
40	Mota, Guillermo	R/R	6-4/205	7-25-73	Ottawa, Montreal	Pitched in 64 games between Ottawa and Montreal in '00.
32	Munoz, Bobby	R/R	6-7/237	3-3-68	Louisville	Hasn't pitched in majors since 1997 when he was with Philadelphia.
45	Pavano, Carl	R/R	6-5/230	1-8-76	Montreal	Was 8-4 with 3.06 ERA before injury ended his season.
68	Reames, Britt	R/R	5-11/170	8-19-73	Arkansas, Memphis, St. Louis	Only pitched eight games in majors, but he will contribute to this rotation.
50	Scanlan, Bob	R/R	6-8/215	8-9-66	Indianapolis, Milwaukee	Had 35 saves for Indianapolis last year.
56	Smart, J.D.	R/R	6-2/180	11-12-73	Ottawa	Only pitched in four games before injuries sidelined him for the rest of the season.
53	Spencer, Sean	L/L	5-11/185	5-29-75	Tacoma, Ottawa, Montreal	Expos used him in lefty situations only, could take over Steve Kline's role.
20	Strickland, Scott	R/R	5-11/180	4-26-76	Montreal, Ottawa	Had four wins and nine saves pitching in short relief.
32	Telford, Anthony	R/R	6-0/195	3-6-66	Montreal	Has pitched in 143 games the last two seasons.
35	Thurman, Mike	R/R	6-5/210	7-22-73	Jupiter, Ott., Mon., Harrisburg	Injuries slowed his progress. He won four times in 17 starts.
52	Tucker, T.J.	R/R	6-3/245	8-20-78	Harrisburg, Montreal	Showed promise in 10 starts before injuries hit.
41	Urbina, Ugueth	R/R	6-0/205	2-15-74	Montreal	Had 8 saves in 13 games before arm trouble hit.
23	Vazquez, Javier	R/R	6-2/195	7-25-76	Montreal	Developing into staff ace. 11 wins and 196 strikeouts in '00.

No.	CATCHERS	B/T	Ht./Wt.	Born	2000 clubs	Projection
13	Henley, Bob	R/R	6-2/205	1-30-73	DID NOT PLAY	Injuries the last two seasons have slowed his development.
14	Martinez, Sandy	L/R	6-2/215	10-3-72	Florida, Calgary	He hit .300 in Class AAA last season.
39	Schneider, Brian	L/R	6-1/180	11-26-76	Ottawa, Montreal	Rushed to majors because of injuries and trades, good defensive catcher.

No.	INFIELDERS	B/T	Ht./Wt.	Born	2000 clubs	Projection
5	Barrett, Michael	R/R	6-2/200	10-22-76	Montreal	Will be in utility role because of Tatis' presence.
11	Blum, Geoff	B/R	6-3/195	4-26-73	Montreal	Utility player hit .283 last season. Provides switch-hitter off bench.
18	Cabrera, Orlando	R/R	5-10/175	11-2-74	Montreal, Ottawa	Everyday shortstop only hit .237. Will need to improve to stay in lineup.
2	De La Rosa, Tomas	R/R	5-10/165	1-28-78	Ottawa, Montreal	Another shortstop prospect in the Expos organization.
	Hodges, Scott	L/R	6-0/185	12-26-78	Jupiter, Harrisburg	Third base prospect will be brought up slowly now that Tatis is in Montreal.
	Mateo, Henry	B/R	5-11/170	10-14-76	Harrisburg	Second base prospect is stuck behind Jose Vidro.
25	Minor, Ryan	R/R	6-7/245	1-5-74	Roch., Balt., Fred., GC Orioles	If he hits, he can make a mark with the club.
12	Mordecai, Mike	R/R	5-10/185	12-13-67	Montreal	Utility guy, proves right handed bat off bench.
56	Nunnari, Talmadge	L/L	6-1/200	4-9-75	Ottawa, Harrisburg, Montreal	Should spend a full year in Class AAA for seasoning.
1	Sasser, Rob	R/R	6-3/205	3-9-75	Toledo	Free-agent brought in to bolster bench. Hit 25 home runs in Class AAA.
19	Seguignol, Fernando	B/R	6-5/230	1-19-75	Ottawa, Montreal	If he hits, he will stay and play first and outfield.
9	Stevens, Lee	L/L	6-4/219	7-10-67	Montreal	Can count on him for at least 20 home runs every season.
23	Tatis, Fernando	R/R	5-10/180	1-1-75	St. Louis, Memphis	Was on pace for monster season before groin injury slowed him down.
46	Tracy, Andy	L/L	6-3/220	12-11-73	Ottawa, Montreal	Can play either corner position and can hold his own at the plate.
3	Vidro, Jose	B/R	5-11/190	8-27-74	Montreal	Some questioned his defense, he only committed 10 errors in 153 games.

No.	OUTFIELDERS	B/T	Ht./Wt.	Born	2000 clubs	Projection
33	Bergeron, Peter	L/R	6-0/185	11-9-77	Montreal	Expos left him in outfield all year for major league experience.
24	Bradley, Milton	B/R	6-0/170	4-15-78	Ottawa, Montreal	Expos will probably use him in left this year, now that Rondell White is gone.
27	Guerrero, Vladimir	R/R	6-3/205	2-9-76	Montreal	All-Star outfielder will post similar numbers this season.
1	Jones, Terry	B/R	5-10/160	2-15-71	Montreal	Used for defense and running ability.
11	Pride, Curtis	L/R	5-11/195	12-17-68	Norfolk, Pawtucket, Bos., Alb.	Will get every chance to show he can contribute.
30	Raines, Tim	B/R	5-8/186	9-16-59	DID NOT PLAY	Veteran trying for one last season in the bigs.
	Ruan, Wilken	R/R	6-0/170	11-18-79	Cape Fear	Expos will give him a look at spring training after 64 stolen bases in '00.

THE COACHING STAFF

Felipe Alou, manager: He finished his ninth season as manager of the team and is remarkably only 15 games under .500 as Expos manager. Even though the Expos lost 90 games for the fourth consecutive season, you can't fault the manager. Nine members of the pitching staff went under the knife and the Expos used 26 different pitchers last season.

Brad Arnsberg: Beginning second season as bullpen coach. Hopefully, the pitchers will stay healthy so he can work some magic.

Pierre Arsenault: Used to throw batting practice for the Expos during home games. After a stint as a broadcaster, he's been the bullpen coordinator for a few seasons.

Jeff Cox: Former AAA manager for Montreal's team was brought in as bench coach midway through last season. Brings 15 years of coaching and managing experience to his position.

Perry Hill: In second season as first base coach. He is also responsible for the infield defense. After last season, no one can argue with the job he did with Jose Vidro.

Pat Roessler: Begins his second season as Expos hitting coach. If he can get Vladimir Guerrero to cut down on strikeouts, consistency for the rest of the lineup can't be far behind.

THE TOP NEWCOMERS

Britt Reames: One of the Cardinals top pitching prospects missed the 1997 and 1998 seasons due to arm injury. Pitched well enough for the Cardinals to recall him late last season. Will be a starter for this team.

Fernando Tatis: When healthy he can be a dangerous player. A severe groin injury put him on the shelf last season. He still hit 18 home runs, but his average dropped over 40 points. He will hit well wherever they put him in the lineup with Vidro, Guerrero and Stevens.

THE TOP PROSPECTS

Donnie Bridges: Former first round pick is starting to learn how to throw in the minors. Had six complete games and four shutouts in just 19 starts in Class AA Harrisburg.

Scott Downs: He was 4-3 with the Cubs before his trade to Montreal. During '99 season was 8-1 with a 1.35 ERA with Class AA West Tenn.

Wilken Ruan: Expos want to give this young outfielder a look. He is speedy with 141 steals after four years in the minor leagues. He also needs to learn discipline at the plate.

NEW YORK METS

NATIONAL LEAGUE EAST DIVISION

2001 SEASON

Mets 2001 SCHEDULE

Home games shaded; D—Day game (games starting before 5 p.m.)
*—All-Star Game at Safeco Field (Seattle)

APRIL

SUN	MON	TUE	WED	THU	FRI	SAT
1	2	3 D ATL	4 ATL	5 ATL	6 MON	7 D MON
8 D MON	9 D ATL	10	11 ATL	12 ATL	13 CIN	14 D CIN
15 D CIN	16 MON	17 MON	18 D MON	19	20 CIN	21 D CIN
22 D CIN	23	24 MIL	25 MIL	26 D MIL	27 STL	28 D STL
29 D STL	30 HOU					

MAY

SUN	MON	TUE	WED	THU	FRI	SAT
		1 HOU	2 HOU	3	4 ARI	5 D ARI
6 D ARI	7 COL	8 COL	9 COL	10 D COL	11 SF	12 D SF
13 D SF	14	15 SD	16 SD	17 SD	18 LA	19 D LA
20 D LA	21 MON	22 MON	23 MON	24 FLA	25 FLA	26 D FLA
27 D FLA	28 D PHI	29 PHI	30 D PHI	31 FLA		

JUNE

SUN	MON	TUE	WED	THU	FRI	SAT
					1 FLA	2 FLA
3 D FLA	4	5 PHI	6 PHI	7 PHI	8 TB	9 D TB
10 D TB	11	12 BAL	13 BAL	14 BAL	15 NYY	16 D NYY
17 NYY	18 MON	19 MON	20 MON	21 MON	22 ATL	23 D ATL
24 D ATL	25 CUB	26 D CUB	27 D CUB	28 ATL	29 ATL	30 D ATL

JULY

SUN	MON	TUE	WED	THU	FRI	SAT
1 D ATL	2	3 CUB	4 D CUB	5 CUB	6 NYY	7 D NYY
8 D NYY	9	10 *	11	12 BOS	13 BOS	14 D BOS
15 D TOR	16 TOR	17 TOR	18 FLA	19 D FLA	20 PHI	21 PHI
22 D PHI	23 FLA	24 FLA	25 FLA	26 PHI	27 PHI	28 D PHI
29 D PHI	30	31 HOU				

AUGUST

SUN	MON	TUE	WED	THU	FRI	SAT
			1 HOU	2 HOU	3 ARI	4 D ARI
5 D ARI	6	7 MIL	8 MIL	9 D MIL	10 STL	11 D STL
12 D STL	13	14 SD	15 SD	16 D SD	17 LA	18 LA
19 D LA	20	21 COL	22 COL	23 COL	24 SF	25 SF
26 D SF	27 D SF	28 PHI	29 PHI	30 PHI	31 FLA	

SEPTEMBER

SUN	MON	TUE	WED	THU	FRI	SAT
						1 FLA
2 D FLA	3 D PHI	4 PHI	5 PHI	6	7 FLA	8 FLA
9 D FLA	10	11 PIT	12 PIT	13 D PIT	14 MON	15 MON
16 D MON	17 PIT	18 PIT	19 PIT	20	21 ATL	22 ATL
23 D ATL	24	25 MON	26 MON	27 MON	28 ATL	29 ATL
30 D ATL						

FRONT-OFFICE DIRECTORY

Chairman of the board .... Nelson Doubleday
President and chief executive officer .... Fred Wilpon
Directors .... Nelson Doubleday, Fred Wilpon, Saul B. Katz, Steve Phillips, Marvin B. Tepper
Special advisor to the board of directors .... Richard Cummins
Senior vice president and general manager .... Steve Phillips
Senior assistant general manager/international scouting director .... Omar Minaya
Senior assistant general manager/player personnel .... Jim Duquette
Assistant general manager/amateur scouting .... Gary Larocque
Assistant general manager/professional scouting .... Carmen Fusco
Assistant directors of amateur scouting .... Jack Bowen, Fred Wright
Assistant director of player personnel .... Kevin Morgan
Senior vice president and treasurer .... Harold W. O'Shaughnessy
Senior vice president of business and legal affairs .... David Howard
Vice president, marketing .... To be announced
Vice president, purchasing and special projects .... Bob Mandt
Vice president, ticket sales and services .... Bill Ianniciello
Senior vice president and consultant .... J. Frank Cashen
Director of marketing .... To be announced
Director of marketing production .... Tim Gunkel
Director of human resources .... Shez Jackson
General counsel .... David Cohen
Director, administrative and data processing .... To be announced
Director, community outreach .... Jill Knee
Director of corporate sales .... Paul Danforth
Controller .... Lennie Labita
Director of media relations .... Jay Horwitz
Director, ticket operations .... Dan DeMato
Manager, customer relations .... Joann Galardy
Director of stadium operations .... Kevin McCarthy
Director of minor league operations .... Kevin Morgan

MINOR LEAGUE AFFILIATES

Class	Team	League	Manager
AAA	Norfolk	International	John Gibbons
AA	Binghamton	Eastern	Howie Freiling
A	Brooklyn	New York-Pennsylvania	Edgar Alfonzo
A	Capital City	South Atlantic	To be announced
A	St. Lucie	Florida State	To be announced
Rookie	Kingsport	Appalachian	Joey Cora

ASSISTANCE STAFF

Club physician
Dr. David Altchek

Club psychologist/Employee Assistance Program
Dr. Allan Lans

Team trainers
Fred Hina, Scott Lawrenson

Advance scouts
Bruce Benedict, Mike Toomey

Professional scouts
Bruce Benedict, Erwin Bryant, Harry Dunlop, Dick Gernert, Roland Johnson, Buddy Kerr, Bill Latham, Harry Minor, Mike Toomey, Tim Teufel

Regional scouting supervisors
Paul Fryer, Gene Kerns, Terry Tripp

Scouting supervisors
Kevin Blankenship, Quincy Boyd, Larry Chase, Joe DelliCarri, Kevin Frady, Chuck Hensley Jr., Dave Lottsfeldt, Fred Mazuca, Marlin McPhail, Randy Milligan, Bob Minor, Greg Morhardt, Joe Morlan, Joe Nigro, Jim Reeves, Junior Roman, Bob Rossi, Joe Salermo, Greg Tubbs

BROADCAST INFORMATION

Radio: WFAN-AM (660).
TV: WPIX (Channel 11).
Cable TV: Fox Sports New York.

SPRING TRAINING

Ballpark (city): Thomas J. White Stadium (Port St. Lucie, Fla.).
Ticket information: 561-871-2115.

BALLPARK INFORMATION

Ballpark (capacity, surface)
Shea Stadium (56,516, grass)

Address
123-01 Roosevelt Ave.
Flushing, NY 11368

Official website
www.mets.com

Business phone
718-507-METS

Ticket information
718-507-TIXX

Ticket prices
$64 (Metropolitan Club gold, inner baseline box)
$60 (Metropolitan Club)
$43 (inner field box, inner loge box, outer baseline box)
$38 (middle field box)
$33 (outer field box, outer loge box, mezz. box)
$29 (loge reserved)
$23 (mezzanine reserved, upper box)
$12 (upper reserved, back rows loge and mezz.)

Field dimensions (from home plate)
To left field at foul line, 338 feet
To center field, 410 feet
To right field at foul line, 338 feet

First game played
April 17, 1964 (Pirates 4, Mets 3)

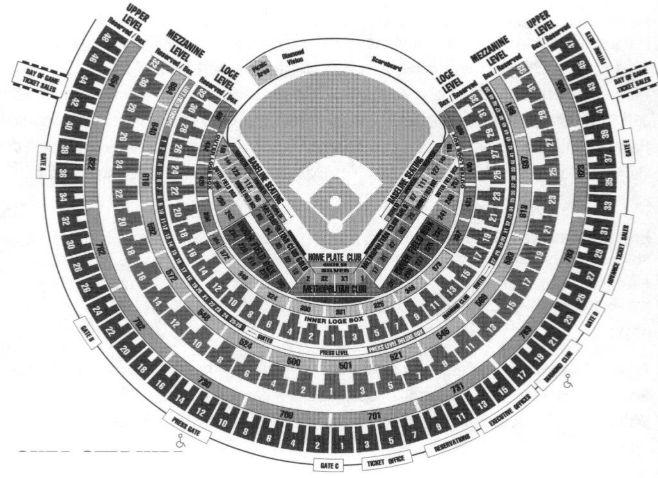

Follow the Mets all season at: www.sportingnews.com/baseball/teams/mets/

METS SPRING ROSTER

No.	PITCHERS	B/T	Ht./Wt.	Born	2000 clubs	Projection
17	Appier, Kevin	R/R	6-2/200	12-6-67	Oakland	Workhorse capable of 15 or more wins when healthy.
49	Benitez, Armando	R/R	6-4/229	11-3-72	New York N.L.	Has developed into a premier closer, saved 41 games in 46 tries last season.
26	Cammack, Eric	R/R	6-1/180	8-14-75	Norfolk, New York N.L.	Bullpen prospect who saw limited action (10 IP) with the big club.
27	Cook, Dennis	L/L	6-3/190	10-4-62	New York N.L.	Situational lefty struggled in '00 but still managed six wins in relief.
45	Franco, John	L/L	5-10/185	9-17-60	New York N.L.	Former closer adjusted well to setup role; provides insurance if Benitez falters.
66	Gonzalez, Dicky	R/R	5-11/170	10-21-78	Binghamton	Waiting his turn while the vets try to win it all; had solid season at Class AA.
21	Jones, Bobby M.	R/L	6-0/178	4-11-72	Norfolk, New York N.L.	Pitched very little with big club last season. Will have hard time making rotation.
22	Leiter, Al	L/L	6-3/220	10-23-65	New York N.L.	First-half ace (10-2 pre-break) and the full-time inspirational leader.
61	Maness, Nick	R/R	6-4/210	10-17-78	St. Lucie, Binghamton	Was 11-7, 3.22 in Class A in '00, but likely won't see majors any time soon.
	Martin, Tom	L/L	6-1/200	5-21-70	Cleveland, Buffalo	Another lefthanded arm out of the bullpen.
35	Reed, Rick	R/R	6-1/195	8-16-65	New York N.L.	Steady No. 3 in rotation with 51 wins in past four seasons.
34	Riggan, Jerrod	R/R	6-3/200	5-16-74	Binghamton, New York N.L.	Got a cup of coffee with the big club last year. Might get bullpen work this season.
36	Roberts, Grant	R/R	6-3/205	9-13-77	Norfolk, New York N.L.	Prospect turning into a suspect; so-so in call-up; work habits, desire questioned.
46	Rodriguez, Rich	L/L	6-0/205	3-1-63	New York N.L., Norfolk	Will have to battle for spot in the bullpen this season.
48	Rusch, Glendon	L/L	6-1/200	11-7-74	New York N.L.	Staff's biggest surprise with 11 wins and a 4.01 ERA out of the fifth spot.
39	Santana, Julio	R/R	6-0/225	1-20-74	Pawtucket, Montreal	Journeyman righthander might fill Pat Mahomes' long-man role.
63	Seo, Jae	R/R	6-1/215	5-24-77	DID NOT PLAY	South Korean righty showed great promise before elbow surgery; still rehabbing.
29	Trachsel, Steve	R/R	6-4/205	10-31-70	Tampa Bay, Toronto	Innings-eater replaces Bobby M. Jones as the fourth starter.
	Walker, Tyler	R/R	6-3/255	5-15-76	Binghamton, Norfolk	Posted a sub-3.00 ERA between AA and AAA last year.
33	Wall, Donne	R/R	6-1/205	7-11-67	San Diego, Las Vegas	Acquired for Bubba Trammell; can set up, likely to be a middle man.
99	Wendell, Turk	L/R	6-2/205	5-19-67	New York N.L.	ERA rose half a point from '99, but still the top righty in bullpen.
51	White, Rick	R/R	6-4/230	12-23-68	Tampa Bay, New York N.L.	Solid deadline pickup last year is fighting to keep his spot on the staff.

No.	CATCHERS	B/T	Ht./Wt.	Born	2000 clubs	Projection
31	Piazza, Mike	R/R	6-3/215	9-4-68	New York N.L.	MVP favorite until September swoon; offense's heart and soul.
7	Pratt, Todd	R/R	6-3/230	2-9-67	New York N.L.	One of the best backups in all of majors; throwing is his strong suit.
3	Wilson, Vance	R/R	5-11/190	3-17-73	Norfolk, New York N.L.	Soon-to-be career minor leaguer stuck in a logjam.

No.	INFIELDERS	B/T	Ht./Wt.	Born	2000 clubs	Projection
13	Alfonzo, Edgardo	R/R	5-11/187	11-8-73	New York N.L.	Many considered him the team's MVP; had big numbers despite injuries.
19	Harris, Lenny	L/R	5-10/220	10-28-64	Arizona, New York N.L.	Top pinch hitter is beloved in the locker room; brings speed to the bench.
47	McEwing, Joe	R/R	5-11/170	10-19-72	Norfolk, New York N.L.	Versatility will keep him in the majors.
10	Ordonez, Rey	R/R	5-9/159	11-11-72	New York N.L.	Bears watching if he can return to Gold Glove form after missing four months.
8	Relaford, Desi	B/R	5-9/174	9-16-73	Philadelphia, San Diego	If he can hit he might everyday starter at shortstop.
30	Toca, Jorge	R/R	6-3/220	1-7-75	Norfolk, Bing., New York N.L.	Cuban first baseman has some pop, but is stuck behind Todd Zeile.
4	Ventura, Robin	L/R	6-1/198	7-14-67	New York N.L.	Looking to rebound from injury-filled season where offense and defense slipped.
9	Zeile, Todd	R/R	6-1/200	9-9-65	New York N.L.	Steady vet, hit well in the clutch and became an adequate defensive first baseman.

No.	OUTFIELDERS	B/T	Ht./Wt.	Born	2000 clubs	Projection
50	Agbayani, Benny	R/R	6-0/225	12-28-71	New York N.L.	Postseason hero is a Valentine favorite; still might have to platoon in left.
60	Cole, Brian	R/R	5-9/170	9-28-78	St. Lucie, Binghamton	Fleet, powerful youngster has sped through the system.
25	Escobar, Alex	R/R	6-1/180	9-6-78	Binghamton	Remains the No. 1 prospect; a Class AA all-star last year with 16 HRs and 24 SBs.
18	Hamilton, Darryl	L/R	6-1/192	12-3-64	New York N.L., St. Lucie, Norfolk	Fourth outfielder if he stays in town; missed most of '00 with toe injury.
44	Payton, Jay	R/R	5-10/185	11-22-72	New York N.L.	Stayed healthy and competed for Rookie of the Year; can he take the next step?
6	Perez, Timo	L/L	5-9/165	4-8-77	St. Lucie, Norfolk, New York N.L.	Late-season sensation showed big-time flaws during the LCS and World Series.
	Shinjo, Tsuyoshi	R/R	6-1/185	1-28-72		Flashed power in Japan and will compete for playing time at all three spots.

THE COACHING STAFF

Bobby Valentine, manager: Showed many last season that '99 season wasn't a fluke. He will have to do it again without some of his better players who left via free agency.

Charlie Hough: Hough brings many years of experince to veteran rotation. Might have to get some younger arms in the bullpen.

John Stearns: Moves to the third base coach position after helping Piazza improve his defense.

Mookie Wilson: One of the most popular players in Mets history stays on as first base coach. As the outfield instructor he has turned Agbayani into a serviceable outfielder. He might work some magic on Timo Perez too.

Randy Niemann: Back with Mets after being fired in '99. Will help to keep bullpen sharp as it was last season.

Dave Engle: Promoted after two-year stint as a minor-league skipper. Will have to help Robin Ventura regain his form at the plate.

Bob Floyd: Has spent nearly two decades as a coordinator/manager in the Mets' minor-league system. As the infield coordinator he won't have too much work to do as long as the four mainstays of the Mets infield stay healthy.

THE TOP NEWCOMERS

Kevin Appier: Rebounded in Oakland after suffering some injured plagued seasons with the Royals. If he stays healthy this year, the Mets should be in the thick of things in the N.L. East.

Steve Trachsel: Won a total of eight games last year with Tampa Bay and Toronto. With a better defense and runs support, he could win 15 games again.

Donne Wall: He was a starter who has been converted to a reliever. He has won 12 games in relief in the past two seasons. Could end up in long relief, if he pitches well this spring.

THE TOP PROSPECTS

Alex Escobar: Mentioned in trade rumors alot. And why not, he can hit for power and average. Could be a Mets outfielder if he has a good spring.

Brian Cole: Another outfield prospect who looks as good as Escobar. He stole 54 bases in St. Lucie in only 91 games. Can hit for average too. Power numbers will come with time.

Tyler Walker: Will need some more work at AAA. Right now, he has to wait for his turn. He is stuck behind five good starters in New York.

PHILADELPHIA PHILLIES

NATIONAL LEAGUE EAST DIVISION

2001 SEASON

Phillies
2001 SCHEDULE
Home games shaded; D—Day game (games starting before 5 p.m.)
*—All-Star Game at Safeco Field (Seattle)

APRIL

SUN	MON	TUE	WED	THU	FRI	SAT
1	2 D FLA	3 FLA	4 FLA	5	6 D CUB	7 D CUB
8 D CUB	9 FLA	10 FLA	11 FLA	12	13 ATL	14 ATL
15 D ATL	16 CUB	17 D CUB	18 D CUB	19	20 ATL	21 ATL
22 D ATL	23 SD	24 SD	25 SD	26 D SD	27 LA	28 LA
29 D LA	30					

MAY

SUN	MON	TUE	WED	THU	FRI	SAT
		1 COL	2 COL	3 D COL	4 SF	5 SF
6 D SF	7 HOU	8 HOU	9 HOU	10	11 ARI	12 ARI
13 D ARI	14	15 MIL	16 MIL	17 MIL	18 STL	19 STL
20 D STL	21	22 PIT	23 PIT	24 PIT	25 MON	26 MON
27 D MON	28 D NYM	29 NYM	30 D NYM	31 MON		

JUNE

SUN	MON	TUE	WED	THU	FRI	SAT
					1 MON	2 MON
3 D MON	4	5 NYM	6 NYM	7 NYM	8 BOS	9 D BOS
10 D BOS	11	12 TB	13 TB	14 D TB	15 BAL	16 BAL
17 D BAL	18	19 PIT	20 PIT	21 PIT	22 FLA	23 FLA
24 D FLA	25 ATL	26 ATL	27 D ATL	28 FLA	29 FLA	30 FLA

JULY

SUN	MON	TUE	WED	THU	FRI	SAT
1 D FLA	2	3 ATL	4 ATL	5 ATL	6 BAL	7 D BAL
8 D BAL	9	10 *	11	12 TOR	13 TOR	14 D TOR
15 D NYY	16 NYY	17 NYY	18 MON	19 D MON	20 NYM	21 NYM
22 D NYM	23 MON	24 MON	25 D MON	26 NYM	27 NYM	28 D NYM
29 D NYM	30	31 COL				

AUGUST

SUN	MON	TUE	WED	THU	FRI	SAT
			1 COL	2 D COL	3 SF	4 D SF
5 D SF	6	7 SD	8 SD	9 D SD	10 LA	11 LA
12 D LA	13	14 MIL	15 MIL	16 D MIL	17 STL	18 STL
19 D STL	20	21 HOU	22 HOU	23 HOU	24 ARI	25 D ARI
26 D ARI	27 ARI	28 NYM	29 NYM	30 NYM	31 MON	

SEPTEMBER

SUN	MON	TUE	WED	THU	FRI	SAT
						1 MON
2 D MON	3 D NYM	4 NYM	5 NYM	6 MON	7 MON	8 MON
9 D MON	10	11 ATL	12 D ATL	13 ATL	14 CIN	15 D CIN
16 D CIN	17 ATL	18 ATL	19 ATL	20 ATL	21 FLA	22 FLA
23 D FLA	24	25 CIN	26 CIN	27 CIN	28 FLA	29 FLA
30 D FLA						

FRONT-OFFICE DIRECTORY

General partner, president, CEO .... David Montgomery
Chairman .... Bill Giles
Partners .... Claire S. Betz, Tri-Play Associates (Alexander K. Buck, J. Mahlon Buck Jr., William C. Buck), Double Play, Inc. (John Middleton, chairman), Giles Limited Partnership (Bill Giles)
Vice president, general counsel and secretary .... Bill Webb
Senior vice president, chief financial officer .... Jerry Clothier
Special assistant to the president .... Sharon Swainson
Director, business development .... Joe Giles
Vice president and general manager .... Ed Wade
Assistant general manager .... Ruben Amaro Jr.
Controller .... John Fusco
Director, minor leagues and scouting .... Mike Arbuckle
Senior advisors to general manager .... Dallas Green, Paul Owens
Director, minor league operations .... Steve Noworyta
Executive assistant to the general manager .... Susan Ingersoll
Vice president, public relations .... Larry Shenk
Manager, media relations .... Leigh Tobin
Director, community relations .... Gene Dias
Vice president, advertising sales .... Dave Buck
Director, information systems .... Brian Lamoreaux
Vice president, ticket operations .... Richard Deats
Director, ticket department .... Dan Goroff
Director, sales .... John Weber
Director, broadcasting and video services .... Rory McNeil
Director, stadium operations .... Mike DiMuzio

MINOR LEAGUE AFFILIATES

Class	Team	League	Manager
AAA	Scranton/Wilkes-Barre	International	Marc Bombard
AA	Reading	Eastern	Gary Varsho
A	Batavia	New York-Pennsylvania	Frank Klebe
A	Clearwater	Florida State	Ramon Aviles
A	Lakewood	South Atlantic	Greg Legg
Rookie	Gulf Coast Phillies	Gulf Coast	Roly de Armas

BROADCAST INFORMATION

Radio: WPHT Talk Radio 1210.
TV: UPN (Channel 57).
Cable TV: Comcast SportsNet.

SPRING TRAINING

Ballpark (city): Jack Russell Stadium (Clearwater, Fla.).
Ticket information: 215-463-1000, 727-442-8496.

ASSISTANCE STAFF

Club physician
Dr. Michael Ciccotti

Club trainers
Jeff Cooper, Mark Andersen

Mgr., equipment and team travel
Frank Coppenbarger

Manager, visiting clubhouse
Kevin Steinhour

National supervisors
Marti Wolever, Sonny Bowers

Director, Florida operations
John Timberlake

Director, Latin American operations
Sal Artiaga

Director, Major League scouts
Gordon Lakey

Major League scout
Jimmy Stewart

Advance scout, Major Leagues
Hank King

Special assignment scout
Dean Jongewaard

Coordinator, professional coverage
Dick Lawlor

Cross-checkers
Scott Trcka, Brian Kohlscheen
Mitch Sokol

Regular scouts
Sal Agostinelli, Emil Belich, Darrell Connor, Steve Gillispie, Ken Hultzapple, Marlon Jones, Tim Kissner, Jerry Lafferty, Matt Lundin, Miguel Machado, Lloyd Merritt, Venice Murray, Dave Owen, Scott Ramsay, Paul Scott, Doug Takaragawa, Roy Tanner

BALLPARK INFORMATION

Ballpark (capacity, surface)
Veterans Stadium (62,418, artificial)

Address
P.O. Box 7575
Philadelphia, PA 19101

Official website
www.phillies.com

Business phone
215-463-6000

Ticket information
215-463-1000

Ticket prices
$24 (field box)
$20 (sections 258-201, terrace box)
$18 (loge box)
$14 (reserved, 600 level)
$8 (reserved, 700 level, adult gen. admission)
$5 (children's general admission)

Field dimensions (from home plate)
To left field at foul line, 330 feet
To center field, 408 feet
To right field at foul line, 330 feet

First game played
April 10, 1971 (Phillies 4, Expos 1)

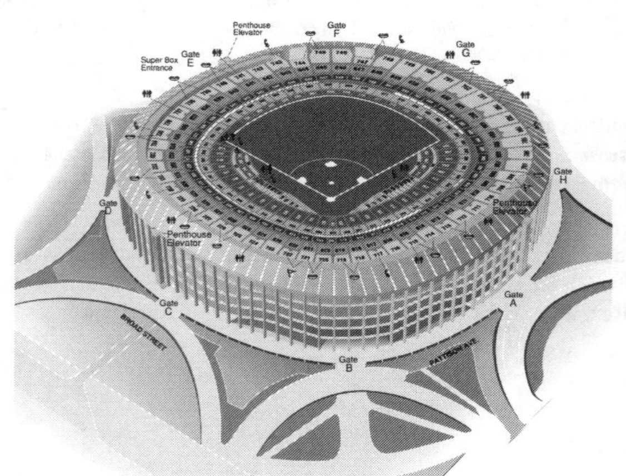

Follow the Phillies all season at: www.sportingnews.com/baseball/teams/phillies/

PHILLIES SPRING ROSTER

No.	PITCHERS	B/T	Ht./Wt.	Born	2000 clubs	Projection
27	Bottalico, Ricky	L/R	6-1/215	8-26-69	Kansas City	Phillies former closer comes back for second tour.
41	Boyd, Jason	R/R	6-3/173	2-23-73	Clearwater, Scranton/W.B., Phila.	Might not be enough room in bullpen to keep on team this year.
62	Brester, Jason	L/L	6-3/190	12-7-76	Reading	Pitched well at Reading last year and could be valueable lefty out of bullpen.
45	Brock, Chris	R/R	6-0/185	2-5-70	Philadelphia	Steady out of bullpen and can start if needed.
39	Chen, Bruce	L/L	6-2/210	6-19-77	Atlanta, Richmond, Philadelphia	Phillies looking for breakthrough season out of this talented lefty.
48	Coggin, Dave	R/R	6-4/205	10-30-76	Clr,. Read., Scranton/W.B., Phila.	Worked his way through minor leagues last year for a shot in rotation.
33	Cormier, Rheal	L/L	5-10/187	4-23-67	Boston	Lefty who can give you innings out of the bullpen in short or long releif.
37	Daal, Omar	L/L	6-3/195	3-1-72	Arizona, Philadelphia	Led league with 19 losses, but pitched better with Phillies after the trade.
62	Duckworth, Brandon	B/R	6-2/185	1-23-76	Reading	Young, talented starter coming off big season at Reading last year.
53	Eaton, Adam	R/R	6-2/190	11-23-77	Mobile, San Diego	Potential to be in Phillies starting rotation, pitched well last year with Padres.
57	Figueroa, Nelson	B/R	6-1/155	5-18-74	Tucson, Arizona, Scranton/W.B.	Shot to make the team, but more likely as reliever than starter.
61	Gomes, Wayne	R/R	6-2/227	1-15-73	Philadelphia, Scranton/W.B.	Showed signs of brillance out of bullpen last year starting the year as closer.
72	Jacquez, Tom	L/L	6-2/195	12-29-75	Reading, Scranton/W.B., Phila.	After strong season in minors, could prove to be solid lefty out of bullpen.
49	Mesa, Jose	R/R	6-3/225	5-22-66	Seattle	Brought in to take over closer duties after Mike Jackson experiment flopped.
51	Nickle, Doug	R/R	6-4/210	10-2-74	Reading, Philadelphia	One of the top prospects in baseball as Reading found out last season.
73	Nunez, Franklin	R/R	6-0/175	1-18-77	Clearwater	Consecutive strong years in the minors hope to get him a spot on the team.
58	Osting, Jimmy	R/L	6-5/180	4-7-77	M. Beach, Green., Rich., Read.	Could become a steal after coming over from the Braves.
44	Padilla, Vicente	R/R	6-2/200	9-27-77	Tucson, Arizona, Philadelphia	Reliable relief pitcher, but struggle at times with Phillies in second half.
31	Person, Robert	R/R	6-0/194	10-6-69	Phila., Clearwater, Reading	Live arm that has potential to be number one pitcher in rotation.
35	Politte, Cliff	R/R	5-11/185	2-27-74	Scranton/Wilkes-Barre, Phila.	Could see time both as starter and reliever after strong season.
68	Silva, Carlos	R/R	6-4/225	4-23-79	Clearwater	Starting pitcher with good stuff, but log jam of pitchers could make it hard for him.
47	Telemaco, Amaury	R/R	6-3/222	1-19-74	Philadelphia, Scranton/W.B.	Versatile pitcher that can be used in short or long relief, spot starter if needed.
70	Thomas, Evan	R/R	5-10/170	6-14-74	Scranton/Wilkes-Barre	Solid starter not likely to make team this year.
43	Wolf, Randy	L/L	6-0/194	8-22-76	Philadelphia	Dependable starter who will be counted on once again to eat up innings.

No.	CATCHERS	B/T	Ht./Wt.	Born	2000 clubs	Projection
4	Bennett, Gary	R/R	6-0/208	4-17-72	Scranton/W.B., Philadelphia	Good offensive player who could be valueable off the bench.
76	Estrada, Johnny	B/R	5-11/210	6-27-76	Reading	Solid offensively. Will compete for back-up catching spot.
24	Lieberthal, Mike	R/R	6-0/190	1-18-72	Philadelphia	Premier catcher in baseball who can do it all defensively and offensively.

No.	INFIELDERS	B/T	Ht./Wt.	Born	2000 clubs	Projection
8	Anderson, Marlon	L/R	5-11/198	1-6-74	Scranton/W.B., Philadelphia	Talented player, but still hasn't earned starting spot.
13	Perez, Tomas	B/R	5-11/177	12-29-73	Reading, Phila., Scranton/W.B.	Versatile infielder who could help off the bench.
75	Punto, Nick	R/R	5-9/170	11-8-77	Reading	Will compete for spot on infield. Has good speed and offensive skills.
17	Rolen, Scott	R/R	6-4/226	4-4-75	Philadelphia	Could be top third baseman with his offensive and defensive skills.
29	Rollins, Jimmy	B/R	5-8/165	11-27-78	Scranton/W.B., Philadelphia	Could have earned himself a spot on the team with strong play last year.

No.	OUTFIELDERS	B/T	Ht./Wt.	Born	2000 clubs	Projection
53	Abreu, Bobby	L/R	6-0/197	3-11-74	Philadelphia	Could put himself in position for MVP if Phillies have strong season.
5	Burrell, Pat	R/R	6-4/225	10-10-76	Scranton/W.B., Philadelphia	Emerged as the real deal last year and will only get better.
2	Ducey, Rob	L/R	6-2/183	5-24-65	Philadelphia, Toronto	More than capable back-up who is coming off poor year at the plate.
6	Glanville, Doug	R/R	6-2/172	8-25-70	Philadelphia	Consistent hitter and durable player with great speed at top of line-up.
	Hunter, Brian L.	R/R	6-3/180	3-5-71	Colorado, Cincinnati	Might see alot of playing time if Travis Lee doesn't rebound.
16	Lee, Travis	L/L	6-3/214	5-26-75	Arizona, El Paso, Tucson, Phila.	Always had the potential, but can he provide offense the Phillies need?
67	Michaels, Jason	R/R	6-0/205	5-4-76	Reading	Showed some pop last year and ability to drive in runs with Reading.
64	Perez, Josue	B/R	6-0/180	8-12-77	Clearwater, Reading	Good speed and hitting ability, but still few years off from making team.
28	Taylor, Reggie	L/R	6-1/178	1-12-77	Scranton/W.B., Philadelphia	Likely to start season in minors, but has good ability with power and speed.
71	Valent, Eric	L/L	6-0/190	4-4-77	Reading	Coming off solid season at Reading and could compete for spot on bench.

THE COACHING STAFF

Larry Bowa, manager: Takes over as Phillies manager after Terry Francona's stint on the bench. Bowa is a stern leader and will be looked to help mold the young, talented Phillies squad into contenders this year. This is Bowa's second time as manager after coaching the Padres from 1986-88.

Greg Gross: Will serve as bench coach in his first season at the major league level. Coached for six years in the Rockies organization before coming to Philadelphia.

Richie Hebner: Gets another shot at hitting coach after coaching with the Red Sox from 1989-91. Hebner has been coaching since serving as manager of Myrtle Beach in 1988 for the Toronto Blue Jays organization.

Ramon Henderson: Continues duties as bullpen coach for third consecutive season. He is a 11-year member of the Phillies organization.

Vern Ruhle: Comes over from the Astros to serve as pitching coach for the Phillies. Ruhle has been dealt some good cards so he will be watched closely this season to see how the young staff performs.

Tony Scott: Takes over as first base coach in his first season coaching in the majors. He has been in the Phillies oranization since 1989.

John Vukovich: Continues his job as third base coach for the fourth straight season.

THE TOP NEWCOMERS

Jose Mesa: He has saved over 30 games three times in his career and will be counted on this year to provide stability to the closer role.

Rheal Cormier: Tough on lefties and has proved over the past few seasons that he is durable out of the bullpen.

Ricky Bottalico: The Phillies are hoping he can regain the form he once had before the arm problems to help their bullpen woes. Bottalico battled back last year to post decent numbers after a sub-par season before in St. Louis.

THE TOP PROSPECTS

Pat Burrell: Played on a regular basis in the outfield for the first time in his career and showed flashes of greatness. Could become and all-star player in this league as soon as this season.

Doug Nickle: While Mesa and Bottalico were brought in to shore up the closer role, Nickle looks like the future closer for the Phillies after back to back solid minor league seasons.

Jimmy Rollins: Finished the season strong with the big league club last year and is the future shortstop of the Phillies with the future being sooner than later.

Brandon Duckworth: Probably the top pitcher in the Phillies organization last year after posting 13-7 record with 3.16 ERA. Duckworth is a hard thrower with good control.

Pittsburgh Pirates

National League Central Division

2001 SEASON

Pirates 2001 SCHEDULE

Home games shaded; D—Day game (games starting before 5 p.m.)
*—All-Star Game at Safeco Field (Seattle)

APRIL

SUN	MON	TUE	WED	THU	FRI	SAT
1	2	3 CIN	4 CIN	5 D CIN	6 HOU	7 D HOU
8 D HOU	9 D CIN	10	11 CIN	12 CIN	13 D CUB	14 D CUB
15 D CUB	16 HOU	17 HOU	18 HOU	19	20 CUB	21 D CUB
22 D CUB	23	24 LA	25 LA	26 LA	27 SD	28 SD
29 D SD	30					

MAY

SUN	MON	TUE	WED	THU	FRI	SAT
		1 SF	2 SF	3 SF	4 COL	5 COL
6 D COL	7 STL	8 STL	9 STL	10 D STL	11 MIL	12 MIL
13 D MIL	14 D MIL	15 STL	16 STL	17 STL	18 MIL	19 MIL
20 D MIL	21	22 PHI	23 PHI	24 PHI	25 ATL	26 ATL
27 D ATL	28 FLA	29 FLA	30 FLA	31		

JUNE

SUN	MON	TUE	WED	THU	FRI	SAT
					1 ATL	2 ATL
3 D ATL	4	5 FLA	6 FLA	7 D FLA	8 MIN	9 MIN
10 D MIN	11	12 DET	13 DET	14 DET	15 CLE	16 CLE
17 D CLE	18	19 PHI	20 PHI	21 PHI	22 MON	23 MON
24 D MON	25 MIL	26 MIL	27 MIL	28 D MIL	29 MON	30 MON

JULY

SUN	MON	TUE	WED	THU	FRI	SAT
1 D MON	2 CIN	3 CIN	4 D CIN	5 D CIN	6 CWS	7 CWS
8 D CWS	9	10 *	11	12 KC	13 KC	14 D KC
15 LA	16 LA	17 LA	18 CUB	19 CUB	20 STL	21 STL
22 D STL	23	24 CUB	25 D CUB	26 HOU	27 HOU	28 HOU
29 D HOU	30	31 SF				

AUGUST

SUN	MON	TUE	WED	THU	FRI	SAT
			1 SF	2 D SF	3 COL	4 COL
5 D COL	6	7 LA	8 LA	9 LA	10 SD	11 SD
12 D SD	13 ARI	14 ARI	15 ARI	16 HOU	17 HOU	18 D HOU
19 D HOU	20	21 ARI	22 ARI	23 ARI	24 HOU	25 HOU
26 D HOU	27 MIL	28 MIL	29 MIL	30	31 CIN	

SEPTEMBER

SUN	MON	TUE	WED	THU	FRI	SAT
						1 CIN
2 D CIN	3 MIL	4 MIL	5 MIL	6 CIN	7 CIN	8 CIN
9 D CIN	10	11 NYM	12 NYM	13 D NYM	14 D CUB	15 D CUB
16 D CUB	17 NYM	18 NYM	19 NYM	20 STL	21 STL	22 STL
23 D STL	24 CUB	25 CUB	26 CUB	27	28 STL	29 D STL
30 D STL						

FRONT-OFFICE DIRECTORY

General partner ..... Kevin S. McClatchy
Board of directors ..... William B. Allen, Donald Beaver, Frank Brenner, Chip Ganassi, Kevin S. McClatchy, Mayor Tom Murphy, G. Ogden Nutting, William E. Springer
Chief operating officer ..... Dick Freeman
Senior vice president and general manager ..... Cam Bonifay
Assistant general manager/baseball operations ..... John Sirignano
Assistant general manager/player personnel ..... Roy Smith
Senior advisor/player personnel ..... Lenny Yochim
Special assistants to the general manager ..... Jon Mercurio, Chet Montgomery, Ken Parker, Willie Stargell
Vice president, finance and administration ..... Jim Plake
Vice president, broadcasting and marketing ..... Vic Gregovits
Vice president, communications and new ballpark development ..... Steven N. Greenberg
Vice president, operations ..... Dennis DaPra
Vice president, special events ..... Nellie Briles
Assistant vice president, communications and new ballpark development ..... Patty Paytas
Controller ..... David Bowman
Director of finance ..... Patti Mistick
Traveling secretary ..... Greg Johnson
Director of corporate sales ..... Mark Ferraco
Director of Florida baseball operations ..... Mike Kennedy
Director of community services and sales ..... Al Gordon
Director of information systems ..... Terry Zeigler
Director of media relations ..... Jim Trdinich
Director of merchandising ..... Joe Billetdeaux
Director of player development ..... Paul Tinnell
Director of community and player relations ..... Kathy Guy
Director of promotions and advertising ..... Rick Orienza
Director of sales ..... Jim Alexander
Director of community development ..... Rod Scott

MINOR LEAGUE AFFILIATES

Class	Team	League	Manager
AAA	Nashville	Pacific Coast	Marty Brown
AA	Altoona	Eastern	Dale Sveum
A	Lynchburg	Carolina	Curtis Wilkerson
A	Hickory	South Atlantic	To be announced
A	Williamsport	New York-Pennsylvania	Tony Beasley
Rookie	Gulf Coast Pirates	Gulf Coast	Woody Huyke

ASSISTANCE STAFF

Club physician
Dr. Joseph Coroso

Team orthopedist
Dr. Jack Failla

Head trainer
Kent Biggerstaff

Equipment manager
Roger Wilson

Director of scouting
Mickey White

Scouting coordinators
Tom Barnard, Dana Brown, Mark McKnight

Special assignment scout
Jim Guinn

Latin America coordinators
Pablo Cruz (advisor), Jose Luna

Scouting supervisors
Jason Angel, Russell Bowen, Grant Brittain, Dan Durst, Duane Gustavson, James House, Mike Kendall, Jose Luna, Greg McClain, Jon Mercurio, Jack Powell, Everett Russell, Delvy Santiago, Rob Sidwell, Charlie Sullivan, Mike Williams, Ted Williams

BROADCAST INFORMATION

Radio: KDKA-AM (1020).
Cable TV: Fox Sports Pittsburgh.

SPRING TRAINING

Ballpark (city): McKechnie Field (Bradenton, Fla.).
Ticket information: 941-748-4610.

BALLPARK INFORMATION

Ballpark (capacity, surface)
PNC Park (38,000, grass)

Address
PNC Park at North Shore
115 Federal Street
Pittsburgh, PA 15212

Official website
www.pittsburghpirates.com

Business phone
412-323-5000

Ticket information
800-BUY-BUCS

Ticket prices
$35 (dugout boxes)
$25 (baseline and IF boxes, club level-group seating)
$23 (LF/RF boxes)
$16 (OF reserved, deck seating, grandstand)
$12 (bleachers)
$9 (LF/RF grandstand)

Field dimensions (from home plate)
To left field at foul line, 325 feet
To center field, 399 feet
To right field at foul line, 320 feet

First game played
Scheduled for April 9, 2001 vs. Cincinnati

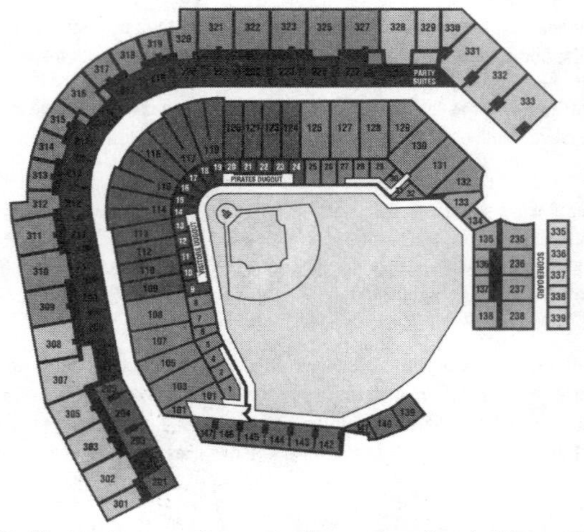

Follow the Pirates all season at: www.sportingnews.com/baseball/teams/pirates/

PIRATES SPRING ROSTER

No.	PITCHERS	B/T	Ht./Wt.	Born	2000 clubs	Projection
55	Anderson, Jimmy	L/L	6-1/215	1-22-76	Nashville, Pittsburgh, Altoona	Faltered in 2000 after showing promise at end of the '99 season.
69	Arroyo, Bronson	R/R	6-5/181	2-24-77	Nashville, Pittsburgh, Lynchburg	Should be only a matter of time before he has success in the major leagues.
53	Beimel, Joe	L/L	6-2/200	4-19-77	Lynchburg, Altoona	Workhorse pitched 180-plus innings last season. Could use more seasoning.
34	Benson, Kris	R/R	6-4/195	11-7-74	Pittsburgh	First pick overall of '96 draft hasn't disappointed.
32	Cordova, Francisco	R/R	6-1/204	4-26-72	Pittsburgh	Only started 17 games before arm injuries ended his 2000 season.
39	Grabow, John	L/L	6-2/190	11-4-78	Altoona	Lefthanded starter will get a look. However, he's still a year away.
46	Guzman, Wilson	L/L	5-9/200	7-14-77	Altoona, Lynchburg	Another lefthander who will get a look during spring training.
51	Loiselle, Rich	R/R	6-5/245	1-12-72	Altoona, Pitt., GC Pirates, Nash.	Injuries have plagued him for the last three seasons.
49	Manzanillo, Josias	R/R	6-0/205	10-16-67	Nashville, Pittsburgh	Pitched well out of the bullpen for the Pirates last season.
45	Mulholland, Terry	R/L	6-3/220	3-9-63	Atlanta	Veteran who can start or relieve. The Pirates are counting on him to start.
41	O'Connor, Brian	L/L	6-2/195	1-4-77	Altoona, Pittsburgh, Nashville	Needs a year of seasoning in Class AAA to be effective in the majors.
53	Pena, Alex	R/R	6-2/205	9-9-77	Hickory	Outfielder-turned-pitcher pitched in three games last season because of injury.
48	Ritchie, Todd	R/R	6-3/220	11-7-71	Pittsburgh	He'll have to win more than nine games for Pirates to be successful.
47	Sauerbeck, Scott	R/L	6-3/197	11-9-71	Pittsburgh, Nashville	Good reliever who can be counted on to pitch one quality inning.
22	Schmidt, Jason	R/R	6-5/220	1-29-73	Pittsburgh, Gulf Coast Pirates	When healthy, he can be counted on to win at least 10 games per season.
38	Serafini, Daniel	B/L	6-1/195	1-25-74	S.D., Las Vegas, Pitt., Nashville	Started 11 games last year out of necessity. Should be in bullpen this season.
56	Silva, Jose	R/R	6-5/235	12-19-73	Pittsburgh	Can spot start if necessary. Did last season and won 11 games.
50	Spurling, Chris	R/R	6-6/240	6-28-77	Tampa, Lynchburg	Relief prospect averaged almost a strikeout per inning in minor leagues.
58	Williams, David	L/L	6-2/205	3-12-79	Hickory, Lynchburg	Won 11 games with Hickory. Will return to minors for more seasoning.
43	Williams, Mike	R/R	6-2/200	7-29-68	Pittsburgh	Has 47 saves over the last two seasons.

No.	CATCHERS	B/T	Ht./Wt.	Born	2000 clubs	Projection
11	Cota, Humberto	R/R	6-0/175	2-7-79	Altoona	Good-hitting catcher, but needs to cut down on errors.
7	Haad, Yamid	R/R	6-2/204	9-2-77	Altoona, Lynchburg	Needs more seasoning in the minors.
18	Kendall, Jason	R/R	6-0/195	6-26-74	Pittsburgh	Came back from gruesome ankle injury to post All-Star numbers last year.
15	Osik, Keith	R/R	6-0/195	10-22-68	Pittsburgh	Backup catcher had decent year and can play elsewhere in the field in a pinch.
36	Wilson, Craig	R/R	6-2/217	11-30-76	Nashville	Might find work is he hits like he did in Class AAA last season.

No.	INFIELDERS	B/T	Ht./Wt.	Born	2000 clubs	Projection
10	Nunez, Abraham	B/R	5-11/185	3-16-76	Nashville, Pittsburgh	Continues to post solid numbers in minors. Needs that to carry over to majors.
6	Benjamin, Mike	R/R	6-0/175	11-22-65	Pittsburgh	Utility infielder will have same role this season.
2	Meares, Pat	R/R	6-0/187	9-6-68	Pittsburgh	Team is counting on him to be a competent shortstop until prospects are ready.
30	Morris, Warren	L/R	5-11/180	1-11-74	Pittsburgh	Regressed a little but should be a solid second baseman for years to come.
16	Ramirez, Aramis	R/R	6-1/219	6-25-78	Pittsburgh, Nashville	Should be ready for the full-time job at third base.
25	Wilson, Enrique	B/R	5-11/195	7-27-75	Cleveland, Nashville, Pittsburgh	Utility infielder likely will get more playing time with Pirates than with Indians.
12	Wilson, Jack	R/R	6-0/175	12-29-77	Potomac, Arkansas, Altoona	Solid shortstop prospect with can hit for average.
29	Young, Kevin	R/R	6-3/225	6-16-69	Pittsburgh	Decent hitter who is not dependable at first base.

No.	OUTFIELDERS	B/T	Ht./Wt.	Born	2000 clubs	Projection
14	Bell, Derek	R/R	6-2/215	12-11-68	New York N.L.	Can hit anywhere in a lineup, which will help the Pirates' offensive attack.
13	Brown, Adrian	B/R	6-0/185	2-7-74	Pittsburgh, Altoona, Nashville	Needs more playing time. He might be leadoff hitter Pirates have been looking for.
17	Brown, Emil	R/R	6-2/193	12-29-74	Nashville, Pittsburgh	Good hitter can draw walks, hit for average and drive in runs.
26	Davis, J.J.	R/R	6-4/250	10-25-78	Lynchburg	Power-hitting prospect still at least two years away.
3	Hermansen, Chad	R/R	6-2/185	9-10-77	Pittsburgh, Nashville	Power-hitting prospect couldn't figure out major league pitching last season.
27	Hernandez, Alex	L/L	6-4/190	5-28-77	Altoona, Nashville, Pittsburgh	Will battle a crowd of prospects for one spot in the outfield.
5	Redman, Tike	L/L	5-11/166	3-10-77	Nashville, Pittsburgh	Speedy outfielder could be Pirates' leadoff hitter in a year or two.
28	Vander Wal, John	L/L	6-1/197	4-29-66	Pittsburgh	Surprised everyone by hitting 24 home runs last season, but back to bench.

THE COACHING STAFF

Lloyd McClendon, manager: After four seasons as the Pirates hitting instructor, McClendon takes over as the team's manager. He has spent his entire coaching career in the Pittsburgh organization, so at least he knows most of the players he'll be managing.

Dave Clark: After retiring in 1999 as a player, he took over as hitting coach for Nashville and now holds the same position with the Pirates. He will be challenged to get young players to hit with consistency.

Trent Jewett: During his fifth season as manager at Class AAA Nashville, the Pirates hired him to handle third-base coaching duties after Jack Lind was reassigned within the franchise.

Tommy Sandt: Sandt is in his second stint as a Pirates coach. He originally coached first base under Jim Leyland and followed Leyland to Florida and Colorado before making his way back to the Steel City.

Bruce Tanner: Son of former Pirates manager Chuck Tanner, Bruce will serve as bullpen coach in his first season with the Pirates. He has been in the team's minor league system for the past seven years.

Bill Virdon: Most recently the Astros' bench coach in 1997, Virdon will bring 40 years of experience to the Pirates as a bench coach.

Spin Williams: The only coach left from Gene Lamont's staff, Williams will be the Pirates' bullpen coach for the eighth straight season. This will be his 20th season overall with the organization.

THE TOP NEWCOMERS

Derek Bell: The well-traveled outfielder played well for the Mets last season. This season he should be able to help the Pirates attack and hit in the five hole.

Terry Mulholland: After spending the past 1½ seasons filling a variety of roles with the Braves, Mulholland brings his years of experience to a young Pittsburgh staff. He will be expected to provide veteran leadership and fill the void for a lefthanded starter.

THE TOP PROSPECTS

Wilson Guzman: Lefty prospect went a combined 14-7 last season in two minor league stops. Had a combined ERA under 3.00 and has the ability to get the strikeout when needed.

David Williams: Williams, who recorded 193 strikeouts in 170 innings in the minors last season, is not expected to arrive in the majors for one or two more seasons.

St. Louis Cardinals

National League Central Division

2001 SEASON

Cardinals 2001 SCHEDULE

Home games shaded; D—Day game (games starting before 5 p.m.)
*—All-Star Game at Safeco Field (Seattle)

APRIL

SUN	MON	TUE	WED	THU	FRI	SAT
1	2 D COL	3	4 COL	5 COL	6 ARI	7 D ARI
8 D ARI	9 D COL	10	11 COL	12 D COL	13 HOU	14 D HOU
15 D HOU	16 ARI	17 ARI	18 ARI	19	20 HOU	21 D HOU
22 HOU	23	24 MON	25 MON	26 D MON	27 NYM	28 D NYM
29 D NYM	30					

MAY

SUN	MON	TUE	WED	THU	FRI	SAT
		1 FLA	2 FLA	3 FLA	4 ATL	5 ATL
6 D ATL	7 PIT	8 PIT	9 PIT	10 D PIT	11 CUB	12 D CUB
13 D CUB	14	15 PIT	16 PIT	17 PIT	18 PHI	19 PHI
20 D PHI	21	22 MIL	23 MIL	24 D MIL	25 CIN	26 CIN
27 D CIN	28 D MIL	29 MIL	30 MIL	31 MIL		

JUNE

SUN	MON	TUE	WED	THU	FRI	SAT
					1 CIN	2 D CIN
3 CIN	4 CIN	5 CUB	6 D CUB	7 D CUB	8 COL	9 COL
10 D COL	11	12 KC	13 KC	14 KC	15 CWS	16 D CWS
17 D CWS	18 CUB	19 CUB	20 CUB	21 D CUB	22 SF	23 SF
24 SF	25	26 CIN	27 CIN	28	29 SF	30 D SF

JULY

SUN	MON	TUE	WED	THU	FRI	SAT
1 D SF	2	3 D MIL	4 MIL	5 D MIL	6 CLE	7 D CLE
8 D CLE	9	10 *	11	12 DET	13 DET	14 D DET
15 D MIN	16 MIN	17 MIN	18 HOU	19 D HOU	20 PIT	21 PIT
22 D PIT	23	24 HOU	25 D HOU	26 D CUB	27 D CUB	28 D CUB
29 CUB	30	31 ATL				

AUGUST

SUN	MON	TUE	WED	THU	FRI	SAT
			1 ATL	2 ATL	3 FLA	4 FLA
5 D FLA	6	7 MON	8 MON	9 MON	10 NYM	11 D NYM
12 D NYM	13 CIN	14 CIN	15 CIN	16 CIN	17 PHI	18 PHI
19 D PHI	20 CIN	21 CIN	22 CIN	23 D CIN	24 D CUB	25 D CUB
26 D CUB	27	28 SD	29 SD	30 D SD	31 LA	

SEPTEMBER

SUN	MON	TUE	WED	THU	FRI	SAT
						1 LA
2 LA	3 SD	4 SD	5 SD	6	7 LA	8 D LA
9 D LA	10 MIL	11 MIL	12 MIL	13 D MIL	14 HOU	15 HOU
16 D HOU	17 MIL	18 MIL	19 D MIL	20 PIT	21 PIT	22 PIT
23 D PIT	24 HOU	25 HOU	26 HOU	27	28 PIT	29 D PIT
30 D PIT						

FRONT-OFFICE DIRECTORY

Chairman of the board/general partner .... William O. DeWitt Jr.
Chairman .... Frederick O. Hanser
Secretary-treasurer .... Andrew N. Baur
President .... Mark C. Lamping
Vice president, general manager .... Walt Jocketty
Admin. assistant to the president .... Julie Laningham
Senior executive assistant to vice president, general manager .... Judy Carpenter-Barada
Vice president/player personnel .... Jerry Walker
Special asst. to the general manager .... Bob Gebhard
Senior vice president, sales and marketing .... Dan Farrell
Vice president, controller .... Brad Wood
Vice president, community relations .... Marty Hendin
Vice president, business development .... Bill DeWitt III
Vice president, stadium operations .... Joe Abernathy
Vice president, ticket operations .... Josie Arnold
Vice president, sales .... Kevin Wade
Director, group sales .... Joe Strohm
Manager, ticket sales .... Mark Murray
Director, corporate sales/marketing .... Thane van Breusegen
Group director, community outreach/ Cardinals Care .... Tim Hanser
Director, target marketing .... Ted Savage
Director, media relations .... Brian Bartow
Manager, media relations & publications .... Steve Zesch
Assistant to director, media relations .... Brad Hainje
Traveling secretary .... C.J. Cherre
Director, player development .... Mike Jorgensen
Director, international operations .... Jeff Scott
Director, baseball operations .... John Mozeliak
Director, minor league operations .... Scott Smulczenski
Director, player procurement .... Marty Maier
Director, professional scouting .... Marteese Robinson
Manager, baseball information/player development .... John Vuch

MINOR LEAGUE AFFILIATES

Class	Team	League	Manager
AAA	Memphis	Pacific Coast	Gaylen Pitts
AA	New Haven	Eastern	Dan Sheaffer
A	New Jersey	New York-Pennsylvania	Brian Rupp
A	Peoria	Midwest	Joe Hall
A	Potomac	Carolina	Joe Cunningham
Rookie	Johnson City	Appalachian	Chris Maloney

ASSISTANCE STAFF

Major league trainer
Barry Weinberg

Assistant major league trainer
Brad Henderson

Medical/rehabilitation coordinator
Mark O'Neal

Equipment manager
Buddy Bates

Assistant equipment manager
Rip Rowan

Special assignment scouts
Bing Devine, Jim Leyland, Fred McAlister, Joe Sparks (advance scout), Mike Squires

Professional scouts
Clark Crist, Marty Keough, Joe Rigoli

National cross-checkers
Mike Roberts, Chuck Fick

Scouts
Randy Benson, Ben Galante, Steve Gossett, Steve Grilli, Manny Guerra, Dave Karaff, Scott Melvin, Scott Nichols, Jay North, Dan Ontiveros, Tommy Shields, Roger Smith, Steve Turco, Dane Walker

International scouts
Jorge Brito, Domingo Carrasquel, Bobby Diaz

BROADCAST INFORMATION

Radio: KMOX-AM (1120).
TV: KPLR-TV (Channel 11).
Cable TV: Fox Sports Midwest.

SPRING TRAINING

Ballpark (city): Roger Dean Stadium (Jupiter, Fla.).
Ticket information: 561-966-3309.

BALLPARK INFORMATION

Ballpark (capacity, surface)
Busch Stadium (49,779, grass)

Address
250 Stadium Plaza
St. Louis, MO 63102

Official website
www.stlcardinals.com

Business phone
314-421-3060

Ticket information
314-421-2400

Ticket prices
$36 (field boxes-infield), $33 (loge boxes-infield)
$31 (field boxes-outfield), $27 (loge boxes-outfield)
$24 (loge reserved-infield), $22 (terrace boxes-infield)
$20 (terrace boxes-outfield, loge reserved-outfield)
$17 (terrace reserved-adults), $10 (bleachers)
$9 (upper terrace-outfield-adults), $8 (terrace reserved-children)
$4 (upper terrace reserved-children)

Field dimensions (from home plate)
To left field at foul line, 330 feet
To center field, 402 feet
To right field at foul line, 330 feet

First game played
May 12, 1966 (Cardinals 4, Braves 3)

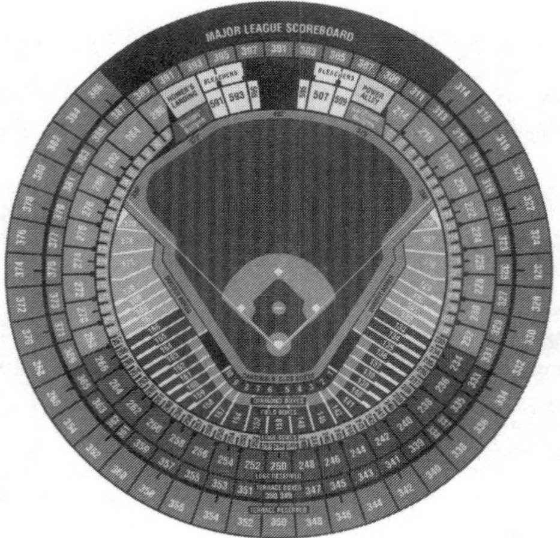

Follow the Cardinals all season at: www.sportingnews.com/baseball/teams/cardinals/

CARDINALS SPRING ROSTER

No.	PITCHERS	B/T	Ht./Wt.	Born	2000 clubs	Projection
66	Ankiel, Rick	L/L	6-1/210	7-19-79	St. Louis	Despite wild ride in playoffs was one of baseball's top rookies in 2000.
31	Benes, Alan	R/R	6-5/235	1-21-72	Memphis, St. Louis	Should be back in the bullpen but could eventually return to the rotation.
40	Benes, Andy	R/R	6-6/245	8-20-67	St. Louis	Should provide plenty of innings and a double-digit win total.
56	Brunette, Justin	L/L	6-1/200	10-7-75	Arkansas, St. Louis, Memphis	He'll have to improve upon his 6.15 ERA in Class AAA to reach the majors.
48	Christiansen, Jason	R/L	6-5/241	9-21-69	Pittsburgh, St. Louis	He'll be counted on as one of the team's two lefthanded specialists.
63	Hackman, Luther	R/R	6-4/195	10-10-74	Memphis, St. Louis	The hard thrower has shown improvement with his control.
30	Hermanson, Dustin	R/R	6-2/200	12-21-72	Montreal	Former Expo should benefit from new scenery and better offensive support.
65	Hutchinson, Chad	R/R	6-5/230	2-21-77	Memphis, Arkansas	Former Stanford QB needs to work out control problems in the minors.
49	James, Mike	R/R	6-3/180	8-15-67	Memphis, St. Louis	Has rebounded nicely from arm troubles; had 2.87 ERA in the second half.
	Karnuth, Jason	R/R	6-2/190	5-15-76	Arkansas, Memphis	He'll need to impress folks at Memphis to reach St. Louis.
57	Kile, Darryl	R/R	6-5/212	12-2-68	St. Louis	Last season's 20-game winner has one of the best curveballs in the majors.
44	Kline, Steve	B/L	6-1/215	8-22-72	Montreal	Workhorse has held lefties to a .207 average over the last three seasons.
50	Matthews, Mike	L/L	6-2/180	10-24-73	Memphis, St. Louis	Had 11.57 ERA in 14 games with Cardinals. Faces uphill battle to make team.
35	Morris, Matt	R/R	6-5/210	8-9-74	Arkansas, Memphis, St. Louis	He has regained his velocity after arm surgery and will be in the starting rotation.
67	Stechschulte, Gene	R/R	6-5/210	8-12-73	Memphis, St. Louis, Arkansas	Has not been able to translate success in the minors to the majors.
55	Stephenson, Garrett	R/R	6-5/208	1-2-72	St. Louis	Surprising 16-game winner from last season may not make rotation.
50	Timlin, Mike	R/R	6-4/210	3-10-66	Baltimore, St. Louis	Will be used in a setup role but could pick up a few saves.
43	Veres, Dave	R/R	6-2/220	10-19-66	St. Louis	Not overpowering but had a 2.88 ERA and 29 saves.
	Walrond, Les	L/L	6-0/195	11-7-76	Potomac	Was exceptional in Class A with 153 strikeouts in 151 innings.
	Weibl, Clint	R/R	6-3/180	3-17-75	Memphis, Arkansas	Decent fastball and good control helped hold batters to .226 in PCL.

No.	CATCHERS	B/T	Ht./Wt.	Born	2000 clubs	Projection
13	Figga, Mike	R/R	6-0/185	7-31-70	Paw., Trenton, Alb., San Antonio	Journeyman has played 46 games in majors; doesn't figure to add to that total.
8	Hernandez, Carlos	R/R	5-11/215	5-24-67	San Diego, St. Louis	If Cardinals don't carry three catchers, he'll compete with Marrero for backup role.
26	Marrero, Eli	R/R	6-1/180	11-17-73	St. Louis, Memphis	Will have to improve upon .219 career average to get more playing time.
44	Matheny, Mike	R/R	6-3/205	9-22-70	St. Louis	The N.L.s best defensive catcher threw out 53 percent of base stealers.
32	McDonald, Keith	R/R	6-2/215	2-8-73	Memphis, St. Louis	Made history by homering in first two at-bats but is ticketed for minors.
	Stefanski, Mike	R/R	6-2/190	9-12-69	Louisville	Would only see action in St. Louis because of injuries to others.

No.	INFIELDERS	B/T	Ht./Wt.	Born	2000 clubs	Projection
	Haas, Chris	L/R	6-2/210	10-15-76	Memphis, Arkansas	Homered 18 times in 347 minor league at-bats but can't stay healthy.
	Lucca, Lou	R/R	5-11/210	10-13-70	Memphis	Hit .284 with 14 homers and 70 RBIs in Class AAA last season.
25	McGwire, Mark	R/R	6-5/250	10-1-63	St. Louis	Was on pace for another 70-homer season before sidelined by knee tendinitis.
21	Paquette, Craig	R/R	6-0/190	3-28-69	St. Louis	He'll see a lot of action at third but can also play second, first and the outfield.
27	Polanco, Placido	R/R	5-10/168	10-10-75	St. Louis	Not much pop, but hit .316 overall in part-time role.
3	Renteria, Edgar	R/R	6-1/180	8-7-75	St. Louis	Last season, he had career high in runs (94), homers (16) and RBIs (76).
28	Sutton, Larry	L/L	6-0/185	5-14-70	Memphis, St. Louis	Could receive a call-up to back up at first if McGwire gets hurt.
4	Vina, Fernando	L/R	5-9/174	4-16-69	St. Louis	He combines great defense with an ability to get on base.

No.	OUTFIELDERS	B/T	Ht./Wt.	Born	2000 clubs	Projection
	Bonilla, Bobby	B/R	6-3/240	2-23-63	Atlanta	Will see plenty of at-bats against lefthanders.
7	Drew, J.D.	L/R	6-1/195	11-20-75	St. Louis	Should see more playing time this season and improve his power numbers.
15	Edmonds, Jim	L/L	6-1/212	6-27-70	St. Louis	Made acrobatic catches in center and led the team in runs, homers and RBIs.
16	Lankford, Ray	L/L	5-11/200	6-5-67	St. Louis	Coming off worst season, needs to cut down on strikeouts and raise average.
	McCracken, Quinton	B/R	5-7/173	3-16-70	Tampa Bay, Durham	He offers the team some speed off the bench.
	Ortega, Bill	R/R	6-4/205	7-24-75	Arkansas	Hit .325 in Class AA, is great defensively and doesn't strike out.
13	Saturria, Luis	R/R	6-2/165	7-21-76	Arkansas, St. Louis	Has above-average power and speed but still needs fine-tuning in the minors.
	Snead, Esix	B/R	5-10/175	6-7-76	Potomac	Stole 109 bases in Class A last season but needs to hit better.

THE COACHING STAFF

Tony La Russa: La Russa, who led St. Louis to its second division title since taking over as manager in 1996, leads all active managers with 1,734 victories and has won six division titles with three different teams. Last season was the first since 1996 that he didn't have to deal with major injuries to his pitching staff. He has taken the Cards to the NLCS twice in five seasons and this year will try to lead them to their first World Series since 1987.

Mark DeJohn: DeJohn has been in the Cardinals' organization since 1986 and on the major league staff since 1996. He has managed minor league teams for the Tigers, Royals and Cardinals.

Dave Duncan: The Duncan-La Russa relationship goes back to 1983 with the White Sox. When La Russa went to Oakland, Duncan followed and helped mold the A's pitching staff into one of the A.L.'s best. Known for helping struggling veterans resurrect their careers.

Mike Easler: This is Easler's third season as hitting coach. Last season was a mixed bag as the team set team marks for home runs (235) and strikeouts (1,253).

Marty Mason: Mason is in his second season as the team's bullpen coach. He has been in the organization for 15 seasons.

Dave McKay: This is McKay's 15th season as a member of La Russa's staff. He has coached first base for him since 1989.

Jose Oquendo: Oquendo, who played for the Cardinals during the 1980s, is in his third season on the St. Louis staff and second as third base coach.

THE TOP NEWCOMERS

Dustin Hermanson: He will be in the rotation and should improve on his 12-14 record from 2000 but his increasing ERA and decreasing strikeout totals are a concern.

Steve Kline: Thanks to Kline, St. Louis has a proven veteran to call upon when a tough lefthanded batter comes to the plate late in the game. Kline was a little overused last season, which explains his poor second half.

THE TOP PROSPECTS

Albert Pujols: The Cardinals confidence in Pujols is one of the reasons they traded Fernando Tatis in the offseason. Last season at Class A Peoria, Pujols hit .324 with 17 homers and 84 RBIs. Could hit .300 with 30 homers and 100 RBIs in the majors; is above-average defensively.

Chad Hutchinson: The former Stanford QB has a mid-90s fastball and an above-average slider but suffered control problems in the minors. If he improves he could be in St. Louis before the end of the summer. The Cardinals envision him as a starter but he could become a closer.

SAN DIEGO PADRES

NATIONAL LEAGUE WEST DIVISION

2001 SEASON

Padres 2001 SCHEDULE

Home games shaded; D—Day game (games starting before 5 p.m.)
*—All-Star Game at Safeco Field (Seattle)

APRIL

SUN	MON	TUE	WED	THU	FRI	SAT
1	2 D SF	3	4 SF	5 SF	6 COL	7 D COL
8 D COL	9	10 D SF	11 SF	12 D SF	13 LA	14 LA
15 D LA	16	17 COL	18 COL	19 D COL	20 LA	21 LA
22 D LA	23 PHI	24 PHI	25 PHI	26 D PHI	27 PIT	28 PIT
29 D PIT	30					

MAY

SUN	MON	TUE	WED	THU	FRI	SAT
		1 CUB	2 CUB	3 D CUB	4 CIN	5 D CIN
6 D CIN	7	8 ATL	9 ATL	10 D ATL	11 FLA	12 FLA
13 D FLA	14	15 NYM	16 NYM	17 NYM	18 MON	19 MON
20 D MON	21 HOU	22 HOU	23 D HOU	24 D ARI	25 ARI	26 ARI
27 D ARI	28	29 HOU	30 HOU	31 D HOU		

JUNE

SUN	MON	TUE	WED	THU	FRI	SAT
					1 ARI	2 ARI
3 D ARI	4 SF	5 SF	6 SF	7 D SF	8 SEA	9 SEA
10 D SEA	11	12 OAK	13 OAK	14 D OAK	15 SEA	16 SEA
17 D SEA	18	19 SF	20 SF	21 D SF	22 LA	23 LA
24 D LA	25 COL	26 COL	27 COL	28 LA	29 LA	30 LA

JULY

SUN	MON	TUE	WED	THU	FRI	SAT
1 D LA	2	3 COL	4 COL	5 D COL	6 TEX	7 D TEX
8 D TEX	9	10 *	11	12 HOU	13 HOU	14 HOU
15 ANA	16 ANA	17 D ANA	18 ARI	19 D ARI	20 MIL	21 MIL
22 D MIL	23 ARI	24 ARI	25 ARI	26	27 MIL	28 MIL
29 D MIL	30	31 CUB				

AUGUST

SUN	MON	TUE	WED	THU	FRI	SAT
			1 CUB	2 D CUB	3 CIN	4 CIN
5 D CIN	6	7 PHI	8 PHI	9 D PHI	10 PIT	11 PIT
12 D PIT	13	14 NYM	15 NYM	16 D NYM	17 MON	18 MON
19 D MON	20	21 ATL	22 ATL	23 ATL	24 FLA	25 FLA
26 D FLA	27 FLA	28 STL	29 STL	30 D STL	31 ARI	

SEPTEMBER

SUN	MON	TUE	WED	THU	FRI	SAT
						1 ARI
2 D ARI	3 STL	4 STL	5 STL	6	7 ARI	8 D ARI
9 D ARI	10 ARI	11 LA	12 LA	13 D LA	14 COL	15 COL
16 D COL	17 LA	18 LA	19 LA	20	21 SF	22 SF
23 D SF	24 COL	25 COL	26 COL	27 D COL	28 SF	29 D SF
30 D SF						

FRONT-OFFICE DIRECTORY

Chairman ....John Moores
President and chief executive officer ....Larry Lucchino
Executive vice president, public affairs ....Charles Steinberg
Exec. vice president, baseball operations and general manager ....Kevin Towers
Senior vice president, corporate marketing ....Michael Dee
Senior vice president, general counsel....................Bob Vizas
Vice president, scouting and player development ....Ted Simmons
Vice president, community relations ....Michele Anderson
Vice president, Hispanic & international marketing....................Enrique Morones
Assistant general manager ....Fred Uhlman Jr.
Director, merchandising....................Michael Babida
Controller ....Steve Fitch
Director, administrative services ....Lucy Freeman
Executive director, ticket operations and services ....Dave Gilmore
Director, sales ....Mark Tilson
Director, entertainment....................George Stieren
Director, ballpark planning ....Erik Judson
Director, baseball operations ....Theo Epstein
Director, Padres Foundation ....Sue Botos
Director, corporate development ....Sam Kennedy
Director, video production....................Tom Catlin
Director, military marketing....................Captain Jack Ensch (Ret.)
Director, stadium operations....................Mark Guglielmo
Director, player development....................Tye Waller
Director, minor league operations ....Priscilla Oppenheimer
Director, team travel ....Brian Prilaman
Director, public relations ....Glenn Geffner
Director, fan services....................Tim Katzman
Director, scouting ....Bill "Chief" Gayton

MINOR LEAGUE AFFILIATES

Class	Team	League	Manager
AAA	Portland	Pacific Coast	Rick Sweet
AA	Mobile	Southern	Tracy Woodson
A	Eugene	Northwest	Randy Whisler
A	Fort Wayne	Midwest	To be announced
A	Lake Elsinore	California	Craig Colbert
Rookie	Idaho Falls	Pioneer	Don Werner

BROADCAST INFORMATION

Radio: KOGO-AM (600), KURS-AM (1040, Spanish).
TV: KUSI (Channel 9).
Cable TV: Channel 4 Padres.

SPRING TRAINING

Ballpark (city): Peoria Stadium (Peoria, Ariz.).
Ticket information: 623-878-4337, 800-409-1511.

ASSISTANCE STAFF

Trainer
Todd Hutcheson

Assistant trainer
Jim Daniel

Strength and conditioning coordinator
Bill Henry

Club physicians
Cliff Colwell
Paul Hirshman
Jan Fronek
Blaine Phillips

Major league scouts
Ken Bracey
Moose Johnson
Ray Crone Sr.

Director of professional scouting
Gary Nickels

Advance scout
Jeff Gardner

International scouting supervisor
Bill Clark

Professional scouts
Brandy Davis
Ben McLure
Craig Shipley
Mal Fichman
Gary Roenicke
Van Smith

Full-time scouts
Joe Bochy
Bob Cummings
Lane Decker
Ronquito Garcia
Don "Trip" Keister
Tim McWilliam
Darryl Milne
Mike Rickard
Jim Woodward
Rich Bordi
Takeo Daigo
Jimmy Dreyer
Chris Gwynn
Don Lyle
Billy Merkel
Rene Mons
Mark Wasinger

BALLPARK INFORMATION

Ballpark (capacity, surface)
Qualcomm Stadium (66,307, grass)
Address
P.O. Box 2000
San Diego, CA 92112-2000
Official website
www.padres.com
Business phone
619-881-6500
Ticket information
888-697-2373
Ticket prices
$26 (field level/IF), $24 (club level/IF)
$22 (field level/OF, plaza level/IF, club level/OF)
$20 (plaza level/OF), $18 (loge level/IF)
$16 (loge level/OF), $14 (press level)
$9 (grandstand/plaza level, view level/lower IF)
$8 (grandstand/club level, view level/IF)
$7 (view level/OF), $5 (outfield bleachers)
Field dimensions (from home plate)
To left field at foul line, 327 feet
To center field, 405 feet
To right field at foul line, 330 feet
First game played
April 8, 1969 (Padres 2, Astros 1)

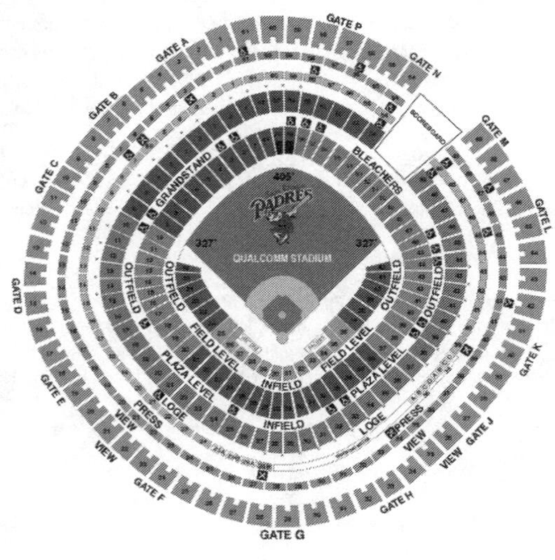

Follow the Padres all season at: www.sportingnews.com/baseball/teams/padres/

PADRES SPRING ROSTER

No.	PITCHERS	B/T	Ht./Wt.	Born	2000 clubs	Projection
40	Almanzar, Carlos	R/R	6-2/200	11-6-73	San Diego, Las Vegas	Pitched 62 games for Padres, mainly in one-inning relief stints.
21	Clement, Matt	R/R	6-3/195	8-12-74	San Diego	Young starter had issues with control. Led league in walks and wild pitches.
44	Davey, Tom	R/R	6-7/230	9-11-73	Tacoma, Las Vegas, San Diego	In 11 games with Padres, had sub-1.00 ERA.
59	Herndon, Harry	R/R	6-1/190	9-11-78	Las Vegas	Won 10 games, might get a shot at Padres rotation.
41	Hitchcock, Sterling	L/L	6-0/205	4-29-71	San Diego	Had "Tommy John surgery." Might miss most of 2001 season due to rehab.
51	Hoffman, Trevor	R/R	6-0/205	10-13-67	San Diego	One of game's top closers; has six consecutive 30-save seasons.
29	Karl, Scott	L/L	6-2/209	8-9-71	Colo., C. Spr., Lake Elsinore, Ana.	Trying to regain the form he once had in Milwaukee.
57	Lawrence, Brian	R/R	6-0/195	5-14-76	Mobile, Las Vegas	Had a miniscule ERA between Mobile and Las Vegas.
46	Loewer, Carlton	R/R	6-6/211	9-24-73	Las Vegas, Rancho Cucamonga	Padres didn't get to see much of what Loewer had. He was injured all season.
60	Lopez, Rodrigo	R/R	6-1/180	12-14-75	Las Vegas, San Diego	Has the ability to strike batters out, just needs experience.
54	Maurer, David	R/L	6-2/205	2-23-75	Mobile, Las Vegas, San Diego	Reliever has good track record in minors. Pitched well briefly with Padres.
48	Myers, Randy	L/L	6-1/210	9-19-62	DID NOT PLAY	Has not pitched since 1998 World Series. Rehabbing rotator cuff injury.
66	Myers, Rodney	R/R	6-1/215	6-26-69	San Diego, Rancho Cucamonga	Injuries limited him to six games the entire season. Could be effective reliever.
64	Serrano, Wascar	R/R	6-2/178	6-2-78	Mobile, Las Vegas	Won nine games in 20 starts with Mobile. Needs seasoning in Class AAA.
58	Slocumb, Heathcliff	R/R	6-3/220	6-7-66	St. Louis, San Diego	Most effective when only pitching one inning of relief.
55	Tollberg, Brian	R/R	6-3/195	9-16-72	Las Vegas, San Diego	Padres scored only 11 runs in his five losses last season.
56	Walker, Kevin	L/L	6-4/190	9-20-76	Mobile, San Diego	Went 7-1 in 70 games out of the bullpen.
49	Watkins, Steve	R/R	6-4/190	7-19-78	Rancho Cucamonga	Strikeout pitcher will likely get a year in Class AAA.
18	Williams, Woody	R/R	6-0/195	8-19-66	S.D., Rancho Cuca., Las Vegas	If he hadn't injured his shoulder likely would have had good year in 2000.
34	Witasick, Jay	R/R	6-4/235	8-28-72	Kansas City, San Diego	Was 3-8 with Kansas City, 3-2 with Padres.

No.	CATCHERS	B/T	Ht./Wt.	Born	2000 clubs	Projection
13	Davis, Ben	B/R	6-4/215	3-10-77	Las Vegas, San Diego	Needs experience in calling games and hitting major league pitchers.
7	Gonzalez, Wiki	R/R	5-11/203	5-17-74	San Diego	Good defensive catcher hit .232 last season.

No.	INFIELDERS	B/T	Ht./Wt.	Born	2000 clubs	Projection
9	Arias, Alex	R/R	6-3/202	11-20-67	Philadelphia	Only played in 70 games last season. Will have chance to win starting job at short.
63	Eberwein, Kevin	R/R	6-4/200	3-30-77	Mobile	First base prospect will get chance in Class AAA.
10	Gomez, Chris	R/R	6-1/195	6-16-71	San Diego	Looks to rebound afer undergoing knee surgery cut last season short.
2	Jackson, Damian	R/R	5-11/185	8-6-73	San Diego	Played primarily at short, but can play second, too. Had 28 stolen bases last season.
30	Klesko, Ryan	L/L	6-3/220	6-12-71	San Diego	First baseman hit 26 home runs and had 23 stolen bases.
17	Mendez, Donaldo	R/R	6-1/155	6-7-78	Michigan	Rule 5 draftee will get long look at spring training.
22	Nady, Xavier	R/R	6-2/205	11-14-78	San Diego	Second-round draft choice in 2000 played in one game with San Diego.
23	Nevin, Phil	R/R	6-2/231	1-19-71	San Diego	Had career highs in every major offensive category.
16	Nicholson, Kevin	B/R	5-10/190	3-29-76	Las Vegas, San Diego	Utility infielder likely will be back in AAA.
1	Perez, Santiago	B/R	6-2/150	12-30-75	Indianapolis, Milwaukee	After decent season in Class AAA, he'll get crack at starting shortstop job.

No.	OUTFIELDERS	B/T	Ht./Wt.	Born	2000 clubs	Projection
60	Colangelo, Mike	R/R	6-1/185	10-22-76	DID NOT PLAY	Injured all of last season but can hit for average.
26	Darr, Mike	L/R	6-3/205	3-21-76	Las Vegas, San Diego	Has a chance to be fourth outfielder this season.
25	DeHaan, Kory	L/R	6-2/187	7-16-76	Rancho Cuca., Las Vegas, S.D.	Utility outfielder brings speed to bench.
19	Gwynn, Tony	L/L	5-11/225	5-9-60	San Diego	Future Hall of Famer keeps on hitting. Age is catching up with him.
8	Owens, Eric	R/R	6-0/198	2-3-71	San Diego	Posted career highs in runs scored and stolen bases.
61	Owens, Jeremy	R/R	6-1/200	12-9-76	Rancho Cucamonga	Could be a power prospect if he hits well in Class AAA.
28	Rivera, Ruben	R/R	6-3/208	11-14-73	San Diego, Las Vegas	Five-tool player can't seem to avoid injuries and slumps.
27	Trammell, Bubba	R/R	6-2/220	11-6-71	Tampa Bay, New York N.L.	Might make team because of versatility and because he's a veteran.

THE COACHING STAFF

Bruce Bochy, manager: He once again had his team playing hard, but lack of talent and injuries to key players hurt the Padres in the end. He gets the most from the players he has to work with.

Greg Booker: Booker heads into his fourth season as bullpen coach after coaching the Indians pitching staff for five years. He has some young arms to work with in the bullpen.

Duane Espy: Espy, the Padres' new hitting coach, has plenty of experience. He has been a minor league manger, coach or hitting instructor since 1979.

Tim Flannery: Enters his sixth season as third-base coach under Bochy after spending most of his playing career with the Padres.

Rob Picciolo: Picciolo returns for his eighth season as bench coach and his 16th year with the Padres organization.

Dave Smith: Smith returns for a second season as Padres pitching coach and will continue to have the tough task of molding a young group of pitchers.

Alan Trammell: The longtime Tigers shortstop is back for his second season as Padres first base coach.

THE TOP NEWCOMERS

Alex Arias: He has a chance to become the starting shortstop if youngsters don't win job from him. Has always hit for pretty good average and plays good defense. He is also a versatile player.

Bubba Trammell: Gives the Padres a good veteran presence off the bench. Can hit for power and plays decent in the outfield.

THE TOP PROSPECTS

Mike Darr: Outstanding hitter waiting for chance to win starting position in the Padres' outfield. Hit .344 last year at Las Vegas.

Brian Lawrence: Compiled a 11-6 record with 2.29 ERA between Mobile and Las Vegas while only walking 35 hitters the entire season. Great control along with a lively fastball give the Padres hope for the future.

Jacob Peavy: A 19-year-old fireballer, he tore up Class A ball last year with a 13-8 record and 2.90 ERA. Peavy also struck out 164 batters in 133 $^{2}/_{3}$ innings.

SAN FRANCISCO GIANTS

NATIONAL LEAGUE WEST DIVISION

2001 SEASON

Giants 2001 SCHEDULE

Home games shaded; D—Day game (games starting before 5 p.m.)
*—All-Star Game at Safeco Field (Seattle)

APRIL

SUN	MON	TUE	WED	THU	FRI	SAT
1	2 D SD	3	4 SD	5 SD	6 LA	7 LA
8 LA	9	10 D SD	11 SD	12 D SD	13 MIL	14 MIL
15 D MIL	16	17 LA	18 LA	19 LA	20 MIL	21 D MIL
22 D MIL	23	24 CIN	25 CIN	26 D CIN	27 CUB	28 D CUB
29 D CUB	30					

MAY

SUN	MON	TUE	WED	THU	FRI	SAT
		1 PIT	2 PIT	3 PIT	4 PHI	5 PHI
6 D PHI	7 MON	8 MON	9 MON	10 D MON	11 NYM	12 D NYM
13 D NYM	14	15 FLA	16 FLA	17 FLA	18 ATL	19 ATL
20 D ATL	21 ARI	22 ARI	23 ARI	24 COL	25 COL	26 D COL
27 D COL	28 D ARI	29 ARI	30 ARI	31		

JUNE

SUN	MON	TUE	WED	THU	FRI	SAT
					1 COL	2 D COL
3 D COL	4 SD	5 SD	6 SD	7 D SD	8 OAK	9 OAK
10 D OAK	11	12 ANA	13 ANA	14 D ANA	15 OAK	16 D OAK
17 D OAK	18	19 SD	20 SD	21 D SD	22 STL	23 STL
24 STL	25 LA	26 LA	27 D LA	28	29 STL	30 D STL

JULY

SUN	MON	TUE	WED	THU	FRI	SAT
1 D STL	2 LA	3 LA	4 LA	5 LA	6 MIL	7 D MIL
8 D MIL	9	10 *	11	12 SEA	13 SEA	14 D SEA
15 TEX	16 TEX	17 TEX	18 COL	19 COL	20 ARI	21 D ARI
22 D ARI	23 COL	24 COL	25 D COL	26 ARI	27 ARI	28 ARI
29 D ARI	30	31 PIT				

AUGUST

SUN	MON	TUE	WED	THU	FRI	SAT
			1 PIT	2 D PIT	3 PHI	4 D PHI
5 D PHI	6	7 CIN	8 CIN	9 CIN	10 D CUB	11 D CUB
12 D CUB	13	14 FLA	15 FLA	16 D FLA	17 ATL	18 D ATL
19 D ATL	20	21 MON	22 MON	23 MON	24 NYM	25 NYM
26 D NYM	27 D NYM	28 ARI	29 ARI	30 ARI	31 COL	

SEPTEMBER

SUN	MON	TUE	WED	THU	FRI	SAT
						1 D COL
2 D COL	3 D COL	4 ARI	5 ARI	6 D ARI	7 COL	8 D COL
9 D COL	10	11 HOU	12 HOU	13 HOU	14 LA	15 D LA
16 D LA	17	18 HOU	19 HOU	20 D HOU	21 SD	22 SD
23 D SD	24 LA	25 LA	26 LA	27	28 SD	29 D SD
30 D SD						

FRONT-OFFICE DIRECTORY

President and managing general partner .... Peter A. Magowan
Executive vice president/COO .... Larry Baer
Senior vice president and general manager .... Brian Sabean
Vice president and assistant general manager .... Ned Colletti
Vice president of player personnel .... Dick Tidrow
Special assistant to the general manager .... Ron Perranoski
Director of player development .... Jack Hiatt
Coordinator of international operations .... Rick Ragazzo
Senior vice president and chief financial officer .... John Yee
Senior vice president, ballpark operations/security .... Jorge Costa
Vice president, communications .... Bob Rose
Senior vice president, corporate marketing .... Mario Alioto
Senior vice president, consumer marketing .... Tom McDonald
General manager, retail .... Connie Kullberg
Director of ballpark operations .... Gene Telucci
Vice president, ticket services .... Russ Stanley
Director of travel .... Reggie Younger Jr.
Senior vice president and general counsel .... Jack Bair
Media relations manager .... Jim Moorehead

MINOR LEAGUE AFFILIATES

Class	Team	League	Manager
AAA	Fresno	Pacific Coast	Shane Turner
AA	Shreveport	Texas	Bill Russell
A	Hagerstown	South Atlantic	Bill Hayes
A	San Jose	California	Lenn Sakata
Rookie	Salem-Keizer	Northwest	Fred Stanley
Rookie	Giants	Arizona	Keith Comstock

BROADCAST INFORMATION

Radio: KNBR-AM (680).
TV: KTVU-TV (Channel 2).
Cable TV: Fox Sports Net.

SPRING TRAINING

Ballpark (city): Scottsdale Stadium (Scottsdale, Ariz.).
Ticket information: 602-990-7972.

ASSISTANCE STAFF

Western regional cross-checker
Doug Mapson

Eastern regional cross-checker
Alan Marr

West Coast cross-checker
Darren Wittcke

East Coast cross-checker
Bobby Myrick

Canadian cross-checker
Steve Arnieri

Major league scouts
Joe DiCarlo, Stan Saleski, Paul Turco, Randy Waddill, Tom Zimmer

Major league advance scout
Pat Dobson

Special assignment scouts
Dick Cole   Bo Osborne

Scouts
Mateo Alou, Jose Cassino, Pedro Chavez, John DiCarlo, Lee Elder, Charlie Gonzalez, Tom Korenek, Doug McMillan, Luis Pena, John Shafer, Jesus Stephens, Joe Strain, Todd Thomas, Alex Torres, Glenn Tufts, Paul Turco Jr., Ciro Villalobos, Cal Webster

BALLPARK INFORMATION

Ballpark (capacity, surface)
Pacific Bell Park (40,800, grass)

Address
24 Willie Mays Plaza
San Francisco, CA 94107

Official website
www.sfgiants.com

Business phone
415-972-2000

Ticket information
415-972-2000

Ticket prices
$26 (lower box)
$20 (view box, arcade)
$16 (view reserved)
$10 (bleachers)

Field dimensions (from home plate)
To left field at foul line, 339 feet
To center field, 399 feet
To right field at foul line, 309 feet

First game played
April 11, 2000 (Dodgers 6, Giants)

Follow the Giants all season at: www.sportingnews.com/baseball/teams/giants/

GIANTS SPRING ROSTER

No.	PITCHERS	B/T	Ht./Wt.	Born	2000 clubs	Projection
51	Andra, Jeff	L/L	6-5/210	9-9-75	Shreveport, Fresno	Struggled in PCL callup last year (0-3, 8.73) after going .500 in Class AA.
58	Brous, David	L/L	6-2/195	3-9-80	San Jose	Has problems with control (23 BB in 33 IP), but opponents hit just .218 against him.
56	Embree, Alan	L/L	6-2/190	1-23-70	San Francisco	Lefty setup man and situational reliever should bounce back after off year in 2000.
55	Estes, Shawn	R/L	6-2/195	2-18-73	Fresno, San Jose, San Francisco	Looks like he finally found consistency.
38	Fultz, Aaron	L/L	6-0/196	9-4-73	San Francisco	Middle reliever has averaged nearly a strikeout per inning over his career.
26	Gardner, Mark	R/R	6-1/220	3-1-62	San Francisco	Steady veteran adds flexibility to staff; can start or pitch in relief.
61	Hernandez, Livan	R/R	6-2/222	2-20-75	San Francisco	Won 17 games in 2000; will inherit ace title if Estes is traded.
43	Jensen, Ryan	R/R	6-0/205	9-17-75	Fresno	Strong-armed righty at least two years away after Class AAA struggles.
49	Johnstone, John	R/R	6-3/210	11-25-68	S.Fran., S.Jose, AZL Giants, Fresno	Had spectacular 1999, but disastrous 2000. Needs to rebound to solidify bullpen.
50	Joseph, Kevin	R/R	6-4/200	8-1-76	Shreveport	Hard-luck pitcher's 3-11 record is deceiving.
36	Nathan, Joe	R/R	6-4/195	11-22-74	S. Fran., S. Jose, Bakers., Fresno	Converted shortstop is work in progress, possesses some of best stuff on staff.
31	Nen, Robb	R/R	6-5/215	11-28-69	San Francisco	Statistically was the best closer in the game last year; was not overworked.
48	Ortiz, Russ	R/R	6-1/210	6-5-74	San Francisco	Enigmatic starter will be in rotation but struggles with consistency, control.
47	Rodriguez, Felix	R/R	6-1/190	12-5-72	San Francisco	One of best-kept secrets in the game.
46	Rueter, Kirk	L/L	6-3/205	12-1-70	San Francisco	Solid veteran lefty doesn't blow people away, just finds a way to win.
40	Urban, Jeff	L/R	6-8/215	1-25-77	DID NOT PLAY	Control pitcher missed last season due to injury.
14	Vogelsong, Ryan	R/R	6-3/195	7-22-77	Shreveport, San Francisco	Top prospect, didn't allow a run in six big-league innings last year.
45	Worrell, Tim	R/R	6-4/231	7-5-67	Baltimore, Iowa, Chicago N.L.	Journeyman reliever provides an extra arm in bullpen.
41	Zerbe, Chad	L/L	6-0/190	3-27-72	Shreveport, Fresno, San Fran.	Top prospect played in an independent league, will battle for roster spot.

No.	CATCHERS	B/T	Ht./Wt.	Born	2000 clubs	Projection
33	Chiaramonte, Giuseppe	R/R	6-0/200	2-19-76	Fresno	Power hitter (24 HR, .512 SLG) needs to show better discipline at plate.
29	Estalella, Bobby	R/R	6-1/205	8-23-74	San Francisco	Best offensive catcher on roster; makes do defensively.
15	Mirabelli, Doug	R/R	6-1/218	10-18-70	San Francisco	Best defensive catcher on roster; doesn't add much with the bat.
9	Torrealba, Yorvit	R/R	5-11/190	7-19-78	Shreveport	Good batting eye resulted in .350 OBP in Class AA last season.

No.	INFIELDERS	B/T	Ht./Wt.	Born	2000 clubs	Projection
35	Aurilia, Rich	R/R	6-1/185	9-2-71	San Francisco	One of best hitting shortstops in the game; much improved in the field.
28	Castro, Nelson	R/R	5-10/190	6-4-76	Bakersfield, Fresno	Terrible eye (14 BB, 51 K in 244 ABs), but decent power potential for middle infielder.
52	Crespo, Felipe	B/R	5-11/200	3-5-73	San Francisco	Not much room in crowed Giants roster for him.
18	Davis, Russ	R/R	6-0/195	9-13-69	San Francisco	Third baseman has 30-homer, 45-error potential if he plays full-time.
39	Feliz, Pedro	R/R	6-1/195	4-27-77	Fresno, San Francisco	Is probably a year away, but wields a highly-touted bat (33 HR, .571 SLG).
2	Guzman, Edwards	L/R	5-11/205	9-11-76	Fresno	Average hitter could use better plate coverage if he wants to make the jump to bigs.
21	Kent, Jeff	R/R	6-1/205	3-7-68	San Francisco	Reigning league MVP will anchor lineup and be top righthanded power threat.
34	Martinez, Ramon	R/R	6-1/187	10-10-72	San Francisco	Versatile infielder has solid bat and made just one error in 88 games.
22	Minor, Damon	L/L	6-7/230	1-9-75	Fresno, San Francisco	Has never lived up to his potential; still a long-shot prospect.
23	Ransom, Cody	R/R	6-2/190	2-17-76	Shreveport	Free swinger with not much to show; 141 Ks in 459 ABs, batted .200.
6	Snow, J.T.	L/L	6-2/205	2-26-68	San Francisco	Slick-fielding first baseman contributed mightily (.296, 19 HR, 96 RBI) last year and should repeat in 2001.

No.	OUTFIELDERS	B/T	Ht./Wt.	Born	2000 clubs	Projection
7	Benard, Marvin	L/L	5-9/185	1-20-70	San Francisco	Disappointing season (.262 BA) has people questioning his plate discipline.
25	Bonds, Barry	L/L	6-2/210	7-24-64	San Francisco	Even at 37, one of the most dangerous hitters in the game; can still field, too.
	Davis, Eric	R/R	6-3/200	5-29-62	St. Louis	Another veteran presence in the outfield, killed lefties (.390 BA, .543 SLG) last year.
	Dunston, Shawon	R/R	6-1/180	3-21-63	St. Louis	Adds outfield depth, will probably play right field against LHPs.
8	Murray, Calvin	R/R	5-11/190	7-30-71	San Francisco	Has speed and glove to play any outfield position, but carries a suspect bat.
1	Rios, Armando	L/L	5-9/185	9-13-71	San Francisco	Solid hitter needs to improve vs. lefties; coming off Tommy John surgery.
53	Valderrama, Carlos	R/R	6-3/186	11-30-77	Bakersfield	Blazing speed (51 SBs) with .370 OBP and .315 AVG; future looks bright.

THE COACHING STAFF

Dusty Baker, manager: Two-time N.L. Manager of the Year; needs 37 wins to surpass Roger Craig's San Francisco record of 586 victories.

Gene Clines: Giants ranked in league's top four in runs scored in each of Clines' three years as hitting coach; only Colorado has scored more.

Sonny Jackson: Begins his third year as third base coach; fourth year on Giants major league staff.

Juan Lopez: Bullpen coach begins his fourth year; has his work cut out for him with several questions at catcher.

Dave Righetti: Entering second year as Giants' pitching coach; former standout closer deserves credit for bullpen's improvement.

Robby Thompson: Former second baseman begins his first year as coach; was one of Giants' most popular players in 11-year career.

Ron Wotus: Bench coach elevated from minors where he was two-time manager of year, reached playoffs in six of seven seasons.

THE TOP NEWCOMERS

Shawon Dunston: Versatile outfielder adds much-needed depth as Rios' return from Tommy John surgery is anything but certain.

Eric Davis: In the same situation as Dunston; won't start much but will be a valuable reserve.

Tim Worrell: With Johnstone's struggles in 2000, every arm will be valuable; could add to league's deepest bullpen.

THE TOP PROSPECTS

Pedro Feliz: Scouts salivate when discussing the potential of this power-hitting third baseman; he should get a late-season look (if not before).

Ryan Vogelsong: Had just six wins, but struck out 147 batters in 155 innings at Class AA Shreveport. Shone in brief callup last year, could see more action this time around.

INFORMATION AND COMPUTATIONS

1999 IMPORTANT DATES

January 4-14—Period in which a player may make submission to arbitration.

January 8—The last day for former clubs to re-sign players who refused arbitration.

January 18—Office of the Commissioner and MLBPA will exchange salary arbitration filing figures.

January 20-21—Office of the Commissioner and MLBPA will schedule arbitration hearing dates.

January 31-February 18—Salary arbiration hearings held.

February 18—The first date in which injured players, pitchers and catchers may be invited to attend spring training workouts.

February 23—The first date all other players may be invited to attend spring training workouts.

March 1—The mandatory date players are required to report for first spring training workout.

March 2—The first date to renew contracts. The 10-day renewal period ends on March 11.

March 9—The first date clubs may ask waivers on draft-excluded players acquired after August 15, 1999, or players chosen in the 1999 Rule 5 draft. Special waivers are required for all outright assignments to the National Association from September 1, 1999, through May 2, 2000.

March 14—The first date that draft-excluded/selected players may be assigned to a National Association club.

March 15—Unconditional release waivers requested today until 2 p.m. (EDT) March 29 will owe 45 days termination pay.

March 16—The first date that draft-excluded/selected players may be assigned to a National Association club.

March 18—The last day to assign an injured player to a National Association club until the close of the championship season provided that: the player has less than three years of Major League service; the assignment would not be the player's second career outright since 3-19-90; the player had no Major League service prior to the season; the player was not selected by the assignor Major League team in the immediately preceding Rule 5 draft.

March 29—The last date to request unconditional release waivers by 2 p.m. (EDT) without incurring full-season salary.

April 3—The official opening of the 2000 championship season. All clubs are required to cut down to 25 players by midnight, April 2, and transmit rosters to the league office by noon on April 3.

May 1—The earliest date former clubs may re-sign free agents who refused arbitration and were unsigned after July 31.

May 2—Waivers secured on or after November 11 expire at 5 p.m. (EDT).

May 3—The new waiver period begins. Waivers secured on or after this date are good through 5 p.m. (ET) July 31.

May 15—The earliest date clubs may re-sign players whom they unconditionally released after midnight August 31, 1999.

May 29—The start of the amateur free agent closed period regarding the summer draft—12:01 a.m.

June 5-7—The summer free-agent draft.

July 11—The All-Star Game at Atlanta's Turner Field.

July 31—Waivers secured on or after May 3, 2000, expire at 5 p.m. (EDT). Players may be traded between Major League clubs until midnight without any waivers in effect.

August 1—New waiver period begins. Beginning this date and ending on the day following the close of the championship season, players may be assigned between Major League clubs only after Major League waivers have been secured during the current waiver period.

August 15—The last date to bring players up for "full trial" to avoid draft-excluded status.

August 31—Any player released after midnight may not be re-signed to a Major League contract by the club that released him until May 15 of the following season.

Post-season rosters are established at midnight. To be eligible, a player must be a bona fide member of a qualifying team on August 31 and must remain a bona fide member until the end of the season.

September 1—The active player limit is increased from 25 to 40. After this date, outright assignments to the National Association can be made only with special waivers in effect.

October 1—Players on optional assignment must be recalled.

October 1—The official closing of the 1999 season.

October 2—Starting on this date, players may be traded between Major League clubs without waivers in effect.

October 9—The last date to request waivers on draft-excluded players until 25 days prior to the opening of the next season.

October 10—The beginning of the closed period for Major League waiver requests. Special waivers may still be requested on players that are not draft excluded for the next Rule 5 draft.

November 10—Waivers secured on or after August 1, 2000, expire at 5 p.m. (ET).

November 11—The new waiver period begins. Major League waiver requests can be withdrawn by a club on a player only once in each waiver period; subsequent Major League waiver requests in that period are irrevocable.

Waivers (exclusive of special waivers) secured on this day and after shall be in effect until the 30th day of the following championship season.

November (TBA)—Dates for filing Rookie, A, AA, AAA and Major League reserve lists will be announced as soon as the dates are determined.

December 20—The last date to tender contracts.

NOTE: The dates will be used unless notified differently.

RULES AND INFORMATION

SUSPENDED GAMES

A game may be suspended and completed at a future date for any of the following reasons:

1. A legally imposed curfew
2. The game is still tied at 1 a.m., local time. No inning may begin after 1 a.m., though an inning already in progress may be completed.
3. Any other mechanical difficulties that make continuing play overly difficult or dangerous.
4. Darkness falls and law prevents the use of lights.
5. Weather conditions make playing overly difficult or dangerous.

DISABLED LISTS

15-day: The player must remain off the active roster for a minimum of 15 calendar days, starting on the day following the player's last game.

60-day: Same rules apply, however, this may only be used when the team's 40-man roster is full. Any player placed on the 60-day disabled list after August 1 may not play for the remaider of the season, including any postseason games.

MAJOR LEAGUE SERVICE

A player gets service time:

1. For every day spent on an active roster, a Major League disabled list or a suspended list.
2. The day he physically reports to the team upon being called up from the minor leagues.
3. For however long it takes him, within reason, to report to his new team following a trade.
4. Up to and including the day he is sent down to the minors.
5. Up to and including the day he was notified of his unconditional release.
6. At the rate of 172 days per season, even though the regular season spans 183 days.

QUALIFICATIONS FOR INDIVIDUAL CHAMPIONSHIPS

Batting championship: It is awarded to the player with the highest batting average and at least 502 plate appearances. A player who falls short of the required 502 plate appearances can still win the title if the difference between his plate appearance total and 502 can be added as hitless at-bats and he still has the highest average.

Pitching championship: Awarded to the pitcher with the lowest ERA and at least 162 innings pitched.

Fielding championship: Awarded to each position player with the highest fielding average. Pitchers need a minimum of 162 innings, catchers 82 games and all other positions 108 games.

Night games: Night games are defined as any game beginning at or after 5 p.m. local time.

Streaks: A consecutive-game hitting streak will continue if the player fails to get a hit, but his at-bats result in a combination of any of the following: a walk, being hit by a pitch, defensive interference or a sacrifice bunt. The streak is terminated if the player's at-bats result only in a sacrifice fly.

A consecutive-games played streak is extended by a half inning of defensive play or a single at-bat, but pinch running will not extend the streak. The player's streak also continues if he is ejected from the game before he can satisfy any of the above requirements.

HOW TO COMPUTE:

Batting average: Divide at-bats into hits.

ERA: Multiply earned runs by 9 and divide the total by innings pitched.

Slugging percentage: Divide total bases by total times at bat (not including walks, hit by pitcher, sacrifices or interference).

On-base percentage: Divide the on-base total (hits, walks and hit by pitcher) by total plate appearances (at-bats, walks, hit by pitcher, sacrifices).

Fielding average: Add putouts and assists, divide the sum by total chances (putouts, assists, and errors).

Winning percentage: Divide the number of games won by the total games played.

Magic number: Determine the number of games yet to be played and add one. Then subtract the number of games the second-place team trails the first-place team in the loss column.

2000 Review

Scott Brosius, Mariano Rivera and Tino Martinez celebrate the fourth World Series championship for the Yankees in the last five years.

INTRODUCTION

It was a season of underdogs, career-defining offensive performances and pitching mastery, punctuated by a three-team playoff chase that re-energized proponents of the wild-card system. It was a season in which names like Helton, Delgado and Erstad overshadowed the more magical names of McGwire, Griffey and Gwynn.

It was a season of new against old, good vs. evil ... and the little guys fared well against the rich Goliaths. But in the end, sanity prevailed. The powerful, intimidating New York Yankees became kings of the baseball universe for a 26th time, the fourth time in five years, and they did it at the expense of the crosstown Mets in the first Subway Series in 44 years.

If the 2000 season didn't measure up to the excitement of the great 1998 home run chase and the 1999 Mark McGwire-Sammy Sosa encore, it at least gave us the element of surprise and the happy sense that baseball's incredible talent pipeline, which has been rejuvenating the game for more than a century, is still pumping full throttle.

Colorado first baseman Todd Helton commanded a fair share of the National League spotlight with a spirited run at .400 and Toronto first baseman Carlos Delgado combined with Anaheim left fielder Darin Erstad to touch off fireworks in the American League. They were joined by such young lions as Jason Giambi, Troy Glaus, Nomar Garciaparra, Vladimir Guerrero, Alex Rodriguez, Johnny Damon, Mike Sweeney, Tim Hudson, Rafael Furcal, Rick Ankiel and Jason Kendall.

There also were familiar faces in key places. Arizona lefthander Randy Johnson was good enough to win his second straight N.L. Cy Young, but Atlanta aces Tom Glavine and Greg Maddux and Los Angeles righthander Kevin Brown weren't far behind. Boston righthander Pedro Martinez carved out a phenomenal 1.74 ERA against A.L. batters en route to a second straight Cy Young and Toronto lefty David Wells became the second oldest pitcher (37) to win 20 games for the first time.

But the greatest rejuvenation was witnessed in the standings. The young Chicago White Sox won 95 games and the A.L. Central—their first division title since 1993. Youth also prevailed in Oakland and Seattle, where the A's and Mariners waged a division battle that wasn't decided until the last day. The Mariners lost that battle but survived the playoff war with a final-day win that eliminated Cleveland from wild-card contention.

Colorado's Todd Helton commanded his fair share of the baseball spotlight in 2000 when he flirted for awhile with .400.

The Atlanta Braves cruised to their ninth consecutive division title in the N.L. East, but St. Louis and San Francisco were surprise winners in the Central and West.

THE WILD, WILD WEST

The spotlight was focused on the A.L. West Division and wild-card chase over the final weeks of the season and the A's, Mariners and Indians played at a frenetic pace. Oakland, fueled by the blazing September bat of A.L. MVP Giambi (.400 with 13 home runs), won 22-of-29 games to hold off the 19-10 Mariners and 22-12 Indians.

The three teams entered the final day of the regular season locked in a complicated playoff scenario that, with the right combination of wins and, losses, could have forced a one or two-day extension to the season. The Indians won an early game and then crossed their fingers that either Seattle or Oakland would lose. But the A's beat Texas 3-0 to clinch the division title and the Mariners won 5-2 at Anaheim, giving them the wild-card. The Indians, winners of five straight Central Division titles, were out.

The excitement of the regular season carried over to the playoffs and both the Mariners and A's gave the defending-champion Yankees tough battles in the Division Series and A.L. Championship Series. But the New Yorkers, who had lost 15 of their last 18 regular-season games and appeared on the verge of collapse, dug deep and put together another postseason run that took them to the World Series.

There they collided with the crosstown Mets in the first Subway Series since the Dodgers and Yankees hooked up in 1956. The Yankees, now playing on cruise control, dispatched the wild-card Mets in a humbling five games.

TAKING OFFENSE

The 27-year-old Helton won two-thirds of a Triple Crown with his .372 average and 147 RBIs, but his 42 home runs were well behind N.L. leader Sammy Sosa's 50. The focus of his season, however, was not the Triple Crown—it was his pursuit of the legendary .400 plateau.

In the sixth inning of an August 21 loss to Atlanta, Helton singled to raise his average to .400 (178-for-445). It marked the latest point in a season that anyone had reached that level since George Brett in 1980. It also capped a blazing 46-for-89 run (.517) over a 24-game stretch. After games of May 31, he had owned a .421 average.

Delgado never heard talk of .400, but he did answer Triple Crown questions until late in the season. He led the A.L. in several offensive categories, but his .344 average, 41 homers and 137 RBIs all ranked fourth. Anaheim third baseman Glaus was the surprise home run leader in the A.L. with 47 and veteran Mariners designated hitter Edgar Martinez led in RBIs with 145. Boston shortstop Garciaparra won his second straight batting title (.372).

Not lost in the shuffle was a big comeback season by White Sox slugger Frank Thomas, who batted .328 with 43 home runs and 143 RBIs.

OTHER NEWS

Erstad, on pace much of the season to break George Sisler's single-season hit record of 257, finished with 240, the most since Wade Boggs got that many in 1985. ... Baltimore third baseman Cal Ripken reached the magical 3,000-hit plateau on April 7, but much of the rest of his season was spent on the disabled list battling back problems. Eight-time N.L. batting champion Tony Gwynn did not play for the Padres after June 23 because of a bad knee. ... Cubs right fielder Sosa captured his first home run title and joined Mark McGwire as the only players to hit 50 home runs in three consecutive seasons. Cardinals first baseman McGwire sat out much of the season with a knee injury and finished with 32 homers after seasons of 70 and 65. ... Martinez (18-6) pitched a one-hitter and a two-hitter and enjoyed games with 17, 15 and 15 strikeouts. He also was on center stage in a wild beanball battle at Tampa Bay. ... Glavine led the Braves with 21 wins and joined teammate Maddux (19-9) in the 200-win club. ... John Rocker reestablished himself as the Braves' closer after an early season suspension, a stint at Class AAA Richmond and much heckling from fans, who took offense at his disparaging offseason comments about gays, minorities and foreigners. Rocker, who recorded 24 saves, triggered a media frenzy when he returned to New York's Shea Stadium in late June. ... For the first time since 1942, no manager was fired during the regular season. ... McGwire, despite his short season, moved up to seventh on the all-time home run list with 554. ... Dodger Dave Hansen set a major league record with seven pinch-hit home runs. ... The Houston Astros, playing half their games in new Enron Field, set a National League record with 249 home runs. ... The Pirates played their final game at 30-year-old Three Rivers Stadium October 1 and 55,351 fans watched them lose to the Chicago Cubs, 10-9.

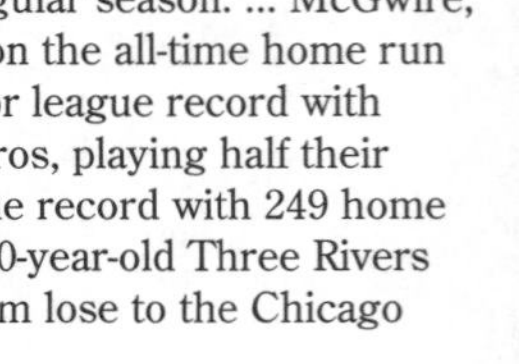

—RON SMITH

FINAL STANDINGS, LEADERS, AWARDS

AMERICAN LEAGUE STANDINGS

FINAL

EAST DIVISION

Team	N.Y.	Bos.	Tor.	Bal.	T.B.	Chi.	Cle.	Det.	K.C.	Min.	Oak.	Sea.	Ana.	Tex.	Atl.	N.Y.	Fla.	Mon.	Phi.	W	L	Pct.	GB
New York	—	7	5	7	6	4	5	4	8	5	6	4	5	10	2-1	4-2	1-1	2-1	2-1	87	74	.540	—
Boston	6	—	4	7	6	7	6	7	4	8	5	5	4	7	2-4	2-1	2-1	3-0	0-3	85	77	.525	2.5
Toronto	7	8	—	6	7	5	4	9	6	4	3	2	7	6	2-1	1-2	1-2	4-2	1-2	83	79	.512	4.5
Baltimore	5	5	7	—	8	4	5	6	3	6	4	3	5	6	0-3	1-2	2-1	0-3	4-2	74	88	.457	13.5
Tampa Bay	6	6	5	5	—	4	2	5	5	6	2	3	6	5	1-2	1-2	3-3	2-1	2-1	69	92	.429	18.0

CENTRAL DIVISION

Team	Chi.	Cle.	Det.	K.C.	Min.	N.Y.	Bos.	Tor.	Bal.	T.B.	Oak.	Sea.	Ana.	Tex.	St.L.	Cin.	Mil.	Hou.	Pit.	Chi.	W	L	Pct.	GB
Chicago	—	8	9	5	7	8	5	5	6	6	6	7	6	5	1-2	3-0	3-0	2-1	—	3-3	95	67	.586	—
Cleveland	5	—	6	5	5	5	6	8	4	8	6	7	6	6	2-1	3-3	3-0	2-1	3-0	—	90	72	.556	5.0
Detroit	3	7	—	5	7	8	5	3	4	4	6	7	5	5	2-1	2-1	1-2	2-1	1-2	2-1	79	83	.488	16.0
Kansas City	7	7	7	—	7	2	6	4	7	5	4	4	6	3	1-2	—	1-2	1-2	4-2	1-2	77	85	.475	18.0
Minnesota	5	8	6	5	—	5	2	5	3	4	5	3	3	8	2-1	0-3	1-2	2-1	1-2	1-2	69	93	.426	26.0

WEST DIVISION

Team	Oak.	Sea.	Ana.	Tex.	N.Y.	Bos.	Tor.	Bal.	T.B.	Chi.	Cle.	Det.	K.C.	Min.	S.F.	L.A.	Ari.	Col.	S.D.	W	L	Pct.	GB
Oakland	—	9	8	5	3	5	7	8	7	3	6	4	8	7	3-3	2-1	2-1	1-2	3-0	91	70	.565	—
Seattle	4	—	8	7	6	5	8	7	9	5	2	2	8	9	2-1	2-1	2-1	2-1	3-3	91	71	.562	0.5
Anaheim	5	5	—	7	5	5	5	7	6	4	3	5	6	7	2-1	4-2	1-2	3-0	2-1	82	80	.506	9.5
Texas	7	5	5	—	2	3	4	6	7	5	4	5	7	4	0-3	1-2	4-2	0-3	2-1	71	91	.438	20.5

Note: Read across for wins, down for losses.

Clinching dates: New York (East)—September 29; Chicago (Central)—September 24; Oakland (West)—October 1; Seattle (wild card)—October 1.

HOME

Team	Cle.	Oak.	Sea.	Ana.	Chi.	Tor.	N.Y.	Bal.	Det.	Bos.	K.C.	Tex.	TB.	Min.	N.L.	W	L	Pct.
Cleveland	..	3	3	5	2	5	2	2	4	3	3	3	3	3	7	48	33	.593
Oakland	3	..	4	5	2	4	1	4	3	2	3	4	3	2	7	47	34	.580
Seattle	2	2	..	4	2	3	3	4	0	3	5	4	4	5	6	47	34	.580
Anaheim	2	3	3	..	2	3	3	3	3	4	4	3	4	2	7	46	35	.568
Chicago	4	2	3	4	..	2	3	4	5	3	3	2	2	3	6	46	35	.568
Toronto	3	1	1	4	1	..	5	4	5	4	4	3	3	3	4	45	36	.556
New York	1	4	1	2	1	4	..	4	3	2	5	5	4	3	5	44	36	.550
Baltimore	4	2	3	2	2	5	3	..	4	1	2	5	5	2	4	44	37	.543
Detroit	4	3	4	2	2	2	5	2	..	2	2	3	2	4	6	43	38	.531
Boston	3	3	2	2	4	2	2	2	3	..	2	3	4	4	6	42	39	.519
Kansas City	4	1	3	4	4	2	1	5	3	2	..	2	2	5	4	42	39	.519
Texas	1	5	3	2	3	3	1	5	2	2	3	..	4	3	5	42	39	.519
Tampa Bay	1	1	1	4	2	2	4	4	1	4	1	3	..	3	5	36	44	.450
Minnesota	4	1	2	1	2	2	2	2	4	0	4	5	3	..	4	36	45	.444
N.L. Clubs	3	5	4	4	3	4	3	6	5	6	5	7	5	6	..	..	..	..
Lost	39	36	37	45	32	43	38	51	45	38	46	52	48	48	..	608	524	.537

ROAD

Team	Chi.	Oak.	Sea.	Bos.	N.Y.	Cle.	Tor.	Ana.	Det.	K.C.	Min.	TB.	Bal.	Tex.	N.L.	W	L	Pct.
Chicago	..	4	4	2	5	4	3	2	4	2	4	4	2	3	6	49	32	.605
Oakland	1	..	5	3	2	3	3	3	1	5	5	4	4	1	4	44	36	.550
Seattle	3	2	..	2	3	0	5	4	2	3	4	5	3	3	5	44	37	.543
Boston	3	2	3	..	4	3	2	2	4	2	4	2	5	4	3	43	38	.531
New York	3	2	3	5	..	4	1	3	1	3	2	2	3	5	6	43	38	.531
Cleveland	3	3	4	3	3	..	3	1	2	2	2	5	2	3	6	42	39	.519
Toronto	4	2	1	4	2	1	..	3	4	2	1	4	2	3	5	38	43	.469
Anaheim	2	2	2	1	2	1	2	..	2	2	5	2	4	4	5	36	45	.444
Detroit	1	3	3	3	3	3	1	3	..	3	3	2	2	2	4	36	45	.444
Kansas City	3	3	1	4	1	3	2	2	4	..	2	3	2	1	4	35	46	.432
Minnesota	3	4	1	2	3	4	3	2	2	1	..	1	1	3	3	33	48	.407
Tampa Bay	2	1	2	2	2	1	3	2	4	4	3	..	1	2	4	33	48	.407
Baltimore	2	2	0	4	2	1	2	3	2	1	4	3	..	1	3	30	51	.370
Texas	2	2	2	1	1	3	1	3	3	4	1	3	1	..	2	29	52	.358
N.L. Clubs	3	2	3	3	3	2	5	2	3	5	5	4	5	4	..	..	..	..
Lost	35	34	34	39	36	33	36	35	38	39	45	44	37	39	..	535	598	.472

MONTHLY

Through April 30

East

Team	W	L	GB
New York	15	8	—
Baltimore	14	10	1.5
Boston	12	9	2.0
Toronto	12	14	4.5
Tampa Bay	9	15	6.5

Central

Team	W	L	GB
Chicago	17	8	—
Cleveland	13	8	2.0
Kansas City	12	13	5.0
Minnesota	11	15	6.5
Detroit	6	17	10.0

West

Team	W	L	GB
Seattle	13	10	—
Anaheim	13	13	1.5
Oakland	12	13	2.0
Texas	9	15	4.5

Through May 31

East

Team	W	L	GB
Boston	29	19	—
New York	28	21	1.5
Toronto	28	26	4.0
Baltimore	23	27	7.0
Tampa Bay	17	34	13.5

Central

Team	W	L	GB
Chicago	30	22	—
Cleveland	27	22	1.5
Kansas City	26	25	3.5
Minnesota	24	29	6.5
Detroit	18	31	10.5

West

Team	W	L	GB
Seattle	26	24	—
Texas	27	25	—
Anaheim	27	26	0.5
Oakland	27	26	0.5

Through June 30

East

Team	W	L	GB
Toronto	44	36	—
New York	38	36	3.0
Boston	38	37	3.5
Baltimore	33	44	9.5
Tampa Bay	32	45	10.5

Central

Team	W	L	GB
Chicago	50	29	—
Cleveland	40	38	9.5
Kansas City	37	409	12.0
Minnesota	36	45	15.0
Detroit	33	43	15.5

West

Team	W	L	GB
Seattle	45	32	—
Oakland	45	33	0.5
Anaheim	41	38	5.0
Texas	37	40	8.0

Through July 31

East

Team	W	L	GB
New York	56	44	—
Boston	54	48	3.0
Toronto	55	52	4.5
Baltimore	46	58	12.0
Tampa Bay	44	59	13.5

Central

Team	W	L	GB
Chicago	64	41	—
Cleveland	52	50	10.5
Detroit	48	56	15.5
Kansas City	47	57	16.5
Minnesota	48	60	17.5

West

Team	W	L	GB
Seattle	61	44	—
Oakland	58	47	3.0
Anaheim	57	50	5.0
Texas	50	53	10.0

Through August 31

East

Team	W	L	GB
New York	74	56	—
Boston	69	61	5.0
Toronto	70	63	5.5
Baltimore	60	73	15.5
Tampa Bay	59	74	16.5

Central

Team	W	L	GB
Chicago	79	54	—
Cleveland	70	60	7.5
Detroit	66	66	12.5
Kansas City	62	71	17.0
Minnesota	59	74	20.0

West

Team	W	L	GB
Seattle	72	61	—
Oakland	69	63	2.5
Anaheim	68	65	4.0
Texas	59	74	13.0

Through October 3 (Final)

East

Team	W	L	GB
New York	57	74	—
Boston	85	77	2.5
Toronto	83	79	4.5
Baltimore	74	88	13.5
Tampa Bay	69	92	18.0

Central

Team	W	L	GB
Chicago	95	67	—
Cleveland	90	72	5.0
Detroit	79	83	16.0
Kansas City	77	85	18.0
Minnesota	69	93	26.0

West

Team	W	L	GB
Oakland	91	70	—
Seattle	91	71	0.5
Anaheim	82	80	9.5
Texas	71	91	20.5

NATIONAL LEAGUE STANDINGS

FINAL

EAST DIVISION

Team	Atl.	N.Y.	Fla.	Mon.	Phi.	St.L.	Cin.	Mil.	Hou.	Pit.	Chi.	S.F.	L.A.	Ari.	Col.	S.D.	N.Y.	Bos.	Tor.	Bal.	T.B.	W	L	Pct.	GB
Atlanta	—	7	6	6	8	3	2	6	5	5	4	6	7	6	5	8	1-2	4-2	1-2	3-0	2-1	95	67	.586	—
New York	6	—	6	9	6	6	4	7	5	7	5	3	5	7	6	3	2-4	1-2	2-1	2-1	2-1	94	68	.580	1.0
Florida	6	6	—	7	9	3	6	3	3	5	6	3	2	5	5	2	1-1	1-2	2-1	1-2	3-3	79	82	.491	15.5
Montreal	7	3	6	—	5	2	3	5	5	3	5	3	3	5	2	3	1-2	0-3	2-4	3-0	1-2	67	95	.414	28.0
Philadelphia	5	7	4	7	—	2	4	5	4	3	3	2	4	1	3	2	1-2	3-0	2-1	2-4	1-2	65	97	.401	30.0

CENTRAL DIVISION

Team	St.L.	Cin.	Mil.	Hou.	Pit.	Chi.	Atl.	N.Y.	Fla.	Mon.	Phi.	S.F.	L.A.	Ari.	Col.	S.D.	Chi.	Cle.	Det.	K.C.	Min.	W	L	Pct.	GB
St. Louis	—	6	7	6	8	10	4	3	6	5	7	4	6	4	3	9	2-1	1-2	1-2	2-1	1-2	95	67	.586	—
Cincinnati	7	—	5	7	7	8	5	5	3	6	3	3	4	5	6	4	0-3	3-3	1-2	—	3-0	85	77	.525	10.0
Milwaukee	5	8	—	6	7	7	3	2	4	4	2	3	4	5	5	2	0-3	0-3	2-1	2-1	2-1	73	89	.451	22.0
Houston	6	5	7	—	10	7	4	2	5	4	5	1	3	1	4	2	1-2	1-2	1-2	2-1	1-2	72	90	.444	23.0
Pittsburgh	4	6	5	3	—	9	2	2	4	4	6	2	5	2	2	7	—	0-3	2-1	2-4	2-1	69	93	.426	26.0
Chicago	3	4	6	5	3	—	5	2	1	4	6	4	3	4	4	3	3-3	—	1-2	2-1	2-1	65	97	.401	30.0

WEST DIVISION

Team	S.F.	L.A.	Ari.	Col.	S.D.	Atl.	N.Y.	Fla.	Mon.	Phi.	St.L.	Cin.	Mil.	Hou.	Pit.	Chi.	Oak.	Sea.	Ana.	Tex.	W	L	Pct.	GB
San Francisco	—	5	7	7	7	3	5	6	6	7	5	6	6	8	6	5	3-3	1-2	1-2	3-0	97	65	.599	—
Los Angeles	7	—	6	9	8	2	4	7	5	5	3	5	3	6	4	6	1-2	1-2	2-4	2-1	86	76	.531	11.0
Arizona	6	7	—	7	9	3	2	4	4	8	5	2	4	6	7	5	1-2	1-2	2-1	2-4	85	77	.525	12.0
Colorado	6	4	6	—	7	4	3	4	7	6	5	3	4	5	7	5	2-1	1-2	0-3	3-0	82	80	.506	15.0
San Diego	5	5	4	6	—	1	6	7	6	5	0	5	7	7	2	5	0-3	3-3	1-2	1-2	76	86	.469	21.0

Note: Read across for wins, down for losses.
Tie game—Milwaukee at Cincinnati, April 3 (5 innings).
Clinching dates: Atlanta (East)—September 26; St. Louis (Central)—September 20; San Francisco (West)—September 21; New York (wild card)—September 27.

HOME

Team	N.Y.	S.F.	Atl.	St.L.	Col.	Ari.	L.A.	Cin.	Fla.	Mil.	S.D.	Hou.	Chi.	Mon.	Pit.	Phi.	A.L.	W	L	Pct.
New York	..	3	4	3	4	5	2	3	4	5	1	2	3	6	3	2	5	55	26	.679
San Francisco	4	..	2	2	6	2	2	5	2	3	3	2	4	3	3	6	6	55	26	.679
Atlanta	4	5	..	1	3	3	5	1	4	2	5	3	2	2	3	4	4	51	30	.630
St. Louis	3	3	1	..	2	2	4	3	4	4	3	3	7	3	3	2	3	50	31	.617
Colorado	1	6	1	3	..	4	3	2	3	1	2	4	4	3	4	2	5	48	33	.593
Arizona	1	1	3	4	5	..	5	1	1	2	5	3	3	1	5	3	4	47	34	.580
Los Angeles	3	3	1	1	5	5	..	2	3	1	4	4	1	3	2	4	2	44	37	.543
Cincinnati	2	2	2	4	2	2	0	..	1	4	4	3	4	3	3	2	5	43	38	.531
Florida	4	2	4	1	2	3	2	1	..	2	1	2	3	3	2	6	5	43	38	.531
Milwaukee	1	3	2	3	3	1	2	5	2	..	1	4	5	3	4	1	2	42	39	.519
San Diego	4	2	0	0	2	3	2	3	2	5	..	4	3	5	0	3	3	41	40	.506
Houston	1	0	4	3	2	0	1	2	3	4	0	..	3	2	7	3	4	39	42	.481
Chicago	1	2	4	3	2	4	1	2	1	5	2	2	..	2	1	3	3	38	43	.469
Montreal	3	0	2	1	2	3	2	0	3	2	2	4	4	..	2	2	5	37	44	.457
Pittsburgh	2	1	2	1	0	1	1	3	3	3	4	3	4	2	..	2	5	37	44	.457
Philadelphia	3	2	3	1	2	1	2	2	3	2	2	1	0	3	2	..	5	34	47	.420
A.L. Clubs	5	4	2	5	5	4	5	4	5	5	7	4	4	7	5	5	..	..	..	..
Lost	42	39	37	36	47	43	39	39	44	50	46	48	54	51	49	50	..	704	592	.543

ROAD

Team	St.L.	Atl.	Cin.	L.A.	S.F.	N.Y.	Ari.	Fla.	S.D.	Col.	Hou.	Pit.	Mil.	Phi.	Mon.	Chi.	A.L.	W	L	Pct.
St. Louis	..	3	3	2	1	0	2	2	6	1	3	5	3	5	2	3	4	45	36	.556
Atlanta	2	..	1	2	1	3	3	2	3	2	2	2	4	4	4	2	7	44	37	.543
Cincinnati	3	3	..	4	1	3	3	2	0	4	4	4	1	1	3	4	2	42	39	.519
Los Angeles	2	1	3	..	4	1	1	4	4	4	2	2	2	1	2	5	4	42	39	.519
San Francisco	3	1	1	3	..	1	5	4	4	1	6	3	3	1	3	1	2	42	39	.519
New York	3	2	1	3	0	..	2	2	2	2	3	4	2	4	3	2	4	39	42	.481
Arizona	1	0	1	2	5	1	..	3	4	2	3	2	2	5	3	2	2	38	43	.469
Florida	2	2	5	0	1	2	2	..	1	3	1	3	1	3	4	3	3	36	44	.450
San Diego	0	1	2	3	3	2	1	5	..	4	3	2	2	2	1	2	2	35	46	.432
Colorado	2	3	1	1	0	2	2	1	5	..	1	3	3	4	4	1	1	34	47	.420
Houston	3	0	3	2	1	1	1	2	2	2	..	3	3	2	2	4	2	33	48	.407
Pittsburgh	3	0	3	4	1	0	1	1	3	2	0	..	2	4	2	5	1	32	49	.395
Milwaukee	2	1	3	2	0	1	4	2	1	2	2	3	..	1	1	2	4	31	50	.383
Philadelphia	1	2	2	2	0	4	0	1	0	1	3	1	3	..	4	3	4	31	50	.383
Montreal	1	5	3	1	3	0	2	3	1	0	1	1	3	3	..	1	2	30	51	.370
Chicago	0	1	2	2	2	1	0	0	1	2	3	2	1	3	2	..	5	27	54	.333
A.L. Clubs	3	5	4	4	3	4	5	4	3	1	5	4	4	4	4	3	..	..	..	..
Lost	31	30	38	37	26	26	34	38	40	33	42	44	39	47	44	43	..	581	714	.449

MONTHLY

Through April 30

Team	W	L	GB
East			
Atlanta	18	6	—
New York	16	10	3.0
Montreal	14	9	3.5
Florida	13	13	6.0
Philadelphia	7	17	11.0
Central			
St. Louis	17	8	—
Cincinnati	12	12	4.5
Houston	9	14	7.0
Pittsburgh	9	15	7.5
Milwaukee	9	15	7.5
Chicago	10	17	8.0
West			
Arizona	16	9	—
Los Angeles	14	10	1.5
San Fran.	10	13	5.0
San Diego	11	14	5.0
Colorado	11	14	5.0

Through May 31

Team	W	L	GB
East			
Atlanta	35	16	—
New York	29	24	7.0
Montreal	26	23	8.0
Florida	24	30	12.5
Philadelphia	18	33	17.0
Central			
St. Louis	30	22	—
Cincinnati	28	23	1.5
Pittsburgh	23	28	6.5
Milwaukee	22	31	8.5
Chicago	20	33	10.5
Houston	19	33	11.0
West			
Arizona	33	19	—
Colorado	28	22	4.0
Los Angeles	28	22	4.0
San Fran.	25	25	7.0
San Diego	24	28	9.0

Through June 30

Team	W	L	GB
East			
Atlanta	48	31	—
New York	45	32	2.0
Montreal	38	37	8.0
Florida	39	41	9.5
Philadelphia	33	44	14.0
Central			
St. Louis	47	32	—
Cincinnati	38	40	8.5
Pittsburgh	34	44	12.5
Chicago	32	46	14.5
Milwaukee	32	47	15.0
Houston	27	52	20.0
West			
Arizona	46	33	—
Colorado	43	32	1.0
Los Angeles	41	37	4.5
San Fran.	38	38	6.5
San Diego	35	43	10.5

Through July 31

Team	W	L	GB
East			
Atlanta	65	40	—
New York	59	45	5.5
Florida	51	54	14.0
Montreal	47	55	16.5
Philadelphia	46	58	18.5
Central			
St. Louis	58	47	—
Cincinnati	54	51	4.0
Chicago	49	55	8.5
Pittsburgh	45	58	12.0
Milwaukee	44	62	14.5
Houston	39	66	19.0
West			
Arizona	58	47	—
San Fran.	57	46	—
Los Angeles	55	49	2.5
Colorado	50	54	7.5
San Diego	47	58	11.0

Through August 31

Team	W	L	GB
East			
New York	79	54	—
Atlanta	79	55	0.5
Florida	64	69	15.0
Philadelphia	56	76	22.0
Montreal	55	75	22.0
Central			
St. Louis	75	58	—
Cincinnati	67	66	8.0
Chicago	58	75	17.0
Milwaukee	58	75	17.0
Houston	55	78	20.0
Pittsburgh	53	79	21.5
West			
San Fran.	75	56	—
Arizona	73	59	2.5
Los Angeles	70	64	6.5
Colorado	68	65	8.0
San Diego	65	69	11.5

Through October 3 (Final)

Team	W	L	GB
East			
Atlanta	95	67	—
New York	94	68	1.0
Florida	79	82	15.5
Montreal	67	95	28.0
Philadelphia	65	97	30.0
Central			
St. Louis	95	67	—
Cincinnati	85	77	10.0
Milwaukee	73	89	22.0
Houston	72	90	23.0
Pittsburgh	69	93	26.0
Chicago	65	97	30.0
West			
San Fran.	97	65	—
Los Angeles	86	76	11.0
Arizona	85	77	12.0
Colorado	82	80	15.0
San Diego	76	86	21.0

AMERICAN LEAGUE MISCELLANEOUS

SHUTOUTS

Team	Chi.	Sea.	Oak.	Bos.	K.C.	Cle.	TB.	N.Y.	Bal.	Tex.	Ana.	Tor.	Min.	Det.	N.L.	W	L	Pct.
Chicago	..	0	2	1	0	1	1	1	0	0	0	0	0	1	0	7	3	.700
Seattle	0	..	0	1	1	0	0	0	1	1	1	0	2	1	2	10	5	.667
Oakland	1	0	..	1	0	0	2	0	2	1	1	2	0	0	1	11	7	.611
Boston	1	1	0	..	0	1	1	2	1	1	0	1	0	3	0	12	8	.600
Kansas City	0	0	0	0	..	1	0	0	1	1	0	0	0	3	0	6	4	.600
Cleveland	0	1	1	0	1	..	0	1	0	1	0	0	0	0	0	5	4	.556
Tampa Bay	0	0	1	1	0	0	..	1	0	0	1	1	2	1	0	8	8	.500
New York	1	0	0	2	0	0	0	..	0	0	0	1	1	1	0	6	7	.462
Baltimore	0	0	1	1	0	1	1	0	..	0	0	0	2	0	0	6	8	.429
Texas	0	0	0	0	0	0	1	1	0	..	0	1	0	0	1	4	6	.400
Anaheim	0	0	1	0	0	0	0	0	0	0	..	1	0	1	0	3	5	.375
Toronto	0	0	0	0	0	0	0	0	1	1	0	..	0	2	0	4	7	.364
Minnesota	0	0	1	0	0	0	0	0	0	0	1	0	..	1	1	4	8	.333
Detroit	0	2	0	0	1	0	1	0	0	0	1	0	1	..	0	6	15	.286
N.L. Clubs	0	1	0	1	1	0	1	1	2	0	0	0	0	1	..	..	..	..
Lost	3	5	7	8	4	4	8	7	8	6	5	7	8	15	..	92	95	.492

A.L. shutouts vs. N.L. clubs (5): Seattle vs. Los Angeles 2; Minnesota vs. Houston; Oakland vs. Los Angeles; Texas vs. Los Angeles.

RECORD VS. DIVISIONS

	vs. A.L. East			vs. A.L. Central			vs. A.L. West			vs. N.L.			Total		
Team	W	L	Pct.	W	L	Pct.	W	L	Pct.	W	L	Pct.	W	L	Pct.
Chicago	30	24	.556	29	20	.592	24	17	.585	12	6	.667	95	67	.586
Oakland	30	20	.600	28	27	.509	22	16	.579	11	7	.611	91	70	.565
Seattle	35	17	.673	26	28	.481	19	19	.500	11	7	.611	91	71	.562
Cleveland	31	22	.585	21	30	.412	25	15	.625	13	5	.722	90	72	.556
New York	25	24	.510	26	28	.481	25	16	.610	11	6	.647	87	74	.540
Boston	23	26	.469	32	24	.571	21	18	.538	9	9	.500	85	77	.525
Toronto	28	21	.571	28	25	.528	18	24	.429	9	9	.500	83	79	.512
Anaheim	28	27	.509	25	26	.490	17	21	.447	12	6	.667	82	80	.506
Detroit	24	31	.436	22	28	.440	23	16	.590	10	8	.556	79	83	.488
Kansas City	24	26	.480	28	20	.583	17	29	.370	8	10	.444	77	85	.475
Baltimore	25	25	.500	24	24	.500	18	28	.391	7	11	.389	74	88	.457
Texas	22	34	.393	25	27	.481	17	19	.472	7	11	.389	71	91	.438
Tampa Bay	22	27	.449	22	27	.449	16	29	.356	9	9	.500	69	92	.429
Minnesota	19	29	.396	24	26	.480	19	27	.413	7	11	.389	69	93	.426
Totals	366	353	.509	360	360	.500	281	294	.489	136	115	.542	1143	1122	.505

ONE-RUN DECISIONS

	W	L	Pct.
Chicago	28	18	.609
Anaheim	32	23	.582
Baltimore	29	25	.537
Detroit	20	18	.526
New York	20	18	.526
Oakland	21	19	.525
Toronto	21	19	.525
Texas	27	25	.519
Tampa Bay	26	26	.500
Boston	20	23	.465
Minnesota	22	26	.458
Kansas City	21	26	.447
Cleveland	17	24	.415
Seattle	15	22	.405
Totals	319	312	.506

DOUBLEHEADERS

	Won	Lost	Split
Seattle	1	0	0
Texas	1	0	0
Baltimore	0	1	0
Chicago	0	1	0
Anaheim	0	0	0
Boston	0	0	0
Cleveland	0	0	0
Detroit	0	0	0
Kansas City	0	0	0
Minnesota	0	0	0
New York	0	0	0
Oakland	0	0	0
Tampa Bay	0	0	0
Toronto	0	0	0
Totals	2	2	0

DAY GAMES

	W	L	Pct.
Cleveland	37	15	.712
Kansas City	29	19	.604
Oakland	35	25	.583
New York	34	25	.576
Seattle	32	24	.571
Toronto	28	28	.500
Boston	22	24	.478
Chicago	26	30	.464
Baltimore	25	30	.455
Minnesota	22	27	.449
Anaheim	18	24	.429
Detroit	21	28	.429
Tampa Bay	22	30	.423
Texas	16	23	.410
Totals	367	352	.510

NIGHT GAMES

	W	L	Pct.
Chicago	69	37	.651
Seattle	59	47	.557
Oakland	56	45	.554
Boston	63	53	.543
Anaheim	64	56	.533
New York	53	49	.520
Toronto	55	51	.519
Detroit	58	55	.513
Cleveland	53	57	.482
Baltimore	49	58	.458
Texas	55	68	.447
Tampa Bay	47	62	.431
Kansas City	48	66	.421
Minnesota	47	66	.416
Totals	776	770	.502

EXTRA-INNING GAMES

	W	L	Pct.
Detroit	8	4	.667
Tampa Bay	9	5	.643
Chicago	7	4	.636
Oakland	8	5	.615
Anaheim	9	7	.563
Cleveland	6	5	.545
New York	4	4	.500
Texas	5	5	.500
Kansas City	7	8	.467
Minnesota	7	9	.438
Seattle	3	4	.429
Boston	5	8	.385
Baltimore	4	7	.364
Toronto	2	6	.250
Totals	84	81	.509

ON GRASS

	W	L	Pct.
Chicago	81	62	.566
New York	80	62	.563
Cleveland	79	62	.560
Oakland	79	67	.541
Boston	77	66	.538
Seattle	77	67	.535
Anaheim	73	71	.507
Detroit	72	71	.503
Kansas City	68	75	.476
Baltimore	63	74	.460
Texas	66	80	.452
Toronto	31	38	.449
Minnesota	28	37	.431
Tampa Bay	25	41	.379
Totals	899	873	.507

ON TURF

	W	L	Pct.
Oakland	12	3	.800
Seattle	14	4	.778
Chicago	14	5	.737
Toronto	52	41	.559
Cleveland	11	10	.524
Anaheim	9	9	.500
Kansas City	9	10	.474
Tampa Bay	44	51	.463
Baltimore	11	14	.440
Minnesota	41	56	.423
Boston	8	11	.421
Detroit	7	12	.368
New York	7	12	.368
Texas	5	11	.313
Totals	244	249	.495

vs. LEFTHANDERS

	W	L	Pct.
Chicago	21	10	.677
Seattle	20	11	.645
Texas	19	15	.559
Detroit	24	21	.533
Baltimore	23	24	.489
New York	22	24	.478
Boston	20	22	.476
Anaheim	21	25	.457
Cleveland	17	21	.447
Oakland	21	26	.447
Toronto	19	24	.442
Kansas City	18	24	.429
Tampa Bay	11	25	.306
Minnesota	11	29	.275
Totals	267	301	.470

vs. RIGHTHANDERS

	W	L	Pct.
Oakland	70	44	.614
Cleveland	73	51	.589
New York	65	50	.565
Chicago	74	57	.565
Seattle	71	60	.542
Boston	65	55	.542
Toronto	64	55	.538
Anaheim	61	55	.526
Kansas City	59	61	.492
Minnesota	58	64	.475
Detroit	55	62	.470
Tampa Bay	58	67	.464
Baltimore	51	64	.443
Texas	52	76	.406
Totals	876	821	.516

NATIONAL LEAGUE MISCELLANEOUS

SHUTOUTS

Team	Cin.	S.F.	St.L.	Atl.	Ari.	N.Y.	L.A.	Mil.	Pit.	Mon.	Phi.	S.D.	Hou.	Chi.	Fla.	Col.	A.L.	W	L	Pct.
Cincinnati	..	0	0	0	0	1	0	0	0	0	1	1	1	2	1	0	0	7	0	1.000
San Francisco	0	..	0	1	0	0	1	1	1	1	1	2	0	1	3	3	0	15	5	.750
St. Louis	0	0	..	1	1	0	0	1	1	1	0	1	0	1	0	0	0	7	5	.583
Atlanta	0	0	0	..	1	1	1	0	0	2	0	0	0	1	1	1	1	9	7	.563
Arizona	0	0	1	1	..	0	0	0	1	1	0	0	0	1	0	2	1	8	7	.533
New York	0	1	0	1	0	..	1	0	2	1	1	0	1	0	0	0	2	10	9	.526
Los Angeles	0	2	1	0	3	0	..	0	0	1	2	2	0	0	0	0	0	11	11	.500
Milwaukee	0	1	0	0	0	0	0	..	1	0	0	0	0	1	2	1	1	7	7	.500
Pittsburgh	0	1	0	1	0	1	2	1	..	0	0	0	0	1	0	0	0	7	7	.500
Montreal	0	0	1	1	1	1	0	0	0	..	2	0	0	0	0	0	1	7	9	.438
Philadelphia	0	0	1	1	0	1	1	1	0	1	..	0	0	0	0	0	0	6	8	.429
San Diego	0	0	0	0	0	2	1	1	0	0	0	..	0	0	1	0	0	5	7	.417
Houston	0	0	0	0	0	0	0	2	0	0	0	0	..	0	0	0	0	2	3	.400
Chicago	0	0	0	0	0	0	0	0	1	1	1	0	0	..	0	1	1	5	8	.385
Florida	0	0	1	0	0	2	0	0	0	0	0	0	0	0	..	0	1	4	8	.333
Colorado	0	0	0	0	1	0	0	0	0	0	0	1	0	0	0	..	0	2	8	.200
A.L. Clubs	0	0	0	0	0	0	4	0	0	0	0	0	1	0	0	0	..	..	..	..
Lost	0	5	5	7	7	9	11	7	7	9	8	7	3	8	8	8	..	112	109	.507

N.L. shutouts vs. A.L. clubs (8): Arizona vs. Seattle; Atlanta vs. Boston; Chicago vs. Detroit; Florida vs. Baltimore; Milwaukee vs. Kansas City; Montreal vs. Baltimore; New York vs. New York A.L.; New York vs. Tampa Bay.

RECORD VS. DIVISIONS

	vs. N.L. East			vs. N.L. Central			vs. N.L. West			vs. A.L.			Total		
Team	W	L	Pct.	W	L	Pct.	W	L	Pct.	W	L	Pct.	W	L	Pct.
San Francisco	27	17	.614	36	17	.679	26	24	.520	8	7	.533	97	65	.599
Atlanta	27	24	.529	25	23	.521	32	13	.711	11	7	.611	95	67	.586
St. Louis	25	16	.610	37	25	.597	26	18	.591	7	8	.467	95	67	.586
New York	27	23	.540	34	16	.680	24	20	.545	9	9	.500	94	68	.580
Los Angeles	23	21	.523	27	25	.519	30	21	.588	6	9	.400	86	76	.531
Arizona	21	24	.467	29	21	.580	29	23	.558	6	9	.400	85	77	.525
Cincinnati	22	19	.537	34	29	.540	22	21	.512	7	8	.467	85	77	.525
Colorado	24	21	.533	29	24	.547	23	29	.442	6	6	.500	82	80	.506
Florida	28	22	.560	26	23	.531	17	28	.378	8	9	.471	79	82	.491
San Diego	25	18	.581	26	27	.491	20	31	.392	5	10	.333	76	86	.469
Milwaukee	15	26	.366	33	30	.524	19	24	.442	6	9	.400	73	89	.451
Houston	20	22	.476	35	27	.565	11	32	.256	6	9	.400	72	90	.444
Pittsburgh	18	23	.439	27	35	.435	18	26	.409	6	9	.400	69	93	.426
Montreal	21	29	.420	23	27	.460	16	28	.364	7	11	.389	67	95	.414
Chicago	18	23	.439	21	41	.339	18	26	.409	8	7	.533	65	97	.401
Philadelphia	23	28	.451	21	29	.420	12	31	.279	9	9	.500	65	97	.401
Totals	364	356	.506	463	419	.525	343	395	.465	115	136	.458	1285	1306	.496

ONE-RUN DECISIONS

	W	L	Pct.
St. Louis	28	16	.636
Florida	32	20	.615
New York	29	20	.592
Milwaukee	26	21	.553
Los Angeles	25	21	.543
Colorado	23	20	.535
Cincinnati	25	23	.521
Atlanta	18	18	.500
Montreal	23	24	.489
San Diego	25	27	.481
Chicago	27	30	.474
San Francisco	18	22	.450
Arizona	22	27	.449
Philadelphia	25	35	.417
Pittsburgh	17	30	.362
Houston	15	31	.326
Totals	378	385	.495

DOUBLEHEADERS

	Won	Lost	Split
New York	3	0	0
Los Angeles	1	0	1
Milwaukee	1	0	1
Pittsburgh	1	0	2
Atlanta	0	0	1
Florida	0	0	1
Philadelphia	0	0	1
Montreal	0	1	1
Chicago	0	2	0
Cincinnati	0	1	0
Colorado	0	1	0
Houston	0	1	0
Arizona	0	0	0
St. Louis	0	0	0
San Diego	0	0	0
San Francisco	0	0	0
Totals	6	6	8

DAY GAMES

	W	L	Pct.
St. Louis	38	20	.655
Atlanta	30	20	.592
New York	33	24	.579
Cincinnati	35	27	.565
San Francisco	37	29	.561
Florida	25	21	.556
Philadelphia	21	20	.512
Los Angeles	23	22	.511
Arizona	22	24	.478
Colorado	27	30	.474
San Diego	23	26	.469
Milwaukee	21	29	.431
Houston	22	31	.415
Chicago	36	56	.391
Montreal	18	29	.383
Pittsburgh	15	33	.306
Totals	426	441	.491

NIGHT GAMES

	W	L	Pct.
San Francisco	60	36	.625
Atlanta	65	47	.584
New York	61	44	.581
St. Louis	57	47	.548
Arizona	63	53	.543
Los Angeles	63	54	.538
Colorado	55	50	.524
Cincinnati	50	50	.500
Pittsburgh	54	60	.478
San Diego	53	60	.469
Florida	54	61	.466
Milwaukee	52	60	.459
Houston	50	59	.459
Montreal	49	66	.426
Chicago	29	41	.414
Philadelphia	44	77	.364
Totals	859	865	.498

EXTRA-INNING GAMES

	W	L	Pct.
St. Louis	5	2	.714
Florida	9	5	.643
Los Angeles	9	5	.643
Milwaukee	13	9	.591
San Fran.	7	5	.583
Cincinnati	9	7	.563
New York	10	8	.556
Colorado	6	5	.545
Montreal	4	4	.500
San Diego	11	13	.458
Pittsburgh	8	11	.421
Chicago	9	13	.409
Houston	6	9	.400
Arizona	5	8	.385
Atlanta	3	5	.375
Philadelphia	4	12	.250
Totals	118	121	.494

ON GRASS

	W	L	Pct.
San Fran.	89	60	.597
Atlanta	82	57	.590
New York	79	56	.585
St. Louis	79	58	.577
Los Angeles	78	71	.523
Arizona	74	70	.514
Cincinnati	34	34	.500
Colorado	70	74	.486
San Diego	69	74	.483
Florida	63	70	.474
Milwaukee	63	77	.450
Houston	62	79	.440
Chicago	53	83	.390
Pittsburgh	23	42	.354
Montreal	21	39	.350
Philadelphia	22	43	.338
Totals	961	987	.493

ON TURF

	W	L	Pct.
Colorado	12	6	.667
St. Louis	16	9	.640
Los Angeles	8	5	.615
San Fran.	8	5	.615
Arizona	11	7	.611
Florida	16	12	.571
Atlanta	13	10	.565
New York	15	12	.556
Cincinnati	51	43	.543
Houston	10	11	.476
Pittsburgh	46	51	.474
Chicago	12	14	.462
Milwaukee	10	12	.455
Montreal	46	56	.451
Philadelphia	43	54	.443
San Diego	7	12	.368
Totals	324	319	.504

vs. LEFTHANDERS

	W	L	Pct.
Cincinnati	25	12	.676
Colorado	24	13	.649
Atlanta	21	14	.600
New York	18	13	.581
Arizona	23	17	.575
San Fran.	19	20	.487
Montreal	19	24	.442
Florida	17	22	.436
Los Angeles	19	25	.432
St. Louis	17	23	.425
Houston	15	21	.417
Pittsburgh	15	22	.405
Chicago	14	21	.400
Milwaukee	14	21	.400
Philadelphia	14	22	.389
San Diego	19	30	.388
Totals	293	320	.478

vs. RIGHTHANDERS

	W	L	Pct.
St. Louis	78	44	.639
San Fran.	78	45	.634
Atlanta	74	53	.583
New York	76	55	.580
Los Angeles	67	51	.568
Arizona	62	60	.508
Florida	62	60	.508
San Diego	57	56	.504
Cincinnati	60	65	.480
Milwaukee	59	68	.465
Colorado	58	67	.464
Houston	57	69	.452
Pittsburgh	54	71	.432
Philadelphia	51	75	.405
Montreal	48	71	.403
Chicago	51	76	.402
Totals	992	986	.502

AMERICAN LEAGUE LEADERS

TOP 15 QUALIFIERS FOR BATTING CHAMPIONSHIP

(502 or more plate appearances)

Batter	Team	BA	G	PA	AB	R	H	TB	2B	3B	HR	RBI	SH	SF	HBP	BB	IBB	SO	SB	CS	GI DP	SLG	OBP
Garciaparra, Nomar	Bos.	.372	140	599	529	104	197	317	51	3	21	96	0	7	2	61	20	50	5	2	8	.599	.434
Erstad, Darin	Ana.	.355	157	747	676	121	240	366	39	6	25	100	2	4	1	64	9	82	28	8	8	.541	.409
Ramirez, Manny	Cle.	.351	118	532	439	92	154	306	34	2	38	122	0	4	3	86	9	117	1	1	9	.697	.457
Delgado, Carlos	Tor.	.344	162	711	569	115	196	378	57	1	41	137	0	4	15	123	18	104	0	1	12	.664	.470
Jeter, Derek	N.Y.	.339	148	679	593	119	201	285	31	4	15	73	3	3	12	68	4	99	22	4	14	.481	.416
Segui, David	Tex.-Cle.	.334	150	634	574	93	192	293	42	1	19	103	0	6	1	53	2	84	0	1	20	.510	.388
Sweeney, Mike	K.C.	.333	159	717	618	105	206	323	30	0	29	144	0	13	15	71	5	67	8	3	15	.523	.407
Giambi, Jason	Oak.	.333	152	664	510	108	170	330	29	1	43	137	0	8	9	137	6	96	2	0	9	.647	.476
Thomas, Frank	Chi.	.328	159	707	582	115	191	364	44	0	43	143	0	8	5	112	18	94	1	3	13	.625	.436
Damon, Johnny	K.C.	.327	159	741	655	136	214	324	42	10	16	88	8	12	1	65	4	60	46	9	7	.495	.382
Martinez, Edgar	Sea.	.324	153	665	556	100	180	322	31	0	37	145	0	8	5	96	8	95	3	0	13	.579	.423
Fryman, Travis	Cle.	.321	155	658	574	93	184	296	38	4	22	106	0	10	1	73	2	111	1	1	15	.516	.392
Dye, Jermaine	K.C.	.321	157	679	601	107	193	337	41	2	33	118	0	6	3	69	6	99	0	1	12	.561	.390
Stewart, Shannon	Tor.	.319	136	631	583	107	186	302	43	5	21	69	1	4	6	37	1	79	20	5	12	.518	.363
Rodriguez, Alex	Sea.	.316	148	672	554	134	175	336	34	2	41	132	0	11	7	100	5	121	15	4	10	.606	.420

TOP 15 QUALIFIERS FOR EARNED-RUN AVERAGE CHAMPIONSHIP

(162 or more innings pitched)

Pitcher	Team	W	L	WP	ERA	G	GS	CG	SHO	GF	SV	IP	H	BFP	R	ER	HR	SH	SF	HBP	BB	IBB	SO	WP	BK
Martinez, Pedro	Bos.	18	6	.750	1.74	29	29	7	4	0	0	217.0	128	817	44	42	17	2	1	14	32	0	284	1	0
Clemens, Roger	N.Y.	13	8	.619	3.70	32	32	1	0	0	0	204.1	184	878	96	84	26	1	2	10	84	0	188	2	1
Mussina, Mike	Bal.	11	15	.423	3.79	34	34	6	1	0	0	237.2	236	987	105	100	28	8	6	3	46	0	210	3	0
Sirotka, Mike	Chi.	15	10	.600	3.79	32	32	1	0	0	0	197.0	203	832	101	83	23	4	3	1	69	1	128	8	2
Colon, Bartolo	Cle.	15	8	.652	3.88	30	30	2	1	0	0	188.0	163	807	86	81	21	2	3	4	98	4	212	4	0
Wells, David	Tor.	20	8	.714	4.11	35	35	9	1	0	0	229.2	266	972	115	105	23	6	7	8	31	0	166	9	1
Heredia, Gil	Oak.	15	11	.577	4.12	32	32	2	0	0	0	198.2	214	860	106	91	24	4	6	4	66	5	101	3	0
Lopez, Albie	T.B.	11	13	.458	4.13	45	24	4	1	10	2	185.1	199	798	95	85	24	6	3	1	70	3	96	4	1
Hudson, Tim	Oak.	20	6	.769	4.14	32	32	2	2	0	0	202.1	169	847	100	93	24	5	7	7	82	5	169	7	0
Finley, Chuck	Cle.	16	11	.593	4.17	34	34	3	0	0	0	218.0	211	936	108	101	23	5	4	2	101	3	189	9	0
Abbott, Paul	Sea.	9	7	.563	4.22	35	27	0	0	2	0	179.0	164	766	89	84	23	1	4	5	80	4	100	3	0
Parque, Jim	Chi.	13	6	.684	4.28	33	32	0	0	0	0	187.0	208	828	105	89	21	5	5	11	71	1	111	2	5
Weaver, Jeff	Det.	11	15	.423	4.32	31	30	2	0	0	0	200.0	205	849	102	96	26	3	9	15	52	2	136	3	2
Suzuki, Mac	K.C.	8	10	.444	4.34	32	29	1	1	0	0	188.2	195	839	100	91	26	2	3	3	94	6	135	11	0
Pettitte, Andy	N.Y.	19	9	.679	4.35	32	32	3	1	0	0	204.2	219	903	111	99	17	7	4	4	80	4	125	2	3

BATTING LEADERS

Games
162 Jose Cruz, Tor.
162 Carlos Delgado, Tor.
161 Mo Vaughn, Ana.
160 Miguel Tejada, Oak.
159 Garret Anderson, Ana.
159 Johnny Damon, K.C.
159 Troy Glaus, Ana.
159 John Olerud, Sea.
159 Mike Sweeney, K.C.
159 Frank Thomas, Chi.

At-bats
676 Darin Erstad, Ana.
655 Johnny Damon, K.C.
647 Garret Anderson, Ana.
632 Gerald Williams, T.B.
631 Cristian Guzman, Min.

Runs scored
136 Johnny Damon, K.C.
134 Alex Rodriguez, Sea.
121 Darin Erstad, Ana.
121 Ray Durham, Chi.
120 Troy Glaus, Ana.

Hits
240 Darin Erstad, Ana.
214 Johnny Damon, K.C.
206 Mike Sweeney, K.C.
201 Derek Jeter, N.Y.
197 N. Garciaparra, Bos.

RBIs
145 Edgar Martinez, Sea.
144 Mike Sweeney, K.C.
143 Frank Thomas, Chi.
137 Carlos Delgado, Tor.
137 Jason Giambi, Oak.

Total bases
378 Carlos Delgado, Tor.
366 Darin Erstad, Ana.
364 Frank Thomas, Chi.
340 Troy Glaus, Ana.
337 Jermaine Dye, K.C.

Doubles
57 Carlos Delgado, Tor.
51 N. Garciaparra, Bos.
46 Deivi Cruz, Det.
45 John Olerud, Sea.
44 Frank Thomas, Chi.
44 Bobby Higginson, Det.
44 Matt Lawton, Min.

Triples
20 Cristian Guzman, Min.
11 Adam Kennedy, Ana.
10 Johnny Damon, K.C.
9 Ray Durham, Chi.
8 Trot Nixon, Bos.
8 Luis Alicea, Tex.

Home runs
47 Troy Glaus, Ana.
43 Jason Giambi, Oak.
43 Frank Thomas, Chi.
41 Alex Rodriguez, Sea.
41 Tony Batista, Tor.
41 Carlos Delgado, Tor.
41 David Justice, Cle.-N.Y.

Walks
137 Jason Giambi, Oak.
123 Carlos Delgado, Tor.
118 Jim Thome, Cle.
112 Troy Glaus, Ana.
112 Frank Thomas, Chi.

On-base percentage
.476 Jason Giambi, Oak.
.470 Carlos Delgado, Tor.
.457 Manny Ramirez, Cle.
.436 Frank Thomas, Chi.
.434 N. Garciaparra, Bos.

Slugging percentage
.697 Manny Ramirez, Cle.
.664 Carlos Delgado, Tor.
.647 Jason Giambi, Oak.
.625 Frank Thomas, Chi.
.606 Alex Rodriguez, Sea.

Stolen bases
46 Johnny Damon, K.C.
39 Roberto Alomar, Cle.
37 Delino DeShields, Bal.
31 Rickey Henderson, Sea.
30 Kenny Lofton, Cle.
30 Mark McLemore, Sea.

Caught stealing
14 Mark McLemore, Sea.
13 Ray Durham, Chi.
12 Gerald Williams, T.B.
11 Troy Glaus, Ana.
10 Delino DeShields, Bal.
10 Cristian Guzman, Min.
10 Omar Vizquel, Cle.

Sacrifice bunts
16 Alex Gonzalez, Tor.
13 Carlos Febles, K.C.
13 Jose Valentin, Chi.
12 Chris Singleton, Chi.
12 Royce Clayton, Tex.
12 Felix Martinez, T.B.

Sacrifice flies
15 Magglio Ordonez, Chi.
13 Mike Sweeney, K.C.
12 Johnny Damon, K.C.
11 Paul O'Neill, N.Y.
11 Alex Rodriguez, Sea.

Strikeouts
181 Mo Vaughn, Ana.
171 Jim Thome, Cle.
163 Troy Glaus, Ana.
151 Jorge Posada, N.Y.
146 Dean Palmer, Det.

Intentional walks
20 N. Garciaparra, Bos.
18 Carlos Delgado, Tor.
18 Frank Thomas, Chi.
17 Rafael Palmeiro, Tex.
11 Mo Vaughn, Ana.
11 John Olerud, Sea.
11 Bernie Williams, N.Y.
11 Albert Belle, Bal.

PITCHING LEADERS

Wins
20 Tim Hudson, Oak.
20 David Wells, Tor.
19 Andy Pettitte, N.Y.
18 Pedro Martinez, Bos.
17 Aaron Sele, Sea.

Losses
16 Brad Radke, Min.
15 Kelvim Escobar, Tor.
15 Joe Mays, Min.
15 Mike Mussina, Bal.
15 Steve Trachsel, T.B.-Tor.
15 Jeff Weaver, Det.

Games
83 Kelly Wunsch, Chi.
77 Mike Venafro, Tex.
76 Bob Wells, Min.
75 Mike Trombley, Bal.
74 Derek Lowe, Bos.

Games started
35 Rick Helling, Tex.
35 David Wells, Tor.
34 Chuck Finley, Cle.
34 Mike Mussina, Bal.
34 Brad Radke, Min.
34 Kenny Rogers, Tex.
34 Aaron Sele, Sea.
34 Steve Trachsel, T.B.-Tor.

Games finished
64 Derek Lowe, Bos.
62 Billy Koch, Tor.
61 Mariano Rivera, N.Y.
60 Todd Jones, Det.
58 Keith Foulke, Chi.
58 Rob. Hernandez, T.B.
58 Kazuhiro Sasaki, Sea.

Complete games
9 David Wells, Tor.
7 Pedro Martinez, Bos.
6 Mike Mussina, Bal.
6 Sidney Ponson, Bal.
4 Albie Lopez, T.B.
4 Brad Radke, Min.

Innings pitched
237.2 Mike Mussina, Bal.
229.2 David Wells, Tor.
227.1 Kenny Rogers, Tex.
226.2 Brad Radke, Min.
222.0 Sidney Ponson, Bal.

Shutouts
4 Pedro Martinez, Bos.
2 Tim Hudson, Oak.
2 Aaron Sele, Sea.
1 26 pitchers tied

Hits allowed
266 David Wells, Tor.
261 Brad Radke, Min.
257 Kenny Rogers, Tex.
240 Jeff Suppan, K.C.
236 Mike Mussina, Bal.

Home runs allowed
36 Jeff Suppan, K.C.
35 Eric Milton, Min.
34 James Baldwin, Chi.
34 Orl. Hernandez, N.Y.
31 Hideo Nomo, Det.
31 Tim Wakefield, Bos.

Runs allowed
130 Chris Carpenter, Tor.
126 Kenny Rogers, Tex.
125 Sidney Ponson, Bal.
125 Pat Rapp, Bal.
124 David Cone, N.Y.

Earned runs allowed
122 Chris Carpenter, Tor.
119 David Cone, N.Y.
119 Sidney Ponson, Bal.
119 Jeff Suppan, K.C.
115 Kenny Rogers, Tex.

Batting average yielded
.167 Pedro Martinez, Bos.
.227 Tim Hudson, Oak.
.233 Bartolo Colon, Cle.
.236 Roger Clemens, N.Y.
.243 Paul Abbott, Sea.

Walks
102 Kevin Appier, Oak.
101 Chuck Finley, Cle.
99 Rick Helling, Tex.
98 Bartolo Colon, Cle.
94 Mac Suzuki, K.C.

Strikeouts
284 Pedro Martinez, Bos.
212 Bartolo Colon, Cle.
210 Mike Mussina, Bal.
189 Chuck Finley, Cle.
188 Roger Clemens, N.Y.

Hit batsmen
15 Jeff Weaver, Det.
14 Pedro Martinez, Bos.
13 E. Loaiza, Tex.-Tor.
11 Jim Parque, Chi.
11 Kenny Rogers, Tex.
11 Esteban Yan, T.B.

Wild pitches
18 Dan Reichert, K.C.
16 Jason Grimsley, N.Y.
16 Hideo Nomo, Det.
14 H. Carrasco, Min.-Bos.
11 David Cone, N.Y.
11 Joe Mays, Min.
11 Mac Suzuki, K.C.

Saves
42 Todd Jones, Det.
42 Derek Lowe, Bos.
37 Kazuhiro Sasaki, Sea.
36 Mariano Rivera, N.Y.
34 Keith Foulke, Chi.
34 John Wetteland, Tex.

NATIONAL LEAGUE LEADERS

TOP 15 QUALIFIERS FOR BATTING CHAMPIONSHIP

(502 or more plate appearances)

Batter	Team	BA	G	PA	AB	R	H	TB	2B	3B	HR	RBI	SH	SF	HBP	BB	IBB	SO	SB	CS	GIDP	SLG	OBP
Helton, Todd	Col.	.372	160	697	580	138	216	405	59	2	42	147	0	10	4	103	22	61	5	3	12	.698	.463
Alou, Moises	Hou.	.355	126	517	454	82	161	283	28	2	30	114	0	9	2	52	4	45	3	3	21	.623	.416
Guerrero, Vladimir	Mon.	.345	154	641	571	101	197	379	28	11	44	123	0	4	8	58	23	74	9	10	15	.664	.410
Hammonds, Jeffrey	Col.	.335	122	511	454	94	152	240	24	2	20	106	2	6	5	44	4	83	14	7	11	.529	.395
Castillo, Luis	Fla.	.334	136	626	539	101	180	209	17	3	2	17	9	0	0	78	0	86	62	22	11	.388	.418
Kent, Jeff	S.F.	.334	159	695	587	114	196	350	41	7	33	125	0	9	9	90	6	107	12	9	17	.596	.424
Vidro, Jose	Mon.	.330	153	663	606	101	200	327	51	2	24	97	0	6	2	49	4	69	5	4	17	.540	.379
Cirillo, Jeff	Col.	.326	157	684	598	111	195	285	53	2	11	115	1	12	6	67	4	72	3	4	19	.477	.392
Sheffield, Gary	L.A.	.325	141	612	501	105	163	322	24	3	43	109	0	6	4	101	7	71	4	6	13	.643	.438
Piazza, Mike	N.Y.	.324	136	545	482	90	156	296	26	0	38	113	0	2	3	58	10	69	4	2	15	.614	.398
Alfonzo, Edgardo	N.Y.	.324	150	650	544	109	176	295	40	2	25	94	0	6	5	95	1	70	3	2	12	.542	.425
Sosa, Sammy	Chi.	.320	156	705	604	106	193	383	38	1	50	138	0	8	2	91	19	168	7	4	12	.634	.406
Kendall, Jason	Pit.	.320	152	678	579	112	185	272	33	6	14	58	1	4	15	79	3	79	22	12	13	.470	.412
Abreu, Bobby	Phi.	.316	154	680	576	103	182	319	42	10	25	79	0	3	1	100	9	116	28	8	12	.554	.416
Giles, Brian S.	Pit.	.315	156	688	559	111	176	332	37	7	35	123	0	8	7	114	13	69	6	0	15	.594	.432

TOP 15 QUALIFIERS FOR EARNED-RUN AVERAGE CHAMPIONSHIP

(162 or more innings pitched)

Pitcher	Team	W	L	WP	ERA	G	GS	CG	SHO	GF	SV	IP	H	BFP	R	ER	HR	SH	SF	HBP	BB	IBB	SO	WP	BK
Brown, Kevin	L.A.	13	6	.684	2.58	33	33	5	1	0	0	230.0	181	921	76	66	21	13	4	9	47	1	216	4	0
Johnson, Randy	Ari.	19	7	.731	2.64	35	35	8	3	0	0	248.2	202	1001	89	73	23	14	5	6	76	1	347	5	2
D'Amico, Jeff C.	Mil.	12	7	.632	2.66	23	23	1	1	0	0	162.1	143	667	55	48	14	10	3	6	46	5	101	5	0
Maddux, Greg	Atl.	19	9	.679	3.00	35	35	6	3	0	0	249.1	225	1012	91	83	19	8	5	10	42	12	190	1	2
Hampton, Mike	N.Y.	15	10	.600	3.14	33	33	3	1	0	0	217.2	194	929	89	76	10	11	5	8	99	5	151	10	0
Leiter, Al	N.Y.	16	8	.667	3.20	31	31	2	1	0	0	208.0	176	874	84	74	19	10	6	11	76	1	200	4	1
Park, Chan Ho	L.A.	18	10	.643	3.27	34	34	3	1	0	0	226.0	173	963	92	82	21	12	5	12	124	4	217	13	0
Glavine, Tom	Atl.	21	9	.700	3.40	35	35	4	2	0	0	241.0	222	992	101	91	24	9	5	4	65	6	152	0	0
Ankiel, Rick	St.L	11	7	.611	3.50	31	30	0	0	0	0	175.0	137	735	80	68	21	8	6	6	90	2	194	12	2
Person, Robert	Phi.	9	7	.563	3.63	28	28	1	1	0	0	173.1	144	743	73	70	13	4	9	6	95	1	164	10	1
Dempster, Ryan	Fla.	14	10	.583	3.66	33	33	2	1	0	0	226.1	210	974	102	92	30	4	5	5	97	7	209	4	0
Hernandez, Livan	S.F.	17	11	.607	3.75	33	33	5	2	0	0	240.0	254	1030	114	100	22	12	9	4	73	3	165	3	0
Williams, Woody	S.D.	10	8	.556	3.75	23	23	4	0	0	0	168.0	152	700	74	70	23	4	3	3	54	2	111	4	0
Schilling, Curt	Phi.-Ari.	11	12	.478	3.81	29	29	8	2	0	0	210.1	204	862	90	89	27	11	4	1	45	4	168	4	0
Benson, Kris	Pit.	10	12	.455	3.85	32	32	2	1	0	0	217.2	206	936	104	93	24	7	6	10	86	5	184	5	0

BATTING LEADERS

Games
162 Luis Gonzalez, Ari.
162 Shawn Green, L.A.
162 Neifi Perez, Col.
161 Jeromy Burnitz, Mil.
161 Andruw Jones, Atl.
161 Preston Wilson, Fla.

At-bats
656 Andruw Jones, Atl.
651 Neifi Perez, Col.
637 Doug Glanville, Phi.
618 Luis Gonzalez, Ari.
617 Mark Grudzielanek, L.A.
617 Tony Womack, Ari.

Runs scored
152 Jeff Bagwell, Hou.
138 Todd Helton, Col.
129 Barry Bonds, S.F.
129 Jim Edmonds, St.L.
122 Andruw Jones, Atl.

Hits
216 Todd Helton, Col.
200 Jose Vidro, Mon.
199 Andruw Jones, Atl.
197 V. Guerrero, Mon.
196 Jeff Kent, S.F.

RBIs
147 Todd Helton, Col.
138 Sammy Sosa, Chi.
132 Jeff Bagwell, Hou.
125 Jeff Kent, S.F.
123 V. Guerrero, Mon.
123 Brian Giles, Pit.

Total bases
405 Todd Helton, Col.
383 Sammy Sosa, Chi.
379 V. Guerrero, Mon.
363 Jeff Bagwell, Hou.
355 Richard Hidalgo, Hou.
355 Andruw Jones, Atl.

Doubles
59 Todd Helton, Col.
53 Jeff Cirillo, Col.
51 Jose Vidro, Mon.
47 Luis Gonzalez, Ari.
44 Shawn Green, L.A.

Triples
14 Tony Womack, Ari.
11 Neifi Perez, Col.
11 V. Guerrero, Mon.
10 Bobby Abreu, Phi.
9 Ron Belliard, Mil.
9 T. Goodwin, Col.-L.A.

Home runs
50 Sammy Sosa, Chi.
49 Barry Bonds, S.F.
47 Jeff Bagwell, Hou.
44 V. Guerrero, Mon.
44 Richard Hidalgo, Hou.

Walks
117 Barry Bonds, S.F.
114 Brian S. Giles, Pit.
107 Jeff Bagwell, Hou.
103 Todd Helton, Col.
103 Jim Edmonds, St.L.

On-base percentage
.463 Todd Helton, Col.
.440 Barry Bonds, S.F.
.438 Gary Sheffield, L.A.
.432 Brian S. Giles, Pit.
.425 Edgardo Alfonzo, N.Y.

Slugging percentage
.698 Todd Helton, Col.
.688 Barry Bonds, S.F.
.664 V. Guerrero, Mon.
.643 Gary Sheffield, L.A.
.636 Richard Hidalgo, Hou.

Stolen bases
62 Luis Castillo, Fla.
55 T. Goodwin, Col.-L.A.
54 Eric Young, Chi.
45 Tony Womack, Ari.
40 Rafael Furcal, Atl.

Caught stealing
22 Luis Castillo, Fla.
14 Rafael Furcal, Atl.
14 Preston Wilson, Fla.
14 Eric Owens, S.D.
13 Edgar Renteria, St.L.
13 Peter Bergeron, Mon.

Sacrifice bunts
16 Ricky Gutierrez, Chi.
14 Peter Bergeron, Mon.
14 Tom Glavine, Atl.
14 Kevin Brown, L.A.
14 Kevin Millwood, Atl.
14 Rick Reed, N.Y.

Sacrifice flies
14 J.T. Snow, S.F.
12 Luis Gonzalez, Ari.
12 Jeff Cirillo, Col.
12 Eric Karros, L.A.
11 Neifi Perez, Col.
11 Mike Lowell, Fla.

Strikeouts
187 Preston Wilson, Fla.
168 Sammy Sosa, Chi.
167 Jim Edmonds, St.L.
148 Ray Lankford, St.L.
139 Pat Burrell, Phi.

Intentional walks
23 V. Guerrero, Mon.
22 Barry Bonds, S.F.
22 Todd Helton, Col.
19 Sammy Sosa, Chi.
17 Ken Griffey, Cin.

PITCHING LEADERS

Wins
21 Tom Glavine, Atl.
20 Darryl Kile, St.L
19 Randy Johnson, Ari.
19 Greg Maddux, Atl.
18 Chan Ho Park, L.A.

Losses
19 Omar Daal, Ari.-Phi.
17 Matt Clement, S.D.
17 Steve Parris, Cin.
16 Chris Holt, Hou.
16 Jose Lima, Hou.

Games
83 Steve Kline, Mon.
79 Scott Sullivan, Cin.
78 Mike Myers, Col.
77 Turk Wendell, N.Y.
76 Armando Benitez, N.Y.
76 Felix Rodriguez, S.F.

Games started
35 Tom Glavine, Atl.
35 Randy Johnson, Ari.
35 Jon Lieber, Chi.
35 Greg Maddux, Atl.
35 Kevin Millwood, Atl.

Games finished
68 Armando Benitez, N.Y.
63 Robb Nen, S.F.
63 Mike Williams, Pit.
62 Antonio Alfonseca, Fla.
61 Dave Veres, St.L

Complete games
8 Randy Johnson, Ari.
8 Curt Schilling, Phi.-Ari.
6 Jon Lieber, Chi.
6 Greg Maddux, Atl.
5 Kevin Brown, L.A.
5 Livan Hernandez, S.F.
5 Darryl Kile, St.L

Innings pitched
251.0 Jon Lieber, Chi.
249.1 Greg Maddux, Atl.
248.2 Randy Johnson, Ari.
241.0 Tom Glavine, Atl.
240.0 Livan Hernandez, S.F.

Shutouts
3 Randy Johnson, Ari.
3 Greg Maddux, Atl.
2 Shawn Estes, S.F.
2 Tom Glavine, Atl.
2 Livan Hernandez, S.F.
2 Jesus Sanchez, Fla.
2 Curt Schilling, Phi.-Ari.
2 G. Stephenson, St.L

Hits allowed
254 Livan Hernandez, S.F.
251 Jose Lima, Hou.
248 Jon Lieber, Chi.
247 Chris Holt, Hou.
247 Javier Vazquez, Mon.

Home runs allowed
48 Jose Lima, Hou.
38 Brian Anderson, Ari.
36 Jon Lieber, Chi.
35 Kevin Tapani, Chi.
33 Darryl Kile, St.L

Runs allowed
152 Jose Lima, Hou.
131 Matt Clement, S.D.
131 Chris Holt, Hou.
130 Jon Lieber, Chi.
128 Omar Daal, Ari.-Phi.
128 Jimmy Haynes, Mil.
128 D. Hermanson, Mon.

Earned runs allowed
145 Jose Lima, Hou.
123 Chris Holt, Hou.
123 Jon Lieber, Chi.
118 Jimmy Haynes, Mil.
117 Matt Clement, S.D.

Batting average yielded
.213 Kevin Brown, L.A.
.214 Chan Ho Park, L.A.
.219 Rick Ankiel, St.L
.224 Randy Johnson, Ari.
.228 Al Leiter, N.Y.

Walks
125 Matt Clement, S.D.
124 Chan Ho Park, L.A.
112 Russ Ortiz, S.F.
108 Shawn Estes, S.F.
100 Jimmy Haynes, Mil.

Strikeouts
347 Randy Johnson, Ari.
217 Chan Ho Park, L.A.
216 Kevin Brown, L.A.
209 Ryan Dempster, Fla.
200 Al Leiter, N.Y.

Hit batsmen
18 Jamey Wright, Mil.
16 Matt Clement, S.D.
15 Pedro Astacio, Col.
13 Darryl Kile, St.L
12 Rolando Arrojo, Col.
12 Darren Dreifort, L.A.
12 Chan Ho Park, L.A.

Wild pitches
23 Matt Clement, S.D.
21 Scott Williamson, Cin.
17 Darren Dreifort, L.A.
13 Chan Ho Park, L.A.
12 Rick Ankiel, St.L

Saves
45 Antonio Alfonseca, Fla.
43 Trevor Hoffman, S.D.
41 Armando Benitez, N.Y.
41 Robb Nen, S.F.
30 Danny Graves, Cin.

1999 BBWAA AWARDS VOTING

AMERICAN LEAGUE MVP

Player, Team	1	2	3	4	5	6	7	8	9	10	Pts.
Jason Giambi, Oakland	14	11	2	-	1	-	-	-	-	-	317
Frank Thomas, Chicago	10	7	7	2	2	-	-	-	-	-	285
Alex Rodriguez, Seattle	4	4	6	7	3	1	1	-	1	-	218
Carlos Delgado, Toronto	-	4	10	9	2	3	-	-	-	-	206
Pedro Martinez, Boston	-	1	1	6	1	5	1	2	-	3	103
Manny Ramirez, Cleveland	-	-	1	-	7	3	4	2	4	2	97
Edgar Martinez, Seattle	-	-	-	-	5	5	3	7	4	1	97
Darin Erstad, Anaheim	-	1	1	1	4	4	3	2	3	2	94
Nomar Garciaparra, Boston	-	-	-	2	-	4	3	3	4	3	66
Derek Jeter, New York	-	-	-	-	-	1	5	4	2	3	44
Mike Sweeney, Kansas City	-	-	-	-	1	-	1	2	5	7	33
Magglio Ordonez, Chicago	-	-	-	-	-	2	1	3	2	1	28
David Justice, Cleveland-New York	-	-	-	1	1	-	1	2	-	-	23
Bernie Williams, New York	-	-	-	-	1	-	3	1	1	-	23
Tim Hudson, Oakland	-	-	-	-	-	-	1	-	1	2	8
Miguel Tejada, Oakland	-	-	-	-	-	-	1	-	-	1	5
Travis Fryman, Cleveland	-	-	-	-	-	-	-	-	1	-	2
David Wells, Toronto	-	-	-	-	-	-	-	-	-	2	2
Johnny Damon, Kansas City	-	-	-	-	-	-	-	-	-	1	1

14 points awarded for a first-place vote, 9 for a second, 8 for a third, 7 for a fourth, etc.

NATIONAL LEAGUE MVP

Player, Team	1	2	3	4	5	6	7	8	9	10	Pts.
Jeff Kent, San Francisco	22	5	4	1	-	-	-	-	-	-	392
Barry Bonds, San Francisco	6	8	8	6	1	1	1	-	1	-	279
Mike Piazza, New York	3	10	11	5	1	2	-	-	-	-	271
Jim Edmonds, St. Louis	-	6	7	5	9	1	-	-	2	-	208
Todd Helton, Colorado	1	3	1	12	5	4	2	2	-	1	198
Vladimir Guerrero, Montreal	-	-	-	1	4	7	7	2	7	3	117
Jeff Bagwell, Houston	-	-	-	-	1	6	8	8	4	2	102
Andruw Jones, Atlanta	-	-	-	1	8	3	-	5	4	2	95
Sammy Sosa, Chicago	-	-	-	1	1	3	3	5	5	6	71
Gary Sheffield, Los Angeles	-	-	-	-	-	2	8	6	4	3	71
Chipper Jones, Atlanta	-	-	1	-	1	-	-	1	2	2	23
Greg Maddux, Atlanta	-	-	-	-	-	2	-	-	1	-	12
Robb Nen, San Francisco	-	-	-	-	-	-	1	2	-	2	12
Tom Glavine, Atlanta	-	-	-	-	-	-	1	-	1	2	8
Ellis Burks, San Francisco	-	-	-	-	1	-	-	-	-	-	6
Edgardo Alfonzo, New York	-	-	-	-	-	1	-	-	-	1	6
Randy Johnson, Arizona	-	-	-	-	-	-	-	1	-	2	5
Darryl Kile, St. Louis	-	-	-	-	-	-	1	-	-	-	4
Brian Giles, Pittsburgh	-	-	-	-	-	-	-	-	-	3	3
Moises Alou, Houston	-	-	-	-	-	-	-	-	1	-	2
Richard Hidalgo, Houston	-	-	-	-	-	-	-	-	-	2	2
Antonio Alfonseca, Florida	-	-	-	-	-	-	-	-	-	1	1

14 points awarded for a first-place vote, 9 for a second, 8 for a third, 7 for a fourth, etc.

A.L. CY YOUNG

Player, Team	1	2	3	Pts.
Pedro Martinez, Boston	28	-	-	140
Tim Hudson, Oakland	-	16	6	54
David Wells, Toronto	-	12	10	46
Andy Pettitte, New York	-	-	7	7
Todd Jones, Detroit	-	-	3	3
Roger Clemens, New York	-	-	1	1
Mike Mussina, Baltimore	-	-	1	1

5 points awarded for a first-place vote, 3 for a second, 1 for a third.

A.L. ROOKIE OF THE YEAR

Player, Team	1	2	3	Pts.
Kazuhiro Sasaki, Seattle	17	5	4	104
Terrence Long, Oakland	7	15	3	83
Mark Quinn, Kansas City	4	8	12	56
Bengie Molina, Anaheim	-	-	3	3
Kelly Wunsch, Chicago	-	-	2	2
Steve Cox, Tampa Bay	-	-	1	1
Adam Kennedy, Anaheim	-	-	1	1
Mark Redman, Minnesota	-	-	1	1
Barry Zito, Oakland	-	-	1	1

5 points awarded for a first-place vote, 3 for a second, 1 for a third.

A.L. MANAGER OF THE YEAR

Manager, Team	1	2	3	Pts.
Jerry Manuel, Chicago	25	3	-	134
Art Howe, Oakland	2	20	4	74
Lou Piniella, Seattle	1	3	14	28
Mike Scioscia, Anaheim	-	1	5	8
Joe Torre, New York	-	1	2	5
Phil Garner, Detroit	-	-	2	2
Jimy Williams, Boston	-	-	1	1

5 points awarded for a first-place vote, 3 for a second, 1 for a third.

Oakland first baseman Jason Giambi hit 43 homers in his MVP season.

Shortstop Rafael Furcal was a rookie godsend for the Braves.

N.L. CY YOUNG

Player, Team	1	2	3	Pts.
Randy Johnson, Arizona	22	7	2	133
Tom Glavine, Atlanta	4	12	8	64
Greg Maddux, Atlanta	3	10	14	59
Robb Nen, San Francisco	2	2	4	20
Darryl Kile, St. Louis	1	-	3	8
Kevin Brown, Los Angeles	-	1	1	4

5 points awarded for a first-place vote, 3 for a second, 1 for a third.

N.L. ROOKIE OF THE YEAR

Player, Team	1	2	3	Pts.
Rafael Furcal, Atlanta	25	6	1	144
Rick Ankiel, St. Louis	6	17	6	87
Jay Payton, New York	1	7	11	37
Pat Burrell, Philadelphia	-	1	7	10
Mitch Meluskey, Houston	-	1	4	7
Lance Berkman, Houston	-	-	1	1
Juan Pierre, Colorado	-	-	1	1
Chuck Smith, Florida	-	-	1	1

5 points awarded for a first-place vote, 3 for a second, 1 for a third.

N.L. MANAGER OF THE YEAR

Manager, Team	1	2	3	Pts.
Dusty Baker, San Francisco	30	1	1	154
Tony La Russa, St. Louis	1	16	6	59
Bobby Cox, Atlanta	1	8	12	41
Bobby Valentine, New York	-	4	4	16
John Boles, Florida	-	3	6	15
Buddy Bell, Colorado	-	-	2	2
Felipe Alou, Montreal	-	-	1	1

5 points awarded for a first-place vote, 3 for a second, 1 for a third.

MISCELLANEOUS AWARDS

GOLD GLOVE WINNERS

First basemen	PO	A	E	Pct.
A.L.: John Olerud, Mariners	1271	132	5	.996
N.L.: J.T. Snow, Giants	1197	91	6	.995
Second basemen				
A.L.: Roberto Alomar, Indians	293	437	15	.980
N.L.: Pokey Reese, Reds	289	393	14	.980
Shortstops				
A.L.: Omar Vizquel, Indians	231	414	3	.995
N.L.: Neifi Perez, Rockies	288	523	18	.978
Third basemen				
A.L.: Travis Fryman, Indians	83	276	8	.978
N.L.: Scott Rolen, Phillies	89	245	10	.971
Outfielders				
A.L.: Jermaine Dye, Royals	277	11	7	.976
A.L.: Darin Erstad, Angels	355	9	3	.992
A.L.: Bernie Williams, Yankees	353	2	0	1.000
N.L.: Jim Edmonds, Cardinals	392	14	4	.990
N.L.: Steve Finley, Diamondbacks	342	10	3	.992
N.L.: Andruw Jones, Braves	438	9	2	.996
Catchers				
A.L.: Ivan Rodriguez, Rangers	507	34	2	.996
N.L.: Mike Matheny, Cardinals	815	76	5	.994
Pitchers				
A.L.: Kenny Rogers, Rangers	18	46	2	
N.L.: Greg Maddux, Braves	25	69	2	.979

Note: Voting by Major League players and managers is conducted by The Sporting News.

SILVER SLUGGERS

First basemen	Avg.	H	HR	RBI
A.L.: Carlos Delgado, Blue Jays	344	196	41	137
N.L.: Todd Helton, Rockies	372	216	42	147
Second basemen				
A.L.: Roberto Alomar, Indians	310	189	19	89
N.L.: Jeff Kent, Giants	334	196	33	125
Shortstops				
A.L.: Alex Rodriguez, Mariners	316	175	41	132
N.L.: Edgar Renteria, Cardinals	278	156	16	76
Third basemen				
A.L.: Troy Glaus, Angels	.284	160	47	102
N.L. Chipper Jones, Braves	.311	180	36	111
Outfielders				
A.L.: Darin Erstad, Angels	.355	240	25	100
A.L.: Manny Ramirez, Indians	.351	154	38	122
A.L.: Magglio Ordonez, White Sox	315	185	32	126
N.L.: Sammy Sosa, Cubs	.320	193	50	138
N.L.: Barry Bonds, Giants	.306	147	49	106
N.L.: Vladimir Guerrero, Expos	345	197	44	123
Catchers				
A.L.: Jorge Posada, Yankees	.287	145	28	86
N.L.: Mike Piazza, Mets	.324	156	38	113
Pitcher				
N.L.: Mike Hampton, Mets	.274	20	0	8
Designated Hitter				
A.L.: Frank Thomas, White Sox	328	191	43	143

Note: Voting by Major League players and managers is conducted by The Sporting News.

PLAYERS OF THE WEEK

March 29-April 9		Position
A.L.:	Frank Thomas, White Sox	designated hitter
N.L.:	Vladimir Guerrero, Expos	outfielder
	Randy Johnson, Diamondbacks	pitcher
April 10-16		
A.L.:	Alex Rodriguez, Mariners	shortstop
N.L.:	Mike Piazza, Mets	catcher
April 17-23		
A.L.:	Chris Singleton, White Sox	outfielder
	Carlos Delgado, Blue Jays	first base
N.L.:	Derek Bell, Mets	outfielder

Darin Erstad, a 240-hit machine for the Anaheim Angels, doubled his pleasure as a Gold Glove and Silver Slugger winner.

April 24-30		
A.L.:	Jermaine Dye, Royals	outfielder
N.L.:	Tom Glavine, Braves	pitcher
May 1-7		
A.L.:	Jose Cruz, Blue Jays	outfielder
N.L.:	Brian Giles, Pirates	outfielder
May 8-14		
A.L.:	Mo Vaughn, Angels	first base
N.L.:	Todd Helton, Rockies	first base
May 15-21		
A.L.:	Edgar Martinez, Mariners	designated hitter
N.L.:	Phil Nevin, Padres	third base
May 22-28		
A.L.:	Darin Erstad, Angels	outfielder
N.L.:	Barry Bonds, Giants	outfielder
May 29-June 4		
A.L.:	Nomar Garciaparra, Red Sox	shortstop
N.L.:	Dante Bichette, Reds	outfielder
June 5-11		
A.L.:	Carlos Delgado, Blue Jays	first base
N.L.:	Luis Gonzalez, Diamondbacks	outfielder
June 12-18		
A.L.:	Bobby Higginson, Tigers	outfielder
N.L.:	Gary Sheffield, Dodgers	outfielder
June 19-25		
A.L.:	Tony Clark, Tigers	first base
N.L.:	Brian Tollberg, Padres	pitcher
June 26-July 2		
A.L.:	Magglio Ordonez, White Sox	outfielder
N.L.:	Jeff Cirillo, Rockies	third base
July 3-9		
A.L.:	Darin Erstad, Angels	outfielder
	Carlos Delgado, Blue Jays	first base
N.L.:	Jon Lieber, Cubs	pitcher
July 10-16		
A.L.:	Frank Thomas, White Sox	designated hitter
N.L.:	Gary Sheffield, Dodgers	outfielder
July 17-23		
A.L.:	Pedro Martinez, Red Sox	pitcher
	Manny Ramirez, Indians	outfielder
N.L.:	Todd Helton, Rockies	first base
	Ryan Klesko, Padres	first base
July 24-30		
A.L.:	Gabe Kapler, Rangers	outfielder
N.L.:	Luis Gonzalez, Diamondbacks	outfielder
	Jeffrey Hammonds, Rockies	outfielder
July 31-August 6		
A.L.:	Tim Salmon, Angels	outfielder
N.L.:	Will Clark, Cardinals	first base
	Scott Elarton, Astros	pitcher
August 7-13		
A.L.:	Albie Lopez, Devil Rays	pitcher
N.L.:	Jeff Bagwell, Astros	first base
August 14-20		
A.L.:	Travis Fryman, Indians	third baseman
N.L.:	Brian Giles, Pirates	outfielder
	Todd Helton, Rockies	first base
August 21-27		
A.L.:	Tim Salmon, Angels	outfielder
N.L.:	Adrian Beltre, Dodgers	third base
August 28-September 3		
A.L.:	Kenny Lofton, Indians	outfielder
N.L.:	Mike Lowell, Marlins	third base
September 4-10		
A.L.:	Carlos Lee, White Sox	outfielder
	Barry Zito, Athletics	pitcher
N.L.:	Richard Hidalgo, Astros	outfielder
	Julio Lugo, Astros	infielder
September 11-17		
A.L.:	Manny Ramirez, Indians	outfielder
	Jason Giambi, Athletics	first base
N.L.:	Alex Ochoa, Reds	outfielder
September 18-24		
A.L.:	Bartolo Colon, Indians	pitcher
N.L.:	Chan Ho Park, Dodgers	pitcher
September 25-October 3		
A.L.	Bobby Higginson, Tigers	outfielder
N.L.:	Cliff Floyd, Marlins	outfielder

PLAYERS OF THE MONTH

April	Avg.	R	HR	RBI
A.L.: Jermaine Dye, Royals	.388	22	11	28
N.L.: Vladimir Guerrero, Expos	.410	16	8	27
May				
A.L.: Edgar Martinez, Mariners	.441	24	10	32
N.L.: Todd Helton, Rockies	.512	32	11	26
June				
A.L.: Albert Belle, Orioles	.364	18	12	37
N.L.: Jeff Kent, Giants	.424	20	8	34
July				
A.L.: Johnny Damon, Royals	.436	25	2	20
N.L.: Sammy Sosa, Cubs	.337	19	11	24
August				
A.L.: Glenallen Hill, Yankees	.411	12	10	19
N.L.: Todd Helton, Rockies	.476	22	7	32
September				
A.L.: Jason Giambi, Athletics	.400	26	14	32
N.L.: Richard Hidalgo, Astros	.476	36	11	31

PITCHER OF THE MONTH

April	W	L	Pct.	ERA
A.L.: Pedro Martinez, Red Sox	5	0	1.000	1.27
N.L.: Randy Johnson, Diamondbacks	6	0	1.000	0.91
May				
A.L.: James Baldwin, White Sox	4	1	.800	3.07
N.L.: Garrett Stephenson, Cardinals	5	0	1.000	1.42
June				
A.L.: Cal Eldred, White Sox	5	0	1.000	3.41
N.L.: Al Leiter, Mets	4	0	1.000	2.38
July				
A.L.: Roger Clemens, Yankees	5	0	1.000	1.91
N.L.: Jeff D'Amico, Brewers	5	0	1.000	0.76
August				
A.L.: Steve Sparks, Tigers	5	0	1.000	1.69
N.L.: Russ Ortiz, Giants	6	0	1.000	1.12
September				
A.L.: Tim Hudson, Athletics	5	0	1.000	1.69
N.L.: Greg Maddux, Braves	5	1	.833	2.03

BATTERS

BATTING AVERAGE
(minimum 3,000 at-bats)

1. Tony Gwynn .344
2. Mike Piazza .329
3. Edgar Martinez .322
4. Frank Thomas .320
5. Paul Molitor .313
   Larry Walker .313
7. Kirby Puckett .312
8. Mark Grace .310
   Kenny Lofton .310
10. Roberto Alomar .308
11. Manny Ramirez .307
    Hal Morris .307
13. Julio Franco .304
    Wade Boggs .304
    Jeff Bagwell .304
    Bernie Williams .304
17. Dante Bichette .303
    Barry Larkin .303
19. Barry Bonds .302
    Will Clark .302
    Ken Griffey Jr. .302

GAMES

1. Rafael Palmeiro 1,526
2. Craig Biggio 1,515
3. Mark Grace 1,491
4. Jay Bell 1,487
5. Cal Ripken 1,475
6. Fred McGriff 1,472
7. Steve Finley 1,457
8. Todd Zeile 1,445
9. Barry Bonds 1,434
10. Roberto Alomar 1,421
11. Paul O'Neill 1,420
12. Marquis Grissom 1,409
13. Ken Griffey Jr. 1,408
14. Robin Ventura 1,399
15. John Olerud 1,390

AT-BATS

1. Rafael Palmeiro 5,848
2. Craig Biggio 5,823
3. Cal Ripken 5,710
4. Mark Grace 5,650
5. Jay Bell 5,619
6. Steve Finley 5,571
7. Marquis Grissom 5,529
8. Roberto Alomar 5,443
9. Fred McGriff 5,399
10. Ken Griffey Jr. 5,377
11. Todd Zeile 5,262
12. Dante Bichette 5,231
13. Matt Williams 5,179
14. Travis Fryman 5,176
15. Paul O'Neill 5,155

RUNS

1. Barry Bonds 1,091
2. Craig Biggio 1,042
3. Ken Griffey Jr. 1,002
4. Frank Thomas 968
5. Rafael Palmeiro 965
6. Roberto Alomar 951
7. Chuck Knoblauch 950
8. Tony Phillips 946
9. Rickey Henderson 932
10. Jeff Bagwell 921
11. Jay Bell 890
12. Larry Walker 882
13. Albert Belle 881
14. Steve Finley 870
15. Edgar Martinez 854

HITS

1. Mark Grace 1,754
2. Rafael Palmeiro 1,747
3. Craig Biggio 1,728
4. Tony Gwynn 1,713
5. Roberto Alomar 1,678
6. Ken Griffey Jr. 1,622
7. Cal Ripken 1,589
8. Dante Bichette 1,584
9. Fred McGriff 1,573
10. Paul Molitor 1,568
11. Frank Thomas 1,564
12. Chuck Knoblauch 1,533
13. Steve Finley 1,532
14. Marquis Grissom 1,531
15. Jay Bell 1,529

DOUBLES

1. Mark Grace 364
2. Craig Biggio 362
3. Edgar Martinez 358
4. Albert Belle 344
5. Rafael Palmeiro 343
6. Dante Bichette 330
   Tony Gwynn 330
8. Paul O'Neill 328
9. John Olerud 322
10. Roberto Alomar 321
11. Thomas, Frank 317
12. Jeff Bagwell 314
    Larry Walker 314
14. Jay Bell 309
15. Cal Ripken 305

TRIPLES

1. Lance Johnson 113
2. Steve Finley 83
3. Delino DeShields 63
4. Jose Offerman 62
5. Kenny Lofton 60
6. Chuck Knoblauch 59
7. Brady Anderson 58
   Brian McRae 58
9. Brett Butler 57
10. Jay Bell 55
11. Paul Molitor 54
12. Roberto Alomar 51
    Barry Larkin 51
14. Mickey Morandini 50
15. Tony Fernandez 48

HOME RUNS

1. Mark McGwire 405
2. Ken Griffey Jr. 382
3. Barry Bonds 361
4. Albert Belle 351
5. Juan Gonzalez 339
6. Sammy Sosa 332
7. Rafael Palmeiro 328
8. Jose Canseco 303
9. Frank Thomas 301
10. Fred McGriff 300
    Matt Williams 300
12. Cecil Fielder 288
13. Greg Vaughn 287
14. Jeff Bagwell 263
    Mo Vaughn 263
16. Larry Walker 262
17. Jay Buhner 260
18. Andres Galarraga 255
19. Joe Carter 245

RUNS BATTED IN

1. Albert Belle 1,099
2. Ken Griffey Jr. 1,091
3. Barry Bonds 1,076
4. Juan Gonzalez 1,068
   Rafael Palmeiro 1,068
6. Frank Thomas 1,040
7. Dante Bichette 979
8. Fred McGriff 975
9. Jeff Bagwell 961
10. Matt Williams 960
11. Mark McGwire 956
12. Sammy Sosa 928
13. Cecil Fielder 924
14. Paul O'Neill 923
15. Joe Carter 914

WALKS

1. Barry Bonds 1,146
2. Frank Thomas 1,076
3. Tony Phillips 977
4. Rickey Henderson 976
5. Mark McGwire 951
6. Jeff Bagwell 885
7. Edgar Martinez 854
8. John Olerud 820
9. Fred McGriff 787
10. Mickey Tettleton 740
11. Robin Ventura 734
12. Craig Biggio 730
13. Brady Anderson 724
14. Gary Sheffield 723
15. Chili Davis 716

STRIKEOUTS

1. Sammy Sosa 1,322
2. Jose Canseco 1,205
3. Cecil Fielder 1,172
4. Jay Buhner 1,145
5. Ray Lankford 1,141
6. Greg Vaughn 1,137
7. Travis Fryman 1,113
8. Jay Bell 1,095
9. Fred McGriff 1,085
10. Dean Palmer 1,082
11. Mo Vaughn 1,081
12. Andres Galarraga 1,080
13. Devon White 1,042
14. Mark McGwire 1,040
15. Tony Phillips 1,009

STOLEN BASES

1. Otis Nixon 478
2. Rickey Henderson 463
3. Kenny Lofton 433
4. Delino DeShields 393
5. Marquis Grissom 381
6. Barry Bonds 343
7. Chuck Knoblauch 335
8. Craig Biggio 319
9. Roberto Alomar 311
10. Lance Johnson 297
11. Eric Young 292
12. Vince Coleman 280
13. Barry Larkin 266
14. Brady Anderson 257
15. Tom Goodwin 252

PITCHERS

EARNED RUN AVERAGE
(minimum 1,000 innings pitched)

1. Greg Maddux 2.58
2. Jose Rijo 2.74
3. Pedro J. Martinez 2.83
4. Roger Clemens 3.02
5. Randy Johnson 3.14
6. Tom Glavine 3.21
   David Cone 3.21
8. Kevin Brown 3.25
9. Curt Schilling 3.31
10. John Smoltz 3.32
11. Dennis Martinez 3.37
12. Ismael Valdes 3.38
13. Bret Saberhagen 3.43
14. Ramon J. Martinez 3.45
15. Kevin Appier 3.47
16. Mike Mussina 3.50
    Mike Hampton 3.50
18. Bill Swift 3.53
19. Zane Smith 3.55
20. Jimmy Key 3.62

WINS

1. Greg Maddux 176
2. Tom Glavine 164
3. Roger Clemens 152
4. Randy Johnson 150
5. Kevin Brown 143
   John Smoltz 143
7. David Cone 141
8. Mike Mussina 136
9. Chuck Finley 135
10. Scott Erickson 130
11. David Wells 127
12. Andy Benes 125
13. Kevin Tapani 124
14. Charles Nagy 121
15. Kevin Appier 120
16. John Burkett 119
    Jack McDowell 119

LOSSES

1. Andy Benes 116
2. Tim Belcher 115
3. Bobby Witt 113
4. Jaime Navarro 112
5. Tom Candiotti 110
6. Scott Erickson 108
   Chuck Finley 108
8. John Burkett 101
   Mike Morgan 101
10. Terry Mulholland 100
11. Kevin Brown 98
    Todd Stottlemyre 98
13. Kevin Tapani 97
14. Jim Abbott 96
15. Doug Drabek 95
    Darryl Kile 95
    John Smoltz 95
18. Kevin Appier 90
19. Roger Clemens 89
    Bob Tewksbury 89

GAMES

1. Paul Assenmacher 644
   Mike Jackson 644
3. Doug Jones 618
4. Dan Plesac 612
5. Jesse Orosco 594
6. Mike Stanton 591
7. Jeff Montgomery 578
8. Eric Plunk 557
9. Rick Aguilera 553
10. Scott Radinsky 552
11. Chuck McElroy 551
12. Randy Myers 543
13. Rod Beck 540
14. Dennis Eckersley 530
15. Mel Rojas 525
    John Wetteland 525

GAMES STARTED

1. Greg Maddux 331
2. Tom Glavine 327
3. Chuck Finley 316
4. John Smoltz 315
5. Andy Benes 314
   Kevin Brown 314
7. John Burkett 308
8. Scott Erickson 306
9. Roger Clemens 305
10. Tim Belcher 302
11. Randy Johnson 290
    Kevin Tapani 290
13. David Cone 287
14. Jaime Navarro 285
15. Todd Stottlemyre 283

COMPLETE GAMES

1. Greg Maddux 75
2. Randy Johnson 65
3. Jack McDowell 61
4. Kevin Brown 58
5. Roger Clemens 57
   Curt Schilling 57
7. Scott Erickson 47
8. Chuck Finley 46
9. John Smoltz 42
10. Doug Drabek 41
    Terry Mulholland 41
12. David Cone 40
13. Mike Mussina 39
14. Tom Glavine 38
15. Dennis Martinez 36
    David Wells 36

SHUTOUTS

1. Randy Johnson 25
2. Roger Clemens 24
3. Greg Maddux 23
4. Ramon J. Martinez 18
5. Kevin Brown 16
   David Cone 16
   Scott Erickson 16
8. Doug Drabek 14
   Tom Glavine 14
   Dennis Martinez 14
   Mike Mussina 14
   John Smoltz 14
13. Chuck Finley 13
    Jack McDowell 13
    Curt Schilling 13

SAVES

1. John Wetteland 295
2. Dennis Eckersley 293
3. Randy Myers 291
4. Jeff Montgomery 285
5. Rick Aguilera 282
6. John Franco 268
7. Rod Beck 260
8. Lee Smith 244
9. Roberto Hernandez 234
10. Trevor Hoffman 228
11. Doug Jones 223
12. Gregg Olson 190
13. Tom Henke 189
14. Robb Nen 185
15. Mike Henneman 156

INNINGS PITCHED

1. Greg Maddux 2,394.2
2. Tom Glavine 2,228.0
3. Kevin Brown 2,211.1
4. Roger Clemens 2,178.2
5. Chuck Finley 2,144.0
6. John Smoltz 2,143.1
7. Andy Benes 2,069.1
8. Randy Johnson 2,064.1
9. David Cone 2,018.0
10. Scott Erickson 2,014.2
11. Tim Belcher 1,959.1
12. John Burkett 1,935.0
13. Jaime Navarro 1,913.1
14. David Wells 1,897.0
15. Kevin Appier 1,868.2

WALKS

1. Randy Johnson 910
2. Chuck Finley 888
3. Bobby Witt 846
4. David Cone 774
5. Darryl Kile 767
6. Tom Glavine 764
7. Roger Clemens 731
8. Tom Gordon 714
9. Wilson Alvarez 706
10. Tim Belcher 700
11. Andy Benes 698
12. Scott Erickson 697
13. Ken Hill 683
    Todd Stottlemyre 683
15. John Smoltz 669

STRIKEOUTS

1. Randy Johnson 2,538
2. Roger Clemens 2,101
3. David Cone 1,928
4. John Smoltz 1,893
5. Chuck Finley 1,784
6. Greg Maddux 1,764
7. Andy Benes 1,655
8. Kevin Brown 1,581
9. Curt Schilling 1,561
10. Pedro J. Martinez 1,534
11. Kevin Appier 1,494
12. Tom Glavine 1,465
13. Todd Stottlemyre 1,369
14. Mike Mussina 1,325
15. Bobby Witt 1,270
16. Tom Gordon 1,260
17. Darryl Kile 1,247
18. David Wells 1,244
19. Juan Guzman 1,240
20. John Burkett 1,233

ANAHEIM ANGELS

DAY BY DAY

Date	Opp.	Res.	Score	(inn.*)	Hits	Opp. hits	Winning pitcher	Losing pitcher	Save	Record	Pos.	GB
4-3	N.Y.	L	2-3		10	6	Hernandez	Hill	Rivera	0-1	T2nd	1.0
4-4	N.Y.	L	3-5		10	9	Mendoza	Percival	Rivera	0-2	T3rd	2.0
4-5	N.Y.	W	12-6		12	13	Schoeneweis	Cone		1-2	4th	1.0
4-7	Bos.	W	7-3		9	6	Dickson	Schourek		2-2	T3rd	1.0
4-8	Bos.	W	7-5		13	7	Hill	Rose	Percival	3-2	T1st	...
4-9	Bos.	L	2-5		7	9	P. Martinez	Bottenfield		3-3	T3rd	1.0
4-10	Tor.	W	6-0		7	3	Schoeneweis	Carpenter		4-3	T2nd	0.5
4-11	Tor.	W	5-4		8	10	Ortiz	Escobar	Percival	5-3	1st	+0.5
4-12	Tor.	L	2-6		9	13	Borbon	Petkovsek		5-4	2nd	0.5
4-14	At Chi.	L	4-9		12	12	Sirotka	Hill		5-5	T2nd	1.0
4-15	At Chi.	W	3-1		7	7	Bottenfield	Wells	Percival	6-5	T2nd	1.0
4-16	At Chi.	W	3-1		13	3	Schoeneweis	Parque	Percival	7-5	2nd	1.0
4-17	At Tor.	L	1-7		8	10	Escobar	Ortiz		7-6	2nd	1.5
4-18	At Tor.	W	16-10		19	17	Dickson	Castillo		8-6	2nd	0.5
4-19	At Tor.	L	4-12		8	17	Wells	Hill		8-7	2nd	0.5
4-20	At Tor.	L	11-12		19	14	Halladay	Bottenfield	Koch	8-8	2nd	1.0
4-21	At T.B.	W	9-6		12	8	Petkovsek	Hernandez	Percival	9-8	2nd	1.0
4-22	At T.B.	L	9-11	(10)	10	12	Lopez	Mercker		9-9	2nd	2.0
4-23	At T.B.	L	0-1		4	5	Eiland	Dickson	Hernandez	9-10	2nd	3.0
4-24	Det.	W	10-4		14	13	Hill	Mlicki		10-10	2nd	2.0
4-25	Det.	L	2-4		8	10	Poole	Bottenfield	Jones	10-11	2nd	3.0
4-26	Det.	W	6-1		11	5	Schoeneweis	Nitkowski		11-11	2nd	2.0
4-27	T.B.	L	3-7		6	12	Gooden	Ortiz		11-12	2nd	2.5
4-28	T.B.	L	2-11		7	19	Yan	Dickson		11-13	2nd	2.5
4-29	T.B.	W	7-6	(13)	13	16	Levine	Sparks		12-13	2nd	2.5
4-30	T.B.	W	5-2		9	7	Bottenfield	Trachsel	Percival	13-13	2nd	1.5
5-2	At Bal.	L	6-7		11	9	Trombley	Percival		13-14	T2nd	2.5
5-3	At Bal.	W	6-5		9	8	Ortiz	Johnson	Percival	14-14	T2nd	1.5
5-4	At Bal.	W	8-5		11	9	Hill	Mussina	Hasegawa	15-14	2nd	1.0
5-5	At Sea.	W	6-5		11	11	Bottenfield	Sele	Percival	16-14	2nd	...
5-6	At Sea.	L	0-1		2	7	Sasaki	Holtz		16-15	2nd	1.0
5-7	At Sea.	L	2-8		7	7	Halama	Schoeneweis		16-16	2nd	2.0
5-8	Oak.	W	9-8		17	10	Petkovsek	Mathews	Percival	17-16	2nd	1.0
5-9	Oak.	L	2-5		9	9	Heredia	Hill	Isringhausen	17-17	2nd	2.0
5-10	Oak.	L	4-7		9	13	Isringhausen	Petkovsek		17-18	3rd	2.0
5-11	Tex.	W	3-2		10	8	Hasegawa	Rogers	Percival	18-18	3rd	1.0
5-12	Tex.	L	11-13		14	14	Davis	Schoeneweis	Wetteland	18-19	3rd	1.5
5-13	Tex.	L	5-6		7	9	Helling	Washburn	Wetteland	18-20	3rd	2.0
5-14	Tex.	W	7-6		8	8	Hasegawa	Cordero		19-20	3rd	1.5
5-16	Bal.	L	3-4		9	7	Erickson	Bottenfield	Timlin	19-21	4th	2.5
5-17	Bal.	W	8-7		11	12	Percival	Timlin		20-21	4th	2.5
5-19	K.C.	W	6-4		12	10	Washburn	Suppan	Percival	21-21	3rd	2.5
5-20	K.C.	W	9-8		11	12	Hasegawa	Reichert	Percival	22-21	3rd	1.5
5-21	K.C.	L	6-10		7	14	Santiago	Bottenfield		22-22	3rd	2.5
5-23	At Min.	W	7-4		12	7	Cooper	Mays	Percival	23-22	3rd	1.5
5-24	At Min.	W	6-5	(10)	18	7	Percival	Wells	Levine	24-22	3rd	0.5
5-25	At Min.	W	3-1		9	7	Schoeneweis	Radke	Percival	25-22	2nd	0.5
5-26	At K.C.	L	4-9		6	14	Fussell	Weaver	Bottalico	25-23	3rd	0.5
5-27	At K.C.	L	5-6	(10)	9	8	Reichert	Weaver		25-24	3rd	1.5
5-28	At K.C.	W	8-4		13	10	Cooper	Batista	Hasegawa	26-24	2nd	0.5
5-29	At Cle.	W	3-2	(10)	4	5	Hasegawa	Karsay	Percival	27-24	2nd	0.5
5-30	At Cle.	L	1-6		9	9	Burba	Schoeneweis		27-25	2nd	0.5
5-31	At Cle.	L	3-7		14	10	Finley	Etherton	Karsay	27-26	T3rd	0.5
6-2	L.A.	W	12-5		18	11	Bottenfield	Dreifort		28-26	T2nd	0.5
6-3	L.A.	L	3-8		12	9	Park	Cooper		28-27	4th	1.0
6-4	L.A.	W	8-7		9	11	Percival	Osuna		29-27	T3rd	0.5
6-5	S.F.	L	4-5	(11)	14	10	Fultz	Hasegawa		29-28	4th	1.5
6-6	S.F.	W	6-5		10	9	Percival	Nen		30-28	4th	1.5
6-7	S.F.	W	10-9		13	15	Hasegawa	Embree		31-28	3rd	1.0
6-9	At Ari.	L	1-4		5	8	Johnson	Cooper	Kim	31-29	3rd	2.0
6-10	At Ari.	W	10-3		13	7	Washburn	Daal		32-29	3rd	1.0
6-11	At Ari.	L	2-3		8	6	Plesac	Schoeneweis	Kim	32-30	3rd	2.0
6-13	At T.B.	W	5-3		10	7	Etherton	Rekar	Percival	33-30	3rd	2.0
6-14	At T.B.	L	2-3		7	8	Lopez	Percival		33-31	3rd	2.5
6-15	At T.B.	L	1-2		6	5	Trachsel	Hasegawa		33-32	3rd	3.0
6-16	At Bal.	L	3-4		9	7	Mussina	Schoeneweis	Timlin	33-33	3rd	4.0
6-17	At Bal.	W	8-3		9	10	Belcher	Johnson		34-33	3rd	4.0
6-18	At Bal.	W	8-6		14	7	Etherton	Erickson	Percival	35-33	3rd	4.0
6-20	K.C.	L	6-8		5	17	Santiago	Percival	Bottalico	35-34	3rd	5.5
6-21	K.C.	W	3-1		6	5	Washburn	Suzuki	Percival	36-34	3rd	5.5
6-22	K.C.	W	4-3		10	3	Belcher	Witasick	Petkovsek	37-34	3rd	5.0
6-23	Min.	W	8-3		11	8	Etherton	Ryan	Levine	38-34	3rd	5.0
6-24	Min.	L	5-11		11	16	Milton	Bottenfield		38-35	3rd	5.0
6-25	Min.	W	7-6	(11)	10	11	Hasegawa	Guardado		39-35	3rd	5.0
6-26	Min.	L	6-10		11	13	Radke	Washburn		39-36	3rd	5.5
6-27	At Sea.	L	3-5		5	8	Sele	Belcher	Sasaki	39-37	3rd	6.5
6-28	At Sea.	W	3-2		8	6	Hill	Moyer	Percival	40-37	3rd	5.5
6-29	At Sea.	L	2-7		7	8	Paniagua	Bottenfield		40-38	3rd	6.0
6-30	Oak.	W	7-0		12	3	Cooper	Mulder		41-38	3rd	5.0

HIGHLIGHTS

High point: A 10-3 stretch in July, including a three-game sweep of the Rockies, pushed the Angels' record to a season-best nine games over .500 (53-44). Starting pitching fueled the run, temporarily alleviating the burden on an overworked bullpen, and the Angels pulled to within four games of first-place Seattle.

Low point: Trailing the Mariners by four after games of August 29, the Angels lost six straight to Toronto, Chicago and Detroit, their longest skid of the season, and fell out of contention. A devastating 13-12 loss to the White Sox might have sealed their fate.

Turning point: Within a three-day period from August 5-7, the Angels lost starting pitchers Jarrod Washburn and Seth Etherton to season-ending injuries. The two youngsters had combined for a 12-3 record before the injuries and their performance was instrumental in the decision to trade veteran righthander Kent Bottenfield.

Most valuable player: Darin Erstad emerged as one of baseball's most exciting young players, amassing a major league-leading 240 hits, batting .355 and setting an all-time record for leadoff hitters with 100 RBIs. The left fielder also won a Gold Glove, hit 25 home runs and stole 28 bases in a breakthrough season after a .253 performance in 1999.

Most valuable pitcher: Japanese righthander Shigetoshi Hasegawa filled a variety of relief roles and excelled in all, going 10-6 with a 3.57 ERA and nine saves in 66 games. Hasegawa was untouchable from July 13-August 29, working 27[1]/[3] straight scoreless innings.

Most improved player: In his second full season, third baseman Troy Glaus led the A.L. with 47 home runs and set a club record with 85 extra-base hits. Glaus hit .284, 44 points higher than 1999, and avoided the prolonged slumps that plagued him in the past.

Most pleasant surprise: The emergence of rookie catcher Bengie Molina. He handled a diverse pitching staff, threw out 33 percent of basestealers and batted .281 with 14 homers, 20 doubles and 71 RBIs.

Key injuries: Shortstop Gary DiSarcina (torn rotator cuff) and pitchers Tim Belcher (elbow) and Jason Dickson (shoulder) missed most of the season. ... Ken Hill (rib cage, elbow) made only 16 starts before being released in August. ... Washburn (shoulder) and Etherton (shoulder) missed the final two months.

Notable: The Angels hit a franchise-record 236 home runs. Sixty-two percent (147) came with the bases empty. ... The Angels became the first team in A.L. history to have four players hit 30 or more homers. Glaus hit 47, Mo Vaughn 36, Garret Anderson 35 and Tim Salmon 34. ... The Angels bullpen ranked second behind Boston in ERA (4.16) and innings (552).

—MIKE DiGIOVANNA

MISCELLANEOUS

RECORDS

2000 regular-season record: 82-80 (3rd in A.L. West); 46-35 at home; 36-45 on road; 28-27 vs. East; 25-26 vs. Central; 29-27 vs. West; 21-25 vs. lefthanded starters; 61-55 vs. righthanded starters; 73-71 on grass; 9-9 on turf; 18-24 in daytime; 64-56 at night; 32-23 in one-run games; 9-7 in extra-inning games; 0-0 in doubleheaders.

Team record past five years: 391-418 (.483, ranks 10th in league in that span).

TEAM LEADERS

Batting average: Darin Erstad (.355).
At-bats: Darin Erstad (676).
Runs: Darin Erstad (121).
Hits: Darin Erstad (240).
Total Bases: Darin Erstad (366).
Doubles: Garret Anderson (40).
Triples: Adam Kennedy (11).
Home runs: Troy Glaus (47).
Runs batted in: Garret Anderson, Mo Vaughn (117).
Stolen bases: Darin Erstad (28).
Slugging percentage: Troy Glaus (.604).
On-base percentage: Darin Erstad (.409).
Wins: Shigetoshi Hasegawa (10).
Earned-run average: Scott Schoeneweis (5.45).
Complete games: Ramon Ortiz (2).
Shutouts: Brian Cooper, Scott Schoeneweis (1).
Saves: Troy Percival (32).
Innings pitched: Scott Schoeneweis (170.0).
Strikeouts: Scott Schoeneweis (78).

Date	Opp.	Res.	Score	(inn.*)	Hits	Opp. hits	Winning pitcher	Losing pitcher	Save	Record	Pos.	GB
7-1	Oak.	W	7-2		8	3	Washburn	Prieto		42-38	3rd	5.0
7-2	Oak.	L	3-10		8	12	Hudson	Belcher		42-39	3rd	6.0
7-3	Sea.	L	6-8		13	13	Moyer	Hill	Sasaki	42-40	3rd	7.0
7-4	Sea.	W	7-6		8	8	Petkovsek	Mesa	Percival	43-40	3rd	6.0
7-5	Sea.	L	4-6		10	11	Halama	Cooper	Sasaki	43-41	3rd	7.0
7-6	Sea.	W	5-1		5	8	Washburn	Abbott		44-41	3rd	6.0
7-7	Col.	W	12-4		13	7	Ortiz	Jarvis		45-41	3rd	5.0
7-8	Col.	W	6-2		11	9	Hill	Bohanon		46-41	3rd	5.0
7-9	Col.	W	10-4		13	10	Bottenfield	Yoshii		47-41	3rd	5.0
7-13	At L.A.	L	3-4	(10)	9	8	Osuna	Levine		47-42	3rd	5.0
7-14	At L.A.	W	5-3		11	3	Bottenfield	Brown	Percival	48-42	3rd	5.0
7-15	At L.A.	W	6-2		10	6	Etherton	Park		49-42	3rd	4.0
7-16	At S.D.	L	5-6	(10)	13	11	Wall	Levine		49-43	3rd	5.0
7-17	At S.D.	W	3-2		6	4	Cooper	Clement	Percival	50-43	3rd	4.0
7-18	At S.D.	W	3-2	(11)	7	8	Levine	Hoffman		51-43	3rd	4.0
7-19	Tex.	L	2-3		13	10	Rogers	Bottenfield	Wetteland	51-44	T2nd	5.0
7-20	Tex.	W	6-1		9	7	Etherton	Oliver	Hasegawa	52-44	3rd	4.0
7-21	At Oak.	W	12-3		16	8	Washburn	Hudson		53-44	2nd	4.0
7-22	At Oak.	L	3-10		5	18	Zito	Cooper		53-45	T2nd	5.0
7-23	At Oak.	L	0-5		6	11	Mulder	Hill		53-46	3rd	5.0
7-24	At Tex.	W	6-5	(12)	11	11	Hasegawa	Crabtree	Percival	54-46	3rd	5.0
7-25	At Tex.	L	6-9		10	10	Davis	Holtz	Wetteland	54-47	3rd	5.0
7-26	At Tex.	L	5-6		7	12	Wetteland	Levine		54-48	3rd	5.0
7-27	Chi.	L	5-6		9	18	Garland	Cooper	Foulke	54-49	3rd	5.0
7-28	Chi.	W	10-7		10	13	Holtz	Beirne	Percival	55-49	3rd	5.0
7-29	Chi.	W	6-5		11	9	Bottenfield	Barcelo	Percival	56-49	3rd	5.0
7-30	Chi.	L	7-11	(10)	12	18	Foulke	Levine		56-50	3rd	6.0
7-31	Det.	W	5-4		7	10	Petkovsek	Jones		57-50	3rd	5.0
8-1	Det.	L	3-6		8	10	Cruz	Cooper	Jones	57-51	3rd	6.0
8-2	Det.	L	3-5		9	9	Moehler	Hill	Jones	57-52	3rd	6.0
8-4	At Cle.	L	10-11		13	13	Wickman	Percival		57-53	3rd	6.0
8-5	At Cle.	L	3-6		6	16	Speier	Schoeneweis		57-54	3rd	7.0
8-6	At Cle.	L	2-5		7	10	Colon	Cooper	Wickman	57-55	3rd	8.0
8-7	Bos.	W	4-1		10	5	Washburn	Ohka	Hasegawa	58-55	3rd	8.0
8-8	Bos.	W	2-1		3	2	Ortiz	P. Martinez		59-55	3rd	8.5
8-9	Bos.	L	2-4		6	8	Fassero	Wise	Lowe	59-56	3rd	8.5
8-11	N.Y.	W	8-3		10	11	Schoeneweis	Hernandez		60-56	3rd	9.0
8-12	N.Y.	W	9-6		12	10	Pote	Neagle	Hasegawa	61-56	3rd	8.0
8-13	N.Y.	L	1-4		4	5	Clemens	Ortiz	Rivera	61-57	3rd	8.0
8-15	At Tor.	W	8-4		12	8	Wise	Wells		62-57	3rd	6.5
8-16	At Tor.	L	6-8		11	10	Koch	Pote		62-58	3rd	6.5
8-17	At N.Y.	L	1-6		11	6	Neagle	Mercker		62-59	3rd	7.0
8-18	At N.Y.	W	9-8	(11)	15	13	Hasegawa	Stanton		63-59	3rd	6.0
8-19	At N.Y.	L	1-9		5	11	Pettitte	Cooper		63-60	3rd	6.0
8-20	At N.Y.	W	5-4		6	9	Wise	Nelson	Hasegawa	64-60	3rd	5.0
8-21	At Bos.	L	6-7	(11)	8	8	Lowe	Hasegawa		64-61	3rd	5.5
8-22	At Bos.	W	11-4		14	9	Mercker	Wakefield		65-61	3rd	5.5
8-23	At Bos.	L	1-3		8	5	Ohka	Ortiz	Lowe	65-62	3rd	5.5
8-25	Cle.	W	4-1		9	4	Wise	Burba	Hasegawa	66-62	3rd	4.0
8-26	Cle.	L	5-9		9	12	Bere	Schoeneweis		66-63	3rd	5.0
8-27	Cle.	W	10-9		16	14	Levine	Finley	Hasegawa	67-63	3rd	4.0
8-28	Tor.	L	2-4		7	5	Loaiza	Ortiz	Koch	67-64	3rd	4.0
8-29	Tor.	W	9-4		12	11	Holtz	Carpenter		68-64	3rd	4.0
8-30	Tor.	L	2-11		9	19	Wells	Wise		68-65	3rd	4.0
9-1	At Chi.	L	8-9		10	14	Ginter	Hasegawa	Foulke	68-66	3rd	4.0
9-2	At Chi.	L	6-13		5	14	Parque	Mercker		68-67	3rd	5.0
9-3	At Chi.	L	12-13		11	15	Wunsch	Hasegawa	Foulke	68-68	3rd	6.0
9-4	At Det.	L	0-5		5	11	Nomo	Karl		68-69	3rd	6.0
9-5	At Det.	L	5-7		10	10	Moehler	Wise	Jones	68-70	3rd	7.0
9-6	At Det.	W	1-0		9	2	Schoeneweis	Sparks	Percival	69-70	3rd	6.0
9-7	At Det.	W	6-4		11	9	Belcher	Mlicki	Hasegawa	70-70	3rd	6.0
9-8	Bal.	W	2-1		7	3	Ortiz	Rapp	Percival	71-70	3rd	5.0
9-9	Bal.	L	3-10		8	14	Mercedes	Karl		71-71	3rd	6.0
9-10	Bal.	W	2-1		5	7	Hasegawa	Mussina	Percival	72-71	3rd	6.0
9-11	Bal.	L	1-3		8	9	Ponson	Schoeneweis		72-72	3rd	6.0
9-12	T.B.	W	5-2		8	5	Belcher	Rekar	Percival	73-72	3rd	6.0
9-13	T.B.	W	8-4		10	7	Ortiz	Lidle		74-72	3rd	6.0
9-15	At Min.	W	16-5		21	9	Karl	Kinney		75-72	3rd	6.0
9-16	At Min.	W	7-6		13	8	Hasegawa	Hawkins	Percival	76-72	3rd	6.0
9-17	At Min.	L	0-1		8	5	Radke	Belcher		76-73	3rd	7.0
9-19	At K.C.	L	1-5		3	10	Stein	Ortiz		76-74	3rd	8.5
9-20	At K.C.	W	7-4	(10)	14	10	Percival	Santiago	Petkovsek	77-74	3rd	8.5
9-21	At K.C.	L	3-8		6	16	Suppan	Schoeneweis		77-75	3rd	8.5
9-22	At Tex.	W	2-1		9	8	Weber	Oliver	Percival	78-75	3rd	7.5
9-23	At Tex.	W	15-4		18	4	Karl	Helling		79-75	3rd	6.5
9-24	At Tex.	W	9-2		5	5	Ortiz	Johnson		80-75	3rd	6.5
9-25	At Oak.	L	5-7		11	10	Zito	Belcher		80-76	3rd	7.0
9-26	At Oak.	L	3-10		7	8	Hudson	Schoeneweis		80-77	3rd	8.0
9-27	At Oak.	L	7-9		13	10	D. Jones	Holtz	Isringhausen	80-78	3rd	9.0
9-28	At Oak.	W	6-3	(14)	12	8	Holtz	Service	Percival	81-78	3rd	8.0
9-29	Sea.	W	9-3		10	5	Ortiz	Abbott	Pote	82-78	3rd	7.5
9-30	Sea.	L	9-21		12	22	Halama	Belcher		82-79	3rd	8.5
10-1	Sea.	L	2-5		7	12	Rhodes	Hasegawa	Sasaki	82-80	3rd	9.5

Monthly records: April (13-13), May (14-13), June (14-12), July (16-12), August (11-15), September (14-14), October (0-1).
*Innings, if other than nine. † First game of a doubleheader. ‡ Second game of a doubleheader.

MEMORABLE GAMES

August 18 at New York

With two out and two on in the bottom of the 10th inning, left fielder Darin Erstad raced toward the wall and made a full-extension, back-handed diving catch to rob Jorge Posada of a game-winning double—a spectacular play that Yankee pitcher Roger Clemens labeled one of the top three he has ever seen. Erstad followed that with an 11th-inning home run off Mike Stanton that lifted the Angels to a dramatic 9-8 win. Erstad's heroics were made possible by a five-run, game-tying rally in the ninth off relievers Jeff Nelson and Mariano Rivera.

Anaheim	AB	R	H	BI	Yankees	AB	R	H	BI
Erstad, lf	5	3	2	3	Jeter, ss	4	1	2	2
Palmeiro, rf	6	1	3	1	Posada, c	6	1	2	0
Vaughn, 1b	6	1	2	3	O'Neill, rf	6	0	2	2
Salmon, dh	5	1	2	1	Williams, cf	5	0	0	0
Anderson, cf	6	0	0	0	Justice, lf	5	0	0	0
Glaus, 3b	4	1	2	0	Martinez, 1b	4	1	1	0
Molina, c	5	0	2	0	Hill, dh	5	2	3	3
Kennedy, 2b	5	1	1	0	Polonia, pr-dh	0	0	0	0
Stocker, ss	4	1	1	0	Sojo, 3b-2b	4	2	1	0
					Vizcaino, 2b	4	1	2	0
					Canseco, ph	1	0	0	0
					Brosius, 3b	0	0	0	0
Totals	**46**	**9**	**15**	**8**	**Totals**	**44**	**8**	**13**	**7**

Anaheim ....1 0 0 1 1 0 0 0 5 0 1—9 15 1
Yankees.........................1 2 0 2 2 1 0 0 0 0 0—8 13 0

E—Kennedy (15). DP—Yankees 2. LOB—Anaheim 8, Yankees 9. 2B—O.Palmeiro (11), O'Neill (25). HR—Erstad (21), Vaughn (30), Salmon (27), Hill 2 (9). CS—Posada (2). SH—Sojo.

Anaheim	IP	H	R	ER	BB	SO
Ortiz	5.2	11	8	8	2	4
J.Alvarez	0.2	1	0	0	1	0
Pote	1.2	0	0	0	0	4
Hasegawa (W 8-2)	3	1	0	0	2	0

Yankees	IP	H	R	ER	BB	SO
Clemens	8	9	5	5	3	4
Nelson	0.1	0	1	1	1	0
Rivera	1.2	3	2	2	0	2
Stanton (L 2-2)	1	3	1	1	0	1

Clemens pitched to 2 batters in 9th.

BK—Ortiz. PB—Posada. U—HP, Cederstro. 1B, Welke. 2B, Scott. 3B, Hudson. T—4:11. A—37,503.

August 21 at Boston

In the most gut-wrenching loss of the season, Scott Schoeneweis, one out away from a complete-game victory, gave up a two-run, game-tying homer to Brian Daubach in the bottom of the ninth at Fenway Park. The Angels took a 6-5 lead in the top of the 11th, but the Red Sox came back to win in the bottom of the inning when Daubach's two-run bloop single to left barely eluded the glove of diving outfielder Orlando Palmeiro.

Anaheim	AB	R	H	BI	Boston	AB	R	H	BI
O.Palmeiro, lf	5	0	0	0	Offerman, 2b	5	0	1	1
Stocker, ss	5	1	1	0	Merloni, 3b	4	0	0	0
Vaughn, 1b	4	1	1	0	Everett, cf	4	1	0	0
Salmon, rf	4	0	2	1	Garciaparra, ss	2	0	0	0
Anderson, cf	5	0	1	0	O'Leary, lf	5	1	2	1
Glaus, 3b	2	2	1	0	Gilkey, dh	4	0	0	0
Molina, c	3	1	0	1	Hatteberg, ph	0	0	0	0
Kennedy, 2b	4	1	1	4	Alexander, pr	0	1	0	0
Gant, dh	5	0	1	0	Varitek, c	4	2	1	0
					Daubach, 1b	5	1	3	4
					Lewis, rf	3	1	1	1
					Nixon, ph-rf	1	0	0	0
Totals	**37**	**6**	**8**	**6**	**Totals**	**37**	**7**	**8**	**7**

Anaheim ....0 0 0 2 0 3 0 0 0 0 1—6 8 0
Boston...........................0 0 2 0 0 1 0 0 2 0 2—7 8 0

DP—Anaheim 3, Boston 2. LOB—Anaheim 6, Boston 5. 2B—Anderson (30), Glaus (26), Gant (1), Lewis (9). HR—Kennedy (8), Daubach (17). SH—B.Molina, Kennedy.

Anaheim	IP	H	R	ER	BB	SO
Schoeneweis	8.2	6	5	5	4	2
Petkovsek	1.1	0	1	1	1	1
Holtz (L 1-3)	0	1	1	1	0	0
Hasegawa	0.2	1	0	0	1	0

Boston	IP	H	R	ER	BB	SO
Arrojo	6	5	5	5	2	4
Cormier	1	0	0	0	0	2
Garces	1	2	0	0	1	0
Lowe (W 4-4)	3	1	1	1	1	1

Petkovsek pitched to 1 batter in the 11th. Holtz pitched to 1 batter in the 11th.

HBP—Vaughn by Arrojo, Everett by Schoeneweis,.Molina by Arrojo. WP—Schoeneweis. BK—Schoeneweis. U—HP, Marquez. 1B, Fichter. 2B, Cousins. 3B, Meals. T—3:26. A—32,795.

INDIVIDUAL STATISTICS

BATTING

Name	G	TPA	AB	R	H	TB	2B	3B	HR	RBI	Avg.	Obp.	Slg.	SH	SF	HP	BB	IBB	SO	SB	CS	GDP	vs RHP AB	vs RHP Avg.	vs RHP HR	vs RHP RBI	vs LHP AB	vs LHP Avg.	vs LHP HR	vs LHP RBI
Erstad, Darin	157	747	676	121	240	366	39	6	25	100	.355	.409	.541	2	4	1	64	9	82	28	8	8	466	.363	16	66	210	.338	9	34
Anderson, Garret	159	681	647	92	185	336	40	3	35	117	.286	.307	.519	1	9	0	24	5	87	7	6	21	458	.266	20	75	189	.333	15	42
Vaughn, Mo	161	712	614	93	167	306	31	0	36	117	.272	.365	.498	0	5	14	79	11	181	2	0	14	423	.303	30	95	191	.204	6	22
Kennedy, Adam	156	641	598	82	159	241	33	11	9	72	.266	.300	.403	8	4	3	28	5	73	22	8	10	456	.263	9	56	142	.275	0	16
Salmon, Tim	158	680	568	108	165	307	36	2	34	97	.290	.404	.540	0	2	6	104	5	139	0	2	14	413	.315	22	75	155	.226	12	22
Glaus, Troy	159	678	563	120	160	340	37	1	47	102	.284	.404	.604	0	1	2	112	6	163	14	11	14	433	.259	30	70	130	.369	17	32
Molina, Ben	130	513	473	59	133	199	20	2	14	71	.281	.318	.421	4	7	6	23	0	33	1	0	17	350	.277	6	43	123	.293	8	28
Gil, Benji	110	343	301	28	72	106	14	1	6	23	.239	.317	.352	5	2	5	30	0	59	10	6	7	188	.202	4	17	113	.301	2	6
Spiezio, Scott	123	345	297	47	72	138	11	2	17	49	.242	.334	.465	1	4	3	40	2	56	1	2	5	241	.241	15	43	56	.250	2	6
Palmeiro, Orlando	108	296	243	38	73	97	20	2	0	25	.300	.395	.399	10	3	2	38	0	20	4	1	4	212	.307	0	22	31	.258	0	3
Stocker, Kevin	70	272	229	21	45	64	13	3	0	16	.197	.299	.279	8	1	2	32	0	54	0	3	8	170	.194	0	12	59	.203	0	4
Walbeck, Matt	47	155	146	17	29	52	5	0	6	12	.199	.240	.356	1	0	1	7	0	22	0	1	2	117	.179	4	9	29	.276	2	3
Gant, Ron	34	103	82	15	19	42	3	1	6	16	.232	.379	.512	0	1	0	20	0	18	1	2	0	43	.256	5	10	39	.205	1	6
Clemente, Edgard	46	80	78	4	17	19	2	0	0	5	.218	.228	.244	1	0	1	0	0	27	0	1	0	12	.167	0	1	66	.227	0	4
DiSarcina, Gary	12	42	38	6	15	20	2	0	1	11	.395	.425	.526	2	0	1	1	0	3	0	1	1	34	.412	1	11	4	.250	0	0
Baughman, Justin	16	23	22	4	5	7	2	0	0	0	.227	.261	.318	0	0	0	1	0	2	3	0	0	9	.333	0	0	13	.154	0	0
Luuloa, Keith	6	19	18	3	6	6	0	0	0	0	.333	.368	.333	0	0	0	1	0	1	0	0	0	14	.214	0	0	4	.750	0	0
Wooten, Shawn	7	9	9	2	5	6	1	0	0	1	.556	.556	.667	0	0	0	0	0	0	0	0	0	3	1.000	0	0	6	.333	0	1
Johnson, Keith	6	7	4	2	2	2	0	0	0	0	.500	.667	.500	1	0	0	2	0	0	0	0	0	1	1.000	0	0	3	.333	0	0
Cooper, Brian	15	4	4	0	0	0	0	0	0	0	.000	.000	.000	0	0	0	0	0	3	0	0	0	3	.000	0	0	1	.000	0	0
Bottenfield, Kent	21	3	3	1	2	2	0	0	0	0	.667	.667	.667	0	0	0	0	0	1	0	0	0	3	.667	0	0	0	.000	0	0
Hill, Ken	16	4	3	0	1	1	0	0	0	0	.333	.333	.333	1	0	0	0	0	0	0	0	0	2	.000	0	0	1	1.000	0	0
Washburn, Jarrod	14	6	3	0	1	1	0	0	0	2	.333	.500	.333	2	0	0	1	0	0	0	0	0	2	.000	0	0	1	1.000	0	2
Schoeneweis, Scott	27	3	3	0	1	1	0	0	0	1	.333	.333	.333	0	0	0	0	0	0	0	0	0	3	.333	0	1	0	.000	0	0
Durrington, Trent	4	3	3	0	0	0	0	0	0	0	.000	.000	.000	0	0	0	0	0	0	0	0	1	0	.000	0	0	3	.000	0	0
Etherton, Seth	11	3	2	1	0	0	0	0	0	0	.000	.333	.000	0	0	0	1	0	0	0	0	0	2	.000	0	0	0	.000	0	0
Hasegawa, Shigetoshi	66	1	1	0	0	0	0	0	0	0	.000	.000	.000	0	0	0	0	0	0	0	0	0	1	.000	0	0	0	.000	0	0
Petkovsek, Mark	64	0	0	0	0	0	0	0	0	0	.000	.000	.000	0	0	0	0	0	0	0	0	0	0	.000	0	0	0	.000	0	0
Percival, Troy	54	0	0	0	0	0	0	0	0	0	.000	.000	.000	0	0	0	0	0	0	0	0	0	0	.000	0	0	0	.000	0	0
Levine, Al	51	0	0	0	0	0	0	0	0	0	.000	.000	.000	0	0	0	0	0	0	0	0	0	0	.000	0	0	0	.000	0	0
Holtz, Mike	61	0	0	0	0	0	0	0	0	0	.000	.000	.000	0	0	0	0	0	0	0	0	0	0	.000	0	0	0	.000	0	0
Fyhrie, Mike	32	0	0	0	0	0	0	0	0	0	.000	.000	.000	0	0	0	0	0	0	0	0	0	0	.000	0	0	0	.000	0	0
Weaver, Eric	17	0	0	0	0	0	0	0	0	0	.000	.000	.000	0	0	0	0	0	0	0	0	0	0	.000	0	0	0	.000	0	0
Pote, Lou	32	0	0	0	0	0	0	0	0	0	.000	.000	.000	0	0	0	0	0	0	0	0	0	0	.000	0	0	0	.000	0	0
Belcher, Tim	9	0	0	0	0	0	0	0	0	0	.000	.000	.000	0	0	0	0	0	0	0	0	0	0	.000	0	0	0	.000	0	0
Mercker, Kent	21	0	0	0	0	0	0	0	0	0	.000	.000	.000	0	0	0	0	0	0	0	0	0	0	.000	0	0	0	.000	0	0
Karl, Scott	6	0	0	0	0	0	0	0	0	0	.000	.000	.000	0	0	0	0	0	0	0	0	0	0	.000	0	0	0	.000	0	0
Dickson, Jason	6	0	0	0	0	0	0	0	0	0	.000	.000	.000	0	0	0	0	0	0	0	0	0	0	.000	0	0	0	.000	0	0
Ward, Bryan	7	0	0	0	0	0	0	0	0	0	.000	.000	.000	0	0	0	0	0	0	0	0	0	0	.000	0	0	0	.000	0	0
Hinchcliffe, Brett	2	0	0	0	0	0	0	0	0	0	.000	.000	.000	0	0	0	0	0	0	0	0	0	0	.000	0	0	0	.000	0	0
Ortiz, Ramon	18	0	0	0	0	0	0	0	0	0	.000	.000	.000	0	0	0	0	0	0	0	0	0	0	.000	0	0	0	.000	0	0
Alvarez, Juan	11	0	0	0	0	0	0	0	0	0	.000	.000	.000	0	0	0	0	0	0	0	0	0	0	.000	0	0	0	.000	0	0
Turnbow, Derrick	24	0	0	0	0	0	0	0	0	0	.000	.000	.000	0	0	0	0	0	0	0	0	0	0	.000	0	0	0	.000	0	0
Weber, Ben	10	0	0	0	0	0	0	0	0	0	.000	.000	.000	0	0	0	0	0	0	0	0	0	0	.000	0	0	0	.000	0	0
Wise, Matt	8	0	0	0	0	0	0	0	0	0	.000	.000	.000	0	0	0	0	0	0	0	0	0	0	.000	0	0	0	.000	0	0

Players with more than one A.L. team

Name	G	TPA	AB	R	H	TB	2B	3B	HR	RBI	Avg.	Obp.	Slg.	SH	SF	HP	BB	IBB	SO	SB	CS	GDP	vs RHP AB	vs RHP Avg.	vs RHP HR	vs RHP RBI	vs LHP AB	vs LHP Avg.	vs LHP HR	vs LHP RBI
Hill, Chi.	2	0	0	0	0	0	0	0	0	0	.000	.000	.000	0	0	0	0	0	0	0	0	0	2	.000	0	0	1	1.000	0	0
Hill, Ana.-Chi.	18	4	3	0	1	1	0	0	0	0	.333	.333	.333	1	0	0	0	0	0	0	0	0	2	.000	0	0	1	1.000	0	0
Stocker, T.B.	40	137	114	20	30	45	7	1	2	8	.263	.378	.395	2	0	2	19	0	27	1	2	3	170	.194	0	12	59	.203	0	4
Stocker, T.B.-Ana.	110	409	343	41	75	109	20	4	2	24	.219	.326	.318	10	1	4	51	0	81	1	5	11	259	.220	2	19	84	.214	0	5

PITCHING

Name	W	L	Pct.	ERA	IP	H	R	ER	HR	SH	SF	HB	BB	IBB	SO	G	GS	CG	ShO	GF	Sv	vs. RH AB	vs. RH Avg.	vs. RH HR	vs. RH RBI	vs. LH AB	vs. LH Avg.	vs. LH HR	vs. LH RBI
Schoeneweis, Scott	7	10	.412	5.45	170.0	183	112	103	21	2	5	6	67	2	78	27	27	1	1	0	0	509	.271	17	72	153	.294	4	24
Bottenfield, Kent	7	8	.467	5.71	127.2	144	82	81	25	2	5	3	56	4	75	21	21	0	0	0	0	249	.249	14	40	256	.320	11	39
Ortiz, Ramon	8	6	.571	5.09	111.1	96	69	63	18	4	4	2	55	0	73	18	18	2	0	0	0	187	.219	7	25	220	.250	11	34
Hasegawa, Shigetoshi	10	6	.625	3.57	95.2	100	43	38	11	2	3	2	38	6	59	66	0	0	0	26	9	199	.291	6	25	171	.246	5	28
Levine, Al	3	4	.429	3.87	95.1	98	44	41	10	3	3	2	49	5	42	51	5	0	0	12	2	209	.268	4	22	160	.263	6	22
Cooper, Brian	4	8	.333	5.90	87.0	105	66	57	18	4	4	2	35	1	36	15	15	1	1	0	0	198	.298	11	33	152	.303	7	26
Washburn, Jarrod	7	2	.778	3.74	84.1	64	38	35	16	1	3	1	37	0	49	14	14	0	0	0	0	233	.215	12	28	65	.215	4	8
Petkovsek, Mark	4	2	.667	4.22	81.0	86	39	38	8	4	1	3	23	6	31	64	1	0	0	21	2	183	.295	5	19	127	.252	3	25
Hill, Ken	5	7	.417	6.52	78.2	102	59	57	16	2	7	2	53	1	50	16	16	0	0	0	0	181	.331	10	25	135	.311	6	30
Etherton, Seth	5	1	.833	5.52	60.1	68	38	37	16	1	1	1	22	0	32	11	11	0	0	0	0	121	.273	6	15	124	.282	10	18
Fyhrie, Mike	0	0	.000	2.39	52.2	54	14	14	4	1	3	0	15	4	43	32	0	0	0	7	0	120	.300	4	15	81	.222	0	6
Pote, Lou	1	1	.500	3.40	50.1	52	23	19	4	1	1	0	17	1	44	32	1	0	0	12	1	110	.245	2	10	85	.294	2	16
Percival, Troy	5	5	.500	4.50	50.0	42	27	25	7	3	2	2	30	4	49	54	0	0	0	45	32	91	.220	4	15	93	.237	3	13
Mercker, Kent	1	3	.250	6.52	48.1	57	35	35	12	3	1	2	29	3	30	21	7	0	0	2	0	139	.324	10	24	51	.235	2	10
Holtz, Mike	3	3	.500	5.05	41.0	37	26	23	4	4	3	2	18	2	40	61	0	0	0	6	0	60	.300	2	8	89	.213	2	12
Belcher, Tim	4	5	.444	6.86	40.2	45	31	31	8	1	1	2	22	1	22	9	9	1	0	0	0	86	.256	6	16	74	.311	2	11
Turnbow, Derrick	0	0	.000	4.74	38.0	36	21	20	7	0	1	2	36	0	25	24	1	0	0	16	0	75	.240	5	15	67	.269	2	9
Wise, Matt	3	3	.500	5.54	37.1	40	23	23	7	0	2	1	13	1	20	8	6	0	0	0	0	63	.302	3	11	84	.250	4	9
Dickson, Jason	2	2	.500	6.11	28.0	39	20	19	5	1	0	1	7	0	18	6	6	0	0	0	0	64	.344	3	11	52	.327	2	7
Karl, Scott	2	2	.500	6.65	21.2	31	21	16	2	1	0	0	12	0	9	6	4	0	0	0	0	58	.345	0	8	34	.324	2	9
Weaver, Eric	0	2	.000	6.87	18.1	20	16	14	5	0	1	0	16	1	8	17	0	0	0	4	0	43	.233	4	10	32	.313	1	5
Weber, Ben	1	0	1.000	1.84	14.2	12	6	3	0	0	1	0	2	1	8	10	0	0	0	1	0	32	.188	0	3	24	.250	0	3
Ward, Bryan	0	0	.000	5.63	8.0	8	6	5	1	0	0	0	2	0	3	7	0	0	0	2	0	24	.208	1	4	10	.300	0	2
Alvarez, Juan	0	0	.000	13.50	6.0	14	9	9	3	0	1	0	7	1	2	11	0	0	0	3	0	13	.462	1	3	17	.471	2	8
Hinchcliffe, Brett	0	0	.000	5.40	1.2	1	1	1	0	0	0	0	1	0	0	2	0	0	0	0	0	3	.000	0	0	3	.333	0	0

PITCHERS WITH MORE THAN ONE A.L. TEAM

Name	W	L	Pct.	ERA	IP	H	R	ER	HR	SH	SF	HB	BB	IBB	SO	G	GS	CG	ShO	GF	Sv	vs. RH AB	vs. RH Avg.	vs. RH HR	vs. RH RBI	vs. LH AB	vs. LH Avg.	vs. LH HR	vs. LH RBI
Hill, Chi.	0	1	.000	24.00	3.0	5	8	8	0	1	1	0	6	0	0	2	1	0	0	0	0	181	.331	10	25	135	.311	6	30
Hill, Ana.-Chi.	5	8	.385	7.16	81.2	107	67	65	16	3	8	2	59	1	50	18	17	0	0	8	0	190	.337	10	30	137	.314	6	30

DESIGNATED HITTERS

Name	AB	Avg.	HR	RBI
Spiezio, Scott	161	.224	6	16
Salmon, Tim	115	.287	5	15
Erstad, Darin	91	.407	5	18
Vaughn, Mo	50	.260	2	9
Palmeiro, Orlando	50	.180	0	4
Anderson, Garret	40	.300	2	10
Gant, Ron	26	.346	3	5
Clemente, Edgard	21	.143	0	1
Glaus, Troy	9	.444	1	1
Gil, Benji	6	.333	1	1
Molina, Ben	6	.167	1	1
Walbeck, Matt	2	.000	0	0
Baughman, Justin	2	.000	0	0

INDIVIDUAL STATISTICS

FIELDING

FIRST BASEMEN

Player	Pct.	G	PO	A	E	TC	DP
Vaughn, Mo	.990	147	1257	69	14	1340	156
Spiezio, Scott	.993	29	141	4	1	146	12
Wooten, Shawn	1.000	3	10	1	0	11	2
Erstad, Darin	1.000	3	5	0	0	5	0
Gil, Benji	1.000	3	4	0	0	4	0
Johnson, Keith	1.000	3	3	0	0	3	0
Walbeck, Matt	1.000	2	1	0	0	1	1
Anderson, Garret	-	1	0	0	0	0	0

SECOND BASEMEN

Player	Pct.	G	PO	A	E	TC	DP
Kennedy, Adam	.976	155	337	425	19	781	106
Gil, Benji	1.000	7	20	19	0	39	10
Baughman, Justin	.958	5	8	15	1	24	4
Luuloa, Keith	1.000	3	6	9	0	15	3
Johnson, Keith	1.000	2	2	7	0	9	0
Spiezio, Scott	-	2	0	0	0	0	0
Durrington, Trent	1.000	1	1	2	0	3	0

THIRD BASEMEN

Player	Pct.	G	PO	A	E	TC	DP
Glaus, Troy	.933	156	111	349	33	493	33
Spiezio, Scott	.929	15	9	17	2	28	4

SHORTSTOPS

Player	Pct.	G	PO	A	E	TC	DP
Gil, Benji	.957	94	140	261	18	419	59
Stocker, Kevin	.978	69	98	210	7	315	49
DiSarcina, Gary	.934	12	24	47	5	76	12
Glaus, Troy	1.000	6	1	4	0	5	1
Baughman, Justin	1.000	5	4	2	0	6	0
Luuloa, Keith	.833	4	2	3	1	6	1
Johnson, Keith	1.000	1	2	2	0	4	0

OUTFIELDERS

Player	Pct.	G	PO	A	E	TC	DP
Anderson, Garret	.990	148	380	5	4	389	0
Erstad, Darin	.992	136	350	9	3	362	2
Salmon, Tim	.979	124	274	12	6	292	4
Palmeiro, Orlando	.984	72	117	6	2	125	0
Clemente, Edgard	1.000	32	36	2	0	38	0
Gant, Ron	.977	21	42	1	1	44	1
Spiezio, Scott	1.000	10	14	0	0	14	0
Vaughn, Mo	-	1	0	0	0	0	0

CATCHERS

Player	Pct.	G	PO	A	E	TC	DP	PB
Molina, Ben	.991	127	683	61	7	751	9	6
Walbeck, Matt	.991	44	200	16	2	218	0	0
Wooten, Shawn	1.000	4	5	0	0	5	0	0

PITCHERS

Player	Pct.	G	PO	A	E	TC	DP
Hasegawa, Shigetoshi	1.000	66	6	10	0	16	1
Petkovsek, Mark	1.000	64	4	12	0	16	0
Holtz, Mike	1.000	61	3	7	0	10	0
Percival, Troy	1.000	54	2	3	0	5	0
Levine, Al	.944	51	4	13	1	18	0
Pote, Lou	1.000	32	2	9	0	11	1
Fyhrie, Mike	1.000	32	1	6	0	7	0
Schoeneweis, Scott	.968	27	5	25	1	31	4
Turnbow, Derrick	1.000	24	0	1	0	1	0
Bottenfield, Kent	1.000	21	7	18	0	25	1
Mercker, Kent	.857	21	1	5	1	7	1
Ortiz, Ramon	1.000	18	1	12	0	13	1
Weaver, Eric	1.000	17	1	4	0	5	0
Hill, Ken	.947	16	5	13	1	19	1
Cooper, Brian	.882	15	3	12	2	17	1
Washburn, Jarrod	1.000	14	1	14	0	15	1
Etherton, Seth	1.000	11	1	11	0	12	1
Alvarez, Juan	1.000	11	2	0	0	2	1
Weber, Ben	1.000	10	1	1	0	2	0
Belcher, Tim	1.000	9	1	5	0	6	0
Wise, Matt	1.000	8	2	5	0	7	0
Ward, Bryan	.500	7	1	0	1	2	0
Dickson, Jason	1.000	6	3	2	0	5	0
Karl, Scott	.500	6	0	1	1	2	0
Hinchliffe, Brett	-	2	0	0	0	0	0

PITCHING AGAINST EACH CLUB

Pitcher	Bal. W-L	Bos. W-L	Chi. W-L	Cle. W-L	Det. W-L	K.C. W-L	Min. W-L	N.Y. W-L	Oak. W-L	Sea. W-L	T.B. W-L	Tex. W-L	Tor. W-L	N.L. W-L	Total W-L
Alvarez, Juan	0-0	0-0	0-0	0-0	0-0	0-0	0-0	0-0	0-0	0-0	0-0	0-0	0-0	0-0	0-0
Belcher, Tim	1-0	0-0	0-0	0-0	1-0	1-0	0-1	0-0	0-2	0-2	1-0	0-0	0-0	0-0	4-5
Bottenfield, Kent	0-1	0-1	2-0	0-0	0-1	0-1	0-1	0-0	0-0	1-1	1-0	0-1	0-1	3-0	7-8
Cooper, Brian	0-0	0-0	0-1	0-1	0-1	1-0	1-0	0-1	1-1	0-1	0-0	0-0	0-0	1-2	4-8
Dickson, Jason	0-0	1-0	0-0	0-0	0-0	0-0	0-0	0-0	0-0	0-0	0-2	0-0	1-0	0-0	2-2
Etherton, Seth	1-0	0-0	0-0	0-1	0-0	0-0	1-0	0-0	0-0	0-0	1-0	1-0	0-0	1-0	5-1
Fyhrie, Mike	0-0	0-0	0-0	0-0	0-0	0-0	0-0	0-0	0-0	0-0	0-0	0-0	0-0	0-0	0-0
Hasegawa, Shigetoshi	1-0	0-1	0-2	1-0	0-0	1-0	2-0	1-0	0-0	0-1	0-1	3-0	0-0	1-1	10-6
Hill, Ken	1-0	1-0	0-1	0-0	1-1	0-0	0-0	0-1	0-2	1-1	0-0	0-0	0-1	1-0	5-7
Hinchliffe, Brett	0-0	0-0	0-0	0-0	0-0	0-0	0-0	0-0	0-0	0-0	0-0	0-0	0-0	0-0	0-0
Holtz, Mike	0-0	0-0	1-0	0-0	0-0	0-0	0-0	0-0	1-1	0-1	0-0	0-1	1-0	0-0	3-3
Karl, Scott	0-1	0-0	0-0	0-0	0-1	0-0	1-0	0-0	0-0	0-0	0-0	1-0	0-0	0-0	2-2
Levine, Al	0-0	0-0	0-1	1-0	0-0	0-0	0-0	0-0	0-0	0-0	1-0	0-1	0-0	1-2	3-4
Mercker, Kent	0-0	1-0	0-1	0-0	0-0	0-0	0-0	0-1	0-0	0-0	0-1	0-0	0-0	0-0	1-3
Ortiz, Ramon	2-0	1-1	0-0	0-0	0-0	0-1	0-0	0-1	0-0	1-0	1-1	1-0	1-2	1-0	8-6
Percival, Troy	1-1	0-0	0-0	0-1	0-0	1-1	1-0	0-1	0-0	0-0	0-1	0-0	0-0	2-0	5-5
Petkovsek, Mark	0-0	0-0	0-0	0-0	1-0	0-0	0-0	0-0	1-1	1-0	1-0	0-0	0-1	0-0	4-2
Pote, Lou	0-0	0-0	0-0	0-0	0-0	0-0	0-0	1-0	0-0	0-0	0-0	0-0	0-1	0-0	1-1
Schoeneweis, Scott	0-2	0-0	1-0	0-3	2-0	0-1	1-0	2-0	0-1	0-1	0-0	0-1	1-0	0-1	7-10
Turnbow, Derrick	0-0	0-0	0-0	0-0	0-0	0-0	0-0	0-0	0-0	0-0	0-0	0-0	0-0	0-0	0-0
Ward, Bryan	0-0	0-0	0-0	0-0	0-0	0-0	0-0	0-0	0-0	0-0	0-0	0-0	0-0	0-0	0-0
Washburn, Jarrod	0-0	1-0	0-0	0-0	0-0	2-0	0-1	0-0	2-0	1-0	0-0	0-1	0-0	1-0	7-2
Weaver, Eric	0-0	0-0	0-0	0-0	0-0	0-2	0-0	0-0	0-0	0-0	0-0	0-0	0-0	0-0	0-2
Weber, Ben	0-0	0-0	0-0	0-0	0-0	0-0	0-0	0-0	0-0	0-0	0-0	1-0	0-0	0-0	1-0
Wise, Matt	0-0	0-1	0-0	1-0	0-1	0-0	0-0	1-0	0-0	0-0	0-0	0-0	1-1	0-0	3-3
Totals	7-5	5-4	4-6	3-6	5-5	6-6	7-3	5-5	5-8	5-8	6-6	7-5	5-7	12-6	82-80

INTERLEAGUE: Bottenfield 2-0, Percival 1-0, Etherton 1-0, Levine 0-1, Cooper 0-1 vs. Dodgers; Levine 1-1, Cooper 1-0 vs. Padres; Hasegawa 1-1, Percival 1-0 vs. Giants; Ortiz 1-0, Hill 1-0, Bottenfield 1-0 vs. Rockies; Washburn 1-0, Cooper 0-1, Schoeneweis 0-1 vs. Diamondbacks. Total: 12-6.

MISCELLANEOUS

HOME RUNS BY PARK

At Anaheim (130): Glaus 24, Anderson 20, Vaughn 18, Salmon 17, Erstad 11, Molina 11, Spiezio 10, Kennedy 7, Gant 5, Gil 4, Walbeck 2, DiSarcina 1.

At Arizona (5): Anderson 2, Salmon 1, Gil 1, Glaus 1.

At Baltimore (13): Vaughn 3, Glaus 3, Salmon 2, Anderson 2, Gil 1, Walbeck 1, Erstad 1.

At Boston (2): Vaughn 1, Kennedy 1.

At Chicago (AL) (9): Anderson 2, Erstad 2, Glaus 2, Vaughn 1, Salmon 1, Spiezio 1.

At Cleveland (3): Salmon 2, Glaus 1.

At Detroit (3): Salmon 1, Spiezio 1, Glaus 1.

At Kansas City (9): Anderson 3, Erstad 3, Vaughn 1, Salmon 1, Molina 1.

At Los Angeles (4): Glaus 3, Erstad 1.

At Minnesota (7): Vaughn 3, Salmon 1, Anderson 1, Erstad 1, Glaus 1.

At New York (AL) (6): Salmon 2, Vaughn 1, Erstad 1, Spiezio 1, Glaus 1.

At Oakland (8): Spiezio 2, Glaus 2, Vaughn 1, Walbeck 1, Anderson 1, Erstad 1.

At San Diego (4): Vaughn 1, Walbeck 1, Anderson 1, Erstad 1.

At Seattle (2): Vaughn 1, Salmon 1.

At Tampa Bay (10): Vaughn 3, Salmon 2, Molina 2, Glaus 2, Spiezio 1.

At Texas (12): Glaus 4, Salmon 3, Anderson 2, Vaughn 1, Erstad 1, Spiezio 1.

At Toronto (9): Erstad 2, Glaus 2, Gant 1, Vaughn 1, Walbeck 1, Anderson 1, Kennedy 1.

LOW-HIT GAMES

No-hitters: None.

One-hitters: None.

Two-hitters: Ramon Ortiz, August 8 vs. Boston, W 2-1.

10-STRIKEOUT GAMES

Total: 0

FOUR OR MORE HITS IN ONE GAME

Darin Erstad 5, Tim Salmon 3, Garret Anderson 3, Ben Molina 3, Orlando Palmeiro 2, Troy Glaus 2, Adam Kennedy 2, Mo Vaughn 1 (including one five-hit game), Total: 21

MULTI-HOMER GAMES

Troy Glaus 6, Mo Vaughn 4, Darin Erstad 3, Scott Spiezio 2, Ron Gant 1, Tim Salmon 1, Garret Anderson 1, Ben Molina 1, Adam Kennedy 1, Total: 20

GRAND SLAMS

4-18: Adam Kennedy (off Toronto's Frank Castillo)
5-21: Garret Anderson (off Kansas City's Chris Fussell)
6-20: Tim Salmon (off Kansas City's Jeff Suppan)
7-7: Ben Molina (off Colorado's Scott Karl)
8-12: Troy Glaus (off New York's Denny Neagle)
9-1: Mo Vaughn (off Chicago's Lorenzo Barcelo)
9-24: Mo Vaughn (off Texas's Mike Venafro)

PINCH HITTERS

(Minimum 5 at-bats)

Name	AB	Avg.	HR	RBI
Spiezio, Scott	28	.286	2	8
Palmeiro, Orlando	20	.250	0	1
Gant, Ron	9	.111	0	2
Clemente, Edgard	8	.125	0	0
Kennedy, Adam	7	.143	0	0

DEBUTS

4-17: Derrick Turnbow, P.
4-17: Keith Johnson, PR.
5-17: Keith Luuloa, PR.
5-26: Seth Etherton, P.
8-2: Matt Wise, P.
8-19: Shawn Wooten, C.

GAMES BY POSITION

Catcher: Ben Molina 127, Matt Walbeck 44, Shawn Wooten 4.

First base: Mo Vaughn 147, Scott Spiezio 29, Benji Gil 3, Darin Erstad 3, Keith Johnson 3, Shawn Wooten 3, Matt Walbeck 2, Garret Anderson 1.

Second base: Adam Kennedy 155, Benji Gil 7, Justin Baughman 5, Keith Luuloa 3, Scott Spiezio 2, Keith Johnson 2, Trent Durrington 1.

Third base: Troy Glaus 156, Scott Spiezio 15.

Shortstop: Benji Gil 94, Kevin Stocker 69, Gary DiSarcina 12, Troy Glaus 6, Justin Baughman 5, Keith Luuloa 4, Keith Johnson 1.

Outfield: Garret Anderson 148, Darin Erstad 136, Tim Salmon 124, Orlando Palmeiro 72, Edgard Clemente 32, Ron Gant 21, Scott Spiezio 10, Mo Vaughn 1.

Designated hitter: Scott Spiezio 50, Tim Salmon 33, Darin Erstad 20, Orlando Palmeiro 19, Mo Vaughn 14, Ron Gant 12, Edgard Clemente 11, Garret Anderson 10, Benji Gil 6, Justin Baughman 4, Troy Glaus 4, Ben Molina 2, Matt Walbeck 1.

STREAKS

Wins: 4 (July 6-9, September 12-16)

Losses: 6 (August 30-September 5)

Consecutive games with at least one hit: 17,Tim Salmon (July 23-August 9)

Wins by pitcher: 5,Seth Etherton (June 13-July 20)

ATTENDANCE

Home: 2,066,977

Road: 2,273,474

Highest (home): 43,619 (June 2 vs. Los Angeles).

Highest (road): 53,115 (July 14 vs. Los Angeles).

Lowest (home): 14,338 (April 10 vs. Toronto).

Lowest (road): 7,231 (September 17 vs. Minnesota).

Baltimore Orioles

DAY BY DAY

Date	Opp.	Res.	Score	(inn.*)	Hits	Opp. hits	Winning pitcher	Losing pitcher	Save	Record	Pos.	GB
4-3	Cle.	L	1-4		6	6	Colon	Mussina	Karsay	0-1	T4th	1.0
4-5	Cle.	W	11-7		12	10	Ryan	Kamieniecki		1-1	T3rd	0.5
4-6	Cle.	W	6-2		10	6	Rapp	Nagy	Groom	2-1	T1st	...
4-7	Det.	W	14-10		13	14	Worrell	Mlicki		3-1	1st	+1.0
4-8	Det.	W	2-1	(10)	8	10	Reyes	Brocail		4-1	1st	+1.0
4-9	Det.	W	11-6		16	10	Mercedes	Nitkowski		5-1	1st	+2.0
4-11	At K.C.	L	5-7	(12)	11	11	Santiago	Worrell		5-2	1st	+1.5
4-12	At K.C.	L	6-7		8	8	Santiago	Trombley		5-3	1st	+0.5
4-13	At K.C.	L	5-6		12	12	Bottalico	Ryan		5-4	T2nd	0.5
4-14	At Min.	L	9-10		16	12	Redman	Groom	Guardado	5-5	T2nd	1.5
4-15	At Min.	W	6-4		15	9	Worrell	Miller	Trombley	6-5	T2nd	1.5
4-16	At Min.	W	5-0		8	4	Ponson	Mays		7-5	T2nd	1.5
4-19	T.B.	W	3-2		7	7	Trombley	Mecir		8-5	2nd	2.5
4-20	T.B.	W	8-4		8	7	Rapp	Rupe		9-5	2nd	2.0
4-21	At Oak.	W	11-9		15	11	Ponson	Olivares	Timlin	10-5	2nd	1.0
4-22	At Oak.	W	4-3		10	9	Mercedes	Heredia	Groom	11-5	T1st	...
4-23	At Oak.	L	2-3	(11)	7	7	Isringhausen	Worrell		11-6	2nd	1.0
4-24	At Chi.	L	2-8		2	9	Eldred	Mussina		11-7	2nd	1.0
4-25	At Chi.	W	12-6		12	11	Rapp	Sirotka		12-7	T1st	...
4-26	At Chi.	L	6-11		10	10	Wells	Ponson		12-8	3rd	1.0
4-27	At Chi.	L	4-13		9	13	Parque	Mercedes		12-9	3rd	1.5
4-28	Tex.	W	4-3		8	9	Groom	Zimmerman		13-9	2nd	1.5
4-29	Tex.	W	3-1		6	9	Mussina	Oliver		14-9	2nd	0.5
4-30	Tex.	L	4-8		9	14	Rogers	Rapp		14-10	2nd	1.5
5-2	Ana.	W	7-6		9	11	Trombley	Percival		15-10	2nd	2.0
5-3	Ana.	L	5-6		8	9	Ortiz	Johnson	Percival	15-11	3rd	3.0
5-4	Ana.	L	5-8		9	11	Hill	Mussina	Hasegawa	15-12	3rd	3.5
5-5	At N.Y.	L	10-12		14	16	Nelson	Ryan		15-13	3rd	4.5
5-6	At N.Y.	L	1-3		6	6	Clemens	Rapp	Rivera	15-14	3rd	5.5
5-7	At N.Y.	W	7-6		12	10	Groom	Rivera	Timlin	16-14	3rd	4.5
5-8	At Tor.	L	5-6		14	12	Escobar	Johnson	Koch	16-15	3rd	5.5
5-9	At Tor.	L	4-6		10	12	Wells	Mussina	Koch	16-16	4th	6.5
5-10	At Tor.	L	2-7		5	14	Painter	Erickson	Quantrill	16-17	4th	7.0
5-11	Bos.	L	4-11		8	16	Cormier	Mercedes		16-18	4th	7.0
5-12	Bos.	L	0-9		2	16	P. Martinez	Ponson		16-19	4th	7.0
5-13	Bos.	L	1-5		11	6	Garces	Trombley		16-20	4th	7.0
5-14	Bos.	L	1-10		6	12	Rose	Mussina		16-21	4th	7.5
5-16	At Ana.	W	4-3		7	9	Erickson	Bottenfield	Timlin	17-21	4th	7.0
5-17	At Ana.	L	7-8		12	11	Percival	Timlin		17-22	4th	8.0
5-18	At Tex.	L	7-8		11	13	Helling	Ryan	Wetteland	17-23	4th	8.5
5-20	At Tex.	L	1-2		7	6	Loaiza	Mussina	Wetteland	17-24	4th	9.0
5-21	At Tex.	L	5-6		14	7	Venafro	Groom	Wetteland	17-25	4th	9.0
5-23	Sea.	W	4-2		6	8	Timlin	Mesa		18-25	4th	8.0
5-24	Sea.	W	4-3		8	7	Groom	Sasaki		19-25	4th	8.0
5-25	Sea.	W	5-1		9	5	Mussina	Rodriguez		20-25	4th	7.0
5-26	Oak.	W	8-3		13	6	Erickson	Mulder		21-25	4th	7.0
5-27	Oak.	L	0-4		2	11	Hudson	Johnson		21-26	4th	7.0
5-29	At T.B.	W	5-1		9	13	Rapp	Trachsel		22-26	4th	7.0
5-30	At T.B.	W	8-7		12	14	Ponson	Yan	Timlin	23-26	4th	7.0
5-31	At T.B.	L	3-4		9	6	Mecir	Groom	Hernandez	23-27	4th	7.0
6-1	At T.B.	L	1-2		6	8	Rekar	Erickson	Hernandez	23-28	4th	7.0
6-2	At Mon.	L	3-5		9	9	Pavano	Johnson	Kline	23-29	4th	7.0
6-3	At Mon.	L	4-7		9	12	Lira	Rapp	Kline	23-30	4th	7.0
6-4	At Mon.	L	0-1		3	6	Armas	Ponson	Kline	23-31	4th	8.0
6-5	At N.Y. (NL)	W	4-2		10	6	Mussina	Hampton	Timlin	24-31	4th	7.0
6-7	At N.Y. (NL)	L	3-11		12	12	Mahomes	Erickson		24-32	4th	8.5
6-8	At N.Y. (NL)	L	7-8	(10)	13	11	Cook	Mercedes		24-33	4th	9.0
6-9	Phi.	L	5-9		9	10	Wolf	Rapp		24-34	4th	9.0
6-10	Phi.	W	11-4		12	6	Ponson	Schilling		25-34	4th	9.0
6-11	Phi.	W	7-2		12	5	Mussina	Ashby		26-34	4th	8.5
6-13	Tex.	W	3-2		6	6	Erickson	Helling	Timlin	27-34	4th	7.5
6-14	Tex.	W	11-10		12	10	Timlin	Crabtree		28-34	4th	7.5
6-15	Tex.	W	10-1		8	5	McElroy	Loaiza		29-34	4th	6.5
6-16	Ana.	W	4-3		7	9	Mussina	Schoeneweis	Timlin	30-34	4th	6.0
6-17	Ana.	L	3-8		10	9	Belcher	Johnson		30-35	4th	6.0
6-18	Ana.	L	6-8		7	14	Etherton	Erickson	Percival	30-36	4th	6.0
6-19	At Oak.	L	12-13	(10)	16	14	Tam	Timlin		30-37	4th	6.5
6-20	At Oak.	L	5-8		9	9	Hudson	Ponson	Isringhausen	30-38	4th	7.5
6-21	At Oak.	L	3-10		8	15	Prieto	Mussina		30-39	4th	7.5
6-22	At Sea.	L	4-11		8	14	Moyer	Johnson		30-40	4th	8.0
6-23	At Sea.	L	3-8		10	11	Meche	Erickson		30-41	4th	8.5
6-24	At Sea.	L	1-2		7	4	Halama	Rapp	Sasaki	30-42	T4th	9.5
6-25	At Sea.	L	2-4		4	4	Rhodes	Timlin	Sasaki	30-43	T4th	10.5
6-27	At Bos.	W	6-3	(10)	11	10	Trombley	Lowe	Groom	31-43	T4th	9.5
6-28	At Bos.	W	8-7	(11)	16	11	Mercedes	Florie	Groom	32-43	4th	9.5
6-29	At Bos.	L	4-12		12	16	Wakefield	Erickson		32-44	4th	10.5
6-30	Tor.	W	8-3		11	7	Rapp	Halladay		33-44	4th	9.5

HIGHLIGHTS

High point: The Orioles ended a difficult season with a three-game sweep of the Yankees. The positive finish was punctuated by a 7-3 win and the sight of a sellout crowd, clearly having bought into the team's youth movement, standing and chanting, "Let's go, Orioles!"
Low point: On July 25, with the inevitability of a salary purge sinking in, the Orioles were embarrassed 19-1 at Camden Yards by the Yankees. Worse than the score was the realization that many voices in the sellout crowd apparently belonged to Yankees fans.
Turning point: On July 28, the Orioles traded shortstop Mike Bordick to the New York Mets for Melvin Mora and three prospects—the first of five trades and a series of callups that would transform the roster and change the way the team played the rest of the season.
Most valuable player: Only a handful of players were with the Orioles the entire season and Delino DeShields was the most productive. His average hovered around .300 for most of the season and he finished third in the league with 37 stolen bases.
Most valuable pitcher: Although Mike Mussina's 11-15 record was the worst of his career, his other numbers were right in line—3.80 ERA, 237 innings, 210 strikeouts. If the Orioles had given him any support, he would have won many more games.
Most improved player: Shortstop Bordick was enjoying a career offensive season when the Orioles traded him to the Mets. Always known for his defense, the 35-year-old Bordick earned his first All-Star berth and hit 16 home runs in 100 games.
Most pleasant surprise: Jose Mercedes, who had been released by three different organizations in 1999, led the team with 14 wins and secured a spot in the front half of the rotation.
Key injuries: Pitchers Scott Erickson and Matt Riley both underwent Tommy John surgery and will miss most of the 2001 season. ... Third baseman Cal Ripken went on the disabled list with a bad back for the third time in two seasons and played only 83 games. ... Right fielder Albert Belle was slowed by a degenerative hip condition during much of the second half.
Notable: Ripken joined the 3,000-hit club with a single in an April 15 game at Minnesota. ... Lefthander Buddy Groom set an A.L. record by making 70 appearances for a fifth straight year. ... Rookie first baseman Chris Richard homered 13 times in his 56 games with the Orioles, surpassing the four-month production of Will Clark before he was traded. ... Ripken made his first career appearance as a D.H. on May 9 at Toronto.

—DAVE SHEININ

MISCELLANEOUS

RECORDS

2000 regular-season record: 74-88 (4th in A.L. East); 44-37 at home; 30-51 on road; 32-36 vs. East; 24-24 vs. Central; 18-28 vs. West; 23-24 vs. lefthanded starters; 51-64 vs. righthanded starters; 63-74 on grass; 11-14 on turf; 25-30 in daytime; 49-58 at night; 29-25 in one-run games; 4-7 in extra-inning games; 0-1-4 in doubleheaders.
Team record past five years: 417-393 (.515, ranks 6th in league in that span).

TEAM LEADERS

Batting average: Delino DeShields (.296).
At-bats: Delino DeShields (561).
Runs: Brady Anderson (89).
Hits: Delino DeShields (166).
Total Bases: Albert Belle (265).
Doubles: Delino DeShields (43).
Triples: Delino DeShields (5).
Home runs: Albert Belle (23).
Runs batted in: Albert Belle (103).
Stolen bases: Delino DeShields (37).
Slugging percentage: Albert Belle (.474).
On-base percentage: Brady Anderson (.375).
Wins: Jose Mercedes (14).
Earned-run average: Mike Mussina (3.79).
Complete games: Mike Mussina, Sidney Ponson (6).
Shutouts: Mike Mussina, Sidney Ponson (1).
Saves: Ryan Kohlmeier (13).
Innings pitched: Mike Mussina (237.2).
Strikeouts: Mike Mussina (210).

Date	Opp.	Res.	Score	(inn.*)	Hits	Opp. hits	Winning pitcher	Losing pitcher	Save	Record	Pos.	GB
7-1	Tor.	W	12-5		13	8	Ponson	Carpenter		34-44	4th	8.5
7-2	Tor.	W	3-2		7	8	Trombley	Quantrill	Mills	35-44	4th	7.5
7-3	Tor.	L	4-6		11	6	Wells	Johnson	Koch	35-45	4th	8.5
7-4	At N.Y.	W	7-6		7	10	Erickson	Cone	Trombley	36-45	4th	7.5
7-5	At N.Y.	L	6-12		10	13	Pettitte	Rapp		36-46	4th	7.5
7-6	At N.Y.	L	9-13		11	10	Stanton	Johnson		36-47	4th	8.5
7-7	At Phi.	W	2-1		7	8	Mussina	Schilling	Timlin	37-47	4th	8.0
7-8	At Phi.	L	4-13		9	15	Ashby	Mercedes		37-48	4th	9.5
7-9	At Phi.	W	5-4		12	8	Mills	Brantley	Timlin	38-48	4th	8.5
7-13	Atl.	L	3-6		8	6	Maddux	Mussina	Kamieniecki	38-49	4th	8.5
7-14	Atl.	L	1-4		7	10	Ashby	Ponson		38-50	4th	9.5
7-15	Atl.	L	3-7		8	11	Glavine	Erickson		38-51	4th	10.0
7-16	Fla.	W	9-5		16	11	Mills	Darensbourg	Timlin	39-51	4th	10.0
7-17	Fla.	W	5-3		8	8	Mercedes	Cornelius	Timlin	40-51	4th	9.0
7-18	Fla.	L	0-7		8	13	Sanchez	Mussina		40-52	4th	10.0
7-20†	Bos.	L	7-11		11	17	R. Martinez	Ponson		40-53		
7-20‡	Bos.	W	9-4		14	4	Erickson	Schourek		41-53	4th	10.0
7-21	At Tor.	W	9-5		16	9	Rapp	Halladay		42-53	4th	10.0
7-22	At Tor.	W	8-2		13	9	Mercedes	Loaiza		43-53	4th	9.0
7-23	At Tor.	L	1-4		5	8	Castillo	Mussina	Koch	43-54	4th	10.0
7-24	N.Y.	L	3-4		6	5	Clemens	Parrish	Rivera	43-55	4th	11.0
7-25	N.Y.	L	1-19		9	20	Pettitte	Erickson		43-56	4th	12.0
7-26	N.Y.	L	1-4		8	8	Gooden	Ponson	Rivera	43-57	4th	13.0
7-29†	Cle.	L	3-14		9	20	Bere	Rapp		43-58		
7-29‡	Cle.	W	4-0		8	10	Mercedes	Woodard		44-58	4th	12.5
7-30	Cle.	W	10-7		12	9	Parrish	Finley		45-58	4th	12.5
7-31	Min.	W	6-5		9	9	Ponson	Romero	Trombley	46-58	4th	12.0
8-1	Min.	W	10-0		13	1	Mussina	Redman		47-58	4th	12.0
8-2	Min.	L	6-10		12	14	Radke	Rapp		47-59	4th	12.0
8-4	At T.B.	W	10-9	(15)	17	12	Johnson	Yan		48-59	4th	12.5
8-5	At T.B.	L	4-5	(10)	6	9	Hernandez	Trombley		48-60	4th	12.5
8-6	At T.B.	L	4-7		10	10	Rupe	Mussina	Hernandez	48-61	4th	12.5
8-7	At Det.	W	4-3		7	11	Groom	Brocail	Kohlmeier	49-61	4th	11.5
8-8	At Det.	L	1-4		8	7	Moehler	Rapp		49-62	4th	12.5
8-9	At Det.	W	5-2		11	7	Mercedes	Blair	Kohlmeier	50-62	4th	12.5
8-10	At Det.	L	3-14		6	14	Sparks	Ponson		50-63	T4th	13.5
8-11	At K.C.	L	6-7		8	11	Reichert	Mussina	Bottalico	50-64	T4th	13.5
8-12	At K.C.	W	12-11		11	14	Groom	Bottalico	Kohlmeier	51-64	4th	12.5
8-13	At K.C.	L	5-10		12	14	Suzuki	Brea		51-65	T4th	13.5
8-14	Chi.	W	8-2		11	10	Mercedes	Sirotka		52-65	4th	13.5
8-15	Chi.	L	4-14		8	16	Biddle	Johnson		52-66	T4th	14.5
8-16	Chi.	L	3-7		5	9	Parque	Mussina		52-67	T4th	14.5
8-17	Chi.	W	5-3		10	4	Parrish	Baldwin		53-67	4th	14.5
8-18	K.C.	L	1-4		8	4	Stein	Rapp		53-68	4th	14.5
8-19	K.C.	L	0-7		4	11	Suzuki	Mercedes		53-69	4th	15.5
8-20	K.C.	W	2-1		9	6	Ponson	Wilson	Kohlmeier	54-69	4th	14.5
8-21	K.C.	W	2-1		7	8	Mussina	Meadows	Kohlmeier	55-69	4th	14.5
8-23	At Chi.	L	4-8		8	7	Barcelo	Parrish		55-70	T4th	15.0
8-24	At Chi.	W	8-5		10	9	Mercedes	Hill		56-70	4th	15.0
8-25	T.B.	W	4-3		7	10	Ryan	Taylor	Kohlmeier	57-70	4th	14.0
8-26†	T.B.	L	1-4		7	7	Eiland	Ponson	Hernandez	57-71		
8-26‡	T.B.	W	2-0		7	4	Groom	Lidle	Trombley	58-71	4th	14.5
8-27	T.B.	W	3-2		10	10	Spurgeon	Rupe	Kohlmeier	59-71	4th	14.5
8-29	Det.	L	2-12		7	16	Weaver	Parrish		59-72	4th	15.0
8-30	Det.	W	5-1		11	2	Mercedes	Nomo		60-72	4th	15.0
8-31	Det.	L	1-6		5	11	Patterson	Trombley		60-73	4th	15.5
9-1	At Cle.	L	2-5		7	11	Finley	Ponson	Wickman	60-74	4th	16.5
9-2	At Cle.	W	8-6		13	9	Rapp	Karsay	Kohlmeier	61-74	4th	16.5
9-3	At Cle.	L	11-12	(13)	16	18	Cairncross	Trombley		61-75	4th	16.5
9-4	At Min.	W	3-2		9	10	Mercedes	Redman	Kohlmeier	62-75	4th	16.5
9-5	At Min.	W	6-5		10	14	Mussina	Romero	Kohlmeier	63-75	4th	16.5
9-6	At Min.	L	1-4		6	9	Radke	Ponson		63-76	4th	16.5
9-8	At Ana.	L	1-2		3	7	Ortiz	Rapp	Percival	63-77	4th	18.0
9-9	At Ana.	W	10-3		14	8	Mercedes	Karl		64-77	4th	18.0
9-10	At Ana.	L	1-2		7	5	Hasegawa	Mussina	Percival	64-78	4th	19.0
9-11	At Ana.	W	3-1		9	8	Ponson	Schoeneweis		65-78	4th	18.0
9-12†	At Tex.	L	1-9		3	16	Helling	Parrish		65-79		
9-12‡	At Tex.	L	5-6		8	5	Rogers	Spurgeon	Wetteland	65-80	4th	19.5
9-13	At Tex.	W	9-4		14	6	Rapp	Glynn		66-80	4th	19.5
9-15	Sea.	L	2-10		8	10	Sele	Mercedes		66-81	4th	19.0
9-16	Sea.	L	0-14		3	16	Moyer	Mussina		66-82	4th	20.0
9-17	Sea.	L	2-3		7	7	Garcia	Ponson	Sasaki	66-83	4th	20.0
9-18	Oak.	L	3-12		8	17	Appier	Rapp		66-84	4th	20.0
9-19†	Oak.	L	4-7		13	8	Mecir	Johnson	Isringhausen	66-85		
9-20†	Oak.	W	2-0		4	4	McElroy	Zito	Kohlmeier	67-85		
9-20‡	Oak.	L	0-4		9	10	Heredia	Mercedes		67-86	4th	19.5
9-22	At Bos.	W	3-1		6	4	Ponson	R. Martinez		68-86	4th	18.0
9-23	At Bos.	L	7-8	(10)	13	12	Carrasco	Kohlmeier		68-87	4th	19.0
9-24	At Bos.	W	1-0		4	8	Mussina	Ohka	Kohlmeier	69-87	4th	19.0
9-26	Tor.	W	2-1		7	5	Mercedes	Wells	Kohlmeier	70-87	4th	17.5
9-27	Tor.	L	0-4		4	7	Castillo	Ponson		70-88	4th	17.5
9-28	Tor.	W	23-1		23	2	Rapp	Carpenter		71-88	4th	16.5
9-29	N.Y.	W	13-2		13	6	McElroy	Pettitte		72-88	4th	15.5
9-30	N.Y.	W	9-1		12	7	Mussina	Cone		73-88	4th	14.5
10-1	N.Y.	W	7-3		10	9	Mercedes	Hernandez		74-88	4th	13.5

Monthly records: April (14-10), May (9-17), June (10-17), July (13-14), August (14-15), September (13-15), October (1-0).
*Innings, if other than nine. † First game of a doubleheader. ‡ Second game of a doubleheader.

MEMORABLE GAMES

June 8 at New York Mets

After commuting back and forth from Baltimore to New York because of a rainout and a scarcity of hotel rooms in New York City, the Orioles suffered a suitably painful 8-7 loss to the Mets in 10 innings. The suffering started when Mike Trombley surrendered a solo home run to Jay Payton in the eighth inning and intensified when Jose Mercedes gave up a game-winning homer in the 10th to Kurt Abbott.

Baltimore	AB	R	H	BI	Mets	AB	R	H	BI
Anderson, cf	4	1	1	1	Tyner, lf	4	0	1	1
Bordick, ss	5	2	2	2	Mora, lf	0	0	0	0
DeShields, 2b	4	0	3	0	Bell, rf	4	0	0	0
Belle, rf	3	0	2	0	Alfonzo, 2b	4	0	2	0
Conine, 1b	3	1	1	0	Piazza, c	5	1	2	0
Clark, ph-1b	0	0	0	1	Ventura, 3b	4	2	1	0
Ripken 3b	5	2	2	1	Zeile, 1b	4	2	2	3
Surhoff, lf	4	1	1	1	J.Franco, p	0	0	0	0
C.Johnson, c	4	0	1	1	Benitez, p	0	0	0	0
J.Johnson, p	2	0	0	0	Pratt, ph	1	0	0	0
Groom, p	0	0	0	0	Cook, p	0	0	0	0
Baines, ph	0	0	0	0	Payton, cf	4	2	2	2
Amaral, ph	1	0	0	0	Abbott, ss	3	1	1	2
Trombley, p	0	0	0	0	Rusch, p	2	0	0	0
.Lewis, ph	1	0	0	0	Mahomes, p	0	0	0	0
Mercedes, p	0	0	0	0	M.Franco, ph	0	0	0	0
					Agbayani, ph	1	0	0	0
					Wendell, p	0	0	0	0
					Harris, 1b	1	0	0	0
Totals	**36**	**7**	**13**	**7**	**Totals**	**37**	**8**	**11**	**8**

Baltimore..........................0 1 0 3 2 0 0 0 1 0—7 13 0
Mets ....0 0 0 3 0 3 0 1 0 1—8 11 0

DP—Mets 2. LOB—Baltimore 8, Mets 8. 2B—Anderson (13), Ventura (12), Payton (7). HR—Bordick (11), Ripken (12), Zeile (11), Payton (5), Abbott (2). SB—DeShields 2 (20). CS—Anderson (6), DeShields (4), Tyner (1). S—C. Johnson, Clark, Abbott. SH—J. Johnson.

Baltimore	IP	H	R	ER	BB	SO
J. Johnson	5.1	6	6	6	5	4
Groom	1.2	1	0	0	1	0
Trombley	2	3	1	1	0	3
Mercedes (L 2-3)	0.1	1	1	1	0	0
Mets	**IP**	**H**	**R**	**ER**	**BB**	**SO**
Rusch	5	10	6	6	3	4
Mahomes	1	0	0	0	1	0
Wendell	1.1	2	0	0	0	0
J.Franco	1	1	1	1	1	0
Benitez	0.2	0	0	0	1	0
Cook (W 5-2)	1	0	0	0	0	2

U—HP, Van Vleet. 1B, Everitt. 2B, DiMuro. 3B, Gorman. T—3:40. A—9,540.

September 28 at Baltimore

The Orioles set a team record for runs in a 23-1 win over Toronto. Entering the game, the Orioles had scored only 15 runs in their previous seven and had been shut out three times in the last two weeks. Brady Anderson's 200th career home run set the tone and the Orioles scored 13 unearned runs, thanks to four Blue Jays errors. The O's performed the rare feat of batting around in back-to-back innings.

Toronto	AB	R	H	BI	Baltimore	AB	R	H	BI
Stewart, lf	3	0	1	0	Anderson, rf	2	4	2	4
Wise, lf	1	0	0	0	Garcia, ph-lf	1	0	0	0
Gonzalez, ss	3	0	0	0	Hairston Jr., 2b6	4	2	2	
Woodward, ss	1	0	0	0	DeShields, lf	4	2	3	5
Martinez, rf	2	0	0	0	Hubbard, pr-lf-rf	1	0	1	0
Mottola, rf	2	0	0	0	Belle, dh	6	0	2	2
Delgado, 1b	2	0	0	0	Richard, 1b	5	2	2	1
Fletcher, dh	2	1	1	1	Minor, 1b	0	1	0	0
Cordova, ph-dh	1	0	0	0	Ripken 3b	4	1	3	1
Batista, 3b	3	0	0	0	Lewis, pr-3b	2	1	1	0
Cruz, cf	2	0	0	0	Mora, ss	2	1	1	0
V.Wells, cf	1	0	0	0	Garcia, ph-ss	2	1	0	0
Grebeck, 2b	3	0	0	0	Fordyce, c	5	4	4	2
Castillo, c	3	0	0	0	Lunar, c	1	0	0	1
					Kingsale, cf	6	2	2	2
Totals	**29**	**1**	**2**	**1**	**Totals**	**47**	**23**	**23**	**20**

Toronto ....0 0 0 0 1 0 0 0 0—1 2 4
Baltimore ....3 3 0 (10) 5 1 0 1 x—23 23 0

E—Grebeck 2 (9), Castillo (1), Batista (17). DP—Toronto 1. LOB—Toronto 2, Baltimore 7. 2B—Anderson (26), Richard (12). HR—Fletcher (20), Anderson (18), DeShields (10), Fordyce (14). S—Anderson.

Toronto	IP	H	R	ER	BB	SO
Carpenter (L 10-12)	3	5	6	4	2	3
Halladay	0.2	5	7	0	1	0
Painter	1	8	8	8	1	1
Frascatore	3.1	5	2	1	1	1
Baltimore	**IP**	**H**	**R**	**ER**	**BB**	**SO**
Rapp (W 9-12)	7	2	1	1	1	7
Spurgeon	1	0	0	0	0	1
Groom	0.1	0	0	0	0	0
Brea	0.2	0	0	0	0	1

HBP—Mora by Carpenter. PB—Castillo. U—HP, Wendelstedt, 1B, Clark. 2B, Bucknor. 3B, Reed. T—2:47. A—32,203.

INDIVIDUAL STATISTICS

BATTING

Name	G	TPA	AB	R	H	TB	2B	3B	HR	RBI	Avg.	Obp.	Slg.	SH	SF	HP	BB	IBB	SO	SB	CS	GDP	vs RHP AB	vs RHP Avg.	vs RHP HR	vs RHP RBI	vs LHP AB	vs LHP Avg.	vs LHP HR	vs LHP RBI
DeShields, Delino	151	643	561	84	166	249	43	5	10	86	.296	.369	.444	3	9	1	69	2	82	37	10	16	407	.278	8	62	154	.344	2	24
Belle, Albert	141	622	559	71	157	265	37	1	23	103	.281	.342	.474	0	7	4	52	11	68	0	5	17	422	.261	13	70	137	.343	10	33
Anderson, Brady	141	618	506	89	130	213	26	0	19	50	.257	.375	.421	5	7	8	92	5	103	16	9	4	360	.256	16	36	146	.260	3	14
Surhoff, B.J.	103	444	411	56	120	186	27	0	13	57	.292	.341	.453	1	1	2	29	3	46	7	2	5	272	.290	7	41	139	.295	6	16
Conine, Jeff	119	452	409	53	116	179	20	2	13	46	.284	.341	.438	0	4	2	36	1	53	4	3	14	289	.263	6	30	120	.333	7	16
Bordick, Mike	100	433	391	70	116	188	22	1	16	59	.297	.350	.481	2	5	1	34	0	71	6	5	12	274	.296	12	44	117	.299	4	15
Ripken Jr., Cal	83	339	309	43	79	140	16	0	15	56	.256	.310	.453	0	4	3	23	0	37	0	0	10	214	.252	13	40	95	.263	2	16
Johnson, Charles	84	320	286	52	84	163	16	0	21	55	.294	.364	.570	1	1	0	32	0	69	2	0	8	202	.317	17	44	84	.238	4	11
Clark, Will	79	310	256	49	77	121	15	1	9	28	.301	.413	.473	0	3	4	47	3	45	4	2	4	182	.330	9	23	74	.230	0	5
Baines, Harold	72	252	222	24	59	97	8	0	10	30	.266	.349	.437	0	1	0	29	6	39	0	0	6	200	.270	10	27	22	.227	0	3
Mora, Melvin	53	222	199	25	58	79	9	3	2	17	.291	.359	.397	2	0	4	17	0	32	5	8	2	159	.283	2	14	40	.325	0	3
Richard, Chris	56	221	199	38	55	112	14	2	13	36	.276	.335	.563	0	3	4	15	3	38	7	5	5	161	.286	12	33	38	.237	1	3
Matos, Luis	72	201	182	21	41	56	6	3	1	17	.225	.281	.308	2	2	3	12	0	30	13	4	7	124	.210	0	10	58	.259	1	7
Hairston Jr., Jerry	49	212	180	27	46	66	5	0	5	19	.256	.353	.367	5	0	6	21	0	22	8	5	8	135	.259	4	13	45	.244	1	6
Fordyce, Brook	53	194	177	23	57	95	11	0	9	28	.322	.361	.537	0	4	2	11	0	27	0	0	3	135	.311	4	15	42	.357	5	13
Lewis, Mark	71	178	163	19	44	67	17	0	2	21	.270	.322	.411	1	1	1	12	0	31	7	2	5	106	.255	2	16	57	.298	0	5
Myers, Greg	43	134	125	9	28	43	6	0	3	12	.224	.271	.344	1	0	0	8	0	29	0	0	7	117	.239	3	12	8	.000	0	0
Kingsale, Gene	26	91	88	13	21	25	2	1	0	9	.239	.253	.284	0	1	0	2	0	14	1	2	4	63	.190	0	5	25	.360	0	4
Minor, Ryan	32	88	84	4	11	12	1	0	0	3	.131	.170	.143	0	0	1	3	0	20	0	0	0	55	.127	0	1	29	.138	0	2
Amaral, Rich	30	67	60	10	13	16	1	1	0	6	.217	.299	.267	0	0	0	7	0	8	6	2	6	15	.333	0	1	45	.178	0	5
Coffie, Ivanon	23	67	60	6	13	19	4	1	0	6	.217	.284	.317	0	1	1	5	0	11	1	0	3	51	.196	0	3	9	.333	0	3
Hubbard, Trenidad	31	27	27	3	5	7	0	1	0	0	.185	.185	.259	0	0	0	0	0	3	2	1	2	17	.176	0	0	10	.200	0	0
Garcia, Jesse	14	19	17	2	1	1	0	0	0	0	.059	.158	.059	0	0	0	2	0	2	0	0	0	13	.077	0	0	4	.000	0	0
Lunar, Fernando	9	17	16	0	2	2	0	0	0	1	.125	.176	.125	0	0	1	0	0	4	0	0	0	14	.143	0	1	2	.000	0	0
Garcia, Karim	8	16	16	0	0	0	0	0	0	0	.000	.000	.000	0	0	0	0	0	6	0	0	0	16	.000	0	0	0	.000	0	0
Morales, Willie	3	11	11	1	3	4	1	0	0	0	.273	.273	.364	0	0	0	0	0	3	0	0	0	8	.250	0	0	3	.333	0	0
Casimiro, Carlos	2	8	8	0	1	2	1	0	0	3	.125	.125	.250	0	0	0	0	0	2	0	0	0	3	.000	0	0	5	.200	0	3
Kinkade, Mike	3	8	7	0	3	4	1	0	0	1	.429	.500	.571	0	0	1	0	0	0	0	0	0	6	.500	0	1	1	.000	0	0
Mussina, Mike	34	6	6	0	0	0	0	0	0	0	.000	.000	.000	0	0	0	0	0	1	0	0	0	3	.000	0	0	3	.000	0	0
Erickson, Scott	17	5	5	2	2	3	1	0	0	1	.400	.400	.600	0	0	0	0	0	0	0	0	0	5	.400	0	1	0	.000	0	0
Rapp, Pat	31	3	3	0	0	0	0	0	0	0	.000	.000	.000	0	0	0	0	0	0	0	0	0	3	.000	0	0	0	.000	0	0
Johnson, Jason	25	5	3	0	0	0	0	0	0	0	.000	.000	.000	2	0	0	0	0	2	0	0	0	1	.000	0	0	2	.000	0	0
Trombley, Mike	75	1	1	0	0	0	0	0	0	0	.000	.000	.000	0	0	0	0	0	1	0	0	0	1	.000	0	0	0	.000	0	0
Mercedes, Jose	36	1	1	0	0	0	0	0	0	0	.000	.000	.000	0	0	0	0	0	0	0	0	0	1	.000	0	0	0	.000	0	0
Ponson, Sidney	32	3	1	0	0	0	0	0	0	0	.000	.000	.000	2	0	0	0	0	1	0	0	0	1	.000	0	0	0	.000	0	0
McElroy, Chuck	43	0	0	0	0	0	0	0	0	0	.000	.000	.000	0	0	0	0	0	0	0	0	0	0	.000	0	0	0	.000	0	0
Mills, Alan	23	0	0	0	0	0	0	0	0	0	.000	.000	.000	0	0	0	0	0	0	0	0	0	0	.000	0	0	0	.000	0	0
Holmes, Darren	5	0	0	0	0	0	0	0	0	0	.000	.000	.000	0	0	0	0	0	0	0	0	0	0	.000	0	0	0	.000	0	0
Timlin, Mike	37	0	0	0	0	0	0	0	0	0	.000	.000	.000	0	0	0	0	0	0	0	0	0	0	.000	0	0	0	.000	0	0
Groom, Buddy	70	0	0	0	0	0	0	0	0	0	.000	.000	.000	0	0	0	0	0	0	0	0	0	0	.000	0	0	0	.000	0	0
Reyes, Al	13	0	0	0	0	0	0	0	0	0	.000	.000	.000	0	0	0	0	0	0	0	0	0	0	.000	0	0	0	.000	0	0
Molina, Gabe	9	0	0	0	0	0	0	0	0	0	.000	.000	.000	0	0	0	0	0	0	0	0	0	0	.000	0	0	0	.000	0	0
Ryan, B.J.	42	0	0	0	0	0	0	0	0	0	.000	.000	.000	0	0	0	0	0	0	0	0	0	0	.000	0	0	0	.000	0	0
Kohlmeier, Ryan	25	0	0	0	0	0	0	0	0	0	.000	.000	.000	0	0	0	0	0	0	0	0	0	0	.000	0	0	0	.000	0	0
Worrell, Tim	5	0	0	0	0	0	0	0	0	0	.000	.000	.000	0	0	0	0	0	0	0	0	0	0	.000	0	0	0	.000	0	0
Maduro, Calvin	15	0	0	0	0	0	0	0	0	0	.000	.000	.000	0	0	0	0	0	0	0	0	0	0	.000	0	0	0	.000	0	0
Rivera, Luis	1	0	0	0	0	0	0	0	0	0	.000	.000	.000	0	0	0	0	0	0	0	0	0	0	.000	0	0	0	.000	0	0
Parrish, John	8	0	0	0	0	0	0	0	0	0	.000	.000	.000	0	0	0	0	0	0	0	0	0	0	.000	0	0	0	.000	0	0
Brea, Leslie	6	0	0	0	0	0	0	0	0	0	.000	.000	.000	0	0	0	0	0	0	0	0	0	0	.000	0	0	0	.000	0	0
Spurgeon, Jay	7	0	0	0	0	0	0	0	0	0	.000	.000	.000	0	0	0	0	0	0	0	0	0	0	.000	0	0	0	.000	0	0

Players with more than one A.L. team

Name	G	TPA	AB	R	H	TB	2B	3B	HR	RBI	Avg.	Obp.	Slg.	SH	SF	HP	BB	IBB	SO	SB	CS	GDP	vs RHP AB	vs RHP Avg.	vs RHP HR	vs RHP RBI	vs LHP AB	vs LHP Avg.	vs LHP HR	vs LHP RBI
Baines, Bal.-Chi.	96	320	283	26	72	118	13	0	11	39	.254	.338	.417	0	1	0	36	7	50	0	0	6	257	.261	11	36	26	.192	0	3
Fordyce, Chi.-Bal.	93	330	302	41	91	153	18	1	14	49	.301	.341	.507	2	5	4	17	0	50	0	0	4	230	.287	8	31	72	.347	6	18
Garcia, Det.-Bal.	16	33	33	1	3	3	0	0	0	0	.091	.091	.091	0	0	0	0	0	10	0	0	1	33	.091	0	0	0	.000	0	0
Johnson, Bal.-Chi.	128	478	421	76	128	245	24	0	31	91	.304	.379	.582	1	3	1	52	0	106	2	0	8	306	.324	25	70	115	.252	6	21

PITCHING

Name	W	L	Pct.	ERA	IP	H	R	ER	HR	SH	SF	HB	BB	IBB	SO	G	GS	CG	ShO	GF	Sv	vs. RH AB	vs. RH Avg.	vs. RH HR	vs. RH RBI	vs. LH AB	vs. LH Avg.	vs. LH HR	vs. LH RBI
Mussina, Mike	11	15	.423	3.79	237.2	236	105	100	28	8	6	3	46	0	210	34	34	6	1	0	0	520	.281	19	59	404	.223	9	42
Ponson, Sidney	9	13	.409	4.82	222.0	223	125	119	30	3	3	1	83	0	152	32	32	6	1	0	0	441	.259	18	57	422	.258	12	53
Rapp, Pat	9	12	.429	5.90	174.0	203	125	114	18	1	7	5	83	5	106	31	30	0	0	0	0	366	.298	14	66	335	.281	4	44
Mercedes, Jose	14	7	.667	4.02	145.2	150	71	65	15	7	7	3	64	1	70	36	20	1	0	7	0	290	.252	7	41	265	.291	8	30
Johnson, Jason	1	10	.091	7.02	107.2	119	95	84	21	3	5	4	61	2	79	25	13	0	0	3	0	233	.288	10	46	195	.267	11	39
Erickson, Scott	5	8	.385	7.87	92.2	127	81	81	14	3	5	5	48	0	41	16	16	1	0	0	0	189	.270	6	25	195	.390	8	46
Trombley, Mike	4	5	.444	4.13	72.0	67	34	33	15	7	2	4	38	8	72	75	0	0	0	32	4	163	.252	10	30	108	.241	5	13
McElroy, Chuck	3	0	1.000	4.69	63.1	60	36	33	6	0	3	2	34	2	50	43	2	0	0	10	0	150	.273	4	23	93	.204	2	12
Groom, Buddy	6	3	.667	4.85	59.1	63	37	32	5	5	5	0	21	2	44	70	0	0	0	14	4	141	.326	3	30	88	.193	2	10
Ryan, B.J.	2	3	.400	5.91	42.2	36	29	28	7	1	1	0	31	1	41	42	0	0	0	9	0	103	.252	6	25	57	.175	1	8
Parrish, John	2	4	.333	7.18	36.1	40	32	29	6	1	4	1	35	0	28	8	8	0	0	0	0	128	.297	6	28	11	.182	0	3
Timlin, Mike	2	3	.400	4.89	35.0	37	22	19	6	5	1	2	15	3	26	37	0	0	0	31	11	73	.233	4	8	61	.328	2	17
Kohlmeier, Ryan	0	1	.000	2.39	26.1	30	9	7	1	1	1	0	15	2	17	25	0	0	0	22	13	49	.245	0	4	54	.333	1	7
Spurgeon, Jay	1	1	.500	6.00	24.0	26	16	16	5	1	0	2	15	0	11	7	4	0	0	1	0	38	.211	1	2	54	.333	4	12
Mills, Alan	2	0	1.000	6.46	23.2	25	17	17	6	0	0	1	19	1	18	23	0	0	0	3	1	53	.264	4	10	42	.262	2	5
Maduro, Calvin	0	0	.000	9.64	23.1	29	25	25	8	1	2	2	16	1	18	15	2	0	0	6	0	50	.340	7	13	42	.286	1	13
Reyes, Al	1	0	1.000	6.92	13.0	13	10	10	2	1	2	0	11	1	10	13	0	0	0	2	0	31	.355	2	13	17	.118	0	0
Molina, Gabe	0	0	.000	9.00	13.0	25	14	13	2	0	2	0	9	0	8	9	0	0	0	3	0	27	.333	2	8	36	.444	0	7
Brea, Leslie	0	1	.000	11.00	9.0	12	11	11	1	0	1	1	10	0	5	6	1	0	0	3	0	25	.240	1	6	12	.500	0	7
Worrell, Tim	2	2	.500	7.36	7.1	12	6	6	3	0	0	0	5	3	5	5	0	0	0	2	0	18	.444	2	5	16	.250	1	1
Holmes, Darren	0	0	.000	25.07	4.2	13	13	13	3	0	0	0	5	0	6	5	0	0	0	0	0	16	.375	2	7	11	.636	1	7
Rivera, Luis	0	0	.000	0.00	0.2	1	0	0	0	0	0	0	1	0	0	1	0	0	0	0	0	2	.500	0	0	1	.000	0	0

DESIGNATED HITTERS

Name	AB	Avg.	HR	RBI
Baines, Harold	215	.265	10	30
Belle, Albert	122	.303	1	12
Conine, Jeff	56	.214	1	5
DeShields, Delino	43	.349	0	6
Ripken Jr., Cal	38	.289	0	6
Anderson, Brady	29	.207	0	2
Myers, Greg	24	.208	2	4
Clark, Will	18	.278	0	3
Garcia, Karim	12	.000	0	0
Casimiro, Carlos	8	.125	0	3
Kinkade, Mike	6	.500	0	1
Surhoff, B.J.	3	.333	0	0
Richard, Chris	3	.000	0	0
Hubbard, Trenidad	2	.000	0	0
Kingsale, Gene	2	.000	0	0
Amaral, Rich	1	.000	0	0
Lewis, Mark	1	.000	0	0
Johnson, Charles	1	.000	0	0
Coffie, Ivanon	1	.000	0	0
Matos, Luis	0	-	0	0

INDIVIDUAL STATISTICS

FIELDING

FIRST BASEMEN

Player	Pct.	G	PO	A	E	TC	DP
Clark, Will	.991	72	583	44	6	633	58
Richard, Chris	.989	53	440	18	5	463	52
Conine, Jeff	.985	39	304	31	5	340	27
Minor, Ryan	1.000	5	26	3	0	29	1
Amaral, Rich	1.000	1	5	4	0	9	4
Kinkade, Mike	1.000	1	1	0	0	1	0

SECOND BASEMEN

Player	Pct.	G	PO	A	E	TC	DP
DeShields, Delino	.975	96	171	254	11	436	46
Hairston Jr., Jerry	.981	49	101	156	5	262	45
Lewis, Mark	.978	21	37	51	2	90	11
Garcia, Jesse	1.000	6	5	18	0	23	3
Mora, Melvin	1.000	1	2	1	0	3	1

THIRD BASEMEN

Player	Pct.	G	PO	A	E	TC	DP
Ripken Jr., Cal	.974	73	56	134	5	195	17
Conine, Jeff	.932	44	21	75	7	103	10
Lewis, Mark	.857	29	8	34	7	49	2
Minor, Ryan	.926	26	18	32	4	54	5
Coffie, Ivanon	.971	15	6	27	1	34	1

SHORTSTOPS

Player	Pct.	G	PO	A	E	TC	DP
Bordick, Mike	.979	100	161	258	9	428	57
Mora, Melvin	.952	52	78	160	12	250	32
Lewis, Mark	.975	14	19	20	1	40	5
Garcia, Jesse	1.000	5	4	4	0	8	2
Coffie, Ivanon	1.000	4	7	5	0	12	1

OUTFIELDERS

Player	Pct.	G	PO	A	E	TC	DP
Anderson, Brady	.997	127	301	1	1	303	1
Belle, Albert	.986	110	211	8	3	222	2
Surhoff, B.J.	.987	102	226	5	3	234	1
Matos, Luis	.988	69	168	3	2	173	0
DeShields, Delino	.975	41	76	3	2	81	1
Kingsale, Gene	.954	24	60	2	3	65	0
Hubbard, Trenidad	.929	24	12	1	1	14	0
Amaral, Rich	1.000	19	45	1	0	46	0
Conine, Jeff	.930	19	38	2	3	43	1
Garcia, Karim	1.000	2	2	0	0	2	0
Richard, Chris	1.000	1	3	0	0	3	0

CATCHERS

Player	Pct.	G	PO	A	E	TC	DP	PB
Johnson, Charles	.994	83	498	30	3	531	4	3
Fordyce, Brook	.988	52	313	20	4	337	2	3
Myers, Greg	1.000	28	166	14	0	180	1	0
Lunar, Fernando	1.000	9	43	2	0	45	0	0
Morales, Willie	1.000	3	22	2	0	24	1	0

PITCHERS

Player	Pct.	G	PO	A	E	TC	DP
Trombley, Mike	1.000	75	3	11	0	14	1
Groom, Buddy	.857	70	2	10	2	14	1
McElroy, Chuck	.900	43	3	6	1	10	1
Ryan, B.J.	1.000	42	0	4	0	4	0
Timlin, Mike	1.000	37	1	10	0	11	1
Mercedes, Jose	1.000	36	2	16	0	18	0
Mussina, Mike	.977	34	17	26	1	44	1
Ponson, Sidney	1.000	32	13	22	0	35	0
Rapp, Pat	.967	31	4	25	1	30	2
Johnson, Jason	1.000	25	3	4	0	7	0
Kohlmeier, Ryan	1.000	25	2	2	0	4	0
Mills, Alan	.800	23	2	2	1	5	0
Erickson, Scott	.800	16	7	5	3	15	0
Maduro, Calvin	1.000	15	1	2	0	3	0
Reyes, Al	1.000	13	0	3	0	3	0
Molina, Gabe	1.000	9	1	1	0	2	0
Parrish, John	.833	8	1	4	1	6	1
Spurgeon, Jay	.667	7	0	2	1	3	0
Brea, Leslie	-	6	0	0	0	0	0
Worrell, Tim	1.000	5	1	0	0	1	0
Holmes, Darren	-	5	0	0	0	0	0
Rivera, Luis	-	1	0	0	0	0	0

PITCHING AGAINST EACH CLUB

Pitcher	Ana. W-L	Bos. W-L	Chi. W-L	Cle. W-L	Det. W-L	K.C. W-L	Min. W-L	N.Y. W-L	Oak. W-L	Sea. W-L	T.B. W-L	Tex. W-L	Tor. W-L	N.L. W-L	Total W-L
Brea, Leslie	0-0	0-0	0-0	0-0	0-0	0-1	0-0	0-0	0-0	0-0	0-0	0-0	0-0	0-0	0-1
Erickson, Scott	1-1	1-1	0-0	0-0	0-0	0-0	0-0	1-1	1-0	0-1	0-1	1-0	0-1	0-2	5-8
Groom, Buddy	0-0	0-0	0-0	0-0	1-0	1-0	0-1	1-0	0-0	1-0	1-1	1-1	0-0	0-0	6-3
Holmes, Darren	0-0	0-0	0-0	0-0	0-0	0-0	0-0	0-0	0-0	0-0	0-0	0-0	0-0	0-0	0-0
Johnson, Jason	0-2	0-0	0-1	0-0	0-0	0-0	0-0	0-1	0-2	0-1	1-0	0-0	0-2	0-1	1-10
Kohlmeier, Ryan	0-0	0-1	0-0	0-0	0-0	0-0	0-0	0-0	0-0	0-0	0-0	0-0	0-0	0-0	0-1
Maduro, Calvin	0-0	0-0	0-0	0-0	0-0	0-0	0-0	0-0	0-0	0-0	0-0	0-0	0-0	0-0	0-0
McElroy, Chuck	0-0	0-0	0-0	0-0	0-0	0-0	0-0	1-0	1-0	0-0	0-0	1-0	0-0	0-0	3-0
Mercedes, Jose	1-0	1-1	2-1	1-0	3-0	0-1	1-0	1-0	1-1	0-1	0-0	0-0	2-0	1-2	14-7
Mills, Alan	0-0	0-0	0-0	0-0	0-0	0-0	0-0	0-0	0-0	0-0	0-0	0-0	0-0	2-0	2-0
Molina, Gabe	0-0	0-0	0-0	0-0	0-0	0-0	0-0	0-0	0-0	0-0	0-0	0-0	0-0	0-0	0-0
Mussina, Mike	1-2	1-1	0-2	0-1	0-0	1-1	2-0	1-0	0-1	1-1	0-1	1-1	0-2	3-2	11-15
Parrish, John	0-0	0-0	1-1	1-0	0-1	0-0	0-0	0-1	0-0	0-0	0-0	0-1	0-0	0-0	2-4
Ponson, Sidney	1-0	1-2	0-1	0-1	0-1	1-0	2-1	0-1	1-1	0-1	1-1	0-0	1-1	1-2	9-13
Rapp, Pat	0-1	0-0	1-0	2-1	0-1	0-1	0-1	0-2	0-1	0-1	2-0	1-1	3-0	0-2	9-12
Reyes, Al	0-0	0-0	0-0	0-0	1-0	0-0	0-0	0-0	0-0	0-0	0-0	0-0	0-0	0-0	1-0
Rivera, Luis	0-0	0-0	0-0	0-0	0-0	0-0	0-0	0-0	0-0	0-0	0-0	0-0	0-0	0-0	0-0
Ryan, B.J.	0-0	0-0	0-0	1-0	0-0	0-1	0-0	0-1	0-0	0-0	1-0	0-1	0-0	0-0	2-3
Spurgeon, Jay	0-0	0-0	0-0	0-0	0-0	0-0	0-0	0-0	0-0	0-0	1-0	0-1	0-0	0-0	1-1
Timlin, Mike	0-1	0-0	0-0	0-0	0-0	0-0	0-0	0-0	0-1	1-1	0-0	1-0	0-0	0-0	2-3
Trombley, Mike	1-0	1-1	0-0	0-1	0-1	0-1	0-0	0-0	0-0	0-0	1-1	0-0	1-0	0-0	4-5
Worrell, Tim	0-0	0-0	0-0	0-0	1-0	0-1	1-0	0-0	0-1	0-0	0-0	0-0	0-0	0-0	2-2
Totals	5-7	5-7	4-6	5-4	6-4	3-7	6-3	5-7	4-8	3-7	8-5	6-6	7-6	7-11	74-88

INTERLEAGUE: Mussina 0-1, Ponson 0-1, Erickson 0-1 vs. Braves; Johnson 0-1, Rapp 0-1, Ponson 0-1 vs. Expos; Mussina 1-0, Erickson 0-1, Mercedes 0-1 vs. Mets; Mussina 2-0, Ponson 1-0, Mills 1-0, Rapp 0-1, Mercedes 0-1 vs. Phillies; Mills 1-0, Mercedes 1-0, Mussina 0-1 vs. Marlins. Total: 7-11.

MISCELLANEOUS

HOME RUNS BY PARK

At Anaheim (5): Richard 2, Belle 1, Bordick 1, Conine 1.
At Baltimore (90): Belle 14, Johnson 12, Anderson 9, Ripken Jr. 8, Clark 6, Surhoff 6, Bordick 6, Conine 6, Fordyce 5, Baines 4, DeShields 4, Richard 4, Hairston Jr. 2, Myers 1, Lewis 1, Mora 1, Matos 1.
At Boston (7): Johnson 2, Myers 1, Belle 1, Conine 1, Hairston Jr. 1, Richard 1.
At Chicago (AL) (10): Conine 2, Baines 1, Surhoff 1, Anderson 1, DeShields 1, Bordick 1, Johnson 1, Hairston Jr. 1, Richard 1.
At Cleveland (4): Fordyce 2, Richard 2.
At Detroit (2): Anderson 1, DeShields 1.
At Kansas City (9): Fordyce 2, Richard 2, Ripken Jr. 1, Anderson 1, Belle 1, Bordick 1, Hairston Jr. 1.
At Minnesota (7): Conine 2, Surhoff 1, Anderson 1, DeShields 1, Bordick 1, Johnson 1.
At Montreal (4): Belle 2, Surhoff 1, Johnson 1.
At New York (AL) (11): Baines 2, Ripken Jr. 2, Anderson 2, Surhoff 1, DeShields 1, Bordick 1, Lewis 1, Johnson 1.
At New York (NL) (4): Ripken Jr. 2, Surhoff 1, Bordick 1.
At Oakland (7): Bordick 2, Baines 1, Ripken Jr. 1, Clark 1, Belle 1, Johnson 1.
At Philadelphia (1): Clark 1.
At Seattle (3): Baines 1, Conine 1, Johnson 1.
At Tampa Bay (12): Surhoff 2, Anderson 2, Belle 2, Ripken Jr. 1, DeShields 1, Bordick 1, Johnson 1, Mora 1, Richard 1.
At Texas (4): Anderson 2, Myers 1, Bordick 1.
At Toronto (4): Baines 1, Clark 1, Belle 1, DeShields 1.

LOW-HIT GAMES

No-hitters: None.
One-hitters: Mike Mussina, August 1 vs. Minnesota, W 10-0.
Two-hitters: Jose Mercedes, August 30 vs. Detroit, W 5-1.

10-STRIKEOUT GAMES

Mike Mussina 4, Sidney Ponson 2, Total: 6

FOUR OR MORE HITS IN ONE GAME

B.J. Surhoff 3 (including one five-hit game), Harold Baines 1, Cal Ripken Jr. 1, Delino DeShields 1, Brook Fordyce 1, Melvin Mora 1, Chris Richard 1, Total: 9

MULTI-HOMER GAMES

Chris Richard 3, Albert Belle 2, Charles Johnson 2, Harold Baines 1, Brook Fordyce 1, Total: 9

GRAND SLAMS

6-14: Albert Belle (off Texas's Kenny Rogers)
6-15: Albert Belle (off Texas's Mark Clark)
7-20: Will Clark (off Boston's Ramon Martinez)

PINCH HITTERS

(Minimum 5 at-bats)

Name	AB	Avg.	HR	RBI
Conine, Jeff	9	.333	1	3
Myers, Greg	9	.222	0	2
Baines, Harold	8	.375	0	0
DeShields, Delino	5	.000	0	0

DEBUTS

4-9: Willie Morales, C.
6-19: Luis Matos, CF.
7-15: Ivanon Coffie, PR.
7-24: John Parrish, P.
7-29: Ryan Kohlmeier, P.
7-31: Carlos Casimiro, PH.
8-13: Leslie Brea, P.
8-15: Jay Spurgeon, P.

GAMES BY POSITION

Catcher: Charles Johnson 83, Brook Fordyce 52, Greg Myers 28, Fernando Lunar 9, Willie Morales 3.
First base: Will Clark 72, Chris Richard 53, Jeff Conine 39, Ryan Minor 5, Rich Amaral 1, Mike Kinkade 1.
Second base: Delino DeShields 96, Jerry Hairston Jr. 49, Mark Lewis 21, Jesse Garcia 6, Melvin Mora 1.
Third base: Cal Ripken Jr. 73, Jeff Conine 44, Mark Lewis 29, Ryan Minor 26, Ivanon Coffie 15.
Shortstop: Mike Bordick 100, Melvin Mora 52, Mark Lewis 14, Jesse Garcia 5, Ivanon Coffie 4.
Outfield: Brady Anderson 127, Albert Belle 110, B.J. Surhoff 102, Luis Matos 69, Delino DeShields 41, Trenidad Hubbard 24, Gene Kingsale 24, Jeff Conine 19, Rich Amaral 19, Karim Garcia 2, Chris Richard 1.
Designated hitter: Harold Baines 62, Albert Belle 31, Jeff Conine 20, Brady Anderson 11, Cal Ripken Jr. 10, Delino DeShields 10, Greg Myers 9, Will Clark 6, Trenidad Hubbard 6, Rich Amaral 5, Mark Lewis 4, Karim Garcia 4, Luis Matos 3, Mike Kinkade 2, Carlos Casimiro 2, B.J. Surhoff 1, Charles Johnson 1, Gene Kingsale 1, Ivanon Coffie 1, Chris Richard 1.

STREAKS

Wins: 6 (April 15-22,June 10-16)
Losses: 9 (June 17-25)
Consecutive games with at least one hit: 21, B.J. Surhoff (June 5-28)
Wins by pitcher: 4, Jose Mercedes (August 24-September 9)

ATTENDANCE

Home: 3,103,122
Road: 2,014,669
Highest (home): 49,013 (July 15 vs. Atlanta).
Highest (road): 54,350 (May 6 vs. New York).
Lowest (home): 30,341 (September 18 vs. Oakland).
Lowest (road): 5,753 (September 6 vs. Minnesota).

BOSTON RED SOX

DAY BY DAY

Date	Opp.	Res.	Score	(inn.*)	Hits	Opp. hits	Winning pitcher	Losing pitcher	Save	Record	Pos.	GB
4-4	At Sea.	W	2-0		7	2	P. Martinez	Moyer	Lowe	1-0	T1st	0.5
4-5	At Sea.	L	3-9		9	9	Garcia	R. Martinez		1-1	T3rd	0.5
4-6	At Sea.	L	2-5		8	7	Mesa	Florie	Sasaki	1-2	5th	1.0
4-7	At Ana.	L	3-7		6	9	Dickson	Schourek		1-3	5th	2.0
4-8	At Ana.	L	5-7		7	13	Hill	Rose	Percival	1-4	5th	3.0
4-9	At Ana.	W	5-2		9	7	P. Martinez	Bottenfield		2-4	4th	3.0
4-11	Min.	W	13-4		16	9	R. Martinez	Mays		3-4	3rd	2.0
4-12	Min.	W	7-3		10	9	Fassero	Santana		4-4	3rd	1.0
4-13	Min.	W	4-3		7	7	Wakefield	Wells	Lowe	5-4	T2nd	0.5
4-14	Oak.	L	6-13		12	11	Appier	Rose		5-5	T2nd	1.5
4-15	Oak.	W	14-2		13	6	P. Martinez	Hudson		6-5	T2nd	1.5
4-16	Oak.	W	5-4		9	10	Lowe	Mathews		7-5	T2nd	1.5
4-17	Oak.	L	0-1		4	10	Heredia	Fassero	Isringhausen	7-6	3rd	2.5
4-18	At Det.	W	7-0		10	6	Schourek	Mlicki	Lowe	8-6	3rd	2.5
4-19	At Det.	W	10-0		15	6	Rose	Nomo		9-6	3rd	2.5
4-24	At Tex.	L	4-5		9	7	Rogers	Wakefield	Wetteland	9-7	3rd	2.0
4-25	At Tex.	W	6-3		9	6	P. Martinez	Helling	Lowe	10-7	3rd	1.0
4-26	At Tex.	W	14-4		21	10	Fassero	Clark		11-7	2nd	1.0
4-28	At Cle.	L	3-4		7	8	Burba	Schourek	Karsay	11-8	3rd	2.0
4-29	At Cle.	L	2-3		5	5	Finley	R. Martinez	Karsay	11-9	3rd	2.0
4-30	At Cle.	W	2-1		7	6	P. Martinez	Nagy	Lowe	12-9	3rd	2.0
5-1	Det.	W	10-6		11	11	Fassero	Nitkowski		13-9	2nd	2.0
5-2	Det.	L	6-7	(12)	10	18	Blair	Wakefield	Jones	13-10	3rd	3.0
5-3	Det.	W	4-2		7	6	Lowe	Weaver		14-10	2nd	3.0
5-5	T.B.	W	5-3		10	8	R. Martinez	Eiland	Lowe	15-10	2nd	3.0
5-6	T.B.	L	0-1		3	6	Trachsel	P. Martinez		15-11	2nd	4.0
5-7	T.B.	W	9-7		12	13	Fassero	Rekar	Lowe	16-11	2nd	3.0
5-8	Chi.	W	3-2		8	8	Rose	Sturtze	Lowe	17-11	2nd	3.0
5-9	Chi.	L	0-6		3	10	Baldwin	Schourek		17-12	2nd	4.0
5-10	Chi.	W	5-3	(7)	7	7	R. Martinez	Eldred	Garces	18-12	2nd	3.5
5-11	At Bal.	W	11-4		16	8	Cormier	Mercedes		19-12	2nd	2.5
5-12	At Bal.	W	9-0		16	2	P. Martinez	Ponson		20-12	2nd	1.5
5-13	At Bal.	W	5-1		6	11	Garces	Trombley		21-12	2nd	0.5
5-14	At Bal.	W	10-1		12	6	Rose	Mussina		22-12	1st	+0.5
5-15	At Tor.	W	8-1		13	6	Schourek	Castillo		23-12	1st	+1.0
5-16	At Tor.	L	6-7		11	14	Munro	Lowe		23-13	1st	+1.0
5-17	At Tor.	W	8-0		15	4	P. Martinez	Carpenter		24-13	1st	+1.0
5-19	Det.	W	3-0		7	5	Fassero	Moehler	Lowe	25-13	1st	+1.0
5-20	Det.	L	1-2		6	9	Mlicki	Wakefield	Jones	25-14	1st	+1.0
5-21	Det.	L	5-7		12	11	Nomo	R. Martinez	Jones	25-15	1st	+1.0
5-23	Tor.	L	2-3		9	7	Carpenter	P. Martinez	Koch	25-16	1st	+1.0
5-24	Tor.	W	6-3	(11)	9	10	Cormier	Frascatore		26-16	1st	+1.0
5-25	Tor.	L	6-11		13	17	Wells	Schourek		26-17	T1st	...
5-26	At N.Y.	W	4-1		8	8	R. Martinez	Cone	Lowe	27-17	1st	+1.0
5-27	At N.Y.	L	3-8		9	11	Stanton	Wasdin		27-18	T1st	...
5-28	At N.Y.	W	2-0		5	4	P. Martinez	Clemens		28-18	1st	+1.0
5-30	K.C.	W	8-2		12	8	Fassero	Suppan		29-18	1st	+1.5
5-31	K.C.	L	7-9		12	14	Suzuki	Schourek	Spradlin	29-19	1st	+1.5
6-1	K.C.	L	11-13		12	19	Santiago	Lowe	Reichert	29-20	1st	+1.0
6-2	At Phi.	L	1-2	(11)	9	9	Brantley	Wasdin		29-21	T1st	...
6-3	At Phi.	L	3-9		3	10	Wolf	Wakefield		29-22	T1st	...
6-4	At Phi.	L	5-6	(12)	8	12	Schrenk	Cormier		29-23	2nd	1.0
6-5	At Fla.	W	3-2		9	6	Wakefield	Bones	Lowe	30-23	T1st	...
6-6	At Fla.	W	4-3		10	9	R. Martinez	Sanchez	Lowe	31-23	T1st	...
6-7	At Fla.	L	2-6		10	5	Darensbourg	Rose		31-24	2nd	1.0
6-8	Cle.	W	3-0		9	2	P. Martinez	Colon	Lowe	32-24	2nd	0.5
6-9	At Atl.	L	4-6		8	9	Maddux	Fassero	Seanez	32-25	2nd	0.5
6-10	At Atl.	L	0-6		5	9	Mulholland	Schourek		32-26	2nd	1.5
6-11	At Atl.	W	5-3		8	7	Garces	Seanez	Lowe	33-26	2nd	1.0
6-13	At N.Y.	W	5-3		10	6	Pichardo	Hernandez	Lowe	34-26	2nd	...
6-14	At N.Y.	L	1-2		10	8	Grimsley	Wakefield	Rivera	34-27	2nd	1.0
6-16	Tor.	W	7-4		12	11	Pichardo	Escobar	Lowe	35-27	1st	+0.5
6-17	Tor.	L	10-11		13	14	Wells	R. Martinez	Koch	35-28	1st	+0.5
6-18	Tor.	L	1-5		6	9	Castillo	Fassero	Koch	35-29	1st	+0.5
6-19	N.Y.	L	1-22		6	19	Mendoza	Rose		35-30	2nd	0.5
6-20	N.Y.	L	0-3		6	5	Pettitte	P. Martinez	Rivera	35-31	2nd	1.5
6-21	N.Y.	W	9-7		11	10	Garces	Grimsley		36-31	2nd	0.5
6-22	N.Y.	W	4-2		8	5	R. Martinez	Westbrook	Lowe	37-31	1st	+0.5
6-23	At Tor.	L	4-5		7	9	Castillo	Wasdin	Koch	37-32	2nd	0.5
6-24	At Tor.	L	4-6		7	9	Halladay	Rose	Koch	37-33	3rd	1.5
6-25	At Tor.	L	5-6	(13)	15	10	DeWitt	Florie		37-34	3rd	2.5
6-27	Bal.	L	3-6	(10)	10	11	Trombley	Lowe	Groom	37-35	3rd	2.5
6-28	Bal.	L	7-8	(11)	11	16	Mercedes	Florie	Groom	37-36	3rd	3.5
6-29	Bal.	W	12-4		16	12	Wakefield	Erickson		38-36	3rd	3.5
6-30	At Chi.	L	4-10		11	13	Parque	Pichardo		38-37	3rd	3.5
7-1	At Chi.	L	2-7		6	5	Sirotka	Crawford		38-38	3rd	3.5
7-2	At Chi.	L	2-8		6	11	Baldwin	Schourek		38-39	3rd	3.5
7-3	At Min.	W	11-8		15	13	Pichardo	Lincoln	Lowe	39-39	3rd	3.5
7-4	At Min.	W	14-4		18	10	Wakefield	Milton	Florie	40-39	3rd	2.5

HIGHLIGHTS

High point: When Pedro Martinez and Roger Clemens hooked up at Yankee Stadium on May 28, both pitched eight shutout innings before the Red Sox prevailed in the ninth, 2-0. At the time, all was rosy for the Red Sox: They were in first place in the A.L. East, Martinez looked phenomenal and new acquisition Carl Everett was playing like an MVP candidate.

Low point: A line drive off the bat of Yankee Ryan Thompson hit Red Sox reliever Bryce Florie squarely in the right eye, horrifying a September 8 crowd at Fenway Park and threatening Florie's career. The fading Red Sox lost that game 4-0 and were swept in the three-game weekend series, falling into third place, nine games behind the Yankees.

Turning point: Carl Everett's July 15 tantrum, during which he bumped the umpire in an argument over where his feet were in the batter's box, cast a distasteful pall over the team. Everett's unpredictable behavior and an inability to find chemistry on a changing roster kept the Red Sox from generating any momentum.

Most valuable player: There's no question about the best player on this team. Shortstop Nomar Garciaparra won his second straight batting title (.372) and ranks among the most dangerous bats in the league.

Most valuable pitcher: Martinez. His astounding 1.74 ERA was nearly two runs lower than the next closest (Roger Clemens, 3.70) in the league and he is fast approaching the mystique of Hall of Famers Sandy Koufax, Steve Carlton and Bob Gibson.

Most improved player: Young righthander Tomo Ohka began showing more aggressiveness to go with his good stuff and excellent control. His 3.12 ERA in 13 appearances bodes well for the future.

Most pleasant surprise: When Martinez went on the D.L. at mid-season, Paxton Crawford jumped from Class AA and made two superb starts. He returned in September and finished 2-1 with a 3.41 ERA in six appearances.

Key injuries: Third baseman John Valentin went down with a serious knee injury in May. ... Second baseman Jose Offerman (groin, knee) went on the D.L. twice and Martinez was sidelined in late June with a strained side muscle. ... Right fielder Trot Nixon strained a hamstring in late June and never returned to form. ... Reliever Rod Beck missed the first few months with neck problems.

Notable: The club set a single-season record for attendance with 2.58 million. ... Martinez became the first unanimous A.L. Cy Young winner in consecutive years. ... Garciaparra became the first righthanded hitter to win back-to-back A.L. batting titles since Joe DiMaggio in 1939-40. ... The club won the league ERA title (4.23) in consecutive seasons for the first time since 1902-04. ... Derek Lowe's 42 saves tied for the league lead.

—MICHAEL SILVERMAN

MISCELLANEOUS

RECORDS

2000 regular-season record: 85-77 (2nd in A.L. East); 42-39 at home; 43-38 on road; 32-35 vs. East; 32-24 vs. Central; 21-18 vs. West; 20-22 vs. lefthanded starters; 65-55 vs. righthanded starters; 77-66 on grass; 8-11 on turf; 22-24 in daytime; 63-53 at night; 20-23 in one-run games; 5-8 in extra-inning games; 0-1-3 in doubleheaders.

Team record past five years: 434-376 (.536, ranks 3rd in league in that span).

TEAM LEADERS

Batting average: Nomar Garciaparra (.372).
At-bats: Nomar Garciaparra (529).
Runs: Nomar Garciaparra (104).
Hits: Nomar Garciaparra (197).
Total Bases: Nomar Garciaparra (317).
Doubles: Nomar Garciaparra (51).
Triples: Trot Nixon (8).
Home runs: Carl Everett (34).
Runs batted in: Carl Everett (108).
Stolen bases: Carl Everett (11).
Slugging percentage: Nomar Garciaparra (.599).
On-base percentage: Nomar Garciaparra (.434).
Wins: Pedro Martinez (18).
Earned-run average: Pedro Martinez (1.74).
Complete games: Pedro Martinez (7).
Shutouts: Pedro Martinez (4).
Saves: Derek Lowe (42).
Innings pitched: Pedro Martinez (217.0).
Strikeouts: Pedro Martinez (284).

Date	Opp.	Res.	Score	(inn.*)	Hits	Opp. hits	Winning pitcher	Losing pitcher	Save	Record	Pos.	GB
7-5	At Min.	W	11-8		12	10	Wasdin	Redman	Lowe	41-39	3rd	1.5
7-6	At Min.	W	8-7		8	12	Crawford	Radke		42-39	3rd	1.5
7-7	Atl.	L	3-5		7	11	Glavine	Schourek	Ligtenberg	42-40	3rd	2.0
7-8	Atl.	L	1-5		7	10	Mulholland	R. Martinez		42-41	3rd	3.5
7-9	Atl.	W	7-2		14	6	Wakefield	Millwood		43-41	3rd	2.5
7-13	N.Y. (NL)	W	4-3		8	8	Garces	Benitez		44-41	3rd	1.5
7-14	N.Y. (NL)	L	4-6		12	12	Mahomes	Lowe	Benitez	44-42	3rd	2.5
7-15	N.Y. (NL)	W	6-4		9	10	R. Martinez	Hampton	Lowe	45-42	3rd	2.0
7-16	Mon.	W	5-2		8	4	Wakefield	Johnson	Wasdin	46-42	3rd	2.0
7-17	Mon.	W	7-3		9	7	Pichardo	Telford		47-42	3rd	1.0
7-18	Mon.	W	3-1		9	6	P. Martinez	Vazquez	Lowe	48-42	2nd	1.0
7-20†	At Bal.	W	11-7		17	11	R. Martinez	Ponson		49-42		
7-20‡	At Bal.	L	4-9		4	14	Erickson	Schourek		49-43	3rd	1.0
7-21	Chi.	L	5-8		11	15	Simas	Pichardo	Howry	49-44	3rd	2.0
7-22	Chi.	W	8-6		11	10	Fassero	Garland		50-44	2nd	1.0
7-23	Chi.	W	1-0		5	6	P. Martinez	Sirotka		51-44	2nd	1.0
7-24	Min.	L	2-4		6	14	Milton	Ohka		51-45	2nd	2.0
7-25	Min.	L	2-4		8	8	Mays	R. Martinez	Guardado	51-46	2nd	3.0
7-27	At Oak.	W	5-4	(10)	8	10	Garces	Tam	Lowe	52-46	3rd	2.5
7-28	At Oak.	W	4-1		7	5	P. Martinez	Mulder	Lowe	53-46	2nd	2.5
7-29	At Oak.	L	1-12		7	11	Appier	Fassero		53-47	2nd	2.5
7-30	At Oak.	L	2-5		6	3	Heredia	Arrojo	Isringhausen	53-48	2nd	3.5
7-31	At Sea.	W	8-5		11	3	Garces	Mesa	Pichardo	54-48	2nd	3.0
8-1	At Sea.	L	4-5	(19)	12	12	Sasaki	Fassero		54-49	2nd	4.0
8-2	At Sea.	W	5-2		8	5	P. Martinez	Garcia		55-49	2nd	3.0
8-4	K.C.	W	5-4		11	8	Garces	Larkin	Lowe	56-49	2nd	3.5
8-5	K.C.	L	5-7		8	13	Meadows	Cormier	Bottalico	56-50	2nd	3.5
8-6	K.C.	L	1-3		10	8	Reichert	Wakefield	Bottalico	56-51	2nd	3.5
8-7	At Ana.	L	1-4		5	10	Washburn	Ohka	Hasegawa	56-52	2nd	3.5
8-8	At Ana.	L	1-2		2	3	Ortiz	P. Martinez		56-53	2nd	4.5
8-9	At Ana.	W	4-2		8	6	Fassero	Wise	Lowe	57-53	2nd	4.5
8-11	At Tex.	W	7-3		11	7	Arrojo	Glynn		58-53	2nd	4.0
8-12	At Tex.	L	3-6		6	6	Helling	Wakefield		58-54	2nd	4.0
8-13	At Tex.	W	4-2		7	6	Ohka	Rogers	Lowe	59-54	2nd	4.0
8-14	T.B.	W	7-3		9	11	Lowe	Taylor		60-54	2nd	4.0
8-15	T.B.	L	1-3		9	11	Sturtze	Fassero	Hernandez	60-55	2nd	5.0
8-16	T.B.	W	4-3		11	7	Arrojo	Wilson	Lowe	61-55	2nd	4.0
8-17	Tex.	W	8-7		18	12	Garces	Wetteland		62-55	2nd	4.0
8-18	Tex.	W	6-4		11	8	Ohka	Rogers	Lowe	63-55	2nd	3.0
8-19	Tex.	W	9-0		11	5	P. Martinez	Perisho		64-55	2nd	3.0
8-20	Tex.	L	2-6		9	9	Davis	Fassero		64-56	2nd	3.0
8-21	Ana.	W	7-6	(11)	8	8	Lowe	Hasegawa		65-56	2nd	3.0
8-22	Ana.	L	4-11		9	14	Mercker	Wakefield		65-57	2nd	3.0
8-23	Ana.	W	3-1		5	8	Ohka	Ortiz	Lowe	66-57	2nd	3.0
8-24	At K.C.	W	9-7	(10)	12	11	Pichardo	Larkin	Lowe	67-57	2nd	3.0
8-25	At K.C.	L	2-6		5	13	Suppan	Florie		67-58	2nd	3.0
8-26	At K.C.	W	5-3		14	9	Arrojo	Meadows	Lowe	68-58	2nd	3.0
8-27	At K.C.	L	7-11		11	10	Reichert	Wakefield		68-59	2nd	4.0
8-28	At T.B.	L	2-5		8	9	Rekar	Pichardo	Hernandez	68-60	2nd	5.0
8-29	At T.B.	W	8-0		12	1	P. Martinez	Eiland		69-60	2nd	4.0
8-30	At T.B.	L	1-3		4	11	Lopez	Fassero	Hernandez	69-61	2nd	5.0
9-1	Sea.	W	6-2		14	6	Arrojo	Halama		70-61	2nd	5.0
9-2	Sea.	L	1-4		3	7	Garcia	Garces	Sasaki	70-62	2nd	6.0
9-3	Sea.	L	0-5		1	9	Abbott	Ohka	Paniagua	70-63	2nd	6.0
9-4	Sea.	W	5-1		7	7	P. Martinez	Moyer		71-63	2nd	6.0
9-5	Oak.	W	10-3		12	6	Schourek	Appier		72-63	2nd	6.0
9-6	Oak.	L	4-6		9	13	Mulder	Arrojo	Mecir	72-64	2nd	6.0
9-7	Min.	W	11-6		16	9	R. Martinez	Milton		73-64	2nd	6.0
9-8	N.Y.	L	0-4		5	8	Clemens	Ohka		73-65	2nd	7.0
9-9	N.Y.	L	3-5		9	7	Pettitte	P. Martinez		73-66	2nd	8.0
9-10	N.Y.	L	2-6		7	11	Keisler	Schourek	Gooden	73-67	3rd	9.0
9-11	At N.Y.	W	4-0		7	5	Arrojo	Hernandez	Lowe	74-67	2nd	8.0
9-12	At Cle.	W	8-6		12	7	R. Martinez	Finley	Lowe	75-67	2nd	8.0
9-13	At Cle.	L	3-10		6	12	Colon	Ohka		75-68	2nd	9.0
9-14	At Cle.	W	7-4		10	7	P. Martinez	Nagy	Lowe	76-68	2nd	8.0
9-15	At Det.	W	7-6		12	9	Beck	Cruz	Lowe	77-68	2nd	7.0
9-16†	At Det.	W	8-5		13	11	Pichardo	Anderson	Lowe	78-68		
9-16‡	At Det.	L	2-12		8	13	Nomo	Ontiveros		78-69	2nd	7.5
9-17	At Det.	L	4-5		8	9	Mlicki	R. Martinez	Jones	78-70	2nd	7.5
9-19	Cle.	W	7-4		12	11	Beck	Nagy	Lowe	79-70	2nd	6.0
9-20†	Cle.	L	1-2		6	7	Woodard	P. Martinez	Wickman	79-71		
9-20‡	Cle.	L	4-5		10	10	Karsay	Cormier	Wickman	79-72	3rd	6.5
9-21†	Cle.	W	9-8		12	12	Ontiveros	Speier	Lowe	80-72		
9-21‡	Cle.	L	5-8		12	15	Finley	Wakefield		80-73	3rd	6.0
9-22	Bal.	L	1-3		4	6	Ponson	R. Martinez		80-74	3rd	6.0
9-23	Bal.	W	8-7	(10)	12	13	Carrasco	Kohlmeier		81-74	3rd	6.0
9-24	Bal.	L	0-1		8	4	Mussina	Ohka	Kohlmeier	81-75	3rd	7.0
9-26	At Chi.	W	4-3		6	5	P. Martinez	Beirne	Lowe	82-75	T2nd	5.5
9-27	At Chi.	W	2-1		7	5	Crawford	Baldwin	Lowe	83-75	T2nd	4.5
9-28	At Chi.	W	7-6		9	8	Beck	Simas	Lowe	84-75	2nd	3.5
9-29	At T.B.	L	6-8		11	11	Yan	Carrasco	Hernandez	84-76	2nd	3.5
9-30	At T.B.	W	4-2		11	5	Cormier	Hernandez	Lowe	85-76	2nd	2.5
10-1	At T.B.	L	2-3	(10)	9	10	Wheeler	Croushore		85-77	2nd	2.5

Monthly records: April (12-9), May (17-10), June (9-18), July (16-11), August (15-13), September (16-15), October (0-1).
*Innings, if other than nine. † First game of a doubleheader. ‡ Second game of a doubleheader.

MEMORABLE GAMES

April 30 at Cleveland

This plunkfest in Cleveland sparked a slap-on-the-wrist suspension for Pedro Martinez and renewed debate over a pitcher's right to work inside. First, Indians batter Einar Diaz, offended by a high and tight pitch, engaged in a staredown contest with Martinez. Then Cleveland pitcher Charles Nagy retaliated by hitting Jose Offerman. When Martinez plunked Robbie Alomar, both benches cleared before order could be restored. It was great theatre—and a 2-1 victory for Martinez and the Red Sox.

Boston	AB	R	H	BI	Cleveland	AB	R	H	BI
Offerman, 2b	3	0	0	0	Cabrera, cf	4	0	1	0
Nixon, rf	4	0	1	1	Whiten, ph	0	0	0	0
Daubach, 1b	4	0	1	0	Vizquel, ss	5	0	0	0
Garciaparra, ss	4	0	0	0	Alomar, 2b	4	0	0	0
O'Leary, lf	4	0	1	0	Ramirez, rf	4	0	1	0
Everett, cf	4	0	1	0	Justice, lf	2	0	0	0
Stanley, dh	4	1	1	1	Thome, dh	3	0	1	0
Varitek, c	3	1	2	0	Fryman, 3b	4	0	0	0
Alexander, 3b	3	0	0	0	Sexson, 1b	3	1	1	1
					Diaz, c	4	0	2	0
Totals	**33**	**2**	**7**	**2**	**Totals**	**33**	**1**	**6**	**1**

Boston.......................................0 0 0 0 0 1 1 0 0—2 7 1
Cleveland...................................0 0 0 0 0 0 0 0 1—1 6 0

E—Garciaparra (4). LOB—Boston 7, Cleveland 11. 2B—O'Leary (6), Diaz 2 (5). HR—Stanley (3), Sexson (1). SB—Everett (1), Alomar 2 (5), Justice (1). SH—Alexander.

Boston	IP	H	R	ER	BB	SO
P. Martinez (W 5-0)	7	5	0	0	3	10
Lowe (S 5)	2	1	1	1	2	1

Cleveland	IP	H	R	ER	BB	SO
Nagy (L 1-4)	8	6	2	2	0	5
DePaula	1	1	0	0	1	2

P. Martinez pitched to 1 batter in 8th.

HBP—Alomar by P. Martinez, Offerman by Nagy. U—HP, Tschida. 1B, Meriwether. 2B, Gibson. 3B, Rippley. T—2:50. A—42,065.

August 29 at Tampa Bay

Martinez took center stage again when Gerald Williams, the first batter in the game for Tampa Bay, charged the mound after being hit by a pitch. After a brawl, the Devil Rays spent the rest of the night throwing pitches at Brian Daubach, whom they believed had thrown a cheap punch in the pileup. Martinez was unfazed. He did not allow another baserunner until John Flaherty singled to lead off the ninth and finished with a one-hit, 13-strikeout 8-0 win.

Boston	AB	R	H	BI	Tampa Bay	AB	R	H	BI
Nixon, rf	5	2	3	0	Williams, cf	0	0	0	0
Daubach, 1b	2	0	0	0	Tyner, pr-cf	3	0	0	0
Brogna, pr-1b	0	2	0	0	Cairo, 2b	4	0	0	0
Everett, cf	5	2	4	6	Vaughn, dh	3	0	0	0
Garciaparra, ss	4	1	1	0	McGriff, 1b	3	0	0	0
O'Leary, lf	4	0	2	1	Cox, lf	3	0	0	0
Hatteberg, dh	4	0	0	0	Huff, 3b	3	0	0	0
Merloni, 3b	1	0	1	0	J.Guillen, rf	3	0	0	0
Alexander, ph-3b	4	0	0	1	Flaherty, c	3	0	1	0
Varitek, c	4	0	0	0	O.Guillen, ss	3	0	0	0
Lansing, 2b	4	1	1	0					
Totals	**37**	**8**	**12**	**8**	**Totals**	**28**	**0**	**1**	**0**

Boston...................................0 0 2 0 1 0 3 0 2—8 12 0
Tampa Bay...............................0 0 0 0 0 0 0 0 0—0 1 0

DP—Tampa Bay 2. LOB—Boston 9, Tampa Bay 2. 2B—Everett (23). 3B—Nixon (7), Everett (4). HR—Everett 2 (32).

Boston	IP	H	R	ER	BB	SO
P. Martinez (W 15-4)	9	1	0	0	0	13

Tampa Bay	IP	H	R	ER	BB	SO
Eiland (L 2-2)	2	5	2	2	0	1
Lidle	4	4	2	2	1	2
Fiore	0	0	1	1	0	0
Creek	2	1	1	1	1	2
Taylor	1	2	2	2	2	0

Eiland pitched to 5 batters in 3rd. Lidle pitched to 1 batter in 7th. Fiore pitched to 1 batter in 7th.

HBP—Williams by P. Martinez, Garciaparra by Eiland, Daubach by Eiland; by Fiore. U—HP, Cuzzi. 1B, Schrieber. 2B, McClelland. 3B, Rapuano. T—2:58. A—17,450.

INDIVIDUAL STATISTICS

BATTING

Name	G	TPA	AB	R	H	TB	2B	3B	HR	RBI	Avg.	Obp.	Slg.	SH	SF	HP	BB	IBB	SO	SB	CS	GDP	vs RHP				vs LHP			
																							AB	Avg.	HR	RBI	AB	Avg.	HR	RBI
Garciaparra, Nomar	140	599	529	104	197	317	51	3	21	96	.372	.434	.599	0	7	2	61	20	50	5	2	8	388	.369	15	67	141	.383	6	29
O'Leary, Troy	138	563	513	68	134	211	30	4	13	70	.261	.320	.411	0	4	2	44	2	76	0	2	12	366	.265	10	47	147	.252	3	23
Everett, Carl	137	561	496	82	149	291	32	4	34	108	.300	.373	.587	0	5	8	52	5	113	11	4	4	364	.283	30	85	132	.348	4	23
Daubach, Brian	142	549	495	55	123	222	32	2	21	76	.248	.315	.448	0	4	6	44	2	130	1	1	6	393	.257	18	65	102	.216	3	11
Offerman, Jose	116	527	451	73	115	162	14	3	9	41	.255	.354	.359	2	3	1	70	0	70	0	8	9	317	.240	5	25	134	.291	4	16
Varitek, Jason	139	519	448	55	111	174	31	1	10	65	.248	.342	.388	1	4	6	60	3	84	1	1	16	318	.245	7	46	130	.254	3	19
Nixon, Trot	123	502	427	66	118	197	27	8	12	60	.276	.368	.461	5	5	2	63	2	85	8	1	11	374	.278	11	54	53	.264	1	6
Lewis, Darren	97	303	270	44	65	83	12	0	2	17	.241	.305	.307	8	0	3	22	0	34	10	5	2	158	.215	1	9	112	.277	1	8
Frye, Jeff	69	273	239	35	69	85	13	0	1	13	.289	.364	.356	4	1	1	28	0	38	1	3	5	171	.263	0	10	68	.353	1	3
Hatteberg, Scott	92	271	230	21	61	100	15	0	8	36	.265	.367	.435	1	2	0	38	3	39	0	1	8	193	.280	8	32	37	.189	0	4
Alexander, Manny	101	209	194	30	41	63	4	3	4	19	.211	.261	.325	2	0	0	13	0	41	2	0	0	137	.204	3	15	57	.228	1	4
Stanley, Mike	58	218	185	22	41	76	5	0	10	28	.222	.327	.411	1	2	0	30	0	44	0	0	1	142	.211	8	20	43	.256	2	8
Veras, Wilton	49	179	164	21	40	49	7	1	0	14	.244	.278	.299	3	3	2	7	0	20	0	0	2	129	.248	0	11	35	.229	0	3
Lansing, Mike	49	148	139	10	27	31	4	0	0	13	.194	.230	.223	0	2	0	7	1	26	0	0	7	109	.202	0	10	30	.167	0	3
Merloni, Lou	40	139	128	10	41	56	11	2	0	18	.320	.341	.438	4	2	1	4	1	22	1	0	8	94	.330	0	13	34	.294	0	5
Bichette, Dante	30	122	114	13	33	59	5	0	7	14	.289	.336	.518	0	0	0	8	0	22	0	0	3	86	.279	3	9	28	.321	4	5
Sprague, Ed	33	123	111	11	24	34	4	0	2	9	.216	.293	.306	0	0	0	12	0	18	0	0	2	74	.243	1	4	37	.162	1	5
Sadler, Donnie	49	112	99	14	22	30	5	0	1	10	.222	.262	.303	5	2	1	5	0	18	3	1	1	74	.270	1	9	25	.080	0	1
Gilkey, Bernard	36	104	91	11	21	31	5	1	1	9	.231	.327	.341	0	0	3	10	0	12	0	0	5	33	.242	1	2	58	.224	0	7
Burkhart, Morgan	25	95	73	16	21	36	3	0	4	18	.288	.442	.493	0	1	4	17	1	25	0	0	1	51	.314	4	14	22	.227	0	4
Brogna, Rico	43	60	56	8	11	17	3	0	1	8	.196	.237	.304	1	0	0	3	0	13	0	0	1	53	.208	1	8	3	.000	0	0
Alcantara, Israel	21	48	45	9	13	26	1	0	4	7	.289	.333	.578	0	0	0	3	0	7	0	0	0	13	.308	1	1	32	.281	3	6
Valentin, John	10	38	35	6	9	16	1	0	2	2	.257	.297	.457	1	0	0	2	0	5	0	1	1	30	.233	2	2	5	.400	0	0
Cummings, Midre	21	31	25	1	7	7	0	0	0	2	.280	.419	.280	0	0	0	6	0	3	0	0	1	25	.280	0	2	0	.000	0	0
Sheets, Andy	12	21	21	1	2	2	0	0	0	1	.095	.095	.095	0	0	0	0	0	3	0	0	1	19	.105	0	1	2	.000	0	0
Pride, Curtis	9	21	20	4	5	6	1	0	0	0	.250	.286	.300	0	0	0	1	0	7	0	0	0	17	.294	0	0	3	.000	0	0
Gaetti, Gary	5	11	10	0	0	0	0	0	0	1	.000	.000	.000	0	1	0	0	0	3	0	0	0	3	.000	0	0	7	.000	0	1
Martinez, Ramon	27	5	5	1	1	1	0	0	0	0	.200	.200	.200	0	0	0	0	0	1	0	0	0	0	.000	0	0	5	.200	0	0
Schourek, Pete	22	4	4	0	2	2	0	0	0	0	.500	.500	.500	0	0	0	0	0	1	0	0	0	3	.667	0	0	1	.000	0	0
Berry, Sean	1	4	4	0	0	0	0	0	0	0	.000	.000	.000	0	0	0	0	0	2	0	0	0	0	.000	0	0	4	.000	0	0
Rose, Brian	15	4	3	0	0	0	0	0	0	0	.000	.250	.000	0	0	0	1	0	1	0	0	0	2	.000	0	0	1	.000	0	0
Fassero, Jeff	38	3	2	1	0	0	0	0	0	0	.000	.000	.000	1	0	0	0	0	2	0	0	0	2	.000	0	0	0	.000	0	0
Wakefield, Tim	52	3	2	0	0	0	0	0	0	0	.000	.000	.000	1	0	0	0	0	2	0	0	0	0	.000	0	0	2	.000	0	0
Pichardo, Hipolito	38	1	1	0	0	0	0	0	0	0	.000	.000	.000	0	0	0	0	0	1	0	0	0	1	.000	0	0	0	.000	0	0
Lowe, Derek	74	1	1	0	0	0	0	0	0	0	.000	.000	.000	0	0	0	0	0	1	0	0	0	1	.000	0	0	0	.000	0	0
Garces, Rich	64	0	0	0	0	0	0	0	0	0	.000	.000	.000	0	0	0	0	0	0	0	0	0	0	.000	0	0	0	.000	0	0
Cormier, Rheal	64	0	0	0	0	0	0	0	0	0	.000	.000	.000	0	0	0	0	0	0	0	0	0	0	.000	0	0	0	.000	0	0
Florie, Bryce	29	0	0	0	0	0	0	0	0	0	.000	.000	.000	0	0	0	0	0	0	0	0	0	0	.000	0	0	0	.000	0	0
Wasdin, John	25	0	0	0	0	0	0	0	0	0	.000	.000	.000	0	0	0	0	0	0	0	0	0	0	.000	0	0	0	.000	0	0
Stanifer, Rob	8	0	0	0	0	0	0	0	0	0	.000	.000	.000	0	0	0	0	0	0	0	0	0	0	.000	0	0	0	.000	0	0
Smith, Dan	2	0	0	0	0	0	0	0	0	0	.000	.000	.000	0	0	0	0	0	0	0	0	0	0	.000	0	0	0	.000	0	0
Ontiveros, Steve	3	0	0	0	0	0	0	0	0	0	.000	.000	.000	0	0	0	0	0	0	0	0	0	0	.000	0	0	0	.000	0	0
Beck, Rod	34	0	0	0	0	0	0	0	0	0	.000	.000	.000	0	0	0	0	0	0	0	0	0	0	.000	0	0	0	.000	0	0
Martinez, Pedro	29	0	0	0	0	0	0	0	0	0	.000	.000	.000	0	0	0	0	0	0	0	0	0	0	.000	0	0	0	.000	0	0
Carrasco, Hector	8	0	0	0	0	0	0	0	0	0	.000	.000	.000	0	0	0	0	0	0	0	0	0	0	.000	0	0	0	.000	0	0
Arrojo, Rolando	13	0	0	0	0	0	0	0	0	0	.000	.000	.000	0	0	0	0	0	0	0	0	0	0	.000	0	0	0	.000	0	0
Croushore, Rick	5	0	0	0	0	0	0	0	0	0	.000	.000	.000	0	0	0	0	0	0	0	0	0	0	.000	0	0	0	.000	0	0
Young, Tim	8	0	0	0	0	0	0	0	0	0	.000	.000	.000	0	0	0	0	0	0	0	0	0	0	.000	0	0	0	.000	0	0
Ohka, Tomokazu	13	0	0	0	0	0	0	0	0	0	.000	.000	.000	0	0	0	0	0	0	0	0	0	0	.000	0	0	0	.000	0	0
Pena, Jesus	2	0	0	0	0	0	0	0	0	0	.000	.000	.000	0	0	0	0	0	0	0	0	0	0	.000	0	0	0	.000	0	0
Lee, Sang-Hoon	9	0	0	0	0	0	0	0	0	0	.000	.000	.000	0	0	0	0	0	0	0	0	0	0	.000	0	0	0	.000	0	0
Crawford, Paxton	7	0	0	0	0	0	0	0	0	0	.000	.000	.000	0	0	0	0	0	0	0	0	0	0	.000	0	0	0	.000	0	0

Players with more than one A.L. team

Name	G	TPA	AB	R	H	TB	2B	3B	HR	RBI	Avg.	Obp.	Slg.	SH	SF	HP	BB	IBB	SO	SB	CS	GDP	vs RHP				vs LHP			
																							AB	Avg.	HR	RBI	AB	Avg.	HR	RBI
Carrasco, Min.-Bos.	69	0	0	0	0	0	0	0	0	0	.000	.000	.000	0	0	0	0	0	0	0	0	0	0	.000	0	0	0	.000	0	0
Cummings, Min.-Bos.	98	227	206	29	57	79	10	0	4	24	.277	.341	.383	1	0	3	17	1	28	0	0	5	181	.265	4	21	25	.360	0	3
Pena, Chi.-Bos.	22	0	0	0	0	0	0	0	0	0	.000	.000	.000	0	0	0	0	0	0	0	0	0	0	.000	0	0	0	.000	0	0
Stanley, Bos.-Oak.	90	331	282	33	67	121	12	0	14	46	.238	.339	.429	1	3	1	44	0	65	0	0	4	199	.211	8	25	83	.301	6	21

PITCHING

Name	W	L	Pct.	ERA	IP	H	R	ER	HR	SH	SF	HB	BB	IBB	SO	G	GS	CG	ShO	GF	Sv	vs. RH				vs. LH			
																						AB	Avg.	HR	RBI	AB	Avg.	HR	RBI
Martinez, Pedro	18	6	.750	1.74	217.0	128	44	42	17	2	1	14	32	0	284	29	29	7	4	0	0	369	.184	12	22	399	.150	5	19
Wakefield, Tim	6	10	.375	5.48	159.1	170	107	97	31	4	8	4	65	3	102	51	17	0	0	13	0	342	.295	20	54	283	.244	11	45
Fassero, Jeff	8	8	.500	4.78	130.0	153	72	69	16	7	2	1	50	2	97	38	23	0	0	4	0	411	.307	14	54	106	.255	2	10
Martinez, Ramon	10	8	.556	6.13	127.2	143	94	87	16	2	7	9	67	3	89	27	27	0	0	0	0	250	.292	8	38	255	.275	8	40
Schourek, Pete	3	10	.231	5.11	107.1	116	67	61	17	4	1	3	38	2	63	21	21	0	0	0	0	338	.266	14	41	80	.325	3	10
Lowe, Derek	4	4	.500	2.56	91.1	90	27	26	6	4	1	2	22	5	79	74	0	0	0	64	42	186	.247	3	17	164	.268	3	16
Garces, Rich	8	1	.889	3.25	74.2	64	28	27	7	1	4	1	23	5	69	64	0	0	0	9	1	165	.242	5	16	115	.209	2	18
Arrojo, Rolando	5	2	.714	5.05	71.1	67	41	40	10	1	0	4	22	0	44	13	13	0	0	0	0	128	.211	3	22	146	.274	7	16
Ohka, Tomokazu	3	6	.333	3.12	69.1	70	25	24	7	1	2	2	26	0	40	13	12	0	0	1	0	107	.243	2	10	159	.277	5	15
Cormier, Rheal	3	3	.500	4.61	68.1	74	40	35	7	5	2	0	17	2	43	64	0	0	0	12	0	182	.280	6	23	87	.264	1	8
Pichardo, Hipolito	6	3	.667	3.46	65.0	63	29	25	1	2	2	3	26	2	37	38	1	0	0	5	1	148	.243	1	18	94	.287	0	14
Rose, Brian	3	5	.375	6.11	53.0	58	37	36	11	1	2	3	21	3	24	15	12	0	0	1	0	112	.250	5	14	100	.300	6	23
Florie, Bryce	0	4	.000	4.56	49.1	57	30	25	5	6	3	1	19	6	34	29	0	0	0	14	1	112	.259	4	22	81	.346	1	12
Wasdin, John	1	3	.250	5.04	44.2	48	25	25	8	0	5	2	15	1	36	25	1	0	0	10	1	107	.290	4	24	69	.246	4	12
Beck, Rod	3	0	1.000	3.10	40.2	34	15	14	2	2	0	2	12	1	35	34	0	0	0	8	0	84	.202	1	10	69	.246	1	8
Crawford, Paxton	2	1	.667	3.41	29.0	25	15	11	0	0	4	2	13	2	17	7	4	0	0	2	0	50	.180	0	8	54	.296	0	5
Stanifer, Rob	0	0	.000	7.62	13.0	22	19	11	3	0	0	0	4	1	3	8	0	0	0	3	0	30	.333	2	9	32	.375	1	7
Lee, Sang-Hoon	0	0	.000	3.09	11.2	11	4	4	2	0	1	1	5	0	6	9	0	0	0	1	0	37	.297	2	4	5	.000	0	0
Young, Tim	0	0	.000	6.43	7.0	7	5	5	3	0	0	1	2	0	6	8	0	0	0	3	0	15	.200	0	0	11	.364	3	6
Carrasco, Hector	1	1	.500	9.45	6.2	15	8	7	2	2	0	1	5	1	7	8	1	0	0	2	0	19	.526	1	4	13	.385	1	4
Ontiveros, Steve	1	1	.500	10.13	5.1	9	6	6	1	0	0	0	4	0	1	3	1	0	0	0	0	11	.364	1	3	13	.385	0	3
Croushore, Rick	0	1	.000	5.79	4.2	4	3	3	0	1	1	1	5	1	3	5	0	0	0	3	0	10	.400	0	1	6	.000	0	2
Smith, Dan	0	0	.000	8.10	3.1	2	3	3	0	1	3	0	3	0	1	2	0	0	0	0	0	5	.400	0	2	3	.000	0	1
Pena, Jesus	0	0	.000	3.00	3.0	3	1	1	1	0	0	0	3	0	1	2	0	0	0	0	0	9	.111	0	0	2	1.000	1	1

PITCHERS WITH MORE THAN ONE A.L. TEAM

Name	W	L	Pct.	ERA	IP	H	R	ER	HR	SH	SF	HB	BB	IBB	SO	G	GS	CG	ShO	GF	Sv	vs. RH				vs. LH			
																						AB	Avg.	HR	RBI	AB	Avg.	HR	RBI
Carrasco, Min.-Bos.	5	4	.556	4.69	78.2	90	46	41	8	8	4	4	38	1	64	69	1	0	0	4	1	195	.297	4	29	115	.278	4	24
Pena, Chi.-Bos.	2	1	.667	5.13	26.1	28	19	15	7	0	2	1	19	0	20	22	0	0	0	2	1	64	.250	5	16	37	.324	2	7

DESIGNATED HITTERS

Name	AB	Avg.	HR	RBI	Name	AB	Avg.	HR	RBI	Name	AB	Avg.	HR	RBI
Daubach, Brian	150	.220	7	22	Gilkey, Bernard	25	.200	0	2	Alexander, Manny	4	.000	0	0
Bichette, Dante	114	.289	7	14	Alcantara, Israel	23	.217	2	5	Frye, Jeff	3	.333	0	0
Stanley, Mike	67	.269	5	13	Everett, Carl	19	.474	1	9	Garciaparra, Nomar	3	.000	0	0
Burkhart, Morgan	62	.274	4	16	Gaetti, Gary	10	.000	0	1	Sheets, Andy	2	.000	0	0
Hatteberg, Scott	56	.232	3	10	Sprague, Ed	6	.000	0	0	Nixon, Trot	1	.000	0	0
Offerman, Jose	39	.205	0	1	Varitek, Jason	5	.200	0	1	Brogna, Rico	1	.000	0	0

INDIVIDUAL STATISTICS

FIELDING

FIRST BASEMEN

Player	Pct.	G	PO	A	E	TC	DP
Daubach, Brian	.996	83	642	51	3	696	49
Stanley, Mike	.997	39	264	31	1	296	26
Offerman, Jose	.986	39	253	29	4	286	19
Brogna, Rico	.983	37	165	9	3	177	13
Burkhart, Morgan	.964	5	26	1	1	28	1
Alcantara, Israel	1.000	5	9	0	0	9	1
Sprague, Ed	1.000	3	17	4	0	21	1
Sheets, Andy	1.000	1	0	1	0	1	0

SECOND BASEMEN

Player	Pct.	G	PO	A	E	TC	DP
Offerman, Jose	.981	80	150	202	7	359	43
Frye, Jeff	.991	53	95	122	2	219	20
Lansing, Mike	1.000	49	73	106	0	179	12
Sadler, Donnie	1.000	12	9	18	0	27	3
Alexander, Manny	1.000	7	5	7	0	12	1

THIRD BASEMEN

Player	Pct.	G	PO	A	E	TC	DP
Alexander, Manny	.944	63	39	79	7	125	5
Veras, Wilton	.907	49	33	94	13	140	11
Merloni, Lou	.928	40	26	64	7	97	3
Sprague, Ed	.972	31	19	50	2	71	1
Valentin, John	1.000	10	6	9	0	15	0
Frye, Jeff	1.000	3	1	2	0	3	0
Sadler, Donnie	1.000	3	0	3	0	3	1
Daubach, Brian	1.000	1	0	1	0	1	0
Berry, Sean	-	1	0	0	0	0	0
Hatteberg, Scott	-	1	0	0	0	0	0
Lansing, Mike	-	1	0	0	0	0	0

SHORTSTOPS

Player	Pct.	G	PO	A	E	TC	DP
Garciaparra, Nomar	.971	136	201	402	18	621	65
Alexander, Manny	1.000	20	16	33	0	49	7
Sadler, Donnie	.958	19	19	50	3	72	7
Sheets, Andy	1.000	10	7	17	0	24	4

OUTFIELDERS

Player	Pct.	G	PO	A	E	TC	DP
O'Leary, Troy	.988	137	243	9	3	255	0
Everett, Carl	.980	126	276	11	6	293	4
Nixon, Trot	.991	118	216	8	2	226	4
Lewis, Darren	.981	89	152	5	3	160	1
Gilkey, Bernard	1.000	22	36	1	0	37	0
Sadler, Donnie	1.000	17	21	0	0	21	0
Frye, Jeff	1.000	15	20	0	0	20	0
Pride, Curtis	1.000	9	15	0	0	15	0
Daubach, Brian	1.000	8	20	0	0	20	0
Alcantara, Israel	.889	8	8	0	1	9	0
Cummings, Midre	1.000	4	7	0	0	7	0
Burkhart, Morgan	-	1	0	0	0	0	0

CATCHERS

Player	Pct.	G	PO	A	E	TC	DP	PB
Varitek, Jason	.992	128	867	46	7	920	3	14
Hatteberg, Scott	.981	48	297	16	6	319	3	12

PITCHERS

Player	Pct.	G	PO	A	E	TC	DP
Lowe, Derek	1.000	74	8	11	0	19	0
Cormier, Rheal	1.000	64	1	14	0	15	0
Garces, Rich	1.000	64	5	6	0	11	0
Wakefield, Tim	.917	51	11	11	2	24	2
Fassero, Jeff	.967	38	11	18	1	30	3
Pichardo, Hipolito	.944	38	7	10	1	18	1
Beck, Rod	1.000	34	0	3	0	3	0
Martinez, Pedro	1.000	29	14	28	0	42	2
Florie, Bryce	1.000	29	7	12	0	19	1
Martinez, Ramon	1.000	27	16	7	0	23	0
Wasdin, John	1.000	25	2	2	0	4	0
Schourek, Pete	.875	21	3	18	3	24	1
Rose, Brian	.889	15	4	4	1	9	0
Arrojo, Rolando	1.000	13	6	10	0	16	1
Ohka, Tomokazu	.938	13	8	7	1	16	1
Lee, Sang-Hoon	1.000	9	0	2	0	2	0
Stanifer, Rob	1.000	8	0	2	0	2	0
Carrasco, Hector	.000	8	0	0	1	1	0
Young, Tim	1.000	8	1	0	0	1	0
Crawford, Paxton	1.000	7	1	0	0	1	0
Croushore, Rick	1.000	5	0	1	0	1	0
Ontiveros, Steve	-	3	0	0	0	0	0
Pena, Jesus	-	2	0	0	0	0	0
Smith, Dan	-	2	0	0	0	0	0

PITCHING AGAINST EACH CLUB

Pitcher	Ana. W-L	Bal. W-L	Chi. W-L	Cle. W-L	Det. W-L	K.C. W-L	Min. W-L	N.Y. W-L	Oak. W-L	Sea. W-L	T.B. W-L	Tex. W-L	Tor. W-L	N.L. W-L	Total W-L
Arrojo, Rolando	0-0	0-0	0-0	0-0	0-0	1-0	0-0	1-0	0-2	1-0	1-0	1-0	0-0	0-0	5-2
Beck, Rod	0-0	0-0	1-0	1-0	1-0	0-0	0-0	0-0	0-0	0-0	0-0	0-0	0-0	0-0	3-0
Carrasco, Hector	0-0	1-0	0-0	0-0	0-0	0-0	0-0	0-0	0-0	0-0	0-1	0-0	0-0	0-0	1-1
Cormier, Rheal	0-0	1-0	0-0	0-1	0-0	0-1	0-0	0-0	0-0	0-0	1-0	0-0	1-0	0-1	3-3
Crawford, Paxton	0-0	0-0	1-1	0-0	0-0	0-0	1-0	0-0	0-0	0-0	0-0	0-0	0-0	0-0	2-1
Croushore, Rick	0-0	0-0	0-0	0-0	0-0	0-0	0-0	0-0	0-0	0-0	0-1	0-0	0-0	0-0	0-1
Fassero, Jeff	1-0	0-0	1-0	0-0	2-0	1-0	1-0	0-0	0-2	0-1	1-2	1-1	0-1	0-1	8-8
Florie, Bryce	0-0	0-1	0-0	0-0	0-0	0-1	0-0	0-0	0-0	0-1	0-0	0-0	0-1	0-0	0-4
Garces, Rich	0-0	1-0	0-0	0-0	0-0	1-0	0-0	1-0	1-0	1-1	0-0	1-0	0-0	2-0	8-1
Lee, Sang-Hoon	0-0	0-0	0-0	0-0	0-0	0-0	0-0	0-0	0-0	0-0	0-0	0-0	0-0	0-0	0-0
Lowe, Derek	1-0	0-1	0-0	0-0	1-0	0-1	0-0	0-0	1-0	0-0	1-0	0-0	0-1	0-1	4-4
Martinez, Pedro	1-1	1-0	2-0	3-1	0-0	0-0	0-0	1-2	2-0	3-0	1-1	2-0	1-1	1-0	18-6
Martinez, Ramon	0-0	1-1	1-0	1-1	0-2	0-0	2-1	2-0	0-0	0-1	1-0	0-0	0-1	2-1	10-8
Ohka, Tomokazu	1-1	0-1	0-0	0-1	0-0	0-0	0-1	0-1	0-0	0-1	0-0	2-0	0-0	0-0	3-6
Ontiveros, Steve	0-0	0-0	0-0	1-0	0-1	0-0	0-0	0-0	0-0	0-0	0-0	0-0	0-0	0-0	1-1
Pena, Jesus	0-0	0-0	0-0	0-0	0-0	0-0	0-0	0-0	0-0	0-0	0-0	0-0	0-0	0-0	0-0
Pichardo, Hipolito	0-0	0-0	0-2	0-0	1-0	1-0	1-0	1-0	0-0	0-0	0-1	0-0	1-0	1-0	6-3
Rose, Brian	0-1	1-0	1-0	0-0	1-0	0-0	0-0	0-1	0-1	0-0	0-0	0-0	0-1	0-1	3-5
Schourek, Pete	0-1	0-1	0-2	0-1	1-0	0-1	0-0	0-1	1-0	0-0	0-0	0-0	1-1	0-2	3-10
Smith, Dan	0-0	0-0	0-0	0-0	0-0	0-0	0-0	0-0	0-0	0-0	0-0	0-0	0-0	0-0	0-0
Stanifer, Rob	0-0	0-0	0-0	0-0	0-0	0-0	0-0	0-0	0-0	0-0	0-0	0-0	0-0	0-0	0-0
Wakefield, Tim	0-1	1-0	0-0	0-1	0-2	0-2	2-0	0-1	0-0	0-0	0-0	0-2	0-0	3-1	6-10
Wasdin, John	0-0	0-0	0-0	0-0	0-0	0-0	1-0	0-1	0-0	0-0	0-0	0-0	0-1	0-1	1-3
Young, Tim	0-0	0-0	0-0	0-0	0-0	0-0	0-0	0-0	0-0	0-0	0-0	0-0	0-0	0-0	0-0
Totals	4-5	7-5	7-5	6-6	7-5	4-6	8-2	6-7	5-5	5-5	6-6	7-3	4-8	9-9	85-77

INTERLEAGUE: Garces 1-0, Wakefield 1-0, Schourek 0-2, Fassero 0-1, Martinez 0-1 vs. Braves; Wakefield 1-0, Pichardo 1-0, Martinez 1-0 vs. Expos; Garces 1-0, Martinez 1-0, Lowe 0-1 vs. Mets; Cormier 0-1, Wasdin 0-1, Wakefield 0-1 vs. Phillies; Wakefield 1-0, Martinez 1-0, Rose 0-1 vs. Marlins. Total: 9-9.

MISCELLANEOUS

HOME RUNS BY PARK

At Anaheim (8): O'Leary 2, Everett 2, Alexander 1, Garciaparra 1, Nixon 1, Daubach 1.
At Atlanta (1): Daubach 1.
At Baltimore (11): Everett 2, Hatteberg 2, Daubach 2, Stanley 1, Offerman 1, Lewis 1, Varitek 1, Sadler 1.
At Boston (66): Everett 17, Daubach 10, O'Leary 7, Garciaparra 7, Stanley 5, Bichette 4, Nixon 4, Offerman 3, Hatteberg 2, Varitek 2, Sprague 1, Brogna 1, Alexander 1, Burkhart 1, Alcantara 1.
At Chicago (AL) (7): Garciaparra 2, Alcantara 2, Bichette 1, Offerman 1, Hatteberg 1.
At Cleveland (6): Stanley 2, Bichette 2, Everett 1, Varitek 1.
At Detroit (10): Nixon 3, Stanley 1, Offerman 1, O'Leary 1, Hatteberg 1, Garciaparra 1, Daubach 1, Alcantara 1.
At Florida (2): Everett 1, Garciaparra 1.
At Kansas City (3): Daubach 2, Everett 1.
At Minnesota (13): O'Leary 2, Garciaparra 2, Offerman 1, Gilkey 1, Frye 1, Alexander 1, Everett 1, Hatteberg 1, Varitek 1, Daubach 1, Burkhart 1.
At New York (AL) (7): Stanley 1, Offerman 1, Valentin 1, Alexander 1, Garciaparra 1, Nixon 1, Varitek 1.
At Oakland (5): Garciaparra 2, Sprague 1, Hatteberg 1, Varitek 1.
At Philadelphia (3): Everett 2, Garciaparra 1.
At Seattle (7): Daubach 2, Lewis 1, Valentin 1, Garciaparra 1, Nixon 1, Varitek 1.
At Tampa Bay (8): Everett 2, Burkhart 2, O'Leary 1, Nixon 1, Varitek 1, Daubach 1.
At Texas (7): Everett 4, Offerman 1, Garciaparra 1, Varitek 1.
At Toronto (3): Everett 1, Garciaparra 1, Nixon 1.

LOW-HIT GAMES

No-hitters: None.
One-hitters: Pedro Martinez, August 29 vs. Tampa Bay, W 8-0.
Two-hitters: Pedro Martinez, May 12 vs. Baltimore, W 9-0.

10-STRIKEOUT GAMES

Pedro Martinez 15, Jeff Fassero 1,Total: 16

FOUR OR MORE HITS IN ONE GAME

Carl Everett 3, Nomar Garciaparra 2, Brian Daubach 2, Mike Stanley 1, Jose Offerman 1, Troy O'Leary 1, Trot Nixon 1, Total: 11

MULTI-HOMER GAMES

Carl Everett 3, Nomar Garciaparra 2, Brian Daubach 2, Jose Offerman 1, Troy O'Leary 1, Total: 9

GRAND SLAMS

4-19: Trot Nixon (off Detroit's Jim Poole)
6-1: Carl Everett (off Kansas City's Chris Fussell)
8-14: Rico Brogna (off Tampa Bay's Billy Taylor)
9-5: Manny Alexander (off Oakland's Kevin Appier)

PINCH HITTERS

(Minimum 5 at-bats)

Name	AB	Avg.	HR	RBI
Hatteberg, Scott	24	.292	2	5
Varitek, Jason	14	.286	0	2
Cummings, Midre	14	.286	0	2
Gilkey, Bernard	11	.182	0	0
Nixon, Trot	9	.111	0	0
Daubach, Brian	9	.111	1	5
Everett, Carl	8	.250	0	1
Alcantara, Israel	7	.143	0	0
Stanley, Mike	5	.600	0	1
Frye, Jeff	5	.400	0	0
Brogna, Rico	5	.000	0	0

DEBUTS

6-25: Israel Alcantara, RF.
6-27: Morgan Burkhart, DH.
6-29: Sang-Hoon Lee, P.
7-1: Paxton Crawford, P.

GAMES BY POSITION

Catcher: Jason Varitek 128, Scott Hatteberg 48.
First base: Brian Daubach 83, Mike Stanley 39, Jose Offerman 39, Rico Brogna 37, Morgan Burkhart 5, Israel Alcantara 5, Ed Sprague 3, Andy Sheets 1.
Second base: Jose Offerman 80, Jeff Frye 53, Mike Lansing 49, Donnie Sadler 12, Manny Alexander 7.
Third base: Manny Alexander 63, Wilton Veras 49, Lou Merloni 40, Ed Sprague 31, John Valentin 10, Jeff Frye 3, Donnie Sadler 3, Sean Berry 1, Mike Lansing 1, Scott Hatteberg 1, Brian Daubach 1.
Shortstop: Nomar Garciaparra 136, Manny Alexander 20, Donnie Sadler 19, Andy Sheets 10.
Outfield: Troy O'Leary 137, Carl Everett 126, Trot Nixon 118, Darren Lewis 89, Bernard Gilkey 22, Donnie Sadler 17, Jeff Frye 15, Curtis Pride 9, Brian Daubach 8, Israel Alcantara 8, Midre Cummings 4, Morgan Burkhart 1.
Designated hitter: Brian Daubach 41, Dante Bichette 30, Scott Hatteberg 20, Morgan Burkhart 19, Mike Stanley 18, Jose Offerman 9, Bernard Gilkey 8, Israel Alcantara 8, Gary Gaetti 5, Darren Lewis 5, Carl Everett 5, Jeff Frye 3, Manny Alexander 3, Rico Brogna 2, Andy Sheets 2, Donnie Sadler 2, Ed Sprague 1, Midre Cummings 1, Curtis Pride 1, Nomar Garciaparra 1, Trot Nixon 1, Jason Varitek 1.

STREAKS

Wins: 6 (May 10-15)
Losses: 5 (May 31-June 4, June 23-28)
Consecutive games with at least one hit: 14, Nomar Garciaparra (April 8-28)
Wins by pitcher: 5, Pedro Martinez (April 4-30)

ATTENDANCE

Home: 2,521,489
Road: 2,447,909
Highest (home): 33,909 (June 20 vs. New York).
Highest (road): 55,671 (May 27 vs. New York).
Lowest (home): 20,313 (April 12 vs. Minnesota).
Lowest (road): 8,488 (July 5 vs. Minnesota).

CHICAGO WHITE SOX

DAY BY DAY

Date	Opp.	Res.	Score	(inn.*)	Hits	Opp. hits	Winning pitcher	Losing pitcher	Save	Record	Pos.	GB
4-3	At Tex.	L	4-10		10	11	Rogers	Sirotka		0-1	T3rd	1.0
4-4	At Tex.	L	8-12		14	12	Cordero	Simas		0-2	T4th	1.5
4-5	At Tex.	W	12-8		15	13	Foulke	Zimmerman		1-2	T3rd	1.0
4-6	At Tex.	W	6-2		11	6	Baldwin	Loaiza		2-2	T1st	...
4-7	At Oak.	W	7-6		9	6	Eyre	Magnante	Foulke	3-2	T1st	...
4-8	At Oak.	W	7-3		13	7	Sirotka	Mahay		4-2	T1st	...
4-9	At Oak.	L	2-14		9	9	Appier	Wells		4-3	T2nd	0.5
4-11	At T.B.	W	13-6		18	10	Parque	Yan		5-3	3rd	1.0
4-12	At T.B.	W	7-1		15	7	Baldwin	Wheeler		6-3	3rd	1.0
4-13	At T.B.	L	5-6	(12)	8	11	Mecir	Sturtze		6-4	3rd	1.5
4-14	Ana.	W	9-4		12	12	Sirotka	Hill		7-4	3rd	0.5
4-15	Ana.	L	1-3		7	7	Bottenfield	Wells	Percival	7-5	3rd	0.5
4-16	Ana.	L	1-3		3	13	Schoeneweis	Parque	Percival	7-6	3rd	1.5
4-18	Sea.	W	18-11		19	13	Sturtze	Sele		8-6	2nd	0.5
4-19	Sea.	W	5-2		6	8	Lowe	Meche	Howry	9-6	1st	+0.5
4-21	Det.	W	7-2		8	8	Wells	Nitkowski		10-6	1st	+0.5
4-22	Det.	W	14-6		14	6	Parque	Weaver		11-6	1st	+1.0
4-23	Det.	W	9-4		9	9	Baldwin	Borkowski		12-6	1st	+1.5
4-24	Bal.	W	8-2		9	2	Eldred	Mussina		13-6	1st	+1.5
4-25	Bal.	L	6-12		11	12	Rapp	Sirotka		13-7	1st	+1.5
4-26	Bal.	W	11-6		10	10	Wells	Ponson		14-7	1st	+1.5
4-27	Bal.	W	13-4		13	9	Parque	Mercedes		15-7	1st	+2.0
4-28	At Det.	W	3-2		10	6	Baldwin	Weaver	Foulke	16-7	1st	+2.0
4-29	At Det.	W	2-1		5	6	Eldred	Mlicki	Foulke	17-7	1st	+2.0
4-30	At Det.	L	3-4	(12)	10	15	Anderson	Eyre		17-8	1st	+2.0
5-1	Tor.	L	3-5		6	9	Carpenter	Wells	Koch	17-9	1st	+2.0
5-2	Tor.	L	1-4		5	7	Castillo	Wunsch	Koch	17-10	1st	+2.0
5-3	Tor.	W	7-3		8	5	Baldwin	Escobar	Foulke	18-10	1st	+3.0
5-5	At K.C.	L	1-5		8	10	Fussell	Eldred		18-11	1st	+3.5
5-6	At K.C.	L	5-11		10	18	Spradlin	Sirotka		18-12	1st	+2.5
5-7	At K.C.	L	8-12		13	13	Bottalico	Wunsch		18-13	1st	+1.5
5-8	At Bos.	L	2-3		8	8	Rose	Sturtze	Lowe	18-14	1st	+0.5
5-9	At Bos.	W	6-0		10	3	Baldwin	Schourek		19-14	1st	+1.5
5-10	At Bos.	L	3-5	(7)	7	7	R. Martinez	Eldred	Garces	19-15	1st	+0.5
5-12	Min.	L	3-4	(10)	9	12	Miller	Lowe	Carrasco	19-16	2nd	...
5-13	Min.	W	4-3		8	8	Wunsch	Wells		20-16	2nd	...
5-14	Min.	W	5-3		10	8	Wunsch	Radke	Foulke	21-16	1st	+1.0
5-16	At N.Y.	W	4-0		7	3	Eldred	Hernandez		22-16	1st	+1.0
5-17	At N.Y.	L	4-9		7	15	Clemens	Parque		22-17	2nd	...
5-19	At Tor.	W	5-3		5	11	Sirotka	Escobar	Foulke	23-17	1st	+1.0
5-20	At Tor.	W	6-2		12	7	Baldwin	Wells		24-17	1st	+1.0
5-21	At Tor.	W	2-1		1	6	Eldred	Castillo	Foulke	25-17	1st	+1.0
5-22	At Tor.	L	3-4		6	11	Koch	Howry		25-18	1st	+0.5
5-23	N.Y.	W	8-2		11	9	Wells	Clemens		26-18	1st	+1.5
5-24	N.Y.	L	4-12		7	18	Pettitte	Sirotka		26-19	1st	+1.5
5-25	N.Y.	L	0-7		4	12	Mendoza	Baldwin		26-20	1st	+0.5
5-26	Cle.	W	5-3		6	8	Eldred	Finley	Foulke	27-20	1st	+1.5
5-27	Cle.	W	14-3		16	9	Parque	Wright		28-20	1st	+2.5
5-28	Cle.	L	3-12		7	15	Colon	Wells		28-21	1st	+1.5
5-29	At Sea.	L	4-5		7	6	Halama	Sirotka	Sasaki	28-22	1st	+1.5
5-30	At Sea.	W	2-1		4	5	Baldwin	Abbott	Foulke	29-22	1st	+1.5
5-31	At Sea.	W	4-3		6	6	Howry	Sasaki	Foulke	30-22	1st	+1.5
6-2	At Hou.	W	7-4		9	10	Parque	Reynolds	Foulke	31-22	1st	+2.5
6-3	At Hou.	L	1-6		8	10	Holt	Wells		31-23	1st	+1.5
6-4	At Hou.	W	7-3		13	5	Sirotka	Dotel		32-23	1st	+1.5
6-5	At Cin.	W	4-3		7	10	Baldwin	Parris	Foulke	33-23	1st	+1.5
6-6	At Cin.	W	17-12		19	12	Eldred	Villone		34-23	1st	+1.5
6-7	At Cin.	W	6-4		11	8	Parque	Bell	Foulke	35-23	1st	+1.5
6-9	Chi. (NL)	W	6-5	(14)	15	8	Pena	Van Poppel		36-23	1st	+2.0
6-10	Chi. (NL)	W	4-3		5	7	Sirotka	Wood	Foulke	37-23	1st	+2.0
6-11	Chi. (NL)	L	5-6		10	8	Van Poppel	Pena	Aguilera	37-24	1st	+2.0
6-12	At Cle.	W	8-7		14	13	Eldred	Rigdon	Foulke	38-24	1st	+3.0
6-13	At Cle.	W	4-3	(10)	8	8	Simas	Speier	Howry	39-24	1st	+4.0
6-14	At Cle.	W	11-4		12	5	Beirne	Brower		40-24	1st	+5.0
6-15	At N.Y.	W	12-3		16	12	Sirotka	Pettitte		41-24	1st	+5.5
6-16	At N.Y.	W	3-1		9	6	Baldwin	Stanton	Howry	42-24	1st	+6.5
6-17	At N.Y.	W	10-9		15	15	Eldred	Westbrook	Foulke	43-24	1st	+7.5
6-18	At N.Y.	W	17-4		18	10	Parque	Hernandez		44-24	1st	+7.5
6-19	Cle.	W	6-1		13	5	Wells	Colon		45-24	1st	+8.5
6-20	Cle.	L	1-4		7	9	Brower	Sirotka	Karsay	45-25	1st	+7.5
6-21	Cle.	L	6-8		14	12	Burba	Baldwin	Karsay	45-26	1st	+6.5
6-22	Cle.	W	6-0		11	7	Eldred	Finley		46-26	1st	+7.5
6-23	N.Y.	W	4-3		8	11	Lowe	Rivera		47-26	1st	+8.5
6-24	N.Y.	L	8-12		13	16	Mendoza	Wells	Rivera	47-27	1st	+8.0
6-25	N.Y.	W	8-7		13	10	Sirotka	Pettitte	Howry	48-27	1st	+8.0
6-27	Min.	L	4-7		9	12	Mays	Baldwin	Wells	48-28	1st	+7.5
6-28	Min.	W	7-3		14	4	Eldred	Lincoln		49-28	1st	+8.5
6-29	Min.	L	1-10		6	15	Milton	Wells		49-29	1st	+8.5
6-30	Bos.	W	10-4		13	11	Parque	Pichardo		50-29	1st	+9.5

HIGHLIGHTS

High point: There were two. One came on a mid-June romp through Cleveland and New York, when the young White Sox won seven straight games and took control of the A.L. Central Division. The other came September 24 when the Sox, despite a loss at Minnesota, clinched their first division title since 1993 and ended Cleveland's five-year reign.

Low point: The Sox entered the playoffs with the best record in the A.L. and high hopes. But a Division Series sweep by the Mariners sent them back to the drawing board. The Sox scored only seven runs on 17 hits in the series—single-game totals in the regular-season.

Turning point: During an April 22 game against the Tigers at Comiskey Park, two separate brawls resulted in the suspension of seven Sox players and manager Jerry Manuel. The team pulled together after the fracas and finished April with a sizzling 17-8 record.

Most valuable player: Frank Thomas was the best player on the league's best team. After two sluggish seasons, Thomas bounced back with a .328 average and career highs in home runs (43) and RBIs (143).

Most valuable pitcher: While James Baldwin and Cal Eldred battled late-season injuries, lefty Mike Sirotka quietly put up solid numbers—a career-high 15 wins and a 3.79 ERA that ranked third in the A.L. In nine starts against the Yankees, A's and Mariners, Sirotka was 6-3 with a 3.08 ERA.

Most improved player: Jim Parque bounced back from an 0-9, 6.95 ERA second half of 1999 to post a 13-6 record and 4.28 ERA. The White Sox gave him plenty of opportunity to win by averaging 8.6 runs for every nine innings he pitched.

Most pleasant surprise: Herbert Perry, a role player for Tampa Bay and Cleveland, started 98 games at third base and delivered nicely. He batted .308, hit 12 homers and drove in 61 runs in 109 games.

Key injuries: Starters Cal Eldred and James Baldwin combined for a 21-6 record in the first half, but injuries took their toll. Baldwin (shoulder) was 3-3 and Eldred (elbow) failed to win a game after the All-Star break. ...Shortstop Jose Valentin stayed in the lineup, even though he was bothered by an inflamed muscle in his pelvic region for much of the second half. ... Center fielder Chris Singleton was a different player after dislocating his right index finger in mid-May. Prior to the injury, Singleton was batting .285. He finished at .254.

Notable: The White Sox reeled off 11 straight road wins in June, the longest streak in baseball since 1984. ... Baldwin has had 10 or more wins and at least 100 strikeouts in each of his first five full seasons. ... Seven pitchers made their major league debuts in 2000 and eight rookies won their first game in the big leagues.

—SCOT GREGOR

MISCELLANEOUS

RECORDS

2000 regular-season record: 95-67 (1st in A.L. Central); 46-35 at home; 49-32 on road; 30-24 vs. East; 41-26 vs. Central; 24-17 vs. West; 21-10 vs. left-handed starters; 74-57 vs. righthanded starters; 81-62 on grass; 14-5 on turf; 26-30 in daytime; 69-37 at night; 28-18 in one-run games; 7-4 in extra-inning games; 0-1-0 in doubleheaders.

Team record past five years: 415-393 (.514, ranks 7th in league in that span).

TEAM LEADERS

Batting average: Frank Thomas (.328).
At-bats: Ray Durham (614).
Runs: Ray Durham (121).
Hits: Frank Thomas (191).
Total Bases: Frank Thomas (364).
Doubles: Frank Thomas (44).
Triples: Ray Durham (9).
Home runs: Frank Thomas (43).
Runs batted in: Frank Thomas (143).
Stolen bases: Ray Durham (25).
Slugging percentage: Frank Thomas (.625).
On-base percentage: Frank Thomas (.436).
Wins: Mike Sirotka (15).
Earned-run average: Mike Sirotka (3.79).
Complete games: James Baldwin, Cal Eldred (2).
Shutouts: James Baldwin, Cal Eldred (1).
Saves: Keith Foulke (34).
Innings pitched: Mike Sirotka (197.0).
Strikeouts: Mike Sirotka (128).

Date	Opp.	Res.	Score	(inn.*)	Hits	Opp. hits	Winning pitcher	Losing pitcher	Save	Record	Pos.	GB
7-1	Bos.	W	7-2		5	6	Sirotka	Crawford		51-29	1st	+10.5
7-2	Bos.	W	8-2		11	6	Baldwin	Schourek		52-29	1st	+10.5
7-3	At K.C.	W	14-10		22	10	Pena	Santiago		53-29	1st	+11.0
7-4	At K.C.	L	7-10		14	12	Spradlin	Garland		53-30	1st	+10.0
7-5	At K.C.	W	6-3	(13)	13	17	Wunsch	Bochtler		54-30	1st	+10.0
7-7	At Chi. (NL)	W	4-2	(12)	11	6	Lowe	Van Poppel	Pena	55-30	1st	+11.5
7-8	At Chi. (NL)	L	2-9		5	14	Lieber	Baldwin		55-31	1st	+11.5
7-9	At Chi. (NL)	L	6-9		8	11	Tapani	Simas	Worrell	55-32	1st	+10.5
7-13	StL.	L	5-13		11	14	An. Benes	Sirotka		55-33	1st	+9.5
7-14	StL.	L	4-9		8	11	Stephenson	Wunsch		55-34	1st	+8.5
7-15	StL.	W	15-7		15	13	Parque	Kile		56-34	1st	+8.5
7-16	Mil.	W	11-5		16	9	Baldwin	Snyder		57-34	1st	+9.5
7-17	Mil.	W	11-2		13	4	Garland	Bere		58-34	1st	+9.5
7-18	Mil.	W	7-5		10	9	Sirotka	Wright	Wunsch	59-34	1st	+9.5
7-19	At Min.	W	3-2		9	8	Buehrle	Milton	Foulke	60-34	1st	+10.5
7-20	At Min.	L	1-5		6	12	Mays	Parque		60-35	1st	+10.5
7-21	At Bos.	W	8-5		15	11	Simas	Pichardo	Howry	61-35	1st	+11.5
7-22	At Bos.	L	6-8		10	11	Fassero	Garland		61-36	1st	+11.5
7-23	At Bos.	L	0-1		6	5	P. Martinez	Sirotka		61-37	1st	+10.5
7-24	K.C.	W	7-6		9	14	Wunsch	Suzuki	Foulke	62-37	1st	+11.0
7-25	K.C.	L	1-6		4	8	Suppan	Parque		62-38	1st	+10.0
7-26	K.C.	L	6-7		9	10	Spradlin	Howry	Bottalico	62-39	1st	+10.0
7-27	At Ana.	W	6-5		18	9	Garland	Cooper	Foulke	63-39	1st	+10.5
7-28	At Ana.	L	7-10		13	10	Holtz	Beirne	Percival	63-40	1st	+10.0
7-29	At Ana.	L	5-6		9	11	Bottenfield	Barcelo	Percival	63-41	1st	+9.5
7-30	At Ana.	W	11-7	(10)	18	12	Foulke	Levine		64-41	1st	+10.5
8-1	At Tex.	W	4-3		12	7	Howry	Wetteland		65-41	1st	+11.5
8-2	At Tex.	L	2-7		4	13	Helling	Garland	Crabtree	65-42	1st	+10.5
8-4	Oak.	L	3-5		8	8	Appier	Sirotka	Isringhausen	65-43	1st	+9.0
8-5	Oak.	W	4-3	(10)	9	7	Foulke	Mathews		66-43	1st	+9.0
8-6	Oak.	W	13-0		15	5	Baldwin	Hudson		67-43	1st	+9.0
8-8†	Sea.	L	4-12		10	17	Pineiro	Garland	Tomko	67-44		
8-8‡	Sea.	L	5-7		8	9	Garcia	Buehrle	Sasaki	67-45	1st	+8.0
8-9	Sea.	W	19-3		24	8	Sirotka	Moyer		68-45	1st	+8.0
8-10	Sea.	L	3-6		11	9	Sele	Biddle	Sasaki	68-46	1st	+7.5
8-11	At T.B.	W	6-5		8	6	Buehrle	Wilson	Foulke	69-46	1st	+8.5
8-12	At T.B.	W	5-4	(10)	11	10	Buehrle	Hernandez	Foulke	70-46	1st	+8.5
8-13	At T.B.	L	3-5		5	8	Lopez	Howry		70-47	1st	+7.5
8-14	At Bal.	L	2-8		10	11	Mercedes	Sirotka		70-48	1st	+7.5
8-15	At Bal.	W	14-4		16	8	Biddle	Johnson		71-48	1st	+8.5
8-16	At Bal.	W	7-3		9	5	Parque	Mussina		72-48	1st	+9.5
8-17	At Bal.	L	3-5		4	10	Parrish	Baldwin		72-49	1st	+9.0
8-18	T.B.	W	5-2		9	7	Garland	Rekar	Foulke	73-49	1st	+9.0
8-19	T.B.	W	7-0		11	3	Sirotka	Lopez		74-49	1st	+9.0
8-20	T.B.	L	11-12		15	15	Yan	Foulke	Hernandez	74-50	1st	+8.0
8-21	T.B.	L	4-11		8	10	Sturtze	Parque		74-51	1st	+7.5
8-23	Bal.	W	8-4		7	8	Barcelo	Parrish		75-51	1st	+7.0
8-24	Bal.	L	5-8		9	10	Mercedes	Hill		75-52	1st	+7.0
8-25	At Sea.	W	4-1		10	4	Sirotka	Sele	Foulke	76-52	1st	+8.0
8-26	At Sea.	L	5-11		8	12	Halama	Biddle		76-53	1st	+7.0
8-27	At Sea.	W	2-1		6	4	Barcelo	Garcia	Foulke	77-53	1st	+8.0
8-28	At Oak.	L	0-3		1	6	Hudson	Parque		77-54	1st	+7.0
8-29	At Oak.	W	3-0		7	5	Baldwin	Zito	Foulke	78-54	1st	+7.0
8-30	At Oak.	W	8-3		11	9	Sirotka	Appier	Howry	79-54	1st	+7.0
9-1	Ana.	W	9-8		14	10	Ginter	Hasegawa	Foulke	80-54	1st	+7.5
9-2	Ana.	W	13-6		14	5	Parque	Mercker		81-54	1st	+8.5
9-3	Ana.	W	13-12		15	11	Wunsch	Hasegawa	Foulke	82-54	1st	+8.5
9-4	Tex.	L	4-5		11	13	Davis	Garland	Wetteland	82-55	1st	+7.5
9-5	Tex.	L	1-2		8	10	Johnson	Howry	Wetteland	82-56	1st	+6.5
9-6	Tex.	W	13-1		13	4	Wells	Helling		83-56	1st	+6.5
9-7	Tex.	W	10-6		12	12	Barcelo	Zimmerman	Foulke	84-56	1st	+7.5
9-8	At Cle.	W	5-4		10	9	Buehrle	Woodard	Foulke	85-56	1st	+8.5
9-9	At Cle.	L	3-9		7	12	Burba	Garland		85-57	1st	+7.5
9-11	Det.	W	10-3		12	7	Sirotka	Moehler	Howry	86-57	1st	+8.0
9-12	Det.	L	3-10		4	11	Mlicki	Wells		86-58	1st	+8.0
9-13	Det.	W	1-0		4	5	Parque	Weaver	Foulke	87-58	1st	+8.0
9-15	Tor.	L	5-6		11	6	Escobar	Garland	Koch	87-59	1st	+7.5
9-16	Tor.	W	6-3		8	11	Wunsch	Escobar	Foulke	88-59	1st	+8.5
9-17	Tor.	L	1-14		6	15	Painter	Wells		88-60	1st	+7.5
9-18	At Det.	L	2-5		3	12	Weaver	Barcelo	Jones	88-61	1st	+6.5
9-19	At Det.	W	6-2		13	7	Lowe	Sparks		89-61	1st	+7.5
9-20	At Det.	W	13-6		15	10	Garland	Moehler		90-61	1st	+7.0
9-21	At Min.	W	9-4		11	11	Sirotka	Santana		91-61	1st	+7.5
9-22	At Min.	W	5-4		10	12	Barcelo	Wells	Foulke	92-61	1st	+8.5
9-23	At Min.	W	5-3		8	8	Parque	Milton	Foulke	93-61	1st	+8.5
9-24	At Min.	L	5-6	(10)	12	10	Guardado	Beirne		93-62	1st	+8.5
9-25	At Cle.	L	2-9		8	13	Burba	Garland		93-63		
9-26	Bos.	L	3-4		5	6	P. Martinez	Beirne	Lowe	93-64	1st	+7.0
9-27	Bos.	L	1-2		5	7	Crawford	Baldwin	Lowe	93-65	1st	+6.0
9-28	Bos.	L	6-7		8	9	Beck	Simas	Lowe	93-66	1st	+6.0
9-29	K.C.	W	6-4		9	14	Bradford	Reichert	Foulke	94-66	1st	+6.0
9-30	K.C.	W	9-1		11	6	Wells	Stein		95-66	1st	+6.0
10-1	K.C.	L	2-6		8	10	Fussell	Baldwin		95-67	1st	+5.0

Monthly records: April (17-8), May (13-14), June (20-7), July (14-12), August (15-13), September (16-12), October (0-1).
*Innings, if other than nine. † First game of a doubleheader. ‡ Second game of a doubleheader.

MEMORABLE GAMES

May 13 at Chicago

Trailing the Twins 3-2 in the bottom of the ninth inning at Comiskey Park, pinch hitter Jeff Abbott launched a two-run homer off Bob Wells to give the White Sox a 4-3 win. If Abbott had not come through, the Sox would have lost for the seventh time in eight games. But buoyed by the key home run, they went on a 26-of-34 tear and took control of the Central Division.

Minnesota	AB	R	H	BI	White Sox	AB	R	H	BI
Guzman, ss	4	1	2	0	Durham, 2b	4	0	1	0
Canizaro, 2b	4	1	1	0	Valentin, ss	4	0	0	0
Lawton, rf	3	0	1	2	Thomas, dh	4	0	1	0
Coomer, 1b	4	0	1	0	Ordonez, rf	4	1	1	1
Huskey, dh	3	0	1	0	Konerko, 1b	4	0	0	0
Ortiz, ph	0	0	0	0	Singleton, cf	3	0	1	0
Hocking, ph-dh	1	0	0	0	Lee, lf	3	2	3	1
Koskie, 3b	3	0	0	0	Perry, 3b	3	0	0	0
LeCroy, c	3	1	1	1	Norton, ph	1	0	0	0
Jones, lf	3	0	0	0	Paul, c	2	0	0	0
Hunter, cf	3	0	1	0	Abbott, ph	1	1	1	2
Totals	**31**	**3**	**8**	**3**	**Totals**	**33**	**4**	**8**	**4**

Minnesota ....0 0 3 0 0 0 0 0 0—3 8 0
White Sox ....0 0 0 0 0 1 1 0 2—4 8 0

DP—Minnesota 1, White Sox 4. LOB—Minnesota 2, White Sox 6. HR—LeCroy (3), Ordonez (7),.Lee (7), Abbott (1). CS—Lawton (2), Huskey (2), Singleton (4).

Minnesota	IP	H	R	ER	BB	SO
Redman	6.1	6	2	2	3	7
Hawkins	1.2	0	0	0	0	2
Guardado	0.1	0	0	0	0	0
Wells (L 0-4)	0.1	2	2	2	0	1

Chi White Sox	IP	H	R	ER	BB	SO
Sirotka	8.1	7	3	3	1	6
Simas	0	1	0	0	0	0
Wunsch (W 1-2)	0.2	0	0	0	0	1

Simas pitched to 1 batter in 9th.

WP—Sirotka. BK—Sirotka. U—HP, Gibson. 1B, Rippley. 2B, Tschida. 3B, Meriwether. T—2:52. A—22,545.

September 8 at Cleveland

The White Sox, facing an opportunity to strengthen their hold on first place in the A.L. Central, traveled to Cleveland for an important two-game series. In the opener, first baseman Paul Konerko hit a two-run homer and robbed Jim Thome of extra bases with a great diving catch, sparking a 5-4 victory. The win lifted the Sox to an $8^1/_2$-game lead and dashed any Cleveland hopes of a sixth straight division title.

White Sox	AB	R	H	BI	Cleveland	AB	R	H	BI
Durham, 2b	3	0	0	0	Lofton, cf	4	2	2	0
Valentin, ss	5	1	1	1	Vizquel, ss	4	0	1	0
Thomas, dh	4	0	1	0	Alomar, 2b	5	1	1	0
Ordonez, rf	5	0	0	0	Ramirez, rf	3	1	3	3
Lee, lf	4	2	3	0	Thome, dh	4	0	1	1
Konerko, 1b	4	1	1	2	Segui, 1b	4	0	0	0
Perry, 3b	4	0	0	0	Fryman, 3b	3	0	0	0
Singleton, cf	4	1	2	1	Cordero, lf	4	0	1	0
Johnson, c	4	0	2	1	Alomar Jr., c	3	0	0	0
					Branyan, ph	1	0	0	0
					Diaz, c	0	0	0	0
Totals	**37**	**5**	**10**	**5**	**Totals**	**35**	**4**	**9**	**4**

White Sox ....0 2 1 2 0 0 0 0 0—5 10 0
Cleveland.................................1 0 0 2 1 0 0 0 0—4 9 1

E—Speier (1). DP—White Sox 1. LOB—White Sox 8, Cleveland 8. 2B—Johnson (22), Ramirez (27). HR—Valentin (22), Konerko (17). SB—Lee (12), Singleton (19), Alomar (33).

White Sox	IP	H	R	ER	BB	SO
Baldwin	4.1	8	4	4	1	2
Buehrle (W 4-1)	1.1	1	0	0	0	0
Lowe	0.1	0	0	0	0	0
Wunsch	0	0	0	0	2	0
Howry	2	0	0	0	1	0
Foulke (S 29)	1	0	0	0	0	0

Cleveland	IP	H	R	ER	BB	SO
Woodard (L 1-3)	4	7	5	5	0	4
Speier	1.2	2	0	0	2	2
Cairncross	0.1	0	0	0	0	0
Reed	1.1	1	0	0	0	0
Rincon	0.1	0	0	0	0	1
Shuey	1.1	0	0	0	1	1

Wunsch pitched to 2 batters in 7th.

WP—Speier. U—HP, Bell. 1B, O'Nora. 2B, Hirschbeck. 3B, Iassogna. T—3:34. A—42,526.

INDIVIDUAL STATISTICS

BATTING

Name	G	TPA	AB	R	H	TB	2B	3B	HR	RBI	Avg.	Obp.	Slg.	SH	SF	HP	BB	IBB	SO	SB	CS	GDP	vs RHP AB	vs RHP Avg.	vs RHP HR	vs RHP RBI	vs LHP AB	vs LHP Avg.	vs LHP HR	vs LHP RBI
Durham, Ray	151	709	614	121	172	276	35	9	17	75	.280	.361	.450	5	8	7	75	0	105	25	13	13	485	.289	13	59	129	.248	4	16
Ordonez, Magglio	153	665	588	102	185	321	34	3	32	126	.315	.371	.546	0	15	2	60	3	64	18	4	28	490	.310	26	99	98	.337	6	27
Thomas, Frank	159	707	582	115	191	364	44	0	43	143	.328	.436	.625	0	8	5	112	18	94	1	3	13	491	.314	33	111	91	.407	10	32
Lee, Carlos	152	619	572	107	172	277	29	2	24	92	.301	.345	.484	1	5	3	38	1	94	13	4	17	474	.295	20	74	98	.327	4	18
Valentin, Jose	144	648	568	107	155	279	37	6	25	92	.273	.343	.491	13	4	4	59	1	106	19	2	11	489	.282	24	82	79	.215	1	10
Konerko, Paul	143	586	524	84	156	252	31	1	21	97	.298	.363	.481	0	5	10	47	0	72	1	0	22	428	.297	19	77	96	.302	2	20
Singleton, Chris	147	566	511	83	130	195	22	5	11	62	.254	.301	.382	12	4	1	35	2	85	22	7	6	443	.262	11	55	68	.206	0	7
Perry, Herbert	109	420	383	69	118	185	29	1	12	61	.308	.356	.483	2	4	9	22	1	68	4	1	13	304	.316	11	51	79	.278	1	10
Abbott, Jeff	80	242	215	31	59	85	15	1	3	29	.274	.343	.395	2	1	2	21	1	38	2	1	2	152	.296	2	23	63	.222	1	6
Johnson, Mark L.	75	251	213	29	48	68	11	0	3	23	.225	.315	.319	10	0	1	27	0	40	3	2	3	190	.232	3	20	23	.174	0	3
Norton, Greg	71	231	201	25	49	75	6	1	6	28	.244	.333	.373	0	2	2	26	0	47	1	0	2	185	.254	5	27	16	.125	1	1
Graffanino, Tony	57	172	148	25	40	53	5	1	2	16	.270	.363	.358	1	1	1	21	0	25	7	4	1	92	.293	0	8	56	.232	2	8
Johnson, Charles	44	158	135	24	44	82	8	0	10	36	.326	.411	.607	0	2	1	20	0	37	0	0	0	104	.337	8	26	31	.290	2	10
Fordyce, Brook	40	136	125	18	34	58	7	1	5	21	.272	.313	.464	2	1	2	6	0	23	0	0	1	95	.253	4	16	30	.333	1	5
Wilson, Craig	28	83	73	12	19	22	3	0	0	4	.260	.316	.301	4	0	1	5	0	11	1	0	5	48	.188	0	1	25	.400	0	3
Paul, Josh	36	79	71	15	20	30	3	2	1	8	.282	.338	.423	2	0	1	5	0	17	1	0	3	50	.260	1	5	21	.333	0	3
Baines, Harold	24	68	61	2	13	21	5	0	1	9	.213	.294	.344	0	0	0	7	1	11	0	0	0	57	.228	1	9	4	.000	0	0
Christensen, McKay	32	22	19	4	2	2	0	0	0	1	.105	.227	.105	0	0	1	2	0	6	1	1	0	17	.059	0	0	2	.500	0	1
Crede, Joe	7	15	14	2	5	6	1	0	0	3	.357	.333	.429	0	1	0	0	0	3	0	0	0	12	.333	0	3	2	.500	0	0
Liefer, Jeff	5	11	11	0	2	2	0	0	0	0	.182	.182	.182	0	0	0	0	0	4	0	0	0	10	.200	0	0	1	.000	0	0
Eldred, Cal	20	6	4	3	1	1	0	0	0	0	.250	.500	.250	0	0	0	2	0	1	0	0	0	4	.250	0	0	0	.000	0	0
Baldwin, James	29	5	4	0	0	0	0	0	0	0	.000	.000	.000	1	0	0	0	0	2	0	0	0	4	.000	0	0	0	.000	0	0
Sirotka, Mike	32	5	4	0	0	0	0	0	0	0	.000	.200	.000	0	0	0	1	0	2	0	0	0	4	.000	0	0	0	.000	0	0
Parque, Jim	33	4	4	0	0	0	0	0	0	0	.000	.000	.000	0	0	0	0	0	3	0	0	0	4	.000	0	0	0	.000	0	0
Wells, Kip	20	2	2	0	0	0	0	0	0	0	.000	.000	.000	0	0	0	0	0	2	0	0	0	2	.000	0	0	0	.000	0	0
Simas, Bill	60	0	0	0	0	0	0	0	0	0	.000	.000	.000	0	0	0	0	0	0	0	0	0	0	.000	0	0	0	.000	0	0
Foulke, Keith	72	0	0	0	0	0	0	0	0	0	.000	.000	.000	0	0	0	0	0	0	0	0	0	0	.000	0	0	0	.000	0	0
Lowe, Sean	50	0	0	0	0	0	0	0	0	0	.000	.000	.000	0	0	0	0	0	0	0	0	0	0	.000	0	0	0	.000	0	0
Howry, Bob	65	0	0	0	0	0	0	0	0	0	.000	.000	.000	0	0	0	0	0	0	0	0	0	0	.000	0	0	0	.000	0	0
Beirne, Kevin	29	0	0	0	0	0	0	0	0	0	.000	.000	.000	0	0	0	0	0	0	0	0	0	0	.000	0	0	0	.000	0	0
Pena, Jesus	20	0	0	0	0	0	0	0	0	0	.000	.000	.000	0	0	0	0	0	0	0	0	0	0	.000	0	0	0	.000	0	0
Garland, Jon	15	0	0	0	0	0	0	0	0	0	.000	.000	.000	0	0	0	0	0	0	0	0	0	0	.000	0	0	0	.000	0	0
Wunsch, Kelly	83	0	0	0	0	0	0	0	0	0	.000	.000	.000	0	0	0	0	0	0	0	0	0	0	.000	0	0	0	.000	0	0
Hill, Ken	2	0	0	0	0	0	0	0	0	0	.000	.000	.000	0	0	0	0	0	0	0	0	0	0	.000	0	0	0	.000	0	0
Sturtze, Tanyon	10	0	0	0	0	0	0	0	0	0	.000	.000	.000	0	0	0	0	0	0	0	0	0	0	.000	0	0	0	.000	0	0
Barcelo, Lorenzo	22	0	0	0	0	0	0	0	0	0	.000	.000	.000	0	0	0	0	0	0	0	0	0	0	.000	0	0	0	.000	0	0
Eyre, Scott	13	0	0	0	0	0	0	0	0	0	.000	.000	.000	0	0	0	0	0	0	0	0	0	0	.000	0	0	0	.000	0	0
Bradford, Chad	12	0	0	0	0	0	0	0	0	0	.000	.000	.000	0	0	0	0	0	0	0	0	0	0	.000	0	0	0	.000	0	0
Myette, Aaron	2	0	0	0	0	0	0	0	0	0	.000	.000	.000	0	0	0	0	0	0	0	0	0	0	.000	0	0	0	.000	0	0
Buehrle, Mark	28	0	0	0	0	0	0	0	0	0	.000	.000	.000	0	0	0	0	0	0	0	0	0	0	.000	0	0	0	.000	0	0
Biddle, Rocky	4	0	0	0	0	0	0	0	0	0	.000	.000	.000	0	0	0	0	0	0	0	0	0	0	.000	0	0	0	.000	0	0
Ginter, Matt	7	0	0	0	0	0	0	0	0	0	.000	.000	.000	0	0	0	0	0	0	0	0	0	0	.000	0	0	0	.000	0	0

Players with more than one A.L. team

Name	G	TPA	AB	R	H	TB	2B	3B	HR	RBI	Avg.	Obp.	Slg.	SH	SF	HP	BB	IBB	SO	SB	CS	GDP	vs RHP AB	vs RHP Avg.	vs RHP HR	vs RHP RBI	vs LHP AB	vs LHP Avg.	vs LHP HR	vs LHP RBI
Baines, Bal.-Chi.	96	320	283	26	72	118	13	0	11	39	.254	.338	.417	0	1	0	36	7	50	0	0	6	257	.261	11	36	26	.192	0	3
Fordyce, Chi.-Bal.	93	330	302	41	91	153	18	1	14	49	.301	.341	.507	2	5	4	17	0	50	0	0	4	230	.287	8	31	72	.347	6	18
Graffanino, T.B.-Chi.	70	194	168	33	46	60	6	1	2	17	.274	.363	.357	1	1	2	22	0	27	7	4	2	110	.300	0	9	58	.224	2	8
Hill, Ana.-Chi.	18	4	3	0	1	1	0	0	0	0	.333	.333	.333	1	0	0	0	0	0	0	0	0	2	.000	0	0	1	1.000	0	0
Johnson, Bal.-Chi.	128	478	421	76	128	245	24	0	31	91	.304	.379	.582	1	3	1	52	0	106	2	0	8	306	.324	25	70	115	.252	6	21
Pena, Chi.-Bos.	22	0	0	0	0	0	0	0	0	0	.000	.000	.000	0	0	0	0	0	0	0	0	0	0	.000	0	0	0	.000	0	0
Perry, T.B.-Chi.	116	450	411	71	124	192	30	1	12	62	.302	.350	.467	2	4	9	24	1	75	4	1	13	330	.303	11	52	81	.296	1	10
Sturtze, Chi.-T.B.	29	0	0	0	0	0	0	0	0	0	.000	.000	.000	0	0	0	0	0	0	0	0	0	0	.000	0	0	0	.000	0	0

PITCHING

Name	W	L	Pct.	ERA	IP	H	R	ER	HR	SH	SF	HB	BB	IBB	SO	G	GS	CG	ShO	GF	Sv	vs. RH AB	vs. RH Avg.	vs. RH HR	vs. RH RBI	vs. LH AB	vs. LH Avg.	vs. LH HR	vs. LH RBI
Sirotka, Mike	15	10	.600	3.79	197.0	203	101	83	23	4	3	1	69	1	128	32	32	1	0	0	0	578	.256	16	60	177	.311	7	28
Parque, Jim	13	6	.684	4.28	187.0	208	105	89	21	5	5	11	71	1	111	33	32	0	0	0	0	549	.271	16	60	187	.316	5	26
Baldwin, James	14	7	.667	4.65	178.0	185	96	92	34	6	5	8	59	3	116	29	28	2	1	0	0	318	.264	17	41	362	.279	17	42
Eldred, Cal	10	2	.833	4.58	112.0	103	61	57	12	3	2	5	59	0	97	20	20	2	1	0	0	214	.252	5	22	209	.234	7	28
Wells, Kip	6	9	.400	6.02	98.2	126	76	66	15	1	3	2	58	4	71	20	20	0	0	0	0	183	.339	6	27	221	.290	9	39
Foulke, Keith	3	1	.750	2.97	88.0	66	31	29	9	5	2	2	22	2	91	72	0	0	0	58	34	156	.192	2	10	163	.221	7	23
Howry, Bob	2	4	.333	3.17	71.0	54	26	25	6	2	4	4	29	2	60	65	0	0	0	29	7	129	.256	4	24	121	.174	2	7
Lowe, Sean	4	1	.800	5.48	70.2	78	47	43	10	4	1	6	39	3	53	50	5	0	0	8	0	162	.241	6	22	113	.345	4	21
Garland, Jon	4	8	.333	6.46	69.2	82	55	50	10	0	2	1	40	0	42	15	13	0	0	1	0	133	.278	7	25	148	.304	3	27
Simas, Bill	2	3	.400	3.46	67.2	69	27	26	9	6	4	1	22	6	49	60	0	0	0	9	0	156	.269	4	21	94	.287	5	16
Wunsch, Kelly	6	3	.667	2.93	61.1	50	22	20	4	0	2	2	29	1	51	83	0	0	0	12	1	120	.275	3	18	106	.160	1	12
Buehrle, Mark	4	1	.800	4.21	51.1	55	27	24	5	1	0	3	19	1	37	28	3	0	0	6	0	129	.279	3	21	73	.260	2	12
Beirne, Kevin	1	3	.250	6.70	49.2	50	41	37	9	1	5	4	20	1	41	29	1	0	0	8	0	98	.245	4	12	92	.283	5	21
Barcelo, Lorenzo	4	2	.667	3.69	39.0	34	17	16	5	0	1	0	9	1	26	22	1	0	0	5	0	81	.259	2	9	66	.197	3	10
Pena, Jesus	2	1	.667	5.40	23.1	25	18	14	6	0	2	1	16	0	19	20	0	0	0	7	1	55	.273	5	16	35	.286	1	6
Biddle, Rocky	1	2	.333	8.34	22.2	31	25	21	5	0	2	0	8	0	7	4	4	0	0	0	0	56	.321	5	14	39	.333	0	9
Eyre, Scott	1	1	.500	6.63	19.0	29	15	14	3	0	2	1	12	0	16	13	1	0	0	3	0	50	.360	2	10	28	.393	1	9
Sturtze, Tanyon	1	2	.333	12.06	15.2	25	23	21	4	0	2	2	15	0	6	10	1	0	0	2	0	27	.333	1	5	39	.410	3	16
Bradford, Chad	1	0	1.000	1.98	13.2	13	4	3	0	0	0	0	1	1	9	12	0	0	0	5	0	32	.125	0	1	19	.474	0	3
Ginter, Matt	1	0	1.000	13.50	9.1	18	14	14	5	0	1	0	7	0	6	7	0	0	0	3	0	15	.533	2	7	29	.345	3	9
Hill, Ken	0	1	.000	24.00	3.0	5	8	8	0	1	1	0	6	0	0	2	1	0	0	0	0	9	.444	0	5	2	.500	0	0
Myette, Aaron	0	0	.000	0.00	2.2	0	0	0	0	0	0	0	4	0	1	2	0	0	0	1	0	7	.000	0	0	1	.000	0	0

PITCHERS WITH MORE THAN ONE A.L. TEAM

Name	W	L	Pct.	ERA	IP	H	R	ER	HR	SH	SF	HB	BB	IBB	SO	G	GS	CG	ShO	GF	Sv	vs. RH AB	vs. RH Avg.	vs. RH HR	vs. RH RBI	vs. LH AB	vs. LH Avg.	vs. LH HR	vs. LH RBI
Hill, Ana.-Chi.	5	8	.385	7.16	81.2	107	67	65	16	3	8	2	59	1	50	18	17	0	0	8	0	190	.337	10	30	137	.314	6	30
Pena, Chi.-Bos.	2	1	.667	5.13	26.1	28	19	15	7	0	2	1	19	0	20	22	0	0	0	2	1	64	.250	5	16	37	.324	2	7
Sturtze, Chi.-T.B.	5	2	.714	4.74	68.1	72	39	36	8	1	2	3	29	1	44	29	6	0	0	2	0	131	.275	4	17	134	.269	4	23

DESIGNATED HITTERS

Name	AB	Avg.	HR	RBI
Thomas, Frank	467	.321	30	102
Baines, Harold	55	.218	1	9
Konerko, Paul	26	.115	0	1
Abbott, Jeff	14	.286	0	2
Lee, Carlos	8	.250	1	3
Norton, Greg	6	.167	0	0
Perry, Herbert	3	.000	0	0
Graffanino, Tony	1	.000	0	0
Johnson, Mark L.	1	.000	0	0
Singleton, Chris	0	-	0	0
Crede, Joe	0	-	0	0

INDIVIDUAL STATISTICS

FIELDING

FIRST BASEMEN

Player	Pct.	G	PO	A	E	TC	DP
Konerko, Paul	.991	122	1051	67	10	1128	118
Thomas, Frank	.996	30	267	15	1	283	38
Norton, Greg	.990	17	94	10	1	105	12
Perry, Herbert	1.000	3	10	0	0	10	1
Liefer, Jeff	.875	1	6	1	1	8	1

SECOND BASEMEN

Player	Pct.	G	PO	A	E	TC	DP
Durham, Ray	.980	151	299	419	15	733	126
Graffanino, Tony	.964	19	27	53	3	83	12
Wilson, Craig	.950	4	11	8	1	20	3

THIRD BASEMEN

Player	Pct.	G	PO	A	E	TC	DP
Perry, Herbert	.969	104	82	200	9	291	17
Norton, Greg	.926	47	32	56	7	95	5
Wilson, Craig	.938	15	6	24	2	32	2
Graffanino, Tony	1.000	12	10	8	0	18	2
Konerko, Paul	.900	7	2	7	1	10	1
Crede, Joe	.933	6	5	9	1	15	1

SHORTSTOPS

Player	Pct.	G	PO	A	E	TC	DP
Valentin, Jose	.950	141	233	456	36	725	117
Graffanino, Tony	.966	21	24	61	3	88	16
Wilson, Craig	1.000	10	14	29	0	43	4

OUTFIELDERS

Player	Pct.	G	PO	A	E	TC	DP
Ordonez, Magglio	.983	152	280	12	5	297	3
Lee, Carlos	.990	149	273	10	3	286	0
Singleton, Chris	.992	145	373	9	3	385	0
Abbott, Jeff	.981	65	101	2	2	105	0
Christensen, McKay	1.000	29	20	1	0	21	0
Liefer, Jeff	1.000	5	2	0	0	2	0
Paul, Josh	-	1	0	0	0	0	0
Valentin, Jose	-	1	0	0	0	0	0

CATCHERS

Player	Pct.	G	PO	A	E	TC	DP	PB
Johnson, Mark L.	.992	74	466	27	4	497	4	7
Johnson, Charles	.987	43	224	12	3	239	3	2
Fordyce, Brook	1.000	40	251	13	0	264	2	2
Paul, Josh	.974	34	130	17	4	151	5	2

PITCHERS

Player	Pct.	G	PO	A	E	TC	DP
Wunsch, Kelly	1.000	83	3	8	0	11	0
Foulke, Keith	1.000	72	7	3	0	10	1
Howry, Bob	1.000	65	3	6	0	9	1
Simas, Bill	1.000	60	1	8	0	9	0
Lowe, Sean	.917	50	3	8	1	12	0
Parque, Jim	.900	33	2	25	3	30	0
Sirotka, Mike	.958	32	5	18	1	24	2
Baldwin, James	.952	29	14	26	2	42	2
Beirne, Kevin	.857	29	2	4	1	7	0
Buehrle, Mark	.909	28	1	9	1	11	2
Barcelo, Lorenzo	1.000	22	0	1	0	1	0
Eldred, Cal	1.000	20	8	13	0	21	2
Wells, Kip	.688	20	6	5	5	16	0
Pena, Jesus	.857	20	0	6	1	7	0
Garland, Jon	.857	15	2	10	2	14	0
Eyre, Scott	1.000	13	0	3	0	3	0
Bradford, Chad	1.000	12	0	2	0	2	0
Sturtze, Tanyon	-	10	0	0	0	0	0
Ginter, Matt	1.000	7	0	1	0	1	0
Biddle, Rocky	.800	4	1	3	1	5	0
Hill, Ken	1.000	2	0	1	0	1	0
Myette, Aaron	-	2	0	0	0	0	0

PITCHING AGAINST EACH CLUB

Pitcher	Ana. W-L	Bal. W-L	Bos. W-L	Cle. W-L	Det. W-L	K.C. W-L	Min. W-L	N.Y. W-L	Oak. W-L	Sea. W-L	T.B. W-L	Tex. W-L	Tor. W-L	N.L. W-L	Total W-L
Baldwin, James	0-0	0-1	2-1	0-1	2-0	0-1	0-1	1-1	2-0	1-0	1-0	1-0	2-0	2-1	14-7
Barcelo, Lorenzo	0-1	1-0	0-0	0-0	0-1	0-0	1-0	0-0	0-0	1-0	0-0	1-0	0-0	0-0	4-2
Beirne, Kevin	0-1	0-0	0-1	1-0	0-0	0-0	0-1	0-0	0-0	0-0	0-0	0-0	0-0	0-0	1-3
Biddle, Rocky	0-0	1-0	0-0	0-0	0-0	0-0	0-0	0-0	0-0	0-2	0-0	0-0	0-0	0-0	1-2
Bradford, Chad	0-0	0-0	0-0	0-0	0-0	1-0	0-0	0-0	0-0	0-0	0-0	0-0	0-0	0-0	1-0
Buehrle, Mark	0-0	0-0	0-0	1-0	0-0	0-0	1-0	0-0	0-0	0-1	2-0	0-0	0-0	0-0	4-1
Eldred, Cal	0-0	1-0	0-1	3-0	1-0	0-1	1-0	2-0	0-0	0-0	0-0	0-0	1-0	1-0	10-2
Eyre, Scott	0-0	0-0	0-0	0-0	0-1	0-0	0-0	0-0	1-0	0-0	0-0	0-0	0-0	0-0	1-1
Foulke, Keith	1-0	0-0	0-0	0-0	0-0	0-0	0-0	0-0	1-0	0-0	0-1	1-0	0-0	0-0	3-1
Garland, Jon	1-0	0-0	0-1	0-2	1-0	0-1	0-0	0-0	0-0	0-1	1-0	0-2	0-1	1-0	4-8
Ginter, Matt	1-0	0-0	0-0	0-0	0-0	0-0	0-0	0-0	0-0	0-0	0-0	0-0	0-0	0-0	1-0
Hill, Ken	0-0	0-1	0-0	0-0	0-0	0-0	0-0	0-0	0-0	0-0	0-0	0-0	0-0	0-0	0-1
Howry, Bob	0-0	0-0	0-0	0-0	0-0	0-1	0-0	0-0	0-0	1-0	0-1	1-1	0-1	0-0	2-4
Lowe, Sean	0-0	0-0	0-0	0-0	1-0	0-0	0-1	1-0	0-0	1-0	0-0	0-0	0-0	1-0	4-1
Myette, Aaron	0-0	0-0	0-0	0-0	0-0	0-0	0-0	0-0	0-0	0-0	0-0	0-0	0-0	0-0	0-0
Parque, Jim	1-1	2-0	1-0	1-0	2-0	0-1	1-1	1-1	0-1	0-0	1-1	0-0	0-0	3-0	13-6
Pena, Jesus	0-0	0-0	0-0	0-0	0-0	1-0	0-0	0-0	0-0	0-0	0-0	0-0	0-0	1-1	2-1
Simas, Bill	0-0	0-0	1-1	1-0	0-0	0-0	0-0	0-0	0-0	0-0	0-0	0-1	0-0	0-1	2-3
Sirotka, Mike	1-0	0-2	1-1	0-1	1-0	0-1	1-0	2-1	2-1	2-1	1-0	0-1	1-0	3-1	15-10
Sturtze, Tanyon	0-0	0-0	0-1	0-0	0-0	0-0	0-0	0-0	0-0	1-0	0-1	0-0	0-0	0-0	1-2
Wells, Kip	0-1	1-0	0-0	1-1	1-1	1-0	0-1	1-1	0-1	0-0	0-0	1-0	0-2	0-1	6-9
Wunsch, Kelly	1-0	0-0	0-0	0-0	0-0	2-1	2-0	0-0	0-0	0-0	0-0	0-0	1-1	0-1	6-3
Totals	6-4	6-4	5-7	8-5	9-3	5-7	7-5	8-4	6-3	7-5	6-4	5-5	5-5	12-6	95-67

INTERLEAGUE: Baldwin 1-0, Garland 1-0, Sirotka 1-0 vs. Brewers; Pena 1-1, Lowe 1-0, Sirotka 1-0, Simas 0-1, Baldwin 0-1 vs. Cubs; Baldwin 1-0, Eldred 1-0, Parque 1-0 vs. Reds; Parque 1-0, Sirotka 1-0, Wells 0-1 vs. Astros; Parque 1-0, Sirotka 0-1, Wunsch 0-1 vs. Cardinals. Total: 12-6.

MISCELLANEOUS

HOME RUNS BY PARK

At Anaheim (4): Valentin 1, Perry 1, Konerko 1, Singleton 1.
At Baltimore (6): Thomas 2, Baines 1, Valentin 1, Graffanino 1, Abbott 1.
At Boston (3): Valentin 1, Fordyce 1, Ordonez 1.
At Chicago (AL) (125): Thomas 30, Ordonez 21, Valentin 16, Lee 12, Konerko 10, Perry 7, Johnson 7, Durham 5, Singleton 5, Norton 4, Fordyce 3, Johnson 2, Graffanino 1, Abbott 1, Paul 1.
At Chicago (NL) (6): Ordonez 2, Lee 2, Thomas 1, Perry 1.
At Cincinnati (4): Thomas 2, Valentin 1, Norton 1.
At Cleveland (5): Durham 2, Thomas 1, Valentin 1, Konerko 1.
At Detroit (7): Konerko 2, Valentin 1, Johnson 1, Durham 1, Ordonez 1, Singleton 1.
At Houston (4): Thomas 1, Durham 1, Lee 1, Singleton 1.
At Kansas City (10): Thomas 2, Durham 2, Valentin 1, Perry 1, Ordonez 1, Konerko 1, Johnson 1, Lee 1.
At Minnesota (5): Valentin 1, Perry 1, Johnson 1, Fordyce 1, Konerko 1.
At New York (AL) (8): Ordonez 3, Valentin 1, Norton 1, Konerko 1, Lee 1, Singleton 1.
At Oakland (4): Durham 2, Thomas 1, Konerko 1.
At Seattle (7): Lee 3, Durham 2, Ordonez 1, Konerko 1.
At Tampa Bay (9): Ordonez 2, Konerko 2, Lee 2, Thomas 1, Durham 1, Singleton 1.
At Texas (6): Lee 2, Thomas 1, Johnson 1, Durham 1, Singleton 1.
At Toronto (3): Thomas 1, Perry 1, Abbott 1.

LOW-HIT GAMES

No-hitters: None.
One-hitters: None.
Two-hitters: Cal Eldred, April 24 vs. Baltimore, W 8-2.

10-STRIKEOUT GAMES

Cal Eldred 1, James Baldwin 1, Mike Sirotka 1, Total: 3

FOUR OR MORE HITS IN ONE GAME

Magglio Ordonez 4, Carlos Lee 4, Paul Konerko 3, Chris Singleton 2 (including one five-hit game), Frank Thomas 1, Jose Valentin 1, Ray Durham 1, Total: 16

MULTI-HOMER GAMES

Frank Thomas 4, Magglio Ordonez 4, Jose Valentin 3, Charles Johnson 1, Brook Fordyce 1, Carlos Lee 1, Total: 14

GRAND SLAMS

4-26: Frank Thomas (off Baltimore's Sidney Ponson)
6-18: Jose Valentin (off New York's Orlando Hernandez)
7-16: Magglio Ordonez (off Milwaukee's Juan Acevedo)
8-9: Tony Graffanino (off Seattle's Rob Ramsay)
9-11: Frank Thomas (off Detroit's Nelson Cruz)
9-20: Ray Durham (off Detroit's Matt Anderson)

PINCH HITTERS

(Minimum 5 at-bats)

Name	AB	Avg.	HR	RBI
bbott, Jeff	15	.133	1	3
Konerko, Paul	10	.500	0	5
Norton, Greg	10	.000	0	0
Baines, Harold	7	.143	0	0
Valentin, Jose	5	.400	1	3
Graffanino, Tony	5	.200	0	1

DEBUTS

4-3: Kelly Wunsch, P.
5-17: Kevin Beirne, P.
7-4: Jon Garland, P.
7-16: Mark Buehrle, P.
7-22: Lorenzo Barcelo, P.
8-10: Rocky Biddle, P.
9-1: Matt Ginter, P.
9-12: Joe Crede, 3B.

GAMES BY POSITION

Catcher: Mark L. Johnson 74, Charles Johnson 43, Brook Fordyce 40, Josh Paul 34.
First base: Paul Konerko 122, Frank Thomas 30, Greg Norton 17, Herbert Perry 3, Jeff Liefer 1.
Second base: Ray Durham 151, Tony Graffanino 19, Craig Wilson 4.
Third base: Herbert Perry 104, Greg Norton 47, Craig Wilson 15, Tony Graffanino 12, Paul Konerko 7, Joe Crede 6.
Shortstop: Jose Valentin 141, Tony Graffanino 21, Craig Wilson 10.
Outfield: Magglio Ordonez 152, Carlos Lee 149, Chris Singleton 145, Jeff Abbott 65, McKay Christensen 29, Jeff Liefer 5, Jose Valentin 1, Josh Paul 1.
Designated hitter: Frank Thomas 127, Harold Baines 16, Jeff Abbott 7, Paul Konerko 7, Herbert Perry 3, Tony Graffanino 3, Greg Norton 3, Carlos Lee 2, Mark L. Johnson 1, Chris Singleton 1, Joe Crede 1.

STREAKS

Wins: 8 (June 12-19)
Losses: 5 (September 24-28)
Consecutive games with at least one hit: 14, Magglio Ordonez (June 9-22)
Wins by pitcher: 6, James Baldwin (April 6-May 9)

ATTENDANCE

Home: 1,947,799
Road: 2,310,637
Highest (home): 44,140 (June 9 vs. Chicago).
Highest (road): 54,053 (June 17 vs. New York).
Lowest (home): 8,425 (April 19 vs. Seattle).
Lowest (road): 6,688 (September 21 vs. Minnesota).

CLEVELAND INDIANS

DAY BY DAY

Date	Opp.	Res.	Score	(inn.*)	Hits	Opp. hits	Winning pitcher	Losing pitcher	Save	Record	Pos.	GB
4-3	At Bal.	W	4-1		6	6	Colon	Mussina	Karsay	1-0	T1st	...
4-5	At Bal.	L	7-11		10	12	Ryan	Kamieniecki		1-1	2nd	0.5
4-6	At Bal.	L	2-6		6	10	Rapp	Nagy	Groom	1-2	T4th	0.5
4-7	At T.B.	W	14-5		15	10	Wright	Guzman		2-2	3rd	0.5
4-8	At T.B.	W	6-4		11	10	Burba	Trachsel	Karsay	3-2	3rd	0.5
4-9	At T.B.	W	17-4		16	11	Colon	Rupe		4-2	1st	+0.5
4-10	At Oak.	W	9-4		14	8	Kamieniecki	Tam		5-2	1st	+0.5
4-11	At Oak.	W	5-1		7	4	Nagy	Olivares		6-2	1st	+0.5
4-12	At Oak.	W	5-0		8	5	Wright	Heredia		7-2	1st	+0.5
4-14	Tex.	L	2-7		4	14	Helling	Burba		7-3	1st	...
4-15	Tex.	L	4-6		6	11	Clark	Colon	Wetteland	7-4	1st	...
4-16	Tex.	W	2-1		4	5	Finley	Wetteland		8-4	1st	+1.0
4-18	Oak.	L	5-8		9	9	Mulder	Nagy	Isringhausen	8-5	1st	+0.5
4-19	Oak.	L	5-10		12	12	Appier	Wright		8-6	2nd	0.5
4-20	Oak.	W	9-5		14	15	Burba	Hudson		9-6	T1st	...
4-24	At Sea.	W	6-0		9	2	Finley	Meche		10-6	2nd	1.5
4-25	At Sea.	L	5-8		11	9	Halama	Nagy		10-7	2nd	1.5
4-26	At Sea.	W	5-3	(10)	13	5	Shuey	Rhodes		11-7	2nd	1.5
4-28	Bos.	W	4-3		8	7	Burba	Schourek	Karsay	12-7	2nd	2.0
4-29	Bos.	W	3-2		5	5	Finley	R. Martinez	Karsay	13-7	2nd	2.0
4-30	Bos.	L	1-2		6	7	P. Martinez	Nagy	Lowe	13-8	2nd	2.0
5-1	N.Y.	L	1-2		7	8	Mendoza	Wright	Rivera	13-9	2nd	2.0
5-2	N.Y.	L	2-4		6	10	Pettitte	Witt	Rivera	13-10	2nd	2.0
5-3	N.Y.	L	5-6		10	9	Grimsley	Karsay	Rivera	13-11	2nd	3.0
5-4	At Tor.	L	1-8		7	10	Wells	Finley		13-12	2nd	3.5
5-5	At Tor.	L	10-11		20	13	Koch	Shuey		13-13	2nd	3.5
5-6	At Tor.	W	8-6		11	10	Rincon	Quantrill	Karsay	14-13	2nd	2.5
5-7	At Tor.	W	10-8	(12)	14	16	Shuey	Gunderson	Karsay	15-13	2nd	1.5
5-8	At Min.	W	3-2	(10)	10	9	Rincon	Wells	Karsay	16-13	2nd	0.5
5-9	At Min.	L	5-6		13	6	Hawkins	Finley	Miller	16-14	2nd	1.5
5-10	At Min.	L	9-10		14	13	Guardado	Karsay		16-15	3rd	1.5
5-11	K.C.	W	16-0		22	5	Wright	Durbin		17-15	2nd	1.0
5-12	K.C.	W	7-3		9	5	Colon	Batista		18-15	1st	...
5-13	K.C.	W	7-6	(12)	12	9	Reed	Reichert		19-15	1st	...
5-14	K.C.	L	4-5		7	8	Suzuki	Finley	Spradlin	19-16	2nd	1.0
5-16	Det.	W	11-9		14	15	Nagy	Nomo	Karsay	20-16	2nd	1.0
5-17	Det.	W	7-2		16	6	Colon	Nitkowski		21-16	1st	...
5-19	N.Y.	L	7-11		9	14	Mendoza	Kamieniecki		21-17	2nd	1.0
5-20	N.Y.	W	3-2		7	9	Shuey	Nelson		22-17	2nd	1.0
5-21	N.Y.	W	6-1		11	4	Rigdon	Hernandez		23-17	2nd	1.0
5-23	At Det.	L	4-10		11	16	Blair	Colon		23-18	2nd	1.5
5-24	At Det.	L	9-10		16	12	Patterson	Watson	Jones	23-19	2nd	1.5
5-25	At Det.	W	4-1		9	5	Burba	Moehler	Karsay	24-19	2nd	0.5
5-26	At Chi.	L	3-5		8	6	Eldred	Finley	Foulke	24-20	2nd	1.5
5-27	At Chi.	L	3-14		9	16	Parque	Wright		24-21	2nd	2.5
5-28	At Chi.	W	12-3		15	7	Colon	Wells		25-21	2nd	1.5
5-29	Ana.	L	2-3	(10)	5	4	Hasegawa	Karsay	Percival	25-22	2nd	1.5
5-30	Ana.	W	6-1		9	9	Burba	Schoeneweis		26-22	2nd	1.5
5-31	Ana.	W	7-3		10	14	Finley	Etherton	Karsay	27-22	2nd	1.5
6-2	At StL.	L	1-5		3	8	Kile	Wright		27-23	2nd	2.5
6-3	At StL.	W	4-2		8	4	Colon	Stephenson	Karsay	28-23	2nd	1.5
6-4	At StL.	W	3-2		7	6	Martin	Morris	Karsay	29-23	2nd	1.5
6-5	At Mil.	W	8-4		9	8	Burba	D'Amico		30-23	2nd	1.5
6-6	At Mil.	W	4-2		7	7	Finley	Snyder		31-23	2nd	1.5
6-7	At Mil.	W	9-5		10	10	Brewington	Bere		32-23	2nd	1.5
6-8	At Bos.	L	0-3		2	9	P. Martinez	Colon	Lowe	32-24	2nd	2.0
6-9	Cin.	W	7-4		12	8	Brower	Neagle	Karsay	33-24	2nd	2.0
6-10	Cin.	W	6-5		12	8	Burba	Parris	Karsay	34-24	2nd	2.0
6-11	Cin.	L	5-7	(13)	14	9	Aybar	Kamieniecki		34-25	2nd	2.0
6-12	Chi.	L	7-8		13	14	Eldred	Rigdon	Foulke	34-26	2nd	3.0
6-13	Chi.	L	3-4	(10)	8	8	Simas	Speier	Howry	34-27	2nd	4.0
6-14	Chi.	L	4-11		5	12	Beirne	Brower		34-28	2nd	5.0
6-16	At Det.	L	2-5		6	8	Moehler	Burba	Jones	34-29	2nd	6.5
6-17	At Det.	L	6-8		6	10	Brocail	Karsay		34-30	2nd	7.5
6-18	At Det.	W	9-4		13	8	Speier	Patterson		35-30	2nd	7.5
6-19	At Chi.	L	1-6		5	13	Wells	Colon		35-31	2nd	8.5
6-20	At Chi.	W	4-1		9	7	Brower	Sirotka	Karsay	36-31	2nd	7.5
6-21	At Chi.	W	8-6		12	14	Burba	Baldwin	Karsay	37-31	2nd	6.5
6-22	At Chi.	L	0-6		7	11	Eldred	Finley		37-32	2nd	7.5
6-23	Det.	L	6-7		9	16	Blair	Navarro	Jones	37-33	2nd	8.5
6-24†	Det.	W	8-1		10	4	Colon	Sparks		38-33		
6-24‡	Det.	L	8-14		12	16	Nitkowski	Mohler		38-34	2nd	8.0
6-25	Det.	W	2-1		9	6	Karsay	Anderson		39-34	2nd	8.0
6-26	Det.	L	2-13		11	16	Moehler	Burba		39-35	2nd	8.5
6-27	At K.C.	W	12-1		13	6	Finley	Suzuki		40-35	2nd	7.5
6-28	At K.C.	L	1-8		4	9	Witasick	Davis		40-36	2nd	8.5
6-29	At K.C.	L	1-6		5	4	Durbin	Colon		40-37	2nd	8.5
6-30	Min.	L	2-7		7	16	Redman	Brower	Hawkins	40-38	2nd	9.5

HIGHLIGHTS

High point: A September 20 matchup between Steve Woodard and Boston's Pedro Martinez looked like a mismatch. But Woodard, the sacrificial lamb, threw six shutout innings and Kenny Lofton's ninth-inning home run was the difference in a 2-1 win. The loss was the first for Martinez in 10 decisions against Cleveland.

Low point: When the Indians were swept by the young White Sox in a three-game series from June 12-14, the five-time defending-champion Indians fell five games behind in the A.L. Central. The sweep sent the Indians into a season-killing skid that lasted two months.

Turning point: With the Indians fighting to stay in the wild-card race, G.M. John Hart added pitchers Bob Wickman, Jason Bere and Woodard, first baseman David Segui and left fielder Wil Cordero at the deadline. The playoff drive came up a game short, but the season would have been over earlier without the deals.

Most valuable player: When Manny Ramirez was out from May 30 to July 12 with a pulled hamstring, the Indians went 19-20. When he returned, they vaulted back into the playoff hunt. Despite playing only 118 games, he batted .351 with 38 homers and 122 RBIs.

Most valuable pitcher: Righthander Dave Burba was steady all season. His 16 wins were a career high and he was 8-2 over the second half—4-0 in September and a 5-0 over his last seven starts.

Most improved player: Third baseman Travis Fryman, a .274 career hitter entering the season, batted .321 with 106 RBIs and 184 hits, all career highs. Fryman also won his first Gold Glove.

Most pleasant surprise: Reliever Justin Speier, not even in the Indians' plans at the beginning of the season, came to the aid of a ravaged staff and compiled a 5-2 record and 3.29 ERA in 47 games as a setup man.

Key injuries: Righthander starters Bartolo Colon, Charles Nagy and Jaret Wright all missed time with long stints on the disabled list. ... Catcher Sandy Alomar Jr. missed three weeks with a pulled hamstring. ... Center fielder Kenny Lofton was on the D.L. with a strained biceps and outfielder Jacob Cruz missed most of the season with a knee injury. ... Ramirez missed 39 games with his hamstring.

Notable: The Indians failed to win the A.L. Central for the first time since baseball went to its three-division format in 1994. ... The Indians spent 17 of 182 days in first and last had a share of the Central lead on May 18. ... The Indians played host to the White Sox and Twins in a day-night doubleheader on September 25. It was the first time a team had played two full games against two different teams in the same day since 1951.

—STEVE HERRICK

MISCELLANEOUS

RECORDS

2000 regular-season record: 90-72 (2nd in A.L. Central); 48-33 at home; 42-39 on road; 31-22 vs. East; 34-35 vs. Central; 25-15 vs. West; 17-21 vs. lefthanded starters; 73-51 vs. righthanded starters; 79-62 on grass; 11-10 on turf; 37-15 in daytime; 53-57 at night; 17-24 in one-run games; 6-5 in extra-inning games; 1-0-3 in doubleheaders.

Team record past five years: 461-347 (.571, ranks 2nd in league in that span).

TEAM LEADERS

Batting average: Manny Ramirez (.351).
At-bats: Omar Vizquel (613).
Runs: Roberto Alomar (111).
Hits: Roberto Alomar (189).
Total Bases: Manny Ramirez (306).
Doubles: Roberto Alomar (40).
Triples: Kenny Lofton (5).
Home runs: Manny Ramirez (38).
Runs batted in: Manny Ramirez (122).
Stolen bases: Roberto Alomar (39).
Slugging percentage: Manny Ramirez (.697).
On-base percentage: Manny Ramirez (.457).
Wins: Dave Burba, Chuck Finley (16).
Earned-run average: Bartolo Colon (3.88).
Complete games: Chuck Finley (3).
Shutouts: Bartolo Colon, Jaret Wright (1).
Saves: Steve Karsay (20).
Innings pitched: Chuck Finley (218.0).
Strikeouts: Bartolo Colon (212).

Date	Opp.	Res.	Score	(inn.*)	Hits	Opp. hits	Winning pitcher	Losing pitcher	Save	Record	Pos.	GB
7-1	Min.	L	3-4	(10)	8	9	Guardado	Karsay	Wells	40-39	2nd	10.5
7-2	Min.	W	7-1		11	6	Finley	Mays		41-39	2nd	10.5
7-4	Tor.	W	9-4		9	9	Colon	Frascatore		42-39	2nd	10.0
7-5	Tor.	W	15-7		16	12	Brewington	Quantrill		43-39	2nd	10.0
7-6	Tor.	L	6-9		15	15	Carpenter	Burba	Koch	43-40	2nd	10.5
7-7	At Cin.	L	1-2		8	7	Neagle	Finley	Graves	43-41	2nd	11.5
7-8	At Cin.	L	5-14		9	17	Parris	Davis		43-42	2nd	11.5
7-9	At Cin.	W	5-3		6	7	Colon	Williamson	Karsay	44-42	2nd	10.5
7-13	Pit.	W	4-3	(10)	10	8	Karsay	Sauerbeck		45-42	2nd	9.5
7-14	Pit.	W	9-3		11	8	Finley	Benson		46-42	2nd	8.5
7-15	Pit.	W	6-4		10	10	Brewington	Silva	Karsay	47-42	2nd	8.5
7-16	Hou.	L	1-5		7	9	Elarton	Colon		47-43	2nd	9.5
7-17	Hou.	W	8-6		9	8	Drew	Miller	Karsay	48-43	2nd	9.5
7-18	Hou.	W	8-2		8	11	Burba	Reynolds		49-43	2nd	9.5
7-19	K.C.	L	5-10		13	12	Suzuki	Finley	Spradlin	49-44	2nd	10.5
7-20	K.C.	L	6-10		11	17	Suppan	Brower		49-45	2nd	10.5
7-21	At Min.	L	1-2		8	8	Redman	Colon	Hawkins	49-46	2nd	11.5
7-22	At Min.	L	6-10		10	18	Santana	Davis	Wells	49-47	2nd	11.5
7-23	At Min.	W	8-3		12	7	Burba	Radke		50-47	2nd	10.5
7-25	At Tor.	W	10-3		10	9	Finley	Escobar		51-47	2nd	10.0
7-26	At Tor.	L	1-8		5	9	Wells	Colon		51-48	2nd	10.0
7-29†	At Bal.	W	14-3		20	9	Bere	Rapp		52-48		
7-29‡	At Bal.	L	0-4		10	8	Mercedes	Woodard		52-49	2nd	9.5
7-30	At Bal.	L	7-10		9	12	Parrish	Finley		52-50	2nd	10.5
8-1	At T.B.	L	5-6		10	7	Creek	Wickman		52-51	2nd	11.5
8-2	At T.B.	W	5-3		12	5	Karsay	Creek	Wickman	53-51	2nd	10.5
8-3	At T.B.	W	5-1		9	6	Bere	Lopez		54-51	2nd	10.0
8-4	Ana.	W	11-10		13	13	Wickman	Percival		55-51	2nd	9.0
8-5	Ana.	W	6-3		16	6	Speier	Schoeneweis		56-51	2nd	9.0
8-6	Ana.	W	5-2		10	7	Colon	Cooper	Wickman	57-51	2nd	9.0
8-7	Tex.	W	2-0		7	5	Reed	Helling	Wickman	58-51	2nd	8.5
8-8	Tex.	L	2-11		9	18	Rogers	Bere		58-52	2nd	8.0
8-9	Tex.	W	6-4		8	7	Speier	Perisho	Wickman	59-52	2nd	8.0
8-11	At Sea.	L	1-7		6	10	Abbott	Finley	Paniagua	59-53	2nd	8.5
8-12	At Sea.	W	5-4		7	7	Colon	Halama	Wickman	60-53	2nd	8.5
8-13	At Sea.	W	10-4		11	8	Speier	Garcia		61-53	2nd	7.5
8-14	At Oak.	L	1-8		8	13	Appier	Bere		61-54	2nd	7.5
8-15	At Oak.	L	3-5		10	6	Mulder	Burba	Isringhausen	61-55	2nd	8.5
8-16	At Oak.	L	6-7		9	12	D. Jones	Wickman		61-56	2nd	9.5
8-18	Sea.	W	9-8		10	14	Karsay	Rhodes		62-56	2nd	9.0
8-19	Sea.	W	10-4		11	8	Bere	Moyer		63-56	2nd	9.0
8-20	Sea.	W	12-4		15	11	Burba	Sele		64-56	2nd	8.0
8-22	Oak.	W	14-6		16	12	Finley	Heredia		65-56	2nd	7.0
8-23	Oak.	W	7-5		12	10	Shuey	Hudson	Wickman	66-56	2nd	7.0
8-24	Oak.	L	7-11		11	12	Zito	Woodard	Mecir	66-57	2nd	7.0
8-25	At Ana.	L	1-4		4	9	Wise	Burba	Hasegawa	66-58	2nd	8.0
8-26	At Ana.	W	9-5		12	9	Bere	Schoeneweis		67-58	2nd	7.0
8-27	At Ana.	L	9-10		14	16	Levine	Finley	Hasegawa	67-59	2nd	8.0
8-28	At Tex.	W	5-2		11	6	Colon	Rogers	Wickman	68-59	2nd	7.0
8-29	At Tex.	W	12-1		14	6	Woodard	Glynn		69-59	2nd	7.0
8-30	At Tex.	W	5-3		13	7	Burba	Davis	Wickman	70-59	2nd	7.0
8-31	At Tex.	L	7-14		14	21	Venafro	Karsay		70-60	2nd	7.5
9-1	Bal.	W	5-2		11	7	Finley	Ponson	Wickman	71-60	2nd	7.5
9-2	Bal.	L	6-8		9	13	Rapp	Karsay	Kohlmeier	71-61	2nd	8.5
9-3	Bal.	W	12-11	(13)	18	16	Cairncross	Trombley		72-61	2nd	8.5
9-4	T.B.	W	5-1		13	7	Burba	Lopez		73-61	2nd	7.5
9-5	T.B.	W	7-4		9	5	Bere	Fiore	Wickman	74-61	2nd	6.5
9-6	T.B.	W	6-2		11	4	Finley	Harper		75-61	2nd	6.5
9-7	T.B.	L	3-4		7	15	Rekar	Karsay	Hernandez	75-62	2nd	7.5
9-8	Chi.	L	4-5		9	10	Buehrle	Woodard	Foulke	75-63	2nd	8.5
9-9	Chi.	W	9-3		12	7	Burba	Garland		76-63	2nd	7.5
9-12	Bos.	L	6-8		7	12	R. Martinez	Finley	Lowe	76-64	2nd	8.0
9-13	Bos.	W	10-3		12	6	Colon	Ohka		77-64	2nd	8.0
9-14	Bos.	L	4-7		7	10	P. Martinez	Nagy	Lowe	77-65	2nd	8.5
9-15	At N.Y.	W	11-1		15	4	Burba	Cone		78-65	2nd	7.5
9-16	At N.Y.	L	3-6		4	12	Hernandez	Bere		78-66	2nd	8.5
9-17	At N.Y.	W	15-4		15	5	Finley	Neagle		79-66	2nd	7.5
9-18	At N.Y.	W	2-0		7	1	Colon	Clemens		80-66	2nd	6.5
9-19	At Bos.	L	4-7		11	12	Beck	Nagy	Lowe	80-67	2nd	7.5
9-20†	At Bos.	W	2-1		7	6	Woodard	P. Martinez	Wickman	81-67		
9-20‡	At Bos.	W	5-4		10	10	Karsay	Cormier	Wickman	82-67	2nd	7.0
9-21†	At Bos.	L	8-9		12	12	Ontiveros	Speier	Lowe	82-68		
9-21‡	At Bos.	W	8-5		15	12	Finley	Wakefield		83-68	2nd	7.5
9-22	At K.C.	L	2-3		10	10	Bottalico	Karsay		83-69	2nd	8.5
9-23	At K.C.	W	11-1		16	4	Colon	Reichert		84-69	2nd	8.5
9-24	At K.C.	L	0-9		6	12	Stein	Nagy		84-70	2nd	8.5
9-25	Chi.	W	9-2		13	8	Burba	Garland		85-70		
9-25	Min.	L	3-4		11	10	Miller	Shuey	Hawkins	85-71	2nd	8.0
9-26	Min.	W	4-2		8	8	Finley	Romero	Wickman	86-71	2nd	7.0
9-27	Min.	W	8-2		13	7	Bere	Radke		87-71	2nd	6.0
9-28	Min.	L	3-4	(10)	9	7	Guardado	Wickman	Hawkins	87-72	2nd	6.0
9-29	Tor.	W	8-4		9	5	Speier	Trachsel	Karsay	88-72	2nd	6.0
9-30	Tor.	W	6-5		11	10	Finley	Loaiza	Wickman	89-72	2nd	6.0
10-1	Tor.	W	11-4		12	8	Woodard	Wells		90-72	2nd	5.0

Monthly records: April (13-8), May (14-14), June (13-16), July (12-12), August (18-10), September (19-12), October (1-0).
*Innings, if other than nine. † First game of a doubleheader. ‡ Second game of a doubleheader.

MEMORABLE GAMES

June 11 at Cleveland

The Indians took a 5-0 lead into the eighth, but starter Chuck Finley didn't retire a batter in the inning and the Reds tied the game on Ken Griffey's three-run homer off Justin Speier. After the Indians loaded the bases with one out in the 10th and failed to score, the Reds scored twice in the 13th for the 7-5 win. The Indians entered the game with a 34-24 record, their season high point until August 23.

Cincinnati	AB	R	H	BI	Cleveland	AB	R	H	BI
Reese, 2b	6	1	0	0	Lofton, cf	4	0	3	1
.Larkin, dh-ss	6	1	1	0	Vizquel, ss	7	0	0	0
Griffey Jr., cf	5	2	2	3	Fryman, 3b-1b	5	1	1	0
Bichette, rf	2	0	1	0	Justice, rf	7	0	1	0
Tucker, rf	4	1	2	0	Sexson, 1b-lf	6	2	2	1
Young, 1b	5	0	0	0	Alomar Jr., c	5	2	2	0
.Boone, 3b	5	1	2	2	Thome, dh	5	0	1	1
Stynes, lf	5	1	1	0	Al.Ramirez, lf	4	0	2	0
Santiago, c	2	0	0	0	Cabrera, pr-lf	0	0	0	0
Taubensee, c	2	0	0	0	Branyan, ph	0	0	0	0
Castro, ss	3	0	0	1	Alomar, pr-2b	1	0	0	0
Casey, ph	1	0	0	0	Wilson, 2b-3b	4	0	2	1
Aybar, p	0	0	0	0					
Totals	**46**	**7**	**9**	**6**	**Totals**	**48**	**5**	**14**	**4**

Cincinnati ....0 0 0 0 0 0 0 5 0 0 0 0 2—7 9 1
Cleveland ....0 2 1 0 0 1 1 0 0 0 0 0 0—5 14 1

E—Boone (6), Alomar (6). DP—Cincinnati 3, Cleveland 1. LOB—Cincinnati 8, Cleveland 14. 2B—Boone (13), Al. Ramirez (3). HR—Griffey Jr. (18), Sexson (13). SB—Wilson (2). S—Castro, Wilson. SH—Stynes, Wilson.

Cincinnati	IP	H	R	ER	BB	SO
Villone	6	8	4	4	5	3
Dessens	1	2	1	1	0	0
Graves	3	3	0	0	2	1
Williamson	1	0	0	0	0	1
Aybar (W 1-2)	2	1	0	0	1	2
Cleveland	**IP**	**H**	**R**	**ER**	**BB**	**SO**
Finley	7	3	3	3	2	2
Reed	0.2	1	1	1	0	0
Speier	1.1	1	1	1	0	0
Brewington	2	1	0	0	1	2
Kamieniecki (L 1-3)	2	3	2	2	3	0

C.Finley pitched to 5 batters in 8th.

WP—Villone 2, Finley. PB—Alomar Jr.. U—HP, McClelland. 1B, Craft. 2B, Schrieber. 3B, Cuzzi. T—4:38. A—43,036.

September 21 at Boston

A day after the Indians had swept the Red Sox in a day-night doubleheader, the teams played another day-night twinbill. The Indians, battling Oakland and Boston for the wild-card spot, scored seven runs in the first inning of the opener. But starter Jason Bere did not retire a batter in the third and the Indians trailed 8-7 by the time the inning was over. The eventual 9-8 loss was a crushing blow to the team's playoff hopes.

Cleveland	AB	R	H	BI	Boston	AB	R	H	BI
Lofton, cf	6	0	2	1	Nixon, rf	4	1	2	2
Vizquel, ss	5	0	1	0	Offerman, 2b	2	2	1	1
Alomar, 2b	5	2	1	0	Sadler, pr-2b	0	0	0	0
M.Ramirez, rf	2	1	0	0	Bichette, dh	4	2	1	0
Thome, dh	1	1	1	0	Garciaparra, ss	4	1	3	2
Segui, 1b	5	1	2	3	O'Leary, lf	4	1	2	4
Fryman, 3b	5	1	2	2	Daubach, 1b	4	0	0	0
Roberts, lf	2	1	1	0	Brogna, 1b	0	0	0	0
Cabrera, ph-lf	1	0	0	0	Merloni, 3b	4	1	1	0
Selby, ph	1	0	0	0	Alexander, 3b	0	0	0	0
Diaz, c	4	1	2	2	Varitek, c	4	0	1	0
Branyan, ph	1	0	0	0	Lewis, cf	3	1	1	0
Totals	**38**	**8**	**12**	**8**	**Totals**	**33**	**9**	**12**	**9**

Cleveland.................................7 0 0 0 0 0 0 1 0—8 12 0
Boston.....................................2 0 6 0 1 0 0 0 x—9 12 2

E—Pichardo (1), Merloni (5). DP—Cleveland 1, Boston 1. LOB—Cleveland 13, Boston 7. 2B—Alomar (38), Segui (39), Fryman (36), Nixon (26), O'Leary (28). HR—Nixon (11), O'Leary (12). SB—Lofton (29), Alomar 3 (38), Fryman (1), Roberts (1). CS—Sadler (1). S—Garciaparra.

Cleveland	IP	H	R	ER	BB	SO
Bere	2	4	6	6	3	0
Cairncross	0.1	1	1	1	0	0
Speier (L 4-2)	0.1	2	1	1	2	1
Brewington	2.2	3	1	1	0	2
Martin	1.2	1	0	0	0	1
Reed	1	1	0	0	0	0
Boston	**IP**	**H**	**R**	**ER**	**BB**	**SO**
Arrojo	0.2	3	7	7	4	1
Ontiveros (W 1-1)	2.1	2	0	0	1	0
J.Pena	1	1	0	0	2	0
Pichardo	1	2	0	0	0	0
Fassero	2	1	0	0	1	2
Beck	1	2	1	1	1	2
Lowe (S 38)	1	1	0	0	1	2

Bere pitched to 4 batters in 3rd.

HBP—Lewis by Brewington. U—HP, Davis. 1B, Barksdale. 2B, Rieker. 3B, Guccione. T—4:03 A—31,404.

INDIVIDUAL STATISTICS

BATTING

																							vs RHP				vs LHP			
Name	G	TPA	AB	R	H	TB	2B	3B	HR	RBI	Avg.	Obp.	Slg.	SH	SF	HP	BB	IBB	SO	SB	CS	GDP	AB	Avg.	HR	RBI	AB	Avg.	HR	RBI
Vizquel, Omar	156	717	613	101	176	230	27	3	7	66	.287	.377	.375	7	5	5	87	0	72	22	10	13	457	.311	6	50	156	.218	1	16
Alomar, Roberto	155	697	610	111	189	290	40	2	19	89	.310	.378	.475	11	6	6	64	4	82	39	4	19	459	.307	16	72	151	.318	3	17
Fryman, Travis	155	658	574	93	184	296	38	4	22	106	.321	.392	.516	0	10	1	73	2	111	1	1	15	456	.327	18	89	118	.297	4	17
Thome, Jim	158	684	557	106	150	296	33	1	37	106	.269	.398	.531	0	5	4	118	4	171	1	0	8	405	.277	31	87	152	.250	6	19
Lofton, Kenny	137	640	543	107	151	229	23	5	15	73	.278	.369	.422	6	8	4	79	3	72	30	7	11	420	.283	13	53	123	.260	2	20
Ramirez, Manny	118	532	439	92	154	306	34	2	38	122	.351	.457	.697	0	4	3	86	9	117	1	1	9	348	.339	31	97	91	.396	7	25
Alomar Jr., Sandy	97	384	356	44	103	144	16	2	7	42	.289	.324	.404	4	4	4	16	1	41	2	2	9	282	.273	6	34	74	.351	1	8
Sexson, Richie	91	356	324	45	83	149	16	1	16	44	.256	.315	.460	0	3	4	25	0	96	1	0	8	249	.253	12	34	75	.267	4	10
Diaz, Einar	75	275	250	29	68	98	14	2	4	25	.272	.323	.392	6	0	8	11	0	29	4	2	7	193	.275	4	20	57	.263	0	5
Justice, David	68	288	249	46	66	145	14	1	21	58	.265	.361	.582	0	1	0	38	2	49	1	1	7	196	.260	15	42	53	.283	6	16
Segui, David	57	245	223	41	74	111	13	0	8	46	.332	.384	.498	0	2	1	19	1	33	0	0	8	161	.335	6	32	62	.323	2	14
Branyan, Russ	67	220	193	32	46	105	7	2	16	38	.238	.327	.544	0	1	4	22	1	76	0	0	2	178	.242	16	37	15	.200	0	1
Cabrera, Jolbert	100	187	175	27	44	55	3	1	2	15	.251	.290	.314	1	1	2	8	0	15	6	4	1	113	.274	1	9	62	.210	1	6
Cordero, Wil	38	158	148	18	39	54	11	2	0	17	.264	.310	.365	0	0	3	7	0	18	0	0	7	108	.250	0	14	40	.300	0	3
Wilson, Enrique	40	127	117	16	38	53	9	0	2	12	.325	.360	.453	2	1	0	7	0	11	2	1	2	84	.321	2	7	33	.333	0	5
Ramirez, Alex	41	117	112	13	32	54	5	1	5	12	.286	.316	.482	0	0	0	5	0	17	1	0	3	56	.286	4	7	56	.286	1	5
Ledee, Ricky	17	71	63	13	14	24	2	1	2	8	.222	.310	.381	0	0	0	8	0	9	0	0	3	49	.245	1	6	14	.143	1	2
Selby, Bill	30	48	46	8	11	12	1	0	0	4	.239	.271	.261	0	0	1	1	0	9	0	0	1	42	.262	0	4	4	.000	0	0
Cruz, Jacob	11	36	29	3	7	10	3	0	0	5	.241	.361	.345	0	1	1	5	0	4	1	0	0	24	.208	0	4	5	.400	0	1
Perry, Chan	13	14	14	1	1	1	0	0	0	0	.071	.071	.071	0	0	0	0	0	5	0	0	1	5	.000	0	0	9	.111	0	0
Roberts, Dave	19	13	10	1	2	2	0	0	0	0	.200	.333	.200	1	0	0	2	0	2	1	1	0	8	.250	0	0	2	.000	0	0
McDonald, John	9	9	9	0	4	4	0	0	0	0	.444	.444	.444	0	0	0	0	0	1	0	0	0	6	.500	0	0	3	.333	0	0
Whiten, Mark	6	10	7	2	2	3	1	0	0	1	.286	.500	.429	0	0	0	3	0	2	0	0	0	6	.333	0	1	1	.000	0	0
Finley, Chuck	34	7	7	0	0	0	0	0	0	0	.000	.000	.000	0	0	0	0	0	4	0	0	0	4	.000	0	0	3	.000	0	0
Colon, Bartolo	30	5	5	0	0	0	0	0	0	0	.000	.000	.000	0	0	0	0	0	5	0	0	0	5	.000	0	0	0	.000	0	0
Brower, Jim	17	3	3	0	0	0	0	0	0	0	.000	.000	.000	0	0	0	0	0	2	0	0	0	1	.000	0	0	2	.000	0	0
Speier, Justin	47	2	2	0	1	1	0	0	0	0	.500	.500	.500	0	0	0	0	0	1	0	0	0	2	.500	0	0	0	.000	0	0
Burba, Dave	32	3	1	0	0	0	0	0	0	0	.000	.000	.000	2	0	0	0	0	1	0	0	0	1	.000	0	0	0	.000	0	0
Karsay, Steve	72	1	1	0	0	0	0	0	0	0	.000	.000	.000	0	0	0	0	0	0	0	0	0	1	.000	0	0	0	.000	0	0
Brewington, Jamie	26	2	1	1	0	0	0	0	0	0	.000	.500	.000	0	0	0	1	0	0	0	0	0	1	.000	0	0	0	.000	0	0
Wright, Jaret	9	2	1	0	0	0	0	0	0	0	.000	.000	.000	1	0	0	0	0	1	0	0	0	1	.000	0	0	0	.000	0	0
Davis, Kane	5	1	1	0	0	0	0	0	0	0	.000	.000	.000	0	0	0	0	0	1	0	0	0	1	.000	0	0	0	.000	0	0
Kamieniecki, Scott	26	0	0	0	0	0	0	0	0	0	.000	.000	.000	0	0	0	0	0	0	0	0	0	0	.000	0	0	0	.000	0	0
Reed, Steve	57	0	0	0	0	0	0	0	0	0	.000	.000	.000	0	0	0	0	0	0	0	0	0	0	.000	0	0	0	.000	0	0
Shuey, Paul	57	0	0	0	0	0	0	0	0	0	.000	.000	.000	0	0	0	0	0	0	0	0	0	0	.000	0	0	0	.000	0	0
Lorraine, Andrew	10	0	0	0	0	0	0	0	0	0	.000	.000	.000	0	0	0	0	0	0	0	0	0	0	.000	0	0	0	.000	0	0
Martin, Tom	31	0	0	0	0	0	0	0	0	0	.000	.000	.000	0	0	0	0	0	0	0	0	0	0	.000	0	0	0	.000	0	0
Watson, Mark	6	0	0	0	0	0	0	0	0	0	.000	.000	.000	0	0	0	0	0	0	0	0	0	0	.000	0	0	0	.000	0	0
Rigdon, Paul	5	0	0	0	0	0	0	0	0	0	.000	.000	.000	0	0	0	0	0	0	0	0	0	0	.000	0	0	0	.000	0	0
Witt, Bobby	7	0	0	0	0	0	0	0	0	0	.000	.000	.000	0	0	0	0	0	0	0	0	0	0	.000	0	0	0	.000	0	0
Navarro, Jaime	7	0	0	0	0	0	0	0	0	0	.000	.000	.000	0	0	0	0	0	0	0	0	0	0	.000	0	0	0	.000	0	0
Nagy, Charles	11	0	0	0	0	0	0	0	0	0	.000	.000	.000	0	0	0	0	0	0	0	0	0	0	.000	0	0	0	.000	0	0
Haney, Chris	1	0	0	0	0	0	0	0	0	0	.000	.000	.000	0	0	0	0	0	0	0	0	0	0	.000	0	0	0	.000	0	0
Williams, Brian	7	0	0	0	0	0	0	0	0	0	.000	.000	.000	0	0	0	0	0	0	0	0	0	0	.000	0	0	0	.000	0	0
Wickman, Bob	26	0	0	0	0	0	0	0	0	0	.000	.000	.000	0	0	0	0	0	0	0	0	0	0	.000	0	0	0	.000	0	0
Mohler, Mike	2	0	0	0	0	0	0	0	0	0	.000	.000	.000	0	0	0	0	0	0	0	0	0	0	.000	0	0	0	.000	0	0
Bere, Jason	11	0	0	0	0	0	0	0	0	0	.000	.000	.000	0	0	0	0	0	0	0	0	0	0	.000	0	0	0	.000	0	0
Nichting, Chris	7	0	0	0	0	0	0	0	0	0	.000	.000	.000	0	0	0	0	0	0	0	0	0	0	.000	0	0	0	.000	0	0
Rincon, Ricky	35	0	0	0	0	0	0	0	0	0	.000	.000	.000	0	0	0	0	0	0	0	0	0	0	.000	0	0	0	.000	0	0
Woodard, Steve	13	0	0	0	0	0	0	0	0	0	.000	.000	.000	0	0	0	0	0	0	0	0	0	0	.000	0	0	0	.000	0	0
Newman, Alan	1	0	0	0	0	0	0	0	0	0	.000	.000	.000	0	0	0	0	0	0	0	0	0	0	.000	0	0	0	.000	0	0
DePaula, Sean	13	0	0	0	0	0	0	0	0	0	.000	.000	.000	0	0	0	0	0	0	0	0	0	0	.000	0	0	0	.000	0	0
Martinez, Willie	1	0	0	0	0	0	0	0	0	0	.000	.000	.000	0	0	0	0	0	0	0	0	0	0	.000	0	0	0	.000	0	0
Drew, Tim	3	0	0	0	0	0	0	0	0	0	.000	.000	.000	0	0	0	0	0	0	0	0	0	0	.000	0	0	0	.000	0	0
Cairncross, Cam	15	0	0	0	0	0	0	0	0	0	.000	.000	.000	0	0	0	0	0	0	0	0	0	0	.000	0	0	0	.000	0	0

Players with more than one A.L. team

																							vs RHP				vs LHP			
Name	G	TPA	AB	R	H	TB	2B	3B	HR	RBI	Avg.	Obp.	Slg.	SH	SF	HP	BB	IBB	SO	SB	CS	GDP	AB	Avg.	HR	RBI	AB	Avg.	HR	RBI
Justice, Cle.-N.Y.	146	606	524	89	150	306	31	1	41	118	.286	.377	.584	0	3	1	77	3	91	2	1	13	390	.279	26	82	134	.306	15	36
Ledee, N.Y.	62	220	191	23	46	80	11	1	7	31	.241	.332	.419	0	2	1	26	2	39	7	3	7	49	.245	1	6	14	.143	1	2
Ledee, Tex.	58	240	213	23	50	74	6	3	4	38	.235	.317	.347	0	1	1	25	2	50	6	3	7	49	.245	1	6	14	.143	1	2
Ledee, N.Y.-Cle.-Tex.	137	531	467	59	110	178	19	5	13	77	.236	.322	.381	0	3	2	59	4	98	13	6	17	384	.234	10	62	83	.241	3	15
Segui, Tex.-Cle.	150	634	574	93	192	293	42	1	19	103	.334	.388	.510	0	6	1	53	2	84	0	1	20	419	.344	15	80	155	.310	4	23

PITCHING

																							vs. RH				vs. LH			
Name	W	L	Pct.	ERA	IP	H	R	ER	HR	SH	SF	HB	BB	IBB	SO	G	GS	CG	ShO	GF	Sv	AB	Avg.	HR	RBI	AB	Avg.	HR	RBI
Finley, Chuck	16	11	.593	4.17	218.0	211	108	101	23	5	4	2	101	3	189	34	34	3	0	0	0	649	.260	19	72	175	.240	4	18
Burba, Dave	16	6	.727	4.47	191.1	199	99	95	19	5	5	2	91	2	180	32	32	0	0	0	0	394	.274	11	47	351	.259	8	39
Colon, Bartolo	15	8	.652	3.88	188.0	163	86	81	21	2	3	4	98	4	212	30	30	2	1	0	0	365	.225	9	39	335	.242	12	35
Karsay, Steve	5	9	.357	3.76	76.2	79	33	32	5	2	2	3	25	4	66	72	0	0	0	46	20	158	.304	3	23	139	.223	2	19
Speier, Justin	5	2	.714	3.29	68.1	57	27	25	9	2	4	4	28	3	69	47	0	0	0	12	0	135	.274	5	17	117	.171	4	14
Shuey, Paul	4	2	.667	3.39	63.2	51	25	24	4	1	3	3	30	3	69	57	0	0	0	12	0	115	.235	2	16	118	.203	2	18
Brower, Jim	2	3	.400	6.24	62.0	80	45	43	11	1	0	2	31	1	32	17	11	0	0	1	0	139	.324	3	23	120	.292	8	17
Nagy, Charles	2	7	.222	8.21	57.0	71	53	52	15	5	2	2	21	2	41	11	11	0	0	0	0	105	.295	8	29	132	.303	7	18
Reed, Steve	2	0	1.000	4.34	56.0	58	30	27	7	4	1	1	21	4	39	57	0	0	0	16	0	157	.268	4	18	59	.271	3	11
Bere, Jason	6	3	.667	6.63	54.1	65	41	40	6	0	3	4	26	0	44	11	11	0	0	0	0	99	.333	4	21	120	.267	2	14
Woodard, Steve	3	3	.500	5.67	54.0	57	35	34	10	1	1	2	11	1	35	13	11	0	0	1	0	96	.313	5	14	116	.233	5	18
Wright, Jaret	3	4	.429	4.70	51.2	44	27	27	6	0	1	1	28	0	36	9	9	1	1	0	0	99	.182	1	10	88	.295	5	13
Brewington, Jamie	3	0	1.000	5.36	45.1	56	28	27	3	2	2	2	19	0	34	26	0	0	0	10	0	98	.245	0	12	82	.390	3	23
Martin, Tom	1	0	1.000	4.05	33.1	32	16	15	3	0	1	1	15	2	21	31	0	0	0	7	0	69	.232	3	8	57	.281	0	9
Kamieniecki, Scott	1	3	.250	5.67	33.1	42	22	21	6	1	0	1	20	5	29	26	0	0	0	7	0	86	.291	3	11	49	.347	3	11
Wickman, Bob	1	3	.250	3.38	26.2	27	12	10	0	3	0	0	12	3	11	26	0	0	0	24	14	47	.277	0	7	53	.264	0	8
Rincon, Ricky	2	0	1.000	2.70	20.0	17	7	6	1	0	0	1	13	1	20	35	0	0	0	4	0	25	.240	1	3	51	.216	0	0
Williams, Brian	0	0	.000	4.00	18.0	23	9	8	2	0	1	1	8	1	6	7	0	0	0	1	0	47	.319	1	8	24	.333	1	2
Rigdon, Paul	1	1	.500	7.64	17.2	21	15	15	4	0	0	0	9	1	15	5	4	0	0	0	0	38	.289	1	6	32	.313	3	9
DePaula, Sean	0	0	.000	5.94	16.2	20	11	11	3	0	1	0	14	2	16	13	0	0	0	3	0	40	.175	1	9	28	.464	2	8
Witt, Bobby	0	1	.000	7.63	15.1	28	13	13	4	0	0	0	6	1	6	7	2	0	0	2	0	45	.378	2	6	26	.423	2	6
Navarro, Jaime	0	1	.000	7.98	14.2	20	13	13	3	0	2	1	5	0	9	7	2	0	0	1	0	38	.289	0	6	23	.391	3	9
Davis, Kane	0	3	.000	14.73	11.0	20	21	18	3	0	0	1	8	0	2	5	2	0	0	0	0	29	.379	2	12	23	.391	1	3
Lorraine, Andrew	0	0	.000	3.86	9.1	8	4	4	1	0	0	0	5	0	5	10	0	0	0	3	0	17	.294	1	3	19	.158	0	2
Cairncross, Cam	1	0	1.000	3.86	9.1	11	4	4	1	0	1	0	3	1	8	15	0	0	0	2	0	16	.313	0	2	20	.300	1	5
Nichting, Chris	0	0	.000	7.00	9.0	13	7	7	0	0	1	2	5	1	7	7	0	0	0	1	0	25	.360	0	6	13	.308	0	3
Drew, Tim	1	0	1.000	10.00	9.0	17	12	10	1	0	2	1	8	0	5	3	3	0	0	0	0	14	.500	1	4	26	.385	0	6
Watson, Mark	0	1	.000	8.53	6.1	12	7	6	0	0	0	1	2	0	4	6	0	0	0	1	0	17	.412	0	3	13	.385	0	2
Martinez, Willie	0	0	.000	3.00	3.0	1	1	1	0	0	1	0	1	0	1	1	0	0	0	0	0	4	.250	0	0	5	.000	0	1
Newman, Alan	0	0	.000	20.25	1.1	6	3	3	1	0	0	0	1	0	0	1	0	0	0	1	0	8	.750	1	4	1	.000	0	0
Haney, Chris	0	0	.000	9.00	1.0	1	1	1	0	0	1	0	1	0	0	1	0	0	0	1	0	3	.333	0	1	0	.000	0	0
Mohler, Mike	0	1	.000	9.00	1.0	1	1	1	1	0	0	0	0	0	2	2	0	0	0	0	0	1	.000	0	0	3	.333	1	2

DESIGNATED HITTERS

Name	AB	Avg.	HR	RBI	Name	AB	Avg.	HR	RBI	Name	AB	Avg.	HR	RBI
Thome, Jim	183	.235	8	32	Justice, David	76	.276	8	20	Wilson, Enrique	21	.286	2	3
Ramirez, Manny	89	.326	11	28	Segui, David	57	.386	3	11	Ramirez, Alex	15	.067	0	1
Branyan, Russ	78	.244	10	20	Sexson, Richie	34	.206	1	1	Selby, Bill	5	.400	0	3

INDIVIDUAL STATISTICS

FIELDING

FIRST BASEMEN

Player	Pct.	G	PO	A	E	TC	DP
Thome, Jim	.995	107	834	91	5	930	101
Segui, David	1.000	35	261	33	0	294	21
Sexson, Richie	.996	27	198	25	1	224	11
Fryman, Travis	1.000	1	4	0	0	4	1
Perry, Chan	1.000	1	3	0	0	3	0

SECOND BASEMEN

Player	Pct.	G	PO	A	E	TC	DP
Alomar, Roberto	.980	155	293	437	15	745	109
Cabrera, Jolbert	1.000	19	13	19	0	32	7
Wilson, Enrique	1.000	7	10	12	0	22	2
Selby, Bill	1.000	6	3	2	0	5	0
McDonald, John	1.000	2	2	2	0	4	0

THIRD BASEMEN

Player	Pct.	G	PO	A	E	TC	DP
Fryman, Travis	.978	154	79	276	8	363	20
Wilson, Enrique	.950	12	2	17	1	20	0
Selby, Bill	1.000	4	0	1	0	1	1
Branyan, Russ	.500	1	0	1	1	2	1
Diaz, Einar	-	1	0	0	0	0	0

SHORTSTOPS

Player	Pct.	G	PO	A	E	TC	DP
Vizquel, Omar	.995	156	231	414	3	648	99
Cabrera, Jolbert	1.000	8	7	17	0	24	2
Wilson, Enrique	1.000	7	8	15	0	23	5
McDonald, John	1.000	7	2	6	0	8	1

OUTFIELDERS

Player	Pct.	G	PO	A	E	TC	DP
Lofton, Kenny	.989	135	348	4	4	356	1
Ramirez, Manny	.986	93	134	7	2	143	1
Cabrera, Jolbert	.989	74	89	3	1	93	1
Sexson, Richie	1.000	58	79	3	0	82	0
Justice, David	.977	47	84	2	2	88	1
Cordero, Wil	1.000	38	79	2	0	81	0
Branyan, Russ	.968	33	59	2	2	63	0
Ramirez, Alex	.978	31	44	1	1	46	0
Ledee, Ricky	1.000	17	39	1	0	40	0
Roberts, Dave	1.000	17	10	0	0	10	0
Selby, Bill	1.000	10	16	0	0	16	0
Cruz, Jacob	1.000	9	16	1	0	17	1
Segui, David	1.000	7	6	0	0	6	0
Perry, Chan	1.000	7	5	0	0	5	0
Whiten, Mark	1.000	5	3	0	0	3	0

CATCHERS

Player	Pct.	G	PO	A	E	TC	DP	PB
Alomar Jr., Sandy	.989	95	661	42	8	711	6	6
Diaz, Einar	.994	74	579	48	4	631	4	4

PITCHERS

Player	Pct.	G	PO	A	E	TC	DP
Karsay, Steve	.957	72	9	13	1	23	0
Reed, Steve	.933	57	6	8	1	15	0
Shuey, Paul	1.000	57	7	8	0	15	0
Speier, Justin	.875	47	1	6	1	8	0
Rincon, Ricky	1.000	35	2	3	0	5	0
Finley, Chuck	.886	34	11	20	4	35	1
Burba, Dave	1.000	32	10	27	0	37	0
Martin, Tom	.889	31	5	3	1	9	0
Colon, Bartolo	.946	30	17	18	2	37	1
Kamieniecki, Scott	.889	26	3	5	1	9	1
Brewington, Jamie	1.000	26	4	4	0	8	1
Wickman, Bob	1.000	26	1	5	0	6	0
Brower, Jim	.955	17	9	12	1	22	1
Cairncross, Cam	.500	15	0	1	1	2	0
Woodard, Steve	1.000	13	7	10	0	17	1
DePaula, Sean	1.000	13	4	2	0	6	0
Nagy, Charles	1.000	11	12	13	0	25	0
Bere, Jason	1.000	11	6	2	0	8	1
Lorraine, Andrew	1.000	10	1	1	0	2	0
Wright, Jaret	1.000	9	5	3	0	8	0
Williams, Brian	1.000	7	2	2	0	4	0
Witt, Bobby	1.000	7	0	3	0	3	0
Nichting, Chris	1.000	7	1	1	0	2	0
Navarro, Jaime	-	7	0	0	0	0	0
Watson, Mark	1.000	6	1	0	0	1	0
Davis, Kane	1.000	5	1	3	0	4	0
Rigdon, Paul	1.000	5	0	2	0	2	0
Drew, Tim	.800	3	1	3	1	5	0
Mohler, Mike	-	2	0	0	0	0	0
Martinez, Willie	1.000	1	0	2	0	2	0
Haney, Chris	1.000	1	0	1	0	1	0
Newman, Alan	-	1	0	0	0	0	0

PITCHING AGAINST EACH CLUB

Pitcher	Ana. W-L	Bal. W-L	Bos. W-L	Chi. W-L	Det. W-L	K.C. W-L	Min. W-L	N.Y. W-L	Oak. W-L	Sea. W-L	T.B. W-L	Tex. W-L	Tor. W-L	N.L. W-L	Total W-L
Bere, Jason	1-0	1-0	0-0	0-0	0-0	0-0	1-0	0-1	0-1	1-0	2-0	0-1	0-0	0-0	6-3
Brewington, Jamie	0-0	0-0	0-0	0-0	0-0	0-0	0-0	0-0	0-0	0-0	0-0	0-0	1-0	2-0	3-0
Brower, Jim	0-0	0-0	0-0	1-1	0-0	0-1	0-1	0-0	0-0	0-0	0-0	0-0	0-0	1-0	2-3
Burba, Dave	1-1	0-0	1-0	3-0	1-2	0-0	1-0	1-0	1-1	1-0	2-0	1-1	0-1	3-0	16-6
Cairncross, Cam	0-0	1-0	0-0	0-0	0-0	0-0	0-0	0-0	0-0	0-0	0-0	0-0	0-0	0-0	1-0
Colon, Bartolo	1-0	1-0	1-1	1-1	2-1	2-1	0-1	1-0	0-0	1-0	1-0	1-1	1-1	2-1	15-8
Davis, Kane	0-0	0-0	0-0	0-0	0-0	0-1	0-1	0-0	0-0	0-0	0-0	0-0	0-0	0-1	0-3
DePaula, Sean	0-0	0-0	0-0	0-0	0-0	0-0	0-0	0-0	0-0	0-0	0-0	0-0	0-0	0-0	0-0
Drew, Tim	0-0	0-0	0-0	0-0	0-0	0-0	0-0	0-0	0-0	0-0	0-0	0-0	0-0	1-0	1-0
Finley, Chuck	1-1	1-1	2-1	0-2	0-0	1-2	2-1	1-0	1-0	1-1	1-0	1-0	2-1	2-1	16-11
Haney, Chris	0-0	0-0	0-0	0-0	0-0	0-0	0-0	0-0	0-0	0-0	0-0	0-0	0-0	0-0	0-0
Kamieniecki, Scott	0-0	0-1	0-0	0-0	0-0	0-0	0-0	0-1	1-0	0-0	0-0	0-0	0-0	0-1	1-3
Karsay, Steve	0-1	0-1	1-0	0-0	1-1	0-1	0-2	0-1	0-0	1-0	1-1	0-1	0-0	1-0	5-9
Lorraine, Andrew	0-0	0-0	0-0	0-0	0-0	0-0	0-0	0-0	0-0	0-0	0-0	0-0	0-0	0-0	0-0
Martin, Tom	0-0	0-0	0-0	0-0	0-0	0-0	0-0	0-0	0-0	0-0	0-0	0-0	0-0	1-0	1-0
Martinez, Willie	0-0	0-0	0-0	0-0	0-0	0-0	0-0	0-0	0-0	0-0	0-0	0-0	0-0	0-0	0-0
Mohler, Mike	0-0	0-0	0-0	0-0	0-1	0-0	0-0	0-0	0-0	0-0	0-0	0-0	0-0	0-0	0-1
Nagy, Charles	0-0	0-1	0-3	0-0	1-0	0-1	0-0	0-0	1-1	0-1	0-0	0-0	0-0	0-0	2-7
Navarro, Jaime	0-0	0-0	0-0	0-0	0-1	0-0	0-0	0-0	0-0	0-0	0-0	0-0	0-0	0-0	0-1
Newman, Alan	0-0	0-0	0-0	0-0	0-0	0-0	0-0	0-0	0-0	0-0	0-0	0-0	0-0	0-0	0-0
Nichting, Chris	0-0	0-0	0-0	0-0	0-0	0-0	0-0	0-0	0-0	0-0	0-0	0-0	0-0	0-0	0-0
Reed, Steve	0-0	0-0	0-0	0-0	0-0	1-0	0-0	0-0	0-0	0-0	0-0	1-0	0-0	0-0	2-0
Rigdon, Paul	0-0	0-0	0-0	0-1	0-0	0-0	0-0	1-0	0-0	0-0	0-0	0-0	0-0	0-0	1-1
Rincon, Ricky	0-0	0-0	0-0	0-0	0-0	0-0	1-0	0-0	0-0	0-0	0-0	0-0	1-0	0-0	2-0
Shuey, Paul	0-0	0-0	0-0	0-0	0-0	0-0	0-1	1-0	1-0	1-0	0-0	0-0	1-1	0-0	4-2
Speier, Justin	1-0	0-0	0-1	0-1	1-0	0-0	0-0	0-0	0-0	1-0	0-0	1-0	1-0	0-0	5-2
Watson, Mark	0-0	0-0	0-0	0-0	0-1	0-0	0-0	0-0	0-0	0-0	0-0	0-0	0-0	0-0	0-1
Wickman, Bob	1-0	0-0	0-0	0-0	0-0	0-0	0-1	0-0	0-1	0-0	0-1	0-0	0-0	0-0	1-3
Williams, Brian	0-0	0-0	0-0	0-0	0-0	0-0	0-0	0-0	0-0	0-0	0-0	0-0	0-0	0-0	0-0
Witt, Bobby	0-0	0-0	0-0	0-0	0-0	0-0	0-0	0-1	0-0	0-0	0-0	0-0	0-0	0-0	0-1
Woodard, Steve	0-0	0-1	1-0	0-1	0-0	0-0	0-0	0-0	0-1	0-0	0-0	1-0	1-0	0-0	3-3
Wright, Jaret	0-0	0-0	0-0	0-1	0-0	1-0	0-0	0-1	1-1	0-0	1-0	0-0	0-0	0-1	3-4
Totals	6-3	4-5	6-6	5-8	6-7	5-7	5-8	5-5	6-6	7-2	8-2	6-4	8-4	13-5	90-72

INTERLEAGUE: Burba 1-0, Finley 1-0, Brewington 1-0 vs. Brewers; Brower 1-0, Burba 1-0, Colon 1-0, Kamieniecki 0-1, Finley 0-1, Davis 0-1 vs. Reds; Drew 1-0, Burba 1-0, Colon 0-1 vs. Astros; Karsay 1-0, Finley 1-0, Brewington 1-0 vs. Pirates; Martin 1-0, Colon 1-0, Wright 0-1 vs. Cardinals. Total: 13-5.

MISCELLANEOUS

HOME RUNS BY PARK

At Anaheim (4): Alomar 1, Vizquel 1, Fryman 1, Lofton 1.
At Baltimore (8): Ramirez 3, Alomar 1, Segui 1, Fryman 1, Thome 1, Lofton 1.
At Boston (1): Lofton 1.
At Chicago (AL) (8): Thome 3, Diaz 2, Alomar 1, Fryman 1, Ramirez 1.
At Cincinnati (4): Vizquel 3, Lofton 1.
At Cleveland (122): Ramirez 22, Thome 21, Branyan 13, Justice 10, Lofton 10, Fryman 9, Alomar 8, Sexson 8, Alomar Jr. 5, Segui 4, Ramirez 3, Diaz 2, Ledee 2, Wilson 2, Cabrera 2, Vizquel 1.
At Detroit (12): Thome 3, Alomar 2, Justice 2, Sexson 2, Fryman 1, Ramirez 1, Branyan 1.
At Kansas City (5): Thome 2, Alomar Jr. 1, Ramirez 1, Sexson 1.
At Milwaukee (6): Justice 3, Fryman 1, Sexson 1, Branyan 1.
At Minnesota (11): Ramirez 3, Fryman 2, Sexson 2, Alomar 1, Vizquel 1, Justice 1, Thome 1.
At New York (AL) (6): Ramirez 3, Segui 1, Fryman 1, Branyan 1.
At Oakland (5): Alomar 2, Fryman 2, Justice 1.
At Seattle (3): Fryman 2, Ramirez 1.
At St. Louis (5): Sexson 2, Justice 1, Thome 1, Lofton 1.
At Tampa Bay (12): Thome 3, Ramirez 3, Justice 2, Alomar 1, Alomar Jr. 1, Vizquel 1, Segui 1.
At Texas (5): Alomar 1, Segui 1, Fryman 1, Thome 1, Ramirez 1.
At Toronto (4): Alomar 1, Justice 1, Thome 1, Ramirez 1.

LOW-HIT GAMES

No-hitters: None.
One-hitters: Bartolo Colon, September 18 vs. New York, W 2-0.
Two-hitters: None.

10-STRIKEOUT GAMES

Bartolo Colon 6, Chuck Finley 3, Dave Burba 1, Total: 10

FOUR OR MORE HITS IN ONE GAME

Roberto Alomar 2, Sandy Alomar Jr. 2, Travis Fryman 2, Kenny Lofton 2, Jolbert Cabrera 2 (including one five-hit game), Omar Vizquel 1, Jim Thome 1, Wil Cordero 1, Einar Diaz 1 (including one five-hit game), Total: 14

MULTI-HOMER GAMES

Jim Thome 4, Manny Ramirez 4, Roberto Alomar 3, Russ Branyan 3, David Justice 2, Travis Fryman 2, Richie Sexson 2, Omar Vizquel 1, Kenny Lofton 1, Total: 22

GRAND SLAMS

4-7: Omar Vizquel (off Tampa Bay's Juan Guzman)
5-11: Manny Ramirez (off Kansas City's Chad Durbin)
6-17: Russ Branyan (off Detroit's Hideo Nomo)
7-22: Richie Sexson (off Minnesota's Mike Lincoln)
7-29: Manny Ramirez (off Baltimore's Pat Rapp)
7-30: David Segui (off Baltimore's John Parrish)
8-19: Manny Ramirez (off Seattle's Jamie Moyer)
8-20: Kenny Lofton (off Seattle's Aaron Sele)
8-27: Roberto Alomar (off Anaheim's Mark Petkovsek)
9-15: David Segui (off New York's Jason Grimsley)

PINCH HITTERS

(Minimum 5 at-bats)

Name	AB	Avg.	HR	RBI
Branyan, Russ	10	.100	0	1
Wilson, Enrique	9	.000	0	0
Selby, Bill	8	.500	0	1
Ramirez, Alex	6	.333	0	0
Sexson, Richie	5	.400	1	3
Cabrera, Jolbert	5	.000	0	0
Perry, Chan	5	.000	0	0

DEBUTS

5-19: Mark Watson, P.
5-21: Paul Rigdon, P.
5-24: Tim Drew, P.
6-12: Kane Davis, P.
6-14: Willie Martinez, P.
7-20: Cam Cairncross, P.
8-5: Chan Perry, RF.

GAMES BY POSITION

Catcher: Sandy Alomar Jr. 95, Einar Diaz 74.
First base: Jim Thome 107, David Segui 35, Richie Sexson 27, Travis Fryman 1, Chan Perry 1.
Second base: Roberto Alomar 155, Jolbert Cabrera 19, Enrique Wilson 7, Bill Selby 6, John McDonald 2.
Third base: Travis Fryman 154, Enrique Wilson 12, Bill Selby 4, Einar Diaz 1, Russ Branyan 1.
Shortstop: Omar Vizquel 156, Jolbert Cabrera 8, Enrique Wilson 7, John McDonald 7.
Outfield: Kenny Lofton 135, Manny Ramirez 93, Jolbert Cabrera 74, Richie Sexson 58, David Justice 47, Wil Cordero 38, Russ Branyan 33, Alex Ramirez 31, Ricky Ledee 17, Dave Roberts 17, Bill Selby 10, Jacob Cruz 9, David Segui 7, Chan Perry 7, Mark Whiten 5.
Designated hitter: Jim Thome 49, Manny Ramirez 25, Russ Branyan 23, David Justice 20, David Segui 15, Richie Sexson 10, Enrique Wilson 8, Bill Selby 6, Alex Ramirez 6, Chan Perry 4, Jacob Cruz 2, Jolbert Cabrera 2, Sandy Alomar Jr. 1, Travis Fryman 1, Kenny Lofton 1.

STREAKS

Wins: 6 (April 7-12, August 2-7)
Losses: 6 (April 30-May 5, June 11-17)
Consecutive games with at least one hit: 20, Manny Ramirez (August 15-September 5)
Wins by pitcher: 4, Dave Burba (May 25-June 10) Dave Burba (August 30-September 15)

ATTENDANCE

Home: 3,370,697
Road: 2,265,708
Highest (home): 43,333 (August 9 vs. Texas).
Highest (road): 55,097 (September 16 vs. New York).
Lowest (home): 40,530 (May 14 vs. Kansas City).
Lowest (road): 7,309 (May 8 vs. Minnesota).

DETROIT TIGERS

DAY BY DAY

Date	Opp.	Res.	Score	(inn.*)	Hits	Opp. hits	Winning pitcher	Losing pitcher	Save	Record	Pos.	GB
4-3	At Oak.	W	7-4		11	4	Nomo	Appier	Jones	1-0	T1st	...
4-4	At Oak.	L	1-3		2	5	Hudson	Nitkowski	Isringhausen	1-1	T2nd	0.5
4-5	At Oak.	L	2-8		6	10	Olivares	Moehler		1-2	T3rd	1.0
4-7	At Bal.	L	10-14		14	13	Worrell	Mlicki		1-3	5th	1.5
4-8	At Bal.	L	1-2	(10)	10	8	Reyes	Brocail		1-4	5th	2.5
4-9	At Bal.	L	6-11		10	16	Mercedes	Nitkowski		1-5	5th	3.0
4-11	Sea.	W	5-2		8	12	Moehler	Garcia	Jones	2-5	5th	3.5
4-12	Sea.	L	0-4		3	9	Sele	Mlicki		2-6	5th	4.5
4-13	Sea.	W	2-0		9	9	Brocail	Rhodes	Jones	3-6	4th	4.0
4-14	T.B.	W	10-5		11	14	Nitkowski	Rupe		4-6	4th	3.0
4-15	T.B.	L	0-7		6	11	Gooden	Weaver		4-7	4th	3.0
4-16	T.B.	L	6-7		8	16	Hernandez	Jones		4-8	4th	4.0
4-18	Bos.	L	0-7		6	10	Schourek	Mlicki	Lowe	4-9	5th	4.0
4-19	Bos.	L	0-10		6	15	Rose	Nomo		4-10	5th	4.5
4-21	At Chi.	L	2-7		8	8	Wells	Nitkowski		4-11	5th	5.5
4-22	At Chi.	L	6-14		6	14	Parque	Weaver		4-12	5th	6.5
4-23	At Chi.	L	4-9		9	9	Baldwin	Borkowski		4-13	5th	7.5
4-24	At Ana.	L	4-10		13	14	Hill	Mlicki		4-14	5th	8.5
4-25	At Ana.	W	4-2		10	8	Poole	Bottenfield	Jones	5-14	5th	7.5
4-26	At Ana.	L	1-6		5	11	Schoeneweis	Nitkowski		5-15	5th	8.5
4-28	Chi.	L	2-3		6	10	Baldwin	Weaver	Foulke	5-16	5th	10.0
4-29	Chi.	L	1-2		6	5	Eldred	Mlicki	Foulke	5-17	5th	11.0
4-30	Chi.	W	4-3	(12)	15	10	Anderson	Eyre		6-17	5th	10.0
5-1	At Bos.	L	6-10		11	11	Fassero	Nitkowski		6-18	5th	10.0
5-2	At Bos.	W	7-6	(12)	18	10	Blair	Wakefield	Jones	7-18	5th	9.0
5-3	At Bos.	L	2-4		6	7	Lowe	Weaver		7-19	5th	10.0
5-4	At Min.	W	8-6	(11)	10	12	Anderson	Wells	Jones	8-19	5th	9.5
5-5	At Min.	W	10-8		14	11	Patterson	Carrasco	Jones	9-19	5th	8.5
5-6	At Min.	L	1-6		10	8	Redman	Nitkowski		9-20	5th	8.5
5-7	At Min.	L	0-4		5	6	Mays	Johnson		9-21	5th	8.5
5-8	K.C.	L	1-4	(11)	3	8	Santiago	Brocail		9-22	5th	8.5
5-10	K.C.	L	0-6		4	9	Fussell	Nomo		9-23	5th	9.0
5-12	N.Y.	W	9-7		16	12	Nitkowski	Clemens	Jones	10-23	5th	8.0
5-13	N.Y.	W	6-3		13	8	Weaver	Pettitte	Jones	11-23	5th	8.0
5-14	N.Y.	W	2-1		8	5	Mlicki	Cone	Jones	12-23	5th	8.0
5-16	At Cle.	L	9-11		15	14	Nagy	Nomo	Karsay	12-24	5th	9.0
5-17	At Cle.	L	2-7		6	16	Colon	Nitkowski		12-25	5th	9.0
5-19	At Bos.	L	0-3		5	7	Fassero	Moehler	Lowe	12-26	5th	10.0
5-20	At Bos.	W	2-1		9	6	Mlicki	Wakefield	Jones	13-26	5th	10.0
5-21	At Bos.	W	7-5		11	12	Nomo	R. Martinez	Jones	14-26	5th	10.0
5-23	Cle.	W	10-4		16	11	Blair	Colon		15-26	5th	9.5
5-24	Cle.	W	10-9		12	16	Patterson	Watson	Jones	16-26	5th	8.5
5-25	Cle.	L	1-4		5	9	Burba	Moehler	Karsay	16-27	5th	8.5
5-26	Tor.	L	2-8		7	12	Frascatore	Brocail		16-28	5th	9.5
5-27	Tor.	W	4-3		7	7	Brocail	Quantrill		17-28	5th	9.5
5-28	Tor.	L	7-12		11	15	Andrews	Blair		17-29	5th	9.5
5-29	Tex.	L	2-3		11	7	Rogers	Weaver	Wetteland	17-30	5th	9.5
5-30	Tex.	W	7-4		13	9	Moehler	Loaiza	Jones	18-30	5th	9.5
5-31	Tex.	L	5-13		11	16	Oliver	Mlicki		18-31	5th	10.5
6-2	At Chi. (NL)	L	0-2		8	5	Downs	Nomo	Aguilera	18-32	5th	11.5
6-3	At Chi. (NL)	W	5-3		7	6	Weaver	Wood	Jones	19-32	5th	10.5
6-4	At Chi. (NL)	W	3-2	(12)	7	9	Anderson	Van Poppel	Jones	20-32	5th	10.5
6-5	At Pit.	L	1-5		7	9	Cordova	Mlicki		20-33	5th	11.5
6-6	At Pit.	W	2-1		5	11	Nitkowski	Anderson	Jones	21-33	5th	11.5
6-7	At Pit.	L	3-4		8	9	Ritchie	Nomo	Williams	21-34	5th	12.5
6-9	StL.	W	4-2		7	4	Weaver	Stephenson	Jones	22-34	5th	12.5
6-10	StL.	W	10-1		13	7	Moehler	Ankiel		23-34	5th	12.5
6-11	StL.	L	3-7		6	11	Hentgen	Mlicki		23-35	5th	12.5
6-12	Tor.	L	2-4		8	10	Castillo	Nomo	Koch	23-36	5th	13.5
6-13	Tor.	W	16-3		21	8	Blair	Andrews		24-36	5th	13.5
6-14	Tor.	L	1-8		9	9	Carpenter	Weaver		24-37	5th	14.5
6-16	Cle.	W	5-2		8	6	Moehler	Burba	Jones	25-37	5th	15.0
6-17	Cle.	W	8-6		10	6	Brocail	Karsay		26-37	5th	15.0
6-18	Cle.	L	4-9		8	13	Speier	Patterson		26-38	5th	16.0
6-20	At Tor.	W	18-6		18	8	Weaver	Carpenter		27-38	5th	15.5
6-21	At Tor.	L	0-6		4	12	Escobar	Moehler		27-39	5th	15.5
6-22	At Tor.	L	4-7		8	8	Wells	Nomo		27-40	5th	16.5
6-23	At Cle.	W	7-6		16	9	Blair	Navarro	Jones	28-40	5th	16.5
6-24†	At Cle.	L	1-8		4	10	Colon	Sparks		28-41		
6-24‡	At Cle.	W	14-8		16	12	Nitkowski	Mohler		29-41	5th	16.0
6-25	At Cle.	L	1-2		6	9	Karsay	Anderson		29-42	5th	17.0
6-26	At Cle.	W	13-2		16	11	Moehler	Burba		30-42	5th	16.5
6-27	N.Y.	W	7-6	(11)	17	15	Cruz	Rivera		31-42	5th	15.5
6-28	N.Y.	W	13-6		12	11	Blair	Ford	Sparks	32-42	4th	15.5
6-29	N.Y.	L	0-8		6	14	Pettitte	Mlicki		32-43	5th	15.5
6-30	At K.C.	W	3-1		5	7	Weaver	Reichert	Jones	33-43	5th	15.5
7-1	At K.C.	W	8-7		15	14	Brocail	Bottalico	Jones	34-43	5th	15.5
7-2	At K.C.	W	2-0		6	3	Nomo	Suzuki	Jones	35-43	4th	15.5
7-3	At T.B.	W	5-4	(10)	11	7	Patterson	Hernandez	Jones	36-43	4th	15.5

HIGHLIGHTS

High point: The Tigers capped a 61-44 run with a 7-5 win over the Angels September 5, pushing their record a season-high three games over .500 (70-67). That eased the pain of a horrible start and put the club on the fringes of the wild-card chase before it suffered a late collapse.

Low point: The team bottomed out at 9-23 with a 6-0 loss to Kansas City on May 10. It marked the sixth shutout against the Tigers in 32 games as the team struggled to adjust to the vast dimensions of new Comerica Park.

Turning point: A three-game sweep of the defending World Series-champion Yankees at Comerica May 12-14 seemed to provide a major psychological boost. Playing with a new confidence, the Tigers suddenly began winning low-scoring games, especially on their home turf.

Most valuable player: Left fielder Bobby Higginson bounced back from two subpar seasons and hit .300 with 30 homers, 102 RBIs, 104 runs and 15 steals. He also led both leagues with 19 assists.

Most valuable pitcher: Aided by the addition of a slider and changeup, All-Star closer Todd Jones set a franchise record with 42 saves. He allowed only two earned runs in 31 appearances from May 2 through July 29.

Most improved player: Righthander Jeff Weaver began looking like a future ace as he rebounded from the terrible second half that spoiled his rookie 1999 season. Weaver won 11 times and would have had four or five more wins with decent support.

Most pleasant surprise: Steve Sparks wasn't doing much at Class AAA Toledo when he was recalled to patch up an injury-plagued rotation. The 35-year-old knuckleballer went 5-0 in August and won six straight starts overall, during which he allowed 10 earned runs.

Key injuries: Right fielder Juan Gonzalez missed 47 games because of hamstring, foot and back problems. ... First baseman Tony Clark had three stints on the disabled list and played only 60 games. ... Second baseman Damion Easley missed 31 of the team's first 49 games with various injuries. ... Third baseman Dean Palmer played the entire season with a painful throwing shoulder. ... Setup man Doug Brocail missed most of September with a sore elbow. ... Righthander Dave Mlicki missed two months with a sinus problem that required surgery. ... Righthander Seth Greisinger, a starting rotation candidate, missed virtually the whole season with arm problems. ... Backup catcher Robert Fick missed eight weeks with a separated shoulder.

Notable: The team was shut out a major league-leading 15 times. ... The pitching staff walked 496 batters, the lowest total in the league and a big accomplishment in the wake of pitching failures in recent years. ... After an April 22 brawl at Comiskey Park, regulars Dean Palmer, Bobby Higginson and Juan Encarnacion were among those who received staggered suspensions, adding another headache to the horrid start.

—REID CREAGER

MISCELLANEOUS

RECORDS

2000 regular-season record: 79-83 (3rd in A.L. Central); 43-38 at home; 36-45 on road; 24-31 vs. East; 32-36 vs. Central; 23-16 vs. West; 24-21 vs. left-handed starters; 55-62 vs. righthanded starters; 72-71 on grass; 7-12 on turf; 21-28 in daytime; 58-55 at night; 20-18 in one-run games; 8-4 in extra-inning games; 0-0-3 in doubleheaders.

Team record past five years: 345-464 (.426, ranks 13th in league in that span).

TEAM LEADERS

Batting average: Deivi Cruz (.302).
At-bats: Bobby Higginson (597).
Runs: Bobby Higginson (104).
Hits: Bobby Higginson (179).
Total Bases: Bobby Higginson (321).
Doubles: Deivi Cruz (46).
Triples: Juan Encarnacion (6).
Home runs: Bobby Higginson (30).
Runs batted in: Bobby Higginson, Dean Palmer (102).
Stolen bases: Juan Encarnacion (16).
Slugging percentage: Bobby Higginson (.538).
On-base percentage: Bobby Higginson (.377).
Wins: Brian Moehler (12).
Earned-run average: Jeff Weaver (4.32).
Complete games: Brian Moehler, Jeff Weaver (2).
Shutouts: Steve W. Sparks (1).
Saves: Todd Jones (42).
Innings pitched: Jeff Weaver (200.0).
Strikeouts: Hideo Nomo (181).

Date	Opp.	Res.	Score	(inn.*)	Hits	Opp. hits	Winning pitcher	Losing pitcher	Save	Record	Pos.	GB
7-4	At T.B.	W	11-0		12	9	Mlicki	Lidle		37-43	4th	14.5
7-5	At T.B.	L	1-4		8	9	Rekar	Weaver	Hernandez	37-44	4th	15.5
7-7	At Mil.	L	3-4		6	9	Haynes	Moehler	Wickman	37-45	4th	16.5
7-8	At Mil.	W	4-2	(15)	12	15	Cruz	de los Santos		38-45	4th	15.5
7-9	At Mil.	L	3-10		10	13	Bere	Blair		38-46	4th	15.5
7-13	Hou.	W	8-2		12	11	Moehler	Reynolds		39-46	3rd	14.5
7-14	Hou.	L	4-9		10	13	Holt	Nomo		39-47	3rd	14.5
7-15	Hou.	W	11-6		15	11	Patterson	Henry		40-47	3rd	14.5
7-16	Cin.	W	6-2		10	10	Weaver	Parris		41-47	3rd	14.5
7-17	Cin.	W	3-1		8	10	Mlicki	Luebbers	Jones	42-47	3rd	14.5
7-18	Cin.	L	4-5		10	15	Dessens	Moehler	Graves	42-48	3rd	15.5
7-19	At N.Y.	L	1-9		6	11	Clemens	Nomo		42-49	3rd	16.5
7-20	At N.Y.	W	5-3		8	8	Blair	Pettitte	Jones	43-49	3rd	15.5
7-21	K.C.	L	0-4		6	9	Reichert	Weaver		43-50	4th	16.5
7-22†	K.C.	L	5-8		9	11	Witasick	Mlicki	Bottalico	43-51		
7-22‡	K.C.	W	10-6		14	8	Cruz	Bochtler		44-51	4th	16.0
7-23	K.C.	W	12-9		14	13	Brocail	Byrdak	Jones	45-51	3rd	15.0
7-24	T.B.	L	2-4		5	10	Lopez	Nomo	Hernandez	45-52	3rd	16.0
7-25	T.B.	W	6-4		10	9	Blair	Trachsel	Jones	46-52	3rd	15.0
7-26	T.B.	L	2-6		5	10	Yan	Weaver	Hernandez	46-53	4th	15.0
7-27	At Tex.	L	3-7		4	11	Glynn	Sparks	Zimmerman	46-54	4th	16.0
7-28	At Tex.	L	5-11		8	14	Helling	Moehler		46-55	4th	16.0
7-29	At Tex.	W	10-2		15	7	Nomo	Rogers		47-55	3rd	15.0
7-30	At Tex.	W	8-7		11	12	Blair	Oliver	Jones	48-55	3rd	15.0
7-31	At Ana.	L	4-5		10	7	Petkovsek	Jones		48-56	3rd	15.5
8-1	At Ana.	W	6-3		10	8	Cruz	Cooper	Jones	49-56	3rd	15.5
8-2	At Ana.	W	5-3		9	9	Moehler	Hill	Jones	50-56	3rd	14.5
8-4	Min.	L	1-3		4	10	Milton	Nitkowski	Wells	50-57	3rd	14.5
8-5	Min.	W	4-3		6	9	Sparks	Mays	Jones	51-57	3rd	14.5
8-6	Min.	L	3-7		10	10	Romero	Weaver		51-58	3rd	15.5
8-7	Bal.	L	3-4		11	7	Groom	Brocail	Kohlmeier	51-59	3rd	16.0
8-8	Bal.	W	4-1		7	8	Moehler	Rapp		52-59	3rd	14.5
8-9	Bal.	L	2-5		7	11	Mercedes	Blair	Kohlmeier	52-60	3rd	15.5
8-10	Bal.	W	14-3		14	6	Sparks	Ponson		53-60	3rd	14.5
8-11	At Oak.	W	11-4		15	9	Weaver	Heredia		54-60	3rd	14.5
8-12	At Oak.	L	5-9		9	11	Hudson	Bernero		54-61	3rd	15.5
8-13	At Oak.	W	5-3		11	10	Moehler	Zito	Jones	55-61	3rd	14.5
8-14	At Sea.	W	15-4		18	12	Blair	Moyer		56-61	3rd	13.5
8-15	At Sea.	W	9-0		17	5	Sparks	Sele		57-61	3rd	13.5
8-16	At Sea.	W	12-8		16	10	Weaver	Tomko		58-61	3rd	13.5
8-18	Oak.	W	10-1		17	3	Nomo	Hudson		59-61	3rd	13.0
8-19	Oak.	W	4-3		9	10	Moehler	Zito	Jones	60-61	3rd	13.0
8-20	Oak.	L	4-5	(11)	10	14	Isringhausen	Cruz	Tam	60-62	3rd	13.0
8-21	Oak.	W	3-1		8	5	Sparks	Mulder	Jones	61-62	3rd	12.0
8-22	Sea.	L	4-8		6	10	Paniagua	Weaver	Sasaki	61-63	3rd	12.5
8-23	Sea.	W	6-5		11	11	Cruz	Rhodes	Jones	62-63	3rd	12.5
8-24	Sea.	W	10-3		12	8	Moehler	Moyer		63-63	3rd	11.5
8-25	At Min.	L	3-8		7	10	Radke	Blair	Wells	63-64	3rd	12.5
8-26	At Min.	W	8-2		11	5	Sparks	Milton		64-64	3rd	11.5
8-27	At Min.	L	6-7	(10)	9	11	Carrasco	Jones		64-65	3rd	12.5
8-29	At Bal.	W	12-2		16	7	Weaver	Parrish		65-65	3rd	12.0
8-30	At Bal.	L	1-5		2	11	Mercedes	Nomo		65-66	3rd	13.0
8-31	At Bal.	W	6-1		11	5	Patterson	Trombley		66-66	3rd	12.5
9-1	Tex.	W	7-5		10	11	Sparks	Helling	Jones	67-66	3rd	12.5
9-2	Tex.	W	5-3		10	10	Blair	Rogers	Anderson	68-66	3rd	12.5
9-3	Tex.	L	1-4		7	11	Glynn	Weaver	Wetteland	68-67	3rd	13.5
9-4	Ana.	W	5-0		11	5	Nomo	Karl		69-67	3rd	12.5
9-5	Ana.	W	7-5		10	10	Moehler	Wise	Jones	70-67	3rd	11.5
9-6	Ana.	L	0-1		2	9	Schoeneweis	Sparks	Percival	70-68	3rd	12.5
9-7	Ana.	L	4-6		9	11	Belcher	Mlicki	Hasegawa	70-69	3rd	13.5
9-8	At Tor.	L	0-3		5	7	Loaiza	Weaver		70-70	3rd	14.5
9-9	At Tor.	L	5-6		10	8	Koch	Nitkowski		70-71	3rd	14.5
9-10	At Tor.	L	2-6		8	7	Carpenter	Sparks	Escobar	70-72	3rd	15.0
9-11	At Chi.	L	3-10		7	12	Sirotka	Moehler	Howry	70-73	3rd	16.0
9-12	At Chi.	W	10-3		11	4	Mlicki	Wells		71-73	3rd	15.0
9-13	At Chi.	L	0-1		5	4	Parque	Weaver	Foulke	71-74	3rd	16.0
9-15	Bos.	L	6-7		9	12	Beck	Cruz	Lowe	71-75	3rd	16.0
9-16†	Bos.	L	5-8		11	13	Pichardo	Anderson	Lowe	71-76		
9-16‡	Bos.	W	12-2		13	8	Nomo	Ontiveros		72-76	3rd	16.5
9-17	Bos.	W	5-4		9	8	Mlicki	R. Martinez	Jones	73-76	3rd	15.5
9-18	Chi.	W	5-2		12	3	Weaver	Barcelo	Jones	74-76	3rd	14.5
9-19	Chi.	L	2-6		7	13	Lowe	Sparks		74-77	3rd	15.5
9-20	Chi.	L	6-13		10	15	Garland	Moehler		74-78	3rd	16.5
9-22	At N.Y.	W	9-6		10	9	Nomo	Neagle	Jones	75-78	3rd	17.0
9-23	At N.Y.	L	8-13		8	18	Nelson	Blair	Rivera	75-79	3rd	18.0
9-24	At N.Y.	L	3-6		7	10	Pettitte	Weaver	Rivera	75-80	3rd	18.0
9-25	At N.Y.	W	15-4		18	11	Sparks	Gooden		76-80	3rd	17.0
9-26	At K.C.	L	6-7		9	10	Bottalico	Blair		76-81	3rd	17.0
9-27	At K.C.	L	0-3		6	9	Suppan	Nomo		76-82	3rd	17.0
9-28	At K.C.	L	5-8		12	12	Santiago	Jones	Bottalico	76-83	T3rd	17.0
9-29	Min.	W	1-0		7	7	Weaver	Mays	Jones	77-83	3rd	17.0
9-30	Min.	W	6-5	(11)	13	13	Jones	Hawkins		78-83	3rd	17.0
10-1	Min.	W	12-11		19	15	Jones	Guardado		79-83	3rd	16.0

Monthly records: April (6-17), May (12-14), June (15-12), July (15-13), August (18-10), September (12-17), October (1-0).
*Innings, if other than nine. † First game of a doubleheader. ‡ Second game of a doubleheader.

MEMORABLE GAMES

April 11 at Detroit

Despite a game-time temperature of 36 degrees, the mood was festive as the Comerica Park era opened with a 5-2 win over Seattle. As in the Tiger Stadium finale at the end of the 1999 season, starter Brian Moehler got the win and Todd Jones finished the game. The stadium opener drew a crowd of 39,168, many of whom departed early because of the cold.

Seattle	AB	R	H	BI	Detroit	AB	R	H	BI
McLemore, lf-2b	5	0	0	0	Polonia, dh	4	2	1	0
Cameron, cf	4	0	0	0	Jefferies, 2b	4	1	2	2
Rodriguez, ss	4	0	2	0	Halter, 2b	1	0	0	0
Olerud, 1b	5	1	3	0	Higginson, lf	4	0	1	2
Martinez, dh	5	0	0	0	Clark, 1b	4	0	1	0
Buhner, rf	5	0	3	0	Ausmus, c	3	0	0	0
Bell, 2b	3	0	0	0	Palmer, 3b	2	0	0	0
Mabry, ph-lf	1	0	0	0	Garcia, rf	4	0	0	0
Wilson, c	4	1	3	0	Encarnacion, cf	3	2	2	0
Guillen, 3b	3	0	1	1	Cruz, ss	1	0	1	0
Totals	**39**	**2**	**12**	**1**	**Totals**	**30**	**5**	**8**	**4**

Seattle ....0 0 0 1 1 0 0 0 0—2 12 2
Detroit ....2 2 0 0 0 1 0 0 x—5 8 3

E—Wilson (1), Cameron (1), Palmer (3), Cruz (1), Encarnacion (3). DP—Detroit 1. LOB—Seattle 13, Detroit 9. 2B—Olerud (1), Wilson (1), Guillen (1), Encarnacion (1), Cruz (3). 3B—Polonia (2), Higginson (1). SH—Cruz 3.

Seattle	IP	H	R	ER	BB	SO
Garcia (L 1-1)	6	6	5	5	5	4
Paniagua	2	2	0	0	0	2

Detroit	IP	H	R	ER	BB	SO
Moehler (W 1-1)	6	10	2	1	1	3
Patterson	0.2	1	0	0	1	0
Brocail	1.1	0	0	0	0	1
Jones (S 2)	1	1	0	0	1	2

BK—Garcia. U—HP, Reed. 1B, Wegner. 2B, Reynolds. 3B, Williams. T—3:12. A—39,168.

August 23 at Detroit

After looking lethargic for much of the game against Paul Abbott, the team overcame a 4-1 deficit with five runs in the seventh and hung on for a 6-5 win over the Mariners. The team's 10th win in 13 games also featured a first-inning attack by flying ants, which swarmed the Comerica Park stands and field and sent fans scurrying for cover

Seattle	AB	R	H	BI	Detroit	AB	R	H	BI
Henderson, lf	5	1	3	0	McMillon, dh	3	1	1	0
Olerud, 1b	4	0	0	1	Magee, ph-dh	1	1	1	0
Rodriguez, ss	3	0	2	1	Encarnacion, cf	4	1	3	3
Martinez, dh	4	1	1	1	Higginson, lf	4	1	1	1
Martin, rf	4	0	0	0	Gonzalez, rf	4	0	2	0
Cameron, cf	4	1	1	1	Palmer, 1b	2	0	0	1
Guillen, 3b	4	1	1	0	Easley, 2b	4	0	0	0
Wilson, c	2	1	2	1	D.Cruz, ss	4	1	1	0
Javier, ph	1	0	0	0	Ausmus, c	4	0	1	0
McLemore, 2b	4	0	1	0	Macias, 3b	4	1	1	1
Totals	**35**	**5**	**11**	**5**	**Totals**	**34**	**6**	**11**	**6**

Seattle....................................0 1 2 0 0 0 1 1 0--5 11 1 5
Detroit....................................0 0 0 0 0 1 5 0 x--6 11 0 6

E—Wilson (5). LOB—Seattle 5, Detroit 6. 2B—Henderson (9), Rodriguez (27), Guillen (8), Wilson 2 (10), McMillon (3), D. Cruz (38). 3B—Encarnacion (5). HR—Martinez (30), Cameron (16). SB—Henderson (29), Encarnacion (10). CS—Rodriguez (4), Wilson (2). S—Palmer.

Seattle	IP	H	R	ER	BB	SO
Abbott	6.1	6	2	2	1	4
Rhodes (L 3-7)	0	4	4	4	0	0
Mesa	1.2	1	0	0	0	1

Detroit	IP	H	R	ER	BB	SO
Nomo	6.1	9	4	4	2	6
Nitkowski	0.1	0	0	0	0	0
N. Cruz (W 5-1)	1.1	1	1	1	0	1
Jones (S 36)	1	1	0	0	0	0

Rhodes pitched to 4 batters in 7th.

U—HP, Barksdale, 1B, Runge. 2B, Lamplugh. 3B, Roe. T—3:07. A—32,356.

INDIVIDUAL STATISTICS

BATTING

																							vs RHP				vs LHP			
Name	**G**	**TPA**	**AB**	**R**	**H**	**TB**	**2B**	**3B**	**HR**	**RBI**	**Avg.**	**Obp.**	**Slg.**	**SH**	**SF**	**HP**	**BB**	**IBB**	**SO**	**SB**	**CS**	**GDP**	**AB**	**Avg.**	**HR**	**RBI**	**AB**	**Avg.**	**HR**	**RBI**
Higginson, Bobby	154	679	597	104	179	321	44	4	30	102	.300	.377	.538	2	3	2	74	6	99	15	3	5	415	.316	26	83	182	.264	4	19
Cruz, Deivi	156	615	583	68	176	262	46	5	10	82	.302	.318	.449	8	7	4	13	2	43	1	4	25	444	.288	5	55	139	.345	5	27
Encarnacion, Juan	141	590	547	75	158	237	25	6	14	72	.289	.330	.433	3	4	7	29	1	90	16	4	15	407	.280	7	45	140	.314	7	27
Palmer, Dean	145	604	524	73	134	247	22	2	29	102	.256	.338	.471	0	10	4	66	2	146	4	2	9	401	.264	23	82	123	.228	6	20
Ausmus, Brad	150	604	523	75	139	191	25	3	7	51	.266	.357	.365	4	2	6	69	0	79	11	5	19	386	.246	4	36	137	.321	3	15
Easley, Damion	126	535	464	76	120	193	27	2	14	58	.259	.350	.416	4	1	11	55	1	79	13	4	11	339	.251	11	45	125	.280	3	13
Gonzalez, Juan	115	496	461	69	133	233	30	2	22	67	.289	.337	.505	0	1	2	32	3	84	1	2	13	347	.265	16	50	114	.360	6	17
Polonia, Luis	80	298	267	37	73	111	10	5	6	25	.273	.325	.416	3	5	1	22	1	25	8	5	2	236	.280	5	19	31	.226	1	6
Halter, Shane	105	265	238	26	62	87	12	2	3	27	.261	.302	.366	10	2	1	14	0	49	5	2	5	147	.245	0	13	91	.286	3	14
Becker, Rich	92	298	238	48	58	91	12	0	7	34	.244	.383	.382	0	4	0	56	0	70	1	2	0	210	.262	7	32	28	.107	0	2
Clark, Tony	60	232	208	32	57	110	14	0	13	37	.274	.349	.529	0	0	0	24	2	51	0	0	10	169	.266	10	28	39	.308	3	9
Magee, Wendell	91	198	186	31	51	80	4	2	7	31	.274	.310	.430	0	1	0	10	0	28	1	0	7	54	.278	5	14	132	.273	2	17
Macias, Jose	73	196	173	25	44	63	3	5	2	24	.254	.328	.364	4	0	1	18	0	24	2	0	3	133	.226	1	14	40	.350	1	10
Fick, Robert	66	188	163	18	41	61	7	2	3	22	.252	.340	.374	0	2	1	22	2	39	2	1	4	132	.265	3	19	31	.194	0	3
Jefferies, Gregg	41	160	142	18	39	53	8	0	2	14	.275	.344	.373	0	2	0	16	1	10	0	2	7	102	.294	2	12	40	.225	0	2
McMillon, Billy	46	150	123	20	37	58	7	1	4	24	.301	.388	.472	2	4	1	19	0	19	1	0	2	108	.306	4	20	15	.267	0	4
Morris, Hal	40	126	106	15	33	43	7	0	1	8	.311	.416	.406	1	0	0	19	1	16	0	0	3	85	.329	1	7	21	.238	0	1
Cardona, Javier	26	42	40	1	7	11	1	0	1	2	.175	.190	.275	0	1	1	0	0	9	0	0	1	34	.206	1	2	6	.000	0	0
Garcia, Karim	8	17	17	1	3	3	0	0	0	0	.176	.176	.176	0	0	0	0	0	4	0	0	1	17	.176	0	0	0	.000	0	0
Allen, Dusty	18	18	16	5	7	15	2	0	2	2	.438	.500	.938	0	0	0	2	0	7	0	0	0	7	.429	0	0	9	.444	2	2
Nomo, Hideo	32	6	6	0	0	0	0	0	0	0	.000	.000	.000	0	0	0	0	0	2	0	0	0	4	.000	0	0	2	.000	0	0
Munson, Eric	3	5	5	0	0	0	0	0	0	1	.000	.000	.000	0	0	0	0	0	1	0	0	0	5	.000	0	1	0	.000	0	0
Moehler, Brian	29	4	4	0	0	0	0	0	0	0	.000	.000	.000	0	0	0	0	0	1	0	0	0	4	.000	0	0	0	.000	0	0
Blair, Willie	47	3	3	0	1	1	0	0	0	0	.333	.333	.333	0	0	0	0	0	2	0	0	0	1	.000	0	0	2	.500	0	0
Lindsey, Rod	11	5	3	6	1	2	1	0	0	0	.333	.500	.667	1	0	1	0	0	1	2	1	0	2	.500	0	0	1	.000	0	0
Weaver, Jeff	31	3	3	0	0	0	0	0	0	0	.000	.000	.000	0	0	0	0	0	2	0	0	0	3	.000	0	0	0	.000	0	0
Mlicki, Dave	24	2	2	0	0	0	0	0	0	0	.000	.000	.000	0	0	0	0	0	1	0	0	0	2	.000	0	0	0	.000	0	0
Cruz, Nelson	27	1	1	0	0	0	0	0	0	0	.000	.000	.000	0	0	0	0	0	0	0	0	0	1	.000	0	0	0	.000	0	0
Alvarez, Gabe	1	3	1	0	0	0	0	0	0	0	.000	.667	.000	0	0	0	2	0	1	0	1	0	1	.000	0	0	0	.000	0	0
Brocail, Doug	49	0	0	0	0	0	0	0	0	0	.000	.000	.000	0	0	0	0	0	0	0	0	0	0	.000	0	0	0	.000	0	0
Jones, Todd	67	0	0	0	0	0	0	0	0	0	.000	.000	.000	0	0	0	0	0	0	0	0	0	0	.000	0	0	0	.000	0	0
Nitkowski, C.J.	67	0	0	0	0	0	0	0	0	0	.000	.000	.000	0	0	0	0	0	0	0	0	0	0	.000	0	0	0	.000	0	0
Patterson, Danny	58	0	0	0	0	0	0	0	0	0	.000	.000	.000	0	0	0	0	0	0	0	0	0	0	.000	0	0	0	.000	0	0
McDill, Allen	13	0	0	0	0	0	0	0	0	0	.000	.000	.000	0	0	0	0	0	0	0	0	0	0	.000	0	0	0	.000	0	0
Anderson, Matt	69	0	0	0	0	0	0	0	0	0	.000	.000	.000	0	0	0	0	0	0	0	0	0	0	.000	0	0	0	.000	0	0
Poole, Jim	18	0	0	0	0	0	0	0	0	0	.000	.000	.000	0	0	0	0	0	0	0	0	0	0	.000	0	0	0	.000	0	0
Sparks, Steve W.	20	0	0	0	0	0	0	0	0	0	.000	.000	.000	0	0	0	0	0	0	0	0	0	0	.000	0	0	0	.000	0	0
Runyan, Sean	3	0	0	0	0	0	0	0	0	0	.000	.000	.000	0	0	0	0	0	0	0	0	0	0	.000	0	0	0	.000	0	0
Kida, Masao	2	0	0	0	0	0	0	0	0	0	.000	.000	.000	0	0	0	0	0	0	0	0	0	0	.000	0	0	0	.000	0	0
Borkowski, Dave	2	0	0	0	0	0	0	0	0	0	.000	.000	.000	0	0	0	0	0	0	0	0	0	0	.000	0	0	0	.000	0	0
Hiljus, Erik	3	0	0	0	0	0	0	0	0	0	.000	.000	.000	0	0	0	0	0	0	0	0	0	0	.000	0	0	0	.000	0	0
Johnson, Mark	9	0	0	0	0	0	0	0	0	0	.000	.000	.000	0	0	0	0	0	0	0	0	0	0	.000	0	0	0	.000	0	0
Villafuerte, Brandon	3	0	0	0	0	0	0	0	0	0	.000	.000	.000	0	0	0	0	0	0	0	0	0	0	.000	0	0	0	.000	0	0
Bernero, Adam	12	0	0	0	0	0	0	0	0	0	.000	.000	.000	0	0	0	0	0	0	0	0	0	0	.000	0	0	0	.000	0	0
Tolar, Kevin	5	0	0	0	0	0	0	0	0	0	.000	.000	.000	0	0	0	0	0	0	0	0	0	0	.000	0	0	0	.000	0	0

Players with more than one A.L. team

																							vs RHP				vs LHP			
Name	**G**	**TPA**	**AB**	**R**	**H**	**TB**	**2B**	**3B**	**HR**	**RBI**	**Avg.**	**Obp.**	**Slg.**	**SH**	**SF**	**HP**	**BB**	**IBB**	**SO**	**SB**	**CS**	**GDP**	**AB**	**Avg.**	**HR**	**RBI**	**AB**	**Avg.**	**HR**	**RBI**
Becker, Oak.	23	59	47	11	11	16	2	0	1	5	.234	.390	.340	0	0	1	11	0	17	1	0	1	210	.262	7	32	28	.107	0	2
Becker, Oak.-Det.	115	357	285	59	69	107	14	0	8	39	.242	.384	.375	0	4	1	67	0	87	2	2	1	253	.257	8	36	32	.125	0	3
Garcia, Bal.	8	16	16	0	0	0	0	0	0	0	.000	.000	.000	0	0	0	0	0	6	0	0	0	17	.176	0	0	0	.000	0	0
Garcia, Det.-Bal.	16	33	33	1	3	3	0	0	0	0	.091	.091	.091	0	0	0	0	0	10	0	0	1	33	.091	0	0	0	.000	0	0
Polonia, N.Y.	37	85	77	11	22	29	4	0	1	5	.286	.341	.377	0	1	0	7	0	7	4	2	2	236	.280	5	19	31	.226	1	6
Polonia, Det.-N.Y.	117	383	344	48	95	140	14	5	7	30	.276	.329	.407	3	6	1	29	1	32	12	7	4	311	.283	6	24	33	.212	1	6

PITCHING

																						vs. RH				vs. LH			
Name	**W**	**L**	**Pct.**	**ERA**	**IP**	**H**	**R**	**ER**	**HR**	**SH**	**SF**	**HB**	**BB**	**IBB**	**SO**	**G**	**GS**	**CG**	**ShO**	**GF**	**Sv**	**AB**	**Avg.**	**HR**	**RBI**	**AB**	**Avg.**	**HR**	**RBI**
Weaver, Jeff	11	15	.423	4.32	200.0	205	102	96	26	3	9	15	52	2	136	31	30	2	0	0	0	367	.264	7	34	402	.269	19	59
Nomo, Hideo	8	12	.400	4.74	190.0	191	102	100	31	6	3	3	89	1	181	32	31	1	0	0	0	370	.284	15	44	357	.241	16	43
Moehler, Brian	12	9	.571	4.50	178.0	222	99	89	20	3	4	2	40	0	103	29	29	2	0	0	0	376	.324	7	46	351	.285	13	40
Blair, Willie	10	6	.625	4.88	156.2	185	89	85	20	1	7	2	35	0	74	47	17	0	0	8	0	337	.329	9	53	288	.257	11	34
Mlicki, Dave	6	11	.353	5.58	119.1	143	79	74	17	3	6	3	44	1	57	24	21	0	0	1	0	256	.301	8	29	235	.281	9	36
Nitkowski, C.J.	4	9	.308	5.25	109.2	124	79	64	13	3	8	4	49	3	81	67	11	0	0	7	0	286	.322	8	41	147	.218	5	34
Sparks, Steve W.	7	5	.583	4.07	104.0	108	55	47	7	1	1	4	29	0	53	20	15	1	1	5	1	195	.262	2	18	216	.264	5	27
Anderson, Matt	3	2	.600	4.72	74.1	61	44	39	8	2	6	3	45	4	71	69	0	0	0	27	1	158	.247	4	24	110	.200	4	22
Jones, Todd	2	4	.333	3.52	64.0	67	28	25	6	1	1	1	25	1	67	67	0	0	0	60	42	117	.256	3	17	126	.294	3	17
Patterson, Danny	5	1	.833	3.97	56.2	69	26	25	4	3	2	2	14	2	29	58	0	0	0	12	0	127	.323	2	16	96	.292	2	10
Brocail, Doug	5	4	.556	4.09	50.2	57	25	23	5	3	3	1	14	2	41	49	0	0	0	10	0	90	.333	0	10	110	.245	5	17
Cruz, Nelson	5	2	.714	3.07	41.0	39	14	14	4	0	2	3	13	3	34	27	0	0	0	12	0	82	.268	2	15	72	.236	2	9
Bernero, Adam	0	1	.000	4.19	34.1	33	18	16	3	2	3	1	13	1	20	12	4	0	0	4	0	60	.300	0	5	62	.242	3	7
Johnson, Mark	0	1	.000	7.50	24.0	25	23	20	3	1	4	1	16	1	11	9	3	0	0	3	0	41	.220	2	9	53	.302	1	11
McDill, Allen	0	0	.000	7.20	10.0	13	9	8	2	0	0	1	1	0	7	13	0	0	0	1	0	21	.333	0	4	20	.300	2	6
Poole, Jim	1	0	1.000	7.27	8.2	13	8	7	4	1	2	1	1	0	5	18	0	0	0	1	0	16	.375	1	6	20	.350	3	14
Borkowski, Dave	0	1	.000	21.94	5.1	11	13	13	2	0	1	0	7	1	1	2	1	0	0	0	0	16	.250	1	6	10	.700	1	4
Villafuerte, Brandon	0	0	.000	10.38	4.1	4	5	5	0	0	0	0	4	0	1	3	0	0	0	2	0	9	.222	0	3	7	.286	0	2
Hiljus, Erik	0	0	.000	7.36	3.2	5	3	3	1	0	0	0	1	0	2	3	0	0	0	2	0	7	.571	0	3	8	.125	1	1
Tolar, Kevin	0	0	.000	3.00	3.0	1	1	1	0	0	0	0	1	0	3	5	0	0	0	1	0	8	.125	0	0	3	.000	0	1
Runyan, Sean	0	0	.000	6.00	3.0	2	2	2	0	0	1	0	2	0	1	3	0	0	0	0	0	3	.000	0	0	6	.333	0	3
Kida, Masao	0	0	.000	10.13	2.2	5	3	3	1	0	0	0	0	0	0	2	0	0	0	0	0	10	.400	1	3	3	.333	0	0
Halter, Shane	0	0	.000	-	0.0	0	0	0	0	0	0	0	1	0	0	1	0	0	0	0	0	0	.000	0	0	0	.000	0	0

DESIGNATED HITTERS

Name	AB	Avg.	HR	RBI	Name	AB	Avg.	HR	RBI	Name	AB	Avg.	HR	RBI
Gonzalez, Juan	200	.305	5	26	Higginson, Bobby	34	.412	2	10	Macias, Jose	1	.000	0	0
Polonia, Luis	181	.287	3	19	Magee, Wendell	7	.286	0	0	Alvarez, Gabe	1	.000	0	0
McMillon, Billy	77	.273	3	17	Becker, Rich	6	.500	0	0	Garcia, Karim	0	-	0	0
Palmer, Dean	46	.239	2	14	Clark, Tony	4	.000	0	0					
Fick, Robert	38	.263	1	5	Jefferies, Gregg	3	.333	0	0					

INDIVIDUAL STATISTICS

FIELDING

FIRST BASEMEN

Player	Pct.	G	PO	A	E	TC	DP
Clark, Tony	.993	58	488	45	4	537	49
Morris, Hal	.990	38	263	23	3	289	27
Fick, Robert	.984	34	222	18	4	244	19
Halter, Shane	.995	29	172	14	1	187	21
Jefferies, Gregg	.994	20	163	15	1	179	18
Palmer, Dean	.984	20	122	5	2	129	13
Allen, Dusty	1.000	17	45	1	0	46	5
Munson, Eric	.941	3	16	0	1	17	2
Ausmus, Brad	1.000	1	2	0	0	2	1

SECOND BASEMEN

Player	Pct.	G	PO	A	E	TC	DP
Easley, Damion	.990	125	198	411	6	615	98
Macias, Jose	.976	39	39	85	3	127	19
Jefferies, Gregg	1.000	14	23	33	0	56	6
Halter, Shane	1.000	10	12	14	0	26	2
Ausmus, Brad	-	1	0	0	0	0	0

THIRD BASEMEN

Player	Pct.	G	PO	A	E	TC	DP
Palmer, Dean	.914	115	66	180	23	269	14
Halter, Shane	.937	55	26	63	6	95	11
Macias, Jose	.976	26	11	29	1	41	3
Jefferies, Gregg	1.000	6	2	4	0	6	1
Allen, Dusty	1.000	1	1	0	0	1	0
Ausmus, Brad	-	1	0	0	0	0	0

SHORTSTOPS

Player	Pct.	G	PO	A	E	TC	DP
Cruz, Deivi	.982	156	222	482	13	717	116
Halter, Shane	.981	17	19	33	1	53	8
Macias, Jose	1.000	1	1	2	0	3	1

OUTFIELDERS

Player	Pct.	G	PO	A	E	TC	DP
Higginson, Bobby	.979	145	307	19	7	333	3
Encarnacion, Juan	.987	141	363	3	5	371	2
Becker, Rich	.956	80	127	3	6	136	3
Magee, Wendell	1.000	76	86	3	0	89	0
Gonzalez, Juan	.992	66	118	2	1	121	1
Polonia, Luis	1.000	27	44	2	0	46	0
McMillon, Billy	.964	15	27	0	1	28	0
Halter, Shane	1.000	8	15	1	0	16	0
Garcia, Karim	1.000	7	8	0	0	8	0
Lindsey, Rod	1.000	7	2	0	0	2	0
Macias, Jose	1.000	3	2	0	0	2	0
Allen, Dusty	1.000	1	1	0	0	1	0
Morris, Hal	1.000	1	1	0	0	1	0
Jefferies, Gregg	-	1	0	0	0	0	0

CATCHERS

Player	Pct.	G	PO	A	E	TC	DP	PB
Ausmus, Brad	.992	150	898	68	8	974	9	3
Cardona, Javier	.973	26	66	7	2	75	0	2
Fick, Robert	.981	16	50	3	1	54	1	2
Halter, Shane	1.000	2	1	0	0	1	0	0

PITCHERS

Player	Pct.	G	PO	A	E	TC	DP
Anderson, Matt	1.000	69	4	6	0	10	0
Nitkowski, C.J.	.966	67	7	21	1	29	2
Jones, Todd	1.000	67	3	2	0	5	0
Patterson, Danny	1.000	58	4	8	0	12	0
Brocail, Doug	.933	49	7	7	1	15	0
Blair, Willie	1.000	47	4	13	0	17	1
Nomo, Hideo	.966	32	12	16	1	29	2
Weaver, Jeff	.978	31	17	28	1	46	0
Moehler, Brian	1.000	29	13	30	0	43	5
Cruz, Nelson	1.000	26	1	6	0	7	1
Mlicki, Dave	1.000	24	12	14	0	26	3
Sparks, Steve W.	.966	20	11	17	1	29	2
Poole, Jim	1.000	18	0	3	0	3	0
McDill, Allen	1.000	13	0	1	0	1	0
Bernero, Adam	1.000	12	2	6	0	8	2
Johnson, Mark	1.000	9	1	5	0	6	0
Tolar, Kevin	-	5	0	0	0	0	0
Runyan, Sean	1.000	3	0	2	0	2	0
Villafuerte, Brandon	1.000	3	1	0	0	1	0
Hiljus, Erik	-	3	0	0	0	0	0
Kida, Masao	1.000	2	2	1	0	3	0
Borkowski, Dave	-	2	0	0	0	0	0
Halter, Shane	-	1	0	0	0	0	0

PITCHING AGAINST EACH CLUB

Pitcher	Ana. W-L	Bal. W-L	Bos. W-L	Chi. W-L	Cle. W-L	K.C. W-L	Min. W-L	N.Y. W-L	Oak. W-L	Sea. W-L	T.B. W-L	Tex. W-L	Tor. W-L	N.L. W-L	Total W-L
Anderson, Matt	0-0	0-0	0-1	1-0	0-1	0-0	1-0	0-0	0-0	0-0	0-0	0-0	0-0	1-0	3-2
Bernero, Adam	0-0	0-0	0-0	0-0	0-0	0-0	0-0	0-0	0-1	0-0	0-0	0-0	0-0	0-0	0-1
Blair, Willie	0-0	0-1	1-0	0-0	2-0	0-1	0-1	2-1	0-0	1-0	1-0	2-0	1-1	0-1	10-6
Borkowski, Dave	0-0	0-0	0-0	0-1	0-0	0-0	0-0	0-0	0-0	0-0	0-0	0-0	0-0	0-0	0-1
Brocail, Doug	0-0	0-2	0-0	0-0	1-0	2-1	0-0	0-0	0-0	1-0	0-0	0-0	1-1	0-0	5-4
Cruz, Nelson	1-0	0-0	0-1	0-0	0-0	1-0	0-0	1-0	0-1	1-0	0-0	0-0	0-0	1-0	5-2
Halter, Shane	0-0	0-0	0-0	0-0	0-0	0-0	0-0	0-0	0-0	0-0	0-0	0-0	0-0	0-0	0-0
Hiljus, Erik	0-0	0-0	0-0	0-0	0-0	0-0	0-0	0-0	0-0	0-0	0-0	0-0	0-0	0-0	0-0
Johnson, Mark	0-0	0-0	0-0	0-0	0-0	0-0	0-1	0-0	0-0	0-0	0-0	0-0	0-0	0-0	0-1
Jones, Todd	0-1	0-0	0-0	0-0	0-0	0-1	2-1	0-0	0-0	0-0	0-1	0-0	0-0	0-0	2-4
Kida, Masao	0-0	0-0	0-0	0-0	0-0	0-0	0-0	0-0	0-0	0-0	0-0	0-0	0-0	0-0	0-0
McDill, Allen	0-0	0-0	0-0	0-0	0-0	0-0	0-0	0-0	0-0	0-0	0-0	0-0	0-0	0-0	0-0
Mlicki, Dave	0-2	0-1	2-1	1-1	0-0	0-1	0-0	1-1	0-0	0-1	1-0	0-1	0-0	1-2	6-11
Moehler, Brian	2-0	1-0	0-1	0-2	2-1	0-0	0-0	0-0	2-1	2-0	0-0	1-1	0-1	2-2	12-9
Nitkowski, C.J.	0-1	0-1	0-1	0-1	1-1	0-0	0-2	1-0	0-1	0-0	1-0	0-0	0-1	1-0	4-9
Nomo, Hideo	1-0	0-1	2-1	0-0	0-1	1-2	0-0	1-1	2-0	0-0	0-1	1-0	0-2	0-3	8-12
Patterson, Danny	0-0	1-0	0-0	0-0	1-1	0-0	1-0	0-0	0-0	0-0	1-0	0-0	0-0	1-0	5-1
Poole, Jim	1-0	0-0	0-0	0-0	0-0	0-0	0-0	0-0	0-0	0-0	0-0	0-0	0-0	0-0	1-0
Runyan, Sean	0-0	0-0	0-0	0-0	0-0	0-0	0-0	0-0	0-0	0-0	0-0	0-0	0-0	0-0	0-0
Sparks, Steve W.	0-1	1-0	0-0	0-1	0-1	0-0	2-0	1-0	1-0	1-0	0-0	1-1	0-1	0-0	7-5
Tolar, Kevin	0-0	0-0	0-0	0-0	0-0	0-0	0-0	0-0	0-0	0-0	0-0	0-0	0-0	0-0	0-0
Villafuerte, Brandon	0-0	0-0	0-0	0-0	0-0	0-0	0-0	0-0	0-0	0-0	0-0	0-0	0-0	0-0	0-0
Weaver, Jeff	0-0	1-0	0-1	1-3	0-0	1-1	1-1	1-1	1-0	1-1	0-3	0-2	1-2	3-0	11-15
Totals	5-5	4-6	5-7	3-9	7-6	5-7	7-6	8-4	6-4	7-2	4-5	5-5	3-9	10-8	79-83

INTERLEAGUE: Cruz 1-0, Moehler 0-1, Blair 0-1 vs. Brewers; Weaver 1-0, Anderson 1-0, Nomo 0-1 vs. Cubs; Weaver 1-0, Mlicki 1-0, Moehler 0-1 vs. Reds; Moehler 1-0, Patterson 1-0, Nomo 0-1 vs. Astros; Nitkowski 1-0, Mlicki 0-1, Nomo 0-1 vs. Pirates; Weaver 1-0, Moehler 1-0, Mlicki 0-1 vs. Cardinals. Total: 10-8.

MISCELLANEOUS

HOME RUNS BY PARK

At Anaheim (8): Gonzalez 3, Encarnacion 2, Easley 1, Higginson 1, Cruz 1.

At Baltimore (12): Palmer 3, Ausmus 2, Encarnacion 2, Higginson 1, Clark 1, Magee 1, Cruz 1, Allen 1.

At Boston (6): Gonzalez 2, Jefferies 1, Clark 1, Magee 1, Halter 1.

At Chicago (AL) (8): Higginson 3, Morris 1, Gonzalez 1, Palmer 1, Magee 1, Encarnacion 1.

At Chicago (NL) (2): Palmer 1, Higginson 1.

At Cleveland (14): Gonzalez 3, Higginson 3, Clark 2, Polonia 1, Jefferies 1, Easley 1, Ausmus 1, Becker 1, Magee 1.

At Detroit (69): Palmer 15, Higginson 12, Gonzalez 8, Clark 6, Easley 5, Encarnacion 4, Polonia 3, Ausmus 3, Becker 3, McMillon 3, Magee 2, Macias 2, Cruz 1, Cardona 1, Allen 1.

At Kansas City (9): Higginson 3, Palmer 2, Fick 2, Polonia 1, Cruz 1.

At Milwaukee (3): Polonia 1, Easley 1, Becker 1.

At Minnesota (7): Easley 2, Ausmus 1, Higginson 1, Cruz 1, Halter 1, Encarnacion 1.

At New York (AL) (7): Easley 2, Higginson 2, McMillon 1, Magee 1, Cruz 1.

At Oakland (6): Palmer 2, Gonzalez 1, Becker 1, Halter 1, Encarnacion 1.

At Pittsburgh (1): Cruz 1.

At Seattle (6): Gonzalez 2, Palmer 1, Higginson 1, Cruz 1, Encarnacion 1.

At Tampa Bay (6): Palmer 2, Easley 2, Higginson 1, Cruz 1.

At Texas (4): Palmer 2, Gonzalez 1, Encarnacion 1.

At Toronto (9): Clark 3, Gonzalez 1, Becker 1, Higginson 1, Cruz 1, Encarnacion 1, Fick 1.

LOW-HIT GAMES

No-hitters: None.
One-hitters: None.
Two-hitters: None.

10-STRIKEOUT GAMES

Jeff Weaver 1, Total: 1

FOUR OR MORE HITS IN ONE GAME

Bobby Higginson 3, Shane Halter 2, Juan Encarnacion 2, Juan Gonzalez 1, Dean Palmer 1, Brad Ausmus 1, Wendell Magee 1, Deivi Cruz 1, Total: 12

MULTI-HOMER GAMES

Bobby Higginson 3, Juan Gonzalez 1, Dean Palmer 1, Tony Clark 1, Billy McMillon 1, Total: 7

GRAND SLAMS

6-27: Dean Palmer (off New York's David Cone)
7-22: Jose Macias (off Kansas City's Tim Byrdak)
9-23: Billy McMillon (off New York's Roger Clemens)

PINCH HITTERS

(Minimum 5 at-bats)

Name	AB	Avg.	HR	RBI
Magee, Wendell	26	.385	1	5
Becker, Rich	19	.263	1	3
Macias, Jose	14	.071	0	3
Polonia, Luis	12	.250	1	1
Fick, Robert	12	.250	0	4
McMillon, Billy	7	.714	0	2

DEBUTS

4-7: Mark Johnson, P.
5-23: Brandon Villafuerte, P.
5-31: Javier Cardona, C.
7-18: Eric Munson, 1B.
8-1: Adam Bernero, P.
9-2: Rod Lindsey, PR.
9-11: Kevin Tolar, P.

GAMES BY POSITION

Catcher: Brad Ausmus 150, Javier Cardona 26, Robert Fick 16, Shane Halter 2.

First base: Tony Clark 58, Hal Morris 38, Robert Fick 34, Shane Halter 29, Gregg Jefferies 20, Dean Palmer 20, Dusty Allen 17, Eric Munson 3, Brad Ausmus 1.

Second base: Damion Easley 125, Jose Macias 39, Gregg Jefferies 14, Shane Halter 10, Brad Ausmus 1.

Third base: Dean Palmer 115, Shane Halter 55, Jose Macias 26, Gregg Jefferies 6, Brad Ausmus 1, Dusty Allen 1.

Shortstop: Deivi Cruz 156, Shane Halter 17, Jose Macias 1.

Outfield: Bobby Higginson 145, Juan Encarnacion 141, Rich Becker 80, Wendell Magee 76, Juan Gonzalez 66, Luis Polonia 27, Billy McMillon 15, Shane Halter 8, Karim Garcia 7, Rod Lindsey 7, Jose Macias 3, Gregg Jefferies 1, Hal Morris 1, Dusty Allen 1.

Designated hitter: Juan Gonzalez 48, Luis Polonia 44, Billy McMillon 24, Dean Palmer 14, Robert Fick 12, Bobby Higginson 10, Wendell Magee 6, Rich Becker 4, Gregg Jefferies 2, Karim Garcia 1, Tony Clark 1, Gabe Alvarez 1, Jose Macias 1.

STREAKS

Wins: 6 (August 13-19)
Losses: 8 (April 15-24)
Consecutive games with at least one hit: 19, Juan Encarnacion (April 16-May 7)
Wins by pitcher: 6, Steve Sparks (August 5-September 1)

ATTENDANCE

Home: 2,462,013
Road: 2,067,434
Highest (home): 40,637 (July 16 vs. Cincinnati).
Highest (road): 53,498 (April 3 vs. Oakland).
Lowest (home): 20,322 (September 5 vs. Anaheim).
Lowest (road): 6,675 (May 4 vs. Minnesota).

Kansas City Royals

DAY BY DAY

Date	Opp.	Res.	Score	(inn.*)	Hits	Opp. hits	Winning pitcher	Losing pitcher	Save	Record	Pos.	GB
4-3	At Tor.	L	4-5		9	8	Koch	Spradlin		0-1	T3rd	1.0
4-4	At Tor.	L	3-6		7	7	Halladay	Witasick	Koch	0-2	T4th	1.5
4-5	At Tor.	W	4-3		7	5	Rosado	Carpenter	Bottalico	1-2	T3rd	1.0
4-6	At Tor.	W	9-3		17	5	Durbin	Escobar	Rigby	2-2	T1st	...
4-7	Min.	W	10-6		15	12	Fussell	Miller		3-2	T1st	...
4-8	Min.	W	5-2		10	6	Suppan	Radke	Santiago	4-2	T1st	...
4-9	Min.	L	7-13		9	16	Milton	Witasick		4-3	T2nd	0.5
4-10	Min.	W	6-5		14	8	Bottalico	Hawkins		5-3	2nd	0.5
4-11	Bal.	W	7-5	(12)	11	11	Santiago	Worrell		6-3	2nd	0.5
4-12	Bal.	W	7-6		8	8	Santiago	Trombley		7-3	2nd	0.5
4-13	Bal.	W	6-5		12	12	Bottalico	Ryan		8-3	2nd	...
4-14	At N.Y.	L	5-7		9	10	Clemens	Witasick	Rivera	8-4	2nd	...
4-15	At N.Y.	L	1-7		2	11	Mendoza	Rosado		8-5	2nd	...
4-16	At N.Y.	L	4-8		9	10	Nelson	Fussell		8-6	2nd	1.0
4-18	At Min.	L	1-3		6	7	Radke	Suppan	Wells	8-7	3rd	1.0
4-19	At Min.	L	6-7		10	9	Carrasco	Santiago		8-8	3rd	1.5
4-20	At Min.	L	7-9		12	13	Bergman	Rosado	Wells	8-9	3rd	2.0
4-21	At Sea.	L	2-10		8	10	Rodriguez	Durbin		8-10	T3rd	3.0
4-22	At Sea.	L	2-4		6	7	Tomko	Witasick	Sasaki	8-11	T3rd	4.0
4-23	At Sea.	L	5-8		10	7	Rhodes	Bottalico		8-12	4th	5.0
4-25	T.B.	W	7-6		13	10	Reichert	Lopez		9-12	4th	4.5
4-26	T.B.	W	7-6		12	8	Bottalico	Lopez		10-12	4th	4.5
4-28	Sea.	W	8-5		12	9	Batista	Tomko	Bottalico	11-12	3rd	5.0
4-29	Sea.	L	3-11		10	17	Sele	Suppan		11-13	3rd	6.0
4-30	Sea.	W	6-3		10	7	Rosado	Meche	Bottalico	12-13	3rd	5.0
5-1	Oak.	L	5-7		9	7	Olivares	Reichert	Isringhausen	12-14	3rd	5.0
5-2	Oak.	W	8-7	(10)	14	10	Rakers	Isringhausen		13-14	3rd	4.0
5-3	Oak.	L	5-14		15	20	Heredia	Suppan		13-15	3rd	5.0
5-5	Chi.	W	5-1		10	8	Fussell	Eldred		14-15	3rd	4.0
5-6	Chi.	W	11-5		18	10	Spradlin	Sirotka		15-15	3rd	3.0
5-7	Chi.	W	12-8		13	13	Bottalico	Wunsch		16-15	3rd	2.0
5-8	At Det.	W	4-1	(11)	8	3	Santiago	Brocail		17-15	3rd	1.0
5-10	At Det.	W	6-0		9	4	Fussell	Nomo		18-15	2nd	0.5
5-11	At Cle.	L	0-16		5	22	Wright	Durbin		18-16	3rd	1.0
5-12	At Cle.	L	3-7		5	9	Colon	Batista		18-17	3rd	1.0
5-13	At Cle.	L	6-7	(12)	9	12	Reed	Reichert		18-18	3rd	2.0
5-14	At Cle.	W	5-4		8	7	Suzuki	Finley	Spradlin	19-18	3rd	2.0
5-15	At Oak.	L	3-6		7	7	Mulder	Fussell	Isringhausen	19-19	3rd	2.5
5-16	At Oak.	W	8-7		11	11	Reichert	D. Jones	Spradlin	20-19	3rd	2.5
5-17	At Oak.	W	4-3		8	3	Batista	Olivares	Spradlin	21-19	3rd	1.5
5-19	At Ana.	L	4-6		10	12	Washburn	Suppan	Percival	21-20	3rd	2.5
5-20	At Ana.	L	8-9		12	11	Hasegawa	Reichert	Percival	21-21	3rd	3.5
5-21	At Ana.	W	10-6		14	7	Santiago	Bottenfield		22-21	3rd	3.5
5-23	Tex.	L	3-4		9	7	Helling	Batista	Wetteland	22-22	3rd	4.0
5-24	Tex.	W	3-0		8	6	Suppan	Rogers	Spradlin	23-22	3rd	3.0
5-25	Tex.	L	3-5		10	8	Loaiza	Santiago	Wetteland	23-23	3rd	3.0
5-26	Ana.	W	9-4		14	6	Fussell	Weaver	Bottalico	24-23	3rd	3.0
5-27	Ana.	W	6-5	(10)	8	9	Reichert	Weaver		25-23	3rd	3.0
5-28	Ana.	L	4-8		10	13	Cooper	Batista	Hasegawa	25-24	3rd	3.0
5-30	At Bos.	L	2-8		8	12	Fassero	Suppan		25-25	3rd	3.5
5-31	At Bos.	W	9-7		14	12	Suzuki	Schourek	Spradlin	26-25	3rd	3.5
6-1	At Bos.	W	13-11		19	12	Santiago	Lowe	Reichert	27-25	3rd	3.0
6-2	At Pit.	L	3-9		4	8	Ritchie	Batista		27-26	3rd	4.0
6-3	At Pit.	W	16-3		18	8	Witasick	Schmidt		28-26	3rd	3.0
6-4	At Pit.	W	7-5	(11)	9	9	Rakers	Christiansen	Reichert	29-26	3rd	3.0
6-5	At StL.	W	7-4		10	6	Suzuki	Hentgen	Spradlin	30-26	3rd	3.0
6-6	At StL.	L	4-5		10	7	An. Benes	Witasick	Veres	30-27	3rd	4.0
6-7	At StL.	L	2-4		7	10	Kile	Batista		30-28	3rd	5.0
6-9	Pit.	W	6-5	(10)	13	9	Spradlin	Christiansen		31-28	3rd	5.0
6-10	Pit.	W	2-1	(12)	10	13	Bottalico	Silva		32-28	3rd	5.0
6-11	Pit.	L	6-10	(10)	11	18	Sauerbeck	Spradlin		32-29	3rd	5.0
6-12	Sea.	L	3-5		7	7	Moyer	Batista	Sasaki	32-30	3rd	6.0
6-13	Sea.	L	0-7	(6)	1	10	Meche	Laxton		32-31	3rd	7.0
6-14	Sea.	W	5-4		11	9	Bottalico	Sasaki		33-31	3rd	7.0
6-16	Oak.	L	3-8		8	11	D. Jones	Reichert	Tam	33-32	3rd	8.5
6-17	Oak.	L	4-10		7	13	Appier	Witasick		33-33	3rd	9.5
6-18	Oak.	L	3-21		8	21	Heredia	D'Amico		33-34	3rd	10.5
6-20	At Ana.	W	8-6		17	5	Santiago	Percival	Bottalico	34-34	3rd	10.0
6-21	At Ana.	L	1-3		5	6	Washburn	Suzuki	Percival	34-35	3rd	10.0
6-22	At Ana.	L	3-4		3	10	Belcher	Witasick	Petkovsek	34-36	3rd	11.0
6-23	At Oak.	L	6-10		12	13	Appier	Durbin		34-37	3rd	12.0
6-24	At Oak.	W	8-3		13	9	Bottalico	Heredia		35-37	3rd	11.0
6-25	At Oak.	L	3-4		7	9	Mulder	Suppan	Isringhausen	35-38	3rd	12.0
6-27	Cle.	L	1-12		6	13	Finley	Suzuki		35-39	3rd	12.0
6-28	Cle.	W	8-1		9	4	Witasick	Davis		36-39	3rd	12.0
6-29	Cle.	W	6-1		4	5	Durbin	Colon		37-39	3rd	11.0
6-30	Det.	L	1-3		7	5	Weaver	Reichert	Jones	37-40	3rd	12.0
7-1	Det.	L	7-8		14	15	Brocail	Bottalico	Jones	37-41	3rd	13.0
7-2	Det.	L	0-2		3	6	Nomo	Suzuki	Jones	37-42	3rd	14.0

HIGHLIGHTS

High point: The Royals plowed through an improbable early season stretch in which the club won six straight home games in its final at-bat. That April magic set a tone for the season and the Royals proved adept at fighting back from deficits and staying in every game.
Low point: The icy relationship between the Royals and outfielder Carlos Beltran, the 1999 Rookie of the Year who was suspended in August for defying team orders to rehabilitate an injured knee at the club's facility in Florida. That led to nasty words from both sides and an arbitration hearing that still hadn't been resolved by the end of the year.
Turning point: The Royals played themselves out of contention in the first month of the season, going 0-9 on a trip from April 14-23. The team never led in any of those nine games.
Most valuable player: First baseman Mike Sweeney edged Jermaine Dye and Johnny Damon. Sweeney batted .333 and drove in a franchise-record 144 runs. He was disciplined, striking out only 67 times, and led the A.L. with a .385 average with runners in scoring position.
Most valuable pitcher: Righthander Jeff Suppan gets the nod by default. He led the club with a modest 10 victories and chewed up more innings (217) than any other pitcher while compiling a 4.94 ERA.
Most improved player: Mac Suzuki, almost a castoff, made slight alterations in his delivery and wound up being one of the club's most consistent pitchers. He led the team in strikeouts (135) while compiling the best ERA (4.34) among all starters. He was just 8-10 overall, but lost a lot of close games.
Most pleasant surprise: The Royals did not expect outfielder Mark Quinn to make a run at Rookie of the Year honors. He batted .294 with 20 home runs and 78 RBIs while displaying uncanny patience for a rookie. He also reined in a brash attitude after a short exile to the minors.
Key injuries: Nothing hurt more than the shoulder injury that robbed Jose Rosado of almost the entire season. He pitched only 27 $^{2}/_{3}$ innings before finally having shoulder surgery to repair the posterior labrum. ... Righthander Blake Stein, who suffered a cracked bone in his forearm, missed most of the first half. ... Beltran's nagging knee injury limited him to 98 games. ... Various injuries to second baseman Carlos Febles (shoulder, ankle) limited him to 100.
Notable: The Royals, for the second year in a row, established a franchise record for runs scored with 879. ... Three players, Sweeney (144), Jermaine Dye (118) and Joe Randa (106), topped 100 RBIs, matching the feat accomplished by the 1999 team.

—STEVE ROCK

MISCELLANEOUS

RECORDS

2000 regular-season record: 77-85 (4th in A.L. Central); 42-39 at home; 35-46 on road; 24-26 vs. East; 36-30 vs. Central; 17-29 vs. West; 18-24 vs. left-handed starters; 59-61 vs. righthanded starters; 68-75 on grass; 9-10 on turf; 29-19 in daytime; 48-66 at night; 21-26 in one-run games; 7-8 in extra-inning games; 0-0-1 in doubleheaders.
Team record past five years: 355-451 (.440, ranks 11th in league in that span).

TEAM LEADERS

Batting average: Mike Sweeney (.333).
At-bats: Johnny Damon (655).
Runs: Johnny Damon (136).
Hits: Johnny Damon (214).
Total Bases: Jermaine Dye (337).
Doubles: Johnny Damon (42).
Triples: Johnny Damon (10).
Home runs: Jermaine Dye (33).
Runs batted in: Mike Sweeney (144).
Stolen bases: Johnny Damon (46).
Slugging percentage: Jermaine Dye (.561).
On-base percentage: Mike Sweeney (.407).
Wins: Jeff Suppan (10).
Earned-run average: Makoto Suzuki (4.34).
Complete games: Jeff Suppan (3).
Shutouts: Dan Reichert, Jeff Suppan, Makoto Suzuki (1).
Saves: Ricky Bottalico (16).
Innings pitched: Jeff Suppan (217.0).
Strikeouts: Makoto Suzuki (135).

Date	Opp.	Res.	Score	(inn.*)	Hits	Opp. hits	Winning pitcher	Losing pitcher	Save	Record	Pos.	GB
7-3	Chi.	L	10-14		10	22	Pena	Santiago		37-43	3rd	15.0
7-4	Chi.	W	10-7		12	14	Spradlin	Garland		38-43	3rd	14.0
7-5	Chi.	L	3-6	(13)	17	13	Wunsch	Bochtler		38-44	3rd	15.0
7-7	At Hou.	L	5-9		6	10	Elarton	Stein		38-45	3rd	16.0
7-8	At Hou.	W	5-2		13	9	Suzuki	Miller		39-45	3rd	15.0
7-9	At Hou.	L	6-9		10	13	Lima	Witasick	Dotel	39-46	3rd	15.0
7-13	Mil.	L	2-5		10	8	Wright	Stein	Wickman	39-47	4th	15.0
7-14	Mil.	L	0-4		4	12	D'Amico	Suzuki		39-48	4th	15.0
7-15	Mil.	W	7-4		11	11	Suppan	Haynes	Bottalico	40-48	4th	15.0
7-16	Chi. (NL)	L	7-10		14	10	Wood	Reichert	Aguilera	40-49	4th	16.0
7-17	Chi. (NL)	L	1-3		7	8	Downs	Durbin	Aguilera	40-50	4th	17.0
7-18	Chi. (NL)	W	12-4		20	8	Stein	Valdes		41-50	4th	17.0
7-19	At Cle.	W	10-5		12	13	Suzuki	Finley	Spradlin	42-50	4th	17.0
7-20	At Cle.	W	10-6		17	11	Suppan	Brower		43-50	4th	16.0
7-21	At Det.	W	4-0		9	6	Reichert	Weaver		44-50	3rd	16.0
7-22†	At Det.	W	8-5		11	9	Witasick	Mlicki	Bottalico	45-50		
7-22‡	At Det.	L	6-10		8	14	Cruz	Bochtler		45-51	3rd	15.5
7-23	At Det.	L	9-12		13	14	Brocail	Byrdak	Jones	45-52	4th	15.5
7-24	At Chi.	L	6-7		14	9	Wunsch	Suzuki	Foulke	45-53	4th	16.5
7-25	At Chi.	W	6-1		8	4	Suppan	Parque		46-53	4th	15.5
7-26	At Chi.	W	7-6		10	9	Spradlin	Howry	Bottalico	47-53	3rd	14.5
7-27	T.B.	L	5-8		14	10	Rupe	Durbin	Hernandez	47-54	3rd	15.5
7-28	T.B.	L	3-10		8	12	Rekar	Stein		47-55	3rd	15.5
7-29	T.B.	L	1-2		7	4	Lopez	Suzuki	Hernandez	47-56	4th	15.5
7-30	T.B.	L	6-7	(10)	12	12	Sturtze	Spradlin	Hernandez	47-57	4th	16.5
8-1	At N.Y.	L	4-5		6	9	Nelson	Bottalico	Rivera	47-58	4th	17.5
8-2	At N.Y.	W	4-1		11	2	Stein	Neagle	Bottalico	48-58	4th	16.5
8-3	At N.Y.	L	2-3		5	6	Rivera	Spradlin		48-59	4th	17.0
8-4	At Bos.	L	4-5		8	11	Garces	Larkin	Lowe	48-60	5th	17.0
8-5	At Bos.	W	7-5		13	8	Meadows	Cormier	Bottalico	49-60	4th	17.0
8-6	At Bos.	W	3-1		8	10	Reichert	Wakefield	Bottalico	50-60	4th	17.0
8-7	Tor.	W	8-7		14	14	Stein	Loaiza	Bottalico	51-60	4th	16.5
8-8	Tor.	L	1-6		4	14	Castillo	Suzuki		51-61	4th	16.0
8-9	Tor.	W	5-3		10	11	Suppan	Trachsel	Larkin	52-61	4th	16.0
8-10	Tor.	L	7-15		14	17	Carpenter	Fussell		52-62	4th	16.0
8-11	Bal.	W	7-6		11	8	Reichert	Mussina	Bottalico	53-62	4th	16.0
8-12	Bal.	L	11-12		14	11	Groom	Bottalico	Kohlmeier	53-63	4th	17.0
8-13	Bal.	W	10-5		14	12	Suzuki	Brea		54-63	4th	16.0
8-15	At Min.	L	2-6		5	11	Milton	Suppan	Wells	54-64	4th	16.5
8-16	At Min.	W	9-3		16	7	Meadows	Romero		55-64	4th	16.5
8-17	At Min.	W	8-4		15	9	Reichert	Redman		56-64	4th	15.5
8-18	At Bal.	W	4-1		4	8	Stein	Rapp		57-64	4th	15.5
8-19	At Bal.	W	7-0		11	4	Suzuki	Mercedes		58-64	4th	15.5
8-20	At Bal.	L	1-2		6	9	Ponson	Wilson	Kohlmeier	58-65	4th	15.5
8-21	At Bal.	L	1-2		8	7	Mussina	Meadows	Kohlmeier	58-66	4th	15.5
8-22	At Tor.	L	5-7		11	10	Escobar	Santiago	Koch	58-67	4th	16.0
8-23	At Tor.	L	8-9		11	13	Escobar	Larkin	Koch	58-68	4th	17.0
8-24	Bos.	L	7-9	(10)	11	12	Pichardo	Larkin	Lowe	58-69	4th	17.0
8-25	Bos.	W	6-2		13	5	Suppan	Florie		59-69	4th	17.0
8-26	Bos.	L	3-5		9	14	Arrojo	Meadows	Lowe	59-70	4th	17.0
8-27	Bos.	W	11-7		10	11	Reichert	Wakefield		60-70	4th	17.0
8-29	Min.	W	7-3		10	5	Stein	Romero		61-70	4th	16.5
8-30	Min.	W	8-7		14	17	Suzuki	Redman	Bottalico	62-70	4th	16.5
8-31	At T.B.	L	1-2		6	7	Fiore	Suppan	Hernandez	62-71	4th	17.0
9-1	At T.B.	W	9-5		15	8	Meadows	Rupe		63-71	4th	17.0
9-2	At T.B.	W	7-5		8	8	Santiago	Hernandez	Bottalico	64-71	4th	17.0
9-3	At T.B.	W	8-2		10	6	Stein	Eiland		65-71	4th	17.0
9-4	N.Y.	L	3-4		12	8	Pettitte	Suzuki	Rivera	65-72	4th	17.0
9-5	N.Y.	L	5-10		10	17	Gooden	Suppan		65-73	4th	17.0
9-6	N.Y.	W	3-2		12	9	Meadows	Stanton		66-73	4th	17.0
9-7	N.Y.	L	3-7		8	7	Neagle	Bottalico	Rivera	66-74	4th	18.0
9-8	Tex.	L	5-6		12	12	Glynn	Stein	Wetteland	66-75	4th	19.0
9-9	Tex.	L	5-6		10	11	Zimmerman	Suzuki	Wetteland	66-76	4th	19.0
9-10	Tex.	W	13-8		14	16	Suppan	Oliver		67-76	4th	18.5
9-11	At Sea.	W	6-3		15	7	Meadows	Halama	Santiago	68-76	4th	18.5
9-12	At Sea.	L	3-11		9	15	Garcia	Reichert		68-77	4th	18.5
9-13	At Sea.	L	1-2	(11)	8	6	Mesa	Bottalico		68-78	4th	19.5
9-14	At Tex.	L	1-8		4	9	Davis	Suzuki	Crabtree	68-79	4th	20.0
9-15	At Tex.	L	11-12	(10)	18	15	Wetteland	Santiago		68-80	4th	20.0
9-16	At Tex.	W	8-5		8	10	Meadows	Sikorski		69-80	4th	20.0
9-17	At Tex.	L	5-6		12	11	Rogers	Reichert	Wetteland	69-81	4th	20.0
9-19	Ana.	W	5-1		10	3	Stein	Ortiz		70-81	4th	19.5
9-20	Ana.	L	4-7	(10)	10	14	Percival	Santiago	Petkovsek	70-82	4th	20.5
9-21	Ana.	W	8-3		16	6	Suppan	Schoeneweis		71-82	4th	20.5
9-22	Cle.	W	3-2		10	10	Bottalico	Karsay		72-82	4th	20.5
9-23	Cle.	L	1-11		4	16	Colon	Reichert		72-83	4th	21.5
9-24	Cle.	W	9-0		12	6	Stein	Nagy		73-83	4th	20.5
9-26	Det.	W	7-6		10	9	Bottalico	Blair		74-83	4th	19.0
9-27	Det.	W	3-0		9	6	Suppan	Nomo		75-83	4th	18.0
9-28	Det.	W	8-5		12	12	Santiago	Jones	Bottalico	76-83	T3rd	17.0
9-29	At Chi.	L	4-6		14	9	Bradford	Reichert	Foulke	76-84	4th	18.0
9-30	At Chi.	L	1-9		6	11	Wells	Stein		76-85	4th	19.0
10-1	At Chi.	W	6-2		10	8	Fussell	Baldwin		77-85	4th	18.0

Monthly records: April (12-13), May (14-12), June (11-15), July (10-17), August (15-14), September (14-14), October (1-0).
*Innings, if other than nine. † First game of a doubleheader. ‡ Second game of a doubleheader.

MEMORABLE GAMES

April 7 at Kansas City

In the Kansas City home opener, played before the biggest opening-day crowd in more than a decade, the Royals stormed back from a 6-0 deficit by scoring four times in both the seventh and eighth innings to post an emotional and pulsating 10-6 victory over Minnesota.

Minnesota	AB	R	H	BI	Kansas City	AB	R	H	BI
Walker, 2b	5	0	2	0	Damon, lf	5	1	2	0
Guzman, ss	5	0	2	3	Febles, 2b	4	2	3	0
Lawton, rf	5	0	1	0	Beltran, cf	5	1	0	0
Huskey, dh	5	0	0	0	Dye, rf	5	3	3	3
Koskie, 3b	3	2	1	0	Sweeney, 1b	5	2	3	4
Coomer, 1b	5	1	1	0	McCarty, 1b	0	0	0	0
Jones, lf	4	1	2	2	Randa, 3b	3	0	1	1
LeCroy, c	3	1	1	0	Quinn, dh	4	0	1	0
Hunter, cf	3	1	2	0	Johnson, c	3	1	1	1
					Zaun, ph-c	2	0	0	0
					Sanchez, ss	4	0	1	0
Totals	**38**	**6**	**12**	**5**	**Totals**	**40**	**10**	**15**	**9**

Minnesota ....0 4 0 0 2 0 0 0 0—6 12 2
Kansas City..........................0 0 0 0 1 1 4 4 x—10 15 1

E—Koskie (1), LeCroy (1), Randa (1). DP—Minnesota 1, Kansas City 1. LOB—Minnesota 9, Kansas City 10. 2B—Koskie (3), Damon (1), Febles (1), Dye (4). 3B—Guzman (1). HR—Jones (1), Dye (2),.Sweeney 2 (3), Johnson (1).

Minnesota	IP	H	R	ER	BB	SO
Santana	5	5	1	1	2	2
Wells	1.1	6	5	5	0	3
Carrasco	0.2	1	0	0	1	0
Miller (L 0-1)	0.1	3	4	3	1	0
Guardado	0.2	0	0	0	0	0

Kansas City	IP	H	R	ER	BB	SO
Suzuki	4	6	4	4	3	5
Fussell (W 1-0)	4	6	2	0	0	2
Reichert	1	0	0	0	1	0

WP—Fussell. U—HP, Gibson. 1B, Rippley. 2B, Tschida. 3B, Meriwether. T—3:11. A—40,474.

April 9 at Kansas City

In the wackiest game of the season, Kansas City was in danger of getting "perfect gamed" by Twins pitcher Eric Milton, who retired the first 20 batters he faced. But suddenly the Royals stormed back, scoring seven runs in the eighth before losing, 13-7. The game marked the first time in major league history that both teams hit back-to-back-to-back home runs.

Minnesota	AB	R	H	BI	Kansas City	AB	R	H	BI
Walker, 2b	4	1	0	0	Damon, lf	3	1	0	0
Maxwell, 2b	0	0	0	0	Febles, 2b	5	1	1	2
Guzman, ss	4	1	1	0	Beltran, cf	5	1	2	3
Lawton, rf	5	2	3	4	Dye, rf	4	1	2	1
Hocking, rf	0	0	0	0	Sweeney, dh	4	1	1	1
Huskey, dh	4	2	2	2	Randa, 3b	4	0	0	0
Cummings, ph-dh	1	0	1	0	McCarty, 1b	4	0	1	0
Koskie, 3b	5	2	2	1	Johnson, c	4	1	1	0
Coomer, 1b	5	2	2	4	Sanchez, ss	3	0	1	0
Jones, lf	5	1	1	1	Ordaz, pr-ss	1	1	0	0
LeCroy, c	4	1	2	1					
Hunter, cf	4	1	2	0					
Totals	**41**	**13**	**16**	**13**	**Totals**	**37**	**7**	**9**	**7**

Minnesota ....2 0 3 0 1 4 3 0 0—13 16 1
Kansas City ....0 0 0 0 0 0 0 7 0—7 9 1

E—Koskie (2), McCarty (1). DP— Kansas City 2. LOB—Minnesota 3, Kansas City 5. 2B—Lawton (1), Huskey (2), Hunter 2 (3), Cummings (2), Beltran (3). HR—Lawton (2), Huskey (1), Coomer 2 (2), Jones (2), LeCroy (1), Beltran (1), Dye (3), Sweeney (4).

Minnesota	IP	H	R	ER	BB	SO
Milton (W 1-0)	7.2	4	2	2	0	3
Guardado	0	3	4	4	1	0
Carrasco	1.1	2	1	1	1	1

Kansas City	IP	H	R	ER	BB	SO
Witasick (L 0-2)	4.2	6	6	5	1	3
Rigby	1.1	8	7	7	0	2
Spradlin	3	2	0	0	1	0

Guardado pitched to 4 batters in 8th. Rigby pitched to 3 batters in 7th.

PB—LeCroy. U—HP, Tschida. 1B, Meriwether. 2B, Gibson. 3B, Rippley. T—2:57. A—20,480.

INDIVIDUAL STATISTICS

BATTING

Name	G	TPA	AB	R	H	TB	2B	3B	HR	RBI	Avg.	Obp.	Slg.	SH	SF	HP	BB	IBB	SO	SB	CS	GDP	vs RHP AB	vs RHP Avg.	vs RHP HR	vs RHP RBI	vs LHP AB	vs LHP Avg.	vs LHP HR	vs LHP RBI
Damon, Johnny	159	741	655	136	214	324	42	10	16	88	.327	.382	.495	8	12	1	65	4	60	46	9	7	484	.316	12	55	171	.357	4	33
Sweeney, Mike	159	717	618	105	206	323	30	0	29	144	.333	.407	.523	0	13	15	71	5	67	8	3	15	487	.322	23	115	131	.374	6	29
Randa, Joe	158	665	612	88	186	268	29	4	15	106	.304	.343	.438	1	10	6	36	3	66	6	3	19	486	.302	15	82	126	.310	0	24
Dye, Jermaine	157	679	601	107	193	337	41	2	33	118	.321	.390	.561	0	6	3	69	6	99	0	1	12	468	.321	26	93	133	.323	7	25
Sanchez, Rey	143	555	509	68	139	164	18	2	1	38	.273	.314	.322	11	3	4	28	0	55	7	3	17	378	.267	1	31	131	.290	0	7
Quinn, Mark	135	544	500	76	147	244	33	2	20	78	.294	.342	.488	3	3	3	35	1	91	5	2	11	397	.277	14	59	103	.359	6	19
Beltran, Carlos	98	413	372	49	92	136	15	4	7	44	.247	.309	.366	2	4	0	35	2	69	13	0	12	301	.233	3	32	71	.310	4	12
Febles, Carlos	100	399	339	59	87	107	12	1	2	29	.257	.345	.316	13	1	10	36	1	48	17	6	10	247	.251	2	17	92	.272	0	12
McCarty, Dave	103	295	270	34	75	129	14	2	12	53	.278	.329	.478	0	3	0	22	1	68	0	0	6	166	.223	7	29	104	.365	5	24
Zaun, Gregg	83	282	234	36	64	96	11	0	7	33	.274	.390	.410	0	2	3	43	3	34	7	3	4	200	.265	5	30	34	.324	2	3
Reboulet, Jeff	66	212	182	29	44	51	7	0	0	14	.242	.325	.280	6	1	0	23	0	32	3	1	8	145	.228	0	10	37	.297	0	4
Dunwoody, Todd	61	195	178	12	37	49	9	0	1	23	.208	.238	.275	2	6	1	8	0	42	3	0	4	161	.211	1	20	17	.176	0	3
Fabregas, Jorge	43	152	142	13	40	53	4	0	3	17	.282	.320	.373	2	0	0	8	1	11	1	0	1	129	.279	3	16	13	.308	0	1
Johnson, Brian	37	132	125	9	26	44	6	0	4	18	.208	.229	.352	1	2	0	4	0	28	0	0	4	83	.217	2	13	42	.190	2	5
Ordaz, Luis	65	117	104	17	23	25	2	0	0	11	.221	.257	.240	4	3	1	5	0	10	4	2	6	75	.240	0	9	29	.172	0	2
Ortiz, Hector	26	99	88	15	34	40	6	0	0	5	.386	.443	.455	2	0	1	8	1	8	0	0	0	45	.444	0	1	43	.326	0	4
Delgado, Wilson	33	90	83	15	22	23	1	0	0	7	.265	.311	.277	0	1	0	6	0	17	1	1	1	61	.262	0	5	22	.273	0	2
Pose, Scott	47	54	48	6	9	9	0	0	0	1	.188	.278	.188	0	0	0	6	0	13	0	1	1	44	.182	0	1	4	.250	0	0
Brown, Dee	15	28	25	4	4	5	1	0	0	4	.160	.250	.200	0	0	0	3	0	9	0	0	0	23	.174	0	4	2	.000	0	0
Suzuki, Makoto	32	6	5	1	1	1	0	0	0	0	.200	.200	.200	1	0	0	0	0	2	0	0	0	5	.200	0	0	0	.000	0	0
Holbert, Ray	3	4	4	0	1	1	0	0	0	0	.250	.250	.250	0	0	0	0	0	2	0	0	0	3	.333	0	0	1	.000	0	0
Witasick, Jay	22	4	4	0	0	0	0	0	0	0	.000	.000	.000	0	0	0	0	0	2	0	0	0	4	.000	0	0	0	.000	0	0
Batista, Miguel	14	3	3	0	0	0	0	0	0	0	.000	.000	.000	0	0	0	0	0	3	0	0	0	3	.000	0	0	0	.000	0	0
Suppan, Jeff	35	3	3	0	0	0	0	0	0	0	.000	.000	.000	0	0	0	0	0	0	0	0	0	3	.000	0	0	0	.000	0	0
Stein, Blake	17	2	2	0	0	0	0	0	0	0	.000	.000	.000	0	0	0	0	0	2	0	0	0	2	.000	0	0	0	.000	0	0
Fussell, Chris	20	2	2	0	0	0	0	0	0	0	.000	.000	.000	0	0	0	0	0	2	0	0	0	2	.000	0	0	0	.000	0	0
Reichert, Dan	44	1	1	0	0	0	0	0	0	0	.000	.000	.000	0	0	0	0	0	0	0	0	1	1	.000	0	0	0	.000	0	0
Spradlin, Jerry	50	0	0	0	0	0	0	0	0	0	.000	.000	.000	0	0	0	0	0	0	0	0	0	0	.000	0	0	0	.000	0	0
Bottalico, Ricky	62	0	0	0	0	0	0	0	0	0	.000	.000	.000	0	0	0	0	0	0	0	0	0	0	.000	0	0	0	.000	0	0
Bochtler, Doug	6	0	0	0	0	0	0	0	0	0	.000	.000	.000	0	0	0	0	0	0	0	0	0	0	.000	0	0	0	.000	0	0
Santiago, Jose	45	0	0	0	0	0	0	0	0	0	.000	.000	.000	0	0	0	0	0	0	0	0	0	0	.000	0	0	0	.000	0	0
Rakers, Jason	11	0	0	0	0	0	0	0	0	0	.000	.000	.000	0	0	0	0	0	0	0	0	0	0	.000	0	0	0	.000	0	0
D'Amico, Jeff M.	7	0	0	0	0	0	0	0	0	0	.000	.000	.000	0	0	0	0	0	0	0	0	0	0	.000	0	0	0	.000	0	0
Spoljaric, Paul	13	0	0	0	0	0	0	0	0	0	.000	.000	.000	0	0	0	0	0	0	0	0	0	0	.000	0	0	0	.000	0	0
Rosado, Jose	5	0	0	0	0	0	0	0	0	0	.000	.000	.000	0	0	0	0	0	0	0	0	0	0	.000	0	0	0	.000	0	0
Larkin, Andy	18	0	0	0	0	0	0	0	0	0	.000	.000	.000	0	0	0	0	0	0	0	0	0	0	.000	0	0	0	.000	0	0
Rigby, Brad	4	0	0	0	0	0	0	0	0	0	.000	.000	.000	0	0	0	0	0	0	0	0	0	0	.000	0	0	0	.000	0	0
Meadows, Brian	11	0	0	0	0	0	0	0	0	0	.000	.000	.000	0	0	0	0	0	0	0	0	0	0	.000	0	0	0	.000	0	0
Byrdak, Tim	12	0	0	0	0	0	0	0	0	0	.000	.000	.000	0	0	0	0	0	0	0	0	0	0	.000	0	0	0	.000	0	0
Laxton, Brett	6	0	0	0	0	0	0	0	0	0	.000	.000	.000	0	0	0	0	0	0	0	0	0	0	.000	0	0	0	.000	0	0
Murray, Dan	10	0	0	0	0	0	0	0	0	0	.000	.000	.000	0	0	0	0	0	0	0	0	0	0	.000	0	0	0	.000	0	0
Durbin, Chad	16	0	0	0	0	0	0	0	0	0	.000	.000	.000	0	0	0	0	0	0	0	0	0	0	.000	0	0	0	.000	0	0
Wilson, Kris	20	0	0	0	0	0	0	0	0	0	.000	.000	.000	0	0	0	0	0	0	0	0	0	0	.000	0	0	0	.000	0	0
Mullen, Scott	11	0	0	0	0	0	0	0	0	0	.000	.000	.000	0	0	0	0	0	0	0	0	0	0	.000	0	0	0	.000	0	0

Players with more than one A.L. team

Name	G	TPA	AB	R	H	TB	2B	3B	HR	RBI	Avg.	Obp.	Slg.	SH	SF	HP	BB	IBB	SO	SB	CS	GDP	vs RHP AB	vs RHP Avg.	vs RHP HR	vs RHP RBI	vs LHP AB	vs LHP Avg.	vs LHP HR	vs LHP RBI
Delgado, N.Y.	31	51	45	6	11	15	1	0	1	4	.244	.314	.333	0	1	0	5	0	9	1	0	1	61	.262	0	5	22	.273	0	2
Delgado, N.Y.-K.C.	64	141	128	21	33	38	2	0	1	11	.258	.312	.297	0	2	0	11	0	26	2	1	2	99	.263	1	9	29	.241	0	2

PITCHING

Name	W	L	Pct.	ERA	IP	H	R	ER	HR	SH	SF	HB	BB	IBB	SO	G	GS	CG	ShO	GF	Sv	vs. RH AB	vs. RH Avg.	vs. RH HR	vs. RH RBI	vs. LH AB	vs. LH Avg.	vs. LH HR	vs. LH RBI
Suppan, Jeff	10	9	.526	4.94	217.0	240	121	119	36	5	6	7	84	3	128	35	33	3	1	0	0	389	.283	21	64	457	.284	15	42
Suzuki, Makoto	8	10	.444	4.34	188.2	195	100	91	26	2	3	3	94	6	135	32	29	1	1	0	0	337	.255	8	39	400	.273	18	51
Reichert, Dan	8	10	.444	4.70	153.1	157	92	80	15	5	7	7	91	1	94	44	18	1	1	11	2	285	.267	10	40	295	.275	5	37
Stein, Blake	8	5	.615	4.68	107.2	98	57	56	19	3	4	3	57	1	78	17	17	1	0	0	0	213	.272	11	34	184	.217	8	20
Witasick, Jay	3	8	.273	5.94	89.1	109	65	59	15	3	3	4	38	0	67	22	14	2	0	2	0	186	.269	6	24	176	.335	9	39
Spradlin, Jerry	4	4	.500	5.52	75.0	81	49	46	9	3	1	3	27	2	54	50	0	0	0	30	7	135	.311	5	20	151	.258	4	27
Bottalico, Ricky	9	6	.600	4.83	72.2	65	40	39	12	3	1	2	41	3	56	62	0	0	0	50	16	139	.237	6	17	133	.241	6	20
Durbin, Chad	2	5	.286	8.21	72.1	91	71	66	14	1	3	0	43	1	37	16	16	0	0	0	0	157	.299	6	26	145	.303	8	32
Meadows, Brian	6	2	.750	4.77	71.2	84	39	38	8	0	3	0	14	0	26	11	10	2	0	0	0	123	.285	4	19	164	.299	4	18
Fussell, Chris	5	3	.625	6.30	70.0	76	52	49	18	3	5	2	44	2	46	20	9	0	0	2	0	128	.313	9	23	138	.261	9	23
Santiago, Jose	8	6	.571	3.91	69.0	70	33	30	7	1	3	3	26	3	44	45	0	0	0	20	2	122	.303	5	25	147	.224	2	25
Batista, Miguel	2	6	.250	7.74	57.0	66	54	49	17	0	1	0	34	2	30	14	9	0	0	2	0	117	.308	10	30	109	.275	7	20
Wilson, Kris	0	1	.000	4.19	34.1	38	16	16	3	1	1	0	11	3	17	20	0	0	0	5	0	60	.267	1	8	72	.306	2	10
Rosado, Jose	2	2	.500	5.86	27.2	29	18	18	4	1	1	4	9	0	15	5	5	0	0	0	0	90	.267	4	13	17	.294	0	3
Rakers, Jason	2	0	1.000	9.14	21.2	33	22	22	5	0	1	0	7	0	16	11	0	0	0	3	0	44	.341	1	8	50	.360	4	12
Murray, Dan	0	0	.000	4.66	19.1	20	10	10	7	2	1	1	10	0	16	10	0	0	0	3	0	40	.300	5	7	32	.250	2	4
Larkin, Andy	0	3	.000	8.84	19.1	29	20	19	5	2	1	0	11	2	17	18	0	0	0	9	1	47	.255	2	12	36	.472	3	12
Laxton, Brett	0	1	.000	8.10	16.2	23	15	15	0	1	0	2	10	1	14	6	1	0	0	1	0	30	.300	0	3	36	.389	0	7
D'Amico, Jeff M.	0	1	.000	9.22	13.2	19	14	14	2	1	0	0	15	1	9	7	1	0	0	1	0	29	.207	0	2	26	.500	2	10
Mullen, Scott	0	0	.000	4.35	10.1	10	5	5	2	0	0	0	3	0	7	11	0	0	0	5	0	20	.350	1	5	21	.143	1	2
Spoljaric, Paul	0	0	.000	6.52	9.2	9	7	7	4	1	0	0	5	0	6	13	0	0	0	4	0	14	.429	2	4	20	.150	2	5
Bochtler, Doug	0	2	.000	6.48	8.1	13	6	6	2	1	0	0	10	4	4	6	0	0	0	2	0	22	.318	1	4	13	.462	1	3
Rigby, Brad	0	0	.000	16.20	8.1	19	16	15	6	0	0	1	5	0	3	4	0	0	0	1	1	21	.476	4	12	24	.375	2	5
Byrdak, Tim	0	1	.000	11.37	6.1	11	8	8	3	0	0	0	4	0	8	12	0	0	0	1	0	13	.385	1	7	17	.353	2	7

DESIGNATED HITTERS

Name	AB	Avg.	HR	RBI
Sweeney, Mike	183	.301	9	41
Quinn, Mark	177	.243	6	21
Damon, Johnny	106	.330	0	10
Dye, Jermaine	40	.325	2	8
Dunwoody, Todd	39	.256	0	7
McCarty, Dave	23	.217	2	6
Beltran, Carlos	22	.273	0	6
Pose, Scott	5	.000	0	0
Randa, Joe	4	.500	0	2
Fabregas, Jorge	1	1.000	0	0
Reboulet, Jeff	0	-	0	0

INDIVIDUAL STATISTICS

FIELDING

FIRST BASEMEN

Player	Pct.	G	PO	A	E	TC	DP
Sweeney, Mike	.991	114	960	88	9	1057	107
McCarty, Dave	.992	63	463	59	4	526	62
Zaun, Gregg	1.000	1	1	0	0	1	0

SECOND BASEMEN

Player	Pct.	G	PO	A	E	TC	DP
Febles, Carlos	.978	99	165	285	10	460	76
Reboulet, Jeff	.982	50	71	143	4	218	36
Ordaz, Luis	1.000	22	27	30	0	57	10
Delgado, Wilson	1.000	19	28	70	0	98	15
Holbert, Ray	1.000	1	3	1	0	4	1
Zaun, Gregg	-	1	0	0	0	0	0

THIRD BASEMEN

Player	Pct.	G	PO	A	E	TC	DP
Randa, Joe	.957	156	132	293	19	444	30
Reboulet, Jeff	.813	11	4	9	3	16	2
Delgado, Wilson	1.000	3	0	2	0	2	0
Holbert, Ray	-	1	0	0	0	0	0

SHORTSTOPS

Player	Pct.	G	PO	A	E	TC	DP
Sanchez, Rey	.994	143	224	446	4	674	106
Ordaz, Luis	.986	38	37	35	1	73	14
Delgado, Wilson	.972	12	10	25	1	36	8
Reboulet, Jeff	.923	5	9	15	2	26	3
Holbert, Ray	1.000	1	1	1	0	2	1

OUTFIELDERS

Player	Pct.	G	PO	A	E	TC	DP
Dye, Jermaine	.976	146	277	11	7	295	3
Damon, Johnny	.986	133	334	6	5	345	1
Beltran, Carlos	.975	88	231	5	6	242	2
Quinn, Mark	.988	81	158	9	2	169	1
Dunwoody, Todd	.976	40	81	0	2	83	0
McCarty, Dave	.955	11	19	2	1	22	1
Pose, Scott	1.000	11	6	0	0	6	0
Brown, Dee	1.000	5	12	0	0	12	0

CATCHERS

Player	Pct.	G	PO	A	E	TC	DP	PB
Zaun, Gregg	.988	76	376	31	5	412	4	2
Fabregas, Jorge	.992	39	219	21	2	242	2	1
Johnson, Brian	.991	37	221	12	2	235	1	4
Ortiz, Hector	.993	26	130	18	1	149	1	0

PITCHERS

Player	Pct.	G	PO	A	E	TC	DP
Bottalico, Ricky	.929	62	6	7	1	14	1
Spradlin, Jerry	.917	50	4	7	1	12	1
Santiago, Jose	.933	45	5	9	1	15	0
Reichert, Dan	1.000	44	14	16	0	30	1
Suppan, Jeff	.944	35	14	20	2	36	0
Suzuki, Makoto	.972	32	20	15	1	36	2
Witasick, Jay	.917	22	5	6	1	12	0
Fussell, Chris	.929	20	9	4	1	14	0
Wilson, Kris	.917	20	2	9	1	12	0
Larkin, Andy	1.000	18	2	1	0	3	0
Stein, Blake	.941	17	8	8	1	17	0
Durbin, Chad	.938	16	8	7	1	16	2
Batista, Miguel	.875	14	3	4	1	8	0
Spoljaric, Paul	1.000	13	1	4	0	5	1
Byrdak, Tim	1.000	12	1	0	0	1	0
Meadows, Brian	1.000	11	6	7	0	13	0
Mullen, Scott	1.000	11	0	1	0	1	0
Rakers, Jason	1.000	11	1	0	0	1	0
Murray, Dan	1.000	10	4	4	0	8	0
D'Amico, Jeff M.	1.000	7	1	1	0	2	0
Bochtler, Doug	-	6	0	0	0	0	0
Laxton, Brett	-	6	0	0	0	0	0
Rosado, Jose	1.000	5	2	4	0	6	0
Rigby, Brad	1.000	4	3	0	0	3	0

PITCHING AGAINST EACH CLUB

Pitcher	Ana. W-L	Bal. W-L	Bos. W-L	Chi. W-L	Cle. W-L	Det. W-L	Min. W-L	N.Y. W-L	Oak. W-L	Sea. W-L	T.B. W-L	Tex. W-L	Tor. W-L	N.L. W-L	Total W-L
Batista, Miguel	0-1	0-0	0-0	0-0	0-1	0-0	0-0	0-0	1-0	1-1	0-0	0-1	0-0	0-2	2-6
Bochtler, Doug	0-0	0-0	0-0	0-1	0-0	0-1	0-0	0-0	0-0	0-0	0-0	0-0	0-0	0-0	0-2
Bottalico, Ricky	0-0	1-1	0-0	1-0	1-0	1-1	1-0	0-2	1-0	1-2	1-0	0-0	0-0	1-0	9-6
Byrdak, Tim	0-0	0-0	0-0	0-0	0-0	0-1	0-0	0-0	0-0	0-0	0-0	0-0	0-0	0-0	0-1
D'Amico, Jeff M.	0-0	0-0	0-0	0-0	0-0	0-0	0-0	0-0	0-1	0-0	0-0	0-0	0-0	0-0	0-1
Durbin, Chad	0-0	0-0	0-0	0-0	1-1	0-0	0-0	0-0	0-1	0-1	0-1	0-0	1-0	0-1	2-5
Fussell, Chris	1-0	0-0	0-0	2-0	0-0	1-0	1-0	0-1	0-1	0-0	0-0	0-0	0-1	0-0	5-3
Larkin, Andy	0-0	0-0	0-2	0-0	0-0	0-0	0-0	0-0	0-0	0-0	0-0	0-0	0-1	0-0	0-3
Laxton, Brett	0-0	0-0	0-0	0-0	0-0	0-0	0-0	0-0	0-0	0-1	0-0	0-0	0-0	0-0	0-1
Meadows, Brian	0-0	0-1	1-1	0-0	0-0	0-0	1-0	1-0	0-0	1-0	1-0	1-0	0-0	0-0	6-2
Mullen, Scott	0-0	0-0	0-0	0-0	0-0	0-0	0-0	0-0	0-0	0-0	0-0	0-0	0-0	0-0	0-0
Murray, Dan	0-0	0-0	0-0	0-0	0-0	0-0	0-0	0-0	0-0	0-0	0-0	0-0	0-0	0-0	0-0
Rakers, Jason	0-0	0-0	0-0	0-0	0-0	0-0	0-0	0-0	1-0	0-0	0-0	0-0	0-0	1-0	2-0
Reichert, Dan	1-1	1-0	2-0	0-1	0-2	1-1	1-0	0-0	1-2	0-1	1-0	0-1	0-0	0-1	8-10
Rigby, Brad	0-0	0-0	0-0	0-0	0-0	0-0	0-0	0-0	0-0	0-0	0-0	0-0	0-0	0-0	0-0
Rosado, Jose	0-0	0-0	0-0	0-0	0-0	0-0	0-1	0-1	0-0	1-0	0-0	0-0	1-0	0-0	2-2
Santiago, Jose	2-1	2-0	1-0	0-1	0-0	2-0	0-1	0-0	0-0	0-0	1-0	0-2	0-1	0-0	8-6
Spoljaric, Paul	0-0	0-0	0-0	0-0	0-0	0-0	0-0	0-0	0-0	0-0	0-0	0-0	0-0	0-0	0-0
Spradlin, Jerry	0-0	0-0	0-0	3-0	0-0	0-0	0-0	0-1	0-0	0-0	0-1	0-0	0-1	1-1	4-4
Stein, Blake	1-0	1-0	0-0	0-1	1-0	0-0	1-0	1-0	0-0	0-0	1-1	0-1	1-0	1-2	8-5
Suppan, Jeff	1-1	0-0	1-1	1-0	1-0	1-0	1-2	0-1	0-2	0-1	0-1	2-0	1-0	1-0	10-9
Suzuki, Makoto	0-1	2-0	1-0	0-1	2-1	0-1	1-0	0-1	0-0	0-0	0-1	0-2	0-1	2-1	8-10
Wilson, Kris	0-0	0-1	0-0	0-0	0-0	0-0	0-0	0-0	0-0	0-0	0-0	0-0	0-0	0-0	0-1
Witasick, Jay	0-1	0-0	0-0	0-0	1-0	1-0	0-1	0-1	0-1	0-1	0-0	0-0	0-1	1-2	3-8
Totals	6-6	7-3	6-4	7-5	7-5	7-5	7-5	2-8	4-8	4-8	5-5	3-7	4-6	8-10	77-85

INTERLEAGUE: Suppan 1-0, Stein 0-1, Suzuki 0-1 vs. Brewers; Stein 1-0, Reichert 0-1, Durbin 0-1 vs. Cubs; Suzuki 1-0, Stein 0-1, Witasick 0-1 vs. Astros; Spradlin 1-1, Rakers 1-0, Witasick 1-0, Bottalico 1-0, Batista 0-1 vs. Pirates; Suzuki 1-0, Witasick 0-1, Batista 0-1 vs. Cardinals. Total: 8-10.

MISCELLANEOUS

HOME RUNS BY PARK

At Anaheim (5): Beltran 2, McCarty 1, Randa 1, Dye 1.
At Baltimore (3): Dye 2, Randa 1.
At Boston (1): McCarty 1.
At Chicago (AL) (5): Dye 3, Sweeney 1, Quinn 1.
At Cleveland (4): McCarty 1, Randa 1, Zaun 1, Damon 1.
At Detroit (2): Zaun 1, Sweeney 1.
At Houston (6): Fabregas 1, Randa 1, Damon 1, Sweeney 1, Dye 1, Quinn 1.
At Kansas City (84): Sweeney 17, Dye 15, Quinn 12, Damon 10, Randa 9, McCarty 6, Beltran 4, Johnson 3, Fabregas 2, Zaun 2, Febles 2, Sanchez 1, Dunwoody 1.
At Minnesota (9): Quinn 4, Sweeney 2, Dye 2, McCarty 1.
At New York (AL) (2): Zaun 1, Sweeney 1.
At Oakland (2): McCarty 1, Quinn 1.
At Pittsburgh (6): Dye 3, Johnson 1, Zaun 1, Sweeney 1.
At Seattle (8): Sweeney 3, Damon 2, Dye 2, McCarty 1.
At St. Louis (1): Dye 1.
At Tampa Bay (3): Sweeney 1, Dye 1, Quinn 1.
At Texas (4): Zaun 1, Damon 1, Dye 1, Beltran 1.
At Toronto (5): Randa 2, Damon 1, Sweeney 1, Dye 1.

LOW-HIT GAMES

No-hitters: None.
One-hitters: None.
Two-hitters: None.

10-STRIKEOUT GAMES

Total: 0

FOUR OR MORE HITS IN ONE GAME

Johnny Damon 9 (including two five-hit games), Mike Sweeney 8, Joe Randa 3, Jermaine Dye 2, Todd Dunwoody 2, Rey Sanchez 1, Dave McCarty 1, Carlos Febles 1, Mark Quinn 1, Total: 28

MULTI-HOMER GAMES

Jermaine Dye 3, Mike Sweeney 2, Mark Quinn 2, Joe Randa 1, Johnny Damon 1, Carlos Beltran 1, Total: 10

GRAND SLAMS

4-26: Jermaine Dye (off Tampa Bay's Ryan Rupe)
7-3: Jorge Fabregas (off Chicago's Kevin Beirne)
7-19: Dave McCarty (off Cleveland's Chuck Finley)
9-1: Jermaine Dye (off Tampa Bay's Ryan Rupe)
9-3: Mark Quinn (off Tampa Bay's Dave Eiland)
9-15: Johnny Damon (off Texas's Jeff Zimmerman)

PINCH HITTERS

(Minimum 5 at-bats)

Name	AB	Avg.	HR	RBI
Pose, Scott	27	.222	0	1
McCarty, Dave	23	.391	1	9
Zaun, Gregg	14	.357	0	2
Dunwoody, Todd	14	.071	0	0
Brown, Dee	11	.273	0	4
Ordaz, Luis	7	.286	0	0
Delgado, Wilson	6	.167	0	0
Quinn, Mark	5	.200	0	2

DEBUTS

6-3: Jeff M. D'Amico, P.
7-28: Kris Wilson, P.
8-31: Scott Mullen, P.

GAMES BY POSITION

Catcher: Gregg Zaun 76, Jorge Fabregas 39, Brian Johnson 37, Hector Ortiz 26.
First base: Mike Sweeney 114, Dave McCarty 63, Gregg Zaun 1.
Second base: Carlos Febles 99, Jeff Reboulet 50, Luis Ordaz 22, Wilson Delgado 19, Ray Holbert 1, Gregg Zaun 1.
Third base: Joe Randa 156, Jeff Reboulet 11, Wilson Delgado 3, Ray Holbert 1.
Shortstop: Rey Sanchez 143, Luis Ordaz 38, Wilson Delgado 12, Jeff Reboulet 5, Ray Holbert 1.
Outfield: Jermaine Dye 146, Johnny Damon 133, Carlos Beltran 88, Mark Quinn 81, Todd Dunwoody 40, Scott Pose 11, Dave McCarty 11, Dee Brown 5.
Designated hitter: Mark Quinn 48, Mike Sweeney 45, Johnny Damon 25, Todd Dunwoody 11, Jermaine Dye 10, Dave McCarty 7, Carlos Beltran 7, Scott Pose 4, Jeff Reboulet 1, Jorge Fabregas 1, Joe Randa 1.

STREAKS

Wins: 5 (May 5-10, July 18-22)
Losses: 9 (April 14-23)
Consecutive games with at least one hit: 16, Johnny Damon (August 5-21) Mike Sweeney (August 13-30)
Wins by pitcher: 4, Brian Meadows (September 1-16)

ATTENDANCE

Home: 1,677,915
Road: 2,286,526
Highest (home): 40,474 (April 7 vs. Minnesota).
Highest (road): 43,827 (August 19 vs. Baltimore).
Lowest (home): 11,442 (September 20 vs. Anaheim).
Lowest (road): 6,630 (April 18 vs. Minnesota).

MINNESOTA TWINS

2000 REVIEW

DAY BY DAY

Date	Opp.	Res.	Score	(inn.*)	Hits	Opp. hits	Winning pitcher	Losing pitcher	Save	Record	Pos.	GB
4-3	T.B.	L	0-7		8	14	Trachsel	Radke		0-1	T3rd	1.0
4-4	T.B.	W	6-5		11	9	Carrasco	Hernandez		1-1	T2nd	0.5
4-5	T.B.	W	10-7		12	13	Guardado	White		2-1	1st	+0.5
4-6	T.B.	L	6-7		13	10	Mecir	Carrasco	Hernandez	2-2	T1st	...
4-7	At K.C.	L	6-10		12	15	Fussell	Miller		2-3	4th	1.0
4-8	At K.C.	L	2-5		6	10	Suppan	Radke	Santiago	2-4	4th	2.0
4-9	At K.C.	W	13-7		16	9	Milton	Witasick		3-4	4th	1.5
4-10	At K.C.	L	5-6		8	14	Bottalico	Hawkins		3-5	4th	2.5
4-11	At Bos.	L	4-13		9	16	R. Martinez	Mays		3-6	4th	3.5
4-12	At Bos.	L	3-7		9	10	Fassero	Santana		3-7	4th	4.5
4-13	At Bos.	L	3-4		7	7	Wakefield	Wells	Lowe	3-8	5th	5.0
4-14	Bal.	W	10-9		12	16	Redman	Groom	Guardado	4-8	5th	4.0
4-15	Bal.	L	4-6		9	15	Worrell	Miller	Trombley	4-9	5th	4.0
4-16	Bal.	L	0-5		4	8	Ponson	Mays		4-10	5th	5.0
4-18	K.C.	W	3-1		7	6	Radke	Suppan	Wells	5-10	4th	4.0
4-19	K.C.	W	7-6		9	10	Carrasco	Santiago		6-10	4th	3.5
4-20	K.C.	W	9-7		13	12	Bergman	Rosado	Wells	7-10	4th	3.0
4-21	At Tex.	W	10-5		12	15	Carrasco	Clark		8-10	T3rd	3.0
4-22	At Tex.	L	3-8		11	11	Loaiza	Santana		8-11	T3rd	4.0
4-23	At Tex.	W	5-4		13	11	Radke	Oliver	Wells	9-11	3rd	4.0
4-24	At N.Y.	W	7-3		6	5	Milton	Clemens		10-11	3rd	4.0
4-25	At N.Y.	W	6-1		10	7	Bergman	Mendoza		11-11	3rd	3.0
4-26	At N.Y.	L	0-2		5	6	Nelson	Mays	Rivera	11-12	3rd	4.0
4-28	Oak.	L	2-5		7	6	Heredia	Radke	Isringhausen	11-13	4th	5.5
4-29	Oak.	L	2-6	(10)	10	7	Mathews	Guardado		11-14	4th	6.5
4-30	Oak.	L	2-8		7	14	Hudson	Bergman		11-15	4th	6.5
5-2	Sea.	L	4-5		10	9	Halama	Mays	Sasaki	11-16	4th	6.0
5-3	Sea.	W	5-4	(10)	10	12	Guardado	Mesa		12-16	4th	6.0
5-4	Det.	L	6-8	(11)	12	10	Anderson	Wells	Jones	12-17	4th	6.5
5-5	Det.	L	8-10		11	14	Patterson	Carrasco	Jones	12-18	4th	6.5
5-6	Det.	W	6-1		8	10	Redman	Nitkowski		13-18	4th	5.5
5-7	Det.	W	4-0		6	5	Mays	Johnson		14-18	4th	4.5
5-8	Cle.	L	2-3	(10)	9	10	Rincon	Wells	Karsay	14-19	4th	4.5
5-9	Cle.	W	6-5		6	13	Hawkins	Finley	Miller	15-19	4th	4.5
5-10	Cle.	W	10-9		13	14	Guardado	Karsay		16-19	4th	3.5
5-12	At Chi.	W	4-3	(10)	12	9	Miller	Lowe	Carrasco	17-19	4th	2.5
5-13	At Chi.	L	3-4		8	8	Wunsch	Wells		17-20	4th	3.5
5-14	At Chi.	L	3-5		8	10	Wunsch	Radke	Foulke	17-21	4th	4.5
5-15	At Sea.	L	0-14		2	16	Sele	Milton		17-22	4th	5.0
5-16	At Sea.	L	5-9		10	9	Meche	Bergman		17-23	4th	6.0
5-17	At Sea.	L	0-4		4	6	Halama	Mays		17-24	4th	6.0
5-18	At Oak.	W	10-5		18	7	Redman	Vizcaino		18-24	4th	5.5
5-19	At Oak.	W	3-2		9	3	Radke	Heredia		19-24	4th	5.5
5-20	At Oak.	W	3-0		9	3	Milton	Mulder	Guardado	20-24	4th	5.5
5-21	At Oak.	L	4-13		11	15	Hudson	Bergman		20-25	4th	6.5
5-23	Ana.	L	4-7		7	12	Cooper	Mays	Percival	20-26	4th	7.0
5-24	Ana.	L	5-6	(10)	7	18	Percival	Wells	Levine	20-27	4th	7.0
5-25	Ana.	L	1-3		7	9	Schoeneweis	Radke	Percival	20-28	4th	7.0
5-26	Tex.	W	10-2		16	5	Milton	Oliver		21-28	4th	7.0
5-27	Tex.	W	10-5		10	8	Mays	Clark		22-28	4th	7.0
5-28	Tex.	W	4-3		7	8	Bergman	Helling	Hawkins	23-28	4th	6.0
5-30	At Tor.	W	4-1		10	5	Redman	Escobar	Hawkins	24-28	4th	5.5
5-31	At Tor.	L	2-4		9	6	Wells	Radke	Koch	24-29	4th	6.5
6-1	At Tor.	W	5-1		6	6	Milton	Castillo		25-29	4th	6.0
6-2	At Cin.	L	3-4		7	10	Bell	Mays	Graves	25-30	4th	7.0
6-3	At Cin.	L	3-9		4	8	Neagle	Bergman		25-31	4th	7.0
6-4	At Cin.	L	2-3	(10)	9	9	Graves	Hawkins		25-32	4th	8.0
6-5	At Hou.	L	2-8		8	11	Elarton	Radke		25-33	4th	9.0
6-6	At Hou.	W	3-1		6	6	Santana	Lima	Guardado	26-33	4th	9.0
6-7	At Hou.	W	2-0		9	6	Mays	Reynolds	Guardado	27-33	4th	9.0
6-9	Mil.	W	9-6		10	10	Bergman	Wright		28-33	4th	9.0
6-10	Mil.	L	3-5		7	13	Haynes	Redman	Wickman	28-34	4th	10.0
6-11	Mil.	L	3-5		10	13	Snyder	Radke	Wickman	28-35	4th	10.0
6-12	Oak.	W	7-2		8	9	Milton	Heredia		29-35	4th	10.0
6-13	Oak.	L	5-6		12	13	Mulder	Mays	Isringhausen	29-36	4th	11.0
6-14	Oak.	L	6-9		8	16	Hudson	Bergman		29-37	4th	12.0
6-15	Sea.	L	5-12		8	18	Ramsay	Redman		29-38	4th	13.0
6-16	Sea.	W	7-2		12	4	Radke	Sele		30-38	4th	13.0
6-17	Sea.	L	3-12		7	17	Moyer	Milton		30-39	4th	14.0
6-18	Sea.	L	2-10		6	12	Meche	Mays		30-40	4th	15.0
6-20	At Tex.	L	2-5		5	13	Rogers	Redman	Wetteland	30-41	4th	15.5
6-21	At Tex.	L	5-7		12	11	Loaiza	Radke	Wetteland	30-42	4th	15.5
6-22	At Tex.	W	3-2		6	9	Hawkins	Crabtree	Wells	31-42	4th	15.5
6-23	At Ana.	L	3-8		8	11	Etherton	Ryan	Levine	31-43	4th	16.5
6-24	At Ana.	W	11-5		16	11	Milton	Bottenfield		32-43	4th	15.5
6-25	At Ana.	L	6-7	(11)	11	10	Hasegawa	Guardado		32-44	4th	16.5
6-26	At Ana.	W	10-6		13	11	Radke	Washburn		33-44	4th	16.0
6-27	At Chi.	W	7-4		12	9	Mays	Baldwin	Wells	34-44	4th	15.0
6-28	At Chi.	L	3-7		4	14	Eldred	Lincoln		34-45	5th	16.0
6-29	At Chi.	W	10-1		15	6	Milton	Wells		35-45	4th	15.0
6-30	At Cle.	W	7-2		16	7	Redman	Brower	Hawkins	36-45	4th	15.0

HIGHLIGHTS

High point: On July 3, the Twins signed pitcher Brad Radke to a $36 million contract extension that could keep him with the club through 2004. That move provided unusual hope for a team that played the 2000 season with a $16.5 million payroll. Radke's signing and the long-term extension signed by shortstop Cristian Guzman appear to be first steps toward keeping together a corps of young players that includes Eric Milton, Corey Koskie, Jacque Jones and Matt Lawton.
Low point: When Todd Walker was sent to the minors on May 4, the former No. 1 pick fired some shots at manager Tom Kelly. Walker ripped Kelly's handling of young players—and several former Twins echoed his criticism. The jabs hurt worse when Walker was traded to Colorado and hit .316 over the final two months.
Turning point: Opening day, when the Twins were blanked 7-0 by Tampa Bay before 43,830 fans at the Metrodome. It only got worse as the Twins suffered through their eighth consecutive losing season.
Most valuable player: No contest. Matt Lawton, the team's only All-Star representative, led the Twins in batting (.305), hits (171), doubles (44), RBIs (88) and multi-hit games (46). Lawton's numbers could have been better if not for a severely bruised toe that bothered him over the final two months.
Most valuable pitcher: After a dismal spring and first three weeks, LaTroy Hawkins righted himself and emerged as the team's leading closer candidate. The righthander recorded a 3.41 ERA in 66 appearances and was a perfect 14-of-14 in save opportunities.
Most improved player: After seeing his average dip to .190 after his recall in late July, Torii Hunter caught fire, providing hope that the organization had found its everyday center fielder. Hunter batted .355 with five homers and 33 RBIs over the final 49 games.
Most pleasant surprise: Mark Redman didn't get his first start until May 6, but the lefthander won 12 of his first 18 and finished with a 12-9 record. Only a season-ending knee injury kept him from making a serious run for Rookie of the Year honors.
Key injuries: The Twins were one of the healthiest teams in baseball. Lawton suffered his toe injury in late July and did not start the next six games. Redman and Eric Milton both suffered September knee injuries, neither of which required surgery.
Notable: Kelly managed his 1,000th victory May 7 against Detroit. ... The Twins finished last in the major leagues with 116 home runs—34 fewer than Kansas City's next-lowest total in the A.L. ... The Twins have played 17 rookies in each of the last two seasons. ... Guzman tied a franchise record with 20 triples.

—DENNIS BRACKIN

MISCELLANEOUS

RECORDS

2000 regular-season record: 69-93 (5th in A.L. Central); 36-45 at home; 33-48 on road; 19-29 vs. East; 31-37 vs. Central; 19-27 vs. West; 11-29 vs. lefthanded starters; 58-64 vs. righthanded starters; 28-37 on grass; 41-56 on turf; 22-27 in daytime; 47-66 at night; 22-26 in one-run games; 7-9 in extra-inning games; 0-0-0 in doubleheaders.
Team record past five years: 348-460 (.431, ranks 12th in league in that span).

TEAM LEADERS

Batting average: Matt Lawton (.305).
At-bats: Cristian Guzman (631).
Runs: Cristian Guzman (89).
Hits: Matt Lawton (171).
Total Bases: Matt Lawton (258).
Doubles: Matt Lawton (44).
Triples: Cristian Guzman (20).
Home runs: Jacque Jones (19).
Runs batted in: Matt Lawton (88).
Stolen bases: Cristian Guzman (28).
Slugging percentage: Jacque Jones (.463).
On-base percentage: Matt Lawton (.405).
Wins: Eric Milton (13).
Earned-run average: Brad Radke (4.45).
Complete games: Brad Radke (4).
Shutouts: Joe Mays, Brad Radke (1).
Saves: LaTroy Hawkins (14).
Innings pitched: Brad Radke (226.2).
Strikeouts: Eric Milton (160).

Date	Opp.	Res.	Score	(inn.*)	Hits	Opp. hits	Winning pitcher	Losing pitcher	Save	Record	Pos.	GB
7-1	At Cle.	W	4-3	(10)	9	8	Guardado	Karsay	Wells	37-45	4th	15.0
7-2	At Cle.	L	1-7		6	11	Finley	Mays		37-46	5th	16.0
7-3	Bos.	L	8-11		13	15	Pichardo	Lincoln	Lowe	37-47	5th	17.0
7-4	Bos.	L	4-14		10	18	Wakefield	Milton	Florie	37-48	5th	17.0
7-5	Bos.	L	8-11		10	12	Wasdin	Redman	Lowe	37-49	5th	18.0
7-6	Bos.	L	7-8		12	8	Crawford	Radke		37-50	5th	18.5
7-7	At Pit.	L	6-8		9	13	Christiansen	Wells	Williams	37-51	5th	19.5
7-8	At Pit.	L	1-4		5	8	Benson	Milton	Williams	37-52	5th	19.5
7-9	At Pit.	W	3-2		8	8	Redman	Silva	Hawkins	38-52	5th	18.5
7-13	Chi. (NL)	W	5-1		11	6	Radke	Valdes	Hawkins	39-52	5th	17.5
7-14	Chi. (NL)	L	2-6		8	12	Lieber	Milton		39-53	5th	17.5
7-15	Chi. (NL)	L	4-8		13	13	Tapani	Mays		39-54	5th	18.5
7-16	StL.	W	5-2		10	6	Redman	Ankiel	Guardado	40-54	5th	18.5
7-17	StL.	L	3-8		11	13	Hentgen	Lincoln		40-55	5th	19.5
7-18	StL.	W	3-2		7	9	Radke	An. Benes	Hawkins	41-55	5th	19.5
7-19	Chi.	L	2-3		8	9	Buehrle	Milton	Foulke	41-56	5th	20.5
7-20	Chi.	W	5-1		12	6	Mays	Parque		42-56	5th	19.5
7-21	Cle.	W	2-1		8	8	Redman	Colon	Hawkins	43-56	5th	19.5
7-22	Cle.	W	10-6		18	10	Santana	Davis	Wells	44-56	5th	18.5
7-23	Cle.	L	3-8		7	12	Burba	Radke		44-57	5th	18.5
7-24	At Bos.	W	4-2		14	6	Milton	Ohka		45-57	5th	18.5
7-25	At Bos.	W	4-2		8	8	Mays	R. Martinez	Guardado	46-57	5th	17.5
7-27	N.Y.	W	9-3		12	9	Redman	Cone		47-57	5th	17.0
7-28	N.Y.	L	5-9		5	17	Rivera	Guardado		47-58	5th	17.0
7-29	N.Y.	W	6-2		8	2	Milton	Mendoza		48-58	5th	16.0
7-30	N.Y.	L	4-7		9	12	Pettitte	Mays		48-59	5th	17.0
7-31	At Bal.	L	5-6		9	9	Ponson	Romero	Trombley	48-60	5th	17.5
8-1	At Bal.	L	0-10		1	13	Mussina	Redman		48-61	5th	18.5
8-2	At Bal.	W	10-6		14	12	Radke	Rapp		49-61	5th	17.5
8-4	At Det.	W	3-1		10	4	Milton	Nitkowski	Wells	50-61	4th	16.5
8-5	At Det.	L	3-4		9	6	Sparks	Mays	Jones	50-62	5th	17.5
8-6	At Det.	W	7-3		10	10	Romero	Weaver		51-62	5th	17.5
8-7	At T.B.	W	4-2		9	6	Redman	Rekar	Guardado	52-62	5th	17.0
8-8	At T.B.	L	0-5		4	10	Lopez	Radke		52-63	5th	16.5
8-9	At T.B.	L	4-5	(10)	13	11	Taylor	Hawkins		52-64	5th	17.5
8-10	At T.B.	L	4-10		9	7	Sturtze	Mays		52-65	5th	17.5
8-11	Tor.	W	9-4		13	8	Romero	Escobar		53-65	5th	17.5
8-12	Tor.	W	6-3		13	10	Redman	Loaiza	Hawkins	54-65	5th	17.5
8-13	Tor.	L	3-13		8	20	Carpenter	Radke		54-66	5th	17.5
8-15	K.C.	W	6-2		11	5	Milton	Suppan	Wells	55-66	5th	17.0
8-16	K.C.	L	3-9		7	16	Meadows	Romero		55-67	5th	18.0
8-17	K.C.	L	4-8		9	15	Reichert	Redman		55-68	5th	18.0
8-18	At Tor.	L	2-3		8	8	Loaiza	Kinney	Koch	55-69	5th	19.0
8-19	At Tor.	W	5-1		8	8	Radke	Guthrie	Guardado	56-69	5th	19.0
8-20	At Tor.	L	3-6		9	10	Wells	Carrasco		56-70	5th	19.0
8-22	T.B.	L	2-3		5	5	Rupe	Romero	Hernandez	56-71	5th	19.0
8-23	T.B.	W	8-2		13	5	Redman	Rekar	Hawkins	57-71	5th	19.0
8-25	Det.	W	8-3		10	7	Radke	Blair	Wells	58-71	5th	18.5
8-26	Det.	L	2-8		5	11	Sparks	Milton		58-72	5th	18.5
8-27	Det.	W	7-6	(10)	11	9	Carrasco	Jones		59-72	5th	18.5
8-29	At K.C.	L	3-7		5	10	Stein	Romero		59-73	5th	19.0
8-30	At K.C.	L	7-8		17	14	Suzuki	Redman	Bottalico	59-74	5th	20.0
9-1	At N.Y.	L	2-4		6	10	Hernandez	Radke	Rivera	59-75	5th	21.0
9-2	At N.Y.	L	4-13	(8)	10	11	Neagle	Milton	Grimsley	59-76	5th	22.0
9-3	At N.Y.	W	2-1	(10)	4	5	Guardado	Rivera	Hawkins	60-76	5th	22.0
9-4	Bal.	L	2-3		10	9	Mercedes	Redman	Kohlmeier	60-77	5th	22.0
9-5	Bal.	L	5-6		14	10	Mussina	Romero	Kohlmeier	60-78	5th	22.0
9-6	Bal.	W	4-1		9	6	Radke	Ponson		61-78	5th	22.0
9-7	At Bos.	L	6-11		9	16	R. Martinez	Milton		61-79	5th	23.0
9-8	At Sea.	W	4-2		10	6	Kinney	Abbott	Hawkins	62-79	5th	23.0
9-9	At Sea.	L	2-7		5	10	Moyer	Redman		62-80	5th	23.0
9-10	At Sea.	L	1-8		7	8	Sele	Romero		62-81	5th	23.5
9-12	At Oak.	L	3-5		6	10	Mulder	Radke	Isringhausen	62-82	5th	24.0
9-13	At Oak.	W	7-6		17	9	Milton	Heredia	Hawkins	63-82	5th	24.0
9-15	Ana.	L	5-16		9	21	Karl	Kinney		63-83	5th	24.0
9-16	Ana.	L	6-7		8	13	Hasegawa	Hawkins	Percival	63-84	5th	25.0
9-17	Ana.	W	1-0		5	8	Radke	Belcher		64-84	5th	24.0
9-18	Tex.	W	3-1		7	10	Mays	Helling	Guardado	65-84	5th	23.0
9-19	Tex.	W	15-7		20	10	Kinney	Glynn		66-84	5th	23.0
9-20	Tex.	L	4-6	(12)	11	10	Wetteland	Miller	Venafro	66-85	5th	24.0
9-21	Chi.	L	4-9		11	11	Sirotka	Santana		66-86	5th	25.0
9-22	Chi.	L	4-5		12	10	Barcelo	Wells	Foulke	66-87	5th	26.0
9-23	Chi.	L	3-5		8	8	Parque	Milton	Foulke	66-88	5th	27.0
9-24	Chi.	W	6-5	(10)	10	12	Guardado	Beirne		67-88	5th	26.0
9-25	At Cle.	W	4-3		10	11	Miller	Shuey	Hawkins	68-88	5th	25.0
9-26	At Cle.	L	2-4		8	8	Finley	Romero	Wickman	68-89	5th	25.0
9-27	At Cle.	L	2-8		7	13	Bere	Radke		68-90	5th	25.0
9-28	At Cle.	W	4-3	(10)	7	9	Guardado	Wickman	Hawkins	69-90	5th	24.0
9-29	At Det.	L	0-1		7	7	Weaver	Mays	Jones	69-91	5th	25.0
9-30	At Det.	L	5-6	(11)	13	13	Jones	Hawkins		69-92	5th	26.0
10-1	At Det.	L	11-12		15	19	Jones	Guardado		69-93	5th	26.0

Monthly records: April (11-15), May (13-14), June (12-16), July (12-15), August (11-14), September (10-18), October (0-1).

*Innings, if other than nine. † First game of a doubleheader. ‡ Second game of a doubleheader.

MEMORABLE GAMES

April 15 at Minneapolis

The biggest Metrodome moment belonged to Baltimore third baseman Cal Ripken, who posted his 3,000th career hit in a 6-4 Orioles' victory. Ripken collected three singles between the fourth and seventh innings to become the 24th major leaguer to reach the 3,000 milestone. His final single of the night, his 3,000th hit, came off Twins reliever Hector Carrasco in a decisive seventh inning.

Baltimore	AB	R	H	BI	Minnesota	AB	R	H	BI
Anderson, cf	5	1	2	0	Walker, 2b	5	0	1	1
Bordick, ss	5	1	2	1	Guzman, ss	3	1	2	0
Surhoff, lf	5	1	3	2	Lawton, rf	2	1	1	0
Belle, rf	4	1	1	0	Huskey, dh	4	0	1	0
Baines, dh	5	1	2	0	Koskie, 3b	4	1	1	2
Ripken 3b	5	0	3	0	Coomer, 1b	4	0	2	1
Conine, 1b	4	0	1	1	LeCroy, c	3	0	0	0
Johnson, c	4	1	1	1	Jones, lf	4	0	0	0
Garcia, 2b	4	0	0	0	Hunter, cf	3	1	1	0
					Cummings, ph	1	0	0	0
Totals	**41**	**6**	**15**	**5**	**Totals**	**33**	**4**	**9**	**4**

Baltimore..............................1 1 0 1 1 0 1 0 1—6 15 0
Minnesota..............................0 0 0 3 1 0 0 0 0—4 9 1

E—Walker (2). DP—Baltimore 2, Minnesota 2. LOB—Baltimore 9, Minnesota 6. 2B—Anderson 2 (2), Bordick (4), Belle (5), Coomer (2). 3B—Koskie (2), Hunter (2). HR—Surhoff (1), Johnson (5). SB—Bordick (2), Guzman (3). SH—Guzman.

Baltimore	IP	H	R	ER	BB	SO
Maduro	5	6	4	4	2	4
Worrell (W 2-1)	1.2	2	0	0	0	1
Ryan	1.1	1	0	0	0	1
Trombley (S 1)	1	0	0	0	0	0

Minnesota	IP	H	R	ER	BB	SO
Bergman	6	12	4	4	0	3
Miller (L 0-2)	0.2	1	1	1	0	1
Carrasco	0.2	1	0	0	0	0
Redman	1.2	1	1	1	0	0

HBP—Belle by Bergman, Lawton by Maduro. PB—LeCroy. U—HP, Froemming. 1B, Winters. 2B, Culbreth. 3B, Welke. T—2:49. A—18,745.

May 7 at Minneapolis

Manager Tom Kelly's 1,000th career victory was delivered by Joe Mays, who tossed a complete-game shutout and defeated Detroit, 4-0. For Mays, who allowed just five hits, it would be a game to remember. He was dispatched to the minors before the season ended.

Detroit	AB	R	H	BI	Minnesota	AB	R	H	BI
Polonia, rf	4	0	1	0	Guzman, ss	3	2	1	0
Ausmus, c	3	0	0	0	Canizaro, 2b	4	1	1	0
Encarnacion, cf	3	0	1	0	Lawton, rf	4	0	1	1
Gonzalez, dh	4	0	0	0	Coomer, 1b	3	0	0	1
Higginson, lf	4	0	0	0	Koskie, 3b	3	1	0	0
Palmer, 3b	4	0	1	0	Huskey, dh	1	0	0	0
Easley, 2b	3	0	0	0	Jones, lf	3	0	1	2
Clark, 1b	3	0	0	0	Jensen, c	3	0	1	0
Cruz, ss	3	0	2	0	Hunter, cf	4	0	1	0
Totals	**31**	**0**	**5**	**0**	**Totals**	**28**	**4**	**6**	**4**

Detroit..............................0 0 0 0 0 0 0 0 0—0 5 0
Minnesota..............................3 0 0 1 0 0 0 0 x—4 6 0

DP—Detroit 1, Minnesota 1. LOB—Detroit 6, Minnesota 10. 3B—Encarnacion (1), Guzman (7). S—Coomer.

Detroit	IP	H	R	ER	BB	SO
Johnson (L 0-1)	3.1	4	4	4	6	1
Blair	4.1	2	0	0	2	2
Anderson	0.1	0	0	0	0	1

Minnesota	IP	H	R	ER	BB	SO
Mays (W 1-4)	9	5	0	0	2	5

HBP—Huskey by Johnson. WP—Johnson, Mays. U—HP, Timmons. 1B, Foster. 2B, Kulpa. 3B, Hernandez. T—2:37. A—8,333.

BATTING

Name	G	TPA	AB	R	H	TB	2B	3B	HR	RBI	Avg.	Obp.	Slg.	SH	SF	HP	BB	IBB	SO	SB	CS	GDP	vs RHP AB	vs RHP Avg.	vs RHP HR	vs RHP RBI	vs LHP AB	vs LHP Avg.	vs LHP HR	vs LHP RBI
Guzman, Cristian	156	690	631	89	156	245	25	20	8	54	.247	.299	.388	7	4	2	46	1	101	28	10	5	459	.261	4	35	172	.209	4	19
Lawton, Matt	156	664	561	84	171	258	44	2	13	88	.305	.405	.460	0	5	7	91	8	63	23	7	10	398	.309	11	60	163	.294	2	28
Coomer, Ron	140	589	544	64	147	226	29	1	16	82	.270	.317	.415	0	5	4	36	2	50	2	0	25	419	.274	11	66	125	.256	5	16
Jones, Jacque	154	552	523	66	149	242	26	5	19	76	.285	.319	.463	1	0	0	26	4	111	7	5	17	449	.294	18	68	74	.230	1	8
Koskie, Corey	146	559	474	79	142	209	32	4	9	65	.300	.400	.441	1	3	4	77	7	104	5	4	11	384	.292	9	53	90	.333	0	12
Ortiz, David	130	478	415	59	117	185	36	1	10	63	.282	.364	.446	0	6	0	57	2	81	1	0	13	337	.249	9	50	78	.423	1	13
Hocking, Denny	134	433	373	52	111	155	24	4	4	47	.298	.373	.416	7	5	0	48	1	77	7	5	2	262	.305	2	27	111	.279	2	20
Canizaro, Jay	102	371	346	43	93	137	21	1	7	40	.269	.318	.396	0	0	1	24	0	57	4	2	8	253	.269	5	25	93	.269	2	15
Hunter, Torii	99	358	336	44	94	137	14	7	5	44	.280	.318	.408	0	2	2	18	2	68	4	3	13	253	.292	3	34	83	.241	2	10
Huskey, Butch	64	245	215	22	48	76	13	0	5	27	.223	.306	.353	0	3	2	25	1	49	0	2	5	135	.193	3	21	80	.275	2	6
Cummings, Midre	77	196	181	28	50	72	10	0	4	22	.276	.328	.398	1	0	3	11	1	25	0	0	4	156	.263	4	19	25	.360	0	3
LeCroy, Matt	56	190	167	18	29	54	10	0	5	17	.174	.254	.323	1	3	2	17	2	38	0	0	6	108	.176	4	15	59	.169	1	2
Jensen, Marcus	52	164	139	16	29	47	7	1	3	14	.209	.325	.338	1	0	0	24	0	36	0	1	3	114	.219	3	11	25	.160	0	3
Moeller, Chad	48	139	128	13	27	35	3	1	1	9	.211	.261	.273	1	1	0	9	0	33	1	0	4	83	.217	1	6	45	.200	0	3
Maxwell, Jason	64	124	111	14	27	36	6	0	1	11	.243	.298	.324	0	3	1	9	0	32	2	1	2	39	.282	1	4	72	.222	0	7
Pierzynski, A.J.	33	96	88	12	27	40	5	1	2	11	.307	.354	.455	0	1	2	5	0	14	1	0	1	84	.321	2	10	4	.000	0	1
Buchanan, Brian	30	93	82	10	19	25	3	0	1	8	.232	.301	.305	0	2	1	8	0	22	0	2	3	49	.184	1	6	33	.303	0	2
Walker, Todd	23	87	77	14	18	25	1	0	2	8	.234	.287	.325	0	3	0	7	0	10	3	0	3	75	.240	2	7	2	.000	0	1
Rivas, Luis	16	64	58	8	18	24	4	1	0	6	.310	.323	.414	2	2	0	2	0	4	2	0	2	39	.308	0	5	19	.316	0	1
Allen, Chad	15	55	50	2	15	18	3	0	0	7	.300	.345	.360	0	1	1	3	0	14	0	2	1	37	.324	0	6	13	.231	0	1
Barnes, John	11	41	37	5	13	17	4	0	0	2	.351	.415	.459	0	0	2	2	0	6	0	1	3	25	.240	0	0	12	.583	0	2
Ardoin, Danny	15	40	32	4	4	8	1	0	1	5	.125	.300	.250	0	0	0	8	0	10	0	0	0	25	.120	1	2	7	.143	0	3
Blake, Casey	7	21	16	1	3	5	2	0	0	1	.188	.333	.313	0	1	1	3	0	7	0	0	1	12	.083	0	0	4	.500	0	1
Mientkiewicz, Doug	3	15	14	0	6	6	0	0	0	4	.429	.400	.429	0	1	0	0	0	0	0	0	1	12	.417	0	1	2	.500	0	3
Mays, Joe	31	6	5	1	2	3	1	0	0	0	.400	.400	.600	1	0	0	0	0	2	0	0	0	5	.400	0	0	0	.000	0	0
Redman, Mark	32	5	4	0	0	0	0	0	0	0	.000	.000	.000	1	0	0	0	0	3	0	0	0	4	.000	0	0	0	.000	0	0
Bergman, Sean	15	2	2	0	1	2	1	0	0	0	.500	.500	1.000	0	0	0	0	0	1	0	0	0	0	.000	0	0	2	.500	0	0
Radke, Brad	34	2	2	0	0	0	0	0	0	0	.000	.000	.000	0	0	0	0	0	2	0	0	0	2	.000	0	0	0	.000	0	0
Milton, Eric	33	2	2	0	0	0	0	0	0	0	.000	.000	.000	0	0	0	0	0	0	0	0	0	2	.000	0	0	0	.000	0	0
Hawkins, LaTroy	66	1	1	0	0	0	0	0	0	0	.000	.000	.000	0	0	0	0	0	1	0	0	0	1	.000	0	0	0	.000	0	0
Santana, Johan	30	1	1	0	0	0	0	0	0	0	.000	.000	.000	0	0	0	0	0	0	0	0	0	1	.000	0	0	0	.000	0	0
Guardado, Eddie	70	0	0	0	0	0	0	0	0	0	.000	.000	.000	0	0	0	0	0	0	0	0	0	0	.000	0	0	0	.000	0	0
Carrasco, Hector	61	0	0	0	0	0	0	0	0	0	.000	.000	.000	0	0	0	0	0	0	0	0	0	0	.000	0	0	0	.000	0	0
Wells, Bob	76	0	0	0	0	0	0	0	0	0	.000	.000	.000	0	0	0	0	0	0	0	0	0	0	.000	0	0	0	.000	0	0
Miller, Travis	67	0	0	0	0	0	0	0	0	0	.000	.000	.000	0	0	0	0	0	0	0	0	0	0	.000	0	0	0	.000	0	0
Lincoln, Mike	8	0	0	0	0	0	0	0	0	0	.000	.000	.000	0	0	0	0	0	0	0	0	0	0	.000	0	0	0	.000	0	0
Ryan, Jason	16	0	0	0	0	0	0	0	0	0	.000	.000	.000	0	0	0	0	0	0	0	0	0	0	.000	0	0	0	.000	0	0
Romero, J.C.	12	0	0	0	0	0	0	0	0	0	.000	.000	.000	0	0	0	0	0	0	0	0	0	0	.000	0	0	0	.000	0	0
Kinney, Matt	8	0	0	0	0	0	0	0	0	0	.000	.000	.000	0	0	0	0	0	0	0	0	0	0	.000	0	0	0	.000	0	0
Cressend, Jack	11	0	0	0	0	0	0	0	0	0	.000	.000	.000	0	0	0	0	0	0	0	0	0	0	.000	0	0	0	.000	0	0
Mota, Danny	4	0	0	0	0	0	0	0	0	0	.000	.000	.000	0	0	0	0	0	0	0	0	0	0	.000	0	0	0	.000	0	0

Players with more than one A.L. team

Name	G	TPA	AB	R	H	TB	2B	3B	HR	RBI	Avg.	Obp.	Slg.	SH	SF	HP	BB	IBB	SO	SB	CS	GDP	vs RHP AB	vs RHP Avg.	vs RHP HR	vs RHP RBI	vs LHP AB	vs LHP Avg.	vs LHP HR	vs LHP RBI
Carrasco, Bos.	8	0	0	0	0	0	0	0	0	0	.000	.000	.000	0	0	0	0	0	0	0	0	0	0	.000	0	0	0	.000	0	0
Carrasco, Min.-Bos.	69	0	0	0	0	0	0	0	0	0	.000	.000	.000	0	0	0	0	0	0	0	0	0	0	.000	0	0	0	.000	0	0
Cummings, Bos.	21	31	25	1	7	7	0	0	0	2	.280	.419	.280	0	0	0	6	0	3	0	0	1	156	.263	4	19	25	.360	0	3
Cummings, Min.-Bos.	98	227	206	29	57	79	10	0	4	24	.277	.341	.383	1	0	3	17	1	28	0	0	5	181	.265	4	21	25	.360	0	3

PITCHING

Name	W	L	Pct.	ERA	IP	H	R	ER	HR	SH	SF	HB	BB	IBB	SO	G	GS	CG	ShO	GF	Sv	vs. RH AB	vs. RH Avg.	vs. RH HR	vs. RH RBI	vs. LH AB	vs. LH Avg.	vs. LH HR	vs. LH RBI
Radke, Brad	12	16	.429	4.45	226.2	261	119	112	27	7	4	5	51	1	141	34	34	4	1	0	0	412	.274	11	45	499	.297	16	63
Milton, Eric	13	10	.565	4.86	200.0	205	123	108	35	4	6	7	44	0	160	33	33	0	0	0	0	638	.265	28	82	149	.242	7	21
Mays, Joe	7	15	.318	5.56	160.1	193	105	99	20	3	5	2	67	1	102	31	28	2	1	1	0	336	.298	10	43	310	.300	10	44
Redman, Mark	12	9	.571	4.76	151.1	168	81	80	22	3	2	3	45	0	117	32	24	0	0	3	0	449	.281	17	63	149	.282	5	20
Hawkins, LaTroy	2	5	.286	3.39	87.2	85	34	33	7	4	1	1	32	1	59	66	0	0	0	38	14	204	.265	3	19	128	.242	4	16
Wells, Bob	0	7	.000	3.65	86.1	80	39	35	14	3	5	4	15	2	76	76	0	0	0	25	10	204	.255	13	41	120	.233	1	10
Santana, Johan	2	3	.400	6.49	86.0	102	64	62	11	1	3	2	54	0	64	30	5	0	0	9	0	243	.317	8	38	95	.263	3	14
Carrasco, Hector	4	3	.571	4.25	72.0	75	38	34	6	6	4	3	33	0	57	61	0	0	0	18	1	176	.273	3	25	101	.267	3	20
Bergman, Sean	4	5	.444	9.66	68.0	111	76	73	18	2	3	2	33	1	35	15	14	0	0	0	0	162	.346	8	36	135	.407	10	32
Miller, Travis	2	3	.400	3.90	67.0	83	35	29	4	1	3	1	32	2	62	67	0	0	0	12	1	174	.328	3	27	105	.248	1	10
Guardado, Eddie	7	4	.636	3.94	61.2	55	27	27	14	3	2	1	25	3	52	70	0	0	0	36	9	144	.208	9	17	87	.287	5	19
Romero, J.C.	2	7	.222	7.02	57.2	72	51	45	8	4	2	1	30	0	50	12	11	0	0	0	0	174	.322	7	33	57	.281	1	10
Kinney, Matt	2	2	.500	5.10	42.1	41	26	24	7	0	4	0	25	1	24	8	8	0	0	0	0	62	.194	3	9	95	.305	4	13
Ryan, Jason	0	1	.000	7.62	26.0	37	24	22	8	0	2	1	10	0	19	16	1	0	0	6	0	63	.286	3	10	49	.388	5	16
Lincoln, Mike	0	3	.000	10.89	20.2	36	25	25	10	0	0	2	13	0	15	8	4	0	0	1	0	49	.388	7	16	45	.378	3	8
Cressend, Jack	0	0	.000	5.27	13.2	20	8	8	0	0	0	0	6	0	6	11	0	0	0	4	0	35	.371	0	11	20	.350	0	1
Mota, Danny	0	0	.000	8.44	5.1	10	5	5	1	0	0	0	1	0	3	4	0	0	0	3	0	15	.333	1	5	12	.417	0	5

PITCHERS WITH MORE THAN ONE A.L. TEAM

Name	W	L	Pct.	ERA	IP	H	R	ER	HR	SH	SF	HB	BB	IBB	SO	G	GS	CG	ShO	GF	Sv	vs. RH AB	vs. RH Avg.	vs. RH HR	vs. RH RBI	vs. LH AB	vs. LH Avg.	vs. LH HR	vs. LH RBI
Carrasco, Bos.	1	1	.500	9.45	6.2	15	8	7	2	2	0	1	5	1	7	8	1	0	0	2	0	176	.273	3	25	101	.267	3	20
Carrasco, Min.-Bos.	5	4	.556	4.69	78.2	90	46	41	8	8	4	4	38	1	64	69	1	0	0	4	1	195	.297	4	29	115	.278	4	24

DESIGNATED HITTERS

Name	AB	Avg.	HR	RBI
Ortiz, David	310	.303	9	50
Huskey, Butch	134	.194	2	16
Cummings, Midre	43	.326	1	6
Coomer, Ron	39	.308	1	5
Lawton, Matt	33	.182	0	2
LeCroy, Matt	8	.250	0	1
Koskie, Corey	4	.250	0	1
Canizaro, Jay	4	.250	0	0
Jensen, Marcus	4	.000	0	0
Walker, Todd	3	.333	0	0
Hocking, Denny	3	.333	0	2
Maxwell, Jason	1	.000	0	0
Blake, Casey	1	.000	0	1
Buchanan, Brian	0	-	0	1
Guzman, Cristian	0	-	0	0

INDIVIDUAL STATISTICS

FIELDING

FIRST BASEMEN

Player	Pct.	G	PO	A	E	TC	DP
Coomer, Ron	.995	124	1020	67	5	1092	102
Ortiz, David	.996	27	210	12	1	223	17
Hocking, Denny	1.000	12	35	5	0	40	6
Huskey, Butch	.971	9	61	5	2	68	2
Mientkiewicz, Doug	1.000	3	22	0	0	22	3
LeCroy, Matt	1.000	3	13	0	0	13	1
Blake, Casey	1.000	1	5	0	0	5	1

SECOND BASEMEN

Player	Pct.	G	PO	A	E	TC	DP
Canizaro, Jay	.982	90	120	199	6	325	41
Hocking, Denny	.978	47	56	75	3	134	19
Maxwell, Jason	.967	30	28	61	3	92	13
Walker, Todd	.946	19	34	36	4	74	12
Rivas, Luis	.983	14	30	28	1	59	8

THIRD BASEMEN

Player	Pct.	G	PO	A	E	TC	DP
Koskie, Corey	.966	139	96	241	12	349	27
Maxwell, Jason	.935	19	5	24	2	31	4
Hocking, Denny	.958	16	3	20	1	24	2
Coomer, Ron	1.000	5	3	15	0	18	2
Blake, Casey	1.000	5	2	5	0	7	0

SHORTSTOPS

Player	Pct.	G	PO	A	E	TC	DP
Guzman, Cristian	.967	151	228	413	22	663	96
Hocking, Denny	.983	15	19	38	1	58	10
Maxwell, Jason	.923	5	2	10	1	13	1
Rivas, Luis	1.000	2	1	1	0	2	1

OUTFIELDERS

Player	Pct.	G	PO	A	E	TC	DP
Jones, Jacque	.994	147	334	9	2	345	1
Lawton, Matt	.983	143	278	4	5	287	1
Hunter, Torii	.989	99	270	12	3	285	3
Hocking, Denny	1.000	51	70	5	0	75	3
Cummings, Midre	1.000	40	58	4	0	62	2
Buchanan, Brian	1.000	25	34	1	0	35	0
Huskey, Butch	.975	15	37	2	1	40	0
Allen, Chad	1.000	15	26	2	0	28	2
Barnes, John	1.000	11	28	2	0	30	2
Maxwell, Jason	1.000	2	3	0	0	3	0

CATCHERS

Player	Pct.	G	PO	A	E	TC	DP	PB
LeCroy, Matt	.988	49	317	16	4	337	8	4
Jensen, Marcus	.993	49	261	13	2	276	3	4
Moeller, Chad	.979	48	266	13	6	285	0	2
Pierzynski, A.J.	1.000	32	160	10	0	170	3	2
Ardoin, Danny	.989	15	80	8	1	89	0	3

PITCHERS

Player	Pct.	G	PO	A	E	TC	DP
Wells, Bob	.846	76	2	9	2	13	2
Guardado, Eddie	1.000	70	0	3	0	3	0
Miller, Travis	1.000	67	2	6	0	8	0
Hawkins, LaTroy	.905	66	3	16	2	21	1
Carrasco, Hector	1.000	61	2	12	0	14	0
Radke, Brad	.982	34	29	25	1	55	5
Milton, Eric	.957	33	7	15	1	23	0
Redman, Mark	.955	32	4	17	1	22	1
Mays, Joe	.943	31	9	24	2	35	2
Santana, Johan	.947	30	5	13	1	19	2
Ryan, Jason	.600	16	2	1	2	5	0
Bergman, Sean	.952	15	8	12	1	21	2
Romero, J.C.	1.000	12	6	10	0	16	0
Cressend, Jack	1.000	11	1	0	0	1	0
Kinney, Matt	.889	8	3	5	1	9	0
Lincoln, Mike	1.000	8	1	2	0	3	0
Mota, Danny	-	4	0	0	0	0	0

PITCHING AGAINST EACH CLUB

Pitcher	Ana. W-L	Bal. W-L	Bos. W-L	Chi. W-L	Cle. W-L	Det. W-L	K.C. W-L	N.Y. W-L	Oak. W-L	Sea. W-L	T.B. W-L	Tex. W-L	Tor. W-L	N.L. W-L	Total W-L
Bergman, Sean	0-0	0-0	0-0	0-0	0-0	0-0	1-0	1-0	0-3	0-1	0-0	1-0	0-0	1-1	4-5
Carrasco, Hector	0-0	0-0	0-0	0-0	0-0	1-1	1-0	0-0	0-0	0-0	1-1	1-0	0-1	0-0	4-3
Cressend, Jack	0-0	0-0	0-0	0-0	0-0	0-0	0-0	0-0	0-0	0-0	0-0	0-0	0-0	0-0	0-0
Guardado, Eddie	0-1	0-0	0-0	1-0	3-0	0-1	0-0	1-1	0-1	1-0	1-0	0-0	0-0	0-0	7-4
Hawkins, LaTroy	0-1	0-0	0-0	0-0	1-0	0-1	0-1	0-0	0-0	0-0	0-1	1-0	0-0	0-1	2-5
Kinney, Matt	0-1	0-0	0-0	0-0	0-0	0-0	0-0	0-0	0-0	1-0	0-0	1-0	0-1	0-0	2-2
Lincoln, Mike	0-0	0-0	0-1	0-1	0-0	0-0	0-0	0-0	0-0	0-0	0-0	0-0	0-0	0-1	0-3
Mays, Joe	0-1	0-1	1-1	2-0	0-1	1-2	0-0	0-2	0-1	0-3	0-1	2-0	0-0	1-2	7-15
Miller, Travis	0-0	0-1	0-0	1-0	1-0	0-0	0-1	0-0	0-0	0-0	0-0	0-1	0-0	0-0	2-3
Milton, Eric	1-0	0-0	1-2	1-2	0-0	1-1	2-0	2-1	3-0	0-2	0-0	1-0	1-0	0-2	13-10
Mota, Danny	0-0	0-0	0-0	0-0	0-0	0-0	0-0	0-0	0-0	0-0	0-0	0-0	0-0	0-0	0-0
Radke, Brad	2-1	2-0	0-1	0-1	0-2	1-0	1-1	0-1	1-2	1-0	0-2	1-1	1-2	2-2	12-16
Redman, Mark	0-0	1-2	0-1	0-0	2-0	1-0	0-2	1-0	1-0	0-2	2-0	0-1	2-0	2-1	12-9
Romero, J.C.	0-0	0-2	0-0	0-0	0-1	1-0	0-2	0-0	0-0	0-1	0-1	0-0	1-0	0-0	2-7
Ryan, Jason	0-1	0-0	0-0	0-0	0-0	0-0	0-0	0-0	0-0	0-0	0-0	0-0	0-0	0-0	0-1
Santana, Johan	0-0	0-0	0-1	0-1	1-0	0-0	0-0	0-0	0-0	0-0	0-0	0-1	0-0	1-0	2-3
Wells, Bob	0-1	0-0	0-1	0-2	0-1	0-1	0-0	0-0	0-0	0-0	0-0	0-0	0-0	0-1	0-7
Totals	3-7	3-6	2-8	5-7	8-5	6-7	5-7	5-5	5-7	3-9	4-6	8-4	5-4	7-11	69-93

INTERLEAGUE: Bergman 1-0, Redman 0-1, Radke 0-1 vs. Brewers; Radke 1-0, Milton 0-1, Mays 0-1 vs. Cubs; Mays 0-1, Bergman 0-1, Hawkins 0-1 vs. Reds; Santana 1-0, Mays 1-0, Radke 0-1 vs. Astros; Redman 1-0, Wells 0-1, Milton 0-1 vs. Pirates; Redman 1-0, Radke 1-0, Lincoln 0-1 vs. Cardinals. Total: 7-11.

MISCELLANEOUS

HOME RUNS BY PARK

At Anaheim (6): Coomer 1, Lawton 1, Canizaro 1, Ortiz 1, Koskie 1, Jones 1.
At Baltimore (1): Coomer 1.
At Boston (4): Coomer 2, Ortiz 1, Koskie 1.
At Chicago (AL) (4): Canizaro 1, Koskie 1, Jones 1, LeCroy 1.
At Cincinnati (2): Canizaro 1, Jones 1.
At Cleveland (5): Lawton 2, Cummings 1, Coomer 1, Hunter 1.
At Detroit (1): Hocking 1.
At Houston (2): Canizaro 1, LeCroy 1.
At Kansas City (12): Jones 3, Coomer 2, Lawton 2, Huskey 1, Hocking 1, Walker 1, Koskie 1, LeCroy 1.
At Minnesota (54): Jones 11, Lawton 8, Ortiz 7, Huskey 4, Hunter 4, Coomer 3, Guzman 3, Cummings 2, Jensen 2, Canizaro 2, LeCroy 2, Hocking 1, Maxwell 1, Pierzynski 1, Koskie 1, Buchanan 1, Moeller 1.
At New York (AL) (5): Coomer 1, Canizaro 1, Walker 1, Ortiz 1, Guzman 1.
At Oakland (4): Jones 2, Hocking 1, Guzman 1.
At Pittsburgh (2): Koskie 2.
At Seattle (2): Coomer 1, Pierzynski 1.
At Tampa Bay (3): Koskie 1, Guzman 1, Ardoin 1.
At Texas (5): Coomer 3, Jensen 1, Koskie 1.
At Toronto (4): Guzman 2, Cummings 1, Coomer 1.

LOW-HIT GAMES

No-hitters: None.
One-hitters: None.
Two-hitters: None.

10-STRIKEOUT GAMES

Eric Milton 2, Total: 2

FOUR OR MORE HITS IN ONE GAME

Cristian Guzman 3, Denny Hocking 2 (including one five-hit game), Corey Koskie 2, Ron Coomer 1, Matt Lawton 1, Jay Canizaro 1, Torii Hunter 1, David Ortiz 1, A.J. Pierzynski 1, Jacque Jones 1, Luis Rivas 1, Total: 15

MULTI-HOMER GAMES

Ron Coomer 2, Matt Lawton 1, Total: 3

GRAND SLAMS

8-25: Jay Canizaro (off Detroit's Willie Blair)
9-7: David Ortiz (off Boston's Ramon Martinez)

PINCH HITTERS

(Minimum 5 at-bats)

Name	AB	Avg.	HR	RBI
Cummings, Midre	33	.333	0	10
Hocking, Denny	24	.333	0	3
Ortiz, David	16	.188	1	4
Jones, Jacque	13	.308	0	1
Canizaro, Jay	10	.200	0	1
Maxwell, Jason	9	.111	0	0
Lawton, Matt	7	.143	0	2
Jensen, Marcus	7	.000	0	0
Koskie, Corey	6	.500	0	0
Guzman, Cristian	5	.200	0	0

DEBUTS

4-3: Matt LeCroy, C.
4-3: Johan Santana, P.
5-19: Brian Buchanan, RF.
6-20: Chad Moeller, C.
8-2: Danny Ardoin, C.
8-18: Matt Kinney, P.
8-26: Jack Cressend, P.
9-15: Danny Mota, P.
9-16: Luis Rivas, 2B.
9-16: John Barnes, CF.

GAMES BY POSITION

Catcher: Marcus Jensen 49, Matt LeCroy 49, Chad Moeller 48, A.J. Pierzynski 32, Danny Ardoin 15.
First base: Ron Coomer 124, David Ortiz 27, Denny Hocking 12, Butch Huskey 9, Doug Mientkiewicz 3, Matt LeCroy 3, Casey Blake 1.
Second base: Jay Canizaro 90, Denny Hocking 47, Jason Maxwell 30, Todd Walker 19, Luis Rivas 14.
Third base: Corey Koskie 139, Jason Maxwell 19, Denny Hocking 16, Ron Coomer 5, Casey Blake 5.
Shortstop: Cristian Guzman 151, Denny Hocking 15, Jason Maxwell 5, Luis Rivas 2.
Outfield: Jacque Jones 147, Matt Lawton 143, Torii Hunter 99, Denny Hocking 51, Midre Cummings 40, Brian Buchanan 25, Butch Huskey 15, Chad Allen 15, John Barnes 11, Jason Maxwell 2.
Designated hitter: David Ortiz 88, Butch Huskey 39, Midre Cummings 15, Ron Coomer 9, Matt Lawton 9, Jason Maxwell 7, Matt LeCroy 3, Denny Hocking 2, Jay Canizaro 2, Todd Walker 2, Brian Buchanan 2, Marcus Jensen 1, Corey Koskie 1, Cristian Guzman 1, Casey Blake 1.

STREAKS

Wins: 4 (April 18-21, May 26-30)
Losses: 7 (July 2-8)
Consecutive games with at least one hit: 16, Matt Lawton (April 13-30)
Wins by pitcher: 4, Mark Redman (July 9-27)

ATTENDANCE

Home: 1,059,715
Road: 2,332,786
Highest (home): 43,830 (April 3 vs. Tampa Bay).
Highest (road): 47,438 (September 2 vs. New York).
Lowest (home): 5,753 (September 6 vs. Baltimore).
Lowest (road): 8,746 (May 18 vs. Oakland).

NEW YORK YANKEES

DAY BY DAY

Date	Opp.	Res.	Score	(inn.*)	Hits	Opp. hits	Winning pitcher	Losing pitcher	Save	Record	Pos.	GB
4-3	At Ana.	W	3-2		6	10	Hernandez	Hill	Rivera	1-0	T1st	...
4-4	At Ana.	W	5-3		9	10	Mendoza	Percival	Rivera	2-0	T1st	...
4-5	At Ana.	L	6-12		13	12	Schoeneweis	Cone		2-1	T1st	...
4-7	At Sea.	L	5-7		9	12	Halama	Pettitte	Sasaki	2-2	2nd	1.0
4-8	At Sea.	W	3-2		10	5	Nelson	Mesa	Rivera	3-2	2nd	1.0
4-9	At Sea.	L	3-9		3	9	Moyer	Clemens		3-3	2nd	2.0
4-12	Tex.	W	8-6		13	10	Nelson	Munoz	Rivera	4-3	2nd	0.5
4-13	Tex.	W	5-1		8	4	Hernandez	Rogers		5-3	1st	+0.5
4-14	K.C.	W	7-5		10	9	Clemens	Witasick	Rivera	6-3	1st	+1.5
4-15	K.C.	W	7-1		11	2	Mendoza	Rosado		7-3	1st	+1.5
4-16	K.C.	W	8-4		10	9	Nelson	Fussell		8-3	1st	+1.5
4-17	At Tex.	W	5-4	(11)	8	11	Rivera	Crabtree	Erdos	9-3	1st	+2.0
4-18	At Tex.	W	6-3		11	8	Hernandez	Rogers		10-3	1st	+2.5
4-19	At Tex.	W	5-4	(10)	12	7	Rivera	Zimmerman		11-3	1st	+2.5
4-21	At Tor.	L	3-8		5	12	Carpenter	Mendoza		11-4	1st	+1.0
4-22	At Tor.	L	2-8		9	10	Escobar	Cone		11-5	T1st	...
4-23	At Tor.	W	10-7		15	8	Hernandez	Andrews	Rivera	12-5	1st	+1.0
4-24	Min.	L	3-7		5	6	Milton	Clemens		12-6	1st	+1.0
4-25	Min.	L	1-6		7	10	Bergman	Mendoza		12-7	T1st	...
4-26	Min.	W	2-0		6	5	Nelson	Mays	Rivera	13-7	1st	+1.0
4-28	Tor.	W	6-0		8	3	Cone	Escobar		14-7	1st	+1.5
4-29	Tor.	L	2-6		11	14	Wells	Hernandez	Koch	14-8	1st	+0.5
4-30	Tor.	W	7-1		12	9	Clemens	Halladay		15-8	1st	+1.5
5-1	At Cle.	W	2-1		8	7	Mendoza	Wright	Rivera	16-8	1st	+2.0
5-2	At Cle.	W	4-2		10	6	Pettitte	Witt	Rivera	17-8	1st	+2.0
5-3	At Cle.	W	6-5		9	10	Grimsley	Karsay	Rivera	18-8	1st	+3.0
5-5	Bal.	W	12-10		16	14	Nelson	Ryan		19-8	1st	+3.0
5-6	Bal.	W	3-1		6	6	Clemens	Rapp	Rivera	20-8	1st	+4.0
5-7	Bal.	L	6-7		10	12	Groom	Rivera	Timlin	20-9	1st	+3.0
5-8	T.B.	W	6-3		8	9	Pettitte	Gooden	Rivera	21-9	1st	+3.0
5-9	T.B.	W	4-3	(10)	7	8	Nelson	White		22-9	1st	+4.0
5-11	T.B.	L	0-1		4	7	Trachsel	Hernandez	Lopez	22-10	1st	+2.5
5-12	At Det.	L	7-9		12	16	Nitkowski	Clemens	Jones	22-11	1st	+1.5
5-13	At Det.	L	3-6		8	13	Weaver	Pettitte	Jones	22-12	1st	+0.5
5-14	At Det.	L	1-2		5	8	Mlicki	Cone	Jones	22-13	2nd	0.5
5-16	Chi.	L	0-4		3	7	Eldred	Hernandez		22-14	2nd	1.0
5-17	Chi.	W	9-4		15	7	Clemens	Parque		23-14	2nd	1.0
5-19	At Cle.	W	11-7		14	9	Mendoza	Kamieniecki		24-14	2nd	1.0
5-20	At Cle.	L	2-3		9	7	Shuey	Nelson		24-15	2nd	1.0
5-21	At Cle.	L	1-6		4	11	Rigdon	Hernandez		24-16	2nd	1.0
5-23	At Chi.	L	2-8		9	11	Wells	Clemens		24-17	2nd	1.0
5-24	At Chi.	W	12-4		18	7	Pettitte	Sirotka		25-17	2nd	1.0
5-25	At Chi.	W	7-0		12	4	Mendoza	Baldwin		26-17	T1st	...
5-26	Bos.	L	1-4		8	8	R. Martinez	Cone	Lowe	26-18	2nd	1.0
5-27	Bos.	W	8-3		11	9	Stanton	Wasdin		27-18	T1st	...
5-28	Bos.	L	0-2		4	5	P. Martinez	Clemens		27-19	2nd	1.0
5-29	Oak.	W	4-1		6	2	Pettitte	Olivares		28-19	2nd	0.5
5-30	Oak.	L	4-7		10	11	Appier	Mendoza	Isringhausen	28-20	2nd	1.5
5-31	Oak.	L	7-8		11	9	Heredia	Cone	Isringhausen	28-21	2nd	1.5
6-2	At Atl.	W	5-2		10	5	Hernandez	Millwood	Rivera	29-21	T1st	...
6-3	At Atl.	L	7-11		13	11	Remlinger	Grimsley		29-22	T1st	...
6-4	At Atl.	W	7-6		16	12	Pettitte	Mulholland	Rivera	30-22	1st	+1.0
6-5	At Mon.	L	4-6		13	8	Johnson	Cone	Kline	30-23	T1st	...
6-6	At Mon.	W	8-1		13	3	Grimsley	Vazquez		31-23	T1st	...
6-7	At Mon.	W	7-2		9	4	Hernandez	Pavano		32-23	1st	+1.0
6-9	N.Y. (NL)	L	2-12		8	15	Leiter	Clemens		32-24	1st	+0.5
6-10	N.Y. (NL)	W	13-5		17	8	Pettitte	B.J. Jones		33-24	1st	+1.5
6-13	Bos.	L	3-5		6	10	Pichardo	Hernandez	Lowe	33-25	1st	...
6-14	Bos.	W	2-1		8	10	Grimsley	Wakefield	Rivera	34-25	1st	+1.0
6-15	Chi.	L	3-12		12	16	Sirotka	Pettitte		34-26	1st	+0.5
6-16	Chi.	L	1-3		6	9	Baldwin	Stanton	Howry	34-27	2nd	0.5
6-17	Chi.	L	9-10		15	15	Eldred	Westbrook	Foulke	34-28	2nd	0.5
6-18	Chi.	L	4-17		10	18	Parque	Hernandez		34-29	2nd	0.5
6-19	At Bos.	W	22-1		19	6	Mendoza	Rose		35-29	1st	+0.5
6-20	At Bos.	W	3-0		5	6	Pettitte	P. Martinez	Rivera	36-29	1st	+1.5
6-21	At Bos.	L	7-9		10	11	Garces	Grimsley		36-30	1st	+0.5
6-22	At Bos.	L	2-4		5	8	R. Martinez	Westbrook	Lowe	36-31	2nd	0.5
6-23	At Chi.	L	3-4		11	8	Lowe	Rivera		36-32	3rd	1.0
6-24	At Chi.	W	12-8		16	13	Mendoza	Wells	Rivera	37-32	2nd	1.0
6-25	At Chi.	L	7-8		10	13	Sirotka	Pettitte	Howry	37-33	2nd	2.0
6-27	At Det.	L	6-7	(11)	15	17	Cruz	Rivera		37-34	2nd	2.0
6-28	At Det.	L	6-13		11	12	Blair	Ford	Sparks	37-35	2nd	3.0
6-29	At Det.	W	8-0		14	6	Pettitte	Mlicki		38-35	2nd	3.0
6-30	At T.B.	L	4-6		7	12	Mecir	Nelson	Hernandez	38-36	2nd	3.0
7-1	At T.B.	W	6-1		12	5	Hernandez	Lopez		39-36	2nd	2.0
7-2	At T.B.	W	5-2		10	4	Clemens	Trachsel	Rivera	40-36	2nd	1.0
7-4	Bal.	L	6-7		10	7	Erickson	Cone	Trombley	40-37	2nd	1.5
7-5	Bal.	W	12-6		13	10	Pettitte	Rapp		41-37	2nd	0.5

HIGHLIGHTS

High point: Mike Piazza's fly ball to deep center field, caught by Bernie Williams, in World Series Game 5 at Shea Stadium. With that out, the Yankees had a third straight World Series crown and distinction as baseball's first three-peaters since the 1972-74 Oakland A's.
Low point: A 17-4 loss to Chicago at Yankee Stadium on June 18. The Bombers were embarrassed at home, getting swept in four games by the upstart White Sox, and starter Orlando Hernandez lasted just two-thirds of an inning before leaving with elbow problems. The team was falling apart and everyone was getting testy.
Turning point: Three positives happened in one weekend: David Justice arrived from Cleveland June 30, ending rampant trade speculation; El Duque pitched well the next day after sitting out 13 days with an injury, and Roger Clemens followed that with a good outing after sitting out with a groin injury.
Most valuable player: Justice. He came through with numerous big hits, both in the regular season and the postseason, and the team played infinitely better with him around.
Most valuable pitcher: A tie between the two setup men, righthander Jeff Nelson and lefty Mike Stanton. They pitched brilliantly in the early going, when the Yanks jumped out to a 22-9 record, before tiring in the second half. After resting in September, both contributed strong postseasons.
Most improved player: In the wake of a disappointing 1999 as a part-time player, Jorge Posada took over full-time catching duties and was fantastic. He woke up at the plate (28 homers, 86 RBIs), rediscovered his cannon arm (nailing 34-of-104 basestealers) and became adept at calling a game.
Most pleasant surprise: Glenallen Hill, acquired to provide righthanded bench power, batted .411 with 10 homers and 19 RBIs in a blazing August. He gave the Yanks far more than they ever could have hoped when they got him from the Cubs.
Key injuries: Numerous Yankees missed significant time: third baseman Scott Brosius (ribs), 19-game winner Andy Pettitte (back), Hernandez (elbow, back), Clemens (groin), outfielder Shane Spencer (knee), second baseman Chuck Knoblauch (elbow, wrist), righthander Ramiro Mendoza (shoulder), outfielder Bernie Williams (ribs) and righthander David Cone (dislocated shoulder). Spencer and Mendoza missed the entire second half.
Notable: Shortstop Derek Jeter, in just his fifth season, reached the 1,000-hit milestone. ... Williams established career highs with 30 homers and 121 RBIs. ...The Yankees' bullpen, mostly reliable, coughed up five potential Clemens victories.

—KEN DAVIDOFF

MISCELLANEOUS

RECORDS

2000 regular-season record: 87-74 (1st in A.L. East); 44-36 at home; 43-38 on road; 36-30 vs. East; 26-28 vs. Central; 25-16 vs. West; 22-24 vs. lefthanded starters; 65-50 vs. righthanded starters; 80-62 on grass; 7-12 on turf; 34-25 in daytime; 53-49 at night; 20-18 in one-run games; 4-4 in extra-inning games; 0-0 in doubleheaders.
Team record past five years: 487-322 (.602, ranks 1st in league in that span).

TEAM LEADERS

Batting average: Derek Jeter (.339).
At-bats: Derek Jeter (593).
Runs: Derek Jeter (119).
Hits: Derek Jeter (201).
Total Bases: Bernie Williams (304).
Doubles: Tino Martinez, Bernie Williams (37).
Triples: Bernie Williams (6).
Home runs: Bernie Williams (30).
Runs batted in: Bernie Williams (121).
Stolen bases: Derek Jeter (22).
Slugging percentage: Bernie Williams (.566).
On-base percentage: Jorge Posada (.417).
Wins: Andy Pettitte (19).
Earned-run average: Roger Clemens (3.70).
Complete games: Orlando Hernandez, Andy Pettitte (3).
Shutouts: Ramiro Mendoza, Andy Pettitte (1).
Saves: Mariano Rivera (36).
Innings pitched: Andy Pettitte (204.2).
Strikeouts: Roger Clemens (188).

Date	Opp.	Res.	Score	(inn.*)	Hits	Opp. hits	Winning pitcher	Losing pitcher	Save	Record	Pos.	GB
7-6	Bal.	W	13-9		10	11	Stanton	Johnson		42-37	2nd	0.5
7-7	At N.Y. (NL)	W	2-1		6	6	Hernandez	Leiter	Rivera	43-37	1st	+0.5
7-8†	At N.Y. (NL)	W	4-2		6	6	Gooden	B.J. Jones	Rivera	44-37		
7-8‡	N.Y. (NL)	W	4-2		5	7	Clemens	Rusch	Rivera	45-37	1st	+1.0
7-9	At N.Y. (NL)	L	0-2		7	6	Hampton	Pettitte	Benitez	45-38	1st	...
7-13	Fla.	L	9-11		12	14	Penny	Hernandez	Alfonseca	45-39	1st	...
7-14	Fla.	W	6-2		9	7	Clemens	Dempster		46-39	1st	...
7-16	Phi.	W	9-8	(10)	13	14	Rivera	Brantley		47-39	1st	+0.5
7-17	Phi.	L	8-10		12	9	Coggin	Cone	Brock	47-40	1st	+0.5
7-18	Phi.	W	3-1		4	5	Neagle	Schilling	Rivera	48-40	1st	+1.0
7-19	Det.	W	9-1		11	6	Clemens	Nomo		49-40	1st	+1.5
7-20	Det.	L	3-5		8	8	Blair	Pettitte	Jones	49-41	1st	+0.5
7-21	T.B.	W	11-1		17	10	Gooden	Yan		50-41	1st	+1.5
7-22	T.B.	L	4-12		12	14	Rupe	Cone		50-42	1st	+1.0
7-23	T.B.	W	5-1		7	4	Neagle	Rekar		51-42	1st	+1.0
7-24	At Bal.	W	4-3		5	6	Clemens	Parrish	Rivera	52-42	1st	+2.0
7-25	At Bal.	W	19-1		20	9	Pettitte	Erickson		53-42	1st	+3.0
7-26	At Bal.	W	4-1		8	8	Gooden	Ponson	Rivera	54-42	1st	+3.0
7-27	At Min.	L	3-9		9	12	Redman	Cone		54-43	1st	+2.0
7-28	At Min.	W	9-5		17	5	Rivera	Guardado		55-43	1st	+2.5
7-29	At Min.	L	2-6		2	8	Milton	Mendoza		55-44	1st	+2.5
7-30	At Min.	W	7-4		12	9	Pettitte	Mays		56-44	1st	+3.5
8-1	K.C.	W	5-4		9	6	Nelson	Bottalico	Rivera	57-44	1st	+4.0
8-2	K.C.	L	1-4		2	11	Stein	Neagle	Bottalico	57-45	1st	+3.0
8-3	K.C.	W	3-2		6	5	Rivera	Spradlin		58-45	1st	+3.5
8-4	Sea.	W	13-6		16	15	Pettitte	Moyer		59-45	1st	+3.5
8-5	Sea.	L	5-6		10	11	Tomko	Gooden	Sasaki	59-46	1st	+3.5
8-6	Sea.	L	1-11		8	16	Abbott	Hernandez		59-47	1st	+3.5
8-7	Sea.	L	5-8		11	13	Halama	Neagle		59-48	1st	+3.5
8-8	Oak.	W	4-3		6	7	Rivera	Isringhausen		60-48	1st	+4.5
8-9	Oak.	W	12-1		12	9	Pettitte	Appier		61-48	1st	+4.5
8-10	Oak.	W	12-6		15	13	Cone	Mulder		62-48	1st	+5.0
8-11	At Ana.	L	3-8		11	10	Schoeneweis	Hernandez		62-49	1st	+4.0
8-12	At Ana.	L	6-9		10	12	Pote	Neagle	Hasegawa	62-50	1st	+4.0
8-13	At Ana.	W	4-1		5	4	Clemens	Ortiz	Rivera	63-50	1st	+4.0
8-14	At Tex.	W	7-3		9	7	Pettitte	Perisho		64-50	1st	+4.0
8-15	At Tex.	W	10-2		17	8	Cone	Davis	Gooden	65-50	1st	+5.0
8-16	At Tex.	L	0-5		4	8	Sikorski	Hernandez		65-51	1st	+4.0
8-17	Ana.	W	6-1		6	11	Neagle	Mercker		66-51	1st	+4.0
8-18	Ana.	L	8-9	(11)	13	15	Hasegawa	Stanton		66-52	1st	+3.0
8-19	Ana.	W	9-1		11	5	Pettitte	Cooper		67-52	1st	+3.0
8-20	Ana.	L	4-5		9	6	Wise	Nelson	Hasegawa	67-53	1st	+3.0
8-21	Tex.	W	12-3		13	8	Hernandez	Sikorski		68-53	1st	+3.0
8-22	Tex.	L	4-5		6	8	Crabtree	Neagle	Wetteland	68-54	1st	+3.0
8-23	Tex.	W	10-9		17	11	Rivera	Crabtree		69-54	1st	+3.0
8-24	Tex.	W	8-7		12	11	Pettitte	Perisho	Rivera	70-54	1st	+3.0
8-25	At Oak.	L	1-8		5	8	Appier	Cone		70-55	1st	+3.0
8-26	At Oak.	W	10-6		14	10	Hernandez	Mulder	Rivera	71-55	1st	+3.0
8-27	At Oak.	W	7-5		10	6	Neagle	Mecir	Rivera	72-55	1st	+4.0
8-28	At Sea.	W	9-1		10	5	Clemens	Abbott		73-55	1st	+5.0
8-29	At Sea.	L	3-5		8	8	Tomko	Pettitte	Sasaki	73-56	1st	+4.0
8-30	At Sea.	W	5-4		10	8	Cone	Sele	Rivera	74-56	1st	+5.0
9-1	Min.	W	4-2		10	6	Hernandez	Radke	Rivera	75-56	1st	+5.0
9-2	Min.	W	13-4	(8)	11	10	Neagle	Milton	Grimsley	76-56	1st	+6.0
9-3	Min.	L	1-2	(10)	5	4	Guardado	Rivera	Hawkins	76-57	1st	+6.0
9-4	At K.C.	W	4-3		8	12	Pettitte	Suzuki	Rivera	77-57	1st	+6.0
9-5	At K.C.	W	10-5		17	10	Gooden	Suppan		78-57	1st	+6.0
9-6	At K.C.	L	2-3		9	12	Meadows	Stanton		78-58	1st	+6.0
9-7	At K.C.	W	7-3		7	8	Neagle	Bottalico	Rivera	79-58	1st	+6.0
9-8	At Bos.	W	4-0		8	5	Clemens	Ohka		80-58	1st	+7.0
9-9	At Bos.	W	5-3		7	9	Pettitte	P. Martinez		81-58	1st	+8.0
9-10	At Bos.	W	6-2		11	7	Keisler	Schourek	Gooden	82-58	1st	+8.5
9-11	Bos.	L	0-4		5	7	Arrojo	Hernandez	Lowe	82-59	1st	+8.0
9-12	Tor.	W	10-2		11	8	Neagle	Hamilton		83-59	1st	+8.0
9-13	Tor.	W	3-2		7	11	Clemens	Loaiza	Rivera	84-59	1st	+9.0
9-14	Tor.	L	2-3	(11)	11	6	Koch	Choate	Escobar	84-60	1st	+8.0
9-15	Cle.	L	1-11		4	15	Burba	Cone		84-61	1st	+7.0
9-16	Cle.	W	6-3		12	4	Hernandez	Bere		85-61	1st	+7.5
9-17	Cle.	L	4-15		5	15	Finley	Neagle		85-62	1st	+7.5
9-18	Cle.	L	0-2		1	7	Colon	Clemens		85-63	1st	+7.0
9-19	At Tor.	L	3-16		4	19	Trachsel	Pettitte		85-64	1st	+6.0
9-20	At Tor.	L	2-7		9	10	Loaiza	Cone		85-65	1st	+5.5
9-21	At Tor.	L	1-3		5	9	Wells	Hernandez		85-66	1st	+4.5
9-22	Det.	L	6-9		9	10	Nomo	Neagle	Jones	85-67	1st	+4.5
9-23	Det.	W	13-8		18	8	Nelson	Blair	Rivera	86-67	1st	+4.5
9-24	Det.	W	6-3		10	7	Pettitte	Weaver	Rivera	87-67	1st	+5.5
9-25	Det.	L	4-15		11	18	Sparks	Gooden		87-68	1st	+5.5
9-26	At T.B.	L	1-2		8	3	Hernandez	Nelson		87-69	1st	+5.5
9-27	At T.B.	L	1-11		7	9	Lidle	Neagle		87-70	1st	+4.5
9-28	At T.B.	L	3-11		10	15	Rekar	Clemens		87-71	1st	+3.5
9-29	At Bal.	L	2-13		6	13	McElroy	Pettitte		87-72	1st	+3.5
9-30	At Bal.	L	1-9		7	12	Mussina	Cone		87-73	1st	+2.5
10-1	At Bal.	L	3-7		9	10	Mercedes	Hernandez		87-74	1st	+2.5

Monthly records: April (15-8), May (13-13), June (10-15), July (18-8), August (18-12), September (13-17), October (0-1).
*Innings, if other than nine. † First game of a doubleheader. ‡ Second game of a doubleheader.

MEMORABLE GAMES

April 17 at Texas

The Yankees squeaked into the playoffs with 87 regular-season wins, thanks largely to a freakish 22-9 start. Their early success was exemplified by this game at Texas, in which the Yanks erased deficits in the seventh and ninth innings, blew a lead in the 10th and regained it in the 11th. The Rangers loaded the bases with no one out in the bottom of the 11th, but Luis Alicea fouled a ball off his leg that was called fair—and catcher Jorge Posada turned it into an unassisted double play. One out later, the Yanks had a 5-4 victory, somehow.

Yankees	AB	R	H	BI	Texas	AB	R	H	BI
Knoblauch, 2b	5	1	1	0	Clayton, ss	4	2	1	0
Jeter, ss	5	1	1	0	Curtis, lf	4	0	3	1
O'Neill, rf	4	1	2	0	Rodriguez, c	5	0	1	1
Williams, cf	4	1	1	2	Palmeiro, 1b	4	1	1	1
Martinez, 1b	5	0	2	2	Segui, dh	5	0	2	1
Spencer, dh	3	0	0	0	McDonald, pr	0	0	0	0
Ledee, ph-dh	2	0	0	0	Mateo, cf	5	0	1	0
Posada, c	4	1	1	1	Kapler, rf	3	0	0	0
Kelly, lf	4	0	0	0	Alicea, 2b	4	0	1	0
Bellinger, 3b	4	0	0	0	Evans, 3b	2	1	1	0
					Catalanotto, ph	1	0	0	0
					Sheldon, 3b	1	0	0	0
Totals	**40**	**5**	**8**	**5**	**Totals**	**38**	**4**	**11**	**4**

Yankees........................0 0 0 0 0 0 2 0 1 1 1—5 8 1
Texas............................0 0 2 0 0 0 0 1 0 1 0—4 11 1

E—Cone (1), Clayton (3). DP—Yankees 3, Texas 2. LOB—Yankees 4, Texas 8. 2B—Curtis (2), Evans (2). HR—Williams (3), Posada (2), Palmeiro (5). SB—Williams (2), Curtis (1). CS—O'Neill (2), Evans (2). SH—Curtis, Kapler, Alicea.

Yankees	IP	H	R	ER	BB	SO
Cone	7	5	2	2	3	3
Nelson	0.2	0	0	0	0	2
Stanton	0.1	1	1	1	0	0
Rivera (W 1-0)	2	3	1	1	0	1
Watson	0	2	0	0	0	0
Erdos (S 1)	1	0	0	0	0	0

Texas	IP	H	R	ER	BB	SO
Oliver	8	2	2	2	1	6
Wetteland	1	3	1	1	0	2
Crabtree (L 0-1)	1	2	2	2	0	0
Venafro	1	1	0	0	1	1

Watson pitched to 3 batters in 11th. Crabtree pitched to 1 batter in 11th.

HBP—Palmeiro by Cone. WP—Cone. U—HP, Kellogg. 1B, Cooper. 2B, Diaz. 3B, Reilly. T—3:52. A—38,166.

August 8 at New York

A crazy day at Yankee Stadium. Before the game, Jose Canseco and Luis Sojo joined the club, and George Steinbrenner publicly tweaked Joe Torre for his negative reaction to the Canseco acquisition. Sojo, starting in place of injured Chuck Knoblauch, received a standing ovation. So did Canseco, who pinch hit in the seventh. Roger Clemens departed with his team down, 3-2, but A's closer Jason Isringhausen threw two pitches in the ninth—home run Bernie Williams, home run David Justice.

Oakland	AB	R	H	BI	Yankees	AB	R	H	BI
Long, cf	4	0	0	0	Jeter, ss	4	0	1	0
Velarde, 2b	5	0	0	0	Posada, c	4	0	0	0
Ja.Giambi, 1b	3	0	1	0	O'Neill, rf	3	1	0	0
Grieve, lf	3	0	1	0	Williams, cf	4	1	1	1
Christenson, pr-lf	0	0	0	0	Justice, lf	4	1	2	2
Stairs, dh	3	0	0	0	Hill, dh	3	0	1	0
Piatt, ph-dh	2	0	0	0	Polonia, pr-dh	0	0	0	0
Tejada, ss	3	0	1	0	Martinez, 1b	2	0	0	0
Je.Giambi, rf	3	1	0	0	Brosius, 3b	2	1	0	0
Chavez, 3b	4	1	2	2	Sojo, 2b	2	0	1	0
Hernandez, c	4	1	2	1	Canseco, ph	1	0	0	0
					Vizcaino, 2b	0	0	0	0
Totals	**34**	**3**	**7**	**3**	**Totals**	**29**	**4**	**6**	**3**

Oakland......................................0 0 0 0 3 0 0 0 0—3 7 1
Yankees......................................0 0 1 0 0 0 1 0 2—4 6 0

E—Ja. Giambi (5). DP—Oakland 2. LOB—Oakland 11, Yankees 4. 2B—Tejada (22), Hill (1). HR—Chavez (16), Hernandez (13), Williams (25), Justice (30).

Oakland	IP	H	R	ER	BB	SO
Zito	6.1	3	2	1	2	4
Mecir	1.2	1	0	0	1	1
Isringhausen (L 5-4)	0	2	2	2	0	0

Yankees	IP	H	R	ER	BB	SO
Clemens	7	5	3	3	4	4
Stanton	1	1	0	0	1	2
Rivera (W 6-3)	1	1	0	0	2	1

Isringhausen pitched to 2 batters in 9th.

WP—Stanton. U—HP, DeMuth. 1B, Eddings. 2B, Reliford. 3B, Carlson. T—3:00. A—36,357.

INDIVIDUAL STATISTICS

BATTING

Name	G	TPA	AB	R	H	TB	2B	3B	HR	RBI	Avg.	Obp.	Slg.	SH	SF	HP	BB	IBB	SO	SB	CS	GDP	vs RHP AB	Avg.	HR	RBI	vs LHP AB	Avg.	HR	RBI
Jeter, Derek	148	679	593	119	201	285	31	4	15	73	.339	.416	.481	3	3	12	68	4	99	22	4	14	446	.321	11	56	147	.395	4	17
Martinez, Tino	155	632	569	69	147	240	37	4	16	91	.258	.328	.422	0	3	8	52	9	74	4	1	16	398	.249	13	63	171	.281	3	28
O'Neill, Paul	142	628	566	79	160	240	26	0	18	100	.283	.336	.424	0	11	0	51	2	90	14	9	17	410	.259	15	72	156	.346	3	28
Williams, Bernie	141	616	537	108	165	304	37	6	30	121	.307	.391	.566	0	3	5	71	11	84	13	5	15	371	.315	21	78	166	.289	9	43
Posada, Jorge	151	624	505	92	145	266	35	1	28	86	.287	.417	.527	0	4	8	107	10	151	2	2	11	346	.272	22	58	159	.321	6	28
Brosius, Scott	135	519	470	57	108	176	20	0	16	64	.230	.299	.374	0	2	2	45	1	73	0	3	17	366	.221	10	44	104	.260	6	20
Knoblauch, Chuck	102	457	400	75	113	154	22	2	5	26	.283	.366	.385	1	2	8	46	0	45	15	7	6	300	.307	3	21	100	.210	2	5
Justice, David	78	318	275	43	84	161	17	0	20	60	.305	.391	.585	0	2	1	39	1	42	1	0	6	194	.299	11	40	81	.321	9	20
Spencer, Shane	73	276	248	33	70	114	11	3	9	40	.282	.330	.460	0	7	2	19	0	45	1	2	4	171	.269	6	27	77	.312	3	13
Ledee, Ricky	62	220	191	23	46	80	11	1	7	31	.241	.332	.419	0	2	1	26	2	39	7	3	7	169	.249	7	28	22	.182	0	3
Bellinger, Clay	98	209	184	33	38	68	8	2	6	21	.207	.288	.370	1	2	5	17	1	48	5	0	1	127	.220	5	15	57	.175	1	6
Vizcaino, Jose	73	191	174	23	48	58	8	1	0	10	.276	.319	.333	3	2	0	12	0	28	5	7	3	141	.284	0	7	33	.242	0	3
Hill, Glenallen	40	143	132	22	44	97	5	0	16	29	.333	.378	.735	0	1	1	9	0	33	0	0	1	73	.315	8	15	59	.356	8	14
Sojo, Luis	34	134	125	19	36	51	7	1	2	17	.288	.321	.408	3	0	0	6	0	6	1	0	5	93	.312	2	16	32	.219	0	1
Canseco, Jose	37	137	111	16	27	48	3	0	6	19	.243	.365	.432	0	3	0	23	1	37	0	0	2	76	.184	3	11	35	.371	3	8
Turner, Chris	37	102	89	9	21	27	3	0	1	7	.236	.320	.303	2	0	1	10	0	21	0	1	2	64	.219	1	5	25	.280	0	2
Polonia, Luis	37	85	77	11	22	29	4	0	1	5	.286	.341	.377	0	1	0	7	0	7	4	2	2	75	.293	1	5	2	.000	0	0
Leyritz, Jim	24	63	55	2	12	15	0	0	1	4	.218	.317	.273	0	0	1	7	0	14	0	0	2	27	.185	1	1	28	.250	0	3
Thompson, Ryan	33	56	50	12	13	25	3	0	3	14	.260	.339	.500	0	0	1	5	0	12	0	1	0	38	.263	3	14	12	.250	0	0
Soriano, Alfonso	22	53	50	5	9	18	3	0	2	3	.180	.196	.360	2	0	0	1	0	15	2	0	0	30	.200	1	2	20	.150	1	1
Delgado, Wilson	31	51	45	6	11	15	1	0	1	4	.244	.314	.333	0	1	0	5	0	9	1	0	1	38	.263	1	4	7	.143	0	0
Johnson, Lance	18	30	30	6	9	10	1	0	0	2	.300	.300	.333	0	0	0	0	0	7	2	0	1	27	.296	0	2	3	.333	0	0
Jose, Felix	20	32	29	4	7	10	0	0	1	5	.241	.281	.345	0	1	0	2	0	9	0	1	1	16	.250	1	4	13	.231	0	1
Kelly, Roberto	10	27	25	4	3	7	1	0	1	1	.120	.185	.280	0	0	1	1	0	6	0	0	0	4	.000	0	0	21	.143	1	1
Hernandez, Orlando	29	10	9	0	0	0	0	0	0	0	.000	.000	.000	1	0	0	0	0	7	0	0	0	6	.000	0	0	3	.000	0	0
Pettitte, Andy	32	5	5	0	0	0	0	0	0	0	.000	.000	.000	0	0	0	0	0	2	0	0	0	0	.000	0	0	5	.000	0	0
Cone, David	30	3	3	0	1	1	0	0	0	0	.333	.333	.333	0	0	0	0	0	1	0	0	0	3	.333	0	0	0	.000	0	0
Clemens, Roger	32	3	3	0	0	0	0	0	0	0	.000	.000	.000	0	0	0	0	0	1	0	0	0	3	.000	0	0	0	.000	0	0
Gooden, Dwight	18	2	2	0	0	0	0	0	0	0	.000	.000	.000	0	0	0	0	0	1	0	0	0	2	.000	0	0	0	.000	0	0
Stanton, Mike	69	1	1	1	1	1	0	0	0	0	1.000	1.000	1.000	0	0	0	0	0	0	0	0	0	1	1.000	0	0	0	.000	0	0
Grimsley, Jason	63	3	1	0	0	0	0	0	0	0	.000	.667	.000	0	0	0	2	0	1	0	0	0	1	.000	0	0	0	.000	0	0
Nelson, Jeff	73	1	1	0	0	0	0	0	0	0	.000	.000	.000	0	0	0	0	0	0	0	0	0	0	.000	0	0	1	.000	0	0
Erdos, Todd	14	1	1	0	0	0	0	0	0	0	.000	.000	.000	0	0	0	0	0	0	0	0	0	1	.000	0	0	0	.000	0	0
Watson, Allen	17	0	0	0	0	0	0	0	0	0	.000	.000	.000	0	0	0	0	0	0	0	0	0	0	.000	0	0	0	.000	0	0
Rivera, Mariano	66	0	0	0	0	0	0	0	0	0	.000	.000	.000	0	0	0	0	0	0	0	0	0	0	.000	0	0	0	.000	0	0
Choate, Randy	22	0	0	0	0	0	0	0	0	0	.000	.000	.000	0	0	0	0	0	0	0	0	0	0	.000	0	0	0	.000	0	0
Neagle, Denny	16	0	0	0	0	0	0	0	0	0	.000	.000	.000	0	0	0	0	0	0	0	0	0	0	.000	0	0	0	.000	0	0
Mendoza, Ramiro	14	0	0	0	0	0	0	0	0	0	.000	.000	.000	0	0	0	0	0	0	0	0	0	0	.000	0	0	0	.000	0	0
Ford, Ben	4	0	0	0	0	0	0	0	0	0	.000	.000	.000	0	0	0	0	0	0	0	0	0	0	.000	0	0	0	.000	0	0
Tessmer, Jay	7	0	0	0	0	0	0	0	0	0	.000	.000	.000	0	0	0	0	0	0	0	0	0	0	.000	0	0	0	.000	0	0
Einertson, Darrell	11	0	0	0	0	0	0	0	0	0	.000	.000	.000	0	0	0	0	0	0	0	0	0	0	.000	0	0	0	.000	0	0
Lilly, Ted	7	0	0	0	0	0	0	0	0	0	.000	.000	.000	0	0	0	0	0	0	0	0	0	0	.000	0	0	0	.000	0	0
Yarnall, Ed	2	0	0	0	0	0	0	0	0	0	.000	.000	.000	0	0	0	0	0	0	0	0	0	0	.000	0	0	0	.000	0	0
Westbrook, Jake	3	0	0	0	0	0	0	0	0	0	.000	.000	.000	0	0	0	0	0	0	0	0	0	0	.000	0	0	0	.000	0	0
Dingman, Craig	10	0	0	0	0	0	0	0	0	0	.000	.000	.000	0	0	0	0	0	0	0	0	0	0	.000	0	0	0	.000	0	0
Keisler, Randy	4	0	0	0	0	0	0	0	0	0	.000	.000	.000	0	0	0	0	0	0	0	0	0	0	.000	0	0	0	.000	0	0

Players with more than one A.L. team

Name	G	TPA	AB	R	H	TB	2B	3B	HR	RBI	Avg.	Obp.	Slg.	SH	SF	HP	BB	IBB	SO	SB	CS	GDP	vs RHP AB	Avg.	HR	RBI	vs LHP AB	Avg.	HR	RBI
Canseco, T.B.-N.Y.	98	401	329	47	83	146	18	0	15	49	.252	.377	.444	0	4	4	64	2	102	2	0	7	252	.242	9	32	77	.286	6	17
Delgado, N.Y.-K.C.	64	141	128	21	33	38	2	0	1	11	.258	.312	.297	0	2	0	11	0	26	2	1	2	99	.263	1	9	29	.241	0	2
Gooden, T.B.-N.Y.	26	2	2	0	0	0	0	0	0	0	.000	.000	.000	0	0	0	0	0	1	0	0	0	2	.000	0	0	0	.000	0	0
Justice, Cle.-N.Y.	146	606	524	89	150	306	31	1	41	118	.286	.377	.584	0	3	1	77	3	91	2	1	13	390	.279	26	82	134	.306	15	36
Ledee, Cle.	17	71	63	13	14	24	2	1	2	8	.222	.310	.381	0	0	0	8	0	9	0	0	3	169	.249	7	28	22	.182	0	3
Ledee, Tex.	58	240	213	23	50	74	6	3	4	38	.235	.317	.347	0	1	1	25	2	50	6	3	7	169	.249	7	28	22	.182	0	3
Ledee, N.Y.-Cle.-Tex.	137	531	467	59	110	178	19	5	13	77	.236	.322	.381	0	3	2	59	4	98	13	6	17	384	.234	10	62	83	.241	3	15
Polonia, Det.-N.Y.	117	383	344	48	95	140	14	5	7	30	.276	.329	.407	3	6	1	29	1	32	12	7	4	311	.283	6	24	33	.212	1	6

PITCHING

Name	W	L	Pct.	ERA	IP	H	R	ER	HR	SH	SF	HB	BB	IBB	SO	G	GS	CG	ShO	GF	Sv	vs. RH AB	Avg.	HR	RBI	vs. LH AB	Avg.	HR	RBI
Pettitte, Andy	19	9	.679	4.35	204.2	219	111	99	17	7	4	4	80	4	125	32	32	3	1	0	0	632	.275	16	73	176	.256	1	16
Clemens, Roger	13	8	.619	3.70	204.1	184	96	84	26	1	2	10	84	0	188	32	32	1	0	0	0	374	.267	15	60	407	.206	11	30
Hernandez, Orlando	12	13	.480	4.51	195.2	186	104	98	34	4	5	6	51	2	141	29	29	3	0	0	0	357	.210	14	41	397	.280	20	55
Cone, David	4	14	.222	6.91	155.0	192	124	119	25	6	8	9	82	3	120	30	29	0	0	0	0	310	.310	14	49	318	.302	11	59
Grimsley, Jason	3	2	.600	5.04	96.1	100	58	54	10	2	6	5	42	1	53	63	4	0	0	18	1	211	.299	5	30	162	.228	5	31
Neagle, Denny	7	7	.500	5.81	91.1	99	61	59	16	6	5	2	31	1	58	16	15	1	0	0	0	256	.266	13	45	100	.310	3	8
Rivera, Mariano	7	4	.636	2.85	75.2	58	26	24	4	5	2	0	25	3	58	66	0	0	0	61	36	136	.206	3	16	143	.210	1	19
Nelson, Jeff	8	4	.667	2.45	69.2	44	24	19	2	6	2	2	45	1	71	73	0	0	0	13	0	159	.157	1	14	82	.232	1	10
Stanton, Mike	2	3	.400	4.10	68.0	68	32	31	5	2	4	2	24	2	75	69	0	0	0	20	0	141	.199	2	13	118	.339	3	19
Mendoza, Ramiro	7	4	.636	4.25	65.2	66	32	31	9	1	2	4	20	1	30	14	9	1	1	0	0	127	.220	4	13	127	.299	5	18
Gooden, Dwight	4	2	.667	3.36	64.1	66	28	24	8	3	2	0	21	3	31	18	5	0	0	3	2	143	.280	4	9	105	.248	4	20
Erdos, Todd	0	0	.000	5.04	25.0	31	14	14	2	0	0	1	11	0	18	14	0	0	0	6	1	52	.385	2	12	50	.220	0	5
Watson, Allen	0	0	.000	10.23	22.0	30	25	25	6	2	2	2	18	0	20	17	0	0	0	9	0	60	.317	4	14	31	.355	2	12
Choate, Randy	0	1	.000	4.76	17.0	14	10	9	3	0	1	1	8	0	12	22	0	0	0	6	0	27	.259	2	5	38	.184	1	4
Einertson, Darrell	0	0	.000	3.55	12.2	16	9	5	1	0	1	0	4	0	3	11	0	0	0	4	0	38	.263	0	8	15	.400	1	4
Dingman, Craig	0	0	.000	6.55	11.0	18	8	8	1	0	0	0	3	0	8	10	0	0	0	4	0	26	.462	1	9	22	.273	0	4
Ford, Ben	0	1	.000	9.00	11.0	14	11	11	1	0	0	3	7	0	5	4	2	0	0	0	0	24	.292	0	4	18	.389	1	7
Keisler, Randy	1	0	1.000	11.81	10.2	16	14	14	1	0	0	0	8	0	6	4	1	0	0	0	0	35	.400	1	10	9	.222	0	0
Lilly, Ted	0	0	.000	5.63	8.0	8	6	5	1	0	0	0	5	0	11	7	0	0	0	1	0	20	.200	1	5	14	.286	0	0
Tessmer, Jay	0	0	.000	6.75	6.2	9	6	5	3	0	0	0	1	1	5	7	0	0	0	5	0	24	.333	2	7	6	.167	1	2
Westbrook, Jake	0	2	.000	13.50	6.2	15	10	10	1	0	2	0	4	1	1	3	2	0	0	1	0	16	.563	1	7	16	.375	0	3
Yarnall, Ed	0	0	.000	15.00	3.0	5	5	5	1	0	0	1	3	0	1	2	1	0	0	1	0	8	.375	0	1	4	.500	1	1

PITCHERS WITH MORE THAN ONE A.L. TEAM

Name	W	L	Pct.	ERA	IP	H	R	ER	HR	SH	SF	HB	BB	IBB	SO	G	GS	CG	ShO	GF	Sv	vs. RH AB	Avg.	HR	RBI	vs. LH AB	Avg.	HR	RBI
Gooden, T.B.-N.Y.	6	5	.545	4.54	101.0	113	60	51	22	4	2	3	41	3	54	26	13	0	0	2	2	218	.303	12	23	179	.263	10	34

DESIGNATED HITTERS

Name	AB	Avg.	HR	RBI
Spencer, Shane	116	.233	4	12
Canseco, Jose	89	.258	5	16
Hill, Glenallen	86	.314	9	14
Knoblauch, Chuck	71	.338	0	6
Justice, David	65	.308	2	12
Leyritz, Jim	44	.250	0	3
Ledee, Ricky	26	.038	0	0
Williams, Bernie	15	.267	1	3
Polonia, Luis	12	.333	0	0
Posada, Jorge	11	.182	0	0
Johnson, Lance	10	.400	0	1
O'Neill, Paul	8	.500	1	3
Jose, Felix	2	1.000	0	0
Brosius, Scott	1	.000	0	1
Vizcaino, Jose	1	.000	0	0
Soriano, Alfonso	0	-	0	0

INDIVIDUAL STATISTICS

FIELDING

FIRST BASEMEN

Player	Pct.	G	PO	A	E	TC	DP
Martinez, Tino	.994	154	1154	88	7	1249	110
Posada, Jorge	.986	12	63	8	1	72	6
Bellinger, Clay	1.000	10	29	1	0	30	3
Sojo, Luis	.960	7	20	4	1	25	0
Brosius, Scott	1.000	2	3	0	0	3	0
Leyritz, Jim	1.000	1	2	0	0	2	0
Turner, Chris	1.000	1	1	0	0	1	0

SECOND BASEMEN

Player	Pct.	G	PO	A	E	TC	DP
Knoblauch, Chuck	.958	82	149	190	15	354	42
Vizcaino, Jose	.990	62	83	120	2	205	28
Sojo, Luis	.989	25	33	59	1	93	7
Bellinger, Clay	1.000	21	19	49	0	68	5
Delgado, Wilson	.950	14	16	22	2	40	3
Soriano, Alfonso	.000	1	0	0	1	1	0

THIRD BASEMEN

Player	Pct.	G	PO	A	E	TC	DP
Brosius, Scott	.968	134	101	231	11	343	23
Bellinger, Clay	.921	18	10	25	3	38	4
Soriano, Alfonso	.846	10	11	11	4	26	2
Sojo, Luis	1.000	10	9	10	0	19	0
Vizcaino, Jose	1.000	6	3	5	0	8	1
Delgado, Wilson	.667	5	1	1	1	3	0

SHORTSTOPS

Player	Pct.	G	PO	A	E	TC	DP
Jeter, Derek	.961	148	237	349	24	610	78
Delgado, Wilson	1.000	11	6	14	0	20	2
Soriano, Alfonso	.875	9	7	7	2	16	1
Bellinger, Clay	1.000	6	9	11	0	20	1
Sojo, Luis	1.000	2	2	2	0	4	0
Vizcaino, Jose	1.000	2	2	2	0	4	2

OUTFIELDERS

Player	Pct.	G	PO	A	E	TC	DP
O'Neill, Paul	.993	140	293	5	2	300	3
Williams, Bernie	1.000	137	353	2	0	355	1
Justice, David	.985	60	127	6	2	135	1
Ledee, Ricky	.979	49	94	1	2	97	0
Bellinger, Clay	.968	46	60	1	2	63	0
Spencer, Shane	.989	40	83	3	1	87	1
Thompson, Ryan	1.000	31	33	0	0	33	0
Polonia, Luis	.970	28	32	0	1	33	0
Jose, Felix	.929	14	13	0	1	14	0
Hill, Glenallen	1.000	12	19	0	0	19	0
Kelly, Roberto	1.000	10	18	0	0	18	0
Canseco, Jose	.818	5	9	0	2	11	0
Johnson, Lance	1.000	4	2	0	0	2	0
Brosius, Scott	-	2	0	0	0	0	0

CATCHERS

Player	Pct.	G	PO	A	E	TC	DP	PB
Posada, Jorge	.993	142	892	56	7	955	7	11
Turner, Chris	1.000	36	171	5	0	176	0	2
Leyritz, Jim	1.000	2	13	0	0	13	0	0

PITCHERS

Player	Pct.	G	PO	A	E	TC	DP
Nelson, Jeff	.909	73	0	10	1	11	1
Stanton, Mike	1.000	69	3	11	0	14	0
Rivera, Mariano	1.000	66	8	15	0	23	0
Grimsley, Jason	.917	63	11	11	2	24	4
Pettitte, Andy	.926	32	17	33	4	54	3
Clemens, Roger	.958	32	14	32	2	48	2
Cone, David	.935	30	9	20	2	31	0
Hernandez, Orlando	1.000	29	12	24	0	36	4
Choate, Randy	.750	22	0	3	1	4	0
Gooden, Dwight	1.000	18	4	14	0	18	3
Watson, Allen	1.000	17	1	2	0	3	0
Neagle, Denny	.900	16	7	11	2	20	1
Mendoza, Ramiro	1.000	14	2	8	0	10	0
Erdos, Todd	1.000	14	1	1	0	2	0
Einertson, Darrell	1.000	11	0	2	0	2	0
Dingman, Craig	-	10	0	0	0	0	0
Lilly, Ted	1.000	7	1	1	0	2	0
Tessmer, Jay	-	7	0	0	0	0	0
Ford, Ben	1.000	4	0	1	0	1	0
Keisler, Randy	-	4	0	0	0	0	0
Westbrook, Jake	1.000	3	1	0	0	1	0
Yarnall, Ed	-	2	0	0	0	0	0

PITCHING AGAINST EACH CLUB

Pitcher	Ana. W-L	Bal. W-L	Bos. W-L	Chi. W-L	Cle. W-L	Det. W-L	K.C. W-L	Min. W-L	Oak. W-L	Sea. W-L	T.B. W-L	Tex. W-L	Tor. W-L	N.L. W-L	Total W-L
Choate, Randy	0-0	0-0	0-0	0-0	0-0	0-0	0-0	0-0	0-0	0-0	0-0	0-0	0-1	0-0	0-1
Clemens, Roger	1-0	2-0	1-1	1-1	0-1	1-1	1-0	0-1	0-0	1-1	1-1	0-0	2-0	2-1	13-8
Cone, David	0-1	0-2	0-1	0-0	0-1	0-1	0-0	0-1	1-2	1-0	0-1	1-0	1-2	0-2	4-14
Dingman, Craig	0-0	0-0	0-0	0-0	0-0	0-0	0-0	0-0	0-0	0-0	0-0	0-0	0-0	0-0	0-0
Einertson, Darrell	0-0	0-0	0-0	0-0	0-0	0-0	0-0	0-0	0-0	0-0	0-0	0-0	0-0	0-0	0-0
Erdos, Todd	0-0	0-0	0-0	0-0	0-0	0-0	0-0	0-0	0-0	0-0	0-0	0-0	0-0	0-0	0-0
Ford, Ben	0-0	0-0	0-0	0-0	0-0	0-1	0-0	0-0	0-0	0-0	0-0	0-0	0-0	0-0	0-1
Gooden, Dwight	0-0	1-0	0-0	0-0	0-0	0-1	1-0	0-0	0-0	0-1	1-0	0-0	0-0	1-0	4-2
Grimsley, Jason	0-0	0-0	1-1	0-0	1-0	0-0	0-0	0-0	0-0	0-0	0-0	0-0	0-0	1-1	3-2
Hernandez, Orlando	1-1	0-1	0-2	0-2	1-1	0-0	0-0	1-0	1-0	0-1	1-1	3-1	1-2	3-1	12-13
Keisler, Randy	0-0	0-0	1-0	0-0	0-0	0-0	0-0	0-0	0-0	0-0	0-0	0-0	0-0	0-0	1-0
Lilly, Ted	0-0	0-0	0-0	0-0	0-0	0-0	0-0	0-0	0-0	0-0	0-0	0-0	0-0	0-0	0-0
Mendoza, Ramiro	1-0	0-0	1-0	2-0	2-0	0-0	1-0	0-2	0-1	0-0	0-0	0-0	0-1	0-0	7-4
Neagle, Denny	1-1	0-0	0-0	0-0	0-1	0-1	1-1	1-0	1-0	0-1	1-1	0-1	1-0	1-0	7-7
Nelson, Jeff	0-1	1-0	0-0	0-0	0-1	1-0	2-0	1-0	0-0	1-0	1-2	1-0	0-0	0-0	8-4
Pettitte, Andy	1-0	2-1	2-0	1-2	1-0	2-2	1-0	1-0	2-0	1-2	1-0	2-0	0-1	2-1	19-9
Rivera, Mariano	0-0	0-1	0-0	0-1	0-0	0-1	1-0	1-1	1-0	0-0	0-0	3-0	0-0	1-0	7-4
Stanton, Mike	0-1	1-0	1-0	0-1	0-0	0-0	0-1	0-0	0-0	0-0	0-0	0-0	0-0	0-0	2-3
Tessmer, Jay	0-0	0-0	0-0	0-0	0-0	0-0	0-0	0-0	0-0	0-0	0-0	0-0	0-0	0-0	0-0
Watson, Allen	0-0	0-0	0-0	0-0	0-0	0-0	0-0	0-0	0-0	0-0	0-0	0-0	0-0	0-0	0-0
Westbrook, Jake	0-0	0-0	0-1	0-1	0-0	0-0	0-0	0-0	0-0	0-0	0-0	0-0	0-0	0-0	0-2
Yarnall, Ed	0-0	0-0	0-0	0-0	0-0	0-0	0-0	0-0	0-0	0-0	0-0	0-0	0-0	0-0	0-0
Totals	5-5	7-5	7-6	4-8	5-5	4-8	8-2	5-5	6-3	4-6	6-6	10-2	5-7	11-6	87-74

INTERLEAGUE: Hernandez 1-0, Pettitte 1-0, Grimsley 0-1 vs. Braves; Grimsley 1-0, Hernandez 1-0, Cone 0-1 vs. Expos; Clemens 1-1, Pettitte 1-1, Hernandez 1-0, Gooden 1-0 vs. Mets; Rivera 1-0, Neagle 1-0, Cone 0-1 vs. Phillies; Clemens 1-0, Hernandez 0-1 vs. Marlins. Total: 11-6.

MISCELLANEOUS

HOME RUNS BY PARK

At Anaheim (9): Williams 2, Spencer 2, Canseco 1, O'Neill 1, Hill 1, Martinez 1, Brosius 1.
At Atlanta (4): Brosius 1, Turner 1, Ledee 1, Bellinger 1.
At Baltimore (6): O'Neill 1, Hill 1, Williams 1, Thompson 1, Jeter 1, Bellinger 1.
At Boston (14): Williams 3, Brosius 3, Jeter 2, Canseco 1, O'Neill 1, Jose 1, Justice 1, Posada 1, Spencer 1.
At Chicago (AL) (5): O'Neill 1, Brosius 1, Posada 1, Delgado 1, Ledee 1.
At Cleveland (5): Ledee 2, O'Neill 1, Williams 1, Spencer 1.
At Detroit (2): O'Neill 1, Williams 1.
At Kansas City (6): Justice 2, O'Neill 1, Brosius 1, Jeter 1, Bellinger 1.
At Minnesota (3): Hill 1, Justice 1, Posada 1.
At Montreal (4): Martinez 1, Williams 1, Posada 1, Ledee 1.
At New York (AL) (117): Posada 18, Williams 15, Justice 14, Martinez 12, Hill 11, O'Neill 10, Jeter 8, Brosius 7, Knoblauch 5, Spencer 4, Canseco 2, Sojo 2, Thompson 2, Ledee 2, Bellinger 2, Polonia 1, Kelly 1, Leyritz 1.
At New York (NL) (1): Martinez 1.
At Oakland (1): Canseco 1.
At Seattle (6): Soriano 2, Canseco 1, Martinez 1, Jeter 1, Spencer 1.
At Tampa Bay (4): Hill 1, Williams 1, Brosius 1, Posada 1.
At Texas (11): Posada 3, Williams 2, Jeter 2, O'Neill 1, Justice 1, Brosius 1, Bellinger 1.
At Toronto (7): Williams 3, Posada 2, Hill 1, Justice 1.

LOW-HIT GAMES

No-hitters: None.
One-hitters: None.
Two-hitters: Andy Pettitte, May 29 vs. Oakland, W 4-1.

10-STRIKEOUT GAMES

Roger Clemens 2, Andy Pettitte 1, Orlando Hernandez 1, Total: 4

FOUR OR MORE HITS IN ONE GAME

Derek Jeter 5, Jorge Posada 4, Scott Brosius 3, Paul O'Neill 2, Jose Vizcaino 2, Bernie Williams 2, Lance Johnson 1, Tino Martinez 1, Total: 20

MULTI-HOMER GAMES

David Justice 3, Bernie Williams 2, Jorge Posada 2, Glenallen Hill 1, Tino Martinez 1, Total: 9

GRAND SLAMS

5-7: Scott Brosius (off Baltimore's Mike Trombley)
5-17: Bernie Williams (off Chicago's Tanyon Sturtze)
7-25: Bernie Williams (off Baltimore's Chuck McElroy)
7-28: Glenallen Hill (off Minnesota's Bob Wells)
8-9: Tino Martinez (off Oakland's Kevin Appier)
9-5: Scott Brosius (off Kansas City's Andy Larkin)

PINCH HITTERS

(Minimum 5 at-bats)

Name	AB	Avg.	HR	RBI
Johnson, Lance	14	.214	0	1
Ledee, Ricky	7	.286	1	4
Bellinger, Clay	6	.333	1	1
Hill, Glenallen	6	.333	2	5
Canseco, Jose	6	.167	0	0
Jose, Felix	6	.000	0	0
Martinez, Tino	5	.400	0	0
Leyritz, Jim	5	.200	0	0

DEBUTS

4-15: Darrell Einertson, P.
6-17: Jake Westbrook, P.
6-30: Craig Dingman, P.
7-1: Randy Choate, P.
9-10: Randy Keisler, P.

GAMES BY POSITION

Catcher: Jorge Posada 142, Chris Turner 36, Jim Leyritz 2.
First base: Tino Martinez 154, Jorge Posada 12, Clay Bellinger 10, Luis Sojo 7, Scott Brosius 2, Jim Leyritz 1, Chris Turner 1.
Second base: Chuck Knoblauch 82, Jose Vizcaino 62, Luis Sojo 25, Clay Bellinger 21, Wilson Delgado 14, Alfonso Soriano 1.
Third base: Scott Brosius 134, Clay Bellinger 18, Luis Sojo 10, Alfonso Soriano 10, Jose Vizcaino 6, Wilson Delgado 5.
Shortstop: Derek Jeter 148, Wilson Delgado 11, Alfonso Soriano 9, Clay Bellinger 6, Jose Vizcaino 2, Luis Sojo 2.
Outfield: Paul O'Neill 140, Bernie Williams 137, David Justice 60, Ricky Ledee 49, Clay Bellinger 46, Shane Spencer 40, Ryan Thompson 31, Luis Polonia 28, Felix Jose 14, Glenallen Hill 12, Roberto Kelly 10, Jose Canseco 5, Lance Johnson 4, Scott Brosius 2.
Designated hitter: Shane Spencer 33, Jose Canseco 26, Glenallen Hill 24, Chuck Knoblauch 20, David Justice 18, Jim Leyritz 15, Ricky Ledee 10, Luis Polonia 7, Jose Vizcaino 4, Bernie Williams 4, Jorge Posada 4, Lance Johnson 3, Paul O'Neill 2, Felix Jose 2, Scott Brosius 1, Alfonso Soriano 1.

STREAKS

Wins: 8 (April 12-19)
Losses: 6 (September 17-22)
Consecutive games with at least one hit: 17, Bernie Williams (June 19-July 7)
Wins by pitcher: 7, Andy Pettitte (July 25-August 24)

ATTENDANCE

Home: 3,227,657
Road: 2,822,341
Highest (home): 55,839 (June 10 vs. New York).
Highest (road): 54,286 (July 9 vs. New York).
Lowest (home): 14,292 (May 11 vs. Tampa Bay).
Lowest (road): 15,025 (September 5 vs. Kansas City).

Oakland Athletics

DAY BY DAY

Date	Opp.	Res.	Score	(inn.*)	Hits	Opp. hits	Winning pitcher	Losing pitcher	Save	Record	Pos.	GB
4-3	Det.	L	4-7		4	11	Nomo	Appier	Jones	0-1	T2nd	1.0
4-4	Det.	W	3-1		5	2	Hudson	Nitkowski	Isringhausen	1-1	2nd	1.0
4-5	Det.	W	8-2		10	6	Olivares	Moehler		2-1	T1st	...
4-7	Chi.	L	6-7		6	9	Eyre	Magnante	Foulke	2-2	T3rd	1.0
4-8	Chi.	L	3-7		7	13	Sirotka	Mahay		2-3	4th	1.0
4-9	Chi.	W	14-2		9	9	Appier	Wells		3-3	T3rd	1.0
4-10	Cle.	L	4-9		8	14	Kamieniecki	Tam		3-4	4th	1.5
4-11	Cle.	L	1-5		4	7	Nagy	Olivares		3-5	4th	2.0
4-12	Cle.	L	0-5		5	8	Wright	Heredia		3-6	4th	2.5
4-14	At Bos.	W	13-6		11	12	Appier	Rose		4-6	4th	2.0
4-15	At Bos.	L	2-14		6	13	P. Martinez	Hudson		4-7	4th	3.0
4-16	At Bos.	L	4-5		10	9	Lowe	Mathews		4-8	4th	4.0
4-17	At Bos.	W	1-0		10	4	Heredia	Fassero	Isringhausen	5-8	4th	3.5
4-18	At Cle.	W	8-5		9	9	Mulder	Nagy	Isringhausen	6-8	T3rd	2.5
4-19	At Cle.	W	10-5		12	12	Appier	Wright		7-8	3rd	1.5
4-20	At Cle.	L	5-9		15	14	Burba	Hudson		7-9	3rd	2.0
4-21	Bal.	L	9-11		11	15	Ponson	Olivares	Timlin	7-10	3rd	3.0
4-22	Bal.	L	3-4		9	10	Mercedes	Heredia	Groom	7-11	4th	4.0
4-23	Bal.	W	3-2	(11)	7	7	Isringhausen	Worrell		8-11	3rd	4.0
4-24	Tor.	L	2-3		10	7	Wells	Appier	Koch	8-12	4th	4.0
4-25	Tor.	W	11-2		12	4	Hudson	Halladay		9-12	3rd	4.0
4-26	Tor.	L	2-4		6	9	Carpenter	Olivares	Koch	9-13	3rd	4.0
4-28	At Min.	W	5-2		6	7	Heredia	Radke	Isringhausen	10-13	3rd	3.0
4-29	At Min.	W	6-2	(10)	7	10	Mathews	Guardado		11-13	3rd	3.0
4-30	At Min.	W	8-2		14	7	Hudson	Bergman		12-13	3rd	2.0
5-1	At K.C.	W	7-5		7	9	Olivares	Reichert	Isringhausen	13-13	T2nd	1.5
5-2	At K.C.	L	7-8	(10)	10	14	Rakers	Isringhausen		13-14	T2nd	2.5
5-3	At K.C.	W	14-5		20	15	Heredia	Suppan		14-14	T2nd	1.5
5-5	At Tex.	L	16-17		16	21	Wetteland	Tam		14-15	3rd	1.5
5-6	At Tex.	L	10-11		14	17	Wetteland	Isringhausen		14-16	3rd	2.5
5-7	At Tex.	W	7-6		9	12	Olivares	Davis	Jones	15-16	3rd	2.5
5-8	At Ana.	L	8-9		10	17	Petkovsek	Mathews	Percival	15-17	3rd	2.5
5-9	At Ana.	W	5-2		9	9	Heredia	Hill	Isringhausen	16-17	3rd	2.5
5-10	At Ana.	W	7-4		13	9	Isringhausen	Petkovsek		17-17	2nd	1.5
5-11	Sea.	W	7-6		10	8	Hudson	Meche	Isringhausen	18-17	2nd	0.5
5-12	Sea.	W	9-7		6	10	Mathews	Sasaki		19-17	1st	+0.5
5-13	Sea.	L	4-6		8	6	Tomko	Appier	Mesa	19-18	2nd	0.5
5-14	Sea.	W	7-2		6	10	Heredia	Abbott		20-18	1st	+0.5
5-15	K.C.	W	6-3		7	7	Mulder	Fussell	Isringhausen	21-18	1st	+0.5
5-16	K.C.	L	7-8		11	11	Reichert	D. Jones	Spradlin	21-19	2nd	0.5
5-17	K.C.	L	3-4		3	8	Batista	Olivares	Spradlin	21-20	2nd	1.5
5-18	Min.	L	5-10		7	18	Redman	Vizcaino		21-21	3rd	2.0
5-19	Min.	L	2-3		3	9	Radke	Heredia		21-22	4th	3.0
5-20	Min.	L	0-3		3	9	Milton	Mulder	Guardado	21-23	4th	3.0
5-21	Min.	W	13-4		15	11	Hudson	Bergman		22-23	4th	3.0
5-23	At T.B.	L	4-6		10	11	Rekar	Olivares	Hernandez	22-24	4th	3.0
5-24	At T.B.	W	9-2		12	6	Appier	Gooden	Tam	23-24	4th	2.0
5-25	At T.B.	W	6-3		8	8	Heredia	Yan	Isringhausen	24-24	4th	2.0
5-26	At Bal.	L	3-8		6	13	Erickson	Mulder		24-25	4th	2.0
5-27	At Bal.	W	4-0		11	2	Hudson	Johnson		25-25	4th	2.0
5-29	At N.Y.	L	1-4		2	6	Pettitte	Olivares		25-26	4th	2.5
5-30	At N.Y.	W	7-4		11	10	Appier	Mendoza	Isringhausen	26-26	4th	1.5
5-31	At N.Y.	W	8-7		9	11	Heredia	Cone	Isringhausen	27-26	T3rd	0.5
6-2	S.F.	W	5-4		8	10	Mulder	Ortiz	Isringhausen	28-26	T2nd	0.5
6-3	S.F.	W	9-7		11	9	D. Jones	Embree	Isringhausen	29-26	1st	+0.5
6-4	S.F.	L	2-18		7	19	Estes	Olivares		29-27	T3rd	0.5
6-5	S.D.	W	3-2	(10)	5	4	Isringhausen	Almanzar		30-27	3rd	0.5
6-6	S.D.	W	5-4		7	7	Heredia	Lopez	Isringhausen	31-27	2nd	0.5
6-7	S.D.	W	10-4		13	10	Service	Clement	Jones	32-27	1st	+0.5
6-9	At L.A.	W	3-1		4	5	Tam	Osuna	Isringhausen	33-27	1st	+1.5
6-10	At L.A.	L	2-7		7	13	Brown	Olivares		33-28	1st	+0.5
6-11	At L.A.	W	6-0		7	7	Appier	Gagne		34-28	1st	+0.5
6-12	At Min.	L	2-7		9	8	Milton	Heredia		34-29	2nd	0.5
6-13	At Min.	W	6-5		13	12	Mulder	Mays	Isringhausen	35-29	2nd	0.5
6-14	At Min.	W	9-6		16	8	Hudson	Bergman		36-29	1st	+0.5
6-16	At K.C.	W	8-3		11	8	D. Jones	Reichert	Tam	37-29	1st	+1.0
6-17	At K.C.	W	10-4		13	7	Appier	Witasick		38-29	1st	+1.0
6-18	At K.C.	W	21-3		21	8	Heredia	D'Amico		39-29	1st	+1.0
6-19	Bal.	W	13-12	(10)	14	16	Tam	Timlin		40-29	1st	+2.0
6-20	Bal.	W	8-5		9	9	Hudson	Ponson	Isringhausen	41-29	1st	+2.0
6-21	Bal.	W	10-3		15	8	Prieto	Mussina		42-29	1st	+2.0
6-23	K.C.	W	10-6		13	12	Appier	Durbin		43-29	1st	+1.5
6-24	K.C.	L	3-8		9	13	Bottalico	Heredia		43-30	1st	+0.5
6-25	K.C.	W	4-3		9	7	Mulder	Suppan	Isringhausen	44-30	1st	+0.5
6-27	Tex.	W	7-6		10	10	Hudson	Perisho	Isringhausen	45-30	1st	+0.5
6-28	Tex.	L	3-5		6	10	Helling	Appier	Wetteland	45-31	1st	+0.5
6-29	Tex.	L	1-3		8	9	Loaiza	Heredia	Wetteland	45-32	2nd	0.5
6-30	At Ana.	L	0-7		3	12	Cooper	Mulder		45-33	2nd	0.5

HIGHLIGHTS

High point: The A's won their first division title since 1992 by beating Texas 3-0 on the final day. Adding spice to the celebration were Tim Hudson's 20th victory and Jason Isringhausen's 33rd save. With the win, Oakland finished a half game ahead of wild-card winner Seattle and avoided having to travel to Tampa for a season-extending makeup game.

Low point: After being swept at New York, the A's came home August 11 and lost 11-4 to Detroit—Oakland's season-high sixth consecutive defeat. The loss pushed the A's seven games behind the first-place Mariners.

Turning point: After missing eight of 13 games with a shoulder injury, Jason Giambi returned to action September 2 and the A's took off. Giambi hit .400 the rest of the way (38-for-95) with 13 homers and 32 RBIs and Oakland finished on a 22-6 tear.

Most valuable player: Giambi, the league's MVP, continued his amazing rise up the star charts. The first baseman established career highs in average (.333), homers (43) and RBIs (137) and his 137 walks and .474 on-base percentage led both leagues.

Most valuable pitcher: In less than two full seasons, Hudson has established himself as one of the league's elite. An All-Star at age 24, Hudson tied for the league lead in wins (20) and raised his career record to 31-8. Opponents batted .227 against him.

Most improved player: Miguel Tejada is being compared to the Big Three of shortstops—Alex Rodriguez Nomar Garciaparra and Derek Jeter. Tejada has cut back on mental errors and his defense is spectacular. So is his bat, which produced 30 homers and 115 RBIs.

Most pleasant surprise: Minor league free-agent pickup Jeff Tam finished with a 2.63 ERA out of the bullpen. The 30-year-old sinkerballer allowed just three homers in $85^2/_3$ innings.

Key injuries: The A's lost D.H. John Jaha, their cleanup hitter, to season-ending shoulder surgery. That took a much-needed righthanded threat out of the lefty-heavy Oakland lineup and left Jason Giambi without much protection. ... Olmedo Saenz, who took over as the A's top righthanded slugger, missed nearly two months with a hamstring injury late in the season.

Notable: The A's won 91 games, an improvement of four over 1999, and spent 26 days in sole possession of first place in the A.L. West. Most of those days were in June. From June 29 until September 29, the A's were in first only once, a brief one-day tie with Seattle. ... The A's set a major league record with 14 grand slams, two more than Atlanta hit in 1997. Jason Giambi had four. ... The A's set Oakland records for average (.270), runs (947), hits (1.501) and RBIs (908).

—SUSAN SLUSSER

MISCELLANEOUS

RECORDS

2000 regular-season record: 91-70 (1st in A.L. West); 47-34 at home; 44-36 on road; 30-20 vs. East; 28-27 vs. Central; 33-23 vs. West; 21-26 vs. lefthanded starters; 70-44 vs. righthanded starters; 79-67 on grass; 12-3 on turf; 35-25 in daytime; 56-45 at night; 21-19 in one-run games; 8-5 in extra-inning games; 0-0-2 in doubleheaders.

Team record past five years: 395-414 (.488, ranks 9th in league in that span).

TEAM LEADERS

Batting average: Jason Giambi (.333).
At-bats: Miguel Tejada (607).
Runs: Jason Giambi (108).
Hits: Jason Giambi (170).
Total Bases: Jason Giambi (330).
Doubles: Ben Grieve (40).
Triples: Adam Piatt (5).
Home runs: Jason Giambi (43).
Runs batted in: Jason Giambi (137).
Stolen bases: Randy Velarde (9).
Slugging percentage: Jason Giambi (.647).
On-base percentage: Jason Giambi (.476).
Wins: Tim Hudson (20).
Earned-run average: Gil Heredia (4.12).
Complete games: Gil Heredia, Tim Hudson (2).
Shutouts: Tim Hudson (2).
Saves: Jason Isringhausen (33).
Innings pitched: Tim Hudson (202.1).
Strikeouts: Tim Hudson (169).

Date	Opp.	Res.	Score	(inn.*)	Hits	Opp. hits	Winning pitcher	Losing pitcher	Save	Record	Pos.	GB
7-1	At Ana.	L	2-7		3	8	Washburn	Prieto		45-34	2nd	1.5
7-2	At Ana.	W	10-3		12	8	Hudson	Belcher		46-34	2nd	1.5
7-3	At Tex.	L	3-8		9	9	Helling	Appier		46-35	2nd	2.5
7-4	At Tex.	L	7-10		11	13	Davis	Service	Wetteland	46-36	2nd	2.5
7-5	At Tex.	L	4-9		11	17	Rogers	Mulder		46-37	2nd	3.5
7-7	Ari.	W	5-4	(11)	11	9	Tam	Daal		47-37	2nd	2.0
7-8	Ari.	W	8-7	(10)	13	9	Isringhausen	Swindell		48-37	2nd	2.0
7-9	Ari.	L	2-4		6	13	Johnson	Heredia	Mantei	48-38	2nd	3.0
7-13	At S.F.	L	2-4		7	6	Ortiz	Mulder	Nen	48-39	2nd	3.0
7-14	At S.F.	L	2-4		5	10	Gardner	Appier	Nen	48-40	2nd	4.0
7-15	At S.F.	W	6-2		16	9	Heredia	Rueter		49-40	2nd	3.0
7-17†	At Col.	W	11-10		13	12	Magnante	White	Isringhausen	50-40		
7-17‡	At Col.	L	9-10	(10)	12	15	DeJean	Isringhausen		50-41	2nd	3.0
7-18	At Col.	L	3-18		8	21	Astacio	Mulder		50-42	2nd	4.0
7-19	Sea.	L	3-6		7	10	Moyer	Appier	Sasaki	50-43	T2nd	5.0
7-20	Sea.	W	5-4		5	9	Heredia	Sele	Isringhausen	51-43	2nd	4.0
7-21	Ana.	L	3-12		8	16	Washburn	Hudson		51-44	3rd	5.0
7-22	Ana.	W	10-3		18	5	Zito	Cooper		52-44	T2nd	5.0
7-23	Ana.	W	5-0		11	6	Mulder	Hill		53-44	2nd	4.0
7-24	At Sea.	L	4-6		9	11	Moyer	Appier	Sasaki	53-45	2nd	5.0
7-25	At Sea.	W	8-7		11	11	Heredia	Sele	Isringhausen	54-45	2nd	4.0
7-26	At Sea.	W	6-1		5	8	Hudson	Abbott		55-45	2nd	3.0
7-27	Bos.	L	4-5	(10)	10	8	Garces	Tam	Lowe	55-46	2nd	3.0
7-28	Bos.	L	1-4		5	7	P. Martinez	Mulder	Lowe	55-47	2nd	4.0
7-29	Bos.	W	12-1		11	7	Appier	Fassero		56-47	2nd	4.0
7-30	Bos.	W	5-2		3	6	Heredia	Arrojo	Isringhausen	57-47	2nd	4.0
7-31	Tor.	W	6-1		12	4	Hudson	Wells		58-47	2nd	3.0
8-1	Tor.	W	3-1	(10)	6	7	Isringhausen	Koch		59-47	2nd	3.0
8-2	Tor.	W	5-4		12	10	Mecir	Guthrie	Isringhausen	60-47	2nd	2.0
8-4	At Chi.	W	5-3		8	8	Appier	Sirotka	Isringhausen	61-47	2nd	1.0
8-5	At Chi.	L	3-4	(10)	7	9	Foulke	Mathews		61-48	2nd	2.0
8-6	At Chi.	L	0-13		5	15	Baldwin	Hudson		61-49	2nd	3.0
8-8	At N.Y.	L	3-4		7	6	Rivera	Isringhausen		61-50	2nd	5.0
8-9	At N.Y.	L	1-12		9	12	Pettitte	Appier		61-51	2nd	5.0
8-10	At N.Y.	L	6-12		13	15	Cone	Mulder		61-52	2nd	6.0
8-11	Det.	L	4-11		9	15	Weaver	Heredia		61-53	2nd	7.0
8-12	Det.	W	9-5		11	9	Hudson	Bernero		62-53	2nd	6.0
8-13	Det.	L	3-5		10	11	Moehler	Zito	Jones	62-54	2nd	6.0
8-14	Cle.	W	8-1		13	8	Appier	Bere		63-54	2nd	5.0
8-15	Cle.	W	5-3		6	10	Mulder	Burba	Isringhausen	64-54	2nd	4.0
8-16	Cle.	W	7-6		12	9	D. Jones	Wickman		65-54	2nd	3.0
8-18	At Det.	L	1-10		3	17	Nomo	Hudson		65-55	2nd	3.0
8-19	At Det.	L	3-4		10	9	Moehler	Zito	Jones	65-56	2nd	3.0
8-20	At Det.	W	5-4	(11)	14	10	Isringhausen	Cruz	Tam	66-56	2nd	2.0
8-21	At Det.	L	1-3		5	8	Sparks	Mulder	Jones	66-57	2nd	2.5
8-22	At Cle.	L	6-14		12	16	Finley	Heredia		66-58	2nd	3.5
8-23	At Cle.	L	5-7		10	12	Shuey	Hudson	Wickman	66-59	2nd	3.5
8-24	At Cle.	W	11-7		12	11	Zito	Woodard	Mecir	67-59	2nd	2.5
8-25	N.Y.	W	8-1		8	5	Appier	Cone		68-59	2nd	1.5
8-26	N.Y.	L	6-10		10	14	Hernandez	Mulder	Rivera	68-60	2nd	2.5
8-27	N.Y.	L	5-7		6	10	Neagle	Mecir	Rivera	68-61	2nd	2.5
8-28	Chi.	W	3-0		6	1	Hudson	Parque		69-61	2nd	1.5
8-29	Chi.	L	0-3		5	7	Baldwin	Zito	Foulke	69-62	2nd	2.5
8-30	Chi.	L	3-8		9	11	Sirotka	Appier	Howry	69-63	2nd	2.5
9-1	At Tor.	L	3-4		10	14	Frascatore	D. Jones		69-64	2nd	2.5
9-2	At Tor.	W	8-0		9	5	Heredia	Trachsel	Mecir	70-64	2nd	2.5
9-3	At Tor.	W	4-3		7	8	Hudson	Loaiza	Mecir	71-64	2nd	2.5
9-4	At Tor.	W	10-0		19	2	Zito	Wells		72-64	2nd	1.5
9-5	At Bos.	L	3-10		6	12	Schourek	Appier		72-65	2nd	2.5
9-6	At Bos.	W	6-4		13	9	Mulder	Arrojo	Mecir	73-65	2nd	1.5
9-8	T.B.	L	0-4		2	5	Lidle	Heredia	Creek	73-66	2nd	2.0
9-9	T.B.	W	10-0		14	2	Hudson	Lopez		74-66	2nd	2.0
9-10	T.B.	W	11-0		12	5	Zito	Wilson		75-66	2nd	2.0
9-11	T.B.	W	5-1		7	6	Appier	Creek		76-66	2nd	1.0
9-12	Min.	W	5-3		10	6	Mulder	Radke	Isringhausen	77-66	2nd	1.0
9-13	Min.	L	6-7		9	17	Milton	Heredia	Hawkins	77-67	2nd	2.0
9-15	At T.B.	W	17-3		20	4	Zito	Lopez		78-67	2nd	2.0
9-16	At T.B.	W	5-2		8	8	Hudson	Wilson	Isringhausen	79-67	2nd	2.0
9-18	At Bal.	W	12-3		17	8	Appier	Rapp		80-67	2nd	2.5
9-19†	At Bal.	W	7-4		8	13	Mecir	Johnson	Isringhausen	81-67		
9-20†	At Bal.	L	0-2		4	4	McElroy	Zito	Kohlmeier	81-68		
9-20‡	At Bal.	W	4-0		10	9	Heredia	Mercedes		82-68	2nd	3.0
9-21	At Sea.	W	5-2		6	5	Hudson	Moyer	Isringhausen	83-68	2nd	2.0
9-22	At Sea.	W	8-3		9	7	Olivares	Garcia	Service	84-68	2nd	1.0
9-23	At Sea.	W	8-2		10	2	Appier	Rhodes		85-68	1st	...
9-24	At Sea.	L	2-3		8	6	Halama	Prieto	Sasaki	85-69	2nd	1.0
9-25	Ana.	W	7-5		10	11	Zito	Belcher		86-69	2nd	0.5
9-26	Ana.	W	10-3		8	7	Hudson	Schoeneweis		87-69	2nd	0.5
9-27	Ana.	W	9-7		10	13	D. Jones	Holtz	Isringhausen	88-69	2nd	0.5
9-28	Ana.	L	3-6	(14)	8	12	Holtz	Service	Percival	88-70	2nd	0.5
9-29	Tex.	W	7-5		8	12	Mecir	Cordero	Isringhausen	89-70	1st	+0.5
9-30	Tex.	W	23-2		24	9	Zito	Oliver		90-70	1st	+0.5
10-1	Tex.	W	3-0		8	6	Hudson	Glynn	Isringhausen	91-70	1st	+0.5

Monthly records: April (12-13), May (15-13), June (18-7), July (13-14), August (11-16), September (21-7), October (1-0).
*Innings, if other than nine. † First game of a doubleheader. ‡ Second game of a doubleheader.

MEMORABLE GAMES

September 21 at Seattle

Trailing the Mariners by three games in the A.L. West Division and the Indians by a half game in the wild-card race, the A's opened a key four-game series at Safeco Field. Tim Hudson, looking for his 18th win, fell behind 2-0 in the first but the A's rallied for a 5-2 win by scoring one run in the fourth and four in the sixth. Miguel Tejada hit a home run in the momentum-saving victory.

Oakland	AB	R	H	BI	Seattle	AB	R	H	BI
Long, cf	4	0	0	0	Henderson, lf	4	0	0	0
Ortiz, 2b	2	1	1	0	Wilson, c	0	0	0	0
Velarde, 2b	1	0	0	0	Martin, ph	0	0	0	0
Ja.Giambi, 1b	3	1	1	0	Cameron, cf	3	1	1	0
Tejada, ss	3	2	1	1	Rodriguez, ss	5	1	1	0
Grieve, lf	4	0	0	0	Martinez, dh	2	0	0	1
Christenson, lf	0	0	0	0	Olerud, 1b	3	0	0	0
Piatt, rf	3	1	0	1	Buhner, rf	3	0	1	0
Porter, rf	0	0	0	0	Bell, 3b	4	0	0	0
Stairs, dh	4	0	2	2	Oliver, c	2	0	0	0
Chavez, 3b	4	0	1	1	Ibanez, ph-lf	2	0	1	0
Hernandez, c	3	0	0	0	McLemore, 2b	4	0	1	0
Totals	**31**	**5**	**6**	**5**	**Totals**	**32**	**2**	**5**	**1**

Oakland ....0 0 0 1 0 4 0 0 0—5 6 1
Seattle ....2 0 0 0 0 0 0 0 0—2 5 0

E—Hudson (4). DP—Seattle 1. LOB—Oakland 3, Seattle 10. 2B—Ja.Giambi (29), Stairs (25), Buhner (20). HR—Tejada (28). SB—Cameron (20), Rodriguez (14). CS—Stairs (2).

Oakland	IP	H	R	ER	BB	SO
Hudson (W 18-6)	6	5	2	1	3	6
Mecir	1.1	0	0	0	2	3
Tam	0.2	0	0	0	0	1
Isringhausen (S 30)	1	0	0	0	1	1

Seattle	IP	H	R	ER	BB	SO
Moyer (L 13-10)	5.2	6	5	5	3	4
Tomko	3.1	0	0	0	1	0

Hudson pitched to 2 batters in 7th.

HBP—Martinez by Hudson. WP--Hudson. U—HP, Bell. 1B, Nelson. 2B, Hirschbeck. 3B, Iassogna.T—3:14. A—44,786.

September 30 at Oakland

The A's set Oakland records with 23 runs and a 21-run margin of victory in a 23-2 win over Texas. The A's batted around three times and scored nine runs in the first and eight in the seventh. Jason Giambi hit his 43rd homer and Miguel Tejada hit his 30th, a grand slam that put the A's in position to claim their first division title in eight years in the season finale the next day.

Texas	AB	R	H	BI	Oakland	AB	R	H	BI
Green, cf	5	0	1	0	Long, cf	4	3	3	3
Clayton, ss	3	0	0	0	Porter, ph-cf	1	1	0	0
Young, 2b	2	0	0	0	Velarde, 2b	5	3	3	2
Palmeiro, 1b	3	0	0	0	Menechino, 2b	2	1	2	2
Dransfeldt, ss	1	0	0	0	JaGiambi, 1b	3	3	3	3
Curtis, lf	3	0	0	0	JeGiambi, pr-1b	2	0	1	0
Valdes, ph-rf	1	0	1	0	Saenz, dh	3	0	1	1
Sierra, dh	4	1	1	0	Ortiz, pr-dh	2	2	1	1
Ledee, rf-lf	2	1	1	0	Hinch, ph-dh	1	0	0	0
Sheldon, 2b-1b	4	0	2	0	Tejada, ss	4	1	1	5
Lamb, 3b	4	0	2	1	Byrnes, ph-rf	1	1	1	0
Knorr, c	3	0	0	0	Grieve, lf	4	1	1	0
Waszgis, c	1	0	1	1	Christ'son, pr-lf	1	2	1	3
					Piatt, rf-3b	6	2	4	0
					Chavez, 3b	0	1	0	0
					Bellhorn, ph-3b-ss	4	0	0	0
					Hernandez, c	2	1	0	1
					Fasano, c	3	1	2	2
Totals	**36**	**2**	**9**	**2**	**Totals**	**48**	**23**	**24**	**23**

Texas ....0 1 0 0 0 0 0 0 1—2 9 0
Oakland ....9 0 1 0 5 0 8 0 x—23 24 0

LOB—Texas 9, Oakland 11. 2B—Long (34), Grieve (39), Piatt (5), Fasano (6), Menechino (9). HR—Velarde (11), Ja.Giambi (43), Tejada (30), Christenson (4).

Texas	IP	H	R	ER	BB	SO
Oliver (L 2-9)	0.2	5	6	6	1	0
Sikorski	3.1	4	4	4	4	2
Perisho	0.1	3	4	4	1	1
Cordero	1.2	3	1	1	2	2
Johnson	0.2	5	7	7	2	2
Davis	0.1	2	1	1	0	1
Zimmerman	1	2	0	0	0	2

Oakland	IP	H	R	ER	BB	SO
Zito (W 7-4)	6	5	1	1	1	7
Service	2	2	0	0	0	2
Belitz	1	2	1	1	1	1

WP—Perisho. U—HP, Shulock. 1B, Runge. 2B, Roe. 3B, Lamplugh. T—3:32. A—35,546.

INDIVIDUAL STATISTICS

BATTING

Name	G	TPA	AB	R	H	TB	2B	3B	HR	RBI	Avg.	Obp.	Slg.	SH	SF	HP	BB	IBB	SO	SB	CS	GDP	vs RHP AB	vs RHP Avg.	vs RHP HR	vs RHP RBI	vs LHP AB	vs LHP Avg.	vs LHP HR	vs LHP RBI
Tejada, Miguel	160	681	607	105	167	291	32	1	30	115	.275	.349	.479	2	2	4	66	6	102	6	0	15	439	.296	20	89	168	.220	10	26
Grieve, Ben	158	675	594	92	166	289	40	1	27	104	.279	.359	.487	0	5	3	73	2	130	3	0	32	404	.285	19	66	190	.268	8	38
Long, Terrence	138	631	584	104	168	264	34	4	18	80	.288	.336	.452	0	3	1	43	1	77	5	0	18	413	.298	17	69	171	.263	1	11
Giambi, Jason	152	664	510	108	170	330	29	1	43	137	.333	.476	.647	0	8	9	137	6	96	2	0	9	334	.338	36	101	176	.324	7	36
Chavez, Eric	153	569	501	89	139	248	23	4	26	86	.277	.355	.495	0	5	1	62	8	94	2	2	9	379	.303	23	70	122	.197	3	16
Velarde, Randy	122	546	485	82	135	194	23	0	12	41	.278	.354	.400	3	1	3	54	0	95	9	3	15	340	.285	9	32	145	.262	3	9
Stairs, Matt	143	562	476	74	108	197	26	0	21	81	.227	.333	.414	1	6	1	78	4	122	5	2	7	362	.235	16	58	114	.202	5	23
Hernandez, Ramon	143	479	419	52	101	162	19	0	14	62	.241	.311	.387	10	5	7	38	1	64	1	0	14	312	.240	10	45	107	.243	4	17
Giambi, Jeremy	104	302	260	42	66	110	10	2	10	50	.254	.338	.423	3	4	3	32	2	61	0	0	7	196	.250	5	33	64	.266	5	17
Saenz, Olmedo	76	247	214	40	67	110	12	2	9	33	.313	.401	.514	0	1	7	25	2	40	1	0	6	120	.308	7	23	94	.319	2	10
Piatt, Adam	60	182	157	24	47	77	5	5	5	23	.299	.392	.490	1	0	1	23	0	44	0	1	1	73	.219	0	6	84	.369	5	17
Menechino, Frank	66	169	145	31	37	66	9	1	6	26	.255	.345	.455	1	2	1	20	0	45	1	4	1	96	.271	4	13	49	.224	2	13
Christenson, Ryan	121	153	129	31	32	50	2	2	4	18	.248	.349	.388	4	0	1	19	0	33	1	2	1	75	.307	2	9	54	.167	2	9
Fasano, Sal	52	144	126	21	27	54	6	0	7	19	.214	.306	.429	0	1	3	14	0	47	0	0	3	88	.227	4	13	38	.184	3	6
Stanley, Mike	32	113	97	11	26	45	7	0	4	18	.268	.363	.464	0	1	1	14	0	21	0	0	3	57	.211	0	5	40	.350	4	13
Jaha, John	33	133	97	14	17	21	1	0	1	5	.175	.398	.216	0	0	3	33	0	38	1	0	4	63	.143	1	4	34	.235	0	1
Becker, Rich	23	59	47	11	11	16	2	0	1	5	.234	.390	.340	0	0	1	11	0	17	1	0	1	43	.233	1	4	4	.250	0	1
Velandia, Jorge	18	25	24	1	3	4	1	0	0	2	.125	.160	.167	0	0	1	0	0	6	0	0	0	18	.167	0	2	6	.000	0	0
Bellhorn, Mark	9	15	13	2	2	2	0	0	0	0	.154	.267	.154	0	0	0	2	0	6	0	0	0	12	.167	0	0	1	.000	0	0
Porter, Bo	17	15	13	3	2	5	0	0	1	2	.154	.267	.385	0	0	0	2	0	5	0	0	0	7	.286	1	2	6	.000	0	0
Valdez, Mario	5	12	12	0	0	0	0	0	0	0	.000	.000	.000	0	0	0	0	0	3	0	0	0	10	.000	0	0	2	.000	0	0
Ortiz, Jose	7	13	11	4	2	2	0	0	0	1	.182	.308	.182	0	0	0	2	0	3	0	0	0	8	.125	0	1	3	.333	0	0
Byrnes, Eric	10	11	10	5	3	3	0	0	0	0	.300	.364	.300	0	0	1	0	0	1	2	1	0	4	.500	0	0	6	.167	0	0
Hinch, A.J.	6	9	8	1	2	2	0	0	0	0	.250	.333	.250	0	0	0	1	0	1	0	0	0	4	.500	0	0	4	.000	0	0
Appier, Kevin	31	6	6	0	1	1	0	0	0	0	.167	.167	.167	0	0	0	0	0	3	0	0	0	5	.200	0	0	1	.000	0	0
Mulder, Mark	27	4	4	0	0	0	0	0	0	0	.000	.000	.000	0	0	0	0	0	3	0	0	1	4	.000	0	0	0	.000	0	0
Hudson, Tim	33	3	3	0	0	0	0	0	0	0	.000	.000	.000	0	0	0	0	0	1	0	0	0	0	.000	0	0	3	.000	0	0
Heredia, Gil	32	3	2	0	1	1	0	0	0	0	.500	.500	.500	1	0	0	0	0	0	0	0	0	0	.000	0	0	2	.500	0	0
Prieto, Ariel	8	2	2	0	0	0	0	0	0	0	.000	.000	.000	0	0	0	0	0	1	0	0	0	2	.000	0	0	0	.000	0	0
Jones, Marcus	1	2	2	0	0	0	0	0	0	0	.000	.000	.000	0	0	0	0	0	0	0	0	0	1	.000	0	0	1	.000	0	0
Olivares, Omar	21	1	1	0	1	1	0	0	0	0	1.000	1.000	1.000	0	0	0	0	0	0	0	0	0	1	1.000	0	0	0	.000	0	0
Magnante, Mike	55	1	1	0	0	0	0	0	0	0	.000	.000	.000	0	0	0	0	0	0	0	0	0	1	.000	0	0	0	.000	0	0
Jones, Doug	54	0	0	0	0	0	0	0	0	0	.000	.000	.000	0	0	0	0	0	0	0	0	0	0	.000	0	0	0	.000	0	0
Sauveur, Rich	10	0	0	0	0	0	0	0	0	0	.000	.000	.000	0	0	0	0	0	0	0	0	0	0	.000	0	0	0	.000	0	0
Service, Scott	20	0	0	0	0	0	0	0	0	0	.000	.000	.000	0	0	0	0	0	0	0	0	0	0	.000	0	0	0	.000	0	0
Mahay, Ron	6	0	0	0	0	0	0	0	0	0	.000	.000	.000	0	0	0	0	0	0	0	0	0	0	.000	0	0	0	.000	0	0
Isringhausen, Jason	66	0	0	0	0	0	0	0	0	0	.000	.000	.000	0	0	0	0	0	0	0	0	0	0	.000	0	0	0	.000	0	0
Mathews, T.J.	50	1	0	0	0	0	0	0	0	0	.000	1.000	.000	0	0	0	1	0	0	0	0	0	0	.000	0	0	0	.000	0	0
Tam, Jeff	72	0	0	0	0	0	0	0	0	0	.000	.000	.000	0	0	0	0	0	0	0	0	0	0	.000	0	0	0	.000	0	0
Mecir, Jim	25	0	0	0	0	0	0	0	0	0	.000	.000	.000	0	0	0	0	0	0	0	0	0	0	.000	0	0	0	.000	0	0
Vizcaino, Luis	12	0	0	0	0	0	0	0	0	0	.000	.000	.000	0	0	0	0	0	0	0	0	0	0	.000	0	0	0	.000	0	0
Zito, Barry	14	0	0	0	0	0	0	0	0	0	.000	.000	.000	0	0	0	0	0	0	0	0	0	0	.000	0	0	0	.000	0	0
Ratliff, Jon	1	0	0	0	0	0	0	0	0	0	.000	.000	.000	0	0	0	0	0	0	0	0	0	0	.000	0	0	0	.000	0	0
Belitz, Todd	5	0	0	0	0	0	0	0	0	0	.000	.000	.000	0	0	0	0	0	0	0	0	0	0	.000	0	0	0	.000	0	0

Players with more than one A.L. team

Name	G	TPA	AB	R	H	TB	2B	3B	HR	RBI	Avg.	Obp.	Slg.	SH	SF	HP	BB	IBB	SO	SB	CS	GDP	vs RHP AB	vs RHP Avg.	vs RHP HR	vs RHP RBI	vs LHP AB	vs LHP Avg.	vs LHP HR	vs LHP RBI
Becker, Det.	92	298	238	48	58	91	12	0	7	34	.244	.383	.382	0	4	0	56	0	70	1	2	0	43	.233	1	4	4	.250	0	1
Becker, Oak.-Det.	115	357	285	59	69	107	14	0	8	39	.242	.384	.375	0	4	1	67	0	87	2	2	1	253	.257	8	36	32	.125	0	3
Mecir, T.B.	38	0	0	0	0	0	0	0	0	0	.000	.000	.000	0	0	0	0	0	0	0	0	0	0	.000	0	0	0	.000	0	0
Mecir, T.B.-Oak.	63	0	0	0	0	0	0	0	0	0	.000	.000	.000	0	0	0	0	0	0	0	0	0	0	.000	0	0	0	.000	0	0
Stanley, Bos.	58	218	185	22	41	76	5	0	10	28	.222	.327	.411	1	2	0	30	0	44	0	0	1	57	.211	0	5	40	.350	4	13
Stanley, Bos.-Oak.	90	331	282	33	67	121	12	0	14	46	.238	.339	.429	1	3	1	44	0	65	0	0	4	199	.211	8	25	83	.301	6	21

PITCHING

Name	W	L	Pct.	ERA	IP	H	R	ER	HR	SH	SF	HB	BB	IBB	SO	G	GS	CG	ShO	GF	Sv	vs. RH AB	vs. RH Avg.	vs. RH HR	vs. RH RBI	vs. LH AB	vs. LH Avg.	vs. LH HR	vs. LH RBI
Hudson, Tim	20	6	.769	4.14	202.1	169	100	93	24	5	7	7	82	5	169	32	32	2	2	0	0	326	.221	7	34	420	.231	17	54
Heredia, Gil	15	11	.577	4.12	198.2	214	106	91	24	4	6	4	66	5	101	32	32	2	0	0	0	385	.294	13	50	395	.256	11	40
Appier, Kevin	15	11	.577	4.52	195.1	200	109	98	23	5	6	9	102	10	129	31	31	1	1	0	0	357	.224	10	36	405	.296	13	57
Mulder, Mark	9	10	.474	5.44	154.0	191	106	93	22	3	8	4	69	3	88	27	27	0	0	0	0	466	.288	18	74	155	.368	4	21
Olivares, Omar	4	8	.333	6.75	108.0	134	86	81	10	0	7	7	60	0	57	21	16	1	0	1	0	239	.314	4	42	195	.303	6	31
Zito, Barry	7	4	.636	2.72	92.2	64	30	28	6	1	0	2	45	2	78	14	14	1	1	0	0	256	.195	6	26	72	.194	0	2
Tam, Jeff	3	3	.500	2.63	85.2	86	30	25	3	2	4	1	23	8	46	72	0	0	0	23	3	196	.209	1	14	125	.360	2	18
Jones, Doug	4	2	.667	3.93	73.1	86	34	32	6	2	2	2	18	4	54	54	0	0	0	22	2	157	.299	2	23	138	.283	4	21
Isringhausen, Jason	6	4	.600	3.78	69.0	67	34	29	6	2	1	3	32	5	57	66	0	0	0	57	33	113	.265	2	15	153	.242	4	19
Mathews, T.J.	2	3	.400	6.03	59.2	73	40	40	10	1	4	2	25	5	42	50	0	0	0	19	0	143	.301	6	26	98	.306	4	14
Magnante, Mike	1	1	.500	4.31	39.2	50	22	19	3	6	0	2	19	7	17	55	0	0	0	6	0	88	.330	1	13	73	.288	2	11
Service, Scott	1	2	.333	6.38	36.2	45	31	26	5	1	2	1	19	1	35	20	0	0	0	6	1	82	.305	4	20	67	.299	1	8
Mecir, Jim	3	1	.750	2.80	35.1	35	14	11	2	0	1	1	14	2	37	25	0	0	0	7	4	68	.309	2	12	69	.203	0	9
Prieto, Ariel	1	2	.333	5.12	31.2	42	21	18	3	2	1	1	13	0	19	8	6	0	0	2	0	58	.397	1	9	73	.260	2	10
Vizcaino, Luis	0	1	.000	7.45	19.1	25	17	16	2	0	1	2	11	0	18	12	0	0	0	1	0	45	.333	1	7	37	.270	1	7
Mahay, Ron	0	1	.000	9.00	16.0	26	18	16	4	1	1	0	9	0	5	5	2	0	0	1	0	53	.415	3	12	18	.222	1	3
Sauveur, Rich	0	0	.000	4.35	10.1	13	5	5	3	0	0	0	1	0	7	10	0	0	0	4	0	25	.280	3	8	17	.353	0	3
Belitz, Todd	0	0	.000	2.70	3.1	4	2	1	0	0	0	0	4	0	3	5	0	0	0	3	0	9	.333	0	2	6	.167	0	2
Jones, Marcus	0	0	.000	15.43	2.1	5	4	4	1	0	0	0	3	0	1	1	1	0	0	0	0	6	.500	1	3	6	.333	0	1
Ratliff, Jon	0	0	.000	0.00	1.0	0	0	0	0	0	0	0	0	0	0	1	0	0	0	1	0	3	.000	0	0	0	.000	0	0
Menechino, Frank	0	0	.000	36.00	1.0	6	4	4	1	0	0	0	0	0	0	1	0	0	0	1	0	5	.600	0	1	3	1.000	1	5

PITCHERS WITH MORE THAN ONE A.L. TEAM

Name	W	L	Pct.	ERA	IP	H	R	ER	HR	SH	SF	HB	BB	IBB	SO	G	GS	CG	ShO	GF	Sv	vs. RH AB	vs. RH Avg.	vs. RH HR	vs. RH RBI	vs. LH AB	vs. LH Avg.	vs. LH HR	vs. LH RBI
Mecir, T.B.	7	2	.778	3.08	49.2	35	17	17	2	1	1	1	22	0	33	38	0	0	0	10	1	68	.309	2	12	69	.203	0	9
Mecir, T.B.-Oak.	10	3	.769	2.96	85.0	70	31	28	4	1	2	2	36	2	70	63	0	0	0	2	5	159	.245	3	22	152	.204	1	13

DESIGNATED HITTERS

Name	AB	Avg.	HR	RBI
Stairs, Matt	124	.226	3	18
Jaha, John	96	.177	1	5
Giambi, Jason	85	.259	5	15
Saenz, Olmedo	84	.310	2	10
Giambi, Jeremy	62	.194	2	6
Grieve, Ben	42	.262	0	2
Piatt, Adam	36	.250	1	6
Stanley, Mike	24	.333	2	4
Byrnes, Eric	4	.500	0	0
Ortiz, Jose	4	.250	0	1
Becker, Rich	1	.000	0	0
Hinch, A.J.	1	.000	0	0
Mahay, Ron	0	-	0	0
Chavez, Eric	0	-	0	0
Menechino, Frank	0	-	0	0
Hudson, Tim	0	-	0	0

INDIVIDUAL STATISTICS

FIELDING

FIRST BASEMEN

Player	Pct.	G	PO	A	E	TC	DP
Giambi, Jason	.995	124	1161	59	6	1226	114
Stanley, Mike	.988	19	146	13	2	161	18
Saenz, Olmedo	.993	17	126	8	1	135	14
Giambi, Jeremy	1.000	15	55	5	0	60	5
Valdez, Mario	1.000	4	26	2	0	28	2
Piatt, Adam	1.000	3	5	0	0	5	0
Stairs, Matt	1.000	1	2	0	0	2	0

SECOND BASEMEN

Player	Pct.	G	PO	A	E	TC	DP
Velarde, Randy	.982	122	243	399	12	654	94
Menechino, Frank	.973	51	83	131	6	220	30
Velandia, Jorge	1.000	14	15	22	0	37	6
Ortiz, Jose	.857	3	2	4	1	7	1
Bellhorn, Mark	1.000	2	0	1	0	1	0

THIRD BASEMEN

Player	Pct.	G	PO	A	E	TC	DP
Chavez, Eric	.951	146	91	256	18	365	17
Saenz, Olmedo	.923	18	11	25	3	39	2
Piatt, Adam	1.000	13	4	11	0	15	0
Menechino, Frank	1.000	4	3	4	0	7	1
Bellhorn, Mark	1.000	2	0	4	0	4	0

SHORTSTOPS

Player	Pct.	G	PO	A	E	TC	DP
Tejada, Miguel	.972	160	233	501	21	755	115
Menechino, Frank	1.000	5	4	4	0	8	0
Velandia, Jorge	1.000	4	2	2	0	4	1
Chavez, Eric	1.000	2	1	0	0	1	0
Bellhorn, Mark	-	1	0	0	0	0	0

OUTFIELDERS

Player	Pct.	G	PO	A	E	TC	DP
Grieve, Ben	.988	144	237	6	3	246	0
Long, Terrence	.971	137	328	2	10	340	1
Christenson, Ryan	.951	114	95	2	5	102	1
Stairs, Matt	.979	103	185	5	4	194	1
Giambi, Jeremy	.966	55	81	3	3	87	0
Piatt, Adam	.950	29	37	1	2	40	0
Becker, Rich	.949	19	35	2	2	39	2
Porter, Bo	1.000	16	13	0	0	13	0
Byrnes, Eric	1.000	4	4	0	0	4	0

CATCHERS

Player	Pct.	G	PO	A	E	TC	DP	PB
Hernandez, Ramon	.984	142	764	43	13	820	7	7
Fasano, Sal	.981	52	231	22	5	258	2	1
Hinch, A.J.	.900	5	9	0	1	10	0	0

PITCHERS

Player	Pct.	G	PO	A	E	TC	DP
Tam, Jeff	.950	72	3	16	1	20	3
Isringhausen, Jason	.923	66	1	11	1	13	0
Magnante, Mike	.944	55	3	14	1	18	1
Jones, Doug	.941	54	6	10	1	17	0
Mathews, T.J.	1.000	50	2	11	0	13	1
Heredia, Gil	.974	32	9	29	1	39	0
Hudson, Tim	.897	32	15	20	4	39	1
Appier, Kevin	.957	31	8	14	1	23	1
Mulder, Mark	.906	27	7	22	3	32	1
Mecir, Jim	1.000	25	2	3	0	5	0
Olivares, Omar	.957	21	6	16	1	23	2
Service, Scott	.833	20	2	3	1	6	0
Zito, Barry	1.000	14	4	9	0	13	0
Vizcaino, Luis	1.000	12	1	3	0	4	0
Sauveur, Rich	1.000	10	0	1	0	1	0
Prieto, Ariel	.900	8	4	5	1	10	0
Mahay, Ron	1.000	5	1	2	0	3	0
Belitz, Todd	-	5	0	0	0	0	0
Jones, Marcus	-	1	0	0	0	0	0
Menechino, Frank	-	1	0	0	0	0	0
Ratliff, Jon	-	1	0	0	0	0	0

PITCHING AGAINST EACH CLUB

Pitcher	Ana. W-L	Bal. W-L	Bos. W-L	Chi. W-L	Cle. W-L	Det. W-L	K.C. W-L	Min. W-L	N.Y. W-L	Sea. W-L	T.B. W-L	Tex. W-L	Tor. W-L	N.L. W-L	Total W-L
Appier, Kevin	0-0	1-0	2-1	2-1	2-0	0-1	2-0	0-0	2-1	1-3	2-0	0-2	0-1	1-1	15-11
Belitz, Todd	0-0	0-0	0-0	0-0	0-0	0-0	0-0	0-0	0-0	0-0	0-0	0-0	0-0	0-0	0-0
Heredia, Gil	1-0	1-1	2-0	0-0	0-2	0-1	2-1	1-3	1-0	3-0	1-1	0-1	1-0	2-1	15-11
Hudson, Tim	2-1	2-0	0-1	1-1	0-2	2-1	0-0	3-0	0-0	3-0	2-0	2-0	3-0	0-0	20-6
Isringhausen, Jason	1-0	1-0	0-0	0-0	0-0	1-0	0-1	0-0	0-1	0-0	0-0	0-1	1-0	2-1	6-4
Jones, Doug	1-0	0-0	0-0	0-0	1-0	0-0	1-1	0-0	0-0	0-0	0-0	0-0	0-1	1-0	4-2
Jones, Marcus	0-0	0-0	0-0	0-0	0-0	0-0	0-0	0-0	0-0	0-0	0-0	0-0	0-0	0-0	0-0
Magnante, Mike	0-0	0-0	0-0	0-1	0-0	0-0	0-0	0-0	0-0	0-0	0-0	0-0	0-0	1-0	1-1
Mahay, Ron	0-0	0-0	0-0	0-1	0-0	0-0	0-0	0-0	0-0	0-0	0-0	0-0	0-0	0-0	0-1
Mathews, T.J.	0-1	0-0	0-1	0-1	0-0	0-0	0-0	1-0	0-0	1-0	0-0	0-0	0-0	0-0	2-3
Mecir, Jim	0-0	1-0	0-0	0-0	0-0	0-0	0-0	0-0	0-1	0-0	0-0	1-0	1-0	0-0	3-1
Menechino, Frank	0-0	0-0	0-0	0-0	0-0	0-0	0-0	0-0	0-0	0-0	0-0	0-0	0-0	0-0	0-0
Mulder, Mark	1-1	0-1	1-1	0-0	2-0	0-1	2-0	2-1	0-2	0-0	0-0	0-1	0-0	1-2	9-10
Olivares, Omar	0-0	0-1	0-0	0-0	0-1	1-0	1-1	0-0	0-1	1-0	0-1	1-0	0-1	0-2	4-8
Prieto, Ariel	0-1	1-0	0-0	0-0	0-0	0-0	0-0	0-0	0-0	0-1	0-0	0-0	0-0	0-0	1-2
Ratliff, Jon	0-0	0-0	0-0	0-0	0-0	0-0	0-0	0-0	0-0	0-0	0-0	0-0	0-0	0-0	0-0
Sauveur, Rich	0-0	0-0	0-0	0-0	0-0	0-0	0-0	0-0	0-0	0-0	0-0	0-0	0-0	0-0	0-0
Service, Scott	0-1	0-0	0-0	0-0	0-0	0-0	0-0	0-0	0-0	0-0	0-0	0-1	0-0	1-0	1-2
Tam, Jeff	0-0	1-0	0-1	0-0	0-1	0-0	0-0	0-0	0-0	0-0	0-0	0-1	0-0	2-0	3-3
Vizcaino, Luis	0-0	0-0	0-0	0-0	0-0	0-0	0-0	0-1	0-0	0-0	0-0	0-0	0-0	0-0	0-1
Zito, Barry	2-0	0-1	0-0	0-1	1-0	0-2	0-0	0-0	0-0	0-0	2-0	1-0	1-0	0-0	7-4
Totals	8-5	8-4	5-5	3-6	6-6	4-6	8-4	7-5	3-6	9-4	7-2	5-7	7-3	11-7	91-70

INTERLEAGUE: Tam 1-0, Appier 1-0, Olivares 0-1 vs. Dodgers; Isringhausen 1-0, Heredia 1-0, Service 1-0 vs. Padres; Mulder 1-1, Jones 1-0, Heredia 1-0, Olivares 0-1, Appier 0-1 vs. Giants; Magnante 1-0, Isringhausen 0-1, Mulder 0-1 vs. Rockies; Isringhausen 1-0, Tam 1-0, Heredia 0-1 vs. Diamondbacks. Total: 11-7.

MISCELLANEOUS

HOME RUNS BY PARK

At Anaheim (10): Grieve 2, Giambi 2, Stairs 1, Saenz 1, Giambi 1, Tejada 1, Christenson 1, Long 1.
At Baltimore (8): Chavez 3, Stairs 2, Giambi 1, Tejada 1, Giambi 1.
At Boston (6): Giambi 2, Stairs 1, Saenz 1, Chavez 1, Menechino 1.
At Chicago (AL) (2): Giambi 1, Grieve 1.
At Cleveland (7): Stairs 2, Giambi 2, Tejada 1, Grieve 1, Long 1.
At Colorado (6): Saenz 1, Giambi 1, Tejada 1, Grieve 1, Giambi 1, Long 1.
At Detroit (1): Grieve 1.
At Kansas City (18): Tejada 3, Hernandez 3, Giambi 2, Grieve 2, Chavez 2, Long 2, Jaha 1, Saenz 1, Fasano 1, Menechino 1.
At Los Angeles (2): Saenz 1, Chavez 1.
At Minnesota (8): Grieve 3, Giambi 2, Stairs 1, Tejada 1, Piatt 1.
At New York (AL) (9): Stairs 2, Chavez 2, Velarde 1, Giambi 1, Fasano 1, Long 1, Hernandez 1.
At Oakland (126): Giambi 23, Tejada 16, Chavez 15, Grieve 13, Velarde 11, Stairs 9, Long 9, Hernandez 7, Fasano 4, Stanley 3, Saenz 3, Christenson 3, Giambi 3, Menechino 3, Piatt 3, Becker 1.
At San Francisco (4): Fasano 1, Tejada 1, Chavez 1, Hernandez 1.
At Seattle (6): Giambi 3, Tejada 1, Grieve 1, Hernandez 1.
At Tampa Bay (7): Stairs 1, Saenz 1, Giambi 1, Tejada 1, Giambi 1, Chavez 1, Porter 1.
At Texas (10): Giambi 2, Giambi 2, Stairs 1, Grieve 1, Long 1, Hernandez 1, Menechino 1, Piatt 1.
At Toronto (9): Tejada 3, Long 2, Stanley 1, Stairs 1, Giambi 1, Grieve 1.

LOW-HIT GAMES

No-hitters: None.
One-hitters: Tim Hudson, August 28 vs. Chicago, W 3-0.
Two-hitters: Tim Hudson, September 9 vs. Tampa Bay, W 10-0.

10-STRIKEOUT GAMES

Tim Hudson 2, Barry Zito 1, Total: 3

FOUR OR MORE HITS IN ONE GAME

Jason Giambi 2, Ben Grieve 2, Terrence Long 2, Mike Stanley 1(including one five-hit game), Matt Stairs 1, Miguel Tejada 1, Jeremy Giambi 1, Eric Chavez 1, Ramon Hernandez 1, Adam Piatt 1, Total: 13

MULTI-HOMER GAMES

Jason Giambi 5, Sal Fasano 1, Miguel Tejada 1, Total: 7

GRAND SLAMS

4-9: Jason Giambi (off Chicago's Tanyon Sturtze)
4-14: Eric Chavez (off Boston's Brian Rose)
4-19: Miguel Tejada (off Cleveland's Sean DePaula)
4-29: Ben Grieve (off Minnesota's Eddie Guardado)
5-21: Jason Giambi (off Minnesota's Sean Bergman)
6-6: Matt Stairs (off San Diego's Rodrigo Lopez)
6-7: Jason Giambi (off San Diego's Matt Clement)
7-8: Jeremy Giambi (off Arizona's Dan Plesac)
7-22: Ben Grieve (off Anaheim's Brian Cooper)
7-30: Sal Fasano (off Boston's Rolando Arrojo)
8-24: Terrence Long (off Cleveland's Steve Woodard)
9-15: Jason Giambi (off Tampa Bay's Albie Lopez)
9-23: Ben Grieve (off Seattle's Jose Paniagua)
9-30: Miguel Tejada (off Texas's Francisco Cordero)

PINCH HITTERS

(Minimum 5 at-bats)

Name	AB	Avg.	HR	RBI
Giambi, Jeremy	24	.250	0	3
Saenz, Olmedo	20	.400	1	4
Hernandez, Ramon	14	.143	1	3
Chavez, Eric	10	.200	0	1
Piatt, Adam	10	.100	0	1
Stairs, Matt	10	.100	0	3
Becker, Rich	7	.286	0	1
Stanley, Mike	5	.000	0	0

DEBUTS

4-18: Mark Mulder, P.
4-24: Adam Piatt, DH.
7-17: Marcus Jones, P.
7-22: Barry Zito, P.
8-22: Eric Byrnes, DH.
9-4: Todd Belitz, P.
9-15: Jose Ortiz, PH.
9-15: Jon Ratliff, P.

GAMES BY POSITION

Catcher: Ramon Hernandez 142, Sal Fasano 52, A.J. Hinch 5.
First base: Jason Giambi 124, Mike Stanley 19, Olmedo Saenz 17, Jeremy Giambi 15, Mario Valdez 4, Adam Piatt 3, Matt Stairs 1.
Second base: Randy Velarde 122, Frank Menechino 51, Jorge Velandia 14, Jose Ortiz 3, Mark Bellhorn 2.
Third base: Eric Chavez 146, Olmedo Saenz 18, Adam Piatt 13, Frank Menechino 4, Mark Bellhorn 2.
Shortstop: Miguel Tejada 160, Frank Menechino 5, Jorge Velandia 4, Eric Chavez 2, Mark Bellhorn 1.
Outfield: Ben Grieve 144, Terrence Long 137, Ryan Christenson 114, Matt Stairs 103, Jeremy Giambi 55, Adam Piatt 29, Rich Becker 19, Bo Porter 16, Eric Byrnes 4.
Designated hitter: Matt Stairs 37, John Jaha 30, Olmedo Saenz 27, Jason Giambi 24, Jeremy Giambi 21, Adam Piatt 13, Ben Grieve 12, Mike Stanley 8, Frank Menechino 4, Jose Ortiz 4, Rich Becker 2, Eric Byrnes 2, Ron Mahay 1, A.J. Hinch 1, Eric Chavez 1, Tim Hudson 1.

STREAKS

Wins: 9 (June 13-23)
Losses: 6 (August 5-11)
Consecutive games with at least one hit: 17, Terrence Long (June 10-29)
Wins by pitcher: 4, Gil Heredia (April 28-May 14) Gil Heredia (July 15-30) Tim Hudson (June 14-July 2)

ATTENDANCE

Home: 1,728,888
Road: 2,363,769
Highest (home): 54,268 (July 8 vs. Arizona).
Highest (road): 49,187 (July 4 vs. Texas).
Lowest (Home): 6,836 (May 15 vs. Kansas City).
Lowest (road): 7,485 (June 13 vs. Minnesota).

SEATTLE MARINERS

DAY BY DAY

Date	Opp.	Res.	Score	(inn.*)	Hits	Opp. hits	Winning pitcher	Losing pitcher	Save	Record	Pos.	GB
4-4	Bos.	L	0-2		2	7	P. Martinez	Moyer	Lowe	0-1	T3rd	1.5
4-5	Bos.	W	9-3		9	9	Garcia	R. Martinez		1-1	3rd	0.5
4-6	Bos.	W	5-2		7	8	Mesa	Florie	Sasaki	2-1	T1st	...
4-7	N.Y.	W	7-5		12	9	Halama	Pettitte	Sasaki	3-1	1st	+0.5
4-8	N.Y.	L	2-3		5	10	Nelson	Mesa	Rivera	3-2	T1st	...
4-9	N.Y.	W	9-3		9	3	Moyer	Clemens		4-2	1st	+0.5
4-11	At Det.	L	2-5		12	8	Moehler	Garcia	Jones	4-3	T2nd	0.5
4-12	At Det.	W	4-0		9	3	Sele	Mlicki		5-3	1st	+0.5
4-13	At Det.	L	0-2		9	9	Brocail	Rhodes	Jones	5-4	T1st	...
4-14	At Tor.	W	11-9		12	16	Moyer	Wells		6-4	1st	+1.0
4-15	At Tor.	W	17-6		16	10	Rodriguez	Halladay	Paniagua	7-4	1st	+1.0
4-16	At Tor.	W	19-7		22	13	Garcia	Carpenter		8-4	1st	+1.0
4-18	At Chi.	L	11-18		13	19	Sturtze	Sele		8-5	1st	+0.5
4-19	At Chi.	L	2-5		8	6	Lowe	Meche	Howry	8-6	1st	+0.5
4-21	K.C.	W	10-2		10	8	Rodriguez	Durbin		9-6	1st	+1.0
4-22	K.C.	W	4-2		7	6	Tomko	Witasick	Sasaki	10-6	1st	+2.0
4-23	K.C.	W	8-5		7	10	Rhodes	Bottalico		11-6	1st	+3.0
4-24	Cle.	L	0-6		2	9	Finley	Meche		11-7	1st	+2.0
4-25	Cle.	W	8-5		9	11	Halama	Nagy		12-7	1st	+3.0
4-26	Cle.	L	3-5	(10)	5	13	Shuey	Rhodes		12-8	1st	+2.0
4-28	At K.C.	L	5-8		9	12	Batista	Tomko	Bottalico	12-9	1st	+2.5
4-29	At K.C.	W	11-3		17	10	Sele	Suppan		13-9	1st	+2.5
4-30	At K.C.	L	3-6		7	10	Rosado	Meche	Bottalico	13-10	1st	+1.5
5-2	At Min.	W	5-4		9	10	Halama	Mays	Sasaki	14-10	1st	+2.5
5-3	At Min.	L	4-5	(10)	12	10	Guardado	Mesa		14-11	1st	+1.5
5-5	Ana.	L	5-6		11	11	Bottenfield	Sele	Percival	14-12	1st	...
5-6	Ana.	W	1-0		7	2	Sasaki	Holtz		15-12	1st	+1.0
5-7	Ana.	W	8-2		7	7	Halama	Schoeneweis		16-12	1st	+2.0
5-8	At Tex.	L	1-10		5	14	Helling	Tomko		16-13	1st	+1.0
5-9	At Tex.	W	13-3		19	6	Abbott	Loaiza		17-13	1st	+2.0
5-10	At Tex.	L	6-7		12	13	Wetteland	Sasaki		17-14	1st	+1.5
5-11	At Oak.	L	6-7		8	10	Hudson	Meche	Isringhausen	17-15	1st	+0.5
5-12	At Oak.	L	7-9		10	6	Mathews	Sasaki		17-16	2nd	0.5
5-13	At Oak.	W	6-4		6	8	Tomko	Appier	Mesa	18-16	1st	+0.5
5-14	At Oak.	L	2-7		10	6	Heredia	Abbott		18-17	2nd	0.5
5-15	Min.	W	14-0		16	2	Sele	Milton		19-17	2nd	0.5
5-16	Min.	W	9-5		9	10	Meche	Bergman		20-17	1st	+0.5
5-17	Min.	W	4-0		6	4	Halama	Mays		21-17	1st	+1.5
5-19	T.B.	W	7-6		13	7	Mesa	Taylor	Sasaki	22-17	1st	+2.0
5-20	T.B.	L	3-4		8	8	Yan	Ramsay	Hernandez	22-18	1st	+1.0
5-21	T.B.	W	8-4		16	10	Sele	Trachsel		23-18	1st	+1.0
5-23	At Bal.	L	2-4		8	6	Timlin	Mesa		23-19	1st	...
5-24	At Bal.	L	3-4		7	8	Groom	Sasaki		23-20	1st	...
5-25	At Bal.	L	1-5		5	9	Mussina	Rodriguez		23-21	3rd	1.0
5-26	At T.B.	W	11-4		15	9	Sele	Trachsel		24-21	1st	...
5-27	At T.B.	W	6-3		11	4	Tomko	Rekar	Sasaki	25-21	1st	+1.0
5-28	At T.B.	L	4-14		5	20	Mecir	Mesa		25-22	1st	+0.5
5-29	Chi.	W	5-4		6	7	Halama	Sirotka	Sasaki	26-22	1st	+0.5
5-30	Chi.	L	1-2		5	4	Baldwin	Abbott	Foulke	26-23	1st	+0.5
5-31	Chi.	L	3-4		6	6	Howry	Sasaki	Foulke	26-24	1st	...
6-2	S.D.	W	7-4		7	8	Moyer	Clement	Sasaki	27-24	1st	+0.5
6-3	S.D.	L	4-7		7	10	Spencer	Halama	Hoffman	27-25	2nd	0.5
6-4	S.D.	W	6-4		5	10	Abbott	Meadows		28-25	1st	...
6-5	Col.	W	6-2		10	6	Sele	Yoshii		29-25	1st	...
6-6	Col.	W	4-1		7	8	Tomko	Bohanon	Sasaki	30-25	1st	+0.5
6-7	Col.	L	1-6		5	13	Arrojo	Moyer		30-26	2nd	0.5
6-9	At S.F.	L	2-9		8	16	Rueter	Halama		30-27	2nd	1.5
6-10	At S.F.	W	5-2		12	6	Abbott	Estes		31-27	2nd	0.5
6-11	At S.F.	W	9-2		13	7	Sele	Hernandez		32-27	2nd	0.5
6-12	At K.C.	W	5-3		7	7	Moyer	Batista	Sasaki	33-27	1st	+0.5
6-13	At K.C.	W	7-0	(6)	10	1	Meche	Laxton		34-27	1st	+0.5
6-14	At K.C.	L	4-5		9	11	Bottalico	Sasaki		34-28	2nd	0.5
6-15	At Min.	W	12-5		18	8	Ramsay	Redman		35-28	1st	...
6-16	At Min.	L	2-7		4	12	Radke	Sele		35-29	2nd	1.0
6-17	At Min.	W	12-3		17	7	Moyer	Milton		36-29	2nd	1.0
6-18	At Min.	W	10-2		12	6	Meche	Mays		37-29	2nd	1.0
6-19	T.B.	L	3-10		7	14	Lopez	Halama		37-30	2nd	2.0
6-20	T.B.	W	4-3		5	6	Abbott	Trachsel	Sasaki	38-30	2nd	2.0
6-21	T.B.	W	8-5		7	7	Sele	Yan	Sasaki	39-30	2nd	2.0
6-22	Bal.	W	11-4		14	8	Moyer	Johnson		40-30	2nd	1.5
6-23	Bal.	W	8-3		11	10	Meche	Erickson		41-30	2nd	1.5
6-24	Bal.	W	2-1		4	7	Halama	Rapp	Sasaki	42-30	2nd	0.5
6-25	Bal.	W	4-2		4	4	Rhodes	Timlin	Sasaki	43-30	2nd	0.5
6-27	Ana.	W	5-3		8	5	Sele	Belcher	Sasaki	44-30	2nd	0.5
6-28	Ana.	L	2-3		6	8	Hill	Moyer	Percival	44-31	2nd	0.5
6-29	Ana.	W	7-2		8	7	Paniagua	Bottenfield		45-31	1st	+0.5
6-30	At Tex.	L	3-13		8	18	Rogers	Halama		45-32	1st	+0.5
7-1	At Tex.	W	6-3		8	8	Abbott	Clark	Sasaki	46-32	1st	+1.5
7-2	At Tex.	W	11-4		11	10	Sele	Perisho		47-32	1st	+1.5

HIGHLIGHTS

High point: After a sluggish start, the Mariners vaulted to the top of the A.L. West Division with a 35-20 record in June and July. They took over first by beating Anaheim on June 29 and held that position until the last week of the season.
Low point: After August 11, when the Mariners held a seven-game lead over second-place Oakland and rested 22 games above .500 for the first time in franchise history, the bottom nearly fell out. The Mariners lost eight straight games and 15-of-18 while watching their lead shrink to $2^1/_2$.
Turning point: The final day of the regular season, when the Mariners earned their third postseason berth with a do-or-die 5-2 win at Anaheim. They failed to win the division title, but the victory gave them the A.L.'s wild-card position.
Most valuable player: Edgar Martinez, a 37-year-old designated hitter playing his 14th season with Seattle, set career highs with 37 home runs and an A.L.-leading 145 RBIs while batting .324. Four of those 37 homers were grand slams.
Most valuable pitcher: A rookie at age 32, closer Kazuhiro Sasaki made the difficult transition from Japanese baseball and stabilized a shaky bullpen. After losing four games in May, Sasaki went on to post 37 saves and blew only three opportunities, the best mark in the A.L. He posted a 0.73 ERA in September.
Most improved player: Manager Lou Piniella talked Jay Buhner out of retirement and the injury-plagued outfielder rewarded him with 26 homers and 82 RBIs in a part-time role. Buhner had only 29 homers and 83 RBIs in the previous two seasons combined.
Most pleasant surprise: Asked to succeed Ken Griffey Jr. in center field, newcomer Mike Cameron turned in a spectacular year defensively and became one of the Mariners' best clutch hitters as well as a fan favorite at Safeco Field.
Key injuries: Opening-night starter Jamie Moyer pulled a muscle in his shoulder and was on the disabled list from April 21 to June 1. ... Righthander Freddy Garcia missed $2^1/_2$ months with a stress fracture in his leg. ... Righthander Gil Meche was slowed by injuries early and never pitched after July. ... Catcher Tom Lampkin began the season recovering from knee surgery and then was lost for the year when he tore an elbow ligament in June. ... Shortstop Alex Rodriguez missed two weeks with a concussion and sprained knee.
Notable: Just one season after using a club-record 28 different pitchers, the Mariners used 15 in 2000—nine as starters. The staff's final 4.49 ERA was second in the A.L. only to Boston. ... The Mariners matched the franchise record with 11 grand slams. ... The Mariners finished 20 games over .500, but they were just 19-19 against A.L. West competition.

—LARRY LaRUE

MISCELLANEOUS

RECORDS

2000 regular-season record: 91-71 (2nd in A.L. West); 47-34 at home; 44-37 on road; 35-17 vs. East; 26-28 vs. Central; 30-26 vs. West; 20-11 vs. lefthanded starters; 71-60 vs. righthanded starters; 77-67 on grass; 14-4 on turf; 32-24 in daytime; 59-47 at night; 15-22 in one-run games; 3-4 in extra-inning games; 1-0-0 in doubleheaders.
Team record past five years: 421-387 (.521, ranks 4th in league in that span).

TEAM LEADERS

Batting average: Edgar Martinez (.324).
At-bats: John Olerud (565).
Runs: Alex Rodriguez (134).
Hits: Edgar Martinez (180).
Total Bases: Alex Rodriguez (336).
Doubles: John Olerud (45).
Triples: Stan Javier (5).
Home runs: Alex Rodriguez (41).
Runs batted in: Edgar Martinez (145).
Stolen bases: Rickey Henderson (31).
Slugging percentage: Alex Rodriguez (.606).
On-base percentage: Edgar Martinez (.423).
Wins: Aaron Sele (17).
Earned-run average: Paul Abbott (4.22).
Complete games: Aaron Sele (2).
Shutouts: Aaron Sele (2).
Saves: Kazuhiro Sasaki (37).
Innings pitched: Aaron Sele (211.2).
Strikeouts: Aaron Sele (137).

Date	Opp.	Res.	Score	(inn.*)	Hits	Opp. hits	Winning pitcher	Losing pitcher	Save	Record	Pos.	GB
7-3	At Ana.	W	8-6		13	13	Moyer	Hill	Sasaki	48-32	1st	+2.5
7-4	At Ana.	L	6-7		8	8	Petkovsek	Mesa	Percival	48-33	1st	+2.5
7-5	At Ana.	W	6-4		11	10	Halama	Cooper	Sasaki	49-33	1st	+3.5
7-6	At Ana.	L	1-5		8	5	Washburn	Abbott		49-34	1st	+3.0
7-7	L.A.	L	2-3	(11)	12	5	Herges	Rhodes	Fetters	49-35	1st	+2.0
7-8	L.A.	W	11-0		10	5	Sele	Gagne		50-35	1st	+2.0
7-9	L.A.	W	2-0		4	7	Moyer	Park	Sasaki	51-35	1st	+3.0
7-13	At S.D.	L	1-2	(10)	6	5	Hoffman	Tomko		51-36	1st	+3.0
7-14	At S.D.	W	7-5		12	9	Moyer	Meadows	Sasaki	52-36	1st	+4.0
7-15	At S.D.	L	1-4		4	6	Williams	Sele	Hoffman	52-37	1st	+3.0
7-16	At Ari.	W	6-3		9	8	Mesa	Springer	Sasaki	53-37	1st	+3.5
7-17	At Ari.	L	0-7		5	13	Guzman	Halama		53-38	1st	+3.0
7-18	At Ari.	W	5-2		11	6	Rhodes	Padilla	Sasaki	54-38	1st	+4.0
7-19	At Oak.	W	6-3		10	7	Moyer	Appier	Sasaki	55-38	1st	+5.0
7-20	At Oak.	L	4-5		9	5	Heredia	Sele	Isringhausen	55-39	1st	+4.0
7-21	Tex.	W	12-3		11	8	Abbott	Perisho		56-39	1st	+4.0
7-22	Tex.	W	13-5		14	9	Halama	Glynn		57-39	1st	+5.0
7-23	Tex.	L	2-3		8	9	Helling	Rhodes	Wetteland	57-40	1st	+4.0
7-24	Oak.	W	6-4		11	9	Moyer	Appier	Sasaki	58-40	1st	+5.0
7-25	Oak.	L	7-8		11	11	Heredia	Sele	Isringhausen	58-41	1st	+4.0
7-26	Oak.	L	1-6		8	5	Hudson	Abbott		58-42	1st	+3.0
7-27	Tor.	L	2-7		7	16	Loaiza	Rhodes		58-43	1st	+3.0
7-28	Tor.	W	7-4		9	6	Garcia	Carpenter	Sasaki	59-43	1st	+4.0
7-29	Tor.	W	6-5	(13)	16	9	Tomko	Halladay		60-43	1st	+4.0
7-30	Tor.	W	10-6		5	10	Sele	Escobar	Paniagua	61-43	1st	+4.0
7-31	Bos.	L	5-8		3	11	Garces	Mesa	Pichardo	61-44	1st	+3.0
8-1	Bos.	W	5-4	(19)	12	12	Sasaki	Fassero		62-44	1st	+3.0
8-2	Bos.	L	2-5		5	8	P. Martinez	Garcia		62-45	1st	+2.0
8-4	At N.Y.	L	6-13		15	16	Pettitte	Moyer		62-46	1st	+1.0
8-5	At N.Y.	W	6-5		11	10	Tomko	Gooden	Sasaki	63-46	1st	+2.0
8-6	At N.Y.	W	11-1		16	8	Abbott	Hernandez		64-46	1st	+3.0
8-7	At N.Y.	W	8-5		13	11	Halama	Neagle		65-46	1st	+3.5
8-8†	At Chi.	W	12-4		17	10	Pineiro	Garland	Tomko	66-46		
8-8‡	At Chi.	W	7-5		9	8	Garcia	Buehrle	Sasaki	67-46	1st	+5.0
8-9	At Chi.	L	3-19		8	24	Sirotka	Moyer		67-47	1st	+5.0
8-10	At Chi.	W	6-3		9	11	Sele	Biddle	Sasaki	68-47	1st	+6.0
8-11	Cle.	W	7-1		10	6	Abbott	Finley	Paniagua	69-47	1st	+7.0
8-12	Cle.	L	4-5		7	7	Colon	Halama	Wickman	69-48	1st	+6.0
8-13	Cle.	L	4-10		8	11	Speier	Garcia		69-49	1st	+6.0
8-14	Det.	L	4-15		12	18	Blair	Moyer		69-50	1st	+5.0
8-15	Det.	L	0-9		5	17	Sparks	Sele		69-51	1st	+4.0
8-16	Det.	L	8-12		10	16	Weaver	Tomko		69-52	1st	+3.0
8-18	At Cle.	L	8-9		14	10	Karsay	Rhodes		69-53	1st	+3.0
8-19	At Cle.	L	4-10		8	11	Bere	Moyer		69-54	1st	+3.0
8-20	At Cle.	L	4-12		11	15	Burba	Sele		69-55	1st	+2.0
8-22	At Det.	W	8-4		10	6	Paniagua	Weaver	Sasaki	70-55	1st	+3.5
8-23	At Det.	L	5-6		11	11	Cruz	Rhodes	Jones	70-56	1st	+3.5
8-24	At Det.	L	3-10		8	12	Moehler	Moyer		70-57	1st	+2.5
8-25	Chi.	L	1-4		4	10	Sirotka	Sele	Foulke	70-58	1st	+1.5
8-26	Chi.	W	11-5		12	8	Halama	Biddle		71-58	1st	+2.5
8-27	Chi.	L	1-2		4	6	Barcelo	Garcia	Foulke	71-59	1st	+2.5
8-28	N.Y.	L	1-9		5	10	Clemens	Abbott		71-60	1st	+1.5
8-29	N.Y.	W	5-3		8	8	Tomko	Pettitte	Sasaki	72-60	1st	+2.5
8-30	N.Y.	L	4-5		8	10	Cone	Sele	Rivera	72-61	1st	+2.5
9-1	At Bos.	L	2-6		6	14	Arrojo	Halama		72-62	1st	+2.5
9-2	At Bos.	W	4-1		7	3	Garcia	Garces	Sasaki	73-62	1st	+2.5
9-3	At Bos.	W	5-0		9	1	Abbott	Ohka	Paniagua	74-62	1st	+2.5
9-4	At Bos.	L	1-5		7	7	P. Martinez	Moyer		74-63	1st	+1.5
9-5	At Tor.	W	4-3		7	6	Rhodes	Escobar	Sasaki	75-63	1st	+2.5
9-6	At Tor.	L	3-7		6	12	Hamilton	Halama		75-64	1st	+1.5
9-7	At Tor.	W	8-1		12	3	Garcia	Trachsel		76-64	1st	+2.0
9-8	Min.	L	2-4		6	10	Kinney	Abbott	Hawkins	76-65	1st	+2.0
9-9	Min.	W	7-2		10	5	Moyer	Redman		77-65	1st	+2.0
9-10	Min.	W	8-1		8	7	Sele	Romero		78-65	1st	+2.0
9-11	K.C.	L	3-6		7	15	Meadows	Halama	Santiago	78-66	1st	+1.0
9-12	K.C.	W	11-3		15	9	Garcia	Reichert		79-66	1st	+1.0
9-13	K.C.	W	2-1	(11)	6	8	Mesa	Bottalico		80-66	1st	+2.0
9-15	At Bal.	W	10-2		10	8	Sele	Mercedes		81-66	1st	+2.0
9-16	At Bal.	W	14-0		16	3	Moyer	Mussina		82-66	1st	+2.0
9-17	At Bal.	W	3-2		7	7	Garcia	Ponson	Sasaki	83-66	1st	+2.5
9-18	At T.B.	W	4-3		10	7	Paniagua	Hernandez		84-66	1st	+2.5
9-19	At T.B.	W	5-2		6	6	Halama	Harper	Paniagua	85-66	1st	+2.5
9-20	At T.B.	W	5-4		10	10	Sele	Lopez	Sasaki	86-66	1st	+3.0
9-21	Oak.	L	2-5		5	6	Hudson	Moyer	Isringhausen	86-67	1st	+2.0
9-22	Oak.	L	3-8		7	9	Olivares	Garcia	Service	86-68	1st	+1.0
9-23	Oak.	L	2-8		2	10	Appier	Rhodes		86-69	2nd	...
9-24	Oak.	W	3-2		6	8	Halama	Prieto	Sasaki	87-69	1st	+1.0
9-26	Tex.	W	5-0		10	6	Sele	Glynn		88-69	1st	+0.5
9-27	Tex.	W	6-4		11	9	Garcia	Davis	Sasaki	89-69	1st	+0.5
9-28	Tex.	L	6-13		9	15	Helling	Tomko		89-70	1st	+0.5
9-29	At Ana.	L	3-9		5	10	Ortiz	Abbott	Pote	89-71	2nd	0.5
9-30	At Ana.	W	21-9		22	12	Halama	Belcher		90-71	2nd	0.5
10-1	At Ana.	W	5-2		12	7	Rhodes	Hasegawa	Sasaki	91-71	2nd	0.5

Monthly records: April (13-10), May (13-14), June (19-8), July (16-12), August (11-17), September (18-10), October (1-0).
*Innings, if other than nine. † First game of a doubleheader. ‡ Second game of a doubleheader.

MEMORABLE GAMES

August 1 at Seattle

This 5-hour, 34-minute marathon, the longest game in team history, was decided when Mike Cameron hit a 19th-inning home run to beat Boston, 5-4. Cameron had started the game on the bench, coming in as a pinch runner. The Mariners got 10 shutout relief innings from Brett Tomko, Robert Ramsay, Jose Mesa and Kazuhiro Sasaki, none of whom pitched in regulation. Cameron's homer was hit off former Mariners pitcher Jeff Fassero.

Boston	AB	R	H	BI	Seattle	AB	R	H	BI
Lansing, 2b	8	0	1	0	Henderson, lf	7	0	1	0
Daubach, 1b	5	1	2	0	Martin, cf	5	0	0	0
Alexander, pr-3b	4	0	0	0	Buhner, ph-rf	2	0	0	0
Varitek, c	9	0	1	1	Rodriguez, ss	7	1	1	0
Garciaparra, ss	7	1	2	0	Martinez, dh	7	1	0	0
O'Leary, lf	8	0	3	1	Olerud, 1b	5	0	2	1
Gilkey, rf	6	0	1	0	Cameron, pr-rf-cf	3	1	1	1
Alcantara, dh	4	0	0	0	Javier, rf-1b	6	1	2	2
Hat'berg, ph-dh	3	0	0	0	Bell, 3b	7	1	1	0
Sprague, 3b-1b	4	1	0	0	Oliver, c	1	0	1	0
Nixon, ph	1	0	0	0	Wilson, c	5	0	0	1
Burkhart, 1b	1	0	0	0	McLemore, 2b	7	0	3	0
Lewis, cf	5	1	2	2					
Totals	**65**	**4**	**12**	**4**	**Totals**	**62**	**5**	**12**	**5**

Boston ....0 0 4 0 0 0 0 0 0 0 0 0 0 0 0 0 0 0 0—4 12 2
Seattle.............0 0 0 0 2 2 0 0 0 0 0 0 0 0 0 0 0 0 1—5 12 0

E—Garciaparra (14), Varitek (5). DP—Boston 1, Seattle 1. LOB—Boston14, Seattle 9. 2B—Daubach (24), Garciaparra (36),.Lewis (8). 3B—Bell (2). HR—Lewis (2), Javier (5), Cameron (13). SB—Rodriguez (10), McLemore (22), Cameron (11). CS—Lewis (3). S—Wilson. SH—Lewis, Henderson.

Boston	IP	H	R	ER	BB	SO
Wakefield	8	8	4	4	1	7
Lowe	3	1	0	0	2	5
Beck	2	0	0	0	0	2
Garces	1	0	0	0	1	0
Cormier	3	2	0	0	0	2
Pichardo	1	0	0	0	0	0
Fassero (L 7-5)	0	1	1	1	0	0
Seattle	**IP**	**H**	**R**	**ER**	**BB**	**SO**
Halama	9	8	4	4	3	2
Tomko	4	1	0	0	0	0
Mesa	3	1	0	0	3	2
Ramsay	2.1	2	0	0	3	0
Sasaki (W 2-5)	0.2	0	0	0	0	1

Fassero pitched to 1 batter in 19th.

U—HP, Reed. 1B, Wendelstedt. 2B, Clark. 3B, Bucknor. T—5:34. A—37,391.

September 30 at Anaheim

Badly needing a win to keep pace with the torrid Athletics in the A.L. West, the Mariners exploded for a 21-9 win over Anaheim that gave them a share of the division lead with two games to play. Shortstop Alex Rodriguez, who entered the game mired in a 3-for-29 slump, broke loose for four hits, two home runs and seven RBIs. The beneficiary was lefty John Halama, who pitched into the sixth inning despite being knocked flat by a line drive.

Seattle	AB	R	H	BI	Anaheim	AB	R	H	BI
Cameron, lf-cf	6	2	2	0	Erstad, cf	4	1	2	0
Sanders, ph-rf	1	1	1	0	Palmeiro, cf	1	0	0	0
Javier, cf	4	3	3	0	Glaus, 3b	4	1	1	2
Ibanez, pr-lf	1	2	0	0	Salmon, dh	5	1	0	0
Rodriguez, ss	6	4	4	7	Vaughn, 1b	3	0	1	0
Guillen, ss	0	0	0	0	Baughman, ss	1	1	1	0
Martinez, dh	3	2	2	2	Gant, lf	5	3	2	2
Olerud, 1b	6	1	4	4	Anderson, rf	3	1	1	2
Lesher, ph-1b	1	0	0	0	Spiezio, rf	1	0	0	0
Buhner, rf	4	1	1	1	Molina, c	3	1	1	1
Gipson, rf-cf	2	0	0	0	Wooten, c	1	0	1	1
Bell, 3b	3	3	1	1	Kennedy, 2b	4	0	1	1
Oliver, c	4	1	1	3	Gil, ss-1b	4	0	1	0
McLemore, 2b	5	1	3	2					
Totals	**46**	**21**	**22**	**20**	**Totals**	**39**	**9**	**12**	**9**

Seattle ....2 1 1 2 0 5 5 1 4—21 22 2
Anaheim ....0 0 2 0 0 4 0 1 2—9 12 1

E—McLemore (8), Bell (15), Molina (7). DP—Seattle 1, Anaheim 1. LOB—Seattle 11, Anaheim 6. 2B—Javier (18), Olerud (45), McLemore 2 (23), Erstad (38), Anderson (39), Molina (20). 3B—Oliver (1). HR—Rodriguez 2 (40), E.Martinez (37), Buhner (26), D.Bell (10), Glaus (47), Gant (6). SB—Cameron (24), Ibanez (2). CS—McLemore (14), Glaus (11). S—Rodriguez. SH—Oliver.

Seattle	IP	H	R	ER	BB	SO
Halama (W 14-9)	5.2	5	5	2	2	1
Mesa	0	3	1	1	0	0
Rhodes	0.1	0	0	0	0	0
Paniagua	1	0	0	0	0	1
Ramsay	1	2	1	1	1	1
Hodges	1	2	2	2	0	0
Anaheim	**IP**	**H**	**R**	**ER**	**BB**	**SO**
Belcher (L 4-5)	2.2	5	4	4	4	3
Fyhrie	2.1	3	2	2	1	4
Mercker	0.1	5	5	5	0	1
Turnbow	1.1	3	5	5	5	1
Ward	1.1	2	1	1	0	0
Alvarez	1	4	4	4	1	0

Mesa pitched to 3 batters in 6th.

WP—Belcher, Alvarez. U—HP, Emmel. 1B, Rieker. 2B, Guccione. 3B, Davis. T—4:02. A—35,238.

INDIVIDUAL STATISTICS

BATTING

																						vs RHP				vs LHP			
Name	**G**	**TPA**	**AB**	**R**	**H**	**TB**	**2B**	**3B**	**HR**	**RBI**	**Avg.**	**Obp.**	**Slg.**	**SH**	**SF**	**HP**	**BB**	**IBB**	**SO**	**SB**	**CS**	**GDP**	**AB**	**Avg.**	**HR**	**RBI**	**AB**	**Avg.**	**HR**	**RBI**
Olerud, John	159	683	565	84	161	248	45	0	14	103	.285	.392	.439	2	10	4	102	11	96	0	2	17	441	.297	14	80	124	.242	0	23
Martinez, Edgar	153	665	556	100	180	322	31	0	37	145	.324	.423	.579	0	8	5	96	8	95	3	0	13	464	.317	28	111	92	.359	9	34
Rodriguez, Alex	148	672	554	134	175	336	34	2	41	132	.316	.420	.606	0	11	7	100	5	121	15	4	10	461	.306	30	103	93	.366	11	29
Cameron, Mike	155	643	543	96	145	238	28	4	19	78	.267	.365	.438	7	6	9	78	0	133	24	7	10	433	.266	16	64	110	.273	3	14
McLemore, Mark	138	578	481	72	118	152	23	1	3	46	.245	.353	.316	11	4	1	81	2	78	30	14	12	406	.236	2	40	75	.293	1	6
Bell, David	133	512	454	57	112	173	24	2	11	47	.247	.316	.381	6	4	6	42	0	66	2	3	11	346	.234	7	32	108	.287	4	15
Buhner, Jay	112	430	364	50	92	190	20	0	26	82	.253	.361	.522	1	2	4	59	3	98	0	2	10	274	.245	20	63	90	.278	6	19
Javier, Stan	105	392	342	61	94	137	18	5	5	40	.275	.351	.401	4	4	0	42	2	64	4	3	7	287	.272	5	33	55	.291	0	7
Henderson, Rickey	92	395	324	58	77	106	13	2	4	30	.238	.362	.327	3	3	2	63	0	55	31	9	9	254	.240	4	23	70	.229	0	7
Guillen, Carlos	90	328	288	45	74	114	15	2	7	42	.257	.324	.396	7	3	2	28	0	53	1	3	6	238	.244	6	35	50	.320	1	7
Wilson, Dan	90	303	268	31	63	90	12	0	5	27	.235	.291	.336	11	2	0	22	0	51	1	2	8	204	.235	3	19	64	.234	2	8
Oliver, Joe	69	219	200	33	53	98	13	1	10	35	.265	.313	.490	5	0	0	14	1	38	2	1	6	161	.286	9	30	39	.179	1	5
Ibanez, Raul	92	156	140	21	32	46	8	0	2	15	.229	.301	.329	0	1	1	14	1	25	2	0	1	131	.221	2	15	9	.333	0	0
Martin, Al	42	145	134	19	31	53	2	4	4	9	.231	.283	.396	0	1	2	8	0	31	4	1	1	133	.233	4	9	1	.000	0	0
Lampkin, Tom	36	117	103	15	26	55	6	1	7	23	.252	.325	.534	0	2	3	9	1	17	0	0	7	93	.269	6	22	10	.100	1	1
Mabry, John	48	115	103	18	25	33	5	0	1	7	.243	.322	.320	0	0	2	10	0	31	0	1	1	90	.278	1	7	13	.000	0	0
Gipson, Charles	59	33	29	7	9	12	1	1	0	3	.310	.394	.414	0	0	0	4	0	9	2	3	0	14	.357	0	1	15	.267	0	2
Machado, Robert	8	15	14	2	3	6	0	0	1	1	.214	.267	.429	0	0	0	1	0	4	0	0	0	13	.154	1	1	1	1.000	0	0
Widger, Chris	10	12	11	1	1	4	0	0	1	1	.091	.167	.364	0	0	0	1	0	2	0	0	0	4	.000	0	0	7	.143	1	1
Lesher, Brian	5	6	5	1	4	7	1	1	0	3	.800	.833	1.400	0	0	0	1	0	0	1	0	0	2	1.000	0	2	3	.667	0	1
Abbott, Paul	35	6	5	1	2	3	1	0	0	0	.400	.400	.600	1	0	0	0	0	1	0	0	0	3	.333	0	0	2	.500	0	0
Garcia, Freddy	21	6	3	0	2	2	0	0	0	0	.667	.667	.667	3	0	0	0	0	0	0	0	0	1	.000	0	0	2	1.000	0	0
Sele, Aaron	34	4	3	0	0	0	0	0	0	0	.000	.000	.000	1	0	0	0	0	0	0	0	0	3	.000	0	0	0	.000	0	0
Halama, John	30	3	2	0	1	1	0	0	0	0	.500	.500	.500	1	0	0	0	0	1	0	0	0	1	1.000	0	0	1	.000	0	0
Moyer, Jamie	26	2	2	0	0	0	0	0	0	0	.000	.000	.000	0	0	0	0	0	1	0	0	0	2	.000	0	0	0	.000	0	0
Sanders, Anthony	1	1	1	1	1	1	0	0	0	0	1.000	1.000	1.000	0	0	0	0	0	0	0	0	0	0	.000	0	0	1	1.000	0	0
Rodriguez, Frank	23	1	1	0	0	0	0	0	0	0	.000	.000	.000	0	0	0	0	0	1	0	0	0	0	.000	0	0	1	.000	0	0
Paniagua, Jose	69	1	1	0	0	0	0	0	0	0	.000	.000	.000	0	0	0	0	0	1	0	0	0	1	.000	0	0	0	.000	0	0
Hernandez, Carlos E.	2	1	1	0	0	0	0	0	0	0	.000	.000	.000	0	0	0	0	0	1	0	1	0	0	.000	0	0	1	.000	0	0
Mesa, Jose	66	0	0	0	0	0	0	0	0	0	.000	.000	.000	0	0	0	0	0	0	0	0	0	0	.000	0	0	0	.000	0	0
Rhodes, Arthur	72	0	0	0	0	0	0	0	0	0	.000	.000	.000	0	0	0	0	0	0	0	0	0	0	.000	0	0	0	.000	0	0
Tomko, Brett	32	0	0	0	0	0	0	0	0	0	.000	.000	.000	0	0	0	0	0	0	0	0	0	0	.000	0	0	0	.000	0	0
Ramsay, Rob	37	0	0	0	0	0	0	0	0	0	.000	.000	.000	0	0	0	0	0	0	0	0	0	0	.000	0	0	0	.000	0	0
Sasaki, Kazuhiro	63	0	0	0	0	0	0	0	0	0	.000	.000	.000	0	0	0	0	0	0	0	0	0	0	.000	0	0	0	.000	0	0
Meche, Gil	15	0	0	0	0	0	0	0	0	0	.000	.000	.000	0	0	0	0	0	0	0	0	0	0	.000	0	0	0	.000	0	0
Hodges, Kevin	13	0	0	0	0	0	0	0	0	0	.000	.000	.000	0	0	0	0	0	0	0	0	0	0	.000	0	0	0	.000	0	0
Pineiro, Joel	8	0	0	0	0	0	0	0	0	0	.000	.000	.000	0	0	0	0	0	0	0	0	0	0	.000	0	0	0	.000	0	0

PITCHING

																					vs. RH				vs. LH			
Name	**W**	**L**	**Pct.**	**ERA**	**IP**	**H**	**R**	**ER**	**HR**	**SH**	**SF**	**HB**	**BB**	**IBB**	**SO**	**G**	**GS**	**CG**	**ShO**	**GF**	**Sv**	**AB**	**Avg.**	**HR**	**RBI**	**AB**	**Avg.**	**HR**	**RBI**
Sele, Aaron	17	10	.630	4.51	211.2	221	110	106	17	5	8	5	74	7	137	34	34	2	2	0	0	373	.265	7	46	443	.275	10	49
Abbott, Paul	9	7	.563	4.22	179.0	164	89	84	23	1	4	5	80	4	100	35	27	0	0	2	0	306	.222	14	40	370	.259	9	42
Halama, John	14	9	.609	5.08	166.2	206	108	94	19	4	6	2	56	0	87	30	30	1	1	0	0	502	.297	15	63	166	.343	4	26
Moyer, Jamie	13	10	.565	5.49	154.0	173	103	94	22	3	3	3	53	2	98	26	26	0	0	0	0	456	.279	17	72	160	.288	5	23
Garcia, Freddy	9	5	.643	3.91	124.1	112	62	54	16	6	1	2	64	4	79	21	20	0	0	0	0	219	.205	4	14	246	.272	12	37
Tomko, Brett	7	5	.583	4.68	92.1	92	53	48	12	5	5	3	40	4	59	32	8	0	0	10	1	195	.262	6	28	153	.268	6	26
Meche, Gil	4	4	.500	3.78	85.2	75	37	36	7	5	4	1	40	0	60	15	15	1	1	0	0	135	.244	1	11	178	.236	6	17
Mesa, Jose	4	6	.400	5.36	80.2	89	48	48	11	2	6	5	41	0	84	66	0	0	0	29	1	169	.296	6	31	149	.262	5	25
Paniagua, Jose	3	0	1.000	3.47	80.1	68	31	31	6	3	5	7	38	3	71	69	0	0	0	26	5	165	.255	5	28	126	.206	1	16
Rhodes, Arthur	5	8	.385	4.28	69.1	51	34	33	6	1	2	0	29	3	77	72	0	0	0	9	0	140	.193	4	18	109	.220	2	17
Sasaki, Kazuhiro	2	5	.286	3.16	62.2	42	25	22	10	2	2	2	31	5	78	63	0	0	0	58	37	112	.170	2	9	116	.198	8	20
Ramsay, Rob	1	1	.500	3.40	50.1	43	22	19	3	2	3	1	40	3	32	37	1	0	0	6	0	106	.236	1	12	78	.231	2	11
Rodriguez, Frank	2	1	.667	6.27	47.1	60	33	33	8	0	3	0	22	2	19	23	0	0	0	5	0	111	.360	6	20	78	.256	2	13
Pineiro, Joel	1	0	1.000	5.59	19.1	25	13	12	3	0	2	0	13	0	10	8	1	0	0	5	0	51	.294	1	7	28	.357	2	8
Hodges, Kevin	0	0	.000	5.19	17.1	18	10	10	4	0	1	2	12	0	7	13	0	0	0	7	0	38	.263	3	10	20	.400	1	3
Mabry, John	0	0	.000	27.00	0.2	3	2	2	0	0	0	0	1	0	0	1	0	0	0	1	0	3	.667	0	3	2	.500	0	1

DESIGNATED HITTERS

Name	AB	Avg.	HR	RBI
Martinez, Edgar	545	.323	37	143
Javier, Stan	12	.333	0	0
Lampkin, Tom	11	.455	1	4
Mabry, John	5	.200	0	1
Buhner, Jay	2	.500	0	1
Ibanez, Raul	1	.000	0	0
Oliver, Joe	1	.000	0	0
Bell, David	0	-	0	0
Henderson, Rickey	0	-	0	0
Widger, Chris	0	-	0	0
Martin, Al	0	-	0	0
Lesher, Brian	0	-	0	0
Gipson, Charles	0	-	0	0

INDIVIDUAL STATISTICS

FIELDING

FIRST BASEMEN

Player	Pct.	G	PO	A	E	TC	DP
Olerud, John	.996	158	1271	132	5	1408	154
Lesher, Brian	1.000	4	4	1	0	5	0
Javier, Stan	1.000	3	21	1	0	22	2
Ibanez, Raul	1.000	3	13	0	0	13	2
Mabry, John	1.000	3	8	1	0	9	1
Martinez, Edgar	1.000	2	12	1	0	13	3
Widger, Chris	1.000	2	9	0	0	9	2
Bell, David	1.000	2	4	0	0	4	0
Oliver, Joe	1.000	1	5	0	0	5	1
Wilson, Dan	1.000	1	3	0	0	3	0

SECOND BASEMEN

Player	Pct.	G	PO	A	E	TC	DP
McLemore, Mark	.987	129	262	346	8	616	87
Bell, David	.984	48	85	102	3	190	33

THIRD BASEMEN

Player	Pct.	G	PO	A	E	TC	DP
Bell, David	.944	93	50	151	12	213	14
Guillen, Carlos	.911	68	57	116	17	190	7
Mabry, John	.862	22	6	19	4	29	3
Gipson, Charles	1.000	5	1	9	0	10	1
Hernandez, Carlos E.	1.000	2	1	0	0	1	0
Wilson, Dan	-	1	0	0	0	0	0

SHORTSTOPS

Player	Pct.	G	PO	A	E	TC	DP
Rodriguez, Alex	.986	148	243	438	10	691	123
Guillen, Carlos	.947	23	28	44	4	76	14
Gipson, Charles	1.000	5	0	2	0	2	0
Bell, David	-	1	0	0	0	0	0

OUTFIELDERS

Player	Pct.	G	PO	A	E	TC	DP
Cameron, Mike	.985	155	399	5	6	410	3
Buhner, Jay	1.000	104	176	4	0	180	0
Henderson, Rickey	.984	88	181	0	3	184	0
Javier, Stan	.993	88	140	6	1	147	0
Ibanez, Raul	.978	76	86	1	2	89	1
Gipson, Charles	1.000	48	22	1	0	23	0
Martin, Al	.963	35	76	3	3	82	0
Mabry, John	1.000	19	23	0	0	23	0
McLemore, Mark	1.000	14	24	0	0	24	0
Sanders, Anthony	1.000	1	1	0	0	1	0
Widger, Chris	-	1	0	0	0	0	0

CATCHERS

Player	Pct.	G	PO	A	E	TC	DP	PB
Wilson, Dan	.990	88	482	30	5	517	5	6
Oliver, Joe	.995	66	354	18	2	374	1	0
Lampkin, Tom	.987	28	138	13	2	153	2	1
Machado, Robert	1.000	8	35	2	0	37	1	0
Widger, Chris	1.000	6	11	0	0	11	0	1

PITCHERS

Player	Pct.	G	PO	A	E	TC	DP
Rhodes, Arthur	1.000	72	2	8	0	10	1
Paniagua, Jose	1.000	69	8	8	0	16	1
Mesa, Jose	1.000	66	7	8	0	15	0
Sasaki, Kazuhiro	1.000	63	2	3	0	5	0
Ramsay, Rob	1.000	37	3	7	0	10	1
Abbott, Paul	.969	35	12	19	1	32	3
Sele, Aaron	.946	34	19	34	3	56	2
Tomko, Brett	1.000	32	6	6	0	12	1
Halama, John	.912	30	4	27	3	34	3
Moyer, Jamie	.974	26	11	27	1	39	1
Rodriguez, Frank	.929	23	6	7	1	14	2
Garcia, Freddy	.889	21	5	19	3	27	1
Meche, Gil	1.000	15	7	7	0	14	0
Hodges, Kevin	1.000	13	1	1	0	2	0
Pineiro, Joel	1.000	8	1	2	0	3	0
Mabry, John	-	1	0	0	0	0	0

PITCHING AGAINST EACH CLUB

Pitcher	Ana. W-L	Bal. W-L	Bos. W-L	Chi. W-L	Cle. W-L	Det. W-L	K.C. W-L	Min. W-L	N.Y. W-L	Oak. W-L	T.B. W-L	Tex. W-L	Tor. W-L	N.L. W-L	Total W-L
Abbott, Paul	0-2	0-0	1-0	0-1	1-0	0-0	0-0	0-1	1-1	0-2	1-0	3-0	0-0	2-0	9-7
Garcia, Freddy	0-0	1-0	2-1	1-1	0-1	0-1	1-0	0-0	0-0	0-1	0-0	1-0	3-0	0-0	9-5
Halama, John	3-0	1-0	0-1	2-0	1-1	0-0	0-1	2-0	2-0	1-0	1-1	1-1	0-1	0-3	14-9
Hodges, Kevin	0-0	0-0	0-0	0-0	0-0	0-0	0-0	0-0	0-0	0-0	0-0	0-0	0-0	0-0	0-0
Mabry, John	0-0	0-0	0-0	0-0	0-0	0-0	0-0	0-0	0-0	0-0	0-0	0-0	0-0	0-0	0-0
Meche, Gil	0-0	1-0	0-0	0-1	0-1	0-0	1-1	2-0	0-0	0-1	0-0	0-0	0-0	0-0	4-4
Mesa, Jose	0-1	0-1	1-1	0-0	0-0	0-0	1-0	0-1	0-1	0-0	1-1	0-0	0-0	1-0	4-6
Moyer, Jamie	1-1	2-0	0-2	0-1	0-1	0-2	1-0	2-0	1-1	2-1	0-0	0-0	1-0	3-1	13-10
Paniagua, Jose	1-0	0-0	0-0	0-0	0-0	1-0	0-0	0-0	0-0	0-0	1-0	0-0	0-0	0-0	3-0
Pineiro, Joel	0-0	0-0	0-0	1-0	0-0	0-0	0-0	0-0	0-0	0-0	0-0	0-0	0-0	0-0	1-0
Ramsay, Rob	0-0	0-0	0-0	0-0	0-0	0-0	0-0	1-0	0-0	0-0	0-1	0-0	0-0	0-0	1-1
Rhodes, Arthur	1-0	1-0	0-0	0-0	0-2	0-2	1-0	0-0	0-0	0-1	0-0	0-1	1-1	1-1	5-8
Rodriguez, Frank	0-0	0-1	0-0	0-0	0-0	0-0	1-0	0-0	0-0	0-0	0-0	0-0	1-0	0-0	2-1
Sasaki, Kazuhiro	1-0	0-1	1-0	0-1	0-0	0-0	0-1	0-0	0-0	0-1	0-0	0-1	0-0	0-0	2-5
Sele, Aaron	1-1	1-0	0-0	1-2	0-1	1-1	1-0	2-1	0-1	0-2	4-0	2-0	1-0	3-1	17-10
Tomko, Brett	0-0	0-0	0-0	0-0	0-0	0-1	1-1	0-0	2-0	1-0	1-0	0-2	1-0	1-1	7-5
Totals	8-5	7-3	5-5	5-7	2-7	2-7	8-4	9-3	6-4	4-9	9-3	7-5	8-2	11-7	91-71

INTERLEAGUE: Sele 1-0, Moyer 1-0, Rhodes 0-1 vs. Dodgers; Moyer 2-0, Abbott 1-0, Tomko 0-1, Halama 0-1, Sele 0-1 vs. Padres; Abbott 1-0, Sele 1-0, Halama 0-1 vs. Giants; Sele 1-0, Tomko 1-0, Moyer 0-1 vs. Rockies; Mesa 1-0, Rhodes 1-0, Halama 0-1 vs. Diamondbacks. Total: 11-7.

MISCELLANEOUS

HOME RUNS BY PARK

At Anaheim (13): Rodriguez 6, Bell 3, Buhner 1, Martinez 1, Oliver 1, Cameron 1.

At Arizona (1): Oliver 1.

At Baltimore (8): Rodriguez 2, Buhner 1, Martinez 1, Oliver 1, Olerud 1, Wilson 1, Bell 1.

At Boston (4): Martinez 1, Rodriguez 1, Cameron 1, Guillen 1.

At Chicago (AL) (11): Buhner 2, Martinez 2, Rodriguez 2, Cameron 2, Lampkin 1, Oliver 1, Widger 1.

At Cleveland (4): Martinez 1, Martin 1, Wilson 1, Guillen 1.

At Detroit (4): Martinez 2, Rodriguez 1, Cameron 1.

At Kansas City (6): Martinez 2, Rodriguez 2, Cameron 2.

At Minnesota (9): Lampkin 3, Olerud 2, Rodriguez 2, Martinez 1, Cameron 1.

At New York (AL) (6): Rodriguez 3, Buhner 1, Martinez 1, Guillen 1.

At Oakland (6): Rodriguez 2, Buhner 1, Martinez 1, Bell 1, Guillen 1.

At San Diego (3): Olerud 2, Cameron 1.

At San Francisco (2): Henderson 1, Rodriguez 1.

At Seattle (92): Martinez 19, Buhner 15, Rodriguez 13, Olerud 8, Oliver 6, Javier 5, Cameron 5, Bell 4, Lampkin 3, Guillen 3, Henderson 2, McLemore 2, Martin 2, Wilson 2, Ibanez 2, Machado 1.

At Tampa Bay (7): Cameron 2, Henderson 1, Buhner 1, Martinez 1, Olerud 1, Bell 1.

At Texas (9): Buhner 2, Martinez 2, Rodriguez 2, Cameron 2, Bell 1.

At Toronto (13): Rodriguez 4, Buhner 2, Martinez 2, McLemore 1, Martin 1, Wilson 1, Mabry 1, Cameron 1.

LOW-HIT GAMES

No-hitters: None.
One-hitters: Gil Meche, June 13 vs. Kansas City, W 7-0.
Two-hitters: None.

10-STRIKEOUT GAMES

Aaron Sele 1, Total: 1

FOUR OR MORE HITS IN ONE GAME

John Olerud 4, Alex Rodriguez 4, Edgar Martinez 3, Stan Javier 1 (including one five-hit game), Jay Buhner 1, Al Martin 1, Mike Cameron 1, Carlos Guillen 1, Total: 16

MULTI-HOMER GAMES

Alex Rodriguez 3, John Olerud 2, Jay Buhner 1, Edgar Martinez 1, Total: 7

GRAND SLAMS

4-15: Edgar Martinez (off Toronto's Pedro Borbon)
4-16: Alex Rodriguez (off Toronto's Pedro Borbon)
6-15: Mike Cameron (off Minnesota's Mark Redman)
6-22: Edgar Martinez (off Baltimore's Buddy Groom)
6-25: Tom Lampkin (off Baltimore's Mike Timlin)
7-22: Joe Oliver (off Texas's Ryan Glynn)
7-31: Jay Buhner (off Boston's Ramon Martinez)
8-7: Carlos Guillen (off New York's Denny Neagle)
8-8: Jay Buhner (off Chicago's Jon Garland)
8-8: Edgar Martinez (off Chicago's Bill Simas)
8-29: Edgar Martinez (off New York's Jeff Nelson)

PINCH HITTERS

(Minimum 5 at-bats)

Name	AB	Avg.	HR	RBI
Javier, Stan	20	.200	0	5
Ibanez, Raul	15	.133	0	1
Buhner, Jay	8	.250	0	1
Mabry, John	8	.125	0	1
Guillen, Carlos	5	.200	0	0
Lampkin, Tom	5	.000	0	0

DEBUTS

4-5: Kazuhiro Sasaki, P.
4-24: Kevin Hodges, P.
8-8: Joel Pineiro, P.

GAMES BY POSITION

Catcher: Dan Wilson 88, Joe Oliver 66, Tom Lampkin 28, Robert Machado 8, Chris Widger 6.

First base: John Olerud 158, Brian Lesher 4, Stan Javier 3, John Mabry 3, Raul Ibanez 3, Edgar Martinez 2, David Bell 2, Chris Widger 2, Joe Oliver 1, Dan Wilson 1.

Second base: Mark McLemore 129, David Bell 48.

Third base: David Bell 93, Carlos Guillen 68, John Mabry 22, Charles Gipson 5, Carlos E. Hernandez 2, Dan Wilson 1.

Shortstop: Alex Rodriguez 148, Carlos Guillen 23, Charles Gipson 5, David Bell 1.

Outfield: Mike Cameron 155, Jay Buhner 104, Rickey Henderson 88, Stan Javier 88, Raul Ibanez 76, Charles Gipson 48, Al Martin 35, John Mabry 19, Mark McLemore 14, Chris Widger 1, Anthony Sanders 1.

Designated hitter: Edgar Martinez 146, John Mabry 5, Stan Javier 4, Raul Ibanez 4, Tom Lampkin 3, Rickey Henderson 2, Al Martin 2, Chris Widger 2, Jay Buhner 1, Joe Oliver 1, David Bell 1, Brian Lesher 1, Charles Gipson 1.

STREAKS

Wins: 8 (September 12-20)
Losses: 8 (August 12-20)
Consecutive games with at least one hit: 17, Alex Rodriguez (May 5-23)
Wins by pitcher: 5,Jamie Moyer (July 3-24)

ATTENDANCE

Home: 3,148,317
Road: 2,208,975
Highest (home): 45,552 (April 4 vs. Boston).
Highest (road): 55,629 (August 5 vs. New York).
Lowest (home): 25,121 (April 6 vs. Boston).
Lowest (road): 6,596 (May 3 vs. Minnesota).

TAMPA BAY DEVIL RAYS

DAY BY DAY

Date	Opp.	Res.	Score	(inn.*)	Hits	Opp. hits	Winning pitcher	Losing pitcher	Save	Record	Pos.	GB
4-3	At Min.	W	7-0		14	8	Trachsel	Radke		1-0	T1st	...
4-4	At Min.	L	5-6		9	11	Carrasco	Hernandez		1-1	4th	1.0
4-5	At Min.	L	7-10		13	12	Guardado	White		1-2	5th	1.0
4-6	At Min.	W	7-6		10	13	Mecir	Carrasco	Hernandez	2-2	T3rd	0.5
4-7	Cle.	L	5-14		10	15	Wright	Guzman		2-3	T3rd	1.5
4-8	Cle.	L	4-6		10	11	Burba	Trachsel	Karsay	2-4	4th	2.5
4-9	Cle.	L	4-17		11	16	Colon	Rupe		2-5	5th	3.5
4-11	Chi.	L	6-13		10	18	Parque	Yan		2-6	5th	3.5
4-12	Chi.	L	1-7		7	15	Baldwin	Wheeler		2-7	5th	3.5
4-13	Chi.	W	6-5	(12)	11	8	Mecir	Sturtze		3-7	5th	3.0
4-14	At Det.	L	5-10		14	11	Nitkowski	Rupe		3-8	5th	4.0
4-15	At Det.	W	7-0		11	6	Gooden	Weaver		4-8	T4th	4.0
4-16	At Det.	W	7-6		16	8	Hernandez	Jones		5-8	4th	4.0
4-19	At Bal.	L	2-3		7	7	Trombley	Mecir		5-9	5th	6.0
4-20	At Bal.	L	4-8		7	8	Rapp	Rupe		5-10	5th	6.5
4-21	Ana.	L	6-9		8	12	Petkovsek	Hernandez	Percival	5-11	5th	6.5
4-22	Ana.	W	11-9	(10)	12	10	Lopez	Mercker		6-11	5th	5.5
4-23	Ana.	W	1-0		5	4	Eiland	Dickson	Hernandez	7-11	5th	5.5
4-25	At K.C.	L	6-7		10	13	Reichert	Lopez		7-12	5th	5.0
4-26	At K.C.	L	6-7		8	12	Bottalico	Lopez		7-13	5th	6.0
4-27	At Ana.	W	7-3		12	6	Gooden	Ortiz		8-13	5th	5.5
4-28	At Ana.	W	11-2		19	7	Yan	Dickson		9-13	5th	5.5
4-29	At Ana.	L	6-7	(13)	16	13	Levine	Sparks		9-14	5th	5.5
4-30	At Ana.	L	2-5		7	9	Bottenfield	Trachsel	Percival	9-15	5th	6.5
5-2	Tex.	L	1-8		2	12	Helling	Rupe		9-16	5th	8.0
5-3	Tex.	L	1-5		11	11	Clark	Gooden	Wetteland	9-17	5th	9.0
5-4	Tex.	W	8-7	(11)	12	12	Lopez	Zimmerman		10-17	5th	8.5
5-5	At Bos.	L	3-5		8	10	R. Martinez	Eiland	Lowe	10-18	5th	9.5
5-6	At Bos.	W	1-0		6	3	Trachsel	P. Martinez		11-18	5th	9.5
5-7	At Bos.	L	7-9		13	12	Fassero	Rekar	Lowe	11-19	5th	9.5
5-8	At N.Y.	L	3-6		9	8	Pettitte	Gooden	Rivera	11-20	5th	10.5
5-9	At N.Y.	L	3-4	(10)	8	7	Nelson	White		11-21	5th	11.5
5-11	At N.Y.	W	1-0		7	4	Trachsel	Hernandez	Lopez	12-21	5th	10.5
5-12	Tor.	W	4-3		8	10	White	Carpenter	Lopez	13-21	5th	9.5
5-13	Tor.	L	4-8		5	12	Escobar	Lidle		13-22	5th	9.5
5-14	Tor.	L	2-3		7	8	Wells	Lopez		13-23	5th	10.0
5-15	At Tex.	L	5-6		6	10	Oliver	White	Wetteland	13-24	5th	11.0
5-16	At Tex.	L	7-9		11	12	Zimmerman	Lopez	Wetteland	13-25	5th	11.0
5-17	At Tex.	L	6-11		8	16	Crabtree	Rekar		13-26	5th	12.0
5-19	At Sea.	L	6-7		7	13	Mesa	Taylor	Sasaki	13-27	5th	13.0
5-20	At Sea.	W	4-3		8	8	Yan	Ramsay	Hernandez	14-27	5th	12.0
5-21	At Sea.	L	4-8		10	16	Sele	Trachsel		14-28	5th	12.0
5-23	Oak.	W	6-4		11	10	Rekar	Olivares	Hernandez	15-28	5th	11.0
5-24	Oak.	L	2-9		6	12	Appier	Gooden	Tam	15-29	5th	12.0
5-25	Oak.	L	3-6		8	8	Heredia	Yan	Isringhausen	15-30	5th	12.0
5-26	Sea.	L	4-11		9	15	Sele	Trachsel		15-31	5th	13.0
5-27	Sea.	L	3-6		4	11	Tomko	Rekar	Sasaki	15-32	5th	13.0
5-28	Sea.	W	14-4		20	5	Mecir	Mesa		16-32	5th	13.0
5-29	Bal.	L	1-5		13	9	Rapp	Trachsel		16-33	5th	13.5
5-30	Bal.	L	7-8		14	12	Ponson	Yan	Timlin	16-34	5th	14.5
5-31	Bal.	W	4-3		6	9	Mecir	Groom	Hernandez	17-34	5th	13.5
6-1	Bal.	W	2-1		8	6	Rekar	Erickson	Hernandez	18-34	5th	12.5
6-2	At N.Y. (NL)	L	3-5		7	5	Rusch	White	Benitez	18-35	5th	12.5
6-3	At N.Y. (NL)	L	0-1		5	6	Leiter	Trachsel	Benitez	18-36	5th	12.5
6-4	At N.Y. (NL)	W	15-5		14	9	Yan	B.J. Jones		19-36	5th	12.5
6-5	At Phi.	W	5-3	(12)	9	5	Guthrie	Boyd	White	20-36	5th	11.5
6-6	At Phi.	W	5-3	(10)	9	8	Hernandez	Brantley	White	21-36	5th	11.5
6-7	At Phi.	L	4-5		8	10	Brock	Guthrie	Brantley	21-37	5th	12.5
6-9	Fla.	W	6-4		9	7	Trachsel	Dempster	Hernandez	22-37	5th	11.5
6-10	Fla.	L	1-5		3	10	Cornelius	Yan	Alfonseca	22-38	5th	12.5
6-11	Fla.	W	7-6		13	13	Mecir	Bones	Hernandez	23-38	5th	12.0
6-13	Ana.	L	3-5		7	10	Etherton	Rekar	Percival	23-39	5th	12.0
6-14	Ana.	W	3-2		8	7	Lopez	Percival		24-39	5th	12.0
6-15	Ana.	W	2-1		5	6	Trachsel	Hasegawa		25-39	5th	11.0
6-16	Tex.	W	9-2		13	8	Yan	Oliver		26-39	5th	10.5
6-17	Tex.	L	0-5		3	13	Perisho	Lidle		26-40	5th	10.5
6-18	Tex.	W	6-1		9	9	White	Helling		27-40	5th	9.5
6-19	At Sea.	W	10-3		14	7	Lopez	Halama		28-40	5th	9.0
6-20	At Sea.	L	3-4		6	5	Abbott	Trachsel	Sasaki	28-41	5th	10.0
6-21	At Sea.	L	5-8		7	7	Sele	Yan	Sasaki	28-42	5th	10.0
6-23	At Tex.	W	7-4		13	9	Lidle	Helling	Hernandez	29-42	5th	9.5
6-24	At Tex.	W	9-7		18	13	White	Crabtree	Hernandez	30-42	T4th	9.5
6-25	At Tex.	L	5-9		10	14	Rogers	Lopez	Loaiza	30-43	T4th	10.5
6-27	Tor.	W	11-1		13	9	Trachsel	Escobar		31-43	T4th	9.5
6-28	Tor.	L	2-5		5	7	Wells	Yan		31-44	5th	10.5
6-29	Tor.	L	3-12		10	14	Castillo	Lidle		31-45	5th	11.5
6-30	N.Y.	W	6-4		12	7	Mecir	Nelson	Hernandez	32-45	5th	10.5

HIGHLIGHTS

High point: The Devil Rays finished with an 8-2 run against playoff contenders Toronto, Boston and New York. It might be inaccurate to say the hot finish saved manager Larry Rothschild's job, but it didn't hurt.
Low point: When the team opened September with a 2-16 collapse (including losing streaks of six and 10 games), it was the low point of the franchise's three-year existence. First baseman Fred McGriff complained the franchise was moving backward and the atmosphere in the clubhouse was as dark as it has ever been.
Turning point: It came early, when lefthander Wilson Alvarez went down with a shoulder injury in spring training and righthander Juan Guzman followed after one regular-season start. Minus its top two starters, the rotation couldn't get back in sync until June.
Most valuable player: Center fielder Gerald Williams hit the first pitch of the season for a home run and went on to hit .274 with 21 homers and 89 RBIs. He became only the seventh player to hit at least 20 homers and drive in 80 runs from the leadoff spot.
Most valuable pitcher: Albie Lopez moved from the bullpen to the rotation and became a No. 1 starter. His 11-13 record and 4.13 ERA were impressive for a team that finished 69-92.
Most improved player: Clearly overmatched in his first major league start on August 4 against Baltimore, Travis Harper went to the minors and returned a month later to better reviews. In his fifth start, he raised eyebrows with a two-hit shutout of Toronto. Harper retired 17 of the last 18 batters in that game.
Most pleasant surprise: The work as a starter by Lopez, who was being groomed as a closer.
Key injuries: Alvarez and Guzman were lost for the year with shoulder injuries. ... Ryan Rupe ended the year on the disabled list after a blood clot was discovered in September. ... Righthander Tanyon Sturtze missed the final month with a muscle injury. ... Third baseman Vinny Castilla made three appearances on the D.L. and hit just six homers in a disappointing season. ... Before being claimed by the Yankees on August 7, D.H. Jose Canseco missed 46 games with a sore heel. ... Vaughn missed 19 games with a hamstring injury and struggled late with a sore shoulder.
Notable: Fred McGriff hit his 400th homer, recorded his 2,000th hit and played in his 2,000th game. He also became the second player to hit 200 homers in both leagues. ... Tampa Bay's 4.43 ERA after June 1 ranked third in the A.L. ... Tampa Bay was the only A.L. East team to improve its winning percentage from 1999.

—CHRIS ANDERSON

MISCELLANEOUS

RECORDS

2000 regular-season record: 69-92 (5th in A.L. East); 36-44 at home; 33-48 on road; 31-36 vs. East; 22-27 vs. Central; 16-29 vs. West; 11-25 vs. lefthanded starters; 58-67 vs. righthanded starters; 25-41 on grass; 44-51 on turf; 22-30 in daytime; 47-62 at night; 26-26 in one-run games; 9-5 in extra-inning games; 0-0-1 in doubleheaders.
Team record past five years: 201-284 in three years (.414, ranks 14th in league in that span).

TEAM LEADERS

Batting average: Fred McGriff (.277).
At-bats: Gerald Williams (632).
Runs: Gerald Williams (87).
Hits: Gerald Williams (173).
Total Bases: Gerald Williams (270).
Doubles: Gerald Williams (30).
Triples: Jose Guillen (5).
Home runs: Greg Vaughn (28).
Runs batted in: Fred McGriff (106).
Stolen bases: Miguel Cairo (28).
Slugging percentage: Greg Vaughn (.499).
On-base percentage: Fred McGriff (.373).
Wins: Albie Lopez (11).
Earned-run average: Albie Lopez (4.13).
Complete games: Albie Lopez (4).
Shutouts: Travis Harper, Albie Lopez, Steve Trachsel (1).
Saves: Roberto Hernandez (32).
Innings pitched: Albie Lopez (185.1).
Strikeouts: Esteban Yan (111).

Date	Opp.	Res.	Score	(inn.*)	Hits	Opp. hits	Winning pitcher	Losing pitcher	Save	Record	Pos.	GB
7-1	N.Y.	L	1-6		5	12	Hernandez	Lopez		32-46	5th	10.5
7-2	N.Y.	L	2-5		4	10	Clemens	Trachsel	Rivera	32-47	5th	10.5
7-3	Det.	L	4-5	(10)	7	11	Patterson	Hernandez	Jones	32-48	5th	11.5
7-4	Det.	L	0-11		9	12	Mlicki	Lidle		32-49	5th	11.5
7-5	Det.	W	4-1		9	8	Rekar	Weaver	Hernandez	33-49	5th	10.5
7-7	At Fla.	W	8-3		11	7	Lopez	Dempster	Mecir	34-49	5th	10.5
7-8	At Fla.	L	5-6		11	13	Looper	White	Alfonseca	34-50	5th	12.0
7-9	At Fla.	L	9-10		11	14	Sanchez	Creek	Alfonseca	34-51	5th	12.0
7-13	Mon.	W	6-4		14	8	Mecir	Lira	Hernandez	35-51	5th	11.0
7-14	Mon.	W	8-5		11	12	Lopez	Armas	Hernandez	36-51	5th	11.0
7-15	Mon.	L	1-4		9	13	Hermanson	Trachsel	Kline	36-52	5th	11.5
7-16	Atl.	L	4-6		5	8	Kamieniecki	Mecir		36-53	5th	12.5
7-17	Atl.	W	8-6		12	10	Rupe	Mulholland	Hernandez	37-53	5th	11.5
7-18	Atl.	L	2-8		7	10	Maddux	Rekar		37-54	5th	12.5
7-19	At Tor.	L	2-5		2	9	Escobar	Lopez	Koch	37-55	5th	13.5
7-20	At Tor.	L	5-6		7	10	Quantrill	White	Koch	37-56	5th	13.5
7-21	At N.Y.	L	1-11		10	17	Gooden	Yan		37-57	5th	14.5
7-22	At N.Y.	W	12-4		14	12	Rupe	Cone		38-57	5th	13.5
7-23	At N.Y.	L	1-5		4	7	Neagle	Rekar		38-58	5th	14.5
7-24	At Det.	W	4-2		10	5	Lopez	Nomo	Hernandez	39-58	5th	14.5
7-25	At Det.	L	4-6		9	10	Blair	Trachsel	Jones	39-59	5th	15.5
7-26	At Det.	W	6-2		10	5	Yan	Weaver	Hernandez	40-59	5th	15.5
7-27	At K.C.	W	8-5		10	14	Rupe	Durbin	Hernandez	41-59	5th	14.5
7-28	At K.C.	W	10-3		12	8	Rekar	Stein		42-59	5th	14.5
7-29	At K.C.	W	2-1		4	7	Lopez	Suzuki	Hernandez	43-59	5th	13.5
7-30	At K.C.	W	7-6	(10)	12	12	Sturtze	Spradlin	Hernandez	44-59	5th	13.5
8-1	Cle.	W	6-5		7	10	Creek	Wickman		45-59	5th	13.5
8-2	Cle.	L	3-5		5	12	Karsay	Creek	Wickman	45-60	5th	13.5
8-3	Cle.	L	1-5		6	9	Bere	Lopez		45-61	5th	14.5
8-4	Bal.	L	9-10	(15)	12	17	Johnson	Yan		45-62	5th	15.5
8-5	Bal.	W	5-4	(10)	9	6	Hernandez	Trombley		46-62	5th	14.5
8-6	Bal.	W	7-4		10	10	Rupe	Mussina	Hernandez	47-62	5th	13.5
8-7	Min.	L	2-4		6	9	Redman	Rekar	Guardado	47-63	5th	13.5
8-8	Min.	W	5-0		10	4	Lopez	Radke		48-63	5th	13.5
8-9	Min.	W	5-4	(10)	11	13	Taylor	Hawkins		49-63	5th	13.5
8-10	Min.	W	10-4		7	9	Sturtze	Mays		50-63	T4th	13.5
8-11	Chi.	L	5-6		6	8	Buehrle	Wilson	Foulke	50-64	T4th	13.5
8-12	Chi.	L	4-5	(10)	10	11	Buehrle	Hernandez	Foulke	50-65	5th	13.5
8-13	Chi.	W	5-3		8	5	Lopez	Howry		51-65	T4th	13.5
8-14	At Bos.	L	3-7		11	9	Lowe	Taylor		51-66	5th	14.5
8-15	At Bos.	W	3-1		11	9	Sturtze	Fassero	Hernandez	52-66	T4th	14.5
8-16	At Bos.	L	3-4		7	11	Arrojo	Wilson	Lowe	52-67	T4th	14.5
8-18	At Chi.	L	2-5		7	9	Garland	Rekar	Foulke	52-68	5th	15.0
8-19	At Chi.	L	0-7		3	11	Sirotka	Lopez		52-69	5th	16.0
8-20	At Chi.	W	12-11		15	15	Yan	Foulke	Hernandez	53-69	5th	15.0
8-21	At Chi.	W	11-4		10	8	Sturtze	Parque		54-69	5th	15.0
8-22	At Min.	W	3-2		5	5	Rupe	Romero	Hernandez	55-69	T4th	14.0
8-23	At Min.	L	2-8		5	13	Redman	Rekar	Hawkins	55-70	T4th	15.0
8-25	At Bal.	L	3-4		10	7	Ryan	Taylor	Kohlmeier	55-71	5th	15.5
8-26†	At Bal.	W	4-1		7	7	Eiland	Ponson	Hernandez	56-71		
8-26‡	At Bal.	L	0-2		4	7	Groom	Lidle	Trombley	56-72	5th	16.0
8-27	At Bal.	L	2-3		10	10	Spurgeon	Rupe	Kohlmeier	56-73	5th	17.0
8-28	Bos.	W	5-2		9	8	Rekar	Pichardo	Hernandez	57-73	5th	17.0
8-29	Bos.	L	0-8		1	12	P. Martinez	Eiland		57-74	5th	17.0
8-30	Bos.	W	3-1		11	4	Lopez	Fassero	Hernandez	58-74	5th	17.0
8-31	K.C.	W	2-1		7	6	Fiore	Suppan	Hernandez	59-74	5th	16.5
9-1	K.C.	L	5-9		8	15	Meadows	Rupe		59-75	5th	17.5
9-2	K.C.	L	5-7		8	8	Santiago	Hernandez	Bottalico	59-76	5th	18.5
9-3	K.C.	L	2-8		6	10	Stein	Eiland		59-77	5th	18.5
9-4	At Cle.	L	1-5		7	13	Burba	Lopez		59-78	5th	19.5
9-5	At Cle.	L	4-7		5	9	Bere	Fiore	Wickman	59-79	5th	20.5
9-6	At Cle.	L	2-6		4	11	Finley	Harper		59-80	5th	20.5
9-7	At Cle.	W	4-3		15	7	Rekar	Karsay	Hernandez	60-80	5th	20.5
9-8	At Oak.	W	4-0		5	0	Lidle	Heredia		61-80	5th	20.5
9-9	At Oak.	L	0-10		2	14	Hudson	Lopez		61-81	5th	21.5
9-10	At Oak.	L	0-11		5	12	Zito	Wilson		61-82	5th	22.5
9-11	At Oak.	L	1-5		6	7	Appier	Creek		61-83	5th	22.5
9-12	At Ana.	L	2-5		5	8	Belcher	Rekar	Percival	61-84	5th	23.5
9-13	At Ana.	L	4-8		7	10	Ortiz	Lidle		61-85	5th	24.5
9-15	Oak.	L	3-17		4	20	Zito	Lopez		61-86	5th	24.0
9-16	Oak.	L	2-5		8	8	Hudson	Wilson	Isringhausen	61-87	5th	25.0
9-18	Sea.	L	3-4		7	10	Paniagua	Hernandez		61-88	5th	24.5
9-19	Sea.	L	2-5		6	6	Halama	Harper	Paniagua	61-89	5th	24.5
9-20	Sea.	L	4-5		10	10	Sele	Lopez	Sasaki	61-90	5th	24.5
9-22	At Tor.	W	3-2		10	7	Lidle	Frascatore	Hernandez	62-90	5th	23.0
9-23	At Tor.	L	6-7		9	13	Koch	Enders		62-91	5th	24.0
9-24	At Tor.	W	6-0		13	2	Harper	Trachsel		63-91	5th	24.0
9-25	At Tor.	W	5-1		10	5	Wilson	Loaiza	Hernandez	64-91	5th	23.0
9-26	N.Y.	W	2-1		3	8	Hernandez	Nelson		65-91	5th	22.0
9-27	N.Y.	W	11-1		9	7	Lidle	Neagle		66-91	5th	21.0
9-28	N.Y.	W	11-3		15	10	Rekar	Clemens		67-91	5th	20.0
9-29	Bos.	W	8-6		11	11	Yan	Carrasco	Hernandez	68-91	5th	19.0
9-30	Bos.	L	2-4		5	11	Cormier	Hernandez	Lowe	68-92	5th	19.0
10-1	Bos.	W	3-2	(10)	10	9	Wheeler	Croushore		69-92	5th	18.0

Monthly records: April (9-15), May (8-19), June (15-11), July (12-14), August (15-15), September (9-18), October (1-0).
*Innings, if other than nine. † First game of a doubleheader. ‡ Second game of a doubleheader.

MEMORABLE GAMES

May 6 at Boston

Boston's Pedro Martinez tied a career high with 17 strikeouts—and lost the game, 1-0. Martinez was beaten by Steve Trachsel, who allowed three hits and set a career high with 11 strikeouts. Trachsel retired the final 11 Boston hitters. Martinez, who struck out the first seven hitters he faced, gave up a run-scoring single to Greg Vaughn in the eighth inning.

Tampa Bay	AB	R	H	BI	Boston	AB	R	H	BI
Williams, cf	4	0	1	0	Offerman, 2b	4	0	0	0
Martinez, rf	4	1	1	0	Nixon, rf	3	0	0	0
Vaughn, lf	4	0	1	1	Daubach, 1b	4	0	2	0
Canseco, dh	4	0	0	0	Everett, cf	4	0	0	0
McGriff, 1b	4	0	1	0	O'Leary, lf	4	0	1	0
Castilla, 3b	4	0	0	0	Stanley, dh	3	0	0	0
Flaherty, c	3	0	1	0	Varitek, c	3	0	0	0
Stocker, ss	3	0	0	0	Alexander, 3b	3	0	0	0
Cairo, 2b	3	0	1	0	Sheets, ss	3	0	0	0
Totals	**33**	**1**	**6**	**1**	**Totals**	**31**	**0**	**3**	**0**

Tampa Bay.................................0 0 0 0 0 0 0 1 0—1 6 1
Boston.......................................0 0 0 0 0 0 0 0 0—0 3 0

E—McGriff (4). LOB—Tampa Bay 6, Boston 7. SB—Martinez (1), Cairo (5).

Tampa Bay	IP	H	R	ER	BB	SO
Trachsel (W 2-2)	9	3	0	0	3	11

Boston	IP	H	R	ER	BB	SO
P .Martinez (L 5-1)	9	6	1	1	1	17

U—HP, Fichter. 1B, Scott. 2B, Welke. 3B, Cederstrom. T—2:36. A—32,497.

September 24 at Toronto

Rookie Travis Harper recorded his first major league victory—and it was a dandy. Harper faced just four batters over the minimum and retired 17 of the last 18 he faced in a two-hit, 6-0 win over Toronto. No runner reached third base and only two reached second. It was the first two-hitter in team history.

Tampa Bay	AB	R	H	BI	Toronto	AB	R	H	BI
Tyner, cf	3	1	2	0	Stewart, lf	4	0	0	0
O.Guillen, ss	5	1	1	0	Gonzalez, ss	4	0	0	0
Cox, 1b	5	1	1	0	Martinez, rf	4	0	0	0
McGriff, dh	3	1	3	1	Delgado, 1b	3	0	0	0
Timmons, lf	5	0	1	1	Fullmer, dh	3	0	0	0
Huff, 3b	4	0	2	1	Batista, 3b	3	0	1	0
Johnson, pr-3b	1	1	0	0	Fletcher, c	3	0	1	0
Flaherty, c	4	1	1	3	Cruz, cf	3	0	0	0
Smith, 2b	4	0	0	0	Morandini, 2b	3	0	0	0
J.Guillen, rf	4	0	2	0					
Totals	**38**	**6**	**13**	**6**	**Totals**	**30**	**0**	**2**	**0**

Tampa Bay.................................0 0 0 0 0 2 0 3 1—6 13 1
Toronto ....0 0 0 0 0 0 0 0 0—0 2 0

E—Smith (8). DP—Toronto 1. LOB—Tampa Bay 9, Toronto 4.2B—J. Guillen (16), Batista (31). HR—Flaherty (10). SB—Tyner (5). SH—Tyner.

Tampa Bay	IP	H	R	ER	BB	SO
Harper (W 1-2)	9	2	0	0	1	3

Toronto	IP	H	R	ER	BB	SO
Trachsel (L 8-14)	7	8	2	2	2	4
Escobar	2	5	4	4	1	1

WP—Harper. U—HP, Guccione. 1B, Davis. 2B, Emmel. 3B, Rieker T—2:44. A—28,172.

BATTING

Name	G	TPA	AB	R	H	TB	2B	3B	HR	RBI	Avg.	Obp.	Slg.	SH	SF	HP	BB	IBB	SO	SB	CS	GDP	vs RHP AB	vs RHP Avg.	vs RHP HR	vs RHP RBI	vs LHP AB	vs LHP Avg.	vs LHP HR	vs LHP RBI
Williams, Gerald	146	682	632	87	173	270	30	2	21	89	.274	.312	.427	9	4	3	34	0	103	12	12	5	509	.277	16	70	123	.260	5	19
McGriff, Fred	158	664	566	82	157	256	18	0	27	106	.277	.373	.452	0	7	0	91	10	120	2	0	16	405	.279	17	63	161	.273	10	43
Vaughn, Greg	127	545	461	83	117	230	27	1	28	74	.254	.365	.499	0	2	2	80	3	128	8	1	10	374	.251	24	63	87	.264	4	11
Flaherty, John	109	418	394	36	103	148	15	0	10	39	.261	.296	.376	2	2	0	20	2	57	0	0	11	305	.259	8	30	89	.270	2	9
Cairo, Miguel	119	417	375	49	98	123	18	2	1	34	.261	.314	.328	6	5	2	29	0	34	28	7	7	301	.259	1	29	74	.270	0	5
Castilla, Vinny	85	354	331	22	73	102	9	1	6	42	.221	.254	.308	0	6	3	14	3	41	1	2	9	262	.225	5	35	69	.203	1	7
Cox, Steve	116	369	318	44	90	144	19	1	11	35	.283	.379	.453	0	1	4	46	2	47	1	2	9	265	.291	8	28	53	.245	3	7
Guillen, Jose	105	349	316	40	80	136	16	5	10	41	.253	.320	.430	2	0	13	18	1	65	3	1	6	229	.275	5	27	87	.195	5	14
Martinez, Felix	106	353	299	42	64	89	11	4	2	17	.214	.305	.298	12	2	8	32	0	68	9	3	4	230	.248	2	16	69	.101	0	1
Canseco, Jose	61	264	218	31	56	98	15	0	9	30	.257	.383	.450	0	1	4	41	1	65	2	0	5	176	.267	6	21	42	.214	3	9
DiFelice, Mike	60	223	204	23	49	82	13	1	6	19	.240	.280	.402	5	2	0	12	0	40	0	0	8	164	.244	6	18	40	.225	0	1
Trammell, Bubba	66	213	189	19	52	88	11	2	7	33	.275	.352	.466	0	1	2	21	0	30	3	0	5	129	.248	3	19	60	.333	4	14
Johnson, Russ	74	215	185	28	47	61	8	0	2	17	.254	.344	.330	3	1	1	25	0	30	4	1	4	111	.243	1	12	74	.270	1	5
Smith, Bobby	49	191	175	21	41	67	8	0	6	26	.234	.293	.383	0	1	1	14	1	59	2	2	6	127	.228	5	19	48	.250	1	7
Winn, Randy	51	190	159	28	40	48	5	0	1	16	.252	.362	.302	2	1	2	26	0	25	6	7	2	116	.250	0	10	43	.256	1	6
Huff, Aubrey	39	129	122	12	35	54	7	0	4	14	.287	.318	.443	0	1	1	5	1	18	0	0	6	110	.291	4	14	12	.250	0	0
Stocker, Kevin	40	137	114	20	30	45	7	1	2	8	.263	.378	.395	2	0	2	19	0	27	1	2	3	89	.270	2	7	25	.240	0	1
Guillen, Ozzie	63	114	107	22	26	36	4	0	2	12	.243	.283	.336	1	0	0	6	0	7	1	0	1	100	.250	2	12	7	.143	0	0
Martinez, Dave	29	117	104	12	27	38	4	2	1	12	.260	.319	.365	1	2	0	10	1	17	1	4	1	96	.260	1	9	8	.250	0	3
Tyner, Jason	37	94	83	6	20	22	2	0	0	8	.241	.281	.265	5	1	1	4	0	12	6	1	1	68	.265	0	7	15	.133	0	1
Timmons, Ozzie	12	42	41	9	14	29	3	0	4	13	.341	.357	.707	0	0	0	1	0	7	0	0	2	33	.303	3	10	8	.500	1	3
McCracken, Quinton	15	37	31	5	4	4	0	0	0	2	.129	.270	.129	0	0	0	6	0	4	0	1	3	19	.053	0	2	12	.250	0	0
Perry, Herbert	7	30	28	2	6	7	1	0	0	1	.214	.267	.250	0	0	0	2	0	7	0	0	0	26	.154	0	1	2	1.000	0	0
Graffanino, Tony	13	22	20	8	6	7	1	0	0	1	.300	.364	.350	0	0	1	1	0	2	0	0	1	18	.333	0	1	2	.000	0	0
Hall, Toby	4	13	12	1	2	5	0	0	1	1	.167	.231	.417	0	0	0	1	0	0	0	0	0	11	.182	1	1	1	.000	0	0
Lopez, Albie	45	7	6	0	0	0	0	0	0	0	.000	.000	.000	1	0	0	0	0	5	0	0	0	4	.000	0	0	2	.000	0	0
Trachsel, Steve	23	5	4	0	1	1	0	0	0	0	.250	.400	.250	0	0	0	1	0	1	0	0	0	1	.000	0	0	3	.333	0	0
Rekar, Bryan	30	3	3	0	1	2	1	0	0	1	.333	.333	.667	0	0	0	0	0	1	0	0	0	3	.333	0	1	0	.000	0	0
Rolls, Damian	4	3	3	0	1	1	0	0	0	0	.333	.333	.333	0	0	0	0	0	1	0	0	0	3	.333	0	0	0	.000	0	0
Lidle, Cory	31	2	2	0	0	0	0	0	0	0	.000	.000	.000	0	0	0	0	0	1	0	0	0	2	.000	0	0	0	.000	0	0
Yan, Esteban	43	2	1	1	1	4	0	0	1	1	1.000	1.000	4.000	1	0	0	0	0	0	0	0	0	1	1.000	1	1	0	.000	0	0
Rupe, Ryan	18	1	1	0	0	0	0	0	0	0	.000	.000	.000	0	0	0	0	0	0	0	0	0	0	.000	0	0	1	.000	0	0
Kelly, Kenny	2	1	1	0	0	0	0	0	0	0	.000	.000	.000	0	0	0	0	0	0	0	0	0	0	.000	0	0	1	.000	0	0
Guthrie, Mark	34	0	0	0	0	0	0	0	0	0	.000	.000	.000	0	0	0	0	0	0	0	0	0	0	.000	0	0	0	.000	0	0
Hernandez, Roberto	68	0	0	0	0	0	0	0	0	0	.000	.000	.000	0	0	0	0	0	0	0	0	0	0	.000	0	0	0	.000	0	0
White, Rick	44	0	0	0	0	0	0	0	0	0	.000	.000	.000	0	0	0	0	0	0	0	0	0	0	.000	0	0	0	.000	0	0
Sturtze, Tanyon	19	0	0	0	0	0	0	0	0	0	.000	.000	.000	0	0	0	0	0	0	0	0	0	0	.000	0	0	0	.000	0	0
Mecir, Jim	38	0	0	0	0	0	0	0	0	0	.000	.000	.000	0	0	0	0	0	0	0	0	0	0	.000	0	0	0	.000	0	0
Creek, Doug	45	0	0	0	0	0	0	0	0	0	.000	.000	.000	0	0	0	0	0	0	0	0	0	0	.000	0	0	0	.000	0	0
Gooden, Dwight	8	0	0	0	0	0	0	0	0	0	.000	.000	.000	0	0	0	0	0	0	0	0	0	0	.000	0	0	0	.000	0	0
Eiland, Dave	17	0	0	0	0	0	0	0	0	0	.000	.000	.000	0	0	0	0	0	0	0	0	0	0	.000	0	0	0	.000	0	0
Guzman, Juan	1	0	0	0	0	0	0	0	0	0	.000	.000	.000	0	0	0	0	0	0	0	0	0	0	.000	0	0	0	.000	0	0
Taylor, Billy	17	0	0	0	0	0	0	0	0	0	.000	.000	.000	0	0	0	0	0	0	0	0	0	0	.000	0	0	0	.000	0	0
Wilson, Paul	11	0	0	0	0	0	0	0	0	0	.000	.000	.000	0	0	0	0	0	0	0	0	0	0	.000	0	0	0	.000	0	0
Duvall, Mike	2	0	0	0	0	0	0	0	0	0	.000	.000	.000	0	0	0	0	0	0	0	0	0	0	.000	0	0	0	.000	0	0
Sparks, Jeff	15	0	0	0	0	0	0	0	0	0	.000	.000	.000	0	0	0	0	0	0	0	0	0	0	.000	0	0	0	.000	0	0
Wheeler, Dan	11	0	0	0	0	0	0	0	0	0	.000	.000	.000	0	0	0	0	0	0	0	0	0	0	.000	0	0	0	.000	0	0
Morris, Jim	16	0	0	0	0	0	0	0	0	0	.000	.000	.000	0	0	0	0	0	0	0	0	0	0	.000	0	0	0	.000	0	0
Harper, Travis	6	0	0	0	0	0	0	0	0	0	.000	.000	.000	0	0	0	0	0	0	0	0	0	0	.000	0	0	0	.000	0	0
Fiore, Tony	11	0	0	0	0	0	0	0	0	0	.000	.000	.000	0	0	0	0	0	0	0	0	0	0	.000	0	0	0	.000	0	0
Enders, Trevor	9	0	0	0	0	0	0	0	0	0	.000	.000	.000	0	0	0	0	0	0	0	0	0	0	.000	0	0	0	.000	0	0

Players with more than one A.L. team

Name	G	TPA	AB	R	H	TB	2B	3B	HR	RBI	Avg.	Obp.	Slg.	SH	SF	HP	BB	IBB	SO	SB	CS	GDP	vs RHP AB	vs RHP Avg.	vs RHP HR	vs RHP RBI	vs LHP AB	vs LHP Avg.	vs LHP HR	vs LHP RBI
Canseco, T.B.-N.Y.	98	401	329	47	83	146	18	0	15	49	.252	.377	.444	0	4	4	64	2	102	2	0	7	252	.242	9	32	77	.286	6	17
Gooden, T.B.-N.Y.	26	2	2	0	0	0	0	0	0	0	.000	.000	.000	0	0	0	0	0	1	0	0	0	2	.000	0	0	0	.000	0	0
Graffanino, T.B.-Chi.	70	194	168	33	46	60	6	1	2	17	.274	.363	.357	1	1	2	22	0	27	7	4	2	110	.300	0	9	58	.224	2	8
Guthrie, T.B.-Tor.	57	0	0	0	0	0	0	0	0	0	.000	.000	.000	0	0	0	0	0	0	0	0	0	0	.000	0	0	0	.000	0	0
Martinez, Tex.	38	134	119	14	32	44	4	1	2	12	.269	.351	.370	0	0	1	14	2	20	2	1	8	96	.260	1	9	8	.250	0	3
Martinez, Tor.	47	206	180	29	56	74	10	1	2	22	.311	.393	.411	0	1	1	24	0	28	4	2	3	96	.260	1	9	8	.250	0	3
Martinez, T.B.-Tex.-Tor.	114	457	403	55	115	156	18	4	5	46	.285	.362	.387	1	3	2	48	3	65	7	7	12	336	.280	4	37	67	.313	1	9
Mecir, T.B.-Oak.	63	0	0	0	0	0	0	0	0	0	.000	.000	.000	0	0	0	0	0	0	0	0	0	0	.000	0	0	0	.000	0	0
Perry, T.B.-Chi.	116	450	411	71	124	192	30	1	12	62	.302	.350	.467	2	4	9	24	1	75	4	1	13	330	.303	11	52	81	.296	1	10
Stocker, T.B.-Ana.	110	409	343	41	75	109	20	4	2	24	.219	.326	.318	10	1	4	51	0	81	1	5	11	259	.220	2	19	84	.214	0	5
Sturtze, Chi.-T.B.	29	0	0	0	0	0	0	0	0	0	.000	.000	.000	0	0	0	0	0	0	0	0	0	0	.000	0	0	0	.000	0	0
Trachsel, T.B.-Tor.	34	5	4	0	1	1	0	0	0	0	.250	.400	.250	0	0	0	1	0	1	0	0	0	1	.000	0	0	3	.333	0	0

PITCHING

Name	W	L	Pct.	ERA	IP	H	R	ER	HR	SH	SF	HB	BB	IBB	SO	G	GS	CG	ShO	GF	Sv	vs. RH AB	vs. RH Avg.	vs. RH HR	vs. RH RBI	vs. LH AB	vs. LH Avg.	vs. LH HR	vs. LH RBI
Lopez, Albie	11	13	.458	4.13	185.1	199	95	85	24	6	3	1	70	3	96	45	24	4	1	10	2	355	.248	14	47	363	.306	10	45
Rekar, Bryan	7	10	.412	4.41	173.1	200	92	85	22	3	9	4	39	0	95	30	27	2	0	2	0	335	.290	11	39	351	.293	11	49
Trachsel, Steve	6	10	.375	4.58	137.2	160	76	70	16	2	5	6	49	1	78	23	23	3	1	0	0	285	.284	12	48	259	.305	4	21
Yan, Esteban	7	8	.467	6.21	137.2	158	98	95	26	4	6	11	42	0	111	43	20	0	0	8	0	302	.258	18	57	253	.316	8	33
Lidle, Cory	4	6	.400	5.03	96.2	114	61	54	13	3	1	3	29	3	62	31	11	0	0	5	0	198	.293	4	26	190	.295	9	35
Rupe, Ryan	5	6	.455	6.92	91.0	121	75	70	19	2	6	9	31	3	61	18	18	0	0	0	0	176	.330	10	36	201	.313	9	33
Hernandez, Roberto	4	7	.364	3.19	73.1	76	33	26	9	7	3	3	23	1	61	68	0	0	0	58	32	148	.223	5	15	131	.328	4	23
White, Rick	3	6	.333	3.41	71.1	57	30	27	7	1	2	5	26	3	47	44	0	0	0	8	2	151	.172	4	15	108	.287	3	11
Creek, Doug	1	3	.250	4.60	60.2	49	33	31	10	2	3	2	39	3	73	45	0	0	0	8	1	131	.260	9	26	88	.170	1	10
Eiland, Dave	2	3	.400	7.24	54.2	77	46	44	8	0	2	4	18	0	17	17	10	0	0	1	0	114	.333	4	25	122	.320	4	17
Sturtze, Tanyon	4	0	1.000	2.56	52.2	47	16	15	4	1	0	1	14	1	38	19	5	0	0	7	0	104	.260	3	12	95	.211	1	7
Wilson, Paul	1	4	.200	3.35	51.0	38	20	19	1	2	2	4	16	2	40	11	7	0	0	0	0	90	.189	1	3	92	.228	0	11
Mecir, Jim	7	2	.778	3.08	49.2	35	17	17	2	1	1	1	22	0	33	38	0	0	0	10	1	91	.198	1	10	83	.205	1	4
Gooden, Dwight	2	3	.400	6.63	36.2	47	32	27	14	1	0	3	20	0	23	8	8	0	0	0	0	75	.347	8	14	74	.284	6	14
Guthrie, Mark	1	1	.500	4.50	32.0	33	18	16	4	1	0	0	18	5	26	34	0	0	0	7	0	79	.278	2	12	47	.234	2	8
Harper, Travis	1	2	.333	4.78	32.0	30	17	17	5	1	1	1	15	0	14	6	5	1	1	0	0	59	.254	1	10	64	.234	4	6
Wheeler, Dan	1	1	.500	5.48	23.0	29	14	14	2	1	1	2	11	2	17	11	2	0	0	6	0	45	.178	1	4	51	.412	1	11
Sparks, Jeff	0	1	.000	3.54	20.1	13	8	8	2	0	0	2	18	1	24	15	0	0	0	4	0	37	.270	1	3	33	.091	1	4
Fiore, Tony	1	1	.500	8.40	15.0	21	16	14	3	0	0	2	9	2	8	11	0	0	0	3	0	38	.289	2	4	25	.400	1	9
Taylor, Billy	1	3	.250	8.56	13.2	13	13	13	2	0	0	2	9	2	13	17	0	0	0	7	0	28	.214	1	6	23	.304	1	6
Morris, Jim	0	0	.000	4.35	10.1	10	9	5	1	1	0	0	7	1	10	16	0	0	0	3	0	22	.318	1	7	18	.167	0	3
Enders, Trevor	0	1	.000	10.61	9.1	14	13	11	2	2	0	0	5	0	5	9	0	0	0	4	0	19	.316	2	5	20	.400	0	9
Duvall, Mike	0	0	.000	7.71	2.1	5	2	2	0	0	0	0	1	0	0	2	0	0	0	0	0	7	.286	0	1	4	.750	0	2
Guzman, Juan	0	1	.000	43.20	1.2	7	8	8	2	1	0	0	2	0	3	1	1	0	0	0	0	4	.750	0	3	7	.571	2	5

PITCHERS WITH MORE THAN ONE A.L. TEAM

Name	W	L	Pct.	ERA	IP	H	R	ER	HR	SH	SF	HB	BB	IBB	SO	G	GS	CG	ShO	GF	Sv	vs. RH AB	vs. RH Avg.	vs. RH HR	vs. RH RBI	vs. LH AB	vs. LH Avg.	vs. LH HR	vs. LH RBI
Gooden, N.Y.	4	2	.667	3.36	64.1	66	28	24	8	3	2	0	21	3	31	18	5	0	0	3	2	75	.347	8	14	74	.284	6	14
Gooden, T.B.-N.Y.	6	5	.545	4.54	101.0	113	60	51	22	4	2	3	41	3	54	26	13	0	0	2	2	218	.303	12	23	179	.263	10	34
Guthrie, Tor.	0	2	.000	4.79	20.2	20	12	11	3	1	1	1	9	0	20	23	0	0	0	5	0	79	.278	2	12	47	.234	2	8
Guthrie, T.B.-Tor.	1	3	.250	4.61	52.2	53	30	27	7	2	1	1	27	5	46	57	0	0	0	1	0	119	.261	5	22	83	.265	2	13
Mecir, Oak.	3	1	.750	2.80	35.1	35	14	11	2	0	1	1	14	2	37	25	0	0	0	7	4	91	.198	1	10	83	.205	1	4
Mecir, T.B.-Oak.	10	3	.769	2.96	85.0	70	31	28	4	1	2	2	36	2	70	63	0	0	0	2	5	159	.245	3	22	152	.204	1	13
Sturtze, Chi.	1	2	.333	12.06	15.2	25	23	21	4	0	2	2	15	0	6	10	1	0	0	2	0	104	.260	3	12	95	.211	1	7
Sturtze, Chi.-T.B.	5	2	.714	4.74	68.1	72	39	36	8	1	2	3	29	1	44	29	6	0	0	2	0	131	.275	4	17	134	.269	4	23
Trachsel, Tor.	2	5	.286	5.29	63.0	72	40	37	10	4	1	0	25	1	32	11	11	0	0	0	0	285	.284	12	48	259	.305	4	21
Trachsel, T.B.-Tor.	8	15	.348	4.80	200.2	232	116	107	26	6	6	6	74	2	110	34	34	3	1	6	0	404	.290	17	67	386	.298	9	39

DESIGNATED HITTERS

Name	AB	Avg.	HR	RBI	Name	AB	Avg.	HR	RBI	Name	AB	Avg.	HR	RBI
Canseco, Jose	217	.258	9	30	Trammell, Bubba	18	.222	0	2	Kelly, Kenny	1	.000	0	0
Vaughn, Greg	184	.212	11	32	Cairo, Miguel	5	.200	0	1	Stocker, Kevin	0	-	0	0
Cox, Steve	63	.365	2	7	Timmons, Ozzie	4	.500	1	3	Winn, Randy	0	-	0	0
McGriff, Fred	39	.282	1	7	Rolls, Damian	1	1.000	0	0					
Williams, Gerald	31	.290	1	6	Tyner, Jason	1	.000	0	0					

INDIVIDUAL STATISTICS

FIELDING

FIRST BASEMEN

Player	Pct.	G	PO	A	E	TC	DP
McGriff, Fred	.993	144	1300	82	10	1392	137
Cox, Steve	.988	24	160	10	2	172	12
Guillen, Ozzie	1.000	5	7	1	0	8	0
Perry, Herbert	1.000	1	2	0	0	2	0

SECOND BASEMEN

Player	Pct.	G	PO	A	E	TC	DP
Cairo, Miguel	.983	108	218	302	9	529	76
Smith, Bobby	.970	45	84	144	7	235	26
Johnson, Russ	.976	18	27	55	2	84	9
Graffanino, Tony	1.000	6	12	16	0	28	4
Guillen, Ozzie	1.000	2	3	2	0	5	0

THIRD BASEMEN

Player	Pct.	G	PO	A	E	TC	DP
Castilla, Vinny	.967	83	50	185	8	243	20
Johnson, Russ	.967	49	14	74	3	91	6
Huff, Aubrey	.939	37	24	53	5	82	3
Guillen, Ozzie	1.000	11	4	22	0	26	2
Perry, Herbert	.938	7	5	10	1	16	1
Smith, Bobby	.875	5	0	7	1	8	0
Graffanino, Tony	1.000	3	2	1	0	3	0
Rolls, Damian	-	1	0	0	0	0	0

SHORTSTOPS

Player	Pct.	G	PO	A	E	TC	DP
Martinez, Felix	.976	106	191	368	14	573	80
Guillen, Ozzie	.948	42	26	65	5	96	12
Stocker, Kevin	.933	40	43	111	11	165	25
Johnson, Russ	1.000	11	4	14	0	18	1
Graffanino, Tony	1.000	1	0	2	0	2	0

OUTFIELDERS

Player	Pct.	G	PO	A	E	TC	DP
Williams, Gerald	.983	138	349	6	6	361	1
Guillen, Jose	.978	99	169	7	4	180	3
Vaughn, Greg	.993	72	145	6	1	152	1
Cox, Steve	.948	56	107	3	6	116	0
Trammell, Bubba	1.000	48	66	2	0	68	1
Winn, Randy	.990	47	92	4	1	97	1
Tyner, Jason	1.000	31	51	4	0	55	0
Martinez, Dave	1.000	28	46	5	0	51	1
McCracken, Quinton	1.000	11	19	0	0	19	0
Timmons, Ozzie	1.000	9	8	0	0	8	0

CATCHERS

Player	Pct.	G	PO	A	E	TC	DP	PB
Flaherty, John	.993	108	611	51	5	667	9	4
DiFelice, Mike	.980	59	351	35	8	394	6	10
Hall, Toby	1.000	4	19	2	0	21	0	0

PITCHERS

Player	Pct.	G	PO	A	E	TC	DP
Hernandez, Roberto	.938	68	4	11	1	16	1
Lopez, Albie	.906	45	12	17	3	32	2
Creek, Doug	1.000	45	2	9	0	11	1
White, Rick	1.000	44	1	7	0	8	1
Yan, Esteban	.905	43	11	8	2	21	1
Mecir, Jim	1.000	38	1	4	0	5	1
Guthrie, Mark	1.000	34	1	6	0	7	0
Lidle, Cory	.962	31	6	19	1	26	1
Rekar, Bryan	.970	30	11	21	1	33	2
Trachsel, Steve	1.000	23	12	18	0	30	4
Sturtze, Tanyon	1.000	19	6	3	0	9	0
Rupe, Ryan	1.000	18	2	10	0	12	0
Eiland, Dave	1.000	17	6	15	0	21	0
Taylor, Billy	1.000	17	1	0	0	1	0
Morris, Jim	-	16	0	0	0	0	0
Sparks, Jeff	1.000	15	1	0	0	1	0
Wilson, Paul	1.000	11	3	4	0	7	1
Wheeler, Dan	1.000	11	1	4	0	5	1
Fiore, Tony	1.000	11	1	1	0	2	0
Enders, Trevor	1.000	9	2	2	0	4	0
Gooden, Dwight	.667	8	0	2	1	3	0
Harper, Travis	1.000	6	1	3	0	4	0
Duvall, Mike	1.000	2	0	1	0	1	0
Guzman, Juan	-	1	0	0	0	0	0

PITCHING AGAINST EACH CLUB

Pitcher	Ana. W-L	Bal. W-L	Bos. W-L	Chi. W-L	Cle. W-L	Det. W-L	K.C. W-L	Min. W-L	N.Y. W-L	Oak. W-L	Sea. W-L	Tex. W-L	Tor. W-L	N.L. W-L	Total W-L
Creek, Doug	0-0	0-0	0-0	0-0	1-1	0-0	0-0	0-0	0-0	0-1	0-0	0-0	0-0	0-1	1-3
Duvall, Mike	0-0	0-0	0-0	0-0	0-0	0-0	0-0	0-0	0-0	0-0	0-0	0-0	0-0	0-0	0-0
Eiland, Dave	1-0	1-0	0-2	0-0	0-0	0-0	0-1	0-0	0-0	0-0	0-0	0-0	0-0	0-0	2-3
Enders, Trevor	0-0	0-0	0-0	0-0	0-0	0-0	0-0	0-0	0-0	0-0	0-0	0-0	0-1	0-0	0-1
Fiore, Tony	0-0	0-0	0-0	0-0	0-1	0-0	1-0	0-0	0-0	0-0	0-0	0-0	0-0	0-0	1-1
Gooden, Dwight	1-0	0-0	0-0	0-0	0-0	1-0	0-0	0-0	0-1	0-1	0-0	0-1	0-0	0-0	2-3
Guthrie, Mark	0-0	0-0	0-0	0-0	0-0	0-0	0-0	0-0	0-0	0-0	0-0	0-0	0-0	1-1	1-1
Guzman, Juan	0-0	0-0	0-0	0-0	0-1	0-0	0-0	0-0	0-0	0-0	0-0	0-0	0-0	0-0	0-1
Harper, Travis	0-0	0-0	0-0	0-0	0-1	0-0	0-0	0-0	0-0	0-0	0-1	0-0	1-0	0-0	1-2
Hernandez, Roberto	0-1	1-0	0-1	0-1	0-0	1-1	0-1	0-1	1-0	0-0	0-1	0-0	0-0	1-0	4-7
Lidle, Cory	0-1	0-1	0-0	0-0	0-0	0-1	0-0	0-0	1-0	1-0	0-0	1-1	1-2	0-0	4-6
Lopez, Albie	2-0	0-0	1-0	1-1	0-2	1-0	1-2	1-0	0-1	0-2	1-1	1-2	0-2	2-0	11-13
Mecir, Jim	0-0	1-1	0-0	1-0	0-0	0-0	0-0	1-0	1-0	0-0	1-0	0-0	0-0	2-1	7-2
Morris, Jim	0-0	0-0	0-0	0-0	0-0	0-0	0-0	0-0	0-0	0-0	0-0	0-0	0-0	0-0	0-0
Rekar, Bryan	0-2	1-0	1-1	0-1	1-0	1-0	1-0	0-2	1-1	1-0	0-1	0-1	0-0	0-1	7-10
Rupe, Ryan	0-0	1-2	0-0	0-0	0-1	0-1	1-1	1-0	1-0	0-0	0-0	0-1	0-0	1-0	5-6
Sparks, Jeff	0-1	0-0	0-0	0-0	0-0	0-0	0-0	0-0	0-0	0-0	0-0	0-0	0-0	0-0	0-1
Sturtze, Tanyon	0-0	0-0	1-0	1-0	0-0	0-0	1-0	1-0	0-0	0-0	0-0	0-0	0-0	0-0	4-0
Taylor, Billy	0-0	0-1	0-1	0-0	0-0	0-0	0-0	1-0	0-0	0-0	0-1	0-0	0-0	0-0	1-3
Trachsel, Steve	1-1	0-1	1-0	0-0	0-1	0-1	0-0	1-0	1-1	0-0	0-3	0-0	1-0	1-2	6-10
Wheeler, Dan	0-0	0-0	1-0	0-1	0-0	0-0	0-0	0-0	0-0	0-0	0-0	0-0	0-0	0-0	1-1
White, Rick	0-0	0-0	0-0	0-0	0-0	0-0	0-0	0-1	0-1	0-0	0-0	2-1	1-1	0-2	3-6
Wilson, Paul	0-0	0-0	0-1	0-1	0-0	0-0	0-0	0-0	0-0	0-2	0-0	0-0	1-0	0-0	1-4
Yan, Esteban	1-0	0-2	1-0	1-1	0-0	1-0	0-0	0-0	0-1	0-1	1-1	1-0	0-1	1-1	7-8
Totals	6-6	5-8	6-6	4-6	2-8	5-4	5-5	6-4	6-6	2-7	3-9	5-7	5-7	9-9	69-92

INTERLEAGUE: Rupe 1-0, Mecir 0-1, Rekar 0-1 vs. Braves; Mecir 1-0, Lopez 1-0, Trachsel 0-1 vs. Expos; Yan 1-0, White 0-1, Trachsel 0-1 vs. Mets; Guthrie 1-1, Hernandez 1-0 vs. Phillies; Trachsel 1-0, Mecir 1-0, Lopez 1-0, Yan 0-1, Creek 0-1, White 0-1 vs. Marlins. Total: 9-9.

MISCELLANEOUS

HOME RUNS BY PARK

At Anaheim (8): Vaughn 4, Castilla 2, McGriff 1, Canseco 1.
At Baltimore (6): McGriff 1, Canseco 1, Vaughn 1, Castilla 1, Williams 1, Huff 1.
At Boston (5): Canseco 1, Castilla 1, Cairo 1, Trammell 1, Cox 1.
At Chicago (AL) (5): Williams 2, DiFelice 1, Martinez 1, Smith 1.
At Cleveland (3): Cox 2, Vaughn 1.
At Detroit (3): Williams 2, Cox 1.
At Florida (5): McGriff 3, Vaughn 1, Williams 1.
At Kansas City (6): Vaughn 2, Williams 2, Flaherty 1, Stocker 1.
At Minnesota (8): McGriff 2, Vaughn 1, Flaherty 1, Williams 1, Stocker 1, Guillen 1, Smith 1.
At New York (AL) (4): Vaughn 2, McGriff 1, Williams 1.
At New York (NL) (4): McGriff 1, Yan 1, Trammell 1, Martinez 1.
At Oakland (1): Vaughn 1.
At Philadelphia (0):
At Seattle (8): McGriff 2, Vaughn 2, Williams 2, Guillen 1, Smith 1.
At Tampa Bay (76): Vaughn 13, McGriff 10, Flaherty 7, Cox 7, Williams 6, Trammell 5, Guillen 5, Canseco 4, DiFelice 4, Timmons 3, Huff 3, Castilla 2, Johnson 2, Smith 2, Guillen 1, Martinez 1, Winn 1.
At Texas (13): McGriff 4, Guillen 3, Williams 2, Guillen 1, Canseco 1, DiFelice 1, Smith 1.
At Toronto (7): McGriff 2, Canseco 1, Flaherty 1, Williams 1, Timmons 1, Hall 1.

LOW-HIT GAMES

No-hitters: None.
One-hitters: None.
Two-hitters: Travis Harper, September 24 vs. Toronto, W 6-0.

10-STRIKEOUT GAMES

Steve Trachsel 1, Total: 1

FOUR OR MORE HITS IN ONE GAME

Greg Vaughn 2, Fred McGriff 1, Gerald Williams 1, Felix Martinez 1, Steve Cox 1, Total: 6

MULTI-HOMER GAMES

Fred McGriff 3, Greg Vaughn 3, Total: 6

GRAND SLAMS

4-3: Fred McGriff (off Minnesota's Brad Radke)
5-17: Fred McGriff (off Texas's Doug Davis)
6-25: Jose Guillen (off Texas's Kenny Rogers)
6-27: Steve Cox (off Toronto's Kelvim Escobar)

PINCH HITTERS

(Minimum 5 at-bats)

Name	AB	Avg.	HR	RBI
Cox, Steve	21	.333	0	2
Trammell, Bubba	14	.286	3	7
Johnson, Russ	12	.417	0	2
Guillen, Jose	8	.375	0	3
Cairo, Miguel	7	.286	0	1

DEBUTS

8-2: Aubrey Huff, 3B.
8-4: Travis Harper, P.
8-27: Tony Fiore, P.
9-2: Trevor Enders, P.
9-3: Damian Rolls, PH.
9-7: Kenny Kelly, PR.
9-15: Toby Hall, C.

GAMES BY POSITION

Catcher: John Flaherty 108, Mike DiFelice 59, Toby Hall 4.
First base: Fred McGriff 144, Steve Cox 24, Ozzie Guillen 5, Herbert Perry 1.
Second base: Miguel Cairo 108, Bobby Smith 45, Russ Johnson 18, Tony Graffanino 6, Ozzie Guillen 2.
Third base: Vinny Castilla 83, Russ Johnson 49, Aubrey Huff 37, Ozzie Guillen 11, Herbert Perry 7, Bobby Smith 5, Tony Graffanino 3, Damian Rolls 1.
Shortstop: Felix Martinez 106, Ozzie Guillen 42, Kevin Stocker 40, Russ Johnson 11, Tony Graffanino 1.
Outfield: Gerald Williams 138, Jose Guillen 99, Greg Vaughn 72, Steve Cox 56, Bubba Trammell 48, Randy Winn 47, Jason Tyner 31, Dave Martinez 28, Quinton McCracken 11, Ozzie Timmons 9.
Designated hitter: Jose Canseco 60, Greg Vaughn 52, Steve Cox 17, Fred McGriff 10, Bubba Trammell 9, Gerald Williams 7, Miguel Cairo 2, Ozzie Timmons 1, Randy Winn 1, Damian Rolls 1, Jason Tyner 1, Kenny Kelly 1.

STREAKS

Wins: 6 (July 26-August 1, September 24-29)
Losses: 10 (September 9-20)
Consecutive games with at least one hit: 14, Fred McGriff (April 28-May 13)
Wins by pitcher: 3, Tanyon Sturtze (August 10-21) Ryan Rupe (July 17-27)

ATTENDANCE

Home: 1,549,440
Road: 2,182,830
Highest (home): 42,823 (June 10 vs. Florida).
Highest (road): 48,256 (June 24 vs. Texas).
Lowest (home): 13,039 (May 24 vs. Oakland).
Lowest (road): 7,020 (April 4 vs. Minnesota).

TEXAS RANGERS

DAY BY DAY

Date	Opp.	Res.	Score	(inn.*)	Hits	Opp. hits	Winning pitcher	Losing pitcher	Save	Record	Pos.	GB
4-3	Chi.	W	10-4		11	10	Rogers	Sirotka		1-0	1st	+0.5
4-4	Chi.	W	12-8		12	14	Cordero	Simas		2-0	1st	+1.0
4-5	Chi.	L	8-12		13	15	Foulke	Zimmerman		2-1	T1st	...
4-6	Chi.	L	2-6		6	11	Baldwin	Loaiza		2-2	3rd	0.5
4-7	Tor.	W	11-5		11	11	Clark	Castillo		3-2	2nd	0.5
4-8	Tor.	L	0-4		9	10	Wells	Rogers		3-3	3rd	0.5
4-9	Tor.	W	7-5		9	7	Helling	Halladay		4-3	2nd	0.5
4-12	At N.Y.	L	6-8		10	13	Nelson	Munoz	Rivera	4-4	3rd	1.0
4-13	At N.Y.	L	1-5		4	8	Hernandez	Rogers		4-5	3rd	1.0
4-14	At Cle.	W	7-2		14	4	Helling	Burba		5-5	T2nd	1.0
4-15	At Cle.	W	6-4		11	6	Clark	Colon	Wetteland	6-5	T2nd	1.0
4-16	At Cle.	L	1-2		5	4	Finley	Wetteland		6-6	3rd	2.0
4-17	N.Y.	L	4-5	(11)	11	8	Rivera	Crabtree	Erdos	6-7	3rd	2.5
4-18	N.Y.	L	3-6		8	11	Hernandez	Rogers		6-8	T3rd	2.5
4-19	N.Y.	L	4-5	(10)	7	12	Rivera	Zimmerman		6-9	4th	2.5
4-21	Min.	L	5-10		15	12	Carrasco	Clark		6-10	4th	3.5
4-22	Min.	W	8-3		11	11	Loaiza	Santana		7-10	3rd	3.5
4-23	Min.	L	4-5		11	13	Radke	Oliver	Wells	7-11	4th	4.5
4-24	Bos.	W	5-4		7	9	Rogers	Wakefield	Wetteland	8-11	3rd	3.5
4-25	Bos.	L	3-6		6	9	P. Martinez	Helling	Lowe	8-12	4th	4.5
4-26	Bos.	L	4-14		10	21	Fassero	Clark		8-13	4th	4.5
4-28	At Bal.	L	3-4		9	8	Groom	Zimmerman		8-14	4th	4.5
4-29	At Bal.	L	1-3		9	6	Mussina	Oliver		8-15	4th	5.5
4-30	At Bal.	W	8-4		14	9	Rogers	Rapp		9-15	4th	4.5
5-2	At T.B.	W	8-1		12	2	Helling	Rupe		10-15	4th	4.5
5-3	At T.B.	W	5-1		11	11	Clark	Gooden	Wetteland	11-15	4th	3.5
5-4	At T.B.	L	7-8	(11)	12	12	Lopez	Zimmerman		11-16	4th	4.0
5-5	Oak.	W	17-16		21	16	Wetteland	Tam		12-16	4th	3.0
5-6	Oak.	W	11-10		17	14	Wetteland	Isringhausen		13-16	4th	3.0
5-7	Oak.	L	6-7		12	9	Olivares	Davis	Jones	13-17	4th	4.0
5-8	Sea.	W	10-1		14	5	Helling	Tomko		14-17	4th	3.0
5-9	Sea.	L	3-13		6	19	Abbott	Loaiza		14-18	4th	4.0
5-10	Sea.	W	7-6		13	12	Wetteland	Sasaki		15-18	4th	3.0
5-11	At Ana.	L	2-3		8	10	Hasegawa	Rogers	Percival	15-19	4th	3.0
5-12	At Ana.	W	13-11		14	14	Davis	Schoeneweis	Wetteland	16-19	4th	2.5
5-13	At Ana.	W	6-5		9	7	Helling	Washburn	Wetteland	17-19	4th	2.0
5-14	At Ana.	L	6-7		8	8	Hasegawa	Cordero		17-20	4th	2.5
5-15	T.B.	W	6-5		10	6	Oliver	White	Wetteland	18-20	4th	2.5
5-16	T.B.	W	9-7		12	11	Zimmerman	Lopez	Wetteland	19-20	3rd	2.0
5-17	T.B.	W	11-6		16	8	Crabtree	Rekar		20-20	3rd	2.0
5-18	Bal.	W	8-7		13	11	Helling	Ryan	Wetteland	21-20	2nd	1.5
5-20	Bal.	W	2-1		6	7	Loaiza	Mussina	Wetteland	22-20	2nd	1.0
5-21	Bal.	W	6-5		7	14	Venafro	Groom	Wetteland	23-20	2nd	1.0
5-23	At K.C.	W	4-3		7	9	Helling	Batista	Wetteland	24-20	2nd	...
5-24	At K.C.	L	0-3		6	8	Suppan	Rogers	Spradlin	24-21	2nd	...
5-25	At K.C.	W	5-3		8	10	Loaiza	Santiago	Wetteland	25-21	1st	+0.5
5-26	At Min.	L	2-10		5	16	Milton	Oliver		25-22	2nd	...
5-27	At Min.	L	5-10		8	10	Mays	Clark		25-23	2nd	1.0
5-28	At Min.	L	3-4		8	7	Bergman	Helling	Hawkins	25-24	3rd	1.0
5-29	At Det.	W	3-2		7	11	Rogers	Weaver	Wetteland	26-24	3rd	1.0
5-30	At Det.	L	4-7		9	13	Moehler	Loaiza	Jones	26-25	3rd	1.0
5-31	At Det.	W	13-5		16	11	Oliver	Mlicki		27-25	2nd	...
6-2	Ari.	L	4-5		7	13	Anderson	Helling	Mantei	27-26	4th	1.0
6-3	Ari.	W	4-3		9	7	Rogers	Figueroa	Wetteland	28-26	3rd	0.5
6-4	Ari.	W	7-6		10	14	Perisho	Kim	Wetteland	29-26	2nd	...
6-5	L.A.	W	2-0		5	2	Glynn	Brown	Wetteland	30-26	2nd	...
6-6	L.A.	L	1-7		6	14	Gagne	Clark		30-27	3rd	1.0
6-7	L.A.	L	6-11		12	15	Dreifort	Helling		30-28	4th	1.5
6-9	At Col.	L	2-3	(12)	10	8	Tavarez	Wetteland		30-29	4th	2.5
6-10	At Col.	L	6-12		11	15	Karl	Loaiza		30-30	4th	2.5
6-11	At Col.	L	8-9		18	13	DeJean	Crabtree	Jimenez	30-31	4th	3.5
6-13	At Bal.	L	2-3		6	6	Erickson	Helling	Timlin	30-32	4th	4.5
6-14	At Bal.	L	10-11		10	12	Timlin	Crabtree		30-33	4th	5.0
6-15	At Bal.	L	1-10		5	8	McElroy	Loaiza		30-34	4th	5.5
6-16	At T.B.	L	2-9		8	13	Yan	Oliver		30-35	4th	6.5
6-17	At T.B.	W	5-0		13	3	Perisho	Lidle		31-35	4th	6.5
6-18	At T.B.	L	1-6		9	9	White	Helling		31-36	4th	7.5
6-20	Min.	W	5-2		13	5	Rogers	Redman	Wetteland	32-36	4th	8.0
6-21	Min.	W	7-5		11	12	Loaiza	Radke	Wetteland	33-36	4th	8.0
6-22	Min.	L	2-3		9	6	Hawkins	Crabtree	Wells	33-37	4th	8.5
6-23	T.B.	L	4-7		9	13	Lidle	Helling	Hernandez	33-38	4th	9.5
6-24	T.B.	L	7-9		13	18	White	Crabtree	Hernandez	33-39	4th	9.5
6-25	T.B.	W	9-5		14	10	Rogers	Lopez	Loaiza	34-39	4th	9.5
6-27	At Oak.	L	6-7		10	10	Hudson	Perisho	Isringhausen	34-40	4th	10.5
6-28	At Oak.	W	5-3		10	6	Helling	Appier	Wetteland	35-40	4th	9.5
6-29	At Oak.	W	3-1		9	8	Loaiza	Heredia	Wetteland	36-40	4th	9.0
6-30	Sea.	W	13-3		18	8	Rogers	Halama		37-40	4th	8.0
7-1	Sea.	L	3-6		8	8	Abbott	Clark	Sasaki	37-41	4th	9.0
7-2	Sea.	L	4-11		10	11	Sele	Perisho		37-42	4th	10.0

HIGHLIGHTS

High point: The deal that sent Juan Gonzalez to the Tigers didn't work out the way either team expected, but the second-half surge of outfielder Gabe Kapler gave the Rangers reason for optimism. Kapler batted .328 over the final 92 games and put together a club-record 28-game hitting streak. That produced the only suspenseful moments after the All-Star Game.
Low point: On the next-to-last day, the Rangers hit rock bottom in a 23-2 loss at Oakland—their 90th defeat of the season. In one fell swoop they allowed the most runs and suffered the worst loss in club history.
Turning point: The Rangers began June tied for first in the A.L. West. But it was all downhill from there. On June 2, dynamic rookie Ruben Mateo broke his leg in a game against Arizona and the Rangers lost 10 of the next 13, including nine in a row from June 6-16.
Most valuable player: Rafael Palmeiro. Although there were more peaks and valleys than usual, the numbers all added up. He hit 39 home runs, including career No. 400, and drove in 120.
Most valuable pitcher: Rick Helling finished with a 16-13 record and 4.48 ERA, but only after wearing down during a horrid September. Helling entered the final month 14-9 and among the A.L. leaders in ERA.
Most improved player: In 1999, righthander Ryan Glynn was a jittery young pitcher with a hurry-up delivery and little command. He was much more poised and relaxed in 2000 and, despite a September struggle, made a favorable impression with the Rangers.
Most pleasant surprise: When the veteran rotation sprung leaks, 24-year-old lefty Doug Davis stepped in and kept the team from jumping into the overpriced free-agent market. Davis unexpectedly made 13 starts and finished 7-6.
Key injuries: Lefthander Justin Thompson (shoulder surgery) did not pitch all season after reinjuring himself during rehabilitation. ... All-Star catcher Ivan Rodriguez (broken thumb) missed the final two months. ... Center fielder Mateo (broken leg) missed the final four months. ... Catcher Bill Haselman (torn rotator cuff) missed the final two weeks. ... Kapler (quadriceps, shoulder) missed six weeks. ... Outfielder Rusty Greer (ankle) missed nearly nine weeks.
Notable: The Rangers suffered their first 90-loss season since 1988. They also became the fourth team in history to sink from first place to last in consecutive seasons. ... The Rangers made 135 errors, the most in the A.L., and allowed a major league-worst 98 unearned runs. The Rangers also ranked last in the A.L. in fielding percentage at .978. ... Righthander John Wetteland topped the 300-save plateau in May. ... Outfielder Scarborough Green set a club record with five stolen bases in a game at Seattle on September 28, the Rangers' last win of the season.

—EVAN GRANT

MISCELLANEOUS

RECORDS

2000 regular-season record: 71-91 (4th in A.L. West); 42-39 at home; 29-52 on road; 22-34 vs. East; 25-27 vs. Central; 24-30 vs. West; 19-15 vs. lefthanded starters; 52-76 vs. righthanded starters; 66-80 on grass; 5-11 on turf; 16-23 in daytime; 55-68 at night; 27-25 in one-run games; 5-5 in extra-inning games; 1-0-0 in doubleheaders.
Team record past five years: 421-389 (.520, ranks 5th in league in that span).

TEAM LEADERS

Batting average: Luis Alicea (.294).
At-bats: Rafael Palmeiro (565).
Runs: Rafael Palmeiro (102).
Hits: Rafael Palmeiro (163).
Total Bases: Rafael Palmeiro (315).
Doubles: Rusty Greer (34).
Triples: Luis Alicea (8).
Home runs: Rafael Palmeiro (39).
Runs batted in: Rafael Palmeiro (120).
Stolen bases: Royce Clayton (11).
Slugging percentage: Rafael Palmeiro (.558).
On-base percentage: Rafael Palmeiro (.397).
Wins: Rick Helling (16).
Earned-run average: Rick Helling (4.48).
Complete games: Kenny Rogers (2).
Shutouts: None.
Saves: John Wetteland (34).
Innings pitched: Kenny Rogers (227.1).
Strikeouts: Rick Helling (146).

Date	Opp.	Res.	Score	(inn.*)	Hits	Opp. hits	Winning pitcher	Losing pitcher	Save	Record	Pos.	GB
7-3	Oak.	W	8-3		9	9	Helling	Appier		38-42	4th	10.0
7-4	Oak.	W	10-7		13	11	Davis	Service	Wetteland	39-42	4th	9.0
7-5	Oak.	W	9-4		17	11	Rogers	Mulder		40-42	4th	9.0
7-7	S.D.	W	5-4	(10)	9	6	Davis	Whiteside		41-42	4th	7.5
7-8	S.D.	W	8-1		12	3	Helling	Eaton		42-42	4th	7.5
7-9	S.D.	L	3-4		8	13	Clement	Rogers	Hoffman	42-43	4th	8.5
7-13	At Ari.	W	6-4		7	11	Zimmerman	Kim	Wetteland	43-43	4th	7.5
7-14	At Ari.	L	1-6		6	10	Reynoso	Rogers		43-44	4th	8.5
7-15	At Ari.	W	6-5	(11)	10	13	Zimmerman	Swindell	Wetteland	44-44	4th	7.5
7-16	At S.F.	L	4-6		8	11	Estes	Loaiza	Nen	44-45	4th	8.5
7-17	At S.F.	L	8-10		12	13	Hernandez	Davis	Nen	44-46	4th	8.5
7-18	At S.F.	L	3-5		11	10	Fultz	Wetteland		44-47	4th	9.5
7-19	At Ana.	W	3-2		10	13	Rogers	Bottenfield	Wetteland	45-47	4th	9.5
7-20	At Ana.	L	1-6		7	9	Etherton	Oliver	Hasegawa	45-48	4th	9.5
7-21	At Sea.	L	3-12		8	11	Abbott	Perisho		45-49	4th	10.5
7-22	At Sea.	L	5-13		9	14	Halama	Glynn		45-50	4th	11.5
7-23	At Sea.	W	3-2		9	8	Helling	Rhodes	Wetteland	46-50	4th	10.5
7-24	Ana.	L	5-6	(12)	11	11	Hasegawa	Crabtree	Percival	46-51	4th	11.5
7-25	Ana.	W	9-6		10	10	Davis	Holtz	Wetteland	47-51	4th	10.5
7-26	Ana.	W	6-5		12	7	Wetteland	Levine		48-51	4th	9.5
7-27	Det.	W	7-3		11	4	Glynn	Sparks	Zimmerman	49-51	4th	8.5
7-28	Det.	W	11-5		14	8	Helling	Moehler		50-51	4th	8.5
7-29	Det.	L	2-10		7	15	Nomo	Rogers		50-52	4th	9.5
7-30	Det.	L	7-8		12	11	Blair	Oliver	Jones	50-53	4th	10.5
8-1	Chi.	L	3-4		7	12	Howry	Wetteland		50-54	4th	11.0
8-2	Chi.	W	7-2		13	4	Helling	Garland	Crabtree	51-54	4th	10.0
8-3	At Tor.	L	1-3		4	12	Castillo	Rogers	Koch	51-55	4th	10.5
8-4	At Tor.	L	8-10		10	14	Quantrill	Venafro	Koch	51-56	4th	10.5
8-5	At Tor.	L	5-8		11	12	Wells	Davis	Koch	51-57	4th	11.5
8-6	At Tor.	W	11-6		16	10	Glynn	Escobar		52-57	4th	11.5
8-7	At Cle.	L	0-2		5	7	Reed	Helling	Wickman	52-58	4th	12.5
8-8	At Cle.	W	11-2		18	9	Rogers	Bere		53-58	4th	13.0
8-9	At Cle.	L	4-6		7	8	Speier	Perisho	Wickman	53-59	4th	13.0
8-11	Bos.	L	3-7		7	11	Arrojo	Glynn		53-60	4th	14.5
8-12	Bos.	W	6-3		6	6	Helling	Wakefield		54-60	4th	13.5
8-13	Bos.	L	2-4		6	7	Ohka	Rogers	Lowe	54-61	4th	13.5
8-14	N.Y.	L	3-7		7	9	Pettitte	Perisho		54-62	4th	13.5
8-15	N.Y.	L	2-10		8	17	Cone	Davis	Gooden	54-63	4th	13.5
8-16	N.Y.	W	5-0		8	4	Sikorski	Hernandez		55-63	4th	12.5
8-17	At Bos.	L	7-8		12	18	Garces	Wetteland		55-64	4th	13.0
8-18	At Bos.	L	4-6		8	11	Ohka	Rogers	Lowe	55-65	4th	13.0
8-19	At Bos.	L	0-9		5	11	P. Martinez	Perisho		55-66	4th	13.0
8-20	At Bos.	W	6-2		9	9	Davis	Fassero		56-66	4th	12.0
8-21	At N.Y.	L	3-12		8	13	Hernandez	Sikorski		56-67	4th	12.5
8-22	At N.Y.	W	5-4		8	6	Crabtree	Neagle	Wetteland	57-67	4th	12.5
8-23	At N.Y.	L	9-10		11	17	Rivera	Crabtree		57-68	4th	12.5
8-24	At N.Y.	L	7-8		11	12	Pettitte	Perisho	Rivera	57-69	4th	12.5
8-25	Tor.	W	1-0	(11)	13	5	Venafro	Koch		58-69	4th	11.5
8-26	Tor.	L	3-9		6	17	Hamilton	Sikorski	Borbon	58-70	4th	12.5
8-27	Tor.	L	4-6		8	14	Trachsel	Helling	Koch	58-71	4th	12.5
8-28	Cle.	L	2-5		6	11	Colon	Rogers	Wickman	58-72	4th	12.5
8-29	Cle.	L	1-12		6	14	Woodard	Glynn		58-73	4th	13.5
8-30	Cle.	L	3-5		7	13	Burba	Davis	Wickman	58-74	4th	13.5
8-31	Cle.	W	14-7		21	14	Venafro	Karsay		59-74	4th	13.0
9-1	At Det.	L	5-7		11	10	Sparks	Helling	Jones	59-75	4th	13.0
9-2	At Det.	L	3-5		10	10	Blair	Rogers	Anderson	59-76	4th	14.0
9-3	At Det.	W	4-1		11	7	Glynn	Weaver	Wetteland	60-76	4th	14.0
9-4	At Chi.	W	5-4		13	11	Davis	Garland	Wetteland	61-76	4th	13.0
9-5	At Chi.	W	2-1		10	8	Johnson	Howry	Wetteland	62-76	4th	13.0
9-6	At Chi.	L	1-13		4	13	Wells	Helling		62-77	4th	13.0
9-7	At Chi.	L	6-10		12	12	Barcelo	Zimmerman	Foulke	62-78	4th	14.0
9-8	At K.C.	W	6-5		12	12	Glynn	Stein	Wetteland	63-78	4th	13.0
9-9	At K.C.	W	6-5		11	10	Zimmerman	Suzuki	Wetteland	64-78	4th	13.0
9-10	At K.C.	L	8-13		16	14	Suppan	Oliver		64-79	4th	14.0
9-12†	Bal.	W	9-1		16	3	Helling	Parrish		65-79		
9-12‡	Bal.	W	6-5		5	8	Rogers	Spurgeon	Wetteland	66-79	4th	13.0
9-13	Bal.	L	4-9		6	14	Rapp	Glynn		66-80	4th	14.0
9-14	K.C.	W	8-1		9	4	Davis	Suzuki	Crabtree	67-80	4th	13.5
9-15	K.C.	W	12-11	(10)	15	18	Wetteland	Santiago		68-80	4th	13.5
9-16	K.C.	L	5-8		10	8	Meadows	Sikorski		68-81	4th	14.5
9-17	K.C.	W	6-5		11	12	Rogers	Reichert	Wetteland	69-81	4th	14.5
9-18	At Min.	L	1-3		10	7	Mays	Helling	Guardado	69-82	4th	15.5
9-19	At Min.	L	7-15		10	20	Kinney	Glynn		69-83	4th	16.5
9-20	At Min.	W	6-4	(12)	10	11	Wetteland	Miller	Venafro	70-83	4th	16.5
9-22	Ana.	L	1-2		8	9	Weber	Oliver	Percival	70-84	4th	16.0
9-23	Ana.	L	4-15		4	18	Karl	Helling		70-85	4th	16.0
9-24	Ana.	L	2-9		5	5	Ortiz	Johnson		70-86	4th	17.0
9-26	At Sea.	L	0-5		6	10	Sele	Glynn		70-87	4th	18.0
9-27	At Sea.	L	4-6		9	11	Garcia	Davis	Sasaki	70-88	4th	19.0
9-28	At Sea.	W	13-6		15	9	Helling	Tomko		71-88	4th	18.0
9-29	At Oak.	L	5-7		12	8	Mecir	Cordero	Isringhausen	71-89	4th	18.5
9-30	At Oak.	L	2-23		9	24	Zito	Oliver		71-90	4th	19.5
10-1	At Oak.	L	0-3		6	8	Hudson	Glynn	Isringhausen	71-91	4th	20.5

Monthly records: April (9-15), May (18-10), June (10-15), July (13-13), August (9-21), September (12-16), October (0-1).
*Innings, if other than nine. † First game of a doubleheader. ‡ Second game of a doubleheader.

MEMORABLE GAMES

July 15 at Arizona

Down three runs in the eighth inning against Randy Johnson, the Rangers rallied to tie on a run-scoring single by lefthanded-hitting Mike Lamb. After the bullpen held Arizona scoreless for three innings, Lamb singled in the 11th and Luis Alicea tripled to give the Rangers a 6-5 win. The 44-44 Rangers would lose the next day and never see the .500 level again.

Texas	AB	R	H	BI	Arizona	AB	R	H	BI
Alicea, 2b-ss	6	0	2	1	Womack, ss	5	1	0	0
Green, rf-cf	5	1	0	0	Bell, 2b	5	0	1	0
Curtis, lf-rf	4	1	1	0	Swindell, p	0	0	0	0
Segui, 1b	5	1	1	0	Durazo, ph	0	0	0	0
Haselman, c	5	1	2	2	Anderson, pr	0	0	0	0
Kapler, cf	3	0	0	0	Gonzalez, lf	5	1	2	1
Greer, ph-lf	2	0	0	1	Williams, 3b	5	1	3	2
Clayton, ss	2	0	0	0	Frias, pr-2b	1	0	0	0
Palmeiro, ph	0	0	0	0	Finley, cf	4	0	2	0
Catalanotto, 2b	1	0	0	0	Colbrunn, 1b	3	0	0	0
Sheldon, 3b	3	1	1	0	Lee, 1b	2	0	0	0
Lamb, ph-3b	2	1	2	1	Miller, c	4	1	2	0
Perisho, p	2	0	0	0	Bautista, rf	2	1	2	0
Cordero, p	0	0	0	0	Conti, ph-rf	2	0	0	0
Dransfeldt, ph	1	0	1	1	Johnson, p	2	0	1	2
Davis, p	0	0	0	0	Padilla, p	0	0	0	0
Rodriguez, ph	1	0	0	0	Counsell, ph-2-3	2	0	0	0
Venafro, p	0	0	0	0					
Zimmerman, p	0	0	0	0					
Martinez, ph	1	0	0	0					
Wetteland, p	0	0	0	0					
Totals	**43**	**6**	**10**	**6**	**Totals**	**42**	**5**	**13**	**5**

Texas............................0 0 0 1 0 0 1 3 0 0 1—6 10 4
Arizona ....1 0 0 2 0 2 0 0 0 0 0—5 13 0

E—Haselman (2), Perisho 2 (2), Lamb (15). DP—Texas 3. LOB—Texas 8, Arizona 11. 2B—Curtis (18), Haselman 2 (4), Dransfeldt (1), Williams (5), Bautista (8), Johnson (2). 3B—Alicea (6). HR—Williams (3). SB—Womack (19), Finley (7). CS—Finley (4). S—Gonzalez. SH—Johnson.

Texas	IP	H	R	ER	BB	SO
Perisho	5.2	9	5	5	2	5
Cordero	0.1	1	0	0	0	0
Davis	1	0	0	0	0	0
Venafro	0.2	1	0	0	0	1
Zimmerman (W 3-4)	2.1	1	0	0	2	4
Wetteland (S 23)	1	1	0	0	1	1
Arizona	**IP**	**H**	**R**	**ER**	**BB**	**SO**
Johnson	7.1	7	5	5	3 12	
Padilla	1.2	1	0	0	1	0
Swindell (L 1-3)	2	2	1	1	0	1

U—HP, Clark. 1B, Bucknor. 2B, Reed. 3B, Wendelstedt. T—3:39. A—37,856.

September 6 at Chicago

After falling behind 7-0 in the first inning, manager Johnny Oates moved up his "Scott Sheldon plan." Sheldon entered the game in the fourth and proceeded to play all nine positions, matching the feat of Bert Campaneris and Cesar Tovar. Sheldon spent an inning at catcher and another at first. He played second for two batters, shortstop (his natural position) for four, right field for three and center for one. After starting the eighth in left field, he came in to pitch and finished the 13-1 loss at third base.

Texas	AB	R	H	BI	White Sox	AB	R	H	BI
Cat'notto, 2b-1b	3	0	0	0	Durham, 2b	4	0	1	2
Curtis, lf	3	0	0	0	Graffanino, 2b	1	0	0	0
Knorr, c	1	0	0	0	Valentin, ss	3	1	0	0
Palmeiro, 1b	2	0	0	0	Wilson, ss	1	0	0	0
Waszgis, c-1b	2	0	0	0	Thomas, dh	3	2	1	2
Kapler, cf-rf	4	1	2	0	Abbott, ph-dh	1	0	0	0
Ledee, rf-lf-cf	4	0	0	0	Ordonez, rf	4	1	1	1
Sierra, dh	3	0	1	0	Liefer, rf	1	0	0	0
Valdes, lf	0	0	0	0	Lee, lf	4	2	3	0
Haselman, c	1	0	0	0	Christensen, ph-cf	1	0	0	0
Sheldon, c-1b-2b-ss-rf-cf-lf-p-3b	2	0	1	0	Konerko, 1b	2	2	1	1
Lamb, 3b	3	0	0	1	Norton, 3b	3	2	1	3
Cordero, p	0	0	0	0	Singleton, cf-lf	4	2	3	2
Dransfeldt, ss-2	3	0	0	0	Johnson, c	4	1	2	2
					Paul, c	0	0	0	0
Totals	**31**	**1**	**4**	**1**	**Totals**	**36**	**13**	**13**	**13**

Texas ....0 1 0 0 0 0 0 0 0— 1 4 1
White Sox ....7 3 0 0 2 1 0 0 x—13 13 2

E—Haselman (4), Valentin 2 (33). DP—Texas 1, White Sox 2. LOB—Texas 4, White Sox 4. 2B—Durham (34). HR—Thomas (41), Ordonez (27), Norton (6), Johnson (27). SB—Lee (11), Singleton (18).

Texas	IP	H	R	ER	BB	SO
Helling (L 14-11)	0.2	5	7	7	3	0
Sikorski	4.1	4	5	5	1	5
Cubillan	1	2	1	1	1	0
Perisho	1.1	2	0	0	0	0
Sheldon	0.1	0	0	0	0	1
Cordero	0.1	0	0	0	0	0
White Sox	**IP**	**H**	**R**	**ER**	**BB**	**SO**
Wells (W 5-7)	7	4	1	0	1	4
Lowe	1	0	0	0	0	1
Simas	1	0	0	0	0	1

U—HP, Miller. 1B, Meals. 2B, Young. 3B, Katzenmeier T—2:41. A—15,622.

BATTING

Name	G	TPA	AB	R	H	TB	2B	3B	HR	RBI	Avg.	Obp.	Slg.	SH	SF	HP	BB	IBB	SO	SB	CS	GDP	vs RHP AB	vs RHP Avg.	vs RHP HR	vs RHP RBI	vs LHP AB	vs LHP Avg.	vs LHP HR	vs LHP RBI
Palmeiro, Rafael	158	678	565	102	163	315	29	3	39	120	.288	.397	.558	0	7	3	103	17	77	2	1	14	421	.276	29	80	144	.326	10	40
Alicea, Luis	139	619	540	85	159	218	25	8	6	63	.294	.365	.404	7	7	5	59	1	75	1	3	13	426	.289	6	54	114	.316	0	9
Clayton, Royce	148	573	513	70	124	197	21	5	14	54	.242	.301	.384	12	3	3	42	1	92	11	7	21	406	.254	10	40	107	.196	4	14
Lamb, Mike	138	538	493	65	137	184	25	2	6	47	.278	.328	.373	5	2	4	34	6	60	0	2	10	409	.276	5	37	84	.286	1	10
Kapler, Gabe	116	491	444	59	134	210	32	1	14	66	.302	.360	.473	2	3	0	42	2	57	8	4	12	346	.306	9	53	98	.286	5	13
Greer, Rusty	105	453	394	65	117	181	34	3	8	65	.297	.377	.459	0	5	3	51	1	61	4	1	14	296	.314	7	53	98	.245	1	12
Rodriguez, Ivan	91	389	363	66	126	242	27	4	27	83	.347	.375	.667	0	6	1	19	5	48	5	5	17	284	.349	19	65	79	.342	8	18
Segui, David	93	389	351	52	118	182	29	1	11	57	.336	.391	.519	0	4	0	34	1	51	0	1	12	258	.349	9	48	93	.301	2	9
Curtis, Chad	108	381	335	48	91	142	25	1	8	48	.272	.343	.424	5	3	1	37	0	71	3	3	12	219	.242	6	31	116	.328	2	17
Catalanotto, Frank	103	326	282	55	82	129	13	2	10	42	.291	.375	.457	3	2	6	33	0	36	6	2	5	263	.293	10	37	19	.263	0	5
Ledee, Ricky	58	240	213	23	50	74	6	3	4	38	.235	.317	.347	0	1	1	25	2	50	6	3	7	166	.217	2	28	47	.298	2	10
Mateo, Ruben	52	222	206	32	60	92	11	0	7	19	.291	.339	.447	1	0	5	10	1	34	6	0	5	162	.284	4	14	44	.318	3	5
Haselman, Bill	62	210	193	23	53	89	18	0	6	26	.275	.329	.461	0	1	1	15	0	36	0	1	1	158	.272	6	21	35	.286	0	5
Sheldon, Scott	58	138	124	21	35	58	11	0	4	19	.282	.336	.468	1	2	1	10	0	37	0	0	2	81	.235	2	7	43	.372	2	12
Green, Scarborough	79	139	124	21	29	32	1	1	0	9	.234	.291	.258	5	0	0	10	0	26	10	6	3	90	.200	0	6	34	.324	0	3
Martinez, Dave	38	134	119	14	32	44	4	1	2	12	.269	.351	.370	0	0	1	14	2	20	2	1	8	110	.282	1	11	9	.111	1	1
McDonald, Jason	38	114	94	15	22	36	5	0	3	13	.234	.357	.383	2	0	1	17	0	25	4	4	2	86	.256	3	13	8	.000	0	0
Sierra, Ruben	20	64	60	5	14	17	0	0	1	7	.233	.281	.283	0	0	0	4	0	9	1	0	1	45	.178	1	5	15	.400	0	2
Valdes, Pedro	30	60	54	4	15	23	5	0	1	5	.278	.350	.426	0	0	0	6	0	7	0	0	0	49	.286	1	5	5	.200	0	0
Evans, Tom	23	67	54	10	15	19	4	0	0	5	.278	.394	.352	1	1	1	10	0	13	0	3	1	34	.324	0	5	20	.200	0	0
Waszgis, B.J.	24	51	45	6	10	11	1	0	0	4	.222	.294	.244	0	1	1	4	0	10	0	0	1	36	.250	0	3	9	.111	0	1
Knorr, Randy	15	37	34	5	10	18	2	0	2	2	.294	.294	.529	3	0	0	0	0	3	0	0	0	30	.300	2	2	4	.250	0	0
Dransfeldt, Kelly	16	27	26	2	3	5	2	0	0	2	.115	.148	.192	0	0	0	1	0	14	0	0	0	19	.105	0	1	7	.143	0	1
Helling, Rick	35	5	5	0	0	0	0	0	0	0	.000	.000	.000	0	0	0	0	0	2	0	0	0	3	.000	0	0	2	.000	0	0
Rogers, Kenny	34	5	4	0	2	2	0	0	0	0	.500	.500	.500	1	0	0	0	0	1	0	0	0	4	.500	0	0	0	.000	0	0
Perisho, Matt	34	4	4	0	0	0	0	0	0	0	.000	.000	.000	0	0	0	0	0	4	0	0	0	1	.000	0	0	3	.000	0	0
Loaiza, Esteban	20	3	3	0	0	0	0	0	0	0	.000	.000	.000	0	0	0	0	0	0	0	0	0	1	.000	0	0	2	.000	0	0
Oliver, Darren	21	3	2	0	0	0	0	0	0	0	.000	.333	.000	0	0	1	0	0	1	0	0	0	0	.000	0	0	2	.000	0	0
Glynn, Ryan	16	2	2	0	0	0	0	0	0	0	.000	.000	.000	0	0	0	0	0	1	0	0	0	2	.000	0	0	0	.000	0	0
Young, Mike	2	2	2	0	0	0	0	0	0	0	.000	.000	.000	0	0	0	0	0	1	0	0	0	1	.000	0	0	1	.000	0	0
Wetteland, John	62	0	0	0	0	0	0	0	0	0	.000	.000	.000	0	0	0	0	0	0	0	0	0	0	.000	0	0	0	.000	0	0
Crabtree, Tim	68	0	0	0	0	0	0	0	0	0	.000	.000	.000	0	0	0	0	0	0	0	0	0	0	.000	0	0	0	.000	0	0
Zimmerman, Jeff	65	0	0	0	0	0	0	0	0	0	.000	.000	.000	0	0	0	0	0	0	0	0	0	0	.000	0	0	0	.000	0	0
Venafro, Mike	77	0	0	0	0	0	0	0	0	0	.000	.000	.000	0	0	0	0	0	0	0	0	0	0	.000	0	0	0	.000	0	0
Davis, Doug	30	0	0	0	0	0	0	0	0	0	.000	.000	.000	0	0	0	0	0	0	0	0	0	0	.000	0	0	0	.000	0	0
Cordero, Francisco	56	0	0	0	0	0	0	0	0	0	.000	.000	.000	0	0	0	0	0	0	0	0	0	0	.000	0	0	0	.000	0	0
Munoz, Mike	7	0	0	0	0	0	0	0	0	0	.000	.000	.000	0	0	0	0	0	0	0	0	0	0	.000	0	0	0	.000	0	0
Clark, Mark	12	0	0	0	0	0	0	0	0	0	.000	.000	.000	0	0	0	0	0	0	0	0	0	0	.000	0	0	0	.000	0	0
Sikorski, Brian	10	0	0	0	0	0	0	0	0	0	.000	.000	.000	0	0	0	0	0	0	0	0	0	0	.000	0	0	0	.000	0	0
Johnson, Jonathan	15	0	0	0	0	0	0	0	0	0	.000	.000	.000	0	0	0	0	0	0	0	0	0	0	.000	0	0	0	.000	0	0
Kolb, Danny	1	0	0	0	0	0	0	0	0	0	.000	.000	.000	0	0	0	0	0	0	0	0	0	0	.000	0	0	0	.000	0	0
Cubillan, Darwin	13	0	0	0	0	0	0	0	0	0	.000	.000	.000	0	0	0	0	0	0	0	0	0	0	.000	0	0	0	.000	0	0

Players with more than one A.L. team

Name	G	TPA	AB	R	H	TB	2B	3B	HR	RBI	Avg.	Obp.	Slg.	SH	SF	HP	BB	IBB	SO	SB	CS	GDP	vs RHP AB	vs RHP Avg.	vs RHP HR	vs RHP RBI	vs LHP AB	vs LHP Avg.	vs LHP HR	vs LHP RBI
Cubillan, Tor.-Tex.	20	1	1	0	0	0	0	0	0	0	.000	.000	.000	0	0	0	0	0	0	0	0	0	1	.000	0	0	0	.000	0	0
Ledee, N.Y.	62	220	191	23	46	80	11	1	7	31	.241	.332	.419	0	2	1	26	2	39	7	3	7	166	.217	2	28	47	.298	2	10
Ledee, Cle.	17	71	63	13	14	24	2	1	2	8	.222	.310	.381	0	0	0	8	0	9	0	0	3	166	.217	2	28	47	.298	2	10
Ledee, N.Y.-Cle.-Tex.	137	531	467	59	110	178	19	5	13	77	.236	.322	.381	0	3	2	59	4	98	13	6	17	384	.234	10	62	83	.241	3	15
Loaiza, Tex.-Tor.	34	3	3	0	0	0	0	0	0	0	.000	.000	.000	0	0	0	0	0	0	0	0	0	1	.000	0	0	2	.000	0	0
Martinez, T.B.	29	117	104	12	27	38	4	2	1	12	.260	.319	.365	1	2	0	10	1	17	1	4	1	110	.282	1	11	9	.111	1	1
Martinez, Tor.	47	206	180	29	56	74	10	1	2	22	.311	.393	.411	0	1	1	24	0	28	4	2	3	110	.282	1	11	9	.111	1	1
Martinez, T.B.-Tex.-Tor.	114	457	403	55	115	156	18	4	5	46	.285	.362	.387	1	3	2	48	3	65	7	7	12	336	.280	4	37	67	.313	1	9
Segui, Tex.-Cle.	150	634	574	93	192	293	42	1	19	103	.334	.388	.510	0	6	1	53	2	84	0	1	20	419	.344	15	80	155	.310	4	23

PITCHING

Name	W	L	Pct.	ERA	IP	H	R	ER	HR	SH	SF	HB	BB	IBB	SO	G	GS	CG	ShO	GF	Sv	vs. RH AB	vs. RH Avg.	vs. RH HR	vs. RH RBI	vs. LH AB	vs. LH Avg.	vs. LH HR	vs. LH RBI
Rogers, Kenny	13	13	.500	4.55	227.1	257	126	115	20	3	4	11	78	2	127	34	34	2	0	0	0	682	.276	14	82	220	.314	6	31
Helling, Rick	16	13	.552	4.48	217.0	212	122	108	29	4	9	9	99	2	146	35	35	0	0	0	0	389	.267	13	54	453	.238	16	56
Oliver, Darren	2	9	.182	7.42	108.0	151	95	89	16	5	4	4	42	3	49	21	21	0	0	0	0	336	.327	15	69	110	.373	1	15
Loaiza, Esteban	5	6	.455	5.37	107.1	133	67	64	21	2	4	3	31	1	75	20	17	0	0	2	1	213	.305	10	29	227	.300	11	29
Perisho, Matt	2	7	.222	7.37	105.0	136	99	86	20	6	5	6	67	3	74	34	13	0	0	4	0	289	.308	16	59	142	.331	4	25
Davis, Doug	7	6	.538	5.38	98.2	109	61	59	14	6	4	3	58	3	66	30	13	1	0	4	0	293	.280	10	38	86	.314	4	23
Glynn, Ryan	5	7	.417	5.58	88.2	107	65	55	15	3	0	3	41	2	33	16	16	0	0	0	0	191	.257	6	27	174	.333	9	32
Crabtree, Tim	2	7	.222	5.15	80.1	86	52	46	7	1	4	2	31	6	54	68	0	0	0	28	2	187	.241	6	29	127	.323	1	26
Cordero, Francisco	1	2	.333	5.35	77.1	87	51	46	11	2	6	4	48	3	49	56	0	0	0	13	0	192	.271	7	42	113	.310	4	20
Zimmerman, Jeff	4	5	.444	5.30	69.2	80	45	41	10	2	5	2	34	3	74	65	0	0	0	17	1	169	.278	4	21	111	.297	6	21
Wetteland, John	6	5	.545	4.20	60.0	67	35	28	10	4	4	2	24	2	53	62	0	0	0	57	34	112	.259	3	14	123	.309	7	25
Venafro, Mike	3	1	.750	3.83	56.1	64	27	24	2	2	4	4	21	4	32	77	0	0	0	21	1	94	.351	1	14	123	.252	1	21
Clark, Mark	3	5	.375	7.98	44.0	66	42	39	10	1	2	3	24	2	16	12	8	0	0	1	0	95	.379	4	23	95	.316	6	16
Sikorski, Brian	1	3	.250	5.73	37.2	46	31	24	9	0	1	1	25	1	32	10	5	0	0	2	0	75	.333	5	15	85	.247	4	17
Johnson, Jonathan	1	1	.500	6.21	29.0	34	23	20	3	0	2	6	19	2	23	15	0	0	0	3	0	75	.293	1	15	42	.286	2	8
Cubillan, Darwin	0	0	.000	10.70	17.2	32	22	21	4	0	3	0	14	0	13	13	0	0	0	5	0	46	.413	2	9	34	.382	2	12
Munoz, Mike	0	1	.000	13.50	4.0	11	6	6	1	1	0	0	3	1	1	7	0	0	0	2	0	10	.600	1	3	11	.455	0	4
Kolb, Danny	0	0	.000	67.50	0.2	5	5	5	0	0	1	0	2	0	0	1	0	0	0	0	0	3	.667	0	3	3	1.000	0	2
Sheldon, Scott	0	0	.000	0.00	0.1	0	0	0	0	0	0	0	0	0	1	1	0	0	0	0	0	0	.000	0	0	1	.000	0	0

PITCHERS WITH MORE THAN ONE A.L. TEAM

Name	W	L	Pct.	ERA	IP	H	R	ER	HR	SH	SF	HB	BB	IBB	SO	G	GS	CG	ShO	GF	Sv	vs. RH AB	vs. RH Avg.	vs. RH HR	vs. RH RBI	vs. LH AB	vs. LH Avg.	vs. LH HR	vs. LH RBI
Cubillan, Tor.-Tex.	1	0	1.000	9.45	33.1	52	36	35	9	0	3	1	25	0	27	20	0	0	0	3	0	86	.372	5	17	57	.351	4	20
Loaiza, Tex.-Tor.	10	13	.435	4.56	199.1	228	112	101	29	4	5	13	57	1	137	34	31	1	1	5	1	377	.289	13	42	415	.287	16	50

DESIGNATED HITTERS

Name	AB	Avg.	HR	RBI
Segui, David	201	.313	6	27
Palmeiro, Rafael	173	.266	9	34
Catalanotto, Frank	70	.300	2	8
Curtis, Chad	56	.357	1	7
Sierra, Ruben	54	.241	1	6
Alicea, Luis	18	.278	0	2
Valdes, Pedro	11	.273	0	0
Lamb, Mike	9	.222	1	1
Greer, Rusty	8	.250	0	0
Rodriguez, Ivan	4	.000	0	0
Sheldon, Scott	1	.000	0	0
Green, Scarborough	1	.000	0	0
McDonald, Jason	0	-	0	0
Evans, Tom	0	-	0	0

INDIVIDUAL STATISTICS

FIELDING

FIRST BASEMEN

Player	Pct.	G	PO	A	E	TC	DP
Palmeiro, Rafael	.995	108	820	56	4	880	86
Segui, David	1.000	38	295	28	0	323	38
Catalanotto, Frank	.973	17	100	7	3	110	12
Sheldon, Scott	1.000	10	42	2	0	44	6
Martinez, Dave	1.000	4	11	0	0	11	0
Waszgis, B.J.	1.000	3	4	0	0	4	1
Evans, Tom	1.000	1	1	2	0	3	0

SECOND BASEMEN

Player	Pct.	G	PO	A	E	TC	DP
Alicea, Luis	.978	130	247	318	13	578	85
Catalanotto, Frank	.966	49	69	103	6	178	21
Sheldon, Scott	.931	12	12	15	2	29	2
Dransfeldt, Kelly	1.000	2	0	1	0	1	0
Young, Mike	-	1	0	0	0	0	0

THIRD BASEMEN

Player	Pct.	G	PO	A	E	TC	DP
Lamb, Mike	.913	135	118	230	33	381	24
Evans, Tom	.909	21	12	38	5	55	5
Sheldon, Scott	.975	15	11	28	1	40	6
Alicea, Luis	.706	8	5	7	5	17	1

SHORTSTOPS

Player	Pct.	G	PO	A	E	TC	DP
Clayton, Royce	.977	148	265	411	16	692	94
Sheldon, Scott	.970	22	25	40	2	67	6
Dransfeldt, Kelly	1.000	14	13	28	0	41	8
Alicea, Luis	1.000	2	1	3	0	4	0

OUTFIELDERS

Player	Pct.	G	PO	A	E	TC	DP
Kapler, Gabe	.969	116	307	5	10	322	4
Greer, Rusty	.985	97	194	3	3	200	0
Curtis, Chad	.965	80	135	4	5	144	0
Green, Scarborough	1.000	65	102	8	0	110	1
Ledee, Ricky	.977	57	128	0	3	131	0
Mateo, Ruben	.980	52	140	4	3	147	0
Martinez, Dave	1.000	35	82	2	0	84	1
McDonald, Jason	.988	32	75	6	1	82	2
Valdes, Pedro	1.000	14	17	0	0	17	0
Sheldon, Scott	-	2	0	0	0	0	0
Catalanotto, Frank	-	1	0	0	0	0	0

CATCHERS

Player	Pct.	G	PO	A	E	TC	DP	PB
Rodriguez, Ivan	.996	87	507	34	2	543	10	2
Haselman, Bill	.989	62	336	20	4	360	4	1
Waszgis, B.J.	1.000	23	66	2	0	68	1	4
Knorr, Randy	.985	15	64	2	1	67	0	1
Sheldon, Scott	1.000	3	3	0	0	3	0	0

PITCHERS

Player	Pct.	G	PO	A	E	TC	DP
Venafro, Mike	.857	77	3	9	2	14	1
Crabtree, Tim	1.000	68	5	11	0	16	3
Zimmerman, Jeff	.900	65	2	7	1	10	0
Wetteland, John	1.000	62	2	5	0	7	0
Cordero, Francisco	.900	55	4	5	1	10	0
Helling, Rick	.962	35	8	17	1	26	1
Rogers, Kenny	.970	34	18	46	2	66	6
Perisho, Matt	.813	34	4	9	3	16	0
Davis, Doug	.952	30	3	17	1	21	0
Oliver, Darren	1.000	21	7	15	0	22	0
Loaiza, Esteban	.963	20	8	18	1	27	3
Glynn, Ryan	1.000	16	9	12	0	21	1
Johnson, Jonathan	1.000	15	1	7	0	8	0
Cubillan, Darwin	1.000	13	1	2	0	3	0
Clark, Mark	1.000	12	1	6	0	7	3
Sikorski, Brian	.833	10	4	1	1	6	0
Munoz, Mike	-	7	0	0	0	0	0
Kolb, Danny	-	1	0	0	0	0	0
Sheldon, Scott	-	1	0	0	0	0	0

PITCHING AGAINST EACH CLUB

Pitcher	Ana. W-L	Bal. W-L	Bos. W-L	Chi. W-L	Cle. W-L	Det. W-L	K.C. W-L	Min. W-L	N.Y. W-L	Oak. W-L	Sea. W-L	T.B. W-L	Tor. W-L	N.L. W-L	Total W-L
Clark, Mark	0-0	0-0	0-1	0-0	1-0	0-0	0-0	0-2	0-0	0-0	0-1	1-0	1-0	0-1	3-5
Cordero, Francisco	0-1	0-0	0-0	1-0	0-0	0-0	0-0	0-0	0-0	0-1	0-0	0-0	0-0	0-0	1-2
Crabtree, Tim	0-1	0-1	0-0	0-0	0-0	0-0	0-0	0-1	1-2	0-0	0-0	1-1	0-0	0-1	2-7
Cubillan, Darwin	0-0	0-0	0-0	0-0	0-0	0-0	0-0	0-0	0-0	0-0	0-0	0-0	0-0	0-0	0-0
Davis, Doug	2-0	0-0	1-0	1-0	0-1	0-0	1-0	0-0	0-1	1-1	0-1	0-0	0-1	1-1	7-6
Glynn, Ryan	0-0	0-1	0-1	0-0	0-1	2-0	1-0	0-1	0-0	0-1	0-2	0-0	1-0	1-0	5-7
Helling, Rick	1-1	2-1	1-1	1-1	1-1	1-1	1-0	0-2	0-0	2-0	3-0	1-2	1-1	1-2	16-13
Johnson, Jonathan	0-1	0-0	0-0	1-0	0-0	0-0	0-0	0-0	0-0	0-0	0-0	0-0	0-0	0-0	1-1
Kolb, Danny	0-0	0-0	0-0	0-0	0-0	0-0	0-0	0-0	0-0	0-0	0-0	0-0	0-0	0-0	0-0
Loaiza, Esteban	0-0	1-1	0-0	0-1	0-0	0-1	1-0	2-0	0-0	1-0	0-1	0-0	0-0	0-2	5-6
Munoz, Mike	0-0	0-0	0-0	0-0	0-0	0-0	0-0	0-0	0-1	0-0	0-0	0-0	0-0	0-0	0-1
Oliver, Darren	0-2	0-1	0-0	0-0	0-0	1-1	0-1	0-2	0-0	0-1	0-0	1-1	0-0	0-0	2-9
Perisho, Matt	0-0	0-0	0-1	0-0	0-1	0-0	0-0	0-0	0-2	0-1	0-2	1-0	0-0	1-0	2-7
Rogers, Kenny	1-1	2-0	1-2	1-0	1-1	1-2	1-1	1-0	0-2	1-0	1-0	1-0	0-2	1-2	13-13
Sheldon, Scott	0-0	0-0	0-0	0-0	0-0	0-0	0-0	0-0	0-0	0-0	0-0	0-0	0-0	0-0	0-0
Sikorski, Brian	0-0	0-0	0-0	0-0	0-0	0-0	0-1	0-0	1-1	0-0	0-0	0-0	0-1	0-0	1-3
Venafro, Mike	0-0	1-0	0-0	0-0	1-0	0-0	0-0	0-0	0-0	0-0	0-0	0-0	1-1	0-0	3-1
Wetteland, John	1-0	0-0	0-1	0-1	0-1	0-0	1-0	1-0	0-0	2-0	1-0	0-0	0-0	0-2	6-5
Zimmerman, Jeff	0-0	0-1	0-0	0-2	0-0	0-0	1-0	0-0	0-1	0-0	0-0	1-1	0-0	2-0	4-5
Totals	5-7	6-6	3-7	5-5	4-6	5-5	7-3	4-8	2-10	7-5	5-7	7-5	4-6	7-11	71-91

INTERLEAGUE: Glynn 1-0, Clark 0-1, Helling 0-1 vs. Dodgers; Davis 1-0, Helling 1-0, Rogers 0-1 vs. Padres; Loaiza 0-1, Davis 0-1, Wetteland 0-1 vs. Giants; Crabtree 0-1, Wetteland 0-1, Loaiza 0-1 vs. Rockies; Zimmerman 2-0, Rogers 1-1, Perisho 1-0, Helling 0-1 vs. Diamondbacks. Total: 7-11.

MISCELLANEOUS

HOME RUNS BY PARK

At Anaheim (10): Rodriguez 3, Clayton 2, Mateo 2, Segui 1, Kapler 1, Lamb 1.
At Arizona (2): Clayton 1, Sheldon 1.
At Baltimore (5): Rodriguez 3, Segui 1, Curtis 1.
At Boston (2): Haselman 1, Catalanotto 1.
At Chicago (AL) (2): Ledee 1, Kapler 1.
At Cleveland (4): Palmeiro 1, Segui 1, Rodriguez 1, Greer 1.
At Colorado (5): Rodriguez 2, Palmeiro 1, Martinez 1, Clayton 1.
At Detroit (4): Palmeiro 2, Alicea 2.
At Kansas City (7): Palmeiro 2, Segui 2, Curtis 1, Greer 1, Catalanotto 1.
At Minnesota (5): Sheldon 2, Palmeiro 1, Segui 1, Mateo 1.
At New York (AL) (6): Palmeiro 2, Greer 2, Haselman 1, Ledee 1.
At Oakland (2): Palmeiro 1, Greer 1.
At San Francisco (1): Palmeiro 1.
At Seattle (4): Sierra 1, Segui 1, Rodriguez 1, Catalanotto 1.
At Tampa Bay (7): Palmeiro 1, Rodriguez 1, Clayton 1, Curtis 1, Catalanotto 1, Mateo 1, Lamb 1.
At Texas (104): Palmeiro 26, Rodriguez 16, Kapler 11, Clayton 9, Catalanotto 6, Curtis 5, Alicea 4, Segui 4, Lamb 4, Haselman 3, Greer 3, McDonald 3, Mateo 3, Knorr 2, Ledee 2, Martinez 1, Valdes 1, Sheldon 1.
At Toronto (3): Palmeiro 1, Haselman 1, Kapler 1.

LOW-HIT GAMES

No-hitters: None.
One-hitters: None.
Two-hitters: None.

10-STRIKEOUT GAMES

Esteban Loaiza 1, Total: 1

FOUR OR MORE HITS IN ONE GAME

Luis Alicea 4, Ivan Rodriguez 2, Rusty Greer 2 (including one five-hit game), Frank Catalanotto 2 (including one five-hit game), Rafael Palmeiro 1, David Segui 1, Royce Clayton 1, Chad Curtis 1, Total: 14

MULTI-HOMER GAMES

Ivan Rodriguez 4, Rafael Palmeiro 1, Royce Clayton 1, Gabe Kapler 1, Total: 7

GRAND SLAMS

5-12: Royce Clayton (off Anaheim's Scott Schoeneweis)
7-7: Ivan Rodriguez (off San Diego's Woody Williams)
8-12: Ricky Ledee (off Boston's Tim Wakefield)
9-10: Frank Catalanotto (off Kansas City's Andy Larkin)

PINCH HITTERS

(Minimum 5 at-bats)

Name	AB	Avg.	HR	RBI
Catalanotto, Frank	28	.357	0	4
Curtis, Chad	18	.389	1	4
Valdes, Pedro	14	.214	0	0
Sierra, Ruben	8	.250	0	1
Greer, Rusty	6	.333	0	1

DEBUTS

4-23: Mike Lamb, 3B.
7-29: B.J. Waszgis, C.
8-16: Brian Sikorski, P.
9-29: Mike Young, PR.

GAMES BY POSITION

Catcher: Ivan Rodriguez 87, Bill Haselman 62, B.J. Waszgis 23, Randy Knorr 15, Scott Sheldon 3.
First base: Rafael Palmeiro 108, David Segui 38, Frank Catalanotto 17, Scott Sheldon 10, Dave Martinez 4, B.J. Waszgis 3, Tom Evans 1.
Second base: Luis Alicea 130, Frank Catalanotto 49, Scott Sheldon 12, Kelly Dransfeldt 2, Mike Young 1.
Third base: Mike Lamb 135, Tom Evans 21, Scott Sheldon 15, Luis Alicea 8.
Shortstop: Royce Clayton 148, Scott Sheldon 22, Kelly Dransfeldt 14, Luis Alicea 2.
Outfield: Gabe Kapler 116, Rusty Greer 97, Chad Curtis 80, Scarborough Green 65, Ricky Ledee 57, Ruben Mateo 52, Dave Martinez 35, Jason McDonald 32, Pedro Valdes 14, Scott Sheldon 2, Frank Catalanotto 1.
Designated hitter: David Segui 52, Rafael Palmeiro 46, Frank Catalanotto 19, Chad Curtis 16, Ruben Sierra 14, Scarborough Green 6, Luis Alicea 5, Pedro Valdes 3, Rusty Greer 2, Mike Lamb 2, Ivan Rodriguez 1, Scott Sheldon 1, Jason McDonald 1, Tom Evans 1.

STREAKS

Wins: 7 (May 15-23)
Losses: 9 (June 6-16)
Consecutive games with at least one hit: 28, Gabe Kapler (July 17-August 15)
Wins by pitcher: 5, Rick Helling (May 2-23)

ATTENDANCE

Home: 2,800,147
Road: 2,406,986
Highest (home): 49,332 (April 3 vs. Chicago).
Highest (road): 48,563 (April 30 vs. Baltimore).
Lowest (home): 21,896 (August 27 vs. Toronto).
Lowest (road): 6,072 (September 20 vs. Minnesota).

TORONTO BLUE JAYS

DAY BY DAY

Date	Opp.	Res.	Score	(inn.*)	Hits	Opp. hits	Winning pitcher	Losing pitcher	Save	Record	Pos.	GB
4-3	K.C.	W	5-4		8	9	Koch	Spradlin		1-0	T1st	...
4-4	K.C.	W	6-3		7	7	Halladay	Witasick	Koch	2-0	T1st	...
4-5	K.C.	L	3-4		5	7	Rosado	Carpenter	Bottalico	2-1	T1st	...
4-6	K.C.	L	3-9		5	17	Durbin	Escobar	Rigby	2-2	T3rd	0.5
4-7	At Tex.	L	5-11		11	11	Clark	Castillo		2-3	T3rd	1.5
4-8	At Tex.	W	4-0		10	9	Wells	Rogers		3-3	3rd	1.5
4-9	At Tex.	L	5-7		7	9	Helling	Halladay		3-4	3rd	2.5
4-10	At Ana.	L	0-6		3	7	Schoeneweis	Carpenter		3-5	3rd	3.0
4-11	At Ana.	L	4-5		10	8	Ortiz	Escobar	Percival	3-6	4th	3.0
4-12	At Ana.	W	6-2		13	9	Borbon	Petkovsek		4-6	4th	2.0
4-14	Sea.	L	9-11		16	12	Moyer	Wells		4-7	4th	3.0
4-15	Sea.	L	6-17		10	16	Rodriguez	Halladay	Paniagua	4-8	T4th	4.0
4-16	Sea.	L	7-19		13	22	Garcia	Carpenter		4-9	5th	5.0
4-17	Ana.	W	7-1		10	8	Escobar	Ortiz		5-9	5th	5.0
4-18	Ana.	L	10-16		17	19	Dickson	Castillo		5-10	5th	6.0
4-19	Ana.	W	12-4		17	8	Wells	Hill		6-10	4th	6.0
4-20	Ana.	W	12-11		14	19	Halladay	Bottenfield	Koch	7-10	4th	5.5
4-21	N.Y.	W	8-3		12	5	Carpenter	Mendoza		8-10	4th	4.5
4-22	N.Y.	W	8-2		10	9	Escobar	Cone		9-10	4th	3.5
4-23	N.Y.	L	7-10		8	15	Hernandez	Andrews	Rivera	9-11	4th	4.5
4-24	At Oak.	W	3-2		7	10	Wells	Appier	Koch	10-11	4th	3.5
4-25	At Oak.	L	2-11		4	12	Hudson	Halladay		10-12	4th	3.5
4-26	At Oak.	W	4-2		9	6	Carpenter	Olivares	Koch	11-12	4th	3.5
4-28	At N.Y.	L	0-6		3	8	Cone	Escobar		11-13	4th	4.5
4-29	At N.Y.	W	6-2		14	11	Wells	Hernandez	Koch	12-13	4th	3.5
4-30	At N.Y.	L	1-7		9	12	Clemens	Halladay		12-14	4th	4.5
5-1	At Chi.	W	5-3		9	6	Carpenter	Wells	Koch	13-14	4th	4.5
5-2	At Chi.	W	4-1		7	5	Castillo	Wunsch	Koch	14-14	4th	4.5
5-3	At Chi.	L	3-7		5	8	Baldwin	Escobar	Foulke	14-15	4th	5.5
5-4	Cle.	W	8-1		10	7	Wells	Finley		15-15	4th	5.0
5-5	Cle.	W	11-10		13	20	Koch	Shuey		16-15	4th	5.0
5-6	Cle.	L	6-8		10	11	Rincon	Quantrill	Karsay	16-16	4th	6.0
5-7	Cle.	L	8-10	(12)	16	14	Shuey	Gunderson	Karsay	16-17	4th	6.0
5-8	Bal.	W	6-5		12	14	Escobar	Johnson	Koch	17-17	4th	6.0
5-9	Bal.	W	6-4		12	10	Wells	Mussina	Koch	18-17	3rd	6.0
5-10	Bal.	W	7-2		14	5	Painter	Erickson	Quantrill	19-17	3rd	5.5
5-12	At T.B.	L	3-4		10	8	White	Carpenter	Lopez	19-18	3rd	5.0
5-13	At T.B.	W	8-4		12	5	Escobar	Lidle		20-18	3rd	4.0
5-14	At T.B.	W	3-2		8	7	Wells	Lopez		21-18	3rd	3.5
5-15	Bos.	L	1-8		6	13	Schourek	Castillo		21-19	3rd	4.5
5-16	Bos.	W	7-6		14	11	Munro	Lowe		22-19	3rd	3.5
5-17	Bos.	L	0-8		4	15	P. Martinez	Carpenter		22-20	3rd	4.5
5-19	Chi.	L	3-5		11	5	Sirotka	Escobar	Foulke	22-21	3rd	5.5
5-20	Chi.	L	2-6		7	12	Baldwin	Wells		22-22	3rd	5.5
5-21	Chi.	L	1-2		6	1	Eldred	Castillo	Foulke	22-23	3rd	5.5
5-22	Chi.	W	4-3		11	6	Koch	Howry		23-23	3rd	5.0
5-23	At Bos.	W	3-2		7	9	Carpenter	P. Martinez	Koch	24-23	3rd	4.0
5-24	At Bos.	L	3-6	(11)	10	9	Cormier	Frascatore		24-24	3rd	5.0
5-25	At Bos.	W	11-6		17	13	Wells	Schourek		25-24	3rd	4.0
5-26	At Det.	W	8-2		12	7	Frascatore	Brocail		26-24	3rd	4.0
5-27	At Det.	L	3-4		7	7	Brocail	Quantrill		26-25	3rd	4.0
5-28	At Det.	W	12-7		15	11	Andrews	Blair		27-25	3rd	4.0
5-30	Min.	L	1-4		5	10	Redman	Escobar	Hawkins	27-26	3rd	5.0
5-31	Min.	W	4-2		6	9	Wells	Radke	Koch	28-26	3rd	4.0
6-1	Min.	L	1-5		6	6	Milton	Castillo		28-27	3rd	4.0
6-2	At Fla.	L	10-11		15	15	Bones	Munro	Alfonseca	28-28	3rd	4.0
6-3	At Fla.	L	1-2		5	7	Looper	Koch	Alfonseca	28-29	3rd	4.0
6-4	At Fla.	W	7-2		12	8	Escobar	Nunez		29-29	3rd	4.0
6-5	At Atl.	W	9-3		12	9	Wells	Burkett		30-29	3rd	3.0
6-6	At Atl.	L	6-7		10	11	Remlinger	Frascatore		30-30	3rd	4.0
6-7	At Atl.	W	12-8		9	16	Cubillan	Millwood	Koch	31-30	3rd	4.0
6-9	Mon.	W	13-3		16	8	Carpenter	Tucker		32-30	3rd	3.0
6-10	Mon.	L	2-11		6	14	Armas	Escobar		32-31	3rd	4.0
6-11	Mon.	W	8-3		9	13	Koch	Mota		33-31	3rd	3.5
6-12	At Det.	W	4-2		10	8	Castillo	Nomo	Koch	34-31	3rd	3.0
6-13	At Det.	L	3-16		8	21	Blair	Andrews		34-32	3rd	3.0
6-14	At Det.	W	8-1		9	9	Carpenter	Weaver		35-32	3rd	3.0
6-16	At Bos.	L	4-7		11	12	Pichardo	Escobar	Lowe	35-33	3rd	3.0
6-17	At Bos.	W	11-10		14	13	Wells	R. Martinez	Koch	36-33	3rd	2.0
6-18	At Bos.	W	5-1		9	6	Castillo	Fassero	Koch	37-33	3rd	1.0
6-20	Det.	L	6-18		8	18	Weaver	Carpenter		37-34	3rd	2.0
6-21	Det.	W	6-0		12	4	Escobar	Moehler		38-34	3rd	1.0
6-22	Det.	W	7-4		8	8	Wells	Nomo		39-34	3rd	0.5
6-23	Bos.	W	5-4		9	7	Castillo	Wasdin	Koch	40-34	1st	+0.5
6-24	Bos.	W	6-4		9	7	Halladay	Rose	Koch	41-34	1st	+1.0
6-25	Bos.	W	6-5	(13)	10	15	DeWitt	Florie		42-34	1st	+2.0
6-27	At T.B.	L	1-11		9	13	Trachsel	Escobar		42-35	1st	+2.0
6-28	At T.B.	W	5-2		7	5	Wells	Yan		43-35	1st	+3.0
6-29	At T.B.	W	12-3		14	10	Castillo	Lidle		44-35	1st	+3.0
6-30	At Bal.	L	3-8		7	11	Rapp	Halladay		44-36	1st	+3.0

HIGHLIGHTS

High point: A three-game sweep of the Red Sox in late June propelled the Blue Jays into the A.L. East Division lead. It would expand briefly to three games.

Low point: Still within striking distance of the first-place Yankees entering September, the Jays opened a 10-game homestand by losing three of four to Oakland and two of three to Seattle, getting outscored 40-18.

Turning point: On July 22, when right fielder and No. 3 hitter Raul Mondesi was placed on the disabled list with an elbow injury—effectively ending his season. Five days later, the club started a 1-6 trip to Seattle and Oakland, after which they never again got closer to first than $4^1/_2$ games.

Most valuable player: Carlos Delgado made a strong run at the A.L.'s first triple crown since 1967. Batting cleanup, he established career highs with a .344 average, 115 runs, 196 hits, 57 doubles, 137 RBIs, 99 extra-base hits, 123 walks and a 22-game hitting streak.

Most valuable pitcher: David Wells led the A.L. with 15 wins at the All-Star break and went on to record the fifth 20-win season in club history. Wells did not walk a batter in 16 of his 35 starts and his strikeout-to-walk ratio of 5.35 set a club record.

Most improved player: Center fielder Jose Cruz Jr., who batted .241 in 106 games in 1999, broke through with career highs in doubles, triples, homers, hits and stolen bases while playing all 162 games.

Most pleasant surprise: Veteran Frank Castillo, perilously close to losing his roster spot, rediscovered his control and posted a 10-5 record, one win shy of his 1995 career high. Castillo, who held opponents to a .220 average, reeled off nine straight wins starting June 12.

Key injuries: Starter Joey Hamilton missed the first $4^1/_2$ months while recovering from 1999 shoulder surgery. ... Castillo missed a month with a sprained forearm. ... Reliever Lance Painter spent three weeks on the D.L. with a strained elbow. ... Mondesi missed 66 games and shortstop Alex Gonzalez (groin) and outfielder Shannon Stewart (hamstring) missed two weeks. ... Second baseman Homer Bush battled a hip injury early and broke his hand July 30, ending his season. ... Catcher Darrin Fletcher missed three weeks with a rotator-cuff tear.

Notable: The Blue Jays hit a franchise-record 244 home runs and put together a club-record 23-game homer streak. ... The Jays posted winning records against the top two teams in the East—7-5 vs. the Yankees and 8-4 vs. the Red Sox. But they were 5-15 against the two West Division playoff teams—Seattle and Oakland. ... The final home attendance of 1,819,886 marked the first time the club failed to draw 2 million fans since the SkyDome opened in 1989.

—TOM MALONEY

MISCELLANEOUS

RECORDS

2000 regular-season record: 83-79 (3rd in A.L. East); 45-36 at home; 38-43 on road; 37-30 vs. East; 28-25 vs. Central; 18-24 vs. West; 19-24 vs. lefthanded starters; 64-55 vs. righthanded starters; 31-38 on grass; 52-41 on turf; 28-28 in daytime; 55-51 at night; 21-19 in one-run games; 2-6 in extra-inning games; 0-0-0 in doubleheaders.

Team record past five years: 405-405 (.500, ranks 8th in league in that span).

TEAM LEADERS

Batting average: Carlos Delgado (.344).
At-bats: Tony Batista (620).
Runs: Carlos Delgado (115).
Hits: Carlos Delgado (196).
Total Bases: Carlos Delgado (378).
Doubles: Carlos Delgado (57).
Triples: Jose Cruz, Shannon Stewart (5).
Home runs: Tony Batista, Carlos Delgado (41).
Runs batted in: Carlos Delgado (137).
Stolen bases: Raul Mondesi (22).
Slugging percentage: Carlos Delgado (.664).
On-base percentage: Carlos Delgado (.470).
Wins: David Wells (20).
Earned-run average: David Wells (4.11).
Complete games: David Wells (9).
Shutouts: Kelvim Escobar, Esteban Loaiza, David Wells (1).
Saves: Billy Koch (33).
Innings pitched: David Wells (229.2).
Strikeouts: David Wells (166).

Date	Opp.	Res.	Score	(inn.*)	Hits	Opp. hits	Winning pitcher	Losing pitcher	Save	Record	Pos.	GB
7-1	At Bal.	L	5-12		8	13	Ponson	Carpenter		44-37	1st	+2.0
7-2	At Bal.	L	2-3		8	7	Trombley	Quantrill	Mills	44-38	1st	+1.0
7-3	At Bal.	W	6-4		6	11	Wells	Johnson	Koch	45-38	1st	+1.5
7-4	At Cle.	L	4-9		9	9	Colon	Frascatore		45-39	1st	+1.5
7-5	At Cle.	L	7-15		12	16	Brewington	Quantrill		45-40	1st	+0.5
7-6	At Cle.	W	9-6		15	15	Carpenter	Burba	Koch	46-40	1st	+0.5
7-7	At Mon.	L	5-10		10	12	Lira	Quantrill		46-41	2nd	0.5
7-8	At Mon.	W	6-3		7	6	Wells	Armas	Koch	47-41	2nd	1.0
7-9	At Mon.	W	13-3		18	8	Castillo	Hermanson		48-41	2nd	...
7-13	Phi.	L	5-8		7	11	Schilling	Carpenter	Brantley	48-42	2nd	...
7-14	Phi.	W	3-2		13	6	Koch	Brantley		49-42	2nd	...
7-15	Phi.	L	3-7		5	11	Chen	Wells		49-43	2nd	0.5
7-16	N.Y. (NL)	W	7-3		8	10	Halladay	Leiter	Koch	50-43	2nd	0.5
7-17	N.Y. (NL)	L	5-7	(11)	5	11	Franco	Borbon	Benitez	50-44	2nd	0.5
7-18	N.Y. (NL)	L	7-11		13	12	B.J. Jones	Carpenter		50-45	3rd	1.5
7-19	T.B.	W	5-2		9	2	Escobar	Lopez	Koch	51-45	3rd	1.5
7-20	T.B.	W	6-5		10	7	Quantrill	White	Koch	52-45	2nd	0.5
7-21	Bal.	L	5-9		9	16	Rapp	Halladay		52-46	2nd	1.5
7-22	Bal.	L	2-8		9	13	Mercedes	Loaiza		52-47	3rd	1.5
7-23	Bal.	W	4-1		8	5	Castillo	Mussina	Koch	53-47	3rd	1.5
7-25	Cle.	L	3-10		9	10	Finley	Escobar		53-48	3rd	3.0
7-26	Cle.	W	8-1		9	5	Wells	Colon		54-48	2nd	3.0
7-27	At Sea.	W	7-2		16	7	Loaiza	Rhodes		55-48	2nd	2.0
7-28	At Sea.	L	4-7		6	9	Garcia	Carpenter	Sasaki	55-49	3rd	3.0
7-29	At Sea.	L	5-6	(13)	9	16	Tomko	Halladay		55-50	3rd	3.0
7-30	At Sea.	L	6-10		10	5	Sele	Escobar	Paniagua	55-51	3rd	4.0
7-31	At Oak.	L	1-6		4	12	Hudson	Wells		55-52	3rd	4.5
8-1	At Oak.	L	1-3	(10)	7	6	Isringhausen	Koch		55-53	3rd	5.5
8-2	At Oak.	L	4-5		10	12	Mecir	Guthrie	Isringhausen	55-54	3rd	5.5
8-3	Tex.	W	3-1		12	4	Castillo	Rogers	Koch	56-54	3rd	5.5
8-4	Tex.	W	10-8		14	10	Quantrill	Venafro	Koch	57-54	3rd	5.5
8-5	Tex.	W	8-5		12	11	Wells	Davis	Koch	58-54	3rd	4.5
8-6	Tex.	L	6-11		10	16	Glynn	Escobar		58-55	3rd	4.5
8-7	At K.C.	L	7-8		14	14	Stein	Loaiza	Bottalico	58-56	3rd	4.5
8-8	At K.C.	W	6-1		14	4	Castillo	Suzuki		59-56	3rd	4.5
8-9	At K.C.	L	3-5		11	10	Suppan	Trachsel	Larkin	59-57	3rd	5.5
8-10	At K.C.	W	15-7		17	14	Carpenter	Fussell		60-57	3rd	5.5
8-11	At Min.	L	4-9		8	13	Romero	Escobar		60-58	3rd	5.5
8-12	At Min.	L	3-6		10	13	Redman	Loaiza	Hawkins	60-59	3rd	5.5
8-13	At Min.	W	13-3		20	8	Carpenter	Radke		61-59	3rd	5.5
8-15	Ana.	L	4-8		8	12	Wise	Wells		61-60	3rd	7.0
8-16	Ana.	W	8-6		10	11	Koch	Pote		62-60	3rd	6.0
8-18	Min.	W	3-2		8	8	Loaiza	Kinney	Koch	63-60	3rd	5.5
8-19	Min.	L	1-5		8	8	Radke	Guthrie	Guardado	63-61	3rd	6.5
8-20	Min.	W	6-3		10	9	Wells	Carrasco		64-61	3rd	5.5
8-22	K.C.	W	7-5		10	11	Escobar	Santiago	Koch	65-61	3rd	5.0
8-23	K.C.	W	9-8		13	11	Escobar	Larkin	Koch	66-61	3rd	5.0
8-25	At Tex.	L	0-1	(11)	5	13	Venafro	Koch		66-62	3rd	5.5
8-26	At Tex.	W	9-3		17	6	Hamilton	Sikorski	Borbon	67-62	3rd	5.5
8-27	At Tex.	W	6-4		14	8	Trachsel	Helling	Koch	68-62	3rd	5.5
8-28	At Ana.	W	4-2		5	7	Loaiza	Ortiz	Koch	69-62	3rd	5.5
8-29	At Ana.	L	4-9		11	12	Holtz	Carpenter		69-63	3rd	5.5
8-30	At Ana.	W	11-2		19	9	Wells	Wise		70-63	3rd	5.5
9-1	Oak.	W	4-3		14	10	Frascatore	D. Jones		71-63	3rd	5.5
9-2	Oak.	L	0-8		5	9	Heredia	Trachsel	Mecir	71-64	3rd	6.5
9-3	Oak.	L	3-4		8	7	Hudson	Loaiza	Mecir	71-65	3rd	6.5
9-4	Oak.	L	0-10		2	19	Zito	Wells		71-66	3rd	7.5
9-5	Sea.	L	3-4		6	7	Rhodes	Escobar	Sasaki	71-67	3rd	8.5
9-6	Sea.	W	7-3		12	6	Hamilton	Halama		72-67	3rd	7.5
9-7	Sea.	L	1-8		3	12	Garcia	Trachsel		72-68	3rd	8.5
9-8	Det.	W	3-0		7	5	Loaiza	Weaver		73-68	3rd	8.5
9-9	Det.	W	6-5		8	10	Koch	Nitkowski		74-68	3rd	8.5
9-10	Det.	W	6-2		7	8	Carpenter	Sparks	Escobar	75-68	2nd	8.5
9-12	At N.Y.	L	2-10		8	11	Neagle	Hamilton		75-69	3rd	9.0
9-13	At N.Y.	L	2-3		11	7	Clemens	Loaiza	Rivera	75-70	3rd	10.0
9-14	At N.Y.	W	3-2	(11)	6	11	Koch	Choate	Escobar	76-70	3rd	9.0
9-15	At Chi.	W	6-5		6	11	Escobar	Garland	Koch	77-70	3rd	8.0
9-16	At Chi.	L	3-6		11	8	Wunsch	Escobar	Foulke	77-71	3rd	9.0
9-17	At Chi.	W	14-1		15	6	Painter	Wells		78-71	3rd	8.0
9-19	N.Y.	W	16-3		19	4	Trachsel	Pettitte		79-71	3rd	6.5
9-20	N.Y.	W	7-2		10	9	Loaiza	Cone		80-71	2nd	5.5
9-21	N.Y.	W	3-1		9	5	Wells	Hernandez		81-71	2nd	4.5
9-22	T.B.	L	2-3		7	10	Lidle	Frascatore	Hernandez	81-72	2nd	4.5
9-23	T.B.	W	7-6		13	9	Koch	Enders		82-72	2nd	4.5
9-24	T.B.	L	0-6		2	13	Harper	Trachsel		82-73	2nd	5.5
9-25	T.B.	L	1-5		5	10	Wilson	Loaiza	Hernandez	82-74	2nd	5.5
9-26	At Bal.	L	1-2		5	7	Mercedes	Wells	Kohlmeier	82-75	T2nd	5.5
9-27	At Bal.	W	4-0		7	4	Castillo	Ponson		83-75	T2nd	4.5
9-28	At Bal.	L	1-23		2	23	Rapp	Carpenter		83-76	3rd	4.5
9-29	At Cle.	L	4-8		5	9	Speier	Trachsel	Karsay	83-77	3rd	4.5
9-30	At Cle.	L	5-6		10	11	Finley	Loaiza	Wickman	83-78	3rd	4.5
10-1	At Cle.	L	4-11		8	12	Woodard	Wells		83-79	3rd	4.5

Monthly records: April (12-14), May (16-12), June (16-10), July (11-16), August (15-11), September (13-15), October (0-1).
*Innings, if other than nine. † First game of a doubleheader. ‡ Second game of a doubleheader.

MEMORABLE GAMES

June 25 at Boston

The Blue Jays fought back from 4-1 and 5-2 deficits against Pedro Martinez, tying the score 5-5 in the seventh inning on Carlos Delgado's two-run homer. Tony Batista, who had homered earlier, delivered the game-winning single in the 13th, giving rookie Matt DeWitt his first major league win. The victory capped a three-game sweep and increased the Jays' lead in the A.L. East Division to two games.

Boston	AB	R	H	BI	Toronto	AB	R	H	BI
Offerman, 1b	5	1	2	0	Stewart, lf	6	2	1	1
Frye, 2b	6	0	1	1	Woodward, ss	7	2	1	0
Everett, cf	5	1	2	0	Batista, 3b	7	1	3	2
Garciaparra, ss	7	0	1	2	Delgado, 1b	5	1	1	2
Daubach, dh	5	1	1	0	Fullmer, dh	6	0	3	1
Alcantara, rf	6	1	1	0	Cruz, cf	4	0	0	0
Hatteberg, c	6	0	3	2	Cordova, rf	5	0	1	0
Veras, 3b	5	0	1	0	Castillo, c	4	0	0	0
Varitek, ph	1	0	0	0	Bush, 2b	6	0	0	0
Alexander, 3b	0	0	0	0					
Pride, lf	6	1	3	0					
Totals	**52**	**5**	**15**	**5**	**Totals**	**50**	**6**	**10**	**6**

Boston ....2 0 2 1 0 0 0 0 0 0 0 0 0—5 15 4
Toronto...............1 0 1 0 1 0 2 0 0 0 0 0 1—6 10 0

E—Offerman (4), Everett (3), Garciaparra (9), Veras (12). DP—Boston 1, Toronto 1. LOB—Boston 14, Toronto 13. 2B—Garciaparra (21), Daubach (16), Hatteberg (6), Veras (7), Pride (1), Batista (15), Fullmer (19). HR—Stewart (10), Batista (19), Delgado (27). SH—Frye, Castillo.

Boston	IP	H	R	ER	BB	SO
P. Martinez	6.2	6	5	4	1	10
Garces	1.1	0	0	0	1	0
Lowe	2	2	0	0	2	2
Beck	0.2	0	0	0	0	0
Cormier	1.1	1	0	0	0	1
Florie (L 0-2)	0.2	1	1	0	0	0

Toronto	IP	H	R	ER	BB	SO
Carpenter	3.1	7	5	5	3	1
Painter	1.2	1	0	0	0	1
Frascatore	2	1	0	0	0	1
Borbon	1	0	0	0	0	2
Koch	1	1	0	0	1	0
Quantrill	3	4	0	0	0	2
DeWitt (W 1-0)	1	1	0	0	1	1

HBP—Cordova by P. Martinez, Stewart by P. Martinez. WP—Painter U—HP, Cederstrom. 1B, Welke. 2B, Scott. 3B, Hudson. T—4:25. A—31,022.

September 21 at Toronto

David Wells, at 37 years, 124 days, became the second-oldest in pitcher in major league history to win 20 games for the first time when he pitched the Blues Jays to a 3-1 victory over the New York Yankees. The win completed the Jays' first three-game sweep of the Yankees since 1992 and pulled them to within $4^1/_2$ games of New York in the A.L. East.

Yankees	AB	R	H	BI	Toronto	AB	R	H	BI
Knoblauch, 2b	4	0	0	0	Stewart, lf	4	1	1	0
Jeter, ss	4	0	1	0	Gonzalez, ss	4	0	1	1
Williams, cf	4	1	1	1	D. Martinez, rf	4	0	1	0
Hill, lf	4	0	0	0	Delgado, 1b	3	1	2	1
Posada, c	3	0	1	0	Fullmer, dh	4	1	2	0
Justice, rf	3	0	0	0	Batista, 3b	4	0	1	0
Canseco, dh	3	0	2	0	Fletcher, c	2	0	1	0
T. Martinez, 1b	3	0	0	0	Cruz, cf	2	0	0	1
Brosius, 3b	3	0	0	0	Morandini, 2b	3	0	0	0
Totals	**31**	**1**	**5**	**1**	**Totals**	**30**	**3**	**9**	**3**

Yankees....................................0 0 0 0 0 0 1 0 0—1 5 0
Toronto ....0 0 1 0 0 2 0 0 x—3 9 0

DP—Yankees 1, Toronto 1. LOB—Yankees 3, Toronto 6. 2B—Stewart (42), Gonzalez (28), Fullmer (29), Batista (30). HR—Williams (29), Delgado (41). S—Cruz.

Yankees	IP	H	R	ER	BB	SO
Hernandez (L 12-12)	7	8	3	3	1	2
Stanton	1	1	0	0	0	1

Toronto	IP	H	R	ER	BB	SO
Wells (W 20-6)	9	5	1	1	0	8

HBP—Delgado by Hernandez. U—HP, Eddings. 1B, Reliford. 2B, Carlson. 3B, Timmons. T—2:33. A—30,074.

INDIVIDUAL STATISTICS

BATTING

Name	G	TPA	AB	R	H	TB	2B	3B	HR	RBI	Avg.	Obp.	Slg.	SH	SF	HP	BB	IBB	SO	SB	CS	GDP	vs RHP AB	vs RHP Avg.	vs RHP HR	vs RHP RBI	vs LHP AB	vs LHP Avg.	vs LHP HR	vs LHP RBI
Batista, Tony	154	664	620	96	163	322	32	2	41	114	.263	.307	.519	0	3	6	35	1	121	5	4	15	458	.273	35	91	162	.235	6	23
Cruz, Jose	162	681	603	91	146	281	32	5	31	76	.242	.323	.466	2	3	2	71	3	129	15	5	11	441	.224	26	57	162	.290	5	19
Stewart, Shannon	136	631	583	107	186	302	43	5	21	69	.319	.363	.518	1	4	6	37	1	79	20	5	12	444	.322	18	60	139	.309	3	9
Delgado, Carlos	162	711	569	115	196	378	57	1	41	137	.344	.470	.664	0	4	15	123	18	104	0	1	12	381	.357	35	101	188	.319	6	36
Gonzalez, Alex S.	141	591	527	68	133	213	31	2	15	69	.252	.313	.404	16	1	4	43	0	113	4	4	14	413	.259	13	61	114	.228	2	8
Fullmer, Brad	133	524	482	76	142	269	29	1	32	104	.295	.340	.558	0	6	6	30	3	68	3	1	14	389	.311	27	85	93	.226	5	19
Fletcher, Darrin	122	445	416	43	133	214	19	1	20	58	.320	.355	.514	0	4	5	20	3	45	1	0	8	337	.315	19	46	79	.342	1	12
Mondesi, Raul	96	426	388	78	105	203	22	2	24	67	.271	.329	.523	0	3	3	32	0	73	22	6	8	314	.261	20	56	74	.311	4	11
Bush, Homer	76	325	297	38	64	75	8	0	1	18	.215	.271	.253	4	1	5	18	0	60	9	4	10	256	.199	1	13	41	.317	0	5
Grebeck, Craig	66	270	241	38	71	99	19	0	3	23	.295	.364	.411	1	1	2	25	0	33	0	0	7	149	.309	1	13	92	.272	2	10
Cordova, Marty	62	221	200	23	49	68	7	0	4	18	.245	.317	.340	0	0	3	18	0	35	3	2	6	134	.261	2	10	66	.212	2	8
Castillo, Alberto	66	211	185	14	39	49	7	0	1	16	.211	.287	.265	2	3	0	21	0	36	0	0	3	114	.219	1	13	71	.197	0	3
Martinez, Dave	47	206	180	29	56	74	10	1	2	22	.311	.393	.411	0	1	1	24	0	28	4	2	3	130	.292	2	17	50	.360	0	5
Morandini, Mickey	35	116	107	10	29	33	2	1	0	7	.271	.316	.308	2	0	0	7	0	23	1	0	2	101	.277	0	6	6	.167	0	1
Woodward, Chris	37	115	104	16	19	35	7	0	3	14	.183	.254	.337	1	0	0	10	3	28	1	0	1	87	.172	2	7	17	.235	1	7
Greene, Todd	34	90	85	11	20	37	2	0	5	10	.235	.278	.435	0	0	0	5	0	18	0	0	4	35	.200	3	4	50	.260	2	6
Wise, Dewayne	28	24	22	3	3	3	0	0	0	0	.136	.208	.136	0	0	1	1	0	5	1	0	0	19	.105	0	0	3	.333	0	0
Ducey, Rob	5	15	13	2	2	3	1	0	0	1	.154	.267	.231	0	0	0	2	0	2	0	0	0	11	.091	0	0	2	.500	0	1
Mottola, Chad	3	10	9	1	2	2	0	0	0	2	.222	.300	.222	0	0	1	0	0	4	0	0	0	3	.333	0	2	6	.167	0	0
Greene, Charlie	3	9	9	0	1	1	0	0	0	0	.111	.111	.111	0	0	0	0	0	5	0	0	0	8	.125	0	0	1	.000	0	0
Castillo, Frank	25	7	7	0	1	1	0	0	0	0	.143	.143	.143	0	0	0	0	0	3	0	0	0	3	.000	0	0	4	.250	0	0
Escobar, Kelvim	43	7	7	0	0	0	0	0	0	0	.000	.000	.000	0	0	0	0	0	4	0	0	0	5	.000	0	0	2	.000	0	0
Wells, David	35	6	6	0	1	1	0	0	0	0	.167	.167	.167	0	0	0	0	0	2	0	0	0	4	.250	0	0	2	.000	0	0
Thompson, Andy	2	9	6	2	1	1	0	0	0	1	.167	.444	.167	0	0	0	3	0	2	0	0	0	3	.000	0	0	3	.333	0	1
Andrews, Clayton	8	3	3	0	0	0	0	0	0	0	.000	.000	.000	0	0	0	0	0	2	0	0	0	3	.000	0	0	0	.000	0	0
Carpenter, Chris	34	2	2	0	0	0	0	0	0	0	.000	.000	.000	0	0	0	0	0	1	0	0	0	2	.000	0	0	0	.000	0	0
Wells, Vernon	3	2	2	0	0	0	0	0	0	0	.000	.000	.000	0	0	0	0	0	0	0	0	0	2	.000	0	0	0	.000	0	0
Munro, Peter	9	1	1	0	0	0	0	0	0	0	.000	.000	.000	0	0	0	0	0	1	0	0	0	1	.000	0	0	0	.000	0	0
Koch, Billy	68	1	1	0	0	0	0	0	0	0	.000	.000	.000	0	0	0	0	0	1	0	0	0	0	.000	0	0	1	.000	0	0
Cubillan, Darwin	7	1	1	0	0	0	0	0	0	0	.000	.000	.000	0	0	0	0	0	0	0	0	0	1	.000	0	0	0	.000	0	0
Phelps, Josh	1	1	1	0	0	0	0	0	0	0	.000	.000	.000	0	0	0	0	0	1	0	0	0	1	.000	0	0	0	.000	0	0
Quantrill, Paul	68	1	0	0	0	0	0	0	0	0	.000	1.000	.000	0	0	0	1	0	0	0	0	0	0	.000	0	0	0	.000	0	0
Borbon, Pedro	59	0	0	0	0	0	0	0	0	0	.000	.000	.000	0	0	0	0	0	0	0	0	0	0	.000	0	0	0	.000	0	0
Painter, Lance	42	0	0	0	0	0	0	0	0	0	.000	.000	.000	0	0	0	0	0	0	0	0	0	0	.000	0	0	0	.000	0	0
Frascatore, John	60	0	0	0	0	0	0	0	0	0	.000	.000	.000	0	0	0	0	0	0	0	0	0	0	.000	0	0	0	.000	0	0
DeWitt, Matt	8	0	0	0	0	0	0	0	0	0	.000	.000	.000	0	0	0	0	0	0	0	0	0	0	.000	0	0	0	.000	0	0
Guthrie, Mark	23	0	0	0	0	0	0	0	0	0	.000	.000	.000	0	0	0	0	0	0	0	0	0	0	.000	0	0	0	.000	0	0
Gunderson, Eric	6	0	0	0	0	0	0	0	0	0	.000	.000	.000	0	0	0	0	0	0	0	0	0	0	.000	0	0	0	.000	0	0
Trachsel, Steve	11	0	0	0	0	0	0	0	0	0	.000	.000	.000	0	0	0	0	0	0	0	0	0	0	.000	0	0	0	.000	0	0
Hamilton, Joey	6	0	0	0	0	0	0	0	0	0	.000	.000	.000	0	0	0	0	0	0	0	0	0	0	.000	0	0	0	.000	0	0
Loaiza, Esteban	14	0	0	0	0	0	0	0	0	0	.000	.000	.000	0	0	0	0	0	0	0	0	0	0	.000	0	0	0	.000	0	0
Halladay, Roy	19	0	0	0	0	0	0	0	0	0	.000	.000	.000	0	0	0	0	0	0	0	0	0	0	.000	0	0	0	.000	0	0
Bale, John	2	0	0	0	0	0	0	0	0	0	.000	.000	.000	0	0	0	0	0	0	0	0	0	0	.000	0	0	0	.000	0	0
Coco, Pasqual	1	0	0	0	0	0	0	0	0	0	.000	.000	.000	0	0	0	0	0	0	0	0	0	0	.000	0	0	0	.000	0	0
Estrella, Leo	2	0	0	0	0	0	0	0	0	0	.000	.000	.000	0	0	0	0	0	0	0	0	0	0	.000	0	0	0	.000	0	0

Players with more than one A.L. team

Name	G	TPA	AB	R	H	TB	2B	3B	HR	RBI	Avg.	Obp.	Slg.	SH	SF	HP	BB	IBB	SO	SB	CS	GDP	vs RHP AB	vs RHP Avg.	vs RHP HR	vs RHP RBI	vs LHP AB	vs LHP Avg.	vs LHP HR	vs LHP RBI
Cubillan, Tor.-Tex.	20	1	1	0	0	0	0	0	0	0	.000	.000	.000	0	0	0	0	0	0	0	0	0	1	.000	0	0	0	.000	0	0
Guthrie, T.B.-Tor.	57	0	0	0	0	0	0	0	0	0	.000	.000	.000	0	0	0	0	0	0	0	0	0	0	.000	0	0	0	.000	0	0
Loaiza, Tex.-Tor.	34	3	3	0	0	0	0	0	0	0	.000	.000	.000	0	0	0	0	0	0	0	0	0	1	.000	0	0	2	.000	0	0
Martinez, T.B.	29	117	104	12	27	38	4	2	1	12	.260	.319	.365	1	2	0	10	1	17	1	4	1	130	.292	2	17	50	.360	0	5
Martinez, Tex.	38	134	119	14	32	44	4	1	2	12	.269	.351	.370	0	0	1	14	2	20	2	1	8	130	.292	2	17	50	.360	0	5
Martinez, T.B.-Tex.-Tor.	114	457	403	55	115	156	18	4	5	46	.285	.362	.387	1	3	2	48	3	65	7	7	12	336	.280	4	37	67	.313	1	9
Trachsel, T.B.-Tor.	34	5	4	0	1	1	0	0	0	0	.250	.400	.250	0	0	0	1	0	1	0	0	0	1	.000	0	0	3	.333	0	0

PITCHING

Name	W	L	Pct.	ERA	IP	H	R	ER	HR	SH	SF	HB	BB	IBB	SO	G	GS	CG	ShO	GF	Sv	vs. RH AB	vs. RH Avg.	vs. RH HR	vs. RH RBI	vs. LH AB	vs. LH Avg.	vs. LH HR	vs. LH RBI
Wells, David	20	8	.714	4.11	229.2	266	115	105	23	6	7	8	31	0	166	35	35	9	1	0	0	723	.289	18	76	197	.289	5	26
Escobar, Kelvim	10	15	.400	5.35	180.0	186	118	107	26	5	4	3	85	3	142	43	24	3	1	8	2	356	.253	11	50	341	.282	15	55
Carpenter, Chris	10	12	.455	6.26	175.1	204	130	122	30	3	1	5	83	1	113	34	27	2	0	1	0	376	.287	18	70	327	.294	12	46
Castillo, Frank	10	5	.667	3.59	138.0	112	58	55	18	5	2	5	56	0	104	25	24	0	0	1	0	255	.216	8	23	253	.225	10	27
Loaiza, Esteban	5	7	.417	3.62	92.0	95	45	37	8	2	1	10	26	0	62	14	14	1	1	0	0	164	.268	3	13	188	.271	5	21
Quantrill, Paul	2	5	.286	4.52	83.2	100	45	42	7	1	3	2	25	1	47	68	0	0	0	24	1	199	.296	1	27	137	.299	6	30
Koch, Billy	9	3	.750	2.63	78.2	78	28	23	6	4	0	2	18	4	60	68	0	0	0	62	33	157	.261	4	16	145	.255	2	14
Frascatore, John	2	4	.333	5.42	73.0	87	51	44	14	2	4	7	33	2	30	60	0	0	0	15	0	187	.289	10	35	102	.324	4	20
Halladay, Roy	4	7	.364	10.64	67.2	107	87	80	14	2	3	2	42	0	44	19	13	0	0	4	0	157	.350	6	34	143	.364	8	36
Painter, Lance	2	0	1.000	4.73	66.2	69	37	35	9	5	1	2	22	1	53	42	2	0	0	11	0	152	.257	5	13	103	.291	4	28
Trachsel, Steve	2	5	.286	5.29	63.0	72	40	37	10	4	1	0	25	1	32	11	11	0	0	0	0	119	.303	5	19	127	.283	5	18
Borbon, Pedro	1	1	.500	6.48	41.2	45	37	30	5	2	7	5	38	5	29	59	0	0	0	6	1	75	.360	3	24	86	.209	2	16
Hamilton, Joey	2	1	.667	3.55	33.0	28	13	13	3	0	1	2	12	0	15	6	6	0	0	0	0	47	.213	2	9	73	.247	1	3
Munro, Peter	1	1	.500	5.96	25.2	38	22	17	1	1	0	3	16	0	16	9	3	0	0	2	0	65	.385	1	14	42	.310	0	5
Guthrie, Mark	0	2	.000	4.79	20.2	20	12	11	3	1	1	1	9	0	20	23	0	0	0	5	0	40	.225	3	10	36	.306	0	5
Andrews, Clayton	1	2	.333	10.02	20.2	34	23	23	6	1	1	0	9	0	12	8	2	0	0	1	0	61	.393	5	16	30	.333	1	6
Cubillan, Darwin	1	0	1.000	8.04	15.2	20	14	14	5	0	0	1	11	0	14	7	0	0	0	1	0	40	.325	3	8	23	.304	2	8
DeWitt, Matt	1	0	1.000	8.56	13.2	20	13	13	4	0	0	2	9	0	6	8	0	0	0	4	0	33	.212	2	5	24	.542	2	14
Gunderson, Eric	0	1	.000	7.11	6.1	15	6	5	0	0	1	1	2	1	2	6	0	0	0	1	0	22	.591	0	5	11	.182	0	2
Estrella, Leo	0	0	.000	5.79	4.2	9	3	3	1	0	1	0	0	0	3	2	0	0	0	1	0	13	.462	0	2	7	.429	1	2
Coco, Pasqual	0	0	.000	9.00	4.0	5	4	4	1	0	0	1	5	0	2	1	1	0	0	0	0	15	.200	1	2	2	1.000	0	0
Bale, John	0	0	.000	14.73	3.2	5	7	6	1	0	1	2	3	0	6	2	0	0	0	0	0	8	.250	0	2	8	.375	1	7

PITCHERS WITH MORE THAN ONE A.L. TEAM

Name	W	L	Pct.	ERA	IP	H	R	ER	HR	SH	SF	HB	BB	IBB	SO	G	GS	CG	ShO	GF	Sv	vs. RH AB	vs. RH Avg.	vs. RH HR	vs. RH RBI	vs. LH AB	vs. LH Avg.	vs. LH HR	vs. LH RBI
Cubillan, Tor.-Tex.	1	0	1.000	9.45	33.1	52	36	35	9	0	3	1	25	0	27	20	0	0	0	3	0	86	.372	5	17	57	.351	4	20
Guthrie, T.B.-Tor.	1	3	.250	4.61	52.2	53	30	27	7	2	1	1	27	5	46	57	0	0	0	1	0	119	.261	5	22	83	.265	2	13
Loaiza, Tex.-Tor.	10	13	.435	4.56	199.1	228	112	101	29	4	5	13	57	1	137	34	31	1	1	5	1	377	.289	13	42	415	.287	16	50
Trachsel, T.B.-Tor.	8	15	.348	4.80	200.2	232	116	107	26	6	6	6	74	2	110	34	34	3	1	6	0	404	.290	17	67	386	.298	9	39

DESIGNATED HITTERS

Name	AB	Avg.	HR	RBI
Fullmer, Brad	478	.295	32	104
Greene, Todd	74	.216	5	9
Cordova, Marty	48	.292	1	6
Fletcher, Darrin	6	.333	1	1
Wise, Dewayne	0	-	0	0

INDIVIDUAL STATISTICS

FIELDING

FIRST BASEMEN

Player	Pct.	G	PO	A	E	TC	DP
Delgado, Carlos	.991	162	1416	82	13	1511	157
Woodward, Chris	1.000	3	6	1	0	7	1
Fullmer, Brad	1.000	1	2	1	0	3	0

SECOND BASEMEN

Player	Pct.	G	PO	A	E	TC	DP
Bush, Homer	.986	75	165	246	6	417	68
Grebeck, Craig	.968	56	100	174	9	283	34
Morandini, Mickey	.993	35	58	92	1	151	28
Woodward, Chris	.941	3	5	11	1	17	1

THIRD BASEMEN

Player	Pct.	G	PO	A	E	TC	DP
Batista, Tony	.963	154	120	318	17	455	35
Woodward, Chris	1.000	9	5	18	0	23	3

SHORTSTOPS

Player	Pct.	G	PO	A	E	TC	DP
Gonzalez, Alex S.	.975	141	213	407	16	636	100
Woodward, Chris	.955	22	26	58	4	88	9
Grebeck, Craig	1.000	8	10	19	0	29	4

OUTFIELDERS

Player	Pct.	G	PO	A	E	TC	DP
Cruz, Jose	.993	162	405	9	3	417	1
Stewart, Shannon	.993	136	298	5	2	305	2
Mondesi, Raul	.967	96	203	5	7	215	3
Martinez, Dave	.982	47	101	8	2	111	2
Cordova, Marty	.982	41	55	1	1	57	1
Wise, Dewayne	1.000	18	20	0	0	20	0
Ducey, Rob	.889	3	8	0	1	9	0
Mottola, Chad	1.000	3	5	0	0	5	0
Wells, Vernon	1.000	3	2	0	0	2	0
Thompson, Andy	1.000	2	2	0	0	2	0
Greene, Todd	-	1	0	0	0	0	0

CATCHERS

Player	Pct.	G	PO	A	E	TC	DP	PB
Fletcher, Darrin	.994	117	621	39	4	664	7	6
Castillo, Alberto	.993	66	372	31	3	406	2	5
Greene, Charlie	1.000	3	13	0	0	13	0	0
Greene, Todd	1.000	2	2	0	0	2	0	0
Phelps, Josh	1.000	1	1	0	0	1	0	0

PITCHERS

Player	Pct.	G	PO	A	E	TC	DP
Koch, Billy	1.000	68	5	8	0	13	2
Quantrill, Paul	1.000	68	3	9	0	12	0
Frascatore, John	.923	60	7	5	1	13	2
Borbon, Pedro	1.000	59	2	9	0	11	1
Escobar, Kelvim	.963	43	11	15	1	27	1
Painter, Lance	1.000	42	4	17	0	21	2
Wells, David	.897	35	8	18	3	29	1
Carpenter, Chris	.950	34	7	12	1	20	2
Castillo, Frank	.964	25	8	19	1	28	4
Guthrie, Mark	1.000	23	0	1	0	1	0
Halladay, Roy	1.000	19	4	7	0	11	0
Loaiza, Esteban	.882	14	4	11	2	17	1
Trachsel, Steve	1.000	11	8	11	0	19	0
Munro, Peter	1.000	9	2	3	0	5	2
DeWitt, Matt	1.000	8	2	1	0	3	0
Andrews, Clayton	1.000	8	0	1	0	1	0
Cubillan, Darwin	1.000	7	1	2	0	3	1
Hamilton, Joey	1.000	6	2	2	0	4	1
Gunderson, Eric	.667	6	0	2	1	3	0
Estrella, Leo	1.000	2	0	1	0	1	0
Bale, John	-	2	0	0	0	0	0
Coco, Pasqual	-	1	0	0	0	0	0

PITCHING AGAINST EACH CLUB

Pitcher	Ana. W-L	Bal. W-L	Bos. W-L	Chi. W-L	Cle. W-L	Det. W-L	K.C. W-L	Min. W-L	N.Y. W-L	Oak. W-L	Sea. W-L	T.B. W-L	Tex. W-L	N.L. W-L	Total W-L
Andrews, Clayton	0-0	0-0	0-0	0-0	0-0	1-1	0-0	0-0	0-1	0-0	0-0	0-0	0-0	0-0	1-2
Bale, John	0-0	0-0	0-0	0-0	0-0	0-0	0-0	0-0	0-0	0-0	0-0	0-0	0-0	0-0	0-0
Borbon, Pedro	1-0	0-0	0-0	0-0	0-0	0-0	0-0	0-0	0-0	0-0	0-0	0-0	0-0	0-1	1-1
Carpenter, Chris	0-2	0-2	1-1	1-0	1-0	2-1	1-1	1-0	1-0	1-0	0-2	0-1	0-0	1-2	10-12
Castillo, Frank	0-1	2-0	2-1	1-1	0-0	1-0	1-0	0-1	0-0	0-0	0-0	1-0	1-1	1-0	10-5
Coco, Pasqual	0-0	0-0	0-0	0-0	0-0	0-0	0-0	0-0	0-0	0-0	0-0	0-0	0-0	0-0	0-0
Cubillan, Darwin	0-0	0-0	0-0	0-0	0-0	0-0	0-0	0-0	0-0	0-0	0-0	0-0	0-0	1-0	1-0
DeWitt, Matt	0-0	0-0	1-0	0-0	0-0	0-0	0-0	0-0	0-0	0-0	0-0	0-0	0-0	0-0	1-0
Escobar, Kelvim	1-1	1-0	0-1	1-3	0-1	1-0	2-1	0-2	1-1	0-0	0-2	2-1	0-1	1-1	10-15
Estrella, Leo	0-0	0-0	0-0	0-0	0-0	0-0	0-0	0-0	0-0	0-0	0-0	0-0	0-0	0-0	0-0
Frascatore, John	0-0	0-0	0-1	0-0	0-1	1-0	0-0	0-0	0-0	1-0	0-0	0-1	0-0	0-1	2-4
Gunderson, Eric	0-0	0-0	0-0	0-0	0-1	0-0	0-0	0-0	0-0	0-0	0-0	0-0	0-0	0-0	0-1
Guthrie, Mark	0-0	0-0	0-0	0-0	0-0	0-0	0-0	0-1	0-0	0-1	0-0	0-0	0-0	0-0	0-2
Halladay, Roy	1-0	0-2	1-0	0-0	0-0	0-0	1-0	0-0	0-1	0-1	0-2	0-0	0-1	1-0	4-7
Hamilton, Joey	0-0	0-0	0-0	0-0	0-0	0-0	0-0	0-0	0-1	0-0	1-0	0-0	1-0	0-0	2-1
Koch, Billy	1-0	0-0	0-0	1-0	1-0	1-0	1-0	0-0	1-0	0-1	0-0	1-0	0-1	2-1	9-3
Loaiza, Esteban	1-0	0-1	0-0	0-0	0-1	1-0	0-1	1-1	1-1	0-1	1-0	0-1	0-0	0-0	5-7
Munro, Peter	0-0	0-0	1-0	0-0	0-0	0-0	0-0	0-0	0-0	0-0	0-0	0-0	0-0	0-1	1-1
Painter, Lance	0-0	1-0	0-0	1-0	0-0	0-0	0-0	0-0	0-0	0-0	0-0	0-0	0-0	0-0	2-0
Quantrill, Paul	0-0	0-1	0-0	0-0	0-2	0-1	0-0	0-0	0-0	0-0	0-0	1-0	1-0	0-1	2-5
Trachsel, Steve	0-0	0-0	0-0	0-0	0-1	0-0	0-1	0-0	1-0	0-1	0-1	0-1	1-0	0-0	2-5
Wells, David	2-1	2-1	2-0	0-1	2-1	1-0	0-0	2-0	2-0	1-2	0-1	2-0	2-0	2-1	20-8
Totals	7-5	6-7	8-4	5-5	4-8	9-3	6-4	4-5	7-5	3-7	2-8	7-5	6-4	9-9	83-79

INTERLEAGUE: Wells 1-0, Cubillan 1-0, Frascatore 0-1 vs. Braves; Carpenter 1-0, Wells 1-0, Koch 1-0, Castillo 1-0, Quantrill 0-1, Escobar 0-1 vs. Expos; Halladay 1-0, Borbon 0-1, Carpenter 0-1 vs. Mets; Koch 1-0, Carpenter 0-1, Wells 0-1 vs. Phillies; Escobar 1-0, Munro 0-1, Koch 0-1 vs. Marlins. Total: 9-9.

MISCELLANEOUS

HOME RUNS BY PARK

At Anaheim (9): Batista 2, Fullmer 2, Martinez 1, Fletcher 1, Mondesi 1, Delgado 1, Cruz 1.

At Atlanta (5): Delgado 2, Woodward 2, Mondesi 1.

At Baltimore (9): Batista 4, Mondesi 2, Fletcher 1, Delgado 1, Stewart 1.

At Boston (11): Mondesi 3, Batista 2, Fullmer 2, Delgado 1, Gonzalez 1, Stewart 1, Greene 1.

At Chicago (AL) (12): Cruz 3, Fletcher 2, Gonzalez 2, Fullmer 2, Mondesi 1, Delgado 1, Cordova 1.

At Cleveland (7): Gonzalez 2, Batista 2, Stewart 1, Greene 1, Cruz 1.

At Detroit (7): Delgado 2, Fullmer 2, Fletcher 1, Batista 1, Cruz 1.

At Florida (4): Mondesi 1, Delgado 1, Stewart 1, Cruz 1.

At Kansas City (6): Stewart 3, Fullmer 2, Batista 1.

At Minnesota (5): Delgado 1, Gonzalez 1, Stewart 1, Cruz 1, Fullmer 1.

At Montreal (5): Mondesi 3, Fletcher 1, Cruz 1.

At New York (AL) (1): Cruz 1.

At Oakland (5): Fullmer 2, Delgado 1, Gonzalez 1, Batista 1.

At Seattle (4): Fletcher 1, Greene 1, Cruz 1, Fullmer 1.

At Tampa Bay (10): Mondesi 2, Gonzalez 2, Batista 2, Cruz 2, Fullmer 2.

At Texas (10): Fletcher 3, Cruz 3, Grebeck 1, Gonzalez 1, Stewart 1, Batista 1.

At Toronto (134): Delgado 30, Batista 25, Fullmer 16, Cruz 15, Stewart 12, Fletcher 10, Mondesi 10, Gonzalez 5, Cordova 3, Grebeck 2, Greene 2, Martinez 1, Castillo 1, Bush 1, Woodward 1.

LOW-HIT GAMES

No-hitters: None.
One-hitters: None.
Two-hitters: None.

10-STRIKEOUT GAMES

David Wells 3, Esteban Loaiza 1, Kelvim Escobar 1, Total: 5

FOUR OR MORE HITS IN ONE GAME

Shannon Stewart 6, Darrin Fletcher 3, Tony Batista 2, Craig Grebeck 1, Marty Cordova 1, Brad Fullmer 1, Total: 14

MULTI-HOMER GAMES

Carlos Delgado 5, Tony Batista 4, Raul Mondesi 2, Brad Fullmer 2, Darrin Fletcher 1, Shannon Stewart 1, Jose Cruz 1, Total: 16

GRAND SLAMS

4-17: Brad Fullmer (off Anaheim's Lou Pote)
4-20: Darrin Fletcher (off Anaheim's Kent Mercker)
5-8: Darrin Fletcher (off Baltimore's Jason Johnson)
5-26: Darrin Fletcher (off Detroit's Doug Brocail)
6-7: Carlos Delgado (off Atlanta's Kevin Millwood)
6-11: Tony Batista (off Montreal's Felipe Lira)
7-3: Tony Batista (off Baltimore's Jason Johnson)
7-16: Marty Cordova (off New York's Al Leiter)
9-17: Carlos Delgado (off Chicago's Jesus Pena)

PINCH HITTERS

(Minimum 5 at-bats)

Name	AB	Avg.	HR	RBI
Fullmer, Brad	14	.214	0	1
Fletcher, Darrin	13	.308	0	2
Greene, Todd	10	.400	0	3
Cordova, Marty	6	.333	0	1

DEBUTS

4-6: Dewayne Wise, CF.
4-16: Clayton Andrews, P.
5-2: Andy Thompson, LF.
5-20: Darwin Cubillan, P.
6-13: Josh Phelps, C.
6-20: Matt DeWitt, P.
7-17: Pasqual Coco, P.
7-18: Leo Estrella, P.

GAMES BY POSITION

Catcher: Darrin Fletcher 117, Alberto Castillo 66, Charlie Greene 3, Todd Greene 2, Josh Phelps 1.

First base: Carlos Delgado 162, Chris Woodward 3, Brad Fullmer 1.

Second base: Homer Bush 75, Craig Grebeck 56, Mickey Morandini 35, Chris Woodward 3.

Third base: Tony Batista 154, Chris Woodward 9.

Shortstop: Alex S. Gonzalez 141, Chris Woodward 22, Craig Grebeck 8.

Outfield: Jose Cruz 162, Shannon Stewart 136, Raul Mondesi 96, Dave Martinez 47, Marty Cordova 41, Dewayne Wise 18, Rob Ducey 3, Chad Mottola 3, Vernon Wells 3, Andy Thompson 2, Todd Greene 1.

Designated hitter: Brad Fullmer 129, Todd Greene 23, Marty Cordova 15, Darrin Fletcher 2, Dewayne Wise 2.

STREAKS

Wins: 5 (June 21-25)
Losses: 6 (July 28-August 2)
Consecutive games with at least one hit: 22, Carlos Delgado (June 4-29)
Wins by pitcher: 6, David Wells (April 19-May 14)

ATTENDANCE

Home: 1,819,885
Road: 2,207,931
Highest (home): 40,898 (April 3 vs. Kansas City).
Highest (road): 45,264 (July 29 vs. Seattle).
Lowest (home): 13,514 (April 4 vs. Kansas City).
Lowest (road): 8,266 (April 25 vs. Oakland).

Arizona Diamondbacks

DAY BY DAY

Date	Opp.	Res.	Score	(inn.*)	Hits	Opp. hits	Winning pitcher	Losing pitcher	Save	Record	Pos.	GB
4-4	Phi.	W	6-4		10	6	Johnson	Ashby	Holmes	1-0	T1st	0.5
4-5	Phi.	W	11-3		12	9	Stottlemyre	Byrd	Morgan	2-0	1st	+0.5
4-6	Phi.	W	3-2	(11)	7	8	Springer	Schrenk		3-0	1st	+1.0
4-7	Pit.	L	2-7		7	12	Christiansen	Reynoso		3-1	T1st	...
4-8	Pit.	W	6-5		12	12	Swindell	Christiansen		4-1	1st	+1.0
4-9	Pit.	W	1-0		4	5	Johnson	Schmidt		5-1	1st	+2.0
4-10	At S.D.	W	8-4		12	11	Stottlemyre	Williams	Morgan	6-1	1st	+2.5
4-11	At S.D.	L	2-3	(13)	7	9	Whisenant	Springer		6-2	1st	+1.5
4-12	At S.D.	L	2-4		6	6	Meadows	Reynoso	Hoffman	6-3	1st	+1.0
4-13	At S.D.	W	5-4		9	10	Anderson	Hitchcock	Morgan	7-3	1st	+0.5
4-14	At S.F	W	3-1		8	5	Johnson	Hernandez		8-3	1st	+0.5
4-15	At S.F	W	7-4		9	8	Stottlemyre	Ortiz	Swindell	9-3	1st	+1.5
4-17	Col.	L	1-9		8	15	Yoshii	Daal		9-4	1st	+1.5
4-18	Col.	W	7-1		12	4	Reynoso	Karl		10-4	1st	+1.5
4-19	Col.	W	8-7		13	12	Morgan	Tavarez	Kim	11-4	1st	+2.5
4-20	Col.	W	3-0		5	4	Johnson	Arrojo		12-4	1st	+3.0
4-21	S.F	L	5-11		12	16	Ortiz	Stottlemyre		12-5	1st	+2.0
4-22	S.F	L	6-8		7	7	Rueter	Daal	Nen	12-6	1st	+1.0
4-23	S.F	L	7-12		11	14	Nathan	Reynoso		12-7	2nd	...
4-25	At Phi.	W	10-2		10	5	Johnson	Brock		13-7	1st	+1.5
4-26	At Phi.	W	10-4		9	6	Stottlemyre	Ashby		14-7	1st	+2.5
4-27	At Phi.	L	4-5		6	10	Gomes	Kim		14-8	1st	+2.5
4-28	At Chi.	L	5-6		7	10	Tapani	Springer	Aguilera	14-9	1st	+1.5
4-29	At Chi.	W	7-4	(10)	10	9	Mantei	Guthrie	Morgan	15-9	1st	+1.5
4-30	At Chi.	W	6-0		12	6	Johnson	Lorraine		16-9	1st	+1.5
5-2	At Mil.	W	5-1		9	4	Stottlemyre	Haynes		17-9	1st	+3.0
5-3	At Mil.	L	1-4		4	10	Estrada	Daal	Wickman	17-10	1st	+2.0
5-4	At Mil.	W	6-2		10	4	Reynoso	Stull	Kim	18-10	1st	+2.5
5-5	S.D.	W	5-3		8	5	Johnson	Hitchcock		19-10	1st	+2.5
5-6	S.D.	W	10-5		12	8	Anderson	Lopez		20-10	1st	+2.5
5-7	S.D.	W	8-1		11	8	Stottlemyre	Clement		21-10	1st	+3.5
5-8	L.A.	W	15-7		20	7	Daal	Park		22-10	1st	+4.0
5-9	L.A.	W	11-7	(12)	15	15	Padilla	Hershiser		23-10	1st	+5.0
5-10	L.A.	W	2-1		9	9	Kim	Adams		24-10	1st	+5.0
5-12	At S.D.	W	6-4		8	9	Anderson	Clement	Kim	25-10	1st	+6.0
5-13	At S.D.	W	6-2		9	9	Stottlemyre	Spencer	Morgan	26-10	1st	+6.5
5-14	At S.D.	L	1-3		2	5	Meadows	Daal	Hoffman	26-11	1st	+6.5
5-16	At Mon.	L	0-2		5	5	Vazquez	Johnson	Hermanson	26-12	1st	+5.5
5-17	At Mon.	L	2-10		6	14	Pavano	Reynoso		26-13	1st	+4.5
5-18	At Mon.	W	8-6		10	8	Kim	Telford		27-13	1st	+5.0
5-19	At N.Y.	L	3-4		9	8	B.J. Jones	Stottlemyre	Benitez	27-14	1st	+4.0
5-20	At N.Y.	L	7-8		13	11	Hampton	Daal	Benitez	27-15	1st	+3.0
5-21	At N.Y.	L	6-7		10	10	Wendell	Kim		27-16	1st	+2.0
5-23	Pit.	W	6-1		11	8	Anderson	Anderson		28-16	1st	+2.5
5-24	Pit.	W	6-5		9	8	Stottlemyre	Schmidt	Kim	29-16	1st	+3.5
5-25	Pit.	W	7-5		12	9	Daal	Benson	Mantei	30-16	1st	+4.0
5-26	Mil.	W	9-2		9	6	Johnson	Snyder		31-16	1st	+4.0
5-27	Mil.	W	7-3		14	6	Reynoso	Acevedo	Kim	32-16	1st	+5.0
5-28	Mil.	L	3-4	(11)	8	11	Wickman	Swindell		32-17	1st	+5.0
5-29	StL.	L	0-3		6	5	Stephenson	Stottlemyre		32-18	1st	+4.0
5-30	StL.	L	1-6		5	10	Ankiel	Daal	Morris	32-19	1st	+4.0
5-31	StL.	W	6-2		8	10	Johnson	Hentgen	Kim	33-19	1st	+4.0
6-1	StL.	W	4-0		7	4	Reynoso	An. Benes		34-19	1st	+4.5
6-2	At Tex.	W	5-4		13	7	Anderson	Helling	Mantei	35-19	1st	+4.5
6-3	At Tex.	L	3-4		7	9	Rogers	Figueroa	Wetteland	35-20	1st	+4.5
6-4	At Tex.	L	6-7		14	10	Perisho	Kim	Wetteland	35-21	1st	+3.5
6-5	At Chi.	L	3-4	(10)	8	10	Heredia	Mantei		35-22	1st	+3.5
6-6	At Chi.	L	1-4		5	8	Tapani	Reynoso		35-23	1st	+3.5
6-7	At Chi.	L	4-9		11	11	Downs	Anderson	Van Poppel	35-24	1st	+2.5
6-9	Ana.	W	4-1		8	5	Johnson	Cooper	Kim	36-24	1st	+2.5
6-10	Ana.	L	3-10		7	13	Washburn	Daal		36-25	1st	+1.5
6-11	Ana.	W	3-2		6	8	Plesac	Schoeneweis	Kim	37-25	1st	+1.5
6-12	At L.A.	W	4-2		5	8	Anderson	Dreifort	Kim	38-25	1st	+2.0
6-13	At L.A.	L	1-6		5	10	Park	Morgan		38-26	1st	+2.0
6-14	At L.A.	W	5-1		11	6	Johnson	Perez		39-26	1st	+3.0
6-15	At L.A.	L	0-4		4	8	Brown	Stottlemyre		39-27	1st	+2.0
6-17	At Col.	L	5-14		8	17	Bohanon	Anderson		39-28	1st	+1.0
6-18	At Col.	L	2-19		8	23	Yoshii	Reynoso		39-29	2nd	...
6-19	S.D.	W	3-2		7	6	Padilla	Kolb		40-29	1st	+0.5
6-20	S.D.	L	1-3		2	7	Tollberg	Stottlemyre	Hoffman	40-30	1st	+0.5
6-21	S.D.	W	11-8		16	8	Morgan	Reyes		41-30	1st	+0.5
6-23	Col.	W	2-0		5	2	Anderson	Bohanon	Kim	42-30	1st	+2.0
6-24	Col.	L	0-4		7	6	Yoshii	Johnson		42-31	1st	+1.0
6-25	Col.	W	8-3		14	8	Morgan	Astacio		43-31	1st	+2.0
6-26	Hou.	W	6-1		8	5	Reynoso	Dotel	Kim	44-31	1st	+2.0
6-27	Hou.	L	4-12		8	13	Elarton	Daal		44-32	1st	+2.0
6-28	Hou.	W	6-2		10	8	Anderson	Lima	Kim	45-32	1st	+2.0
6-29	Hou.	W	7-1		10	5	Johnson	Reynolds		46-32	1st	+2.0
6-30	Cin.	L	4-5		7	11	Harnisch	Morgan	Graves	46-33	1st	+1.0

HIGHLIGHTS

High point: On May 13, the Diamondbacks recorded their team-record ninth straight victory, a 6-2 decision over San Diego. That lifted their major league-best mark to 26-10 and gave them a $6\frac{1}{2}$-game lead over the Dodgers in the N.L. West.

Low point: Having fallen out of contention for a division title, the Diamondbacks watched their wild-card hopes evaporate during a six-game losing streak in mid-September. The final loss was a tough one to take. The Giants' 8-7 win at San Francisco on September 21 clinched the N.L. West title.

Turning point: Milwaukee's three-game sweep at Bank One Ballpark from August 21-23 dropped Arizona from a half-game behind the Giants to $2\frac{1}{2}$ games back, a deficit that would only grow.

Most valuable player: Steve Finley carried the club over the first half, hitting 27 homers and driving in 75 runs by July 21. His 35 homers were a career high and only late injuries kept his RBI total (96) below 100.

Most valuable pitcher: Randy Johnson won his second straight Cy Young, improving in many ways on his remarkable 1999 season. He went 19-7 with a 2.64 ERA, second best in the N.L., and struck out a major league-high 347 batters. Johnson, dominating over the first half, was 15-2 with a 2.01 ERA at the break.

Most improved player: Lefthander Brian Anderson compiled a so-so 11-7 record and 4.05 ERA, but those numbers were deceptive. He made 10 starts in which he allowed two or fewer earned runs but did not win, and led the N.L. with 14 no-decisions. Anderson set a career high with $213\frac{1}{3}$ innings and finished second in the league in walks per nine innings (1.6)

Most pleasant surprise: Veteran Greg Colbrunn, who was supposed to be a part-time player and pinch hitter, was pressed into duty as the regular first baseman and, with Matt Williams struggling, the cleanup hitter. Over his final 50 starts, Colbrunn batted .349 with nine homers and 38 RBIs.

Key injuries: Third baseman Matt Williams missed half the season with a broken foot and strained quadriceps and played the other half with a sore foot. ... First baseman Erubiel Durazo had two operations on his wrist. ... Righthander Todd Stottlemyre missed a third of the season with elbow tendinitis. ... Shortstop Tony Womack was hampered by a sore knee. ... Closer Matt Mantei was bothered by biceps and shoulder trouble.

Notable: Johnson's three Cy Young Awards leave him second among lefthanders to Steve Carlton (four). ... Luis Gonzalez, the only National Leaguer to start all 162 games, became the first Arizona batter to hit for the cycle. He did it July 5 at Houston. ... Arizona became the first team to fall from 100 or more wins to fewer than 90 since the 1991 Athletics, who followed their 1990 A.L. pennant (103-59) by going 84-78.

—ED PRICE

MISCELLANEOUS

RECORDS

2000 regular-season record: 85-77 (3rd in N.L. West); 47-34 at home; 38-43 on road; 21-24 vs. East; 29-21 vs. Central; 35-32 vs. West; 23-17 vs. lefthanded starters; 62-60 vs. righthanded starters; 74-70 on grass; 11-7 on turf; 22-24 in daytime; 63-53 at night; 22-27 in one-run games; 5-8 in extra-inning games; 0-0-1 in doubleheaders.

Team record past five years: 250-236 in three years (.514, ranks 6th in league in that span).

TEAM LEADERS

Batting average: Luis Gonzalez (.311).
At-bats: Luis Gonzalez (618).
Runs: Luis Gonzalez (106).
Hits: Luis Gonzalez (192).
Total Bases: Luis Gonzalez (336).
Doubles: Luis Gonzalez (47).
Triples: Tony Womack (14).
Home runs: Steve Finley (35).
Runs batted in: Luis Gonzalez (114).
Stolen bases: Tony Womack (45).
Slugging percentage: Luis Gonzalez (.544).
On-base percentage: Luis Gonzalez (.392).
Wins: Randy Johnson (19).
Earned-run average: Randy Johnson (2.64).
Complete games: Randy Johnson (8).
Shutouts: Randy Johnson (3).
Saves: Matt Mantei (17).
Innings pitched: Randy Johnson (248.2).
Strikeouts: Randy Johnson (347).

Date	Opp.	Res.	Score	(inn.*)	Hits	Opp. hits	Winning pitcher	Losing pitcher	Save	Record	Pos.	GB
7-1	Cin.	W	9-6		12	6	Springer	Fernandez	Kim	47-33	1st	+2.0
7-2	Cin.	L	2-14		9	20	Neagle	Daal		47-34	1st	+1.0
7-3	Cin.	L	2-3		9	8	Parris	Anderson	Graves	47-35	2nd	...
7-4	At Hou.	W	10-4		11	6	Johnson	Lima		48-35	1st	+1.5
7-5	At Hou.	W	12-9		16	10	Morgan	Valdes	Kim	49-35	1st	+2.5
7-6	At Hou.	W	2-1		4	4	Guzman	Holt	Mantei	50-35	1st	+3.5
7-7	At Oak.	L	4-5	(11)	9	11	Tam	Daal		50-36	1st	+3.5
7-8	At Oak.	L	7-8	(10)	9	13	Isringhausen	Swindell		50-37	1st	+2.5
7-9	At Oak.	W	4-2		13	6	Johnson	Heredia	Mantei	51-37	1st	+3.5
7-13	Tex.	L	4-6		11	7	Zimmerman	Kim	Wetteland	51-38	1st	+2.5
7-14	Tex.	W	6-1		10	6	Reynoso	Rogers		52-38	1st	+2.5
7-15	Tex.	L	5-6	(11)	13	10	Zimmerman	Swindell	Wetteland	52-39	1st	+2.5
7-16	Sea.	L	3-6		8	9	Mesa	Springer	Sasaki	52-40	1st	+1.5
7-17	Sea.	W	7-0		13	5	Guzman	Halama		53-40	1st	+1.5
7-18	Sea.	L	2-5		6	11	Rhodes	Padilla	Sasaki	53-41	1st	+0.5
7-19	StL.	W	4-3		9	6	Reynoso	Stephenson	Mantei	54-41	1st	+1.5
7-20	StL.	W	3-2		4	6	Johnson	Veres		55-41	1st	+1.5
7-21	At Cin.	W	5-4		14	11	Swindell	Sullivan	Mantei	56-41	1st	+2.5
7-22	At Cin.	L	3-7		8	14	Villone	Guzman		56-42	1st	+1.5
7-23	At Cin.	L	3-5		9	10	Dessens	Anderson	Graves	56-43	1st	+1.5
7-25	At StL.	L	3-7		5	7	Stephenson	Johnson		56-44	1st	+1.0
7-26	At StL.	L	4-8		10	11	Kile	Reynoso		56-45	2nd	...
7-27	At StL.	W	17-5		19	10	Guzman	Ankiel		57-45	1st	+0.5
7-28	At Fla.	W	4-1		6	6	Schilling	Cornelius	Mantei	58-45	1st	+0.5
7-29	At Fla.	L	2-4		2	7	Miceli	Kim	Alfonseca	58-46	1st	+0.5
7-30	At Fla.	L	3-4		6	10	Almanza	Morgan	Alfonseca	58-47	1st	+0.5
8-1	Atl.	L	2-4		2	8	Millwood	Swindell	Remlinger	58-48	2nd	1.0
8-2	Atl.	W	2-0		6	6	Schilling	Maddux		59-48	2nd	...
8-3	Atl.	W	8-4		11	10	Anderson	Ashby		60-48	2nd	...
8-4	N.Y.	L	1-6		6	11	Reed	Johnson	Cook	60-49	2nd	1.0
8-5	N.Y.	L	2-6		11	14	B.J. Jones	Guzman	White	60-50	2nd	1.0
8-6	N.Y.	W	9-5		12	13	Reynoso	Rusch	Mantei	61-50	2nd	1.0
8-7	Mon.	W	5-2		9	8	Schilling	Moore		62-50	2nd	1.0
8-8	Mon.	L	3-9		9	16	Lira	Anderson		62-51	2nd	2.0
8-9	Mon.	L	3-4		8	15	Strickland	Guzman	Telford	62-52	2nd	3.0
8-11	At Pit.	W	6-1		10	4	Reynoso	Serafini		63-52	2nd	2.0
8-12	At Pit.	L	6-9		10	11	Sauerbeck	Schilling		63-53	2nd	2.0
8-13	At Pit.	W	7-6		14	12	Morgan	Arroyo	Mantei	64-53	2nd	1.0
8-14	At Phi.	W	4-3	(11)	7	6	Plesac	Brantley	Mantei	65-53	2nd	1.0
8-15	At Phi.	W	11-6		16	13	Kim	Gomes		66-53	2nd	1.0
8-16	At Phi.	W	5-1		10	7	Reynoso	Chen		67-53	2nd	1.0
8-18	Chi.	W	11-2		12	6	Schilling	Quevedo		68-53	2nd	1.5
8-19	Chi.	W	11-3		15	7	Anderson	Lieber		69-53	2nd	1.5
8-20	Chi.	W	5-4		10	4	Johnson	Rain		70-53	2nd	0.5
8-21	Mil.	L	8-16		13	19	Stull	Reynoso		70-54	2nd	1.5
8-22	Mil.	L	3-4		8	8	D'Amico	Guzman	Leskanic	70-55	2nd	1.5
8-23	Mil.	L	5-8		11	9	Haynes	Schilling	Leskanic	70-56	2nd	2.5
8-25	At N.Y.	L	3-13		6	16	Reed	Johnson		70-57	2nd	3.5
8-26	At N.Y.	W	5-1	(10)	11	5	Plesac	White		71-57	2nd	2.5
8-27	At N.Y.	L	1-2		3	4	Hampton	Reynoso	Benitez	71-58	2nd	2.5
8-28	At Mon.	L	5-9		9	14	Thurman	Schilling	Telford	71-59	2nd	3.5
8-29	At Mon.	W	8-7		8	12	Plesac	Forster	Mantei	72-59	2nd	2.5
8-30	At Mon.	W	7-0		10	5	Johnson	Lira		73-59	2nd	2.5
9-1	Fla.	L	7-8	(11)	13	15	Darensbourg	Swindell	Alfonseca	73-60	2nd	4.0
9-2	Fla.	L	1-10		9	17	Dempster	Schilling		73-61	2nd	5.0
9-3	Fla.	W	10-5		18	11	Kim	Burnett		74-61	2nd	5.0
9-5	At Atl.	L	2-5		7	6	Glavine	Johnson	Rocker	74-62	2nd	6.5
9-6	At Atl.	L	1-7		6	7	Millwood	Reynoso		74-63	2nd	7.5
9-7	At Atl.	L	0-4		4	12	Maddux	Schilling		74-64	2nd	8.5
9-8	At Fla.	W	2-1		8	6	Kim	Bones	Mantei	75-64	2nd	7.5
9-9	At Fla.	W	4-1		9	5	Stottlemyre	Burnett	Mantei	76-64	2nd	6.5
9-10	At Fla.	L	3-4	(12)	4	9	Looper	Springer		76-65	2nd	7.5
9-11	L.A.	L	3-6		6	11	Gagne	Reynoso		76-66	2nd	8.5
9-12	L.A.	W	5-4		8	7	Kim	Masaoka	Mantei	77-66	2nd	8.5
9-13	L.A.	W	3-2		9	5	Plesac	Adams		78-66	2nd	8.5
9-15	Atl.	W	2-1		8	7	Johnson	Glavine	Mantei	79-66	2nd	7.5
9-16	Atl.	L	10-12		14	14	Burkett	Stottlemyre	Rocker	79-67	2nd	8.5
9-17	Atl.	L	1-7		4	16	Millwood	Schilling		79-68	2nd	9.5
9-18	At L.A.	L	1-2		9	6	Shaw	Swindell		79-69	2nd	9.5
9-19	At L.A.	L	0-1		6	7	Park	Anderson	Shaw	79-70	2nd	10.5
9-20	At L.A.	L	0-1		9	7	Herges	Kim		79-71	3rd	11.5
9-21	At S.F	L	7-8		9	9	Henry	Morgan	Nen	79-72	3rd	12.5
9-22	At S.F	W	7-1		11	4	Schilling	Gardner		80-72	2nd	11.5
9-23†	At S.F	W	7-5		9	8	Guzman	Estes	Mantei	81-72		
9-23‡	At S.F	L	5-9		9	10	del Toro	Reynoso		81-73	3rd	11.5
9-24	At S.F	W	8-3		10	7	Anderson	Hernandez		82-73	3rd	10.5
9-25	At Col.	W	6-4		13	10	Johnson	Rose	Mantei	83-73	T2nd	10.0
9-26	At Col.	L	6-7		7	10	Chouinard	Morgan	Jimenez	83-74	3rd	10.0
9-27	At Col.	L	4-6		6	14	White	Plesac	Jimenez	83-75	3rd	11.0
9-28	At Col.	W	12-3		13	7	Reynoso	Wasdin		84-75	T2nd	11.0
9-29	S.F	L	3-4		9	7	Hernandez	Anderson	Nen	84-76	3rd	12.0
9-30	S.F	W	5-1		11	5	Guzman	Embree		85-76	3rd	11.0
10-1	S.F	L	4-11		8	12	Ortiz	Johnson		85-77	3rd	12.0

Monthly records: April (16-9), May (17-10), June (13-14), July (12-14), August (15-12), September (12-17), October (0-1).
*Innings, if other than nine. † First game of a doubleheader. ‡ Second game of a doubleheader.

MEMORABLE GAMES

May 9 at Arizona

Catcher Damian Miller capped a five-run, 12th-inning rally with a dramatic grand slam that gave the Diamondbacks their sixth straight win—a come-from-behind 11-7 win over Los Angeles.

Los Angeles	AB	R	H	BI	Arizona	AB	R	H	BI
Hollandsworth, cf	7	1	2	2	Womack, ss	6	1	2	0
Grudzielanek, 2b	6	1	1	0	Bell, 2b	6	3	3	0
Hershiser, p	0	0	0	0	Gonzalez, lf	4	2	1	2
Sheffield, lf	4	2	2	1	Colbrunn, 1b	3	0	0	0
Green, rf	3	2	2	0	Durazo, ph-1b	2	1	1	0
Karros, 1b	4	0	1	1	Finley, cf	5	0	2	3
Hundley, c	5	0	2	2	Lee, rf	4	0	1	0
Beltre, 3b	6	0	1	1	Kim, p	0	0	0	0
Cora, ss	6	1	3	0	Frias, ph	0	0	0	0
Perez, p	3	0	0	0	Padilla, p	0	0	0	0
Berroa, ph	0	0	0	0	Stinnett, ph	0	1	0	0
Adams, p	0	0	0	0	Miller, c	6	2	2	5
Shaw, p	0	0	0	0	Klassen, 3b	5	1	2	0
Hansen, ph	1	0	0	0	Reynoso, p	1	0	0	0
Osuna, p	0	0	0	0	Springer, p	0	0	0	0
Vizcaino, ph-2b	1	0	1	0	Gilkey, ph	1	0	0	0
					Morgan, p	0	0	0	0
					Harris, ph	1	0	0	0
					Swindell, p	0	0	0	0
					Fox, rf	2	0	1	1
Totals	**46**	**7**	**15**	**7**	**Totals**	**46**	**11**	**15**	**11**

Los Angeles ....3 0 2 0 1 0 0 0 0 0 0 1— 7 15 0
Arizona ....2 1 0 0 0 0 0 2 1 0 0 5—11 15 0

DP—Los Angeles 2, Arizona 3. LOB—Los Angeles 13, Arizona 7. 2B—Grudzielanek (4), Green (11), Finley (5), Klassen (2). 3B—Bell (1). HR—Hollandsworth (4), Sheffield (11), Gonzalez (9), Miller 2 (4). SB—Hollandsworth (3), Sheffield (1), Green 2 (7). S—Karros, Finley. HBP—Gonzalez by Perez, Stinnett by Hershiser.

Los Angeles	IP	H	R	ER	BB	SO
Perez	7	6	3	3	0	2
Adams	1	3	2	2	1	1
Shaw	1	2	1	1	0	0
Osuna	2	1	0	0	1	3
Hershiser (L 1- 0).	1	3	5	5	1	0
Arizona	**IP**	**H**	**R**	**ER**	**BB**	**SO**
Reynoso	4.1	7	6	6	4	1
Springer	0.2	1	0	0	0	0
Morgan	2	1	0	0	2	2
Swindell	1.1	2	0	0	2	2
Kim	1.2	1	0	0	0	4
Padilla (W 1-0)	2	3	1	1	1	1

WP—Perez. PB—Hundley. T—4:12. A—32,326.

September 10 at Florida

Randy Johnson reached two milestones during Arizona's 4-3 loss to the Marlins. Johnson's first of 14 strikeouts gave him distinction as the second pitcher to record four straight 300 seasons and he became the 12th member of the 3,000 club.

Arizona	AB	R	H	BI	Florida	AB	R	H	BI
Womack, ss	4	0	0	0	Castillo, 2b	5	0	1	0
Bell, 2b	4	1	1	0	Berg, ss	3	0	2	2
Gonzalez, lf	3	0	0	1	Rodriguez, ph	1	0	0	0
Colbrunn, 1b	4	1	1	2	A.Gonzalez, ss	1	0	0	0
Finley, cf	5	0	0	0	Millar, lf	2	0	0	0
Williams, 3b	4	0	2	0	Floyd, ph-lf	2	0	0	0
Counsell, pr-3b	0	0	0	0	Wilson, cf	5	0	1	1
Mieske, ph	0	0	0	0	Lowell, 3b	3	0	0	0
Springer, p	0	0	0	0	Lee, 1b	5	0	0	0
Bautista, rf	4	0	0	0	M.Smith, rf	5	1	1	0
Stinnett, c	3	0	0	0	Almanza, p	0	0	0	0
Ryan, ph	1	0	0	0	Looper, p	0	0	0	0
Miller, c	0	0	0	0	Redmond, c	3	1	2	0
Johnson, p	1	1	0	0	Fox, pr	0	0	0	0
Dellucci, ph	1	0	0	0	Castro, c	0	0	0	0
Kim, p	0	0	0	0	Ozuna, pr	0	0	0	0
Conti, ph	1	0	0	0	Martinez, c	1	0	0	0
Swindell, p	0	0	0	0	C.Smith, p	2	1	1	1
Morgan, p	0	0	0	0	Clapinski, ph	1	0	0	0
Plesac, p	0	0	0	0	Miceli, p	0	0	0	0
Frias, ph-3b	1	0	0	0	Rolison, ph	1	0	0	0
					Alfonseca, p	0	0	0	0
					Kotsay, rf	1	1	1	0
Totals	**36**	**3**	**4**	**3**	**Totals**	**41**	**4**	**9**	**4**

Arizona ....0 0 0 0 0 3 0 0 0 0 0 0—3 4 1
Florida.........................0 0 0 0 3 0 0 0 0 0 0 1—4 9 0

E—Johnson (3). DP—Florida 2. LOB—Arizona 6, Florida 10. 2B—Bell (27), Berg (12). HR—Colbrunn (12). SB—Lowell (1). CS—Castillo (20), Fox (3). S—Gonzalez. SH—Bautista, Castillo, Gonzalez.

Arizona	IP	H	R	ER	BB	SO
Johnson	7	6	3	1	2	14
Kim	2	0	0	0	2	4
Swindell	0.2	1	0	0	0	0
Morgan	1	0	0	0	1	1
Plesac	0.1	0	0	0	0	1
Springer (L 2-4)	0.2	2	1	1	1	1
Florida	**IP**	**H**	**R**	**ER**	**BB**	**SO**
C. Smith	7	3	3	3	4	7
Miceli	2	0	0	0	0	0
Alfonseca	2	1	0	0	1	2
Almanza	0.1	0	0	0	0	0
Looper (W 5-1)	0.2	0	0	0	2	2

PB—Stinnett. T—4:07. A—13,117.

INDIVIDUAL STATISTICS

BATTING

Name	G	TPA	AB	R	H	TB	2B	3B	HR	RBI	Avg.	Obp.	Slg.	SH	SF	HP	BB	IBB	SO	SB	CS	GDP	vs RHP AB	vs RHP Avg.	vs RHP HR	vs RHP RBI	vs LHP AB	vs LHP Avg.	vs LHP HR	vs LHP RBI
Gonzalez, Luis	162	722	618	106	192	336	47	2	31	114	.311	.392	.544	2	12	12	78	6	85	2	4	12	441	.333	23	83	177	.254	8	31
Womack, Tony	146	659	617	95	167	237	21	14	7	57	.271	.307	.384	2	5	5	30	0	74	45	11	6	494	.269	6	40	123	.276	1	17
Bell, Jay	149	649	565	87	151	247	30	6	18	68	.267	.348	.437	6	5	3	70	0	88	7	3	7	418	.239	12	47	147	.347	6	21
Finley, Steve	152	623	539	100	151	293	27	5	35	96	.280	.361	.544	2	9	8	65	7	87	12	6	9	382	.283	24	62	157	.274	11	34
Williams, Matt	96	397	371	43	102	160	18	2	12	47	.275	.315	.431	0	3	3	20	1	51	1	2	11	265	.260	7	33	106	.311	5	14
Colbrunn, Greg	116	385	329	48	103	172	22	1	15	57	.313	.405	.523	0	3	10	43	2	45	0	1	13	192	.333	9	32	137	.285	6	25
Miller, Damian	100	364	324	43	89	143	24	0	10	44	.275	.347	.441	1	2	1	36	4	74	2	2	6	220	.277	7	34	104	.269	3	10
Bautista, Danny	87	294	262	45	83	134	16	7	7	47	.317	.366	.511	4	5	3	20	4	30	5	2	10	180	.322	4	36	82	.305	3	11
Stinnett, Kelly	76	265	240	22	52	83	7	0	8	33	.217	.291	.346	0	0	6	19	4	56	0	1	5	192	.208	7	29	48	.250	1	4
Lee, Travis	72	250	224	34	52	89	13	0	8	40	.232	.308	.397	0	1	0	25	1	46	5	1	6	176	.233	8	34	48	.229	0	6
Durazo, Erubiel	67	233	196	35	52	87	11	0	8	33	.265	.373	.444	0	2	1	34	2	43	1	0	3	174	.259	8	31	22	.318	0	2
Counsell, Craig	67	177	152	23	48	64	8	1	2	11	.316	.400	.421	1	1	2	20	0	18	3	3	4	137	.321	2	11	15	.267	0	0
Frias, Hanley	75	129	112	18	23	34	5	0	2	6	.205	.310	.304	0	0	0	17	0	18	2	2	3	64	.219	1	2	48	.188	1	4
Conti, Jason	47	99	91	11	21	34	4	3	1	15	.231	.293	.374	0	0	1	7	2	30	3	0	2	83	.229	1	13	8	.250	0	2
Fox, Andy	31	90	86	10	18	25	4	0	1	10	.209	.244	.291	0	0	0	4	1	16	2	1	1	72	.194	1	9	14	.286	0	1
Harris, Lenny	36	91	85	9	16	22	1	1	1	13	.188	.209	.259	0	3	0	3	1	5	5	0	3	72	.194	1	10	13	.154	0	3
Johnson, Randy	35	92	83	4	13	15	2	0	0	8	.157	.195	.181	5	0	1	3	0	35	0	0	1	64	.141	0	3	19	.211	0	5
Cabrera, Alex	31	87	80	10	21	40	2	1	5	14	.263	.299	.500	0	2	1	4	0	21	0	0	3	54	.259	0	6	26	.269	5	8
Klassen, Danny	29	87	76	13	18	27	3	0	2	8	.237	.318	.355	2	0	1	8	0	24	1	1	0	39	.231	1	5	37	.243	1	3
Gilkey, Bernard	38	81	73	6	8	15	1	0	2	6	.110	.185	.205	0	1	0	7	2	16	0	0	3	27	.111	0	1	46	.109	2	5
Anderson, Brian	37	81	69	4	13	16	3	0	0	4	.188	.194	.232	9	2	0	1	0	10	0	0	1	44	.159	0	4	25	.240	0	0
Ward, Turner	15	59	52	5	9	13	4	0	0	4	.173	.241	.250	1	1	0	5	0	7	1	1	3	47	.170	0	4	5	.200	0	0
Dellucci, David	34	54	50	2	15	18	3	0	0	2	.300	.352	.360	0	0	0	4	0	9	0	2	1	50	.300	0	2	0	.000	0	0
Reynoso, Armando	31	57	48	0	5	5	0	0	0	0	.104	.140	.104	7	0	0	2	0	24	0	0	0	30	.100	0	0	18	.111	0	0
Schilling, Curt	13	38	31	2	8	10	2	0	0	3	.258	.258	.323	7	0	0	0	0	11	0	1	0	26	.231	0	3	5	.400	0	0
Stottlemyre, Todd	18	37	31	6	6	11	2	0	1	4	.194	.265	.355	3	0	0	3	0	14	0	0	0	29	.207	1	4	2	.000	0	0
Ryan, Rob	27	32	27	4	8	11	1	1	0	2	.296	.406	.407	0	0	1	4	0	7	0	0	0	27	.296	0	2	0	.000	0	0
Daal, Omar	20	31	27	2	7	11	1	0	1	4	.259	.286	.407	3	0	0	1	0	3	0	0	1	18	.278	1	4	9	.222	0	0
Guzman, Geraldo	13	22	19	0	0	0	0	0	0	0	.000	.000	.000	3	0	0	0	0	13	0	0	0	11	.000	0	0	8	.000	0	0
Morgan, Mike	60	17	16	0	7	7	0	0	0	1	.438	.438	.438	1	0	0	0	0	5	0	0	0	14	.357	0	1	2	1.000	0	0
Barajas, Rod	5	13	13	1	3	6	0	0	1	3	.231	.231	.462	0	0	0	0	0	4	0	0	0	12	.167	0	1	1	1.000	1	2
Mieske, Matt	11	10	8	3	2	5	0	0	1	2	.250	.300	.625	0	1	0	1	0	1	0	0	0	1	1.000	0	0	7	.143	1	2
Springer, Russ	52	5	5	0	1	1	0	0	0	0	.200	.200	.200	0	0	0	0	0	1	0	0	0	3	.333	0	0	2	.000	0	0
Figueroa, Nelson	3	4	3	1	1	1	0	0	0	0	.333	.333	.333	1	0	0	0	0	1	0	0	0	3	.333	0	0	0	.000	0	0
Kim, Byung-Hyun	61	4	3	0	0	0	0	0	0	0	.000	.250	.000	0	0	0	1	0	2	0	0	0	3	.000	0	0	0	.000	0	0
Padilla, Vicente	27	1	1	0	1	1	0	0	0	0	1.000	1.000	1.000	0	0	0	0	0	0	0	0	0	1	1.000	0	0	0	.000	0	0
Swindell, Greg	64	2	1	0	0	0	0	0	0	0	.000	.000	.000	1	0	0	0	0	1	0	0	0	0	.000	0	0	1	.000	0	0
Plesac, Dan	62	0	0	0	0	0	0	0	0	0	.000	.000	.000	0	0	0	0	0	0	0	0	0	0	.000	0	0	0	.000	0	0
Holmes, Darren	8	0	0	0	0	0	0	0	0	0	.000	.000	.000	0	0	0	0	0	0	0	0	0	0	.000	0	0	0	.000	0	0
Ruffin, Johnny	5	0	0	0	0	0	0	0	0	0	.000	.000	.000	0	0	0	0	0	0	0	0	0	0	.000	0	0	0	.000	0	0
Mantei, Matt	47	0	0	0	0	0	0	0	0	0	.000	.000	.000	0	0	0	0	0	0	0	0	0	0	.000	0	0	0	.000	0	0

Players with more than one N.L. team

Name	G	TPA	AB	R	H	TB	2B	3B	HR	RBI	Avg.	Obp.	Slg.	SH	SF	HP	BB	IBB	SO	SB	CS	GDP	vs RHP AB	vs RHP Avg.	vs RHP HR	vs RHP RBI	vs LHP AB	vs LHP Avg.	vs LHP HR	vs LHP RBI
Bautista, Fla.-Ari.	131	388	351	54	100	167	20	7	11	59	.285	.333	.476	4	5	3	25	4	50	6	2	11	220	.295	7	46	131	.267	4	13
Daal, Ari.-Phi.	32	54	45	3	12	18	3	0	1	6	.267	.327	.400	5	0	0	4	0	8	0	0	1	34	.294	1	6	11	.182	0	0
Fox, Ari.-Fla.	100	275	250	29	58	82	8	2	4	20	.232	.302	.328	0	0	3	22	4	53	10	4	2	226	.230	4	19	24	.250	0	1
Harris, Ari.-N.Y.	112	248	223	31	58	85	7	4	4	26	.260	.317	.381	2	3	0	20	2	22	13	1	7	204	.270	4	23	19	.158	0	3
Holmes, Ari.-StL.	13	1	1	0	0	0	0	0	0	0	.000	.000	.000	0	0	0	0	0	1	0	0	0	1	.000	0	0	0	.000	0	0
Lee, Ari.-Phi.	128	473	404	53	95	148	24	1	9	54	.235	.342	.366	0	2	2	65	1	79	8	1	12	331	.242	9	46	73	.205	0	8
Mieske, Hou.-Ari.	73	99	89	10	16	27	1	2	2	7	.180	.253	.303	0	1	1	8	0	18	0	0	2	43	.233	1	1	46	.130	1	6
Padilla, Ari.-Phi.	55	1	1	0	1	1	0	0	0	0	1.000	1.000	1.000	0	0	0	0	0	0	0	0	0	1	1.000	0	0	0	.000	0	0
Schilling, Phi.-Ari.	29	71	61	2	13	16	3	0	0	4	.213	.226	.262	9	0	0	1	0	15	0	1	0	44	.205	0	4	17	.235	0	0

PITCHING

Name	W	L	Pct.	ERA	IP	H	R	ER	HR	SH	SF	HB	BB	IBB	SO	G	GS	CG	ShO	GF	Sv	vs. RH AB	vs. RH Avg.	vs. RH HR	vs. RH RBI	vs. LH AB	vs. LH Avg.	vs. LH HR	vs. LH RBI
Johnson, Randy	19	7	.731	2.64	248.2	202	89	73	23	14	5	6	76	1	347	35	35	8	3	0	0	817	.224	23	74	83	.229	0	4
Anderson, Brian	11	7	.611	4.05	213.1	226	101	96	38	6	6	3	39	7	104	33	32	2	0	0	0	634	.278	31	77	188	.266	7	19
Reynoso, Armando	11	12	.478	5.27	170.2	179	102	100	22	11	5	6	52	5	89	31	30	2	0	0	0	341	.276	11	39	315	.270	11	46
Morgan, Mike	5	5	.500	4.87	101.2	123	55	55	10	7	4	1	40	5	56	60	4	0	0	15	5	257	.331	7	49	139	.273	3	15
Schilling, Curt	5	6	.455	3.69	97.2	94	41	40	10	6	3	0	13	0	72	13	13	4	1	0	0	151	.291	7	21	215	.233	3	19
Daal, Omar	2	10	.167	7.22	96.0	127	88	77	17	3	5	7	42	11	45	20	16	0	0	1	0	314	.315	12	54	89	.315	5	24
Stottlemyre, Todd	9	6	.600	4.91	95.1	98	55	52	18	3	2	2	36	2	76	18	18	0	0	0	0	222	.266	8	31	143	.273	10	21
Swindell, Greg	2	6	.250	3.20	76.0	71	29	27	7	6	3	1	20	5	64	64	0	0	0	21	1	181	.298	5	23	107	.159	2	8
Kim, Byung-Hyun	6	6	.500	4.46	70.2	52	39	35	9	2	3	9	46	5	111	61	1	0	0	30	14	147	.170	6	19	113	.239	3	17
Springer, Russ	2	4	.333	5.08	62.0	63	36	35	11	2	3	2	34	6	59	52	0	0	0	10	0	171	.269	8	33	70	.243	3	15
Guzman, Geraldo	5	4	.556	5.37	60.1	66	36	36	8	3	1	2	22	0	52	13	10	0	0	0	0	128	.250	3	13	103	.330	5	18
Mantei, Matt	1	1	.500	4.57	45.1	31	24	23	4	2	0	2	35	1	53	47	0	0	0	38	17	90	.200	2	10	71	.183	2	12
Plesac, Dan	5	1	.833	3.15	40.0	34	21	14	4	6	1	0	26	2	45	62	0	0	0	14	0	72	.194	1	10	77	.260	3	14
Padilla, Vicente	2	1	.667	2.31	35.0	32	10	9	0	0	1	0	10	2	30	27	0	0	0	12	0	87	.241	0	5	45	.244	0	5
Figueroa, Nelson	0	1	.000	7.47	15.2	17	13	13	4	1	2	0	5	0	7	3	3	0	0	0	0	31	.258	3	8	29	.310	1	4
Ruffin, Johnny	0	0	.000	9.00	9.0	14	9	9	4	0	0	0	3	1	5	5	0	0	0	2	0	22	.409	2	7	18	.278	2	4
Holmes, Darren	0	0	.000	8.53	6.1	12	6	6	1	0	1	1	1	0	5	8	0	0	0	3	1	21	.429	1	9	8	.375	0	2

PITCHERS WITH MORE THAN ONE N.L. TEAM

Name	W	L	Pct.	ERA	IP	H	R	ER	HR	SH	SF	HB	BB	IBB	SO	G	GS	CG	ShO	GF	Sv	vs. RH AB	vs. RH Avg.	vs. RH HR	vs. RH RBI	vs. LH AB	vs. LH Avg.	vs. LH HR	vs. LH RBI
Daal, Phi.	2	9	.182	4.69	71.0	81	40	37	9	3	1	2	30	0	51	12	12	0	0	0	0	314	.315	12	54	89	.315	5	24
Daal, Ari.-Phi.	4	19	.174	6.14	167.0	208	128	114	26	6	6	9	72	11	96	32	28	0	0	6	0	561	.307	20	90	121	.298	6	28
Holmes, StL.	0	1	.000	9.72	8.1	12	9	9	2	0	2	1	3	0	5	5	0	0	0	1	0	21	.429	1	9	8	.375	0	2
Holmes, Ari.-StL.	0	1	.000	9.20	14.2	24	15	15	3	0	3	2	4	0	10	13	0	0	0	3	1	44	.386	2	18	18	.389	1	6
Padilla, Phi.	2	6	.250	5.34	30.1	40	23	18	3	5	2	1	18	5	21	28	0	0	0	4	2	87	.241	0	5	45	.244	0	5
Padilla, Ari.-Phi.	4	7	.364	3.72	65.1	72	33	27	3	5	3	1	28	7	51	55	0	0	0	3	2	159	.252	1	15	95	.337	2	19
Schilling, Phi.	6	6	.500	3.91	112.2	110	49	49	17	5	1	1	32	4	96	16	16	4	1	0	0	151	.291	7	21	215	.233	3	19
Schilling, Phi.-Ari.	11	12	.478	3.81	210.1	204	90	89	27	11	4	1	45	4	168	29	29	8	2	4	0	373	.268	17	45	428	.243	10	43

DESIGNATED HITTERS

Name	AB	Avg.	HR	RBI
Finley, Steve	8	.250	0	1
Colbrunn, Greg	7	.429	0	0
Bell, Jay	5	.800	1	1
Williams, Matt	5	.400	0	0
Ryan, Rob	3	.333	0	0

INDIVIDUAL STATISTICS

FIELDING

FIRST BASEMEN

Player	Pct.	G	PO	A	E	TC	DP
Colbrunn, Greg	.989	99	649	52	8	709	60
Durazo, Erubiel	.989	60	422	23	5	450	36
Lee, Travis	.984	23	112	8	2	122	16
Cabrera, Alex	1.000	15	101	6	0	107	9
Miller, Damian	.667	2	2	0	1	3	0
Fox, Andy	1.000	1	7	0	0	7	3

SECOND BASEMEN

Player	Pct.	G	PO	A	E	TC	DP
Bell, Jay	.988	145	290	345	8	643	86
Counsell, Craig	.974	25	32	43	2	77	12
Frias, Hanley	.960	15	11	13	1	25	3

THIRD BASEMEN

Player	Pct.	G	PO	A	E	TC	DP
Williams, Matt	.964	94	68	172	9	249	19
Klassen, Danny	.962	25	11	39	2	52	4
Counsell, Craig	.952	23	3	37	2	42	6
Harris, Lenny	.909	20	11	29	4	44	1
Fox, Andy	.952	20	11	29	2	42	3
Frias, Hanley	1.000	7	0	3	0	3	1
Colbrunn, Greg	-	1	0	0	0	0	0

SHORTSTOPS

Player	Pct.	G	PO	A	E	TC	DP
Womack, Tony	.970	143	217	365	18	600	72
Frias, Hanley	.938	21	18	43	4	65	12
Counsell, Craig	.900	6	3	15	2	20	2
Klassen, Danny	1.000	3	3	3	0	6	0

OUTFIELDERS

Player	Pct.	G	PO	A	E	TC	DP
Gonzalez, Luis	.990	162	293	4	3	300	1
Finley, Steve	.992	148	342	10	3	355	2
Bautista, Danny	.987	82	142	6	2	150	0
Lee, Travis	.983	55	115	3	2	120	1
Conti, Jason	.983	35	53	4	1	58	2
Gilkey, Bernard	1.000	17	29	1	0	30	0
Ward, Turner	1.000	15	35	0	0	35	0
Cabrera, Alex	.957	12	21	1	1	23	0
Dellucci, David	1.000	12	15	0	0	15	0
Fox, Andy	1.000	6	3	0	0	3	0
Harris, Lenny	-	3	0	0	0	0	0
Ryan, Rob	1.000	2	1	0	0	1	0
Womack, Tony	1.000	2	1	0	0	1	0
Mieske, Matt	1.000	1	2	0	0	2	0

CATCHERS

Player	Pct.	G	PO	A	E	TC	DP	PB
Miller, Damian	.992	97	681	47	6	734	4	3
Stinnett, Kelly	.990	74	539	40	6	585	4	1
Barajas, Rod	1.000	5	23	0	0	23	0	0

PITCHERS

Player	Pct.	G	PO	A	E	TC	DP
Swindell, Greg	1.000	64	1	12	0	13	0
Plesac, Dan	1.000	62	0	2	0	2	0
Kim, Byung-Hyun	.900	61	2	7	1	10	0
Morgan, Mike	1.000	60	5	13	0	18	1
Springer, Russ	.833	52	1	4	1	6	1
Mantei, Matt	.857	47	4	2	1	7	1
Johnson, Randy	.900	35	5	22	3	30	1
Anderson, Brian	.984	33	13	47	1	61	4
Reynoso, Armando	.979	31	13	34	1	48	3
Padilla, Vicente	1.000	27	3	3	0	6	0
Daal, Omar	.852	20	5	18	4	27	0
Stottlemyre, Todd	.955	18	4	17	1	22	1
Schilling, Curt	1.000	13	5	11	0	16	0
Guzman, Geraldo	1.000	13	0	3	0	3	0
Holmes, Darren	1.000	8	2	0	0	2	0
Ruffin, Johnny	1.000	5	1	3	0	4	0
Figueroa, Nelson	1.000	3	1	2	0	3	0

PITCHING AGAINST EACH CLUB

Pitcher	Atl. W-L	Chi. W-L	Cin. W-L	Col. W-L	Fla. W-L	Hou. W-L	L.A. W-L	Mil. W-L	Mon. W-L	N.Y. W-L	Phi. W-L	Pit. W-L	S.D. W-L	S.F. W-L	StL. W-L	A.L. W-L	Total W-L
Anderson, B.	1-0	1-1	0-2	1-1	0-0	1-0	1-1	0-0	0-1	0-0	0-0	1-0	3-0	1-1	0-0	1-0	11-7
Daal, Omar	0-0	0-0	0-1	0-1	0-0	0-1	1-0	0-1	0-0	0-1	0-0	1-0	0-1	0-1	0-1	0-2	2-10
Figueroa, N.	0-0	0-0	0-0	0-0	0-0	0-0	0-0	0-0	0-0	0-0	0-0	0-0	0-0	0-0	0-0	0-1	0-1
Guzman, G.	0-0	0-0	0-1	0-0	0-0	1-0	0-0	0-1	0-1	0-1	0-0	0-0	0-0	2-0	1-0	1-0	5-4
Holmes, D.	0-0	0-0	0-0	0-0	0-0	0-0	0-0	0-0	0-0	0-0	0-0	0-0	0-0	0-0	0-0	0-0	0-0
Johnson, R.	1-1	2-0	0-0	2-1	0-0	2-0	1-0	1-0	1-1	0-2	2-0	1-0	1-0	1-1	2-1	2-0	19-7
Kim, Byung-H.	0-0	0-0	0-0	0-0	2-1	0-0	2-1	0-0	1-0	0-1	1-1	0-0	0-0	0-0	0-0	0-2	6-6
Mantei, Matt	0-0	1-1	0-0	0-0	0-0	0-0	0-0	0-0	0-0	0-0	0-0	0-0	0-0	0-0	0-0	0-0	1-1
Morgan, Mike	0-0	0-0	0-1	2-1	0-1	1-0	0-1	0-0	0-0	0-0	0-0	1-0	1-0	0-1	0-0	0-0	5-5
Padilla, Vicente	0-0	0-0	0-0	0-0	0-0	0-0	1-0	0-0	0-0	0-0	0-0	0-0	1-0	0-0	0-0	0-1	2-1
Plesac, Dan	0-0	0-0	0-0	0-1	0-0	0-0	1-0	0-0	1-0	1-0	1-0	0-0	0-0	0-0	0-0	1-0	5-1
Reynoso, A.	0-1	0-1	0-0	2-1	0-0	1-0	0-1	2-1	0-1	1-1	1-0	1-1	0-1	0-2	2-1	1-0	11-12
Ruffin, Johnny	0-0	0-0	0-0	0-0	0-0	0-0	0-0	0-0	0-0	0-0	0-0	0-0	0-0	0-0	0-0	0-0	0-0
Schilling, Curt	1-2	1-0	0-0	0-0	1-1	0-0	0-0	0-1	1-1	0-0	0-0	0-1	0-0	1-0	0-0	0-0	5-6
Springer, Russ	0-0	0-1	1-0	0-0	0-1	0-0	0-0	0-0	0-0	0-0	1-0	0-0	0-1	0-0	0-0	0-1	2-4
Stottlemyre, T.	0-1	0-0	0-0	0-0	1-0	0-0	0-1	1-0	0-0	0-1	2-0	1-0	3-1	1-1	0-1	0-0	9-6
Swindell, Greg	0-1	0-0	1-0	0-0	0-1	0-0	0-1	0-1	0-0	0-0	0-0	1-0	0-0	0-0	0-0	0-2	2-6
Totals	3-6	5-4	2-5	7-6	4-5	6-1	7-6	4-5	4-5	2-7	8-1	7-2	9-4	6-7	5-4	6-9	85-77

INTERLEAGUE: Johnson 1-0, Swindell 0-1, Daal 0-1 vs. Athletics; Guzman 1-0, Springer 0-1, Padilla 0-1 vs. Mariners; Anderson 1-0, Reynoso 1-0, Kim 0-2, Figueroa 0-1, Swindell 0-1 vs. Rangers; Johnson 1-0, Plesac 1-0, Daal 0-1 vs. Angels. Total: 6-9.

MISCELLANEOUS

HOME RUNS BY PARK

At Arizona (84): Finley 17, Gonzalez 14, Bell 9, Colbrunn 6, Miller 6, Williams 5, Bautista 4, Womack 4, Durazo 3, Stinnett 2, Frias 2, Klassen 2, Cabrera 2, Harris 1, Gilkey 1, Daal 1, Mieske 1, Fox 1, Lee 1, Barajas 1, Conti 1.
At Atlanta (1): Colbrunn 1.
At Chicago (NL) (9): Gonzalez 3, Bell 1, Finley 1, Gilkey 1, Colbrunn 1, Stinnett 1, Counsell 1.
At Cincinnati (3): Finley 1, Durazo 1, Cabrera 1.
At Colorado (8): Bell 2, Colbrunn 2, Williams 1, Gonzalez 1, Bautista 1, Womack 1.
At Florida (6): Gonzalez 2, Williams 1, Finley 1, Colbrunn 1, Miller 1.
At Houston (4): Miller 2, Gonzalez 1, Lee 1.
At Los Angeles (4): Williams 1, Colbrunn 1, Miller 1, Lee 1.
At Milwaukee (5): Finley 2, Bell 1, Lee 1, Durazo 1.
At Montreal (7): Finley 4, Gonzalez 1, Colbrunn 1, Womack 1.
At New York (NL) (4): Finley 2, Colbrunn 1, Lee 1.
At Oakland (1): Finley 1.
At Philadelphia (10): Gonzalez 2, Stinnett 2, Bell 1, Williams 1, Stottlemyre 1, Finley 1, Lee 1, Durazo 1.
At Pittsburgh (5): Gonzalez 2, Bell 1, Williams 1, Colbrunn 1.
At San Diego (11): Finley 4, Bell 2, Durazo 2, Womack 1, Stinnett 1, Lee 1.
At San Francisco (8): Williams 2, Gonzalez 2, Stinnett 2, Lee 1, Cabrera 1.
At St. Louis (5): Gonzalez 2, Bautista 2, Cabrera 1.
At Texas (4): Bell 1, Finley 1, Gonzalez 1, Counsell 1.

LOW-HIT GAMES

No-hitters: None.
One-hitters: None.
Two-hitters: None.

10-STRIKEOUT GAMES

Randy Johnson 23, Curt Schilling 2, Todd Stottlemyre 1, Total: 26

FOUR OR MORE HITS IN ONE GAME

Luis Gonzalez 3, Greg Colbrunn 2, Jay Bell 1, Steve Finley 1, Tony Womack 1, Craig Counsell 1, Andy Fox 1, Damian Miller 1, Total: 11

MULTI-HOMER GAMES

Steve Finley 3, Jay Bell 2, Luis Gonzalez 2, Kelly Stinnett 2, Danny Bautista 1, Damian Miller 1, Erubiel Durazo 1, Total: 12

GRAND SLAMS

4-5: Lenny Harris (off Philadelphia's Paul Byrd)
5-9: Damian Miller (off Los Angeles's Orel Hershiser)
9-24: Matt Williams (off San Francisco's Livan Hernandez)

PINCH HITTERS

(Minimum 5 at-bats)

Name	AB	Avg.	HR	RBI
Arias, Hanley	25	.280	0	2
Colbrunn, Greg	24	.250	0	4
Counsell, Craig	23	.261	0	1
Dellucci, David	20	.350	0	2
Gilkey, Bernard	20	.100	0	0
Ryan, Rob	19	.316	0	2
Harris, Lenny	16	.250	0	1
Conti, Jason	13	.154	0	2
Bautista, Danny	10	.300	0	0
Durazo, Erubiel	9	.111	0	2
Mieske, Matt	8	.250	1	2
Cabrera, Alex	7	.143	1	2
Fox, Andy	5	.000	0	0

DEBUTS

6-3: Nelson Figueroa, P.
6-26: Alex Cabrera, PH.
6-29: Jason Conti, PH.
7-6: Geraldo Guzman, P.

GAMES BY POSITION

Catcher: Damian Miller 97, Kelly Stinnett 74, Rod Barajas 5.
First base: Greg Colbrunn 99, Erubiel Durazo 60, Travis Lee 23, Alex Cabrera 15, Damian Miller 2, Andy Fox 1.
Second base: Jay Bell 145, Craig Counsell 25, Hanley Frias 15.
Third base: Matt Williams 94, Danny Klassen 25, Craig Counsell 23, Lenny Harris 20, Andy Fox 20, Hanley Frias 7, Greg Colbrunn 1.
Shortstop: Tony Womack 143, Hanley Frias 21, Craig Counsell 6, Danny Klassen 3.
Outfield: Luis Gonzalez 162, Steve Finley 148, Danny Bautista 82, Travis Lee 55, Jason Conti 35, Bernard Gilkey 17, Turner Ward 15, David Dellucci 12, Alex Cabrera 12, Andy Fox 6, Lenny Harris 3, Tony Womack 2, Rob Ryan 2, Matt Mieske 1.
Designated hitter: Steve Finley 2, Greg Colbrunn 2, Jay Bell 1, Matt Williams 1, Rob Ryan 1.

STREAKS

Wins: 9 (May 4-13)
Losses: 6 (September 16-21)
Consecutive games with at least one hit: 24, Tony Womack (May 2-29)
Wins by pitcher: 7, Randy Johnson (April 4-May 5)

ATTENDANCE

Home: 2,942,517
Road: 2,379,767
Highest (home): 47,404 (August 19 vs. Chicago).
Highest (road): 60,021 (April 10 vs. San Diego).
Lowest (home): 28,774 (April 6 vs. Philadelphia).
Lowest (road): 6,029 (August 29 vs. Montreal).

ATLANTA BRAVES

DAY BY DAY

Date	Opp.	Res.	Score	(inn.*)	Hits	Opp. hits	Winning pitcher	Losing pitcher	Save	Record	Pos.	GB
4-3	Col.	W	2-0		7	6	Maddux	Astacio	Remlinger	1-0	T1st	...
4-4	Col.	L	3-5		6	11	Tavarez	Burkett	Jimenez	1-1	T2nd	0.5
4-5	Col.	W	9-6		12	9	Chen	Aybar	Ligtenberg	2-1	1st	+0.5
4-7	S.F	L	2-6		10	8	Gardner	Mulholland		2-2	T2nd	0.5
4-8	S.F	W	7-5		11	10	Maddux	Hernandez	Ligtenberg	3-2	1st	+0.5
4-9	S.F	W	9-3		12	7	Glavine	Ortiz		4-2	1st	+0.5
4-10	At Chi.	L	3-4		7	10	Guthrie	Ligtenberg		4-3	T1st	...
4-12	At Chi.	L	4-11		6	12	Farnsworth	Mulholland		4-4	T3rd	0.5
4-13	At Chi.	L	2-3		8	7	Guthrie	Remlinger		4-5	T3rd	0.5
4-14	At Mil.	W	6-3		14	7	Glavine	Woodard	Remlinger	5-5	3rd	0.5
4-15	At Mil.	L	3-6		5	9	Weathers	Burkett	Wickman	5-6	3rd	1.0
4-16	At Mil.	W	2-1		6	8	Mulholland	Stull	Remlinger	6-6	T2nd	0.5
4-18	Phi.	W	4-3	(12)	9	9	Rivera	Reyes		7-6	T2nd	1.0
4-19	Phi.	W	10-1		12	4	Glavine	Wolf		8-6	T1st	...
4-20	Phi.	W	6-4		8	8	Millwood	Aldred	Rocker	9-6	1st	...
4-21	Pit.	W	6-2		12	8	Mulholland	Garcia		10-6	1st	+1.0
4-22	Pit.	W	4-2		9	9	Chen	Benson	Rocker	11-6	1st	+0.5
4-23	Pit.	W	5-3		7	7	Maddux	Cordova	Rocker	12-6	1st	+0.5
4-25	L.A.	W	1-0		6	3	Glavine	Brown		13-6	1st	...
4-26	L.A.	W	5-1		9	5	Millwood	Gagne		14-6	1st	+1.0
4-27	L.A.	W	6-3		9	9	Mulholland	Park	Rocker	15-6	1st	+2.0
4-28	At S.D.	W	7-2		7	8	Maddux	Meadows	Remlinger	16-6	1st	+2.5
4-29	At S.D.	W	7-4	(12)	10	10	Chen	Palacios	Rocker	17-6	1st	+3.0
4-30	At S.D.	W	7-4		8	6	Glavine	Hitchcock		18-6	1st	+3.0
5-1	At L.A.	W	2-1		6	6	Millwood	Gagne	Rocker	19-6	1st	+4.0
5-2	At L.A.	W	5-3		6	11	Chen	Adams	Rocker	20-6	1st	+5.0
5-3	At L.A.	L	4-6		6	9	Perez	Maddux	Shaw	20-7	1st	+5.0
5-5	Phi.	W	6-5		9	9	Seanez	Gomes		21-7	1st	+5.5
5-6	Phi.	L	0-6		11	13	Schilling	Millwood		21-8	1st	+4.5
5-7	Phi.	L	4-7		11	14	Ashby	Mulholland	Gomes	21-9	1st	+4.5
5-8	At Fla.	L	2-3		7	9	Miceli	Seanez		21-10	1st	+4.0
5-9	At Fla.	W	10-5		12	9	Burkett	Penny		22-10	1st	+4.0
5-10	At Fla.	L	3-5		10	9	Sanchez	Glavine	Alfonseca	22-11	1st	+4.0
5-11	At Fla.	L	4-5		12	8	Grilli	Millwood	Alfonseca	22-12	1st	+4.0
5-12	At Phi.	W	8-7		12	9	Ligtenberg	Gomes	Rocker	23-12	1st	+4.0
5-13	At Phi.	W	3-2	(10)	8	6	Seanez	Aldred	Rocker	24-12	1st	+4.0
5-14	At Phi.	W	11-2		16	8	Burkett	Byrd		25-12	1st	+5.0
5-16	S.F	W	9-7		15	14	Glavine	Ortiz	Mulholland	26-12	1st	+5.0
5-17	S.F	W	5-4		12	7	Millwood	Rueter	Seanez	27-12	1st	+5.0
5-18	S.F	W	3-2		10	7	Maddux	Estes	Rocker	28-12	1st	+6.0
5-19	S.D.	L	7-11		15	12	Whiteside	Mulholland	Hoffman	28-13	1st	+5.0
5-20	S.D.	W	10-6		10	13	Burkett	Cunnane		29-13	1st	+5.0
5-21	S.D.	W	12-6		16	11	Glavine	Hitchcock		30-13	1st	+5.0
5-23	At Mil.	L	6-7		5	7	Wright	Millwood	Wickman	30-14	1st	+4.0
5-24	At Mil.	W	11-2		17	5	Maddux	Haynes		31-14	1st	+5.0
5-25	At Mil.	W	7-3		12	6	Mulholland	D'Amico		32-14	1st	+6.0
5-26	At Hou.	L	4-5	(10)	11	10	Henry	Seanez		32-15	1st	+6.0
5-27	At Hou.	W	6-5		9	10	Burkett	Reynolds	Ligtenberg	33-15	1st	+6.5
5-28	At Hou.	L	3-4		8	5	Valdes	Seanez	Wagner	33-16	1st	+5.5
5-29	At Chi.	W	1-0		2	6	Maddux	Lieber		34-16	1st	+6.5
5-30	At Chi.	W	5-2		9	9	Mulholland	Quevedo	Remlinger	35-16	1st	+6.5
6-1	At Chi.	L	3-5		6	9	Tapani	Glavine	Aguilera	35-17	1st	+6.5
6-2	N.Y. (AL)	L	2-5		5	10	Hernandez	Millwood	Rivera	35-18	1st	+5.5
6-3	N.Y. (AL)	W	11-7		11	13	Remlinger	Grimsley		36-18	1st	+5.5
6-4	N.Y. (AL)	L	6-7		12	16	Pettitte	Mulholland	Rivera	36-19	1st	+5.0
6-5	Tor.	L	3-9		9	12	Wells	Burkett		36-20	1st	+4.0
6-6	Tor.	W	7-6		11	10	Remlinger	Frascatore		37-20	1st	+5.0
6-7	Tor.	L	8-12		16	9	Cubillan	Millwood	Koch	37-21	1st	+5.0
6-9	Bos.	W	6-4		9	8	Maddux	Fassero	Seanez	38-21	1st	+4.5
6-10	Bos.	W	6-0		9	5	Mulholland	Schourek		39-21	1st	+5.5
6-11	Bos.	L	3-5		7	8	Garces	Seanez	Lowe	39-22	1st	+5.0
6-12	At Pit.	W	10-8		13	9	Ligtenberg	Christiansen	Remlinger	40-22	1st	+5.5
6-13	At Pit.	L	6-7	(10)	14	10	Silva	Wengert		40-23	1st	+5.5
6-14	At Pit.	W	8-4		7	9	Maddux	Anderson	Ligtenberg	41-23	1st	+5.5
6-15	At Pit.	L	0-2		6	7	Benson	Millwood		41-24	1st	+5.0
6-16	At Phi.	L	1-2		5	4	Schilling	Glavine	Brantley	41-25	1st	+4.0
6-17	At Phi.	L	3-9		7	16	Politte	Mulholland		41-26	1st	+4.0
6-18	At Phi.	W	5-3		8	6	Burkett	Schrenk	Rocker	42-26	1st	+4.0
6-19	At Phi.	L	2-5		5	8	Brock	Remlinger	Brantley	42-27	1st	+3.5
6-20	Chi.	W	11-4		14	9	Millwood	Tapani		43-27	1st	+4.5
6-21	Chi.	L	1-8		5	11	Wood	Glavine		43-28	1st	+4.5
6-22	Chi.	W	6-4		11	14	Mulholland	Downs	Remlinger	44-28	1st	+4.5
6-23	Mil.	W	3-2		6	7	Marquis	Weathers	Rocker	45-28	1st	+4.5
6-24	Mil.	L	1-2		5	6	Wright	Maddux	Wickman	45-29	1st	+3.5
6-25	Mil.	W	5-4		4	8	Rocker	Leskanic		46-29	1st	+3.5
6-27	At Mon.	L	4-6		5	9	Armas	Glavine	Kline	46-30	1st	+2.0
6-28	At Mon.	W	7-4		10	12	Mulholland	Hermanson	Ligtenberg	47-30	1st	+2.0
6-29	At N.Y.	W	6-4		11	7	Burkett	Reed	Ligtenberg	48-30	1st	+3.0
6-30	At N.Y.	L	8-11		11	12	Benitez	Mulholland		48-31	1st	+2.0

HIGHLIGHTS

High point: The Braves defeated the Mets 7-1 on September 26 at Shea Stadium to clinch their ninth straight division title. They didn't even know they had secured the title until the next day when they were informed of a tie-breaker advantage over the Mets.

Low point: After blowing a two-run lead in the seventh inning of an August 29 loss to Cincinnati, the Braves were locked in a first-place tie with the Mets. The loss was their season-high fourth straight.

Turning point: On September 18, the Braves opened a pivotal series against the second-place Mets in Atlanta with a 6-3 win, upping their division lead to four games with 12 remaining.

Most valuable player: Rafael Furcal. The rookie shortstop made the jump from Class A to the majors look easy, hitting .294 and stealing 40 bases. Furcal took over the leadoff job in July and ignited the offense, compiling a .382 on-base percentage while leading N.L. rookies in runs (87) and walks (73).

Most valuable pitcher: Tom Glavine. In addition to recording his 200th victory, he reached 20 wins for the fifth time and pitched a career-high 241 innings. He was clearly the club's clutch pitcher, going 10-2 following Atlanta losses.

Most improved player: Andruw Jones. In his fourth full season, Jones blossomed into a legitimate slugger, reaching career-highs in average (.303), home runs (36), RBIs (103), runs (122) and hits (199). He became just the second Braves player (joining Hank Aaron) to post three straight 20-20 seasons and the fifth-fastest player in history to reach 100 home runs.

Most pleasant surprise: Andres Galarraga. After missing all of the 1999 season while recovering from cancer, Galarraga made a remarkable comeback at age 39, hitting .302 and driving in 100 runs.

Key injuries: The Braves were devastated by the March loss of John Smoltz to Tommy John surgery, which eventually forced the club to trade for Andy Ashby. ... Backup catcher Eddie Perez was diagnosed with a torn rotator cuff in May and missed the remainder of the season. ... Second baseman Quilvio Veras suffered a torn ACL in July. ... The bullpen was depleted by the losses of relievers Greg McMichael (shoulder surgery) and Rudy Seanez (elbow surgery).

Notable: The Braves became only the third team in major league history to post 90-plus wins in nine straight full seasons. ... Greg Maddux hurled 391/3 consecutive scoreless innings, the third-longest streak in the majors since Orel Hershiser set the record with 59 shutout innings in 1988. ... Chipper Jones became only the second third baseman in major league history to post five straight 100-RBI seasons.

—BILL ZACK

MISCELLANEOUS

RECORDS

2000 regular-season record: 95-67 (1st in N.L. East); 51-30 at home; 44-37 on road; 38-31 vs. East; 25-23 vs. Central; 32-13 vs. West; 21-14 vs. lefthanded starters; 74-53 vs. righthanded starters; 82-57 on grass; 13-10 on turf; 30-20 in daytime; 65-47 at night; 18-18 in one-run games; 3-5 in extra-inning games; 0-0-1 in doubleheaders.

Team record past five years: 501-309 (.619, ranks 1st in league in that span).

TEAM LEADERS

Batting average: Chipper Jones (.311).
At-bats: Andruw Jones (656).
Runs: Andruw Jones (122).
Hits: Andruw Jones (199).
Total Bases: Andruw Jones (355).
Doubles: Chipper Jones (38).
Triples: Andruw Jones (6).
Home runs: Andruw Jones, Chipper Jones (36).
Runs batted in: Chipper Jones (111).
Stolen bases: Rafael Furcal (40).
Slugging percentage: Chipper Jones (.566).
On-base percentage: Chipper Jones (.404).
Wins: Tom Glavine (21).
Earned-run average: Greg Maddux (3.00).
Complete games: Greg Maddux (6).
Shutouts: Greg Maddux (3).
Saves: John Rocker (24).
Innings pitched: Greg Maddux (249.1).
Strikeouts: Greg Maddux (190).

Date	Opp.	Res.	Score	(inn.*)	Hits	Opp. hits	Winning pitcher	Losing pitcher	Save	Record	Pos.	GB
7-1	At N.Y.	L	1-9		6	11	Leiter	Maddux		48-32	1st	+1.0
7-2	At N.Y.	W	10-2		17	5	Glavine	Rusch		49-32	1st	+2.0
7-3	Mon.	L	1-17		6	18	Armas	Mulholland		49-33	1st	+2.0
7-4	Mon.	W	7-3		10	7	Maddux	Hermanson		50-33	1st	+3.0
7-5	Mon.	L	5-6		10	13	Vazquez	Millwood	Kline	50-34	1st	+2.0
7-6	Mon.	L	2-4		6	14	Johnson	Burkett	Kline	50-35	1st	+1.5
7-7	At Bos.	W	5-3		11	7	Glavine	Schourek	Ligtenberg	51-35	1st	+2.5
7-8	At Bos.	W	5-1		10	7	Mulholland	R. Martinez		52-35	1st	+4.0
7-9	At Bos.	L	2-7		6	14	Wakefield	Millwood		52-36	1st	+3.0
7-13	At Bal.	W	6-3		6	8	Maddux	Mussina	Kamieniecki	53-36	1st	+4.0
7-14	At Bal.	W	4-1		10	7	Ashby	Ponson		54-36	1st	+4.0
7-15	At Bal.	W	7-3		11	8	Glavine	Erickson		55-36	1st	+5.0
7-16	At T.B.	W	6-4		8	5	Kamieniecki	Mecir		56-36	1st	+6.0
7-17	At T.B.	L	6-8		10	12	Rupe	Mulholland	Hernandez	56-37	1st	+5.0
7-18	At T.B.	W	8-2		10	7	Maddux	Rekar		57-37	1st	+5.0
7-20†	At Fla.	W	5-3		9	10	Glavine	Dempster	Ligtenberg	58-37		
7-20‡	At Fla.	L	1-6		3	8	Burnett	Kamieniecki		58-38	1st	+5.0
7-21	N.Y.	W	6-3		7	7	Burkett	Leiter	Remlinger	59-38	1st	+6.0
7-22	N.Y.	L	0-4		4	5	Reed	Maddux		59-39	1st	+5.0
7-23	N.Y.	W	1-0		7	4	Ashby	B.J. Jones		60-39	1st	+6.0
7-25	Fla.	W	6-5		6	15	Glavine	Dempster	Ligtenberg	61-39	1st	+6.0
7-26	Fla.	W	6-3		10	9	Millwood	Burnett	Rocker	62-39	1st	+6.5
7-27	Fla.	L	4-12		8	15	Smith	Maddux		62-40	1st	+5.0
7-28	Hou.	W	5-2		8	7	Ashby	Miller	Rocker	63-40	1st	+5.0
7-29	Hou.	W	13-5		14	12	Burkett	Reynolds		64-40	1st	+5.0
7-30	Hou.	W	6-3		10	8	Glavine	Holt	Remlinger	65-40	1st	+5.0
8-1	At Ari.	W	4-2		8	2	Millwood	Swindell	Remlinger	66-40	1st	+5.5
8-2	At Ari.	L	0-2		6	6	Schilling	Maddux		66-41	1st	+4.5
8-3	At Ari.	L	4-8		10	11	Anderson	Ashby		66-42	1st	+4.0
8-4	At StL.	W	6-4		10	10	Glavine	An. Benes	Kamieniecki	67-42	1st	+4.0
8-5	At StL.	L	0-5		5	8	Stephenson	Burkett		67-43	1st	+3.0
8-6	At StL.	W	6-4		10	9	Remlinger	Kile	Ligtenberg	68-43	1st	+4.0
8-7	At Cin.	L	2-3	(10)	12	11	Sullivan	Ligtenberg		68-44	1st	+3.0
8-8	At Cin.	W	5-4		11	9	Ashby	Dessens	Remlinger	69-44	1st	+4.0
8-9	At Cin.	L	6-10		9	12	Harnisch	Glavine		69-45	1st	+3.0
8-11	L.A.	W	7-2		12	5	Remlinger	Adams		70-45	1st	+2.5
8-12	L.A.	W	4-1		6	7	Maddux	Valdes	Ligtenberg	71-45	1st	+2.5
8-13	L.A.	L	2-7		14	11	Dreifort	Ashby		71-46	1st	+1.5
8-14	S.D.	W	9-2		14	6	Glavine	Witasick		72-46	1st	+2.5
8-15	S.D.	W	3-1		7	7	Remlinger	Williams	Rocker	73-46	1st	+2.0
8-16	S.D.	W	4-1		5	5	Kamieniecki	Walker	Rocker	74-46	1st	+3.0
8-18	At S.F	L	0-2		4	7	Hernandez	Maddux		74-47	1st	+1.5
8-19	At S.F	L	3-12		8	12	Ortiz	Ashby		74-48	1st	+1.5
8-20	At S.F	W	8-5		15	4	Glavine	Rueter		75-48	1st	+1.5
8-21	At Col.	W	7-4		13	10	Millwood	Bohanon	Rocker	76-48	1st	+2.5
8-22	At Col.	L	6-7	(12)	14	16	Mayne	Rocker		76-49	1st	+2.5
8-23	At Col.	W	5-2		10	8	Maddux	Rose	Remlinger	77-49	1st	+2.5
8-24	StL.	L	5-12		9	13	Hentgen	Ashby		77-50	1st	+2.0
8-25	StL.	W	7-4		9	8	Glavine	Timlin	Ligtenberg	78-50	1st	+2.0
8-26	StL.	L	3-6		10	10	Stephenson	Millwood		78-51	1st	+2.0
8-27	StL.	L	2-7		8	9	Kile	Ligtenberg		78-52	1st	+1.0
8-28	Cin.	L	3-6		5	11	Villone	Maddux		78-53	T1st	...
8-29	Cin.	L	2-4		9	11	Parris	Remlinger	Graves	78-54	T1st	...
8-30	Cin.	W	5-2		14	3	Glavine	Dessens		79-54	T1st	...
8-31	Cin.	L	3-4		4	8	Riedling	Millwood	Graves	79-55	2nd	0.5
9-1	At Hou.	L	2-3		7	6	Lima	Burkett	Dotel	79-56	2nd	0.5
9-2	At Hou.	W	8-6		10	10	Maddux	Elarton	Rocker	80-56	1st	+0.5
9-3	At Hou.	L	3-9		11	15	Miller	Ashby		80-57	1st	+0.5
9-5	Ari.	W	5-2		6	7	Glavine	Johnson	Rocker	81-57	1st	+1.0
9-6	Ari.	W	7-1		7	6	Millwood	Reynoso		82-57	1st	+2.0
9-7	Ari.	W	4-0		12	4	Maddux	Schilling		83-57	1st	+2.5
9-8	Mon.	W	3-2		9	10	Ashby	Moore	Rocker	84-57	1st	+3.5
9-9	Mon.	L	5-7	(12)	15	14	Santana	Seelbach		84-58	1st	+3.5
9-10	Mon.	L	0-4		6	7	Vazquez	Glavine		84-59	1st	+2.5
9-12	Fla.	L	4-5		12	11	Sanchez	Millwood	Alfonseca	84-60	1st	+2.0
9-13	Fla.	W	4-0		8	4	Maddux	Dempster		85-60	1st	+2.0
9-14	Fla.	W	5-3		10	8	Ashby	Cornelius	Rocker	86-60	1st	+2.0
9-15	At Ari.	L	1-2		7	8	Johnson	Glavine	Mantei	86-61	1st	+2.0
9-16	At Ari.	W	12-10		14	14	Burkett	Stottlemyre	Rocker	87-61	1st	+2.0
9-17	At Ari.	W	7-1		16	4	Millwood	Schilling		88-61	1st	+3.0
9-18	N.Y.	W	6-3		7	9	Maddux	Hampton	Rocker	89-61	1st	+4.0
9-19	N.Y.	W	12-4		13	7	Ashby	Rusch		90-61	1st	+5.0
9-20	N.Y.	L	3-6		6	9	Leiter	Glavine	Benitez	90-62	1st	+4.0
9-22	At Mon.	L	4-6		6	9	Armas	Millwood	Strickland	90-63	1st	+3.5
9-23	At Mon.	W	10-0		9	5	Maddux	Lira		91-63	1st	+3.5
9-24	At Mon.	W	14-5		21	10	Ashby	Thurman		92-63	1st	+3.5
9-25	At Mon.	W	6-0		12	8	Glavine	Vazquez		93-63	1st	+4.0
9-26	At N.Y.	W	7-1		9	7	Burkett	Leiter		94-63	1st	+5.0
9-27	At N.Y.	L	2-6		6	9	Reed	Millwood		94-64	1st	+4.0
9-28	At N.Y.	L	2-8		7	10	B.J. Jones	Maddux		94-65	1st	+3.0
9-29	Col.	L	2-4		6	6	Bohanon	Ashby	Jimenez	94-66	1st	+2.0
9-30	Col.	W	5-2		8	6	Glavine	Rose	Rocker	95-66	1st	+2.0
10-1	Col.	L	5-10		7	17	Tavarez	Rocker		95-67	1st	+1.0

Monthly records: April (18-6), May (17-10), June (13-15), July (17-9), August (14-15), September (16-11), October (0-1).
*Innings, if other than nine. † First game of a doubleheader. ‡ Second game of a doubleheader.

MEMORABLE GAMES

May 2 at Los Angeles

Andruw Jones delivered a two-run single in the eighth to lift the Braves to their 15th straight win, a 5-3 victory over the Dodgers at Los Angeles. The streak, the longest in the major leagues since the Twins won 15 straight in 1991, ended the next day when Carlos Perez bested Greg Maddux 6-4—the first loss of the season by one of the Braves' top three starters.

Atlanta	AB	R	H	BI	Los Angeles	AB	R	H	BI
Furcal, ss	2	0	0	0	White, cf	3	0	0	0
Veras, 2b	3	0	0	0	Santangelo, ph	1	0	0	0
C.Jones, 3b	5	0	0	0	Grudzielanek, 2b	4	0	2	0
Joyner, 1b	3	1	1	1	Green, rf	3	0	2	1
B.Jordan, pr-rf	1	1	1	0	Sheffield, lf	5	0	1	0
Bonilla, lf	1	1	1	0	Berroa, 1b	3	0	0	0
Weiss, pr	0	1	0	0	Hansen, 1b	1	0	0	0
Remlinger, p	0	0	0	0	Beltre, 3b	4	2	3	0
Glavine, ph	1	0	0	0	Hundley, c	4	0	2	1
Rocker, p	0	0	0	0	Elster, ss	4	0	0	1
A.Jones, cf	4	0	1	2	Mills, p	0	0	0	0
Lopez, c	4	1	2	1	Park, p	3	1	1	0
Hubbard, rf-lf	2	0	0	0	Adams, p	0	0	0	0
Mulholland, p	2	0	0	0	Fetters, p	0	0	0	0
Lockhart, ph	1	0	0	0	J.Vizcaino, ss	0	0	0	0
Chen, p	0	0	0	0					
Galarraga, ph-1b	1	0	0	0					
Totals	**30**	**5**	**6**	**4**	**Totals**	**35**	**3**	**11**	**3**

Atlanta ....0 0 0 1 0 1 0 3 0—5 6 1
Los Angeles ....0 1 0 0 1 1 0 0 0—3 11 2

E—Furcal (3), Hansen (1), Park (1). DP—Atlanta 4, Los Angeles 2. LOB—Atlanta 9, Los Angeles 10. 2B—Lopez (3), Jordan (3), Beltre (7), Hundley 2 (4), Park (2). HR—Joyner (1). SB—Furcal (6). SH—Hubbard.

Atlanta	IP	H	R	ER	BB	SO
Mulholland	6	10	3	3	1	2
Chen (W 4-0)	1	0	0	0	2	1
Remlinger	1	0	0	0	0	1
Rocker (S 7)	1	1	0	0	2	0

Los Angeles	IP	H	R	ER	BB	SO
Park	6.2	3	2	2	7	5
Adams (L 2-2)	0.1	2	3	2	2	0
Fetters	1	0	0	0	0	0
Mills	1	1	0	0	1	0

Adams pitched to 6 batters in 8th.

WP—Rocker, Adams. PB—Hundley. U—HP, Meals, 1B, Young. 2B, Higgins. 3B, Katzenmeier. T—3:11. A—30,246.

May 8 at Florida

John Rocker dropped the ball while standing on the rubber in the bottom of the ninth inning and was charged with a balk, allowing the Marlins to pull out a 3-2 victory. With former Brave Danny Bautista on third with two out, the ball slipped from Rocker's hand and it took the stunned umpires several moments to make the call and allow Bautista to trot home. It was the first game-ending balk in the National League since 1993.

Atlanta	AB	R	H	BI	Florida	AB	R	H	BI
Veras, 2b	2	1	1	0	Castillo, 2b	5	0	0	0
A.Jones, cf	3	0	1	0	Kotsay, rf	4	1	1	0
C.Jones, 3b	3	0	1	0	Smith, ph	0	0	0	0
Galarraga, 1b	3	0	1	0	Floyd, lf	3	1	1	0
Jordan, rf	4	0	0	0	Wilson, cf	4	0	1	0
Bonilla, lf	3	0	0	0	Lowell, 3b	4	0	0	1
Furcal, ss	2	1	1	0	Lee, 1b	4	0	0	0
Lunar, c	3	0	0	0	Gonzalez, ss	4	0	2	0
Lopez, c	1	0	0	0	Bako, c	4	0	3	0
Maddux, p	2	0	1	1	Bautista, pr	0	1	0	0
Hubbard, ph	1	0	1	0	Nunez, p	1	0	0	0
Remlinger, p	0	0	0	0	Brown, ph	1	0	1	0
Joyner, ph	1	0	0	0	Almanza, p	0	0	0	0
Seanez, p	0	0	0	0	Miceli, p	0	0	0	0
Rocker, p	0	0	0	0	Berg, ph	1	0	0	0
Totals	**28**	**2**	**7**	**1**	**Totals**	**35**	**3**	**9**	**1**

Atlanta ....0 0 0 0 1 1 0 0 0—2 7 3
Florida ....2 0 0 0 0 0 0 0 1—3 9 0

E—Galarraga (3), C. Jones (5), Furcal (5). DP—Florida 2. LOB—Atlanta 7, Florida 9. 2B—Brown (5). SB—A. Jones (4), Kotsay (5), Wilson (4). CS—Furcal (2), Maddux (1), Floyd (1). SH—Veras, Nunez.

Atlanta	IP	H	R	ER	BB	SO
Maddux	7	8	2	0	1	10
Remlinger	1	0	0	0	0	1
Seanez (L 1-1)	0.2	1	1	0	0	0
Rocker	0	0	0	0	1	0

Florida	IP	H	R	ER	BB	SO
Nunez	6	4	2	2	5	5
Almanza	1.2	2	0	0	1	2
Miceli (W 3-1)	1.1	1	0	0	1	0

Rocker pitched to 3 batters in 9th.

WP—Nunez. BK—Rocker. U—HP, Everett, 1B, Crawford. 2B, DiMuro. 3B, Gorman. T—3:09. A—14,024.

INDIVIDUAL STATISTICS

BATTING

Name	G	TPA	AB	R	H	TB	2B	3B	HR	RBI	Avg.	Obp.	Slg.	SH	SF	HP	BB	IBB	SO	SB	CS	GDP	vs RHP AB	vs RHP Avg.	vs RHP HR	vs RHP RBI	vs LHP AB	vs LHP Avg.	vs LHP HR	vs LHP RBI
Jones, Andruw	161	729	656	122	199	355	36	6	36	104	.303	.366	.541	0	5	9	59	0	100	21	6	12	522	.301	32	91	134	.313	4	13
Jones, Chipper	156	686	579	118	180	328	38	1	36	111	.311	.404	.566	0	10	2	95	10	64	14	7	14	449	.281	24	78	130	.415	12	33
Galarraga, Andres	141	548	494	67	149	260	25	1	28	100	.302	.369	.526	0	1	17	36	5	126	3	5	15	376	.287	25	82	118	.347	3	18
Jordan, Brian	133	537	489	71	129	206	26	0	17	77	.264	.320	.421	0	5	5	38	1	80	10	2	12	377	.223	12	50	112	.402	5	27
Lopez, Javy	134	525	481	60	138	233	21	1	24	89	.287	.337	.484	0	5	4	35	3	80	0	0	20	380	.289	19	67	101	.277	5	22
Furcal, Rafael	131	542	455	87	134	174	20	4	4	37	.295	.394	.382	9	2	3	73	0	80	40	14	2	359	.306	4	32	96	.250	0	5
Sanders, Reggie	103	377	340	43	79	137	23	1	11	37	.232	.302	.403	3	0	2	32	2	78	21	4	9	268	.224	9	24	72	.264	2	13
Veras, Quilvio	84	364	298	56	92	122	15	0	5	37	.309	.413	.409	6	4	5	51	0	50	25	12	8	222	.293	2	21	76	.355	3	16
Lockhart, Keith	113	313	275	32	73	97	12	3	2	32	.265	.331	.353	5	4	0	29	7	31	4	1	10	243	.251	2	27	32	.375	0	5
Bonilla, Bobby	114	278	239	23	61	95	13	3	5	28	.255	.356	.397	0	1	1	37	2	51	0	0	3	196	.230	4	20	43	.372	1	8
Joyner, Wally	119	260	224	24	63	90	12	0	5	32	.281	.365	.402	0	4	1	31	3	31	0	0	2	209	.282	5	29	15	.267	0	3
Weiss, Walt	80	227	192	29	50	60	6	2	0	18	.260	.353	.313	3	3	3	26	1	32	1	1	2	125	.240	0	8	67	.299	0	10
Surhoff, B.J.	44	143	128	13	37	53	9	2	1	11	.289	.352	.414	1	1	1	12	0	12	3	0	5	118	.288	1	9	10	.300	0	2
Hubbard, Trenidad	61	96	81	15	15	22	2	1	1	6	.185	.290	.272	3	0	1	11	0	20	2	1	1	50	.140	1	3	31	.258	0	3
Maddux, Greg	35	90	80	2	15	19	2	1	0	5	.188	.217	.238	7	0	1	2	0	19	0	1	1	61	.246	0	5	19	.000	0	0
Glavine, Tom	37	89	68	5	10	11	1	0	0	2	.147	.227	.162	14	0	0	7	0	20	0	0	0	50	.140	0	1	18	.167	0	1
Millwood, Kevin	36	75	59	1	7	9	2	0	0	2	.119	.148	.153	14	0	0	2	0	30	0	0	3	50	.100	0	2	9	.222	0	0
Bako, Paul	24	63	58	8	11	21	4	0	2	6	.190	.254	.362	0	0	0	5	3	15	0	0	2	47	.191	1	5	11	.182	1	1
Lunar, Fernando	22	60	54	5	10	11	1	0	0	5	.185	.267	.204	0	0	3	3	1	15	0	2	2	37	.054	0	1	17	.471	0	4
Burkett, John	31	51	42	2	6	7	1	0	0	3	.143	.200	.167	6	0	0	3	0	15	0	0	0	37	.135	0	2	5	.200	0	1
Lombard, George	27	41	39	8	4	4	0	0	0	2	.103	.146	.103	0	0	1	1	0	14	4	0	2	34	.118	0	1	5	.000	0	1
Mulholland, Terry	54	45	36	3	9	12	3	0	0	4	.250	.250	.333	9	0	0	0	0	16	0	0	0	25	.240	0	3	11	.273	0	1
Ashby, Andy	16	37	33	2	4	4	0	0	0	1	.121	.121	.121	4	0	0	0	0	12	0	0	1	21	.143	0	1	12	.083	0	0
Sisco, Steve	25	30	27	4	5	8	0	0	1	2	.185	.267	.296	0	0	0	3	0	4	0	0	1	16	.125	0	0	11	.273	1	2
Perez, Eddie	7	22	22	0	4	5	1	0	0	3	.182	.182	.227	0	0	0	0	0	2	0	0	0	17	.235	0	3	5	.000	0	0
DeRosa, Mark	22	15	13	9	4	5	1	0	0	3	.308	.400	.385	0	0	0	2	0	1	0	0	0	7	.286	0	0	6	.333	0	3
Helms, Wes	6	5	5	0	1	1	0	0	0	0	.200	.200	.200	0	0	0	0	0	2	0	0	0	5	.200	0	0	0	.000	0	0
Unroe, Tim	4	7	5	0	0	0	0	0	0	0	.000	.167	.000	1	0	0	1	0	2	0	0	0	4	.000	0	0	1	.000	0	0
Chen, Bruce	22	7	5	0	0	0	0	0	0	0	.000	.000	.000	2	0	0	0	0	3	0	0	0	2	.000	0	0	3	.000	0	0
Remlinger, Mike	71	4	3	0	0	0	0	0	0	0	.000	.250	.000	0	0	0	1	0	2	0	0	0	2	.000	0	0	1	.000	0	0
Hunter, Brian	2	2	2	1	1	4	0	0	1	1	.500	.500	2.000	0	0	0	0	0	0	0	0	0	1	1.000	1	1	1	.000	0	0
Marquis, Jason	15	2	2	0	0	0	0	0	0	0	.000	.000	.000	0	0	0	0	0	0	0	0	0	2	.000	0	0	0	.000	0	0
Swann, Pedro	4	2	2	0	0	0	0	0	0	0	.000	.000	.000	0	0	0	0	0	2	0	0	0	2	.000	0	0	0	.000	0	0
Stevens, Dave	2	1	1	0	0	0	0	0	0	0	.000	.000	.000	0	0	0	0	0	0	0	0	0	1	.000	0	0	0	.000	0	0
Hubbard, Mike	2	1	1	0	0	0	0	0	0	0	.000	.000	.000	0	0	0	0	0	1	0	0	0	1	.000	0	0	0	.000	0	0
Villegas, Ismael	1	1	1	0	0	0	0	0	0	0	.000	.000	.000	0	0	0	0	0	0	0	0	0	1	.000	0	0	0	.000	0	0
Seanez, Rudy	23	0	0	0	0	0	0	0	0	0	.000	.000	.000	0	0	0	0	0	0	0	0	0	0	.000	0	0	0	.000	0	0
Belinda, Stan	10	0	0	0	0	0	0	0	0	0	.000	.000	.000	0	0	0	0	0	0	0	0	0	0	.000	0	0	0	.000	0	0
Kamieniecki, Scott	26	0	0	0	0	0	0	0	0	0	.000	.000	.000	0	0	0	0	0	0	0	0	0	0	.000	0	0	0	.000	0	0
McMichael, Greg	15	0	0	0	0	0	0	0	0	0	.000	.000	.000	0	0	0	0	0	0	0	0	0	0	.000	0	0	0	.000	0	0
Wengert, Don	10	0	0	0	0	0	0	0	0	0	.000	.000	.000	0	0	0	0	0	0	0	0	0	0	.000	0	0	0	.000	0	0
Seelbach, Chris	2	0	0	0	0	0	0	0	0	0	.000	.000	.000	0	0	0	0	0	0	0	0	0	0	.000	0	0	0	.000	0	0
Ligtenberg, Kerry	59	0	0	0	0	0	0	0	0	0	.000	.000	.000	0	0	0	0	0	0	0	0	0	0	.000	0	0	0	.000	0	0
Rocker, John	59	0	0	0	0	0	0	0	0	0	.000	.000	.000	0	0	0	0	0	0	0	0	0	0	.000	0	0	0	.000	0	0
McGlinchy, Kevin	10	0	0	0	0	0	0	0	0	0	.000	.000	.000	0	0	0	0	0	0	0	0	0	0	.000	0	0	0	.000	0	0
Molina, Gabe	2	0	0	0	0	0	0	0	0	0	.000	.000	.000	0	0	0	0	0	0	0	0	0	0	.000	0	0	0	.000	0	0
Rivera, Luis	5	0	0	0	0	0	0	0	0	0	.000	.000	.000	0	0	0	0	0	0	0	0	0	0	.000	0	0	0	.000	0	0

Players with more than one N.L. team

Name	G	TPA	AB	R	H	TB	2B	3B	HR	RBI	Avg.	Obp.	Slg.	SH	SF	HP	BB	IBB	SO	SB	CS	GDP	vs RHP AB	vs RHP Avg.	vs RHP HR	vs RHP RBI	vs LHP AB	vs LHP Avg.	vs LHP HR	vs LHP RBI
Ashby, Phi.-Atl.	32	72	61	2	9	9	0	0	0	6	.148	.175	.148	9	0	0	2	0	22	0	0	1	45	.156	0	4	16	.125	0	2
Bako, Hou.	1	2	2	0	0	0	0	0	0	0	.000	.000	.000	0	0	0	0	0	1	0	0	0	47	.191	1	5	11	.182	1	1
Bako, Fla.	56	186	161	10	39	47	6	1	0	14	.242	.335	.292	1	1	1	22	7	48	0	0	4	47	.191	1	5	11	.182	1	1
Bako, Hou.-Fla.-Atl.	81	251	221	18	50	68	10	1	2	20	.226	.312	.308	1	1	1	27	10	64	0	0	6	194	.237	1	19	27	.148	1	1
Belinda, Col.-Atl.	57	1	1	0	0	0	0	0	0	0	.000	.000	.000	0	0	0	0	0	1	0	0	0	1	.000	0	0	0	.000	0	0
Chen, Atl.-Phi.	37	38	30	0	1	1	0	0	0	1	.033	.065	.033	7	0	0	1	0	20	0	0	0	21	.048	0	0	9	.000	0	1
Hunter, Atl.-Phi.	87	160	140	14	30	59	5	0	8	23	.214	.313	.421	0	0	0	20	1	39	0	1	2	69	.217	8	19	71	.211	0	4

PITCHING

Name	W	L	Pct.	ERA	IP	H	R	ER	HR	SH	SF	HB	BB	IBB	SO	G	GS	CG	ShO	GF	Sv	vs. RH AB	vs. RH Avg.	vs. RH HR	vs. RH RBI	vs. LH AB	vs. LH Avg.	vs. LH HR	vs. LH RBI
Maddux, Greg	19	9	.679	3.00	249.1	225	91	83	19	8	5	10	42	12	190	35	35	6	3	0	0	546	.214	9	50	401	.269	10	35
Glavine, Tom	21	9	.700	3.40	241.0	222	101	91	24	9	5	4	65	6	152	35	35	4	2	0	0	719	.245	20	66	190	.242	4	18
Millwood, Kevin	10	13	.435	4.66	212.2	213	115	110	26	8	5	3	62	2	168	36	35	0	0	0	0	468	.235	15	56	357	.289	11	50
Mulholland, Terry	9	9	.500	5.11	156.2	198	96	89	24	10	5	4	41	7	78	54	20	1	0	14	1	523	.312	22	79	119	.294	2	18
Burkett, John	10	6	.625	4.89	134.1	162	79	73	13	8	5	4	51	2	110	31	22	0	0	4	0	317	.309	9	47	218	.294	4	25
Ashby, Andy	8	6	.571	4.13	98.0	103	49	45	12	7	1	1	23	4	55	15	15	2	1	0	0	192	.203	4	19	188	.340	8	28
Remlinger, Mike	5	3	.625	3.47	72.2	55	29	28	6	3	2	3	37	1	72	71	0	0	0	18	12	187	.209	5	21	79	.203	1	15
Rocker, John	1	2	.333	2.89	53.0	42	25	17	5	1	0	2	48	4	77	59	0	0	0	41	24	163	.202	3	12	37	.243	2	6
Ligtenberg, Kerry	2	3	.400	3.61	52.1	43	21	21	7	2	1	0	24	5	51	59	0	0	0	19	12	127	.236	5	19	63	.206	2	4
Chen, Bruce	4	0	1.000	2.50	39.2	35	15	11	4	3	2	1	19	2	32	22	0	0	0	4	0	112	.241	4	14	39	.205	0	2
Kamieniecki, Scott	2	1	.667	5.47	24.2	22	18	15	3	0	0	0	22	1	17	26	0	0	0	4	2	51	.255	2	7	41	.220	1	6
Marquis, Jason	1	0	1.000	5.01	23.1	23	16	13	4	1	1	1	12	1	17	15	0	0	0	7	0	57	.281	3	14	31	.226	1	5
Seanez, Rudy	2	4	.333	4.29	21.0	15	11	10	3	1	0	1	9	1	20	23	0	0	0	8	2	44	.114	1	4	34	.294	2	5
McMichael, Greg	0	0	.000	4.41	16.1	12	8	8	3	0	1	0	4	1	14	15	0	0	0	3	0	33	.152	0	0	23	.304	3	6
Belinda, Stan	0	0	.000	9.82	11.0	16	12	12	4	0	2	1	5	1	11	10	0	0	0	7	0	27	.370	2	6	19	.316	2	9
Wengert, Don	0	1	.000	7.20	10.0	12	9	8	2	0	0	0	5	0	7	10	0	0	0	6	0	32	.250	2	4	10	.400	0	5
McGlinchy, Kevin	0	0	.000	2.16	8.1	11	4	2	1	1	0	0	6	1	9	10	0	0	0	6	0	22	.364	1	6	13	.231	0	0
Rivera, Luis	1	0	1.000	1.35	6.2	4	1	1	0	2	0	0	5	1	5	5	0	0	0	3	0	12	.083	0	1	9	.333	0	1
Stevens, Dave	0	0	.000	12.00	3.0	5	4	4	2	0	0	0	1	0	4	2	0	0	0	2	0	8	.375	1	3	6	.333	1	1
Villegas, Ismael	0	0	.000	13.50	2.2	4	4	4	2	0	0	1	2	0	2	1	0	0	0	0	0	8	.375	2	6	4	.250	0	0
Molina, Gabe	0	0	.000	9.00	2.0	3	4	2	1	0	1	1	1	0	1	2	0	0	0	1	0	4	.250	1	2	4	.500	0	1
Seelbach, Chris	0	1	.000	10.80	1.2	3	2	2	0	0	1	0	0	0	1	2	0	0	0	2	0	4	.500	0	1	2	.500	0	1

PITCHERS WITH MORE THAN ONE N.L. TEAM

Name	W	L	Pct.	ERA	IP	H	R	ER	HR	SH	SF	HB	BB	IBB	SO	G	GS	CG	ShO	GF	Sv	vs. RH AB	vs. RH Avg.	vs. RH HR	vs. RH RBI	vs. LH AB	vs. LH Avg.	vs. LH HR	vs. LH RBI
Ashby, Phi.-Atl.	12	13	.480	4.92	199.1	216	124	109	29	18	10	6	61	9	106	31	31	3	1	0	0	401	.249	13	57	371	.313	16	54
Belinda, Col.-Atl.	1	3	.250	7.71	46.2	55	44	40	14	4	4	3	22	5	51	56	0	0	0	4	1	121	.322	10	32	66	.242	4	22
Chen, Atl.-Phi.	7	4	.636	3.29	134.0	116	54	49	18	8	3	2	46	4	112	37	15	0	0	3	0	388	.235	15	42	112	.223	3	9

DESIGNATED HITTERS

Name	AB	Avg.	HR	RBI
Joyner, Wally	30	.267	0	1
Galarraga, Andres	4	.250	0	0
Bonilla, Bobby	2	.500	0	0
Sisco, Steve	0	-	0	0

INDIVIDUAL STATISTICS

FIELDING

FIRST BASEMEN

Player	Pct.	G	PO	A	E	TC	DP
Galarraga, Andres	.988	132	1105	61	14	1180	98
Joyner, Wally	.992	55	353	30	3	386	33
Unroe, Tim	1.000	2	12	2	0	14	0
Bako, Paul	1.000	1	2	0	0	2	1

SECOND BASEMEN

Player	Pct.	G	PO	A	E	TC	DP
Veras, Quilvio	.984	82	146	223	6	375	42
Lockhart, Keith	.979	74	103	177	6	286	32
Furcal, Rafael	.992	31	45	72	1	118	18
Sisco, Steve	1.000	5	3	4	0	7	2

THIRD BASEMEN

Player	Pct.	G	PO	A	E	TC	DP
Jones, Chipper	.944	152	90	297	23	410	23
Lockhart, Keith	.946	18	8	27	2	37	2
Helms, Wes	.833	5	1	4	1	6	1
Sisco, Steve	1.000	2	1	1	0	2	0
Bonilla, Bobby	-	1	0	0	0	0	0

SHORTSTOPS

Player	Pct.	G	PO	A	E	TC	DP
Furcal, Rafael	.950	110	147	290	23	460	54
Weiss, Walt	.949	69	83	197	15	295	38
DeRosa, Mark	1.000	10	6	7	0	13	2
Jones, Chipper	.875	6	6	8	2	16	2

OUTFIELDERS

Player	Pct.	G	PO	A	E	TC	DP
Jones, Andruw	.996	161	438	9	2	449	2
Jordan, Brian	.990	130	287	7	3	297	0
Sanders, Reggie	.964	96	155	7	6	168	1
Bonilla, Bobby	.929	64	51	1	4	56	0
Hubbard, Trenidad	1.000	43	39	1	0	40	0
Surhoff, B.J.	1.000	32	50	1	0	51	0
Lombard, George	1.000	15	17	1	0	18	0
Sisco, Steve	1.000	6	3	1	0	4	0
Swann, Pedro	-	3	0	0	0	0	0
Unroe, Tim	-	1	0	0	0	0	0

CATCHERS

Player	Pct.	G	PO	A	E	TC	DP	PB
Lopez, Javy	.993	132	817	62	6	885	6	8
Bako, Paul	.992	23	116	9	1	126	1	0
Lunar, Fernando	.993	22	125	12	1	138	2	0
Perez, Eddie	.976	7	39	2	1	42	0	1
Hubbard, Mike	1.000	1	3	0	0	3	0	0

PITCHERS

Player	Pct.	G	PO	A	E	TC	DP
Remlinger, Mike	.909	71	2	8	1	11	1
Rocker, John	1.000	59	1	6	0	7	0
Ligtenberg, Kerry	1.000	59	0	4	0	4	1
Mulholland, Terry	.889	54	6	18	3	27	1
Millwood, Kevin	1.000	36	4	19	0	23	1
Maddux, Greg	.979	35	25	69	2	96	5
Glavine, Tom	1.000	35	11	42	0	53	5
Burkett, John	.962	31	10	15	1	26	1
Kamieniecki, Scott	1.000	26	0	9	0	9	0
Seanez, Rudy	1.000	23	1	1	0	2	0
Chen, Bruce	1.000	22	0	3	0	3	1
Ashby, Andy	.920	15	8	15	2	25	0
Marquis, Jason	1.000	15	1	4	0	5	0
McMichael, Greg	1.000	15	1	2	0	3	0
McGlinchy, Kevin	1.000	10	0	2	0	2	0
Belinda, Stan	1.000	10	0	1	0	1	0
Wengert, Don	1.000	10	0	1	0	1	0
Rivera, Luis	1.000	5	0	1	0	1	0
Stevens, Dave	1.000	2	0	1	0	1	0
Molina, Gabe	-	2	0	0	0	0	0
Seelbach, Chris	-	2	0	0	0	0	0
Villegas, Ismael	1.000	1	0	1	0	1	0

PITCHING AGAINST EACH CLUB

Pitcher	Ari. W-L	Chi. W-L	Cin. W-L	Col. W-L	Fla. W-L	Hou. W-L	L.A. W-L	Mil. W-L	Mon. W-L	N.Y. W-L	Phi. W-L	Pit. W-L	S.D. W-L	S.F. W-L	StL. W-L	A.L. W-L	Total W-L
Ashby, Andy	0-1	0-0	1-0	0-1	1-0	1-1	0-1	0-0	2-0	2-0	0-0	0-0	0-0	0-1	0-1	1-0	8-6
Belinda, Stan	0-0	0-0	0-0	0-0	0-0	0-0	0-0	0-0	0-0	0-0	0-0	0-0	0-0	0-0	0-0	0-0	0-0
Burkett, John	1-0	0-0	0-0	0-1	1-0	2-1	0-0	0-1	0-1	3-0	2-0	0-0	1-0	0-0	0-1	0-1	10-6
Chen, Bruce	0-0	0-0	0-0	1-0	0-0	0-0	1-0	0-0	0-0	0-0	0-0	1-0	1-0	0-0	0-0	0-0	4-0
Glavine, Tom	1-1	0-2	1-1	1-0	2-1	1-0	1-0	1-0	1-2	1-1	1-1	0-0	3-0	3-0	2-0	2-0	21-9
Kamieniecki, S.	0-0	0-0	0-0	0-0	0-1	0-0	0-0	0-0	0-0	0-0	0-0	0-0	1-0	0-0	0-0	1-0	2-1
Ligtenberg, K.	0-0	0-1	0-1	0-0	0-0	0-0	0-0	0-0	0-0	0-0	1-0	1-0	0-0	0-0	0-1	0-0	2-3
Maddux, Greg	1-1	1-0	0-1	2-0	1-1	1-0	1-1	1-1	2-0	1-3	0-0	2-0	1-0	2-1	0-0	3-0	19-9
Marquis, J.	0-0	0-0	0-0	0-0	0-0	0-0	0-0	1-0	0-0	0-0	0-0	0-0	0-0	0-0	0-0	0-0	1-0
McGlinchy, K.	0-0	0-0	0-0	0-0	0-0	0-0	0-0	0-0	0-0	0-0	0-0	0-0	0-0	0-0	0-0	0-0	0-0
McMichael, G.	0-0	0-0	0-0	0-0	0-0	0-0	0-0	0-0	0-0	0-0	0-0	0-0	0-0	0-0	0-0	0-0	0-0
Millwood, K.	3-0	1-0	0-1	1-0	1-2	0-0	2-0	0-1	0-2	0-1	1-1	0-1	0-0	1-0	0-1	0-3	10-13
Molina, Gabe	0-0	0-0	0-0	0-0	0-0	0-0	0-0	0-0	0-0	0-0	0-0	0-0	0-0	0-0	0-0	0-0	0-0
Mulholland, T.	0-0	2-1	0-0	0-0	0-0	0-0	1-0	2-0	1-1	0-1	0-2	1-0	0-1	0-1	0-0	2-2	9-9
Remlinger, M.	0-0	0-1	0-1	0-0	0-0	0-0	1-0	0-0	0-0	0-0	0-1	0-0	1-0	0-0	1-0	2-0	5-3
Rivera, Luis	0-0	0-0	0-0	0-0	0-0	0-0	0-0	0-0	0-0	0-0	1-0	0-0	0-0	0-0	0-0	0-0	1-0
Rocker, John	0-0	0-0	0-0	0-2	0-0	0-0	0-0	1-0	0-0	0-0	0-0	0-0	0-0	0-0	0-0	0-0	1-2
Seanez, Rudy	0-0	0-0	0-0	0-0	0-1	0-2	0-0	0-0	0-0	0-0	2-0	0-0	0-0	0-0	0-0	0-1	2-4
Seelbach, C.	0-0	0-0	0-0	0-0	0-0	0-0	0-0	0-0	0-1	0-0	0-0	0-0	0-0	0-0	0-0	0-0	0-1
Stevens, Dave	0-0	0-0	0-0	0-0	0-0	0-0	0-0	0-0	0-0	0-0	0-0	0-0	0-0	0-0	0-0	0-0	0-0
Villegas, I.	0-0	0-0	0-0	0-0	0-0	0-0	0-0	0-0	0-0	0-0	0-0	0-0	0-0	0-0	0-0	0-0	0-0
Wengert, Don	0-0	0-0	0-0	0-0	0-0	0-0	0-0	0-0	0-0	0-0	0-0	0-1	0-0	0-0	0-0	0-0	0-1
Totals	6-3	4-5	2-5	5-4	6-6	5-4	7-2	6-3	6-7	7-6	8-5	5-2	8-1	6-3	3-4	11-7	95-67

INTERLEAGUE: Maddux 1-0, Ashby 1-0, Glavine 1-0 vs. Orioles; Mulholland 2-0, Maddux 1-0, Glavine 1-0, Seanez 0-1, Millwood 0-1 vs. Red Sox; Remlinger 1-0, Millwood 0-1, Mulholland 0-1 vs. Yankees; Remlinger 1-0, Burkett 0-1, Millwood 0-1 vs. Blue Jays; Kamieniecki 1-0, Maddux 1-0, Mulholland 0-1 vs. Devil Rays. Total: 11-7.

MISCELLANEOUS

HOME RUNS BY PARK

At Arizona (10): Sanders 2, Jordan 2, Jones 2, Galarraga 1, Joyner 1, Jones 1, Furcal 1.

At Atlanta (84): Jones 18, Jones 15, Galarraga 14, Lopez 12, Jordan 7, Bonilla 4, Sanders 4, Joyner 2, Veras 2, Bako 2, Surhoff 1, Hunter 1, Lockhart 1, Furcal 1.

At Baltimore (3): Galarraga 1, Lopez 1, Jones 1.

At Boston (4): Galarraga 1, Sanders 1, Lopez 1, Jones 1.

At Chicago (NL) (8): Galarraga 4, Jones 3, Lopez 1.

At Cincinnati (0):

At Colorado (5): Jones 2, Jones 2, Jordan 1.

At Florida (3): Sanders 1, Jordan 1, Lopez 1.

At Houston (9): Jones 3, Lopez 2, Sanders 1, Jordan 1, Jones 1, Furcal 1.

At Los Angeles (2): Joyner 1, Veras 1.

At Milwaukee (4): Galarraga 1, Lopez 1, Lockhart 1, Veras 1.

At Montreal (8): Jones 3, Bonilla 1, Sanders 1, Lopez 1, Jones 1, Furcal 1.

At New York (NL) (7): Galarraga 2, Lopez 2, Jordan 1, Jones 1, Jones 1.

At Philadelphia (13): Jones 4, Jones 3, Jordan 2, Galarraga 1, Sanders 1, Veras 1, Sisco 1.

At Pittsburgh (5): Jones 3, Jordan 1, Jones 1.

At San Diego (5): Galarraga 2, Jordan 1, Hubbard 1, Jones 1.

At San Francisco (3): Jones 2, Lopez 1.

At St. Louis (1): Galarraga 1.

At Tampa Bay (5): Jones 2, Joyner 1, Lopez 1, Jones 1.

LOW-HIT GAMES

No-hitters: None.
One-hitters: None.
Two-hitters: None.

10-STRIKEOUT GAMES

Greg Maddux 2, Kevin Millwood 1, Total: 3

FOUR OR MORE HITS IN ONE GAME

Andres Galarraga 2 (including one five-hit game), Chipper Jones 2, Quilvio Veras 2, Andruw Jones 2, Walt Weiss 1, Brian Jordan 1, Total: 10

MULTI-HOMER GAMES

Chipper Jones 6, Brian Jordan 3, Andruw Jones 3, Andres Galarraga 1, Reggie Sanders 1, Javy Lopez 1, Total: 15

GRAND SLAMS

4-8: Andres Galarraga (off San Francisco's Livan Hernandez)
5-9: Javy Lopez (off Florida's Brad Penny)

PINCH HITTERS

(Minimum 5 at-bats)

Name	AB	Avg.	HR	RBI
Joyner, Wally	55	.236	1	5
Bonilla, Bobby	39	.308	0	10
Lockhart, Keith	25	.040	0	1
Sisco, Steve	15	.200	1	2
Galarraga, Andres	13	.538	0	5
Hubbard, Trenidad	12	.333	0	1
Surhoff, B.J.	11	.000	0	0
Sanders, Reggie	9	.222	0	0
Weiss, Walt	6	.167	0	0
Lopez, Javy	6	.167	0	1
Lombard, George	6	.000	0	0

DEBUTS

4-4: Luis Rivera, P.
4-4: Rafael Furcal, SS.
5-6: Steve Sisco, PH.
5-8: Fernando Lunar, C.
6-6: Jason Marquis, P.
7-3: Ismael Villegas, P.
9-9: Chris Seelbach, P.
9-9: Pedro Swann, PH.

GAMES BY POSITION

Catcher: Javy Lopez 132, Paul Bako 23, Fernando Lunar 22, Eddie Perez 7, Mike Hubbard 1.

First base: Andres Galarraga 132, Wally Joyner 55, Tim Unroe 2, Paul Bako 1.

Second base: Quilvio Veras 82, Keith Lockhart 74, Rafael Furcal 31, Steve Sisco 5.

Third base: Chipper Jones 152, Keith Lockhart 18, Wes Helms 5, Steve Sisco 2, Bobby Bonilla 1.

Shortstop: Rafael Furcal 110, Walt Weiss 69, Mark DeRosa 10, Chipper Jones 6.

Outfield: Andruw Jones 161, Brian Jordan 130, Reggie Sanders 96, Bobby Bonilla 64, Trenidad Hubbard 43, B.J. Surhoff 32, George Lombard 15, Steve Sisco 6, Pedro Swann 3, Tim Unroe 1.

Designated hitter: Wally Joyner 7, Andres Galarraga 1, Bobby Bonilla 1, Steve Sisco 1.

STREAKS

Wins: 15 (April 16-May 2)
Losses: 4 (August 26-29)
Consecutive games with at least one hit: 19, Chipper Jones (June 1-21)
Wins by pitcher: 7, Tom Glavine (July 2-August 4)

ATTENDANCE

Home: 3,229,082
Road: 2,533,903
Highest (home): 49,802 (June 24 vs. Milwaukee).
Highest (road): 52,831 (June 30 vs. New York).
Lowest (home): 25,529 (September 6 vs. Arizona).
Lowest (road): 5,267 (June 1 vs. Chicago).

CHICAGO CUBS

DAY BY DAY

Date	Opp.	Res.	Score	(inn.*)	Hits	Opp. hits	Winning pitcher	Losing pitcher	Save	Record	Pos.	GB
3-29	At N.Y.§	W	5-3		12	7	Lieber	Hampton	Aguilera	1-0	1st	+0.5
3-30	N.Y.§	L	1-5	(11)	5	6	Cook	Young		1-1	1st	...
4-3	At StL.	L	1-7		3	10	Kile	Tapani		1-2	2nd	1.0
4-5	At StL.	L	4-10		9	12	Hentgen	Lieber		1-3	4th	2.0
4-6	At StL.	L	3-13		6	11	Stephenson	Farnsworth		1-4	6th	3.0
4-7	At Cin.	W	10-6		8	8	Lorraine	Harnisch	Aguilera	2-4	5th	2.0
4-8	At Cin.	L	3-4	(11)	4	11	Graves	Guthrie		2-5	6th	3.0
4-9	At Cin.	L	7-8	(11)	13	9	Graves	Karchner		2-6	6th	4.0
4-10	Atl.	W	4-3		10	7	Guthrie	Ligtenberg		3-6	T5th	4.0
4-12	Atl.	W	11-4		12	6	Farnsworth	Mulholland		4-6	5th	3.5
4-13	Atl.	W	3-2		7	8	Guthrie	Remlinger		5-6	3rd	2.5
4-14	Fla.	L	4-9		8	10	Fernandez	Lorraine		5-7	4th	2.5
4-15	Fla.	W	4-2		6	4	Downs	Dempster	Aguilera	6-7	3rd	2.0
4-16	Fla.	L	5-6	(10)	10	8	Miceli	Quevedo	Alfonseca	6-8	4th	2.5
4-17	Fla.	L	5-6		6	12	Sanchez	Farnsworth	Alfonseca	6-9	6th	3.0
4-18	At Mon.	L	3-4		7	9	Strickland	Tapani	Urbina	6-10	6th	4.0
4-19	At Mon.	L	3-7		7	11	Pavano	Quevedo		6-11	6th	5.0
4-20	At Mon.	W	10-6		10	13	Williams	Blank		7-11	6th	5.0
4-22†	At N.Y.	L	3-8		8	12	Rusch	Lieber		7-12		
4-22‡	At N.Y.	L	6-7		11	10	Cook	Farnsworth	Benitez	7-13	6th	5.0
4-23	At N.Y.	L	8-15		10	18	Hampton	Tapani		7-14	T5th	6.0
4-25	At Hou.	L	7-11		10	16	Reynolds	Downs		7-15	6th	7.0
4-26	At Hou.	W	13-8		16	11	Karchner	Maddux	Aguilera	8-15	6th	7.0
4-27	At Hou.	W	12-3		14	5	Lieber	Lima		9-15	5th	6.0
4-28	Ari.	W	6-5		10	7	Tapani	Springer	Aguilera	10-15	4th	6.0
4-29	Ari.	L	4-7	(10)	9	10	Mantei	Guthrie	Morgan	10-16	5th	7.0
4-30	Ari.	L	0-6		6	12	Johnson	Lorraine		10-17	6th	8.0
5-2	Hou.	W	11-1		16	4	Wood	Lima	Williams	11-17	5th	7.0
5-3	Hou.	W	4-3		7	8	Lieber	Holt	Aguilera	12-17	4th	6.0
5-4	Hou.	L	2-6		9	9	Elarton	Valdes	Wagner	12-18	5th	7.0
5-5	Pit.	L	2-4		8	7	Ritchie	Tapani	Williams	12-19	5th	7.0
5-6	Pit.	L	9-11		16	16	Wallace	Farnsworth	Williams	12-20	5th	8.0
5-7	Pit.	L	3-11		9	13	Schmidt	Wood		12-21	5th	8.0
5-8	Mil.	W	12-11	(10)	16	13	Heredia	Wickman		13-21	5th	7.0
5-9	Mil.	L	3-4		5	8	D'Amico	Guthrie	Weathers	13-22	5th	8.0
5-10	Mil.	W	9-8	(11)	10	9	Aguilera	de los Santos		14-22	5th	7.0
5-11	Mil.	L	8-14		17	18	Woodard	Williams		14-23	5th	7.5
5-12	At Mon.	L	3-8		7	10	Thurman	Wood	Hermanson	14-24	6th	7.5
5-13	At Mon.	W	2-1		6	8	Lieber	Armas		15-24	5th	7.0
5-14	At Mon.	L	15-16		21	16	Hermanson	Aguilera		15-25	5th	7.5
5-16	L.A.	L	5-6		7	9	Mills	Tapani	Shaw	15-26	6th	8.5
5-17	L.A.	L	6-8		7	9	Mills	Heredia	Shaw	15-27	6th	8.5
5-19	Cin.	W	4-1		7	6	Valdes	Parris	Van Poppel	16-27	6th	8.0
5-20	Cin.	L	3-5		10	8	Villone	Lieber	Graves	16-28	6th	9.0
5-21	Cin.	W	4-2		5	10	Tapani	Bell	Heredia	17-28	5th	9.0
5-23	At Col.	L	7-10		9	10	Bohanon	Garibay		17-29	5th	10.0
5-24	At Col.	L	4-9		12	8	Astacio	Farnsworth	Jimenez	17-30	5th	11.0
5-25	At Col.	W	6-5		9	10	Lieber	DeJean	Aguilera	18-30	5th	11.0
5-26	At S.F	L	3-5		8	10	Gardner	Tapani		18-31	6th	11.0
5-27	At S.F	W	3-2	(11)	4	9	Garibay	Fultz	Aguilera	19-31	5th	10.0
5-28	At S.F	W	4-1		8	5	Wood	Rueter	Aguilera	20-31	5th	9.0
5-29	Atl.	L	0-1		6	2	Maddux	Lieber		20-32	5th	10.0
5-30	Atl.	L	2-5		9	9	Mulholland	Quevedo	Remlinger	20-33	5th	11.0
6-1	Atl.	W	5-3		9	6	Tapani	Glavine	Aguilera	21-33	5th	9.5
6-2	Det.	W	2-0		5	8	Downs	Nomo	Aguilera	22-33	5th	9.5
6-3	Det.	L	3-5		6	7	Weaver	Wood	Jones	22-34	5th	9.5
6-4	Det.	L	2-3	(12)	9	7	Anderson	Van Poppel	Jones	22-35	5th	10.0
6-5	Ari.	W	4-3	(10)	10	8	Heredia	Mantei		23-35	5th	9.0
6-6	Ari.	W	4-1		8	5	Tapani	Reynoso		24-35	4th	8.5
6-7	Ari.	W	9-4		11	11	Downs	Anderson	Van Poppel	25-35	4th	8.5
6-9	At Chi. (AL)	L	5-6	(14)	8	15	Pena	Van Poppel		25-36	4th	8.5
6-10	At Chi. (AL)	L	3-4		7	5	Sirotka	Wood	Foulke	25-37	4th	8.5
6-11	At Chi. (AL)	W	6-5		8	10	Van Poppel	Pena	Aguilera	26-37	4th	8.5
6-13	N.Y.	W	4-3		11	5	Heredia	Franco	Aguilera	27-37	4th	9.0
6-14	N.Y.	L	8-10		14	14	Rusch	Garibay	Benitez	27-38	T4th	10.0
6-16	Mon.	W	9-8		9	8	Van Poppel	Armas	Aguilera	28-38	4th	10.0
6-17	Mon.	W	1-0		4	8	Rain	Hermanson	Aguilera	29-38	4th	10.0
6-18	Mon.	L	3-4	(11)	9	9	Telford	Garibay	Rigby	29-39	4th	10.0
6-20	At Atl.	L	4-11		9	14	Millwood	Tapani		29-40	4th	11.0
6-21	At Atl.	W	8-1		11	5	Wood	Glavine		30-40	4th	10.0
6-22	At Atl.	L	4-6		14	11	Mulholland	Downs	Remlinger	30-41	4th	11.0
6-23	At Fla.	L	1-6		8	12	Penny	Lieber		30-42	4th	12.0
6-24	At Fla.	L	4-7		12	9	Strong	Heredia	Alfonseca	30-43	5th	13.0
6-25	At Fla.	L	7-8	(10)	9	10	Alfonseca	Heredia		30-44	5th	14.0
6-27	At Pit.	L	0-6		3	5	Ritchie	Wood		30-45	5th	14.5
6-28	At Pit.	W	5-4		8	9	Lieber	Cordova	Aguilera	31-45	4th	13.5
6-29	At Pit.	L	4-5	(10)	7	7	Wilkins	Worrell		31-46	5th	14.5
6-30	At Mil.	W	7-4	(15)	13	12	Garibay	Levrault	Aguilera	32-46	4th	14.5

HIGHLIGHTS

High point: The highlight came before the Cubs even played a game in North America. They opened a two-game series against the Mets in Tokyo with a win, accounting for their only above-.500 record of the year. The series was the first in the regular season featuring major league teams outside North America.

Low point: Before the Cubs played Arizona on June 6, right fielder Sammy Sosa ripped manager Don Baylor for "lack of respect," touching off a month-long trade watch. The two men eventually mended fences and Sosa went on to an outstanding season.

Turning point: The Cubs were 53-60 and climbing when Cincinnati came to Wrigley Field August 11. Reliever Steve Rain, trying to protect Kevin Tapani's 4-0 eighth-inning lead, surrendered a three-run homer to Ken Griffey Jr., a two-run shot to Dmitri Young and a solo homer to Pokey Reese in a stunning 6-4 loss. The Reds would go on to a three-game sweep.

Most valuable player: Sosa won his first home run crown with 50 and enjoyed his best all-around year at the plate. He batted a career-best .320 and finished with 193 hits, 138 RBIs and a career-high 91 walks.

Most valuable pitcher: Jon Lieber led the N.L. in innings pitched (251) and starts (35) and finished third with six complete games. With a good team, his record probably would have been much better than 12-11.

Most improved player: Todd Van Poppel didn't make the club out of spring training, but he came up May 12 and enjoyed the best year of his career. He pitched in 51 games, compiling a 4-5 record and 3.75 ERA, and excelled as a middle-to-late-inning reliever.

Most pleasant surprise: The Cubs found unexpected shortstop stability from Ricky Gutierrez, a free-agent pickup from Houston. Gutierrez batted .276 and posted career bests in home runs (11) and RBIs (56) and led both leagues with 16 sacrifice bunts.

Key injuries: Mark Grace broke the middle finger of his right hand in spring training and it affected his swing. Grace also missed three weeks with a hamstring injury. ... Tapani had his second straight season cut short, this time with a knee problem that required surgery. ... Rondell White dislocated his shoulder August 26 and missed the rest of the season. ... Third baseman Shane Andrews missed three months because of a herniated disk in his lower back. ... Closer Rick Aguilera suffered a thumb fracture and missed the final three weeks.

Notable: The Cubs finished in last place for the third time in four seasons and posted back-to-back 95-plus-loss marks for the first time in history. ... The Cubs played 22 extra-inning games, one short of the club record. They were 9-13. ... Sosa finished with a club-record 179 homers over three seasons.

—BRUCE MILES

MISCELLANEOUS

RECORDS

2000 regular-season record: 65-97 (6th in N.L. Central); 38-43 at home; 27-54 on road; 18-23 vs. East; 29-48 vs. Central; 18-26 vs. West; 14-21 vs. lefthanded starters; 51-76 vs. righthanded starters; 53-83 on grass; 12-14 on turf; 36-56 in daytime; 29-41 at night; 27-30 in one-run games; 9-13 in extra-inning games; 0-2-0 in doubleheaders.

Team record past five years: 366-445 (.451, ranks 15th in league in that span).

TEAM LEADERS

Batting average: Sammy Sosa (.320).
At-bats: Eric Young (607).
Runs: Sammy Sosa (106).
Hits: Sammy Sosa (193).
Total Bases: Sammy Sosa (383).
Doubles: Mark Grace (41).
Triples: Damon Buford, Jose Nieves (3).
Home runs: Sammy Sosa (50).
Runs batted in: Sammy Sosa (138).
Stolen bases: Eric Young (54).
Slugging percentage: Sammy Sosa (.634).
On-base percentage: Sammy Sosa (.406).
Wins: Jon Lieber (12).
Earned-run average: Jon Lieber (4.41).
Complete games: Jon Lieber (6).
Shutouts: Jon Lieber (1).
Saves: Rick Aguilera (29).
Innings pitched: Jon Lieber (251.0).
Strikeouts: Jon Lieber (192).

Date	Opp.	Res.	Score	(inn.*)	Hits	Opp. hits	Winning pitcher	Losing pitcher	Save	Record	Pos.	GB
7-1	At Mil.	L	0-4		2	11	D'Amico	Valdes		32-47	5th	15.5
7-2	At Mil.	L	2-4		6	7	Haynes	Wood	Wickman	32-48	5th	15.5
7-3	Pit.	W	3-0		9	2	Lieber	Cordova		33-48	5th	15.0
7-4	Pit.	L	4-10		8	12	Wilkins	Aguilera		33-49	5th	16.0
7-5	Pit.	L	6-9		10	12	Anderson	Downs		33-50	5th	17.0
7-7	Chi. (AL)	L	2-4	(12)	6	11	Lowe	Van Poppel	Pena	33-51	5th	16.5
7-8	Chi. (AL)	W	9-2		14	5	Lieber	Baldwin		34-51	5th	15.5
7-9	Chi. (AL)	W	9-6		11	8	Tapani	Simas	Worrell	35-51	5th	15.5
7-13	At Min.	L	1-5		6	11	Radke	Valdes	Hawkins	35-52	5th	16.5
7-14	At Min.	W	6-2		12	8	Lieber	Milton		36-52	5th	16.5
7-15	At Min.	W	8-4		13	13	Tapani	Mays		37-52	5th	15.5
7-16	At K.C.	W	10-7		10	14	Wood	Reichert	Aguilera	38-52	T4th	14.5
7-17	At K.C.	W	3-1		8	7	Downs	Durbin	Aguilera	39-52	3rd	14.5
7-18	At K.C.	L	4-12		8	20	Stein	Valdes		39-53	T3rd	14.5
7-19	Phi.	W	5-4		10	9	Heredia	Holzemer		40-53	3rd	13.5
7-20	Phi.	L	2-3		8	6	Brownson	Tapani	Brantley	40-54	T3rd	13.5
7-21	Mil.	W	4-2		7	5	Wood	Snyder	Aguilera	41-54	T3rd	13.5
7-22	Mil.	W	3-2	(13)	7	10	Heredia	Woodard		42-54	T3rd	12.5
7-23	Mil.	W	5-4		4	7	Valdes	Wright	Aguilera	43-54	3rd	11.5
7-25	At Phi.	W	8-7		7	14	Worrell	Brock	Aguilera	44-54	3rd	11.5
7-26	At Phi.	W	14-9		14	9	Heredia	Byrd		45-54	3rd	11.5
7-27	At Phi.	W	4-1		12	7	Rain	Padilla	Aguilera	46-54	3rd	10.5
7-28	S.F	L	0-2		7	5	Hernandez	Worrell	Nen	46-55	3rd	10.5
7-29	S.F	W	8-1		13	6	Wood	Ortiz	Farnsworth	47-55	3rd	9.5
7-30	S.F	W	3-1		10	4	Lieber	Rueter		48-55	3rd	8.5
7-31	Col.	W	2-0		8	4	Tapani	Bohanon	Aguilera	49-55	3rd	8.5
8-1	Col.	L	1-2		2	7	Astacio	Farnsworth	White	49-56	3rd	8.5
8-2	Col.	W	3-2		8	4	Rain	Wasdin	Aguilera	50-56	3rd	8.5
8-3	At S.D.	L	5-6		10	8	Walker	Worrell	Hoffman	50-57	3rd	9.0
8-4	At S.D.	L	9-11		13	13	Almanzar	Rain	Hoffman	50-58	3rd	9.0
8-5	At S.D.	W	6-3		10	8	Tapani	Williams	Aguilera	51-58	3rd	9.0
8-6	At S.D.	L	6-8		12	11	Eaton	Garibay	Hoffman	51-59	3rd	9.0
8-7	At L.A.	W	7-3		10	7	Quevedo	Herges		52-59	3rd	9.0
8-8	At L.A.	L	5-7		8	13	Dreifort	Norton	Shaw	52-60	3rd	9.0
8-9	At L.A.	W	5-4	(10)	10	8	Worrell	Osuna	Aguilera	53-60	3rd	8.0
8-11	Cin.	L	4-6		6	11	Wohlers	Rain	Graves	53-61	3rd	8.5
8-12	Cin.	L	0-3		5	7	Williamson	Garibay	Graves	53-62	3rd	9.5
8-13	Cin.	L	0-3		7	6	Parris	Quevedo	Sullivan	53-63	3rd	10.5
8-14	StL.	W	7-3		11	8	Lieber	An. Benes		54-63	3rd	9.5
8-15	StL.	L	2-4		7	11	Stephenson	Arnold	Veres	54-64	3rd	10.5
8-16	StL.	L	1-5		6	9	Kile	Tapani		54-65	3rd	11.5
8-18	At Ari.	L	2-11		6	12	Schilling	Quevedo		54-66	3rd	12.5
8-19	At Ari.	L	3-11		7	15	Anderson	Lieber		54-67	3rd	13.5
8-20	At Ari.	L	4-5		4	10	Johnson	Rain		54-68	3rd	13.5
8-21	At Hou.	L	4-5		8	6	Elarton	Tapani	Slusarski	54-69	3rd	14.5
8-22	At Hou.	L	7-10		8	9	Valdes	Farnsworth	Cabrera	54-70	3rd	14.5
8-23	At Hou.	W	15-5		19	4	Quevedo	Miller		55-70	3rd	14.5
8-25†	L.A.	L	3-5		10	13	Osuna	Lieber	Shaw	55-71		
8-25‡	L.A.	L	1-3		9	5	Perez	Garibay	Shaw	55-72	T3rd	15.5
8-26	L.A.	W	6-4		8	9	Worrell	Olson	Aguilera	56-72	T3rd	15.5
8-27	L.A.	L	6-7	(10)	13	9	Fetters	Van Poppel	Shaw	56-73	T3rd	16.5
8-28	S.D.	L	2-8		3	11	Clement	Quevedo		56-74	T3rd	17.5
8-29	S.D.	W	7-6	(13)	10	10	Heredia	Hoffman		57-74	3rd	16.5
8-30	S.D.	W	5-1		10	4	Lieber	Tollberg		58-74	3rd	16.5
8-31	S.D.	L	5-11		8	16	Witasick	Tapani		58-75	T3rd	17.0
9-1	At S.F	L	2-7		6	10	Gardner	Wood		58-76	T3rd	18.0
9-2	At S.F	L	2-13		8	10	Estes	Quevedo		58-77	4th	19.0
9-3	At S.F	L	2-5		5	13	Hernandez	Garibay	Nen	58-78	4th	20.0
9-4	At Col.	L	2-6		8	12	Rose	Lieber		58-79	4th	21.0
9-5	At Col.	L	2-10		4	13	Tavarez	Arnold		58-80	T5th	22.0
9-6	At Col.	W	8-5	(11)	13	11	Van Poppel	White	Aguilera	59-80	T5th	21.0
9-8	Hou.	L	10-13		10	20	Miller	Tapani	Dotel	59-81	6th	21.5
9-9	Hou.	L	4-14		9	19	Holt	Quevedo		59-82	6th	22.5
9-10	Hou.	L	6-7		13	10	McKnight	Lieber	Dotel	59-83	6th	22.5
9-11	At Cin.	L	6-7		14	9	Harnisch	Garibay	Graves	59-84	6th	23.5
9-12	At Cin.	W	2-1		6	4	Wood	Fernandez		60-84	6th	23.5
9-13	At Cin.	L	3-13		6	16	Bell	Arnold		60-85	6th	24.5
9-14	At StL.	L	0-4		3	5	Hentgen	Quevedo		60-86	6th	25.5
9-15	At StL.	L	2-3		6	4	James	Lieber	Veres	60-87	6th	26.5
9-16	At StL.	L	6-7		11	10	Timlin	Spradlin	Veres	60-88	6th	27.5
9-17	At StL.	L	2-4		7	4	Kile	Worrell	Morris	60-89	6th	28.5
9-18	At Mil.	L	1-2		4	5	D'Amico	Van Poppel	Leskanic	60-90	6th	29.0
9-19	At Mil.	L	8-9		7	9	King	Farnsworth		60-91	6th	29.0
9-20	At Mil.	L	2-3	(10)	8	9	Leskanic	Farnsworth		60-92	6th	30.0
9-22	StL.	W	5-4		10	5	Ohman	Veres		61-92	6th	28.5
9-23	StL.	L	5-6		7	10	Reames	Nation	Morris	61-93	6th	29.5
9-24	StL.	W	10-5		12	8	Van Poppel	Hentgen	Heredia	62-93	6th	28.5
9-25	Phi.	W	4-3		4	8	Quevedo	Person	Worrell	63-93	6th	28.0
9-26	Phi.	L	4-10		14	14	Daal	Lieber		63-94	6th	29.0
9-27	Phi.	W	1-0		6	8	Wood	Wolf	Worrell	64-94	6th	29.0
9-28	Phi.	L	2-4		7	7	Politte	Nation	Padilla	64-95	6th	30.0
9-29	At Pit.	L	4-8		10	13	Wilkins	Rain		64-96	6th	30.0
9-30	At Pit.	L	2-4		11	7	Ritchie	Quevedo	Williams	64-97	6th	30.0
10-1	At Pit.	W	10-9		12	14	Farnsworth	Sauerbeck	Arnold	65-97	6th	30.0

Monthly records: March (1-1), April (9-16), May (10-16), June (12-13), July (17-9), August (9-20), September (6-22), October (1-0).

*Innings, if other than nine. † First game of a doubleheader. ‡ Second game of a doubleheader. § Game played in Tokyo, Japan.

MEMORABLE GAMES

May 2 at Chicago

After missing all of 1999 and the first month of 2000 while recovering from reconstructive elbow surgery, Kerry Wood returned to the mound against Houston and recorded an 11-1 victory, allowing one run and three hits over six innings. As if that wasn't enough, Wood hit the first pitch he saw as a batter for a home run off Astros starter Jose Lima.

Houston	AB	R	H	BI	Cubs	AB	R	H	BI
Biggio, 2b	3	0	0	0	Young, 2b	5	0	0	0
Ru.Johnson, ph	1	0	0	0	Gutierrez, ss	5	1	2	0
Cedeno, cf	2	0	1	0	Grace, 1b	4	1	3	1
Bagwell, 1b	4	0	0	0	Sosa, rf	5	0	1	0
Caminiti, 3b	3	0	0	0	Rodriguez, lf	3	3	2	0
Ward, lf	3	1	1	1	Greene, 3b	4	2	4	4
Hidalgo, rf	4	0	0	0	Williams, p	1	0	1	1
Meluskey, c	4	0	0	0	Buford, cf	4	2	1	0
Spiers, ss	3	0	0	0	Girardi, c	4	1	1	3
Lima, p	2	0	1	0	Wood, p	3	1	1	2
Cabrera, p	0	0	0	0	S.Andrews, 3b	1	0	0	0
Berkman, ph	0	0	0	0					
Powell, p	0	0	0	0					
Henry, p	0	0	0	0					
Eusebio, ph	1	0	1	0					
Totals	**30**	**1**	**4**	**1**	**Totals**	**39**	**11**	**16**	**11**

Houston..............................0 0 0 0 0 1 0 0 0—1 4 1
Cubs ....0 4 1 0 5 0 0 1 x—11 16 0

E—Bagwell (1). LOB—Houston 9, Cubs 8. 2B—Eusebio (2), Grace (5), Rodriguez 2 (6), Greene (1), Williams (1). HR—Ward (6), Greene (1), Girardi (1), Wood (1). SB—Cedeno (10), Grace (1), Rodriguez (1). CS—Sosa (2). SH—Cedeno, Buford.

Houston	IP	H	R	ER	BB	SO
Lima (L, 1-5)	4.2	13	10	9	3	5
Cabrera	1.1	1	0	0	0	0
Powell	1	0	0	0	0	1
Henry	1	2	1	1	0	0

Cubs	IP	H	R	ER	BB	SO
Wood (W, 1-0)	6	3	1	1	4	4
Williams (S, 1)	3	1	0	0	2	2

WP—Wood. U—HP, Fichter, 1B, Scott. 2B, Welke. 3B, Cederstrom. T—2:39. A—38,121.

May 29 at Chicago

Jon Lieber allowed two hits while striking out a career-best 12 batters in an outstanding performance at Wrigley Field, but all he had to show for his effort was a 1-0 loss to Atlanta. Lieber's only mistake resulted in a two-out, seventh-inning home run by Andres Galarraga—the Braves' first hit of the game. Atlanta ace Greg Maddux pitched a six-hit shutout to gain the win.

Atlanta	AB	R	H	BI	Cubs	AB	R	H	BI
Veras, 2b	3	0	0	0	Young, 2b	4	0	1	0
A.Jones, cf	4	0	0	0	Martinez, 1b	4	0	2	0
C.Jones, 3b	3	0	0	0	Sosa, rf	4	0	0	0
Lockhart, 3b	1	0	0	0	Rodriguez, lf	4	0	1	0
Galarraga, 1b	3	1	1	1	Reed, c	3	0	0	0
Jordan, rf	3	0	0	0	Greene, 3b	4	0	1	0
Sanders, lf	3	0	0	0	Buford, cf	2	0	1	0
Furcal, ss	3	0	1	0	Nieves, ss	3	0	0	0
Lunar, c	3	0	0	0	Hill, ph	1	0	0	0
Maddux, p	3	0	0	0	Lieber, p	3	0	0	0
					Van Poppel, p	0	0	0	0
Totals	**29**	**1**	**2**	**1**	**Totals**	**32**	**0**	**6**	**0**

Atlanta ....0 0 0 0 0 0 1 0 0—1 2 0
Cubs ....0 0 0 0 0 0 0 0 0—0 6 0

DP—Atlanta 1. LOB—Atlanta 2, Cubs 8. 2B—Martinez (1), Rodriguez (11). HR—Galarraga (13).

Atlanta	IP	H	R	ER	BB	SO
Maddux (W 7-1)	9	6	0	0	2	8

Cubs	IP	H	R	ER	BB	SO
Lieber (L 5-4)	8	2	1	1	1	12
Van Poppel	1	0	0	0	0	1

HBP—Buford by Maddux. U—HP, Eddings. 1B, Relliford. 2B, Carlson. 3B, DeMuth. T—2:21. A—40,123.

INDIVIDUAL STATISTICS

BATTING

Name	G	TPA	AB	R	H	TB	2B	3B	HR	RBI	Avg.	Obp.	Slg.	SH	SF	HP	BB	IBB	SO	SB	CS	GDP	vs RHP AB	vs RHP Avg.	vs RHP HR	vs RHP RBI	vs LHP AB	vs LHP Avg.	vs LHP HR	vs LHP RBI
Young, Eric	153	690	607	98	180	242	40	2	6	47	.297	.367	.399	7	5	8	63	1	39	54	7	12	469	.284	4	39	138	.341	2	8
Sosa, Sammy	156	705	604	106	193	383	38	1	50	138	.320	.406	.634	0	8	2	91	19	168	7	4	12	480	.313	42	115	124	.347	8	23
Grace, Mark	143	621	510	75	143	219	41	1	11	82	.280	.394	.429	2	8	6	95	11	28	1	2	7	379	.272	5	59	131	.305	6	23
Buford, Damon	150	556	495	64	124	193	18	3	15	48	.251	.324	.390	4	2	8	47	3	118	4	6	9	360	.222	11	28	135	.326	4	20
Gutierrez, Ricky	125	542	449	73	124	180	19	2	11	56	.276	.375	.401	16	4	7	66	0	58	8	2	10	359	.256	10	43	90	.356	1	13
Girardi, Joe	106	407	363	47	101	136	15	1	6	40	.278	.339	.375	6	3	3	32	3	61	1	0	12	249	.313	4	33	114	.202	2	7
Greene, Willie	105	339	299	34	60	109	15	2	10	37	.201	.289	.365	0	2	2	36	2	69	4	0	5	254	.193	10	34	45	.244	0	3
Rodriguez, Henry	76	287	259	37	65	136	15	1	18	51	.251	.314	.525	0	3	3	22	2	76	1	2	4	220	.245	16	47	39	.282	2	4
Reed, Jeff	90	277	229	26	49	71	10	0	4	25	.214	.342	.310	2	1	1	44	2	68	0	1	5	204	.225	4	24	25	.120	0	1
Nieves, Jose	82	213	198	17	42	69	6	3	5	24	.212	.251	.348	2	2	0	11	1	43	1	1	8	118	.212	4	12	80	.213	1	12
Andrews, Shane	66	222	192	25	44	91	5	0	14	39	.229	.329	.474	0	1	2	27	1	59	1	1	9	131	.198	7	18	61	.295	7	21
Hill, Glenallen	64	178	168	23	44	83	4	1	11	29	.262	.303	.494	0	0	0	10	2	43	0	1	5	87	.253	6	13	81	.272	5	16
Matthews Jr., Gary	80	175	158	24	30	47	1	2	4	14	.190	.264	.297	1	0	1	15	1	28	3	0	2	118	.169	2	10	40	.250	2	4
Huson, Jeff	70	144	130	19	28	37	7	1	0	11	.215	.287	.285	1	0	0	13	1	9	2	1	6	112	.250	0	11	18	.000	0	0
Brown, Roosevelt	45	98	91	11	32	49	8	0	3	14	.352	.378	.538	0	2	1	4	0	22	0	1	0	87	.356	3	14	4	.250	0	0
Brown, Brant	54	102	89	7	14	24	1	0	3	10	.157	.248	.270	1	1	1	10	0	29	2	1	2	76	.145	3	9	13	.231	0	1
Lieber, Jon	36	94	82	3	18	22	4	0	0	4	.220	.238	.268	10	0	0	2	0	28	0	0	0	59	.271	0	4	23	.087	0	0
Ojeda, Augie	28	89	77	10	17	28	3	1	2	8	.221	.307	.364	1	1	0	10	1	9	0	1	1	53	.208	2	5	24	.250	0	3
Zuleta, Julio	30	73	68	13	20	37	8	0	3	12	.294	.342	.544	0	0	3	2	0	19	0	1	2	48	.250	1	9	20	.400	2	3
White, Rondell	19	74	67	7	22	30	2	0	2	7	.328	.392	.448	0	0	2	5	0	12	0	2	0	57	.333	2	7	10	.300	0	0
Tapani, Kevin	30	68	56	3	10	15	2	0	1	4	.179	.220	.268	9	0	0	3	0	20	0	1	1	45	.178	1	4	11	.182	0	0
Martinez, Dave	18	56	54	5	10	13	1	1	0	1	.185	.214	.241	0	0	0	2	0	8	1	0	0	49	.204	0	1	5	.000	0	0
Meyers, Chad	36	57	52	8	9	11	2	0	0	5	.173	.228	.212	0	1	1	3	0	11	1	0	0	34	.147	0	3	18	.222	0	2
Patterson, Corey	11	47	42	9	7	14	1	0	2	2	.167	.239	.333	1	0	1	3	0	14	1	1	0	36	.194	2	2	6	.000	0	0
Wood, Kerry	25	46	40	6	10	13	0	0	1	4	.250	.286	.325	4	0	0	2	0	10	0	0	0	29	.207	1	4	11	.364	0	0
Gload, Ross	18	35	31	4	6	11	0	1	1	3	.194	.257	.355	0	1	0	3	0	10	0	0	1	29	.207	1	3	2	.000	0	0
Quevedo, Ruben	21	31	30	1	4	4	0	0	0	1	.133	.133	.133	1	0	0	0	0	10	0	0	1	28	.107	0	0	2	.500	0	1
Downs, Scott	18	32	26	2	2	2	0	0	0	1	.077	.143	.077	4	0	0	2	0	10	0	0	0	15	.133	0	1	11	.000	0	0
Garibay, Daniel	30	19	15	1	2	2	0	0	0	1	.133	.133	.133	4	0	0	0	0	6	0	0	0	10	.100	0	1	5	.200	0	0
Valdes, Ismael	13	20	14	1	4	6	2	0	0	2	.286	.333	.429	5	0	0	1	0	3	0	0	0	14	.286	0	2	0	.000	0	0
Farnsworth, Kyle	46	16	14	0	1	2	1	0	0	0	.071	.071	.143	2	0	0	0	0	6	0	0	0	7	.143	0	0	7	.000	0	0
Brock, Tarrik	13	16	12	1	2	2	0	0	0	0	.167	.375	.167	0	0	0	4	0	4	1	1	0	11	.091	0	0	1	1.000	0	0
Arnold, Jamie	12	10	9	0	1	2	1	0	0	0	.111	.200	.222	0	0	1	0	0	3	0	0	0	9	.111	0	0	0	.000	0	0
Van Poppel, Todd	51	11	9	0	0	0	0	0	0	0	.000	.000	.000	2	0	0	0	0	4	0	0	0	7	.000	0	0	2	.000	0	0
Lorraine, Andrew	8	11	8	2	1	1	0	0	0	0	.125	.222	.125	2	0	0	1	0	4	0	0	0	7	.143	0	0	1	.000	0	0
Mahoney, Mike	4	9	7	1	2	3	1	0	0	1	.286	.444	.429	0	0	1	1	0	0	0	0	0	7	.286	0	1	0	.000	0	0
Nation, Joey	2	4	4	0	2	2	0	0	0	0	.500	.500	.500	0	0	0	0	0	1	0	0	0	4	.500	0	0	0	.000	0	0
Norton, Phil	2	4	3	1	2	2	0	0	0	0	.667	.667	.667	1	0	0	0	0	0	0	0	0	3	.667	0	0	0	.000	0	0
Liniak, Cole	3	3	3	0	0	0	0	0	0	0	.000	.000	.000	0	0	0	0	0	2	0	0	0	0	.000	0	0	3	.000	0	0
Williams, Brian	22	2	2	0	1	2	1	0	0	1	.500	.500	1.000	0	0	0	0	0	0	0	0	0	2	.500	0	1	0	.000	0	0
Guthrie, Mark	19	2	2	0	0	0	0	0	0	0	.000	.000	.000	0	0	0	0	0	1	0	0	0	2	.000	0	0	0	.000	0	0
Worrell, Tim	54	2	2	0	0	0	0	0	0	0	.000	.000	.000	0	0	0	0	0	1	0	0	0	2	.000	0	0	0	.000	0	0
Heredia, Felix	74	2	2	0	0	0	0	0	0	0	.000	.000	.000	0	0	0	0	0	1	0	0	0	2	.000	0	0	0	.000	0	0
Rain, Steve	37	3	2	0	0	0	0	0	0	0	.000	.333	.000	0	0	0	1	0	2	0	0	0	2	.000	0	0	0	.000	0	0
Gonzalez, Raul	3	2	2	0	0	0	0	0	0	0	.000	.000	.000	0	0	0	0	0	2	0	0	0	0	.000	0	0	2	.000	0	0
Spradlin, Jerry	8	1	1	0	0	0	0	0	0	0	.000	.000	.000	0	0	0	0	0	1	0	0	0	0	.000	0	0	1	.000	0	0
Aguilera, Rick	54	0	0	0	0	0	0	0	0	0	.000	.000	.000	0	0	0	0	0	0	0	0	0	0	.000	0	0	0	.000	0	0
Karchner, Matt	13	2	0	0	0	0	0	0	0	0	.000	1.000	.000	1	0	0	1	0	0	0	0	0	0	.000	0	0	0	.000	0	0
Young, Danny	4	0	0	0	0	0	0	0	0	0	.000	.000	.000	0	0	0	0	0	0	0	0	0	0	.000	0	0	0	.000	0	0
Mairena, Oswaldo	2	0	0	0	0	0	0	0	0	0	.000	.000	.000	0	0	0	0	0	0	0	0	0	0	.000	0	0	0	.000	0	0
Ohman, Will	6	0	0	0	0	0	0	0	0	0	.000	.000	.000	0	0	0	0	0	0	0	0	0	0	.000	0	0	0	.000	0	0

Players with more than one N.L. team

Name	G	TPA	AB	R	H	TB	2B	3B	HR	RBI	Avg.	Obp.	Slg.	SH	SF	HP	BB	IBB	SO	SB	CS	GDP	vs RHP AB	vs RHP Avg.	vs RHP HR	vs RHP RBI	vs LHP AB	vs LHP Avg.	vs LHP HR	vs LHP RBI
Arnold, L.A.-Chi.	14	10	9	0	1	2	1	0	0	0	.111	.200	.222	0	0	1	0	0	3	0	0	0	9	.111	0	0	0	.000	0	0
Brown, Fla.-Chi.	95	178	162	11	28	50	7	0	5	16	.173	.237	.309	1	1	1	13	0	62	3	1	3	146	.164	5	14	16	.250	0	2
Downs, Chi.-Mon.	19	34	28	2	2	2	0	0	0	1	.071	.133	.071	4	0	0	2	0	10	0	0	0	15	.133	0	1	13	.000	0	0
Rodriguez, Chi.-Fla.	112	410	367	47	94	177	21	1	20	61	.256	.327	.482	0	3	4	36	2	99	1	2	5	314	.258	18	57	53	.245	2	4
Valdes, Chi.-L.A.	22	33	25	2	5	10	2	0	1	3	.200	.231	.400	7	0	0	1	0	10	0	0	0	21	.190	0	2	4	.250	1	1
White, Mon.-Chi.	94	396	357	59	111	176	26	0	13	61	.311	.374	.493	0	2	4	33	0	79	5	3	4	283	.304	10	50	74	.338	3	11

PITCHING

Name	W	L	Pct.	ERA	IP	H	R	ER	HR	SH	SF	HB	BB	IBB	SO	G	GS	CG	ShO	GF	Sv	vs. RH AB	vs. RH Avg.	vs. RH HR	vs. RH RBI	vs. LH AB	vs. LH Avg.	vs. LH HR	vs. LH RBI
Lieber, Jon	12	11	.522	4.41	251.0	248	130	123	36	9	7	10	54	3	192	35	35	6	1	0	0	530	.234	18	61	436	.284	18	64
Tapani, Kevin	8	12	.400	5.01	195.2	208	113	109	35	4	3	8	47	1	150	30	30	2	0	0	0	455	.299	26	74	312	.231	9	32
Wood, Kerry	8	7	.533	4.80	137.0	112	77	73	17	7	5	9	87	0	132	23	23	1	0	0	0	271	.229	11	42	224	.223	6	27
Downs, Scott	4	3	.571	5.17	94.0	117	59	54	13	2	4	5	37	1	63	18	18	0	0	0	0	312	.317	8	38	66	.273	5	12
Quevedo, Ruben	3	10	.231	7.47	88.0	96	81	73	21	4	3	3	54	4	65	21	15	1	0	1	0	209	.287	12	51	145	.248	9	24
Van Poppel, Todd	4	5	.444	3.75	86.1	80	38	36	10	4	3	2	48	2	77	51	2	0	0	13	2	176	.261	7	27	145	.234	3	15
Farnsworth, Kyle	2	9	.182	6.43	77.0	90	58	55	14	4	4	4	50	8	74	46	5	0	0	8	1	185	.314	5	36	124	.258	9	24
Garibay, Daniel	2	8	.200	6.03	74.2	88	54	50	9	5	6	1	39	1	46	30	8	0	0	6	0	228	.320	9	40	66	.227	0	9
Valdes, Ismael	2	4	.333	5.37	67.0	71	40	40	17	0	2	2	27	2	45	12	12	0	0	0	0	145	.248	8	17	115	.304	9	16
Worrell, Tim	3	4	.429	2.47	62.0	60	20	17	7	4	1	1	24	8	52	54	0	0	0	27	3	134	.276	6	17	104	.221	1	7
Heredia, Felix	7	3	.700	4.76	58.2	46	31	31	6	4	2	2	33	4	52	74	0	0	0	24	2	127	.236	4	20	82	.195	2	15
Rain, Steve	3	4	.429	4.35	49.2	46	25	24	10	1	1	1	27	0	54	37	0	0	0	6	0	110	.273	7	21	74	.216	3	8
Aguilera, Rick	1	2	.333	4.91	47.2	47	28	26	11	1	0	4	18	2	38	54	0	0	0	44	29	113	.248	8	22	74	.257	3	11
Arnold, Jamie	0	3	.000	6.61	32.2	34	28	24	1	2	3	3	19	0	13	12	4	0	0	3	1	73	.274	0	15	51	.275	1	8
Lorraine, Andrew	1	2	.333	6.47	32.0	36	25	23	5	2	2	0	18	1	25	8	5	0	0	0	0	110	.300	5	22	16	.188	0	1
Williams, Brian	1	1	.500	9.62	24.1	28	27	26	4	3	1	3	23	2	14	22	0	0	0	5	1	67	.373	3	25	25	.120	1	5
Guthrie, Mark	2	3	.400	4.82	18.2	17	11	10	1	2	3	1	10	4	17	19	0	0	0	3	0	51	.235	1	11	15	.333	0	2
Spradlin, Jerry	0	1	.000	8.40	15.0	20	15	14	2	1	2	1	5	1	13	8	1	0	0	2	0	41	.317	1	10	20	.350	1	5
Karchner, Matt	1	1	.500	6.14	14.2	19	11	10	3	2	1	0	11	0	5	13	0	0	0	5	0	47	.362	3	14	14	.143	0	1
Nation, Joey	0	2	.000	6.94	11.2	12	9	9	2	1	1	2	8	0	8	2	2	0	0	0	0	43	.279	2	7	0	.000	0	0
Norton, Phil	0	1	.000	9.35	8.2	14	10	9	5	0	0	0	7	0	6	2	2	0	0	0	0	34	.382	4	7	6	.167	1	2
Ohman, Will	1	0	1.000	8.10	3.1	4	3	3	0	0	0	0	4	1	2	6	0	0	0	2	0	4	.250	0	0	9	.333	0	0
Young, Danny	0	1	.000	21.00	3.0	5	7	7	1	0	0	0	6	0	0	4	0	0	0	2	0	9	.444	1	4	5	.200	0	0
Mairena, Oswaldo	0	0	.000	18.00	2.0	7	4	4	1	0	0	0	2	0	0	2	0	0	0	1	0	9	.667	0	2	3	.333	1	2

PITCHERS WITH MORE THAN ONE N.L. TEAM

Name	W	L	Pct.	ERA	IP	H	R	ER	HR	SH	SF	HB	BB	IBB	SO	G	GS	CG	ShO	GF	Sv	vs. RH AB	vs. RH Avg.	vs. RH HR	vs. RH RBI	vs. LH AB	vs. LH Avg.	vs. LH HR	vs. LH RBI
Arnold, L.A.-Chi.	0	3	.000	6.18	39.1	38	31	27	1	2	4	4	24	0	16	14	4	0	0	4	1	88	.250	0	17	59	.271	1	10
Downs, Chi.-Mon.	4	3	.571	5.29	97.0	122	62	57	13	2	4	5	40	1	63	19	19	0	0	4	0	321	.321	8	40	70	.271	5	12
Valdes, Chi.-L.A.	2	7	.222	5.64	107.0	124	69	67	22	0	4	3	40	2	74	21	20	0	0	4	0	220	.264	8	26	202	.327	14	35

DESIGNATED HITTERS

Name	AB	Avg.	HR	RBI
Hill, Glenallen	42	.262	2	6

INDIVIDUAL STATISTICS

FIELDING

FIRST BASEMEN

Player	Pct.	G	PO	A	E	TC	DP
Grace, Mark	.997	140	1098	103	4	1205	99
Zuleta, Julio	.966	14	77	8	3	88	9
Martinez, Dave	.986	9	65	5	1	71	3
Brown, Brant	.958	7	20	3	1	24	0
Andrews, Shane	1.000	6	36	7	0	43	3
Gload, Ross	1.000	2	6	0	0	6	2
Huson, Jeff	1.000	1	1	0	0	1	0

SECOND BASEMEN

Player	Pct.	G	PO	A	E	TC	DP
Young, Eric	.979	150	313	400	15	728	86
Huson, Jeff	.952	17	19	21	2	42	7
Meyers, Chad	1.000	8	9	14	0	23	4
Nieves, Jose	1.000	7	2	11	0	13	4
Ojeda, Augie	1.000	4	2	2	0	4	1

THIRD BASEMEN

Player	Pct.	G	PO	A	E	TC	DP
Greene, Willie	.967	90	46	158	7	211	18
Andrews, Shane	.907	58	23	94	12	129	10
Nieves, Jose	.949	39	17	58	4	79	2
Huson, Jeff	1.000	18	10	16	0	26	1
Meyers, Chad	.778	8	2	5	2	9	1

SHORTSTOPS

Player	Pct.	G	PO	A	E	TC	DP
Gutierrez, Ricky	.986	121	190	290	7	487	60
Ojeda, Augie	.989	25	28	63	1	92	11
Nieves, Jose	.984	24	27	34	1	62	10
Huson, Jeff	.982	17	23	33	1	57	7

OUTFIELDERS

Player	Pct.	G	PO	A	E	TC	DP
Sosa, Sammy	.970	156	318	3	10	331	1
Buford, Damon	.986	148	336	4	5	345	1
Rodriguez, Henry	.983	70	110	5	2	117	2
Matthews Jr., Gary	.978	61	84	3	2	89	1
Hill, Glenallen	.955	29	39	3	2	44	2
Brown, Roosevelt	1.000	28	38	1	0	39	0
Brown, Brant	1.000	28	38	0	0	38	0
White, Rondell	1.000	18	41	0	0	41	0
Patterson, Corey	.963	11	26	0	1	27	0
Martinez, Dave	1.000	10	12	0	0	12	0
Brock, Tarrik	.889	10	8	0	1	9	0
Gload, Ross	1.000	8	9	0	0	9	0
Zuleta, Julio	1.000	6	6	0	0	6	0
Gonzalez, Raul	-	2	0	0	0	0	0

CATCHERS

Player	Pct.	G	PO	A	E	TC	DP	PB
Girardi, Joe	.993	103	706	43	5	754	5	3
Reed, Jeff	.990	71	469	19	5	493	7	3
Mahoney, Mike	1.000	4	9	0	0	9	0	0

PITCHERS

Player	Pct.	G	PO	A	E	TC	DP
Heredia, Felix	1.000	74	2	4	0	6	0
Aguilera, Rick	1.000	54	6	7	0	13	0
Worrell, Tim	1.000	54	0	6	0	6	0
Van Poppel, Todd	1.000	51	9	11	0	20	1
Farnsworth, Kyle	.833	46	4	6	2	12	1
Rain, Steve	1.000	37	2	2	0	4	0
Lieber, Jon	.984	35	30	31	1	62	1
Tapani, Kevin	1.000	30	11	19	0	30	1
Garibay, Daniel	1.000	30	8	19	0	27	0
Wood, Kerry	.917	23	8	14	2	24	1
Williams, Brian	1.000	22	1	2	0	3	0
Quevedo, Ruben	.938	21	6	9	1	16	2
Guthrie, Mark	1.000	19	0	2	0	2	0
Downs, Scott	1.000	18	3	11	0	14	1
Karchner, Matt	1.000	13	2	3	0	5	0
Valdes, Ismael	1.000	12	7	9	0	16	1
Arnold, Jamie	1.000	12	1	2	0	3	0
Spradlin, Jerry	1.000	8	0	2	0	2	0
Lorraine, Andrew	1.000	8	0	1	0	1	0
Ohman, Will	1.000	6	0	2	0	2	0
Young, Danny	-	4	0	0	0	0	0
Nation, Joey	1.000	2	0	3	0	3	0
Norton, Phil	1.000	2	1	2	0	3	0
Mairena, Oswaldo	-	2	0	0	0	0	0

PITCHING AGAINST EACH CLUB

Pitcher	Ari. W-L	Atl. W-L	Cin. W-L	Col. W-L	Fla. W-L	Hou. W-L	L.A. W-L	Mil. W-L	Mon. W-L	N.Y. W-L	Phi. W-L	Pit. W-L	S.D. W-L	S.F. W-L	StL. W-L	A.L. W-L	Total W-L
Aguilera, Rick	0-0	0-0	0-0	0-0	0-0	0-0	0-0	1-0	0-1	0-0	0-0	0-1	0-0	0-0	0-0	0-0	1-2
Arnold, Jamie	0-0	0-0	0-1	0-1	0-0	0-0	0-0	0-0	0-0	0-0	0-0	0-0	0-0	0-0	0-1	0-0	0-3
Downs, Scott	1-0	0-1	0-0	0-0	1-0	0-1	0-0	0-0	0-0	0-0	0-0	0-1	0-0	0-0	0-0	2-0	4-3
Farnsworth, K.	0-0	1-0	0-0	0-2	0-1	0-1	0-0	0-2	0-0	0-1	0-0	1-1	0-0	0-0	0-1	0-0	2-9
Garibay, D.	0-0	0-0	0-2	0-1	0-0	0-0	0-1	1-0	0-1	0-1	0-0	0-0	0-1	1-1	0-0	0-0	2-8
Guthrie, Mark	0-1	2-0	0-1	0-0	0-0	0-0	0-0	0-1	0-0	0-0	0-0	0-0	0-0	0-0	0-0	0-0	2-3
Heredia, Felix	1-0	0-0	0-0	0-0	0-2	0-0	0-1	2-0	0-0	1-0	2-0	0-0	1-0	0-0	0-0	0-0	7-3
Karchner, Matt	0-0	0-0	0-1	0-0	0-0	1-0	0-0	0-0	0-0	0-0	0-0	0-0	0-0	0-0	0-0	0-0	1-1
Lieber, Jon	0-1	0-1	0-1	1-1	0-1	2-1	0-1	0-0	1-0	1-1	0-1	2-0	1-0	1-0	1-2	2-0	12-11
Lorraine, A.	0-1	0-0	1-0	0-0	0-1	0-0	0-0	0-0	0-0	0-0	0-0	0-0	0-0	0-0	0-0	0-0	1-2
Mairena, O.	0-0	0-0	0-0	0-0	0-0	0-0	0-0	0-0	0-0	0-0	0-0	0-0	0-0	0-0	0-0	0-0	0-0
Nation, Joey	0-0	0-0	0-0	0-0	0-0	0-0	0-0	0-0	0-0	0-0	0-1	0-0	0-0	0-0	0-1	0-0	0-2
Norton, Phil	0-0	0-0	0-0	0-0	0-0	0-0	0-1	0-0	0-0	0-0	0-0	0-0	0-0	0-0	0-0	0-0	0-1
Ohman, Will	0-0	0-0	0-0	0-0	0-0	0-0	0-0	0-0	0-0	0-0	0-0	0-0	0-0	0-0	1-0	0-0	1-0
Quevedo, R.	0-1	0-1	0-1	0-0	0-1	1-1	1-0	0-0	0-1	0-0	1-0	0-1	0-1	0-1	0-1	0-0	3-10
Rain, Steve	0-1	0-0	0-1	1-0	0-0	0-0	0-0	0-0	1-0	0-0	1-0	0-1	0-1	0-0	0-0	0-0	3-4
Spradlin, J.	0-0	0-0	0-0	0-0	0-0	0-0	0-0	0-0	0-0	0-0	0-0	0-0	0-0	0-0	0-1	0-0	0-1
Tapani, Kevin	2-0	1-1	1-0	1-0	0-0	0-2	0-1	0-0	0-1	0-1	0-1	0-1	1-1	0-1	0-2	2-0	8-12
Valdes, Ismael	0-0	0-0	1-0	0-0	0-0	0-1	0-0	1-1	0-0	0-0	0-0	0-0	0-0	0-0	0-0	0-2	2-4
Van Poppel, T.	0-0	0-0	0-0	1-0	0-0	0-0	0-1	0-1	1-0	0-0	0-0	0-0	0-0	0-0	1-0	1-3	4-5
Williams, B.	0-0	0-0	0-0	0-0	0-0	0-0	0-0	0-1	1-0	0-0	0-0	0-0	0-0	0-0	0-0	0-0	1-1
Wood, Kerry	0-0	1-0	1-0	0-0	0-0	1-0	0-0	1-1	0-1	0-0	1-0	0-2	0-0	2-1	0-0	1-2	8-7
Worrell, Tim	0-0	0-0	0-0	0-0	0-0	0-0	2-0	0-0	0-0	0-0	1-0	0-1	0-1	0-1	0-1	0-0	3-4
Young, Danny	0-0	0-0	0-0	0-0	0-0	0-0	0-0	0-0	0-0	0-1	0-0	0-0	0-0	0-0	0-0	0-0	0-1
Totals	4-5	5-4	4-8	4-5	1-6	5-7	3-6	6-7	4-5	2-5	6-3	3-9	3-5	4-5	3-10	8-7	65-97

INTERLEAGUE: Van Poppel 1-2, Lieber 1-0, Tapani 1-0, Wood 0-1 vs. White Sox; Downs 1-0, Wood 0-1, Van Poppel 0-1 vs. Tigers; Wood 1-0, Downs 1-0, Valdes 0-1 vs. Royals; Lieber 1-0, Tapani 1-0, Valdes 0-1 vs. Twins. Total: 8-7.

MISCELLANEOUS

HOME RUNS BY PARK

At Arizona (4): Sosa 4.
At Atlanta (3): Hill 1, Nieves 1, Matthews Jr. 1.
At Chicago (AL) (4): Hill 1, Grace 1, Sosa 1, Brown 1.
At Chicago (NL) (84): Sosa 22, Buford 9, Greene 7, Gutierrez 7, Andrews 7, Hill 6, Rodriguez 6, Young 5, Girardi 4, Grace 3, Matthews Jr. 2, Wood 1, Nieves 1, Brown 1, Zuleta 1, Patterson 1, Ojeda 1.
At Cincinnati (8): Sosa 3, Grace 2, Hill 1, Buford 1, Andrews 1.
At Colorado (11): Sosa 3, Greene 2, Reed 1, Hill 1, Girardi 1, Buford 1, Zuleta 1, Gload 1.
At Florida (3): Buford 1, Brown 1, Nieves 1.
At Houston (14): Rodriguez 3, Gutierrez 3, Sosa 2, White 2, Young 1, Greene 1, Buford 1, Andrews 1.
At Kansas City (3): Sosa 3.
At Los Angeles (3): Reed 1, Sosa 1, Gutierrez 1.
At Milwaukee (5): Rodriguez 2, Reed 1, Brown 1, Patterson 1.
At Minnesota (3): Sosa 2, Hill 1.
At Montreal (8): Rodriguez 3, Sosa 2, Reed 1, Tapani 1, Buford 1.
At New York (NL) (5): Grace 1, Sosa 1, Rodriguez 1, Buford 1, Andrews 1.
At Philadelphia (5): Grace 2, Sosa 2, Rodriguez 1.
At Pittsburgh (4): Sosa 1, Brown 1, Nieves 1, Brown 1.
At San Diego (3): Grace 1, Girardi 1, Sosa 1.
At San Francisco (5): Rodriguez 2, Sosa 1, Nieves 1, Zuleta 1.
At St. Louis (6): Andrews 3, Sosa 1, Matthews Jr. 1, Ojeda 1.

LOW-HIT GAMES

No-hitters: None.
One-hitters: None.
Two-hitters: Jon Lieber, July 3 vs. Pittsburgh, W 3-0.

10-STRIKEOUT GAMES

Jon Lieber 4, Kerry Wood 2, Kevin Tapani 1, Total: 7

FOUR OR MORE HITS IN ONE GAME

Eric Young 4, Mark Grace 3 (including one five-hit game), Sammy Sosa 3 (including one five-hit game), Damon Buford 3, Joe Girardi 2, Jeff Huson 1, Henry Rodriguez 1, Willie Greene 1, Rondell White 1, Total: 19

MULTI-HOMER GAMES

Sammy Sosa 5, Henry Rodriguez 2, Rondell White 1, Shane Andrews 1, Total: 9

GRAND SLAMS

4-20: Sammy Sosa (off Montreal's Miguel Batista)
4-27: Henry Rodriguez (off Houston's Jose Lima)
7-26: Mark Grace (off Philadelphia's Paul Byrd)
9-19: Roosevelt Brown (off Milwaukee's Juan Acevedo)

PINCH HITTERS

(Minimum 5 at-bats)

Name	AB	Avg.	HR	RBI
Matthews Jr., Gary	25	.240	2	3
Hill, Glenallen	25	.200	1	5
Nieves, Jose	20	.200	0	3
Huson, Jeff	19	.158	0	1
Reed, Jeff	18	.389	0	5
Brown, Brant	18	.111	0	1
Meyers, Chad	16	.188	0	2
Brown, Roosevelt	14	.286	1	5
Greene, Willie	14	.143	0	1
Andrews, Shane	11	.091	1	3
Zuleta, Julio	9	.222	1	2
Gload, Ross	8	.250	0	0
Buford, Damon	6	.000	0	0
Rodriguez, Henry	5	.400	2	6

DEBUTS

3-29: Tarrik Brock, LF.
3-30: Danny Young, P.
4-6: Julio Zuleta, PH.
4-9: Scott Downs, P.
4-9: Daniel Garibay, P.
4-14: Ruben Quevedo, P.
5-25: Raul Gonzalez, PH.
6-4: Augie Ojeda, SS.
8-3: Phil Norton, P.
8-31: Ross Gload, LF.
9-5: Oswaldo Mairena, P.
9-8: Mike Mahoney, C.
9-18: Corey Patterson, PH.
9-19: Will Ohman, P.
9-23: Joey Nation, P.

GAMES BY POSITION

Catcher: Joe Girardi 103, Jeff Reed 71, Mike Mahoney 4.
First base: Mark Grace 140, Julio Zuleta 14, Dave Martinez 9, Brant Brown 7, Shane Andrews 6, Ross Gload 2, Jeff Huson 1.
Second base: Eric Young 150, Jeff Huson 17, Chad Meyers 8, Jose Nieves 7, Augie Ojeda 4.
Third base: Willie Greene 90, Shane Andrews 58, Jose Nieves 39, Jeff Huson 18, Chad Meyers 8.
Shortstop: Ricky Gutierrez 121, Augie Ojeda 25, Jose Nieves 24, Jeff Huson 17.
Outfield: Sammy Sosa 156, Damon Buford 148, Henry Rodriguez 70, Gary Matthews Jr. 61, Glenallen Hill 29, Brant Brown 28, Roosevelt Brown 28, Rondell White 18, Corey Patterson 11, Dave Martinez 10, Tarrik Brock 10, Ross Gload 8, Julio Zuleta 6, Raul Gonzalez 2.
Designated hitter: Glenallen Hill 9.

STREAKS

Wins: 6 (July 21-27)
Losses: 8 (September 13-20)
Consecutive games with at least one hit: 15, Sammy Sosa (July 4-22)
Wins by pitcher: 4, Jon Lieber (June 28-July 14)

ATTENDANCE

Home: 2,789,511
Road: 2,764,792
Highest (home): 55,000 (March 30 vs. New York).
Highest (road): 55,351 (October 1 vs. Pittsburgh).
Lowest (home): 5,267 (June 1 vs. Atlanta).
Lowest (road): 9,975 (April 18 vs. Montreal).

CINCINNATI REDS

DAY BY DAY

Date	Opp.	Res.	Score	(inn.*)	Hits	Opp. hits	Winning pitcher	Losing pitcher	Save	Record	Pos.	GB
4-3	Mil.	T	3-3	(6)	5	7				0-0	T3rd	0.5
4-4	Mil.	L	1-5		4	10	Bruske	Williamson		0-1	T5th	1.0
4-5	Mil.	L	5-8		13	10	Haynes	Parris	Wickman	0-2	T5th	2.0
4-6	Mil.	W	5-1		7	8	Villone	Navarro		1-2	T4th	2.0
4-7	Chi.	L	6-10		8	8	Lorraine	Harnisch	Aguilera	1-3	6th	2.0
4-8	Chi.	W	4-3	(11)	11	4	Graves	Guthrie		2-3	T4th	2.0
4-9	Chi.	W	8-7	(11)	9	13	Graves	Karchner		3-3	T2nd	2.0
4-10	At Col.	L	5-7		10	13	Arrojo	Parris	Belinda	3-4	T3rd	3.0
4-11	At Col.	W	10-3		14	6	Villone	Bohanon		4-4	3rd	3.0
4-12	At Col.	L	5-7		9	9	Jimenez	Reyes	Tavarez	4-5	T3rd	3.0
4-14	At L.A.	L	1-8		9	9	Hershiser	Bell		4-6	T5th	2.5
4-15	At L.A.	W	5-4		8	7	Williamson	Mills	Graves	5-6	T4th	2.0
4-16	At L.A.	W	5-3		7	6	Parris	Park	Graves	6-6	T2nd	1.5
4-18	S.F	L	9-13		8	16	Rueter	Williamson		6-7	T2nd	2.5
4-19	S.F	W	5-4		9	8	Bell	Estes	Graves	7-7	2nd	2.5
4-20	S.F	W	11-1		15	6	Neagle	Hernandez		8-7	2nd	2.5
4-21	L.A.	L	2-9		10	11	Herges	Parris	Adams	8-8	2nd	2.5
4-22	L.A.	L	2-16		5	15	Park	Harnisch	Mills	8-9	2nd	2.5
4-23	L.A.	L	3-11		13	11	Perez	Villone		8-10	2nd	3.5
4-25	At N.Y.	L	5-6		8	8	Wendell	Sullivan	Benitez	8-11	2nd	4.5
4-26	At N.Y.	W	12-1		18	4	Neagle	Springer		9-11	2nd	4.5
4-27	At N.Y.	W	2-1	(12)	8	6	Graves	Benitez	Sullivan	10-11	2nd	3.5
4-28	At Pit.	L	1-2		5	6	Benson	Harnisch	Williams	10-12	2nd	4.5
4-29	At Pit.	W	6-5		8	8	Williamson	Christiansen	Graves	11-12	2nd	4.5
4-30	At Pit.	W	6-2		10	6	Bell	Ritchie	Williamson	12-12	2nd	4.5
5-2	At Phi.	W	7-0		12	3	Neagle	Ashby	Sullivan	13-12	2nd	3.5
5-3	At Phi.	L	2-5		4	9	Byrd	Parris		13-13	2nd	3.5
5-4	At Phi.	L	1-14		7	21	Person	Harnisch		13-14	2nd	4.5
5-5	StL.	W	3-2		8	7	Villone	Benes	Williamson	14-14	2nd	3.5
5-6	StL.	L	1-3		6	5	Kile	Bell	Veres	14-15	2nd	4.5
5-7	StL.	W	9-7		8	10	Neagle	Holmes	Williamson	15-15	2nd	3.5
5-9	S.D.	W	2-0		7	8	Parris	Meadows	Graves	16-15	2nd	3.0
5-10	S.D.	W	5-1		8	6	Villone	Hitchcock	Williamson	17-15	2nd	2.0
5-11	S.D.	W	11-9		16	11	Graves	Whisenant		18-15	2nd	1.5
5-12	At Hou.	W	7-3	(11)	10	9	Graves	Maddux		19-15	2nd	0.5
5-13	At Hou.	W	8-7		12	10	Reyes	Wagner	Williamson	20-15	1st	+0.5
5-14	At Hou.	L	3-10		6	13	Elarton	Parris		20-16	2nd	0.5
5-15	At Hou.	W	4-3		9	4	Villone	Lima	Graves	21-16	T1st	...
5-16	Pit.	W	6-2		12	9	Bell	Ritchie		22-16	T1st	...
5-17	Pit.	L	6-9		12	13	Silva	Sullivan		22-17	T1st	...
5-18	Pit.	W	4-3	(10)	9	10	Graves	Garcia		23-17	T1st	...
5-19	At Chi.	L	1-4		6	7	Valdes	Parris	Van Poppel	23-18	T1st	...
5-20	At Chi.	W	5-3		8	10	Villone	Lieber	Graves	24-18	T1st	...
5-21	At Chi.	L	2-4		10	5	Tapani	Bell	Heredia	24-19	2nd	1.0
5-22	At L.A.	L	3-4	(14)	10	9	Herges	Aybar		24-20	2nd	1.5
5-23	At L.A.	W	3-1		7	3	Fernandez	Gagne	Graves	25-20	2nd	1.5
5-24	At L.A.	W	10-3		11	7	Sullivan	Park		26-20	2nd	1.5
5-26	Fla.	W	3-2		8	8	Graves	Miceli		27-20	2nd	1.0
5-27	Fla.	L	6-8	(10)	8	12	Alfonseca	Williamson		27-21	2nd	1.0
5-28	Fla.	L	1-3		10	8	Dempster	Sullivan	Alfonseca	27-22	2nd	1.0
5-30	Mon.	W	4-2		5	3	Fernandez	Armas	Williamson	28-22	2nd	1.5
5-31	Mon.	L	4-10		6	16	Johnson	Parris		28-23	2nd	1.5
6-1	Mon.	L	7-9		16	17	Vazquez	Villone	Kline	28-24	2nd	1.5
6-2	Min.	W	4-3		10	7	Bell	Mays	Graves	29-24	2nd	1.5
6-3	Min.	W	9-3		8	4	Neagle	Bergman		30-24	2nd	0.5
6-4	Min.	W	3-2	(10)	9	9	Graves	Hawkins		31-24	1st	+0.5
6-5	Chi. (AL)	L	3-4		10	7	Baldwin	Parris	Foulke	31-25	1st	+0.5
6-6	Chi. (AL)	L	12-17		12	19	Eldred	Villone		31-26	2nd	0.5
6-7	Chi. (AL)	L	4-6		8	11	Parque	Bell	Foulke	31-27	2nd	1.5
6-9	At Cle.	L	4-7		8	12	Brower	Neagle	Karsay	31-28	2nd	1.5
6-10	At Cle.	L	5-6		8	12	Burba	Parris	Karsay	31-29	2nd	1.5
6-11	At Cle.	W	7-5	(13)	9	14	Aybar	Kamieniecki		32-29	2nd	1.5
6-12	At S.F	L	3-10		9	11	Nathan	Bell		32-30	2nd	2.5
6-13	At S.F	L	2-3		8	7	Nen	Graves		32-31	2nd	3.5
6-14	At S.F	L	2-6		8	12	Rueter	Neagle	Rodriguez	32-32	2nd	4.5
6-16	At S.D.	L	5-8		10	11	Reyes	Parris	Hoffman	32-33	2nd	5.5
6-17	At S.D.	L	1-3		5	6	Walker	Villone	Hoffman	32-34	2nd	6.5
6-18	At S.D.	L	7-8		11	8	Clement	Bell	Hoffman	32-35	2nd	6.5
6-20	Col.	W	3-2		11	7	Graves	Astacio		33-35	2nd	6.5
6-21	Col.	L	4-6		8	11	Tavarez	Williamson	Jimenez	33-36	2nd	6.5
6-22	Col.	W	5-3		10	6	Parris	Jarvis	Graves	34-36	2nd	6.5
6-23	S.D.	L	7-10	(10)	14	12	Hoffman	Williamson	Reyes	34-37	2nd	7.5
6-24	S.D.	W	11-5		15	14	Villone	Clement	Dessens	35-37	2nd	7.5
6-25	S.D.	L	4-5		12	7	Tollberg	Fernandez	Hoffman	35-38	2nd	8.5
6-26	StL.	W	3-2		10	7	Neagle	Stephenson	Graves	36-38	2nd	7.5
6-27	StL.	L	3-4		11	9	Kile	Parris	Veres	36-39	2nd	8.5
6-28	StL.	W	7-3		8	7	Reyes	Al. Benes		37-39	2nd	7.5
6-29	StL.	L	3-12		4	15	An. Benes	Villone		37-40	2nd	8.5
6-30	At Ari.	W	5-4		11	7	Harnisch	Morgan	Graves	38-40	2nd	8.5

HIGHLIGHTS

High point: June 4. Pokey Reese's one-out, 10th-inning single drove in the winning run in a 3-2 win over Minnesota and completed a three-game sweep at Cinergy Field. The win gave the Reds a half game lead over the Cardinals in the Central Division and closer Danny Graves an 8-0 record.

Low point: August 16. The Brewers completed their first-ever sweep of the Reds and put a serious damper on Cincinnati's playoff hopes. The Reds, fresh off five wins in six games against Atlanta and the Cubs, fell one game below .500 and $6^1/_2$ behind St. Louis.

Turning point: When the Reds were swept out of first place by the White Sox in a June 5-7 series at Cinergy Field. In one game, Reds pitchers surrendered 17 runs. In another, the team blew a 3-0 lead. The series started a 12-game stretch in which the Reds lost 11 times.

Most valuable player: Switch-hitting Dmitri Young batted a solid .303 and led the team with 166 hits and 37 doubles. He was second with 88 RBIs and third with 18 home runs, both of which were career highs.

Most valuable pitcher: Veteran Pete Harnisch struggled early when weakness in his rotator cuff contributed to an 0-4 start. After a stint on the D.L., he made 16 starts, recording an 8-2 record and 3.49 ERA. The team was 43-44 when Harnisch was ineffective and out of action, 42-33 when he was healthy.

Most improved player: Juan Castro came from the Dodgers with a good-field, no-hit reputation. He lived up to it as a slick glove man at short and second, but his .241 average and four home runs over 82 games was much better than expected.

Most pleasant surprise: Journeyman Elmer Dessens moved into the rotation spot vacated by the mid-season trade of Denny Neagle and posted 11 wins in 16 starts. He was 5-0 with a 2.55 ERA in September.

Key injuries: The broken thumb suffered by Sean Casey in the last exhibition game before Opening Day cost the first baseman 28 games but plagued him through a difficult first half. ... Harnisch's weak rotator cuff left the Reds without an ace for the first half. ... Aaron Boone's torn anterior cruciate ligament forced utilityman Chris Stynes into the lineup and hurt the Reds' bench strength for much of the second half.

Notable: The Reds became only the second team to go through an entire season without being shut out. ... Reds pitchers set a major league record with 96 wild pitches, led by Scott Williamson's club-record 21. ... Reds pitchers also handed out a club-record 659 walks. ... Shortstop Barry Larkin became the fourth player in Reds history to collect 2,000 career hits. He joined Pete Rose, Dave Concepcion and Johnny Bench.

—MARK SCHMETZER

MISCELLANEOUS

RECORDS

2000 regular-season record: 85-77 (2nd in N.L. Central); 43-38 at home; 42-39 on road; 22-19 vs. East; 41-37 vs. Central; 22-21 vs. West; 25-12 vs. left-handed starters; 60-65 vs. righthanded starters; 34-34 on grass; 51-43 on turf; 35-27 in daytime; 50-50 at night; 25-23 in one-run games; 9-7 in extra-inning games; 0-1-0 in doubleheaders.

Team record past five years: 415-396 (.512, ranks 9th in league in that span).

TEAM LEADERS

Batting average: Sean Casey (.315).
At-bats: Dmitri Young (548).
Runs: Ken Griffey Jr. (100).
Hits: Dmitri Young (166).
Total Bases: Ken Griffey Jr. (289).
Doubles: Dmitri Young (37).
Triples: Pokey Reese, Dmitri Young (6).
Home runs: Ken Griffey Jr. (40).
Runs batted in: Ken Griffey Jr. (118).
Stolen bases: Pokey Reese (29).
Slugging percentage: Ken Griffey Jr. (.556).
On-base percentage: Ken Griffey Jr. (.387).
Wins: Steve Parris (12).
Earned-run average: Steve Parris (4.81).
Complete games: Pete Harnisch (3).
Shutouts: Pete Harnisch (1).
Saves: Danny Graves (30).
Innings pitched: Steve Parris (192.2).
Strikeouts: Scott Williamson (136).

Date	Opp.	Res.	Score	(inn.*)	Hits	Opp. hits	Winning pitcher	Losing pitcher	Save	Record	Pos.	GB
7-1	At Ari.	L	6-9		6	12	Springer	Fernandez	Kim	38-41	2nd	9.5
7-2	At Ari.	W	14-2		20	9	Neagle	Daal		39-41	2nd	8.5
7-3	At Ari.	W	3-2		8	9	Parris	Anderson	Graves	40-41	2nd	8.0
7-4	At StL.	L	3-14		9	13	An. Benes	Villone		40-42	2nd	9.0
7-5	At StL.	L	3-4		6	5	Hentgen	Harnisch	Veres	40-43	2nd	10.0
7-6	At StL.	W	12-6		13	13	Dessens	Ankiel		41-43	2nd	9.0
7-7	Cle.	W	2-1		7	8	Neagle	Finley	Graves	42-43	2nd	8.0
7-8	Cle.	W	14-5		17	9	Parris	Davis		43-43	2nd	7.0
7-9	Cle.	L	3-5		7	6	Colon	Williamson	Karsay	43-44	2nd	8.0
7-13	At Col.	W	15-6		13	9	Dessens	Astacio		44-44	2nd	8.0
7-14	At Col.	W	9-2		14	5	Harnisch	Arrojo		45-44	2nd	8.0
7-15	At Col.	W	7-4		12	8	Williamson	Yoshii	Graves	46-44	2nd	7.0
7-16	At Det.	L	2-6		10	10	Weaver	Parris		46-45	2nd	7.0
7-17	At Det.	L	1-3		10	8	Mlicki	Luebbers	Jones	46-46	2nd	8.0
7-18	At Det.	W	5-4		15	10	Dessens	Moehler	Graves	47-46	2nd	7.0
7-19	At Hou.	W	4-0		7	4	Harnisch	Holt		48-46	2nd	6.0
7-20	At Hou.	L	2-6		8	8	Lima	Williamson		48-47	2nd	6.0
7-21	Ari.	L	4-5		11	14	Swindell	Sullivan	Mantei	48-48	2nd	7.0
7-22	Ari.	W	7-3		14	8	Villone	Guzman		49-48	2nd	6.0
7-23	Ari.	W	5-3		10	9	Dessens	Anderson	Graves	50-48	2nd	5.0
7-24	Hou.	L	5-7	(10)	7	15	Dotel	Graves		50-49	2nd	5.5
7-25	Hou.	L	4-7		6	12	Valdes	Villone		50-50	2nd	6.5
7-26	Hou.	L	2-3		6	11	Elarton	Parris	Dotel	50-51	2nd	7.5
7-28	At Mon.	W	8-3		12	8	Dessens	Johnson		51-51	2nd	6.0
7-29	At Mon.	W	4-3	(11)	11	11	Graves	Santana		52-51	2nd	5.0
7-30	At Mon.	W	7-4		11	8	Bell	Hermanson	Graves	53-51	2nd	4.0
7-31	At N.Y.	W	6-0		10	8	Williamson	Rusch	Luebbers	54-51	2nd	4.0
8-1	At N.Y.	L	2-3		9	9	Hampton	Parris	Benitez	54-52	2nd	4.0
8-2	At N.Y.	L	1-2		5	7	Leiter	Dessens	Benitez	54-53	2nd	5.0
8-4	Fla.	L	1-2		8	10	Dempster	Harnisch	Alfonseca	54-54	2nd	5.0
8-5	Fla.	L	5-10	(11)	15	13	Alfonseca	Wohlers		54-55	2nd	6.0
8-6	Fla.	L	6-9		12	9	Aybar	Graves	Looper	54-56	2nd	6.0
8-7	Atl.	W	3-2	(10)	11	12	Sullivan	Ligtenberg		55-56	2nd	6.0
8-8	Atl.	L	4-5		9	11	Ashby	Dessens	Remlinger	55-57	2nd	6.0
8-9	Atl.	W	10-6		12	9	Harnisch	Glavine		56-57	2nd	5.0
8-11	At Chi.	W	6-4		11	6	Wohlers	Rain	Graves	57-57	2nd	4.5
8-12	At Chi.	W	3-0		7	5	Williamson	Garibay	Graves	58-57	2nd	4.5
8-13	At Chi.	W	3-0		6	7	Parris	Quevedo	Sullivan	59-57	2nd	4.5
8-14	At Mil.	L	3-4		8	8	Rigdon	Dessens	Leskanic	59-58	2nd	4.5
8-15	At Mil.	L	1-2	(10)	5	7	Leskanic	Wohlers		59-59	2nd	5.5
8-16	At Mil.	L	1-5		9	9	D'Amico	Bell		59-60	2nd	6.5
8-18	Pit.	L	3-6		6	11	Ritchie	Sullivan	Williams	59-61	2nd	7.5
8-19	Pit.	W	7-1		7	8	Parris	Anderson		60-61	2nd	7.5
8-20	Pit.	L	3-7		9	8	Silva	Dessens		60-62	2nd	7.5
8-21	Phi.	W	7-4		13	11	Harnisch	Wolf	Graves	61-62	2nd	7.5
8-22	Phi.	L	4-5		6	9	Padilla	Luebbers	Brantley	61-63	2nd	7.5
8-23	Phi.	L	3-4		5	7	Brock	Graves	Padilla	61-64	2nd	8.5
8-24	Phi.	W	8-3		11	11	Parris	Daal		62-64	2nd	8.5
8-25	At Fla.	W	6-0		13	8	Dessens	Cornelius		63-64	2nd	7.5
8-26	At Fla.	W	3-2		5	9	Harnisch	Darensbourg	Graves	64-64	2nd	7.5
8-27	At Fla.	L	6-7		13	10	Miceli	Graves		64-65	2nd	8.5
8-28	At Atl.	W	6-3		11	5	Villone	Maddux		65-65	2nd	8.5
8-29	At Atl.	W	4-2		11	9	Parris	Remlinger	Graves	66-65	2nd	7.5
8-30	At Atl.	L	2-5		3	14	Glavine	Dessens		66-66	2nd	8.5
8-31	At Atl.	W	4-3		8	4	Riedling	Millwood	Graves	67-66	2nd	8.0
9-1	Mon.	W	8-2		10	7	Bell	Hermanson		68-66	2nd	8.0
9-2	Mon.	L	5-9		6	12	Lira	Villone		68-67	2nd	9.0
9-3	Mon.	W	8-1		12	11	Parris	Thurman		69-67	2nd	9.0
9-4	N.Y.	W	6-2		8	6	Dessens	Leiter		70-67	2nd	9.0
9-5	N.Y.	L	2-3	(10)	8	6	Wendell	Sullivan	Benitez	70-68	2nd	10.0
9-6	N.Y.	W	11-8		13	6	Riedling	Franco	Graves	71-68	2nd	9.0
9-8†	At Pit.	L	3-7		7	11	Ritchie	Williamson		71-69		
9-8‡	At Pit.	L	1-3		9	6	Wilkins	Villone	Williams	71-70	2nd	10.0
9-9	At Pit.	W	6-4		14	9	Parris	Benson	Graves	72-70	2nd	10.0
9-10	At Pit.	W	6-4		8	6	Dessens	Anderson	Graves	73-70	2nd	9.0
9-11	Chi.	W	7-6		9	14	Harnisch	Garibay	Graves	74-70	2nd	9.0
9-12	Chi.	L	1-2		4	6	Wood	Fernandez		74-71	2nd	10.0
9-13	Chi.	W	13-3		16	6	Bell	Arnold		75-71	2nd	10.0
9-14	Mil.	L	4-6		12	8	Haynes	Villone	Leskanic	75-72	2nd	11.0
9-15	Mil.	W	6-4		11	7	Parris	Wright	Graves	76-72	2nd	11.0
9-16	Mil.	W	7-3		9	10	Dessens	Rigdon	Riedling	77-72	2nd	11.0
9-17	Mil.	W	8-4		7	5	Harnisch	Snyder		78-72	2nd	11.0
9-18	At S.F	W	7-1		12	4	Fernandez	Estes		79-72	2nd	10.5
9-19	At S.F	L	3-7		7	14	Hernandez	Bell		79-73	2nd	10.5
9-20	At S.F	L	2-4		4	5	Ortiz	Parris	Nen	79-74	2nd	11.5
9-22	Hou.	W	12-5		14	12	Dessens	Lima		80-74	2nd	10.0
9-23	Hou.	W	6-4		12	11	Riedling	Slusarski	Graves	81-74	2nd	10.0
9-24	Hou.	W	4-3		7	6	Sullivan	Dotel		82-74	2nd	9.0
9-26	At Mil.	L	4-7		9	13	Wright	Parris	Leskanic	82-75	2nd	10.0
9-27	At Mil.	L	6-10		11	8	de los Santos	Riedling		82-76	2nd	11.0
9-28	At Mil.	W	8-1		14	2	Dessens	D'Amico		83-76	2nd	11.0
9-29	At StL.	W	8-1		15	2	Villone	Stephenson		84-76	2nd	10.0
9-30	At StL.	W	8-4		12	9	Fernandez	Hentgen		85-76	2nd	9.0
10-1	At StL.	L	2-6		8	8	An. Benes	Parris		85-77	2nd	10.0

Monthly records: April (12-12), May (16-11), June (10-17), July (16-11), August (13-15), September (18-10), October (0-1).
*Innings, if other than nine. † First game of a doubleheader. ‡ Second game of a doubleheader.

MEMORABLE GAMES

August 9 at Cincinnati

Pete Harnisch survived a five-run Atlanta third and went the distance in a 10-6 victory that snapped the Reds' eight-series losing streak to Atlanta. Harnisch also contributed a two-run homer to the assault on Braves starter Tom Glavine, who had been 14-3 in his career at Cinergy Field. The win came in the rubber game of a three-game series.

Atlanta	AB	R	H	BI	Cincinnati	AB	R	H	BI
Furcal, 2b	5	1	1	0	Stynes, 3b	4	1	0	1
A.Jones, cf	4	0	0	0	Castro, ss	4	0	1	0
C.Jones, 3b	4	0	1	0	Griffey Jr., cf	4	3	3	2
Joyner, 1b	4	2	2	2	Bichette, rf	4	1	1	0
Surhoff, lf	4	1	2	0	Tucker, rf	0	0	0	0
Bonilla, rf	4	1	2	2	Young, 1b	3	1	1	1
Burkett, p	0	0	0	0	Ochoa, lf	4	2	3	3
Bako, c	3	0	0	1	Reese, 2b	4	1	1	0
Weiss, ss	4	0	0	0	LaRue, c	4	0	1	1
Glavine, p	2	1	1	0	Harnisch, p	3	1	1	2
Belinda, p	0	0	0	0					
Lockhart, ph	1	0	0	0					
Mulholland, p	0	0	0	0					
Lombard, rf	1	0	0	0					
Totals	**36**	**6**	**9**	**5**	**Totals**	**34**	**10**	**12**	**10**

Atlanta ....0 1 5 0 0 0 0 0 0— 6 9 1
Cincinnati...............................2 0 1 2 5 0 0 0 x—10 12 0

E—C. Jones (17). DP—Atlanta 1, LOB—Atlanta 4, Cincinnati 3. 2B—Young (24), Ochoa (9). 3B—C.Jones (1), Bonilla (3), Ochoa (1). HR—Griffey Jr. (33), Harnisch (1). CS—Castro (1). SH—Harnisch.

Atlanta	IP	H	R	ER	BB	SO
Glavine (L 14-6)	4	9	8	8	2	0
Belinda	1	2	2	2	0	1
Mulholland	2	1	0	0	0	1
Burkett	1	0	0	0	0	1

Cincinnati	IP	H	R	ER	BB	SO
Harnisch (W 4-6)	9	9	6	6	1	3

Glavine pitched to 4 batters in 5th.

WP—Harnisch. U—HP, Foster. 1B, Van Vleet. 2B, Marsh. 3B, Hernandez. T—2:22. A—31,098.

September 29 at St. Louis

Ron Villone ended his season with a flourish, stopping the Cardinals in a two-hit, 8-1 victory at Busch Stadium. The two-hitter matched the previous day's effort of Elmer Dessens against Milwaukee, also an 8-1 win. Villone set a club record for lefthanders with 16 strikeouts and tied the overall club record for strikeouts by one pitcher in a nine-inning game. He benefited from homers by Michael Tucker, Sean Casey and Alex Ochoa.

Cincinnati	AB	R	H	BI	St. Louis	AB	R	H	BI
Tucker, cf-rf	4	2	2	1	Vina, 2b	3	0	1	0
Sexton, 2b	3	0	0	1	Saturria, cf	0	0	0	0
Young, lf	4	1	1	0	Dunston, lf-cf-lf	4	0	0	0
Hunter, cf	0	0	0	1	Edmonds, cf	2	0	0	0
Casey, 1b	5	2	3	2	Paquette, ph-lf-2b	2	0	0	0
Ochoa, rf-lf	5	1	2	3	Davis, rf	4	0	1	0
Stynes, 3b	5	0	2	0	Tatis, 3b	4	0	0	0
Castro, ss	3	0	0	0	Clark, 1b	2	0	0	0
LaRue, c	4	1	2	0	Perez, 1b	2	0	0	0
Villone, p	4	1	3	0	Renteria, ss	1	1	0	0
					Marrero, c	2	0	0	0
					Stephenson, p	1	0	0	0
					McGwire, ph	1	0	0	0
					Reames, p	0	0	0	0
					Polanco, ph	1	0	0	0
					Stechschulte, p	0	0	0	0
					Al.Benes, p	0	0	0	0
					Hernandez, ph	1	0	0	0
Totals	**37**	**8**	**15**	**8**	**Totals**	**30**	**1**	**2**	**0**

Cincinnati ....3 0 2 0 0 0 0 0 3—8 15 1
St. Louis ....0 0 0 0 1 0 0 0 0—1 2 0

E—Tucker (5). DP—St. Louis 4. LOB—Cincinnati 7, St. Louis 8. 2B—Casey (33). 3B—Vina (6). HR—Tucker (15), Casey (20), Ochoa (13). CS—Castro (2). S—Hunter.

Cincinnati	IP	H	R	ER	BB	SO
Villone (W 10-10)	9	2	1	0	5	16

St. Louis	IP	H	R	ER	BB	SO
Stephenson (L 16-9)	5	9	5	5	1	3
Reames	2	3	0	0	1	0
Stechschulte	1	2	3	3	2	0
Al.Benes	1	1	0	0	0	0

Stechschulte pitched to 4 batters in 9th.

WP—Villone. HBP—Vina by Villone. U—HP, Reliford. 1B, -Carlson.2B, Timmons. 3B, DeMuth. T—2:59. A—46,152.

INDIVIDUAL STATISTICS

BATTING

Name	G	TPA	AB	R	H	TB	2B	3B	HR	RBI	Avg.	Obp.	Slg.	SH	SF	HP	BB	IBB	SO	SB	CS	GDP	vs RHP AB	vs RHP Avg.	vs RHP HR	vs RHP RBI	vs LHP AB	vs LHP Avg.	vs LHP HR	vs LHP RBI
Young, Dmitri	152	593	548	68	166	269	37	6	18	88	.303	.346	.491	1	5	3	36	6	80	0	3	16	407	.292	13	62	141	.333	5	26
Griffey Jr., Ken	145	631	520	100	141	289	22	3	40	118	.271	.387	.556	0	8	9	94	17	117	6	4	7	368	.274	29	86	152	.263	11	32
Reese, Pokey	135	577	518	76	132	200	20	6	12	46	.255	.319	.386	3	5	6	45	5	86	29	3	8	409	.254	11	37	109	.257	1	9
Casey, Sean	133	545	480	69	151	248	33	2	20	85	.315	.385	.517	0	6	7	52	4	80	1	0	16	376	.332	19	67	104	.250	1	18
Bichette, Dante	125	514	461	67	136	215	27	2	16	76	.295	.353	.466	1	7	4	41	3	69	5	2	18	362	.298	12	55	99	.283	4	21
Larkin, Barry	102	447	396	71	124	193	26	5	11	41	.313	.389	.487	2	0	1	48	0	31	14	6	10	321	.315	8	32	75	.307	3	9
Stynes, Chris	119	420	380	71	127	189	24	1	12	40	.334	.386	.497	3	3	2	32	2	54	5	2	5	292	.315	9	28	88	.398	3	12
Boone, Aaron	84	332	291	44	83	137	18	0	12	43	.285	.356	.471	2	4	10	24	1	52	6	1	5	238	.282	11	34	53	.302	1	9
Tucker, Michael	148	323	270	55	72	138	13	4	15	36	.267	.381	.511	0	2	7	44	1	64	13	6	6	246	.276	13	34	24	.167	2	2
Taubensee, Eddie	81	291	266	29	71	101	12	0	6	24	.267	.324	.380	1	1	2	21	1	44	0	0	7	228	.254	5	20	38	.342	1	4
Santiago, Benito	89	277	252	22	66	103	11	1	8	45	.262	.310	.409	0	5	1	19	8	45	2	2	7	170	.259	6	35	82	.268	2	10
Ochoa, Alex	118	275	244	50	77	143	21	3	13	58	.316	.378	.586	0	4	3	24	3	27	8	4	7	154	.325	8	32	90	.300	5	26
Castro, Juan	82	244	224	20	54	82	12	2	4	23	.241	.283	.366	4	2	0	14	1	33	0	2	9	183	.240	4	21	41	.244	0	2
Sexton, Chris	35	118	100	9	21	25	4	0	0	10	.210	.310	.250	2	1	2	13	1	12	4	2	5	81	.235	0	8	19	.105	0	2
LaRue, Jason	31	107	98	12	23	41	3	0	5	12	.235	.299	.418	0	0	4	5	2	19	0	0	1	78	.218	3	5	20	.300	2	7
Morris, Hal	59	78	63	9	14	24	2	1	2	6	.222	.351	.381	1	1	1	12	3	10	0	0	3	58	.224	2	6	5	.200	0	0
Parris, Steve	35	62	55	4	7	9	2	0	0	4	.127	.155	.164	4	1	0	2	0	19	0	1	0	44	.136	0	4	11	.091	0	0
Cromer, D.T.	35	51	47	7	16	26	4	0	2	8	.340	.360	.553	1	1	1	1	1	14	0	0	0	38	.368	2	7	9	.222	0	1
Bell, Rob	26	49	45	1	3	4	1	0	0	0	.067	.087	.089	3	0	0	1	0	27	0	0	1	38	.079	0	0	7	.000	0	0
Harnisch, Pete	24	49	43	4	8	13	2	0	1	8	.186	.186	.302	6	0	0	0	0	14	0	0	1	35	.143	1	6	8	.375	0	2
Villone, Ron	35	45	43	2	7	8	1	0	0	4	.163	.163	.186	2	0	0	0	0	9	0	0	1	32	.125	0	2	11	.273	0	2
Dawkins, Gookie	14	44	41	5	9	11	2	0	0	3	.220	.256	.268	1	0	0	2	1	7	0	0	3	27	.222	0	2	14	.214	0	1
Hunter, Brian L.	32	48	40	11	9	10	1	0	0	1	.225	.319	.250	1	1	0	6	0	9	5	0	0	21	.286	0	1	19	.158	0	0
Dessens, Elmer	40	48	40	6	4	4	0	0	0	0	.100	.234	.100	1	0	0	7	0	16	0	0	0	29	.138	0	0	11	.000	0	0
Neagle, Denny	19	46	37	1	7	9	2	0	0	3	.189	.231	.243	7	0	0	2	0	9	0	0	0	25	.160	0	2	12	.250	0	1
Bell, Mike	19	31	27	5	6	12	0	0	2	4	.222	.323	.444	0	0	0	4	0	7	0	0	0	18	.222	1	3	9	.222	1	1
Fernandez, Osvaldo	15	29	22	0	2	2	0	0	0	1	.091	.167	.091	5	0	0	2	0	10	0	0	0	17	.118	0	0	5	.000	0	1
Lewis, Mark	11	20	19	1	2	3	1	0	0	3	.105	.150	.158	0	0	0	1	0	3	0	0	1	11	.091	0	1	8	.125	0	2
Williamson, Scott	48	22	16	1	1	1	0	0	0	0	.063	.167	.063	4	0	0	2	0	8	0	0	0	12	.083	0	0	4	.000	0	0
Kieschnick, Brooks	14	13	12	0	0	0	0	0	0	0	.000	.077	.000	0	0	0	1	0	5	0	0	0	12	.000	0	0	0	.000	0	0
Clark, Brady	11	11	11	1	3	4	1	0	0	2	.273	.273	.364	0	0	0	0	0	2	0	0	0	9	.222	0	2	2	.500	0	0
Sullivan, Scott	80	7	7	0	2	2	0	0	0	0	.286	.286	.286	0	0	0	0	0	2	0	0	0	6	.167	0	0	1	1.000	0	0
Aybar, Manny	32	9	6	1	0	0	0	0	0	0	.000	.250	.000	1	0	0	2	0	3	0	0	0	3	.000	0	0	3	.000	0	0
Bartee, Kimera	11	5	4	2	0	0	0	0	0	0	.000	.200	.000	0	0	1	0	0	2	1	0	0	2	.000	0	0	2	.000	0	0
Graves, Danny	66	3	2	1	1	4	0	0	1	1	.500	.667	2.000	0	0	0	1	0	0	0	0	0	2	.500	1	1	0	.000	0	0
Reyes, Dennys	62	3	2	0	0	0	0	0	0	0	.000	.333	.000	0	0	0	1	0	1	0	0	0	1	.000	0	0	1	.000	0	0
Riedling, John	13	2	2	0	0	0	0	0	0	0	.000	.000	.000	0	0	0	0	0	2	0	0	0	2	.000	0	0	0	.000	0	0
Larkin, Andy	3	1	1	0	0	0	0	0	0	0	.000	.000	.000	0	0	0	0	0	1	0	0	0	0	.000	0	0	1	.000	0	0
Glauber, Keith	4	1	1	0	0	0	0	0	0	0	.000	.000	.000	0	0	0	0	0	1	0	0	0	0	.000	0	0	1	.000	0	0
Mercado, Hector	12	1	1	0	0	0	0	0	0	0	.000	.000	.000	0	0	0	0	0	1	0	0	0	1	.000	0	0	0	.000	0	0
Charlton, Norm	2	0	0	0	0	0	0	0	0	0	.000	.000	.000	0	0	0	0	0	0	0	0	0	0	.000	0	0	0	.000	0	0
Wohlers, Mark	20	0	0	0	0	0	0	0	0	0	.000	.000	.000	0	0	0	0	0	0	0	0	0	0	.000	0	0	0	.000	0	0
Luebbers, Larry	14	1	0	0	0	0	0	0	0	1	.000	.000	.000	0	1	0	0	0	0	0	0	0	0	.000	0	1	0	.000	0	0
White, Gabe	1	0	0	0	0	0	0	0	0	0	.000	.000	.000	0	0	0	0	0	0	0	0	0	0	.000	0	0	0	.000	0	0
Winchester, Scott	5	0	0	0	0	0	0	0	0	0	.000	.000	.000	0	0	0	0	0	0	0	0	0	0	.000	0	0	0	.000	0	0

Players with more than one N.L. team

Name	G	TPA	AB	R	H	TB	2B	3B	HR	RBI	Avg.	Obp.	Slg.	SH	SF	HP	BB	IBB	SO	SB	CS	GDP	vs RHP AB	vs RHP Avg.	vs RHP HR	vs RHP RBI	vs LHP AB	vs LHP Avg.	vs LHP HR	vs LHP RBI
Aybar, Col.	1	0	0	0	0	0	0	0	0	0	.000	.000	.000	0	0	0	0	0	0	0	0	0	3	.000	0	0	3	.000	0	0
Aybar, Fla.	21	0	0	0	0	0	0	0	0	0	.000	.000	.000	0	0	0	0	0	0	0	0	0	3	.000	0	0	3	.000	0	0
Aybar, Col.-Cin.-Fla.	54	9	6	1	0	0	0	0	0	0	.000	.250	.000	1	0	0	2	0	3	0	0	0	3	.000	0	0	3	.000	0	0
Hunter, Col.	72	226	200	36	55	64	4	1	1	13	.275	.347	.320	4	0	1	21	0	31	15	3	2	21	.286	0	1	19	.158	0	0
Hunter, Col.-Cin.	104	274	240	47	64	74	5	1	1	14	.267	.342	.308	5	1	1	27	0	40	20	3	2	146	.295	1	10	94	.223	0	4
White, Col.	67	10	9	1	2	5	0	0	1	2	.222	.222	.556	1	0	0	0	0	5	0	0	0	0	.000	0	0	0	.000	0	0
White, Cin.-Col.	68	10	9	1	2	5	0	0	1	2	.222	.222	.556	1	0	0	0	0	5	0	0	0	4	.250	0	1	5	.200	1	1

PITCHING

Name	W	L	Pct.	ERA	IP	H	R	ER	HR	SH	SF	HB	BB	IBB	SO	G	GS	CG	ShO	GF	Sv	vs. RH AB	vs. RH Avg.	vs. RH HR	vs. RH RBI	vs. LH AB	vs. LH Avg.	vs. LH HR	vs. LH RBI
Parris, Steve	12	17	.414	4.81	192.2	227	109	103	30	10	3	4	71	5	117	33	33	0	0	0	0	389	.278	13	52	383	.311	17	46
Dessens, Elmer	11	5	.688	4.28	147.1	170	73	70	10	12	7	3	43	7	85	40	16	1	0	6	1	316	.269	5	28	259	.328	5	40
Villone, Ron	10	10	.500	5.43	141.0	154	95	85	22	10	8	9	78	3	77	35	23	2	0	5	0	421	.295	16	68	117	.256	6	18
Bell, Rob	7	8	.467	5.00	140.1	130	84	78	32	8	2	1	73	6	112	26	26	1	0	0	0	300	.257	20	45	234	.226	12	28
Harnisch, Pete	8	6	.571	4.74	131.0	133	76	69	23	1	4	1	46	1	71	22	22	3	1	0	0	284	.257	17	45	226	.265	6	23
Neagle, Denny	8	2	.800	3.52	117.2	111	48	46	15	2	1	3	50	3	88	18	18	0	0	0	0	350	.237	9	39	100	.280	6	8
Williamson, Scott	5	8	.385	3.29	112.0	92	45	41	7	4	2	3	75	7	136	48	10	0	0	13	6	240	.204	2	21	171	.251	5	25
Sullivan, Scott	3	6	.333	3.47	106.1	87	44	41	14	2	5	9	38	8	96	79	0	0	0	22	3	226	.235	9	28	159	.214	5	15
Graves, Danny	10	5	.667	2.56	91.1	81	31	26	8	6	4	3	42	7	53	66	0	0	0	57	30	167	.222	4	22	166	.265	4	22
Fernandez, Osvaldo	4	3	.571	3.62	79.2	69	33	32	6	1	3	2	31	2	36	15	14	1	0	0	0	149	.262	2	16	141	.213	4	14
Aybar, Manny	1	1	.500	4.83	50.1	51	31	27	7	4	3	2	22	2	31	32	0	0	0	10	0	132	.288	6	21	63	.206	1	6
Reyes, Dennys	2	1	.667	4.53	43.2	43	31	22	5	3	3	1	29	0	36	62	0	0	0	15	0	91	.330	3	18	73	.178	2	13
Wohlers, Mark	1	2	.333	4.50	28.0	19	14	14	3	2	1	0	17	0	20	20	0	0	0	7	0	60	.183	1	8	39	.205	2	2
Luebbers, Larry	0	2	.000	6.20	20.1	27	15	14	1	1	0	0	12	2	9	14	1	0	0	4	1	57	.351	1	8	24	.292	0	4
Riedling, John	3	1	.750	2.35	15.1	11	7	4	1	1	0	1	8	0	18	13	0	0	0	5	1	28	.143	0	0	25	.280	1	5
Mercado, Hector	0	0	.000	4.50	14.0	12	7	7	2	1	1	0	8	0	13	12	0	0	0	4	0	30	.233	0	2	20	.250	2	4
Winchester, Scott	0	0	.000	3.68	7.1	10	4	3	1	0	1	0	2	0	3	5	0	0	0	3	0	23	.304	1	4	9	.333	0	0
Glauber, Keith	0	0	.000	3.68	7.1	5	3	3	0	0	0	1	2	0	4	4	0	0	0	0	0	18	.222	0	3	9	.111	0	0
Larkin, Andy	0	0	.000	5.40	6.2	6	4	4	1	0	0	0	5	0	7	3	0	0	0	2	0	17	.353	1	5	8	.000	0	0
Charlton, Norm	0	0	.000	27.00	3.0	6	9	9	1	0	0	0	6	0	1	2	0	0	0	2	0	8	.625	1	8	6	.167	0	1
White, Gabe	0	0	.000	18.00	1.0	2	2	2	1	0	0	0	1	0	2	1	0	0	0	0	0	2	.000	0	0	3	.667	1	2

PITCHERS WITH MORE THAN ONE N.L. TEAM

Name	W	L	Pct.	ERA	IP	H	R	ER	HR	SH	SF	HB	BB	IBB	SO	G	GS	CG	ShO	GF	Sv	vs. RH AB	vs. RH Avg.	vs. RH HR	vs. RH RBI	vs. LH AB	vs. LH Avg.	vs. LH HR	vs. LH RBI
Aybar, Col.	0	1	.000	16.20	1.2	5	3	3	1	0	0	0	0	0	0	1	0	0	0	0	0	132	.288	6	21	63	.206	1	6
Aybar, Fla.	1	0	1.000	2.63	27.1	18	8	8	3	1	1	0	13	1	14	21	0	0	0	10	0	132	.288	6	21	63	.206	1	6
Aybar, Col.-Cin.-Fla.	2	2	.500	4.31	79.1	74	42	38	11	5	4	2	35	3	45	54	0	0	0	4	0	197	.264	9	30	106	.208	2	10
White, Col.	11	2	.846	2.17	83.0	62	21	20	5	2	6	3	14	2	82	67	0	0	0	17	5	2	.000	0	0	3	.667	1	2
White, Cin.-Col.	11	2	.846	2.36	84.0	64	23	22	6	2	6	3	15	2	84	68	0	0	0	6	5	198	.217	2	19	105	.200	4	20

DESIGNATED HITTERS

Name	AB	Avg.	HR	RBI
Young, Dmitri	15	.400	2	4
Larkin, Barry	6	.167	0	0
Morris, Hal	4	.000	0	0

INDIVIDUAL STATISTICS

FIELDING

FIRST BASEMEN

Player	Pct.	G	PO	A	E	TC	DP
Casey, Sean	.995	129	1064	60	6	1130	106
Young, Dmitri	.984	36	229	16	4	249	18
Morris, Hal	1.000	16	50	12	0	62	6
Cromer, D.T.	.964	13	50	3	2	55	8
Kieschnick, Brooks	1.000	1	1	0	0	1	0

SECOND BASEMEN

Player	Pct.	G	PO	A	E	TC	DP
Reese, Pokey	.980	133	289	393	14	696	88
Castro, Juan	.989	21	47	46	1	94	13
Stynes, Chris	.978	15	19	25	1	45	9
Sexton, Chris	1.000	12	17	26	0	43	6
Tucker, Michael	-	1	0	0	0	0	0

THIRD BASEMEN

Player	Pct.	G	PO	A	E	TC	DP
Boone, Aaron	.964	84	62	154	8	224	21
Stynes, Chris	.966	77	53	119	6	178	14
Bell, Mike	.900	13	2	16	2	20	2
Castro, Juan	1.000	7	0	2	0	2	0
Lewis, Mark	.909	5	2	8	1	11	0
Sexton, Chris	1.000	3	2	4	0	6	0

SHORTSTOPS

Player	Pct.	G	PO	A	E	TC	DP
Larkin, Barry	.973	102	153	249	11	413	43
Castro, Juan	.994	57	55	117	1	173	27
Sexton, Chris	.954	14	25	37	3	65	6
Dawkins, Gookie	.965	14	21	34	2	57	13
Boone, Aaron	1.000	2	1	3	0	4	0

OUTFIELDERS

Player	Pct.	G	PO	A	E	TC	DP
Griffey Jr., Ken	.987	141	375	9	5	389	3
Bichette, Dante	.969	121	235	11	8	254	3
Tucker, Michael	.969	120	153	5	5	163	0
Young, Dmitri	.978	111	172	4	4	180	1
Ochoa, Alex	.977	95	125	4	3	132	0
Hunter, Brian L.	.971	25	30	4	1	35	0
Stynes, Chris	1.000	8	11	1	0	12	0
Clark, Brady	1.000	5	6	0	0	6	0
Bartee, Kimera	1.000	3	1	0	0	1	0
Morris, Hal	-	1	0	0	0	0	0

CATCHERS

Player	Pct.	G	PO	A	E	TC	DP	PB
Santiago, Benito	.994	84	428	36	3	467	4	5
Taubensee, Eddie	.989	76	420	26	5	451	8	6
LaRue, Jason	.991	31	190	22	2	214	3	1

PITCHERS

Player	Pct.	G	PO	A	E	TC	DP
Sullivan, Scott	.938	79	5	10	1	16	0
Graves, Danny	.967	66	5	24	1	30	4
Reyes, Dennys	.900	62	4	5	1	10	0
Williamson, Scott	1.000	48	4	10	0	14	0
Dessens, Elmer	1.000	40	10	26	0	36	3
Villone, Ron	.871	35	4	23	4	31	1
Parris, Steve	.974	33	15	22	1	38	4
Aybar, Manny	1.000	32	5	8	0	13	0
Bell, Rob	.917	26	8	14	2	24	0
Harnisch, Pete	1.000	22	6	17	0	23	1
Wohlers, Mark	.833	20	2	3	1	6	0
Neagle, Denny	1.000	18	3	12	0	15	1
Fernandez, Osvaldo	.889	15	6	10	2	18	3
Luebbers, Larry	1.000	14	1	6	0	7	0
Riedling, John	-	13	0	0	0	0	0
Mercado, Hector	1.000	12	0	1	0	1	0
Winchester, Scott	1.000	5	1	1	0	2	0
Glauber, Keith	1.000	4	1	0	0	1	1
Larkin, Andy	1.000	3	1	0	0	1	0
Charlton, Norm	1.000	2	0	1	0	1	0
White, Gabe	-	1	0	0	0	0	0

PITCHING AGAINST EACH CLUB

Pitcher	Ari. W-L	Atl. W-L	Chi. W-L	Col. W-L	Fla. W-L	Hou. W-L	L.A. W-L	Mil. W-L	Mon. W-L	N.Y. W-L	Phi. W-L	Pit. W-L	S.D. W-L	S.F. W-L	StL. W-L	A.L. W-L	Total W-L
Aybar, Manny	0-0	0-0	0-0	0-0	0-0	0-0	0-1	0-0	0-0	0-0	0-0	0-0	0-0	0-0	0-0	1-0	1-1
Bell, Rob	0-0	0-0	1-1	0-0	0-0	0-0	0-1	0-1	2-0	0-0	0-0	2-0	0-1	1-2	0-1	1-1	7-8
Charlton, N.	0-0	0-0	0-0	0-0	0-0	0-0	0-0	0-0	0-0	0-0	0-0	0-0	0-0	0-0	0-0	0-0	0-0
Dessens, E.	1-0	0-2	0-0	1-0	1-0	1-0	0-0	2-1	1-0	1-1	0-0	1-1	0-0	0-0	1-0	1-0	11-5
Fernandez, O.	0-1	0-0	0-1	0-0	0-0	0-0	1-0	0-0	1-0	0-0	0-0	0-0	0-1	1-0	1-0	0-0	4-3
Glauber, Keith	0-0	0-0	0-0	0-0	0-0	0-0	0-0	0-0	0-0	0-0	0-0	0-0	0-0	0-0	0-0	0-0	0-0
Graves, Danny	0-0	0-0	2-0	1-0	1-2	1-1	0-0	0-0	1-0	1-0	0-1	1-0	1-0	0-1	0-0	1-0	10-5
Harnisch, Pete	1-0	1-0	1-1	1-0	1-1	1-0	0-1	1-0	0-0	0-0	1-1	0-1	0-0	0-0	0-1	0-0	8-6
Larkin, Andy	0-0	0-0	0-0	0-0	0-0	0-0	0-0	0-0	0-0	0-0	0-0	0-0	0-0	0-0	0-0	0-0	0-0
Luebbers, L.	0-0	0-0	0-0	0-0	0-0	0-0	0-0	0-0	0-0	0-0	0-1	0-0	0-0	0-0	0-0	0-1	0-2
Mercado, H.	0-0	0-0	0-0	0-0	0-0	0-0	0-0	0-0	0-0	0-0	0-0	0-0	0-0	0-0	0-0	0-0	0-0
Neagle, Denny	1-0	0-0	0-0	0-0	0-0	0-0	0-0	0-0	0-0	1-0	1-0	0-0	0-0	1-1	2-0	2-1	8-2
Parris, Steve	1-0	1-0	1-1	1-1	0-0	0-2	1-1	1-2	1-1	0-1	1-1	2-0	1-1	0-1	0-2	1-3	12-17
Reyes, D.	0-0	0-0	0-0	0-1	0-0	1-0	0-0	0-0	0-0	0-0	0-0	0-0	0-0	0-0	1-0	0-0	2-1
Riedling, John	0-0	1-0	0-0	0-0	0-0	1-0	0-0	0-1	0-0	1-0	0-0	0-0	0-0	0-0	0-0	0-0	3-1
Sullivan, Scott	0-1	1-0	0-0	0-0	0-1	1-0	1-0	0-0	0-0	0-2	0-0	0-2	0-0	0-0	0-0	0-0	3-6
Villone, Ron	1-0	1-0	1-0	1-0	0-0	1-1	0-1	1-1	0-2	0-0	0-0	0-1	2-1	0-0	2-2	0-1	10-10
White, Gabe	0-0	0-0	0-0	0-0	0-0	0-0	0-0	0-0	0-0	0-0	0-0	0-0	0-0	0-0	0-0	0-0	0-0
Williamson, S.	0-0	0-0	1-0	1-1	0-1	0-1	1-0	0-1	0-0	1-0	0-0	1-1	0-1	0-1	0-0	0-1	5-8
Winchester, S.	0-0	0-0	0-0	0-0	0-0	0-0	0-0	0-0	0-0	0-0	0-0	0-0	0-0	0-0	0-0	0-0	0-0
Wohlers, Mark	0-0	0-0	1-0	0-0	0-1	0-0	0-0	0-1	0-0	0-0	0-0	0-0	0-0	0-0	0-0	0-0	1-2
Totals	5-2	5-2	8-4	6-3	3-6	7-5	4-5	5-8	6-3	5-4	3-4	7-6	4-5	3-6	7-6	7-8	85-77

INTERLEAGUE: Parris 0-1, Villone 0-1, Bell 0-1 vs. White Sox; Neagle 1-1, Parris 1-1, Aybar 1-0, Williamson 0-1 vs. Indians; Dessens 1-0, Parris 0-1, Luebbers 0-1 vs. Tigers; Bell 1-0, Graves 1-0, Neagle 1-0 vs. Twins. Total: 7-8.

MISCELLANEOUS

HOME RUNS BY PARK

At Arizona (4): Boone 2, Bichette 1, Ochoa 1.
At Atlanta (3): Young 1, Reese 1, LaRue 1.
At Chicago (NL) (9): Young 2, Boone 2, LaRue 2, Griffey Jr. 1, Reese 1, Casey 1.
At Cincinnati (98): Griffey Jr. 22, Bichette 11, Ochoa 9, Casey 9, Stynes 8, Santiago 7, Tucker 7, Larkin 6, Young 6, Boone 5, Reese 3, Morris 1, Harnisch 1, Castro 1, LaRue 1, Bell 1.
At Cleveland (5): Griffey Jr. 2, Tucker 1, Young 1, Reese 1.
At Colorado (13): Griffey Jr. 4, Reese 2, Casey 2, Larkin 1, Bichette 1, Morris 1, Young 1, Cromer 1.
At Detroit (1): Young 1.
At Florida (3): Larkin 1, Bichette 1, Ochoa 1.
At Houston (10): Griffey Jr. 3, Boone 2, Larkin 1, Tucker 1, Graves 1, Young 1, Reese 1.
At Los Angeles (8): Taubensee 2, Tucker 2, Larkin 1, Griffey Jr. 1, Reese 1, Boone 1.
At Milwaukee (7): Castro 2, Casey 2, Tucker 1, Stynes 1, Bell 1.
At Montreal (4): Taubensee 2, Griffey Jr. 1, Young 1.
At New York (NL) (3): Griffey Jr. 1, Taubensee 1, Young 1.
At Philadelphia (2): Taubensee 1, Casey 1.
At Pittsburgh (8): Griffey Jr. 2, Casey 2, Tucker 1, Castro 1, Ochoa 1, Young 1.
At San Diego (9): Bichette 2, Griffey Jr. 2, Reese 2, Stynes 1, Young 1, Casey 1.
At San Francisco (4): Larkin 1, Santiago 1, Griffey Jr. 1, Young 1.
At St. Louis (9): Tucker 2, Stynes 2, Casey 2, Ochoa 1, LaRue 1, Cromer 1.

LOW-HIT GAMES

No-hitters: None.
One-hitters: None.
Two-hitters: Elmer Dessens, September 28 vs. Milwaukee, W 8-1. Ron Villone, September 29 vs. St. Louis, W 8-1.

10-STRIKEOUT GAMES

Ron Villone 1, Total: 1

FOUR OR MORE HITS IN ONE GAME

Eddie Taubensee 3, Dmitri Young 3, Pokey Reese 3(including one five-hit game), Barry Larkin 2(including one five-hit game), Dante Bichette 2(including one five-hit game), Chris Stynes 2 (including one five-hit game), Alex Ochoa 2, Sean Casey 2, Benito Santiago 1, Ken Griffey Jr. 1, Total: 21

MULTI-HOMER GAMES

Ken Griffey Jr. 5, Barry Larkin 1, Dante Bichette 1, Eddie Taubensee 1, Sean Casey 1, Jason LaRue 1, Total: 10

GRAND SLAMS

4-11: Ken Griffey Jr. (off Colorado's Gabe White)
6-6: Dante Bichette (off Chicago's Jesus Pena)
7-28: Ken Griffey Jr. (off Montreal's Mike Johnson)
8-21: Dmitri Young (off Philadelphia's Randy Wolf)
8-22: Alex Ochoa (off Philadelphia's Bruce Chen)
9-6: Benito Santiago (off New York's Armando Benitez)

PINCH HITTERS

(Minimum 5 at-bats)

Name	AB	Avg.	HR	RBI
Morris, Hal	36	.333	2	6
Ochoa, Alex	34	.176	0	4
Tucker, Michael	26	.231	1	5
Cromer, D.T.	23	.348	0	2
Stynes, Chris	22	.318	1	5
Santiago, Benito	12	.333	0	7
Young, Dmitri	11	.455	0	5
Kieschnick, Brooks	11	.000	0	0
Taubensee, Eddie	10	.300	0	1
Bell, Mike	8	.250	1	1
Clark, Brady	8	.250	0	0
Lewis, Mark	5	.200	0	3
Sexton, Chris	5	.200	0	0
Hunter, Brian L.	5	.200	0	0
Bichette, Dante	5	.000	0	1

DEBUTS

4-4: Hector Mercado, P.
4-5: D.T. Cromer, PH.
4-8: Rob Bell, P.
7-20: Mike Bell, PH.
8-30: John Riedling, P.
9-3: Brady Clark, PH.

GAMES BY POSITION

Catcher: Benito Santiago 84, Eddie Taubensee 76, Jason LaRue 31.
First base: Sean Casey 129, Dmitri Young 36, Hal Morris 16, D.T. Cromer 13, Brooks Kieschnick 1.
Second base: Pokey Reese 133, Juan Castro 21, Chris Stynes 15, Chris Sexton 12, Michael Tucker 1.
Third base: Aaron Boone 84, Chris Stynes 77, Mike Bell 13, Juan Castro 7, Mark Lewis 5, Chris Sexton 3.
Shortstop: Barry Larkin 102, Juan Castro 57, Chris Sexton 14, Gookie Dawkins 14, Aaron Boone 2.
Outfield: Ken Griffey Jr. 141, Dante Bichette 121, Michael Tucker 120, Dmitri Young 111, Alex Ochoa 95, Brian L. Hunter 25, Chris Stynes 8, Brady Clark 5, Kimera Bartee 3, Hal Morris 1.
Designated hitter: Dmitri Young 4, Barry Larkin 1, Hal Morris 1.

STREAKS

Wins: 6 (May 7-13)
Losses: 6 (June 12-18)
Consecutive games with at least one hit: 21, Sean Casey (July 4-30)
Wins by pitcher: 7, Steve Parris (August 13-September 15)

ATTENDANCE

Home: 2,599,318
Road: 3,016,074
Highest (home): 55,596 (April 3 vs. Milwaukee).
Highest (road): 60,767 (June 16 vs. San Diego).
Lowest (home): 16,761 (April 4 vs. Milwaukee).
Lowest (road): 11,547 (July 28 vs. Montreal).

Colorado Rockies

DAY BY DAY

Date	Opp.	Res.	Score	(inn.*)	Hits	Opp. hits	Winning pitcher	Losing pitcher	Save	Record	Pos.	GB
4-3	At Atl.	L	0-2		6	7	Maddux	Astacio	Remlinger	0-1	T2nd	1.0
4-4	At Atl.	W	5-3		11	6	Tavarez	Burkett	Jimenez	1-1	T3rd	1.0
4-5	At Atl.	L	6-9		9	12	Chen	Aybar	Ligtenberg	1-2	5th	1.5
4-7	At Fla.	L	3-4		7	5	Penny	Yoshii	Alfonseca	1-3	5th	2.0
4-8	At Fla.	W	4-2		10	9	Jimenez	Fernandez	Lee	2-3	5th	2.0
4-9	At Fla.	L	6-7		10	9	Dempster	Astacio	Alfonseca	2-4	5th	3.0
4-10	Cin.	W	7-5		13	10	Arrojo	Parris	Belinda	3-4	T3rd	3.0
4-11	Cin.	L	3-10		6	14	Villone	Bohanon		3-5	T4th	3.0
4-12	Cin.	W	7-5		9	9	Jimenez	Reyes	Tavarez	4-5	4th	2.0
4-13	StL.	W	12-6		14	11	Croushore	Kile		5-5	T3rd	2.0
4-14	StL.	W	6-2		9	6	Astacio	Ankiel		6-5	3rd	2.0
4-16†	StL.	L	3-9		9	11	Hentgen	Arrojo		6-6		
4-16‡	StL.	W	14-13		15	17	Jimenez	Mohler	White	7-6	T3rd	2.5
4-17	At Ari.	W	9-1		15	8	Yoshii	Daal		8-6	3rd	1.5
4-18	At Ari.	L	1-7		4	12	Reynoso	Karl		8-7	3rd	2.5
4-19	At Ari.	L	7-8		12	13	Morgan	Tavarez	Kim	8-8	3rd	3.5
4-20	At Ari.	L	0-3		4	5	Johnson	Arrojo		8-9	3rd	4.5
4-21	At StL.	W	6-4		10	12	Jarvis	Hentgen	Jimenez	9-9	3rd	3.5
4-22	At StL.	W	7-6		11	6	Croushore	James	Jimenez	10-9	3rd	2.5
4-23	At StL.	L	3-6	(7)	4	8	An. Benes	Karl	Slocumb	10-10	4th	2.5
4-25	At Mon.	L	4-10		11	14	Pavano	Bohanon		10-11	4th	3.5
4-26	At Mon.	L	2-9		5	12	Hermanson	Jarvis	Urbina	10-12	4th	4.5
4-28	N.Y.	W	12-5		14	12	Astacio	Hampton		11-12	T3rd	3.0
4-29	N.Y.	L	6-13		10	23	Reed	Yoshii		11-13	T3rd	4.0
4-30	N.Y.	L	11-14		10	15	Leiter	Bohanon		11-14	T3rd	5.0
5-1	Mon.	W	15-8		18	15	White	Hermanson		12-14	3rd	4.5
5-2	Mon.	W	12-6		13	11	Karl	Powell		13-14	3rd	4.5
5-3	Mon.	W	16-7		24	12	Astacio	Irabu		14-14	T3rd	3.5
5-5	At S.F	L	0-5		3	6	Nathan	Yoshii		14-15	4th	5.0
5-6	At S.F	L	0-6		9	9	Estes	Arrojo		14-16	4th	6.0
5-8	At Hou.	W	3-1		6	3	Astacio	Holt		15-16	4th	6.5
5-9	At Hou.	L	8-13		10	11	Perez	Tavarez		15-17	4th	7.5
5-10	At Hou.	L	1-5		5	7	Reynolds	Yoshii		15-18	4th	8.5
5-12	S.F	W	15-7		15	10	Bohanon	Nathan		16-18	4th	8.5
5-13	S.F	W	10-9		15	10	White	Johnstone	Jimenez	17-18	4th	8.5
5-14	S.F	W	11-7		15	13	White	Hernandez		18-18	4th	7.5
5-16	At N.Y.	W	4-3	(11)	9	12	Tavarez	Wendell	Jimenez	19-18	3rd	6.5
5-17	At N.Y.	L	2-4		5	10	Leiter	Arrojo	Franco	19-19	3rd	6.5
5-19	At Phi.	W	10-2		14	6	Astacio	Ashby		20-19	3rd	6.0
5-20	At Phi.	W	4-3		6	2	Tavarez	Brock	Jimenez	21-19	3rd	5.0
5-21	At Phi.	L	3-4		7	6	Person	Yoshii	Brantley	21-20	3rd	5.0
5-23	Chi.	W	10-7		10	9	Bohanon	Garibay		22-20	3rd	5.0
5-24	Chi.	W	9-4		8	12	Astacio	Farnsworth	Jimenez	23-20	3rd	5.0
5-25	Chi.	L	5-6		10	9	Lieber	DeJean	Aguilera	23-21	3rd	6.0
5-26	Pit.	L	1-2		6	8	Cordova	Yoshii	Williams	23-22	3rd	7.0
5-27	Pit.	W	7-6		10	12	White	Christiansen		24-22	3rd	7.0
5-28	Pit.	W	11-2		17	7	Arrojo	Anderson		25-22	3rd	6.0
5-29	Hou.	W	8-7		15	12	White	Cabrera	Jimenez	26-22	3rd	5.0
5-30	Hou.	W	10-7		12	12	Belinda	Valdes	Jimenez	27-22	T2nd	4.0
5-31	Hou.	W	8-6		12	14	White	Slusarski	Jimenez	28-22	T2nd	4.0
6-2	At Mil.	W	8-6		12	9	Arrojo	Bere	Myers	29-22	2nd	4.5
6-3	At Mil.	L	1-2	(12)	3	6	de los Santos	Belinda		29-23	T2nd	4.5
6-4	At Mil.	W	7-1		12	5	Jarvis	Haynes		30-23	2nd	3.5
6-5	At Sea.	L	2-6		6	10	Sele	Yoshii		30-24	2nd	3.5
6-6	At Sea.	L	1-4		8	7	Tomko	Bohanon	Sasaki	30-25	T2nd	3.5
6-7	At Sea.	W	6-1		13	5	Arrojo	Moyer		31-25	T2nd	2.5
6-9	Tex.	W	3-2	(12)	8	10	Tavarez	Wetteland		32-25	2nd	2.5
6-10	Tex.	W	12-6		15	11	Karl	Loaiza		33-25	2nd	1.5
6-11	Tex.	W	9-8		13	18	DeJean	Crabtree	Jimenez	34-25	2nd	1.5
6-13	Hou.	L	3-6		10	15	Reynolds	Arrojo	Wagner	34-26	2nd	2.0
6-14	Hou.	L	4-8		8	11	Slusarski	Astacio		34-27	2nd	3.0
6-15	Hou.	W	5-4		8	10	Jimenez	Wagner		35-27	2nd	2.0
6-17	Ari.	W	14-5		17	8	Bohanon	Anderson		36-27	2nd	1.0
6-18	Ari.	W	19-2		23	8	Yoshii	Reynoso		37-27	1st	...
6-20	At Cin.	L	2-3		7	11	Graves	Astacio		37-28	2nd	0.5
6-21	At Cin.	W	6-4		11	8	Tavarez	Williamson	Jimenez	38-28	2nd	0.5
6-22	At Cin.	L	3-5		6	10	Parris	Jarvis	Graves	38-29	2nd	1.0
6-23	At Ari.	L	0-2		2	5	Anderson	Bohanon	Kim	38-30	2nd	2.0
6-24	At Ari.	W	4-0		6	7	Yoshii	Johnson		39-30	2nd	1.0
6-25	At Ari.	L	3-8		8	14	Morgan	Astacio		39-31	2nd	2.0
6-26	S.F	W	15-6		16	9	Arrojo	Gardner		40-31	2nd	2.0
6-27	S.F	L	7-12		9	15	Estes	Jarvis		40-32	2nd	2.0
6-28	S.F	W	17-13		17	13	DeJean	Johnstone		41-32	2nd	2.0
6-29	S.F	W	11-4		15	13	Yoshii	Nathan		42-32	2nd	2.0
6-30	At S.D.	W	5-4		10	7	Astacio	Almanzar	Jimenez	43-32	2nd	1.0
7-1	At S.D.	L	3-5		9	7	Meadows	Arrojo	Hoffman	43-33	2nd	2.0
7-2	At S.D.	W	3-2	(10)	10	7	DeJean	Hoffman	Jimenez	44-33	2nd	1.0
7-3	At S.D.	W	3-1		4	4	Bohanon	Montgomery	Jimenez	45-33	1st	...
7-4†	At S.F	L	1-4		4	9	Hernandez	Yoshii	Nen	45-34		

HIGHLIGHTS

High point: July 3. After Jeffrey Hammonds delivered a 3-1 win at San Diego with a two-run, eighth-inning home run, the Rockies stood a season-best 12 games over .500 (45-33) and in sole possession of first in the N.L. West. It would only go downhill from there.
Low point: Most of the month of July. From July 4-31, the Rockies were locked in a 5-21 slide that destroyed any playoff hopes. Eleven of those losses came in quick succession and nine in the thin air of Coors Field.
Turning point: The 11-game losing streak, which started at San Francisco and wrapped around the All-Star break. Not only did the four-game San Francisco series send the Rockies spiraling out of contention, it propelled the struggling Giants toward an N.L. West title—and the best record in the N.L.
Most valuable player: First baseman Todd Helton was a one-man wrecking machine. Helton led the league with his .372 average and 147 RBIs and he led the N.L. in numerous other offensive category while ranking seventh with 42 home runs. Helton even flirted with .400, lifting his average to .397 as late as August 28—the team's 131st game.
Most valuable pitcher: Righthander Julian Tavarez opened the season in the bullpen and finished as the team's most dependable starter, compiling an 11-5 record and 4.43 ERA. Tavarez, who made 12 starts and worked a career-high 120 innings, enjoyed one four-month stretch in which he was 9-0 with a 3.22 ERA.
Most improved player: Hammonds, who has struggled in his inconsistent career with injuries, enjoyed a breakout season. He batted .335 with 20 homers and 106 RBIs in 122 games. The left fielder added serious punch to the middle of the Rockies' lineup.
Most pleasant surprise: Reliever Gabe White, a journeyman pickup, pitched in 67 games and compiled an 11-2 record and 2.17 ERA. His 2.36 relief ERA ranked second in the N.L.
Key injuries: Right fielder Larry Walker played only 87 games because of a problem with his throwing elbow. The injury visibly affected Walker's swing when he did play, forcing him to settle for opposite-field singles and dropping him from 37 to 9 home runs. ... Hammonds missed 17 of the first 18 games with a hamstring injury and the final 12 games with a shoulder problem. ... Staff ace Pedro Astacio and No. 4 starter Masato Yoshii both missed their last three starts. Astacio suffered a strained oblique muscle and Yoshii needed season-ending surgery on his elbow.
Notables: Helton (59) and Jeff Cirillo (53) finished 1-2 in the N.L. in doubles. ... Helton led the N.L. with a club-record .463 on-base percentage. His road batting average of .353 ranked third in the N.L. ... Recovering slowly from offseason elbow surgery, Brian Bohanon was 0-3 with a 9.67 ERA in April. From June 6, when he was inserted into the rotation, he was 10-7 with a 4.08 ERA.

—MIKE KLIS

MISCELLANEOUS

RECORDS

2000 regular-season record: 82-80 (4th in N.L. West); 48-33 at home; 34-47 on road; 24-21 vs. East; 29-24 vs. Central; 29-35 vs. West; 24-13 vs. lefthanded starters; 58-67 vs. righthanded starters; 70-74 on grass; 12-6 on turf; 27-30 in daytime; 55-50 at night; 23-20 in one-run games; 6-5 in extra-inning games; 0-2-2 in doubleheaders.
Team record past five years: 397-413 (.490, ranks 10th in league in that span).

TEAM LEADERS

Batting average: Todd Helton (.372).
At-bats: Neifi Perez (651).
Runs: Todd Helton (138).
Hits: Todd Helton (216).
Total Bases: Todd Helton (405).
Doubles: Todd Helton (59).
Triples: Neifi Perez (11).
Home runs: Todd Helton (42).
Runs batted in: Todd Helton (147).
Stolen bases: Tom Goodwin (39).
Slugging percentage: Todd Helton (.698).
On-base percentage: Todd Helton (.463).
Wins: Pedro Astacio, Brian Bohanon (12).
Earned-run average: Brian Bohanon (4.68).
Complete games: Pedro Astacio (3).
Shutouts: Brian Bohanon (1).
Saves: Jose Jimenez (24).
Innings pitched: Pedro Astacio (196.1).
Strikeouts: Pedro Astacio (193).

Date	Opp.	Res.	Score	(inn.*)	Hits	Opp. hits	Winning pitcher	Losing pitcher	Save	Record	Pos.	GB
7-4‡	At S.F	L	0-3		6	7	Gardner	Karl	Nen	45-35	2nd	1.5
7-5	At S.F	L	2-4		7	9	Nathan	Belinda	Rodriguez	45-36	2nd	2.5
7-6	At S.F	L	5-6		7	12	Nen	Myers		45-37	2nd	3.5
7-7	At Ana.	L	4-12		7	13	Ortiz	Jarvis		45-38	T2nd	3.5
7-8	At Ana.	L	2-6		9	11	Hill	Bohanon		45-39	3rd	3.5
7-9	At Ana.	L	4-10		10	13	Bottenfield	Yoshii		45-40	3rd	4.5
7-13	Cin.	L	6-15		9	13	Dessens	Astacio		45-41	3rd	4.5
7-14	Cin.	L	2-9		5	14	Harnisch	Arrojo		45-42	3rd	5.5
7-15	Cin.	L	4-7		8	12	Williamson	Yoshii	Graves	45-43	3rd	5.5
7-17†	Oak.	L	10-11		12	13	Magnante	White	Isringhausen	45-44		
7-17‡	Oak.	W	10-9	(10)	15	12	DeJean	Isringhausen		46-44	4th	5.5
7-18	Oak.	W	18-3		21	8	Astacio	Mulder		47-44	3rd	4.5
7-19	At L.A.	L	1-9		1	9	Brown	Arrojo		47-45	4th	5.5
7-20	At L.A.	L	3-6		5	10	Park	Yoshii	Fetters	47-46	4th	6.5
7-21	S.D.	L	1-5		7	12	Eaton	Bohanon		47-47	4th	7.5
7-22	S.D.	W	9-4		16	11	White	Clement		48-47	4th	6.5
7-23	S.D.	L	4-6	(10)	7	11	Hoffman	Belinda	Wall	48-48	4th	6.5
7-24	L.A.	L	1-4		5	11	Brown	Arrojo	Fetters	48-49	4th	7.0
7-25	L.A.	L	4-6		11	8	Park	Chouinard	Shaw	48-50	4th	7.0
7-26	L.A.	W	11-4		14	6	Bohanon	Perez		49-50	4th	6.0
7-27	L.A.	L	11-16		15	20	Masaoka	Carrara		49-51	4th	7.0
7-28	At Mil.	L	0-5		8	8	Wright	Astacio		49-52	4th	8.0
7-29	At Mil.	W	10-2		14	6	Tavarez	Rigdon		50-52	4th	7.0
7-30	At Mil.	L	2-3		7	5	D'Amico	Yoshii	Leskanic	50-53	4th	7.0
7-31	At Chi.	L	0-2		4	8	Tapani	Bohanon	Aguilera	50-54	4th	7.5
8-1	At Chi.	W	2-1		7	2	Astacio	Farnsworth	White	51-54	4th	7.5
8-2	At Chi.	L	2-3		4	8	Rain	Wasdin	Aguilera	51-55	4th	7.5
8-4	Phi.	W	8-1		13	7	Tavarez	Bottenfield		52-55	4th	8.0
8-5	Phi.	W	7-6		15	9	Jimenez	Brantley		53-55	4th	7.0
8-6	Phi.	L	9-10		16	13	Chen	Astacio		53-56	4th	8.0
8-7	Pit.	L	7-8		12	13	Sauerbeck	Jimenez	Williams	53-57	4th	9.0
8-8	Pit.	W	6-1		15	10	Rose	Silva		54-57	4th	9.0
8-9	Pit.	W	4-3		7	7	White	Williams		55-57	4th	9.0
8-10	At StL.	L	4-5		10	12	Timlin	Jimenez		55-58	4th	9.5
8-11	At Mon.	W	10-3		13	11	Bohanon	Hermanson		56-58	4th	8.5
8-12	At Mon.	W	14-2		22	6	Yoshii	Moore		57-58	4th	7.5
8-13	At Mon.	W	5-3		12	7	Chouinard	Strickland	White	58-58	4th	6.5
8-14	At Mon.	W	4-3		12	10	House	Strickland	Jimenez	59-58	4th	6.5
8-15†	At N.Y.	L	5-7		9	9	Cook	House	Benitez	59-59		
8-15‡	At N.Y.	L	3-4		4	10	B.J. Jones	Chouinard	Benitez	59-60	4th	8.0
8-16	At N.Y.	W	7-5		11	8	Bohanon	Rusch	White	60-60	4th	8.0
8-17	At N.Y.	L	2-13		4	15	Wendell	Yoshii		60-61	4th	9.0
8-18	Fla.	L	8-9		18	12	Smith	Rose	Alfonseca	60-62	4th	10.0
8-19	Fla.	W	10-3		10	10	Tavarez	Cornelius		61-62	4th	10.0
8-20	Fla.	W	13-4		14	8	Astacio	Sanchez		62-62	4th	9.0
8-21	Atl.	L	4-7		10	13	Millwood	Bohanon	Rocker	62-63	4th	10.0
8-22	Atl.	W	7-6	(12)	16	14	Mayne	Rocker		63-63	4th	9.0
8-23	Atl.	L	2-5		8	10	Maddux	Rose	Remlinger	63-64	4th	10.0
8-25	At Pit.	W	6-3		13	9	Tavarez	Anderson		64-64	4th	10.0
8-26	At Pit.	W	11-4		19	10	Astacio	Silva		65-64	4th	9.0
8-27	At Pit.	W	9-2		16	4	Bohanon	Serafini		66-64	4th	8.0
8-28	At Phi.	L	2-3		8	8	Person	Yoshii	Brantley	66-65	4th	9.0
8-29	At Phi.	W	2-1		9	3	Rose	Daal	Jimenez	67-65	4th	8.0
8-30	At Phi.	W	5-4	(11)	7	10	White	Gomes	Jimenez	68-65	4th	8.0
9-1	Mil.	W	5-3		11	7	Astacio	Snyder	White	69-65	4th	8.5
9-2	Mil.	L	3-8		10	14	D'Amico	DeJean		69-66	4th	9.5
9-3	Mil.	L	4-6	(11)	8	13	Acevedo	DeJean	Leskanic	69-67	4th	10.5
9-4	Chi.	W	6-2		12	8	Rose	Lieber		70-67	4th	10.5
9-5	Chi.	W	10-2		13	4	Tavarez	Arnold		71-67	4th	10.5
9-6	Chi.	L	5-8	(11)	11	13	Van Poppel	White	Aguilera	71-68	4th	11.5
9-8	L.A.	W	8-5		14	9	Bohanon	Brown		72-68	4th	11.0
9-9	L.A.	W	7-6		13	7	White	Park	Jimenez	73-68	3rd	10.0
9-10	L.A.	L	1-12		5	12	Dreifort	Astacio	Herges	73-69	4th	11.0
9-11	At S.D.	L	2-7		6	10	Williams	Tavarez		73-70	4th	12.0
9-12	At S.D.	W	6-3		12	6	Yoshii	Clement	Jimenez	74-70	4th	12.0
9-13	At S.D.	W	11-0		16	9	Bohanon	Eaton		75-70	3rd	12.0
9-14	At L.A.	W	5-4		9	8	Rose	Park	Jimenez	76-70	3rd	11.5
9-15	At L.A.	L	3-4	(10)	5	5	Herges	DeJean		76-71	3rd	11.5
9-16	At L.A.	L	4-5		13	7	Gagne	Tavarez	Shaw	76-72	4th	12.5
9-17	At L.A.	L	6-12		11	12	Prokopec	Yoshii		76-73	4th	13.5
9-19	S.D.	L	2-7		6	12	Clement	Bohanon		76-74	4th	14.0
9-20	S.D.	L	11-15		11	15	Eaton	Rose	Hoffman	76-75	4th	15.0
9-21	S.D.	W	13-4		17	4	Jarvis	Tollberg		77-75	4th	15.0
9-22	Fla.	L	4-8		7	13	Penny	Tavarez		77-76	4th	15.0
9-23	Fla.	L	1-3	(7)	4	6	Smith	Wasdin		77-77	4th	15.5
9-24	Fla.	W	9-3		14	8	Bohanon	Sanchez		78-77	4th	14.5
9-25	Ari.	L	4-6		10	13	Johnson	Rose	Mantei	78-78	4th	15.0
9-26	Ari.	W	7-6		10	7	Chouinard	Morgan	Jimenez	79-78	4th	14.0
9-27	Ari.	W	6-4		14	6	White	Plesac	Jimenez	80-78	4th	14.0
9-28	Ari.	L	3-12		7	13	Reynoso	Wasdin		80-79	4th	15.0
9-29	At Atl.	W	4-2		6	6	Bohanon	Ashby	Jimenez	81-79	4th	15.0
9-30	At Atl.	L	2-5		6	8	Glavine	Rose	Rocker	81-80	4th	15.0
10-1	At Atl.	W	10-5		17	7	Tavarez	Rocker		82-80	4th	15.0

Monthly records: April (11-14), May (17-8), June (15-10), July (7-22), August (18-11), September (13-15), October (1-0).
*Innings, if other than nine. † First game of a doubleheader. ‡ Second game of a doubleheader.

MEMORABLE GAMES

August 22 at Colorado

After 11 innings of frustration, Rockies manager Buddy Bell sent catcher Brent Mayne out to face Atlanta with the score tied 6-6 in the top of the 12th. After allowing a hit, walk and wild pitch, Mayne got Chipper Jones on a two-out ground ball. Mayne was rewarded in the bottom of the inning when Adam Melhuse singled off John Rocker to drive in the winning run.

Atlanta	AB	R	H	BI	Colorado	AB	R	H	BI
Furcal, ss-2b	6	0	1	0	Pierre, cf	5	1	2	1
A.Jones, cf	6	2	2	1	Perez, ss	6	1	4	2
C.Jones, 3b	7	2	3	1	Helton, 1b	4	0	1	0
Surhoff, lf	2	2	1	2	Hammonds, rf	5	1	0	0
Galarraga, 1b	4	0	2	1	Walker, 2b	3	0	1	2
Ashby, pr	0	0	0	0	Shumpert, ph-2b	2	0	0	0
Bako, 1b	0	0	0	0	Cirillo, 3b	5	1	1	0
B.Jordan, rf	5	0	0	0	Hollandsworth, lf	5	2	2	0
Lopez, c	6	0	2	1	Wasdin, p	0	0	0	0
Lockhart, 2b	5	0	3	0	Bohanon, p	0	0	0	0
Sanders, pr	0	0	0	0	Mayne, p	0	0	0	0
Kamieniecki, p	0	0	0	0	Melhuse, ph	1	0	1	1
Glavine, ph	1	0	0	0	Petrick, c	5	1	3	1
Rocker, p	0	0	0	0	Yoshii, p	0	0	0	0
Belinda, p	0	0	0	0	DeJean, p	1	0	0	0
Burkett, p	3	0	0	0	Jimenez, p	0	0	0	0
Mulholland, p	0	0	0	0	G.White, p	0	0	0	0
Joyner, ph	1	0	0	0	Frye, ph	1	0	1	0
Remlinger, p	0	0	0	0	House, p	0	0	0	0
Ligtenberg, p	0	0	0	0	Chouinard, p	0	0	0	0
Bonilla, ph	0	0	0	0	Myers, p	0	0	0	0
Weiss, pr-ss	1	0	0	0	Huskey, lf	1	0	0	0
Totals	**47**	**6**	**14**	**6**	**Totals**	**44**	**7**	**16**	**7**

Atlanta ....001 030 200 000—6 14 0

Colorado....................................210 300 000 001—7 16 1

E—Petrick (1). DP—Atlanta 3, Colorado 1. LOB—Atlanta 15, Colorado 10. 2B—Surhoff (5), Perez (27), Cirillo (42). 3B—Walker (2). R—A. Jones (28), C. Jones (29). SB—Furcal (27), A. Jones (14), Surhoff (1), Pierre (5). CS—Pierre (2). S—Surhoff, Pierre. SH—Surhoff, Yoshii 2.

Atlanta	IP	H	R	ER	BB	SO
Burkett	5.2	9	6	6	2	3
Mulholland	1.1	1	0	0	0	1
Remlinger	1	0	0	0	0	1
Ligtenberg	1	2	0	0	1	0
Kamieniecki	2	1	0	0	1	1
Rocker (L 1-1)	0.1	2	1	1	0	0
Belinda	0.1	1	0	0	1	1
Colorado	**IP**	**H**	**R**	**ER**	**BB**	**SO**
Yoshii	5	8	4	4	2	1
DeJean	1.1	2	2	2	1	2
Jimenez .	1.2	1	0	0	0	0
White	1	1	0	0	1	0
House	0.1	1	0	0	1	0
Chouinard	0.2	0	0	0	0	0
Myers	0.2	0	0	0	0	1
Wasdin	0	0	0	0	0	0
Bohanon	0.1	0	0	0	1	0
Mayne (W 1-0)	1	1	0	0	1	0

Wasdin pitched to 1 batter in 11th.
HBP—Galarraga by Wasdin. WP—Mayne. U—HP, Montague. 1B, Layne. 2B—Barrett. 3B, Randazzo. T—4:26. A—41,707.

October 1 at Atlanta

Todd Helton capped his amazing offensive season with a three-run homer off John Rocker that triggered a seven-run ninth-inning rally and dashed Atlanta's hopes of hosting their Division Series opener against St. Louis. Helton delivered the big blow in Colorado's 10-5 season-ending win.

Colorado	AB	R	H	BI	Atlanta	AB	R	H	BI
Pierre, cf	4	0	1	0	Furcal, 2b	4	2	2	0
Frye, ph-2b	2	1	1	0	A.Jones, cf	4	0	0	1
Perez, ss	5	1	2	1	C.Jones, 3b	3	2	1	2
Cirillo, 3b	5	2	2	0	Galarraga, 1b	4	0	0	0
Helton, 1b	5	1	2	3	Lopez, c	4	1	1	2
Walker, 2b	4	1	1	1	Sanders, lf	4	0	2	0
Jimenez, p	0	0	0	0	Jordan, rf	4	0	1	0
Hol'dsworth, r-c	5	1	4	0	Weiss, ss	3	0	0	0
Shumpert, lf	4	1	1	1	Surhoff, ph	1	0	0	0
Mayne, c	4	2	2	2	Burkett, p	2	0	0	0
Jarvis, p	1	0	0	0	Millwood, p	1	0	0	0
Dipoto, p	0	0	0	0	Rocker, p	0	0	0	0
Pena, ph	0	0	0	0	Kamieniecki, p	0	0	0	0
DeJean, p	0	0	0	0	Mulholland, p	0	0	0	0
Tavarez, p	0	0	0	0					
Petrick, ph	2	0	1	1					
Huskey, rf	0	0	0	0					
Totals	**41**	**10**	**17**	**9**	**Totals**	**34**	**5**	**7**	**5**

Colorado ....0 0 1 0 0 2 0 0 7—10 17 1

Atlanta ....0 0 0 2 0 3 0 0 0— 5 7 1

E—Walker (5), C. Jones (25). DP—Atlanta 1. LOB—Colorado 9, Atlanta 3. 2B—Sanders (23). 3B—Furcal (4). HR—Helton (42), C. Jones (36), Lopez (24). SB—Sanders (21). CS—Hollandsworth (7). SH—Jarvis.

Colorado	IP	H	R	ER	BB	SO
Jarvis	5.2	6	5	5	1	3
Dipoto	0.1	0	0	0	0	0
DeJean	1	1	0	0	0	2
Tavarez (W 11-5)	1	0	0	0	0	0
Jimenez	1	0	0	0	0	0
Atlanta	**IP**	**H**	**R**	**ER**	**BB**	**SO**
Burkett	5.2	10	3	3	0	3
Millwood	2.1	2	0	0	1	4
Rocker (L 1-2)	0.2	3	6	0	2	2
Kamieniecki	0	0	1	1	1	0
Mulholland	0.1	2	0	0	0	0

Kamieniecki pitched to 1 batter in 9th. U—HP, Katzenmeier. 1B, Miller. 2B, Meals. 3B, Young.T—3:22. A—45,794.

INDIVIDUAL STATISTICS

BATTING

Name	G	TPA	AB	R	H	TB	2B	3B	HR	RBI	Avg.	Obp.	Slg.	SH	SF	HP	BB	IBB	SO	SB	CS	GDP	vs RHP AB	vs RHP Avg.	vs RHP HR	vs RHP RBI	vs LHP AB	vs LHP Avg.	vs LHP HR	vs LHP RBI
Perez, Neifi	162	699	651	92	187	278	39	11	10	71	.287	.314	.427	7	11	0	30	6	63	3	6	9	497	.266	3	45	154	.357	7	26
Cirillo, Jeff	157	684	598	111	195	285	53	2	11	115	.326	.392	.477	1	12	6	67	4	72	3	4	19	466	.311	9	83	132	.379	2	32
Helton, Todd	160	697	580	138	216	405	59	2	42	147	.372	.463	.698	0	10	4	103	22	61	5	3	12	437	.387	35	116	143	.329	7	31
Hammonds, Jeffrey	122	511	454	94	152	240	24	2	20	106	.335	.395	.529	2	6	5	44	4	83	14	7	11	356	.323	14	75	98	.378	6	31
Lansing, Mike	90	400	365	62	94	153	14	6	11	47	.258	.315	.419	3	1	0	31	1	49	8	2	13	280	.261	10	38	85	.247	1	9
Mayne, Brent	117	395	335	36	101	140	21	0	6	64	.301	.381	.418	4	8	1	47	13	48	1	3	12	289	.318	5	52	46	.196	1	12
Goodwin, Tom	91	377	317	65	86	125	8	8	5	47	.271	.368	.394	5	4	1	50	2	76	39	7	3	266	.252	3	32	51	.373	2	15
Walker, Larry	87	372	314	64	97	159	21	7	9	51	.309	.409	.506	0	3	9	46	4	40	5	5	12	229	.297	7	34	85	.341	2	17
Shumpert, Terry	115	300	263	52	68	120	11	7	9	40	.259	.340	.456	0	3	6	28	1	40	8	4	3	169	.249	6	25	94	.277	3	15
Pierre, Juan	51	219	200	26	62	64	2	0	0	20	.310	.353	.320	4	1	1	13	0	15	7	6	2	176	.284	0	15	24	.500	0	5
Hunter, Brian L.	72	226	200	36	55	64	4	1	1	13	.275	.347	.320	4	0	1	21	0	31	15	3	2	125	.296	1	9	75	.240	0	4
Walker, Todd	57	196	171	28	54	93	10	4	7	36	.316	.385	.544	1	3	1	20	0	19	4	1	2	159	.308	6	32	12	.417	1	4
Hollandsworth, Todd	56	178	167	39	54	95	8	0	11	23	.323	.365	.569	0	0	0	11	1	38	7	3	4	145	.331	11	22	22	.273	0	1
Bragg, Darren	71	169	149	16	33	51	7	1	3	21	.221	.296	.342	0	3	0	17	1	41	4	1	3	133	.241	3	20	16	.063	0	1
Petrick, Ben	52	173	146	32	47	68	10	1	3	20	.322	.401	.466	1	4	2	20	2	33	1	2	1	98	.306	2	16	48	.354	1	4
Servais, Scott	33	110	101	6	22	29	4	0	1	13	.218	.273	.287	0	1	1	7	2	16	0	1	1	55	.182	0	6	46	.261	1	7
Huskey, Butch	45	111	92	18	32	52	8	0	4	18	.348	.432	.565	0	3	0	16	1	14	1	1	5	52	.327	3	11	40	.375	1	7
Frye, Jeff	37	98	87	14	31	37	6	0	0	3	.356	.412	.425	1	1	1	8	0	16	4	0	3	38	.342	0	1	49	.367	0	2
Astacio, Pedro	32	84	82	2	8	8	0	0	0	6	.098	.108	.098	1	0	0	1	0	25	0	0	1	65	.123	0	6	17	.000	0	0
Bohanon, Brian	35	67	53	6	11	20	3	0	2	11	.208	.232	.377	11	1	0	2	0	14	0	0	0	37	.216	2	8	16	.188	0	3
Yoshii, Masato	29	64	50	4	9	13	1	0	1	8	.180	.212	.260	12	0	0	2	0	13	1	0	3	40	.125	1	7	10	.400	0	1
Ledesma, Aaron	32	43	40	4	9	11	2	0	0	3	.225	.279	.275	0	0	1	2	0	9	0	0	1	25	.240	0	3	15	.200	0	0
Tavarez, Julian	51	38	35	1	3	3	0	0	0	0	.086	.086	.086	3	0	0	0	0	14	0	0	0	28	.071	0	0	7	.143	0	0
Jarvis, Kevin	25	40	34	4	3	4	1	0	0	0	.088	.162	.118	3	0	1	2	0	11	0	0	0	34	.088	0	0	0	.000	0	0
Arrojo, Rolando	19	32	28	2	3	4	1	0	0	3	.107	.138	.143	3	0	0	1	0	13	0	0	0	20	.050	0	0	8	.250	0	3
Carpenter, Bubba	15	31	27	4	6	15	0	0	3	5	.222	.323	.556	0	0	0	4	0	13	0	0	0	26	.231	3	5	1	.000	0	0
Melhuse, Adam	23	26	23	3	4	6	0	1	0	4	.174	.269	.261	0	0	0	3	0	5	0	0	1	12	.250	0	1	11	.091	0	3
Rose, Brian	12	24	21	1	1	1	0	0	0	0	.048	.048	.048	3	0	0	0	0	10	0	0	1	16	.063	0	0	5	.000	0	0
Karl, Scott	17	18	14	3	4	4	0	0	0	0	.286	.375	.286	2	0	1	1	0	5	0	1	0	12	.333	0	0	2	.000	0	0
Mendoza, Carlos	13	11	10	0	1	1	0	0	0	0	.100	.182	.100	0	0	0	1	0	4	0	1	0	10	.100	0	0	0	.000	0	0
Pena, Elvis	10	10	9	1	3	4	1	0	0	1	.333	.400	.444	0	0	0	1	0	1	1	0	3	8	.375	0	1	1	.000	0	0
White, Gabe	67	10	9	1	2	5	0	0	1	2	.222	.222	.556	1	0	0	0	0	5	0	0	0	4	.250	0	1	5	.200	1	1
Echevarria, Angel	10	9	9	0	1	1	0	0	0	2	.111	.111	.111	0	0	0	0	0	2	0	0	0	7	.000	0	2	2	.500	0	0
Wasdin, John	14	9	8	0	2	2	0	0	0	0	.250	.250	.250	1	0	0	0	0	2	0	0	0	8	.250	0	0	0	.000	0	0
Manto, Jeff	7	7	5	2	4	9	2	0	1	4	.800	.857	1.800	0	0	0	2	0	0	0	0	0	1	1.000	1	3	4	.750	0	1
Jimenez, Jose	72	5	4	0	2	2	0	0	0	1	.500	.500	.500	1	0	0	0	0	2	0	0	0	2	.500	0	1	2	.500	0	0
Chouinard, Bobby	31	3	3	1	1	1	0	0	0	0	.333	.333	.333	0	0	0	0	0	1	0	0	0	2	.500	0	0	1	.000	0	0
DeJean, Mike	54	2	2	0	0	0	0	0	0	0	.000	.000	.000	0	0	0	0	0	0	0	0	0	2	.000	0	0	0	.000	0	0
Croushore, Rick	6	2	1	0	1	1	0	0	0	0	1.000	1.000	1.000	1	0	0	0	0	0	0	0	0	0	.000	0	0	1	1.000	0	0
Belinda, Stan	47	1	1	0	0	0	0	0	0	0	.000	.000	.000	0	0	0	0	0	1	0	0	0	1	.000	0	0	0	.000	0	0
Dipoto, Jerry	17	1	1	0	0	0	0	0	0	0	.000	.000	.000	0	0	0	0	0	1	0	0	0	1	.000	0	0	0	.000	0	0
Carrara, Giovanni	8	1	1	0	0	0	0	0	0	0	.000	.000	.000	0	0	0	0	0	1	0	0	0	1	.000	0	0	0	.000	0	0
Myers, Mike	78	0	0	0	0	0	0	0	0	0	.000	.000	.000	0	0	0	0	0	0	0	0	0	0	.000	0	0	0	.000	0	0
Walker, Pete	3	0	0	0	0	0	0	0	0	0	.000	.000	.000	0	0	0	0	0	0	0	0	0	0	.000	0	0	0	.000	0	0
Beltran, Rigo	1	0	0	0	0	0	0	0	0	0	.000	.000	.000	0	0	0	0	0	0	0	0	0	0	.000	0	0	0	.000	0	0
Aybar, Manny	1	0	0	0	0	0	0	0	0	0	.000	.000	.000	0	0	0	0	0	0	0	0	0	0	.000	0	0	0	.000	0	0
Lee, David	7	0	0	0	0	0	0	0	0	0	.000	.000	.000	0	0	0	0	0	0	0	0	0	0	.000	0	0	0	.000	0	0
Moraga, David	1	0	0	0	0	0	0	0	0	0	.000	.000	.000	0	0	0	0	0	0	0	0	0	0	.000	0	0	0	.000	0	0
House, Craig	16	0	0	0	0	0	0	0	0	0	.000	.000	.000	0	0	0	0	0	0	0	0	0	0	.000	0	0	0	.000	0	0

Players with more than one N.L. team

Name	G	TPA	AB	R	H	TB	2B	3B	HR	RBI	Avg.	Obp.	Slg.	SH	SF	HP	BB	IBB	SO	SB	CS	GDP	vs RHP AB	vs RHP Avg.	vs RHP HR	vs RHP RBI	vs LHP AB	vs LHP Avg.	vs LHP HR	vs LHP RBI
Aybar, Cin.	32	9	6	1	0	0	0	0	0	0	.000	.250	.000	1	0	0	2	0	3	0	0	0	0	.000	0	0	0	.000	0	0
Aybar, Fla.	21	0	0	0	0	0	0	0	0	0	.000	.000	.000	0	0	0	0	0	0	0	0	0	0	.000	0	0	0	.000	0	0
Aybar, Col.-Cin.-Fla.	54	9	6	1	0	0	0	0	0	0	.000	.250	.000	1	0	0	2	0	3	0	0	0	3	.000	0	0	3	.000	0	0
Belinda, Col.-Atl.	57	1	1	0	0	0	0	0	0	0	.000	.000	.000	0	0	0	0	0	1	0	0	0	1	.000	0	0	0	.000	0	0
Echevarria, Col.-Mil.	41	58	51	3	10	15	2	0	1	6	.196	.293	.294	0	0	0	7	0	11	0	0	1	29	.241	1	4	22	.136	0	2
Goodwin, Col.-L.A.	147	606	528	94	139	186	11	9	6	58	.263	.346	.352	5	4	1	68	2	117	55	10	7	422	.244	4	43	106	.340	2	15
Hollandsworth, L.A.-Col.	137	471	428	81	115	192	20	0	19	47	.269	.333	.449	0	1	1	41	3	99	18	7	8	372	.272	19	41	56	.250	0	6
Hunter, Col.-Cin.	104	274	240	47	64	74	5	1	1	14	.267	.342	.308	5	1	1	27	0	40	20	3	2	146	.295	1	10	94	.223	0	4
Melhuse, L.A.-Col.	24	27	24	3	4	6	0	1	0	4	.167	.259	.250	0	0	0	3	0	6	0	0	1	13	.231	0	1	11	.091	0	3
Moraga, Mon.-Col.	4	0	0	0	0	0	0	0	0	0	.000	.000	.000	0	0	0	0	0	0	0	0	0	0	.000	0	0	0	.000	0	0
Servais, Col.-S.F.	40	120	109	7	24	31	4	0	1	13	.220	.283	.284	0	1	1	9	3	17	0	1	1	62	.194	0	6	47	.255	1	7
White, Cin.-Col.	68	10	9	1	2	5	0	0	1	2	.222	.222	.556	1	0	0	0	0	5	0	0	0	4	.250	0	1	5	.200	1	1

PITCHING

Name	W	L	Pct.	ERA	IP	H	R	ER	HR	SH	SF	HB	BB	IBB	SO	G	GS	CG	ShO	GF	Sv	vs. RH AB	vs. RH Avg.	vs. RH HR	vs. RH RBI	vs. LH AB	vs. LH Avg.	vs. LH HR	vs. LH RBI
Astacio, Pedro	12	9	.571	5.27	196.1	217	119	115	32	7	4	15	77	5	193	32	32	3	0	0	0	414	.273	15	52	358	.291	17	57
Bohanon, Brian	12	10	.545	4.68	177.0	181	101	92	24	4	3	6	79	4	98	34	26	2	1	0	0	517	.288	19	64	163	.196	5	24
Yoshii, Masato	6	15	.286	5.86	167.1	201	112	109	32	8	7	2	53	6	88	29	29	0	0	0	0	351	.328	18	59	305	.282	14	42
Tavarez, Julian	11	5	.688	4.43	120.0	124	68	59	11	3	4	7	53	9	62	51	12	1	0	8	1	283	.272	8	31	180	.261	3	28
Jarvis, Kevin	3	4	.429	5.95	115.0	138	83	76	26	6	2	4	33	3	60	24	19	0	0	0	0	255	.271	16	39	205	.337	10	33
Arrojo, Rolando	5	9	.357	6.04	101.1	120	77	68	14	3	7	12	46	6	80	19	19	0	0	0	0	216	.282	4	26	186	.317	10	46
White, Gabe	11	2	.846	2.17	83.0	62	21	20	5	2	6	3	14	2	82	67	0	0	0	17	5	196	.219	2	19	102	.186	3	18
Jimenez, Jose	5	2	.714	3.18	70.2	63	27	25	4	4	2	3	28	6	44	72	0	0	0	55	24	159	.239	2	18	105	.238	2	10
Karl, Scott	2	3	.400	7.68	65.2	95	56	56	14	3	3	3	33	3	29	17	9	0	0	1	0	209	.364	11	45	68	.279	3	16
Rose, Brian	4	5	.444	5.51	63.2	72	41	39	10	2	2	3	30	6	40	12	12	0	0	0	0	123	.228	5	18	132	.333	5	19
DeJean, Mike	4	4	.500	4.89	53.1	54	31	29	9	3	1	0	30	6	34	54	0	0	0	15	0	126	.254	4	15	75	.293	5	10
Myers, Mike	0	1	.000	1.99	45.1	24	10	10	2	1	0	2	24	3	41	78	0	0	0	22	1	59	.220	1	7	91	.121	1	7
Wasdin, John	0	3	.000	5.80	35.2	42	23	23	6	1	2	3	9	2	35	14	3	1	0	2	0	88	.295	4	17	51	.314	2	6
Belinda, Stan	1	3	.250	7.07	35.2	39	32	28	10	4	2	2	17	4	40	46	0	0	0	10	1	94	.309	8	26	47	.213	2	13
Chouinard, Bobby	2	2	.500	3.86	32.2	35	17	14	4	1	1	1	9	2	23	31	0	0	0	6	0	79	.304	3	12	49	.224	1	4
Dipoto, Jerry	0	0	.000	3.95	13.2	16	6	6	1	1	2	0	5	2	9	17	0	0	0	7	0	32	.375	0	6	19	.211	1	3
House, Craig	1	1	.500	7.24	13.2	13	11	11	3	0	1	2	17	0	8	16	0	0	0	3	0	27	.296	2	7	22	.227	1	5
Carrara, Giovanni	0	1	.000	12.83	13.1	21	19	19	5	0	1	1	11	2	15	8	0	0	0	2	0	34	.412	1	7	25	.280	4	10
Croushore, Rick	2	0	1.000	8.74	11.1	15	11	11	1	0	1	1	6	1	11	6	0	0	0	1	0	35	.286	0	11	13	.385	1	3
Lee, David	0	0	.000	11.12	5.2	10	9	7	3	0	0	1	6	0	6	7	0	0	0	3	1	13	.385	1	1	15	.333	2	5
Walker, Pete	0	0	.000	17.36	4.2	10	9	9	1	0	0	0	4	0	2	3	0	0	0	1	0	10	.200	0	1	13	.615	1	8
Aybar, Manny	0	1	.000	16.20	1.2	5	3	3	1	0	0	0	0	0	0	1	0	0	0	0	0	6	.667	1	3	4	.250	0	0
Beltran, Rigo	0	0	.000	40.50	1.1	6	6	6	2	0	0	0	3	0	1	1	1	0	0	0	0	7	.571	1	2	3	.667	1	3
Mayne, Brent	1	0	1.000	0.00	1.0	1	0	0	0	0	0	0	1	0	0	1	0	0	0	1	0	0	.000	0	0	4	.250	0	0
Moraga, David	0	0	.000	45.00	1.0	4	5	5	1	0	1	1	0	0	0	1	0	0	0	1	0	5	.800	1	4	1	.000	0	1

PITCHERS WITH MORE THAN ONE N.L. TEAM

Name	W	L	Pct.	ERA	IP	H	R	ER	HR	SH	SF	HB	BB	IBB	SO	G	GS	CG	ShO	GF	Sv	vs. RH AB	vs. RH Avg.	vs. RH HR	vs. RH RBI	vs. LH AB	vs. LH Avg.	vs. LH HR	vs. LH RBI
Aybar, Cin.	1	1	.500	4.83	50.1	51	31	27	7	4	3	2	22	2	31	32	0	0	0	10	0	6	.667	1	3	4	.250	0	0
Aybar, Fla.	1	0	1.000	2.63	27.1	18	8	8	3	1	1	0	13	1	14	21	0	0	0	10	0	6	.667	1	3	4	.250	0	0
Aybar, Col.-Cin.-Fla.	2	2	.500	4.31	79.1	74	42	38	11	5	4	2	35	3	45	54	0	0	0	4	0	197	.264	9	30	106	.208	2	10
Belinda, Col.-Atl.	1	3	.250	7.71	46.2	55	44	40	14	4	4	3	22	5	51	56	0	0	0	4	1	121	.322	10	32	66	.242	4	22
Moraga, Mon.-Col.	0	0	.000	40.50	2.2	10	12	12	1	1	2	1	2	0	2	4	0	0	0	2	0	11	.727	1	9	5	.400	0	4
White, Cin.-Col.	11	2	.846	2.36	84.0	64	23	22	6	2	6	3	15	2	84	68	0	0	0	6	5	198	.217	2	19	105	.200	4	20

DESIGNATED HITTERS

Name	AB	Avg.	HR	RBI
Walker, Larry	9	.111	0	0
Carpenter, Bubba	7	.143	0	0
Shumpert, Terry	3	.000	0	0

INDIVIDUAL STATISTICS

FIELDING

FIRST BASEMEN

Player	Pct.	G	PO	A	E	TC	DP
Helton, Todd	.995	160	1328	148	7	1483	143
Huskey, Butch	1.000	8	24	1	0	25	6
Shumpert, Terry	.818	6	8	1	2	11	2
Ledesma, Aaron	1.000	3	28	4	0	32	6
Melhuse, Adam	1.000	3	11	1	0	12	1
Echevarria, Angel	1.000	2	3	0	0	3	1
Manto, Jeff	1.000	1	1	0	0	1	1

SECOND BASEMEN

Player	Pct.	G	PO	A	E	TC	DP
Lansing, Mike	.983	88	175	221	7	403	57
Walker, Todd	.975	52	81	118	5	204	25
Frye, Jeff	.990	27	37	58	1	96	15
Shumpert, Terry	1.000	23	33	35	0	68	10
Pena, Elvis	-	1	0	0	0	0	0

THIRD BASEMEN

Player	Pct.	G	PO	A	E	TC	DP
Cirillo, Jeff	.963	155	92	303	15	410	41
Shumpert, Terry	1.000	15	8	13	0	21	0
Ledesma, Aaron	1.000	5	0	2	0	2	0
Frye, Jeff	1.000	1	0	2	0	2	1
Manto, Jeff	1.000	1	0	1	0	1	0

SHORTSTOPS

Player	Pct.	G	PO	A	E	TC	DP
Perez, Neifi	.978	162	288	522	18	828	120
Shumpert, Terry	1.000	7	4	7	0	11	3
Pena, Elvis	1.000	4	1	2	0	3	1

OUTFIELDERS

Player	Pct.	G	PO	A	E	TC	DP
Hammonds, Jeffrey	.991	118	207	8	2	217	0
Goodwin, Tom	.986	88	208	3	3	214	1
Walker, Larry	.994	83	161	11	1	173	4
Hunter, Brian L.	.981	63	103	3	2	108	0
Pierre, Juan	.975	50	115	1	3	119	0
Hollandsworth, Todd	.988	48	74	6	1	81	0
Bragg, Darren	1.000	43	53	0	0	53	0
Shumpert, Terry	.967	40	56	2	2	60	0
Huskey, Butch	1.000	23	36	1	0	37	0
Carpenter, Bubba	1.000	6	3	0	0	3	0
Mendoza, Carlos	.000	3	0	0	1	1	0
Echevarria, Angel	-	1	0	0	0	0	0
Melhuse, Adam	-	1	0	0	0	0	0

CATCHERS

Player	Pct.	G	PO	A	E	TC	DP	PB
Mayne, Brent	.990	106	582	35	6	623	2	5
Petrick, Ben	.985	48	248	19	4	271	4	8
Servais, Scott	.987	32	204	17	3	224	1	1
Melhuse, Adam	1.000	1	0	1	0	1	0	1

PITCHERS

Player	Pct.	G	PO	A	E	TC	DP
Myers, Mike	1.000	78	3	7	0	10	3
Jimenez, Jose	.867	72	5	8	2	15	1
White, Gabe	1.000	67	2	6	0	8	1
DeJean, Mike	1.000	54	2	8	0	10	1
Tavarez, Julian	.974	51	14	23	1	38	1
Belinda, Stan	.833	46	3	2	1	6	0
Bohanon, Brian	.971	34	11	23	1	35	3
Astacio, Pedro	1.000	32	20	22	0	42	0
Chouinard, Bobby	1.000	31	2	2	0	4	0
Yoshii, Masato	1.000	29	16	20	0	36	2
Jarvis, Kevin	1.000	24	14	12	0	26	4
Arrojo, Rolando	.875	19	10	18	4	32	4
Karl, Scott	.941	17	4	12	1	17	2
Dipoto, Jerry	1.000	17	0	2	0	2	0
House, Craig	1.000	16	0	3	0	3	0
Wasdin, John	1.000	14	2	3	0	5	1
Rose, Brian	1.000	12	6	8	0	14	0
Carrara, Giovanni	1.000	8	3	0	0	3	0
Lee, David	.000	7	0	0	1	1	0
Croushore, Rick	-	6	0	0	0	0	0
Walker, Pete	1.000	3	0	1	0	1	0
Mayne, Brent	1.000	1	0	1	0	1	0
Moraga, David	1.000	1	1	0	0	1	0
Aybar, Manny	-	1	0	0	0	0	0
Beltran, Rigo	-	1	0	0	0	0	0

PITCHING AGAINST EACH CLUB

Pitcher	Ari. W-L	Atl. W-L	Chi. W-L	Cin. W-L	Fla. W-L	Hou. W-L	L.A. W-L	Mil. W-L	Mon. W-L	N.Y. W-L	Phi. W-L	Pit. W-L	S.D. W-L	S.F. W-L	StL. W-L	A.L. W-L	Total W-L
Arrojo, R.	0-1	0-0	0-0	1-1	0-0	0-1	0-2	1-0	0-0	0-1	0-0	1-0	0-1	1-1	0-1	1-0	5-9
Astacio, P.	0-1	0-1	2-0	0-2	1-1	1-1	0-1	1-1	1-0	1-0	1-1	1-0	1-0	0-0	1-0	1-0	12-9
Aybar, Manny	0-0	0-1	0-0	0-0	0-0	0-0	0-0	0-0	0-0	0-0	0-0	0-0	0-0	0-0	0-0	0-0	0-1
Belinda, Stan	0-0	0-0	0-0	0-0	0-0	1-0	0-0	0-1	0-0	0-0	0-0	0-0	0-1	0-1	0-0	0-0	1-3
Beltran, Rigo	0-0	0-0	0-0	0-0	0-0	0-0	0-0	0-0	0-0	0-0	0-0	0-0	0-0	0-0	0-0	0-0	0-0
Bohanon, B.	1-1	1-1	1-1	0-1	1-0	0-0	2-0	0-0	1-1	1-1	0-0	1-0	2-2	1-0	0-0	0-2	12-10
Carrara, G.	0-0	0-0	0-0	0-0	0-0	0-0	0-1	0-0	0-0	0-0	0-0	0-0	0-0	0-0	0-0	0-0	0-1
Chouinard, B.	1-0	0-0	0-0	0-0	0-0	0-0	0-1	0-0	1-0	0-1	0-0	0-0	0-0	0-0	0-0	0-0	2-2
Croushore, R.	0-0	0-0	0-0	0-0	0-0	0-0	0-0	0-0	0-0	0-0	0-0	0-0	0-0	0-0	2-0	0-0	2-0
DeJean, Mike	0-0	0-0	0-1	0-0	0-0	0-0	0-1	0-2	0-0	0-0	0-0	0-0	1-0	1-0	0-0	2-0	4-4
Dipoto, Jerry	0-0	0-0	0-0	0-0	0-0	0-0	0-0	0-0	0-0	0-0	0-0	0-0	0-0	0-0	0-0	0-0	0-0
House, Craig	0-0	0-0	0-0	0-0	0-0	0-0	0-0	0-0	1-0	0-1	0-0	0-0	0-0	0-0	0-0	0-0	1-1
Jarvis, Kevin	0-0	0-0	0-0	0-1	0-0	0-0	0-0	1-0	0-1	0-0	0-0	0-0	1-0	0-1	1-0	0-1	3-4
Jimenez, Jose	0-0	0-0	0-0	1-0	1-0	1-0	0-0	0-0	0-0	0-0	1-0	0-1	0-0	0-0	1-1	0-0	5-2
Karl, Scott	0-1	0-0	0-0	0-0	0-0	0-0	0-0	0-0	1-0	0-0	0-0	0-0	0-0	0-1	0-1	1-0	2-3
Lee, David	0-0	0-0	0-0	0-0	0-0	0-0	0-0	0-0	0-0	0-0	0-0	0-0	0-0	0-0	0-0	0-0	0-0
Mayne, Brent	0-0	1-0	0-0	0-0	0-0	0-0	0-0	0-0	0-0	0-0	0-0	0-0	0-0	0-0	0-0	0-0	1-0
Moraga, David	0-0	0-0	0-0	0-0	0-0	0-0	0-0	0-0	0-0	0-0	0-0	0-0	0-0	0-0	0-0	0-0	0-0
Myers, Mike	0-0	0-0	0-0	0-0	0-0	0-0	0-0	0-0	0-0	0-0	0-0	0-0	0-0	0-1	0-0	0-0	0-1
Rose, Brian	0-1	0-2	1-0	0-0	0-1	0-0	1-0	0-0	0-0	0-0	1-0	1-0	0-1	0-0	0-0	0-0	4-5
Tavarez, Julian	0-1	2-0	1-0	1-0	1-1	0-1	0-1	1-0	0-0	1-0	2-0	1-0	0-1	0-0	0-0	1-0	11-5
Walker, Pete	0-0	0-0	0-0	0-0	0-0	0-0	0-0	0-0	0-0	0-0	0-0	0-0	0-0	0-0	0-0	0-0	0-0
Wasdin, John	0-1	0-0	0-1	0-0	0-1	0-0	0-0	0-0	0-0	0-0	0-0	0-0	0-0	0-0	0-0	0-0	0-3
White, Gabe	1-0	0-0	0-1	0-0	0-0	2-0	1-0	0-0	1-0	0-0	1-0	2-0	1-0	2-0	0-0	0-1	11-2
Yoshii, M.	3-0	0-0	0-0	0-1	0-1	0-1	0-2	0-1	1-0	0-2	0-2	0-1	1-0	1-2	0-0	0-2	6-15
Totals	6-7	4-5	5-4	3-6	4-5	5-4	4-9	4-5	7-2	3-6	6-3	7-2	7-6	6-7	5-3	6-6	82-80

INTERLEAGUE: DeJean 1-0, Astacio 1-0, White 0-1 vs. Athletics; Arrojo 1-0, Yoshii 0-1, Bohanon 0-1 vs. Mariners; Tavarez 1-0, Karl 1-0, DeJean 1-0 vs. Rangers; Jarvis 0-1, Bohanon 0-1, Yoshii 0-1 vs. Angels. Total: 6-6.

MISCELLANEOUS

HOME RUNS BY PARK

At Anaheim (1): Shumpert 1.
At Arizona (0):
At Atlanta (6): Helton 3, Shumpert 1, Goodwin 1, Hollandsworth 1.
At Chicago (NL) (1): Walker 1.
At Cincinnati (2): Helton 2.
At Colorado (112): Helton 27, Hammonds 14, Lansing 9, Cirillo 9, Walker 7, Shumpert 7, Hollandsworth 7, Perez 7, Walker 5, Goodwin 4, Mayne 3, Bragg 3, Huskey 2, Petrick 2, Bohanon 1, Servais 1, White 1, Hunter 1, Yoshii 1, Carpenter 1.
At Florida (3): Lansing 2, Manto 1.
At Houston (4): Helton 3, Cirillo 1.
At Los Angeles (4): Mayne 1, Huskey 1, Perez 1, Helton 1.
At Milwaukee (3): Hammonds 2, Helton 1.
At Montreal (5): Helton 2, Walker 1, Bohanon 1, Perez 1.
At New York (NL) (3): Perez 1, Helton 1, Carpenter 1.
At Philadelphia (2): Petrick 1, Carpenter 1.
At Pittsburgh (4): Hammonds 1, Huskey 1, Walker 1, Helton 1.
At San Diego (6): Hollandsworth 3, Mayne 1, Hammonds 1, Cirillo 1.
At San Francisco (0):
At Seattle (2): Mayne 1, Hammonds 1.
At St. Louis (3): Walker 1, Hammonds 1, Helton 1.

LOW-HIT GAMES

No-hitters: None.
One-hitters: None.
Two-hitters: None.

10-STRIKEOUT GAMES

Pedro Astacio 7, John Wasdin 1, Total: 8

FOUR OR MORE HITS IN ONE GAME

Jeff Cirillo 6 (including one five-hit game), Todd Helton 6 (including one five-hit game), Larry Walker 3, Jeffrey Hammonds 3, Neifi Perez 3, Brent Mayne 2, Juan Pierre 2 (including one five-hit game), Tom Goodwin 1, Jeff Frye 1, Mike Lansing 1, Brian L. Hunter 1, Todd Hollandsworth 1, Todd Walker 1, Total: 31

MULTI-HOMER GAMES

Todd Helton 8, Jeffrey Hammonds 3, Mike Lansing 1, Jeff Cirillo 1, Todd Hollandsworth 1, Total: 14

GRAND SLAMS

4-30: Tom Goodwin (off New York's Dennis Cook)
5-2: Jeffrey Hammonds (off Montreal's Jeremy Powell)
7-17: Tom Goodwin (off Oakland's Mike Magnante)
8-11: Larry Walker (off Montreal's Scott Forster)
9-13: Todd Hollandsworth (off San Diego's Adam Eaton)

PINCH HITTERS

(Minimum 5 at-bats)

Name	AB	Avg.	HR	RBI
Shumpert, Terry	45	.333	1	10
Bragg, Darren	27	.185	1	5
Ledesma, Aaron	23	.217	0	0
Melhuse, Adam	19	.211	0	3
Mayne, Brent	18	.056	0	1
Frye, Jeff	14	.500	0	0
Huskey, Butch	13	.231	0	2
Hollandsworth, Todd	12	.333	1	3
Walker, Todd	10	.300	0	1
Mendoza, Carlos	8	.125	0	0
Carpenter, Bubba	7	.286	1	1
Hunter, Brian L.	7	.143	0	0
Goodwin, Tom	7	.143	0	1
Echevarria, Angel	7	.000	0	2
Manto, Jeff	5	.800	1	4
Hammonds, Jeffrey	5	.200	0	1

DEBUTS

5-13: Bubba Carpenter, PH.
8-6: Craig House, P.
8-7: Juan Pierre, PR.
9-2: Elvis Pena, PH.

GAMES BY POSITION

Catcher: Brent Mayne 106, Ben Petrick 48, Scott Servais 32, Adam Melhuse 1.
First base: Todd Helton 160, Butch Huskey 8, Terry Shumpert 6, Aaron Ledesma 3, Adam Melhuse 3, Angel Echevarria 2, Jeff Manto 1.
Second base: Mike Lansing 88, Todd Walker 52, Jeff Frye 27, Terry Shumpert 23, Elvis Pena 1.
Third base: Jeff Cirillo 155, Terry Shumpert 15, Aaron Ledesma 5, Jeff Manto 1, Jeff Frye 1.
Shortstop: Neifi Perez 162, Terry Shumpert 7, Elvis Pena 4.
Outfield: Jeffrey Hammonds 118, Tom Goodwin 88, Larry Walker 83, Brian L. Hunter 63, Juan Pierre 50, Todd Hollandsworth 48, Darren Bragg 43, Terry Shumpert 40, Butch Huskey 23, Bubba Carpenter 6, Carlos Mendoza 3, Angel Echevarria 1, Adam Melhuse 1.
Designated hitter: Larry Walker 3, Bubba Carpenter 2, Terry Shumpert 1.

STREAKS

Wins: 6 (May 27-June 2)
Losses: 11 (July 4-17)
Consecutive games with at least one hit: 18, Jeffrey Hammonds (May 29-June 21)
Wins by pitcher: 3, Pedro Astacio (April 28-May 8) Pedro Astacio (August 20-September 1) Gabe White (May 27-31) Rolando Arrojo (May 28-June 7) Masato Yoshii (June 18-29)

ATTENDANCE

Home: 3,202,562
Road: 2,191,214
Highest (home): 48,735 (July 13 vs. Cincinnati).
Highest (road): 48,933 (September 30 vs. Atlanta).
Lowest (home): 35,071 (September 24 vs. Florida).
Lowest (road): 6,924 (August 14 vs. Montreal).

Florida Marlins

DAY BY DAY

Date	Opp.	Res.	Score	(inn.*)	Hits	Opp. hits	Winning pitcher	Losing pitcher	Save	Record	Pos.	GB
4-3	S.F	W	6-4		12	10	Fernandez	Hernandez	Alfonseca	1-0	T1st	...
4-4	S.F	L	0-3		4	7	Ortiz	Dempster	Nen	1-1	T2nd	0.5
4-5	S.F	L	9-11		12	15	Johnstone	Alfonseca	Nen	1-2	T3rd	1.0
4-6	S.F	W	5-4		8	7	Miceli	Johnstone		2-2	T2nd	0.5
4-7	Col.	W	4-3		5	7	Penny	Yoshii	Alfonseca	3-2	1st	+0.5
4-8	Col.	L	2-4		9	10	Jimenez	Fernandez	Lee	3-3	T2nd	0.5
4-9	Col.	W	7-6		9	10	Dempster	Astacio	Alfonseca	4-3	T2nd	0.5
4-10	At Mil.	L	3-4		9	6	Haynes	Nunez	Wickman	4-4	3rd	0.5
4-12	At Mil.	W	11-4		11	8	Sanchez	Navarro		5-4	T1st	...
4-13	At Mil.	L	0-4		4	6	Bere	Penny		5-5	T1st	...
4-14	At Chi.	W	9-4		10	8	Fernandez	Lorraine		6-5	T1st	...
4-15	At Chi.	L	2-4		4	6	Downs	Dempster	Aguilera	6-6	2nd	0.5
4-16	At Chi.	W	6-5	(10)	8	10	Miceli	Quevedo	Alfonseca	7-6	1st	+0.5
4-17	At Chi.	W	6-5		12	6	Sanchez	Farnsworth	Alfonseca	8-6	1st	+1.0
4-18	Pit.	W	12-5		17	10	Penny	Cordova		9-6	1st	+1.0
4-19	Pit.	L	1-5		8	8	Ritchie	Fernandez		9-7	3rd	...
4-20	Pit.	W	3-2	(14)	10	11	Darensbourg	Williams		10-7	2nd	...
4-21	Phi.	L	3-4		7	8	Ashby	Nunez		10-8	4th	1.0
4-22	Phi.	W	4-2		6	8	Sanchez	Byrd	Alfonseca	11-8	3rd	1.0
4-23	Phi.	W	5-2		5	6	Penny	Person	Alfonseca	12-8	3rd	1.0
4-24	Phi.	W	3-1		7	7	Fernandez	Wolf	Alfonseca	13-8	3rd	0.5
4-25	S.F	L	4-6	(11)	7	13	Gardner	Miceli		13-9	3rd	1.5
4-26	S.F	L	7-8	(12)	16	11	Fultz	Alfonseca		13-10	4th	2.5
4-28	At L.A.	L	3-5		7	9	Adams	Penny	Shaw	13-11	4th	4.0
4-29	At L.A.	L	12-13		12	17	Shaw	Alfonseca		13-12	4th	5.0
4-30	At L.A.	L	1-7		3	9	Brown	Fernandez		13-13	4th	6.0
5-1	At S.D.	W	5-2		9	8	Dempster	Williams	Alfonseca	14-13	4th	6.0
5-2	At S.D.	L	3-8		6	11	Clement	Nunez		14-14	4th	7.0
5-3	At S.D.	L	1-3		5	5	Meadows	Penny	Hoffman	14-15	4th	7.0
5-5	N.Y.	L	1-4		4	5	Leiter	Sanchez	Franco	14-16	4th	8.0
5-6	N.Y.	W	9-1		12	8	Fernandez	Pulsipher		15-16	4th	7.0
5-7	N.Y.	W	3-0		9	1	Dempster	Rusch		16-16	4th	6.0
5-8	Atl.	W	3-2		9	7	Miceli	Seanez		17-16	T3rd	5.0
5-9	Atl.	L	5-10		9	12	Burkett	Penny		17-17	4th	6.0
5-10	Atl.	W	5-3		9	10	Sanchez	Glavine	Alfonseca	18-17	T3rd	5.0
5-11	Atl.	W	5-4		8	12	Grilli	Millwood	Alfonseca	19-17	T3rd	4.0
5-12	At N.Y.	W	6-4		12	10	Dempster	Rusch	Alfonseca	20-17	3rd	4.0
5-13	At N.Y.	W	7-6		8	12	Mahay	Cook	Alfonseca	21-17	2nd	4.0
5-14	At N.Y.	L	1-5		8	5	Hampton	Penny		21-18	3rd	5.0
5-16	S.D.	L	3-7		7	9	Hitchcock	Sanchez		21-19	3rd	6.0
5-17	S.D.	W	4-2		9	8	Dempster	Clement	Alfonseca	22-19	3rd	6.0
5-18	S.D.	L	2-6		6	15	Spencer	Fernandez		22-20	3rd	7.0
5-19	L.A.	L	3-5		7	8	Herges	Looper	Shaw	22-21	4th	7.0
5-20	L.A.	L	6-12		14	15	Perez	Penny		22-22	4th	8.0
5-21	L.A.	L	3-12		7	17	Brown	Sanchez		22-23	4th	9.0
5-23	At StL.	L	3-10		5	13	Kile	Dempster		22-24	4th	9.0
5-24	At StL.	L	1-5		5	11	Stephenson	Nunez		22-25	4th	10.0
5-25	At StL.	L	6-7		11	9	Ankiel	Cornelius	Veres	22-26	4th	11.0
5-26	At Cin.	L	2-3		8	8	Graves	Miceli		22-27	4th	11.0
5-27	At Cin.	W	8-6	(10)	12	8	Alfonseca	Williamson		23-27	4th	11.0
5-28	At Cin.	W	3-1		8	10	Dempster	Sullivan	Alfonseca	24-27	4th	10.0
5-29	At Pit.	L	4-10		11	13	Schmidt	Nunez		24-28	4th	11.0
5-30	At Pit.	L	2-3	(10)	5	11	Williams	Alfonseca		24-29	4th	12.0
5-31	At Pit.	L	2-5		12	5	Cordova	Sanchez	Williams	24-30	4th	12.5
6-2	Tor.	W	11-10		15	15	Bones	Munro	Alfonseca	25-30	4th	11.0
6-3	Tor.	W	2-1		7	5	Looper	Koch	Alfonseca	26-30	4th	11.0
6-4	Tor.	L	2-7		8	12	Escobar	Nunez		26-31	4th	11.0
6-5	Bos.	L	2-3		6	9	Wakefield	Bones	Lowe	26-32	4th	11.0
6-6	Bos.	L	3-4		9	10	R. Martinez	Sanchez	Lowe	26-33	4th	12.0
6-7	Bos.	W	6-2		5	10	Darensbourg	Rose		27-33	4th	11.0
6-9	At T.B.	L	4-6		7	9	Trachsel	Dempster	Hernandez	27-34	4th	12.0
6-10	At T.B.	W	5-1		10	3	Cornelius	Yan	Alfonseca	28-34	4th	12.0
6-11	At T.B.	L	6-7		13	13	Mecir	Bones	Hernandez	28-35	4th	12.0
6-12	At Phi.	W	5-2		10	6	Darensbourg	Politte	Alfonseca	29-35	4th	12.0
6-13	At Phi.	L	3-4		9	10	Gomes	Strong	Brantley	29-36	4th	12.0
6-14	At Phi.	W	8-1		13	4	Dempster	Wolf		30-36	4th	12.0
6-16	At Pit.	W	8-3		10	8	Cornelius	Cordova	Looper	31-36	4th	10.5
6-17	At Pit.	W	4-3	(11)	10	12	Alfonseca	Loiselle	Strong	32-36	4th	9.5
6-18	At Pit.	W	5-4		10	8	Bones	Christiansen	Alfonseca	33-36	4th	9.5
6-19	Mil.	L	0-2		3	5	Wright	Smith	Wickman	33-37	4th	9.5
6-20	Mil.	W	8-2		13	5	Dempster	Woodard		34-37	4th	9.5
6-21	Mil.	W	5-4		9	11	Looper	Haynes	Alfonseca	35-37	4th	8.5
6-22	Mil.	L	1-6		6	10	Snyder	Sanchez		35-38	4th	9.5
6-23	Chi.	W	6-1		12	8	Penny	Lieber		36-38	4th	9.5
6-24	Chi.	W	7-4		9	12	Strong	Heredia	Alfonseca	37-38	4th	8.5
6-25	Chi.	W	8-7	(10)	10	9	Alfonseca	Heredia		38-38	4th	8.5
6-26	At N.Y.	L	5-10		11	12	Leiter	Cornelius		38-39	4th	9.0
6-27	At N.Y.	L	2-5		6	7	Rusch	Sanchez	Benitez	38-40	4th	9.0
6-28	At N.Y.	L	5-6		10	13	B.J. Jones	Penny	Franco	38-41	4th	10.0
6-30	At Mon.	W	5-4		12	7	Almanza	Kline	Alfonseca	39-41	4th	9.5

HIGHLIGHTS

High point: After a 5-11 finish in July, the Marlins needed a confidence boost. They got it during a six-game swing through Cincinnati and St. Louis that produced five wins—the last a come-from-behind triumph that was sealed by Mike Lowell's three-run, eighth-inning home run. The Marlins played the rest of the season with a bit of a swagger.
Low point: The Marlins hit bottom shortly after the All-Star break when they fell under .500 with three ugly losses to the Expos—7-3, 17-7 and 7-6. The next day, they committed five errors in the first of two straight losses to the Braves. Gone was the premature talk of the Marlins contending for the playoffs.
Turning point: Can it occur at the end of a season? A six-game season-ending win streak set a positive tone for the young Marlins, who exceeded expectations with their third-place finish in the N.L. East and recorded a 15-win improvement over 1999.
Most valuable player: Luis Castillo, a scrappy little second baseman, was the undisputed spark in the line-up. He set five club records—average (.334), hits (180), singles (158), multi-hit games (55) and stolen bases (62). His steals total was the best in baseball.
Most valuable pitcher: Ryan Dempster was the undisputed staff ace, but the most valuable pitcher was closer Antonio Alfonseca. The big righthander saved a major league-high 45 games and won five, meaning he figured in 63.3 percent of the team's 79 wins.
Most improved player: After batting .206 in 70 games in 1999, Derrek Lee lost the starting first base job to Kevin Millar in the spring. By mid-April, Lee was back in the lineup and he went on to bat .281 with 28 homers and 70 RBIs in the No. 6 slot.
Most pleasant surprise: Chuck Smith, a 30-year-old journeyman minor leaguer, arrived as a trade throw-in and helped stabilize the rotation. His 6-6 record was deceiving, but not the 3.23 ERA or the 118 batters he struck out in $122^{2}/_{3}$ innings.
Key injuries: The biggest loss was Alex Fernandez, the expected staff ace who was 4-4 when he finally shut it down in May because of a sore shoulder and elbow. ... Brian Edmondson, the workhorse of the 1999 bullpen, missed the entire 2000 season with a bad shoulder... Righthanders Dan Miceli and Brad Penny missed action with sore arms. ... Lefty Michael Tejera missed the season with a torn ligament in his elbow.
Notable: The 79-82 Marlins became just the second N.L. team in 50 years to post a 10-win improvement in back-to-back seasons. ... By hitting 31 homers and stealing 36 bases, center fielder Preston Wilson joined a select club. He became the 23rd player in history to accomplish the feat and the first for the Marlins. ... Dempster broke the club record with 209 strikeouts .

—JOE CAPOZZI

MISCELLANEOUS

RECORDS

2000 regular-season record: 79-82 (3rd in N.L. East); 43-38 at home; 36-44 on road; 36-31 vs. East; 26-23 vs. Central; 17-28 vs. West; 17-22 vs. lefthanded starters; 62-60 vs. righthanded starters; 63-70 on grass; 16-12 on turf; 25-21 in daytime; 54-61 at night; 32-20 in one-run games; 9-5 in extra-inning games; 0-0-1 in doubleheaders.
Team record past five years: 369-440 (.456, ranks 12th in league in that span).

TEAM LEADERS

Batting average: Luis Castillo (.334).
At-bats: Preston Wilson (605).
Runs: Luis Castillo (101).
Hits: Luis Castillo (180).
Total Bases: Preston Wilson (294).
Doubles: Mike Lowell (38).
Triples: Mark Kotsay (5).
Home runs: Preston Wilson (31).
Runs batted in: Preston Wilson (121).
Stolen bases: Luis Castillo (62).
Slugging percentage: Derrek Lee (.507).
On-base percentage: Luis Castillo (.418).
Wins: Ryan Dempster (14).
Earned-run average: Ryan Dempster (3.66).
Complete games: Ryan Dempster, Jesus Sanchez (2).
Shutouts: Jesus Sanchez (2).
Saves: Antonio Alfonseca (45).
Innings pitched: Ryan Dempster (226.1).
Strikeouts: Ryan Dempster (209).

Date	Opp.	Res.	Score	(inn.*)	Hits	Opp. hits	Winning pitcher	Losing pitcher	Save	Record	Pos.	GB
7-1	At Mon.	W	6-5		10	13	Dempster	Johnson	Alfonseca	40-41	4th	8.5
7-2	At Mon.	W	2-1		5	4	Cornelius	Santana	Alfonseca	41-41	3rd	8.5
7-3	N.Y.	W	2-0		6	4	Almanza	Wendell		42-41	3rd	7.5
7-4	N.Y.	W	9-8		10	9	Darensbourg	B.M. Jones	Alfonseca	43-41	3rd	7.5
7-5	N.Y.	L	2-11		6	15	Hampton	Smith		43-42	3rd	7.5
7-7	T.B.	L	3-8		7	11	Lopez	Dempster	Mecir	43-43	4th	8.0
7-8	T.B.	W	6-5		13	11	Looper	White	Alfonseca	44-43	T3rd	8.0
7-9	T.B.	W	10-9		14	11	Sanchez	Creek	Alfonseca	45-43	3rd	7.0
7-13	At N.Y. (AL)	W	11-9		14	12	Penny	Hernandez	Alfonseca	46-43	3rd	7.0
7-14	At N.Y. (AL)	L	2-6		7	9	Clemens	Dempster		46-44	3rd	8.0
7-16	At Bal.	L	5-9		11	16	Mills	Darensbourg	Timlin	46-45	3rd	9.5
7-17	At Bal.	L	3-5		8	8	Mercedes	Cornelius	Timlin	46-46	3rd	9.5
7-18	At Bal.	W	7-0		13	8	Sanchez	Mussina		47-46	3rd	9.5
7-20†	Atl.	L	3-5		10	9	Glavine	Dempster	Ligtenberg	47-47		
7-20‡	Atl.	W	6-1		8	3	Burnett	Kamieniecki		48-47	3rd	9.5
7-21	Mon.	L	3-7		8	9	Thurman	Smith		48-48	3rd	10.5
7-22	Mon.	L	7-17		7	19	Johnson	Cornelius		48-49	3rd	10.5
7-23	Mon.	L	6-7		11	17	Vazquez	Sanchez	Strickland	48-50	4th	11.5
7-25	At Atl.	L	5-6		15	6	Glavine	Dempster	Ligtenberg	48-51	4th	12.5
7-26	At Atl.	L	3-6		9	10	Millwood	Burnett	Rocker	48-52	4th	13.5
7-27	At Atl.	W	12-4		15	8	Smith	Maddux		49-52	3rd	12.5
7-28	Ari.	L	1-4		6	6	Schilling	Cornelius	Mantei	49-53	3rd	13.5
7-29	Ari.	W	4-2		7	2	Miceli	Kim	Alfonseca	50-53	3rd	13.5
7-30	Ari.	W	4-3		10	6	Almanza	Morgan	Alfonseca	51-53	3rd	13.5
7-31	Hou.	L	2-4		9	8	Lima	Burnett	Dotel	51-54	3rd	14.0
8-1	Hou.	L	3-4		6	2	Elarton	Smith	Dotel	51-55	3rd	15.0
8-2	Hou.	W	5-4		8	11	Miceli	Valdes		52-55	3rd	14.0
8-3	Hou.	W	4-3		11	6	Looper	Slusarski	Alfonseca	53-55	3rd	13.0
8-4	At Cin.	W	2-1		10	8	Dempster	Harnisch	Alfonseca	54-55	3rd	13.0
8-5	At Cin.	W	10-5	(11)	13	15	Alfonseca	Wohlers		55-55	3rd	12.0
8-6	At Cin.	W	9-6		9	12	Aybar	Graves	Looper	56-55	3rd	12.0
8-7	At StL.	L	1-2	(11)	4	9	Timlin	Darensbourg		56-56	3rd	12.0
8-8	At StL.	W	7-0		10	6	Sanchez	Hentgen		57-56	3rd	12.0
8-9	At StL.	W	5-3		7	11	Almanza	Morris	Alfonseca	58-56	3rd	11.0
8-11	S.D.	L	0-3		7	5	Eaton	Burnett	Hoffman	58-57	3rd	12.0
8-12	S.D.	L	1-2	(10)	5	9	Walker	Alfonseca	Hoffman	58-58	3rd	13.0
8-13	S.D.	L	3-7		11	8	Walker	Almanza	Hoffman	58-59	3rd	13.0
8-14	L.A.	W	11-2		12	10	Sanchez	Brown		59-59	3rd	13.0
8-15	L.A.	W	7-3		12	6	Dempster	Herges		60-59	3rd	13.0
8-16	L.A.	L	4-10		13	11	Adams	Miceli		60-60	3rd	14.0
8-18	At Col.	W	9-8		12	18	Smith	Rose	Alfonseca	61-60	3rd	13.0
8-19	At Col.	L	3-10		10	10	Tavarez	Cornelius		61-61	3rd	13.0
8-20	At Col.	L	4-13		8	14	Astacio	Sanchez		61-62	3rd	14.0
8-21	At S.F	L	0-6		6	10	Gardner	Dempster		61-63	3rd	15.0
8-22	At S.F	W	7-5		13	8	Burnett	Estes	Alfonseca	62-63	3rd	14.0
8-23	At S.F	L	0-5		4	7	Hernandez	Smith		62-64	3rd	15.0
8-25	Cin.	L	0-6		8	13	Dessens	Cornelius		62-65	3rd	15.5
8-26	Cin.	L	2-3		9	5	Harnisch	Darensbourg	Graves	62-66	3rd	15.5
8-27	Cin.	W	7-6		10	13	Miceli	Graves		63-66	3rd	14.5
8-28	StL.	L	2-5		5	12	James	Almanza	Veres	63-67	3rd	14.5
8-29	StL.	W	3-1		7	4	Smith	Hentgen	Alfonseca	64-67	3rd	13.5
8-30	StL.	L	2-4		8	7	Morris	Alfonseca	Veres	64-68	3rd	14.5
9-1	At Ari.	W	8-7	(11)	15	13	Darensbourg	Swindell	Alfonseca	65-68	3rd	13.5
9-2	At Ari.	W	10-1		17	9	Dempster	Schilling		66-68	3rd	13.0
9-3	At Ari.	L	5-10		11	18	Kim	Burnett		66-69	3rd	13.0
9-4	At Hou.	W	5-2		11	5	Smith	Holt	Alfonseca	67-69	3rd	12.5
9-5	At Hou.	L	5-9		9	15	McKnight	Cornelius		67-70	3rd	13.5
9-6	At Hou.	L	5-13		7	14	Lima	Sanchez		67-71	3rd	14.5
9-7	At Hou.	L	3-7		7	9	Elarton	Miceli		67-72	3rd	15.5
9-8	Ari.	L	1-2		6	8	Kim	Bones	Mantei	67-73	3rd	16.5
9-9	Ari.	L	1-4		5	9	Stottlemyre	Burnett	Mantei	67-74	3rd	16.5
9-10	Ari.	W	4-3	(12)	9	4	Looper	Springer		68-74	3rd	15.5
9-12	At Atl.	W	5-4		11	12	Sanchez	Millwood	Alfonseca	69-74	3rd	14.5
9-13	At Atl.	L	0-4		4	8	Maddux	Dempster		69-75	3rd	15.5
9-14	At Atl.	L	3-5		8	10	Ashby	Cornelius	Rocker	69-76	3rd	16.5
9-15	At Phi.	L	4-7		7	8	Person	Burnett		69-77	3rd	16.5
9-16	At Phi.	W	3-2		7	4	Penny	Daal	Alfonseca	70-77	3rd	16.5
9-17	At Phi.	L	5-6		10	9	Wolf	Smith	Jacquez	70-78	3rd	17.5
9-18	At Mon.	L	4-11		6	9	Lira	Sanchez		70-79	3rd	18.5
9-19	At Mon.	W	3-1		7	5	Dempster	Thurman	Alfonseca	71-79	3rd	18.5
9-20	At Mon.	L	2-4		9	9	Vazquez	Cornelius	Strickland	71-80	3rd	18.5
9-21	At Mon.	L	3-10		7	14	Hermanson	Burnett		71-81	3rd	19.0
9-22	At Col.	W	8-4		13	7	Penny	Tavarez		72-81	3rd	18.0
9-23	At Col.	W	3-1	(7)	6	4	Smith	Wasdin		73-81	3rd	18.0
9-24	At Col.	L	3-9		8	14	Bohanon	Sanchez		73-82	3rd	19.0
9-26	Mon.	W	5-4	(10)	8	8	Alfonseca	Kline		74-82	3rd	19.5
9-27	Mon.	W	6-3		9	5	Burnett	Armas	Alfonseca	75-82	3rd	18.5
9-28	Mon.	W	7-4		9	8	Penny	Lira	Alfonseca	76-82	3rd	17.5
9-29	Phi.	W	7-1		10	4	Smith	Chen		77-82	3rd	16.5
9-30	Phi.	W	11-5		17	10	Cornelius	Person		78-82	3rd	16.5
10-1	Phi.	W	7-5		11	9	Dempster	Telemaco	Alfonseca	79-82	3rd	15.5

Monthly records: April (13-13), May (11-17), June (15-11), July (12-13), August (13-14), September (14-14), October (1-0).
*Innings, if other than nine. † First game of a doubleheader. ‡ Second game of a doubleheader.

MEMORABLE GAMES

May 11 at Florida

The Marlins's 5-4 win over Atlanta provided the first spark in what would become an interesting season. Emergency starter Jason Grilli worked $6\frac{2}{3}$ innings for his first major league victory and lefty Joe Strong,making his big-league debut at age 37, worked $1\frac{1}{3}$ scoreless innings in relief. The final out sparked a championship-style celebration with Grilli and Strong crying in each others' arms.

Atlanta	AB	R	H	BI	Florida	AB	R	H	BI
Veras, 2b	4	0	2	1	Castillo, 2b	4	1	2	1
A.Jones, cf	3	1	1	0	Kotsay, rf	4	1	1	0
C.Jones, 3b	5	0	2	0	Floyd, lf	2	0	0	1
Galarraga, 1b	5	0	2	0	Alfonseca, p	0	0	0	0
Jordan, rf	5	0	0	1	Wilson, cf	2	1	2	2
Bonilla, lf	5	0	1	0	Lowell, 3b	3	1	0	0
Furcal, ss	3	2	1	0	Lee, 1b	4	1	1	0
Lunar, c	3	1	1	0	Gonzalez, ss	3	0	0	0
Millwood, p	2	0	2	2	Strong, p	0	0	0	0
McMichael, p	0	0	0	0	Bautista, lf	0	0	0	0
Joyner, ph	1	0	0	0	Bako, c	3	0	1	0
Remlinger, p	0	0	0	0	Grilli, p	2	0	1	1
					Berg, ss	1	0	0	0
Totals	**36**	**4**	**12**	**4**	**Totals**	**28**	**5**	**8**	**5**

Atlanta ....1 0 0 2 1 0 0 0 0—4 12 0
Florida ....3 0 0 2 0 0 0 0 x—5 8 0

DP—Florida 1. TP—Atlanta 1. LOB—Atlanta 12, Florida 4. 2B—C.Jones (9), Millwood (1). HR—Wilson (6). SB—Furcal (9). CS—Wilson (3). S—Floyd. SH—Furcal, Millwood.

Atlanta	IP	H	R	ER	BB	SO
Millwood (L 3-2)	4	8	5	5	2	2
McMichael	2	0	0	0	0	1
Remlinger	2	0	0	0	1	2

Florida	IP	H	R	ER	BB	SO
Grilli (W 1-0)	6.2	11	4	4	2	3
Strong	1.1	0	0	0	1	0
Alfonseca (S 11)	1	1	0	0	0	0

Millwood pitched to 2 batters in 5th.

HBP—A. Jones by Grilli, Wilson by Millwood, Lunarby Grilli. U—HP, Gorman. 1B, Everett. 2B, Crawford. 3B, DiMuro. T—2:48. A—14,587.

May 28 at Cincinnati

Ryan Dempster, ignoring the pressure of 36,754 screaming fans at Cincinnati's Cinergy Field, struck out Ken Griffey Jr. with the bases loaded in the bottom of the seventh inning and then watched his inspired teammates score three times in the eighth for a 3-1 victory. Outfielder Danny Bautista provided the muscle with a three-run homer off Scott Sullivan.

Florida	AB	R	H	BI	Cincinnati	AB	R	H	BI
Castillo, 2b	5	0	2	0	Reese, 2b	5	0	0	0
Berg, ss-3b	4	0	1	0	Larkin, ss	4	1	3	0
Floyd, lf	4	1	2	0	Griffey Jr., cf	3	0	0	0
Alfonseca, p	0	0	0	0	Bichette, rf	4	0	1	0
Wilson, cf	4	0	0	0	Young, lf	3	0	1	1
Millar, 3b	3	1	1	0	Taubensee, c	4	0	1	0
Gonzalez, ss	0	0	0	0	Casey, 1b	4	0	1	0
Lee, 1b	4	0	0	0	Boone, 3b	4	0	1	0
Bautista, rf-lf	4	1	1	3	Neagle, p	3	0	1	0
Redmond, c	3	0	0	0	Sullivan, p	0	0	0	0
Dempster, p	3	0	0	0	Tucker, ph	1	0	1	0
Darensbourg, p	0	0	0	0					
Kotsay, ph-rf	1	0	1	0					
Totals	**35**	**3**	**8**	**3**	**Totals**	**35**	**1**	**10**	**1**

Florida ....0 0 0 0 0 0 0 3 0—3 8 1
Cincinnati ....1 0 0 0 0 0 0 0 0—1 10 0

E—Wilson (1). DP—Florida 1. LOB—Florida 10, Cincinnati 9. 2B—Kotsay (6), Young (11). HR—Bautista (4). SB—L.Castillo 3 (22), Berg (3).

Florida	IP	H	R	ER	BB	SO
Dempster (W 6-3)	7.2	9	1	1	2	6
Darensbourg	0.1	0	0	0	0	1
Alfonseca (S 15)	1	1	0	0	0	1

Cincinnati	IP	H	R	ER	BB	SO
Neagle	7	5	1	1	4	7
Sullivan (L 1-3)	2	3	2	2	1	4

Neagle pitched to 1 batter in 8th.

PB—Taubensee. U—HP, Wegner. 1B, Van Vleet. 2B, Williams. 3B, Reynolds. T—2:52. A—36,754.

INDIVIDUAL STATISTICS

BATTING

Name	G	TPA	AB	R	H	TB	2B	3B	HR	RBI	Avg.	Obp.	Slg.	SH	SF	HP	BB	IBB	SO	SB	CS	GDP	vs RHP AB	vs RHP Avg.	vs RHP HR	vs RHP RBI	vs LHP AB	vs LHP Avg.	vs LHP HR	vs LHP RBI
Wilson, Preston	161	674	605	94	160	294	35	3	31	121	.264	.331	.486	0	6	8	55	1	187	36	14	11	461	.269	22	90	144	.250	9	31
Castillo, Luis	136	626	539	101	180	209	17	3	2	17	.334	.418	.388	9	0	0	78	0	86	62	22	11	391	.350	0	14	148	.291	2	3
Kotsay, Mark	152	578	530	87	158	235	31	5	12	57	.298	.347	.443	2	4	0	42	2	46	19	9	17	426	.296	11	44	104	.308	1	13
Lowell, Mike	140	583	508	73	137	241	38	0	22	91	.270	.344	.474	0	11	9	54	4	75	4	0	4	403	.273	17	75	105	.257	5	16
Lee, Derrek	158	546	477	70	134	242	18	3	28	70	.281	.368	.507	0	2	4	63	6	123	0	3	14	376	.295	22	62	101	.228	6	8
Floyd, Cliff	121	487	420	75	126	222	30	0	22	91	.300	.378	.529	0	9	8	50	5	82	24	3	4	294	.286	17	65	126	.333	5	26
Gonzalez, Alex	109	407	385	35	77	123	17	4	7	42	.200	.229	.319	5	2	2	13	0	77	7	1	7	287	.185	5	32	98	.245	2	10
Millar, Kevin	123	305	259	36	67	129	14	3	14	42	.259	.364	.498	0	2	8	36	0	47	0	0	5	188	.261	8	28	71	.254	6	14
Berg, Dave	82	245	210	23	53	72	14	1	1	21	.252	.340	.343	1	4	5	25	0	46	3	0	5	147	.245	1	17	63	.270	0	4
Redmond, Mike	87	235	210	17	53	63	8	1	0	15	.252	.316	.300	1	3	8	13	3	19	0	0	5	129	.209	0	11	81	.321	0	4
Smith, Mark	104	213	192	22	47	72	8	1	5	27	.245	.310	.375	0	2	2	17	1	54	2	0	2	117	.291	4	22	75	.173	1	5
Fox, Andy	69	185	164	19	40	57	4	2	3	10	.244	.330	.348	0	0	3	18	3	37	8	3	1	154	.247	3	10	10	.200	0	0
Bako, Paul	56	186	161	10	39	47	6	1	0	14	.242	.335	.292	1	1	1	22	7	48	0	0	4	146	.253	0	14	15	.133	0	0
Castro, Ramon	50	157	138	10	33	43	4	0	2	14	.239	.318	.312	0	2	1	16	7	36	0	0	1	113	.248	2	12	25	.200	0	2
Rodriguez, Henry	36	123	108	10	29	41	6	0	2	10	.269	.358	.380	0	0	1	14	0	23	0	0	1	94	.287	2	10	14	.143	0	0
Bautista, Danny	44	94	89	9	17	33	4	0	4	12	.191	.234	.371	0	0	0	5	0	20	1	0	1	40	.175	3	10	49	.204	1	2
Dempster, Ryan	33	82	77	3	6	8	2	0	0	2	.078	.090	.104	4	0	0	1	0	29	0	0	0	51	.098	0	1	26	.038	0	1
Brown, Brant	41	76	73	4	14	26	6	0	2	6	.192	.224	.356	0	0	0	3	0	33	1	0	1	70	.186	2	5	3	.333	0	1
Sanchez, Jesus	45	60	56	6	13	13	0	0	0	4	.232	.246	.232	3	0	0	1	0	15	0	0	1	38	.263	0	3	18	.167	0	1
Clapinski, Chris	34	55	49	12	15	24	4	1	1	7	.306	.370	.490	1	0	0	5	0	7	0	0	1	31	.323	1	6	18	.278	0	1
Penny, Brad	24	46	45	2	5	5	0	0	0	2	.111	.111	.111	1	0	0	0	0	17	0	0	0	33	.121	0	2	12	.083	0	0
Smith, Chuck	21	41	40	2	4	4	0	0	0	2	.100	.100	.100	1	0	0	0	0	19	0	0	1	33	.091	0	1	7	.143	0	1
Cornelius, Reid	23	41	37	1	5	7	2	0	0	1	.135	.135	.189	4	0	0	0	0	12	0	0	1	29	.172	0	1	8	.000	0	0
Burnett, A.J.	13	30	25	3	7	13	1	1	1	3	.280	.357	.520	2	0	0	3	0	10	0	0	0	20	.200	0	2	5	.600	1	1
Ozuna, Pablo	14	26	24	2	8	9	1	0	0	0	.333	.333	.375	2	0	0	0	0	2	1	0	0	18	.278	0	0	6	.500	0	0
Martinez, Sandy	10	18	18	1	4	6	2	0	0	0	.222	.222	.333	0	0	0	0	0	8	0	0	0	16	.250	0	0	2	.000	0	0
Fernandez, Alex	9	20	17	1	2	3	1	0	0	3	.118	.250	.176	0	0	0	3	0	10	0	0	2	8	.125	0	1	9	.111	0	2
Nunez, Vladimir	17	21	17	2	2	5	0	0	1	3	.118	.118	.294	4	0	0	0	0	5	0	0	0	16	.125	1	2	1	.000	0	1
Rolison, Nate	8	16	13	0	1	1	0	0	0	2	.077	.125	.077	0	2	0	1	0	4	0	0	0	13	.077	0	1	0	.000	0	1
Darensbourg, Vic	56	8	8	0	2	2	0	0	0	0	.250	.250	.250	0	0	0	0	0	2	0	0	0	7	.286	0	0	1	.000	0	0
Mahay, Ron	18	4	4	0	2	3	1	0	0	0	.500	.500	.750	0	0	0	0	0	1	0	0	0	3	.333	0	0	1	1.000	0	0
Lopez, Mendy	4	4	3	0	0	0	0	0	0	0	.000	.250	.000	0	0	0	1	0	1	0	0	0	3	.000	0	0	0	.000	0	0
Grilli, Jason	1	2	2	0	1	1	0	0	0	1	.500	.500	.500	0	0	0	0	0	0	0	0	0	2	.500	0	1	0	.000	0	0
Bones, Ricky	56	4	2	1	0	0	0	0	0	1	.000	.250	.000	0	1	0	1	0	0	0	0	0	2	.000	0	0	0	.000	0	1
Looper, Braden	73	2	2	0	0	0	0	0	0	0	.000	.000	.000	0	0	0	0	0	2	0	0	0	1	.000	0	0	1	.000	0	0
Almanza, Armando	67	2	1	0	0	0	0	0	0	0	.000	.000	.000	1	0	0	0	0	0	0	0	0	0	.000	0	0	1	.000	0	0
Strong, Joe	18	1	1	0	0	0	0	0	0	0	.000	.000	.000	0	0	0	0	0	1	0	0	0	0	.000	0	0	1	.000	0	0
Miceli, Dan	45	0	0	0	0	0	0	0	0	0	.000	.000	.000	0	0	0	0	0	0	0	0	0	0	.000	0	0	0	.000	0	0
Alfonseca, Antonio	68	0	0	0	0	0	0	0	0	0	.000	.000	.000	0	0	0	0	0	0	0	0	0	0	.000	0	0	0	.000	0	0
Aybar, Manny	21	0	0	0	0	0	0	0	0	0	.000	.000	.000	0	0	0	0	0	0	0	0	0	0	.000	0	0	0	.000	0	0

Players with more than one N.L. team

Name	G	TPA	AB	R	H	TB	2B	3B	HR	RBI	Avg.	Obp.	Slg.	SH	SF	HP	BB	IBB	SO	SB	CS	GDP	vs RHP AB	vs RHP Avg.	vs RHP HR	vs RHP RBI	vs LHP AB	vs LHP Avg.	vs LHP HR	vs LHP RBI
Aybar, Col.	1	0	0	0	0	0	0	0	0	0	.000	.000	.000	0	0	0	0	0	0	0	0	0	0	.000	0	0	0	.000	0	0
Aybar, Cin.	32	9	6	1	0	0	0	0	0	0	.000	.250	.000	1	0	0	2	0	3	0	0	0	0	.000	0	0	0	.000	0	0
Aybar, Col.-Cin.-Fla.	54	9	6	1	0	0	0	0	0	0	.000	.250	.000	1	0	0	2	0	3	0	0	0	3	.000	0	0	3	.000	0	0
Bako, Hou.	1	2	2	0	0	0	0	0	0	0	.000	.000	.000	0	0	0	0	0	1	0	0	0	146	.253	0	14	15	.133	0	0
Bako, Atl.	24	63	58	8	11	21	4	0	2	6	.190	.254	.362	0	0	0	5	3	15	0	0	2	146	.253	0	14	15	.133	0	0
Bako, Hou.-Fla.-Atl.	81	251	221	18	50	68	10	1	2	20	.226	.312	.308	1	1	1	27	10	64	0	0	6	194	.237	1	19	27	.148	1	1
Bautista, Ari.	87	294	262	45	83	134	16	7	7	47	.317	.366	.511	4	5	3	20	4	30	5	2	10	40	.175	3	10	49	.204	1	2
Bautista, Fla.-Ari.	131	388	351	54	100	167	20	7	11	59	.285	.333	.476	4	5	3	25	4	50	6	2	11	220	.295	7	46	131	.267	4	13
Brown, Chi.	54	102	89	7	14	24	1	0	3	10	.157	.248	.270	1	1	1	10	0	29	2	1	2	70	.186	2	5	3	.333	0	1
Brown, Fla.-Chi.	95	178	162	11	28	50	7	0	5	16	.173	.237	.309	1	1	1	13	0	62	3	1	3	146	.164	5	14	16	.250	0	2
Fox, Ari.	31	90	86	10	18	25	4	0	1	10	.209	.244	.291	0	0	0	4	1	16	2	1	1	154	.247	3	10	10	.200	0	0
Fox, Ari.-Fla.	100	275	250	29	58	82	8	2	4	20	.232	.302	.328	0	0	3	22	4	53	10	4	2	226	.230	4	19	24	.250	0	1
Rodriguez, Chi.	76	287	259	37	65	136	15	1	18	51	.251	.314	.525	0	3	3	22	2	76	1	2	4	94	.287	2	10	14	.143	0	0
Rodriguez, Chi.-Fla.	112	410	367	47	94	177	21	1	20	61	.256	.327	.482	0	3	4	36	2	99	1	2	5	314	.258	18	57	53	.245	2	4

PITCHING

Name	W	L	Pct.	ERA	IP	H	R	ER	HR	SH	SF	HB	BB	IBB	SO	G	GS	CG	ShO	GF	Sv	vs. RH AB	vs. RH Avg.	vs. RH HR	vs. RH RBI	vs. LH AB	vs. LH Avg.	vs. LH HR	vs. LH RBI
Dempster, Ryan	14	10	.583	3.66	226.1	210	102	92	30	4	5	5	97	7	209	33	33	2	1	0	0	484	.242	14	53	379	.245	16	40
Sanchez, Jesus	9	12	.429	5.34	182.0	197	118	108	32	9	12	4	76	4	123	32	32	2	2	0	0	592	.285	29	96	112	.250	3	15
Cornelius, Reid	4	10	.286	4.82	125.0	135	74	67	19	9	6	4	50	4	50	22	21	0	0	0	0	266	.282	8	33	212	.283	11	30
Smith, Chuck	6	6	.500	3.23	122.2	111	53	44	6	4	5	3	54	2	118	19	19	1	0	0	0	268	.254	4	26	179	.240	2	21
Penny, Brad	8	7	.533	4.81	119.2	120	70	64	13	6	2	5	60	4	80	23	22	0	0	0	0	263	.274	11	46	193	.249	2	16
Burnett, A.J.	3	7	.300	4.79	82.2	80	46	44	8	6	3	2	44	3	57	13	13	0	0	0	0	160	.219	6	22	149	.302	2	13
Bones, Ricky	2	3	.400	4.54	77.1	94	43	39	6	6	6	3	27	8	59	56	0	0	0	13	0	199	.271	3	22	111	.360	3	21
Alfonseca, Antonio	5	6	.455	4.24	70.0	82	35	33	7	3	1	1	24	3	47	68	0	0	0	62	45	152	.303	5	19	130	.277	2	16
Nunez, Vladimir	0	6	.000	7.90	68.1	88	63	60	12	5	5	2	34	2	45	17	12	0	0	3	0	164	.305	6	36	112	.339	6	22
Looper, Braden	5	1	.833	4.41	67.1	71	41	33	3	3	2	5	36	6	29	73	0	0	0	23	2	187	.230	1	30	78	.359	2	17
Darensbourg, Vic	5	3	.625	4.06	62.0	61	32	28	7	3	6	2	28	1	59	56	0	0	0	17	0	156	.295	5	24	79	.190	2	6
Fernandez, Alex	4	4	.500	4.13	52.1	59	25	24	7	3	1	0	16	1	27	8	8	0	0	0	0	118	.322	4	12	84	.250	3	11
Miceli, Dan	6	4	.600	4.25	48.2	45	23	23	4	1	1	1	18	2	40	45	0	0	0	9	0	97	.216	2	12	89	.270	2	11
Almanza, Armando	4	2	.667	4.86	46.1	38	27	25	3	2	2	2	43	6	46	67	0	0	0	8	0	100	.260	2	23	67	.179	1	10
Aybar, Manny	1	0	1.000	2.63	27.1	18	8	8	3	1	1	0	13	1	14	21	0	0	0	10	0	59	.169	2	6	39	.205	1	4
Mahay, Ron	1	0	1.000	6.04	25.1	31	17	17	6	0	1	0	16	1	27	18	0	0	0	6	0	76	.316	6	13	24	.292	0	5
Strong, Joe	1	1	.500	7.32	19.2	26	16	16	3	1	0	2	12	1	18	18	0	0	0	5	1	57	.368	2	16	23	.217	1	5
Grilli, Jason	1	0	1.000	5.40	6.2	11	4	4	0	2	0	2	2	0	3	1	1	0	0	0	0	15	.333	0	3	14	.429	0	1

PITCHERS WITH MORE THAN ONE N.L. TEAM

Name	W	L	Pct.	ERA	IP	H	R	ER	HR	SH	SF	HB	BB	IBB	SO	G	GS	CG	ShO	GF	Sv	vs. RH AB	vs. RH Avg.	vs. RH HR	vs. RH RBI	vs. LH AB	vs. LH Avg.	vs. LH HR	vs. LH RBI
Aybar, Col.	0	1	.000	16.20	1.2	5	3	3	1	0	0	0	0	0	0	1	0	0	0	0	0	59	.169	2	6	39	.205	1	4
Aybar, Cin.	1	1	.500	4.83	50.1	51	31	27	7	4	3	2	22	2	31	32	0	0	0	10	0	59	.169	2	6	39	.205	1	4
Aybar, Col.-Cin.-Fla.	2	2	.500	4.31	79.1	74	42	38	11	5	4	2	35	3	45	54	0	0	0	4	0	197	.264	9	30	106	.208	2	10

DESIGNATED HITTERS

Name	AB	Avg.	HR	RBI
Millar, Kevin	21	.286	1	7
Smith, Mark	5	.200	0	0
Floyd, Cliff	4	.500	0	1

INDIVIDUAL STATISTICS

FIELDING

FIRST BASEMEN

Player	Pct.	G	PO	A	E	TC	DP
Lee, Derrek	.993	147	1101	102	8	1211	104
Millar, Kevin	.989	34	233	29	3	265	18
Brown, Brant	1.000	5	30	3	0	33	2
Rolison, Nate	1.000	4	21	2	0	23	1
Kotsay, Mark	1.000	2	1	0	0	1	0

SECOND BASEMEN

Player	Pct.	G	PO	A	E	TC	DP
Castillo, Luis	.983	136	282	365	11	658	83
Clapinski, Chris	.933	14	25	31	4	60	5
Berg, Dave	1.000	11	17	25	0	42	3
Ozuna, Pablo	.967	7	12	17	1	30	3
Fox, Andy	1.000	2	4	6	0	10	1

THIRD BASEMEN

Player	Pct.	G	PO	A	E	TC	DP
Lowell, Mike	.968	136	102	260	12	374	19
Millar, Kevin	.944	13	11	23	2	36	1
Berg, Dave	.933	13	2	12	1	15	1
Fox, Andy	.963	12	4	22	1	27	4
Clapinski, Chris	1.000	3	2	2	0	4	0

SHORTSTOPS

Player	Pct.	G	PO	A	E	TC	DP
Gonzalez, Alex	.957	104	139	288	19	446	63
Berg, Dave	.957	49	52	105	7	164	27
Fox, Andy	.932	33	37	86	9	132	12
Clapinski, Chris	-	1	0	0	0	0	0

OUTFIELDERS

Player	Pct.	G	PO	A	E	TC	DP
Wilson, Preston	.988	158	387	9	5	401	2
Kotsay, Mark	.990	142	288	14	3	305	3
Floyd, Cliff	.951	108	168	7	9	184	0
Smith, Mark	1.000	49	65	4	0	69	1
Bautista, Danny	.980	38	46	2	1	49	1
Rodriguez, Henry	1.000	29	40	1	0	41	0
Millar, Kevin	1.000	18	25	0	0	25	0
Fox, Andy	.875	14	6	1	1	8	0
Brown, Brant	.923	13	12	0	1	13	0
Clapinski, Chris	1.000	3	1	0	0	1	0

CATCHERS

Player	Pct.	G	PO	A	E	TC	DP	PB
Redmond, Mike	.996	85	446	40	2	488	9	6
Bako, Paul	.991	56	318	21	3	342	2	3
Castro, Ramon	.980	50	274	24	6	304	4	3
Martinez, Sandy	1.000	9	43	2	0	45	0	0

PITCHERS

Player	Pct.	G	PO	A	E	TC	DP
Looper, Braden	.941	73	6	10	1	17	1
Alfonseca, Antonio	.938	68	1	14	1	16	1
Almanza, Armando	1.000	67	1	3	0	4	0
Darensbourg, Vic	1.000	56	6	12	0	18	1
Bones, Ricky	1.000	56	3	11	0	14	0
Miceli, Dan	1.000	45	6	1	0	7	0
Dempster, Ryan	.909	33	11	29	4	44	2
Sanchez, Jesus	.921	32	7	28	3	38	3
Penny, Brad	.933	23	11	17	2	30	1
Cornelius, Reid	1.000	22	8	26	0	34	3
Aybar, Manny	1.000	21	4	6	0	10	0
Smith, Chuck	.926	19	11	14	2	27	1
Strong, Joe	1.000	18	2	4	0	6	0
Mahay, Ron	1.000	18	1	4	0	5	0
Nunez, Vladimir	.909	17	9	11	2	22	0
Burnett, A.J.	.909	13	2	8	1	11	1
Fernandez, Alex	1.000	8	6	8	0	14	1
Grilli, Jason	1.000	1	0	1	0	1	0

PITCHING AGAINST EACH CLUB

Pitcher	Ari. W-L	Atl. W-L	Chi. W-L	Cin. W-L	Col. W-L	Hou. W-L	L.A. W-L	Mil. W-L	Mon. W-L	N.Y. W-L	Phi. W-L	Pit. W-L	S.D. W-L	S.F. W-L	StL. W-L	A.L. W-L	Total W-L
Alfonseca, A.	0-0	0-0	1-0	2-0	0-0	0-0	0-1	0-0	1-0	0-0	0-0	1-1	0-1	0-2	0-1	0-0	5-6
Almanza, A.	1-0	0-0	0-0	0-0	0-0	0-0	0-0	0-0	1-0	1-0	0-0	0-0	0-1	0-0	1-1	0-0	4-2
Aybar, Manny	0-0	0-0	0-0	1-0	0-0	0-0	0-0	0-0	0-0	0-0	0-0	0-0	0-0	0-0	0-0	0-0	1-0
Bones, Ricky	0-1	0-0	0-0	0-0	0-0	0-0	0-0	0-0	0-0	0-0	0-0	1-0	0-0	0-0	0-0	1-2	2-3
Burnett, A.J.	0-2	1-1	0-0	0-0	0-0	0-1	0-0	0-0	1-1	0-0	0-1	0-0	0-1	1-0	0-0	0-0	3-7
Cornelius, R.	0-1	0-1	0-0	0-1	0-1	0-1	0-0	0-0	1-2	0-1	1-0	1-0	0-0	0-0	0-1	1-1	4-10
Darensbourg, V.	1-0	0-0	0-0	0-1	0-0	0-0	0-0	0-0	0-0	1-0	1-0	1-0	0-0	0-0	0-1	1-1	5-3
Dempster, R.	1-0	0-3	0-1	2-0	1-0	0-0	1-0	1-0	2-0	2-0	2-0	0-0	2-0	0-2	0-1	0-3	14-10
Fernandez, A.	0-0	0-0	1-0	0-0	0-1	0-0	0-1	0-0	0-0	1-0	1-0	0-1	0-1	1-0	0-0	0-0	4-4
Grilli, Jason	0-0	1-0	0-0	0-0	0-0	0-0	0-0	0-0	0-0	0-0	0-0	0-0	0-0	0-0	0-0	0-0	1-0
Looper, B.	1-0	0-0	0-0	0-0	0-0	1-0	0-1	1-0	0-0	0-0	0-0	0-0	0-0	0-0	0-0	2-0	5-1
Mahay, Ron	0-0	0-0	0-0	0-0	0-0	0-0	0-0	0-0	0-0	1-0	0-0	0-0	0-0	0-0	0-0	0-0	1-0
Miceli, Dan	1-0	1-0	1-0	1-1	0-0	1-1	0-1	0-0	0-0	0-0	0-0	0-0	0-0	1-1	0-0	0-0	6-4
Nunez, V.	0-0	0-0	0-0	0-0	0-0	0-0	0-0	0-1	0-0	0-0	0-1	0-1	0-1	0-0	0-1	0-1	0-6
Penny, Brad	0-0	0-1	1-0	0-0	2-0	0-0	0-2	0-1	1-0	0-2	2-0	1-0	0-1	0-0	0-0	1-0	8-7
Sanchez, J.	0-0	2-0	1-0	0-0	0-2	0-1	1-1	1-1	0-2	0-2	1-0	0-1	0-1	0-0	1-0	2-1	9-12
Smith, Chuck	0-0	1-0	0-0	0-0	2-0	1-1	0-0	0-1	0-1	0-1	1-1	0-0	0-0	0-1	1-0	0-0	6-6
Strong, Joe	0-0	0-0	1-0	0-0	0-0	0-0	0-0	0-0	0-0	0-0	0-1	0-0	0-0	0-0	0-0	0-0	1-1
Totals	5-4	6-6	6-1	6-3	5-4	3-5	2-7	3-4	7-6	6-6	9-4	5-4	2-7	3-6	3-6	8-9	79-82

INTERLEAGUE: Sanchez 1-0, Darensbourg 0-1, Cornelius 0-1 vs. Orioles; Darensbourg 1-0, Bones 0-1, Sanchez 0-1 vs. Red Sox; Penny 1-0, Dempster 0-1 vs. Yankees; Bones 1-0, Looper 1-0, Nunez 0-1 vs. Blue Jays; Looper 1-0, Cornelius 1-0, Sanchez 1-0, Dempster 0-2, Bones 0-1 vs. Devil Rays. Total: 8-9.

MISCELLANEOUS

HOME RUNS BY PARK

At Arizona (5): Wilson 2, Lowell 2, Lee 1.
At Atlanta (4): Floyd 2, Wilson 1, Lowell 1.
At Baltimore (2): Millar 1, Wilson 1.
At Chicago (NL) (4): Bautista 1, Floyd 1, Millar 1, Gonzalez 1.
At Cincinnati (10): Floyd 2, Lee 2, Kotsay 2, Bautista 1, Fox 1, Wilson 1, Lowell 1.
At Colorado (5): Wilson 2, Rodriguez 1, Kotsay 1, Castro 1.
At Florida (71): Floyd 13, Wilson 12, Lowell 11, Lee 9, Millar 6, Kotsay 5, Gonzalez 5, Smith 2, Brown 2, Rodriguez 1, Bautista 1, Fox 1, Castillo 1, Berg 1, Burnett 1.
At Houston (6): Lee 1, Clapinski 1, Millar 1, Wilson 1, Gonzalez 1, Lowell 1.
At Los Angeles (4): Lee 3, Lowell 1.
At Milwaukee (2): Bautista 1, Lee 1.
At Montreal (8): Smith 2, Wilson 2, Fox 1, Lee 1, Kotsay 1, Castro 1.
At New York (AL) (3): Lee 1, Wilson 1, Lowell 1.
At New York (NL) (8): Lee 2, Wilson 2, Lowell 2, Floyd 1, Millar 1.
At Philadelphia (7): Wilson 3, Lee 2, Kotsay 1, Millar 1.
At Pittsburgh (5): Lee 3, Floyd 1, Wilson 1.
At San Diego (4): Floyd 1, Kotsay 1, Wilson 1, Nunez 1.
At San Francisco (1): Millar 1.
At St. Louis (8): Millar 2, Floyd 1, Smith 1, Lee 1, Kotsay 1, Wilson 1, Lowell 1.
At Tampa Bay (3): Castillo 1, Lee 1, Lowell 1.

LOW-HIT GAMES

No-hitters: None.
One-hitters: Ryan Dempster, May 7 vs. New York, W 3-0.
Two-hitters: None.

10-STRIKEOUT GAMES

Chuck Smith 3, Ryan Dempster 1, A.J. Burnett 1, Total: 5

FOUR OR MORE HITS IN ONE GAME

Mark Kotsay 3, Cliff Floyd 2, Luis Castillo 2, Kevin Millar 1, Total: 8

MULTI-HOMER GAMES

Derrek Lee 3, Preston Wilson 2, Cliff Floyd 1, Mark Smith 1, Alex Gonzalez 1, Mike Lowell 1, Total: 9

GRAND SLAMS

5-6: Preston Wilson (off New York's Armando Benitez)
6-16: Derrek Lee (off Pittsburgh's Francisco Cordova)
6-21: Mark Kotsay (off Milwaukee's Valerio de los Santos)
7-27: Mike Lowell (off Atlanta's Jason Marquis)
9-30: Cliff Floyd (off Philadelphia's Tom Jacquez)

PINCH HITTERS

(Minimum 5 at-bats)

Name	AB	Avg.	HR	RBI
Smith, Mark	48	.229	0	4
Millar, Kevin	43	.209	0	5
Brown, Brant	26	.231	0	1
Berg, Dave	12	.417	1	1
Kotsay, Mark	11	.273	0	0
Floyd, Cliff	11	.273	2	5
Lee, Derrek	11	.182	1	1
Fox, Andy	11	.091	0	0
Clapinski, Chris	9	.444	1	4
Rodriguez, Henry	6	.333	0	0
Bautista, Danny	6	.167	0	0

DEBUTS

4-7: Brad Penny, P.
4-23: Pablo Ozuna, 2B.
5-11: Jason Grilli, P.
5-11: Joe Strong, P.
6-13: Chuck Smith, P.
9-5: Nate Rolison, 1B.

GAMES BY POSITION

Catcher: Mike Redmond 85, Paul Bako 56, Ramon Castro 50, Sandy Martinez 9.
First base: Derrek Lee 147, Kevin Millar 34, Brant Brown 5, Nate Rolison 4, Mark Kotsay 2.
Second base: Luis Castillo 136, Chris Clapinski 14, Dave Berg 11, Pablo Ozuna 7, Andy Fox 2.
Third base: Mike Lowell 136, Dave Berg 13, Kevin Millar 13, Andy Fox 12, Chris Clapinski 3.
Shortstop: Alex Gonzalez 104, Dave Berg 49, Andy Fox 33, Chris Clapinski 1.
Outfield: Preston Wilson 158, Mark Kotsay 142, Cliff Floyd 108, Mark Smith 49, Danny Bautista 38, Henry Rodriguez 29, Kevin Millar 18, Andy Fox 14, Brant Brown 13, Chris Clapinski 3.
Designated hitter: Kevin Millar 6, Cliff Floyd 1, Mark Smith 1.

STREAKS

Wins: 5 (June 30-July 4, August 2-6)
Losses: 8 (May 18-26)
Consecutive games with at least one hit: 19, Luis Castillo (July 3-28)
Wins by pitcher: 4, Ryan Dempster (May 1-17)

ATTENDANCE

Home: 1,218,326
Road: 2,306,316
Highest (home): 35,392 (August 26 vs. Cincinnati).
Highest (road): 53,509 (April 10 vs. Milwaukee).
Lowest (home): 6,955 (May 17 vs. San Diego).
Lowest (road): 4,769 (September 18 vs. Montreal).

HOUSTON ASTROS

DAY BY DAY

Date	Opp.	Res.	Score	(inn.*)	Hits	Opp. hits	Winning pitcher	Losing pitcher	Save	Record	Pos.	GB
4-4	At Pit.	W	5-2		5	6	Reynolds	Schmidt	Wagner	1-0	T1st	...
4-5	At Pit.	W	11-2		10	9	Lima	Benson		2-0	T1st	...
4-6	At Pit.	L	1-10		2	16	Cordova	Holt		2-1	T2nd	1.0
4-7	Phi.	L	1-4		5	6	Wolf	Dotel	Gomes	2-2	T3rd	1.0
4-8	Phi.	W	8-5		11	11	Maddux	Brock	Wagner	3-2	T2nd	1.0
4-9	Phi.	L	2-3		5	7	Schrenk	J. Powell	Gomes	3-3	T2nd	2.0
4-10	StL.	L	7-8		7	13	Hentgen	Lima	Veres	3-4	T3rd	3.0
4-11	StL.	L	6-10		8	9	Stephenson	Holt		3-5	4th	4.0
4-12	StL.	W	7-5		9	9	Perez	Wainhouse	Wagner	4-5	T3rd	3.0
4-14	At S.D.	W	10-4		11	13	Reynolds	Boehringer		5-5	T2nd	1.5
4-15	At S.D.	L	3-5		7	9	Williams	Lima	Hoffman	5-6	T4th	2.0
4-16	At S.D.	L	3-13		8	18	Clement	Holt		5-7	T5th	2.5
4-18	At L.A.	L	3-5		5	8	Dreifort	Dotel	Shaw	5-8	T4th	3.5
4-19	At L.A.	W	10-3		14	7	Reynolds	Hershiser		6-8	T3rd	3.5
4-21	S.D.	L	2-7		6	11	Williams	Lima		6-9	3rd	4.0
4-22	S.D.	L	6-8	(10)	6	14	Cunnane	Perez	Hoffman	6-10	4th	4.0
4-23	S.D.	L	10-11		10	14	Whisenant	Wagner	Hoffman	6-11	4th	5.0
4-25	Chi.	W	11-7		16	10	Reynolds	Downs		7-11	3rd	5.0
4-26	Chi.	L	8-13		11	16	Karchner	Maddux	Aguilera	7-12	4th	6.0
4-27	Chi.	L	3-12		5	14	Lieber	Lima		7-13	6th	6.0
4-28	At Mil.	W	7-0		8	1	Holt	Navarro		8-13	5th	6.0
4-29	At Mil.	W	10-3		5	7	Maddux	Stull		9-13	3rd	6.0
4-30	At Mil.	L	3-4		7	7	Weathers	Henry		9-14	3rd	7.0
5-1	At Mil.	W	5-0		11	2	Dotel	Woodard		10-14	3rd	6.5
5-2	At Chi.	L	1-11		4	16	Wood	Lima	Williams	10-15	T3rd	6.5
5-3	At Chi.	L	3-4		8	7	Lieber	Holt	Aguilera	10-16	5th	6.5
5-4	At Chi.	W	6-2		9	9	Elarton	Valdes	Wagner	11-16	T3rd	6.5
5-5	At L.A.	L	2-3		4	9	Shaw	Henry		11-17	4th	6.5
5-6	At L.A.	L	6-9		12	7	Dreifort	Dotel		11-18	4th	7.5
5-7	At L.A.	W	14-8	(10)	17	12	Wagner	Shaw		12-18	4th	6.5
5-8	Col.	L	1-3		3	6	Astacio	Holt		12-19	4th	6.5
5-9	Col.	W	13-8		11	10	Perez	Tavarez		13-19	4th	6.5
5-10	Col.	W	5-1		7	5	Reynolds	Yoshii		14-19	4th	5.5
5-12	Cin.	L	3-7	(11)	9	10	Graves	Maddux		14-20	4th	5.5
5-13	Cin.	L	7-8		10	12	Reyes	Wagner	Williamson	14-21	4th	6.0
5-14	Cin.	W	10-3		13	6	Elarton	Parris		15-21	4th	5.5
5-15	Cin.	L	3-4		4	9	Villone	Lima	Graves	15-22	4th	6.0
5-16	At Mil.	L	5-6	(16)	14	11	Estrada	Holt		15-23	4th	7.0
5-19	At Mon.	L	2-3	(10)	8	8	Hermanson	Slusarski		15-24	5th	7.0
5-20	At Mon.	L	7-8		10	15	Irabu	Elarton	Hermanson	15-25	5th	8.0
5-21	At Mon.	L	3-8		7	11	Vazquez	Lima		15-26	6th	9.0
5-22†	At Mil.	L	9-10	(10)	13	14	Weathers	Slusarski		15-27		
5-22‡	At Mil.	L	1-6		7	8	Bere	Gross		15-28	6th	10.0
5-23	Phi.	W	10-2		13	8	Holt	Wolf		16-28	6th	10.0
5-24	Phi.	L	7-9		9	13	Gomes	Wagner	Brantley	16-29	6th	11.0
5-25	Phi.	W	10-6		11	8	Elarton	Ashby	Slusarski	17-29	6th	11.0
5-26	Atl.	W	5-4	(10)	10	11	Henry	Seanez		18-29	5th	10.0
5-27	Atl.	L	5-6		10	9	Burkett	Reynolds	Ligtenberg	18-30	6th	10.0
5-28	Atl.	W	4-3		5	8	Valdes	Seanez	Wagner	19-30	6th	9.0
5-29	At Col.	L	7-8		12	15	White	Cabrera	Jimenez	19-31	6th	10.0
5-30	At Col.	L	7-10		12	12	Belinda	Valdes	Jimenez	19-32	6th	11.0
5-31	At Col.	L	6-8		14	12	White	Slusarski	Jimenez	19-33	6th	11.0
6-2	Chi. (AL)	L	4-7		10	9	Parque	Reynolds	Foulke	19-34	6th	11.5
6-3	Chi. (AL)	W	6-1		10	8	Holt	Wells		20-34	6th	10.5
6-4	Chi. (AL)	L	3-7		5	13	Sirotka	Dotel		20-35	6th	11.0
6-5	Min.	W	8-2		11	8	Elarton	Radke		21-35	6th	10.0
6-6	Min.	L	1-3		6	6	Santana	Lima	Guardado	21-36	6th	10.5
6-7	Min.	L	0-2		6	9	Mays	Reynolds	Guardado	21-37	6th	11.5
6-8	At L.A.	L	2-5		6	9	Park	Holt	Fetters	21-38	6th	12.0
6-9	At S.D.	W	7-6		10	11	Wagner	Hoffman		22-38	6th	11.0
6-10	At S.D.	L	3-13		12	12	Meadows	Elarton		22-39	6th	11.0
6-11	At S.D.	L	1-4		4	11	Walker	Lima	Hoffman	22-40	6th	12.0
6-13	At Col.	W	6-3		15	10	Reynolds	Arrojo	Wagner	23-40	6th	12.5
6-14	At Col.	W	8-4		11	8	Slusarski	Astacio		24-40	6th	12.5
6-15	At Col.	L	4-5		10	8	Jimenez	Wagner		24-41	6th	13.0
6-16	At S.F	L	4-7		9	12	Estes	Elarton	Nen	24-42	6th	14.0
6-17	At S.F	L	4-6		10	8	Hernandez	Lima	Nen	24-43	6th	15.0
6-18	At S.F	W	4-2	(11)	6	6	J. Powell	Nen	Henry	25-43	6th	14.0
6-20	L.A.	L	6-9	(10)	13	18	Herges	Slusarski		25-44	6th	15.0
6-21	L.A.	L	6-7		7	13	Herges	Cabrera		25-45	6th	15.0
6-22	L.A.	W	6-3		7	6	Elarton	Dreifort	Valdes	26-45	6th	15.0
6-23	S.F	L	3-10		10	14	Hernandez	Lima		26-46	6th	16.0
6-24	S.F	L	4-13		12	22	Nathan	Reynolds		26-47	6th	17.0
6-25	S.F	L	2-4		8	14	Ortiz	Holt	Nen	26-48	6th	18.0
6-26	At Ari.	L	1-6		5	8	Reynoso	Dotel	Kim	26-49	6th	18.0
6-27	At Ari.	W	12-4		13	8	Elarton	Daal		27-49	6th	18.0
6-28	At Ari.	L	2-6		8	10	Anderson	Lima	Kim	27-50	6th	18.0
6-29	At Ari.	L	1-7		5	10	Johnson	Reynolds		27-51	6th	19.0
6-30	At StL.	L	4-5		6	13	Al. Benes	Holt	Veres	27-52	6th	20.0

HIGHLIGHTS

High point: The Astros won five straight games in mid-August and went on to complete a 7-2 homestand—their first serious home winning streak. Suddenly the 315-foot left field fence and the monster power alleys didn't seem so adversarial at new Enron Field.

Low point: A 9-7 May 24 loss to the Phillies in which the Astros blew a seven-run lead. The game marked Billy Wagner's fourth straight blown save and dropped the team's record to 16-29. Three weeks later, Wagner was diagnosed with a partially torn flexor muscle in his elbow and eventually submitted to surgery.

Turning point: September 1-3, when the Astros took two of three from the Braves, kicking off a 17-12 final month and raising hopes for a 2001 rebound.

Most valuable player: Jeff Bagwell batted .310 with 132 RBIs and posted club records for home runs (47) and runs scored (152). More importantly, Bagwell hit .331 with 68 RBIs after the All-Star break, triggering the team's late resurgence.

Most valuable pitcher: Scott Elarton's 17-7 record was remarkable for a team that finished 18 games below .500. Elarton struck out 131 batters in $192\frac{2}{3}$ innings, his top numbers as a major leaguer. Elarton won 11 of 12 decisions in one midseason stretch.

Most improved player: Richard Hidalgo, a .259 hitter in three partial seasons, skied to a .314 average with 44 homers and 122 RBIs. His move from right field to center was an important reason for the Astros' second-half defensive improvement.

Most pleasant surprise: Backup catcher Tony Eusebio stepped in for injured starter Mitch Meluskey and put together a club-record 24-game hitting streak in late August and September. Eusebio's sterling relief duty was a big factor in the Astros' second-half rebound.

Key injuries: The once-dominant Wagner blew nine saves in 15 opportunities before admitting to his elbow problem and opting for the season-ending surgery. ... Third baseman Ken Caminiti went down for the season after 208 at-bats with a wrist injury. ... Reliever Jay Powell was on the D.L. twice before shoulder surgery ended his season in August. ... Second baseman Craig Biggio missed the last 56 games because of knee surgery, his first time ever on the disabled list. ... Outfielder Roger Cedeno missed 75 games with a broken hand. ... Righthander Shane Reynolds missed the last six weeks with back problems.

Notable: For the first time in Larry Dierker's four years as manager, the team did not win the Central Division. ... Jose Lima allowed an N.L.-record 48 home runs, beating his old club record of 34 by mid-July. Lima, who finished 7-16, also set a club mark with 13 straight losses. ... Bagwell (47) and Hidalgo (44) both broke Bagwell's former franchise record of 43 home runs in a season. ... The team's 249 homers were an N.L. record, topping Colorado's 239 in 1997.

—JIM CARLEY

MISCELLANEOUS

RECORDS

2000 regular-season record: 72-90 (4th in N.L. Central); 39-42 at home; 33-48 on road; 20-22 vs. East; 41-36 vs. Central; 11-32 vs. West; 15-21 vs. left-handed starters; 57-69 vs. righthanded starters; 62-79 on grass; 10-11 on turf; 22-31 in daytime; 50-59 at night; 15-31 in one-run games; 6-9 in extra-inning games; 0-1-0 in doubleheaders.

Team record past five years: 437-373 (.540, ranks 3rd in league in that span).

TEAM LEADERS

Batting average: Moises Alou (.355).
At-bats: Jeff Bagwell (590).
Runs: Jeff Bagwell (152).
Hits: Jeff Bagwell (183).
Total Bases: Jeff Bagwell (363).
Doubles: Richard Hidalgo (42).
Triples: Craig Biggio, Roger Cedeno, Julio Lugo (5).
Home runs: Jeff Bagwell (47).
Runs batted in: Jeff Bagwell (132).
Stolen bases: Roger Cedeno (25).
Slugging percentage: Richard Hidalgo (.636).
On-base percentage: Jeff Bagwell (.424).
Wins: Scott Elarton (17).
Earned-run average: Scott Elarton (4.81).
Complete games: Chris Holt (3).
Shutouts: Chris Holt (1).
Saves: Octavio Dotel (16).
Innings pitched: Chris Holt (207.0).
Strikeouts: Octavio Dotel (142).

Date	Opp.	Res.	Score	(inn.*)	Hits	Opp. hits	Winning pitcher	Losing pitcher	Save	Record	Pos.	GB
7-1	At StL.	L	9-10		15	11	Thompson	Slusarski	Veres	27-53	6th	21.0
7-2	At StL.	W	6-3		10	8	Elarton	Kile	Valdes	28-53	6th	20.0
7-4	Ari.	L	4-10		6	11	Johnson	Lima		28-54	6th	21.0
7-5	Ari.	L	9-12		10	16	Morgan	Valdes	Kim	28-55	6th	22.0
7-6	Ari.	L	1-2		4	4	Guzman	Holt	Mantei	28-56	6th	22.0
7-7	K.C.	W	9-5		10	6	Elarton	Stein		29-56	6th	21.0
7-8	K.C.	L	2-5		9	13	Suzuki	Miller		29-57	6th	21.0
7-9	K.C.	W	9-6		13	10	Lima	Witasick	Dotel	30-57	6th	21.0
7-13	At Det.	L	2-8		11	12	Moehler	Reynolds		30-58	6th	22.0
7-14	At Det.	W	9-4		13	10	Holt	Nomo		31-58	6th	22.0
7-15	At Det.	L	6-11		11	15	Patterson	Henry		31-59	6th	22.0
7-16	At Cle.	W	5-1		9	7	Elarton	Colon		32-59	6th	21.0
7-17	At Cle.	L	6-8		8	9	Drew	Miller	Karsay	32-60	6th	22.0
7-18	At Cle.	L	2-8		11	8	Burba	Reynolds		32-61	6th	22.0
7-19	Cin.	L	0-4		4	7	Harnisch	Holt		32-62	6th	22.0
7-20	Cin.	W	6-2		8	8	Lima	Williamson		33-62	6th	21.0
7-21	StL.	L	1-12		6	16	Ankiel	Elarton		33-63	6th	22.0
7-22	StL.	W	10-5		17	6	Miller	Hentgen		34-63	6th	21.0
7-23	StL.	W	15-7		14	10	Reynolds	An. Benes		35-63	6th	20.0
7-24	At Cin.	W	7-5	(10)	15	7	Dotel	Graves		36-63	6th	19.5
7-25	At Cin.	W	7-4		12	6	Valdes	Villone		37-63	6th	19.5
7-26	At Cin.	W	3-2		11	6	Elarton	Parris	Dotel	38-63	6th	19.5
7-28	At Atl.	L	2-5		7	8	Ashby	Miller	Rocker	38-64	6th	19.0
7-29	At Atl.	L	5-13		12	14	Burkett	Reynolds		38-65	6th	19.0
7-30	At Atl.	L	3-6		8	10	Glavine	Holt	Remlinger	38-66	6th	19.0
7-31	At Fla.	W	4-2		8	9	Lima	Burnett	Dotel	39-66	6th	19.0
8-1	At Fla.	W	4-3		2	6	Elarton	Smith	Dotel	40-66	6th	18.0
8-2	At Fla.	L	4-5		11	8	Miceli	Valdes		40-67	6th	19.0
8-3	At Fla.	L	3-4		6	11	Looper	Slusarski	Alfonseca	40-68	6th	19.5
8-4	Mon.	W	7-6		12	14	Green	Kline	Dotel	41-68	6th	18.5
8-5	Mon.	L	9-10	(10)	15	14	Strickland	Valdes	Kline	41-69	6th	19.5
8-6	Mon.	W	8-1		12	4	Elarton	Thurman		42-69	6th	18.5
8-7	N.Y.	L	5-6	(11)	12	8	Benitez	Green		42-70	6th	19.5
8-8	N.Y.	W	9-3		10	11	B. Powell	Leiter		43-70	6th	18.5
8-9	N.Y.	L	5-12		9	16	Reed	Lima		43-71	6th	18.5
8-10	N.Y.	L	3-10		12	14	B.J. Jones	McKnight		43-72	6th	19.5
8-11	At Phi.	W	7-2		12	7	Valdes	Padilla		44-72	6th	18.5
8-12	At Phi.	L	2-3		7	6	Person	Miller	Brantley	44-73	6th	19.5
8-13	At Phi.	W	14-7		19	8	Cabrera	Daal		45-73	6th	19.5
8-14	Pit.	W	16-2		19	5	Holt	Silva		46-73	6th	18.5
8-15	Pit.	W	5-4		7	9	Lima	Benson	Dotel	47-73	6th	18.5
8-16	Pit.	W	11-10		9	12	Elarton	Serafini	Dotel	48-73	6th	18.5
8-18	Mil.	W	5-4		12	6	Miller	Haynes	Dotel	49-73	6th	18.5
8-19	Mil.	W	10-8		11	8	Cabrera	Acevedo	Dotel	50-73	6th	18.5
8-20	Mil.	L	5-6		7	14	Leskanic	Cabrera		50-74	6th	18.5
8-21	Chi.	W	5-4		6	8	Elarton	Tapani	Slusarski	51-74	6th	18.5
8-22	Chi.	W	10-7		9	8	Valdes	Farnsworth	Cabrera	52-74	6th	17.5
8-23	Chi.	L	5-15		4	19	Quevedo	Miller		52-75	6th	18.5
8-25	At Mon.	W	3-1		7	8	Holt	Lira	Dotel	53-75	5th	18.0
8-26	At Mon.	L	4-5		10	9	Hermanson	Lima	Kline	53-76	5th	19.0
8-27	At Mon.	W	7-3		10	6	Elarton	Moore		54-76	5th	19.0
8-28	At N.Y.	L	2-4		8	6	Rusch	B. Powell	Wendell	54-77	5th	20.0
8-29	At N.Y.	W	11-1		16	5	Miller	Leiter		55-77	5th	19.0
8-30	At N.Y.	L	0-1		3	9	Reed	Holt	Benitez	55-78	5th	20.0
9-1	Atl.	W	3-2		6	7	Lima	Burkett	Dotel	56-78	5th	20.0
9-2	Atl.	L	6-8		10	10	Maddux	Elarton	Rocker	56-79	5th	21.0
9-3	Atl.	W	9-3		15	11	Miller	Ashby		57-79	5th	21.0
9-4	Fla.	L	2-5		5	11	Smith	Holt	Alfonseca	57-80	6th	22.0
9-5	Fla.	W	9-5		15	9	McKnight	Cornelius		58-80	T5th	22.0
9-6	Fla.	W	13-5		14	7	Lima	Sanchez		59-80	T5th	21.0
9-7	Fla.	W	7-3		9	7	Elarton	Miceli		60-80	4th	21.0
9-8	At Chi.	W	13-10		20	10	Miller	Tapani	Dotel	61-80	5th	20.0
9-9	At Chi.	W	14-4		19	9	Holt	Quevedo		62-80	3rd	20.0
9-10	At Chi.	W	7-6		10	13	McKnight	Lieber	Dotel	63-80	3rd	19.0
9-11	S.F	L	7-8	(10)	9	12	Nen	Valdes		63-81	4th	20.0
9-12	S.F	L	5-9		11	12	Estes	Elarton		63-82	4th	21.0
9-13	S.F	L	2-3		8	9	Hernandez	Miller	Nen	63-83	4th	22.0
9-14	Pit.	W	8-7		11	12	Slusarski	Skrmetta		64-83	4th	22.0
9-15	Pit.	W	16-7		19	12	B. Powell	Skrmetta	Slusarski	65-83	3rd	22.0
9-16	Pit.	W	10-9	(10)	9	16	Valdes	Sauerbeck		66-83	3rd	22.0
9-17	Pit.	W	5-3		9	8	Elarton	Serafini	Dotel	67-83	3rd	22.0
9-19	At StL.	W	8-6	(10)	13	8	Dotel	Al. Benes	Cabrera	68-83	3rd	21.0
9-20	At StL.	L	6-11		9	11	Ankiel	Holt		68-84	3rd	22.0
9-21	At StL.	W	7-5		12	11	McKnight	An. Benes	Dotel	69-84	3rd	21.0
9-22	At Cin.	L	5-12		12	14	Dessens	Lima		69-85	3rd	21.0
9-23	At Cin.	L	4-6		11	12	Riedling	Slusarski	Graves	69-86	T3rd	22.0
9-24	At Cin.	L	3-4		6	7	Sullivan	Dotel		69-87	4th	22.0
9-26	At Pit.	L	4-9		7	10	Benson	Holt		69-88	4th	23.0
9-27	At Pit.	W	10-1		10	4	McKnight	Anderson		70-88	4th	23.0
9-28	At Pit.	L	2-3		10	3	Silva	Dotel		70-89	4th	24.0
9-29	Mil.	L	3-13		7	15	Estrada	Elarton		70-90	4th	24.0
9-30	Mil.	W	7-6		11	11	Miller	Haynes	Dotel	71-90	4th	23.0
10-1	Mil.	W	6-1		8	7	Holt	Wright		72-90	4th	23.0

Monthly records: April (9-14), May (10-19), June (8-19), July (12-14), August (16-12), September (16-12), October (1-0).
*Innings, if other than nine. † First game of a doubleheader. ‡ Second game of a doubleheader.

MEMORABLE GAMES

August 29 at New York

Rookie Wade Miller scattered five hits, retiring 17 of the last 20 Mets he faced, in a complete-game 11-1 victory.over Al Leiter at Shea Stadium. The 23-year-old Miller, making only his 12th big-league start, raised eyebrows with an inspiring performance that his teammates supported with 16 hits.

Houston	AB	R	H	BI	NY Mets	AB	R	H	BI
Cedeno, lf	4	2	1	0	D.Hamilton, lf-cf	3	0	0	0
Berkman, ph-lf	1	0	0	0	Bell, rf	3	0	1	0
Lugo, 2b	6	2	2	1	Agbayani, rf	1	0	0	0
Bagwell, 1b	4	2	2	3	Alfonzo, 2b	4	1	1	1
Ward, 1b	1	0	1	0	Piazza, c	3	0	0	0
Hidalgo, cf	2	1	1	1	Riggan, p	0	0	0	0
Barker, cf	2	1	0	0	Cook, p	0	0	0	0
Alou, rf	4	2	2	1	Ventura, ph	1	0	0	0
Eusebio, c	4	1	0	0	Harris, 3b	4	0	0	0
Truby, 3b	5	0	3	2	Zeile, 1b	3	0	1	0
Bogar, ss	5	0	3	2	Payton, cf	2	0	1	0
Miller, p	5	0	1	1	Trammell, ph-lf	1	0	0	0
					Bordick, ss	2	0	1	0
					Abbott, ss	1	0	0	0
					Leiter, p	0	0	0	0
					Mahomes, ph-p	2	0	0	0
					Pratt, c	1	0	0	0
Totals	**43**	**11**	**16**	**11**	**Totals**	**31**	**1**	**5**	**1**

Houston..............................0 0 4 2 0 3 0 2 0—11 16 0
Mets ....0 0 0 1 0 0 0 0 0— 1 5 3

E—Harris (13), Abbott (6), Alfonzo (8). DP—Houston 1, Mets 2. LOB—Houston 12, Mets 4. 2B—Lugo (16), Bell (29). HR—Bagwell (40), Alfonzo (18). SB—Cedeno (22), Lugo (13), Bagwell (8), Truby (1). S—Hidalgo.

Houston	IP	H	R	ER	BB	SO
Miller (W 3-5)	9	5	1	1	1	7

Mets	IP	H	R	ER	BB	SO
Leiter (L 14-6)	3	6	4	4	3	5
Mahomes	3	6	5	5	3	2
Riggan	2	3	2	0	0	1
Cook	1	1	0	0	0	1

U—HP, O'Nora. 1B, Hirschbeck. 2B, Iassogna. 3B, Hollowell. T—3:07. A—39,967.

September 9 at Chicago

The Astros set a club record with seven home runs, six off rookie Ruben Quevedo in the first four innings of a 14-4 win. Included in the onslaught were two homers by light-hitting shortstop Tim Bogar as well as two apiece by Richard Hidalgo and Lance Berkman. Daryle Ward's 19th home run in the seventh put the capper on the Astros' fifth straight win.

Houston	AB	R	H	BI	Cubs	AB	R	H	BI
Lugo, 2b	6	2	3	1	Young, 2b	5	2	3	0
Bogar, ss	6	2	4	5	Gutierrez, ss	3	1	1	0
Bagwell, 1b	4	3	1	0	Sosa, rf	4	0	2	1
Barker, cf	1	0	0	0	Grace, 1b	4	1	1	1
Berkman, rf	4	2	2	4	Van Poppel, p	0	0	0	0
Hidalgo, cf-lf	5	2	3	3	Mairena, p	0	0	0	0
Ward, lf-1b	5	1	2	1	Brown, lf	3	0	2	2
Truby, 3b	5	0	2	0	Matthews Jr., ph-lf	1	0	0	0
Chavez, c	5	0	0	0	Buford, cf	4	0	0	0
Holt, p	3	1	1	0	Greene, 3b	3	0	0	0
Franklin, p	0	0	0	0	Andrews, ph-3	1	0	0	0
Charles, ph	1	1	1	0	Reed, c	3	0	0	0
Meacham, p	0	0	0	0	Mahoney, c	1	0	0	0
					Quevedo, p	1	0	0	0
					Rain, p	0	0	0	0
					Nieves, ph	1	0	0	0
					Spradlin, p	0	0	0	0
					Meyers, ph	1	0	0	0
					Zuleta, 1b	1	0	0	0
Totals	**45**	**14**	**19**	**14**	**Totals**	**36**	**4**	**9**	**4**

Houston..............................2 0 2 5 0 0 1 3 1—14 19 1
Cubs ....0 0 0 0 0 3 1 0 0— 4 9 0

E—Truby (9). DP—Houston 1, Cubs 1. LOB—Houston 7, Cubs 6. 2B—Lugo (19), Bagwell (32), Truby (12), Charles (1), Sosa (34), Brown (4). 3B—Young (2). HR—Bogar 2 (6), Berkman 2 (19), Hidalgo 2 (35), Ward (19).

Houston	IP	H	R	ER	BB	SO
Holt (W 7-14)	6.2	9	4	4	1	2
Franklin	1.1	0	0	0	0	1
Meacham	1	0	0	0	0	0

Cubs	IP	H	R	ER	BB	SO
Quevedo (L 2-8)	3.2	10	9	9	1	6
Rain	1.1	2	0	0	0	2
Spradlin	2	1	1	1	1	2
Van Poppel	1	2	3	3	1	1
Mairena	1	4	1	1	0	0

U—HP, Barrett. 1B, Randazzo. 2B, Montague. 3B, Layne. T—2:53. A—38,203.

BATTING

Name	G	TPA	AB	R	H	TB	2B	3B	HR	RBI	Avg.	Obp.	Slg.	SH	SF	HP	BB	IBB	SO	SB	CS	GDP	vs RHP AB	vs RHP Avg.	vs RHP HR	vs RHP RBI	vs LHP AB	vs LHP Avg.	vs LHP HR	vs LHP RBI
Bagwell, Jeff	159	719	590	152	183	363	37	1	47	132	.310	.424	.615	0	7	15	107	11	116	9	6	19	478	.297	38	93	112	.366	9	39
Hidalgo, Richard	153	644	558	118	175	355	42	3	44	122	.314	.391	.636	0	9	21	56	3	110	13	6	13	441	.308	39	108	117	.333	5	14
Alou, Moises	126	517	454	82	161	283	28	2	30	114	.355	.416	.623	0	9	2	52	4	45	3	3	21	354	.350	22	87	100	.370	8	27
Lugo, Julio	116	465	420	78	119	181	22	5	10	40	.283	.346	.431	3	1	4	37	0	93	22	9	9	307	.300	9	32	113	.239	1	8
Biggio, Craig	101	466	377	67	101	148	13	5	8	35	.268	.388	.393	7	5	16	61	3	73	12	2	10	309	.275	8	32	68	.235	0	3
Spiers, Bill	124	409	355	41	107	139	17	3	3	43	.301	.386	.392	2	2	1	49	3	38	7	4	8	323	.307	3	40	32	.250	0	3
Berkman, Lance	114	417	353	76	105	198	28	1	21	67	.297	.388	.561	0	7	1	56	1	73	6	2	6	275	.320	19	56	78	.218	2	11
Meluskey, Mitch	117	400	337	47	101	164	21	0	14	69	.300	.401	.487	1	3	4	55	10	74	1	0	7	280	.321	14	59	57	.193	0	10
Bogar, Tim	110	351	304	32	63	97	9	2	7	33	.207	.292	.319	5	4	3	35	7	56	1	1	15	223	.179	5	23	81	.284	2	10
Ward, Daryle	119	281	264	36	68	142	10	2	20	47	.258	.295	.538	0	2	0	15	2	61	0	0	6	241	.253	18	39	23	.304	2	8
Cedeno, Roger	74	305	259	54	73	103	2	5	6	26	.282	.383	.398	2	1	0	43	0	47	25	11	6	211	.275	3	16	48	.313	3	10
Truby, Chris	78	279	258	28	67	123	15	4	11	59	.260	.295	.477	1	5	5	10	1	56	2	1	4	182	.220	7	37	76	.355	4	22
Eusebio, Tony	74	249	218	24	61	100	18	0	7	33	.280	.361	.459	0	2	4	25	2	45	0	0	8	155	.303	5	24	63	.222	2	9
Caminiti, Ken	59	253	208	42	63	121	13	0	15	45	.303	.419	.582	0	2	1	42	8	37	3	0	7	168	.304	14	34	40	.300	1	11
Mieske, Matt	62	89	81	7	14	22	1	2	1	5	.173	.247	.272	0	0	1	7	0	17	0	0	2	42	.214	1	1	39	.128	0	4
Barker, Glen	84	77	67	18	15	25	2	1	2	6	.224	.307	.373	2	0	1	7	0	23	9	6	0	47	.234	1	5	20	.200	1	1
Elarton, Scott	30	72	63	6	10	12	2	0	0	0	.159	.197	.190	6	0	2	1	0	20	0	0	2	46	.174	0	0	17	.118	0	0
Lima, Jose	33	69	60	6	10	12	2	0	0	2	.167	.180	.200	8	0	0	1	0	17	0	0	1	49	.184	0	2	11	.091	0	0
Holt, Chris	34	70	60	3	6	7	1	0	0	3	.100	.169	.117	5	0	1	4	0	33	0	0	0	50	.100	0	1	10	.100	0	2
Johnson, Russ	26	48	45	4	8	8	0	0	0	3	.178	.213	.178	1	0	0	2	0	10	1	1	3	32	.156	0	3	13	.231	0	0
Chavez, Raul	14	47	43	3	11	16	2	0	1	5	.256	.298	.372	0	1	0	3	2	6	0	0	5	32	.281	1	3	11	.182	0	2
Reynolds, Shane	22	46	40	2	9	13	1	0	1	2	.225	.262	.325	4	0	1	1	0	13	0	0	1	31	.258	1	1	9	.111	0	1
Miller, Wade	16	41	40	1	4	5	1	0	0	3	.100	.100	.125	1	0	0	0	0	16	0	0	1	36	.111	0	3	4	.000	0	0
Dotel, Octavio	50	40	32	1	1	1	0	0	0	0	.031	.061	.031	7	0	0	1	0	16	0	0	0	25	.040	0	0	7	.000	0	0
McKnight, Tony	6	14	13	1	0	0	0	0	0	0	.000	.000	.000	1	0	0	0	0	6	0	0	0	11	.000	0	0	2	.000	0	0
Powell, Brian	9	10	9	2	2	3	1	0	0	0	.222	.300	.333	0	0	0	1	0	4	0	0	0	2	.000	0	0	7	.286	0	0
Slusarski, Joe	54	9	9	1	1	1	0	0	0	1	.111	.111	.111	0	0	0	0	0	5	0	0	0	7	.000	0	1	2	.500	0	0
Ginter, Keith	5	10	8	3	2	5	0	0	1	3	.250	.300	.625	0	1	0	1	0	3	0	0	0	8	.250	1	2	0	.000	0	1
Cromer, Tripp	9	10	8	2	1	1	0	0	0	0	.125	.222	.125	1	0	0	1	0	1	0	0	0	6	.000	0	0	2	.500	0	0
Charles, Frank	4	7	7	1	3	4	1	0	0	2	.429	.429	.571	0	0	0	0	0	2	0	0	0	5	.400	0	2	2	.500	0	0
Ensberg, Morgan	4	7	7	0	2	2	0	0	0	0	.286	.286	.286	0	0	0	0	0	1	0	0	0	6	.167	0	0	1	1.000	0	0
Zosky, Eddie	4	4	4	0	0	0	0	0	0	0	.000	.000	.000	0	0	0	0	0	1	0	0	0	1	.000	0	0	3	.000	0	0
Valdes, Marc	53	3	3	0	0	0	0	0	0	0	.000	.000	.000	0	0	0	0	0	2	0	0	0	2	.000	0	0	1	.000	0	0
Maddux, Mike	21	2	2	0	0	0	0	0	0	0	.000	.000	.000	0	0	0	0	0	2	0	0	0	2	.000	0	0	0	.000	0	0
Wagner, Billy	28	2	2	0	0	0	0	0	0	0	.000	.000	.000	0	0	0	0	0	2	0	0	0	2	.000	0	0	0	.000	0	0
Bako, Paul	1	2	2	0	0	0	0	0	0	0	.000	.000	.000	0	0	0	0	0	1	0	0	0	1	.000	0	0	1	.000	0	0
Franklin, Wayne	25	2	2	0	0	0	0	0	0	0	.000	.000	.000	0	0	0	0	0	1	0	0	0	2	.000	0	0	0	.000	0	0
Linebrink, Scott	8	1	1	0	1	1	0	0	0	0	1.000	1.000	1.000	0	0	0	0	0	0	0	0	0	0	.000	0	0	1	1.000	0	0
Gooden, Dwight	1	1	1	0	0	0	0	0	0	0	.000	.000	.000	0	0	0	0	0	1	0	0	0	1	.000	0	0	0	.000	0	0
Gross, Kip	2	1	1	0	0	0	0	0	0	0	.000	.000	.000	0	0	0	0	0	0	0	0	0	1	.000	0	0	0	.000	0	0
Henry, Doug	45	1	1	0	0	0	0	0	0	0	.000	.000	.000	0	0	0	0	0	0	0	0	0	1	.000	0	0	0	.000	0	0
Perez, Yorkis	33	1	1	0	0	0	0	0	0	0	.000	.000	.000	0	0	0	0	0	1	0	0	0	1	.000	0	0	0	.000	0	0
Powell, Jay	30	1	1	0	0	0	0	0	0	0	.000	.000	.000	0	0	0	0	0	1	0	0	0	0	.000	0	0	1	.000	0	0
Cabrera, Jose	52	1	1	0	0	0	0	0	0	0	.000	.000	.000	0	0	0	0	0	1	0	0	0	1	.000	0	0	0	.000	0	0
Green, Jason	14	1	1	0	0	0	0	0	0	0	.000	.000	.000	0	0	0	0	0	0	0	0	0	1	.000	0	0	0	.000	0	0
Meacham, Rusty	5	0	0	0	0	0	0	0	0	0	.000	.000	.000	0	0	0	0	0	0	0	0	0	0	.000	0	0	0	.000	0	0

Players with more than one N.L. team

Name	G	TPA	AB	R	H	TB	2B	3B	HR	RBI	Avg.	Obp.	Slg.	SH	SF	HP	BB	IBB	SO	SB	CS	GDP	vs RHP AB	vs RHP Avg.	vs RHP HR	vs RHP RBI	vs LHP AB	vs LHP Avg.	vs LHP HR	vs LHP RBI
Bako, Fla.	56	186	161	10	39	47	6	1	0	14	.242	.335	.292	1	1	1	22	7	48	0	0	4	1	.000	0	0	1	.000	0	0
Bako, Atl.	24	63	58	8	11	21	4	0	2	6	.190	.254	.362	0	0	0	5	3	15	0	0	2	1	.000	0	0	1	.000	0	0
Bako, Hou.-Fla.-Atl.	81	251	221	18	50	68	10	1	2	20	.226	.312	.308	1	1	1	27	10	64	0	0	6	194	.237	1	19	27	.148	1	1
Henry, Hou.-S.F.	72	1	1	0	0	0	0	0	0	0	.000	.000	.000	0	0	0	0	0	0	0	0	0	1	.000	0	0	0	.000	0	0
Linebrink, S.F.-Hou.	11	1	1	0	1	1	0	0	0	0	1.000	1.000	1.000	0	0	0	0	0	0	0	0	0	0	.000	0	0	1	1.000	0	0
Mieske, Hou.-Ari.	73	99	89	10	16	27	1	2	2	7	.180	.253	.303	0	1	1	8	0	18	0	0	2	43	.233	1	1	46	.130	1	6

PITCHING

Name	W	L	Pct.	ERA	IP	H	R	ER	HR	SH	SF	HB	BB	IBB	SO	G	GS	CG	ShO	GF	Sv	vs. RH AB	vs. RH Avg.	vs. RH HR	vs. RH RBI	vs. LH AB	vs. LH Avg.	vs. LH HR	vs. LH RBI
Holt, Chris	8	16	.333	5.35	207.0	247	131	123	22	7	12	8	75	2	136	34	32	3	1	1	0	434	.279	9	52	378	.333	13	68
Lima, Jose	7	16	.304	6.65	196.1	251	152	145	48	12	12	2	68	3	124	33	33	0	0	0	0	441	.272	23	69	360	.364	25	69
Elarton, Scott	17	7	.708	4.81	192.2	198	117	103	29	5	7	6	84	1	131	30	30	2	0	0	0	397	.264	13	57	356	.261	16	47
Reynolds, Shane	7	8	.467	5.22	131.0	150	86	76	20	6	8	6	45	2	93	22	22	0	0	0	0	289	.294	14	47	234	.278	6	29
Dotel, Octavio	3	7	.300	5.40	125.0	127	80	75	26	7	8	7	61	3	142	50	16	0	0	25	16	264	.250	14	40	216	.282	12	38
Miller, Wade	6	6	.500	5.14	105.0	104	66	60	14	3	1	3	42	1	89	16	16	2	0	0	0	239	.222	4	24	165	.309	10	30
Slusarski, Joe	2	7	.222	4.21	77.0	80	36	36	8	2	2	3	22	3	54	54	0	0	0	16	3	163	.227	7	29	135	.319	1	22
Cabrera, Jose	2	3	.400	5.92	59.1	74	40	39	10	3	3	3	17	2	41	52	0	0	0	22	2	135	.304	6	25	105	.314	4	20
Valdes, Marc	5	5	.500	5.08	56.2	69	41	32	3	3	2	5	25	1	35	53	0	0	0	20	2	140	.300	3	26	89	.303	0	20
Henry, Doug	1	3	.250	4.42	53.0	39	26	26	10	2	1	3	28	2	46	45	0	0	0	13	1	114	.193	4	17	77	.221	6	11
McKnight, Tony	4	1	.800	3.86	35.0	35	19	15	4	1	1	2	9	0	23	6	6	1	0	0	0	83	.241	2	11	60	.250	2	7
Powell, Brian	2	1	.667	5.74	31.1	34	21	20	8	2	2	1	13	0	14	9	5	0	0	1	0	78	.269	6	14	44	.295	2	6
Wagner, Billy	2	4	.333	6.18	27.2	28	19	19	6	0	0	1	18	0	28	28	0	0	0	19	6	82	.232	3	10	28	.321	3	13
Maddux, Mike	2	2	.500	6.26	27.1	31	20	19	6	3	1	2	12	0	17	21	0	0	0	6	0	69	.290	6	15	41	.268	0	3
Powell, Jay	1	1	.500	5.67	27.0	29	18	17	1	1	0	0	19	1	16	29	0	0	0	10	0	64	.297	0	11	43	.233	1	7
Perez, Yorkis	2	1	.667	5.16	22.2	25	18	13	4	1	2	0	14	2	21	33	0	0	0	9	0	55	.255	3	14	39	.282	1	5
Franklin, Wayne	0	0	.000	5.48	21.1	24	14	13	2	0	2	4	12	1	21	25	0	0	0	4	0	46	.304	2	8	39	.256	0	6
Green, Jason	1	1	.500	6.62	17.2	15	16	13	3	2	0	1	20	1	19	14	0	0	0	1	0	34	.147	1	6	30	.333	2	7
Linebrink, Scott	0	0	.000	4.66	9.2	11	5	5	3	0	0	3	6	0	6	8	0	0	0	3	0	21	.238	0	0	17	.353	3	5
Meacham, Rusty	0	0	.000	11.57	4.2	8	6	6	3	0	0	0	2	0	3	5	0	0	0	2	0	15	.267	1	3	6	.667	2	4
Gross, Kip	0	1	.000	10.38	4.1	9	8	5	2	0	0	0	2	0	3	2	1	0	0	0	0	17	.353	1	3	4	.750	1	3
Gooden, Dwight	0	0	.000	9.00	4.0	6	4	4	1	0	0	0	3	0	1	1	1	0	0	0	0	12	.250	1	3	5	.600	0	1
Bogar, Tim	0	0	.000	4.50	2.0	2	1	1	1	0	0	0	1	0	1	2	0	0	0	2	0	5	.200	0	0	3	.333	1	1

PITCHERS WITH MORE THAN ONE N.L. TEAM

Name	W	L	Pct.	ERA	IP	H	R	ER	HR	SH	SF	HB	BB	IBB	SO	G	GS	CG	ShO	GF	Sv	vs. RH AB	vs. RH Avg.	vs. RH HR	vs. RH RBI	vs. LH AB	vs. LH Avg.	vs. LH HR	vs. LH RBI
Henry, Hou.-S.F.	4	4	.500	3.79	78.1	57	36	33	12	5	2	4	49	3	62	72	0	0	0	2	1	176	.199	5	23	99	.222	7	16
Linebrink, S.F.-Hou.	0	0	.000	6.00	12.0	18	8	8	4	0	0	3	8	0	6	11	0	0	0	0	0	28	.357	0	4	24	.333	4	7

DESIGNATED HITTERS

Name	AB	Avg.	HR	RBI
Ward, Daryle	16	.250	1	3
Alou, Moises	4	.250	0	2
Bagwell, Jeff	3	.333	0	0

INDIVIDUAL STATISTICS

FIELDING

FIRST BASEMEN

Player	Pct.	G	PO	A	E	TC	DP
Bagwell, Jeff	.994	158	1264	116	9	1389	128
Ward, Daryle	1.000	19	55	3	0	58	5
Berkman, Lance	1.000	2	2	1	0	3	0

SECOND BASEMEN

Player	Pct.	G	PO	A	E	TC	DP
Biggio, Craig	.987	100	181	280	6	467	57
Lugo, Julio	.976	45	92	108	5	205	26
Spiers, Bill	.979	26	40	53	2	95	13
Johnson, Russ	.875	3	5	2	1	8	0
Ginter, Keith	1.000	2	4	5	0	9	2
Bogar, Tim	.750	2	1	2	1	4	1
Cromer, Tripp	-	1	0	0	0	0	0

THIRD BASEMEN

Player	Pct.	G	PO	A	E	TC	DP
Truby, Chris	.926	74	51	125	14	190	15
Caminiti, Ken	.915	58	37	81	11	129	8
Spiers, Bill	.959	51	33	85	5	123	8
Johnson, Russ	1.000	4	1	4	0	5	0
Cromer, Tripp	.500	2	0	1	1	2	0
Ensberg, Morgan	.667	1	1	1	1	3	0
Meluskey, Mitch	.000	1	0	0	1	1	0
Bogar, Tim	-	1	0	0	0	0	0

SHORTSTOPS

Player	Pct.	G	PO	A	E	TC	DP
Bogar, Tim	.971	95	120	243	11	374	55
Lugo, Julio	.951	60	93	141	12	246	30
Spiers, Bill	.990	27	40	57	1	98	18
Johnson, Russ	1.000	5	5	8	0	13	2
Cromer, Tripp	1.000	1	0	1	0	1	0

OUTFIELDERS

Player	Pct.	G	PO	A	E	TC	DP
Hidalgo, Richard	.984	151	425	7	7	439	2
Alou, Moises	.970	121	191	5	6	202	0
Berkman, Lance	.968	96	174	6	6	186	0
Barker, Glen	.985	69	64	1	1	66	0
Cedeno, Roger	.978	67	135	1	3	139	0
Ward, Daryle	.986	47	70	1	1	72	1
Mieske, Matt	.933	18	14	0	1	15	0
Spiers, Bill	1.000	10	5	1	0	6	0
Lugo, Julio	1.000	6	4	0	0	4	0

CATCHERS

Player	Pct.	G	PO	A	E	TC	DP	PB
Meluskey, Mitch	.982	103	623	31	12	666	6	3
Eusebio, Tony	.988	68	411	17	5	433	2	3
Chavez, Raul	.986	14	67	6	1	74	1	0
Charles, Frank	1.000	1	7	2	0	9	1	0
Bako, Paul	1.000	1	2	1	0	3	0	0

PITCHERS

Player	Pct.	G	PO	A	E	TC	DP
Slusarski, Joe	1.000	54	5	6	0	11	0
Valdes, Marc	1.000	53	6	9	0	15	2
Cabrera, Jose	1.000	52	4	5	0	9	0
Dotel, Octavio	.947	50	4	14	1	19	1
Henry, Doug	1.000	45	4	6	0	10	1
Holt, Chris	.930	34	13	27	3	43	4
Lima, Jose	.974	33	16	22	1	39	3
Perez, Yorkis	.667	33	0	2	1	3	0
Elarton, Scott	1.000	30	14	21	0	35	4
Powell, Jay	1.000	29	4	2	0	6	0
Wagner, Billy	1.000	28	1	2	0	3	0
Franklin, Wayne	1.000	25	1	1	0	2	0
Reynolds, Shane	1.000	22	9	20	0	29	0
Maddux, Mike	1.000	21	1	6	0	7	0
Miller, Wade	1.000	16	9	11	0	20	4
Green, Jason	.500	14	0	2	2	4	0
Powell, Brian	1.000	9	3	2	0	5	0
Linebrink, Scott	-	8	0	0	0	0	0
McKnight, Tony	1.000	6	1	6	0	7	1
Meacham, Rusty	1.000	5	1	0	0	1	1
Gross, Kip	.000	2	0	0	1	1	0
Bogar, Tim	-	2	0	0	0	0	0
Gooden, Dwight	1.000	1	0	1	0	1	0

PITCHING AGAINST EACH CLUB

Pitcher	Ari. W-L	Atl. W-L	Chi. W-L	Cin. W-L	Col. W-L	Fla. W-L	L.A. W-L	Mil. W-L	Mon. W-L	N.Y. W-L	Phi. W-L	Pit. W-L	S.D. W-L	S.F. W-L	StL. W-L	A.L. W-L	Total W-L
Bogar, Tim	0-0	0-0	0-0	0-0	0-0	0-0	0-0	0-0	0-0	0-0	0-0	0-0	0-0	0-0	0-0	0-0	0-0
Cabrera, Jose	0-0	0-0	0-0	0-0	0-1	0-0	0-1	1-1	0-0	0-0	1-0	0-0	0-0	0-0	0-0	0-0	2-3
Dotel, Octavio	0-1	0-0	0-0	1-1	0-0	0-0	0-2	1-0	0-0	0-0	0-1	0-1	0-0	0-0	1-0	0-1	3-7
Elarton, Scott	1-0	0-1	2-0	2-0	0-0	2-0	1-0	0-1	2-1	0-0	1-0	2-0	0-1	0-2	1-1	3-0	17-7
Franklin, W.	0-0	0-0	0-0	0-0	0-0	0-0	0-0	0-0	0-0	0-0	0-0	0-0	0-0	0-0	0-0	0-0	0-0
Gooden, D.	0-0	0-0	0-0	0-0	0-0	0-0	0-0	0-0	0-0	0-0	0-0	0-0	0-0	0-0	0-0	0-0	0-0
Green, Jason	0-0	0-0	0-0	0-0	0-0	0-0	0-0	0-0	1-0	0-1	0-0	0-0	0-0	0-0	0-0	0-0	1-1
Gross, Kip	0-0	0-0	0-0	0-0	0-0	0-0	0-0	0-1	0-0	0-0	0-0	0-0	0-0	0-0	0-0	0-0	0-1
Henry, Doug	0-0	1-0	0-0	0-0	0-0	0-0	0-1	0-1	0-0	0-0	0-0	0-0	0-0	0-0	0-0	0-1	1-3
Holt, Chris	0-1	0-1	1-1	0-1	0-1	0-1	0-1	2-1	1-0	0-1	1-0	1-2	0-1	0-1	0-3	2-0	8-16
Lima, Jose	0-2	1-0	0-2	1-2	0-0	2-0	0-0	0-0	0-2	0-1	0-0	2-0	0-3	0-2	0-1	1-1	7-16
Linebrink, S.	0-0	0-0	0-0	0-0	0-0	0-0	0-0	0-0	0-0	0-0	0-0	0-0	0-0	0-0	0-0	0-0	0-0
Maddux, Mike	0-0	0-0	0-1	0-1	0-0	0-0	0-0	1-0	0-0	0-0	1-0	0-0	0-0	0-0	0-0	0-0	2-2
McKnight, T.	0-0	0-0	1-0	0-0	0-0	1-0	0-0	0-0	0-0	0-1	0-0	1-0	0-0	0-0	1-0	0-0	4-1
Meacham, R.	0-0	0-0	0-0	0-0	0-0	0-0	0-0	0-0	0-0	0-0	0-0	0-0	0-0	0-0	0-0	0-0	0-0
Miller, Wade	0-0	1-1	1-1	0-0	0-0	0-0	0-0	2-0	0-0	1-0	0-1	0-0	0-0	0-1	1-0	0-2	6-6
Perez, Yorkis	0-0	0-0	0-0	0-0	1-0	0-0	0-0	0-0	0-0	0-0	0-0	0-0	0-1	0-0	1-0	0-0	2-1
Powell, Brian	0-0	0-0	0-0	0-0	0-0	0-0	0-0	0-0	0-0	1-1	0-0	1-0	0-0	0-0	0-0	0-0	2-1
Powell, Jay	0-0	0-0	0-0	0-0	0-0	0-0	0-0	0-0	0-0	0-0	0-1	0-0	0-0	1-0	0-0	0-0	1-1
Reynolds, S.	0-1	0-2	1-0	0-0	2-0	0-0	1-0	0-0	0-0	0-0	0-0	1-0	1-0	0-1	1-0	0-4	7-8
Slusarski, Joe	0-0	0-0	0-0	0-1	1-1	0-1	0-1	0-1	0-1	0-0	0-0	1-0	0-0	0-0	0-1	0-0	2-7
Valdes, Marc	0-1	1-0	1-0	1-0	0-1	0-1	0-0	0-0	0-1	0-0	1-0	1-0	0-0	0-1	0-0	0-0	5-5
Wagner, Billy	0-0	0-0	0-0	0-1	0-1	0-0	1-0	0-0	0-0	0-0	0-1	0-0	1-1	0-0	0-0	0-0	2-4
Totals	1-6	4-5	7-5	5-7	4-5	5-3	3-6	7-6	4-5	2-5	5-4	10-3	2-7	1-8	6-6	6-9	72-90

INTERLEAGUE: Holt 1-0, Reynolds 0-1, Dotel 0-1 vs. White Sox; Elarton 1-0, Miller 0-1, Reynolds 0-1 vs. Indians; Holt 1-0, Reynolds 0-1, Henry 0-1 vs. Tigers; Elarton 1-0, Lima 1-0, Miller 0-1 vs. Royals; Elarton 1-0, Lima 0-1, Reynolds 0-1 vs. Twins. Total: 6-9.

MISCELLANEOUS

HOME RUNS BY PARK

At Arizona (1): Berkman 1.

At Atlanta (1): Eusebio 1.

At Chicago (NL) (15): Hidalgo 6, Bogar 2, Ward 2, Berkman 2, Cedeno 1, Chavez 1, Lugo 1.

At Cincinnati (11): Bagwell 3, Hidalgo 3, Lugo 2, Biggio 1, Alou 1, Berkman 1.

At Cleveland (5): Ward 2, Biggio 1, Eusebio 1, Hidalgo 1.

At Colorado (12): Berkman 3, Caminiti 2, Alou 2, Bagwell 2, Hidalgo 2, Eusebio 1.

At Detroit (5): Hidalgo 2, Eusebio 1, Meluskey 1, Berkman 1.

At Florida (4): Biggio 1, Alou 1, Bagwell 1, Berkman 1.

At Houston (135): Bagwell 28, Alou 17, Hidalgo 16, Ward 13, Meluskey 11, Berkman 10, Caminiti 9, Truby 9, Lugo 6, Bogar 3, Cedeno 3, Biggio 2, Spiers 2, Eusebio 2, Barker 2, Mieske 1, Ginter 1.

At Los Angeles (9): Caminiti 2, Bagwell 2, Biggio 1, Alou 1, Cedeno 1, Hidalgo 1, Berkman 1.

At Milwaukee (9): Hidalgo 3, Caminiti 1, Alou 1, Bagwell 1, Bogar 1, Ward 1, Meluskey 1.

At Montreal (7): Caminiti 1, Spiers 1, Alou 1, Eusebio 1, Hidalgo 1, Ward 1, Meluskey 1.

At New York (NL) (3): Bagwell 1, Cedeno 1, Hidalgo 1.

At Philadelphia (7): Alou 3, Bagwell 2, Hidalgo 1, Truby 1.

At Pittsburgh (5): Bagwell 1, Bogar 1, Hidalgo 1, Ward 1, Lugo 1.

At San Diego (6): Bagwell 3, Biggio 1, Alou 1, Reynolds 1.

At San Francisco (2): Biggio 1, Alou 1.

At St. Louis (12): Hidalgo 6, Bagwell 3, Alou 1, Berkman 1, Truby 1.

LOW-HIT GAMES

No-hitters: None.

One-hitters: Chris Holt, April 28 vs. Milwaukee, W 7-0.

Two-hitters: None.

10-STRIKEOUT GAMES

Octavio Dotel 2, Total: 2

FOUR OR MORE HITS IN ONE GAME

Moises Alou 3, Jeff Bagwell 3, Tim Bogar 2, Roger Cedeno 2(including one five-hit game), Ken Caminiti 1 (including one five-hit game), Tony Eusebio 1, Richard Hidalgo 1, Mitch Meluskey 1 (including one five-hit game), Julio Lugo 1 (including one five-hit game), Total: 15

MULTI-HOMER GAMES

Jeff Bagwell 4, Richard Hidalgo 4, Moises Alou 3, Lance Berkman 3, Ken Caminiti 1, Bill Spiers 1, Tim Bogar 1, Daryle Ward 1, Mitch Meluskey 1, Chris Truby 1, Total: 20

GRAND SLAMS

4-4: Richard Hidalgo (off Pittsburgh's Jason Schmidt)
4-14: Jeff Bagwell (off San Diego's Kevin Walker)
5-9: Ken Caminiti (off Colorado's Scott Karl)
7-23: Bill Spiers (off St. Louis's Heathcliff Slocumb)
8-6: Chris Truby (off Montreal's Mike Thurman)

PINCH HITTERS

(Minimum 5 at-bats)

Name	AB	Avg.	HR	RBI
Ward, Daryle	52	.212	2	5
Mieske, Matt	45	.133	1	5
Spiers, Bill	33	.303	0	4
Berkman, Lance	18	.056	0	0
Meluskey, Mitch	16	.125	0	1
Johnson, Russ	13	.077	0	1
Bogar, Tim	12	.167	0	0
Cedeno, Roger	9	.222	0	0
Lugo, Julio	8	.375	0	1
Eusebio, Tony	7	.143	0	0
Barker, Glen	5	.000	0	0

DEBUTS

4-15: Julio Lugo, PR.
6-16: Chris Truby, 3B.
7-23: Jason Green, P.
7-24: Wayne Franklin, P.
8-10: Tony McKnight, P.
9-5: Frank Charles, PH.
9-20: Keith Ginter, PH.
9-20: Morgan Ensberg, PH.

GAMES BY POSITION

Catcher: Mitch Meluskey 103, Tony Eusebio 68, Raul Chavez 14, Paul Bako 1, Frank Charles 1.

First base: Jeff Bagwell 158, Daryle Ward 19, Lance Berkman 2.

Second base: Craig Biggio 100, Julio Lugo 45, Bill Spiers 26, Russ Johnson 3, Tim Bogar 2, Keith Ginter 2, Tripp Cromer 1.

Third base: Chris Truby 74, Ken Caminiti 58, Bill Spiers 51, Russ Johnson 4, Tripp Cromer 2, Tim Bogar 1, Mitch Meluskey 1, Morgan Ensberg 1.

Shortstop: Tim Bogar 95, Julio Lugo 60, Bill Spiers 27, Russ Johnson 5, Tripp Cromer 1.

Outfield: Richard Hidalgo 151, Moises Alou 121, Lance Berkman 96, Glen Barker 69, Roger Cedeno 67, Daryle Ward 47, Matt Mieske 18, Bill Spiers 10, Julio Lugo 6.

Designated hitter: Daryle Ward 4, Moises Alou 1, Jeff Bagwell 1.

STREAKS

Wins: 6 (August 13-19, September 5-10)
Losses: 7 (May 15-22)
Consecutive games with at least one hit: 24, Tony Eusebio (July 9-August 28)
Wins by pitcher: 5, Scott Elarton (June 22-July 16)

ATTENDANCE

Home: 3,056,139
Road: 2,401,585
Highest (home): 43,189 (September 2 vs. Atlanta).
Highest (road): 52,806 (May 7 vs. Los Angeles).
Lowest (home): 27,408 (September 5 vs. Florida).
Lowest (road): 3,913 (May 22 vs. Milwaukee).

Los Angeles Dodgers

DAY BY DAY

Date	Opp.	Res.	Score	(inn.*)	Hits	Opp. hits	Winning pitcher	Losing pitcher	Save	Record	Pos.	GB
4-3	At Mon.	W	10-4		9	9	Brown	Hermanson	Adams	1-0	1st	+0.5
4-4	At Mon.	W	10-4		17	6	Park	Irabu		2-0	T1st	+0.5
4-5	At Mon.	L	5-6		12	10	Telford	Shaw		2-1	T2nd	0.5
4-6	At Mon.	L	3-11		6	14	Pavano	Perez		2-2	T3rd	1.5
4-7	At N.Y.	L	1-2		4	2	Reed	Dreifort	Benitez	2-3	4th	1.5
4-8	At N.Y.	W	6-5	(10)	9	11	Fetters	Benitez	Shaw	3-3	T3rd	1.5
4-11	At S.F	W	6-5		12	8	Park	Rueter	Shaw	4-3	2nd	1.5
4-12	At S.F	W	6-5		8	7	Adams	Weber	Shaw	5-3	2nd	1.0
4-13	At S.F	W	11-7		13	11	Perez	Gardner	Shaw	6-3	2nd	0.5
4-14	Cin.	W	8-1		9	9	Hershiser	Bell		7-3	2nd	0.5
4-15	Cin.	L	4-5		7	8	Williamson	Mills	Graves	7-4	2nd	1.5
4-16	Cin.	L	3-5		6	7	Parris	Park	Graves	7-5	2nd	2.0
4-18	Hou.	W	5-3		8	5	Dreifort	Dotel	Shaw	8-5	2nd	1.5
4-19	Hou.	L	3-10		7	14	Reynolds	Hershiser		8-6	2nd	2.5
4-21	At Cin.	W	9-2		11	10	Herges	Parris	Adams	9-6	2nd	2.0
4-22	At Cin.	W	16-2		15	5	Park	Harnisch	Mills	10-6	2nd	1.0
4-23	At Cin.	W	11-3		11	13	Perez	Villone		11-6	1st	...
4-24	At N.Y.	L	0-1		3	8	Benitez	Adams		11-7	2nd	0.5
4-25	At Atl.	L	0-1		3	6	Glavine	Brown		11-8	2nd	1.5
4-26	At Atl.	L	1-5		5	9	Millwood	Gagne		11-9	2nd	2.5
4-27	At Atl.	L	3-6		9	9	Mulholland	Park	Rocker	11-10	2nd	2.5
4-28	Fla.	W	5-3		9	7	Adams	Penny	Shaw	12-10	2nd	1.5
4-29	Fla.	W	13-12		17	12	Shaw	Alfonseca		13-10	2nd	1.5
4-30	Fla.	W	7-1		9	3	Brown	Fernandez		14-10	2nd	1.5
5-1	Atl.	L	1-2		6	6	Millwood	Gagne	Rocker	14-11	2nd	2.0
5-2	Atl.	L	3-5		11	6	Chen	Adams	Rocker	14-12	2nd	3.0
5-3	Atl.	W	6-4		9	6	Perez	Maddux	Shaw	15-12	2nd	2.0
5-5	Hou.	W	3-2		9	4	Shaw	Henry		16-12	2nd	2.5
5-6	Hou.	W	9-6		7	12	Dreifort	Dotel		17-12	2nd	2.5
5-7	Hou.	L	8-14	(10)	12	17	Wagner	Shaw		17-13	2nd	3.5
5-8	At Ari.	L	7-15		7	20	Daal	Park		17-14	3rd	4.5
5-9	At Ari.	L	7-11	(12)	15	15	Padilla	Hershiser		17-15	3rd	5.5
5-10	At Ari.	L	1-2		9	9	Kim	Adams		17-16	3rd	6.5
5-12	At StL.	W	13-0		13	2	Dreifort	Kile		18-16	3rd	6.5
5-13	At StL.	W	3-1		7	3	Park	Veres	Shaw	19-16	2nd	6.5
5-14	At StL.	L	10-12		11	17	Slocumb	Perez	Veres	19-17	2nd	6.5
5-16	At Chi.	W	6-5		9	7	Mills	Tapani	Shaw	20-17	2nd	5.5
5-17	At Chi.	W	8-6		9	7	Mills	Heredia	Shaw	21-17	2nd	4.5
5-19	At Fla.	W	5-3		8	7	Herges	Looper	Shaw	22-17	2nd	4.0
5-20	At Fla.	W	12-6		15	14	Perez	Penny		23-17	2nd	3.0
5-21	At Fla.	W	12-3		17	7	Brown	Sanchez		24-17	2nd	2.0
5-22	Cin.	W	4-3	(14)	9	10	Herges	Aybar		25-17	2nd	1.5
5-23	Cin.	L	1-3		3	7	Fernandez	Gagne	Graves	25-18	2nd	2.5
5-24	Cin.	L	3-10		7	11	Sullivan	Park		25-19	2nd	3.5
5-26	Phi.	W	11-4		10	8	Brown	Byrd		26-19	2nd	4.0
5-27	Phi.	L	6-7		10	9	Person	Dreifort	Brantley	26-20	2nd	5.0
5-28	Phi.	L	2-4		6	12	Wolf	Osuna		26-21	2nd	5.0
5-29	N.Y.	W	4-1		8	4	Park	Leiter		27-21	2nd	4.0
5-30	N.Y.	L	5-10		13	13	Franco	Shaw		27-22	T2nd	4.0
5-31	N.Y.	W	4-3		6	8	Fetters	Wendell		28-22	T2nd	4.0
6-2	At Ana.	L	5-12		11	18	Bottenfield	Dreifort		28-23	3rd	5.5
6-3	At Ana.	W	8-3		9	12	Park	Cooper		29-23	T2nd	4.5
6-4	At Ana.	L	7-8		11	9	Percival	Osuna		29-24	3rd	4.5
6-5	At Tex.	L	0-2		2	5	Glynn	Brown	Wetteland	29-25	3rd	4.5
6-6	At Tex.	W	7-1		14	6	Gagne	Clark		30-25	T2nd	3.5
6-7	At Tex.	W	11-6		15	12	Dreifort	Helling		31-25	T2nd	2.5
6-8	Hou.	W	5-2		9	6	Park	Holt	Fetters	32-25	2nd	2.0
6-9	Oak.	L	1-3		5	4	Tam	Osuna	Isringhausen	32-26	3rd	3.0
6-10	Oak.	W	7-2		13	7	Brown	Olivares		33-26	3rd	2.0
6-11	Oak.	L	0-6		7	7	Appier	Gagne		33-27	3rd	3.0
6-12	Ari.	L	2-4		8	5	Anderson	Dreifort	Kim	33-28	3rd	4.0
6-13	Ari.	W	6-1		10	5	Park	Morgan		34-28	3rd	3.0
6-14	Ari.	L	1-5		6	11	Johnson	Perez		34-29	3rd	4.0
6-15	Ari.	W	4-0		8	4	Brown	Stottlemyre		35-29	3rd	3.0
6-16	StL.	L	3-6		7	9	Hentgen	Hershiser	Veres	35-30	3rd	3.5
6-17	StL.	L	3-4		8	13	An. Benes	Dreifort	Veres	35-31	3rd	3.5
6-18	StL.	W	6-3		8	7	Park	Kile	Shaw	36-31	3rd	2.5
6-20	At Hou.	W	9-6	(10)	18	13	Herges	Slusarski		37-31	3rd	2.0
6-21	At Hou.	W	7-6		13	7	Herges	Cabrera		38-31	3rd	2.0
6-22	At Hou.	L	3-6		6	7	Elarton	Dreifort	Valdes	38-32	3rd	2.5
6-23	At StL.	L	6-9	(12)	10	9	Stechschulte	Shaw		38-33	3rd	3.5
6-24	At StL.	L	1-6		6	9	Al. Benes	Hershiser		38-34	3rd	3.5
6-25	At StL.	L	1-2		6	6	Slocumb	Osuna		38-35	4th	4.5
6-26	S.D.	L	5-9		7	9	Meadows	Hershiser		38-36	4th	5.5
6-27	S.D.	W	5-4	(10)	10	7	Fetters	Whiteside		39-36	T3rd	4.5
6-28	S.D.	W	5-4		7	6	Adams	Montgomery		40-36	3rd	4.5
6-29	S.D.	L	4-5		6	7	Clement	Dreifort	Hoffman	40-37	3rd	5.5
6-30	At S.F	W	9-2		13	6	Brown	Ortiz		41-37	3rd	4.5

HIGHLIGHTS

High point: A six-game winning streak put the Dodgers a season-high eight games above .500 (25-17) on May 22. The rotation, bullpen, everyday lineup and bench were productive, providing fans with hope after several disappointing seasons. It wouldn't last long.

Low point: After going 2-8, including losing streaks of five and three games, the Dodgers dropped to fourth place (a season-high 13 games out of first) on September 14. They also were out of the wild-card race and the season couldn't end soon enough.

Turning point: Chairman Bob Daly criticized Davey Johnson in the *Los Angeles Times* at the All-Star break, eroding whatever team confidence remained for the embattled manager. From that point, the focus was taken off the field and put on Johnson, who was fired after the season.

Most valuable player: Left fielder Gary Sheffield. The six-time All-Star became the first player in franchise history to twice bat at least .300 with 30 home runs, 100 runs batted in, 100 runs and 100 walks. Sheffield's consistency was impressive.

Most valuable pitcher: Kevin Brown. Don't be fooled by the righthander's seemingly mediocre 13-6 record. Brown led the N. L. with a 2.58 earned-run average. He gave up three or fewer earned runs in 28 of 33 starts, and one or less in 14.

Most improved player: Chan Ho Park. The righthander had a breakthrough season, going 18-10 with a 3.27 ERA and 217 strikeouts in 226 innings. He benefited from the tutelage of veteran catcher Chad Kreuter.

Most pleasant surprise: Matt Herges. The 30-year-old rookie reliever was 11-3 with a 3.17 ERA, pitching 110 2/3 innings in 59 appearances. Herges won his first eight decisions, the best start by a Dodger since Fernando Valenzuela won his first eight in 1981.

Key injuries: Pitcher Kevin Brown was on the disabled list 15 days in April because of a broken pinky finger. ... Catcher Todd Hundley played in only 90 games because of a strained oblique muscle and broken thumb. ... Lefthander Carlos Perez underwent arthroscopic surgery on his pitching shoulder in September. ... Closer Jeff Shaw went on the disabled list (elbow tendinitis) for the first time in his career.

Notable: Sheffield's 43 home runs set a Los Angeles record and matched Duke Snider's single-season franchise mark. ... First baseman Eric Karros became the all-time Los Angeles franchise leader with 242 homers, eclipsing Ron Cey's previous mark of 228. ... Infielder Dave Hansen broke baseball's single-season pinch-hit home run record with seven. ... The bullpen had a 3.76 ERA—the lowest in the majors. ... The Dodgers were 42-39 on the road. Only the Atlanta Braves and St. Louis Cardinals had more road wins in the N.L.

—JASON REID

MISCELLANEOUS

RECORDS

2000 regular-season record: 86-76 (2nd in N.L. West); 44-37 at home; 42-39 on road; 23-21 vs. East; 27-25 vs. Central; 36-30 vs. West; 19-25 vs. lefthanded starters; 67-51 vs. righthanded starters; 78-71 on grass; 8-5 on turf; 23-22 in daytime; 63-54 at night; 25-21 in one-run games; 9-5 in extra-inning games; 1-0-1 in doubleheaders.

Team record past five years: 424-386 (.523, ranks 5th in league in that span).

TEAM LEADERS

Batting average: Gary Sheffield (.325).
At-bats: Mark Grudzielanek (617).
Runs: Gary Sheffield (105).
Hits: Mark Grudzielanek (172).
Total Bases: Gary Sheffield (322).
Doubles: Shawn Green (44).
Triples: Alex Cora, Mark Grudzielanek (6).
Home runs: Gary Sheffield (43).
Runs batted in: Gary Sheffield (109).
Stolen bases: Shawn Green (24).
Slugging percentage: Gary Sheffield (.643).
On-base percentage: Gary Sheffield (.438).
Wins: Chan Ho Park (18).
Earned-run average: Kevin Brown (2.58).
Complete games: Kevin Brown (5).
Shutouts: Kevin Brown, Darren Dreifort, Chan Ho Park (1).
Saves: Jeff Shaw (27).
Innings pitched: Kevin Brown (230.0).
Strikeouts: Chan Ho Park (217).

Date	Opp.	Res.	Score	(inn.*)	Hits	Opp. hits	Winning pitcher	Losing pitcher	Save	Record	Pos.	GB
7-1	At S.F	L	1-4		9	10	Rueter	Perez	Nen	41-38	3rd	5.5
7-2	At S.F	L	5-6		13	10	Nen	Fetters		41-39	4th	5.5
7-4	At S.D.	L	2-7		4	9	Clement	Park		41-40	4th	6.0
7-5	At S.D.	W	7-5		11	11	Osuna	Whiteside	Fetters	42-40	4th	6.0
7-6	At S.D.	W	9-3		14	5	Brown	Meadows		43-40	4th	6.0
7-7	At Sea.	W	3-2	(11)	5	12	Herges	Rhodes	Fetters	44-40	4th	5.0
7-8	At Sea.	L	0-11		5	10	Sele	Gagne		44-41	4th	5.0
7-9	At Sea.	L	0-2		7	4	Moyer	Park	Sasaki	44-42	4th	6.0
7-13	Ana.	W	4-3	(10)	8	9	Osuna	Levine		45-42	4th	5.0
7-14	Ana.	L	3-5		3	11	Bottenfield	Brown	Percival	45-43	4th	6.0
7-15	Ana.	L	2-6		6	10	Etherton	Park		45-44	4th	6.0
7-16	Pit.	W	7-3		8	7	Adams	Williams		46-44	T3rd	5.0
7-17	Pit.	W	9-6		12	10	Dreifort	Arroyo	Shaw	47-44	3rd	5.0
7-18	Pit.	L	6-8		12	8	Manzanillo	Judd	Williams	47-45	4th	5.0
7-19	Col.	W	9-1		9	1	Brown	Arrojo		48-45	3rd	5.0
7-20	Col.	W	6-3		10	5	Park	Yoshii	Fetters	49-45	3rd	5.0
7-21	S.F	W	6-5		7	11	Herges	Rodriguez	Shaw	50-45	3rd	5.0
7-22	S.F	L	2-5		5	6	Hernandez	Gagne	Nen	50-46	3rd	5.0
7-23	S.F	W	5-0		10	2	Dreifort	Ortiz		51-46	3rd	4.0
7-24	At Col.	W	4-1		11	5	Brown	Arrojo	Fetters	52-46	3rd	3.5
7-25	At Col.	W	6-4		8	11	Park	Chouinard	Shaw	53-46	3rd	2.5
7-26	At Col.	L	4-11		6	14	Bohanon	Perez		53-47	3rd	2.5
7-27	At Col.	W	16-11		20	15	Masaoka	Carrara		54-47	3rd	2.5
7-28	At Phi.	W	2-0		7	2	Dreifort	Daal	Shaw	55-47	3rd	2.5
7-29	At Phi.	L	0-3		6	7	Politte	Brown	Brantley	55-48	3rd	2.5
7-30	At Phi.	L	2-3		4	9	Wolf	Park	Brantley	55-49	3rd	2.5
8-1†	At Pit.	L	0-6		6	12	Anderson	Perez		55-50		
8-1‡	At Pit.	W	5-3		7	8	Herges	Wilkins	Shaw	56-50	3rd	3.0
8-2	At Pit.	W	11-5		11	10	Dreifort	Silva		57-50	3rd	2.0
8-4	Mil.	W	2-1		7	6	Fetters	Acevedo		58-50	3rd	2.5
8-5	Mil.	L	2-4	(10)	7	10	Acevedo	Fetters	Leskanic	58-51	3rd	2.5
8-6	Mil.	L	6-9		12	15	Haynes	Valdes	Leskanic	58-52	3rd	3.5
8-7	Chi.	L	3-7		7	10	Quevedo	Herges		58-53	3rd	4.5
8-8	Chi.	W	7-5		13	8	Dreifort	Norton	Shaw	59-53	3rd	4.5
8-9	Chi.	L	4-5	(10)	8	10	Worrell	Osuna	Aguilera	59-54	3rd	5.5
8-11	At Atl.	L	2-7		5	12	Remlinger	Adams		59-55	3rd	5.5
8-12	At Atl.	L	1-4		7	6	Maddux	Valdes	Ligtenberg	59-56	3rd	5.5
8-13	At Atl.	W	7-2		11	14	Dreifort	Ashby		60-56	3rd	4.5
8-14	At Fla.	L	2-11		10	12	Sanchez	Brown		60-57	3rd	5.5
8-15	At Fla.	L	3-7		6	12	Dempster	Herges		60-58	3rd	6.5
8-16	At Fla.	W	10-4		11	13	Adams	Miceli		61-58	3rd	6.5
8-18	N.Y.	L	3-5		8	10	White	Adams	Benitez	61-59	3rd	8.0
8-19	N.Y.	W	4-1		9	4	Park	Reed		62-59	3rd	8.0
8-20	N.Y.	L	6-9		11	10	Wendell	Adams	Benitez	62-60	3rd	8.0
8-21	Mon.	L	1-4		8	9	Hermanson	Herges	Strickland	62-61	3rd	9.0
8-22	Mon.	W	14-6		16	13	Adams	Santana		63-61	3rd	8.0
8-23	Mon.	W	5-1		6	4	Brown	Thurman		64-61	3rd	8.0
8-24	Mon.	W	7-0		11	5	Park	Vazquez		65-61	3rd	7.5
8-25†	At Chi.	W	5-3		13	10	Osuna	Lieber	Shaw	66-61		
8-25‡	At Chi.	W	3-1		5	9	Perez	Garibay	Shaw	67-61	3rd	7.0
8-26	At Chi.	L	4-6		9	8	Worrell	Olson	Aguilera	67-62	3rd	7.0
8-27	At Chi.	W	7-6	(10)	9	13	Fetters	Van Poppel	Shaw	68-62	3rd	6.0
8-28	At Mil.	W	5-3		10	7	Brown	D'Amico	Shaw	69-62	3rd	6.0
8-29	At Mil.	W	7-2		8	1	Park	Haynes		70-62	3rd	5.0
8-30	At Mil.	L	2-3		6	6	King	Adams		70-63	3rd	6.0
8-31	At Mil.	L	2-8		8	14	Rigdon	Perez		70-64	3rd	7.0
9-1	Phi.	W	2-1		7	4	Fetters	Brock	Shaw	71-64	3rd	7.0
9-2	Phi.	W	1-0	(10)	6	6	Herges	Padilla		72-64	3rd	7.0
9-3	Phi.	W	6-1		9	4	Park	Person	Shaw	73-64	3rd	7.0
9-4	Pit.	L	1-12		10	13	Anderson	Dreifort		73-65	3rd	8.0
9-5	Pit.	L	0-8		6	15	Silva	Perez		73-66	3rd	9.0
9-6	Pit.	L	3-8		6	12	Serafini	Valdes		73-67	3rd	10.0
9-8	At Col.	L	5-8		9	14	Bohanon	Brown		73-68	3rd	10.5
9-9	At Col.	L	6-7		7	13	White	Park	Jimenez	73-69	4th	10.5
9-10	At Col.	W	12-1		12	5	Dreifort	Astacio	Herges	74-69	3rd	10.5
9-11	At Ari.	W	6-3		11	6	Gagne	Reynoso		75-69	3rd	10.5
9-12	At Ari.	L	4-5		7	8	Kim	Masaoka	Mantei	75-70	3rd	11.5
9-13	At Ari.	L	2-3		5	9	Plesac	Adams		75-71	4th	12.5
9-14	Col.	L	4-5		8	9	Rose	Park	Jimenez	75-72	4th	13.0
9-15	Col.	W	4-3	(10)	5	5	Herges	DeJean		76-72	4th	12.0
9-16	Col.	W	5-4		7	13	Gagne	Tavarez	Shaw	77-72	3rd	12.0
9-17	Col.	W	12-6		12	11	Prokopec	Yoshii		78-72	3rd	12.0
9-18	Ari.	W	2-1		6	9	Shaw	Swindell		79-72	3rd	11.0
9-19	Ari.	W	1-0		7	6	Park	Anderson	Shaw	80-72	3rd	11.0
9-20	Ari.	W	1-0		7	9	Herges	Kim		81-72	2nd	11.0
9-22	S.D.	L	2-3		8	7	Maurer	Osuna	Hoffman	81-73	3rd	11.5
9-23	S.D.	W	2-1		5	2	Brown	Williams		82-73	2nd	11.0
9-24	S.D.	W	1-0		3	2	Park	Clement	Shaw	83-73	2nd	10.0
9-26	S.F	W	9-0		9	2	Dreifort	Ortiz		84-73	2nd	9.0
9-27	S.F	L	0-4		6	5	Rueter	Prokopec		84-74	2nd	10.0
9-28	S.F	L	3-5		5	10	Fultz	Adams	Nen	84-75	T2nd	11.0
9-29	At S.D.	W	3-0		6	2	Park	Williams		85-75	2nd	11.0
9-30	At S.D.	W	10-2		9	6	Gagne	Clement		86-75	2nd	10.0
10-1	At S.D.	L	0-4		7	7	Eaton	Dreifort	Hoffman	86-76	2nd	11.0

Monthly records: April (14-10), May (14-12), June (13-15), July (14-12), August (15-15), September (16-11), October (0-1).
*Innings, if other than nine. † First game of a doubleheader. ‡ Second game of a doubleheader.

MEMORABLE GAMES

April 14 at Los Angeles

In the Dodger Stadium opener, veteran Orel Hershiser gave up one run in six innings to earn his first victory as a Dodger since August 7, 1994—8-1 over the Rockies at Colorado. The emotional victory before a sellout crowd of 53,223 also featured a big performance by left fielder Gary Sheffield, who was 3-for-3 with a homer and two RBIs.

Cincinnati	AB	R	H	BI	Los Angeles	AB	R	H	BI
Reese, 2b	4	0	4	0	White, cf	5	2	2	1
Larkin, ss	5	0	1	0	Grud'lanek, 2b	5	1	0	0
Griffey Jr., cf	3	0	0	0	Sheffield, lf	3	2	3	2
Bichette, rf	3	0	1	0	Herges, p	0	0	0	0
D.Young, lf-1b	4	0	1	0	Green, rf	4	1	2	2
Taubensee, c	3	0	0	0	Karros, 1b	4	1	1	2
Morris, 1b	4	0	0	0	Hundley, c	3	0	0	0
Mercado, p	0	0	0	0	Beltre, 3b	3	0	1	1
Boone, 3b	4	1	1	1	Elster, ss	3	1	0	0
Bell, p	2	0	0	0	Hershiser, p	2	0	0	0
Williamson, p	0	0	0	0	Adams, p	0	0	0	0
Cromer, ph	1	0	1	0	Hol'dsworth, ph-lf1	0	0	0	
Sullivan, p	0	0	0	0					
D.Reyes, p	0	0	0	0					
Aybar, p	0	0	0	0					
Tucker, lf	1	0	0	0					
Totals	**34**	**1**	**9**	**1**	**Totals**	**33**	**8**	**9**	**8**

Cincinnati..................................0 0 1 0 0 0 0 0 0—1 9 1
Los Angeles...............................1 0 1 0 0 0 6 0 x—8 9 1

E—Bell (1), Beltre (3). DP—Cincinnati 1, Los Angeles 2. LOB—Cincinnati 10, Los Angeles 6. 2B—Reese (4), Green (4), Karros (2). HR—Boone (3), Sheffield (3). SB—Reese (4).

Cincinnati	IP	H	R	ER	BB	SO
Bell (L 0-1)	5.1	4	2	1	1	6
Williamson	0.2	0	0	0	0	0
Sullivan	0.2	1	4	4	2	0
Reyes	0	3	2	2	1	0
Aybar	0.1	0	0	0	0	1
Mercado	1	1	0	0	0	1

Los Angeles	IP	H	R	ER	BB	SO
Hershiser (W 1-0)	6	6	1	1	2	2
Adams	1	3	0	0	0	1
Herges	2	0	0	0	1	3

Reyes pitched to 4 batters in 7th.

HBP—Bichette by Herges, Hollandsworth by Sullivan. U—HP, Carlson. 1B, DeMuth. 2B, Reliford. 3B, Eddings. T—2:44. A—53,223.

August 29 at Milwaukee

Chan Ho Park struck out a career-high 14 and gave up only two runs in eight innings of a 7-2 victory over the Brewers. The right-hander's 14 strikeouts were the most by a Dodger since Hideo Nomo fanned 17 on April 13, 1996, vs. the Florida Marlins. Mark Grudzielanek was 3-for-5 with a double, triple and career-high four RBIs.

Los Angeles	AB	R	H	BI	Milwaukee	AB	R	H	BI
Goodwin, cf	4	0	0	0	J.Mouton, cf	3	1	1	2
Grud'lanek, 2b	5	1	3	4	Loretta, ss	4	0	0	0
Green, rf	4	0	1	0	Jenkins, lf	4	0	0	0
Karros, 1b	3	0	0	0	Sexson, 1b	3	0	0	0
Beltre, 3b	4	1	0	0	Houston, 3b	4	0	0	0
Leyritz, lf	4	1	1	0	Echevarria, rf	2	0	0	0
Kreuter, c	4	1	1	1	Belliard, 2b	3	0	0	0
Cora, ss	4	2	2	1	Blanco, c	3	0	0	0
Park, p	1	1	0	0	Haynes, p	1	0	0	0
Hansen, ph	1	0	0	0	Stull, p	0	0	0	0
Fetters, p	0	0	0	0	Sweeney, ph	0	1	0	0
					Weathers, p	0	0	0	0
					Casanova, ph	1	0	0	0
					V.de los Santos, p0	0	0	0	
Totals	**34**	**7**	**8**	**6**	**Totals**	**28**	**2**	**1**	**2**

Los Angeles ....0 4 0 2 0 0 0 0 1—7 8 1 5
Milwaukee...........................0 0 0 0 0 2 0 0 0—2 1 2 3

E—Karros (6), Blanco (5), Sexson (3). DP—Los Angeles 1, LOB—Los Angeles 5, Milwaukee 3. 2B—Grudzielanek (29), Cora (14). 3B—Grudzielanek (5). HR—J.Mouton (2). SB—Green (19). SH—Park.

Los Angeles	IP	H	R	ER	BB	SO
Park (W 14-8)	8	1	2	2	3	14
Fetters	1	0	0	0	0	1

Milwaukee	IP	H	R	ER	BB	SO
Haynes (L 11-12)	4	5	6	4	3	3
Stull	2	1	0	0	1	1
Weathers	2	1	0	0	0	1
V.de los Santos	1	1	1	0	0	1

HBP—Sexson by Park. U—HP, Diaz. 1B, Cooper. 2B, Van Vleet.3B, Kellogg. T—2:57. A—14,179.

INDIVIDUAL STATISTICS

BATTING

Name	G	TPA	AB	R	H	TB	2B	3B	HR	RBI	Avg.	Obp.	Slg.	SH	SF	HP	BB	IBB	SO	SB	CS	GDP	vs RHP AB	vs RHP Avg.	vs RHP HR	vs RHP RBI	vs LHP AB	vs LHP Avg.	vs LHP HR	vs LHP RBI
Grudzielanek, Mark	148	676	617	101	172	240	35	6	7	49	.279	.335	.389	2	3	9	45	0	81	12	3	16	449	.290	5	37	168	.250	2	12
Green, Shawn	162	714	610	98	164	288	44	4	24	99	.269	.367	.472	0	6	8	90	9	121	24	5	18	425	.273	20	75	185	.259	4	24
Karros, Eric	155	663	584	84	146	268	29	0	31	106	.250	.321	.459	0	12	4	63	2	122	4	3	18	444	.239	26	84	140	.286	5	22
Beltre, Adrian	138	575	510	71	148	242	30	2	20	85	.290	.360	.475	3	4	2	56	2	80	12	5	13	391	.294	16	64	119	.277	4	21
Sheffield, Gary	141	612	501	105	163	322	24	3	43	109	.325	.438	.643	0	6	4	101	7	71	4	6	13	378	.339	36	92	123	.285	7	17
Cora, Alex	109	394	353	39	84	126	18	6	4	32	.238	.302	.357	6	2	7	26	4	53	4	1	6	291	.241	4	27	62	.226	0	5
Hundley, Todd	90	353	299	49	85	173	16	0	24	70	.284	.375	.579	1	6	2	45	6	69	0	1	5	223	.300	20	53	76	.237	4	17
Hollandsworth, Todd	81	293	261	42	61	97	12	0	8	24	.234	.314	.372	0	1	1	30	2	61	11	4	4	227	.233	8	19	34	.235	0	5
Elster, Kevin	80	259	220	29	50	100	8	0	14	32	.227	.341	.455	1	0	0	38	5	52	0	0	0	131	.206	6	16	89	.258	8	16
Kreuter, Chad	80	271	212	32	56	87	13	0	6	28	.264	.416	.410	2	1	2	54	0	48	1	0	6	153	.255	2	20	59	.288	4	8
Goodwin, Tom	56	229	211	29	53	61	3	1	1	11	.251	.310	.289	0	0	0	18	0	41	16	3	4	156	.231	1	11	55	.309	0	0
White, Devon	47	168	158	26	42	61	5	1	4	13	.266	.310	.386	0	0	1	9	0	30	3	6	3	93	.237	2	6	65	.308	2	7
Santangelo, F.P.	81	177	142	19	28	35	4	0	1	9	.197	.322	.246	6	2	6	21	0	33	3	2	5	85	.235	1	5	57	.140	0	4
Hansen, Dave	102	147	121	18	35	69	6	2	8	26	.289	.415	.570	0	0	0	26	0	32	0	1	3	113	.310	8	26	8	.000	0	0
Vizcaino, Jose	40	106	93	9	19	23	2	1	0	4	.204	.288	.247	2	0	1	10	3	15	1	0	3	53	.189	0	4	40	.225	0	0
Park, Chan Ho	34	78	70	6	15	25	4	0	2	6	.214	.236	.357	6	0	0	2	0	16	0	0	0	51	.255	2	6	19	.105	0	0
Dreifort, Darren	32	71	68	5	11	23	3	0	3	8	.162	.186	.338	1	0	1	1	0	25	0	0	0	51	.157	2	6	17	.176	1	2
Brown, Kevin	33	84	66	2	5	5	0	0	0	3	.076	.129	.076	14	0	2	2	0	29	0	0	0	50	.100	0	3	16	.000	0	0
LoDuca, Paul	34	75	65	6	16	24	2	0	2	8	.246	.301	.369	2	2	0	6	0	8	0	2	2	40	.250	2	5	25	.240	0	3
Leyritz, Jim	41	68	60	3	12	16	1	0	1	8	.200	.294	.267	0	0	1	7	0	12	0	0	2	30	.233	0	2	30	.167	1	6
Perez, Carlos	32	50	43	0	2	5	1	1	0	3	.047	.047	.116	7	0	0	0	0	15	0	0	1	27	.037	0	1	16	.063	0	2
Donnels, Chris	27	41	34	8	10	25	3	0	4	9	.294	.390	.735	0	1	0	6	1	7	0	0	3	30	.333	4	9	4	.000	0	0
Berroa, Geronimo	24	35	31	2	8	10	0	1	0	5	.258	.343	.323	0	0	0	4	1	8	0	0	2	10	.200	0	0	21	.286	0	5
Gagne, Eric	20	34	28	1	4	4	0	0	0	0	.143	.143	.143	6	0	0	0	0	5	0	0	0	24	.042	0	0	4	.750	0	0
Aven, Bruce	9	23	20	2	5	11	0	0	2	4	.250	.348	.550	0	0	0	3	0	8	0	0	0	13	.231	2	4	7	.286	0	0
Gilbert, Shawn	15	23	20	5	3	7	1	0	1	3	.150	.227	.350	1	0	0	2	0	7	0	0	0	6	.167	0	2	14	.143	1	1
Branson, Jeff	18	18	17	3	4	5	1	0	0	0	.235	.278	.294	0	0	0	1	0	6	0	0	1	12	.333	0	0	5	.000	0	0
Herges, Matt	59	14	13	0	1	1	0	0	0	0	.077	.077	.077	1	0	0	0	0	8	0	0	0	12	.083	0	0	1	.000	0	0
Metcalfe, Mike	4	13	12	0	1	1	0	0	0	0	.083	.154	.083	0	0	0	1	0	2	0	0	0	8	.000	0	0	4	.250	0	0
Valdes, Ismael	9	13	11	1	1	4	0	0	1	1	.091	.091	.364	2	0	0	0	0	7	0	0	0	7	.000	0	0	4	.250	1	1
Bocachica, Hiram	8	10	10	2	3	3	0	0	0	0	.300	.300	.300	0	0	0	0	0	2	0	0	0	3	.667	0	0	7	.143	0	0
Hershiser, Orel	10	7	7	0	0	0	0	0	0	0	.000	.000	.000	0	0	0	0	0	2	0	0	0	7	.000	0	0	0	.000	0	0
Prokopec, Luke	6	6	5	0	0	0	0	0	0	0	.000	.000	.000	1	0	0	0	0	2	0	0	0	4	.000	0	0	1	.000	0	0
Mills, Alan	18	4	3	0	0	0	0	0	0	1	.000	.250	.000	0	0	0	1	0	2	0	0	0	1	.000	0	0	2	.000	0	1
Osuna, Antonio	46	2	2	0	0	0	0	0	0	0	.000	.000	.000	0	0	0	0	0	1	0	0	1	2	.000	0	0	0	.000	0	0
Adams, Terry	66	3	2	0	0	0	0	0	0	0	.000	.000	.000	1	0	0	0	0	1	0	0	0	1	.000	0	0	1	.000	0	0
Judd, Mike	1	2	1	1	1	1	0	0	0	0	1.000	1.000	1.000	1	0	0	0	0	0	0	0	0	1	1.000	0	0	0	.000	0	0
Melhuse, Adam	1	1	1	0	0	0	0	0	0	0	.000	.000	.000	0	0	0	0	0	1	0	0	0	1	.000	0	0	0	.000	0	0
Olson, Gregg	13	0	0	0	0	0	0	0	0	0	.000	.000	.000	0	0	0	0	0	0	0	0	0	0	.000	0	0	0	.000	0	0
Fetters, Mike	51	0	0	0	0	0	0	0	0	0	.000	.000	.000	0	0	0	0	0	0	0	0	0	0	.000	0	0	0	.000	0	0
Shaw, Jeff	60	0	0	0	0	0	0	0	0	0	.000	.000	.000	0	0	0	0	0	0	0	0	0	0	.000	0	0	0	.000	0	0
Reyes, Al	6	0	0	0	0	0	0	0	0	0	.000	.000	.000	0	0	0	0	0	0	0	0	0	0	.000	0	0	0	.000	0	0
Miller, Trever	2	0	0	0	0	0	0	0	0	0	.000	.000	.000	0	0	0	0	0	0	0	0	0	0	.000	0	0	0	.000	0	0
Masaoka, Onan	29	0	0	0	0	0	0	0	0	0	.000	.000	.000	0	0	0	0	0	0	0	0	0	0	.000	0	0	0	.000	0	0
Arnold, Jamie	2	0	0	0	0	0	0	0	0	0	.000	.000	.000	0	0	0	0	0	0	0	0	0	0	.000	0	0	0	.000	0	0
Williams, Jeff	7	0	0	0	0	0	0	0	0	0	.000	.000	.000	0	0	0	0	0	0	0	0	0	0	.000	0	0	0	.000	0	0

Players with more than one N.L. team

Name	G	TPA	AB	R	H	TB	2B	3B	HR	RBI	Avg.	Obp.	Slg.	SH	SF	HP	BB	IBB	SO	SB	CS	GDP	vs RHP AB	vs RHP Avg.	vs RHP HR	vs RHP RBI	vs LHP AB	vs LHP Avg.	vs LHP HR	vs LHP RBI
Arnold, L.A.-Chi.	14	10	9	0	1	2	1	0	0	0	.111	.200	.222	0	0	1	0	0	3	0	0	0	9	.111	0	0	0	.000	0	0
Aven, Pit.-L.A.	81	176	168	20	42	74	11	0	7	29	.250	.284	.440	0	0	0	8	0	39	2	3	4	105	.238	5	21	63	.270	2	8
Goodwin, Col.-L.A.	147	606	528	94	139	186	11	9	6	58	.263	.346	.352	5	4	1	68	2	117	55	10	7	422	.244	4	43	106	.340	2	15
Hollandsworth, L.A.-Col.	137	471	428	81	115	192	20	0	19	47	.269	.333	.449	0	1	1	41	3	99	18	7	8	372	.272	19	41	56	.250	0	6
Melhuse, L.A.-Col.	24	27	24	3	4	6	0	1	0	4	.167	.259	.250	0	0	0	3	0	6	0	0	1	13	.231	0	1	11	.091	0	3
Miller, Phi.-L.A.	16	0	0	0	0	0	0	0	0	0	.000	.000	.000	0	0	0	0	0	0	0	0	0	0	.000	0	0	0	.000	0	0
Valdes, Chi.-L.A.	22	33	25	2	5	10	2	0	1	3	.200	.231	.400	7	0	0	1	0	10	0	0	0	21	.190	0	2	4	.250	1	1

PITCHING

Name	W	L	Pct.	ERA	IP	H	R	ER	HR	SH	SF	HB	BB	IBB	SO	G	GS	CG	ShO	GF	Sv	vs. RH AB	vs. RH Avg.	vs. RH HR	vs. RH RBI	vs. LH AB	vs. LH Avg.	vs. LH HR	vs. LH RBI
Brown, Kevin	13	6	.684	2.58	230.0	181	76	66	21	13	4	9	47	1	216	33	33	5	1	0	0	437	.201	16	39	411	.226	5	33
Park, Chan Ho	18	10	.643	3.27	226.0	173	92	82	21	12	5	12	124	4	217	34	34	3	1	0	0	410	.200	9	39	399	.228	12	41
Dreifort, Darren	12	9	.571	4.16	192.2	175	105	89	31	9	0	12	87	1	164	32	32	1	1	0	0	378	.214	12	35	356	.264	19	57
Perez, Carlos	5	8	.385	5.56	144.0	192	95	89	25	6	2	8	33	1	64	30	22	0	0	1	0	450	.333	19	68	142	.296	6	21
Herges, Matt	11	3	.786	3.17	110.2	100	43	39	7	9	4	6	40	5	75	59	4	0	0	17	1	232	.237	3	33	170	.265	4	24
Gagne, Eric	4	6	.400	5.15	101.1	106	62	58	20	5	3	3	60	1	79	20	19	0	0	0	0	203	.276	9	26	190	.263	11	33
Adams, Terry	6	9	.400	3.52	84.1	80	42	33	6	3	0	0	39	0	56	66	0	0	0	18	2	168	.262	5	25	159	.226	1	12
Osuna, Antonio	3	6	.333	3.74	67.1	57	30	28	7	4	3	2	35	2	70	46	0	0	0	16	0	139	.230	6	20	110	.227	1	13
Shaw, Jeff	3	4	.429	4.24	57.1	61	29	27	7	2	0	1	16	3	39	60	0	0	0	51	27	118	.229	4	13	112	.304	3	10
Fetters, Mike	6	2	.750	3.24	50.0	35	18	18	7	3	0	2	25	2	40	51	0	0	0	20	5	76	.224	1	7	95	.189	6	11
Valdes, Ismael	0	3	.000	6.08	40.0	53	29	27	5	0	2	1	13	0	29	9	8	0	0	1	0	75	.293	0	9	87	.356	5	19
Masaoka, Onan	1	1	.500	4.00	27.0	23	12	12	2	0	0	1	15	1	27	29	0	0	0	3	0	55	.255	2	6	45	.200	0	5
Mills, Alan	2	1	.667	4.21	25.2	31	12	12	3	0	0	1	16	0	18	18	0	0	0	9	1	61	.262	2	4	41	.366	1	10
Hershiser, Orel	1	5	.167	13.14	24.2	42	36	36	5	0	3	11	14	1	13	10	6	0	0	1	0	60	.367	4	16	48	.417	1	12
Prokopec, Luke	1	1	.500	3.00	21.0	19	10	7	2	1	1	2	9	0	12	5	3	0	0	1	0	27	.296	1	5	48	.229	1	3
Olson, Gregg	0	1	.000	5.09	17.2	21	11	10	4	1	1	1	7	0	15	13	0	0	0	9	0	44	.409	2	11	26	.115	2	2
Reyes, Al	0	0	.000	0.00	6.2	2	0	0	0	0	0	0	1	0	8	6	0	0	0	4	0	13	.077	0	0	10	.100	0	0
Arnold, Jamie	0	0	.000	4.05	6.2	4	3	3	0	0	1	1	5	0	3	2	0	0	0	2	0	15	.133	0	2	8	.250	0	2
Williams, Jeff	0	0	.000	15.88	5.2	12	11	10	1	0	1	0	8	0	3	7	0	0	0	0	0	16	.500	0	3	10	.400	1	3
Judd, Mike	0	1	.000	15.75	4.0	4	7	7	2	0	0	1	3	0	5	1	1	0	0	0	0	11	.364	2	7	5	.000	0	0
Miller, Trever	0	0	.000	23.14	2.1	8	6	6	0	0	0	1	3	0	1	2	0	0	0	0	0	7	.714	0	3	7	.429	0	3

PITCHERS WITH MORE THAN ONE N.L. TEAM

Name	W	L	Pct.	ERA	IP	H	R	ER	HR	SH	SF	HB	BB	IBB	SO	G	GS	CG	ShO	GF	Sv	vs. RH AB	vs. RH Avg.	vs. RH HR	vs. RH RBI	vs. LH AB	vs. LH Avg.	vs. LH HR	vs. LH RBI
Arnold, L.A.-Chi.	0	3	.000	6.18	39.1	38	31	27	1	2	4	4	24	0	16	14	4	0	0	4	1	88	.250	0	17	59	.271	1	10
Miller, Phi.-L.A.	0	0	.000	10.47	16.1	27	22	19	3	1	1	2	12	1	11	16	0	0	0	1	0	44	.409	2	12	30	.300	1	8
Valdes, Chi.-L.A.	2	7	.222	5.64	107.0	124	69	67	22	0	4	3	40	2	74	21	20	0	0	4	0	220	.264	8	26	202	.327	14	35

DESIGNATED HITTERS

Name	AB	Avg.	HR	RBI
Hansen, Dave	15	.267	0	2
Sheffield, Gary	7	.143	0	0
Karros, Eric	4	.250	0	1
Hundley, Todd	3	.333	0	0
Vizcaino, Jose	1	.000	0	0

INDIVIDUAL STATISTICS

FIELDING

FIRST BASEMEN

Player	Pct.	G	PO	A	E	TC	DP
Karros, Eric	.995	153	1296	138	7	1441	123
Hansen, Dave	.980	16	44	5	1	50	5
Leyritz, Jim	1.000	8	27	2	0	29	3
Donnels, Chris	.950	4	19	0	1	20	2
Berroa, Geronimo	.929	2	11	2	1	14	3
Elster, Kevin	.000	1	0	0	1	1	0
Vizcaino, Jose	1.000	1	1	0	0	1	0

SECOND BASEMEN

Player	Pct.	G	PO	A	E	TC	DP
Grudzielanek, Mark	.976	148	286	414	17	717	97
Cora, Alex	1.000	8	11	13	0	24	5
Santangelo, F.P.	.971	7	18	15	1	34	2
Branson, Jeff	.900	3	3	6	1	10	2
Vizcaino, Jose	1.000	3	0	1	0	1	0
Bocachica, Hiram	1.000	2	3	9	0	12	2
Donnels, Chris	1.000	1	1	0	0	1	0
Metcalfe, Mike	1.000	1	0	1	0	1	0

THIRD BASEMEN

Player	Pct.	G	PO	A	E	TC	DP
Beltre, Adrian	.944	138	116	273	23	412	30
Hansen, Dave	.955	16	4	17	1	22	2
Vizcaino, Jose	.931	12	8	19	2	29	2
Elster, Kevin	.917	8	6	16	2	24	0
Branson, Jeff	1.000	3	0	2	0	2	0
Donnels, Chris	1.000	2	1	1	0	2	0
LoDuca, Paul	1.000	1	0	1	0	1	0

SHORTSTOPS

Player	Pct.	G	PO	A	E	TC	DP
Cora, Alex	.972	101	152	260	12	424	70
Elster, Kevin	.946	55	60	133	11	204	25
Vizcaino, Jose	1.000	19	15	43	0	58	6
Branson, Jeff	1.000	7	5	5	0	10	0
Grudzielanek, Mark	1.000	1	2	2	0	4	1
Beltre, Adrian	1.000	1	1	0	0	1	0

OUTFIELDERS

Player	Pct.	G	PO	A	E	TC	DP
Green, Shawn	.980	161	280	9	6	295	3
Sheffield, Gary	.954	139	203	5	10	218	0
Hollandsworth, Todd	.987	77	143	6	2	151	0
Goodwin, Tom	1.000	55	138	2	0	140	2
Santangelo, F.P.	.983	50	58	0	1	59	0
White, Devon	.972	41	68	2	2	72	0
Gilbert, Shawn	.941	14	15	1	1	17	1
Aven, Bruce	1.000	9	12	0	0	12	0
LoDuca, Paul	1.000	8	8	0	0	8	0
Donnels, Chris	1.000	6	8	0	0	8	0
Berroa, Geronimo	1.000	6	7	0	0	7	0
Leyritz, Jim	1.000	6	4	0	0	4	0
Metcalfe, Mike	1.000	4	5	0	0	5	0
Hansen, Dave	1.000	3	3	0	0	3	0

CATCHERS

Player	Pct.	G	PO	A	E	TC	DP	PB
Hundley, Todd	.979	84	554	38	13	605	3	8
Kreuter, Chad	.994	78	483	35	3	521	1	7
LoDuca, Paul	.992	20	114	13	1	128	0	0
Leyritz, Jim	1.000	3	10	1	0	11	0	0

PITCHERS

Player	Pct.	G	PO	A	E	TC	DP
Adams, Terry	.946	66	14	21	2	37	0
Shaw, Jeff	.947	60	4	14	1	19	2
Herges, Matt	.960	59	4	20	1	25	2
Fetters, Mike	1.000	51	7	7	0	14	2
Osuna, Antonio	.917	46	4	7	1	12	0
Park, Chan Ho	.952	34	20	39	3	62	4
Brown, Kevin	.944	33	35	33	4	72	1
Dreifort, Darren	.982	32	19	36	1	56	2
Perez, Carlos	.966	30	8	20	1	29	2
Masaoka, Onan	1.000	29	1	2	0	3	0
Gagne, Eric	1.000	20	6	8	0	14	1
Mills, Alan	1.000	18	4	2	0	6	0
Olson, Gregg	1.000	13	2	2	0	4	0
Hershiser, Orel	1.000	10	1	6	0	7	0
Valdes, Ismael	.875	9	3	4	1	8	1
Williams, Jeff	-	7	0	0	0	0	0
Reyes, Al	1.000	6	0	1	0	1	0
Prokopec, Luke	1.000	5	0	3	0	3	1
Arnold, Jamie	1.000	2	0	2	0	2	0
Miller, Trever	-	2	0	0	0	0	0
Judd, Mike	-	1	0	0	0	0	0

PITCHING AGAINST EACH CLUB

Pitcher	Ari. W-L	Atl. W-L	Chi. W-L	Cin. W-L	Col. W-L	Fla. W-L	Hou. W-L	Mil. W-L	Mon. W-L	N.Y. W-L	Phi. W-L	Pit. W-L	S.D. W-L	S.F. W-L	StL. W-L	A.L. W-L	Total W-L
Adams, Terry	0-2	0-2	0-0	0-0	0-0	2-0	0-0	0-1	1-0	0-3	0-0	1-0	1-0	1-1	0-0	0-0	6-9
Arnold, Jamie	0-0	0-0	0-0	0-0	0-0	0-0	0-0	0-0	0-0	0-0	0-0	0-0	0-0	0-0	0-0	0-0	0-0
Brown, Kevin	1-0	0-1	0-0	0-0	2-1	2-1	0-0	1-0	2-0	0-0	1-1	0-0	2-0	1-0	0-0	1-2	13-6
Dreifort, D.	0-1	1-0	1-0	0-0	1-0	0-0	2-1	0-0	0-0	0-1	1-1	2-1	0-2	2-0	1-1	1-1	12-9
Fetters, Mike	0-0	0-0	1-0	0-0	0-0	0-0	0-0	1-1	0-0	2-0	1-0	0-0	1-0	0-1	0-0	0-0	6-2
Gagne, Eric	1-0	0-2	0-0	0-1	1-0	0-0	0-0	0-0	0-0	0-0	0-0	0-0	1-0	0-1	0-0	1-2	4-6
Herges, Matt	1-0	0-0	0-1	2-0	1-0	1-1	2-0	0-0	0-1	0-0	1-0	1-0	0-0	1-0	0-0	1-0	11-3
Hershiser, Orel	0-1	0-0	0-0	1-0	0-0	0-0	0-1	0-0	0-0	0-0	0-0	0-0	0-1	0-0	0-2	0-0	1-5
Judd, Mike	0-0	0-0	0-0	0-0	0-0	0-0	0-0	0-0	0-0	0-0	0-0	0-1	0-0	0-0	0-0	0-0	0-1
Masaoka, O.	0-1	0-0	0-0	0-0	1-0	0-0	0-0	0-0	0-0	0-0	0-0	0-0	0-0	0-0	0-0	0-0	1-1
Miller, Trever	0-0	0-0	0-0	0-0	0-0	0-0	0-0	0-0	0-0	0-0	0-0	0-0	0-0	0-0	0-0	0-0	0-0
Mills, Alan	0-0	0-0	2-0	0-1	0-0	0-0	0-0	0-0	0-0	0-0	0-0	0-0	0-0	0-0	0-0	0-0	2-1
Olson, Gregg	0-0	0-0	0-1	0-0	0-0	0-0	0-0	0-0	0-0	0-0	0-0	0-0	0-0	0-0	0-0	0-0	0-1
Osuna, A.	0-0	0-0	1-1	0-0	0-0	0-0	0-0	0-0	0-0	0-0	0-1	0-0	1-1	0-0	0-1	1-2	3-6
Park, Chan Ho	2-1	0-1	0-0	1-2	2-2	0-0	1-0	1-0	2-0	2-0	1-1	0-0	2-1	1-0	2-0	1-2	18-10
Perez, Carlos	0-1	1-0	1-0	1-0	0-1	1-0	0-0	0-1	0-1	0-0	0-0	0-2	0-0	1-1	0-1	0-0	5-8
Prokopec, L.	0-0	0-0	0-0	0-0	1-0	0-0	0-0	0-0	0-0	0-0	0-0	0-0	0-0	0-1	0-0	0-0	1-1
Reyes, Al	0-0	0-0	0-0	0-0	0-0	0-0	0-0	0-0	0-0	0-0	0-0	0-0	0-0	0-0	0-0	0-0	0-0
Shaw, Jeff	1-0	0-0	0-0	0-0	0-0	1-0	1-1	0-0	0-1	0-1	0-0	0-0	0-0	0-0	0-1	0-0	3-4
Valdes, Ismael	0-0	0-1	0-0	0-0	0-0	0-0	0-0	0-1	0-0	0-0	0-0	0-1	0-0	0-0	0-0	0-0	0-3
Williams, Jeff	0-0	0-0	0-0	0-0	0-0	0-0	0-0	0-0	0-0	0-0	0-0	0-0	0-0	0-0	0-0	0-0	0-0
Totals	6-7	2-7	6-3	5-4	9-4	7-2	6-3	3-4	5-3	4-5	5-4	4-5	8-5	7-5	3-6	6-9	86-76

INTERLEAGUE: Brown 1-0, Osuna 0-1, Gagne 0-1 vs. Athletics; Herges 1-0, Gagne 0-1, Park 0-1 vs. Mariners; Gagne 1-0, Dreifort 1-0, Brown 0-1 vs. Rangers; Park 1-1, Osuna 1-1, Dreifort 0-1, Brown 0-1 vs. Angels. Total: 6-9.

MISCELLANEOUS

HOME RUNS BY PARK

At Anaheim (7): Sheffield 2, Karros 2, Elster 1, Kreuter 1, LoDuca 1.

At Arizona (8): Hundley 2, Beltre 2, Sheffield 1, Hansen 1, Goodwin 1, Hollandsworth 1.

At Atlanta (5): Elster 1, Sheffield 1, Hundley 1, Karros 1, Green 1.

At Chicago (NL) (7): Aven 2, Beltre 2, Hundley 1, Hansen 1, Green 1.

At Cincinnati (8): Elster 2, Hundley 2, Sheffield 1, Karros 1, Green 1, Hollandsworth 1.

At Colorado (12): Sheffield 2, Cora 2, Beltre 2, Hundley 1, Hansen 1, Donnels 1, Karros 1, Green 1, Grudzielanek 1.

At Florida (7): Sheffield 2, Beltre 2, Karros 1, Green 1, Santangelo 1.

At Houston (5): Sheffield 4, Karros 1.

At Los Angeles (108): Sheffield 23, Karros 16, Green 15, Hundley 10, Elster 7, Beltre 7, Hollandsworth 6, Kreuter 4, Hansen 4, Grudzielanek 4, Donnels 3, White 2, Dreifort 2, Cora 2, Leyritz 1, Park 1, Valdes 1.

At Milwaukee (1): Beltre 1.

At Montreal (6): White 1, Sheffield 1, Hundley 1, Hansen 1, Karros 1, Beltre 1.

At New York (NL) (5): Karros 2, White 1, Sheffield 1, Grudzielanek 1.

At Philadelphia (0).

At Pittsburgh (2): Green 1, Beltre 1.

At San Diego (11): Hundley 3, Kreuter 1, Sheffield 1, Karros 1, Green 1, Park 1, Dreifort 1, Grudzielanek 1, Beltre 1.

At San Francisco (7): Elster 3, Sheffield 2, Hundley 1, Green 1.

At Seattle (1): Karros 1.

At St. Louis (11): Karros 3, Sheffield 2, Hundley 2, Green 1, Gilbert 1, LoDuca 1, Beltre 1.

At Texas (0).

LOW-HIT GAMES

No-hitters: None.

One-hitters: None.

Two-hitters: Darren Dreifort, May 12 vs. St. Louis, W 13-0. Kevin Brown, September 23 vs. San Diego, W 2-1. Chan Ho Park, September 29 vs. San Diego, W 3-0.

10-STRIKEOUT GAMES

Chan Ho Park 5, Kevin Brown 4, Darren Dreifort 1, Total: 10

FOUR OR MORE HITS IN ONE GAME

Mark Grudzielanek 3, Adrian Beltre 2, Devon White 1, Gary Sheffield 1, Tom Goodwin 1, Eric Karros 1, Alex Cora 1, Total: 10

MULTI-HOMER GAMES

Gary Sheffield 6, Eric Karros 3, Todd Hundley 2, Shawn Green 2, Kevin Elster 1, Darren Dreifort 1, Bruce Aven 1, Alex Cora 1, Adrian Beltre 1, Total: 18

GRAND SLAMS

4-3: Eric Karros (off Montreal's Scott Strickland)
4-21: Kevin Elster (off Cincinnati's Norm Charlton)
5-6: Todd Hundley (off Houston's Octavio Dotel)
5-20: Gary Sheffield (off Florida's Joe Strong)
5-21: Adrian Beltre (off Florida's Jesus Sanchez)
5-21: Shawn Green (off Florida's Antonio Alfonseca)
5-29: Shawn Green (off New York's Al Leiter)
7-27: Adrian Beltre (off Colorado's Kevin Jarvis)
9-30: Todd Hundley (off San Diego's Matt Clement)

PINCH HITTERS

(Minimum 5 at-bats)

Name	AB	Avg.	HR	RBI
Hansen, Dave	55	.273	7	14
Leyritz, Jim	21	.286	0	5
Santangelo, F.P.	21	.143	1	1
Elster, Kevin	17	.294	2	3
Donnels, Chris	15	.400	1	3
Berroa, Geronimo	15	.267	0	4
Hollandsworth, Todd	13	.077	0	0
Vizcaino, Jose	11	.273	0	2
White, Devon	9	.000	0	0
Bocachica, Hiram	6	.333	0	0
Hundley, Todd	6	.000	0	1

DEBUTS

6-16: Adam Melhuse, PH.
9-4: Luke Prokopec, P.
9-13: Hiram Bocachica, PR.

GAMES BY POSITION

Catcher: Todd Hundley 84, Chad Kreuter 78, Paul LoDuca 20, Jim Leyritz 3.

First base: Eric Karros 153, Dave Hansen 16, Jim Leyritz 8, Chris Donnels 4, Geronimo Berroa 2, Kevin Elster 1, Jose Vizcaino 1.

Second base: Mark Grudzielanek 148, Alex Cora 8, F.P. Santangelo 7, Jose Vizcaino 3, Jeff Branson 3, Hiram Bocachica 2, Chris Donnels 1, Mike Metcalfe 1.

Third base: Adrian Beltre 138, Dave Hansen 16, Jose Vizcaino 12, Kevin Elster 8, Jeff Branson 3, Chris Donnels 2, Paul LoDuca 1.

Shortstop: Alex Cora 101, Kevin Elster 55, Jose Vizcaino 19, Jeff Branson 7, Mark Grudzielanek 1, Adrian Beltre 1.

Outfield: Shawn Green 161, Gary Sheffield 139, Todd Hollandsworth 77, Tom Goodwin 55, F.P. Santangelo 50, Devon White 41, Shawn Gilbert 14, Bruce Aven 9, Paul LoDuca 8, Geronimo Berroa 6, Jim Leyritz 6, Chris Donnels 6, Mike Metcalfe 4, Dave Hansen 3.

Designated hitter: Dave Hansen 5, Gary Sheffield 2, Jose Vizcaino 1, Todd Hundley 1, Eric Karros 1.

STREAKS

Wins: 6 (May 16-22, September 15-20)
Losses: 5 (June 22-26, September 4-9)
Consecutive games with at least one hit: 14, Tom Goodwin (August 30-September 13)
Wins by pitcher: 6, Darren Dreifort (July 17-August 13)

ATTENDANCE

Home: 3,010,765
Road: 2,699,054
Highest (home): 53,563 (July 21 vs. San Francisco).
Highest (road): 51,285 (July 4 vs. San Diego).
Lowest (home): 22,780 (September 5 vs. Pittsburgh).
Lowest (road): 8,345 (August 14 vs. Florida).

MILWAUKEE BREWERS

DAY BY DAY

Date	Opp.	Res.	Score	(inn.*)	Hits	Opp. hits	Winning pitcher	Losing pitcher	Save	Record	Pos.	GB
4-3	At Cin.	T	3-3	(6)	7	5				0-0	T3rd	0.5
4-4	At Cin.	W	5-1		10	4	Bruske	Williamson		1-0	T1st	...
4-5	At Cin.	W	8-5		10	13	Haynes	Parris	Wickman	2-0	T1st	...
4-6	At Cin.	L	1-5		8	7	Villone	Navarro		2-1	T2nd	1.0
4-7	At StL.	W	9-1		11	6	Bere	An. Benes		3-1	T1st	...
4-8	At StL.	L	8-10		9	15	Kile	Woodard	Veres	3-2	T2nd	1.0
4-9	At StL.	L	2-11		6	16	Ankiel	de los Santos		3-3	T2nd	2.0
4-10	Fla.	W	4-3		6	9	Haynes	Nunez	Wickman	4-3	2nd	2.0
4-12	Fla.	L	4-11		8	11	Sanchez	Navarro		4-4	2nd	2.5
4-13	Fla.	W	4-0		6	4	Bere	Penny		5-4	2nd	1.5
4-14	Atl.	L	3-6		7	14	Glavine	Woodard	Remlinger	5-5	T2nd	1.5
4-15	Atl.	W	6-3		9	5	Weathers	Burkett	Wickman	6-5	2nd	1.0
4-16	Atl.	L	1-2		8	6	Mulholland	Stull	Remlinger	6-6	T2nd	1.5
4-18	At N.Y.	L	7-10		9	11	Hampton	Navarro	Benitez	6-7	T2nd	2.5
4-19	At N.Y.	L	1-3		8	8	Reed	Bere	Benitez	6-8	T3rd	3.5
4-20	At N.Y.	L	4-5	(10)	9	7	Wendell	Leskanic		6-9	T4th	4.5
4-21	At Mon.	L	1-5		8	8	Hermanson	Haynes	Urbina	6-10	T5th	4.5
4-22	At Mon.	W	7-3		15	5	Stull	Irabu		7-10	3rd	3.5
4-23	At Mon.	L	4-6		7	10	Vazquez	Navarro	Urbina	7-11	3rd	4.5
4-25	At StL.	L	2-7		7	10	Kile	Bere		7-12	T4th	5.5
4-26	At StL.	L	0-7		4	9	Ankiel	Woodard		7-13	5th	6.5
4-27	At StL.	W	8-4		10	6	Haynes	Hentgen		8-13	T3rd	5.5
4-28	Hou.	L	0-7		1	8	Holt	Navarro		8-14	6th	6.5
4-29	Hou.	L	3-10		7	5	Maddux	Stull		8-15	6th	7.5
4-30	Hou.	W	4-3		7	7	Weathers	Henry		9-15	T4th	7.5
5-1	Hou.	L	0-5		2	11	Dotel	Woodard		9-16	6th	8.0
5-2	Ari.	L	1-5		4	9	Stottlemyre	Haynes		9-17	6th	8.0
5-3	Ari.	W	4-1		10	4	Estrada	Daal	Wickman	10-17	6th	7.0
5-4	Ari.	L	2-6		4	10	Reynoso	Stull	Kim	10-18	6th	8.0
5-5	Mon.	L	2-10		7	14	Vazquez	Bere		10-19	6th	8.0
5-6	Mon.	L	2-3		4	11	Telford	Weathers	Urbina	10-20	6th	9.0
5-7	Mon.	W	9-4		13	8	Haynes	Hermanson		11-20	6th	8.0
5-8	At Chi.	L	11-12	(10)	13	16	Heredia	Wickman		11-21	6th	8.0
5-9	At Chi.	W	4-3		8	5	D'Amico	Guthrie	Weathers	12-21	6th	8.0
5-10	At Chi.	L	8-9	(11)	9	10	Aguilera	de los Santos		12-22	6th	8.0
5-11	At Chi.	W	14-8		18	17	Woodard	Williams		13-22	6th	7.5
5-12	At Pit.	W	6-1		11	4	Haynes	Schmidt		14-22	5th	6.5
5-13	At Pit.	L	8-11		10	16	Sauerbeck	Acevedo	Williams	14-23	6th	7.0
5-14	At Pit.	L	0-3		4	7	Benson	D'Amico	Christiansen	14-24	6th	7.5
5-16	Hou.	W	6-5	(16)	11	14	Estrada	Holt		15-24	5th	7.5
5-19	S.F	W	11-10	(10)	11	15	Wickman	Nen		16-24	4th	6.5
5-20	S.F	W	7-0		6	4	D'Amico	Gardner		17-24	4th	6.5
5-21	S.F	L	10-16		9	20	Ortiz	Ramirez		17-25	4th	7.5
5-22†	Hou.	W	10-9	(10)	14	13	Weathers	Slusarski		18-25		
5-22‡	Hou.	W	6-1		8	7	Bere	Gross		19-25	4th	6.5
5-23	Atl.	W	7-6		7	5	Wright	Millwood	Wickman	20-25	3rd	6.5
5-24	Atl.	L	2-11		5	17	Maddux	Haynes		20-26	3rd	7.5
5-25	Atl.	L	3-7		6	12	Mulholland	D'Amico		20-27	3rd	8.5
5-26	At Ari.	L	2-9		6	9	Johnson	Snyder		20-28	4th	8.5
5-27	At Ari.	L	3-7		6	14	Reynoso	Acevedo	Kim	20-29	4th	8.5
5-28	At Ari.	W	4-3	(11)	11	8	Wickman	Swindell		21-29	3rd	7.5
5-29	At S.D.	W	8-3		10	8	Haynes	Meadows		22-29	3rd	7.5
5-30	At S.D.	L	3-6		9	11	Eaton	D'Amico	Hoffman	22-30	4th	8.5
5-31	At S.D.	L	5-9		10	9	Almanzar	Weathers		22-31	4th	8.5
6-2	Col.	L	6-8		9	12	Arrojo	Bere	Myers	22-32	4th	9.0
6-3	Col.	W	2-1	(12)	6	3	de los Santos	Belinda		23-32	4th	8.0
6-4	Col.	L	1-7		5	12	Jarvis	Haynes		23-33	4th	8.5
6-5	Cle.	L	4-8		8	9	Burba	D'Amico		23-34	4th	8.5
6-6	Cle.	L	2-4		7	7	Finley	Snyder		23-35	5th	9.0
6-7	Cle.	L	5-9		10	10	Brewington	Bere		23-36	5th	10.0
6-9	At Min.	L	6-9		10	10	Bergman	Wright		23-37	5th	10.0
6-10	At Min.	W	5-3		13	7	Haynes	Redman	Wickman	24-37	5th	9.0
6-11	At Min.	W	5-3		13	10	Snyder	Radke	Wickman	25-37	5th	9.0
6-12	Mon.	W	8-1		12	5	Bere	Vazquez		26-37	T4th	9.0
6-13	Mon.	L	4-9		10	12	Pavano	Woodard		26-38	5th	10.0
6-14	Mon.	W	11-2		12	8	Wright	Johnson		27-38	T4th	10.0
6-16	N.Y.	L	1-7		3	15	Leiter	Haynes		27-39	5th	11.0
6-17	N.Y.	W	3-2		4	9	Snyder	Rusch	Wickman	28-39	5th	11.0
6-18	N.Y.	L	3-7		7	10	Reed	Bere		28-40	5th	11.0
6-19	At Fla.	W	2-0		5	3	Wright	Smith	Wickman	29-40	5th	10.5
6-20	At Fla.	L	2-8		5	13	Dempster	Woodard		29-41	5th	11.5
6-21	At Fla.	L	4-5		11	9	Looper	Haynes	Alfonseca	29-42	5th	11.5
6-22	At Fla.	W	6-1		10	6	Snyder	Sanchez		30-42	5th	11.5
6-23	At Atl.	L	2-3		7	6	Marquis	Weathers	Rocker	30-43	5th	12.5
6-24	At Atl.	W	2-1		6	5	Wright	Maddux	Wickman	31-43	4th	12.5
6-25	At Atl.	L	4-5		8	4	Rocker	Leskanic		31-44	4th	13.5
6-27	At Phi.	L	0-7		6	8	Schilling	Haynes		31-45	4th	14.0
6-28	At Phi.	L	7-9		11	13	Brock	Acevedo	Brantley	31-46	5th	14.0
6-29	At Phi.	W	8-6		12	10	Bere	Schrenk	Leskanic	32-46	4th	14.0
6-30	Chi.	L	4-7	(15)	12	13	Garibay	Levrault	Aguilera	32-47	5th	15.0

HIGHLIGHTS

High point: The Brewers were 8-2 during County Stadium's final homestand and that late spurt against Central Division rivals secured a third-place finish. That completed a respectable August and September that gave the team something to build on.
Low point: The Brewers lost eight of nine games in mid-July and were on pace to set a team record for losses when the month ended. Their frustration compounded when Jeromy Burnitz halted contract negotiations because he didn't think the Brewers would change their losing ways while he was in his prime.
Turning point: On July 28, the Brewers acquired first baseman Richie Sexson from Cleveland and the entire outlook changed. It was uncanny how much Sexson's bat meant to the middle of the lineup. Hitting between Geoff Jenkins and Burnitz, Sexson batted .296 with 14 home runs and 47 RBIs over the final two months.
Most valuable player: Jenkins, despite missing three weeks with a broken finger, was a consistent run producer. He hit .303 with 34 home runs and 94 RBIs even though he played the second half of the season in pain.
Most valuable pitcher: Jeff D'Amico. After missing almost two entire seasons with shoulder problems, D'Amico won a rotation spot in May, brought stability to the rotation and finished 12-7 with a 2.66 ERA that ranked third in the league.
Most improved player: After going 6-2 with a 5.08 ERA for Colorado in 1999, Curtis Leskanic developed into one of the top setup men in the league. When Bob Wickman was traded to Cleveland in late July, Leskanic inherited the closer's job and finished 9-3, converting 12 of 13 save opportunities. He allowed just eight earned runs after the break.
Biggest surprise: Lefty Ray King, recalled from the minors for the third time on July 6, became a dominant setup man over the second half. King finished with a 1.26 ERA and held opponents to a .180 average.
Key injuries: Shortstop Mark Loretta missed more than two months with a broken foot. ... Jenkins missed three weeks with his broken finger. ... Jamey Wright, counted on as the team's No. 2 starter, suffered a partial tear of his rotator cuff and didn't pitch until June. ... Righthander John Snyder missed two months with a strained muscle. ... Catcher Henry Blanco missed most of September with a sore throwing shoulder.
Notable: Brewers pitchers set a club record for walks with 728. ... Sexson (30), Jenkins (34) and Burnitz (31) became the first Brewers' trio to finish the season with 30 or more home runs since Gorman Thomas, Ben Oglivie and Cecil Cooper accomplished the feat in 1982. Sexson hit 16 homers for Cleveland and 14 for Milwaukee. ... Burnitz topped 30 home runs for the third straight year, despite hitting just .232.

—EMMETT PROSSER

MISCELLANEOUS

RECORDS

2000 regular-season record: 73-89 (3rd in N.L. Central); 42-39 at home; 31-50 on road; 15-26 vs. East; 39-39 vs. Central; 19-24 vs. West; 14-21 vs. left-handed starters; 59-68 vs. righthanded starters; 63-77 on grass; 10-12 on turf; 21-29 in daytime; 52-60 at night; 26-21 in one-run games; 13-9 in extra-inning games; 1-0-1 in doubleheaders.
Team record past five years: 379-429 (.469, ranks 11th in league in that span).

TEAM LEADERS

Batting average: Geoff Jenkins (.303).
At-bats: Marquis Grissom (595).
Runs: Geoff Jenkins (100).
Hits: Geoff Jenkins (155).
Total Bases: Geoff Jenkins (301).
Doubles: Geoff Jenkins (36).
Triples: Ron Belliard (9).
Home runs: Geoff Jenkins (34).
Runs batted in: Jeromy Burnitz (98).
Stolen bases: Marquis Grissom (20).
Slugging percentage: Geoff Jenkins (.588).
On-base percentage: Geoff Jenkins (.360).
Wins: Jeff D'Amico, Jimmy Haynes (12).
Earned-run average: Jeff D'Amico (2.66).
Complete games: Jeff D'Amico, Steve Woodard (1).
Shutouts: Jeff D'Amico (1).
Saves: Bob Wickman (16).
Innings pitched: Jimmy Haynes (199.1).
Strikeouts: Jeff D'Amico (101).

Date	Opp.	Res.	Score	(inn.*)	Hits	Opp. hits	Winning pitcher	Losing pitcher	Save	Record	Pos.	GB
7-1	Chi.	W	4-0		11	2	D'Amico	Valdes		33-47	4th	15.0
7-2	Chi.	W	4-2		7	6	Haynes	Wood	Wickman	34-47	4th	14.0
7-3	Phi.	L	3-5		6	10	Ashby	Snyder	Brantley	34-48	4th	14.5
7-4	Phi.	L	4-7		10	11	Brock	Wickman	Brantley	34-49	4th	15.5
7-5	Phi.	L	2-5		7	12	Wolf	Wright	Gomes	34-50	4th	16.5
7-6	Phi.	W	4-2		8	11	D'Amico	Byrd	Wickman	35-50	4th	15.5
7-7	Det.	W	4-3		9	6	Haynes	Moehler	Wickman	36-50	4th	14.5
7-8	Det.	L	2-4	(15)	15	12	Cruz	de los Santos		36-51	4th	14.5
7-9	Det.	W	10-3		13	10	Bere	Blair		37-51	4th	14.5
7-13	At K.C.	W	5-2		8	10	Wright	Stein	Wickman	38-51	4th	14.5
7-14	At K.C.	W	4-0		12	4	D'Amico	Suzuki		39-51	3rd	14.5
7-15	At K.C.	L	4-7		11	11	Suppan	Haynes	Bottalico	39-52	3rd	14.5
7-16	At Chi. (AL)	L	5-11		9	16	Baldwin	Snyder		39-53	3rd	14.5
7-17	At Chi. (AL)	L	2-11		4	13	Garland	Bere		39-54	4th	15.5
7-18	At Chi. (AL)	L	5-7		9	10	Sirotka	Wright	Wunsch	39-55	5th	15.5
7-19	Pit.	W	6-0		5	5	D'Amico	Benson		40-55	4th	14.5
7-20	Pit.	L	2-9		5	12	Silva	Haynes		40-56	5th	14.5
7-21	At Chi.	L	2-4		5	7	Wood	Snyder	Aguilera	40-57	5th	15.5
7-22	At Chi.	L	2-3	(13)	10	7	Heredia	Woodard		40-58	5th	15.5
7-23	At Chi.	L	4-5		7	4	Valdes	Wright	Aguilera	40-59	5th	15.5
7-25	At Pit.	W	4-1	(11)	10	6	Leskanic	Christiansen	Wickman	41-59	5th	15.5
7-26	At Pit.	L	4-5		8	10	Silva	Haynes	Williams	41-60	5th	16.5
7-27	At Pit.	W	4-3		9	7	Leskanic	Manzanillo	Wickman	42-60	5th	15.5
7-28	Col.	W	5-0		8	8	Wright	Astacio		43-60	5th	14.5
7-29	Col.	L	2-10		6	14	Tavarez	Rigdon		43-61	5th	14.5
7-30	Col.	W	3-2		5	7	D'Amico	Yoshii	Leskanic	44-61	5th	13.5
7-31	S.F	L	3-4	(11)	4	5	Rodriguez	Weathers	Nen	44-62	5th	14.5
8-1	S.F	L	8-13		10	17	Henry	King		44-63	5th	14.5
8-2	S.F	W	6-4		8	6	Acevedo	Hernandez	Leskanic	45-63	5th	14.5
8-4	At L.A.	L	1-2		6	7	Fetters	Acevedo		45-64	5th	14.5
8-5	At L.A.	W	4-2	(10)	10	7	Acevedo	Fetters	Leskanic	46-64	5th	14.5
8-6	At L.A.	W	9-6		15	12	Haynes	Valdes	Leskanic	47-64	5th	13.5
8-7	At S.F	L	1-8		9	8	Hernandez	Snyder		47-65	5th	14.5
8-8	At S.F	L	0-1		2	6	Ortiz	Wright	Nen	47-66	5th	14.5
8-9	At S.F	L	3-9		6	13	Rueter	Rigdon		47-67	5th	14.5
8-11	StL.	W	6-2		8	7	D'Amico	Kile		48-67	5th	14.0
8-12	StL.	L	1-2	(12)	7	9	Morris	Leskanic	James	48-68	5th	15.0
8-13	StL.	L	4-6		8	13	Hentgen	Wright	Veres	48-69	5th	16.0
8-14	Cin.	W	4-3		8	8	Rigdon	Dessens	Leskanic	49-69	5th	15.0
8-15	Cin.	W	2-1	(10)	7	5	Leskanic	Wohlers		50-69	4th	15.0
8-16	Cin.	W	5-1		9	9	D'Amico	Bell		51-69	4th	15.0
8-18	At Hou.	L	4-5		6	12	Miller	Haynes	Dotel	51-70	4th	16.0
8-19	At Hou.	L	8-10		8	11	Cabrera	Acevedo	Dotel	51-71	4th	17.0
8-20	At Hou.	W	6-5		14	7	Leskanic	Cabrera		52-71	4th	16.0
8-21	At Ari.	W	16-8		19	13	Stull	Reynoso		53-71	4th	16.0
8-22	At Ari.	W	4-3		8	8	D'Amico	Guzman	Leskanic	54-71	4th	15.0
8-23	At Ari.	W	8-5		9	11	Haynes	Schilling	Leskanic	55-71	4th	15.0
8-25	S.D.	L	0-4		6	12	Tollberg	Wright		55-72	T3rd	15.5
8-26	S.D.	W	6-5	(10)	8	14	Leskanic	Hoffman		56-72	T3rd	15.5
8-27	S.D.	L	1-2		8	7	Williams	Weathers	Hoffman	56-73	T3rd	16.5
8-28	L.A.	L	3-5		7	10	Brown	D'Amico	Shaw	56-74	T3rd	17.5
8-29	L.A.	L	2-7		1	8	Park	Haynes		56-75	4th	17.5
8-30	L.A.	W	3-2		6	6	King	Adams		57-75	4th	17.5
8-31	L.A.	W	8-2		14	8	Rigdon	Perez		58-75	T3rd	17.0
9-1	At Col.	L	3-5		7	11	Astacio	Snyder	White	58-76	T3rd	18.0
9-2	At Col.	W	8-3		14	10	D'Amico	DeJean		59-76	3rd	18.0
9-3	At Col.	W	6-4	(11)	13	8	Acevedo	DeJean	Leskanic	60-76	3rd	18.0
9-4	At S.D.	L	3-4		5	7	Davey	King	Hoffman	60-77	3rd	19.0
9-5	At S.D.	L	1-3		3	5	Witasick	Rigdon	Hoffman	60-78	3rd	20.0
9-6	At S.D.	L	6-7		9	11	Williams	Snyder	Hoffman	60-79	3rd	20.0
9-8	StL.	W	6-5		12	8	Leskanic	Veres		61-79	T3rd	19.5
9-9	StL.	L	6-7		12	15	Veres	Acevedo		61-80	T4th	20.5
9-10	StL.	W	4-3	(10)	9	8	King	An. Benes		62-80	4th	19.5
9-11	At N.Y.	W	8-2		12	7	Rigdon	Reed		63-80	3rd	19.5
9-12	At N.Y.	L	2-10		7	13	B.J. Jones	Snyder		63-81	3rd	20.5
9-13	At N.Y.	L	1-4	(10)	5	9	Benitez	Acevedo		63-82	3rd	21.5
9-14	At Cin.	W	6-4		8	12	Haynes	Villone	Leskanic	64-82	3rd	21.5
9-15	At Cin.	L	4-6		7	11	Parris	Wright	Graves	64-83	4th	22.5
9-16	At Cin.	L	3-7		10	9	Dessens	Rigdon	Riedling	64-84	4th	23.5
9-17	At Cin.	L	4-8		5	7	Harnisch	Snyder		64-85	4th	24.5
9-18	Chi.	W	2-1		5	4	D'Amico	Van Poppel	Leskanic	65-85	4th	24.0
9-19	Chi.	W	9-8		9	7	King	Farnsworth		66-85	4th	23.0
9-20	Chi.	W	3-2	(10)	9	8	Leskanic	Farnsworth		67-85	4th	23.0
9-21	Pit.	W	12-2		14	5	Rigdon	Anderson		68-85	4th	22.0
9-23†	Pit.	L	2-4		5	14	Silva	D'Amico	Williams	68-86		
9-23‡	Pit.	W	5-4	(10)	8	10	Leskanic	Arroyo		69-86	T3rd	22.0
9-24	Pit.	W	8-5		9	6	Leskanic	Williams		70-86	3rd	21.0
9-26	Cin.	W	7-4		13	9	Wright	Parris	Leskanic	71-86	3rd	21.0
9-27	Cin.	W	10-6		8	11	de los Santos	Riedling		72-86	3rd	21.0
9-28	Cin.	L	1-8		2	14	Dessens	D'Amico		72-87	3rd	22.0
9-29	At Hou.	W	13-3		15	7	Estrada	Elarton		73-87	3rd	21.0
9-30	At Hou.	L	6-7		11	11	Miller	Haynes	Dotel	73-88	3rd	21.0
10-1	At Hou.	L	1-6		7	8	Holt	Wright		73-89	3rd	22.0

Monthly records: April (9-15), May (13-16), June (10-16), July (12-15), August (14-13), September (15-13), October (0-1).
*Innings, if other than nine. † First game of a doubleheader. ‡ Second game of a doubleheader.

MEMORABLE GAMES

May 11 at Chicago

The Brewers tied the record for the longest nine-inning game in National League history when they defeated the Cubs, 14-8, at Wrigley Field. The two pitching staffs allowed a combined 35 hits and 18 walks. Ten pitchers threw a total of 437 pitches. Mark Loretta, Lyle Mouton and Jose Hernandez combined to reach base 16 times with Loretta garnering five singles and a walk. .

Milwaukee	AB	R	H	BI	Cubs	AB	R	H	BI
Belliard, 2b	6	3	3	1	Huson, 2b	2	0	0	0
Loretta, ss	5	1	5	0	Nieves, ph-2b	4	0	2	1
Burnitz, rf	4	2	1	3	Gutierrez, ss	4	1	2	0
Hayes, 1b	4	1	0	0	Sosa, rf	5	0	1	0
Grissom, cf	4	2	0	1	Greene, 3b	3	0	1	1
Hernandez, 3b	4	2	3	2	Lorraine, p	0	0	0	0
L.Mouton, lf	4	2	3	3	Guthrie, p	0	0	0	0
Blanco, c	4	1	2	2	Rodriguez, ph	1	0	0	0
Woodard, p	4	0	1	1	Heredia, p	0	0	0	0
Acevedo, p	0	0	0	0	Hill, lf	3	2	2	1
Leskanic, p	1	0	0	0	Zuleta, 1b	5	1	1	1
Weathers, p	0	0	0	0	Buford, cf	4	2	4	0
					Girardi, c	4	1	3	1
					Downs, p	0	0	0	0
					Garibay, ph-p	1	0	0	0
					Williams, p	0	0	0	0
					Andrews, ph-3b	3	1	1	3
Totals	**40**	**14**	**18**	**13**	**Totals**	**39**	**8**	**17**	**8**

Milwaukee ....2 1 1 0 0 4 1 5 0—14 18 0
Cubs ....0 1 0 2 1 3 0 0 1— 8 17 3

E—Huson (1), Buford (2), Zuleta (1). DP—Milwaukee 2, Cubs 2. LOB—Milwaukee 11, Cubs 13. 2B—Belliard 2 (8), Burnitz (6), Hernandez (2), L. Mouton (2), Blanco (2), Greene (2), Hill (3). HR—Hill (5), Andrews (10). SB—L. Mouton (1). CS—Burnitz (2), Grissom (6). S—Burnitz, Grissom. SH—Garibay.

Milwaukee	IP	H	R	ER	BB	SO
Woodard (W 1-4)	5	13	7	6	1	4
Acevedo	1	1	0	0	5	1
Leskanic	2.2	3	1	1	2	3
Weathers	0.1	0	0	0	0	1
Cubs	**IP**	**H**	**R**	**ER**	**BB**	**SO**
Downs	3	7	4	4	3	0
Garibay	2	2	0	0	2	0
B.Williams (L 1-1)	1	3	4	4	3	0
Lorraine	1	4	5	4	2	0
Guthrie	1	2	1	1	0	2
Heredia	1	0	0	0	0	0

Woodard pitched to 3 batters in 6th. Acevedo pitched to 2 batters in 7th. Lorraine pitched to 5 batters in 8th.
WP—Woodard, Acevedo, Leskanic, Guthrie. PB—Blanco. U—HP, Tschida. 1B, Meriwether. 2B, Gibson. 3B, Rippley. T—4:22. A—21,995.

May 22 at Milwaukee

Trailing 9-2 in the first game of a doubleheader, the Brewers rallied for seven runs in the bottom of the ninth and won in the 10th on a home run by Jose Hernandez. It was the largest ninth-inning comeback in team history and the largest ninth-inning comeback in baseball since May 10, 1994. The last three runs in the ninth scored with two out off Houston closer Billy Wagner.

Houston	AB	R	H	BI	Milwaukee	AB	R	H	BI
Cedeno, rf	5	1	3	0	Belliard, 2b	4	0	1	0
Biggio, 2b	3	1	3	2	Loretta, ss	5	1	2	1
Bagwell, 1b	6	1	2	0	Burnitz, rf	4	2	2	2
Caminiti, 3b	5	1	1	0	Hayes, 1b	5	2	2	0
Hidalgo, cf	5	2	1	3	L.Mouton, lf	5	1	3	3
Ward, lf	3	0	0	0	Hernandez, 3b	5	2	2	3
Bogar, ss	1	0	0	0	Grissom, cf	4	1	1	1
Eusebio, c	4	2	2	1	Blanco, c	3	0	1	0
Spiers, ss-lf	4	1	1	2	Casanova, pr-c	0	1	0	0
Reynolds, p	3	0	0	0	Woodard, p	2	0	0	0
Alou, ph	1	0	0	0	Acevedo, p	0	0	0	0
Henry, p	1	0	0	0	Sweeney, ph	1	0	0	0
Cabrera, p	0	0	0	0	Ramirez, p	0	0	0	0
Wagner, p	0	0	0	0	J.Mouton, ph	1	0	0	0
Slusarski, p	0	0	0	0	Weathers, p	0	0	0	0
Totals	**41**	**9**	**13**	**8**	**Totals**	**39**	**10**	**14**	**10**

Houston ....1 0 3 0 0 0 0 3 2 0— 9 13 1
Milwaukee.......................2 0 0 0 0 0 0 0 7 1—10 14 1

E—Caminiti (6), Hernandez (8). DP—Houston 4, LOB—Houston 11, Milwaukee 4. 2B—Bagwell 2 (11), Caminiti (10), Spiers (6), L. Mouton 2 (5), Hernandez (3). 3B—Cedeno (4). HR—Hidalgo (13), Hernandez (6). S—Biggio. SH—Biggio.

Houston	IP	H	R	ER	BB	SO
Reynolds	7	6	2	2	0	4
Henry	1	4	4	4	2	0
Cabrera	0	1	1	1	0	0
Wagner	1	2	2	2	1	2
Slusarski (L 0-2)	0.1	1	1	1	0	0
Milwaukee	**IP**	**H**	**R**	**ER**	**BB**	**SO**
Woodard	7	8	4	4	1	4
Acevedo	1	3	3	1	2	0
Ramirez	1	1	2	2	2	0
Weathers (W 3-1)	1	1	0	0	1	1

Henry pitched to 4 batters in 9th. Cabrera to 2 batters in 9th.
HBP—Biggio by Woodard. WP—J.Cabrera, Wagner. U—HP, Cousins. 1B, Marquez. 2B, Van Vleet. 3B, Nelson. T—3:38.

INDIVIDUAL STATISTICS

BATTING

Name	G	TPA	AB	R	H	TB	2B	3B	HR	RBI	Avg.	Obp.	Slg.	SH	SF	HP	BB	IBB	SO	SB	CS	GDP	vs RHP AB	vs RHP Avg.	vs RHP HR	vs RHP RBI	vs LHP AB	vs LHP Avg.	vs LHP HR	vs LHP RBI
Grissom, Marquis	146	640	595	67	145	209	18	2	14	62	.244	.288	.351	2	4	0	39	2	99	20	10	9	470	.228	12	44	125	.304	2	18
Belliard, Ron	152	667	571	83	150	222	30	9	8	54	.263	.354	.389	4	7	3	82	4	84	7	5	12	447	.257	7	45	124	.282	1	9
Burnitz, Jeromy	161	686	564	91	131	257	29	2	31	98	.232	.356	.456	0	9	14	99	10	121	6	4	12	404	.230	24	67	160	.238	7	31
Jenkins, Geoff	135	564	512	100	155	301	36	4	34	94	.303	.360	.588	0	4	15	33	6	135	11	1	9	392	.309	29	73	120	.283	5	21
Hernandez, Jose	124	496	446	51	109	166	22	1	11	59	.244	.315	.372	0	3	6	41	3	125	3	7	12	333	.255	9	49	113	.212	2	10
Hayes, Charlie	121	435	370	46	93	137	17	0	9	46	.251	.348	.370	0	6	1	57	4	84	1	1	11	253	.249	5	32	117	.256	4	14
Loretta, Mark	91	399	352	49	99	143	21	1	7	40	.281	.350	.406	8	1	1	37	2	38	0	3	9	274	.266	6	29	78	.333	1	11
Houston, Tyler	101	305	284	30	71	140	15	0	18	43	.250	.292	.493	4	0	0	17	3	72	2	1	13	262	.256	16	35	22	.182	2	8
Blanco, Henry	93	324	284	29	67	112	24	0	7	31	.236	.318	.394	0	4	0	36	6	60	0	3	9	222	.216	5	23	62	.306	2	8
Casanova, Raul	86	265	231	20	57	94	13	3	6	36	.247	.331	.407	2	2	4	26	1	48	1	2	5	174	.247	5	24	57	.246	1	12
Sexson, Richie	57	251	213	44	63	119	14	0	14	47	.296	.398	.559	0	1	3	34	2	63	1	0	3	170	.335	13	38	43	.140	1	9
Lopez, Luis	78	225	201	24	53	85	14	0	6	27	.264	.309	.423	8	2	5	9	1	35	1	2	2	154	.266	4	22	47	.255	2	5
Mouton, James	87	197	159	28	37	52	7	1	2	17	.233	.363	.327	4	1	3	30	0	43	13	4	5	91	.209	1	10	68	.265	1	7
Barker, Kevin	40	122	100	14	22	33	5	0	2	9	.220	.352	.330	0	1	1	20	0	21	1	0	1	89	.191	2	9	11	.455	0	0
Mouton, Lyle	42	109	97	14	27	42	7	1	2	16	.278	.349	.433	0	1	1	10	0	29	1	0	2	70	.286	2	13	27	.259	0	3
Sweeney, Mark	71	87	73	9	16	25	6	0	1	6	.219	.337	.342	1	0	1	12	1	18	0	0	1	72	.222	1	6	1	.000	0	0
Haynes, Jimmy	33	70	64	3	8	12	4	0	0	4	.125	.138	.188	5	0	0	1	0	30	0	0	0	58	.138	0	3	6	.000	0	1
Perez, Santiago	24	63	52	8	9	11	2	0	0	2	.173	.290	.212	1	1	1	8	2	9	4	0	1	38	.158	0	2	14	.214	0	0
Berry, Sean	32	50	46	1	7	12	2	0	1	2	.152	.220	.261	0	0	0	4	0	13	0	1	1	25	.120	0	0	21	.190	1	2
Wright, Jamey	26	50	46	0	3	4	1	0	0	0	.065	.065	.087	4	0	0	0	0	17	0	0	0	38	.079	0	0	8	.000	0	0
D'Amico, Jeff	23	54	44	2	4	8	1	0	1	2	.091	.146	.182	6	1	0	3	0	19	0	0	3	39	.077	1	2	5	.200	0	0
Echevarria, Angel	31	49	42	3	9	14	2	0	1	4	.214	.327	.333	0	0	0	7	0	9	0	0	1	22	.318	1	2	20	.100	0	2
Bere, Jason	20	40	39	3	8	10	0	1	0	2	.205	.205	.256	1	0	0	0	0	17	0	0	1	36	.194	0	2	3	.333	0	0
Snyder, John	24	42	38	1	3	4	1	0	0	0	.079	.146	.105	1	0	1	2	0	7	0	0	1	26	.115	0	0	12	.000	0	0
Collier, Lou	14	39	32	9	7	11	1	0	1	2	.219	.333	.344	0	1	0	6	0	4	0	0	1	21	.238	0	0	11	.182	1	2
Woodard, Steve	27	26	22	0	1	1	0	0	0	2	.045	.125	.045	2	0	1	1	0	6	0	0	1	12	.000	0	1	10	.100	0	1
Brown, Kevin L.	5	18	17	3	4	7	3	0	0	1	.235	.278	.412	0	0	0	1	0	5	0	0	0	10	.200	0	0	7	.286	0	1
Jones, Chris	12	17	16	3	3	5	2	0	0	1	.188	.235	.313	0	0	0	1	0	4	0	0	0	7	.143	0	1	9	.222	0	0
Rigdon, Paul	12	25	16	3	3	6	0	0	1	1	.188	.278	.375	7	0	0	2	0	6	0	0	1	12	.167	1	1	4	.250	0	0
Stull, Everett	20	10	9	0	0	0	0	0	0	0	.000	.100	.000	0	0	0	1	0	9	0	0	0	5	.000	0	0	4	.000	0	0
Estrada, Horacio	7	8	7	1	1	1	0	0	0	0	.143	.143	.143	1	0	0	0	0	2	0	0	0	4	.250	0	0	3	.000	0	0
de los Santos, Valerio	66	6	6	0	0	0	0	0	0	0	.000	.000	.000	0	0	0	0	0	4	0	0	0	3	.000	0	0	3	.000	0	0
Navarro, Jaime	5	5	5	0	0	0	0	0	0	0	.000	.000	.000	0	0	0	0	0	2	0	0	0	1	.000	0	0	4	.000	0	0
Levrault, Allen	5	3	3	0	0	0	0	0	0	0	.000	.000	.000	0	0	0	0	0	2	0	0	0	3	.000	0	0	0	.000	0	0
Leskanic, Curtis	73	2	2	0	0	0	0	0	0	0	.000	.000	.000	0	0	0	0	0	2	0	0	0	1	.000	0	0	1	.000	0	0
Ramirez, Hector	6	1	1	0	1	1	0	0	0	0	1.000	1.000	1.000	0	0	0	0	0	0	0	0	0	0	.000	0	0	1	1.000	0	0
Weathers, Dave	69	1	1	0	0	0	0	0	0	0	.000	.000	.000	0	0	0	0	0	1	0	0	0	1	.000	0	0	0	.000	0	0
Acevedo, Juan	62	2	1	1	0	0	0	0	0	0	.000	.500	.000	0	0	0	1	0	1	0	0	0	1	.000	0	0	0	.000	0	0
Bruske, Jim	15	1	1	0	0	0	0	0	0	0	.000	.000	.000	0	0	0	0	0	0	0	0	0	1	.000	0	0	0	.000	0	0
Williams, Matt T.	11	1	1	0	0	0	0	0	0	0	.000	.000	.000	0	0	0	0	0	1	0	0	0	1	.000	0	0	0	.000	0	0
Scanlan, Bob	2	0	0	0	0	0	0	0	0	0	.000	.000	.000	0	0	0	0	0	0	0	0	0	0	.000	0	0	0	.000	0	0
Wickman, Bob	43	0	0	0	0	0	0	0	0	0	.000	.000	.000	0	0	0	0	0	0	0	0	0	0	.000	0	0	0	.000	0	0
Buddie, Mike	5	0	0	0	0	0	0	0	0	0	.000	.000	.000	0	0	0	0	0	0	0	0	0	0	.000	0	0	0	.000	0	0
Roque, Rafael	4	0	0	0	0	0	0	0	0	0	.000	.000	.000	0	0	0	0	0	0	0	0	0	0	.000	0	0	0	.000	0	0
King, Ray	36	0	0	0	0	0	0	0	0	0	.000	.000	.000	0	0	0	0	0	0	0	0	0	0	.000	0	0	0	.000	0	0
Davis, Kane	3	0	0	0	0	0	0	0	0	0	.000	.000	.000	0	0	0	0	0	0	0	0	0	0	.000	0	0	0	.000	0	0

Players with more than one N.L. team

Name	G	TPA	AB	R	H	TB	2B	3B	HR	RBI	Avg.	Obp.	Slg.	SH	SF	HP	BB	IBB	SO	SB	CS	GDP	vs RHP AB	vs RHP Avg.	vs RHP HR	vs RHP RBI	vs LHP AB	vs LHP Avg.	vs LHP HR	vs LHP RBI
Echevarria, Col.	10	9	9	0	1	1	0	0	0	2	.111	.111	.111	0	0	0	0	0	2	0	0	0	22	.318	1	2	20	.100	0	2
Echevarria, Col.-Mil.	41	58	51	3	10	15	2	0	1	6	.196	.293	.294	0	0	0	7	0	11	0	0	1	29	.241	1	4	22	.136	0	2

PITCHING

Name	W	L	Pct.	ERA	IP	H	R	ER	HR	SH	SF	HB	BB	IBB	SO	G	GS	CG	ShO	GF	Sv	vs. RH AB	vs. RH Avg.	vs. RH HR	vs. RH RBI	vs. LH AB	vs. LH Avg.	vs. LH HR	vs. LH RBI
Haynes, Jimmy	12	13	.480	5.33	199.1	228	128	118	21	10	6	7	100	7	88	33	33	0	0	0	0	445	.276	10	61	329	.319	11	48
Wright, Jamey	7	9	.438	4.10	164.2	157	81	75	12	4	6	18	88	5	96	26	25	0	0	1	0	355	.256	6	39	247	.267	6	31
D'Amico, Jeff	12	7	.632	2.66	162.1	143	55	48	14	10	3	6	46	5	101	23	23	1	1	0	0	354	.234	9	23	248	.242	5	27
Snyder, John	3	10	.231	6.17	127.0	147	95	87	8	6	7	9	77	10	69	23	23	0	0	0	0	280	.304	3	52	217	.286	5	29
Bere, Jason	6	7	.462	4.93	115.0	115	66	63	19	12	3	1	63	7	98	20	20	0	0	0	0	275	.262	14	37	161	.267	5	21
Woodard, Steve	1	7	.125	5.96	93.2	125	70	62	16	7	3	4	33	4	65	27	11	1	0	6	0	229	.323	10	36	156	.327	6	37
Acevedo, Juan	3	7	.300	3.81	82.2	77	38	35	11	1	1	1	31	9	51	62	0	0	0	18	0	191	.220	7	30	122	.287	4	15
Leskanic, Curtis	9	3	.750	2.56	77.1	58	23	22	7	1	4	3	51	5	75	73	0	0	0	39	12	171	.211	5	12	103	.214	2	13
Weathers, Dave	3	5	.375	3.07	76.1	73	29	26	7	4	1	2	32	8	50	69	0	0	0	23	1	187	.278	6	24	94	.223	1	10
de los Santos, Valerio	2	3	.400	5.13	73.2	72	43	42	15	2	1	1	33	7	70	66	2	0	0	15	0	173	.243	10	31	110	.273	5	19
Rigdon, Paul	4	4	.500	4.52	69.2	68	37	35	14	3	5	1	26	4	48	12	12	0	0	0	0	164	.262	9	25	103	.243	5	9
Wickman, Bob	2	2	.500	2.93	46.0	37	18	15	1	0	1	1	20	2	44	43	0	0	0	36	16	93	.183	1	8	79	.253	0	7
Stull, Everett	2	3	.400	5.82	43.1	41	30	28	7	2	3	4	30	3	33	20	4	0	0	3	0	93	.237	4	12	67	.284	3	13
King, Ray	3	2	.600	1.26	28.2	18	7	4	1	0	1	0	10	1	19	36	0	0	0	8	0	51	.157	0	4	49	.204	1	2
Estrada, Horacio	3	0	1.000	6.29	24.1	30	18	17	5	0	1	2	20	4	13	7	4	0	0	2	0	76	.329	5	12	24	.208	0	4
Navarro, Jaime	0	5	.000	12.54	18.2	34	31	26	6	2	2	0	18	3	7	5	5	0	0	0	0	49	.490	3	17	34	.294	3	10
Bruske, Jim	1	0	1.000	6.48	16.2	22	15	12	5	0	1	2	12	1	8	15	0	0	0	1	0	36	.361	2	8	34	.265	3	11
Levrault, Allen	0	1	.000	4.50	12.0	10	7	6	0	1	1	0	7	0	9	5	1	0	0	2	0	26	.308	0	6	16	.125	0	1
Williams, Matt T.	0	0	.000	7.00	9.0	7	7	7	2	0	0	1	13	0	7	11	0	0	0	1	0	24	.208	2	8	8	.250	0	3
Ramirez, Hector	0	1	.000	10.00	9.0	11	10	10	1	0	0	0	5	0	4	6	0	0	0	1	0	20	.350	0	4	18	.222	1	4
Buddie, Mike	0	0	.000	4.50	6.0	8	3	3	0	1	0	0	1	1	5	5	0	0	0	2	0	17	.353	0	3	8	.250	0	1
Roque, Rafael	0	0	.000	10.13	5.1	7	6	6	1	0	1	0	7	1	4	4	0	0	0	1	0	14	.286	1	3	7	.429	0	2
Davis, Kane	0	0	.000	6.75	4.0	7	3	3	1	0	0	1	5	0	2	3	0	0	0	1	0	10	.500	1	2	8	.250	0	1
Scanlan, Bob	0	0	.000	27.00	1.2	6	6	5	0	1	1	1	0	0	1	2	0	0	0	1	0	5	.600	0	2	5	.600	0	4

DESIGNATED HITTERS

Name	AB	Avg.	HR	RBI
Sweeney, Mark	15	.267	0	2
Casanova, Raul	12	.417	0	2

Name	AB	Avg.	HR	RBI
Hayes, Charlie	3	.667	1	2
Burnitz, Jeromy	3	.333	0	1

INDIVIDUAL STATISTICS

FIELDING

FIRST BASEMEN

Player	Pct.	G	PO	A	E	TC	DP
Sexson, Richie	.991	57	470	66	5	541	50
Hayes, Charlie	.991	57	407	30	4	441	57
Houston, Tyler	.982	35	257	21	5	283	30
Barker, Kevin	.993	32	250	15	2	267	24
Echevarria, Angel	1.000	9	27	3	0	30	4
Sweeney, Mark	1.000	2	3	0	0	3	0

SECOND BASEMEN

Player	Pct.	G	PO	A	E	TC	DP
Belliard, Ron	.976	151	336	437	19	792	130
Lopez, Luis	.987	22	31	44	1	76	11
Loretta, Mark	1.000	1	1	0	0	1	0

THIRD BASEMEN

Player	Pct.	G	PO	A	E	TC	DP
Hernandez, Jose	.950	95	81	165	13	259	23
Hayes, Charlie	.976	59	31	89	3	123	6
Houston, Tyler	.939	28	12	50	4	66	6
Berry, Sean	1.000	9	3	4	0	7	1
Lopez, Luis	1.000	6	2	8	0	10	2
Collier, Lou	-	1	0	0	0	0	0

SHORTSTOPS

Player	Pct.	G	PO	A	E	TC	DP
Loretta, Mark	.995	90	121	254	2	377	54
Lopez, Luis	.959	45	68	94	7	169	27
Hernandez, Jose	.968	37	59	93	5	157	32
Perez, Santiago	.917	20	21	45	6	72	11

OUTFIELDERS

Player	Pct.	G	PO	A	E	TC	DP
Burnitz, Jeromy	.979	158	317	12	7	336	2
Grissom, Marquis	.992	142	352	3	3	358	1
Jenkins, Geoff	.975	131	263	12	7	282	3
Mouton, James	.989	46	84	3	1	88	0
Mouton, Lyle	.978	27	41	4	1	46	1
Collier, Lou	1.000	10	16	2	0	18	0
Echevarria, Angel	1.000	5	2	1	0	3	0
Sweeney, Mark	1.000	3	8	0	0	8	0
Jones, Chris	1.000	2	6	0	0	6	0
Hernandez, Jose	.500	2	1	0	1	2	0

CATCHERS

Player	Pct.	G	PO	A	E	TC	DP	PB
Blanco, Henry	.991	88	506	58	5	569	13	5
Casanova, Raul	.990	72	358	28	4	390	6	3
Houston, Tyler	.972	23	130	9	4	143	1	4
Brown, Kevin L.	.957	5	20	2	1	23	0	0

PITCHERS

Player	Pct.	G	PO	A	E	TC	DP
Leskanic, Curtis	1.000	73	12	11	0	23	0
Weathers, Dave	1.000	69	5	7	0	12	0
de los Santos, Valerio	1.000	66	4	8	0	12	1
Acevedo, Juan	1.000	62	8	8	0	16	0
Wickman, Bob	1.000	43	3	9	0	12	2
King, Ray	1.000	36	2	6	0	8	0
Haynes, Jimmy	.962	33	16	34	2	52	5
Woodard, Steve	1.000	27	4	15	0	19	0
Wright, Jamey	.952	26	17	23	2	42	0
Snyder, John	.938	23	12	18	2	32	0
D'Amico, Jeff	1.000	23	9	13	0	22	1
Bere, Jason	1.000	20	11	17	0	28	1
Stull, Everett	1.000	20	1	7	0	8	1
Bruske, Jim	1.000	15	1	1	0	2	0
Rigdon, Paul	1.000	12	7	7	0	14	0
Williams, Matt T.	1.000	11	0	2	0	2	0
Estrada, Horacio	.875	7	1	6	1	8	0
Ramirez, Hector	1.000	6	0	1	0	1	0
Levrault, Allen	1.000	5	1	0	0	1	0
Navarro, Jaime	1.000	5	1	0	0	1	0
Buddie, Mike	-	5	0	0	0	0	0
Roque, Rafael	-	4	0	0	0	0	0
Davis, Kane	-	3	0	0	0	0	0
Scanlan, Bob	.000	2	0	0	1	1	0

PITCHING AGAINST EACH CLUB

Pitcher	Ari. W-L	Atl. W-L	Chi. W-L	Cin. W-L	Col. W-L	Fla. W-L	Hou. W-L	L.A. W-L	Mon. W-L	N.Y. W-L	Phi. W-L	Pit. W-L	S.D. W-L	S.F. W-L	StL. W-L	A.L. W-L	Total W-L
Acevedo, Juan	0-1	0-0	0-0	0-0	1-0	0-0	0-1	1-1	0-0	0-1	0-1	0-1	0-0	1-0	0-1	0-0	3-7
Bere, Jason	0-0	0-0	0-0	0-0	0-1	1-0	1-0	0-0	1-1	0-2	1-0	0-0	0-0	0-0	1-1	1-2	6-7
Bruske, Jim	0-0	0-0	0-0	1-0	0-0	0-0	0-0	0-0	0-0	0-0	0-0	0-0	0-0	0-0	0-0	0-0	1-0
Buddie, Mike	0-0	0-0	0-0	0-0	0-0	0-0	0-0	0-0	0-0	0-0	0-0	0-0	0-0	0-0	0-0	0-0	0-0
D'Amico, Jeff	1-0	0-1	3-0	1-1	2-0	0-0	0-0	0-1	0-0	0-0	1-0	1-2	0-1	1-0	1-0	1-1	12-7
Davis, Kane	0-0	0-0	0-0	0-0	0-0	0-0	0-0	0-0	0-0	0-0	0-0	0-0	0-0	0-0	0-0	0-0	0-0
de los Santos, V.	0-0	0-0	0-1	1-0	1-0	0-0	0-0	0-0	0-0	0-0	0-0	0-0	0-0	0-0	0-1	0-1	2-3
Estrada, H.	1-0	0-0	0-0	0-0	0-0	0-0	2-0	0-0	0-0	0-0	0-0	0-0	0-0	0-0	0-0	0-0	3-0
Haynes, J.	1-1	0-1	1-0	2-0	0-1	1-1	0-2	1-1	1-1	0-1	0-1	1-2	1-0	0-0	1-0	2-1	12-13
King, Ray	0-0	0-0	1-0	0-0	0-0	0-0	0-0	1-0	0-0	0-0	0-0	0-0	0-1	0-1	1-0	0-0	3-2
Leskanic, C.	0-0	0-1	1-0	1-0	0-0	0-0	1-0	0-0	0-0	0-1	0-0	4-0	1-0	0-0	1-1	0-0	9-3
Levrault, Allen	0-0	0-0	0-1	0-0	0-0	0-0	0-0	0-0	0-0	0-0	0-0	0-0	0-0	0-0	0-0	0-0	0-1
Navarro, J.	0-0	0-0	0-0	0-1	0-0	0-1	0-1	0-0	0-1	0-1	0-0	0-0	0-0	0-0	0-0	0-0	0-5
Ramirez, H.	0-0	0-0	0-0	0-0	0-0	0-0	0-0	0-0	0-0	0-0	0-0	0-0	0-0	0-1	0-0	0-0	0-1
Rigdon, Paul	0-0	0-0	0-0	1-1	0-1	0-0	0-0	1-0	0-0	1-0	0-0	1-0	0-1	0-1	0-0	0-0	4-4
Roque, Rafael	0-0	0-0	0-0	0-0	0-0	0-0	0-0	0-0	0-0	0-0	0-0	0-0	0-0	0-0	0-0	0-0	0-0
Scanlan, Bob	0-0	0-0	0-0	0-0	0-0	0-0	0-0	0-0	0-0	0-0	0-0	0-0	0-0	0-0	0-0	0-0	0-0
Snyder, John	0-1	0-0	0-1	0-1	0-1	1-0	0-0	0-0	0-0	1-1	0-1	0-0	0-1	0-1	0-0	1-2	3-10
Stull, Everett	1-1	0-1	0-0	0-0	0-0	0-0	0-1	0-0	1-0	0-0	0-0	0-0	0-0	0-0	0-0	0-0	2-3
Weathers, D.	0-0	1-1	0-0	0-0	0-0	0-0	2-0	0-0	0-1	0-0	0-0	0-0	0-2	0-1	0-0	0-0	3-5
Wickman, B.	1-0	0-0	0-1	0-0	0-0	0-0	0-0	0-0	0-0	0-0	0-1	0-0	0-0	1-0	0-0	0-0	2-2
Williams, M. T.	0-0	0-0	0-0	0-0	0-0	0-0	0-0	0-0	0-0	0-0	0-0	0-0	0-0	0-0	0-0	0-0	0-0
Woodard, S.	0-0	0-1	1-1	0-0	0-0	0-1	0-1	0-0	0-1	0-0	0-0	0-0	0-0	0-0	0-2	0-0	1-7
Wright, Jamey	0-0	2-0	0-1	1-1	1-0	1-0	0-1	0-0	1-0	0-0	0-1	0-0	0-1	0-1	0-1	1-2	7-9
Totals	5-4	3-6	7-6	8-5	5-4	4-3	6-7	4-3	4-5	2-7	2-5	7-5	2-7	3-6	5-7	6-9	73-89

INTERLEAGUE: Snyder 0-1, Bere 0-1, Wright 0-1 vs. White Sox; D'Amico 0-1, Snyder 0-1, Bere 0-1 vs. Indians; Haynes 1-0, Bere 1-0, de los Santos 0-1 vs. Tigers; Wright 1-0, D'Amico 1-0, Haynes 0-1 vs. Royals; Haynes 1-0, Snyder 1-0, Wright 0-1 vs. Twins. Total: 6-9.

MISCELLANEOUS

HOME RUNS BY PARK

At Arizona (10): Houston 3, Sexson 3, Loretta 2, Burnitz 1, Lopez 1.
At Atlanta (4): Grissom 2, Burnitz 1, Houston 1.
At Chicago (AL) (4): Hayes 2, Houston 1, Jenkins 1.
At Chicago (NL) (7): Burnitz 5, Hernandez 1, Loretta 1.
At Cincinnati (14): Jenkins 4, Burnitz 3, Grissom 1, Sweeney 1, Houston 1, Belliard 1, Collier 1, Sexson 1, Barker 1.
At Colorado (5): Grissom 1, Lopez 1, Houston 1, Sexson 1, Jenkins 1.
At Florida (7): Jenkins 2, Hayes 1, Grissom 1, Burnitz 1, Lopez 1, Houston 1.
At Houston (6): Jenkins 3, Burnitz 2, Belliard 1.
At Kansas City (4): Burnitz 2, Grissom 1, Hernandez 1.
At Los Angeles (4): Jenkins 3, Blanco 1.
At Milwaukee (78): Jenkins 15, Burnitz 12, Hernandez 8, Sexson 7, Houston 6, Grissom 4, Casanova 4, Belliard 4, Lopez 3, Loretta 3, Blanco 3, Hayes 2, Mouton 2, Berry 1, Mouton 1, D'Amico 1, Echevarria 1, Rigdon 1.
At Minnesota (3): Grissom 2, Hernandez 1.
At Montreal (4): Jenkins 3, Belliard 1.
At New York (NL) (5): Hayes 2, Mouton 1, Sexson 1, Jenkins 1.
At Philadelphia (3): Grissom 1, Burnitz 1, Casanova 1.
At Pittsburgh (5): Houston 2, Blanco 2, Hayes 1.
At San Diego (5): Grissom 1, Loretta 1, Houston 1, Casanova 1, Sexson 1.
At San Francisco (0):
At St. Louis (9): Burnitz 3, Hayes 1, Houston 1, Belliard 1, Blanco 1, Jenkins 1, Barker 1.

LOW-HIT GAMES

No-hitters: None.
One-hitters: None.
Two-hitters: None.

10-STRIKEOUT GAMES

Jason Bere 1, Jeff D'Amico 1, Total: 2

FOUR OR MORE HITS IN ONE GAME

Ron Belliard 2, Geoff Jenkins 2, Marquis Grissom 1, Luis Lopez 1, James Mouton 1, Mark Loretta 1 (including one five-hit game), Total: 8

MULTI-HOMER GAMES

Jeromy Burnitz 3, Tyler Houston 2, Geoff Jenkins 2, Total: 7

GRAND SLAMS

5-12: Henry Blanco (off Pittsburgh's Jason Schmidt)
5-20: Jose Hernandez (off San Francisco's Mark Gardner)
5-23: Jose Hernandez (off Atlanta's Kevin Millwood)
6-13: Raul Casanova (off Montreal's Steve Kline)
9-27: Raul Casanova (off Cincinnati's Danny Graves)

PINCH HITTERS

(Minimum 5 at-bats)

Name	AB	Avg.	HR	RBI
Sweeney, Mark	54	.185	1	3
Mouton, James	24	.250	0	3
Berry, Sean	22	.091	0	0
Echevarria, Angel	21	.190	0	1
Houston, Tyler	20	.200	1	3
Mouton, Lyle	16	.250	0	2
Hayes, Charlie	15	.333	0	6
Casanova, Raul	12	.417	0	2
Lopez, Luis	10	.300	1	4
Jones, Chris	9	.222	0	1
Barker, Kevin	8	.125	0	1
Blanco, Henry	5	.200	0	0

DEBUTS

4-5: Matt T. Williams, P.
6-3: Santiago Perez, PH.
6-13: Allen Levrault, P.

GAMES BY POSITION

Catcher: Henry Blanco 88, Raul Casanova 72, Tyler Houston 23, Kevin L. Brown 5.
First base: Charlie Hayes 57, Richie Sexson 57, Tyler Houston 35, Kevin Barker 32, Angel Echevarria 9, Mark Sweeney 2.
Second base: Ron Belliard 151, Luis Lopez 22, Mark Loretta 1.
Third base: Jose Hernandez 95, Charlie Hayes 59, Tyler Houston 28, Sean Berry 9, Luis Lopez 6, Lou Collier 1.
Shortstop: Mark Loretta 90, Luis Lopez 45, Jose Hernandez 37, Santiago Perez 20.
Outfield: Jeromy Burnitz 158, Marquis Grissom 142, Geoff Jenkins 131, James Mouton 46, Lyle Mouton 27, Lou Collier 10, Angel Echevarria 5, Mark Sweeney 3, Chris Jones 2, Jose Hernandez 2.
Designated hitter: Mark Sweeney 4, Raul Casanova 3, Charlie Hayes 1, Jeromy Burnitz 1.

STREAKS

Wins: 4 (August 20-23, September 18-21, September 23-27)
Losses: 5 (April 16-21, June 4-9)
Consecutive games with at least one hit: 13, Ron Belliard (May 9-23)
Wins by pitcher: 4, Jeff D'Amico (July 1-19)

ATTENDANCE

Home: 1,573,621
Road: 2,217,518
Highest (home): 56,354 (September 28 vs. Cincinnati).
Highest (road): 55,596 (April 3 vs. Cincinnati).
Lowest (home): 3,913 (May 22 vs. Houston).
Lowest (road): 7,612 (June 19 vs. Florida).

MONTREAL EXPOS

DAY BY DAY

Date	Opp.	Res.	Score	(inn.*)	Hits	Opp. hits	Winning pitcher	Losing pitcher	Save	Record	Pos.	GB
4-3	L.A.	L	4-10		9	9	Brown	Hermanson	Adams	0-1	T4th	1.0
4-4	L.A.	L	4-10		6	17	Park	Irabu		0-2	T4th	1.5
4-5	L.A.	W	6-5		10	12	Telford	Shaw		1-2	T3rd	1.0
4-6	L.A.	W	11-3		14	6	Pavano	Perez		2-2	T2nd	0.5
4-7	S.D.	L	5-10		12	13	Meadows	Powell		2-3	4th	1.0
4-8	S.D.	W	10-9		11	11	Telford	Wall	Urbina	3-3	T2nd	0.5
4-9	S.D.	W	2-1		4	7	Irabu	Boehringer	Urbina	4-3	T2nd	0.5
4-11	At Pit.	W	7-3		9	4	Vazquez	Benson	Kline	5-3	1st	+0.5
4-12	At Pit.	L	4-6		7	10	Silva	Batista	Williams	5-4	T1st	...
4-13	At Pit.	L	3-4		8	10	Silva	Urbina		5-5	T1st	...
4-14	At Phi.	W	4-0		9	6	Hermanson	Brock		6-5	T1st	...
4-16	At Phi.	L	4-5		7	9	Aldred	Telford		6-6	T2nd	0.5
4-18	Chi.	W	4-3		9	7	Strickland	Tapani	Urbina	7-6	T2nd	1.0
4-19	Chi.	W	7-3		11	7	Pavano	Quevedo		8-6	T1st	...
4-20	Chi.	L	6-10		13	10	Williams	Blank		8-7	4th	1.0
4-21	Mil.	W	5-1		8	8	Hermanson	Haynes	Urbina	9-7	T2nd	1.0
4-22	Mil.	L	3-7		5	15	Stull	Irabu		9-8	4th	2.0
4-23	Mil.	W	6-4		10	7	Vazquez	Navarro	Urbina	10-8	4th	2.0
4-25	Col.	W	10-4		14	11	Pavano	Bohanon		11-8	4th	2.0
4-26	Col.	W	9-2		12	5	Hermanson	Jarvis	Urbina	12-8	3rd	2.0
4-28	At S.F	W	9-3		8	11	Telford	Ortiz		13-8	2nd	2.5
4-29	At S.F	L	1-2		3	9	Johnstone	Telford	Nen	13-9	3rd	3.5
4-30	At S.F	W	4-3		6	6	Strickland	Johnstone	Urbina	14-9	3rd	3.5
5-1	At Col.	L	8-15		15	18	White	Hermanson		14-10	3rd	4.5
5-2	At Col.	L	6-12		11	13	Karl	Powell		14-11	3rd	5.5
5-3	At Col.	L	7-16		12	24	Astacio	Irabu		14-12	3rd	5.5
5-5	At Mil.	W	10-2		14	7	Vazquez	Bere		15-12	2nd	5.5
5-6	At Mil.	W	3-2		11	4	Telford	Weathers	Urbina	16-12	2nd	4.5
5-7	At Mil.	L	4-9		8	13	Haynes	Hermanson		16-13	2nd	4.5
5-9	Phi.	W	3-2		8	6	Kline	Gomes		17-13	2nd	4.0
5-10	Phi.	L	0-8		4	13	Person	Vazquez		17-14	2nd	4.0
5-11	Phi.	L	4-6		8	8	Wolf	Pavano	Gomes	17-15	2nd	4.0
5-12	Chi.	W	8-3		10	7	Thurman	Wood	Hermanson	18-15	2nd	4.0
5-13	Chi.	L	1-2		8	6	Lieber	Armas		18-16	3rd	5.0
5-14	Chi.	W	16-15		16	21	Hermanson	Aguilera		19-16	2nd	5.0
5-16	Ari.	W	2-0		5	5	Vazquez	Johnson	Hermanson	20-16	2nd	5.0
5-17	Ari.	W	10-2		14	6	Pavano	Reynoso		21-16	2nd	5.0
5-18	Ari.	L	6-8		8	10	Kim	Telford		21-17	2nd	6.0
5-19	Hou.	W	3-2	(10)	8	8	Hermanson	Slusarski		22-17	2nd	5.0
5-20	Hou.	W	8-7		15	10	Irabu	Elarton	Hermanson	23-17	2nd	5.0
5-21	Hou.	W	8-3		11	7	Vazquez	Lima		24-17	2nd	5.0
5-23	At S.F	W	3-2		11	8	Pavano	Rueter	Hermanson	25-17	2nd	4.0
5-24	At S.F	L	0-18		7	18	Estes	Thurman		25-18	2nd	5.0
5-25	At S.F	L	1-4		6	9	Hernandez	Armas	Nen	25-19	2nd	6.0
5-26	At S.D.	L	2-6		6	11	Whiteside	Irabu		25-20	2nd	6.0
5-27	At S.D.	L	2-4		7	10	Wall	Kline	Hoffman	25-21	3rd	7.0
5-28	At S.D.	L	3-4		8	6	Walker	Pavano	Hoffman	25-22	3rd	7.0
5-30	At Cin.	L	2-4		3	5	Fernandez	Armas	Williamson	25-23	3rd	8.5
5-31	At Cin.	W	10-4		16	6	Johnson	Parris		26-23	3rd	8.0
6-1	At Cin.	W	9-7		17	16	Vazquez	Villone	Kline	27-23	3rd	7.0
6-2	Bal.	W	5-3		9	9	Pavano	Johnson	Kline	28-23	3rd	6.0
6-3	Bal.	W	7-4		12	9	Lira	Rapp	Kline	29-23	3rd	6.0
6-4	Bal.	W	1-0		6	3	Armas	Ponson	Kline	30-23	2nd	5.0
6-5	N.Y. (AL)	W	6-4		8	13	Johnson	Cone	Kline	31-23	2nd	4.0
6-6	N.Y. (AL)	L	1-8		3	13	Grimsley	Vazquez		31-24	2nd	5.0
6-7	N.Y. (AL)	L	2-7		4	9	Hernandez	Pavano		31-25	2nd	5.0
6-9	At Tor.	L	3-13		8	16	Carpenter	Tucker		31-26	3rd	6.0
6-10	At Tor.	W	11-2		14	6	Armas	Escobar		32-26	3rd	6.0
6-11	At Tor.	L	3-8		13	9	Koch	Mota		32-27	3rd	6.0
6-12	At Mil.	L	1-8		5	12	Bere	Vazquez		32-28	3rd	7.0
6-13	At Mil.	W	9-4		12	10	Pavano	Woodard		33-28	3rd	6.0
6-14	At Mil.	L	2-11		8	12	Wright	Johnson		33-29	3rd	7.0
6-16	At Chi.	L	8-9		8	9	Van Poppel	Armas	Aguilera	33-30	3rd	6.5
6-17	At Chi.	L	0-1		8	4	Rain	Hermanson	Aguilera	33-31	3rd	6.5
6-18	At Chi.	W	4-3	(11)	9	9	Telford	Garibay	Rigby	34-31	3rd	6.5
6-19	Pit.	W	2-1		7	6	Pavano	Loiselle	Kline	35-31	3rd	5.5
6-20	Pit.	L	1-2		6	4	Benson	Johnson	Williams	35-32	3rd	6.5
6-21	Pit.	L	3-8		9	10	Cordova	Armas	Peters	35-33	3rd	6.5
6-22	Pit.	W	6-5		8	11	Hermanson	Ritchie	Telford	36-33	3rd	6.5
6-23	Phi.	L	6-13		9	17	Coggin	Vazquez		36-34	3rd	7.5
6-24	Phi.	L	1-8		7	11	Wolf	Pavano		36-35	3rd	7.5
6-25	Phi.	W	3-1		9	8	Johnson	Byrd	Kline	37-35	3rd	7.5
6-27	Atl.	W	6-4		9	5	Armas	Glavine	Kline	38-35	3rd	6.5
6-28	Atl.	L	4-7		12	10	Mulholland	Hermanson	Ligtenberg	38-36	3rd	7.5
6-30	Fla.	L	4-5		7	12	Almanza	Kline	Alfonseca	38-37	3rd	8.0
7-1	Fla.	L	5-6		13	10	Dempster	Johnson	Alfonseca	38-38	3rd	8.0
7-2	Fla.	L	1-2		4	5	Cornelius	Santana	Alfonseca	38-39	4th	9.0
7-3	At Atl.	W	17-1		18	6	Armas	Mulholland		39-39	4th	8.0
7-4	At Atl.	L	3-7		7	10	Maddux	Hermanson		39-40	4th	9.0

HIGHLIGHTS

High point: Having dropped below .500 for the first time since the opening week, the Expos went to Atlanta and posted a surprising 17-1 victory behind young Tony Armas Jr. After losing Game 2 of the series to Greg Maddux, the Expos rebounded to win the next two and lift their head above .500 for the last time.
Low point: Only one win away from matching their 1999 win total (68), the Expos lost their final nine games and faded quietly into the sunset. The final six defeats were administered on the road by the Marlins and the Mets.
Turning point: The club was eight games over .500 after beating the Yankees on June 5 at Olympic Stadium. But the roof began caving in on a promising season the next day when the Yanks battered the Montreal bullpen for six runs in the eighth inning of an 8-1 loss. It was all downhill after that.
Most valuable player: Vladimir Guerrero continued to rewrite the club's record book as he batted .345 with 44 home runs and 123 RBIs. Guerrero joined Joe DiMaggio, Ted Williams and Jimmie Foxx as the only players to bat .300 with 35 homers and 100 RBIs in three straight seasons before age 25.
Most valuable pitcher: In the absence of a bona fide No. 1 starter, 24-year-old Javier Vazquez emerged as the rotation leader. Vazquez led the team in wins (11), innings ($217^2/_3$), strikeouts (196), ERA (4.05) and starts (33) and was dominant for extended periods.
Most improved player: Second baseman Jose Vidro, shaking off the challenge of veteran Mickey Morandini, recorded unexpectedly high marks for homers (24), runs (101) and RBIs (97) in addition to batting .331.
Most pleasant surprise: Pitching through a suspected rotator cuff tear, 24-year-old Scott Strickland enjoyed a breakout second half and became the late-season closer, converting 9 of 12 save opportunities and finishing with a scoreless streak of $15^2/_3$ innings. A September MRI showed no tear in his shoulder.
Key injuries: Starters Carl Pavano (triceps), Mike Thurman (elbow), Armas (elbow, shoulder) and Hideki Irabu (elbow, knee) all went down for extended periods. ... Closer Ugueth Urbina (elbow) appeared in only 13 games. ... Lefty specialist Graeme Lloyd (shoulder) didn't throw a pitch for his new team after May surgery. ... Workhorse reliever Anthony Telford (rotator cuff) didn't appear in a game after September 8.
Notable: Vladimir Guerrero set team records in eight categories and finished in the top five in nine N.L. categories. He led both leagues in intentional walks with 23. ... Vladimir Guerrero and Vidro combined for 397 hits, a team record for two hitters combined. ... Armas was dominant against the Braves, going 3-0 with a 2.95 ERA. ... Steve Kline's 83 appearances tied Chicago White Sox reliever Kelly Wunsch for the major league lead. He has a two-year total of 165.

—STEPHANIE MYLES

MISCELLANEOUS

RECORDS

2000 regular-season record: 67-95 (4th in N.L. East); 37-44 at home; 30-51 on road; 28-40 vs. East; 23-27 vs. Central; 16-28 vs. West; 19-24 vs. lefthanded starters; 48-71 vs. righthanded starters; 21-39 on grass; 46-56 on turf; 18-29 in daytime; 49-66 at night; 23-24 in one-run games; 4-4 in extra-inning games; 0-1-1 in doubleheaders.
Team record past five years: 366-444 (.452, ranks 14th in league in that span).

TEAM LEADERS

Batting average: Vladimir Guerrero (.345).
At-bats: Jose Vidro (606).
Runs: Vladimir Guerrero, Jose Vidro (101).
Hits: Jose Vidro (200).
Total Bases: Vladimir Guerrero (379).
Doubles: Jose Vidro (51).
Triples: Vladimir Guerrero (11).
Home runs: Vladimir Guerrero (44).
Runs batted in: Vladimir Guerrero (123).
Stolen bases: Peter Bergeron (11).
Slugging percentage: Vladimir Guerrero (.664).
On-base percentage: Vladimir Guerrero (.410).
Wins: Dustin Hermanson (12).
Earned-run average: Javier Vazquez (4.05).
Complete games: Dustin Hermanson, Javier Vazquez (2).
Shutouts: Dustin Hermanson, Javier Vazquez (1).
Saves: Steve Kline (14).
Innings pitched: Javier Vazquez (217.2).
Strikeouts: Javier Vazquez (196).

Date	Opp.	Res.	Score	(inn.*)	Hits	Opp. hits	Winning pitcher	Losing pitcher	Save	Record	Pos.	GB
7-5	At Atl.	W	6-5		13	10	Vazquez	Millwood	Kline	40-40	4th	8.0
7-6	At Atl.	W	4-2		14	6	Johnson	Burkett	Kline	41-40	T3rd	7.0
7-7	Tor.	W	10-5		12	10	Lira	Quantrill		42-40	3rd	7.0
7-8	Tor.	L	3-6		6	7	Wells	Armas	Koch	42-41	T3rd	8.0
7-9	Tor.	L	3-13		8	18	Castillo	Hermanson		42-42	4th	8.0
7-13	At T.B.	L	4-6		8	14	Mecir	Lira	Hernandez	42-43	4th	9.0
7-14	At T.B.	L	5-8		12	11	Lopez	Armas	Hernandez	42-44	4th	10.0
7-15	At T.B.	W	4-1		13	9	Hermanson	Trachsel	Kline	43-44	4th	10.0
7-16	At Bos.	L	2-5		4	8	Wakefield	Johnson	Wasdin	43-45	4th	11.0
7-17	At Bos.	L	3-7		7	9	Pichardo	Telford		43-46	4th	11.0
7-18	At Bos.	L	1-3		6	9	P. Martinez	Vazquez	Lowe	43-47	4th	12.0
7-19	N.Y.	L	3-5		9	11	Mahomes	Kline	Benitez	43-48	4th	12.5
7-20	N.Y.	W	4-1		8	7	Hermanson	Hampton	Strickland	44-48	4th	12.0
7-21	At Fla.	W	7-3		9	8	Thurman	Smith		45-48	4th	12.0
7-22	At Fla.	W	17-7		19	7	Johnson	Cornelius		46-48	4th	11.0
7-23	At Fla.	W	7-6		17	11	Vazquez	Sanchez	Strickland	47-48	3rd	11.0
7-25	At N.Y.	L	0-5		5	12	Rusch	Hermanson		47-49	3rd	12.0
7-27†	At N.Y.	L	8-9		9	15	Franco	Strickland	Benitez	47-50		
7-27‡	At N.Y.	L	3-4		7	7	Hampton	Irabu		47-51	4th	13.0
7-28	Cin.	L	3-8		8	12	Dessens	Johnson		47-52	4th	14.0
7-29	Cin.	L	3-4	(11)	11	11	Graves	Santana		47-53	4th	15.0
7-30	Cin.	L	4-7		8	11	Bell	Hermanson	Graves	47-54	4th	16.0
7-31	StL.	L	0-4		6	10	Kile	Thurman		47-55	4th	16.5
8-1	StL.	W	4-0		9	5	Moore	Ankiel		48-55	4th	16.5
8-2	StL.	L	7-10		11	11	Hentgen	Johnson		48-56	4th	16.5
8-4	At Hou.	L	6-7		14	12	Green	Kline	Dotel	48-57	4th	17.0
8-5	At Hou.	W	10-9	(10)	14	15	Strickland	Valdes	Kline	49-57	4th	16.0
8-6	At Hou.	L	1-8		4	12	Elarton	Thurman		49-58	4th	17.0
8-7	At Ari.	L	2-5		8	9	Schilling	Moore		49-59	4th	17.0
8-8	At Ari.	W	9-3		16	9	Lira	Anderson		50-59	4th	17.0
8-9	At Ari.	W	4-3		15	8	Strickland	Guzman	Telford	51-59	4th	16.0
8-11	Col.	L	3-10		11	13	Bohanon	Hermanson		51-60	4th	17.0
8-12	Col.	L	2-14		6	22	Yoshii	Moore		51-61	4th	18.0
8-13	Col.	L	3-5		7	12	Chouinard	Strickland	White	51-62	4th	18.0
8-14	Col.	L	3-4		10	12	House	Strickland	Jimenez	51-63	4th	19.0
8-15	S.F	L	7-9		9	11	del Toro	Lira	Nen	51-64	4th	20.0
8-16	S.F	L	1-4		8	7	Gardner	Hermanson	Nen	51-65	4th	21.0
8-17	S.F	L	4-5		7	11	Estes	Moore	Rodriguez	51-66	4th	21.5
8-18	At S.D.	W	6-3		11	7	Thurman	Clement	Strickland	52-66	4th	20.5
8-19	At S.D.	L	3-4	(11)	8	12	Walker	Santana		52-67	4th	20.5
8-20	At S.D.	L	4-5		10	7	Witasick	Lira	Hoffman	52-68	4th	21.5
8-21	At L.A.	W	4-1		9	8	Hermanson	Herges	Strickland	53-68	4th	21.5
8-22	At L.A.	L	6-14		13	16	Adams	Santana		53-69	4th	21.5
8-23	At L.A.	L	1-5		4	6	Brown	Thurman		53-70	4th	22.5
8-24	At L.A.	L	0-7		5	11	Park	Vazquez		53-71	4th	22.5
8-25	Hou.	L	1-3		8	7	Holt	Lira	Dotel	53-72	4th	23.5
8-26	Hou.	W	5-4		9	10	Hermanson	Lima	Kline	54-72	4th	22.5
8-27	Hou.	L	3-7		6	10	Elarton	Moore		54-73	5th	22.5
8-28	Ari.	W	9-5		14	9	Thurman	Schilling	Telford	55-73	5th	21.5
8-29	Ari.	L	7-8		12	8	Plesac	Forster	Mantei	55-74	5th	21.5
8-30	Ari.	L	0-7		5	10	Johnson	Lira		55-75	5th	22.5
9-1	At Cin.	L	2-8		7	10	Bell	Hermanson		55-76	5th	22.5
9-2	At Cin.	W	9-5		12	6	Lira	Villone		56-76	4th	22.0
9-3	At Cin.	L	1-8		11	12	Parris	Thurman		56-77	4th	22.0
9-4	At StL.	L	2-4		9	6	Hentgen	Vazquez	Veres	56-78	4th	22.5
9-5	At StL.	L	6-7		4	7	Reames	Santana	Timlin	56-79	4th	23.5
9-6	At StL.	W	7-2		12	8	Hermanson	Stephenson		57-79	4th	23.5
9-7	At StL.	L	1-6		5	11	Kile	Armas		57-80	4th	24.5
9-8	At Atl.	L	2-3		10	9	Ashby	Moore	Rocker	57-81	4th	25.5
9-9	At Atl.	W	7-5	(12)	14	15	Santana	Seelbach		58-81	4th	24.5
9-10	At Atl.	W	4-0		7	6	Vazquez	Glavine		59-81	4th	23.5
9-11†	At Phi.	L	2-5		7	8	Politte	Hermanson	Brantley	59-82		
9-11‡	At Phi.	W	7-6		12	10	Mota	Padilla	Strickland	60-82	4th	23.5
9-12	At Phi.	W	1-0		3	3	Armas	Telemaco	Strickland	61-82	4th	22.5
9-13	At Phi.	L	5-15		8	19	Chen	Lira		61-83	4th	23.5
9-14	N.Y.	L	4-10		10	12	Rusch	Thurman		61-84	4th	24.5
9-15	N.Y.	W	4-3		10	9	Vazquez	Wendell	Strickland	62-84	4th	23.5
9-16	N.Y.	L	4-10		11	14	Reed	Hermanson		62-85	4th	24.5
9-17	N.Y.	W	5-0		7	4	Armas	B.J. Jones		63-85	4th	24.5
9-18	Fla.	W	11-4		9	6	Lira	Sanchez		64-85	4th	24.5
9-19	Fla.	L	1-3		5	7	Dempster	Thurman	Alfonseca	64-86	4th	25.5
9-20	Fla.	W	4-2		9	9	Vazquez	Cornelius	Strickland	65-86	4th	24.5
9-21	Fla.	W	10-3		14	7	Hermanson	Burnett		66-86	4th	24.0
9-22	Atl.	W	6-4		9	6	Armas	Millwood	Strickland	67-86	4th	23.0
9-23	Atl.	L	0-10		5	9	Maddux	Lira		67-87	4th	24.0
9-24	Atl.	L	5-14		10	21	Ashby	Thurman		67-88	4th	25.0
9-25	Atl.	L	0-6		8	12	Glavine	Vazquez		67-89	4th	26.0
9-26	At Fla.	L	4-5	(10)	8	8	Alfonseca	Kline		67-90	4th	27.0
9-27	At Fla.	L	3-6		5	9	Burnett	Armas	Alfonseca	67-91	4th	27.0
9-28	At Fla.	L	4-7		8	9	Penny	Lira	Alfonseca	67-92	4th	27.0
9-29	At N.Y.	L	2-11		7	11	Hampton	Thurman		67-93	4th	27.0
9-30	At N.Y.	L	2-4		4	7	Wendell	Vazquez	Benitez	67-94	4th	28.0
10-1	At N.Y.	L	2-3	(13)	9	9	Mahomes	Powell		67-95	4th	28.0

Monthly records: April (14-9), May (12-14), June (12-14), July (9-18), August (8-20), September (12-19), October (0-1).
*Innings, if other than nine. † First game of a doubleheader. ‡ Second game of a doubleheader.

MEMORABLE GAMES

June 6 at Montreal

Javier Vazquez worked six inspired innings against the New York Yankees, giving up only two runs. But Guillermo Mota, Matt Skrmetta and Felipe Lira,all of whom opened the season in the minor leagues, were pounded over the next three innings in a tough 8-1 loss. The defeat, which pointed out the vulnerability of the Expos' thin staff, began a 2-8 slide that removed the luster of a 31-24 start. .

Yankees	AB	R	H	BI	Montreal	AB	R	H	BI
Ledee, lf	4	1	2	1	Bergeron, cf	3	0	0	0
Jeter, ss	4	1	0	1	Mordecai, 3b	3	1	1	1
Delgado, ss	0	0	0	0	White, lf	3	0	0	0
O'Neill, rf	4	0	1	1	Jones, lf	0	0	0	0
Spencer, pr-rf	0	1	0	0	V. Guerrero, rf	3	0	0	0
Williams, cf	4	1	2	4	W. Guerrero, rf	1	0	0	0
Martinez, 1b	4	1	2	1	Stevens, 1b	3	0	0	0
Posada, c	5	0	0	0	Blum, 2b-ss	4	0	0	0
Brosius, 3b	5	2	4	0	Cabrera, ss	3	0	0	0
Bellinger, 2b	2	0	1	0	Skrmetta, p	0	0	0	0
Grimsley, p	1	0	0	0	Lira, p	0	0	0	0
Jose, ph	1	0	0	0	Webster, c	3	0	0	0
Stanton, p	1	1	1	0	Schneider, c	0	0	0	0
Erdos, p	1	0	0	0	Vazquez, p	2	0	2	0
					Mota, p	0	0	0	0
					Coquillette, 2b	1	0	0	0
Totals	**36**	**8**	**13**	**8**	**Totals**	**29**	**1**	**3**	**1**

Yankees ....0 1 0 1 0 0 0 6 0—8 13 1
Montreal ....0 0 1 0 0 0 0 0 0—1 3 0

E—Jeter (6). DP—Montreal 2. LOB—Yankees 11, Montreal 5. 2B—Williams (14), Brosius (6), Vazquez (2). HR—Williams (12), Martinez (6), Mordecai (3). SB—Ledee (5), Martinez (2). CS—O'Neill (5), .White (1). S—Ledee. SH—Bellinger. HBP—Martinez by Vazquez.

Yankees	IP	H	R	ER	BB	SO
Grimsley (W 2-1)	5	3	1	1	3	3
Stanton	2.2	0	0	0	1	5
Erdos	1.1	0	0	0	0	1

Montreal	IP	H	R	ER	BB	SO
Vazquez (L 6-2)	6	7	2	2	4	7
Mota	1.2	3	3	3	0	1
Skrmetta	0	0	2	2	2	0
Lira	1.1	3	1	1	1	1

Skrmetta pitched to 3 batters in 8th. WP—Skrmetta. U—HP, Emmel. 1B, Davis. 2B, Joyce. 3B, Rieker. T—3:33. A—24,453.

July 18 at Boston

Former Expo Pedro Martinez, the only Cy Young Award winner, in team history, struck out 12 and allowed only five hits in eight innings of a highly anticipated reunion victory at Boston's Fenway Park. Martinez won a pitcher's duel against Javier Vazquez, 3-1, when Darren Lewis squeezed home the winning run in the seventh inning. Martinez pitched Vladimir Guerrero, the player he calls his little brother, very carefully, walking him twice and striking him out twice.

Montreal	AB	R	H	BI	Boston	AB	R	H	BI
Bergeron, cf	4	0	1	0	Offerman, 1b	4	0	1	1
W.Guerrero, rf	4	0	1	0	Frye, 2b	4	0	0	0
Vidro, 2b	4	0	0	0	Daubach, dh	4	0	0	0
V.Guerrero, dh	2	0	0	0	Garciaparra, ss	3	1	1	0
de la Rosa, pr-dh	0	0	0	0	O'Leary, lf	4	0	3	1
Stevens, 1b	4	0	0	0	Varitek, c	4	0	0	0
Blum, ss	4	1	1	0	Gilkey, rf	3	1	2	0
Seguignol, lf	4	0	1	1	Sprague, 3b	3	1	1	0
Barrett, 3b	4	0	1	0	Alexander, 3b	0	0	0	0
Webster, c	2	0	1	0	Lewis, cf	2	0	1	1
Tracy, ph	1	0	0	0					
Totals	**33**	**1**	**6**	**1**	**Totals**	**31**	**3**	**9**	**3**

Montreal ....0 0 0 0 0 0 1 0 0—1 6 1
Boston ....0 0 1 0 0 0 1 1 x—3 9 1

E—Stevens (9), Frye (2). DP—Montreal 2, Boston 1. LOB—Montreal 8, Boston 6. 2B—Bergeron (15), Seguignol (2), Garciaparra (31), O'Leary (15), Gilkey (3). 3B—Blum (1). SH—Lewis.

Montreal	IP	H	R	ER	BB	SO
Vazquez (L 7-5)	8	9	3	3	1	5

Boston	IP	H	R	ER	BB	SO
Martinez (W 10-3)	8	5	1	1	3	12
Lowe (S 21)	1	1	0	0	0	0

U—HP, Rieker. 1B, Emmel. 2B, Davis. 3B, Guccione. T—2:39. A—32,629.

INDIVIDUAL STATISTICS

BATTING

Name	G	TPA	AB	R	H	TB	2B	3B	HR	RBI	Avg.	Obp.	Slg.	SH	SF	HP	BB	IBB	SO	SB	CS	GDP	vs RHP AB	vs RHP Avg.	vs RHP HR	vs RHP RBI	vs LHP AB	vs LHP Avg.	vs LHP HR	vs LHP RBI
Vidro, Jose	153	663	606	101	200	327	51	2	24	97	.330	.379	.540	0	6	2	49	4	69	5	4	17	445	.315	17	72	161	.373	7	25
Guerrero, Vladimir	154	641	571	101	197	379	28	11	44	123	.345	.410	.664	0	4	8	58	23	74	9	10	15	438	.336	32	91	133	.376	12	32
Bergeron, Peter	148	592	518	80	127	181	25	7	5	31	.245	.320	.349	14	2	0	58	0	100	11	13	4	431	.251	5	29	87	.218	0	2
Stevens, Lee	123	501	449	60	119	216	27	2	22	75	.265	.337	.481	0	2	2	48	6	105	0	0	10	335	.260	15	47	114	.281	7	28
Cabrera, Orlando	125	454	422	47	100	166	25	1	13	55	.237	.279	.393	3	3	1	25	3	28	4	4	12	317	.221	11	46	105	.286	2	9
Blum, Geoff	124	379	343	40	97	154	20	2	11	45	.283	.335	.449	3	4	3	26	2	60	1	4	4	271	.280	6	33	72	.292	5	12
White, Rondell	75	322	290	52	89	146	24	0	11	54	.307	.370	.503	0	2	2	28	0	67	5	1	4	226	.296	8	43	64	.344	3	11
Guerrero, Wilton	127	314	288	30	77	94	7	2	2	23	.267	.312	.326	6	1	0	19	0	41	8	1	6	182	.253	0	10	106	.292	2	13
Widger, Chris	86	312	281	31	67	124	17	2	12	34	.238	.311	.441	0	1	1	29	3	61	1	2	5	211	.227	8	23	70	.271	4	11
Barrett, Michael	89	297	271	28	58	78	15	1	1	22	.214	.277	.288	1	1	1	23	5	35	0	1	7	190	.237	1	17	81	.160	0	5
Tracy, Andy	83	218	192	29	50	93	8	1	11	32	.260	.339	.484	0	2	2	22	1	61	1	0	3	162	.272	10	27	30	.200	1	5
Mordecai, Mike	86	183	169	20	48	76	16	0	4	16	.284	.335	.450	1	0	1	12	0	34	2	2	1	101	.267	4	11	68	.309	0	5
Jones, Terry	108	181	168	30	42	54	8	2	0	13	.250	.292	.321	3	0	0	10	1	32	7	2	3	94	.255	0	7	74	.243	0	6
Seguignol, Fernando	76	175	162	22	45	83	8	0	10	22	.278	.326	.512	0	1	3	9	0	46	0	1	5	81	.198	4	10	81	.358	6	12
Bradley, Milton	42	172	154	20	34	50	8	1	2	15	.221	.288	.325	1	1	1	14	0	32	2	1	3	108	.204	1	6	46	.261	1	9
Schneider, Brian	45	123	115	6	27	33	6	0	0	11	.235	.276	.287	0	1	0	7	2	24	0	1	1	93	.204	0	9	22	.364	0	2
Webster, Lenny	39	87	81	6	17	20	3	0	0	5	.210	.264	.247	0	0	0	6	1	14	0	0	5	52	.212	0	3	29	.207	0	2
de la Rosa, Tomas	32	77	66	7	19	30	3	1	2	9	.288	.365	.455	3	0	1	7	0	11	2	1	2	36	.361	1	7	30	.200	1	2
Vazquez, Javier	33	80	65	4	15	17	2	0	0	1	.231	.254	.262	13	0	0	2	0	15	0	0	0	43	.256	0	0	22	.182	0	1
Coquillette, Trace	34	67	59	6	12	19	4	0	1	8	.203	.284	.322	0	1	0	7	0	19	0	0	2	41	.171	1	4	18	.278	0	4
Hermanson, Dustin	38	65	55	1	8	10	2	0	0	1	.145	.175	.182	8	0	0	2	0	21	0	0	0	47	.149	0	1	8	.125	0	0
Pavano, Carl	15	38	35	2	5	6	1	0	0	0	.143	.143	.171	3	0	0	0	0	16	0	0	0	19	.105	0	0	16	.188	0	0
Armas Jr., Tony	17	30	26	1	1	1	0	0	0	1	.038	.074	.038	3	0	0	1	0	12	0	0	0	21	.000	0	0	5	.200	0	1
Thurman, Mike	17	32	24	3	1	1	0	0	0	0	.042	.115	.042	6	0	0	2	0	17	0	0	0	20	.050	0	0	4	.000	0	0
Johnson, Mike	41	26	22	1	4	4	0	0	0	3	.182	.217	.182	3	0	0	1	0	8	0	0	1	16	.188	0	2	6	.167	0	1
O'Brien, Charlie	9	21	19	1	4	8	1	0	1	2	.211	.286	.421	0	0	0	2	1	7	0	0	0	15	.200	0	0	4	.250	1	2
Lira, Felipe	54	21	19	3	4	10	0	0	2	3	.211	.200	.526	1	1	0	0	0	13	0	0	0	11	.091	0	0	8	.375	2	3
Irabu, Hideki	11	18	16	1	2	2	0	0	0	1	.125	.125	.125	2	0	0	0	0	7	0	0	1	13	.154	0	1	3	.000	0	0
Valera, Yohanny	7	13	10	1	0	0	0	0	0	1	.000	.167	.000	1	0	1	1	0	5	0	0	0	6	.000	0	0	4	.000	0	1
Moore, Trey	8	11	8	0	1	1	0	0	0	0	.125	.222	.125	2	0	0	1	0	2	0	0	0	7	.143	0	0	1	.000	0	0
Santana, Julio	36	7	7	0	0	0	0	0	0	0	.000	.000	.000	0	0	0	0	0	4	0	0	0	4	.000	0	0	3	.000	0	0
Powell, Jeremy	11	5	5	1	3	4	1	0	0	1	.600	.600	.800	0	0	0	0	0	1	0	0	0	2	.500	0	0	3	.667	0	1
Nunnari, Talmadge	18	12	5	2	1	1	0	0	0	1	.200	.583	.200	0	1	0	6	1	2	0	0	0	3	.333	0	1	2	.000	0	0
Telford, Anthony	64	3	2	0	0	0	0	0	0	0	.000	.000	.000	1	0	0	0	0	0	0	0	0	1	.000	0	0	1	.000	0	0
Kline, Steve	83	2	2	0	0	0	0	0	0	0	.000	.000	.000	0	0	0	0	0	1	0	0	0	0	.000	0	0	2	.000	0	0
Strickland, Scott	49	2	2	0	0	0	0	0	0	0	.000	.000	.000	0	0	0	0	0	2	0	0	0	1	.000	0	0	1	.000	0	0
Downs, Scott	1	2	2	0	0	0	0	0	0	0	.000	.000	.000	0	0	0	0	0	0	0	0	0	0	.000	0	0	2	.000	0	0
Tucker, T.J.	2	1	1	1	1	1	0	0	0	0	1.000	1.000	1.000	0	0	0	0	0	0	0	0	0	1	1.000	0	0	0	.000	0	0
Batista, Miguel	4	2	1	0	0	0	0	0	0	0	.000	.500	.000	0	0	0	1	0	0	0	0	0	1	.000	0	0	0	.000	0	0
Urbina, Ugueth	13	1	1	0	0	0	0	0	0	0	.000	.000	.000	0	0	0	0	0	1	0	0	0	1	.000	0	0	0	.000	0	0
Rigby, Brad	6	1	1	0	0	0	0	0	0	0	.000	.000	.000	0	0	0	0	0	0	0	0	0	1	.000	0	0	0	.000	0	0
Mota, Guillermo	29	1	1	0	0	0	0	0	0	0	.000	.000	.000	0	0	0	0	0	0	0	0	0	0	.000	0	0	1	.000	0	0
Blank, Matt	13	1	1	0	0	0	0	0	0	0	.000	.000	.000	0	0	0	0	0	1	0	0	0	0	.000	0	0	1	.000	0	0
Poole, Jim	5	0	0	0	0	0	0	0	0	0	.000	.000	.000	0	0	0	0	0	0	0	0	0	0	.000	0	0	0	.000	0	0
Spencer, Sean	8	0	0	0	0	0	0	0	0	0	.000	.000	.000	0	0	0	0	0	0	0	0	0	0	.000	0	0	0	.000	0	0
Skrmetta, Matt	6	0	0	0	0	0	0	0	0	0	.000	.000	.000	0	0	0	0	0	0	0	0	0	0	.000	0	0	0	.000	0	0
Moraga, David	3	0	0	0	0	0	0	0	0	0	.000	.000	.000	0	0	0	0	0	0	0	0	0	0	.000	0	0	0	.000	0	0
Forster, Scott	42	0	0	0	0	0	0	0	0	0	.000	.000	.000	0	0	0	0	0	0	0	0	0	0	.000	0	0	0	.000	0	0
Lara, Yovanny	6	0	0	0	0	0	0	0	0	0	.000	.000	.000	0	0	0	0	0	0	0	0	0	0	.000	0	0	0	.000	0	0

Players with more than one N.L. team

Name	G	TPA	AB	R	H	TB	2B	3B	HR	RBI	Avg.	Obp.	Slg.	SH	SF	HP	BB	IBB	SO	SB	CS	GDP	vs RHP AB	vs RHP Avg.	vs RHP HR	vs RHP RBI	vs LHP AB	vs LHP Avg.	vs LHP HR	vs LHP RBI
Downs, Chi.-Mon.	19	34	28	2	2	2	0	0	0	1	.071	.133	.071	4	0	0	2	0	10	0	0	0	15	.133	0	1	13	.000	0	0
Moraga, Mon.-Col.	4	0	0	0	0	0	0	0	0	0	.000	.000	.000	0	0	0	0	0	0	0	0	0	0	.000	0	0	0	.000	0	0
Skrmetta, Mon.-Pit.	14	2	2	0	0	0	0	0	0	0	.000	.000	.000	0	0	0	0	0	1	0	0	0	2	.000	0	0	0	.000	0	0
White, Mon.-Chi.	94	396	357	59	111	176	26	0	13	61	.311	.374	.493	0	2	4	33	0	79	5	3	4	283	.304	10	50	74	.338	3	11

PITCHING

Name	W	L	Pct.	ERA	IP	H	R	ER	HR	SH	SF	HB	BB	IBB	SO	G	GS	CG	ShO	GF	Sv	vs. RH AB	vs. RH Avg.	vs. RH HR	vs. RH RBI	vs. LH AB	vs. LH Avg.	vs. LH HR	vs. LH RBI
Vazquez, Javier	11	9	.550	4.05	217.2	247	104	98	24	11	3	5	61	10	196	33	33	2	1	0	0	471	.291	17	57	394	.279	7	38
Hermanson, Dustin	12	14	.462	4.77	198.0	226	128	105	26	10	9	4	75	5	94	38	30	2	1	7	4	460	.270	9	51	318	.321	17	60
Lira, Felipe	5	8	.385	5.40	101.2	129	71	61	11	3	9	4	36	6	51	53	7	0	0	8	0	262	.309	6	49	154	.312	5	28
Johnson, Mike	5	6	.455	6.39	101.1	107	73	72	18	4	2	9	53	1	70	41	13	0	0	5	0	220	.245	7	35	178	.298	11	37
Pavano, Carl	8	4	.667	3.06	97.0	89	40	33	8	4	3	8	34	1	64	15	15	0	0	0	0	186	.188	1	10	173	.312	7	22
Armas Jr., Tony	7	9	.438	4.36	95.0	74	49	46	10	7	3	3	50	2	59	17	17	0	0	0	0	197	.183	4	15	143	.266	6	22
Thurman, Mike	4	9	.308	6.42	88.1	112	69	63	9	5	6	3	46	4	52	17	17	0	0	0	0	218	.303	6	43	137	.336	3	20
Kline, Steve	1	5	.167	3.50	82.1	88	36	32	8	2	1	3	27	2	64	83	0	0	0	42	14	209	.297	7	33	107	.243	1	12
Telford, Anthony	5	4	.556	3.79	78.1	76	38	33	10	2	4	5	23	1	68	64	0	0	0	18	3	175	.240	3	13	121	.281	7	20
Santana, Julio	1	5	.167	5.67	66.2	69	45	42	11	1	2	2	33	2	58	36	4	0	0	9	0	157	.236	6	21	98	.327	5	18
Irabu, Hideki	2	5	.286	7.24	54.2	77	45	44	9	3	2	1	14	0	42	11	11	0	0	0	0	137	.328	4	19	90	.356	5	19
Strickland, Scott	4	3	.571	3.00	48.0	38	18	16	3	3	3	1	16	2	48	49	0	0	0	20	9	115	.174	1	14	62	.290	2	10
Moore, Trey	1	5	.167	6.62	35.1	55	31	26	7	2	0	4	21	1	24	8	8	0	0	0	0	114	.333	6	23	37	.459	1	6
Forster, Scott	0	1	.000	7.88	32.0	28	31	28	5	2	3	2	25	1	23	42	0	0	0	10	0	77	.195	2	14	45	.289	3	12
Mota, Guillermo	1	1	.500	6.00	30.0	27	21	20	3	1	1	2	12	0	24	29	0	0	0	7	0	69	.246	0	13	41	.244	3	5
Powell, Jeremy	0	3	.000	7.96	26.0	35	27	23	6	2	1	0	9	0	19	11	4	0	0	6	0	63	.270	4	18	46	.391	2	6
Blank, Matt	0	1	.000	5.14	14.0	12	8	8	1	2	1	1	5	1	4	13	0	0	0	3	0	32	.188	0	0	21	.286	1	5
Urbina, Ugueth	0	1	.000	4.05	13.1	11	6	6	1	0	0	0	5	0	22	13	0	0	0	11	8	23	.174	0	3	26	.269	1	4
Batista, Miguel	0	1	.000	14.04	8.1	19	14	13	2	1	1	2	3	0	7	4	0	0	0	0	0	27	.444	1	9	15	.467	1	7
Tucker, T.J.	0	1	.000	11.57	7.0	11	9	9	5	0	0	0	3	0	2	2	2	0	0	0	0	19	.474	3	5	13	.154	2	3
Spencer, Sean	0	0	.000	5.40	6.2	7	4	4	2	0	1	0	3	0	6	8	0	0	0	1	0	17	.294	1	4	7	.286	1	4
Lara, Yovanny	0	0	.000	6.35	5.2	5	4	4	0	0	1	0	8	0	3	6	0	0	0	2	0	14	.286	0	5	6	.167	0	1
Rigby, Brad	0	0	.000	5.06	5.1	8	5	3	0	0	0	1	3	0	2	6	0	0	0	4	1	14	.429	0	7	9	.222	0	2
Skrmetta, Matt	0	0	.000	15.19	5.1	6	10	9	1	0	1	0	6	0	4	6	0	0	0	3	0	11	.182	0	4	11	.364	1	3
Downs, Scott	0	0	.000	9.00	3.0	5	3	3	0	0	0	0	3	0	0	1	1	0	0	0	0	9	.444	0	2	4	.250	0	0
Poole, Jim	0	0	.000	27.00	2.0	8	6	6	1	0	0	0	3	1	3	5	0	0	0	1	0	5	.400	0	0	9	.667	1	4
Moraga, David	0	0	.000	37.80	1.2	6	7	7	0	1	1	0	2	0	2	3	0	0	0	1	0	6	.667	0	5	4	.500	0	3

PITCHERS WITH MORE THAN ONE N.L. TEAM

Name	W	L	Pct.	ERA	IP	H	R	ER	HR	SH	SF	HB	BB	IBB	SO	G	GS	CG	ShO	GF	Sv	vs. RH AB	vs. RH Avg.	vs. RH HR	vs. RH RBI	vs. LH AB	vs. LH Avg.	vs. LH HR	vs. LH RBI
Downs, Chi.-Mon.	4	3	.571	5.29	97.0	122	62	57	13	2	4	5	40	1	63	19	19	0	0	4	0	321	.321	8	40	70	.271	5	12
Moraga, Mon.-Col.	0	0	.000	40.50	2.2	10	12	12	1	1	2	1	2	0	2	4	0	0	0	2	0	11	.727	1	9	5	.400	0	4
Skrmetta, Mon.-Pit.	2	2	.500	11.66	14.2	19	22	19	3	1	1	1	9	0	11	14	0	0	0	1	0	41	.317	2	11	20	.300	1	6

DESIGNATED HITTERS

Name	AB	Avg.	HR	RBI	Name	AB	Avg.	HR	RBI
Guerrero, Wilton	25	.400	0	3	Seguignol, Fernando	4	.000	0	0
Guerrero, Vladimir	6	.000	0	0	de la Rosa, Tomas	0	-	0	0

INDIVIDUAL STATISTICS

FIELDING

FIRST BASEMEN

Player	Pct.	G	PO	A	E	TC	DP
Stevens, Lee	.991	123	1072	85	11	1168	99
Seguignol, Fernando	.987	30	144	11	2	157	16
Tracy, Andy	1.000	28	177	11	0	188	15
Nunnari, Talmadge	1.000	14	23	2	0	25	1
Blum, Geoff	1.000	11	33	2	0	35	2
Mordecai, Mike	.875	3	6	1	1	8	3

SECOND BASEMEN

Player	Pct.	G	PO	A	E	TC	DP
Vidro, Jose	.986	153	260	442	10	712	102
Blum, Geoff	1.000	13	20	26	0	46	6
Mordecai, Mike	1.000	9	8	6	0	14	2
Coquillette, Trace	1.000	8	1	6	0	7	0
Cabrera, Orlando	-	1	0	0	0	0	0
Guerrero, Wilton	-	1	0	0	0	0	0

THIRD BASEMEN

Player	Pct.	G	PO	A	E	TC	DP
Mordecai, Mike	.937	58	21	68	6	95	9
Blum, Geoff	.952	55	26	93	6	125	6
Barrett, Michael	.891	55	23	83	13	119	10
Tracy, Andy	.882	34	10	35	6	51	2
Coquillette, Trace	.958	19	2	21	1	24	2

SHORTSTOPS

Player	Pct.	G	PO	A	E	TC	DP
Cabrera, Orlando	.981	124	167	338	10	515	77
Blum, Geoff	.978	44	43	89	3	135	22
de la Rosa, Tomas	.980	29	39	58	2	99	7
Mordecai, Mike	.952	10	7	13	1	21	2

OUTFIELDERS

Player	Pct.	G	PO	A	E	TC	DP
Guerrero, Vladimir	.969	151	299	12	10	321	3
Bergeron, Peter	.985	146	303	16	5	324	3
Jones, Terry	.971	78	95	4	3	102	0
Guerrero, Wilton	.967	75	115	4	4	123	1
White, Rondell	.994	74	158	4	1	163	1
Bradley, Milton	.979	41	88	6	2	96	0
Seguignol, Fernando	.857	31	17	1	3	21	0
Coquillette, Trace	1.000	2	2	0	0	2	0

CATCHERS

Player	Pct.	G	PO	A	E	TC	DP	PB
Widger, Chris	.985	85	503	38	8	549	4	4
Schneider, Brian	.974	43	205	19	6	230	2	5
Webster, Lenny	1.000	32	126	9	0	135	1	4
Barrett, Michael	.989	28	163	12	2	177	1	5
O'Brien, Charlie	1.000	9	25	2	0	27	0	0
Valera, Yohanny	1.000	7	24	2	0	26	0	1

PITCHERS

Player	Pct.	G	PO	A	E	TC	DP
Kline, Steve	.933	83	4	10	1	15	1
Telford, Anthony	1.000	64	5	9	0	14	1
Lira, Felipe	1.000	53	4	17	0	21	3
Strickland, Scott	.900	49	2	7	1	10	0
Forster, Scott	1.000	42	3	5	0	8	0
Johnson, Mike	.941	41	4	12	1	17	1
Hermanson, Dustin	.925	38	10	27	3	40	2
Santana, Julio	1.000	36	3	10	0	13	1
Vazquez, Javier	.955	33	10	32	2	44	2
Mota, Guillermo	1.000	29	1	3	0	4	1
Armas Jr., Tony	1.000	17	7	12	0	19	1
Thurman, Mike	.800	17	0	12	3	15	0
Pavano, Carl	.909	15	7	13	2	22	1
Blank, Matt	1.000	13	1	1	0	2	0
Urbina, Ugueth	1.000	13	1	0	0	1	0
Irabu, Hideki	1.000	11	2	6	0	8	0
Powell, Jeremy	1.000	11	2	3	0	5	0
Moore, Trey	.800	8	2	2	1	5	0
Spencer, Sean	-	8	0	0	0	0	0
Skrmetta, Matt	.500	6	0	1	1	2	0
Lara, Yovanny	-	6	0	0	0	0	0
Rigby, Brad	-	6	0	0	0	0	0
Poole, Jim	.000	5	0	0	1	1	0
Batista, Miguel	1.000	4	1	0	0	1	0
Moraga, David	-	3	0	0	0	0	0
Tucker, T.J.	1.000	2	0	1	0	1	0
Downs, Scott	-	1	0	0	0	0	0

PITCHING AGAINST EACH CLUB

Pitcher	Ari. W-L	Atl. W-L	Chi. W-L	Cin. W-L	Col. W-L	Fla. W-L	Hou. W-L	L.A. W-L	Mil. W-L	N.Y. W-L	Phi. W-L	Pit. W-L	S.D. W-L	S.F. W-L	StL. W-L	A.L. W-L	Total W-L
Armas Jr., T.	0-0	3-0	0-2	0-1	0-0	0-1	0-0	0-0	0-0	1-0	1-0	0-1	0-0	0-1	0-1	2-2	7-9
Batista, M.	0-0	0-0	0-0	0-0	0-0	0-0	0-0	0-0	0-0	0-0	0-0	0-1	0-0	0-0	0-0	0-0	0-1
Blank, Matt	0-0	0-0	0-1	0-0	0-0	0-0	0-0	0-0	0-0	0-0	0-0	0-0	0-0	0-0	0-0	0-0	0-1
Downs, Scott	0-0	0-0	0-0	0-0	0-0	0-0	0-0	0-0	0-0	0-0	0-0	0-0	0-0	0-0	0-0	0-0	0-0
Forster, Scott	0-1	0-0	0-0	0-0	0-0	0-0	0-0	0-0	0-0	0-0	0-0	0-0	0-0	0-0	0-0	0-0	0-1
Hermanson, D.	0-0	0-2	1-1	0-2	1-2	1-0	2-0	1-1	1-1	1-2	1-1	1-0	0-0	0-1	1-0	1-1	12-14
Irabu, Hideki	0-0	0-0	0-0	0-0	0-1	0-0	1-0	0-1	0-1	0-1	0-0	0-0	1-1	0-0	0-0	0-0	2-5
Johnson, Mike	0-0	1-0	0-0	1-1	0-0	1-1	0-0	0-0	0-1	0-0	1-0	0-1	0-0	0-0	0-1	1-1	5-6
Kline, Steve	0-0	0-0	0-0	0-0	0-0	0-2	0-1	0-0	0-0	0-1	1-0	0-0	0-1	0-0	0-0	0-0	1-5
Lara, Yovanny	0-0	0-0	0-0	0-0	0-0	0-0	0-0	0-0	0-0	0-0	0-0	0-0	0-0	0-0	0-0	0-0	0-0
Lira, Felipe	1-1	0-1	0-0	1-0	0-0	1-1	0-1	0-0	0-0	0-0	0-1	0-0	0-1	0-1	0-0	2-1	5-8
Moore, Trey	0-1	0-1	0-0	0-0	0-1	0-0	0-1	0-0	0-0	0-0	0-0	0-0	0-0	0-1	1-0	0-0	1-5
Moraga, David	0-0	0-0	0-0	0-0	0-0	0-0	0-0	0-0	0-0	0-0	0-0	0-0	0-0	0-0	0-0	0-0	0-0
Mota, G.	0-0	0-0	0-0	0-0	0-0	0-0	0-0	0-0	0-0	0-0	1-0	0-0	0-0	0-0	0-0	0-1	1-1
Pavano, Carl	1-0	0-0	1-0	0-0	1-0	0-0	0-0	1-0	1-0	0-0	0-2	1-0	0-1	1-0	0-0	1-1	8-4
Poole, Jim	0-0	0-0	0-0	0-0	0-0	0-0	0-0	0-0	0-0	0-0	0-0	0-0	0-0	0-0	0-0	0-0	0-0
Powell, J.	0-0	0-0	0-0	0-0	0-1	0-0	0-0	0-0	0-0	0-1	0-0	0-0	0-1	0-0	0-0	0-0	0-3
Rigby, Brad	0-0	0-0	0-0	0-0	0-0	0-0	0-0	0-0	0-0	0-0	0-0	0-0	0-0	0-0	0-0	0-0	0-0
Santana, Julio	0-0	1-0	0-0	0-1	0-0	0-1	0-0	0-1	0-0	0-0	0-0	0-0	0-1	0-0	0-1	0-0	1-5
Skrmetta, M.	0-0	0-0	0-0	0-0	0-0	0-0	0-0	0-0	0-0	0-0	0-0	0-0	0-0	0-0	0-0	0-0	0-0
Spencer, Sean	0-0	0-0	0-0	0-0	0-0	0-0	0-0	0-0	0-0	0-0	0-0	0-0	0-0	0-0	0-0	0-0	0-0
Strickland, S.	1-0	0-0	1-0	0-0	0-2	0-0	1-0	0-0	0-0	0-1	0-0	0-0	0-0	1-0	0-0	0-0	4-3
Telford, A.	0-1	0-0	1-0	0-0	0-0	0-0	0-0	1-0	1-0	0-0	0-1	0-0	1-0	1-1	0-0	0-1	5-4
Thurman, M.	1-0	0-1	1-0	0-1	0-0	1-1	0-1	0-1	0-0	0-2	0-0	0-0	1-0	0-1	0-1	0-0	4-9
Tucker, T.J.	0-0	0-0	0-0	0-0	0-0	0-0	0-0	0-0	0-0	0-0	0-0	0-0	0-0	0-0	0-0	0-1	0-1
Urbina, U.	0-0	0-0	0-0	0-0	0-0	0-0	0-0	0-0	0-0	0-0	0-0	0-1	0-0	0-0	0-0	0-0	0-1
Vazquez, J.	1-0	2-1	0-0	1-0	0-0	2-0	1-0	0-1	2-1	1-1	0-2	1-0	0-0	0-0	0-1	0-2	11-9
Totals	5-4	7-6	5-4	3-6	2-7	6-7	5-4	3-5	5-4	3-9	5-7	3-4	3-6	3-6	2-5	7-11	67-95

INTERLEAGUE: Pavano 1-0, Lira 1-0, Armas Jr. 1-0 vs. Orioles; Johnson 0-1, Telford 0-1, Vazquez 0-1 vs. Red Sox; Johnson 1-0, Vazquez 0-1, Pavano 0-1 vs. Yankees; Armas Jr. 1-1, Lira 1-0, Tucker 0-1, Hermanson 0-1, Mota 0-1 vs. Blue Jays; Hermanson 1-0, Lira 0-1, Armas Jr. 0-1 vs. Devil Rays. Total: 7-11.

MISCELLANEOUS

HOME RUNS BY PARK

At Arizona (4): Guerrero 3, Stevens 1.
At Atlanta (10): Guerrero 2, Vidro 2, Cabrera 2, Tracy 2, White 1, Seguignol 1.
At Boston (2): Guerrero 1, Seguignol 1.
At Chicago (NL) (3): White 2, Guerrero 1.
At Cincinnati (6): Guerrero 3, O'Brien 1, White 1, Tracy 1.
At Colorado (8): Widger 2, Stevens 1, White 1, Mordecai 1, Vidro 1, Coquillette 1, Bergeron 1.
At Florida (7): Blum 3, Guerrero 1, Seguignol 1, Tracy 1, de la Rosa 1.
At Houston (5): Stevens 1, Vidro 1, Seguignol 1, Blum 1, Tracy 1.
At Los Angeles (2): Cabrera 1, Seguignol 1.
At Milwaukee (7): Vidro 2, Stevens 1, White 1, Widger 1, Guerrero 1, Cabrera 1.
At Montreal (88): Guerrero 25, Stevens 14, Vidro 11, Cabrera 7, Widger 6, Tracy 6, Blum 5, White 3, Bergeron 3, Mordecai 2, Guerrero 2, Lira 1, Seguignol 1, Bradley 1, de la Rosa 1.
At New York (NL) (3): Seguignol 2, Vidro 1.
At Philadelphia (11): Guerrero 3, Vidro 2, White 1, Mordecai 1, Lira 1, Cabrera 1, Blum 1, Bergeron 1.
At Pittsburgh (3): Vidro 2, Stevens 1.
At San Diego (3): Vidro 2, Stevens 1.
At San Francisco (4): White 1, Widger 1, Cabrera 1, Barrett 1.
At St. Louis (6): Guerrero 2, Seguignol 2, Blum 1, Bradley 1.
At Tampa Bay (3): Stevens 1, Widger 1, Guerrero 1.
At Toronto (3): Stevens 1, Widger 1, Guerrero 1.

LOW-HIT GAMES

No-hitters: None.
One-hitters: None.
Two-hitters: None.

10-STRIKEOUT GAMES

Javier Vazquez 5, Total: 5

FOUR OR MORE HITS IN ONE GAME

Lee Stevens 2, Rondell White 2, Vladimir Guerrero 2, Jose Vidro 1, Orlando Cabrera 1, Peter Bergeron 1, Total: 9

MULTI-HOMER GAMES

Vladimir Guerrero 8, Lee Stevens 2, Jose Vidro 2, Rondell White 1, Chris Widger 1, Orlando Cabrera 1, Total: 15

GRAND SLAMS

7-22: Andy Tracy (off Florida's Reid Cornelius)

PINCH HITTERS

(Minimum 5 at-bats)

Name	AB	Avg.	HR	RBI
Guerrero, Wilton	46	.283	0	9
Tracy, Andy	28	.250	1	5
Seguignol, Fernando	23	.348	2	5
Blum, Geoff	21	.143	0	3
Jones, Terry	20	.250	0	1
Barrett, Michael	7	.286	0	1
Mordecai, Mike	7	.143	0	0
Coquillette, Trace	6	.333	0	2
Webster, Lenny	6	.167	0	0

DEBUTS

4-3: Matt Blank, P.
4-25: Andy Tracy, PH.
5-26: Brian Schneider, C.
6-3: T.J. Tucker, P.
6-6: Matt Skrmetta, P.
6-11: David Moraga, P.
6-18: Scott Forster, P.
6-28: Yovanny Lara, P.
7-17: Tomas de la Rosa, SS.
7-19: Milton Bradley, CF.
9-7: Talmadge Nunnari, 1B.
9-13: Yohanny Valera, C.

GAMES BY POSITION

Catcher: Chris Widger 85, Brian Schneider 43, Lenny Webster 32, Michael Barrett 28, Charlie O'Brien 9, Yohanny Valera 7.
First base: Lee Stevens 123, Fernando Seguignol 30, Andy Tracy 28, Talmadge Nunnari 14, Geoff Blum 11, Mike Mordecai 3.
Second base: Jose Vidro 153, Geoff Blum 13, Mike Mordecai 9, Trace Coquillette 8, Wilton Guerrero 1, Orlando Cabrera 1.
Third base: Mike Mordecai 58, Michael Barrett 55, Geoff Blum 55, Andy Tracy 34, Trace Coquillette 19.
Shortstop: Orlando Cabrera 124, Geoff Blum 44, Tomas de la Rosa 29, Mike Mordecai 10.
Outfield: Vladimir Guerrero 151, Peter Bergeron 146, Terry Jones 78, Wilton Guerrero 75, Rondell White 74, Milton Bradley 41, Fernando Seguignol 31, Trace Coquillette 2.
Designated hitter: Wilton Guerrero 6, Vladimir Guerrero 2, Fernando Seguignol 1, Tomas de la Rosa 1.

STREAKS

Wins: 6 (May 24-30)
Losses: 11 (September 23-October 1)
Consecutive games with at least one hit: 14, Jose Vidro (June 16-July 1)
Wins by pitcher: 3, Dustin Hermanson (April 14-26) Javier Vazquez (September 10-20) Tony Armas Jr. (September 12-22)

ATTENDANCE

Home: 926,213
Road: 2,219,547
Highest (home): 51,249 (April 3 vs. Los Angeles).
Highest (road): 56,779 (August 19 vs. San Diego).
Lowest (home): 4,769 (September 18 vs. Florida).
Lowest (road): 7,864 (September 28 vs. Florida).

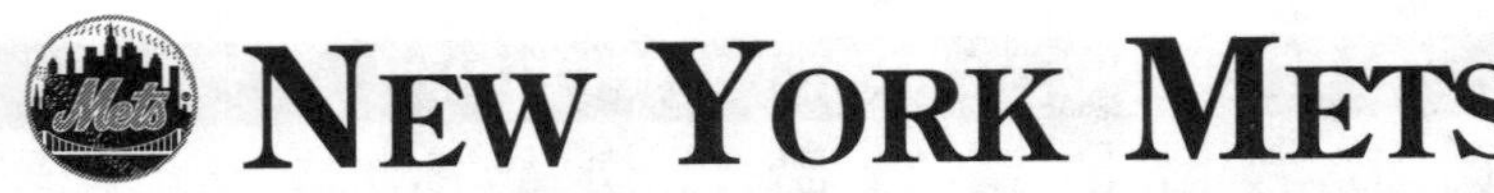

DAY BY DAY

Date	Opp.	Res.	Score	(inn.*)	Hits	Opp. hits	Winning pitcher	Losing pitcher	Save	Record	Pos.	GB
3-29	Chi.§	L	3-5		7	12	Lieber	Hampton	Aguilera	0-1	T1st	0.5
3-30	At Chi.§	W	5-1	(11)	6	5	Cook	Young		1-1	1st	...
4-3	S.D.	W	2-1		4	5	Leiter	Wall	Benitez	2-1	3rd	...
4-5	S.D.	L	0-4		7	11	Williams	B.J. Jones		2-2	2nd	0.5
4-6	S.D.	L	5-8		8	10	Clement	Hampton		2-3	4th	1.0
4-7	L.A.	W	2-1		2	4	Reed	Dreifort	Benitez	3-3	T2nd	0.5
4-8	L.A.	L	5-6	(10)	11	9	Fetters	Benitez	Shaw	3-4	4th	1.0
4-10	At Phi.	L	7-9		9	9	Telemaco	Rodriguez	Gomes	3-5	5th	1.5
4-12	At Phi.	L	5-8		7	12	Person	Hampton	Gomes	3-6	5th	2.0
4-13	At Phi.	W	2-1		8	5	Cook	Aldred	Benitez	4-6	5th	1.0
4-14	At Pit.	W	8-5	(12)	20	11	Franco	Silva		5-6	4th	1.0
4-15	At Pit.	L	0-2		5	4	Anderson	Rusch	Williams	5-7	4th	1.5
4-16	At Pit.	W	12-9		15	11	Mahomes	Peters	Benitez	6-7	4th	1.0
4-18	Mil.	W	10-7		11	9	Hampton	Navarro	Benitez	7-7	4th	1.5
4-19	Mil.	W	3-1		8	8	Reed	Bere	Benitez	8-7	4th	0.5
4-20	Mil.	W	5-4	(10)	7	9	Wendell	Leskanic		9-7	3rd	0.5
4-22†	Chi.	W	8-3		12	8	Rusch	Lieber		10-7		
4-22‡	Chi.	W	7-6		10	11	Cook	Farnsworth	Benitez	11-7	2nd	0.5
4-23	Chi.	W	15-8		18	10	Hampton	Tapani		12-7	2nd	0.5
4-24	L.A.	W	1-0		8	3	Benitez	Adams		13-7	2nd	...
4-25	Cin.	W	6-5		8	8	Wendell	Sullivan	Benitez	14-7	2nd	...
4-26	Cin.	L	1-12		4	18	Neagle	Springer		14-8	2nd	1.0
4-27	Cin.	L	1-2	(12)	6	8	Graves	Benitez	Sullivan	14-9	2nd	2.0
4-28	At Col.	L	5-12		12	14	Astacio	Hampton		14-10	3rd	3.0
4-29	At Col.	W	13-6		23	10	Reed	Yoshii		15-10	2nd	3.0
4-30	At Col.	W	14-11		15	10	Leiter	Bohanon		16-10	2nd	3.0
5-1	At S.F	L	3-10		7	11	Estes	Pulsipher		16-11	2nd	4.0
5-2	At S.F	L	1-7		8	11	Hernandez	Rusch		16-12	2nd	5.0
5-3	At S.F	L	5-8	(11)	14	12	Rodriguez	Wendell		16-13	2nd	5.0
5-4	At S.F	L	2-7		4	7	Rodriguez	Reed		16-14	3rd	5.5
5-5	At Fla.	W	4-1		5	4	Leiter	Sanchez	Franco	17-14	3rd	5.5
5-6	At Fla.	L	1-9		8	12	Fernandez	Pulsipher		17-15	3rd	5.5
5-7	At Fla.	L	0-3		1	9	Dempster	Rusch		17-16	3rd	5.5
5-9	At Pit.	W	2-0		8	6	Hampton	Benson	Benitez	18-16	3rd	5.0
5-10	At Pit.	L	9-13		13	20	Silva	Cook		18-17	T3rd	5.0
5-11	At Pit.	W	3-2		6	8	Leiter	Anderson		19-17	T3rd	4.0
5-12	Fla.	L	4-6		10	12	Dempster	Rusch	Alfonseca	19-18	4th	5.0
5-13	Fla.	L	6-7		12	8	Mahay	Cook	Alfonseca	19-19	4th	6.0
5-14	Fla.	W	5-1		5	8	Hampton	Penny		20-19	4th	6.0
5-16	Col.	L	3-4	(11)	12	9	Tavarez	Wendell	Jimenez	20-20	4th	7.0
5-17	Col.	W	4-2		10	5	Leiter	Arrojo	Franco	21-20	4th	7.0
5-19	Ari.	W	4-3		8	9	B.J. Jones	Stottlemyre	Benitez	22-20	3rd	6.5
5-20	Ari.	W	8-7		11	13	Hampton	Daal	Benitez	23-20	3rd	6.5
5-21	Ari.	W	7-6		10	10	Wendell	Kim		24-20	3rd	6.5
5-22	At S.D.	L	0-1		5	5	Clement	Franco	Hoffman	24-21	3rd	7.0
5-23	At S.D.	W	5-3	(10)	6	7	Wendell	Hoffman	Benitez	25-21	3rd	6.0
5-24	At S.D.	L	4-5		7	11	Wall	Mahomes	Hoffman	25-22	3rd	7.0
5-26	At StL.	W	5-2		9	9	Hampton	Thompson	Benitez	26-22	3rd	6.5
5-27	At StL.	W	12-8		15	11	Cook	Veres		27-22	2nd	6.5
5-28	At StL.	W	6-2		11	6	Rusch	Kile		28-22	2nd	5.5
5-29	At L.A.	L	1-4		4	8	Park	Leiter		28-23	2nd	6.5
5-30	At L.A.	W	10-5		13	13	Franco	Shaw		29-23	2nd	6.5
5-31	At L.A.	L	3-4		8	6	Fetters	Wendell		29-24	2nd	7.0
6-2	T.B.	W	5-3		5	7	Rusch	White	Benitez	30-24	2nd	5.5
6-3	T.B.	W	1-0		6	5	Leiter	Trachsel	Benitez	31-24	2nd	5.5
6-4	T.B.	L	5-15		9	14	Yan	B.J. Jones		31-25	3rd	5.5
6-5	Bal.	L	2-4		6	10	Mussina	Hampton	Timlin	31-26	3rd	5.5
6-7	Bal.	W	11-3		12	12	Mahomes	Erickson		32-26	3rd	5.0
6-8	Bal.	W	8-7	(10)	11	13	Cook	Mercedes		33-26	2nd	4.5
6-9	At N.Y. (AL)	W	12-2		15	8	Leiter	Clemens		34-26	2nd	4.5
6-10	At N.Y. (AL)	L	5-13		8	17	Pettitte	B.J. Jones		34-27	2nd	5.5
6-13	At Chi.	L	3-4		5	11	Heredia	Franco	Aguilera	34-28	2nd	5.5
6-14	At Chi.	W	10-8		14	14	Rusch	Garibay	Benitez	35-28	2nd	5.5
6-16	At Mil.	W	7-1		15	3	Leiter	Haynes		36-28	2nd	4.0
6-17	At Mil.	L	2-3		9	4	Snyder	Rusch	Wickman	36-29	2nd	4.0
6-18	At Mil.	W	7-3		10	7	Reed	Bere		37-29	2nd	4.0
6-20	Phi.	L	2-3	(10)	7	7	Brock	Benitez	Brantley	37-30	2nd	4.5
6-21	Phi.	L	5-10		10	12	Gomes	Franco		37-31	2nd	4.5
6-22	Phi.	W	5-4		7	8	Rusch	Politte	Cook	38-31	2nd	4.5
6-23	Pit.	W	12-2		14	7	B.J. Jones	Arroyo		39-31	2nd	4.5
6-24	Pit.	W	10-8		12	15	Franco	Loiselle	Benitez	40-31	2nd	3.5
6-25	Pit.	W	9-0		12	5	Hampton	Benson		41-31	2nd	3.5
6-26	Fla.	W	10-5		12	11	Leiter	Cornelius		42-31	2nd	3.0
6-27	Fla.	W	5-2		7	6	Rusch	Sanchez	Benitez	43-31	2nd	2.0
6-28	Fla.	W	6-5		13	10	B.J. Jones	Penny	Franco	44-31	2nd	2.0
6-29	Atl.	L	4-6		7	11	Burkett	Reed	Ligtenberg	44-32	2nd	3.0
6-30	Atl.	W	11-8		12	11	Benitez	Mulholland		45-32	2nd	2.0

HIGHLIGHTS

High point: One day after watching Atlanta clinch the N.L. East title at Shea Stadium, the Mets clinched a wild-card berth with a 6-2 September 27 win over the Braves. Tired of playing second fiddle to the Braves, the Mets would get the last laugh in the playoffs.
Low point: Following a sloppy 12-4 loss at Atlanta on September 19, manager Bobby Valentine ripped into his club. "We're a great team, a playoff team. And we need to show it," he said. The loss crippled the Mets' hope of wresting the N.L. East title from the Braves.
Turning point: On September 20 in Atlanta, Al Leiter beat the Braves, 6-3, to salvage the final game of a critical three-game series. The win over Tom Glavine provided a boost to the club's psyche and it went on to win nine of its final 11 regular-season games.
Most valuable player: Mike Piazza (.324, 38 homers, 113 RBIs) was the N.L. MVP until he hit a September slide—and the Mets slid right with him. Second baseman Edgardo Alfonzo was the club's all-around best player, but Piazza's game-affecting presence made him most valuable to a lineup short on offensive threats.
Most valuable pitcher: Al Leiter and Mike Hampton provided a dominant one-two punch, but time and again Leiter won the meaningful games. The Mets' 34-year-old lefty posted the league's fifth-best ERA (3.20).
Most improved player: With two major elbow surgeries robbing him of about 700 minor league at-bats, center fielder Jay Payton was forced to learn on the job. He learned well, batting .291 with 17 homers and 62 RBIs while rising from 25th on the Mets' roster to third in Rookie of the Year balloting.
Most pleasant surprise: The emergence of speedy outfielder Timo Perez in September and October helped the Mets claim their fourth N.L. pennant. But an honorable mention has to go to lefty Glendon Rusch, who rose from a murky pool of fifth starters to stabilize the back of the rotation.
Key injuries: Rey Ordonez broke his left forearm in Los Angeles May 29, costing him the rest of the season. ... Darryl Hamilton had a second operation on an arthritic big toe and was out from April until August 10. He still played in pain. ... Derek Bell sprained his ankle in Division Series Game 1 and was lost for the year.
Notable: When the Mets claimed sole possession of first place on August 31, it marked the latest date they had been atop the N.L. East since 1988. Their first-place stay lasted two days. ... By winning their second straight wild-card, the Mets earned consecutive playoff bids for the first time in club history .... The Mets had five starters with double-digit wins for the first time since 1988: Leiter (16), Hampton (15), Rusch (11), Rick Reed (11) and Bobby J. Jones (11).

—PETE CALDERA

MISCELLANEOUS

RECORDS

2000 regular-season record: 94-68 (2nd in N.L. East); 55-26 at home; 39-42 on road; 36-32 vs. East; 34-16 vs. Central; 24-20 vs. West; 18-13 vs. lefthanded starters; 76-55 vs. righthanded starters; 79-56 on grass; 15-12 on turf; 33-24 in daytime; 61-44 at night; 29-20 in one-run games; 10-8 in extra-inning games; 3-0-0 in doubleheaders.
Team record past five years: 438-373 (.540, ranks 2nd in league in that span).

TEAM LEADERS

Batting average: Mike Piazza (.324).
At-bats: Derek Bell (546).
Runs: Edgardo Alfonzo (109).
Hits: Edgardo Alfonzo (176).
Total Bases: Mike Piazza (296).
Doubles: Edgardo Alfonzo (40).
Triples: Lenny Harris, Todd Zeile (3).
Home runs: Mike Piazza (38).
Runs batted in: Mike Piazza (113).
Stolen bases: Derek Bell, Lenny Harris (8).
Slugging percentage: Mike Piazza (.614).
On-base percentage: Edgardo Alfonzo (.425).
Wins: Al Leiter (16).
Earned-run average: Mike Hampton (3.14).
Complete games: Mike Hampton (3).
Shutouts: Mike Hampton, Al Leiter (1).
Saves: Armando Benitez (41).
Innings pitched: Mike Hampton (217.2).
Strikeouts: Al Leiter (200).

Date	Opp.	Res.	Score	(inn.*)	Hits	Opp. hits	Winning pitcher	Losing pitcher	Save	Record	Pos.	GB
7-1	Atl.	W	9-1		11	6	Leiter	Maddux		46-32	2nd	1.0
7-2	Atl.	L	2-10		5	17	Glavine	Rusch		46-33	2nd	2.0
7-3	At Fla.	L	0-2		4	6	Almanza	Wendell		46-34	2nd	2.0
7-4	At Fla.	L	8-9		9	10	Darensbourg	B.M. Jones	Alfonseca	46-35	2nd	3.0
7-5	At Fla.	W	11-2		15	6	Hampton	Smith		47-35	2nd	2.0
7-7	N.Y. (AL)	L	1-2		6	6	Hernandez	Leiter	Rivera	47-36	2nd	2.5
7-8†	N.Y. (AL)	L	2-4		6	6	Gooden	B.J. Jones	Rivera	47-37		
7-8‡	At N.Y. (AL)	L	2-4		7	5	Clemens	Rusch	Rivera	47-38	2nd	4.0
7-9	N.Y. (AL)	W	2-0		6	7	Hampton	Pettitte	Benitez	48-38	2nd	3.0
7-13	At Bos.	L	3-4		8	8	Garces	Benitez		48-39	2nd	4.0
7-14	At Bos.	W	6-4		12	12	Mahomes	Lowe	Benitez	49-39	2nd	4.0
7-15	At Bos.	L	4-6		10	9	R. Martinez	Hampton	Lowe	49-40	2nd	5.0
7-16	At Tor.	L	3-7		10	8	Halladay	Leiter	Koch	49-41	2nd	6.0
7-17	At Tor.	W	7-5	(11)	11	5	Franco	Borbon	Benitez	50-41	2nd	5.0
7-18	At Tor.	W	11-7		12	13	B.J. Jones	Carpenter		51-41	2nd	5.0
7-19	At Mon.	W	5-3		11	9	Mahomes	Kline	Benitez	52-41	2nd	4.5
7-20	At Mon.	L	1-4		7	8	Hermanson	Hampton	Strickland	52-42	2nd	5.0
7-21	At Atl.	L	3-6		7	7	Burkett	Leiter	Remlinger	52-43	2nd	6.0
7-22	At Atl.	W	4-0		5	4	Reed	Maddux		53-43	2nd	5.0
7-23	At Atl.	L	0-1		4	7	Ashby	B.J. Jones		53-44	2nd	6.0
7-25	Mon.	W	5-0		12	5	Rusch	Hermanson		54-44	2nd	6.0
7-27†	Mon.	W	9-8		15	9	Franco	Strickland	Benitez	55-44		
7-27‡	Mon.	W	4-3		7	7	Hampton	Irabu		56-44	2nd	5.0
7-28	StL.	W	3-2		9	5	Leiter	Hentgen	Benitez	57-44	2nd	5.0
7-29	StL.	W	4-3		5	7	White	James	Benitez	58-44	2nd	5.0
7-30	StL.	W	4-2		7	4	B.J. Jones	Stephenson		59-44	2nd	5.0
7-31	Cin.	L	0-6		8	10	Williamson	Rusch	Luebbers	59-45	2nd	5.5
8-1	Cin.	W	3-2		9	9	Hampton	Parris	Benitez	60-45	2nd	5.5
8-2	Cin.	W	2-1		7	5	Leiter	Dessens	Benitez	61-45	2nd	4.5
8-4	At Ari.	W	6-1		11	6	Reed	Johnson	Cook	62-45	2nd	4.0
8-5	At Ari.	W	6-2		14	11	B.J. Jones	Guzman	White	63-45	2nd	3.0
8-6	At Ari.	L	5-9		13	12	Reynoso	Rusch	Mantei	63-46	2nd	4.0
8-7	At Hou.	W	6-5	(11)	8	12	Benitez	Green		64-46	2nd	3.0
8-8	At Hou.	L	3-9		11	10	B. Powell	Leiter		64-47	2nd	4.0
8-9	At Hou.	W	12-5		16	9	Reed	Lima		65-47	2nd	3.0
8-10	At Hou.	W	10-3		14	12	B.J. Jones	McKnight		66-47	2nd	2.5
8-11	S.F	W	4-1		7	5	Rusch	Gardner	Benitez	67-47	2nd	2.5
8-12	S.F	W	3-2		6	6	Hampton	Rodriguez	Benitez	68-47	2nd	2.5
8-13	S.F	W	2-0		7	2	Leiter	Hernandez	Franco	69-47	2nd	1.5
8-14	S.F	L	1-11		2	14	Ortiz	Reed		69-48	2nd	2.5
8-15†	Col.	W	7-5		9	9	Cook	House	Benitez	70-48		
8-15‡	Col.	W	4-3		10	4	B.J. Jones	Chouinard	Benitez	71-48	2nd	2.0
8-16	Col.	L	5-7		8	11	Bohanon	Rusch	White	71-49	2nd	3.0
8-17	Col.	W	13-2		15	4	Wendell	Yoshii		72-49	2nd	2.5
8-18	At L.A.	W	5-3		10	8	White	Adams	Benitez	73-49	2nd	1.5
8-19	At L.A.	L	1-4		4	9	Park	Reed		73-50	2nd	1.5
8-20	At L.A.	W	9-6		10	11	Wendell	Adams	Benitez	74-50	2nd	1.5
8-21	At S.D.	L	4-5	(10)	10	8	Hoffman	Cook		74-51	2nd	2.5
8-22	At S.D.	L	1-16		7	12	Eaton	Mahomes	Erdos	74-52	2nd	2.5
8-23	At S.D.	W	4-1		7	3	Leiter	Clement	Benitez	75-52	2nd	2.5
8-25	Ari.	W	13-3		16	6	Reed	Johnson		76-52	2nd	2.0
8-26	Ari.	L	1-5	(10)	5	11	Plesac	White		76-53	2nd	2.0
8-27	Ari.	W	2-1		4	3	Hampton	Reynoso	Benitez	77-53	2nd	1.0
8-28	Hou.	W	4-2		6	8	Rusch	B. Powell	Wendell	78-53	T1st	...
8-29	Hou.	L	1-11		5	16	Miller	Leiter		78-54	T1st	...
8-30	Hou.	W	1-0		9	3	Reed	Holt	Benitez	79-54	T1st	...
9-1	At StL.	L	5-6		9	11	Veres	Mahomes		79-55	1st	+0.5
9-2	At StL.	L	1-2		5	9	Kile	Hampton		79-56	2nd	0.5
9-3	At StL.	L	3-4	(11)	5	7	Morris	White		79-57	2nd	0.5
9-4	At Cin.	L	2-6		6	8	Dessens	Leiter		79-58	2nd	1.0
9-5	At Cin.	W	3-2	(10)	6	8	Wendell	Sullivan	Benitez	80-58	2nd	1.0
9-6	At Cin.	L	8-11		6	13	Riedling	Franco	Graves	80-59	2nd	2.0
9-8	Phi.	L	0-2		9	4	Padilla	Hampton	Brantley	80-60	2nd	3.5
9-9	Phi.	L	3-6		6	13	Person	Wendell		80-61	2nd	3.5
9-10	Phi.	W	3-0		6	5	Leiter	Daal		81-61	2nd	2.5
9-11	Mil.	L	2-8		7	12	Rigdon	Reed		81-62	2nd	3.0
9-12	Mil.	W	10-2		13	7	B.J. Jones	Snyder		82-62	2nd	2.0
9-13	Mil.	W	4-1	(10)	9	5	Benitez	Acevedo		83-62	2nd	2.0
9-14	At Mon.	W	10-4		12	10	Rusch	Thurman		84-62	2nd	2.0
9-15	At Mon.	L	3-4		9	10	Vazquez	Wendell	Strickland	84-63	2nd	2.0
9-16	At Mon.	W	10-4		14	11	Reed	Hermanson		85-63	2nd	2.0
9-17	At Mon.	L	0-5		4	7	Armas	B.J. Jones		85-64	2nd	3.0
9-18	At Atl.	L	3-6		9	7	Maddux	Hampton	Rocker	85-65	2nd	4.0
9-19	At Atl.	L	4-12		7	13	Ashby	Rusch		85-66	2nd	5.0
9-20	At Atl.	W	6-3		9	6	Leiter	Glavine	Benitez	86-66	2nd	4.0
9-21	At Phi.	L	5-6		11	12	Brantley	White		86-67	2nd	4.5
9-22	At Phi.	W	9-6		8	8	B.J. Jones	Wolf	Benitez	87-67	2nd	3.5
9-23	At Phi.	W	7-3		10	6	Hampton	Politte		88-67	2nd	3.5
9-24	At Phi.	W	3-2		4	7	Rusch	Chen	Benitez	89-67	2nd	3.5
9-26	Atl.	L	1-7		7	9	Burkett	Leiter		89-68	2nd	5.0
9-27	Atl.	W	6-2		9	6	Reed	Millwood		90-68	2nd	4.0
9-28	Atl.	W	8-2		10	7	B.J. Jones	Maddux		91-68	2nd	3.0
9-29	Mon.	W	11-2		11	7	Hampton	Thurman		92-68	2nd	2.0
9-30	Mon.	W	4-2		7	4	Wendell	Vazquez	Benitez	93-68	2nd	2.0
10-1	Mon.	W	3-2	(13)	9	9	Mahomes	Powell		94-68	2nd	1.0

Monthly records: March (1-1), April (15-9), May (13-14), June (16-8), July (14-13), August (20-9), September (14-14), October (1-0).

*Innings, if other than nine. † First game of a doubleheader. ‡ Second game of a doubleheader. § Game played in Tokyo, Japan.

MEMORABLE GAMES

June 9 at Yankee Stadium

Mike Piazza's grand slam off Yankees righthander Roger Clemens sparked a 12-2 Mets victory that illustrated how thoroughly Piazza had dominated Clemens over the past two seasons.Piazza was 3-for-4 in the game and Edgardo Alfonzo also connected off Clemens. Al Leiter worked seven innings to raise his record to 7-1.

Mets	AB	R	H	BI	Yankees	AB	R	H	BI
Tyner, lf-cf	6	2	2	0	Jeter, ss	5	1	3	0
Bell, rf	4	3	3	5	B.Williams, cf	2	0	1	0
Alfonzo, 2b	4	2	1	2	O'Neill, rf	3	0	0	0
McEwing, 2b	0	0	0	0	Jose, ph-rf	1	0	0	0
Piazza, c	4	2	3	4	Spencer, lf	3	0	0	1
Pratt, c	1	0	0	0	Posada, c	3	0	0	0
Ventura, 3b	5	0	0	0	Turner, c	1	0	0	0
Wendell, p	0	0	0	0	Martinez, 1b	3	1	1	0
Rodriguez, p	0	0	0	0	Delgado, 2b	1	0	0	0
Zeile, 1b	5	0	1	1	Leyritz, dh	4	0	1	0
Harris, dh	3	0	0	0	Brosius, 3b	3	0	1	1
M.Franco, ph-dh-3b	2	0	1	0	Bellinger, 2b-1b	4	0	1	0
Payton, cf	4	1	3	0					
Agbayani, ph-lf	1	0	0	0					
Abbott, ss	1	0	0	0					
Mora, ss	3	2	1	0					
Totals	**43**	**12**	**15**	**12**	**Totals**	**33**	**2**	**8**	**2**

Mets ....0 0 4 1 1 3 3 0 0—12 15 0
Yankees ....0 0 0 1 1 0 0 0 0— 2 8 2

E—Clemens (2), Posada (4). DP—Yankees 1. LOB—Mets 7, Yankees 8. 2B—Tyner (1), Bell (15), Martinez (13). HR—Bell (8), Alfonzo (12), Piazza (16). SB—Mora (3), Williams (7).S—Spencer.

Mets	IP	H	R	ER	BB	SO
Leiter (W 7-1)	7	7	2	2	3	4
Wendell	1	0	0	0	0	0
Rodriguez	1	1	0	0	0	0

Yankees	IP	H	R	ER	BB	SO
Clemens (L 4-6)	5	10	9	8	3	4
Erdos	3	4	3	3	0	2
Watson	1	1	0	0	0	1

Clemens pitched to 4 batters in the 6th. BK—Clemens. PB—Posada. U—HP, Hernandez. 1B, Foster. 2B, Kulpa. 3B, Marsh. T—3:30. A—55,822.

July 8 at Shea Stadium

After Dwight Gooden had pitcfhed the Yankees to a 4-2 victory in his emotional return to Shea Stadium, the teams moved to Yankee Stadium for the nightcap of a special New York-style day-night doubleheader. The Yankees recorded another 4-2 win over the Mets, but the focus of this game revolved around the second-inning Roger Clemens pitch that hit Mets catcher Mike Piazza in the head. Piazza and the Mets complained bitterly that the beaning was intentional, a result of Piazza's past success against Clemens. The rift would carry over into the postseason and flare up again with a nationally televised bat-flinging incident in the World Series.

Mets	AB	R	H	BI	Yankees	AB	R	H	BI
Harris, lf	3	1	0	0	Knoblauch, 2b	4	1	1	3
Bell, rf	4	0	3	1	Vizcaino, 2b	0	0	0	0
Alfonzo, 2b	4	0	2	1	Jeter, ss	4	0	0	0
Piazza, dh	0	0	0	0	O'Neill, rf	4	0	1	0
Franco, pr-dh	2	0	1	0	Williams, cf	3	0	0	0
Agbayani, ph-dh	1	0	0	0	Martinez, 1b	2	0	0	0
Ventura, 3b	4	0	0	0	Justice, dh	3	1	1	0
Zeile, 1b	4	0	0	0	Spencer, lf	3	1	1	0
Payton, cf	4	0	0	0	Turner, c	2	0	0	0
Pratt, c	4	0	0	0	Brosius, 3b	3	1	1	1
Mora, ss	3	1	1	0					
Johnson, ph	1	0	0	0					
Totals	**34**	**2**	**7**	**2**	**Totals**	**28**	**4**	**5**	**4**

Mets ....0 0 0 0 2 0 0 0 0—2 7 0
Yankees ....0 0 0 0 4 0 0 0 x—4 5 1

E—Jeter (11). DP—Yankees 1. LOB— Mets 7, Yankees 2. 2B—Bell (23). HR—Knoblauch (4). SB—Mora (7). SH—Turner.

Mets	IP	H	R	ER	BB	SO
Rusch (L 6-7)	8	5	4	4	0	10

Yankees	IP	H	R	ER	BB	SO
Clemens (W 6-6)	7.1	7	2	2	1	4
Stanton	0.2	0	0	0	0	1
Rivera (S 21)	1	0	0	0	0	0

HBP—Martinez by Rusch, Piazza by Clemens. U—HP, Eddings. 1B, Drake. 2B, Welke. 3B, Cook. T—2:36. A—55,821.

INDIVIDUAL STATISTICS

BATTING

Name	G	TPA	AB	R	H	TB	2B	3B	HR	RBI	Avg.	Obp.	Slg.	SH	SF	HP	BB	IBB	SO	SB	CS	GDP	vs RHP AB	vs RHP Avg.	vs RHP HR	vs RHP RBI	vs LHP AB	vs LHP Avg.	vs LHP HR	vs LHP RBI
Bell, Derek	144	622	546	87	145	232	31	1	18	69	.266	.348	.425	2	3	6	65	0	125	8	4	14	437	.293	18	64	109	.156	0	5
Alfonzo, Edgardo	150	650	544	109	176	295	40	2	25	94	.324	.425	.542	0	6	5	95	1	70	3	2	12	440	.330	20	77	104	.298	5	17
Zeile, Todd	153	623	544	67	146	254	36	3	22	79	.268	.356	.467	0	3	2	74	4	85	3	4	15	427	.274	12	58	117	.248	10	21
Payton, Jay	149	529	488	63	142	218	23	1	17	62	.291	.331	.447	0	8	3	30	0	60	5	11	9	384	.271	12	48	104	.365	5	14
Piazza, Mike	136	545	482	90	156	296	26	0	38	113	.324	.398	.614	0	2	3	58	10	69	4	2	15	403	.318	27	93	79	.354	11	20
Ventura, Robin	141	551	469	61	109	206	23	1	24	84	.232	.338	.439	1	4	2	75	12	91	3	5	14	367	.234	19	62	102	.225	5	22
Agbayani, Benny	119	415	350	59	101	168	20	1	15	60	.289	.391	.480	0	3	7	54	2	68	5	5	6	259	.293	12	49	91	.275	3	11
Mora, Melvin	79	242	215	35	56	91	13	2	6	30	.260	.317	.423	2	5	2	18	3	48	7	3	3	162	.265	3	20	53	.245	3	10
Bordick, Mike	56	211	192	18	50	70	8	0	4	21	.260	.321	.365	2	0	2	15	0	28	3	1	4	156	.244	3	15	36	.333	1	6
Pratt, Todd	80	190	160	33	44	74	6	0	8	25	.275	.378	.463	2	1	5	22	1	31	0	0	5	117	.282	7	20	43	.256	1	5
Abbott, Kurt	79	173	157	22	34	61	7	1	6	12	.217	.283	.389	0	1	1	14	2	51	1	1	2	118	.237	4	8	39	.154	2	4
McEwing, Joe	87	169	153	20	34	56	14	1	2	19	.222	.248	.366	8	2	1	5	0	29	3	1	2	104	.250	1	9	49	.163	1	10
Harris, Lenny	76	157	138	22	42	63	6	3	3	13	.304	.381	.457	2	0	0	17	1	17	8	1	4	132	.311	3	13	6	.167	0	0
Franco, Matt	101	157	134	9	32	42	4	0	2	14	.239	.340	.313	1	1	0	21	3	22	0	0	3	124	.242	2	13	10	.200	0	1
Ordonez, Rey	45	155	133	10	25	30	5	0	0	9	.188	.278	.226	4	1	0	17	2	16	0	0	4	107	.187	0	5	26	.192	0	4
Hamilton, Darryl	43	120	105	20	29	38	4	1	1	6	.276	.358	.362	0	1	0	14	0	20	2	0	0	104	.279	1	6	1	.000	0	0
Henderson, Rickey	31	124	96	17	21	22	1	0	0	2	.219	.387	.229	0	1	2	25	1	20	5	2	2	76	.250	0	2	20	.100	0	0
Nunnally, Jon	48	92	74	16	14	27	5	1	2	6	.189	.337	.365	0	1	0	17	0	26	3	1	1	72	.194	2	6	2	.000	0	0
Hampton, Mike	35	84	73	7	20	20	0	0	0	8	.274	.313	.274	4	2	0	5	0	20	0	1	0	62	.290	0	6	11	.182	0	2
Leiter, Al	31	71	58	1	3	3	0	0	0	0	.052	.113	.052	9	0	0	4	0	33	0	0	1	41	.073	0	0	17	.000	0	0
Trammell, Bubba	36	65	56	9	13	24	2	0	3	12	.232	.323	.429	0	1	0	8	0	19	1	0	3	34	.235	3	9	22	.227	0	3
Rusch, Glendon	31	57	50	2	3	3	0	0	0	1	.060	.113	.060	4	0	0	3	0	19	0	0	0	36	.083	0	1	14	.000	0	0
Perez, Timoniel	24	54	49	11	14	23	4	1	1	3	.286	.333	.469	0	1	1	3	0	5	1	1	0	41	.317	0	2	8	.125	1	1
Reed, Rick	30	67	49	6	10	10	0	0	0	2	.204	.226	.204	14	2	1	1	0	11	0	0	0	39	.231	0	1	10	.100	0	1
Jones, Bobby J.	27	55	44	4	2	2	0	0	0	0	.045	.125	.045	7	0	1	3	0	21	0	0	0	36	.028	0	0	8	.125	0	0
Tyner, Jason	13	48	41	3	8	10	2	0	0	5	.195	.222	.244	3	2	1	1	0	4	1	1	1	36	.194	0	4	5	.200	0	1
Johnson, Mark P.	21	27	22	2	4	7	0	0	1	6	.182	.333	.318	0	0	0	5	0	9	0	0	1	19	.211	1	6	3	.000	0	0
Mahomes, Pat	53	20	17	1	4	5	1	0	0	1	.235	.278	.294	2	0	0	1	0	5	0	0	0	16	.250	0	1	1	.000	0	0
Toca, Jorge	8	7	7	1	3	4	1	0	0	4	.429	.429	.571	0	0	0	0	0	1	0	0	0	3	1.000	0	3	4	.000	0	1
Velandia, Jorge	15	9	7	1	0	0	0	0	0	0	.000	.222	.000	0	0	0	2	0	2	0	0	0	7	.000	0	0	0	.000	0	0
White, Rick	24	5	5	0	1	1	0	0	0	0	.200	.200	.200	0	0	0	0	0	1	0	0	0	5	.200	0	0	0	.000	0	0
Lamb, David	7	6	5	1	1	1	0	0	0	0	.200	.333	.200	0	0	0	1	0	1	0	0	0	3	.333	0	0	2	.000	0	0
Wendell, Turk	77	4	4	0	1	1	0	0	0	0	.250	.250	.250	0	0	0	0	0	0	0	0	0	4	.250	0	0	0	.000	0	0
Springer, Dennis	2	4	4	0	0	0	0	0	0	0	.000	.000	.000	0	0	0	0	0	3	0	0	0	2	.000	0	0	2	.000	0	0
Wilson, Vance	4	4	4	0	0	0	0	0	0	0	.000	.000	.000	0	0	0	0	0	2	0	0	0	3	.000	0	0	1	.000	0	0
Jones, Bobby M.	11	4	2	0	1	1	0	0	0	0	.500	.667	.500	1	0	0	1	0	1	0	0	0	2	.500	0	0	0	.000	0	0
Pulsipher, Bill	2	2	2	0	0	0	0	0	0	0	.000	.000	.000	0	0	0	0	0	1	0	0	0	1	.000	0	0	1	.000	0	0
McGuire, Ryan	1	3	2	0	0	0	0	0	0	0	.000	.333	.000	0	0	0	1	0	0	0	0	1	2	.000	0	0	0	.000	0	0
Kinkade, Mike	2	2	2	0	0	0	0	0	0	0	.000	.000	.000	0	0	0	0	0	1	0	0	0	1	.000	0	0	1	.000	0	0
Cammack, Eric	8	1	1	0	1	3	0	1	0	1	1.000	1.000	3.000	0	0	0	0	0	0	0	0	0	0	.000	0	0	1	1.000	0	1
Franco, John	62	1	1	0	0	0	0	0	0	0	.000	.000	.000	0	0	0	0	0	1	0	0	0	0	.000	0	0	1	.000	0	0
Rodriguez, Rich	32	1	1	0	0	0	0	0	0	0	.000	.000	.000	0	0	0	0	0	1	0	0	0	1	.000	0	0	0	.000	0	0
Cook, Dennis	68	1	0	0	0	0	0	0	0	0	.000	.000	.000	1	0	0	0	0	0	0	0	0	0	.000	0	0	0	.000	0	0
Benitez, Armando	76	0	0	0	0	0	0	0	0	0	.000	.000	.000	0	0	0	0	0	0	0	0	0	0	.000	0	0	0	.000	0	0
Roberts, Grant	4	1	0	0	0	0	0	0	0	0	.000	.000	.000	1	0	0	0	0	0	0	0	0	0	.000	0	0	0	.000	0	0
Mann, Jim	2	0	0	0	0	0	0	0	0	0	.000	.000	.000	0	0	0	0	0	0	0	0	0	0	.000	0	0	0	.000	0	0
Riggan, Jerrod	1	0	0	0	0	0	0	0	0	0	.000	.000	.000	0	0	0	0	0	0	0	0	0	0	.000	0	0	0	.000	0	0

Players with more than one N.L. team

Name	G	TPA	AB	R	H	TB	2B	3B	HR	RBI	Avg.	Obp.	Slg.	SH	SF	HP	BB	IBB	SO	SB	CS	GDP	vs RHP AB	vs RHP Avg.	vs RHP HR	vs RHP RBI	vs LHP AB	vs LHP Avg.	vs LHP HR	vs LHP RBI
Harris, Ari.	36	91	85	9	16	22	1	1	1	13	.188	.209	.259	0	3	0	3	1	5	5	0	3	132	.311	3	13	6	.167	0	0
Harris, Ari.-N.Y.	112	248	223	31	58	85	7	4	4	26	.260	.317	.381	2	3	0	20	2	22	13	1	7	204	.270	4	23	19	.158	0	3

PITCHING

Name	W	L	Pct.	ERA	IP	H	R	ER	HR	SH	SF	HB	BB	IBB	SO	G	GS	CG	ShO	GF	Sv	vs. RH AB	vs. RH Avg.	vs. RH HR	vs. RH RBI	vs. LH AB	vs. LH Avg.	vs. LH HR	vs. LH RBI
Hampton, Mike	15	10	.600	3.14	217.2	194	89	76	10	11	5	8	99	5	151	33	33	3	1	0	0	658	.236	7	63	148	.264	3	16
Leiter, Al	16	8	.667	3.20	208.0	176	84	74	19	10	6	11	76	1	200	31	31	2	1	0	0	653	.248	16	67	118	.119	3	12
Rusch, Glendon	11	11	.500	4.01	190.2	196	91	85	18	10	7	6	44	2	157	31	30	2	0	0	0	577	.256	15	64	158	.304	3	19
Reed, Rick	11	5	.688	4.11	184.0	192	90	84	28	3	5	5	34	3	121	30	30	0	0	0	0	377	.260	15	41	344	.273	13	40
Jones, Bobby J.	11	6	.647	5.06	154.2	171	90	87	25	7	6	5	49	3	85	27	27	1	0	0	0	306	.297	10	34	303	.264	15	46
Mahomes, Pat	5	3	.625	5.46	94.0	96	63	57	15	3	3	2	66	4	76	53	5	0	0	12	0	209	.268	11	53	156	.256	4	23
Wendell, Turk	8	6	.571	3.59	82.2	60	36	33	9	6	3	5	41	7	73	77	0	0	0	17	1	189	.196	6	21	102	.225	3	6
Benitez, Armando	4	4	.500	2.61	76.0	39	24	22	10	2	1	0	38	2	106	76	0	0	0	68	41	143	.161	9	27	120	.133	1	10
Cook, Dennis	6	3	.667	5.34	59.0	63	35	35	8	0	0	5	31	4	53	68	0	0	0	15	2	143	.238	5	26	90	.322	3	15
Franco, John	5	4	.556	3.40	55.2	46	24	21	6	3	0	2	26	6	56	62	0	0	0	14	4	141	.227	6	17	67	.209	0	2
Rodriguez, Rich	0	1	.000	7.78	37.0	59	40	32	7	0	5	3	15	0	18	32	0	0	0	13	0	117	.393	4	26	45	.289	3	12
White, Rick	2	3	.400	3.81	28.1	26	14	12	2	0	1	2	12	2	20	22	0	0	0	6	1	67	.239	0	11	45	.222	2	6
Jones, Bobby M.	0	1	.000	4.15	21.2	18	11	10	2	0	1	3	14	1	20	11	1	0	0	4	0	62	.226	2	6	19	.211	0	2
Springer, Dennis	0	1	.000	8.74	11.1	20	11	11	2	0	0	1	5	0	5	2	2	0	0	0	0	24	.333	0	1	29	.414	2	9
Cammack, Eric	0	0	.000	6.30	10.0	7	7	7	1	0	1	1	10	1	9	8	0	0	0	2	0	25	.160	1	6	11	.273	0	2
Roberts, Grant	0	0	.000	11.57	7.0	11	10	9	0	0	2	0	4	1	6	4	1	0	0	0	0	15	.333	0	2	17	.353	0	7
Pulsipher, Bill	0	2	.000	12.15	6.2	12	9	9	1	1	0	1	6	0	7	2	2	0	0	0	0	23	.391	1	6	8	.375	0	2
Mann, Jim	0	0	.000	10.13	2.2	6	3	3	1	0	0	0	1	0	0	2	0	0	0	2	0	8	.625	1	3	6	.167	0	0
Riggan, Jerrod	0	0	.000	0.00	2.0	3	2	0	0	0	0	0	0	0	1	1	0	0	0	0	0	7	.429	0	2	3	.000	0	0
Bell, Derek	0	0	.000	36.00	1.0	3	5	4	0	0	0	0	3	0	0	1	0	0	0	1	0	3	.333	0	0	4	.500	0	4

DESIGNATED HITTERS

Name	AB	Avg.	HR	RBI
Piazza, Mike	18	.333	2	4
Alfonzo, Edgardo	7	.429	0	2
Franco, Matt	3	.333	0	0
Harris, Lenny	3	.000	0	0
Pratt, Todd	2	.500	0	1
Johnson, Mark P.	2	.000	0	0
Agbayani, Benny	1	.000	0	0

INDIVIDUAL STATISTICS

FIELDING

FIRST BASEMEN

Player	Pct.	G	PO	A	E	TC	DP
Zeile, Todd	.992	151	1205	95	10	1310	88
Franco, Matt	.990	28	89	8	1	98	10
Harris, Lenny	.955	10	36	6	2	44	3
Toca, Jorge	1.000	5	9	0	0	9	0
Johnson, Mark P.	1.000	4	9	0	0	9	1
Ventura, Robin	1.000	1	1	0	0	1	0

SECOND BASEMEN

Player	Pct.	G	PO	A	E	TC	DP
Alfonzo, Edgardo	.985	146	316	362	10	688	84
Abbott, Kurt	.981	23	23	29	1	53	3
McEwing, Joe	.939	16	16	15	2	33	4
Velandia, Jorge	1.000	8	3	1	0	4	0
Mora, Melvin	1.000	4	3	11	0	14	1
Harris, Lenny	1.000	3	2	3	0	5	0
Lamb, David	-	2	0	0	0	0	0
Franco, Matt	-	1	0	0	0	0	0

THIRD BASEMEN

Player	Pct.	G	PO	A	E	TC	DP
Ventura, Robin	.954	137	95	261	17	373	27
Franco, Matt	.900	22	9	18	3	30	0
McEwing, Joe	.914	19	6	26	3	35	1
Harris, Lenny	.854	16	15	26	7	48	2
Mora, Melvin	1.000	4	1	0	0	1	0
Velandia, Jorge	.800	3	2	2	1	5	0
Lamb, David	1.000	3	0	1	0	1	0
Abbott, Kurt	1.000	2	4	1	0	5	0

SHORTSTOPS

Player	Pct.	G	PO	A	E	TC	DP
Bordick, Mike	.968	56	71	140	7	218	24
Ordonez, Rey	.965	44	58	108	6	172	20
Mora, Melvin	.958	44	56	104	7	167	16
Abbott, Kurt	.953	39	47	75	6	128	10
Velandia, Jorge	1.000	7	3	2	0	5	0
McEwing, Joe	1.000	4	3	3	0	6	0
Lamb, David	1.000	2	2	2	0	4	0

OUTFIELDERS

Player	Pct.	G	PO	A	E	TC	DP
Payton, Jay	.981	146	311	7	6	324	2
Bell, Derek	.988	143	252	5	3	260	1
Agbayani, Benny	.975	110	155	3	4	162	0
McEwing, Joe	1.000	52	42	1	0	43	0
Nunnally, Jon	.977	34	38	4	1	43	2
Hamilton, Darryl	1.000	33	41	1	0	42	2
Henderson, Rickey	.946	29	35	0	2	37	0
Mora, Melvin	.967	28	29	0	1	30	0
Trammell, Bubba	.963	25	25	1	1	27	0
Perez, Timoniel	.970	19	30	2	1	33	0
Tyner, Jason	.920	12	22	1	2	25	1
Harris, Lenny	.882	11	14	1	2	17	0
Franco, Matt	1.000	3	2	0	0	2	0
Abbott, Kurt	-	2	0	0	0	0	0
McGuire, Ryan	1.000	1	3	0	0	3	0
Johnson, Mark P.	1.000	1	1	1	0	2	0
Kinkade, Mike	-	1	0	0	0	0	0
Toca, Jorge	-	1	0	0	0	0	0

CATCHERS

Player	Pct.	G	PO	A	E	TC	DP	PB
Piazza, Mike	.997	124	862	38	3	903	10	3
Pratt, Todd	.997	71	314	24	1	339	4	5
Wilson, Vance	1.000	3	14	0	0	14	0	0

PITCHERS

Player	Pct.	G	PO	A	E	TC	DP
Wendell, Turk	.917	77	12	10	2	24	0
Benitez, Armando	1.000	76	2	2	0	4	0
Cook, Dennis	1.000	68	4	10	0	14	2
Franco, John	.900	62	1	8	1	10	0
Mahomes, Pat	1.000	53	9	15	0	24	2
Hampton, Mike	.965	33	10	45	2	57	2
Rodriguez, Rich	1.000	32	3	5	0	8	1
Leiter, Al	1.000	31	5	34	0	39	2
Rusch, Glendon	1.000	31	5	25	0	30	1
Reed, Rick	.923	30	8	16	2	26	0
Jones, Bobby J.	.957	27	9	13	1	23	0
White, Rick	1.000	22	1	3	0	4	0
Jones, Bobby M.	1.000	11	3	3	0	6	0
Cammack, Eric	1.000	8	1	1	0	2	0
Roberts, Grant	-	4	0	0	0	0	0
Pulsipher, Bill	1.000	2	2	2	0	4	0
Springer, Dennis	1.000	2	1	2	0	3	0
Mann, Jim	-	2	0	0	0	0	0
Bell, Derek	-	1	0	0	0	0	0
Riggan, Jerrod	-	1	0	0	0	0	0

PITCHING AGAINST EACH CLUB

Pitcher	Ari. W-L	Atl. W-L	Chi. W-L	Cin. W-L	Col. W-L	Fla. W-L	Hou. W-L	L.A. W-L	Mil. W-L	Mon. W-L	Phi. W-L	Pit. W-L	S.D. W-L	S.F. W-L	StL. W-L	A.L. W-L	Total W-L
Bell, Derek	0-0	0-0	0-0	0-0	0-0	0-0	0-0	0-0	0-0	0-0	0-0	0-0	0-0	0-0	0-0	0-0	0-0
Benitez, A.	0-0	1-0	0-0	0-1	0-0	0-0	1-0	1-1	1-0	0-0	0-1	0-0	0-0	0-0	0-0	0-1	4-4
Cammack, E.	0-0	0-0	0-0	0-0	0-0	0-0	0-0	0-0	0-0	0-0	0-0	0-0	0-0	0-0	0-0	0-0	0-0
Cook, Dennis	0-0	0-0	2-0	0-0	1-0	0-1	0-0	0-0	0-0	0-0	1-0	0-1	0-1	0-0	1-0	1-0	6-3
Franco, John	0-0	0-0	0-1	0-1	0-0	0-0	0-0	1-0	0-0	1-0	0-1	2-0	0-1	0-0	0-0	1-0	5-4
Hampton, M.	2-0	0-1	1-1	1-0	0-1	2-0	0-0	0-0	1-0	2-1	1-2	2-0	0-1	1-0	1-1	1-2	15-10
Jones, B. J.	2-0	1-1	0-0	0-0	1-0	1-0	1-0	0-0	1-0	0-1	1-0	1-0	0-1	0-0	1-0	1-3	11-6
Jones, B. M.	0-0	0-0	0-0	0-0	0-0	0-1	0-0	0-0	0-0	0-0	0-0	0-0	0-0	0-0	0-0	0-0	0-1
Leiter, Al	0-0	2-2	0-0	1-1	2-0	2-0	0-2	0-1	1-0	0-0	1-0	1-0	2-0	1-0	1-0	2-2	16-8
Mahomes, Pat	0-0	0-0	0-0	0-0	0-0	0-0	0-0	0-0	0-0	2-0	0-0	1-0	0-2	0-0	0-1	2-0	5-3
Mann, Jim	0-0	0-0	0-0	0-0	0-0	0-0	0-0	0-0	0-0	0-0	0-0	0-0	0-0	0-0	0-0	0-0	0-0
Pulsipher, Bill	0-0	0-0	0-0	0-0	0-0	0-1	0-0	0-0	0-0	0-0	0-0	0-0	0-0	0-1	0-0	0-0	0-2
Reed, Rick	2-0	2-1	0-0	0-0	1-0	0-0	2-0	1-1	2-1	1-0	0-0	0-0	0-0	0-2	0-0	0-0	11-5
Riggan, Jerrod	0-0	0-0	0-0	0-0	0-0	0-0	0-0	0-0	0-0	0-0	0-0	0-0	0-0	0-0	0-0	0-0	0-0
Roberts, Grant	0-0	0-0	0-0	0-0	0-0	0-0	0-0	0-0	0-0	0-0	0-0	0-0	0-0	0-0	0-0	0-0	0-0
Rodriguez, R.	0-0	0-0	0-0	0-0	0-0	0-0	0-0	0-0	0-0	0-0	0-1	0-0	0-0	0-0	0-0	0-0	0-1
Rusch, G.	0-1	0-2	2-0	0-1	0-1	1-2	1-0	0-0	0-1	2-0	2-0	0-1	0-0	1-1	1-0	1-1	11-11
Springer, D.	0-0	0-0	0-0	0-1	0-0	0-0	0-0	0-0	0-0	0-0	0-0	0-0	0-0	0-0	0-0	0-0	0-1
Wendell, Turk	1-0	0-0	0-0	2-0	1-1	0-1	0-0	1-1	1-0	1-1	0-1	0-0	1-0	0-1	0-0	0-0	8-6
White, Rick	0-1	0-0	0-0	0-0	0-0	0-0	0-0	1-0	0-0	0-0	0-1	0-0	0-0	0-0	1-1	0-0	2-3
Totals	7-2	6-7	5-2	4-5	6-3	6-6	5-2	5-4	7-2	9-3	6-7	7-2	3-6	3-5	6-3	9-9	94-68

INTERLEAGUE: Cook 1-0, Mahomes 1-0, Hampton 0-1 vs. Orioles; Mahomes 1-0, Benitez 0-1, Hampton 0-1 vs. Red Sox; Leiter 1-1, Hampton 1-0, Jones 0-2, Rusch 0-1 vs. Yankees; Franco 1-0, Jones 1-0, Leiter 0-1 vs. Blue Jays; Rusch 1-0, Leiter 1-0, Jones 0-1 vs. Devil Rays. Total: 9-9.

MISCELLANEOUS

HOME RUNS BY PARK

At Arizona (2): Ventura 1, Bordick 1.
At Atlanta (5): Bell 2, Zeile 1, Piazza 1, Alfonzo 1.
At Boston (5): Piazza 3, Payton 1, Mora 1.
At Chicago (NL) (4): Agbayani 2, Ventura 1, Piazza 1.
At Cincinnati (4): Zeile 1, Pratt 1, Piazza 1, Franco 1.
At Colorado (4): Zeile 1, Pratt 1, Alfonzo 1, Mora 1.
At Florida (6): Bell 3, Zeile 1, Piazza 1, Alfonzo 1.
At Houston (8): Payton 2, Hamilton 1, Ventura 1, Bell 1, Piazza 1, Abbott 1, Agbayani 1.
At Los Angeles (8): Alfonzo 2, Harris 1, Bell 1, Pratt 1, Piazza 1, Abbott 1, Trammell 1.
At Milwaukee (4): Ventura 1, Piazza 1, Abbott 1, Agbayani 1.
At Montreal (8): Zeile 2, Ventura 2, Alfonzo 2, Piazza 1, Payton 1.
At New York (AL) (5): Ventura 1, Bell 1, Piazza 1, Alfonzo 1, Payton 1.
At New York (NL) (92): Piazza 16, Alfonzo 13, Ventura 12, Payton 9, Agbayani 9, Zeile 8, Bell 8, Mora 4, Bordick 3, Abbott 3, Pratt 2, Harris 1, Johnson 1, Franco 1, Trammell 1, McEwing 1.
At Philadelphia (8): Zeile 2, Piazza 2, Payton 2, Alfonzo 1, Perez 1.
At Pittsburgh (10): Ventura 3, Piazza 3, Zeile 1, Bell 1, Nunnally 1, Alfonzo 1.
At San Diego (5): Zeile 1, Pratt 1, Piazza 1, Alfonzo 1, Agbayani 1.
At San Francisco (3): Zeile 1, Piazza 1, Nunnally 1.
At St. Louis (10): Zeile 3, Ventura 2, Pratt 1, Piazza 1, Alfonzo 1, Trammell 1, Payton 1.
At Toronto (5): Harris 1, Bell 1, Pratt 1, Piazza 1, McEwing 1.

LOW-HIT GAMES

No-hitters: None.
One-hitters: None.
Two-hitters: None.

10-STRIKEOUT GAMES

Al Leiter 3, Rick Reed 1, Glendon Rusch 1, Total: 5

FOUR OR MORE HITS IN ONE GAME

Derek Bell 3, Edgardo Alfonzo 3, Mike Piazza 2 (including one five-hit game), Todd Pratt 1, Jay Payton 1, Benny Agbayani 1, Melvin Mora 1, Total: 12

MULTI-HOMER GAMES

Mike Piazza 3, Benny Agbayani 2, Todd Zeile 1, Robin Ventura 1, Total: 7

GRAND SLAMS

3-30: Benny Agbayani (off Chicago's Danny Young)
4-18: Robin Ventura (off Milwaukee's Jaime Navarro)
5-14: Mike Piazza (off Florida's Brad Penny)
5-27: Todd Zeile (off St. Louis's Dave Veres)
5-30: Todd Pratt (off Los Angeles's Terry Adams)
6-9: Mike Piazza (off New York's Roger Clemens)
7-18: Mike Piazza (off Toronto's Chris Carpenter)
9-29: Jay Payton (off Montreal's Mike Thurman)

PINCH HITTERS

(Minimum 5 at-bats)

Name	AB	Avg.	HR	RBI
Franco, Matt	48	.208	0	5
Harris, Lenny	40	.275	0	1
Nunnally, Jon	19	.211	0	1
Agbayani, Benny	18	.444	1	9
Trammell, Bubba	18	.167	1	1
Abbott, Kurt	14	.286	0	0
Hamilton, Darryl	13	.385	1	3
Pratt, Todd	13	.077	1	4
Johnson, Mark P.	12	.250	1	3
McEwing, Joe	11	.182	0	3
Payton, Jay	8	.125	0	0
Piazza, Mike	6	.500	1	3

DEBUTS

4-28: Eric Cammack, P.
5-29: Jim Mann, P.
6-5: Jason Tyner, LF.
7-27: Grant Roberts, P.
8-29: Jerrod Riggan, P.
9-1: Timoniel Perez, PH.

GAMES BY POSITION

Catcher: Mike Piazza 124, Todd Pratt 71, Vance Wilson 3.
First base: Todd Zeile 151, Matt Franco 28, Lenny Harris 10, Jorge Toca 5, Mark P. Johnson 4, Robin Ventura 1.
Second base: Edgardo Alfonzo 146, Kurt Abbott 23, Joe McEwing 16, Jorge Velandia 8, Melvin Mora 4, Lenny Harris 3, David Lamb 2, Matt Franco 1.
Third base: Robin Ventura 137, Matt Franco 22, Joe McEwing 19, Lenny Harris 16, Melvin Mora 4, Jorge Velandia 3, David Lamb 3, Kurt Abbott 2.
Shortstop: Mike Bordick 56, Rey Ordonez 44, Melvin Mora 44, Kurt Abbott 39, Jorge Velandia 7, Joe McEwing 4, David Lamb 2.
Outfield: Jay Payton 146, Derek Bell 143, Benny Agbayani 110, Joe McEwing 52, Jon Nunnally 34, Darryl Hamilton 33, Rickey Henderson 29, Melvin Mora 28, Bubba Trammell 25, Timoniel Perez 19, Jason Tyner 12, Lenny Harris 11, Matt Franco 3, Kurt Abbott 2, Mark P. Johnson 1, Ryan McGuire 1, Mike Kinkade 1, Jorge Toca 1.
Designated hitter: Mike Piazza 5, Edgardo Alfonzo 2, Matt Franco 2, Lenny Harris 1, Todd Pratt 1, Mark P. Johnson 1, Benny Agbayani 1.

STREAKS

Wins: 9 (April 16-25)
Losses: 4 (May 1-4, September 1-4)
Consecutive games with at least one hit: 21, Mike Piazza (June 7-July 3)
Wins by pitcher: 4, Al Leiter (April 30-May 17) Mike Hampton (May 9-26) Bobby J. Jones (July 30-August 15)

ATTENDANCE

Home: 2,766,365
Road: 2,575,283
Highest (home): 55,000 (March 29 vs. Chicago).
Highest (road): 55,839 (June 10 vs. New York).
Lowest (home): 9,540 (June 8 vs. Baltimore).
Lowest (road): 6,219 (September 14 vs. Montreal).

PHILADELPHIA PHILLIES

DAY BY DAY

Date	Opp.	Res.	Score	(inn.*)	Hits	Opp. hits	Winning pitcher	Losing pitcher	Save	Record	Pos.	GB
4-4	At Ari.	L	4-6		6	10	Johnson	Ashby	Holmes	0-1	T4th	1.0
4-5	At Ari.	L	3-11		9	12	Stottlemyre	Byrd	Morgan	0-2	5th	1.5
4-6	At Ari.	L	2-3	(11)	8	7	Springer	Schrenk		0-3	5th	2.0
4-7	At Hou.	W	4-1		6	5	Wolf	Dotel	Gomes	1-3	5th	1.5
4-8	At Hou.	L	5-8		11	11	Maddux	Brock	Wagner	1-4	5th	2.0
4-9	At Hou.	W	3-2		7	5	Schrenk	J. Powell	Gomes	2-4	5th	2.0
4-10	N.Y.	W	9-7		9	9	Telemaco	Rodriguez	Gomes	3-4	4th	1.0
4-12	N.Y.	W	8-5		12	7	Person	Hampton	Gomes	4-4	T3rd	0.5
4-13	N.Y.	L	1-2		5	8	Cook	Aldred	Benitez	4-5	T3rd	0.5
4-14	Mon.	L	0-4		6	9	Hermanson	Brock		4-6	5th	1.5
4-16	Mon.	W	5-4		9	7	Aldred	Telford		5-6	5th	1.0
4-18	At Atl.	L	3-4	(12)	9	9	Rivera	Reyes		5-7	5th	2.5
4-19	At Atl.	L	1-10		4	12	Glavine	Wolf		5-8	5th	2.5
4-20	At Atl.	L	4-6		8	8	Millwood	Aldred	Rocker	5-9	5th	3.5
4-21	At Fla.	W	4-3		8	7	Ashby	Nunez		6-9	5th	3.5
4-22	At Fla.	L	2-4		8	6	Sanchez	Byrd	Alfonseca	6-10	5th	4.5
4-23	At Fla.	L	2-5		6	5	Penny	Person	Alfonseca	6-11	5th	5.5
4-24	At Fla.	L	1-3		7	7	Fernandez	Wolf	Alfonseca	6-12	5th	6.0
4-25	Ari.	L	2-10		5	10	Johnson	Brock		6-13	5th	7.0
4-26	Ari.	L	4-10		6	9	Stottlemyre	Ashby		6-14	5th	8.0
4-27	Ari.	W	5-4		10	6	Gomes	Kim		7-14	5th	8.0
4-28	StL.	L	4-7		9	10	Stephenson	Reyes	Veres	7-15	5th	9.0
4-29	StL.	L	6-7	(10)	10	9	Mohler	Gomes		7-16	5th	10.0
4-30	StL.	L	3-4		8	9	Kile	Schilling	James	7-17	5th	11.0
5-2	Cin.	L	0-7		3	12	Neagle	Ashby	Sullivan	7-18	5th	12.5
5-3	Cin.	W	5-2		9	4	Byrd	Parris		8-18	5th	11.5
5-4	Cin.	W	14-1		21	7	Person	Harnisch		9-18	5th	11.0
5-5	At Atl.	L	5-6		9	9	Seanez	Gomes		9-19	5th	12.0
5-6	At Atl.	W	6-0		13	11	Schilling	Millwood		10-19	5th	11.0
5-7	At Atl.	W	7-4		14	11	Ashby	Mulholland	Gomes	11-19	5th	10.0
5-9	At Mon.	L	2-3		6	8	Kline	Gomes		11-20	5th	10.5
5-10	At Mon.	W	8-0		13	4	Person	Vazquez		12-20	5th	9.5
5-11	At Mon.	W	6-4		8	8	Wolf	Pavano	Gomes	13-20	5th	8.5
5-12	Atl.	L	7-8		9	12	Ligtenberg	Gomes	Rocker	13-21	5th	9.5
5-13	Atl.	L	2-3	(10)	6	8	Seanez	Aldred	Rocker	13-22	5th	10.5
5-14	Atl.	L	2-11		8	16	Burkett	Byrd		13-23	5th	11.5
5-16	StL.	L	2-8		10	9	An. Benes	Person		13-24	5th	12.5
5-17	StL.	W	5-4		11	9	Wolf	Slocumb	Brantley	14-24	5th	12.5
5-18	StL.	L	2-7		10	13	Stephenson	Schilling		14-25	5th	13.5
5-19	Col.	L	2-10		6	14	Astacio	Ashby		14-26	5th	13.5
5-20	Col.	L	3-4		2	6	Tavarez	Brock	Jimenez	14-27	5th	14.5
5-21	Col.	W	4-3		6	7	Person	Yoshii	Brantley	15-27	5th	14.5
5-23	At Hou.	L	2-10		8	13	Holt	Wolf		15-28	5th	14.5
5-24	At Hou.	W	9-7		13	9	Gomes	Wagner	Brantley	16-28	5th	14.5
5-25	At Hou.	L	6-10		8	11	Elarton	Ashby	Slusarski	16-29	5th	15.5
5-26	At L.A.	L	4-11		8	10	Brown	Byrd		16-30	5th	15.5
5-27	At L.A.	W	7-6		9	10	Person	Dreifort	Brantley	17-30	5th	15.5
5-28	At L.A.	W	4-2		12	6	Wolf	Osuna		18-30	5th	14.5
5-29	At S.F	L	2-7		4	13	Estes	Schilling	Embree	18-31	5th	15.5
5-30	At S.F	L	3-7		8	12	Hernandez	Ashby	Nen	18-32	5th	16.5
5-31	At S.F	L	4-10		9	14	Gardner	Byrd		18-33	5th	17.0
6-2	Bos.	W	2-1	(11)	9	9	Brantley	Wasdin		19-33	5th	15.5
6-3	Bos.	W	9-3		10	3	Wolf	Wakefield		20-33	5th	15.5
6-4	Bos.	W	6-5	(12)	12	8	Schrenk	Cormier		21-33	5th	14.5
6-5	T.B.	L	3-5	(12)	5	9	Guthrie	Boyd	White	21-34	5th	14.5
6-6	T.B.	L	3-5	(10)	8	9	Hernandez	Brantley	White	21-35	5th	15.5
6-7	T.B.	W	5-4		10	8	Brock	Guthrie	Brantley	22-35	5th	14.5
6-9	At Bal.	W	9-5		10	9	Wolf	Rapp		23-35	5th	14.5
6-10	At Bal.	L	4-11		6	12	Ponson	Schilling		23-36	5th	15.5
6-11	At Bal.	L	2-7		5	12	Mussina	Ashby		23-37	5th	15.5
6-12	Fla.	L	2-5		6	10	Darensbourg	Politte	Alfonseca	23-38	5th	16.5
6-13	Fla.	W	4-3		10	9	Gomes	Strong	Brantley	24-38	5th	15.5
6-14	Fla.	L	1-8		4	13	Dempster	Wolf		24-39	5th	16.5
6-16	Atl.	W	2-1		4	5	Schilling	Glavine	Brantley	25-39	5th	15.0
6-17	Atl.	W	9-3		16	7	Politte	Mulholland		26-39	5th	14.0
6-18	Atl.	L	3-5		6	8	Burkett	Schrenk	Rocker	26-40	5th	15.0
6-19	Atl.	W	5-2		8	5	Brock	Remlinger	Brantley	27-40	5th	14.0
6-20	At N.Y.	W	3-2	(10)	7	7	Brock	Benitez	Brantley	28-40	5th	14.0
6-21	At N.Y.	W	10-5		12	10	Gomes	Franco		29-40	5th	13.0
6-22	At N.Y.	L	4-5		8	7	Rusch	Politte	Cook	29-41	5th	14.0
6-23	At Mon.	W	13-6		17	9	Coggin	Vazquez		30-41	5th	14.0
6-24	At Mon.	W	8-1		11	7	Wolf	Pavano		31-41	5th	13.0
6-25	At Mon.	L	1-3		8	9	Johnson	Byrd	Kline	31-42	5th	14.0
6-27	Mil.	W	7-0		8	6	Schilling	Haynes		32-42	5th	13.0
6-28	Mil.	W	9-7		13	11	Brock	Acevedo	Brantley	33-42	5th	13.0
6-29	Mil.	L	6-8		10	12	Bere	Schrenk	Leskanic	33-43	5th	14.0
6-30	Pit.	L	3-8		11	13	Benson	Wolf		33-44	5th	14.0
7-1	Pit.	W	4-3		10	5	Byrd	Arroyo	Brantley	34-44	5th	13.0
7-2	Pit.	W	9-1		15	9	Schilling	Ritchie		35-44	5th	13.0

HIGHLIGHTS

High point: A 10-5 victory over the eventual N.L. champion Mets on June 21 at Shea Stadium provided one of the few highs in a down season. The game was decided on a ninth-inning grand slam by rookie first baseman Pat Burrell off Mets closer Armando Benitez.

Low point: The most crushing defeat, a 9-8 setback in 10 innings, took place July 16 at Yankee Stadium. The Yankees scored five runs in the bottom of the ninth to force extra innings and, after the Phillies took an 8-6 lead against Mariano Rivera in the 10th, they scored three more off closer Jeff Brantley for the win.

Turning point: Free-agent closer Mike Jackson reported stiffness in his throwing shoulder while warming up in the third game of the season. Unable to battle through the pain, the talented veteran underwent season-ending shoulder surgery and watched the bullpen blow 20-of-54 save opportunities.

Most valuable player: Right fielder Bobby Abreu. The 26-year-old Venezuelan batted .316, scored 103 runs and was the only National Leaguer to reach double figures in doubles, triples, homers and stolen bases.

Most valuable pitcher: After nearly losing his job in the spring, lefthander Randy Wolf made every scheduled start, pitched a team-high $206^1/_3$ innings and compiled an 11-9 record that suffered from poor run support.

Most improved player: Righthander Cliff Politte added a changeup to his fastball/slider repertoire and made a valuable contribution as a spot starter. Politte was 4-3 with a 3.66 ERA in 12 games.

Most pleasant surprise: Unable to crack Atlanta's rotation, lefty Bruce Chen was acquired in a three-player trade July 12 and made 15 starts, going 3-4 with a 3.63 ERA. Chen allowed only 81 hits in 94 1/3 innings and posted a team-best $20^2/_3$-inning scoreless streak.

Key injuries: Jackson was one of five significant pitchers to experience shoulder problems. Curt Schilling did not return to the rotation until late April and Scott Aldred (season-ending surgery in June), Robert Person (one month on the D.L.) and Paul Byrd (season-ending surgery in August) all missed major chunks of time. ... First baseman Rico Brogna suffered a broken wrist May 10 in Montreal and was never the same.

Notable: The team used a franchise-record 27 pitchers ... The Phillies were 12-31 against N.L. West opposition (a .279 winning percentage). ... The team's .983 fielding percentage tied for third in the N.L. and the Phillies matched their 1999 record-low of 100 errors. ... Outfielder Rob Ducey led the N.L. with 81 pinch-hit appearances. ... At age 25, third baseman Scott Rolen came within one hit of his first .300 season and became the second-youngest Phillies player to reach 100 career homers (behind Del Ennis).

—CHRIS EDWARDS

MISCELLANEOUS

RECORDS

2000 regular-season record: 65-97 (5th in N.L. East); 34-47 at home; 31-50 on road; 32-37 vs. East; 21-29 vs. Central; 12-31 vs. West; 14-22 vs. lefthanded starters; 51-75 vs. righthanded starters; 22-43 on grass; 43-54 on turf; 21-20 in daytime; 44-77 at night; 25-35 in one-run games; 4-12 in extra-inning games; 0-0-1 in doubleheaders.

Team record past five years: 352-458 (.435, ranks 16th in league in that span).

TEAM LEADERS

Batting average: Bobby Abreu (.316).
At-bats: Doug Glanville (637).
Runs: Bobby Abreu (103).
Hits: Bobby Abreu (182).
Total Bases: Bobby Abreu (319).
Doubles: Bobby Abreu (42).
Triples: Bobby Abreu (10).
Home runs: Scott Rolen (26).
Runs batted in: Scott Rolen (89).
Stolen bases: Doug Glanville (31).
Slugging percentage: Bobby Abreu (.554).
On-base percentage: Bobby Abreu (.416).
Wins: Randy Wolf (11).
Earned-run average: Robert Person (3.63).
Complete games: Curt Schilling (4).
Shutouts: Kent Bottenfield, Robert Person, Curt Schilling (1).
Saves: Jeff Brantley (23).
Innings pitched: Randy Wolf (206.1).
Strikeouts: Robert Person (164).

Date	Opp.	Res.	Score	(inn.*)	Hits	Opp. hits	Winning pitcher	Losing pitcher	Save	Record	Pos.	GB
7-3	At Mil.	W	5-3		10	6	Ashby	Snyder	Brantley	36-44	5th	12.0
7-4	At Mil.	W	7-4		11	10	Brock	Wickman	Brantley	37-44	5th	12.0
7-5	At Mil.	W	5-2		12	7	Wolf	Wright	Gomes	38-44	5th	11.0
7-6	At Mil.	L	2-4		11	8	D'Amico	Byrd	Wickman	38-45	5th	11.0
7-7	Bal.	L	1-2		8	7	Mussina	Schilling	Timlin	38-46	5th	12.0
7-8	Bal.	W	13-4		15	9	Ashby	Mercedes		39-46	5th	12.0
7-9	Bal.	L	4-5		8	12	Mills	Brantley	Timlin	39-47	5th	12.0
7-13	At Tor.	W	8-5		11	7	Schilling	Carpenter	Brantley	40-47	5th	12.0
7-14	At Tor.	L	2-3		6	13	Koch	Brantley		40-48	5th	13.0
7-15	At Tor.	W	7-3		11	5	Chen	Wells		41-48	5th	13.0
7-16	At N.Y. (AL)	L	8-9	(10)	14	13	Rivera	Brantley		41-49	5th	14.0
7-17	At N.Y. (AL)	W	10-8		9	12	Coggin	Cone	Brock	42-49	5th	13.0
7-18	At N.Y. (AL)	L	1-3		5	4	Neagle	Schilling	Rivera	42-50	5th	14.0
7-19	At Chi.	L	4-5		9	10	Heredia	Holzemer		42-51	5th	14.5
7-20	At Chi.	W	3-2		6	8	Brownson	Tapani	Brantley	43-51	5th	14.0
7-21	At Pit.	L	2-9		4	11	Anderson	Byrd		43-52	5th	15.0
7-22	At Pit.	L	1-2		4	5	Arroyo	Person	Williams	43-53	5th	15.0
7-23	At Pit.	W	4-1		7	3	Schilling	Ritchie		44-53	5th	15.0
7-25	Chi.	L	7-8		14	7	Worrell	Brock	Aguilera	44-54	5th	16.0
7-26	Chi.	L	9-14		9	14	Heredia	Byrd		44-55	5th	17.0
7-27	Chi.	L	1-4		7	12	Rain	Padilla	Aguilera	44-56	5th	17.0
7-28	L.A.	L	0-2		2	7	Dreifort	Daal	Shaw	44-57	5th	18.0
7-29	L.A.	W	3-0		7	6	Politte	Brown	Brantley	45-57	5th	18.0
7-30	L.A.	W	3-2		9	4	Wolf	Park	Brantley	46-57	5th	18.0
7-31	At S.D.	L	1-4		4	7	Williams	Chen		46-58	5th	18.5
8-1	At S.D.	L	9-10	(10)	11	13	Almanzar	Brantley		46-59	5th	19.5
8-2	At S.D.	L	2-5		8	9	Clement	Daal	Hoffman	46-60	5th	19.5
8-4	At Col.	L	1-8		7	13	Tavarez	Bottenfield		46-61	5th	20.0
8-5	At Col.	L	6-7		9	15	Jimenez	Brantley		46-62	5th	20.0
8-6	At Col.	W	10-9		13	16	Chen	Astacio		47-62	5th	20.0
8-7	S.D.	L	4-6		11	8	Clement	Person	Hoffman	47-63	5th	20.0
8-8	S.D.	W	10-4		14	8	Daal	Tollberg		48-63	5th	20.0
8-9	S.D.	W	3-2		9	6	Brock	Slocumb		49-63	5th	19.0
8-10	S.D.	L	3-15		8	19	Williams	Wolf		49-64	5th	19.5
8-11	Hou.	L	2-7		7	12	Valdes	Padilla		49-65	5th	20.5
8-12	Hou.	W	3-2		6	7	Person	Miller	Brantley	50-65	5th	20.5
8-13	Hou.	L	7-14		8	19	Cabrera	Daal		50-66	5th	20.5
8-14	Ari.	L	3-4	(11)	6	7	Plesac	Brantley	Mantei	50-67	5th	21.5
8-15	Ari.	L	6-11		13	16	Kim	Gomes		50-68	5th	22.5
8-16	Ari.	L	1-5		7	10	Reynoso	Chen		50-69	5th	23.5
8-18	At StL.	L	6-7		7	7	Christiansen	Brock		50-70	5th	23.5
8-19	At StL.	L	3-6		7	9	Hentgen	Daal		50-71	5th	23.5
8-20	At StL.	W	6-0		10	5	Bottenfield	Reames		51-71	5th	23.5
8-21	At Cin.	L	4-7		11	13	Harnisch	Wolf	Graves	51-72	5th	24.5
8-22	At Cin.	W	5-4		9	6	Padilla	Luebbers	Brantley	52-72	5th	23.5
8-23	At Cin.	W	4-3		7	5	Brock	Graves	Padilla	53-72	5th	23.5
8-24	At Cin.	L	3-8		11	11	Parris	Daal		53-73	5th	23.5
8-25	S.F	L	3-16		11	21	Ortiz	Bottenfield		53-74	5th	24.5
8-26	S.F	W	5-2		11	8	Wolf	Rueter	Brantley	54-74	5th	23.5
8-27	S.F	W	2-1	(10)	7	3	Vosberg	Fultz		55-74	4th	22.5
8-28	Col.	W	3-2		8	8	Person	Yoshii	Brantley	56-74	4th	21.5
8-29	Col.	L	1-2		3	9	Rose	Daal	Jimenez	56-75	4th	21.5
8-30	Col.	L	4-5	(11)	10	7	White	Gomes	Jimenez	56-76	4th	22.5
9-1	At L.A.	L	1-2		4	7	Fetters	Brock	Shaw	56-77	4th	22.5
9-2	At L.A.	L	0-1	(10)	6	6	Herges	Padilla		56-78	5th	23.0
9-3	At L.A.	L	1-6		4	9	Park	Person	Shaw	56-79	5th	23.0
9-4	At S.F	L	0-3		4	5	Ortiz	Daal	Nen	56-80	5th	23.5
9-5	At S.F	L	5-8		8	11	Johnstone	Vosberg	Nen	56-81	5th	24.5
9-6	At S.F	L	4-5		11	6	Fultz	Padilla	Embree	56-82	5th	25.5
9-8	At N.Y..	W	2-0		4	9	Padilla	Hampton	Brantley	57-82	5th	3.5
9-9	At N.Y.	W	6-3		13	6	Person	Wendell		58-82	5th	25.0
9-10	At N.Y.	L	0-3		5	6	Leiter	Daal		58-83	5th	25.0
9-11†	Mon.	W	5-2		8	7	Politte	Hermanson	Brantley	59-83	5th	25.0
9-11‡	Mon.	L	6-7		10	12	Mota	Padilla	Strickland	59-84	5th	25.0
9-12	Mon.	L	0-1		3	3	Armas	Telemaco	Strickland	59-85	5th	25.0
9-13	Mon.	W	15-5		19	8	Chen	Lira		60-85	5th	25.0
9-15	Fla.	W	7-4		8	7	Person	Burnett		61-85	5th	24.5
9-16	Fla.	L	2-3		4	7	Penny	Daal	Alfonseca	61-86	5th	25.5
9-17	Fla.	W	6-5		9	10	Wolf	Smith	Jacquez	62-86	5th	25.5
9-18	Pit.	L	5-6		10	11	Loiselle	Padilla	Williams	62-87	5th	26.5
9-19	Pit.	L	8-12		6	13	Skrmetta	Telemaco	Williams	62-88	5th	27.5
9-20	Pit.	L	6-7	(10)	7	12	Loiselle	Brock	Williams	62-89	5th	27.5
9-21	N.Y.	W	6-5		12	11	Brantley	White		63-89	5th	27.0
9-22	N.Y.	L	6-9		8	8	B.J. Jones	Wolf	Benitez	63-90	5th	27.0
9-23	N.Y.	L	3-7		6	10	Hampton	Politte		63-91	5th	28.0
9-24	N.Y.	L	2-3		7	4	Rusch	Chen	Benitez	63-92	5th	29.0
9-25	At Chi.	L	3-4		8	4	Quevedo	Person	Worrell	63-93	5th	30.0
9-26	At Chi.	W	10-4		14	14	Daal	Lieber		64-93	5th	30.0
9-27	At Chi.	L	0-1		8	6	Wood	Wolf	Worrell	64-94	5th	30.0
9-28	At Chi.	W	4-2		7	7	Politte	Nation	Padilla	65-94	5th	29.0
9-29	At Fla.	L	1-7		4	10	Smith	Chen		65-95	5th	29.0
9-30	At Fla.	L	5-11		10	17	Cornelius	Person		65-96	5th	30.0
10-1	At Fla.	L	5-7		9	11	Dempster	Telemaco	Alfonseca	65-97	5th	30.0

Monthly records: April (7-17), May (11-16), June (15-11), July (13-14), August (10-18), September (9-20), October (0-1).
*Innings, if other than nine. † First game of a doubleheader. ‡ Second game of a doubleheader.

MEMORABLE GAMES

May 6 at Atlanta

In his second start since returning to the rotation after a month-long minor league rehabilitation, Curt Schilling tossed an 11-hit shutout at Atlanta's Turner Field for his 100th career victory. The win was Schilling's14th complete-game shutout and it required 125 pitches. The game ended with bases-loaded drama, as Atlanta pinch hitter Andres Galarraga struck out for the 19th time in 40 career at-bats against Schilling.

Philadelphia	AB	R	H	BI	Atlanta	AB	R	H	BI
Glanville, cf	5	0	2	2	Veras, 2b	4	0	2	0
Gant, lf	5	0	2	1	Burkett, p	0	0	0	0
Abreu, rf	2	1	0	0	Galarraga, ph	1	0	0	0
Rolen, 3b	5	1	2	1	A.Jones, cf	3	0	1	0
Brogna, 1b	5	0	1	0	C.Jones, 3b	4	0	2	0
Lieberthal, c	5	1	2	1	Joyner, 1b	4	0	0	0
Morandini, 2b	5	2	2	0	Bonilla, lf	4	0	2	0
Relaford, ss	4	1	1	1	Lopez, c	4	0	3	0
Schilling, p	3	0	1	0	Hubbard, rf	4	0	0	0
					Furcal, ss	4	0	0	0
					Millwood, p	1	0	0	0
					Sisco, ph	1	0	0	0
					McMichael, p	0	0	0	0
					Ligtenberg, p	0	0	0	0
					Lockhart, ph-2b2		0	1	0
Totals	**39**	**6**	**13**	**6**	**Totals**	**36**	**0**	**11**	**0**

Philadelphia..............................0 3 1 0 0 1 0 0 1—6 13 1
Atlanta ....0 0 0 0 0 0 0 0 0—0 11 0

E—Rolen (4). DP—Philadelphia 2, Atlanta 1. LOB—Philadelphia 10, Atlanta 10. 2B—Glanville 2 (8), Lieberthal (7), Relaford (2). HR—Rolen (9). SB—Veras (8). CS—A. Jones (3). SH—Schilling.

Philadelphia	IP	H	R	ER	BB	SO
Schilling (W 1-1)	9	11	0	0	1	9

Atlanta	IP	H	R	ER	BB	SO
Millwood (L 3-1)	6	9	5	5	3	4
McMichael	1	0	0	0	0	1
Ligtenberg	1	2	0	0	0	1
Burkett	1	2	1	1	0	0

U—HP, Reilly, 1B, Kellogg.2B, Cooper. 3B, Diaz. T—2:40. A—48,610.

September 26 at Chicago

Trying to avoid becoming the first major league pitcher to lose 20 games since Oakland's Brian Kingman in 1980, lefthander Omar Daal limited the Cubs to two runs over six innings of a 10-4 victory. With Kingman watching from the Wrigley stands, the Phillies scored six runs in the ninth inning to expand on a 4-2 lead, a rally highlighted by Kevin Jordan's inside-the-park home run that became lodged in ivy on the left field wall. Daal helped his own cause with a two-run double.

Philadelphia	AB	R	H	BI	Cubs	AB	R	H	BI
Rollins, ss	5	1	2	1	Young, 2b	5	0	4	0
Glanville, cf	5	1	2	2	Gutierrez, ss	5	0	0	0
Abreu, rf	3	1	1	0	Sosa, rf	4	0	1	0
Rolen, 3b	1	0	0	0	Grace, 1b	4	1	1	0
Jordan, 3b	4	1	2	4	Zuleta, lf	4	1	3	1
Burrell, lf	5	0	1	0	Andrews, 3b	4	1	1	1
Brantley, p	0	0	0	0	Buford, cf	3	0	1	1
T.Lee, 1b	4	0	0	0	Reed, ph	1	1	1	0
Newhan, 2b	4	2	1	0	Girardi, c	3	0	0	0
Prince, c	4	2	4	1	Greene, ph	1	0	0	0
Taylor, pr	0	1	0	0	Lieber, p	2	0	1	0
Bennett, c	0	0	0	0	Huson, ph	1	0	0	0
Daal, p	3	0	1	2	Spradlin, p	0	0	0	0
C.Brock, p	0	0	0	0	Brown, ph	1	0	1	1
Padilla, p	0	0	0	0					
Ducey, ph	0	1	0	0					
Sefcik, lf	0	0	0	0					
Totals	**38**	**10**	**14**	**10**	**Totals**	**38**	**4**	**14**	**4**

Philadelphia..............................0 2 0 0 2 0 0 0 6—10 14 0
Cubs ....0 0 0 1 0 1 0 0 2— 4 14 1

E—Sosa (9). DP—Philadelphia 3, Cubs 2. LOB—Philadelphia 5, Cubs 7. 2B—Glanville (25), Prince (9), Daal (3), Grace (40). HR—Jordan (4), Zuleta (3), Andrews (14). SB—Rollins (3), Prince (1). CS—Glanville (8).

Philadelphia	IP	H	R	ER	BB	SO
Daal (W 4-19)	6	10	2	2	0	2
Brock	1	0	0	0	0	1
Padilla	1	0	0	0	0	0
Brantley	1	4	2	2	0	1

Cubs	IP	H	R	ER	BB	SO
Lieber (L 12-11)	7	10	4	4	2	5
Spradlin	2	4	6	6	2	2

U—HP, Carlson. 1B, Timmons. 2B, DeMuth. 3B, Barksdale. T—2:44. A—6,055.

INDIVIDUAL STATISTICS

BATTING

Name	G	TPA	AB	R	H	TB	2B	3B	HR	RBI	Avg.	Obp.	Slg.	SH	SF	HP	BB	IBB	SO	SB	CS	GDP	vs RHP AB	vs RHP Avg.	vs RHP HR	vs RHP RBI	vs LHP AB	vs LHP Avg.	vs LHP HR	vs LHP RBI
Glanville, Doug	154	689	637	89	175	238	27	6	8	52	.275	.307	.374	12	7	2	31	1	76	31	8	11	498	.285	7	39	139	.237	1	13
Abreu, Bobby	154	680	576	103	182	319	42	10	25	79	.316	.416	.554	0	3	1	100	9	116	28	8	12	440	.339	22	69	136	.243	3	10
Rolen, Scott	128	541	483	88	144	266	32	6	26	89	.298	.370	.551	0	2	5	51	9	99	8	1	4	377	.302	18	69	106	.283	8	20
Burrell, Pat	111	474	408	57	106	189	27	1	18	79	.260	.359	.463	0	2	1	63	2	139	0	0	5	323	.254	13	58	85	.282	5	21
Lieberthal, Mike	108	438	389	55	108	183	30	0	15	71	.278	.352	.470	0	3	6	40	3	53	2	0	12	309	.259	11	52	80	.350	4	19
Gant, Ron	89	384	343	54	87	167	16	2	20	38	.254	.324	.487	1	3	1	36	1	73	5	4	7	258	.217	14	30	85	.365	6	8
Jordan, Kevin	109	358	337	30	74	109	16	2	5	36	.220	.257	.323	0	3	1	17	0	41	0	1	11	224	.223	4	22	113	.212	1	14
Morandini, Mickey	91	341	302	31	76	95	13	3	0	22	.252	.324	.315	5	1	4	29	1	54	5	2	11	252	.262	0	21	50	.200	0	1
Relaford, Desi	83	313	253	29	56	83	12	3	3	30	.221	.363	.328	2	1	9	48	7	45	5	0	7	206	.218	2	25	47	.234	1	5
Lee, Travis	56	223	180	19	43	59	11	1	1	14	.239	.381	.328	0	1	2	40	0	33	3	0	6	155	.252	1	12	25	.160	0	2
Anderson, Marlon	41	174	162	10	37	50	8	1	1	15	.228	.282	.309	0	0	0	12	0	22	2	2	5	141	.234	1	15	21	.190	0	0
Arias, Alex	70	180	155	17	29	44	9	0	2	15	.187	.271	.284	3	3	3	16	2	28	1	0	1	105	.162	1	10	50	.240	1	5
Sefcik, Kevin	99	171	153	15	36	46	6	2	0	10	.235	.300	.301	1	2	2	13	0	19	4	2	4	92	.228	0	6	61	.246	0	4
Ducey, Rob	112	183	152	24	30	54	4	1	6	25	.197	.322	.355	0	2	0	29	1	47	1	0	1	142	.211	6	25	10	.000	0	0
Perez, Tomas	45	152	140	17	31	43	7	1	1	13	.221	.278	.307	1	0	0	11	2	30	1	1	3	117	.205	1	12	23	.304	0	1
Hunter, Brian	85	158	138	13	29	55	5	0	7	22	.210	.310	.399	0	0	0	20	1	39	0	1	2	68	.206	7	18	70	.214	0	4
Brogna, Rico	38	139	129	12	32	49	14	0	1	13	.248	.295	.380	0	1	2	7	1	28	1	0	4	94	.298	0	7	35	.114	1	6
Prince, Tom	46	140	122	14	29	44	9	0	2	16	.238	.321	.361	3	0	2	13	0	31	1	0	6	98	.245	2	13	24	.208	0	3
Bennett, Gary	31	89	74	8	18	29	5	0	2	5	.243	.371	.392	0	0	2	13	0	15	0	0	0	52	.192	1	2	22	.364	1	3
Wolf, Randy	32	71	57	5	11	13	2	0	0	4	.193	.230	.228	10	1	0	3	0	19	0	0	0	46	.217	0	4	11	.091	0	0
Rollins, Jimmy	14	55	53	5	17	20	1	1	0	5	.321	.345	.377	0	0	0	2	0	7	3	0	0	41	.317	0	5	12	.333	0	0
Person, Robert	28	65	53	1	7	10	3	0	0	2	.132	.175	.189	8	1	0	3	0	29	0	0	0	44	.114	0	1	9	.222	0	1
Schilling, Curt	16	33	30	0	5	6	1	0	0	1	.167	.194	.200	2	0	0	1	0	4	0	0	0	18	.167	0	1	12	.167	0	0
Ashby, Andy	16	35	28	0	5	5	0	0	0	5	.179	.233	.179	5	0	0	2	0	10	0	0	0	24	.167	0	3	4	.250	0	2
Chen, Bruce	15	31	25	0	1	1	0	0	0	1	.040	.077	.040	5	0	0	1	0	17	0	0	0	19	.053	0	0	6	.000	0	1
Byrd, Paul	17	24	20	2	3	3	0	0	0	0	.150	.227	.150	2	0	1	1	0	6	0	0	0	14	.143	0	0	6	.167	0	0
Daal, Omar	12	23	18	1	5	7	2	0	0	2	.278	.381	.389	2	0	0	3	0	5	0	0	0	16	.313	0	2	2	.000	0	0
Newhan, David	10	19	17	3	3	3	0	0	0	0	.176	.263	.176	0	0	0	2	0	6	0	0	2	17	.176	0	0	0	.000	0	0
Politte, Cliff	12	19	15	1	2	3	1	0	0	2	.133	.176	.200	2	1	0	1	0	4	0	0	0	10	.200	0	1	5	.000	0	1
Bottenfield, Kent	8	17	14	2	0	0	0	0	0	0	.000	.000	.000	3	0	0	0	0	3	0	0	0	12	.000	0	0	2	.000	0	0
Pritchett, Chris	5	12	11	0	1	1	0	0	0	0	.091	.167	.091	0	0	0	1	0	3	0	0	1	11	.091	0	0	0	.000	0	0
Taylor, Reggie	9	11	11	1	1	1	0	0	0	0	.091	.091	.091	0	0	0	0	0	8	1	0	0	10	.100	0	0	1	.000	0	0
Brock, Chris	63	11	9	1	2	6	1	0	1	2	.222	.222	.667	2	0	0	0	0	2	0	0	0	8	.250	1	2	1	.000	0	0
Coggin, Dave	5	8	7	0	0	0	0	0	0	0	.000	.000	.000	1	0	0	0	0	4	0	0	0	7	.000	0	0	0	.000	0	0
Alvarez, Clemente	2	5	5	1	1	1	0	0	0	0	.200	.200	.200	0	0	0	0	0	1	0	0	0	4	.250	0	0	1	.000	0	0
Telemaco, Amaury	13	5	4	0	0	0	0	0	0	0	.000	.200	.000	0	0	0	1	0	1	0	0	0	4	.000	0	0	0	.000	0	0
Holzemer, Mark	25	1	1	0	0	0	0	0	0	0	.000	.000	.000	0	0	0	0	0	0	0	0	0	1	.000	0	0	0	.000	0	0
Vosberg, Ed	31	0	0	0	0	0	0	0	0	0	.000	.000	.000	0	0	0	0	0	0	0	0	0	0	.000	0	0	0	.000	0	0
Brantley, Jeff	55	0	0	0	0	0	0	0	0	0	.000	.000	.000	0	0	0	0	0	0	0	0	0	0	.000	0	0	0	.000	0	0
Aldred, Scott	23	0	0	0	0	0	0	0	0	0	.000	.000	.000	0	0	0	0	0	0	0	0	0	0	.000	0	0	0	.000	0	0
Reyes, Carlos	10	0	0	0	0	0	0	0	0	0	.000	.000	.000	0	0	0	0	0	0	0	0	0	0	.000	0	0	0	.000	0	0
Miller, Trever	14	0	0	0	0	0	0	0	0	0	.000	.000	.000	0	0	0	0	0	0	0	0	0	0	.000	0	0	0	.000	0	0
Gomes, Wayne	65	0	0	0	0	0	0	0	0	0	.000	.000	.000	0	0	0	0	0	0	0	0	0	0	.000	0	0	0	.000	0	0
Ward, Bryan	20	0	0	0	0	0	0	0	0	0	.000	.000	.000	0	0	0	0	0	0	0	0	0	0	.000	0	0	0	.000	0	0
Brownson, Mark	2	1	0	0	0	0	0	0	0	0	.000	1.000	.000	0	0	0	1	0	0	0	0	0	0	.000	0	0	0	.000	0	0
Bullinger, Kirk	3	0	0	0	0	0	0	0	0	0	.000	.000	.000	0	0	0	0	0	0	0	0	0	0	.000	0	0	0	.000	0	0
Padilla, Vicente	28	0	0	0	0	0	0	0	0	0	.000	.000	.000	0	0	0	0	0	0	0	0	0	0	.000	0	0	0	.000	0	0
Schrenk, Steve	20	0	0	0	0	0	0	0	0	0	.000	.000	.000	0	0	0	0	0	0	0	0	0	0	.000	0	0	0	.000	0	0
Boyd, Jason	30	0	0	0	0	0	0	0	0	0	.000	.000	.000	0	0	0	0	0	0	0	0	0	0	.000	0	0	0	.000	0	0
Jacquez, Tom	9	0	0	0	0	0	0	0	0	0	.000	.000	.000	0	0	0	0	0	0	0	0	0	0	.000	0	0	0	.000	0	0
Nickle, Doug	4	0	0	0	0	0	0	0	0	0	.000	.000	.000	0	0	0	0	0	0	0	0	0	0	.000	0	0	0	.000	0	0

Players with more than one N.L. team

Name	G	TPA	AB	R	H	TB	2B	3B	HR	RBI	Avg.	Obp.	Slg.	SH	SF	HP	BB	IBB	SO	SB	CS	GDP	vs RHP AB	vs RHP Avg.	vs RHP HR	vs RHP RBI	vs LHP AB	vs LHP Avg.	vs LHP HR	vs LHP RBI
Ashby, Phi.-Atl.	32	72	61	2	9	9	0	0	0	6	.148	.175	.148	9	0	0	2	0	22	0	0	1	45	.156	0	4	16	.125	0	2
Chen, Atl.-Phi.	37	38	30	0	1	1	0	0	0	1	.033	.065	.033	7	0	0	1	0	20	0	0	0	21	.048	0	0	9	.000	0	1
Daal, Ari.-Phi.	32	54	45	3	12	18	3	0	1	6	.267	.327	.400	5	0	0	4	0	8	0	0	1	34	.294	1	6	11	.182	0	0
Hunter, Atl.-Phi.	87	160	140	14	30	59	5	0	8	23	.214	.313	.421	0	0	0	20	1	39	0	1	2	69	.217	8	19	71	.211	0	4
Lee, Ari.-Phi.	128	473	404	53	95	148	24	1	9	54	.235	.342	.366	0	2	2	65	1	79	8	1	12	331	.242	9	46	73	.205	0	8
Miller, Phi.-L.A.	16	0	0	0	0	0	0	0	0	0	.000	.000	.000	0	0	0	0	0	0	0	0	0	0	.000	0	0	0	.000	0	0
Newhan, S.D.-Phi.	24	45	37	8	6	10	1	0	1	2	.162	.311	.270	0	0	0	8	1	13	0	0	2	32	.188	1	1	5	.000	0	1
Padilla, Ari.-Phi.	55	1	1	0	1	1	0	0	0	0	1.000	1.000	1.000	0	0	0	0	0	0	0	0	0	1	1.000	0	0	0	.000	0	0
Relaford, Phi.-S.D.	128	502	410	55	88	123	14	3	5	46	.215	.351	.300	3	2	12	75	7	71	13	0	10	317	.221	3	36	93	.194	2	10
Reyes, Phi.-S.D.	22	1	1	0	0	0	0	0	0	0	.000	.000	.000	0	0	0	0	0	0	0	0	0	1	.000	0	0	0	.000	0	0
Schilling, Phi.-Ari.	29	71	61	2	13	16	3	0	0	4	.213	.226	.262	9	0	0	1	0	15	0	1	0	44	.205	0	4	17	.235	0	0

PITCHING

Name	W	L	Pct.	ERA	IP	H	R	ER	HR	SH	SF	HB	BB	IBB	SO	G	GS	CG	ShO	GF	Sv	vs. RH AB	vs. RH Avg.	vs. RH HR	vs. RH RBI	vs. LH AB	vs. LH Avg.	vs. LH HR	vs. LH RBI
Wolf, Randy	11	9	.550	4.36	206.1	210	107	100	25	10	8	8	83	2	160	32	32	1	0	0	0	670	.276	24	89	110	.227	1	12
Person, Robert	9	7	.563	3.63	173.1	144	73	70	13	4	9	6	95	1	164	28	28	1	1	0	0	342	.272	7	40	287	.178	6	24
Schilling, Curt	6	6	.500	3.91	112.2	110	49	49	17	5	1	1	32	4	96	16	16	4	1	0	0	222	.252	10	24	213	.254	7	24
Ashby, Andy	4	7	.364	5.68	101.1	113	75	64	17	11	9	5	38	5	51	16	16	1	0	0	0	209	.292	9	38	183	.284	8	26
Chen, Bruce	3	4	.429	3.63	94.1	81	39	38	14	5	1	1	27	2	80	15	15	0	0	0	0	276	.232	11	28	73	.233	3	7
Brock, Chris	7	8	.467	4.34	93.1	85	48	45	21	1	2	3	41	0	69	63	5	0	0	17	1	230	.248	17	35	126	.222	4	11
Byrd, Paul	2	9	.182	6.51	83.0	89	67	60	17	3	1	3	35	2	53	17	15	0	0	0	0	185	.222	6	31	144	.333	11	32
Gomes, Wayne	4	6	.400	4.40	73.2	72	41	36	6	7	4	3	35	3	49	65	0	0	0	26	7	167	.234	4	23	108	.306	2	20
Daal, Omar	2	9	.182	4.69	71.0	81	40	37	9	3	1	2	30	0	51	12	12	0	0	0	0	247	.296	8	36	32	.250	1	4
Politte, Cliff	4	3	.571	3.66	59.0	55	24	24	8	1	1	0	27	1	50	12	8	0	0	1	0	134	.261	7	19	88	.227	1	3
Brantley, Jeff	2	7	.222	5.86	55.1	64	36	36	12	1	2	2	29	0	57	55	0	0	0	47	23	119	.286	10	17	103	.291	2	19
Bottenfield, Kent	1	2	.333	4.50	44.0	41	24	22	5	0	2	0	21	0	31	8	8	1	1	0	0	75	.213	3	10	96	.260	2	14
Boyd, Jason	0	1	.000	6.55	34.1	39	28	25	2	3	0	1	24	4	32	30	0	0	0	11	0	87	.299	0	18	46	.283	2	5
Padilla, Vicente	2	6	.250	5.34	30.1	40	23	18	3	5	2	1	18	5	21	28	0	0	0	4	2	72	.264	1	10	50	.420	2	14
Coggin, Dave	2	0	1.000	5.33	27.0	35	20	16	2	2	0	1	12	0	17	5	5	0	0	0	0	67	.299	0	9	44	.341	2	8
Holzemer, Mark	0	1	.000	7.71	25.2	36	23	22	4	5	0	1	8	1	19	25	0	0	0	9	0	71	.380	3	16	36	.250	1	9
Telemaco, Amaury	1	3	.250	6.66	24.1	25	22	18	6	0	2	0	14	0	22	13	2	0	0	2	0	48	.313	3	14	43	.233	3	7
Vosberg, Ed	1	1	.500	4.13	24.0	21	11	11	4	1	0	0	18	0	23	31	0	0	0	5	0	45	.200	1	5	42	.286	3	5
Schrenk, Steve	2	3	.400	7.33	23.1	25	20	19	3	1	1	1	13	0	19	20	0	0	0	6	0	57	.281	2	9	36	.250	1	8
Aldred, Scott	1	3	.250	5.75	20.1	23	14	13	3	1	2	1	10	0	21	23	0	0	0	5	0	48	.271	2	7	33	.303	1	7
Ward, Bryan	0	0	.000	2.33	19.1	14	5	5	2	1	2	0	8	0	11	20	0	0	0	8	0	38	.184	2	6	30	.233	0	3
Miller, Trever	0	0	.000	8.36	14.0	19	16	13	3	1	1	1	9	1	10	14	0	0	0	2	0	37	.351	2	9	23	.261	1	5
Reyes, Carlos	0	2	.000	5.23	10.1	10	6	6	2	2	0	0	5	0	4	10	0	0	0	5	0	30	.300	2	8	7	.143	0	0
Jacquez, Tom	0	0	.000	11.05	7.1	10	9	9	2	0	1	0	3	1	6	9	0	0	0	2	1	20	.400	1	7	10	.200	1	6
Brownson, Mark	1	0	1.000	7.20	5.0	7	4	4	1	1	0	0	3	0	3	2	0	0	0	0	0	16	.313	1	3	5	.400	0	1
Bullinger, Kirk	0	0	.000	5.40	3.1	4	2	2	0	0	1	0	0	0	4	3	0	0	0	1	0	7	.143	0	2	6	.500	0	2
Nickle, Doug	0	0	.000	13.50	2.2	5	4	4	0	0	0	1	2	0	0	4	0	0	0	3	0	9	.333	0	1	3	.667	0	1

PITCHERS WITH MORE THAN ONE N.L. TEAM

Name	W	L	Pct.	ERA	IP	H	R	ER	HR	SH	SF	HB	BB	IBB	SO	G	GS	CG	ShO	GF	Sv	vs. RH AB	vs. RH Avg.	vs. RH HR	vs. RH RBI	vs. LH AB	vs. LH Avg.	vs. LH HR	vs. LH RBI
Ashby, Phi.-Atl.	12	13	.480	4.92	199.1	216	124	109	29	18	10	6	61	9	106	31	31	3	1	0	0	401	.249	13	57	371	.313	16	54
Chen, Atl.-Phi.	7	4	.636	3.29	134.0	116	54	49	18	8	3	2	46	4	112	37	15	0	0	3	0	388	.235	15	42	112	.223	3	9
Daal, Ari.-Phi.	4	19	.174	6.14	167.0	208	128	114	26	6	6	9	72	11	96	32	28	0	0	6	0	561	.307	20	90	121	.298	6	28
Miller, Phi.-L.A.	0	0	.000	10.47	16.1	27	22	19	3	1	1	2	12	1	11	16	0	0	0	1	0	44	.409	2	12	30	.300	1	8
Padilla, Ari.-Phi.	4	7	.364	3.72	65.1	72	33	27	3	5	3	1	28	7	51	55	0	0	0	3	2	159	.252	1	15	95	.337	2	19
Reyes, Phi.-S.D.	1	3	.250	5.72	28.1	25	18	18	7	2	0	1	13	0	17	22	0	0	0	0	1	58	.259	3	10	47	.213	4	11
Schilling, Phi.-Ari.	11	12	.478	3.81	210.1	204	90	89	27	11	4	1	45	4	168	29	29	8	2	4	0	373	.268	17	45	428	.243	10	43

DESIGNATED HITTERS

Name	AB	Avg.	HR	RBI	Name	AB	Avg.	HR	RBI
Burrell, Pat	14	.143	0	1	Sefcik, Kevin	2	1.000	0	0
Ducey, Rob	14	.000	0	0	Hunter, Brian	2	.000	0	0

INDIVIDUAL STATISTICS

FIELDING

FIRST BASEMEN

Player	Pct.	G	PO	A	E	TC	DP
Burrell, Pat	.988	58	460	22	6	488	37
Lee, Travis	1.000	47	338	35	0	373	42
Hunter, Brian	.994	40	159	16	1	176	12
Brogna, Rico	.996	34	248	17	1	266	22
Jordan, Kevin	.967	9	54	5	2	61	11
Pritchett, Chris	1.000	3	15	4	0	19	1

SECOND BASEMEN

Player	Pct.	G	PO	A	E	TC	DP
Morandini, Mickey	.987	85	179	196	5	380	45
Jordan, Kevin	.988	47	67	97	2	166	16
Anderson, Marlon	.989	41	87	100	2	189	32
Newhan, David	1.000	5	9	15	0	24	5
Arias, Alex	1.000	1	2	4	0	6	0

THIRD BASEMEN

Player	Pct.	G	PO	A	E	TC	DP
Rolen, Scott	.971	128	89	245	10	344	14
Jordan, Kevin	.967	39	26	61	3	90	8
Arias, Alex	1.000	10	2	6	0	8	1

SHORTSTOPS

Player	Pct.	G	PO	A	E	TC	DP
Relaford, Desi	.930	81	116	202	24	342	46
Perez, Tomas	.976	44	76	89	4	169	20
Arias, Alex	.963	39	41	88	5	134	19
Rollins, Jimmy	.978	13	23	22	1	46	9

OUTFIELDERS

Player	Pct.	G	PO	A	E	TC	DP
Abreu, Bobby	.989	152	337	13	4	354	2
Glanville, Doug	.990	150	380	9	4	393	4
Gant, Ron	.968	84	175	4	6	185	0
Sefcik, Kevin	1.000	50	74	0	0	74	0
Burrell, Pat	.975	48	73	6	2	81	0
Ducey, Rob	.938	33	44	1	3	48	0
Lee, Travis	1.000	10	9	0	0	9	0
Hunter, Brian	1.000	9	8	0	0	8	0
Taylor, Reggie	.750	3	3	0	1	4	0

CATCHERS

Player	Pct.	G	PO	A	E	TC	DP	PB
Lieberthal, Mike	.993	106	724	40	5	769	4	2
Prince, Tom	.996	46	250	20	1	271	2	2
Bennett, Gary	.995	31	173	11	1	185	2	0
Alvarez, Clemente	1.000	2	10	0	0	10	0	0

PITCHERS

Player	Pct.	G	PO	A	E	TC	DP
Gomes, Wayne	.889	65	2	6	1	9	0
Brock, Chris	1.000	63	4	7	0	11	0
Brantley, Jeff	1.000	55	3	2	0	5	0
Wolf, Randy	.970	32	4	28	1	33	2
Vosberg, Ed	1.000	31	1	8	0	9	0
Boyd, Jason	1.000	30	2	5	0	7	0
Person, Robert	1.000	28	6	11	0	17	1
Padilla, Vicente	.875	28	3	4	1	8	0
Holzemer, Mark	1.000	25	0	4	0	4	0
Aldred, Scott	1.000	23	1	2	0	3	0
Schrenk, Steve	1.000	20	2	1	0	3	0
Ward, Bryan	1.000	20	0	3	0	3	0
Byrd, Paul	.938	17	6	9	1	16	1
Ashby, Andy	.955	16	6	15	1	22	0
Schilling, Curt	1.000	16	6	8	0	14	0
Chen, Bruce	1.000	15	1	11	0	12	0
Miller, Trever	1.000	14	3	1	0	4	1
Telemaco, Amaury	1.000	13	2	0	0	2	0
Daal, Omar	1.000	12	3	13	0	16	1
Politte, Cliff	1.000	12	5	8	0	13	0
Reyes, Carlos	1.000	10	0	1	0	1	0
Jacquez, Tom	1.000	9	1	1	0	2	0
Bottenfield, Kent	.909	8	2	8	1	11	0
Coggin, Dave	.800	5	0	4	1	5	0
Nickle, Doug	1.000	4	1	1	0	2	0
Bullinger, Kirk	1.000	3	0	1	0	1	0
Brownson, Mark	1.000	2	1	1	0	2	0

PITCHING AGAINST EACH CLUB

Pitcher	Ari. W-L	Atl. W-L	Chi. W-L	Cin. W-L	Col. W-L	Fla. W-L	Hou. W-L	L.A. W-L	Mil. W-L	Mon. W-L	N.Y. W-L	Pit. W-L	S.D. W-L	S.F. W-L	StL. W-L	A.L. W-L	Total W-L
Aldred, Scott	0-0	0-2	0-0	0-0	0-0	0-0	0-0	0-0	0-0	1-0	0-1	0-0	0-0	0-0	0-0	0-0	1-3
Ashby, Andy	0-2	1-0	0-0	0-1	0-1	1-0	0-1	0-0	1-0	0-0	0-0	0-0	0-0	0-1	0-0	1-1	4-7
Bottenfield, K.	0-0	0-0	0-0	0-0	0-1	0-0	0-0	0-0	0-0	0-0	0-0	0-0	0-0	0-1	1-0	0-0	1-2
Boyd, Jason	0-0	0-0	0-0	0-0	0-0	0-0	0-0	0-0	0-0	0-0	0-0	0-0	0-0	0-0	0-0	0-1	0-1
Brantley, Jeff	0-1	0-0	0-0	0-0	0-1	0-0	0-0	0-0	0-0	0-0	1-0	0-0	0-1	0-0	0-0	1-4	2-7
Brock, Chris	0-1	1-0	0-1	1-0	0-1	0-0	0-1	0-1	2-0	0-1	1-0	0-1	1-0	0-0	0-1	1-0	7-8
Brownson, M.	0-0	0-0	1-0	0-0	0-0	0-0	0-0	0-0	0-0	0-0	0-0	0-0	0-0	0-0	0-0	0-0	1-0
Bullinger, Kirk	0-0	0-0	0-0	0-0	0-0	0-0	0-0	0-0	0-0	0-0	0-0	0-0	0-0	0-0	0-0	0-0	0-0
Byrd, Paul	0-1	0-1	0-1	1-0	0-0	0-1	0-0	0-1	0-1	0-1	0-0	1-1	0-0	0-1	0-0	0-0	2-9
Chen, Bruce	0-1	0-0	0-0	0-0	1-0	0-1	0-0	0-0	0-0	1-0	0-1	0-0	0-1	0-0	0-0	1-0	3-4
Coggin, Dave	0-0	0-0	0-0	0-0	0-0	0-0	0-0	0-0	0-0	1-0	0-0	0-0	0-0	0-0	0-0	1-0	2-0
Daal, Omar	0-0	0-0	1-0	0-1	0-1	0-1	0-1	0-1	0-0	0-0	0-1	0-0	1-1	0-1	0-1	0-0	2-9
Gomes, Wayne	1-1	0-2	0-0	0-0	0-1	1-0	1-0	0-0	0-0	0-1	1-0	0-0	0-0	0-0	0-1	0-0	4-6
Holzemer, M.	0-0	0-0	0-1	0-0	0-0	0-0	0-0	0-0	0-0	0-0	0-0	0-0	0-0	0-0	0-0	0-0	0-1
Jacquez, Tom	0-0	0-0	0-0	0-0	0-0	0-0	0-0	0-0	0-0	0-0	0-0	0-0	0-0	0-0	0-0	0-0	0-0
Miller, Trever	0-0	0-0	0-0	0-0	0-0	0-0	0-0	0-0	0-0	0-0	0-0	0-0	0-0	0-0	0-0	0-0	0-0
Nickle, Doug	0-0	0-0	0-0	0-0	0-0	0-0	0-0	0-0	0-0	0-0	0-0	0-0	0-0	0-0	0-0	0-0	0-0
Padilla, V.	0-0	0-0	0-1	1-0	0-0	0-0	0-1	0-1	0-0	0-1	1-0	0-1	0-0	0-1	0-0	0-0	2-6
Person, R.	0-0	0-0	0-1	1-0	2-0	1-2	1-0	1-1	0-0	1-0	2-0	0-1	0-1	0-0	0-1	0-0	9-7
Politte, Cliff	0-0	1-0	1-0	0-0	0-0	0-1	0-0	1-0	0-0	1-0	0-2	0-0	0-0	0-0	0-0	0-0	4-3
Reyes, Carlos	0-0	0-1	0-0	0-0	0-0	0-0	0-0	0-0	0-0	0-0	0-0	0-0	0-0	0-0	0-1	0-0	0-2
Schilling, Curt	0-0	2-0	0-0	0-0	0-0	0-0	0-0	0-0	1-0	0-0	0-0	2-0	0-0	0-1	0-2	1-3	6-6
Schrenk, S.	0-1	0-1	0-0	0-0	0-0	0-0	1-0	0-0	0-1	0-0	0-0	0-0	0-0	0-0	0-0	1-0	2-3
Telemaco, A.	0-0	0-0	0-0	0-0	0-0	0-1	0-0	0-0	0-0	0-1	1-0	0-1	0-0	0-0	0-0	0-0	1-3
Vosberg, Ed	0-0	0-0	0-0	0-0	0-0	0-0	0-0	0-0	0-0	0-0	0-0	0-0	0-0	1-1	0-0	0-0	1-1
Ward, Bryan	0-0	0-0	0-0	0-0	0-0	0-0	0-0	0-0	0-0	0-0	0-0	0-0	0-0	0-0	0-0	0-0	0-0
Wolf, Randy	0-0	0-1	0-1	0-1	0-0	1-2	1-1	2-0	1-0	2-0	0-1	0-1	0-1	1-0	1-0	2-0	11-9
Totals	1-8	5-8	3-6	4-3	3-6	4-9	4-5	4-5	5-2	7-5	7-6	3-6	2-5	2-7	2-7	9-9	65-97

INTERLEAGUE: Ashby 1-1, Wolf 1-0, Schilling 0-2, Brantley 0-1 vs. Orioles; Brantley 1-0, Wolf 1-0, Schrenk 1-0 vs. Red Sox; Coggin 1-0, Brantley 0-1, Schilling 0-1 vs. Yankees; Schilling 1-0, Chen 1-0, Brantley 0-1 vs. Blue Jays; Brock 1-0, Boyd 0-1, Brantley 0-1 vs. Devil Rays. Total: 9-9.

MISCELLANEOUS

HOME RUNS BY PARK

At Arizona (3): Rolen 2, Relaford 1.
At Atlanta (7): Rolen 3, Gant 1, Lieberthal 1, Abreu 1, Brock 1.
At Baltimore (5): Ducey 1, Lieberthal 1, Glanville 1, Rolen 1, Abreu 1.
At Chicago (NL) (6): Jordan 2, Gant 1, Arias 1, Glanville 1, Abreu 1.
At Cincinnati (3): Lieberthal 1, Rolen 1, Abreu 1.
At Colorado (3): Perez 1, Bennett 1, Rolen 1.
At Florida (3): Gant 1, Abreu 1, Burrell 1.
At Houston (9): Abreu 3, Glanville 2, Gant 1, Relaford 1, Rolen 1, Burrell 1.
At Los Angeles (4): Ducey 1, Lieberthal 1, Relaford 1, Burrell 1.
At Milwaukee (2): Hunter 1, Lieberthal 1.
At Montreal (3): Gant 1, Lieberthal 1, Rolen 1.
At New York (AL) (6): Abreu 2, Gant 1, Hunter 1, Lieberthal 1, Burrell 1.
At New York (NL) (7): Burrell 3, Rolen 2, Gant 1, Hunter 1.
At Philadelphia (66): Abreu 14, Rolen 12, Gant 9, Lieberthal 8, Burrell 7, Ducey 4, Hunter 3, Glanville 3, Jordan 2, Arias 1, Brogna 1, Lee 1, Anderson 1.
At Pittsburgh (4): Prince 2, Bennett 1, Abreu 1.
At San Diego (4): Burrell 2, Hunter 1, Rolen 1.
At San Francisco (4): Gant 2, Jordan 1, Burrell 1.
At St. Louis (1): Glanville 1.
At Toronto (4): Gant 2, Rolen 1, Burrell 1.

LOW-HIT GAMES

No-hitters: None.
One-hitters: None.
Two-hitters: None.

10-STRIKEOUT GAMES

Robert Person 3, Curt Schilling 2, Chris Brock 1, Total: 6

FOUR OR MORE HITS IN ONE GAME

Bobby Abreu 3, Doug Glanville 2 (including one five-hit game), Ron Gant 1, Tom Prince 1, Mike Lieberthal 1, Travis Lee 1, Pat Burrell 1, Total: 10

MULTI-HOMER GAMES

Bobby Abreu 2, Pat Burrell 2, Rob Ducey 1, Ron Gant 1, Tom Prince 1, Mike Lieberthal 1, Scott Rolen 1, Total: 9

GRAND SLAMS

5-12: Scott Rolen (off Atlanta's Rudy Seanez)
5-21: Brian Hunter (off Colorado's Masato Yoshii)
6-21: Pat Burrell (off New York's Armando Benitez)
7-17: Bobby Abreu (off New York's Jason Grimsley)
8-8: Pat Burrell (off San Diego's Kevin Walker)

PINCH HITTERS

(Minimum 5 at-bats)

Name	AB	Avg.	HR	RBI
Ducey, Rob	69	.203	0	6
Sefcik, Kevin	44	.159	0	2
Hunter, Brian	40	.225	1	4
Jordan, Kevin	24	.167	0	2
Arias, Alex	14	.286	0	1
Morandini, Mickey	6	.333	0	0
Brogna, Rico	5	.200	0	1
Glanville, Doug	5	.200	1	1

DEBUTS

5-24: Pat Burrell, 1B.
6-23: Dave Coggin, P.
9-9: Tom Jacquez, P.
9-17: Jimmy Rollins, SS.
9-17: Reggie Taylor, CF.
9-18: Doug Nickle, P.
9-19: Clemente Alvarez, PH.

GAMES BY POSITION

Catcher: Mike Lieberthal 106, Tom Prince 46, Gary Bennett 31, Clemente Alvarez 2.
First base: Pat Burrell 58, Travis Lee 47, Brian Hunter 40, Rico Brogna 34, Kevin Jordan 9, Chris Pritchett 3.
Second base: Mickey Morandini 85, Kevin Jordan 47, Marlon Anderson 41, David Newhan 5, Alex Arias 1.
Third base: Scott Rolen 128, Kevin Jordan 39, Alex Arias 10.
Shortstop: Desi Relaford 81, Tomas Perez 44, Alex Arias 39, Jimmy Rollins 13.
Outfield: Bobby Abreu 152, Doug Glanville 150, Ron Gant 84, Kevin Sefcik 50, Pat Burrell 48, Rob Ducey 33, Travis Lee 10, Brian Hunter 9, Reggie Taylor 3.
Designated hitter: Rob Ducey 5, Pat Burrell 4, Brian Hunter 1, Kevin Sefcik 1.

STREAKS

Wins: 5 (July 1-5)
Losses: 8 (August 29-September 6)
Consecutive games with at least one hit: 14, Scott Rolen (June 21-July 6)
Wins by pitcher: 3, Randy Wolf (May 28-June 9)

ATTENDANCE

Home: 1,612,769
Road: 2,467,356
Highest (home): 48,406 (July 1 vs. Pittsburgh).
Highest (road): 53,775 (September 10 vs. New York).
Lowest (home): 11,310 (September 11 vs. Montreal).
Lowest (road): 8,197 (June 23 vs. Montreal)

Pittsburgh Pirates

DAY BY DAY

Date	Opp.	Res.	Score	(inn.*)	Hits	Opp. hits	Winning pitcher	Losing pitcher	Save	Record	Pos.	GB
4-4	Hou.	L	2-5		6	5	Reynolds	Schmidt	Wagner	0-1	T5th	1.0
4-5	Hou.	L	2-11		9	10	Lima	Benson		0-2	T5th	2.0
4-6	Hou.	W	10-1		16	2	Cordova	Holt		1-2	T4th	2.0
4-7	At Ari.	W	7-2		12	7	Christiansen	Reynoso		2-2	T3rd	1.0
4-8	At Ari.	L	5-6		12	12	Swindell	Christiansen		2-3	T4th	2.0
4-9	At Ari.	L	0-1		5	4	Johnson	Schmidt		2-4	5th	3.0
4-11	Mon.	L	3-7		4	9	Vazquez	Benson	Kline	2-5	6th	4.5
4-12	Mon.	W	6-4		10	7	Silva	Batista	Williams	3-5	6th	3.5
4-13	Mon.	W	4-3		10	8	Silva	Urbina		4-5	T4th	2.5
4-14	N.Y.	L	5-8	(12)	11	20	Franco	Silva		4-6	T5th	2.5
4-15	N.Y.	W	2-0		4	5	Anderson	Rusch	Williams	5-6	T4th	2.0
4-16	N.Y.	L	9-12		11	15	Mahomes	Peters	Benitez	5-7	T5th	2.5
4-18	At Fla.	L	5-12		10	17	Penny	Cordova		5-8	T4th	3.5
4-19	At Fla.	W	5-1		8	8	Ritchie	Fernandez		6-8	T3rd	3.5
4-20	At Fla.	L	2-3	(14)	11	10	Darensbourg	Williams		6-9	T4th	4.5
4-21	At Atl.	L	2-6		8	12	Mulholland	Garcia		6-10	T5th	4.5
4-22	At Atl.	L	2-4		9	9	Chen	Benson	Rocker	6-11	5th	4.5
4-23	At Atl.	L	3-5		7	7	Maddux	Cordova	Rocker	6-12	T5th	5.5
4-25	S.D.	W	4-3	(11)	9	13	Sauerbeck	Almanzar		7-12	T4th	5.5
4-26	S.D.	W	9-8		12	10	Williams	Whisenant		8-12	3rd	5.5
4-27	S.D.	L	4-12		4	15	Clement	Parra		8-13	T3rd	5.5
4-28	Cin.	W	2-1		6	5	Benson	Harnisch	Williams	9-13	3rd	5.5
4-29	Cin.	L	5-6		8	8	Williamson	Christiansen	Graves	9-14	4th	6.5
4-30	Cin.	L	2-6		6	10	Bell	Ritchie	Williamson	9-15	T4th	7.5
5-2	At StL.	W	10-7		13	9	Wallace	Slocumb		10-15	T3rd	6.5
5-3	At StL.	W	8-2		13	5	Benson	Hentgen		11-15	3rd	5.5
5-4	At StL.	L	0-5		4	9	Stephenson	Cordova		11-16	T3rd	6.5
5-5	At Chi.	W	4-2		7	8	Ritchie	Tapani	Williams	12-16	3rd	5.5
5-6	At Chi.	W	11-9		16	16	Wallace	Farnsworth	Williams	13-16	3rd	5.5
5-7	At Chi.	W	11-3		13	9	Schmidt	Wood		14-16	3rd	4.5
5-9	N.Y.	L	0-2		6	8	Hampton	Benson	Benitez	14-17	3rd	5.0
5-10	N.Y.	W	13-9		20	13	Silva	Cook		15-17	3rd	4.0
5-11	N.Y.	L	2-3		8	6	Leiter	Anderson		15-18	3rd	4.5
5-12	Mil.	L	1-6		4	11	Haynes	Schmidt		15-19	3rd	4.5
5-13	Mil.	W	11-8		16	10	Sauerbeck	Acevedo	Williams	16-19	3rd	4.0
5-14	Mil.	W	3-0		7	4	Benson	D'Amico	Christiansen	17-19	3rd	3.5
5-16	At Cin.	L	2-6		9	12	Bell	Ritchie		17-20	3rd	4.5
5-17	At Cin.	W	9-6		13	12	Silva	Sullivan		18-20	3rd	3.5
5-18	At Cin.	L	3-4	(10)	10	9	Graves	Garcia		18-21	3rd	4.5
5-19	StL.	W	13-1		15	3	Benson	Ankiel		19-21	3rd	3.5
5-20	StL.	L	4-19		9	19	Hentgen	Cordova		19-22	3rd	4.5
5-21	StL.	L	5-7		9	10	An. Benes	Ritchie	Veres	19-23	3rd	5.5
5-23	At Ari.	L	1-6		8	11	Anderson	Anderson		19-24	4th	6.5
5-24	At Ari.	L	5-6		8	9	Stottlemyre	Schmidt	Kim	19-25	4th	7.5
5-25	At Ari.	L	5-7		9	12	Daal	Benson	Mantei	19-26	4th	8.5
5-26	At Col.	W	2-1		8	6	Cordova	Yoshii	Williams	20-26	3rd	7.5
5-27	At Col.	L	6-7		12	10	White	Christiansen		20-27	3rd	7.5
5-28	At Col.	L	2-11		7	17	Arrojo	Anderson		20-28	4th	7.5
5-29	Fla.	W	10-4		13	11	Schmidt	Nunez		21-28	4th	7.5
5-30	Fla.	W	3-2	(10)	11	5	Williams	Alfonseca		22-28	3rd	7.5
5-31	Fla.	W	5-2		5	12	Cordova	Sanchez	Williams	23-28	3rd	6.5
6-2	K.C.	W	9-3		8	4	Ritchie	Batista		24-28	3rd	6.0
6-3	K.C.	L	3-16		8	18	Witasick	Schmidt		24-29	3rd	6.0
6-4	K.C.	L	5-7	(11)	9	9	Rakers	Christiansen	Reichert	24-30	3rd	6.5
6-5	Det.	W	5-1		9	7	Cordova	Mlicki		25-30	3rd	5.5
6-6	Det.	L	1-2		11	5	Nitkowski	Anderson	Jones	25-31	3rd	6.0
6-7	Det.	W	4-3		9	8	Ritchie	Nomo	Williams	26-31	3rd	6.0
6-9	At K.C.	L	5-6	(10)	9	13	Spradlin	Christiansen		26-32	3rd	6.0
6-10	At K.C.	L	1-2	(12)	13	10	Bottalico	Silva		26-33	3rd	6.0
6-11	At K.C.	W	10-6	(10)	18	11	Sauerbeck	Spradlin		27-33	3rd	6.0
6-12	Atl.	L	8-10		9	13	Ligtenberg	Christiansen	Remlinger	27-34	3rd	7.0
6-13	Atl.	W	7-6	(10)	10	14	Silva	Wengert		28-34	3rd	7.0
6-14	Atl.	L	4-8		9	7	Maddux	Anderson	Ligtenberg	28-35	3rd	8.0
6-15	Atl.	W	2-0		7	6	Benson	Millwood		29-35	3rd	7.5
6-16	Fla.	L	3-8		8	10	Cornelius	Cordova	Looper	29-36	3rd	8.5
6-17	Fla.	L	3-4	(11)	12	10	Alfonseca	Loiselle	Strong	29-37	3rd	9.5
6-18	Fla.	L	4-5		8	10	Bones	Christiansen	Alfonseca	29-38	3rd	9.5
6-19	At Mon.	L	1-2		6	7	Pavano	Loiselle	Kline	29-39	T3rd	10.0
6-20	At Mon.	W	2-1		4	6	Benson	Johnson	Williams	30-39	3rd	10.0
6-21	At Mon.	W	8-3		10	9	Cordova	Armas	Peters	31-39	3rd	9.0
6-22	At Mon.	L	5-6		11	8	Hermanson	Ritchie	Telford	31-40	3rd	10.0
6-23	At N.Y.	L	2-12		7	14	B.J. Jones	Arroyo		31-41	3rd	11.0
6-24	At N.Y.	L	8-10		15	12	Franco	Loiselle	Benitez	31-42	3rd	12.0
6-25	At N.Y.	L	0-9		5	12	Hampton	Benson		31-43	3rd	13.0
6-27	Chi.	W	6-0		5	3	Ritchie	Wood		32-43	3rd	12.5
6-28	Chi.	L	4-5		9	8	Lieber	Cordova	Aguilera	32-44	3rd	12.5
6-29	Chi.	W	5-4	(10)	7	7	Wilkins	Worrell		33-44	3rd	12.5
6-30	At Phi.	W	8-3		13	11	Benson	Wolf		34-44	3rd	12.5

HIGHLIGHTS

High point: An eight-game winning streak to open September offered hope that the team was getting better and would finish strong. But it was another false alarm. That streak was preceded by a 2-7 fade and followed by a nine-game losing skid.
Low point: An 8-21 August doomed the team to its eighth consecutive losing season and probably sealed the fate of manager Gene Lamont, whose contract was not renewed after four seasons with the team.
Turning point: Jason Schmidt went on the disabled list June 10 with inflammation in his shoulder. The condition eventually required surgery and Schmidt, the team's opening night starter, had his season end after just 11 starts. Schmidt's injury, combined with Francisco Cordova's ongoing elbow problems, was an irreparable blow to the starting staff.
Most valuable player: Brian Giles was indispensable, especially after he moved back to left field. Giles matched his 1999 average (.315) and improved on his RBI total (123) despite hitting four fewer home runs (35) and drawing a team-high 114 walks.
Most valuable pitcher: With Schmidt and Cordova injured, the No. 1 starter job fell to second-year man Kris Benson. It was still a learning experience, but Benson provided some consistency and missed posting a winning record (10-12) only because of weak offensive and defensive support.
Most improved player: Adrian Brown started as the sixth outfielder and finished as the starting center fielder. Brown, a switch-hitter, improved his upper-body strength and spent hours in the cage working on his lefthanded swing. He has transformed himself from a lightly regarded prospect into a valuable leadoff man.
Most pleasant surprise: The Pirates knew they were acquiring a premier pinch hitter when they traded for John Vander Wal. But the 34-year-old veteran forced his way into the lineup and batted .299 with 24 home runs and 94 RBIs.
Key injuries: Schmidt didn't appear in a game after June 9 and Cordova made one appearance over the last two months. Their absences blew a hole in a rotation that had been overappraised by management. ... Adrian Brown was sidelined six weeks with a recurring hamstring injury.
Notable: Pittsburgh's last streak of eight losing seasons occurred from 1949-57. ... The team ERA of 4.94 was the highest since 1953, when the Pirates checked in at 5.22. ... Giles became the franchise's first player to top .300 with 30 home runs and 100 RBIs in consecutive seasons. ... Pitchers issued a team-record 711 walks.

—JOHN MEHNO

MISCELLANEOUS

RECORDS

2000 regular-season record: 69-93 (5th in N.L. Central); 37-44 at home; 32-49 on road; 18-23 vs. East; 33-44 vs. Central; 18-26 vs. West; 15-22 vs. lefthanded starters; 54-71 vs. righthanded starters; 23-42 on grass; 46-51 on turf; 15-33 in daytime; 54-60 at night; 17-30 in one-run games; 8-11 in extra-inning games; 1-0-2 in doubleheaders.
Team record past five years: 368-441 (.455, ranks 13th in league in that span).

TEAM LEADERS

Batting average: Jason Kendall (.320).
At-bats: Jason Kendall (579).
Runs: Jason Kendall (112).
Hits: Jason Kendall (185).
Total Bases: Brian Giles (332).
Doubles: Brian Giles (37).
Triples: Brian Giles (7).
Home runs: Brian Giles (35).
Runs batted in: Brian Giles (123).
Stolen bases: Jason Kendall (22).
Slugging percentage: Brian Giles (.594).
On-base percentage: Brian Giles (.432).
Wins: Jose Silva (11).
Earned-run average: Kris Benson (3.85).
Complete games: Kris Benson (2).
Shutouts: Kris Benson, Todd Ritchie (1).
Saves: Mike Williams (24).
Innings pitched: Kris Benson (217.2).
Strikeouts: Kris Benson (184).

Date	Opp.	Res.	Score	(inn.*)	Hits	Opp. hits	Winning pitcher	Losing pitcher	Save	Record	Pos.	GB
7-1	At Phi.	L	3-4		5	10	Byrd	Arroyo	Brantley	34-45	3rd	13.5
7-2	At Phi.	L	1-9		9	15	Schilling	Ritchie		34-46	3rd	13.5
7-3	At Chi.	L	0-3		2	9	Lieber	Cordova		34-47	3rd	14.0
7-4	At Chi.	W	10-4		12	8	Wilkins	Aguilera		35-47	3rd	14.0
7-5	At Chi.	W	9-6		12	10	Anderson	Downs		36-47	3rd	14.0
7-7	Min.	W	8-6		13	9	Christiansen	Wells	Williams	37-47	3rd	12.5
7-8	Min.	W	4-1		8	5	Benson	Milton	Williams	38-47	3rd	11.5
7-9	Min.	L	2-3		8	8	Redman	Silva	Hawkins	38-48	3rd	12.5
7-13	At Cle.	L	3-4	(10)	8	10	Karsay	Sauerbeck		38-49	3rd	13.5
7-14	At Cle.	L	3-9		8	11	Finley	Benson		38-50	4th	14.5
7-15	At Cle.	L	4-6		10	10	Brewington	Silva	Karsay	38-51	4th	14.5
7-16	At L.A.	L	3-7		7	8	Adams	Williams		38-52	T4th	14.5
7-17	At L.A.	L	6-9		10	12	Dreifort	Arroyo	Shaw	38-53	5th	15.5
7-18	At L.A.	W	8-6		8	12	Manzanillo	Judd	Williams	39-53	T3rd	14.5
7-19	At Mil.	L	0-6		5	5	D'Amico	Benson		39-54	5th	14.5
7-20	At Mil.	W	9-2		12	5	Silva	Haynes		40-54	T3rd	13.5
7-21	Phi.	W	9-2		11	4	Anderson	Byrd		41-54	T3rd	13.5
7-22	Phi.	W	2-1		5	4	Arroyo	Person	Williams	42-54	T3rd	12.5
7-23	Phi.	L	1-4		3	7	Schilling	Ritchie		42-55	4th	12.5
7-25	Mil.	L	1-4	(11)	6	10	Leskanic	Christiansen	Wickman	42-56	4th	13.5
7-26	Mil.	W	5-4		10	8	Silva	Haynes	Williams	43-56	4th	13.5
7-27	Mil.	L	3-4		7	9	Leskanic	Manzanillo	Wickman	43-57	4th	13.5
7-28	S.D.	W	16-5		14	9	Arroyo	Clement		44-57	4th	12.5
7-29	S.D.	W	10-2		16	6	Cordova	Tollberg		45-57	4th	11.5
7-30	S.D.	L	8-9		13	14	Wall	Wilkins	Hoffman	45-58	4th	11.5
8-1†	L.A.	W	6-0		12	6	Anderson	Perez		46-58		
8-1‡	L.A.	L	3-5		8	7	Herges	Wilkins	Shaw	46-59	4th	11.5
8-2	L.A.	L	5-11		10	11	Dreifort	Silva		46-60	4th	12.5
8-3	At S.F	L	2-10		7	12	Ortiz	Cordova		46-61	4th	13.0
8-4	At S.F	L	3-5		11	10	Henry	Benson	Nen	46-62	4th	13.0
8-5	At S.F	W	7-2		13	9	Serafini	Gardner		47-62	4th	13.0
8-6	At S.F	L	1-7		10	9	Estes	Arroyo		47-63	4th	13.0
8-7	At Col.	W	8-7		13	12	Sauerbeck	Jimenez	Williams	48-63	4th	13.0
8-8	At Col.	L	1-6		10	15	Rose	Silva		48-64	4th	13.0
8-9	At Col.	L	3-4		7	7	White	Williams		48-65	4th	13.0
8-11	Ari.	L	1-6		4	10	Reynoso	Serafini		48-66	4th	13.5
8-12	Ari.	W	9-6		11	10	Sauerbeck	Schilling		49-66	4th	13.5
8-13	Ari.	L	6-7		12	14	Morgan	Arroyo	Mantei	49-67	4th	14.5
8-14	At Hou.	L	2-16		5	19	Holt	Silva		49-68	4th	14.5
8-15	At Hou.	L	4-5		9	7	Lima	Benson	Dotel	49-69	5th	15.5
8-16	At Hou.	L	10-11		12	9	Elarton	Serafini	Dotel	49-70	5th	16.5
8-18	At Cin.	W	6-3		11	6	Ritchie	Sullivan	Williams	50-70	5th	16.5
8-19	At Cin.	L	1-7		8	7	Parris	Anderson		50-71	5th	17.5
8-20	At Cin.	W	7-3		8	9	Silva	Dessens		51-71	5th	16.5
8-21	At StL.	L	4-7		6	8	Stephenson	Benson	Veres	51-72	5th	17.5
8-22	At StL.	W	6-2		11	10	Manzanillo	Kile		52-72	5th	16.5
8-23	At StL.	L	2-5		8	10	Ankiel	Ritchie	Veres	52-73	5th	17.5
8-25	Col.	L	3-6		9	13	Tavarez	Anderson		52-74	6th	18.0
8-26	Col.	L	4-11		10	19	Astacio	Silva		52-75	6th	19.0
8-27	Col.	L	2-9		4	16	Bohanon	Serafini		52-76	6th	20.0
8-28	S.F	L	4-5		6	8	Embree	Sauerbeck	Nen	52-77	6th	21.0
8-29	S.F	W	8-0		10	1	Benson	Hernandez		53-77	6th	20.0
8-30	S.F	L	0-2		4	5	Ortiz	Anderson	Nen	53-78	6th	21.0
8-31	S.F	L	2-10		10	13	Rueter	Silva		53-79	6th	21.5
9-1	At S.D.	W	3-2	(10)	10	6	Williams	Hoffman		54-79	6th	21.5
9-2	At S.D.	W	6-3		8	8	Ritchie	Clement	Sauerbeck	55-79	6th	21.5
9-3	At S.D.	W	8-6	(13)	11	16	Skrmetta	Almanzar	Williams	56-79	6th	21.5
9-4	At L.A.	W	12-1		13	10	Anderson	Dreifort		57-79	5th	21.5
9-5	At L.A.	W	8-0		15	6	Silva	Perez		58-79	4th	21.5
9-6	At L.A.	W	8-3		12	6	Serafini	Valdes		59-79	4th	20.5
9-8†	Cin.	W	7-3		11	7	Ritchie	Williamson		60-79		
9-8‡	Cin.	W	3-1		6	9	Wilkins	Villone	Williams	61-79	T3rd	19.5
9-9	Cin.	L	4-6		9	14	Parris	Benson	Graves	61-80	T4th	20.5
9-10	Cin.	L	4-6		6	8	Dessens	Anderson	Graves	61-81	5th	20.5
9-11	StL.	L	4-8		7	12	Stephenson	Manzanillo		61-82	5th	21.5
9-12	StL.	L	1-11		7	16	Kile	Serafini		61-83	5th	22.5
9-13	StL.	L	5-9		10	13	Ankiel	Ritchie		61-84	5th	23.5
9-14	At Hou.	L	7-8		12	11	Slusarski	Skrmetta		61-85	5th	24.5
9-15	At Hou.	L	7-16		12	19	B. Powell	Skrmetta	Slusarski	61-86	5th	25.5
9-16	At Hou.	L	9-10	(10)	16	9	Valdes	Sauerbeck		61-87	5th	26.5
9-17	At Hou.	L	3-5		8	9	Elarton	Serafini	Dotel	61-88	5th	27.5
9-18	At Phi.	W	6-5		11	10	Loiselle	Padilla	Williams	62-88	5th	27.0
9-19	At Phi.	W	12-8		13	6	Skrmetta	Telemaco	Williams	63-88	5th	26.0
9-20	At Phi.	W	7-6	(10)	12	7	Loiselle	Brock	Williams	64-88	5th	26.0
9-21	At Mil.	L	2-12		5	14	Rigdon	Anderson		64-89	5th	26.0
9-23†	At Mil.	W	4-2		14	5	Silva	D'Amico	Williams	65-89		
9-23‡	At Mil.	L	4-5	(10)	10	8	Leskanic	Arroyo		65-90	5th	26.0
9-24	At Mil.	L	5-8		6	9	Leskanic	Williams		65-91	5th	26.0
9-26	Hou.	W	9-4		10	7	Benson	Holt		66-91	5th	26.0
9-27	Hou.	L	1-10		4	10	McKnight	Anderson		66-92	5th	27.0
9-28	Hou.	W	3-2		3	10	Silva	Dotel		67-92	5th	27.0
9-29	Chi.	W	8-4		13	10	Wilkins	Rain		68-92	5th	26.0
9-30	Chi.	W	4-2		7	11	Ritchie	Quevedo	Williams	69-92	5th	25.0
10-1	Chi.	L	9-10		14	12	Farnsworth	Sauerbeck	Arnold	69-93	5th	26.0

Monthly records: April (9-15), May (14-13), June (11-16), July (11-14), August (8-21), September (16-13), October (0-1).
*Innings, if other than nine. † First game of a doubleheader. ‡ Second game of a doubleheader.

MEMORABLE GAMES

May 6 at Chicago

Trailing 9-5 in the ninth, the Pirates rallied for six runs and an 11-9 win over the Cubs. Wil Cordero tripled in the game-tying run and Pat Meares drove in the go-ahead run with a bloop double. It was the Pirates' biggest ninth-inning win since 1991.

Pittsburgh	AB	R	H	BI	Cubs	AB	R	H	BI
Hermansen, cf	4	1	1	0	E.Young, 2b	5	2	3	1
Morris, ph	1	0	0	0	Gutierrez, ss	4	2	1	0
Aven, ph-rf	1	0	0	0	Sosa, rf	4	1	4	4
Sojo, 3b	5	2	3	2	Hill, lf	4	1	2	3
Kendall, c	4	1	2	1	B. Williams, p	0	0	0	0
Giles, rf-cf	4	2	2	3	Huson, ph	1	0	0	0
K.Young, 1b	5	0	1	1	Aguilera, p	0	0	0	0
Cordero, lf	5	2	3	1	Farnsworth, p	0	0	0	0
Meares, ss	4	1	1	1	Heredia, p	0	0	0	0
Benjamin, 2b	5	1	3	2	Andrews, 1b-3b	4	0	1	0
Anderson, p	2	0	0	0	Nieves, 3b	3	0	1	0
Silva, p	0	0	0	0	Rodriguez, lf	1	0	0	0
Parra, p	0	0	0	0	Buford, cf	5	1	2	1
Brown, ph	1	0	0	0	Girardi, c	4	1	1	0
Sauerbeck, p	0	0	0	0	Greene, ph	1	0	0	0
Wallace, p	0	0	0	0	Downs, p	2	0	0	0
Vander Wal, ph	0	1	0	0	Grace, ph-1b	2	1	1	0
M. Williams, p	0	0	0	0					
Totals	**41**	**11**	**16**	**11**	**Totals**	**40**	**9**	**16**	**9**

Pittsburgh ....1 1 1 0 0 1 1 0 6—11 16 0
Cubs ....2 0 0 0 1 6 0 0 0— 9 16 0

DP—Pittsburgh 2, Cubs 2. LOB—Pittsburgh 8, Cubs 9. 2B—Hermansen (3), K. Young (9), Cordero (7), Meares (7), Benjamin (4), E. Young (13), Buford (4). 3B—Cordero (2). HR—Sojo (2), Giles (7), Sosa (11), Hill (4), Buford (5). CS—Andrews (1).

Pittsburgh	IP	H	R	ER	BB	SO
Anderson	5	8	3	3	2	3
Silva	0.1	4	4	4	0	0
Parra	0.2	2	2	2	1	0
Sauerbeck	1	1	0	0	1	1
Wallace (W 2-0)	1	1	0	0	0	1
M.Williams (S 5)	1	0	0	0	1	2
Cubs	**IP**	**H**	**R**	**ER**	**BB**	**SO**
Downs	6	8	4	4	1	3
B.Williams	2	3	1	1	1	0
Aguilera	0.1	2	4	4	2	0
Farnsworth (L	0.1	3	2	2	1	0
FHeredia	0.1	0	0	0	0	0

U—HP, Katzenmeier. 1B, Meals. 2B, Young. 3B, Bonin. T—3:26. A—38,957.

October 1 at Pittsburgh

The last game at Three Rivers Stadium almost had a storybook ending as John Wehner, the only Pittsburgh native on the roster, hit a two-run homer to give the Pirates an 8-5 lead in a four-run fifth inning.But in typical 2000 fashion, the bullpen blew the lead and the Three Rivers finale turned into a 10-9 Cubs win. Wehner grounded out with two runners on base in the ninth.

Cubs	AB	R	H	BI	Pittsburgh	AB	R	H	BI
Huson, 2b-3b	5	2	2	0	A.Brown, cf	5	2	1	1
Patterson, cf	6	2	2	0	M.Williams, p	0	0	0	0
Sosa, rf	5	2	2	1	Kendall, c	5	1	1	0
Grace, 1b	3	1	2	3	Giles, lf	5	2	3	0
R.Brown, lf	2	0	0	1	Vander Wal, rf	5	1	3	3
Zuleta, ph	0	0	0	0	Young, 1b	4	1	0	1
Farnsworth, p	0	0	0	0	Morris, 2b	5	1	2	2
Nieves, ph	1	0	0	0	Wehner, 3b	5	1	3	2
Buford, lf	1	0	0	0	Meares, ss	3	0	0	0
Greene, 3b	2	0	1	1	Wilkins, p	0	0	0	0
Andrews, ph-3b	3	1	1	2	Manzanillo, p	0	0	0	0
Arnold, p	0	0	0	0	Wallace, p	0	0	0	0
Reed, c	5	0	0	0	Loiselle, p	0	0	0	0
Ojeda, ss-2b	3	1	1	1	Sauerbeck, p	0	0	0	0
Lieber, p	2	0	0	0	Osik, ph	1	0	1	0
Gload, ph	0	1	0	0	E.Brown, pr-cf	0	0	0	0
Matthews Jr., lf	1	0	1	0	Benson, p	2	0	0	0
Worrell, p	0	0	0	0	Benjamin, ss	1	0	0	0
Heredia, p	0	0	0	0					
Gutierrez, ss	0	0	0	0					
Totals	**39**	**10**	**12**	**9**	**Totals**	**41**	**9**	**14**	**9**

Cubs ....2 0 2 0 1 2 0 3 0—10 12 2
Pittsburgh ....1 0 3 0 4 0 0 0 1— 9 14 1

E—Huson (3), Ojeda (1), Wehner (1). DP—Cubs 1, LOB—Cubs 14, Pittsburgh 7. 2B—Sosa (38), Grace (41), Ojeda (3), Andrews (5), Vander Wal 2 (29), Morris (31). HR—A. Brown (4), Wehner (1). SB—Patterson (1). S—A. Brown. HBP—Young by Lieber, Zuleta by Wallace.

Cubs	IP	H	R	ER	BB	SO
Lieber	5	9	8	7	0	3
Farnsworth (W 2-9)	2	0	0	0	0	3
Worrell	0.1	2	0	0	1	1
Heredia	1.1	3	1	1	0	1
Arnold (S 1)	0.1	0	0	0	0	0
Pittsburgh	**IP**	**H**	**R**	**ER**	**BB**	**SO**
Benson	5	7	5	4	2	9
Wilkins	0	0	2	2	3	0
Manzanillo	0.2	0	0	0	1	1
Wallace	0	0	0	0	0	0
Loiselle	1.1	1	0	0	1	1
Sauerbeck (L 5-4)	1	3	3	3	2	1
Williams	1	1	0	0	1	0

Wilkins pitched to 3 batters in 6th. Wallace pitched to 1 batter in 6th. WP—Manzanillo. U—HP, Layne. 1B, Barrett. 2B, Randazzo. 3B, Montague. T—3:39. A—55,351.

INDIVIDUAL STATISTICS

BATTING

																							vs RHP				vs LHP			
Name	G	TPA	AB	R	H	TB	2B	3B	HR	RBI	Avg.	Obp.	Slg.	SH	SF	HP	BB	IBB	SO	SB	CS	GDP	AB	Avg.	HR	RBI	AB	Avg.	HR	RBI
Kendall, Jason	152	678	579	112	185	272	33	6	14	58	.320	.412	.470	1	4	15	79	3	79	22	12	13	452	.316	12	44	127	.331	2	14
Giles, Brian	156	688	559	111	176	332	37	7	35	123	.315	.432	.594	0	8	7	114	13	69	6	0	15	409	.323	30	95	150	.293	5	28
Morris, Warren	144	606	528	68	137	181	31	2	3	43	.259	.341	.343	8	3	2	65	3	78	7	10	7	441	.265	3	35	87	.230	0	8
Young, Kevin	132	541	496	77	128	215	27	0	20	88	.258	.311	.433	0	5	8	32	1	96	8	3	15	367	.256	13	74	129	.264	7	14
Meares, Pat	132	514	462	55	111	176	22	2	13	47	.240	.305	.381	5	3	8	36	6	91	1	0	13	341	.243	10	38	121	.231	3	9
Vander Wal, John	134	461	384	74	115	216	29	0	24	94	.299	.410	.563	0	3	2	72	5	92	11	2	7	334	.314	22	87	50	.200	2	7
Cordero, Wil	89	378	348	46	98	176	24	3	16	51	.282	.336	.506	0	1	4	25	1	58	1	2	11	261	.264	11	30	87	.333	5	21
Brown, Adrian	104	340	308	64	97	133	18	3	4	28	.315	.373	.432	2	1	0	29	1	34	13	1	1	256	.305	3	24	52	.365	1	4
Ramirez, Aramis	73	274	254	19	65	102	15	2	6	35	.256	.293	.402	1	4	5	10	0	36	0	0	9	191	.262	5	31	63	.238	1	4
Benjamin, Mike	93	255	233	28	63	91	18	2	2	19	.270	.313	.391	6	1	3	12	0	45	5	4	4	153	.242	2	9	80	.325	0	10
Sojo, Luis	61	189	176	14	50	76	11	0	5	20	.284	.328	.432	0	1	1	11	3	16	1	0	6	124	.298	3	10	52	.250	2	10
Aven, Bruce	72	153	148	18	37	63	11	0	5	25	.250	.275	.426	0	0	0	5	0	31	2	3	4	92	.239	3	17	56	.268	2	8
Osik, Keith	46	143	123	11	36	56	6	1	4	22	.293	.387	.455	1	0	5	14	0	11	3	0	2	88	.261	1	13	35	.371	3	9
Wilson, Enrique	40	136	122	11	32	49	6	1	3	15	.262	.321	.402	2	1	0	11	2	13	0	1	4	92	.228	1	11	30	.367	2	4
Brown, Emil	50	135	119	13	26	40	5	0	3	16	.218	.299	.336	1	1	3	11	0	34	3	1	3	87	.218	3	14	32	.219	0	2
Ramirez, Alex	43	123	115	13	24	44	6	1	4	18	.209	.254	.383	1	0	0	7	2	32	1	0	6	74	.216	4	13	41	.195	0	5
Hermansen, Chad	33	117	108	12	20	32	4	1	2	8	.185	.226	.296	2	1	0	6	0	37	0	0	3	60	.183	1	5	48	.188	1	3
Nunez, Abraham	40	99	91	10	20	24	1	0	1	8	.220	.283	.264	0	0	0	8	1	14	0	0	3	81	.222	1	7	10	.200	0	1
Benson, Kris	32	79	65	3	6	8	2	0	0	1	.092	.157	.123	9	0	1	4	0	29	0	0	0	49	.061	0	1	16	.188	0	0
Ritchie, Todd	31	64	60	4	13	15	2	0	0	2	.217	.242	.250	2	0	0	2	0	22	0	0	1	48	.188	0	2	12	.333	0	0
Hernandez, Alex	20	60	60	4	12	18	3	0	1	5	.200	.200	.300	0	0	0	0	0	13	1	1	0	55	.200	1	4	5	.200	0	1
Wehner, John	21	55	50	10	15	21	3	0	1	9	.300	.352	.420	1	0	0	4	0	6	0	0	1	40	.325	1	7	10	.200	0	2
Anderson, Jimmy	27	54	50	5	7	8	1	0	0	1	.140	.140	.160	4	0	0	0	0	11	0	0	0	35	.086	0	1	15	.267	0	0
Cordova, Francisco	18	37	35	0	4	4	0	0	0	3	.114	.162	.114	0	0	0	2	0	15	0	0	1	28	.143	0	2	7	.000	0	1
Silva, Jose	51	41	34	0	6	6	0	0	0	2	.176	.222	.176	5	0	1	1	0	12	0	0	1	27	.148	0	2	7	.286	0	0
Serafini, Dan	11	27	24	1	2	2	0	0	0	2	.083	.083	.083	3	0	0	0	0	9	0	0	1	23	.087	0	2	1	.000	0	0
Arroyo, Bronson	21	23	21	2	3	5	2	0	0	0	.143	.143	.238	2	0	0	0	0	10	0	0	0	16	.125	0	0	5	.200	0	0
Schmidt, Jason	11	22	19	1	0	0	0	0	0	0	.000	.050	.000	2	0	0	1	0	9	0	0	1	15	.000	0	0	4	.000	0	0
Hyzdu, Adam	12	18	18	2	7	12	2	0	1	4	.389	.389	.667	0	0	0	0	0	4	0	0	0	14	.357	1	3	4	.500	0	1
Redman, Tike	9	19	18	2	6	10	1	0	1	1	.333	.368	.556	0	0	0	1	0	7	1	0	0	15	.333	1	1	3	.333	0	0
Cruz, Ivan	8	11	11	0	1	1	0	0	0	0	.091	.091	.091	0	0	0	0	0	8	0	0	1	11	.091	0	0	0	.000	0	0
Wilkins, Marc	52	6	6	0	1	1	0	0	0	0	.167	.167	.167	0	0	0	0	0	4	0	0	0	4	.000	0	0	2	.500	0	0
Peters, Chris	18	6	6	1	1	1	0	0	0	1	.167	.167	.167	0	0	0	0	0	1	0	0	0	5	.200	0	1	1	.000	0	0
Garcia, Mike	13	3	3	1	1	1	0	0	0	0	.333	.333	.333	0	0	0	0	0	2	0	0	0	2	.500	0	0	1	.000	0	0
Manzanillo, Josias	43	4	3	0	0	0	0	0	0	0	.000	.000	.000	1	0	0	0	0	2	0	0	0	3	.000	0	0	0	.000	0	0
O'Connor, Brian	6	2	2	0	1	1	0	0	0	0	.500	.500	.500	0	0	0	0	0	1	0	0	0	1	.000	0	0	1	1.000	0	0
Skrmetta, Matt	8	2	2	0	0	0	0	0	0	0	.000	.000	.000	0	0	0	0	0	1	0	0	0	2	.000	0	0	0	.000	0	0
Williams, Mike	72	1	1	0	0	0	0	0	0	0	.000	.000	.000	0	0	0	0	0	0	0	0	0	1	.000	0	0	0	.000	0	0
Wallace, Jeff	38	1	1	0	0	0	0	0	0	0	.000	.000	.000	0	0	0	0	0	0	0	0	0	1	.000	0	0	0	.000	0	0
Sauerbeck, Scott	75	1	1	0	0	0	0	0	0	0	.000	.000	.000	0	0	0	0	0	0	0	0	0	0	.000	0	0	1	.000	0	0
Clontz, Brad	5	1	0	1	0	0	0	0	0	0	.000	1.000	.000	0	0	1	0	0	0	0	0	0	0	.000	0	0	0	.000	0	0
Christiansen, Jason	44	0	0	0	0	0	0	0	0	0	.000	.000	.000	0	0	0	0	0	0	0	0	0	0	.000	0	0	0	.000	0	0
Parra, Jose	6	2	0	0	0	0	0	0	0	0	.000	1.000	.000	0	0	0	2	0	0	0	0	0	0	.000	0	0	0	.000	0	0
Loiselle, Rich	40	0	0	0	0	0	0	0	0	0	.000	.000	.000	0	0	0	0	0	0	0	0	0	0	.000	0	0	0	.000	0	0
Sparks, Steve	3	0	0	0	0	0	0	0	0	0	.000	.000	.000	0	0	0	0	0	0	0	0	0	0	.000	0	0	0	.000	0	0
Smith, Brian	3	0	0	0	0	0	0	0	0	0	.000	.000	.000	0	0	0	0	0	0	0	0	0	0	.000	0	0	0	.000	0	0

Players with more than one N.L. team

																							vs RHP				vs LHP			
Name	G	TPA	AB	R	H	TB	2B	3B	HR	RBI	Avg.	Obp.	Slg.	SH	SF	HP	BB	IBB	SO	SB	CS	GDP	AB	Avg.	HR	RBI	AB	Avg.	HR	RBI
Aven, Pit.-L.A.	81	176	168	20	42	74	11	0	7	29	.250	.284	.440	0	0	0	8	0	39	2	3	4	105	.238	5	21	63	.270	2	8
Christiansen, Pit.-StL.	65	0	0	0	0	0	0	0	0	0	.000	.000	.000	0	0	0	0	0	0	0	0	0	0	.000	0	0	0	.000	0	0
Serafini, S.D.-Pit.	14	27	24	1	2	2	0	0	0	2	.083	.083	.083	3	0	0	0	0	9	0	0	1	23	.087	0	2	1	.000	0	0
Skrmetta, Mon.-Pit.	14	2	2	0	0	0	0	0	0	0	.000	.000	.000	0	0	0	0	0	1	0	0	0	2	.000	0	0	0	.000	0	0

PITCHING

																						vs. RH				vs. LH			
Name	W	L	Pct.	ERA	IP	H	R	ER	HR	SH	SF	HB	BB	IBB	SO	G	GS	CG	ShO	GF	Sv	AB	Avg.	HR	RBI	AB	Avg.	HR	RBI
Benson, Kris	10	12	.455	3.85	217.2	206	104	93	24	7	6	10	86	5	184	32	32	2	1	0	0	432	.225	8	39	395	.276	16	53
Ritchie, Todd	9	8	.529	4.81	187.0	208	111	100	26	8	5	3	51	1	124	31	31	1	1	0	0	403	.258	13	54	334	.311	13	51
Anderson, Jimmy	5	11	.313	5.25	144.0	169	94	84	13	5	3	7	58	2	73	27	26	1	0	0	0	456	.292	8	62	119	.303	5	19
Silva, Jose	11	9	.550	5.56	136.0	178	96	84	16	9	5	5	50	7	98	51	19	1	0	12	0	331	.290	6	43	231	.355	10	43
Cordova, Francisco	6	8	.429	5.21	95.0	107	63	55	12	3	3	2	38	4	66	18	17	0	0	0	0	203	.232	8	32	172	.349	4	18
Sauerbeck, Scott	5	4	.556	4.04	75.2	76	36	34	4	3	3	1	61	8	83	75	0	0	0	13	1	164	.305	2	25	117	.222	2	12
Williams, Mike	3	4	.429	3.50	72.0	56	34	28	8	2	4	4	40	3	71	72	0	0	0	63	24	153	.209	2	14	104	.231	6	20
Arroyo, Bronson	2	6	.250	6.40	71.2	88	61	51	10	5	2	4	36	6	50	20	12	0	0	1	0	181	.304	8	33	110	.300	2	20
Schmidt, Jason	2	5	.286	5.40	63.1	71	43	38	6	1	2	1	41	2	51	11	11	0	0	0	0	150	.307	5	25	100	.250	1	10
Serafini, Dan	2	5	.286	4.91	62.1	70	35	34	9	8	2	4	26	1	32	11	11	0	0	0	0	205	.278	8	30	35	.371	1	4
Wilkins, Marc	4	2	.667	5.07	60.1	54	34	34	4	3	7	6	43	3	37	52	0	0	0	8	0	138	.246	4	24	80	.250	0	12
Manzanillo, Josias	2	2	.500	3.38	58.2	50	23	22	6	4	2	0	32	4	39	43	0	0	0	11	0	140	.236	5	23	68	.250	1	4
Loiselle, Rich	2	3	.400	5.10	42.1	43	27	24	5	3	3	3	30	5	32	40	0	0	0	13	0	114	.263	4	26	50	.260	1	7
Christiansen, Jason	2	8	.200	4.97	38.0	28	22	21	2	3	1	0	25	4	41	44	0	0	0	17	1	93	.204	0	11	42	.214	2	4
Wallace, Jeff	2	0	1.000	7.07	35.2	42	32	28	5	0	2	4	34	1	27	38	0	0	0	6	0	96	.292	2	25	49	.286	3	12
Peters, Chris	0	1	.000	2.86	28.1	23	9	9	2	2	0	1	14	2	16	18	0	0	0	4	1	64	.203	0	5	40	.250	2	5
O'Connor, Brian	0	0	.000	5.11	12.1	12	11	7	2	1	1	1	11	0	7	6	1	0	0	2	0	38	.289	2	10	10	.100	0	0
Parra, Jose	0	1	.000	6.94	11.2	17	9	9	3	1	0	1	7	0	9	6	2	0	0	1	0	35	.343	3	9	13	.385	0	2
Garcia, Mike	0	2	.000	11.12	11.1	21	15	14	1	0	3	0	7	1	9	13	0	0	0	2	0	38	.368	1	11	11	.636	0	1
Skrmetta, Matt	2	2	.500	9.64	9.1	13	12	10	2	1	0	1	3	0	7	8	0	0	0	0	0	30	.367	2	7	9	.222	0	3
Clontz, Brad	0	0	.000	5.14	7.0	7	4	4	1	0	0	0	11	2	8	5	0	0	0	0	0	23	.174	1	3	3	1.000	0	0
Smith, Brian	0	0	.000	10.38	4.1	6	5	5	1	1	1	0	2	0	3	3	0	0	0	1	0	9	.333	1	3	7	.429	0	2
Sparks, Steve	0	0	.000	6.75	4.0	4	3	3	0	0	0	0	5	0	2	3	0	0	0	2	0	10	.100	0	1	5	.600	0	4
Osik, Keith	0	0	.000	45.00	1.0	5	5	5	1	0	0	2	0	0	1	1	0	0	0	1	0	5	.600	0	2	3	.667	1	2

PITCHERS WITH MORE THAN ONE N.L. TEAM

																						vs. RH				vs. LH			
Name	W	L	Pct.	ERA	IP	H	R	ER	HR	SH	SF	HB	BB	IBB	SO	G	GS	CG	ShO	GF	Sv	AB	Avg.	HR	RBI	AB	Avg.	HR	RBI
Christiansen, Pit.-StL.	3	8	.273	5.06	48.0	41	29	27	3	4	1	2	27	5	53	65	0	0	0	1	1	111	.225	0	13	65	.246	3	12
Serafini, S.D.-Pit.	2	5	.286	5.51	65.1	79	41	40	11	8	2	4	28	1	35	14	11	0	0	2	0	211	.289	10	34	47	.383	1	5
Skrmetta, Mon.-Pit.	2	2	.500	11.66	14.2	19	22	19	3	1	1	1	9	0	11	14	0	0	0	1	0	41	.317	2	11	20	.300	1	6

DESIGNATED HITTERS

Name	AB	Avg.	HR	RBI	Name	AB	Avg.	HR	RBI
Vander Wal, John	13	.231	0	1	Cordero, Wil	5	.400	1	1
Young, Kevin	6	.333	0	1	Osik, Keith	3	.667	0	0

INDIVIDUAL STATISTICS

FIELDING

FIRST BASEMEN

Player	Pct.	G	PO	A	E	TC	DP
Young, Kevin	.986	129	1109	59	17	1185	121
Vander Wal, John	.996	33	251	10	1	262	21
Hernandez, Alex	.992	12	123	3	1	127	14
Osik, Keith	1.000	5	29	0	0	29	3
Cruz, Ivan	1.000	1	6	0	0	6	0
Benjamin, Mike	1.000	1	4	0	0	4	0
Ramirez, Alex	-	1	0	0	0	0	0

SECOND BASEMEN

Player	Pct.	G	PO	A	E	TC	DP
Morris, Warren	.979	134	291	414	15	720	92
Benjamin, Mike	1.000	27	57	71	0	128	18
Wilson, Enrique	.970	11	10	22	1	33	4
Nunez, Abraham	1.000	6	12	8	0	20	4
Sojo, Luis	-	1	0	0	0	0	0

THIRD BASEMEN

Player	Pct.	G	PO	A	E	TC	DP
Ramirez, Aramis	.917	72	26	128	14	168	7
Sojo, Luis	.960	50	24	97	5	126	5
Benjamin, Mike	.974	34	13	61	2	76	5
Wilson, Enrique	.925	16	7	30	3	40	1
Wehner, John	.973	16	14	22	1	37	0
Osik, Keith	.958	12	9	14	1	24	2

SHORTSTOPS

Player	Pct.	G	PO	A	E	TC	DP
Meares, Pat	.967	126	191	401	20	612	99
Benjamin, Mike	.981	30	30	74	2	106	13
Nunez, Abraham	.978	21	31	57	2	90	10
Wilson, Enrique	.933	8	7	21	2	30	7

OUTFIELDERS

Player	Pct.	G	PO	A	E	TC	DP
Giles, Brian	.982	155	316	14	6	336	1
Brown, Adrian	.976	92	154	7	4	165	1
Cordero, Wil	.983	85	110	3	2	115	0
Vander Wal, John	.965	78	134	2	5	141	0
Aven, Bruce	.980	41	49	0	1	50	0
Brown, Emil	1.000	38	54	3	0	57	1
Ramirez, Alex	.949	31	55	1	3	59	0
Hermansen, Chad	.979	31	44	2	1	47	0
Redman, Tike	1.000	6	12	1	0	13	0
Hernandez, Alex	1.000	5	4	1	0	5	0
Hyzdu, Adam	1.000	5	5	0	0	5	0
Wehner, John	-	1	0	0	0	0	0

CATCHERS

Player	Pct.	G	PO	A	E	TC	DP	PB
Kendall, Jason	.991	147	990	81	10	1081	12	11
Osik, Keith	.992	26	118	9	1	128	1	1

PITCHERS

Player	Pct.	G	PO	A	E	TC	DP
Sauerbeck, Scott	1.000	75	5	10	0	15	2
Williams, Mike	1.000	72	4	11	0	15	2
Wilkins, Marc	1.000	52	2	9	0	11	2
Silva, Jose	.909	51	4	16	2	22	1
Christiansen, Jason	1.000	44	1	8	0	9	0
Manzanillo, Josias	1.000	43	2	5	0	7	0
Loiselle, Rich	.875	40	2	5	1	8	0
Wallace, Jeff	.833	38	2	3	1	6	0
Benson, Kris	.947	32	8	28	2	38	0
Ritchie, Todd	.977	31	8	35	1	44	2
Anderson, Jimmy	.973	27	5	31	1	37	2
Arroyo, Bronson	.889	20	3	5	1	9	0
Cordova, Francisco	.897	18	6	20	3	29	1
Peters, Chris	1.000	18	1	5	0	6	0
Garcia, Mike	1.000	13	0	1	0	1	0
Schmidt, Jason	1.000	11	2	7	0	9	0
Serafini, Dan	1.000	11	1	6	0	7	0
Skrmetta, Matt	1.000	8	1	1	0	2	0
Parra, Jose	1.000	6	0	3	0	3	0
O'Connor, Brian	-	6	0	0	0	0	0
Clontz, Brad	1.000	5	0	1	0	1	0
Sparks, Steve	1.000	3	1	1	0	2	1
Smith, Brian	1.000	3	0	1	0	1	0
Osik, Keith	-	1	0	0	0	0	0

PITCHING AGAINST EACH CLUB

Pitcher	Ari. W-L	Atl. W-L	Chi. W-L	Cin. W-L	Col. W-L	Fla. W-L	Hou. W-L	L.A. W-L	Mil. W-L	Mon. W-L	N.Y. W-L	Phi. W-L	S.D. W-L	S.F. W-L	StL. W-L	A.L. W-L	Total W-L
Anderson, J.	0-1	0-1	1-0	0-2	0-2	0-0	0-1	2-0	0-1	0-0	1-1	1-0	0-0	0-1	0-0	0-1	5-11
Arroyo, B.	0-1	0-0	0-0	0-0	0-0	0-0	0-0	0-1	0-1	0-0	0-1	1-1	1-0	0-1	0-0	0-0	2-6
Benson, Kris	0-1	1-1	0-0	1-1	0-0	0-0	1-2	0-0	1-1	1-1	0-2	1-0	0-0	1-1	2-1	1-1	10-12
Christiansen, J.	1-1	0-1	0-0	0-1	0-1	0-1	0-0	0-0	0-1	0-0	0-0	0-0	0-0	0-0	0-0	1-2	2-8
Clontz, Brad	0-0	0-0	0-0	0-0	0-0	0-0	0-0	0-0	0-0	0-0	0-0	0-0	0-0	0-0	0-0	0-0	0-0
Cordova, F.	0-0	0-1	0-2	0-0	1-0	1-2	1-0	0-0	0-0	1-0	0-0	0-0	1-0	0-1	0-2	1-0	6-8
Garcia, Mike	0-0	0-1	0-0	0-1	0-0	0-0	0-0	0-0	0-0	0-0	0-0	0-0	0-0	0-0	0-0	0-0	0-2
Loiselle, Rich	0-0	0-0	0-0	0-0	0-0	0-1	0-0	0-0	0-0	0-1	0-1	2-0	0-0	0-0	0-0	0-0	2-3
Manzanillo, J.	0-0	0-0	0-0	0-0	0-0	0-0	0-0	1-0	0-1	0-0	0-0	0-0	0-0	0-0	1-1	0-0	2-2
O'Connor, B.	0-0	0-0	0-0	0-0	0-0	0-0	0-0	0-0	0-0	0-0	0-0	0-0	0-0	0-0	0-0	0-0	0-0
Osik, Keith	0-0	0-0	0-0	0-0	0-0	0-0	0-0	0-0	0-0	0-0	0-0	0-0	0-0	0-0	0-0	0-0	0-0
Parra, Jose	0-0	0-0	0-0	0-0	0-0	0-0	0-0	0-0	0-0	0-0	0-0	0-0	0-1	0-0	0-0	0-0	0-1
Peters, Chris	0-0	0-0	0-0	0-0	0-0	0-0	0-0	0-0	0-0	0-0	0-1	0-0	0-0	0-0	0-0	0-0	0-1
Ritchie, Todd	0-0	0-0	3-0	2-2	0-0	1-0	0-0	0-0	0-0	0-1	0-0	0-2	1-0	0-0	0-3	2-0	9-8
Sauerbeck, S.	1-0	0-0	0-1	0-0	1-0	0-0	0-1	0-0	1-0	0-0	0-0	0-0	1-0	0-1	0-0	1-1	5-4
Schmidt, J.	0-2	0-0	1-0	0-0	0-0	1-0	0-1	0-0	0-1	0-0	0-0	0-0	0-0	0-0	0-0	0-1	2-5
Serafini, Dan	0-1	0-0	0-0	0-0	0-1	0-0	0-2	1-0	0-0	0-0	0-0	0-0	0-0	1-0	0-1	0-0	2-5
Silva, Jose	0-0	1-0	0-0	2-0	0-2	0-0	1-1	1-1	3-0	2-0	1-1	0-0	0-0	0-1	0-0	0-3	11-9
Skrmetta, M.	0-0	0-0	0-0	0-0	0-0	0-0	0-2	0-0	0-0	0-0	0-0	1-0	1-0	0-0	0-0	0-0	2-2
Smith, Brian	0-0	0-0	0-0	0-0	0-0	0-0	0-0	0-0	0-0	0-0	0-0	0-0	0-0	0-0	0-0	0-0	0-0
Sparks, Steve	0-0	0-0	0-0	0-0	0-0	0-0	0-0	0-0	0-0	0-0	0-0	0-0	0-0	0-0	0-0	0-0	0-0
Wallace, Jeff	0-0	0-0	1-0	0-0	0-0	0-0	0-0	0-0	0-0	0-0	0-0	0-0	0-0	0-0	1-0	0-0	2-0
Wilkins, Marc	0-0	0-0	3-0	1-0	0-0	0-0	0-0	0-1	0-0	0-0	0-0	0-0	0-1	0-0	0-0	0-0	4-2
Williams, M.	0-0	0-0	0-0	0-0	0-1	1-1	0-0	0-1	0-1	0-0	0-0	0-0	2-0	0-0	0-0	0-0	3-4
Totals	2-7	2-5	9-3	6-7	2-7	4-5	3-10	5-4	5-7	4-3	2-7	6-3	7-2	2-6	4-8	6-9	69-93

INTERLEAGUE: Sauerbeck 0-1, Benson 0-1, Silva 0-1 vs. Indians; Cordova 1-0, Ritchie 1-0, Anderson 0-1 vs. Tigers; Ritchie 1-0, Sauerbeck 1-0, Christiansen 0-2, Schmidt 0-1, Silva 0-1 vs. Royals; Christiansen 1-0, Benson 1-0, Silva 0-1 vs. Twins. Total: 6-9.

MISCELLANEOUS

HOME RUNS BY PARK

At Arizona (5): Giles 2, Vander Wal 1, Meares 1, Aven 1.
At Atlanta (1): Ramirez 1.
At Chicago (NL) (13): Cordero 4, Sojo 3, Giles 2, Young 1, Meares 1, Kendall 1, Ramirez 1.
At Cincinnati (3): Benjamin 1, Giles 1, Kendall 1.
At Cleveland (6): Young 2, Vander Wal 1, Cordero 1, Kendall 1, Redman 1.
At Colorado (2): Cordero 1, Giles 1.
At Florida (1): Osik 1.
At Houston (10): Giles 3, Vander Wal 2, Young 1, Meares 1, Brown 1, Nunez 1, Ramirez 1.
At Kansas City (4): Giles 3, Young 1.
At Los Angeles (9): Cordero 2, Meares 2, Giles 2, Vander Wal 1, Young 1, Kendall 1.
At Milwaukee (4): Benjamin 1, Vander Wal 1, Young 1, Giles 1.
At Montreal (4): Vander Wal 3, Kendall 1.
At New York (NL) (3): Vander Wal 1, Young 1, Giles 1.
At Philadelphia (4): Osik 1, Brown 1, Brown 1, Hyzdu 1.
At Pittsburgh (86): Giles 16, Vander Wal 13, Young 11, Cordero 8, Meares 7, Kendall 7, Aven 4, Ramirez 4, Morris 3, Sojo 2, Brown 2, Brown 2, Hermansen 2, Wehner 1, Osik 1, Wilson 1, Ramirez 1, Hernandez 1.
At San Diego (1): Kendall 1.
At San Francisco (3): Meares 1, Wilson 1, Ramirez 1.
At St. Louis (9): Giles 3, Vander Wal 1, Young 1, Kendall 1, Osik 1, Wilson 1, Ramirez 1.

LOW-HIT GAMES

No-hitters: None.
One-hitters: None.
Two-hitters: None.

10-STRIKEOUT GAMES

Kris Benson 3, Total: 3

FOUR OR MORE HITS IN ONE GAME

Jason Kendall 4, Warren Morris 4 (including one five-hit game), Brian Giles 3 (including two five-hit games), Kevin Young 2, John Vander Wal 1, Wil Cordero 1 (including one five-hit game), Adrian Brown 1, Total: 16

MULTI-HOMER GAMES

Brian Giles 2, John Vander Wal 1, Kevin Young 1, Wil Cordero 1, Bruce Aven 1, Aramis Ramirez 1, Total: 7

GRAND SLAMS

4-26: Pat Meares (off San Diego's Woody Williams)
4-27: John Vander Wal (off San Diego's Matt Clement)
6-21: John Vander Wal (off Montreal's Tony Armas Jr.)
7-28: Aramis Ramirez (off San Diego's Matt Clement)
8-12: Aramis Ramirez (off Arizona's Johnny Ruffin)
9-4: Brian Giles (off Los Angeles's Darren Dreifort)

PINCH HITTERS

(Minimum 5 at-bats)

Name	AB	Avg.	HR	RBI
Aven, Bruce	35	.114	0	3
Vander Wal, John	23	.348	3	10
Brown, Adrian	20	.200	0	0
Ramirez, Alex	13	.308	2	5
Brown, Emil	13	.154	0	0
Nunez, Abraham	12	.250	0	1
Sojo, Luis	10	.500	0	1
Wilson, Enrique	9	.333	0	2
Osik, Keith	9	.222	0	1
Morris, Warren	9	.000	0	0
Benjamin, Mike	8	.500	0	0
Hyzdu, Adam	8	.375	1	4
Cruz, Ivan	7	.000	0	0
Wehner, John	6	.333	0	2
Kendall, Jason	5	.400	0	1
Young, Kevin	5	.200	0	1

DEBUTS

5-13: Brian O'Connor, P.
6-12: Bronson Arroyo, PH.
6-30: Tike Redman, RF.
7-19: Steve Sparks, P.
9-1: Alex Hernandez, 1B.
9-8: Adam Hyzdu, LF.
9-11: Brian Smith, P.

GAMES BY POSITION

Catcher: Jason Kendall 147, Keith Osik 26.
First base: Kevin Young 129, John Vander Wal 33, Alex Hernandez 12, Keith Osik 5, Mike Benjamin 1, Ivan Cruz 1, Alex Ramirez 1.
Second base: Warren Morris 134, Mike Benjamin 27, Enrique Wilson 11, Abraham Nunez 6, Luis Sojo 1.
Third base: Aramis Ramirez 72, Luis Sojo 50, Mike Benjamin 34, John Wehner 16, Enrique Wilson 16, Keith Osik 12.
Shortstop: Pat Meares 126, Mike Benjamin 30, Abraham Nunez 21, Enrique Wilson 8.
Outfield: Brian Giles 155, Adrian Brown 92, Wil Cordero 85, John Vander Wal 78, Bruce Aven 41, Emil Brown 38, Alex Ramirez 31, Chad Hermansen 31, Tike Redman 6, Alex Hernandez 5, Adam Hyzdu 5, John Wehner 1.
Designated hitter: John Vander Wal 3, Kevin Young 1, Wil Cordero 1, Keith Osik 1.

STREAKS

Wins: 8 (September 1-8)
Losses: 9 (September 9-17)
Consecutive games with at least one hit: 15, Wil Cordero (April 29-May 23)
Wins by pitcher: 3, Francisco Cordova (May 26-June 5)

ATTENDANCE

Home: 1,709,119
Road: 2,453,149
Highest (home): 55,351 (October 1 vs. Chicago).
Highest (road): 48,406 (July 1 vs. Philadelphia).
Lowest (home): 10,290 (April 12 vs. Montreal).
Lowest (road): 7,483 (June 19 vs. Montreal).

St. Louis Cardinals

DAY BY DAY

Date	Opp.	Res.	Score	(inn.*)	Hits	Opp. hits	Winning pitcher	Losing pitcher	Save	Record	Pos.	GB
4-3	Chi.	W	7-1		10	3	Kile	Tapani		1-0	1st	+1.0
4-5	Chi.	W	10-4		12	9	Hentgen	Lieber		2-0	T1st	...
4-6	Chi.	W	13-3		11	6	Stephenson	Farnsworth		3-0	1st	+1.0
4-7	Mil.	L	1-9		6	11	Bere	An. Benes		3-1	T1st	...
4-8	Mil.	W	10-8		15	9	Kile	Woodard	Veres	4-1	1st	+1.0
4-9	Mil.	W	11-2		16	6	Ankiel	de los Santos		5-1	1st	+2.0
4-10	At Hou.	W	8-7		13	7	Hentgen	Lima	Veres	6-1	1st	+2.0
4-11	At Hou.	W	10-6		9	8	Stephenson	Holt		7-1	1st	+2.5
4-12	At Hou.	L	5-7		9	9	Perez	Wainhouse	Wagner	7-2	1st	+2.5
4-13	At Col.	L	6-12		11	14	Croushore	Kile		7-3	1st	+1.5
4-14	At Col.	L	2-6		6	9	Astacio	Ankiel		7-4	1st	+1.5
4-16†	At Col.	W	9-3		11	9	Hentgen	Arrojo		8-4		
4-16‡	At Col.	L	13-14		17	15	Jimenez	Mohler	White	8-5	1st	+1.5
4-18	S.D.	W	5-4		10	9	An. Benes	Meadows	Veres	9-5	1st	+2.5
4-19	S.D.	W	4-3		9	6	Kile	Hitchcock	Veres	10-5	1st	+2.5
4-20	S.D.	W	14-1		14	6	Ankiel	Boehringer		11-5	1st	+2.5
4-21	Col.	L	4-6		12	10	Jarvis	Hentgen	Jimenez	11-6	1st	+2.5
4-22	Col.	L	6-7		6	11	Croushore	James	Jimenez	11-7	1st	+2.5
4-23	Col.	W	6-3	(7)	8	4	An. Benes	Karl	Slocumb	12-7	1st	+3.5
4-25	Mil.	W	7-2		10	7	Kile	Bere		13-7	1st	+4.5
4-26	Mil.	W	7-0		9	4	Ankiel	Woodard		14-7	1st	+4.5
4-27	Mil.	L	4-8		6	10	Haynes	Hentgen		14-8	1st	+3.5
4-28	At Phi.	W	7-4		10	9	Stephenson	Reyes	Veres	15-8	1st	+4.5
4-29	At Phi.	W	7-6	(10)	9	10	Mohler	Gomes		16-8	1st	+4.5
4-30	At Phi.	W	4-3		9	8	Kile	Schilling	James	17-8	1st	+4.5
5-2	Pit.	L	7-10		9	13	Wallace	Slocumb		17-9	1st	+3.5
5-3	Pit.	L	2-8		5	13	Benson	Hentgen		17-10	1st	+3.5
5-4	Pit.	W	5-0		9	4	Stephenson	Cordova		18-10	1st	+4.5
5-5	At Cin.	L	2-3		7	8	Villone	An. Benes	Williamson	18-11	1st	+3.5
5-6	At Cin.	W	3-1		5	6	Kile	Bell	Veres	19-11	1st	+4.5
5-7	At Cin.	L	7-9		10	8	Neagle	Holmes	Williamson	19-12	1st	+3.5
5-8	At S.F	L	4-6		9	8	Hernandez	Hentgen	Nen	19-13	1st	+3.0
5-9	At S.F	W	13-6		15	11	Stephenson	Ortiz		20-13	1st	+3.0
5-10	At S.F	L	3-4		7	7	Rodriguez	Slocumb	Nen	20-14	1st	+2.0
5-12	L.A.	L	0-13		2	13	Dreifort	Kile		20-15	1st	+0.5
5-13	L.A.	L	1-3		3	7	Park	Veres	Shaw	20-16	2nd	0.5
5-14	L.A.	W	12-10		17	11	Slocumb	Perez	Veres	21-16	1st	+0.5
5-16	At Phi.	W	8-2		9	10	An. Benes	Person		22-16	T1st	...
5-17	At Phi.	L	4-5		9	11	Wolf	Slocumb	Brantley	22-17	T1st	...
5-18	At Phi.	W	7-2		13	10	Stephenson	Schilling		23-17	T1st	...
5-19	At Pit.	L	1-13		3	15	Benson	Ankiel		23-18	T1st	...
5-20	At Pit.	W	19-4		19	9	Hentgen	Cordova		24-18	T1st	...
5-21	At Pit.	W	7-5		10	9	An. Benes	Ritchie	Veres	25-18	1st	+1.0
5-23	Fla.	W	10-3		13	5	Kile	Dempster		26-18	1st	+1.5
5-24	Fla.	W	5-1		11	5	Stephenson	Nunez		27-18	1st	+1.5
5-25	Fla.	W	7-6		9	11	Ankiel	Cornelius	Veres	28-18	1st	+2.0
5-26	N.Y.	L	2-5		9	9	Hampton	Thompson	Benitez	28-19	1st	+1.0
5-27	N.Y.	L	8-12		11	15	Cook	Veres		28-20	1st	+1.0
5-28	N.Y.	L	2-6		6	11	Rusch	Kile		28-21	1st	+1.0
5-29	At Ari.	W	3-0		5	6	Stephenson	Stottlemyre		29-21	1st	+1.5
5-30	At Ari.	W	6-1		10	5	Ankiel	Daal	Morris	30-21	1st	+1.5
5-31	At Ari.	L	2-6		10	8	Johnson	Hentgen	Kim	30-22	1st	+1.5
6-1	At Ari.	L	0-4		4	7	Reynoso	An. Benes		30-23	1st	+1.5
6-2	Cle.	W	5-1		8	3	Kile	Wright		31-23	1st	+1.5
6-3	Cle.	L	2-4		4	8	Colon	Stephenson	Karsay	31-24	1st	+0.5
6-4	Cle.	L	2-3		6	7	Martin	Morris	Karsay	31-25	2nd	0.5
6-5	K.C.	L	4-7		6	10	Suzuki	Hentgen	Spradlin	31-26	2nd	0.5
6-6	K.C.	W	5-4		7	10	An. Benes	Witasick	Veres	32-26	1st	+0.5
6-7	K.C.	W	4-2		10	7	Kile	Batista		33-26	1st	+1.5
6-9	At Det.	L	2-4		4	7	Weaver	Stephenson	Jones	33-27	1st	+1.5
6-10	At Det.	L	1-10		7	13	Moehler	Ankiel		33-28	1st	+1.5
6-11	At Det.	W	7-3		11	6	Hentgen	Mlicki		34-28	1st	+1.5
6-12	At S.D.	W	7-3		10	8	An. Benes	Clement		35-28	1st	+2.5
6-13	At S.D.	W	8-3		16	11	Kile	Lopez	Veres	36-28	1st	+3.5
6-14	At S.D.	W	3-1		7	6	Stephenson	Spencer	Morris	37-28	1st	+4.5
6-16	At L.A.	W	6-3		9	7	Hentgen	Hershiser	Veres	38-28	1st	+5.5
6-17	At L.A.	W	4-3		13	8	An. Benes	Dreifort	Veres	39-28	1st	+6.5
6-18	At L.A.	L	3-6		7	8	Park	Kile	Shaw	39-29	1st	+6.5
6-20	S.F	W	7-2		8	4	Ankiel	Ortiz		40-29	1st	+6.5
6-21	S.F	L	1-4		5	7	Rueter	Stephenson	Nen	40-30	1st	+6.5
6-22	S.F	W	11-10		12	15	Veres	Gardner		41-30	1st	+6.5
6-23	L.A.	W	9-6	(12)	9	10	Stechschulte	Shaw		42-30	1st	+7.5
6-24	L.A.	W	6-1		9	6	Al. Benes	Hershiser		43-30	1st	+7.5
6-25	L.A.	W	2-1		6	6	Slocumb	Osuna		44-30	1st	+8.5
6-26	At Cin.	L	2-3		7	10	Neagle	Stephenson	Graves	44-31	1st	+7.5
6-27	At Cin.	W	4-3		9	11	Kile	Parris	Veres	45-31	1st	+8.5
6-28	At Cin.	L	3-7		7	8	Reyes	Al. Benes		45-32	1st	+7.5
6-29	At Cin.	W	12-3		15	4	An. Benes	Villone		46-32	1st	+8.5
6-30	Hou.	W	5-4		13	6	Al. Benes	Holt	Veres	47-32	1st	+8.5

HIGHLIGHTS

High point: After beating the Atlanta Braves three times in a four-game late August showdown, the Cardinals swept the Braves in the Division Series, never trailing after any complete inning. They won that series even though only one of their three starting pitchers lasted past the fourth inning.
Low point: After their impressive romp past the Braves, the Cardinals dropped four of five games to the Mets in the N.L. Championship Series. The Cardinals played shorthanded against the Mets, one starting pitcher (Garrett Stephenson) lost to injury and another (Rick Ankiel) rendered ineffective because of wildness.
Turning point: The Cardinals fought off their biggest challenger and extended their N.L. Central lead by taking four of seven games from Cincinnati over an 11-day span in late June and early July. Their lead never dipped below four games the rest of the way.
Most valuable player: It's hard to ignore the 167 strikeouts, but center fielder Jim Edmonds still posted career highs in home runs (42) and runs batted in (108) while playing Gold Glove defense in his first St. Louis season.
Most valuable pitcher: Having posted 21 wins over his previous two seasons in Colorado, Darryl Kile became a 20-game winner in his first season with the Cardinals. And he never missed a turn in the rotation.
Most improved player: Utility infielder Placido Polanco might have been the most improved player in all of baseball. Polanco batted .316 and played in sometimes spectacular, fashion at second, shortstop and third.
Most pleasant surprise: Stephenson, who never had won in double figures as a major leaguer, finished second behind Kile with 16 wins. He made good in his first big-league shot as a rotation regular.
Key injuries: Mark McGwire missed virtually the entire second half with tendinitis in his knee and hit only two home runs after the All-Star break. ... Third baseman Fernando Tatis missed two months early in the season because of a torn groin muscle and he never regained top form, hitting only .204 after the break. ... Andy Benes missed almost a month because of torn cartilage in his knee but still won 12 games. ... Gold Glove catcher Mike Matheny missed all of the postseason after slashing his finger in a freak home accident.
Notable: The Cardinals were in first place for all but four days, one of which was the result of a Chicago victory before they played their first game. The Cardinals' biggest lead was $11\frac{1}{2}$ on September 20 and their peak of 28 games over .500 was reached four times in September. ... Despite the absence of McGwire, the Cardinals set a team record with 235 home runs. ... Ankiel, despite his playoff problems, completed his rookie season at 11-7 with an impressive 3.50 ERA.

—RICK HUMMEL

MISCELLANEOUS

RECORDS

2000 regular-season record: 95-67 (1st in N.L. Central); 50-31 at home; 45-36 on road; 25-16 vs. East; 44-33 vs. Central; 26-18 vs. West; 17-23 vs. left-handed starters; 78-44 vs. righthanded starters; 79-58 on grass; 16-9 on turf; 38-20 in daytime; 57-47 at night; 28-16 in one-run games; 5-2 in extra-inning games; 0-0-1 in doubleheaders.
Team record past five years: 414-395 (.512, ranks 8th in league in that span).

TEAM LEADERS

Batting average: Fernando Vina (.300).
At-bats: Edgar Renteria (562).
Runs: Jim Edmonds (129).
Hits: Edgar Renteria (156).
Total Bases: Jim Edmonds (306).
Doubles: Edgar Renteria (32).
Triples: Fernando Vina (6).
Home runs: Jim Edmonds (42).
Runs batted in: Jim Edmonds (108).
Stolen bases: Edgar Renteria (21).
Slugging percentage: Jim Edmonds (.583).
On-base percentage: Jim Edmonds (.411).
Wins: Darryl Kile (20).
Earned-run average: Rick Ankiel (3.50).
Complete games: Darryl Kile (5).
Shutouts: Garrett Stephenson (2).
Saves: Dave Veres (29).
Innings pitched: Darryl Kile (232.1).
Strikeouts: Rick Ankiel (194).

Date	Opp.	Res.	Score	(inn.*)	Hits	Opp. hits	Winning pitcher	Losing pitcher	Save	Record	Pos.	GB
7-1	Hou.	W	10-9		11	15	Thompson	Slusarski	Veres	48-32	1st	+9.5
7-2	Hou.	L	3-6		8	10	Elarton	Kile	Valdes	48-33	1st	+8.5
7-4	Cin.	W	14-3		13	9	An. Benes	Villone		49-33	1st	+9.0
7-5	Cin.	W	4-3		5	6	Hentgen	Harnisch	Veres	50-33	1st	+10.0
7-6	Cin.	L	6-12		13	13	Dessens	Ankiel		50-34	1st	+9.0
7-7	S.F	L	2-4		9	9	Embree	Morris	Nen	50-35	1st	+8.0
7-8	S.F	L	6-7		14	11	Estes	Stephenson	Nen	50-36	1st	+7.0
7-9	S.F	W	8-7		10	8	Hentgen	Hernandez	Veres	51-36	1st	+8.0
7-13	At Chi. (AL)	W	13-5		14	11	An. Benes	Sirotka		52-36	1st	+8.0
7-14	At Chi. (AL)	W	9-4		11	8	Stephenson	Wunsch		53-36	1st	+8.0
7-15	At Chi. (AL)	L	7-15		13	15	Parque	Kile		53-37	1st	+7.0
7-16	At Min.	L	2-5		6	10	Redman	Ankiel	Guardado	53-38	1st	+7.0
7-17	At Min.	W	8-3		13	11	Hentgen	Lincoln		54-38	1st	+8.0
7-18	At Min.	L	2-3		9	7	Radke	An. Benes	Hawkins	54-39	1st	+7.0
7-19	At Ari.	L	3-4		6	9	Reynoso	Stephenson	Mantei	54-40	1st	+6.0
7-20	At Ari.	L	2-3		6	4	Johnson	Veres		54-41	1st	+6.0
7-21	At Hou.	W	12-1		16	6	Ankiel	Elarton		55-41	1st	+7.0
7-22	At Hou.	L	5-10		6	17	Miller	Hentgen		55-42	1st	+6.0
7-23	At Hou.	L	7-15		10	14	Reynolds	An. Benes		55-43	1st	+5.0
7-25	Ari.	W	7-3		7	5	Stephenson	Johnson		56-43	1st	+6.5
7-26	Ari.	W	8-4		11	10	Kile	Reynoso		57-43	1st	+7.5
7-27	Ari.	L	5-17		10	19	Guzman	Ankiel		57-44	1st	+7.0
7-28	At N.Y.	L	2-3		5	9	Leiter	Hentgen	Benitez	57-45	1st	+6.0
7-29	At N.Y.	L	3-4		7	5	White	James	Benitez	57-46	1st	+5.0
7-30	At N.Y.	L	2-4		4	7	B.J. Jones	Stephenson		57-47	1st	+4.0
7-31	At Mon.	W	4-0		10	6	Kile	Thurman		58-47	1st	+4.0
8-1	At Mon.	L	0-4		5	9	Moore	Ankiel		58-48	1st	+4.0
8-2	At Mon.	W	10-7		11	11	Hentgen	Johnson		59-48	1st	+5.0
8-4	Atl.	L	4-6		10	10	Glavine	An. Benes	Kamieniecki	59-49	1st	+5.0
8-5	Atl.	W	5-0		8	5	Stephenson	Burkett		60-49	1st	+6.0
8-6	Atl.	L	4-6		9	10	Remlinger	Kile	Ligtenberg	60-50	1st	+6.0
8-7	Fla.	W	2-1	(11)	9	4	Timlin	Darensbourg		61-50	1st	+6.0
8-8	Fla.	L	0-7		6	10	Sanchez	Hentgen		61-51	1st	+6.0
8-9	Fla.	L	3-5		11	7	Almanza	Morris	Alfonseca	61-52	1st	+5.0
8-10	Col.	W	5-4		12	10	Timlin	Jimenez		62-52	1st	+5.5
8-11	At Mil.	L	2-6		7	8	D'Amico	Kile		62-53	1st	+4.5
8-12	At Mil.	W	2-1	(12)	9	7	Morris	Leskanic	James	63-53	1st	+4.5
8-13	At Mil.	W	6-4		13	8	Hentgen	Wright	Veres	64-53	1st	+4.5
8-14	At Chi.	L	3-7		8	11	Lieber	An. Benes		64-54	1st	+4.5
8-15	At Chi.	W	4-2		11	7	Stephenson	Arnold	Veres	65-54	1st	+5.5
8-16	At Chi.	W	5-1		9	6	Kile	Tapani		66-54	1st	+6.5
8-18	Phi.	W	7-6		7	7	Christiansen	Brock		67-54	1st	+7.5
8-19	Phi.	W	6-3		9	7	Hentgen	Daal		68-54	1st	+7.5
8-20	Phi.	L	0-6		5	10	Bottenfield	Reames		68-55	1st	+7.5
8-21	Pit.	W	7-4		8	6	Stephenson	Benson	Veres	69-55	1st	+7.5
8-22	Pit.	L	2-6		10	11	Manzanillo	Kile		69-56	1st	+7.5
8-23	Pit.	W	5-2		10	8	Ankiel	Ritchie	Veres	70-56	1st	+8.5
8-24	At Atl.	W	12-5		13	9	Hentgen	Ashby		71-56	1st	+8.5
8-25	At Atl.	L	4-7		8	9	Glavine	Timlin	Ligtenberg	71-57	1st	+7.5
8-26	At Atl.	W	6-3		10	10	Stephenson	Millwood		72-57	1st	+7.5
8-27	At Atl.	W	7-2		9	8	Kile	Ligtenberg		73-57	1st	+8.5
8-28	At Fla.	W	5-2		12	5	James	Almanza	Veres	74-57	1st	+8.5
8-29	At Fla.	L	1-3		4	7	Smith	Hentgen	Alfonseca	74-58	1st	+7.5
8-30	At Fla.	W	4-2		7	8	Morris	Alfonseca	Veres	75-58	1st	+8.5
9-1	N.Y.	W	6-5		11	9	Veres	Mahomes		76-58	1st	+8.0
9-2	N.Y.	W	2-1		9	5	Kile	Hampton		77-58	1st	+9.0
9-3	N.Y.	W	4-3	(11)	7	5	Morris	White		78-58	1st	+9.0
9-4	Mon.	W	4-2		6	9	Hentgen	Vazquez	Veres	79-58	1st	+9.0
9-5	Mon.	W	7-6		7	4	Reames	Santana	Timlin	80-58	1st	+10.0
9-6	Mon.	L	2-7		8	12	Hermanson	Stephenson		80-59	1st	+9.0
9-7	Mon.	W	6-1		11	5	Kile	Armas		81-59	1st	+9.5
9-8	At Mil.	L	5-6		8	12	Leskanic	Veres		81-60	1st	++10.0
9-9	At Mil.	W	7-6		15	12	Veres	Acevedo		82-60	1st	+10.0
9-10	At Mil.	L	3-4	(10)	8	9	King	An. Benes		82-61	1st	+9.0
9-11	At Pit.	W	8-4		12	7	Stephenson	Manzanillo		83-61	1st	+9.0
9-12	At Pit.	W	11-1		16	7	Kile	Serafini		84-61	1st	+10.0
9-13	At Pit.	W	9-5		13	10	Ankiel	Ritchie		85-61	1st	+10.0
9-14	Chi.	W	4-0		5	3	Hentgen	Quevedo		86-61	1st	+11.0
9-15	Chi.	W	3-2		4	6	James	Lieber	Veres	87-61	1st	+11.0
9-16	Chi.	W	7-6		10	11	Timlin	Spradlin	Veres	88-61	1st	+11.0
9-17	Chi.	W	4-2		4	7	Kile	Worrell	Morris	89-61	1st	+11.0
9-19	Hou.	L	6-8	(10)	8	13	Dotel	Al. Benes	Cabrera	89-62	1st	+10.5
9-20	Hou.	W	11-6		11	9	Ankiel	Holt		90-62	1st	+11.5
9-21	Hou.	L	5-7		11	12	McKnight	An. Benes	Dotel	90-63	1st	+11.0
9-22	At Chi.	L	4-5		5	10	Ohman	Veres		90-64	1st	+10.0
9-23	At Chi.	W	6-5		10	7	Reames	Nation	Morris	91-64	1st	+10.0
9-24	At Chi.	L	5-10		8	12	Van Poppel	Hentgen	Heredia	91-65	1st	+9.0
9-26	At S.D.	W	7-1		11	6	An. Benes	Eaton		92-65	1st	+10.0
9-27	At S.D.	W	3-0		7	7	Ankiel	Tollberg	Veres	93-65	1st	+11.0
9-28	At S.D.	W	7-6		8	7	Kile	Davey	Veres	94-65	1st	+11.0
9-29	Cin.	L	1-8		2	15	Villone	Stephenson		94-66	1st	+10.0
9-30	Cin.	L	4-8		9	12	Fernandez	Hentgen		94-67	1st	+9.0
10-1	Cin.	W	6-2		8	8	An. Benes	Parris		95-67	1st	+10.0

Monthly records: April (17-8), May (13-14), June (17-10), July (11-15), August (17-11), September (19-9), October (1-0).
*Innings, if other than nine. † First game of a doubleheader. ‡ Second game of a doubleheader.

MEMORABLE GAMES

May 18 at Philadelphia

Mark McGwire drove in a career-high seven runs while hitting three home runs in a 7-2 Cardinals win at Philadelphia. McGwire became the only player to hit three home runs in a game twice at Veterans Stadium. His previous three-homer effort at Philadelphia had come on the same date—May 18—in 1998.

St. Louis	AB	R	H	BI	Philadelphia	AB	R	H	BI
Vina, 2b	4	2	2	0	Glanville, cf	5	0	1	0
Polanco, ss	1	0	0	0	Gant, lf	5	0	2	0
Renteria, ss	3	0	2	0	Abreu, rf	5	0	0	0
Edmonds, cf	4	2	2	0	Rolen, 3b	5	0	0	0
McGwire, 1b	4	3	3	7	Lieberthal, c	4	1	1	0
Lankford, lf	3	0	0	0	Jordan, 1b	4	1	1	0
James, p	0	0	0	0	Morandini, 2b	3	0	3	1
Howard, ph	1	0	0	0	Relaford, ss	2	0	2	1
Rodriguez, p	0	0	0	0	Schilling, p	2	0	0	0
Thompson, p	0	0	0	0	Pritchett, ph	1	0	0	0
Veres, p	0	0	0	0	Boyd, p	0	0	0	0
Drew, rf	4	0	1	0	Aldred, p	0	0	0	0
Paquette, 3b	5	0	2	0	Gomes, p	0	0	0	0
Matheny, c	4	0	1	0	Arias, ph	1	0	0	0
Stephenson, p	3	0	0	0	Brock, p	0	0	0	0
Dunston, lf	1	0	0	0					
Totals	**37**	**7**	**13**	**7**	**Totals**	**37**	**2**	**10**	**2**

St. Louis ....3 2 0 0 0 0 0 2 0—7 13 0
Philadelphia.............................0 1 0 0 0 1 0 0 0—2 10 2

E—Jordan (2), Relaford (7). DP—Philadelphia 3. LOB—St. Louis 10, Philadelphia 11. 2B—Vina (9), Paquette 2 (12), Matheny (8), Renteria (8), Lieberthal (9), Morandini 2 (5). HR—McGwire 3 (17). SB—Glanville (9), Gant (2). SH—Polanco.

St. Louis	IP	H	R	ER	BB	SO
Stephenson (W 6-0)	5.2	9	2	2	0	3
James	1.1	1	0	0	0	2
Rodriguez	0.1	0	0	0	1	0
Thompson	0.2	0	0	0	0	1
Veres	1	0	0	0	0	1
Philadelphia	**IP**	**H**	**R**	**ER**	**BB**	**SO**
Schilling (L 1-2)	6	9	5	5	5	5
Boyd	1	1	0	0	0	0
Aldred	0.2	1	1	1	0	0
Gomes	0.1	1	1	1	0	0
Brock	1	1	0	0	0	0

HBP—Morandini by Rodriguez, Vina by Aldred, Relaford by Stephenson. U—HP, Crawford. 1B, Wegner. 2B, Williams. 3B, Reynolds. T—3:11. A—17,137.

September 3 at St. Louis

Jim Edmonds' 11th-inning home run off Rick White capped a remarkable weekend sweep of the Mets at Busch Stadium. Each game was decided in the Cardinals' final at-bat. Edmonds homered in the ninth to win the first game and Fernando Vina singled in the ninth to win the second. The three wins were the Cardinals' only ones over the Mets in the regular season.

Mets	AB	R	H	BI	St. Louis	AB	R	H	BI
Agbayani, lf	2	0	0	0	Vina, 2b	5	0	1	0
Perez, pr-lf	1	0	0	0	Dunston, lf	5	0	0	0
Bordick, ss	4	0	2	0	Edmonds, cf	4	1	2	1
Alfonzo, 2b	3	0	1	0	Tatis, 3b	4	0	0	0
Piazza, c	4	0	0	0	Paquette, 1b	3	0	0	0
Pratt, c	0	0	0	0	Timlin, p	0	0	0	0
Zeile, 1b	3	0	0	0	Christiansen, p	0	0	0	0
Toca, pr-1b	0	1	0	0	Veres, p	0	0	0	0
Franco, ph-1b	1	0	0	0	Lankford, ph	1	0	0	0
Ventura, 3b	5	0	0	0	Morris, p	0	0	0	0
Payton, cf	4	1	0	0	Drew, rf	4	0	0	0
Trammell, rf	4	1	2	3	Renteria, ss	3	1	1	0
Rusch, p	2	0	0	0	Matheny, c	3	1	2	0
Harris, ph	1	0	0	0	Marrero, pr-c	0	0	0	0
Wendell, p	0	0	0	0	Ankiel, p	2	0	0	0
Cook, p	0	0	0	0	E.Perez, 1b	0	0	0	0
White, p	1	0	0	0	Howard, ph	0	0	0	0
					Polanco, ph	1	1	1	3
					W.Clark, 1b	1	0	0	0
Totals	**35**	**3**	**5**	**3**	**Totals**	**36**	**4**	**7**	**4**

Mets ....0 0 0 0 1 0 0 0 2 0 0—3 5 0
St. Louis ....0 0 0 0 0 0 0 3 0 0 1—4 7 0

DP—Mets 1, St. Louis 2. LOB—Mets 7, St. Louis 5. 2B—Bordick (6). HR—Trammell (3), Edmonds (38), Polanco (4). SB—Payton (5).

Mets	IP	H	R	ER	BB	SO
Rusch	7	4	0	0	0	7
Wendell	0	1	2	2	1	0
Cook	0.2	1	1	1	1	0
White (L 2-2)	2.1	1	1	1	0	1
St. Louis	**IP**	**H**	**R**	**ER**	**BB**	**SO**
Ankiel	7	2	1	1	5	8
Timlin	1	0	1	1	3	2
Christiansen	0.1	0	0	0	0	0
Veres	0.2	1	1	1	0	1
Morris (W 3-3)	2	2	0	0	0	1

Wendell pitched to 2 batters in 8th. White pitched to 1 batter in 11th. Timlin pitched to 1 batter in 9th. HBP—Matheny by White. U—HP, Cooper. 1B, Van Vleet. 2B, Kellogg. 3B. Diaz. T—3:36. A—42,133.

BATTING

Name	G	TPA	AB	R	H	TB	2B	3B	HR	RBI	Avg.	Obp.	Slg.	SH	SF	HP	BB	IBB	SO	SB	CS	GDP	vs RHP AB	Avg.	HR	RBI	vs LHP AB	Avg.	HR	RBI
Renteria, Edgar	150	643	562	94	156	238	32	1	16	76	.278	.346	.423	8	9	1	63	3	77	21	13	19	423	.284	11	60	139	.259	5	16
Edmonds, Jim	152	643	525	129	155	306	25	0	42	108	.295	.411	.583	1	8	6	103	3	167	10	3	5	373	.306	31	77	152	.270	11	31
Vina, Fernando	123	554	487	81	146	194	24	6	4	31	.300	.380	.398	2	1	28	36	0	36	10	8	5	367	.311	4	28	120	.267	0	3
Matheny, Mike	128	464	417	43	109	151	22	1	6	47	.261	.317	.362	7	4	4	32	8	96	0	0	11	313	.265	4	33	104	.250	2	14
Drew, J.D.	135	486	407	73	120	195	17	2	18	57	.295	.401	.479	5	1	6	67	4	99	17	9	3	333	.303	18	53	74	.257	0	4
Lankford, Ray	128	472	392	73	99	199	16	3	26	65	.253	.367	.508	0	6	4	70	1	148	5	6	6	318	.280	24	55	74	.135	2	10
Paquette, Craig	134	420	384	47	94	167	24	2	15	61	.245	.294	.435	1	6	2	27	1	83	4	3	5	271	.255	13	47	113	.221	2	14
Tatis, Fernando	96	394	324	59	82	159	21	1	18	64	.253	.379	.491	1	2	10	57	1	94	2	3	13	236	.250	10	48	88	.261	8	16
Polanco, Placido	118	350	323	50	102	135	12	3	5	39	.316	.347	.418	7	3	1	16	0	26	4	4	8	236	.309	1	22	87	.333	4	17
Davis, Eric	92	293	254	38	77	109	14	0	6	40	.303	.389	.429	0	2	1	36	0	60	1	1	7	149	.242	3	22	105	.390	3	18
McGwire, Mark	89	321	236	60	72	176	8	0	32	73	.305	.483	.746	0	2	7	76	12	78	1	0	5	183	.301	24	60	53	.321	8	13
Dunston, Shawon	98	231	216	28	54	105	11	2	12	43	.250	.278	.486	4	2	3	6	0	47	3	1	11	110	.273	6	19	106	.226	6	24
Clark, Will	51	197	171	29	59	112	15	1	12	42	.345	.426	.655	0	1	3	22	0	24	1	0	3	132	.364	10	38	39	.282	2	4
Howard, Thomas	86	141	133	13	28	52	4	1	6	28	.211	.255	.391	0	0	1	7	0	34	1	0	3	122	.230	6	27	11	.000	0	1
Marrero, Eli	53	116	102	21	23	43	3	1	5	17	.225	.302	.422	0	2	3	9	0	16	5	0	3	82	.232	3	11	20	.200	2	6
Perez, Eduardo	35	102	91	9	27	40	4	0	3	10	.297	.350	.440	2	1	3	5	0	19	1	0	2	61	.344	2	9	30	.200	1	1
Kile, Darryl	34	91	73	5	9	10	1	0	0	3	.123	.229	.137	8	0	0	10	0	38	0	0	0	57	.140	0	3	16	.063	0	0
Ankiel, Rick	35	73	68	8	17	26	1	1	2	9	.250	.292	.382	1	0	0	4	0	20	0	0	1	55	.291	2	9	13	.077	0	0
Hentgen, Pat	33	72	60	4	8	8	0	0	0	0	.133	.188	.133	8	0	0	4	0	17	0	0	1	48	.104	0	0	12	.250	0	0
Stephenson, Garrett	32	76	59	0	3	3	0	0	0	4	.051	.111	.051	13	0	0	4	0	23	0	0	2	40	.050	0	3	19	.053	0	1
Hernandez, Carlos	17	58	51	7	14	21	4	0	1	10	.275	.345	.412	0	1	1	5	0	9	1	0	0	41	.244	1	9	10	.400	0	1
Benes, Andy	30	60	50	1	4	7	0	0	1	1	.080	.148	.140	6	0	0	4	0	19	0	0	3	38	.079	1	1	12	.083	0	0
Sutton, Larry	23	33	25	5	8	11	0	0	1	6	.320	.406	.440	1	2	0	5	0	7	0	0	0	23	.348	1	5	2	.000	0	1
Richard, Chris	6	18	16	1	2	5	0	0	1	1	.125	.222	.313	0	0	0	2	0	2	0	0	0	15	.067	1	1	1	1.000	0	0
Reames, Britt	10	13	12	1	2	2	0	0	0	0	.167	.167	.167	1	0	0	0	0	2	0	0	0	8	.000	0	0	4	.500	0	0
Wilkins, Rick	4	13	11	3	3	3	0	0	0	1	.273	.385	.273	0	0	0	2	0	2	0	0	0	10	.300	0	1	1	.000	0	0
McDonald, Keith	6	9	7	3	3	12	0	0	3	5	.429	.556	1.714	0	0	0	2	0	1	0	0	0	5	.400	2	3	2	.500	1	2
Saturria, Luis	12	6	5	1	0	0	0	0	0	0	.000	.167	.000	0	0	0	1	0	3	0	0	0	2	.000	0	0	3	.000	0	0
Benes, Alan	30	4	4	0	2	3	1	0	0	0	.500	.500	.750	0	0	0	0	0	1	0	0	0	1	1.000	0	0	3	.333	0	0
Morris, Matt	32	6	3	0	1	1	0	0	0	0	.333	.333	.333	3	0	0	0	0	1	0	0	0	3	.333	0	0	0	.000	0	0
Thompson, Mark	20	3	3	0	0	0	0	0	0	0	.000	.000	.000	0	0	0	0	0	1	0	0	0	2	.000	0	0	1	.000	0	0
Mohler, Mike	22	1	1	0	1	1	0	0	0	0	1.000	1.000	1.000	0	0	0	0	0	0	0	0	0	1	1.000	0	0	0	.000	0	0
Brunette, Justin	4	1	1	0	1	1	0	0	0	0	1.000	1.000	1.000	0	0	0	0	0	0	0	0	0	0	.000	0	0	1	1.000	0	0
Holmes, Darren	5	1	1	0	0	0	0	0	0	0	.000	.000	.000	0	0	0	0	0	1	0	0	0	1	.000	0	0	0	.000	0	0
Slocumb, Heathcliff	44	1	1	0	0	0	0	0	0	0	.000	.000	.000	0	0	0	0	0	1	0	0	0	1	.000	0	0	0	.000	0	0
Veres, Dave	71	1	1	0	0	0	0	0	0	0	.000	.000	.000	0	0	0	0	0	0	0	0	0	1	.000	0	0	0	.000	0	0
James, Mike	52	1	1	1	0	0	0	0	0	0	.000	.000	.000	0	0	0	0	0	0	0	0	0	0	.000	0	0	1	.000	0	0
Rodriguez, Jose	6	1	1	0	0	0	0	0	0	0	.000	.000	.000	0	0	0	0	0	1	0	0	0	1	.000	0	0	0	.000	0	0
Orosco, Jesse	6	0	0	0	0	0	0	0	0	0	.000	.000	.000	0	0	0	0	0	0	0	0	0	0	.000	0	0	0	.000	0	0
Radinsky, Scott	1	0	0	0	0	0	0	0	0	0	.000	.000	.000	0	0	0	0	0	0	0	0	0	0	.000	0	0	0	.000	0	0
Timlin, Mike	25	0	0	0	0	0	0	0	0	0	.000	.000	.000	0	0	0	0	0	0	0	0	0	0	.000	0	0	0	.000	0	0
Wainhouse, Dave	9	0	0	0	0	0	0	0	0	0	.000	.000	.000	0	0	0	0	0	0	0	0	0	0	.000	0	0	0	.000	0	0
Christiansen, Jason	21	0	0	0	0	0	0	0	0	0	.000	.000	.000	0	0	0	0	0	0	0	0	0	0	.000	0	0	0	.000	0	0
Matthews, Mike	14	0	0	0	0	0	0	0	0	0	.000	.000	.000	0	0	0	0	0	0	0	0	0	0	.000	0	0	0	.000	0	0
Hackman, Luther	1	0	0	0	0	0	0	0	0	0	.000	.000	.000	0	0	0	0	0	0	0	0	0	0	.000	0	0	0	.000	0	0
Stechschulte, Gene	20	0	0	0	0	0	0	0	0	0	.000	.000	.000	0	0	0	0	0	0	0	0	0	0	.000	0	0	0	.000	0	0

Players with more than one N.L. team

Name	G	TPA	AB	R	H	TB	2B	3B	HR	RBI	Avg.	Obp.	Slg.	SH	SF	HP	BB	IBB	SO	SB	CS	GDP	vs RHP AB	Avg.	HR	RBI	vs LHP AB	Avg.	HR	RBI
Christiansen, Pit.-StL.	65	0	0	0	0	0	0	0	0	0	.000	.000	.000	0	0	0	0	0	0	0	0	0	0	.000	0	0	0	.000	0	0
Hernandez, S.D.-StL.	75	270	242	23	62	86	15	0	3	35	.256	.322	.355	0	3	4	21	1	35	2	3	4	174	.270	3	29	68	.221	0	6
Holmes, Ari.-StL.	13	1	1	0	0	0	0	0	0	0	.000	.000	.000	0	0	0	0	0	1	0	0	0	1	.000	0	0	0	.000	0	0
Slocumb, StL.-S.D.	66	1	1	0	0	0	0	0	0	0	.000	.000	.000	0	0	0	0	0	1	0	0	0	1	.000	0	0	0	.000	0	0

PITCHING

Name	W	L	Pct.	ERA	IP	H	R	ER	HR	SH	SF	HB	BB	IBB	SO	G	GS	CG	ShO	GF	Sv	vs. RH AB	Avg.	HR	RBI	vs. LH AB	Avg.	HR	RBI
Kile, Darryl	20	9	.690	3.91	232.1	215	109	101	33	11	8	13	58	1	192	34	34	5	1	0	0	464	.263	18	57	406	.229	15	44
Stephenson, Garrett	16	9	.640	4.49	200.1	209	105	100	31	6	7	7	63	0	123	32	31	3	2	0	0	398	.231	21	58	377	.310	10	40
Hentgen, Pat	15	12	.556	4.72	194.1	202	107	102	24	13	8	3	89	4	118	33	33	1	1	0	0	396	.295	17	55	337	.252	7	40
Ankiel, Rick	11	7	.611	3.50	175.0	137	80	68	21	8	6	6	90	2	194	31	30	0	0	0	0	530	.213	20	65	95	.253	1	5
Benes, Andy	12	9	.571	4.88	166.0	174	95	90	30	9	8	1	68	0	137	30	27	1	0	1	0	368	.280	15	51	265	.268	15	39
Veres, Dave	3	5	.375	2.85	75.2	65	26	24	6	5	2	6	25	2	67	71	0	0	0	61	29	153	.261	5	30	119	.210	1	6
Morris, Matt	3	3	.500	3.57	53.0	53	22	21	3	3	1	2	17	1	34	31	0	0	0	12	4	109	.266	1	10	94	.255	2	10
James, Mike	2	2	.500	3.16	51.1	40	22	18	7	2	1	3	24	2	41	51	0	0	0	10	2	119	.227	4	13	64	.203	3	10
Slocumb, Heathcliff	2	3	.400	5.44	49.2	50	32	30	9	3	2	1	24	1	34	43	0	0	0	11	1	120	.233	3	11	68	.324	6	14
Benes, Alan	2	2	.500	5.67	46.0	54	33	29	7	2	1	2	23	2	26	30	0	0	0	16	0	109	.303	3	18	77	.273	4	11
Reames, Britt	2	1	.667	2.88	40.2	30	17	13	4	0	1	1	23	1	31	8	7	0	0	0	0	68	.206	2	11	77	.208	2	3
Timlin, Mike	3	1	.750	3.34	29.2	30	11	11	2	2	1	2	20	3	26	25	0	0	0	9	1	67	.254	1	5	46	.283	1	8
Stechschulte, Gene	1	0	1.000	6.31	25.2	24	22	18	6	0	2	0	17	1	12	20	0	0	0	7	0	53	.283	3	15	44	.205	3	7
Thompson, Mark	1	1	.500	5.04	25.0	24	21	14	4	1	1	3	15	0	19	20	0	0	0	4	0	70	.229	2	12	26	.308	2	5
Mohler, Mike	1	1	.500	9.00	19.0	26	20	19	1	0	0	2	15	1	8	22	0	0	0	7	0	47	.298	1	7	34	.353	0	10
Christiansen, Jason	1	0	1.000	5.40	10.0	13	7	6	1	1	0	2	2	1	12	21	0	0	0	2	0	18	.333	0	2	23	.304	1	8
Matthews, Mike	0	0	.000	11.57	9.1	15	12	12	2	0	0	1	10	2	8	14	0	0	0	4	0	21	.476	2	11	22	.227	0	6
Wainhouse, Dave	0	1	.000	9.35	8.2	13	10	9	2	1	0	2	4	1	5	9	0	0	0	4	0	27	.296	1	8	10	.500	1	1
Holmes, Darren	0	1	.000	9.72	8.1	12	9	9	2	0	2	1	3	0	5	5	0	0	0	1	0	23	.348	1	9	10	.400	1	4
Brunette, Justin	0	0	.000	5.79	4.2	8	3	3	0	0	0	0	5	0	2	4	0	0	0	2	0	14	.357	0	1	8	.375	0	3
Rodriguez, Jose	0	0	.000	0.00	4.0	2	2	0	0	0	1	1	3	0	2	6	0	0	0	1	0	9	.222	0	0	5	.000	0	1
Hackman, Luther	0	0	.000	10.13	2.2	4	3	3	0	2	0	1	4	1	0	1	0	0	0	0	0	9	.333	0	2	1	1.000	0	1
Orosco, Jesse	0	0	.000	3.86	2.1	3	3	1	1	0	0	2	3	2	4	6	0	0	0	0	0	5	.000	0	0	6	.500	1	2
Radinsky, Scott	0	0	.000	-	0.0	0	0	0	0	0	0	0	1	0	0	1	0	0	0	0	0	0	.000	0	0	0	.000	0	0

PITCHERS WITH MORE THAN ONE N.L. TEAM

Name	W	L	Pct.	ERA	IP	H	R	ER	HR	SH	SF	HB	BB	IBB	SO	G	GS	CG	ShO	GF	Sv	vs. RH AB	Avg.	HR	RBI	vs. LH AB	Avg.	HR	RBI
Christiansen, Pit.-StL.	3	8	.273	5.06	48.0	41	29	27	3	4	1	2	27	5	53	65	0	0	0	1	1	111	.225	0	13	65	.246	3	12
Holmes, Ari.-StL.	0	1	.000	9.20	14.2	24	15	15	3	0	3	2	4	0	10	13	0	0	0	3	1	44	.386	2	18	18	.389	1	6
Slocumb, StL.-S.D.	2	4	.333	4.98	68.2	69	43	38	9	4	5	3	37	4	46	65	0	0	0	5	1	153	.242	3	22	107	.299	6	19

DESIGNATED HITTERS

Name	AB	Avg.	HR	RBI
Davis, Eric	12	.583	0	4
Howard, Thomas	10	.200	1	2
Tatis, Fernando	8	.250	1	2
Dunston, Shawon	3	.667	1	4
Lankford, Ray	2	.500	0	0

INDIVIDUAL STATISTICS

FIELDING

FIRST BASEMEN

Player	Pct.	G	PO	A	E	TC	DP
McGwire, Mark	.998	70	535	23	1	559	49
Clark, Will	.992	50	364	27	3	394	34
Paquette, Craig	.993	28	129	9	1	139	15
Perez, Eduardo	1.000	24	156	13	0	169	18
Matheny, Mike	1.000	8	12	1	0	13	0
Marrero, Eli	1.000	7	16	0	0	16	1
Edmonds, Jim	1.000	6	40	4	0	44	6
Sutton, Larry	1.000	6	26	2	0	28	2
Dunston, Shawon	.955	6	21	0	1	22	3
Richard, Chris	1.000	2	3	0	0	3	0
Tatis, Fernando	1.000	1	7	1	0	8	2
Howard, Thomas	1.000	1	4	0	0	4	0
Polanco, Placido	1.000	1	2	1	0	3	0

SECOND BASEMEN

Player	Pct.	G	PO	A	E	TC	DP
Vina, Fernando	.988	122	261	325	7	593	85
Polanco, Placido	.984	51	80	107	3	190	18
Paquette, Craig	.915	13	19	24	4	47	7

THIRD BASEMEN

Player	Pct.	G	PO	A	E	TC	DP
Tatis, Fernando	.953	91	35	128	8	171	15
Paquette, Craig	.942	86	41	88	8	137	9
Polanco, Placido	1.000	35	18	41	0	59	8
Dunston, Shawon	1.000	5	0	3	0	3	1
Perez, Eduardo	-	2	0	0	0	0	0

SHORTSTOPS

Player	Pct.	G	PO	A	E	TC	DP
Renteria, Edgar	.958	149	231	379	27	637	79
Polanco, Placido	1.000	29	31	53	0	84	11
Dunston, Shawon	1.000	8	4	6	0	10	2

OUTFIELDERS

Player	Pct.	G	PO	A	E	TC	DP
Edmonds, Jim	.989	146	352	10	4	366	2
Drew, J.D.	.966	127	248	6	9	263	2
Lankford, Ray	.973	117	179	4	5	188	0
Davis, Eric	.968	69	120	1	4	125	0
Dunston, Shawon	.989	58	85	1	1	87	0
Paquette, Craig	.935	31	27	2	2	31	2
Howard, Thomas	.960	27	23	1	1	25	1
Saturria, Luis	1.000	9	3	0	0	3	0
Perez, Eduardo	1.000	4	11	0	0	11	0
Sutton, Larry	1.000	4	5	0	0	5	0
Richard, Chris	1.000	3	7	0	0	7	0

CATCHERS

Player	Pct.	G	PO	A	E	TC	DP	PB
Matheny, Mike	.994	124	803	75	5	883	7	4
Marrero, Eli	1.000	38	196	14	0	210	2	2
Hernandez, Carlos	.963	16	96	9	4	109	0	2
McDonald, Keith	1.000	4	13	1	0	14	0	0
Wilkins, Rick	1.000	3	28	3	0	31	0	0

PITCHERS

Player	Pct.	G	PO	A	E	TC	DP
Veres, Dave	.800	71	3	9	3	15	0
James, Mike	1.000	51	2	5	0	7	0
Slocumb, Heathcliff	1.000	43	3	5	0	8	0
Kile, Darryl	.977	34	12	30	1	43	3
Hentgen, Pat	.974	33	14	23	1	38	1
Stephenson, Garrett	.975	32	9	30	1	40	0
Ankiel, Rick	.759	31	8	14	7	29	2
Morris, Matt	1.000	31	3	3	0	6	1
Benes, Andy	1.000	30	4	17	0	21	1
Benes, Alan	1.000	30	2	4	0	6	0
Timlin, Mike	1.000	25	1	5	0	6	0
Mohler, Mike	1.000	22	1	0	0	1	0
Christiansen, Jason	1.000	21	0	1	0	1	0
Thompson, Mark	1.000	20	2	4	0	6	0
Stechschulte, Gene	1.000	20	1	3	0	4	0
Matthews, Mike	1.000	14	0	1	0	1	0
Wainhouse, Dave	1.000	9	0	2	0	2	0
Reames, Britt	1.000	8	4	4	0	8	2
Orosco, Jesse	-	6	0	0	0	0	0
Rodriguez, Jose	-	6	0	0	0	0	0
Holmes, Darren	1.000	5	1	0	0	1	0
Brunette, Justin	1.000	4	0	1	0	1	0
Hackman, Luther	1.000	1	0	1	0	1	0
Radinsky, Scott	-	1	0	0	0	0	0

PITCHING AGAINST EACH CLUB

Pitcher	Ari. W-L	Atl. W-L	Chi. W-L	Cin. W-L	Col. W-L	Fla. W-L	Hou. W-L	L.A. W-L	Mil. W-L	Mon. W-L	N.Y. W-L	Phi. W-L	Pit. W-L	S.D. W-L	S.F. W-L	A.L. W-L	Total W-L
Ankiel, Rick	1-1	0-0	0-0	0-1	0-1	1-0	2-0	0-0	2-0	0-1	0-0	0-0	2-1	2-0	1-0	0-2	11-7
Benes, Alan	0-0	0-0	0-0	0-1	0-0	0-0	1-1	1-0	0-0	0-0	0-0	0-0	0-0	0-0	0-0	0-0	2-2
Benes, Andy	0-1	0-1	0-1	3-1	1-0	0-0	0-2	1-0	0-2	0-0	0-0	1-0	1-0	3-0	0-0	2-1	12-9
Brunette, J.	0-0	0-0	0-0	0-0	0-0	0-0	0-0	0-0	0-0	0-0	0-0	0-0	0-0	0-0	0-0	0-0	0-0
Christiansen, J.	0-0	0-0	0-0	0-0	0-0	0-0	0-0	0-0	0-0	0-0	0-0	1-0	0-0	0-0	0-0	0-0	1-0
Hackman, L.	0-0	0-0	0-0	0-0	0-0	0-0	0-0	0-0	0-0	0-0	0-0	0-0	0-0	0-0	0-0	0-0	0-0
Hentgen, Pat	0-1	1-0	2-1	1-1	1-1	0-2	1-1	1-0	1-1	2-0	0-1	1-0	1-1	0-0	1-1	2-1	15-12
Holmes, D.	0-0	0-0	0-0	0-1	0-0	0-0	0-0	0-0	0-0	0-0	0-0	0-0	0-0	0-0	0-0	0-0	0-1
James, Mike	0-0	0-0	1-0	0-0	0-1	1-0	0-0	0-0	0-0	0-0	0-1	0-0	0-0	0-0	0-0	0-0	2-2
Kile, Darryl	1-0	1-1	3-0	2-0	0-1	1-0	0-1	0-2	2-1	2-0	1-1	1-0	1-1	3-0	0-0	2-1	20-9
Matthews, M.	0-0	0-0	0-0	0-0	0-0	0-0	0-0	0-0	0-0	0-0	0-0	0-0	0-0	0-0	0-0	0-0	0-0
Mohler, Mike	0-0	0-0	0-0	0-0	0-1	0-0	0-0	0-0	0-0	0-0	0-0	1-0	0-0	0-0	0-0	0-0	1-1
Morris, Matt	0-0	0-0	0-0	0-0	0-0	1-1	0-0	0-0	1-0	0-0	1-0	0-0	0-0	0-0	0-1	0-1	3-3
Orosco, Jesse	0-0	0-0	0-0	0-0	0-0	0-0	0-0	0-0	0-0	0-0	0-0	0-0	0-0	0-0	0-0	0-0	0-0
Radinsky, S.	0-0	0-0	0-0	0-0	0-0	0-0	0-0	0-0	0-0	0-0	0-0	0-0	0-0	0-0	0-0	0-0	0-0
Reames, Britt	0-0	0-0	1-0	0-0	0-0	0-0	0-0	0-0	0-0	1-0	0-0	0-1	0-0	0-0	0-0	0-0	2-1
Rodriguez, J.	0-0	0-0	0-0	0-0	0-0	0-0	0-0	0-0	0-0	0-0	0-0	0-0	0-0	0-0	0-0	0-0	0-0
Slocumb, H.	0-0	0-0	0-0	0-0	0-0	0-0	0-0	2-0	0-0	0-0	0-0	0-1	0-1	0-0	0-1	0-0	2-3
Stechschulte, G.	0-0	0-0	0-0	0-0	0-0	0-0	0-0	1-0	0-0	0-0	0-0	0-0	0-0	0-0	0-0	0-0	1-0
Stephenson, G.	2-1	2-0	2-0	0-2	0-0	1-0	1-0	0-0	0-0	0-1	0-1	2-0	3-0	1-0	1-2	1-2	16-9
Thompson, M.	0-0	0-0	0-0	0-0	0-0	0-0	1-0	0-0	0-0	0-0	0-1	0-0	0-0	0-0	0-0	0-0	1-1
Timlin, Mike	0-0	0-1	1-0	0-0	1-0	1-0	0-0	0-0	0-0	0-0	0-0	0-0	0-0	0-0	0-0	0-0	3-1
Veres, Dave	0-1	0-0	0-1	0-0	0-0	0-0	0-0	0-1	1-1	0-0	1-1	0-0	0-0	0-0	1-0	0-0	3-5
Wainhouse, D.	0-0	0-0	0-0	0-0	0-0	0-0	0-1	0-0	0-0	0-0	0-0	0-0	0-0	0-0	0-0	0-0	0-1
Totals	4-5	4-3	10-3	6-7	3-5	6-3	6-6	6-3	7-5	5-2	3-6	7-2	8-4	9-0	4-5	7-8	95-67

INTERLEAGUE: Benes 1-0, Stephenson 1-0, Kile 0-1 vs. White Sox; Kile 1-0, Stephenson 0-1, Morris 0-1 vs. Indians; Hentgen 1-0, Stephenson 0-1, Ankiel 0-1 vs. Tigers; Benes 1-0, Kile 1-0, Hentgen 0-1 vs. Royals; Hentgen 1-0, Ankiel 0-1, Benes 0-1 vs. Twins. Total: 7-8.

MISCELLANEOUS

HOME RUNS BY PARK

At Arizona (3): Dunston 1, McGwire 1, Perez 1.
At Atlanta (7): Clark 2, Lankford 2, Edmonds 2, Renteria 1.
At Chicago (AL) (8): Tatis 3, Dunston 1, Perez 1, Edmonds 1, Renteria 1, McDonald 1.
At Chicago (NL) (4): Dunston 1, Clark 1, Renteria 1, Polanco 1.
At Cincinnati (12): Davis 3, Edmonds 2, Renteria 2, Dunston 1, McGwire 1, Lankford 1, Marrero 1, Drew 1.
At Colorado (8): Edmonds 2, Polanco 2, Davis 1, Howard 1, Tatis 1, Marrero 1.
At Detroit (4): McGwire 1, Howard 1, Edmonds 1, Drew 1.
At Florida (3): Clark 1, Paquette 1, Renteria 1.
At Houston (13): Edmonds 3, Renteria 3, Howard 2, McGwire 1, Lankford 1, Vina 1, Perez 1, Drew 1.
At Los Angeles (5): McGwire 2, Edmonds 2, Drew 1.
At Milwaukee (3): Dunston 1, Lankford 1, Matheny 1.
At Minnesota (3): Edmonds 1, Tatis 1, Richard 1.
At Montreal (5): Edmonds 2, Clark 1, Tatis 1, Drew 1.
At New York (NL) (3): Lankford 2, Edmonds 1.
At Philadelphia (9): McGwire 4, Edmonds 2, Benes 1, Paquette 1, Renteria 1.
At Pittsburgh (8): McGwire 2, Matheny 2, Dunston 1, Howard 1, Vina 1, Tatis 1.
At San Diego (6): McGwire 1, Clark 1, Edmonds 1, Matheny 1, Marrero 1, Drew 1.
At San Francisco (7): Renteria 2, McGwire 1, Lankford 1, Vina 1, Sutton 1, Drew 1.
At St. Louis (124): Edmonds 22, McGwire 18, Lankford 18, Paquette 13, Tatis 11, Drew 11, Dunston 6, Clark 6, Renteria 4, Davis 2, Matheny 2, Marrero 2, Polanco 2, Ankiel 2, McDonald 2, Hernandez 2, Howard 1, Vina 1.

LOW-HIT GAMES

No-hitters: None.
One-hitters: None.
Two-hitters: None.

10-STRIKEOUT GAMES

Rick Ankiel 6, Darryl Kile 5, Andy Benes 3, Total: 14

FOUR OR MORE HITS IN ONE GAME

Fernando Vina 2 (including one five-hit game), Eric Davis 1 (including one five-hit game), Craig Paquette 1 (including one five-hit game), Jim Edmonds 1, Placido Polanco 1, J.D. Drew 1, Total: 7

MULTI-HOMER GAMES

Ray Lankford 4, Jim Edmonds 4, Mark McGwire 2, Fernando Tatis 2, J.D. Drew 2, Shawon Dunston 1, Will Clark 1, Craig Paquette 1, Eli Marrero 1, Total: 18

GRAND SLAMS

4-6: J.D. Drew (off Chicago's Brian Williams)
4-11: Thomas Howard (off Houston's Chris Holt)
4-20: Eli Marrero (off San Diego's Brian Boehringer)
4-23: Placido Polanco (off Colorado's Scott Karl)
5-7: Eric Davis (off Cincinnati's Denny Neagle)
5-30: Shawon Dunston (off Arizona's Omar Daal)
7-13: Shawon Dunston (off Chicago's Jesus Pena)
7-14: Eduardo Perez (off Chicago's Bob Howry)
7-25: Fernando Tatis (off Arizona's Russ Springer)
9-16: Fernando Tatis (off Chicago's Daniel Garibay)
9-20: Jim Edmonds (off Houston's Chris Holt)
9-24: Will Clark (off Chicago's Todd Van Poppel)

PINCH HITTERS

(Minimum 5 at-bats)

Name	AB	Avg.	HR	RBI
Howard, Thomas	53	.208	2	11
Dunston, Shawon	33	.091	2	3
Davis, Eric	21	.286	0	2
Polanco, Placido	14	.286	1	6
Sutton, Larry	12	.417	1	4
Lankford, Ray	12	.083	0	2
Paquette, Craig	12	.083	0	0
McGwire, Mark	10	.300	1	2
Drew, J.D.	8	.375	0	1
Perez, Eduardo	7	.143	0	0
Marrero, Eli	6	.000	0	0

DEBUTS

4-13: Justin Brunette, P.
4-20: Gene Stechschulte, P.
5-18: Jose Rodriguez, P.
5-31: Mike Matthews, P.
7-4: Keith McDonald, PH.
7-17: Chris Richard, LF.
8-20: Britt Reames, P.
9-11: Luis Saturria, PR.

GAMES BY POSITION

Catcher: Mike Matheny 124, Eli Marrero 38, Carlos Hernandez 16, Keith McDonald 4, Rick Wilkins 3.
First base: Mark McGwire 70, Will Clark 50, Craig Paquette 28, Eduardo Perez 24, Mike Matheny 8, Eli Marrero 7, Shawon Dunston 6, Jim Edmonds 6, Larry Sutton 6, Chris Richard 2, Thomas Howard 1, Fernando Tatis 1, Placido Polanco 1.
Second base: Fernando Vina 122, Placido Polanco 51, Craig Paquette 13.
Third base: Fernando Tatis 91, Craig Paquette 86, Placido Polanco 35, Shawon Dunston 5, Eduardo Perez 2.
Shortstop: Edgar Renteria 149, Placido Polanco 29, Shawon Dunston 8.
Outfield: Jim Edmonds 146, J.D. Drew 127, Ray Lankford 117, Eric Davis 69, Shawon Dunston 58, Craig Paquette 31, Thomas Howard 27, Luis Saturria 9, Eduardo Perez 4, Larry Sutton 4, Chris Richard 3.
Designated hitter: Eric Davis 4, Thomas Howard 3, Fernando Tatis 2, Shawon Dunston 1, Ray Lankford 1.

STREAKS

Wins: 7 (September 11-17)
Losses: 4 (July 27-30)
Consecutive games with at least one hit: 17, Fernando Vina (August 8-25)
Wins by pitcher: 5, Darryl Kile (August 27-September 17)

ATTENDANCE

Home: 3,336,493
Road: 2,680,778
Highest (home): 48,901 (August 4 vs. Atlanta).
Highest (road): 50,726 (July 29 vs. New York).
Lowest (home): 27,997 (April 19 vs. San Diego).
Lowest (road): 9,558 (July 31 vs. Montreal).

SAN DIEGO PADRES

DAY BY DAY

Date	Opp.	Res.	Score	(inn.*)	Hits	Opp. hits	Winning pitcher	Losing pitcher	Save	Record	Pos.	GB
4-3	At N.Y.	L	1-2		5	4	Leiter	Wall	Benitez	0-1	T2nd	1.0
4-5	At N.Y.	W	4-0		11	7	Williams	B.J. Jones		1-1	4th	1.0
4-6	At N.Y.	W	8-5		10	8	Clement	Hampton		2-1	2nd	1.0
4-7	At Mon.	W	10-5		13	12	Meadows	Powell		3-1	T1st	...
4-8	At Mon.	L	9-10		11	11	Telford	Wall	Urbina	3-2	2nd	1.0
4-9	At Mon.	L	1-2		7	4	Irabu	Boehringer	Urbina	3-3	T2nd	2.0
4-10	Ari.	L	4-8		11	12	Stottlemyre	Williams	Morgan	3-4	T3rd	3.0
4-11	Ari.	W	3-2	(13)	9	7	Whisenant	Springer		4-4	3rd	2.0
4-12	Ari.	W	4-2		6	6	Meadows	Reynoso	Hoffman	5-4	3rd	1.0
4-13	Ari.	L	4-5		10	9	Anderson	Hitchcock	Morgan	5-5	T3rd	2.0
4-14	Hou.	L	4-10		13	11	Reynolds	Boehringer		5-6	4th	3.0
4-15	Hou.	W	5-3		9	7	Williams	Lima	Hoffman	6-6	4th	3.0
4-16	Hou.	W	13-3		18	8	Clement	Holt		7-6	T3rd	2.5
4-18	At StL.	L	4-5		9	10	An. Benes	Meadows	Veres	7-7	4th	3.0
4-19	At StL.	L	3-4		6	9	Kile	Hitchcock	Veres	7-8	4th	4.0
4-20	At StL.	L	1-14		6	14	Ankiel	Boehringer		7-9	4th	5.0
4-21	At Hou.	W	7-2		11	6	Williams	Lima		8-9	4th	4.0
4-22	At Hou.	W	8-6	(10)	14	6	Cunnane	Perez	Hoffman	9-9	4th	3.0
4-23	At Hou.	W	11-10		14	10	Whisenant	Wagner	Hoffman	10-9	3rd	2.0
4-25	At Pit.	L	3-4	(11)	13	9	Sauerbeck	Almanzar		10-10	3rd	3.0
4-26	At Pit.	L	8-9		10	12	Williams	Whisenant		10-11	3rd	4.0
4-27	At Pit.	W	12-4		15	4	Clement	Parra		11-11	3rd	3.0
4-28	Atl.	L	2-7		8	7	Maddux	Meadows	Remlinger	11-12	T3rd	3.0
4-29	Atl.	L	4-7	(12)	10	10	Chen	Palacios	Rocker	11-13	T3rd	4.0
4-30	Atl.	L	4-7		6	8	Glavine	Hitchcock		11-14	T3rd	5.0
5-1	Fla.	L	2-5		8	9	Dempster	Williams	Alfonseca	11-15	5th	5.5
5-2	Fla.	W	8-3		11	6	Clement	Nunez		12-15	5th	5.5
5-3	Fla.	W	3-1		5	5	Meadows	Penny	Hoffman	13-15	5th	4.5
5-5	At Ari.	L	3-5		5	8	Johnson	Hitchcock		13-16	5th	6.0
5-6	At Ari.	L	5-10		8	12	Anderson	Lopez		13-17	5th	7.0
5-7	At Ari.	L	1-8		8	11	Stottlemyre	Clement		13-18	5th	8.0
5-9	At Cin.	L	0-2		8	7	Parris	Meadows	Graves	13-19	5th	9.5
5-10	At Cin.	L	1-5		6	8	Villone	Hitchcock	Williamson	13-20	5th	10.5
5-11	At Cin.	L	9-11		11	16	Graves	Whisenant		13-21	5th	11.0
5-12	Ari.	L	4-6		9	8	Anderson	Clement	Kim	13-22	5th	12.0
5-13	Ari.	L	2-6		9	9	Stottlemyre	Spencer	Morgan	13-23	5th	13.0
5-14	Ari.	W	3-1		5	2	Meadows	Daal	Hoffman	14-23	5th	12.0
5-16	At Fla.	W	7-3		9	7	Hitchcock	Sanchez		15-23	5th	11.0
5-17	At Fla.	L	2-4		8	9	Dempster	Clement	Alfonseca	15-24	5th	11.0
5-18	At Fla.	W	6-2		15	6	Spencer	Fernandez		16-24	5th	11.0
5-19	At Atl.	W	11-7		12	15	Whiteside	Mulholland	Hoffman	17-24	5th	10.0
5-20	At Atl.	L	6-10		13	10	Burkett	Cunnane		17-25	5th	10.0
5-21	At Atl.	L	6-12		11	16	Glavine	Hitchcock		17-26	5th	10.0
5-22	N.Y.	W	1-0		5	5	Clement	Franco	Hoffman	18-26	5th	9.5
5-23	N.Y.	L	3-5	(10)	7	6	Wendell	Hoffman	Benitez	18-27	5th	10.5
5-24	N.Y.	W	5-4		11	7	Wall	Mahomes	Hoffman	19-27	5th	10.5
5-26	Mon.	W	6-2		11	6	Whiteside	Irabu		20-27	5th	11.0
5-27	Mon.	W	4-2		10	7	Wall	Kline	Hoffman	21-27	5th	11.0
5-28	Mon.	W	4-3		6	8	Walker	Pavano	Hoffman	22-27	5th	10.0
5-29	Mil.	L	3-8		8	10	Haynes	Meadows		22-28	5th	10.0
5-30	Mil.	W	6-3		11	9	Eaton	D'Amico	Hoffman	23-28	5th	9.0
5-31	Mil.	W	9-5		9	10	Almanzar	Weathers		24-28	5th	9.0
6-2	At Sea.	L	4-7		8	7	Moyer	Clement	Sasaki	24-29	5th	10.5
6-3	At Sea.	W	7-4		10	7	Spencer	Halama	Hoffman	25-29	5th	9.5
6-4	At Sea.	L	4-6		10	5	Abbott	Meadows		25-30	5th	9.5
6-5	At Oak.	L	2-3	(10)	4	5	Isringhausen	Almanzar		25-31	5th	9.5
6-6	At Oak.	L	4-5		7	7	Heredia	Lopez	Isringhausen	25-32	5th	9.5
6-7	At Oak.	L	4-10		10	13	Service	Clement	Jones	25-33	5th	9.5
6-9	Hou.	L	6-7		11	10	Wagner	Hoffman		25-34	5th	10.5
6-10	Hou.	W	13-3		12	12	Meadows	Elarton		26-34	5th	9.5
6-11	Hou.	W	4-1		11	4	Walker	Lima	Hoffman	27-34	5th	9.5
6-12	StL.	L	3-7		8	10	An. Benes	Clement		27-35	5th	10.5
6-13	StL.	L	3-8		11	16	Kile	Lopez	Veres	27-36	5th	10.5
6-14	StL.	L	1-3		6	7	Stephenson	Spencer	Morris	27-37	5th	11.5
6-16	Cin.	W	8-5		11	10	Reyes	Parris	Hoffman	28-37	5th	10.5
6-17	Cin.	W	3-1		6	5	Walker	Villone	Hoffman	29-37	5th	9.5
6-18	Cin.	W	8-7		8	11	Clement	Bell	Hoffman	30-37	5th	8.5
6-19	At Ari.	L	2-3		6	7	Padilla	Kolb		30-38	5th	9.5
6-20	At Ari.	W	3-1		7	2	Tollberg	Stottlemyre	Hoffman	31-38	5th	8.5
6-21	At Ari.	L	8-11		8	16	Morgan	Reyes		31-39	5th	9.5
6-23	At Cin.	W	10-7	(10)	12	14	Hoffman	Williamson	Reyes	32-39	5th	9.5
6-24	At Cin.	L	5-11		14	15	Villone	Clement	Dessens	32-40	5th	9.5
6-25	At Cin.	W	5-4		7	12	Tollberg	Fernandez	Hoffman	33-40	5th	9.5
6-26	At L.A.	W	9-5		9	7	Meadows	Hershiser		34-40	5th	9.5
6-27	At L.A.	L	4-5	(10)	7	10	Fetters	Whiteside		34-41	5th	9.5
6-28	At L.A.	L	4-5		6	7	Adams	Montgomery		34-42	5th	10.5
6-29	At L.A.	W	5-4		7	6	Clement	Dreifort	Hoffman	35-42	5th	10.5
6-30	Col.	L	4-5		7	10	Astacio	Almanzar	Jimenez	35-43	5th	10.5

HIGHLIGHTS

High point: Rookie reliever Kevin Walker improved his record to 6-0 August 13 in a 7-3 victory at Pro Player Stadium. The win completed the franchise's first three-game sweep in Florida and brought the Padres to within four games of .500 for the first time since June 3.
Low point: The Padres rolled into Atlanta after their Marlins sweep and lost three straight to the Braves. They fell to the bottom of the N.L. West standings, 11½ games out of first place, and remained there the rest of the season.
Turning point: The Padres were 13-15 in early May when they embarked on a six-game trip to Arizona and Cincinnati. They lost all six games and returned to San Diego 11 games out of first.
Most valuable player: Cleanup man Phil Nevin led the team in home runs (31), doubles (34) and RBIs (107). He batted .394 with nine home runs and 29 RBIs in 104 August at-bats.
Most valuable pitcher: Trevor Hoffman stabilized a bullpen that suffered from inconsistent set-up work over several prolonged stretches. The veteran righthander totaled 43 saves, pitched in 70 games and served as mentor to several young teammates.
Most improved player: Speedy Damian Jackson blossomed after replacing injured Bret Boone at second base. Jackson made huge strides at the plate, where he learned to hit the ball to all fields.
Most pleasant surprise: Walker, who opened at the Class AA level, became the most reliable lefthanded reliever in Bruce Bochy's six seasons as manager. The 24-year-old, who appeared in 70 games, was more resilient and poised than many veteran teammates.
Key injuries: Projected No. 1 starter Sterling Hitchcock underwent elbow surgery after making 11 starts. ... June knee surgery limited right fielder Tony Gwynn to 36 games. The eight-time batting champion finished at .323, topping .300 for the 18th straight season. ... Randy Myers, a $13.6-million addition in 1998, has missed the 1999 and 2000 seasons. ... Starter Woody Williams made an inspirational return to the mound July 2 when he faced the Rockies after being sidelined for two months by an aneurysm. Williams went on to win 10 games and post a 3.75 ERA over 168 innings.
Notable: Rookie Adam Eaton came up from Class AA and showed why the club views him as a future staff ace. Over his first 16 starts, Eaton posted a 2.89 ERA. ... The club led both leagues in errors (141). ... Center fielder Ruben Rivera, touted as a future star, batted .208—an improvement over his .195 average in 1999. ... The Padres lost all nine of their games against the N.L. Central-champion Cardinals, and eight of nine games to East-champion Atlanta.

—TOM KRASOVIC

MISCELLANEOUS

RECORDS

2000 regular-season record: 76-86 (5th in N.L. West); 41-40 at home; 35-46 on road; 25-18 vs. East; 26-27 vs. Central; 25-41 vs. West; 19-30 vs. lefthanded starters; 57-56 vs. righthanded starters; 69-74 on grass; 7-12 on turf; 23-26 in daytime; 53-60 at night; 25-27 in one-run games; 11-13 in extra-inning games; 0-0-0 in doubleheaders.
Team record past five years: 415-395 (.512, ranks 7th in league in that span).

TEAM LEADERS

Batting average: Phil Nevin (.303).
At-bats: Eric Owens (583).
Runs: Ryan Klesko (88).
Hits: Eric Owens (171).
Total Bases: Phil Nevin (292).
Doubles: Phil Nevin (34).
Triples: Eric Owens (7).
Home runs: Phil Nevin (31).
Runs batted in: Phil Nevin (107).
Stolen bases: Eric Owens (29).
Slugging percentage: Phil Nevin (.543).
On-base percentage: Ryan Klesko (.393).
Wins: Matt Clement (13).
Earned-run average: Woody Williams (3.75).
Complete games: Woody Williams (4).
Shutouts: None.
Saves: Trevor Hoffman (43).
Innings pitched: Matt Clement (205.0).
Strikeouts: Matt Clement (170).

Date	Opp.	Res.	Score	(inn.*)	Hits	Opp. hits	Winning pitcher	Losing pitcher	Save	Record	Pos.	GB
7-1	Col.	W	5-3		7	9	Meadows	Arrojo	Hoffman	36-43	5th	10.5
7-2	Col.	L	2-3	(10)	7	10	DeJean	Hoffman	Jimenez	36-44	5th	10.5
7-3	Col.	L	1-3		4	4	Bohanon	Montgomery	Jimenez	36-45	5th	10.5
7-4	L.A.	W	7-2		9	4	Clement	Park		37-45	5th	10.5
7-5	L.A.	L	5-7		11	11	Osuna	Whiteside	Fetters	37-46	5th	11.5
7-6	L.A.	L	3-9		5	14	Brown	Meadows		37-47	5th	12.5
7-7	At Tex.	L	4-5	(10)	6	9	Davis	Whiteside		37-48	5th	12.5
7-8	At Tex.	L	1-8		3	12	Helling	Eaton		37-49	5th	12.5
7-9	At Tex.	W	4-3		13	8	Clement	Rogers	Hoffman	38-49	5th	12.5
7-13	Sea.	W	2-1	(10)	5	6	Hoffman	Tomko		39-49	5th	11.5
7-14	Sea.	L	5-7		9	12	Moyer	Meadows	Sasaki	39-50	5th	12.5
7-15	Sea.	W	4-1		6	4	Williams	Sele	Hoffman	40-50	5th	11.5
7-16	Ana.	W	6-5	(10)	11	13	Wall	Levine		41-50	5th	10.5
7-17	Ana.	L	2-3		4	6	Cooper	Clement	Percival	41-51	5th	11.5
7-18	Ana.	L	2-3	(11)	8	7	Levine	Hoffman		41-52	5th	11.5
7-19	At S.F	W	4-3	(10)	13	10	Wall	Embree		42-52	5th	11.5
7-20	At S.F	L	3-7		5	8	Rueter	Williams	Fultz	42-53	5th	12.5
7-21	At Col.	W	5-1		12	7	Eaton	Bohanon		43-53	5th	12.5
7-22	At Col.	L	4-9		11	16	White	Clement		43-54	5th	12.5
7-23	At Col.	W	6-4	(10)	11	7	Hoffman	Belinda	Wall	44-54	5th	11.5
7-24	S.F	L	0-3		6	6	Gardner	Meadows	Nen	44-55	5th	12.0
7-25	S.F	W	3-2		10	7	Williams	Rueter	Hoffman	45-55	5th	11.0
7-26	S.F	L	1-3		5	5	Estes	Eaton	Nen	45-56	5th	11.0
7-28	At Pit.	L	5-16		9	14	Arroyo	Clement		45-57	5th	12.5
7-29	At Pit.	L	2-10		6	16	Cordova	Tollberg		45-58	5th	12.5
7-30	At Pit.	W	9-8		14	13	Wall	Wilkins	Hoffman	46-58	5th	11.5
7-31	Phi.	W	4-1		7	4	Williams	Chen		47-58	5th	11.0
8-1	Phi.	W	10-9	(10)	13	11	Almanzar	Brantley		48-58	5th	11.0
8-2	Phi.	W	5-2		9	8	Clement	Daal	Hoffman	49-58	5th	10.0
8-3	Chi.	W	6-5		8	10	Walker	Worrell	Hoffman	50-58	5th	10.0
8-4	Chi.	W	11-9		13	13	Almanzar	Rain	Hoffman	51-58	5th	10.0
8-5	Chi.	L	3-6		8	10	Tapani	Williams	Aguilera	51-59	5th	10.0
8-6	Chi.	W	8-6		11	12	Eaton	Garibay	Hoffman	52-59	5th	10.0
8-7	At Phi.	W	6-4		8	11	Clement	Person	Hoffman	53-59	5th	10.0
8-8	At Phi.	L	4-10		8	14	Daal	Tollberg		53-60	5th	11.0
8-9	At Phi.	L	2-3		6	9	Brock	Slocumb		53-61	5th	12.0
8-10	At Phi.	W	15-3		19	8	Williams	Wolf		54-61	5th	11.5
8-11	At Fla.	W	3-0		5	7	Eaton	Burnett	Hoffman	55-61	5th	10.5
8-12	At Fla.	W	2-1	(10)	9	5	Walker	Alfonseca	Hoffman	56-61	5th	9.5
8-13	At Fla.	W	7-3		8	11	Walker	Almanza	Hoffman	57-61	5th	8.5
8-14	At Atl.	L	2-9		6	14	Glavine	Witasick		57-62	5th	9.5
8-15	At Atl.	L	1-3		7	7	Remlinger	Williams	Rocker	57-63	5th	10.5
8-16	At Atl.	L	1-4		5	5	Kamieniecki	Walker	Rocker	57-64	5th	11.5
8-18	Mon.	L	3-6		7	11	Thurman	Clement	Strickland	57-65	5th	13.0
8-19	Mon.	W	4-3	(11)	12	8	Walker	Santana		58-65	5th	13.0
8-20	Mon.	W	5-4		7	10	Witasick	Lira	Hoffman	59-65	5th	12.0
8-21	N.Y.	W	5-4	(10)	8	10	Hoffman	Cook		60-65	5th	12.0
8-22	N.Y.	W	16-1		12	7	Eaton	Mahomes	Erdos	61-65	5th	11.0
8-23	N.Y.	L	1-4		3	7	Leiter	Clement	Benitez	61-66	5th	12.0
8-25	At Mil.	W	4-0		12	6	Tollberg	Wright		62-66	5th	12.0
8-26	At Mil.	L	5-6	(10)	14	8	Leskanic	Hoffman		62-67	5th	12.0
8-27	At Mil.	W	2-1		7	8	Williams	Weathers	Hoffman	63-67	5th	11.0
8-28	At Chi.	W	8-2		11	3	Clement	Quevedo		64-67	5th	11.0
8-29	At Chi.	L	6-7	(13)	10	10	Heredia	Hoffman		64-68	5th	11.0
8-30	At Chi.	L	1-5		4	10	Lieber	Tollberg		64-69	5th	12.0
8-31	At Chi.	W	11-5		16	8	Witasick	Tapani		65-69	5th	12.0
9-1	Pit.	L	2-3	(10)	6	10	Williams	Hoffman		65-70	5th	13.0
9-2	Pit.	L	3-6		8	8	Ritchie	Clement	Sauerbeck	65-71	5th	14.0
9-3	Pit.	L	6-8	(13)	16	11	Skrmetta	Almanzar	Williams	65-72	5th	15.0
9-4	Mil.	W	4-3		7	5	Davey	King	Hoffman	66-72	5th	15.0
9-5	Mil.	W	3-1		5	3	Witasick	Rigdon	Hoffman	67-72	5th	15.0
9-6	Mil.	W	7-6		11	9	Williams	Snyder	Hoffman	68-72	5th	15.0
9-7	At S.F	L	0-13		5	16	Estes	Clement		68-73	5th	16.0
9-8	At S.F.	W	10-7		16	13	Almanzar	Embree	Hoffman	69-73	5th	15.0
9-9	At S.F	W	7-3		8	11	Tollberg	Ortiz		70-73	5th	14.0
9-10	At S.F	L	2-10		5	10	Rueter	Witasick		70-74	5th	15.0
9-11	Col.	W	7-2		10	6	Williams	Tavarez		71-74	5th	15.0
9-12	Col.	L	3-6		6	12	Yoshii	Clement	Jimenez	71-75	5th	16.0
9-13	Col.	L	0-11		9	16	Bohanon	Eaton		71-76	5th	17.0
9-15	S.F	W	5-4		9	9	Davey	Henry	Hoffman	72-76	5th	16.0
9-16	S.F	L	3-4	(13)	10	16	Embree	Almanzar	Nen	72-77	5th	17.0
9-17	S.F	L	1-5		5	9	Gardner	Williams		72-78	5th	18.0
9-19	At Col.	W	7-2		12	6	Clement	Bohanon		73-78	5th	17.5
9-20	At Col.	W	15-11		15	11	Eaton	Rose	Hoffman	74-78	5th	17.5
9-21	At Col.	L	4-13		4	17	Jarvis	Tollberg		74-79	5th	18.5
9-22	At L.A.	W	3-2		7	8	Maurer	Osuna	Hoffman	75-79	5th	17.5
9-23	At L.A.	L	1-2		2	5	Brown	Williams		75-80	5th	18.0
9-24	At L.A.	L	0-1		2	3	Park	Clement	Shaw	75-81	5th	18.0
9-26	StL.	L	1-7		6	11	An. Benes	Eaton		75-82	5th	18.0
9-27	StL.	L	0-3		7	7	Ankiel	Tollberg	Veres	75-83	5th	19.0
9-28	StL.	L	6-7		7	8	Kile	Davey	Veres	75-84	5th	20.0
9-29	L.A.	L	0-3		2	6	Park	Williams		75-85	5th	21.0
9-30	L.A.	L	2-10		6	9	Gagne	Clement		75-86	5th	21.0
10-1	L.A.	W	4-0		7	7	Eaton	Dreifort	Hoffman	76-86	5th	21.0

Monthly records: April (11-14), May (13-14), June (11-15), July (12-15), August (18-11), September (10-17), October (1-0).
*Innings, if other than nine. † First game of a doubleheader. ‡ Second game of a doubleheader.

MEMORABLE GAMES

April 3 at New York Mets

Padres cleanup man Phil Nevin ripped a home run off Mets ace Al Leiter, but the Mets claimed a 2-1 victory in the season opener when former Padre Derek Bell homered off Donne Wall. Nevin went on to have a big year, but the contest also provided an omen for the club, which fumbled away several winnable games in the first half.

San Diego	AB	R	H	BI	Mets	AB	R	H	BI
Martin, lf	4	0	0	0	Henderson, lf	4	0	0	0
Jackson, ss	4	0	0	0	Benitez, p	0	0	0	0
Gwynn, rf	3	0	0	0	Bell, rf	3	1	1	1
Nevin, 3b	4	1	3	1	Alfonzo, 2b	3	1	0	0
Klesko, 1b	4	0	0	0	Piazza, c	3	0	1	0
Boone, 2b	4	0	0	0	Zeile, 1b	2	0	1	1
Rivera, cf	3	0	0	0	Ventura, 3b	2	0	1	0
Hernandez, c	3	0	2	0	Mora, cf	2	0	0	0
Hitchcock, p	2	0	0	0	Hamilton, ph-cf	1	0	0	0
Wall, p	0	0	0	0	Ordonez, ss	3	0	0	0
					Leiter, p	2	0	0	0
					Nunnally, ph-lf	1	0	0	0
Totals	**31**	**1**	**5**	**1**	**Totals**	**26**	**2**	**4**	**2**

San Diego ....0 1 0 0 0 0 0 0 0—1 5 0
Mets..0 0 0 0 0 0 1 1 x—2 4 1

E—Alfonzo (1). DP—San Diego 1. LOB—San Diego 5, Mets 4. 2B—Zeile (1). HR—Nevin (1), Bell (1). CS—Hernandez (1). S—Zeile. SH—Hitchcock.

San Diego	IP	H	R	ER	BB	SO
Hitchcock	6.1	3	1	1	2	4
Wall (L 0-1)	1.2	1	1	1	0	3

Mets	IP	H	R	ER	BB	SO
Leiter (W 1-0)	8	5	1	1	0	7
Benitez (S 1)	1	0	0	0	0	1

HBP—Gwynn by Leiter, Ventura by Hitchcock. U—HP-Hirschbeck, 1B, Bell. 2B, O'Nora. 3B, Iossugna. T—2:24. A—52,308.

August 11 at Florida

Rookie pitcher Adam Eaton, drilled by a line drive in his last outing, fired fastballs in the mid-90s to lead the club to a 3-0 victory over the Marlins. Padres players and coaches said it was an inspiring performance that solidified their belief that Eaton could become a top starter. Marlins manager John Boles rated it the best pitching performance he had seen all season.

San Diego	AB	R	H	BI	Florida	AB	R	H	BI
Owens, lf	4	2	1	0	Castillo, 2b	4	0	1	0
Darr, rf	3	0	2	0	Kotsay, rf	4	0	2	0
Klesko, 1b	4	0	0	0	Rodriguez, lf	3	0	1	0
Nevin, 3b	3	1	1	1	Clapinski, pr-lf	0	0	0	0
Boone, 2b	3	0	0	1	Wilson, cf	3	0	0	0
Davis, c	4	0	0	0	Lowell, 3b	4	0	0	0
Rivera, cf	2	0	1	0	Lee, 1b	4	0	1	0
Jackson, ss	3	0	0	0	Fox, ss	4	0	1	0
Eaton, p	3	0	0	0	Castro, c	4	0	1	0
Mabry, ph	0	0	0	0	Burnett, p	2	0	0	0
Vitiello, ph	1	0	0	0	Almanza, p	0	0	0	0
Hoffman, p	0	0	0	0	Bones, p	0	0	0	0
					Smith, ph	1	0	0	0
					Aybar, p	0	0	0	0
					Darensbourg, p0	0	0	0	
Totals	**30**	**3**	**5**	**2**	**Totals**	**33**	**0**	**7**	**0**

San Diego ....1 0 0 1 0 0 0 1 0—3 5 1
Florida ....0 0 0 0 0 0 0 0 0—0 7 2

E—Rivera (4), Fox (8), Castro (3). LOB—San Diego 6, Florida 8. 2B—Kotsay (25). HR—Nevin (25). SB—Owens (23), Darr 2 (2), Rivera (5). CS—Rivera 2 (4), Wilson (7). S—Boone.

San Diego	IP	H	R	ER	BB	SO
Eaton (W 4-2)	8	6	0	0	2	6
Hoffman (S 31)	1	1	0	0	0	2

Florida	IP	H	R	ER	BB	SO
Burnett (L 1-3)	7	4	3	2	3	4
Almanza	0.1	1	0	0	1	1
Bones	0.2	0	0	0	0	1
Aybar	0.1	0	0	0	1	0
Darensbourg	0.2	0	0	0	0	1

Burnett pitched to 1 batter in 8th. WP—Eaton. PB—Davis. U—HP, Timmons. 1B, Craft. 2B, Morrison. 3B—Fletcher. T—2:43. A—14,663.

INDIVIDUAL STATISTICS

BATTING

Name	G	TPA	AB	R	H	TB	2B	3B	HR	RBI	Avg.	Obp.	Slg.	SH	SF	HP	BB	IBB	SO	SB	CS	GDP	vs RHP				vs LHP			
																							AB	Avg.	HR	RBI	AB	Avg.	HR	RBI
Owens, Eric	145	636	583	87	171	222	19	7	6	51	.293	.346	.381	0	4	4	45	4	63	29	14	16	404	.287	2	39	179	.307	4	12
Nevin, Phil	143	605	538	87	163	292	34	1	31	107	.303	.374	.543	0	4	4	59	9	121	2	0	17	392	.288	18	72	146	.342	13	35
Klesko, Ryan	145	590	494	88	140	255	33	2	26	92	.283	.393	.516	0	4	1	91	9	81	23	7	10	373	.292	24	76	121	.256	2	16
Jackson, Damian	138	541	470	68	120	177	27	6	6	37	.255	.345	.377	4	2	3	62	2	108	28	6	7	349	.266	5	31	121	.223	1	6
Boone, Bret	127	525	463	61	116	195	18	2	19	74	.251	.326	.421	0	7	5	50	7	97	8	4	11	331	.257	14	56	132	.235	5	18
Rivera, Ruben	135	479	423	62	88	169	18	6	17	57	.208	.296	.400	0	2	10	44	1	137	8	4	8	274	219	12	41	149	.188	5	16
Martin, Al	93	378	346	62	106	164	13	6	11	27	.306	.360	.474	0	2	2	28	5	54	6	8	2	270	.348	11	24	76	.158	0	3
Gonzalez, Wiki	95	319	284	25	66	98	15	1	5	30	.232	.311	.345	1	1	3	30	4	31	1	2	5	201	.214	4	22	83	.277	1	8
Darr, Mike	58	228	205	21	55	80	14	4	1	30	.268	.342	.390	0	0	0	23	1	45	9	1	9	153	.268	1	23	52	.269	0	7
Hernandez, Carlos	58	212	191	16	48	65	11	0	2	25	.251	.316	.340	0	2	3	16	1	26	1	3	4	133	.278	2	20	58	.190	0	5
Sprague, Ed	73	175	157	19	41	83	12	0	10	27	.261	.326	.529	0	2	3	13	2	40	0	0	1	57	.123	2	7	100	.340	8	20
Relaford, Desi	45	189	157	26	32	40	2	0	2	16	.204	.330	.255	1	1	3	27	0	26	8	0	3	111	.225	1	11	46	.152	1	5
Magadan, Dave	95	166	132	13	36	49	7	0	2	21	.273	.410	.371	0	2	0	32	1	23	0	0	4	112	.277	2	19	20	.250	0	2
Davis, Ben	43	148	130	12	29	44	6	0	3	14	.223	.297	.338	3	1	0	14	1	35	1	1	2	94	.234	1	9	36	.194	2	5
Gwynn, Tony	36	140	127	17	41	56	12	0	1	17	.323	.364	.441	0	3	1	9	2	4	0	1	4	91	.286	0	11	36	.417	1	6
Mabry, John	48	129	123	17	28	57	8	0	7	25	.228	.256	.463	0	1	0	5	0	38	0	0	3	111	.252	7	24	12	.000	0	1
DeHaan, Kory	90	110	103	19	21	34	7	0	2	13	.204	.239	.330	1	1	0	5	0	39	4	2	2	85	.212	2	13	18	.167	0	0
Nicholson, Kevin	37	105	97	7	21	32	6	1	1	8	.216	.255	.330	3	0	1	4	0	31	1	0	2	60	.233	0	6	37	.189	1	2
Clement, Matt	34	69	60	3	4	6	0	1	0	2	.067	.125	.100	5	0	0	4	0	33	0	0	0	43	.070	0	2	17	.059	0	0
Williams, Woody	30	66	58	10	15	22	4	0	1	9	.259	.308	.379	1	2	1	4	0	26	0	0	1	39	.231	0	6	19	.316	1	3
Gomez, Chris	33	64	54	4	12	12	0	0	0	3	.222	.306	.222	1	1	0	7	0	5	0	0	1	32	.219	0	2	22	.227	0	1
Vitiello, Joe	39	63	52	7	13	22	3	0	2	8	.250	.365	.423	0	1	0	10	0	9	0	0	1	11	.182	0	1	41	.268	2	7
Meadows, Brian	22	44	40	2	6	6	0	0	0	2	.150	.150	.150	4	0	0	0	0	17	0	0	1	31	.129	0	2	9	.222	0	0
Eaton, Adam	23	45	38	6	11	13	2	0	0	4	.289	.400	.342	0	0	1	6	0	10	2	0	1	27	.222	0	4	11	.455	0	0
Tollberg, Brian	19	38	32	1	3	3	0	0	0	1	.094	.094	.094	6	0	0	0	0	11	0	0	1	27	.074	0	1	5	.200	0	0
LaRocca, Greg	13	30	27	1	6	8	2	0	0	2	.222	.250	.296	2	0	0	1	0	4	0	0	1	13	.154	0	0	14	.286	0	2
Roskos, John	14	30	27	0	1	2	1	0	0	1	.037	.133	.074	0	0	0	3	0	7	0	0	1	7	.143	0	1	20	.000	0	0
Witasick, Jay	11	25	22	0	3	3	0	0	0	3	.136	.174	.136	2	0	0	1	0	10	0	0	1	17	.176	0	3	5	.000	0	0
Hitchcock, Sterling	11	23	22	0	0	0	0	0	0	1	.000	.000	.000	1	0	0	0	0	12	0	0	1	8	.000	0	1	14	.000	0	0
Newhan, David	14	26	20	5	3	7	1	0	1	2	.150	.346	.350	0	0	0	6	1	7	0	0	0	15	.200	1	1	5	.000	0	1
Williams, George	11	17	16	2	3	6	0	0	1	2	.188	.235	.375	0	0	1	0	0	4	0	0	0	14	.143	1	2	2	.500	0	0
Alvarez, Gabe	11	14	13	1	2	3	1	0	0	0	.154	.214	.231	0	0	0	1	0	1	0	0	0	7	.000	0	0	6	.333	0	0
Spencer, Stan	9	14	12	0	4	5	1	0	0	1	.333	.333	.417	2	0	0	0	0	6	0	0	0	7	.571	0	1	5	.000	0	0
Allen, Dusty	9	14	12	0	0	0	0	0	0	0	.000	.143	.000	0	0	0	2	0	5	0	0	1	3	.000	0	0	9	.000	0	0
Lopez, Rodrigo	6	9	9	1	1	1	0	0	0	0	.111	.111	.111	0	0	0	0	0	4	0	0	0	8	.125	0	0	1	.000	0	0
Cunnane, Will	27	7	7	0	1	2	1	0	0	0	.143	.143	.286	0	0	0	0	0	3	0	0	0	7	.143	0	0	0	.000	0	0
Boehringer, Brian	7	5	4	0	1	2	1	0	0	2	.250	.250	.500	1	0	0	0	0	0	0	0	1	3	.333	0	2	1	.000	0	0
Walker, Kevin	70	4	4	0	1	1	0	0	0	0	.250	.250	.250	0	0	0	0	0	1	0	0	0	1	.000	0	0	3	.333	0	0
Almanzar, Carlos	62	3	3	0	0	0	0	0	0	0	.000	.000	.000	0	0	0	0	0	2	0	0	1	2	.000	0	0	1	.000	0	0
Nady, Xavier	1	1	1	1	1	1	0	0	0	0	1.000	1.000	1.000	0	0	0	0	0	0	0	0	0	0	.000	0	0	1	1.000	0	0
Reyes, Carlos	12	1	1	0	0	0	0	0	0	0	.000	.000	.000	0	0	0	0	0	0	0	0	0	1	.000	0	0	0	.000	0	0
Wall, Donne	44	2	1	0	0	0	0	0	0	0	.000	.000	.000	1	0	0	0	0	1	0	0	0	0	.000	0	0	1	.000	0	0
Erdos, Todd	22	1	1	0	0	0	0	0	0	0	.000	.000	.000	0	0	0	0	0	0	0	0	0	1	.000	0	0	0	.000	0	0
Kolb, Brandon	11	1	1	1	0	0	0	0	0	0	.000	.000	.000	0	0	0	0	0	0	0	0	0	0	.000	0	0	1	.000	0	0
Palacios, Vicente	7	0	0	0	0	0	0	0	0	0	.000	.000	.000	0	0	0	0	0	0	0	0	0	0	.000	0	0	0	.000	0	0
Slocumb, Heathcliff	22	0	0	0	0	0	0	0	0	0	.000	.000	.000	0	0	0	0	0	0	0	0	0	0	.000	0	0	0	.000	0	0
Whiteside, Matt	28	0	0	0	0	0	0	0	0	0	.000	.000	.000	0	0	0	0	0	0	0	0	0	0	.000	0	0	0	.000	0	0
Hoffman, Trevor	70	0	0	0	0	0	0	0	0	0	.000	.000	.000	0	0	0	0	0	0	0	0	0	0	.000	0	0	0	.000	0	0
Montgomery, Steve	7	0	0	0	0	0	0	0	0	0	.000	.000	.000	0	0	0	0	0	0	0	0	0	0	.000	0	0	0	.000	0	0
Myers, Rodney	3	0	0	0	0	0	0	0	0	0	.000	.000	.000	0	0	0	0	0	0	0	0	0	0	.000	0	0	0	.000	0	0
Serafini, Dan	3	0	0	0	0	0	0	0	0	0	.000	.000	.000	0	0	0	0	0	0	0	0	0	0	.000	0	0	0	.000	0	0
Whisenant, Matt	24	0	0	0	0	0	0	0	0	0	.000	.000	.000	0	0	0	0	0	0	0	0	0	0	.000	0	0	0	.000	0	0
Davey, Tom	11	0	0	0	0	0	0	0	0	0	.000	.000	.000	0	0	0	0	0	0	0	0	0	0	.000	0	0	0	.000	0	0
Carlyle, Buddy	4	0	0	0	0	0	0	0	0	0	.000	.000	.000	0	0	0	0	0	0	0	0	0	0	.000	0	0	0	.000	0	0
Maurer, Dave	14	0	0	0	0	0	0	0	0	0	.000	.000	.000	0	0	0	0	0	0	0	0	0	0	.000	0	0	0	.000	0	0
Guzman, Domingo	1	0	0	0	0	0	0	0	0	0	.000	.000	.000	0	0	0	0	0	0	0	0	1	0	.000	0	0	0	.000	0	0

Players with more than one N.L. team

Name	G	TPA	AB	R	H	TB	2B	3B	HR	RBI	Avg.	Obp.	Slg.	SH	SF	HP	BB	IBB	SO	SB	CS	GDP	vs RHP				vs LHP			
																							AB	Avg.	HR	RBI	AB	Avg.	HR	RBI
Hernandez, S.D.-StL.	75	270	242	23	62	86	15	0	3	35	.256	.322	.355	0	3	4	21	1	35	2	3	4	174	.270	3	29	68	.221	0	6
Newhan, S.D.-Phi.	24	45	37	8	6	10	1	0	1	2	.162	.311	.270	0	0	0	8	1	13	0	0	2	32	.188	1	1	5	.000	0	1
Relaford, Phi.-S.D.	128	502	410	55	88	123	14	3	5	46	.215	.351	.300	3	2	12	75	7	71	13	0	10	317	.221	3	36	93	.194	2	10
Reyes, Phi.-S.D.	22	1	1	0	0	0	0	0	0	0	.000	.000	.000	0	0	0	0	0	0	0	0	0	1	.000	0	0	0	.000	0	0
Serafini, S.D.-Pit.	14	27	24	1	2	2	0	0	0	2	.083	.083	.083	3	0	0	0	0	9	0	0	1	23	.087	0	2	1	.000	0	0
Slocumb, StL.-S.D.	66	1	1	0	0	0	0	0	0	0	.000	.000	.000	0	0	0	0	0	1	0	0	0	1	.000	0	0	0	.000	0	0

PITCHING

Name	W	L	Pct.	ERA	IP	H	R	ER	HR	SH	SF	HB	BB	IBB	SO	G	GS	CG	ShO	GF	Sv	vs. RH				vs. LH			
																						AB	Avg.	HR	RBI	AB	Avg.	HR	RBI
Clement, Matt	13	17	.433	5.14	205.0	194	131	117	22	12	5	16	125	4	170	34	34	0	0	0	0	370	.227	8	29	412	.267	14	78
Williams, Woody	10	8	.556	3.75	168.0	152	74	70	23	4	3	3	54	2	111	23	23	4	0	0	0	347	.248	19	52	289	.228	4	19
Eaton, Adam	7	4	.636	4.13	135.0	134	63	62	14	1	3	2	61	3	90	22	22	0	0	0	0	247	.215	6	22	269	.301	8	35
Meadows, Brian	7	8	.467	5.34	124.2	150	80	74	24	7	2	8	50	6	53	22	22	0	0	0	0	267	.288	9	32	231	.316	15	39
Tollberg, Brian	4	5	.444	3.58	118.0	126	58	47	13	6	0	5	35	4	76	19	19	1	0	0	0	230	.265	7	23	230	.283	6	26
Hoffman, Trevor	4	7	.364	2.99	72.1	61	29	24	7	3	5	0	11	4	85	70	0	0	0	59	43	142	.246	5	18	130	.200	2	12
Almanzar, Carlos	4	5	.444	4.39	69.2	73	35	34	12	2	3	4	25	2	56	62	0	0	0	11	0	170	.300	10	33	104	.212	2	19
Walker, Kevin	7	1	.875	4.19	66.2	49	35	31	5	4	2	5	38	6	56	70	0	0	0	14	0	133	.165	4	25	105	.257	1	9
Hitchcock, Sterling	1	6	.143	4.93	65.2	69	38	36	12	2	1	5	26	1	61	11	11	0	0	0	0	208	.279	9	28	50	.220	3	8
Witasick, Jay	3	2	.600	5.64	60.2	69	42	38	9	5	1	3	35	5	54	11	11	0	0	0	0	121	.281	3	14	122	.287	6	23
Wall, Donne	5	2	.714	3.35	53.2	36	20	20	4	3	0	0	21	1	29	44	0	0	0	14	1	96	.177	2	7	91	.209	2	13
Spencer, Stan	2	2	.500	3.26	49.2	44	22	18	7	2	1	2	19	1	40	8	8	0	0	0	0	99	.263	6	13	85	.212	1	7
Cunnane, Will	1	1	.500	4.23	38.1	35	21	18	2	1	1	1	21	0	34	27	3	0	0	4	0	71	.239	1	6	74	.243	1	11
Whiteside, Matt	2	3	.400	4.14	37.0	32	21	17	6	2	1	1	17	3	27	28	0	0	0	9	0	85	.212	5	18	53	.264	1	6
Erdos, Todd	0	0	.000	6.67	29.2	32	24	22	5	1	4	6	17	1	16	22	0	0	0	8	1	58	.276	2	10	60	.267	3	16
Lopez, Rodrigo	0	3	.000	8.76	24.2	40	24	24	5	0	1	0	13	0	17	6	6	0	0	0	0	61	.328	1	7	45	.444	4	12
Whisenant, Matt	2	2	.500	3.80	21.1	16	12	9	1	1	2	0	17	1	12	24	0	0	0	12	0	40	.275	1	12	35	.143	0	4
Slocumb, Heathcliff	0	1	.000	3.79	19.0	19	11	8	0	1	3	2	13	3	12	22	0	0	0	6	0	33	.273	0	11	39	.256	0	5
Reyes, Carlos	1	1	.500	6.00	18.0	15	12	12	5	0	0	1	8	0	13	12	0	0	0	4	1	28	.214	1	2	40	.225	4	11
Boehringer, Brian	0	3	.000	5.74	15.2	18	15	10	4	0	1	0	10	0	9	7	3	0	0	1	0	38	.289	3	8	25	.280	1	2
Maurer, Dave	1	0	1.000	3.68	14.2	15	8	6	2	0	0	2	5	1	13	14	0	0	0	1	0	30	.233	1	2	27	.296	1	3
Kolb, Brandon	0	1	.000	4.50	14.0	16	8	7	0	0	1	0	11	1	12	11	0	0	0	5	0	29	.379	0	5	25	.200	0	5
Davey, Tom	2	1	.667	0.71	12.2	12	1	1	0	0	0	0	2	0	6	11	0	0	0	2	0	26	.269	0	0	22	.227	0	2
Palacios, Vicente	0	1	.000	6.75	10.2	12	10	8	4	1	1	0	5	1	8	7	0	0	0	2	0	21	.238	3	8	18	.389	1	4
Montgomery, Steve	0	2	.000	7.94	5.2	6	6	5	3	1	0	0	4	0	3	7	0	0	0	1	0	11	.364	2	4	11	.182	1	1
Serafini, Dan	0	0	.000	18.00	3.0	9	6	6	2	0	0	0	2	0	3	3	0	0	0	1	0	6	.667	2	4	12	.417	0	1
Carlyle, Buddy	0	0	.000	21.00	3.0	6	7	7	0	0	0	0	3	0	2	4	0	0	0	2	0	6	.333	0	2	9	.444	0	1
Myers, Rodney	0	0	.000	4.50	2.0	2	1	1	0	0	0	0	0	0	3	3	0	0	0	1	0	4	.250	0	0	4	.250	0	0
Guzman, Domingo	0	0	.000	9.00	1.0	1	1	1	0	0	0	2	1	0	0	1	0	0	0	0	0	0	.000	0	0	3	.333	0	0

PITCHERS WITH MORE THAN ONE N.L. TEAM

Name	W	L	Pct.	ERA	IP	H	R	ER	HR	SH	SF	HB	BB	IBB	SO	G	GS	CG	ShO	GF	Sv	vs. RH				vs. LH			
																						AB	Avg.	HR	RBI	AB	Avg.	HR	RBI
Reyes, Phi.-S.D.	1	3	.250	5.72	28.1	25	18	18	7	2	0	1	13	0	17	22	0	0	0	0	1	58	.259	3	10	47	.213	4	11
Serafini, S.D.-Pit.	2	5	.286	5.51	65.1	79	41	40	11	8	2	4	28	1	35	14	11	0	0	2	0	211	.289	10	34	47	.383	1	5
Slocumb, StL.-S.D.	2	4	.333	4.98	68.2	69	43	38	9	4	5	3	37	4	46	65	0	0	0	5	1	153	.242	3	22	107	.299	6	19

DESIGNATED HITTERS

Name	AB	Avg.	HR	RBI
Gwynn, Tony	24	.375	0	2
Davis, Ben	4	.250	0	0
Magadan, Dave	3	.000	0	0
Allen, Dusty	1	.000	0	0
DeHaan, Kory	1	.000	0	0

INDIVIDUAL STATISTICS

FIELDING

FIRST BASEMEN

Player	Pct.	G	PO	A	E	TC	DP
Klesko, Ryan	.992	136	1029	90	9	1128	104
Sprague, Ed	.965	25	181	10	7	198	14
Vitiello, Joe	.966	17	77	7	3	87	11
Magadan, Dave	1.000	8	47	10	0	57	7
Mabry, John	1.000	2	8	1	0	9	0
Roskos, John	1.000	2	0	1	0	1	0
Hernandez, Carlos	1.000	1	2	0	0	2	0
Allen, Dusty	-	1	0	0	0	0	0

SECOND BASEMEN

Player	Pct.	G	PO	A	E	TC	DP
Boone, Bret	.977	126	292	334	15	641	83
Jackson, Damian	.972	36	70	104	5	179	24
Nicholson, Kevin	.833	4	2	8	2	12	2
Gomez, Chris	1.000	3	3	3	0	6	2
Newhan, David	1.000	3	3	3	0	6	0
LaRocca, Greg	.818	2	3	6	2	11	0
Sprague, Ed	1.000	1	0	1	0	1	0
Owens, Eric	-	1	0	0	0	0	0

THIRD BASEMEN

Player	Pct.	G	PO	A	E	TC	DP
Nevin, Phil	.929	142	96	242	26	364	22
Magadan, Dave	.952	29	11	29	2	42	2
Sprague, Ed	1.000	10	3	9	0	12	1
LaRocca, Greg	1.000	8	3	3	0	6	0
Alvarez, Gabe	1.000	3	0	1	0	1	0
Newhan, David	1.000	2	0	1	0	1	0

SHORTSTOPS

Player	Pct.	G	PO	A	E	TC	DP
Jackson, Damian	.955	88	144	258	19	421	50
Relaford, Desi	.965	45	73	120	7	200	33
Nicholson, Kevin	.983	30	37	79	2	118	11
Gomez, Chris	.928	17	24	40	5	69	10
LaRocca, Greg	1.000	4	4	3	0	7	1
Magadan, Dave	1.000	2	0	2	0	2	1

OUTFIELDERS

Player	Pct.	G	PO	A	E	TC	DP
Owens, Eric	1.000	144	315	6	0	321	2
Rivera, Ruben	.984	133	303	10	5	318	3
Martin, Al	.950	89	128	4	7	139	0
DeHaan, Kory	1.000	60	50	3	0	53	1
Darr, Mike	1.000	57	124	7	0	131	1
Mabry, John	.980	32	49	1	1	51	0
Gwynn, Tony	1.000	26	31	1	0	32	0
Jackson, Damian	.952	17	20	0	1	21	0
Sprague, Ed	1.000	8	10	1	0	11	0
Roskos, John	.875	6	7	0	1	8	0
Newhan, David	1.000	5	6	0	0	6	0
Klesko, Ryan	1.000	4	2	0	0	2	0
Allen, Dusty	1.000	2	2	0	0	2	0
Vitiello, Joe	1.000	2	1	0	0	1	0
Alvarez, Gabe	-	2	0	0	0	0	0

CATCHERS

Player	Pct.	G	PO	A	E	TC	DP	PB
Gonzalez, Wiki	.991	87	525	42	5	572	13	7
Hernandez, Carlos	.987	54	343	33	5	381	3	3
Davis, Ben	.996	38	236	17	1	254	2	3
Williams, George	1.000	6	16	2	0	18	0	0

PITCHERS

Player	Pct.	G	PO	A	E	TC	DP
Walker, Kevin	1.000	70	2	8	0	10	0
Hoffman, Trevor	1.000	70	2	7	0	9	0
Almanzar, Carlos	1.000	62	3	11	0	14	0
Wall, Donne	1.000	44	1	5	0	6	0
Clement, Matt	.929	34	27	25	4	56	4
Whiteside, Matt	.917	28	4	7	1	12	0
Cunnane, Will	1.000	27	4	4	0	8	0
Whisenant, Matt	1.000	24	1	3	0	4	0
Williams, Woody	.905	23	7	12	2	21	1
Meadows, Brian	.964	22	9	18	1	28	2
Eaton, Adam	.962	22	7	18	1	26	2
Slocumb, Heathcliff	1.000	22	2	4	0	6	0
Erdos, Todd	1.000	22	1	4	0	5	0
Tollberg, Brian	.960	19	9	15	1	25	1
Maurer, Dave	1.000	14	2	0	0	2	0
Reyes, Carlos	1.000	12	1	1	0	2	0
Witasick, Jay	1.000	11	5	10	0	15	1
Hitchcock, Sterling	1.000	11	0	9	0	9	0
Davey, Tom	1.000	11	0	4	0	4	0
Kolb, Brandon	.500	11	0	1	1	2	0
Spencer, Stan	1.000	8	5	4	0	9	0
Palacios, Vicente	1.000	7	0	3	0	3	1
Montgomery, Steve	1.000	7	0	1	0	1	0
Boehringer, Brian	-	7	0	0	0	0	0
Lopez, Rodrigo	1.000	6	4	3	0	7	1
Carlyle, Buddy	1.000	4	1	0	0	1	0
Serafini, Dan	1.000	3	1	0	0	1	0
Myers, Rodney	-	3	0	0	0	0	0
Guzman, Domingo	-	1	0	0	0	0	0

PITCHING AGAINST EACH CLUB

Pitcher	Ari. W-L	Atl. W-L	Chi. W-L	Cin. W-L	Col. W-L	Fla. W-L	Hou. W-L	L.A. W-L	Mil. W-L	Mon. W-L	N.Y. W-L	Phi. W-L	Pit. W-L	S.F. W-L	StL. W-L	A.L. W-L	Total W-L
Almanzar, C.	0-0	0-0	1-0	0-0	0-1	0-0	0-0	0-0	1-0	0-0	0-0	1-0	0-2	1-1	0-0	0-1	4-5
Boehringer, B.	0-0	0-0	0-0	0-0	0-0	0-0	0-1	0-0	0-0	0-1	0-0	0-0	0-0	0-0	0-1	0-0	0-3
Carlyle, Buddy	0-0	0-0	0-0	0-0	0-0	0-0	0-0	0-0	0-0	0-0	0-0	0-0	0-0	0-0	0-0	0-0	0-0
Clement, Matt	0-2	0-0	1-0	1-1	1-2	1-1	1-0	2-2	0-0	0-1	2-1	2-0	1-2	0-1	0-1	1-3	13-17
Cunnane, Will	0-0	0-1	0-0	0-0	0-0	0-0	1-0	0-0	0-0	0-0	0-0	0-0	0-0	0-0	0-0	0-0	1-1
Davey, Tom	0-0	0-0	0-0	0-0	0-0	0-0	0-0	0-0	1-0	0-0	0-0	0-0	0-0	1-0	0-1	0-0	2-1
Eaton, Adam	0-0	0-0	1-0	0-0	2-1	1-0	0-0	1-0	1-0	0-0	1-0	0-0	0-0	0-1	0-1	0-1	7-4
Erdos, Todd	0-0	0-0	0-0	0-0	0-0	0-0	0-0	0-0	0-0	0-0	0-0	0-0	0-0	0-0	0-0	0-0	0-0
Guzman, D.	0-0	0-0	0-0	0-0	0-0	0-0	0-0	0-0	0-0	0-0	0-0	0-0	0-0	0-0	0-0	0-0	0-0
Hitchcock, S.	0-2	0-2	0-0	0-1	0-0	1-0	0-0	0-0	0-0	0-0	0-0	0-0	0-0	0-0	0-1	0-0	1-6
Hoffman, T.	0-0	0-0	0-1	1-0	1-1	0-0	0-1	0-0	0-1	0-0	1-1	0-0	0-1	0-0	0-0	1-1	4-7
Kolb, Brandon	0-1	0-0	0-0	0-0	0-0	0-0	0-0	0-0	0-0	0-0	0-0	0-0	0-0	0-0	0-0	0-0	0-1
Lopez, R.	0-1	0-0	0-0	0-0	0-0	0-0	0-0	0-0	0-0	0-0	0-0	0-0	0-0	0-0	0-1	0-1	0-3
Maurer, Dave	0-0	0-0	0-0	0-0	0-0	0-0	0-0	1-0	0-0	0-0	0-0	0-0	0-0	0-0	0-0	0-0	1-0
Meadows, B.	2-0	0-1	0-0	0-1	1-0	1-0	1-0	1-1	0-1	1-0	0-0	0-0	0-0	0-1	0-1	0-2	7-8
Montgomery, S.	0-0	0-0	0-0	0-0	0-1	0-0	0-0	0-1	0-0	0-0	0-0	0-0	0-0	0-0	0-0	0-0	0-2
Myers, R.	0-0	0-0	0-0	0-0	0-0	0-0	0-0	0-0	0-0	0-0	0-0	0-0	0-0	0-0	0-0	0-0	0-0
Palacios, V.	0-0	0-1	0-0	0-0	0-0	0-0	0-0	0-0	0-0	0-0	0-0	0-0	0-0	0-0	0-0	0-0	0-1
Reyes, Carlos	0-1	0-0	0-0	1-0	0-0	0-0	0-0	0-0	0-0	0-0	0-0	0-0	0-0	0-0	0-0	0-0	1-1
Serafini, Dan	0-0	0-0	0-0	0-0	0-0	0-0	0-0	0-0	0-0	0-0	0-0	0-0	0-0	0-0	0-0	0-0	0-0
Slocumb, H.	0-0	0-0	0-0	0-0	0-0	0-0	0-0	0-0	0-0	0-0	0-0	0-1	0-0	0-0	0-0	0-0	0-1
Spencer, Stan	0-1	0-0	0-0	0-0	0-0	1-0	0-0	0-0	0-0	0-0	0-0	0-0	0-0	0-0	0-1	1-0	2-2
Tollberg, Brian	1-0	0-0	0-1	1-0	0-1	0-0	0-0	0-0	1-0	0-0	0-0	0-1	0-1	1-0	0-1	0-0	4-5
Walker, Kevin	0-0	0-1	1-0	1-0	0-0	2-0	1-0	0-0	0-0	2-0	0-0	0-0	0-0	0-0	0-0	0-0	7-1
Wall, Donne	0-0	0-0	0-0	0-0	0-0	0-0	0-0	0-0	0-0	1-1	1-1	0-0	1-0	1-0	0-0	1-0	5-2
Whisenant, M.	1-0	0-0	0-0	0-1	0-0	0-0	1-0	0-0	0-0	0-0	0-0	0-0	0-1	0-0	0-0	0-0	2-2
Whiteside, M.	0-0	1-0	0-0	0-0	0-0	0-0	0-0	0-2	0-0	1-0	0-0	0-0	0-0	0-0	0-0	0-1	2-3
Williams, W.	0-1	0-1	0-1	0-0	1-0	0-1	2-0	0-2	2-0	0-0	1-0	2-0	0-0	1-2	0-0	1-0	10-8
Witasick, Jay	0-0	0-1	1-0	0-0	0-0	0-0	0-0	0-0	1-0	1-0	0-0	0-0	0-0	0-1	0-0	0-0	3-2
Totals	4-9	1-8	5-3	5-4	6-7	7-2	7-2	5-8	7-2	6-3	6-3	5-2	2-7	5-7	0-9	5-10	76-86

INTERLEAGUE: Almanzar 0-1, Lopez 0-1, Clement 0-1 vs. Athletics; Spencer 1-0, Hoffman 1-0, Williams 1-0, Meadows 0-2, Clement 0-1 vs. Mariners; Clement 1-0, Whiteside 0-1, Eaton 0-1 vs. Rangers; Wall 1-0, Hoffman 0-1, Clement 0-1 vs. Angels. Total: 5-10.

MISCELLANEOUS

HOME RUNS BY PARK

At Arizona (9): Sprague 3, Klesko 3, Boone 1, Owens 1, Nevin 1.
At Atlanta (9): Nevin 3, Hernandez 1, Sprague 1, Martin 1, Boone 1, Mabry 1, Rivera 1.
At Chicago (NL) (3): Nevin 2, DeHaan 1.
At Cincinnati (10): Boone 5, Rivera 2, Klesko 1, Owens 1, Nicholson 1.
At Colorado (9): Klesko 2, Davis 2, Magadan 1, Mabry 1, Nevin 1, Rivera 1, Gonzalez 1.
At Florida (6): Nevin 3, Klesko 2, Mabry 1.
At Houston (2): Martin 1, Klesko 1.
At Los Angeles (6): Boone 1, Klesko 1, Nevin 1, Rivera 1, Relaford 1, Gonzalez 1.
At Milwaukee (2): Nevin 1, Gonzalez 1.
At Montreal (5): Klesko 2, Boone 1, Nevin 1, Rivera 1.
At New York (NL) (2): Sprague 1, Nevin 1.
At Oakland (2): Sprague 1, Rivera 1.
At Philadelphia (6): Nevin 2, Boone 1, Vitiello 1, Rivera 1, Relaford 1.
At Pittsburgh (5): Klesko 2, Nevin 1, Rivera 1, Jackson 1.
At San Diego (72): Nevin 13, Klesko 9, Martin 8, Boone 8, Rivera 8, Jackson 5, Sprague 4, Owens 4, Mabry 3, Gwynn 1, Magadan 1, Hernandez 1, Vitiello 1, Williams 1, Davis 1, Darr 1, Newhan 1, Gonzalez 1, DeHaan 1.
At San Francisco (3): Klesko 1, Williams 1, Mabry 1.
At Seattle (3): Martin 1, Klesko 1, Nevin 1.
At St. Louis (2): Klesko 1, Gonzalez 1.
At Texas (1): Boone 1.

LOW-HIT GAMES

No-hitters: None.
One-hitters: None.
Two-hitters: None.

10-STRIKEOUT GAMES

Sterling Hitchcock 1, Jay Witasick 1, Adam Eaton 1, Total: 3

FOUR OR MORE HITS IN ONE GAME

Eric Owens 2, Ed Sprague 1, Al Martin 1, Phil Nevin 1, Damian Jackson 1, Total: 6

MULTI-HOMER GAMES

Bret Boone 3, Ed Sprague 2, Ryan Klesko 2, Phil Nevin 2, Total: 9

GRAND SLAMS

5-19: Phil Nevin (off Atlanta's Kevin McGlinchy)
6-10: Bret Boone (off Houston's Scott Elarton)
7-30: Ruben Rivera (off Pittsburgh's Josias Manzanillo)
8-22: Damian Jackson (off New York's Pat Mahomes)

PINCH HITTERS

(Minimum 5 at-bats)

Name	AB	Avg.	HR	RBI
Magadan, Dave	55	.200	1	9
Sprague, Ed	35	.200	1	8
DeHaan, Kory	23	.261	1	5
Vitiello, Joe	17	.294	0	2
Klesko, Ryan	12	.167	2	4
Mabry, John	11	.182	0	2
Gomez, Chris	8	.625	0	0
Gonzalez, Wiki	8	.125	0	1
Alvarez, Gabe	7	.143	0	0
Martin, Al	6	.333	1	2
Roskos, John	6	.000	0	1
Davis, Ben	5	.000	0	0
Allen, Dusty	5	.000	0	0
Williams, George	5	.000	0	0

DEBUTS

4-14: Kevin Walker, P.
4-25: Kory DeHaan, PH.
4-29: Rodrigo Lopez, P.
5-12: Brandon Kolb, P.
5-30: Adam Eaton, P.
6-20: Brian Tollberg, P.
6-23: Kevin Nicholson, SS.
7-1: Dusty Allen, PH.
7-22: Dave Maurer, P.
9-7: Greg LaRocca, 3B.
9-30: Xavier Nady, PH.

GAMES BY POSITION

Catcher: Wiki Gonzalez 87, Carlos Hernandez 54, Ben Davis 38, George Williams 6.
First base: Ryan Klesko 136, Ed Sprague 25, Joe Vitiello 17, Dave Magadan 8, John Mabry 2, John Roskos 2, Carlos Hernandez 1, Dusty Allen 1.
Second base: Bret Boone 126, Damian Jackson 36, Kevin Nicholson 4, Chris Gomez 3, David Newhan 3, Greg LaRocca 2, Ed Sprague 1, Eric Owens 1.
Third base: Phil Nevin 142, Dave Magadan 29, Ed Sprague 10, Greg LaRocca 8, Gabe Alvarez 3, David Newhan 2.
Shortstop: Damian Jackson 88, Desi Relaford 45, Kevin Nicholson 30, Chris Gomez 17, Greg LaRocca 4, Dave Magadan 2.
Outfield: Eric Owens 144, Ruben Rivera 133, Al Martin 89, Kory DeHaan 60, Mike Darr 57, John Mabry 32, Tony Gwynn 26, Damian Jackson 17, Ed Sprague 8, John Roskos 6, David Newhan 5, Ryan Klesko 4, Joe Vitiello 2, Gabe Alvarez 2, Dusty Allen 2.
Designated hitter: Tony Gwynn 6, Dave Magadan 2, Ben Davis 1, Kory DeHaan 1, Dusty Allen 1.

STREAKS

Wins: 6 (July 30-August 4)
Losses: 8 (May 5-13)
Consecutive games with at least one hit: 13, Eric Owens (April 5-19) Damian Jackson (August 22-September 4)
Wins by pitcher: 3, Matt Clement (June 29-July 9)

ATTENDANCE

Home: 2,423,149
Road: 2,419,947
Highest (home): 60,767 (June 16 vs. Cincinnati).
Highest (road): 52,308 (April 3 vs. New York).
Lowest (home): 13,777 (September 6 vs. Milwaukee).
Lowest (road): 6,955 (May 17 vs. Florida).

SAN FRANCISCO GIANTS

DAY BY DAY

Date	Opp.	Res.	Score	(inn.*)	Hits	Opp. hits	Winning pitcher	Losing pitcher	Save	Record	Pos.	GB
4-3	At Fla.	L	4-6		10	12	Fernandez	Hernandez	Alfonseca	0-1	T2nd	1.0
4-4	At Fla.	W	3-0		7	4	Ortiz	Dempster	Nen	1-1	T3rd	1.0
4-5	At Fla.	W	11-9		15	12	Johnstone	Alfonseca	Nen	2-1	T2nd	0.5
4-6	At Fla.	L	4-5		7	8	Miceli	Johnstone		2-2	T3rd	1.5
4-7	At Atl.	W	6-2		8	10	Gardner	Mulholland		3-2	3rd	0.5
4-8	At Atl.	L	5-7		10	11	Maddux	Hernandez	Ligtenberg	3-3	T3rd	1.5
4-9	At Atl.	L	3-9		7	12	Glavine	Ortiz		3-4	4th	2.5
4-11	L.A.	L	5-6		8	12	Park	Rueter	Shaw	3-5	T4th	3.0
4-12	L.A.	L	5-6		7	8	Adams	Weber	Shaw	3-6	5th	2.5
4-13	L.A.	L	7-11		11	13	Perez	Gardner	Shaw	3-7	5th	4.0
4-14	Ari.	L	1-3		5	8	Johnson	Hernandez		3-8	5th	5.0
4-15	Ari.	L	4-7		8	9	Stottlemyre	Ortiz	Swindell	3-9	5th	6.0
4-18	At Cin.	W	13-9		16	8	Rueter	Williamson		4-9	5th	5.5
4-19	At Cin.	L	4-5		8	9	Bell	Estes	Graves	4-10	5th	6.5
4-20	At Cin.	L	1-11		6	15	Neagle	Hernandez		4-11	5th	7.5
4-21	At Ari.	W	11-5		16	12	Ortiz	Stottlemyre		5-11	5th	6.5
4-22	At Ari.	W	8-6		7	7	Rueter	Daal	Nen	6-11	5th	5.5
4-23	At Ari.	W	12-7		14	11	Nathan	Reynoso		7-11	5th	4.5
4-25	At Fla.	W	6-4	(11)	13	7	Gardner	Miceli		8-11	5th	4.5
4-26	At Fla.	W	8-7	(12)	11	16	Fultz	Alfonseca		9-11	5th	4.5
4-28	Mon.	L	3-9		11	8	Telford	Ortiz		9-12	5th	4.0
4-29	Mon.	W	2-1		9	3	Johnstone	Telford	Nen	10-12	5th	4.0
4-30	Mon.	L	3-4		6	6	Strickland	Johnstone	Urbina	10-13	5th	5.0
5-1	N.Y.	W	10-3		11	7	Estes	Pulsipher		11-13	4th	4.5
5-2	N.Y.	W	7-1		11	8	Hernandez	Rusch		12-13	4th	4.5
5-3	N.Y.	W	8-5	(11)	12	14	Rodriguez	Wendell		13-13	T3rd	3.5
5-4	N.Y.	W	7-2		7	4	Rodriguez	Reed		14-13	3rd	3.5
5-5	Col.	W	5-0		6	3	Nathan	Yoshii		15-13	3rd	3.5
5-6	Col.	W	6-0		9	9	Estes	Arrojo		16-13	3rd	3.5
5-8	StL.	W	6-4		8	9	Hernandez	Hentgen	Nen	17-13	2nd	4.0
5-9	StL.	L	6-13		11	15	Stephenson	Ortiz		17-14	2nd	5.0
5-10	StL.	W	4-3		7	7	Rodriguez	Slocumb	Nen	18-14	2nd	5.0
5-12	At Col.	L	7-15		10	15	Bohanon	Nathan		18-15	2nd	6.0
5-13	At Col.	L	9-10		10	15	White	Johnstone	Jimenez	18-16	3rd	7.0
5-14	At Col.	L	7-11		13	15	White	Hernandez		18-17	3rd	7.0
5-16	At Atl.	L	7-9		14	15	Glavine	Ortiz	Mulholland	18-18	4th	7.0
5-17	At Atl.	L	4-5		7	12	Millwood	Rueter	Seanez	18-19	4th	7.0
5-18	At Atl.	L	2-3		7	10	Maddux	Estes	Rocker	18-20	4th	8.0
5-19	At Mil.	L	10-11	(10)	15	11	Wickman	Nen		18-21	4th	8.0
5-20	At Mil.	L	0-7		4	6	D'Amico	Gardner		18-22	4th	8.0
5-21	At Mil.	W	16-10		20	9	Ortiz	Ramirez		19-22	4th	7.0
5-23	Mon.	L	2-3		8	11	Pavano	Rueter	Hermanson	19-23	4th	8.0
5-24	Mon.	W	18-0		18	7	Estes	Thurman		20-23	4th	8.0
5-25	Mon.	W	4-1		9	6	Hernandez	Armas	Nen	21-23	4th	8.0
5-26	Chi.	W	5-3		10	8	Gardner	Tapani		22-23	4th	8.0
5-27	Chi.	L	2-3	(11)	9	4	Garibay	Fultz	Aguilera	22-24	4th	9.0
5-28	Chi.	L	1-4		5	8	Wood	Rueter	Aguilera	22-25	4th	9.0
5-29	Phi.	W	7-2		13	4	Estes	Schilling	Embree	23-25	4th	8.0
5-30	Phi.	W	7-3		12	8	Hernandez	Ashby	Nen	24-25	4th	7.0
5-31	Phi.	W	10-4		14	9	Gardner	Byrd		25-25	4th	7.0
6-2	At Oak.	L	4-5		10	8	Mulder	Ortiz	Isringhausen	25-26	4th	8.5
6-3	At Oak.	L	7-9		9	11	D. Jones	Embree	Isringhausen	25-27	4th	8.5
6-4	At Oak.	W	18-2		19	7	Estes	Olivares		26-27	4th	7.5
6-5	At Ana.	W	5-4	(11)	10	14	Fultz	Hasegawa		27-27	4th	6.5
6-6	At Ana.	L	5-6		9	10	Percival	Nen		27-28	4th	6.5
6-7	At Ana.	L	9-10		15	13	Hasegawa	Embree		27-29	4th	6.5
6-9	Sea.	W	9-2		16	8	Rueter	Halama		28-29	4th	6.5
6-10	Sea.	L	2-5		6	12	Abbott	Estes		28-30	4th	6.5
6-11	Sea.	L	2-9		7	13	Sele	Hernandez		28-31	4th	7.5
6-12	Cin.	W	10-3		11	9	Nathan	Bell		29-31	4th	7.5
6-13	Cin.	W	3-2		7	8	Nen	Graves		30-31	4th	6.5
6-14	Cin.	W	6-2		12	8	Rueter	Neagle	Rodriguez	31-31	4th	6.5
6-16	Hou.	W	7-4		12	9	Estes	Elarton	Nen	32-31	4th	5.5
6-17	Hou.	W	6-4		8	10	Hernandez	Lima	Nen	33-31	4th	4.5
6-18	Hou.	L	2-4	(11)	6	6	J. Powell	Nen	Henry	33-32	4th	4.5
6-20	At StL.	L	2-7		4	8	Ankiel	Ortiz		33-33	4th	5.0
6-21	At StL.	W	4-1		7	5	Rueter	Stephenson	Nen	34-33	4th	5.0
6-22	At StL.	L	10-11		15	12	Veres	Gardner		34-34	4th	5.5
6-23	At Hou.	W	10-3		14	10	Hernandez	Lima		35-34	4th	5.5
6-24	At Hou.	W	13-4		22	12	Nathan	Reynolds		36-34	4th	4.5
6-25	At Hou.	W	4-2		14	8	Ortiz	Holt	Nen	37-34	3rd	4.5
6-26	At Col.	L	6-15		9	16	Arrojo	Gardner		37-35	3rd	5.5
6-27	At Col.	W	12-7		15	9	Estes	Jarvis		38-35	T3rd	4.5
6-28	At Col.	L	13-17		13	17	DeJean	Johnstone		38-36	4th	5.5
6-29	At Col.	L	4-11		13	15	Yoshii	Nathan		38-37	4th	6.5
6-30	L.A.	L	2-9		6	13	Brown	Ortiz		38-38	4th	6.5
7-1	L.A.	W	4-1		10	9	Rueter	Perez	Nen	39-38	4th	6.5
7-2	L.A.	W	6-5		10	13	Nen	Fetters		40-38	3rd	5.5

HIGHLIGHTS

High point: On September 21, the Giants beat Arizona, 8-7, to clinch their second N.L. West Division title in four years. It was a joyous conclusion to a celebratory season that began with the opening of Pacific Bell Park.

Low point: On April 20, the Giants suffered a taxing 11-1 loss at Cincnnati, dropping their record to 4-11—an unexpected and horrifying start that included five straight losses in their new ballpark. Some fans were only half joking when they called for a return to 3Com Park.

Turning point: On May 4, the Giants beat the New York Mets, 7-2, and concluded a four-game sweep that asserted their superiority at Pac Bell and catapulted them back into the N.L. West race. The Giants would go on to finish 55-26 in their home park.

Most valuable player: Not only was second baseman Jeff Kent the team's MVP, he also was the league MVP after hitting .334 with 33 homers and 125 RBIs—his fourth straight season with at least 100 runs batted in. His clutch first-half hitting helped the Giants overcome their terrible start and he continued in his clutch role throughout the season.

Most valuable pitcher: Livan Hernandez was touted as the staff ace before the season and he did not disappoint. Hernandez won 17 games (he was 12-3 at home) and set the tone for a rotation that rated among the best in baseball.

Most improved player: At age 38, Mark Gardner rebounded from offseason shoulder surgery and posted an 11-7 record—a vast improvement over his 5-11 mark of 1999. Gardner also bailed out the Giants when heralded youngster Joe Nathan spent most of the second half on the disabled list.

Most pleasant surprise: Felix Rodriguez stepped in for injured John Johnstone and became one of the most reliable setup men in the majors. He appeared in 76 games and struck out 95 batters while setting the stage for closer Robb Nen.

Key injuries: Nathan spent 56 days on the disabled list with a shoulder injury that would require postseason surgery. ... Johnstone needed postseason surgery to repair a bad back. Although he did not go on the disabled list until mid-July, Johnstone clearly was affected and struggled through a lost season.

Notable: The Giants finished with baseball's best record for the first time since 1962. ... The team's season run total of 925 was second in franchise history only to the 959 scored by the New York Giants in 1930. ... Kent's total of 475 RBIs from 1997 to 2000 is the most ever by a second baseman over a four-year span. ... Barry Bonds finished the season with 494 home runs, 17th on baseball's all-time list.

—HENRY SCHULMAN

MISCELLANEOUS

RECORDS

2000 regular-season record: 97-65 (1st in N.L. West); 55-26 at home; 42-39 on road; 27-17 vs. East; 36-17 vs. Central; 34-31 vs. West; 19-20 vs. lefthanded starters; 78-45 vs. righthanded starters; 89-60 on grass; 8-5 on turf; 37-29 in daytime; 60-36 at night; 18-22 in one-run games; 7-5 in extra-inning games; 1-0-1 in doubleheaders.

Team record past five years: 430-381 (.530, ranks 4th in league in that span).

TEAM LEADERS

Batting average: Jeff Kent (.334).
At-bats: Jeff Kent (587).
Runs: Barry Bonds (129).
Hits: Jeff Kent (196).
Total Bases: Jeff Kent (350).
Doubles: Jeff Kent (41).
Triples: Jeff Kent (7).
Home runs: Barry Bonds (49).
Runs batted in: Jeff Kent (125).
Stolen bases: Marvin Benard (22).
Slugging percentage: Barry Bonds (.688).
On-base percentage: Barry Bonds (.440).
Wins: Livan Hernandez (17).
Earned-run average: Livan Hernandez (3.75).
Complete games: Livan Hernandez (5).
Shutouts: Shawn Estes, Livan Hernandez (2).
Saves: Robb Nen (41).
Innings pitched: Livan Hernandez (240.0).
Strikeouts: Russ Ortiz (167).

Date	Opp.	Res.	Score	(inn.*)	Hits	Opp. hits	Winning pitcher	Losing pitcher	Save	Record	Pos.	GB
7-4†	Col.	W	4-1		9	4	Hernandez	Yoshii	Nen	41-38		
7-4‡	Col.	W	3-0		7	6	Gardner	Karl	Nen	42-38	3rd	4.5
7-5	Col.	W	4-2		9	7	Nathan	Belinda	Rodriguez	43-38	3rd	4.5
7-6	Col.	W	6-5		12	7	Nen	Myers		44-38	3rd	4.5
7-7	At StL.	W	4-2		9	9	Embree	Morris	Nen	45-38	T2nd	3.5
7-8	At StL.	W	7-6		11	14	Estes	Stephenson	Nen	46-38	2nd	2.5
7-9	At StL.	L	7-8		8	10	Hentgen	Hernandez	Veres	46-39	2nd	3.5
7-13	Oak.	W	4-2		6	7	Ortiz	Mulder	Nen	47-39	2nd	2.5
7-14	Oak.	W	4-2		10	5	Gardner	Appier	Nen	48-39	2nd	2.5
7-15	Oak.	L	2-6		9	16	Heredia	Rueter		48-40	2nd	2.5
7-16	Tex.	W	6-4		11	8	Estes	Loaiza	Nen	49-40	2nd	1.5
7-17	Tex.	W	10-8		13	12	Hernandez	Davis	Nen	50-40	2nd	1.5
7-18	Tex.	W	5-3		10	11	Fultz	Wetteland		51-40	2nd	0.5
7-19	S.D.	L	3-4	(10)	10	13	Wall	Embree		51-41	2nd	1.5
7-20	S.D.	W	7-3		8	5	Rueter	Williams	Fultz	52-41	2nd	1.5
7-21	At L.A.	L	5-6		11	7	Herges	Rodriguez	Shaw	52-42	2nd	2.5
7-22	At L.A.	W	5-2		6	5	Hernandez	Gagne	Nen	53-42	2nd	1.5
7-23	At L.A.	L	0-5		2	10	Dreifort	Ortiz		53-43	2nd	1.5
7-24	At S.D.	W	3-0		6	6	Gardner	Meadows	Nen	54-43	2nd	1.0
7-25	At S.D.	L	2-3		7	10	Williams	Rueter	Hoffman	54-44	2nd	1.0
7-26	At S.D.	W	3-1		5	5	Estes	Eaton	Nen	55-44	1st	...
7-28	At Chi.	W	2-0		5	7	Hernandez	Worrell	Nen	56-44	2nd	0.5
7-29	At Chi.	L	1-8		6	13	Wood	Ortiz	Farnsworth	56-45	2nd	0.5
7-30	At Chi.	L	1-3		4	10	Lieber	Rueter		56-46	2nd	0.5
7-31	At Mil.	W	4-3	(11)	5	4	Rodriguez	Weathers	Nen	57-46	1st	...
8-1	At Mil.	W	13-8		17	10	Henry	King		58-46	1st	+1.0
8-2	At Mil.	L	4-6		6	8	Acevedo	Hernandez	Leskanic	58-47	1st	...
8-3	Pit.	W	10-2		12	7	Ortiz	Cordova		59-47	1st	...
8-4	Pit.	W	5-3		10	11	Henry	Benson	Nen	60-47	1st	+1.0
8-5	Pit.	L	2-7		9	13	Serafini	Gardner		60-48	1st	+1.0
8-6	Pit.	W	7-1		9	10	Estes	Arroyo		61-48	1st	+1.0
8-7	Mil.	W	8-1		8	9	Hernandez	Snyder		62-48	1st	+1.0
8-8	Mil.	W	1-0		6	2	Ortiz	Wright	Nen	63-48	1st	+2.0
8-9	Mil.	W	9-3		13	6	Rueter	Rigdon		64-48	1st	+3.0
8-11	At N.Y.	L	1-4		5	7	Rusch	Gardner	Benitez	64-49	1st	+2.0
8-12	At N.Y.	L	2-3		6	6	Hampton	Rodriguez	Benitez	64-50	1st	+2.0
8-13	At N.Y.	L	0-2		2	7	Leiter	Hernandez	Franco	64-51	1st	+1.0
8-14	At N.Y.	W	11-1		14	2	Ortiz	Reed		65-51	1st	+1.0
8-15	At Mon.	W	9-7		11	9	del Toro	Lira	Nen	66-51	1st	+1.0
8-16	At Mon.	W	4-1		7	8	Gardner	Hermanson	Nen	67-51	1st	+1.0
8-17	At Mon.	W	5-4		11	7	Estes	Moore	Rodriguez	68-51	1st	+1.5
8-18	Atl.	W	2-0		7	4	Hernandez	Maddux		69-51	1st	+1.5
8-19	Atl.	W	12-3		12	8	Ortiz	Ashby		70-51	1st	+1.5
8-20	Atl.	L	5-8		4	15	Glavine	Rueter		70-52	1st	+0.5
8-21	Fla.	W	6-0		10	6	Gardner	Dempster		71-52	1st	+1.5
8-22	Fla.	L	5-7		8	13	Burnett	Estes	Alfonseca	71-53	1st	+1.5
8-23	Fla.	W	5-0		7	4	Hernandez	Smith		72-53	1st	+2.5
8-25	At Phi.	W	16-3		21	11	Ortiz	Bottenfield		73-53	1st	+3.5
8-26	At Phi.	L	2-5		8	11	Wolf	Rueter	Brantley	73-54	1st	+2.5
8-27	At Phi.	L	1-2	(10)	3	7	Vosberg	Fultz		73-55	1st	+2.5
8-28	At Pit.	W	5-4		8	6	Embree	Sauerbeck	Nen	74-55	1st	+3.5
8-29	At Pit.	L	0-8		1	10	Benson	Hernandez		74-56	1st	+2.5
8-30	At Pit.	W	2-0		5	4	Ortiz	Anderson	Nen	75-56	1st	+2.5
8-31	At Pit.	W	10-2		13	10	Rueter	Silva		76-56	1st	+3.0
9-1	Chi.	W	7-2		10	6	Gardner	Wood		77-56	1st	+4.0
9-2	Chi.	W	13-2		10	8	Estes	Quevedo		78-56	1st	+5.0
9-3	Chi.	W	5-2		13	5	Hernandez	Garibay	Nen	79-56	1st	+5.0
9-4	Phi.	W	3-0		5	4	Ortiz	Daal	Nen	80-56	1st	+5.5
9-5	Phi.	W	8-5		11	8	Johnstone	Vosberg	Nen	81-56	1st	+6.5
9-6	Phi.	W	5-4		6	11	Fultz	Padilla	Embree	82-56	1st	+7.5
9-7	S.D.	W	13-0		16	5	Estes	Clement		83-56	1st	+8.5
9-8	S.D.	L	7-10		13	16	Almanzar	Embree	Hoffman	83-57	1st	+7.5
9-9	S.D.	L	3-7		11	8	Tollberg	Ortiz		83-58	1st	+6.5
9-10	S.D.	W	10-2		10	5	Rueter	Witasick		84-58	1st	+7.5
9-11	At Hou.	W	8-7	(10)	12	9	Nen	Valdes		85-58	1st	+8.5
9-12	At Hou.	W	9-5		12	11	Estes	Elarton		86-58	1st	+8.5
9-13	At Hou.	W	3-2		9	8	Hernandez	Miller	Nen	87-58	1st	+8.5
9-15	At S.D.	L	4-5		9	9	Davey	Henry	Hoffman	87-59	1st	+7.5
9-16	At S.D.	W	4-3	(13)	16	10	Embree	Almanzar	Nen	88-59	1st	+8.5
9-17	At S.D.	W	5-1		9	5	Gardner	Williams		89-59	1st	+9.5
9-18	Cin.	L	1-7		4	12	Fernandez	Estes		89-60	1st	+9.5
9-19	Cin.	W	7-3		14	7	Hernandez	Bell		90-60	1st	+10.5
9-20	Cin.	W	4-2		5	4	Ortiz	Parris	Nen	91-60	1st	+11.0
9-21	Ari.	W	8-7		9	9	Henry	Morgan	Nen	92-60	1st	+11.5
9-22	Ari.	L	1-7		4	11	Schilling	Gardner		92-61	1st	+11.5
9-23†	Ari.	L	5-7		8	9	Guzman	Estes	Mantei	92-62		
9-23‡	Ari.	W	9-5		10	9	del Toro	Reynoso		93-62	1st	+11.0
9-24	Ari.	L	3-8		7	10	Anderson	Hernandez		93-63	1st	+10.0
9-26	At L.A.	L	0-9		2	9	Dreifort	Ortiz		93-64	1st	+9.0
9-27	At L.A.	W	4-0		5	6	Rueter	Prokopec		94-64	1st	+10.0
9-28	At L.A.	W	5-3		10	5	Fultz	Adams	Nen	95-64	1st	+11.0
9-29	At Ari.	W	4-3		7	9	Hernandez	Anderson	Nen	96-64	1st	+11.0
9-30	At Ari.	L	1-5		5	11	Guzman	Embree		96-65	1st	+10.0
10-1	At Ari.	W	11-4		12	8	Ortiz	Johnson		97-65	1st	+11.0

Monthly records: April (10-13), May (15-12), June (13-13), July (19-8), August (19-10), September (20-9), October (1-0).
*Innings, if other than nine. † First game of a doubleheader. ‡ Second game of a doubleheader.

MEMORABLE GAMES

April 21 at Arizona

On the night of April 20, after the Giants had lost in Cincinnati to fall to 4-11, the players held an impromptu team meeting in the bar at their hotel in Phoenix—a reminder that they were better than they were playing. The next night, they destroyed the defending N.L. West-champion Diamondbacks 11-5 to start a three-game road sweep. That prevented the Giants from being knocked out of the divison race early.

San Francisco	AB	R	H	BI	Arizona	AB	R	H	BI
Benard, cf-rf	4	3	3	4	Womack, ss	4	0	2	0
Mueller, 3b	4	1	2	1	Morgan, p	0	0	0	0
Bonds, lf	3	1	1	0	Gilkey, ph	1	0	0	0
Rios, pr-lf	2	1	1	1	Swindell, p	0	0	0	0
Kent, 2b	5	1	3	5	Bell, 2b	5	1	1	1
Crespo, 2b	0	0	0	0	Gonzalez, lf	5	1	3	0
Snow, 1b	4	1	1	0	Durazo, 1b	4	1	2	1
Burks, rf	3	0	0	0	Finley, cf	4	1	2	0
Murray, cf	0	0	0	0	Lee, rf	5	0	1	1
Aurilia, ss	5	1	2	0	Stinnett, c	4	1	1	1
Embree, p	0	0	0	0	Harris, 3b	2	0	0	0
Johnstone, p	0	0	0	0	Plesac, p	0	0	0	0
Mirabelli, c	4	0	0	0	Colbrunn, ph	1	0	0	0
Ortiz, p	3	2	2	0	Frias, ss	1	0	0	0
Martinez, ss	1	0	1	0	Stottlemyre, p	1	0	0	0
					Springer, p	0	0	0	0
					Fox, 3b	1	0	0	1
					Klassen, ph-3b	1	0	0	0
Totals	**38**	**11**	**16**	**11**	**Totals**	**39**	**5**	**12**	**5**

San Francisco ....1 0 3 3 2 0 2 0 0—11 16 1
Arizona ....0 1 0 0 0 1 2 0 1— 5 12 1

E—Murray (1), Durazo (3). DP—Arizona 2. LOB—San Francisco 10, Arizona 11. 2B—Kent (5), Ortiz (1), Rios (3), Womack (1), Gonzalez 2 (8), Durazo 2 (2), Lee (1). HR—Benard (2), Mueller (1), Kent (3), Bell (4), Stinnett (4). CS—Kent (1), Womack (2). SH—Mueller.

San Francisco	IP	H	R	ER	BB	SO
Ortiz (W 2-2)	7	10	4	4	4	5
Embree	1	0	0	0	0	1
Johnstone	1	2	1	1	0	1
Arizona	**IP**	**H**	**R**	**ER**	**BB**	**SO**
Stottlemyre (L 3-1)	3.2	8	7	7	3	1
Springer	1	1	2	1	3	1
Plesac	1.1	1	0	0	2	1
Morgan	2	4	2	2	1	1
Swindell	1	2	0	0	0	1

U—HP, Froemming. 1B, Winters. 2B, Culbreth. 3B, Welke. T—3:07. A—40,929.

July 2 at San Francisco

In a nationally televised game against the Dodgers at Pacific Bell Park, Marvin Benard hit a ninth-inning home run to give the Giants a 6-5 victory after Robb Nen had blown a save. The emotional win keyed an eight-game winning streak that brought the Giants to the brink of first place. Nen's blown save would be his last until late September, after the Giants already had clinched the division title.

Los Angeles	AB	R	H	BI	San Francisco	AB	R	H	BI
Santangelo, cf-rf	4	1	1	0	Benard, cf-lf	5	2	2	1
Grudzielanek, 2b	5	1	1	1	Mueller, 3b	3	0	0	1
Sheffield, lf	4	0	3	1	Snow, 1b	4	1	1	0
Karros, 1b	4	0	2	0	Kent, 2b	4	3	3	2
Beltre, 3b	3	1	0	0	Burks, rf	2	0	1	0
Hundley, c	4	1	1	0	Rios, lf	3	0	0	1
Elster, ss	3	0	0	0	Nen, p	0	0	0	0
Hansen, ph	1	0	1	1	Aurilia, ss	4	0	2	1
Cora, ss	1	0	0	0	Estalella, c	3	0	1	0
Gilbert, rf	3	0	1	0	Estes, p	2	0	0	0
Herges, p	0	0	0	0	Fultz, p	1	0	0	0
Green, ph	1	0	0	0	F.Rodriguez, p	0	0	0	0
Osuna, p	0	0	0	0	Murray, cf	1	0	0	0
Leyritz, ph	1	0	1	0					
Fetters, p	0	0	0	0					
Gagne, p	2	1	2	0					
Hollandsworth, ph-cf	3	0	0	0					
Totals	**39**	**5**	**13**	**3**	**Totals**	**32**	**6**	**10**	**6**

Los Angeles ....0 0 0 1 0 0 2 2 0—5 13 1 13
San Francisco ....1 0 0 2 1 0 1 0 1—6 10 1 7

E—Hundley (3), Estalella (1). LOB—Los Angeles 13, San Francisco 7. 2B—Santangelo (3), Estalella (13). HR—Benard (6), Kent 2 (23). SB—Benard (11). S—Mueller, Rios. SH—Hundley.

Los Angeles	IP	H	R	ER	BB	SO
Gagne	5	6	4	3	3	3
Herges	1	1	0	0	0	1
Osuna	2	2	1	1	0	1
Fetters (L 3-1)	0	1	1	1	0	0
San Francisco	**IP**	**H**	**R**	**ER**	**BB**	**SO**
Estes	5	7	1	1	4	3
Fultz	1.2	2	2	2	0	2
Rodriguez (HOLD 10	0.2	3	2	2	1	1
Nen (W 2-3)	1.2	1	0	0	0	3

Fetters pitched to 1 batter in 9th. WP—Rodriguez, Nen 2. U—HP, Foster. 1B, Kulpa. 2B. Marsh. 3B, Hernandez. T—3:24. A—40,930.

INDIVIDUAL STATISTICS

BATTING

Name	G	TPA	AB	R	H	TB	2B	3B	HR	RBI	Avg.	Obp.	Slg.	SH	SF	HP	BB	IBB	SO	SB	CS	GDP	vs RHP AB	vs RHP Avg.	vs RHP HR	vs RHP RBI	vs LHP AB	vs LHP Avg.	vs LHP HR	vs LHP RBI
Kent, Jeff	159	695	587	114	196	350	41	7	33	125	.334	.424	.596	0	9	9	90	6	107	12	9	17	442	.337	28	101	145	.324	5	24
Mueller, Bill	153	631	560	97	150	217	29	4	10	55	.268	.333	.388	7	6	6	52	0	62	4	2	16	452	.259	7	44	108	.306	3	11
Benard, Marvin	149	633	560	102	147	222	27	6	12	55	.263	.342	.396	2	2	6	63	0	97	22	7	4	458	.273	11	50	102	.216	1	5
Snow, J.T.	155	627	536	82	152	246	33	2	19	96	.284	.365	.459	0	14	11	66	6	129	1	3	20	407	.292	15	69	129	.256	4	27
Aurilia, Rich	141	571	509	67	138	226	24	2	20	79	.271	.339	.444	4	4	0	54	2	90	1	2	15	390	.267	13	54	119	.286	7	25
Bonds, Barry	143	607	480	129	147	330	28	4	49	106	.306	.440	.688	0	7	3	117	22	77	11	3	6	332	.340	37	74	148	.230	12	32
Burks, Ellis	122	458	393	74	135	238	21	5	24	96	.344	.419	.606	0	8	1	56	5	49	5	1	10	293	.338	20	75	100	.360	4	21
Estalella, Bobby	106	361	299	45	70	140	22	3	14	53	.234	.357	.468	0	3	2	57	9	92	3	0	4	227	.229	10	34	72	.250	4	19
Rios, Armando	115	269	233	38	62	117	15	5	10	50	.266	.347	.502	1	4	0	31	4	43	3	2	9	191	.288	8	40	42	.167	2	10
Mirabelli, Doug	82	273	230	23	53	85	10	2	6	28	.230	.337	.370	3	2	2	36	2	57	1	0	6	182	.231	5	20	48	.229	1	8
Murray, Calvin	108	229	194	35	47	67	12	1	2	22	.242	.348	.345	2	1	3	29	0	33	9	3	0	79	.203	0	4	115	.270	2	18
Martinez, Ramon E.	88	210	189	30	57	92	13	2	6	25	.302	.354	.487	4	1	1	15	1	22	3	2	6	125	.304	4	19	64	.297	2	6
Davis, Russ	80	192	180	27	47	79	5	0	9	24	.261	.302	.439	0	1	2	9	0	29	0	3	1	77	.195	2	7	103	.311	7	17
Crespo, Felipe	89	150	131	17	38	58	6	1	4	29	.290	.351	.443	2	3	4	10	2	23	3	2	3	108	.315	4	27	23	.174	0	2
Hernandez, Livan	34	99	89	6	21	27	3	0	1	9	.236	.244	.303	9	0	0	1	0	14	0	0	4	64	.281	1	9	25	.120	0	0
Estes, Shawn	32	81	68	4	14	21	4	0	1	10	.206	.229	.309	11	0	0	2	0	28	0	0	2	56	.214	1	9	12	.167	0	1
Ortiz, Russ	33	75	61	7	12	14	2	0	0	5	.197	.290	.230	6	0	0	8	0	16	0	0	2	42	.214	0	2	19	.158	0	3
Rueter, Kirk	34	71	60	5	12	15	3	0	0	5	.200	.213	.250	10	0	0	1	0	11	0	0	2	47	.191	0	5	13	.231	0	0
Gardner, Mark	30	50	43	1	5	5	0	0	0	0	.116	.116	.116	7	0	0	0	0	22	0	0	0	34	.118	0	0	9	.111	0	0
Lowery, Terrell	24	42	34	13	15	22	4	0	1	5	.441	.548	.647	0	0	1	7	0	8	1	0	1	18	.389	0	1	16	.500	1	4
Nathan, Joe	20	38	32	3	5	13	2	0	2	3	.156	.176	.406	4	1	0	1	0	9	0	0	1	22	.136	1	2	10	.200	1	1
Melo, Juan	11	13	13	0	1	1	0	0	0	1	.077	.077	.077	0	0	0	0	0	5	0	0	0	10	.100	0	1	3	.000	0	0
Minor, Damon	10	11	9	3	4	13	0	0	3	6	.444	.545	1.444	0	0	0	2	0	1	0	0	0	9	.444	3	6	0	.000	0	0
Servais, Scott	7	10	8	1	2	2	0	0	0	0	.250	.400	.250	0	0	0	2	1	1	0	0	0	7	.286	0	0	1	.000	0	0
Feliz, Pedro	8	7	7	1	2	2	0	0	0	0	.286	.286	.286	0	0	0	0	0	1	0	0	0	6	.333	0	0	1	.000	0	0
Fultz, Aaron	58	7	6	0	2	2	0	0	0	0	.333	.333	.333	1	0	0	0	0	1	0	0	2	5	.200	0	0	1	1.000	0	0
Rodriguez, Felix	76	4	4	0	0	0	0	0	0	0	.000	.000	.000	0	0	0	0	0	3	0	0	0	3	.000	0	0	1	.000	0	0
del Toro, Miguel	9	2	2	1	1	1	0	0	0	2	.500	.500	.500	0	0	0	0	0	0	0	0	0	2	.500	0	2	0	.000	0	0
Johnstone, John	47	2	2	0	0	0	0	0	0	0	.000	.000	.000	0	0	0	0	0	2	0	0	0	2	.000	0	0	0	.000	0	0
Henry, Doug	27	0	0	0	0	0	0	0	0	0	.000	.000	.000	0	0	0	0	0	0	0	0	0	0	.000	0	0	0	.000	0	0
Nen, Robb	68	0	0	0	0	0	0	0	0	0	.000	.000	.000	0	0	0	0	0	0	0	0	0	0	.000	0	0	0	.000	0	0
Embree, Alan	63	0	0	0	0	0	0	0	0	0	.000	.000	.000	0	0	0	0	0	0	0	0	0	0	.000	0	0	0	.000	0	0
Weber, Ben	9	0	0	0	0	0	0	0	0	0	.000	.000	.000	0	0	0	0	0	0	0	0	0	0	.000	0	0	0	.000	0	0
Linebrink, Scott	3	0	0	0	0	0	0	0	0	0	.000	.000	.000	0	0	0	0	0	0	0	0	0	0	.000	0	0	0	.000	0	0
Vogelsong, Ryan	4	0	0	0	0	0	0	0	0	0	.000	.000	.000	0	0	0	0	0	0	0	0	0	0	.000	0	0	0	.000	0	0
Zerbe, Chad	4	0	0	0	0	0	0	0	0	0	.000	.000	.000	0	0	0	0	0	0	0	0	0	0	.000	0	0	0	.000	0	0

Players with more than one N.L. team

Name	G	TPA	AB	R	H	TB	2B	3B	HR	RBI	Avg.	Obp.	Slg.	SH	SF	HP	BB	IBB	SO	SB	CS	GDP	vs RHP AB	vs RHP Avg.	vs RHP HR	vs RHP RBI	vs LHP AB	vs LHP Avg.	vs LHP HR	vs LHP RBI
Henry, Hou.	45	1	1	0	0	0	0	0	0	0	.000	.000	.000	0	0	0	0	0	0	0	0	0	0	.000	0	0	0	.000	0	0
Henry, Hou.-S.F.	72	1	1	0	0	0	0	0	0	0	.000	.000	.000	0	0	0	0	0	0	0	0	0	1	.000	0	0	0	.000	0	0
Linebrink, Hou.	8	1	1	0	1	1	0	0	0	0	1.000	1.000	1.000	0	0	0	0	0	0	0	0	0	0	.000	0	0	0	.000	0	0
Linebrink, S.F.-Hou.	11	1	1	0	1	1	0	0	0	0	1.000	1.000	1.000	0	0	0	0	0	0	0	0	0	0	.000	0	0	1	1.000	0	0
Servais, Col.	33	110	101	6	22	29	4	0	1	13	.218	.273	.287	0	1	1	7	2	16	0	1	1	7	.286	0	0	1	.000	0	0
Servais, Col.-S.F.	40	120	109	7	24	31	4	0	1	13	.220	.283	.284	0	1	1	9	3	17	0	1	1	62	.194	0	6	47	.255	1	7

PITCHING

Name	W	L	Pct.	ERA	IP	H	R	ER	HR	SH	SF	HB	BB	IBB	SO	G	GS	CG	ShO	GF	Sv	vs. RH AB	vs. RH Avg.	vs. RH HR	vs. RH RBI	vs. LH AB	vs. LH Avg.	vs. LH HR	vs. LH RBI
Hernandez, Livan	17	11	.607	3.75	240.0	254	114	100	22	12	9	4	73	3	165	33	33	5	2	0	0	518	.274	13	54	414	.271	9	46
Ortiz, Russ	14	12	.538	5.01	195.2	192	117	109	28	10	6	7	112	1	167	33	32	0	0	0	0	378	.257	20	59	358	.265	8	37
Estes, Shawn	15	6	.714	4.26	190.1	194	99	90	11	7	6	3	108	1	136	30	30	4	2	0	0	603	.285	10	62	102	.216	1	13
Rueter, Kirk	11	9	.550	3.96	184.0	205	92	81	23	19	9	2	62	5	71	32	31	0	0	0	0	572	.301	19	73	135	.244	4	14
Gardner, Mark	11	7	.611	4.05	149.0	155	72	67	16	6	6	5	42	2	92	30	20	0	0	3	0	335	.245	9	41	240	.304	7	31
Nathan, Joe	5	2	.714	5.21	93.1	89	63	54	12	5	5	4	63	4	61	20	15	0	0	0	0	169	.219	8	32	180	.289	4	26
Rodriguez, Felix	4	2	.667	2.64	81.2	65	29	24	5	2	3	3	42	2	95	76	0	0	0	19	3	163	.270	5	26	133	.158	0	11
Fultz, Aaron	5	2	.714	4.67	69.1	67	38	36	8	7	6	3	28	0	62	58	0	0	0	18	1	169	.284	5	30	86	.221	3	14
Nen, Robb	4	3	.571	1.50	66.0	37	15	11	4	4	3	2	19	1	92	68	0	0	0	63	41	109	.128	1	5	119	.193	3	11
Embree, Alan	3	5	.375	4.95	60.0	62	34	33	4	4	5	3	25	2	49	63	0	0	0	21	2	135	.267	2	18	91	.286	2	24
Johnstone, John	3	4	.429	6.30	50.0	64	35	35	11	4	4	2	13	2	37	47	0	0	0	9	0	122	.287	6	25	77	.377	5	16
Henry, Doug	3	1	.750	2.49	25.1	18	10	7	2	3	1	1	21	1	16	27	0	0	0	8	0	62	.210	1	6	22	.227	1	5
del Toro, Miguel	2	0	1.000	5.19	17.1	17	10	10	3	1	0	2	6	2	16	9	1	0	0	4	0	39	.231	2	5	29	.276	1	3
Weber, Ben	0	1	.000	14.63	8.0	16	13	13	0	0	0	0	4	0	6	9	0	0	0	2	0	26	.385	0	7	14	.429	0	1
Vogelsong, Ryan	0	0	.000	0.00	6.0	4	0	0	0	0	0	0	2	0	6	4	0	0	0	3	0	16	.250	0	0	6	.000	0	0
Zerbe, Chad	0	0	.000	4.50	6.0	6	3	3	1	1	0	0	1	0	5	4	0	0	0	2	0	13	.308	1	2	9	.222	0	1
Linebrink, Scott	0	0	.000	11.57	2.1	7	3	3	1	0	0	0	2	0	0	3	0	0	0	1	0	7	.714	0	4	7	.286	1	2

PITCHERS WITH MORE THAN ONE N.L. TEAM

Name	W	L	Pct.	ERA	IP	H	R	ER	HR	SH	SF	HB	BB	IBB	SO	G	GS	CG	ShO	GF	Sv	vs. RH AB	vs. RH Avg.	vs. RH HR	vs. RH RBI	vs. LH AB	vs. LH Avg.	vs. LH HR	vs. LH RBI
Henry, Hou.	1	3	.250	4.42	53.0	39	26	26	10	2	1	3	28	2	46	45	0	0	0	13	1	62	.210	1	6	22	.227	1	5
Henry, Hou.-S.F.	4	4	.500	3.79	78.1	57	36	33	12	5	2	4	49	3	62	72	0	0	0	2	1	176	.199	5	23	99	.222	7	16
Linebrink, Hou.	0	0	.000	4.66	9.2	11	5	5	3	0	0	3	6	0	6	8	0	0	0	3	0	7	.714	0	4	7	.286	1	2
Linebrink, S.F.-Hou.	0	0	.000	6.00	12.0	18	8	8	4	0	0	3	8	0	6	11	0	0	0	0	0	28	.357	0	4	24	.333	4	7

DESIGNATED HITTERS

Name	AB	Avg.	HR	RBI
Davis, Russ	12	.417	1	2
Burks, Ellis	9	.000	0	0
Lowery, Terrell	4	.250	0	0
Crespo, Felipe	1	1.000	0	0

INDIVIDUAL STATISTICS

FIELDING

FIRST BASEMEN

Player	Pct.	G	PO	A	E	TC	DP
Snow, J.T.	.995	153	1197	91	6	1294	135
Kent, Jeff	.973	16	73	0	2	75	10
Crespo, Felipe	1.000	11	30	1	0	31	1
Davis, Russ	.923	6	23	1	2	26	4
Minor, Damon	1.000	4	5	0	0	5	0
Martinez, Ramon E.	1.000	2	1	0	0	1	1
Rios, Armando	-	1	0	0	0	0	0

SECOND BASEMEN

Player	Pct.	G	PO	A	E	TC	DP
Kent, Jeff	.986	150	302	394	10	706	96
Martinez, Ramon E.	1.000	32	43	35	0	78	11
Crespo, Felipe	1.000	7	2	3	0	5	0
Melo, Juan	1.000	6	3	4	0	7	0
Mueller, Bill	1.000	2	1	0	0	1	0

THIRD BASEMEN

Player	Pct.	G	PO	A	E	TC	DP
Mueller, Bill	.974	145	99	244	9	352	24
Davis, Russ	.933	43	14	42	4	60	3
Feliz, Pedro	-	4	0	0	0	0	0
Martinez, Ramon E.	1.000	2	1	1	0	2	0

SHORTSTOPS

Player	Pct.	G	PO	A	E	TC	DP
Aurilia, Rich	.967	140	218	403	21	642	110
Martinez, Ramon E.	.991	44	43	72	1	116	20

OUTFIELDERS

Player	Pct.	G	PO	A	E	TC	DP
Benard, Marvin	.997	141	323	11	1	335	1
Bonds, Barry	.989	141	255	8	3	266	4
Burks, Ellis	.982	108	215	4	4	223	1
Murray, Calvin	.980	106	143	2	3	148	1
Rios, Armando	.959	93	133	6	6	145	1
Crespo, Felipe	.962	26	25	0	1	26	0
Lowery, Terrell	.917	20	11	0	1	12	0

CATCHERS

Player	Pct.	G	PO	A	E	TC	DP	PB
Estalella, Bobby	.993	106	654	49	5	708	14	10
Mirabelli, Doug	.985	80	429	38	7	474	4	5
Servais, Scott	1.000	6	18	0	0	18	0	0

PITCHERS

Player	Pct.	G	PO	A	E	TC	DP
Rodriguez, Felix	.750	76	0	3	1	4	0
Nen, Robb	.800	68	2	6	2	10	0
Embree, Alan	1.000	63	0	9	0	9	3
Fultz, Aaron	1.000	58	5	17	0	22	2
Johnstone, John	1.000	47	3	6	0	9	1
Hernandez, Livan	1.000	33	18	44	0	62	4
Ortiz, Russ	1.000	33	11	33	0	44	4
Rueter, Kirk	1.000	32	8	44	0	52	4
Estes, Shawn	.964	30	11	43	2	56	7
Gardner, Mark	.938	30	5	10	1	16	1
Henry, Doug	.750	27	0	3	1	4	0
Nathan, Joe	1.000	20	8	11	0	19	0
del Toro, Miguel	1.000	9	0	3	0	3	0
Weber, Ben	-	9	0	0	0	0	0
Zerbe, Chad	1.000	4	1	2	0	3	0
Vogelsong, Ryan	-	4	0	0	0	0	0
Linebrink, Scott	1.000	3	0	1	0	1	0

PITCHING AGAINST EACH CLUB

Pitcher	Ari. W-L	Atl. W-L	Chi. W-L	Cin. W-L	Col. W-L	Fla. W-L	Hou. W-L	L.A. W-L	Mil. W-L	Mon. W-L	N.Y. W-L	Phi. W-L	Pit. W-L	S.D. W-L	StL. W-L	A.L. W-L	Total W-L
del Toro, M.	1-0	0-0	0-0	0-0	0-0	0-0	0-0	0-0	0-0	1-0	0-0	0-0	0-0	0-0	0-0	0-0	2-0
Embree, Alan	0-1	0-0	0-0	0-0	0-0	0-0	0-0	0-0	0-0	0-0	0-0	0-0	1-0	1-2	1-0	0-2	3-5
Estes, Shawn	0-1	0-1	1-0	0-2	2-0	0-1	2-0	0-0	0-0	2-0	1-0	1-0	1-0	2-0	1-0	2-1	15-6
Fultz, Aaron	0-0	0-0	0-1	0-0	0-0	1-0	0-0	1-0	0-0	0-0	0-0	1-1	0-0	0-0	0-0	2-0	5-2
Gardner, Mark	0-1	1-0	2-0	0-0	1-1	2-0	0-0	0-1	0-1	1-0	0-1	1-0	0-1	2-0	0-1	1-0	11-7
Henry, Doug	1-0	0-0	0-0	0-0	0-0	0-0	0-0	0-0	1-0	0-0	0-0	0-0	1-0	0-1	0-0	0-0	3-1
Hernandez, L.	1-2	1-1	2-0	1-1	1-1	1-1	3-0	1-0	1-1	1-0	1-1	1-0	0-1	0-0	1-1	1-1	17-11
Johnstone, J.	0-0	0-0	0-0	0-0	0-2	1-1	0-0	0-0	0-0	1-1	0-0	1-0	0-0	0-0	0-0	0-0	3-4
Linebrink, S.	0-0	0-0	0-0	0-0	0-0	0-0	0-0	0-0	0-0	0-0	0-0	0-0	0-0	0-0	0-0	0-0	0-0
Nathan, Joe	1-0	0-0	0-0	1-0	2-2	0-0	1-0	0-0	0-0	0-0	0-0	0-0	0-0	0-0	0-0	0-0	5-2
Nen, Robb	0-0	0-0	0-0	1-0	1-0	0-0	1-1	1-0	0-1	0-0	0-0	0-0	0-0	0-0	0-0	0-1	4-3
Ortiz, Russ	2-1	1-2	0-1	1-0	0-0	1-0	1-0	0-3	2-0	0-1	1-0	2-0	2-0	0-1	0-2	1-1	14-12
Rodriguez, F.	0-0	0-0	0-0	0-0	0-0	0-0	0-0	0-1	1-0	0-0	2-1	0-0	0-0	0-0	1-0	0-0	4-2
Rueter, Kirk	1-0	0-2	0-2	2-0	0-0	0-0	0-0	2-1	1-0	0-1	0-0	0-1	1-0	2-1	1-0	1-1	11-9
Vogelsong, R.	0-0	0-0	0-0	0-0	0-0	0-0	0-0	0-0	0-0	0-0	0-0	0-0	0-0	0-0	0-0	0-0	0-0
Weber, Ben	0-0	0-0	0-0	0-0	0-0	0-0	0-0	0-1	0-0	0-0	0-0	0-0	0-0	0-0	0-0	0-0	0-1
Zerbe, Chad	0-0	0-0	0-0	0-0	0-0	0-0	0-0	0-0	0-0	0-0	0-0	0-0	0-0	0-0	0-0	0-0	0-0
Totals	7-6	3-6	5-4	6-3	7-6	6-3	8-1	5-7	6-3	6-3	5-3	7-2	6-2	7-5	5-4	8-7	97-65

INTERLEAGUE: Ortiz 1-1, Estes 1-0, Gardner 1-0, Rueter 0-1, Embree 0-1 vs. Athletics; Rueter 1-0, Estes 0-1, Hernandez 0-1 vs. Mariners; Estes 1-0, Hernandez 1-0, Fultz 1-0 vs. Rangers; Fultz 1-0, Nen 0-1, Embree 0-1 vs. Angels. Total: 8-7.

MISCELLANEOUS

HOME RUNS BY PARK

At Anaheim (6): Bonds 2, Kent 1, Aurilia 1, Benard 1, Rios 1.

At Arizona (13): Bonds 2, Kent 2, Aurilia 2, Mueller 2, Benard 1, Crespo 1, Estalella 1, Murray 1, Minor 1.

At Atlanta (6): Kent 3, Bonds 1, Crespo 1, Estalella 1.

At Chicago (NL) (2): Aurilia 1, Rios 1.

At Cincinnati (4): Mirabelli 2, Bonds 1, Martinez 1.

At Colorado (17): Kent 3, Rios 3, Bonds 2, Mueller 2, Estalella 2, Davis 1, Aurilia 1, Hernandez 1, Lowery 1, Nathan 1.

At Florida (8): Burks 3, Kent 2, Bonds 1, Davis 1, Aurilia 1.

At Houston (14): Bonds 4, Snow 2, Benard 2, Burks 1, Kent 1, Mueller 1, Mirabelli 1, Estalella 1, Rios 1.

At Los Angeles (7): Bonds 2, Snow 1, Aurilia 1, Crespo 1, Estalella 1, Rios 1.

At Milwaukee (6): Bonds 3, Burks 1, Kent 1, Snow 1.

At Montreal (7): Bonds 2, Snow 2, Aurilia 1, Benard 1, Estalella 1.

At New York (NL) (0):

At Oakland (10): Bonds 3, Kent 3, Burks 1, Davis 1, Mueller 1, Martinez 1.

At Philadelphia (1): Rios 1.

At Pittsburgh (4): Bonds 1, Kent 1, Davis 1, Mueller 1.

At San Diego (4): Burks 1, Kent 1, Benard 1, Estalella 1.

At San Francisco (110): Bonds 25, Burks 15, Kent 14, Aurilia 12, Snow 10, Benard 6, Estalella 6, Davis 5, Martinez 4, Mueller 3, Mirabelli 2, Rios 2, Minor 2, Estes 1, Crespo 1, Nathan 1, Murray 1.

At St. Louis (7): Snow 3, Burks 2, Kent 1, Mirabelli 1.

LOW-HIT GAMES

No-hitters: None.
One-hitters: None.
Two-hitters: None.

10-STRIKEOUT GAMES

Russ Ortiz 4, Shawn Estes 1, Livan Hernandez 1, Total: 6

FOUR OR MORE HITS IN ONE GAME

Marvin Benard 4, Jeff Kent 2, J.T. Snow 2, Barry Bonds 1, Ellis Burks 1, Doug Mirabelli 1 (including one five-hit game), Terrell Lowery 1 (including one five-hit game), Total: 12

MULTI-HOMER GAMES

Barry Bonds 4, Ellis Burks 2, Jeff Kent 2, J.T. Snow 2, Doug Mirabelli 1, Bobby Estalella 1, Armando Rios 1, Total: 13

GRAND SLAMS

5-2: Bobby Estalella (off New York's Glendon Rusch)
5-21: J.T. Snow (off Milwaukee's Valerio de los Santos)
5-24: Shawn Estes (off Montreal's Mike Johnson)
8-9: Jeff Kent (off Milwaukee's Paul Rigdon)
8-15: J.T. Snow (off Montreal's Mike Johnson)
8-21: Russ Davis (off Florida's Armando Almanza)
10-1: Calvin Murray (off Arizona's Randy Johnson)

PINCH HITTERS

(Minimum 5 at-bats)

Name	AB	Avg.	HR	RBI
Crespo, Felipe	51	.294	1	13
Davis, Russ	31	.161	2	6
Rios, Armando	23	.174	1	7
Benard, Marvin	15	.133	0	2
Martinez, Ramon E.	12	.000	0	1
Mueller, Bill	11	.455	0	1
Burks, Ellis	9	.444	0	3
Murray, Calvin	8	.375	1	5
Minor, Damon	7	.429	2	4
Lowery, Terrell	7	.143	0	0

DEBUTS

4-3: Ben Weber, P.
4-5: Aaron Fultz, P.
4-15: Scott Linebrink, P.
9-2: Ryan Vogelsong, P.
9-2: Damon Minor, PH.
9-2: Juan Melo, PH.
9-5: Pedro Feliz, PH.
9-18: Chad Zerbe, P.

GAMES BY POSITION

Catcher: Bobby Estalella 106, Doug Mirabelli 80, Scott Servais 6.

First base: J.T. Snow 153, Jeff Kent 16, Felipe Crespo 11, Russ Davis 6, Damon Minor 4, Ramon E. Martinez 2, Armando Rios 1.

Second base: Jeff Kent 150, Ramon E. Martinez 32, Felipe Crespo 7, Juan Melo 6, Bill Mueller 2.

Third base: Bill Mueller 145, Russ Davis 43, Pedro Feliz 4, Ramon E. Martinez 2.

Shortstop: Rich Aurilia 140, Ramon E. Martinez 44.

Outfield: Barry Bonds 141, Marvin Benard 141, Ellis Burks 108, Calvin Murray 106, Armando Rios 93, Felipe Crespo 26, Terrell Lowery 20.

Designated hitter: Russ Davis 3, Ellis Burks 2, Felipe Crespo 1, Terrell Lowery 1.

STREAKS

Wins: 9 (August 30-September 7)
Losses: 8 (May 12-20)
Consecutive games with at least one hit: 15, Bill Mueller (May 1-19)
Wins by pitcher: 7, Russ Ortiz (August 3-September 4)

ATTENDANCE

Home: 3,233,470
Road: 2,595,222
Highest (home): 40,930 (April 11 vs. Los Angeles).
Highest (road): 55,695 (September 16 vs. San Diego).
Lowest (home): 40,930 (April 11 vs. Los Angeles).
Lowest (road): 7,165 (August 15 vs. Montreal).

TEAM STATISTICS

AMERICAN LEAGUE

BATTING

Team	Avg.	G	PA	AB	R	H	TB	2B	3B	HR	RBI	SH	SF	HP	BB	IBB	SO	SB	CS	GI DP	LOB	SHO	SLG	OBP
Cleveland	.288	162	6512	5683	950	1639	2672	310	30	221	889	41	52	51	685	27	1057	113	34	134	1260	4	.470	.367
Kansas City	.288	162	6394	5709	879	1644	2429	281	27	150	831	56	70	48	511	28	840	121	35	139	1184	4	.425	.348
Chicago	.286	162	6406	5646	978	1615	2654	325	33	216	926	55	61	53	591	28	960	119	42	140	1127	3	.470	.356
Texas	.283	162	6363	5648	848	1601	2520	330	35	173	806	48	48	39	580	39	922	69	47	161	1198	6	.446	.352
Anaheim	.280	162	6373	5628	864	1574	2659	309	34	236	837	47	43	47	608	43	1024	93	52	126	1173	5	.472	.352
New York	.277	161	6310	5556	871	1541	2500	294	25	205	833	16	50	57	631	42	1007	99	48	134	1189	7	.450	.354
Detroit	.275	162	6340	5644	823	1553	2473	307	41	177	785	42	49	43	562	22	982	83	38	142	1185	15	.438	.343
Toronto	.275	162	6326	5677	861	1562	2664	328	21	244	826	29	34	60	526	32	1026	89	34	130	1152	7	.469	.341
Baltimore	.272	162	6237	5549	794	1508	2414	310	22	184	750	27	54	49	558	34	900	126	65	148	1129	8	.435	.341
Minnesota	.270	162	6281	5615	748	1516	2287	325	49	116	711	24	51	35	556	31	1021	90	45	143	1198	8	.407	.337
Oakland	.270	161	6432	5560	947	1501	2545	281	23	239	908	26	44	52	750	32	1159	40	15	147	1210	7	.458	.360
Seattle	.269	162	6444	5497	907	1481	2427	300	26	198	869	63	61	48	775	34	1073	122	56	129	1247	5	.442	.361
Boston	.267	162	6371	5630	792	1503	2384	316	32	167	755	40	48	42	611	40	1019	43	30	115	1226	8	.423	.341
Tampa Bay	.257	161	6206	5505	733	1414	2197	253	22	162	692	52	40	51	558	25	1022	90	46	126	1140	8	.399	.329
Totals	.276	1133	88995	78547	11995	21652	34825	4269	420	2688	11418	566	705	675	8502	457	14012	1297	587	1914	16618	95	.443	.349

PITCHING

Team	W	L	Pct.	ERA	G	ShO	Rel.	Sv.	IP	H	TBF	R	ER	HR	SH	SF	HB	BB	IBB	SO	WP	Bk.
Boston	85	77	.525	4.23	162	12	425	46	1452.2	1433	6225	745	683	173	46	49	58	498	40	1121	33	2
Seattle	91	71	.562	4.49	162	10	383	44	1441.2	1442	6269	780	720	167	39	55	38	634	37	998	43	6
Oakland	91	70	.565	4.58	161	11	381	43	1435.1	1535	6355	813	730	158	35	51	48	615	57	963	46	1
Chicago	95	67	.586	4.66	162	7	466	43	1450.1	1509	6337	839	751	195	39	49	54	614	27	1037	43	8
Detroit	79	83	.488	4.71	162	6	429	44	1443.1	1583	6295	827	755	177	33	63	47	496	22	978	51	5
New York	87	74	.540	4.76	161	6	382	40	1424.1	1458	6256	814	753	177	45	48	52	577	23	1040	49	6
Cleveland	90	72	.556	4.84	162	5	462	34	1442.1	1511	6380	816	775	173	34	42	42	666	45	1213	50	3
Tampa Bay	69	92	.429	4.86	161	8	401	38	1431.1	1553	6283	842	773	198	42	45	66	533	33	955	57	3
Anaheim	82	80	.506	5.00	162	3	441	46	1448.0	1534	6401	869	805	228	40	53	36	662	44	846	47	10
Toronto	83	79	.512	5.14	162	4	388	37	1437.1	1615	6377	908	821	195	44	40	64	560	19	978	37	3
Minnesota	69	93	.426	5.14	162	4	412	35	1432.2	1634	6336	880	819	212	41	46	35	516	12	1042	68	4
Baltimore	74	88	.457	5.37	162	6	396	33	1433.1	1547	6433	913	855	202	48	57	36	665	32	1017	51	1
Kansas City	77	85	.475	5.48	162	6	329	29	1439.1	1585	6443	930	876	239	39	45	42	693	35	927	77	5
Texas	71	91	.438	5.52	162	4	415	39	1429.0	1683	6559	974	876	202	42	62	63	661	40	918	40	6
Totals	1143	1122	.505	4.91	1133	92	5710	551	20141.0	21622	88949	11950	10992	2696	567	705	681	8390	466	14033	692	63

FIELDING

Team	PCT	G	PO	A	E	TC	DP	TP	PB
Cleveland	.988	162	4327	1665	72	6064	147	0	10
Seattle	.984	162	4325	1629	99	6053	176	0	8
Toronto	.984	162	4312	1679	100	6091	176	0	11
Kansas City	.983	162	4318	1751	102	6171	185	0	7
Detroit	.983	162	4330	1754	105	6189	171	0	7
Minnesota	.983	162	4298	1526	102	5926	155	0	13
Boston	.982	162	4358	1647	109	6114	120	0	26
New York	.981	161	4273	1487	109	5869	132	0	13
Tampa Bay	.981	161	4294	1814	118	6226	169	0	14
Baltimore	.981	162	4300	1578	116	5994	151	1	6
Anaheim	.978	162	4344	1746	134	6224	182	0	6
Chicago	.978	162	4351	1686	133	6170	190	0	13
Oakland	.978	161	4306	1726	134	6166	164	1	8
Texas	.978	162	4287	1594	135	6016	162	0	8
Totals	.982	1133	60423	23282	1568	85273	2280	2	150

PINCH HITTING

Team	BA	AB	R	H	2B	3B	HR	RBI	BB	SO	SLG
Texas	.340	103	13	35	8	2	4	22	16	16	.573
Toronto	.333	51	6	17	3	0	0	8	6	7	.392
Detroit	.299	107	15	32	3	1	3	19	14	22	.430
Tampa Bay	.265	98	8	26	1	1	3	18	11	19	.388
Boston	.256	133	10	34	4	0	3	19	20	32	.353
Minnesota	.253	146	14	37	6	1	1	25	27	39	.329
Kansas City	.250	120	13	30	0	0	1	18	11	26	.275
New York	.237	76	10	18	2	0	4	15	7	23	.421
Anaheim	.232	82	12	19	3	0	2	11	22	19	.341
Cleveland	.231	65	5	15	3	0	1	5	6	17	.323
Baltimore	.213	61	5	13	6	0	1	9	10	17	.361
Oakland	.212	137	14	29	3	0	2	20	21	41	.277
Seattle	.202	94	10	19	3	1	0	12	11	26	.255
Chicago	.192	73	7	14	1	1	3	16	9	19	.356
Totals	.251	1346	142	338	46	7	28	217	191	323	.358

DESIGNATED HITTING

Team	Avg.	AB	R	H	2B	3B	HR	RBI	BB	SO	Slg.
Seattle	.324	577	110	187	32	0	38	149	101	101	.577
Chicago	.296	581	99	172	43	0	32	117	104	101	.535
Detroit	.293	598	89	175	34	5	16	91	72	87	.446
Texas	.288	607	92	175	33	2	21	88	64	86	.453
Toronto	.285	606	92	173	33	1	39	120	38	93	.536
Kansas City	.283	600	91	170	35	0	19	101	58	93	.437
Anaheim	.275	579	93	159	27	0	26	81	86	96	.456
New York	.274	558	88	153	23	3	22	71	79	132	.444
Minnesota	.269	588	79	158	35	0	13	85	58	116	.395
Cleveland	.266	579	103	154	30	0	43	117	88	153	.541
Baltimore	.261	586	71	153	32	2	14	72	63	101	.394
Tampa Bay	.260	565	86	147	36	0	25	89	89	145	.457
Boston	.242	591	72	143	28	1	29	94	64	151	.440
Oakland	.242	563	95	136	23	3	16	67	103	153	.378
Totals	.276	8178	1260	2255	444	17	353	1342	1067	1608	.464

NATIONAL LEAGUE

BATTING

Team	Avg.	G	PA	AB	R	H	TB	2B	3B	HR	RBI	SH	SF	HP	BB	IBB	SO	SB	CS	GIDP	LOB	SHO	SLG	OBP
Colorado	.294	162	6453	5660	968	1664	2573	320	53	161	905	75	75	42	601	64	907	131	61	126	1198	8	.455	.362
San Francisco	.278	162	6418	5519	925	1535	2605	304	44	226	889	73	66	51	709	60	1032	79	39	131	1213	5	.472	.362
Houston	.278	162	6444	5570	938	1547	2655	289	36	249	900	57	61	83	673	57	1129	114	52	154	1171	3	.477	.361
Cincinnati	.274	163	6372	5635	825	1545	2519	302	36	200	794	56	58	64	559	60	995	100	38	137	1189	0	.447	.343
Atlanta	.271	162	6275	5489	810	1490	2353	274	26	179	758	87	45	59	595	38	1010	148	56	127	1192	7	.429	.346
St. Louis	.270	162	6369	5478	887	1481	2495	259	25	235	841	79	53	84	675	33	1253	87	51	116	1214	5	.455	.356
Pittsburgh	.267	162	6369	5643	793	1506	2392	320	31	168	749	59	37	66	564	41	1032	86	40	133	1202	7	.424	.339
Montreal	.266	162	6152	5535	738	1475	2389	310	35	178	705	78	34	29	476	53	1048	58	48	111	1100	9	.432	.326
Arizona	.265	162	6240	5527	792	1466	2373	282	44	179	756	61	58	59	535	37	975	97	44	114	1128	7	.429	.333
New York	.263	162	6327	5486	807	1445	2360	281	20	198	761	70	51	45	675	42	1037	66	46	122	1214	9	.430	.346
Florida	.262	161	6202	5509	731	1441	2253	274	29	160	691	42	51	60	540	39	1184	168	55	100	1168	8	.409	.331
Los Angeles	.257	162	6312	5481	798	1408	2362	265	28	211	756	66	46	51	668	42	1083	95	42	129	1188	11	.431	.341
Chicago	.256	162	6397	5577	764	1426	2293	272	23	183	722	89	45	54	632	50	1120	93	37	114	1215	8	.411	.335
San Diego	.254	162	6290	5560	752	1413	2237	279	37	157	714	39	43	46	602	50	1177	131	53	123	1155	7	.402	.330
Philadelphia	.251	162	6273	5511	708	1386	2202	304	40	144	668	70	37	44	611	40	1117	102	30	115	1209	8	.400	.329
Milwaukee	.246	163	6354	5563	740	1366	2244	297	25	177	708	61	49	61	620	47	1245	72	44	126	1183	7	.403	.325
Totals	.266	1297	101247	88743	12976	23594	38305	4632	532	3005	12317	1062	809	898	9735	753	17344	1627	736	1978	18939	109	.432	.342

PITCHING

Team	W	L	Pct.	ERA	G	ShO	Rel.	Sv.	IP	H	TBF	R	ER	HR	SH	SF	HB	BB	IBB	SO	WP	Bk.
Atlanta	95	67	.586	4.05	162	9	376	53	1440.1	1428	6165	714	648	165	64	37	37	484	52	1093	23	6
Los Angeles	86	76	.531	4.10	162	11	371	36	1445.0	1379	6249	729	659	176	68	30	75	600	22	1154	60	6
New York	94	68	.580	4.16	162	10	411	49	1450.0	1398	6276	738	670	164	56	46	60	574	42	1164	34	7
San Francisco	97	65	.599	4.21	162	15	384	47	1444.1	1452	6270	747	675	151	85	63	41	623	26	1076	43	4
Cincinnati	85	77	.525	4.33	163	7	387	42	1456.1	1446	6362	765	700	190	68	48	43	659	53	1015	96	5
Arizona	85	77	.525	4.35	162	8	390	38	1443.2	1441	6158	754	698	190	72	45	42	500	53	1220	30	10
St. Louis	95	67	.586	4.38	162	7	386	37	1433.2	1403	6200	771	698	196	69	52	62	606	28	1100	49	9
San Diego	76	86	.469	4.52	162	5	443	46	1459.1	1443	6414	815	733	191	59	41	68	649	50	1071	66	7
Florida	79	82	.491	4.59	161	4	429	48	1429.2	1477	6307	797	729	169	68	59	43	650	56	1051	49	10
Milwaukee	73	89	.451	4.63	163	7	433	29	1466.1	1501	6497	826	755	174	67	52	65	728	87	967	60	6
Philadelphia	65	97	.401	4.77	162	6	414	34	1438.2	1458	6314	830	763	201	74	53	42	640	32	1123	54	3
Pittbsurgh	69	93	.426	4.94	162	7	466	27	1449.0	1554	6514	888	795	163	70	55	60	711	61	1070	67	6
Montreal	67	95	.414	5.13	162	7	452	39	1424.2	1575	6340	902	812	181	66	58	60	579	40	1011	55	7
Chicago	65	97	.401	5.25	162	5	421	39	1454.2	1505	6451	904	849	231	62	54	62	658	45	1143	45	4
Colorado	82	80	.506	5.26	162	2	479	33	1430.0	1568	6340	897	835	221	53	52	72	588	72	1001	40	5
Houston	72	90	.444	5.42	162	2	410	30	1437.2	1596	6455	944	865	234	60	64	60	598	25	1064	55	3
Totals	1285	1306	.496	4.63	1297	112	6652	627	23103.1	23624	101312	13021	11884	2997	1061	809	892	9847	744	17323	826	98

FIELDING

Team	PCT	G	PO	A	E	TC	DP	TP	PB
San Francisco	.985	162	4333	1644	93	6070	173	0	15
Colorado	.985	162	4290	1727	94	6111	176	0	15
Chicago	.983	162	4364	1574	100	6038	139	0	6
Philadelphia	.983	162	4316	1491	100	5907	136	0	4
Arizona	.982	162	4331	1541	107	5979	138	1	4
Cincinnati	.982	163	4369	1639	111	6119	156	0	12
St. Louis	.981	162	4301	1524	111	5936	148	0	8
Milwaukee	.981	163	4399	1747	118	6264	187	0	12
New York	.980	162	4350	1582	118	6050	121	0	8
Florida	.980	161	4289	1710	125	6124	144	0	12
Atlanta	.979	162	4321	1733	129	6183	138	1	9
Pittsburgh	.979	162	4347	1828	132	6307	169	0	12
Montreal	.978	162	4274	1703	132	6109	151	1	19
Los Angeles	.978	162	4335	1717	135	6187	151	0	15
Houston	.978	162	4313	1561	133	6007	149	0	6
San Diego	.977	162	4378	1670	141	6189	155	0	13
Totals	.981	1297	69310	26391	1879	97580	2431	3	170

PINCH HITTING

Team	BA	AB	R	H	2B	3B	HR	RBI	BB	SO	SLG
Cincinnati	.258	233	24	60	10	0	6	42	23	51	.378
Pittsburgh	.246	211	29	52	14	1	7	34	21	54	.422
Colorado	.246	248	35	61	7	2	5	36	28	54	.351
Montreal	.246	179	21	44	8	1	3	27	24	34	.352
New York	.245	249	32	61	11	1	7	37	36	68	.382
Atlanta	.236	216	19	51	10	1	3	30	24	48	.333
San Francisco	.235	196	25	46	10	0	7	48	30	41	.393
Arizona	.234	214	22	50	8	0	2	20	30	44	.299
Los Angeles	.233	206	27	48	5	0	12	37	32	56	.432
Florida	.230	217	19	50	13	0	5	23	31	57	.359
Milwaukee	.224	232	25	52	12	0	3	31	38	64	.315
San Diego	.224	232	23	52	12	0	7	43	36	65	.366
Philadelphia	.199	231	22	46	5	2	2	19	37	63	.264
St. Louis	.199	206	24	41	6	1	9	36	24	67	.369
Chicago	.188	234	32	44	3	1	8	38	27	68	.312
Houston	.184	244	20	45	10	2	3	20	22	67	.279
Totals	.226	3548	399	803	144	12	89	521	463	901	.349

DESIGNATED HITTING

Team	Avg.	AB	R	H	2B	3B	HR	RBI	BB	SO	Slg.
Arizona	.429	28	6	12	0	0	1	2	0	7	.536
St. Louis	.400	35	5	14	3	0	3	12	3	7	.743
Milwaukee	.364	33	4	12	1	0	1	7	5	8	.485
Pittsburgh	.333	27	2	9	0	0	1	3	2	7	.444
New York	.306	36	7	11	2	0	2	7	4	8	.528
San Diego	.303	33	4	10	1	0	0	2	8	3	.333
Florida	.300	30	7	9	2	1	1	8	2	1	.533
Montreal	.286	35	3	10	0	0	0	3	4	5	.286
Cincinnati	.280	25	4	7	2	0	2	4	1	2	.600
Atlanta	.278	36	5	10	2	0	0	1	3	8	.333
San Francisco	.269	26	5	7	2	0	1	2	1	3	.462
Chicago	.262	42	3	11	1	0	2	6	0	6	.429
Houston	.261	23	2	6	1	0	1	5	3	4	.435
Los Angeles	.233	30	4	7	2	0	0	3	10	6	.300
Philadelphia	.125	32	2	4	0	0	0	1	6	9	.125
Colorado	.105	19	1	2	0	0	0	0	5	7	.105
Totals	.288	490	64	141	19	1	15	66	57	91	.422

TRANSACTIONS

JANUARY 1, 2000–DECEMBER 31, 2000

January 3

Orioles organization signed P Jose Mercedes.
Astros organization signed P Travis Driskill, P Rick Huisman, P Brad Kaufman, P Rusty Meacham, P Joe Slusarski, P Bryan Wolff, P Eric Plantenberg and OF Marc Sagmoen.
Mets released OF Bobby Bonilla.

January 4

Twins organization signed C Marcus Jensen.

January 5

Angels organization signed P Greg Cadaret.
Astros organization signed C Raul Chavez, 1B Mike Robertson and P Don Wengert.
Dodgers signed P Gregg Olson.
Mets organization signed IF Domingo Cedeno.

January 6

Dodgers traded OF Terry Jones to Yankees for a player to be named.
Rangers organization signed IF Jon Shave.
Astros organization signed P Dwight Gooden.

January 7

Angels signed 2B Scott Spiezio, 2B Pat Kelly and 2B Jason Bates.
Devil Rays signed P Juan Guzman and P Norm Chartlon.
Blue Jays signed P Pedro Borbon.
Braves organization signed P Bobby St. Pierre.
Cubs signed P Brian Williams.
Dodgers signed OF-IF F.P. Santangelo.
Cardinals signed P Andy Benes.

January 8

Indians organization signed P Chris Haney.

January 10

Indians organization signed C Matt Nokes.
Tigers organization signed OF Billy McMillon.
Mariners signed P Aaron Sele.
Rangers organization signed OF Jason McDonald and IF Luis Ortiz.
Giants signed P John Johnstone.

January 11

Padres organization signed P Nobuaki Yoshida.

January 12

Royals organization signed C Jorge Fabregas.
Rangers signed P Darren Oliver.
White Sox traded P Jaime Navarro and P John Snyder to Brewers for P Cal Eldred and IF Jose Valentin.

January 13

White Sox organization signed IF Esteban Beltre, OF Yamil Benitez, OF Steve Gibralter and P Kelly Wunsch.
Indians organization signed OF Lance Johnson and C Jesse Levis.
Devil Rays signed P Steve Trachsel.

January 14

Royals signed P Ricky Bottalico.
Twins organization signed P Bobby Ayala.
Devil Rays organization signed IF Dave Hollins, C John Marzano and 1B-OF Ryan Jackson.
Diamondbacks organization signed P Mike Morgan.
Cubs organization signed IF Jeff Huson.
Brewers traded OF Alex Ochoa to Reds for OF Mark Sweeney and a player to be named; Reds sent P Gene Altman to complete deal (May 15).
Mets traded P Masato Yoshii to Rockies for P Bobby M. Jones and P Lariel Gonzalez.

January 17

Devil Rays organization signed P John Burkett.
Brewers signed C Tyler Houston.
Padres organization signed IF Jed Hansen.

January 19

Angels organization signed IF Archi Cianfrocco and P Brett Hinchliffe.
Red Sox organization signed OF Marty Cordova.
Indians organization signed P Bobby Witt.
Mariners signed C Joe Oliver.
Cubs signed 3B-OF Willie Greene.
Mets organization signed 3B Charlie Hayes.
Pirates organization signed IF Luis Sojo.
Cardinals organization signed P Jim Dougherty, P John Hudek, C Steve Bieser, C Henry Mercedes, C Marc Ronan, IF Casey Candaele, IF Luis Garcia and OF Ernie Young.

January 20

Devil Rays organization signed P Terry Mathews.
Braves organization signed OF Trenidad Hubbard.
Reds organization signed OF Deion Sanders, P Mark Portugal and P Johnny Ruffin.
Dodgers organization signed C Chad Kreuter.
Mets organization signed OF Curtis Pride.

January 21

Tigers signed P Hideo Nomo.
Mets traded IF Luis Lopez to Brewers for P Bill Pulsipher and signed P Rich Rodriguez.
Pirates organization signed P John Smiley.

January 24

Angels organization signed P Tom Candiotti and P Steve Mintz.
Rockies signed P Billy Taylor.
Giants organization signed 3B Russ Davis.

January 25

Astros organization signed C Frank Charles and C Pedro Lopez.

January 26

Angels organization signed P Kent Mercker and P Eric Weaver.
Indians organization signed P Alan Newman, P Curtis King and P Steve Falteisek.
Royals organization signed 1B Paul Sorrento.
Mets organization signed IF Kurt Abbott.

January 27

Indians organization signed P Scott Sanders.
Devil Rays organization signed C Pat Borders.
Expos organization signed 2B Mickey Morandini.

January 28

Orioles signed P Pat Rapp.
Devil Rays signed P Steve Trachsel.
Braves organization signed OF Bobby Bonilla.
Reds organization signed P Mark Wohlers.
Padres organization signed OF Danny Tartabull.

January 31

Angels organization signed IF Carlos Garcia.
Twins organization signed OF Butch Huskey.
Yankees organization signed P Mike Grace.

February 1

Angels organization signed IF Benji Gil.
Yankees organization signed OF Tim Raines.
Devil Rays organization signed P Doug Creek.
Reds organization signed P Javier Martinez and P Willis Roberts.
Astros organization signed P Mike Maddux and P Kip Gross.
Dodgers organization signed OF Geronimo Berroa.

February 2

Red Sox organization signed P Julio Santana.
Yankees organization signed IF Rafael Bournigal.
Diamondbacks released P Bobby Chouinard.
Rockies signed OF Darren Bragg.
Phillies organization signed P Steve Sparks.

February 3

Royals organization signed P Edwin Hurtado.
Cardinals organization signed IF-OF Shawon Dunston, OF Brian McRae, 1B Eduardo Perez and C Rick Wilkins.
Padres organization signed 3B Ed Sprague.

February 4

Orioles organization signed P Tim Worrell and P Rick Krivda.
Rangers organization signed OF Scarborough Green.
Braves organization signed P Paul Assenmacher.
Expos organization signed C Charlie O'Brien.
Mets organization signed P Dennis Springer.

February 7

Mets claimed IF David Lamb on waivers from Devil Rays.

February 8

Indians organization signed P Chris Nichting, P Marc Pisciotta, P Mike Bovee, C Matt Curtis, C Cesar Devarez, IF Kelcey Mucker, IF Jeff Patzke and OF Andy Tomberlin.
Yankees organization signed OF Luke Wilcox.
Cubs organization signed P Greg McMichael.

February 9

Pirates organization signed P Mark Leiter, P Danilo Leon, P Josias Manzanillo and P Dave Stevens.

February 10

Mariners traded OF Ken Griffey Jr. to Reds for P Brett Tomko, OF Mike Cameron, IF Antonio Perez and P Jake Meyer.

February 14

Cubs released P Andy Larkin.

February 15

Reds organization signed P Osvaldo Fernandez.

February 16

Red Sox organization signed P Hipolito Pichardo.
Athletics organization signed P Doug Johns.
Blue Jays organization signed P Eric Gunderson.
Expos organization signed OF Patrick Lennon and P Felipe Lira.

February 18

Indians organization signed OF Mark Whiten.
Royals traded OF Jeremy Giambi to Athletics for P Brett Laxton.
Diamondbacks released P Al Garcia.

February 19

Diamondbacks organization signed OF Turner Ward and P Jim Corsi.
Brewers organization signed P Jim Bruske.

February 22

Braves organization signed P Steve Avery.
Mets organization signed 1B Mark Johnson.

February 23

Pirates traded OF Al Martin and cash to Padres for OF-1B John Vander Wal, P Geraldo Padua and P James Sak.

February 24

Devil Rays organization signed IF Carlos Baerga.
Reds organization signed C Benito Santiago.
Rockies announced retirement of P Roger Pavlik.

March 1

Pirates released P Pep Harris.

March 6

Tigers released OF Marc Newfield.

March 7

Tigers traded C Gregg Zaun to Royals for a player to be named or cash.
Yankees released P Jeff Juden.
Devil Rays released OF Danny Clyburn.

March 9

Mets released IF Shane Halter.

March 10

Phillies traded OF Wendell Magee Jr. to Tigers for P Bobby Sismondo.

March 11

Tigers released P Mike Oquist.
Royals released P Carl Dale.

March 13

Indians released P Brian Barber.
Braves traded IF-OF Freddy Garcia to Reds for P Dennis Russo.
Mets organization signed P Rene Arocha.

March 15

Red Sox released OF Jermaine Allensworth.
Tigers released P Ramon Tatis.

March 16

Angels released P Greg Cadaret.
Rangers traded IF Lee Stevens to Expos, Expos traded 1B Brad Fullmer to Blue Jays, Blue Jays traded 1B David Segui and cash to Rangers.

March 17

Angels released IF Archi Cianfrocco and IF Carlos Garcia.
Diamondbacks organization signed IF Craig Counsell.
Mets organization signed OF Timoniel Perez.

March 18

Indians announced retirement of P Mark Langston and released OF Ruben Sierra.
Mets traded P Jesse Orosco to Cardinals for IF-OF Joe McEwing.

March 20

Braves released P Everett Stull.
Mets released IF Charlie Hayes.

March 21

Yankees released P Mike Grace.
Mariners traded C Carlos Maldonado to Astros for IF Carlos Hernandez.

March 22

Angels announced retirement of IF Pat Kelly and released IF Jason Bates.
Brewers organization signed IF Charlie Hayes.
Mets traded IF Jersen Perez to Blue Jays to keep the rights to P Jim Mann.

March 23

Angels traded OF Jim Edmonds to Cardinals for P Kent Bottenfield and 2B Adam Kennedy.
Yankees announced retirement of OF Tim Raines and traded IF Juan Melo to Giants for IF Wilson Delgado.
Cubs released P Greg McMichael.
Rockies released P Billy Taylor.
Pirates released P Mark Leiter.
Cubs traded P Rodney Myers to Padres for OF Gary Matthews Jr.

March 24

Athletics traded 1B-OF David McCarty to Royals for cash.
Yankees organization signed IF Carlos Garcia.
Marlins claimed Derrick Gibson on waivers from Rockies.
Rockies released C Raul Casanova.

March 25

Red Sox released OF Marty Cordova.
Yankees released IF Rafael Bournigal.
Braves organization signed P Greg McMichael.

March 27

Indians traded SS Jose Olmeda to White Sox for future considerations and traded P Steve Falteisek to Marlins for SS Victor Rodriguez.
Twins released P Bobby Ayala.
Mariners released OF Brian L. Hunter.
Blue Jays organization signed OF Marty Cordova.
Rockies released IF David Howard.

March 28

Indians organization signed P Clint Sodowsky, P Joe Roa and P Brian Looney.
Royals released P Ken Ryan and P Billy Brewer.
Brewers released C Bobby Hughes and C Brian Banks.
Expos traded IF Mickey Morandini to the Phillies for cash.
Mets claimed P Nerio Rodriguez on waivers from Blue Jays.

March 29

Angels released C-DH Todd Greene.
White Sox released P Carlos Castillo.
Indians released P Scott Sanders.
Yankees released catcher Tom Pagnozzi.
Devil Rays released C Mike Figga, P John Burkett and P Chad Ogea and signed IF Rafael Bournigal.
Blue Jays claimed P Mike Kusiewicz on waivers from Minnesota.
Diamondbacks released P Brad Clontz.
Braves released 1B Randall Simon and P Rafael Medina and signed P John Burkett.
Reds released P Mark Portugal.
Rockies traded OF Edgard Clemente to Anaheim for OF Norm Hutchins and C Jason Dewey.
Astros traded P Trever Miller to Phillies for P Yorkis Perez.
Brewers claimed P Jason Boyd on waivers from Pirates.
Pirates released P Pete Schourek.
Giants released IF Jay Canizaro.

March 30

Indians released OF Lance Johnson.
Royals traded C Sal Fasano to Athletics for cash.
Mariners organization signed C Alberto Hernandez.
Devil Rays organization signed P Julio Cesar Villalon.
Braves organization signed OF Nataniel Reinoso.
Rockies signed OF Brian L. Hunter.
Cardinals released OF Brian McRae.

March 31

Yankees organization signed OF Lance Johnson.
Mariners claimed OF Anthony Sanders on waivers from Blue Jays.
Braves released SS Ozzie Guillen and P Paul Assenmacher.

April 1

Angels released P Tom Candiotti.
Indians organization signed P Scott Sanders.
Yankees released OF Ryan Thompson and IF Jason Bates.
Dodgers traded IF Juan Castro to Reds for a player to be named.
Expos claimed OF Terry Jones on waivers from Yankees.

April 3

Red Sox signed P Pete Schourek.
Indians organization signed C Bobby Hughes.
Royals organization signed P Paul Spoljaric and 3B Kevin Orie.
Diamondbacks organization signed P Jim Corsi.

April 4

Cubs organization signed P Bobby Ayala.

April 5

Royals claimed IF Luis Ordaz on waivers from Diamondbacks.
Devil Rays signed SS Ozzie Guillen.
Rangers organization signed OF Monty Lee and IF Matt Halloran.

April 6

Rangers organization signed P Terry Mathews.
Mets claimed P Radhames Dykhoff on waivers from Orioles.
Pirates organization signed P Brad Clontz.
Padres signed 1B Young-Jin Jung.

April 7

Athletics organization signed OF Bo Porter.
Reds traded P Gabe White to Rockies for P Manny Aybar.

April 8

Reds organization signed P Norm Charlton.

April 11

Astros traded C Paul Bako to Marlins for cash and a player to be named.
Mets organization signed IF Rafael Bournigal.

April 12

Indians organization signed P Chad Ogea.
Mets claimed P Anthony Shumaker on waivers from Phillies.

April 13

Astros traded P Dwight Gooden to Devil Rays for cash.
Cubs traded C Pat Cline to Brewers for a player to be named.

April 14

Red Sox announced retirement of 3B Gary Gaetti.

April 19

Red Sox organization signed IF Freddy Garcia. Diamondbacks traded OF Garry Maddox Jr. to Red Sox for IF Javier Fuentes.

April 20

Indians traded OF Dan McKinley to Expos for OF Scott Hunter.

April 21

White Sox claimed 3B Herbert Perry on waivers from Devil Rays.
Mariners released OF Shane Monahan.
Phillies claimed OF Brian R. Hunter on waivers from Braves.

April 25

Red Sox organization signed P Mel Rojas and C Mike Figga.
Expos traded P Miguel Batista to Royals for P Brad Rigby.

April 26

Orioles claimed IF Mark Lewis on waivers from Reds.

April 27

Mets traded OF Curtis Pride to Red Sox for a player to be named.

April 28

Angels claimed OF Scott Morgan on waivers from Indians.
Reds released P Norm Charlton.
Brewers organization signed C Mark Dalesandro.

April 29

Indians signed IF-OF Jeff Manto.
Yankees signed OF-DH Felix Jose.
Brewers released P Jamie Navarro.

May 3

Orioles released P Tim Worrell.
Rangers organization signed IF Scott Livingstone.

May 4

Cardinals signed P Darren Holmes.

May 8

Cubs organization signed P Tim Worrell and released RHP Bobby Ayala.

May 10

Tigers signed OF Rich Becker.
Phillies claimed C Cesar King on waivers from Rangers.

May 12

Cubs traded P Mark Guthrie and cash to Devil Rays for 1B-OF Dave Martinez.

May 13

Mets released OF Rickey Henderson.

May 17

Indians signed P Jason Davis.
Tigers released P Jim Poole.
Mariners signed OF Rickey Henderson.

May 18

Indians released P Bobby Witt.

May 19

Braves organization signed C Brayan Pena.
Dodgers claimed P Trever Miller on waivers from Phillies.

May 22

Mets traded P Richie Lewis to Indians for a player to be named.
Cubs released P Andrew Lorraine.
Padres organization signed P Carlos Reyes.

May 24

Mets organization signed IF Jed Hansen.
Phillies signed OF Lawrence Alexander.

May 25

Devil Rays released SS Kevin Stocker and P Dwight Gooden.

May 26

Cubs released P Brian Williams.

May 27

Astros traded IF Russ Johnson to Devil Rays for P Marc Valdes.

May 30

Angels signed IF Kevin Stocker.

May 31

Angels released P Cody Salter.
White Sox traded P Tanyon Sturtze to Devil Rays for IF Tony Graffanino.
Diamondbacks released P Doug Kohl and OF Justin Graham.

June 1

Blue Jays signed P Brandon Lyon.

June 2

Diamondbacks traded OF-IF Lenny Harris to Mets for P Bill Pulsipher.

June 5

Indians signed P Brian Williams and P Tyler Green.

June 7

White Sox signed P Kevin Zaug.
Expos released P Jim Poole.

June 8

Tigers sold P Masao Kida to Orix of the Japanese Pacific League.
Mets sold OF Jon Nunnally to Orix of the Japanese Pacific League.

June 9

Indians organization signed P Jim Poole.
Rangers traded P Chuck Smith to Marlins, Marlins traded OF Brant Brown to Cubs, Cubs traded OF Dave Martinez to Texas.
Diamondbacks traded IF Andy Fox to Marlins for OF Danny Bautista.

June 10

Yankees organization signed P Dwight Gooden.

June 12

Tigers traded OF Karim Garcia to Orioles for future considerations.

June 13

Orioles traded P Al Reyes to Dodgers for P Alan Mills and cash.

June 14

Rangers claimed P Scott Randall on waivers from Twins.

June 15

Rockies released P Jaime Navarro.
Indians signed P Jaime Navarro.

June 16

Rangers claimed P Jared Camp on waivers from Indians.

June 17

Marlins organization signed pitcher Scott Sanders.
Dodgers traded C Adam Melhuse to Rockies for a player to be named.

June 19

Blue Jays organization signed P Mark Eichhorn.

June 20

Twins released P Sean Bergman.
Yankees traded DH Jim Leyritz to Dodgers for IF Jose Vizcaino and cash.

June 22

Expos released C Charlie O'Brien.

June 23

Mariners claimed P Mark Watson on waivers from Indians.

June 27

Dodgers released P Orel Hershiser.

June 28

Cardinals traded P Darren Holmes to Orioles for future considerations.
Rockies traded P Ed Vosberg to Phillies for a player to be named.

June 29

Yankees traded OF Ricky Ledee and two players to be named to Indians for OF David Justice; Yankees sent P Jake Westbrook and Zach Day to complete deal (July 25).

June 30

Padres traded 3B Ed Sprague to Red Sox for P Dennis Tankersley and IF Cesar Saba.

July 3

Rangers released P Mark Clark.

July 4

Red Sox signed OF Bernard Gilkey.

July 5

Braves signed P Scott Kamieniecki.
Astros released P Mike Maddux.

July 7

Reds claimed P Jason Sekany on waivers from Red Sox.

July 12

Reds traded P Denny Neagle and OF Mike Frank to Yankees for 3B Drew Henson, OF Jackson Melian, P Brian Reith and P Ed Yarnall.
Mets organization signed P Willie Banks and P Oscar Henriquez.
Phillies traded P Andy Ashby to Braves for P Bruce Chen and P Jim Osting.
Padres claimed P Todd Erdos on waivers from Yankees.

July 13

Orioles organization signed 3B Dave Hollins.

July 15

Rockies traded 1B Todd Sears and cash to Twins for 2B Todd Walker and OF Butch Huskey.

July 17

Tigers traded IF Gabe Alvarez to Padres for 1B-OF Dusty Allen.
Rangers released P Jared Camp.

July 18

Reds traded 1B Hal Morris to Tigers for cash.

July 19

Orioles released P Darren Holmes.
Royals claimed P Andy Larkin on waivers from Reds.
Rangers traded P Esteban Loaiza to Blue Jays for P Darwin Dubillan and IF Mike Young.
Brewers claimed OF Angel Echevarria on waivers from Rockies.

July 21

Braves claimed C Paul Bako on waivers from Marlins.
Cubs traded OF Glenallen Hill to Yankees for P Ben Ford and P Ozwaldo Mairena.

July 22

Astros released P Yorkis Perez.

July 25

Blue Jays traded C Kevin Brown to Brewers for OF Alvin Morrow.

July 26

Phillies traded P Curt Schilling to Diamondbacks for 1B-OF Travis Lee, P Omar Daal, P Vicente Padilla and P Nelson Figueroa.
Reds traded P Manny Aybar to Marlins for P Jorge Cordova.
Rockies released OF Darren Bragg.
Cubs traded P Ismael Valdes to Dodgers for P Jamie Arnold, OF Jorge Piedra and cash considerations.
Phillies traded OF Rob Ducey to Blue Jays for a player to be named; Blue Jays sent P John Sneed to complete deal (July 31).

July 27

Rockies traded P Rolando Arrojo, P Rick Croushore, IF Mike Lansing and cash to Red Sox for P Brian Rose, P John Wasdin, P Jeff Taglienti and IF Jeff Frye.

July 28

Angels traded P Brett Hinchcliffe and IF Keith Luuloa to Cubs for OF Chris Hatcher, P Mike Heathcott and IF Brett King.
Brewers traded P Bob Wickman, P Steve Woodard and P Jason Bere to Indians for OF Richie Sexson, P Paul Rigdon, P Kane Davis and a player to be named; Indians sent 2B Marcos Scutaro to complete deal (August 30).
Indians traded OF Alex Ramirez and IF Enrique Wilson to Pirates for OF Wil Cordero.
Devil Rays traded P Jim Mecir and P Todd Belitz to Athletics for P Jesus Colome and a player to be named later.
Rangers traded 1B David Segui to Indians for OF Ricky Ledee.
Orioles traded SS Mike Bordick to Mets for IF Melvin Mora, IF Mike Kinkade, P Lesli Brea and P Pat Gorman.
Mets traded OF Jason Tyner and P Paul Wilson to Devil Rays for P Rick White and OF Bubba Trammell.

July 29

Orioles traded C Charles Johnson and DH Harold Baines to White Sox for C Brook Fordyce, P Miguel Felix, P Juan Figueroa and P Jason Lakman.
Cardinals traded 1B Chris Richard and P Mark Nussbeck to Orioles for P Mike Timlin and cash.
Braves signed P Stan Belinda.
Astros traded P Doug Henry to Giants for P Scott Linebrink.
Phillies traded OF Ron Gant to Angels for P Kent Bottenfield.
Pirates traded P Jason Christiansen to Cardinals for SS Jack Wilson.

July 31

Orioles traded OF B.J. Surhoff and P Gabe Molina to Braves for OF Trenidad Hubbard, C Fernando Lunar and P Luis Rivera.
Cardinals traded 3B Jose Leon to Orioles for 1B Will Clark and cash.
Tigers released OF Luis Polonia.
Royals traded P Jay Witasick to Padres for P Brian Meadows.
Twins traded 1B Mario Valdez to Athletics for C Danny Ardoin.
Mariners traded 1B-OF John Mabry and P Tom Davey to Padres for OF Al Martin.
Devil Rays traded P Steve Trachsel and P Mark Guthrie to Blue Jays for 2B Brent Abernathy and a player to be named.
Cubs traded OF Henry Rodriguez to Marlins for 1B-OF Ross Gload and P Dave Noyce. Montreal traded OF Rondell White to Cubs for P Scott Downs.
Dodgers traded OF Todd Hollandsworth, OF Kevin Gibbs and P Randey Dorame to Rockies for OF Tom Goodwin and cash.
Orioles traded P Juan Aracena to Mets for P Anthony Shumaker.
Cardinals traded P Heathcliff Slocumb and OF Ben Johnson to Padres for C Carlos Hernandez and IF-OF Nate Tebbs.

August 3

Red Sox claimed 1B Rico Brogna on waivers from Phillies.
Yankees signed OF Luis Polonia.

August 4

Athletics signed DH-1B Mike Stanley.
Rangers traded OF Dave Martinez to Blue Jays for a player to be named; Blue Jays sent P Pete Munro to complete deal (August 8).
Marlins organization signed P Jack Armstrong.
Phillies traded SS Desi Relaford to Padres for a player to be named; Padres sent IF David Newhan to complete deal (August 7).

August 5

Reds traded P Robert Averette to Rockies for OF Brian L. Hunter.
Phillies traded 2B Mickey Morandini to Blue Jays for a player to be named; Blue Jays sent Rob Ducey to complete deal (August 7).
Pirates traded OF Bruce Aven to Dodgers for a player to be named.

August 7

Angels released pitcher Ken Hill.
Yankees claimed OF-DH Jose Canseco off waivers from Devil Rays.
Pirates traded IF Luis Sojo to Yankees for P Chris Spurling.
Marlins organization signed IF-OF Casey Candaele.
Padres claimed IF David Newhan on waivers.

August 8

Expos traded C Chris Widger to Mariners for a player to be named; Mariners sent to OF Terrmel Sledge to complete deal (September 28).

August 11

Indians organization signed 3B Dave Hollins.
Yankees traded IF Wilson Delgado to Royals for SS Nick Ortiz.

August 16

Angels organization signed P Bryan Ward and claimed 2B David Eckstein on waivers from Red Sox.

August 18

White Sox organization signed P Ken Hill.
Astros released OF Matt Mieske.

August 22

Rockies traded P Scott Karl and cash to Angels for a player to be named.

August 23

Blue Jays claimed P Pat Daneker on waivers from White Sox.

August 24

Indians organization signed IF Sean Berry.
Tigers organization signed C Brad Wise.

August 25

Braves organization signed OF Rich Amaral.

August 30

Angels claimed P Ben Weber on waivers from Giants.
White Sox released P Ken Hill.
Royals released P Jerry Spradlin.
Athletics traded IF Jorge Velandia to Tigers for OF Nelson Cruz.

August 31

Twins traded OF Midre Cummings to Red Sox for IF Hector De Los Santos.
Reds traded OF Dante Bichette to Red Sox for P Chris Reitsma and P John Curtice.
Giants claimed C Scott Servais on waivers from Rockies.

September 8

Indians claimed P Eric Dubose on waivers from Athletics.
Cubs signed P Jerry Spradlin.

September 9

Red Sox traded OF Lew Ford to Twins for P Hector Carrasco.

September 11

Red Sox signed P Steve Ontiveros.
Athletics released IF Joey Espada.

September 20

White Sox traded P Jesus Pena to Red Sox for a player to be named.

September 22

Tigers claimed P Eric DuBose on waivers from Indians.

October 3

Blue Jays claimed P John Sneed on waivers from Phillies.

October 5

Orioles released OF Trenidad Hubbard.
Mets claimed P Jason Middlebrook on waivers from Padres.

October 11

Angels claimed P Mark Lukasiewicz on waivers from Blue Jays.
Indians released P Chris Haney.
Rangers claimed OF Bo Porter on waivers from Athletics.
Pirates released P Brad Clontz.

October 12

Mets claimed SS Desi Relaford on waivers from Padres.
Padres organization signed IF Greg LaRocca, IF John Roskos and IF Joe Vitiello.

October 13

Athletics claimed P Marc Wilkins on waivers from Pirates.
Diamondbacks organization signed P Kennie Steenstra.
Rockies claimed P Jason Green on waivers from Astros.

October 17

Padres claimed OF Mike Colangelo on waivers from Diamondbacks.

October 19

Mariners organization signed P Kenny Rayborn and OF Chad Alexander.

October 24

Tigers organization signed P Sean Runyan.

November 2

Tigers released P Hideo Nomo.
Devil Rays organization signed P Bill Pulsipher, OF Norm Hutchins and P Juan Rosario.
Diamondbacks signed C Ken Huckaby.
Cardinals announced retirement of 1B Will Clark.

November 6

Rangers signed C Mike Hubbard.
Expos organization signed P Scott Stewart.

November 7

Blue Jays traded P Gary Glover to White Sox for P Scott Eyre.
White Sox released IF Craig Wilson.

November 8

Reds traded P Ron Villone to Rockies for two players to be named.

November 10

Devil Rays organization signed 1B-OF Chris Hatcher and 1B Ron Wright.

November 13

Rangers organization signed P Jayson Durocher.
Blue Jays organization signed P Jason Dickson.

November 15

Indians organization signed IF Ralph Milliard and P Dan Smith.
Yankees released OF Ryan Thompson.
Devil Rays organization signed IF Andy Sheets, P Jim Pittsley and C Yohanny Valera.
Diamondbacks signed P Miguel Batista.
Phillies signed P Joel Adamson, IF P.J. Forbes, P Eddie Oropesa, IF Pete Rose Jr., 1B Gene Schall and OF Ken Woods.
Cardinals organization signed IF Lou Lucca, C Mike Stefanski, C Mike Figga and SS Kevin Polkovich.

November 16

Orioles organization signed P Willis Roberts.
Reds traded C Eddie Taubensee to Indians for P Jim Brower and P Robert Purgmire.
Mariners released P Todd Williams and 1B Brian Lesher.
Cubs signed P Julian Tavarez.
Reds traded IF Chris Stynes to Red Sox for OF Michael Coleman and IF Donnie Sadler.

November 17

Angels signed C Jorge Fabregas.
Athletics traded 2B Randy Velarde to Rangers for P Ryan Cullen and P Aaron Harang.
Rangers released OF Scarborough Green.
Expos organization signed P Felipe Lira, P Pat Flury, P Scott Stewart, C Randy Knorr, C Sandy Martinez, 3B Rob Sasser and OF Mark Smith and released P J.D. Smart.
Mets organization signed P Nerio Rodriguez, P Manny Barrios and OF Ray Montgomery.
Phillies signed P Jose Mesa.

November 18

Indians signed OF Ellis Burks.
Mariners signed OF Ichiro Suzuki.
Cubs traded P Tim Worrell to Giants for 3B Bill Mueller.

November 20

Yankees released P Jason Grimsley.
Cubs claimed P Eric Ireland on waivers from Astros.
Athletics traded OF Matt Stairs to Cubs for P Eric Ireland.
Astros signed IF Jose Vizcaino.
Padres organization signed P Bryan Corey, P Matt Miller, P Ron Mahay, OF Ernie Young, IF Keith Luuloa and C Charlie Greene.

November 21

Yankees signed C Joe Oliver and released C Chris Turner.
Marlins organization signed C Matt Treanor, C B.J. Waszgis and P Pat Ahearne.

November 22

Devil Rays organization signed P Sean Bergman, P Dwayne Jacobs, IF Ray Holbert and IF Mike Metcalfe.
Reds traded P Steve Parris to Blue Jays for P Clayton Andrews and P Leo Estrella.
Padres claimed P Jason Middlebrook on waivers from Mets.

November 24

Expos signed P Luis Herrera and P Lenin Aragon.

November 27

Devil Rays released P Jim Morris, P Jeff Sparks, IF Miguel Cairo, OF Quinton McCracken and OF Ozzie Timmons.
Cubs released P Ben Ford and P Jerry Spradlin.
Marlins traded IF Amaury Garcia to White Sox for a player to be named; White Sox sent P Mark Roberts to complete deal (December 11).
Brewers released OF Lyle Mouton.

November 28

Brewers signed P Curtis Leskanic.

November 29

Phillies signed P Rheal Cormier.

November 30

Yankees signed P Mike Mussina.
Phillies organization signed P Brian R. Hunter.

December 1

Reds claimed P Jeff Wallace on waivers from Pirates and released OF Kimera Bartee.
Padres traded P Brandon Kolb to Brewers for SS Santiago Perez and a player to be named or cash and signed P Scott Karl.

December 4

Mariners signed P Jeff Nelson.
Braves claimed P Trey Moore on waivers from Expos.
Rockies signed P Denny Neagle.

December 5

Mets organization signed IF-OF David Howard, P Brett Hinchliffe, P Joe Crawford and SS Kevin Baez.

December 6

Athletics organization signed P Dave Eiland, P Eric Hiljus, P Frank Lankford, P Jon Ratliff, P Steve Schrenk and C Tom Wilson.
Blue Jays organization signed 2B Mickey Morandini.
Diamondbacks signed P Armando Reynoso.
Dodgers signed P Andy Ashby.

December 7

Red Sox signed P Frank Castillo and P Pete Schourek.
White Sox traded P Chad Bradford to Athletics for a player to be named; Athletics sent C Miguel Olivo to complete deal (December 13).
Diamondbacks signed P Jason Jacome and sold the contract of 1B Alex Cabrera to Seibu of the Japanese Pacific League.
Brewers signed OF James Mouton.
Mets organization signed P Scott Forster.

December 8

Rangers signed 1B Andres Galarraga.
Blue Jays signed P Dan Plesac.
Diamondbacks signed 1B Mark Grace.
Cubs signed P Jeff Fassero.
Mets signed OF Bubba Carpenter.
Giants signed OF-IF Shawon Dunston.

December 9

Reds traded SS Wilmy Caceres to Angels for P Seth Etherton.
Rangers signed 3B Ken Caminiti and P Mark Petkovsek.
Braves signed OF Dave Martinez.
Reds signed P Dennys Reyes.
Rockies signed P Mike Hampton and OF Ron Gant.
Marlins traded OF Julio Ramirez to White Sox for OF Jeff Abbott.
Pirates signed P Terry Mulholland and OF Derek Bell.

December 11

Angels signed P Pat Rapp and OF Kimera Bartee.
Orioles traded C Jayson Werth to Blue Jays for P John Bale.
Tigers traded C Brad Ausmus, P Doug Brocail and P Nelson Cruz to Astros for OF Roger Cedeno, C Mitch Meluskey and P Chris Holt.
Royals signed P Doug Henry.
Twins released P Jason Ryan.
Rangers signed SS Alex Rodriguez.
Blue Jays signed IF Jeff Frye.
Mets signed P Kevin Appier, P Steve Trachsel and OF Tsuyoshi Shinjo.
Padres traded P Donne Wall to Mets for OF Bubba Trammell.

December 13

Red Sox signed OF Manny Ramirez.
Blue Jays organization signed P Jaime Navarro, OF Ryan Thompson, C Izzy Molina, IF Aaron Holbert, OF Chris Latham and P Chris Michalak.
Rangers organization signed P Kevin Foster, P Mike Munoz and OF Ruben Sierra.
Braves signed IF Rico Brogna and IF Kurt Abbott.
Cubs signed C Todd Hundley, OF Scarborough Green, C Brian Banks, C Robert Machado, IF Chris Snopek, IF Trace Coquillette, P Rob Stanifer, P Dave Wainhouse and P Brian Barkley.
Padres signed 3B Alex Arias.

December 14

Yankees organization signed P Brian Boehringer.
Mariners claimed IF Mike Caruso on waivers from White Sox.
Rangers traded SS Royce Clayton to White Sox for P Aaron Myette and P Brian Schmack.
Cubs signed P Tom Gordon and P Jason Bere.
Astros signed P Mike Jackson.
Dodgers organization signed P Jim Morris and P Matt Whisenant.
Cardinals traded 3B Fernando Tatis and P Britt Reames to Expos for P Dustin Hermanson and P Steve Kline.

December 15

Red Sox signed P Hideo Nomo.
Rangers traded P Matt Perisho to Tigers for P Kevin Mobley and P Brandon Villafuerte.
Athletics released P Marc Wilkins.
Diamondbacks signed OF Midre Cummings.
Expos organization signed P Bobby Munoz and P Terry Burrows.
Phillies signed P Ricky Bottalico.
Padres organization signed OF-1B Kevin Witt, 2B Adam Riggs and P Jeremy Powell.

December 18

Braves traded 3B Steve Sisco to Orioles for INF Jesse Garcia.
White Sox signed C Sandy Alomar Jr.
Cubs signed P Jason Bere.
Marlins signed C Charles Johnson.
Dodgers organization signed P Eddie Priest, P Todd Rizzo, IF Keith Johnson, OF Jeff Barry.

December 19

Orioles signed P Pat Hentgen.
Twins organization signed C Tom Prince and IF Edwin Diaz.
Mariners organization signed P Norm Charlton.

December 20

Orioles signed SS Mike Bordick.
Red Sox released OF Izzy Alcantara.
Indians organization signed P Scott Aldred, P Eric Gunderson, C Tim Laker, P Tim Kubinski, OF Marty Cordova and OF Scott Krause.
Phillies organization signed P Edwin Hurtado, P Rigo Beltran, IF Kevin Orie, P Eddie Oropesa, C Eric Schreimann, P Clint Sodowsky and OF Turner Ward.

December 21

Orioles signed 1B David Segui.
Expos organization signed OF Tim Raines, OF Curtis Pride and P Bob Scanlan.

December 22

Expos traded P Jorge Julio to Orioles for 3B Ryan Minor.
Indians organization signed OF Karim Garcia.
Mariners signed 2B Bret Boone.
Brewers signed OF Jeffrey Hammonds.
Cardinals signed OF Quinton McCracken.

December 23

Indians organization signed P Tim Byrdak.

ALL-STAR GAME

AT TURNER FIELD, ATLANTA, JULY 11, 2000

AMERICAN LEAGUE 6, NATIONAL LEAGUE 3

Why the American League won: A combination of timely hitting, clutch pitching and poor N.L. defense lifted the Americans to their fourth straight All-Star victory and 10th in 13 games. The A.L., dominating the midsummer classic in the era of power baseball, won without the aid of a home run against eight N.L. pitchers. Much of the damage was perpetrated by Yankees shortstop Derek Jeter, who collected three hits, drove in two runs and scored another en route to MVP honors.

Why the National League lost: The N.L. stars managed nine hits off eight A.L. hurlers, but they couldn't break through in key situations. Defensively, they contributed to their own downfall with two errors and a difficult third inning during which Dodgers righthander Kevin Brown walked three batters. One bright spot for the National Leaguers was the hitting of Atlanta's Jones boys, Chipper and Andruw, who combined for four hits and two RBIs before their home fans at Turner Field.

TURNING POINTS:

1. The Americans broke on top in the third inning when Brown inexplicably lost his control, walking Roberto Alomar, surrendering a single to Jeter and walking Jason Giambi and Carl Everett to force in a run. The damage would have been worse if not for a twisting, back-to-the-infield catch by N.L. center fielder Jim Edmonds on a drive hit by Mike Bordick.

2. After Chipper Jones had hit a pitch by Chicago White Sox righthander James Baldwin over the left-center field fence to tie the game in the bottom of the third, the Americans came right back in the fourth. Jermaine Dye drew a walk off Al Leiter and Travis Fryman singled to center. Shortstop Barry Larkin's error on a Mike Sweeney grounder loaded the bases and set the stage for the opportunistic Jeter. After Alomar had popped out, the Yankee shortstop stepped in against the Mets lefthander and won the New York matchup by driving a two-run single to center.

3. Leading only 3-2 after a fifth-inning RBI single by Andruw Jones, the A.L. put the game away with three runs in the ninth. Singles by Ray Durham, Nomar Garciaparra and Matt Lawton produced one run and a sacrifice fly by Chicago's Magglio Ordonez netted another. The finale crossed the plate on second baseman Jose Vidro's error.

WORTH NOTING:

The game opened without seven of the players voted to starting lineups by the fans. Missing from the lineups were such names as Mark McGwire, Ken Griffey Jr., Barry Bonds and Mike Piazza. Pitchers Pedro Martinez and Greg Maddux also were unavailable because of injury. ... Jeter's All-Star MVP award was the first ever earned by a New York Yankee. The talented shortstop had struck out in his previous two All-Star at-bats. ... With the victory, the A.L. cut its overall deficit to 40-30-1. ... Yankee boss Joe Torre joined Tony La Russa and Tommy Lasorda as the only managers to win their first three All-Star Games. ... Chipper Jones became the 13th player to hit an All-Star home run in his home ballpark.

WORTH QUOTING:

Jeter, when informed he was the first Yankee ever to win an All-Star MVP: "You have to play for a lot of years before you can be considered a Yankee great. I've only played four years. This is my fifth. Hopefully, I can play for a few more years, then start that debate."... Chipper Jones, commenting on the performance of Jeter, who had worn out the Braves in the 1996 and 1999 World Series: "That really is a shocker. Derek Jeter stealing all the headlines. It's good to see no one else in the National League can get him out, either."... Braves first baseman Andres Galarraga, the recovered cancer patient who received a rousing ovation from his home fans: "Probably no words to explain how happy, how excited I am feeling."

PLAY BY PLAY

First Inning

A.L.—R. Alomar grounded out, Larkin to Galarraga. Jeter doubled to left. Williams grounded out, Larkin to Galarraga. Giambi struck out.

N.L.—Larkin popped to Giambi. C. Jones singled to center. V. Guerrero lined to R. Alomar. Sosa struck out.

Second Inning

A.L.—Graves now pitching. Everett flied to Edmonds. Rodriguez singled to right. Dye flied to Guerrero. Fryman struck out.

N.L.—Kent grounded out to Giambi, unassisted. Galarraga lined to Everett. Edmonds singled to right. Kendall struck out.

Third Inning

A.L.—Bordick pinch hit for Wells. Brown now pitching. Bordick flied to Edmonds. R. Alomar walked. Jeter singled to center as R. Alomar advanced to second. Williams forced R. Alomar at third, C. Jones, unassisted, as Jeter advanced to second. Giambi walked. Everett walked, scoring Jeter. Rodriguez lined to Edmonds. A.L. 1, N.L. 0.

N.L.—Baldwin now pitching. Hammonds, pinch-hitting for Brown, flied to Dye. Larkin popped to R. Alomar. C. Jones homered to left. Guerrero singled to left. Sosa popped to R. Alomar. A.L. 1, N.L. 1.

Fourth Inning

A.L.—Sheffield now in left and Leiter pitching. Dye walked. Fryman singled to center as Dye advanced to second. Sweeney pinch hit for Baldwin. Sweeney forced Fryman at second, but Fryman was safe on Larkin's error. R. Alomar popped to Galarraga. Jeter singled to left, scoring Dye and Fryman as Sweeney advanced to third and Jeter to second. Giambi struck out. A.L. 3, N.L. 1.

N.L.—Glaus now at third, Delgado at first and Sele pitching. Kent grounded out, R. Alomar to Delgado. Galarraga singled to center. Helton now pinch-running for Galarraga. Edmonds popped to Glaus in foul territory. Kendall grounded out, Jeter to Delgado.

Fifth Inning

A.L.—A. Jones now in center, Alfonzo at second, Helton at first, Lieberthal catching and Glavine pitching. Everett grounded out, Alfonzo to Helton. Rodriguez flied to Sosa. Dye struck out.

N.L.—Durham now at second, Garciaparra at shortstop, Ordonez in right, Erstad in left and Isringhausen pitching. Sheffield walked. Larkin popped to Rodriguez in foul territory. C. Jones singled to right as Sheffield advanced to second. A. Jones singled to center, scoring Sheffield as C. Jones advanced to second. Sosa flied to Ordonez as C. Jones advanced to third. Alfonzo popped to Delgado in foul territory. A.L. 3, N.L. 2.

Sixth Inning

A.L.—Renteria now at short, Cirillo at third, Giles in right and Kile pitching. Glaus grounded out, Renteria to Helton. Delgado doubled to right. Durham popped to Cirillo in foul territory. Garciaparra lined to Sheffield.

N.L.—Lawton now in center, Posada catching and Lowe pitching. Helton lined to Garciaparra. Lieberthal popped to Glaus in foul territory. Giles reached first on an error by Garciaparra. Sheffield grounded out, Garciaparra to Delgado.

Seventh Inning

A.L.—S. Finley now in left. Lawton grounded out, Kile to Helton. Ordonez doubled to right. Erstad grounded out, Renteria to Helton, as Ordonez advanced to third. Posada grounded out, Cirillo to Helton.

N.L.—McGriff now at first and T. Jones pitching. Renteria grounded out, Durham to McGriff. Cirillo popped to McGriff in foul territory. A. Jones struck out.

Eighth Inning

A.L.—Wickman now pitching. McGriff popped to Cirillo in foul territory. Batista, pinch-hitting for Glaus, struck out. Martinez, pinch-hitting for T. Jones, lined to A. Jones.

N.L.—Batista now at third and Hudson pitching. Vidro, pinch-hitting for Wickman, popped to Garciaparra. Alfonzo struck out. Helton grounded out, Durham to McGriff.

Ninth Inning

A.L.—Vidro now at second and Hoffman pitching. Durham singled to right. Garciaparra singled to left as Durham advanced to third. Lawton singled to right, scoring Durham as Garciaparra advanced to third. Lawton stole second. Ordonez hit a sacrifice fly to A. Jones, scoring Garciaparra as Lawton advanced to third. Erstad reached first on Vidro's error as Lawton scored. Posada and McGriff struck out. A.L. 6, N.L. 2.

N.L.—Rivera now pitching. Lieberthal singled to short and advanced to second on a wild-throw error by Garciaparra. Giles grounded out, Rivera to McGriff. S. Finley singled to center, scoring Lieberthal. Renteria grounded into a double play, Garciaparra to Durham to McGriff. Final score: A.L. 6, N.L. 3.

BOX SCORE

American League	AB	R	H	RBI	PO	A
R. Alomar, 2b (Indians)	2	0	0	0	3	1
Durham, 2b (White Sox)	2	1	1	0	1	3
Jeter, ss (Yankees)	3	1	3	2	0	1
Garciaparra, ss (Red Sox)	2	1	1	0	2	2
Williams, cf (Yankees)	3	0	0	0	0	0
Lawton, cf (Twins)	2	1	1	1	0	0
Ja. Giambi, 1b (Athletics)	2	0	0	0	2	0
Sele, p (Mariners)	0	0	0	0	0	0
Ordonez, rf (White Sox)	1	0	1	1	1	0
Everett, lf (Red Sox)	2	0	0	1	1	0
Erstad, lf (Angels)	2	0	0	1	0	0
Rodriguez, c (Rangers)	3	0	1	0	3	0
Posada, c (Yankees)	2	0	0	0	2	0
Dye, rf (Royals)	2	1	0	0	1	0
Isringhausen, p (Athletics)	0	0	0	0	0	0
Lowe, p (Red Sox)	0	0	0	0	0	0
McGriff, 1b (Devil Rays)	2	0	0	0	5	0
Fryman, 3b (Indians)	2	1	1	0	0	0
Glaus, 3b (Angels)	1	0	0	0	2	0
∞Batista, ph-3b (Blue Jays)	1	0	0	0	0	0
Wells, p (Blue Jays)	0	0	0	0	0	0
*Bordick, ph (Orioles)	1	0	0	0	0	0
Baldwin, p (White Sox)	0	0	0	0	0	0
‡Sweeney, ph (Royals)	1	0	0	0	0	0
Delgado, 1b (Blue Jays)	1	0	1	0	4	0
T. Jones, p (Tigers)	0	0	0	0	0	0
▲Martinez, ph (Mariners)	1	0	0	0	0	0
Hudson, p (Athletics)	0	0	0	0	0	0
Rivera, p (Yankees)	0	0	0	0	0	1
Totals	38	6	10	6	27	8

National League	AB	R	H	RBI	PO	A
Larkin, ss (Reds)	3	0	0	0	0	2
Renteria, ss (Cardinals)	2	0	0	0	0	2
C. Jones, 3b (Braves)	3	1	3	1	1	0
Cirillo, 3b (Rockies)	1	0	0	0	2	1
V. Guerrero, lf (Expos)	2	0	1	0	1	0
Leiter, p (Mets)	0	0	0	0	0	0
A. Jones, cf (Braves)	2	0	1	1	2	0
Sosa, rf (Cubs)	3	0	0	0	1	0
Kile, p (Cardinals)	0	0	0	0	0	1
Wickman, p (Brewers)	0	0	0	0	0	0
◆Vidro, ph-2b (Expos)	1	0	0	0	0	0
Kent, 2b (Giants)	2	0	0	0	0	0
Alfonzo, 2b (Mets)	2	0	0	0	0	1
Hoffman, p (Padres)	0	0	0	0	0	0
Galarraga, 1b (Braves)	2	0	1	0	4	0
§Helton, pr-1b (Rockies)	2	0	0	0	5	0
Edmonds, cf (Cardinals)	2	0	1	0	3	0
Lieberthal, c (Phillies)	2	1	1	0	4	0
Kendall, c (Pirates)	2	0	0	0	3	1
Glavine, p (Braves)	0	0	0	0	0	0
Giles, rf (Pirates)	2	0	0	0	0	0
Johnson, p (Diamondbacks)	0	0	0	0	0	0
Graves, p (Reds)	0	0	0	0	0	0
Brown, p (Dodgers)	0	0	0	0	0	0
†Hammonds, ph (Rockies)	1	0	0	0	0	0
Sheffield, lf (Dodgers)	1	1	0	0	1	0
S. Finley, lf (Diamondbacks)	1	0	1	1	0	0
Totals	36	3	9	3	27	8

American League	0 0 1	2 0 0	0 0 3	—6
National League	0 0 1	0 1 0	0 0 1	—3

American League	IP	H	R	ER	BB	SO
Wells (Blue Jays)	2.0	2	0	0	0	2
Baldwin (White Sox) (W)	1.0	2	1	1	0	0
Sele (Mariners)	1.0	1	0	0	0	0
Isringhausen (Athletics)	1.0	2	1	1	1	0
Lowe (Red Sox)	1.0	0	0	0	0	0
T. Jones (Tigers)	1.0	0	0	0	0	1
Hudson (Athletics)	1.0	0	0	0	0	1
Rivera (Yankees)	1.0	2	1	0	0	0

National League	IP	H	R	ER	BB	SO
Johnson (Diamondbacks)	1.0	1	0	0	0	1
Graves (Reds)	1.0	1	0	0	0	1
Brown (Dodgers)	1.0	1	1	1	3	0
Leiter (Mets) (L)	1.0	2	2	1	1	1
Glavine (Braves)	1.0	0	0	0	0	1
Kile (Cardinals)	2.0	2	0	0	0	0
Wickman (Brewers)	1.0	0	0	0	0	1
Hoffman (Padres)	1.0	3	3	3	0	2

Bases on balls—Off Isringhausen 1 (Sheffield), off Brown 3 (R. Alomar, Ja. Giambi, Everett), off Leiter 1 (Dye).

Strikeouts—By Wells 2 (Sosa, Kendall), by T. Jones 1 (A. Jones), by Hudson 1 (Alfonzo), by Johnson 1 (Ja. Giambi), by Graves 1 (Fryman), by Leiter 1 (Ja. Giambi), by Glavine 1 (Dye), by Wickman 1 (Batista), by Hoffman 2 (Posada, McGriff).

*Flied out for Wells in third. †Flied out for Brown in third. ‡Reached on a fielder's choice for Baldwin in the 4th. §Ran for Galarraga in fourth. ∞Struck out for Glaus in eighth. ▲Lined out for T. Jones in eighth. ◆Popped out for Wickman in eighth. E—Garciaparra 2, Larkin, Vidro. DP—A.L. 1. LOB—A.L. 10, N.L. 7. 2B—Jeter, Delgado, Ordonez. HR—C. Jones. SB—Lawton. SF—Ordonez. T—2:56. A—51,323. U—Reilly, plate; Hirschbeck, first; Ford, second; Schrieber, third; O'Nora, left field; Diaz, right field. Official scorer—Mark Fredericksson, Charlie Scoggins and Bill Zack.

Players listed on rosters but not used: A.L.—C. Finley (Indians); N.L.—Dempster (Marlins), Girardi (Cubs), Reynolds (Astros).

SEATTLE VS. CHICAGO

The bottom line: The A.L. Central Division-champion Chicago White Sox, unable to get key hits from the middle of its lineup or solve Seattle's bullpen, were swept out of their first postseason appearance since 1993 and denied a shot at their first World Series appearance since 1959. The wild-card Mariners, who didn't clinch a playoff berth until the final day of the regular season, outpitched, outhit and outplayed the American League's winningest team while claiming the second ALCS berth in franchise history. Seattle's surprising success was achieved in the first season after longtime star Ken Griffey Jr. was traded to Cincinnati and the clincher was recorded, appropriately, in the first playoff game at Safeco Field.

Why the Mariners won: Pitching, defense and timely hitting—baseball's traditional winning mix. Seattle pitchers limited the highest scoring team in the major leagues to seven runs and 17 hits over three games and held Chicago's Big Four offensive guns—Frank Thomas, Magglio Ordonez, Carlos Lee and Paul Konerko—to a dismal 3-for-40, two-RBI performance. The Mariners' starting pitching was solid, but their bullpen—Brett Tomko, Jose Paniagua, Arthur Rhodes, Jose Mesa and Kazuhiro Sasaki—was spectacular, working $11^{2}/_{3}$ scoreless innings and allowing the team to post two last-at-bat victories. The first two wins came at Chicago's Comiskey Park and continued a late-season trend—the Mariners won eight of their final nine road games while fighting for a playoff spot.

TURNING POINTS:

Game 1: The Mariners took control of the series in the 10th inning, a rally set up by former White Sox center fielder Mike Cameron. After singling home the tying run in the seventh, Cameron led off the 10th with a single off Chicago closer Keith Foulke. When Alex Rodriguez popped out, Cameron began stretching his lead, drawing Foulke into a cat-and-mouse pickoff game that finally ended with a stolen base. Obviously distracted, Foulke fired a pitch that Edgar Martinez pounded over the left field wall to give the Mariners a 6-4 lead and John Olerud hit his next pitch over the center field fence for the final 7-4 margin. When Sasaki shut down the White Sox in the bottom of the inning, he completed $6^{2}/_{3}$ scoreless innings for the bullpen and a win for Mesa. The loss was particularly difficult for the White Sox, who had rallied from a 3-0 deficit to a 4-3 advantage on a home run by Ray Durham and RBI triples by Ordonez and Chris Singleton.

Game 2: The bottom of the first inning provided a microcosm of the frustration the White Sox would experience in this series. Chicago leadoff man Durham doubled over center fielder Cameron's head and scored when No. 2 hitter Jose Valentin doubled into the right field corner. Valentin set the White Sox up for more when he stole third base off pitcher Paul Abbott. But just as they had in Game 1, Chicago's top offensive guns misfired. Thomas, who hit 43 homers and drove in 143 runs during an outstanding regular season, hit a fly ball to shallow left field as Valentin held. Ordonez walked, but Abbott retired Lee on a popup and Konerko on a soft grounder back to the mound. Having escaped with minimal damage, the Mariners scored twice in the top of the second on third baseman David Bell's single and catcher Dan Wilson's sacrifice fly and took the lead for good on Jay Buhner's fourth-inning home run off loser Mike Sirotka. Seattle's 5-2 victory also featured a superb run-saving defensive play by second baseman Mark McLemore and another $3^{1}/_{3}$ scoreless innings by the Mariners bullpen.

Game 3: The game—and the series—ended in an unlikely manner with one out in the bottom of the ninth inning when pinch hitter Carlos Guillen successfully squeezed home the winning run in a 2-1 Seattle victory. The White Sox's surprising season came to a sudden halt when Guillen, with Rickey Henderson stationed at third, dragged a hard safety squeeze bunt that eluded diving first baseman Thomas. Henderson was pinch running for Olerud, who had opened the inning by lining a ball off the stomach of pitcher Kelly Wunsch and moved to second when Wunsch made a wild throw. Henderson was sacrificed to third by Stan Javier before Bell drew a four-pitch walk from closer Foulke. Guillen's hit ended a tense battle that opened with Chicago's James Baldwin and Seattle's Aaron Sele matching pitches and ended after yeoman work by both bullpens. Sele, Rhodes and Paniagua, the winner, stopped the White Sox on three hits and stretched Thomas' frustration in an 0-for-9 postseason.

WORTH NOTING:

White Sox: Before surrendering the two 10th-inning home runs to Seattle in Game 1, relief ace Foulke had been on a roll. The righthander, who saved 34 games, had allowed only one run in his final $14^{2}/_{3}$ regular-season innings. ... The Game 2 loss at Comiskey Park stretched the White Sox's postseason home losing streak to nine games. The last home playoff victory came in Game 1 of the 1959 World Series against Los Angeles. ... After losing the first two games, the White Sox were understandably optimistic about their comeback chances in Seattle. Chicago recorded a major league-best 49-32 road record in 2000.

Mariners: Seattle claimed its second ALCS appearance in its third postseason venture. The Mariners defeated the New York Yankees in the 1995 Division Series before losing to the Indians in the ALCS. They lost a Division Series to Baltimore in 1997. ... Five players picked up in the trades for Randy Johnson and Ken Griffey Jr. played key roles in the Mariners' regular-season and postseason success. Guillen and Cameron provided key hits during the season and in the series against the White Sox. Freddy Garcia and John Halama were members of the rotation and Tomko worked successfully out of the bullpen. ... Temporary bleachers were added to Safeco Field for the playoffs and 48,010 attended the first postseason game in the stadium's history.

WORTH QUOTING:

White Sox: Thomas, lamenting his first-inning failure in Game 2: "A guy on third with less than two out. I've got to get him home. That's what I get paid for. That's what I've made my living doing." ... Manager Jerry Manuel after watching his Sox lose their third straight game: "We played good baseball. They played magnificent baseball. It took that kind of effort to beat us. They pitched extremely well; they played great defense. They did everything you have to do to win."

Mariners: Cameron, referring to the surprise visit he received from manager Lou Piniella after he was almost picked off three times by Foulke in the 10th inning of Game 1: "I didn't know what he was going to say to me. The only time you see something like that is in Little League. I can't tell you what he said. It's a baseball secret we keep under the sheets." ... Piniella, when assessing the Mariners' 2-1 Game 3-clinching win: "This was a trademark game for us. We pitched well, we played really good defense."

Shortstop Alex Rodriguez and his fired up Seattle teammates were too much for the stumbling White Sox in an A.L. Division Series.

Game 1 at Chicago

SEATTLE 7, CHICAGO 4 (10 INNINGS)

HOW THEY SCORED

First Inning

Mariners—Rickey Henderson singled to right-center field. Mike Cameron was hit by a pitch, moving Henderson to second. Alex Rodriguez singled to right, scoring Henderson and moving Cameron to third. Edgar Martinez lined to shortstop. John Olerud grounded into a 4-6 forceout, scoring Cameron. Jay Buhner walked, moving Olerud to second. David Bell flied to center. Two runs. Mariners 2, White Sox 0.

Second Inning

Mariners—Joe Oliver homered to left. Mark McLemore singled to left center. Henderson flied to right. Cameron grounded into a 4-6-3 double play. One run. Mariners 3, White Sox 0.

White Sox—Carlos Lee flied to center. Paul Konerko walked. Herbert Perry grounded to second, moving Konerko to second. Chris Singleton tripled to right, scoring Konerko. Singleton scored on Freddy Garcia's wild pitch. Charles Johnson grounded to third. Two runs. Mariners 3, White Sox 2.

Third Inning

White Sox—Ray Durham homered to left center. Jose Valentin walked. Frank Thomas fouled out to the catcher. Maggio Ordonez tripled to right, scoring Valentin. Lee struck out. Konerko flied to left center. Two runs. White Sox 4, Mariners 3.

Seventh Inning

Mariners—Bob Howry relieved Jim Parque. Buhner walked. Bell doubled to left center, moving Buhner to third. Raul Ibanez pinch ran for Buhner. Al Martin batted for Joe Oliver and grounded to second, both runners holding. McLemore walked, loading the bases. Stan Javier batted for Henderson and struck out. Chad Bradford relieved Howry. Cameron singled to right, scoring Ibanez. Bell was thrown out trying to score. One run. White Sox 4, Mariners 4.

Tenth Inning

Mariners—Cameron singled to left. Rodriguez flied to left. Cameron stole second. Martinez homered to left, scoring Cameron. Olerud homered to center. Ibanez flied to right. Bell walked. Dan Wilson struck out. Three runs. Mariners 7, White Sox 4.

BOX SCORE

Seattle	AB	R	H	RBI	PO	A
Henderson, lf	3	1	1	0	1	0
Javier, ph-lf	2	0	0	0	3	0
Cameron, cf	4	2	2	1	4	0
Rodriguez, ss	5	0	3	1	1	2
Martinez, dh	5	1	2	2	0	0
Olerud, 1b	5	1	1	2	8	0
Buhner, rf	1	0	0	0	2	0
Ibanez, pr-rf	2	1	1	0	1	0
Bell, 3b	4	0	1	0	0	3
Oliver, c	2	1	1	1	3	0
Martin, ph	1	0	0	0	0	0
Wilson, c	2	0	0	0	4	0
McLemore, 2b	3	0	1	0	3	3
Garcia, p	0	0	0	0	0	2
Tomko, p	0	0	0	0	0	0
Paniagua, p	0	0	0	0	0	0
Rhodes, p	0	0	0	0	0	1
Mesa, p	0	0	0	0	0	0
Sasaki, p	0	0	0	0	0	0
Totals	39	7	13	7	30	11

Chicago	AB	R	H	RBI	PO	A
Durham, 2b	3	1	1	1	4	4
Valentin, ss	4	1	1	0	5	6
Thomas, dh	3	0	0	0	0	0
Ordonez, rf	5	0	1	1	4	1
Lee, lf	5	0	1	0	2	0
Konerko, 1b	4	1	0	0	6	0
Perry, 3b	4	0	1	0	1	1
Singleton, cf	5	1	1	1	2	0
Johnson, c	4	0	3	0	5	1
Paul, pr-c	0	0	0	0	1	0
Parque, p	0	0	0	0	0	0
Howry, p	0	0	0	0	0	0
Bradford, p	0	0	0	0	0	0
Wunsch, p	0	0	0	0	0	0
Simas, p	0	0	0	0	0	0
Foulke, p	0	0	0	0	0	0
Totals	37	4	9	3	30	13

Seattle	210	000	100 3—7
Chicago	022	000	000 0—4

Seattle	IP	H	R	ER	BB	SO
Garcia	3.1	6	4	4	3	2
Tomko	2.2	1	0	0	1	0
Paniagua	*2.0	1	0	0	1	2
Rhodes	0.2	0	0	0	0	0
Mesa (W)	0.1	0	0	0	1	0
Sasaki (S)	1.0	1	0	0	0	2

Chicago	IP	H	R	ER	BB	SO
Parque	6.0	6	3	3	1	2
Howry	0.2	1	1	1	2	1
Bradford	0.2	2	0	0	0	0
Wunsch	0.1	1	0	0	0	0
Simas	0.1	0	0	0	0	0
Foulke (L)	2.0	3	3	3	1	2

*Pitched to one batter in ninth.

DP—Seattle 1, Chicago 2. LOB—Seattle 7, Chicago 10. 2B—Bell, Valentin, Lee. 3B—Singleton, Ordonez. HR—Olerud, Martinez, Durham, Oliver. SH—Durham. SB—Cameron, Valentin. CS—Rodriguez. HBP—By Parque (Cameron). WP—Garcia, Tomko. T—4:12. A—45,290. U—Reliford, plate; Danley, first; Reilly, second; Winters, third; Reed, left field; Eddings, right field.

Game 2 at Chicago

SEATTLE 5, CHICAGO 2

HOW THEY SCORED

First Inning

White Sox—Ray Durham doubled to center. Jose Valentin doubled to right, scoring Durham. Valentin stole third. Frank Thomas flied to shallow left. Magglio Ordonez walked. Carlos Lee popped to first. Paul Konerko grounded to the pitcher. One run. White Sox 1, Mariners 0.

Second Inning

Mariners—Edgar Martinez doubled to right. John Olerud was hit by a pitch. Jay Buhner was safe on an error by the shortstop, loading the bases. David Bell singled to left, scoring Martinez and reloading the bases. Dan Wilson flied to center, scoring Olerud. McLemore grounded to third, Buhner moving to third and Bell to second. Rickey Henderson popped to second. Two runs. Mariners 2, White Sox 1.

Third Inning

White Sox—Valentin reached on a bunt single. Thomas popped to third. Valentin stole second and went to third on catcher Dan Wilson's throwing error. Ordonez walked. Lee flied to deep right, scoring Valentin. Ordonez stole second. Konerko fouled out to first. One run. Mariners 2, White Sox 2.

Fourth Inning

Mariners—Olerud popped to third. Buhner homered to left. Bell grounded to shortstop. Wilson walked. McLemore grounded into a 6-4 forceout. One run. Mariners 3, White Sox 2.

Fifth Inning

Mariners—Henderson walked. Mike Cameron sacrificed Henderson to second. Henderson stole third. Alex Rodriguez grounded to third, scoring Henderson. Martinez flied to right. One run. Mariners 4, White Sox 2.

Ninth Inning

Mariners—Bell struck out. Javier struck out. McLemore walked. Mark Buehrle relieved Bill Simas. Raul Ibanez singled to right, moving McLemore to third. Cameron singled to right center, scoring McLemore and moving Ibanez to third. Rodriguez struck out. One run. Mariners 5, White Sox 2.

BOX SCORE

Seattle	AB	R	H	RBI	PO	A
Henderson, lf	2	1	1	0	1	0
Ibanez, lf-rf	2	0	1	0	2	0
Cameron, cf	4	0	1	1	2	0
Rodriguez, ss	5	0	1	1	4	4
Martinez, dh	3	1	1	0	0	0
Olerud, 1b	3	1	1	0	7	0
Buhner, rf	4	1	1	1	2	0
Oliver, c	0	0	0	0	5	0
Bell, 3b	4	0	2	1	1	1
Wilson, c	1	0	0	1	1	0
Javier, lf	1	0	0	0	0	0
McLemore, 2b	3	1	0	0	2	3
P. Abbott, p	0	0	0	0	0	1
Rhodes, p	0	0	0	0	0	0
Mesa, p	0	0	0	0	0	1
Sasaki, p	0	0	0	0	0	0
Totals	32	5	9	5	27	10

Chicago	AB	R	H	RBI	PO	A
Durham, 2b	4	1	1	0	4	1
Valentin, ss	3	1	2	1	4	7
Thomas, dh	4	0	0	0	0	0
Ordonez, rf	2	0	0	0	1	0
Lee, lf	3	0	0	1	1	0
Konerko, 1b	4	0	0	0	11	1
Perry, 3b	4	0	2	0	1	4
Singleton, cf	2	0	0	0	1	0
J. Abbott, ph-cf	1	0	0	0	1	0
Baines, ph	1	0	0	0	0	0
Johnson, c	2	0	0	0	3	1
Sirotka, p	0	0	0	0	0	1
Barcelo, p	0	0	0	0	0	0
Wunsch, p	0	0	0	0	0	0
Simas, p	0	0	0	0	0	0
Buehrle, p	0	0	0	0	0	0
Totals	30	2	5	2	27	15

Seattle	020	110	001—5
Chicago	101	000	000—2

Seattle	IP	H	R	ER	BB	SO
P. Abbott (W)	5.2	5	2	1	3	1
Rhodes	0.2	0	0	0	2	0
Mesa	1.2	0	0	0	0	2
Sasaki (S)	1.0	0	0	0	0	3

Chicago	IP	H	R	ER	BB	SO
Sirotka (L)	5.2	7	4	3	2	0
Barcelo	1.2	0	0	0	1	0
Wunsch	0.1	0	0	0	0	0
Simas	1.0	0	1	1	1	2
Buehrle	0.1	2	0	0	0	1

E—Wilson, Valentin. DP—Seattle 1, Chicago 3. LOB—Seattle 7, Chicago 8. 2B—Martinez, Durham, Valentin, Perry. HR—Buhner. SH—Cameron. SF—Wilson, Lee. SB—Henderson, Valentin 2, Ordonez. HBP—By P. Abbott (Johnson), by Sirotka (Olerud). T—3:16. A—45,383. U—Danley, plate; Reilly, first; Winters, second; Reed, third; Eddings, left field; Reliford, right field.

Game 3 at Seattle

SEATTLE 2, CHICAGO 1

HOW THEY SCORED

Second Inning

White Sox—Harold Baines doubled to left. Charles Johnson flied to right center, moving Baines to third. Herbert Perry flied to center, scoring Baines. Carlos Lee flied to center. One run. White Sox 1, Mariners 0.

Fourth Inning

Mariners—Raul Ibanez singled to left. Alex Rodriguez sacrificed Ibanez to second. Edgar Martinez grounded to shortstop, advancing Ibanez to third. John Olerud walked. Stan Javier reached on an infield single, scoring Ibanez and moving Olerud to second. David Bell grounded into a fielder's choice forceout at third. One run. White Sox 1, Mariners 1.

Ninth Inning

Mariners—Kelly Wunsch relieved Bob Howry. Olerud reached on an infield single and moved to second on Wunsch's throwing error. Keith Foulke relieved Wunsch. Rickey Henderson ran for Olerud. and Javier sacrificed him to third. Bell walked. Carlos Guillen batted for Joe Oliver and bunted safely, scoring Henderson. One run. Mariners 2, White Sox 1.

BOX SCORE

Chicago	AB	R	H	RBI	PO	A
Durham, 2b	3	0	0	0	2	1
Valentin, ss	3	0	0	0	1	4
Thomas, 1b	2	0	0	0	8	0
Ordonez, rf	4	0	1	0	3	0
Baines, dh	3	1	1	0	0	0
Johnson, c	3	0	0	0	5	0
Perry, 3b	1	0	1	1	3	2
Graffanino, pr-3b	0	0	0	0	0	1
Lee, lf	3	0	0	0	3	0
Singleton, cf	2	0	0	0	0	0
Konerko, ph	1	0	0	0	0	0
Christensen, cf	0	0	0	0	0	0
Baldwin, p	0	0	0	0	0	1
Howry, p	0	0	0	0	0	1
Wunsch, p	0	0	0	0	0	0
Foulke, p	0	0	0	0	0	0
Totals	25	1	3	1	25	10

Seattle	AB	R	H	RBI	PO	A
Cameron, cf	4	0	0	0	6	0
Ibanez, rf	4	1	1	0	1	0
Rodriguez, ss	3	0	0	0	3	3
Martinez, dh	3	0	1	0	0	0
Olerud, 1b	2	0	1	0	10	0
Henderson, pr	0	1	0	0	0	0
Javier, lf	3	0	1	1	1	0
Bell, 3b	3	0	1	0	1	0
Oliver, c	2	0	0	0	4	0
Guillen, ph	1	0	1	1	0	0
McLemore, 2b	3	0	0	0	1	3
Sele, p	0	0	0	0	0	1
Rhodes, p	0	0	0	0	0	0
Paniagua, p	0	0	0	0	0	0
Totals	28	2	6	2	27	7

Chicago	010	000	00—1
Seattle	000	100	01—2

One out when winning run scored.

Chicago	IP	H	R	ER	BB	SO
Baldwin	6.0	3	1	1	3	2
Howry	2.0	1	0	0	0	3
Wunsch (L)	*0.0	1	1	0	0	0
Foulke	0.1	1	0	0	1	0

Seattle	IP	H	R	ER	BB	SO
Sele	7.1	3	1	1	3	1
Rhodes	1.1	0	0	0	0	2
Paniagua (W)	0.1	0	0	0	1	1

*Pitched to one batter in ninth.

E—Wunsch. DP—Seattle 3. LOB—Chicago 3, Seattle 8. 2B—Baines. SH—Valentin, Rodriguez, Javier, Oliver. SF—Perry. T—2:40. A—48,010. U—McClelland, plate; Schrieber, first; Clark, second; Nelson, third; Welke, left field; Meriwether, right field.

COMPOSITE

BATTING AVERAGES

Seattle Mariners

Player, position	G	AB	R	H	2B	3B	HR	RBI	Avg.
Guillen, ph	1	1	0	1	0	0	0	1	1.000
Henderson, lf-pr	3	5	3	2	0	0	0	0	.400
Ibanez, pr-rf-lf	3	8	2	3	0	0	0	0	.375
Bell, 3b	3	11	0	4	1	0	0	1	.364
Martinez, dh	3	11	2	4	1	0	1	2	.364
Rodriguez, ss	3	13	0	4	0	0	0	2	.308
Olerud, 1b	3	10	2	3	0	0	1	2	.300
Cameron, cf	3	12	2	3	0	0	0	2	.250
Oliver, c	3	4	1	1	0	0	1	1	.250
Buhner, rf	2	5	1	1	0	0	1	1	.200
Javier, ph-lf	3	6	0	1	0	0	0	1	.167
McLemore, 2b	3	9	1	1	0	0	0	0	.111
P. Abbott, p	1	0	0	0	0	0	0	0	.000
Garcia, p	1	0	0	0	0	0	0	0	.000
Mesa, p	2	0	0	0	0	0	0	0	.000
Paniagua, p	2	0	0	0	0	0	0	0	.000
Rhodes, p	3	0	0	0	0	0	0	0	.000
Sasaki, p	2	0	0	0	0	0	0	0	.000
Sele, p	1	0	0	0	0	0	0	0	.000
Tomko, p	1	0	0	0	0	0	0	0	.000
Martin, ph	1	1	0	0	0	0	0	0	.000
Wilson, c	2	3	0	0	0	0	0	1	.000
Totals	3	99	14	28	2	0	4	14	.283

Chicago White Sox

Player, position	G	AB	R	H	2B	3B	HR	RBI	Avg.
Perry, 3b	3	9	0	4	1	0	0	1	.444
Johnson, c	3	9	0	3	0	0	0	0	.333
Valentin, ss	3	10	2	3	2	0	0	1	.300
Baines, ph-dh	2	4	1	1	1	0	0	0	.250
Durham, 2b	3	10	2	2	1	0	1	1	.200
Ordonez, rf	3	11	0	2	0	1	0	1	.182
Singleton, cf	3	9	1	1	0	1	0	1	.111
Lee, lf	3	11	0	1	1	0	0	1	.091
Baldwin, p	1	0	0	0	0	0	0	0	.000
Barcelo, p	1	0	0	0	0	0	0	0	.000
Bradford, p	1	0	0	0	0	0	0	0	.000
Buehrle, p	1	0	0	0	0	0	0	0	.000
Christensen, cf	1	0	0	0	0	0	0	0	.000
Foulke, p	2	0	0	0	0	0	0	0	.000
Graffanino, pr-3b	1	0	0	0	0	0	0	0	.000
Howry, p	2	0	0	0	0	0	0	0	.000
Parque, p	1	0	0	0	0	0	0	0	.000
Paul, pr-c	1	0	0	0	0	0	0	0	.000
Simas, p	2	0	0	0	0	0	0	0	.000
Sirotka, p	1	0	0	0	0	0	0	0	.000
Wunsch, p	3	0	0	0	0	0	0	0	.000
J. Abbott, ph-cf	1	1	0	0	0	0	0	0	.000
Konerko, 1b-ph	3	9	1	0	0	0	0	0	.000
Thomas, dh-1b	3	9	0	0	0	0	0	0	.000
Totals	3	92	7	17	6	2	1	6	.185

PITCHING AVERAGES

Seattle Mariners

Pitcher	G	IP	H	R	ER	BB	SO	W	L	ERA
Rhodes	3	2.2	0	0	0	2	2	0	0	0.00
Tomko	1	2.2	1	0	0	1	0	0	0	0.00
Paniagua	2	2.1	1	0	0	2	3	1	0	0.00
Mesa	2	2.0	0	0	0	1	2	1	0	0.00
Sasaki	2	2.0	1	0	0	0	5	0	0	0.00
Sele	1	7.1	3	1	1	3	1	0	0	1.23
P. Abbott	1	5.2	5	2	1	3	1	1	0	1.59
Garcia	1	3.1	6	4	4	3	2	0	0	10.80
Totals	3	28.0	17	7	6	15	16	3	0	1.93

No shutouts. Saves—Sasaki 2.

Chicago White Sox

Pitcher	G	IP	H	R	ER	BB	SO	W	L	ERA
Barcelo	1	1.2	0	0	0	1	0	0	0	0.00
Bradford	1	0.2	2	0	0	0	0	0	0	0.00
Wunsch	3	0.2	2	1	0	0	0	0	1	0.00
Buehrle	1	0.1	2	0	0	0	1	0	0	0.00
Baldwin	1	6.0	3	1	1	3	2	0	0	1.50
Howry	2	2.2	2	1	1	2	4	0	0	3.38
Parque	1	6.0	6	3	3	1	2	0	0	4.50
Sirotka	1	5.2	7	4	3	2	0	0	1	4.76
Simas	2	1.1	0	1	1	1	2	0	0	6.75
Foulke	2	2.1	4	3	3	2	2	0	1	11.57
Totals	3	27.1	28	14	12	12	13	0	3	3.95

No shutouts or saves.

A.L. DIVISION SERIES

NEW YORK VS. OAKLAND

The bottom line: The "too old, too tired, inconsistent" New York Yankees, looking for their third straight World Series title and fourth in five years, slipped past the young and restless Oakland Athletics in a tough five-game Division Series that seriously tested their championship resolve. After ending the regular season with seven straight losses and 15 in 18 games, the Yankees lost the series opener to Oakland and seemed to be reeling. But lefthander Andy Pettitte righted the ship with a Game 2 shutout and the A.L. East Division champions came up with big plays and rallies every time they needed them. The A.L. West-champion A's, making their first postseason appearance since 1992, pushed the Yankees to the brink before falling into a 6-0 Game 5 hole they couldn't climb out of. The win completed a Bay Area sweep for New York teams—the Yankees beating the A's a few hours after the Mets had dispatched the Giants.

Why the Yankees won: Because of experience, their ability to turn on a sputtering offense and the Game 5 rescue work of their much-maligned bullpen. Pettitte was outstanding in a must-win Game 2 and Orlando Hernandez followed his lead in Game 3. The Yankees showed old offensive flashes throughout the series and they took control of Game 5 with a six-run, first-inning outburst that shocked the A's and quieted 41,170 fired-up Oakland fans. When the relentless A's kept coming, the bullpen stepped up to deliver $5^1/_3$ scoreless innings and a 7-5 victory.

TURNING POINTS:

Game 1: After being dominated for four innings by Yankees starter Roger Clemens, the A's broke through for four runs in the fifth and sixth innings and went on to record a 5-3 win at Network Associates Coliseum. Clemens, who allowed only one hit and struck out five through four innings, carried a 2-0 lead into the fifth, thanks to back-to-back RBI doubles by Luis Sojo and Scott Brosius in the second. But the A's struck for three runs on RBI singles by Ramon Hernandez and Randy Velarde and a wild pitch by Clemens, and broke a 3-3 deadlock in the sixth on a run-scoring double by Hernandez. The Yankees, who lost for the eighth straight game and 16th in 19 outings, managed only three hits over the last seven innings off winning pitcher Gil Heredia and relievers Jeff Tam, Jim Mecir and Jason Isringhausen.

Game 2: With their backs planted firmly against the wall and their hopes for a third straight World Series championship at stake, the Yankees turned to Pettitte and snapped their eight-game losing streak. The 19-game winner shut down the free-swinging A's, allowing five hits over $7\ ^2/_3$ innings en route to a 4-0 victory that evened the Division Series at a game apiece. Pettitte, who was helped by double plays in the first and seventh innings, kept Oakland at bay until the Yankees could get their offense going in the top of the sixth against Kevin Appier. The A's righthander was cruising with two out and a runner on second when manager Art Howe ordered slumping Paul O'Neill, a lefthanded hitter, to be walked intentionally. Righthander Glenallen Hill spoiled the strategy with an RBI single and Sojo's double scored two more. Pettitte left with two out and two runners on base in the eighth and Yankees closer Mariano Rivera finished for his 14th postseason save.

Game 3: The A's inability to handle struggling Orlando Hernandez, combined with a popgun Yankees attack, lifted New York to within one win of the ALCS. El Duque needed 130 pitches to get through seven innings, allowing only four hits but walking five and allowing two runs. He was aided by good defensive plays by left fielder David Justice and second baseman Sojo en route to his sixth win in as many postseason decisions. Playing before a roaring Yankee Stadium crowd of 55,606, the young A's committed two errors and made several more defensive lapses that contributed to Yankee runs. Two scored in the second on infield choppers by Hill and Derek Jeter and another came home in the fourth on Jeter's groundout after a throwing error by catcher Ramon Hernandez. That was all the support needed by Orlando Hernandez and Rivera, who earned his record-tying 15th postseason save. One of the A's runs came on a fifth-inning home run by Terrence Long—the first homer in the series.

Eric Chavez had a big postseason, batting .333 with four RBIs. His performance helped the A's push the Yankees to a five-game series.

Game 4: The A's, facing elimination at pressure-packed Yankee Stadium, delivered a first-inning message that this series was far from over. The unlikely messenger was backup DH Olmedo Saenz, who pounded the first Clemens pitch he saw over the left field fence after the big righthander had walked Long and Jason Giambi. The 3-0 advantage held up until the sixth, when the A's struck for three more runs, two on a single by Ben Grieve, en route to an 11-1 win. While the 38-year-old Clemens, a five-time Cy Young winner, was faltering, 22-year-old A's rookie lefthander Barry Zito was slamming the door on the Yankees, working $5^2/_3$ innings in his postseason debut. The win forced the series back to Oakland and put the Yankees on the brink of elimination for the first time since their 1997 Division Series loss to Cleveland.

Game 5: As if shooing away an annoying fly, the Yankees jumped on Oakland starter Gil Heredia for six first-inning runs en route to a 7-5 Division Series-clinching victory. But what should have been easy turned into a tense struggle before the two-time defending World Series champs could claim their fourth ALCS berth in five years. Chuck Knoblauch singled twice, stole a base, scored a run and drove in another in the big first inning that featured a bases-loaded triple by first baseman Tino Martinez. But Pettitte, unable to match his Game 2 performance, surrendered 10 hits and five runs over $3\ ^2/_3$ spotty innings. Only a solo home run by Justice—the Yankees' only homer of the series—and outstanding work by Mike Stanton, Jeff Nelson, Hernandez and Rivera kept the A's from wiping out their deficit and ending the Yankees' postseason series win streak at six. Rivera's 16th postseason save broke the record he had shared with Dennis Eckersley since Game 3.

WORTH NOTING:

Athletics: The A's, unlike the Yankees, entered the playoff series on a high, having won eight of their last 10 regular-season games to overtake Seattle for the A.L. West title. ... The A's win in Game 1 was the first postseason managerial victory for Art Howe. ... Game 2 starter Kevin Appier, making his first postseason appearance in 12 major league seasons, allowed three runs on six hits over $6^1/_3$ innings. ... In Oakland's Game 3 loss to Orlando Hernandez, the A's Nos. 2-7 hitters were a combined 0-for-19. ... That Game 3 loss marked the first time since September 1 that the A's had lost two games in a row. ... After the A's Game 4 win at New York, both teams made the long flight to Oakland, arriving about 4 a.m.—13 hours before game time.

Yankees: Entering the series, the Yankees had won 18 of the last 19 postseason games and 22 of 25. ... When the Yankees took a 2-0 lead in Game 1, it broke a streak of 63 innings in which they trailed or were tied. ... Justice set a major league record in Game 1 when he appeared in his 78th postseason game, breaking a tie with Reggie Jackson. ... Rivera stretched his postseason scoreless-innings streak to $30^2/_3$ over 21 appearances, moving him within range of Whitey Ford's major league record of 33. ... The six-run first in Game 5 was the Yankees' biggest inning since September 7, when they scored seven in the ninth at Kansas City.

WORTH QUOTING:

Athletics: First baseman Jason Giambi, after the A's had routed the Yankees in Game 4 to force the series back to Oakland: "Shoot, we won the division on the last day of the season, we are going to a fifth game. They make movies about this stuff. We are in the middle of a 'Rocky' movie right now."... Game 4 starter Zito, after his first postseason win: "It was an awesome experience. The crowd was great. The fans were loud. I just tried not to get caught up in the hype and throw my pitches. My stuff was working pretty well today."... Manager Howe, after the Game 5 loss: "We let them get a running start on us tonight, that's the difference in the ballgame."

Yankees: Pettitte, after his Game 2 shutout: "We've been down. We've been on a terrible skid. I hope this will get us going. This is a big game for us, obviously. We've really been struggling."... Justice, after watching the young A's self-destruct in Game 3: "We knew we were coming home to our crowd and our crowd could be very overwhelming to the opposing team. I don't think they're afraid. I think they just made a couple of misplays that we took advantage of."... Jeter, after the Game 5 clincher: "A lot of people were trying to say

Roger Clemens had two forgettable starts in the Division Series.

that our run was over, but you're not going to beat us that easily. We're still the champs until someone beats us."

Game 1 at Oakland

OAKLAND 5, NEW YORK 3

HOW THEY SCORED

Second Inning

Yankees—David Justice flied to center. Tino Martinez grounded to first. Jorge Posada singled to right. Luis Sojo doubled to left-center, scoring Posada. Scott Brosius doubled to left, scoring Sojo. Chuck Knoblauch struck out. Two runs. Yankees 2, A's 0.

Fifth Inning

Athletics—Eric Chavez singled to right. Jeremy Giambi walked, moving Chavez to second. Ramon Hernandez singled to right, scoring Chavez and moving Jeremy Giambi to second. Terrence Long grounded to second, moving Jeremy Giambi to third and Hernandez to second. Randy Velarde singled to left, scoring Jeremy Giambi and moving Hernandez to third. Hernandez scored and Velarde moved to second on a wild pitch. Jason Giambi was walked intentionally. Ben Grieve grounded into a 4-6-3 double play. Three runs. A's 3, Yankees 2.

Sixth Inning

Yankees—Bernie Williams doubled to right. Justice grounded to first, moving Williams to third. Martinez flied to left, scoring Williams. Posada walked. Sojo flied to left-center. One run. A's 3, Yankees 3.

Athletics—Miguel Tejada grounded to shortstop. Matt Stairs grounded to second. Chavez singled to left. Jeremy Giambi singled to right, moving Jeremy Giambi to third. Hernandez doubled to right, scoring Chavez. Jeremy Giambi was thrown out trying to score. One run. A's 4, Yankees 3.

Eighth Inning

Athletics—Tejada singled to left. Stairs flied to left. Tejada moved to second on a wild pitch. Chavez singled to center, scoring Tejada. Olmedo Saenz batted for Jeremy Giambi. Jeff Nelson relieved Mike Stanton. Saenz flied to right. Hermandez flied to left. One run. A's 5, Yankees 3.

BOX SCORE

New York	AB	R	H	RBI	PO	A
Knoblauch, dh	4	0	1	0	0	0
Jeter, ss	3	0	0	0	2	3
O'Neill, rf	4	0	0	0	1	1
Williams, cf	4	1	2	0	2	0
Justice, lf	4	0	0	0	2	0
Martinez, 1b	3	0	1	1	7	1
Posada, c	3	1	1	0	6	0
Sojo, 2b	3	1	1	1	0	4
Hill, ph	1	0	0	0	0	0
Brosius, 3b	4	0	1	1	3	1
Clemens, p	0	0	0	0	1	0
Stanton, p	0	0	0	0	0	0
Nelson, p	0	0	0	0	0	0
Totals	33	3	7	3	24	10

Oakland	AB	R	H	RBI	PO	A
Long, cf	4	0	1	0	2	0
Velarde, 2b	3	0	1	1	3	3
Ja. Giambi, 1b	2	0	1	0	9	0
Grieve, lf	3	0	0	0	2	0
Christenson, lf	0	0	0	0	0	0
Tejada, ss	4	1	1	0	1	3
Stairs, rf	4	0	0	0	3	0
Chavez, 3b	4	2	3	1	0	1
Je. Giambi, dh	2	1	1	0	0	0
Saenz, ph-dh	1	0	0	0	0	0
R. Hernandez, c	4	1	2	2	7	0
Heredia, p	0	0	0	0	0	0
Tam, p	0	0	0	0	0	0
Mecir, p	0	0	0	0	0	0
Isringhausen, p	0	0	0	0	0	0
Totals	31	5	10	4	27	7

New York	0 2 0	0 0 1	0 0 0—3
Oakland	0 0 0	0 3 1	0 1 x—5

New York	IP	H	R	ER	BB	SO
Clemens (L)	6.0	7	4	4	4	5
Stanton	1.1	3	1	1	1	0
Nelson	0.2	0	0	0	0	0

Oakland	IP	H	R	ER	BB	SO
Heredia (W)	6.0	7	3	3	1	3
Tam	0.2	0	0	0	0	1
Mecir	1.1	0	0	0	0	1
Isringhausen (S)	1.0	0	0	0	0	2

E—Long, Velarde. DP—New York 2, Oakland 1. LOB—New York 6, Oakland 7. 2B—Williams, Sojo, Brosius, R. Hernandez. SF—Martinez. SB—Velarde, Ja. Giambi. HBP—By Heredia (Jeter). WP—Clemens, Stanton. T—3:16. A—47,360. U—Welke, plate; Meriwether, first; McClelland, second; Schrieber, third; Clark, left field; Nelson, right field.

Game 2 at Oakland

NEW YORK 4, OAKLAND 0

HOW THEY SCORED

Sixth Inning

Yankees—David Justice grounded to second. Bernie Williams doubled to right. Tino Martinez struck out. Paul O'Neill was walked intentionally. Glenallen Hill singled to center, scoring Williams and moving O'Neill to second. Luis Sojo doubled to right, scoring O'Neill and Hill. Scott Brosius grounded to third. Three runs. Yankees 3, A's 0.

Ninth Inning

Yankees—Jeff Tam relieved Mike Magnante. Sojo was safe on Jason Giambi's error. Jose Vizcaino ran for Sojo. Brosius sacrificed Vizcaino to second. Derek Jeter grounded to second, moving Vizcaino to third. Jorge Posada was walked intentionally. Clay Bellinger doubled to right, scoring Vizcaino and moving Posada to third. Doug Jones relieved Tam. Williams grounded to first. One run. Yankees 4, A's 0.

BOX SCORE

New York	AB	R	H	RBI	PO	A
Jeter, ss	5	0	0	0	0	5
Posada, c	3	0	1	0	3	0
Justice, lf	3	0	0	0	1	0
Bellinger, lf	1	0	1	1	0	0
Williams, cf	5	1	2	0	2	0
Martinez, 1b	4	0	2	0	16	1
O'Neill, rf	2	1	0	0	1	0
Hill, dh	4	1	1	1	0	0
Sojo, 2b	3	0	1	2	3	4
Vizcaino, pr-2b	0	1	0	0	0	1
Brosius, 3b	3	0	0	0	0	5
Pettitte, p	0	0	0	0	0	1
Rivera, p	0	0	0	0	1	0
Totals	33	4	8	4	27	17

Oakland	AB	R	H	RBI	PO	A
Long, cf	4	0	0	0	1	0
Velarde, 2b	3	0	0	0	0	4
Ja. Giambi, 1b	4	0	2	0	12	0
Saenz, dh	4	0	0	0	0	0
Tejada, ss	4	0	2	0	3	2
Grieve, lf	4	0	0	0	0	0
Piatt, rf	3	0	0	0	3	0
Chavez, 3b	3	0	1	0	1	3
R. Hernandez, c	3	0	1	0	7	2
Appier, p	0	0	0	0	0	0
Magnante, p	0	0	0	0	0	0
Tam, p	0	0	0	0	0	0
Jones, p	0	0	0	0	0	0
Totals	32	0	6	0	27	11

New York	0 0 0	0 0 3	0 0 1—4
Oakland	0 0 0	0 0 0	0 0 0—0

New York	IP	H	R	ER	BB	SO
Pettitte (W)	7.2	5	0	0	1	3
Rivera (S)	1.1	1	0	0	0	0

Oakland	IP	H	R	ER	BB	SO
Appier (L)	6.1	6	3	3	5	7
Magnante	1.2	1	0	0	0	1
Tam	0.2	1	1	0	1	0
Jones	0.1	0	0	0	0	0

E—Sojo, Ja. Giambi. DP—New York 2, Oakland 1. LOB—New York 9, Oakland 6. 2B—Posada, Bellinger, Williams, Sojo, Tejada, Chavez, R. Hernandez. SH—Brosius. CS—Williams. T—3:15. A—47,860. U—Meriwether, plate; McClelland, first; Schrieber, second; Clark, third; Nelson, left field; Welke, right field.

Game 3 at New York

NEW YORK 4, OAKLAND 2

HOW THEY SCORED

Second Inning

Athletics—Eric Chavez flied to left. Miguel Tejada walked. Matt Stairs fouled to right. Ben Grieve walked, moving Tejada to second. Jeremy Giambi singled to right, scoring Tejada and moving Grieve to third. Ramon Hernandez struck out. One run. A's 1, Yankees 0.

Yankees—Bernie Williams doubled to left-center. Tino Martinez struck out. Paul O'Neill reached on an infield single, moving Williams to third. Glenallen Hill grounded to the pitcher, who threw late to home with Williams scoring and O'Neill moving to second. Luis Sojo flied to center. Scott Brosius walked, loading the bases. Derek Jeter reached on an infield single, scoring O'Neill and reloading the bases. Jorge Posada struck out. Two runs. Yankees 2, A's 1.

Fourth Inning

Yankees—Sojo walked. Brosius bunted and catcher Hernandez threw wildly to second, Sojo moving to third. Jeter grounded into 6-4 forceout, scoring Sojo. Jeter was caught stealing. Posada flied to right-center. One run. Yankees 3, A's 1.

Fifth Inning

Athletics—Terrence Long homered to right. Randy Velarde flied to right. Jason Giambi walked. Chavez grounded into 6-4-3 double play. One run. Yankees 3, A's 2.

Eighth Inning

Yankees—Williams lined to third. Martinez singled to right. O'Neill grounded to third, moving Martinez to second. Hill walked. Chuck Knoblauch ran for Hill. Sojo singled to center, scoring Martinez and moving Knoblauch to third. Sojo was thrown out attempting to advance to second on the throw to third. One run. Yankees 4, A's 2.

BOX SCORE

Oakland	AB	R	H	RBI	PO	A
Long, cf	4	1	2	1	3	1
Velarde, 2b	4	0	0	0	3	3
Ja. Giambi, 1b	2	0	0	0	7	0
Chavez, 3b	4	0	0	0	1	2
Tejada, ss	3	1	0	0	2	5
Stairs, rf	4	0	0	0	3	0
Grieve, lf	2	0	0	0	0	0
Je. Giambi, dh	4	0	1	1	0	0
R. Hernandez, c	3	0	1	0	5	1
Hudson, p	0	0	0	0	0	1
Totals	30	2	4	2	24	13

New York	AB	R	H	RBI	PO	A
Jeter, ss	4	0	1	2	2	3
Posada, c	4	0	0	0	6	1
Justice, lf	4	0	1	0	3	0
Williams, cf	4	1	1	0	2	0
Martinez, 1b	3	1	1	0	7	0
O'Neill, rf	4	1	1	0	3	0
Hill, dh	3	0	0	1	0	0
Knoblauch, pr-dh	0	0	0	0	0	0
Sojo, 2b	3	1	1	1	2	3
Brosius, 3b	2	0	0	0	2	0
O. Hernandez, p	0	0	0	0	0	0
Rivera, p	0	0	0	0	0	0
Totals	31	4	6	4	27	7

Oakland	0 1 0	0 1 0	0 0 0—2
New York	0 2 0	1 0 0	0 1 x—4

Oakland	IP	H	R	ER	BB	SO
Hudson (L)	8.0	6	4	3	4	5

New York	IP	H	R	ER	BB	SO
O. Hernandez (W)	7.0	4	2	2	5	4
Rivera (S)	2.0	0	0	0	0	1

E—Velarde, R. Hernandez, Martinez. DP—New York 2. LOB—Oakland 6, New York 7. 2B—Williams. HR—Long. CS—Jeter. T—3:12. A—56,606. U—Reilly, plate; Winters, first; Reed, second; Eddings, third; Reliford, left field; Danley, right field.

Game 4 at New York

OAKLAND 11, NEW YORK 1

HOW THEY SCORED

First Inning

Athletics—Terrence Long walked. Randy Velarde grounded into 5-4 forceout. Jason Giambi walked, moving Velarde to second. Olmedo Saenz homered to left, scoring Velarde and Jason Giambi. Eric Chavez grounded to second. Miguel Tejada struck out. A's 3, Yankees 0.

Sixth Inning

Athletics—Chavez singled to center. Tejada doubled to left, moving Chavez to third. Ben Grieve singled to right, scoring Chavez and Tejada. Mike Stanton relieved Roger Clemens. Jeremy Giambi singled to right, moving Grieve to third. Ryan Christenson ran for Jeremy Giambi. Ramon Hernandez grounded into 6-4 forceout, scoring Grieve. Long grounded to first, moving Hernandez to second. Velarde flied to center. Three runs. A's 6, Yankees 0.

Seventh Inning

Yankees—Paul O'Neill reached on an infield single. Bernie Williams flied to right-center. David Justice singled to right, moving O'Neill to second. Glenallen Hill flied to right. Jorge Posada doubled to left, scoring O'Neill and moving Justice to third. Jim Mecir relieved Barry Zito. Tino Martinez popped to second. One run. A's 6, Yankees 1.

Eighth Inning

Athletics—Tejada walked and stole second. Grieve struck out. Dwight Gooden relieved Randy Choate. Christenson singled to right, scoring Tejada. Hernandez was hit by a pitch, moving Christenson to second. Long grounded into a 4-6-3 double play. One run. A's 7, Yankees 1.

Ninth Inning

A's—Velarde doubled to left. Jason Giambi walked. Saenz was hit by a pitch, loading the bases. Adam Piatt ran for Saenz. Chavez doubled to right, scoring Velarde and Jason Giambi and moving Piatt to third. Tejada grounded to second, scoring Piatt and moving Chavez to third. Bo Porter reached on an infield single, scoring Chavez. Christenson struck out. Hernandez grounded to second. Four runs. A's 11, Yankees 1.

BOX SCORE

Oakland	AB	R	H	RBI	PO	A
Long, cf	4	0	0	0	2	0
Velarde, 2b	5	2	1	0	3	2
Menechino, 2b	0	0	0	0	2	0
Ja. Giambi, 1b	2	2	0	0	4	0
Saenz, dh	4	1	2	3	0	0
Piatt, pr-dh	0	1	0	0	0	0
Chavez, 3b	5	2	2	2	0	1
Tejada, ss	4	2	1	1	2	2
Grieve, lf	4	1	2	2	2	0
Porter, rf	1	0	1	1	1	0
Je. Giambi, rf	2	0	1	0	1	0
Christenson, pr-rf-lf	2	0	1	1	2	0
R. Hernandez, c	3	0	0	1	7	0
Zito, p	0	0	0	0	0	0
Mecir, p	0	0	0	0	1	0
Magnante, p	0	0	0	0	0	0
Jones, p	0	0	0	0	0	0
Totals	36	11	11	11	27	5

New York	AB	R	H	RBI	PO	A
Jeter, ss	3	0	2	0	1	2
Sojo, 2b	4	0	0	0	4	7
O'Neill, rf	4	1	1	0	1	0
Williams, cf	3	0	0	0	2	0
Justice, lf	4	0	2	0	1	0
Hill, dh	4	0	0	0	0	0
Posada, c	3	0	1	1	8	0
Polonia, ph	1	0	1	0	0	0
Martinez, 1b	4	0	1	0	8	2
Brosius, 3b	4	0	0	0	0	2
Clemens, p	0	0	0	0	0	2
Stanton, p	0	0	0	0	1	0
Choate, p	0	0	0	0	1	0
Gooden, p	0	0	0	0	0	0
Totals	34	1	8	1	27	15

Oakland .... 3 0 0 0 0 3 0 1 4—11
New York .... 0 0 0 0 0 1 0 0 0— 1

Oakland	IP	H	R	ER	BB	SO
Zito (W)	5.2	7	1	1	2	5
Mecir	1.0	0	0	0	0	0
Magnante	1.1	0	0	0	0	1
Jones	1.0	1	0	0	0	1

New York	IP	H	R	ER	BB	SO
Clemens (L)	*5.0	6	6	6	4	5
Stanton	1.0	1	0	0	0	0
Choate	1.1	0	1	1	1	1
Gooden	1.2	4	4	4	1	1

*Pitched to three batters in sixth.

DP—Oakland 1, New York 1. LOB—Oakland 7, New York 8. 2B—Velarde, Chavez, Tejada, Posada. HR—Saenz. SH—R. Hernandez. SB—Tejada. HBP—By Gooden (Saenz, R. Hernandez). T—3:42. A—56,915. U—Winters, plate; Reed, first; Eddings, second; Reliford, third; Danley, left field; Reilly, right field.

Game 5 at Oakland

NEW YORK 7, OAKLAND 5

HOW THEY SCORED

First Inning

Yankees—Chuck Knoblauch singled to right. Derek Jeter walked, moving Knoblauch to second. Paul O'Neill reached on an infield single, loading the bases. Bernie Williams flied to right, scoring Knoblauch. David Justice walked, loading the bases. Tino Martinez doubled to center, scoring Jeter, O'Neill and Justice. Jorge Posada reached on an infield single, moving Martinez to third. Jeff Tam relieved Gil Heredia. Luis Sojo flied to center, scoring Martinez. Scott Brosius singled to center, moving Posada to second. Knoblauch singled to right, scoring Posada and moving Brosius to third. Knoblauch stole second. Jeter flied to right. Six runs. Yankees 6, A's 0.

Second Inning

Athletics—Eric Chavez struck out. Adam Piatt singled to center. Ben Grieve struck out. Ramon Hernandez singled to center, moving Piatt to second. Terrence Long walked, loading the bases. Randy Velarde singled to left, scoring Piatt and Hernandez and moving Long to second. Jason Giambi flied to center. Two runs. Yankees 6, A's 2.

Third Inning

Athletics—Olmedo Saenz flied to right-center. Miguel Tejada singled to center. Chavez doubled to left-center, scoring Tejada. Piatt flied to left. Grieve struck out. One run. Yankees 6, A's 3.

Fourth Inning

Yankees—Williams struck out. Justice homered to right. Martinez struck out. Posada popped to third. One run. Yankees 7, A's 3.

Athletics—Hernandez singled to center. Long walked, moving Hernandez to second. Velarde singled to right, loading the bases. Jason Giambi flied to center, scoring Hernandez and moving Long to third. Saenz flied to left, scoring Long. Tejada singled to left, moving Velarde to second. Mike Stanton relieved Andy Pettitte. Chavez grounded to second. Two runs. Yankees 7, A's 5.

BOX SCORE

New York	AB	R	H	RBI	PO	A
Knoblauch, dh	5	1	2	1	0	0
Jeter, ss	4	1	1	0	1	2
O'Neill, rf	5	1	2	0	2	0
Williams, cf	4	0	0	1	2	0
Justice, lf	3	2	1	1	3	0
Bellinger, lf	0	0	0	0	0	0
Martinez, 1b	5	1	3	3	7	1
Posada, c	4	1	1	0	11	0
Sojo, 2b	3	0	0	1	0	4
Brosius, 3b	4	0	2	0	0	0
Pettitte, p	0	0	0	0	0	0
Stanton, p	0	0	0	0	1	0
Nelson, p	0	0	0	0	0	0
O. Hernandez, p	0	0	0	0	0	0
Rivera, p	0	0	0	0	0	0
Totals	37	7	12	7	27	7

Oakland	AB	R	H	RBI	PO	A
Long, cf	3	1	0	0	3	0
Fasano, c	0	0	0	0	1	0
Velarde, 2b	5	0	3	2	0	2
Ja. Giambi, 1b	4	0	1	1	8	0
Saenz, dh	4	0	1	1	0	0
Tejada, ss	5	1	3	0	0	2
Chavez, 3b	5	0	1	1	2	1
Piatt, rf	3	1	1	0	2	0
Je. Giambi, ph-rf	1	0	0	0	0	0
Grieve, lf	4	0	0	0	3	0
R. Hernandez, c	3	2	2	0	8	0
Stairs, ph	1	0	1	0	0	0
Porter, pr-cf	0	0	0	0	0	0
Heredia, p	0	0	0	0	0	0
Tam, p	0	0	0	0	0	0
Appier, p	0	0	0	0	0	0
Mecir, p	0	0	0	0	0	1
Isringhausen, p	0	0	0	0	0	0
Totals	38	5	13	5	27	6

New York .... 6 0 0 1 0 0 0 0 0—7
Oakland .... 0 2 1 2 0 0 0 0 0—5

New York	IP	H	R	ER	BB	SO
Pettitte	3.2	10	5	5	2	4
Stanton (W)	2.0	1	0	0	0	3
Nelson	1.1	0	0	0	0	2
O. Hernandez	0.1	1	0	0	0	1
Rivera (S)	1.2	1	0	0	0	1

Oakland	IP	H	R	ER	BB	SO
Heredia (L)	0.1	4	6	6	2	0
Tam	0.2	2	0	0	0	0
Appier	4.0	4	1	1	1	6
Mecir	3.0	1	0	0	0	1
Isringhausen	1.0	1	0	0	0	1

LOB—New York 8, Oakland 10. 2B—O'Neill, Martinez 2, Chavez, Stairs. HR—Justice. SF—Williams, Sojo, Ja. Giambi, Saenz. SB—Knoblauch. T—3:50. A—41,170. U—Reed, plate; Eddings, first; Reliford, second; Danley, third; Reilly, left field; Winters, right field.

COMPOSITE

BATTING AVERAGES

New York Yankees

Player, position	G	AB	R	H	2B	3B	HR	RBI	Avg.
Bellinger, lf	2	1	0	1	1	0	0	1	1.000
Polonia, ph	1	1	0	1	0	0	0	0	1.000
Martinez, 1b	5	19	2	8	2	0	0	4	.421
Knoblauch, dh-pr	3	9	1	3	0	0	0	1	.333
Williams, cf	5	20	3	5	3	0	0	1	.250
Posada, c	5	17	2	4	2	0	0	1	.235
Justice, lf	5	18	2	4	0	0	1	1	.222
Jeter, ss	5	19	1	4	0	0	0	2	.211
O'Neill, rf	5	19	4	4	1	0	0	0	.211
Sojo, 2b	5	16	2	3	2	0	0	5	.188
Brosius, 3b	5	17	0	3	1	0	0	1	.176
Hill, ph-dh	4	12	1	1	0	0	0	2	.083
Choate, p	1	0	0	0	0	0	0	0	.000
Clemens, p	2	0	0	0	0	0	0	0	.000
Gooden, p	1	0	0	0	0	0	0	0	.000
O. Hernandez, p	2	0	0	0	0	0	0	0	.000
Nelson, p	2	0	0	0	0	0	0	0	.000
Pettitte, p	2	0	0	0	0	0	0	0	.000
Rivera, p	3	0	0	0	0	0	0	0	.000
Stanton, p	3	0	0	0	0	0	0	0	.000
Vizcaino, pr-2b	1	0	1	0	0	0	0	0	.000
Totals	5	168	19	41	12	0	1	19	.244

Oakland Athletics

Player, position	G	AB	R	H	2B	3B	HR	RBI	Avg.
Porter, rf-pr-cf	2	1	0	1	0	0	0	1	1.000
Christenson, lf-pr-rf	2	2	0	1	0	0	0	1	.500
R. Hernandez, c	5	16	3	6	2	0	0	3	.375
Tejada, ss	5	20	5	7	2	0	0	1	.350
Chavez, 3b	5	21	4	7	3	0	0	4	.333
Je. Giambi, dh-rf-ph	4	9	1	3	0	0	0	1	.333
Ja. Giambi, 1b	5	14	2	4	0	0	0	1	.286
Velarde, 2b	5	20	2	5	1	0	0	3	.250
Saenz, ph-dh	4	13	1	3	0	0	1	4	.231
Piatt, rf-pr-dh	3	6	2	1	0	0	0	0	.167
Long, cf	5	19	2	3	0	0	1	1	.158
Grieve, lf	5	17	1	2	0	0	0	2	.118
Stairs, rf-ph	3	9	0	1	1	0	0	0	.111
Appier, p	2	0	0	0	0	0	0	0	.000
Fasano, c	1	0	0	0	0	0	0	0	.000
Heredia, p	2	0	0	0	0	0	0	0	.000
Hudson, p	1	0	0	0	0	0	0	0	.000
Isringhausen, p	2	0	0	0	0	0	0	0	.000
Jones, p	2	0	0	0	0	0	0	0	.000
Magnante, p	2	0	0	0	0	0	0	0	.000
Mecir, p	3	0	0	0	0	0	0	0	.000
Menechino, 2b	1	0	0	0	0	0	0	0	.000
Tam, p	3	0	0	0	0	0	0	0	.000
Zito, p	1	0	0	0	0	0	0	0	.000
Totals	5	167	23	44	9	0	2	22	.263

PITCHING AVERAGES

New York Yankees

Pitcher	G	IP	H	R	ER	BB	SO	W	L	ERA
Rivera	3	5.0	2	0	0	0	2	0	0	0.00
Nelson	2	2.0	0	0	0	0	2	0	0	0.00
Stanton	3	4.1	5	1	1	1	3	1	0	2.08
O. Hernandez	2	7.1	5	2	2	5	5	1	0	2.45
Pettitte	2	11.1	15	5	5	3	7	1	0	3.97
Choate	1	1.1	0	1	1	1	1	0	0	6.75
Clemens	2	11.0	13	10	10	8	10	0	2	8.18
Gooden	1	1.2	4	4	4	1	1	0	0	21.60
Totals	5	44.0	44	23	23	19	31	3	2	4.70

Shutouts—Pettitte and Rivera (combined). Saves—Rivera 3.

Oakland Athletics

Pitcher	G	IP	H	R	ER	BB	SO	W	L	ERA
Mecir	3	5.1	1	0	0	0	2	0	0	0.00
Magnante	2	3.0	1	0	0	0	2	0	0	0.00
Isringhausen	2	2.0	1	0	0	0	3	0	0	0.00
Tam	3	2.0	3	1	0	1	1	0	0	0.00
Jones	2	1.1	1	0	0	0	1	0	0	0.00
Zito	1	5.2	7	1	1	2	5	1	0	1.59
Hudson	1	8.0	6	4	3	4	5	0	1	3.38
Appier	2	10.1	10	4	4	6	13	0	1	3.48
Heredia	2	6.1	11	9	9	3	3	1	1	12.79
Totals	5	44.0	41	19	17	16	35	2	3	3.48

N.L. Division Series

NEW YORK VS. SAN FRANCISCO

Livan Hernandez and his teammates celebrate the Giants' Game 1 victory. Unfortunately for the Giants, they never experienced that winning feeling again.

The bottom line: The New York Mets, looking for their fourth World Series appearance and third championship, advanced to the National League Championship Series for the first time since 1986 with a surprising three-games-to-one win over the San Francisco Giants. The wild-card Mets dispatched baseball's best regular-season team in dramatic fashion, surviving a ninth-inning Giants rally for a 10-inning win in Game 2 at Pacific Bell Park and prevailing in a 13-inning Game 3 marathon at New York's Shea Stadium. After falling quietly in the first game, the Mets rebounded to hand the Giants their first three-game losing streak since early August and end hopes for their first N.L. pennant since 1989.

Why the Mets won: Pitching and timely hitting were the difference after a 5-1 Game 1 loss. Showing the ability to overcome adversity, the Mets shrugged off a three-run, game-tying, ninth-inning home run by J.T. Snow in Game 3 and prevailed in the 10th on Jay Payton's clutch hit. Then they fought valiantly to win Game 3 on a 13th-inning home run by Benny Agbayani. Over the series' final 18 innings, the Mets bullpen combined with starters Rick Reed and Bobby J. Jones to shut out the high-scoring Giants; over the final two games, the Giants' Big Three of Barry Bonds, Jeff Kent and Ellis Burks were a combined 3-for-15 with no RBIs and one run scored.

TURNING POINTS:

Game 1: Any hope the Mets had of winning the first playoff game at new Pac Bell Park was shot down in a long third inning in which the Giants scored four times. Bill Mueller triggered the rally with a two-out single off Mets lefthander Mike Hampton and Bonds, who entered the series with a history of postseason failure, followed with a ground-ball triple into the right field corner, breaking a 1-1 deadlock. Suddenly trailing, Hampton was forced to wait about five minutes as manager Bobby Valentine and the trainer examined right fielder Derek Bell, who sprained his ankle while chasing Bonds' hit. Then, after walking Kent, he had to wait again as Darryl Hamilton replaced Bell. When Burks followed with a line drive off the left field foul pole for a three-run homer, Giants ace Livan Hernandez had all the support he needed to improve his playoff record to 5-0. The Cuban righthander worked 7 $^{2}/_{3}$ innings and allowed only five hits before turning matters over to Felix Rodriguez and Robb Nen. The 5-1 win was the first in the postseason for Baker, and Hampton suffered his first career loss to the Giants after nine victories.

Game 2: The Mets showed their character in the 10th inning of a critical game, after the Giants had risen from the dead with a shocking game-tying rally in the ninth inning off closer Armando Benitez. Facing the prospect of going down two-games-to-none with no momentum, the New Yorkers scored a 10th-inning run on a two-out double by Hamilton and a run-scoring single by rookie center fielder Jay Payton to claim a 5-4 victory. The Mets had carried a 2-1 lead into the ninth behind the pitching of lefthander Al Leiter and they stretched their margin on Edgardo Alfonzo's two-run homer. But the Giants sent the Pac Bell Park faithful into a towel-waving frenzy in the bottom of the ninth when they tied the game on a shocking three-run homer by Snow—his first career pinch-hit home run. After the Mets had regained the lead in the top of the 10th, veteran lefty John Franco came on to record his first career postseason save in the bottom of the inning.

Game 3: If Game 2 was the momentum shifter, this one was the backbreaker. The Mets treated 56,270 Shea Stadium fans to an exhausting and emotional 3-2 victory in a game that lasted 5 hours and 22 minutes before left fielder Agbayani drove an Aaron Fultz pitch over the left-center field fence in the bottom of the 13th inning. The Mets' second straight dramatic win was made possible by the outstanding work of starter Rick Reed, who allowed two runs in six innings, and five relievers, who allowed only four hits over seven shutout frames. After the Mets had tied the game in the eighth on Alfonzo's RBI double off dependable Giants closer Nen, both teams squandered good scoring opportunities before the Mets finally broke through. The Giants' leadoff hitter reached base in the ninth, 10th and 12th innings; the Mets had runners in scoring position in the ninth and 11th. The Giants missed on a chance in the top of the 13th when winning pitcher Rick White retired Bonds on a popup with two runners on base. Agbayani, 0-for-5 before the home run, ended the marathon moments later against Fultz, the Giants' sixth pitcher.

Game 4: This one belonged to Bobby J. Jones—and a raucous Shea Stadium crowd that cheered every pitch of his 4-0 Division Series masterpiece. Jones, confusing the Giants with his 84-mph fastballs and big-breaking curves, pitched the first one-hit shutout in postseason play since 1967 and gave the Mets a berth in the NLCS opposite the St. Louis Cardinals. Jones, who had been demoted to Class AAA Tidewater earlier in the season, retired the Giants in eight of his nine innings and allowed only a fifth-inning double by Kent—a line drive that ticked the top of leaping third baseman Robin Ventura's glove. That fifth inning was Jones' moment of truth as he retired opposing pitcher Mark Gardner on a popup with the bases loaded after surrendering Kent's hit and two walks. The Mets gave Jones all the support he needed with Ventura's two-run homer in the first and a two-run, fifth-inning double by Alfonzo.

WORTH NOTING:

Giants: After bashing their way through the regular season with a San Francisco-record 925 runs and a franchise-record 226 home runs, the Giants managed only 11 runs and two homers against the Mets. ... Bonds continued his disappointing play with a .176 series average and one RBI. Kent batted .375, but he, too, drove in only one run. ... To add insult to injury, Bonds made the final out in all three Mets wins. ... Before Game 1, two-time Manager of the Year Dusty Baker had never managed a postseason victory. His 1997 Giants were swept in the Division Series by the eventual World Series-champion Florida Marlins.

Mets: The Mets became only the second N.L. team in the six years of Division Series play to lose the first game and still advance to the NLCS. ... In Game 1, the Giants threesome of Bonds, Kent and Burks were 4-for-9 with five RBIs. They combined for eight hits and one RBI in the other three games. ... In his three starts after taking over in right field for the injured Bell, Timo Perez collected five hits and drove in three runs from the leadoff spot in the Mets lineup. He also played well defensively. ... Jones' one-hit series clincher came on the 44th anniversary of Don Larsen's World Series perfect game at Yankee Stadium.

WORTH QUOTING:

Giants: Bonds, after watching Hernandez post his Game 1 win: "Livan was phenomenal. He's been doing it for us now for quite awhile. You've got to go with your big dog in the big games, and that's him."... Baker, on his controversial Game 4 decision not to pinch hit for pitcher Gardner with the bases loaded and the Mets leading 2-0 in the fifth inning: "I don't regret the decision. We were short on pitching and it was only the fifth inning. It was too early to pinch hit. I figured we'd get some more runs."

Mets: Backup outfielder Hamilton, after the Mets had coughed up a ninth-inning Game 2 lead and recovered in the 10th for a dramatic win: "Stuff like this seems to happen to the Mets. Last year, you always wondered what crazy thing was going to happen next. It's hard on the fans and it's hard on us, (but) it's great when we win." ... Valentine, after the 13th-inning win in Game 3: "Brilliant finish, gutted it out. Everyone did their little parts."... Catcher Mike Piazza on Jones in Game 4: "Just text-book pitching. He really knew how to work the hitters. As the game wore on, he just got tougher and tougher."

Game 1 at San Francisco

SAN FRANCISCO 5, NEW YORK 1

HOW THEY SCORED

First Inning

Giants—Marvin Benard struck out. Bill Mueller doubled to left. Barry Bonds singled to center, moving Mueller to third. Bonds advanced to second on the throw. Jeff Kent grounded to shortstop, scoring Mueller and moving Bonds to third. Ellis Burks grounded to first. One run. Giants 1, Mets 0.

Third Inning

Mets—Derek Bell flied to center. Mike Bordick singled to right. Mike Hampton singled to right, moving Bordick to second. Benny Agbayani walked, loading the bases. Jay Payton flied to right-center, scoring Bordick and moving Hampton to third. Edgardo Alfonzo flied to right. One run. Giants 1, Mets 1.

Giants—Livan Hernandez grounded to second. Benard grounded to the pitcher. Mueller singled to left-center. Bonds tripled to right, scoring Mueller. Kent walked. Burks homered to left, scoring Bonds and Kent. Rich Aurilia struck out. Four runs. Giants 5, Mets 1.

BOX SCORE

New York	AB	R	H	RBI	PO	A
Agbayani, lf	3	0	1	0	3	0
Cook, p	0	0	0	0	0	0
White, p	0	0	0	0	0	1
McEwing, lf	0	0	0	0	0	0
Harris, ph	1	0	0	0	0	0
Payton, cf	3	0	0	1	0	0
Alfonzo, 2b	4	0	1	0	1	3
Piazza, c	3	0	0	0	7	0
Ventura, 3b	4	0	0	0	1	1
Zeile, 1b	3	0	1	0	7	2
Bell, rf	1	0	0	0	0	0
Hamilton, rf-lf	2	0	0	0	0	0
Rusch, p	0	0	0	0	0	0
Bordick, ss	3	1	1	0	2	3
Hampton, p	2	0	1	0	3	0
Wendell, p	0	0	0	0	0	0
Perez, ph-rf	2	0	0	0	0	0
Totals	31	1	5	1	24	10

San Francisco	AB	R	H	RBI	PO	A
Benard, cf	4	0	0	0	5	0
Davis, ph	1	0	0	0	0	0
Nen, p	0	0	0	0	0	0
Mueller, 3b	5	2	2	0	2	0
Bonds, lf	3	1	2	1	3	0
Kent, 2b	3	1	1	1	2	2
Burks, rf	3	1	1	3	2	0
Aurilia, ss	4	0	2	0	2	2
Snow, 1b	3	0	1	0	5	0
Estalella, c	4	0	0	0	6	0
Hernandez, p	3	0	0	0	0	0
Rodriguez, p	0	0	0	0	0	0
Crespo, ph	1	0	1	0	0	0
Murray, cf	0	0	0	0	0	0
Totals	34	5	10	5	27	4

New York	0 0 1	0 0 0	0 0 0	—1
San Francisco	1 0 4	0 0 0	0 0 x	—5

New York	IP	H	R	ER	BB	SO
Hampton (L)	5.1	6	5	5	3	2
Wendell	0.2	0	0	0	0	2
Cook	0.2	0	0	0	1	1
White	0.2	4	0	0	0	0
Rusch	0.2	0	0	0	0	2

San Francisco	IP	H	R	ER	BB	SO
Hernandez (W)	7.2	5	1	1	5	5
Rodriguez	0.1	0	0	0	0	1
Nen	1.0	0	0	0	0	0

LOB—New York 9, San Francisco 9. 2B—Zeile, Mueller, Aurilia. 3B—Bonds. HR—Burks. SF—Payton. SB—Bonds. T—3:06. A—40,430. U—Kellogg, home; Cederstrom, first; Montague, second; Morrison, third; Young, left field; Barrett, right field.

Game 2 at San Francisco

NEW YORK 5, SAN FRANCISCO 4 (10 INNINGS)

HOW THEY SCORED

Second Inning

Mets—Robin Ventura was hit by a pitch. Benny Agbayani walked, moving Ventura to second. Jay Payton grounded into a 4-6 forceout, Ventura moving to third. Mike Bordick walked, loading the bases. Al Leiter bunted into a 3-2 fielder's-choice force at home, Payton moving to third and Bordick to second. Timo Perez singled to center, scoring Payton and Bordick and moving Leiter to second. Edgardo Alfonzo struck out. Two runs. Mets 2, Giants 0.

Giants—Jeff Kent singled to right and stole second. Ellis Burks doubled to left, scoring Kent. Ramon Martinez flied to center. Rich Aurilia grounded to third. Bobby Estalella fouled to the catcher. One run. Mets 2, Giants 1.

Ninth Inning

Mets—Felix Rodriguez relieved Doug Henry. Bordick struck out. Leiter struck out. Perez singled to left. Alfonzo homered to left-center, scoring Perez. Mike Piazza fouled to the catcher. Two runs. Mets 4, Giants 1.

Giants—Barry Bonds doubled to right-center. Armando Benitez relieved Leiter. Kent reached on an infield single, Bonds holding. Burks flied to right. J.T. Snow batted for Martinez and homered to right, scoring Bonds and Kent. Aurilia grounded to shortstop. Estalella popped to left. Three runs. Mets 4, Giants 4.

John Franco gives a fist pump after collecting his first postseason save in Game 2.

10th Inning

Mets—Todd Zeile grounded to second. Ventura fouled to left. Darryl Hamilton batted for Joe McEwing and doubled to center. Jay Payton singled to center, scoring Hamilton. Mike Bordick struck out. One run. Mets 5, Giants 4.

BOX SCORE

New York	AB	R	H	RBI	PO	A
Perez, rf	5	1	3	2	2	0
Alfonzo, 2b	5	1	1	2	2	0
Piazza, c	4	0	2	0	8	0
Zeile, 1b	5	0	0	0	5	0
Ventura, 3b	3	0	0	0	5	1
Agbayani, lf	2	0	1	0	3	0
McEwing, pr-lf	0	0	0	0	0	0
Hamilton, ph-lf	1	1	1	0	0	0
Payton, cf	5	1	1	1	2	0
Bordick, ss	4	1	1	0	3	4
Leiter, p	4	0	0	0	0	1
Benitez, p	0	0	0	0	0	0
J. Franco, p	0	0	0	0	0	1
Totals	38	5	10	5	30	7

San Francisco	AB	R	H	RBI	PO	A
Murray, cf	4	0	1	0	3	0
Benard, ph	0	0	0	0	0	0
Mueller, 3b	5	0	1	0	0	3
Bonds, lf	5	1	1	0	1	0
Kent, 1b-2b	4	2	2	0	6	3
Burks, rf	3	0	1	1	2	0
Martinez, 2b	3	0	0	0	3	5
Snow, ph-1b	1	1	1	3	1	0
Aurilia, ss	4	0	0	0	3	3
Estalella, c	4	0	0	0	9	1
Estes, p	0	0	0	0	1	0
Rueter, p	0	0	0	0	1	0
Henry, p	0	0	0	0	0	0
Crespo, ph	1	0	0	0	0	0
Rodriguez, p	0	0	0	0	0	0
Rios, ph	1	0	1	0	0	0
Totals	35	4	8	4	30	15

New York	0 2 0	0 0 0	0 0 2	1	—5
San Francisco	0 1 0	0 0 0	0 0 3	0	—4

New York	IP	H	R	ER	BB	SO
Leiter	*8.0	5	2	2	3	6
Benitez (W)	†1.0	3	2	2	0	0
J. Franco (S)	1.0	0	0	0	0	1

San Francisco	IP	H	R	ER	BB	SO
Estes	3.0	3	2	2	3	3
Rueter	4.1	3	0	0	1	1
Henry	0.2	0	0	0	1	0
Rodriguez (L)	2.0	4	3	3	0	3

*Pitched to one batter in ninth.
†Pitched to one batter in 10th.

DP—New York 1, San Francisco 2. LOB—New York 9, San Francisco 5. 2B—Piazza, Hamilton, Bonds, Burks. HR—Snow, Alfonzo. SH—Benard. SB—Kent. HBP—By Estes (Ventura). T—3:41. A—40,430. U—Cederstrom, plate; Montague, first; Morrison, second; Young, third; Barrett, left field; Kellogg, right field.

Game 3 at New York

NEW YORK 3, SAN FRANCISCO 2 (13 INNINGS)

HOW THEY SCORED

Fourth Inning

Giants—Ellis Burks singled to center. J.T. Snow singled to center, moving Burks to second. Rich Aurilia fouled to first. Bobby Estalella singled to left, scoring Burks and moving Snow to second. Russ Ortiz bunted into 1-6 fielder's choice, moving Estalella to second. Marvin Benard singled to right, scoring Estalella and moving Ortiz to third. Bill Mueller flied to center. Two runs. Giants 2, Mets 0.

Sixth Inning

Mets—Mike Bordick walked. Darryl Hamilton batted for Rick Reed and singled to right, moving Bordick to third. Timo Perez singled to left, scoring Bordick and moving Hamilton to second. Edgardo Alfonzo grounded to shortstop, moving Hamilton to third and Perez to second. Mike Piazza was intentionally walked. Alan Embree relieved Ortiz. Robin Ventura grounded into a 4-6-3 double play. One run. Giants 2, Mets 1.

Eighth Inning

Mets—Bordick was hit by a pitch. Lenny Harris batted for Turk Wendell and grounded into a 4-6 fielder's choice. Perez popped to shortstop. Robb Nen relieved Doug Henry. Harris stole second. Alfonzo doubled to left, scoring Harris. Piazza struck out. One run. Giants 2, Mets 2.

13th Inning

Mets—Ventura grounded to second. Benny Agbayani homered to left-center. One run. Mets 3, Giants 2.

BOX SCORE

San Francisco	AB	R	H	RBI	PO	A
Benard, cf-rf	6	0	1	1	4	0
Mueller, 3b	6	0	2	0	0	1
Bonds, lf	5	0	0	0	4	0
Kent, 2b	6	0	2	0	1	6
Burks, rf	4	1	1	0	5	0
Fultz, p	0	0	0	0	0	0
Snow, 1b	4	0	2	0	9	0
Aurilia, ss	4	0	0	0	4	4
Nen, p	0	0	0	0	0	0
Rios, ph	1	0	0	0	0	0
Mirabelli, c	1	0	0	0	2	0
Estalella, c	4	1	1	1	8	1
Crespo, ph	1	0	0	0	0	0
Rodriguez, p	0	0	0	0	0	0
Murray, cf	1	0	0	0	0	0
Ortiz, p	3	0	0	0	0	0
Embree, p	0	0	0	0	0	0
Henry, p	0	0	0	0	0	0
Martinez, ss	3	0	2	0	0	2
Totals	49	2	11	2	37	14

New York	AB	R	H	RBI	PO	A
Perez, rf	6	0	1	1	5	0
Alfonzo, 2b	5	0	2	1	2	0
Piazza, c	4	0	1	0	12	1

Edgardo Alfonzo provided a two-run double to help ensure a Mets victory in Game 4.

New York	AB	R	H	RBI	PO	A
McEwing, pr-3b	1	0	1	0	0	0
Ventura, 3b-1b	5	0	1	0	1	3
Agbayani, lf	6	1	1	1	2	0
Payton, cf	5	0	1	0	4	0
Zeile, 1b	3	0	0	0	7	1
White, p	0	0	0	0	0	0
Bordick, ss	2	1	0	0	2	2
Benitez, p	0	0	0	0	0	0
Pratt, ph-c	1	0	0	0	4	0
Reed, p	1	0	0	0	0	1
Hamilton, ph	1	0	1	0	0	0
Cook, p	0	0	0	0	0	0
Wendell, p	0	0	0	0	0	0
Harris, ph	1	1	0	0	0	0
J. Franco, p	0	0	0	0	0	0
Abbott, ss	2	0	0	0	0	0
Totals	43	3	9	3	39	8

San Francisco	0 0 0	2 0 0	0 0 0	0 0 0	0—2
New York	0 0 0	0 0 1	0 1 0	0 0 0	1—3

One out when winning run scored.

San Francisco	IP	H	R	ER	BB	SO
Ortiz	5.1	2	1	1	4	4
Embree	0.2	0	0	0	0	0
Henry	1.2	0	1	1	0	1
Nen	1.1	2	0	0	1	3
Rodriguez	2.0	2	0	0	1	2
Fultz (L)	1.1	3	1	1	0	0

New York	IP	H	R	ER	BB	SO
Reed	6.0	7	2	2	2	6
Cook	0.2	0	0	0	1	0
Wendell	1.1	0	0	0	1	3
J. Franco	1.0	1	.0	0	0	1
Benitez	2.0	1	0	0	1	3
White (W)	2.0	2	0	0	2	4

DP—San Francisco 2. LOB—San Francisco 16, New York 10. 2B—Mueller, Alfonzo. HR—Agbayani. SH—Mueller. SB—Payton, Harris. CS—Alfonzo. HBP—By Henry (Bordick). T—5:22. A—56,270. U—Crawford, plate; Gorman, first; Roe, second; DiMuro, third; Rieker, left field; Craft, right field.

Game 4 at New York

NEW YORK 4, SAN FRANCISCO 0

HOW THEY SCORED

First Inning

Mets—Timo Perez struck out. Edgardo Alfonzo flied to right. Mike Piazza walked. Robin Ventura homered to right-center, scoring Piazza. Benny Agbayani fouled to third. Two runs. Mets 2, Giants 0.

Fifth Inning

Mets—Mike Bordick grounded to shortstop. Bobby Jones struck out on a Mark Gardner wild pitch and reached first safely. Perez doubled to right, moving Jones to third. Alfonzo doubled to center scoring Jones and Perez. Doug Henry relieved Gardner. Piazza flied to center. Ventura was walked intentionally. Agbayani flied to center. Two runs. Mets 4, Giants 0.

BOX SCORE

San Francisco	AB	R	H	RBI	PO	A
Benard, cf	4	0	0	0	3	0
Mueller, 3b	4	0	0	0	1	1
Bonds, lf	4	0	0	0	2	0
Kent, 2b	3	0	1	0	0	2
Burks, rf	3	0	0	0	3	0
Snow, 1b	2	0	0	0	8	0
Aurilia, ss	3	0	0	0	1	2
Mirabelli, c	1	0	0	0	4	1
Crespo, ph	1	0	0	0	0	0
Del Toro, p	0	0	0	0	0	0
Gardner, p	2	0	0	0	0	1
Henry, p	0	0	0	0	0	0
Embree, p	0	0	0	0	0	0
Davis, ph	1	0	0	0	0	0
Estalella, c	0	0	0	0	2	0
Totals	28	0	1	0	24	7

New York	AB	R	H	RBI	PO	A
Perez, rf	4	1	1	0	3	0
Alfonzo, 2b	4	0	1	2	1	4
Piazza, c	3	1	0	0	5	1
Ventura, 3b	2	1	1	2	0	1
Agbayani, lf	4	0	2	0	2	0
McEwing, pr-lf	0	0	0	0	0	0
Payton, cf	4	0	1	0	4	0
Zeile, 1b	3	0	0	0	11	1
Bordick, ss	3	0	0	0	0	1
B.J. Jones, p	4	1	0	0	1	0
Totals	31	4	6	4	27	8

San Francisco	0 0 0	0 0 0	0 0 0—0
New York	2 0 0	0 2 0	0 0 x—4

San Francisco	IP	H	R	ER	BB	SO
Gardner (L)	4.1	4	4	4	2	5
Henry	1.2	1	0	0	2	0
Embree	1.0	0	0	0	0	0
Del Toro	1.0	1	0	0	0	2

New York	IP	H	R	ER	BB	SO
B.J. Jones (W)	9.0	1	0	0	2	5

E—Aurilia. LOB—San Francisco 3, New York 8. 2B—Kent, Perez, Alfonzo, Agbayani. HR—Ventura. SB—Perez. CS—Payton. HBP—By Del Toro (Bordick). WP—Gardner. T—2:48. A—52,888. U—Gorman, plate; Roe, first; DiMuro, second; Rieker, third; Craft, left field; Crawford, right field.

COMPOSITE

BATTING AVERAGES

New York Mets

Player, position	G	AB	R	H	2B	3B	HR	RBI	Avg.
McEwing, lf-pr-3b	4	1	0	1	0	0	0	0	1.000
Hamilton, rf-lf-ph	3	4	1	2	1	0	0	0	.500
Hampton, p	1	2	0	1	0	0	0	0	.500
Agbayani, lf	4	15	1	5	1	0	1	1	.333
Perez, ph-rf	4	17	2	5	1	0	0	3	.294
Alfonzo, 2b	4	18	1	5	2	0	1	5	.278
Piazza, c	4	14	1	3	1	0	0	0	.214
Payton, cf	4	17	1	3	0	0	0	2	.176
Bordick, ss	4	12	3	2	0	0	0	0	.167
Ventura, 3b-1b	4	14	1	2	0	0	1	2	.143
Zeile, 1b	4	14	0	1	1	0	0	0	.071
Benitez, p	2	0	0	0	0	0	0	0	.000
Cook, p	2	0	0	0	0	0	0	0	.000
J. Franco, p	2	0	0	0	0	0	0	0	.000
Rusch, p	1	0	0	0	0	0	0	0	.000
Wendell, p	2	0	0	0	0	0	0	0	.000
White, p	2	0	0	0	0	0	0	0	.000
Bell, rf	1	1	0	0	0	0	0	0	.000
Pratt, ph-c	1	1	0	0	0	0	0	0	.000
Reed, p	1	1	0	0	0	0	0	0	.000
Abbott, ss	1	2	0	0	0	0	0	0	.000
Harris, ph	2	2	1	0	0	0	0	0	.000
B.J. Jones, p	1	4	1	0	0	0	0	0	.000
Leiter, p	1	4	0	0	0	0	0	0	.000
Totals	4	143	13	30	7	0	3	13	.210

San Francisco Giants

Player, position	G	AB	R	H	2B	3B	HR	RBI	Avg.
Rios, ph	2	2	0	1	0	0	0	0	.500
Snow, 1b-ph	4	10	1	4	0	0	1	3	.400
Kent, 2b-1b	4	16	3	6	1	0	0	1	.375
Martinez, 2b-ss	2	6	0	2	0	0	0	0	.333
Mueller, 3b	4	20	2	5	2	0	0	0	.250
Crespo, ph	4	4	0	1	0	0	0	0	.250
Burks, rf	4	13	2	3	1	0	1	4	.231
Murray, cf	3	5	0	1	0	0	0	0	.200
Bonds, lf	4	17	2	3	1	1	0	1	.176
Aurilia, ss	4	15	0	2	1	0	0	0	.133
Estalella, c	4	12	1	1	0	0	0	1	.083
Benard, cf-ph-rf	4	14	0	1	0	0	0	1	.071
Del Toro, p	1	0	0	0	0	0	0	0	.000
Embree, p	2	0	0	0	0	0	0	0	.000
Estes, p	1	0	0	0	0	0	0	0	.000
Fultz, p	1	0	0	0	0	0	0	0	.000
Henry, p	3	0	0	0	0	0	0	0	.000
Nen, p	2	0	0	0	0	0	0	0	.000
Rodriguez, p	3	0	0	0	0	0	0	0	.000
Rueter, p	1	0	0	0	0	0	0	0	.000
Davis, ph	2	2	0	0	0	0	0	0	.000
Mirabelli, c	2	2	0	0	0	0	0	0	.000
Gardner, p	1	2	0	0	0	0	0	0	.000
Hernandez, p	1	3	0	0	0	0	0	0	.000
Ortiz, p	1	3	0	0	0	0	0	0	.000
Totals	4	146	11	30	6	1	2	11	.205

PITCHING AVERAGES

New York Mets

Pitcher	G	IP	H	R	ER	BB	SO	W	L	ERA
B.J. Jones	1	9.0	1	0	0	2	5	1	0	0.00
White	2	2.2	6	0	0	2	4	1	0	0.00
J. Franco	2	2.0	1	0	0	0	2	0	0	0.00
Wendell	2	2.0	0	0	0	1	5	0	0	0.00
Cook	2	1.1	0	0	0	2	1	0	0	0.00
Rusch	1	0.2	0	0	0	0	2	0	0	0.00
Leiter	1	8.0	5	2	2	3	6	0	0	2.25
Reed	1	6.0	7	2	2	2	6	0	0	3.00
Benitez	2	3.0	4	2	2	1	3	1	0	6.00
Hampton	1	5.1	6	5	5	3	2	0	1	8.44
Totals	4	40.0	30	11	11	16	36	3	1	2.48

Shutout—B.J. Jones. Save—J. Franco.

San Francisco Giants

Pitcher	G	IP	H	R	ER	BB	SO	W	L	ERA
Rueter	1	4.1	3	0	0	1	1	0	0	0.00
Nen	2	2.1	2	0	0	1	3	0	0	0.00
Embree	2	1.2	0	0	0	0	0	0	0	0.00
Del Toro	1	1.0	1	0	0	0	2	0	0	0.00
Hernandez	1	7.2	5	1	1	5	5	1	0	1.17
Ortiz	1	5.1	2	1	1	4	4	0	0	1.69
Henry	3	4.0	1	1	1	3	1	0	0	2.25
Estes	1	3.0	3	2	2	3	3	0	0	6.00
Rodriguez	3	4.1	6	3	3	1	6	0	1	6.23
Fultz	1	1.1	3	1	1	0	0	0	1	6.75
Gardner	1	4.1	4	4	4	2	5	0	1	8.31
Totals	4	39.1	30	13	13	20	30	1	3	2.97

No shutouts or saves.

N.L. DIVISION SERIES

ST. LOUIS VS. ATLANTA

The bottom line: In a shocking reversal of form, the St. Louis Cardinals swept past the "Team of the '90s" and snapped the Braves' unprecedented string of NLCS appearances at eight. The opportunistic Cardinals dominated their playoff-seasoned opponents in a three-game blitz that rocked one of the game's outstanding pitching staffs for 24 runs and avenged a 1996 NLCS loss to the Braves. The Cardinals pounded away with the big bat of center fielder Jim Edmonds, who was 8-of-14 with two home runs, seven RBIs and a Division Series-record four doubles, and they kept Atlanta hitters at bay with a sterling effort from their normally suspect bullpen. The Braves, who compiled a 15-2 Division Series record and made five World Series appearances in the 1990s, saw their playoff losing streak stretch to seven games—four straight to the Yankees in the 1999 fall classic and three to the Cardinals.

Why the Cardinals won: They showed a quick-strike ability that put two of the game's top pitchers in a hole from which they could not recover. Righthander Greg Maddux, a four-time Cy Young Award winner who posted a 19-9 regular-season record, was rocked for six first-inning runs in the opener at Busch Stadium and 21-game winner Tom Glavine, a two-time Cy Young winner, surrendered seven runs over the first three innings of Game 2. While Edmonds and his Cardinals teammates were pounding the Braves with their bats, relievers Britt Reames, Mike James, Matt Morris and Dave Veres were providing timely interference in relief of shaky Cardinals starters.

TURNING POINTS:

Game 1: The opener was decided in the first inning on five singles, two Braves errors and a misplayed fly ball. Before Maddux could even catch his breath, the Braves were trailing 6-0 and the series pattern had been set. An error by third baseman Chipper Jones on Ray Lankford's grounder and a throwing error by catcher Paul Bako contributed to the onslaught, which was a lot worse than it should have been. The Cardinals were thankful for the generosity when 21-year-old Rick Ankiel, a surprise Game 1 starter, self-destructed and allowed the Braves to crawl back into the game. Ankiel, a lefthander who was 3-0 with a 1.65 ERA over his last five regular-season starts, gave up four third-inning runs while walking four batters and throwing a modern major league-record five wild pitches in a bizarre breakdown that gave new meaning to the term "wild." Not only did Ankiel start missing the strike zone, he bounced several pitches past catcher Carlos Hernandez and fired others well over his head, off the backstop. Ankiel was replaced by James, who combined with Mike Timlin, Reames and Veres to allow only one run over the final 6 1/3 innings. The Cardinals' 7-5 victory was punctuated by Edmonds' fourth-inning home run off Maddux.

Game 2: This, too, was decided in the bottom of the first inning. The Braves, shaken by their first-game collapse, jumped on 20-game winner Darryl Kile for two quick runs on Chipper Jones' RBI single and a groundout by Brian Jordan, temporarily quieting the expectant Busch Stadium crowd. But the Cardinals responded in the bottom of the inning on Fernando Vina's leadoff single, a walk to Edmonds and a dramatic home run by first baseman Will Clark. Having surrendered his early advantage, Glavine surrendered a solo home run to catcher Hernandez in the second and a two-run double to Lankford in a three-run third. When Glavine was relieved by Andy Ashby with one out in the third, it marked his shortest outing since 1993 and his worst postseason start since the 1992 NLCS against Pittsburgh. Kile did not surrender another run while working seven innings in the Cardinals' eventual 10-4 win and Mark McGwire, relegated to pinch-hit duty because of a sore knee, provided the coup de grace with an eighth-inning homer that sent the crowd into ecstasy. Edmonds continued his torrid assault with three doubles, a Division Series single-game record.

Game 3: The turning point for the Cardinals was as easy as 1-2-3. Second baseman Vina, the setup man for St. Louis' offense, provided the "1" on the game's second pitch when he muscled up on a Kevin Millwood fastball and hit a shocking home run. Edmonds took care of the "2" in the third inning, launching a pitch from Millwood 418 feet over the right field wall for a two-run homer, breaking a 1-1 tie. Vina's two-run single highlighted a three-run sixth inning that destroyed any hopes for a Braves comeback. Again the Cardinals' bullpen stepped front and center in relief of Garrett Stephenson, who had to leave the game in the fourth inning with a stiff elbow. Reames, James, Morris and Veres finished off a three-hitter that left long-spoiled Atlanta fans scratching their heads.

Shortstop Edgar Renteria scored three times and stole a base during the Cardinals' Game 2 Division Series victory over the reeling Braves.

WORTH NOTING:

Braves: Payback was not so sweet for the Braves, many of whom could remember their comeback from a three-games-to-one deficit to beat the Cardinals in the 1996 NLCS. Atlanta outscored St. Louis, 32-1, over the final three games of that series. ... After five straight Division Series wins, the Braves failed to reach the NLCS for the first time since 1990. ... Atlanta's playoff failure was a continuation of a late regular-season collapse. The Braves lost four of their last five games and a season-ending ninth-inning loss to Colorado cost them home-field advantage in the first round of the playoffs. ... A less-than-capacity crowd of 49,898 in Game 3, the only contest at Turner Field, included many red-clad Cardinals fans. ... The one bright spot for Millwood was his success against Clark, who struck out and popped up against him in Game 3. Entering the game, Clark was 5-for-8 with four career home runs against the righthander.

Cardinals: The underdog Cardinals outscored the Braves 24-10, outhit them .275-.189 and outhomered them 6-1. ... The Cardinals have never lost a game in a best-of-five series, sweeping the Braves in 1982, the Padres in 1996 and the Braves in 2000. ... The Cardinals were 6-for-12 against Game 2 starter Tom Glavine, who had finished the regular season with 14 consecutive scoreless innings. ... Edmonds punctuated his Game 2 performance with a spectacular over-the-shoulder warning-track catch on a drive hit by Braves shortstop Rafael Furcal. ... The Cardinals committed only one error in the three-game series. The Braves committed five.

WORTH QUOTING:

Braves: Chipper Jones, on the error-filled first inning that allowed the Cardinals to take a 6-0 lead in Game 1: "I'd like to get a do-over on that first inning. We were like the Bad News Bears out there. We have nobody to blame but ourselves for this loss." ... Pitching coach Leo Mazzone, after watching Maddux and Glavine get manhandled in Games 1 and 2: "It's hard to believe what you're seeing with the way these two games have gone. We're so spoiled with the great pitching we've had over the years."

Cardinals: Catcher Hernandez, when asked if he could have caught any of Ankiel's wild pitches in Game 1: "A couple of them were too high. If I'm Superman, maybe. But I don't think I can fly." ... Clark, on the Cardinals' in-your-face offensive approach: "It was awesome. It was a special series because we took it to 'em. There was no fear, there was no hesitation. We took it to 'em and beat 'em."

Game 1 at St. Louis

ST. LOUIS 7, ATLANTA 5

HOW THEY SCORED

First Inning

Cardinals—Fernando Vina reached on an infield single. J.D. Drew singled to right, Vina taking third. Jim Edmonds singled to left center, Vina scoring and Drew moving to second. Will Clark singled to right center, Drew scoring and Edmonds going to third. Ray Lankford was safe on third baseman Chipper Jones' error, Edmonds scoring and Clark moving to second. Edgar Renteria sacrificed the runners to second and third. Carlos Hernandez was walked intentionally. Placido Polanco singled to center, scoring Clark and Lankford and moving Hernandez to third. A wild throw by catcher Paul Bako trying to get Polanco at second allowed Hernandez to score and Polanco to go to third. Rick Ankiel popped to shortstop. Vina grounded to first. Six runs. Cardinals 6, Braves 0.

Third Inning

Braves—Greg Maddux walked. Rafael Furcal fouled to first. Maddux moved to second and third on consecutive wild pitches. Andruw Jones walked and advanced to second on a wild pitch. Chipper Jones struck

Cardinals lefthander Rick Ankiel gets some stern words of encouragement from catcher Carlos Hernandez after running into control problems during Game 1 against the Braves.

out. Andres Galarraga walked. Maddux scored and Andruw Jones moved to third on a wild pitch. Brian Jordan singled to left, scoring Andruw Jones and moving Galarraga to second. Galarraga moved to third and Jordan to second on a wild pitch. Reggie Sanders walked, loading the bases. Walt Weiss singled to left, scoring Galarraga and Jordan and moving Sanders to second. Mike James relieved Ankiel. Javy Lopez flied to center. Four runs. Cardinals 6, Braves 4.

Fourth Inning

Cardinals—Edmonds homered to right field. Clark grounded to second. Lankford struck out. Renteria walked. Hernandez grounded to third. One run. Cardinals 7, Braves 4.

Ninth Inning

Braves—Dave Veres relieved Britt Reames. Andruw Jones reached on shortstop Renteria's error. Chipper Jones struck out. Andruw Jones moved to second on fielder indifference. Galarraga was hit by a pitch. Jordan singled to left, scoring Andruw Jones and moving Galarraga to second. Sanders struck out. Keith Lockhart flied to center. One run. Cardinals 7, Braves 5.

BOX SCORE

Atlanta	AB	R	H	RBI	PO	A
Furcal, 2b-ss	5	0	1	0	1	1
A. Jones, cf	2	2	0	0	2	0
C. Jones, 3b	4	0	1	0	2	2
Galarraga, 1b	2	1	0	0	8	1
Jordan, rf	4	1	3	2	3	0
Sanders, lf	4	0	0	0	3	0
Weiss, ss	3	0	2	2	2	1
Bonilla, ph	1	0	0	0	0	0
Lockhart, 2b	1	0	0	0	0	1
Bako, c	0	0	0	0	0	0
Lopez, ph-c	4	0	0	0	3	0
Maddux, p	1	1	0	0	0	2
Remlinger, p	0	0	0	0	0	0
Joyner, ph	1	0	1	0	0	0
Mulholland, p	0	0	0	0	0	0
Surhoff, ph	1	0	0	0	0	0
Rocker, p	0	0	0	0	0	0
Ligtenberg, p	0	0	0	0	0	0
Totals	33	5	8	4	24	8

St. Louis	AB	R	H	RBI	PO	A
Vina, 2b	5	1	1	0	3	4
Drew, rf	4	1	1	0	0	0
Edmonds, cf	5	2	3	2	1	0
Clark, 1b	5	1	1	1	8	2
Lankford, lf	3	1	0	1	1	0
Reames, p	0	0	0	0	2	0
McGwire, ph	0	0	0	0	0	0
Kile, pr	0	0	0	0	0	0
Veres, p	0	0	0	0	0	0
Renteria, ss	2	0	0	0	3	2
Hernandez, c	3	1	1	0	7	2
Polanco, 3b	4	0	3	2	0	1
Ankiel, p	1	0	0	0	0	0
James, p	1	0	0	0	0	0
Dunston, ph	1	0	1	0	0	0
Timlin, p	0	0	0	0	0	0
Paquette, lf	1	0	0	0	2	0
Totals	35	7	11	6	27	11

Atlanta .... 0 0 4 0 0 0 0 0 1—5
St. Louis .... 6 0 0 1 0 0 0 0 x—7

Atlanta	IP	H	R	ER	BB	SO
Maddux (L)	4.0	9	7	5	3	2
Remlinger	1.0	2	0	0	0	1
Mulholland	2.0	0	0	0	1	0
Rocker	0.2	0	0	0	1	0
Ligtenberg	0.1	0	0	0	1	0
St. Louis	**IP**	**H**	**R**	**ER**	**BB**	**SO**
Ankiel	2.2	4	4	4	6	3
James (W)	2.1	1	0	0	1	0
Timlin	*1.0	2	0	0	1	1
Reames	2.0	0	0	0	1	1
Veres (S)	1.0	1	1	0	0	2

*Pitched to two batters in seventh.

E—C. Jones, Bako, Rocker, Renteria. DP—St. Louis 1. LOB—Atlanta 11, St. Louis 11. 2B—Jordan, Weiss, Joyner. HR—Edmonds. SH—Renteria. SB—Drew, Edmonds. CS—Furcal, A. Jones. HBP—By Veres (Galarraga). WP—Ankiel 5. T—3:34. A—52,378. U—Rieker, plate; Craft, first; Crawford, second; Gorman, third; Roe, left field; DiMuro, right field.

Game 2 at St. Louis

ST. LOUIS 10, ATLANTA 4

HOW THEY SCORED

First Inning

Braves—Rafael Furcal walked. Andruw Jones grounded to third, Furcal advancing to second. Chipper Jones singled to left, scoring Furcal. Andres Galarraga doubled to right, moving Chipper Jones to third. Brian Jordan grounded to second, scoring Chipper Jones. Javy Lopez lined to left. Two runs. Braves 2, Cardinals 0.

Cardinals—Fernando Vina singled to center. Vina was forced out at second on Edgar Renteria's grounder to third. Jim Edmonds walked, moving Renteria to second. Will Clark homered to right-center field, scoring Renteria and Edmonds. Eric Davis grounded to second. Ray Lankford struck out. Three runs. Cardinals 3, Braves 2.

Second Inning

Cardinals—Carlos Hernandez homered to left. Placido Polanco lined to center. Darryl Kile struck out. Vina grounded to second. One run. Cardinals 4, Braves 2.

Third Inning

Cardinals—Renteria singled to left. Edmonds doubled to right, moving Renteria to third. Clark was hit by a pitch, loading the bases. Davis flied to left center, scoring Renteria and advancing Edmonds to third. Lankford doubled to right center, scoring Edmonds and Clark. Andy Ashby relieved Tom Glavine. Lankord moved to third on a wild pitch. Hernandez struck out. Polanco was walked intentionally. Kile grounded to shortstop. Three runs. Cardinals 7, Braves 2.

Fourth Inning

Cardinals—Vina lined to first. Renteria walked and stole second base. Edmonds doubled to left, scoring Renteria. Clark was walked intentionally. Davis struck out. Lankford grounded to second. One run. Cardinals 8, Braves 2.

Sixth Inning

Cardinals—Vina was hit by a pitch. Renteria lined out to right. Edmonds doubled to right center, scoring Vina. Edmonds moved to third on Furcal's throwing error. Terry Mulholland relieved John Burkett. Clark was thrown out by the catcher on a swinging bunt. Davis grounded to shortstop. One run. Cardinals 9, Braves 2.

Eighth Inning

Braves—Jason Christiansen relieved Kile. Furcal flied to center. Mike Timlin relieved Christiansen. Andruw Jones homered to left. Chipper Jones doubled to left. Galarraga struck out. Jordan singled to right, scoring Chipper Jones. Lopez lined to shortstop. Two runs. Cardinals 9, Braves 4.

Cardinals—Mike Remlinger relieved Kerry Ligtenberg. Mark McGwire batted for Timlin and homered to center. Vina grounded to shortstop. Renteria struck out. Edmonds popped to shortstop. One run. Cardinals 10, Braves 4.

BOX SCORE

Atlanta	AB	R	H	RBI	PO	A
Furcal, ss	4	1	0	0	1	5
A. Jones, cf	3	1	1	1	3	0
C. Jones, 3b	4	2	2	1	0	1
Galarraga, 1b	4	0	1	0	11	0
Jordan, rf	4	0	1	2	1	0
Lopez, c	4	0	0	0	7	1
Sanders, lf	4	0	0	0	0	0
Lockhart, 2b	4	0	1	0	1	4
Glavine, p	1	0	0	0	0	0
Ashby, p	0	0	0	0	0	0
Surhoff, ph	1	0	1	0	0	0
Maddux, pr	0	0	0	0	0	0
Burkett, p	0	0	0	0	0	0
Mulholland, p	0	0	0	0	0	0
Joyner, ph	1	0	0	0	0	0
Ligtenberg, p	0	0	0	0	0	0
Remlinger, p	0	0	0	0	0	0
Bonilla, ph	0	0	0	0	0	0
Totals	34	4	7	4	24	11

St. Louis	AB	R	H	RBI	PO	A
Vina, 2b	4	1	1	0	1	6
Renteria, ss	4	3	1	0	1	0
Edmonds, cf	4	2	3	2	4	0
Clark, 1b	2	2	1	3	10	0
Davis, rf	3	0	0	1	0	0
Lankford, lf	4	0	1	2	4	0
Hernandez, c	4	1	1	1	7	0
Polanco, 3b	3	0	0	0	0	3
Kile, p	3	0	0	0	0	1
Christiansen, p	0	0	0	0	0	0
Timlin, p	0	0	0	0	0	0
McGwire, ph	1	1	1	1	0	0
Morris, p	0	0	0	0	0	0
Totals	32	10	9	10	27	10

Atlanta .... 2 0 0 0 0 0 0 2 0— 4
St. Louis .... 3 1 3 1 0 1 0 1 x—10

Atlanta	IP	H	R	ER	BB	SO
Glavine (L)	2.1	6	7	7	1	2
Ashby	1.2	1	1	1	3	2
Burkett	1.1	1	1	1	0	0
Mulholland	0.2	0	0	0	0	0
Ligtenberg	1.0	0	0	0	0	2
Remlinger	1.0	1	1	1	0	1

St. Louis	IP	H	R	ER	BB	SO
Kile (W)	7.0	4	2	2	2	6
Christiansen	0.1	0	0	0	0	0
Timlin	0.2	3	2	2	0	1
Morris	1.0	0	0	0	1	0

E—Furcal. LOB—Atlanta 6, St. Louis 5. 2B—C. Jones, Galarraga, Edmonds 3, Lankford. HR—McGwire, A. Jones, Hernandez, Clark. SF—Davis. SB—Renteria. HBP—By Burkett (Vina), by Glavine (Clark). WP—Ashby. T—3:02. A—52,389. U—Craft, plate; Crawford, first; Gorman, second; Roe, third; DiMuro, left field; Rieker, right field.

Game 3 at Atlanta

ST. LOUIS 7, ATLANTA 1

HOW THEY SCORED

First Inning

Cardinals—Fernando Vina homered to right. Edgar Renteria flied to center. Jim Edmonds flied to left. Will Clark struck out. One run. Cardinals 1, Braves 0.

Braves—Rafael Furcal walked. Andruw Jones fouled out to first. Furcal stole second base. Chipper Jones flied to right, moving Furcal to third. Andres Galarraga singled to center, scoring Furcal. Javy Lopez bounced into a 4-6 fielder's choice. One run. Cardinals 1, Braves 1.

Third Inning

Cardinals—Vina grounded to shortstop. Renteria singled to right. Edmonds homered to right center, scoring Renteria. Clark popped to third. Ray Lankford struck out. Two runs. Cardinals 3, Braves 1.

Fifth Inning

Cardinals—Britt Reames flied to right. Vina walked. Vina was out trying to steal second. Renteria walked and stole second. Renteria moved to third on a balk by Kevin Millwood. Edmonds doubled to left, scoring Renteria. Terry Mulholland relieved Millwood. Clark struck out. One run. Cardinals 4, Braves 1.

Sixth Inning

Cardinals—Lankford walked. Carlos Hernandez singled to center, moving Lankford to second. J.D. Drew sacrificed Lankford to third and Hernandez to second. Kerry Ligtenberg relieved Mulholland. Placido Polanco grounded to second and Lankford beat the throw home, Hernandez moving to third and Polanco safe at first. Eric Davis batted for Reames. Polanco stole second. Davis struck out. Mike Remlinger relieved Ligtenberg. Vina singled to center, scoring Hernandez and Polanco. Renteria popped to second. Three runs. Cardinals 7, Braves 1.

BOX SCORE

St. Louis	AB	R	H	RBI	PO	A
Vina, 2b	4	1	2	3	3	3
Renteria, ss	4	2	1	0	2	2
Edmonds, c	5	1	2	3	2	0
Clark, 1b	5	0	1	0	8	0
Lankford, lf	3	1	1	0	3	0
Hernandez, c	4	1	1	0	6	2
Drew, rf	2	0	0	0	2	0
Polanco, 3b	3	1	0	1	1	1
Paquette, 3b	1	0	0	0	0	0
Stephenson, p	1	0	0	0	0	0
Reames, p	1	0	0	0	0	0
Davis, ph	1	0	0	0	0	0
James, p	0	0	0	0	0	0
McGwire, ph	1	0	0	0	0	0
Morris, p	0	0	0	0	0	0
Veres, p	0	0	0	0	0	0
Totals	35	7	8	7	27	8

Atlanta	AB	R	H	RBI	PO	A
Furcal, ss	2	1	0	0	1	5
A. Jones, cf	4	0	0	0	3	0
C. Jones, 3b	4	0	1	0	1	2
Galarraga, 1b	4	0	1	1	7	0
Lopez, c	3	0	1	0	5	1
Bako, c	1	0	0	0	4	0
Jordan, rf	3	0	0	0	2	0
Sanders, lf	1	0	0	0	1	0
Mulholland, p	0	0	0	0	0	0
Ligtenberg, p	0	0	0	0	0	0
Remlinger, p	0	0	0	0	0	0
Joyner, ph	1	0	0	0	0	0
Ashby, p	0	0	0	0	0	0
Lockhart, 2b	3	0	0	0	3	1
Millwood, p	1	0	0	0	0	0
Bonilla, lf	1	0	0	0	0	0
Totals	28	1	3	1	27	9

St. Louis .... 1 0 2 0 1 3 0 0 0—7
Atlanta .... 1 0 0 0 0 0 0 0 0—1

St. Louis	IP	H	R	ER	BB	SO
Stephenson	3.2	3	1	1	2	2
Reames (W)	1.1	0	0	0	2	1
James	2.0	0	0	0	0	1
Morris	1.0	0	0	0	0	0
Veres	1.0	0	0	0	0	2
Atlanta	**IP**	**H**	**R**	**ER**	**BB**	**SO**
Millwood (L)	4.2	4	4	4	3	3
Mulholland	0.2	1	2	2	1	1
Ligtenberg	0.1	0	1	1	0	1
Remlinger	1.1	3	0	0	0	1
Ashby	2.0	0	0	0	0	3

E—C. Jones. DP—St. Louis 2. LOB—St. Louis 6, Atlanta 4. 2B—Edmonds. HR—Vina, Edmonds. SH—Drew. SB—Renteria, Drew, Polanco, Furcal. CS—Vina, Lopez. Balk—Millwood. T—3:09. A—49,898. U—Montague, plate; Morrison, first; Young, second; Barrett, third; Kellogg, left field; Cederstrom, right field.

COMPOSITE

BATTING AVERAGES

St. Louis Cardinals

Player, position	G	AB	R	H	2B	3B	HR	RBI	Avg.
Dunston, ph	1	1	0	1	0	0	0	0	1.000
Edmonds, cf	3	14	5	8	4	0	2	7	.571
McGwire, ph	3	2	1	1	0	0	1	1	.500
Vina, 2b	3	13	3	4	0	0	1	3	.308
Polanco, 3b	3	10	1	3	0	0	0	3	.300
Hernandez, c	3	11	3	3	0	0	1	1	.273
Clark, 1b	3	12	3	3	0	0	1	4	.250
Lankford, lf	3	10	2	2	1	0	0	3	.200
Renteria, ss	3	10	5	2	0	0	0	0	.200
Drew, rf	2	6	1	1	0	0	0	0	.167
Christiansen, p	1	0	0	0	0	0	0	0	.000
Morris, p	2	0	0	0	0	0	0	0	.000
Timlin, p	2	0	0	0	0	0	0	0	.000
Veres, p	2	0	0	0	0	0	0	0	.000
Ankiel, p	1	1	0	0	0	0	0	0	.000
James, p	2	1	0	0	0	0	0	0	.000
Reames, p	2	1	0	0	0	0	0	0	.000
Stephenson, p	1	1	0	0	0	0	0	0	.000
Paquette, lf-3b	2	2	0	0	0	0	0	0	.000
Kile, pr-p	2	3	0	0	0	0	0	0	.000
Davis, rf-ph	2	4	0	0	0	0	0	1	.000
Totals	**3**	**102**	**24**	**28**	**5**	**0**	**6**	**23**	**.275**

Atlanta Braves

Player, position	G	AB	R	H	2B	3B	HR	RBI	Avg.
Weiss, ss	1	3	0	2	1	0	0	2	.667
Surhoff, ph	2	2	0	1	0	0	0	0	.500
Jordan, rf	3	11	1	4	1	0	0	4	.364
C. Jones, 3b	3	12	2	4	1	0	0	1	.333
Joyner, ph	3	3	0	1	1	0	0	0	.333
Galarraga, 1b	3	10	1	2	1	0	0	1	.200
Lockhart, 2b	3	8	0	1	0	0	0	0	.125
A. Jones, cf	3	9	3	1	0	0	1	1	.111
Furcal, 2b-ss	3	11	2	1	0	0	0	0	.091
Lopez, ph-c	3	11	0	1	0	0	0	0	.091
Ashby, p	2	0	0	0	0	0	0	0	.000
Burkett, p	1	0	0	0	0	0	0	0	.000
Ligtenberg, p	3	0	0	0	0	0	0	0	.000
Mulholland, p	3	0	0	0	0	0	0	0	.000
Remlinger, p	3	0	0	0	0	0	0	0	.000
Rocker, p	1	0	0	0	0	0	0	0	.000
Bako, c	2	1	0	0	0	0	0	0	.000
Glavine, p	1	1	0	0	0	0	0	0	.000
Maddux, p-pr	2	1	1	0	0	0	0	0	.000
Millwood, p	1	1	0	0	0	0	0	0	.000
Bonilla, ph-lf	3	2	0	0	0	0	0	0	.000
Sanders, lf	3	9	0	0	0	0	0	0	.000
Totals	**3**	**95**	**10**	**18**	**5**	**0**	**1**	**9**	**.189**

Cardinals center fielder Jim Edmonds goes back for an over-the-shoulder catch on a Game 2 drive hit by Rafael Furcal.

PITCHING AVERAGES

St. Louis Cardinals

Pitcher	G	IP	H	R	ER	BB	SO	W	L	ERA
James	2	4.1	1	0	0	1	1	1	0	0.00
Reames	2	3.1	0	0	0	3	2	1	0	0.00
Morris	2	2.0	0	0	0	1	0	0	0	0.00
Veres	2	2.0	1	1	0	0	4	0	0	0.00
Christiansen	1	0.1	0	0	0	0	0	0	0	0.00
Stephenson	1	3.2	3	1	1	2	2	0	0	2.45
Kile	1	7.0	4	2	2	2	6	1	0	2.57
Timlin	2	1.2	5	2	2	1	2	0	0	10.80
Ankiel	1	2.2	4	4	4	6	3	0	0	13.50
Totals	3	27.0	18	10	9	16	20	3	0	3.00

No shutouts. Save—Veres.

Atlanta Braves

Pitcher	G	IP	H	R	ER	BB	SO	W	L	ERA
Rocker	1	0.2	0	0	0	1	0	0	0	0.00
Ashby	2	3.2	1	1	1	3	5	0	0	2.45
Remlinger	3	3.1	6	1	1	0	3	0	0	2.70
Mulholland	3	3.1	1	2	2	2	1	0	0	5.40
Ligtenberg	3	1.2	0	1	1	1	3	0	0	5.40
Burkett	1	1.1	1	1	1	0	0	0	0	6.75
Millwood	1	4.2	4	4	4	3	3	0	1	7.71
Maddux	1	4.0	9	7	5	3	2	0	1	11.25
Glavine	1	2.1	6	7	7	1	2	0	1	27.00
Totals	3	25.0	28	24	22	14	19	0	3	7.92

No shutouts or saves.

N.L. Championship Series

St. Louis vs. New York

Edgardo Alfonzo feasted on Cardinals pitching. Alfonzo hit .444 in the NLCS after batting just .278 in the Division Series.

The bottom line: The New York Mets, fulfilling their half of the all-New York World Series equation, posted a surprisingly easy five-game NLCS win over the St. Louis Cardinals and claimed their first pennant since 1986. With the victory, New York joined the 1997 Florida Marlins as the only wild-card teams to reach the World Series and denied the N.L. Central Division-champion Cardinals their first fall classic appearance since 1987. The Mets showed their superiority in every facet of the game, winning Games 1 and 2 in St. Louis and closing out the series with consecutive wins at Shea Stadium after the Cardinals had rebounded in Game 3. The Cardinals did not even resemble the team that had rolled over the defending N.L.-champion Atlanta Braves in a shocking Division Series.

Why the Mets won: Because their lefthanded starters, Mike Hampton and Al Leiter, were able to shut down the Cardinals' lefty-dominated lineup. Hampton worked seven shutout innings in Game 1 and fired a three-hit shutout in Game 5, striking out Jim Edmonds three times in the clincher. Leiter worked seven solid innings in a Game 2 Mets win that was decided in the ninth inning. The Mets also were able to avoid critical game situations in which they would have to deal with super pinch hitter Mark McGwire, who was forced into that role by a knee injury. Cardinals starting pitchers other than Game 3 winner Andy Benes worked just $14^1/_3$ innings with a whopping 11.30 ERA and the normally reliable St. Louis defense collapsed at inopportune moments.

TURNING POINTS:

Game 1: The first inning provided a double lift for the Mets, who stormed past the Cardinals, 6-2, before 52,225 red-clad fans at Busch Stadium. First, the Mets' sometimes-sluggish offense got a boost when top gun Mike Piazza, a career .211 postseason hitter, broke out of a slump with a double off Darryl Kile that keyed a two-run outburst. Then Hampton, a failure in four previous postseason starts, escaped a bases-loaded jam by getting Carlos Hernandez on a ground ball. Piazza signaled his return to prominence with a 2-for-4 performance and Hampton worked seven shutout innings en route to his first postseason victory. Hampton's biggest scare came in the seventh when, with the Mets leading 3-0, Edmonds drove left fielder Benny Agbayani to the left-center field fence with two men on base. The Mets secured victory by scoring three ninth-inning runs on a solo home run by Todd Zeile and a two-run shot by Jay Payton.

Game 2: The Mets took control of the series when center fielder Payton delivered his second game-winning hit of the postseason—a run-scoring, ninth-inning single that produced a 6-5 win and a two-games-to-none lead. Payton's winner was set up when normally sure-handed Cardinals first baseman Will Clark booted Robin Ventura's ground ball. The Mets, who got a solo home run from Piazza, needed Payton's heroics because they blew a pair of two-run leads. The Cardinals struck for two runs off Leiter in the fifth to tie the game at 3-3 and two more in the eighth off John Franco after the Mets had scored twice in the top of the inning. The Mets broke on top with two first-inning runs, courtesy of Rick Ankiel's wildness. The 21-year-old Cardinals rookie, bringing back memories of his five-wild pitch-inning in a Division Series start against Atlanta, walked three batters, threw two wild pitches and fired several more pitches to the backstop before being relieved with two out by Britt Reames.

Game 3: After falling behind 2-0 before they even batted in Games 1 and 2, the Cardinals turned the tables and went on to claim a face-saving 8-2 victory before a hostile crowd at Shea Stadium. Fernando Vina opened the game with a single and Edgar Renteria reached on an error by third baseman Ventura. Before Rick Reed could record his first out, Edmonds lined a two-run double to left. Starter Andy Benes, pitching for the first time in 13 days because of knee problems, escaped a first-inning jam with one run and went on to work eight six-hit innings. The Cardinals supported him with 14 hits and put the game away by scoring six runs in the third, fourth and fifth innings.

Game 4: Trying to duplicate their Game 2 victory formula, the Cardinals broke on top on Edmonds' two-run, first-inning home run off Bobby J. Jones. But this time the Mets answered back in record-setting fashion and went on to claim a 10-6 victory that put them within one win of an N.L. pennant. Cardinals ace Darryl Kile, working on three days rest, felt the brunt of a New York offensive explosion that produced a 7-2 lead after two innings. The Mets scored four first-inning runs on an LCS-record five doubles and added three runs in the second, two on Zeile's double. The Cardinals knocked out Jones after four innings and fought back to 8-6, but they could never catch up. Piazza contributed a solo home run to the nine-hit Mets attack.

Game 5: The Mets gave Hampton another first-inning boost and he turned the fifth game into one long Shea Stadium victory celebration. The three-run first was a combination of timely New York hitting and shoddy St. Louis defense and the result was a hole out of which the Cardinals could not climb. Edgardo Alfonzo and Ventura delivered RBI hits off starter Pat Hentgen; catcher Carlos Hernandez and first baseman Clark contributed costly errors. Zeile's three-run, fourth-inning double was icing for Hampton, who completed his NLCS scoreless-innings streak at 16 innings and walked away with MVP honors.

WORTH NOTING:

Cardinals: After going 3-for-28 with runners in scoring position at St. Louis, the Cardinals were 7-for-16 in their Game 3 victory over the Mets. ... The ability of lefties Hampton, Leiter, Franco and Glendon Rusch to shut down the Cardinals was not surprising. During the regular season, St. Louis was 17-23 against lefthanders. ... After outscoring the Braves 10-3 in their Division Series sweep, the Cardinals were outscored in the first inning by the Mets 12-4. ... Much of the Cardinals' first-inning woes could be traced to Mets right fielder Timo Perez, who replaced injured Derek Bell in right field. Perez scored an LCS-tying eight runs from his leadoff spot in the lineup.

Mets: When the Mets won both games in St. Louis, they had to feel good about their chances of winning the series. No team in LCS play has ever come back to win after dropping the first two games at home. ... Second baseman Alfonzo singled twice in the Game 5 finale, extending his postseason hitting streak to 11 games. ... The NLCS win gave the 40-year-old Franco his first World Series opportunity at age 40. ... Center fielder Payton was hit on the helmet by a Dave Veres pitch in the eighth inning of Game 5, but order was quickly restored after both benches emptied. Payton seemed to accept Veres' assurance that the beaning was unintentional.

WORTH QUOTING:

Cardinals: Will Clark, on his ninth-inning error in Game 2: "It's a shame. I misplayed a ball and it caused us to lose the game."... Kile, referring to those who blamed the short rest on his Game 4 collapse: "That has nothing to do with it. If you make good pitches, it doesn't matter if you're pitching on one day rest. I didn't make good pitches."... McGwire, on why the Cardinals lost: "In a short series, it comes down to pitching. They shut us down."

Mets: Hampton, recalling Edmonds' deep seventh-inning Game 1 drive that came within a few feet of tying the game: "I didn't breathe, I'll tell you that. I was going to breathe, but I thought I might push the ball over the fence."... Zeile, on the prospects of a Subway Series after the Mets had finished off the Cardinals: "I'm rooting for the Yankees, to be perfectly honest. I'd love to see a Subway Series. We have some unfinished business with the Yankees."... Mets manager Bobby Valentine on Hampton's Game 5 performance: "He did a fabulous job. He pitched the game of his life—and mine."

Game 1 at St. Louis

NEW YORK 6, ST. LOUIS 2

HOW THEY SCORED

First Inning

Mets—Timo Perez doubled to right. Perez moved to third on a wild pitch. Edgardo Alfonzo walked. Mike Piazza, doubled to left, scoring Perez and moving Alfonzo to third. Robin Ventura flied to left, scoring Alfonzo. Todd Zeile struck out. Benny Agbayani grounded to shortstop. Two runs. Mets 2, Cardinals 0.

Fifth Inning

Mets—Mike Bordick grounded to third. Mike Hampton reached on an infield single. Perez grounded to the pitcher, Hampton moving to second. Alfonzo singled to left, scoring Hampton. Piazza fouled to first. One run. Mets 3, Cardinals 0.

Ninth Inning

Mets—Zeile homered to left-center. Agbayani singled to left. Joe McEwing ran for Agbayani. Jay Payton homered to left, scoring McEwing. Bordick was hit by a pitch. Kurt Abbott ran for Bordick. Darryl Hamilton batted for John Franco and Jason Christiansen relieved Mike James. Bubba Trammell batted for Hamilton and struck out. Perez grounded into a 1-6-3 double play. Three runs. Mets 6, Cardinals 0.

Cardinals—Armando Benitez relieved Franco. Ray Lankford batted for Christiansen and doubled to right. Fernando Tatis flied to left. Fernando Vina flied to right. Edgar Renteria was safe at first on shortstop Abbott's throwing error, Lankford scoring. Jim Edmonds singled to right, and Renteria scored on right fielder Perez's error as Edmonds moved to third. Eric Davis grounded to third. Two runs. Mets 6, Cardinals 2.

BOX SCORE

New York	AB	R	H	RBI	PO	A
Perez, rf	5	1	1	0	2	0
Alfonzo, 2b	3	1	1	1	0	4
Piazza, c	4	0	2	1	5	0
Ventura, 3b	2	0	0	1	0	2
Zeile, 1b	4	1	1	1	11	1
Agbayani, lf	4	0	1	0	2	0
McEwing, pr-lf	0	1	0	0	1	0
Payton, cf	4	1	1	2	2	0
Bordick, ss	3	0	0	0	3	4
Abbott, pr-ss	0	0	0	0	0	0
Hampton, p	3	1	1	0	1	0
J. Franco, p	0	0	0	0	0	0
Hamilton, ph	0	0	0	0	0	0
Trammell, ph	1	0	0	0	0	0
Benitez, p	0	0	0	0	0	0
Totals	33	6	8	6	27	11
St. Louis	**AB**	**R**	**H**	**RBI**	**PO**	**A**
Vina, 2b	4	0	1	0	2	2
Renteria, ss	5	1	1	0	1	3
Edmonds, cf	5	0	2	0	2	0
Davis, rf	5	0	1	0	4	0
Clark, 1b	3	0	1	0	10	1
Hernandez, c	4	0	1	0	3	0
Marrero, pr-c	0	0	0	0	1	0
Drew, lf	3	0	0	0	2	0
Dunston, ph-lf	1	0	0	0	0	0
Polanco, 3b	3	0	1	0	0	4
James, p	0	0	0	0	1	0
Christiansen, p	0	0	0	0	0	1
Lankford, ph	1	1	1	0	0	0
Kile, p	1	0	0	0	1	3
Tatis, ph-3b	2	0	0	0	0	0
Totals	37	2	9	0	27	14

New York	2 0 0	0 1 0	0 0 3	—6
St. Louis	0 0 0	0 0 0	0 0 2	—2

New York	IP	H	R	ER	BB	SO
Hampton (W)	7.0	6	0	0	3	4
J. Franco	1.0	1	0	0	0	1
Benitez	1.0	2	2	0	0	0
St. Louis	**IP**	**H**	**R**	**ER**	**BB**	**SO**
Kile (L)	7.0	5	3	3	2	1
James	*1.0	3	3	3	0	0
Christiansen	1.0	0	0	0	0	1

*Pitched to four batters in ninth.

E—Agbayani, Abbott, Perez. DP—St. Louis 1. LOB—New York 4, St. Louis 11. 2B—Perez, Piazza, Clark, Lankford. HR—Zeile, Payton. SF—Ventura. HBP—By James (Bordick). WP—Hampton, Kile. T—3:08. A—52,255. U—Froemming, plate; Tschida, first; Rapuano, second; Scott, third; DeMuth, left field; Rippley, right field.

Game 2 at St. Louis

NEW YORK 6, ST. LOUIS 5

HOW THEY SCORED

First Inning

Mets—Timo Perez struck out. Edgardo Alfonzo walked and moved to second on a wild pitch. Mike Piazza walked as Alfonzo moved to third on a wild pitch. Todd Zeile flied to center, scoring Alfonzo. Robin Ventura walked, moving Piazza to second. Benny Agbayani doubled to left-center, scoring Piazza and moving Ventura to third. Britt Reames relieved Rick Ankiel. Jay Payton struck out. Two runs. Mets 2, Cardinals 0.

Second Inning

Cardinals—Will Clark flied to left. Shawon Dunston doubled to left. Ray Lankford singled to left, moving Dunston to third. Eli Marrero grounded to second, scoring Dunston and moving Lankford to second. Reames struck out. One run. Mets 2, Cardinals 1.

Third Inning

Mets—Piazza homered to right. Zeile flied to left. Ventura singled to right-center. Agbayani flied to right. Ventura moved to second on a passed ball. Payton walked. Kurt Abbott grounded into a 6 unassisted forceout at third. One run. Mets 3, Cardinals 1.

Fifth Inning

Cardinals—Eric Davis batted for Reames and fouled to right. Fernando Vina reached on a bunt single. Edgar Renteria doubled to left, scoring Vina. Renteria stole third. Jim Edmonds flied to right. Fernando Tatis doubled to left, scoring Renteria. Clark flied to left. Two runs. Mets 3, Cardinals 3.

Eighth Inning

Mets—Matt Franco batted for Abbott and grounded to second. Darryl Hamilton batted for Al Leiter and flied to left. Perez singled to left. Alfonzo singled to right-center, scoring Perez with Alfonzo moving to second on the throw. Piazza was walked intentionally. Dave Veres relieved Matt Morris. Zeile singled to left, scoring Alfonzo and moving Piazza to second. Piazza was tagged out trying to advance to third on the throw. Two runs. Mets 5, Cardinals 3.

Cardinals—John Franco relieved Leiter. Edmonds grounded to first. Carlos Hernandez walked. Clark singled to right, Hernandez moving to third. Hernandez scored and Clark moved to second on a wild pitch. Dunston grounded to third. Placido Polanco batted for Lankford. Turk Wendell relieved John Franco. J.D. Drew batted for Polanco. Drew doubled to center, scoring Clark. Mark McGwire batted for Veres and was walked intentionally. Darryl Kile ran for McGwire. Craig Paquette struck out. Two runs. Mets 5, Cardinals 5.

Ninth Inning

Mets—Mike Timlin relieved Veres. Ventura was safe on first baseman Clark's error. Agbayani sacrificed Ventura to second. Joe McEwing ran for Ventura. Payton singled to center, scoring McEwing as Payton moved to third on center fielder Edmonds' error. Matt Franco grounded to second. Mike Bordick grounded to shortstop. One run. Mets 6, Cardinals 5.

BOX SCORE

New York	AB	R	H	RBI	PO	A
Perez, rf	5	1	1	0	4	0
Alfonzo, 2b	3	2	2	1	1	1
Piazza, c	2	2	1	1	11	0
Zeile, 1b	3	0	2	2	3	0
J. Franco, p	0	0	0	0	0	0
Wendell, p	0	0	0	0	0	0
Benitez, p	0	0	0	0	0	0
Ventura, 3b	4	0	1	0	0	2
McEwing, pr-3b	0	1	0	0	0	0
Agbayani, lf	4	0	1	1	2	0
Payton, cf	4	0	1	1	3	0
Abbott, ss	3	0	0	0	1	0
M. Franco, ph-1b	2	0	0	0	2	0
Leiter, p	3	0	0	0	0	0
Hamilton, ph	1	0	0	0	0	0
Bordick, ss	1	0	0	0	0	0
Totals	35	6	9	6	27	3

St. Louis	AB	R	H	RBI	PO	A
Vina, 2b	5	1	1	0	3	4
Renteria, ss	5	1	3	1	0	4
Edmonds, cf	4	0	0	0	2	0
Tatis, 3b	3	0	1	1	3	0
Morris, p	0	0	0	0	0	0
Hernandez, c	1	1	0	0	0	0
Clark, 1b	4	1	2	0	7	1
Dunston, rf-lf	3	1	1	0	1	0
Lankford, lf	3	0	1	0	2	1
Polanco, ph	0	0	0	0	0	0
Drew, ph-rf	1	0	1	1	0	0
Marrero, c	3	0	0	1	9	0
Veres, p	0	0	0	0	0	0
McGwire, ph	0	0	0	0	0	0
Kile, pr	0	0	0	0	0	0
Timlin, p	0	0	0	0	0	0
Ankiel, p	0	0	0	0	0	0
Reames, p	1	0	0	0	0	0
Davis, ph	1	0	0	0	0	0
Paquette, 3b	2	0	0	0	0	1
Totals	36	5	10	4	27	11

New York	2 0 1 0 0 0 0 2 1—6
St. Louis	0 1 0 0 2 0 0 2 0—5

New York	IP	H	R	ER	BB	SO
Leiter	7.0	8	3	3	0	9
J. Franco	0.2	1	2	2	1	0
Wendell (W)	0.1	1	0	0	1	1
Benitez (S)	1.0	0	0	0	1	1

St. Louis	IP	H	R	ER	BB	SO
Ankiel	0.2	1	2	2	3	1
Reames	4.1	3	1	1	3	6
Morris	3.0	3	2	2	2	2
Veres	0.0	1	0	0	0	0
Timlin (L)	1.0	1	1	0	0	0

E—Vina, Clark, Edmonds. LOB—New York 12, St. Louis 8. 2B—Zeile, Agbayani, Renteria, Tatis, Clark, Dunston, Drew. 3B—Alfonzo. HR—Piazza. SH—Agbayani, Dunston. SF—Zeile. SB—Renteria 3. WP—J. Franco, Ankiel 2. PB—Marrero. T—3:59. A—52,250. U—Tschida, plate; Rapuano, first; Scott, second; DeMuth, third; Rippley, left field; Froemming, right field.

Game 3 at New York

ST. LOUIS 8, NEW YORK 2

HOW THEY SCORED

First Inning

Cardinals—Fernando Vina singled to left. Edgar Renteria sacrificed Vina to second and was safe on third baseman Robin Ventura's error. Jim Edmonds doubled to left, scoring Vina and Renteria. Will Clark singled to right, moving Edmonds to third. Ray Lankford struck out. Fernando Tatis struck out. J.D. Drew struck out. Two runs. Cardinals 2, Mets 0.

Mets—Timo Perez singled to center. Edgardo Alfonzo singled to right, moving Perez to third. Mike Piazza grounded into a 6-4-3 double play, scoring Perez. Ventura lined to the pitcher. One run. Cardinals 2, Mets 1.

Third Inning

Cardinals—Renteria singled to left-center. Edmonds flied to left. Clark walked, moving Renteria to second. Lankford singled to right-center, scoring Renteria and moving Clark to third. Tatis flied to right, scoring Clark. Drew fouled to the catcher. Two runs. Cardinals 4, Mets 1.

Fourth Inning

Cardinals—Carlos Hernandez flied to center. Andy Benes singled to left-center. Vina singled to left-center, moving Benes to second. Renteria singled to left-center, scoring Benes and moving Vina to second. Glendon Rusch relieved Rick Reed. Edmonds struck out. Clark was hit by a pitch, loading the bases. Mark McGwire batted for Lankford and flied to left. One run. Cardinals 5, Mets 1.

Mets—Ventura walked. Todd Zeile singled to right, moving Ventura to second. Benny Agbayani singled to center, loading the bases. Jay Payton grounded into a 4-3-6 double play, scoring Ventura and moving Zeile to third. Mike Bordick walked. Darryl Hamilton batted for Rusch and flied to center. One run. Cardinals 5, Mets 2.

Fifth Inning

Cardinals—Rick White relieved Rusch. Tatis doubled to left. Drew singled to right, moving Tatis to third. Hernandez singled to left-center, scoring Tatis and moving Drew to second. Benes sacrificed Drew to third and Hernandez to second. Vina was safe on a fielder's choice grounder to second, Drew beating the late throw to the plate and Hernandez moving to third. Renteria grounded to shortstop, scoring Hernandez and moving Vina to second. Edmonds flied to right. Three runs. Cardinals 8, Mets 2.

BOX SCORE

St. Louis	AB	R	H	RBI	PO	A
Vina, 2b	5	1	2	1	3	2
Renteria, ss	4	2	2	2	0	1
Edmonds, cf	5	0	1	2	4	0
Clark, 1b	3	1	2	0	7	0
Lankford, lf	2	0	1	1	2	0
McGwire, ph	1	0	0	0	0	0
Paquette, lf	2	0	1	0	1	0
Tatis, 3b	3	1	1	1	0	1
Drew, rf	5	1	2	0	1	0
Hernandez, c	5	1	1	1	8	0
Benes, p	3	1	1	0	1	0
Wilkins, ph	1	0	0	0	0	0
James, p	0	0	0	0	0	0
Veres, p	0	0	0	0	0	0
Totals	39	8	14	8	27	4

New York	AB	R	H	RBI	PO	A
Perez, rf	4	1	1	0	3	1
Alfonzo, 2b	4	0	2	0	1	1
Piazza, c	4	0	1	0	11	0
Ventura, 3b	3	1	0	0	1	2
Zeile, 1b	4	0	2	0	6	0
Agbayani, lf	3	0	1	0	2	0
Payton, cf	3	0	0	0	1	0
Bordick, ss	2	0	0	0	2	4
M. Franco, ph	1	0	0	0	0	0
Reed, p	1	0	0	0	0	0
Rusch, p	0	0	0	0	0	0
Hamilton, ph	1	0	0	0	0	0
White, p	0	0	0	0	0	0
Harris, ph	1	0	0	0	0	0
Cook, p	0	0	0	0	0	0
Wendell, p	0	0	0	0	0	0
Trammell, ph	1	0	0	0	0	0
Totals	32	2	7	0	27	8

St. Louis	2 0 2 1 3 0 0 0 0—8
New York	1 0 0 1 0 0 0 0 0—2

St. Louis	IP	H	R	ER	BB	SO
Benes (W)	8.0	6	2	2	3	5
James	*0.0	1	0	0	1	0
Veres	1.0	0	0	0	0	3

New York	IP	H	R	ER	BB	SO
Reed (L)	3.1	8	5	4	1	4
Rusch	0.2	0	0	0	0	1
White	3.0	5	3	3	1	1
Cook	1.0	1	0	0	0	2
Wendell	1.0	0	0	0	0	1

*Pitched to two batters in ninth.

E—Ventura. DP—St. Louis 2. LOB—St. Louis 10, New York 7. 2B—Edmonds, Tatis. SH—Renteria, Benes. SF—Tatis. HBP—By Rusch (Clark). T—3:23. A—55,693. U—Rapuano, plate; Scott, first; DeMuth, second; Rippley, third; Froemming, left field; Tschida, right field.

Mike Piazza not only hit well in the NLCS, he provided steady, if not spectacular, defense, too.

Game 4 at New York

NEW YORK 10, ST. LOUIS 6

HOW THEY SCORED

First Inning

Cardinals—Fernando Vina doubled to right. Edgar Renteria sacrificed Vina to third. Jim Edmonds homered to right-center, scoring Vina. Will Clark flied to center. Ray Lankford struck out. Two runs. Cardinals 2, Mets 0.

Mets—Timo Perez doubled to right-center. Edgardo Alfonzo doubled to right, scoring Perez. Mike Piazza doubled to right, moving Alfonzo to third. Robin Ventura doubled to right-center, scoring Alfonzo and Piazza. Todd Zeile grounded to third. Benny Agbayani doubled to center, scoring Ventura. Jay Payton struck out. Mike Bordick grounded to second. Four runs. Mets 4, Cardinals 2.

Second Inning

Mets—Bobby Jones lined to center. Perez singled to left-center. Perez stole second. Alfonzo flied to center, moving Perez to third. Piazza was walked intentionally. Ventura walked, loading the bases. Zeile doubled to left, scoring Perez and Piazza and moving Ventura to third. Agbayani singled to center, scoring Ventura. Zeile was thrown out at the plate trying to score. Three runs. Mets 7, Cardinals 2.

Fourth Inning

Cardinals—Edmonds flied to left-center. Clark homered to left-center. Lankford flied to left. Fernando Tatis grounded to third. One run. Mets 7, Cardinals 3.

Mets—Perez walked. Mike James relieved Darryl Kile. Alfonzo flied to right-center. Perez was caught stealing, 2-4. Piazza homered to left. Ventura grounded to third. One run. Mets 8, Cardinals 3.

Because of a knee injury, Mark McGwire was limited to pinch-hit duty in the postseason.

Fifth Inning

Cardinals—J.D. Drew singled to right. Carlos Hernandez singled to center, Drew moving to second. Eric Davis batted for James and doubled to left, scoring Drew and moving Hernandez to third. Glendon Rusch relieved Bobby Jones. Vina struck out. Renteria flied to right, scoring Hernandez and moving Davis to third. Edmonds singled to right, scoring Davis. Clark grounded to first. Three runs. Mets 8, Cardinals 6.

Sixth Inning

Mets—Mike Bordick walked. Rusch sacrificed Bordick to second. Perez was safe on third baseman Tatis' throwing error. Alfonzo was hit by a pitch, loading the bases. Piazza was safe at first on Tatis' error, scoring Bordick and reloading the bases. Ventura flied to left, scoring Perez. Zeile flied to left-center. Two runs. Mets 10, Cardinals 6.

BOX SCORE

St. Louis	AB	R	H	RBI	PO	A
Vina, 2b	5	1	1	0	3	1
Renteria, ss	3	0	0	1	0	2
Edmonds, cf	5	1	2	3	3	1
Clark, 1b	4	1	1	1	10	0
Lankford, lf	3	0	1	0	2	0
Tatis, 3b	4	0	1	0	0	4
Drew, rf	3	1	1	0	3	0
Paquette, ph-rf	1	0	0	0	1	0
Hernandez, c	4	1	2	0	2	2
Marrero, pr	0	0	0	0	0	0
Kile, p	1	0	0	0	0	1
James, p	0	0	0	0	0	0
Davis, ph	1	1	1	1	0	0
Timlin, p	0	0	0	0	0	2
Dunston, ph	1	0	1	0	0	0
Morris, p	0	0	0	0	0	0
Christiansen, p	0	0	0	0	0	0
Polanco, ph	0	0	0	0	0	0
Totals	35	6	11	6	24	13

New York	AB	R	H	RBI	PO	A
Perez, rf	4	3	2	0	5	1
Alfonzo, 2b	4	1	1	1	1	1
Piazza, c	3	3	2	2	6	0
Ventura, 3b	2	2	1	3	0	2
Zeile, 1b	4	0	1	2	6	0
Agbayani, lf	4	0	2	2	3	0
McEwing, lf	0	0	0	0	0	0
Payton, cf	4	0	0	0	3	0
Bordick, ss	3	1	0	0	3	1
B.J. Jones, p	2	0	0	0	0	1
Rusch, p	0	0	0	0	0	0
J. Franco, p	0	0	0	0	0	0
Harris, ph	0	0	0	0	0	0
Trammell, ph	1	0	0	0	0	0
Benitez, p	0	0	0	0	0	0
Totals	31	10	9	10	27	6

St. Louis .... 2 0 0 1 3 0 0 0 0— 6
New York .... 4 3 0 1 0 2 0 0 x—10

St. Louis	IP	H	R	ER	BB	SO
Kile (L)	*3.0	8	7	7	3	2
James	1.0	1	1	1	0	0
Timlin	2.0	0	2	0	1	0
Morris	1.0	0	0	0	0	0
Christiansen	1.0	0	0	0	0	0

New York	IP	H	R	ER	BB	SO
B.J. Jones	†4.0	6	6	6	0	2
Rusch (W)	3.0	3	0	0	0	2
J. Franco	1.0	1	0	0	1	1
Benitez	1.0	1	0	0	1	1

*Pitched to one batter in fourth.

†Pitched to three batters in fifth.

E—Tatis 2. DP—New York 1. LOB—St. Louis 6, New York 4. 2B—Vina, Davis, Perez, Alfonzo, Piazza, Ventura, Zeile, Agbayani. HR—Edmonds, Clark, Piazza. SH—Renteria, Rusch. SF—Renteria, Ventura. SB—Perez. CS—Perez. HBP—By Timlin (Alfonzo). T—3:14. A—55,665. U—Scott, plate; DeMuth, first; Rippley, second; Froemming, third; Tschida, left field; Rapuano, right field.

Game 5 at New York

NEW YORK 7, ST. LOUIS 0

HOW THEY SCORED

First Inning

Mets—Timo Perez singled to center and stole second. Perez moved to third on catcher Carlos Hernandez's throwing error. Edgardo Alfonzo singled to left, scoring Perez. Mike Piazza walked, moving Alfonzo to second. Robin Ventura singled to right, scoring Alfonzo and moving Piazza to third. Todd Zeile grounded into 4-6 fielder's choice and was safe at first on first baseman Will Clark's error as Piazza scored. Benny Agbayani walked, moving Zeile to second. Jay Payton singled to right, loading the bases. Mike Bordick popped to first. Mike Hampton struck out. Three runs. Mets 3, Cardinals 0.

Fourth Inning

Mets—Hampton flied to left. Perez reached on an infield single. Alfonzo popped to third. Piazza doubled to left, moving Perez to third. Ventura walked, loading the bases. Zeile doubled to right-center, scoring Perez, Piazza and Ventura. Mike Timlin relieved Pat Hentgen. Agbayani walked. Payton grounded into a 6-4 forceout. Three runs. Mets 6, Cardinals 0.

Seventh Inning

Mets—Rick Ankiel relieved Britt Reames. Bordick walked. Hampton sacrificed Bordick to second. Perez struck out. Bordick moved to third on a wild pitch. Bordick scored on a wild pitch. Alfonzo walked. Mike James relieved Ankiel. Piazza popped to second. One run. Mets 7, Cardinals 0.

BOX SCORE

St. Louis	AB	R	H	RBI	PO	A
Vina, 2b	4	0	1	0	3	1
Polanco, 3b	2	0	0	0	2	0
Paquette, ph	1	0	0	0	0	0
Edmonds, cf	3	0	0	0	2	0
McGwire, ph	1	0	0	0	0	0
Davis, rf	3	0	0	0	1	0
Drew, rf	0	0	0	0	1	0
Wilkins, ph	1	0	0	0	0	0
Clark, 1b	3	0	1	0	4	2
Renteria, ss	3	0	0	0	4	2
Lankford, lf	3	0	0	0	4	0
Hernandez, c	2	0	0	0	2	0
Marrero, c	1	0	0	0	1	0
Hentgen, p	1	0	1	0	0	1
Timlin, p	0	0	0	0	0	0
Tatis, ph	1	0	0	0	0	0
Reames, p	0	0	0	0	0	1
Ankiel, p	0	0	0	0	0	0
James, p	0	0	0	0	0	0
Dunston, ph	1	0	0	0	0	0
Veres, p	0	0	0	0	0	0
Totals	30	0	3	0	24	7

New York	AB	R	H	RBI	PO	A
Perez, rf-cf	5	2	2	0	2	0
Alfonzo, 2b	4	1	2	1	0	3
Piazza, c	4	2	1	0	7	1
Ventura, 3b	3	1	1	1	1	5
Zeile, 1b	4	0	1	3	12	0
Agbayani, lf	2	0	1	0	2	0
Payton, cf	4	0	1	0	1	0
McEwing, pr-rf	0	0	0	0	0	0
Bordick, ss	4	1	1	0	2	2
Hampton, p	3	0	0	0	0	0
Totals	33	7	10	5	27	11

St. Louis .... 0 0 0 0 0 0 0 0 0—0
New York .... 3 0 0 3 0 0 1 0 x—7

St. Louis	IP	H	R	ER	BB	SO
Hentgen (L)	3.2	7	6	6	5	2
Timlin	0.1	0	0	0	1	0
Reames	2.0	2	0	0	1	0
Ankiel	0.2	0	1	1	2	1
James	0.1	0	0	0	0	0
Veres	1.0	1	0	0	0	0

New York	IP	H	R	ER	BB	SO
Hampton (W)	9.0	3	0	0	1	8

E—Hernandez, Clark. LOB—St. Louis 4, New York 13. 2B—Piazza, Zeile. SH—Hampton. HBP—By Veres (Payton). WP—Ankiel 2. T—3:17. A—55,695. U—DeMuth, plate; Rippley, first; Froemming, second; Tschida, third; Rapuano, left field; Scott, right field.

COMPOSITE

BATTING AVERAGES

New York Mets

Player, position	G	AB	R	H	2B	3B	HR	RBI	Avg.
Alfonzo, 2b	5	18	5	8	1	1	0	4	.444
Piazza, c	5	17	7	7	3	0	2	4	.412
Zeile, 1b	5	19	1	7	3	0	1	8	.368
Agbayani, lf	5	17	0	6	2	0	0	3	.353
Perez, rf-cf	5	23	8	7	2	0	0	0	.304
Ventura, 3b	5	14	4	3	1	0	0	5	.214
Hampton, p	2	6	1	1	0	0	0	0	.167
Payton, cf	5	19	1	3	0	0	1	3	.158
Bordick, ss	5	13	2	1	0	0	0	0	.077
Benitez, p	3	0	0	0	0	0	0	0	.000
Cook, p	1	0	0	0	0	0	0	0	.000
J. Franco, p	3	0	0	0	0	0	0	0	.000
McEwing, pr-lf-3b-rf	4	0	2	0	0	0	0	0	.000
Rusch, p	2	0	0	0	0	0	0	0	.000
Wendell, p	2	0	0	0	0	0	0	0	.000
White, p	1	0	0	0	0	0	0	0	.000
Harris, ph	2	1	0	0	0	0	0	0	.000
Reed, p	1	1	0	0	0	0	0	0	.000
Hamilton, ph	3	2	0	0	0	0	0	0	.000
B.J. Jones, p	1	2	0	0	0	0	0	0	.000
Abbott, pr-ss	2	3	0	0	0	0	0	0	.000
M. Franco, ph-1b	2	3	0	0	0	0	0	0	.000
Leiter, p	1	3	0	0	0	0	0	0	.000
Trammell, ph	3	3	0	0	0	0	0	0	.000
Totals	5	164	31	43	12	1	4	27	.262

St. Louis Cardinals

Player, position	G	AB	R	H	2B	3B	HR	RBI	Avg.
Hentgen, p	1	1	0	1	0	0	0	0	1.000
Clark, 1b	5	17	3	7	2	0	1	1	.412
Drew, lf-ph-rf	5	12	2	4	1	0	0	1	.333
Lankford, ph-lf	5	12	1	4	1	0	0	1	.333
Dunston, ph-lf-rf	4	6	1	2	1	0	0	0	.333
An. Benes, p	1	3	1	1	0	0	0	0	.333
Renteria, ss	5	20	4	6	1	0	0	4	.300
Vina, 2b	5	23	3	6	1	0	0	1	.261
Hernandez, c	5	16	3	4	0	0	0	1	.250
Tatis, ph-3b	5	13	1	3	2	0	0	2	.231
Edmonds, cf	5	22	1	5	1	0	1	5	.227
Davis, rf-ph	4	10	1	2	1	0	0	1	.200
Polanco, 3b-ph	4	5	0	1	0	0	0	0	.200
Paquette, 3b-lf-ph-rf	4	6	0	1	0	0	0	0	.167
James, p	4	0	0	0	0	0	0	0	.000
Ankiel, p	2	0	0	0	0	0	0	0	.000
Christiansen, p	2	0	0	0	0	0	0	0	.000
Morris, p	2	0	0	0	0	0	0	0	.000
Timlin, p	3	0	0	0	0	0	0	0	.000
Veres, p	3	0	0	0	0	0	0	0	.000
Reames, p	2	1	0	0	0	0	0	0	.000
McGwire, ph	3	2	0	0	0	0	0	0	.000
Wilkins, ph	2	2	0	0	0	0	0	0	.000
Kile, p-pr	3	2	0	0	0	0	0	0	.000
Marrero, pr-c	4	4	0	0	0	0	0	1	.000
Totals	5	177	21	47	11	0	2	18	.266

PITCHING AVERAGES

New York Mets

Pitcher	G	IP	H	R	ER	BB	SO	W	L	ERA
Hampton	2	16.0	9	0	0	4	12	2	0	0.00
Rusch	2	3.2	3	0	0	0	3	1	0	0.00
Benitez	3	3.0	3	2	0	2	2	0	0	0.00
Wendell	2	1.1	1	0	0	1	2	1	0	0.00
Cook	1	1.0	1	0	0	0	2	0	0	0.00
Leiter	1	7.0	8	3	3	0	9	0	0	3.86
J. Franco	3	2.2	3	2	2	2	2	0	0	6.75
White	1	3.0	5	3	3	1	1	0	0	9.00
Reed	1	3.1	8	5	4	1	4	0	1	10.80
B.J. Jones	1	4.0	6	6	6	0	2	0	0	13.50
Totals	5	45.0	47	21	18	11	39	4	1	3.60

Shutout—Hampton. Save—Benitez.

St. Louis Cardinals

Pitcher	G	IP	H	R	ER	BB	SO	W	L	ERA
Timlin	3	3.1	1	3	0	2	0	0	1	0.00
Veres	3	2.1	2	0	0	0	3	0	0	0.00
Christiansen	2	2.0	0	0	0	0	1	0	0	0.00
Reames	2	6.1	5	1	1	4	6	0	0	1.42
An. Benes	1	8.0	6	2	2	3	5	1	0	2.25
Morris	2	3.2	3	2	2	2	2	0	0	4.91
Kile	2	10.0	13	10	10	5	3	0	2	9.00
Hentgen	1	3.2	7	6	6	5	2	0	1	14.73
James	4	2.1	5	4	4	1	0	0	0	15.43
Ankiel	2	1.1	1	3	3	5	2	0	0	20.25
Totals	5	43.0	43	31	28	27	24	1	4	5.86

No shutouts or saves.

A.L. Championship Series

SEATTLE VS. NEW YORK

The bottom line: The Yankees, shaking off the cobwebs of a late-season slump, claimed their third straight A.L. pennant and joined the cross-town Mets in an all-New York World Series—the first Subway Series in 44 years. The six-game ALCS win over the Seattle Mariners gave New York a fall classic monopoly for the first time since 1956, when the Yankees defeated the Brooklyn Dodgers. The Bronx Bombers became the first team since the 1988-90 Oakland Athletics to win three straight pennants and they extended their record pennant total to 37. The Mariners were trying to win their first pennant in their third postseason appearance. If they had succeeded, baseball would have had its first wild-card World Series—the Mariners vs. the Mets—and a trans-continental nightmare.

Why the Yankees won: Because of starting pitchers Orlando Hernandez, Andy Pettitte and Roger Clemens, who revived the Yankees after a Game 1 loss at Yankee Stadium. That trio held the hot-hitting Mariners to three runs over the next three games as the New Yorkers took control with 7-1, 8-2 and 5-0 wins—two of them at Seattle's Safeco Field. The Yankees also brushed off their late-season doldrums (15 losses in the last 18 games; seven straight losses to end the season) and showed the character that had allowed them to win 22 of their last 25 postseason games entering the 2000 playoffs. As the suddenly-rejuvenated offense began delivering in clutch situations, the Yankees began looking more and more like a baseball machine rolling toward a third consecutive championship.

TURNING POINTS:

Game 1: For Freddy Garcia, the moment of truth came in the sixth inning when he was faced with a two-on, nobody-out situation while protecting a 2-0 lead. Manager Lou Piniella trudged to the mound and the sellout Yankee Stadium crowd braced for a pitching change. But Piniella decided to stay with his 24-year-old righthander and he wasn't sorry. Garcia struck out Paul O'Neill and Bernie Williams and retired David Justice on a long fly ball. Garcia went on to work 6²/₃ three-hit innings and relievers Jose Paniagua, Arthur Rhodes and Kazuhiro Sasaki held the Yankees scoreless the rest of the way. It was deja vu for the veteran Yankees, who continued their late-season funk with an 0-for-8 effort with runners in scoring position. The Mariners touched tough-luck loser Denny Neagle for Rickey Henderson's RBI single in the fifth and Alex Rodriguez's solo home run an inning later.

Game 2: Trailing 1-0 entering the bottom of the eighth and in danger of going down two games to none, the Yankees' dormant offense finally exploded. Justice greeted reliever Rhodes with a leadoff double, setting the stage for cleanup hitter Bernie Williams. The Yankees were 0-for-5 in the game and 0-for-13 in the series with runners in scoring position when Williams slapped a single to center, scoring Justice and tying the game. The Yankees would go on to collect eight consecutive hits (an LCS single-inning record) and score seven runs—two on Derek Jeter's home run. As the crowd of 55,317 roared, Mariano Rivera came out of the bullpen to close out Hernandez's seventh straight postseason victory. El Duque, pitching on his birthday, worked eight six-hit innings, allowing only one run on Stan Javier's third-inning single. The Mariners wasted a six-inning scoreless outing by New York-born lefthander John Halama.

Game 3: The Yankees took control of the series in the second inning of this game, when Bernie Williams and Tino Martinez hit back-to-back solo home runs to wipe out a 1-0 deficit. Suddenly that old Yankee strut was back—and so was the sense that the Bronx Bombers' title ship was back on course. Pettitte, who lifted his postseason record to 8-4, wasn't exactly overpowering in the 8-2 victory, but he spread out nine hits over 6²/₃ innings and limited the Mariners to solo runs in the first and fifth. Jeff Nelson and Rivera were perfect in relief. Of special note for the Yankees were a sixth-inning RBI single by O'Neill, who had been 0-for-8 in the series and 4-for-27 without an RBI in the postseason, and the continued hot hitting of Justice, who drove in three runs with a double and single.

Game 4: Unsuccessful through most of his postseason career, Clemens blew away the Mariners in one of the most dominating playoff performances in history. Attacking hitters relentlessly with his 97 mph fastball, The Rocket allowed only one hit, struck out 15 and posted a 5-0 victory that lifted the Yankees to within one win of the pennant. And he did it with his usual menacing edge. After retiring the first two Mariners in the first inning, Clemens buzzed Seattle star Rodriguez with two chin-high fastballs that angered the Mariners dugout and prompted Seattle starter Paul Abbott to respond with a second-inning pitch near the head of Yankees catcher Jorge Posada. Clemens walked Rodriguez and one other Seattle batter and the only hit was Al Martin's line-drive double in the seventh inning—a ball that tipped off the glove of leaping first baseman Tino Martinez. The Yankees got a three-run, fifth-inning homer from Jeter and a two-run, eighth-inning shot from Justice to account for all the scoring.

Game 5: Trailing 2-1 in the fifth inning and facing elimination, the Mariners blitzed Yankees starter Denny Neagle and reliever Nelson for five runs and went on to record a 6-2 victory that forced the series back to New York. The uprising started with a Mark McLemore bunt single and Neagle departed with runners on second and third with one out. Rodriguez greeted Nelson with a two-run single and Edgar Martinez and John Olerud followed with home runs. The beneficiary of the uprising was Garcia, who worked five strong innings to earn his second win of the series.

Game 6: Down 4-3 in the seventh inning and facing the prospect of having to play a seventh game, the Yankees got a dramatic three-run homer from Justice in a six-run outburst that keyed a 9-7 pennant-clinching victory. Yankee Stadium went into a delirious frenzy when Justice drove a Rhodes pitch high into the upper-deck and the celebration really started moments later when O'Neill added a two-run single and Jose Vizcaino added a sacrifice fly. Orlando Hernandez was far from his usual playoff self, but he struggled through seven innings and became the first pitcher to go 8-0 in the postseason. The Mariners scored two first-inning runs off El Duque and stretched their lead to 4-0 in the fourth on Carlos Guillen's upper-deck home run, but the Yankees fought back with three in the fourth and broke it open in the seventh. Rodriguez, possibly playing his final game in a Mariners uniform, collected four hits, including a solo eighth-inning home run.

WORTH NOTING:

Mariners: When the Yankees broke through for seven eighth-inning runs in Game 2, they snapped a string of 15 scoreless innings by the Seattle bullpen in the playoffs. ... Game 3 loser Aaron Sele saw his postseason record drop to 0-3. ... Entering the playoffs, the Mariners had lost to Clemens 21 times—his most wins over any team. The 15 strikeouts Clemens recorded in Game 4 were a nine-inning LCS record. ... Before scoring five runs in the fifth inning of Game 5, the Mariners were batting .180 against Yankee pitching in the series. ... Dan Wilson's single to right in the fifth inning of Game 6 snapped a record 42-at-bat postseason hitless streak.

Yankees: Before erupting for seven runs in the eighth inning of Game 2, the Yankees had suffered through a 21-inning postseason scoreless streak. ... When closer Mariano Rivera worked 1 ²/₃ innings to save Game 3, he broke the consecutive-innings postseason record held by former Yankee Whitey Ford. Rivera lifted his streak to 33¹/₃ innings, one-third more than Ford. Rivera's streak was snapped in Game 6. ... The Yankees stranded an ALCS-record 15 runners in Game 5. ... Before Game 6, Hernandez had never allowed more than three earned runs in a postseason game.

WORTH QUOTING:

Mariners: Rodriguez, after the Mariners had defeated the Yankees in Game 1: "We have to attack them, attack them early and be ready to go to war. They're going to come out real hungry and be ready to go to war tomorrow."... Piniella, after his Mariners had forced a Game 6 at New York: "All of the pressure is on them. They are supposed to win and they are going home. The onus is on them."... McLemore, when asked how he felt when the Mariners had a 4-0 Game 6 lead: "The bottom line is they scored more runs than we did. It doesn't matter if we started off 15-0."

Yankees: Nelson, after watching Garcia and three relievers stop the Yankees 2-0 in Game 1: "If they pitch like they pitched tonight, then we're not going to win the series."... Manager Joe Torre, after watching his team snap a scoring slump with seven eighth-inning runs in Game 2: "It was just a great relief for us to score the runs. I just sense we relieved a lot of pressure today."... Clemens, after his Game 4 masterpiece: "Tonight was special. The ball was jumping out of my hand."... Justice, after his Game 6 home run: "It was magical. It was unbelievable when I rounded the bases, to see this place erupt."

Derek Jeter continued his strong postseason play by hitting .318 with two home runs and five RBIs.

Game 1 at New York

SEATTLE 2, NEW YORK 0

HOW THEY SCORED

Fifth Inning

Mariners—Joe Oliver flied to left-center. David Bell flied to left. Mark McLemore doubled to left. Rickey Henderson singled to right, scoring McLemore. Mike Cameron flied to right. One run. Mariners 1, Yankees 0.

Sixth Inning

Mariners—Alex Rodriguez homered to left. Edgar Martinez grounded to shortstop. John Olerud grounded to second. Jeff Nelson relieved Denny Neagle. Jay Buhner struck out. One run. Mariners 2, Yankees 0.

BOX SCORE

Seattle	AB	R	H	RBI	PO	A
Henderson, lf	2	0	1	1	0	0
Ibanez, lf-rf	1	0	0	0	1	0
Cameron, cf	4	0	0	0	5	0
Rodriguez, ss	3	1	1	1	1	1
E. Martinez, dh	4	0	0	0	0	0
Olerud, 1b	4	0	0	0	6	1
Buhner, rf	3	0	0	0	0	0
Gipson, lf	0	0	0	0	0	0
Oliver, c	3	0	0	0	13	0
Bell, 3b	4	0	2	0	0	2
McLemore, 2b	4	1	1	0	0	3
Garcia, p	0	0	0	0	1	1
Paniagua, p	0	0	0	0	0	0
Rhodes, p	0	0	0	0	0	0
Sasaki, p	0	0	0	0	0	0
Totals	32	2	5	2	27	8
New York	**AB**	**R**	**H**	**RBI**	**PO**	**A**
Knoblauch, dh	4	0	2	0	0	0
Jeter, ss	3	0	0	0	2	2
O'Neill, rf	3	0	0	0	1	0
Hill, ph	1	0	0	0	0	0
Bellinger, lf	0	0	0	0	0	0
Williams, cf	4	0	1	0	3	0
Justice, lf-rf	4	0	0	0	2	0
T. Martinez, 1b	4	0	1	0	5	0
Vizcaino, pr	0	0	0	0	0	0
Posada, c	2	0	0	0	10	1
Sojo, 2b	4	0	2	0	4	3

Alex Rodriguez stares at Yankees pitcher Roger Clemens after diving away from a first-inning fastball that was high and inside.

New York	AB	R	H	RBI	PO	A
Brosius, 3b	3	0	0	0	0	0
Neagle, p	0	0	0	0	0	1
Nelson, p	0	0	0	0	0	0
Choate, p	0	0	0	0	0	0
Grimsley, p	0	0	0	0	0	0
Totals	32	0	6	0	27	7

Seattle	0 0 0	0 1 1	0 0 0—2
New York	0 0 0	0 0 0	0 0 0—0

Seattle	IP	H	R	ER	BB	SO
Garcia (W)	6.2	3	0	0	2	8
Paniagua	1.0	1	0	0	0	3
Rhodes	0.1	0	0	0	0	1
Sasaki (S)	1.0	2	0	0	0	1

New York	IP	H	R	ER	BB	SO
Neagle (L)	5.2	3	2	2	3	3
Nelson	2.1	1	0	0	0	4
Choate	0.1	0	0	0	0	1
Grimsley	0.2	1	0	0	1	1

E—Brosius. DP—Seattle 1, New York 1. LOB—Seattle 7, New York 8. 2B—McLemore, Knoblauch. HR—Rodriguez. CS—Henderson. HBP—By Garcia (Posada). T—3:45. A—54,481. U—J. Hirschbeck, plate; Hernandez, first; Bell, second; M. Hirschbeck, third; Davis, left field; Marsh, right field.

Game 2 at New York

NEW YORK 7, SEATTLE 1

HOW THEY SCORED

Third Inning

Mariners—Dan Wilson struck out. Mark McLemore grounded to shortstop. Mike Cameron walked and stole second. Stan Javier singled to center, scoring Cameron. Alex Rodriguez popped to third. One run. Mariners 1, Yankees 0.

Eighth Inning

Yankees—Arthur Rhodes relieved Jose Paniagua. David Justice doubled to left-center. Bernie Williams singled to right-center, scoring Justice. Tino Martinez singled to left, moving Williams to second. Jorge Posada singled to right, scoring Williams and moving Martinez to third. Paul O'Neill flied to left-center, scoring Martinez. Jose Mesa relieved Rhodes. Luis Sojo singled to center, moving Posada to third. Posada was caught stealing, 2-6. Jose Vizcaino doubled to left-center, scoring Sojo. Vizcaino moved to third on a passed ball. Chuck Knoblauch singled to center, scoring Vizcaino. Derek Jeter homered to right, scoring Knoblauch. Justice flied to center. Seven runs. Yankees 7, Mariners 1.

BOX SCORE

Seattle	AB	R	H	RBI	PO	A
Cameron, cf	3	1	0	0	3	0
Javier, rf	4	0	1	1	1	0
Rodriguez, ss	4	0	1	0	0	1
E. Martinez, dh	3	0	1	0	0	0
Olerud, 1b	4	0	2	0	11	1
Martin, lf	3	0	1	0	2	0
Bell, 3b	4	0	0	0	1	2
Wilson, c	3	0	0	0	4	3
Ibanez, ph	1	0	0	0	0	0
McLemore, 2b	3	0	1	0	1	4
Halama, p	0	0	0	0	1	2
Paniagua, p	0	0	0	0	0	0
Rhodes, p	0	0	0	0	0	0
Mesa, p	0	0	0	0	0	0
Totals	32	1	7	1	24	13

New York	AB	R	H	RBI	PO	A
Knoblauch, dh	4	1	2	1	0	0
Jeter, ss	4	1	2	2	2	2
Justice, lf	4	1	1	0	2	0
Williams, cf	4	1	1	1	2	0
T. Martinez, 1b	4	1	3	0	8	1
Posada, c	4	0	1	1	8	0
O'Neill, rf	3	0	0	1	2	0
Sojo, 2b-3b	4	1	1	0	0	2
Brosius, 3b	3	0	2	0	1	1
Vizcaino, pr-2b	1	1	1	1	0	1
Hernandez, p	0	0	0	0	1	1
Rivera, p	0	0	0	0	1	1
Totals	35	7	14	7	27	9

Seattle	0 0 1	0 0 0	0 0 0—1
New York	0 0 0	0 0 0	0 7 x—7

Seattle	IP	H	R	ER	BB	SO
Halama	6.0	5	0	0	3	2
Paniagua	1.0	1	0	0	0	1
Rhodes (L)	0.1	4	3	3	0	0
Mesa	0.2	4	4	4	0	0

New York	IP	H	R	ER	BB	SO
Hernandez (W)	8.0	6	1	1	3	7
Rivera	1.0	1	0	0	0	0

E—McLemore, Wilson. DP—Seattle 1, New York 2. LOB—Seattle 7, New York 8. 2B—Olerud, Martin, McLemore, Knoblauch, Justice, Vizcaino. HR—Jeter. SF—O'Neill. SB—Cameron, Vizcaino. CS—Posada. PB—Wilson. T—3:36. A—55,317. U—Hernandez, plate; Bell, first; M. Hirschbeck, second; Davis, third; Marsh, left field; J. Hirschbeck, right field.

Game 3 at Seattle

NEW YORK 8, SEATTLE 2

HOW THEY SCORED

First Inning

Mariners—Rickey Henderson grounded to second. Mike Cameron reached on an infield single. Alex Rodriguez singled to center, moving Cameron to second. Edgar Martinez singled to left, scoring Cameron and moving Rodriguez to second. Jay Buhner grounded to first, moving Rodriguez to third and Martinez to second. John Olerud popped to shortstop. One run. Mariners 1, Yankees 0.

Second Inning

Yankees—Bernie Williams homered to right. Tino Martinez homered to center. Jorge Posada struck out. Paul O'Neill popped to third. Luis Sojo grounded to second. Two runs. Yankees 2, Mariners 1.

Third Inning

Yankees—Scott Brosius singled to left. Chuck Knoblauch flied to right. Derek Jeter grounded into a 6-4 forceout. David Justice doubled to left-center, scoring Jeter. Williams grounded to second. One run. Yankees 3, Mariners 1.

Fifth Inning

Mariners—Mark McLemore flied to right. Henderson doubled to right-center. Cameron singled to left-center, scoring Henderson. Rodriguez flied to left. Martinez grounded into 6-4 forceout. One run. Yankees 3, Mariners 2.

Sixth Inning

Yankees—Justice struck out. Williams singled to center. Martinez reached on an infield single, moving Williams to second. Posada flied to right, moving Williams to third. O'Neill singled to right, scoring Williams and moving Martinez to second. Luis Sojo flied to right. One run. Yankees 4, Mariners 2.

Ninth Inning

Yankees—O'Neill grounded to first. Sojo singled to right-center. Jose Vizcaino ran for Sojo and stole second. Brosius walked. Vizcaino moved to third on a wild pitch. Knoblauch singled to center, scoring Vizcaino and moving Brosius to second. Jeter walked, loading the bases. Robert Ramsay relieved Brett Tomko. Justice singled to right, scoring Brosius and Knoblauch and moving Jeter to third. Clay Bellinger ran for Justice. Williams flied to left, scoring Jeter. Bellinger advanced to second on the throw. Martinez flied to center. Four runs. Yankees 8, Mariners 2.

BOX SCORE

New York	AB	R	H	RBI	PO	A
Knoblauch, dh	5	1	2	1	0	0
Jeter, ss	4	2	1	0	3	3
Justice, lf	5	0	2	3	2	0
Bellinger, pr-lf	0	0	0	0	0	0
Williams, cf	4	2	3	2	3	0
T. Martinez, 1b	5	1	2	1	12	0
Posada, c	4	0	0	0	4	1
O'Neill, rf	4	0	1	1	1	0
Sojo, 2b	4	0	1	0	1	2
Vizcaino, pr-2b	0	1	0	0	0	1
Brosius, 3b	3	1	1	0	1	3
Pettitte, p	0	0	0	0	0	1
Nelson, p	0	0	0	0	0	0
Rivera, p	0	0	0	0	0	0
Totals	38	8	13	8	27	11

Seattle	AB	R	H	RBI	PO	A
Henderson, lf	4	1	1	0	2	0
Cameron, cf	4	1	2	1	1	0
Rodriguez, ss	4	0	2	0	3	2
E. Martinez, dh	4	0	2	1	0	0
Buhner, rf	3	0	0	0	4	0
Javier, ph-rf	1	0	0	0	0	0
Olerud, 1b	4	0	1	0	6	3
Bell, 3b	3	0	1	0	1	0
Martin, ph	1	0	0	0	0	0
Oliver, c	3	0	1	0	7	1
Ibanez, ph	1	0	0	0	0	0
McLemore, 2b	2	0	0	0	1	5
Sele, p	0	0	0	0	0	0
Tomko, p	0	0	0	0	2	0
Ramsay, p	0	0	0	0	0	0
Totals	34	2	10	2	27	11

New York	0 2 1	0 0 1	0 0 4—8
Seattle	1 0 0	0 1 0	0 0 0—2

New York	IP	H	R	ER	BB	SO
Pettitte (W)	6.2	9	2	2	1	2
Nelson	0.2	1	0	0	0	2
Rivera (S)	1.2	0	0	0	0	0

Seattle	IP	H	R	ER	BB	SO
Sele (L)	*6.0	9	4	4	0	4
Tomko	2.1	3	4	4	2	3
Ramsay	0.2	1	0	0	0	0

*Pitched to one batter in seventh.

E—McLemore. DP—New York 1, Seattle 1. LOB—New York 6, Seattle 7. 2B—Justice, Henderson. HR—Williams, T. Martinez. SH—McLemore. SF—Williams. SB—Vizcaino, Rodriguez. CS—Brosius. WP—Tomko. T—3:35. A—47,827. U—M. Hirschbeck, plate; Bell, first; Davis, second; J. Hirschbeck, third; Hernandez, left field; Culbreth, right field.

Game 4 at Seattle

NEW YORK 5, SEATTLE 0

HOW THEY SCORED

Fifth Inning

Yankees—Paul O'Neill struck out. Luis Sojo flied to center. Scott Brosius singled to right. Chuck Knoblauch walked, moving Brosius to second. Derek Jeter homered to center, scoring Brosius and Knoblauch. Justice grounded to the pitcher. Three runs. Yankees 3, Mariners 0.

Eighth Inning

Yankees—Jeter walked. Justice homered to center, scoring Jeter. Bernie Williams grounded to third. Tino Martinez flied to left-center. Jorge Posada lined to shortstop. Two runs. Yankees 5, Mariners 0.

BOX SCORE

New York	AB	R	H	RBI	PO	A
Knoblauch, dh	3	1	0	0	0	0
Jeter, ss	3	2	1	3	1	3
Justice, lf	3	1	1	2	1	0
Bellinger, lf	0	0	0	0	1	0
Williams, cf	4	0	1	0	0	0
T. Martinez, 1b	4	0	0	0	4	2
Posada, c	3	0	0	0	15	0
O'Neill, rf	4	0	1	0	1	0
Sojo, 2b	4	0	0	0	1	0
Brosius, 3b	4	1	1	0	1	0
Clemens, p	0	0	0	0	2	0
Totals	32	5	5	5	27	5

Seattle	AB	R	H	RBI	PO	A
Javier, rf	4	0	0	0	2	0
Martin, lf	4	0	1	0	6	0
Rodriguez, ss	3	0	0	0	3	0
E. Martinez, dh	3	0	0	0	0	0
Olerud, 1b	2	0	0	0	5	0
Cameron, cf	3	0	0	0	5	0
Guillen, 3b	3	0	0	0	0	2
Bell, 2b	3	0	0	0	2	2
Wilson, c	2	0	0	0	4	0
Ibanez, ph	1	0	0	0	0	0
Oliver, c	0	0	0	0	0	0
Abbott, p	0	0	0	0	0	1
Ramsay, p	0	0	0	0	0	0
Mesa, p	0	0	0	0	0	0
Paniagua, p	0	0	0	0	0	0
Totals	28	0	1	0	27	5

New York	0 0 0	0 3 0	0 2 0—5
Seattle	0 0 0	0 0 0	0 0 0—0

New York	IP	H	R	ER	BB	SO
Clemens (W)	9.0	1	0	0	2	15

Seattle	IP	H	R	ER	BB	SO
Abbott (L)	5.0	3	3	3	3	3
Ramsay	1.0	1	0	0	0	1
Mesa	2.0	1	2	2	1	0
Paniagua	1.0	0	0	0	0	0

LOB—New York 4, Seattle 3. 2B—Martin. HR—Jeter, Justice. SB—Williams. T—2:59. A—47,803. U—Bell, plate; Davis, first; J. Hirschbeck, second; Hernandez, third; Culbreth, left field; M. Hirschbeck, right field.

Game 5 at Seattle

SEATTLE 6, NEW YORK 2

HOW THEY SCORED

First Inning

Mariners—Rickey Henderson struck out. Mike Cameron walked. Alex Rodriguez walked, moving Cameron to second. Edgar Martinez walked, loading the bases. John Olerud flied to right, scoring Cameron. Jay Buhner struck out. One run. Mariners 1, Yankees 0.

Fourth Inning

Yankees—Tino Martinez doubled to right-center. Jorge Posada singled to left, moving Martinez to third. Paul O'Neill walked, loading the bases. Luis Sojo doubled to left-center, scoring Martinez and Posada and moving O'Neill to third. Scott Brosius popped to third. Chuck Knoblauch struck out. Derek Jeter grounded to shortstop. Two runs. Yankees 2, Mariners 1.

Fifth Inning

Mariners—Mark McLemore reached on a bunt single. Henderson walked, moving McLemore to second. Cameron sacrificed McLemore to third and Henderson to second. Jeff Nelson relieved Denny Neagle. Rodriguez singled to left, scoring McLemore and Henderson. Martinez homered to center, scoring Rodriguez. Olerud homered to right. Jason Grimsley relieved Nelson. Buhner singled to right. David Bell flied to center. Buhner moved to second on a wild pitch. Dan Wilson walked. McLemore walked, loading the bases. Dwight Gooden relieved Grimsley. Henderson popped to second. Five runs. Mariners 6, Yankees 2.

BOX SCORE

New York	AB	R	H	RBI	PO	A
Knoblauch, dh	4	0	0	0	0	0
Jeter, ss	4	0	2	0	0	2
Justice, lf-rf	5	0	0	0	0	0
Williams, cf	3	0	1	0	4	0
T. Martinez, 1b	4	1	1	0	11	1
Posada, c	3	1	1	0	5	0
O'Neill, rf	2	0	1	0	1	0
Hill, ph	1	0	0	0	0	0
Bellinger, lf	1	0	0	0	0	0
Sojo, 2b	5	0	2	2	3	6
Brosius, 3b	3	0	0	0	0	2
Neagle, p	0	0	0	0	0	0
Nelson, p	0	0	0	0	0	0
Grimsley, p	0	0	0	0	0	0
Gooden, p	0	0	0	0	0	0
Cone, p	0	0	0	0	0	0
Totals	35	2	8	2	24	11

Seattle	AB	R	H	RBI	PO	A
Henderson, lf	3	1	0	0	0	0
Ibanez, lf	1	0	0	0	0	0
Cameron, cf	3	1	0	0	1	0
Rodriguez, ss	3	1	1	2	1	5
E. Martinez, dh	3	1	1	2	0	0
Olerud, 1b	3	1	2	2	12	1
Buhner, rf	4	0	2	0	0	0
Gipson, rf	0	0	0	0	0	0
Bell, 3b	4	0	1	0	1	3
Wilson, c	3	0	0	0	9	0
McLemore, 2b	3	1	1	0	2	4
Garcia, p	0	0	0	0	1	0
Paniagua, p	0	0	0	0	0	0
Rhodes, p	0	0	0	0	0	0
Sasaki, p	0	0	0	0	0	0
Totals	30	6	8	6	27	13

New York .... 0 0 0 2 0 0 0 0 0—2
Seattle .... 1 0 0 0 5 0 0 0 x—6

New York	IP	H	R	ER	BB	SO
Neagle (L)	4.1	3	3	3	4	4
Nelson	*0.0	3	3	3	0	0
Grimsley	0.1	1	0	0	2	0
Gooden	2.1	1	0	0	0	1
Cone	1.0	0	0	0	0	0

Seattle	IP	H	R	ER	BB	SO
Garcia (W)	5.0	7	2	2	2	3
Paniagua	†1.0	0	0	0	1	0
Rhodes	1.1	0	0	0	3	4
Sasaki	1.2	1	0	0	1	2

*Pitched to three batters in fifth.

†Pitched to one batter in seventh.

LOB—New York 15, Seattle 8. 2B—Williams, T. Martinez, Sojo. HR—E. Martinez, Olerud. SH—Cameron. SF—Olerud. SB—Olerud. HBP—By Garcia (Knoblauch), by Sasaki (Williams). WP—Grimsley, Sasaki. T—4:14. A—47,802. U—Davis, plate; J. Hirschbeck, first; Hernandez, second; Culbreth, third; M. Hirschbeck, left field; Bell, right field.

Game 6 at New York

NEW YORK 9, SEATTLE 7

HOW THEY SCORED

First Inning

Mariners—Stan Javier grounded to third. Al Martin walked. Alex Rodriguez doubled to left, scoring Martin. Edgar Martinez doubled to left, scoring Rodriguez. John Olerud flied to center, moving Martinez to third. Raul Ibanez struck out. Two runs. Mariners 2, Yankees 0.

Fourth Inning

Mariners—Martinez struck out. Olerud doubled to right-center. Ibanez flied to left. Carlos Guillen homered to right, scoring Olerud. Mark McLemore grounded to second. Two runs. Mariners 4, Yankees 0.

Yankees—Derek Jeter flied to right. David Justice singled to right. Bernie Williams singled to left, moving Justice to second. Tino Martinez walked, loading the bases. Jorge Posada doubled to right-center, scoring Justice and Williams and moving Martinez to third. Paul O'Neill singled to center, scoring Martinez and moving Posada to third. Brett Tomko relieved John Halama. Luis Sojo flied to right. Scott Brosius grounded to third. Three runs. Mariners 4, Yankees 3.

Seventh Inning

Yankees—Jose Paniagua relieved Tomko. Jose Vizcaino batted for Brosius and reached on an infield single. Chuck Knoblauch sacrificed Vizcaino to second. Jeter singled to left, moving Vizcaino to third. Arthur Rhodes relieved Paniagua. Justice homered to right, scoring Vizcaino and Jeter. Williams singled to right. Martinez doubled to left, moving Williams to third. Posada was walked intentionally, loading the bases. O'Neill singled to right, scoring Williams and Martinez and moving Posada to second. Jose Mesa relieved Rhodes. Sojo walked, loading the bases. Vizcaino flied to left, scoring Posada. Knoblauch walked, loading the bases. Jeter struck out. Six runs. Yankees 9, Mariners 4.

Eighth Inning

Mariners—Rodriguez homered to left. Martinez walked. Mariano Rivera relieved Orlando Hernandez. Olerud doubled to right, moving Martinez to third. Ibanez flied to right. Guillen grounded to the pitcher. McLemore doubled to right, scoring Martinez and Olerud. Jay Buhner batted for Dan Wilson and struck out. Three runs. Yankees 9, Mariners 7.

BOX SCORE

Seattle	AB	R	H	RBI	PO	A
Javier, cf-lf	5	0	0	0	1	0
Martin, lf	3	1	0	0	1	0
Cameron, cf	1	0	0	0	1	0
Rodriguez, ss	5	2	4	2	1	2
E. Martinez, dh	4	1	1	1	0	0
Olerud, 1b	3	2	2	0	5	1
Ibanez, rf	4	0	0	0	5	0
Guillen, 3b	2	1	1	2	1	1
McLemore, 2b	4	0	1	2	2	2
Wilson, c	3	0	1	0	3	1
Buhner, ph	1	0	0	0	0	0
Oliver, c	0	0	0	0	2	0
Halama, p	0	0	0	0	0	1
Tomko, p	0	0	0	0	2	0
Paniagua, p	0	0	0	0	0	0
Rhodes, p	0	0	0	0	0	0
Mesa, p	0	0	0	0	0	0
Totals	35	7	10	7	24	8

New York	AB	R	H	RBI	PO	A
Knoblauch, dh	3	0	0	0	0	0
Jeter, ss	4	1	1	0	1	4
Justice, lf	5	2	2	3	2	0
Bellinger, lf	0	0	0	0	0	0
Williams, cf	4	2	3	0	2	0
T. Martinez, 1b	4	2	1	0	7	2
Posada, c	3	1	1	2	9	1
O'Neill, rf	4	0	2	3	2	0
Sojo, 2b-3b	2	0	0	0	1	2
Brosius, 3b	2	0	0	0	1	1
Vizcaino, ph-2b	1	1	1	1	0	0
Hernandez, p	0	0	0	0	1	0
Rivera, p	0	0	0	0	1	1
Totals	32	9	11	9	27	11

Seattle .... 2 0 0 2 0 0 0 3 0—7
New York .... 0 0 0 3 0 0 6 0 x—9

Seattle	IP	H	R	ER	BB	SO
Halama	3.1	5	3	3	2	1
Tomko	2.2	0	0	0	2	1
Paniagua (L)	0.1	2	2	2	0	0
Rhodes	0.0	4	4	4	1	0
Mesa	1.2	0	0	0	2	3

New York	IP	H	R	ER	BB	SO
Hernandez (W)	*7.0	7	6	6	5	7
Rivera	2.0	3	1	1	0	1

*Pitched to two batters in eighth.

DP—Seattle 1, New York 1. LOB—Seattle 6, New York 8. 2B—Rodriguez 2, Olerud 2, E. Martinez, McLemore, T. Martinez, Posada. HR—Rodriguez, Guillen, Justice. SH—Knoblauch. SF—Vizcaino. SB—Jeter. CS—Guillen. T—4:03. A—56,598. U—J. Hirschbeck, plate; Hernandez, first; Culbreth, second; M. Hirschbeck, third; Bell, left field; Davis, right field.

COMPOSITE

BATTING AVERAGES

New York Yankees

Player, position	G	AB	R	H	2B	3B	HR	RBI	Avg.
Vizcaino, pr-2b	4	2	3	2	1	0	0	2	1.000
Williams, cf	6	23	5	10	1	0	1	3	.435
T. Martinez, 1b	6	25	5	8	2	0	1	1	.320
Jeter, ss	6	22	6	7	0	0	2	5	.318
Knoblauch, dh	6	23	3	6	2	0	0	2	.261
Sojo, 2b-3b	6	23	1	6	1	0	0	2	.261
O'Neill, rf	6	20	0	5	0	0	0	5	.250
Justice, lf-rf	6	26	4	6	2	0	2	8	.231
Brosius, 3b	6	18	2	4	0	0	0	0	.222
Posada, c	6	19	2	3	1	0	0	3	.158
Choate, p	1	0	0	0	0	0	0	0	.000
Clemens, p	1	0	0	0	0	0	0	0	.000
Cone, p	1	0	0	0	0	0	0	0	.000
Gooden, p	1	0	0	0	0	0	0	0	.000
Grimsley, p	2	0	0	0	0	0	0	0	.000
Hernandez, p	2	0	0	0	0	0	0	0	.000
Neagle, p	2	0	0	0	0	0	0	0	.000
Nelson, p	3	0	0	0	0	0	0	0	.000
Pettitte, p	1	0	0	0	0	0	0	0	.000
Rivera, p	3	0	0	0	0	0	0	0	.000
Bellinger, lf-pr	5	1	0	0	0	0	0	0	.000
Hill, ph	2	2	0	0	0	0	0	0	.000
Totals	6	204	31	57	10	0	6	31	.279

Yankees manager Joe Torre (left) gives Roger Clemens a victory hug after his one-hit, 15-strike-out Game 4 masterpiece.

Seattle Mariners

Player, position	G	AB	R	H	2B	3B	HR	RBI	Avg.
Rodriguez, ss	6	22	4	9	2	0	2	5	.409
Olerud, 1b	6	20	3	7	3	0	1	2	.350
McLemore, 2b	5	16	2	4	3	0	0	2	.250
E. Martinez, dh	6	21	2	5	1	0	1	4	.238
Bell, 3b	5	18	0	4	0	0	0	0	.222
Henderson, lf	3	9	2	2	1	0	0	1	.222
Guillen, 3b	2	5	1	1	0	0	1	2	.200
Buhner, rf-ph	4	11	0	2	0	0	0	0	.182
Martin, lf-ph	4	11	1	2	2	0	0	0	.182
Oliver, c	4	6	0	1	0	0	0	0	.167
Cameron, cf	6	18	3	2	0	0	0	1	.111
Wilson, c	4	11	0	1	0	0	0	0	.091
Javier, rf-ph-cf-lf	4	14	0	1	0	0	0	1	.071
Abbott, p	1	0	0	0	0	0	0	0	.000
Garcia, p	2	0	0	0	0	0	0	0	.000
Gipson, lf	2	0	0	0	0	0	0	0	.000
Halama, p	2	0	0	0	0	0	0	0	.000
Mesa, p	3	0	0	0	0	0	0	0	.000
Paniagua, p	5	0	0	0	0	0	0	0	.000
Ramsay, p	2	0	0	0	0	0	0	0	.000
Rhodes, p	4	0	0	0	0	0	0	0	.000
Sasaki, p	2	0	0	0	0	0	0	0	.000
Sele, p	1	0	0	0	0	0	0	0	.000
Tomko, p	2	0	0	0	0	0	0	0	.000
Ibanez, lf-rf-ph	6	9	0	0	0	0	0	0	.000
Totals	6	191	18	41	12	0	5	18	.215

PITCHING AVERAGES

New York Yankees

Pitcher	G	IP	H	R	ER	BB	SO	W	L	ERA
Clemens	1	9.0	1	0	0	2	15	1	0	0.00
Gooden	1	2.1	1	0	0	0	1	0	0	0.00
Cone	1	1.0	0	0	0	0	0	0	0	0.00
Grimsley	2	1.0	2	0	0	3	1	0	0	0.00
Choate	1	0.1	0	0	0	0	1	0	0	0.00
Rivera	3	4.2	4	1	1	0	1	0	0	1.93
Pettitte	1	6.2	9	2	2	1	2	1	0	2.70
Hernandez	2	15.0	13	7	7	8	14	2	0	4.20
Neagle	2	10.0	6	5	5	7	7	0	2	4.50
Nelson	3	3.0	5	3	3	0	6	0	0	9.00
Totals	6	53.0	41	18	18	21	48	4	2	3.06

Shutout—Clemens. Save—Rivera.

Seattle Mariners

Pitcher	G	IP	H	R	ER	BB	SO	W	L	ERA
Sasaki	2	2.2	3	0	0	1	3	0	0	0.00
Ramsay	2	1.2	2	0	0	0	1	0	0	0.00
Garcia	2	11.2	10	2	2	4	11	2	0	1.54
Halama	2	9.1	10	3	3	5	3	0	0	2.89
Paniagua	5	4.1	4	2	2	1	4	0	1	4.15
Abbott	1	5.0	3	3	3	3	3	0	1	5.40
Sele	1	6.0	9	4	4	0	4	0	1	6.00
Tomko	2	5.0	3	4	4	4	4	0	0	7.20
Mesa	3	4.1	5	6	6	3	3	0	0	12.46
Rhodes	4	2.0	8	7	7	4	5	0	1	31.50
Totals	6	52.0	57	31	31	25	41	2	4	5.37

Shutout—Garcia, Paniagua, Rhodes and Sasaki (combined). Save—Sasaki.

WORLD SERIES

NEW YORK A.L. VS. NEW YORK N.L.

Yankee Chuck Knoblauch evades Mets catcher Mike Piazza to score the first run of the 2000 Series.

Game 1 at Yankee Stadium

YANKEES 4, METS 3 (12 INNINGS)

Why the Yankees won: Jose Vizcaino, making his first start of the postseason, went 4-for-6 and singled home the winning run with two out in the 12th inning. Yankees manager Joe Torre started Vizcaino because he was 10-for-19 (.526) against Mets lefthanded starter Al Leiter. However, Vizcaino's biggest hits came in the ninth against righthander reliever Armando Benitez when the Yankees rallied to tie the game, and in the 12th, when he knocked in the game-winning run off Turk Wendell.

Why the Mets lost: Timo Perez was thrown out at home in the sixth inning when he slowed to a jog before reaching second because he thought a ball hit by Todd Zeile would go for a home run. Instead, the ball hit off the top of the left-field wall for a double. If Perez had run hard, he would have scored easily and given New York a 1-0 lead. And perhaps this game never would have gone into extra innings.

TURNING POINT:

Benitez, who was 41-for-46 in save opportunities during the regular season, couldn't preserve a 3-2 lead in the ninth against the bottom of the Yankees' order. He walked Paul O'Neill with one out and then allowed singles to Luis Polonia and Vizcaino to load the bases. Chuck Knoblauch tied the game with a sacrifice fly.

WORTH NOTING:

The victory was the Yankees' record 13th straight in World Series play. They lost the first two games of the 1996 World Series before winning the next four. They then swept the Series in both 1998 and 1999. ... It was the longest World Series game by time at 4 hours and 51 minutes. ... The Yankees' bullpen pitched 5$^1/_3$ scoreless innings. ... The Yankees had only two hits—a pair of second-inning singles—in the first five innings against Leiter. ... The Yankees had a great chance to win the game in the 10th with runners at first and third and nobody out. However, Tino Martinez popped out and O'Neill grounded into a double play. ... Benitez blew his sixth postseason save—the most in baseball history—and dropped to 3-for-9 in postseason save opportunities. ... No Met reached base after the ninth inning. ... Leiter and Andy Pettitte became the first two lefthanders to start World Series Game 1 since October 17, 1987, when Minnesota's Frank Viola beat St. Louis' Joe Magrane.

WORTH QUOTING:

Mets manager Bobby Valentine: "We came in with very little World Series experience and got a lot in one night." . ... Zeile, on his double that just missed being a homer: "We needed Jeffrey Maier. Where was he when we needed him?" Maier was the 12-year-old boy who got the Yankees a tainted homer against Baltimore in the 1996 ALCS by reaching over the wall at Yankee Stadium to catch a ball that replays indicated would not have gotten over the wall. Zeile was a member of that Orioles team. ... Vizcaino, on his game-winning hit off Wendell in the 12th: "I knew what was coming. His best pitch is the fastball. I knew he was going to come with the fastball." . ... Torre, on what he said to Vizcaino after the game: "I kissed him on the cheek and said, 'Thanks for making me look smart.' "

BOX SCORE

New York Mets	AB	R	H	RBI	PO	A
Perez, rf	6	0	1	0	3	0
Alfonzo, 2b	6	0	1	1	1	3
Piazza, dh	5	0	1	0	0	0
Zeile, 1b	5	0	2	0	9	1
Ventura, 3b	5	0	0	0	0	3
Agbayani, lf	4	1	2	0	2	0
McEwing, lf	1	0	0	0	2	0
Payton, cf	5	1	1	0	5	0
Pratt, c	2	1	0	0	10	0
Bordick, ss	1	0	0	0	2	2
†Trammell, ph	1	0	1	2	0	0
Abbott, ss	2	0	1	0	1	1
Leiter, p	0	0	0	0	0	2
J. Franco, p	0	0	0	0	0	0
Benitez, p	0	0	0	0	0	0
Cook, p	0	0	0	0	0	0
Rusch, p	0	0	0	0	0	0
Wendell, p	0	0	0	0	0	0
Totals	43	3	10	3	35	12

New York Yankees	AB	R	H	RBI	PO	A
Knoblauch, dh	4	1	0	1	0	0
Jeter, ss	4	1	1	0	1	2
Justice, lf	4	0	1	2	0	1
§Bellinger, pr-lf	0	0	0	0	0	0
∞Hill, ph-lf	1	0	0	0	0	0
Williams, cf	4	0	0	0	6	0
Martinez, 1b	6	1	2	0	8	1
Posada, c	5	0	1	0	13	0
O'Neill, rf	4	1	1	0	4	0
Brosius, 3b	3	0	1	0	1	1
‡Polonia, ph	1	0	1	0	0	0
Sojo, 3b	2	0	0	0	0	1
Vizcaino, 2b	6	0	4	1	3	2
Pettitte, p	0	0	0	0	0	4
Nelson, p	0	0	0	0	0	0
Rivera, p	0	0	0	0	0	0
Stanton, p	0	0	0	0	0	0
Totals	44	4	12	4	36	12

New York Mets..............................0 0 0 0 0 0 3 0 0 0 0 0—3
New York Yankees ....0 0 0 0 0 2 0 0 1 0 0 1—4

New York Mets	IP	H	R	ER	BB	SO
Leiter	7.0	5	2	2	3	7
J. Franco	1.0	1	0	0	0	0
Benitez	1.0	2	1	1	1	1
Cook	*0.0	0	0	0	2	0
Rusch	1.2	1	0	0	2	0
Wendell (L)	1.0	3	1	1	1	0

New York Yankees	IP	H	R	ER	BB	SO
Pettitte	6.2	8	3	3	1	4
Nelson	1.1	1	0	0	0	0
Rivera	2.0	1	0	0	0	3
Stanton (W)	2.0	0	0	0	0	3

*Pitched to two batters in 10th.

Bases on balls—Off Leiter 3 (Knoblauch, Jeter, Williams), off Benitez 1 (O'Neill), off Cook 2 (Justice, Williams), off Rusch 2 (Posada, Jeter), off Wendell 1 (O'Neill), off Pettitte 1 (Pratt).

Strikeouts—By Leiter 7 (Jeter, Vizcaino, Williams, Martinez, Posada, O'Neill, Knoblauch), by Benitez 1 (Jeter), by Pettitte 4 (Ventura, Agbayani, Pratt, Bordick), by Rivera 3 (Alfonzo, Piazza, Zeile), by Stanton 3 (Pratt, Perez, Alfonzo).

†Singled for Bordick in seventh. ‡Singled for Brosius in ninth. §Ran for Justice in 10th. ∞Flied out for Bellinger in 11th.

DP—Mets 1. LOB—Mets 8, Yankees 15. 2B—Zeile, Agbayani, Abbott, Justice, Posada. SH—Bordick. SF—Knoblauch. CS—Piazza, Knoblauch. HBP—By Pettitte (Pratt), by Rivera (Pratt). WP—Rusch 2. T—4:51. A—55,913. U—Montague, plate: Reliford, first; Kellogg, second; Welke, third; McClelland, left field; Crawford, right field.

PLAY BY PLAY

FIRST INNING

Mets—Perez grounded out, Vizcaino to Martinez. Alfonzo lined to O'Neill. Piazza flied to O'Neill.

Yankees—Knoblauch flied to Payton. Jeter struck out. Justice flied to Agbayani.

SECOND INNING

Mets—Zeile singled to left. Ventura and Agbayani struck out. Payton flied to Williams.

Yankees—Williams grounded out, Bordick to Zeile. Martinez singled to center. Posada forced Martinez at second, Ventura to Alfonzo. O'Neill singled to center as Posada advanced to third. Brosius grounded out to Zeile.

THIRD INNING

Mets—Pratt hit by a pitch. Bordick sacrificed Pratt to second. Bordick was out on the play, Pettitte to Martinez. Perez popped to Brosius. Alfonzo grounded out, Jeter to Martinez.

Yankees—Vizcaino struck out. Knoblauch walked. Knoblauch caught attempting to steal, Leiter to Zeile to Bordick. Jeter grounded out, Ventura to Zeile.

FOURTH INNING

Mets—Piazza singled to left-center. Piazza caught attempting to steal, Pettitte to Martinez to Jeter. Zeile grounded out, Brosius to Martinez. Ventura grounded out, Pettitte to Martinez.

Yankees—Justice flied to Perez. Williams and Martinez struck out.

FIFTH INNING

Mets—Agbayani doubled to left. Payton grounded out to Posada, unassisted. Pratt and Bordick struck out.

Yankees—Posada struck out. O'Neill flied to Agbayani. Brosius grounded out, Bordick to Zeile.

SIXTH INNING

Mets—Perez singled to center. Alfonzo popped to Vizcaino. Piazza flied to Williams. Zeile doubled to left, but Perez was tagged out at home on the play, Justice to Jeter to Posada.

Yankees—Vizcaino singled to left. Knoblauch forced Vizcaino at second, Leiter to Bordick. Jeter walked. Justice doubled to left-center, scoring Knoblauch and Jeter. Williams was intentionally walked. Martinez grounded to Zeile as Justice advanced to third and Williams to second. Posada flied to Payton. Yankees 2, Mets 0.

SEVENTH INNING

Mets—Ventura popped to Vizcaino. Agbayani singled to right. Payton singled to center as Agbayani advanced to second. Pratt walked. Trammell, pinch-hitting for Bordick, singled to left, scoring Agbayani and Payton as Pratt advanced to second. Perez grounded out, Pettitte to Martinez, as Pratt advanced to third and Trammell to second. Nelson now pitching. Alfonzo singled to third, scoring Pratt as Trammell advanced to third. Piazza flied to Williams. Mets 3, Yankees 2.

Yankees—Abbott now at shortstop. O'Neill struck out. Brosius singled to center. Vizcaino grounded out, Ventura to Zeile, as Brosius advanced to second. Knoblauch struck out.

EIGHTH INNING

Mets—Zeile popped to Vizcaino. Ventura fouled to Posada. Agbayani flied to O'Neill.

Yankees—J. Franco now pitching and McEwing in left field. Jeter singled to center. Justice flied to Payton. Williams flied to Perez. Martinez flied to Payton.

NINTH INNING

Mets—Rivera now pitching. Payton flied to O'Neill. Pratt hit by a pitch. Abbott doubled to right as Pratt advanced to third. Perez grounded out, Vizcaino to Martinez. Alfonzo struck out.

Yankees—Benitez now pitching. Posada flied to Payton. O'Neill walked. Polonia, pinch-hitting for Brosius, singled to right as O'Neill advanced to second. Vizcaino singled to left as O'Neill advanced to third and Polonia to second. Knoblauch hit a sacrifice fly to McEwing, scoring O'Neill. Jeter struck out. Mets 3, Yankees 3.

10TH INNING

Mets—Sojo now at third base. Piazza and Zeile struck out. Ventura flied to Williams.

Yankees—Cook now pitching. Justice and Williams walked. Bellinger now pinch-running for Justice. Rusch now pitching. Bellinger advanced to third and Williams to second on a wild pitch. Martinez flied to McEwing. Posada was intentionally walked. O'Neill grounded into a double play, Alfonzo to Abbott to Zeile.

11TH INNING

Mets—Stanton now pitching and Bellinger in left field. McEwing flied to Williams. Payton grounded out, Sojo to Martinez. Pratt struck out.

Yankees—Sojo grounded out, Alfonzo to Zeile. Vizcaino singled to right-center. Knoblauch fouled to Pratt. Jeter walked on a wild pitch and advanced to second as Vizcaino advanced to third. Wendell now pitching. Hill, pinch-hitting for Bellinger, flied to Perez.

12TH INNING

Mets—Hill now in left field. Abbott flied to Williams. Perez and Alfonzo struck out.

Yankees—Williams grounded out, Alfonzo to Zeile. Martinez singled to right-center. Posada doubled to right-center as Martinez advanced to third. O'Neill was intentionally walked. Sojo fouled to Pratt. Vizcaino singled to left, scoring Martinez as Posada advanced to third and O'Neill to second. Final score: Yankees 4, Mets 3.

Game 2 at Yankee Stadium

YANKEES 6, METS 5

Why the Yankees won: Roger Clemens, making his first start since throwing a one-hitter against Seattle in the ALCS, was magnificent. He pitched eight scoreless innings and allowed only two singles. He walked none and struck out nine. The Yankees got to Mets lefthander Mike Hampton early, scoring twice in the first and once in the second. The Yankees built a 6-0 lead and needed every run as the Mets rallied for five runs in the ninth.

Why the Mets lost: They needed a great start from Hampton—who pitched 15 scoreless innings in the NLCS—and didn't get it. Hampton struggled with his control early and fell behind in the count to the first six hitters. He retired the first two batters but then walked two and gave up hits to Tino Martinez and Jorge Posada. Hampton allowed four runs in six innings and the bullpen gave up two more. The Mets made a great rally in the ninth but came up short.

TURNING POINT:

This game might have been over as soon as the Yankees scored two runs in the first because it was clear Clemens had his best stuff. The Mets got a single in the second and didn't get another hit until one out in the seventh. The Mets had only one runner reach second against Clemens and that was because he granted permission to advance from first via a wild pitch. Of Clemens' 112 pitches, 78 were for strikes. In the ninth, when the Mets had closed the gap to 6-2, Todd Zeile hit a ball over the left-field wall that Clay Bellinger, who was brought into the game for his defense, brought back for an out. It was a huge catch as the Mets' rally fell one run short.

WORTH NOTING:

Most of the headlines stemming from this game concerned the first inning, when Clemens faced Mike Piazza. Piazza hit a foul ball and shattered his bat. Not knowing the ball was foul, Piazza ran toward first and Clemens then tossed the barrel of the bat toward Piazza, with the jagged piece of lumber cartwheeling dangerously close to the Mets catcher. Piazza glared at Clemens, and the two players exchanged words as both benches cleared. Clemens later was fined $50,000 for his actions. ... It was the Yankees' 14th consecutive World Series victory. ... Hampton threw 124 pitches but only 65 strikes. ... Yankees reliever Jeff Nelson faced three batters in the ninth and allowed all three to reach base. ... Mariano Rivera allowed two runs in the ninth inning, snapping a streak of 14 1/3 scoreless innings in World Series competition. ... Yankees shortstop Derek Jeter went 3-for-5 to extend his World Series hitting streak to 11 games. He had reached base in 53 of 58 career postseason games. ... Benny Agbayani singled in the ninth inning for the Mets to hit safely in all 11 of their postseason games. ... Clemens improved to 2-0 with a 1.67 ERA in four career World Series starts. ... In the first two games of the Series the Yankees left a combined 27 men on base.

WORTH QUOTING:

Clemens, on the bat-throwing incident: "There was no intent. I was fired up and emotional and flung the bat toward the on-deck circle where the batboy was. I had no idea that Mike was running." Piazza: "If he (Clemens) says anything that was, like, derogatory or obscene to me, that would have been a problem. But he seemed extremely apologetic and unsure and confused and unstable." . . . .Piazza, on why he wouldn't be seeking an apology from Clemens: "An apology is only as good as the source it comes from." . ... Hampton on his performance: "It took a while to settle in. They're a great team. If you make a mistake they capitalize on it." . ... Yankees left fielder David Justice, on the media coverage of the bat-throwing incident: "They've made this into a freak show. Roger threw a two-hitter, one of best playoff performances I've ever seen, and all anyone's talking about is him tossing the end of a bat."

BOX SCORE

New York Mets	AB	R	H	RBI	PO	A
Perez, rf	4	0	0	0	1	1
Alfonzo, 2b	3	1	1	0	1	5
Piazza, c	4	1	1	2	6	1
Ventura, 3b	4	0	1	0	0	2
Zeile, 1b	4	0	2	0	9	0
Agbayani, lf	4	1	1	0	0	0
Harris, dh	4	1	0	0	0	0
Payton, cf	4	1	1	3	5	0
Bordick, ss	2	0	0	0	1	3
†Hamilton, ph	1	0	0	0	0	0
Abbott, ss	1	0	0	0	1	1
Hampton, p	0	0	0	0	0	0
Rusch, p	0	0	0	0	0	0
White, p	0	0	0	0	0	0
Cook, p	0	0	0	0	0	0
Totals	35	5	7	5	24	13

New York Yankees	AB	R	H	RBI	PO	A
Knoblauch, dh	4	0	0	0	0	0
Jeter, ss	5	1	3	0	1	4
Justice, lf	3	1	0	0	2	0
Bellinger, lf	0	0	0	0	1	0
Williams, cf	3	1	0	0	1	0
Martinez, 1b	5	1	3	2	11	0
Posada, c	3	1	2	1	10	1
O'Neill, rf	4	0	3	1	0	0
Brosius, 3b	3	1	1	2	0	2
Vizcaino, 2b	4	0	0	0	1	2
Clemens, p	0	0	0	0	0	2
Nelson, p	0	0	0	0	0	0
Rivera, p	0	0	0	0	0	1
Totals	34	6	12	6	27	12

New York Mets	0 0 0	0 0 0	0 0 5	—5
New York Yankees	2 1 0	0 1 0	1 1 x	—6

New York Mets	IP	H	R	ER	BB	SO
Hampton (L)	6.0	8	4	4	5	4
Rusch	0.1	2	1	1	0	0
White	1.1	1	1	1	1	1
Cook	0.1	1	0	0	0	0

New York Yankees	IP	H	R	ER	BB	SO
Clemens (W)	8.0	2	0	0	0	9
Nelson	*0.0	3	3	3	0	0
Rivera	1.0	2	2	2	0	1

*Pitched to three batters in ninth.

Bases on balls—Off Hampton 5 (Justice, Williams, Knoblauch, Posada 2), off White 1 (Williams).

Strikeouts—By Hampton 4 (Jeter, O'Neill, Brosius, Justice), by White 1 (Vizcaino), by Clemens 9 (Perez, Alfonzo, Agbayani 2, Harris, Payton, Ventura, Bordick, Hamilton), by Rivera 1 (Abbott).

†Struck out for Bordick in eighth.

E—Payton, Bordick, Perez, Clemens. LOB—Mets 4, Yankees 12. 2B—Jeter 2, Martinez, O'Neill. HR—Piazza, Payton, Brosius. SF—Brosius. CS—Vizcaino. HBP—By Hampton (Justice), by Clemens (Alfonzo). WP—Clemens. PB—Posada. T—3:30. A—56,059. U—Reliford, plate; Kellogg, first; Welke, second; McClelland, third; Crawford, left field; Montague, right field.

PLAY BY PLAY

FIRST INNING

Mets—Perez struck out. Alfonzo struck out and was put out at first after a dropped third strike, Posada to Martinez. Piazza grounded out, Vizcaino to Martinez.

Yankees—Knoblauch lined to Payton. Jeter struck out. Justice walked. Martinez singled to left, scoring Justice as Williams advanced to second. Posada singled to center and reached second on a fielding error by Payton as Williams scored and Martinez advanced to third. O'Neill struck out. Yankees 2, Mets 0.

SECOND INNING

Mets—Ventura grounded out, Clemens to Martinez. Zeile singled to center. Agbayani and Harris struck out.

Yankees—Brosius homered to left. Vizcaino reached first on a fielding error by Bordick. Vizcaino caught attempting to steal second, Piazza to Bordick. Knoblauch walked. Jeter singled to right and reached second on a fielding error by Perez. On the play, Knoblauch was tagged out at home, Perez to Alfonzo to Piazza. Justice grounded out, Alfonzo to Zeile. Yankees 3, Mets 0.

THIRD INNING

Mets—Payton struck out. Bordick popped to Jeter. Perez grounded to Martinez.

Yankees—Williams flied to Payton. Martinez grounded out, Alfonzo to Zeile. Posada walked. O'Neill singled to center as Posada advanced to second. Brosius struck out.

FOURTH INNING

Mets—Alfonzo hit by a pitch. Piazza fouled to Martinez. Ventura struck out. Zeile forced Alfonzo at second, Jeter to Vizcaino.

Yankees—Vizcaino grounded out, Bordick to Zeile. Knoblauch flied to Payton. Jeter grounded out, Ventura to Zeile.

FIFTH INNING

Mets—Agbayani grounded out, Jeter to Martinez. Harris and Payton grounded out, Brosius to Martinez.

Yankees—Justice struck out. Williams grounded out, Bordick to Zeile. Martinez doubled to right-center. Posada was intentionally walked. O'Neill singled to right, scoring Martinez as Posada advanced to third. Brosius popped to Alfonzo. Yankees 4, Mets 0.

SIXTH INNING

Mets—Bordick struck out. Perez bunted and reached first on a throwing error by Clemens. Alfonzo flied to Williams. Piazza flied to Justice.

Yankees—Vizcaino grounded out, Ventura to Zeile. Knoblauch flied to Payton. Jeter doubled to left-center. Justice was hit by a pitch. Williams flied to Payton.

SEVENTH INNING

Mets—Ventura flied to Justice. Zeile singled to left. Zeile advanced to second on a wild pitch. Agbayani struck out and was put out at first after a dropped third strike, Posada to Martinez. Harris grounded out, Clemens to Martinez.

Yankees—Rusch now pitching. Martinez grounded out, Bordick to Zeile. Posada singled to right-center. O'Neill doubled to right as Posada advanced to third. White now pitching. Brosius hit a sacrifice fly to Perez, scoring Posada as O'Neill advanced to third. Vizcaino struck out. Yankees 5, Mets 0.

EIGHTH INNING

Mets—Payton grounded out, Vizcaino to Martinez. Hamilton, pinch-hitting for Bordick, struck out. Perez grounded out, Jeter to Martinez.

Yankees—Abbott now at shortstop. Knoblauch grounded out, Alfonzo to Zeile. Jeter doubled to right. Justice grounded out, Abbott to Zeile. Williams was intentionally walked. Cook now pitching. Martinez singled to left, scoring Jeter as Williams advanced to second. Posada forced Martinez at second, Alfonzo to Abbott. Yankees 6, Mets 0.

NINTH INNING

Mets—Nelson now pitching and Bellinger in left field. Alfonzo singled to left-center. Piazza homered, scoring Alfonzo. Ventura singled to center. Rivera now pitching. Zeile flied to Bellinger. Agbayani singled to left as Ventura advanced to second. Ventura advanced to third and Agbayani to second on a passed ball. Harris reached first on a fielder's choice as Ventura was tagged out at the plate, Rivera to Jeter to Posada. Agbayani advanced to third on the play. Harris advanced to second on defensive indifference. Payton homered to right, scoring Agbayani and Harris. Abbott struck out. Final score: Yankees 6, Mets 5.

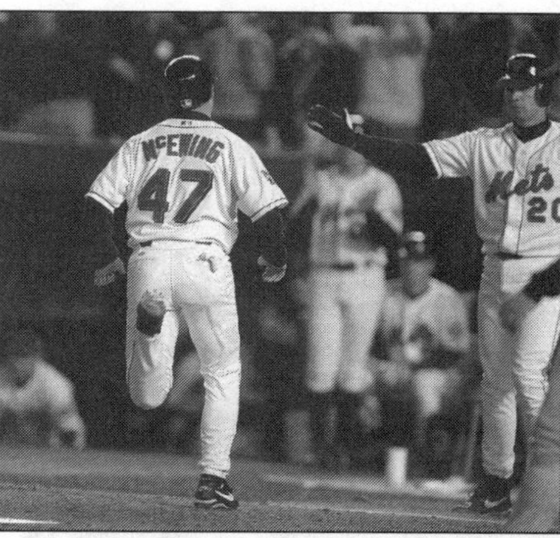

Joe McEwing crosses the plate with an insurance run in the Mets' 4-2 victory in Game 3.

Game 3 at Shea Stadium

METS 4, YANKEES 2

Why the Mets won: They got some clutch hits for the first time in the Series. With the game tied 2-2 in the eighth, the Mets got an RBI double from Benny Agbayani to take the lead, and Bubba Trammell added another run with a sacrifice fly to center. The Mets bullpen, which had been scored upon in each of the first two games, pitched three scoreless innings and Armando Benitez picked up the save.

Why the Yankees lost: They were too patient at the plate against Mets starter Rick Reed, who walked only 34 batters in 30 regular season starts. Five Yankees struck out looking in the first four innings alone. The Bronx Bombers never got going on offense. They had only three hits after the fifth inning and for the game went 0-for-5 with runners in scoring position. The top four spots in the Yankee order went 3-for-16 (.188).

TURNING POINT:

With the Yankees leading 2-1 in the sixth, the Mets had runners at first and second, nobody out and Todd Zeile at the plate. Mets manager Bobby Valentine had Zeile bunting despite the fact Zeile had no sacrifice bunts all season and only seven in his 12-year career. After one miserable attempt by Zeile, Valentine had Zeile swing away. Zeile came through with an RBI double to tie the game.

WORTH NOTING:

Yankees starter Orlando Hernandez struck out the side in each of the first two innings. His 12 strikeouts for the game were the most by a Yankee in a World Series game, breaking Bob Turley's mark of 11 set in 1956. ... Hernandez suffered his first postseason loss. He entered the game with a postseason record of 8-0 and a 1.90 ERA. ... Mets reliever John Franco, 40, picked up the victory in relief, becoming the second-oldest pitcher to win a World Series game. Dolph Luque was 43 when he won a World Series game for the Giants against the Senators in 1933. ... The Mets' victory snapped the Yankees' 14-game World Series winning streak. ... Yankees right fielder Paul O'Neill doubled and tripled in his first two at-bats to give him five consecutive hits—two short of the Series record of seven set by Cincinnati's Billy Hatcher in 1990. O'Neill grounded out in his next at-bat. ... The Mets had the bases loaded and nobody out in the sixth but failed to score.

WORTH QUOTING:

Franco, noting that the win was the Mets' first in World Series play at Shea Stadium since Game 7 of the 1986 series: "Our fans have been waiting 14 years for this. They're very loud, and

Game 2 will be remembered for the bat-throwing incident between Roger Clemens (right) and Mike Piazza. Lost in the glare is the two-hit, eight-inning shutout Clemens threw at the Mets.

we just love being in this ballpark because of the noise." . ... Yankees manager Joe Torre, on why he left Hernandez in the game with the go-ahead run at the plate in the eighth: "He deserved the right to get a decision in this one. I thought he was great.". ... Agbayani, on the end of Hernandez's streak: "All we ever heard was how he won all those games and had never lost. There's the first time for everyone." . ... Valentine: "We were a couple of swings and a couple of pitches away from winning the first two games in Yankee Stadium. We got the swings and we got the pitches this time. We played the same game, minus a couple of mistakes. You know, it seems light years of difference between 0-3 and 1-2, and it's 1-2."

BOX SCORE

New York Yankees	AB	R	H	RBI	PO	A
Vizcaino, 2b	4	0	0	0	3	0
tPolonia, ph	1	0	0	0	0	0
Jeter, ss	4	1	2	0	0	1
Justice, lf	3	0	1	1	3	0
Williams, cf	4	0	0	0	1	0
Martinez, 1b	3	1	1	0	2	1
Posada, c	4	0	0	0	14	0
O'Neill, rf	4	0	3	1	1	0
Brosius, 3b	2	0	0	0	0	1
‡Hill, ph	1	0	0	0	0	0
Sojo, 3b	0	0	0	0	0	0
Hernandez, p	2	0	0	0	0	0
Stanton, p	0	0	0	0	0	0
nKnoblauch, ph	1	0	1	0	0	0
Totals	33	2	8	2	24	3

New York Mets	AB	R	H	RBI	PO	A
Perez, rf	3	0	0	0	2	0
Alfonzo, 2b	4	0	0	0	4	3
Piazza, c	4	1	1	0	12	0
Ventura, 3b	3	1	2	1	0	1
Zeile, 1b	4	1	2	1	5	0
Agbayani, lf	3	0	1	1	1	0
§McEwing, pr-lf	0	1	0	0	0	0
Payton, cf	4	0	1	0	3	0
Bordick, ss	3	0	1	0	0	1
∞Harris, ph	0	0	0	0	0	0
sTrammell, ph	0	0	0	1	0	0
Benitez, p	0	0	0	0	0	0
Reed, p	1	0	1	0	0	1
†Hamilton, ph	1	0	0	0	0	0
Wendell, p	0	0	0	0	0	0
Cook, p	0	0	0	0	0	0
J. Franco, p	0	0	0	0	0	0
uAbbott, ph-ss	1	0	0	0	0	0
Totals	31	4	9	4	27	6

New York Yankees .... 0 0 1 1 0 0 0 0 0—2
New York Mets............................... 0 1 0 0 0 1 0 2 x—4

New York Yankees	IP	H	R	ER	BB	SO
Hernandez (L)	7.1	9	4	4	3	12
Stanton	0.2	0	0	0	0	1

New York Mets	IP	H	R	ER	BB	SO
Reed	6.0	6	2	2	1	8
Wendell	0.2	0	0	0	1	2
Cook	*0.1	0	0	0	1	1
J. Franco (W)	1.0	1	0	0	0	0
Benitez (S)	1.0	1	0	0	0	1

*Pitched to one batter in eighth.

Bases on balls—Off Hernandez 3 (Perez, Ventura, Agbayani), off Reed 1 (Justice), off Wendell 1 (Jeter), off Cook 1 (Martinez).

Strikeouts—By Hernandez 12 (Perez, Alfonzo 2, Piazza 2, Zeile 2, Agbayani, Payton 2, Bordick, Ventura), by Stanton 1 (Abbott), by Reed 8 (Jeter, Williams, Martinez, Posada 2, Brosius, Hernandez, Vizcaino), by Wendell 2 (Hernandez, Vizcaino), by Cook 1 (Williams), by Benitez 1 (Jeter).

†Reached on a fielder's choice for Reed in sixth. ‡Flied out for Brosius in eighth. §Ran for Agbayani in eighth. ∞Announced for Bordick in eighth. sHit sacrifice fly for Harris in eighth. uStruck out for J. Franco in eighth. nSingled for Stanton in ninth. tFlied out for Vizcaino in ninth.

DP—Mets 1. LOB—Yankees 10, Mets 8. 2B—Justice, O'Neill, Piazza, Ventura, Zeile, Agbayani. 3B—O'Neill. HR—Ventura. SH—Hernandez, Reed. SF—Trammell. HBP—By Reed (Brosius), by Cook (Justice). T—3:39. A—55,299. U—Kellogg, plate; Welke, first; McClelland, second; Crawford, third; Montague, left field; Reliford, right field.

PLAY BY PLAY

FIRST INNING

Yankees—Vizcaino flied to Perez, Jeter struck out. Justice walked. Williams struck out.

Mets—Perez, Alfonzo and Piazza struck out.

SECOND INNING

Yankees—Martinez and Posada struck out. O'Neill doubled to left. Brosius struck out.

Mets—Ventura homered to right-center. Zeile, Agbayani and Payton struck out. Mets 1, Yankees 0.

THIRD INNING

Yankees—Hernandez struck out. Vizcaino grounded out, Bordick to Zeile. Jeter singled to left-center. Justice doubled to right, scoring Jeter, and Justice advanced to third on the throw from the outfield. Williams grounded out, Alfonzo to Zeile. Mets 1, Yankees 1.

Mets—Bordick flied to Justice. Reed singled to left. Perez flied to Justice. Alfonzo popped to Vizcaino.

FOURTH INNING

Yankees—Martinez singled to right. Posada struck out. O'Neill tripled to right-center, scoring Martinez. Brosius was hit by a pitch. Hernandez sacrificed Brosius to second. Hernandez was out on the play, Reed, to Alfonzo, covering first. Vizcaino struck out. Yankees 2, Mets 1.

Mets—Piazza struck out. Ventura doubled to right. Zeile struck out. Agbayani flied to O'Neill.

FIFTH INNING

Yankees—Jeter singled to short. Justice flied to Payton. Williams grounded to Zeile as Jeter advanced to second. Martinez flied to Payton.

Mets—Payton fouled to Posada. Bordick singled to center. Reed sacrificed Bordick to second. Reed was out on the play, Martinez to Vizcaino, covering first. Perez walked. Alfonzo struck out.

SIXTH INNING

Yankees—Posada flied to Agbayani. O'Neill grounded out, Alfonzo to Zeile. Brosius popped to Alfonzo.

Mets—Piazza doubled to left. Ventura walked. Zeile doubled to left, scoring Piazza as Ventura advanced to third. Agbayani walked. Payton and Bordick struck out. Hamilton, pinch-hitting for Reed, forced Agbayani at second, Jeter to Vizcaino. Yankees 2, Mets 2.

SEVENTH INNING

Yankees—Wendell now pitching. Hernandez and Vizcaino struck out. Jeter walked. Cook now pitching. Justice was hit by a pitch. Williams struck out.

Mets—Perez flied to Justice. Alfonzo grounded out, Brosius to Martinez. Piazza popped to Martinez.

EIGHTH INNING

Yankees—Martinez walked. J. Franco now pitching. Posada grounded into a double play, Ventura to Alfonzo to Zeile. O'Neill singled to center. Hill, pinch-hitting for Brosius, flied to Perez.

Mets—Sojo now at third base. Ventura struck out. Zeile singled to left-center. Agbayani doubled to left-center, scoring Zeile. McEwing now pinch-running for Agbayani. Payton singled to second as McEwing advanced to third. Harris now pinch-hitting for Bordick. Stanton now pitching. Trammell, pinch-hitting for Harris, hit a sacrifice fly to Williams, scoring McEwing. Abbott, pinch-hitting for J. Franco, struck out. Mets 4, Yankees 2.

NINTH INNING

Yankees—Benitez now pitching, McEwing in left field and Abbott at shortstop. Knoblauch, pinch-hitting for Stanton, singled to center. Polonia, pinch-hitting for Vizcaino, flied to Payton. Jeter struck out. Knoblauch advanced to second on defensive indifference. Justice popped to Alfonzo. Final score: Mets 4, Yankees 2.

Game 4 at Shea Stadium

YANKEES 3, METS 2

Why the Yankees won: They made the most of their scoring opportunities to build an early 3-0 lead. When the Mets cut it to 3-2, the bullpen came in and pitched $4\frac{1}{3}$ scoreless innings, allowing only two hits. The Yankees got a home run from Derek Jeter on the first pitch of the game, a sacrifice fly by Scott Brosius in the second and an RBI groundout by Luis Sojo in the third. Through three innings, the Yankees had three runs on only three hits, but it was all they would need.

Why the Mets lost: Despite having runners on base in every inning except for the fifth and the ninth, their only runs came on a two-run homer by Mike Piazza in the third. Edgardo Alfonzo, the Mets' No. 2 hitter, was held hitless for a second consecutive game, and No. 5 hitter Robin Ventura went 0-for-4. The bottom three spots in the Mets' order went 3-for-14 (.214).

TURNING POINT:

Jeter hit in the leadoff spot for the first time in the Series and quickly quieted the crowd by homering on the first pitch from Mets righthander Bobby Jones. Jeter led off the third with a triple to right center and scored on a RBI groundout. In the fifth, Piazza, who had homered off Denny Neagle in the third, came up to the plate with two outs and nobody on. Torre didn't want Neagle to face Piazza so he took him out and brought in David Cone, who got Piazza to pop out to end the inning.

WORTH NOTING:

Jeter's homer and triple in his first two at-bats put him in a position to become the first player to hit for the cycle in World Series history. However, in his next three at-bats, he struck out, grounded out and reached on a error. ... Paul O'Neill tripled in the second, his second consecutive game with a triple. Before the World Series, O'Neill hadn't hit a triple since July 23, 1999. ... Yankees center fielder Bernie Williams went 0-for-4 to remain hitless in the Series (0-for-15) and lower his career World Series average to .118 (8-for-68). ... Mets left fielder Benny Agbayani went 0-for-3, failing to get a hit for the first time in his team's 13 postseason games. ... By pulling Neagle in the fifth with the Yankees up 3-2, manager Joe Torre prevented him from getting the victory. After the game, Torre admitted Neagle was upset when he went to take him out of the game. ... The Yankees had runners on in every inning after the third but never got one past second base. The 2-3-4 hitters in the Yankees' lineup went 1-for-11.

WORTH QUOTING:

Jeter, on his leadoff homer: "I've been known to swing at the first pitch. When you play games like this, you want to score early. I got a good pitch to hit, and I hit it well." . . . Jones, in his first pitch to Jeter: "I wasn't expecting him to swing." . ...

Mets manager Bobby Valentine, whose team fell behind in the series three games to one: "It's not frustrating. We're giving everything we have out there. They're giving just a little extra." . . . Torre on why he took Neagle out of the game when Piazza came to the plate in the fifth: "Denny did a terrific job for us, but when you're managing in a short series, you have to do what you think is right at that moment to get you out of the situation. Mike had two pretty good swings against Denny, and I wouldn't have been able to forgive myself if something bad would have happened there."

BOX SCORE

New York Yankees	AB	R	H	RBI	PO	A
Jeter, ss	5	2	2	1	1	3
Sojo, 2b	4	0	1	1	4	0
Justice, lf	5	0	0	0	2	0
Bellinger, lf	0	0	0	0	1	0
Williams, cf	4	0	0	0	0	0
Martinez, 1b	4	0	2	0	7	0
O'Neill, rf	4	1	2	0	3	0
Posada, c	3	0	0	0	8	0
Brosius, 3b	1	0	1	1	0	1
Neagle, p	2	0	0	0	0	0
Cone, p	0	0	0	0	0	0
†Canseco, ph	1	0	0	0	0	0
Nelson, p	0	0	0	0	1	1
Stanton, p	0	0	0	0	0	0
Rivera, p	1	0	0	0	0	0
Totals	34	3	8	3	27	5

New York Mets	AB	R	H	RBI	PO	A
Perez, rf	3	1	1	0	2	0
sAbbott, ph-ss	1	0	0	0	1	1
Alfonzo, 2b	3	0	0	0	1	5
Piazza, c	4	1	1	2	6	0
Zeile, 1b	4	0	2	0	6	1
uMcEwing, pr	0	0	0	0	0	0
Benitez, p	0	0	0	0	0	0
Ventura, 3b	4	0	0	0	0	2
Agbayani, lf	3	0	0	0	1	0
Payton, cf	4	0	2	0	4	0
Bordick, ss	2	0	0	0	1	1
‡Harris, ph	0	0	0	0	0	0
J. Franco, p	0	0	0	0	1	0
M. Franco, 1b	1	0	0	0	1	0
B.J. Jones, p	2	0	0	0	1	0
Rusch, p	0	0	0	0	0	0
§Hamilton, ph	0	0	0	0	0	0
∞Trammell, ph-rf	1	0	0	0	2	0
Totals	32	2	6	2	27	10

New York Yankees .... 1 1 1 0 0 0 0 0 0—3
New York Mets.............................. 0 0 2 0 0 0 0 0 0—2

New York Yankees	IP	H	R	ER	BB	SO
Neagle	4.2	4	2	2	2	3
Cone	0.1	0	0	0	0	0
Nelson (W)	1.1	1	0	0	1	1
Stanton	0.2	0	0	0	0	2
Rivera (S)	2.0	1	0	0	0	2

New York Mets	IP	H	R	ER	BB	SO
B.J. Jones (L)	5.0	4	3	3	3	3
Rusch	2.0	3	0	0	0	2
J. Franco	1.0	1	0	0	0	1
Benitez	1.0	0	0	0	1	0

Bases on balls—Off Neagle 2 (Alfonzo, Agbayani), off Nelson 1 (Harris), off B.J. Jones 3 (Posada, Brosius, Sojo), off Benitez 1 (Brosius).

Strikeouts—By Neagle 3 (Perez, Piazza, B.J. Jones), by Nelson 1 (Payton), by Stanton 2 (Trammell, Abbott), by Rivera 2 (Agbayani, M. Franco), by B.J. Jones 3 (Martinez, Neagle, Jeter), by Rusch 2 (Canseco, Williams), by J. Franco (Posada).

†Struck out for Cone in sixth. ‡Walked for Bordick in seventh. §Announced for Rusch in seventh. ∞Struck out for Hamilton in seventh. sStruck out for Perez in seventh. uRan for Zeile in eighth.

E—Trammell. DP—Yankees 1, Mets 1. LOB—Yankees 9, Mets 6. 3B—Jeter, O'Neill. HR—Jeter, Piazza. SF—Brosius. SB—Sojo. T—3:20. A—55,290. U—Welke, plate; McClelland, first; Crawford, second; Montague, third; Reliford, left field; Kellogg, right field.

PLAY BY PLAY

FIRST INNING

Yankees—Jeter homered to left. Sojo grounded out, Ventura to Zeile. Justice flied to Perez. Williams lined to Payton. Yankees 1, Mets 0.

Mets—Perez struck out. Alfonzo walked. Piazza struck out. Zeile forced Alfonzo at second, Jeter to Sojo.

SECOND INNING

Yankees—Martinez struck out. O'Neill tripled to right. Posada was intentionally walked. Brosius hit a sacrifice fly to Payton, scoring O'Neill. Neagle struck out. Yankees 2, Mets 0.

Mets—Ventura grounded out, Jeter to Martinez. Agbayani walked. Payton singled to right as Agbayani advanced to second. Bordick popped to Sojo. B.J. Jones popped to Martinez.

THIRD INNING

Yankees—Jeter tripled to right-center. Sojo grounded out, Alfonzo to Zeile, as Jeter scored. Justice grounded to Zeile. Williams flied to Payton. Yankees 3, Mets 0.

Mets—Perez singled to center. Alfonzo grounded out, Brosius to Martinez, as Perez advanced to second. Piazza homered to left, scoring Perez. Zeile popped to Sojo. Ventura grounded to Martinez. Yankees 3, Mets 2.

FOURTH INNING

Yankees—Martinez singled to right-center. O'Neill forced Martinez at second, Ventura to Alfonzo. Posada grounded out, Alfonzo to B.J. Jones, as O'Neill advanced to second. Brosius was intentionally walked. Neagle flied to Perez.

Mets—Agbayani fouled to Martinez. Payton singled to center. Bordick flied to Justice. B.J. Jones struck out.

FIFTH INNING

Yankees—Jeter struck out. Sojo walked. Justice grounded out, Alfonzo to Zeile, as Sojo advanced to second. Williams lined to Bordick.

Mets—Perez and Alfonzo flied to O'Neill. Cone now pitching. Piazza popped to Sojo.

SIXTH INNING

Yankees—Rusch now pitching. Martinez grounded out, Bordick to Zeile. O'Neill singled to center. Posada flied to Agbayani. Brosius singled to left as O'Neill advanced to second. Canseco, pinch-hitting for Cone, struck out.

Mets—Nelson now pitching. Zeile singled to center. Ventura flied to Justice. Agbayani lined into a double play, Nelson to Martinez.

SEVENTH INNING

Yankees—Jeter grounded out, Alfonzo to Zeile. Sojo singled to right. Justice lined to Payton. Sojo stole second. Williams struck out.

Mets—Payton struck out. Harris, pinch-hitting for Bordick, walked. Hamilton now pinch-hitting for Rusch. Stanton now pitching. Trammell, pinch-hitting for Hamilton, struck out. Abbott, pinch-hitting for Perez, struck out.

EIGHTH INNING

Yankees—J. Franco now pitching, Abbott at shortstop and Trammell in right field. Martinez singled to right. O'Neill grounded into a double play, Zeile to Abbott to J. Franco. Posada struck out.

Mets—Rivera now pitching. Alfonzo flied to O'Neill. Piazza grounded out, Jeter to Martinez. Zeile singled to center. McEwing now pinch-running for Zeile. Ventura popped to Jeter.

NINTH INNING

Yankees—Benitez now pitching and M. Franco at first base. Brosius walked. Rivera flied to Trammell. Jeter reached first on Trammell's fielding error as Brosius advanced to second. Sojo grounded out, Alfonzo to M. Franco, as Brosius advanced to third and Jeter to second. Justice flied to Trammell.

Mets—Bellinger now in left field. Agbayani struck out. Payton flied to Bellinger. M. Franco struck out. Final score: Yankees 3, Mets 2.

Game 5 at Shea Stadium

YANKEES 4, METS 2

Why the Yankees won: Bernie Williams, hitless in his last 22 World Series at-bats, got his first hit of the 2000 Series in the second inning with a solo homer down the left field line to give the Yankees a 1-0 lead. With the game tied 2-2 in the top of the ninth, the Yankees scored two runs with the bottom of the order doing most of the damage. The big hit was delivered by No. 9 hitter Luis Sojo, whose two-out single scored two runs.

Why the Mets lost: Once again, they couldn't get the big hit. The Mets had runners on base in seven of the nine innings but were just 1-for-7 with runners in scoring position. The top five spots in the order went 3-for-21. Also, manager Bobby Valentine may have stuck with his starter, Al Leiter, too long. The pitch Sojo smacked for the decisive hit was Leiter's 142nd of the game.

TURNING POINT:

The Mets scored both their runs thanks to poor defense by the Yankees. Leiter came up with runners at second and third and two outs and hit a dribbler to first baseman Tino Martinez. Pitcher Andy Pettitte, who was covering first, dropped the throw for an error to hand the Mets their first run. The next batter, Benny Agbayani, hit a grounder to third that Scott Brosius unsuccessfully tried to grab with his bare hand. It was ruled a RBI single but was a play Brosius normally makes. In the fourth with the Mets up 2-1 and a chance to extend their lead, Kurt Abbott walked to put runners at first and second and only one out, but then he got picked off.

WORTH NOTING:

The Yankees became the first team since the Oakland A's (1972-74) to win three consecutive World Series. ... Yankees manager Joe Torre improved his World Series record to 16-3. His .842 winning percentage is the highest of any manager. ... Derek Jeter, who hit .409 (9-for-22) with two doubles, one triple, two homers and six runs, was named World Series MVP. ... When Jeter homered in the sixth to tie the game 2-2, he also extended his World Series hitting streak to 14 games. ... Leiter retired 16 of the first 19 hitters he faced. Before the

Although Edgardo Alfonzo played strong defense in the World Series, he only hit .143 in the five games.

ninth the only two Yankees to get past second were Jeter and Williams on the solo homers. ... Mariano Rivera pitched a scoreless ninth for the save, the 18th consecutive postseason save opportunity he successfully converted. ... The Yankees set a five-game World Series record by leaving 52 men on base, easily shattering the previous record of 42 set by the 1941 Yankees. ... . Leiter's 8 $^{2}/_{3}$ innings in Game 5 was the longest start by a pitcher in a World Series game since Atlanta's Greg Maddux pitched a nine-inning complete game in Game 1 of the 1995 Series against Cleveland. Leiter's record dropped to 0-3 in 11 postseason starts, the most starts in postseason history without a win. ... Despite being ousted in five games, the Mets were only outscored 19-16 in the Series. ... . It was the Yankees' 26th World Series championship. No other franchise has more than nine.

WORTH QUOTING:

Paul O'Neill, on the Yankees winning the World Series after losing 13 of their last 15 regular season games, many by lopsided scores: "Whether you like us or not, we're winners. Everybody was ready for the collapse. Everybody was waiting for us to lose." . ... Torre: "We may not have the greatest players, but we have the greatest team." . ... Jeter, on the Mets: "In my opinion, the Mets were the toughest team we have played in my five years here. Every one of these games could have gone either way. They could have given up after (losing) the first two games, but they never quit. You can't say enough about the New York Mets." . . . Mets reliever Turk Wendell on Leiter's performance: "Al deserved to win this game. In many ways, he deserved to be out there to lose this game, too. It doesn't even need to be questioned. Al deserved to be the deciding factor." . ... Valentine, with a touch of sarcasm lacing his comments when asked why he left Leiter in the game: "It was the wrong decision, obviously. If I brought somebody else in, they definitely would have gotten the guy out, and we'd still be playing."

BOX SCORE

New York Yankees	AB	R	H	RBI	PO	A
Vizcaino, 2b	3	0	0	0	2	2
†Knoblauch, ph	1	0	0	0	0	0
Stanton, p	0	0	0	0	0	0
‡Hill, ph	1	0	0	0	0	0
Rivera, p	0	0	0	0	0	0
Jeter, ss	4	1	1	1	2	5
Justice, lf	4	0	1	0	1	0
Bellinger, lf	0	0	0	0	0	0
Williams, cf	3	1	2	1	2	0
Martinez, 1b	4	0	0	0	11	2
O'Neill, rf	3	0	0	0	2	0
Posada, c	3	1	1	0	7	0
Brosius, 3b	4	1	1	0	0	4
Pettitte, p	3	0	0	0	0	1
Sojo, 2b	1	0	1	1	0	0
Totals	34	4	7	3	27	14

New York Mets	AB	R	H	RBI	PO	A
Agbayani, lf	4	0	1	1	5	0
Alfonzo, 2b	5	0	1	0	0	3
Piazza, c	5	0	2	0	10	0
Zeile, 1b	3	0	0	0	10	0
Ventura, 3b	4	0	0	0	1	0
Trammell, rf	3	1	1	0	1	0
Perez, rf	0	0	0	0	0	0
Payton, cf	4	1	2	0	0	0
Abbott, ss	3	0	1	0	0	2
Leiter, p	2	0	0	0	0	1

Yankees manager Joe Torre embraces the World Series trophy for a fourth time in five years.

New York Mets	AB	R	H	RBI	PO	A
J. Franco, p	0	0	0	0	0	0
§Hamilton, ph	1	0	0	0	0	0
Totals	34	2	8	1	27	6

New York Yankees	0 1 0 0 0 1 0 0 2—4
New York Mets................................	0 2 0 0 0 0 0 0 0—2

New York Yankees	IP	H	R	ER	BB	SO
Pettitte	7.0	8	2	0	3	5
Stanton (W)	1.0	0	0	0	0	1
Rivera (S)	1.0	0	0	0	1	1

New York Mets	IP	H	R	ER	BB	SO
Leiter (L)	8.2	7	4	3	3	9
J. Franco	0.1	0	0	0	0	0

Bases on balls—Off Pettitte 3 (Trammell, Abbott, Zeile), off Rivera 1 (Agbayani), off Leiter 3 (Williams, O'Neill, Posada).

Strikeouts—By Pettitte 5 (Ventura 2, Zeile 2, Agbayani), by Stanton 1 (Payton), by Rivera 1 (Hamilton), by Leiter 9 (Jeter 2, O'Neill 2, Pettitte, Vizcaino, Justice, Williams, Martinez).

†Fouled out for Vizcaino in eighth. ‡Flied out for Stanton in ninth. §Struck out for J. Franco in ninth.

E—Pettitte, Payton. LOB—Yankees 6, Mets 10. 2B—Piazza. HR—Jeter, Williams. SH—Leiter. T—3:32. A—55,292. U—McClelland, plate; Crawford, first; Montague, second; Reliford, third; Kellogg, left field; Welke, right field.

PLAY BY PLAY

FIRST INNING

Yankees—Vizcaino grounded out, Alfonzo to Zeile. Jeter struck out. Justice grounded to Zeile.

Mets—Agbayani and Alfonzo grounded out, Brosius to Martinez. Piazza singled to center. Zeile forced Piazza at second, Jeter, unassisted.

SECOND INNING

Yankees—Williams homered to left. Martinez flied to Agbayani. O'Neill struck out. Posada grounded out, Alfonzo to Zeile. Yankees 1, Mets 0.

Mets—Ventura struck out. Trammell walked. Payton singled to right-center as Trammell advanced to second. Abbott grounded out, Jeter to Martinez, as Trammell advanced to third and Payton to second. Leiter reached first base on Pettitte's fielding error (assist by Martinez), scoring Trammell as Payton advanced to third. Agbayani singled to third, scoring Payton as Leiter advanced to second. Alfonzo popped to Vizcaino. Mets 2, Yankees 1.

THIRD INNING

Yankees—Brosius fouled to Zeile. Pettitte and Vizcaino struck out.

Mets—Piazza grounded out, Brosius to Martinez. Zeile struck out. Ventura grounded out, Vizcaino to Martinez.

FOURTH INNING

Yankees—Jeter and Justice flied to Agbayani. Williams singled to left. Martinez fouled to Ventura.

Mets—Trammell singled to right. Payton forced Trammell at second, Vizcaino to Jeter. Abbott walked. Abbott picked off first base, Pettitte to Martinez. Leiter grounded out, Jeter to Martinez.

FIFTH INNING

Yankees—O'Neill grounded out, Abbott to Zeile. Posada singled to left. Brosius grounded to Zeile as Posada advanced to second. Pettitte grounded out, Alfonzo to Zeile.

Mets—Agbayani struck out. Alfonzo grounded out, Jeter to Martinez. Piazza doubled to left-center. Zeile was intentionally walked. Ventura flied to Justice.

SIXTH INNING

Yankees—Vizcaino grounded out, Leiter to Zeile. Jeter homered to left. Justice struck out. Williams walked. Martinez grounded out, Abbott to Zeile. Mets 2, Yankees 2.

Mets—Trammell grounded out, Jeter to Martinez. Payton singled to third. Abbott singled to center as Payton advanced to second. Leiter sacrificed Payton to third and Abbott to second. Leiter was out on the play, Martinez to Vizcaino, covering first. Agbayani grounded out, Jeter to Martinez.

SEVENTH INNING

Yankees—O'Neill walked. Posada flied out to Agbayani. Brosius flied to Trammell. Pettitte grounded to Zeile.

Mets—Alfonzo singled to left. Piazza flied to Williams. Zeile and Ventura struck out.

EIGHTH INNING

Yankees—Knoblauch, pinch-hitting for Vizcaino, fouled to Piazza. Jeter struck out. Justice singled to short. Williams struck out.

Mets—Stanton now pitching and Sojo at second base. Trammell grounded out, Brosius to Martinez. Payton struck out. Abbott flied to O'Neill.

NINTH INNING

Yankees—Perez now in right field. Martinez and O'Neill struck out. Posada walked. Brosius singled to left as Posada advanced to second. Sojo singled to center, scoring Posada. During the play, Sojo advanced to second on the throw in from the outfield and reached third and then scored on Payton's throwing error. Hill now pinch-hitting for Stanton. J. Franco now pitching. Hill flied to Agbayani. Yankees 4, Mets 2.

Mets—Rivera now pitching and Bellinger in left field. Hamilton, pinch-hitting for J. Franco, struck out. Agbayani walked. Agbayani advanced to second on defensive indifference. Alfonzo flied to O'Neill as Agbayani advanced to third. Piazza flied to Williams. Final score: Yankees 4, Mets 2.

COMPOSITE

BATTING AVERAGES

New York Yankees

Player, position	G	AB	R	H	2B	3B	HR	RBI	Avg.
Polonia, ph	2	2	0	1	0	0	0	0	.500
O'Neill, rf	5	19	2	9	2	2	0	2	.474
Jeter, ss	5	22	6	9	2	1	2	2	.409
Martinez, 1b	5	22	3	8	1	0	0	2	.364
Brosius, 3b	5	13	2	4	0	0	1	3	.308
Sojo, 3b-2b	4	7	0	2	0	0	0	2	.286
Vizcaino, 2b	4	17	0	4	0	0	0	1	.235
Posada, c	5	18	2	4	1	0	0	1	.222
Justice, lf	5	19	1	3	2	0	0	3	.158
Williams, cf	5	18	2	2	0	0	1	1	.111
Knoblauch, dh-ph	4	10	1	1	0	0	0	1	.100
Bellinger, pr-lf	4	0	0	0	0	0	0	0	.000
Clemens, p	1	0	0	0	0	0	0	0	.000
Cone, p	1	0	0	0	0	0	0	0	.000
Nelson, p	3	0	0	0	0	0	0	0	.000
Stanton, p	4	0	0	0	0	0	0	0	.000
Canseco, ph	1	1	0	0	0	0	0	0	.000
Rivera, p	4	1	0	0	0	0	0	0	.000
Hernandez, p	1	2	0	0	0	0	0	0	.000
Neagle, p	1	2	0	0	0	0	0	0	.000
Hill, ph-lf	3	3	0	0	0	0	0	0	.000
Pettitte, p	2	3	0	0	0	0	0	0	.000
Totals	5	179	19	47	8	3	4	18	.263

New York Mets

Player, position	G	AB	R	H	2B	3B	HR	RBI	Avg.
Reed, p	1	1	0	1	0	0	0	0	1.000
Zeile, 1b	5	20	1	8	2	0	0	1	.400
Trammell, ph-rf	4	5	1	2	0	0	0	3	.400
Payton, cf	5	21	3	7	0	0	1	3	.333
Agbayani, lf	5	18	2	5	2	0	0	2	.278
Piazza, dh-c	5	22	3	6	2	0	2	4	.273
Abbott, ss-ph	5	8	0	2	1	0	0	0	.250
Ventura, 3b	5	20	1	3	1	0	1	1	.150
Alfonzo, 2b	5	21	1	3	0	0	0	1	.143
Perez, rf	5	16	1	2	0	0	0	0	.125
Bordick, ss	4	8	0	1	0	0	0	0	.125
Benitez, p	3	0	0	0	0	0	0	0	.000
Cook, p	3	0	0	0	0	0	0	0	.000
Hampton, p	1	0	0	0	0	0	0	0	.000
J. Franco, p	4	0	0	0	0	0	0	0	.000
Rusch, p	3	0	0	0	0	0	0	0	.000
Wendell p	2	0	0	0	0	0	0	0	.000
White, p	1	0	0	0	0	0	0	0	.000
M. Franco, 1b	1	1	0	0	0	0	0	0	.000
McEwing, lf-pr	3	1	1	0	0	0	0	0	.000
B.J. Jones, p	1	2	0	0	0	0	0	0	.000
Leiter, p	2	2	0	0	0	0	0	0	.000
Pratt, c	1	2	1	0	0	0	0	0	.000
Hamilton, ph	4	3	0	0	0	0	0	0	.000
Harris, dh-ph	3	4	1	0	0	0	0	0	.000
Totals	5	175	16	40	8	0	4	15	.229

PITCHING AVERAGES

New York Yankees

Pitcher	G	IP	H	R	ER	BB	SO	W	L	ERA
Clemens	1	8.0	2	0	0	0	9	1	0	0.00
Stanton	4	4.1	0	0	0	0	7	2	0	0.00
Cone	1	0.1	0	0	0	0	0	0	0	0.00
Pettitte	2	13.2	16	5	3	4	9	0	0	1.98
Rivera	4	6.0	4	2	2	1	7	0	0	3.00
Neagle	1	4.2	4	2	2	2	3	0	0	3.86
Hernandez	1	7.1	9	4	4	3	12	0	1	4.91
Nelson	3	2.2	5	3	3	1	1	1	0	10.13
Totals	5	47.0	40	16	14	11	48	4	1	2.68

No shutouts. Saves—Rivera 2.

New York Mets

Pitcher	G	IP	H	R	ER	BB	SO	W	L	ERA
J. Franco	4	3.1	3	0	0	0	1	1	0	0.00
Cook	3	0.2	1	0	0	3	1	0	0	0.00
Rusch	3	4.0	6	1	1	2	2	0	0	2.25
Leiter	2	15.2	12	6	5	6	16	0	1	2.87
Reed	1	6.0	6	2	2	1	8	0	0	3.00
Benitez	3	3.0	3	1	1	2	2	0	0	3.00
B.J. Jones	1	5.0	4	3	3	3	3	0	1	5.40
Wendell	2	1.2	3	1	1	2	2	0	1	5.40
Hampton	1	6.0	8	4	4	5	4	0	1	6.00
White	1	1.1	1	1	1	1	1	0	0	6.75
Totals	5	46.2	47	19	18	25	40	1	4	3.47

No shutouts. Save—Benitez.

Who's Who

This Hall of Fame gathering at the 1939 Cooperstown induction ceremonies included (front row from left) Eddie Collins, Babe Ruth, Connie Mack, Cy Young and (back row) Honus Wagner, Grover Alexander, Tris Speaker, Nap Lajoie, George Sisler and Walter Johnson.

Introduction

NO EASY TICKET TO COOPERSTOWN

It's not easy to join this club—just ask Don Sutton.

Winning 300 games as a big-league pitcher is a remarkable feat—worthy, it seems, of a ticket into the Hall of Fame in the first year of eligibility. Occasionally, though, all it means is a rain check. Try again some time in the future.

Sutton, elected in 1998, knows all about that. Winner of 324 games, he didn't gain the necessary votes until his fifth year on the ballot. Phil Niekro and Gaylord Perry are other 1990s inductees who could speak to the issue. Niekro posted 318 victories but he, too, wasn't elected until his fifth year of eligibility, 1997. And Perry, who won 314 games, made the Hall in 1991—his third try.

Winning 500 games is another story, right? Automatic induction, to be sure. Denton True "Cy" Young must have thought so, anyway, as the Hall—destined for Cooperstown, N.Y., but not yet a physical reality—prepared to take in its first class in 1936. Young had finished his career with a record 511 victories and tossed 76 shutouts.

But not even the great Cy Young, who eventually had baseball's preeminent pitching award named in his honor, was a Hall of Fame first-timer. When the balloting for the first Hall enshrinement was announced, those receiving the votes necessary for election—75 percent or more of the ballots cast—were Ty Cobb (the leading vote-getter), Babe Ruth, Honus Wagner, Christy Mathewson and Walter Johnson. Young's pitching brethren Mathewson and Johnson had won 373 and 417 games, respectively.

The skills of The Select Five, as reported at the time by the Spalding Official Base Ball Guide:

"He (Mathewson, who died in 1925) alone, of the five so far chosen, has been called to the great beyond, brought low before his time. ... Who is there who approaches him in daring when, at a critical stage of the game, he never hesitated to put the ball 'across the plate'? Over it would come, but never, if he could help it, at the place where the batter hoped it would.

"Cobb, most elusive of batters as well as most effective, who did not rely on strength alone ... was as clever with the short, powerful hit as with the long and ground-covering one.

"Ruth, possessor of the stout arms, the stout heart, the sharp eye that picked only the best of the pitched balls to hit; Wagner, who has never been equaled as batter and fielder, not even in the five who have been selected as worthy of being put in this Hall of Fame, which is to recognize the greatest of the base ball world since 1900; and Walter Johnson, of fabulous pitching speed, round up the first five chosen."

The Spalding publication also noted that "only the fact there have been so many good second basemen kept the vote divided so that (Nap) Lajoie did not get a higher count," with Rogers Hornsby and Eddie Collins being the spoilers. Tris Speaker and Willie Keeler were "highly placed" in the voting, the guide said, with Grover Cleveland Alexander and Young earning mention along with Mickey Cochrane and Roger Bresnahan.

It was obvious, from the initial balloting in '36, that baseball's Hall of Fame would be a truly selective shrine. Cy Young could have expounded on that.

No, the Hall didn't yet have a gleaming building to house its plaques and myriad treasures. But it did have a lustrous membership of five.

THE ROSTER GROWS

Young and seven other baseball notables were elected to the Hall in the second year of balloting—but baseball's winningest pitcher was named on only 76.1 percent of the ballots. Others in the second class of honorees were Nap Lajoie, Tris Speaker, John McGraw, Connie Mack, George Wright and the first presidents of the National and American leagues, Morgan Bulkeley and Ban Johnson. The Hall, whose special-election procedures and waiting-period rules would vary over the years, was already well on its way to including a wide range of baseball personalities in its mix—players, managers, executives, organizers, founders and umpires. Voting for the honorees was being done by the nation's baseball writers and various special committees—much the same as it is today (with the Baseball Writers' Association of America and the Hall's Committee on Veterans currently holding forth). ... Grover Cleveland Alexander, whose career victory total matched Mathewson's, was voted into the Hall in 1938, along with Alexander J. Cartwright, considered by some as the game's real founder and by most as its foremost organizer, and Henry Chadwick, baseball's leading chronicler in its formative years. ... Lou Gehrig was the headliner and sentimental choice in a 10-man addition in 1939, the year the Hall of Fame and Museum became part of the Cooperstown landscape in June dedication ceremonies. Gehrig, forced to retire during the '39 season because of an illness that would take his life within two years, was joined by such luminaries as Willie Keeler, Eddie Collins and George Sisler. ... Rogers Hornsby and the late commissioner Kenesaw Mountain Landis (enshrined shortly after his death in 1944) were the only new inductees from 1940-44. ... Hugh Duffy, who compiled the highest single-season batting average in big-league history (.440, in 1894), was among 10 new members in 1945, and the Tinker-to-Evers-to-Chance double-play unit accounted for three of the 11 enshrinees the next year. ... The Hall classes were downsized in the ensuing six years, with a total of only 13 players winning admission. ... In 1953, Bill Klem gained the distinction of being the first umpire to reach Cooperstown. ... In 1962, Jackie Robinson, the first black player in modern big-league baseball, became the first black to make the Hall. ... Satchel Paige, confined to the Negro leagues, the barnstorming circuit and foreign leagues for most of his career because of the color barrier, was the first player voted to the shrine (1971) by the Special Committee on Negro Leagues, which was formed to honor players whose careers were victimized by racial policies in existence for nearly half of this century. ... Roberto Clemente, killed in an airplane crash on December 31, 1972, and Gehrig are the only players for whom waiting-period guidelines have been waived. Clemente was enshrined in 1973. ... It took until 1979 for Hack Wilson, who holds the big-league record for RBIs in one year and owned the N.L. season homer mark until Mark McGwire broke it in 1998, to achieve induction. ... Defensive skills and leadership qualities seemed to be appreciated more than usual in 1984 when Luis Aparicio, Pee Wee Reese and Rick Ferrell were among those selected. ... Nellie Fox missed election to the Hall by the slimmest margin in history. He was named on 74.7 percent of the ballots in 1985, just short of the 75 percent required. But Fox made it in March 1997, thanks to the veterans committee. ... Voters paid tribute to the age of the relief specialist in 1992, adding Rollie Fingers to the pantheon. Also in '92, Tom Seaver set a record for the highest percentage of votes received, 98.84. ... Nolan Ryan, the majors' runaway leader in career strikeouts (5,714) and no-hitters (seven), threatened Seaver's mark in 1999, being named on 491 of 497 ballots, or 98.79 percent. Besides electing Ryan, who like Sutton won 324 games, writers also made George Brett (named on 488 ballots) and Robin Yount members of the '99 class. All three players were ballot first-timers, bringing the total of those reaching the Hall in their initial attempt to 29. ... The 2000 class provided another tribute to perseverance—Tony Perez was elected in his ninth try, Carlton Fisk in his second. ... And, proving that Hall voters attempt to honor anyone truly deserving, regardless of the time frame, the veterans committee chose William Hulbert in 1995—119 years after the Chicago businessman played a pivotal role in the founding of the National League.

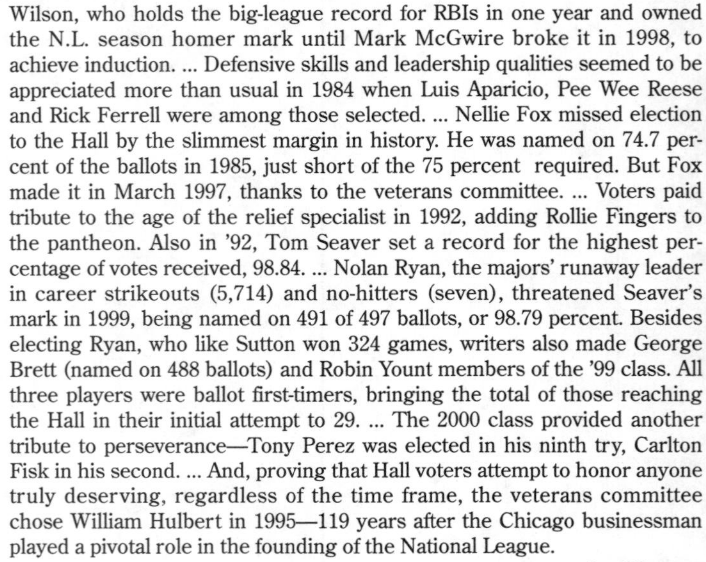

—Joe Hoppel

Detroit's Ty Cobb, the game's premier batsman of the early century, was the leading vote-getter for the first Hall of Fame enshrinement.

HALL OF FAMERS

CLASS BY CLASS

1936

TY COBB **OF**
6-1, 175. **B:** L. **T:** R.
Born: Dec. 18, 1886. **Died:** July 17, 1961.
Career: .366 avg., 1st on all-time list; 117 HR; 1,937 RBIs; 4,189 hits; 891 SB.
Teams: Tigers 1905-26; Athletics 1927-28.
How elected: 98.2 percent of vote.

WALTER JOHNSON **P**
6-1, 200. **B:** R. **T:** R.
Born: Nov. 6, 1887. **Died:** Dec. 10, 1946.
Career: 417-279; 2.16 ERA; 3,509 SO.
Team: Senators 1907-27.
How elected: 83.6 percent of vote.

CHRISTY MATHEWSON **P**
6-1, 195. **B:** R. **T:** R.
Born: Aug. 12, 1880. **Died:** Oct. 7, 1925.
Career: 373-188; 2.13 ERA; 2,502 SO.
Teams: Giants 1900-16; Reds 1916.
How elected: 90.7 percent of vote.

BABE RUTH **OF**
6-2, 215. **B:** L. **T:** L.
Born: Feb. 6, 1895. **Died:** Aug. 16, 1948.
Career: .342 avg.; 714 HR; 2,213 RBIs.
Teams: Red Sox 1914-19; Yankees 1920-34; Braves 1935.
How elected: 95.1 percent of vote.

HONUS WAGNER **SS**
5-11, 200. **B:** R. **T:** R.
Born: Feb. 24, 1874. **Died:** Dec. 6, 1955.
Career: .327 avg.; 101 HR; 1,732 RBIs; 3,415 hits.
Teams: Louisville (Nat.) 1897-99; Pirates 1900-17.
How elected: 95.1 percent of vote.

1937

MORGAN BULKELEY **EXECUTIVE**
First president of N.L.
Born: Dec. 26, 1837. **Died:** Nov. 6, 1922.
Career: Former Connecticut governor and U.S. senator; helped N.L. organize its first league.
How elected: Centennial Commission.

BAN JOHNSON **EXECUTIVE**
A.L. founder/president.
Born: Jan. 5, 1864. **Died:** March 28, 1931.
Career: A former sportswriter who revived the old Western League and later renamed it the American League; A.L. president 1901-27.
How elected: Centennial Commission.

NAPOLEON LAJOIE **2B**
6-1, 195. **B:** R. **T:** R.
Born: Sept. 5, 1874. **Died:** Feb. 7, 1959.
Career: .338 avg.; 83 HR; 1,599 RBIs; 3,242 hits.
Teams: Phillies 1896-1900; Athletics 1901-02, 1915-16; Indians 1902-14.
How elected: 83.6 percent of vote.

CONNIE MACK **C, MAN.**
6-1, 150. **B:** R. **T:** R.
Born: Dec. 22, 1862. **Died:** Feb. 8, 1956.
Managing career: 3,731-3,948, 53 years; 3 World Series championships.
Teams: Pirates 1894-96; Athletics 1901-50.
How elected: Centennial Commission.

JOHN MCGRAW **IF, MAN.**
5-7, 155 **B:** L. **T:** R.
Born: April 7, 1873. **Died:** Feb. 25, 1934.
Playing career: .334 avg.; 13 HR; 462 RBIs.
Managing career: 2,784-1,959, 33 years; 3 World Series championships.
Teams (player): Baltimore (A.A.) 1891; Baltimore (Nat.) 1892-99; St. Louis (Nat.) 1900; Baltimore (Amer.) 1901-02; Giants 1902-06.
Teams (manager): Baltimore (Nat.) 1899; Baltimore (Amer.) 1901-02; Giants 1902-32.
How elected: Centennial Commission.

TRIS SPEAKER **OF**
5-11, 193. **B:** L. **T:** L.
Born: April 4, 1888. **Died:** Dec. 8, 1958.
Career: .345 avg.; 117 HR; 1,529 RBIs; 3,514 hits.
Teams: Red Sox 1907-15; Indians 1916-26; Senators 1927; Athletics 1928.
How elected: 82.1 percent of vote.

GEORGE WRIGHT **SS**
5-9, 150. **B:** R. **T:** R.
Born: Jan. 28, 1847. **Died:** Aug. 21, 1937.
Career: .256 avg.; 2 HR; 132 RBIs.
Teams: Boston (Nat.) 1876-78, 1880-81; Providence (Nat.) 1879, 1882.
How elected: Centennial Commission.

CY YOUNG **P**
6-2, 210. **B:** R. **T:** R.
Born: March 29, 1867. **Died:** Nov. 4, 1955.
Career: 511-316, 1st on all-time win list; 2.63 ERA; 2,800 SO.
Teams: Cleveland (Nat.) 1890-98; St. Louis (Nat.) 1899-1900; Red Sox 1901-08; Indians 1909-11; Braves 1911.
How elected: 76.1 percent of vote.

1938

GROVER CLEVELAND ALEXANDER **P**
6-1, 185. **B:** R. **T:** R.
Born: Feb. 26, 1887. **Died:** Nov. 4, 1950.
Career: 373-208; 2.56 ERA; 2,198 SO.
Teams: Phillies 1911-17, 1930; Cubs 1918-26; Cardinals 1926-29.
How elected: 80.9 percent of vote.

ALEXANDER CARTWRIGHT **ORGANIZER**
Organized 1st baseball club in 1845.
Born: April 17, 1820. **Died:** July 12, 1892.
Career: Formed the Knickerbocker Ball Club in 1845 and taught the new game to Americans from coast to coast; served as unofficial ambassador for the game until his death.
How elected: Centennial Commission.

HENRY CHADWICK **ORGANIZER**
Known as "Father of Baseball."
Born: Oct. 5, 1824. **Died:** April 29, 1908.
Career: A longtime New York baseball writer and contributor to numerous statistical publications dealing with the game; longtime chairman of baseball's committee on rules and author of many significant rules changes during the game's formative years.
How elected: Centennial Commission.

Pirates shortstop Honus Wagner was a member of baseball's first Hall of Fame class.

1939

Cap Anson — 1B
6-1, 227. **B:** R. **T:** R.
Born: April 17, 1852. **Died:** April 14, 1922.
Career: .329 avg.; 97 HR; 1,879 RBIs.
Team: Chicago (Nat.) 1876-97.
How elected: Committee old-time players and writers.

Eddie Collins — 2B
5-9, 175. **B:** L. **T:** R.
Born: May 2, 1887. **Died:** March 25, 1951.
Career: .333 avg.; 47 HR; 1,300 RBIs; 3,312 hits.
Teams: Athletics 1906-14; White Sox 1915-26; Athletics 1927-30.
How elected: 77.7 percent of vote.

Charles Comiskey — 1B, Man., Exec.
Founder/owner of Chicago White Sox.
6-0, 180. **B:** R. **T:** R.
Born: Aug. 15, 1859. **Died:** Oct. 26, 1931.
Playing career: .264 avg.; 29 HR; revolutionized art of playing first base by playing off the bag.
Managing career: 839-542, 12 years.
Teams: St. Louis (A.A.) 1882-89, 1891; Chicago (P.L.) 1890; Cincinnati (Nat.) 1892-94.
How elected: Committee old-time players and writers.

Candy Cummings — P
5-9, 120. **B:** R. **T:** R.
Born: Oct. 17, 1948. **Died:** May 17, 1924.
Career: 21-22; 2.78 ERA; credited with throwing the first curveball.
Teams: Hartford (Nat.) 1876; Cincinnati (Nat.) 1877.
How elected: Committee old-time players and writers.

Buck Ewing — C, IF, Man.
5-10, 188. **B:** R. **T:** R.
Born: Oct. 27, 1859. **Died:** Oct. 20, 1906.
Playing career: .303 avg.; 71 HR; 883 RBIs.
Managing career: 489-395, 7 years.
Teams (player): Troy (Nat.) 1880-82; New York (Nat.) 1883-89, 1891-92; New York (P.L.) 1890; Cleveland (Nat.) 1893-94; Cincinnati (Nat.) 1895-97.
Teams (manager): New York (P.L.) 1890; Cincinnati (Nat.) 1895-99; New York (Nat.) 1900.
How elected: Committee old-time players and writers.

Lou Gehrig — 1B
6-1, 200. **B:** L. **T:** L.
Born: June 19, 1903. **Died:** June 2, 1941.
Career: .340 avg.; 493 HR; 1,995 RBIs.
Team: Yankees 1923-39.
How elected: Special election Baseball Writers.

Willie Keeler — OF
5-4, 140. **B:** L. **T:** L.
Born: March 3, 1872. **Died:** Jan. 1, 1923.
Career: .341 avg.; 33 HR; 810 RBIs; 495 SB.
Teams: New York (Nat.) 1892-93, 1910; Brooklyn (Nat.) 1893, 1899-1902; Baltimore (Nat.) 1894-98; Yankees 1903-09.
How elected: 75.5 percent of vote.

Hoss Radbourn — P
5-9, 168. **B:** R. **T:** R.
Born: Dec. 9, 1853. **Died:** Feb. 5, 1897.
Career: 309-195; 2.67 ERA; 1,830 SO.
Teams: Providence (Nat.) 1881-85; Boston (Nat.) 1886-90; Cincinnati (Nat.) 1891.
How elected: Committee old-time players and writers.

George Sisler — 1B
5-11, 170. **B:** L. **T:** L.
Born: March 24, 1893. **Died:** March 26, 1973.
Career: .340 avg.; 102 HR; 1,175 RBIs.
Teams: Browns 1915-27; Senators 1928; Braves 1928-30.
How elected: 85.8 percent of vote.

Al Spalding — P, Man., Owner
Founder A.G. Spalding & Bros. sporting goods.
6-1, 170. **B:** R. **T:** R.
Born: Sept. 2, 1850. **Died:** Sept. 9, 1915.
Career: 48-12; 1.78 ERA.
Team (player): Chicago (Nat.) 1876-77.
Team (manager): Chicago (Nat.) 1876-78.
Team (owner): Chicago (Nat.) 1882-91.
How elected: Committee old-time players and writers.

1942

Rogers Hornsby — 2B
5-11, 200. **B:** R. **T:** R.
Born: April 27, 1896. **Died:** Jan. 5, 1963.
Career: .358 avg.; 301 HR; 1,584 RBIs.
Teams: Cardinals 1915-26, 1933; Giants 1927; Braves 1928; Cubs 1929-32; Browns 1933-37.
How elected: 78.1 percent of vote.

1944

Kenesaw Mountain Landis — Exec.
First baseball commissioner.
Born: Nov. 20, 1866. **Died:** Nov. 25, 1944.
Career: Former U.S. District judge; became baseball's first commissioner in 1921 and served until his death.
How elected: Committee on Old-Timers.

1945

Roger Bresnahan — C
5-9, 190. **B:** R. **T:** R.
Born: June 11, 1879. **Died:** Dec. 4, 1944.
Career: .279 avg.; 26 HR; 530 RBIs; credited with introducing shinguards for catchers.
Teams: Washington (Nat.) 1897; Chicago (Nat.) 1900; Orioles 1901-02; Giants 1902-08; Cardinals 1909-12; Cubs 1913-15.
How elected: Committee on Old-Timers.

Dan Brouthers — 1B
6-2, 200. **B:** L. **T:** L.
Born: May 8, 1858. **Died:** Aug. 3, 1932.
Career: .342 avg.; 106 HR; 1,296 RBIs.
Teams: Troy (Nat.) 1879-80; Buffalo (Nat.) 1881-85; Detroit (Nat.) 1886-88; Boston (Nat.) 1889; Boston (P.L.) 1890; Boston (A.A.) 1891; Brooklyn (Nat.) 1892-93; Baltimore (Nat.) 1894-95; Louisville (Nat.) 1895; Philadelphia (Nat.) 1896; Giants 1904.
How elected: Committee on Old-Timers.

Fred Clarke — OF, Man.
5-10, 165. **B:** L. **T:** R.
Born: Oct. 3, 1872. **Died:** Aug. 14, 1960.
Playing career: .312 avg.; 67 HR; 1,015 RBIs.
Managing career: 1,602-1,181, 19 years.
Teams (player): Louisville (Nat.) 1894-99; Pirates 1900-15.
Teams (manager): Louisville (Nat.) 1897-99; Pirates 1900-15.
How elected: Committee on Old-Timers.

Jimmy Collins — 3B
5-9, 178. **B:** R. **T:** R.
Born: Jan. 16, 1873. **Died:** March 6, 1943.
Career: .294 avg.; 65 HR; 983 RBIs.
Teams: Boston (Nat.) 1895, 1896-1900; Louisville 1895; Red Sox 1901-07; Athletics 1907-08.
How elected: Committee on Old-Timers.

Ed Delahanty — 1B, OF
6-1, 170. **B:** R. **T:** R.
Born: Oct. 30, 1867. **Died:** July 2, 1903.
Career: .346 avg.; 101 HR; 1,464 RBIs.
Teams: Philadelphia (Nat.) 1888-89, 1891-1901; Cleveland (P.L) 1890; Senators 1902-03.
How elected: Committee on Old-Timers.

Hugh Duffy — OF
5-7, 168. **B:** R. **T:** R.
Born: Nov. 26, 1866. **Died:** Oct. 19, 1954.
Career: .324 avg.; 106 HR; 1,302 RBIs.
Teams: Chicago (Nat.) 1888-89; Chicago (P.L.) 1890; Boston (A.A.) 1891; Boston (Nat.) 1892-1900; Milwaukee (Amer.) 1901; Phillies 1904-06.
How elected: Committee on Old-Timers.

Hugh Jennings — IF
5-8, 165. **B:** R. **T:** R.
Born: April 2, 1869. **Died:** Feb. 1, 1928.
Career: .311 avg.; 18 HR; 840 RBIs.
Teams: Louisville (A.A.) 1891; Louisville (Nat.) 1892-93; Baltimore (Nat.) 1893-99; Brooklyn (Nat.) 1899-1900, 1903; Phillies 1901-02; Tigers 1907-1909, 1912, 1918.
How elected: Committee on Old-Timers.

Mike (King) Kelly — C, IF
5-10, 180. **B:** R. **T:** R.
Born: Dec. 31, 1857. **Died:** Nov. 8, 1894.
Career: .308 avg.; 69 HR; 950 RBIs.
Teams: Cincinnati (Nat.) 1878-79; Chicago (Nat.) 1880-86; Boston (Nat.) 1887-90, 1891-92; Cincinnati (A.A.) 1891; New York (Nat.) 1893.
How elected: Committee on Old-Timers.

Jim O'Rourke — OF, IF
5-8, 185. **B:** R. **T:** R.
Born: Aug. 24, 1852. **Died:** Jan. 8, 1919.
Career: .310 avg.; 50 HR; 1,010 RBIs.
Teams: Boston (Nat.) 1876-78, 1880; Providence (Nat.) 1879; Buffalo (Nat.) 1881-84; New York (Nat.) 1885-89, 1891-92, 1904; New York (P.L.) 1890; Washington (Nat.) 1893.
How elected: Committee on Old-Timers.

Wilbert Robinson — C, Man.
5-8, 215. **B:** R. **T:** R.
Born: June 2, 1864. **Died:** Aug. 8, 1934.
Playing career: .273 avg.; 18 HR; 622 RBIs.
Managing career: 1,399-1,398, 19 years.
Teams (player): Philadelphia (A.A.) 1886-90; Baltimore (A.A.) 1890-91; Baltimore (Nat.) 1892-99; St. Louis (Nat.) 1900; Baltimore (Amer.) 1901-02.
Teams (manager): Baltimore (Amer.) 1902; Dodgers 1914-31.
How elected: Committee on Old-Timers.

1946

Jesse Burkett — OF
5-8, 155. **B:** L. **T:** L.
Born: Dec. 4, 1868. **Died:** May 27, 1953.
Career: .338 avg.; 75 HR; 952 RBIs.
Teams: New York (Nat.) 1890; Cleveland (Nat.) 1891-98; St. Louis (Nat.) 1899-1901; Browns 1902-04; Red Sox 1905.
How elected: Committee on Old-Timers.

Frank Chance — 1B, Man.
6-0, 190. **B:** R. **T:** R.
Born: Sept. 9, 1877. **Died:** Sept. 15, 1924.
Playing career: .296 avg.; 20 HR; 596 RBIs.
Managing career: 946-648, 11 years.
Teams (player): Cubs 1898-1912; Yankees 1913-14.
Teams (manager): Cubs 1905-12; Yankees 1913-14; Red Sox 1923.
How elected: Committee on Old-Timers.

Jack Chesbro — P
5-9, 180. **B:** R. **T:** R.
Born: June 5, 1874. **Died:** Nov. 6, 1931.
Career: 198-132; 2.68 ERA; 1,265 SO.
Teams: Pirates 1899-1902; Yankees 1903-09; Red Sox 1909.
How elected: Committee on Old-Timers.

Johnny Evers — 2B
5-9, 130. **B:** R. **T:** R.
Born: July 21, 1881. **Died:** March 28, 1947.
Career: .270 avg.; 12 HR; 538 RBIs.
Teams: Cubs 1902-13; Braves 1914-17, 1929; Phillies 1917; White Sox 1922.
How elected: Committee on Old-Timers.

Clark Griffith — P, Man., Exec.
5-7, 156. **B:** R. **T:** R.
Born: Nov. 20, 1869. **Died:** Oct. 27, 1955.
Playing career: 237-146; 3.31 ERA; 955 SO.
Managing career: 1,491-1,367, 20 years.
Teams (player): St. Louis (A.A.) 1891; Boston (A.A.) 1891; Chicago (Nat.) 1893-1900; White Sox 1901-02; Yankees 1903-07; Reds 1909-10; Senators 1912-14.
Teams (manager): White Sox 1901-02; Yankees 1903-08; Reds 1909-11; Senators 1912-20.
How elected: Committee on Old-Timers.

Tommy McCarthy — **OF, IF**
5-7, 170. **B:** R. **T:** R.
Born: July 24, 1864 **Died:** Aug. 5, 1922.
Career: .292 avg.; 44 HR, 666 RBIs.
Teams: Boston (U.A.) 1884; Boston (Nat.) 1885; Philadelphia (Nat.) 1886-87; St. Louis (A.A.) 1888-91; Boston (Nat.) 1892-95; Brooklyn (Nat.) 1896.
How elected: Committee on Old-Timers.

Joe McGinnity — **P**
5-11, 206. **B:** R. **T:** R.
Born: March 19, 1871. **Died:** Nov. 14, 1929.
Career: 246-142; 2.66 ERA; 1,068 SO.
Teams: Baltimore (Nat.) 1899; Brooklyn (Nat.) 1900; Orioles 1901-02; Giants 1902-08.
How elected: Committee on Old-Timers.

Eddie Plank — **P**
5-11, 175. **B:** L. **T:** L.
Born: Aug. 31, 1875. **Died:** Feb. 24, 1926.
Career: 326-194; 2.35 ERA; 2,246 SO.
Teams: Athletics 1901-14; St. Louis (Fed.) 1915; Browns 1916-17.
How elected: Committee on Old-Timers.

Joe Tinker — **SS**
5-9, 175. **B:** R. **T:** R.
Born: July 27, 1880. **Died:** July 27, 1948.
Career: .262 avg.; 31 HR; 782 RBIs.
Teams: Cubs 1902-13, 1916; Chicago (Fed.) 1914-15.
How elected: Committee on Old-Timers.

Rube Waddell — **P**
6-1, 196. **B:** L. **T:** L.
Born: Oct. 13, 1876. **Died:** April 1, 1914.
Career: 193-143; 2.16 ERA; 2,316 SO.
Teams: Louisville (Nat.) 1897, 1899; Pirates 1900-01; Cubs 1901; Athletics 1902-07; Browns 1908-10.
How elected: Committee on Old-Timers.

Ed Walsh — **P**
6-1, 193. **B:** R. **T:** R.
Born: May 14, 1881. **Died:** May 26, 1959.
Career: 195-126; 1.82 ERA; 1,736 SO.
Teams: White Sox 1904-16; Braves 1917.
How elected: Committee on Old-Timers.

1947

Mickey Cochrane — **C**
5-10, 180. **B:** L. **T:** R.
Born: April 6, 1903. **Died:** June 28, 1962.
Career: .320 avg.; 119 HR; 832 RBIs.
Teams: Athletics 1925-33; Tigers 1934-37.
How elected: 79.5 percent of vote.

Frank Frisch — **2B, Man.**
5-11, 165. **B:** B. **T:** R.
Born: Sept. 9, 1898. **Died:** March 12, 1973.
Playing career: .316 avg.; 105 HR; 1,244 RBIs.
Managing career: 1,138-1,078, 16 years.
Teams (player): Giants 1919-26; Cardinals 1927-37.
Teams (manager): Cardinals 1933-38; Pirates 1940-46; Cubs 1949-51.
How elected: 84.5 percent of vote.

Lefty Grove — **P**
6-3, 200. **B:** L. **T:** L.
Born: March 6, 1900. **Died:** May 22, 1975.
Career: 300-141; 3.06 ERA; 2,266 SO.
Teams: Athletics 1925-33; Red Sox 1934-41.
How elected: 76.4 percent of vote.

Carl Hubbell — **P**
6-0, 170. **B:** R. **T:** L.
Born: June 22, 1903. **Died:** Nov. 21, 1988.
Career: 253-154; 2.98 ERA; 1,677 SO.
Teams: Giants 1928-43.
How elected: 87 percent of vote.

1948

Herb Pennock — **P**
6-0, 160. **B:** B. **T:** L.
Born: Feb. 10, 1894. **Died:** Jan. 30, 1948.
Career: 240-162; 3.60 ERA; 1,227 SO.
Teams: Athletics 1912-15; Red Sox 1915-22; Yankees 1923-33; Red Sox 1934.
How elected: 77.7 percent of vote.

Pie Traynor — **3B**
6-0, 170. **B:** R. **T:** R.
Born: Nov. 11, 1899. **Died:** March 16, 1972.
Career: .320 avg.; 58 HR; 1,273 RBIs.
Team: Pirates 1920-37.
How elected: 76.9 percent of vote.

1949

Mordecai (Three Finger) Brown — **P**
5-10, 175. **B:** B. **T:** R.
Born: Oct. 19, 1876. **Died:** Feb. 14, 1948.
Career: 239-130; 2.06 ERA; 1,375 SO.
Teams: Cardinals 1903; Cubs 1904-12, 1916; Reds 1913; St. Louis (Fed.) 1914; Brooklyn (Fed.) 1914; Chicago (Fed.) 1915.
How elected: Committee on Old-Timers.

Charley Gehringer — **2B**
5-11, 180. **B:** L. **T:** R.
Born: May 11, 1903. **Died:** Jan. 21, 1993.
Career: .320 avg.; 184 HR; 1,427 RBIs.
Team: Tigers 1924-42.
How elected: 85 percent of vote.

Kid Nichols — **P**
5-10, 175. **B:** R. **T:** R.
Born: Sept. 14, 1869. **Died:** April 11, 1953.
Career: 361-208; 2.95 ERA; 1,868 SO.
Teams: Boston (Nat.) 1890-1901; Cardinals 1904-05; Phillies 1905-06.
How elected: Committee on Old-Timers.

1951

Jimmie Foxx — **C, 3B, 1B**
6-0, 195. **B:** R. **T:** R.
Born: Oct. 22, 1907. **Died:** July 21, 1967.
Career: .325 avg.; 534 HR; 1,922 RBIs.
Teams: Athletics 1925-35; Red Sox 1936-42; Cubs 1942, 1944; Phillies 1945.
How elected: 79.2 percent of vote.

Mel Ott — **OF**
5-9, 170. **B:** L. **T:** R.
Born: March 2, 1909. **Died:** Nov. 21, 1958.
Career: .304 avg.; 511 HR; 1,860 RBIs.
Team: Giants 1926-47.
How elected: 87.2 percent of vote.

1952

Harry Heilmann — **OF, 1B**
6-1, 195. **B:** R. **T:** R.
Born: Aug. 3, 1894. **Died:** July 9, 1951.
Career: .342 avg.; 183 HR; 1,539 RBIs.
Teams: Tigers 1914-29; Reds 1930-32.
How elected: 86.8 percent of vote.

Paul Waner — **OF**
5-8, 153. **B:** L. **T:** L.
Born: April 16, 1903. **Died:** Aug. 29, 1965.
Career: .333 avg.; 113 HR; 1,309 RBIs; 3,152 hits.
Teams: Pirates 1926-40; Dodgers 1941, 1943-44; Braves 1941-42; Yankees 1944-45.
How elected: 83.3 percent of vote.

1953

Ed Barrow — **Man., Exec.**
Born: May 10, 1868. **Died:** Dec. 15, 1953.
Managing career: 310-320, 5 years.
Executive career: Architect of Yankees dynasty that produced 14 A.L. pennants and 10 World Series championships as business manager and president from 1921-45; managed Red Sox to 1918 World Series title and started conversion of Babe Ruth from a pitcher to an outfielder.
How elected: Committee on Veterans.

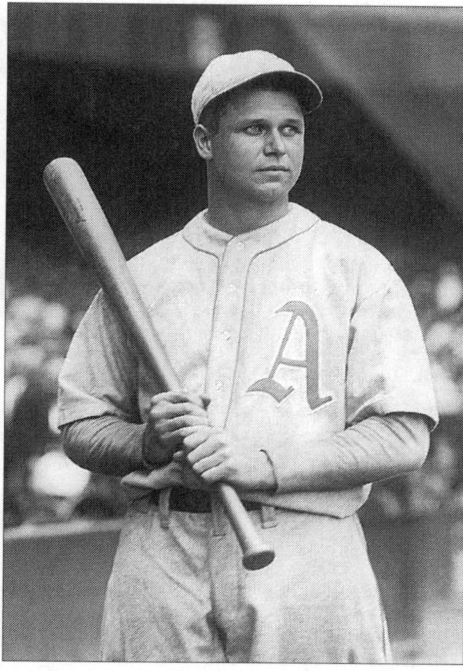

Athletics slugger Jimmie Foxx was the second player to reach the 500-home run plateau.

Chief Bender — **P**
6-2, 185. **B:** R. **T:** R.
Born: May 5, 1884. **Died:** May 22, 1954.
Career: 212-127; 2.46 ERA; 1,711 SO.
Teams: Athletics 1903-14; Baltimore (Fed.) 1915; Phillies 1916-17; White Sox 1925.
How elected: Committee on Veterans.

Tommy Connolly — **Umpire**
Born: Dec. 31, 1870. **Died:** April 28, 1961.
Career: Umpired from 1901, the A.L.'s first season, until 1931; served as A.L. umpires' chief of staff until retirement in 1954; an influential member of baseball's rules committee for many years.
How elected: Committee on Veterans.

Dizzy Dean — **P**
6-2, 200. **B:** R. **T:** R.
Born: Jan. 16, 1911. **Died:** July 17, 1974.
Career: 150-83; 3.03 ERA; 1,155 SO.
Teams: Cardinals 1930, 1932-37; Cubs 1938-41; Browns 1947.
How elected: 79.2 percent of vote.

Bill Klem — **Umpire**
Born: Feb. 22, 1874. **Died:** Sept. 1, 1951.
Career: Joined N.L. as an umpire in 1905 and served with distinction until 1941; called 18 World Series, more than any other umpire; served as N.L. umpires' chief of staff from 1941 until death; responsible for many umpiring innovations; generally considered the greatest arbiter of all time.
How elected: Committee on Veterans.

Al Simmons — **OF**
5-11, 190. **B:** R. **T:** R.
Born: May 22, 1902. **Died:** May 26, 1956.
Career: .334 avg.; 307 HR; 1,827 RBIs.
Teams: Athletics 1924-32, 1940-41, 1944; White Sox 1933-35; Tigers 1936; Senators 1937-38; Braves 1939; Reds 1939; Red Sox 1943.
How elected: 75.4 percent of vote.

Bobby Wallace — **SS**
5-8, 170. **B:** R. **T:** R.
Born: Nov. 4, 1874. **Died:** Nov. 3, 1960.
Career: .268 avg.; 34 HR; 1,121 RBIs.
Teams: Cleveland (Nat.) 1894-98; St. Louis (Nat.) 1899-1901, 1917-18; Browns 1902-16;
How elected: Committee on Veterans.

Harry Wright **Manager**
Born: Jan. 10, 1835. **Died:** Oct. 3, 1895.
Career: 933-660, 18 years.
Teams: Boston (Nat.) 1876-81; Providence (Nat.) 1882-83; Philadelphia (Nat.) 1884-93.
How elected: Committee on Veterans.

1954

Bill Dickey **C**
6-1, 185. **B:** L. **T:** R.
Born: June 6, 1907. **Died:** Nov. 12, 1993.
Career: .313 avg.; 202 HR; 1,210 RBIs.
Teams: Yankees 1928-43, 1946.
How elected: 80.2 percent of vote.

Rabbit Maranville **SS**
5-5, 155. **B:** R. **T:** R.
Born: Nov. 11, 1891. **Died:** Jan. 5, 1954.
Career: .258 avg.; 28 HR; 884 RBIs.
Teams: Braves 1912-20, 1929-35; Pirates 1921-24; Cubs 1925; Dodgers 1926; Cardinals 1927-28.
How elected: 82.9 percent of vote.

Bill Terry **1B, Man.**
6-1, 200. **B:** L. **T:** L.
Born: Oct. 30, 1898. **Died:** Jan. 9, 1989.
Playing career: .341 avg.; 154 HR; 1,078 RBIs.
Managing career: 823-661, 10 years.
Team (player): Giants 1923-36.
Team (manager): Giants 1932-41.
How elected: 77.4 percent of vote.

1955

Frank (Home Run) Baker **3B**
5-11, 173. **B:** L. **T:** R.
Born: March 13, 1886. **Died:** June 28, 1963.
Career: .307 avg.; 96 HR; 987 RBIs.
Teams: Athletics 1908-14; Yankees 1916-19, 1921-22.
How elected: Committee on Veterans.

Joe DiMaggio **OF**
6-2, 193. **B:** R. **T:** R.
Born: Nov. 25, 1914. **Died:** March 8, 1999.
Career: .325 avg.; 361 HR; 1,537 RBIs.
Team: Yankees 1936-42, 1946-51.
How elected: 88.8 percent of vote.

Gabby Hartnett **C**
6-1, 200. **B:** R. **T:** R.
Born: Dec. 20, 1900. **Died:** Dec. 20, 1972.
Career: .297 avg.; 236 HR; 1,179 RBIs.
Teams: Cubs 1922-40; Giants 1941.
How elected: 77.7 percent of vote.

Ted Lyons **P**
5-11, 200. **B:** B. **T:** R.
Born: Dec. 28, 1900. **Died:** July 25, 1986.
Career: 260-230; 3.67 ERA; 1,073 SO.
Team: White Sox 1923-42, 1946.
How elected: 86.5 percent of vote.

Ray Schalk **C**
5-9, 165. **B:** R. **T:** R.
Born: Aug. 12, 1892. **Died:** May 19, 1970.
Career: .253 avg.; 11 HR; 594 RBIs.
Teams: White Sox 1912-28; Giants 1929.
How elected: Committee on Veterans.

Dazzy Vance **P**
6-2, 200. **B:** R. **T:** R.
Born: March 4, 1891. **Died:** Feb. 16, 1961.
Career: 197-140; 3.24 ERA; 2,045 SO.
Teams: Pirates 1915; Yankees 1915, 1918; Dodgers 1922-32, 1935; Cardinals 1933, 1934; Reds 1934.
How elected: 81.7 percent of vote.

1956

Joe Cronin **IF, Man., Exec.**
6-0, 180. **B:** R. **T:** R.
Born: Oct. 12, 1906. **Died:** Sept. 7, 1984.
Playing career: .301 avg.; 170 HR; 1,424 RBIs.
Managing career: 1,236-1,055, 15 years.
Teams (player): Pirates 1926-27; Senators 1928-34; Red Sox 1935-45.
Teams (manager): Senators 1933-34; Red Sox 1935-47.
Executive career: President of A.L. 1959-73.
How elected: 78.8 percent of vote.

Hank Greenberg **1B, OF**
6-3, 210. **B:** R. **T:** R.
Born: Jan. 1, 1911. **Died:** Sept. 4, 1986.
Career: .313 avg.; 331 HR; 1,276 RBIs.
Teams: Tigers 1930, 1933-41, 1945-46; Pirates 1947.
How elected: 85.0 percent of vote.

1957

Sam Crawford **OF**
6-0, 190. **B:** L. **T:** L.
Born: April 18, 1880. **Died:** June 15, 1968.
Career: .309 avg.; 98 HR; 1,525 RBIs.
Teams: Reds 1899-1902; Tigers 1903-17.
How elected: Committee on Veterans.

Joe McCarthy **Manager**
Born: April 21, 1887. **Died:** Jan. 13, 1978.
Career: 2,125-1,333, 24 years; 7 World Series championships.
Teams: Cubs 1926-30; Yankees 1931-46; Red Sox 1948-50.
How elected: Committee on Veterans.

1959

Zack Wheat **OF**
5-10, 170. **B:** L. **T:** R.
Born: May 23, 1888. **Died:** March 11, 1972.
Career: .317 avg.; 132 HR; 1,248 RBIs.
Teams: Dodgers 1909-26; Athletics 1927.
How elected: Committee on Veterans.

1961

Max Carey **OF**
5-11, 170. **B:** B. **T:** R.
Born: Jan. 11, 1890. **Died:** May 30, 1976.
Career: .285 avg.; 69 HR; 800 RBIs.
Teams: Pirates 1910-26; Dodgers 1926-29.
How elected: Committee on Veterans.

Billy Hamilton **OF**
5-6, 165. **B:** L. **T:** R.
Born: Feb. 16, 1866. **Died:** Dec. 16, 1940.
Career: .344 avg.; 40 HR; 736 RBIs; 912 SB.
Teams: Kansas City (A.A.) 1888-89; Philadelphia (Nat.) 1890-95; Boston (Nat.) 1896-1901.
How elected: Committee on Veterans.

1962

Bob Feller **P**
6-0, 185. **B:** R. **T:** R.
Born: Nov. 3, 1918.
Career: 266-162; 3.25 ERA; 2,581 SO.
Team: Indians 1936-41, 1945-56.
How elected: 93.8 percent of vote.

Bill McKechnie **Manager**
Born: Aug. 7, 1887. **Died:** Oct. 29, 1965.
Career: 1,896-1,723, 25 years; 2 World Series championships.
Teams: Newark (Fed.) 1915; Pirates 1922-26; Cardinals 1928-29; Braves 1930-37; Reds 1938-46.
How elected: Committee on Veterans.

Jackie Robinson **IF**
5-11, 195. **B:** R. **T:** R.
Born: Jan. 31, 1919. **Died:** Oct. 24, 1972.
Career: .311 avg.; 137 HR; 734 RBIs.
Team: Dodgers 1947-56.
How elected: 77.5 percent of vote.

Edd Roush **OF**
5-11, 170. **B:** L. **T:** L.
Born: May 8, 1893. **Died:** March 21, 1988.
Career: .323 avg.; 67 HR; 981 RBIs.
Teams: White Sox 1913; Indianapolis (Fed.) 1914; Newark (Fed.) 1915; Giants 1916, 1927-29; Reds 1916-26, 1931.
How elected: Committee on Veterans.

1963

John Clarkson **P**
5-10, 165. **B:** R. **T:** R.
Born: July 1, 1861. **Died:** Feb. 4, 1909.
Career: 328-178; 2.81 ERA; 1,978 SO.
Teams: Worcester (Nat.) 1882; Chicago (Nat.) 1884-87; Boston (Nat.) 1888-92; Cleveland (Nat.) 1892-94.
How elected: Committee on Veterans.

Elmer Flick **OF**
5-9, 168. **B:** L. **T:** R.
Born: Jan. 11, 1876. **Died:** Jan. 9, 1971.
Career: .313 avg.; 48 HR; 756 RBIs.
Teams: Philadelphia (Nat.) 1898-1902; Indians 1902-10.
How elected: Committee on Veterans.

Sam Rice **OF**
5-9, 150. **B:** L. **T:** L.
Born: Feb. 20, 1890. **Died:** Oct. 13, 1974.
Career: .322 avg.; 34 HR; 1,078 RBIs.
Teams: Senators 1915-33; Indians 1934.
How elected: Committee on Veterans.

Eppa Rixey **P**
6-5, 210. **B:** R: **T:** L.
Born: May 3, 1891. **Died:** Feb. 28, 1963.
Career: 266-251; 3.15 ERA; 1,350 SO.
Teams: Phillies 1912-1917, 1919-20; Reds 1921-33.
How elected: Committee on Veterans.

1964

Luke Appling **SS**
5-10, 183. **B:** R. **T:** R.
Born: April 2, 1907. **Died:** Jan. 3, 1991.
Career: .310 avg.; 45 HR; 1,116 RBIs.
Team: White Sox 1930-43, 1945-50.
How elected: 84 percent of vote.

Red Faber **P**
6-2, 180. **B:** B. **T:** R.
Born: Sept. 6, 1888. **Died:** Sept. 25, 1976.
Career: 254-213; 3.15 ERA; 1,471 SO.
Team: White Sox 1914-33.
How elected: Committee on Veterans.

Burleigh Grimes **P**
5-10, 175. **B:** R. **T:** R.
Born: Aug. 18, 1893. **Died:** Dec. 6, 1985.
Career: 270-212; 3.53 ERA; 1,512 SO.
Teams: Pirates 1916-17, 1928-29, 1934; Dodgers 1918-26; Giants 1927; Braves 1930; Cardinals 1930-31, 1933-34; Cubs 1932-33; Yankees 1934.
How elected: Committee on Veterans.

Miller Huggins **Manager**
Born: March 27, 1880. **Died:** Sept. 25, 1929.
Career: 1,413-1,134, 17 years.
Teams: Cardinals 1913-17; Yankees 1918-29.
How elected: Committee on Veterans.

Tim Keefe **P**
5-10, 185. **B:** R. **T:** R.
Born: Jan. 1, 1857. **Died:** April 23, 1933.
Career: 342-225; 2.62 ERA; 2,527 SO.
Teams: Troy (Nat.) 1880-82; Metropolitan (A.A.) 1883-84; New York (Nat.) 1885-91; Philadelphia (Nat.) 1891-93.
How elected: Committee on Veterans.

Heinie Manush **OF**
6-1, 200. **B:** L. **T:** L.
Born: July 20, 1901. **Died:** May 12, 1971.
Career: .330 avg.; 110 HR; 1,183 RBIs.
Teams: Tigers 1923-27; Browns 1928-30; Senators 1930-35; Red Sox 1936; Dodgers 1937-38; Pirates 1938-39.
How elected: Committee on Veterans.

John Montgomery Ward — IF, P
5-9, 165. **B:** L. **T:** R.
Born: March 3, 1860. **Died:** March 4, 1925.
Playing career: .275 avg.; 26 HR; 867 RBIs.
Pitching career: 164-102; 2.10 ERA; 920 SO.
Teams: Providence (Nat.) 1878-82; New York (Nat.) 1883-89, 1893-94; Brooklyn 1890-92.
How elected: Committee on Veterans.

1965

Pud Galvin — P
5-8, 190. **B:** R. **T:** R.
Born: Dec. 25, 1856. **Died:** March 7, 1902.
Career: 360-308; 2.87 ERA; 1,799 SO.
Teams: Buffalo (Nat.) 1879-85; Allegheny (A.A.) 1885-86; Pittsburgh (Nat.) 1887-89, 1891-92; Pittsburgh (P.L.) 1890; St. Louis (Nat.) 1892.
How elected: Committee on Veterans.

1966

Casey Stengel — OF, Man.
5-11, 175. **B:** L. **T:** L.
Born: July 30, 1890. **Died:** Sept. 29, 1975.
Playing career: .284 avg.; 60 HR; 535 RBIs.
Managing career: 1,905-1,842, 25 years; 7 World Series championships.
Teams (player): Dodgers 1912-17; Pirates 1918-19; Phillies 1920-21; Giants 1921-23; Braves 1924-25.
Teams (manager): Dodgers 1934-36; Braves 1938-43; Yankees 1949-60; Mets 1962-65.
How elected: Committee on Veterans.

Ted Williams — OF
6-3, 205. **B:** L. **T:** R.
Born: Aug. 30, 1918.
Career: .344 avg.; 521 HR; 1,839 RBIs.
Team: Red Sox 1939-42, 1946-60.
How elected: 93.4 percent of vote.

1967

Branch Rickey — Executive
Born: Dec. 20, 1881. **Died:** Dec. 9, 1965.
Career: Began baseball association as a minor league catcher in 1903 and played briefly for the Cardinals in three seasons; advanced through the chains of the Browns, Cardinals, Dodgers and Pirates in various front-office positions; introduced concept of a farm system as a member of Cardinals organization; broke baseball's color barrier when he brought Jackie Robinson to the Dodgers in 1947.
How elected: Committee on Veterans.

Red Ruffing — P
6-1, 205. **B:** R. **T:** R.
Born: May 5, 1905. **Died:** Feb. 17, 1986.
Career: 273-225; 3.80 ERA; 1,987 SO.
Teams: Red Sox 1924-30; Yankees 1930-42, 1945-46; White Sox 1947.
How elected: 86.9 percent of vote.

Lloyd Waner — OF
5-9, 150. **B:** L. **T:** R.
Born: March 16, 1906. **Died:** July 22, 1982.
Career: .316 avg.; 27 HR; 598 RBIs.
Teams: Pirates 1927-41, 1944-45; Braves 1941; Reds 1941; Phillies 1942; Dodgers 1944.
How elected: Committee on Veterans.

1968

Kiki Cuyler — OF
5-10, 180. **B:** R. **T:** R.
Born: Aug. 30, 1899. **Died:** Feb. 11, 1950.
Career: .321 avg.; 128 HR; 1,065 RBIs.
Teams: Pirates 1921-27; Cubs 1928-35; Reds 1935-37; Dodgers 1938.
How elected: Committee on Veterans.

Goose Goslin — OF
5-11, 185. **B:** L. **T:** R.
Born: Oct. 16, 1900. **Died:** May 15, 1971.
Career: .316 avg.; 248 HR; 1,609 RBIs.
Teams: Senators 1921-30, 1933, 1938; Browns 1930-32; Tigers 1934-37.
How elected: Committee on Veterans.

Joe Medwick — OF
5-10, 187. **B:** R. **T:** R.
Born: Nov. 24, 1911. **Died:** March 21, 1975.
Career: .324 avg.; 205 HR; 1,383 RBIs.
Teams: Cardinals 1932-40, 1947-48; Dodgers 1940-43, 1946; Giants 1943-45; Braves 1945.
How elected: 84.8 percent of vote.

1969

Roy Campanella — C
5-9, 200. **B:** R. **T:** R.
Born: Nov. 19, 1921. **Died:** June 26, 1993.
Career: .276 avg.; 242 HR; 856 RBIs.
Team: Dodgers 1948-57.
How elected: 79.4 percent of vote.

Stan Coveleski — P
5-11, 166. **B:** R. **T:** R.
Born: July 13, 1890. **Died:** March 20, 1984.
Career: 215-142; 2.89 ERA; 981 SO.
Teams: Athletics 1912; Indians 1916-24; Senators 1925-27; Yankees 1928.
How elected: Committee on Veterans.

Waite Hoyt — P
6-0, 180. **B:** R. **T:** R.
Born: Sept. 9, 1899. **Died:** Aug. 25, 1984.
Career: 237-182; 3.59 ERA; 1,206 SO.
Teams: Giants 1918, 1932; Red Sox 1919-20; Yankees 1921-30; Tigers 1930-31; Athletics 1931; Dodgers 1932, 1937-38; Pirates 1933-37.
How elected: Committee on Veterans.

Stan Musial — OF, 1B
6-0, 175. **B:** L. **T:** L.
Born: Nov. 21, 1920.
Career: .331 avg.; 475 HR; 1,951 RBIs; 3,630 hits.
Team: Cardinals 1941-44, 1946-63.
How elected: 93.2 percent of vote.

1970

Lou Boudreau — SS, Man.
5-11, 185. **B:** R. **T:** R.
Born: July 17, 1917.
Playing career: .295 avg.; 68 HR; 789 RBIs.
Managing career: 1,162-1,224, 16 years.
Teams (player): Indians 1938-50; Red Sox 1951-52.
Teams (manager): Indians 1942-50; Red Sox 1952-54; Athletics 1955-57; Cubs 1960.
How elected: 77.3 percent of vote.

Earle Combs — OF
6-0, 185. **B:** L. **T:** R.
Born: May 14, 1899. **Died:** July 21, 1976.
Career: .325 avg.; 58 HR; 632 RBIs.
Team: Yankees 1924-35.
How elected: Committee on Veterans.

Ford Frick — Executive
Baseball's third commissioner.
Born: Dec. 19, 1894. **Died:** April 8, 1978.
Career: Newspaper reporter and sportswriter; N.L. president from 1934-51; elected as baseball's third commissioner following resignation of Happy Chandler in 1951; served until retirement Dec. 14, 1965.
How elected: Committee on Veterans.

Jesse Haines — P
6-0, 190. **B:** R. **T:** R.
Born: July 22, 1893. **Died:** Aug. 5, 1978.
Career: 210-158; 3.64 ERA; 981 SO.
Teams: Reds 1918; Cardinals 1920-37.
How elected: Committee on Veterans.

Red Sox left fielder Ted Williams compiled a lofty .344 career batting average.

1971

Dave Bancroft — SS
5-9, 160. **B:** B. **T:** R.
Born: April 20, 1892. **Died:** Oct. 9, 1972.
Career: .279 avg.; 32 HR; 591 RBIs.
Teams: Phillies 1915-20; Giants 1920-23, 1930; Braves 1924-27; Dodgers 1928-29.
How elected: Committee on Veterans.

Jake Beckley — 1B
5-10, 200. **B:** L. **T:** L.
Born: Aug. 4, 1867. **Died:** June 25, 1918.
Career: .308 avg.; 86 HR; 1,575 RBIs.
Teams: Pittsburgh (Nat.) 1888-89, 1891-96; Pittsburgh (P.L.) 1890; New York (Nat.) 1896-97; Cincinnati (Nat.) 1897-1903; Cardinals 1904-07.
How elected: Committee on Veterans.

Chick Hafey — OF
6-0, 185. **B:** R. **T:** R.
Born: Feb. 12, 1903. **Died:** July 2, 1973.
Career: .317 avg.; 164 HR; 833 RBIs.
Teams: Cardinals 1924-31; Reds 1932-35, 1937.
How elected: Committee on Veterans.

Harry Hooper — OF
5-10, 168. **B:** L. **T:** R.
Born: Aug. 24, 1887. **Died:** Dec. 18, 1974.
Career: .281 avg.; 75 HR; 817 RBIs.
Teams: Red Sox 1909-20; White Sox 1921-25.
How elected: Committee on Veterans.

Joe Kelley — OF
5-11, 190. **B:** R. **T:** R.
Born: Dec. 9, 1871. **Died:** Aug. 14, 1943.
Career: .317 avg.; 65 HR; 1,194 RBIs.
Teams: Boston (Nat.) 1891; Pittsburgh (Nat.) 1891-92; Baltimore (Nat.) 1892-98; Brooklyn (Nat.) 1899-1901; Orioles 1902; Reds 1902-06; Braves 1908.
How elected: Committee on Veterans.

Rube Marquard — P
6-3, 180. **B:** B. **T:** L.
Born: Oct. 9, 1889. **Died:** June 1, 1980.
Career: 201-177; 3.08 ERA; 1,593 SO.
Teams: Giants 1908-15; Dodgers 1915-20; Reds 1921; Braves 1922-25.
How elected: Committee on Veterans.

Satchel Paige — P
6-3, 180. **B:** R. **T:** R.
Born: July 7, 1906. **Died:** June 8, 1982.
Career: 28-31; 3.29 ERA; 290 SO.
Teams: Indians 1948-49; Browns 1951-53; Athletics 1965.
How elected: Special Committee on Negro Leagues.

GEORGE WEISS EXECUTIVE
Born: June 23, 1895. **Died:** Aug. 13, 1972.
Career: Joined Yankees as farm director in 1932 after impressive career as minor league executive; built Yankees farm system that stocked pennant-winning machines of the 1930s, '40s and '50s; became general manager in 1948 and led Yankees to 10 pennants and seven World Series championships in 13 seasons; the man who hired Casey Stengel as manager; president of the expansion Mets from 1961-66.
How elected: Committee on Veterans.

1972

YOGI BERRA C
5-8, 194. **B:** L. **T:** R.
Born: May 12, 1925.
Career: .285 avg.; 358 HR; 1,430 RBIs.
Teams: Yankees 1946-63; Mets 1965.
How elected: 85.6 percent of vote.

JOSH GIBSON C
6-1, 215. **B:** R. **T:** R.
Born: Dec. 21, 1911. **Died:** Jan. 20, 1947.
Career: Negro League star; statistics not available.
How elected: Special Committee on Negro Leagues.

LEFTY GOMEZ P
6-2, 173. **B:** L. **T:** L.
Born: Nov. 26, 1910. **Died:** Feb. 17, 1989.
Career: 189-102; 3.34 ERA; 1,468 SO.
Teams: Yankees 1930-42; Senators 1943.
How elected: Committee on Veterans.

WILL HARRIDGE EXECUTIVE
Born: Oct. 16, 1883. **Died:** April 9, 1971.
Career: Private secretary to A.L. President Ban Johnson; A.L. secretary after Johnson's retirement; became A.L. president when Ernest Barnard died suddenly in 1931; served with distinction until retirement in 1958.
How elected: Committee on Veterans.

SANDY KOUFAX P
6-2, 210. **B:** R. **T:** L.
Born: Dec. 30, 1935.
Career: 165-87; 2.76 ERA; 2,396 SO.
Team: Dodgers 1955-66.
How elected: 86.9 percent of vote.

WALTER (BUCK) LEONARD 1B
5-10, 185 **B:** L. **T:** L.
Born: Sept. 8, 1907. **Died:** Nov. 27, 1997.
Career: Negro League star; statistics not available.
How elected: Special Committee on Negro Leagues.

EARLY WYNN P
6-0, 200. **B:** B. **T:** R.
Born: Jan. 6, 1920. **Died:** April 4, 1999.
Career: 300-244; 3.54 ERA; 2,334 SO.
Teams: Senators 1939, 1941-44, 1946-48; Indians 1949-57, 1963; White Sox 1958-62.
How elected: 76.0 percent of vote.

ROSS YOUNGS OF
5-8, 162. **B:** B. **T:** R.
Born: April 10, 1897. **Died:** Oct. 22, 1927.
Career: .322 avg.; 42 HR; 592 RBIs.
Team: Giants 1917-26.
How elected: Committee on Veterans.

1973

ROBERTO CLEMENTE OF
5-11, 175. **B:** R. **T:** R.
Born: Aug. 18, 1934. **Died:** Dec. 31, 1972.
Career: .317 avg.; 240 HR; 1,305 RBIs; 3,000 hits.
Team: Pirates 1955-72.
How elected: 92.7 percent of vote.

BILLY EVANS UMPIRE
Born: Feb. 10, 1884. **Died:** Jan. 23, 1956.
Career: A.L. umpire from 1906-27; considered a master of the rules book and an expert at rules applications on tricky plays; front-office executive for the Indians, Red Sox and Tigers; president of Southern League from 1942-46.
How elected: Committee on Veterans.

MONTE IRVIN OF
6-1, 195. **B:** R. **T:** R.
Born: Feb. 25, 1919.
Career: .293 avg.; 99 HR; 443 RBIs; Negro League statistics not available.
Teams: Giants 1949-55; Cubs 1956.
How elected: Special Committee on Negro Leagues.

GEORGE KELLY 1B
6-4, 190. **B:** R. **T:** R.
Born: Sept. 10, 1895. **Died:** Oct. 13, 1984.
Career: .297 avg.; 148 HR; 1,020 RBIs.
Teams: Giants 1915-17, 1919-26; Pirates 1917; Reds 1927-30; Cubs 1930; Dodgers 1932.
How elected: Committee on Veterans.

WARREN SPAHN P
6-0, 175. **B:** L. **T:** L.
Born: April 23, 1921.
Career: 363-245; 3.09 ERA; 2,583 SO.
Teams: Braves 1942, 1946-64; Mets 1965; Giants 1965.
How elected: 83.2 percent of vote.

MICKEY WELCH P
5-8, 160. **B:** R. **T:** R.
Born: July 4, 1859. **Died:** July 30, 1941.
Career: 307-210; 2.71 ERA; 1,850 SO.
Teams: Troy (Nat.) 1880-82; New York (Nat.) 1883-92.
How elected: Committee on Veterans.

1974

COOL PAPA BELL OF
6-0, 143. **B:** B. **T:** L.
Born: May 17, 1903. **Died:** March 7, 1991.
Career: Negro League star; statistics not available.
How elected: Special Committee on Negro Leagues.

JIM BOTTOMLEY 1B
6-0, 180. **B:** L. **T:** L.
Born: April 23, 1900. **Died:** Dec. 11, 1959.
Career: .310 avg.; 219 HR; 1,422 RBIs.
Teams: Cardinals 1922-32; Reds 1933-35; Browns 1936-37.
How elected: Committee on Veterans.

JOCKO CONLAN UMPIRE
Born: Dec. 6, 1899. **Died:** April 1, 1989.
Career: N.L. umpire from 1941-64; worked 5 World Series and 6 All-Star Games; a master of the rules book known for fair and impartial decisions.
How elected: Committee on Veterans.

WHITEY FORD P
5-10, 181. **B:** L. **T:** L.
Born: Oct. 21, 1928.
Career: 236-106; 2.75 ERA; 1,956 SO.
Team: Yankees 1950, 1953-67.
How elected: 77.8 percent of vote.

MICKEY MANTLE OF
6-0, 198. **B:** B. **T:** R.
Born: Oct. 20, 1931. **Died:** Aug. 13, 1995.
Career: .298 avg.; 536 HR; 1,509 RBIs.
Team: Yankees 1951-68.
How elected: 88.2 percent of vote.

SAM THOMPSON OF
6-2, 207. **B:** L. **T:** L.
Born: March 5, 1860. **Died:** Nov. 7, 1922.
Career: .331 avg.; 127 HR; 1,299 RBIs.
Teams: Detroit (Nat.) 1885-88; Philadelphia (Nat.) 1889-98; Tigers 1906.
How elected: Committee on Veterans.

1975

EARL AVERILL OF
5-9, 172. **B:** L. **T:** R.
Born: May 21, 1902. **Died:** Aug. 16, 1983.
Career: .318 avg.; 238 HR; 1,164 RBIs.
Teams: Indians 1929-39; Tigers 1939-40; Braves 1941.
How elected: Committee on Veterans.

BUCKY HARRIS 2B, MAN.
5-9, 156. **B:** R. **T:** R.
Born: Nov. 8, 1896. **Died:** Nov. 8, 1977.
Playing career: .274 avg.; 9 HR; 506 RBIs.
Managing career: 2,157-2,218, 29 years; 2 World Series championships.
Teams (player): Senators 1919-28; Tigers 1929, 1931.
Teams (manager): Senators 1924-28, 1935-42, 1950-54; Tigers 1929-33, 1955-56; Red Sox 1934; Phillies 1943; Yankees 1947-48.
How elected: Committee on Veterans.

BILLY HERMAN 2B
5-11, 180. **B:** R. **T:** R.
Born: July 7, 1909. **Died:** Sept. 5, 1992.
Career: .304 avg.; 47 HR; 839 RBIs.
Teams: Cubs 1931-41; Dodgers 1941-43, 1946; Braves 1946; Pirates 1947.
How elected: Committee on Veterans.

JUDY JOHNSON 3B
5-11, 150. **B:** R. **T:** R.
Born: Oct. 26, 1899. **Died:** June 14, 1989.
Career: Negro League star; statistics not available.
How elected: Special Committee on Negro Leagues.

RALPH KINER OF
6-2, 195. **B:** R. **T:** R.
Born: Oct. 27, 1922.
Career: .279 avg.; 369 HR; 1,015 RBIs.
Teams: Pirates 1946-53; Cubs 1953-54; Indians 1955.
How elected: 75.4 percent of vote.

1976

OSCAR CHARLESTON OF
5-11, 190. **B:** L. **T:** L.
Born: Oct. 14, 1896. **Died:** Oct. 5, 1954.
Career: Negro League star; statistics not available.
How elected: Special Committee on Negro Leagues.

ROGER CONNOR 1B
6-3, 220. **B:** L. **T:** L.
Born: July 1, 1857. **Died:** Jan. 4, 1931.
Career: .317 avg.; 138 HR; 1,322 RBIs.
Teams: Troy (Nat.) 1880-82; New York (Nat.) 1883-89, 1891, 1893-94; New York (P.L.) 1890; Philadelphia (Nat.) 1892; St. Louis (Nat.) 1894-97.
How elected: Committee on Veterans.

CAL HUBBARD UMPIRE
Born: Oct. 31, 1900. **Died:** Oct. 17, 1977.
Career: A.L. umpire from 1936-50; assistant to A.L. supervisor of umpires 1952-53; supervisor of umpires 1954-69; a former pro football player and a member of the National Football League Hall of Fame.
How elected: Committee on Veterans.

BOB LEMON P
6-0, 185. **B:** L. **T:** R.
Born: Sept. 22, 1920. **Died:** Jan. 11, 2000.
Career: 207-128; 3.23 ERA; 1,277 SO.
Team: Indians 1946-58.
How elected: 78.6 percent of vote.

FRED LINDSTROM 3B
5-11, 170. **B:** R. **T:** R.
Born: Nov. 21, 1905. **Died:** Oct. 4, 1981.
Career: .311 avg.; 103 HR; 779 RBIs.
Teams: Giants 1924-32; Pirates 1933-34; Cubs 1935; Dodgers 1936.
How elected: Committee on Veterans.

ROBIN ROBERTS P
6-0, 190. **B:** B. **T:** R.
Born: Sept. 30, 1926.
Career: 286-245; 3.41 ERA; 2,357 SO.
Teams: Phillies 1948-61; Orioles 1962-65; Astros 1965-66; Cubs 1966.
How elected: 86.9 percent of vote.

1977

Ernie Banks SS
6-1, 180. **B:** R. **T:** R.
Born: Jan. 31, 1931.
Career: .274 avg.; 512 HR; 1,636 RBIs.
Team: Cubs 1953-71.
How elected: 83.8 percent of vote.

Martin Dihigo P, IF, OF
6-3, 225. **B:** R. **T:** R.
Born: May 24, 1905. **Died:** May 20, 1971.
Career: Negro League star; statistics not available.
How elected: Special Committee on Negro Leagues.

John Henry Lloyd SS
5-11, 180. **B:** L. **T:** R.
Born: April 25, 1884. **Died:** March 19, 1965.
Career: Negro League star; statistics not available.
How elected: Special Committee on Negro Leagues.

Al Lopez C, Man.
5-11, 165. **B:** R. **T:** R.
Born: Aug. 20, 1908.
Playing career: .261 avg.; 51 HR; 652 RBIs.
Managing career: 1,410-1,004, 17 years.
Teams (player): Dodgers 1928, 1930-35; Braves 1936-40; Pirates 1940-46; Indians 1947.
Teams (manager): Indians 1951-56; White Sox 1957-65, 1968-69.
How elected: Committee on Veterans.

Amos Rusie P
6-1, 200. **B:** R. **T:** R.
Born: May 30, 1871. **Died:** Dec. 6, 1942.
Career: 245-174; 3.07 ERA; 1,934 SO.
Teams: Indianapolis (Nat.) 1889; New York (Nat.) 1890-95, 1897-98; Reds 1901.
How elected: Committee on Veterans.

Joe Sewell SS, 3B
5-7, 155. **B:** L. **T:** R.
Born: Oct. 9, 1898. **Died:** March 6, 1990.
Career: .312 avg.; 49 HR; 1,055 RBIs.
Teams: Indians 1920-30; Yankees 1931-33.
How elected: Committee on Veterans.

1978

Addie Joss P
6-3, 185. **B:** R. **T:** R.
Born: April 12, 1880. **Died:** April 14, 1911.
Career: 160-97; 1.89 ERA; 920 SO.
Team: Indians 1902-10.
How elected: Committee on Veterans.

Larry MacPhail Executive
Born: Feb. 3, 1890. **Died:** Oct. 1, 1975.
Career: A franchise builder and innovator; built championship teams for the Reds, Dodgers and Yankees; introduced night baseball in 1935 at Cincinnati; first to use radio broadcasts to increase revenues for his teams.
How elected: Committee on Veterans.

Eddie Mathews 3B
6-1, 200. **B:** L. **T:** R.
Born: Oct. 13, 1931.
Career: .271 avg.; 512 HR; 1,453 RBIs.
Teams: Braves 1952-66; Astros 1967; Tigers 1967-68.
How elected: 79.4 percent of vote.

1979

Warren Giles Executive
Born: May 28, 1896. **Died:** Feb. 7, 1979.
Career: Reds general manager from 1937-47; Reds president from 1947-52; N.L. president from 1952-69.
How elected: Committee on Veterans.

Willie Mays OF
5-11, 180. **B:** R. **T:** R.
Born: May 6, 1931.
Career: .302 avg.; 660 HR; 1,903 RBIs; 3,283 hits.
Teams: Giants 1951-52, 1954-72; Mets 1972-73.
How elected: 94.7 percent of vote.

Hack Wilson OF
5-6, 190. **B:** R. **T:** R.
Born: April 26, 1900. **Died:** Nov. 23, 1948.
Career: .307 avg.; 244 HR; 1,062 RBIs.
Teams: Giants 1923-25; Cubs 1926-31; Dodgers 1932-34; Phillies 1934.
How elected: Committee on Veterans.

1980

Al Kaline OF
6-2, 180. **B:** R. **T:** R.
Born: Dec. 19, 1934.
Career: .297 avg.; 399 HR; 1,583 RBIs; 3,007 hits.
Team: Tigers 1953-74.
How elected: 88.3 percent of vote.

Chuck Klein OF
6-0, 185. **B:** L. **T:** R.
Born: Oct. 7, 1905. **Died:** March 28, 1958.
Career: .320 avg.; 300 HR; 1,201 RBIs.
Teams: Phillies 1928-33, 1936-39, 1940-44; Cubs 1934-36; Pirates 1939.
How elected: Committee on Veterans.

Duke Snider OF
6-0, 190. **B:** L. **T:** R.
Born: Sept. 19, 1926.
Career: .295 avg.; 407 HR; 1,333 RBIs.
Teams: Dodgers 1947-62; Mets 1963; Giants 1964.
How elected: 86.5 percent of vote

Tom Yawkey Executive
Born: Feb. 21, 1903. **Died:** July 9, 1976.
Career: Owner of Red Sox franchise from 1933 until death; longtime champion of the A.L. and one of the most respected figures in the game.
How elected: Committee on Veterans.

1981

Rube Foster P, Man., Exec.
6-4, 240.
Born: Sept. 17, 1879. **Died:** Dec. 9, 1930.
Playing career: Negro League star; statistics not available.
Executive career: Founder of Negro American and Negro National leagues; owner of Chicago-based American Giants, the model from which all other Negro clubs were built.
How elected: Committee on Veterans.

Bob Gibson P
6-1, 195. **B:** R. **T:** R.
Born: Nov. 9, 1935.
Career: 251-174; 2.91 ERA; 3,117 SO.
Team: Cardinals 1959-75.
How elected: 84 percent of vote.

Johnny Mize 1B
6-2, 215. **B:** L. **T:** R.
Born: Jan. 7, 1913. **Died:** June 2, 1993.
Career: .312 avg.; 359 HR; 1,337 RBIs.
Teams: Cardinals 1936-41; Giants 1942, 1946-49; Yankees 1949-53.
How elected: Committee on Veterans.

1982

Hank Aaron OF
6-0, 180. **B:** R. **T:** R.
Born: Feb. 5, 1934.
Career: .305 avg.; 755 HR, 1st on all-time list; 2,297 RBIs, 1st on all-time list; 3,771 hits.
Teams: Braves 1954-74; Brewers 1975-76.
How elected: 97.8 percent of vote.

Happy Chandler Executive
Second commissioner of baseball.
Born: July 14, 1898. **Died:** June 15, 1991.

Hank Aaron's Hall of Fame credentials include record totals of 755 home runs and 2,297 RBIs.

Career: Former U.S. senator from Kentucky; was elected commissioner in 1945 after the death of Kenesaw Mountain Landis; served until his forced retirement in 1950; returned to Kentucky and won two terms as the state's governor.
How elected: Committee on Veterans.

Travis Jackson SS
5-11, 160. **B:** R. **T:** R.
Born: Nov. 2, 1903. **Died:** July 17, 1987.
Career: .291 avg.; 135 HR; 929 RBIs.
Team: Giants 1922-36.
How elected: Committee on Veterans.

Frank Robinson OF
6-1, 195. **B:** R. **T:** R.
Born: Aug. 31, 1935.
Career: .294 avg.; 586 HR; 1,812 RBIs.
Teams: Reds 1956-65; Orioles 1966-71; Dodgers 1972; Angels 1973-74; Indians 1974-76.
How elected: 89.2 percent of vote.

1983

Walter Alston Manager
Born: Dec. 1, 1911. **Died:** Oct. 1, 1984.
Career: 2,040-1,613, 23 years; 4 World Series championships.
Team: Dodgers 1954-76.
How elected: Committee on Veterans.

George Kell 3B
5-9, 175. **B:** R. **T:** R.
Born: Aug. 23, 1922.
Career: .306 avg.; 78 HR; 870 RBIs.
Teams: Athletics 1943-46; Tigers 1946-52; Red Sox 1952-54; White Sox 1954-56; Orioles 1956-57.
How elected: Committee on Veterans.

Juan Marichal P
6-0, 185. **B:** R. **T:** R.
Born: Oct. 20, 1938.
Career: 243-142; 2.89 ERA; 2,303 SO.
Teams: Giants 1960-73; Red Sox 1974; Dodgers 1975.
How elected: 83.7 percent of vote.

Brooks Robinson 3B
6-1, 190. **B:** R. **T:** R.
Born: May 18, 1937.
Career: .267 avg.; 268 HR; 1,357 RBIs.
Team: Orioles 1955-77.
How elected: 92 percent of vote

Shortstop Pee Wee Reese anchored the Dodgers infield through two glorious decades.

1984

LUIS APARICIO SS
5-9, 160. **B:** R. **T:** R.
Born: April 29, 1934.
Career: .262 avg.; 83 HR; 791 RBIs.
Teams: White Sox 1956-62, 1968-70; Orioles 1963-67; Red Sox 1971-73.
How elected: 84.6 percent of vote.

DON DRYSDALE P
6-6, 216. **B:** R. **T:** R.
Born: July 23, 1936. **Died:** July 3, 1993.
Career: 209-166; 2.95 ERA; 2,486 SO.
Team: Dodgers 1956-69.
How elected: 78.4 percent of vote.

RICK FERRELL C
5-10, 160. **B:** R. **T:** R.
Born: Oct. 12, 1906. **Died:** July 27, 1995.
Career: .281 avg.; 28 HR; 734 RBIs.
Teams: Browns 1929-33, 1941-43; Red Sox 1933-37; Senators 1937-41, 1944-45, 1947.
How elected: Committee on Veterans.

HARMON KILLEBREW 3B, 1B
5-11, 213. **B:** R. **T:** R.
Born: June 29, 1936.
Career: .256 avg.; 573 HR; 1,584 RBIs.
Teams: Senators 1954-60; Twins 1961-74; Royals 1975.
How elected: 83.1 percent of vote.

PEE WEE REESE SS
5-10, 175. **B:** R. **T:** R.
Born: July 23, 1918. **Died:** August 14, 1999.
Career: .269 avg.; 126 HR; 885 RBIs.
Teams: Dodgers 1940-42, 1946-58.
How elected: Committee on Veterans.

1985

LOU BROCK OF
5-11, 170. **B:** L. **T:** L.
Born: June 18, 1939.
Career: .293 avg.; 149 HR; 900 RBIs; 3,023 hits; 938 SB.
Teams: Cubs 1961-64; Cardinals 1964-79.
How elected: 79.7 percent of vote.

ENOS SLAUGHTER OF
5-9, 192. **B:** L. **T:** R.
Born: April 27, 1916.
Career: .300 avg.; 169 HR; 1,304 RBIs.
Teams: Cardinals 1938-42, 1946-53; Yankees 1954-55, 1956-59; Athletics 1955-56; Braves 1959.
How elected: Committee on Veterans.

ARKY VAUGHAN IF
5-11, 175. **B:** L. **T:** R.
Born: March 9, 1912. **Died:** Aug. 30, 1952.
Career: .318 avg.; 96 HR; 926 RBIs.
Teams: Pirates 1932-41; Dodgers 1942-43, 1947-48.
How elected: Committee on Veterans.

HOYT WILHELM P
6-0, 195. **B:** R. **T:** R.
Born: July 26, 1923.
Career: 143-122; 2.52 ERA; 1,610 SO; 1,070 games, 1st on all-time list; 227 saves.
Teams: Giants 1952-56; Cardinals 1957; Indians 1957-58; Orioles 1958-62; White Sox 1963-68; Angels 1969; Braves 1969-70, 1971; Cubs 1970; Dodgers 1971-72.
How elected: 83.8 percent of vote.

1986

BOBBY DOERR 2B
5-11, 175. **B:** R. **T:** R.
Born: April 7, 1918.
Career: .288 avg.; 223 HR; 1,247 RBIs.
Team: Red Sox 1937-44, 1946-51.
How elected: Committee on Veterans.

ERNIE LOMBARDI C
6-3, 230. **B:** R. **T:** R.
Born: April 6, 1908. **Died:** Sept. 26, 1977.
Career: .306 avg.; 190 HR; 990 RBIs.
Teams: Dodgers 1931; Reds 1932-41; Braves 1942; Giants 1943-47.
How elected: Committee on Veterans.

WILLIE MCCOVEY 1B
6-4, 210. **B:** L. **T:** L.
Born: Jan. 10, 1938.
Career: .270 avg.; 521 HR; 1,555 RBIs.
Teams: Giants 1959-73, 1977-80; Padres 1974-76; Athletics 1976.
How elected: 81.4 percent of vote.

1987

RAY DANDRIDGE 3B
5-7, 175. **B:** R. **T:** R.
Born: Aug. 31, 1913. **Died:** Feb. 12, 1994.
Career: Negro League star; statistics not available.
How elected: Committee on Veterans.

JIM (CATFISH) HUNTER P
6-0, 195. **B:** R. **T:** R.
Born: April 8, 1946. **Died:** September 9, 1999.
Career: 224-166; 3.26 ERA; 2,012 SO.
Teams: Athletics 1965-74; Yankees 1975-79.
How elected: 76.3 percent of vote.

BILLY WILLIAMS OF
6-1, 175. **B:** L. **T:** R.
Born: June 15, 1938.
Career: .290 avg.; 426 HR; 1,475 RBIs.
Teams: Cubs 1959-74; Athletics 1975-76.
How elected: 85.7 percent of vote.

1988

WILLIE STARGELL OF, 1B
6-2, 225. **B:** L. **T:** L.
Born: March 6, 1940.
Career: .282 avg.; 475 HR; 1,540 RBIs.
Team: Pirates 1962-82.
How elected: 82.4 percent of vote.

1989

AL BARLICK UMPIRE
Born: April 2, 1915. **Died:** December 27, 1995.
Career: N.L. umpire from 1940-1971; worked as N.L. umpire supervisor after retirement.
How elected: Committee on Veterans.

JOHNNY BENCH C
6-1, 208. **B:** R. **T:** R.
Born: Dec. 7, 1947.
Career: .267 avg.; 389 HR; 1,376 RBIs.
Team: Reds 1967-83.
How elected: 96.4 percent of vote.

RED SCHOENDIENST 2B
6-0, 170. **B:** B. **T:** R.
Born: Feb. 2, 1923.
Career: .289 avg.; 84 HR; 773 RBIs.
Teams: Cardinals 1945-56, 1961-63; Giants 1956-57; Braves 1957-60.
How elected: Committee on Veterans.

CARL YASTRZEMSKI OF
5-11, 182. **B:** L. **T:** R.
Born: Aug. 22, 1939.
Career: .285 avg.; 452 HR; 1,844 RBIs; 3,419 hits.
Team: Red Sox 1961-83.
How elected: 94.6 percent of vote.

1990

JOE MORGAN 2B
5-7, 160. **B:** L. **T:** R.
Born: Sept. 19, 1943.
Career: .271 avg.; 268 HR; 1,133 RBIs.
Teams: Astros 1963-71, 1980; Reds 1972-79; Giants 1981-82; Phillies 1983; Athletics 1984.
How elected: 81.8 percent of vote.

JIM PALMER P
6-3, 196. **B:** R. **T:** R.
Born: Oct. 15, 1945.
Career: 268-152; 2.86 ERA; 2,212 SO.
Team: Orioles 1965-67; 1969-84.
How elected: 92.6 percent of vote.

1991

ROD CAREW 2B, 1B
6-0, 182. **B:** L. **T:** R.
Born: Oct. 1, 1945.
Career: .328 avg.; 92 HR; 1,015 RBIs; 3,053 hits.
Teams: Twins 1967-78; Angels 1979-85.
How elected: 89.7 percent of vote.

FERGUSON JENKINS P
6-5, 210. **B:** R. **T:** R.
Born: Dec. 13, 1943.
Career: 284-226; 3.34 ERA; 3,192 SO.
Teams: Phillies 1965-66; Cubs 1966-73, 1982-83; Rangers 1974-75, 1978-81; Red Sox 1976-77.
How elected: 74.7 percent of vote.

TONY LAZZERI 2B
6-0, 170. **B:** R. **T:** R.
Born: Dec. 6, 1903. **Died:** Aug. 6, 1946.
Career: .292 avg.; 178 HR; 1,191 RBIs.
Teams: Yankees 1926-37; Cubs 1938; Dodgers 1939; Giants 1939.
How elected: Committee on Veterans.

GAYLORD PERRY P
6-4, 215. **B:** R. **T:** R.
Born: Sept. 15, 1938.
Career: 314-265; 3.11 ERA; 3,534 SO.
Teams: Giants 1962-71; Indians 1972-75; Rangers 1975-77, 1980; Padres 1978-79; Yankees 1980; Braves 1981; Mariners 1982-83; Royals 1983.
How elected: 76.5 percent of vote.

BILL VEECK EXECUTIVE
Born: Feb. 9, 1914. **Died:** Jan. 2, 1986.
Career: A three-time major league owner best known for his showmanship and promotional stunts; owned Indians, Browns and White Sox franchises; broke A.L. color barrier in 1947 by signing Larry Doby to an Indians contract; remembered as the man who sent a midget to the plate for the Browns in a 1951 promotional stunt.
How elected: Committee on Veterans.

1992

Rollie Fingers **P**
6-4, 195. **B:** R. **T:** R.
Born: Aug. 25, 1946.
Career: 114-118; 2.90 ERA; 1,299 SO; 341 saves.
Teams: Athletics 1968-76; Padres 1977-80; Brewers 1981-82, 1984-85.
How elected: 81.2 percent of vote.

Bill McGowan **Umpire**
Born: Jan. 18, 1896. **Died:** Dec. 9, 1954.
Career: Served as an A.L. umpire from 1925-53; worked 8 World Series and 4 All-Star Games; worked 2,541 consecutive games over a 16½-year period.
How elected: Committee on Veterans.

Hal Newhouser **P**
6-2, 192. **B:** L. **T:** L.
Born: May 20, 1921. **Died:** November 10, 1998.
Career: 207-150; 3.06 ERA; 1,796 SO.
Teams: Tigers 1939-53; Indians 1954-55.
How elected: Committee on Veterans.

Tom Seaver **P**
6-1, 206. **B:** R. **T:** R.
Born: Nov. 17, 1944.
Career: 311-205; 2.86 ERA; 3,640 SO.
Teams: Mets 1967-77, 1983; Reds 1977-82; White Sox 1984-86; Red Sox 1986.
How elected: 98.8 percent of vote.

1993

Reggie Jackson **OF**
6-0, 200. **B:** L. **T:** L.
Born: May 18, 1946.
Career: .262 avg.; 563 HR; 1,702 RBIs.
Teams: Athletics 1967-75, 1987; Orioles 1976; Yankees 1977-81; Angels 1982-86.
How elected: 93.6 percent of vote.

1994

Steve Carlton **P**
6-4, 210. **B:** L. **T:** L.
Born: Dec. 22, 1944.
Career: 329-244; 3.22 ERA; 4,136 SO.
Teams: Cardinals 1965-71; Phillies 1972-86; Giants 1986; White Sox 1986; Indians 1987; Twins 1987-88.
How elected: 95.8 percent of vote.

Leo Durocher **SS, Man.**
5-10, 160. **B:** R. **T:** R.
Born: July 27, 1905. **Died:** Oct. 7, 1991.
Playing career: .247 avg.; 24 HR; 567 RBIs.
Managing career: 2,008-1,709, 24 years; 1 World Series championship.
Teams (player): Yankees 1925, 1928-29; Reds 1930-33; Cardinals 1933-37; Dodgers 1938-41, 1943, 1945.
Teams (manager): Dodgers 1939-46, 1948; Giants 1948-55; Cubs 1966-72; Astros 1972-73.
How elected: Committee on Veterans.

Phil Rizzuto **SS**
5-6, 160. **B:** R. **T:** R.
Born: Sept. 25, 1917.
Career: .273 avg.; 38 HR; 563 RBIs.
Team: Yankees 1941-42, 1946-56.
How elected: Committee on Veterans.

1995

Richie Ashburn **OF**
5-10, 170 **B:** L. **T:** R.
Born: March 19, 1927. **Died:** September 9, 1997.
Career: .308 avg.; 29 HR; 586 RBIs.
Teams: Phillies 1948-59; Cubs 1960-61; Mets 1962.
How elected: Committee on Veterans.

More than a decade of Tom Seaver's outstanding career was spent in New York.

Leon Day **P**
5-10, 180. **B:** R. **T:** R.
Born: Oct. 30, 1916. **Died:** March 13, 1995.
Career: Negro League star; statistics not available.
How elected: Committee on Veterans.

William Hulbert **Executive**
Born: Oct. 23, 1832. **Died:** April 10, 1882.
Career: A former National Association executive and founder of the National League in 1876; served as second president of the new circuit when Morgan Bulkeley left the job after 10 months; he also is credited with hiring baseball's first umpiring staff.
How elected: Committee on Veterans.

Mike Schmidt **3B**
6-2, 203. **B:** R. **T:** R.
Born: Sept. 27, 1949.
Career: .267 avg.; 548 HR; 1,595 RBIs.
Team: Phillies 1972-89.
How elected: 96.5 percent of vote.

Vic Willis **P**
6-2, 185. **B:** R. **T:** R.
Born: April 12, 1876. **Died:** Aug. 3, 1947.
Career: 249-205; 2.63 ERA; 1,651 SO.
Teams: Braves 1898-1905; Pirates 1906-09; Cardinals 1910.
How elected: Committee on Veterans.

1996

Jim Bunning **P**
6-3, 195. **B:** R. **T:** R.
Born: Oct. 23, 1931.
Career: 224-184; 3.27 ERA; 2,855 SO.
Teams: Tigers 1955-63; Phillies 1964-67, 1970-71; Pirates 1968-69; Dodgers 1969.
How elected: Committee on Veterans.

Bill Foster **P**
6-1, 196. **B:** B. **T:** L.
Born: June 12, 1904. **Died:** Sept. 16, 1978.
Career: Negro League star; statistics not available.
How elected: Committee on Veterans.

Ned Hanlon **OF, Man.**
5-10, 170. **B:** L. **T:** R.
Born: Aug. 22, 1857. **Died:** April 14, 1937.
Playing career: .260 avg.; 30 HR; 517 RBIs.
Managing career: 1,313-1,164, 19 years; 5 championships.
Teams (player): Cleveland 1880; Detroit 1881-88; Pittsburgh (N.L.) 1889, 1891; Pittsburgh (P.L.) 1890; Baltimore (N.L.) 1892.
Teams (manager): Pittsburgh (N.L.) 1889, 1891; Pittsburgh (P.L.) 1890; Baltimore (N.L.) 1892-98; Dodgers 1899-1905; Reds 1906-07.
How elected: Committee on Veterans.

Earl Weaver **Manager**
Born: Aug. 14, 1930.
Career: 1,480-1,060, 17 years; 1 World Series championship.
Team: Orioles 1968-82, 1985-86.
How elected: Committee on Veterans.

1997

Nellie Fox **2B**
5-9,150. **B:** L. **T:** R
Born: Dec. 25, 1927. **Died:** Dec. 1, 1975.
Career: .288 avg.; 35 HR; 790 RBIs.
Teams: Athletics 1947-49; White Sox 1950-63; Astros 1964-65.
How elected: Committee on Veterans.

Larry Doby, baseball's second black player, began his career in 1947 under Hall of Fame Cleveland player-manager Lou Boudreau (left).

TOM LASORDA **MANAGER**
Born: September 22, 1927.
Career: 1,599-1,439, 21 years; 2 World Series championships.
Team: Dodgers 1976-96.
How elected: Committee on Veterans.

PHIL NIEKRO **P**
6-1,180. **B:** R. **T:** R
Born: April 1, 1939.
Career: 318-274; 3.35 ERA; 3,342 strikeouts.
Teams: Braves 1964-83, 1987; Yankees 1984-85; Indians 1986, 1987; Blue Jays 1987.
How elected: 80.3 percent of vote.

WILLIE WELLS **SS, 3B, 2B, P**
5-8, 160. **B:** R. **T:** R.
Born: Aug. 10, 1905. **Died:** Jan. 22, 1989.
Career: Negro League star; statistics not available.
How elected: Committee on Veterans.

1998

GEORGE DAVIS **3B, OF, SS**
5-9, 180. **B:** B. **T:** R.
Born: Aug. 23, 1870. **Died:** Oct. 17, 1940.
Career: .295 avg.; 73 HR; 1,437 RBIs.
Teams: Cleveland N.L. 1890-92; Giants 1893-1901, 1903; White Sox 1902, 1904-09.
How elected: Committee on Veterans.

LARRY DOBY **OF**
6-1, 182. **B:** L. **T:** R.
Born: Dec. 13, 1924.
Career: .283 avg.; 253 HR; 970 RBIs.
Teams: Indians 1947-55, 1958; White Sox 1956-57, 1959; Tigers 1959.
How elected: Committee on Veterans.

LEE MACPHAIL **EXECUTIVE**
Born: Oct. 25, 1917.
Career: A former minor league executive, major league executive and president of the American League (1974-83); as director of player personnel for the New York Yankees, he helped build the farm system that fueled seven World Series titles in 10 years; as general manager of the Baltimore Orioles, he helped build another championship organization; the son of Larry MacPhail, a Hall of Fame executive and innovator who paved the way for his son's career.
How elected: Committee on Veterans.

JOE ROGAN **P, OF, IF**
5-7, 180. **B:** R. **T:** R.
Born: July 28, 1889. **Died:** March 4, 1967.
Career: Negro League star; statistics not available.
How elected: Committee on Veterans.

DON SUTTON **P**
6-1, 185. **B:** R. **T:** R.
Born: April 2, 1945.
Career: 324-256; 3.26 ERA; 3,574 strikeouts.
Teams: Dodgers 1966-80, 1988; Astros 1981-82; Brewers 1982-84; Athletics 1985; Angels 1985-87.
How elected: 81.6 percent of vote.

1999

GEORGE BRETT **3B**
6-0, 200. **B:** L. **T:** R.
Born: May 15, 1953.
Career: .305 avg.; 317 HR; 1,595 RBIs.
Teams: Royals 1973-93.
How elected: 98.2 percent of vote.

ORLANDO CEPEDA **1B, OF**
6-2, 210. **B:** R. **T:** R.
Born: September 17, 1937.
Career: .297 avg.; 379 HR; 1,365 RBIs.
Teams: Giants 1958-66, Cardinals 1966-68, Braves 1969-72, Athletics 1972, Red Sox 1973, Royals 1974.
How elected: Committee on Veterans.

NESTOR CHYLAK **UMPIRE**
Born: May 11, 1922. **Died:** February 17, 1982.
Career: Served as an A.L. umpire from 1954-78; worked 5 World Series and 6 All-Star Games; known as an excellent teacher of umpires.
How elected: Committee on Veterans.

NOLAN RYAN **P**
6-2, 195 **B:** R. **T:** R.
Born: January 31, 1947.
Career: 324-292; 3.19 ERA; 5,714 strikeouts.
Teams: Mets 1966-71, Angels 1972-79, Astros 1980-88; Rangers 1989-93.
How elected: 98.8 percent of vote.

FRANK SELEE **MANAGER**
Born: Oct. 26, 1859. **Died:** July 5, 1909.
Career: 1,284-862, 16 years.
Teams: Braves 1890-1901, Cubs 1902-1905.
How elected: Committee on Veterans.

SMOKEY JOE WILLIAMS **P, OF, 1B, MAN.**
6-4, 200. **B:** R. **T:** R.
Born: April 6, 1885. **Died:** March 12, 1946.
Career: Negro League star; statistics not available.
How elected: Committee on Veterans.

ROBIN YOUNT **SS, OF**
6-0, 170. **B:** R. **T:** R.
Born: September 16, 1955.
Career: .285 avg.; 251 HR; 1,406 RBIs.
Teams: Brewers 1974-93.
How elected: 77.5 percent of vote.

2000

SPARKY ANDERSON **MANAGER**
Born: February 22, 1934.
Career: 2,194-1,834, 26 years; 3 World Series championships.
Team: Reds 1970-78; Tigers 1979-95.
How elected: Committee on Veterans.

CARLTON FISK **C**
6-2, 220. **B:** R. **T:** R.
Born: December 26, 1947.
Career: .269 avg.; 376 HR; 1,330 RBIs.
Teams: Red Sox 1969-80; White Sox 1982-93.
How elected: 79.6 percent of vote.

JOHN (BID) MCPHEE **2B**
5-8, 152. **B:** R. **T:** R.
Born: Nov. 1, 1859. **Died:** Jan. 3, 1943.
Career: .271 avg.; 53 HR; 1,067 RBIs.
Teams: Cincinnati (A.A.) 1882-89; Cincinnati (Nat.) 1890-99.
How elected: Committee on Veterans.

TONY PEREZ **1B**
6-2, 190. **B:** R. **T:** R.
Born: May 14, 1942.
Career: .279 avg.; 379 HR; 1,652 RBIs.
Teams: Reds 1964-76, 1984-86; Expos 1977-79; Red Sox 1980-82; Phillies 1983.
How elected: 77.15 percent of vote.

NORMAN (TURKEY) STEARNES **OF, 1B**
6-0, 175. **B:** L. **T:** L.
Born: May 8, 1901. **Died:** Sept. 4, 1979.
Career: Negro League star; statistics not available.
How elected: Committee on Veterans.

2001

KIRBY PUCKETT **OF**
5-8, 210. **B:** R. **T:** R.
Born: March 14, 1961.
Career: .318 avg.; 207 HR; 1,085 RBIs.
Teams: Twins 1984-95.
How elected: 82.1 percent of vote.

DAVE WINFIELD **OF**
6-6, 220. **B:** R. **T:** R.
Born: October 3, 1951.
Career: .283 avg.; 465 HR; 1,833 RBIs.
Teams: Padres 1973-80; Yankees 1981-90; Angels 1990-91; Blue Jays 1992; Twins 1993-94; Indians 1995.
How elected: 84.5 percent of vote.

Award Winners

BASEBALL WRITERS' ASSOCIATION OF AMERICA

1931

Lefty Grove — **A.L. MVP**
Team: Athletics. **Position:** Pitcher.
Season: 31-4; 2.06 ERA; 175 SO.
(See Hall of Fame section, 1947.)

Frank Frisch — **N.L. MVP**
Team: Cardinals. **Position:** Second base.
Season: .311 avg.; 4 HR; 82 RBIs; 28 SB.
(See Hall of Fame section, 1947.)

1932

Jimmie Foxx — **A.L. MVP**
Team: Athletics. **Position:** First base.
Season: .364 avg.; 58 HR; 169 RBIs.
(See Hall of Fame section, 1951.)

Chuck Klein — **N.L. MVP**
Team: Phillies. **Position:** Outfield.
Season: .348 avg.; 38 HR; 137 RBIs.
(See Hall of Fame section, 1980.)

1933

Jimmie Foxx — **A.L. MVP**
Team: Athletics. **Position:** First base.
Season: .356 avg.; 48 HR; 163 RBIs.
(See Hall of Fame section, 1951.)

Carl Hubbell — **N.L. MVP**
Team: Giants. **Position:** Pitcher.
Season: 23-12; 1.66 ERA; 156 SO.
(See Hall of Fame section, 1947.)

1934

Mickey Cochrane — **A.L. MVP**
Team: Tigers. **Position:** Catcher.
Season: .320 avg.; 2 HR; 76 RBIs.
(See Hall of Fame section, 1947.)

Dizzy Dean — **N.L. MVP**
Team: Cardinals. **Position:** Pitcher.
Season: 30-7; 2.66 ERA; 195 SO.
(See Hall of Fame section, 1953.)

1935

Hank Greenberg — **A.L. MVP**
Team: Tigers. **Position:** First base.
Season: .328 avg.; 36 HR; 170 RBIs.
(See Hall of Fame section, 1956.)

Gabby Hartnett — **N.L. MVP**
Team: Cubs. **Position:** Catcher.
Season: .344 avg.; 13 HR; 91 RBIs.
(See Hall of Fame section, 1955.)

1936

Lou Gehrig — **A.L. MVP**
Team: Yankees. **Position:** First base.
Season: .354 avg.; 49 HR; 152 RBIs.
(See Hall of Fame section, 1939.)

Carl Hubbell — **N.L. MVP**
Team: Giants. **Position:** Pitcher.
Season: 26-6; 2.31 ERA; 123 SO.
(See Hall of Fame section, 1947.)

Hank Greenberg (left) and Charley Gehringer were Tigers teammates for 10 seasons.

1937

Charley Gehringer — **A.L. MVP**
Team: Tigers. **Position:** Second base.
Season: .371 avg.; 14 HR; 96 RBIs.
(See Hall of Fame section, 1949.)

Joe Medwick — **N.L. MVP**
Team: Cardinals. **Position:** Outfield.
Season: .374 avg.; 31 HR; 154 RBIs; Triple Crown winner.
(See Hall of Fame section, 1968.)

1938

Jimmie Foxx — **A.L. MVP**
Team: Red Sox. **Position:** First base.
Season: .349 avg.; 50 HR; 175 RBIs.
(See Hall of Fame section, 1951.)

Ernie Lombardi — **N.L. MVP**
Team: Reds. **Position:** Catcher.
Season: .342 avg.; 19 HR; 95 RBIs.
(See Hall of Fame section, 1986.)

1939

Joe DiMaggio — **A.L. MVP**
Team: Yankees. **Position:** Outfield.
Season: .381 avg.; 30 HR; 126 RBIs.
(See Hall of Fame section, 1955.)

Bucky Walters — **N.L. MVP**
Team: Reds. **Position:** Pitcher.
6-1, 180. **B:** R. **T:** R.
Born: April 19, 1909.
Season: 27-11; 2.29 ERA; 137 SO.
Career: 198-160; 3.30 ERA; 1,107 SO.
Teams: Phillies 1934-38; Reds 1938-48; Braves 1950.

1940

Hank Greenberg — **A.L. MVP**
Team: Tigers. **Position:** Outfield.
Season: .340 avg.; 41 HR; 150 RBIs.
(See Hall of Fame section, 1956.)

Frank McCormick — **N.L. MVP**
Team: Reds. **Position:** First base.
6-4, 205. **B:** R. **T.** R.
Born: June 9, 1911. **Died:** Nov. 21, 1982.
Season: .309 avg.; 19 HR; 127 RBIs.
Career: .299 avg.; 128 HR; 951 RBIs.
Teams: Reds 1934, 1937-45; Phillies 1946-47; Braves 1947-48.

1941

Joe DiMaggio — **A.L. MVP**
Team: Yankees. **Position:** Outfield.
Season: .357 avg.; 30 HR; 125 RBIs.
(See Hall of Fame section, 1955.)

Dolph Camilli — **N.L. MVP**
Team: Dodgers. **Position:** First base.
5-10, 185. **B:** L. **T:** L.
Born: April 23, 1907.
Season: .285 avg.; 34 HR; 120 RBIs.
Career: .277 avg.; 239 HR; 950 RBIs.
Teams: Cubs 1933-34; Phillies 1934-37; Dodgers 1938-43; Red Sox 1945.

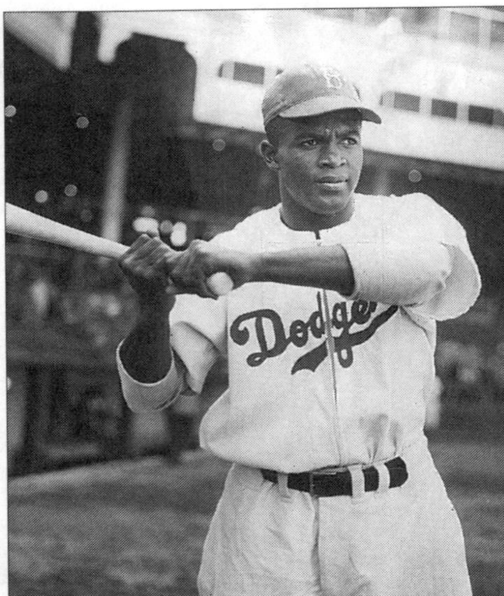

Jackie Robinson was the first Rookie of the Year after his barrier-breaking 1947 season.

1942

JOE GORDON — **A.L. MVP**
Team: Yankees. **Position:** Second base.
5-10, 180. **B:** R. **T:** R.
Born: Feb. 18, 1915. **Died:** April 14, 1978.
Season: .322 avg.; 18 HR; 103 RBIs.
Career: .268 avg.; 253 HR; 975 RBIs.
Teams: Yankees 1938-43, 1946; Indians 1947-50.

MORT COOPER — **N.L. MVP**
Team: Cardinals. **Position:** Pitcher.
6-2, 210. **B:** R. **T:** R.
Born: March 2, 1913. **Died:** Nov. 17, 1958.
Season: 22-7; 1.78 ERA; 152 SO.
Career: 128-75; 2.97 ERA; 913 SO.
Teams: Cardinals 1938-45; Braves 1945-47; Giants 1947; Cubs 1949.

1943

SPUD CHANDLER — **A.L. MVP**
Team: Yankees. **Position:** Pitcher.
6-0, 181. **B:** R. **T:** R.
Born: Sept. 12, 1907. **Died:** Jan. 9, 1990.
Season: 20-4; 1.64 ERA; 134 SO.
Career: 109-43; 2.84 ERA; 614 SO.
Team: Yankees 1937-47.

STAN MUSIAL — **N.L. MVP**
Team: Cardinals. **Position:** Outfield.
Season: .357 avg.; 13 HR; 81 RBIs.
(See Hall of Fame section, 1969.)

1944

HAL NEWHOUSER — **A.L. MVP**
Team: Tigers. **Position:** Pitcher.
Season: 29-9; 2.22 ERA; 187 SO.
(See Hall of Fame section, 1992.)

MARTY MARION — **N.L. MVP**
Team: Cardinals. **Position:** Shortstop.
6-2, 170. **B:** R. **T:** R.
Born: Dec. 1, 1917.
Season: .267 avg.; 6 HR; 63 RBIs.
Career: .263 avg.; 36 HR; 624 RBIs.
Team: Cardinals 1940-50, 1952-53.

1945

HAL NEWHOUSER — **A.L. MVP**
Team: Tigers. **Position:** Pitcher.
Season: 25-9; 1.81 ERA; 212 SO.
(See Hall of Fame section, 1992.)

PHIL CAVARRETTA — **N.L. MVP**
Team: Cubs. **Position:** First base.
5-11, 175. **B:** L. **T:** L.
Born: July 19, 1916.
Season: .355 avg.; 6 HR; 97 RBIs.
Career: .293 avg.; 95 HR; 920 RBIs.
Team: Cubs 1934-55.

1946

TED WILLIAMS — **A.L. MVP**
Team: Red Sox. **Position:** Outfield.
Season: .342 avg.; 38 HR; 123 RBIs.
(See Hall of Fame section, 1966.)

STAN MUSIAL — **N.L. MVP**
Team: Cardinals. **Position:** First base.
Season: .365 avg.; 16 HR; 103 RBIs.
(See Hall of Fame section, 1969.)

1947

JOE DIMAGGIO — **A.L. MVP**
Team: Yankees. **Position:** Outfield.
Season: .315 avg.; 20 HR; 97 RBIs.
(See Hall of Fame section, 1955.)

BOB ELLIOTT — **N.L. MVP**
Team: Braves. **Position:** Third base.
6-0, 185. **B:** R. **T:** R.
Born: Nov. 26, 1916. **Died:** May 4, 1966.
Season: .317 avg.; 22 HR; 113 RBIs.
Career: .289 avg.; 170 HR; 1,195 RBIs.
Teams: Pirates 1939-46; Braves 1947-51; Giants 1952; Browns 1953; White Sox 1953.

JACKIE ROBINSON — **ROOKIE**
Team: Dodgers. **Position:** First base.
Season: .297 avg.; 12 HR; 48 RBIs; 29 SB.
(See Hall of Fame section, 1962.)

1948

LOU BOUDREAU — **A.L. MVP**
Team: Indians. **Position:** Shortstop.
Season: .355 avg.; 18 HR; 106 RBIs.
(See Hall of Fame section, 1970.)

STAN MUSIAL — **N.L. MVP**
Team: Cardinals. **Position:** Outfield.
Season: .376 avg.; 39 HR; 131 RBIs.
(See Hall of Fame section, 1969.)

ALVIN DARK — **ROOKIE**
Team: Braves. **Position:** Shortstop.
5-11, 185. **B:** R. **T:** R.
Born: Jan. 7, 1922.
Season: .322 avg.; 3 HR; 48 RBIs.
Career: .289 avg.; 126 HR; 757 RBIs.
Teams: Braves 1946, 1948-49, 1960; Giants 1950-56; Cardinals 1956-58; Cubs 1958-59; Phillies 1960.

1949

TED WILLIAMS — **A.L. MVP**
Team: Red Sox. **Position:** Outfield.
Season: .343 avg.; 43 HR; 159 RBIs.
(See Hall of Fame section, 1966.)

JACKIE ROBINSON — **N.L. MVP**
Team: Dodgers. **Position:** Second base.
Season: .342 avg.; 16 HR; 124 RBIs; 37 SB.
(See Hall of Fame section, 1962.)

ROY SIEVERS — **A.L. ROOKIE**
Team: Browns. **Position:** Outfield.
6-1, 195. **B:** R. **T:** R.
Born: Nov. 18, 1926.
Season: .306 avg.; 16 HR; 91 RBIs.
Career: .267 avg.; 318 HR; 1,147 RBIs.
Teams: Browns 1949-53; Senators 1954-59, 1964-65; White Sox 1960-61; Phillies 1962-64.

DON NEWCOMBE — **N.L. ROOKIE**
Team: Dodgers. **Position:** Pitcher.
6-4, 225. **B:** L. **T:** R.
Born: June 14, 1926.
Season: 17-8; 3.17 ERA; 149 SO.
Career: 149-90; 3.56 ERA; 1,129 SO.
Teams: Dodgers 1949-51, 1954-58; Reds 1958-60; Indians 1960.

1950

PHIL RIZZUTO — **A.L. MVP**
Team: Yankees. **Position:** Shortstop.
Season: .324 avg.; 7 HR; 66 RBIs.
(See Hall of Fame section, 1994.)

JIM KONSTANTY — **N.L. MVP**
Team: Phillies. **Position:** Pitcher.
6-2, 202. **B:** R. **T:** R.
Born: March 2, 1917. **Died:** June 11, 1976.
Season: 16-7; 2.66 ERA; 56 SO.
Career: 66-48; 3.46 ERA; 268 SO.
Teams: Reds 1944; Braves 1946; Phillies 1948-54; Yankees 1954-56; Cardinals 1956.

WALT DROPO — **A.L. ROOKIE**
Team: Red Sox. **Position:** First base.
6-5, 220. **B:** R. **T:** R.
Born: Jan. 30, 1923.
Season: .322 avg.; 34 HR; 144 RBIs.
Career: .270 avg.; 152 HR; 704 RBIs.
Teams: Red Sox 1949-52; Tigers 1952-54; White Sox 1955-58; Reds 1958-59; Orioles 1959-61.

SAM JETHROE — **N.L. ROOKIE**
Team: Braves. **Position:** Outfield.
6-1, 178. **B:** B. **T:** R.
Born: Jan. 20, 1922.
Season: .273 avg.; 18 HR; 58 RBIs.
Career: .261 avg.; 49 HR; 181 RBIs.
Teams: Braves 1950-52; Pirates 1954.

1951

YOGI BERRA — **A.L. MVP**
Team: Yankees. **Position:** Catcher.
Season: .294 avg.; 27 HR; 88 RBIs.
(See Hall of Fame section, 1972.)

ROY CAMPANELLA — **N.L. MVP**
Team: Dodgers. **Position:** Catcher.
Season: .325 avg.; 33 HR; 108 RBIs.
(See Hall of Fame section, 1969.)

GIL MCDOUGALD — **A.L. ROOKIE**
Team: Yankees. **Position:** Third base.
6-1, 180. **B:** R. **T:** R.
Born: May 19, 1928.
Season: .306 avg.; 14 HR; 63 RBIs.
Career: .276 avg.; 112 HR; 576 RBIs.
Team: Yankees 1951-60.

WILLIE MAYS — **N.L. ROOKIE**
Team: Giants. **Position:** Outfield.
Season: .274 avg.; 20 HR; 68 RBIs.
(See Hall of Fame section, 1979.)

1952

BOBBY SHANTZ — **A.L. MVP**
Team: Athletics. **Position:** Pitcher.
5-6, 142. **B:** R. **T:** L.
Born: Sept. 26, 1925.
Season: 24-7; 2.48 ERA; 152 SO.
Career: 119-99; 3.38 ERA; 1,072 SO.
Teams: Athletics 1949-56; Yankees 1957-60; Pirates 1961; Colt .45s 1962; Cardinals 1962-64; Cubs 1964; Phillies 1964.

Hank Sauer — N.L. MVP
Team: Cubs. **Position:** Outfield.
6-4, 199. **B:** R. **T:** R.
Born: March 17, 1919.
Season: .270 avg.; 37 HR; 121 RBIs.
Career: .266 avg.; 288 HR; 876 RBIs.
Teams: Reds 1941-42, 1945, 1948-49; Cubs 1949-55; Cardinals 1956; Giants 1957-59.

Harry Byrd — A.L. Rookie
Team: Athletics. **Position:** Pitcher.
6-1, 188. **B:** R. **T:** R.
Born: Feb. 3, 1925. **Died:** May 14, 1985.
Season: 15-15; 3.31 ERA; 116 SO.
Career: 46-54; 4.35 ERA; 381 SO.
Teams: Athletics 1950, 1952-53; Yankees 1954; Orioles 1955; White Sox 1955-56; Tigers 1957.

Joe Black — N.L. Rookie
Team: Dodgers. **Position:** Pitcher.
6-2, 220. **B:** R. **T:** R.
Born: Feb. 8, 1924.
Season: 15-4; 2.15 ERA; 85 SO.
Career: 30-12; 3.91 ERA; 222 SO.
Teams: Dodgers 1952-55; Reds 1955-56; Senators 1957.

1953

Al Rosen — A.L. MVP
Team: Indians. **Position:** Third base.
5-11, 180. **B:** R. **T:** R.
Born: Feb. 29, 1924.
Season: .336 avg.; 43 HR; 145 RBIs.
Career: .285 avg.; 192 HR; 717 RBIs.
Team: Indians 1947-56.

Roy Campanella — N.L. MVP
Team: Dodgers. **Position:** Catcher.
Season: .312 avg.; 41 HR; 142 RBIs.
(See Hall of Fame section, 1969.)

Harvey Kuenn — A.L. Rookie
Team: Tigers. **Position:** Shortstop.
6-2, 190. **B:** R. **T:** R.
Born: Dec. 4, 1930. **Died:** Feb. 28, 1988.
Season: .308 avg.; 2 HR; 48 RBIs.
Career: .303 avg.; 87 HR; 671 RBIs.
Teams: Tigers 1952-59; Indians 1960; Giants 1961-65; Cubs 1965-66; Phillies 1966.

Jim Gilliam — N.L. Rookie
Team: Dodgers. **Position:** Second base.
5-11, 175. **B:** B. **T:** R.
Born: Oct. 17, 1928. **Died:** Oct. 8, 1978.
Season: .278 avg.; 6 HR; 63 RBIs; 21 SB.
Career: .265 avg.; 65 HR; 558 RBIs; 203 SB.
Team: Dodgers 1953-66.

1954

Yogi Berra — A.L. MVP
Team: Yankees. **Position:** Catcher.
Season: .307 avg.; 22 HR; 125 RBIs.
(See Hall of Fame section, 1972.)

Willie Mays — N.L. MVP
Team: Giants. **Position:** Outfield.
Season: .345 avg.; 41 HR; 110 RBIs.
(See Hall of Fame section, 1979.)

Bob Grim — A.L. Rookie
Team: Yankees. **Position:** Pitcher.
6-1, 185. **B:** R. **T:** R.
Born: March 8, 1930.
Season: 20-6; 3.26 ERA; 108 SO.
Career: 61-41; 3.61 ERA; 443 SO.
Teams: Yankees 1954-58; Athletics 1958-59, 1962; Indians 1960; Reds 1960; Cardinals 1960.

Wally Moon — N.L. Rookie
Team: Cardinals. **Position:** Outfield.
6-0, 175. **B:** L. **T:** R.
Born: April 3, 1930.
Season: .304 avg.; 12 HR; 76 RBIs.
Career: .289 avg.; 142 HR; 661 RBIs.
Teams: Cardinals 1954-58; Dodgers 1959-65.

1955

Yogi Berra — A.L. MVP
Team: Yankees. **Position:** Catcher.
Season: .272 avg.; 27 HR; 108 RBIs.
(See Hall of Fame section, 1972.)

Roy Campanella — N.L. MVP
Team: Dodgers. **Position:** Catcher.
Season: .318 avg.; 32 HR; 107 RBIs.
(See Hall of Fame section, 1969.)

Herb Score — A.L. Rookie
Team: Indians. **Position:** Pitcher.
6-2, 185. **B:** L. **T:** L.
Born: June 7, 1933.
Season: 16-10; 2.85 ERA; 245 SO.
Career: 55-46; 3.36 ERA; 837 SO.
Teams: Indians 1955-59; White Sox 1960-62.

Bill Virdon — N.L. Rookie
Team: Cardinals. **Position:** Outfield.
6-0, 175. **B:** L. **T:** R.
Born: June 9, 1931.
Season: .281 avg.; 17 HR; 68 RBIs.
Career: .267 avg.; 91 HR; 502 RBIs.
Teams: Cardinals 1955-56; Pirates 1956-65, 1968.

1956

Mickey Mantle — A.L. MVP
Team: Yankees. **Position:** Outfield.
Season: .353 avg.; 52 HR; 130 RBIs; Triple Crown winner.
(See Hall of Fame section, 1974.)

Don Newcombe — N.L. MVP, Cy Young
Team: Dodgers. **Position:** Pitcher.
Season: 27-7; 3.06 ERA; 139 SO.
(See 1949 N.L. Rookie of Year.)

Luis Aparicio — A.L. Rookie
Team: White Sox. **Position:** Shortstop.
Season: .266 avg.; 3 HR; 56 RBIs; 21 SB.
(See Hall of Fame section, 1984.)

Frank Robinson — N.L. Rookie
Team: Reds. **Position:** Outfield.
Season: .290 avg.; 38 HR; 83 RBIs.
(See Hall of Fame section, 1982.)

1957

Mickey Mantle — A.L. MVP
Team: Yankees. **Position:** Outfield.
Season: .365 avg.; 34 HR; 94 RBIs.
(See Hall of Fame section, 1974.)

Hank Aaron — N.L. MVP
Team: Braves. **Position:** Outfield.
Season: .322 avg.; 44 HR; 132 RBIs.
(See Hall of Fame section, 1982.)

Warren Spahn — Cy Young
Team: Braves.
Season: 21-11; 2.69 ERA; 111 SO.
(See Hall of Fame section, 1973.)

Tony Kubek — A.L. Rookie
Team: Yankees. **Position:** Infield, outfield.
6-3, 190. **B:** L. **T:** R.
Born: Oct. 12, 1936.

Giants star Willie Mays was named N.L. MVP after his second full Major League season.

Season: .297 avg.; 3 HR; 39 RBIs.
Career: .266 avg.; 57 HR; 373 RBIs.
Team: Yankees 1957-65.

Jack Sanford — N.L. Rookie
Team: Phillies. **Position:** Pitcher.
6-0, 190. **B:** R. **T:** R.
Born: May 18, 1929.
Season: 19-8; 3.08 ERA; 188 SO.
Career: 137-101; 3.69 ERA; 1,182 SO.
Teams: Phillies 1956-58; Giants 1959-65; Angels 1965-67; Athletics 1967.

1958

Jackie Jensen — A.L. MVP
Team: Red Sox. **Position:** Outfield.
5-11, 190. **B:** R. **T:** R.
Born: March 9, 1927. **Died:** July 14, 1982.
Season: .286 avg.; 35 HR; 122 RBIs.
Career: .279 avg.; 199 HR; 929 RBIs.
Teams: Yankees 1950-52; Senators 1952-53; Red Sox 1954-59, 1961.

Ernie Banks — N.L. MVP
Team: Cubs. **Position:** Shortstop.
Season: .313 avg.; 47 HR; 129 RBIs.
(See Hall of Fame section, 1977.)

Bob Turley — Cy Young
Team: Yankees.
6-2, 215. **B:** R. **T:** R.
Born: Sept. 19, 1930.
Season: 21-7; 2.97 ERA; 168 SO.
Career: 101-85; 3.64 ERA; 1,265 SO.
Teams: Browns 1951, 1953; Orioles 1954; Yankees 1955-62; Angels 1963; Red Sox 1963.

Albie Pearson — A.L. Rookie
Team: Senators. **Position:** Outfield.
5-5, 140. **B:** L. **T:** L.
Born: Sept. 12, 1934.
Season: .275 avg.; 3 HR; 33 RBIs.
Career: .270 avg.; 28 HR; 214 RBIs.
Teams: Senators 1958-59; Orioles 1959-60; Angels 1961-66.

Orlando Cepeda — N.L. Rookie
Team: Giants. **Position:** First base.
Season: .312 avg.; 25 HR; 96 RBIs.
(See Hall of Fame section, 1999.)

Dodgers ace Sandy Koufax swept N.L. Cy Young and MVP honors in 1963.

1959

NELLIE FOX — A.L. MVP
Team: White Sox. **Position:** Second base.
Season: .306 avg.; 2 HR; 70 RBIs.
(See Hall of Fame section, 1999.)

ERNIE BANKS — N.L. MVP
Team: Cubs. **Position:** Shortstop.
Season: .304 avg.; 45 HR; 143 RBIs.
(See Hall of Fame section, 1977.)

EARLY WYNN — CY YOUNG
Team: White Sox.
Season: 22-10; 3.17 ERA; 179 SO.
(See Hall of Fame section, 1972.)

BOB ALLISON — A.L. ROOKIE
Team: Senators. **Position:** Outfield.
6-4, 215. **B:** R. **T:** R.
Born: July 11, 1934.
Season: .261 avg.; 30 HR; 85 RBIs.
Career: .255 avg.; 256 HR; 796 RBIs.
Teams: Senators 1958-60; Twins 1961-70.

WILLIE McCOVEY — N.L. ROOKIE
Team: Giants. **Position:** First base.
Season: .354 avg.; 13 HR; 38 RBIs.
(See Hall of Fame section, 1986.)

1960

ROGER MARIS — A.L. MVP
Team: Yankees. **Position:** Outfield.
6-0, 203. **B:** L. **T:** R.
Born: Sept. 10, 1934. **Died:** Dec. 14, 1985.
Season: .283 avg.; 39 HR; 112 RBIs.
Career: .260 avg.; 275 HR; 851 RBIs.
Teams: Indians 1957-58; Athletics 1958-59; Yankees 1960-66; Cardinals 1967-68.

DICK GROAT — N.L. MVP
Team: Pirates. **Position:** Shortstop.
6-0, 180. **B:** R. **T:** R.
Born: Nov. 4, 1930.
Season: .325 avg.; 2 HR; 50 RBIs.
Career: .286 avg.; 39 HR; 707 RBIs.
Teams: Pirates 1952, 1955-62; Cardinals 1963-65; Phillies 1966-67; Giants 1967.

VERNON LAW — CY YOUNG
Team: Pirates.
6-2, 195. **B:** R. **T:** R.
Born: March 12, 1930.
Season: 20-9; 3.08 ERA; 120 SO.
Career: 162-147; 3.77 ERA; 1,092 SO.
Team: Pirates 1950-51, 1954-67.

RON HANSEN — A.L. ROOKIE
Team: Orioles. **Position:** Shortstop.
6-3, 200. **B:** R. **T:** R.
Born: April 5, 1938.
Season: .255 avg.; 22 HR; 86 RBIs.
Career: .234 avg.; 106 HR; 501 RBIs.
Teams: Orioles 1958-62; White Sox 1963-67, 1968-69; Senators 1968; Yankees 1970-71; Royals 1972.

FRANK HOWARD — N.L. ROOKIE
Team: Dodgers. **Position:** Outfield.
6-7, 255. **B:** R. **T:** R.
Born: Aug. 8, 1936.
Season: .268 avg.; 23 HR; 77 RBIs.
Career: .273 avg.; 382 HR; 1,119 RBIs.
Teams: Dodgers 1958-64; Senators 1965-71; Rangers 1972; Tigers 1972-73.

1961

ROGER MARIS — A.L. MVP
Team: Yankees. **Position:** Outfield.
Season: .269 avg.; 61 HR; 142 RBIs.
(See 1960 A.L. MVP.)

FRANK ROBINSON — N.L. MVP
Team: Reds. **Position:** Outfield.
Season: .323 avg.; 37 HR; 124 RBIs.
(See Hall of Fame section, 1982.)

WHITEY FORD — CY YOUNG
Team: Yankees.
Season: 25-4; 3.21 ERA; 209 SO.
(See Hall of Fame section, 1974.)

DON SCHWALL — A.L. ROOKIE
Team: Red Sox. **Position:** Pitcher.
6-6, 200. **B:** R. **T:** R.
Born: March 2, 1936.
Season: 15-7; 3.22 ERA; 91 SO.
Career: 49-48; 3.72 ERA; 408 SO.
Teams: Red Sox 1961-62; Pirates 1963-66; Braves 1966-67.

BILLY WILLIAMS — N.L. ROOKIE
Team: Cubs. **Position:** Outfield.
Season: .278 avg.; 25 HR; 86 RBIs.
(See Hall of Fame section, 1987.)

1962

MICKEY MANTLE — A.L. MVP
Team: Yankees. **Position:** Outfield.
Season: .321 avg.; 30 HR; 89 RBIs.
(See Hall of Fame section, 1974.)

MAURY WILLS — N.L. MVP
Team: Dodgers. **Position:** Shortstop.
5-11, 170. **B:** B. **T:** R.
Born: Oct. 2, 1932.
Season: .299 avg.; 6 HR; 48 RBIs; 104 SB.
Career: .281 avg.; 20 HR; 458 RBIs; 586 SB.
Teams: Dodgers 1959-66, 1969-72; Pirates 1967-68; Expos 1969.

DON DRYSDALE — CY YOUNG
Team: Dodgers.
Season: 25-9; 2.83 ERA; 232 SO.
(See Hall of Fame section, 1984.)

TOM TRESH — A.L. ROOKIE
Team: Yankees. **Position:** Shortstop, Outfield.
6-1, 190. **B:** B. **T:** R.
Born: Sept. 20, 1937.
Season: .286 avg.; 20 HR; 93 RBIs.
Career: .245 avg.; 153 HR; 530 RBIs.
Teams: Yankees 1961-69; Tigers 1969.

KEN HUBBS — N.L. ROOKIE
Team: Cubs. **Position:** Second base.
6-2, 175. **B:** R. **T:** R.
Born: Dec. 23, 1941. **Died:** Feb. 13, 1964.
Season: .260 avg.; 5 HR; 49 RBIs.
Career: .247 avg.; 14 HR; 98 RBIs.
Team: Cubs 1961-63.

1963

ELSTON HOWARD — A.L. MVP
Team: Yankees. **Position:** Catcher.
6-2, 200. **B:** R. **T:** R.
Born: Feb. 23, 1929. **Died:** Dec. 14, 1980.
Season: .287 avg.; 28 HR; 85 RBIs.
Career: .274 avg.; 167 HR; 762 RBIs.
Teams: Yankees 1955-67; Red Sox 1967-68.

SANDY KOUFAX — N.L. MVP, CY YOUNG
Team: Dodgers. **Position:** Pitcher.
Season: 25-5; 1.88 ERA; 306 SO.
(See Hall of Fame section, 1972.)

GARY PETERS — A.L. ROOKIE
Team: White Sox. **Position:** Pitcher.
6-2, 200. **B:** L. **T:** L.
Born: April 21, 1937.
Season: 19-8; 2.33 ERA; 189 SO.
Career: 124-103; 3.25 ERA; 1,420 SO.
Teams: White Sox 1959-69; Red Sox 1970-72.

PETE ROSE — N.L. ROOKIE
Team: Reds. **Position:** Second base.
5-11, 200. **B:** B. **T:** R.
Born: April 14, 1941.
Season: .273 avg.; 6 HR; 41 RBIs.
Career: .303 avg.; 160 HR; 1,314 RBIs; 4,256 hits, 1st on all-time list.
Teams: Reds 1963-78, 1984-86; Phillies 1979-83; Expos 1984.

1964

BROOKS ROBINSON — A.L. MVP
Team: Orioles. **Position:** Third base.
Season: .317 avg.; 28 HR; 118 RBIs.
(See Hall of Fame section, 1983.)

KEN BOYER — N.L. MVP
Team: Cardinals. **Position:** Third base.
6-2, 200. **B:** R. **T:** R.
Born: May 20, 1931. **Died:** Sept. 7, 1982.
Season: .295 avg.; 24 HR; 119 RBIs.
Career: .287 avg.; 282 HR; 1,141 RBIs.
Teams: Cardinals 1955-65; Mets 1966-67; Cubs 1967-68; Dodgers 1968-69.

DEAN CHANCE — CY YOUNG
Team: Angels.
6-3, 200. **B:** R. **T:** R.
Born: June 1, 1941.
Season: 20-9; 1.65 ERA; 207 SO.
Career: 128-115; 2.92 ERA; 1,534 SO.
Teams: Angels 1961-66; Twins 1967-69; Indians 1970; Mets 1970; Tigers 1971.

TONY OLIVA — A.L. ROOKIE
Team: Twins. **Position:** Outfield.
6-2, 190. **B:** L. **T:** R.
Born: July 20, 1940.
Season: .323 avg.; 32 HR; 94 RBIs; 217 hits.
Career: .304 avg.; 220 HR; 947 RBIs.
Team: Twins 1962-76.

DICK ALLEN — N.L. ROOKIE
Team: Phillies. **Position:** Third base.
5-11, 190. **B:** R. **T:** R.
Born: March 8, 1942.
Season: .318 avg.; 29 HR; 91 RBIs.

Career: .292 avg.; 351 HR; 1,119 RBIs.
Teams: Phillies 1963-69, 1975-76; Cardinals 1970; Dodgers 1971; White Sox 1972-74; Athletics 1977.

1965

ZOILO VERSALLES — **A.L. MVP**
Team: Twins. **Position:** Shortstop.
5-10, 150. **B:** R. **T:** R.
Born: Dec. 18, 1939.
Season: .273 avg.; 19 HR; 77 RBIs; 27 SB.
Career: .242 avg.; 95 HR; 471 RBIs.
Teams: Senators 1959-60, 1969; Twins 1961-67; Dodgers 1968; Indians 1969; Braves 1971.

WILLIE MAYS — **N.L. MVP**
Team: Giants. **Position:** Outfield.
Season: .317 avg.; 52 HR; 112 RBIs.
(See Hall of Fame section, 1979.)

SANDY KOUFAX — **CY YOUNG**
Team: Dodgers.
Season: 26-8; 2.04 ERA; 382 SO.
(See Hall of Fame section, 1972.)

CURT BLEFARY — **A.L. ROOKIE**
Team: Orioles. **Position:** Outfield.
6-2, 195. **B:** L. **T:** R.
Born: July 5, 1943.
Season: .260 avg.; 22 HR; 70 RBIs.
Career: .237 avg.; 112 HR; 382 RBIs.
Teams: Orioles 1965-68; Astros 1969; Yankees 1970-71; Athletics 1971-72; Padres 1972.

JIM LEFEBVRE — **N.L. ROOKIE**
Team: Dodgers. **Position:** Second base.
6-0, 185. **B:** B. **T:** R.
Born: Jan. 7, 1942.
Season: .250 avg.; 12 HR; 69 RBIs.
Career: .251 avg.; 74 HR; 404 RBIs.
Team: Dodgers 1965-72.

1966

FRANK ROBINSON — **A.L. MVP**
Team: Orioles. **Position:** Outfield.
Season: .316 avg.; 49 HR; 122 RBIs.
(See Hall of Fame section, 1982.)

ROBERTO CLEMENTE — **N.L. MVP**
Team: Pirates. **Position:** Outfield.
Season: .317 avg.; 29 HR; 119 RBIs.
(See Hall of Fame section, 1973.)

SANDY KOUFAX — **CY YOUNG**
Team: Dodgers.
Season: 27-9; 1.73 ERA; 317 SO.
(See Hall of Fame section, 1972.)

TOMMIE AGEE — **A.L. ROOKIE**
Team: White Sox. **Position:** Outfield.
5-11, 195. **B:** R. **T:** R.
Born: Aug. 9, 1942.
Season: .273 avg.; 22 HR; 86 RBIs.
Career: .255 avg.; 130 HR; 433 RBIs.
Teams: Indians 1962-64; White Sox 1965-67; Mets 1968-72; Astros 1973; Cardinals 1973.

TOMMY HELMS — **N.L. ROOKIE**
Team: Reds. **Position:** Third base.
5-10, 175. **B:** R. **T:** R.
Born: May 5, 1941.
Season: .284 avg.; 9 HR; 49 RBIs.
Career: .269 avg.; 34 HR; 477 RBIs.
Teams: Reds 1964-71; Astros 1972-75; Pirates 1976-77; Red Sox 1977.

1967

CARL YASTRZEMSKI — **A.L. MVP**
Team: Red Sox. **Position:** Outfield.
Season: .326 avg.; 44 HR; 121 RBIs; Triple Crown winner.
(See Hall of Fame section, 1989.)

ORLANDO CEPEDA — **N.L. MVP**
Team: Cardinals. **Position:** First base.
Season: .325 avg.; 25 HR; 111 RBIs.
(See Hall of Fame section, 1999.)

JIM LONBORG — **A.L. CY YOUNG**
Team: Red Sox.
6-5, 210. **B:** R. **T:** R.
Born: April 16, 1942.
Season: 22-9; 3.16 ERA; 246 SO.
Career: 157-137; 3.86 ERA; 1,475 SO.
Teams: Red Sox 1965-71; Brewers 1972; Phillies 1973-79.

MIKE MCCORMICK — **N.L. CY YOUNG**
Team: Giants.
6-2, 195. **B:** L. **T:** L.
Born: Sept. 29, 1938.
Season: 22-10; 2.85 ERA; 150 SO.
Career: 134-128; 3.73 ERA; 1.321 SO.
Teams: Giants 1956-62, 1967-70; Orioles 1963-64; Senators 1965-66; Yankees 1970; Royals 1971.

ROD CAREW — **A.L. ROOKIE**
Team: Twins. **Position:** Second base.
Season: .292 avg.; 8 HR; 51 RBIs.
(See Hall of Fame section, 1991.)

TOM SEAVER — **N.L. ROOKIE**
Team: Mets. **Position:** Pitcher.
Season: 16-13; 2.76 ERA; 170 SO.
(See Hall of Fame section, 1992.)

1968

DENNY MCLAIN — **A.L. MVP, CY YOUNG**
Team: Tigers. **Position:** Pitcher.
6-1, 185. **B:** R. **T:** R.
Born: March 29, 1944.
Season: 31-6; 1.96 ERA; 280 SO.
Career: 131-91; 3.39 ERA; 1,282 SO.
Teams: Tigers 1963-70; Senators 1971; Athletics 1972; Braves 1972.

BOB GIBSON — **N.L. MVP, CY YOUNG**
Team: Cardinals. **Position:** Pitcher.
Season: 22-9; 1.12 ERA; 268 SO.
(See Hall of Fame section, 1981.)

STAN BAHNSEN — **A.L. ROOKIE**
Team: Yankees. **Position:** Pitcher.
6-2, 203. **B:** R. **T:** R.
Born: Dec. 15, 1944.
Season: 17-12; 2.05 ERA; 162 SO.
Career: 146-149; 3.60 ERA; 1,359 SO.
Teams: Yankees 1966, 1968-71; White Sox 1972-75; Athletics 1975-77; Expos 1977-81; Angels 1982; Phillies 1982.

JOHNNY BENCH — **N.L. ROOKIE**
Team: Reds. **Position:** Catcher.
Season: .275 avg.; 15 HR; 82 RBIs.
(See Hall of Fame section, 1989.)

1969

HARMON KILLEBREW — **A.L. MVP**
Team: Twins. **Position:** First base, third base.
Season: .276 avg.; 49 HR; 140 RBIs.
(See Hall of Fame section, 1984.)

WILLIE MCCOVEY — **N.L. MVP**
Team: Giants. **Position:** First base.
Season: .320 avg.; 45 HR; 126 RBIs.
(See Hall of Fame section, 1986.)

DENNY MCLAIN — **A.L. CO-CY YOUNG**
Team: Tigers.
Season: 24-9; 2.80 ERA; 181 SO.
(See 1968 A.L. MVP.)

MIKE CUELLAR — **A.L. CO-CY YOUNG**
Team: Orioles.
5-11, 175. **B:** L. **T:** L.
Born: May 8, 1937.
Season: 23-11; 2.38 ERA; 182 SO.
Career: 185-130; 3.14 ERA; 1,632 SO.
Teams: Reds 1959; Cardinals 1964; Astros 1965-68; Orioles 1969-76; Angels 1977.

TOM SEAVER — **N.L. CY YOUNG**
Team: Mets.
Season: 25-7; 2.21 ERA; 208 SO.
(See Hall of Fame section, 1992.)

LOU PINIELLA — **A.L. ROOKIE**
Team: Royals. **Position:** Outfield.
6-2, 198. **B:** R. **T:** R.
Born: Aug. 28, 1943.
Season: .282 avg.; 11 HR; 68 RBIs.
Career: .291 avg.; 102 HR; 766 RBIs.
Teams: Orioles 1964; Indians 1968; Royals 1969-73; Yankees 1974-84.

TED SIZEMORE — **N.L. ROOKIE**
Team: Dodgers. **Position:** Second base.
5-10, 165. **B:** R. **T:** R.
Born: April 15, 1945.
Season: .271 avg.; 4 HR; 46 RBIs.
Career: .262 avg.; 23 HR; 430 RBIs.
Teams: Dodgers 1969-70, 1976; Cardinals 1971-75; Phillies 1977-78; Cubs 1979; Red Sox 1979-80.

1970

BOOG POWELL — **A.L. MVP**
Team: Orioles. **Position:** First base.
6-4, 240. **B:** L. **T:** R.
Born: Aug. 17, 1941.
Season: .297 avg.; 35 HR; 114 RBIs.
Career: .266 avg.; 339 HR; 1,187 RBIs.
Teams: Orioles 1961-74; Indians 1975-76; Dodgers 1977.

JOHNNY BENCH — **N.L. MVP**
Team: Reds. **Position:** Catcher.
Season: .293 avg.; 45 HR; 148 RBIs.
(See Hall of Fame section, 1989.)

JIM PERRY — **A.L. CY YOUNG**
Team: Twins.
6-4, 200. **B:** B. **T:** R.
Born: Oct. 30, 1936.
Season: 24-12; 3.04 ERA; 168 SO.
Career: 215-174; 3.45 ERA; 1,576.
Teams: Indians 1959-63, 1974-75; Twins 1963-72; Tigers 1973; Athletics 1975.

BOB GIBSON — **N.L. CY YOUNG**
Team: Cardinals.
Season: 23-7; 3.12 ERA; 274 SO.
(See Hall of Fame section, 1981.)

THURMAN MUNSON — **A.L. ROOKIE**
Team: Yankees. **Position:** Catcher.
5-11, 190. **B:** R. **T:** R.
Born: June 7, 1947. **Died:** Aug. 2, 1979.
Season: .302 avg.; 6 HR; 53 RBIs.
Career: .292 avg.; 113 HR; 701 RBIs.
Team: Yankees 1969-79.

CARL MORTON — **N.L. ROOKIE**
Team: Expos. **Position:** Pitcher.
6-0, 200. **B:** R. **T:** R.
Born: Jan. 18, 1944. **Died:** April 12, 1983.
Season: 18-11; 3.60 ERA; 154 SO.
Career: 87-92; 3.73 ERA; 650 SO.
Teams: Expos 1969-72; Braves 1973-76.

Cincinnati catcher Johnny Bench won the first of two N.L. MVP awards in 1970.

1971

Vida Blue — **A.L. MVP, Cy Young**
Team: Athletics. **Position:** Pitcher.
6-0, 189. **B:** B. **T:** L.
Born: July 28, 1949.
Season: 24-8; 1.82 ERA; 301 SO.
Career: 209-161; 3.27 ERA; 2,175 SO.
Teams: Athletics 1969-77; Giants 1978-81, 1985-86; Royals 1982-83.

Joe Torre — **N.L. MVP**
Team: Cardinals. **Position:** Third base.
6-2, 212. **B:** R. **T:** R.
Born: July 18, 1940.
Season: .363 avg.; 24 HR; 137 RBIs.
Career: .297 avg.; 252 HR; 1,185 RBIs.
Teams: Braves 1960-68; Cardinals 1969-74; Mets 1975-77.

Ferguson Jenkins — **N.L. Cy Young**
Team: Cubs.
Season: 24-13; 2.77 ERA; 263 SO.
(See Hall of Fame section, 1991.)

Chris Chambliss — **A.L. Rookie**
Team: Indians. **Position:** First base.
6-1, 215. **B:** L. **T:** R.
Born: Dec. 26, 1948.
Season: .275 avg.; 9 HR; 48 RBIs.
Career: .279 avg.; 185 HR; 972 RBIs.
Teams: Indians 1971-74; Yankees 1974-79, 1988; Braves 1980-86.

Earl Williams — **N.L. Rookie**
Team: Braves. **Position:** Catcher.
6-3, 220. **B:** R. **T:** R.
Born: July 14, 1948.
Season: .260 avg.; 33 HR; 87 RBIs.
Career: .247 avg.; 138 HR; 457 RBIs.
Teams: Braves 1970-72, 1975-76; Orioles 1973-74; Expos 1976; Athletics 1977.

1972

Dick Allen — **A.L. MVP**
Team: White Sox. **Position:** First base.
Season: .308 avg.; 37 HR; 113 RBIs.
(See 1964 N.L. Rookie of Year.)

Johnny Bench — **N.L. MVP**
Team: Reds. **Position:** Catcher.
Season: .270 avg.; 40 HR; 125 RBIs.
(See Hall of Fame section, 1989.)

Gaylord Perry — **A.L. Cy Young**
Team: Indians.
Season: 24-16; 1.92 ERA; 234 SO.
(See Hall of Fame section, 1991.)

Steve Carlton — **N.L. Cy Young**
Team: Phillies.
Season: 27-10; 1.97 ERA; 310 SO.
(See Hall of Fame section, 1994.)

Carlton Fisk — **A.L. Rookie**
Team: Red Sox. **Position:** Catcher.
6-2, 220. **B:** R. **T:** R.
Born: Dec. 26, 1947.
Season: .293 avg.; 22 HR; 61 RBIs.
Career: .269 avg.; 376 HR; 1,330 RBIs.
Teams: Red Sox 1969, 1971-80; White Sox 1981-93.

Jon Matlack — **N.L. Rookie**
Team: Mets. **Position:** Pitcher.
6-3, 205. **B:** L. **T:** L.
Born: Jan. 19, 1950.
Season: 15-10; 2.32 ERA; 169 SO.
Career: 125-126; 3.18 ERA; 1,516 SO.
Teams: Mets 1971-77; Rangers 1978-83.

1973

Reggie Jackson — **A.L. MVP**
Team: Athletics. **Position:** Outfield.
Season: .293 avg.; 32 HR; 117 RBIs.
(See Hall of Fame section, 1993.)

Pete Rose — **N.L. MVP**
Team: Reds. **Position:** Outfield.
Season: .338 avg.; 5 HR; 64 RBIs; 230 hits.
(See 1963 N.L. Rookie of Year.)

Jim Palmer — **A.L. Cy Young**
Team: Orioles.
Season: 22-9; 2.40 ERA; 158 SO.
(See Hall of Fame section, 1990.)

Tom Seaver — **N.L. Cy Young**
Team: Mets.
Season: 19-10; 2.08 ERA; 251 SO.
(See Hall of Fame section, 1992.)

Al Bumbry — **A.L. Rookie**
Team: Orioles. **Position:** Outfield.
5-8, 175. **B:** L. **T:** R.
Born: April 21, 1947.
Season: .337 avg.; 7 HR; 34 RBIs; 23 SB.
Career: .281 avg.; 54 HR; 402 RBIs; 254 SB.
Teams: Orioles 1972-84; Padres 1985.

Gary Matthews — **N.L. Rookie**
Team: Giants. **Position:** Outfield.
6-3, 190. **B:** R. **T:** R.
Born: July 5, 1950.
Season: .300 avg.; 12 HR; 58 RBIs.
Career: .281 avg.; 234 HR; 978 RBIs.
Teams: Giants 1972-76; Braves 1977-80; Phillies 1981-83; Cubs 1984-87; Mariners 1987.

1974

Jeff Burroughs — **A.L. MVP**
Team: Rangers. **Position:** Outfield.
6-1, 200. **B:** R. **T:** R.
Born: March 7, 1951.
Season: .301 avg.; 25 HR; 118 RBIs.
Career: .261 avg.; 240 HR; 882 RBIs.
Teams: Senators 1970-71; Rangers 1972-76; Braves 1977-80; Mariners 1981; Athletics 1982-84; Blue Jays 1985.

Steve Garvey — **N.L. MVP**
Team: Dodgers. **Position:** First base.
5-10, 192. **B:** R. **T:** R.
Born: Dec. 22, 1948.
Season: .312 avg.; 21 HR; 111 RBIs.
Career: .294 avg.; 272 HR; 1,308 RBIs.
Teams: Dodgers 1969-82; Padres 1983-87.

Jim (Catfish) Hunter — **A.L. Cy Young**
Team: Athletics.
Season: 25-12; 2.49 ERA; 143 SO.
(See Hall of Fame section, 1987.)

Mike Marshall — **N.L. Cy Young**
Team: Dodgers.
5-10, 180. **B:** R. **T:** R.
Born: Jan. 15, 1943.
Season: 15-12; 2.42 ERA; 143 SO; 21 saves; 106 games.
Career: 97-112; 3.14 ERA; 880 SO; 188 saves.
Teams: Tigers 1967; Mariners 1969; Astros 1970; Expos 1970-73; Dodgers 1974-76; Braves 1976-77; Rangers 1977; Twins 1978-80; Mets 1981.

Mike Hargrove — **A.L. Rookie**
Team: Rangers. **Position:** First base.
6-0, 195. **B:** L. **T:** L.
Born: Oct. 26, 1949.
Season: .323 avg.; 4 HR; 66 RBIs.
Career: .290 avg.; 80 HR; 686 RBIs.
Teams: Rangers 1974-78; Padres 1979; Indians 1979-85.

Bake McBride — **N.L. Rookie**
Team: Cardinals. **Position:** Outfield.
6-2, 190. **B:** L. **T:** R.
Born: Feb. 3, 1949.
Season: .309 avg.; 6 HR; 56 RBIs.
Career: .299 avg.; 63 HR; 430 RBIs.
Teams: Cardinals 1973-77; Phillies 1977-81; Indians 1982-83.

1975

Fred Lynn — **A.L. MVP, Rookie**
Team: Red Sox. **Position:** Outfield.
6-1, 190. **B:** L. **T:** L.
Born: Feb. 3, 1952.
Season: .331 avg.; 21 HR; 105 RBIs.
Career: .283 avg.; 306 HR; 1,111 RBIs.
Teams: Red Sox 1974-80; Angels 1981-84; Orioles 1985-88; Tigers 1988-89; Padres 1990.

Joe Morgan — **N.L. MVP**
Team: Reds. **Position:** Second base.
Season: .327 avg.; 17 HR; 94 RBIs; 67 SB.
(See Hall of Fame section, 1990.)

Jim Palmer — **A.L. Cy Young**
Team: Orioles.
Season: 23-11; 2.09 ERA; 193 SO.
(See Hall of Fame section, 1990.)

Tom Seaver — **N.L. Cy Young**
Team: Mets.
Season: 22-9; 2.38 ERA; 243 SO.
(See Hall of Fame section, 1992.)

John Montefusco — **N.L. Rookie**
Team: Giants. **Position:** Pitcher.
6-1, 180. **B:** R. **T:** R.
Born: May 25, 1950.
Season: 15-9; 2.88 ERA; 215 SO.
Career: 90-83; 3.54 ERA; 1,081 SO.
Teams: Giants 1974-80; Braves 1981; Padres 1982-83; Yankees 1983-86.

1976

Thurman Munson — **A.L. MVP**
Team: Yankees. **Position:** Catcher.
Season: .302 avg.; 17 HR; 105 RBIs.
(See 1970 A.L. Rookie of Year.)

Joe Morgan — **N.L. MVP**
Team: Reds. **Position:** Second base.
Season: .320 avg.; 27 HR; 111 RBIs; 60 SB.
(See Hall of Fame section, 1990.)

Jim Palmer **A.L. Cy Young**
Team: Orioles.
Season: 22-13; 2.51 ERA; 159 SO.
(See Hall of Fame section, 1990.)

Randy Jones **N.L. Cy Young**
Team: Padres.
6-0, 178. **B:** R. **T:** L.
Born: Jan. 12, 1950.
Season: 22-14; 2.74 ERA; 93 SO.
Career: 100-123; 3.42 ERA; 735 SO.
Teams: Padres 1973-80; Mets 1981-82.

Mark Fidrych **A.L. Rookie**
Team: Tigers. **Position:** Pitcher.
6-3, 175. **B:** R. **T:** R.
Born: Aug. 14, 1954.
Season: 19-9; 2.34 ERA; 97 SO.
Career: 29-19; 3.10 ERA; 170 SO.
Team: Tigers 1976-80.

Butch Metzger **N.L. co-Rookie**
Team: Padres. **Position:** Pitcher.
6-1, 185. **B:** R. **T:** R.
Born: May 23, 1952.
Season: 11-4; 2.92 ERA; 89 SO.
Career: 18-9; 3.74 ERA; 175 SO.
Teams: Giants 1974; Padres 1975-77; Cardinals 1977; Mets 1978.

Pat Zachry **N.L. co-Rookie**
Team: Reds. **Position:** Pitcher.
6-5, 180. **B:** R. **T:** R.
Born: April 24, 1952.
Season: 14-7; 2.74 ERA; 143 SO.
Career: 69-67; 3.52 ERA; 669 SO.
Teams: Reds 1976-77; Mets 1977-82; Dodgers 1983-84; Phillies 1985.

1977

Rod Carew **A.L. MVP**
Team: Twins. **Position:** First base.
Season: .388 avg.; 14 HR; 100 RBIs; 239 hits.
(See Hall of Fame section, 1991.)

George Foster **N.L. MVP**
Team: Reds. **Position:** Outfield.
6-1, 185. **B:** R. **T:** R.
Born: Dec. 1, 1948.
Season: .320 avg.; 52 HR; 149 RBIs.
Career: .274 avg.; 348 HR; 1,239 RBIs.
Teams: Giants 1969-71; Reds 1971-81; Mets 1982-86; White Sox 1986.

Sparky Lyle **A.L. Cy Young**
Team: Yankees.
6-1, 192. **B:** L. **T:** L.
Born: July 22, 1944.
Season: 13-5; 2.17 ERA; 68 SO; 26 saves.
Career: 99-76; 2.88 ERA; 873 SO; 238 saves.
Teams: Red Sox 1967-71; Yankees 1972-78; Rangers 1979-80; Phillies 1980-82; White Sox 1982.

Steve Carlton **N.L. Cy Young**
Team: Phillies.
Season: 23-10; 2.64 ERA; 198 SO.
(See Hall of Fame section, 1994.)

Eddie Murray **A.L. Rookie**
Team: Orioles. **Position:** First base.
6-2, 200. **B:** B. **T:** R.
Born: Feb. 24, 1956.
Season: .283 avg.; 27 HR; 88 RBIs.
Career: .287 avg.; 504 HR; 1,917 RBIs.
Teams: Orioles 1977-88, 1996; Dodgers 1989-91, 1997; Mets 1992-93; Indians 1994-96; Angels 1997.

Andre Dawson **N.L. Rookie**
Team: Expos. **Position:** Outfield.
6-3, 195. **B:** R. **T:** R.
Born: July 10, 1954.
Season: .282 avg.; 19 HR; 65 RBIs.
Career: .279 avg.; 438 HR; 1,591 RBIs; still active.
Teams: Expos 1976-86; Cubs 1987-92; Red Sox 1993-94; Marlins 1995-96.

1978

Jim Rice **A.L. MVP**
Team: Red Sox. **Position:** Outfield.
6-2, 205. **B:** R. **T:** R.
Born: March 8, 1953.
Season: .315 avg.; 46 HR; 139 RBIs.
Career: .298 avg.; 382 HR; 1,451 RBIs.
Team: Red Sox 1974-89.

Dave Parker **N.L. MVP**
Team: Pirates. **Position:** Outfield.
6-5, 230. **B:** L. **T:** R.
Born: June 9, 1951.
Season: .334 avg.; 30 HR; 117 RBIs.
Career: .290 avg.; 339 HR; 1,493 RBIs.
Teams: Pirates 1973-83; Reds 1984-87; Athletics 1988-89; Brewers 1990; Angels 1991; Blue Jays 1991.

Ron Guidry **A.L. Cy Young**
Team: Yankees.
5-11, 161. **B:** L. **T:** L.
Born: Aug. 28, 1950.
Season: 25-3; 1.74 ERA; 248 SO.
Career: 170-91; 3.29 ERA; 1,778 SO.
Team: Yankees 1975-88.

Gaylord Perry **N.L. Cy Young**
Team: Padres.
Season: 21-6; 2.73 ERA; 154 SO.
(See Hall of Fame section, 1991.)

Lou Whitaker **A.L. Rookie**
Team: Tigers. **Position:** Second base.
5-11, 160. **B:** L. **T:** R.
Born: May 12, 1957.
Season: .285 avg.; 3 HR; 58 RBIs.
Career: .276 avg.; 244 HR; 1,084 RBIs.
Team: Tigers 1977-95.

Bob Horner **N.L. Rookie**
Team: Braves. **Position:** Third base.
6-1, 210. **B:** R. **T:** R.
Born: Aug. 6, 1957.
Season: .266 avg.; 23 HR; 63 RBIs.
Career: .277 avg.; 218 HR; 685 RBIs.
Teams: Braves 1978-86; Cardinals 1988.

1979

Don Baylor **A.L. MVP**
Team: Angels. **Position:** Outfield.
6-1, 200. **B:** R. **T:** R.
Born: June 28, 1949.
Season: .296 avg.; 36 HR; 139 RBIs.
Career: .260 avg.; 338 HR; 1,276 RBIs.
Teams: Orioles 1970-75; Athletics 1976, 1988; Angels 1977-82; Yankees 1983-85; Red Sox 1986-87; Twins 1987.

Willie Stargell **N.L. co-MVP**
Team: Pirates. **Position:** First base.
Season: .281 avg.; 32 HR; 82 RBIs.
(See Hall of Fame section, 1988.)

Keith Hernandez **N.L. co-MVP**
Team: Cardinals. **Position:** First base.
6-0, 195. **B:** L. **T:** L.
Born: Oct. 20, 1953.
Season: .344 avg.; 11 HR; 105 RBIs.
Career: .296 avg.; 162 HR; 1,071 RBIs.
Teams: Cardinals 1974-83; Mets 1983-89; Indians 1990.

Mike Flanagan **A.L. Cy Young**
Team: Orioles.
6-0, 195. **B:** L. **T:** L.

Pittsburgh first baseman Willie Stargell had to share N.L. MVP honors in 1979.

Born: Dec. 16, 1951.
Season: 23-9; 3.08 ERA; 190 SO.
Career: 167-143; 3.90 ERA; 1,491 SO.
Teams: Orioles 1975-87, 1991-92; Blue Jays 1987-90.

Bruce Sutter **N.L. Cy Young**
Team: Cubs.
6-2, 190. **B:** R. **T:** R.
Born: Jan. 8, 1953.
Season: 6-6; 2.22 ERA; 110 SO; 37 saves.
Career: 68-71; 2.83 ERA; 861 SO; 300 saves.
Teams: Cubs 1976-80; Cardinals 1981-84; Braves 1985-88.

John Castino **A.L. co-Rookie**
Team: Twins. **Position:** Third base.
5-11, 175. **B:** R. **T:** R.
Born: Oct. 23, 1954.
Season: .285 avg.; 5 HR; 52 RBIs.
Career: .278 avg.; 41 HR; 249 RBIs.
Team: Twins 1979-84.

Alfredo Griffin **A.L. co-Rookie**
Team: Blue Jays. **Position:** Shortstop.
5-11, 165. **B:** B. **T:** R.
Born: Oct. 6, 1957.
Season: .287 avg.; 2 HR; 31 RBIs; 21 SB.
Career: .249 avg.; 24 HR; 527 RBIs.
Teams: Indians 1976-78; Blue Jays 1979-84, 1992-93; Athletics 1985-87; Dodgers 1988-91.

Rick Sutcliffe **N.L. Rookie**
Team: Dodgers. **Position:** Pitcher.
6-7, 220. **B:** L. **T:** R.
Born: June 21, 1956.
Season: 17-10; 3.46 ERA; 117 SO.
Career: 171-139; 4.08 ERA; 1,679 SO.
Teams: Dodgers 1976, 1978-81; Indians 1982-84; Cubs 1984-91; Orioles 1992-93; Cardinals 1994.

1980

George Brett **A.L. MVP**
Team: Royals. **Position:** Third base.
Season: .390 avg.; 24 HR; 118 RBIs.
(See Hall of Fame section, 1999.)

Mike Schmidt **N.L. MVP**
Team: Phillies. **Position:** Third base.
Season: .286 avg.; 48 HR; 121 RBIs.
(See Hall of Fame section, 1995.)

Steve Stone **A.L. Cy Young**
Team: Orioles.

Atlanta outfielder Dale Murphy won consecutive MVP awards in 1982 and '83.

5-10, 175. **B:** R. **T:** R.
Born: July 14, 1947.
Season: 25-7; 3.23 ERA; 149 SO.
Career: 107-93; 3.97 ERA; 1,065 SO.
Teams: Giants 1971-72; White Sox 1973, 1977-78; Cubs 1974-76; Orioles 1979-81.

Steve Carlton — **N.L. Cy Young**
Team: Phillies.
Season: 24-9; 2.34 ERA; 286 SO.
(See Hall of Fame section, 1994.)

Joe Charboneau — **A.L. Rookie**
Team: Indians. **Position:** Outfield.
6-2, 205. **B:** R. **T:** R.
Born: June 17, 1955.
Season: .289 avg.; 23 HR; 87 RBIs.
Career: .266 avg.; 29 HR; 114 RBIs.
Team: Indians 1980-82.

Steve Howe — **N.L. Rookie**
Team: Dodgers. **Position:** Pitcher.
6-1, 180. **B:** L. **T:** L.
Born: March 10, 1958.
Season: 7-9; 2.66 ERA; 39 SO; 17 saves.
Career: 47-41; 3.03 ERA; 328 SO; 91 saves.
Teams: Dodgers 1980-83, 1985; Twins 1985; Rangers 1987; Yankees 1991-95.

1981

Rollie Fingers — **A.L. MVP, Cy Young**
Team: Brewers. **Position:** Pitcher.
Season: 6-3; 1.04 ERA; 61 SO; 28 saves.
(See Hall of Fame section, 1992.)

Mike Schmidt — **N.L. MVP**
Team: Phillies. **Position:** Third base.
Season: .316 avg.; 31 HR; 91 RBIs.
(See Hall of Fame section, 1995.)

Fernando Valenzuela — **N.L. Rookie, Cy Young**
Team: Dodgers.
5-11, 195. **B:** L. **T:** L.
Born: Nov. 1, 1960.
Season: 13-7; 2.48 ERA; 180 SO.
Career: 173-153; 3.54 ERA; 2,074 SO.
Teams: Dodgers 1980-90; Angels 1991; Orioles 1993; Phillies 1994; Padres 1995-97; Cardinals 1997.

Dave Righetti — **A.L. Rookie**
Team: Yankees. **Position:** Pitcher.
6-3, 205. **B:** L. **T:** L.
Born: Nov. 28, 1958.
Season: 8-4; 2.05 ERA; 89 SO.
Career: 82-79; 3.46 ERA; 1,112 SO.
Teams: Yankees 1979, 1981-90; Giants 1991-93; Athletics 1994; White Sox 1995.

1982

Robin Yount — **A.L. MVP**
Team: Brewers. **Position:** Shortstop.
Season: .331 avg.; 29 HR; 114 RBIs.
(See Hall of Fame section, 1999.)

Dale Murphy — **N.L. MVP**
Team: Braves. **Position:** Outfield.
6-4, 215. **B:** R. **T:** R.
Born: March 12, 1956.
Season: .281 avg; 36 HR; 109 RBIs.
Career: .265 avg.; 398 HR; 1,266 RBIs.
Teams: Braves 1976-90; Phillies 1990-92; Rockies 1993.

Pete Vuckovich — **A.L. Cy Young**
Team: Brewers.
6-4, 220. **B:** R. **T:** R.
Born: Oct. 27, 1952.
Season: 18-6; 3.34 ERA; 105 SO.
Career: 93-69; 3.66 ERA; 882 SO.
Teams: White Sox 1975-76; Blue Jays 1977; Cardinals 1978-80; Brewers 1981-83, 1985-86.

Steve Carlton — **N.L. Cy Young**
Team: Phillies.
Season: 23-11; 3.10 ERA; 286 SO.
(See Hall of Fame section, 1994.)

Cal Ripken — **A.L. Rookie**
Team: Orioles. **Position:** Shortstop, third base.
6-4, 210. **B:** R. **T:** R.
Born: Aug. 24, 1960.
Season: .264 avg.; 28 HR; 93 RBIs.
Career: .278 avg.; 402 HR; 1,571 RBIs; still active.
Team: Orioles 1981-99.

Steve Sax — **N.L. Rookie**
Team: Dodgers. **Position:** Second base.
5-11, 185. **B:** R. **T:** R.
Born: Jan. 29, 1960.
Season: .282 avg.; 4 HR; 47 RBIs; 49 SB.
Career: .281 avg.; 54 HR; 550 RBIs; 444 SB.
Teams: Dodgers 1981-88; Yankees 1989-91; White Sox 1992-93; Athletics 1994.

1983

Cal Ripken — **A.L. MVP**
Team: Orioles. **Position:** Shortstop.
Season: .318 avg.; 27 HR; 102 RBIs.
(See 1982 A.L. Rookie.)

Dale Murphy — **N.L. MVP**
Team: Braves. **Position:** Outfield.
Season: .302 avg.; 36 HR; 121 RBIs.
(See 1982 N.L. MVP.)

LaMarr Hoyt — **A.L. Cy Young**
Team: White Sox.
6-1, 222. **B:** R. **T:** R.
Born: Jan. 1, 1955.
Season: 24-10; 3.66 ERA; 148 SO.
Career: 98-68; 3.99 ERA; 681 SO.
Teams: White Sox 1979-84; Padres 1985-86.

John Denny — **N.L. Cy Young**
Team: Phillies.
6-3, 190. **B:** R. **T:** R.
Born: Nov. 8, 1952.
Season: 19-6; 2.37 ERA; 139 SO.
Career: 123-108; 3.59 ERA; 1,146 SO.
Teams: Cardinals 1974-79; Indians 1980-82; Phillies 1982-85; Reds 1986.

Ron Kittle — **A.L. Rookie**
Team: White Sox. **Position:** Outfield.
6-4, 220. **B:** R. **T:** R.
Born: Jan. 5, 1958.
Season: .254 avg.; 35 HR; 100 RBIs.
Career: .239 avg.; 176 HR; 460 RBIs.
Teams: White Sox 1982-86, 1989-91; Yankees 1986-87; Indians 1988; Orioles 1990.

Darryl Strawberry — **N.L. Rookie**
Team: Mets. **Position:** Outfield.
6-6, 200. **B:** L. **T:** L.
Born: March 12, 1962.
Season: .257 avg.; 26 HR; 74 RBIs.
Career: .259 avg.; 335 HR; 1,000 RBIs; still active.
Teams: Mets 1983-90; Dodgers 1991-93; Giants 1994; Yankees 1995-99.

1984

Willie Hernandez — **A.L. MVP, Cy Young**
Team: Tigers. **Position:** Pitcher.
6-3, 180. **B:** L. **T:** L.
Born: Nov. 14, 1954.
Season: 9-3; 1.92 ERA; 112 SO; 32 saves.
Career: 70-63; 3.38 ERA; 788 SO; 147 saves.
Teams: Cubs 1977-83; Phillies 1983; Tigers 1984-89.

Ryne Sandberg — **N.L. MVP**
Team: Cubs. **Position:** Second base.
6-2, 180. **B:** R. **T:** R.
Born: Sept. 18, 1959.
Season: .314 avg.; 19 HR; 84 RBIs.
Career: .285 avg.; 282 HR; 1,061 RBIs.
Teams: Phillies 1981; Cubs 1982-94, 1996-97.

RICK SUTCLIFFE — **N.L. CY YOUNG**
Team: Cubs.
Season: 16-1; 2.69 ERA; 155 SO.
(See 1979 N.L. Rookie of Year.)

ALVIN DAVIS — **A.L. ROOKIE**
Team: Mariners. **Position:** First base.
6-1, 195. **B:** L. **T:** R.
Born: Sept. 9, 1960.
Season: .284 avg.; 27 HR; 116 RBIs.
Career: .280 avg.; 160 HR; 683 RBIs.
Team: Mariners 1984-91; Angels 1992.

DWIGHT GOODEN — **N.L. ROOKIE**
Team: Mets. **Position:** Pitcher.
6-3, 200. **B:** R. **T:** R.
Born: Nov. 16, 1964.
Season: 17-9; 2.60 ERA; 276 SO.
Career: 188-107; 3.46 ERA; 2,238 SO; still active.
Team: Mets 1984-94; Yankees 1996-97; Indians 1998-99.

1985

DON MATTINGLY — **A.L. MVP**
Team: Yankees. **Position:** First base.
6-0, 185. **B:** L. **T:** L.
Born: April 20, 1961.
Season: .324 avg.; 35 HR; 145 RBIs.
Career: .307 avg.; 222 HR; 1,099 RBIs.
Team: Yankees 1982-95.

WILLIE MCGEE — **N.L. MVP**
Team: Cardinals. **Position:** Outfield.
6-1, 185. **B:** B. **T:** R.
Born: Nov. 2, 1958.
Season: .353 avg.; 10 HR; 82 RBIs; 216 hits; 56 SB.
Career: .295 avg.; 79 HR; 856 RBIs; 352 SB.
Teams: Cardinals 1982-90, 1996-99; Athletics 1990; Giants 1991-94; Red Sox 1995.

BRET SABERHAGEN — **A.L. CY YOUNG**
Team: Royals.
6-1, 195. **B:** R. **T:** R.
Born: April 11, 1964.
Season: 20-6; 2.87 ERA; 158 SO.
Career: 166-115; 3.33 ERA; 1,705 SO; still active.
Teams: Royals 1984-91; Mets 1992-95; Rockies 1995-96; Red Sox 1997-99.

DWIGHT GOODEN — **N.L. CY YOUNG**
Team: Mets.
Season: 24-4; 1.53 ERA; 268 SO.
(See 1984 N.L. Rookie of Year.)

OZZIE GUILLEN — **A.L. ROOKIE**
Team: White Sox. **Position:** Shortstop.
5-11, 160. **B:** L. **T:** R.
Born: Jan. 20, 1964.
Season: .273 avg.; 1 HR; 33 RBIs.
Career: .264 avg.; 26 HR; 607 RBIs; still active.
Team: White Sox 1985-97; Orioles 1998; Braves 1998-99.

VINCE COLEMAN — **N.L. ROOKIE**
Team: Cardinals. **Position:** Outfield
6-0, 170. **B:** B. **T:** R.
Born: Sept. 22, 1961.
Season: .267 avg.; 1 HR; 40 RBIs; 110 SB.
Career: .264 avg.; 28 HR; 346 RBIs; 752 SB.
Teams: Cardinals 1985-90; Mets 1991-93; Royals 1994-95; Mariners 1995; Reds 1996; Tigers 1997.

1986

ROGER CLEMENS — **A.L. MVP, CY YOUNG**
Team: Red Sox. **Position:** Pitcher.
6-4, 215. **B:** R. **T:** R.
Born: Aug. 4, 1962.
Season: 24-4; 2.48 ERA; 238 SO.

Willie McGee's .353 average, 56 stolen bases and outstanding defense in center field for the '85 pennant-winning Cardinals won him the N.L. MVP award.

Career: 247-134; 3.04 ERA; 3,316 SO; still active.
Team: Red Sox 1984-96; Blue Jays 1997-98; Yankees 1999.

MIKE SCHMIDT — **N.L. MVP**
Team: Phillies. **Position:** Third base.
Season: .290 avg.; 37 HR; 119 RBIs.
(See Hall of Fame section, 1995.)

MIKE SCOTT — **N.L. CY YOUNG**
Team: Astros.
6-3, 215. **B:** R. **T:** R.
Born: April 26, 1955.
Season: 18-10; 2.22 ERA; 306 SO.
Career: 124-108; 3.54 ERA; 1,469 SO.
Teams: Mets 1979-82; Astros 1983-91.

JOSE CANSECO — **A.L. ROOKIE**
Team: Athletics. **Position:** Outfield.
6-4, 240. **B:** R. **T:** R.
Born: July 2, 1964.
Season: .240 avg.; 33 HR; 117 RBIs.
Career: .267 avg.; 431 HR; 1,309 RBIs; still active.
Teams: Athletics 1985-92, 1997; Rangers 1992-94; Red Sox 1995-96; Blue Jays 1998; Devil Rays 1999.

TODD WORRELL — **N.L. ROOKIE**
Team: Cardinals. **Position:** Pitcher.
6-5, 215. **B:** R. **T:** R.
Born: Sept. 28, 1959.
Season: 9-10; 2.08 ERA; 73 SO; 36 saves.
Career: 50-52; 3.09 ERA; 628 SO; 256 saves.
Teams: Cardinals 1985-89, 1992; Dodgers 1993-97.

1987

GEORGE BELL — **A.L. MVP**
Team: Blue Jays. **Position:** Outfield.
6-1, 200. **B:** R. **T:** R.
Born: Oct. 21, 1959.
Season: .308 avg.; 47 HR; 134 RBIs.
Career: .278 avg.; 265 HR; 1,002 RBIs.
Teams: Blue Jays 1981, 1983-90; Cubs 1991; White Sox 1992-93.

ANDRE DAWSON — **N.L. MVP**
Team: Cubs. **Position:** Outfield.
Season: .287 avg.; 49 HR; 137 RBIs.
(See 1977 N.L. Rookie of Year.)

ROGER CLEMENS — **A.L. CY YOUNG**
Team: Red Sox.
Season: 20-9; 2.97 ERA; 256 SO.
(See 1986 A.L. MVP.)

STEVE BEDROSIAN — **N.L. CY YOUNG**
Team: Phillies.
6-3, 200. **B:** R. **T:** R.
Born: Dec. 6, 1957.
Season: 5-3; 2.83 ERA; 74 SO; 40 saves.
Career: 76-79; 3.38 ERA; 921 SO; 184 saves.
Teams: Braves 1981-85, 1993-95; Phillies 1986-89; Giants 1989-90; Twins 1991.

MARK MCGWIRE — **A.L. ROOKIE**
Team: Athletics. **Position:** First base.
6-5, 225. **B:** R. **T:** R.
Born: Oct. 1, 1963.
Season: .289 avg.; 49 HR; 118 RBIs.
Career: .265 avg.; 522 HR; 1,277 RBIs; still active.
Team: Athletics 1986-97; Cardinals 1997-99.

BENITO SANTIAGO — **N.L. ROOKIE**
Team: Padres. **Position:** Catcher.
6-1, 185. **B:** R. **T:** R.
Born: March 9, 1965.
Season: .300 avg.; 18 HR; 79 RBIs.
Career: .260 avg.; 170 HR; 677 RBIs; still active.
Teams: Padres 1986-92; Marlins 1993-94; Reds 1995; Phillies 1996; Blue Jays 1997-98; Cubs 1999.

Red Sox ace Roger Clemens won the first of five Cy Youngs in 1986.

1988

Jose Canseco — **A.L. MVP**
Team: Athletics. **Position:** Outfield.
Season: .307 avg.; 42 HR; 124 RBIs; 40 SB.
(See 1986 A.L. Rookie of Year.)

Kirk Gibson — **N.L. MVP**
Team: Dodgers. **Position:** Outfield.
6-3, 215. **B:** L. **T:** L.
Born: May 28, 1957.
Season: .290 avg.; 25 HR; 76 RBIs; 31 SB.
Career: .268 avg.; 255 HR; 870 RBIs.
Teams: Tigers 1979-87, 1993-95; Dodgers 1988-90; Royals 1991; Pirates 1992.

Frank Viola — **A.L. Cy Young**
Team: Twins.
6-4, 210. **B:** L. **T:** L.
Born: April 19, 1960.
Season: 24-7; 2.64 ERA; 193 SO.
Career: 176-150; 3.73 ERA; 1,844 SO.
Teams: Twins 1982-89; Mets 1989-91; Red Sox 1992-94; Reds 1995; Blue Jays 1996.

Orel Hershiser — **N.L. Cy Young**
Team: Dodgers.
6-3, 190. **B:** R. **T:** R.
Born: Sept. 16, 1958.
Season: 23-8; 2.26 ERA; 178 SO.
Career: 203-145; 3.41 ERA; 2,001 SO; still active.
Team: Dodgers 1983-94; Indians 1995-97; Giants 1998; Mets 1999.

Walt Weiss — **A.L. Rookie**
Team: Athletics. **Position:** Shortstop.
6-0, 175. **B:** B. **T:** R.
Born: Nov. 28, 1963.
Season: .250 avg.; 3 HR; 39 RBIs.
Career: .257 avg.; 25 HR; 368 RBIs; still active.
Teams: Athletics 1987-92; Marlins 1993; Rockies 1994-97.

Chris Sabo — **N.L. Rookie**
Team: Reds. **Position:** Third base.
5-11, 185. **B:** R. **T:** R.
Born: Jan. 19, 1962.
Season: .271 avg.; 11 HR; 44 RBIs; 46 SB.
Career: .268 avg.; 116 HR; 426 RBIs; 120 SB.
Teams: Reds 1988-93, 1996; Orioles 1994; White Sox 1995; Cardinals 1995.

1989

Robin Yount — **A.L. MVP**
Team: Brewers. **Position:** Outfield.
Season: .318 avg.; 21 HR; 103 RBIs.
(See Hall of Fame section, 1999.)

Kevin Mitchell — **N.L. MVP**
Team: Giants. **Position:** Outfield.
5-11, 220. **B:** R. **T:** R.
Born: Jan. 13, 1962.
Season: .291 avg.; 47 HR; 125 RBIs.
Career: .284 avg.; 234 HR; 760 RBIs.
Teams: Mets 1984, 1986; Padres 1987; Giants 1987-91; Mariners 1992; Reds 1993-94, 1996; Red Sox 1996; Indians 1997; Athletics 1998.

Bret Saberhagen — **A.L. Cy Young**
Team: Royals.
Season: 23-6, 2.16 ERA; 193 SO.
(See 1985 A.L. Cy Young.)

Mark Davis — **N.L. Cy Young**
Team: Padres.
6-4, 205. **B:** L. **T:** L.
Born: Oct. 19, 1960.
Season: 4-3; 1.85 ERA; 92 SO; 44 saves.
Career: 51-84; 4.15 ERA; 993 SO; 96 saves.
Teams: Phillies 1980-81; Giants 1983-87; Padres 1987-89, 1993-94; Royals 1990-92; Braves 1992; Phillies 1993.

Gregg Olson — **A.L. Rookie**
Team: Orioles. **Position:** Pitcher.
6-4, 210. **B:** R. **T:** R.
Born: Oct. 11, 1966.
Season: 5-2; 1.69 ERA; 90 SO; 27 saves.
Career: 40-37; 3.23 ERA; 549 SO; 217 saves; still active.
Teams: Orioles 1988-93; Braves 1994; Indians 1995; Royals 1995, 1997; Tigers 1996; Astros 1996; Twins 1997; Diamondbacks 1998-99.

Jerome Walton — **N.L. Rookie**
Team: Cubs. **Position:** Outfield.
6-1, 175. **B:** R. **T:** R.
Born: July 8, 1965.
Season: .293 avg.; 5 HR; 46 RBIs; 24 SB.
Career: .268 avg.; 25 HR; 129 RBIs; still active.
Teams: Cubs 1989-92; Angels 1993; Reds 1994-95; Braves 1996; Orioles 1997.

1990

Rickey Henderson — **A.L. MVP**
Team: Athletics. **Position:** Outfield.
5-10, 195. **B:** R. **T:** L.
Born: Dec. 25, 1958.
Season: .325 avg.; 28 HR; 61 RBIs; 65 SB.
Career: .284 avg.; 278 HR; 1,020 RBIs; 1,334 SB; still active.
Teams: Athletics 1979-84, 1989-93, 1994-95, 1998; Yankees 1985-89; Blue Jays 1993; Padres 1996-97; Angels 1997; Mets 1999.

Barry Bonds — **N.L. MVP**
Team: Pirates. **Position:** Outfield.
6-1, 185. **B:** L. **T:** L.
Born: July 24, 1964.
Season: .301 avg.; 33 HR; 114 RBIs; 52 SB.
Career: .288 avg.; 445 HR; 1,299 RBIs; 460 SB; still active.
Teams: Pirates 1986-92; Giants 1993-99.

Bob Welch — **A.L. Cy Young**
Team: Athletics.
6-3, 190. **B:** R. **T:** R.
Born: Nov. 3, 1956.
Season: 27-6; 2.95 ERA; 127 SO.
Career: 211-146; 3.47 ERA; 1,969 SO.
Teams: Dodgers 1978-87; Athletics 1988-94.

Doug Drabek — **N.L. Cy Young**
Team: Pirates.
6-1, 185. **B:** R. **T:** R.
Born: July 25, 1962.
Season: 22-6; 2.76 ERA; 131 SO.
Career: 155-134; 3.73 ERA; 1,594 SO.
Teams: Yankees 1986; Pirates 1987-92; Astros 1993-96; White Sox 1997; Orioles 1998.

Sandy Alomar Jr. — **A.L. Rookie**
Team: Indians. **Position:** Catcher.
6-5, 200. **B:** R. **T:** R.
Born: June 18, 1966.
Season: .290 avg.; 9 HR; 66 RBIs.
Career: .275 avg.; 86 HR; 417 RBIs; still active.
Teams: Padres 1988-89; Indians 1990-99.

David Justice — **N.L. Rookie**
Team: Braves. **Position:** Outfield.
6-3, 195. **B:** L. **T:** L.
Born: April 14, 1966.
Season: .282 avg.; 28 HR; 78 RBIs.
Career: .283 avg.; 235 HR; 799 RBIs; still active.
Team: Braves 1989-96; Indians 1997-99.

1991

Cal Ripken — **A.L. MVP**
Team: Orioles. **Position:** Shortstop.
Season: .323 avg.; 34 HR; 114 RBIs.
(See 1982 A.L. Rookie of Year.)

Terry Pendleton — **N.L. MVP**
Team: Braves. **Position:** Third base.
5-9, 190. **B:** B. **T:** R.
Born: July 16, 1960.
Season: .319 avg.; 22 HR; 86 RBIs.
Career: .270 avg.; 140 HR; 946 RBIs.
Teams: Cardinals 1984-90; Braves 1991-94, 1996; Marlins 1995-96; Reds 1997; Royals 1998.

Roger Clemens — **A.L. Cy Young**
Team: Red Sox.
Season: 18-10; 2.62 ERA; 241 SO.
(See 1986 A.L. MVP.)

Tom Glavine — **N.L. Cy Young**
Team: Braves.
6-1, 190. **B:** L. **T:** L.
Born: March 25, 1966.
Season: 20-11; 2.55 ERA; 192 SO.
Career: 187-116; 3.38 ERA; 1,659 SO; still active.
Team: Braves 1987-99.

Chuck Knoblauch — **A.L. Rookie**
Team: Twins. **Position:** Second base.
5-9, 175. **B:** R. **T:** R.
Born: July 7, 1968.
Season: .281 avg.; 1 HR; 50 RBIs; 25 SB.
Career: .298 avg.; 78 HR; 523 RBIs; 335 SB; still active.
Team: Twins 1991-97; Yankees 1998-99.

Jeff Bagwell — **N.L. Rookie**
Team: Astros. **Position:** First base.
6-0, 195. **B:** R. **T:** R.
Born: May 27, 1968.
Season: .294 avg.; 15 HR; 82 RBIs.
Career: .304 avg.; 263 HR; 961 RBIs; still active.
Team: Astros 1991-99.

1992

Dennis Eckersley — **A.L. MVP, Cy Young**
Team: Athletics. **Position:** Pitcher.
6-2, 190. **B:** R. **T:** R.
Born: Oct. 3, 1954.

Season: 7-1; 1.91 ERA; 93 SO; 51 saves.
Career: 197-171; 3.50 ERA; 2,401 SO; 390 saves; still active.
Teams: Indians 1975-77; Red Sox 1978-84, 1998; Cubs 1984-86; Athletics 1987-95; Cardinals 1996-97.

BARRY BONDS **N.L. MVP**
Team: Pirates. **Position:** Outfield.
Season: .311 avg.; 34 HR; 103 RBIs; 39 SB.
(See 1990 N.L. MVP.)

GREG MADDUX **N.L. CY YOUNG**
Team: Cubs.
6-0, 175. **B:** R. **T:** R.
Born: April 14, 1966.
Season: 20-11; 2.18 ERA; 199 SO.
Career: 221-126; 2.81 ERA; 2,160 SO.
Teams: Cubs 1986-92; Braves 1993-99.

PAT LISTACH **A.L. ROOKIE**
Team: Brewers. **Position:** Shortstop.
5-9, 170. **B:** B. **T:** R.
Born: Sept. 12, 1967.
Season: .290 avg.; 1 HR; 47 RBIs; 54 SB.
Career: .251 avg.; 5 HR; 143 RBIs; 116 SB; still active.
Team: Brewers 1992-96; Astros 1997.

ERIC KARROS **N.L. ROOKIE**
Team: Dodgers. **Position:** First base.
6-4, 216. **B:** R. **T:** R.
Born: Nov. 4, 1967.
Season: .257 avg.; 20 HR; 88 RBIs.
Career: .273 avg.; 211 HR; 734 RBIs; still active.
Team: Dodgers 1991-99.

1993

FRANK THOMAS **A.L. MVP**
Team: White Sox. **Position:** First base.
6-5, 240. **B:** R. **T:** R.
Born: May 27, 1968.
Season: .317 avg.; 41 HR; 128 RBIs.
Career: .320 avg.; 301 HR; 1,040 RBIs; still active.
Team: White Sox 1990-99.

BARRY BONDS **N.L. MVP**
Team: Giants. **Position:** Outfield.
Season: .336 avg.; 46 HR; 123 RBIs; 29 SB.
(See 1990 N.L. MVP.)

JACK MCDOWELL **A.L. CY YOUNG**
Team: White Sox.
6-5, 188. **B:** R. **T:** R.
Born: Jan. 16, 1966.
Season: 22-10; 3.37 ERA; 158 SO.
Career: 127-87; 3.85 ERA; 1,311 SO; still active.
Teams: White Sox 1987-88, 1990-94; Yankees 1995; Indians 1996-97; Angels 1998-99.

GREG MADDUX **N.L. CY YOUNG**
Team: Braves.
Season: 20-10; 2.36 ERA; 197 SO.
(See 1992 N.L. Cy Young.)

TIM SALMON **A.L. ROOKIE**
Team: Angels. **Position:** Outfield.
6-3, 220. **B:** R. **T:** R.
Born: Aug. 24, 1968.
Season: .283 avg.; 31 HR; 95 RBIs.
Career: .291 avg.; 196 HR; 660 RBIs; still active.
Team: Angels 1992-99.

MIKE PIAZZA **N.L. ROOKIE**
Team: Dodgers. **Position:** Catcher.
6-3, 197. **B:** R. **T:** R.
Born: Sept. 4, 1968.
Season: .318 avg.; 35 HR; 112 RBIs.
Career: .328 avg.; 240 HR; 768 RBIs; still active.
Team: Dodgers 1992-98; Marlins 1998; Mets 1998-99.

Arizona's Randy Johnson overpowered hitters in his first full season in the National League. He struck out 364 hitters, recorded a 2.48 ERA and brought home his second Cy Young Award.

1994

FRANK THOMAS **A.L. MVP**
Team: White Sox. **Position:** First base.
Season: .353 avg.; 38 HR; 101 RBIs.
(See 1993 A.L. MVP.)

JEFF BAGWELL **N.L. MVP**
Team: Astros. **Position:** First base.
Season: .368 avg.; 39 HR; 116 RBIs.
(See 1991 N.L. Rookie of Year.)

DAVID CONE **A.L. CY YOUNG**
Team: Royals.
6-1, 190. **B:** L. **T:** R.
Born: Jan. 2, 1963.
Season: 16-5; 2.94 ERA; 132 SO.
Career: 180-102; 3.19 ERA; 2,420 SO; still active.
Teams: Royals 1986, 1993-94; Mets 1987-92; Blue Jays 1992, 1995; Yankees 1995-99.

GREG MADDUX **N.L. CY YOUNG**
Team: Braves.
Season: 16-6; 1.56 ERA; 156 SO.
(See 1992 N.L. Cy Young.)

BOB HAMELIN **A.L. ROOKIE**
Team: Royals. **Position:** Designated hitter.
6-0, 235. **B:** L. **T:** L.
Born: Nov. 29, 1967.
Season: .282 avg.; 24 HR; 65 RBIs.
Career: .246 avg.; 67 HR; 209 RBIs; still active.
Team: Royals 1993-96; Tigers 1997; Brewers 1998.

RAUL MONDESI **N.L. ROOKIE**
Team: Dodgers. **Position:** Outfield.
5-11, 202. **B:** R. **T:** R.
Born: March 12, 1971.
Season: .306 avg.; 16 HR; 56 RBIs.
Career: .288 avg.; 163 HR; 518 RBIs; still active.
Team: Dodgers 1993-99.

1995

MO VAUGHN **A.L. MVP**
Team: Red Sox. **Position:** First base.
6-1, 230. **B:** L. **T:** R.
Born: Dec. 15, 1967.
Season: .300 avg.; 39 HR; 126 RBIs.
Career: .301 avg.; 263 HR; 860 RBIs; still active.
Team: Red Sox 1991-98; Angels 1999.

BARRY LARKIN **N.L. MVP**
Team: Reds. **Position:** Shortstop.
6-0, 196. **B:** R. **T:** R.
Born: April 28, 1964.
Season: .319 avg.; 15 HR; 66 RBIs; 51 SBs.
Career: .299 avg.; 168 HR; 793 RBIs; 345 SBs; still active.
Team: Reds 1986-99.

RANDY JOHNSON **A.L. CY YOUNG**
Team: Mariners.
6-10, 225. **B:** R. **T:** L.
Born: Sept. 10, 1963
Season: 18-2; 2.48 ERA; 294 SO.
Career: 160-88; 3.26 ERA; 2,693 SO; still active.
Teams: Expos 1988-89; Mariners 1989-98; Astros 1998; Diamondbacks 1999.

GREG MADDUX **N.L. CY YOUNG**
Team: Braves.
Season: 19-2; 1.63 ERA; 181 SO.
(See 1992 N.L. Cy Young.)

MARTY CORDOVA **A.L. ROOKIE**
Team: Twins. **Position:** Outfield.
6-0, 200. **B:** R. **T:** R.
Born: July 10, 1969.
Season: .277 avg.; 24 HR; 84 RBIs.
Career: .277 avg.; 79 HR; 385 RBIs; still active.
Team: Twins 1995-99.

Boston Red Sox shortstop Nomar Garciaparra.

Hideo Nomo **N.L. Rookie**
Team: Dodgers. **Position:** Pitcher.
6-2, 210. **B:** R. **T:** R.
Born: Aug. 31, 1968.
Season: 13-6; 2.54 ERA; 236 SO.
Career: 61-49; 3.82 ERA; 1,031 SO; still active.
Team: Dodgers 1995-98; Mets 1998; Brewers 1999.

1996

Juan Gonzalez **A.L. MVP**
Team: Rangers. **Position:** Outfield.
6-3, 215 **B:** R. **T:** R.
Born: Oct. 16, 1969.
1996 season: .314 avg.; 47 HR; 144 RBIs.
Career: .294 avg.; 340 HR; 1,075 RBIs.
Teams: Rangers 1989-99.

Ken Caminiti **N.L. MVP**
Team: Padres. **Position:** Third base.
6-0, 200. **B:** B. **T:** R.
Born: April 21, 1963.
Season: .326 avg.; 40 HR; 130 RBIs.
Career: .274 avg.; 209 HR; 897 RBIs; still active.
Teams: Astros 1987-94, 1999; Padres 1995-98.

Pat Hentgen **A.L. Cy Young**
Team: Blue Jays.
6-2, 200. **B:** R. **T:** R.
Born: Nov. 13, 1968
Season: 20-10; 3.22 ERA; 177 SO.
Career: 105-76; 4.14 ERA; 995 SO; still active.
Teams: Blue Jays 1991-99.

John Smoltz **N.L. Cy Young**
Team: Braves.
6-3, 185. **B:** R. **T:** R.
Born: May 15, 1967.
Season: 24-8; 2.94 ERA; 276 SO.
Career: 157-113; 3.35 ERA; 2,098 SO; still active.
Teams: Braves 1988-99.

Derek Jeter **A.L. Rookie**
Team: Yankees. **Position:** Shortstop.
6-3, 185. **B:** R. **T:** R.
Born: June 26, 1974.
Season: .314 avg.; 10 HR; 78 RBIs.
Career: .318 avg.; 63 HR; 341 RBIs; still active.
Team: Yankees 1995-99.

Todd Hollandsworth **N.L. Rookie**
Team: Dodgers. **Position:** Outfield.
6-2, 193. **B:** L. **T:** L.
Born: April 20, 1973.
Season: .291 avg.; 12 HR; 59 RBIs.
Career: .272 avg.; 33 HR; 155 RBIs; still active.
Team: Dodgers 1995-99.

1997

Ken Griffey Jr. **A.L. MVP**
Team: Mariners. **Position:** Outfield.
6-3, 205. **B:** L. **T:** L.
Born: November 21, 1969.
Season: .304 avg.; 56 HR; 147 RBIs.
Career: .299 avg.; 398 HR; 1,152 RBIs; still active.
Team: Mariners 1989-99.

Larry Walker **N.L. MVP**
Team: Rockies. **Position:** Outfield.
6-3, 225. **B:** L. **T:** R.
Born: December 1, 1966.
Season: .366 avg.; 49 HR; 130 RBIs; 33 SBs.
Career: .312 avg.; 262 HR; 855 RBIs; still active.
Team: Expos 1989-94; Rockies 1995-99.

Roger Clemens **A.L. Cy Young**
Team: Blue Jays.
Season: 21-7; 2.05 ERA; 292 SO.
(See 1986 A.L. MVP.)

Pedro Martinez **N.L. Cy Young**
Team: Expos.
5-11, 175. **B:** R. **T:** R.
Born: October 25, 1971.
Season: 17-8; 1.90 ERA; 305 SO.
Career: 107-50; 2.83 ERA; 1,534 SO; still active.
Team: Dodgers 1992-93; Expos 1994-97; Red Sox 1998-99.

Nomar Garciaparra **A.L. Rookie**
Team: Red Sox. **Position:** Shortstop.
6-0, 167. **B:** R. **T:** R.
Born: July 23, 1973.
Season: .306 avg.; 30 HR; 98 RBIs; 22 SB.
Career: .322 avg.; 96 HR; 340 RBIs; 53 SB; still active.
Team: Red Sox 1996-99.

Scott Rolen **N.L. Rookie**
Team: Phillies. **Position:** Third base.
6-4, 195. **B:** R. **T:** R.
Born: April 4, 1975.
Season: .283 avg.; 21 HR; 92 RBIs.
Career: .280 avg.; 82 HR; 297 RBIs; still active.
Team: Phillies 1996-99.

1998

Juan Gonzalez **A.L. MVP**
Team: Rangers. **Position:** Outfield.
Season: .318 avg.; 45 HR; 157 RBIs.
(See 1997 A.L. MVP.)

Sammy Sosa **N.L. MVP**
Team: Cubs. **Position:** Outfield.
6-0, 200. **B:** R. **T:** R.
Born: November 12, 1968.
Season: .307 avg.; 66 HR; 158 RBIs.
Career: .267 avg.; 336 HR; 941 RBIs; still active.
Team: Rangers 1989; White Sox 1989-91; Cubs 1992-99.

Roger Clemens **A.L. Cy Young**
Team: Blue Jays.
Season: 20-6; 2.65 ERA; 271 SO.
(See 1986 A.L. MVP.)

Tom Glavine **N.L. Cy Young**
Team: Braves.
Season: 20-6; 2.47 ERA; 157 SO.
(See 1991 N.L. Cy Young.)

Ben Grieve **A.L. Rookie**
Team: Athletics. **Position:** Outfield.
6-4, 200. **B:** L. **T:** R.
Born: May 4, 1976.
Season: .288 avg.; 18 HR; 89 RBIs.
Career: .281 avg.; 49 HR; 199 RBIs; still active
Team: Athletics 1997-99.

Kerry Wood **N.L. Rookie**
Team: Cubs. **Position:** Pitcher.
6-5, 195. **B:** R. **T:** R.
Born: June 16, 1977.
Season: 13-6; 3.40 ERA; 233 SO.
Career: 13-6; 3.40 ERA; 233 SO; still active.
Team: Cubs 1998.

1999

Ivan Rodriguez **A.L. MVP**
Team: Rangers. **Position:** Catcher.
5-9, 205. **B:** R. **T:** R.
Born: November 30, 1971.
Season: .332 avg.; 35 HR; 113 RBIs; 25 SBs.
Career: .300 avg.; 144 HR; 621 RBIs; 60 SBs; still active.
Team: Rangers 1991-99.

Chipper Jones **N.L. MVP**
Team: Braves. **Position:** Third base.
6-4, 210. **B:** B. **T:** R.
Born: April 24, 1972.
Season: .319 avg.; 45 HR; 110 RBIs; 25 SBs.
Career: .301 avg.; 153 HR; 524 RBIs; 83 SBs; still active.
Team: Braves 1993-99.

Pedro Martinez **A.L. Cy Young**
Team: Red Sox.
Season: 23-4; 2.07 ERA; 313 SO.
(See 1997 N.L. Cy Young.)

Randy Johnson **N.L. Cy Young**
Team: Diamondbacks.
Season: 17-9; 2.48 ERA; 364 SO.
(See 1995 A.L. Cy Young.)

Carlos Beltran **A.L. Rookie**
Team: Royals. **Position:** Outfield.
6-0, 175. **B:** B. **T:** R.
Born: April 24, 1977.
Season: .293 avg.; 22 HR; 108 RBIs; 27 SBs.
Career: .291 avg.; 22 HR; 115 RBIs; 27 SBs; still active
Team: Royals 1998-99.

Scott Williamson **N.L. Rookie**
Team: Reds. **Position:** Pitcher.
6-2, 210. **B:** R. **T:** R.
Born: February 17, 1976.
Season: .12-7, 2.41 ERA, 107 SO; 19 saves.
Career: .12-7; 2.41 ERA, 107 SO; 19 saves.
Team: Reds 1999.

2000

Jason Giambi **A.L. MVP**
Team: Athletics. **Position:** First baseman.
6-3, 235 **B:** L. **T:** R.
Born: January 8, 1971.

Season: .333 avg.; 43 HR; 137 RBIs.
Career: .302 avg.; 149 HRs; 555 RBIs.
Teams: Athletics 1995-2000.

JEFF KENT — N.L. MVP

6-1, 205 **B:** R. **T:** R.
Team: Giants. **Position:** Second base.
Born: March 7, 1968.
Season: .334 avg.; 33 HR; 125 RBIs.
Career: .284 avg.; 194 HRs; 793 RBIs.
Teams: Blue Jays 1992; Mets 1992-96; Indians 1996; Giants 1997-2000.

PEDRO MARTINEZ — A.L. CY YOUNG

Team: Red Sox.
Season: 18-6; 1.74 ERA; 284 SO.
(See 1997 N.L. Cy Young.)

RANDY JOHNSON — N.L. CY YOUNG

Team: Diamondbacks.
Season: 19-7; 2.64 ERA; 347 SO.
(See 1995 A.L. Cy Young.)

KAZUHIRO SASAKI — A.L. ROOKIE

Team: Mariners. **Position:** Pitcher.
6-4, 209 **B:** R. **T:** R.
Born: February 22, 1968.
Season: 2-5; 3.16 ERA; 37 saves.
Career: 2-5; 3.16 ERA; 37 saves.
Team: Mariners 2000.

RAFAEL FURCAL — N.L. ROOKIE

Team: Braves. **Position:** Second base, shortstop.
5-10, 165 **B:** B. **T:** R.
Born: August 24, 1980.
Season: .294 avg.; 4 HR; 37 RBIs; 40 SB.
Career: .294 avg.; 4 HR; 37 RBIs; 40 SB.
Team: Braves 2000.

San Francisco Giants second baseman Jeff Kent.

2001 Prominent Faces

Players

Balltimore Orioles' outfielder Albert Belle.

Batters

Bobby Abreu — **Phillies**
6-0, 197 **B:** L. **T:** R.
Position: Outfield.
Born: March 11, 1974.
2000 season: .316 avg.; 25 HR; 79 RBIs.
Career: .313 avg.; 65 HR; 273 RBIs.
Teams: Astros 1996-97; Phillies 1998-2000.

Benny Agbayani — **Mets**
5-11, 225 **B:** R. **T:** R.
Position: Outfield.
Born: December 28, 1971.
2000 season: .289 avg.; 15 HR; 60RBIs.
Career: .284 avg.; 29 HR; 102 RBIs.
Teams: Mets 1998-2000.

Edgardo Alfonzo — **Mets**
5-11, 187 **B:** R. **T:** R.
Position: Second base.
Born: November 8, 1973.
2000 season: .324 avg.; 25 HR; 94 RBIs.
Career: .296 avg.; 87 HR; 433 RBIs.
Teams: Mets 1995-2000.

Roberto Alomar — **Indians**
6-0, 185 B:B. T:R.
Position: Second base.
Born: February 5, 1968.
2000 season: .310 avg.; 19 HR; 89 RBIs.
Career: .304 avg.; 170 HR; 918 RBIs.
Teams: Padres 1988-90; Blue Jays 1991-95; Orioles 1996-98; Indians 1999-2000.

Sandy Alomar Jr. — **White Sox**
6-5, 220 B:R. T:R.
Position: Catcher.
2000 season: .289 avg.; 7 HR; 42 RBIs.
Awards: See A.L. Rookie of the Year 1990.

Moises Alou — **Astros**
6-3, 195 **B:** R. **T:** R.
Position: Outfield.
Born: July 3, 1966.
2000 season: .355 avg.; 30 HR; 114 RBIs.
Career: .303 avg.; 175 HR; 726 RBIs.
Teams: Pirates 1990; Expos 1990, 1992-96; Marlins 1997; Astros 1998-2000.

Brady Anderson — **Orioles**
6-1, 190 **B:** L. **T:** L.
Position: Outfield.
Born: January 18, 1964.
2000 season: .257 avg.; 19 HR; 50 RBIs; 16 SB.
Career: .261 avg.; 201 HR; 711 RBIs; 299 SB.
Teams: Red Sox 1988; Orioles 1988-2000.

Garret Anderson — **Angels**
6-3, 220 **B:** L. **T:** L.
Position: Outfield.
Born: June 30, 1972.
2000 season: .286 avg.; 35 HR; 117 RBIs.
Career: .297 avg.; 107 HR; 510 RBIs.
Teams: Angels 1994-2000.

Rich Aurilla — **Giants**
6-1, 185 **B:** R. **T:** R.
Position: Shortstop.
Born: September 2, 1971.
2000 season: .271 avg.; 20 HR; 79 RBIs.
Career: .270 avg.; 61 HR; 257 RBIs.
Teams: Giants 1995-2000.

Brad Ausmus — **Astros**
5-11, 195 **B:** R. **T:** R.
Position: Catcher.
Born: April 14, 1969.
2000 season: .266 avg.; 7 HR; 51 RBIs.
Career: .263 avg.; 48 HR; 299 RBIs.
Teams: Padres 1993-96; Tigers 1996, 1999-2000; Astros 1997-98.

Jeff Bagwell — **Astros**
Position: First base.
2000 season: .310 avg.; 47 HR; 132 RBIs.
Awards: See N.L. Rookie of the Year 1991; N.L. MVP 1994.

Harold Baines — **White Sox**
6-2, 195 **B:** L. **T:** L.
Position: Designated hitter.
Born: March 15, 1959.
2000 season: .254 avg.; 11 HR; 39 RBIs.
Career: .291 avg.; 384 HR; 1,622 RBIs.
Teams: White Sox 1980-89, 2000; Rangers 1989-90; Athletics 1990-92; Orioles 1993-95, 1997-2000; Indians 1999.

Tony Batista — **Blue Jays**
6-0, 185 **B:** R. **T:** R.
Position: Shortstop.
Born: December 9, 1973.
2000 season: .263 avg.; 41 HR; 114 RBIs.
Career: .267 avg.; 100 HR; 298 RBIs.
Teams: Athletics 1996-97; Diamondbacks 1998-99; Blue Jays 1999-2000.

Jay Bell — **Diamondbacks**
6-0, 184 **B:** R. **T:** R.
Position: Third base.
Born: December 11, 1965.
2000 season: .267 avg.; 18 HR; 68 RBIs.
Career: .269 avg.; 180 HR; 800 RBIs.
Teams: Indians 1986-88; 1989-96; Royals 1997; Diamondbacks 1998-2000.

Albert Belle — **Orioles**
6-2, 225 **B:** R. **T:** R.
Position: Outfield.
Born: August 25, 1966.
2000 season: .281 avg.; 23 HR; 103 RBIs.
Career: .295 avg.; 381 HR; 1,239 RBIs.
Teams: Indians 1989-96; White Sox 1997-98; Orioles 1999-2000.

Carlos Beltran — **Royals**
Position: Outfield.
2000 season: .247 avg.; 7 HR; 44 RBIs.
Awards: See A.L. Rookie of the Year 1999.

Adrian Beltre — **Dodgers**
5-11, 170 **B:** R. **T:** R.
Position: Third base.
Born: April 7, 1979.
2000 season: .290 avg.; 20 HR; 85 RBIs.
Career: .272 avg.; 42 HR; 174 RBIs.
Teams: Dodgers 1998-2000.

Lance Berkman — **Astros**
6-1, 205 **B:** B. **T:** R.
Position: Outfield.
Born: February 10, 1976.
2000 season: .297 avg.; 21 HR; 67 RBIs.
Career: .285 avg.; 25 HR; 82 RBIs.
Teams: Astros 1999-2000.

Dante Bichette — **Red Sox**
6-3, 238 **B:** R. **T:** R.
Position: Outfield.
Born: November 18, 1963.
2000 season: .294 avg.; 23 HR; 90 RBIs.
Career: .299 avg.; 262 HR; 1,092 RBIs.
Teams: Angels 1988-90; Brewers 1991-92; Rockies 1993-99; Reds 2000; Red Sox 2000.

Craig Biggio — **Astros**
5-11, 180 **B:** R. **T:** R.
Position: Second base.
Born: December 14, 1965
2000 season: .268 avg.; 8 HR; 35 RBIs.
Career: .291 avg.; 160 HR; 741 RBIs.
Teams: Astros 1988-2000.

Barry Bonds — **Giants**
Position: Outfield.
2000 season: .306 avg.; 49 HR; 106 RBIs.
Awards: See N.L. MVP 1990, 1992, 1993.

Aaron Boone — **Reds**
6-2, 200 **B:** R. **T:** R.
Position: Third base.
Born: March 9, 1973.
2000 season: .285 avg.; 12 HR; 43 RBIs.
Career: .280 avg.; 28 HR; 148 RBIs.
Teams: Reds 1997-2000.

Bret Boone — **Mariners**
5-10, 180 **B:** R. **T:** R.
Position: Second base.
Born: April 6, 1969.
2000 season: .251 avg.; 19 HR; 74 RBIs.
Career: .255 avg.; 125 HR; 536 RBIs.
Teams: Mariners 1992-93; Reds 1994-98; Braves 1999; Padres 2000.

Mike Bordick — **Orioles**
5-11, 175 **B:** R. **T:** R.
Position: Shortstop.
Born: July 21, 1965.
2000 season: .285 avg.; 20 HR; 80 RBIs.
Career: .264 avg.; 71 HR; 506 RBIs.

Teams: Athletics 1990-96; Orioles 1997-2000; Mets 2000.

RICO BROGNA **RED SOX**
6-2, 205 **B:** L. **T:** L.
Position: First base.
Born: April 18, 1970.
2000 season: .232 avg.; 2 HR; 21 RBIs.
Career: .270 avg.; 103 HR; 437 RBIs.
Teams: Tigers 1992; Mets 1994-96; Phillies 1997-2000; Red Sox 2000.

ADRIAN BROWN **PIRATES**
6-0, 185 **B:** B. **T:** R.
Position: Outfield.
Born: February 7, 1974.
2000 season: .315 avg.; 4 HR; 28 RBIs; 13 SB.
Career: .275 avg.; 9 HR; 60 RBIs; 30 SB.
Teams: Pirates 1997-2000.

JAY BUHNER **MARINERS**
6-3, 215 **B:** R. **T:** R.
Position: Outfield.
Born: August 13, 1964.
2000 season: .253 avg.; 26 HR; 82 RBIs.
Career: .254 avg.; 308 HR; 960 RBIs.
Teams: Yankees 1987-88; 1988-2000.

ELLIS BURKS **INDIANS**
6-2, 205 **B:** R. **T:** R.
Position: Outfield.
Born: September 11, 1964.
2000 season: .344 avg.; 24 HR; 96 RBIs.
Career: .293 avg.; 285 HR; 1012 RBIs.
Teams: Red Sox 1987-92; White Sox 1993; Rockies 1994-98; Giants 1998-2000.

JEROMY BURNITZ **BREWERS**
6-0, 205 **B:** L. **T:** R.
Position: Outfield.
Born: April 15, 1969.
2000 season: .232 avg.; 31 HR; 98 RBIs.
Career: .259 avg.; 154 HR; 504 RBIs.
Teams: Mets 1993-94; Indians 1995-96; Brewers 1996-2000.

PAT BURRELL **PHILLIES**
6-4, 222 **B:** R. **T:** R.
Position: Outfield.
Born: October 10, 1976.
2000 season: .260 avg.; 18 HR; 79 RBIs.
Career: .260 avg.; 18 HR; 79 RBIs.
Teams: Phillies 2000.

MIKE CAMERON **MARINERS**
6-2, 190 **B:** R. **T:** R.
Position: Outfield.
Born: January 8, 1973.
2000 season: .267 avg.; 19 HR; 78 RBIs.
Career: .248 avg.; 63 HR; 244 RBIs.
Teams: White Sox 1995-98; Reds 1999; Mariners 2000.

KEN CAMINITI **RANGERS**
Position: Third base.
2000 season: .303 avg.; 15 HR; 45 RBIs.
Awards: See N.L. MVP 1996.

SEAN CASEY **REDS**
6-4, 225 **B:** L. **T:** R.
Position: First base.
Born: July 2, 1974.
2000 season: .315 avg.; 20 HR; 85 RBIs.
Career: .312 avg.; 52 HR; 237 RBIs.
Teams: Indians 1997; Reds 1998-2000.

LUIS CASTILLO **MARLINS**
5-11, 175 **B:** B. **T:** R.
Position: Second base.
Born: September 12, 1975.
2000 season: .334 avg.; 2 HR; 17 RBIs.
Career: .289 avg.; 4 HR; 71 RBIs.
Teams: Marlins 1996-2000.

RODGER CEDENO **TIGERS**
6-1, 205 **B:** B. **T:** R.
Position: Outfield.
Born: August 16, 1974.
2000 season: .282 avg.; 6 HR; 26 RBIs.
Career: .277 avg.; 17 HR; 117 RBIs.
Teams: Dodgers 1995-98; Mets 1999; Astros 2000.

ERIC CHAVEZ **ATHLETICS**
6-0, 204 **B:** L. **T:** R.
Position: Third base.
Born: December 7, 1977.
2000 season: .277 avg.; 26 HR; 86 RBIs.
Career: .267 avg.; 39 HR; 142 RBIs.
Teams: Athletics 1998-2000.

JEFF CIRILLO **ROCKIES**
6-1, 195 **B:** R. **T:** R.
Position: Third base.
Born: September 23, 1969.
2000 season: .326 avg.; 11 HR; 115 RBIs.
Career: .311 avg.; 77 HR; 487 RBIs.
Teams: Brewers 1994-99; Rockies 2000.

JEFF CONINE **ORIOLES**
6-1, 220 **B:** R. **T:** R.
Position: Third base, first base.
Born: June 27, 1966.
2000 season: .284 avg.; 13 HR; 46 RBIs.
Career: .286 avg.; 132 HR; 597 RBIs.
Teams: Royals 1990, 1992, 1998; Marlins 1993-97; Orioles 1999-2000.

STEVE COX **DEVIL RAYS**
6-4, 222 **B:** L. **T:** L.
Position: First base, outfield.
Born: October 31, 1974.
2000 season: .283 avg.; 11 HR; 35 RBIs.
Career: .279 avg.; 11 HR; 35 RBIs.
Teams: Devil Rays 1999-2000.

DEVI CRUZ **TIGERS**
6-0, 184 **B:** R. **T:** R.
Position: Shortstop.
Born: November 6, 1975.
2000 season: .302 avg.; 10 HR; 82 RBIs.
Career: .274 avg.; 30 HR; 225 RBIs.
Teams: Tigers 1997-2000.

JOSE CRUZ JR. **BLUE JAYS**
6-0, 200 **B:** B. **T:** R.
Position: Outfield.
Born: April 19, 1974.
2000 season: .242 avg.; 31 HR; 76 RBIs.
Career: .245 avg.; 82 HR; 231 RBIs.
Teams: Marniers 1997; Blue Jays 1997-2000.

JOHNNY DAMON **ATHLETICS**
6-2, 190 **B:** L. **T:** L.
Position: Outfield.
Born: November 5, 1973.
2000 season: .327 avg.; 16 HR; 88 RBIs.
Career: .292 avg.; 65 HR; 352 RBIs.
Teams: Royals 1995-2000.

ERIC DAVIS **GIANTS**
6-3, 185 **B:** R. **T:** R.
Position: Outfield.
Born: May 29, 1962.
2000 season: .303 avg.; 6 HR; 40 RBIs.
Career: .271 avg.; 278 HR; 912 RBIs.
Teams: Reds 1984-91; Dodgers 1992-93; Tigers 1993-94; Orioles 1997-98; Cardinals 1999-2000.

CARLOS DELGADO **BLUE JAYS**
6-3, 225 **B:** L. **T:** R.
Position: First base.
Born: June 25, 1972.
2000 season: .344 avg.; 41 HR; 137 RBIs.
Career: .282 avg.; 190 HR; 604 RBIs.
Teams: Blue Jays 1993-2000.

Oakland Athletics outfielder Johnny Damon.

DELINO DESHIELDS **ORIOLES**
6-1, 175 **B:** L. **T:** R.
Position: Second base, outfield.
Born: January 15, 1969.
2000 season: .296 avg.; 10 HR; 86 RBIs; 37 SB.
Career: .272 avg.; 72 HR; 514 RBI; 430 SB.
Teams: Expos 1990-93; Dodgers 1994-96; Cardinals 1997-98; Orioles 1999-2000.

J.D. DREW **CARDINALS**
6-1, 195 **B:** L. **T:** R.
Position: Outfield.
Born: November 20, 1975.
2000 season: .295 avg.; 18 HR; 57 RBIs.
Career: .276 avg.; 36 HR; 109 RBIs.
Teams: Cardinals 1998-2000.

RAY DURHAM **WHITE SOX**
5-8, 170 **B:** B. **T:** R.
Position: Second base.
Born: November 30, 1971.
2000 season: .280 avg.; 17 HR; 75 RBIs.
Career: .278 avg.; 77 HR; 371 RBIs.
Teams: White Sox 1995-2000.

JERMAINE DYE **ROYALS**
6-5, 220 **B:** R. **T:** R.
Position: Outfield.
Born: January 28, 1974.
2000 season: .321 avg.; 33 HR; 118 RBIs.
Career: .286 avg.; 84 HR; 319 RBIs.
Teams: Braves 1996; Royals 1997-2000.

DAMION EASLEY **TIGERS**
5-11, 185 **B:** R. **T:** R.
Position: Second base.
Born: November 11, 1969.
2000 season: .259 avg.; 14 HR; 58 RBIs.
Career: .258 avg.; 100 HR; 411 RBIs.
Teams: Angels 1992-96; Tigers 1996-2000.

JIM EDMONDS **CARDINALS**
6-1, 212 **B:** L. **T:** L.
Position: Outfield.
Born: June 27, 1970.
2000 season: .295 avg.; 42 HR; 108 RBIs.

Anaheim Angels third baseman Troy Glaus.

Career: .291 avg.; 163 HR; 516 RBIs.
Teams: Angels 1993-99; Cardinals 2000.

JUAN ENCARNACION **TIGERS**
6-3, 187 **B:** R. **T:** R.
Position: Outfield.
Born: March 8, 1976.
2000 season: .289 avg.; 14 HR; 72 RBIs.
Career: .279 avg.; 41 HR; 172 RBIs.
Teams: Tigers 1997-2000.

CARL EVERETT **RED SOX**
6-0, 215 **B:** B. **T:** R.
Position: Outfield.
Born: June 3, 1971.
2000 season: .300 avg.; 34 HR; 108 RBIs.
Career: .282 avg.; 103 HR; 425 RBIs.
Teams: Marlins 1993-94; Mets 1995-97; Astros 1998-99; Red Sox 2000.

STEVE FINLEY **DIAMONDBACKS**
6-2, 180 **B:** L. **T:** L.
Position: Outfield.
Born: March 12, 1965.
2000 season: .280 avg.; 35 HR; 96 RBIs.
Career: .275 avg.; 188 HR; 745 RBIs.
Teams: Orioles 1989-90; Astros 1991-94; Padres 1995-98; Diamondbacks 1999-2000.

DARRIN FLETCHER **BLUE JAYS**
6-2, 205 **B:** L. **T:** R.
Position: Catcher.
Born: October 3, 1966.
2000 season: .320 avg.; 20 HR; 58 RBIs.
Career: .276 avg.; 110 HR; 505 RBIs.
Teams: Dodgers 1989-90; Phillies 1990-91; Expos 1992-97; Blue Jays 1998-2000.

CLIFF FLOYD **MARLINS**
6-4, 235 **B:** L. **T:** R.
Position: Outfield.
Born: December 5, 1972.
2000 season: .300 avg.; 22 HR; 91 RBIs.
Career: .275 avg.; 73 HR; 326 RBIs.
Teams: Expos 1993-96; Marlins 1997-2000.

TRAVIS FRYMAN **INDIANS**
6-1, 195 **B:** R. **T:** R.
Position: Third base.
Born: March 25, 1969.
2000 season: .321 avg.; 22 HR; 106 RBIs.
Career: .279 avg.; 208 HRs; 929 RBIs.
Teams: Tigers 1990-97; Indians 1998-2000.

BRAD FULLMER **BLUE JAYS**
6-0, 215 **B:** L. **T:** R.
Position: First base.
Born: January 17, 1975.
2000 season: .295 avg.; 32 HR; 104 RBIs.
Career: .282 avg.; 57 HRs; 232 RBIs.
Teams: Expos 1997-99; Blue Jays 2000.

RAFAEL FURCAL **BRAVES**
Position: Second base, shortstop.
2000 season: .295 avg.; 4 HR; 37 RBIs.
Awards: See N.L. Rookie of the Year 2000.

ANDRES GALARRAGA **RANGERS**
6-3, 235 **B:** R. **T:** R.
Position: First base.
Born: June 18, 1961.
2000 season: .302 avg.; 28 HR; 100 RBIs.
Career: .291 avg.; 360 HR; 1,272 RBIs.
Teams: Expos 1985-91; Cardinals 1992; Rockies 1993-97; Braves 1998-2000.

NOMAR GARCIAPARRA **RED SOX**
Position: Shortstop.
2000 season: .372 avg.; 21 HR; 96 RBIs.
Awards: See A.L. Rookie of the Year 1997.

JASON GIAMBI **ATHLETICS**
Position: First base.
2000 season: .333 avg.; 43 HR; 137 RBIs.
Awards: See N.L. MVP 2000.

BRIAN GILES **PIRATES**
5-10, 200 **B:** L. **T:** L.
Position: Outfield.
Born: January 20, 1971.
2000 season: .315 avg.; 35 HR; 123 RBIs.
Career: .301 avg.; 113 HR; 395 RBIs.
Teams: Indians 1995-98; Pirates 1999-2000.

TROY GLAUS **ANGELS**
6-5, 229 **B:** R. **T:** R.
Position: Third base.
Born: August 3, 1976.
2000 season: .284 avg.; 47 HR; 102 RBIs.
Career: .256 avg.; 77 HR; 204 RBIs.
Teams: Angels 1998-2000.

ALEX GONZALEZ **BLUE JAYS**
6-0, 195 **B:** R. **T:** R.
Position: Shortstop.
Born: April 8, 1973.
2000 season: .252 avg.; 15 HR; 69 RBIs.
Career: .243 avg.; 66 HR; 274 RBIs.
Teams: Blue Jays 1994-2000.

ALEX GONZALEZ **MARLINS**
6-0, 170 **B:** R. **T:** R.
Position: Shortstop.
Born: February 15, 1977.
2000 season: .200 avg.; 7 HR; 42 RBIs.
Career: .238 avg.; 24 HR; 108 RBIs.
Teams: Marlins 1998-2000.

JUAN GONZALEZ **INDIANS**
Position: Outfield, designated hitter.
2000 season: .289 avg.; 22 HR; 67 RBIs.
Awards: See A.L. MVP 1996, 1998.

LUIS GONZALEZ **DIAMONDBACKS**
6-2, 190 **B:** L. **T:** R.
Position: Outfield.
Born: September 2, 1967.
2000 season: .311 avg.; 31 HR; 114 RBIs.
Career: .281 avg.; 164 HR; 775 RBIs.
Teams: Astros 1990-95, 1997; Cubs 1995-96; Tigers 1998; Diamondbacks 1999-2000.

MARK GRACE **DIAMONDBACKS**
6-2, 200 **B:** L. **T:** L.
Position: First base.
Born: June 28, 1964.
2000 season: .280 avg.; 11 HR; 82 RBIs.
Career: .308 avg.; 148 HR; 1004 RBIs.
Teams: Cubs 1988-2000.

SHAWN GREEN **DODGERS**
6-4, 195 **B:** L. **T:** L.
Position: Outfield.
Born: November 10, 1972.
2000 season: .269 avg.; 24 HR; 99 RBIs.
Career: .282 avg.; 143 HR; 475 RBIs.
Teams: Blue Jays 1993-99; Dodgers 2000.

RUSTY GREER **RANGERS**
6-0, 190 **B:** L. **T:** L.
Position: Outfield.
Born: January 21, 1969.
2000 season: .297 avg.; 8 HR; 65 RBIs.
Career: .307 avg.; 111 HR; 568 RBIs.
Teams: Rangers 1994-2000.

BEN GRIEVE **DEVIL RAYS**
6-4, 230 **B:** L. **T:** R.
Position: Outfield.
Born: May 4, 1976.
2000 season: .279 avg; 27 HR; 104 RBIs.
Career: .280 avg.; 76 HR; 303 RBIs.
Teams: Athletics 1997-2000.

KEN GRIFFEY JR. **REDS**
Position: Outfield.
2000 season: .271 avg.; 40 HR; 118 RBIs.
Awards: See A.L. MVP 1997.

MARK GRUDZIELANEK **DODGERS**
6-1, 185 **B:** R. **T:** R.
Position: Shortstop/second base.
Born: June 30, 1970.
2000 season: .279 avg.; 7 HR; 49 RBIs.
Career: .286 avg.; 35 HR; 277 RBIs.
Teams: Expos 1995-98; Dodgers 1998-2000.

VLADIMIR GUERRERO **EXPOS**
6-3, 205 **B:** R. **T:** R.
Position: Outfield.
Born: February 9, 1976.
2000 season: .345 avg.; 44 HR; 123 RBIs.
Career: .322 avg.; 136 HR; 404 RBIs.
Teams: Expos 1996-2000.

CRISTIAN GUZMAN **TWINS**
6-0, 195 **B:** B. **T:** R.
Position: Shortstop.
Born: March 21, 1978.
2000 season: .247 avg.; 8 HR; 54 RBIs.
Career: .239 avg.; 9 HR; 80 RBIs.
Teams: Twins 1999-2000.

TONY GWYNN **PADRES**
5-11, 225 **B:** L. **T:** L.
Position: Outfield.
Born: May 9, 1960.
2000 season: .323 avg.; 1 HR; 17 RBIs.
Career: .338 avg.; 134 HR; 1,121 RBIs.
Teams: Padres 1982-2000.

TODD HELTON **ROCKIES**
6-2, 206 **B:** L. **T:** L.
Position: First base.
Born: August 20, 1973.
2000 season: .372 avg.; 42 HR; 147 RBIs.
Career: .334 avg.; 107 HR; 368 RBIs.
Teams: Rockies 1997-2000.

RICKY HENDERSON
Position: Outfield.
2000 season: .233 avg.; 4 HR; 32 RBIs.
Awards: See A.L. MVP 1990.

RAMON HERNANDEZ **ATHLETICS**
6-0, 227 **B:** R. **T:** R.
Position: Catcher.
Born: May 20, 1976.
2000 season: .241 avg.; 14 HR; 62 RBIs.
Career: .250 avg.; 17 HR; 83 RBIs.
Teams: Oakland 1999-2000.

Richard Hidalgo **Astros**
6-3, 190 **B:** R. **T:** R.
Position: Outfield.
Born: July 2, 1975.
2000 season: .314 avg.; 44 HR; 122 RBIs.
Career: .284 avg.; 68 HR; 219 RBIs.
Teams: Astros 1997-2000.

Bobby Higginson **Tigers**
5-11, 195 **B:** L. **T:** R.
Position: Outfield.
Born: August 18, 1970.
2000 season: .300 avg.; 30 HR; 102 RBIs.
Career: .281 avg.; 134 HR; 458 RBIs.
Teams: Tigers 1995-2000.

Glenallen Hill **Yankees**
6-3, 230 **B:** R. **T:** R.
Position: Outfield.
Born: March 22, 1965.
2000 season: .293 avg.; 27 HR; 58 RBIs.
Career: .273 avg.; 185 HR; 584 RBIs.
Teams: Blue Jays 1989-91; Indians 1991-93; Cubs 1993-94, 1998-2000; Giants 1995-97; Mariners 1998; Yankees 2000.

Todd Hundley **Cubs**
5-11, 199 **B:** B. **T:** R.
Position: Catcher.
Born: May 27, 1969.
2000 season: .284 avg.; 24 HR; 70 RBIs.
Career: .240 avg.; 172 HR; 522 RBIs.
Teams: Mets 1991-98; Dodgers 1999-2000.

Brian L. Hunter **Phillies**
6-3, 180 **B:** R. **T:** R.
Position: Outfield.
Born: March 5, 1971.
2000 season: .267 avg.; 1 HR; 14 RBIs; 19 SB.
Career: .264 avg.; 20 HR; 192 RBIs; 241 SB.
Teams: Astros 1994-96; Tigers 1997-99; Mariners 1999-2000.

Geoff Jenkins **Brewers**
6-1, 204 **B:** L. **T:** R.
Position: Outfield.
Born: July 21, 1974.
2000 season: .303 avg.; 34 HR; 94 RBIs.
Career: .291 avg.; 64 HR; 204 RBIs.
Teams: Brewers 1998-2000.

Derek Jeter **Yankees**
Position: Shortstop.
2000 season: .339 avg.; 15 HR; 73 RBIs.
Awards: See A.L. Rookie of the Year 1996.

Charles Johnson **Marlins**
6-2, 220 **B:** R. **T:** R.
Position: Outfield.
Born: July 20, 1971.
2000 season: .304 avg.; 31 HR; 91 RBIs.
Career: .249 avg.; 110 HR; 346 RBIs.
Teams: Marlins 1994-98; Dodgers 1998; Orioles 1999-2000; White Sox 2000.

Andruw Jones **Braves**
6-1, 210 **B:** R. **T:** R.
Position: Outfield.
Born: April 23, 1977.
2000 season: .303 avg.; 36 HR; 104 RBIs.
Career: .272 avg.; 116 HR; 361 RBIs.
Teams: Braves 1996-2000.

Chipper Jones **Braves**
Position: Third base.
2000 season: .311 avg.; 36 HR; 111 RBIs.
Awards: See N.L. MVP 1999.

Brian Jordan **Braves**
6-1, 205 **B:** R. **T:** R.
Position: Outfield.
Born: March 29, 1967.
2000 season: .264 avg.; 17 HR; 77 RBIs.
Career: .286 avg.; 124 HR; 559 RBIs.
Teams: Cardinals 1992-98; Braves 1999-2000.

David Justice **Yankees**
Position: Outfield.
2000 season: .286 avg.; 41 HR; 118 RBIs.
Awards: See N.L. Rookie of the Year 1990.

Gabe Kapler **Rangers**
6-2, 208 **B:** R. **T:** R.
Position: Outfield.
Born: August 31, 1975.
2000 season: .302 avg.; 14 HR; 66 RBIs.
Career: .272 avg.; 32 HR; 115 RBIs.
Teams: Tigers 1998-99; Rangers 2000.

Eric Karros **Dodgers**
Position: First base.
2000 season: .250 avg.; 31 HR; 106 RBIs.
Awards: See N.L. Rookie of the Year 1992.

Jason Kendall **Pirates**
6-0, 190 **B:** R. **T:** R.
Position: Catcher.
Born: June 26, 1974.
2000 season: .320 avg.; 14 HR; 58 RBIs.
Career: .314 avg.; 45 HR; 265 RBIs.
Teams: Pirates 1996-2000.

Adam Kennedy **Angels**
6-1, 180 **B:** L. **T:** R.
Position: Second base.
Born: January 10, 1976.
2000 season: .266 avg.; 9 HR; 72 RBIs.
Career: .264 avg.; 10 HR; 88 RBIs.
Teams: Cardinals 1999; Angels 2000.

Jeff Kent **Giants**
Position: Second base.
2000 season: .334 avg.; 33 HR; 125 RBIs.
Awards: See N.L. MVP 2000.

Ryan Klesko **Padres**
6-3, 220 **B:** L. **T:** L.
Position: First base, outfield.
Born: June 12, 1971.
2000 season: .283 avg.; 26 HR; 92 RBIs.
Career: .282 avg.; 165 HR; 542 RBIs.
Teams: Braves 1992-99; Padres 2000.

Chuck Knoblauch **Yankees**
Position: Second base.
2000 season: .283 avg.; 5 HR; 26 RBIs.
Awards: See A.L. Rookie of the Year 1991.

Paul Konerko **White Sox**
6-3, 211 **B:** R. **T:** R.
Position: Third base.
Born: March 5, 1976.
2000 season: .298 avg.; 21 HR; 97 RBIs.
Career: .282 avg.; 52 HR; 207 RBIs.
Teams: Dodgers 1997-98; Reds 1998; White Sox 1999-2000.

Ray Lankford **Cardinals**
5-11, 198 **B:** L. **T:** L.
Position: Outfield.
Born: June 5, 1967.
2000 season: .253 avg.; 26 HR; 65 RBIs.
Career: .276 avg.; 207 HR; 768 RBIs.
Teams: Cardinals 1990-2000.

Barry Larkin **Reds**
Position: Shortstop.
2000 season: .313 avg.; 11 HR; 41 RBIs.
Awards: See N.L. MVP 1995.

Matt Lawton **Twins**
5-10, 186 **B:** L. **T:** R.
Position: Outfield.
Born: November 3, 1971.
2000 season: .305 avg.; 13 HR; 88 RBIs.
Career: .274 avg.; 62 HR; 333 RBIs.
Teams: Twins 1995-2000.

Pittsburgh Pirates catcher Jason Kendall.

Carlos Lee **White Sox**
6-2, 220 **B:** R. **T:** R.
Position: Outfield.
Born: June 20, 1976.
2000 season: .301 avg.; 24 HR; 92 RBIs.
Career: .297 avg.; 40 HR; 176 RBIs.
Teams: White Sox 1999-2000.

Travis Lee **Phillies**
6-3, 210 **B:** L. **T:** L.
Position: First base.
Born: May 26, 1975.
2000 season: .235 avg.; 9 HR; 54 RBIs.
Career: .250 avg.; 40 HR; 176 RBIs.
Teams: Diamondbacks 1998-2000; Phillies 2000.

Mike Lieberthal **Phillies**
6-0, 186 **B:** R. **T:** R.
Position: Catcher.
Born: January 18, 1972.
2000 season: .278 avg.; 15 HR; 71 RBIs.
Career: .270 avg.; 82 HR; 321 RBIs.
Teams: Phillies 1994-2000.

Kenny Lofton **Indians**
6-0, 180 **B:** L. **T:** L.
Position: Outfield.
Born: May 31, 1967.
2000 season: .278 avg.; 15 HR; 73 RBIs.
Career: .306 avg.; 78 HR; 485 RBIs.
Teams: Astros 1991; Indians 1992-96, 1998-2000; Braves 1997.

Terrence Long **Athletics**
6-1, 190 **B:** L. **T:** L.
Position: Outfield.
Born: February 29, 1976.
2000 season: .288 avg.; 18 HR; 80 RBIs.
Career: .286 avg.; 18 HR; 80 RBIs.
Teams: Mets 1999; Athletics 2000.

Javy Lopez **Braves**
6-3, 200 **B:** R. **T:** R.
Position: Catcher.
Born: November 5, 1970.
2000 season: .287 avg.; 24 HR; 89 RBIs.
Career: .290 avg.; 143 HR; 467 RBIs.
Teams: Braves 1992-2000.

Mark Loretta **Brewers**
6-0, 189 **B:** R. **T:** R.

Seattle Mariners designated hitter Edgar Martinez.

Position: Shortstop.
Born: August 14, 1971.
2000 season: .281 avg.; 7 HR; 40 RBIs.
Career: .292 avg.; 25 HR; 224 RBIs.
Teams: Brewers 1995-2000.

AL MARTIN — **MARINERS**
6-2, 210 **B:** L. **T:** L.
Position: Outfield.
Born: November 24, 1967.
2000 season: .285 avg; 15 HR; 36 RBIs.
Career: .280 avg.; 122 HR; 417 RBIs.
Teams: Pirates 1992-99; Mariners 2000.

EDGAR MARTINEZ — **MARINERS**
5-11, 200 **B:** R. **T:** R.
Position: Designated hitter.
Born: January 2, 1963.
2000 season: .324 avg.; 37 HR; 145 RBIs.
Career: .320 avg.; 235 HR; 925 RBIs.
Teams: Mariners 1987-2000.

TINO MARTINEZ — **YANKEES**
6-2, 210 **B:** L. **T:** R.
Position: First base.
Born: December 7, 1967.
2000 season: .258 avg.; 16 HR; 91 RBIs.
Career: .273 avg.; 229 HR; 889 RBIs.
Teams: Mariners 1990-95; Yankees 1996-2000.

MIKE MATHENY — **CARDINALS**
6-3, 205 **B:** R. **T:** R.
Position: Catcher.
Born: September 22, 1970.
2000 season: .261 avg,; 6 HR; 47 RBIs.
Career: .237 avg.; 28 HR; 192 RBIs.
Teams: Brewers 1994-98; Blue Jays 1999; Cardinals 2000.

FRED MCGRIFF — **DEVIL RAYS**
6-3, 215 **B:** L. **T:** L.
Position: First base, designated hitter.
Born: October 31, 1963.
2000 season: .277 avg.; 27 HR; 106 RBIs.
Career: .286 avg.; 417 HR; 1,298 RBIs.
Teams: Blue Jays 1986-90; Padres 1991-93; Braves 1993-97; Devil Rays 1998-2000.

MARK MCGWIRE — **CARDINALS**
Position: First base.
2000 season: .305 avg.; 32 HR; 73 RBIs.
Awards: See A.L. Rookie of the Year 1987.

MITCH MELUSKEY — **TIGERS**
6-0, 185 **B:** B. **T:** R.
Position: Catcher.
Born: September 18, 1973.
2000 season: .300 avg.; 14 HR; 69 RBIs.
Career: .291 avg.; 15 HR; 72 RBIs.
Teams: Astros 1998-2000.

BENJI MOLINA — **ANGELS**
5-11, 200 **B:** R. **T:** R.
Position: Catcher.
Born: July 20, 1974.
2000 season: .281 avg.; 14 HR; 71 RBIs.
Career: .277 avg.; 15 HR; 81 RBIs.
Teams: Angels 1998-2000.

RAUL MONDESI — **BLUE JAYS**
Position: Outfield.
2000 season: .271 avg.; 24 HR; 67 RBIs.
Awards: See N.L. Rookie of the Year 1994.

WARREN MORRIS — **PIRATES**
5-11, 175 **B:** L. **T:** R.
Position: Second base.
Born: January 11, 1974.
2000 season: .259 avg.; 3 HR; 43 RBIs.
Career: .273 avg.; 18 HR; 116 RBIs.
Teams: Pirates 1999-2000.

PHIL NEVIN — **PADRES**
6-2, 231 **B:** R. **T:** R.
Position: Third base, catcher.
Born: January 19, 1971.
2000 season: .303 avg.; 31 HR; 107 RBIs.
Career: .262 avg.; 82 HR; 286 RBIs.
Teams: Astros 1995; Tigers 1995-97; Angels 1998; Padres 1999-2000.

TROY O'LEARY — **RED SOX**
6-0, 198 **B:** L. **T:** L.
Position: Outfield.
Born: August 4, 1969.
2000 season: .261 avg.; 13 HR; 70 RBIs.
Career: .280 avg.; 106 HR; 476 RBIs.
Teams: Brewers 1993-94; Red Sox 1995-2000.

JOHN OLERUD — **MARINERS**
6-5, 220 **B:** L. **T:** L.
Position: First base.
Born: August 5, 1968.
2000 season: .285 avg.; 14 HR; 103 RBIs.
Career: .299 avg.; 186 HR; 865 RBIs.
Teams: Blue Jays 1989-96; Mets 1997-99; Mariners 2000.

PAUL O'NEILL — **YANKEES**
6-4, 215 **B:** L. **T:** L.
Position: Outfield.
Born: February 25, 1963.
2000 season: .283 avg.; 18 HR; 100 RBIs.
Career: .289 avg.; 260 HR; 1,199 RBIs.
Teams: Reds 1985-92; Yankees 1993-2000.

MAGGLIO ORDONEZ — **WHITE SOX**
6-0, 200 **B:** R. **T:** R.
Position: Outfield.
Born: January 24, 1974.
2000 season: .315 avg.; 32 HR; 126 RBIs.
Career: .301 avg.; 80 HR; 319 RBIs.
Teams: White Sox 1997-2000.

REY ORDONEZ — **METS**
5-9, 159 **B:** R. **T:** R.
Position: Shortstop.
Born: November 11, 1972.
2000 season: .188 avg.; 0 HR; 9 RBIs.
Career: .243 avg.; 4 HR; 174 RBIs.
Teams: Mets 1996-2000.

DAVID ORTIZ — **TWINS**
6-4, 230 **B:** L. **T:** L.
Position: First base.
Born: November 18, 1975.
2000 season: .282 avg.; 10 HR; 63 RBIs.
Career: .276 avg.; 20 HR; 115 RBIs.
Teams: Twins 1997-2000.

ERIC OWENS — **PADRES**
6-0, 198 **B:** R. **T:** R.
Position: Outfield.
Born: February 3, 1971.
2000 season: .293 avg.; 6 HR; 51 RBIs.
Career: .265 avg.; 16 HR; 129 RBIs.
Teams: Reds 1995-97; Brewers 1998; Padres 1999-2000.

RAFAEL PALMEIRO — **RANGERS**
6-0, 190 **B:** L. **T:** L.
Position: Designated hitter, first base.
Born: September 24, 1964.
2000 season: .288 avg.; 39 HR; 120 RBIs.
Career: .296 avg.; 400 HR; 1,347 RBIs.
Teams: Cubs 1986-88; Rangers 1989-93, 1999-2000; Orioles 1994-98.

DEAN PALMER — **TIGERS**
6-1, 210 **B:** R. **T:** R.
Position: Third base.
Born: December 27, 1968.
2000 season: .256 avg.; 29 HR; 102 RBIs.
Career: .255 avg.; 264 HR; 803 RBIs.
Teams: Rangers 1989-97; Royals 1997-98; Tigers 1999-2000.

JAY PAYTON — **METS**
5-10, 185 **B:** R. **T:** R.
Position: Outfield.
Born: November 22, 1972.
2000 season: .291 avg.; 17 HR; 62 RBIs.
Career: .292 avg.; 17 HR; 63 RBIs.
Teams: Mets 1998-2000.

TIMO PEREZ — **METS**
5-9, 167 **B:** L. **T:** L.
Position: Outfield.
Born: April 8, 1977.
2000 season: .286 avg.; 1 HR; 3 RBIs.
Career: .286 avg.; 1 HR; 3 RBIs.
Teams: Mets 2000.

BEN PETRICK — **ROCKIES**
6-0, 200 **B:** R. **T:** R.
Position: Catcher.
Born: April 7, 1977.
2000 season: .322 avg.; 3 HR; 20 RBIs.
Career: .322 avg.; 7 HR; 32 RBIs.
Teams: Rockies 1999-2000.

MIKE PIAZZA — **METS**
Position: Catcher.
2000 season: .324 avg.; 38 HR; 113 RBIs.
Awards: See N.L. Rookie of the Year 1993.

JUAN PIERRE — **ROCKIES**
6-0, 165 **B:** L. **T:** L.
Position: Outfielder.
Born: August 14, 1977.
2000 season: .310 avg.; 0 HR; 20 RBIs; 7 SB.
Career: .310 avg.; 0 HR; 20 RBIs; 7 SB.
Teams: Rockies 2000.

JORGE POSADA — **YANKEES**
6-2, 205 **B:** B. **T:** R.
Position: Catcher.
Born: August 17, 1971.
2000 season: .287 avg.; 28 HR; 86 RBIs.
Career: .265 avg.; 63 HR; 231 RBIs.
Teams: Yankees 1995-2000.

MARK QUINN — **ROYALS**
6-1, 195 **B:** R. **T:** R.
Position: Outfield.

Born: May 21, 1974.
2000 season: .294 avg.; 20 HR; 78 RBIs.
Career: .298 avg.; 26 HR; 96 RBIs.
Teams: Royals 1999-2000.

MANNY RAMIREZ — **RED SOX**
6-0, 215 **B:** R. **T:** R.
Position: Outfield.
Born: May 30, 1972.
2000 season: .351 avg.; 38 HR; 122 RBIs.
Career: .313 avg.; 236 HR; 804 RBIs.
Teams: Indians 1993-2000.

JOE RANDA — **ROYALS**
5-11, 190 **B:** R. **T:** R.
Position: Third base.
Born: December 18, 1969.
2000 season: .304 avg.; 15 HR; 106 RBIs.
Career: .293 avg.; 54 HR; 352 RBIs.
Teams: Royals 1995-96, 1999-2000; Pirates 1997; Tigers 1998.

POKEY REESE — **REDS**
5-11, 180 **B:** R. **T:** R.
Position: Second base.
Born: June 10, 1973.
2000 season: .255 avg.; 12 HR; 46 RBIs.
Career: .257 avg.; 27 HR; 140 RBIs.
Teams: Reds 1997-2000.

EDGAR RENTERIA — **CARDINALS**
6-1, 180 **B:** R. **T:** R.
Position: Shortstop.
Born: August 7, 1975.
2000 season: .278 avg.; 16 HR; 76 RBIs.
Career: .283 avg.; 39 HR; 253 RBIs.
Teams: Marlins 1996-98; Cardinals 1999-2000.

CHRIS RICHARD — **ORIOLES**
6-2, 190 **B:** L. **T:** L.
Position: First base.
Born: June 7, 1974.
2000 season: .266 avg.; 14 HR; 37 RBIs.
Career: .265 avg.; 14 HR; 37 RBIs.
Teams: Cardinals 2000; Orioles 2000.

CAL RIPKEN — **ORIOLES**
Position: Third base.
2000 season: .256 avg.; 15 HR; 56 RBIs.
Awards: See A.L. Rookie of the Year 1982; A.L. MVP 1983, 1991.

ALEX RODRIGUEZ — **RANGERS**
6-3, 190 **B:** R. **T:** R.
Position: Shortstop.
Born: July 27, 1975.
2000 season: .316 avg.; 41 HR; 132 RBIs.
Career: .309 avg.; 189 HR; 595 RBIs.
Teams: Mariners 1994-2000.

HENRY RODRIGUEZ
6-2, 225 **B:** L. **T:** L.
Position: Outfield.
Born: November 8, 1967.
2000 season: .256 avg.; 20 HR; 61 RBIs.
Career: .261 avg.; 160 HR; 520 RBIs.
Teams: Dodgers 1992-95; Expos 1995-97; Cubs 1998-2000.

IVAN RODRIGUEZ — **RANGERS**
Position: Catcher.
2000 season: .347 avg.; 27 HR; 83 RBIs.
Awards: See A.L. MVP 1999.

SCOTT ROLEN — **PHILLIES**
Position: Third base.
2000 season: .298 avg.; 26 HR; 89 RBIs.
Awards: See N.L. Rookie of the Year 1997.

TIM SALMON — **ANGELS**
Position: Outfield.
2000 season: .290 avg.; 34 HR; 97 RBIs.
Awards: See A.L. Rookie of the Year 1993.

DAVID SEGUI — **ORIOLES**
6-1, 202 **B:** B. **T:** L.
Position: First base.
Born: July 19, 1966.
2000 season: .334 avg.; 19 HR; 103 RBIs.
Career: .292 avg.; 121 HR; 590 RBIs.
Teams: Orioles 1990-93; Mets 1994-95; Expos 1995-97; Mariners 1998-99; Blue Jays 1999-2000; Indians 2000.

RICHIE SEXSON — **BREWERS**
6-7, 225 **B:** R. **T:** R.
Position: First base, outfield.
Born: December 29, 1974.
2000 season: .272 avg.; 30 HR; 91 RBIs.
Career: .271 avg.; 72 HR; 242 RBIs.
Teams: Indians 1997-2000; Brewers 2000.

GARY SHEFFIELD — **DODGERS**
5-11, 205 **B:** R. **T:** R.
Position: Outfield.
Born: November 18, 1968.
2000 season: .325 avg.; 43 HR; 109 RBIs.
Career: .293 avg.; 279 HR; 916 RBIs.
Teams: Brewers 1988-91; Padres 1992-93; Marlins 1993-98; Dodgers 1998-2000.

CHRIS SINGLETON — **WHITE SOX**
6-2, 195 **B:** L. **T:** L.
Position: Outfield.
Born: August 15, 1972.
2000 season: .254 avg.; 11 HR; 62 RBIs.
Career: .277 avg.; 28 HR; 134 RBIs.
Teams: White Sox 1999-2000.

J.T. SNOW — **GIANTS**
6-2, 205 **B:** L. **T:** L.
Position: First base.
Born: February 26, 1968.
2000 season: .284 avg.; 19 HR; 96 RBIs.
Career: .266 avg.; 151 HR; 635 RBIs.
Teams: Yankees 1992; Angels 1993-96; Giants 1997-2000.

SAMMY SOSA — **CUBS**
Position: Outfield.
2000 season: .320 avg.; 50 HR; 138 RBIs.
Awards: See N.L. MVP 1998.

SHANNON STEWART — **BLUE JAYS**
6-1, 205 **B:** R. **T:** R.
Position: Outfield.
Born: February 25, 1974.
2000 season: .319 avg.; 21 HR; 69 RBIs.
Career: .297 avg.; 44 HR; 216 RBIs.
Teams: Blue Jays 1995-2000.

B.J. SURHOFF — **BRAVES**
6-1, 200 **B:** L. **T:** R.
Position: Outfield.
Born: August 4, 1964.
2000 season: .291 avg; 14 HR; 68 RBIs.
Career: .281 avg.; 160 HR; 961 RBIs.
Teams: Brewers 1987-95; Orioles 1996-2000; Braves 2000.

MIKE SWEENEY — **ROYALS**
6-2, 215 **B:** R. **T:** R.
Position: First base, designated hitter.
Born: July 22, 1973.
2000 season: .333 avg.; 29 HR; 144 RBIs.
Career: .302 avg.; 70 HR; 336 RBIs.
Teams: Royals 1995-2000.

FERNANDO TATIS — **EXPOS**
5-10, 175 **B:** R. **T:** R.
Position: Third base.
Born: January 1, 1975.
2000 season: .253 avg.; 18 HR; 64 RBIs.
Career: .276 avg; 71 HR; 258 RBIs.
Teams: Rangers 1997-98; Cardinals 1998-2000.

EDDIE TAUBENSEE — **INDIANS**
6-3, 230 **B:** L. **T:** R.

Milwaukee Brewers first baseman Richie Sexson.

Position: Catcher.
Born: October 31, 1968.
2000 season: .267 avg.; 6 HR; 24 RBIs.
Career: .274 avg.; 91 HR; 408 RBIs.
Teams: Indians 1991; Astros 1992-94; Reds 1994-2000.

MIGUEL TEJADA — **ATHLETICS**
5-9, 192 **B:** R. **T:** R.
Position: Shortstop.
Born: May 25, 1976.
2000 season: .275 avg.; 30 HR; 115 RBIs.
Career: .253 avg.; 64 HR; 254 RBIs.
Teams: Athletics 1997-2000.

FRANK THOMAS — **WHITE SOX**
Position: Designated hitter, first base.
2000 season: .328 avg.; 43 HR; 143 RBIs.
Awards: See A.L. MVP 1993, 1994.

JIM THOME — **INDIANS**
6-4, 225 **B:** L. **T:** R.
Position: First base.
Born: August 27, 1970.
2000 season: .269 avg.; 37 HR; 106 RBIs.
Career: .284 avg.; 233 HR; 685 RBIs.
Teams: Indians 1991-2000.

JOSE VALENTIN — **WHITE SOX**
5-10, 190 **B:** B. **T:** R.
Position: Infield.
Born: October 12, 1969.
2000 season: .273 avg.; 25 HR; 92 RBIs.
Career: .246 avg.; 115 HR; 435 RBIs.
Teams: Brewers 1992-1999; White Sox 2000.

JOHN VANDER WAL — **PIRATES**
6-2, 197 **B:** L. **T:** L.
Position: Outfield, first base.
Born: April 29, 1966.
2000 season: .299 avg.; 24 HR; 94 RBIs.
Career: .263 avg.; 61 HR; 291 RBIs.
Teams: Expos 1991-93; Rockies 1994-98; Padres 1998-99; Pirates 2000.

JASON VARITEK — **RED SOX**
6-2, 220 **B:** R. **T:** R.
Position: Catcher.
Born: April 11, 1972.
2000 season: .248 avg.; 10 HR; 65 RBIs.
Career: .258 avg.; 37 HR; 174 RBIs.
Teams: Red Sox 1997-2000.

St. Louis Cardinals second baseman Fernando Vina scoring a run against Milwaukee.

Greg Vaughn — **Devil Rays**
6-0, 202 **B:** R. **T:** R.
Position: Outfield.
Born: July 3, 1965.
2000 season: .254 avg.; 28 HR; 74 RBIs.
Career: .247 avg.; 320 HR; 956 RBIs.
Teams: Brewers 1989-96; Padres 1996-98; Reds 1999; Devil Rays 2000.

Mo Vaughn — **Angels**
Position: First base, designated hitter.
2000 season: .272 avg.; 36 HR; 117 RBIs.
Awards: See A.L. MVP 1995.

Randy Velarde — **Rangers**
6-0, 200 **B:** R. **T:** R.
Position: Second base.
Born: November 24, 1962.
2000 season: .278 avg.; 12 HR; 41 RBIs.
Career: .278 avg.; 89 HR; 405 RBIs.
Teams: Yankees 1987-95; Angels 1996-99; Athletics 1999-2000.

Robin Ventura — **Mets**
6-1, 198 **B:** L. **T:** R.
Position: Third base.
Born: July 14, 1967.
2000 season: .232 avg.; 24 HR; 84 RBIs.
Career: .273 avg.; 227 HR; 945 RBIs.
Teams: White Sox 1989-98; Mets 1999-2000.

Quilvio Veras — **Braves**
5-10, 183 **B:** B. **T:** R.
Position: Second base.
Born: April 3, 1971.
2000 season: .309 avg; 5 HR; 37 RBIs.
Career: .272 avg.; 29 HR; 214 RBIs.
Teams: Marlins 1995-96; Padres 1997-99; Braves 2000.

Jose Vidro — **Expos**
5-11, 190 **B:** B. **T:** R.
Position: Second base.
Born: August 27, 1974.
2000 season: .330 avg.; 24 HR; 97 RBIs.
Career: .297 avg.; 38 HR; 191 RBIs.
Teams: Expos 1997-2000.

Fernando Vina — **Cardinals**
5-9, 170 **B:** L. **T:** R.
Position: Second base.
Born: April 16, 1969.
2000 season: .300 avg.; 4 HR; 31 RBIs.
Career: .285 avg.; 26 HR; 203 RBIs.
Teams: Mariners 1993; Mets 1994; Brewers 1995-99; Cardinals 2000.

Omar Vizquel — **Indians**
5-9, 175 **B:** B. **T:** R.
Position: Shortstop.
Born: April 24, 1967.
2000 season: .287 avg.; 7 HR; 66 RBIs.
Career: .276 avg.; 41 HR; 515 RBIs.
Teams: Mariners 1989-93; Indians 1994-2000.

Larry Walker — **Rockies**
Position: Outfield.
2000 season: .309 avg.; 9 HR; 51 RBIs.
Awards: See N.L. MVP 1997.

Rondell White — **Cubs**
6-0, 210 **B:** R. **T:** R.
Position: Outfield.
Born: February 23, 1972.
2000 season: .311 avg.; 13 HR; 61 RBIs.
Career: .294 avg.; 103 HR; 391 RBIs.
Teams: Expos 1993-2000.

Bernie Williams — **Yankees**
6-2, 205 **B:** B. **T:** R.
Position: Outfield.
Born: September 13, 1968.
2000 season: .307 avg.; 30 HR; 121 RBIs.
Career: .304 avg.; 181 HR; 802 RBIs.
Teams: Yankees 1991-2000.

Gerald Williams — **Devil Rays**
6-2, 187 **B:** R. **T:** R.
Position: Outfield.
Born: August 10, 1966.
2000 season: .274 avg; 21 HR; 89 RBIs.
Career: .265 avg.; 76 HR; 329 RBIs.
Teams: Yankees 1992-96; Brewers 1996-97; Braves 1998-99; Devil Rays 2000.

Matt Williams — **Diamondbacks**
6-2, 214 **B:** R. **T:** R.
Position: Third base.
Born: November 28, 1965.
2000 season: .275 avg.; 12 HR; 47 RBIs.
Career: .269 avg.; 346 HR; 1,097 RBIs.
Teams: Giants 1987-96; Indians 1997; Diamondbacks 1998-2000.

Preston Wilson — **Marlins**
6-2, 193 **B:** R. **T:** R.
Position: Outfield.
Born: July 19, 1974.
2000 season: .264 avg.; 31 HR; 121 RBIs.
Career: .266 avg.; 58 HR; 195 RBIs.
Teams: Mets 1998; Marlins 1998-2000.

Tony Womack — **Diamondbacks**
5-9, 155 **B:** L. **T:** R.
Position: Outfield, shortstop, second base.
Born: September 25, 1969.
2000 season: .271 avg.; 7 HR; 57 RBIs.
Career: .276 avg.; 20 HR; 201 RBIs.
Teams: Pirates 1993-98; Diamondbacks 1999-2000.

Dmitri Young — **Reds**
6-2, 235 **B:** B. **T:** R.
Position: Outfield.
Born: October 11, 1973.
2000 season: .303 avg.; 18 HR; 88 RBIs.
Career: .295 avg.; 51 HR; 263 RBIs.
Teams: Cardinals 1996-97; Reds 1998-2000.

Eric Young — **Cubs**
5-8, 175 **B:** R. **T:** R.
Position: Second base.
Born: May 18, 1967.
2000 season: .297 avg.; 6 HR; 47 RBIs.
Career: .290 avg.; 49 HR; 385 RBIs.
Teams: Dodgers 1991, 1997-99; Rockies 1993-97; Cubs 2000.

Kevin Young — **Pirates**
6-3, 221 **B:** R. **T:** R.
Position: First base.
Born: June 16, 1969.
2000 season: .258 avg.; 20 HR; 88 RBIs.
Career: .266 avg.; 112 HR; 483 RBIs.
Teams: Pirates 1992-95, 1997-2000; Royals 1996.

Todd Zeile — **Mets**
6-1, 205 **B:** R. **T:** R.
Position: First base.
Born: September 9, 1965.
2000 season: .268 avg.; 22 HR; 79 RBIs.
Career: .268 avg.; 205 HR; 884 RBIs.
Teams: Cardinals 1989-95; Cubs 1995; Phillies 1996; Orioles 1996; Dodgers 1997-98; Marlins 1998; Rangers 1998-99; Mets 2000.

PITCHERS

Antonio Alfonseca — **Marlins**
6-5, 235 **Throws:** Right.
Status: Reliever.
Born: April 16, 1972.
2000 season: 5-6; 4.24 ERA; 45 saves.
Career: 14-20; 3.95 ERA; 74 saves.
Teams: Marlins 1997-2000.

Rick Ankiel — **Cardinals**
6-1, 210 **Throws:** Left.
Status: Starter.
Born: July 19, 1979.
2000 season: 11-7; 3.50 ERA; 194 SO.
Career: 11-8; 3.46 ERA; 233 SO.
Team: Cardinals 1999-2000.

Kevin Appier — **Mets**
6-2, 200 **Throws:** Right
Status: Starter.
Born: December 6, 1967.

2000 season: 15-11; 4.52 ERA; 129 SO.
Career: 136-105; 3.63 ERA; 1633 SO.
Teams: Royals 1989-99; Athletics 1999-2000.

Rolando Arrojo **Red Sox**
6-4, 220 **Throws:** Right.
Status: Starter.
Born: July 18, 1968.
2000 season: 10-11; 5.63 ERA; 124 SO.
Career: 31-35; 4.70 ERA; 383 RBIs.
Teams: Devil Rays 1998-99; Rockies 2000; Red Sox 2000.

Andy Ashby **Dodgers**
6-5, 190 **Throws:** Right.
Status: Starter.
Born: July 11, 1967.
2000 season: 12-13; 4.92 ERA; 106 SO.
Career: 84-87; 4.10 ERA; 1016 SO.
Teams: Phillies 1991-92; Rockies 1993; Padres 1993-99; Phillies 2000; Braves 2000.

Pedro Astacio **Rockies**
6-2, 208 **Throws:** Right.
Status: Starter.
Born: November 28, 1969.
2000 season: 12-9; 5.27 ERA; 193 SO.
Career: 95-82; 4.44 ERA; 1,222 SO.
Teams: Dodgers 1992-96; Rockies 1997-2000.

Rob Bell **Reds**
6-5, 225 **Throws:** Right.
Status: Starter.
Born: January 17, 1977.
2000 season: 7-8; 5.00 ERA; 112 SO.
Career: 7-8; 5.00 ERA; 112 SO.
Teams: Reds 2000.

Matt Anderson **Tigers**
6-4, 200 **Throws:** Right.
Status: Reliever.
Born: August 17, 1976.
2000 season: 3-2; 4.72 ERA; 71 SO.
Career: 10-4; 4.55 ERA; 147 SO.
Teams: Tigers 1998-2000.

Andy Benes **Cardinals**
6-6, 245 **Throws:** Right.
Status: Starter.
Born: August 20, 1967.
2000 season: 12-9; 4.88 ERA; 137 SO.
Career: 143-128; 3.86 ERA; 1858 SO.
Teams: Padres 1989-95; Mariners 1995; Cardinals 1996-97, 2000; Diamondbacks 1998-99.

Armando Benitez **Mets**
6-4, 229 **Throws:** Right.
Status: Reliever.
Born: November 3, 1972.
2000 season: 4-4; 2.61 ERA; 41 saves.
Career: 19-23; 3.04 ERA; 100 saves.
Teams: Orioles 1994-98; Mets 1999-2000.

Kris Benson **Pirates**
6-4, 195 **Throws:** Right.
Status: Starter.
Born: November 7, 1974.
2000 season: 10-12; 3.85 ERA; 184 SO.
Career: 21-26; 3.95 ERA; 323 SO.
Teams: Pirates 1999-2000.

Brian Bohanon **Rockies**
6-2, 250 **Throws:** Left.
Status: Starter.
Born: August 1, 1968.
2000 season: 12-10; 4.68 ERA; 98 SO.
Career: 49-52; 5.00 ERA; 624 SO.
Teams: Rangers 1990-94; Tigers 1995; Blue Jays 1996; Mets 1997-98; Dodgers 1998; Rockies 1999-2000.

Kent Bottenfield **Astros**
6-3, 240 **Throws:** Right.
Status: Starter.
Born: November 14, 1968.
2000 season: 8-10; 5.40 ERA; 106 SO.
Career: 44-44; 4.43 ERA; 527 SO.
Teams: Expos 1992-93; Rockies 1993-94; Giants 1994; Cubs 1996-97; Cardinals 1998-99; Angels 2000; Phillies 2000.

Kevin Brown **Dodgers**
6-4, 200 **Throws:** Right.
Status: Starter.
Born: March 14, 1965.
2000 season: 13-6; 2.58 ERA; 216 SO.
Career: 170-114; 3.21 ERA; 1,917 SO.
Teams: Rangers 1986-94; Orioles 1995; Marlins 1996-97; Padres 1998; Dodgers 1999-2000.

Dave Burba **Indians**
6-4, 240 **Throws:** Right.
Status: Starter.
Born: July 7, 1966.
2000 season: 16-6; 4.47 ERA; 180 SO.
Career: 95-70; 4.26 ERA; 1,100 SO.
Teams: Mariners 1990-91; Giants 1992-95; Reds 1995-97; Indians 1998-2000.

Frank Castillo **Red Sox**
6-1, 194 **Throws:** Right.
Status: Starter.
Born: April 1, 1969.
2000 season: 10-5; 3.59 ERA; 104 SO.
Career: 66-79; 4.52 ERA; 896 SO.
Teams: Cubs 1991-1997; Rockies 1997; Tigers 1998; Blue Jays 2000.

Bruce Chen **Phillies**
6-1, 180 **Throws:** Left.
Status: Starter/reliever.
Born: June 19, 1977.
2000 season: 7-4; 3.29 ERA; 112 SO.
Career: 11-6; 3.90 ERA; 174 SO.
Teams: Braves 1998-2000; Phillies 2000.

Roger Clemens **Yankees**
Status: Starter.
2000 season: 13-8; 3.70 ERA; 188 SO.
Awards: See A.L. Cy Young 1986, 1987, 1991, 1997, 1998; A.L. MVP 1986.

Bartolo Colon **Indians**
6-0, 230 **Throws:** Right.
Status: Starter.
Born: May 24, 1975.
2000 season: 15-8; 3.88 ERA; 212 SO.
Career: 51-29; 4.09 ERA; 597 SO.
Teams: Indians 1997-2000.

David Cone **Red Sox**
Status: Starter.
2000 season: 4-14; 6.91 ERA; 120 SO.
Awards: See A.L. Cy Young 1994.

Francisco Cordova **Pirates**
6-1, 197 **Throws:** Right.
Status: Starter.
Born: April 26, 1972.
2000 season: 6-8; 5.21 ERA; 66 SO.
Career: 42-47; 3.96 ERA; 537 SO.
Teams: Pirates 1996-2000.

Omar Daal **Phillies**
6-3, 195 **Throws:** Left.
Status: Starter.
Born: March 1, 1972.
2000 season: 4-19; 6.14 ERA; 96 SO.
Career: 40-51; 4.49 ERA; 541 SO.
Teams: Dodgers 1993-95; Expos 1996-97; Blue Jays 1997; Diamondbacks 1998-2000; Phillies 2000.

Jeff D'Amico **Brewers**
6-7, 250 **Throws:** Right.
Status: Starter.
Born: December 27, 1975.
2000 season: 12-7; 2.66 ERA; 101 SO.

Los Angeles Dodgers pitcher Kevin Brown.

Career: 27-20; 4.00 ERA; 249 SO.
Teams: Brewers 1996-2000.

Ryan Demptser **Marlins**
6-1, 211 **Throws:** Right.
Status: Starter.
Born: May 3, 1977.
2000 season: 14-10; 3.66 ERA; 209 SO.
Career: 22-23; 4.46 ERA; 370 SO.
Teams: Marlins 1998-2000.

Octavio Dotel **Astros**
6-0, 175 **Throws:** Right.
Status: Starter, reliever.
Born: November 25, 1975.
2000 season: 3-7; 5.40 ERA; 142 SO, 16 saves.
Career: 11-10; 5.39 ERA; 227 SO; 16 saves.
Teams: Mets 1999; Astros 2000.

Darren Dreifort **Dodgers**
6-2, 211 **Throws:** Right.
Status: Starter.
Born: May 3, 1972.
2000 season: 12-9; 4.16 ERA; 164 SO.
Career: 39-45; 4.28 ERA; 581 SO.
Teams: Dodgers 1996-2000.

Chad Durbin **Royals**
6-2, 200 **Throws:** Right.
Status: Starter.
Born: December 3, 1977.
2000 season: 2-5; 8.21 ERA; 37 SO.
Career: 2-5; 7.96 ERA; 40 SO.
Teams: Royals 1999-2000.

Adam Eaton **Padres**
6-2, 190 **Throws:** Right.
Status: Starter.
Born: November 23, 1977.
2000 season: 7-4; 4.13 ERA; 90 SO.
Career: 7-4; 4.13 ERA; 90 SO.
Teams: Padres 2000.

Scott Elarton **Astros**
6-7, 240 **Throws:** Right.
Status: Starter.
Born: February 23, 1976.
2000 season: 17-7; 4.81 ERA; 131 SO.
Career: 28-13; 4.14 ERA; 308 SO.
Teams: Astros 1998-2000.

Oakland Athletics pitcher Tim Hudson.

SCOTT ERICKSON **ORIOLES**
6-4, 230 **Throws:** Right.
Status: Starter.
Born: February 2, 1968.
2000 season: 5-8; 7.87 ERA; 41 SO.
Career: 135-116; 4.43 ERA; 1,152 SO.
Teams: Twins 1990-95; Orioles 1996-2000.

KELVIM ESCOBAR **BLUE JAYS**
6-1, 195 **Throws:** Right.
Status: Starter.
Born: April 11, 1976.
2000 season: 10-15; 5.35 ERA; 142 SO.
Career: 34-31; 5.04 ERA; 379 SO.
Teams: Blue Jays 1997-2000.

SHAWN ESTES **GIANTS**
6-2, 192 **Throws:** Left.
Status: Starter.
Born: February 18, 1973.
2000 season: 15-6; 4.26 ERA; 136 SO.
Career: 55-42; 4.30 ERA; 686 SO.
Teams: Giants 1995-2000.

CHUCK FINLEY **INDIANS**
6-6, 226 **Throws:** Left.
Status: Starter.
Born: November 26, 1962.
2000 season: 16-11; 4.17; 189 SO.
Career: 181-151; 3.76 ERA; 2,340 SO.
Teams: Angels 1986-99; Indians 2000.

JOHN FRANCO **METS**
5-10, 185 **Throws:** Left.
Status: Reliever.
Born: September 17, 1960.
2000 season: 5-4; 3.40 ERA; 4 saves.
Career: 82-74; 2.68 ERA; 420 saves.
Teams: Reds 1984-89; Mets 1990-2000.

FREDDY GARCIA **MARINERS**
6-4, 235 **Throws:** Right.
Status: Starter.
Born: October 6, 1976.
2000 season: 9-5; 3.91 ERA; 79 SO.
Career: 26-13; 4.01 ERA; 249 SO.
Teams: Mariners 1999-2000.

TOM GLAVINE **BRAVES**
Status: Starter.
2000 season: 21-9; 3.40 ERA; 152 SO.
Awards: See N.L. Cy Young 1991, 1998.

DANNY GRAVES **REDS**
5-11, 185 **Throws:** Right.
Status: Reliever.
Born: August 7, 1973.
2000 season: 10-5; 2.56 ERA; 30 saves.
Career: 22-13; 3.32 ERA; 65 saves.
Teams: Indians 1996-97; Reds 1997-2000.

JOHN HALAMA **MARINERS**
6-5, 220 **Throws:** Right.
Status: Starter.
Born: February 22, 1972.
2000 season: 14-9; 5.08 ERA; 87 SO.
Career: 26-20; 4.74 ERA; 213 SO.
Teams: Astros 1998; Mariners 1999-2000.

JOEY HAMILTON **BLUE JAYS**
6-4, 230 **Throws:** Right.
Status: Starter.
Born: September 9, 1970.
2000 season: 2-1; 3.55 ERA; 15 SO.
Career: 64-53; 4.07 ERA; 710 SO.
Teams: Padres 1994-98; Blue Jays 1999-2000.

MIKE HAMPTON **ROCKIES**
5-10, 180 **Throws:** Left.
Status: Starter.
Born: September 9, 1972.
2000 season: 15-10; 3.14 ERA; 151 SO.
Career: 85-53; 3.44 ERA; 852 SO.
Teams: Mariners 1993; Astros 1994-99; Mets 2000.

PETE HARNISCH **REDS**
6-0, 228 **Throws:** Right.
Status: Starter.
Born: September 23, 1966.
2000 season: 8-6; 4.74 ERA; 71 SO.
Career: 110-100; 3.84 ERA; 1,351 SO.
Teams: Orioles 1988-90; Astros 1991-94; Mets 1995-97; Brewers 1997; Reds 1998-2000.

RICK HELLING **RANGERS**
6-3, 220 **Throws:** Right.
Status: Starter.
Born: December 15, 1970.
2000 season: 16-13; 4.48 ERA; 146 SO.
Career: 60-47; 4.65 ERA; 612 SO.
Teams: Rangers 1994-2000; Marlins 1996-97.

DOUG HENRY **ROYALS**
6-4, 205 **Throws:** Right.
Status: Reliever.
Born: December 10, 1963.
2000 season: 4-4; 3.79 ERA; 62 SO.
Career: 32-40; 3.95 ERA; 484 SO; 82 saves.
Teams: Brewers 1991-94; Mets 1995-96; Giants 1997, 2000; Astros 1998-2000.

PAT HENTGEN **ORIOLES**
6-2, 195 **Throws:** Right.
Status: Starter.
Born: November 13, 1968.
2000 season: 15-12; 4.72 ERA; 118 SO.
Career: 120-88; 4.21 ERA; 1113 SO.
Teams: Blue Jays 1991-99; Cardinals 2000.

DUSTIN HERMANSON **CARDINALS**
6-2, 200 **Throws:** Right.
Status: Starter.
Born: December 21, 1972.
2000 season: 12-14; 4.77 ERA; 94 SO.
Career: 47-48; 4.17 ERA; 559 SO.
Teams: Padres 1995-96; Expos 1997-2000.

LIVAN HERNANDEZ **GIANTS**
6-2, 222 **Throws:** Right.
Status: Starter.
Born: February 20, 1975.
2000 season: 17-11; 3.75 ERA; 165 SO.
Career: 44-38; 4.19 ERA; 545 SO.
Teams: Marlins 1996-99; Giants 1999-2000.

ORLANDO HERNANDEZ **YANKEES**
6-2, 210 **Throws:** Right.
Status: Starter.
Born: October 11, 1965.
2000 season: 12-13; 4.51 ERA; 141 SO.
Career: 41-26; 4.00 ERA; 429 SO.
Teams: Yankees 1998-2000.

ROBERTO HERNANDEZ **ROYALS**
6-4, 235 **Throws:** Right.
Status: Reliever.
Born: November 11, 1964.
2000 season: 4-7; 3.19 ERA; 32 saves.
Career: 42-42; 3.04 ERA; 266 saves.
Teams: White Sox 1991-97; Giants 1997; Devil Rays 1998-2000.

TREVOR HOFFMAN **PADRES**
6-0, 205 **Throws:** Right.
Status: Reliever.
Born: October 13, 1967.
2000 season: 4-7; 2.99 ERA; 43 saves.
Career: 40-35; 2.72 ERA; 271 saves.
Teams: Marlins 1993; Padres 1993-2000.

TIM HUDSON **ATHLETICS**
6-0, 160 **Throws:** Right.
Status: Starter.
Born: July 14, 1975.
2000 season: 20-6; 4.14 ERA; 169 SO.
Career: 31-8; 3.77 ERA; 301 SO.
Teams: Athletics 1999-2000.

JASON ISRINGHAUSEN **ATHLETICS**
6-3, 210 **Throws:** Right.
Status: Reliever.
Born: September 7, 1972.
2000 season: 6-4; 3.78 ERA; 33 saves.
Career: 24-26; 4.37 ERA; 42 saves.
Teams: Mets 1995-99; Athletics 1999-2000

JOSE JIMENEZ **ROCKIES**
6-3, 190 **Throws:** Right.
Status: Reliever.
Born: July 7, 1973.
2000 season: 5-2; 3.18 ERA; 24 saves.
Career: 13-16; 4.87 ERA; 24 saves.
Teams: Cardinals 1998-99; Rockies 2000.

RANDY JOHNSON **DIAMONDBACKS**
Status: Starter.
2000 season: 19-7; 2.64 ERA; 347 SO.
Awards: See A.L. Cy Young 1995; N.L. Cy Young 1999, 2000.

TODD JONES **TIGERS**
6-3, 230 **Throws:** Right.
Status: Reliever.
Born: April 24, 1968.
2000 season: 2-4; 3.52 ERA; 42 saves.
Career: 30-28; 3.54 ERA; 170 saves.
Teams: Astros 1993-96; Tigers 1997-2000.

DARRYL KILE **CARDINALS**
6-5, 212 **Throws:** Right.
Status: Starter.
Born: December 2, 1968.
2000 season: 20-9; 3.91 ERA; 192 SO.
Career: 112-104; 4.27 ERA; 1439 SO.
Teams: Astros 1991-97; Rockies 1998-99; Cardinals 2000.

BILLY KOCH **BLUE JAYS**
6-3, 206 **Throws:** Right.
Status: Reliever.
Born: December 14, 1974.
2000 season: 9-3; 2.63 ERA; 33 saves.
Career: 9-8; 2.97 ERA; 64 saves.
Teams: Blue Jays 1999-2000.

RYAN KOHLMEIER **ORIOLES**
6-2, 197 **Throws:** Right.
Status: Reliever.
Born: June 25, 1977.
2000 season: 0-1; 2.39 ERA; 13 saves.
Career: 0-1; 2.39 ERA; 13 saves.
Teams: Orioles 2000.

AL LEITER **METS**
6-3, 220 **Throws:** Left.
Status: Starter.
Born: October 23, 1965.
2000 season: 16-8; 3.20 ERA; 200 SO.
Career: 106-79; 3.73 ERA; 1,307 SO.
Teams: Yankees 1987-89; Blue Jays 1989-95; Marlins 1996-97; Mets 1998-2000.

JON LIEBER **CUBS**
6-3, 225 **Throws:** Right.
Status: Starter.
Born: April 2, 1970.
2000 season: 12-11; 4.41 ERA; 192 SO.
Career: 60-69; 4.32 ERA; 886 SO.
Teams: Pirates 1994-98; Cubs 1999-2000.

KERRY LIGTENBERG **BRAVES**
6-2, 205 **Throws:** Right.
Status: Reliever.
Born: May 11, 1971.
2000 season: 2-3; 3.61 ERA; 12 saves.
Career: 6-5; 3.08 ERA; 43 saves.
Teams: Braves 1997-2000.

JOSE LIMA **ASTROS**
6-2, 205 **Throws:** Right.
Status: Starter.
Born: September 30, 1972.
2000 season: 7-16; 6.65 ERA; 124 SO.
Career: 53-56; 4.87 ERA; 646 SO.
Teams: Tigers 1994-96; Astros 1997-2000.

ESTEBAN LOAIZA **BLUE JAYS**
6-3, 210 **Throws:** Right.
Status: Starter.
Born: December 31, 1971.
2000 season: 10-13; 4.56 ERA; 137 SO.
Career: 49-52; 4.72 ERA; 561 SO.
Teams: Pirates 1995-98; Rangers 1998-2000; Blue Jays 2000.

ALBIE LOPEZ **DEVIL RAYS**
6-2, 240 **Throws:** Right.
Status: Starter.
Born: August 18, 1971.
2000 season: 11-13; 4.13 ERA; 96 SO.
Career: 33-33; 4.73 ERA; 368 SO.
Teams: Indians 1993-97; Devil Rays 1998-2000.

DEREK LOWE **RED SOX**
6-6, 200 **Throws:** Right.
Status: Reliever.
Born: June 1, 1973.
2000 season: 4-4; 2.56 ERA; 42 saves.
Career: 15-22; 3.67 ERA; 61 saves.
Teams: Mariners 1997; Red Sox 1997-2000.

GREG MADDUX **BRAVES**
Status: Starter.
2000 season: 19-9; 3.00 ERA; 190 SO.
Awards: See N.L. Cy Young 1992, 1993, 1994, 1995.

MATT MANTEI **DIAMONDBACKS**
6-1, 190 **Throws:** Right.
Status: Reliever.
Born: July 7, 1973.
2000 season: 1-1; 4.57 ERA; 17 saves.
Career: 6-9; 3.70 ERA; 58 saves.
Teams: Marlins 1995-99; Diamondbacks 1999-2000.

PEDRO MARTINEZ **RED SOX**
Status: Starter.
2000 season: 18-6; 1.74 ERA; 284 saves.
Awards: See N.L. Cy Young 1997; A.L. Cy Young 1999, 2000.

RAMON MARTINEZ **DODGERS**
6-4, 184 **Throws:** Right.
Status: Starter.
Born: March 22, 1968.
2000 season: 10-8; 6.13 ERA; 89 SO.
Career: 135-86; 3.62 ERA; 1,418 SO.
Teams: Dodgers 1988-98; Red Sox 1999-2000.

BRIAN MEADOWS **ROYALS**
6-4, 210 **Throws:** Right.
Status: Starter.
Born: November 21, 1975.
2000 season: 13-10; 5.13 ERA; 79 SO.
Career: 35-38; 5.31 ERA; 239 SO.
Teams: Marlins 1998-99; Padres 2000; Royals 2000.

GIL MECHE **MARINERS**
6-3, 200 **Throws:** Right.
Status: Starter.
Born: September 8, 1978.
2000 season: 4-4; 3.78 ERA; 60 SO.
Career: 12-8; 4.25 ERA; 107 SO.
Teams: Mariners 1999-2000.

RAMIRO MENDOZA **YANKEES**
6-2, 195 **Throws:** Right.
Status: Starter, reliever.
Born: June 15, 1972.
2000 season: 7-4; 4.25 ERA; 30 SO.
Career: 38-26; 4.27 ERA; 282 SO.
Teams: Yankees 1996-2000.

JOSE MERCEDES **ORIOLES**
6-1, 180 **Throws:** Right.
Status: Starter.
Born: March 5, 1971.
2000 season: 14-7; 4.02 ERA; 70 SO.
Career: 25-22; 4.34 ERA; 184 SO.
Teams: Brewers 1994-98; Orioles 2000.

KEVIN MILLWOOD **BRAVES**
6-4, 220 **Throws:** Right.
Status: Starter.
Born: December 24, 1974.
2000 season: 10-13; 4.66 ERA; 168 SO.
Career: 50-31; 3.78 ERA; 578 SO.
Teams: Braves 1997-2000.

ERIC MILTON **TWINS**
6-3, 220 **Throws:** Left.
Status: Starter.
Born: August 4, 1975.
2000 season: 13-10; 4.86 ERA; 160 SO.
Career: 28-35; 4.96 ERA; 430 SO.
Teams: Twins 1998-2000.

BRIAN MOEHLER **TIGERS**
6-3, 235 **Throws:** Right.
Status: Starter.
Born: December 31, 1971.
2000 season: 12-9; 4.50 ERA; 103 SO.
Career: 47-51; 4.50 ERA; 431 SO.
Teams: Tigers 1996-2000.

MATT MORRIS **CARDINALS**
6-5, 210 **Throws:** Right.
Status: Starter, reliever.
Born: August 9, 1974.
2000 season: 3-3; 3.57 ERA; 34 SO.
Career: 22-17; 3.05 ERA; 262 SO.
Teams: Cardinals 1997-2000.

JAMIE MOYER **MARINERS**
6-0, 170 **Throws:** Left.
Status: Starter.
Born: November 18, 1962.
2000 season: 13-10; 5.49 ERA; 98 SO.
Career: 131-111; 4.30 ERA; 1,262 SO.
Teams: Cubs 1986-88; Rangers 1989-90; Cardinals 1991; Orioles 1993-95; Red Sox 1996; Mariners 1996-2000.

MARK MULDER **ATHLETICS**
6-6, 200 **Throws:** Left.
Status: Starter.
Born: August 5, 1977.
2000 season: 9-10; 5.44 ERA; 88 SO.
Career: 9-10; 5.44 ERA; 88 SO.
Teams: Athletics 2000.

New York Mets pitcher Al Leiter.

MIKE MUSSINA **YANKEES**
6-2, 185 **Throws:** Right.
Status: Starter.
Born: December 8, 1968.
2000 season: 11-15; 3.79 ERA; 210 SO.
Career: 147-81; 3.53 ERA; 1,535 SO.
Teams: Orioles 1991-2000.

CHARLES NAGY **INDIANS**
6-3, 200 **Throws:** Right.
Status: Starter.
Born: May 5, 1967.
2000 season: 2-7; 8.21 ERA; 41 SO.
Career: 123-93; 4.32 ERA; 1,184 SO.
Teams: Indians 1990-2000.

JOE NATHAN **GIANTS**
6-4, 195 **Throws:** Right.
Status: Starter.
Born: November 22, 1974.
2000 season: 5-2; 5.21 ERA; 61 SO.
Career: 12-6; 4.70 ERA; 115 SO.
Teams: Giants 1999-2000.

DENNY NEAGLE **ROCKIES**
6-3, 225 **Throws:** Left.
Status: Starter.
Born: September 13, 1968.
2000 season: 15-9; 4.52 ERA; 146 SO.
Career: 105-69; 3.92 ERA; 1144 SO.
Teams: Twins 1991; Pirates 1992-96; Braves 1996-98; Reds 1999-2000; Yankees 2000.

ROBB NEN **GIANTS**
6-5, 215 **Throws:** Right.
Status: Reliever.
Born: November 28, 1969.
2000 season: 4-3; 1.50 ERA; 41 saves.
Career: 35-35; 3.08 ERA; 226 saves.
Teams: Rangers 1993; Marlins 1993-97; Giants 1998-2000.

HIDEO NOMO **RED SOX**
Status: Starter.
2000 season: 8-12; 4.74 ERA; 181 SO.
Awards: See N.L. Rookie of the Year 1995.

OMAR OLIVARES **ATHLETICS**
6-0, 205 **Throws:** Right.

Minnesota Twins pitcher Brad Radke.

Status: Starter.
Born: July 6, 1967.
2000 season: 4-8; 6.75 ERA; 57 SO.
Career: 71-77; 4.53 ERA; 784 SO.
Teams: Cardinals 1990-94; Rockies 1995; Phillies 1995; Tigers 1996-97; Mariners 1997; Angels 1998-99; Athletics 1999-2000.

Darren Oliver — Rangers
6-2, 210 **Throws:** Left.
Status: Starter.
Born: October 6, 1970.
2000 season: 2-9; 7.42 ERA; 49 SO.
Career: 56-49; 4.88 ERA; 564 SO.
Teams: Rangers 1993-98, 2000; Cardinals 1998-99.

Ramon Ortiz — Angels
6-0, 175 **Throws:** Right.
Status: Starter.
Born: March 23, 1976.
2000 season: 8-6; 5.09 ERA; 73 SO.
Career: 10-9; 5.52 ERA; 117 SO.
Teams: Angels 1999-2000.

Russ Ortiz — Giants
6-1, 210 **Throws:** Right.
Status: Starter.
Born: June 5, 1974.
2000 season: 14-12; 5.01 ERA; 167 SO.
Career: 36-25; 4.50 ERA; 406 SO.
Teams: Giants 1998-2000.

Chan Ho Park — Dodgers
6-2, 204 **Throws:** Right.
Status: Starter.
Born: June 30, 1973.
2000 season: 18-10; 3.27 ERA; 217 SO.
Career: 65-43; 3.88 ERA; 880 SO.
Teams: Dodgers 1994-2000.

Brad Penny — Marlins
6-4, 200 **Throws:** Right.
Status: Starter.
Born: May 24, 1978.
2000 season: 8-7; 4.81 ERA; 80 SO.
Career: 8-7; 4.81 ERA; 80 SO.
Teams: Marlins 2000.

Troy Percival — Angels
6-3, 230 **Throws:** Right.
Status: Reliever.
Born: August 9, 1969.
2000 season: 5-5; 4.50 ERA; 32 saves
Career: 19-27; 3.16 ERA; 171 saves.
Teams: Angels 1995-2000.

Robert Person — Phillies
6-0, 193 **Throws:** Right.
Status: Starter.
Born: October 6, 1969.
2000 season: 9-7; 3.63 ERA; 164 SO.
Career: 32-30; 4.62 ERA; 519 SO.
Teams: Mets 1995-96; Blue Jays 1997-99; Phillies 1999-2000.

Andy Pettitte — Yankees
6-5, 225 **Throws:** Left.
Status: Starter.
Born: June 15, 1972.
2000 season: 19-9; 4.35 ERA; 125 SO.
Career: 100-55; 3.99 ERA; 834 SO.
Teams: Yankees 1995-2000.

Sidney Ponson — Orioles
6-1, 220 **Throws:** Right.
Status: Starter.
Born: November 2, 1976.
2000 season: 9-13; 4.82 ERA; 152 SO.
Career: 29-34; 4.89 ERA; 349 SO.
Teams: Orioles 1998-2000.

Brad Radke — Twins
6-2, 184 **Throws:** Right.
Status: Starter.
Born: October 27, 1972.
2000 season: 12-16; 4.45 ERA; 141 SO.
Career: 78-84; 4.32 ERA; 805 SO.
Teams: Twins 1995-2000.

Rick Reed — Mets
6-1, 195 **Throws:** Right.
Status: Starter.
Born: August 16, 1965.
2000 season: 11-5; 4.11 ERA; 121 SO.
Career: 60-45; 3.93 ERA; 636 SO.
Teams: Pirates 1988-91; Royals 1992-93; Rangers 1993-94; Reds 1995; Mets 1997-2000.

Shane Reynolds — Astros
6-3, 210 **Throws:** Right.
Status: Starter.
Born: March 26, 1968.
2000 season: 7-8; 5.22 ERA; 93 SO.
Career: 86-69; 3.85 ERA; 1,160 SO.
Teams: Astros 1992-2000.

Armando Reynoso — Diamondbacks
6-0, 204 **Throws:** Right.
Status: Starter.
Born: May 1, 1966.
2000 season: 11-12; 5.27 ERA; 89 SO.
Career: 67-56; 4.68 ERA; 537 SO.
Teams: Braves 1991-92; Rockies 1993-96; Mets 1997-98; Diamondbacks 1999-2000.

Todd Ritchie — Pirates
6-3, 219 **Throws:** Right.
Status: Starter.
Born: November 7, 1971.
2000 season: 9-8; 4.81 ERA; 124 SO.
Career: 26-20; 4.32 ERA; 296 SO.
Teams: Twins 1997-98; Pirates 1999-2000.

Mariano Rivera — Yankees
6-2, 170 **Throws:** Right.
Status: Reliever.
Born: November 29, 1969.
2000 season: 7-4; 2.85 ERA; 36 saves.
Career: 33-17; 2.63 ERA; 165 saves.
Teams: Yankees 1995-2000.

John Rocker — Braves
6-4, 225 **Throws:** Left.
Status: Reliever.
Born: October 17, 1974.
2000 season: 1-2; 2.89 ERA; 24 saves.
Career: 6-10; 2.53 ERA; 64 saves.
Teams: Braves 1998-2000.

Kenny Rogers — Rangers
6-1, 217 **Throws:** Left.
Status: Starter.
Born: November 10, 1964.
2000 season: 13-13; 4.55 ERA; 127 SO.
Career: 127-91; 4.11 ERA; 1,241 SO.
Teams: Rangers 1989-95, 2000; Yankees 1996-97; Athletics 1998-99; Mets 1999.

Jose Rosado — Royals
6-0, 185 **Throws:** Left.
Status: Starter.
Born: November 9, 1974.
2000 season: 2-2; 5.86 ERA; 15 SO.
Career: 37-45; 4.27 ERA; 484 SO.
Teams: Royals 1996-2000.

Brian Rose — Rockies
6-3, 212 **Throws:** Right.
Status: Starter.
Born: February 13, 1976.
2000 season: 7-10; 5.79 ERA; 64 SO.
Career: 15-20; 5.67 ERA; 136 SO.
Teams: Red Sox 1996-2000; Rockies 2000.

Kirk Rueter — Giants
6-2, 205 **Throws:** Left.
Status: Starter.
Born: December 1, 1970.
2000 season: 11-9; 3.96 ERA; 71 SO.
Career: 81-48; 4.16 ERA; 537 SO.
Teams: Expos 1993-96; Giants 1996-2000.

Ryan Rupe — Devil Rays
6-5, 230 **Throws:** Right.
Status: Starter.
Born: March 31, 1975.
2000 season: 5-6; 6.92 ERA; 61 SO.
Career: 13-15; 5.48 ERA; 158 SO.
Teams: Devil Rays 1999-2000.

Bret Saberhagen — Red Sox
Status: Starter.
2000 season: Did not pitch due to injury.
Awards: See A.L. Cy Young 1985, 1989.

Kazuhiro Sasaki — Mariners
Status: Reliever.
2000 season: 2-5; 3.16 ERA; 37 saves.
Awards: See A.L. Rookie of the Year 2000.

Curt Schilling — Diamondbacks
6-4, 228 **Throws:** Right.
Status: Starter.
Born: November 14, 1966.
2000 season: 11-12; 3.81 ERA; 168 SO.
Career: 110-95; 3.43 ERA; 1,739.
Teams: Orioles 1988-90; Astros 1991; Phillies 1992-2000; Diamondbacks 2000.

Jason Schmidt — Pirates
6-5, 211 **Throws:** Right.
Status: Starter.
Born: January 29, 1973.
2000 season: 2-5; 5.40 ERA; 51 SO.
Career: 43-47; 4.58 ERA; 586 SO.
Teams: Braves 1995-96; Pirates 1996-2000.

Aaron Sele — Mariners
6-5, 215 **Throws:** Right.
Status: Starter.
Born: June 25, 1970.
2000 season: 17-10; 4.51 ERA; 137 SO.
Career: 92-63; 4.46 ERA; 968 SO.

Teams: Red Sox 1993-97; Rangers 1998-99; Mariners 2000.

JEFF SHAW **DODGERS**
6-2, 200 **Throws:** Right.
Status: Reliever.
Born: July 7, 1966.
2000 season: 3-4; 4.24 ERA; 27 saves.
Career: 31-49; 3.54 ERA; 160 saves.
Teams: Indians 1990-92; Expos 1993-95; White Sox 1995; Reds 1996-98; Dodgers 1998-2000.

JOHN SMOLTZ **BRAVES**
Status: Starter.
2000 season: Did not pitch due to injury.
Awards: See N.L. Cy Young 1996.

STEVE SPARKS **TIGERS**
6-0, 180 **Throws:** Right.
Status: Starter.
Born: July 2, 1965.
2000 season: 7-5; 4.07 ERA; 53 SO.
Career: 34-38; 4.92 ERA; 333 SO.
Teams: Brewers 1995-96; Angels 1998-99; Tigers 2000.

TODD STOTTLEMYRE **DIAMONDBACKS**
6-3, 200 **Throws:** Right.
Status: Starter.
Born: May 20, 1965.
2000 season: 9-6; 4.91 ERA; 76 SO.
Career: 138-119; 4.25 ERA; 1,575.
Teams: Blue Jays 1988-94; Athletics 1995; Cardinals 1996-98; Rangers 1998; Diamondbacks 1999-2000.

JUSTIN THOMPSON **RANGERS**
6-4, 215 **Throws:** Left.
Status: Starter.
Born: March 8, 1973.
2000 season: Did not pitch due to injury.
Career: 36-43; 3.98 ERA; 427 SO.
Teams: Tigers 1996-99; Rangers 2000.

MIKE TIMLIN **CARDINALS**
6-4, 210 **Throws:** Right
Status: Reliever
Born: March 10, 1966
2000 Season: 5-4; 4.18 ERA; 12 saves.
Career: 37-40; 3.59 ERA; 111 saves.
Teams: Blue Jays 1991-97; Mariners 1997-98; Orioles 1999-2000; Cardinals 2000.

BRETT TOMKO **MARINERS**
6-4, 215 **Throws:** Right.
Status: Starter.
Born: April 7, 1973.
2000 season: 7-5; 4.68 ERA; 59 SO.
Career: 36-31; 4.40 ERA; 448 SO.
Teams: Reds 1997-99; Mariners 2000.

STEVE TRACHSEL **METS**
6-4, 205 **Throws:** Right.
Status: Starter.
Born: October 31, 1970.
2000 season: 8-15; 4.80 ERA; 110 SO.
Career: 68-84; 4.42 ERA; 939 SO.
Teams: Cubs 1993-99; Devil Rays 2000; Blue Jays 2000.

MIKE TROMBLEY **ORIOLES**
6-2, 210 **Throws:** Right.
Status: Reliever.
Born: April 14, 1967.
2000 season: 4-5; 4.13 ERA; 4 saves.
Career: 34-38; 4.43 ERA; 38 saves.
Teams: Twins 1992-99; Orioles 2000.

UGUETH URBINA **EXPOS**
6-2, 205 **Throws:** Right.
Status: Reliever.
Born: February 15, 1974.
2000 season: 0-1; 4.05; 8 saves.
Career: 29-25; 3.43 ERA; 110 saves.
Teams: Expos 1995-2000.

ISMAEL VALDES **ANGELS**
6-3, 215 **Throws:** Right.
Status: Starter.
Born: August 21, 1973.
2000 season: 2-7; 5.64 ERA; 74 SO.
Career: 63-61; 3.59 ERA; 830 SO.
Teams: Dogers 1994-2000; Cubs 2000.

JAVIER VAZQUEZ **EXPOS**
6-2, 195 **Throws:** Right.
Status: Starter.
Born: July 25, 1976.
2000 season: 11-9; 4.05 ERA; 196 SO.
Career: 25-32; 4.96 ERA; 448 SO
Teams: Expos 1998-2000.

DAVE VERES **CARDINALS**
6-2, 220 **Throws:** Right.
Status: Reliever.
Born: October 19, 1966.
2000 season: 3-5; 2.85 ERA; 29 Saves.
Career: 26-24; 3.32 ERA; 75 saves.
Teams: Astros 1994-95; Expos 1996-97; Rockies 1998-99; Cardinals 2000.

BILLY WAGNER **ASTROS**
5-11, 180 **Throws:** Left.
Status: Reliever.
Born: July 25, 1971.
2000 season: 2-4; 6.18 ERA; 6 saves.
Career: 19-18; 2.73 ERA; 107 saves.
Teams: Astros 1995-2000.

JEFF WEAVER **TIGERS**
6-5, 200 **Throws:** Right.
Status: Starter.
Born: August 22, 1976.
2000 season: 11-15; 4.32 ERA; 136 SO.
Career: 20-27; 4.88 ERA; 250 SO.
Teams: Tigers 1999-2000.

DAVID WELLS **WHITE SOX**
6-4, 235 **Throws:** Left.
Status: Starter.
Born: May 20, 1963.
2000 season: 20-8; 4.11 ERA; 166 SO.
Career: 161-107; 4.06 ERA; 1,576 SO.
Teams: Blue Jays 1987-92, 1999-2000; Tigers 1993-95; Reds 1995; Orioles 1996; Yankess 1997-98.

JOHN WETTELAND
6-2, 215 **Throws:** Right.
Status: Reliever.
Born: August 21, 1966.
2000 season: 6-5; 4.20 ERA; 34 saves.
Career: 48-45; 2.93 ERA; 330 saves.
Teams: Dodgers 1989-91; Expos 1992-94; Yankees 1995-96; Rangers 1997-2000.

GABE WHITE **ROCKIES**
6-2, 204 **Throws:** Left.
Status: Reliever.
Born: November 20, 1971.
2000 season: 11-2; 2.36 ERA; 82 SO.
Career: 21-14; 4.10 ERA; 295 SO.
Teams: Expos 1994-95; Reds 1997-2000; Rockies 2000.

MIKE WILLIAMS **PIRATES**
6-2, 200 **Throws:** Right.
Status: Reliever.
Born: July 29, 1968.
2000 season: 3-4; 3.50 ERA; 24 saves.

Chicago White Sox pitcher David Wells.

Career: 23-37; 4.50 ERA; 48 saves.
Teams: Phillies 1992-96; Royals 1997; Pirates 1998-2000.

SCOTT WILLIAMSON **REDS**
Status: Reliever.
2000 season: 5-8; 3.29 ERA; 6 saves.
Awards: See N.L. Rookie of the Year 1999.

JARET WRIGHT **INDIANS**
6-2, 230 **Throws:** Right.
Status: Starter.
Born: December 29, 1975.
2000 season: 3-4; 4.70 ERA; 36 SO.
Career: 31-27; 5.03 ERA; 330 SO.
Teams: Indians 1997-2000.

MASATO YOSHII **ROCKIES**
6-2, 210 **Throws:** Right.
Status: Starter.
Born: April 20, 1965.
2000 season: 6-15; 5.86 ERA; 88 SO.
Career: 24-31; 4.72 ERA; 310 SO.
Teams: Mets 1998-99; Rockies 2000.

JEFF ZIMMERMAN **RANGERS**
6-1, 200 **Throws:** Right.
Status: Reliever.
Born: August 9, 1972.
2000 season: 4-5; 5.30 ERA; 1 save.
Career: 13-8; 3.66 ERA; 4 saves.
Teams: Rangers 1999-2000.

BARRY ZITO **ATHLETICS**
6-4, 205 **Throws:** Left
Status: Starter.
Born: May 13, 1978.
2000 season: 7-4; 2.72 ERA; 78 SO.
Career: 7-4; 2.72 ERA; 78 SO.
Teams: Athletics 2000.

MANAGERS

AMERICAN LEAGUE

PHIL GARNER — **TIGERS**
5-10, 177 **Born:** April 30, 1949.
2000 record: 79-83, 3rd place, A.L. Central.
Career: 563-617 Brewers 1992-99; 79-83 Tigers 2000.
Position as player: Second base, third base.

MIKE HARGROVE — **ORIOLES**
6-0, 195 **Born:** October 26, 1949.
2000 record: 74-88, 4th place, A.L. East.
Career: 721-591 Indians 1991-99; 74-88 Orioles 2000.
Position as player: First base, DH.

ART HOWE — **ATHLETICS**
6-1, 200 **Born:** December 15, 1946.
2000 record: 91-70, 1st place, A.L. West.
Career: 391-418 Astros 1989-93; 395-414 Athletics 1996-2000.
Position as player: Third base, first base.

TOM KELLY — **TWINS**
5-11, 205 **Born:** August 15, 1950.
2000 record: 69-93, 5th place, A.L. Central.
Career: 1055-1167 Twins 1986-2000.
Position as player: First base, outfield.

CHARLIE MANUEL — **INDIANS**
6-4, 220 **Born:** January 4, 1944.
2000 record: 90-72, 2nd place, A.L. Central.
Career: 90-72 Indians 2000.
Position as player: Outfield.

JERRY MANUEL — **WHITE SOX**
5-11, 180 **Born:** December 23, 1953.
2000 record: 95-67, 1st place, A.L. Central.
Career: 250-235 White Sox 1998-2000.
Position as player: Second base, shortstop.

BUCK MARTINEZ — **BLUE JAYS**
5-11, 200 **Born:** November 7, 1948.
2000 record: Did not manage.
Career: Beginning first year as manager.
Position as player: Catcher.

Chicago White Sox manager Jerry Manuel.

TONY MUSER — **ROYALS**
6-2, 190 **Born:** August 1, 1947.
2000 record: 77-85, 4th place, A.L. Central.
Career: 244-319 Royals 1997-2000.
Position as player: First base, outfield.

JOHNNY OATES — **RANGERS**
5-11, 185 **Born:** January 21, 1946.
2000 record: 71-91, 4th place, A.L. West.
Career: 291-270 Orioles 1991-94; 495-459 Rangers 1995-2000.
Position as player: Catcher.

LOU PINIELLA — **MARINERS**
6-2, 225 **Born:** August 28, 1943.
2000 record: 91-71, 2nd place, A.L. West.
Career: 224-193 Yankees 1986-88; 255-231 Reds 1990-92; 631-596 Mariners 1993-2000.
Position as player: Outfield, DH.

LARRY ROTHSCHILD — **DEVIL RAYS**
6-2, 185 **Born:** March 12, 1954.
2000 record: 69-92, 5th place, A.L. East.
Career: 201-284 Devil Rays 1998-2000.
Position as player: Pitcher.

MIKE SCIOSCIA — **ANGELS**
6-2, 220 **Born:** November 27, 1958.
2000 record: 82-80, 3rd place, A.L. West.
Career: 82-80 Angels 2000.
Position as player: Catcher.

JOE TORRE — **YANKEES**
6-1, 210 **Born:** July 18, 1940.
2000 record: 87-74, 1st place, A.L. East.
Career: 286-420 Mets 1977-81; 257-229 Braves 1982-84; 351-354 Cardinals 1990-95; 487-322 Yankees 1996-2000.
Position as player: Catcher, first base, third base.

JIMY WILLIAMS — **RED SOX**
5-11, 170 **Born:** October 4, 1943.
2000 record: 85-77, 2nd place, A.L. East.
Career: 281-241 Blue Jays 1986-89; 349-299 Red Sox 1997-2000.
Position as player: Shortstop.

NATIONAL LEAGUE

FELIPE ALOU — **EXPOS**
6-1, 195 **Born:** May 12, 1935.
2000 record: 67-95, 4th place, N.L. East.
Career: 670-685 Expos 1992-2000.
Position as player: Outfield, first base.

DUSTY BAKER — **GIANTS**
6-2, 200 **Born:** June 15, 1949.
2000 record: 97-65, 1st place, N.L. West.
Career: 655-577 Giants 1993-2000.
Position as player: Outfield.

DON BAYLOR — **CUBS**
6-1, 220 **Born:** June 28, 1949.
2000 record: 65-97, 6th place, N.L. Central.
Career: 440-469 Rockies 1993-98; 65-97 Cubs 2000.
Position as player: Outfield, DH.

BUDDY BELL — **ROCKIES**
6-3, 200 **Born:** August 27, 1951.
2000 record: 82-80, 4th place, N.L. West.
Career: 184-277 Tigers 1996-98; 82-80 Rockies 2000.
Position as player: Third base, first base.

BRUCE BOCHY — **PADRES**
6-4, 215 **Born:** April 16, 1955.
2000 record: 76-86, 5th place, N.L. West.
Career: 485-469 Padres 1995-2000.
Position as player: Catcher.

JOHN BOLES — **MARLINS**
5-10, 165 **Born:** August 19, 1948.
2000 record: 79-82, 3rd place, N.L. East.
Career: 40-35 Marlins 1996; 143-180 Marlins 1999-2000.
Position as player: No Major League Experience.

BOB BOONE — **REDS**
6-2, 207 **Born:** November 11, 1947.
2000 record: Did not manage.
Career: 181-206 Royals 1995-97.
Postion as player: Catcher.

LARRY BOWA — **PHILLIES**
5-10, 155 **Born:** December 6, 1945.
2000 record: Did not manage.
Career: 81-127 Padres 1986-88.
Position as player: Shortstop.

BOB BRENLY — **DIAMONDBACKS**
6-2, 205 **Born:** February 25, 1954.
2000 record: Did not manage.
Career: Beginning first year as manager.
Position as player: Catcher.

BOBBY COX — **BRAVES**
6-0, 185 **Born:** May 21, 1941.
2000 record: 95-67, 1st place, N.L. East.
Career: 266-323 Braves 1978-81, 995-656 1990-2000; 355-292 Blue Jays 1982-85.
Position as player: Third base, second base.

LARRY DIERKER — **ASTROS**
6-4, 215 **Born:** September 22, 1946.
2000 record: 72-90, 4th place, N.L. Central.
Career: 355-293 Astros 1997-2000.
Position as player: Pitcher.

TONY LARUSSA — **CARDINALS**
6-0, 185 **Born:** October 4, 1944.
2000 record: 95-67, 1st place, N.L. Central.
Career: 522-510 White Sox 1979-86; 798-673 Athletics 1986-95; 414-395 Cardinals 1996-2000.
Position as player: Infield.

DAVEY LOPES — **BREWERS**
5-9, 170 **Born:** May 3, 1945.
2000 record: 73-89, 3rd place, N.L. Central.
Career: 73-89 Brewers 2000.
Position as player: Second base.

LLOYD MCCLENDON — **PIRATES**
6-2, 208 **Born:** November 11, 1959.
2000 record: Did not manage.
Career: Beginning first year as manager.
Position as player: Outfield, first base, third base.

JIM TRACY — **DODGERS**
6-3, 205 **Born:** December 31, 1955.
2000 record: Did not manage.
Career: Beginning first year as manager.
Position as player: Outfield, first base.

BOBBY VALENTINE — **METS**
5-10, 189 **Born:** May 13, 1950.
2000 record: 94-68, 2nd place, N.L. East.
Career: 581-605 Rangers 1985-92; 379-301 Mets 1996-2000.
Position as player: Infield, outfield.

GENERAL MANAGERS

AMERICAN LEAGUE

GORD ASH — BLUE JAYS
Born: December 20, 1951.
Blue Jays general manager: 1994-2000.
Career path: Joined the Blue Jays organization in 1978; Blue Jays assistant director, operations 1980-84; Blue Jays administrator, player personnel 1984-89; Blue Jays assistant G.M. 1989-94; Blue Jays V.P. baseball and G.M. 1994-2000.

BILLY BEANE — ATHLETICS
Born: March 29, 1962.
Athletics general manager: 1996-2000.
Career path: Major League player with Mets, Twins, Tigers and Athletics 1984-89; joined Athletics as advance scout in 1990; Athletics assistant general manager 1993-96; Athletics general manager 1996-2000.

BRIAN CASHMAN — YANKEES
Born: July 3, 1967.
Yankees general manager: 1998-2000.
Career path: Joined Yankees as a college intern in 1986; became a full-time assistant in baseball operations department in 1989; served as assistant G.M. 1992-98; Yankees G.M. 1998-2000.

DAN DUQUETTE — RED SOX
Born: May 26, 1958.
Red Sox general manager: 1994-2000.
Career path: Joined Brewers front office in 1980 as assistant in scouting and player development; Brewers scouting director 1986-87; joined Expos organization in 1987 as director of player development; named Expos assistant G.M. 1990; Expos vice-president and general manager 1991-94; Red Sox G.M. 1994-2000.

PAT GILLICK — MARINERS
Born: August 22, 1937.
Mariners general manager: 2000.
Career path: Joined Astros organization as assistant farm director in 1964; advanced to director of scouting in 10 years with Houston; joined the Yankees as coordinator of player development and scouting in 1974; joined Blue Jays front office in the expansion season of 1976 as vice-president of player personnel; Blue Jays vice-president of baseball operations 1977-84; Blue Jays executive vice-president/baseball 1984-94; Orioles G.M. 1995-98; Mariners executive vice president and general manager of baseball operations 1999-2000.

JOHN HART — INDIANS
Born: July 21, 1948.
Indians general manager: 1991-2000.
Career path: Minor league manager in Orioles organization 1982-87; Orioles third base coach 1988; joined Indians front office in 1989 and served as director of baseball operations 1990-91; Indians executive V.P. and G.M. 1991-2000.

CHUCK LAMAR — DEVIL RAYS
Born: July 22, 1956.
Devil Rays general manager: 1995-2000.
Career path: Scouting supervisor for Reds 1985-89; director of minor league operations for Pirates 1989-90; director of scouting and player development for Braves 1990-93; assistant G.M. for player personnel for Braves 1993-95; Devil Rays senior V.P. for Baseball Operations and G.M. 1995-2000.

DOUG MELVIN — RANGERS
Born: August 8, 1952.
Rangers general manager: 1994-2000.
Career path: Coordinator of advance scouting reports for Yankees 1979-85; Yankees scouting director 1985; Orioles special assistant to club owner 1986-87; Orioles director of player personnel 1987-88; Orioles assistant G.M. 1988-94; Rangers V.P. and G.M. 1994-2000.

HERK ROBINSON — ROYALS
Born: June 25, 1940.
Royals general manager: 1990-2000.
Career path: Began career in Reds organization 1962-67; Orioles organization 1968; Royals assistant scouting director 1969-73; Royals director of stadium operations 1973-75; Royals vice-president 1975-81; Royals executive V.P. for administration 1981-90; Royals executive V.P. and G.M. 1990-2000.

TERRY RYAN — TWINS
Born: October 26, 1953.
Twins general manager: 1994-2000.
Career path: Mets Midwest scouting supervisor 1980-86; Twins scouting director 1986-91; Twins V.P. of player personnel 1991-94; Twins V.P. and G.M. 1994-2000.

RON SCHUELER — WHITE SOX
Born: April 18, 1948.
White Sox general manager: 1990-2000.
Career path: Major League pitcher with Braves, Phillies, Twins and White Sox 1972-79; White Sox pitching coach 1979-81; A's pitching coach 1982-84; Pirates pitching coach 1986; A's special assistant to G.M. 1986-89; White Sox V.P., Major League operations 1990-2000.

RANDY SMITH — TIGERS
Born: June 15, 1953.
Tigers general manager: 1995-2000.
Career path: Administrative assistant in Padres minor league system 1984; Padres assistant director of scouting 1985-88; Rockies assistant G.M. 1991-93; Padres V.P. baseball operations and G.M. 1993-95; Tigers V.P. baseball operations and G.M. 1995-2000.

BILL STONEMAN — ANGELS
Born: April 7, 1944.
Angels general manager: 2000.
Career path: Major League pitcher with Cubs, Expos and Angels 1967-74; Expos assistant to the President 1983; Expos vice president, baseball administration 1984-99; Angels vice president and general manager 1999-2000.

SYD THRIFT — ORIOLES
Born: February 25, 1929.
Orioles general manager: 2000.
Career path: Pitcher/first baseman in Yankees farm system 1949-50; part-time scout with Pirates and Yankees 1953-56; Pirates scouting supervisor and spring training instructor 1957-67; Royals scouting director and founding director of Royals Baseball Academy 1967-75; worked with Athletics scouting department 1975-76; Pirates general manager 1985-88; Yankees senior vice president, baseball operations 1989; consultant to the Dodgers, Mets and Giants organizations 1991; Cubs assistant general manager 1991-94; Orioles director of player development 1995-98; Orioles director of player personnel 1999-2000.

NATIONAL LEAGUE

JIM BEATTIE — EXPOS
Born: July 4, 1954.
Expos general manager: 1995-2000.
Career path: Major League pitcher with Yankees and Mariners 1978-86; Mariners director of player development 1989-95; Expos V.P and G.M. 1995-2000.

CAM BONIFAY — PIRATES
Born: February 12, 1952.
Pirates general manager: 1993-2000.
Career path: Served as a scout in Reds organization 1976-77; Cardinals scout 1978-80; Reds scouting supervisor 1982-87; Pirates scout 1988-90; Pirates assistant G.M. 1990-93; Pirates senior V.P. and G.M. 1993-2000.

Manager Bobby Cox (right) and general manager John Schuerholz call the shots for the Braves.

Jim Bowden **Reds**
Born: May 18, 1961.
Reds general manager: 1992-2000.
Career path: Joined Pirates organization in 1984; Pirates assistant director of player development 1985-88; Yankees assistant to the senior V.P. 1989; Reds administrative assistant for scouting 1990; Reds director of player development 1991-92; Reds G.M. 1992-2000.

Dave Dombrowski **Marlins**
Born: July 27, 1956.
Marlins general manager: 1991-2000.
Career path: Joined White Sox organization in 1978 as a minor league administrative assistant; White Sox assistant director of player development 1979-81; White Sox assistant G.M. 1981-85; White Sox V.P., baseball operations 1985-86; joined Expos front office 1986; Expos assistant to the G.M. 1987-88; Expos V.P./player personnel 1988-90; Expos G.M. 1990-91; Marlins executive V.P. and G.M. 1991-2000.

Joe Garagiola Jr. **Diamondbacks**
Born: August 6, 1950.
Diamondbacks general manager: 1995-2000.
Career path: Began baseball association in 1970s as general counsel and assistant to the president for the Yankees; practiced law with a Phoenix firm from 1982-95; chairman of Phoenix Metropolitan Sports Foundation 1985-87; vice chairman of Governor's Cactus League Task Force 1988-90; as member of Mayor's Professional Baseball Committee, he helped get an expansion team for Phoenix; Diamondbacks V.P. and G.M. 1995-2000.

Gerry Hunsicker **Astros**
Born: June 10, 1950.
Astros general manager: 1995-2000.
Career path: Held a variety of jobs in Astros organization 1978-81, including assistant to the G.M.; Mets director of minor league operations 1988-90; Mets director of baseball operations 1990-91; Mets assistant to the executive V.P. 1991-95; Astros G.M. 1995-2000.

Walt Jocketty **Cardinals**
Born: February 19, 1951.
Cardinals general manager: 1994-2000.
Career path: A's director of minor league operations and scouting 1980-83; A's director of baseball administration 1983-93; Rockies assistant G.M./player personnel 1993-94; Cardinals V.P./G.M. 1994-2000.

Ed Lynch **Cubs**
Born: February 25, 1956.
Cubs general manager: 1994-2000.
Career path: Major League pitcher with Mets and Cubs 1980-87; Padres director of minor leagues 1990-93; Mets special assistant to executive V.P. of baseball operations 1993-94; Cubs G.M. 1994-2000.

Kevin Malone **Dodgers**
Born: Aug. 6, 1957.
Dodgers general manager: 1999-2000.
Career path: Served as the Angels' Southern California scout from 1985-87; worked as Expos' Southern California scout and a minor league instructor in 1988; worked as Twins' East Coast scouting supervisor from 1989-91; Expos' director of scouting from 1991-94; Expos' G.M. from 1994-95; Orioles' assistant G.M. from 1995-98; Dodgers' executive V.P and G.M. September 1998-2000.

Dan O'Dowd **Rockies**
Born: 1959.
Rockies general manager: 2000.
Career path: Worked in Orioles broadcasting and marketing departments 1983-85; Orioles assistant director of player development and scouting 1985-87; Indians director of player development 1988-92; Indians director of baseball operations and assistant general manager 1993-98; Rockies executive vice president-general manager, 1999-2000.

Steve Phillips **Mets**
Born: May 18, 1963, 1949.
Mets general manager: 1998-2000.
Career path: Mets administrative assistant to the minor leagues and scouting 1990-91; Mets director of minor leagues 1991-97; Mets senior vice president and G.M. 1998-2000.

Brian Sabean **Giants**
Born: July 1, 1956.
Giants general manager: 1996-2000.
Career path: Former college baseball coach at St. Leo College and University of Tampa; head coach at Tampa 1983-84; joined Yankees organization and served as director of scouting 1986-90; Yankees vice president player development/scouting 1990-92; joined Giants and served as assistant general manager and vice president of scouting/player personnel 1993-95; served as senior vice president, player personnel 1995-96; Giants senior V.P. and G.M. 1996-2000.

John Schuerholz **Braves**
Born: October 1, 1940.
Braves general manager: 1990-2000.
Career path: Worked in Orioles organization 1966-68; Royals administrative assistant 1968-70; Royals assistant farm director 1970-75; Royals farm director 1975-76; Royals director of player procurement 1976-79; Royals V.P. /player personnel 1979-81; Royals executive V.P and G.M. 1981-90; Braves executive V.P. and G.M. 1990-2000.

Dean Taylor **Brewers**
Born: April 19, 1951.
Brewers general manager: 2000.
Career path: Minor league general manager 1976-80; Royals administrative assistant for minor league operations and assistant director of scouting and player development 1980-85; Royals assistant to the general manager 1985-90; Braves assistant general manager 1990-99; Brewers senior vice president/baseball operations and G.M. 1999-2000.

Kevin Towers **Padres**
Born: November 11, 1961.
Padres general manager: 1995-2000.
Career path: Padres scout 1989-91; Padres scouting director 1993-95; Padres senior V.P. and G.M. 1995-2000.

Ed Wade **Phillies**
Born: January 31, 1956.
Phillies general manager: 1997-2000.
Career path: Began baseball career as public relations assistant 1977-79; Astros public relations director 1979-81; joined Pirates as public relations director 1981-85; became an associate for Tal Smith Enterprises 1985-89; Phillies assistant general manager 1989-97; Phillies G.M. 1997-2000.

History

The year before Jackie Robinson became the first black player in modern baseball history, he performed his magic for the Montreal Royals, Brooklyn's Class AAA farm team.

INTRODUCTION

IN THE BEGINNING

When Chicago businessman William Ambrose Hulbert set out to cure the ills that had afflicted his favorite sport in its formative years, he called a meeting in New York.

And what a meeting it turned out to be. When all was said and done, Major League Baseball—in the form of the National League—had become a part of the American sports landscape.

It all happened at the Grand Central Hotel on February 2, 1876. Hulbert, a baseball fan of the first rank, was determined to end the rowdyism, alcohol abuse and gambling that had troubled baseball. What he ended up with was the founding of the National League of Professional Baseball Clubs, with franchises awarded to Chicago, Cincinnati, St. Louis, Louisville, New York, Hartford, Boston and Philadelphia.

Hulbert, who had headed the Chicago club in baseball's first professional league, the wild and woolly National Association (1871-75), wanted the new league to exhibit a higher caliber of play and, just as important, be beyond reproach in terms of integrity and orderliness. To help achieve his goals, Hulbert named prominent businessman Morgan Bulkeley—the son of the founder of the Aetna Insurance Co.—as the National League's first president.

Bulkeley indicated his reign would be brief, and it was. His one year on the job was long enough, though, to get the National League off on a firm footing. And this new league, with strong leadership and outstanding talent, won billing as baseball's first major league.

Franchises came and went in the National League's first 24 years, but the alignment in place for 1900—Brooklyn, Boston, New York, Philadelphia, Pittsburgh, Chicago, Cincinnati and St. Louis—remained intact through the 1952 season.

Commissioner Kenesaw Mountain Landis, pictured with American League president Will Harridge (left), brought order to the game after the Black Sox scandal.

Rivals to the N.L. came and went, too, with only the American League surviving. The A.L., with Ban Johnson as its first president, was founded in 1901. And, from 1903 through 1953, the American League was another model of stability, with its membership (New York, Boston, Washington, Cleveland, Detroit, Chicago, Philadelphia and St. Louis) holding firm.

Spurred by franchise shifts and expansion, the major league landscape has changed dramatically since '52. The leagues have grown from two entities of eight teams each to two of 16 and 14 clubs, and the majors have moved into Milwaukee, Baltimore, Kansas City, Los Angeles, San Francisco, Minneapolis-St. Paul, Houston, Anaheim, Atlanta, Oakland, Seattle, Montreal, San Diego, Arlington, Toronto, Miami, Denver, Tampa-St. Petersburg and Phoenix. The latter two areas were new to the big-league map in 1998.

Major League Baseball's growth since that 1876 meeting in New York has mirrored that of the nation. It has been an exhilarating and frenetic 125 years in America's ballparks—and as season No. 126 unfolds in 2001, fans are expecting more of the same.

THE WAY IT WAS ... AND IS

When the first pitch in major league history was thrown on April 22, 1876 (in a game matching the Boston and Philadelphia teams in the fledgling National League), Ulysses S. Grant was serving as the 18th president of the United States, the Union consisted of 37 states, George Armstrong Custer and his troops had yet to meet their fate at the Battle of the Little Bighorn, the Statue of Liberty was eight years away from completion in France and aviation's Wright brothers were 9 and 4 years old. In that first game, another Wright—Harry, known as the "father of professional baseball" because he organized the first pro team, the 1869 Cincinnati Red Stockings—managed Boston to a 6-5 victory. ... The Boston franchise, later to be known as the Braves, lives on today in Atlanta and is one of only two big-league clubs to have been in continuous operation since the start of major league ball. Of course, the franchise has bounced from Beantown to Milwaukee to Atlanta, leaving Chicago's N.L. team as the only franchise to be operated continuously in one city from Day One of the majors' inception. ... Other "big leagues" sprung up in 1882 (the American Association, which lasted through 1891), 1884 (the Union Association), 1890 (the Players League, like the UA, a one-season operation), 1901 (the American League) and 1914 (the Federal League, which lasted two years). ... Although the Cubs and Red Sox will be among teams hoping to end long World Series droughts in 2001, those clubs were among the scourges of baseball in the early part of the 20th century. The Cubs, who haven't even played in a Series since 1945 and last won one in 1908, took two consecutive Series crowns while making four fall classic appearances in five years (1906-1910). The Red Sox, who haven't claimed a Series title since 1918, won the first-ever fall classic in 1903 and were champions in their first five Series ('03, 1912, 1915, 1916, 1918). Boston has lost in its last four Series. The Red Sox qualified for the playoffs for the second consecutive year in 1999 (the first time they had made back-to-back postseason appearances since '15-'16), but New England fans were disappointed once more when the Sox were eliminated in the League Championship Series by the Yankees. ... The Yankees, who won their 37th A.L. pennant in 2000, won their first flag in the club's pre-Bronx Bombers days. Yes, the Yanks had Babe Ruth and other robust hitters when they copped their first pennant in 1921, but the club was still playing at the Polo Grounds—in the borough of Manhattan—in those days. The move to the Bronx and Yankee Stadium came in 1923, the year the Yankees won their first of 26 World Series championships. ... The Athletics and Giants also fielded powerhouse teams in the century's first three decades. Connie Mack's A's were World Series champions three times in a four-year span (1910-13) and ruled again in 1929 and 1930. John McGraw's Giants won it all in 1905, 1921 and 1922 and appeared in six other Series. ... Commissioner Kenesaw Mountain Landis' unyielding stewardship, Ruth's slugging (and accompanying gate appeal) and the presence of great Yankees teams helped baseball overcome the Black Sox mess of 1919. Starting in '23, the Yanks won eight Series titles in 17 years. ... In the 18 seasons from 1947 through 1964, the Yankees rolled to 15 pennants in a run that included a record-setting five consecutive Series championships (1949-53). ... Since '64, the Oakland A's (three straight Series crowns in the early 1970s) and Cincinnati's Big Red Machine (1975 and 1976 Series championships and strong clubs before and after) have been in the spotlight, joined in recent years by the Series-winning Toronto Blue Jays of 1992 and 1993 and the Yankees, whose 2000 Series title was their fourth in five years. Also rating mention are the Atlanta Braves, who have won divisional crowns in the last nine non-strike seasons; the Florida Marlins, who won the World Series in only the fifth season in franchise history, 1997, before being dismantled in a payroll-reduction move; and the Arizona Diamondbacks, who won a division title in 1999, their second year of existence.

—JOE HOPPEL

1876

FINAL STANDINGS

National League

Team	W	L	Pct.	GB
Chicago	52	14	.788	...
St. Louis	45	19	.703	6
Hartford	47	21	.691	6
Boston	39	31	.557	15
Louisville	30	36	.455	22
New York	21	35	.375	26
Philadelphia	14	45	.237	34.5
Cincinnati	9	56	.138	42.5

SIGNIFICANT EVENTS

■ William Hulbert, president of the National Association's Chicago franchise, presided over a February meeting that signaled the official beginning of a new National League. Morgan Bulkeley was selected as the new circuit's first president.

■ The New York Mutuals, following the lead of the Philadelphia Athletics, announced they would not make their season-ending Western trip, forcing cancellation of a major chunk of the N.L.'s September schedule.

■ During a December meeting in Cleveland, the Athletics and Mutuals were expelled from the N.L. lineup and William Hulbert was elected president.

MEMORABLE MOMENTS

■ Boston 6, Philadelphia 5 in the first N.L. game. Jim O'Rourke entered the record books as the first player to get a hit in the April 22 battle at Athletic Park.

■ Chicago's Ross Barnes became the first N.L. player to hit a home run—an inside-the-park drive in a game at Cincinnati.

■ St. Louis' George Bradley pitched the first no-hitter in N.L. history, defeating Hartford, 2-0.

■ Hartford 14-8, Cincinnati 4-1 in baseball's first doubleheader.

■ Chicago clinched the N.L.'s first pennant with a victory over Hartford.

LEADERS

BA: Ross Barnes, Chi., .403.
Runs: Ross Barnes, Chi., 126.
Hits: Ross Barnes, Chi., 138.
TB: Ross Barnes, Chi., 190.
HR: George Hall, Phil., 5.
RBI: Deacon White, Chi., 60.
Wins: Al Spalding, Chi., 47.
ERA: George Bradley, St.L., 1.23.
CG: Jim Devlin, Lou., 66.
IP: Jim Devlin, Lou., 622.
SO: Jim Devlin, Lou., 122.

20-game winners

Al Spalding, Chi., 47-12
George Bradley, St.L., 45-19
Tommy Bond, Hart., 31-13
Jim Devlin, Lou., 30-35
Bobby Mathews, N.Y., 21-34

THE RULES

■ The new National League adopted a detailed rule book that included these interesting variations to the rules we use today:

■ The Strike Zone: The batter, upon stepping into position, had to call for a high or low pitch and the umpire notified the pitcher to deliver the ball as requested, making his calls accordingly.

■ The Strikeout: When a batter with two strikes failed to swing at the next good pitch, the umpire warned him by calling "good ball." If the batter swung and missed or failed to swing at the next "good ball", the umpire called "three strikes" and the batter was expected to run to first as if he had hit a fair ball.

■ Substitutions: No player could be replaced after the fourth inning, except those giving way temporarily for a pinch runner.

■ Batter/Position: When batters stepped outside the box while striking at the ball, the umpire would call "foul balk and out," allowing all runners to return to their bases.

■ Pitchers threw underhanded from a box with a front line that was 45 feet from the center of home base.

1877

FINAL STANDINGS

National League

Team	W	L	Pct.	GB
Boston	42	18	.700	...
Louisville	35	25	.583	7
Hartford	31	27	.534	10
St. Louis	28	32	.467	14
Chicago	26	33	.441	15.5
Cincinnati	15	42	.263	25.5

SIGNIFICANT EVENTS

■ The Hartford club announced in March that it would play its 1877 "home games" in Brooklyn while retaining its "home base" of Hartford.

■ Without enough money to finance a mid-season trip, the Cincinnati club disbanded. It was reorganized three days later under new ownership.

■ The Louisville team expelled players George Hall, Jim Devlin, Al Nichols and Bill Craver for fixing games, a move that later would be supported by league officials.

■ At its December meeting, the N.L. dropped franchises in Hartford and St. Louis and admitted teams in Indianapolis and Milwaukee.

MEMORABLE MOMENTS

■ Boston and Hartford opened the N.L.'s second season with an 11-inning 1-1 tie at Brooklyn.

■ Boston clinched the N.L. pennant with a victory over Hartford.

LEADERS

BA: Deacon White, Bos., .387.
Runs: Jim O'Rourke, Bos., 68.
Hits: Deacon White, Bos., 103.
TB: Deacon White, Bos., 145.
HR: Lip Pike, Cin., 4.
RBI: Deacon White, Bos., 49.
Wins: Tommy Bond, Bos., 40.
ERA: Tommy Bond, Bos., 2.11.
CG: Jim Devlin, Lou., 61.
IP: Jim Devlin, Lou., 559.
SO: Tommy Bond, Bos., 170.

20-game winners

Tommy Bond, Bos., 40-17
Jim Devlin, Lou., 35-25
Terry Larkin, Hart., 29-25

MAJOR RULES CHANGES

■ Any batted ball that bounced into foul territory before passing first or third base became a "foul" ball instead of a "fair" ball.

■ Home base was repositioned entirely in fair territory, two sides laying flush with the foul lines. The 17-inch move forward forced a corresponding move back of the pitcher's box.

■ The batter's box was changed to 6 feet in length—3 feet in front and 3 feet in back of the home-base line.

■ The size of bases was enlarged to 15 square inches, with their sides positioned parallel to the base lines.

■ An at-bat was not charged when a batter drew a base on balls.

1878

FINAL STANDINGS

National League

Team	W	L	Pct.	GB
Boston	41	19	.683	...
Cincinnati	37	23	.617	4
Providence	33	27	.550	8
Chicago	30	30	.500	11
Indianapolis	24	36	.400	17
Milwaukee	15	45	.250	26

SIGNIFICANT EVENTS

■ The N.L. increased its membership to seven with the addition of the Grays, a new franchise in Providence, R.I., but the field was reduced back to six when Louisville, unable to put together a competitive roster, resigned from the league.

■ At its winter meetings, the N.L. admitted new members Syracuse, Buffalo and Cleveland while dropping Indianapolis and Milwaukee.

MEMORABLE MOMENTS

■ Defending-champion Boston spoiled the Major League debut of the Grays, 1-0, in an opening day game at Providence's new Messer Street Park.

■ Tommy Bond defeated Providence for his 40th victory and brought Boston within range of its second consecutive pennant.

LEADERS

BA: Abner Dalrymple, Mil., .354.
Runs: Dick Higham, Pro., 60.
Hits: Joe Start, Chi., 100.
TB: Paul Hines, Pro.; Joe Start, Chi.; Tom York, Pro., 125.
HR: Paul Hines, Pro., 4.
RBI: Paul Hines, Pro., 50.
Wins: Tommy Bond, Bos., 40.
ERA: Monte Ward, Pro., 1.51.
CG: Tommy Bond, Bos., 57.
IP: Tommy Bond, Bos., 532.2.
SO: Tommy Bond, Bos., 182.

20-game winners

Tommy Bond, Bos., 40-19
Will White, Cin., 30-21
Terry Larkin, Chi. 29-26
Monte Ward, Pro., 22-13

MAJOR RULES CHANGES

■ Captains were required to position their players and after one at-bat, the batting order could no longer be changed.

■ Pinch runners were not allowed except in cases of illness or injury. The emergency substitute could enter the game only after the original player had reached base.

1879

FINAL STANDINGS

National League

Team	W	L	Pct.	GB
Providence	59	25	.702	...
Boston	54	30	.643	5
Buffalo	46	32	.590	10
Chicago	46	33	.582	10.5
Cincinnati	43	37	.538	14
Cleveland	27	55	.329	31
Syracuse	22	48	.314	30
Troy	19	56	.253	35.5

SIGNIFICANT EVENTS

■ The N.L. beefed up its preseason roster by admitting a new Troy franchise.

■ The Syracuse Stars, facing bankruptcy in mid-September, resigned from the N.L., leaving the league with an incomplete schedule.

■ The financially strapped Cincinnati club ended the season and folded operation, refusing to pay its players their final month's salary.

■ A new Cincinnati club gained quick N.L. acceptance during the annual winter meetings.

MEMORABLE MOMENTS

■ John Montgomery Ward's streak of having pitched every inning of 73 consecutive Providence games ended in mid-July when he was relieved in the fourth inning of a 9-0 loss to Cincinnati.

■ The Providence Grays scored a ninth-inning run and claimed a pennant-clinching victory over Boston.

■ Cincinnati pitcher Will White completed the season with 75 complete games and 680 innings—still-standing Major League records.

LEADERS

BA: Cap Anson, Chi., .317.
Runs: Charley Jones, Bos., 85.
Hits: Paul Hines, Pro., 146.
TB: Paul Hines, Pro., 197.
HR: Charley Jones, Bos., 9.
RBI: Charley Jones, Bos.; Jim O'Rourke, Bos., 62.
Wins: Monte Ward, Pro., 47.
ERA: Tommy Bond, Bos., 1.96.
CG: Will White, Cin., 75.
IP: Will White, Cin., 680.
SO: Monte Ward, Pro., 239.

20-game winners

Monte Ward, Pro., 47-19
Tommy Bond, Bos., 43-19
Will White, Cin., 43-31
Pud Galvin, Buf., 37-27
Terry Larkin, Chi., 31-23
Jim McCormick, Cle., 20-40

MAJOR RULES CHANGES

■ The size of the pitcher's box was enlarged to 4-by-6 feet.

■ A batter was declared out after three strikes if the pitch was caught before touching the ground.

■ Any pitcher who, in the opinion of the umpire, intentionally hit a batter with a pitch was fined from $10 to $50.

■ The "Spalding League Ball" was adopted as the official ball.

1880

FINAL STANDINGS

National League

Team	W	L	Pct.	GB
Chicago	67	17	.798	...
Providence	52	32	.619	15
Cleveland	47	37	.560	20
Troy	41	42	.494	25.5
Worcester	40	43	.482	26.5
Boston	40	44	.476	27
Buffalo	24	58	.293	42
Cincinnati	21	59	.263	44

SIGNIFICANT EVENTS

- The preseason addition of a team in Worcester brought the N.L. field back to eight.
- After kicking Cincinnati out of the league for rules violations, the N.L. admitted a new franchise from Detroit.

MEMORABLE MOMENTS

- A Major League first—Worcester's Lee Richmond was perfect in a 1-0 victory over Cleveland.
- Providence ace John Montgomery Ward matched the perfect-game feat of Lee Richmond five days earlier, retiring all 27 Buffalo batters he faced in a 5-0 victory.
- Fred Dunlap's ninth-inning home run broke a scoreless tie and gave Cleveland a victory over Chicago, snapping the White Stockings' record 21-game inning streak.
- Chicago completed its season with a 67-17 record and a 15-game bulge over second-place Providence.

LEADERS

BA: George Gore, Chi., .360.
Runs: Abner Dalrymple, Chi., 91.
Hits: Abner Dalrymple, Chi., 126.
TB: Abner Dalrymple, Chi., 175.
HR: Jim O'Rourke, Bos.; Harry Stovey, Wor., 6.
RBI: Cap Anson, Chi., 74.
Wins: Jim McCormick, Cle., 45.
ERA: Tim Keefe, Troy, 0.86.
CG: Jim McCormick, Cle., 72.
IP: Jim McCormick, Cle., 657.2.
SO: Larry Corcoran, Chi., 268.

20-game winners

Jim McCormick, Cle., 45-28
Larry Corcoran, Chi., 43-14
Monte Ward, Pro., 39-24
Mickey Welch, Troy, 34-30
Lee Richmond, Wor., 32-32
Tommy Bond, Bos., 26-29
Fred Goldsmith, Chi., 21-3
Pud Galvin, Buf., 20-35

MAJOR RULES CHANGES

- A walk was awarded after eight balls instead of nine.
- A runner was declared out if hit by a batted ball, and no run was allowed to score on the play.
- The batter was required to run for first base immediately after "strike three" was called by the umpire.

1881

FINAL STANDINGS

National League

Team	W	L	Pct.	GB
Chicago	56	28	.667	...
Providence	47	37	.560	9
Buffalo	45	38	.542	10.5
Detroit	41	43	.488	15
Troy	39	45	.464	17
Boston	38	45	.458	17.5
Cleveland	36	48	.429	20
Worcester	32	50	.390	23

SIGNIFICANT EVENTS

- One month after the 1881 season had ended, officials announced the formation of the American Association, a rival Major League with franchises in St. Louis, Cincinnati, Louisville, Philadelphia, Pittsburgh and Brooklyn.
- American Association officials voted to ignore N.L. rules against Sunday games, liquor sales and 25-cent ticket prices. They also announced their decision not to abide by the N.L.'s restrictive reserve clause in player contracts.

MEMORABLE MOMENTS

- Troy's Roger Connor hit the first grand slam in N.L. history—a bottom-of-the-ninth blow that handed Worcester an 8-7 defeat.
- Chicago clinched its second straight pennant with a victory over Boston and White Stockings star Cap Anson put the finishing touches on his league-leading .399 average.

LEADERS

BA: Cap Anson, Chi., .399.
Runs: George Gore, Chi., 86.
Hits: Cap Anson, Chi., 137.
TB: Cap Anson, Chi., 175.
HR: Dan Brouthers, Buf., 8.
RBI: Cap Anson, Chi., 82.
Wins: Larry Corcoran, Chi.; Jim Whitney, Bos., 31.
ERA: Stump Weidman, Det., 1.80.
CG: Jim McCormick, Cle.; Jim Whitney, Bos., 57.
IP: Jim Whitney, Bos., 552.1.
SO: George Derby, Det., 212.

20-game winners

Larry Corcoran, Chi., 31-14
Jim Whitney, Bos., 31-33
George Derby, Det., 29-26
Pud Galvin, Buf., 28-24
Jim McCormick, Cle., 26-30
Hoss Radbourn, Pro., 25-11
Lee Richmond, Wor., 25-26
Fred Goldsmith, Chi., 24-13
Mickey Welch, Troy, 21-18

MAJOR RULES CHANGES

- The front line of the pitcher's box was moved from 45 to 50 feet from the center of home base.
- A batter was awarded first base after seven balls.
- No substitutes were permitted except in the cases of illness or injury.
- Umpires no longer gave players the "good ball" warning on called third strikes.

1882

FINAL STANDINGS

American Association

Team	W	L	Pct.	GB
Cincinnati	55	25	.688	...
Philadelphia	41	34	.547	11.5
Louisville	42	38	.525	13
Pittsburgh	39	39	.500	15
St. Louis	37	43	.463	18
Baltimore	19	54	.260	32.5

SIGNIFICANT EVENTS

- After completing its first season as a six-team circuit, the American Association added franchises in Columbus and New York.
- A baseball first: The Association formed the first permanent staff of umpires.

MEMORABLE MOMENTS

- Opening day for the new American Association: St. Louis 9, Louisville 7; Philadelphia 10, Baltimore 7; Allegheny 10, Cincinnati 9.
- Louisville ace Tony Mullane recorded the league's first no-hitter, beating the Red Stockings 2-0 at Cincinnati.
- Cincinnati clinched the first A.A. pennant with a 6-1 mid-September victory over Louisville as the second-place Athletics dropped a game at Pittsburgh.
- In the first post-season matchup of Major League champions, the Red Stockings split a two-game series with N.L. pennant winner Chicago.

LEADERS

BA: Pete Browning, Lou., .378.
Runs: Ed Swartwood, Pit., 86.
Hits: Hick Carpenter, Cin., 120.
TB: Ed Swartwood, Pit., 159.
HR: Oscar Walker, St.L., 7.
Wins: Will White, Cin., 40.
ERA: Denny Driscoll, Pit., 1.21.
CG: Will White, Cin., 52.
IP: Will White, Cin., 480.
SO: Tony Mullane, Lou., 170.

20-game winners

Will White, Cin., 40-12
Tony Mullane, Lou., 30-24
Sam Weaver, Phil., 26-15
George McGinnis, St.L., 25-18
Harry Salisbury, Pit., 20-18

THE RULES

- The new American Association began its first season with several modifications to the existing rules book. Among the variations:
- Sunday games were allowed.
- Teams could charge 25 cents for admission rather than the N.L. price of 50 cents.
- Liquor could be sold at the ballparks.
- Pitchers judged to be intentionally throwing at batters were not subject to immediate fines.

FINAL STANDINGS

National League

Team	W	L	Pct.	GB
Chicago	55	29	.655	...
Providence	52	32	.619	3
Boston	45	39	.536	10
Buffalo	45	39	.536	10
Cleveland	42	40	.512	12
Detroit	42	41	.506	12.5
Troy	35	48	.422	19.5
Worcester	18	66	.214	37

SIGNIFICANT EVENTS

- When N.L. President William Hulbert died of a heart attack in April, Boston team president A.H. Soden was named as his replacement.
- At the winter meetings, N.L. officials replaced the Troy and Worcester franchises with teams from New York and Philadelphia, keeping the league roster at eight.

MEMORABLE MOMENTS

- Chicago 35, Cleveland 4: a record rout in which seven White Stockings got four or more hits.
- Chicago ace Larry Corcoran pitched his second career no-hitter, beating Worcester, 5-0.
- Chicago finished with a 55-29 record and claimed its third straight N.L. pennant by three games over Providence.

LEADERS

BA: Dan Brouthers, Buf., .368.
Runs: George Gore, Chi., 99.
Hits: Dan Brouthers, Buf., 129.
TB: Dan Brouthers, Buf., 192.
HR: George Wood, Det., 7.
RBI: Cap Anson, Chi., 83.
Wins: Jim McCormick, Cle., 36.
ERA: Larry Corcoran, Chi., 1.95.
CG: Jim McCormick, Cle., 65.
IP: Jim McCormick, Cle., 595.2.
SO: Hoss Radbourn, Pro., 201.

20-game winners

Jim McCormick, Cle., 36-30
Hoss Radbourn, Pro., 33-20
Fred Goldsmith, Chi., 28-17
Pud Galvin, Buf., 28-23
Larry Corcoran, Chi., 27-12
George Weidman, Det., 25-20
Jim Whitney, Bos., 24-21

MAJOR RULES CHANGES

- Umpires could call for a new ball at the end of even innings, provided the old ball was unfit for fair use.
- The home team was required to provide a players' bench, 12 feet in length and fastened to the ground. Racks that held at least 20 bats became mandatory.
- A baserunner obstructing a player attempting to field a batted ball was called out for interference.
- Spectators caught hissing or hooting at the umpire were ejected from the park.

1883

FINAL STANDINGS

American Association

Team	W	L	Pct.	GB
Philadelphia	66	32	.673	...
St. Louis	65	33	.663	1
Cincinnati	61	37	.622	5
New York	54	42	.563	11
Louisville	52	45	.536	13.5
Columbus	32	65	.330	33.5
Pittsburgh	31	67	.316	35
Baltimore	28	68	.292	37

SIGNIFICANT EVENTS

■ In a significant February meeting, baseball officials drafted the first National Agreement, ensuring peaceful co-existence and respect for player contracts between the N.L. and American Association. Both leagues embraced the controversial reserve clause.

■ The Association announced post-season plans to expand to 12 teams with new franchises in Brooklyn, Washington, Indianapolis and Toledo.

MEMORABLE MOMENTS

■ New York's Tim Keefe celebrated Independence Day by winning both ends of a doubleheader against Columbus. Keefe allowed only three total hits.

■ The Athletics posted a late-September victory over Louisville and claimed the American Association's second pennant.

LEADERS

BA: Ed Swartwood, Pit., .357.
Runs: Harry Stovey, Phil., 110.
Hits: Ed Swartwood, Pit., 147.
TB: Harry Stovey, Phil., 213.
HR: Harry Stovey, Phil., 14.
Wins: Will White, Cin., 43.
ERA: Will White, Cin., 2.09.
CG: Tim Keefe, N.Y., 68.
IP: Tim Keefe, N.Y., 619.
SO: Tim Keefe, N.Y., 359.

20-game winners

Will White, Cin., 43-22
Tim Keefe, N.Y., 41-27
Tony Mullane, St.L., 35-15
Bobby Mathews, Phil., 30-13
George McGinnis, St.L., 28-16
Sam Weaver, Lou., 26-22
Guy Hecker, Lou., 26-23
Frank Mountain, Col., 26-33

MAJOR RULES CHANGES

■ Pitchers were allowed to deliver the ball from a shoulder-length position instead of the former below-the-waist position.

■ A runner touching and overrunning first base put himself at risk of being tagged out if he turned to his left while returning to the bag.

■ Pinch runners were allowed in cases of illness and injury.

FINAL STANDINGS

National League

Team	W	L	Pct.	GB
Boston	63	35	.643	...
Chicago	59	39	.602	4
Providence	58	40	.592	5
Cleveland	55	42	.567	7.5
Buffalo	52	45	.536	10.5
New York	46	50	.479	16
Detroit	40	58	.408	23
Philadelphia	17	81	.173	46

SIGNIFICANT EVENTS

■ Peace prevails: The N.L. and American Association signed a new National Agreement, ensuring respect for player contracts under the controversial reserve system.

MEMORABLE MOMENTS

■ Philadelphia 28, Providence 0—the most lopsided shutout in Major League history.

■ The White Stockings exploded for a record 18 runs in the seventh inning of a victory over Detroit.

■ Boston broke Chicago's three-year stranglehold on the N.L. pennant with a clinching victory over Cleveland.

LEADERS

BA: Dan Brouthers, Buf., .374.
Runs: Joe Hornung, Bos., 107.
Hits: Dan Brouthers, Buf., 159.
TB: Dan Brouthers, Buf., 243.
HR: Buck Ewing, N.Y., 10.
RBI: Dan Brouthers, Buf., 97.
Wins: Hoss Radbourn, Pro., 48.
ERA: Jim McCormick, Cle., 1.84.
CG: Pud Galvin, Buf., 72.
IP: Pud Galvin, Buf., 656.1.
SO: Jim Whitney, Bos., 345.

20-game winners

Hoss Radbourn, Pro., 48-25
Pud Galvin, Buf., 46-29
Jim Whitney, Bos., 37-21
Larry Corcoran, Chi., 34-20
Jim McCormick, Cle., 28-12
Charlie Buffinton, Bos., 25-14
Fred Goldsmith, Chi., 25-19
Mickey Welch, N.Y., 25-23
Hugh Daily, Cle., 23-19

MAJOR RULES CHANGES

■ Pitchers working within the confines of the box and facing the batter could deliver the ball with more forceful motion. The ball, on delivery, had to pass below the line of the pitcher's shoulder instead of below his waist.

■ A batted ball caught in foul territory was declared an out. Previously, balls caught on one bounce in foul territory were outs.

■ A player batting out of order was declared out.

■ Umpires became salaried employees.

1884

FINAL STANDINGS

Union Association

Team	W	L	Pct.	GB
St. Louis	94	19	.832	...
Milwaukee	8	4	.667	35.5
Cincinnati	69	36	.657	21
Baltimore	58	47	.552	32
Boston	58	51	.532	34
Chicago-Pitt.	41	50	.451	42
Washington	47	65	.420	46.5
Philadelphia	21	46	.313	50
St. Paul	2	6	.250	39.5
Altoona	6	19	.240	44
Kansas City	16	63	.203	61
Wilmington	2	16	.111	44.5

SIGNIFICANT EVENTS

■ The new Union Association, organized the previous September as a third Major League, added a Boston team to its roster while preparing for its first season.

■ U.A. casualties: Altoona (6-19) ceased operations in May, Philadelphia (21-46) disbanded in August and Chicago transferred operations in late August to Pittsburgh. Wilmington and Pittsburgh later were replaced by Milwaukee and Omaha—a franchise that lasted eight days and was replaced by St. Paul.

■ Only five teams attended the U.A.'s winter meetings, setting the stage for the league to disband in January.

MEMORABLE MOMENTS

■ Boston defeated St. Louis and ended the Maroons' 20-game winning streak

■ Boston's Fred Shaw held St. Louis to one hit and struck out 18, but he still lost a 1-0 decision to the pennant-bound Maroons.

LEADERS

BA: Fred Dunlap, St.L., .412.
Runs: Fred Dunlap, St.L., 160.
Hits: Fred Dunlap, St.L., 185.
TB: Fred Dunlap, St.L., 279.
HR: Fred Dunlap, St.L., 13.
Wins: Bill Sweeney, Bal., 40.
ERA: Jim McCormick, Cin., 1.54.
CG: Bill Sweeney, Bal., 58.
IP: Bill Sweeney, Bal., 538.
SO: Hugh Daily, CP-Wash., 483.

20-game winners

Bill Sweeney, Bal., 40-21
Hugh Daily, C-W-P, 28-28
Billy Taylor, St.L., 25-4
George Bradley, Cin., 25-15
Charlie Sweeney, St.L., 24-7
Dick Burns, Cin., 23-15
Bill Wise, Wash., 23-18
Jim McCormick, Cin., 21-3
Fred Shaw, Bos., 21-15

THE RULES

■ The Union Association, in its only Major League season, adopted the American Association rules book, which still included the shoulder-length restriction on pitching deliveries and seven-ball walks. The U.A., however, did adopt the N.L. rule on foul flies. The A.A.'s new hit-by-pitch rule was not adopted by the U.A.

FINAL STANDINGS

American Association

Team	W	L	Pct.	GB
New York	75	32	.701	...
Columbus	69	39	.639	6.5
Louisville	68	40	.630	7.5
St. Louis	67	40	.626	8
Cincinnati	68	41	.624	8
Baltimore	63	43	.594	11.5
Philadelphia	61	46	.570	14
Toledo	46	58	.442	27.5
Brooklyn	40	64	.385	33.5
Richmond	12	30	.286	30.5
Pittsburgh	30	78	.278	45.5
Indianapolis	29	78	.271	46
Washington	12	51	.190	41

SIGNIFICANT EVENTS

■ Toledo's Fleetwood Walker became the Major League's first black player when he went 0-for-3 in an opening day loss to Louisville.

■ Columbus, a second-place finisher in its only season, sold its players and dropped out of the league.

MEMORABLE MOMENTS

■ Louisville ace Guy Hecker, en route to Association season-high totals of 52 wins and 72 complete games, pitched both ends of a Fourth of July doubleheader sweep of Brooklyn.

■ The Metropolitans captured their first A.A. pennant with a 4-1 victory over Columbus.

■ The N.L.'s Providence Grays posted a 6-0 victory over New York in a post-season matchup of pennant winners. The Grays would go on to win three straight games and an unofficial world championship.

LEADERS

BA: Dude Esterbrook, N.Y., .314.
Runs: Harry Stovey, Phil., 124.
Hits: Dave Orr, N.Y., 162.
TB: Dave Orr, N.Y.; John Reilly, Cin., 247.
HR: John Reilly, Cin., 11.
Wins: Guy Hecker, Lou., 52.
ERA: Guy Hecker, Lou., 1.80.
CG: Guy Hecker, Lou., 72.
IP: Guy Hecker, Lou., 670.2.
SO: Guy Hecker, Lou., 385.

20-game winners

Guy Hecker, Lou., 52-20
Jack Lynch, N.Y., 37-15
Tim Keefe, N.Y., 37-17
Tony Mullane, Tol., 36-26
Ed Morris, Col., 34-13
Will White, Cin., 34-18
Bob Emslie, Bal., 32-17
Bobby Mathews, Phil., 30-18
Hardie Henderson, Bal., 27-23
George McGinnis, St.L., 24-16
Frank Mountain, Col., 23-17

MAJOR RULES CHANGES

■ Any batter hit by a pitch after trying to avoid the ball was awarded first base.

■ Each team was allowed an extra person on the field to take charge of bats—the equivalent of a modern-day bat boy.

1884

FINAL STANDINGS

National League

Team	W	L	Pct.	GB
Providence	84	28	.750	...
Boston	73	38	.658	10.5
Buffalo	64	47	.577	19.5
Chicago	62	50	.554	22
New York	62	50	.554	22
Philadelphia	39	73	.348	45
Cleveland	35	77	.313	49
Detroit	28	84	.250	56

SIGNIFICANT EVENTS

■ N.L. officials legalized overhand pitching, stipulating that pitchers must keep both feet on the ground through their delivery.

MEMORABLE MOMENTS

■ Providence pitcher Charlie Sweeney struck out a record 19 Boston batters in a 2-1 victory over the Red Stockings.

■ Chicago ace Larry Corcoran pitched his record third career no-hitter, ending a 10-game Providence winning streak with a 6-0 victory.

■ New York's Mickey Welch opened a game against Philadelphia with a record nine consecutive strikeouts.

■ September 11: Hoss Radbourn, who would finish the season with a record 59 wins, pitched pennant-bound Providence to a victory over Cleveland—the Grays' 20th consecutive triumph.

■ Providence completed a three-game sweep of the American Association's New York Metropolitans with an 12-2 victory, punctuating baseball's second post-season matchup between pennant winners.

LEADERS

BA: Jim O'Rourke, Buf., .347.
Runs: King Kelly, Chi., 120.
Hits: Jim O'Rourke, Buf.; Ezra Sutton, Bos., 162.
TB: Abner Dalrymple, Chi., 263.
HR: Ned Williamson, Chi., 27.
RBI: Cap Anson, Chi., 102.
Wins: Hoss Radbourn, Pro., 59.
ERA: Hoss Radbourn, Pro., 1.38.
CG: Hoss Radbourn, Pro., 73.
IP: Hoss Radbourn, Pro., 678.2.
SO: Hoss Radbourn, Pro., 441.

20-game winners

Hoss Radbourn, Pro., 59-12
Charlie Buffinton, Bos., 48-16
Pud Galvin, Buf., 46-22
Mickey Welch, N.Y., 39-21
Larry Corcoran, Chi., 35-23
Jim Whitney, Bos., 23-14
Charlie Ferguson, Phil., 21-25

POST-SEASON PLAYOFF

(Providence N.L. 3, New York A.A. 0)

Game 1—Providence 6, New York 0

Game 2—Providence 3, New York 1

Game 3—Providence 12, New York 2 (6 innings, darkness)

MAJOR RULES CHANGES

■ All restrictions against pitching deliveries were lifted, meaning pitchers could throw overhand for the first time.

■ Batters were awarded first base after six balls.

■ Any ball leaving the park was declared either fair or foul, depending on its position within the foul lines.

1885

FINAL STANDINGS

American Association

Team	W	L	Pct.	GB
St. Louis	79	33	.705	...
Cincinnati	63	49	.563	16
Pittsburgh	56	55	.505	22.5
Philadelphia	55	57	.491	24
Louisville	53	59	.473	26
Brooklyn	53	59	.473	26
New York	44	64	.407	33
Baltimore	41	68	.376	36.5

SIGNIFICANT EVENTS

■ The reorganized American Association began play with teams located in St. Louis, Philadelphia, Cincinnati, Pittsburgh, Brooklyn, Louisville, New York and Baltimore.

MEMORABLE MOMENTS

■ St. Louis jumped into first place with an early May victory over Philadelphia—a position the Browns would hold the remainder of the season.

■ Baltimore snapped St. Louis' A.A.-record 17-game winning streak with a 7-1 victory.

■ The Browns, refusing to acknowledge a controversial Game 2 forfeit loss to N.L.-champion Chicago, "claimed" status as baseball world champions after beating the White Stockings and knotting the post-season series at three games apiece.

LEADERS

BA: Pete Browning, Lou., .362.
Runs: Harry Stovey, Phil., 130.
Hits: Pete Browning, Phil., 174.
TB: Pete Browning, Lou., 255.
HR: Harry Stovey, Phil., 13.
Wins: Bob Caruthers, St.L., 40.
ERA: Bob Caruthers, St.L., 2.07.
CG: Ed Morris, Pit., 63.
IP: Ed Morris, Pit., 581.
SO: Ed Morris, Pit., 298.

20-game winners

Bob Caruthers, St.L., 40-13
Ed Morris, Pit., 39-24
Dave Foutz, St.L., 33-14
Henry Porter, Brk., 33-21
Bobby Mathews, Phil., 30-17
Guy Hecker, Lou., 30-23
Hardie Henderson, Bal., 25-35
Jack Lynch, N.Y., 23-21
Larry McKeon, Cin., 20-13

MAJOR RULES CHANGES

■ The one-bounce rule was dropped and fielders were required to catch foul balls on the fly to record an out.

■ Home-team captains were given the option of batting first or second.

■ The overhand delivery was permitted, bringing league pitchers in line with their N.L. counterparts.

■ Every team was required to wear a neat and attractive uniform.

FINAL STANDINGS

National League

Team	W	L	Pct.	GB
Chicago	87	25	.777	...
New York	85	27	.759	2
Philadelphia	56	54	.509	30
Providence	53	57	.482	33
Boston	46	66	.411	41
Detroit	41	67	.380	44
Buffalo	38	74	.339	49
St. Louis	36	72	.333	49

SIGNIFICANT EVENTS

■ Providence ace Hoss Radbourn, the N.L.'s highest paid player, was suspended for poor pitching after a lopsided loss to New York.

■ The Washington Nationals were accepted into the league, replacing Providence.

MEMORABLE MOMENTS

■ Philadelphia snapped Chicago's 18-game winning streak—the White Stockings' first loss at new West Side Park.

■ John Clarkson, en route to a Major League-high 53 wins, held Providence hitless in an 4-0 victory.

■ Game 2 of a post-season "World's Series" between Chicago and American Association-champion St. Louis ended in controversy when the Browns refused to continue the game in the sixth inning because of umpiring decisions. The White Stockings were declared forfeit winners.

■ The Browns defeated the White Stockings 13-4 in the championship finale, tying the series at 3-3. The Browns claimed victory, refusing to accept the forfeit decision.

LEADERS

BA: Roger Connor, N.Y., .371.
Runs: King Kelly, Chi., 124.
Hits: Roger Connor, N.Y., 169.
TB: Roger Connor, N.Y., 225.
HR: Abner Dalrymple, Chi., 11.
RBI: Cap Anson, Chi., 108.
Wins: John Clarkson, Chi., 53.
ERA: Tim Keefe, N.Y., 1.58.
CG: John Clarkson, Chi., 68.
IP: John Clarkson, Chi., 623.
SO: John Clarkson, Chi., 308.

20-game winners

John Clarkson, Chi., 53-16
Mickey Welch, N.Y., 44-11
Tim Keefe, N.Y., 32-13
Hoss Radbourn, Pro., 28-21
Charlie Ferguson, Phil., 26-20
Ed Daily, Phil., 26-23
Fred Shaw, Pro., 23-26
Charlie Buffinton, Bos., 22-27
Jim McCormick, Pro.-Chi., 21-7

POST-SEASON PLAYOFF

(Chicago N.L. 3, St. Louis A.A. 3; 1 tie)

Game 1—Chicago 5, St. Louis 5 (8 innings, darkness)

Game 2—Chicago awarded 5-4 forfeit victory

Game 3—St. Louis 7, Chicago 4

Game 4—St. Louis 3, Chicago 2

Game 5—Chicago 9, St. Louis 2 (7 innings, darkness)

Game 6—Chicago 9, St. Louis 2

Game 7—St. Louis 13, Chicago 4 (8 innings, darkness)

MAJOR RULES CHANGES

■ The batter's box was resized to 4 feet wide by 6 feet long and moved a foot closer to home base.

■ Pitchers were required to keep both feet in contact with the ground during delivery. Batters were awarded first base after two "foul balks," a rule that was eliminated at midseason.

■ Players were permitted to use bats with one flat side.

■ Any ball leaving the park at a distance of less than 210 feet was declared an automatic double.

1886

FINAL STANDINGS

American Association

Team	W	L	Pct.	GB
St. Louis	93	46	.669	...
Pittsburgh	80	57	.584	12
Brooklyn	76	61	.555	16
Louisville	66	70	.485	25.5
Cincinnati	65	73	.471	27.5
Philadelphia	63	72	.467	28
New York	53	82	.393	38
Baltimore	48	83	.366	41

SIGNIFICANT EVENTS

■ When Pittsburgh defected to the rival N.L. in November, the American Association filled the void with a new Cleveland franchise.

MEMORABLE MOMENTS

■ Louisville pitcher Guy Hecker belted a record-tying three home runs and scored a Major League-record seven times in a victory over Brooklyn.

■ The St. Louis Browns posted a 4-3 victory over the N.L.'s Chicago White Stockings in Game 6 of the "World's Series," staking their undisputed claim as king of baseball.

LEADERS

BA: Dave Orr, N.Y., .338.
Runs: Arlie Latham, St.L., 152.
Hits: Dave Orr, N.Y., 193.
TB: Dave Orr, N.Y., 301.
HR: Bid McPhee, Cin., 8.
SB: Harry Stovey, Phil., 68.
Wins: Dave Foutz, St.L.; Ed Morris, Pit., 41.
ERA: Dave Foutz, St.L., 2.11.
CG: Matt Kilroy, Bal.; Toad Ramsey, Lou., 66.
IP: Toad Ramsey, Lou., 588.2.
SO: Matt Kilroy, Bal., 513.

20-game winners

Dave Foutz, St.L., 41-16
Ed Morris, Pit., 41-20
Tom Ramsey, Lou., 38-27
Tony Mullane, Cin., 33-27
Bob Caruthers, St.L., 30-14
Pud Galvin, Pit., 29-21
Matt Kilroy, Bal., 29-34
Henry Porter, Brk., 27-19
Guy Hecker, Lou., 26-23
Al Atkinson, Phil., 25-17
Jack Lynch, N.Y., 20-30

MAJOR RULES CHANGES

■ A 4-by-1 foot smooth stone slab was placed at the front end of the pitcher's box, helping umpires determine if the pitcher had stepped beyond the front line.

■ The number of balls required for a walk was decreased from seven to six.

■ The A.A. adopted the reshaped 6-by-3 foot batter's box and 4-by-7 foot pitcher's box.

■ Stolen bases were credited for any base a runner was able to gain on his own volition, such as a first-to-third dash on a single.

1886

FINAL STANDINGS

National League

Team	W	L	Pct.	GB
Chicago	90	34	.726	...
Detroit	87	36	.707	2.5
New York	75	44	.630	12.5
Philadelphia	71	43	.623	14
Boston	56	61	.479	30.5
St. Louis	43	79	.352	46
Kansas City	30	91	.248	58.5
Washington	28	92	.233	60

SIGNIFICANT EVENTS

- The N.L. increased its preseason roster to eight with the addition of a Kansas City team on a one-year trial basis.
- The N.L. adopted the stolen base as an official statistic and reshaped the pitcher's box to 4-by-7 feet.
- New rules: 4 strikes for an out; 5 balls for a walk; a standardized strike zone from the knees to the shoulders, and a 55½-foot pitching distance.
- Pittsburgh made a November jump from the American Association to the N.L., replacing Kansas City.

MEMORABLE MOMENTS

- The White Stockings clinched another N.L. pennant with a final-day victory over Boston. The final lead was 2½ games over Detroit.
- Chicago dropped a 4-3 decision to the American Association-champion Browns and lost the best-of-seven "World's Series" in six games.

LEADERS

BA: King Kelly, Chi., .388.
Runs: King Kelly, Chi., 155.
Hits: Hardy Richardson, Det., 189.
TB: Dan Brouthers, Det., 284.
HR: Dan Brouthers, Det.; Hardy Richardson, Det., 11.
RBI: Cap Anson, Chi., 147.
SB: Ed Andrews, Phil., 56.
Wins: Lady Baldwin, Det.; Tim Keefe, N.Y., 42.
ERA: Henry Boyle, St.L., 1.76.
CG: Tim Keefe, N.Y., 62.
IP: Tim Keefe, N.Y., 535.
SO: Lady Baldwin, Det., 323.

20-game winners

Lady Baldwin, Det., 42-13
Tim Keefe, N.Y., 42-20
John Clarkson, Chi., 36-17]
Mickey Welch, N.Y., 33-22
Charlie Ferguson, Phil., 30-9
Charlie Getzien, Det., 30-11
Jim McCormick, Chi., 31-11
Hoss Radbourn, Bos., 27-31
Dan Casey, Phil., 24-18
Jocko Flynn, Chi., 23-6
Bill Stemmeyer, Bos., 22-18

POST-SEASON PLAYOFF

(St. Louis A.A. 4, Chicago N.L. 2)

Game 1—Chicago 6, St. Louis 0
Game 2—St. Louis 12, Chicago 0 (8 innings, darkness)
Game 3—Chicago 11, St. Louis 4 (8 innings, darkness)
Game 4—St. Louis 8, Chicago 5 (7 innings, darkness)
Game 5—St. Louis 10, Chicago 3 (8 innings, darkness)
Game 6—St. Louis 4, Chicago 3 (10 innings)

MAJOR RULES CHANGES

- The number of balls required for a walk was increased from six to seven.
- The shape of the pitcher's box was changed from 6-by-6 to 4-by-7 feet.
- Pitchers no longer were required to keep both feet on the ground during delivery. "Foul balks" were eliminated.
- The batter's box was reshaped to its 6-by-3 shape, 12 inches from home base.
- Stolen bases were credited for any base a runner was able to gain on his own volition, such as a first-to-third dash on a single.

1887

FINAL STANDINGS

American Association

Team	W	L	Pct.	GB
St. Louis	95	40	.704	...
Cincinnati	81	54	.600	14
Baltimore	77	58	.570	18
Louisville	76	60	.559	19.5
Philadelphia	64	69	.481	30
Brooklyn	60	74	.448	34.5
New York	44	89	.331	50
Cleveland	39	92	.298	54

SIGNIFICANT EVENTS

- The 4-strike rule was eliminated in a November meeting and officials reversed their preseason decision to count walks as "hits."

MEMORABLE MOMENTS

- St. Louis, en route to 95 victories and its third straight A.A. pennant, defeated the Athletics for its 15th consecutive victory.
- The 52-game hitting streak of Athletics star Denny Lyons came to an end in late August. Lyons' streak included two games in which he managed only walks, which were counted as hits in the 1887 season.
- The Browns defeated New York for their 12th straight victory and increased their lead over second-place Cincinnati to a whopping 19½ games.
- The Browns closed their best-of-15 "World's Series" battle against Detroit with a 9-2 victory, but they still lost the war, 10 games to 5.

LEADERS

BA: Tip O'Neill, St.L., .485.
Runs: Tip O'Neill, St.L., 167.
Hits: Tip O'Neill, St.L., 275.
TB: Tip O'Neill, St.L., 407.
HR: Tip O'Neill, St.L., 14.
SB: Hugh Nicol, Cin., 138.
Wins: Matt Kilroy, Bal., 46.
ERA: Elmer Smith, Cin., 2.94.
CG: Matt Kilroy, Bal., 66.
IP: Matt Kilroy, Bal., 589.1.
SO: Toad Ramsey, Lou., 355.

20-game winners

Matt Kilroy, Bal., 46-19
Toad Ramsey, Lou., 37-27
Silver King, St.L., 32-12
Elmer Smith, Cin., 34-17
Tony Mullane, Cin., 31-17
Bob Caruthers, St.L., 29-9
John Smith, Bal., 25-30
Gus Weyhing, Phil., 26-28
Ed Seward, Phil., 25-25
Dave Foutz, St.L., 25-12

MAJOR RULES CHANGES

- The National League and American Association agreed to abide by a uniform rules book and several rules were rewritten. Here are some of the more significant changes:
- Batters no longer were allowed to call for high or low pitches and the strike zone was defined as the area between the top of the shoulder and the bottom of the knees.
- The pitcher's box was reshaped to 4-by-5½ feet.
- Batters hit by a pitch were awarded first base and not charged with an at-bat.
- The number of balls required for a walk was dropped to five.
- The batter was declared out after four strikes.
- Batters drawing a base on balls were credited with a hit and charged with a time at-bat.

FINAL STANDINGS

National League

Team	W	L	Pct.	GB
Detroit	79	45	.637	...
Philadelphia	75	48	.610	3.5
Chicago	71	50	.587	6.5
New York	68	55	.553	10.5
Boston	61	60	.504	16.5
Pittsburgh	55	69	.444	24
Washington	46	76	.377	32
Indianapolis	37	89	.294	43

SIGNIFICANT EVENTS

- The N.L.'s St. Louis franchise was sold to Indianapolis interests.
- The Phillies christened their new ballpark, which would remain in use as the "Baker Bowl" until 1938.
- N.L. officials held a November meeting with the Brotherhood of Professional Base Ball Players, an organization set up to protect players' contract interests.

MEMORABLE MOMENTS

- Detroit posted a doubleheader sweep of Chicago, increasing its N.L. lead to seven games and putting the city on the verge of its first pennant.
- The best-of-15 "World's Series" opened with the Browns posting a 6-1 victory over Detroit.
- The post-season title series ended with Detroit holding a commanding 10 games to 5 advantage.

LEADERS

BA: Cap Anson, Chi., .421.
Runs: Dan Brouthers, Det., 153.
Hits: Sam Thompson, Det., 235.
TB: Sam Thompson, Det., 340.
HR: Billy O'Brien, Wash., 19.
RBI: Sam Thompson, Det., 166.
SB: Monte Ward, N.Y., 111.
Wins: John Clarkson, Chi., 38.
ERA: Dan Casey, Phil., 2.86.
CG: John Clarkson, Chi., 56.
IP: John Clarkson, Chi., 523.
SO: John Clarkson, Chi., 237.

20-game winners

John Clarkson, Chi., 38-21
Tim Keefe, N.Y., 35-19
Charlie Getzien, Det., 29-13
Dan Casey, Phil., 28-13
Pud Galvin, Pit., 28-21
Jim Whitney, Wash., 24-21
Hoss Radbourn, Bos., 24-23
Charlie Ferguson, Phil., 22-10
Mickey Welch, N.Y., 22-15
Kid Madden, Bos., 21-14
Charlie Buffinton, Phil., 21-17

POST-SEASON PLAYOFF

(Detroit N.L. 10, St. Louis A.A. 5)

Game 1—St. Louis 6, Detroit 1
Game 2—Detroit 5, St. Louis 3
Game 3—Detroit 2, St. Louis 1(13 innings)
Game 4—Detroit 8, St. Louis 0
Game 5—St. Louis 5, Detroit 2
Game 6—Detroit 9, St. Louis 0
Game 7—Detroit 3, St. Louis 1
Game 8—Detroit 9, St. Louis 2
Game 9—Detroit 4, St. Louis 2
Game 10—St. Louis 11, Detroit 4
Game 11—Detroit 13, St. Louis 3
Game 12—St. Louis 5, Detroit 1 (7 innings, darkness)
Game 13—Detroit 6, St. Louis 3
Game 14—Detroit 4, St. Louis 3
Game 15—St. Louis 9, Detroit 2 (6 innings, cold)

MAJOR RULES CHANGES

- The National League and American Association agreed to abide by a uniform rules book and several rules were rewritten. Here are some of the more significant changes:
- Batters no longer were allowed to call for high or low pitches and the strike zone was defined as the area between the top of the shoulder and the bottom of the knees.
- The pitcher's box was reshaped to 4-by-5½ feet.
- Batters hit by a pitch were awarded first base and not charged with an at-bat.
- The number of balls required for a walk was dropped to five.
- The batter was declared out after four strikes.
- Batters drawing a base on balls were credited with a hit and charged with a time at-bat.

1888

FINAL STANDINGS

American Association

Team	W	L	Pct.	GB
St. Louis	92	43	.681	...
Brooklyn	88	52	.629	6.5
Philadelphia	81	52	.609	10
Cincinnati	80	54	.597	11.5
Baltimore	57	80	.416	36
Cleveland	50	82	.379	40.5
Louisville	48	87	.356	44
Kansas City	43	89	.326	47.5

SIGNIFICANT EVENTS

- Columbus became a member of the American Association roster in December, replacing Cleveland.

MEMORABLE MOMENTS

- The St. Louis Browns, seeking their fourth straight A.A. pennant, moved into first place with a mid-July victory over Kansas City—a position they would not relinquish the rest of the season.
- St. Louis ace Silver King posted his 45th victory and raised his league-leading totals in games (66), innings (585⅔), complete games (64) and ERA (1.64).
- The Browns fell to N.L.-champion New York in a best-of-10 "World's Series," despite winning the finale, 18-7.

LEADERS

BA: Tip O'Neill, St.L., .335.
Runs: George Pinkney, Brk., 134.
Hits: Tip O'Neill, St.L., 177.
TB: John Reilly, Cin., 264.
HR: John Reilly, Cin., 13.
RBI: John Reilly, Cin., 103.
SB: Arlie Latham, St.L., 109.
Wins: Silver King, St.L., 45.
ERA: Silver King, St.L., 1.64.
CG: Silver King, St.L., 64.
IP: Silver King, St.L., 585.2.
SO: Ed Seward, Phil., 272.

20-game winners

Silver King, St.L., 45-21
Ed Seward, Phil., 35-19
Bob Caruthers, Brk., 29-15
Gus Weyhing, Phil., 28-18
Lee Viau, Cin., 27-14
Tony Mullane, Cin., 26-16
Nat Hudson, St.L., 25-10
Elton Chamberlain, Lou.-St.L., 25-11
Mickey Hughes, Brk., 25-13
Ed Bakely, Cle., 25-33
Elmer Smith, Cin., 22-17
Bert Cunningham, Bal., 22-29

MAJOR RULES CHANGES

- The rule awarding the batter a hit on a base on balls was reversed.
- The batter was credited with a "hit" on any batted ball that struck a baserunner, even though the runner was declared out.
- The number of strikes required for a strikeout was reduced to three.
- Pitchers were charged with an error for walks, wild pitches, hit batters and balks.

1888

FINAL STANDINGS

National League

Team	W	L	Pct.	GB
New York	84	47	.641	...
Chicago	77	58	.570	9
Philadelphia	69	61	.531	14.5
Boston	70	64	.522	15.5
Detroit	68	63	.519	16
Pittsburgh	66	68	.493	19.5
Indianapolis	50	85	.370	36
Washington	48	86	.358	37.5

SIGNIFICANT EVENTS

■ Rules changes: 4 balls for a walk and 3 strikes for a strikeout—standards that would hold up for more than a century.

■ Cleveland, a former American Association franchise, was admitted to the N.L., replacing Detroit.

MEMORABLE MOMENTS

■ With more than 10,000 fans watching at New York's Polo Grounds, Giants pitcher Tim Keefe dropped a 4-2 decision to Pittsburgh, snapping his record 19-game winning streak.

■ Pittsburgh ace Ed Morris pitched his record fourth consecutive shutout—a 1-0 victory over New York.

■ The Giants clinched the first of many N.L. pennants.

■ The Giants clinched their best-of-10 "World's Series" against St. Louis in Game 8 with an 11-3 victory.

LEADERS

BA: Cap Anson, Chi., .344.
Runs: Dan Brouthers, Det., 118.
Hits: Jimmy Ryan, Chi., 182.
TB: Jimmy Ryan, Chi., 283.
HR: Jimmy Ryan, Chi., 16.
RBI: Cap Anson, Chi., 84.
SB: Dummy Hoy, Wash., 82.
Wins: Tim Keefe, N.Y., 35.
ERA: Tim Keefe, N.Y., 1.74.
CG: Ed Morris, Pit., 54.
IP: John Clarkson, Bos., 483.1.
SO: Tim Keefe, N.Y., 333.

20-game winners

Tim Keefe, N.Y., 35-12
John Clarkson, Bos., 33-20
Pete Conway, Det., 30-14
Ed Morris, Pit., 29-23
Charlie Buffinton, Phil., 28-17
Mickey Welch, N.Y., 26-19
Gus Krock, Chi., 25-14
Pud Galvin, Pit., 23-25

POST-SEASON PLAYOFF

(New York N.L. 6, St. Louis A.A. 4)

Game 1—New York 2, St. Louis 1
Game 2—St. Louis 3, New York 0
Game 3—New York 4, St. Louis 2
Game 4—New York 6, St. Louis 3
Game 5—St. Louis 6, New York 4 (8 innings, darkness)
Game 6—New York 12, St. Louis 5 (8 innings, darkness)
Game 7—St. Louis 7, New York 5 (8 innings, darkness)
Game 8—New York 11, St. Louis 3
Game 9—St. Louis 14, New York 11 (10 innings)
Game 10—St. Louis 18, New York 7

MAJOR RULES CHANGES

■ The rule awarding the batter a hit on a base on balls was reversed.

■ The batter was credited with a "hit" on any batted ball that struck a baserunner, even though the runner was declared out.

■ Pitchers were charged with an error for walks, wild pitches, hit batters and balks.

1889

FINAL STANDINGS

American Association

Team	W	L	Pct.	GB
Brooklyn	93	44	.679	...
St. Louis	90	45	.667	2
Philadelphia	75	58	.564	16
Cincinnati	76	63	.547	18
Baltimore	70	65	.519	22
Columbus	60	78	.435	33.5
Kansas City	55	82	.401	38
Louisville	27	111	.196	66.5

SIGNIFICANT EVENTS

■ A record Association crowd of 22,122 showed up for a May 30 game in Brooklyn to watch the Bridegrooms play the Browns.

■ Baltimore, following the lead of Brooklyn, Cincinnati and Kansas City, dropped out of the American Association.

MEMORABLE MOMENTS

■ Toad Ramsey pitched Louisville to a victory over St. Louis, snapping the Colonels' Major League-record losing streak at 26 games.

■ The Browns, leading 4-2 in the ninth inning of a September 7 game, walked off the field in Brooklyn, claiming it was too dark to continue. The Bridegrooms were declared forfeit winners, a ruling that later would be reversed.

■ The Browns, claiming they feared for the personal safety amid unruly Brooklyn fans, forfeited their September 8 game to the Bridegrooms—a defeat that would help Brooklyn claim the A.A. pennant.

■ The Bridegrooms dropped a 3-2 decision to the N.L.-champion Giants in the decisive Game 9 of the "World's Series."

LEADERS

BA: Tommy Tucker, Bal., .372.
Runs: Mike Griffin, Bal.; Harry Stovey, Phil., 152.
Hits: Tommy Tucker, Bal., 196.
TB: Harry Stovey, Phil., 292.
HR: Bug Holliday, Cin.; Harry Stovey, Phil., 19.
RBI: Harry Stovey, Phil., 119.
SB: Billy Hamilton, K.C., 111.
Wins: Bob Caruthers, Brk., 40.
ERA: Jack Stivetts, St.L., 2.25.
CG: Matt Kilroy, Bal., 55.
IP: Mark Baldwin, Col., 513.2.
SO: Mark Baldwin, Col., 368.

20-game winners

Bob Caruthers, Brk., 40-11
Silver King, St.L., 35-16
Elton Chamberlain, St.L., 32-15
Jesse Duryea, Cin., 32-19
Gus Weyhing, Phil., 30-21
Matt Kilroy, Bal., 29-25
Mark Baldwin, Col., 27-34
Frank Foreman, Bal., 23-21
Adonis Terry, Brk., 22-15
Lee Viau, Cin., 22-20
Ed Seward, Phil., 21-15

MAJOR RULES CHANGES

■ The number of balls required for a walk was reduced to four.

■ A foul tip was defined as a foul hit that did not rise above the batter's head and was caught within 10 feet of home base. Batters could not be declared out on a caught foul tip and runners were permitted to return safely to their bases.

■ Pitchers were required to get into pitching position by placing one foot on the back line of the pitching box and only one step was allowed during delivery.

■ One "extra player" could be substituted at the end of any complete inning, but the player leaving the game could not return. Substitutions could be made at any time for a disabled player.

■ Pitchers no longer were charged with errors for walks, wild pitches, hit batsmen and balks.

■ The sacrifice bunt was recognized for the first time, although the hitter still was charged with an at-bat.

FINAL STANDINGS

National League

Team	W	L	Pct.	GB
New York	83	43	.659	...
Boston	83	45	.648	1
Chicago	67	65	.508	19
Philadelphia	63	64	.496	20.5
Pittsburgh	61	71	.462	25
Cleveland	61	72	.459	25.5
Indianapolis	59	75	.440	28
Washington	41	83	.331	41

SIGNIFICANT EVENTS

■ Brooklyn and Cincinnati made a November jump from the American Association to the N.L., creating a 10-team circuit.

■ A threat becomes official: The Brotherhood of Professional Base Ball Players formally organized the Players League, a third major circuit partially operated by the players themselves.

MEMORABLE MOMENTS

■ The Giants christened their new Polo Grounds with a victory over Pittsburgh.

■ The New York Giants captured their second straight pennant on the final day of the season, beating Cleveland while Boston was losing to Pittsburgh.

■ The Giants reigned as world champions again, thanks to a 6 games to 3 post-season victory over the American Association's Brooklyn Bridegrooms. New York won Game 9, 3-2.

LEADERS

BA: Dan Brouthers, Bos., .373.
Runs: Mike Tiernan, N.Y., 147.
Hits: Jack Glasscock, Ind., 205.
TB: Jimmy Ryan, Chi., 287.
HR: Sam Thompson, Phil., 20.
RBI: Roger Connor, N.Y., 130.
SB: Jim Fogarty, Phil., 99.
Wins: John Clarkson, Bos., 49.
ERA: John Clarkson, Bos., 2.73.
CG: John Clarkson, Bos., 68.
IP: John Clarkson, Bos., 620.
SO: John Clarkson, Bos., 284.

20-game winners

John Clarkson, Bos., 49-19
Tim Keefe, N.Y., 28-13
Charlie Buffinton, Phil., 28-16
Mickey Welch, N.Y., 27-12
Pud Galvin, Pit., 23-16
Darby O'Brien, Cle., 22-17
Henry Boyle, Ind., 21-23
Harry Staley, Pit., 21-26
Hoss Radbourn, Bos., 20-11
Ed Beatin, Cle., 20-15

POST-SEASON PLAYOFF

(New York N.L. 6, Brooklyn A.A. 3)

Game 1—Brooklyn 12, New York 10 (8 innings, darkness)
Game 2—New York 6, Brooklyn 2
Game 3—Brooklyn 8, New York 7 (8 innings, darkness)
Game 4—Brooklyn 10, New York 7 (6 innings, darkness)
Game 5—New York 11, Brooklyn 3
Game 6—New York 2, Brooklyn 1 (11 innings)
Game 7—New York 11, Brooklyn 7
Game 8—New York 16, Brooklyn 7
Game 9—New York 3, Brooklyn 2

MAJOR RULES CHANGES

■ The number of balls required for a walk was reduced to four.

■ A foul tip was defined as a foul hit that did not rise above the batter's head and was caught within 10 feet of home base. Batters could not be declared out on a caught foul tip and runners were permitted to return safely to their bases.

■ Pitchers were required to get into pitching position by placing one foot on the back line of the pitching box and only one step was allowed during delivery.

■ One "extra player" could be substituted at the end of any complete inning, but the player leaving the game could not return. Substitutions could be made at any time for a disabled player.

■ Pitchers no longer were charged with errors for walks, wild pitches, hit batsmen and balks.

■ The sacrifice bunt was recognized for the first time, although the hitter still was charged with an at-bat.

1890

FINAL STANDINGS

Players League

Team	W	L	Pct.	GB
Boston	81	48	.628	...
Brooklyn	76	56	.576	6.5
New York	74	57	.565	8
Chicago	75	62	.547	10
Philadelphia	68	63	.519	14
Pittsburgh	60	68	.469	20.5
Cleveland	55	75	.423	26.5
Buffalo	36	96	.273	46.5

SIGNIFICANT EVENTS

■ The new Players League won the first of many lawsuits it would have to endure when a judge refused to grant a January injunction against Brotherhood president John Montgomery Ward.

■ The Players League began its inaugural season in a war-like atmosphere, thanks to the league-jumping antics of many big-name stars from the National League and American Association.

■ The New York and Pittsburgh teams combined with the same-city franchises from the N.L., pronouncing last rites for the one-year circuit. The December defections would prompt Players League backers to seek their own deals in a scramble to remain solvent.

MEMORABLE MOMENTS

■ Willie McGill, a 16-year-old Cleveland hurler, became the youngest Major League pitcher to throw a complete game when he defeated Buffalo.

■ Boston closed out the first and last Players League season with an 81-48 record, capturing the pennant by 6½ games over Brooklyn.

LEADERS

BA: Pete Browning, Cle., .373.
Runs: Hugh Duffy, Chi., 161.
Hits: Hugh Duffy, Chi., 191.
TB: Billy Shindle, Phil., 281.
HR: Roger Connor, N.Y., 14.
RBI: Hardy Richardson, Bos., 146.
SB: Harry Stovey, Bos., 97.
Wins: Mark Baldwin, Chi., 34.
ERA: Silver King, Chi., 2.69.
CG: Mark Baldwin, Chi., 54.
IP: Mark Baldwin, Chi., 501.
SO: Mark Baldwin, Chi., 211.

20-game winners

Mark Baldwin, Chi., 34-24
Gus Weyhing, Brk., 30-16
Silver King, Chi., 30-22
Hoss Radbourn, Bos., 27-12
Addison Gumbert, Bos., 23-12
Phil Knell, Phil., 22-11
Hank O'Day, N.Y., 22-13
Henry Gruber, Cle., 22-23
Harry Staley, Pit., 21-25

THE RULES

■ The one-season Players League adopted its own rules book with only slight variations to the ones used by the American Association and National League. The most significant was a resized pitcher's box that reverted to the 6-by-4 foot rectangle last used in 1885 with a front line 51 feet from the center of home base. Other key variations:

■ If a team failed to begin play within one minute after the umpire called "play" at the start of a game, a forfeit was declared.

■ Each corner of the reshaped pitcher's box was marked by a wooden peg, a variation from the flat rubber plates used by the other leagues.

■ Two umpires were required for each championship game, one behind the plate and the other standing in the field.

1890

FINAL STANDINGS

American Association

Team	W	L	Pct.	GB
Louisville	88	44	.667	...
Columbus	79	55	.590	10
St. Louis	78	58	.574	12
Toledo	68	64	.515	20
Rochester	63	63	.500	22
Baltimore	15	19	.441	24
Syracuse	55	72	.433	30.5
Philadelphia	54	78	.409	34
Brooklyn	26	73	.263	45.5

SIGNIFICANT EVENTS

■ Brooklyn joined Syracuse, Rochester and Toledo as new American Association cities.

■ The bankrupt Athletics disbanded, releasing and selling their players. A patchwork Philadelphia club would close the season with 22 consecutive losses.

■ The Athletics were expelled, a new Philadelphia franchise was admitted and new teams from Boston, Washington and Chicago replaced Syracuse, Rochester and Toledo in action at the winter meetings.

MEMORABLE MOMENT

■ Louisville defeated N.L.-champion Brooklyn 6-2 to salvage a "World's Series" split. Each team won three games and one ended in a tie.

LEADERS

BA: Jimmy Wolf, Lou., .363.
Runs: Jim McTamany, Col., 140.
Hits: Jimmy Wolf, Lou., 197.
TB: Jimmy Wolf, Lou., 260.
HR: Count Campau, St.L., 9.
SB: Tommy McCarthy, St.L., 83.
Wins: Sadie McMahon, Phil.-Bal., 36.
ERA: Scott Stratton, Lou., 2.36.
CG: Sadie McMahon, Phil.-Bal., 55.
IP: Sadie McMahon, Phil.-Bal., 509.
SO: Sadie McMahon, Phil.-Bal., 291.

20-game winners

Sadie McMahon, Phil.-Bal., 36-21
Scott Stratton, Lou., 34-14
Hank Gastright, Col., 30-14
Bob Barr, Rch., 28-24
Jack Stivetts, St.L., 27-21
Red Ehret, Lou., 25-14
Toad Ramsey, St.L., 24-17
John Healy, Tol., 22-21

MAJOR RULES CHANGES

■ Pitchers and other players were no longer allowed to discolor the ball by rubbing it with soil or other foreign substances.

■ Each team was allowed a second "extra player" and substitutions could be made at any time with retiring players unable to return.

FINAL STANDINGS

National League

Team	W	L	Pct.	GB
Brooklyn	86	43	.667	...
Chicago	84	53	.613	6
Philadelphia	78	54	.591	9.5
Cincinnati	77	55	.583	10.5
Boston	76	57	.571	12
New York	63	68	.481	24
Cleveland	44	88	.333	43.5
Pittsburgh	23	113	.169	66.5

SIGNIFICANT EVENTS

■ Committees from the three rival Major Leagues began October peace negotiations that eventually would signal the end of the Players League.

MEMORABLE MOMENTS

■ N.L. newcomer Brooklyn moved into first place with a victory over Cincinnati. The Bridegrooms would win the pennant with a six-game edge over Chicago.

■ Brooklyn swept a tripleheader from hapless Pittsburgh and stretched its losing streak to 22 games. Pittsburgh would finish the season with a record 113 losses.

■ Brooklyn (N.L.) and Louisville (A.A.) began play in a "World's Series" that did not include Players League champion Boston. The Bridegrooms won the opener, 9-0, but the series would end in a 3-3 deadlock with one tie.

LEADERS

BA: Jack Glasscock, N.Y., .336.
Runs: Hub Collins, Brk., 148.
Hits: Jack Glasscock, N.Y.; Sam Thompson, Phil., 172.
TB: Mike Tiernan, N.Y., 274.
HR: Oyster Burns, Brk.; Mike Tiernan, N.Y.; Walt Wilmot, Chi., 13.
RBI: Oyster Burns, Brk., 128.
SB: Billy Hamilton, Phil., 102.
Wins: Bill Hutchinson, Chi., 42.
ERA: Billy Rhines, Cin., 1.95.
CG: Bill Hutchinson, Chi., 65.
IP: Bill Hutchinson, Chi., 603.
SO: Amos Rusie, N.Y., 341.

20-game winners

Bill Hutchison, Chi., 42-25
Kid Gleason, Phil., 38-17
Tom Lovett, Brk., 30-11
Amos Rusie, N.Y., 29-34
Billy Rhines, Cin., 28-17
Kid Nichols, Bos., 27-19
Adonis Terry, Brk., 26-16
John Clarkson, Bos., 26-18
Tom Vickery, Phil., 24-22
Bob Caruthers, Brk., 23-11
Charlie Getzien, Bos., 23-17
Ed Beatin, Cle., 22-30
Pat Luby, Chi., 20-9

POST-SEASON PLAYOFF

(Brooklyn N.L. 3, Louisville A.A. 3; 1 tie)

Game 1—Brooklyn 9, Louisville 0 (8 innings, darkness)

Game 2—Brooklyn 5, Louisville 3

Game 3—Brooklyn 7, Louisville 7 (8 innings, darkness)

Game 4—Louisville 5, Brooklyn 4

Game 5—Brooklyn 7, Louisville 2

Game 6—Louisville 9, Brooklyn 8

Game 7—Louisville 6, Brooklyn 2

MAJOR RULES CHANGES

■ Pitchers and other players were no longer allowed to discolor the ball by rubbing it with soil or other foreign substances.

■ Each team was allowed a second "extra player" and substitutions could be made at any time with retiring players unable to return.

1891

FINAL STANDINGS

American Association

Team	W	L	Pct.	GB
Boston	93	42	.689	...
St. Louis	86	52	.623	8.5
Milwaukee	21	15	.583	22.5
Baltimore	71	64	.526	22
Philadelphia	73	66	.525	22
Columbus	61	76	.445	33
Cincinnati	43	57	.430	32.5
Louisville	55	84	.396	40
Washington	44	91	.326	49

SIGNIFICANT EVENTS

■ In a February declaration of war, the American Association withdrew from the National Agreement and moved its Chicago franchise to Cincinnati to compete with the N.L.'s Reds.

■ The Association's Cincinnati franchise folded in mid-August and was replaced by the Western Association's Milwaukee Brewers.

■ The Boston Reds, en route to the A.A. pennant, were shocked by the August defection of star King Kelly to their Boston N.L. rival.

■ A "World's Series" challenge by Reds owners was turned down by the the N.L.-champion Boston team. N.L. officials cited the A.A.'s withdrawal from the National Agreement.

■ After 10 Major League seasons, the Association died when four of its eight teams joined the N.L. and the other four accepted buyouts.

MEMORABLE MOMENTS

■ The Boston Reds defeated Baltimore and clinched the final A.A. pennant.

■ Browns rookie Ted Breitenstein, making his first Major League start on the final day of the season, pitched an 8-0 no-hitter against Louisville.

LEADERS

BA: Dan Brouthers, Bos., .350.
Runs: Tom Brown, Bos., 177.
Hits: Tom Brown, Bos., 189.
TB: Tom Brown, Bos., 276.
HR: Duke Farrell, Bos., 12.
RBI: Hugh Duffy, Bos.; Duke Farrell, Bos., 110.
SB: Tom Brown, Bos., 106.
Wins: Sadie McMahon, Bal., 35.
ERA: Ed Crane, Cin., 2.45.
CG: Sadie McMahon, Bal., 53.
IP: Sadie McMahon, Bal., 503.
SO: Jack Stivetts, St.L., 259.

20-game winners

Sadie McMahon, Bal., 35-24
George Haddock, Bos., 34-11
Jack Stivetts, St.L., 33-22
Gus Weyhing, Phil., 31-20
Charlie Buffinton, Bos., 29-9
Phil Knell, Col., 28-27
Elton Chamberlain, Phil., 22-23
Willie McGill, Cin.-St.L., 21-15

MAJOR RULES CHANGE

■ All teams were required to have one or more substitutes available for each game.

FINAL STANDINGS

National League

Team	W	L	Pct.	GB
Boston	87	51	.630	...
Chicago	82	53	.607	3.5
New York	71	61	.538	13
Philadelphia	68	69	.496	18.5
Cleveland	65	74	.468	22.5
Brooklyn	61	76	.445	25.5
Cincinnati	56	81	.409	30.5
Pittsburgh	55	80	.407	30.5

SIGNIFICANT EVENTS

■ The American Association withdrew from the National Agreement in February and declared war, moving its Chicago franchise to Cincinnati to compete with the N.L.'s Reds.

■ Pittsburgh secured its nickname as "Pirates" when it lured stars Pete Browning and Scott Stratton away from the A.A.'s Louisville team.

■ With August peace talks between the National League and American Association in progress, the N.L. Boston team shattered the calm by pirating King Kelly away from its A.A. Boston rival.

■ The American Association ceased operations in December when four A.A. clubs (St. Louis, Louisville, Washington and Baltimore) joined the N.L., creating "The National League and American Association of Professional Base Ball Clubs."

MEMORABLE MOMENTS

■ Cy Young christened Cleveland's new League Park, pitching the Spiders to an easy victory over the Reds.

■ Chicago's Wild Bill Hutchison defeated Boston for his 40th victory en route to a Major League-high 44.

■ Boston clinched the N.L. pennant with a victory over Philadelphia—its 17th in a row.

LEADERS

BA: Billy Hamilton, Phil., .340.
Runs: Billy Hamilton, Phil., 141.
Hits: Billy Hamilton, Phil., 179.
TB: Harry Stovey, Bos., 271.
HR: Harry Stovey, Bos.; Mike Tiernan, N.Y., 16.
RBI: Cap Anson, Chi., 120.
SB: Billy Hamilton, Phil., 111.
Wins: Bill Hutchinson, Chi., 44.
ERA: John Ewing, N.Y., 2.27.
CG: Bill Hutchinson, Chi., 56.
IP: Bill Hutchinson, Chi., 561.
SO: Amos Rusie, N.Y., 337.

20-game winners

Bill Hutchison, Chi., 44-19
John Clarkson, Bos., 33-19
Amos Rusie, N.Y., 33-20
Kid Nichols, Bos., 30-17
Cy Young, Cle., 27-22
Harry Staley, Pit.-Bos., 24-13
Kid Gleason, Phil., 24-22
Tom Lovett, Brk., 23-19
Tony Mullane, Cin., 23-26
Mark Baldwin, Pit., 22-28
John Ewing, N.Y., 21-8
Duke Esper, Phil., 20-15

MAJOR RULES CHANGE

■ All teams were required to have one or more substitutes available for each game.

1892

FINAL STANDINGS

National League

Team	W	L	Pct.	GB
Boston	102	48	.680	...
Cleveland	93	56	.624	8.5
Brooklyn	95	59	.617	9
Philadelphia	87	66	.569	16.5
Cincinnati	82	68	.547	20
Pittsburgh	80	73	.523	23.5
Chicago	70	76	.479	30
New York	71	80	.470	31.5
Louisville	63	89	.414	40
Washington	58	93	.384	44.5
St. Louis	56	94	.373	46
Baltimore	46	101	.313	54.5

SIGNIFICANT EVENTS

■ The new 12-team N.L. adopted a 154-game split schedule featuring first-half and second-half champions.
■ Cincinnati, playing host to the first Sunday game in N.L. history, defeated the Browns, 5-1.
■ N.L. owners, holding a mid-November meeting in Chicago, shortened the 1893 schedule to 132 games and dropped the split-season format.

MEMORABLE MOMENTS

■ Baltimore catcher Wilbert Robinson collected a record seven hits during a 25-7 victory over the Browns.
■ Cincinnati's Bumpus Jones made his Major League debut a spectacular one, holding Pittsburgh hitless in a 7-1 victory.
■ First-half champion Boston swept aside second-half champion Cleveland in a post-season playoff. The Beaneaters won five of the six games and the other ended in a tie.

LEADERS

BA: Dan Brouthers, Brk., .335.
Runs: Cupid Childs, Cle., 136.
Hits: Dan Brouthers, Brk., 197.
TB: Dan Brouthers, Brk., 282.
HR: Bug Holliday, Cin., 13.
RBI: Dan Brouthers, Brk., 124.
SB: Monte Ward, Brk., 88.
Wins: Bill Hutchinson, Chi.; Cy Young, Cle., 36.
ERA: Cy Young, Cle., 1.93.
CG: Bill Hutchinson, Chi., 67.
IP: Bill Hutchinson, Chi., 627.
SO: Bill Hutchinson, Chi., 316.

20-game winners

Bill Hutchinson, Chi., 36-36
Cy Young, Cle., 36-12
Kid Nichols, Bos., 35-16
Jack Stivetts, Bos., 35-16
Gus Weyhing, Phil., 32-21
Amos Rusie, N.Y., 31-31
George Haddock, Brk., 29-13
Frank Killen, Wash., 29-26
George Cuppy, Cle., 28-13
Ed Stein, Brk., 27-16
Mark Baldwin, Pit., 26-27
John Clarkson, Bos.-Cle., 25-16
Silver King, N.Y., 23-24
Harry Staley, Bos., 22-10
Ad Gumbert, Chi., 22-19
Tony Mullane, Cin., 21-13
Frank Dwyer, St.L.-Cin., 21-18
Scott Stratton, Lou., 21-19
Kid Gleason, St.L., 20-24

POST-SEASON PLAYOFF

(Boston 5, Cleveland 0; 1 tie)
Game 1—Boston 0, Cleveland 0 (11 innings, darkness)
Game 2—Boston 4, Cleveland 3
Game 3—Boston 3, Cleveland 2
Game 4—Boston 4, Cleveland 0
Game 5—Boston 12, Cleveland 7
Game 6—Boston 8, Cleveland 3

MAJOR RULES CHANGES

■ Games were declared "official" after five full innings or 4½ if the home team was leading.

■ An umpire was given authority to declare a forfeit when he believed players were using delay tactics to gain suspension of a game.

■ Any ball hit over an outfield fence was declared a home run, except in cases where the distance was less than 235 feet from home base. Such drives were called ground-rule doubles.

■ Any batter obstructing or interfering with a catcher's throw was declared out.

1893

FINAL STANDINGS

National League

Team	W	L	Pct.	GB
Boston	86	43	.667	...
Pittsburgh	81	48	.628	5
Cleveland	73	55	.570	12.5
Philadelphia	72	57	.558	14
New York	68	64	.515	19.5
Brooklyn	65	63	.508	20.5
Cincinnati	65	63	.508	20.5
Baltimore	60	70	.462	26.5
Chicago	56	71	.441	29
St. Louis	57	75	.432	30.5
Louisville	50	75	.400	34
Washington	40	89	.310	46

SIGNIFICANT EVENT

■ A revolutionary rules change: The pitching box was eliminated and a pitcher's rubber was placed 5 feet behind the back line of the box—60 feet, 6 inches from home plate.

MEMORABLE MOMENTS

■ Boston defeated Baltimore 6-2 in a late July game and took over permanent posession of first place en route to its third consecutive pennant.
■ Cleveland ended the 33-game hitting streak of George Davis during an 8-6 victory over the Giants.

LEADERS

BA: Hugh Duffy, Bos., .363.
Runs: Herman Long, Bos., 149.
Hits: Sam Thompson, Phil., 222.
TB: Ed Delahanty, Phil., 347.
HR: Ed Delahanty, Phil., 19.
RBI: Ed Delahanty, Phil., 146.
SB: Tom Brown, Lou., 66.
Wins: Frank Killen, Pit., 36.
ERA: Ted Breitenstein, St.L., 3.18.
CG: Amos Rusie, N.Y., 50.
IP: Amos Rusie, N.Y., 482.
SO: Amos Rusie, N.Y., 208.

20-game winners

Frank Killen, Pit., 36-14
Kid Nichols, Bos., 34-14
Cy Young, Cle., 34-16
Amos Rusie, N.Y., 33-21
Brickyard Kennedy, Brk., 25-20
Gus Weyhing, Phil., 23-16
Sadie McMahon, Bal., 23-18
Kid Gleason, St.L., 21-22
Jack Stivetts, Bos., 20-12

MAJOR RULES CHANGES

■ The pitcher's box was eliminated and the pitching distance was lengthened to 60 feet, 6 inches from the outer corner of home base. The distance was marked by a rubber slab (a pitching rubber) 12 inches long and 4 inches wide.

■ Pitchers were required to deliver the ball with one foot remaining in contact with the rubber.

■ Bats with a flat surface were outlawed. Bats were required to be completely round.

■ Lineups were submitted before each game and the batting order was followed throughout the contest. Each new inning started with the batter whose name followed the man who had made the final out of the previous inning.

1894

FINAL STANDINGS

National League

Team	W	L	Pct.	GB
Baltimore	89	39	.695	...
New York	88	44	.667	3
Boston	83	49	.629	8
Philadelphia	71	57	.555	18
Brooklyn	70	61	.534	20.5
Cleveland	68	61	.527	21.5
Pittsburgh	65	65	.500	25
Chicago	57	75	.432	34
St. Louis	56	76	.424	35
Cincinnati	55	75	.423	35
Washington	45	87	.341	46
Louisville	36	94	.277	54

SIGNIFICANT EVENT

■ Rules changes: Foul bunts became strikes and the infield fly rule was entered into the books.

MEMORABLE MOMENTS

■ Boston second baseman Bobby Lowe became baseball's first four-homer man when he connected in consecutive at-bats during a rout of Cincinnati.
■ Chicago shortstop Bill Dahlen failed to get a hit in six at-bats against Cincinnati, ending his 42-game hitting streak.
■ Philadelphia star Billy Hamilton tied a Major League record with seven stolen bases in a victory over Washington.
■ The Orioles clinched the first of three consecutive pennants with a victory over Cleveland.
■ Second-place New York defeated regular-season champion Baltimore 16-3 and concluded its sweep of the best-of-seven Temple Cup series—a new post-season playoff.

LEADERS

BA: Hugh Duffy, Bos., .440.
Runs: Billy Hamilton, Phil., 192.
Hits: Hugh Duffy, Bos., 237.
TB: Hugh Duffy, Bos., 374.
HR: Hugh Duffy, Bos., 18.
RBI: Hugh Duffy, Bos., 145.
SB: Billy Hamilton, Phil., 98.
Wins: Amos Rusie, N.Y., 36.
ERA: Amos Rusie, N.Y., 2.78.
CG: Ted Breitenstein, St.L., 46.
IP: Ted Breitenstein, St.L., 447.1.
SO: Amos Rusie, N.Y., 195.

20-game winners

Amos Rusie, N.Y., 36-13
Jouett Meekin, N.Y., 33-9
Kid Nichols, Bos., 32-13
Ted Breitenstein, St.L., 27-23
Ed Stein, Brk., 26-14
Jack Stivetts, Bos., 26-14
Cy Young, Cle., 26-21
Sadie McMahon, Bal., 25-8
George Cuppy, Cle., 24-15
Brickyard Kennedy, Brk., 24-20
Jack Taylor, Phil., 23-13
Clark Griffith, Chi., 21-14

TEMPLE CUP

(New York 4, Baltimore 0)
Game 1—New York 4, Baltimore 1
Game 2—New York 9, Baltimore 6
Game 3—New York 4, Baltimore 1
Game 4—New York 16, Baltimore 3

MAJOR RULES CHANGES

■ Batters were charged with a strike when bunting the ball into foul territory.

■ Batters who advanced a runner with a bunt while being put out were credited with a sacrifice and not charged with an at-bat.

1895

FINAL STANDINGS

National League

Team	W	L	Pct.	GB
Baltimore	87	43	.669	...
Cleveland	84	46	.646	3
Philadelphia	78	53	.595	9.5
Chicago	72	58	.554	15
Boston	71	60	.542	16.5
Brooklyn	71	60	.542	16.5
Pittsburgh	71	61	.538	17
Cincinnati	66	64	.508	21
New York	66	65	.504	21.5
Washington	43	85	.336	43
St. Louis	39	92	.298	48.5
Louisville	35	96	.267	52.5

SIGNIFICANT EVENT

■ N.L. officials, reacting to player complaints, restricted the size of gloves for everybody but first basemen and catchers to 10 ounces and 14 inches in circumference around the palm.

MEMORABLE MOMENTS

■ Louisville defeated Washington, but Colonels star Fred Clarke saw his 35-game hitting streak come to an end.
■ Baltimore clinched its second straight pennant with a victory over New York—two days before the regular season ended.
■ Cleveland captured the Temple Cup with a fifth-game, 5-2 victory over Baltimore.

LEADERS

BA: Jesse Burkett, Cle., .409.
Runs: Billy Hamilton, Phil., 166.
Hits: Jesse Burkett, Cle., 225.
TB: Sam Thompson, Phil., 352.
HR: Sam Thompson, Phil., 18.
RBI: Sam Thompson, Phil., 165.
SB: Billy Hamilton, Phil., 97.
Wins: Cy Young, Cle., 35.
ERA: Al Maul, Wash., 2.45.
CG: Ted Breitenstein, St.L., 46.
IP: Pink Hawley, Pit., 444.1.
SO: Amos Rusie, N.Y., 201.

20-game winners

Cy Young, Cle., 35-10
Bill Hoffer, Bal., 31-6
Pink Hawley, Pit., 31-22
George Cuppy, Cle., 26-14
Clark Griffith, Chi., 26-14
Jack Taylor, Phil., 26-14
Kid Nichols, Bos., 26-16
Kid Carsey, Phil., 24-16
Amos Rusie, N.Y., 23-23
Adonis Terry, Chi., 21-14
George Hemming, Bal., 20-13

TEMPLE CUP

(Cleveland 4, Baltimore 1)
Game 1—Cleveland 5, Baltimore 4
Game 2—Cleveland 7, Baltimore 2
Game 3—Cleveland 7, Baltimore 1
Game 4—Baltimore 5, Cleveland 0
Game 5—Cleveland 5, Baltimore 2

MAJOR RULES CHANGES

■ The pitching rubber was enlarged to 24-by-6 inches, its current size.

■ A foul tip caught by the catcher became a strike.

■ The infield fly rule became official.

■ Bats were limited to 2¾ inches in diameter.

■ Catchers and first basemen were given permission to use oversized gloves. Other fielders still were restricted to gloves weighing 10 ounces with a hand size not more than 14 inches.

1896

FINAL STANDINGS

National League

Team	W	L	Pct.	GB
Baltimore	90	39	.698	...
Cleveland	80	48	.625	9.5
Cincinnati	77	50	.606	12
Boston	74	57	.565	17
Chicago	71	57	.555	18.5
Pittsburgh	66	63	.512	24
New York	64	67	.489	27
Philadelphia	62	68	.477	28.5
Brooklyn	58	73	.443	33
Washington	58	73	.443	33
St. Louis	40	90	.308	50.5
Louisville	38	93	.290	53

SIGNIFICANT EVENT

■ Cleveland's Jesse Burkett collected three final-day hits and finished with a league-leading .410 average—his record second consecutive .400 season.

MEMORABLE MOMENTS

■ Philadelphia star Ed Delahanty matched Bobby Lowe's 1894 record of four home runs in a game—all inside-the-park shots in a loss to Chicago.
■ Baltimore clinched its third straight pennant with a victory over Brooklyn.
■ Regular-season champion Baltimore defeated Cleveland 5-0 and capped its four-game sweep of the Temple Cup series.

LEADERS

BA: Jesse Burkett, Cle., .410.
Runs: Jesse Burkett, Cle., 160.
Hits: Jesse Burkett, Cle., 240.
TB: Jesse Burkett, Cle., 317.
HR: Ed Delahanty, Phil.;
Bill Joyce, Wash.-N.Y., 13.
RBI: Ed Delahanty, Phil., 126.
SB: Joe Kelley, Bal., 87.
Wins: Frank Killen, Pit.; Kid Nichols, Bos., 30.
ERA: Billy Rhines, Cin., 2.45.
CG: Frank Killen, Pit., 44.
IP: Frank Killen, Pit., 432.1.
SO: Cy Young, Cle., 140.

20-game winners

Kid Nichols, Bos., 30-14
Frank Killen, Pit., 30-18
Cy Young, Cle., 28-15
Jouett Meekin, N.Y., 26-14
Bill Hoffer, Bal., 25-7
George Cuppy, Cle., 25-14
George Mercer, Wash., 25-18
Frank Dwyer, Cin., 24-11
Clark Griffith, Chi., 23-11
Jack Stivetts, Bos., 22-14
Pink Hawley, Pit., 22-21
Jack Taylor, Phil., 20-21

TEMPLE CUP

(Baltimore 4, Cleveland 0)

Game 1—Baltimore 7, Cleveland 1
Game 2—Baltimore 7, Cleveland 2 (8 innings, darkness)
Game 3—Baltimore 6, Cleveland 2
Game 4—Baltimore 5, Cleveland 0

MAJOR RULES CHANGES

■ Pitchers were no longer required to hold the ball in full sight of the umpire up to delivery.
■ Umpires were given authority to eject players using vulgar language and fine them $25. Umpires also were allowed to fine players $5 to $10 for specified misconduct.
■ Home teams were required to have at least 12 regulation balls available for each game.

1897

FINAL STANDINGS

National League

Team	W	L	Pct.	GB
Boston	93	39	.705	...
Baltimore	90	40	.692	2
New York	83	48	.634	9.5
Cincinnati	76	56	.576	17
Cleveland	69	62	.527	23.5
Brooklyn	61	71	.462	32
Washington	61	71	.462	32
Pittsburgh	60	71	.458	32.5
Chicago	59	73	.447	34
Philadelphia	55	77	.417	38
Louisville	52	78	.400	40
St. Louis	29	102	.221	63.5

SIGNIFICANT EVENT

■ The 4-year-old Temple Cup series, which failed to attract fan interest, died a quiet death after regular-season champion Boston lost a five-game series to second-place Baltimore.

MEMORABLE MOMENTS

■ Pittsburgh pitcher Frank Killen defeated Baltimore and ended Willie Keeler's 44-game hitting streak.
■ Chicago set an N.L. single-game scoring record during a 36-7 demolition of Louisville.
■ Boston's victory over Brooklyn, coupled with Baltimore's same-day loss to Washington, gave the Beaneaters the N.L. pennant.

LEADERS

BA: Willie Keeler, Bal., .424.
Runs: Billy Hamilton, Bos., 152.
Hits: Willie Keeler, Bal., 239.
TB: Nap Lajoie, Phil., 310.
HR: Hugh Duffy, Bos., 11.
RBI: George Davis, N.Y., 136.
SB: Bill Lange, Chi., 73.
Wins: Kid Nichols, Bos., 31.
ERA: Amos Rusie, N.Y., 2.54.
CG: Red Donahue, St.L.; Clark Griffith, Chi.;
Frank Killen, Pit., 38.
IP: Kid Nichols, Bos., 368.
SO: Doc McJames, Wash., 156.

20-game winners

Kid Nichols, Bos., 31-11
Amos Rusie, N.Y., 28-10
Fred Klobedanz, Bos., 26-7
Joe Corbett, Bal., 24-8
Ted Breitenstein, Cin., 23-12
Bill Hoffer, Bal., 22-11
Ted Lewis, Bos., 21-12
Bill Rhines, Cin., 21-15
Clark Griffith, Chi., 21-18
Cy Young, Cle., 21-19
Jerry Nops, Bal., 20-6
Jouett Meekin, N.Y., 20-11
George Mercer, Wash., 20-20

TEMPLE CUP

(Baltimore 4, Boston 1)

Game 1—Boston 13, Baltimore 12
Game 2—Baltimore 13, Boston 11
Game 3—Baltimore 8, Boston 3 (7 innings, rain)
Game 4—Baltimore 12, Boston 11
Game 5—Baltimore 9, Boston 3

MAJOR RULES CHANGES

■ Runners who were held or obstructed by fielders without the ball were given the base they were trying to reach. Any fielder stopping a ball in any way other than with his hands was guilty of obstruction and runners were allowed to advance.
■ Runners returning to their original base after a caught fly ball were required to retouch all bases they had passed in reverse order.
■ Any judgement call by the umpire was final and could not be reversed.
■ Earned runs were defined as runs scored without the aid of errors.

1898

FINAL STANDINGS

National League

Team	W	L	Pct.	GB
Boston	102	47	.685	...
Baltimore	96	53	.644	6
Cincinnati	92	60	.605	11.5
Chicago	85	65	.567	17.5
Cleveland	81	68	.544	21
Philadelphia	78	71	.523	24
New York	77	73	.513	25.5
Pittsburgh	72	76	.486	29.5
Louisville	70	81	.464	33
Brooklyn	54	91	.372	46
Washington	51	101	.336	52.5
St. Louis	39	111	.260	63.5

SIGNIFICANT EVENT

■ Cap Anson, who compiled a 1,293-932 record over 19 seasons as a Chicago manager, was fired.

MEMORABLE MOMENTS

■ A Major League first: Baltimore's Jim Hughes and Cincinnati's Ted Breitenstein pitched nine-inning no-hitters on the same day.
■ Philadelphia pitcher Bill Duggleby hit a grand slam in his first Major League at-bat—a feat never since duplicated.
■ Boston, en route to a record-tying 102 wins, clinched its second straight pennant with a victory over Washington.

LEADERS

BA: Willie Keeler, Bal., .385.
Runs: John McGraw, Bal., 143.
Hits: Willie Keeler, Bal., 216.
TB: Jimmy Collins, Bos., 286.
HR: Jimmy Collins, Bos., 15.
RBI: Nap Lajoie, Phil., 127.
SB: Ed Delahanty, Phil., 58.
Wins: Kid Nichols, Bos., 31.
ERA: Clark Griffith, Chi., 1.88.
CG: Jack Taylor, St.L., 42.
IP: Jack Taylor, St.L., 397.1.
SO: Cy Seymour, N.Y., 239.

20-game winners

Kid Nichols, Bos., 31-12
Bert Cunningham, Lou., 28-15
Pink Hawley, Cin., 27-11
Doc McJames, Bal., 27-15
Ted Lewis, Bos., 26-8
Jesse Tannehill, Pit., 25-13
Vic Willis, Bos., 25-13
Cy Young, Cle., 25-13
Cy Seymour, N.Y., 25-19
Clark Griffith, Chi., 24-10
Wiley Piatt, Phil., 24-14
Jim Hughes, Bal., 23-12
Jack Powell, Cle., 23-15
Al Maul, Bal., 20-7
Jim Callahan, Chi., 20-10
Amos Rusie, N.Y., 20-11
Ted Breitenstein, Cin., 20-14

MAJOR RULES CHANGES

■ Penalties were specified for teams batting out of order.
■ Detailed definitions were provided for pitchers committing balks, including illegal motions to home base and to the bases.
■ Stolen bases were awarded for bases attained without the aid of batted balls or errors.

1899

FINAL STANDINGS

National League

Team	W	L	Pct.	GB
Brooklyn	101	47	.682	...
Boston	95	57	.625	8
Philadelphia	94	58	.618	9
Baltimore	86	62	.581	15
St. Louis	84	67	.556	18.5
Cincinnati	83	67	.553	19
Pittsburgh	76	73	.510	25.5
Chicago	75	73	.507	26
Louisville	75	77	.493	28
New York	60	90	.400	42
Washington	54	98	.355	49
Cleveland	20	134	.130	84

SIGNIFICANT EVENTS

■ John McGraw made his managerial debut a successful one, leading Baltimore to a victory over New York.
■ The Western League changed its name to the American Baseball League, setting the stage for Ban Johnson's circuit to gain "Major League" credibility.

MEMORABLE MOMENTS

■ Cleveland defeated Washington and snapped its 24-game losing streak.
■ The Brooklyn Superbas, en route to 101 victories, clinched the pennant with a win over New York.
■ Cincinnati posted a season-closing sweep of Cleveland, handing the Spiders their 133rd and 134th losses.

LEADERS

BA: Ed Delahanty, Phil., .410.
Runs: Willie Keeler, Brk.;
John McGraw, Bal., 140.
Hits: Ed Delahanty, Phil., 238.
TB: Ed Delahanty, Phil., 338.
HR: Buck Freeman, Wash., 25.
RBI: Ed Delahanty, Phil., 137.
SB: Jimmy Sheckard, Bal., 77.
Wins: Jim Hughes, Brk.; Joe McGinnity, Bal., 28.
ERA: Vic Willis, Bos., 2.50.
CG: Bill Carrick, N.Y.; Jack Powell, St.L.;
Cy Young, St.L., 40.
IP: Sam Leever, Pit., 379.
SO: Noodles Hahn, Cin., 145.

20-game winners

Jim Hughes, Brk., 28-6
Joe McGinnity, Bal., 28-16
Vic Willis, Bos., 27-8
Cy Young, St.L., 26-16
Jesse Tannehill, Pit., 24-14
Noodles Hahn, Cin., 23-8
Jack Dunn, Brk., 23-13
Wiley Piatt, Phil., 23-15
Jack Powell, St.L., 23-19
Brickyard Kennedy, Brk., 22-9
Clark Griffith, Chi., 22-14
Frank Kitson, Bal., 22-16
Red Donahue, Phil., 21-8
Jim Callahan, Chi., 21-12
Chick Fraser, Phil., 21-12
Deacon Phillippe, Lou., 21-17
Kid Nichols, Bos., 21-19
Sam Leever, Pit., 21-23

MAJOR RULES CHANGES

■ The score of any game suspended or called before the full nine innings had been played reverted back to the last full inning completed.
■ Batters were awarded first base for catcher's interference.
■ The 1898 balk rules were further defined.
■ Each team was required to wear uniforms that conformed in color and style.

1900

FINAL STANDINGS

National League

Team	W	L	Pct.	GB
Brooklyn	82	54	.603	...
Pittsburgh	79	60	.568	4.5
Philadelphia	75	63	.543	8
Boston	66	72	.478	17
Chicago	65	75	.464	19
St. Louis	65	75	.464	19
Cincinnati	62	77	.446	21.5
New York	60	78	.435	23

SIGNIFICANT EVENTS

■ **March 8:** The National League streamlined its product, reducing from 12 to eight teams.
■ **March 9:** N.L. officials expanded the strike zone by reshaping home plate from a 12-inch square to a 17-inch-wide, five-sided figure.
■ **March 16:** Ban Johnson announced formation of a franchise in Chicago, giving his young American League teams in eight cities. The others were Kansas City, Minneapolis, Milwaukee, Indianapolis, Detroit, Cleveland and Buffalo.
■ **October 11:** Ban Johnson's new American League, claiming status as an equal to the National League, announced plans to locate franchises in Baltimore and Washington.
■ **November 14:** The N.L. declared war when it rejected the A.L. as an equal and pronounced it an "outlaw league" outside the National Agreement.
■ **December 15:** The Giants traded aging Amos Rusie to the Reds for a young pitcher named Christy Mathewson.

MEMORABLE MOMENTS

■ **April 19:** Ban Johnson's new American League opened with a bang when Buffalo's Doc Amole pitched an 8-0 no-hitter against the Tigers.
■ **July 7:** Boston's Kid Nichols defeated the Cubs 11-4 for his 300th career victory.
■ **October 3:** Brooklyn clinched the N.L. pennant with a 6-4, 5-4 sweep at Boston, giving manager Ned Hanlon his fifth championship in seven years.

LEADERS

BA: Honus Wagner, Pit., .381.
Runs: Roy Thomas, Phil., 132.
Hits: Willie Keeler, Brk., 204.
TB: Honus Wagner, Pit., 302.
HR: Herman Long, Bos., 12.
RBI: Elmer Flick, Phil., 110.
SB: Patsy Donovan, St.L.; George Van Haltren, N.Y., 45.
Wins: Joe McGinnity, Brk., 28.
ERA: Rube Waddell, Pit., 2.37.
CG: Pink Hawley, N.Y., 34.
IP: Joe McGinnity, Brk., 343.
SO: Noodles Hahn, Cin., 132.

20-game winners
Joe McGinnity, Brk., 28-8
Jesse Tannehill, Pit., 20-6
Brickyard Kennedy, Brk., 20-13
Deacon Phillippe, Pit., 20-13
Bill Dinneen, Bos., 20-14

100 RBIs
Elmer Flick, Phil., 110
Ed Delahanty, Phil., 109
Honus Wagner, Pit., 100

CHRONICLE-TELEGRAPH CUP

(Brooklyn 3, Pittsburgh 1)
Game 1—Brooklyn 5, Pittsburgh 2
Game 2—Brooklyn 4, Pittsburgh 2
Game 3—Pittsburgh 10, Brooklyn 0
Game 4—Brooklyn 6, Pittsburgh 1

MAJOR RULES CHANGES

■ Home "base" became home "plate" when its shape was changed from a 12-inch square to a five-sided flat surface 17 inches wide.
■ A batter was not awarded first base on a pitcher's balk.

1901

FINAL STANDINGS

American League

Team	W	L	Pct.	GB
Chicago	83	53	.610	...
Boston	79	57	.581	4
Detroit	74	61	.548	8.5
Philadelphia	74	62	.544	9
Baltimore	68	65	.511	13.5
Washington	61	72	.459	20.5
Cleveland	54	82	.397	29
Milwaukee	48	89	.350	35.5

National League

Team	W	L	Pct.	GB
Pittsburgh	90	49	.647	...
Philadelphia	83	57	.593	7.5
Brooklyn	79	57	.581	9.5
St. Louis	76	64	.543	14.5
Boston	69	69	.500	20.5
Chicago	53	86	.381	37
New York	52	85	.380	37
Cincinnati	52	87	.374	38

SIGNIFICANT EVENTS

■ **January 28:** When the A.L. formally organized as an eight-team "Major League," it placed franchises in Chicago, Philadelphia and Boston—N.L. strongholds.
■ **February 27:** Among a series of N.L. rules changes was the declaration that all foul balls will count as strikes, except when the batter already has two.
■ **March 28:** In a move to keep Napoleon Lajoie from jumping to the A.L.'s Athletics, the Phillies filed for an injunction to keep him from playing for any other team.
■ **September 19:** The baseball schedule was canceled because of the funeral of President William McKinley, who was killed by an assassin's bullet.
■ **October 20:** Seven Cardinals, including top hitters Jesse Burkett and Bobby Wallace, jumped to the American League's new St. Louis franchise.
■ **November 20:** A.L. President Ban Johnson shifted his Milwaukee franchise to St. Louis for a head-to-head battle with the N.L.'s Cardinals.

MEMORABLE MOMENTS

■ **April 24:** Chicago played host to the A.L.'s first Major League game, defeating Cleveland, 8-2.
■ **April 25:** Detroit celebrated its A.L. debut by scoring 10 ninth-inning runs and beating Milwaukee, 14-13.
■ **July 15:** Christy Mathewson, the Giants' 21-year-old rookie righthander, held the Cardinals hitless in a 5-0 New York victory at St. Louis.
■ **September 29:** The White Stockings captured the first A.L. pennant, but Philadelphia's Napoleon Lajoie compiled Triple Crown totals of .426, 14 homers and 125 RBI.

LEADERS

American League
BA: Nap Lajoie, Phil., .426.
Runs: Nap Lajoie, Phil., 145.
Hits: Lajoie, Phil., 232.
TB: Nap Lajoie, Phil., 350.
HR: Nap Lajoie, Phil., 14.
RBI: Nap Lajoie, Phil., 125.
SB: Frank Isbell, Chi., 52.
Wins: Cy Young, Bos., 33
ERA: Cy Young, Bos., 1.62
CG: Joe McGinnity, Balt., 39.
IP: Joe McGinnity, Balt., 382.
SO: Cy Young, Bos., 158.

National League
BA: Jesse Burkett, St.L., .376.
Runs: Jesse Burkett, St.L., 142.
Hits: Jesse Burkett, St.L., 226.
TB: Jesse Burkett, St.L., 306.
HR: Sam Crawford, Cin., 16.
RBI: Honus Wagner, Pit., 126.
SB: Honus Wagner, Pit., 49.
Wins: Bill Donovan, Brk., 25.
ERA: Jesse Tannehill, Pit., 2.18.
CG: Noodles Hahn, Cin., 41.
IP: Noodles Hahn, Cin., 375.1.
SO: Noodles Hahn, Cin., 239.

A.L. 20-game winners
Cy Young, Bos., 33-10
Joe McGinnity, Bal., 26-20
Clark Griffith, Chi., 24-7
Roscoe Miller, Det., 23-13
Chick Fraser, Phil., 22-16
Roy Patterson, Chi., 20-15
Red Donahue, Phil., 21-13
Al Orth, Phil., 20-12

N.L. 20-game winners
Bill Donovan, Brk., 25-15
Jack Harper, St.L., 23-13
Deacon Phillippe, Pit., 22-12
Noodles Hahn, Cin., 22-19
Jack Chesbro, Pit., 21-10
Christy Mathewson, N.Y., 20-17
Vic Willis, Bos., 20-17

A.L. 100 RBIs
Nap Lajoie, Phil., 125
Buck Freeman, Bos., 114

N.L. 100 RBIs
Honus Wagner, Pit., 126
Ed Delahanty, Phil., 108
Jimmy Sheckard, Brk., 104
Sam Crawford, Cin., 104

1902

FINAL STANDINGS

American League

Team	W	L	Pct.	GB
Philadelphia	83	53	.610	...
St. Louis	78	58	.574	5
Boston	77	60	.562	6.5
Chicago	74	60	.552	8
Cleveland	69	67	.507	14
Washington	61	75	.449	22
Detroit	52	83	.385	30.5
Baltimore	50	88	.362	34

National League

Team	W	L	Pct.	GB
Pittsburgh	103	36	.741	...
Brooklyn	75	63	.543	27.5
Boston	73	64	.533	29
Cincinnati	70	70	.500	33.5
Chicago	68	69	.496	34
St. Louis	56	78	.418	44.5
Philadelphia	56	81	.409	46
New York	48	88	.353	53.5

SIGNIFICANT EVENTS

■ **April 21:** The Pennsylvania Supreme Court granted an injunction barring league-jumper Napoleon Lajoie from playing for any team but the Phillies.
■ **May 27:** To keep Lajoie from returning to the N.L., A.L. president Ban Johnson shifted his contract from the Athletics to the Indians, getting him out of Pennsylvania.
■ **July 8:** The A.L. lost Baltimore manager John McGraw, who jumped to the N.L. as manager of the Giants and took five players with him.
■ **September 28:** Philadelphia Athletics star Socks Seybold completed the American League season with a Major League single-season record 16 home runs.
■ **December 9:** The A.L. announced plans to locate a franchise in New York for the 1903 season.
■ **December 12:** Owners elected Harry Pulliam as N.L. president.

MEMORABLE MOMENTS

■ **April 26:** In a stirring Major League debut, Cleveland's Addie Joss fired a one-hitter and beat the Browns, 3-0.
■ **July 19:** The New York Giants, en route to a last-place finish in the N.L., dropped a 5-3 decision to Philadelphia in the managerial debut of John McGraw.
■ **October 4:** The Pirates completed their 103-36 season with a 27½-game lead over second-place Brooklyn in the N.L.

LEADERS

American League
BA: Nap Lajoie, Phil-Cle., .378.
Runs: Dave Fultz, Phil.; Topsy Hartsel, Phil., 109.
Hits: Charlie Hickman, Bos.-Cle., 193.
TB: Charlie Hickman, Bos.-Cle., 288.
HR: Socks Seybold, Phil., 16.
RBI: Buck Freeman, Bos., 121.
SB: Topsy Hartsel, Phil., 47.
Wins: Cy Young, Bos., 32.
ERA: Ed Siever, Det., 1.91.
CG: Cy Young, Bos., 41.
IP: Cy Young, Bos., 384.2
SO: Rube Waddell, Phil., 210.

National League
BA: Ginger Beaumont, Pit., .357.
Runs: Honus Wagner, Pit., 105.
Hits: Ginger Beaumont, Pit., 193.
TB: Sam Crawford, Cin., 256.
HR: Tommy Leach, Pit., 6.
RBI: Honus Wagner, Pit., 91.
SB: Honus Wagner, Pit., 42.
Wins: Jack Chesbro, Pit., 28.
ERA: Jack Taylor, Chi., 1.33.
CG: Vic Willis, Bos., 45
IP: Vic Willis, Bos., 410.
SO: Vic Willis, Bos., 225.

A.L. 20-game winners
Cy Young, Bos., 32-11
Rube Waddell, Phil., 24-7
Red Donahue, St.L., 22-11
Jack Powell, St.L., 22-17
Bill Dinneen, Bos., 21-21
Eddie Plank, Phil., 20-15

N.L. 20-game winners
Jack Chesbro, Pit., 28-6
Togie Pittinger, Bos., 27-16
Vic Willis, Bos., 27-20
Jack Taylor, Chi., 23-11
Noodles Hahn, Cin., 23-12
Jesse Tannehill, Pit., 20-6
Deacon Phillippe, Pit., 20-9

A.L./N.L. 20-game winner
Joe McGinnity, Bal.-Pit., 21

A.L. 100 RBIs
Buck Freeman, Bos., 121
Charlie Hickman, Bos.-Cle., 110
Lave Cross, Phil., 108

1903

FINAL STANDINGS

American League

Team	W	L	Pct.	GB
Boston	91	47	.659	...
Philadelphia	75	60	.556	14.5
Cleveland	77	63	.550	15
New York	72	62	.537	17
Detroit	65	71	.478	25
St. Louis	65	74	.468	26.5
Chicago	60	77	.438	30.5
Washington	43	94	.314	47.5

National League

Team	W	L	Pct.	GB
Pittsburgh	91	49	.650	...
New York	84	55	.604	6.5
Chicago	82	56	.594	8
Cincinnati	74	65	.532	16.5
Brooklyn	70	66	.515	19
Boston	58	80	.420	32
Philadelphia	49	86	.363	39.5
St. Louis	43	94	.314	46.5

SIGNIFICANT EVENTS

■ **January 9:** A peace treaty was signed with the N.L. agreeing to recognize the A.L. as a Major League and both parties agreeing to honor the reserve clause in player contracts.
■ **July 2:** Washington star Ed Delahanty died when he fell off a railroad bridge spanning the Niagara River at Fort Erie, Ontario.
■ **August 8:** A bleacher overhang at Philadelphia's N.L. park collapsed, killing 12 and injuring 282.
■ **September 16:** The presidents of the A.L. Boston and N.L. Pittsburgh teams agreed to a best-of-nine championship playoff—baseball's first World Series.

MEMORABLE MOMENTS

■ **April 22:** The A.L.'s new New York team officially opened play, but the Highlanders dropped a 3-1 decision at Washington.
■ **April 30:** The A.L.'s New York team opened new Hilltop Park with a 6-2 victory over Washington.
■ **September 17:** Boston clinched the A.L. pennant with a victory over Cleveland and set up a championship showdown with N.L.-winner Pittsburgh.

LEADERS

American League

BA: Nap Lajoie, Cle., .344.
Runs: Patsy Dougherty, Bos., 107.
Hits: Patsy Dougherty, Bos., 195.
TB: Buck Freeman, Bos., 281.
HR: Buck Freeman, Bos., 13.
RBI: Buck Freeman, Bos., 104.
SB: Harry Bay, Cle., 45.
Wins: Cy Young, Bos., 28.
ERA: Earl Moore, Cle., 1.74.
CG: Bill Donovan, Det.; Rube Waddell, Phil.; Cy Young, Bos., 34.
IP: Cy Young, Bos., 341.2.
SO: Rube Waddell, Phil., 302.

National League

BA: Honus Wagner, Pit., .355.
Runs: Ginger Beaumont, Pit., 137.
Hits: Ginger Beaumont, Pit., 209.
TB: Ginger Beaumont, Pit., 272.
HR: Jimmy Sheckard, Brk., 9.
RBI: Sam Mertes, N.Y., 104.
SB: Frank Chance, Chi.; Jimmy Sheckard, Brk., 67.
Wins: Joe McGinnity, N.Y., 31.
ERA: Sam Leever, Pit., 2.06.
CG: Joe McGinnity, N.Y., 44.
IP: Joe McGinnity, N.Y., 434.
SO: Christy Mathewson, N.Y., 267.

A.L. 20-game winners

Cy Young, Bos., 28-9
Eddie Plank, Phil., 23-16
Bill Dinneen, Bos., 21-13
Jack Chesbro, N.Y., 21-15
Willie Sudhoff, St.L., 21-15
Rube Waddell, Phil., 21-16
Tom Hughes, Bos., 20-7
Earl Moore, Cle., 20-8

N.L. 20-game winners

Joe McGinnity, N.Y., 31-20
Christy Mathewson, N.Y., 30-13
Sam Leever, Pit., 25-7
Deacon Phillippe, Pit., 25-9
Noodles Hahn, Cin., 22-12
Henry Schmidt, Brk., 22-13
Jack Taylor, Chi., 21-14
Jake Weimer, Chi., 20-8
Bob Wicker, St.L.-Chi., 20-9

A.L. 100 RBIs

Buck Freeman, Bos., 104

N.L. 100 RBIs

Sam Mertes, N.Y., 104
Honus Wagner, Pit., 101

WORLD SERIES

■ **Winner:** The Red Sox captured the first modern World Series with a five-games-to-three victory over the N.L.-champion Pirates.

■ **Turning point:** A 7-3 Game 7 victory in which the Red Sox claimed a 4-3 Series lead and finally showed they could beat Pirates starter Deacon Phillippe.

■ **Memorable moments:** Pirates right fielder Jimmy Sebring's Game 1 home run—the first in World Series history.

■ **Top guns:** Bill Dinneen (35 IP, 3-1, 2.06 ERA), Cy Young (34 IP, 2-1, 1.59), Red Sox; Phillippe (44 IP, 3-2), Pirates.

Linescores

Game 1—October 1, at Boston
Pittsburgh...... 401 100 100 — 7 12 2
Boston........... 000 000 201 — 3 6 4
Phillippe; Young. W—Phillippe. L—Young. HR—Sebring (Pit.).

Game 2—October 2, at Boston
Pittsburgh...... 000 000 000 — 0 3 2
Boston........... 200 001 00x — 3 9 0
Leever, Veil (2); Dinneen. W—Dinneen. L—Leever. HR—Dougherty 2 (Bos.).

Game 3—October 3, at Boston
Pittsburgh...... 012 000 010 — 4 7 0
Boston........... 000 100 010 — 2 4 2
Phillippe; Hughes, Young (3). W—Phillippe. L—Hughes.

Game 4—October 6, at Pittsburgh
Boston........... 000 010 003 — 4 9 1
Pittsburgh...... 100 010 30x — 5 12 1
Dinneen; Phillippe. W—Phillippe. L—Dinneen.

Game 5—October 7, at Pittsburgh
Boston........... 000 006 410 — 11 14 2
Pittsburgh...... 000 000 020 — 2 6 4
Young; Kennedy, Thompson (8). W—Young. L—Kennedy.

Game 6—October 8, at Pittsburgh
Boston........... 003 020 100 — 6 10 1
Pittsburgh...... 000 000 300 — 3 10 3
Dinneen; Leever. W—Dinneen. L—Leever.

Game 7—October 10, at Pittsburgh
Boston........... 200 202 010 — 7 11 4
Pittsburgh...... 000 101 001 — 3 10 3
Young; Phillippe. W—Young. L—Phillippe.

Game 8—October 13, at Boston
Pittsburgh...... 000 000 000 — 0 4 3
Boston........... 000 201 00x — 3 8 0
Phillippe; Dinneen. W—Dinneen. L—Phillippe.

1904

FINAL STANDINGS

American League

Team	W	L	Pct.	GB
Boston	95	59	.617	...
New York	92	59	.609	1.5
Chicago	89	65	.578	6
Cleveland	86	65	.570	7.5
Philadelphia	81	70	.536	12.5
St. Louis	65	87	.428	29
Detroit	62	90	.408	32
Washington	38	113	.252	55.5

National League

Team	W	L	Pct.	GB
New York	106	47	.693	...
Chicago	93	60	.608	13
Cincinnati	88	65	.575	18
Pittsburgh	87	66	.569	19
St. Louis	75	79	.487	31.5
Brooklyn	56	97	.366	50
Boston	55	98	.359	51
Philadelphia	52	100	.342	53.5

SIGNIFICANT EVENT

■ **October 10:** Chastising the A.L. as a "minor circuit," Giants owner John T. Brush and manager John McGraw refused to meet the A.L.-champion Red Sox in a second "World Series."

MEMORABLE MOMENTS

■ **May 5:** Boston great Cy Young pitched the century's first perfect game, retiring all 27 Athletics he faced in a 3-0 victory.
■ **July 5:** The Phillies defeated the Giants 6-5 in 10 innings, ending New York's winning streak at 18 games.
■ **October 6:** Cardinals pitcher Jack Taylor pitched his Major League-record 39th consecutive complete game, but dropped a 6-3 decision to Pittsburgh.
■ **October 10:** The Red Sox captured their second straight A.L. pennant when New York's Jack Chesbro uncorked a final-day wild pitch that allowed the winning run to score in a 3-2 victory.

LEADERS

American League

BA: Nap Lajoie, Cle., .376.
Runs: Patsy Dougherty, Bos.-N.Y., 113.
Hits: Nap Lajoie, Cle., 208.
TB: Nap Lajoie, Cle., 305.
HR: Harry Davis, Phil., 10.
RBI: Nap Lajoie, Cle., 102.
SB: Harry Bay, Cle.; Elmer Flick, Cle., 38.
Wins: Jack Chesbro, N.Y., 41.
ERA: Addie Joss, Cle., 1.59.
CG: Jack Chesbro, N.Y., 48.
IP: Jack Chesbro, N.Y., 454.2.
SO: Rube Waddell, Phil., 349.

National League

BA: Honus Wagner, Pit., .349.
Runs: George Browne, N.Y., 99.
Hits: Ginger Beaumont, Pit., 185.
TB: Honus Wagner, Pit., 255.
HR: Harry Lumley, Brk., 9.
RBI: Bill Dahlen, N.Y., 80.
SB: Honus Wagner, Pit., 53.
Wins: Joe McGinnity, N.Y., 35.
ERA: Joe McGinnity, N.Y., 1.61.
CG: Jack Taylor, St.L.; Vic Willis, Bos., 39.
IP: Joe McGinnity, N.Y., 408.
SO: Christy Mathewson, N.Y., 212.

A.L. 20-game winners

Jack Chesbro, N.Y., 41-12
Cy Young, Bos., 26-16
Eddie Plank, Phil., 26-17
Rube Waddell, Phil., 25-19
Bill Bernhard, Cle., 23-13
Bill Dinneen, Bos., 23-14
Jack Powell, N.Y., 23-19
Jesse Tannehill, Bos., 21-11
Frank Owen, Chi., 21-15

N.L. 20-game winners

Joe McGinnity, N.Y., 35-8
Christy Mathewson, N.Y., 33-12
Jack Harper, Cin., 23-9
Kid Nichols, St.L., 21-13
Dummy Taylor, N.Y., 21-15
Jake Weimer, Chi., 20-14
Jack Taylor, St.L., 20-19

A.L./N.L. 20-game winner

Patsy Flaherty, Chi.-Pit., 20

A.L. 100 RBIs

Nap Lajoie, Cle., 102

No World Series in 1904.

Cleveland's Nap Lajoie won his fourth consecutive A.L. batting championship in 1904.

HISTORY

1905

FINAL STANDINGS

American League

Team	W	L	Pct.	GB
Philadelphia	92	56	.622	...
Chicago	92	60	.605	2
Detroit	79	74	.516	15.5
Boston	78	74	.513	16
Cleveland	76	78	.494	19
New York	71	78	.477	21.5
Washington	64	87	.424	29.5
St. Louis	54	99	.353	40.5

National League

Team	W	L	Pct.	GB
New York	105	48	.686	...
Pittsburgh	96	57	.627	9
Chicago	92	61	.601	13
Philadelphia	83	69	.546	21.5
Cincinnati	79	74	.516	26
St. Louis	58	96	.377	47.5
Boston	51	103	.331	54.5
Brooklyn	48	104	.316	56.5

SIGNIFICANT EVENTS

■ **October 3:** The National Commission adopted the John T. Brush rules for World Series play: a seven-game format, four umpires, two from each league, to work the Series and a revenue-sharing formula for the teams involved.

MEMORABLE MOMENTS

■ **June 13:** New York's Christy Mathewson pitched his second career no-hitter, but the Giants needed a ninth-inning run off Chicago's Mordecai Brown to post a 1-0 victory.

■ **August 30:** Detroit's Ty Cobb made his Major League debut, doubling off New York's Jack Chesbro in a 5-3 Tigers victory.

■ **September 27:** Boston's Bill Dinneen pitched the fourth no-hitter of the season, beating Chicago 2-0 in the first game of a doubleheader.

■ **October 6:** Despite losing to Washington 10-4, the Athletics clinched the A.L. pennant when the Browns defeated the White Sox 6-2 on the next-to-last day of the season.

LEADERS

American League

BA: Elmer Flick, Cle., .308
Runs: Harry Davis, Phil., 93.
Hits: George Stone, St.L., 187.
TB: George Stone, St.L., 259.
HR: Harry Davis, Phil., 8.
RBI: Harry Davis, Phil., 83.
SB: Danny Hoffman, Phil., 46.
Wins: Rube Waddell, Phil., 27.
ERA: Rube Waddell, Phil., 1.48.
CG: Harry Howell, St.L.; George Mullin, Det.; Eddie Plank, Phil., 35.
IP: George Mullin, Det., 347.2.
SO: Rube Waddell, Phil., 287.

National League

BA: Cy Seymour, Cin., .377.
Runs: Mike Donlin, N.Y., 124.
Hits: Cy Seymour, Cin., 219.
TB: Cy Seymour, Cin., 325.
HR: Fred Odwell, Cin., 9.
RBI: Cy Seymour, Cin., 121.
SB: Art Devlin, N.Y.; Billy Maloney, Chi., 59.
Wins: Christy Mathewson, N.Y., 31.
ERA: Christy Mathewson, N.Y., 1.28.
CG: Irv Young, Bos., 41.
IP: Irv Young, Bos., 378.
SO: Christy Mathewson, N.Y., 206.

A.L. 20-game winners
Rube Waddell, Phil., 27-10
Eddie Plank, Phil., 24-12
Nick Altrock, Chi., 23-12
Ed Killian, Det., 23-14
Jesse Tannehill, Bos., 22-9
Frank Owen, Chi., 21-13
George Mullin, Det., 21-21
Addie Joss, Cle., 20-12
Frank Smith, Chi., 20-14

N.L. 20-game winners
Christy Mathewson, N.Y., 31-9
Togie Pittinger, Phil., 23-14
Red Ames, N.Y., 22-8
Joe McGinnity, N.Y., 21-15
Sam Leever, Pit., 20-5
Bob Ewing, Cin., 20-11
Deacon Phillippe, Pit., 20-13
Irv Young, Bos., 20-21

N.L. 100 RBIs
Cy Seymour, Cin., 121
Sam Mertes, N.Y., 108
Honus Wagner, Pit., 101

WORLD SERIES

■ **Winner:** The Giants prevailed over the Athletics in an all-shutout fall classic.

■ **Turning point:** Joe McGinnity's five-hit, 1-0 victory over Athletics lefthander Eddie Plank in Game 4. Plank allowed only four hits.

■ **Memorable moment:** New York's John McGraw and Philadelphia's Connie Mack exchanging lineups before Game 1. The two managers would dominate baseball for more than three decades.

■ **Top guns:** Christy Mathewson (3 shutouts, 0.00 ERA), Joe McGinnity, (17 IP, 0.00), Giants; Chief Bender (17 IP, 1.06), Athletics.

Linescores

Game 1—October 9, at Philadelphia
New York........ 0 0 0 0 2 0 0 0 1 — 3 10 1
Philadelphia.... 0 0 0 0 0 0 0 0 0 — 0 4 0
Mathewson; Plank. W—Mathewson. L—Plank.

Game 2—October 10, at New York
Philadelphia.... 0 0 1 0 0 0 0 2 0 — 3 6 2
New York........ 0 0 0 0 0 0 0 0 0 — 0 4 2
Bender; McGinnity, Ames (9). W—Bender. L—McGinnity.

Game 3—October 12, at Philadelphia
New York........ 2 0 0 0 5 0 0 0 2 — 9 9 1
Philadelphia.... 0 0 0 0 0 0 0 0 0 — 0 4 5
Mathewson; Coakley. W—Mathewson. L—Coakley.

Game 4—October 13, at New York
Philadelphia.... 0 0 0 0 0 0 0 0 0 — 0 5 2
New York........ 0 0 0 1 0 0 0 0 x — 1 4 1
Plank; McGinnity. W—McGinnity. L—Plank.

Game 5—October 14, at New York
Philadelphia.... 0 0 0 0 0 0 0 0 0 — 0 6 0
New York........ 0 0 0 0 1 0 0 1 x — 2 5 1
Bender; Mathewson. W—Mathewson. L—Bender.

1906

FINAL STANDINGS

American League

Team	W	L	Pct.	GB
Chicago	93	58	.616	...
New York	90	61	.596	3
Cleveland	89	64	.582	5
Philadelphia	78	67	.538	12
St. Louis	76	73	.510	16
Detroit	71	78	.477	21
Washington	55	95	.367	37.5
Boston	49	105	.318	45.5

National League

Team	W	L	Pct.	GB
Chicago	116	36	.763	...
New York	96	56	.632	20
Pittsburgh	93	60	.608	23.5
Philadelphia	71	82	.464	45.5
Brooklyn	66	86	.434	50
Cincinnati	64	87	.424	51.5
St. Louis	52	98	.347	63
Boston	49	102	.325	66.5

SIGNIFICANT EVENTS

■ **August 13:** When Chicago's Jack Taylor failed to last through the third inning of a game against Brooklyn, it ended his record complete-game streak at 187.

■ **October 7:** The Cubs ended an amazing regular season with a Major League-record 116 victories and a team ERA of 1.76.

MEMORABLE MOMENTS

■ **May 25:** Jesse Tannehill snapped Boston's A.L.-record 20-game losing streak with a 3-0 victory over the White Sox.

■ **June 9:** The Boston Beaneaters ended their 19-game losing streak with a 6-3 victory over the Cardinals.

■ **August 23:** Washington ended the Chicago White Stockings' A.L.-record winning streak at 19 games.

■ **September 1:** The Athletics scored three times in the top of the 24th inning and claimed a 4-1 victory over Boston in the longest game in Major League history.

■ **October 3:** Chicago's "Hitless Wonders" clinched the A.L. pennant when the Athletics posted a 3-0 victory over New York in the second game of a doubleheader.

LEADERS

American League

BA: George Stone, St.L.,.358.
Runs: Elmer Flick, Cle., 98.
Hits: Nap Lajoie, Cle., 214.
TB: George Stone, St.L., 291.
HR: Harry Davis, Phil., 12.
RBI: Harry Davis, Phil., 96.
SB: John Anderson, Wash.; Elmer Flick, Cle., 39.
Wins: Al Orth, N.Y., 27.
ERA: Doc White, Chi., 1.52.
CG: Al Orth, N.Y., 36.
IP: Al Orth, N.Y., 338.2.
SO: Rube Waddell, Phil., 196.

National League

BA: Honus Wagner, Pit., .339.
Runs: Frank Chance, Chi.; Honus Wagner, Pit., 103.
Hits: Harry Steinfeldt, Chi., 176.
TB: Honus Wagner, Pit., 237.
HR: Tim Jordan, Brk., 12.
RBI: Jim Nealon, Pit.; Harry Steinfeldt, Chi., 83.
SB: Frank Chance, Chi., 57.
Wins: Joe McGinnity, N.Y., 27.
ERA: Mordecai Brown, Chi., 1.04.
CG: Irv Young, Bos., 37.
IP: Irv Young, Bos., 358.1.
SO: Fred Beebe, Chi.-St.L., 171.

A.L. 20-game winners
Al Orth, N.Y., 27-17
Jack Chesbro, N.Y., 23-17
Bob Rhoades, Cle., 22-10
Frank Owen, Chi., 22-13
Addie Joss, Cle., 21-9
George Mullin, Det., 21-18
Nick Altrock, Chi., 20-13
Otto Hess, Cle., 20-17

N.L. 20-game winners
Joe McGinnity, N.Y., 27-12
Mordecai Brown, Chi., 26-6
Vic Willis, Pit., 23-13
Sam Leever, Pit., 22-7
Christy Mathewson, N.Y., 22-12
Jack Pfiester, Chi., 20-8
Jack Taylor, St.L.-Chi., 20-12
Jake Weimer, Cin., 20-14

WORLD SERIES

■ **Winner:** Chicago's "Hitless Wonders" pulled an intra-city shocker with a six-game victory over the powerful Cubs.

■ **Turning point:** An eight-run Game 5 explosion by the light-hitting White Sox, which was spiced by Frank Isbell's four doubles and two RBIs.

■ **Memorable moment:** Big Ed Walsh's two-hit Game 3 shutout. The Cubs were held hitless after getting a first-inning single and double.

■ **Top guns:** Walsh (2-0, 1.80 ERA), George Rohe (.333, 4 RBIs), White Sox; Ed Reulbach (Game 2 1-hitter), Cubs.

Linescores

Game 1—October 9, at Chicago Cubs
White Sox....... 0 0 0 0 1 1 0 0 0 — 2 4 1
Cubs.............. 0 0 0 0 0 1 0 0 0 — 1 4 2
Altrock; Brown. W—Altrock. L—Brown.

Game 2—October 10, at Chicago White Sox
Cubs.............. 0 3 1 0 0 1 0 2 0 — 7 10 2
White Sox....... 0 0 0 0 1 0 0 0 0 — 1 1 2
Reulbach; White, Owen (4). W—Reulbach. L—White.

Game 3—October 11, at Chicago Cubs
White Sox....... 0 0 0 0 0 3 0 0 0 — 3 4 1
Cubs.............. 0 0 0 0 0 0 0 0 0 — 0 2 2
Walsh; Pfiester. W—Walsh. L—Pfiester.

Game 4—October 12, at Chicago White Sox
Cubs.............. 0 0 0 0 0 0 1 0 0 — 1 7 1
White Sox....... 0 0 0 0 0 0 0 0 0 — 0 2 1
Brown; Altrock. W—Brown. L—Altrock.

Game 5—October 13, at Chicago Cubs
White Sox....... 1 0 2 4 0 1 0 0 0 — 8 12 6
Cubs.............. 3 0 0 1 0 2 0 0 0 — 6 6 0
Walsh, White (7); Reulbach, Pfiester (3), Overall (4). W—Walsh. L—Pfiester.

Game 6—October 14, at Chicago White Sox
Cubs.............. 1 0 0 0 1 0 0 0 1 — 3 7 0
White Sox....... 3 4 0 0 0 0 0 1 x — 8 14 3
Brown, Overall (2); White. W—White. L—Brown.

1907

FINAL STANDINGS

American League

Team	W	L	Pct.	GB
Detroit	92	58	.613	...
Philadelphia	88	57	.607	1.5
Chicago	87	64	.576	5.5
Cleveland	85	67	.559	8
New York	70	78	.473	21
St. Louis	69	83	.454	24
Boston	59	90	.396	32.5
Washington	49	102	.325	43.5

National League

Team	W	L	Pct.	GB
Chicago	107	45	.704	...
Pittsburgh	91	63	.591	17
Philadelphia	83	64	.565	21.5
New York	82	71	.536	25.5
Brooklyn	65	83	.439	40
Cincinnati	66	87	.431	41.5
Boston	58	90	.392	47
St. Louis	52	101	.340	55.5

SIGNIFICANT EVENTS

■ **April 11:** Giants catcher Roger Bresnahan introduced his newest innovation in a game against the Phillies: wooden shinguards to protect his legs and knees.

■ **August 2:** Washington fireballer Walter Johnson dropped a 3-2 decision to Detroit in his Major League debut.

MEMORABLE MOMENTS

■ **May 20:** The Cardinals ended New York's 17-game winning streak with a 6-4 victory at the Polo Grounds.

■ **October 3:** The seventh-place Boston Red Sox edged sixth-place St. Louis 1-0 and ended their 16-game losing streak.

■ **October 5:** The Tigers, locked in a tight A.L. pennant race with Philadelphia, clinched the title with a 10-2 victory over St. Louis.

LEADERS

American League

BA: Ty Cobb, Det., .350.
Runs: Sam Crawford, Det., 102.
Hits: Ty Cobb, Det., 212.
TB: Ty Cobb, Det., 283.
HR: Harry Davis, Phil., 8.
RBI: Ty Cobb, Det., 119.
SB: Ty Cobb, Det., 49.
Wins: Addie Joss, Cle.; Doc White, Chi., 27.
ERA: Ed Walsh, Chi., 1.60.
CG: Ed Walsh, Chi., 37.
IP: Ed Walsh, Chi., 422.1.
SO: Rube Waddell, Phil., 232.

National League

BA: Honus Wagner, Pit., .350.
Runs: Spike Shannon, N.Y., 104.
Hits: Ginger Beaumont, Bos., 187.
TB: Honus Wagner, Pit., 264.
HR: Dave Brain, Bos., 10.
RBI: Sherry Magee, Phil., 85.
SB: Honus Wagner, Pit., 61.
Wins: Christy Mathewson, N.Y., 24.
ERA: Jack Pfiester, Chi., 1.15.
CG: Stoney McGlynn, St.L., 33.
IP: Stoney McGlynn, St.L., 352.1.
SO: Christy Mathewson, N.Y., 178.

A.L. 20-game winners

Addie Joss, Cle., 27-11
Doc White, Chi., 27-13
Bill Donovan, Det., 25-4
Ed Killian, Det., 25-13
Eddie Plank, Phil., 24-16
Ed Walsh, Chi., 24-18
Frank Smith, Chi., 23-10
Jimmy Dygert, Phil., 21-8
Cy Young, Bos., 21-15
George Mullin, Det., 20-20

N.L. 20-game winners

Christy Mathewson, N.Y., 24-12
Orval Overall, Chi., 23-7
Tully Sparks, Phil., 22-8
Vic Willis, Pit., 21-11
Mordecai Brown, Chi., 20-6
Lefty Leifield, Pit., 20-16

A.L. 100 RBIs

Ty Cobb, Det., 119

WORLD SERIES

■ **Winner:** The powerful Cubs, atoning for their shocking loss to the White Sox in 1906, made short work of the A.L.-champion Tigers.

■ **Turning point:** A ninth-inning passed ball by Tigers catcher Charlie Schmidt that allowed the Cubs to score the tying run in a Game 1 battle that would end in a 3-3 deadlock.

■ **Memorable moment:** Schmidt's passed ball, which awoke the Cubs and set the stage for their sweeping finish.

■ **Top guns:** Harry Steinfeldt (.471), Johnny Evers (.350), Cubs; Claude Rossman (.400), Tigers.

Linescores

Game 1—October 8, at Chicago
Detroit...0 0 0 0 0 0 0 3 0 0 0 0 — 3 9 3
Chicago .0 0 0 1 0 0 0 0 2 0 0 0 — 3 10 5
Donovan; Overall, Reulbach (10). Game called after 12 innings because of darkness.

Game 2—October 9, at Chicago
Detroit............ 0 1 0 0 0 0 0 0 0 — 1 9 1
Chicago.......... 0 1 0 2 0 0 0 0 x — 3 9 1
Mullin; Pfiester. W—Pfiester. L—Mullin.

Game 3—October 10, at Chicago
Detroit............ 0 0 0 0 0 1 0 0 0 — 1 6 1
Chicago.......... 0 1 0 3 1 0 0 0 x — 5 10 1
Siever, Killian (5); Reulbach. W—Reulbach. L—Siever.

Game 4—October 11, at Detroit
Chicago.......... 0 0 0 0 2 0 3 0 1 — 6 7 2
Detroit............ 0 0 0 1 0 0 0 0 0 — 1 5 2
Overall; Donovan. W—Overall. L—Donovan.

Game 5—October 12, at Detroit
Chicago.......... 1 1 0 0 0 0 0 0 0 — 2 7 1
Detroit............ 0 0 0 0 0 0 0 0 0 — 0 7 2
Brown; Mullin. W—Brown. L—Mullin.

1908

FINAL STANDINGS

American League

Team	W	L	Pct.	GB
Detroit	90	63	.588	...
Cleveland	90	64	.584	.5
Chicago	88	64	.579	1.5
St. Louis	83	69	.546	6.5
Boston	75	79	.487	15.5
Philadelphia	68	85	.444	22
Washington	67	85	.441	22.5
New York	51	103	.331	39.5

National League

Team	W	L	Pct.	GB
Chicago	99	55	.643	...
New York	98	56	.636	1
Pittsburgh	98	56	.636	1
Philadelphia	83	71	.539	16
Cincinnati	73	81	.474	26
Boston	63	91	.409	36
Brooklyn	53	101	.344	46
St. Louis	49	105	.318	50

SIGNIFICANT EVENTS

■ **February 27:** Baseball adopted the sacrifice fly rule, stating that a batter will not be charged with an at-bat if a runner tags up and scores after the catch of his fly ball.

MEMORABLE MOMENTS

■ **June 30:** Boston's 41-year-old Cy Young became the first pitcher to notch three career no-hitters when he defeated New York, 8-0.

■ **September 23:** The outcome of an important Giants-Cubs game was thrown into confusion when New York baserunner Fred Merkle failed to touch second base on an apparent game-ending hit, prompting the Cubs' claims of a game-prolonging forceout.

■ **September 24:** N.L. President Harry Pulliam declared the September 23 Cubs-Giants game a tie.

■ **September 26:** Chicago's Ed Reulbach made baseball history when he shut out Brooklyn twice—5-0 and 3-0—on the same day.

■ **October 2:** Cleveland's Addie Joss became the second modern-era pitcher to throw a perfect game, retiring all 27 Chicago batters he faced in a 1-0 victory.

■ **October 6:** The Tigers defeated the White Sox, 7-0, and claimed the A.L. pennant on the season's final day.

■ **October 8:** In an N.L. pennant-deciding matchup dictated by the controversial September 23 tie game, Chicago defeated the Giants, 4-2.

LEADERS

American League

BA: Ty Cobb, Det., .324.
Runs: Matty McIntyre, Det., 105.
Hits: Ty Cobb, Det., 188.
TB: Ty Cobb, Det., 276.
HR: Sam Crawford, Det., 7.
RBI: Ty Cobb, Det., 108.
SB: Patsy Dougherty, Chi., 47.
Wins: Ed Walsh, Chi., 40.
ERA: Addie Joss, Cle., 1.16.
CG: Ed Walsh, Chi., 42.
IP: Ed Walsh, Chi., 464.
SO: Ed Walsh, Chi., 269.

National League

BA: Honus Wagner, Pit., .354.
Runs: Fred Tenney, N.Y., 101.
Hits: Honus Wagner, Pit., 201.
TB: Honus Wagner, Pit., 308.
HR: Tim Jordan, Brk., 12.
RBI: Honus Wagner, Pit., 109.
SB: Honus Wagner, Pit., 53.
Wins: Christy Mathewson, N.Y., 37.
ERA: Christy Mathewson, N.Y., 1.43.
CG: Christy Mathewson, N.Y., 34.
IP: Christy Mathewson, N.Y., 390.2.
SO: Christy Mathewson, N.Y., 259.

A.L. 20-game winners

Ed Walsh, Chi., 40-15
Addie Joss, Cle., 24-11
Ed Summers, Det., 24-12
Cy Young, Bos., 21-11

N.L. 20-game winners

Christy Mathewson, N.Y., 37-11
Mordecai Brown, Chi., 29-9
Ed Reulbach, Chi., 24-7
Nick Maddox, Pit., 23-8
Vic Willis, Pit. 23-11
Hooks Wiltse, N.Y., 23-14
George McQuillan, Phil., 23-17

A.L. 100 RBIs

Ty Cobb, Det., 108

N.L. 100 RBIs

Honus Wagner, Pit., 109
Mike Donlin, N.Y., 106

WORLD SERIES

■ **Winner:** The Cubs became the first two-time Series champs by defeating Detroit for the second consecutive year.

■ **Turning point:** A five-run ninth-inning rally that turned a 6-5 Game 1 deficit into a 10-6 Cubs victory.

■ **Memorable moment:** A two-run eighth-inning home run by Chicago's Joe Tinker that broke up a scoreless Game 2 pitching duel and gave Orval Overall a 6-1 victory over Bill Donovan.

■ **Top guns:** Overall (2-0, 0.98 ERA), Frank Chance (.421), Cubs; Ty Cobb (.368), Tigers.

Linescores

Game 1—October 10, at Detroit
Chicago.......... 0 0 4 0 0 0 1 0 5 — 10 14 2
Detroit............ 1 0 0 0 0 0 3 2 0 — 6 10 4
Reulbach, Overall (7), Brown (8); Killian, Summers (3). W—Brown. L—Summers.

Game 2—October 11, at Chicago
Detroit............ 0 0 0 0 0 0 0 0 1 — 1 4 1
Chicago.......... 0 0 0 0 0 0 0 6 x — 6 7 1
Donovan; Overall. W—Overall. L—Donovan. HR—Tinker (Chi.).

Game 3—October 12, at Chicago
Detroit............ 1 0 0 0 0 5 0 2 0 — 8 11 4
Chicago.......... 0 0 0 3 0 0 0 0 0 — 3 7 2
Mullin; Pfiester, Reulbach (9). W—Mullin. L—Pfiester.

Game 4—October 13, at Detroit
Chicago.......... 0 0 2 0 0 0 0 0 1 — 3 10 0
Detroit............ 0 0 0 0 0 0 0 0 0 — 0 4 1
Brown; Summers, Winter (9). W—Brown. L—Summers.

Game 5—October 14, at Detroit
Chicago.......... 1 0 0 0 1 0 0 0 0 — 2 10 0
Detroit............ 0 0 0 0 0 0 0 0 0 — 0 3 0
Overall; Donovan. W—Overall. L—Donovan.

1909

FINAL STANDINGS

American League

Team	W	L	Pct.	GB
Detroit	98	54	.645	...
Philadelphia	95	58	.621	3.5
Boston	88	63	.583	9.5
Chicago	78	74	.513	20
New York	74	77	.490	23.5
Cleveland	71	82	.464	27.5
St. Louis	61	89	.407	36
Washington	42	110	.276	56

National League

Team	W	L	Pct.	GB
Pittsburgh	110	42	.724	...
Chicago	104	49	.680	6.5
New York	92	61	.601	18.5
Cincinnati	77	76	.503	33.5
Philadelphia	74	79	.484	36.5
Brooklyn	55	98	.359	55.5
St. Louis	54	98	.355	56
Boston	45	108	.294	65.5

SIGNIFICANT EVENTS

■ **April 12:** The Athletics and pitcher Eddie Plank christened Philadelphia's new Shibe Park with an 8-1 victory over Boston.

■ **June 30:** The Cubs spoiled Pittsburgh's opening of new Forbes Field, posting a 3-2 victory over the Pirates.

■ **July 29:** N.L. President Harry Pulliam shocked the baseball world when he shot himself to death.

■ **October 5:** Detroit's Ty Cobb finished his Triple Crown season with a .377 average, 9 home runs and 107 RBIs.

MEMORABLE MOMENTS

■ **April 15:** New York's Red Ames lost his Opening Day no-hit bid in the 10th inning and the game in the 13th when Brooklyn scored a 3-0 victory.

■ **July 16:** A Detroit-Washington game ended 0-0 after 18 innings—the longest scoreless tie in A.L. history.

■ **July 19:** Cleveland shortstop Neal Ball pulled off the first unassisted triple play of the century in a game against the Red Sox.

LEADERS

American League

BA: Ty Cobb, Det., .377.
Runs: Ty Cobb, Det., 116.
Hits: Ty Cobb, Det., 216.
TB: Ty Cobb, Det., 296.
HR: Ty Cobb, Det., 9.
RBI: Ty Cobb, Det., 107.
SB: Ty Cobb, Det., 76.
Wins: George Mullin, Det., 29.
ERA: Harry Krause, Phil., 1.39.
CG: Frank Smith, Chi., 37.
IP: Frank Smith, Chi., 365.
SO: Frank Smith, Chi., 177.

National League

BA: Honus Wagner, Pit., .339.
Runs: Tommy Leach, Pit., 126.
Hits: Larry Doyle, N.Y., 172.
TB: Honus Wagner, Pit., 242.
HR: Red Murray, N.Y., 7.
RBI: Honus Wagner, Pit., 100.
SB: Bob Bescher, Cin., 54.
Wins: Mordecai Brown, Chi., 27.
ERA: Christy Mathewson, N.Y., 1.14.
CG: Mordecai Brown, Chi., 32.
IP: Mordecai Brown, Chi., 342.2.
SO: Orval Overall, Chi., 205.

A.L. 20-game winners

George Mullin, Det., 29-8
Frank Smith, Chi., 25-17
Ed Willett, Det., 21-10

N.L. 20-game winners

Mordecai Brown, Chi., 27-9
Howie Camnitz, Pit., 25-6
Christy Mathewson, N.Y., 25-6
Vic Willis, Pit., 22-11
Orval Overall, Chi., 20-11
Hooks Wiltse, N.Y., 20-11

A.L. 100 RBIs

Ty Cobb, Det., 107

N.L. 100 RBIs

Honus Wagner, Pit., 100

WORLD SERIES

■ **Winner:** The Pirates, losers in baseball's first World Series, bounced back to hand the Tigers their third straight post-season loss.

■ **Turning point:** A tie-breaking three-run homer by Pirates player/manager Fred Clarke that keyed an 8-4 victory in the pivotal fifth game.

■ **Memorable moment:** When Pirates pitcher Babe Adams retired the final Tiger in Game 7 and ended the first Series to go the distance.

■ **Top guns:** Adams (3-0, 1.33 ERA), Honus Wagner (.333, 7 RBIs, 6 SB), Pirates; Jim Delahanty (.346), Tigers.

Linescores

Game 1—October 8, at Pittsburgh
Detroit............ 1 0 0 0 0 0 0 0 0 — 1 6 4
Pittsburgh...... 0 0 0 1 2 1 0 0 x — 4 5 0
Mullin; Adams. W—Adams. L—Mullin. HR—Clarke (Pit.).

Game 2—October 9, at Pittsburgh
Detroit............ 0 2 3 0 2 0 0 0 0 — 7 9 3
Pittsburgh...... 2 0 0 0 0 0 0 0 0 — 2 5 1
Donovan; Camnitz, Willis (3). W—Donovan. L—Camnitz.

Game 3—October 11, at Detroit
Pittsburgh...... 5 1 0 0 0 0 0 0 2 — 8 10 3
Detroit............ 0 0 0 0 0 0 4 0 2 — 6 10 5
Maddox; Summers, Willett (1), Works (8). W—Maddox. L—Summers.

Game 4—October 12, at Detroit
Pittsburgh...... 0 0 0 0 0 0 0 0 0 — 0 5 6
Detroit............ 0 2 0 3 0 0 0 0 x — 5 8 0
Leifield, Phillippe (5); Mullin. W—Mullin. L—Leifield.

Game 5—October 13, at Pittsburgh
Detroit............ 1 0 0 0 0 2 0 1 0 — 4 6 1
Pittsburgh...... 1 1 1 0 0 0 4 1 x — 8 10 1
Summers, Willett (8); Adams. W—Adams. L—Summers. HR—D. Jones, Crawford (Det.); Clarke (Pit.).

Game 6—October 14, at Detroit
Pittsburgh...... 3 0 0 0 0 0 0 0 1 — 4 7 3
Detroit............ 1 0 0 2 1 1 0 0 x — 5 10 3
Willis, Camnitz (6), Phillippe (7); Mullin. W—Mullin. L—Willis.

Game 7—October 16, at Detroit
Pittsburgh...... 0 2 0 2 0 3 0 1 0 — 8 7 0
Detroit............ 0 0 0 0 0 0 0 0 0 — 0 6 3
Adams; Donovan, Mullin (4). W—Adams. L—Donovan.

1910

FINAL STANDINGS

American League

Team	W	L	Pct.	GB
Philadelphia	102	48	.680	...
New York	88	63	.583	14.5
Detroit	86	68	.558	18
Boston	81	72	.529	22.5
Cleveland	71	81	.467	32
Chicago	68	85	.444	35.5
Washington	66	85	.437	36.5
St. Louis	47	107	.305	57

National League

Team	W	L	Pct.	GB
Chicago	104	50	.675	...
New York	91	63	.591	13
Pittsburgh	86	67	.562	17.5
Philadelphia	78	75	.510	25.5
Cincinnati	75	79	.487	29
Brooklyn	64	90	.416	40
St. Louis	63	90	.412	40.5
Boston	53	100	.346	50.5

SIGNIFICANT EVENTS

■ **February 18:** The N.L. approved a 154-game schedule, a plan already adopted by the A.L.

■ **April 14:** William Howard Taft became the first U.S. President to throw out the first ball at a season opener in Washington.

■ **April 21:** Detroit spoiled the opening of Cleveland's League Park with a 5-0 victory over the Indians.

■ **July 1:** Chicago unveiled White Sox Park (Comiskey Park), but the Browns spoiled the occasion with a 2-0 victory.

MEMORABLE MOMENTS

■ **July 19:** The incredible Cy Young earned his 500th career victory when he pitched Cleveland to an 11-inning, 5-2 win over Washington.

■ **August 30:** The Highlanders' Tom Hughes lost his no-hit bid against Cleveland with one out in the 10th and lost the game, 5-0, in the 11th.

■ **September 25:** The scoreless streak of Philadelphia's Jack Coombs ended at 53 innings in a darkness-shortened 5-2 loss to Chicago in the second game of a doubleheader.

■ **October 9:** Cleveland's Napoleon Lajoie collected eight final-day hits, seven of them bunt singles, in a doubleheader against the Browns and lifted his final average to .384—one point ahead of Detroit's Ty Cobb.

■ **October 15:** A.L. President Ban Johnson adjusted Cobb's final average to .385 and declared him winner of the A.L. batting title.

LEADERS

American League

BA: Ty Cobb, Det., .383.
Runs: Ty Cobb, Det., 106.
Hits: Nap Lajoie, Cle., 227.
TB: Nap Lajoie, Cle., 304.
HR: Jake Stahl, Bos., 10.
RBI: Sam Crawford, Det., 120.
SB: Eddie Collins, Phil., 81.
Wins: Jack Coombs, Phil., 31.
ERA: Ed Walsh, Chi., 1.27.
CG: Walter Johnson, Wash., 38.
IP: Walter Johnson, Wash., 370.
SO: Walter Johnson, Wash., 313.

National League

BA: Sherry Magee, Phil., .331.
Runs: Sherry Magee, Phil., 110.
Hits: Bobby Byrne, Pit.; Honus Wagner, Pit., 178.
TB: Sherry Magee, Phil., 263.
HR: Fred Beck, Bos.; Frank Schulte, Chi., 10.
RBI: Sherry Magee, Phil., 123.
SB: Bob Bescher, Cin., 70.
Wins: Christy Mathewson, N.Y., 27.
ERA: King Cole, Chi., 1.80.
CG: Mordecai Brown, Chi.; Christy Mathewson, N.Y.; Nap Rucker, Brk., 27
IP: Nap Rucker, Brk., 320.1.
SO: Earl Moore, Phil., 185.

A.L. 20-game winners

Jack Coombs, Phil., 31-9
Russ Ford, N.Y., 26-6
Walter Johnson, Wash., 25-17
Chief Bender, Phil., 23-5
George Mullin, Det., 21-12

N.L. 20-game winners

Christy Mathewson, N.Y., 27-9
Mordecai Brown, Chi., 25-14
Earl Moore, Phil., 22-15
King Cole, Chi., 20-4
George Suggs, Cin., 20-12

A.L. 100 RBIs

Sam Crawford, Det., 120

N.L. 100 RBIs

Sherry Magee, Phil., 123

WORLD SERIES

■ **Winner:** Philadelphia won their first Series championship and thwarted the Cubs' bid to become a three-time winner.

■ **Turning point:** The Cubs' failure to take advantage of the less-than-artistic Jack Coombs in Game 2. Coombs allowed eight hits and nine walks but still won, 9-3.

■ **Memorable moment:** A three-run homer by Danny Murphy that broke up a tight Game 3 and helped Philadelphia to a 12-5 victory.

■ **Top guns:** Eddie Collins (.429), Murphy (.350, 8 RBIs), Frank Baker (.409), Athletics; Frank Chance (.353), Frank Schulte (.353), Cubs.

Linescores

Game 1—October 17, at Philadelphia
Chicago.......... 0 0 0 0 0 0 0 0 1 — 1 3 1
Philadelphia.... 0 2 1 0 0 0 0 1 x — 4 7 2
Overall, McIntire (4); Bender. W—Bender. L—Overall.

Game 2—October 18, at Philadelphia
Chicago.......... 1 0 0 0 0 0 1 0 1 — 3 8 3
Philadelphia.... 0 0 2 0 1 0 6 0 x — 9 14 4
Brown, Richie (8); Coombs. W—Coombs. L—Brown.

Game 3—October 20, at Chicago
Philadelphia.... 1 2 5 0 0 0 4 0 0 — 12 15 1
Chicago.......... 1 2 0 0 0 0 0 2 0 — 5 6 5
Coombs; Reulbach, McIntire (3), Pfiester (3). W—Coombs. L—McIntire. HR—Murphy (Phil.).

Game 4—October 22, at Chicago
Philadelphia 0 0 1 2 0 0 0 0 0 0 — 3 11 3
Chicago 1 0 0 1 0 0 0 0 1 1 — 4 9 1
Bender; Cole, Brown (9). W—Brown. L—Bender.

Game 5—October 23, at Chicago
Philadelphia.... 1 0 0 0 1 0 0 5 0 — 7 9 1
Chicago.......... 0 1 0 0 0 0 0 1 0 — 2 9 2
Coombs; Brown. W—Coombs. L—Brown.

1911

FINAL STANDINGS

American League

Team	W	L	Pct.	GB
Philadelphia	101	50	.669	...
Detroit	89	65	.578	13.5
Cleveland	80	73	.523	22
Chicago	77	74	.510	24
Boston	78	75	.510	24
New York	76	76	.500	25.5
Washington	64	90	.416	38.5
St. Louis	45	107	.296	56.5

National League

Team	W	L	Pct.	GB
New York	99	54	.647	...
Chicago	92	62	.597	7.5
Pittsburgh	85	69	.552	14.5
Philadelphia	79	73	.520	19.5
St. Louis	75	74	.503	22
Cincinnati	70	83	.458	29
Brooklyn	64	86	.427	33.5
Boston	44	107	.291	54

SIGNIFICANT EVENTS

- **April 14:** New York's Polo Grounds burned down, forcing the Giants to play a big stretch of their schedule at the Highlanders' Hilltop Park.
- **June 28:** The Giants defeated the Braves, 3-0, in the first game at the new Polo Grounds.
- **October 11:** Chalmers automobile recipients as baseball's first MVPs: Detroit's Ty Cobb in the A.L. and Chicago's Frank Schulte in the N.L.

MEMORABLE MOMENTS

- **May 13:** The Giants exploded for a record 13 first-inning runs, 10 before the first out was recorded, in a 19-5 victory over St. Louis.
- **July 4:** Chicago ace Ed Walsh stopped Detroit, 7-3, and ended Ty Cobb's hitting streak at 40 games.
- **September 29:** Phillies righthander Grover Cleveland Alexander defeated Pittsburgh 7-4 and claimed his rookie-record 28th victory.
- **September 22:** Cy Young, ending his career with the Braves, won his 511th and final game, beating Pittsburgh 1-0.

LEADERS

American League

BA: Ty Cobb, Det., .420.
Runs: Ty Cobb, Det., 147.
Hits: Ty Cobb, Det., 248.
TB: Ty Cobb, Det., 367.
HR: Frank Baker, Phil., 11.
RBI: Ty Cobb, Det., 127.
SB: Ty Cobb, Det., 83.
Wins: Jack Coombs, Phil., 28.
ERA: Vean Gregg, Cle., 1.80.
CG: Walter Johnson, Wash., 36.
IP: Ed Walsh, Chi., 368.2.
SO: Ed Walsh, Chi., 255.

National League

BA: Honus Wagner, Pit., .334.
Runs: Jimmy Sheckard, Chi., 121.
Hits: Doc Miller, Bos., 192.
TB: Frank Schulte, Chi., 308.
HR: Frank Schulte, Chi., 21.
RBI: Frank Schulte, Chi.; Chief Wilson, Pit., 107.
SB: Bob Bescher, Cin., 80.
Wins: Grover Alexander, Phil., 28.
ERA: Christy Mathewson, N.Y., 1.99.
CG: Grover Alexander, Phil., 31.
IP: Grover Alexander, Phil., 367.
SO: Rube Marquard, N.Y., 237.

A.L. 20-game winners

Jack Coombs, Phil., 28-12
Ed Walsh, Chi., 27-18
Walter Johnson, Wash., 25-13
Vean Gregg, Cle., 23-7
Eddie Plank, Phil., 23-8
Joe Wood, Bos., 23-17
Russ Ford, N.Y., 22-11

N.L. 20-game winners

Grover Alexander, Phil., 28-13
Christy Mathewson, N.Y., 26-13
Rube Marquard, N.Y., 24-7
Bob Harmon, St.L., 23-16
Babe Adams, Pit., 22-12
Nap Rucker, Brk., 22-18
Mordecai Brown, Chi., 21-11
Howie Camnitz, Pit., 20-15

A.L. 100 RBIs

Ty Cobb, Det., 127
Frank Baker, Phil., 115
Sam Crawford, Det., 115

N.L. 100 RBIs

Frank Schulte, Chi., 107
Chief Wilson, Pit., 107

Chalmers MVP

A.L.: Ty Cobb, OF, Det.
N.L.: Frank Schulte, OF, Chi.

WORLD SERIES

- **Winner:** The Athletics became baseball's second back-to-back winners and gained revenge for their 1905 loss to the Giants.
- **Turning point:** A ninth-inning Game 3 homer by Frank Baker off Christy Mathewson. The solo shot tied the game at 1-1 and the A's won in 11 innings, 3-2.
- **Memorable moment:** Baker's homer off Mathewson.
- **Top guns:** Chief Bender (2-1, 1.04 ERA), Baker (.375, 2 HR), Jack Barry (.368), Athletics; Mathewson (27 IP, 2.00), Giants.

Linescores

Game 1—October 14, at New York
Philadelphia.... 0 1 0 0 0 0 0 0 0 — 1 6 2
New York........ 0 0 0 1 0 0 1 0 x — 2 5 0
Bender; Mathewson. W—Mathewson. L—Bender.

Game 2—October 16, at Philadelphia
New York........ 0 1 0 0 0 0 0 0 0 — 1 5 3
Philadelphia.... 1 0 0 0 0 2 0 0 x — 3 4 0
Marquard, Crandall (8); Plank. W—Plank. L—Marquard. HR—Baker (Phil.).

Game 3—October 17, at New York
Philadelphia ....0 0 0 0 0 0 0 0 1 0 2—3 9 2
New York ....0 0 1 0 0 0 0 0 0 0 1—2 3 5
Coombs; Mathewson. W—Coombs. L—Mathewson. HR—Baker (Phil.).

Game 4—October 24, at Philadelphia
New York........ 2 0 0 0 0 0 0 0 0 — 2 7 3
Philadelphia.... 0 0 0 3 1 0 0 0 x — 4 1 1
Mathewson, Wiltse (8); Bender. W—Bender. L—Mathewson.

Game 5—October 25, at New York
Philadelphia.... 0 0 3 0 0 0 0 0 0 0 — 3 7 1
New York........ 0 0 0 0 0 0 1 0 2 1 — 4 9 2
Coombs, Plank (10); Marquard, Ames (4), Crandall (8). W—Crandall. L—Plank. HR—Oldring (Phil.).

Game 6—October 26, at Philadelphia
New York........ 1 0 0 0 0 0 0 0 1 — 2 4 3
Philadelphia.... 0 0 1 4 0 1 7 0 x — 13 3 5
Ames, Wiltse (5), Marquard (7); Bender. W—Bender. L—Ames.

1912

FINAL STANDINGS

American League

Team	W	L	Pct.	GB
Boston	105	47	.691	...
Washington	91	61	.599	14
Philadelphia	90	62	.592	15
Chicago	78	76	.506	28
Cleveland	75	78	.490	30.5
Detroit	69	84	.451	36.5
St. Louis	53	101	.344	53
New York	50	102	.329	55

National League

Team	W	L	Pct.	GB
New York	103	48	.682	...
Pittsburgh	93	58	.616	10
Chicago	91	59	.607	11.5
Cincinnati	75	78	.490	29
Philadelphia	73	79	.480	30.5
St. Louis	63	90	.412	41
Brooklyn	58	95	.379	46
Boston	52	101	.340	52

SIGNIFICANT EVENTS

- **April 11:** Cincinnati celebrated the opening of new Redland Field with a 10-6 victory over the Cubs.
- **April 20:** The Red Sox christened Fenway Park with an 11-inning 7-6 victory over New York and the Tigers opened Navin Field with an 11-inning 6-5 victory over Cleveland.
- **May 16:** A.L. President Ban Johnson handed Detroit's Ty Cobb an indefinite suspension after Cobb entered the stands at New York's Hilltop Park to fight a heckler.
- **May 18:** A team of amateur Tigers dropped a 24-2 decision to the Athletics when the regular Tigers went on strike to protest Cobb's suspension.
- **May 20:** The Tigers, facing the threat of lifetime suspensions from Johnson, returned to uniform.

MEMORABLE MOMENTS

- **June 13:** New York's Christy Mathewson earned his 300th career victory and 20th win of the season when he defeated the Cubs, 3-2.
- **July 3:** Giants lefty Rube Marquard earned his record 19th consecutive victory of the season and 21st straight over two years, stopping Brooklyn, 2-1.
- **August 26:** The Browns handed Washington's Walter Johnson a 3-2 loss and ended his A.L.-record winning streak at 16 games.
- **September 20:** Joe Wood's record-tying 16-game winning streak ended when Detroit handed Boston a 6-4 loss.
- **September 22:** For the second time in 11 days, Athletics star Eddie Collins stole a modern-record six bases in a game—an 8-2 victory over the Browns.

LEADERS

American League

BA: Ty Cobb, Det., .409.
Runs: Eddie Collins, Phil., 137.
Hits: Ty Cobb, Det.; Joe Jackson, Cle., 226.
TB: Joe Jackson, Cle., 331.
HR: Frank Baker, Phil.; Tris Speaker, Bos., 10.
RBI: Frank Baker, Phil., 130.
SB: Clyde Milan, Wash., 88.
Wins: Joe Wood, Bos., 34.
ERA: Walter Johnson, Wash., 1.39.
CG: Joe Wood, Bos., 35.
IP: Ed Walsh, Chi., 393.
SO: Walter Johnson, Wash., 303.

National League

BA: Heinie Zimmerman, Chi., .372.
Runs: Bob Bescher, Cin., 120.
Hits: Heinie Zimmerman, Chi., 207.
TB: Heinie Zimmerman, Chi., 318.
HR: Heinie Zimmerman, Chi., 14.
RBI: Honus Wagner, Pit., 102.
SB: Bob Bescher, Cin., 67.
Wins: Larry Cheney, Chi.; Rube Marquard, N.Y., 26.
ERA: Jeff Tesreau, N.Y., 1.96.
CG: Larry Cheney, Chi., 28.
IP: Grover Alexander, Phil., 310.1.
SO: Grover Alexander, Phil., 195.

A.L. 20-game winners

Joe Wood, Bos., 34-5
Walter Johnson, Wash., 33-12
Ed Walsh, Chi., 27-17
Eddie Plank, Phil., 26-6
Bob Groom, Wash., 24-13
Jack Coombs, Phil., 21-10
Hugh Bedient, Bos., 20-9
Vean Gregg, Cle., 20-13
Buck O'Brien, Bos., 20-13

N.L. 20-game winners

Larry Cheney, Chi., 26-10
Rube Marquard, N.Y., 26-11
Claude Hendrix, Pit., 24-9
Christy Mathewson, N.Y., 23-12
Howie Camnitz, Pit., 22-12

A.L. 100 RBIs

Frank Baker, Phil., 130
Sam Crawford, Det., 109
Duffy Lewis, Bos., 109
Stuffy McInnis, Phil., 101

N.L. 100 RBIs

Honus Wagner, Pit., 102
Bill Sweeney, Bos., 100

Chalmers MVP

A.L.: Tris Speaker, OF, Bos.
N.L.: Larry Doyle, 2B, N.Y.

WORLD SERIES

- **Winners:** The Red Sox, who had not made a Series appearance since beating Pittsburgh in the 1903 inaugural, made it two for two with a victory over the Giants.
- **Turning point:** A dropped fly ball by Giants center fielder Fred Snodgrass in the Series-deciding eighth game. The Red Sox wiped out a 2-1 deficit against Christy Mathewson and claimed a 3-2 victory.
- **Memorable moment:** Snodgrass' muff and the failure of catcher Chief Meyers and first baseman Fred Merkle to catch a foul pop in the same inning.
- **Top guns:** Joe Wood (3-1), Red Sox; Buck Herzog (.400), Meyers (.357), Giants.

Linescores

Game 1—October 8, at New York
Boston....................0 0 0 0 0 1 3 0 0 — 4 6 1
New York.................0 0 2 0 0 0 0 0 1 — 3 8 1
Wood; Tesreau, Crandall (8). W—Wood. L—Tesreau.

Game 2—October 9, at Boston
New York......0 1 0 1 0 0 0 3 0 1 0 — 6 11 5
Boston..........3 0 0 0 1 0 0 1 0 1 0 — 6 10 1
Mathewson; Collins, Hall (8), Bedient (11). Game called after 11 innings because of darkness.

Game 3—October 10, at Boston
New York................0 1 0 0 1 0 0 0 0 — 2 7 1
Boston....................0 0 0 0 0 0 0 0 1 — 1 7 0
Marquard; O'Brien, Bedient (9). W—Marquard. L—O'Brien.

Game 4—October 11, at New York
Boston....................0 1 0 1 0 0 0 0 1 — 3 8 1
New York................0 0 0 0 0 0 1 0 0 — 1 9 1
Wood; Tesreau, Ames (8). W—Wood. L—Tesreau.

Game 5—October 12, at Boston
New York...............0 0 0 0 0 0 1 0 0 — 1 3 1
Boston...................0 0 2 0 0 0 0 0 x — 2 5 1
Mathewson; Bedient. W—Bedient. L—Mathewson.

Game 6—October 14, at New York
Boston...................0 2 0 0 0 0 0 0 0 — 2 7 2
New York...............5 0 0 0 0 0 0 0 x — 5 11 2
O'Brien, Collins (2); Marquard. W—Marquard. L—O'Brien.

Game 7—October 15, at Boston
New York............6 1 0 0 0 2 1 0 1 — 11 16 4
Boston................0 1 0 0 0 0 2 1 0 — 4 9 3
Tesreau; Wood, Hall (2). W—Tesreau. L—Wood. HR—Doyle (N.Y.); Gardner (Bos.).

Game 8—October 16, at Boston
New York..........0 0 1 0 0 0 0 0 0 1 — 2 9 2
Boston..............0 0 0 0 0 0 1 0 0 2 — 3 8 5
Mathewson; Bedient, Wood (8). W—Wood. L—Mathewson.

1913

FINAL STANDINGS

American League

Team	W	L	Pct.	GB
Philadelphia	96	57	.627	...
Washington	90	64	.584	6.5
Cleveland	86	66	.566	9.5
Boston	79	71	.527	15.5
Chicago	78	74	.513	17.5
Detroit	66	87	.431	30
New York	57	94	.377	38
St. Louis	57	96	.373	39

National League

Team	W	L	Pct.	GB
New York	101	51	.664	...
Philadelphia	88	63	.583	12.5
Chicago	88	65	.575	13.5
Pittsburgh	78	71	.523	21.5
Boston	69	82	.457	31.5
Brooklyn	65	84	.436	34.5
Cincinnati	64	89	.418	37.5
St. Louis	51	99	.340	49

SIGNIFICANT EVENTS

■ **January 22:** The Yankees, no longer tenants of Hilltop Park, received permission from the New York Giants to use the Polo Grounds as co-tenants.
■ **April 9:** The Dodgers lost their Ebbets Field debut to the Phillies, 1-0.
■ **April 10:** The A.L.'s New York team began life anew as the "Yankees," losing to Washington, 2-1, in the season opener.
■ **November 2:** The outlaw Federal League began its challenge as a third Major League when its Kansas City entry enticed Browns manager George Stovall to jump.
■ **December 9:** N.L. owners elected Pennsylvania Governor John K. Tener as their new president.

MEMORABLE MOMENTS

■ **May 14:** Walter Johnson's Major League-record 56-inning scoreless streak ended when the Washington righthander yielded a fourth-inning run to the Browns.
■ **August 28:** Johnson's 14-game winning streak came to an end when the Senators fell to Boston, 1-0, in 11 innings.
■ **September 29:** Johnson defeated the Athletics, 1-0, and closed his incredible season with a 36-7 record, 11 shutouts and a 1.14 ERA.

LEADERS

American League

BA: Ty Cobb, Det., .390.
Runs: Eddie Collins, Phil., 125.
Hits: Joe Jackson, Cle., 197.
TB: Sam Crawford, Det., 298.
HR: Frank Baker, Phil., 12.
RBI: Frank Baker, Phil., 117.
SB: Clyde Milan, Wash., 75.
Wins: Walter Johnson, Wash., 36.
ERA: Walter Johnson, Wash., 1.14.
CG: Walter Johnson, Wash., 29.
IP: Walter Johnson, Wash., 346.
SO: Walter Johnson, Wash., 243.

National League

BA: Jake Daubert, Brk., .350.
Runs: Max Carey, Pit.; Tommy Leach, Chi., 99.
Hits: Gavvy Cravath, Phil., 179.
TB: Gavvy Cravath, Phil., 298.
HR: Gavvy Cravath, Phil., 19.
RBI: Gavvy Cravath, Phil., 128.
SB: Max Carey, Pit., 61.
Wins: Tom Seaton, Phil., 27.
ERA: Christy Mathewson, N.Y., 2.06.
CG: Lefty Tyler, Bos., 28.
IP: Tom Seaton, Phil., 322.1.
SO: Tom Seaton, Phil., 168.

A.L. 20-game winners

Walter Johnson, Wash., 36-7
Cy Falkenberg, Cle., 23-10
Reb Russell, Chi., 22-16
Chief Bender, Phil., 21-10
Vean Gregg, Cle., 20-13
Jim Scott, Chi., 20-21

N.L. 20-game winners

Tom Seaton, Phil., 27-12
Christy Mathewson, N.Y., 25-11
Rube Marquard, N.Y., 23-10
Grover Alexander, Phil., 22-8
Jeff Tesreau, N.Y., 22-13
Babe Adams, Pit., 21-10
Larry Cheney, Chi., 21-14

A.L. 100 RBIs

Frank Baker, Phil., 117

N.L. 100 RBIs

Gavvy Cravath, Phil., 128

Chalmers MVP

A.L.: Walter Johnson, P, Wash.
N.L.: Jake Daubert, 1B, Brk.

WORLD SERIES

■ **Winner:** The Athletics needed only five games to win their third Series in four years and hand the Giants their third straight loss.

■ **Turning point:** Complete-game victories by A's pitchers Joe Bush and Chief Bender in Games 3 and 4, setting up Eddie Plank for the kill.

■ **Memorable moment:** A Game 2 pitching duel between Plank and Christy Mathewson. The Giants scored three runs in the 10th for a 3-0 win.

■ **Top guns:** Frank Baker (.450, 7 RBIs), Eddie Collins (.421), Athletics; Mathewson (19 IP, 0.95 ERA), Giants.

Linescores

Game 1—October 7, at New York
Philadelphia........0 0 0 3 2 0 0 1 0 — 6 11 1
New York...........0 0 1 0 3 0 0 0 0 — 4 11 0
Bender; Marquard, Crandall (6), Tesreau (8). W—Bender. L—Marquard. HR—Baker (Phil.).

Game 2—October 8, at Philadelphia
New York..........0 0 0 0 0 0 0 0 0 3 — 3 7 2
Philadelphia......0 0 0 0 0 0 0 0 0 0 — 0 8 2
Mathewson; Plank. W—Mathewson. L—Plank.

Game 3—October 9, at New York
Philadelphia........3 2 0 0 0 0 2 1 0 — 8 12 1
New York...........0 0 0 0 1 0 1 0 0 — 2 5 1
Bush; Tesreau, Crandall (7). W—Bush. L—Tesreau. HR—Schang (Phil.).

Game 4—October 10, at Philadelphia
New York.............0 0 0 0 0 0 3 2 0 — 5 8 2
Philadelphia..........0 1 0 3 2 0 0 0 x — 6 9 0
Demaree, Marquard (5); Bender. W—Bender. L—Demaree. HR—Merkle (N.Y.).

Game 5—October 11, at New York
Philadelphia..........1 0 2 0 0 0 0 0 0 — 3 6 1
New York..............0 0 0 0 1 0 0 0 0 — 1 2 2
Plank; Mathewson. W—Plank. L—Mathewson.

1914

FINAL STANDINGS

American League

Team	W	L	Pct.	GB
Philadelphia	99	53	.651	...
Boston	91	62	.595	8.5
Washington	81	73	.526	19
Detroit	80	73	.523	19.5
St. Louis	71	82	.464	28.5
Chicago	70	84	.455	30
New York	70	84	.455	30
Cleveland	51	102	.333	48.5

National League

Team	W	L	Pct.	GB
Boston	94	59	.614	...
New York	84	70	.545	10.5
St. Louis	81	72	.529	13
Chicago	78	76	.506	16.5
Brooklyn	75	79	.487	19.5
Philadelphia	74	80	.481	20.5
Pittsburgh	69	85	.448	25.5
Cincinnati	60	94	.390	34.5

SIGNIFICANT EVENTS

■ **April 13:** The outlaw Federal League, claiming to be a Major League equal, opened play with Baltimore defeating Buffalo, 3-2.
■ **November 1:** Philadelphia's Connie Mack began dismantling his powerful Athletics team by asking waivers on Jack Coombs, Eddie Plank and Chief Bender.
■ **December 8:** Connie Mack continued his housecleaning by selling star second baseman Eddie Collins to the White Sox for $50,000.

MEMORABLE MOMENTS

■ **May 14:** Chicago's Jim Scott lost his no-hit bid and the game when the Senators scored on two 10th-inning hits for a 1-0 victory.
■ **July 11:** Young Babe Ruth pitched the Red Sox to a 4-3 victory over Cleveland in his Major League debut.
■ **July 17:** Giants 3, Pirates 1 as Rube Marquard outpitched Babe Adams in a 21-inning marathon.
■ **September 23:** The Reds snapped their team-record 19-game losing streak with a 3-0 victory over the Braves.
■ **September 27:** Cleveland's Napoleon Lajoie collected career hit No. 3,000, a double, and the Indians defeated the Yankees, 5-3.
■ **September 29:** The Miracle Braves, who would finish with an incredible 68-19 rush, clinched their first N.L. pennant with a 3-2 victory over the Cubs.
■ **October 7:** The Indianapolis Hoosiers defeated St. Louis, 4-0, and claimed the Federal League pennant.

LEADERS

American League

BA: Ty Cobb, Det., .368.
Runs: Eddie Collins, Phil., 122.
Hits: Tris Speaker, Bos., 193.
TB: Tris Speaker, Bos., 287.
HR: Frank Baker, Phil., 9.
RBI: Sam Crawford, Det., 104.
SB: Fritz Maisel, N.Y., 74.
Wins: Walter Johnson, Wash., 28.
ERA: Dutch Leonard, Bos., 0.96.
CG: Walter Johnson, Wash., 33.
IP: Walter Johnson, Wash., 371.2.
SO: Walter Johnson, Wash., 225.

National League

BA: Jake Daubert, Brk., .329.
Runs: George Burns, N.Y., 100.
Hits: Sherry Magee, Phil., 171.
TB: Sherry Magee, Phil., 277.
HR: Gavvy Cravath, Phil., 19.
RBI: Sherry Magee, Phil., 103.
SB: George Burns, N.Y., 62.
Wins: Grover Alexander, Phil., 27.
ERA: Bill Doak, St.L., 1.72.
CG: Grover Alexander, Phil., 32.
IP: Grover Alexander, Phil., 355.
SO: Grover Alexander, Phil., 214.

A.L. 20-game winners

Walter Johnson, Wash., 28-18
Harry Coveleski, Det., 22-12
Ray Collins, Bos., 20-13

N.L. 20-game winners

Grover Alexander, Phil., 27-15
Bill James, Bos., 26-7
Dick Rudolph, Bos., 26-10
Jeff Tesreau, N.Y., 26-10
Christy Mathewson, N.Y., 24-13
Jeff Pfeffer, Brk., 23-12
Hippo Vaughn, Chi., 21-13
Erskine Mayer, Phil., 21-19
Larry Cheney, Chi., 20-18

A.L. 100 RBIs

Sam Crawford, Det., 104

N.L. 100 RBIs

Sherry Magee, Phil., 103
Gavvy Cravath, Phil., 100

Chalmers MVP

A.L.: Eddie Collins, 2B, Phil.
N.L.: Johnny Evers, 2B, Bos.

WORLD SERIES

■ **Winner:** The Braves punctuated their miracle pennant run with a shocking four-game sweep of the powerful Athletics.

■ **Turning point:** Boston's come-from-behind effort in Game 3 that produced a 5-4 victory in 12 innings. The Braves stayed alive by scoring two 10th-inning runs after falling behind in the top of the inning.

■ **Memorable moment:** A dramatic Game 2 pitching duel between Boston's Bill James and Eddie Plank. James won 1-0 on Les Mann's ninth-inning single.

■ **Top guns:** James (2-0, 0.00 ERA), Dick Rudolph (2-0, 0-50), Hank Gowdy (.545), Johnny Evers (.438), Braves.

Linescores

Game 1—October 9, at Philadelphia
Boston............ 0 2 0 0 1 3 0 1 0 — 7 11 2
Phil................. 0 1 0 0 0 0 0 0 0 — 1 5 0
Rudolph; Bender, Wyckoff (6). W—Rudolph. L—Bender.

Game 2—October 10, at Philadelphia
Boston............ 0 0 0 0 0 0 0 0 1 — 1 7 1
Phil................. 0 0 0 0 0 0 0 0 0 — 0 2 1
James; Plank. W—James. L—Plank.

Game 3—October 12, at Boston
Phil..........1 0 0 1 0 0 0 0 0 2 0 0 — 4 8 2
Boston......0 1 0 1 0 0 0 0 0 2 0 1 — 5 9 1
Bush; Tyler, James (11). W—James. L—Bush. HR—Gowdy (Bos.).

Game 4—October 13, at Boston
Phil. ....0 0 0 0 1 0 0 0 0 — 1 7 0
Boston ....0 0 0 1 2 0 0 0 x — 3 6 0
Shawkey, Pennock (6); Rudolph. W—Rudolph. L—Shawkey.

1914—Federal League

FINAL STANDINGS

Team	W	L	Pct.	GB
Indianapolis	88	65	.575	...
Chicago	87	67	.565	1.5
Baltimore	84	70	.545	4.5
Buffalo	80	71	.530	7
Brooklyn	77	77	.500	11.5
Kansas City	67	84	.444	20
Pittsburgh	64	86	.427	22.5
St. Louis	62	89	.411	25

SIGNIFICANT EVENT

■ **November 1:** After being released by A's boss Connie Mack, pitchers Eddie Plank (St. Louis) and Chief Bender (Baltimore) signed contracts to play in the second-year Federal League.

MEMORABLE MOMENTS

■ **April 13:** Baltimore pitcher Jack Quinn, working before an estimated crowd of 28,000 at new Terrapin Park, posted a 3-2 victory over Buffalo in the Federal League inaugural.

■ **April 23:** The Chicago Whales christened new Weeghman Park—the future Wrigley Field—with a 9-1 victory over the Kansas City Packers.

■ **September 19:** Brooklyn's Ed Lafitte pitched the Federal League's first no-hitter, beating the Packers 6-2.

■ **October 6:** An Indianapolis victory over St. Louis combined with a Chicago loss to Kansas City clinched the first Federal League pennant for the Hoosiers, who finished with an 88-65 record.

LEADERS

BA: Benny Kauff, Ind., .370
Runs: Benny Kauff, Ind., 120
Hits: Benny Kauff, Ind., 211
TB: Benny Kauff, Ind., 305
HR: Dutch Zwilling, Chi., 16
RBI: Frank LaPorte, Ind., 107
SB: Benny Kauff, Ind., 75
Wins: Claude Hendrix, Chi., 29
ERA: Claude Hendrix, Chi., 1.69
CG: Claude Hendrix, Chi., 34
IP: Cy Falkenberg, Ind., 377.1
SO: Cy Falkenberg, Ind., 236

20-game winners
Claude Hendrix, Chi., 29-10
Jack Quinn, Bal., 26-14
Tom Seaton, Brk., 25-14
Cy Falkenberg, Ind., 25-16
George Suggs, Bal., 24-14
Russ Ford, Buf., 21-6
Elmer Knetzer, Pit., 20-12
Gene Packard, K.C., 20-14

100 RBIs
Frank LaPorte, Ind., 107

1915—Federal League

FINAL STANDINGS

Team	W	L	Pct.	GB
Chicago	86	66	.566	...
St. Louis	87	67	.565	...
Pittsburgh	86	67	.562	0.5
Kansas City	81	72	.529	5.5
Newark	80	72	.526	6
Buffalo	74	78	.487	12
Brooklyn	70	82	.461	16
Baltimore	47	107	.305	40

SIGNIFICANT EVENTS

■ **January 5:** The Federal League filed a lawsuit challenging Organized Baseball as an illegal trust that should be dissolved.
■ **December 22:** Organized Baseball's costly two-year battle against the Federal League ended when a peace treaty was arranged and the outlaw circuit was disbanded.

MEMORABLE MOMENTS

■ **April 24:** Pittsburgh's Frank Allen held St. Louis hitless in the Rebels' 2-0 victory.
■ **May 15:** Chicago's Claude Hendrix pitched a Whale of a game—a 10-0 no-hitter against Pittsburgh.
■ **July 31:** St. Louis' Dave Davenport pitched a pair of 1-0 games on the same day against Buffalo, winning the opener and dropping the nightcap.
■ **August 16, September 7:** Kansas City's Miles Main and St. Louis' Dave Davenport joined the no-hit fraternity. Main stopped Buffalo 5-0 and Davenport beat Chicago 3-0.
■ **October 3:** Chicago's season-ending victory over Pittsburgh clinched the second Federal League pennant—by an incredible .001 over St. Louis and a half game over the Rebels.

LEADERS

BA: Benny Kauff, Brk., .342
Runs: Babe Borton, St.L., 97
Hits: Jack Tobin, St.L., 184
TB: Ed Konetchy, Pit., 278
HR: Hal Chase, Buf., 17
RBI: Dutch Zwilling, Chi., 94
SB: Benny Kauff, Brk., 55
Wins: George McConnell, Chi., 25
ERA: Earl Moseley, New., 1.91
CG: Dave Davenport, St.L., 30
IP: Dave Davenport, St.L., 392.2
SO: Dave Davenport, St.L., 229

20-game winners
George McConnell, Chi., 25-10
Frank Allen, Pit., 23-13
Nick Cullop, K.C., 22-11
Dave Davenport, St.L., 22-18
Ed Reulbach, New., 21-10
Eddie Plank, St.L., 21-11
Al Schulz, Buf., 21-14
Doc Crandall, St.L., 21-15
Gene Packard, K.C., 20-12

1915

FINAL STANDINGS

American League

Team	W	L	Pct.	GB
Boston	101	50	.669	...
Detroit	100	54	.649	2.5
Chicago	93	61	.604	9.5
Washington	85	68	.556	17
New York	69	83	.454	32.5
St. Louis	63	91	.409	39.5
Cleveland	57	95	.375	44.5
Philadelphia	43	109	.283	58.5

National League

Team	W	L	Pct.	GB
Philadelphia	90	62	.592	...
Boston	83	69	.546	7
Brooklyn	80	72	.526	10
Chicago	73	80	.477	17.5
Pittsburgh	73	81	.474	18
St. Louis	72	81	.471	18.5
Cincinnati	71	83	.461	20
New York	69	83	.454	21

SIGNIFICANT EVENTS

■ **August 18:** Boston defeated St. Louis, 3-1, in the first game at new Braves Field.
■ **December 22:** Organized Baseball's costly two-year battle against the Federal League ended when a peace treaty was arranged and the outlaw circuit was disbanded.

MEMORABLE MOMENTS

■ **September 29:** Grover Cleveland Alexander pitched a one-hitter and his 12th shutout of the season as the Phillies clinched their first N.L. pennant with a 5-0 victory over the Braves.
■ **September 30:** The Red Sox clinched the A.L. pennant when the St. Louis Browns handed the Tigers an 8-2 loss in a game at Detroit.
■ **October 3:** Detroit's Ty Cobb, on his way to a record ninth consecutive A.L. batting title, stole his record 96th base in a 6-5 victory over Cleveland.

LEADERS

American League
BA: Ty Cobb, Det., .369.
Runs: Ty Cobb, Det., 144.
Hits: Ty Cobb, Det., 208.
TB: Ty Cobb, Det., 274.
HR: Braggo Roth, Chi.-Cle., 7.
RBI: Sam Crawford, Det.; Bobby Veach, Det., 112.
SB: Ty Cobb, Det., 96.
Wins: Walter Johnson, Wash., 27.
ERA: Joe Wood, Bos., 1.49.
CG: Walter Johnson, Wash., 35.
IP: Walter Johnson, Wash., 336.2.
SO: Walter Johnson, Wash., 203.

National League
BA: Larry Doyle, N.Y., .320.
Runs: Gavvy Cravath, Phil., 89.
Hits: Larry Doyle, N.Y., 189.
TB: Gavvy Cravath, Phil., 266.
HR: Gavvy Cravath, Phil., 24.
RBI: Gavvy Cravath, Phil., 115.
SB: Max Carey, Pit., 36.
Wins: Grover Alexander, Phil., 31.
ERA: Grover Alexander, Phil., 1.22.
CG: Grover Alexander, Phil., 36.
IP: Grover Alexander, Phil, 376.1
SO: Grover Alexander, Phil., 241.

A.L. 20-game winners
Walter Johnson, Wash., 27-13
Jim Scott, Chi., 24-11
Hooks Dauss, Det., 24-13
Red Faber, Chi., 24-14
Harry Coveleski, Det., 22-13

N.L. 20-game winners
Grover Alexander, Phil., 31-10
Dick Rudolph, Bos., 22-19
Al Mamaux, Pit., 21-8
Erskine Mayer, Phil., 21-15
Hippo Vaughn, Chi., 20-12

A.L. 100 RBIs
Sam Crawford, Det., 112
Bobby Veach, Det., 112

N.L. 100 RBIs
Gavvy Cravath, Phil., 115

WORLD SERIES

■ **Winner:** The Red Sox matched the Athletics as three-time Series winners with a five-game romp past another Philadelphia team — the Phillies.

■ **Turning point:** Dutch Leonard's 2-1 Game 3 victory over Phillies ace Grover Cleveland Alexander. The game was decided in the ninth inning on Duffy Lewis' RBI single.

■ **Memorable moment:** Harry Hooper's Series-deciding ninth-inning home run in Game 5 off Philadelphia reliever Eppa Rixey.

■ **Top guns:** Rube Foster (2-0, 2.00 ERA), Lewis (.444), Red Sox; Fred Luderus (.438), Phillies.

Linescores

Game 1—October 8, at Philadelphia

					R	H	E
Boston	0 0 0	0 0 0	0 1 0	—	1	8	1
Philadelphia	0 0 0	1 0 0	0 2 x	—	3	5	1

Shore; Alexander. W—Alexander. L—Shore.

Game 2—October 9, at Philadelphia

					R	H	E
Boston	1 0 0	0 0 0	0 0 1	—	2	10	0
Philadelphia	0 0 0	0 1 0	0 0 0	—	1	3	1

Foster; Mayer. W—Foster. L—Mayer.

Game 3—October 11, at Boston

					R	H	E
Philadelphia	0 0 1	0 0 0	0 0 0	—	1	3	0
Boston	0 0 0	1 0 0	0 0 1	—	2	6	1

Alexander; Leonard. W—Leonard. L—Alexander.

Game 4—October 12, at Boston

					R	H	E
Philadelphia	0 0 0	0 0 0	0 1 0	—	1	7	0
Boston	0 0 1	0 0 1	0 0 x	—	2	8	1

Chalmers; Shore. W—Shore. L—Chalmers.

Game 5—October 13, at Philadelphia

					R	H	E
Boston	0 1 1	0 0 0	0 2 1	—	5	10	1
Philadelphia	2 0 0	2 0 0	0 0 0	—	4	9	1

Foster; Mayer, Rixey (3). W—Foster. L—Rixey. HR—Hooper 2, Lewis (Bos.); Luderus (Phil.).

1916

FINAL STANDINGS

American League

Team	W	L	Pct.	GB
Boston	91	63	.591	...
Chicago	89	65	.578	2
Detroit	87	67	.565	4
New York	80	74	.519	11
St. Louis	79	75	.513	12
Cleveland	77	77	.500	14
Washington	76	77	.497	14.5
Philadelphia	36	117	.235	54.5

National League

Team	W	L	Pct.	GB
Brooklyn	94	60	.610	...
Philadelphia	91	62	.595	2.5
Boston	89	63	.586	4
New York	86	66	.566	7
Chicago	67	86	.438	26.5
Pittsburgh	65	89	.422	29
Cincinnati	60	93	.392	33.5
St. Louis	60	93	.392	33.5

SIGNIFICANT EVENTS

■ **July 20:** Giants great Christy Mathewson was traded to Cincinnati in a career-prolonging deal that allowed him to become manager of the Reds.
■ **November 1:** Harry Frazee, a New York theater owner and producer, bought the Red Sox for $675,000.

MEMORABLE MOMENTS

■ **August 9:** The Athletics' 20-game losing streak came to a merciful end when they defeated the Tigers, 7-1.
■ **September 30:** The Braves ended New York's winning streak at a Major League-record 26 games with an 8-3 victory in the second game of a doubleheader.
■ **October 2:** Grover Cleveland Alexander pitched the Phillies to a 2-0 victory over the Braves—his modern record 16th shutout of the season.

LEADERS

American League
BA: Tris Speaker, Cle., .386.
Runs: Ty Cobb, Det., 113.
Hits: Tris Speaker, Cle., 211.
TB: Joe Jackson, Chi., 293.
HR: Wally Pipp, N.Y., 12.
RBI: Del Pratt, St.L., 103.
SB: Ty Cobb, Det., 68.
Wins: Walter Johnson, Wash., 25.
ERA: Babe Ruth, Bos., 1.75.
CG: Walter Johnson, Wash., 36.
IP: Walter Johnson, Wash., 369.2.
SO: Walter Johnson, Wash., 228.

National League
BA: Hal Chase, Cin., .339.
Runs: George Burns, N.Y., 105.
Hits: Hal Chase, Cin., 184.
TB: Zack Wheat, Brk., 262.
HR: Dave Robertson, N.Y.; Cy Williams, Chi., 12.
RBI: Heinie Zimmerman, Chi.-N.Y., 83.
SB: Max Carey, Pit., 63.
Wins: Grover Alexander, Phil., 33.
ERA: Grover Alexander, Phil., 1.55.
CG: Grover Alexander, Phil., 38.
IP: Grover Alexander, Phil., 389.
SO: Grover Alexander, Phil., 167.

A.L. 20-game winners
Walter Johnson, Wash., 25-20
Bob Shawkey, N.Y., 24-14
Babe Ruth, Bos., 23-12
Harry Coveleski, Det., 21-11

N.L. 20-game winners
Grover Alexander, Phil., 33-12
Jeff Pfeffer, Brk., 25-11
Eppa Rixey, Phil., 22-10
Al Mamaux, Pit., 21-15

A.L. 100 RBIs
Del Pratt, St.L., 103

WORLD SERIES

■ **Winner:** Stingy Boston pitchers allowed only eight earned runs and the Red Sox closed down the Dodgers to become the first four-time Series winners.

■ **Turning point:** Larry Gardner's three-run Game 4 homer propelled Dutch Leonard to a 6-2 victory and the Red Sox to a 3-1 Series advantage.

■ **Memorable moment:** A 14-inning Game 2 pitching duel between Boston's Babe Ruth and Brooklyn's Sherry Smith. Ruth won 2-1 on Del Gainor's pinch-hit single.

■ **Top guns:** Ernie Shore (2-0, 1.53 ERA), Duffy Lewis (.353), Red Sox; Casey Stengel (.364), Dodgers.

Linescores

Game 1—October 7, at Boston

					R	H	E
Brooklyn	0 0 0	1 0 0	0 0 4	—	5	10	4
Boston	0 0 1	0 1 0	3 1 x	—	6	8	1

Marquard, Pfeffer (8); Shore, Mays (9). W—Shore. L—Marquard.

Game 2—October 9, at Boston

							R	H	E
Brooklyn	1 0 0	0 0 0	0 0 0	0 0 0	0 0	—	1	6	2
Boston	0 0 1	0 0 0	0 0 0	0 0 0	0 1	—	2	7	1

Smith; Ruth. W—Ruth. L—Smith. HR—Myers (Brk.).

Game 3—October 10, at Brooklyn

					R	H	E
Boston	0 0 0	0 0 2	1 0 0	—	3	7	1
Brooklyn	0 0 1	1 2 0	0 0 x	—	4	10	0

Mays, Foster (6); Coombs, Pfeffer (7). W—Coombs. L—Mays. HR—Gardner (Bos.).

Game 4—October 11, at Brooklyn

					R	H	E
Boston	0 3 0	1 1 0	1 0 0	—	6	10	1
Brooklyn	2 0 0	0 0 0	0 0 0	—	2	5	4

Leonard; Marquard, Cheney (5), Rucker (8). W—Leonard. L—Marquard. HR—Gardner (Bos.).

Game 5—October 12, at Boston

					R	H	E
Brooklyn	0 1 0	0 0 0	0 0 0	—	1	3	3
Boston	0 1 2	0 1 0	0 0 x	—	4	7	2

Pfeffer, Dell (8); Shore. W—Shore. L—Pfeffer.

1917

FINAL STANDINGS

American League

Team	W	L	Pct.	GB
Chicago	100	54	.649	...
Boston	90	62	.592	9
Cleveland	88	66	.571	12
Detroit	78	75	.510	21.5
Washington	74	79	.484	25.5
New York	71	82	.464	28.5
St. Louis	57	97	.370	43
Philadelphia	55	98	.359	44.5

National League

Team	W	L	Pct.	GB
New York	98	56	.636	...
Philadelphia	87	65	.572	10
St. Louis	82	70	.539	15
Cincinnati	78	76	.506	20
Chicago	74	80	.481	24
Boston	72	81	.471	25.5
Brooklyn	70	81	.464	26.5
Pittsburgh	51	103	.331	47

SIGNIFICANT EVENTS

■ **October 26:** New York owner Jacob Ruppert took a dynastic step when he signed former Cardinals manager Miller Huggins to manage the Yankees.

MEMORABLE MOMENTS

■ **April 14:** Chicago ace Eddie Cicotte kicked off the season's no-hitter parade with an 11-0 victory over St. Louis. Cicotte's no-hitter was the first of five in the American League.
■ **May 2:** Cincinnati's Fred Toney and Chicago's Hippo Vaughn matched no-hitters for an unprecedented nine innings before Vaughn wilted in the 10th and the Reds scored a 1-0 victory.
■ **May 6:** Browns pitcher Bob Groom pitched a 3-0 no-hitter against the White Sox, matching the previous-day feat of teammate Ernie Koob in a 1-0 victory over Chicago.
■ **June 23:** Boston's Ernie Shore retired 27 consecutive Senators after replacing starter Babe Ruth, who was ejected after walking the first batter of the game. The runner was thrown out trying to steal and Shore went on to claim a 4-0 victory.
■ **September 3:** Grover Alexander, en route to a Major League-leading 30 victories, pitched both ends of the Phillies' 6-0 and 9-3 doubleheader sweep of Brooklyn.

LEADERS

American League
BA: Ty Cobb, Det., .383.
Runs: Donie Bush, Det., 112.
Hits: Ty Cobb, Det., 225.
TB: Ty Cobb, Det., 335.
HR: Wally Pipp, N.Y., 9.
RBI: Bobby Veach, Det., 103.
SB: Ty Cobb, Det., 55.
Wins: Eddie Cicotte, Chi., 28.
ERA: Eddie Cicotte, Chi., 1.53.
CG: Babe Ruth, Bos., 35.
IP: Eddie Cicotte, Chi., 346.2.
SO: Walter Johnson, Wash., 188.

National League
BA: Edd Roush, Cin., .341.
Runs: George Burns, N.Y., 103.
Hits: Heinie Groh, Cin., 182.
TB: Rogers Hornsby, St.L., 253.
HR: Gavvy Cravath, Phil.; Dave Robertson, N.Y., 12.
RBI: Heinie Zimmerman, N.Y., 102.
SB: Max Carey, Pit., 46.
Wins: Grover Alexander, Phil., 30.
ERA: Fred Anderson, N.Y., 1.44.
CG: Grover Alexander, Phil., 34.
IP: Grover Alexander, Phil., 388.
SO: Grover Alexander, Phil., 200.

A.L. 20-game winners
Ed Cicotte, Chi., 28-12
Babe Ruth, Bos., 24-13
Jim Bagby, Cle., 23-13
Walter Johnson, Wash., 23-16
Carl Mays, Bos., 22-9

N.L. 20-game winners
Grover Alexander, Phil., 30-13
Fred Toney, Cin., 24-16
Hippo Vaughn, Chi., 23-13
Ferdie Schupp, N.Y., 21-7
Pete Schneider, Cin., 20-19

A.L. 100 RBIs
Bobby Veach, Det., 103
Ty Cobb, Det., 102
Happy Felsch, Chi., 102

N.L. 100 RBIs
Heinie Zimmerman, N.Y., 102

WORLD SERIES

■ **Winner:** The White Sox, making their first Series appearance since 1906, took advantage of the Giants' sloppy play for a six-game victory.

■ **Turning point:** The White Sox rallied for six seventh and eighth-inning runs to claim an 8-5 victory in the pivotal fifth game.

■ **Memorable moment:** Third baseman Heinie Zimmerman giving futile chase to Chicago's Eddie Collins as he bolted toward the uncovered plate on one of several Game 6 fielding gaffes by the Giants. The White Sox closed out the Series with a 4-2 victory.

■ **Top guns:** Red Faber (3-1), Collins (.409), White Sox; Dave Robertson (.500), Giants.

Linescores

Game 1—October 6, at Chicago
New York........ 0 0 0 0 1 0 0 0 0 — 1 7 1
Chicago.......... 0 0 1 1 0 0 0 0 x — 2 7 1
Sallee; Cicotte. W—Cicotte. L—Sallee.
HR—Felsch (Chi.).

Game 2—October 7, at Chicago
New York........ 0 2 0 0 0 0 0 0 0 — 2 8 1
Chicago.......... 0 2 0 5 0 0 0 0 x — 7 14 1
Schupp, Anderson (2), Perritt (4), Tesreau (8); Faber. W—Faber. L—Anderson.

Game 3—October 10, at New York
Chicago.......... 0 0 0 0 0 0 0 0 0 — 0 5 3
New York........ 0 0 0 2 0 0 0 0 x — 2 8 2
Cicotte; Benton. W—Benton. L—Cicotte.

Game 4—October 11, at New York
Chicago.......... 0 0 0 0 0 0 0 0 0 — 0 7 0
New York........ 0 0 0 1 1 0 1 2 x — 5 10 1
Faber, Danforth (8); Schupp. W—Schupp. L—Faber. HR—Kauff 2 (N.Y.).

Game 5—October 13, at Chicago
New York........ 2 0 0 2 0 0 1 0 0 — 5 12 3
Chicago.......... 0 0 1 0 0 1 3 3 x — 8 14 6
Sallee, Perritt (8); Russell, Cicotte (1), Williams (7), Faber (8). W—Faber. L—Sallee.

Game 6—October 15, at New York
Chicago.......... 0 0 0 3 0 0 0 0 1 — 4 7 1
New York........ 0 0 0 0 2 0 0 0 0 — 2 6 3
Faber; Benton, Perritt (6). W—Faber. L—Benton.

1918

FINAL STANDINGS

American League

Team	W	L	Pct.	GB
Boston	75	51	.595	...
Cleveland	73	54	.575	2.5
Washington	72	56	.563	4
New York	60	63	.488	13.5
St. Louis	58	64	.475	15
Chicago	57	67	.460	17
Detroit	55	71	.437	20
Philadelphia	52	76	.406	24

National League

Team	W	L	Pct.	GB
Chicago	84	45	.651	...
New York	71	53	.573	10.5
Cincinnati	68	60	.531	15.5
Pittsburgh	65	60	.520	17
Brooklyn	57	69	.452	25.5
Philadelphia	55	68	.447	26
Boston	53	71	.427	28.5
St. Louis	51	78	.395	33

SIGNIFICANT EVENTS

■ **April 30:** Cubs great Grover Cleveland Alexander answered the draft call and reported for World War I duty with the Army.
■ **May 14:** Washington D.C. officials repealed the ban against night baseball in the nation's capital, citing the need for more wartime recreational outlets.
■ **July 19:** U.S. Secretary of War Newton Baker issued a "Work or Fight" order forcing all able-bodied Americans into jobs considered essential to the war.
■ **August 2:** A.L. and N.L. officials voted to close down the regular season by September 2 (Labor Day) with the World Series to follow immediately.
■ **October 5:** Infielder Eddie Grant became baseball's first war casualty when he was killed during action in France.
■ **December 10:** N.L. secretary John Heydler was selected to replace John K. Tener as the league's new president.

MEMORABLE MOMENTS

■ **April 15:** Babe Ruth got the Red Sox' s season off to a rousing start with an opening day 7-1 victory over the A's.
■ **June 3:** Boston's Dutch Leonard pitched the season's only no-hitter, beating the Tigers 5-0 with the aide of a Babe Ruth home run.
■ **August 31:** Babe Ruth pitched the Red Sox to an A.L. pennant-clinching 6-1 victory over the Athletics.

LEADERS

American League
BA: Ty Cobb, Det., .382.
Runs: Ray Chapman, Cle., 84.
Hits: George Burns, Phil., 178.
TB: George Burns, Phil., 236.
HR: Babe Ruth, Bos.; Tilly Walker, Phil., 11.
RBI: Bobby Veach, Det., 78.
SB: George Sisler, St.L., 45.
Wins: Walter Johnson, Wash., 23.
ERA: Walter Johnson, Wash., 1.27.
CG: Carl Mays, Bos.; Scott Perry, Phil., 30.
IP: Scott Perry, Phil., 332.1.
SO: Walter Johnson, Wash., 162.

National League
BA: Zack Wheat, Brk., .335.
Runs: Heinie Groh, Cin., 86.
Hits: Charlie Hollocher, Chi., 161.
TB: Charlie Hollocher, Chi., 202.
HR: Gavvy Cravath, Phil., 8.
RBI: Sherry Magee, Cin., 76.
SB: Max Carey, Pit., 58.
Wins: Hippo Vaughn, Chi., 22.
ERA: Hippo Vaughn, Chi., 1.74.
CG: Art Nehf, Bos., 28.
IP: Hippo Vaughn, Chi., 290.1.
SO: Hippo Vaughn, Chi., 148.

A.L. 20-game winners
Walter Johnson, Wash., 23-13
Stan Coveleski, Cle., 22-13
Carl Mays, Bos., 21-13
Scott Perry, Phil., 20-19

N.L. 20-game winners
Hippo Vaughn, Chi., 22-10
Claude Hendrix, Chi., 20-7

WORLD SERIES

■ **Winner:** The Red Sox ended baseball's war-depleted season by defeating the Cubs and winning their fifth Series in as many tries.

■ **Turning point:** Babe Ruth's second victory, a 3-2 Game 4 decision that gave the Red Sox a three games to one advantage.

■ **Memorable moment:** A Game 6 delay while players haggled with the owners over gate receipts. The Red Sox closed out the Cubs with a 2-1 victory.

■ **Top guns:** Carl Mays (2-0, 1.00 ERA), Ruth (2-0, 1.06), Red Sox; Charlie Pick (.389), Cubs.

Linescores

Game 1—September 5, at Chicago
Boston ....0 0 0 1 0 0 0 0 0 — 1 5 0
Chicago..........0 0 0 0 0 0 0 0 0 — 0 6 0
Ruth; Vaughn. W—Ruth. L—Vaughn.

Game 2—September 6, at Chicago
Boston ....0 0 0 0 0 0 0 0 1 — 1 6 1
Chicago..........0 3 0 0 0 0 0 0 x — 3 7 1
Bush; Tyler. W—Tyler. L—Bush.

Game 3—September 7, at Chicago
Boston ....0 0 0 2 0 0 0 0 0 — 2 7 0
Chicago..........0 0 0 0 1 0 0 0 0 — 1 7 1
Mays; Vaughn. W—Mays. L—Vaughn.

Game 4—September 9, at Boston
Chicago..........0 0 0 0 0 0 0 2 0 — 2 7 1
Boston............0 0 0 2 0 0 0 1 x — 3 4 0
Tyler, Douglas (8); Ruth, Bush (9). W—Ruth. L—Douglas.

Game 5—September 10, at Boston
Chicago..........0 0 1 0 0 0 0 2 0 — 3 7 0
Boston ....0 0 0 0 0 0 0 0 0 — 0 5 0
Vaughn; Jones. W—Vaughn. L—Jones.

Game 6—September 11, at Boston
Chicago..........0 0 0 1 0 0 0 0 0 — 1 3 2
Boston............0 0 2 0 0 0 0 0 x — 2 5 0
Tyler, Hendrix (8); Mays. W—Mays. L—Tyler.

1919

FINAL STANDINGS

American League

Team	W	L	Pct.	GB
Chicago	88	52	.629	...
Cleveland	84	55	.604	3.5
New York	80	59	.576	7.5
Detroit	80	60	.571	8
St. Louis	67	72	.482	20.5
Boston	66	71	.482	20.5
Washington	56	84	.400	32
Philadelphia	36	104	.257	52

National League

Team	W	L	Pct.	GB
Cincinnati	96	44	.686	...
New York	87	53	.621	9
Chicago	75	65	.536	21
Pittsburgh	71	68	.511	24.5
Brooklyn	69	71	.493	27
Boston	57	82	.410	38.5
St. Louis	54	83	.394	40.5
Philadelphia	47	90	.343	47.5

SIGNIFICANT EVENTS

- **April 19:** New York Governor Al Smith signed a bill permitting Sunday baseball throughout the state.
- **April 23:** The slimmed-down 140-game Major League schedule opened in Washington, where Walter Johnson shut out the A's, 1-0.
- **September 2:** Major League officials approved a best-of-nine World Series format, replacing the long-running seven-game format.

MEMORABLE MOMENTS

- **September 16:** The Reds defeated the Giants, 4-3, and clinched their first N.L. pennant of the century.
- **September 24:** The White Sox captured their second A.L. pennant in three years when they defeated St. Louis, 6-5.
- **September 27:** Boston's Babe Ruth stretched his one-season home run record to 29 in a game at Washington.

LEADERS

American League

BA: Ty Cobb, Det., .384.
Runs: Babe Ruth, Bos., 103.
Hits: Ty Cobb, Det.; Bobby Veach, Det., 191.
TB: Babe Ruth, Bos., 284.
HR: Babe Ruth, Bos., 29.
RBI: Babe Ruth, Bos., 114.
SB: Eddie Collins, Chi., 33.
Wins: Eddie Cicotte, Chi., 29.
ERA: Walter Johnson, Wash., 1.49.
CG: Eddie Cicotte, Chi., 30.
IP: Eddie Cicotte, Chi.; Jim Shaw, Wash., 306.2.
SO: Walter Johnson, Wash., 147.

National League

BA: Gavvy Cravath, Phil., .341.
Runs: George Burns, N.Y., 86.
Hits: Ivy Olson, Brk., 164.
TB: Hy Myers, Brk., 223.
HR: Gavvy Cravath, Phil., 12.
RBI: Hy Myers, Brk., 73.
SB: George Burns, N.Y., 40.
Wins: Jesse Barnes, N.Y., 25.
ERA: Grover Alexander, Chi., 1.72.
CG: Wilbur Cooper, Pit., 27.
IP: Hippo Vaughn, Chi., 306.2.
SO: Hippo Vaughn, Chi., 141.

A.L. 20-game winners
Ed Cicotte, Chi., 29-7
Stan Coveleski, Cle., 24-12
Lefty Williams, Chi., 23-11
Hooks Dauss, Det., 21-9
Allen Sothoron, St.L., 20-12
Bob Shawkey, N.Y., 20-11
Walter Johnson, Wash., 20-14

N.L. 20-game winners
Jess Barnes, N.Y., 25-9
Slim Sallee, Cin., 21-7
Hippo Vaughn, Chi., 21-14

A.L. 100 RBIs
Babe Ruth, Bos., 114
Bobby Veach, Det., 101

WORLD SERIES

- **Winner:** The Reds earned their first Series victory amid suspicions the White Sox were consorting with gamblers in a fall classic fix.
- **Turning point:** The Series' first pitch, when Chicago starter Eddie Cicotte hit Cincinnati leadoff man Morrie Rath, reportedly signaling to bettors the fix was on.
- **Memorable moment:** White Sox lefthander Dickey Kerr, suspecting something was brewing among his teammates, fired a heroic three-hit shutout in Game 3.
- **Top guns:** Hod Eller (2-0, 2.00 ERA), Greasy Neale (.357), Reds; Kerr (2-0, 1.42), White Sox.

Linescores

Game 1—October 1, at Cincinnati
Chicago.......... 0 1 0 0 0 0 0 0 0 — 1 6 1
Cincinnati....... 1 0 0 5 0 0 2 1 x — 9 14 1
Cicotte, Wilkinson (4), Lowdermilk (8); Ruether. W—Ruether. L—Cicotte.

Game 2—October 2, at Cincinnati
Chicago.......... 0 0 0 0 0 0 2 0 0 — 2 10 1
Cincinnati....... 0 0 0 3 0 1 0 0 x — 4 4 2
Williams; Sallee. W—Sallee. L—Williams.

Game 3—October 3, at Chicago
Cincinnati....... 0 0 0 0 0 0 0 0 0 — 0 3 1
Chicago.......... 0 2 0 1 0 0 0 0 x — 3 7 0
Fisher, Luque (8); Kerr. W—Kerr. L—Fisher.

Game 4—October 4, at Chicago
Cincinnati....... 0 0 0 0 2 0 0 0 0—2 5 2
Chicago.......... 0 0 0 0 0 0 0 0 0—0 3 2
Ring; Cicotte. W—Ring. L—Cicotte.

Game 5—October 6, at Chicago
Cincinnati....... 0 0 0 0 0 4 0 0 1 — 5 4 0
Chicago.......... 0 0 0 0 0 0 0 0 0 — 0 3 3
Eller; Williams, Mayer (9). W—Eller. L—Williams.

Game 6—October 7, at Cincinnati
Chicago.......... 0 0 0 0 1 3 0 0 0 1—5 10 3
Cincinnati....... 0 0 2 2 0 0 0 0 0 0—4 11 0
Kerr; Ruether, Ring (6). W—Kerr. L—Ring.

Game 7—October 8, at Cincinnati
Chicago.......... 1 0 1 0 2 0 0 0 0 — 4 10 1
Cincinnati....... 0 0 0 0 0 1 0 0 0 — 1 7 4
Cicotte; Sallee, Fisher (5), Luque (6). W—Cicotte. L—Sallee.

Game 8—October 9, at Chicago
Cincinnati....... 4 1 0 0 1 3 0 1 0 —10 16 2
Chicago.......... 0 0 1 0 0 0 0 4 0 — 5 10 1
Eller; Williams, James (1), Wilkinson (6). W—Eller. L—Williams. HR—Jackson (Chi.).

1920

FINAL STANDINGS

American League

Team	W	L	Pct.	GB
Cleveland	98	56	.636	...
Chicago	96	58	.623	2
New York	95	59	.617	3
St. Louis	76	77	.497	21.5
Boston	72	81	.471	25.5
Washington	68	84	.447	29
Detroit	61	93	.396	37
Philadelphia	48	106	.312	50

National League

Team	W	L	Pct.	GB
Brooklyn	93	61	.604	...
New York	86	68	.558	7
Cincinnati	82	71	.536	10.5
Pittsburgh	79	75	.513	14
Chicago	75	79	.487	18
St. Louis	75	79	.487	18
Boston	62	90	.408	30
Philadelphia	62	91	.405	30.5

SIGNIFICANT EVENTS

- **January 5:** The New York Yankees acquired pitcher-outfielder Babe Ruth from Boston Red Sox owner Harry Frazee for the incredible price of $125,000.
- **February 9:** Baseball's joint rules committee banned the use of all foreign substances and ball-doctoring methods used by pitchers.
- **September 28:** A Chicago grand jury indicted eight White Sox players, including star center fielder Joe Jackson, for conspiring to fix the 1919 World Series. All eight were immediately suspended by Chicago owner Charles Comiskey.

MEMORABLE MOMENTS

- **May 1:** Boston's Joe Oeschger and Brooklyn's Leon Cadore traded pitches for a Major League-record 26 innings in a game that ended in a 1-1 tie at Braves Field.
- **May 14:** Washington great Walter Johnson defeated Detroit for his 300th career victory.
- **August 17:** Cleveland shortstop Ray Chapman died a day after he was hit on the head by a pitch from Yankee righthander Carl Mays.
- **October 2:** Pittsburgh and Cincinnati played the century's only tripleheader.
- **October 3:** Browns first baseman George Sisler collected his record-setting 257th hit of the season.

LEADERS

American League

BA: George Sisler, St.L., .407.
Runs: Babe Ruth, N.Y., 158.
Hits: George Sisler, St.L., 257.
TB: George Sisler, St.L., 399.
HR: Babe Ruth, N.Y., 54.
RBI: Babe Ruth, N.Y., 137.
SB: Sam Rice, Wash., 63.
Wins: Jim Bagby, Cle., 31.
ERA: Bob Shawkey, N.Y., 2.45.
CG: Jim Bagby, Cle., 30.
IP: Jim Bagby, Cle., 339.2.
SO: Stan Coveleski, Cle., 133.

National League

BA: Rogers Hornsby, St.L., .370.
Runs: George Burns, N.Y., 115.
Hits: Rogers Hornsby, St.L., 218.
TB: Rogers Hornsby, St.L., 329.
HR: Cy Williams, Phil., 15.
RBI: Rogers Hornsby, St.L.; George Kelly, N.Y., 94.
SB: Max Carey, Pit., 52.
Wins: Grover Alexander, Chi., 27.
ERA: Grover Alexander, Chi., 1.91.
CG: Grover Alexander, Chi., 33.
IP: Grover Alexander, Chi., 363.1.
SO: Grover Alexander, Chi., 173.

A.L. 20-game winners
Jim Bagby, Cle., 31-12
Carl Mays, N.Y., 26-11
Stan Coveleski, Cle., 24-14
Red Faber, Chi., 23-13
Lefty Williams, Chi., 22-14
Dickie Kerr, Chi., 21-9
Ed Cicotte, Chi., 21-10
Ray Caldwell, Cle., 20-10
Urban Shocker, St.L., 20-10
Bob Shawkey, N.Y., 20-13

N.L. 20-game winners
Grover Alexander, Chi., 27-14
Wilbur Cooper, Pit., 24-15
Burleigh Grimes, Brk., 23-11
Fred Toney, N.Y., 21-11
Art Nehf, N.Y., 21-12
Bill Doak, St.L., 20-12
Jess Barnes, N.Y., 20-15

A.L. 100 RBIs
Babe Ruth, N.Y., 137
Bill Jacobson, St.L., 122
George Sisler, St.L., 122
Joe Jackson, Chi., 121
Larry Gardner, Cle., 118
Happy Felsch, Chi., 115
Bobby Veach, Det., 113
Tris Speaker, Cle., 107
Elmer Smith, Cle., 103

A.L. 40 homers
Babe Ruth, N.Y., 54

WORLD SERIES

- **Winner:** The Indians, Series newcomers, held off the Dodgers in a seven-game fall classic filled with memorable firsts.
- **Turning point:** Stan Coveleski's second win, a 5-1 Game 4 decision, that knotted the Series at two and set up a dramatic Game 5.
- **Memorable moments:** There were several for the Indians in Game 5. Elmer Smith hit the first grand slam in Series history, Jim Bagby became the first pitcher to hit a Series homer and second baseman Bill Wambsganss pulled off the first Series triple play — unassisted.
- **Top guns:** Coveleski (3-0, 0.67 ERA), Smith (.308, 5 RBIs), Indians; Zack Wheat (.333), Dodgers.

Linescores

Game 1—October 5, at Brooklyn
Cleveland........ 0 2 0 1 0 0 0 0 0 — 3 5 0
Brooklyn......... 0 0 0 0 0 0 1 0 0 — 1 5 1
Coveleski; Marquard, Mamaux (7), Cadore (9). W—Coveleski. L—Marquard.

Game 2—October 6, at Brooklyn
Cleveland........ 0 0 0 0 0 0 0 0 0 — 0 7 1
Brooklyn......... 1 0 1 0 1 0 0 0 x — 3 7 0
Bagby, Uhle (7); Grimes. W—Grimes. L—Bagby.

Game 3—October 7, at Brooklyn
Cleveland........ 0 0 0 1 0 0 0 0 0 — 1 3 1
Brooklyn......... 2 0 0 0 0 0 0 0 x — 2 6 1
Caldwell, Mails (1), Uhle (8); S. Smith. W—S. Smith. L—Caldwell.

Game 4—October 9, at Cleveland
Brooklyn......... 0 0 0 1 0 0 0 0 0 — 1 5 1
Cleveland........ 2 0 2 0 0 1 0 0 x — 5 12 2
Cadore, Mamaux (2), Marquard (3), Pfeffer (6); Coveleski. W—Coveleski. L—Cadore.

Game 5—October 10, at Cleveland
Brooklyn......... 0 0 0 0 0 0 0 0 1 — 1 13 1
Cleveland........ 4 0 0 3 1 0 0 0 x — 8 12 2
Grimes, Mitchell (4); Bagby. W—Bagby. L—Grimes. HR—E. Smith, Bagby (Cle.).

Game 6—October 11, at Cleveland
Brooklyn......... 0 0 0 0 0 0 0 0 0 — 0 3 0
Cleveland........ 0 0 0 0 0 1 0 0 x — 1 7 3
S. Smith; Mails. W—Mails. L—S. Smith.

Game 7—October 12, at Cleveland
Brooklyn......... 0 0 0 0 0 0 0 0 0 — 0 5 2
Cleveland........ 0 0 0 1 1 0 1 0 x — 3 7 3
Grimes, Mamaux (8); Coveleski. W—Coveleski. L—Grimes.

1921

FINAL STANDINGS

American League

Team	W	L	Pct.	GB
New York	98	55	.641	...
Cleveland	94	60	.610	4.5
St. Louis	81	73	.526	17.5
Washington	80	73	.523	18
Boston	75	79	.487	23.5
Detroit	71	82	.464	27
Chicago	62	92	.403	36.5
Philadelphia	53	100	.346	45

National League

Team	W	L	Pct.	GB
New York	94	59	.614	...
Pittsburgh	90	63	.588	4
St. Louis	87	66	.569	7
Boston	79	74	.516	15
Brooklyn	77	75	.507	16.5
Cincinnati	70	83	.458	24
Chicago	64	89	.418	30
Philadelphia	51	103	.331	43.5

SIGNIFICANT EVENTS

- **January 21:** Federal Judge Kenesaw Mountain Landis began his seven-year contract as baseball's first commissioner.
- **August 3:** Commissioner Landis banned eight Chicago White Sox players from baseball for life, even though a Chicago jury had cleared them of charges that they conspired to fix the 1919 World Series.
- **August 5:** Pittsburgh radio station KDKA did the first Major League baseball broadcast—a Pirates-Phillies game at Forbes Field.
- **October 5:** Pittsburgh radio station KDKA broadcast the opening game of the Yankees-Giants World Series.
- **October 21:** Commissioner Landis suspended Babe Ruth and Yankee teammates Bob Meusel and Bill Piercy for their illegal barnstorming tour after the 1921 World Series.

MEMORABLE MOMENTS

- **August 19:** Detroit's Ty Cobb collected career hit No. 3,000 off Boston pitcher Elmer Myers.
- **October 2:** Babe Ruth connected for record home run No. 59 off Boston's Curt Fullerton.

LEADERS

American League

BA: Harry Heilmann, Det., .394.
Runs: Babe Ruth, N.Y., 177.
Hits: Harry Heilmann, Det., 237.
TB: Babe Ruth, N.Y., 457.
HR: Babe Ruth, N.Y., 59.
RBI: Babe Ruth, N.Y., 171.
SB: George Sisler, St.L., 35.
Wins: Carl Mays, N.Y.; Urban Shocker, St.L., 27.
ERA: Red Faber, Chi., 2.48.
CG: Red Faber, Chi., 32.
IP: Carl Mays, N.Y., 336.2.
SO: Walter Johnson, Wash., 143.

National League

BA: Rogers Hornsby, St.L., .397.
Runs: Rogers Hornsby, St.L., 131.
Hits: Rogers Hornsby, St.L., 235.
TB: Rogers Hornsby, St.L., 378.
HR: George Kelly, N.Y., 23.
RBI: Rogers Hornsby, St.L., 126.
SB: Frank Frisch, N.Y., 49.
Wins: Wilbur Cooper, Pit.; Burleigh Grimes, Brk., 22.
ERA: Bill Doak, St.L., 2.59.
CG: Burleigh Grimes, Brk., 30.
IP: Wilbur Cooper, Pit., 327.
SO: Burleigh Grimes, Brk., 136.

A.L. 20-game winners

Carl Mays, N.Y., 27-9
Urban Shocker, St.L., 27-12
Red Faber, Chi., 25-15
Stan Coveleski, Cle., 23-13
Sam Jones, Bos., 23-16

N.L. 20-game winners

Burleigh Grimes, Brk., 22-13
Wilbur Cooper, Pit., 22-14
Art Nehf, N.Y., 20-10
Joe Oeschger, Bos., 20-14

A.L. 100 RBIs

Babe Ruth, N.Y., 170
Harry Heilmann, Det., 139
Bob Meusel, N.Y., 135
Bobby Veach, Det., 128
Ken Williams, St.L., 117
Larry Gardner, Cle., 115
George Sisler, St.L., 104
Ty Cobb, Det., 101
Tilly Walker, Phil., 101
Del Pratt, Bos., 100

N.L. 100 RBIs

Rogers Hornsby, St.L., 126
George Kelly, N.Y., 122
Austin McHenry, St.L., 102
Ross Youngs, N.Y., 102
Frank Frisch, N.Y., 100

A.L. 40 homers

Babe Ruth, N.Y., 59

WORLD SERIES

- **Winner:** The Giants shook the ghosts of Series past and rallied for an eight-game victory in the battle of New York.
- **Turning point:** Down two games to none and trailing 4-0 in the third inning of Game 3, the Giants rallied for a 13-5 victory.
- **Memorable moment:** An unusual 4-3-5 double play that finished off Art Nehf's 1-0 Game 8 victory over Yankee Waite Hoyt and provided a dramatic conclusion to the Series.
- **Top guns:** Jesse Barnes (2-0, 1.65 ERA), Frank Snyder (.364), Irish Meusel (.345, 7 RBIs), Giants; Hoyt (2-1, 0.00), Yankees.

Linescores

Game 1—October 5, at Polo Grounds
Yankees.......... 1 0 0 0 1 1 0 0 0 — 3 7 0
Giants............ 0 0 0 0 0 0 0 0 0 — 0 5 0
Mays; Douglas, Barnes (9). W—Mays. L—Douglas.

Game 2—October 6, at Polo Grounds
Giants............ 0 0 0 0 0 0 0 0 0 — 0 2 3
Yankees.......... 0 0 0 1 0 0 0 2 x — 3 3 0
Nehf; Hoyt. W—Hoyt. L—Nehf.

Game 3—October 7, at Polo Grounds
Yankees.......... 0 0 4 0 0 0 0 1 0 — 5 8 0
Giants............ 0 0 4 0 0 0 8 1 x — 13 20 0
Shawkey, Quinn (3), Collins (7), Rogers (7); Toney, Barnes (3). W—Barnes. L—Quinn.

Game 4—October 9, at Polo Grounds
Giants............ 0 0 0 0 0 0 0 3 1 — 4 9 1
Yankees.......... 0 0 0 0 1 0 0 0 1 — 2 7 1
Douglas; Mays. W—Douglas. L—Mays. HR—Ruth (NYY).

Game 5—October 10, at Polo Grounds
Yankees.......... 0 0 1 2 0 0 0 0 0 — 3 6 1
Giants............ 1 0 0 0 0 0 0 0 0 — 1 10 1
Hoyt; Nehf. W—Hoyt. L—Nehf.

Game 6—October 11, at Polo Grounds
Giants............ 0 3 0 4 0 1 0 0 0 — 8 13 0
Yankees.......... 3 2 0 0 0 0 0 0 0 — 5 7 2
Toney, Barnes (1); Harper, Shawkey (2), Piercy (9). W—Barnes. L—Shawkey. HR—E. Meusel, Snyder (NYG); Fewster (NYY).

Game 7—October 12, at Polo Grounds
Yankees.......... 0 1 0 0 0 0 0 0 0 — 1 8 1
Giants............ 0 0 0 1 0 0 1 0 x — 2 6 0
Mays; Douglas. W—Douglas. L—Mays.

Game 8—October 13, at Polo Grounds
Giants............ 1 0 0 0 0 0 0 0 0 — 1 6 0
Yankees.......... 0 0 0 0 0 0 0 0 0 — 0 4 1
Nehf; Hoyt. W—Nehf. L—Hoyt.

1922

FINAL STANDINGS

American League

Team	W	L	Pct.	GB
New York	94	60	.610	...
St. Louis	93	61	.604	1
Detroit	79	75	.513	15
Cleveland	78	76	.506	16
Chicago	77	77	.500	17
Washington	69	85	.448	25
Philadelphia	65	89	.422	29
Boston	61	93	.396	33

National League

Team	W	L	Pct.	GB
New York	93	61	.604	...
Cincinnati	86	68	.558	7
Pittsburgh	85	69	.552	8
St. Louis	85	69	.552	8
Chicago	80	74	.519	13
Brooklyn	76	78	.494	17
Philadelphia	57	96	.373	35.5
Boston	53	100	.346	39.5

SIGNIFICANT EVENTS

- **March 5:** Babe Ruth signed a three-year Yankee contract for a record $52,000 per season.
- **September 21:** Browns first baseman George Sisler, a .420 hitter, was the choice of A.L. baseball writers for the first MVP award presented since 1914.
- **October:** The World Series returned to a best-of-seven format and the entire Series was broadcast over the radio.

MEMORABLE MOMENTS

- **April 30:** Chicago rookie Charlie Robertson became the third modern-era pitcher to throw a perfect game, retiring all 27 Tigers he faced in a 2-0 victory at Detroit.
- **May 7:** Giants righthander Jesse Barnes pitched a 6-0 no-hitter against Philadelphia, an effort blemished only by a fifth-inning walk.
- **June 28:** Washington fireballer Walter Johnson outdueled New York ace Waite Hoyt and recorded his 95th career shutout with a 1-0 victory at Griffith Stadium.
- **August 25:** Chicago and Philadelphia combined for a record 49 runs and 51 hits in the Cubs' 26-23 victory at Wrigley Field.
- **September 18:** The New York Yankees ended George Sisler's modern-era record hitting streak at 41 games during a 3-2 victory over the Browns.
- **October 1:** Cardinals second baseman Rogers Hornsby became baseball's third Triple Crown winner when he finished the season at .401 with 42 homers and 152 RBI.

LEADERS

American League

BA: George Sisler, St.L., .420.
Runs: George Sisler, St.L., 134.
Hits: George Sisler, St.L., 246.
TB: Ken Williams, St.L., 367.
HR: Ken Williams, St.L., 39.
RBI: Ken Williams, St.L., 155.
SB: George Sisler, St.L., 51.
Wins: Eddie Rommel, Phil., 27.
ERA: Red Faber, Chi., 2.81.
CG: Red Faber, Chi., 31.
IP: Red Faber, Chi., 352.
SO: Urban Shocker, St.L., 149.

National League

BA: Rogers Hornsby, St.L., .401.
Runs: Rogers Hornsby, St.L., 141.
Hits: Rogers Hornsby, St.L., 250.
TB: Rogers Hornsby, St.L., 450.
HR: Rogers Hornsby, St.L., 42.
RBI: Rogers Hornsby, St.L., 152.
SB: Max Carey, Pit., 51.
Wins: Eppa Rixey, Cin., 25.
ERA: Phil Douglas, N.Y., 2.63.
CG: Wilbur Cooper, Pit., 27.
IP: Eppa Rixey, Cin., 313.1.
SO: Dazzy Vance, Brk., 134.

A.L. 20-game winners

Eddie Rommel, Phil., 27-13
Joe Bush, N.Y., 26-7
Urban Shocker, St.L., 24-17
George Uhle, Cle., 22-16
Red Faber, Chi., 21-17
Bob Shawkey, N.Y., 20-12

N.L. 20-game winners

Eppa Rixey, Cin., 25-13
Wilbur Cooper, Pit., 23-14
Dutch Ruether, Brk., 21-12

A.L. 100 RBIs

Ken Williams, St.L., 155
Bobby Veach, Det., 126
Marty McManus, St.L., 109
George Sisler, St.L., 105
Bill Jacobson, St.L., 102

N.L. 100 RBIs

Rogers Hornsby, St.L., 152
Irish Meusel, N.Y., 132
Zack Wheat, Brk., 112
George Kelly, N.Y., 107

N.L 40 homers

Rogers Hornsby, St.L., 42

League MVP

A.L.: George Sisler, 1B, St.L.
N.L.: No selection.

WORLD SERIES

- **Winner:** The all-New York rematch had the same result, the Giants winning this time in five games.
- **Turning point:** A 3-3 Game 2 tie that took away the Yankees' best hope for a victory.
- **Memorable moment:** Giants lefthander Art Nehf closing out the Yankees in the Series finale for the second straight year.
- **Top guns:** Heinie Groh (.474), Frankie Frisch (.471), Irish Meusel (7 RBIs), Giants.

Linescores

Game 1—October 4, at Polo Grounds
Yankees.......... 0 0 0 0 0 1 1 0 0 — 2 7 0
Giants............ 0 0 0 0 0 0 0 3 x — 3 11 3
Bush, Hoyt (8); Nehf, Ryan (8). W—Ryan. L—Bush.

Game 2—October 5, at Polo Grounds
Giants............ 3 0 0 0 0 0 0 0 0 0 — 3 8 1
Yankees.......... 1 0 0 1 0 0 0 1 0 0 — 3 8 0
J. Barnes; Shawkey. HR—E. Meusel (NYG); Ward (NYY). Game called after 10 innings because of darkness.

Game 3—October 6, at Polo Grounds
Yankees.......... 0 0 0 0 0 0 0 0 0 — 0 4 1
Giants............ 0 0 2 0 0 0 1 0 x — 3 12 1
Hoyt, Jones (8); J. Scott. W—J. Scott. L—Hoyt.

Game 4—October 7, at Polo Grounds
Giants............ 0 0 0 0 4 0 0 0 0 — 4 9 1
Yankees.......... 2 0 0 0 0 0 1 0 0 — 3 8 0
McQuillan; Mays, Jones (9). W—McQuillan. L—Mays. HR—Ward (NYY).

Game 5—October 8, at Polo Grounds
Yankees.......... 1 0 0 0 1 0 1 0 0 — 3 5 0
Giants............ 0 2 0 0 0 0 0 3 x — 5 10 0
Bush; Nehf. W—Nehf. L—Bush.

1923

FINAL STANDINGS

American League

Team	W	L	Pct.	GB
New York	98	54	.645	...
Detroit	83	71	.539	16
Cleveland	82	71	.536	16.5
Washington	75	78	.490	23.5
St. Louis	74	78	.487	24
Philadelphia	69	83	.454	29
Chicago	69	85	.448	30
Boston	61	91	.401	37

National League

Team	W	L	Pct.	GB
New York	95	58	.621	...
Cincinnati	91	63	.591	4.5
Pittsburgh	87	67	.565	8.5
Chicago	83	71	.539	12.5
St. Louis	79	74	.516	16
Brooklyn	76	78	.494	19.5
Boston	54	100	.351	41.5
Philadelphia	50	104	.325	45.5

SIGNIFICANT EVENTS

■ **April 18:** A Major League-record 74,217 fans watched Babe Ruth christen new Yankee Stadium with a three-run homer that sparked a 4-1 victory over Boston.

MEMORABLE MOMENTS

■ **May 2:** New York Yankee shortstop Everett Scott was honored when his ironman streak reached 1,000 games.
■ **May 11:** The Phillies defeated the Cardinals 20-14 in a game that featured 10 homers—three by Philadelphia's Cy Williams.
■ **July 7:** Cleveland, scoring in each of its eight at-bats, set an A.L. record for runs in a 27-3 victory over Boston.
■ **July 22:** Washington's Walter Johnson fanned five Indians and became the first pitcher to record 3,000 career strikeouts.
■ **September 7:** Boston's Howard Ehmke, duplicating the no-hit feat of New York Yankee Sam Jones three days earlier in the same stadium, stopped the Athletics 4-0 at Philadelphia.
■ **October 7:** St. Louis ended the regular season with a doubleheader split against the Cubs and Cardinals star Rogers Hornsby captured his fourth straight batting title with a .384 average.

LEADERS

American League
BA: Harry Heilmann, Det., .403.
Runs: Babe Ruth, N.Y., 151.
Hits: Charlie Jamieson, Cle., 222.
TB: Babe Ruth, N.Y., 399.
HR: Babe Ruth, N.Y., 41.
RBI: Babe Ruth, N.Y., 131.
SB: Eddie Collins, Chi., 49.
Wins: George Uhle, Cle., 26.
ERA: Stan Coveleski, Cle., 2.76.
CG: George Uhle, Cle., 29.
IP: George Uhle, Cle., 357.2.
SO: Walter Johnson, Wash., 130.

National League
BA: Rogers Hornsby, St.L., .384.
Runs: Ross Youngs, N.Y., 121.
Hits: Frank Frisch, N.Y., 223.
TB: Frank Frisch, N.Y., 311.
HR: Cy Williams, Phil., 41.
RBI: Irish Meusel, N.Y., 125.
SB: Max Carey, Pit., 51.
Wins: Dolf Luque, Cin., 27.
ERA: Dolf Luque, Cin., 1.93.
CG: Burleigh Grimes, Brk., 33.
IP: Burleigh Grimes, Brk., 327.
SO: Dazzy Vance, Brk., 197.

A.L. 20-game winners
George Uhle, Cle., 26-16
Sam Jones, N.Y., 21-8
Hooks Dauss, Det., 21-13
Urban Shocker, St.L., 20-12
Howard Ehmke, Bos., 20-17

N.L. 20-game winners
Dolf Luque, Cin., 27-8
Johnny Morrison, Pit., 25-13
Grover Alexander, Chi., 22-12
Pete Donohue, Cin., 21-15
Burleigh Grimes, Brk., 21-18
Jesse Haines, St.L., 20-13
Eppa Rixey, Cin., 20-15

A.L. 100 RBIs
Babe Ruth, N.Y., 130
Tris Speaker, Cle., 130
Harry Heilmann, Det., 115
Joe Sewell, Cle., 109
Wally Pipp, N.Y., 108

N.L. 100 RBIs
Irish Meusel, N.Y., 125
Cy Williams, Phil., 114
Frank Frisch, N.Y., 111
George Kelly, N.Y., 103
Jack Fournier, Brk., 102
Pie Traynor, Pit., 101

A.L. 40 homers
Babe Ruth, N.Y., 41

N.L. 40 homers
Cy Williams, Phil., 41

League MVP
A.L.: Babe Ruth, OF, N.Y.
N.L.: No selection.

WORLD SERIES

■ **Winner:** The third Series was a charm for the Yankees, who ascended to baseball's throne with a six-game victory over the Giants.

■ **Turning point:** A three-hit Game 5 performance by Joe Bush that helped the Yankees claim an 8-1 victory and a 3-2 Series lead.

■ **Memorable moment:** Veteran Casey Stengel chugging around the bases on a ninth-inning inside-the-park home run that gave the Giants a 5-4 Game 1 victory in the first Series contest at new Yankee Stadium.

■ **Top guns:** Aaron Ward (.417), Babe Ruth (.368, 3 HR), Yankees; Stengel (.417, 2 HR), Giants.

Linescores

Game 1—October 10, at Yankee Stadium
Giants............ 0 0 4 0 0 0 0 0 1 — 5 8 0
Yankees.......... 1 2 0 0 0 0 1 0 0 — 4 12 1
Watson, Ryan (3); Hoyt, Bush (3). W—Ryan. L—Bush. HR—Stengel (NYG).

Game 2—October 11, at Polo Grounds
Yankees.......... 0 1 0 2 1 0 0 0 0 — 4 10 0
Giants............ 0 1 0 0 0 1 0 0 0 — 2 9 2
Pennock; McQuillan, Bentley (4). W—Pennock. L—McQuillan. HR—Ward, Ruth 2 (NYY); E. Meusel (NYG).

Game 3—October 12, at Yankee Stadium
Giants............ 0 0 0 0 0 0 1 0 0 — 1 4 0
Yankees.......... 0 0 0 0 0 0 0 0 0 — 0 6 1
Nehf; Jones, Bush (9). W—Nehf. L—Jones. HR—Stengel (NYG).

Game 4—October 13, at Polo Grounds
Yankees.......... 0 6 1 1 0 0 0 0 0 — 8 13 1
Giants............ 0 0 0 0 0 0 0 3 1 — 4 13 1
Shawkey, Pennock (8); J. Scott, Ryan (2), McQuillan (2), Jonnard (8), Barnes (9). W—Shawkey. L—J. Scott. HR—Youngs (NYG).

Game 5—October 14, at Yankee Stadium
Giants............ 0 1 0 0 0 0 0 0 0 — 1 3 2
Yankees.......... 3 4 0 1 0 0 0 0 x — 8 14 0
Bentley, J. Scott (2), Barnes (4), Jonnard (8); Bush. W—Bush. L—Bentley. HR—Dugan (NYY).

Game 6—October 15, at Polo Grounds
Yankees.......... 1 0 0 0 0 0 0 5 0 — 6 5 0
Giants............ 1 0 0 1 1 1 0 0 0 — 4 10 1
Pennock, Jones (8); Nehf, Ryan (8). W—Pennock. L—Nehf. HR—Ruth (NYY); Snyder (NYG).

1924

FINAL STANDINGS

American League

Team	W	L	Pct.	GB
Washington	92	62	.597	...
New York	89	63	.586	2
Detroit	86	68	.558	6
St. Louis	74	78	.487	17
Philadelphia	71	81	.467	20
Cleveland	67	86	.438	24.5
Boston	67	87	.435	25
Chicago	66	87	.431	25.5

National League

Team	W	L	Pct.	GB
New York	93	60	.608	...
Brooklyn	92	62	.597	1.5
Pittsburgh	90	63	.588	3
Cincinnati	83	70	.542	10
Chicago	81	72	.529	12
St. Louis	65	89	.422	28.5
Philadelphia	55	96	.364	37
Boston	53	100	.346	40

SIGNIFICANT EVENTS

■ **March 7:** Reds manager Pat Moran died of Bright's disease at a hospital in Orlando, Fla., the team's spring training home.
■ **December 10:** National League owners accepted a proposal to go to a 2-3-2 World Series format.

MEMORABLE MOMENTS

■ **June 13:** The Yankees were awarded a 9-0 forfeit victory over the Tigers when a ninth-inning players' fight escalated into a full-scale fan riot at Detroit's Navin Field, creating a life-threatening situation for players, umpires and police.
■ **July 16:** Giants first baseman George Kelly set a Major League record when he homered in his sixth consecutive game—an 8-7 victory over the Pirates.
■ **September 16:** Jim Bottomley collected six hits, belted two homers and drove in a single-game record 12 runs in St. Louis' 17-3 victory over Brooklyn.
■ **September 28:** Cardinals second baseman Rogers Hornsby finished the season with the highest average in baseball history—.424.

LEADERS

American League
BA: Babe Ruth, N.Y., .378.
Runs: Babe Ruth, N.Y., 143.
Hits: Sam Rice, Wash., 216.
TB: Babe Ruth, N.Y., 391.
HR: Babe Ruth, N.Y., 46.
RBI: Goose Goslin, Wash., 129.
SB: Eddie Collins, Chi., 42.
Wins: Walter Johnson, Wash., 23.
ERA: Walter Johnson, Wash., 2.72.
CG: Sloppy Thurston, Chi., 28.
IP: Howard Ehmke, Bos., 315.
SO: Walter Johnson, Wash., 158.

National League
BA: Rogers Hornsby, St.L., .424.
Runs: Frank Frisch, N.Y.; Rogers Hornsby, St.L., 121.
Hits: Rogers Hornsby, St.L., 227.
TB: Rogers Hornsby, St.L., 373.
HR: Jack Fournier, Brk., 27.
RBI: George Kelly, N.Y., 136.
SB: Max Carey, Pit., 49.
Wins: Dazzy Vance, Brk., 28.
ERA: Dazzy Vance, Brk., 2.16.
CG: Burleigh Grimes, Brk.; Dazzy Vance, Brk., 30.
IP: Burleigh Grimes, Brk., 310.2.
SO: Dazzy Vance, Brk., 262.

A.L. 20-game winners
Walter Johnson, Wash., 23-7
Herb Pennock, N.Y., 21-9
Sloppy Thurston, Chi., 20-14
Joe Shaute, Cle., 20-17

N.L. 20-game winners
Dazzy Vance, Brk., 28-6
Burleigh Grimes, Brk., 22-13
Carl Mays, Cin., 20-9
Wilbur Cooper, Pit., 20-14

A.L. 100 RBIs
Goose Goslin, Wash., 129
Babe Ruth, N.Y., 121
Bob Meusel, N.Y., 120
Joe Hauser, Phil., 115
Harry Heilmann, Det., 113
Wally Pipp, N.Y., 113
Joe Sewell, Cle., 104
Earl Sheely, Chi., 103
Al Simmons, Phil., 102

N.L. 100 RBIs
George Kelly, N.Y., 136
Jack Fournier, Brk., 116
Jim Bottomley, St.L., 111
Glenn Wright, Pit., 111
Irish Meusel, N.Y., 102

A.L. 40 homers
Babe Ruth, N.Y., 46

League MVP
A.L.: Walter Johnson, P, Wash.
N.L.: Dazzy Vance, P, Brk.

WORLD SERIES

■ **Winner:** The Senators made their first appearance in baseball's fall classic a successful one.

■ **Turning point:** A dramatic 2-1 Game 6 victory that kept Washington's hopes alive. Tom Zachary allowed seven hits and player/manager Bucky Harris drove in both runs with a fifth-inning single.

■ **Memorable moment:** Earl McNeely's 12th-inning Game 7 ground ball that took an inexplicable hop over third baseman Fred Lindstrom's head and gave the Senators a Series-ending 4-3 victory.

■ **Top guns:** Zachary (2-0, 2.04 ERA), Goose Goslin (.344, 3 HR, 7 RBIs), Harris (.333, 7 RBIs), Senators; Bill Terry (.429), Giants.

Linescores

Game 1—October 4, at Washington
N,Y,.........0 1 0 1 0 0 0 0 0 0 0 2 — 4 14 1
Wash.....0 0 0 0 0 1 0 0 1 0 0 1 — 3 10 1
Nehf; Johnson. W—Nehf. L—Johnson. HR—Kelly, Terry (N.Y.).

Game 2—October 5, at Washington
N.Y. .... 0 0 0 0 0 0 1 0 2 — 3 6 0
Wash............. 2 0 0 0 1 0 0 0 1 — 4 6 1
Bentley; Zachary, Marberry (9). W—Zachary. L—Bentley. HR—Goslin, Harris (Wash.).

Game 3—October 6, at New York
Wash............. 0 0 0 2 0 0 0 1 1 — 4 9 2
N.Y. .... 0 2 1 1 0 1 0 1 x — 6 12 0
Marberry, Russell (4), Martina (7), Speece (8); McQuillan, Ryan (4), Jonnard (9), Watson (9). W—McQuillan. L—Marberry. HR—Ryan (N.Y.).

Game 4—October 7, at New York
Wash............. 0 0 3 0 2 0 0 2 0 — 7 13 3
N.Y. .... 1 0 0 0 0 1 0 1 1 — 4 6 1
Mogridge, Marberry (8); Barnes, Baldwin (6), Dean (8). W—Mogridge. L—Barnes. HR—Goslin (Wash.).

Game 5—October 8, at New York
Wash............. 0 0 0 1 0 0 0 1 0 — 2 9 1
N.Y. .... 0 0 1 0 2 0 0 3 x — 6 13 0
Johnson; Bentley, McQuillan (8). W—Bentley. L—Johnson. HR—Bentley (N.Y.); Goslin (Wash.).

Game 6—October 9, at Washington
N.Y. .... 1 0 0 0 0 0 0 0 0 — 1 7 1
Wash............. 0 0 0 0 2 0 0 0 x — 2 4 0
Nehf, Ryan (8); Zachary. W—Zachary. L—Nehf.

Game 7—October 10, at Washington
N.Y.........0 0 0 0 0 3 0 0 0 0 0 0 — 3 8 3
Wash.....0 0 0 1 0 0 0 2 0 0 0 1 — 4 10 4
Barnes, Nehf (8), McQuillan (9), Bentley (11); Ogden, Mogridge (1), Marberry (6), Johnson (9). W—Johnson. L—Bentley. HR—Harris (Wash.).

1925

FINAL STANDINGS

American League

Team	W	L	Pct.	GB
Washington	96	55	.636	...
Philadelphia	88	64	.579	8.5
St. Louis	82	71	.536	15
Detroit	81	73	.526	16.5
Chicago	79	75	.513	18.5
Cleveland	70	84	.455	27.5
New York	69	85	.448	28.5
Boston	47	105	.309	49.5

National League

Team	W	L	Pct.	GB
Pittsburgh	95	58	.621	...
New York	86	66	.566	8.5
Cincinnati	80	73	.523	15
St. Louis	77	76	.503	18
Boston	70	83	.458	25
Brooklyn	68	85	.444	27
Philadelphia	68	85	.444	27
Chicago	68	86	.442	27.5

SIGNIFICANT EVENTS

■ **April 17:** Yankee slugger Babe Ruth underwent surgery for an intestinal abscess, an injury that would sideline him until June 1.

■ **April 18:** Brooklyn owner Charles Ebbets died on the morning of his Dodgers' home opener against the Giants at Ebbets Field.

■ **October 7:** Christy Mathewson, considered by many the greatest pitcher in history, died after a five-year bout with tuberculosis at age 45.

MEMORABLE MOMENTS

■ **May 5:** Detroit's Ty Cobb enjoyed a six-hit, three-homer game against the Browns, setting a modern Major League record with 16 total bases.

■ **May 6:** Yankee manager Miller Huggins benched shortstop Everett Scott, ending his record consecutive-games streak at 1,307.

■ **May 17:** Cleveland's Tris Speaker collected career hit No. 3,000 off Washington lefthander Tom Zachary.

■ **June 3:** White Sox manager Eddie Collins joined baseball's select 3,000-hit circle in a game against Detroit.

■ **June 15:** The Philadelphia Athletics, trailing 15-4 in the eighth inning, exploded for 13 runs and a 17-15 victory over the Indians.

■ **October 4:** St. Louis manager Rogers Hornsby matched his 1922 Triple Crown feat when he finished with a .403 average, 39 home runs and 143 RBIs.

LEADERS

American League

BA: Harry Heilmann, Det., .393.
Runs: Johnny Mostil, Chi., 135.
Hits: Al Simmons, Phil., 253.
TB: Al Simmons, Phil., 392.
HR: Bob Meusel, N.Y., 33.
RBI: Bob Meusel, N.Y., 138.
SB: Johnny Mostil, Chi., 43.
Wins: Ted Lyons, Chi.; Eddie Rommel, Phil., 21.
ERA: Stan Coveleski, Wash., 2.84.
CG: Howard Ehmke, Bos.; Sherry Smith, Cle., 22.
IP: Herb Pennock, N.Y., 277.
SO: Lefty Grove, Phil., 116.

National League

BA: Rogers Hornsby, St.L., .403.
Runs: Kiki Cuyler, Pit., 144.
Hits: Jim Bottomley, St.L., 227.
TB: Rogers Hornsby, St.L., 381.
HR: Rogers Hornsby, St.L., 39.
RBI: Rogers Hornsby, St.L., 143.
SB: Max Carey, Pit., 46.
Wins: Dazzy Vance, Brk., 22.
ERA: Dolf Luque, Cin., 2.63.
CG: Pete Donohue, Cin., 27.
IP: Pete Donohue, Cin., 301.
SO: Dazzy Vance, Brk., 221.

A.L. 20-game winners

Eddie Rommel, Phil., 21-10
Ted Lyons, Chi., 21-11
Stan Coveleski, Wash., 20-5
Walter Johnson, Wash., 20-7

N.L. 20-game winners

Dazzy Vance, Brk., 22-9
Eppa Rixey, Cin., 21-11
Pete Donohue, Cin., 21-14

A.L. 100 RBIs

Bob Meusel, N.Y., 138
Harry Heilmann, Det., 133
Al Simmons, Phil., 129
Goose Goslin, Wash., 113
Earl Sheely, Chi., 111
George Sisler, St.L., 105
Ken Williams, St.L., 105
Ty Cobb, Det., 102

N.L. 100 RBIs

Rogers Hornsby, St.L., 143
Jack Fournier, Brk., 130
Jim Bottomley, St.L., 128
Glenn Wright, Pit., 121
Clyde Barnhart, Pit., 114
Irish Meusel, N.Y., 111
Pie Traynor, Pit., 106
Zack Wheat, Brk., 103
Kiki Cuyler, Pit., 102

League MVP

A.L.: Roger Peckinpaugh, SS, Wash.
N.L.: Rogers Hornsby, 2B, St.L.

WORLD SERIES

■ **Winner:** The Pirates became the first team to rally from a three-games-to-one Series deficit and ruined Washington's hopes for a repeat victory.

■ **Turning point:** A Game 6 home run by Eddie Moore that gave Pittsburgh a 3-2 victory and knotted the Series at three games apiece.

■ **Memorable moment:** Washington's 37-year-old Walter Johnson battling valiantly but coming up short in Pittsburgh's 9-7 Game 7 victory.

■ **Top guns:** Max Carey (.458), Pirates; Joe Harris (.440, 3 HR, 6 RBIs), Goose Goslin (3 HR, 6 RBIs), Senators.

Linescores

Game 1—October 7, at Pittsburgh
Washington.... 0 1 0 0 2 0 0 0 1 — 4 8 1
Pittsburgh...... 0 0 0 0 1 0 0 0 0 — 1 5 0
Johnson; Meadows, Morrison (9). W—Johnson. L—Meadows. HR—J. Harris (Wash.); Traynor (Pit.).

Game 2—October 8, at Pittsburgh
Washington.... 0 1 0 0 0 0 0 0 1 — 2 8 2
Pittsburgh...... 0 0 0 1 0 0 0 2 x — 3 7 0
Coveleski; Aldridge. W—Aldridge. L—Coveleski. HR—Judge (Wash.); Wright, Cuyler (Pit.).

Game 3—October 10, at Washington
Pittsburgh...... 0 1 0 1 0 1 0 0 0 — 3 8 3
Washington.... 0 0 1 0 0 1 2 0 x — 4 10 1
Kremer; Ferguson, Marberry (8). W—Ferguson. L—Kremer. HR—Goslin (Wash.).

Game 4—October 11, at Washington
Pittsburgh...... 0 0 0 0 0 0 0 0 0 — 0 6 1
Washington.... 0 0 4 0 0 0 0 0 x — 4 12 0
Yde, Morrison (3), C. Adams (8); Johnson. W—Johnson. L—Yde. HR—Goslin, J. Harris (Wash.).

Game 5—October 12, at Washington
Pittsburgh...... 0 0 2 0 0 0 2 1 1 — 6 13 0
Washington.... 1 0 0 1 0 0 1 0 0 — 3 8 1
Aldridge; Coveleski, Ballou (7), Zachary (8), Marberry (9). W—Aldridge. L—Coveleski. HR—J. Harris (Wash.).

Game 6—October 13, at Pittsburgh
Washington.... 1 1 0 0 0 0 0 0 0 — 2 6 2
Pittsburgh...... 0 0 2 0 1 0 0 0 x — 3 7 1
Ferguson, Ballou (8); Kremer. W—Kremer. L—Ferguson. HR—Goslin (Wash.); Moore (Pit.).

Game 7—October 15, at Pittsburgh
Washington.... 4 0 0 2 0 0 0 1 0 — 7 7 2
Pittsburgh...... 0 0 3 0 1 0 2 3 x — 9 15 2
Johnson; Aldridge, Morrison (1), Kremer (5), Oldham (9). W—Kremer. L—Johnson. HR—Peckinpaugh (Wash.).

1926

FINAL STANDINGS

American League

Team	W	L	Pct.	GB
New York	91	63	.591	...
Cleveland	88	66	.571	3
Philadelphia	83	67	.553	6
Washington	81	69	.540	8
Chicago	81	72	.529	9.5
Detroit	79	75	.513	12
St. Louis	62	92	.403	29
Boston	46	107	.301	44.5

National League

Team	W	L	Pct.	GB
St. Louis	89	65	.578	...
Cincinnati	87	67	.565	2
Pittsburgh	84	69	.549	4.5
Chicago	82	72	.532	7
New York	74	77	.490	13.5
Brooklyn	71	82	.464	17.5
Boston	66	86	.434	22
Philadelphia	58	93	.384	29.5

SIGNIFICANT EVENTS

■ **January 30:** The Major League rules committee granted pitchers permission to use a resin bag during the course of games.

■ **October 13:** Cleveland first baseman George Burns, who batted .358 with a record 64 doubles, captured A.L. MVP honors, even though the Yankees' Babe Ruth batted .372 with 47 homers and 146 RBIs.

■ **December 16:** Commissioner Kenesaw Mountain Landis was elected to a second seven-year term.

■ **December 20:** In a trade billed as the biggest in baseball history, Cardinals manager Rogers Hornsby was dealt to the Giants for second baseman Frank Frisch and pitcher Jimmy Ring.

■ **December 22:** Baseball greats Ty Cobb and Tris Speaker denied accusations by former Detroit pitcher Dutch Leonard that they had conspired to throw 1919 Tigers-Indians games and had bet on their outcome. The charges would be investigated by Commissioner Kenesaw Mountain Landis and later dismissed for lack of evidence.

MEMORABLE MOMENTS

■ **May 12:** Washington fireballer Walter Johnson defeated St. Louis, 7-4, and became baseball's second 400-game winner.

■ **May 21:** Chicago's Earl Sheely belted a home run and three doubles in a game against Boston, giving him a record seven consecutive extra-base hits.

LEADERS

American League

BA: Heinie Manush, Det., .378.
Runs: Babe Ruth, N.Y., 139.
Hits: George Burns, Cle.; Sam Rice, Wash., 216.
TB: Babe Ruth, N.Y., 365.
HR: Babe Ruth, N.Y., 47.
RBI: Babe Ruth, N.Y., 146.
SB: Johnny Mostil, Chi., 35.
Wins: George Uhle, Cle., 27.
ERA: Lefty Grove, Phil., 2.51.
CG: George Uhle, Cle., 32.
IP: George Uhle, Cle., 318.1.
SO: Lefty Grove, Phil., 194.

National League

BA: Bubbles Hargrave, Cin., .353.
Runs: Kiki Cuyler, Pit., 113.
Hits: Eddie Brown, Bos., 201.
TB: Jim Bottomley, St.L., 305.
HR: Hack Wilson, Chi., 21.
RBI: Jim Bottomley, St.L., 120.
SB: Kiki Cuyler, Pit., 35.
Wins: Pete Donohue, Cin.; Ray Kremer, Pit.; Lee Meadows, Pit.; Flint Rhem, St.L., 20.
ERA: Ray Kremer, Pit., 2.61.
CG: Carl Mays, Cin., 24.
IP: Pete Donohue, Cin., 285.2.
SO: Dazzy Vance, Brk., 140.

A.L. 20-game winners

George Uhle, Cle., 27-11
Herb Pennock, N.Y., 23-11

N.L. 20-game winners

Remy Kremer, Pit., 20-6
Flint Rhem, St.L., 20-7
Lee Meadows, Pit., 20-9
Pete Donohue, Cin., 20-14

A.L. 100 RBIs

Babe Ruth, N.Y., 146
George Burns, Cle., 114
Tony Lazzeri, N.Y., 114
Al Simmons, Phil., 109
Bibb Falk, Chi., 108
Goose Goslin, Wash., 108
Lou Gehrig, N.Y., 107
Harry Heilmann, Det., 103

N.L. 100 RBIs

Jim Bottomley, St.L., 120
Hack Wilson, Chi., 109
Les Bell, St.L., 100

A.L. 40 homers

Babe Ruth, N.Y., 47

League MVP

A.L.: George Burns, 1B, Cle.
N.L.: Bob O'Farrell, C, St.L.

WORLD SERIES

■ **Winner:** The Cardinals, making their first Series appearance, outlasted the Yankees in a seven-game classic.

■ **Turning point:** A Series-squaring 10-2 Cardinals victory in Game 6. Lester Bell homered and drove in four runs.

■ **Memorable moment:** The aging Grover Cleveland Alexander striking out Yankee slugger Tony Lazzeri with the bases loaded in the seventh inning of Game 7, saving the Cardinals.

■ **Top guns:** Jesse Haines (2-0, 1.08 ERA), Alexander (2-0, 1.33), Tommy Thevenow (.417), Cardinals; Babe Ruth (4 HR), Yankees.

Linescores

Game 1—October 2, at New York
St. Louis......... 1 0 0 0 0 0 0 0 0 — 1 3 1
New York........ 1 0 0 0 0 1 0 0 x — 2 6 0
Sherdel, Haines (8); Pennock. W—Pennock. L—Sherdel.

Game 2—October 3, at New York
St. Louis......... 0 0 2 0 0 0 3 0 1 — 6 12 1
New York........ 0 2 0 0 0 0 0 0 0 — 2 4 0
Alexander; Shocker, Shawkey (8), Jones (9). W—Alexander. L—Shawkey. HR—Southworth, Thevenow (St.L.).

Game 3—October 5, at St. Louis
New York........ 0 0 0 0 0 0 0 0 0 — 0 5 1
St. Louis......... 0 0 0 3 1 0 0 0 x — 4 8 0
Ruether, Shawkey (5), Thomas (8); Haines. W—Haines. L—Ruether. HR—Haines (St.L.).

Game 4—October 6, at St. Louis
New York........ 1 0 1 1 4 2 1 0 0 — 10 14 1
St. Louis......... 1 0 0 3 0 0 0 0 1 — 5 14 0
Hoyt; Rhem, Reinhart (5), H. Bell (5), Hallahan (7), Keen (9). W—Hoyt. L—Reinhart. HR—Ruth 3 (N.Y.).

Game 5—October 7, at St. Louis
New York........ 0 0 0 0 0 10 0 1 1—3 9 1
St. Louis......... 0 0 0 1 0 01 0 0 0—2 7 1
Pennock; Sherdel. W—Pennock. L—Sherdel.

Game 6—October 9, at New York
St. Louis......... 3 0 0 0 1 0 5 0 1 — 10 13 2
New York........ 0 0 0 1 0 0 1 0 0 — 2 8 1
Alexander; Shawkey, Shocker (7), Thomas (8). W—Alexander. L—Shawkey. HR—L. Bell (St.L.).

Game 7—October 10, at New York
St. Louis......... 0 0 0 3 0 0 0 0 0 — 3 8 0
New York........ 0 0 1 0 0 1 0 0 0 — 2 8 3
Haines, Alexander (7); Hoyt, Pennock (7). W—Haines. L—Hoyt. HR—Ruth (N.Y.).

1927

FINAL STANDINGS

American League

Team	W	L	Pct.	GB
New York	110	44	.714	...
Philadelphia	91	63	.591	19
Washington	85	69	.552	25
Detroit	82	71	.536	27.5
Chicago	70	83	.458	39.5
Cleveland	66	87	.431	43.5
St. Louis	59	94	.386	50.5
Boston	51	103	.331	59

National League

Team	W	L	Pct.	GB
Pittsburgh	94	60	.610	...
St. Louis	92	61	.601	1.5
New York	92	62	.597	2
Chicago	85	68	.556	8.5
Cincinnati	75	78	.490	18.5
Brooklyn	65	88	.425	28.5
Boston	60	94	.390	34
Philadelphia	51	103	.331	43

SIGNIFICANT EVENTS

- **March 3:** The Yankees made slugger Babe Ruth the highest paid player in baseball history, signing him for three years at a reported $70,000 per season.
- **October 17:** A.L. founder and 28-year president Ban Johnson retired, three days after 416-game winner Walter Johnson called it quits after 21 seasons with Washington.
- **October 22:** Ross Youngs, a .322 hitter over 10 seasons with the Giants, died of Bright's disease at age 30.
- **November 2:** E.S. Barnard was named new A.L. president, replacing Ban Johnson.

MEMORABLE MOMENTS

- **May 30-31:** Cubs shortstop Jimmy Cooney and Detroit first baseman Johnny Neun pulled off rare unassisted triple plays on consecutive days.
- **July 18:** Philadelphia's Ty Cobb opened a new club when he doubled against his former Detroit teammates for hit No. 4,000.
- **July 19:** The Cubs spoiled John McGraw Day at the Polo Grounds by beating the Giants. But fans enjoyed festivities honoring McGraw for his 25 years as New York manager.
- **September 30:** Yankee slugger Babe Ruth broke his own one-season record when he blasted home run No. 60 off Washington lefty Tom Zachary.

LEADERS

American League

BA: Harry Heilmann, Det., .398.
Runs: Babe Ruth, N.Y., 158.
Hits: Earle Combs, N.Y., 231.
TB: Lou Gehrig, N.Y., 447.
HR: Babe Ruth, N.Y., 60.
RBI: Lou Gehrig, N.Y., 175.
SB: George Sisler, St.L., 27.
Wins: Waite Hoyt, N.Y.; Ted Lyons, Chi., 22.
ERA: Wilcy Moore, N.Y., 2.28.
CG: Ted Lyons, Chi., 30.
IP: Ted Lyons, Chi.; Tommy Thomas, Chi., 307.2
SO: Lefty Grove, Phil., 174.

National League

BA: Paul Waner, Pit., .380.
Runs: Rogers Hornsby, N.Y.; Lloyd Waner, Pit., 133.
Hits: Paul Waner, Pit., 237.
TB: Paul Waner, Pit., 342.
HR: Cy Williams, Phil.; Hack Wilson, Chi., 30.
RBI: Paul Waner, Pit., 131.
SB: Frank Frisch, St.L., 48.
Wins: Charlie Root, Chi., 26.
ERA: Ray Kremer, Pit., 2.47.
CG: Jesse Haines, St.L.; Lee Meadows, Pit.; Dazzy Vance, Brk., 25.
IP: Charlie Root, Chi., 309.
SO: Dazzy Vance, Brk., 184.

A.L. 20-game winners
Waite Hoyt, N.Y., 22-7
Ted Lyons, Chi., 22-14
Lefty Grove, Phil., 20-13

N.L. 20-game winners
Charlie Root, Chi., 26-15
Jesse Haines, St.L., 24-10
Carmen Hill, Pit., 22-11
Grover Alexander, St.L., 21-10

A.L. 100 RBIs
Lou Gehrig, N.Y., 175
Babe Ruth, N.Y., 164
Goose Goslin, Wash., 120
Harry Heilmann, Det., 120
Bob Fothergill, Det., 114
Al Simmons, Phil., 108
Bob Meusel, N.Y., 103
Tony Lazzeri, N.Y., 102

N.L. 100 RBIs
Paul Waner, Pit., 131
Hack Wilson, Chi., 129
Rogers Hornsby, N.Y., 125
Jim Bottomley, St.L., 124
Bill Terry, N.Y., 121
Pie Traynor, Pit., 106
Glenn Wright, Pit., 105

A.L. 40 homers
Babe Ruth, N.Y., 60
Lou Gehrig, N.Y., 47

League MVP
A.L.: Lou Gehrig, 1B, N.Y.
N.L.: Paul Waner, OF, Pit.

WORLD SERIES

- **Winner:** The powerful Yankees made short work of the overmatched Pirates.
- **Turning point:** When the Pirates watched the Yankees take batting practice before Game 1.
- **Memorable moment:** Yankee Earle Combs dancing across the plate with the Series-ending run after a John Miljus wild pitch.
- **Top guns:** Wilcy Moore (1-0, 0.84 ERA), Herb Pennock (1-0, 1.00), Mark Koenig (.500), Babe Ruth (.400, 2 HR, 7 RBIs), Yankees; Lloyd Waner (.400), Pirates.

Linescores

Game 1—October 5, at Pittsburgh
New York........ 103 010 000 — 5 6 1
Pittsburgh...... 101 010 010 — 4 9 2
Hoyt, Moore (8); Kremer, Miljus (6). W—Hoyt. L—Kremer.

Game 2—October 6, at Pittsburgh
New York........ 003 000 030 — 6 11 0
Pittsburgh...... 100 000 010 — 2 7 2
Pipgras; Aldridge, Cvengros (8), Dawson (9). W—Pipgras. L—Aldridge.

Game 3—October 7, at New York
Pittsburgh...... 000 000 010 — 1 3 1
New York........ 200 000 60x — 8 9 0
Meadows, Cvengros (7); Pennock. W—Pennock. L—Meadows. HR—Ruth (N.Y.).

Game 4—October 8, at New York
Pittsburgh...... 100 000 200 — 3 10 1
New York........ 100 020 001 — 4 12 2
Hill, Miljus (7); Moore. W—Moore. L—Miljus. HR—Ruth (N.Y.).

1928

FINAL STANDINGS

American League

Team	W	L	Pct.	GB
New York	101	53	.656	...
Philadelphia	98	55	.641	2.5
St. Louis	82	72	.532	19
Washington	75	79	.487	26
Chicago	72	82	.468	29
Detroit	68	86	.442	33
Cleveland	62	92	.403	39
Boston	57	96	.373	43.5

National League

Team	W	L	Pct.	GB
St. Louis	95	59	.617	...
New York	93	61	.604	2
Chicago	91	63	.591	4
Pittsburgh	85	67	.559	9
Cincinnati	78	74	.513	16
Brooklyn	77	76	.503	17.5
Boston	50	103	.327	44.5
Philadelphia	43	109	.283	51

SIGNIFICANT EVENTS

- **May 14:** Giants manager John McGraw was hit by a car while crossing a street outside Chicago's Wrigley Field, an injury that would sideline him for six weeks.
- **September 9:** Urban Shocker, a 187-game winner for the Yankees and Browns, died of pneumonia at age 38.
- **November 7:** Massachusetts voters cleared the way for Sunday baseball in Boston, leaving Pennsylvania as the only state still enforcing the blue law.
- **December 13:** National League President John Heydler, contending fans were tired of watching weak-hitting pitchers try to bat, proposed a designated hitter rule that was voted down at the annual winter meetings.

MEMORABLE MOMENTS

- **July 21:** Philadelphia's Jimmie Foxx became the first player to hit a ball over the double-decked left-field stands of Shibe Park during a game against St. Louis.
- **September 3:** Athletics pinch-hitter Ty Cobb stroked his 724th career double and final career hit—No. 4,191—in a game against Washington.
- **September 28-29:** The New York Yankees clinched the A.L. pennant with a victory over the Tigers and the Cardinals closed out a tight N.L. race with a next-day win over the Braves.

LEADERS

American League

BA: Goose Goslin, Wash., .379.
Runs: Babe Ruth, N.Y., 163.
Hits: Heinie Manush, St.L., 241.
TB: Babe Ruth, N.Y., 380.
HR: Babe Ruth, N.Y., 54.
RBI: Lou Gehrig, N.Y.; Babe Ruth, N.Y., 142.
SB: Buddy Myer, Bos., 30.
Wins: Lefty Grove, Phil.; George Pipgras, N.Y., 24.
ERA: Garland Braxton, Wash., 2.51.
CG: Red Ruffing, Bos., 25.
IP: George Pipgras, N.Y., 300.2.
SO: Lefty Grove, Phil., 183.

National League

BA: Rogers Hornsby, Bos., .387.
Runs: Paul Waner, Pit., 142.
Hits: Fred Lindstrom, N.Y., 231.
TB: Jim Bottomley, St.L., 362.
HR: Jim Bottomley, St.L.; Hack Wilson, Chi., 31.
RBI: Jim Bottomley, St.L., 136.
SB: Kiki Cuyler, Chi., 37.
Wins: Larry Benton, N.Y.; Burleigh Grimes, Pit., 25.
ERA: Dazzy Vance, Brk., 2.09.
CG: Larry Benton, N.Y.; Burleigh Grimes, Pit., 28.
IP: Burleigh Grimes, Pit., 330.2.
SO: Dazzy Vance, Brk., 200.

A.L. 20-game winners
Lefty Grove, Phil., 24-8
George Pipgras, N.Y., 24-13
Waite Hoyt, N.Y., 23-7
General Crowder, St.L., 21-5
Sam Gray, St.L., 20-12

N.L. 20-game winners
Larry Benton, N.Y., 25-9
Burleigh Grimes, Pit., 25-14
Dazzy Vance, Brk., 22-10
Bill Sherdel, St.L., 21-10
Jesse Haines, St.L., 20-8
Fred Fitzsimmons, N.Y., 20-9

A.L. 100 RBIs
Lou Gehrig, N.Y., 142
Babe Ruth, N.Y., 142
Bob Meusel, N.Y., 113
Heinie Manush, St.L., 108
Harry Heilmann, Det., 107
Al Simmons, Phil., 107
Goose Goslin, Wash., 102

N.L. 100 RBIs
Jim Bottomley, St.L., 136
Pie Traynor, Pit., 124
Hack Wilson, Chi., 120
Chick Hafey, St.L., 111
Fred Lindstrom, N.Y., 107
Del Bissonette, Brk., 106
Pinky Whitney, Phil., 103
Bill Terry, N.Y., 101

A.L. 40 homers
Babe Ruth, N.Y., 54

League MVP
A.L.: Mickey Cochrane, C, Phil.
N.L.: Jim Bottomley, 1B, St.L.

WORLD SERIES

- **Winner:** The muscular Yankees swept aside St. Louis for their third Series victory of the decade.
- **Turning point:** A 9-3 second-game romp that made it clear the Cardinals were overmatched.
- **Memorable moment:** Babe Ruth's show-stealing three-home run performance in Game 4 at St. Louis' Sportsman's Park.
- **Top guns:** Waite Hoyt (2-0, 1.50 ERA), Ruth (.625, 3 HR), Lou Gehrig, (.545, 4 HR, 9 RBIs).

Linescores

Game 1—October 4, at New York
St. Louis......... 000 000 100 — 1 3 1
New York........ 100 200 01x — 4 7 0
Sherdel, Johnson (8); Hoyt. W—Hoyt. L—Sherdel. HR—Meusel (N.Y.); Bottomley (St.L.).

Game 2—October 5, at New York
St. Louis......... 030 000 000 — 3 4 1
New York........ 314 000 10x — 9 8 2
Alexander, Mitchell (3); Pipgras. W—Pipgras. L—Alexander. HR—Gehrig (N.Y.).

Game 3—October 7, at St. Louis
New York........ 010 203 100 — 7 7 2
St. Louis......... 200 010 000 — 3 9 3
Zachary; Haines, Johnson (7), Rhem (8). W—Zachary. L—Haines. HR—Gehrig 2 (N.Y.).

Game 4—October 9, at St. Louis
New York........ 000 100 420 — 7 15 2
St. Louis......... 001 100 001 — 3 11 0
Hoyt; Sherdel, Alexander (7). W—Hoyt. L—Sherdel. HR—Ruth 3, Durst, Gehrig (N.Y.).

HISTORY

1929

FINAL STANDINGS

American League

Team	W	L	Pct.	GB
Philadelphia	104	46	.693	...
New York	88	66	.571	18
Cleveland	81	71	.533	24
St. Louis	79	73	.520	26
Washington	71	81	.467	34
Detroit	70	84	.455	36
Chicago	59	93	.388	46
Boston	58	96	.377	48

National League

Team	W	L	Pct.	GB
Chicago	98	54	.645	...
Pittsburgh	88	65	.575	10.5
New York	84	67	.556	13.5
St. Louis	78	74	.513	20
Philadelphia	71	82	.464	27.5
Brooklyn	70	83	.458	28.5
Cincinnati	66	88	.429	33
Boston	56	98	.364	43

SIGNIFICANT EVENTS

- **January 22:** The Yankees announced an innovation: permanent numbers on the backs of uniforms corresponding to players' positions in the batting order.
- **September 25:** New York manager Miller Huggins, who led the Yankees to six pennants and three World Series championships in 12 seasons, died suddenly of blood poisoning at age 49.

MEMORABLE MOMENTS

- **July 6:** The Cardinals set a modern Major League record for runs and an N.L. record for hits (28) when they pounded the Phillies, 28-6.
- **August 10:** Cardinals great Grover Cleveland Alexander shut out Philadelphia in four innings of relief and was credited with an 11-9 victory—the 373rd and last of his career.
- **August 11:** Yankee Babe Ruth drove a Willis Hudlin pitch out of Cleveland's League Park for career homer No. 500.
- **October 5:** Philadelphia slugger Chuck Klein hit home run No. 43 in a final-day doubleheader against New York, setting a one-season N.L. record and edging Giants outfielder Mel Ott by one.
- **October 6:** Cleveland third baseman Joe Sewell finished the season with an amazing four strikeouts in 578 official at-bats.

LEADERS

American League

BA: Lew Fonseca, Cle., .369.
Runs: Charley Gehringer, Det., 131.
Hits: Dale Alexander, Det.; Charley Gehringer, Det., 215.
TB: Al Simmons, Phil., 373.
HR: Babe Ruth, N.Y., 46.
RBI: Al Simmons, Phil., 157.
SB: Charley Gehringer, Det., 27.
Wins: George Earnshaw, Phil., 24.
ERA: Lefty Grove, Phil., 2.81.
CG: Tommy Thomas, Chi., 24.
IP: Sam Gray, St.L., 305.
SO: Lefty Grove, Phil., 170.

National League

BA: Lefty O'Doul, Phil., .398.
Runs: Rogers Hornsby, Chi., 156.
Hits: Lefty O'Doul, Phil., 254.
TB: Rogers Hornsby, Chi., 409.
HR: Chuck Klein, Phil., 43.
RBI: Hack Wilson, Chi., 159.
SB: Kiki Cuyler, Chi., 43.
Wins: Pat Malone, Chi., 22.
ERA: Bill Walker, N.Y., 3.09.
CG: Red Lucas, Cin., 28.
IP: Watty Clark, Brk., 279.
SO: Pat Malone, Chi., 166.

A.L. 20-game winners
George Earnshaw, Phil., 24-8
Wes Ferrell, Cle., 21-10
Lefty Grove, Phil., 20-6

N.L. 20-game winners
Pat Malone, Chi., 22-10

A.L. 100 RBIs
Al Simmons, Phil., 157
Babe Ruth, N.Y., 154
Dale Alexander, Det., 137
Lou Gehrig, N.Y., 126
Harry Heilmann, Det., 120
Jimmie Foxx, Phil., 117
Red Kress, St.L., 107
Charlie Gehringer, Det., 106
Tony Lazzeri, N.Y., 106
Lew Fonseca, Cle., 103

N.L. 100 RBIs
Hack Wilson, Chi., 159
Mel Ott, N.Y., 151
Rogers Hornsby, Chi., 149
Chuck Klein, Phil., 145
Jim Bottomley, St.L., 137
Chick Hafey, St.L., 125
Don Hurst, Phil., 125
Lefty O'Doul, Phil., 122
Bill Terry, N.Y., 117
Pinky Whitney, Phil., 115
Babe Herman, Brk., 113
Riggs Stephenson, Chi., 110
Pie Traynor, Pit., 108
George Kelly, Cin., 103
Kiki Cuyler, Chi., 102
Paul Waner, Pit., 100

A.L. 40 homers
Babe Ruth, N.Y., 46

N.L. 40 homers
Chuck Klein, Phil., 43
Mel Ott, N.Y., 42

League MVP
A.L.: No selection.
N.L.: Rogers Hornsby, 2B, Chi.

WORLD SERIES

- **Winner:** The Athletics, an A.L. doormat since their last Series appearance in 1914, re-emerged as baseball's dominant team.
- **Turning point:** The seventh inning of Game 4. Leading the Series two games to one but trailing the Cubs 8-0, the A's exploded for an incredible 10 runs.
- **Memorable moments:** Mule Haas' three-run inside-the-park home run in the 10-run seventh inning and his ninth-inning game-tying homer in the Series-ending fifth game; surprise starter Howard Ehmke's record 13 strikeouts in Game 1.
- **Top guns:** Jimmie Dykes (.421), Jimmie Foxx (.350, 2 HR, 5 RBIs), Haas (2 HR, 6 RBIs), Athletics; Hack Wilson (.471), Cubs.

Linescores

Game 1—October 8, at Chicago
Philadelphia.... 0 0 0 0 0 0 1 0 2 — 3 6 1
Chicago.......... 0 0 0 0 0 0 0 0 1 — 1 8 2
Ehmke; Root, Bush (8). W—Ehmke. L—Root. HR—Foxx (Phil.).

Game 2—October 9, at Chicago
Philadelphia.... 0 0 3 3 0 0 1 2 0 — 9 12 0
Chicago.......... 0 0 0 0 3 0 0 0 0 — 3 11 1
Earnshaw, Grove (5); Malone, Blake (4), Carlson (6), Nehf (9). W—Earnshaw. L—Malone. HR—Simmons, Foxx (Phil.).

Game 3—October 11, at Philadelphia
Chicago.......... 0 0 0 0 0 3 0 0 0 — 3 6 1
Philadelphia.... 0 0 0 0 1 0 0 0 0 — 1 9 1
Bush; Earnshaw. W—Bush. L—Earnshaw.

Game 4—October 12, at Philadelphia
Chicago.......... 0 0 0 2 0 5 1 0 0 — 8 10 2
Philadelphia.... 0 0 0 0 0 0 10 0 x — 10 15 2
Root, Nehf (7), Blake (7), Malone (7), Carlson (8); Quinn, Walberg (6), Rommel (7), Grove (8). W—Rommel. L—Blake. HR—Grimm (Chi.); Haas, Simmons (Phil.).

Game 5—October 14, at Philadelphia
Chicago.......... 0 0 0 2 0 0 0 0 0 — 2 8 1
Philadelphia.... 0 0 0 0 0 0 0 0 3 — 3 6 0
Malone; Ehmke, Walberg (4). W—Walberg. L—Malone. HR—Haas (Phil.).

1930

FINAL STANDINGS

American League

Team	W	L	Pct.	GB
Philadelphia	102	52	.662	...
Washington	94	60	.610	8
New York	86	68	.558	16
Cleveland	81	73	.526	21
Detroit	75	79	.487	27
St. Louis	64	90	.416	38
Chicago	62	92	.403	40
Boston	52	102	.338	50

National League

Team	W	L	Pct.	GB
St. Louis	92	62	.597	...
Chicago	90	64	.584	2
New York	87	67	.565	5
Brooklyn	86	68	.558	6
Pittsburgh	80	74	.519	12
Boston	70	84	.455	22
Cincinnati	59	95	.383	33
Philadelphia	52	102	.338	40

SIGNIFICANT EVENTS

- **March 8:** Yankee slugger Babe Ruth signed a record two-year contract at $80,000 per season.
- **December 11:** Major League officials granted the Baseball Writers Association of America permission to conduct future MVP balloting—a practice that would continue without interruption.
- **December 12:** Rules changes: The sacrifice fly was eliminated and balls bouncing into the stands were classified as ground-rule doubles instead of home runs.

MEMORABLE MOMENTS

- **May 2:** Commissioner Kenesaw Mountain Landis attended Organized Baseball's first game under permanently installed lights at Des Moines (Iowa) of the Western League.
- **September 27:** Chicago's Hack Wilson hit home runs 55 and 56—an N.L. record—in a game against the Reds.
- **September 28:** Wilson drove in his Major League-record 189th and 190th runs in Chicago's season-finale victory over the Reds.
- **September 28:** New York's Bill Terry finished with a .401 average and N.L. hitters closed with a composite .303 mark.

LEADERS

American League

BA: Al Simmons, Phil., .381.
Runs: Al Simmons, Phil., 152.
Hits: Johnny Hodapp, Cle., 225.
TB: Lou Gehrig, N.Y., 419.
HR: Babe Ruth, N.Y., 49.
RBI: Lou Gehrig, N.Y., 174.
SB: Marty McManus, Det., 23.
Wins: Lefty Grove, Phil., 28.
ERA: Lefty Grove, Phil., 2.54.
CG: Ted Lyons, Chi., 29.
IP: Lyons, Chi., 297.2.
SO: Lefty Grove, Phil., 209.

National League

BA: Bill Terry, N.Y., .401.
Runs: Chuck Klein, Phil., 158.
Hits: Bill Terry, N.Y., 254.
TB: Chuck Klein, Phil., 445.
HR: Hack Wilson, Chi., 56.
RBI: Hack Wilson, Chi., 190.
SB: Kiki Cuyler, Chi., 37.
Wins: Ray Kremer, Pit.; Pat Malone, Chi., 20.
ERA: Dazzy Vance, Brk., 2.61.
CG: Erv Brame, Pit.; Pat Malone, Chi., 22.
IP: Ray Kremer, Pit., 276.
SO: Bill Hallahan, St.L., 177.

A.L. 20-game winners
Lefty Grove, Phil., 28-5
Wes Ferrell, Cle., 25-13
George Earnshaw, Phil., 22-13
Ted Lyons, Chi., 22-15
Lefty Stewart, St.L., 20-12

N.L. 20-game winners
Pat Malone, Chi., 20-9
Remy Kremer, Pit., 20-12

A.L. 100 RBIs
Lou Gehrig, N.Y., 174
Al Simmons, Phil., 165
Jimmie Foxx, Phil., 156
Babe Ruth, N.Y., 153
Goose Goslin, Wash.-St.L., 138
Ed Morgan, Cle., 136
Dale Alexander, Det., 135
Joe Cronin, Wash., 126
Johnny Hodapp, Cle., 121
Tony Lazzeri, N.Y., 121
Earl Averill, Cle., 119
Smead Jolley, Chi., 114
Red Kress, St.L., 112
Carl Reynolds, Chi., 104
Bing Miller, Phil., 100

N.L. 100 RBIs
Hack Wilson, Chi., 190
Chuck Klein, Phil., 170
Kiki Cuyler, Chi., 134
Babe Herman, Brk., 130
Bill Terry, N.Y., 129
Glenn Wright, Brk., 126
Gabby Hartnett, Chi., 122
Wally Berger, Bos., 119
Adam Comorosky, Pit., 119
Mel Ott, N.Y., 119
Pie Traynor, Pit., 119
Pinky Whitney, Pit., 117
Frank Frisch, St.L., 114
Del Bissonette, Brk., 113
Chick Hafey, St.L., 107
Gus Suhr, Pit., 107
Fred Lindstrom, N.Y., 106

A.L. 40 homers
Babe Ruth, N.Y., 49
Lou Gehrig, N.Y., 41

N.L. 40 homers
Hack Wilson, Chi., 56
Chuck Klein, Phil., 40

WORLD SERIES

- **Winner:** The Athletics became the first team to win back-to-back Series twice.
- **Turning point:** Jimmie Foxx's two-run ninth-inning home run off Burleigh Grimes, which broke open a scoreless Game 5 and put Philadelphia in the driver's seat.
- **Memorable moment:** Foxx's Game 5-winning home run.
- **Top guns:** George Earnshaw (2-0, 0.72 ERA), Al Simmons (.364, 2 HR, 4 RBIs), Athletics; Jesse Haines (1-0, 1.00), Cardinals.

Linescores

Game 1—October 1, at Philadelphia
St. Louis ....0 0 2 0 0 0 0 0 0—2 9 0
Philadelphia........0 1 0 1 0 1 1 1 x—5 5 0
Grimes; Grove. W—Grove. L—Grimes. HR—Cochrane, Simmons (Phil.).

Game 2—October 2, at Philadelphia
St. Louis ....0 1 0 0 0 0 0 0 0—1 6 2
Philadelphia........2 0 2 2 0 0 0 0 x—6 7 2
Rhem, Lindsey (4), Johnson (7); Earnshaw. W—Earnshaw. L—Rhem. HR—Cochrane (Phil.); Watkins (St.L.).

Game 3—October 4, at St. Louis
Philadelphia......0 0 0 0 0 0 0 0 0—0 7 0
St. Louis ....0 0 0 1 1 0 2 1 x—5 10 0
Walberg, Shores (5), Quinn (7); Hallahan. W—Hallahan. L—Walberg. HR—Douthit (St.L.).

Game 4—October 5, at St. Louis
Philadelphia........1 0 0 0 0 0 0 0 0—1 4 1
St. Louis ....0 0 1 2 0 0 0 0 x—3 5 1
Grove; Haines. W—Haines. L—Grove.

Game 5—October 6, at St. Louis
Philadelphia........0 0 0 0 0 0 0 0 2—2 5 0
St. Louis ....0 0 0 0 0 0 0 0 0—0 3 1
Earnshaw, Grove (8); Grimes. W—Grove. L—Grimes. HR—Foxx (Phil.).

Game 6—October 8, at Philadelphia
St. Louis ....0 0 0 0 0 0 0 0 1—1 5 1
Philadelphia........2 0 1 2 1 1 0 0 x—7 7 0
Hallahan, Johnson (3), Lindsey (6), Bell (8); Earnshaw. W—Earnshaw. L—Hallahan. HR—Dykes, Simmons (Phil.).

1931

FINAL STANDINGS

American League				
Team	W	L	Pct.	GB
Philadelphia	107	45	.704	...
New York	94	59	.614	13.5
Washington	92	62	.597	16
Cleveland	78	76	.506	30
St. Louis	63	91	.409	45
Boston	62	90	.408	45
Detroit	61	93	.396	47
Chicago	56	97	.366	51.5

National League				
Team	W	L	Pct.	GB
St. Louis	101	53	.656	...
New York	87	65	.572	13
Chicago	84	70	.545	17
Brooklyn	79	73	.520	21
Pittsburgh	75	79	.487	26
Philadelphia	66	88	.429	35
Boston	64	90	.416	37
Cincinnati	58	96	.377	43

SIGNIFICANT EVENTS

■ **March 27-28:** Former A.L. president and founder Ban Johnson died at age 67, 16 hours after E.S. Barnard, the man who succeeded him, died of a heart attack at age 56.
■ **October 20, 28:** The Baseball Writers Association of America named its first MVPs: Cardinals infielder Frank Frisch and Athletics 31-game winner Lefty Grove.
■ **October 26:** Charles Comiskey, one of the A.L.'s founding fathers and longtime owner of the White Sox, died at age 72.

MEMORABLE MOMENTS

■ **May 26:** The Yankees ended Philadelphia's winning streak at 17 games with a 6-2 victory.
■ **August 21:** Yankee Babe Ruth belted his historic 600th career home run off Browns righthander George Blaeholder.
■ **August 23:** Philadelphia's Lefty Grove, bidding to break the A.L. record of 16 straight victories, dropped a 1-0 decision to the Browns.
■ **September 1:** Yankee Lou Gehrig, en route to an A.L.-record 184 RBIs, became the third player to hit home runs in six straight games —a streak that included three grand slams in five days.

LEADERS

American League
BA: Al Simmons, Phil., .390.
Runs: Lou Gehrig, N.Y., 163.
Hits: Lou Gehrig, N.Y., 211.
TB: Lou Gehrig, N.Y., 410.
HR: Lou Gehrig, N.Y.; Babe Ruth, N.Y., 46.
RBI: Lou Gehrig, N.Y., 184.
SB: Ben Chapman, N.Y., 61.
Wins: Lefty Grove, Phil., 31.
ERA: Lefty Grove, Phil., 2.06.
CG: Wes Ferrell, Cle.; Lefty Grove, Phil., 27.
IP: Rube Walberg, Phil., 291.
SO: Lefty Grove, Phil., 175.

National League
BA: Chick Hafey, St.L., .349.
Runs: Chuck Klein, Phil.; Bill Terry, N.Y., 121.
Hits: Lloyd Waner, Pit., 214.
TB: Chuck Klein, Phil., 347.
HR: Chuck Klein, Phil., 31.
RBI: Chuck Klein, Phil., 121.
SB: Frank Frisch, St.L., 28.
Wins: Jumbo Elliott, Phil.; Bill Hallahan, St.L.; Heinie Meine, Pit., 19.
ERA: Bill Walker, N.Y., 2.26.
CG: Red Lucas, Cin., 24.
IP: Heinie Meine, Pit., 284.
SO: Bill Hallahan, St.L., 159.

A.L. 20-game winners
Lefty Grove, Phil., 31-4
Wes Ferrell, Cle., 22-12
George Earnshaw, Phil., 21-7
Lefty Gomez, N.Y., 21-9
Rube Walberg, Phil., 20-12

A.L. 100 RBIs
Lou Gehrig, N.Y., 184
Babe Ruth, N.Y., 163
Earl Averill, Cle., 143
Al Simmons, Phil., 128
Joe Cronin, Wash., 126
Ben Chapman, N.Y., 122
Jimmie Foxx, Phil., 120
Joe Vosmik, Cle., 117
Red Kress, St.L., 114
Lyn Lary, N.Y., 107
Goose Goslin, St.L., 105
Earl Webb, Bos., 103

N.L. 100 RBIs
Chuck Klein, Phil., 121
Mel Ott, N.Y., 115
Bill Terry, N.Y., 112
Pie Traynor, Pit., 103

A.L. 40 homers
Lou Gehrig, N.Y., 46
Babe Ruth, N.Y., 46

Most Valuable Player
A.L.: Lefty Grove, P, Phil.
N.L.: Frank Frisch, 2B, St.L.

WORLD SERIES

■ **Winner:** The Cardinals spoiled Philadelphia's bid to win a record third consecutive Series.

■ **Turning point:** A pair of two-run innings that staked Cardinals spitballer Burleigh Grimes to a 4-0 lead in Game 7.

■ **Memorable moment:** The Series-long do-everything performance of exciting Cardinals center fielder Pepper Martin.

■ **Top guns:** Grimes (2-0, 2.04 ERA), Bill Hallahan (2-0, 0.49), Martin (.500, 12 hits, 5 RBIs, 5 SB), Cardinals; Al Simmons (.333, 2 HR, 8 RBIs), Athletics.

Linescores

Game 1—October 1, at St. Louis
Philadelphia......0 0 4 0 0 0 2 0 0—6 11 0
St. Louis ....2 0 0 0 0 0 0 0 0—2 12 0
Grove; Derringer, Johnson (8). W—Grove. L—Derringer. HR—Simmons (Phil.).

Game 2—October 2, at St. Louis
Philadelphia........0 0 0 0 0 0 0 0 0—0 3 0
St. Louis ....0 1 0 0 0 0 1 0 x—2 6 1
Earnshaw; Hallahan. W—Hallahan. L—Earnshaw.

Game 3—October 5, at Philadelphia
St. Louis ....0 2 0 2 0 0 0 0 1—5 12 0
Philadelphia......0 0 0 0 0 0 0 0 2—2 2 0
Grimes; Grove, Mahaffey (9). W—Grimes. L—Grove. HR—Simmons (Phil).

Game 4—October 6, at Philadelphia
St. Louis ....0 0 0 0 0 0 0 0 0—0 2 1
Philadelphia......1 0 0 0 0 2 0 0 x—3 10 0
Johnson, Lindsey (6), Derringer (8); Earnshaw. W—Earnshaw. L—Johnson. HR—Foxx (Phil.).

Game 5—October 7, at Philadelphia
St. Louis ....1 0 0 0 0 2 0 1 1—5 12 0
Philadelphia......0 0 0 0 0 0 1 0 0—1 9 0
Hallahan; Hoyt, Walberg (7), Rommel (9). W—Hallahan. L—Hoyt. HR—Martin (St.L.).

Game 6—October 9, at St. Louis
Philadelphia........0 0 0 0 4 0 4 0 0—8 8 1
St. Louis ....0 0 0 0 0 1 0 0 0—1 5 2
Grove; Derringer, Johnson (5), Lindsey (7), Rhem (9). W—Grove. L—Derringer.

Game 7—October 10, at St. Louis
Philadelphia........0 0 0 0 0 0 0 0 2—2 7 1
St. Louis ....2 0 2 0 0 0 0 0 x—4 5 0
Earnshaw, Walberg (8); Grimes, Hallahan (9). W—Grimes. L—Earnshaw. HR—Watkins (St.L.).

1932

FINAL STANDINGS

American League				
Team	W	L	Pct.	GB
New York	107	47	.695	...
Philadelphia	94	60	.610	13
Washington	93	61	.604	14
Cleveland	87	65	.572	19
Detroit	76	75	.503	29.5
St. Louis	63	91	.409	44
Chicago	49	102	.325	56.5
Boston	43	111	.279	64

National League				
Team	W	L	Pct.	GB
Chicago	90	64	.584	...
Pittsburgh	86	68	.558	4
Brooklyn	81	73	.526	9
Philadelphia	78	76	.506	12
Boston	77	77	.500	13
New York	72	82	.468	18
St. Louis	72	82	.468	18
Cincinnati	60	94	.390	30

SIGNIFICANT EVENTS

■ **June 22:** N.L. officials, after a long holdout, approved the use of numbers to identify their players.
■ **July 31:** The 76,979 fans who turned out for Cleveland's unveiling of Municipal Stadium watched the Indians lose a 1-0 decision to the Athletics and Lefty Grove.
■ **September 28:** Connie Mack began dismantling his powerful Athletics with the sale of Al Simmons, Jimmie Dykes and Mule Haas to the White Sox for $150,000.
■ **October 19:** A Philadelphia double: Athletics slugger Jimmie Foxx earned A.L. MVP honors and Phillies slugger Chuck Klein captured the N.L. award.

MEMORABLE MOMENTS

■ **June 3:** An historic day: Yankee Lou Gehrig belted four home runs in a game at Philadelphia and John McGraw retired after 31 seasons as manager of the Giants.
■ **July 4:** In a Fourth of July battle between the Yankees and Senators, New York catcher Bill Dickey punched Washington outfielder Carl Reynolds and broke his jaw, a tantrum that would cost him a 30-day suspension and $1,000.
■ **September 25:** Athletics slugger Jimmie Foxx hit home run No. 58 in the season finale against Washington, falling two short of Babe Ruth's single-season record.

LEADERS

American League
BA: Dale Alexander, Det.-Bos., .367.
Runs: Jimmie Foxx, Phil., 151.
Hits: Al Simmons, Phil., 216.
TB: Jimmie Foxx, Phil., 438.
HR: Jimmie Foxx, Phil., 58.
RBI: Jimmie Foxx, Phil., 169.
SB: Ben Chapman, N.Y., 38.
Wins: General Crowder, Wash., 26.
ERA: Lefty Grove, Phil., 2.84.
CG: Lefty Grove, Phil., 27.
IP: General Crowder, Wash., 327.
SO: Red Ruffing, N.Y., 190.

National League
BA: Lefty O'Doul, Brk., .368.
Runs: Chuck Klein, Phil., 152.
Hits: Chuck Klein, Phil., 226.
TB: Chuck Klein, Phil., 420.
HR: Chuck Klein, Phil.; Mel Ott, N.Y., 38.
RBI: Don Hurst, Phil., 143.
SB: Chuck Klein, Phil., 20.
Wins: Lon Warneke, Chi., 22.
ERA: Lon Warneke, Chi., 2.37.
CG: Red Lucas, Cin., 28.
IP: Dizzy Dean, St.L., 286.
SO: Dizzy Dean, St.L., 191.

A.L. 20-game winners
General Crowder, Wash., 26-13
Lefty Grove, Phil., 25-10
Lefty Gomez, N.Y., 24-7
Wes Ferrell, Cle., 23-13
Monte Weaver, Wash., 22-10

N.L. 20-game winners
Lon Warneke, Chi., 22-6
Watty Clark, Brk., 20-12

A.L. 100 RBIs
Jimmie Foxx, Phil., 169
Lou Gehrig, N.Y., 151
Al Simmons, Phil., 151
Babe Ruth, N.Y., 137
Earl Averill, Cle., 124
Joe Cronin, Wash., 116
Heinie Manush, Wash., 116
Tony Lazzeri, N.Y., 113
Mickey Cochrane, Phil., 112
John Stone, Det., 108
Ben Chapman, N.Y., 107
Charlie Gehringer, Det., 107
Smead Jolley, Chi.-St.L., 106
Goose Goslin, St.L., 104

N.L. 100 RBIs
Don Hurst, Phil., 143
Chuck Klein, Phil., 137
Pinky Whitney, Phil., 124
Mel Ott, N.Y., 123
Hack Wilson, Brk., 123
Bill Terry, N.Y., 117

A.L. 40 homers
Jimmie Foxx, Phil., 58
Babe Ruth, N.Y., 41

Most Valuable Player
A.L.: Jimmie Foxx, 1B, Phil.
N.L.: Chuck Klein, OF, Phil.

WORLD SERIES

■ **Winner:** The Yankees played long ball in their sweep of the Cubs.

■ **Turning point:** A fourth-inning Game 1 homer by Lou Gehrig that gave the Yankees a 3-2 lead and propelled them to their sweep.

■ **Memorable moment:** Babe Ruth's second homer in Game 3 off Cubs righthander Charlie Root — whether it was a "called shot" or not.

■ **Top guns:** Gehrig (.529, 3 HR, 8 RBIs), Ruth (.333, 2 HR, 6 RBIs), Yankees; Riggs Stephenson (.444), Cubs.

Linescores

Game 1—September 28, at New York
Chicago..........2 0 0 0 0 0 2 2 0— 6 10 1
New York........0 0 0 3 0 5 3 1 x—12 8 2
Bush, Grimes (6), Smith (8); Ruffing. W—Ruffing. L—Bush. HR—Gehrig (N.Y.).

Game 2—September 29, at New York
Chicago............1 0 1 0 0 0 0 0 0—2 9 0
New York..........2 0 2 0 1 0 0 0 x—5 10 1
Warneke; Gomez. W—Gomez. L—Warneke.

Game 3—October 1, at Chicago
New York ....3 0 1 0 2 0 0 0 1—7 8 1
Chicago.............1 0 2 1 0 0 0 0 1—5 9 4
Pipgras, Pennock (9); Root, Malone (5), May (8), Tinning (9). W—Pipgras. L—Root. HR—Ruth 2, Gehrig 2 (N.Y.); Cuyler, Hartnett (Chi.).

Game 4—October 2, at Chicago
New York ......1 0 2 0 0 2 4 0 4—13 19 4
Chicago..........4 0 0 0 0 1 0 0 1— 6 9 1
Allen, W. Moore (1), Pennock (7); Bush, Warneke (1), May (4), Tinning (7), Grimes (9). W—W. Moore. L—May. HR—Demaree (Chi.); Lazzeri 2, Combs (N.Y.).

1933

FINAL STANDINGS

American League

Team	W	L	Pct.	GB
Washington	99	53	.651	...
New York	91	59	.607	7
Philadelphia	79	72	.523	19.5
Cleveland	75	76	.497	23.5
Detroit	75	79	.487	25
Chicago	67	83	.447	31
Boston	63	86	.423	34.5
St. Louis	55	96	.364	43.5

National League

Team	W	L	Pct.	GB
New York	91	61	.599	...
Pittsburgh	87	67	.565	5
Chicago	86	68	.558	6
Boston	83	71	.539	9
St. Louis	82	71	.536	9.5
Brooklyn	65	88	.425	26.5
Philadelphia	60	92	.395	31
Cincinnati	58	94	.382	33

SIGNIFICANT EVENTS

■ **January 7:** Commissioner Kenesaw Mountain Landis, sending a Depression-era message to owners and players, took a voluntary $25,000 cut in salary.
■ **November 7:** A referendum was passed by Pennsylvania voters legalizing Sunday baseball for Pittsburgh and Philadelphia — the only Major League cities still observing the blue law.

MEMORABLE MOMENTS

■ **July 30:** Cardinals ace Dizzy Dean set a modern record with 17 strikeouts in an 8-2 victory over Chicago.
■ **July 2:** Giants pitchers Carl Hubbell (18) and Roy Parmelee (9) combined for 27 scoreless innings in a doubleheader shutout of the St. Louis Cardinals. Both games ended 1-0.
■ **August 1:** Giants lefty Carl Hubbell extended his N.L.-record scoreless-innings streak to 45 in a game eventually won by Boston, 3-1.
■ **August 17:** Yankee Lou Gehrig broke Everett Scott's Major League record when he played in his 1,308th consecutive game — a 7-6 loss at St. Louis.
■ **October 1:** Philadelphia stars Jimmie Foxx (.356, 48 homers, 163 RBIs) and Chuck Klein (.368, 28, 120) completed an unprecedented one-season double, becoming the fifth and sixth Triple Crown winners of the century.

LEADERS

American League
BA: Jimmie Foxx, Phil., .356.
Runs: Lou Gehrig, N.Y., 138.
Hits: Heinie Manush, Wash., 221.
TB: Jimmie Foxx, Phil., 403.
HR: Jimmie Foxx, Phil., 48.
RBI: Jimmie Foxx, Phil., 163.
SB: Ben Chapman, N.Y., 27.
Wins: General Crowder, Wash.; Lefty Grove, Phil., 24.
ERA: Mel Harder, Cle., 2.95.
CG: Lefty Grove, Phil., 21.
IP: Bump Hadley, St.L., 316.2.
SO: Lefty Gomez, N.Y., 163.

National League
BA: Chuck Klein, Phil., .368.
Runs: Pepper Martin, St.L., 122.
Hits: Chuck Klein, Phil., 223.
TB: Chuck Klein, Phil., 365.
HR: Chuck Klein, Phil., 28.
RBI: Chuck Klein, Phil., 120.
SB: Pepper Martin, St.L., 26.
Wins: Carl Hubbell, N.Y., 23.
ERA: Carl Hubbell, N.Y., 1.66.
CG: Dizzy Dean, St.L.; Lon Warneke, Chi., 26.
IP: Carl Hubbell, N.Y., 308.2.
SO: Dizzy Dean, St.L., 199.

A.L. 20-game winners
Lefty Grove, Phil., 24-8
General Crowder, Wash., 24-15
Earl Whitehill, Wash., 22-8

N.L. 20-game winners
Carl Hubbell, N.Y., 23-12
Ben Cantwell, Bos., 20-10
Guy Bush, Chi., 20-12
Dizzy Dean, St.L., 20-18

A.L. 100 RBIs
Jimmie Foxx, Phil., 163
Lou Gehrig, N.Y., 139
Al Simmons, Chi., 119
Joe Cronin, Wash., 118
Joe Kuhel, Wash., 107
Bruce Campbell, St.L., 106
Charlie Gehringer, Det., 105
Tony Lazzeri, N.Y., 104
Babe Ruth, N.Y., 103

N.L. 100 RBIs
Chuck Klein, Phil., 120
Wally Berger, Bos., 106
Mel Ott, N.Y., 103

A.L. 40 homers
Jimmie Foxx, Phil., 48

Most Valuable Player
A.L.: Jimmie Foxx, 1B, Phil.
N.L.: Carl Hubbell, P, N.Y.

ALL-STAR GAME

■ **Winner:** The American League prevailed 4-2 in baseball's "Game of the Century," which gathered the biggest stars from both leagues for an unprecedented meeting at Chicago's Comiskey Park.

■ **Key inning:** The third, when Yankee slugger Babe Ruth pounded a two-run homer and gave the A.L. a 3-0 lead.

■ **Memorable moment:** The star-studded pregame introductions for baseball's first All-Star classic.

■ **Top guns:** Lefty Gomez (Yankees), Ruth (Yankees), Jimmie Dykes (White Sox), A.L.; Frank Frisch (Cardinals), Bill Terry (Giants), N.L.

■ **MVP:** Ruth.

Linescore

July 6, at Chicago's Comiskey Park
N.L. ....0 0 0 0 0 2 0 0 0—2 8 0
A.L. ....0 1 2 0 0 1 0 0 x—4 9 1
Hallahan (Cardinals), Warneke (Cubs) 3, Hubbell (Giants) 7; Gomez (Yankees), Crowder (Senators) 4, Grove (Athletics) 7. W—Gomez. L—Hallahan. HR—Ruth, A.L.; Frisch (N.L.).

WORLD SERIES

■ **Winner:** The pitching-rich Giants, now under the direction of player/manager Bill Terry, captured their first Series without John McGraw at the helm.

■ **Turning point:** Carl Hubbell's 2-1, 11-inning victory that gave the Giants a three-games-to-one edge.

■ **Memorable moment:** A 10th-inning home run by Mel Ott that gave the Giants a Series-ending 4-3 victory.

■ **Top guns:** Hubbell (2-0, 0.00 ERA), Ott (.389, 2 HR, 4 RBIs), Giants; Fred Schulte (.333), Senators.

Linescores

Game 1—October 3, at New York
Washington..............0 0 0 1 0 0 0 0 1—2 5 3
New York..................2 0 2 0 0 0 0 0 x—4 10 2
Stewart, Russell (3), Thomas (8); Hubbell. W—Hubbell. L—Stewart. HR—Ott (N.Y.).

Game 2—October 4, at New York
Washington..............0 0 1 0 0 0 0 0 0—1 5 0
New York..................0 0 0 0 0 6 0 0 x—6 10 0
Crowder, Thomas (6), McColl (7); Schumacher. W—Schumacher. L—Crowder. HR—Goslin (Wash.).

Game 3—October 5, at Washington
New York...................0 0 0 0 0 0 0 0 0—0 5 0
Washington...............2 1 0 0 0 0 1 0 x—4 9 1
Fitzsimmons, Bell (8); Whitehill. W—Whitehill. L—Fitzsimmons.

Game 4—October 6, at Washington
New York........0 0 0 1 0 0 0 0 0 0 1—2 11 1
Washington....0 0 0 0 0 0 1 0 0 0 0—1 8 0
Hubbell; Weaver, Russell (11). W—Hubbell. L—Weaver. HR—Terry (N.Y.).

Game 5—October 7, at Washington
New York...........0 2 0 0 0 1 0 0 0 1—4 11 1
Washington........0 0 0 0 0 3 0 0 0 0—3 10 0
Schumacher, Luque (6); Crowder, Russell (6). W—Luque. L—Russell. HR—Schulte (Wash.); Ott (N.Y.).

1934

FINAL STANDINGS

American League

Team	W	L	Pct.	GB
Detroit	101	53	.656	...
New York	94	60	.610	7
Cleveland	85	69	.552	16
Boston	76	76	.500	24
Philadelphia	68	82	.453	31
St. Louis	67	85	.441	33
Washington	66	86	.434	34
Chicago	53	99	.349	47

National League

Team	W	L	Pct.	GB
St. Louis	95	58	.621	...
New York	93	60	.608	2
Chicago	86	65	.570	8
Boston	78	73	.517	16
Pittsburgh	74	76	.493	19.5
Brooklyn	71	81	.467	23.5
Philadelphia	56	93	.376	37
Cincinnati	52	99	.344	42

SIGNIFICANT EVENTS

■ **February 25:** John McGraw, considered by many the greatest manager of all time, died of cancer at age 60.
■ **November 9:** N.L. officials selected Ford Frick as league president, six days after John Heydler resigned for health reasons.
■ **December 12:** The N.L., acting independently of the A.L., voted to allow night baseball on a limited basis.

MEMORABLE MOMENTS

■ **July 13:** Yankee outfielder Babe Ruth opened the 700-homer club when he connected off righthander Tommy Bridges in a game at Detroit.
■ **August 25:** Detroit rookie Schoolboy Rowe defeated Washington 4-2 for his A.L. record-tying 16th consecutive victory.
■ **September 21:** Cardinals ace Dizzy Dean shut out Brooklyn on three hits in the first game of a doubleheader and brother Paul pitched a no-hitter against the Dodgers in the nightcap.

LEADERS

American League
BA: Lou Gehrig, N.Y., .363.
Runs: Charley Gehringer, Det., 134.
Hits: Charley Gehringer, Det., 214.
TB: Lou Gehrig, N.Y., 409.
HR: Lou Gehrig, N.Y., 49.
RBI: Lou Gehrig, N.Y., 165.
SB: Billy Werber, Bos., 40.
Wins: Lefty Gomez, N.Y., 26.
ERA: Lefty Gomez, N.Y., 2.33.
CG: Lefty Gomez, N.Y., 25.
IP: Lefty Gomez, N.Y., 281.2.
SO: Lefty Gomez, N.Y., 158.

National League
BA: Paul Waner, Pit., .362.
Runs: Paul Waner, Pit., 122.
Hits: Paul Waner, Pit., 217.
TB: Ripper Collins, St.L., 369.
HR: Ripper Collins, St.L.; Mel Ott, N.Y., 35.
RBI: Mel Ott, N.Y., 135.
SB: Pepper Martin, St.L., 23.
Wins: Dizzy Dean, St.L., 30.
ERA: Carl Hubbell, N.Y., 2.30.
CG: Carl Hubbell, N.Y., 25.
IP: Van Lingle Mungo, Brk., 315.1.
SO: Dizzy Dean, St.L., 195.

A.L. 20-game winners
Lefty Gomez, N.Y., 26-5
Schoolboy Rowe, Det., 24-8
Tommy Bridges, Det., 22-11
Mel Harder, Cle., 20-12

N.L. 20-game winners
Dizzy Dean, St.L., 30-7
Hal Schumacher, N.Y., 23-10
Lon Warneke, Chi., 22-10
Carl Hubbell, N.Y., 21-12

A.L. 100 RBIs
Lou Gehrig, N.Y., 165
Hal Trosky, Cle., 142
Hank Greenberg, Det., 139
Jimmie Foxx, Phil., 130
Charlie Gehringer, Det., 127
Roy Johnson, Bos., 119
Earl Averill, Cle., 113
Zeke Bonura, Chi., 110
Al Simmons, Chi., 104
Joe Cronin, Wash., 101
Odell Hale, Cle., 101
Roy Pepper, St.L., 101
Goose Goslin, Det., 100
Billy Rogell, Det., 100

N.L. 100 RBIs
Mel Ott, N.Y., 135
Ripper Collins, St.L., 128
Wally Berger, Bos., 121
Joe Medwick, St.L., 106
Gus Suhr, Pit., 103
Sam Leslie, Brk., 102
Travis Jackson, N.Y., 101

A.L. 40 homers
Lou Gehrig, N.Y., 49
Jimmie Foxx, Phil., 44

Most Valuable Player
A.L.: Mickey Cochrane, C, Det.
N.L.: Dizzy Dean, P, St.L.

ALL-STAR GAME

■ **Winner:** The A.L. made it two in a row by roaring back from a 4-0 deficit for a 9-7 victory.

■ **Key inning:** The fifth, when the A.L. scored six times to take command. Cleveland's Earl Averill doubled home two runs and Yankee pitcher Red Ruffing singled in two more.

■ **Memorable moment:** The first- and second-inning performance of Giants lefthander Carl Hubbell, who struck out A.L. bashers Babe Ruth (Yankees), Lou Gehrig (Yankees), Jimmie Foxx (Athletics), Al Simmons (White Sox) and Joe Cronin (Senators) consecutively.

■ **Top guns:** Mel Harder (Indians), Averill (Indians), Cronin (Senators), Simmons (White Sox), A.L.; Hubbell (Giants), Joe Medwick (Cardinals), Frank Frisch (Cardinals), N.L.

■ **MVP:** Averill.

Linescore

July 10, at New York's Polo Grounds
A.L. ....0 0 0 2 6 1 0 0 0—9 14 1
N.L. ....1 0 3 0 3 0 0 0 0—7 8 1
Gomez (Yankees), Ruffing (Yankees) 4, Harder (Indians) 5, A.L.; Hubbell (Giants), Warneke (Cubs) 4, Mungo (Dodgers) 5, Dean (Cardinals) 6, Frankhouse (Braves) 9. W—Harder. L—Mungo. HR—Frisch, Medwick, N.L.

WORLD SERIES

■ **Winner:** St. Louis' Gas House Gang defeated the Tigers in the infamous "Garbage" World Series.

■ **Turning point:** Paul Dean's pitching and hitting gave the Cardinals a 4-3 Game 6 victory that set up a winner-take-all seventh game.

■ **Memorable moment:** A seventh-game outburst by frustrated Tigers fans who pelted Cardinals left fielder Joe Medwick with garbage and other debris, forcing a long delay. The Cardinals were leading 9-0 en route to an 11-0 victory.

■ **Top guns:** Paul Dean (2-0, 1.00 ERA), Dizzy Dean (2-1, 1.73), Medwick (.379, 5 RBIs), Cardinals; Charley Gehringer (.379), Tigers.

Linescores

Game 1—October 3, at Detroit
St. Louis ....0 2 1 0 1 4 0 0 0—8 13 2
Detroit......................0 0 1 0 0 1 0 1 0—3 8 5
D. Dean; Crowder, Marberry (6), Hogsett (6). W—D. Dean. L—Crowder. HR—Medwick (St.L.); Greenberg (Det.).

Game 2—October 4, at Detroit
St. Louis ......0 1 1 0 0 0 0 0 0 0 0 0—2 7 3
Detroit..........0 0 0 1 0 0 0 0 1 0 0 1—3 7 0
Hallahan, W. Walker (9); Rowe. W—Rowe. L—W. Walker.

Game 3—October 5, at St. Louis
Detroit........................0 0 0 0 0 0 0 0 1—1 8 2
St. Louis ....1 1 0 0 2 0 0 0 x—4 9 1
Bridges, Hogsett (5); P. Dean. W—P. Dean. L—Bridges.

Game 4—October 6, at St. Louis
Detroit...................0 0 3 1 0 0 1 5 0—10 13 1
St. Louis ....0 1 1 2 0 0 0 0 0— 4 10 5
Auker; Carleton, Vance (3), W. Walker (5), Haines (8), Mooney (9). W—Auker. L—W. Walker.

Game 5—October 7, at St. Louis
Detroit........................0 1 0 0 0 2 0 0 0—3 7 0
St. Louis ....0 0 0 0 0 0 1 0 0—1 7 1
Bridges; D. Dean, Carleton (9). W—Bridges. L—D. Dean. HR—Gehringer (Det.); DeLancey (St.L.).

Game 6—October 8, at Detroit
St. Louis ....1 0 0 0 2 0 1 0 0—4 10 2
Detroit.....................0 0 1 0 0 2 0 0 0—3 7 1
P. Dean; Rowe. W—P. Dean. L—Rowe.

Game 7—October 9, at Detroit
St. Louis ....0 0 7 0 0 2 2 0 0—11 17 1
Detroit.....................0 0 0 0 0 0 0 0 0— 0 6 3
D. Dean; Auker, Rowe (3), Hogsett (3), Bridges (3), Marberry (8), Crowder (9). W—D. Dean. L—Auker.

1935

FINAL STANDINGS

American League

Team	W	L	Pct.	GB
Detroit	93	58	.616	...
New York	89	60	.597	3
Cleveland	82	71	.536	12
Boston	78	75	.510	16
Chicago	74	78	.487	19.5
Washington	67	86	.438	27
St. Louis	65	87	.428	28.5
Philadelphia	58	91	.389	34

National League

Team	W	L	Pct.	GB
Chicago	100	54	.649	...
St. Louis	96	58	.623	4
New York	91	62	.595	8.5
Pittsburgh	86	67	.562	13.5
Brooklyn	70	83	.458	29.5
Cincinnati	68	85	.444	31.5
Philadelphia	64	89	.418	35.5
Boston	38	115	.248	61.5

SIGNIFICANT EVENTS

■ **February 26:** Babe Ruth ended his long love affair with New York fans when the Yankees granted him a release to sign with the Braves.

■ **December 10:** A.L. owners attending the winter meetings voted not to sanction night baseball.

MEMORABLE MOMENTS

■ **May 24:** Larry MacPhail's Reds staged the first night game in Major League history and defeated the Phillies, 2-1, at Crosley Field.

■ **June 2:** Braves slugger Babe Ruth retired, eight days after a three-homer game at Pittsburgh had raised his career total to 714.

■ **August 31:** Chicago pitcher Vern Kennedy pitched the first no-hitter in Comiskey Park history and punctuated his 5-0 victory over Cleveland with a bases-loaded triple.

■ **September 22:** The lowly Braves lost their Major League-record 110th game en route to 115 losses.

■ **September 27:** The Cubs clinched the N.L. pennant with a 6-2 victory over St. Louis — their 20th straight win in a streak that would end at 21.

LEADERS

American League

BA: Buddy Myer, Wash., .349.
Runs: Lou Gehrig, N.Y., 125.
Hits: Joe Vosmik, Cle., 216.
TB: Hank Greenberg, Det., 389.
HR: Jimmie Foxx, Phil.; Hank Greenberg, Det., 36.
RBI: Hank Greenberg, Det., 170.
SB: Billy Werber, Bos., 29.
Wins: Wes Ferrell, Bos., 25.
ERA: Lefty Grove, Bos., 2.70.
CG: Wes Ferrell, Bos., 31.
IP: Wes Ferrell, Bos., 322.1.
SO: Tommy Bridges, Det., 163.

National League

BA: Arky Vaughan, Pit., .385.
Runs: Augie Galan, Chi., 133.
Hits: Billy Herman, Chi., 227.
TB: Joe Medwick, St.L., 365.
HR: Wally Berger, Bos., 34.
RBI: Wally Berger, Bos., 130.
SB: Augie Galan, Chi., 22.
Wins: Dizzy Dean, St.L., 28.
ERA: Cy Blanton, Pit., 2.58.
CG: Dizzy Dean, St.L., 29.
IP: Dizzy Dean, St.L., 325.1
SO: Dizzy Dean, St.L., 190.

A.L. 20-game winners
Wes Ferrell, Bos., 25-14
Mel Harder, Cle., 22-11
Tommy Bridges, Det., 21-10
Lefty Grove, Bos., 20-12

N.L. 20-game winners
Dizzy Dean, St.L., 28-12
Carl Hubbell, N.Y., 23-12
Paul Derringer, Cin., 22-13
Bill Lee, Chi., 20-6
Lon Warneke, Chi., 20-13

A.L. 100 RBIs
Hank Greenberg, Det., 170
Lou Gehrig, N.Y., 119
Jimmie Foxx, Phil., 115
Hal Trosky, Cle., 113
Moose Solters, Bos.-St.L., 112
Joe Vosmik, Cle., 110
Goose Goslin, Det., 109
Bob Johnson, Phil., 109
Charlie Gehringer, Det., 108
Odell Hale, Cle., 101
Buddy Myer, Wash., 100

N.L. 100 RBIs
Wally Berger, Bos., 130
Joe Medwick, St.L., 126
Ripper Collins, St.L., 122
Mel Ott, N.Y., 114
Hank Leiber, N.Y., 107

Most Valuable Player
A.L.: Hank Greenberg, 1B, Det.
N.L.: Gabby Hartnett, C, Chi.

ALL-STAR GAME

■ **Winner:** New York's Lefty Gomez and Cleveland's Mel Harder combined on a four-hitter and the A.L. recorded its third straight All-Star victory, 4-1.

■ **Key inning:** The first, when Athletics slugger Jimmie Foxx belted a two-run homer off Bill Walker, giving Gomez and Harder all the runs they would need.

■ **Memorable moment:** The ovation for hometown favorite Harder after his three-inning, one-hit pitching to close out the N.L.

■ **Top guns:** Gomez (Yankees), Harder (Indians), Foxx (Athletics), Charley Gehringer (Tigers), A.L.; Bill Terry (Giants), N.L.

■ **MVP:** Foxx.

Linescore

July 8, at Cleveland Stadium
N.L. ....0 0 0 1 0 0 0 0 0—1 4 1
A.L. ....2 1 0 0 1 0 0 0 x—4 8 0
Walker (Cardinals), Schumacher (Giants) 3, Derringer (Reds) 7, Dean (Cardinals) 8; Gomez (Yankees), Harder (Indians) 7. W—Gomez. L—Walker. HR—Foxx, A.L.

WORLD SERIES

■ **Winner:** The Tigers, four-time Series losers, won their first in a six-game battle with the Cubs.

■ **Turning point:** Detroit's 6-5 Game 3 victory. Jo Jo White drove in the game-winner with an 11th-inning single, giving the Tigers a two-games-to-one edge.

■ **Memorable moment:** Detroit pitcher Tommy Bridges' dramatic ninth-inning escape in Game 7 after giving up a leadoff triple to Stan Hack with the game tied, 3-3. The Tigers ended the Series in the bottom of the inning.

■ **Top guns:** Bridges (2-0, 2.50 ERA), Pete Fox (.385), Tigers; Lon Warneke (2-0, 0.54), Billy Herman (.333, 6 RBIs), Cubs.

Linescores

Game 1—October 2, at Detroit
Chicago.....................2 0 0 0 0 0 0 0 1—3 7 0
Detroit......................0 0 0 0 0 0 0 0 0—0 4 3
Warneke; Rowe. W—Warneke. L—Rowe. HR—Demaree (Chi.).

Game 2—October 3, at Detroit
Chicago.....................0 0 0 0 1 0 2 0 0—3 6 1
Detroit......................4 0 0 3 0 0 1 0 x—8 9 2
Root, Henshaw (1), Kowalik (4); Bridges. W—Bridges. L—Root. HR—Greenberg (Det.).

Game 3—October 4, at Chicago
Detroit...........0 0 0 0 0 1 0 4 0 0 1—6 12 2
Chicago..........0 2 0 0 1 0 0 0 2 0 0—5 10 3
Auker, Hogsett (7), Rowe (8); Lee, Warneke (8), French (10). W—Rowe. L—French. HR—Demaree (Chi.).

Game 4—October 5, at Chicago
Detroit......................0 0 1 0 0 1 0 0 0—2 7 0
Chicago.....................0 1 0 0 0 0 0 0 0—1 5 2
Crowder; Carleton, Root (8). W—Crowder. L—Carleton. HR—Hartnett (Chi.).

Game 5—October 6, at Chicago
Detroit......................0 0 0 0 0 0 0 0 1—1 7 1
Chicago.....................0 0 2 0 0 0 1 0 x—3 8 0
Rowe; Warneke, Lee (7). W—Warneke. L—Rowe. HR—Klein (Chi.).

Game 6—October 7, at Detroit
Chicago.....................0 0 1 0 2 0 0 0 0—3 12 0
Detroit......................1 0 0 1 0 1 0 0 1—4 12 1
French; Bridges. W—Bridges. L—French. HR—Herman (Chi.).

1936

FINAL STANDINGS

American League

Team	W	L	Pct.	GB
New York	102	51	.667	...
Detroit	83	71	.539	19.5
Chicago	81	70	.536	20
Washington	82	71	.536	20
Cleveland	80	74	.519	22.5
Boston	74	80	.481	28.5
St. Louis	57	95	.375	44.5
Philadelphia	53	100	.346	49

National League

Team	W	L	Pct.	GB
New York	92	62	.597	...
Chicago	87	67	.565	5
St. Louis	87	67	.565	5
Pittsburgh	84	70	.545	8
Cincinnati	74	80	.481	18
Boston	71	83	.461	21
Brooklyn	67	87	.435	25
Philadelphia	54	100	.351	38

SIGNIFICANT EVENTS

■ **February 2:** Ty Cobb, Babe Ruth, Honus Wagner, Walter Johnson and Christy Mathewson were named charter members of baseball's new Hall of Fame.

■ **June 4:** Detroit player/manager Mickey Cochrane collapsed in a Shibe Park dugout and was hospitalized on the threshhold of a career-threatening nervous breakdown.

■ **December 9:** A.L. owners granted the Browns permission to play night baseball in St. Louis and ruled that players must have at least 400 at-bats to qualify for a batting championship.

MEMORABLE MOMENTS

■ **May 24:** Tony Lazzeri drilled three home runs, including a single-game record two grand slams, and drove in an A.L.-record 11 runs in the Yankees' 25-2 pounding of the Athletics.

■ **July 10:** Philadelphia's Chuck Klein became the fourth Major Leaguer to hit four homers in one game, completing his big day with a solo blast leading off the 10th inning of a 9-6 victory over Pittsburgh.

■ **September 13:** Cleveland 17-year-old Bob Feller tied a Major League record when he struck out 17 Athletics in a 5-2 victory.

LEADERS

American League

BA: Luke Appling, Chi., .388.
Runs: Lou Gehrig, N.Y., 167.
Hits: Earl Averill, Cle., 232.
TB: Hal Trosky, Cle., 405.
HR: Lou Gehrig, N.Y., 49.
RBI: Hal Trosky, Cle., 162.
SB: Lyn Lary, St.L., 37.
Wins: Tommy Bridges, Det., 23.
ERA: Lefty Grove, Bos., 2.81.
CG: Wes Ferrell, Bos., 28.
IP: Wes Ferrell, Bos., 301.
SO: Tommy Bridges, Det., 175.

National League

BA: Paul Waner, Pit., .373.
Runs: Arky Vaughan, Pit., 122.
Hits: Joe Medwick, St.L., 223.
TB: Joe Medwick, St.L., 367.
HR: Mel Ott, N.Y., 33.
RBI: Joe Medwick, St.L., 138.
SB: Pepper Martin, St.L., 23.
Wins: Carl Hubbell, N.Y., 26.
ERA: Carl Hubbell, N.Y., 2.31.
CG: Dizzy Dean, St.L., 28.
IP: Dizzy Dean, St.L., 315.
SO: Van Lingle Mungo, Brk., 238.

A.L. 20-game winners
Tommy Bridges, Det., 23-11
Vern Kennedy, Chi., 21-9
Johnny Allen, Cle., 20-10
Red Ruffing, N.Y., 20-12
Wes Ferrell, Bos., 20-15

N.L. 20-game winners
Carl Hubbell, N.Y., 26-6
Dizzy Dean, St.L., 24-13

A.L. 100 RBIs
Hal Trosky, Cle., 162
Lou Gehrig, N.Y., 152
Jimmie Foxx, Bos., 143
Zeke Bonura, Chi., 138
Moose Solters, St.L., 134
Luke Appling, Chi., 128
Earl Averill, Cle., 126
Joe DiMaggio, N.Y., 125
Goose Goslin, Det., 125
Beau Bell, St.L., 123
Bob Johnson, Phil., 121
Joe Kuhel, Wash., 118
Charlie Gehringer, Det., 116
Al Simmons, Det., 112
Tony Lazzeri, N.Y., 109
Bill Dickey, N.Y., 107
George Selkirk, N.Y., 107
Marv Owen, Det., 105

N.L. 100 RBIs
Joe Medwick, St.L., 138
Mel Ott, N.Y., 135
Gus Suhr, Pit., 118
Chuck Klein, Chi.-Phil.,, 104
Bill Brubaker, Pit., 102
Dolph Camilli, Phil., 102

A.L. 40 homers
Lou Gehrig, N.Y., 49
Hal Trosky, Cle., 42
Jimmie Foxx, Bos., 41

Most Valuable Player
A.L.: Lou Gehrig, 1B, N.Y.
N.L.: Carl Hubbell, P, N.Y.

Hall of Fame additions

Charter Class
Ty Cobb, OF, 1905-28
Walter Johnson, P, 1907-27
Christy Mathewson, P, 1900-16
Babe Ruth, P/OF, 1914-35
Honus Wagner, SS, 1897-1917

ALL-STAR GAME

■ **Winner:** The N.L. recorded its first All-Star victory, thanks to the work of three Cubs — Gabby Hartnett (a run-scoring triple), Augie Galan (a solo home run) and pitcher Lon Warneke.

■ **Key inning:** After the A.L. had cut its deficit to 4-3 in the seventh, Warneke retired Yankee slugger Joe DiMaggio on a line drive with the bases loaded.

■ **Memorable moment:** Galan's fifth-inning blast into the right-field bleachers. It drew a vehement protest from A.L. manager Joe McCarthy, who thought it was foul.

■ **Top guns:** Dizzy Dean (Cardinals), Warneke (Cubs), Galan (Cubs), Hartnett (Cubs), N.L.; Lou Gehrig (Yankees), Luke Appling (White Sox), A.L.

■ **MVP:** Warneke.

Linescore

July 7, at Boston's Braves Field
A.L. ....0 0 0 0 0 0 3 0 0—3 7 1
N.L. ....0 2 0 0 2 0 0 0 x—4 9 0
Grove (Red Sox), Rowe (Tigers) 4, Harder (Indians) 7; D. Dean (Cardinals), Hubbell (Giants) 4, Davis (Cubs) 7, Warneke (Cubs) 7. W—D. Dean. L—Grove. HR—Galan, N.L.; Gehrig, A.L.

WORLD SERIES

■ **Winner:** Renewing an old New York rivalry, the Yankees prevailed in their first Series without Babe Ruth.

■ **Turning point:** Lou Gehrig's two-run Game 4 homer off Giants ace Carl Hubbell propelled the Yankees to a 5-2 victory and a three-games-to-one Series lead.

■ **Memorable moment:** Yankee slugger Tony Lazzeri's Game 2 grand slam, only the second in Series history.

■ **Top guns:** Jake Powell (.455), Gehrig (2 HR, 7 RBIs), Red Rolfe (.400), Yankees; Dick Bartell (.381), Giants.

Linescores

Game 1—September 30, at Polo Grounds
Yankees.....................0 0 1 0 0 0 0 0 0—1 7 2
Giants ....0 0 0 0 1 1 0 4 x—6 9 1
Ruffing; Hubbell. W—Hubbell. L—Ruffing. HR—Bartell (NYG); Selkirk (NYY).

Game 2—October 2, at Polo Grounds
Yankees.................2 0 7 0 0 1 2 0 6—18 17 0
Giants ....0 1 0 3 0 0 0 0 0— 4 6 1
Gomez; Schumacher, Smith (3), Coffman (3), Gabler (5), Gumbert (9). W—Gomez. L—Schumacher. HR—Dickey, Lazzeri (NYY).

Game 3—October 3, at Yankee Stadium
Giants ....0 0 0 0 1 0 0 0 0—1 11 0
Yankees...................0 1 0 0 0 0 0 1 x—2 4 0
Fitzsimmons; Hadley, Malone (9). W—Hadley. L—Fitzsimmons. HR—Gehrig (NYY); Ripple (NYG).

Game 4—October 4, at Yankee Stadium
Giants ....0 0 0 1 0 0 0 1 0—2 7 1
Yankees...................0 1 3 0 0 0 0 1 x—5 10 1
Hubbell, Gabler (8); Pearson. W—Pearson. L—Hubbell. HR—Gehrig (NYY).

Game 5—October 5, at Yankee Stadium
Giants ....3 0 0 0 0 1 0 0 0 1—5 8 3
Yankees...............0 1 1 0 0 2 0 0 0 0—4 10 1
Schumacher; Ruffing, Malone (7). W—Schumacher. L—Malone. HR—Selkirk (NYY).

Game 6—October 6, at Polo Grounds
Yankees.................0 2 1 2 0 0 0 1 7—13 17 2
Giants ....2 0 0 0 1 0 1 1 0— 5 9 1
Gomez, Murphy (7); Fitzsimmons, Castleman (4), Coffman (9), Gumbert (9). W—Gomez. L—Fitzsimmons. HR—Moore, Ott (NYG); Powell (NYY).

HISTORY

1937

FINAL STANDINGS

American League

Team	W	L	Pct.	GB
New York	102	52	.662	...
Detroit	89	65	.578	13
Chicago	86	68	.558	16
Cleveland	83	71	.539	19
Boston	80	72	.526	21
Washington	73	80	.477	28.5
Philadelphia	54	97	.358	46.5
St. Louis	46	108	.299	56

National League

Team	W	L	Pct.	GB
New York	95	57	.625	...
Chicago	93	61	.604	3
Pittsburgh	86	68	.558	10
St. Louis	81	73	.526	15
Boston	79	73	.520	16
Brooklyn	62	91	.405	33.5
Philadelphia	61	92	.399	34.5
Cincinnati	56	98	.364	40

SIGNIFICANT EVENTS

■ **May 25:** Detroit player/manager Mickey Cochrane suffered a career-ending skull fracture when he was struck by a pitch from Yankee Bump Hadley.

■ **May 26:** Commissioner Kenesaw Mountain Landis took the All-Star vote away from the fans and decreed that the two managers would select future teams.

MEMORABLE MOMENTS

■ **April 20:** Detroit outfielder Gee Walker carved out his own piece of the Major League record book when he hit a single, double, triple and home run in a season-opening victory over Cleveland—the first player to hit for the cycle on Opening Day.

■ **May 27:** Giants lefty Carl Hubbell, asked to make a rare relief appearance, pitched two scoreless innings and earned a 3-2 victory over the Reds, his record 24th straight over two seasons.

■ **August 31:** Detroit rookie Rudy York hit two home runs against Washington, capping the biggest home run-hitting month in baseball history with 18.

■ **October 3:** Cleveland's Johnny Allen, 15-0 and one win from tying the A.L. record for consecutive victories, dropped a 1-0 final-day decision to Detroit.

■ **October 3:** St. Louis' Joe Medwick captured an N.L. Triple Crown, batting .374, driving in 154 runs and tying New York's Mel Ott with 31 homers.

LEADERS

American League

BA: Charley Gehringer, Det., .371.
Runs: Joe DiMaggio, N.Y., 151.
Hits: Beau Bell, St.L., 218.
TB: Joe DiMaggio, N.Y., 418.
HR: Joe DiMaggio, N.Y., 46.
RBI: Hank Greenberg, Det., 183.
SB: Ben Chapman, Wash.-Bos.; Billy Werber, Phil., 35.
Wins: Lefty Gomez, N.Y., 21.
ERA: Lefty Gomez, N.Y., 2.33.
CG: Wes Ferrell, Wash.-Bos., 26.
IP: Wes Ferrell, Wash.-Bos., 281.
SO: Lefty Gomez, N.Y., 194.

National League

BA: Joe Medwick, St.L., .374.
Runs: Joe Medwick, St.L., 111.
Hits: Joe Medwick, St.L., 237.
TB: Joe Medwick, St.L., 406.
HR: Joe Medwick, St.L.; Mel Ott, N.Y., 31.
RBI: Joe Medwick, St.L., 154.
SB: Augie Galan, Chi., 23.
Wins: Carl Hubbell, N.Y., 22.
ERA: Jim Turner, Bos., 2.38.
CG: Jim Turner, Bos., 24.
IP: Claude Passeau, Phil., 292.1.
SO: Carl Hubbell, N.Y., 159.

A.L. 20-game winners

Lefty Gomez, N.Y., 21-11
Red Ruffing, N.Y., 20-7

N.L. 20-game winners

Carl Hubbell, N.Y., 22-8
Cliff Melton, N.Y., 20-9
Lou Fette, Bos., 20-10
Jim Turner, Bos., 20-11

A.L. 100 RBIs

Hank Greenberg, Det., 183
Joe DiMaggio, N.Y., 167
Lou Gehrig, N.Y., 159
Bill Dickey, N.Y., 133
Hal Trosky, Cle., 128
Jimmie Foxx, Bos., 127
Harlond Clift, St.L., 118
Beau Bell, St.L., 117
Gee Walker, Det., 113
Joe Cronin, Bos., 110
Moose Solters, Cle., 109
Bob Johnson, Phil., 108
Pinky Higgins, Bos., 106
Rudy York, Det., 103
Zeke Bonura, Chi., 100

N.L. 100 RBIs

Joe Medwick, St.L., 154
Frank Demaree, Chi., 115
Johnny Mize, St.L., 113

A.L. 40 homers

Joe DiMaggio, N.Y., 46
Hank Greenberg, Det., 40

Most Valuable Player

A.L.: Charley Gehringer, 2B, Det.
N.L.: Joe Medwick, OF, St.L.

Hall of Fame additions

Morgan Bulkeley, executive
Ban Johnson, executive
Napoleon Lajoie, 2B, 1896-1916
Connie Mack, manager/owner
John McGraw, manager
Tris Speaker, OF, 1907-28
George Wright, player/manager
Cy Young, P, 1890-1911

ALL-STAR GAME

■ **Winner:** Yankees Lou Gehrig, Red Rolfe and Bill Dickey combined for seven RBIs and teammate Lefty Gomez claimed his third All-Star victory as the A.L. won for the fourth time in five years.

■ **Key inning:** The third, when Gehrig blasted a Dizzy Dean pitch for a two-run homer. The Yankee first baseman later added a two-run double.

■ **Memorable moment:** A third-inning Earl Averill line drive that deflected off the foot of Dean. The Cardinals' righthander suffered a broken toe that would begin to unravel his outstanding career.

■ **Top guns:** Gomez (Yankees), Gehrig (Yankees), Rolfe (Yankees), Dickey (Yankees), Charley Gehringer (Tigers), A.L.; Joe Medwick (Cardinals), Billy Herman (Cubs), N.L.

■ **MVP:** Gehrig.

Linescore

July 7, at Washington's Griffith Stadium
N.L. ....0 0 0 1 1 1 0 0 0—3 13 0
A.L. ....0 0 2 3 1 2 0 0 x—8 13 2
D. Dean (Cardinals), Hubbell (Giants) 4, Blanton (Pirates) 4, Grissom (Reds) 5, Mungo (Dodgers) 6, Walters (Phillies) 8; Gomez (Yankees), Bridges (Tigers) 4, Harder (Indians) 7. W—Gomez. L—D. Dean. HR—Gehrig, A.L.

WORLD SERIES

■ **Winner:** Two in a row. The first of several big Yankee World Series runs began to take shape.

■ **Turning point:** The Yankees' 8-1 pounding of Giants ace Carl Hubbell in Game 1.

■ **Memorable moment:** Yankee pitcher Lefty Gomez, a notoriously poor hitter, driving in the Game 5 winner with a fifth-inning single.

■ **Top guns:** Gomez (2-0, 1.50 ERA), Tony Lazzeri (.400), Yankees; Joe Moore (.391), Giants.

Linescores

Game 1—October 6, at Yankee Stadium
Giants ....0 0 0 0 1 0 0 0 0—1 6 2
Yankees ....0 0 0 0 0 7 0 1 x—8 7 0
Hubbell, Gumbert (6), Coffman (6), Smith (8); Gomez. W—Gomez. L—Hubbell. HR—Lazzeri (NYY).

Game 2—October 7, at Yankee Stadium
Giants ....1 0 0 0 0 0 0 0 0—1 7 0
Yankees ....0 0 0 0 2 4 2 0 x—8 12 0
Melton, Gumbert (5), Coffman (6); Ruffing. W—Ruffing. L—Melton.

Game 3—October 8, at Polo Grounds
Yankees ....0 1 2 1 1 0 0 0 0—5 9 0
Giants ....0 0 0 0 0 0 1 0 0—1 5 4
Pearson, Murphy (9); Schumacher, Melton (7), Brennan (9). W—Pearson. L—Schumacher.

Game 4—October 9, at Polo Grounds
Yankees ....1 0 1 0 0 0 0 0 1—3 6 0
Giants ....0 6 0 0 0 0 1 0 x—7 12 3
Hadley, Andrews (2), Wicker (8); Hubbell. W—Hubbell. L—Hadley. HR—Gehrig (NYY).

Game 5—October 10, at Polo Grounds
Yankees ....0 1 1 0 2 0 0 0 0—4 8 0
Giants ....0 0 2 0 0 0 0 0 0—2 10 0
Gomez; Melton, Smith (6), Brennan (8). W—Gomez. L—Melton. HR—DiMaggio, Hoag (NYY); Ott (NYG).

1938

FINAL STANDINGS

American League

Team	W	L	Pct.	GB
New York	99	53	.651	...
Boston	88	61	.591	9.5
Cleveland	86	66	.566	13
Detroit	84	70	.545	16
Washington	75	76	.497	23.5
Chicago	65	83	.439	32
St. Louis	55	97	.362	44
Philadelphia	53	99	.349	46

National League

Team	W	L	Pct.	GB
Chicago	89	63	.586	...
Pittsburgh	86	64	.573	2
New York	83	67	.553	5
Cincinnati	82	68	.547	6
Boston	77	75	.507	12
St. Louis	71	80	.470	17.5
Brooklyn	69	80	.463	18.5
Philadelphia	45	105	.300	43

SIGNIFICANT EVENTS

■ **April 16:** The Cardinals sent shockwaves through baseball when they traded ace Dizzy Dean to the Cubs for two pitchers and an outfielder.

■ **May 31:** Yankee Lou Gehrig stretched his ironman streak to an incredible 2,000 games during a victory over Boston.

■ **December 14:** The N.L. granted Cincinnati, baseball's first professional team, permission to play its traditional season opener.

MEMORABLE MOMENTS

■ **June 15:** Cincinnati's Johnny Vander Meer pitched his record second consecutive no-hitter, a 6-0 victory that stole the spotlight from the Dodgers in the first night game at Brooklyn's Ebbets Field.

■ **June 21:** Boston third baseman Pinky Higgins etched his name in the record books when he collected 12 consecutive hits over a two-day, four-game stretch against Chicago and Detroit.

■ **September 28:** Moments away from a suspended game, Chicago catcher Gabby Hartnett stroked a ninth-inning homer into the thickening darkness of Wrigley Field, giving the Cubs a crucial 6-5 victory over Pittsburgh and half-game lead in the tense N.L. pennant race.

■ **October 2:** Cleveland's Bob Feller struck out a Major League-record 18 batters while losing a 4-1 decision to the Tigers.

LEADERS

American League

BA: Jimmie Foxx, Bos., .349.
Runs: Hank Greenberg, Det., 144.
Hits: Joe Vosmik, Bos., 201.
TB: Jimmie Foxx, Bos., 398.
HR: Hank Greenberg, Det., 58.
RBI: Jimmie Foxx, Bos., 175.
SB: Frank Crosetti, N.Y., 27.
Wins: Red Ruffing, N.Y., 21.
ERA: Lefty Grove, Bos., 3.08.
CG: Bobo Newsom, St.L., 31.
IP: Bobo Newsom, St.L., 329.2.
SO: Bob Feller, Cle., 240.

National League

BA: Ernie Lombardi, Cin., .342.
Runs: Mel Ott, N.Y., 116.
Hits: Frank McCormick, Cin., 209.
TB: Johnny Mize, St.L., 326.
HR: Mel Ott, N.Y., 36.
RBI: Joe Medwick, St.L., 122.
SB: Stan Hack, Chi., 16.
Wins: Bill Lee, Chi., 22.
ERA: Bill Lee, Chi., 2.66.
CG: Paul Derringer, Cin., 26.
IP: Paul Derringer, Cin., 307.
SO: Clay Bryant, Chi., 135.

A.L. 20-game winners

Red Ruffing, N.Y., 21-7
Bobo Newsom, St.L., 20-16

N.L. 20-game winners

Bill Lee, Chi., 22-9
Paul Derringer, Cin., 21-14

A.L. 100 RBIs

Jimmie Foxx, Bos., 175
Hank Greenberg, Det., 146
Joe DiMaggio, N.Y., 140
Rudy York, Det., 127
Harlond Clift, St.L., 118
Bill Dickey, N.Y., 115
Zeke Bonura, Wash., 114
Lou Gehrig, N.Y., 114
Bob Johnson, Phil., 113
Ken Keltner, Cle., 113
Jeff Heath, Cle., 112
Hal Trosky, Cle., 110
Charlie Gehringer, Det., 107
Pinky Higgins, Bos., 106

N.L. 100 RBIs

Joe Medwick, St.L., 122
Mel Ott, N.Y., 116
Johnny Rizzo, Pit., 111
Frank McCormick, Cin., 106
Johnny Mize, St.L., 102
Dolph Camilli, Brk., 100

A.L. 40 homers

Hank Greenberg, Det., 58
Jimmie Foxx, Bos., 50

Most Valuable Player

A.L.: Jimmie Foxx, 1B, Bos.
N.L.: Ernie Lombardi, C, Cin.

Hall of Fame additions

Grover Alexander, P, 1911-30
Alexander Cartwright, executive
Henry Chadwick, historian, executive

ALL-STAR GAME

■ **Winner:** Cincinnati's Johnny Vander Meer, Chicago's Bill Lee and Pittsburgh's Mace Brown held the A.L. to seven hits as the N.L. claimed its second All-Star victory.

■ **Key inning:** The first, when the N.L. took a lead it never surrendered on Red Sox shortstop Joe Cronin's error.

■ **Memorable moment:** A seventh-inning sacrifice bunt by Brooklyn's Leo Durocher that resulted in two N.L. runs. Durocher circled the bases when third baseman Jimmie Foxx and right fielder Joe DiMaggio made wild throws on the play.

■ **Top guns:** Vander Meer (Reds), Lee (Cubs), Ernie Lombardi (Reds), N.L.; Cronin (Red Sox), A.L.

■ **MVP:** Vander Meer.

Linescore

July 6, at Cincinnati's Crosley Field
A.L. ....0 0 0 0 0 0 0 0 1—1 7 4
N.L. ....1 0 0 1 0 0 2 0 x—4 8 0
Gomez (Yankees), Allen (Indians) 4, Grove (Red Sox) 7; Vander Meer (Reds), Lee (Cubs) 4, Brown (Pirates) 7. W—Vander Meer. L—Gomez.

WORLD SERIES

■ **Winner:** Three in a row. Another Series first for the vaunted Yankee machine of Joe McCarthy.

■ **Turning point:** Light-hitting Frankie Crosetti hit an eighth-inning Game 2 homer, helping the Yankees rally to a 6-3 victory over Chicago veteran Dizzy Dean.

■ **Memorable moment:** Lou Gehrig's fourth-game single — his last hit in World Series competition.

■ **Top guns:** Red Ruffing (2-0, 1.50 ERA), Bill Dickey (.400), Joe Gordon (.400, 6 RBIs), Crosetti (6 RBIs), Yankees; Stan Hack (.471), Cubs.

Linescores

Game 1—October 5, at Chicago
New York ....0 2 0 0 0 0 1 0 0—3 12 1
Chicago ....0 0 1 0 0 0 0 0 0—1 9 1
Ruffing; Lee, Russell (9). W—Ruffing. L—Lee.

Game 2—October 6, at Chicago
New York ....0 2 0 0 0 0 0 2 2—6 7 2
Chicago ....1 0 2 0 0 0 0 0 0—3 11 0
Gomez, Murphy (8); Dean, French (9). W—Gomez. L—Dean. HR—Crosetti, DiMaggio (N.Y.).

Game 3—October 8, at New York
Chicago ....0 0 0 0 1 0 0 1 0—2 5 1
New York ....0 0 0 0 2 2 0 1 x—5 7 2
Bryant, Russell (6), French (7); Pearson. W—Pearson. L—Bryant. HR—Dickey, Gordon (N.Y.); Marty (Chi.).

Game 4—October 9, at New York
Chicago ....0 0 0 1 0 0 0 2 0—3 8 1
New York ....0 3 0 0 0 1 0 4 x—8 11 1
Lee, Root (4), Page (7), French (8), Carleton (8), Dean (8); Ruffing. W—Ruffing. L—Lee. HR—Henrich (N.Y.); O'Dea (Chi.).

1939

FINAL STANDINGS

American League

Team	W	L	Pct.	GB
New York	106	45	.702	...
Boston	89	62	.589	17
Cleveland	87	67	.565	20.5
Chicago	85	69	.552	22.5
Detroit	81	73	.526	26.5
Washington	65	87	.428	41.5
Philadelphia	55	97	.362	51.5
St. Louis	43	111	.279	64.5

National League

Team	W	L	Pct.	GB
Cincinnati	97	57	.630	...
St. Louis	92	61	.601	4.5
Brooklyn	84	69	.549	12.5
Chicago	84	70	.545	13
New York	77	74	.510	18.5
Pittsburgh	68	85	.444	28.5
Boston	63	88	.417	32.5
Philadelphia	45	106	.298	50.5

SIGNIFICANT EVENTS

■ **June 12:** Baseball dignitaries, gathering in Cooperstown, N.Y., for a centennial celebration, dedicated the sport's new Hall of Fame museum and inducted its first four classes of Hall of Famers.

■ **August 26:** Red Barber handled the play-by-play as experimental station W2XBS presented Major League baseball's first telecast, a game between the Dodgers and Reds at Ebbets Field.

MEMORABLE MOMENTS

■ **May 16:** The visiting Indians recorded a 10-inning 8-3 victory in the A.L.'s first night game at Philadelphia's Shibe Park.

■ **June 27:** Brooklyn and Boston battled for 23 innings and more than five hours before settling for a 2-2 tie in a marathon game at Braves Field.

■ **June 28:** The New York Yankees rocketed a doubleheader-record 13 home runs out of Shibe Park in a 23-2 and 10-0 sweep of the Athletics.

■ **July 4:** Lou Gehrig, forced to end his incredible ironman streak at 2,130 games and retire because of a life-threatening disease, was honored in an emotional farewell at Yankee Stadium.

■ **July 4:** Boston's Jim Tabor tied a Major League record with two grand slams during an 18-12 victory over the Athletics.

LEADERS

American League

BA: Joe DiMaggio, N.Y., .381.
Runs: Red Rolfe, N.Y., 139.
Hits: Red Rolfe, N.Y., 213.
TB: Ted Williams, Bos., 344.
HR: Jimmie Foxx, Bos., 35.
RBI: Ted Williams, Bos., 145.
SB: George Case, Wash., 51.
Wins: Bob Feller, Cle., 24.
ERA: Lefty Grove, Bos., 2.54.
CG: Bob Feller, Cle.; Bobo Newsom, St.L.-Det., 24.
IP: Bob Feller, Cle., 296.2.
SO: Bob Feller, Cle., 246.

National League

BA: Johnny Mize, St.L., .349.
Runs: Billy Werber, Cin., 115.
Hits: Frank McCormick, Cin., 209.
TB: Johnny Mize, St.L., 353.
HR: Johnny Mize, St.L., 28.
RBI: Frank McCormick, Cin., 128.
SB: Stan Hack, Chi.; Lee Handley, Pit., 17.
Wins: Bucky Walters, Cin., 27.
ERA: Bucky Walters, Cin., 2.29.
CG: Bucky Walters, Cin., 31.
IP: Bucky Walters, Cin., 319.
SO: Claude Passeau, Phil.-Chi.; Bucky Walters, Cin., 137.

A.L. 20-game winners
Bob Feller, Cle., 24-9
Red Ruffing, N.Y., 21-7
Dutch Leonard, Wash., 20-8
Bobo Newsom, St.L.-Det., 20-11

N.L. 20-game winners
Bucky Walters, Cin., 27-11
Paul Derringer, Cin., 25-7
Curt Davis, St.L., 22-16
Luke Hamlin, Brk., 20-13

A.L. 100 RBIs
Ted Williams, Bos., 145
Joe DiMaggio, N.Y., 126
Bob Johnson, Phil., 114
Hank Greenberg, Det., 112
Joe Gordon, N.Y., 111
Gee Walker, Chi., 111
Joe Cronin, Bos., 107
Bill Dickey, N.Y., 105
Jimmie Foxx, Bos., 105
Hal Trosky, Cle., 104
George Selkirk, N.Y., 101

N.L. 100 RBIs
Frank McCormick, Cin., 128
Joe Medwick, St.L., 117
Johnny Mize, St.L., 108
Dolph Camilli, Brk., 104

Most Valuable Player
A.L.: Joe DiMaggio, OF, N.Y.
N.L.: Bucky Walters, P, Cin.

Hall of Fame additions
Cap Anson, 1B, 1876-97
Eddie Collins, 2B, 1906-30
Charles Comiskey, manager/exec.
Candy Cummings, P, 1872-77
Buck Ewing, C, 1880-97
Lou Gehrig, 1B, 1923-39
Willie Keeler, OF, 1892-1910
Hoss Radbourn, P, 1880-91
George Sisler, 1B, 1915-30
Al Spalding, pitcher/executive

ALL-STAR GAME

■ **Winner:** The A.L.'s Yankee-studded lineup posted a ho-hum 3-1 victory before 62,892 fans at Yankee Stadium.

■ **Key inning:** The sixth, when the N.L. loaded the bases with one out. Indians fireballer Bob Feller was summoned and got Pittsburgh's Arky Vaughan to hit into a first-pitch double play. Feller allowed one hit the rest of the way.

■ **Memorable moment:** Joe DiMaggio's fifth-inning home run, which touched off a celebration among ecstatic Yankee fans.

■ **Top guns:** Tommy Bridges (Tigers), Feller (Indians), George Selkirk (Yankees), DiMaggio (Yankees), A.L.; Paul Derringer (Reds), Lonny Frey (Reds), N.L.

■ **MVP:** Feller.

Linescore

July 11, at New York's Yankee Stadium
N.L. ....0 0 1 0 0 0 0 0 0 — 1 7 1
A.L. ....0 0 0 2 1 0 0 0 x — 3 6 1
Derringer (Reds), Lee (Cubs) 4, Fette (Braves) 7; Ruffing (Yankees), Bridges (Tigers) 4, Feller (Indians) 6. W—Bridges. L—Lee. HR—DiMaggio, A.L.

WORLD SERIES

■ **Winner:** Four in a row. The Yankees recorded their second straight sweep and 13th victory in 14 Series games.

■ **Turning point:** Bill Dickey's ninth-inning single gave New York a 2-1 victory in Game 1 and momentum the Reds could not stop.

■ **Memorable moment:** A strange Game 4 play that helped produce three 10th-inning Yankee runs. Joe DiMaggio singled to right with two runners aboard and circled the bases when Reds catcher Ernie Lombardi lay dazed after a home-plate collision with Yankee runner Charlie Keller. "Lombardi's Snooze."

■ **Top guns:** Keller (.438, 3 HR, 6 RBIs), Dickey (2 HR, 5 RBIs), Yankees; Frank McCormick (.400), Reds.

Linescores

Game 1—October 4, at New York
Cincinnati 0 0 0 1 0 0 0 0 0 — 1 4 0
New York 0 0 0 0 1 0 0 0 1 — 2 6 0
Derringer; Ruffing. W—Ruffing. L—Derringer.

Game 2—October 5, at New York
Cincinnati 0 0 0 0 0 0 0 0 0 — 0 2 0
New York 0 0 3 1 0 0 0 0 x — 4 9 0
Walters; Pearson. W—Pearson. L—Walters. HR—Dahlgren (N.Y.).

Game 3—October 7, at Cincinnati
New York 2 0 2 0 3 0 0 0 0 — 7 5 1
Cincinnati 1 2 0 0 0 0 0 0 0 — 3 10 0
Gomez, Hadley (2); Thompson, Grissom (5), Moore (7). W—Hadley. L—Thompson. HR—Keller 2, DiMaggio, Dickey (N.Y.).

Game 4—October 8, at Cincinnati
New York 0 0 0 0 0 0 2 0 2 3—7 7 1
Cincinnati 0 0 0 0 0 0 3 1 0 0—4 11 4
Hildebrand, Sundra (5), Murphy (7); Derringer, Walters (8). W—Murphy. L—Walters. HR—Keller, Dickey (N.Y.).

1940

FINAL STANDINGS

American League

Team	W	L	Pct.	GB
Detroit	90	64	.584	...
Cleveland	89	65	.578	1
New York	88	66	.571	2
Boston	82	72	.532	8
Chicago	82	72	.532	8
St. Louis	67	87	.435	23
Washington	64	90	.416	26
Philadelphia	54	100	.351	36

National League

Team	W	L	Pct.	GB
Cincinnati	100	53	.654	...
Brooklyn	88	65	.575	12
St. Louis	84	69	.549	16
Pittsburgh	78	76	.506	22.5
Chicago	75	79	.487	25.5
New York	72	80	.474	27.5
Boston	65	87	.428	34.5
Philadelphia	50	103	.327	50

SIGNIFICANT EVENTS

■ **January 14:** In the biggest free-agency ruling ever handed down, Commissioner Kenesaw Mountain Landis freed 91 members of the Tigers organization, citing player-movement coverup.

■ **May 7:** The Dodgers became the first N.L. team to travel by air, flying in two planes from St. Louis to Chicago.

■ **May 24, June 4:** The first night games were played at New York's Polo Grounds, St. Louis' Sportsman's Park and Pittsburgh's Forbes Field.

■ **August 3:** Reds catcher Willard Hershberger, despondent over what he considered inadequate play, committed suicide in his Boston hotel room.

MEMORABLE MOMENTS

■ **April 16:** Cleveland's Bob Feller fired the first Opening Day no-hitter in baseball history, beating the White Sox, 1-0, at Chicago's Comiskey Park.

■ **September 24:** Jimmie Foxx became baseball's second 500-homer man when he hit one of Boston's four sixth-inning blasts in a 16-8 victory over the Athletics.

■ **September 27:** Detroit rookie Floyd Giebell ignored near-riotous Cleveland fans and outpitched Bob Feller in an A.L. pennant-clinching 2-0 Tigers victory.

LEADERS

American League

BA: Joe DiMaggio, N.Y., .352.
Runs: Ted Williams, Bos., 134.
Hits: Doc Cramer, Bos.; Barney McCosky, Det.; Rip Radcliff, St.L., 200.
TB: Hank Greenberg, Det., 384.
HR: Hank Greenberg, Det., 41.
RBI: Hank Greenberg, Det., 150.
SB: George Case, Wash., 35.
Wins: Bob Feller, Cle., 27.
ERA: Bob Feller, Cle., 2.61.
CG: Bob Feller, Cle., 31.
IP: Bob Feller, Cle., 320.1.
SO: Bob Feller, Cle., 261.

National League

BA: Debs Garms, Pit., .355.
Runs: Arky Vaughan, Pit., 113.
Hits: Stan Hack, Chi.; Frank McCormick, Cin., 191.
TB: Johnny Mize, St.L., 368.
HR: Johnny Mize, St.L., 43.
RBI: Johnny Mize, St.L., 137.
SB: Lonny Frey, Cin., 22.
Wins: Bucky Walters, Cin., 22.
ERA: Bucky Walters, Cin., 2.48.
CG: Bucky Walters, Cin., 29.
IP: Bucky Walters, Cin., 305.
SO: Kirby Higbe, Phil., 137.

A.L. 20-game winners
Bob Feller, Cle., 27-11
Bobo Newsom, Det., 21-5

N.L. 20-game winners
Bucky Walters, Cin., 22-10
Paul Derringer, Cin., 20-12
Claude Passeau, Chi., 20-13

A.L. 100 RBIs
Hank Greenberg, Det., 150
Rudy York, Det., 134
Joe DiMaggio, N.Y., 133
Jimmie Foxx, Bos., 119
Ted Williams, Bos., 113
Joe Cronin, Bos, 111
Bobby Doerr, Bos., 105
Joe Gordon, N.Y., 103
Bob Johnson, Phil., 103
Lou Boudreau, Cle., 101

N.L. 100 RBIs
Johnny Mize, St.L., 137
Frank McCormick, Cin., 127
Maurice Van Robays, Pit., 116
Elbie Fletcher, Pit., 104
Babe Young, N.Y., 101

A.L. 40 homers
Hank Greenberg, Det., 41

N.L. 40 homers
Johnny Mize, St.L., 43

Most Valuable Player
A.L.: Hank Greenberg, OF, Det.
N.L.: Frank McCormick, 1B, Cin.

ALL-STAR GAME

■ **Winner:** Five N.L. pitchers shut down the A.L. on three hits and recorded the first shutout in All-Star Game history.

■ **Key inning:** The first, when Boston's Max West connected with a Red Ruffing delivery for a three-run homer.

■ **Memorable moment:** An inning after his home run, West crashed into the outfield wall while chasing a fly ball and had to be helped off the field.

■ **Top guns:** Paul Derringer (Reds), Bucky Walters (Reds), Whitlow Wyatt (Dodgers), Larry French (Cubs), Carl Hubbell (Giants), West (Braves), Billy Herman (Cubs), N.L.; Luke Appling (White Sox), A.L.

■ **MVP:** West.

Linescore

July 9, at St. Louis' Sportsman's Park
A.L. ....0 0 0 0 0 0 0 0 0—0 3 1
N.L. ....3 0 0 0 0 0 0 1 x—4 7 0
Ruffing (Yankees), Newsom (Tigers) 4, Feller (Indians) 7; Derringer (Reds), Walters (Reds) 3, Wyatt (Dodgers) 5, French (Cubs) 7, Hubbell (Giants) 9. W—Derringer. L—Ruffing. HR—West, N.L.

WORLD SERIES

■ **Winner:** The Reds needed seven games to dispatch the Tigers and capture their first non-tainted World Series.

■ **Turning point:** The Reds' Game 6 victory in which Bucky Walters pitched a 4-0 shutout and also hit a home run.

■ **Memorable moment:** Reds pitcher Paul Derringer retiring Detroit in order in a tense ninth inning of Game 7.

■ **Top guns:** Walters (2-0, 1.50 ERA), Jimmy Ripple (.333, 6 RBIs), Reds; Hank Greenberg (.357, 6 RBIs), Pinky Higgins (.333, 6 RBIs), Tigers.

Linescores

Game 1—October 2, at Cincinnati
Detroit ....0 5 0 0 2 0 0 0 0—7 10 1
Cincinnati.................0 0 0 1 0 0 0 1 0—2 8 3
Newsom; Derringer, Moore (2), Riddle (9). W—Newsom. L—Derringer. HR—Campbell (Det.).

Game 2—October 3, at Cincinnati
Detroit ....2 0 0 0 0 1 0 0 0—3 3 1
Cincinnati..................0 2 2 1 0 0 0 0 x—5 9 0
Rowe, Gorsica (4); Walters. W—Walters. L—Rowe. HR—Ripple (Cin.).

Game 3—October 4, at Detroit
Cincinnati................1 0 0 0 0 0 0 1 2—4 10 1
Detroit ....0 0 0 1 0 0 4 2 x—7 13 1
Turner, Moore (7), Beggs (8); Bridges. W—Bridges. L—Turner. HR—York, Higgins (Det.).

Game 4—October 5, at Detroit
Cincinnati................2 0 1 1 0 0 0 1 0—5 11 1
Detroit ....0 0 1 0 0 1 0 0 0—2 5 1
Derringer; Trout, Smith (3), McKain (7). W—Derringer. L—Trout.

Game 5—October 6, at Detroit
Cincinnati................0 0 0 0 0 0 0 0 0—0 3 0
Detroit ....0 0 3 4 0 0 0 1 x—8 13 0
Thompson, Moore (4), Vander Meer (5), Hutchings (8); Newsom. W—Newsom. L—Thompson. HR—Greenberg (Det.).

Game 6—October 7, at Cincinnati
Detroit ....0 0 0 0 0 0 0 0 0—0 5 0
Cincinnati................2 0 0 0 0 1 0 1 x—4 10 2
Rowe, Gorsica (1), Hutchinson (8); Walters. W—Walters. L—Rowe. HR—Walters (Cin.).

Game 7—October 8, at Cincinnati
Detroit ....0 0 1 0 0 0 0 0 0—1 7 0
Cincinnati..................0 0 0 0 0 0 2 0 x—2 7 1
Newsom; Derringer. W—Derringer. L—Newsom.

1941

FINAL STANDINGS

American League

Team	W	L	Pct.	GB
New York	101	53	.656	...
Boston	84	70	.545	17
Chicago	77	77	.500	24
Cleveland	75	79	.487	26
Detroit	75	79	.487	26
St. Louis	70	84	.455	31
Washington	70	84	.455	31
Philadelphia	64	90	.416	37

National League

Team	W	L	Pct.	GB
Brooklyn	100	54	.649	...
St. Louis	97	56	.634	2.5
Cincinnati	88	66	.571	12
Pittsburgh	81	73	.526	19
New York	74	79	.484	25.5
Chicago	70	84	.455	30
Boston	62	92	.403	38
Philadelphia	43	111	.279	57

SIGNIFICANT EVENTS

- **May 1:** Dodgers President Larry MacPhail submitted a patent application on the "Brooklyn Safety Cap," a hat lined with plastic to protect players from bean balls.
- **May 7:** Detroit slugger Hank Greenberg reported for duty in the U.S. Army—one of many Major Leaguers who would leave baseball to fight in World War II.
- **June 2:** Former Yankee great Lou Gehrig died at age 37 from the incurable disease that had forced his retirement two years earlier.
- **May 28:** The Senators dropped a 6-5 decision to the Yankees in the first night game at Washington's Griffith Stadium.

MEMORABLE MOMENTS

- **July 17:** Yankee center fielder Joe DiMaggio's record 56-game hitting streak was stopped by pitchers Al Smith and Jim Bagby Jr. at Cleveland Stadium.
- **July 25:** Boston's Lefty Grove joined the 300-victory club when he staggered to a 10-6 victory over Cleveland at Fenway Park.
- **September 4:** The Yankees recorded the earliest pennant-clinching date in history when they defeated Boston, 6-3.
- **November 27:** Yankee Joe DiMaggio won the A.L. MVP by a slim 37-point margin over Boston's Ted Williams, baseball's first .400 hitter (.406) since 1930.

LEADERS

American League

BA: Ted Williams, Bos., .406.
Runs: Ted Williams, Bos., 135.
Hits: Cecil Travis, Wash., 218.
TB: Joe DiMaggio, N.Y., 348.
HR: Ted Williams, Bos., 37.
RBI: Joe DiMaggio, N.Y., 125.
SB: George Case, Wash., 33.
Wins: Bob Feller, Cle., 25.
ERA: Thornton Lee, Chi., 2.37.
CG: Thornton Lee, Chi., 30.
IP: Bob Feller, Cle., 343.
SO: Bob Feller, Cle., 260.

National League

BA: Pete Reiser, Brk., .343.
Runs: Pete Reiser, Brk., 117.
Hits: Stan Hack, Chi., 186.
TB: Pete Reiser, Brk., 299.
HR: Dolph Camilli, Brk., 34.
RBI: Dolph Camilli, Brk., 120.
SB: Danny Murtaugh, Phil., 18.
Wins: Kirby Higbe, Brk.; Whitlow Wyatt, Brk., 22.
ERA: Elmer Riddle, Cin., 2.24.
CG: Bucky Walters, Cin., 27.
IP: Bucky Walters, Cin., 302.
SO: Johnny Vander Meer, Cin., 202.

A.L. 20-game winners
Bob Feller, Cle., 25-13
Thornton Lee, Chi., 22-11

N.L. 20-game winners
Kirby Higbe, Brk., 22-9
Whitlow Wyatt, Brk., 22-10

A.L. 100 RBIs
Joe DiMaggio, N.Y., 125
Jeff Heath, Cle., 123
Charlie Keller, N.Y., 122
Ted Williams, Bos., 120
Rudy York, Det., 111
Bob Johnson, Phil., 107
Sam Chapman, Phil., 106
Jimmie Foxx, Bos., 105
Jim Tabor, Bos., 101
Cecil Travis, Wash., 101

N.L. 100 RBIs
Dolph Camilli, Brk., 120
Babe Young, N.Y., 104
Vince DiMaggio, Pit., 100
Johnny Mize, St.L., 100

Most Valuable Player
A.L.: Joe DiMaggio, OF, N.Y.
N.L.: Dolf Camilli, 1B, Brk.

ALL-STAR GAME

- **Winner:** The A.L. scored four ninth-inning runs and overcame a pair of home runs by Pittsburgh's Arky Vaughan for a 7-5 victory in the most exciting All-Star Game in the classic's nine-year history.
- **Key inning:** The ninth, when the A.L. overcame a 5-3 deficit to claim its sixth victory in nine All-Star Games.
- **Memorable moment:** A dramatic game-ending, three-run homer by Boston slugger Ted Williams with two out in the ninth. Williams connected off Chicago's Claude Passeau after the N.L. had botched what could have been a game-ending double play.
- **Top guns:** Bob Feller (Indians), Williams (Red Sox), Lou Boudreau (Indians), A.L.; Vaughan (Pirates), N.L.
- **MVP:** Williams.

Linescore

July 8, at Detroit's Briggs Stadium
N.L. ....0 0 0 0 0 1 2 2 0—5 10 2
A.L. ....0 0 0 1 0 1 0 1 4—7 11 3
Wyatt (Dodgers), Derringer (Reds) 3, Walters (Reds) 5, Passeau (Cubs) 7; Feller (Indians), Lee (White Sox) 4, Hudson (Senators) 7, Smith (White Sox) 8. W—Smith. L—Passeau. HR—Vaughan 2, N.L.; Williams, A.L.

WORLD SERIES

- **Winner:** The Yankees returned to the top and won the first of many memorable meetings with the Dodgers.
- **Turning point:** A two-out, ninth-inning passed ball by Dodgers catcher Mickey Owen that could have finished off a 4-3 Brooklyn victory in Game 4. Given new life, the Yanks scored four times and took a three-games-to-one Series lead.
- **Memorable moment:** Owen's passed ball.
- **Top guns:** Joe Gordon (.500, 5 RBIs), Charlie Keller (.389, 5 RBIs), Yankees.

Linescores

Game 1—October 1, at New York
Brooklyn ....0 0 0 0 1 0 1 0 0—2 6 0
New York....................0 1 0 1 0 1 0 0 x—3 6 1
Davis, Casey (6), Allen (7); Ruffing. W—Ruffing. L—Davis. HR—Gordon (N.Y.).

Game 2—October 2, at New York
Brooklyn ....0 0 0 0 2 1 0 0 0—3 6 2
New York....................0 1 1 0 0 0 0 0 0—2 9 1
Wyatt; Chandler, Murphy (6). W—Wyatt. L—Chandler.

Game 3—October 4, at Brooklyn
New York....................0 0 0 0 0 0 0 2 0—2 8 0
Brooklyn ....0 0 0 0 0 0 0 1 0—1 4 0
Russo; Fitzsimmons, Casey (8), French (8), Allen (9). W—Russo. L—Casey.

Game 4—October 5, at Brooklyn
New York....................1 0 0 2 0 0 0 0 4—7 12 0
Brooklyn ....0 0 0 2 2 0 0 0 0—4 9 1
Donald, Breuer (5), Murphy (8); Higbe, French (4), Allen (5), Casey (5). W—Murphy. L—Casey. HR—Reiser (Brk.).

Game 5—October 6, at Brooklyn
New York....................0 2 0 0 1 0 0 0 0—3 6 0
Brooklyn ....0 0 1 0 0 0 0 0 0—1 4 1
Bonham; Wyatt. W—Bonham. L—Wyatt. HR—Henrich (N.Y.).

1942

FINAL STANDINGS

American League

Team	W	L	Pct.	GB
New York	103	51	.669	...
Boston	93	59	.612	9
St. Louis	82	69	.543	19.5
Cleveland	75	79	.487	28
Detroit	73	81	.474	30
Chicago	66	82	.446	34
Washington	62	89	.411	39.5
Philadelphia	55	99	.357	48

National League

Team	W	L	Pct.	GB
St. Louis	106	48	.688	...
Brooklyn	104	50	.675	2
New York	85	67	.559	20
Cincinnati	76	76	.500	29
Pittsburgh	66	81	.449	36.5
Chicago	68	86	.442	38
Boston	59	89	.399	44
Philadelphia	42	109	.278	62.5

SIGNIFICANT EVENTS

- **January 6:** Cleveland ace Bob Feller became the second high-profile star to leave baseball for the armed services when he enlisted in the Navy and reported for duty.
- **January 16:** U.S. President Franklin D. Roosevelt gave baseball the "green light" to continue wartime play as a needed diversion for hard-working Americans.
- **February 3:** In response to President Roosevelt's request for more night games, baseball owners softened restrictions and more than doubled the nocturnal schedule.
- **October 29:** Cardinals Vice-President Branch Rickey resigned to become president of the Dodgers.
- **November 4:** Yankee second baseman Joe Gordon edged out Boston Triple Crown winner Ted Williams by 21 votes for A.L. MVP.

MEMORABLE MOMENTS

- **June 19:** Boston's Paul Waner became baseball's seventh 3,000-hit man when he singled off Pittsburgh's Rip Sewell.
- **July 7:** One day after defeating the N.L. in the annual All-Star Game, the A.L. beat Mickey Cochrane's Armed Service All-Stars, 5-0, in a game to raise money for the war effort.
- **September 27:** The Cardinals recorded a final-day sweep of the Cubs and finished with 106 victories, two more than the Dodgers in an amazing N.L. pennant battle.

LEADERS

American League

BA: Ted Williams, Bos., .356.
Runs: Ted Williams, Bos., 141.
Hits: Johnny Pesky, Bos., 205.
TB: Ted Williams, Bos., 338.
HR: Ted Williams, Bos., 36.
RBI: Ted Williams, Bos., 137.
SB: George Case, Wash., 44.
Wins: Tex Hughson, Bos., 22.
ERA: Ted Lyons, Chi., 2.10.
CG: Tiny Bonham, N.Y.; Tex Hughson, Bos., 22.
IP: Tex Hughson, Bos., 281.
SO: Tex Hughson, Bos.; Bobo Newsom, Wash., 113.

National League

BA: Ernie Lombardi, Cin., .330.
Runs: Mel Ott, N.Y., 118.
Hits: Enos Slaughter, St.L., 188.
TB: Enos Slaughter, St.L., 292.
HR: Mel Ott, N.Y., 30.
RBI: Johnny Mize, N.Y., 110.
SB: Pete Reiser, Brk., 20.
Wins: Mort Cooper, St.L., 22.
ERA: Mort Cooper, St.L., 1.78.
CG: Jim Tobin, Bos., 28.
IP: Jim Tobin, Bos., 287.2.
SO: Johnny Vander Meer, Cin., 186.

A.L. 20-game winners
Tex Hughson, Bos., 22-6
Tiny Bonham, N.Y., 21-5

N.L. 20-game winners
Mort Cooper, St.L., 22-7
Johnny Beazley, St.L., 21-6

A.L. 100 RBIs
Ted Williams, Bos., 137
Joe DiMaggio, N.Y., 114
Charlie Keller, N.Y., 108
Joe Gordon, N.Y., 103
Bobby Doerr, Bos., 102

N.L. 100 RBIs
Johnny Mize, N.Y., 110
Dolph Camilli, Brk., 109

Most Valuable Player
A.L.: Joe Gordon, 2B, N.Y.
N.L.: Mort Cooper, P, St.L.

Hall of Fame addition
Rogers Hornsby, 2B, 1915-37

ALL-STAR GAME

- **Winner:** Spud Chandler and Al Benton combined on a six-hitter and the A.L. made it 7 for 10 with a rainy-day victory in an All-Star Game played with war-depleted rosters.
- **Key inning:** The first, when the A.L. scored all of its runs, one coming on a leadoff home run by Cleveland's Lou Boudreau.
- **Memorable moment:** After New York's Tommy Henrich had followed Boudreau's home run with a double, Detroit slugger Rudy York lined an opposite-field shot that settled into the right-field bleachers for a two-run homer.
- **Top guns:** Chandler (Yankees), Benton (Tigers), Boudreau (Indians), York (Tigers), A.L.; Johnny Vander Meer (Reds), Mickey Owen (Dodgers), N.L.
- **MVP:** York.

Linescore

July 7, at New York's Polo Grounds
A.L. ....3 0 0 0 0 0 0 0 0—3 7 0
N.L. ....0 0 0 0 0 0 0 1 0—1 6 1
Chandler (Yankees), Benton (Tigers) 5; M. Cooper (Cardinals), Vander Meer (Reds) 4, Passeau (Cubs) 7, Walters (Reds) 9. W—Chandler. L—M. Cooper. HR—Boudreau, York, A.L.; Owen, N.L.

WORLD SERIES

- **Winner:** After losing the opener, the Cardinals tamed the powerful Yankees with four consecutive victories.
- **Turning point:** The ninth inning of Game 1. Although the Cardinals' four-run rally fell short in a 7-4 Yankee victory, they delivered a message that would become more clear as the Series progressed.
- **Memorable moment:** A two-run, ninth-inning home run by Whitey Kurowski that gave St. Louis a Series-ending 4-2 victory.
- **Top guns:** Johnny Beazley (2-0, 2.50 ERA), Kurowski (5 RBIs), Cardinals; Phil Rizzuto (.381), Yankees.

Linescores

Game 1—September 30, at St. Louis
New York.................0 0 0 1 1 0 0 3 2—7 11 0
St. Louis ....0 0 0 0 0 0 0 0 4—4 7 4
Ruffing, Chandler (9); M. Cooper, Gumbert (8), Lanier (9). W—Ruffing. L—M. Cooper.

Game 2—October 1, at St. Louis
New York.................0 0 0 0 0 0 0 3 0—3 10 2
St. Louis ....2 0 0 0 0 0 1 1 x—4 6 0
Bonham; Beazley. W—Beazley. L—Bonham. HR—Keller (N.Y.).

Game 3—October 3, at New York
St. Louis ....0 0 1 0 0 0 0 0 1—2 5 1
New York...................0 0 0 0 0 0 0 0 0—0 6 1
White; Chandler, Breuer (9), Turner (9). W—White. L—Chandler.

Game 4—October 4, at New York
St. Louis ....0 0 0 6 0 0 2 0 1—9 12 1
New York...................1 0 0 0 0 5 0 0 0—6 10 1
M. Cooper, Gumbert (6), Pollet (6), Lanier (7); Borowy, Donald (4), Bonham (7). W—Lanier. L—Donald. HR—Keller (N.Y.).

Game 5—October 5, at New York
St. Louis ....0 0 0 1 0 1 0 0 2—4 9 4
New York...................1 0 0 1 0 0 0 0 0—2 7 1
Beazley; Ruffing. W—Beazley. L—Ruffing. HR—Rizzuto (N.Y.); Slaughter, Kurowski (St.L.).

1943

FINAL STANDINGS

American League

Team	W	L	Pct.	GB
New York	98	56	.636	...
Washington	84	69	.549	13.5
Cleveland	82	71	.536	15.5
Chicago	82	72	.532	16
Detroit	78	76	.506	20
St. Louis	72	80	.474	25
Boston	68	84	.447	29
Philadelphia	49	105	.318	49

National League

Team	W	L	Pct.	GB
St. Louis	105	49	.682	...
Cincinnati	87	67	.565	18
Brooklyn	81	72	.529	23.5
Pittsburgh	80	74	.519	25
Chicago	74	79	.484	30.5
Boston	68	85	.444	36.5
Philadelphia	64	90	.416	41
New York	55	98	.359	49.5

SIGNIFICANT EVENTS

- **January 5:** In concessions to the war and travel restrictions, Major League owners agreed to open the season a week late and to conduct spring training in northern cities.
- **February 28:** The Texas League suspended operations, cutting the minor league ranks to nine circuits—down from the 41 that operated in 1941.
- **April 20:** Boston Braves manager Casey Stengel suffered a broken leg when he was hit by a Boston taxicab—an injury that would sideline him for much of the season.
- **May 8:** Baseball's two-week "dead ball" era came to an end when A.G. Spalding's "war ball" was replaced with a more lively ball.

MEMORABLE MOMENTS

- **June 4:** Cardinals ace Mort Cooper stopped Philadelphia 5-0 at Sportsman's Park—his second consecutive one-hit shutout.
- **June 17:** Boston player-manager Joe Cronin made history when he blasted three-run pinch-hit homers in both ends of a doubleheader against Philadelphia at Fenway Park.
- **August 24:** The Athletics ended their A.L. record-tying losing streak at 20 with an 8-1 victory in the second game of a doubleheader at Chicago.

LEADERS

American League

BA: Luke Appling, Chi., .328.
Runs: George Case, Wash., 102.
Hits: Dick Wakefield, Det., 200.
TB: Rudy York, Det., 301.
HR: Rudy York, Det., 34.
RBI: Rudy York, Det., 118.
SB: George Case, Wash., 61.
Wins: Spud Chandler, N.Y.; Dizzy Trout, Det., 20.
ERA: Spud Chandler, N.Y., 1.64.
CG: Spud Chandler, N.Y.; Tex Hughson, Bos., 20.
IP: Jim Bagby, Cle., 273.
SO: Allie Reynolds, Cle., 151.

National League

BA: Stan Musial, St.L., .357.
Runs: Arky Vaughan, Brk., 112.
Hits: Stan Musial, St.L., 220.
TB: Stan Musial, St.L., 347.
HR: Bill Nicholson, Chi., 29.
RBI: Bill Nicholson, Chi., 128.
SB: Arky Vaughan, Brk., 20.
Wins: Mort Cooper, St.L.; Elmer Riddle, Cin.; Rip Sewell, Pit., 21.
ERA: Max Lanier, St.L., 1.90.
CG: Rip Sewell, Pit., 25.
IP: Al Javery, Bos., 303.
SO: Johnny Vander Meer, Cin., 174.

A.L. 20-game winners
Spud Chandler, N.Y., 20-4
Dizzy Trout, Det., 20-12

N.L. 20-game winners
Mort Cooper, St.L., 21-8
Rip Sewell, Pit., 21-9
Elmer Riddle, Cin., 21-11

A.L. 100 RBIs
Rudy York, Det., 118
Nick Etten, N.Y., 107

N.L. 100 RBIs
Bill Nicholson, Chi., 128
Bob Elliott, Pit., 101
Billy Herman, Brk., 100

Most Valuable Player
A.L.: Spud Chandler, P, N.Y.
N.L.: Stan Musial, OF, St.L.

ALL-STAR GAME

- **Winner:** A.L. manager Joe McCarthy, tired of complaints that he favored his own Yankee players in All-Star competition, guided his team to a Yankeeless victory.
- **Key inning:** The second, when Boston's Bobby Doerr belted a three-run homer that gave the A.L. a lead it never relinquished.
- **Memorable moments:** A seventh-inning run-scoring triple and a ninth-inning home run by Pittsburgh's Vince DiMaggio, brother of Yankee great Joe DiMaggio.
- **Top guns:** Hal Newhouser (Tigers), Doerr (Red Sox), Dick Wakefield (Tigers), A.L.; V. DiMaggio (Pirates), Stan Hack (Cubs), N.L.
- **MVP:** Doerr.

Linescore

July 13, at Philadelphia's Shibe Park
N.L. ....1 0 0 0 0 0 1 0 1—3 10 3
A.L. ....0 3 1 0 1 0 0 0 x—5 8 1
M. Cooper (Cardinals), Vander Meer (Reds) 3, Sewell (Pirates) 6, Javery (Braves) 7; Leonard (Senators), Newhouser (Tigers) 4, Hughson (Red Sox) 7. W—Leonard. L—M. Cooper. HR—Doerr, A.L.; DiMaggio, N.L.

WORLD SERIES

- **Winner:** Joe McCarthy managed his seventh and final Series champion as the Yankees avenged their 1942 loss to the Cardinals.
- **Turning point:** Billy Johnson's bases-loaded triple that keyed a five-run eighth inning and helped the Yankees to a 6-2 victory in Game 3.
- **Memorable moment:** Bill Dickey's two-run, sixth-inning home run in New York's 2-0 Series-ending victory.
- **Top guns:** Spud Chandler (2-0, 0.50 ERA), Dickey (4 RBIs), Yankees; Marty Marion (.357), Cardinals.

Linescores

Game 1—October 5, at New York
St. Louis ....0 1 0 0 1 0 0 0 0—2 7 2
New York ....0 0 0 2 0 2 0 0 x—4 8 2
Lanier, Brecheen (8); Chandler. W—Chandler. L—Lanier. HR—Gordon (N.Y.).

Game 2—October 6, at New York
St. Louis ....0 0 1 3 0 0 0 0 0—4 7 2
New York ....0 0 0 1 0 0 0 0 2—3 6 0
M. Cooper; Bonham, Murphy (9). W—M. Cooper. L—Bonham. HR—Marion, Sanders (St.L.).

Game 3—October 7, at New York
St. Louis ....0 0 0 2 0 0 0 0 0—2 6 4
New York ....0 0 0 0 0 1 0 5 x—6 8 0
Brazle, Krist (8), Brecheen (8); Borowy, Murphy (9). W—Borowy. L—Brazle.

Game 4—October 10, at St. Louis
New York ....0 0 0 1 0 0 0 1 0—2 6 2
St. Louis ....0 0 0 0 0 0 1 0 0—1 7 1
Russo; Lanier, Brecheen (8). W—Russo. L—Brecheen.

Game 5—October 11, at St. Louis
New York ....0 0 0 0 0 2 0 0 0—2 7 1
St. Louis ....0 0 0 0 0 0 0 0 0—0 10 1
Chandler; M. Cooper, Lanier (8), Dickson (9). W—Chandler. L—M. Cooper. HR—Dickey (N.Y.).

1944

FINAL STANDINGS

American League

Team	W	L	Pct.	GB
St. Louis	89	65	.578	...
Detroit	88	66	.571	1
New York	83	71	.539	6
Boston	77	77	.500	12
Cleveland	72	82	.468	17
Philadelphia	72	82	.468	17
Chicago	71	83	.461	18
Washington	64	90	.416	25

National League

Team	W	L	Pct.	GB
St. Louis	105	49	.682	...
Pittsburgh	90	63	.588	14.5
Cincinnati	89	65	.578	16
Chicago	75	79	.487	30
New York	67	87	.435	38
Boston	65	89	.422	40
Brooklyn	63	91	.409	42
Philadelphia	61	92	.399	43.5

SIGNIFICANT EVENTS

- **June 6:** Baseball canceled its schedule as Americans braced for D-day—the invasion of Europe on the beaches of Normandy, France.
- **October:** Major League baseball raised $329,555 for the National War Fund Inc. and the American Red Cross through its 16 war relief games.
- **November 25:** Kenesaw Mountain Landis, baseball's first commissioner, died of a heart attack at age 78.

MEMORABLE MOMENTS

- **April 30:** Giants first baseman Phil Weintraub drove in 11 runs, one short of the Major League record, in a 26-8 victory over the Dodgers.
- **June 10:** Reds pitcher Joe Nuxhall, at 15 years and 10 months, became the youngest player to compete in a Major League game when he worked 2/3 of an inning against the Cardinals.
- **August 10:** Braves righthander Red Barrett threw a record-low 58 pitches in a 2-0 victory over the Reds.
- **October 1:** The Browns recorded a final-day 5-2 victory over the Yankees and clinched the first pennant of their frustrating 44-year history.

LEADERS

American League

BA: Lou Boudreau, Cle., .327.
Runs: Snuffy Stirnweiss, N.Y., 125.
Hits: Snuffy Stirnweiss, N.Y., 205.
TB: Johnny Lindell, N.Y., 297.
HR: Nick Etten, N.Y., 22.
RBI: Vern Stephens, St.L., 109.
SB: Snuffy Stirnweiss, N.Y., 55.
Wins: Hal Newhouser, Det., 29.
ERA: Dizzy Trout, Det., 2.12.
CG: Dizzy Trout, Det., 33.
IP: Dizzy Trout, Det., 352.1.
SO: Hal Newhouser, Det., 187.

National League

BA: Dixie Walker, Brk., .357.
Runs: Bill Nicholson, Chi., 116.
Hits: Phil Cavarretta, Chi.; Stan Musial, St.L., 197.
TB: Bill Nicholson, Chi., 317.
HR: Bill Nicholson, Chi., 33.
RBI: Bill Nicholson, Chi., 122.
SB: Johnny Barrett, Pit., 28.
Wins: Bucky Walters, Cin., 23.
ERA: Ed Heusser, Cin., 2.38.
CG: Jim Tobin, Bos., 28.
IP: Bill Voiselle, N.Y., 312.2.
SO: Bill Voiselle, N.Y., 161.

A.L. 20-game winners
Hal Newhouser, Det., 29-9
Dizzy Trout, Det., 27-14

N.L. 20-game winners
Bucky Walters, Cin., 23-8
Mort Cooper, St.L., 22-7
Rip Sewell, Pit., 21-12
Bill Voiselle, N.Y., 21-16

A.L. 100 RBIs
Vern Stephens, St.L., 109
Bob Johnson, Bos., 106
Johnny Lindell, N.Y., 103
Stan Spence, Wash., 100

N.L. 100 RBIs
Bill Nicholson, Chi., 122
Bob Elliott, Pit., 108
Ron Northey, Phil., 104
Frank McCormick, Cin., 102
Ray Sanders, St.L., 102
Babe Dahlgren, Pit., 101

Most Valuable Player
A.L.: Hal Newhouser, P, Det.
N.L.: Marty Marion, SS, St.L.

Hall of Fame addition
Kenesaw M. Landis, commissioner

ALL-STAR GAME

- **Winner:** With many of baseball's stars serving their country in World War II, four pitchers held the A.L. to six hits and the N.L. claimed a 7-1 victory.
- **Key inning:** The fifth, when the N.L. scored four times on RBI hits by Chicago's Bill Nicholson, St. Louis' Walker Cooper and Dodgers' Augie Galan and Dixie Walker.
- **Memorable moment:** Pittsburgh's Rip Sewell threw two "ephus pitches" to Browns first baseman George McQuinn, who took one for a called strike and bunted the other for an out.
- **Top guns:** Sewell (Pirates), Phil Cavarretta (Cubs), Cooper (Cardinals), Walker (Dodgers), Whitey Kurowski (Cardinals), Nicholson (Cubs), N.L.; Hank Borowy (Yankees), A.L.
- **MVP:** Sewell.

Linescore

July 11, at Pittsburgh's Forbes Field
A.L. ....0 1 0 0 0 0 0 0 0—1 6 3
N.L. ....0 0 0 0 4 0 2 1 x—7 12 1
Borowy (Yankees), Hughson (Red Sox) 4, Muncrief (Browns) 5, Newhouser (Tigers) 7, Newsom (Athletics) 8; Walters (Reds), Raffensberger (Phillies) 4, Sewell (Pirates) 6, Tobin (Braves) 9. W—Raffensberger. L—Hughson.

WORLD SERIES

- **Winner:** Playing with a war-depleted roster, the Cardinals won the all-Sportsman's Park Series and the Battle of St. Louis.
- **Turning point:** Game 5 homers by Ray Sanders and Danny Litwhiler that gave the Cardinals a 2-0 victory and a three-games-to-two edge.
- **Memorable moment:** A two-run George McQuinn homer that gave the long-suffering Browns a 2-1 victory in their first-ever Series game.
- **Top guns:** Emil Verban (.412), Walker Cooper (.318), Cardinals; McQuinn (.438, 5 RBIs), Browns.

Linescores

Game 1—October 4, at St. Louis
Browns ....0 0 0 2 0 0 0 0 0—2 2 0
Cardinals ....0 0 0 0 0 0 0 0 1—1 7 0
Galehouse; M. Cooper, Donnelly (8). W—Galehouse. L—M. Cooper. HR—McQuinn (Browns).

Game 2—October 5, at St. Louis
Browns ....0 0 0 0 0 0 2 0 0 0 0—2 7 4
Cardinals ....0 0 1 1 0 0 0 0 0 0 1—3 7 0
Potter, Muncrief (7); Lanier, Donnelly (8). W—Donnelly. L—Muncrief.

Game 3—October 6, at St. Louis
Cardinals ....1 0 0 0 0 0 1 0 0—2 7 0
Browns ....0 0 4 0 0 0 2 0 x—6 8 2
Wilks, Schmidt (3), Jurisich (7), Byerly (7); Kramer. W—Kramer. L—Wilks.

Game 4—October 7, at St. Louis
Cardinals ....2 0 2 0 0 1 0 0 0—5 12 0
Browns ....0 0 0 0 0 0 0 1 0—1 9 1
Brecheen; Jakucki, Hollingsworth (4), Shirley (8). W—Brecheen. L—Jakucki. HR—Musial (Cardinals).

Game 5—October 8, at St. Louis
Cardinals ....0 0 0 0 0 1 0 1 0—2 6 1
Browns ....0 0 0 0 0 0 0 0 0—0 7 1
M. Cooper; Galehouse. W—M. Cooper. L—Galehouse. HR—Sanders, Litwhiler (Cardinals).

Game 6—October 9, at St. Louis
Browns ....0 1 0 0 0 0 0 0 0—1 3 2
Cardinals ....0 0 0 3 0 0 0 0 0—3 10 0
Potter, Muncrief (4), Kramer (7); Lanier, Wilks (6). W—Lanier. L—Potter.

1945

FINAL STANDINGS

American League

Team	W	L	Pct.	GB
Detroit	88	65	.575	...
Washington	87	67	.565	1.5
St. Louis	81	70	.536	6
New York	81	71	.533	6.5
Cleveland	73	72	.503	11
Chicago	71	78	.477	15
Boston	71	83	.461	17.5
Philadelphia	52	98	.347	34.5

National League

Team	W	L	Pct.	GB
Chicago	98	56	.636	...
St. Louis	95	59	.617	3
Brooklyn	87	67	.565	11
Pittsburgh	82	72	.532	16
New York	78	74	.513	19
Boston	67	85	.441	30
Cincinnati	61	93	.396	37
Philadelphia	46	108	.299	52

SIGNIFICANT EVENTS

■ **January 26:** The Yankees were sold to the triumvirate of Larry MacPhail, Dan Topping and Del Webb for $2.8 million.

■ **April 24:** Kentucky Senator Albert B. (Happy) Chandler was the unanimous selection as baseball's second commissioner.

■ **July 10:** The All-Star Game, a baseball fixture since 1933, was not played because of wartime travel restrictions.

■ **October 23:** Brooklyn President Branch Rickey signed Jackie Robinson to a minor league contract, giving Organized Baseball its first black player since the turn of the century.

MEMORABLE MOMENTS

■ **April 18:** One-armed St. Louis outfielder Pete Gray collected one hit in his Major League debut—a 7-1 Browns victory over Detroit.

■ **July 12:** Boston's Tommy Holmes failed to get a hit during a 6-1 loss to the Cubs, ending his modern-era N.L.-record 37-game hitting streak.

■ **August 1:** Giants slugger Mel Ott became baseball's third 500-homer man when he connected off Boston's Johnny Hutchings.

■ **September 9:** Philadelphia's Dick Fowler, released from military duty nine days earlier, pitched a 1-0 no-hitter against the Browns in his first post-war appearance.

LEADERS

American League

BA: Snuffy Stirnweiss, N.Y., .309.
Runs: Snuffy Stirnweiss, N.Y., 107.
Hits: Snuffy Stirnweiss, N.Y., 195.
TB: Snuffy Stirnweiss, N.Y., 301.
HR: Vern Stephens, St.L., 24.
RBI: Nick Etten, N.Y., 111.
SB: Snuffy Stirnweiss, N.Y., 33.
Wins: Hal Newhouser, Det., 25.
ERA: Hal Newhouser, Det., 1.81.
CG: Hal Newhouser, Det., 29.
IP: Hal Newhouser, Det., 313.1.
SO: Hal Newhouser, Det., 212.

National League

BA: Phil Cavarretta, Chi., .355.
Runs: Eddie Stanky, Brk., 128.
Hits: Tommy Holmes, Bos., 224.
TB: Tommy Holmes, Bos., 367.
HR: Tommy Holmes, Bos., 28.
RBI: Dixie Walker, Brk., 124.
SB: Red Schoendienst, St.L., 26.
Wins: Red Barrett, Bos.-St.L., 23.
ERA: Ray Prim, Chi., 2.40.
CG: Red Barrett, Bos.-St.L., 24.
IP: Red Barrett, Bos.-St.L., 284.2.
SO: Preacher Roe, Pit., 148.

A.L. 20-game winners

Hal Newhouser, Det., 25-9
Boo Ferriss, Bos., 21-10
Roger Wolff, Wash., 20-10

N.L. 20-game winners

Red Barrett, Bos.-St.L., 23-12
Hank Wyse, Chi., 22-10

A.L./N.L. 20-game winner

Hank Borowy, N.Y.-Chi., 21

A.L. 100 RBIs

Nick Etten, N.Y., 111

N.L. 100 RBIs

Dixie Walker, Brk., 124
Tommy Holmes, Bos., 117
Luis Olmo, Brk., 110
Andy Pafko, Chi., 110
Buster Adams, Phil.-St.L., 109
Bob Elliott, Pit., 108
Whitey Kurowski, St.L., 102

Most Valuable Player

A.L.: Hal Newhouser, P, Det.
N.L.: Phil Cavarretta, 1B, Chi.

Hall of Fame additions

Roger Bresnahan, C, 1897-1915
Dan Brouthers, 1B, 1879-1904
Fred Clarke, OF, 1894-1915
Jimmy Collins, 3B, 1895-1908
Ed Delahanty, OF, 1888-1903
Hugh Duffy, OF, 1888-1906
Hugh Jennings, SS, 1891-1918
Mike (King) Kelly, C, 1878-93
Jim O'Rourke, OF, 1876-1904
Wilbert Robinson, manager

ALL-STAR GAME

The scheduled 13th All-Star Game was called off because of wartime travel restrictions.

WORLD SERIES

■ **Winner:** The Tigers won only their second Series and the Cubs lost their seventh straight in the last of the wartime fall classics.

■ **Turning point:** A four-run, sixth-inning explosion that broke a 1-1 tie and helped the Tigers to an 8-4 victory in the pivotal fifth game.

■ **Memorable moment:** Stan Hack's 12th-inning bad-hop double that gave the Cubs an 8-7 victory in a must-win sixth game.

■ **Top guns:** Roger Cramer (.379), Hank Greenberg (.304, 2 HR, 7 RBIs), Tigers; Phil Cavarretta (.423, 5 RBIs), Cubs.

Linescores

Game 1—October 3, at Detroit
Chicago....................4 0 3 0 0 0 2 0 0—9 13 0
Detroit....................0 0 0 0 0 0 0 0 0—0 6 0
Borowy; Newhouser, Benton (3), Tobin (5), Mueller (8). W—Borowy. L—Newhouser. HR—Cavarretta (Chi.).

Game 2—October 4, at Detroit
Chicago....................0 0 0 1 0 0 0 0 0—1 7 0
Detroit....................0 0 0 0 4 0 0 0 x—4 7 0
Wyse, Erickson (7); Trucks. W—Trucks. L—Wyse. HR—Greenberg (Det.).

Game 3—October 5, at Detroit
Chicago....................0 0 0 2 0 0 1 0 0—3 8 0
Detroit....................0 0 0 0 0 0 0 0 0—0 1 2
Passeau; Overmire, Benton (7). W—Passeau. L—Overmire.

Game 4—October 6, at Chicago
Detroit....................0 0 0 4 0 0 0 0 0—4 7 1
Chicago....................0 0 0 0 0 1 0 0 0—1 5 1
Trout; Prim, Derringer (4), Vandenberg (6), Erickson (8). W—Trout. L—Prim.

Game 5—October 7, at Chicago
Detroit....................0 0 1 0 0 4 1 0 2—8 11 0
Chicago....................0 0 1 0 0 0 2 0 1—4 7 2
Newhouser; Borowy, Vandenberg (6), Chipman (6), Derringer (7), Erickson (9). W—Newhouser. L—Borowy.

Game 6—October 8, at Chicago
Detroit........0 1 0 0 0 0 2 4 0 0 0 0—7 13 1
Chicago......0 0 0 0 4 1 2 0 0 0 0 1—8 15 3
Trucks, Caster (5), Bridges (6), Benton (7), Trout (8); Passeau, Wyse (7), Prim (8), Borowy (9). W—Borowy. L—Trout. HR—Greenberg (Det.).

Game 7—October 10, at Chicago
Detroit....................5 1 0 0 0 0 1 2 0—9 9 1
Chicago....................1 0 0 1 0 0 0 1 0—3 10 0
Newhouser; Borowy, Derringer (1), Vandenberg (2), Erickson (6), Passeau (8), Wyse (9). W—Newhouser. L—Borowy.

1946

FINAL STANDINGS

American League

Team	W	L	Pct.	GB
Boston	104	50	.675	...
Detroit	92	62	.597	12
New York	87	67	.565	17
Washington	76	78	.494	28
Chicago	74	80	.481	30
Cleveland	68	86	.442	36
St. Louis	66	88	.429	38
Philadelphia	49	105	.318	55

National League

Team	W	L	Pct.	GB
*St. Louis	98	58	.628	...
Brooklyn	96	60	.615	2
Chicago	82	71	.536	14.5
Boston	81	72	.529	15.5
Philadelphia	69	85	.448	28
Cincinnati	67	87	.435	30
Pittsburgh	63	91	.409	34
New York	61	93	.396	36

*Defeated Brooklyn 2-0 in pennant playoff.

SIGNIFICANT EVENTS

■ **February 19:** Giants outfielder Danny Gardella jumped to the outlaw Mexican League, the first in a group of Major Leaguers who would fall victim to big-money inducements.

■ **April 18:** Jackie Robinson broke Organized Baseball's color barrier with a four-hit debut for the International League's Montreal Royals.

■ **September 16:** Among the benefits awarded players in a history-making New York meeting were a $5,000 minimum salary, upgraded hospital and medical expenses and salary-cut guarantees.

■ **December 6:** Baseball owners decided to return the All-Star vote to the fans.

MEMORABLE MOMENTS

■ **July 27:** Boston's Rudy York belted a record-tying two grand slams and drove in 10 runs in a 13-6 victory over the Browns.

■ **October 3:** The Cardinals capped their two-game sweep of the Dodgers with an 8-4 victory in baseball's first pennant playoff.

LEADERS

American League

BA: Mickey Vernon, Wash., .353.
Runs: Ted Williams, Bos., 142.
Hits: Johnny Pesky, Bos., 208.
TB: Ted Williams, Bos., 343.
HR: Hank Greenberg, Det., 44.
RBI: Hank Greenberg, Det., 127.
SB: George Case, Cle., 28.
Wins: Bob Feller, Cle.; Hal Newhouser, Det., 26.
ERA: Hal Newhouser, Det., 1.94.
CG: Bob Feller, Cle., 36.
IP: Bob Feller, Cle., 371.1.
SO: Bob Feller, Cle., 348.

National League

BA: Stan Musial, St.L., .365.
Runs: Stan Musial, St.L., 124.
Hits: Stan Musial, St.L., 228.
TB: Stan Musial, St.L., 366.
HR: Ralph Kiner, Pit., 23.
RBI: Enos Slaughter, St.L., 130.
SB: Pete Reiser, Brk., 34.
Wins: Howie Pollet, St.L., 21.
ERA: Howie Pollet, St.L., 2.10.
CG: Johnny Sain, Bos., 24.
IP: Howie Pollet, St.L., 266.
SO: Johnny Schmitz, Chi., 135.

A.L. 20-game winners

Hal Newhouser, Det., 26-9
Bob Feller, Cle., 26-15
Boo Ferriss, Bos., 25-6
Spud Chandler, N.Y., 20-8
Tex Hughson, Bos., 20-11

N.L. 20-game winners

Howie Pollet, St.L., 21-10
Johnny Sain, Bos., 20-14

A.L. 100 RBIs

Hank Greenberg, Det., 127
Ted Williams, Bos., 123
Rudy York, Bos., 119
Bobby Doerr, Bos., 116
Charlie Keller, N.Y., 101

N.L. 100 RBIs

Enos Slaughter, St.L., 130
Dixie Walker, Brk., 116
Stan Musial, St.L., 103

A.L. 40 homers

Hank Greenberg, Det., 44

Most Valuable Player

A.L.: Ted Williams, OF, Bos.
N.L.: Stan Musial, 1B, St.L.

Hall of Fame additions

Jesse Burkett, OF, 1890-1905
Frank Chance, 1B, 1898-1914
Jack Chesbro, P, 1899-1909
Johnny Evers, 2B, 1902-29
Clark Griffith, P/Man./Exec.
Tommy McCarthy, OF, 1884-96
Joe McGinnity, P, 1899-1908
Eddie Plank, P, 1901-17
Joe Tinker, SS, 1902-16
Rube Waddell, P, 1897-1910
Ed Walsh, P, 1904-17

ALL-STAR GAME

■ **Winner:** War hero Ted Williams rewarded his home fans with a four-hit, two-homer, five-RBI performance and three pitchers — Cleveland's Bob Feller, Detroit's Hal Newhouser and St. Louis' Jack Kramer — combined on a three-hitter that produced a 12-0 victory.

■ **Key inning:** The first, when Yankee Charlie Keller hit a two-run homer that ignited the A.L. charge.

■ **Memorable moment:** Williams' three-run, eighth-inning homer off Rip Sewell's famed "ephus pitch"—one of the All-Star Game's classic moments.

■ **Top guns:** Feller (Indians), Newhouser (Tigers), Kramer (Browns), Williams (Red Sox), Keller (Yankees), Vern Stephens (Browns), A.L.

■ **MVP:** Williams.

Linescore

July 9, at Boston's Fenway Park
N.L.........................0 0 0 0 0 0 0 0 0— 0 3 0
A.L.........................2 0 0 1 3 0 2 4 x—12 14 1
Passeau (Cubs), Higbe (Dodgers) 4, Blackwell (Reds) 5, Sewell (Pirates) 8; Feller (Indians), Newhouser (Tigers) 4, Kramer (Browns) 7. W—Feller. L—Passeau. HR—Keller, Williams 2, A.L.

WORLD SERIES

■ **Winner:** The Cardinals celebrated the end of wartime baseball with seven-game victory over the Red Sox.

■ **Turning point:** Harry Brecheen's seven-hit pitching gave the Cardinals a 4-1 victory in a must-win sixth game.

■ **Memorable moments:** The eighth inning of Game 7, when Enos Slaughter made his game-winning "Mad Dash" around the bases on Harry Walker's double. The ninth inning of Game 7, when Brecheen pitched out of a two-on, nobody out jam to secure the victory.

■ **Top guns:** Brecheen (3-0, 0.45 ERA), Slaughter (.320), Walker (.412, 6 RBIs), Cardinals; Bobby Doerr (.409), Rudy York (2 HR, 5 RBIs), Red Sox.

Linescores

Game 1—October 6, at St. Louis
Boston ....0 1 0 0 0 0 0 0 1 1—3 9 2
St. Louis ....0 0 0 0 0 1 0 1 0 0—2 7 0
Hughson, Johnson (9); Pollet. W—Johnson. L—Pollet. HR—York (Bos.).

Game 2—October 7, at St. Louis
Boston ....0 0 0 0 0 0 0 0 0—0 4 1
St. Louis ....0 0 1 0 2 0 0 0 x—3 6 0
Harris, Dobson (8); Brecheen. W—Brecheen. L—Harris.

Game 3—October 9, at Boston
St. Louis ....0 0 0 0 0 0 0 0 0—0 6 1
Boston.......................3 0 0 0 0 0 0 1 x—4 8 0
Dickson, Wilks (8); Ferriss. W—Ferriss. L—Dickson. HR—York (Bos.).

Game 4—Ocotber 10, at Boston
St. Louis ....0 3 3 0 1 0 1 0 4—12 20 1
Boston ....0 0 0 1 0 0 0 2 0— 3 9 4
Munger; Hughson, Bagby (3), Zuber (6), Brown (8), Ryba (9), Driesewerd (9). W—Munger. L—Hughson. HR—Slaughter (St.L.); Doerr (Bos.).

Game 5—October 11, at Boston
St. Louis ....0 1 0 0 0 0 0 0 2—3 4 1
Boston.....................1 1 0 0 0 1 3 0 x—6 11 3
Pollet, Brazle (1), Beazley (8); Dobson. W—Dobson. L—Brazle. HR—Culberson (Bos.).

Game 6—October 13, at St. Louis
Boston ....0 0 0 0 0 0 1 0 0—1 7 0
St. Louis ....0 0 3 0 0 0 0 1 x—4 8 0
Harris, Hughson (3), Johnson (8); Brecheen. W—Brecheen. L—Harris.

Game 7—October 15, at St. Louis
Boston ....1 0 0 0 0 0 0 2 0—3 8 0
St. Louis ....0 1 0 0 2 0 0 1 x—4 9 1
Ferriss, Dobson (5), Klinger (8), Johnson (8); Dickson, Brecheen (8). W—Brecheen. L—Klinger.

1947

FINAL STANDINGS

American League

Team	W	L	Pct.	GB
New York	97	57	.630	...
Detroit	85	69	.552	12
Boston	83	71	.539	14
Cleveland	80	74	.519	17
Philadelphia	78	76	.506	19
Chicago	70	84	.455	27
Washington	64	90	.416	33
St. Louis	59	95	.383	38

National League

Team	W	L	Pct.	GB
Brooklyn	94	60	.610	...
St. Louis	89	65	.578	5
Boston	86	68	.558	8
New York	81	73	.526	13
Cincinnati	73	81	.474	21
Chicago	69	85	.448	25
Philadelphia	62	92	.403	32
Pittsburgh	62	92	.403	32

SIGNIFICANT EVENTS

■ **April 9:** Brooklyn manager Leo Durocher was suspended by Commissioner Happy Chandler for the entire 1947 season for "conduct detrimental to baseball."
■ **April 15:** The Major League color barrier came tumbling down when Jackie Robinson went hitless in the Dodgers' 5-3 Opening Day victory over the Braves at Ebbets Field.
■ **April 27:** Cancer-stricken Babe Ruth was honored throughout baseball on "Babe Ruth Day" and in special ceremonies at Yankee Stadium.
■ **July 5:** Cleveland's Larry Doby became the A.L.'s first black player when he struck out as a pinch-hitter in a 6-5 loss at Chicago.
■ **November 12:** Dodgers first baseman Jackie Robinson capped his historic season by capturing the first Rookie of the Year award.

MEMORABLE MOMENTS

■ **June 22:** Cincinnati's Ewell Blackwell fell two outs short of matching Johnny Vander Meer's back-to-back no-hitter feat when Brooklyn's Eddie Stanky stroked a ninth-inning single.
■ **September 28:** The greatest home run battle in history ended with neither Pittsburgh's Ralph Kiner nor New York's Johnny Mize adding to their 51-homer totals.

LEADERS

American League
BA: Ted Williams, Bos., .343.
Runs: Ted Williams, Bos., 125.
Hits: Johnny Pesky, Bos., 207.
TB: Ted Williams, Bos., 335.
HR: Ted Williams, Bos., 32.
RBI: Ted Williams, Bos., 114.
SB: Bob Dillinger, St.L., 34.
Wins: Bob Feller, Cle., 20.
ERA: Joe Haynes, Chi., 2.42.
CG: Hal Newhouser, Det., 24.
IP: Bob Feller, Cle., 299.
SO: Bob Feller, Cle., 196.

National League
BA: Harry Walker, St.L.-Phil., .363.
Runs: Johnny Mize, N.Y., 137.
Hits: Tommy Holmes, Bos., 191.
TB: Ralph Kiner, Pit., 361.
HR: Ralph Kiner, Pit.; Johnny Mize, N.Y., 51.
RBI: Johnny Mize, N.Y., 138.
SB: Jackie Robinson, Brk., 29.
Wins: Ewell Blackwell, Cin., 22.
ERA: Warren Spahn, Bos., 2.33.
CG: Ewell Blackwell, Cin., 23.
IP: Warren Spahn, Bos., 289.2.
SO: Ewell Blackwell, Cin., 193.

A.L. 20-game winners
Bob Feller, Cle., 20-11

N.L. 20-game winners
Ewell Blackwell, Cin., 22-8
Larry Jansen, N.Y., 21-5
Warren Spahn, Bos., 21-10
Ralph Branca, Brk., 21-12
Johnny Sain, Bos., 21-12

A.L. 100 RBIs
Ted Williams, Bos., 114

N.L. 100 RBIs
Johnny Mize, N.Y., 138
Ralph Kiner, Pit., 127
Walker Cooper, N.Y., 122
Bob Elliott, Bos., 113
Willard Marshall, N.Y., 107
Whitey Kurowski, St.L., 104

N.L. 40 homers
Ralph Kiner, Pit., 51
Johnny Mize, N.Y., 51

Most Valuable Player
A.L.: Joe DiMaggio, OF, N.Y.
N.L.: Bob Elliott, 3B, Bos.

Rookie of the Year
A.L.-N.L.: Jackie Robinson, 1B, Brk.

Hall of Fame additions
Mickey Cochrane, C, 1925-37
Frank Frisch, 2B, 1919-37
Lefty Grove, P, 1925-41
Carl Hubbell, P, 1928-43

ALL-STAR GAME

■ **Winner:** The A.L. won its 10th All-Star Game in 14 tries with a 2-1 decision at windswept Wrigley Field.

■ **Key inning:** The seventh, when Washington pinch-hitter Stan Spence singled home Boston's Bobby Doerr with the eventual winning run.

■ **Memorable moment:** A game-saving defensive play by Cleveland shortstop Lou Boudreau in the eighth inning on a ball hit by St. Louis' Enos Slaughter with two men on base.

■ **Top guns:** Hal Newhouser (Tigers), Spec Shea (Yankees), Ted Williams (Red Sox), Spence (Senators), A.L.; Ewell Blackwell (Reds), Johnny Mize (Giants), N.L.

■ **MVP:** Spence.

Linescore

July 8, at Chicago's Wrigley Field
A.L. ....0 0 0 0 0 1 1 0 0—2 8 0
N.L. ....0 0 0 1 0 0 0 0 0—1 5 1
Newhouser (Tigers), Shea (Yankees) 4, Masterson (Senators) 7, Page (Yankees) 8; Blackwell (Reds), Brecheen (Cardinals) 4, Sain (Braves) 7, Spahn (Braves) 8. W—Shea. L—Sain. HR—Mize, N.L.

WORLD SERIES

■ **Winner:** After a three-year drought, the Yankees returned to the top in a memorable seven-game battle against the Dodgers.

■ **Turning point:** Spec Shea's 2-1 Game 5 victory — the day after teammate Bill Bevens, one out away from victory and the first no-hitter in Series history, had surrendered a game-deciding two-run double to Dodgers pinch-hitter Cookie Lavagetto.

■ **Memorable moments:** Lavagetto's Game 4 hit and a spectacular Game 6 catch by Dodgers left fielder Al Gionfriddo that robbed Joe DiMaggio of a three-run homer and helped secure an 8-6 must victory for Brooklyn.

■ **Top guns:** Shea (2-0, 2.35 ERA), Johnny Lindell (.500, 7 RBIs), Yankees; Hugh Casey (2-0, 0.87), Carl Furillo (.353), Dodgers.

Linescores

Game 1—September 30, at New York
Brooklyn ....1 0 0 0 0 1 1 0 0—3 6 0
New York....................0 0 0 0 5 0 0 0 x—5 4 0
Branca, Behrman (5), Casey (7); Shea, Page (6). W—Shea. L—Branca.

Game 2—October 1, at New York
Brooklyn ....0 0 1 1 0 0 0 0 1— 3 9 2
New York................1 0 1 1 2 1 4 0 x—10 15 1
Lombardi, Gregg (5), Behrman (7), Barney (7); Reynolds. W—Reynolds. L—Lombardi. HR—Walker (Brk.); Henrich (N.Y.).

Game 3—October 2, at Brooklyn
New York.................0 0 2 2 2 1 1 0 0—8 13 0
Brooklyn ....0 6 1 2 0 0 0 0 x—9 13 1
Newsom, Raschi (2), Drews (3), Chandler (4), Page (6); Hatten, Branca (5), Casey (7). W—Casey. L—Newsom. HR—DiMaggio, Berra (N.Y.).

Game 4—October 3, at Brooklyn
New York....................1 0 0 1 0 0 0 0 0—2 8 1
Brooklyn ....0 0 0 0 1 0 0 0 2—3 1 3
Bevens; Taylor, Gregg (1), Behrman (8), Casey (9). W—Casey. L—Bevens.

Game 5—October 4, at Brooklyn
New York....................0 0 0 1 1 0 0 0 0—2 5 0
Brooklyn ....0 0 0 0 0 1 0 0 0—1 4 1
Shea; Barney, Hatten (5), Behrman (7), Casey (8). W—Shea. L—Barney. HR—DiMaggio (N.Y.).

Game 6—October 5, at New York
Brooklyn ....2 0 2 0 0 4 0 0 0—8 12 1
New York..................0 0 4 1 0 0 0 0 1—6 15 2
Lombardi, Branca (3), Hatten (6), Casey (9); Reynolds, Drews (3), Page (5), Newsom (6), Raschi (7), Wensloff (8). W—Branca. L—Page.

Game 7—October 6, at New York
Brooklyn ....0 2 0 0 0 0 0 0 0—2 7 0
New York....................0 1 0 2 0 1 1 0 x—5 7 0
Gregg, Behrman (4), Hatten (6), Barney (6), Casey (7); Shea, Bevens (2), Page (5). W—Page. L—Gregg.

1948

FINAL STANDINGS

American League

Team	W	L	Pct.	GB
*Cleveland	97	58	.626	...
Boston	96	59	.619	1
New York	94	60	.610	2.5
Philadelphia	84	70	.545	12.5
Detroit	78	76	.506	18.5
St. Louis	59	94	.386	37
Washington	56	97	.366	40
Chicago	51	101	.336	44.5

*Defeated Boston in one-game pennant playoff.

National League

Team	W	L	Pct.	GB
Boston	91	62	.595	...
St. Louis	85	69	.552	6.5
Brooklyn	84	70	.545	7.5
Pittsburgh	83	71	.539	8.5
New York	78	76	.506	13.5
Philadelphia	66	88	.429	25.5
Cincinnati	64	89	.418	27
Chicago	64	90	.416	27.5

SIGNIFICANT EVENTS

■ **June 15:** The Tigers became the final A.L. team to host a night game when they posted a 4-1 victory over the Athletics at Briggs Stadium.
■ **August 16:** Babe Ruth, whose uniform No. 3 had been retired by the Yankees two months earlier, died of throat cancer at age 53.
■ **October 3:** The Indians finished the season with a record attendance of 2,620,627.
■ **October 12:** Casey Stengel brought his colorful antics to New York when he signed a two-year contract to manage the Yankees.

MEMORABLE MOMENTS

■ **July 18:** Chicago's Pat Seerey joined a select club when he pounded an 11th-inning home run, his fourth of the game, to give the White Sox a 12-11 victory over the Athletics.
■ **October 4:** Player-manager Lou Boudreau belted two home runs and the Indians posted an 8-3 victory over Boston in a one-game playoff to decide the A.L. pennant.

LEADERS

American League
BA: Ted Williams, Bos., .369.
Runs: Tommy Henrich, N.Y., 138.
Hits: Bob Dillinger, St.L., 207.
TB: Joe DiMaggio, N.Y., 355.
HR: Joe DiMaggio, N.Y., 39.
RBI: Joe DiMaggio, N.Y., 155.
SB: Bob Dillinger, St.L., 28.
Wins: Hal Newhouser, Det., 21.
ERA: Gene Bearden, Cle., 2.43.
CG: Bob Lemon, Cle., 20.
IP: Bob Lemon, Cle., 293.2.
SO: Bob Feller, Cle., 164.

National League
BA: Stan Musial, St.L., .376.
Runs: Stan Musial, St.L., 135.
Hits: Stan Musial, St.L., 230.
TB: Stan Musial, St.L., 429.
HR: Ralph Kiner, Pit.; Johnny Mize, N.Y., 40.
RBI: Stan Musial, St.L., 131.
SB: Richie Ashburn, Phil., 32.
Wins: Johnny Sain, Bos., 24.
ERA: Harry Brecheen, St.L., 2.24.
CG: Johnny Sain, Bos., 28.
IP: Johnny Sain, Bos., 314.2.
SO: Harry Brecheen, St.L., 149.

A.L. 20-game winners
Hal Newhouser, Det., 21-12
Gene Bearden, Cle., 20-7
Bob Lemon, Cle., 20-14

N.L. 20-game winners
Johnny Sain, Bos., 24-15
Harry Brecheen, St.L., 20-7

A.L. 100 RBIs
Joe DiMaggio, N.Y., 155
Vern Stephens, Bos., 137
Ted Williams, Bos., 127
Joe Gordon, Cle., 124
Hank Majeski, Phil., 120
Ken Keltner, Cle., 119
Bobby Doerr, Bos., 111
Lou Boudreau, Cle., 106
Hoot Evers, Det., 103
Tommy Henrich, N.Y., 100

N.L. 100 RBIs
Stan Musial, St.L., 131
Johnny Mize, N.Y., 125
Ralph Kiner, Pit., 123
Sid Gordon, N.Y., 107
Andy Pafko, Chi., 101
Bob Elliott, Bos., 100

N.L. 40 homers
Ralph Kiner, Pit., 40
Johnny Mize, N.Y., 40

Most Valuable Player
A.L.: Lou Boudreau, SS, Cle.
N.L.: Stan Musial, OF, St.L.

Rookie of the Year
A.L.-N.L.: Alvin Dark, SS, Bos. (N.L.).

Hall of Fame additions
Herb Pennock, P, 1912-34
Pie Traynor, 3B, 1920-37

ALL-STAR GAME

■ **Winner:** Yankee Vic Raschi and Philadelphia's Joe Coleman pitched six innings of shutout relief and the A.L. won for the 11th time in 15 All-Star classics.

■ **Key inning:** The fourth, when the A.L. broke a 2-2 tie with three runs. Two scored on a bases-loaded single by pitcher Raschi.

■ **Memorable moment:** A first-inning home run by hometown favorite Stan Musial — the first of a record six All-Star homers he would hit.

■ **Top guns:** Raschi (Yankees), Coleman (Athletics), Hoot Evers (Tigers), A.L.; Musial (Cardinals), Richie Ashburn (Phillies).

■ **MVP:** Raschi.

Linescore

July 13, at St. Louis' Sportsman's Park
N.L. ....2 0 0 0 0 0 0 0 0—2 8 0
A.L. ....0 1 1 3 0 0 0 0 x—5 6 0
Branca (Dodgers), Schmitz (Cubs) 4, Sain (Braves) 4, Blackwell (Reds) 6; Masterson (Senators), Raschi (Yankees) 4, Coleman (Athletics) 7. W—Raschi. L—Schmitz. HR—Musial, N.L.; Evers, A.L.

WORLD SERIES

■ **Winner:** The Indians, survivors of a pennant playoff against the Red Sox, needed six games to dispatch Boston's other team in the Series.

■ **Turning point:** Gene Bearden's 2-0 Game 3 shutout, which put the Indians in the driver's seat.

■ **Memorable moment:** The Game 5 appearance of Indians pitcher Satchel Paige, the 42-year-old former Negro Leagues legend. Paige became the first black pitcher in Series history.

■ **Top guns:** Bob Lemon (2-0, 1.65 ERA), Larry Doby (.318), Indians; Bob Elliott (.333, 2 HR, 5 RBIs), Braves.

Linescores

Game 1—October 6, at Boston
Cleveland ....0 0 0 0 0 0 0 0 0—0 4 0
Boston........................0 0 0 0 0 0 0 1 x—1 2 2
Feller; Sain. W—Sain. L—Feller.

Game 2—October 7, at Boston
Cleveland ....0 0 0 2 1 0 0 0 1—4 8 1
Boston ....1 0 0 0 0 0 0 0 0—1 8 3
Lemon; Spahn, Barrett (5), Potter (8). W—Lemon. L—Spahn.

Game 3—October 8, at Cleveland
Boston ....0 0 0 0 0 0 0 0 0—0 5 1
Cleveland....................0 0 1 1 0 0 0 0 x—2 5 0
Bickford, Voiselle (4), Barrett (8); Bearden. W—Bearden. L—Bickford.

Game 4—October 9, at Cleveland
Boston ....0 0 0 0 0 0 1 0 0—1 7 0
Cleveland....................1 0 1 0 0 0 0 0 x—2 5 0
Sain; Gromek. W—Gromek. L—Sain. HR—Doby (Cle.); Rickert (Bos.).

Game 5—October 10, at Cleveland
Boston ....3 0 1 0 0 1 6 0 0—11 12 0
Cleveland ....1 0 0 4 0 0 0 0 0— 5 6 2
Potter, Spahn (4); Feller, Klieman (7), Christopher (7), Paige (7), Muncrief (8). W—Spahn. L—Feller. HR—Elliott 2, Salkeld (Bos.); Mitchell, Hegan (Cle.).

Game 6—October 11, at Boston
Cleveland ....0 0 1 0 0 2 0 1 0—4 10 0
Boston ....0 0 0 1 0 0 0 2 0—3 9 0
Lemon, Bearden (8); Voiselle, Spahn (8). W—Lemon. L—Voiselle. HR—Gordon (Cle.).

HISTORY

1949

FINAL STANDINGS

American League

Team	W	L	Pct.	GB
New York	97	57	.630	...
Boston	96	58	.623	1
Cleveland	89	65	.578	8
Detroit	87	67	.565	10
Philadelphia	81	73	.526	16
Chicago	63	91	.409	34
St. Louis	53	101	.344	44
Washington	50	104	.325	47

National League

Team	W	L	Pct.	GB
Brooklyn	97	57	.630	...
St. Louis	96	58	.623	1
Philadelphia	81	73	.526	16
Boston	75	79	.487	22
New York	73	81	.474	24
Pittsburgh	71	83	.461	26
Cincinnati	62	92	.403	35
Chicago	61	93	.396	36

SIGNIFICANT EVENTS

■ **February 7:** Yankee star Joe DiMaggio signed baseball's first $100,000 contract.

■ **April 19:** In ceremonies at Yankee Stadium, the Yankees unveiled center-field granite monuments honoring Babe Ruth, Lou Gehrig and Miller Huggins.

■ **June 5:** Commissioner Happy Chandler lifted the five-year suspensions of the 18 players who jumped to the outlaw Mexican League in 1946.

■ **June 15:** Phillies star Eddie Waitkus was shot and seriously wounded in a Chicago hotel room by a 19-year-old woman who professed to having a secret crush on him.

■ **December 12:** Baseball's Rules Committee redefined the strike zone as the area over home plate between the batter's armpits and the top of his knees.

MEMORABLE MOMENTS

■ **September 30:** Pittsburgh's Ralph Kiner, the first N.L. player to top the 50-homer plateau twice, blasted No. 54 in a 3-2 victory over the Reds.

■ **October 2:** The Yankees posted a 5-3 final-day victory over Boston in a pennant-deciding battle at Yankee Stadium.

■ **October 2:** The Dodgers held off the Cardinals and claimed the N.L. pennant with a 10-inning, 9-7 final-day victory over Philadelphia.

LEADERS

American League

BA: George Kell, Det., .343.
Runs: Ted Williams, Bos., 150.
Hits: Dale Mitchell, Cle., 203.
TB: Ted Williams, Bos., 368.
HR: Ted Williams, Bos., 43.
RBI: Vern Stephens, Bos.,; Ted Williams, Bos., 159.
SB: Bob Dillinger, St.L., 20.
Wins: Mel Parnell, Bos., 25.
ERA: Mike Garcia, Cle., 2.36.
CG: Mel Parnell, Bos., 27.
IP: Mel Parnell, Bos., 295.1.
SO: Virgil Trucks, Det., 153.

National League

BA: Jackie Robinson, Brk., .342.
Runs: Pee Wee Reese, Brk., 132.
Hits: Stan Musial, St.L., 207.
TB: Stan Musial, St.L., 382.
HR: Ralph Kiner, Pit., 54.
RBI: Ralph Kiner, Pit., 127.
SB: Jackie Robinson, Brk., 37.
Wins: Warren Spahn, Bos., 21.
ERA: Dave Koslo, N.Y., 2.50.
CG: Warren Spahn, Bos., 25.
IP: Warren Spahn, Bos., 302.1.
SO: Warren Spahn, Bos., 151.

A.L. 20-game winners
Mel Parnell, Bos., 25-7
Ellis Kinder, Bos., 23-6
Bob Lemon, Cle., 22-10
Vic Raschi, N.Y., 21-10
Alex Kellner, Phil., 20-12

N.L. 20-game winners
Warren Spahn, Bos., 21-14
Howie Pollet, St.L., 20-9

A.L. 100 RBIs
Vern Stephens, Bos., 159
Ted Williams, Bos., 159
Vic Wertz, Det., 133
Bobby Doerr, Bos., 109
Sam Chapman, Phil., 108

N.L. 100 RBIs
Ralph Kiner, Pit., 127
Jackie Robinson, Brk., 124
Stan Musial, St.L., 123
Gil Hodges, Brk., 115
Del Ennis, Phil., 110
Bobby Thomson, N.Y., 109
Carl Furillo, Brk., 106
Wally Westlake, Pit., 104

A.L. 40 homers
Ted Williams, Bos., 43

N.L. 40 homers
Ralph Kiner, Pit., 54

Most Valuable Player
A.L.: Ted Williams, OF, Bos.
N.L.: Jackie Robinson, 2B, Brk.

Rookie of the Year
A.L.: Roy Sievers, OF, St.L.
N.L.: Don Newcombe, P, Brk.

Hall of Fame additions
Three Finger Brown, P, 1903-16
Charley Gehringer, 2B, 1924-42
Kid Nichols, P, 1890-1906

ALL-STAR GAME

■ **Winner:** The DiMaggios, Boston's Dom and New York's Joe, combined for four RBIs and Yankee pitcher Vic Raschi shut down the N.L. over the last three innings as the A.L. prevailed in a sloppy game at Brooklyn.

■ **Key inning:** The seventh, when the A.L. broke open a close game with a three-run rally.

■ **Memorable moment:** Jackie Robinson's first-inning double — the first hit by a black player in the first integrated All-Star Game.

■ **Top guns:** Raschi (Yankees), D. DiMaggio (Red Sox), J. DiMaggio (Yankees), George Kell (Tigers), A.L.; Stan Musial (Cardinals), Ralph Kiner (Pirates), N.L.

■ **MVP:** Joe DiMaggio.

Linescore

July 12, at Brooklyn's Ebbets Field
A.L. ....4 0 0 2 0 2 3 0 0—1 13 1
N.L. ....2 1 2 0 0 2 0 0 0—7 12 5
Parnell (Red Sox), Trucks (Tigers) 2, Brissie (Athletics) 4, Raschi (Yankees) 7; Spahn (Braves), Newcombe (Dodgers) 2, Munger (Cardinals) 5, Bickford (Braves) 6, Pollet (Cardinals) 7, Blackwell (Reds) 8, Roe (Dodgers) 9. W—Trucks. L—Newcombe. HR—Musial, Kiner, N.L.

WORLD SERIES

■ **Winner:** The Yankee machine was back, this time with a new driver. Casey Stengel made his Series managerial debut a successful one.

■ **Turning point:** A three-run ninth inning that produced a 4-3 Yankee victory in Game 3.

■ **Memorable moment:** Tommy Henrich's leadoff ninth-inning home run that decided a 1-0 pitching duel between Dodgers ace Don Newcombe and Yankee righthander Allie Reynolds in Game 1.

■ **Top guns:** Reynolds (12⅓ IP, 0.00 ERA), Bobby Brown (.500, 5 RBIs), Yankees; Pee Wee Reese (.316), Dodgers.

Linescores

Game 1—Oct. 5, at New York
Brooklyn ....0 0 0 0 0 0 0 0 0—0 2 0
New York....................0 0 0 0 0 0 0 0 1—1 5 1
Newcombe; Reynolds. W—Reynolds. L—Newcombe. HR—Henrich (N.Y.).

Game 2—October 6, at New York
Brooklyn ....0 1 0 0 0 0 0 0 0—1 7 2
New York....................0 0 0 0 0 0 0 0 0—0 6 1
Roe; Raschi, Page (9). W—Roe. L—Raschi.

Game 3—October 7, at Brooklyn
New York....................0 0 1 0 0 0 0 0 3—4 5 0
Brooklyn ....0 0 0 1 0 0 0 0 2—3 5 0
Byrne, Page (4); Branca, Banta (9). W—Page. L—Branca. HR—Reese, Olmo, Campanella (Brk.).

Game 4—October 8, at Brooklyn
New York..................0 0 0 3 3 0 0 0 0—6 10 0
Brooklyn ....0 0 0 0 0 4 0 0 0—4 9 1
Lopat, Reynolds (6); Newcombe, Hatten (4), Erskine (6), Banta (7). W—Lopat. L—Newcombe.

Game 5—October 9, at Brooklyn
New York...............2 0 3 1 1 3 0 0 0—10 11 1
Brooklyn ....0 0 1 0 0 1 4 0 0— 6 11 2
Raschi, Page (7); Barney, Banta (3), Erskine (6), Hatten (6), Palica (7), Minner (9). W—Raschi. L—Barney. HR—DiMaggio (N.Y.); Hodges (Brk.).

1950

FINAL STANDINGS

American League

Team	W	L	Pct.	GB
New York	98	56	.636	...
Detroit	95	59	.617	3
Boston	94	60	.610	4
Cleveland	92	62	.597	6
Washington	67	87	.435	31
Chicago	60	94	.390	38
St. Louis	58	96	.377	40
Philadelphia	52	102	.338	46

National League

Team	W	L	Pct.	GB
Philadelphia	91	63	.591	...
Brooklyn	89	65	.578	2
New York	86	68	.558	5
Boston	83	71	.539	8
St. Louis	78	75	.510	12.5
Cincinnati	66	87	.431	24.5
Chicago	64	89	.418	26.5
Pittsburgh	57	96	.373	33.5

SIGNIFICANT EVENTS

■ **January 31:** Pittsburgh made 18-year-old pitcher Paul Pettit baseball's first $100,000 bonus baby.

■ **October 18:** Connie Mack retired after 50 years as manager and owner of the Athletics, the team he built in 1901 when the American League was organized.

■ **December 11:** Major League owners pulled a shocker when they voted not to renew the contract of Commissioner Happy Chandler.

■ **December 26:** Chandler announced that the Gillette Safety Razor Company had agreed to pay a six-year fee of $6 million for rights to the World Series and All-Star Game.

MEMORABLE MOMENTS

■ **June 8:** The Red Sox, in the biggest single-game explosion in history, defeated the Browns 29-4 at Boston's Fenway Park.

■ **August 31:** Brooklyn's Gil Hodges became the sixth player to hit four home runs in a game during a 19-3 rout of the Braves at Ebbets Field. Hodges also singled and tied the single-game record of 17 total bases.

■ **October 1:** Dick Sisler crashed a three-run 10th-inning home run to give the Phillies a 4-1 victory over the Dodgers and their first N.L. pennant in 35 years.

LEADERS

American League

BA: Billy Goodman, Bos., .354.
Runs: Dom DiMaggio, Bos., 131.
Hits: George Kell, Det., 218.
TB: Walt Dropo, Bos., 326.
HR: Al Rosen, Cle., 37.
RBI: Walt Dropo, Bos.; Vern Stephens, Bos., 144.
SB: Dom DiMaggio, Bos., 15.
Wins: Bob Lemon, Cle., 23.
ERA: Early Wynn, Cle., 3.20.
CG: Ned Garver, St.L.; Bob Lemon, Cle., 22.
IP: Bob Lemon, Cle., 288.
SO: Bob Lemon, Cle., 170.

National League

BA: Stan Musial, St.L., .346.
Runs: Earl Torgeson, Bos., 120.
Hits: Duke Snider, Brk., 199.
TB: Duke Snider, Brk., 343.
HR: Ralph Kiner, Pit., 47.
RBI: Del Ennis, Phil., 126.
SB: Sam Jethroe, Bos., 35.
Wins: Warren Spahn, Bos., 21.
ERA: Sal Maglie, N.Y., 2.71.
CG: Vern Bickford, Bos., 27.
IP: Vern Bickford, Bos., 311.2.
SO: Warren Spahn, Bos., 191.

A.L. 20-game winners
Bob Lemon, Cle., 23-11
Vic Raschi, N.Y., 21-8

N.L. 20-game winners
Warren Spahn, Bos., 21-17
Robin Roberts, Phil., 20-11
Johnny Sain, Bos., 20-13

A.L. 100 RBIs
Walt Dropo, Bos., 144
Vern Stephens, Bos., 144
Yogi Berra, N.Y., 124
Vic Wertz, Det., 123
Joe DiMaggio, N.Y., 122
Bobby Doerr, Bos., 120
Al Rosen, Cle., 116
Luke Easter, Cle., 107
Hoot Evers, Det., 103
Larry Doby, Cle., 102
George Kell, Det., 101

N.L. 100 RBIs
Del Ennis, Phil., 126
Ralph Kiner, Pit., 118
Gil Hodges, Brk., 113
Ted Kluszewski, Cin., 111
Stan Musial, St.L., 109
Bob Elliott, Bos., 107
Duke Snider, Brk., 107
Carl Furillo, Brk., 106
Sid Gordon, Bos., 103
Hank Sauer, Chi., 103
Enos Slaughter, St.L., 101

N.L. 40 homers
Ralph Kiner, Pit., 47

Most Valuable Player
A.L.: Phil Rizzuto, SS, N.Y.
N.L.: Jim Konstanty, P, Phil.

Rookie of the Year
A.L.: Walt Dropo, 1B, Bos.
N.L.: Sam Jethroe, OF, Bos.

ALL-STAR GAME

■ **Winner:** The N.L. broke a four-game losing streak with a 4-3 victory in the first extra-inning All-Star Game.

■ **Key inning:** The ninth, when Tigers pitcher Art Houtteman, trying to close out a 3-2 A.L. victory, surrendered a game-tying home run to Pirates slugger Ralph Kiner.

■ **Memorable moment:** A dramatic 14th-inning home run by Cardinals second baseman Red Schoendienst that gave the N.L. its first win since 1944. Schoendienst was an 11th-inning defensive replacement.

■ **Top guns:** Larry Jansen (Giants), Ewell Blackwell (Reds), Kiner (Pirates), Schoendienst (Cardinals), N.L.; Bob Lemon (Indians), Larry Doby (Indians), A.L.

■ **MVP:** Schoendienst.

Linescore

July 11, at Chicago's Comiskey Park
N.L.......0 2 0 0 0 0 0 0 1 0 0 0 0 1—4 10 0
A.L.......0 0 1 0 2 0 0 0 0 0 0 0 0 0—3 8 1
Roberts (Phillies), Newcombe (Dodgers) 4, Konstanty (Phillies) 6, Jansen (Giants) 7, Blackwell (Reds) 12; Raschi (Yankees), Lemon (Indians) 4, Houtteman (Tigers) 7, Reynolds (Yankees) 10, Gray (Tigers) 13, Feller (Indians) 14. W—Blackwell. L—Gray. HR—Kiner, Schoendienst, N.L.

WORLD SERIES

■ **Winner:** Rekindling memories of New York's 1936-39 machine, the Bronx Bombers captured their second straight Series with a sweep of the Phillies.

■ **Turning point:** Joe DiMaggio's 10th-inning homer that gave the Yankees and Allie Reynolds a 2-1 victory in Game 2.

■ **Memorable moment:** Rookie Whitey Ford's first Series victory — a 5-2 Game 4 decision.

■ **Top guns:** Gene Woodling (.429), Bobby Brown (.333), Yankees; Granny Hamner (.429), Phillies.

Linescores

Game 1—October 4, at Philadelphia
New York ....0 0 0 1 0 0 0 0 0—1 5 0
Philadelphia ....0 0 0 0 0 0 0 0 0—0 2 1
Raschi; Konstanty, Meyer (9). W—Raschi. L—Konstanty.

Game 2—October 5, at Philadelphia
New York ....0 1 0 0 0 0 0 0 0 1—2 10 0
Philadelphia ....0 0 0 0 1 0 0 0 0 0—1 7 0
Reynolds; Roberts. W—Reynolds. L—Roberts. HR—DiMaggio (N.Y.).

Game 3—October 6, at New York
Philadelphia ....0 0 0 0 0 1 1 0 0—2 10 2
New York ....0 0 1 0 0 0 0 1 1—3 7 0
Heintzelman, Konstanty (8), Meyer (9); Lopat, Ferrick (9). W—Ferrick. L—Meyer.

Game 4—October 7, at New York
Philadelphia ....0 0 0 0 0 0 0 0 2—2 7 1
New York ....2 0 0 0 0 3 0 0 x—5 8 2
Miller, Konstanty (1), Roberts (8); Ford, Reynolds (9). W—Ford. L—Miller. HR—Berra (N.Y.).

1951

FINAL STANDINGS

American League

Team	W	L	Pct.	GB
New York	98	56	.636	...
Cleveland	93	61	.604	5
Boston	87	67	.565	11
Chicago	81	73	.526	17
Detroit	73	81	.474	25
Philadelphia	70	84	.455	28
Washington	62	92	.403	36
St. Louis	52	102	.338	46

National League

Team	W	L	Pct.	GB
*New York	98	59	.624	...
Brooklyn	97	60	.618	1
St. Louis	81	73	.526	15.5
Boston	76	78	.494	20.5
Philadelphia	73	81	.474	23.5
Cincinnati	68	86	.442	28.5
Pittsburgh	64	90	.416	32.5
Chicago	62	92	.403	34.5

*Defeated Brooklyn 2-1 in pennant playoff.

SIGNIFICANT EVENTS

■ **August 19:** Browns owner Bill Veeck pulled off a wild promotional stunt when he sent midget Eddie Gaedel to the plate as a surprise pinch-hitter in a Sportsman's Park game against the Tigers.
■ **September 20:** N.L. President Ford Frick was selected as baseball's third commissioner during a marathon meeting in Chicago.
■ **December 11:** Yankee center fielder Joe DiMaggio, a three-time A.L. MVP, announced his retirement.

MEMORABLE MOMENTS

■ **September 14:** Browns outfielder Bob Nieman became the first player to hit home runs in his first two big-league at-bats. Both came off Mickey McDermott in a game at Boston.
■ **September 28:** New York's Allie Reynolds fired his record-tying second no-hitter of the season in the opener of a doubleheader against Boston, earning an 8-0 decision and clinching at least a tie for the A.L. pennant. The Yankees clinched their third straight flag with an 11-3 win in the nightcap.
■ **October 3:** Bobby Thomson smashed a three-run, ninth-inning homer—giving the Giants a dramatic 5-4 victory over the Dodgers in the decisive third game of an N.L. pennant playoff.

LEADERS

American League

BA: Ferris Fain, Phil., .344.
Runs: Dom DiMaggio, Bos., 113.
Hits: George Kell, Det., 191.
TB: Ted Williams, Bos., 295.
HR: Gus Zernial, Chi.-Phil., 33.
RBI: Gus Zernial, Chi.-Phil., 129.
SB: Minnie Minoso, Cle.-Chi., 31.
Wins: Bob Feller, Cle., 22.
ERA: Saul Rogovin, Det.-Chi., 2.78.
CG: Ned Garver, St.L., 24.
IP: Early Wynn, Cle., 274.1.
SO: Vic Raschi, N.Y., 164.

National League

BA: Stan Musial, St.L., .355.
Runs: Ralph Kiner, Pit.; Stan Musial, St.L., 124.
Hits: Richie Ashburn, Phil., 221.
TB: Stan Musial, St.L., 355.
HR: Ralph Kiner, Pit., 42.
RBI: Monte Irvin, N.Y., 121.
SB: Sam Jethroe, Bos., 35.
Wins: Larry Jansen, N.Y.; Sal Maglie, N.Y., 23.
ERA: Chet Nichols, Bos., 2.88.
CG: Warren Spahn, Bos., 26.
IP: Robin Roberts, Phil., 315.
SO: Don Newcombe, Brk.; Warren Spahn, Bos., 164.

A.L. 20-game winners
Bob Feller, Cle., 22-8
Eddie Lopat, N.Y., 21-9
Vic Raschi, N.Y., 21-10
Ned Garver, St.L., 20-12
Mike Garcia, Cle., 20-13
Early Wynn, Cle., 20-13

N.L. 20-game winners
Sal Maglie, N.Y., 23-6
Larry Jansen, N.Y., 23-11
Preacher Roe, Brk., 22-3
Warren Spahn, Bos., 22-14
Robin Roberts, Phil., 21-15
Don Newcombe, Brk., 20-9
Murry Dickson, Pit., 20-16

A.L. 100 RBIs
Gus Zernial, Chi.-Phil., 129
Ted Williams, Bos., 126
Eddie Robinson, Chi., 117
Luke Easter, Cle., 103
Al Rosen, Cle., 102

N.L. 100 RBIs
Monte Irvin, N.Y., 121
Sid Gordon, Bos., 109
Ralph Kiner, Pit., 109
Roy Campanella, Brk., 108
Stan Musial, St.L., 108
Gil Hodges, Brk., 103
Duke Snider, Brk., 101
Bobby Thomson, N.Y., 101

N.L. 40 homers
Ralph Kiner, Pit., 42
Gil Hodges, Brk., 40

Most Valuable Player
A.L.: Yogi Berra, C, N.Y.
N.L.: Roy Campanella, C, Brk.

Rookie of the Year
A.L.: Gil McDougald, 3B, N.Y.
N.L.: Willie Mays, OF, N.Y.

Hall of Fame additions
Jimmie Foxx, 1B, 1925-45
Mel Ott, OF, 1926-47

ALL-STAR GAME

■ **Winner:** The N.L. hit an All-Star Game-record four home runs in an 8-3 victory. It marked the first time the senior circuit had recorded back-to-back wins.
■ **Key inning:** A three-run fourth, when St. Louis' Stan Musial and Boston's Bob Elliott connected off Yankee lefty Eddie Lopat.
■ **Memorable moments:** A.L. home runs by Vic Wertz and George Kell before their home fans at Detroit's Briggs Stadium.
■ **Top guns:** Don Newcombe (Dodgers), Musial (Cardinals), Elliott (Braves), Jackie Robinson (Dodgers), Ralph Kiner (Pirates), Gil Hodges (Dodgers), N.L.; Wertz (Tigers), Kell (Tigers), A.L.
■ **MVP:** Elliott.

Linescore

July 10, at Detroit's Briggs Stadium
N.L. ....1 0 0 3 0 2 1 1 0—8 12 1
A.L. ....0 1 0 1 1 0 0 0 0—3 10 2
Roberts (Phillies), Maglie (Giant) 3, Newcombe (Dodgers) 6, Blackwell (Reds) 9; Garver (Browns), Lopat (Yankees) 4, Hutchinson (Tigers) 5, Parnell (Red Sox) 8, Lemon (Indians) 9. W—Maglie. L—Lopat. HR—Musial, Elliott, Hodges, Kiner, N.L.; Wertz, Kell, A.L.

WORLD SERIES

■ **Winner:** The Yankees' third straight Series victory came at the expense of the torrid Giants, who had beaten Brooklyn in a memorable pennant playoff series.
■ **Turning point:** Infielder Gil McDougald's Game 5 grand slam, which sparked a momentum-turning 13-1 Yankee victory.
■ **Memorable moment:** Yankee right fielder Hank Bauer's Game 6 heroics: a bases-loaded triple and a spectacular Series-ending catch in a 4-3 victory.
■ **Top guns:** Eddie Lopat (2-0, 0.50 ERA), Bobby Brown (.357), McDougald (7 RBIs), Yankees; Monte Irvin (.458), Alvin Dark (.417), Giants.

Linescores

Game 1—October 4, at Yankee Stadium
Giants ....2 0 0 0 0 3 0 0 0—5 10 1
Yankees ....0 1 0 0 0 0 0 0 0—1 7 1
Koslo; Reynolds, Hogue (7), Morgan (8). W—Koslo. L—Reynolds. HR—Dark (Giants).

Game 2—October 5, at Yankee Stadium
Giants ....0 0 0 0 0 0 1 0 0—1 5 1
Yankees ....1 1 0 0 0 0 0 1 x—3 6 0
Jansen, Spencer (7); Lopat. W—Lopat. L—Jansen. HR—Collins (Yankees).

Game 3—October 6, at Polo Grounds
Yankees ....0 0 0 0 0 0 0 1 1—2 5 2
Giants ....0 1 0 0 5 0 0 0 x—6 7 2
Raschi, Hogue (5), Ostrowski (8); Hearn, Jones (8). W—Hearn. L—Raschi. HR—Lockman (Giants); Woodling (Yankees).

Game 4—October 8, at Polo Grounds
Yankees ....0 1 0 1 2 0 2 0 0—6 12 0
Giants ....1 0 0 0 0 0 0 0 1—2 8 2
Reynolds; Maglie, Jones (6), Kennedy (9). W—Reynolds. L—Maglie. HR—DiMaggio (Yankees).

Game 5—October 9, at Polo Grounds
Yankees ....0 0 5 2 0 2 4 0 0—13 12 1
Giants ....1 0 0 0 0 0 0 0 0— 1 5 3
Lopat; Jansen, Kennedy (4), Spencer (6), Corwin (7), Konikowski (9). W—Lopat. L—Jansen. HR—McDougald, Rizzuto (Yankees).

Game 6—October 10, at Yankee Stadium
Giants ....0 0 0 0 1 0 0 0 2—3 11 1
Yankees ....1 0 0 0 0 3 0 0 x—4 7 0
Koslo, Hearn (7), Jansen (8); Raschi, Sain (7), Kuzava (9). W—Raschi. L—Koslo.

1952

FINAL STANDINGS

American League

Team	W	L	Pct.	GB
New York	95	59	.617	...
Cleveland	93	61	.604	2
Chicago	81	73	.526	14
Philadelphia	79	75	.513	16
Washington	78	76	.506	17
Boston	76	78	.494	19
St. Louis	64	90	.416	31
Detroit	50	104	.325	45

National League

Team	W	L	Pct.	GB
Brooklyn	96	57	.627	...
New York	92	62	.597	4.5
St. Louis	88	66	.571	8.5
Philadelphia	87	67	.565	9.5
Chicago	77	77	.500	19.5
Cincinnati	69	85	.448	27.5
Boston	64	89	.418	32
Pittsburgh	42	112	.273	54.5

SIGNIFICANT EVENTS

■ **May 2:** Boston's Ted Williams, who lost three years to military service in World War II, returned to a 17-month tour of duty with the U.S. Marines as a fighter pilot in Korea.
■ **May-June-July:** Joining Williams on the Korean front were such name players as Don Newcombe, Willie Mays, Jerry Coleman, Bob Kennedy, Bobby Brown and Tom Morgan.

MEMORABLE MOMENTS

■ **April 23:** Browns lefty Bob Cain outdueled Cleveland ace Bob Feller, 1-0, in a record-tying battle of one-hitters at St. Louis' Sportsman's Park.
■ **May 21:** The Dodgers exploded for a Major League-record 15 first-inning runs and coasted to a 19-1 victory over the Reds at Ebbets Field.
■ **July 15:** Detroit first baseman Walt Dropo doubled in the second game of a doubleheader against Washington for his 12th consecutive hit, tying the 1938 record set by Boston's Pinky Higgins.
■ **August 25:** Detroit's Virgil Trucks became the third pitcher to throw two no-hitters in one season when he stopped New York, 1-0, at Yankee Stadium.

LEADERS

American League

BA: Ferris Fain, Phil., .327.
Runs: Larry Doby, Cle., 104.
Hits: Nellie Fox, Chi., 192.
TB: Al Rosen, Cle., 297.
HR: Larry Doby, Cle., 32.
RBI: Al Rosen, Cle., 105.
SB: Minnie Minoso, Chi., 22.
Wins: Bobby Shantz, Phil., 24.
ERA: Allie Reynolds, N.Y., 2.06.
CG: Bob Lemon, Cle., 28.
IP: Bob Lemon, Cle., 309.2.
SO: Allie Reynolds, N.Y., 160.

National League

BA: Stan Musial, St.L., .336.
Runs: Solly Hemus, St.L.; Stan Musial, St.L., 105.
Hits: Stan Musial, St.L., 194.
TB: Stan Musial, St.L., 311.
HR: Ralph Kiner, Pit.; Hank Sauer, Chi., 37.
RBI: Hank Sauer, Chi., 121.
SB: Pee Wee Reese, Brk., 30.
Wins: Robin Roberts, Phil., 28.
ERA: Hoyt Wilhelm, N.Y., 2.43.
CG: Robin Roberts, Phil., 30.
IP: Robin Roberts, Phil., 330.
SO: Warren Spahn, Bos., 183.

A.L. 20-game winners
Bobby Shantz, Phil., 24-7
Early Wynn, Cle., 23-12
Mike Garcia, Cle., 22-11
Bob Lemon, Cle., 22-11
Allie Reynolds, N.Y., 20-8

N.L. 20-Game Winner
Robin Roberts, Phil., 28-7

A.L. 100 RBIs
Al Rosen, Cle., 105
Larry Doby, Cle., 104
Eddie Robinson, Chi., 104
Gus Zernial, Phil., 100

N.L. 100 RBIs
Hank Sauer, Chi., 121
Bobby Thomson, N.Y., 108
Del Ennis, Phil., 107
Gil Hodges, Brk., 102
Enos Slaughter, St.L., 101

Most Valuable Player
A.L.: Bobby Shantz, P, Phil.
N.L.: Hank Sauer, OF, Chi.

Rookie of the Year
A.L.: Harry Byrd, P, Phil.
N.L.: Joe Black, P, Brk.

Hall of Fame additions
Harry Heilmann, OF/1B, 1914-32
Paul Waner, OF, 1926-45

ALL-STAR GAME

■ **Winner:** The N.L. recorded a rain-shortened 3-2 victory and closed its All-Star deficit to 12-7.
■ **Key inning:** The fourth, when the A.L. scored twice for a 2-1 lead and the N.L. answered with a two-run homer by the Cubs' Hank Sauer.
■ **Memorable moments:** The pitching of Philadelphia stars Curt Simmons (Phillies) and Bobby Shantz (Athletics) before their home fans. Simmons pitched three scoreless innings for the N.L. and Shantz struck out all three batters he faced in a scoreless fifth.
■ **Top guns:** Simmons (Phillies), Jackie Robinson (Dodgers), Sauer (Cubs), N.L.; Shantz (Athletics), Bobby Avila (Indians), A.L.
■ **MVP:** Sauer.

Linescore

July 8, at Philadelphia's Shibe Park
A.L. ....0 0 0 2 0—2 5 0
N.L. ....1 0 0 2 0—3 3 0
Raschi (Yankees), Lemon (Indians) 3, Shantz (Athletics) 5; Simmons (Phillies), Rush (Cubs) 4. W—Rush. L—Lemon. HR—J. Robinson, Sauer, N.L.

WORLD SERIES

■ **Winner:** The Yankees tied their own previous best run of four consecutive Series championships with a seven-game thriller against the Dodgers.
■ **Turning point:** Game 6 home runs by Yogi Berra and Mickey Mantle that keyed a 3-2 victory and tied the Series at three games apiece.
■ **Memorable moment:** Yankee second baseman Billy Martin's Series-saving shoetop catch of Jackie Robinson's bases-loaded infield popup, which appeared destined to fall untouched. Martin's mad-dash catch saved a 4-2 victory.
■ **Top guns:** Vic Raschi (2-0, 1.59 ERA), Johnny Mize (.400, 3 HR, 6 RBIs), Mantle (.345, 2 HR), Yankees; Duke Snider (.345, 4 HR, 8 RBIs), Pee Wee Reese (.345), Dodgers.

Linescores

Game 1—October 1, at Brooklyn
New York ....0 0 1 0 0 0 0 1 0—2 6 2
Brooklyn ....0 1 0 0 0 2 0 1 x—4 6 0
Reynolds, Scarborough (8); Black. W—Black. L—Reynolds. HR—Robinson, Snider, Reese (Brk.); McDougald (N.Y.).

Game 2—October 2, at Brooklyn
New York ....0 0 0 1 1 5 0 0 0—7 10 0
Brooklyn ....0 0 1 0 0 0 0 0 0—1 3 1
Raschi; Erskine, Loes (6), Lehman (8). W—Raschi. L—Erskine. HR—Martin (N.Y.).

Game 3—October 3, at New York
Brooklyn ....0 0 1 0 1 0 0 1 2—5 11 0
New York ....0 1 0 0 0 0 0 1 1—3 6 2
Roe; Lopat, Gorman (9). W—Roe. L—Lopat. HR—Berra, Mize (N.Y.).

Game 4—October 4, at New York
Brooklyn ....0 0 0 0 0 0 0 0 0—0 4 1
New York ....0 0 0 1 0 0 0 1 x—2 4 1
Black, Rutherford (8); Reynolds. W—Reynolds. L—Black. HR—Mize (N.Y.).

Game 5—October 5, at New York
Brooklyn ....0 1 0 0 3 0 1 0 0 0 1—6 10 0
New York ....0 0 0 0 5 0 0 0 0 0 0—5 5 1
Erskine; Blackwell, Sain (6). W—Erskine. L—Sain. HR—Snider (Brk.); Mize (N.Y.).

Game 6—October 6, at Brooklyn
New York ....0 0 0 0 0 0 2 1 0—3 9 0
Brooklyn ....0 0 0 0 0 1 0 1 0—2 8 1
Raschi, Reynolds (8); Loes, Roe (9). W—Raschi. L—Loes. HR—Mantle, Berra (N.Y.); Snider 2 (Brk.).

Game 7—October 7, at Brooklyn
New York ....0 0 0 1 1 1 1 0 0—4 10 4
Brooklyn ....0 0 0 1 1 0 0 0 0—2 8 1
Lopat, Reynolds (4), Raschi (7), Kuzava (7); Black, Roe (6), Erskine (8). W—Reynolds. L—Black. HR—Woodling, Mantle (N.Y.).

1953

FINAL STANDINGS

American League

Team	W	L	Pct.	GB
New York	99	52	.656	...
Cleveland	92	62	.597	8.5
Chicago	89	65	.578	11.5
Boston	84	69	.549	16
Washington	76	76	.500	23.5
Detroit	60	94	.390	40.5
Philadelphia	59	95	.383	41.5
St. Louis	54	100	.351	46.5

National League

Team	W	L	Pct.	GB
Brooklyn	105	49	.682	...
Milwaukee	92	62	.597	13
Philadelphia	83	71	.539	22
St. Louis	83	71	.539	22
New York	70	84	.455	35
Cincinnati	68	86	.442	37
Chicago	65	89	.422	40
Pittsburgh	50	104	.325	55

SIGNIFICANT EVENTS

■ **March 18:** The Braves, a fixture in Boston for 77 years, received unanimous approval for a move to Milwaukee—baseball's first franchise shift since 1903.

■ **September 29:** Bill Veeck sold his St. Louis Browns to a syndicate that received quick approval to move the franchise to Baltimore.

■ **November 9:** Baseball won a major victory when the U.S. Supreme Court ruled that it is a sport, not an interstate business, and therefore not subject to federal antitrust laws.

MEMORABLE MOMENTS

■ **May 6:** Browns rookie Bobo Holloman made baseball history when he pitched a 6-0 no-hitter against Philadelphia in his first Major League start.

■ **May 25:** Milwaukee's Max Surkont struck out a modern-record eight consecutive Reds en route to a 10-3 victory.

■ **June 18:** The Red Sox scored a record 17 runs in the seventh inning of a 23-3 victory over the Tigers.

LEADERS

American League

BA: Mickey Vernon, Wash., .337.
Runs: Al Rosen, Cle., 115.
Hits: Harvey Kuenn, Det., 209.
TB: Al Rosen, Cle., 367.
HR: Al Rosen, Cle., 43.
RBI: Al Rosen, Cle., 145.
SB: Minnie Minoso, Chi., 25.
Wins: Bob Porterfield, Wash., 22.
ERA: Eddie Lopat, N.Y., 2.42.
CG: Bob Porterfield, Wash., 24.
IP: Bob Lemon, Cle., 286.2.
SO: Billy Pierce, Chi., 186.

National League

BA: Carl Furillo, Brk., .344.
Runs: Duke Snider, Brk., 132.
Hits: Richie Ashburn, Phil., 205.
TB: Duke Snider, Brk., 370.
HR: Eddie Mathews, Mil., 47.
RBI: Roy Campanella, Brk., 142.
SB: Bill Bruton, Mil., 26.
Wins: Robin Roberts, Phil.; Warren Spahn, Mil., 23.
ERA: Warren Spahn, Mil., 2.10.
CG: Robin Roberts, Phil., 33.
IP: Robin Roberts, Phil., 346.2.
SO: Robin Roberts, Phil., 198.

A.L. 20-game winners
Bob Porterfield, Wash., 22-10
Mel Parnell, Bos., 21-8
Bob Lemon, Cle., 21-15
Virgil Trucks, St.L.-Chi., 20-10

N.L. 20-game winners
Warren Spahn, Mil., 23-7
Robin Roberts, Phil., 23-16
Carl Erskine, Brk., 20-6
Harvey Haddix, St.L., 20-9

A.L. 100 RBIs
Al Rosen, Cle., 145
Mickey Vernon, Wash., 115
Ray Boone, Cle.-Det., 114
Yogi Berra, N.Y., 108
Gus Zernial, Phil., 108
Minnie Minoso, Chi., 104
Larry Doby, Cle., 102
Eddie Robinson, Phil., 102

N.L. 100 RBIs
Roy Campanella, Brk., 142
Eddie Mathews, Mil., 135
Duke Snider, Brk., 126
Del Ennis, Phil., 125
Gil Hodges, Brk., 122
Ralph Kiner, Pit.-Chi., 116
Stan Musial, St.L., 113
Ray Jablonski, St.L., 112
Ted Kluszewski, Cin., 108
Bobby Thomson, N.Y., 106
Gus Bell, Cin., 105
Frank Thomas, Pit., 102
Jim Greengrass, Cin., 100

A.L. 40 homers
Al Rosen, Cle., 43
Gus Zernial, Phil., 42

N.L. 40 homers
Eddie Mathews, Mil., 47
Duke Snider, Brk., 42
Roy Campanella, Brk., 41
Ted Kluszewski, Cin., 40

Most Valuable Player
A.L.: Al Rosen, 3B, Cle.
N.L.: Roy Campanella, C, Brk.

Rookie of the Year
A.L.: Harvey Kuenn, SS, Det.
N.L.: Jim Gilliam, 2B, Brk.

Hall of Fame additions
Ed Barrow, manager/executive
Chief Bender, P, 1903-25
Tommy Connolly, umpire
Dizzy Dean, P, 1930-47
Bill Klem, umpire
Al Simmons, OF, 1924-44
Bobby Wallace, SS, 1894-1918
Harry Wright, manager

ALL-STAR GAME

■ **Winner:** Robin Roberts (Phillies), Warren Spahn (Braves), Curt Simmons (Phillies) and Murry Dickson (Pirates) combined on a six-hitter and the N.L. rolled to its fourth consecutive victory.

■ **Key inning:** The N.L.'s two-run fifth, when Philadelphia's Richie Ashburn and Brooklyn's Pee Wee Reese singled home runs.

■ **Memorable moment:** The eighth-inning appearance of Browns righthander Satchel Paige, a former Negro League legend and the oldest man (47) ever to play in an All-Star Game.

■ **Top guns:** Roberts (Phillies), Spahn (Braves), Simmons (Phillies), Reese (Dodgers), N.L.; Billy Pierce (White Sox), Minnie Minoso (White Sox), A.L.

■ **MVP:** Reese.

Linescore

July 14, at Cincinnati's Crosley Field
A.L. ....0 0 0 0 0 0 0 0 1—1 5 0
N.L. ....0 0 0 0 2 0 1 2 x—5 10 0
Pierce (White Sox), Reynolds (Yankees) 4, Garcia (Indians) 6, Paige (Browns) 8; Roberts (Phillies), Spahn (Braves) 4, Simmons (Phillies) 6, Dickson (Pirates) 8. W—Spahn. L—Reynolds.

WORLD SERIES

■ **Winner:** The Yankees earned their record fifth consecutive Series victory and remained perfect in post-season play under manager Casey Stengel.

■ **Turning point:** Billy Martin's two-run homer and Mickey Mantle's grand slam in the Yankees' 11-7 fifth-game Series-turning triumph.

■ **Memorable moment:** Martin's ninth-inning Series-ending single in Game 6 — his record-tying 12th hit of the fall classic.

■ **Top guns:** Martin (.500, 12 hits, 2 HR, 8 RBIs), Mantle (2 HR, 7 RBIs), Yankees; Gil Hodges (.364), Carl Furillo (.333), Dodgers.

Linescores

Game 1—September 30, at New York
Brooklyn ....0 0 0 0 1 3 1 0 0—5 12 2
New York..................4 0 0 0 1 0 1 3 x—9 12 0
Erskine, Hughes (2), Labine (6), Wade (7); Reynolds, Sain (6). W—Sain. L—Labine. HR—Berra, Collins (N.Y.); Gilliam, Hodges, Shuba (Brk.).

Game 2—October 1, at New York
Brooklyn ....0 0 0 2 0 0 0 0 0—2 9 1
New York....................1 0 0 0 0 0 1 2 x—4 5 0
Roe; Lopat. W—Lopat. L—Roe. HR—Martin, Mantle (N.Y.).

Game 3—October 2, at Brooklyn
New York....................0 0 0 0 1 0 0 1 0—2 6 0
Brooklyn ....0 0 0 0 1 1 0 1 x—3 9 0
Raschi; Erskine. W—Erskine. L—Raschi. HR—Campanella (Brk.).

Game 4—October 3, at Brooklyn
New York..................0 0 0 0 2 0 0 0 1—3 9 0
Brooklyn ....3 0 0 1 0 2 1 0 x—7 12 0
Ford, Gorman (2), Sain (5), Schallock (7); Loes, Labine (9). W—Loes. L—Ford. HR—McDougald (N.Y.); Snider (Brk.).

Game 5—October 4, at Brooklyn
New York................1 0 5 0 0 0 3 1 1—11 11 1
Brooklyn ....0 1 0 0 1 0 0 4 1— 7 14 1
McDonald, Kuzava (8), Reynolds (9); Podres, Meyer (3), Wade (8), Black (9). W—McDonald. L—Podres. HR—Woodling, Mantle, Martin, McDougald (N.Y.); Cox, Gilliam (Brk.).

Game 6—October 5, at New York
Brooklyn ....0 0 0 0 0 1 0 0 2—3 8 3
New York..................2 1 0 0 0 0 0 0 1—4 13 0
Erskine, Milliken (5), Labine (7); Ford, Reynolds (8). W—Reynolds. L—Labine. HR—Furillo (Brk.).

1954

FINAL STANDINGS

American League

Team	W	L	Pct.	GB
Cleveland	111	43	.721	...
New York	103	51	.669	8
Chicago	94	60	.610	17
Boston	69	85	.448	42
Detroit	68	86	.442	43
Washington	66	88	.429	45
Baltimore	54	100	.351	57
Philadelphia	51	103	.331	60

National League

Team	W	L	Pct.	GB
New York	97	57	.630	...
Brooklyn	92	62	.597	5
Milwaukee	89	65	.578	8
Philadelphia	75	79	.487	22
Cincinnati	74	80	.481	23
St. Louis	72	82	.468	25
Chicago	64	90	.416	33
Pittsburgh	53	101	.344	44

SIGNIFICANT EVENTS

■ **July 12:** Big league players organized into a group called the Major League Baseball Players Association and hired J. Norman Lewis to represent it in negotiations with owners.

■ **November 8:** A.L. owners approved the sale of the Athletics to Chicago industrialist Arnold Johnson and transfer of the team to Kansas City.

■ **December 1:** The finishing touches were put on a record 17-player trade between the Orioles and Yankees.

MEMORABLE MOMENTS

■ **April 15:** Baltimore welcomed its new Orioles with a huge celebration and the team responded with a 3-1 victory over Chicago at Memorial Stadium.

■ **May 2:** Cardinals slugger Stan Musial hit a doubleheader-record five home runs in a split with the Giants at Busch Stadium.

■ **July 31:** Milwaukee's Joe Adcock joined the exclusive four-homer club in a 15-7 victory over Brooklyn and set a record for total bases (18) when he added a double to his offensive explosion.

■ **September 25:** Early Wynn fired a two-hitter and the Indians defeated Detroit, 11-1, for their A.L.-record 111th victory of the season.

LEADERS

American League

BA: Bobby Avila, Cle., .341.
Runs: Mickey Mantle, N.Y., 129.
Hits: Nellie Fox, Chi.; Harvey Kuenn, Det., 201.
TB: Minnie Minoso, Chi., 304.
HR: Larry Doby, Cle., 32.
RBI: Larry Doby, Cle., 126.
SB: Jackie Jensen, Bos., 22.
Wins: Bob Lemon, Cle.; Early Wynn, Cle., 23.
ERA: Mike Garcia, Cle., 2.64.
CG: Bob Lemon, Cle.; Bob Porterfield, Wash., 21.
IP: Early Wynn, Cle., 270.2.
SO: Bob Turley, Bal., 185.

National League

BA: Willie Mays, N.Y., .345.
Runs: Stan Musial, St.L.; Duke Snider, Brk., 120.
Hits: Don Mueller, N.Y., 212.
TB: Duke Snider, Brk., 378.
HR: Ted Kluszewski, Cin., 49.
RBI: Ted Kluszewski, Cin., 141.
SB: Bill Bruton, Mil., 34.
Wins: Robin Roberts, Phil., 23.
ERA: Johnny Antonelli, N.Y., 2.30.
CG: Robin Roberts, Phil., 29.
IP: Robin Roberts, Phil., 336.2.
SO: Robin Roberts, Phil., 185.

A.L. 20-game winners
Bob Lemon, Cle., 23-7
Early Wynn, Cle., 23-11
Bob Grim, N.Y., 20-6

N.L. 20-game winners
Robin Roberts, Phil., 23-15
Johnny Antonelli, N.Y., 21-7
Warren Spahn, Mil., 21-12

A.L. 100 RBIs
Larry Doby, Cle., 126
Yogi Berra, N.Y., 125
Jackie Jensen, Bos., 117
Minnie Minoso, Chi., 116
Mickey Mantle, N.Y., 102
Al Rosen, Cle., 102
Roy Sievers, Wash., 102

N.L. 100 RBIs
Ted Kluszewski, Cin., 141
Gil Hodges, Brk., 130
Duke Snider, Brk., 130
Stan Musial, St.L., 126
Del Ennis, Phil., 119
Willie Mays, N.Y., 110
Ray Jablonski, St.L., 104
Eddie Mathews, Mil., 103
Hank Sauer, Chi., 103
Gus Bell, Cin., 101

N.L. 40 homers
Ted Kluszewski, Cin., 49
Gil Hodges, Brk., 42
Willie Mays, N.Y., 41
Hank Sauer, Chi., 41
Eddie Mathews, Mil., 40
Duke Snider, Brk., 40

Most Valuable Player
A.L.: Yogi Berra, C, N.Y.
N.L.: Willie Mays, OF, N.Y.

Rookie of the Year
A.L.: Bob Grim, P, N.Y.
N.L.: Wally Moon, OF, St.L.

Hall of Fame additions
Bill Dickey, C, 1928-46
Rabbit Maranville, SS, 1912-35
Bill Terry, 1B, 1923-36

ALL-STAR GAME

■ **Winner:** Chicago's Nellie Fox looped a two-run eighth-inning single to spark the A.L. in a game that featured two home runs and five RBIs by Cleveland fan favorite Al Rosen.

■ **Key inning:** The eighth. Before Fox's game-winning single, Cleveland's Larry Doby excited the home fans with a game-tying home run.

■ **Memorable moment:** Senators lefthander Dean Stone's no-pitch victory. Stone entered the game with two out in the eighth and retired St. Louis' Red Schoendienst trying to steal home.

■ **Top guns:** Rosen (Indians), Bobby Avila (Indians), Doby (Indians), Ray Boone (Tigers), Fox (White Sox), Yogi Berra (Yankees), A.L.; Duke Snider (Dodgers), Ted Kluszewski (Reds), Gus Bell (Reds), N.L.

■ **MVP:** Rosen.

Linescore

July 13, at Cleveland Stadium
N.L. ....0 0 0 5 2 0 0 2 0— 9 14 0
A.L. ....0 0 4 1 2 1 0 3 x—11 17 1
Roberts (Phillies), Antonelli (Giants) 4, Spahn (Braves) 6, Grissom (Giants) 6, Conley (Braves) 8, Erskine (Dodgers) 8; Ford (Yankees), Consuegra (White Sox) 4, Lemon (Indians) 4, Porterfield (Senators) 5, Keegan (White Sox) 8, Stone (Senators) 8, Trucks (White Sox) 9. W—Stone. L—Conley. HR—Rosen 2, Boone, Doby, A.L.; Kluszewski, Bell, N.L.

WORLD SERIES

■ **Winner:** The Giants pulled off a surprising sweep of the Indians, who had won an A.L.-record 111 games.

■ **Turning point:** A three-run 10th-inning home run by pinch-hitter Dusty Rhodes that decided Game 1. Rhodes' pop-fly homer traveled 260 feet.

■ **Memorable moment:** Center fielder Willie Mays' over-the-shoulder catch of a Game 1 blast by Cleveland's Vic Wertz — perhaps the greatest defensive play in Series history.

■ **Top guns:** Rhodes (.667, 2 HR, 7 RBIs), Alvin Dark (.412), Don Mueller (.389), Giants; Wertz (.500), Indians.

Linescores

Game 1—September 29, at New York
Cleveland ....2 0 0 0 0 0 0 0 0 0—2 8 0
New York..............0 0 2 0 0 0 0 0 0 3—5 9 3
Lemon; Maglie, Liddle (8), Grissom (8). W—Grissom. L—Lemon. HR—Rhodes (N.Y.).

Game 2—September 30, at New York
Cleveland ....1 0 0 0 0 0 0 0 0—1 8 0
New York....................0 0 0 0 2 0 1 0 x—3 4 0
Wynn, Mossi (8); Antonelli. W—Antonelli. L—Wynn. HR—Smith (Cle.); Rhodes (N.Y.).

Game 3—October 1, at Cleveland
New York..................1 0 3 0 1 1 0 0 0—6 10 1
Cleveland ....0 0 0 0 0 0 1 1 0—2 4 2
Gomez, Wilhelm (8); Garcia, Houtteman (4), Narleski (6), Mossi (9). W—Gomez. L—Garcia. HR—Wertz (Cle.).

Game 4—October 2, at Cleveland
New York..................0 2 1 0 4 0 0 0 0—7 10 3
Cleveland ....0 0 0 0 3 0 1 0 0—4 6 2
Liddle, Wilhelm (7), Antonelli (8); Lemon, Newhouser (5), Narleski (5), Mossi (6), Garcia (8). W—Liddle. L—Lemon. HR—Majeski (Cle.).

1955

FINAL STANDINGS

American League

Team	W	L	Pct.	GB
New York	96	58	.623	...
Cleveland	93	61	.604	3
Chicago	91	63	.591	5
Boston	84	70	.545	12
Detroit	79	75	.513	17
Kansas City	63	91	.409	33
Baltimore	57	97	.370	39
Washington	53	101	.344	43

National League

Team	W	L	Pct.	GB
Brooklyn	98	55	.641	...
Milwaukee	85	69	.552	13.5
New York	80	74	.519	18.5
Philadelphia	77	77	.500	21.5
Cincinnati	75	79	.487	23.5
Chicago	72	81	.471	26
St. Louis	68	86	.442	30.5
Pittsburgh	60	94	.390	38.5

SIGNIFICANT EVENT

■ **April 14:** The New York Yankees, one of four non-integrated teams, broke the color barrier when Elston Howard singled in his first big-league at-bat in a game at Boston.

MEMORABLE MOMENTS

■ **April 12:** The Athletics made their Kansas City debut with a 6-2 victory over the Tigers.
■ **April 23:** The White Sox hit seven home runs and tied a modern run-scoring record with a 29-6 victory at Kansas City.
■ **September 25:** Giants slugger Willie Mays, baseball's seventh 50-homer man, belted No. 51 in a 5-2 victory over the Phillies.
■ **September 25:** 20-year-old Tigers outfielder Al Kaline became baseball's youngest batting champ when he finished with an A.L.-best .340 average.

LEADERS

American League
BA: Al Kaline, Det., .340.
Runs: Al Smith, Cle., 123.
Hits: Al Kaline, Det., 200.
TB: Al Kaline, Det., 321.
HR: Mickey Mantle, N.Y., 37.
RBI: Ray Boone, Det.; Jackie Jensen, Bos., 116.
SB: Jim Rivera, Chi., 25.
Wins: Whitey Ford, N.Y.; Bob Lemon, Cle.; Frank Sullivan, Bos., 18.
ERA: Billy Pierce, Chi., 1.97.
CG: Whitey Ford, N.Y., 18.
IP: Frank Sullivan, Bos., 260.
SO: Herb Score, Cle., 245.

National League
BA: Richie Ashburn, Phil., .338.
Runs: Duke Snider, Brk., 126.
Hits: Ted Kluszewski, Cin., 192.
TB: Willie Mays, N.Y., 382.
HR: Willie Mays, N.Y., 51.
RBI: Duke Snider, Brk., 136.
SB: Bill Bruton, Mil., 25.
Wins: Robin Roberts, Phil., 23.
ERA: Bob Friend, Pit., 2.83.
CG: Robin Roberts, Phil., 26.
IP: Robin Roberts, Phil., 305.
SO: Sam Jones, Chi., 198.

N.L. 20-game winners
Robin Roberts, Phil., 23-14
Don Newcombe, Brk., 20-5

A.L. 100 RBIs
Ray Boone, Det., 116
Jackie Jensen, Bos., 116
Yogi Berra, N.Y., 108
Roy Sievers, Wash., 106
Al Kaline, Det., 102

N.L. 100 RBIs
Duke Snider, Brk., 136
Willie Mays, N.Y., 127
Del Ennis, Phil., 120
Ernie Banks, Chi., 117
Ted Kluszewski, Cin., 113
Wally Post, Cin., 109
Stan Musial, St.L., 108
Roy Campanella, Brk., 107
Hank Aaron, Mil., 106
Gus Bell, Cin., 104
Gil Hodges, Brk., 102
Eddie Mathews, Mil., 101

N.L. 40 homers
Willie Mays, N.Y., 51
Ted Kluszewski, Cin., 47
Ernie Banks, Chi., 44
Duke Snider, Brk., 42
Eddie Mathews, Mil., 41
Wally Post, Cin., 40

Most Valuable Player
A.L.: Yogi Berra, C, N.Y.
N.L.: Roy Campanella, C, Brk.

Rookie of the Year
A.L.: Herb Score, P, Cle.
N.L.: Bill Virdon, OF, St.L.

Hall of Fame additions
Home Run Baker, 3B, 1908-22
Joe DiMaggio, OF, 1936-51
Gabby Hartnett, C, 1922-41
Ted Lyons, P, 1923-46
Ray Schalk, C, 1912-29
Dazzy Vance, P, 1915-35

ALL-STAR GAME

■ **Winner:** The N.L., down 5-0 entering the seventh inning, rallied for a 6-5 victory in 12 innings — the second longest All-Star Game.

■ **Key inning:** The N.L.'s three-run eighth, which tied the score and forced extra innings. The tying run scored on right fielder Al Kaline's wild throw.

■ **Memorable moment:** Stan Musial's first-pitch home run in the 12th off Boston's Frank Sullivan. It was Musial's record fourth All-Star homer.

■ **Top guns:** Joe Nuxhall (Reds), Gene Conley (Braves), Willie Mays (Giants), Hank Aaron (Braves), Musial (Cardinals), N.L.; Billy Pierce (White Sox), Chico Carrasquel (White Sox), Mickey Mantle (Yankees), A.L.

■ **MVP:** Musial.

Linescore

July 12, at Milwaukee's County Stadium
A.L. ....4 0 0 0 0 1 0 0 0 0 0 0—5 10 2
N.L. ....0 0 0 0 0 0 2 3 0 0 0 1—6 13 1
Pierce (White Sox), Wynn (Indians) 4, Ford (Yankees) 7, Sullivan (Red Sox) 8; Roberts (Phillies), Haddix (Cardinals) 4, Newcombe (Dodgers) 7, Jones (Cubs) 8, Nuxhall (Reds) 8, Conley (Braves) 12. W—Conley. L—Sullivan. HR—Mantle, A.L.; Musial, N.L.

WORLD SERIES

■ **Winner:** Brooklyn's long wait finally ended as the Dodgers won a Series on their eighth try — beating the hated Yankees in the process.
Turning point: Hot-hitting Duke Snider's two home runs powered the Dodgers to within a game of their first championship in a 5-3 Game 5 victory.

■ **Memorable moment:** A spectacular Series-saving catch by Dodgers outfielder Sandy Amoros in the sixth inning of Game 7. The two-on, nobody-out catch of Yogi Berra's line drive resulted in a double play and preserved Johnny Podres' 2-0 shutout.

■ **Top guns:** Podres (2-0, 1.00 ERA), Snider (.320, 4 HR, 7 RBIs), Dodgers; Whitey Ford (2-0, 2.12), Hank Bauer (.429), Berra (.417), Yankees.

■ **MVP:** Podres.

Linescores

Game 1—September 28, at New York
Brooklyn ....0 2 1 0 0 0 0 2 0—5 10 0
New York..................0 2 1 1 0 2 0 0 x—6 9 1
Newcombe, Bessent (6), Labine (8); Ford, Grim (9). W—Ford. L—Newcombe. HR—Collins 2, Howard (N.Y.); Furillo, Snider (Brk.).

Game 2—September 29, at New York
Brooklyn ....0 0 0 1 1 0 0 0 0—2 5 2
New York..................0 0 0 4 0 0 0 0 x—4 8 0
Loes, Bessent (4), Spooner (5), Labine (8); Byrne. W—Byrne. L—Loes.

Game 3—September 30, at Brooklyn
New York..................0 2 0 0 0 0 1 0 0—3 7 0
Brooklyn ....2 2 0 2 0 0 2 0 x—8 11 1
Turley, Morgan (2), Kucks (5), Sturdivant (7); Podres. W—Podres. L—Turley. HR—Campanella (Brk.); Mantle (N.Y.).

Game 4—October 1, at Brooklyn
New York..................1 1 0 1 0 2 0 0 0—5 9 0
Brooklyn ....0 0 1 3 3 0 1 0 x—8 14 0
Larsen, Kucks (5), R. Coleman (6), Morgan (7), Sturdivant (8); Erskine, Bessent (4), Labine (5). W—Labine. L—Larsen. HR—McDougald (N.Y.); Campanella, Hodges, Snider (Brk).

Game 5—October 2, at Brooklyn
New York..................0 0 0 1 0 0 1 1 0—3 6 0
Brooklyn ....0 2 1 0 1 0 0 1 x—5 9 2
Grim, Turley (7); Craig, Labine (7). W—Craig. L—Grim. HR—Snider 2, Amoros (Brk.); Cerv, Berra (N.Y.).

Game 6—October 3, at New York
Brooklyn ....0 0 0 1 0 0 0 0 0—1 4 1
New York..................5 0 0 0 0 0 0 0 x—5 8 0
Spooner, Meyer (1), Roebuck (7); Ford. W—Ford. L—Spooner. HR—Skowron (N.Y.).

Game 7—October 4, at New York
Brooklyn ....0 0 0 1 0 1 0 0 0—2 5 0
New York..................0 0 0 0 0 0 0 0 0—0 8 1
Podres; Byrne, Grim (6), Turley (8). W—Podres. L—Byrne.

1956

FINAL STANDINGS

American League

Team	W	L	Pct.	GB
New York	97	57	.630	...
Cleveland	88	66	.571	9
Chicago	85	69	.552	12
Boston	84	70	.545	13
Detroit	82	72	.532	15
Baltimore	69	85	.448	28
Washington	59	95	.383	38
Kansas City	52	102	.338	45

National League

Team	W	L	Pct.	GB
Brooklyn	93	61	.604	...
Milwaukee	92	62	.597	1
Cincinnati	91	63	.591	2
St. Louis	76	78	.494	17
Philadelphia	71	83	.461	22
New York	67	87	.435	26
Pittsburgh	66	88	.429	27
Chicago	60	94	.390	33

SIGNIFICANT EVENTS

■ **April 19:** The Dodgers played the first of seven "home-away-from-home" games at Jersey City's Roosevelt Stadium and posted a 10-inning, 5-4 victory over the Phillies.
■ **September 30:** Yankee slugger Mickey Mantle finished his Triple Crown journey with a .353 average, 52 home runs and 130 RBIs.
■ **November 21:** N.L. MVP Don Newcombe, who finished 27-7 for the Dodgers, captured the inaugural Cy Young Award as baseball's top pitcher.

MEMORABLE MOMENTS

■ **May 28:** Pittsburgh first baseman Dale Long hit a home run in his record eighth consecutive game as the Pirates defeated Brooklyn, 3-2.
■ **September 11:** Cincinnati's Frank Robinson tied the rookie home run record when he hit No. 38 in an 11-5 victory over the Giants.
■ **September 30:** The Dodgers posted a final-day 8-6 victory over Pittsburgh and captured their second straight N.L. pennant by one game over Milwaukee.

LEADERS

American League
BA: Mickey Mantle, N.Y., .353.
Runs: Mickey Mantle, N.Y., 132.
Hits: Harvey Kuenn, Det., 196.
TB: Mickey Mantle, N.Y., 376.
HR: Mickey Mantle, N.Y., 52.
RBI: Mickey Mantle, N.Y., 130.
SB: Luis Aparicio, Chi., 21.
Wins: Frank Lary, Det., 21.
ERA: Whitey Ford, N.Y., 2.47.
CG: Bob Lemon, Cle.; Billy Pierce, Chi., 21.
IP: Frank Lary, Det., 294.
SO: Herb Score, Cle., 263.

National League
BA: Hank Aaron, Mil., .328.
Runs: Frank Robinson, Cin., 122.
Hits: Hank Aaron, Mil., 200.
TB: Hank Aaron, Mil., 340.
HR: Duke Snider, Brk., 43.
RBI: Stan Musial, St.L., 109.
SB: Willie Mays, N.Y., 40.
Wins: Don Newcombe, Brk., 27.
ERA: Lew Burdette, Mil., 2.70.
CG: Robin Roberts, Phil., 22.
IP: Bob Friend, Pit., 314.1
SO: Sam Jones, Chi., 176.

A.L. 20-game winners
Frank Lary, Det., 21-13
Herb Score, Cle., 20-9
Early Wynn, Cle., 20-9
Billy Pierce, Chi., 20-9
Bob Lemon, Cle., 20-14
Billy Hoeft, Det., 20-14

N.L. 20-game winners
Don Newcombe, Brk., 27-7
Warren Spahn, Mil., 20-11
Johnny Antonelli, N.Y., 20-13

A.L. 100 RBIs
Mickey Mantle, N.Y., 130
Al Kaline, Det., 128
Vic Wertz, Cle., 106
Yogi Berra, N.Y., 105
Harry Simpson, K.C., 105
Larry Doby, Chi., 102

N.L. 100 RBIs
Stan Musial, St.L., 109
Joe Adcock, Mil., 103
Ted Kluszewski, Cin., 102
Duke Snider, Brk., 101

A.L. 40 homers
Mickey Mantle, N.Y., 52

N.L. 40 homers
Duke Snider, Brk., 43

Most Valuable Player
A.L.: Mickey Mantle, OF, N.Y.
N.L.: Don Newcombe, P, Brk.

Cy Young Award
A.L.-N.L.: Don Newcombe, Brk.

Rookie of the Year
A.L.: Luis Aparicio, SS, Chi.
N.L.: Frank Robinson, OF, Cin.

Hall of Fame additions
Joe Cronin, SS/Man./Exec.
Hank Greenberg, 1B, 1930-47

ALL-STAR GAME

■ **Winner:** Third baseman Ken Boyer singled three times and made three outstanding defensive plays to lead the N.L. to victory — its sixth in seven years.

■ **Key inning:** The fourth, when the N.L. stretched its 1-0 lead on a two-run pinch-hit homer by Willie Mays.

■ **Memorable moment:** Stan Musial's fifth All-Star home run, a seventh-inning shot that offset sixth-inning blasts by A.L. stars Ted Williams and Mickey Mantle.

■ **Top guns:** Bob Friend (Pirates), Boyer (Cardinals), Mays (Giants), Ted Kluszewski (Reds), Musial (Cardinals), N.L.; Williams (Red Sox), Mantle (Yankees), Yogi Berra (Yankees), A.L.

■ **MVP:** Boyer.

Linescore

July 10, at Washington's Griffith Stadium
N.L. ....0 0 1 2 1 1 2 0 0—7 11 0
A.L. ....0 0 0 0 0 3 0 0 0—3 11 0
Friend (Pirates), Spahn (Braves) 4, Antonelli (Giants) 6; Pierce (White Sox), Ford (Yankees) 4, Wilson (White Sox) 5, Brewer (Red Sox) 6, Score (Indians) 8, Wynn (Indians) 9. W—Friend. L—Pierce. HR—Mays, Musial, N.L.; Williams, Mantle, A.L.

WORLD SERIES

■ **Winner:** The Yankees turned the tables on the Dodgers in a Series featuring one of baseball's most incredible pitching performances.

■ **Turning point:** 5-3 and 6-2 Yankee victories in Games 3 and 4 after the Dodgers had won the first two games.

■ **Memorable moment:** The final pitch of Yankee righthander Don Larsen's Game 5 perfect game — the first no-hitter in Series history. Larsen struck out pinch-hitter Dale Mitchell to complete his 2-0 shutout.

■ **Top guns:** Larsen (1-0, 0.00 ERA), Yogi Berra (.360, 3 HR, 10 RBIs), Enos Slaughter (.350), Yankees; Gil Hodges (.304, 8 RBIs), Dodgers.

■ **MVP:** Larsen.

Linescores

Game 1—October 3, at Brooklyn
New York....................2 0 0 1 0 0 0 0 0—3 9 1
Brooklyn ....0 2 3 1 0 0 0 0 x—6 9 0
Ford, Kucks (4), Morgan (6), Turley (8); Maglie. W—Maglie. L—Ford. HR—Mantle, Martin (N.Y.); Robinson, Hodges (Brk.).

Game 2—October 5, at Brooklyn
New York................1 5 0 1 0 0 0 0 1— 8 12 2
Brooklyn ....0 6 1 2 2 0 0 2 x—13 12 0
Larsen, Kucks (2), Byrne (2), Sturdivant (3), Morgan (3), Turley (5), McDermott (6); Newcombe, Roebuck (2), Bessent (3). W—Bessent. L—Morgan. HR—Berra (N.Y.); Snider (Brk.).

Game 3—October 6, at New York
Brooklyn ....0 1 0 0 0 1 1 0 0—3 8 1
New York....................0 1 0 0 0 3 0 1 x—5 8 1
Craig, Labine (7); Ford. W—Ford. L—Craig. HR—Martin, Slaughter (N.Y.).

Game 4—October 7, at New York
Brooklyn ....0 0 0 1 0 0 0 0 1—2 6 0
New York....................1 0 0 2 0 1 2 0 x—6 7 2
Erskine, Roebuck (5), Drysdale (7); Sturdivant. W—Sturdivant. L—Erskine. HR—Mantle, Bauer (N.Y.).

Game 5—October 8, at New York
Brooklyn ....0 0 0 0 0 0 0 0 0—0 0 0
New York....................0 0 0 1 0 1 0 0 x—2 5 0
Maglie; Larsen. W—Larsen. L—Maglie. HR—Mantle (N.Y.).

Game 6—October 9, at Brooklyn
New York.............0 0 0 0 0 0 0 0 0 0—0 7 0
Brooklyn ....0 0 0 0 0 0 0 0 0 1—1 4 0
Turley; Labine. W—Labine. L—Turley.

Game 7—October 10, at Brooklyn
New York..................2 0 2 1 0 0 4 0 0—9 10 0
Brooklyn ....0 0 0 0 0 0 0 0 0—0 3 1
Kucks; Newcombe, Bessent (4), Craig (7), Roebuck (7), Erskine (9). W—Kucks. L—Newcombe. HR—Berra 2, Howard, Skowron (N.Y.).

HISTORY

1957

FINAL STANDINGS

American League

Team	W	L	Pct.	GB
New York	98	56	.636	...
Chicago	90	64	.584	8
Boston	82	72	.532	16
Detroit	78	76	.506	20
Baltimore	76	76	.500	21
Cleveland	76	77	.497	21.5
Kansas City	59	94	.386	38.5
Washington	55	99	.357	43

National League

Team	W	L	Pct.	GB
Milwaukee	95	59	.617	...
St. Louis	87	67	.565	8
Brooklyn	84	70	.545	11
Cincinnati	80	74	.519	15
Philadelphia	77	77	.500	18
New York	69	85	.448	26
Chicago	62	92	.403	33
Pittsburgh	62	92	.403	33

SIGNIFICANT EVENTS

■ **February 2:** Baseball owners approved a five-year pension plan offering more liberal benefits to players, coaches and trainers.
■ **April 22:** The Phillies became the final N.L. team to break the color barrier when John Kennedy was inserted as a pinch-runner in a 5-1 loss to Brooklyn.
■ **May 28:** N.L. owners approved the proposed moves of the Dodgers and Giants to the West Coast, opening the door for relocations that would become official in the fall.
■ **June 28:** Commissioner Ford Frick infuriated ballot-stuffing Cincinnati fans when he replaced three members of an all-Reds starting lineup for the All-Star Game.

MEMORABLE MOMENTS

■ **May 7:** Young Cleveland ace Herb Score suffered a career-threatening injury when he was hit in the eye by Yankee Gil McDougald's line drive.
■ **September 23:** Hank Aaron belted a two-run, 11th-inning homer to give the Braves a 4-2 victory over St. Louis and their first pennant since moving to Milwaukee.

LEADERS

American League
BA: Ted Williams, Bos., .388.
Runs: Mickey Mantle, N.Y., 121.
Hits: Nellie Fox, Chi., 196.
TB: Roy Sievers, Wash., 331.
HR: Roy Sievers, Wash., 42.
RBI: Roy Sievers, Wash., 114.
SB: Luis Aparicio, Chi., 28.
Wins: Jim Bunning, Det.; Billy Pierce, Chi., 20.
ERA: Bobby Shantz, N.Y., 2.45.
CG: Dick Donovan, Chi.; Billy Pierce, Chi., 16.
IP: Jim Bunning, Det., 267.1.
SO: Early Wynn, Cle., 184.

National League
BA: Stan Musial, St.L., .351.
Runs: Hank Aaron, Mil., 118.
Hits: Red Schoendienst, N.Y.-Mil., 200.
TB: Hank Aaron, Mil., 369.
HR: Hank Aaron, Mil., 44.
RBI: Hank Aaron, Mil., 132.
SB: Willie Mays, N.Y., 38.
Wins: Warren Spahn, Mil., 21.
ERA: Johnny Podres, Brk., 2.66.
CG: Warren Spahn, Mil., 18.
IP: Bob Friend, Pit., 277.
SO: Jack Sanford, Phil., 188.

A.L. 20-game winners
Jim Bunning, Det., 20-8
Billy Pierce, Chi., 20-12

N.L. 20-game winners
Warren Spahn, Mil., 21-11

A.L. 100 RBIs
Roy Sievers, Wash., 114
Vic Wertz, Cle., 105
Jackie Jensen, Bos., 103
Frank Malzone, Bos., 103
Minnie Minoso, Chi., 103

N.L. 100 RBIs
Hank Aaron, Mil., 132
Del Ennis, St.L., 105
Ernie Banks, Chi., 102
Stan Musial, St.L., 102

A.L. 40 homers
Roy Sievers, Wash., 42

N.L. 40 homers
Hank Aaron, Mil., 44
Ernie Banks, Chi., 43
Duke Snider, Brk., 40

Most Valuable Player
A.L.: Mickey Mantle, OF, N.Y.
N.L.: Hank Aaron, OF, Mil.

Cy Young Award
A.L.-N.L.: Warren Spahn, Mil.

Rookie of the Year
A.L.: Tony Kubek, IF/OF, N.Y.
N.L.: Jack Sanford, P, Phil.

Hall of Fame additions
Sam Crawford, OF, 1899-1917
Joe McCarthy, manager

ALL-STAR GAME

■ **Winner:** Minnie Minoso, who had doubled home a run in the top of the ninth, made two outstanding defensive plays in the bottom of the inning to preserve the A.L.'s victory.

■ **Key inning:** The ninth. After the A.L. had scored three times in the top of the frame for a 6-2 lead, the N.L. answered with three runs and had the tying run on second when the game ended.

■ **Memorable moment:** Left fielder Minoso, who had just thrown out a runner trying to advance to third, made an outstanding game-ending catch of a Gil Hodges drive into left-center field.

■ **Top guns:** Jim Bunning (Tigers), Al Kaline (Tigers), Bill Skowron (Yankees), Minoso (White Sox), A.L.; Lew Burdette (Braves), Willie Mays (Giants), Gus Bell (Reds), N.L.

■ **MVP:** Minoso.

Linescore

July 9, at St. Louis' Busch Stadium
A. L. .... 0 2 0 0 0 1 0 0 3—6 10 0
N.L. .... 0 0 0 0 0 0 2 0 3—5 9 1
Bunning (Tigers), Loes (Orioles) 4, Wynn (Indians) 7, Pierce (White Sox) 7, Mossi (Indians) 9, Grim (Yankees) 9; Simmons (Phillies), Burdette (Braves) 2, Sanford (Phillies) 6, Jackson (Cardinals) 7, Labine (Dodgers) 9. W—Bunning. L—Simmons.

WORLD SERIES

■ **Winner:** The Braves' fifth Milwaukee season produced the franchise's first Series winner since the miracle of 1914.

■ **Turning point:** A two-run 10th-inning home run by Eddie Mathews that gave Milwaukee a 7-5 victory in Game 4 and evened the Series at two games apiece.

■ **Memorable moment:** The final pitch of Milwaukee righthander Lew Burdette's 5-0 seventh-game shutout, giving Milwaukee its first Series championship.

■ **Top guns:** Burdette (3-0, 0-67 ERA), Hank Aaron (.393, 3 HR, 7 RBIs), Frank Torre (.300, 2 HR), Braves; Jerry Coleman (.364), Yankees.

■ **MVP:** Burdette.

Linescores

Game 1—October 2, at New York
Milwaukee .... 0 0 0 0 0 0 1 0 0—1 5 0
New York .... 0 0 0 0 1 2 0 0 x—3 9 1
Spahn, Johnson (6), McMahon (7); Ford. W—Ford. L—Spahn.

Game 2—October 3, at New York
Milwaukee .... 0 1 1 2 0 0 0 0 0—4 8 0
New York .... 0 1 1 0 0 0 0 0 0—2 7 2
Burdette; Shantz, Ditmar (4), Grim (8). W—Burdette. L—Shantz. HR—Logan (Mil.); Bauer (N.Y.).

Game 3—October 5, at Milwaukee
New York .... 3 0 2 2 0 0 5 0 0—12 9 0
Milwaukee .... 0 1 0 0 2 0 0 0 0—3 8 1
Turley, Larsen (2); Buhl, Pizarro (1), Conley (3), Johnson (5), Trowbridge (7), McMahon (8). W—Larsen. L—Buhl. HR—Kubek 2, Mantle (N.Y.); Aaron (Mil.).

Game 4—October 6, at Milwaukee
New York .... 1 0 0 0 0 0 0 0 3 1—5 11 0
Milwaukee .... 0 0 0 4 0 0 0 0 0 3—7 7 0
Sturdivant, Shantz (5), Kucks (8), Byrne (8), Grim (10); Spahn. W—Spahn. L—Grim. HR—Aaron, Torre, Mathews (Mil.); Howard (N.Y.).

Game 5—October 7, at Milwaukee
New York .... 0 0 0 0 0 0 0 0 0—0 7 0
Milwaukee .... 0 0 0 0 0 1 0 0 x—1 6 1
Ford, Turley (8); Burdette. W—Burdette. L—Ford.

Game 6—October 9, at New York
Milwaukee .... 0 0 0 0 1 0 1 0 0—2 4 0
New York .... 0 0 2 0 0 0 1 0 x—3 7 0
Buhl, Johnson (3), McMahon (8); Turley. W—Turley. L—Johnson. HR—Berra, Bauer (N.Y.); Torre, Aaron (Mil.).

Game 7—October 10, at New York
Milwaukee .... 0 0 4 0 0 0 0 1 0—5 9 1
New York .... 0 0 0 0 0 0 0 0 0—0 7 3
Burdette; Larsen, Shantz (3), Ditmar (4), Sturdivant (6), Byrne (8). W—Burdette. L—Larsen. HR—Crandall (Mil.).

1958

FINAL STANDINGS

American League

Team	W	L	Pct.	GB
New York	92	62	.597	...
Chicago	82	72	.532	10
Boston	79	75	.513	13
Cleveland	77	76	.503	14.5
Detroit	77	77	.500	15
Baltimore	74	79	.484	17.5
Kansas City	73	81	.474	19
Washington	61	93	.396	31

National League

Team	W	L	Pct.	GB
Milwaukee	92	62	.597	...
Pittsburgh	84	70	.545	8
San Francisco	80	74	.519	12
Cincinnati	76	78	.494	16
Chicago	72	82	.468	20
St. Louis	72	82	.468	20
Los Angeles	71	83	.461	21
Philadelphia	69	85	.448	23

SIGNIFICANT EVENTS

■ **January 28:** Dodgers catcher Roy Campanella suffered a broken neck and paralysis from his shoulders down when the car he was driving overturned on a slippery road in Glen Cove, N.Y.
■ **January 29:** Stan Musial became the N.L.'s first six-figure star when he signed with the Cardinals for $100,000.
■ **January 30:** Commissioner Ford Frick took the All-Star vote away from the fans, handing it back to the players, coaches and managers.
■ **September 28:** Boston's 40-year-old Ted Williams used a 7-for-11 closing surge to win his sixth A.L. batting title with a .328 average.
■ **December 3:** Will Harridge, who served as A.L. president for more than 27 years, retired at age 72.

MEMORABLE MOMENTS

■ **April 15:** The Giants rolled to an 8-0 victory over the Dodgers in the first West Coast game at San Francisco's Seals Stadium.
■ **April 18:** The Dodgers rewarded a record Los Angeles Coliseum crowd of 78,672 with a 6-5 victory over the Giants in their West Coast home debut.
■ **May 13:** Stan Musial became the eighth member of baseball's 3,000-hit club when he stroked a pinch-hit double off Moe Drabowsky in a 5-3 Cardinals' victory at Chicago.

LEADERS

American League
BA: Ted Williams, Bos., .328.
Runs: Mickey Mantle, N.Y., 127.
Hits: Nellie Fox, Chi., 187.
TB: Mickey Mantle, N.Y., 307.
HR: Mickey Mantle, N.Y., 42.
RBI: Jackie Jensen, Bos., 122.
SB: Luis Aparicio, Chi., 29.
Wins: Bob Turley, N.Y., 21.
ERA: Whitey Ford, N.Y., 2.01.
CG: Frank Lary, Det.; Billy Pierce, Chi.; Bob Turley, N.Y., 19.
IP: Frank Lary, Det., 260.1.
SO: Early Wynn, Chi., 179.

National League
BA: Richie Ashburn, Phil., .350.
Runs: Willie Mays, S.F., 121.
Hits: Richie Ashburn, Phil., 215.
TB: Ernie Banks, Chi., 379.
HR: Ernie Banks, Chi., 47.
RBI: Ernie Banks, Chi., 129.
SB: Willie Mays, S.F., 31.
Wins: Bob Friend, Pit.; Warren Spahn, Mil., 22.
ERA: Stu Miller, S.F., 2.47.
CG: Warren Spahn, Mil., 23.
IP: Warren Spahn, Mil., 290.
SO: Sam Jones, St.L., 225.

A.L. 20-game winners
Bob Turley, N.Y., 21-7

N.L. 20-game winners
Warren Spahn, Mil., 22-11
Bob Friend, Pit., 22-14
Lew Burdette, Mil., 20-10

A.L. 100 RBIs
Jackie Jensen, Bos., 122
Rocky Colavito, Cle., 113
Roy Sievers, Wash., 108
Bob Cerv, K.C., 104

N.L. 100 RBIs
Ernie Banks, Chi., 129
Frank Thomas, Pit., 109

A.L. 40 homers
Mickey Mantle, N.Y., 42
Rocky Colavito, Cle., 41

N.L. 40 homers
Ernie Banks, Chi., 47

Most Valuable Player
A.L.: Jackie Jensen, OF, Bos.
N.L.: Ernie Banks, SS, Chi.

Cy Young Award
A.L.-N.L.: Bob Turley, N.Y. (AL).

Rookie of the Year
A.L.: Albie Pearson, OF, Wash.
N.L.: Orlando Cepeda, 1B, S.F.

ALL-STAR GAME

■ **Winner:** After spotting the N.L. a 3-1 lead, the A.L. rallied for a 4-3 victory in the first All-Star Game without an extra-base hit. Ray Narleski, Early Wynn and Billy O'Dell allowed one hit over the final 7 1/3 innings.

■ **Key inning:** The sixth, when the A.L. scored the go-ahead run on a single by Gil McDougald.

■ **Memorable moment:** The last out of the game — the ninth consecutive batter retired by hometown favorite O'Dell.

■ **Top guns:** Narleski (Indians), Wynn (White Sox), O'Dell (Orioles), Nellie Fox (White Sox), McDougald (Yankees), A.L.; Willie Mays (Giants), N.L.

■ **MVP:** O'Dell.

Linescore

July 8, at Baltimore's Memorial Stadium
N.L. .... 2 1 0 0 0 0 0 0 0—3 4 2
A.L. .... 1 1 0 0 1 1 0 0 x—4 9 2
Spahn (Braves), Friend (Pirates) 4, Jackson (Cardinals) 6, Farrell (Phillies) 7; Turley (Yankees), Narleski (Indians) 2, Wynn (White Sox) 6, O'Dell (Orioles) 7. W—Wynn. L—Friend.

WORLD SERIES

■ **Winner:** The Yankees became only the second team to recover from a three-games to-one deficit en route to their seventh Series victory in 10 years under manager Casey Stengel.

■ **Turning point:** Bob Turley's five-hit 7-0 victory in Game 5 with his Yankees on the brink of elimination.

■ **Memorable moment:** A 10th-inning Game 6 home run by Gil McDougald that lifted the Yankees to a 4-3 victory and forced a seventh game.

■ **Top guns:** Turley (2-1, 2.76 ERA), Hank Bauer (.323, 4 HR, 8 RBIs), McDougald (.321, 2 HR, 4 RBIs), Yankees; Bill Bruton (.412), Braves.

■ **MVP:** Turley.

Linescores

Game 1—October 1, at Milwaukee
New York .... 0 0 0 1 2 0 0 0 0 0—3 8 1
Milwaukee .... 0 0 0 2 0 0 0 1 0 1—4 10 0
Ford, Duren (8); Spahn. W—Spahn. L—Duren. HR—Skowron, Bauer (N.Y.).

Game 2—October 2, at Milwaukee
New York .... 1 0 0 1 0 0 0 0 3—5 7 0
Milwaukee .... 7 1 0 0 0 0 2 3 x—13 15 1
Turley, Maas (1), Kucks (1), Dickson (5), Monroe (8); Burdette. W—Burdette. L—Turley. HR—Bruton, Burdette (Mil.); Mantle 2, Bauer (N.Y.).

Game 3—October 4, at New York
Milwaukee .... 0 0 0 0 0 0 0 0 0—0 6 0
New York .... 0 0 0 0 2 0 2 0 x—4 4 0
Rush, McMahon (7); Larsen, Duren (8). W—Larsen. L—Rush. HR—Bauer (N.Y.).

Game 4—October 5, at New York
Milwaukee .... 0 0 0 0 0 1 1 1 0—3 9 0
New York .... 0 0 0 0 0 0 0 0 0—0 2 1
Spahn; Ford, Kucks (8), Dickson (9). W—Spahn. L—Ford.

Game 5—October 6, at New York
Milwaukee .... 0 0 0 0 0 0 0 0 0—0 5 0
New York .... 0 0 1 0 0 6 0 0 x—7 10 0
Burdette, Pizarro (6), Willey (8); Turley. W—Turley. L—Burdette. HR—McDougald (N.Y.).

Game 6—October 8, at Milwaukee
New York .... 1 0 0 0 0 1 0 0 0 2—4 10 1
Milwaukee .... 1 1 0 0 0 0 0 0 0 1—3 10 4
Ford, Ditmar (2), Duren (6), Turley (10); Spahn, McMahon (10). W—Duren. L—Spahn. HR—Bauer, McDougald (N.Y.).

Game 7—October 9, at Milwaukee
New York .... 0 2 0 0 0 0 0 4 0—6 8 0
Milwaukee .... 1 0 0 0 0 0 0 0 0—2 5 2
Larsen, Turley (3); Burdette, McMahon (9). W—Turley. L—Burdette. HR—Crandall (Mil.); Skowron (N.Y.).

1959

FINAL STANDINGS

American League

Team	W	L	Pct.	GB
Chicago	94	60	.610	...
Cleveland	89	65	.578	5
New York	79	75	.513	15
Detroit	76	78	.494	18
Boston	75	79	.487	19
Baltimore	74	80	.481	20
Kansas City	66	88	.429	28
Washington	63	91	.409	31

National League

Team	W	L	Pct.	GB
*Los Angeles	88	68	.564	...
Milwaukee	86	70	.551	2
San Francisco	83	71	.539	4
Pittsburgh	78	76	.506	9
Chicago	74	80	.481	13
Cincinnati	74	80	.481	13
St. Louis	71	83	.461	16
Philadelphia	64	90	.416	23

*Defeated Milwaukee 2-0 in pennant playoff.

SIGNIFICANT EVENT

■ **July 21:** The Red Sox became the last Major League team to break the color barrier when infielder Pumpsie Green played briefly in a game at Chicago.

MEMORABLE MOMENTS

■ **May 26:** In an amazing pitching exhibition, Pittsburgh's Harvey Haddix worked 12 perfect innings before losing to the Braves, 1-0, in the 13th.

■ **June 10:** Cleveland's Rocky Colavito became the eighth member of an exclusive club when he belted four home runs during the Indians' 11-8 victory over Baltimore.

■ **September 11:** The Dodgers ended the two-year, 22-game winning streak of Pittsburgh reliever Elroy Face when they scored two ninth-inning runs for a 5-4 victory.

■ **September 29:** The Dodgers completed their two-game sweep of a pennant-playoff series against Milwaukee with a 12-inning, 6-5 victory at Los Angeles.

LEADERS

American League

BA: Harvey Kuenn, Det., .353.
Runs: Eddie Yost, Det., 115.
Hits: Harvey Kuenn, Det., 198.
TB: Rocky Colavito, Cle., 301.
HR: Rocky Colavito, Cle.; Harmon Killebrew, Wash., 42.
RBI: Jackie Jensen, Bos., 112.
SB: Luis Aparicio, Chi., 56.
Wins: Early Wynn, Chi., 22.
ERA: Hoyt Wilhelm, Bal., 2.19.
CG: Camilo Pascual, Wash., 17.
IP: Early Wynn, Chi., 255.2.
SO: Jim Bunning, Det., 201.

National League

BA: Hank Aaron, Mil., .355.
Runs: Vada Pinson, Cin., 131.
Hits: Hank Aaron, Mil., 223.
TB: Hank Aaron, Mil., 400.
HR: Eddie Mathews, Mil., 46.
RBI: Ernie Banks, Chi., 143.
SB: Willie Mays, S.F., 27.
Wins: Lew Burdette, Mil.; Sam Jones, S.F.; Warren Spahn, Mil., 21.
ERA: Sam Jones, S.F., 2.83.
CG: Warren Spahn, Mil., 21.
IP: Warren Spahn, Mil., 292.
SO: Don Drysdale, L.A., 242.

A.L. 20-game winners
Early Wynn, Chi., 22-10

N.L. 20-game winners
Lew Burdette, Mil., 21-15
Warren Spahn, Mil., 21-15
Sam Jones, S.F., 21-15

A.L. 100 RBIs
Jackie Jensen, Bos., 112
Rocky Colavito, Cle., 111
Harmon Killebrew, Wash., 105
Jim Lemon, Wash., 100

N.L. 100 RBIs
Ernie Banks, Chi., 143
Frank Robinson, Cin., 125
Hank Aaron, Mil., 123
Gus Bell, Cin., 115
Eddie Mathews, Mil., 114
Orlando Cepeda, S.F., 105
Willie Mays, S.F., 104

A.L. 40 homers
Rocky Colavito, Cle., 42
Harmon Killebrew, Wash., 42

N.L. 40 homers
Eddie Mathews, Mil., 46
Ernie Banks, Chi., 45

Most Valuable Player
A.L.: Nellie Fox, 2B, Chi.
N.L.: Ernie Banks, SS, Chi.

Cy Young Award
A.L.-N.L.: Early Wynn, Chi. (AL)

Rookie of the Year
A.L.: Bob Allison, OF, Wash.
N.L.: Willie McCovey, 1B, S.F.

Hall of Fame addition
Zack Wheat, OF, 1909-27

ALL-STAR GAMES

■ **Winner:** Home runs by Frank Malzone, Yogi Berra and Rocky Colavito helped the A.L. to a 5-3 victory and a split of the first All-Star doubleheader. The N.L. had won the first game four weeks earlier, 5-4.

■ **Key Innings:** The eighth in Game 1, when San Francisco's Willie Mays tripled home the winning run. The third in Game 2, when Berra pounded a two-run homer to give the A.L. a lead it never relinquished.

■ **Memorable moment:** The final out of Game 2. With hometown favorite Jim Gilliam at bat and the potential tying runs on second and third, Los Angeles fans roared. But Gilliam grounded out.

■ **Top guns:** Game 1: Don Drysdale (Dodgers), Eddie Mathews (Braves), Hank Aaron (Braves), N.L.; Al Kaline (Tigers), Gus Triandos (Orioles), A.L.; Game 2: Berra (Yankees), Malzone (Red Sox), Colavito (Indians), A.L.; Frank Robinson (Reds), Gilliam (Dodgers), N.L.

■ **MVPs:** Game 1: Drysdale. Game 2: Berra.

Linescores

Game 1, July 7, at Pittsburgh's Forbes Field
A.L. ....0 0 0 1 0 0 0 3 0—4 8 0
N.L. ....1 0 0 0 0 0 2 2 x—5 9 1
Wynn (White Sox), Duren (Yankees) 4, Bunning (Tigers) 7, Ford (Yankees) 8, Daley (Athletics) 8; Drysdale (Dodgers), Burdette (Braves) 4, Face (Pirates) 7, Antonelli (Giants) 8, Elston (Cubs) 9. W—Antonelli. L—Ford. HR—Mathews, N.L.; Kaline, A.L.

Game 2, August 3, at Los Angeles Coliseum
A.L. ....0 1 2 0 0 0 1 1 0—5 6 0
N.L. ....1 0 0 0 1 0 1 0 0—3 6 3
Walker (Orioles), Wynn (White Sox) 4, Wilhelm (Orioles) 6, O'Dell (Orioles) 7, McLish (Indians) 8; Drysdale (Dodgers), Conley (Phillies) 4, Jones (Giants) 6, Face (Pirates) 8. W—Walker. L—Drysdale. HR—Malzone, Berra, Colavito, A.L.; Robinson, Gilliam, N.L.

WORLD SERIES

■ **Winner:** The Dodgers, winners of a pennant playoff against Milwaukee, defeated the "Go-Go" White Sox for their first Series victory in Los Angeles.

■ **Turning point:** The Dodgers' 5-4 fourth-game victory, which was decided by Gil Hodges' home run.

■ **Memorable moment:** The first West Coast World Series contest — a 3-1 Dodger victory in Game 3.

■ **Top guns:** Larry Sherry (2-0, 0.71 ERA), Charlie Neal (.370, 2 HR, 6 RBIs), Chuck Essegian (2 PH HR), Dodgers; Ted Kluszewski (.391, 3 HR, 10 RBIs), Nellie Fox (.375), White Sox.

■ **MVP:** Sherry.

Linescores

Game 1—October 1, at Chicago
Los Angeles ....0 0 0 0 0 0 0 0 0— 0 8 3
Chicago ....2 0 7 2 0 0 0 0 x—11 11 0
Craig, Churn (3), Labine (4), Koufax (5), Klippstein (7); Wynn, Staley (8). W—Wynn. L—Craig. HR—Kluszewski 2 (Chi.).

Game 2—October 2, at Chicago
Los Angeles ....0 0 0 0 1 0 3 0 0—4 9 1
Chicago ....2 0 0 0 0 0 0 1 0—3 8 0
Podres, Sherry (7); Shaw, Lown (7). W—Podres. L—Shaw. HR—Neal 2, Essegian (L.A.).

Game 3—October 4, at Los Angeles.
Chicago ....0 0 0 0 0 0 0 1 0—1 12 0
Los Angeles ....0 0 0 0 0 0 2 1 x—3 5 0
Donovan, Staley (7); Drysdale, Sherry (8). W—Drysdale. L—Donovan.

Game 4—October 5, at Los Angeles
Chicago ....0 0 0 0 0 0 4 0 0—4 10 3
Los Angeles ....0 0 4 0 0 0 0 1 x—5 9 0
Wynn, Lown (3), Pierce (4), Staley (7); Craig, Sherry (8). W—Sherry. L—Staley. HR—Lollar (Chi.); Hodges (L.A.).

Game 5—October 6, at Los Angels
Chicago ....0 0 0 1 0 0 0 0 0—1 5 0
Los Angeles ....0 0 0 0 0 0 0 0 0—0 9 0
Shaw, Pierce (8), Donovan (8); Koufax, Williams (8). W—Shaw. L—Koufax.

Game 6—October 8, at Chicago
Los Angeles ....0 0 2 6 0 0 0 0 1—9 13 0
Chicago ....0 0 0 3 0 0 0 0 0—3 6 1
Podres, Sherry (4); Wynn, Donovan (4), Lown (4), Staley (5), Pierce (8), Moore (9). W—Sherry. L—Wynn. HR—Snider, Moon, Essegian (L.A.); Kluszewski (Chi.).

1960

FINAL STANDINGS

American League

Team	W	L	Pct.	GB
New York	97	57	.630	...
Baltimore	89	65	.578	8
Chicago	87	67	.565	10
Cleveland	76	78	.494	21
Washington	73	81	.474	24
Detroit	71	83	.461	26
Boston	65	89	.422	32
Kansas City	58	96	.377	39

National League

Team	W	L	Pct.	GB
Pittsburgh	95	59	.617	...
Milwaukee	88	66	.571	7
St. Louis	86	68	.558	9
Los Angeles	82	72	.532	13
San Francisco	79	75	.513	16
Cincinnati	67	87	.435	28
Chicago	60	94	.390	35
Philadelphia	59	95	.383	36

SIGNIFICANT EVENTS

■ **August 3:** In baseball's most bizarre trade, the Indians swapped manager Joe Gordon to Detroit for manager Jimmie Dykes.

■ **October 18:** Casey Stengel, who managed the Yankees to 10 pennants and seven World Series titles in 12 years, was fired.

■ **October 26:** The A.L. announced relocation of the Senators to Minneapolis-St. Paul and 1961 expansion to Los Angeles and Washington.

MEMORABLE MOMENTS

■ **June 17:** Ted Williams became the fourth member of the 500-homer fraternity when he connected off Cleveland's Wynn Hawkins in a 3-1 Boston victory.

■ **September 28:** Williams belted career homer No. 521 in Boston's 5-4 victory over Baltimore and promptly retired.

LEADERS

American League

BA: Pete Runnels, Bos., .320.
Runs: Mickey Mantle, N.Y., 119.
Hits: Minnie Minoso, Chi., 184.
TB: Mickey Mantle, N.Y., 294.
HR: Mickey Mantle, N.Y., 40.
RBI: Roger Maris, N.Y., 112.
SB: Luis Aparicio, Chi., 51.
Wins: Chuck Estrada, Bal.; Jim Perry, Cle., 18.
ERA: Frank Baumann, Chi., 2.67.
CG: Frank Lary, Det., 15.
IP: Frank Lary, Det., 274.1.
SO: Jim Bunning, Det., 201.

National League

BA: Dick Groat, Pit., .325.
Runs: Bill Bruton, Mil., 112.
Hits: Willie Mays, S.F., 190.
TB: Hank Aaron, Mil., 334.
HR: Ernie Banks, Chi., 41.
RBI: Hank Aaron, Mil., 126.
SB: Maury Wills, L.A., 50.
Wins: Ernie Broglio, St.L.; Warren Spahn, Mil., 21.
ERA: Mike McCormick, S.F., 2.70.
CG: Lew Burdette, Mil.; Vernon Law, Pit.; Warren Spahn, Mil., 18.
IP: Larry Jackson, St.L., 282.
SO: Don Drysdale, L.A., 246.

N.L. 20-game winners
Ernie Broglio, St.L., 21-9
Warren Spahn, Mil., 21-10
Vernon Law, Pit., 20-9

A.L. 100 RBIs
Roger Maris, N.Y., 112
Minnie Minoso, Chi., 105
Vic Wertz, Bos., 103
Jim Lemon, Wash., 100

N.L. 100 RBIs
Hank Aaron, Mil., 126
Eddie Mathews, Mil., 124
Ernie Banks, Chi., 117
Willie Mays, S.F., 103

A.L. 40 homers
Mickey Mantle, N.Y., 40

N.L. 40 homers
Ernie Banks, Chi., 41
Hank Aaron, Mil., 40

Most Valuable Player
A.L.: Roger Maris, OF, N.Y.
N.L.: Dick Groat, SS, Pit.

Cy Young Award
A.L.-N.L.: Vernon Law, Pit.

Rookie of the Year
A.L.: Ron Hansen, SS, Bal.
N.L.: Frank Howard, OF, L.A.

ALL-STAR GAMES

■ **Winner:** In a three-day All-Star doubleheader, the N.L. pulled off a 5-3 and 6-0 sweep and narrowed its once-embarrassing overall deficit to 16-13.

■ **Key Innings:** The first in Game 1, when a Willie Mays triple and an Ernie Banks homer sparked the N.L. to a 3-0 lead; the second in Game 2, when Eddie Mathews opened the N.L. scoring with a two-run homer.

■ **Memorable moment:** A third-inning Game 2 home run by Mays, who was 6 for 8 in the two games. The homer gave Mays a perfect 6-for-6 All-Star ledger against Yankee great Ford.

■ **Top guns:** Game 1: Bob Friend (Pirates), Mays (Giants), Banks (Cubs), N.L.; Al Kaline (Tigers), A.L.; Game 2: Vernon Law (Pirates), Mays (Giants), Mathews (Braves), Ken Boyer (Cardinals), N.L.

■ **MVPs:** Games 1 and 2 : Mays.

Linescores

Game 1, July 11, at Kansas City's Municipal Stadium
N.L. ....3 1 1 0 0 0 0 0 0—5 12 4
A.L. ....0 0 0 0 0 1 0 2 0—3 6 1
Friend (Pirates), McCormick (Giants) 4, Face (Pirates) 6, Buhl (Braves) 8, Law (Pirates) 9; Monbouquette (Red Sox), Estrada (Orioles) 3, Coates (Yankees) 4, Bell (Indians) 6, Lary (Tigers) 8, Daley (Athletics) 9. W—Friend. L—Monbouquette. HR—Banks, Crandall, N.L.; Kaline, A.L.

Game 2, July 13, at New York's Yankee Stadium
N.L. ....0 2 1 0 0 0 1 0 2—6 10 0
A.L. ....0 0 0 0 0 0 0 0 0—0 8 0
Law (Pirates), Podres (Dodgers) 3, S. Williams (Dodgers) 5, Jackson (Cardinals) 7, Henry (Reds) 8, McDaniel (Cardinals) 9; Ford (Yankees), Wynn (White Sox) 4, Staley (White Sox) 6, Lary (Tigers) 8, Bell (Indians) 9. W—Law. L—Ford. HR—Mathews, Mays, Musial, Boyer, N.L.

WORLD SERIES

■ **Winner:** Despite being outscored 55-27, the Pirates edged the Yankees in a seven-game Series that will be long remembered for its classic ending.

■ **Turning point:** The Pirates' 3-2 fourth-game victory after suffering successive 16-3 and 10-0 losses to the hard-hitting Yankees.

■ **Memorable moment:** Bill Mazeroski's Series-ending ninth-inning home run that broke a 9-9 tie after the Yankees had rallied for two runs in the top of the frame. One of the classic moments in Series history.

■ **Top guns:** Vernon Law (2-0), Mazeroski (.320, 2 HR, 5 RBIs), Pirates; Whitey Ford (2-0, 0.00 ERA), Mickey Mantle (.400, 3 HR, 11 RBIs), Bobby Richardson (.367, 12 RBIs), Yankees.

■ **MVP:** Richardson.

Linescores

Game 1—October 5, at Pittsburgh
New York ....1 0 0 1 0 0 0 0 2—4 13 2
Pittsburgh ....3 0 0 2 0 1 0 0 x—6 8 0
Ditmar, Coates (1), Maas (5), Duren (7); Law, Face (8). W—Law. L—Ditmar. HR—Maris, Howard (N.Y.); Mazeroski (Pit.).

Game 2—October 6, at Pittsburgh
New York ....0 0 2 1 2 7 3 0 1—16 19 1
Pittsburgh ....0 0 0 1 0 0 0 0 2— 3 13 1
Turley, Shantz (9); Friend, Green (5), Labine (6), Witt (6), Gibbon (7), Cheney (9). W—Turley. L—Friend. HR—Mantle 2 (N.Y.).

Game 3—October 8, at New York
Pittsburgh ....0 0 0 0 0 0 0 0 0— 0 4 0
New York ....6 0 0 4 0 0 0 0 x—10 16 1
Mizell, Labine (1), Green (1), Witt (4), Cheney (6), Gibbon (8); Ford. W—Ford. L—Mizell. HR—Richardson, Mantle (N.Y.).

Game 4—October 9, at New York
Pittsburgh ....0 0 0 0 3 0 0 0 0—3 7 0
New York ....0 0 0 1 0 0 1 0 0—2 8 0
Law, Face (7); Terry, Shantz (7), Coates (8). W—Law. L—Terry. HR—Skowron (N.Y.).

Game 5—October 10, at New York
Pittsburgh ....0 3 1 0 0 0 0 0 1—5 10 2
New York ....0 1 1 0 0 0 0 0 0—2 5 2
Haddix, Face (7); Ditmar, Arroyo (2), Stafford (3), Duren (8). W—Haddix. L—Ditmar. HR—Maris (N.Y.).

Game 6—October 12, at Pittsburgh
New York ....0 1 5 0 0 2 2 2 0—12 17 1
Pittsburgh ....0 0 0 0 0 0 0 0 0— 0 7 1
Ford; Friend, Cheney (3), Mizell (4), Green (6), Labine (6), Witt (9). W—Ford. L—Friend.

Game 7—October 13, at Pittsburgh
New York ....0 0 0 0 1 4 0 2 2— 9 13 1
Pittsburgh ....2 2 0 0 0 0 0 5 1—10 11 0
Turley, Stafford (2), Shantz (3), Coates (8), Terry (8); Law, Face (6), Friend (9), Haddix (9). W—Haddix. L—Terry. HR—Skowron, Berra (N.Y.); Nelson, Smith, Mazeroski (Pit.).

1961

FINAL STANDINGS

American League

Team	W	L	Pct.	GB
New York	109	53	.673	...
Detroit	101	61	.623	8
Baltimore	95	67	.586	14
Chicago	86	76	.531	23
Cleveland	78	83	.484	30.5
Boston	76	86	.469	33
Minnesota	70	90	.438	38
Los Angeles	70	91	.435	38.5
Kansas City	61	100	.379	47.5
Washington	61	100	.379	47.5

National League

Team	W	L	Pct.	GB
Cincinnati	93	61	.604	...
Los Angeles	89	65	.578	4
San Francisco	85	69	.552	8
Milwaukee	83	71	.539	10
St. Louis	80	74	.519	13
Pittsburgh	75	79	.487	18
Chicago	64	90	.416	29
Philadelphia	47	107	.305	46

SIGNIFICANT EVENTS

■ **April 6:** The Cubs designated Vedie Himsl as the first of nine coaches who would rotate as the team's manager during the season.

■ **July 17:** Commissioner Ford Frick ruled that nobody could be credited with breaking Babe Ruth's 60-homer record unless he did it in the first 154 games of a season.

■ **October 10:** The Mets and Colt .45s combined to pick 45 players in the N.L.'s first expansion draft.

MEMORABLE MOMENTS

■ **April 30:** Willie Mays became the ninth player to hit four homers in a game during the Giants' 14-4 victory at Milwaukee.

■ **August 11:** Warren Spahn pitched Milwaukee to a 2-1 victory over Chicago and claimed his 300th career victory.

■ **August 20:** The Phillies defeated Milwaukee, 7-4, and ended their modern-era record losing streak at 23.

■ **October 1:** Roger Maris drove a pitch from Boston's Tracy Stallard for his record-setting 61st home run, giving New York a 1-0 victory at Yankee Stadium.

LEADERS

American League

BA: Norm Cash, Det., .361.
Runs: Mickey Mantle, N.Y.; Roger Maris, N.Y., 132.
Hits: Norm Cash, Det., 193.
TB: Roger Maris, N.Y., 366.
HR: Roger Maris, N.Y., 61.
RBI: Roger Maris, N.Y., 142.
SB: Luis Aparicio, Chi., 53.
Wins: Whitey Ford, N.Y., 25.
ERA: Dick Donovan, Wash., 2.40.
CG: Frank Lary, Det., 22.
IP: Whitey Ford, N.Y., 283.
SO: Camilo Pascual, Min., 221.

National League

BA: Roberto Clemente, Pit., .351.
Runs: Willie Mays, S.F., 129.
Hits: Vada Pinson, Cin., 208.
TB: Hank Aaron, Mil., 358.
HR: Orlando Cepeda, S.F., 46.
RBI: Orlando Cepeda, S.F., 142.
SB: Maury Wills, L.A., 35.
Wins: Joey Jay, Cin.; Warren Spahn, Mil., 21.
ERA: Warren Spahn, Mil., 3.02.
CG: Warren Spahn, Mil., 21.
IP: Lew Burdette, Mil., 272.1.
SO: Sandy Koufax, L.A., 269.

A.L. 20-game winners
Whitey Ford, N.Y., 25-4
Frank Lary, Det., 23-9

N.L. 20-game winners
Joey Jay, Cin., 21-10
Warren Spahn, Mil., 21-13

A.L. 100 RBIs
Roger Maris, N.Y., 142
Jim Gentile, Bal., 141
Rocky Colavito, Det., 140
Norm Cash, Det., 132
Mickey Mantle, N.Y., 128
Harmon Killebrew, Min., 122
Bob Allison, Min., 105

N.L. 100 RBIs
Orlando Cepeda, S.F., 142
Frank Robinson, Cin., 124
Willie Mays, S.F., 123
Hank Aaron, Mil., 120
Dick Stuart, Pit., 117
Joe Adcock, Mil., 108

A.L. 40 homers
Roger Maris, N.Y., 61
Mickey Mantle, N.Y., 54
Jim Gentile, Bal., 46
Harmon Killebrew, Min., 46
Rocky Colavito, Det., 45
Norm Cash, Det., 41

N.L. 40 homers
Orlando Cepeda, S.F., 46
Willie Mays, S.F., 40

Most Valuable Player
A.L.: Roger Maris, OF, N.Y.
N.L.: Frank Robinson, OF, Cin.

Cy Young Award
A.L.-N.L.: Whitey Ford, N.Y. (AL)

Rookie of the Year
A.L.: Don Schwall, P, Bos.
N.L.: Billy Williams, OF, Chi.

Hall of Fame additions
Max Carey, OF, 1910-29
Billy Hamilton, OF, 1888-1901

ALL-STAR GAMES

■ **Winner:** The N.L. captured a wind-blown 5-4 victory in the All-Star opener at Candlestick Park and played to a 1-1 tie in a second game that was halted by a Boston rainstorm after nine innings.

■ **Key inning:** The 10th in Game 1, when the A.L. took a 4-3 lead and the N.L. answered with two runs. The winner was driven home by a Roberto Clemente single.

■ **Memorable moment:** The ninth inning of Game 1 when the A.L's two-run, game-tying rally received a big assist from a gust of wind that blew Giants reliever Stu Miller off the mound in mid delivery for a balk.

■ **Top guns:** Game 1: Warren Spahn (Braves), Willie Mays (Giants), Clemente (Pirates), N.L.; Harmon Killebrew (Twins), A.L.; Game 2: Jim Bunning (Tigers), Camilo Pascual (Twins), Rocky Colavito (Tigers), A.L.; Miller (Giants), Bill White (Cardinals), N.L.

■ **MVPs:** Game 1: Clemente; Game 2: Bunning.

Linescores

Game 1, July 11, at San Francisco's Candlestick Park
A.L. ....0 0 0 0 0 1 0 0 2 1—4 4 2
N.L. ....0 1 0 1 0 0 0 1 0 2—5 11 5
Ford (Yankees), Lary (Tigers) 4, Donovan (Senators) 4, Bunning (Tigers) 6, Fornieles (Red Sox) 8, Wilhelm (Orioles) 8; Spahn (Braves), Purkey (Reds) 4, McCormick (Giants) 6, Face (Pirates) 9, Koufax (Dodgers) 9, Miller (Giants) 9. W—Miller. L—Wilhelm. HR—Killebrew, A.L.; Altman, N.L.

Game 2, July 31, at Boston's Fenway Park
N.L. ....0 0 0 0 0 1 0 0 0—1 5 1
A.L. ....1 0 0 0 0 0 0 0 0—1 4 0
Purkey (Reds), Mahaffey (Phillies) 3, Koufax (Dodgers) 5, Miller (Giants) 7; Bunning (Tigers), Schwall (Red Sox) 4, Pascual (Twins) 7. HR—Colavito, A.L.

WORLD SERIES

■ **Winner:** The Yankee machine, powered by 61-homer man Roger Maris, earned its first Series championship since 1947 without Casey Stengel at the helm.

■ **Turning point:** A ninth-inning Maris home run that lifted the Yankees to a 3-2 victory in Game 3.

■ **Memorable moment:** Yankee lefthander Whitey Ford's five shutout innings in Game 4, which lifted his consecutive-inning scoreless streak to a Series-record 32.

■ **Top guns:** Ford (2-0, 0.00 ERA), John Blanchard (.400, 2 HR), Bill Skowron (.353, 5 RBIs), Hector Lopez (.333, 7 RBIs), Yankees; Wally Post (.333), Reds.

■ **MVP:** Ford.

Linescores

Game 1—October 4, at New York
Cincinnati ....0 0 0 0 0 0 0 0 0—0 2 0
New York.....................0 0 0 1 0 1 0 0 x—2 6 0
O'Toole, Brosnan (8); Ford. W—Ford. L—O'Toole. HR—Howard, Skowron (N.Y.).

Game 2—October 5, at New York
Cincinnati ....0 0 0 2 1 1 0 2 0—6 9 0
New York.....................0 0 0 2 0 0 0 0 0—2 4 3
Jay; Terry, Arroyo (8). W—Jay. L—Terry. HR—Coleman (Cin.); Berra (N.Y.).

Game 3—October 7, at Cincinnati
New York.....................0 0 0 0 0 0 1 1 1—3 6 1
Cincinnati ....0 0 1 0 0 0 1 0 0—2 8 0
Stafford, Daley (7), Arroyo (8); Purkey. W—Arroyo. L—Purkey. HR—Blanchard, Maris (N.Y.).

Game 4—October 8, at Cincinnati
New York...................0 0 0 1 1 2 3 0 0—7 11 0
Cincinnati ....0 0 0 0 0 0 0 0 0—0 5 1
Ford, Coates (6); O'Toole, Brosnan (6), Henry (9). W—Ford. L—O'Toole.

Game 5—October 9, at Cincinnati
New York................5 1 0 5 0 2 0 0 0—13 15 1
Cincinnati ....0 0 3 0 2 0 0 0 0— 5 11 3
Terry, Daley (3); Jay, Maloney (1), K. Johnson (2), Henry (3), Jones (4), Purkey (5), Brosnan (7), Hunt (9). W—Daley. L—Jay. HR—Blanchard, Lopez (N.Y.); Robinson, Post (Cin.).

1962

FINAL STANDINGS

American League

Team	W	L	Pct.	GB
New York	96	66	.593	...
Minnesota	91	71	.562	5
Los Angeles	86	76	.531	10
Detroit	85	76	.528	10.5
Chicago	85	77	.525	11
Cleveland	80	82	.494	16
Baltimore	77	85	.475	19
Boston	76	84	.475	19
Kansas City	72	90	.444	24
Washington	60	101	.373	35.5

National League

Team	W	L	Pct.	GB
*San Francisco	103	62	.624	...
Los Angeles	102	63	.618	1
Cincinnati	98	64	.605	3.5
Pittsburgh	93	68	.578	8
Milwaukee	86	76	.531	15.5
St. Louis	84	78	.519	17.5
Philadelphia	81	80	.503	20
Houston	64	96	.400	36.5
Chicago	59	103	.364	42.5
New York	40	120	.250	60.5

*Defeated Los Angeles 2-1 in pennant playoff.

SIGNIFICANT EVENTS

■ **April 9-10:** The Senators christened their $20-million D.C. Stadium with a 4-1 victory over Detroit, but Cincinnati beat Los Angeles 6-3 in the first game at Dodger Stadium.

■ **November 23:** Dodgers shortstop Maury Wills, who ran his way to a record 104 stolen bases, walked away with the N.L. MVP.

MEMORABLE MOMENTS

■ **September 12:** Washington's Tom Cheney set a single-game record when he struck out 21 batters in a 16-inning 2-1 victory over the Orioles.

■ **October 3:** The Giants captured the N.L. pennant with a 6-4 victory over the Dodgers in the third game of a three-game playoff.

LEADERS

American League

BA: Pete Runnels, Bos., .326.
Runs: Albie Pearson, L.A., 115.
Hits: Bobby Richardson, N.Y., 209.
TB: Rocky Colavito, Det., 309.
HR: Harmon Killebrew, Min., 48.
RBI: Harmon Killebrew, Min., 126.
SB: Luis Aparicio, Chi., 31.
Wins: Ralph Terry, N.Y., 23.
ERA: Hank Aguirre, Det., 2.21.
CG: Camilo Pascual, Min., 18.
IP: Ralph Terry, N.Y., 298.2.
SO: Camilo Pascual, Min., 206.

National League

BA: Tommy Davis, L.A., .346.
Runs: Frank Robinson, Cin., 134.
Hits: Tommy Davis, L.A., 230.
TB: Willie Mays, S.F., 382.
HR: Willie Mays, S.F., 49.
RBI: Tommy Davis, L.A., 153.
SB: Maury Wills, L.A., 104.
Wins: Don Drysdale, L.A., 25.
ERA: Sandy Koufax, L.A., 2.54.
CG: Warren Spahn, Mil., 22.
IP: Don Drysdale, L.A., 314.1.
SO: Don Drysdale, L.A., 232.

A.L. 20-game winners
Ralph Terry, N.Y., 23-12
Ray Herbert, Chi., 20-9
Dick Donovan, Cle., 20-10
Camilo Pascual, Min., 20-11

N.L. 20-game winners
Don Drysdale, L.A., 25-9
Jack Sanford, S.F., 24-7
Bob Purkey, Cin., 23-5
Joey Jay, Cin., 21-14

A.L. 100 RBIs
Harmon Killebrew, Min., 126
Norm Siebern, K.C., 117
Rocky Colavito, Det., 112
Floyd Robinson, Chi., 109
Leon Wagner, L.A., 107
Lee Thomas, L.A., 104
Bob Allison, Min., 102
Roger Maris, N.Y., 100

N.L. 100 RBIs
Tommy Davis, L.A., 153
Willie Mays, S.F., 141
Frank Robinson, Cin., 136
Hank Aaron, Mil., 128
Frank Howard, L.A., 119
Orlando Cepeda, S.F., 114
Don Demeter, Phil., 107
Ernie Banks, Chi., 104
Bill White, St.L., 102
Vada Pinson, Cin., 100

N.L. 40 homers
Willie Mays, S.F., 49
Hank Aaron, Mil., 45

A.L. 40 homers
Harmon Killebrew, Min., 48

Most Valuable Player
A.L.: Mickey Mantle, OF, N.Y.
N.L.: Maury Wills, SS, L.A.

Cy Young Award
A.L.-N.L.: Don Drysdale, L.A. (NL)

Rookie of the Year
A.L.: Tom Tresh, SS, N.Y.
N.L.: Ken Hubbs, 2B, Chi.

Hall of Fame additions
Bob Feller, P, 1936-56
Bill McKechnie, manager
Jackie Robinson, 2B, 1947-56
Edd Roush, OF, 1913-31

ALL-STAR GAMES

■ **Winner:** The N.L. narrowed its series deficit to 16-15 with a 3-1 victory in the All-Star opener, but the A.L. pulled out its heavy artillery in a 9-4 second-game rout.

■ **Key Innings:** The sixth in Game 1, when pinch-runner Maury Wills sparked a two-run rally with a stolen base; the seventh in Game 2, when Rocky Colavito belted a three-run homer.

■ **Memorable moment:** The final out of the second game. The A.L. would not win again in the 1960s.

■ **Top guns:** Game 1: Don Drysdale (Dodgers), Juan Marichal (Giants), Roberto Clemente (Pirates), Wills (Dodgers), N.L.; Game 2: Leon Wagner (Angels), Pete Runnels (Red Sox), Colavito (Tigers), A.L.

■ **MVPs:** Game 1: Wills; Game 2: Wagner.

Linescores

Game 1, July 10, at Washington's D.C. Stadium
N.L. ....0 0 0 0 0 2 0 1 0—3 8 0
A.L. ....0 0 0 0 0 1 0 0 0—1 4 0
Drysdale (Dodgers), Marichal (Giants) 4, Purkey (Reds) 6, Shaw (Braves) 8; Bunning (Tigers), Pascual (Twins) 4, Donovan (Indians) 7, Pappas (Orioles) 9. W—Marichal. L—Pascual.

Game 2, July 30, at Chicago's Wrigley Field
A.L. ....0 0 1 2 0 1 3 0 2—9 10 0
N.L. ....0 1 0 0 0 0 1 1 1—4 10 4
Stenhouse (Senators), Herbert (White Sox) 3, Aguirre (Tigers) 6, Pappas (Orioles) 9; Podres (Dodgers), Mahaffey (Phillies) 3, Gibson (Cardinals) 5, Farrell (Colts) 7, Marichal (Giants) 8. W—Herbert. L—Mahaffey. HR—Runnels, Wagner, Colavito, A.L.; Roseboro, N.L.

WORLD SERIES

■ **Winner:** The Yankees prevailed over the Giants, who were making their first Series appearance since moving from New York to San Francisco.

■ **Turning point:** A three-run eighth-inning homer by rookie Tom Tresh that lifted Ralph Terry and the Yankees to a 5-3 Game 5 victory.

■ **Memorable moment:** Yankee second baseman Bobby Richardson snagging Willie McCovey's vicious seventh-game line drive with runners on second and third base, preserving Terry's 1-0 shutout and ending the Series. A slight variation in the path of McCovey's shot would have given the Giants a championship.

■ **Top guns:** Terry (2-1, 1.80 ERA), Tresh (.321, 4 RBIs), Yankees; Jose Pagan (.368), Giants.

■ **MVP:** Terry.

Linescores

Game 1—October 4, at San Francisco
New York..................2 0 0 0 0 0 1 2 1—6 11 0
San Francisco ....0 1 1 0 0 0 0 0 0—2 10 0
Ford; O'Dell, Larsen (8), Miller (9). W—Ford. L—O'Dell. HR—Boyer (N.Y.).

Game 2—October 5, at San Francisco
New York....................0 0 0 0 0 0 0 0 0—0 3 1
San Francisco ....1 0 0 0 0 0 1 0 x—2 6 0
Terry, Daley (8); Sanford. W—Sanford. L—Terry. HR—McCovey (S.F.).

Game 3—October 7, at New York
San Francisco ....0 0 0 0 0 0 0 0 2—2 4 3
New York....................0 0 0 0 0 0 3 0 x—3 5 1
Pierce, Larsen (7), Bolin (8); Stafford. W—Stafford. L—Pierce. HR—Bailey (S.F.).

Game 4—October 8, at New York
San Francisco ....0 2 0 0 0 0 4 0 1—7 9 1
New York....................0 0 0 0 0 2 0 0 1—3 9 1
Marichal, Bolin (5), Larsen (6), O'Dell (7); Ford, Coates (7), Bridges (7). W—Larsen. L—Coates. HR—Haller, Hiller (S.F.).

Game 5—October 10, at New York
San Francisco ....0 0 1 0 1 0 0 0 1—3 8 2
New York....................0 0 0 1 0 1 0 3 x—5 6 0
Sanford, Miller (8); Terry. W—Terry. L—Sanford. HR—Pagan (S.F.); Tresh (N.Y.).

Game 6—October 15, at San Francisco
New York..................0 0 0 0 1 0 0 1 0—2 3 2
San Francisco ....0 0 0 3 2 0 0 0 x—5 10 1
Ford, Coates (5), Bridges (8); Pierce. W—Pierce. L—Ford. HR—Maris (N.Y.).

Game 7—October 16, at San Francisco
New York....................0 0 0 0 1 0 0 0 0—1 7 0
San Francisco ....0 0 0 0 0 0 0 0 0—0 4 1
Terry; Sanford, O'Dell (8). W—Terry. L—Sanford.

1963

FINAL STANDINGS

American League

Team	W	L	Pct.	GB
New York	104	57	.646	...
Chicago	94	68	.580	10.5
Minnesota	91	70	.565	13
Baltimore	86	76	.531	18.5
Cleveland	79	83	.488	25.5
Detroit	79	83	.488	25.5
Boston	76	85	.472	28
Kansas City	73	89	.451	31.5
Los Angeles	70	91	.435	34
Washington	56	106	.346	48.5

National League

Team	W	L	Pct.	GB
Los Angeles	99	63	.611	...
St. Louis	93	69	.574	6
San Francisco	88	74	.543	11
Philadelphia	87	75	.537	12
Cincinnati	86	76	.531	13
Milwaukee	84	78	.519	15
Chicago	82	80	.506	17
Pittsburgh	74	88	.457	25
Houston	66	96	.407	33
New York	51	111	.315	48

SIGNIFICANT EVENTS

■ **January 26:** Baseball's Rules Committee expanded the strike zone—from the top of the shoulders to the bottom of the knees.

■ **September 29:** Cardinals great Stan Musial retired with N.L. records for hits (3,630) and RBIs (1,951).

■ **November 7:** Yankee catcher Elston Howard became the first black MVP in A.L. history.

MEMORABLE MOMENTS

■ **July 13:** Cleveland's Early Wynn struggled through five rocky innings but still won his 300th career game, a 7-4 victory over Kansas City.

■ **August 21:** Pittsburgh's Jerry Lynch hit his record-setting 15th career pinch-hit homer in a 7-6 victory at Chicago.

■ **September 8:** 42-year-old Braves lefty Warren Spahn tied the N.L. record when he stopped Philadelphia 3-2, becoming a 20-game winner for the 13th time.

LEADERS

American League

BA: Carl Yastrzemski, Bos., .321.
Runs: Bob Allison, Min., 99.
Hits: Carl Yastrzemski, Bos., 183.
TB: Dick Stuart, Bos., 319.
HR: Harmon Killebrew, Min., 45.
RBI: Dick Stuart, Bos., 118.
SB: Luis Aparicio, Bal., 40.
Wins: Whitey Ford, N.Y., 24.
ERA: Gary Peters, Chi., 2.33.
CG: Camilo Pascual, Min.; Ralph Terry, N.Y., 18.
IP: Whitey Ford, N.Y., 269.1.
SO: Camilo Pascual, Min., 202.

National League

BA: Tommy Davis, L.A., .326.
Runs: Hank Aaron, Mil., 121.
Hits: Vada Pinson, Cin., 204.
TB: Hank Aaron, Mil., 370.
HR: Hank Aaron, Mil.; Willie McCovey, S.F., 44.
RBI: Hank Aaron, Mil., 130.
SB: Maury Wills, L.A., 40.
Wins: Sandy Koufax, L.A.; Juan Marichal, S.F., 25.
ERA: Sandy Koufax, L.A., 1.88.
CG: Warren Spahn, Mil., 22.
IP: Juan Marichal, S.F., 321.1.
SO: Sandy Koufax, L.A., 306.

A.L. 20-game winners

Whitey Ford, N.Y., 24-7
Jim Bouton, N.Y., 21-7
Camilo Pascual, Min., 21-9
Bill Monbouquette, Bos., 20-10
Steve Barber, Bal., 20-13

N.L. 20-game winners

Sandy Koufax, L.A., 25-5
Juan Marichal, S.F., 25-8
Jim Maloney, Cin., 23-7
Warren Spahn, Mil., 23-7
Dick Ellsworth, Chi., 22-10

A.L. 100 RBIs

Dick Stuart, Bos., 118
Al Kaline, Det., 101

N.L. 100 RBIs

Hank Aaron, Mil., 130
Ken Boyer, St.L., 111
Bill White, St.L., 109
Vada Pinson, Cin., 106
Willie Mays, S.F., 103
Willie McCovey, S.F., 102

A.L. 40 homers

Harmon Killebrew, Min., 45
Dick Stuart, Bos., 42

N.L. 40 homers

Hank Aaron, Mil., 44
Willie McCovey, S.F., 44

Most Valuable Player

A.L.: Elston Howard, C, N.Y.
N.L.: Sandy Koufax, P, L.A.

Cy Young Award

A.L.-N.L.: Sandy Koufax, L.A. (NL)

Rookie of the Year

A.L.: Gary Peters, P, Chi.
N.L.: Pete Rose, 2B, Cin.

Hall of Fame additions

John Clarkson, P, 1882-94
Elmer Flick, OF, 1898-1910
Sam Rice, OF, 1915-35
Eppa Rixey, P, 1912-33

ALL-STAR GAME

■ **Winner:** The N.L. unleashed secret weapon Willie Mays on the A.L. again and claimed a 5-3 victory in a return to the single All-Star Game format.

■ **Key inning:** The third, when Mays singled home a run, stole his second base and scored on a single by Dick Groat. Mays scored two runs, drove in two and made an outstanding catch.

■ **Memorable moment:** Pinch-hitter Stan Musial lining out to right field in his 24th, and last, All-Star appearance. Musial batted .317 and hit a record six home runs.

■ **Top guns:** Mays (Giants), Ron Santo (Cubs), N.L.; Albie Pearson (Angels), Leon Wagner (Angels), A.L.

■ **MVP:** Mays.

Linescore

July 9, at Cleveland Stadium
N.L. .... 0 1 2 0 1 0 0 1 0—5 6 0
A.L. .... 0 1 2 0 0 0 0 0 0—3 11 1
O'Toole (Reds), Jackson (Cubs) 3, Culp (Phillies) 5, Woodeshick (Colts) 6, Drysdale (Dodgers) 8; McBride (Angels), Bunning (Tigers) 4, Bouton (Yankees) 6, Pizarro (White Sox) 7, Radatz (Red Sox) 8. W—Jackson. L—Bunning.

WORLD SERIES

■ **Winner:** The Dodgers cut down their old nemesis in an impressive pitching-dominated sweep.

■ **Turning point:** The first two innings of Game 1. Dodgers lefthander Sandy Koufax set the tone for the Series when he struck out the first five Yankees he faced en route to a record-setting 15-strikeout performance.

■ **Memorable moment:** The first World Series game at new Dodger Stadium — a three-hit 1-0 victory for Los Angeles righthander Don Drysdale in Game 3.

■ **Top guns:** Koufax (2-0, 1.50 ERA), Tommy Davis (.400), Bill Skowron (.385), Dodgers; Elston Howard (.333), Yankees.

■ **MVP:** Koufax.

Linescores

Game 1—October 2, at New York
Los Angeles .... 0 4 1 0 0 0 0 0 0—5 9 0
New York.................... 0 0 0 0 0 0 0 2 0—2 6 0
Koufax; Ford, Williams (6), Hamilton (9). W—Koufax. L—Ford. HR—Roseboro (L.A.); Tresh (N.Y.).

Game 2—October 3, at New York
Los Angeles .... 2 0 0 1 0 0 0 1 0—4 10 1
New York.................. 0 0 0 0 0 0 0 0 1—1 7 0
Podres, Perranoski (9); Downing, Terry (6), Reniff (9). W—Podres. L—Downing. HR—Skowron (L.A.).

Game 3—October 5, at Los Angeles
New York.................. 0 0 0 0 0 0 0 0 0—0 3 0
Los Angeles .... 1 0 0 0 0 0 0 0 x—1 4 1
Bouton, Reniff (8); Drysdale. W—Drysdale. L—Bouton.

Game 4—October 6, at Los Angeles
New York.................. 0 0 0 0 0 0 1 0 0—1 6 1
Los Angeles................ 0 0 0 0 1 0 1 0 x—2 2 1
Ford, Reniff (8); Koufax. W—Koufax. L—Ford. HR—F. Howard (L.A.); Mantle (N.Y.).

1964

FINAL STANDINGS

American League

Team	W	L	Pct.	GB
New York	99	63	.611	...
Chicago	98	64	.605	1
Baltimore	97	65	.599	2
Detroit	85	77	.525	14
Los Angeles	82	80	.506	17
Cleveland	79	83	.488	20
Minnesota	79	83	.488	20
Boston	72	90	.444	27
Washington	62	100	.383	37
Kansas City	57	105	.352	42

National League

Team	W	L	Pct.	GB
St. Louis	93	69	.574	...
Cincinnati	92	70	.568	1
Philadelphia	92	70	.568	1
San Francisco	90	72	.556	3
Milwaukee	88	74	.543	5
Los Angeles	80	82	.494	13
Pittsburgh	80	82	.494	13
Chicago	76	86	.469	17
Houston	66	96	.407	27
New York	53	109	.327	40

SIGNIFICANT EVENTS

■ **February 13:** Ken Hubbs, the Cubs' 22-year-old second baseman, died when the single-engine plane he was flying crashed near Provo, Utah.

■ **April 17:** The Mets opened $25-million Shea Stadium with a 4-3 loss to the Pirates.

■ **November 7:** The Braves received N.L. permission to move their sagging franchise from Milwaukee to Atlanta after the 1965 season.

MEMORABLE MOMENTS

■ **April 23:** Houston's Ken Johnson became the first pitcher to lose a game in which he had thrown a complete-game no-hitter. Johnson dropped a 1-0 decision to the Reds.

■ **June 4:** Dodgers lefty Sandy Koufax joined Bob Feller as the only three-time no-hit pitchers of the 20th Century when he stopped the Phillies, 3-0.

■ **June 21:** Philadelphia's Jim Bunning fired baseball's first regular-season perfect game in 42 years, beating the Mets, 6-0.

LEADERS

American League

BA: Tony Oliva, Min., .323.
Runs: Tony Oliva, Min., 109.
Hits: Tony Oliva, Min., 217.
TB: Tony Oliva, Min., 374.
HR: Harmon Killebrew, Min., 49.
RBI: Brooks Robinson, Bal., 118.
SB: Luis Aparicio, Bal., 57.
Wins: Dean Chance, L.A.; Gary Peters, Chi., 20.
ERA: Dean Chance, L.A., 1.65.
CG: Dean Chance, L.A., 15.
IP: Dean Chance, L.A., 278.1.
SO: Al Downing, N.Y., 217.

National League

BA: Roberto Clemente, Pit., .339.
Runs: Dick Allen, Phil., 125.
Hits: Roberto Clemente, Pit.; Curt Flood, St.L., 211.
TB: Dick Allen, Phil., 352.
HR: Willie Mays, S.F., 47.
RBI: Ken Boyer, St.L., 119.
SB: Maury Wills, L.A., 53.
Wins: Larry Jackson, Chi., 24.
ERA: Sandy Koufax, L.A., 1.74.
CG: Juan Marichal, S.F., 22.
IP: Don Drysdale, L.A., 321.1.
SO: Bob Veale, Pit., 250.

A.L. 20-game winners

Dean Chance, L.A., 20-9
Gary Peters, Chi., 20-8

N.L. 20-game winners

Larry Jackson, Chi., 24-11
Juan Marichal, S.F., 21-8
Ray Sadecki, St.L., 20-11

A.L. 100 RBIs

Brooks Robinson, Bal., 118
Dick Stuart, Bos., 114
Harmon Killebrew, Min., 111
Mickey Mantle, N.Y., 111
Rocky Colavito, K.C., 102
Joe Pepitone, N.Y., 100
Leon Wagner, Cle., 100

N.L. 100 RBIs

Ken Boyer, St.L., 119
Ron Santo, Chi., 114
Willie Mays, S.F., 111
Joe Torre, Mil., 109
Johnny Callison, Phil., 104
Bill White, St.L., 102

A.L. 40 homers

Harmon Killebrew, Min., 49

N.L. 40 homers

Willie Mays, S.F., 47

Most Valuable Player

A.L.: Brooks Robinson, 3B, Bal.
N.L.: Ken Boyer, 3B, St.L.

Cy Young Award

A.L.-N.L.: Dean Chance, L.A. (AL)

Rookie of the Year

A.L.: Tony Oliva, OF, Min.
N.L.: Dick Allen, 3B, Phil.

Hall of Fame additions

Luke Appling, SS, 1930-50
Red Faber, P, 1914-33
Burleigh Grimes, P, 1916-34
Miller Huggins, manager
Tim Keefe, P, 1880-93
Heinie Manush, OF, 1923-39
Monte Ward, IF/P, 1878-94

ALL-STAR GAME

■ **Winner:** In a game that rekindled memories of 1941, the N.L. struck for four ninth-inning runs and escaped with a stunning 7-4 victory.

■ **Key inning:** The ninth, when Willie Mays walked, stole second moved to third on Orlando Cepeda's bloop single and scored the tying run on a wild throw. But the N.L. was far from finished.

■ **Memorable moment:** Johnny Callison's stunning three-run homer that finished off the A.L. in the ninth. The blast was hit off Boston relief ace Dick Radatz.

■ **Top guns:** Billy Williams (Cubs), Ken Boyer (Cardinals), Callison (Phillies), N.L.; Dean Chance (Angels), Harmon Killebrew (Twins), A.L.

■ **MVP:** Callison.

Linescore

July 7, at New York's Shea Stadium
A.L. .... 1 0 0 0 0 2 1 0 0—4 9 1
N.L. .... 0 0 0 2 1 0 0 0 4—7 8 0
Chance (Angels), Wyatt (Athletics) 4, Pascual (Twins) 5, Radatz (Red Sox) 7; Drysdale (Dodgers), Bunning (Phillies) 4, Short (Phillies) 6, Farrell (Colts) 7, Marichal (Giants) 9. W—Marichal. L—Radatz. HR—Williams, Boyer, Callison, N.L.

WORLD SERIES

■ **Winner:** The Cardinals brought down the curtain on the Yankee dynasty with a seven-game triumph.

■ **Turning point:** Trailing two games to one and 3-0 in the sixth inning of Game 4, the Cardinals rallied to a 4-3 victory when Ken Boyer connected for a grand slam.

■ **Memorable moment:** A dramatic Game 3-ending homer by Mickey Mantle on the first ninth-inning pitch by St. Louis reliever Barney Schultz.

■ **Top guns:** Bob Gibson (2-1, 3.00 ERA), Tim McCarver (.478, 5 RBIs), Boyer (2 HR, 6 RBIs), Lou Brock (.300, 5 RBIs), Cardinals; Bobby Richardson (13 hits, .406), Mantle (.333, 3 HR, 8 RBIs), Yankees.

■ **MVP:** Gibson.

Linescores

Game 1—October 7, at St. Louis
New York.................. 0 3 0 0 1 0 0 1 0—5 12 2
St. Louis .... 1 1 0 0 0 4 0 3 x—9 12 0
Ford, Downing (6), Sheldon (8), Mikkelsen (8); Sadecki, Schultz (7). W—Sadecki. L—Ford. HR—Tresh (N.Y.); Shannon (St.L.).

Game 2—October 8, at St. Louis
New York.................. 0 0 0 1 0 1 2 0 4—8 12 0
St. Louis .... 0 0 1 0 0 0 0 1 1—3 7 0
Stottlemyre; Gibson, Schultz (9); G. Richardson (9); Craig (9). W—Stottlemyre. L—Gibson. HR—Linz (N.Y.).

Game 3—October 10, at New York
St. Louis .... 0 0 0 0 1 0 0 0 0—1 6 0
New York.................. 0 1 0 0 0 0 0 0 1—2 5 2
Simmons, Schultz (9); Bouton. W—Bouton. L—Schultz. HR—Mantle (N.Y.).

Game 4—October 11, at New York
St. Louis .... 0 0 0 0 0 4 0 0 0—4 6 1
New York.................. 3 0 0 0 0 0 0 0 0—3 6 1
Sadecki, Craig (1), Taylor (6); Downing, Mikkelsen (7), Terry (8). W—Craig. L—Downing. HR—K. Boyer (St.L.).

Game 5—October 12, at New York
St. Louis .... 0 0 0 0 2 0 0 0 3—5 10 1
New York.................. 0 0 0 0 0 0 0 0 2—2 6 2
Gibson; Stottlemyre, Reniff (8), Mikkelsen (8). W—Gibson. L—Mikkelsen. HR—Tresh (N.Y.); McCarver (St.L.).

Game 6—October 14, at St. Louis
New York.................. 0 0 0 0 1 2 0 5 0—8 10 0
St. Louis .... 1 0 0 0 0 0 0 1 1—3 10 1
Bouton, Hamilton (9); Simmons, Taylor (7), Schultz (8), G. Richardson (8), Humphreys (9). W—Bouton. L—Simmons. HR—Maris, Mantle, Pepitone (N.Y.).

Game 7—October 15, at St. Louis
New York.................. 0 0 0 0 0 3 0 0 2—5 9 2
St. Louis .... 0 0 0 3 3 0 1 0 x—7 10 1
Stottlemyre, Downing (5), Sheldon (5), Hamilton (7), Mikkelsen (8); Gibson. W—Gibson. L—Stottlemyre. HR—Brock, K. Boyer (St.L.); Mantle, C. Boyer, Linz (N.Y.).

1965

FINAL STANDINGS

American League

Team	W	L	Pct.	GB
Minnesota	102	60	.630	...
Chicago	95	67	.586	7
Baltimore	94	68	.580	8
Detroit	89	73	.549	13
Cleveland	87	75	.537	15
New York	77	85	.475	25
California	75	87	.463	27
Washington	70	92	.432	32
Boston	62	100	.383	40
Kansas City	59	103	.364	43

National League

Team	W	L	Pct.	GB
Los Angeles	97	65	.599	...
San Francisco	95	67	.586	2
Pittsburgh	90	72	.556	7
Cincinnati	89	73	.549	8
Milwaukee	86	76	.531	11
Philadelphia	85	76	.528	11.5
St. Louis	80	81	.497	16.5
Chicago	72	90	.444	25
Houston	65	97	.401	32
New York	50	112	.309	47

SIGNIFICANT EVENTS

■ **April 9:** The Houston Astrodome, baseball's first domed stadium, was unveiled for an exhibition game between the Astros and Yankees.

■ **August 22:** Giants pitcher Juan Marichal touched off a wild 14-minute brawl when he attacked Dodgers catcher John Roseboro with a bat.

■ **August 29:** Citing poor health, Casey Stengel stepped down as Mets manager and ended his 56-year baseball career.

■ **September 2:** The Los Angeles Angels, preparing to move to Anaheim, changed their name to the California Angels.

MEMORABLE MOMENTS

■ **August 19:** Cincinnati's Jim Maloney, who had no-hit the Mets two months earlier only to lose in the 11th, fired another 10-inning no-hitter and beat the Cubs, 1-0.

■ **September 13:** San Francisco's Willie Mays, en route to his second 50-homer season, became the fifth member of the 500 club when he connected off Houston's Don Nottebart in a game at the Astrodome.

■ **September 29:** Dodgers ace Sandy Koufax reached perfection when he retired all 27 Cubs he faced in a 1-0 victory—his record fourth career no-hitter.

LEADERS

American League

BA: Tony Oliva, Min., .321.
Runs: Zoilo Versalles, Min., 126.
Hits: Tony Oliva, Min., 185.
TB: Zoilo Versalles, Min., 308.
HR: Tony Conigliaro, Bos., 32.
RBI: Rocky Colavito, Cle., 108.
SB: Campy Campaneris, K.C., 51.
Wins: Jim (Mudcat) Grant, Min., 21.
ERA: Sam McDowell, Cle., 2.18.
CG: Mel Stottlemyre, N.Y., 18.
IP: Mel Stottlemyre, N.Y., 291.
SO: Sam McDowell, Cle., 325.

National League

BA: Roberto Clemente, Pit., .329.
Runs: Tommy Harper, Cin., 126.
Hits: Pete Rose, Cin., 209.
TB: Willie Mays, S.F., 360.
HR: Willie Mays, S.F., 52.
RBI: Deron Johnson, Cin., 130.
SB: Maury Wills, L.A., 94.
Wins: Sandy Koufax, L.A., 26.
ERA: Sandy Koufax, L.A., 2.04.
CG: Sandy Koufax, L.A., 27.
IP: Sandy Koufax, L.A., 335.2.
SO: Sandy Koufax, L.A., 382.

A.L. 20-game winners
Jim (Mudcat) Grant, Min., 21-7
Mel Stottlemyre, N.Y., 20-9

N.L. 20-game winners
Sandy Koufax, L.A., 26-8
Tony Cloninger, Mil., 24-11
Don Drysdale, L.A., 23-12
Sammy Ellis, Cin., 22-10
Juan Marichal, S.F., 22-13
Jim Maloney, Cin., 20-9
Bob Gibson, St.L., 20-12

A.L. 100 RBIs
Rocky Colavito, Cle., 108
Willie Horton, Det., 104

N.L. 100 RBIs
Deron Johnson, Cin., 130
Frank Robinson, Cin., 113
Willie Mays, S.F., 112
Billy Williams, Chi., 108
Willie Stargell, Pit., 107
Ernie Banks, Chi., 106
Johnny Callison, Phil., 101
Ron Santo, Chi., 101

N.L. 40 homers
Willie Mays, S.F., 52

Most Valuable Player
A.L.: Zoilo Versalles, SS, Min.
N.L.: Willie Mays, OF, S.F.

Cy Young Award
A.L.-N.L.: Sandy Koufax, L.A. (NL)

Rookie of the Year
A.L.: Curt Blefary, OF, Bal.
N.L.: Jim Lefebvre, 2B, L.A.

Hall of Fame addition
Pud Galvin, P, 1879-92

ALL-STAR GAME

■ **Winner:** The N.L. took its first All-Star lead when Ron Santo drove home Willie Mays with a seventh-inning infield single that produced the winning run.

■ **Key Innings:** An N.L. first that featured home runs by Mays and Joe Torre and an A.L. fifth that featured Dick McAuliffe and Harmon Killebrew homers.

■ **Memorable moment:** Bob Gibson striking out Killebrew and New York's Joe Pepitone in the ninth inning with the tying run on second base.

■ **Top guns:** Juan Marichal (Giants), Mays (Giants), Willie Stargell (Pirates), Joe Torre (Braves), N.L.; McAuliffe (Tigers), Killebrew (Twins), A.L.

■ **MVP:** Marichal.

Linescore

July 13, at Minnesota's Metropolitan Stadium
N.L. ....3 2 0 0 0 0 1 0 0—6 11 0
A.L. ....0 0 0 1 4 0 0 0 0—5 8 0
Marichal (Giants), Maloney (Reds) 4, Drysdale (Dodgers) 5, Koufax (Dodgers) 6, Farrell (Astros) 7, Gibson (Cardinals) 8; Pappas (Orioles), Grant (Twins) 2, Richert (Senators) 4, McDowell (Indians) 6, Fisher (White Sox) 8. W—Koufax. L—McDowell. HR—Mays, Torre, Stargell, N.L.; McAuliffe, Killebrew, A.L.

WORLD SERIES

■ **Winner:** The pitching-rich Dodgers prevailed after dropping the first two games to the Twins — Minnesota's first World Series representative.

■ **Turning point:** A 4-0 shutout by Dodgers lefthander Claude Osteen in Game 3, after the Twins had beaten Don Drysdale and Sandy Koufax in Games 1 and 2.

■ **Memorable moment:** A three-hit seventh-game shutout by Koufax, who struck out 10 in his 2-0 victory.

■ **Top guns:** Koufax (2-1, 0.38 ERA), Ron Fairly (2 HR, 6 RBIs), Dodgers; Jim Grant (2-1, 2.74), Twins.

■ **MVP:** Koufax.

Linescores

Game 1—October 6, at Minnesota
Los Angeles ....0 1 0 0 0 0 0 0 1—2 10 1
Minnesota ....0 1 6 0 0 1 0 0 x—8 10 0
Drysdale, Reed (3), Brewer (5), Perranoski (7); Grant. W—Grant. L—Drysdale. HR—Fairly (L.A.); Mincher, Versalles (Min.).

Game 2—October 7, at Minnesota
Los Angeles ....0 0 0 0 0 0 1 0 0—1 7 3
Minnesota ....0 0 0 0 0 2 1 2 x—5 9 0
Koufax, Perranoski (7), Miller (8); Kaat. W—Kaat. L—Koufax.

Game 3—October 9, at Los Angeles
Minnesota ....0 0 0 0 0 0 0 0 0—0 5 0
Los Angeles.............0 0 0 2 1 1 0 0 x—4 10 1
Pascual, Merritt (6), Klippstein (8); Osteen. W—Osteen. L—Pascual.

Game 4—October 10, at Los Angeles
Minnesota ....0 0 0 1 0 1 0 0 0—2 5 2
Los Angeles.............1 1 0 1 0 3 0 1 x—7 10 0
Grant, Worthington (6), Pleis (8); Drysdale. W—Drysdale. L—Grant. HR—Killebrew, Oliva (Min.); Parker, Johnson (L.A.).

Game 5—October 11, at Los Angeles
Minnesota ....0 0 0 0 0 0 0 0 0—0 4 1
Los Angeles.............2 0 2 1 0 0 2 0 x—7 14 0
Kaat, Boswell (3), Perry (6); Koufax. W—Koufax. L—Kaat.

Game 6—October 13, at Minnesota
Los Angeles ....0 0 0 0 0 0 1 0 0—1 6 1
Minnesota ....0 0 0 2 0 3 0 0 x—5 6 1
Osteen, Reed (6), Miller (8); Grant. W—Grant. L—Osteen. HR—Fairly (L.A.); Allison, Grant (Min.).

Game 7—October 14, at Minnesota
Los Angeles ....0 0 0 2 0 0 0 0 0—2 7 0
Minnesota ....0 0 0 0 0 0 0 0 0—0 3 1
Koufax; Kaat, Worthington (4), Klippstein (6), Merritt (7), Perry (9). W—Koufax. L—Kaat. HR—Johnson (L.A.).

1966

FINAL STANDINGS

American League

Team	W	L	Pct.	GB
Baltimore	97	63	.606	...
Minnesota	89	73	.549	9
Detroit	88	74	.543	10
Chicago	83	79	.512	15
Cleveland	81	81	.500	17
California	80	82	.494	18
Kansas City	74	86	.463	23
Washington	71	88	.447	25.5
Boston	72	90	.444	26
New York	70	89	.440	26.5

National League

Team	W	L	Pct.	GB
Los Angeles	95	67	.586	...
San Francisco	93	68	.578	1.5
Pittsburgh	92	70	.568	3
Philadelphia	87	75	.537	8
Atlanta	85	77	.525	10
St. Louis	83	79	.512	12
Cincinnati	76	84	.475	18
Houston	72	90	.444	23
New York	66	95	.410	28.5
Chicago	59	103	.364	36

SIGNIFICANT EVENTS

■ **March 30:** The joint 32-day holdout of Dodger pitchers Sandy Koufax and Don Drysdale ended when they agreed to a combined package worth more than $210,000.

■ **April 11:** Another barrier fell when Emmett Ashford, baseball's first black umpire, worked the season opener at Washington.

■ **April 12:** The Braves dropped a 3-2 verdict to the Pirates in their debut at the new $18-million Atlanta Stadium.

■ **November 18:** Sandy Koufax, baseball's only three-time Cy Young Award winner, stunned the Dodgers when he announced his retirement at age 30 because of an arthritic elbow.

MEMORABLE MOMENTS

■ **June 9:** Rich Rollins, Zoilo Versalles, Tony Oliva, Don Mincher and Harmon Killebrew hit home runs in a seventh-inning explosion against Kansas City, matching a Major League record.

■ **August 17:** San Francisco's Willie Mays belted career homer No. 535 off St. Louis' Ray Washburn and moved into second place on the all-time list.

■ **September 22:** The Orioles clinched their first A.L. pennant with a 6-1 victory over Kansas City.

■ **October 2:** Sandy Koufax, working on two days rest, beat Philadelphia 6-3 for his 27th victory and clinched the Dodgers' third pennant in four years.

■ **November 8:** Baltimore's Frank Robinson, baseball's 13th Triple Crown winner, became the first player to win MVP honors in both leagues.

LEADERS

American League

BA: Frank Robinson, Bal., .316.
Runs: Frank Robinson, Bal., 122.
Hits: Tony Oliva, Min., 191.
TB: Frank Robinson, Bal., 367.
HR: Frank Robinson, Bal., 49.
RBI: Frank Robinson, Bal., 122.
SB: Campy Campaneris, K.C., 52.
Wins: Jim Kaat, Min., 25.
ERA: Gary Peters, Chi., 1.98.
CG: Jim Kaat, Min., 19.
IP: Jim Kaat, Min., 304.2.
SO: Sam McDowell, Cle., 225.

National League

BA: Matty Alou, Pit., .342.
Runs: Felipe Alou, Atl., 122.
Hits: Felipe Alou, Atl., 218.
TB: Felipe Alou, Atl., 355.
HR: Hank Aaron, Atl., 44.
RBI: Hank Aaron, Atl., 127.
SB: Lou Brock, St.L., 74.
Wins: Sandy Koufax, L.A., 27.
ERA: Sandy Koufax, L.A., 1.73.
CG: Sandy Koufax, L.A., 27.
IP: Sandy Koufax, L.A., 323.
SO: Sandy Koufax, L.A., 317.

A.L. 20-game winners
Jim Kaat, Min., 25-13
Denny McLain, Det., 20-14

N.L. 20-game winners
Sandy Koufax, L.A., 27-9
Juan Marichal, S.F., 25-6
Gaylord Perry, S.F., 21-8
Bob Gibson, St.L., 21-12
Chris Short, Phil., 20-10

A.L. 100 RBIs
Frank Robinson, Bal., 122
Harmon Killebrew, Min., 110
Boog Powell, Bal., 109
Willie Horton, Det., 100
Brooks Robinson, Bal., 100

N.L. 100 RBIs
Hank Aaron, Atl., 127
Roberto Clemente, Pit., 119
Dick Allen, Phil., 110
Willie Mays, S.F., 103
Bill White, Phil., 103
Willie Stargell, Pit., 102
Joe Torre, Atl., 101

A.L. 40 homers
Frank Robinson, Bal., 49

N.L. 40 homers
Hank Aaron, Atl., 44
Dick Allen, Phil., 40

Most Valuable Player
A.L.: Frank Robinson, OF, Bal.
N.L.: Roberto Clemente, OF, Pit.

Cy Young Award
A.L.-N.L.: Sandy Koufax, L.A. (NL)

Rookie of the Year
A.L.: Tommie Agee, OF, Chi.
N.L.: Tommy Helms, 3B, Cin.

Hall of Fame additions
Casey Stengel, manager
Ted Williams, OF, 1939-60

ALL-STAR GAME

■ **Winner:** The N.L. needed 10 innings to win its fourth consecutive All-Star Game in the blistering 105-degree heat of St. Louis.

■ **Key inning:** The 10th, when Maury Wills singled home Tim McCarver with the game-ending run.

■ **Memorable moment:** The almost-constant sight of fans being helped in the stands after passing out because of the heat.

■ **Top guns:** Gaylord Perry (Giants), Roberto Clemente (Pirates), Wills (Dodgers), N.L.; Denny McLain (Tigers), Brooks Robinson (Orioles), A.L.

■ **MVP:** Robinson.

Linescore

July 12, at St. Louis' Busch Stadium
A.L. ....0 1 0 0 0 0 0 0 0 0—1 6 0
N.L. ....0 0 0 1 0 0 0 0 0 1—2 6 0
McLain (Tigers), Kaat (Twins) 4, Stottlemyre (Yankees) 6, Siebert (Indians) 8, Richert (Senators) 10; Koufax (Dodgers), Bunning (Phillies) 4, Marichal (Giants) 6, Perry (Giants) 9. W—Perry. L—Richert.

WORLD SERIES

■ **Winner:** The Orioles, making only the second Series appearance in franchise history and first since moving from St. Louis to Baltimore, allowed only two Dodger runs — none after the third inning of Game 1.

■ **Turning point:** Game 1, when Moe Drabowsky relieved Baltimore lefty Dave McNally with the bases loaded in the third inning. Drabowsky worked 6⅔ innings of shutout relief and struck out 11 Dodgers in a 5-2 victory.

■ **Memorable moments:** Series-ending 1-0 victories by Wally Bunker (six-hitter) and McNally (four-hitter).

■ **Top guns:** Boog Powell (.357), Frank Robinson (2 HR, 3 RBIs), Orioles.

■ **MVP:** Frank Robinson.

Linescores

Game 1—October 5, at Los Angeles
Baltimore ....3 1 0 1 0 0 0 0 0—5 9 0
Los Angeles ....0 1 1 0 0 0 0 0 0—2 3 0
McNally, Drabowsky (3); Drysdale, Moeller (3), R. Miller (5), Perranoski (8). W—Drabowsky. L—Drysdale. HR—F. Robinson, B. Robinson (Bal.); Lefebvre (L.A.).

Game 2—October 6, at Los Angeles
Baltimore ....0 0 0 0 3 1 0 2 0—6 8 0
Los Angeles ....0 0 0 0 0 0 0 0 0—0 4 6
Palmer; Koufax, Perranoski (7), Regan (8), Brewer (9). W—Palmer. L—Koufax.

Game 3—October 8, at Baltimore
Los Angeles ....0 0 0 0 0 0 0 0 0—0 6 0
Baltimore...................0 0 0 0 1 0 0 0 x—1 3 0
Osteen, Regan (8); Bunker. W—Bunker. L—Osteen. HR—Blair (Bal.).

Game 4—October 9, at Baltimore
Los Angeles ....0 0 0 0 0 0 0 0 0—0 4 0
Baltimore...................0 0 0 1 0 0 0 0 x—1 4 0
Drysdale; McNally. W—McNally. L—Drysdale. HR—F. Robinson.

1967

FINAL STANDINGS

American League	W	L	Pct.	GB
Boston	92	70	.568	...
Detroit	91	71	.562	1
Minnesota	91	71	.562	1
Chicago	89	73	.549	3
California	84	77	.522	7.5
Baltimore	76	85	.472	15.5
Washington	76	85	.472	15.5
Cleveland	75	87	.463	17
New York	72	90	.444	20
Kansas City	62	99	.385	29.5

National League	W	L	Pct.	GB
St. Louis	101	60	.627	...
San Francisco	91	71	.562	10.5
Chicago	87	74	.540	14
Cincinnati	87	75	.537	14.5
Philadelphia	82	80	.506	19.5
Pittsburgh	81	81	.500	20.5
Atlanta	77	85	.475	24.5
Los Angeles	73	89	.451	28.5
Houston	69	93	.426	32.5
New York	61	101	.377	40.5

SIGNIFICANT EVENT

■ **October 18:** The A.L. approved the Athletics' move to Oakland and 1969 expansion to Kansas City and Seattle.

MEMORABLE MOMENTS

■ **April 14:** Boston lefthander Bill Rohr, making his Major League debut, lost a no-hit bid when Yankee Elston Howard singled with two out in the ninth inning of a 3-0 Red Sox victory.
■ **April 30:** Baltimore's Steve Barber and Stu Miller combined to pitch a no-hitter, but the Orioles lost, 2-1, when Detroit scored two ninth-inning runs.
■ **May 14, July 14:** New York's Mickey Mantle and Houston's Eddie Mathews became the sixth and seventh members of the 500-homer club exactly two months apart.

LEADERS

American League
BA: Carl Yastrzemski, Bos., .326.
Runs: Carl Yastrzemski, Bos., 112.
Hits: Carl Yastrzemski, Bos., 189.
TB: Carl Yastrzemski, Bos., 360.
HR: Harmon Killebrew, Min.; Carl Yastrzemski, Bos., 44.
RBI: Carl Yastrzemski, Bos., 121.
SB: Campy Campaneris, K.C., 55.
Wins: Jim Lonborg, Bos.; Earl Wilson, Det., 22.
ERA: Joel Horlen, Chi., 2.06.
CG: Dean Chance, Min., 18.
IP: Dean Chance, Min., 283.2.
SO: Jim Lonborg, Bos., 246.

National League
BA: Roberto Clemente, Pit., .357.
Runs: Hank Aaron, Atl.; Lou Brock, St.L., 113.
Hits: Roberto Clemente, Pit., 209.
TB: Hank Aaron, Atl., 344.
HR: Hank Aaron, Atl., 39.
RBI: Orlando Cepeda, St.L., 111.
SB: Lou Brock, St.L., 52.
Wins: Mike McCormick, S.F., 22.
ERA: Phil Niekro, Atl., 1.87.
CG: Ferguson Jenkins, Chi., 20.
IP: Jim Bunning, Phil., 302.1.
SO: Jim Bunning, Phil., 253.

A.L. 20-game winners
Jim Lonborg, Bos., 22-9
Earl Wilson, Det., 22-11
Dean Chance, Min., 20-14

N.L. 20-game winners
Mike McCormick, S.F., 22-10
Ferguson Jenkins, Chi., 20-13

A.L. 100 RBIs
Carl Yastrzemski, Bos., 121
Harmon Killebrew, Min., 113

N.L. 100 RBIs
Orlando Cepeda, St.L., 111
Roberto Clemente, Pit., 110
Hank Aaron, Atl., 109
Jim Wynn, Hou., 107
Tony Perez, Cin., 102

A.L. 40 homers
Harmon Killebrew, Min., 44
Carl Yastrzemski, Bos., 44

Most Valuable Player
A.L.: Carl Yastrzemski, OF, Bos.
N.L.: Orlando Cepeda, 1B, St.L.

Cy Young Award
A.L.: Jim Lonborg, Bos.
N.L.: Mike McCormick, S.F.

Rookie of the Year
A.L.: Rod Carew, 2B, Min.
N.L.: Tom Seaver, P, N.Y.

Hall of Fame additions
Branch Rickey, executive
Red Ruffing, P, 1924-47
Lloyd Waner, OF, 1927-45

ALL-STAR GAME

■ **Winner:** The N.L. continued its All-Star hex with a pulsating 15-inning 2-1 victory — the longest game in the classic's 35-year history.
■ **Key inning:** The 15th, when Cincinnati's Tony Perez deposited a Catfish Hunter pitch over the left-field fence, ending the N.L.'s 12-inning scoreless run.
■ **Memorable moment:** The overall performance of 12 pitchers, who gave up only 17 hits and two bases on balls while recording 30 strikeouts.
■ **Top guns:** Juan Marichal (Giants), Don Drysdale (Dodgers), Richie Allen (Phillies), Perez (Reds), N.L.; Gary Peters (White Sox), Hunter (Athletics), Carl Yastrzemski (Red Sox), Brooks Robinson (Orioles), A.L.
■ **MVP:** Perez.

Linescore
July 11, at California's Anaheim Stadium
N.L. ..0 1 0 000 000 000 001—2 9 0
A.L. ..0 0 0 001 000 000 000—1 8 0
Marichal (Giants), Jenkins (Cubs) 4, Gibson (Cardinals) 7, Short (Phillies) 9, Cuellar (Astros) 11, Drysdale (Dodgers) 13, Seaver (Mets) 15; Chance (Twins), McGlothlin (Angels) 4, Peters (White Sox) 6, Downing (Yankees) 9, Hunter (Athletics) 11. W—Drysdale. L—Hunter. HR—Allen, Perez, N.L.; Robinson, A.L.

WORLD SERIES

■ **Winner:** It took seven games for the Cardinals to ruin Boston's "impossible dream" of winning its first Series championship since 1918.
■ **Turning point:** The seventh-game heroics of Bob Gibson, who belted a home run and pitched the Cardinals to a 7-2 victory.
■ **Memorable moment:** A two-out eighth-inning double by St. Louis' Julian Javier in Game 2, ending Boston righthander Jim Lonborg's no-hit bid. Lonborg finished with a one-hit 5-0 victory.
■ **Top guns:** Gibson (3-0, 1.00 ERA), Lou Brock (.414), Roger Maris (.385, 7 RBIs), Cardinals; Lonborg (2-1), Carl Yastrzemski (.400, 3 HR, 5 RBIs), Red Sox.
■ **MVP:** Gibson.

Linescores

Game 1—October 4, at Boston
St. Louis ....0 0 1 0 0 0 1 0 0—2 10 0
Boston ....0 0 1 0 0 0 0 0 0—1 6 0
Gibson; Santiago, Wyatt (8). W—Gibson. L—Santiago. HR—Santiago (Bos.).

Game 2—October 5, at Boston
St. Louis ....0 0 0 0 0 0 0 0 0—0 1 1
Boston......................0 0 0 1 0 1 3 0 x—5 9 0
Hughes, Willis (6), Hoerner (7), Lamabe (7); Lonborg. W—Lonborg. L—Hughes. HR—Yastrzemski 2 (Bos.).

Game 3—Ocotber 7, at St. Louis
Boston ....0 0 0 0 0 1 1 0 0—2 7 1
St. Louis ....1 2 0 0 0 1 0 1 x—5 10 0
Bell, Waslewski (3), Stange (6), Osinski (8); Briles. W—Briles. L—Bell. HR—Shannon (St.L.); Smith (Bos.).

Game 4—October 8, at St. Louis
Boston ....0 0 0 0 0 0 0 0 0—0 5 0
St. Louis ....4 0 2 0 0 0 0 0 x—6 9 0
Santiago, Bell (1), Stephenson (3), Morehead (5), Brett (8); Gibson. W—Gibson. L—Santiago.

Game 5—October 9, at St. Louis
Boston ....0 0 1 0 0 0 0 0 2—3 6 1
St. Louis ....0 0 0 0 0 0 0 0 1—1 3 2
Lonborg; Carlton, Washburn (7), Willis (9), Lamabe (9). W—Lonborg. L—Carlton. HR—Maris.

Game 6—October 11, at Boston
St. Louis ....0 0 2 0 0 0 2 0 0— 4 8 0
Boston......................0 1 0 3 0 0 4 0 x—8 12 1
Hughes, Willis (4), Briles (5), Lamabe (7), Hoerner (7), Jaster (7), Washburn (7), Woodeshick (8); Waslewski, Wyatt (6), Bell (8). W—Wyatt. L—Lamabe. HR—Petrocelli 2, Yastrzemski, Smith (Bos.); Brock (St.L.).

Game 7—October 12, at Boston
St. Louis ....0 0 2 0 2 3 0 0 0—7 10 1
Boston ....0 0 0 0 1 0 0 1 0—2 3 1
Gibson; Lonborg, Santiago (7), Morehead (9), Osinski (9), Brett (9). W—Gibson. L—Lonborg. HR—Gibson, Javier (St.L.).

1968

FINAL STANDINGS

American League	W	L	Pct.	GB
Detroit	103	59	.636	...
Baltimore	91	71	.562	12
Cleveland	86	75	.534	16.5
Boston	86	76	.531	17
New York	83	79	.512	20
Oakland	82	80	.506	21
Minnesota	79	83	.488	24
California	67	95	.414	36
Chicago	67	95	.414	36
Washington	65	96	.404	37.5

National League	W	L	Pct.	GB
St. Louis	97	65	.599	...
San Francisco	88	74	.543	9
Chicago	84	78	.519	13
Cincinnati	83	79	.512	14
Atlanta	81	81	.500	16
Pittsburgh	80	82	.494	17
Los Angeles	76	86	.469	21
Philadelphia	76	86	.469	21
New York	73	89	.451	24
Houston	72	90	.444	25

SIGNIFICANT EVENTS

■ **May 27:** The N.L. crossed the Canadian border when it awarded 1969 expansion franchises to Montreal and San Diego.
■ **July 10:** A.L. and N.L. officials agreed to uniformity in their 1969 expansions: two-division formats, 162-game schedules and best-of-five League Championship Series.
■ **December 3:** The Rules Committee lowered the mound, shrunk the strike zone and cracked down on illegal pitches in an effort to increase offense.
■ **December 6:** Baseball owners forced William Eckert to resign as commissioner.

MEMORABLE MOMENTS

■ **May 8:** A's righthander Catfish Hunter fired baseball's ninth perfect game, retiring all 27 Twins he faced in a 4-0 victory at Oakland.
■ **July 30:** Washington shortstop Ron Hansen pulled off baseball's eighth unassisted triple play in the first inning of a 10-1 loss at Cleveland.
■ **September 14:** The Tigers rallied for two ninth-inning runs and defeated Oakland 5-4, allowing Denny McLain to become baseball's first 30-game winner since 1934.

LEADERS

American League
BA: Carl Yastrzemski, Bos., .301.
Runs: Dick McAuliffe, Det., 95.
Hits: Campy Campaneris, Oak., 177.
TB: Frank Howard, Wash., 330.
HR: Frank Howard, Wash., 44.
RBI: Ken Harrelson, Bos., 109.
SB: Campy Campaneris, Oak., 62.
Wins: Denny McLain, Det., 31.
ERA: Luis Tiant, Cle., 1.60.
CG: Denny McLain, Det., 28.
IP: Denny McLain, Det., 336.
SO: Sam McDowell, Cle., 283.

National League
BA: Pete Rose, Cin., .335.
Runs: Glenn Beckert, Chi., 98.
Hits: Felipe Alou, Atl.; Pete Rose, Cin., 210.
TB: Billy Williams, Chi., 321.
HR: Willie McCovey, S.F., 36.
RBI: Willie McCovey, S.F., 105.
SB: Lou Brock, St.L., 62.
Wins: Juan Marichal, S.F., 26.
ERA: Bob Gibson, St.L., 1.12.
CG: Juan Marichal, S.F., 30.
IP: Juan Marichal, S.F., 326.
SO: Bob Gibson, St.L., 268.

A.L. 20-game winners
Denny McLain, Det., 31-6
Dave McNally, Bal., 22-10
Luis Tiant, Cle., 21-9
Mel Stottlemyre, N.Y., 21-12

N.L. 20-game winners
Juan Marichal, S.F., 26-9
Bob Gibson, St.L., 22-9
Ferguson Jenkins, Chi., 20-15

A.L. 100 RBIs
Ken Harrelson, Bos., 109
Frank Howard, Wash., 106

N.L. 100 RBIs
Willie McCovey, S.F., 105

A.L. 40 homers
Frank Howard, Wash., 44

Most Valuable Player
A.L.: Denny McLain, P, Det.
N.L.: Bob Gibson, P, St.L.

Cy Young Award
A.L.: Denny McLain, Det.
N.L.: Bob Gibson, St.L.

Rookie of the Year
A.L.: Stan Bahnsen, P, N.Y.
N.L.: Johnny Bench, C, Cin.

Hall of Fame additions
Kiki Cuyler, OF, 1921-38
Goose Goslin, OF, 1921-38
Joe Medwick, OF, 1932-48

ALL-STAR GAME

■ **Winner:** The N.L. stretched its winning streak to six with the first 1-0 game in All-Star history. It also was the first played indoors and on an artificial surface.
■ **Key inning:** The first, when the N.L. scored the game's only run on a double-play grounder.
■ **Memorable moment:** The performance of a six-man N.L. staff that held the A.L. to three hits.
■ **Top guns:** Don Drysdale (Dodgers), Juan Marichal (Giants), Steve Carlton (Cardinals), Tom Seaver (Mets), Willie Mays (Giants), N.L.; Blue Moon Odom (Athletics), Denny McLain (Tigers), A.L.
■ **MVP:** Mays.

Linescore
July 9, at Houston's Astrodome
A.L. ....0 0 0 0 0 0 0 0 0—0 3 1
N.L. ....1 0 0 0 0 0 0 0 x—1 5 0
Tiant (Indians), Odom (Athletics) 3, McLain (Tigers) 5, McDowell (Indians) 7, Stottlemyre (Yankees) 8, John (White Sox) 8; Drysdale (Dodgers), Marichal (Giants) 4, Carlton (Cardinals) 6, Seaver (Mets) 7, Reed (Braves) 9, Koosman (Mets) 9. W—Drysdale. L—Tiant.

WORLD SERIES

■ **Winner:** The Tigers, down three games to one, rallied to win their first World Series since 1945.
■ **Turning point:** With the Tigers on the brink of elimination entering Game 5, lefthander Mickey Lolich pitched them to a 5-3 victory.
■ **Memorable moments:** Bob Gibson striking out 17 Tigers in Game 1. Cardinals center fielder Curt Flood misjudging Jim Northrup's seventh-game fly ball, which became a Series-deciding two-run triple.
■ **Top guns:** Lolich (3-0, 1.67 ERA), Norm Cash (.385, 5 RBIs); Al Kaline (.379, 2 HR, 8 RBIs), Tigers; Gibson (2-1, 1.67), Lou Brock (.464, 2 HR, 5 RBIs), Cardinals.
■ **MVP:** Lolich.

Linescores

Game 1—October 2, at St. Louis
Detroit........................0 0 0 0 0 0 0 0 0—0 5 3
St. Louis ....0 0 0 3 0 0 1 0 x—4 6 0
McLain, Dobson (6), McMahon (8); Gibson. W—Gibson. L—McLain. HR—Brock (St.L.).

Game 2—October 3, at St. Louis
Detroit......................0 1 1 0 0 3 1 0 2—8 13 1
St. Louis ....0 0 0 0 0 1 0 0 0—1 6 1
Lolich; Briles, Carlton (6), Willis (7), Hoerner (9). W—Lolich. L—Briles. HR—Horton, Lolich, Cash (Det.).

Game 3—October 5, at Detroit
St. Louis ....0 0 0 0 4 0 3 0 0—7 13 0
Detroit......................0 0 2 0 1 0 0 0 0—3 4 0
Washburn, Hoerner (6); Wilson, Dobson (5), McMahon (6), Patterson (7), Hiller (8). W—Washburn. L—Wilson. HR—Kaline, McAuliffe (Det.); McCarver, Cepeda (St.L.).

Game 4—October 6, at Detroit
St. Louis ....2 0 2 2 0 0 0 4 0—10 13 0
Detroit.....................0 0 0 1 0 0 0 0 0— 1 5 4
Gibson; McLain, Sparma (3), Patterson (4), Lasher (6), Hiller (8), Dobson (8). W—Gibson. L—McLain. HR—Brock, Gibson (St.L.); Northrup (Det.).

Game 5—October 7, at Detroit
St. Louis ....3 0 0 0 0 0 0 0 0—3 9 0
Detroit ....0 0 0 2 0 0 3 0 x—5 9 1
Briles, Hoerner (7), Willis (7); Lolich. W—Lolich. L—Hoerner. HR—Cepeda (St.L.).

Game 6—October 9, at St. Louis
Detroit..................0 2 10 0 1 0 0 0 0—13 12 1
St. Louis ....0 0 0 0 0 0 0 0 1— 1 9 1
McLain; Washburn, Jaster (3), Willis (3), Hughes (3), Carlton (4), Granger (7), Nelson (9). W—McLain. L—Washburn. HR—Northrup, Kaline (Det.).

Game 7—October 10, at St. Louis
Detroit.......................0 0 0 0 0 0 3 0 1—4 8 1
St. Louis ....0 0 0 0 0 0 0 0 1—1 5 0
Lolich; Gibson. W—Lolich. L—Gibson. HR—Shannon (St.L.).

FINAL STANDINGS

American League

East Division

Team	Bal.	Det.	Bos.	Wash.	N.Y.	Cle.	Min.	Oak.	Cal.	K.C.	Chi.	Sea.	W	L	Pct.	GB
Baltimore	...	11	10	13	11	13	8	8	6	11	9	9	109	53	.673	...
Detroit	7	...	8	7	10	11	6	7	7	8	9	10	90	72	.556	19
Boston	8	10	...	6	11	12	7	4	8	10	5	6	87	75	.537	22
Washington	5	11	12	...	8	15	6	4	7	5	8	5	86	76	.531	23
New York	7	8	7	10	...	8	2	6	9	7	9	7	80	81	.497	28.5
Cleveland	5	7	6	3	9	...	5	5	4	7	4	7	62	99	.385	46.5

West Division

Team	Min.	Oak.	Cal.	K.C.	Chi.	Sea.	Bal.	Det.	Bos.	Wash.	N.Y.	Cle.	W	L	Pct.	GB
Minnesota	...	13	11	10	13	12	4	6	5	6	10	7	97	65	.599	...
Oakland	5	...	12	10	10	13	4	5	8	8	6	7	88	74	.543	9
California	7	6	...	9	9	9	6	5	4	5	3	8	71	91	.438	26
Kansas City	8	8	9	...	10	10	1	4	2	7	5	5	69	93	.426	28
Chicago	5	8	9	8	...	10	3	3	7	4	3	8	68	94	.420	29
Seattle	6	5	9	8	8	...	3	2	6	7	5	5	64	98	.395	33

National League

East Division

Team	N.Y.	Chi.	Pit.	St.L.	Phi.	Mon.	Atl.	S.F.	Cin.	L.A.	Hou.	S.D.	W	L	Pct.	GB
New York	...	10	10	12	12	13	8	8	6	8	2	11	100	62	.617	...
Chicago	8	...	7	9	12	10	9	6	6	6	8	11	92	70	.568	8
Pittsburgh	8	11	...	9	8	13	4	5	7	4	9	10	88	74	.543	12
St. Louis	6	9	9	...	11	11	6	9	4	9	5	8	87	75	.537	13
Philadelphia	6	6	10	7	...	7	6	3	2	4	4	8	63	99	.389	37
Montreal	5	8	5	7	11	...	4	1	4	2	1	4	52	110	.321	48

West Division

Team	Atl.	S.F.	Cin.	L.A.	Hou.	S.D.	N.Y.	Chi.	Pit.	St.L	Phi.	Mon.	W	L	Pct.	GB
Atlanta	...	9	12	9	15	13	4	3	8	6	6	8	93	69	.574	...
San Fran.	9	...	8	13	8	12	4	6	7	3	9	11	90	72	.556	3
Cincinnati	6	10	...	10	9	11	6	6	5	8	10	8	89	73	.549	4
Los Angeles	9	5	8	...	12	12	4	6	8	3	8	10	85	77	.525	8
Houston	3	10	9	6	...	10	10	4	3	7	8	11	81	81	.500	12
San Diego	5	6	7	6	8	...	1	1	2	4	4	8	52	110	.321	41

SIGNIFICANT EVENTS

■ **February 4:** Bowie Kuhn, a little-known attorney, was handed a one-year term as a compromise choice to succeed William Eckert as commissioner.

■ **February 25:** Baseball owners avoided a strike by increasing player pension plan contributions and granting improvements in other important benefits.

■ **April 8:** The four expansion teams—Kansas City, Seattle, Montreal and San Diego—recorded Opening Day victories.

■ **April 14:** The first Major League game on foreign soil: Montreal defeated the Cardinals, 8-7, at Jarry Park.

■ **December 4:** Chub Feeney was named to succeed Warren Giles as N.L. president.

MEMORABLE MOMENTS

■ **April 30-May 1:** Cincinnati's Jim Maloney and Houston's Don Wilson fired back-to-back no-hitters at Crosley Field, matching the Gaylord Perry-Ray Washburn feat of 1968.

■ **September 15:** Cardinals lefty Steve Carlton struck out a record 19 batters, but the Mets won the game 4-3 on a pair of two-run homers by Ron Swoboda.

■ **September 22:** San Francisco's Willie Mays became the second batter to hit 600 home runs when he connected off Mike Corkins in a 4-2 victory over San Diego.

LEADERS

American League
BA: Rod Carew, Min., .332.
Runs: Reggie Jackson, Oak., 123.
Hits: Tony Oliva, Min., 197.
TB: Frank Howard, Wash., 340.
HR: Harmon Killebrew, Min., 49.
RBI: Harmon Killebrew, Min., 140.
SB: Tommy Harper, Sea., 73.
Wins: Denny McLain, Det., 24.
ERA: Dick Bosman, Wash., 2.19.
CG: Mel Stottlemyre, N.Y., 24.
IP: Denny McLain, Det., 325.
SO: Sam McDowell, Cle., 279.
SV: Ron Perranoski, Min., 31.

National League
BA: Pete Rose, Cin., .348.
Runs: Bobby Bonds, S.F.; Pete Rose, Cin., 120.
Hits: Matty Alou, Pit., 231.
TB: Hank Aaron, Atl., 332.
HR: Willie McCovey, S.F., 45.
RBI: Willie McCovey, S.F., 126.
SB: Lou Brock, St.L., 53.
Wins: Tom Seaver, N.Y., 25.
ERA: Juan Marichal, S.F., 2.10.
CG: Bob Gibson, St.L., 28.
IP: Gaylord Perry, S.F., 325.1.
SO: Ferguson Jenkins, Chi., 273.
SV: Fred Gladding, Hou., 29.

A.L. 20-game winners
Denny McLain, Det., 24-9
Mike Cuellar, Bal., 23-11
Jim Perry, Min., 20-6
Dave McNally, Bal., 20-7
Dave Boswell, Min., 20-12
Mel Stottlemyre, N.Y., 20-14

N.L. 20-game winners
Tom Seaver, N.Y., 25-7
Phil Niekro, Atl., 23-13
Juan Marichal, S.F., 21-11
Ferguson Jenkins, Chi., 21-15
Bill Singer, L.A., 20-12
Larry Dierker, Hou., 20-13
Bob Gibson, St.L., 20-13
Bill Hands, Chi., 20-14
Claude Osteen, L.A., 20-15

A.L. 100 RBIs
Harmon Killebrew, Min., 140
Boog Powell, Bal., 121
Reggie Jackson, Oak., 118
Sal Bando, Oak., 113
Frank Howard, Wash., 111
Carl Yastrzemski, Bos., 111
Tony Oliva, Min., 101
Frank Robinson, Bal., 100

N.L. 100 RBIs
Willie McCovey, S.F., 126
Ron Santo, Chi., 123
Tony Perez, Cin., 122
Lee May, Cin., 110
Ernie Banks, Chi., 106
Joe Torre, St.L., 101

A.L. 40 homers
Harmon Killebrew, Min., 49
Frank Howard, Wash., 48
Reggie Jackson, Oak., 47
Rico Petrocelli, Bos., 40
Carl Yastrzemski, Bos., 40

N.L. 40 homers
Willie McCovey, S.F., 45
Hank Aaron, Atl., 44

Most Valuable Player
A.L.: Harmon Killebrew, 3B, Min.
N.L.: Willie McCovey, 1B, S.F.

Cy Young Award
A.L.: Denny McLain, Det.
Mike Cuellar, Bal.
N.L.: Tom Seaver, N.Y.

Rookie of the Year
A.L.: Lou Piniella, OF, K.C.
N.L.: Ted Sizemore, 2B, L.A.

Hall of Fame additions
Roy Campanella, C, 1948-57
Stan Coveleski, P, 1912-28
Waite Hoyt, P, 1918-38
Stan Musial, OF/1B, 1941-63

ALL-STAR GAME

■ **Winner:** Willie McCovey belted a pair of home runs and Johnny Bench hit another as the N.L. stretched its winning streak to seven.

■ **Key inning:** A five-run N.L. third, fueled by the first of McCovey's two blasts. The explosion broke open a 3-1 contest.

■ **Memorable moment:** A sensational leaping catch by A.L. left fielder Carl Yastrzemski in the sixth inning, robbing Bench of another home run.

■ **Top guns:** McCovey (Giants), Bench (Reds), Cleon Jones (Mets), Felix Millan (Braves), N.L.; Frank Howard (Senators), Bill Freehan (Tigers), A.L.

■ **MVP:** McCovey.

Linescore
July 22, at Washington's RFK Stadium
N.L.............1 2 5 1 0 0 0 0 0—9 11 0
A.L.............0 1 1 1 0 0 0 0 0—3 6 2
Carlton (Cardinals), Gibson (Cardinals) 4, Singer (Dodgers) 5, Koosman (Mets) 7, Dierker (Astros) 8, Niekro (Braves) 9; Stottlemyre (Yankees), Odom (Athletics) 3, Knowles (Senators) 3, McLain (Tigers) 4, McNally (Orioles) 5, McDowell (Indians) 7, Culp (Red Sox) 9. W—Carlton. L—Stottlemyre. HR—McCovey 2, Bench, N.L.; Howard, Freehan, A.L.

ALCS

■ **Winner:** The Baltimore Orioles, hailed by many as the best A.L. team since the Yankee pennant-winning machines of yesteryear, swept past Minnesota in baseball's first season of League Championship Series play.

■ **Turning point:** Paul Blair's 12th-inning squeeze bunt gave the Orioles a 4-3 Game 1 victory after Boog Powell had tied the contest with a ninth-inning home run.

■ **Memorable moment:** An 11th-inning Curt Motton pinch-hit single that put the capper on a second-game, three-hit, 1-0 shutout by Orioles lefthander Dave McNally.

■ **Top guns:** McNally (1-0, 0.00 ERA), Brooks Robinson (.500), Blair (.400, 6 RBIs), Orioles; Tony Oliva (.385), Twins.

■ **MVP:** McNally.

Linescores

Game 1—October 4, at Baltimore
Minn. 0 0 0 0 1 0 2 0 0 0 0 0—3 4 2
Balt. ..0 0 0 1 1 0 0 0 1 0 0 1—4 10 1
Perry, Perranoski (9); Cuellar, Richert (9), Watt (10), Lopez (12), Hall (12). W—Hall. L—Perranoski. HR—F. Robinson, Belanger, Powell (Bal.); Oliva (Min.).

Game 2—October 5, at Baltimore
Minn. ....0 0 0 0 0 0 0 0 0 0 0—0 3 1
Balt. ......0 0 0 0 0 0 0 0 0 0 1—1 8 0
Boswell, Perranoski (11); McNally. W—McNally. L—Boswell.

Game 3—October 6, at Minnesota
Balt. ....0 3 0 2 0 1 0 2 3—11 18 0
Minn. ......1 0 0 0 1 0 0 0 0— 2 10 2
Palmer; Miller, Woodson (2), Hall (4), Worthington (5), Grzenda (6), Chance (7), Perranoski (9). W—Palmer. L—Miller. HR—Blair (Bal.).

NLCS

■ **Winner:** The Mets completed their stunning pennant run by sweeping the Braves in the N.L.'s first League Championship Series.

■ **Turning point:** A five-run eighth-inning rally that produced a 9-5 Mets victory in Game 1 and set the tone for the rest of the series.

■ **Memorable moment:** Young Nolan Ryan's Game 3 heroics. Ryan took over for starter Gary Gentry in the third inning with runners on second and third, none out and the Braves leading 2-0. He pitched out of the jam and recorded the series-ending victory with seven innings of three-hit pitching.

■ **Top guns:** Art Shamsky (.538), Cleon Jones (.429), Ken Boswell (.333, 2 HR, 5 RBIs), Mets; Orlando Cepeda (.455), Hank Aaron (.357, 3 HR, 7 RBIs), Braves.

■ **MVP:** Boswell.

Linescores

Game 1—October 4, at Atlanta
New York ..0 2 0 2 0 0 0 5 0—9 10 1
Atlanta ......0 1 2 0 1 0 1 0 0—5 10 2
Seaver, Taylor (8); Niekro, Upshaw (9). W—Seaver. L—Niekro. S—Taylor. HR—Gonzalez, H. Aaron (Atl.).

Game 2—October 5, at Atlanta
New York 1 3 2 2 1 0 2 0 0—11 13 1
Atlanta ....0 0 0 1 5 0 0 0 0— 6 9 3
Koosman, Taylor (5), McGraw (7); Reed, Doyle (2), Pappas (3), Britton (6), Upshaw (6), Neibauer (9). W—Taylor. L—Reed. S—McGraw. HR—Agee, Boswell, Jones (N.Y.); H. Aaron (Atl.).

Game 3—October 6, at New York
Atlanta ......2 0 0 0 2 0 0 0 0—4 8 1
New York ..0 0 1 2 3 1 0 0 x—7 14 0
Jarvis, Stone (5), Upshaw (6); Gentry, Ryan (3). W—Ryan. L—Jarvis. HR—H. Aaron, Cepeda (Atl.); Agee, Boswell, Garrett (N.Y.).

WORLD SERIES

■ **Winner:** The Amazing Mets completed their Cinderella season with a shocking five-game victory over the powerful Orioles.

■ **Turning point:** A ninth-inning RBI single by light-hitting Al Weis that gave the Mets and Jerry Koosman a Series-evening 2-1 victory in Game 2.

■ **Memorable moments:** Tommie Agee's Game 3 performance. Center fielder Agee hit a first-inning home run and made two spectacular catches that saved five runs and preserved a 5-0 victory.

■ **Top guns:** Koosman (2-0, 2.04 ERA), Weis (.455), Donn Clendenon (.357, 3 HR, 4 RBIs), Mets.

■ **MVP:** Clendenon.

Linescores

Game 1—October 11, at Baltimore
NY................0 0 0 0 0 0 1 0 0—1 6 1
Balt. ....1 0 0 3 0 0 0 0 x—4 6 0
Seaver, Cardwell (6), Taylor (7); Cuellar. W—Cuellar. L—Seaver. HR—Buford (Bal.).

Game 2—October 12, at Baltimore
NY................0 0 0 1 0 0 0 0 1—2 6 0
Balt. ....0 0 0 0 0 0 1 0 0—1 2 0
Koosman, Taylor (9); McNally. W—Koosman. L—McNally. HR—Clendenon (N.Y.).

Game 3—October 14, at New York
Balt. ....0 0 0 0 0 0 0 0 0—0 4 1
NY................1 2 0 0 0 1 0 1 x—5 6 0
Palmer, Leonhard (7); Gentry, Ryan (7). W—Gentry. L—Palmer. S—Ryan. HR—Agee, Kranepool (N.Y.).

Game 4—Ocotber 15, at New York
Balt. ....0 0 0 0 0 0 0 0 1 0—1 6 1
NY ....0 1 0 0 0 0 0 0 0 1—2 10 1
Cuellar, Watt (8), Hall (10), Richert (10); Seaver. W—Seaver. L—Hall. HR—Clendenon (N.Y.).

Game 5—October 16, at New York
Balt. ....0 0 3 0 0 0 0 0 0—3 5 2
NY................0 0 0 0 0 2 1 2 x—5 7 0
McNally, Watt (8); Koosman. W—Koosman. L—Watt. HR—McNally, F. Robinson (Bal.); Clendenon, Weis (N.Y.).

FINAL STANDINGS

American League

East Division

Team	Bal.	N.Y.	Bos.	Det.	Cle.	Wsh.	Min.	Oak.	Cal.	K.C.	Mil.	Chi.	W	L	Pct.	GB
Baltimore	...	11	13	11	14	12	5	7	7	12	7	9	108	54	.667	...
New York	7	...	8	11	10	10	7	6	7	11	9	7	93	69	.574	15
Boston	5	10	...	9	12	12	7	7	5	7	5	8	87	75	.537	21
Detroit	7	7	9	...	11	9	4	6	6	6	8	6	79	83	.488	29
Cleveland	4	8	6	7	...	11	6	7	6	8	7	6	76	86	.469	32
Washington	6	8	6	9	7	...	6	2	5	6	7	8	70	92	.432	38

West Division

Team	Min.	Oak.	Cal.	K.C.	Mil.	Chi.	Bal.	N.Y.	Bos.	Det.	Cle.	Wsh.	W	L	Pct.	GB
Minnesota	...	13	10	13	13	12	7	5	5	8	6	6	98	64	.605	...
Oakland	5	...	10	11	10	16	5	6	5	6	5	10	89	73	.549	9
California	8	8	...	10	12	12	5	5	7	6	6	7	86	76	.531	12
Kansas City	5	7	8	...	12	11	0	1	5	6	4	6	65	97	.401	33
Milwaukee	5	8	6	6	...	11	5	3	7	4	5	5	65	97	.401	33
Chicago	6	2	6	7	7	...	3	5	4	6	6	4	56	106	.346	42

National League

East Division

Team	Pit.	Chi.	N.Y.	St.L.	Phi.	Mon.	Cin.	L.A.	S.F.	Hou.	Atl.	S.D.	W	L	Pct.	GB
Pittsburgh	...	10	12	12	14	9	4	6	4	6	6	6	89	73	.549	...
Chicago	8	...	7	7	9	13	7	6	7	7	4	9	84	78	.519	5
New York	6	11	...	12	13	8	4	5	6	6	6	6	83	79	.512	6
St. Louis	6	11	6	...	10	11	3	5	5	6	5	8	76	86	.469	13
Philadelphia	4	9	5	8	...	7	5	5	8	8	5	9	73	88	.453	15.5
Montreal	9	5	10	7	11	...	5	4	6	4	6	6	73	89	.451	16

West Division

Team	Cin.	L.A.	S.F.	Hou.	Atl.	S.D.	Pit.	Chi.	N.Y.	St.L.	Phi.	Mon.	W	L	Pct.	GB
Cincinnati	...	13	9	15	13	8	8	5	8	9	7	7	102	60	.630	...
Los Angeles	5	...	9	10	12	11	6	6	7	7	6	8	87	74	.540	14.5
San Fran.	9	9	...	8	11	13	8	5	6	7	4	6	86	76	.531	16
Houston	3	8	10	...	9	14	6	5	6	6	4	8	79	83	.488	23
Atlanta	5	6	7	9	...	9	6	8	6	7	7	6	76	86	.469	26
San Diego	10	7	5	4	9	...	6	3	6	4	3	6	63	99	.389	39

LEADERS

American League
BA: Alex Johnson, Cal., .329.
Runs: Carl Yastrzemski, Bos., 125.
Hits: Tony Oliva, Min., 204.
TB: Carl Yastrzemski, Bos., 335.
HR: Frank Howard, Wash., 44.
RBI: Frank Howard, Wash., 126.
SB: Campy Campaneris, Oak., 42.
Wins: Mike Cuellar, Bal.; Dave McNally, Bal.; Jim Perry, Min., 24.
ERA: Diego Segui, Oak., 2.56.
CG: Mike Cuellar, Bal., 21.
IP: Sam McDowell, Cle.; Jim Palmer, Bal., 305.
SO: Sam McDowell, Cle., 304.
SV: Ron Perranoski, Min., 34.

National League
BA: Rico Carty, Atl., .366.
Runs: Billy Williams, Chi., 137.
Hits: Pete Rose, Cin.; Billy Williams, Chi., 205.
TB: Billy Williams, Chi., 373.
HR: Johnny Bench, Cin., 45.
RBI: Johnny Bench, Cin., 148.
SB: Bobby Tolan, Cin., 57.
Wins: Bob Gibson, St.L.; Gaylord Perry, S.F., 23.
ERA: Tom Seaver, N.Y., 2.82.
CG: Ferguson Jenkins, Chi., 24.
IP: Gaylord Perry, S.F., 328.2.
SO: Tom Seaver, N.Y., 283.
SV: Wayne Granger, Cin., 35.

A.L. 20-game winners
Mike Cuellar, Bal., 24-8
Dave McNally, Bal., 24-9
Jim Perry, Min., 24-12
Clyde Wright, Cal., 22-12
Jim Palmer, Bal., 20-10
Fritz Peterson, N.Y., 20-11
Sam McDowell, Cle., 20-12

N.L. 20-game winners
Bob Gibson, St.L., 23-7
Gaylord Perry, S.F., 23-13
Ferguson Jenkins, Chi., 22-16
Jim Merritt, Cin., 20-12

A.L. 100 RBIs
Frank Howard, Wash., 126
Tony Conigliaro, Bos., 116
Boog Powell, Bal., 114
Harmon Killebrew, Min., 113
Tony Oliva, Min., 107
Rico Petrocelli, Bos., 103
Carl Yastrzemski, Bos., 102

N.L. 100 RBIs
Johnny Bench, Cin., 148
Tony Perez, Cin., 129
Billy Williams, Chi., 129
Willie McCovey, S.F., 126
Hank Aaron, Atl., 118
Jim Hickman, Chi., 115
Ron Santo, Chi., 114
Orlando Cepeda, Atl., 111
Wes Parker, L.A., 111
Dick Dietz, S.F., 107
Dick Allen, St.L., 101
Rico Carty, Atl., 101
Joe Torre, St.L., 100

A.L. 40 homers
Frank Howard, Wash., 44
Harmon Killebrew, Min., 41
Carl Yastrzemski, Bos., 40

N.L. 40 homers
Johnny Bench, Cin., 45
Billy Williams, Chi., 42
Tony Perez, Cin., 40

Most Valuable Player
A.L.: Boog Powell, 1B, Bal.
N.L.: Johnny Bench, C, Cin.

Cy Young Award
A.L.: Jim Perry, Min.
N.L.: Bob Gibson, St.L.

Rookie of the Year
A.L.: Thurman Munson, C, N.Y.
N.L.: Carl Morton, P, Mon.

Hall of Fame additions
Lou Boudreau, SS, 1938-52
Earle Combs, OF, 1924-35
Ford Frick, exec./commissioner
Jesse Haines, P, 1918-37

SIGNIFICANT EVENTS

■ **January 16:** Outfielder Curt Flood, who refused to report to Philadelphia after being traded by the Cardinals, filed a federal lawsuit challenging baseball's reserve clause.

■ **March 28:** Commissioner Bowie Kuhn returned the All-Star selection to the fans, with voting to be done on punch cards and processed by computer.

■ **March 31:** The financially strapped Pilots ended their one-year Seattle existence when the team was sold and moved to Milwaukee.

■ **June 30, July 16:** The Reds lost in their Riverfront Stadium debut to Atlanta, 8-2, but spoiled the Pirates' Three Rivers Stadium inaugural, 3-2.

■ **September 3:** Exhausted Cubs star Billy Williams ended his N.L.-record ironman streak at 1,117 games.

■ **October 4:** Umpires ended their unprecedented one-day strike when they accepted a four-year contract and returned to work for the second games of the League Championship Series.

MEMORABLE MOMENTS

■ **April 22:** Mets righthander Tom Seaver tied the Major League record when he struck out 19 Padres, including a record 10 in succession, during a 2-1 victory at Shea Stadium.

■ **May 10:** Atlanta knuckleballer Hoyt Wilhelm became the first pitcher to appear in 1,000 Major League games.

■ **May 12:** Cubs shortstop Ernie Banks hit his 500th career home run off Atlanta's Pat Jarvis in a 4-3 victory at Wrigley Field.

■ **May 17, July 18:** Two new members of baseball's 3,000-hit club: Atlanta's Hank Aaron and San Francisco's Willie Mays.

■ **June 21:** Detroit's Cesar Gutierrez performed a 20th Century first when he collected seven hits (six singles and a double) in a 12-inning 9-8 victory over Cleveland.

■ **June 26:** Baltimore's Frank Robinson belted a record-tying two grand slams in the Orioles' 12-2 victory over the Senators.

■ **October 1:** California's Alex Johnson collected two final-day hits and edged Boston's Carl Yastrzemski, .3289 to .3286, in the tightest A.L. batting race since 1946.

ALL-STAR GAME

■ **Winner:** Chicago's Jim Hickman singled home Pete Rose in the 12th inning, giving the N.L. a come-from-behind victory that pushed its All-Star winning streak to eight games.
■ **Key inning:** The bottom of the ninth, when a Dick Dietz home run, an RBI single by Willie McCovey and Roberto Clemente's sacrifice fly brought the N.L. back from a 4-1 deficit and forced extra innings.
■ **Memorable moment:** A game-ending collision between Rose and A.L. catcher Ray Fosse. Rose, playing before his home fans, jarred the ball free and sent Fosse sprawling with a nasty body block.
■ **Top guns:** Tom Seaver (Mets), Bud Harrelson (Mets), Dietz (Giants), McCovey (Giants), Rose (Reds), Hickman (Cubs), N.L.; Jim Palmer (Orioles), Sam McDowell (Indians), Carl Yastrzemski (Red Sox), Brooks Robinson (Orioles), A.L.
■ **MVP:** Yastrzemski

Linescore
July 14, at Cincinnati's Riverfront Stadium
A.L...0 0 0 0 0 1 1 2 0 0 0 0—4 12 0
N.L. 0 0 0 0 0 0 1 0 3 0 0 1—5 10 0
Palmer (Orioles), McDowell (Indians) 4, J. Perry (Twins) 7, Hunter (Athletics) 9, Peterson (Yankees) 9, Stottlemyre (Yankees) 9, Wright (Angels) 11; Seaver (Mets), Merritt (Reds) 4, G. Perry (Giants) 6, Gibson (Cardinals) 8, Osteen (Dodgers) 10. W—Osteen. L—Wright. HR—Dietz, N.L.

ALCS

■ **Winner:** Powerful Baltimore made it two straight over the Twins, who were outscored by an average of almost six runs per game.
■ **Turning point:** The fourth inning of Game 1. The Orioles scored seven times and broke the only tie the Twins could manage in the entire series.
■ **Memorable moment:** A fourth-inning Game 1 grand slam homer by light-hitting pitcher Mike Cuellar. He pulled the pitch down the right-field line, clearly foul, but a gusty wind brought the ball back inside the foul pole.
■ **Top guns:** Jim Palmer (1-0, 1.00 ERA), Brooks Robinson (.583), Boog Powell (.429, 6 RBIs), Don Buford (.429), Orioles; Tony Oliva (.500), Twins.
■ **MVP:** Powell.

Linescores
Game 1—October 3, at Minnesota
Balt. ....0 2 0 7 0 1 0 0 0—10 13 0
Minn. ......1 1 0 1 3 0 0 0 0— 6 11 2
Cuellar, Hall (5); Perry, Zepp (4), Woodson (5), Williams (6), Perranoski (9). W—Hall. L—Perry. HR—Cuellar, Buford, Powell (Bal.); Killebrew (Min.).

Game 2—October 4, at Minnesota
Balt. ....1 0 2 1 0 0 0 0 7—11 13 0
Minn. ......0 0 0 3 0 0 0 0 0— 3 6 2
McNally; Hall, Zepp (4), Williams (5), Perranoski (8), Tiant (9). W—McNally. L—Hall. HR—F. Robinson, Johnson (Bal.); Killebrew, Oliva (Min.).

Game 3—October 5, at Baltimore
Minn. ....0 0 0 0 1 0 0 0 0—1 7 2
Balt. ....1 1 3 0 0 0 1 0 x—6 10 0
Kaat, Blyleven (3), Hall (5), Perry (7); Palmer. W—Palmer. L—Kaat. HR—Johnson (Bal.).

NLCS

■ **Winner:** Power-packed Cincinnati's sweep of Pittsburgh was orchestrated by an oft-maligned pitching staff that recorded a 0.96 series ERA.
■ **Turning point:** Don Gullett's 3⅓ innings of hitless relief in Game 2. He secured a 3-1 Cincinnati victory and struck out the side in an impressive seventh inning.
■ **Memorable moment:** Back-to-back Game 3 homers by Tony Perez and Johnny Bench — the Reds' only power display of the series.
■ **Top guns:** Gary Nolan (1-0, 0-00 ERA), Bobby Tolan (.417), Reds; Richie Hebner (.667), Willie Stargell (.500), Pirates.
■ **MVP:** Reds' pitching staff (0.96 ERA).

Linescores
Game 1—October 3, at Pittsburgh
Cin. ....0 0 0 0 0 0 0 0 0 3—3 9 0
Pitt. ....0 0 0 0 0 0 0 0 0 0—0 8 0
Nolan, Carroll (10); Ellis, Gibbon (10). W—Nolan. L—Ellis S—Carroll.

Game 2—October 4, at Pittsburgh
Cincinnati ....0 0 1 0 1 0 0 1 0—3 8 1
Pittsburgh....0 0 0 0 0 1 0 0 0—1 5 2
Merritt, Carroll (6), Gullett (6); Walker, Giusti (8). W—Merritt. L—Walker. HR—Tolan (Cin.).

Game 3—October 5, at Cincinnati
Pittsburgh..1 0 0 0 1 0 0 0 0—2 10 0
Cincinnati ..2 0 0 0 0 0 0 1 x—3 5 0
Moose, Gibbon (8), Giusti (8); Cloninger, Wilcox (6), Granger (9), Gullett (9). W—Wilcox. L—Moose. S—Gullett. HR—Perez, Bench (Cin.).

WORLD SERIES

■ **Winner:** The Orioles, still reeling from their five-game 1969 loss to the Mets, turned the tables on the young Reds.
■ **Turning point:** Game 1. The Orioles, down 3-0 in the first Series game at new Riverfront Stadium, rallied on home runs by Boog Powell, Brooks Robinson and Elrod Hendricks for a 4-3 victory.
■ **Memorable moments:** The incredible fielding artistry of Orioles third baseman Brooks Robinson, who constantly foiled the Reds with big plays, and Baltimore pitcher Dave McNally's third-game grand slam.
■ **Top guns:** Brooks Robinson (.429, 6 RBIs), Paul Blair (.474), Orioles; Hal McRae (.455), Lee May (.389, 2 HR, 8 RBIs), Reds.
■ **MVP:** Brooks Robinson.

Linescores
Game 1—October 10, at Cincinnati
Balt. ....0 0 0 2 1 0 1 0 0—4 7 2
Cin. ....1 0 2 0 0 0 0 0 0—3 5 0
Palmer, Richert (9); Nolan, Carroll (7). W—Palmer. L—Nolan. S—Richert. HR—May (Cin.); Powell, Hendricks, B. Robinson (Bal.).

Game 2—October 11, at Cincinnati
Balt. ....0 0 0 1 5 0 0 0 0—6 10 2
Cin. ....3 0 1 0 0 1 0 0 0—5 7 0
Cuellar, Phoebus (3), Drabowsky (5), Lopez (7), Hall (7); McGlothlin, Wilcox (5), Carroll (5), Gullett (8). W—Phoebus. L—Wilcox. S—Hall. HR—Tolan, Bench (Cin.); Powell (Bal.).

Game 3—October 13, at Baltimore
Cin. ....0 1 0 0 0 0 2 0 0—3 9 0
Balt. ....2 0 1 0 1 4 1 0 x—9 10 1
Cloninger, Granger (6), Gullett (7); McNally. W—McNally. L—Cloninger. HR—F. Robinson, Buford, McNally (Bal.).

Game 4—October 14, at Baltimore
Cin. ....0 1 1 0 1 0 0 3 0—6 8 3
Balt. ....0 1 3 0 0 1 0 0 0—5 8 0
Nolan, Gullett (3), Carroll (6); Palmer, Watt (8), Drabowsky (9). W—Carroll. L—Watt. HR—B. Robinson (Bal.); Rose, May (Cin.).

Game 5—October 15, at Baltimore
Cin. ....3 0 0 0 0 0 0 0 0—3 6 0
Balt. ....2 2 2 0 1 0 0 2 x—9 15 0
Merritt, Granger (2), Wilcox (3), Cloninger (5), Washburn (7), Carroll (8); Cuellar. W—Cuellar. L—Merritt. HR—F. Robinson, Rettenmund (Bal.).

FINAL STANDINGS

American League

East Division

Team	Bal.	Det.	Bos.	N.Y.	Wash.	Cle.	Oak.	K.C.	Chi.	Cal.	Min.	Mil.	W	L	Pct.	GB
Baltimore	...	8	9	11	13	13	7	6	8	7	10	9	101	57	.639	...
Detroit	10	...	6	10	14	12	4	8	5	6	6	10	91	71	.562	12
Boston	9	12	...	7	12	11	3	1	10	6	8	6	85	77	.525	18
New York	7	8	11	...	7	10	5	7	7	6	4	10	82	80	.506	21
Washington	3	4	6	11	...	11	3	3	2	8	6	6	63	96	.396	38.5
Cleveland	5	6	7	8	7	...	4	2	9	4	4	4	60	102	.370	43

West Division

Team	Oak.	K.C.	Chi.	Cal.	Min.	Mil.	Bal.	Det.	Bos.	N.Y.	Wash.	Cle.	W	L	Pct.	GB
Oakland	...	13	7	11	10	15	4	8	9	7	9	8	101	60	.627	...
Kansas City	5	...	9	10	9	8	5	4	11	5	9	10	85	76	.528	16
Chicago	11	9	...	10	7	11	4	7	2	5	10	3	79	83	.488	22.5
California	7	8	8	...	12	6	5	6	6	6	4	8	76	86	.469	25.5
Minnesota	8	9	11	6	...	7	2	6	4	8	5	8	74	86	.463	26.5
Milwaukee	3	10	7	12	10	...	3	2	6	2	6	8	69	92	.429	32

National League

East Division

Team	Pit.	St.L.	Chi.	N.Y.	Mon.	Phi.	S.F.	L.A.	Atl.	Cin.	Hou.	S.D.	W	L	Pct.	GB
Pittsburgh	...	11	12	8	11	12	3	8	8	7	8	9	97	65	.599	...
St. Louis	7	...	9	8	14	11	7	6	6	4	10	8	90	72	.556	7
Chicago	6	9	...	11	8	11	3	8	7	6	5	9	83	79	.512	14
New York	10	10	7	...	9	13	4	7	5	4	7	7	83	79	.512	14
Montreal	7	4	10	9	...	6	7	4	5	5	8	6	71	90	.441	25.5
Philadelphia	6	7	7	5	12	...	6	5	4	7	4	4	67	95	.414	30

West Division

Team	S.F.	L.A.	Atl.	Cin.	Hou.	S.D.	Pit.	St.L.	Chi.	N.Y.	Mon.	Phi.	W	L	Pct.	GB
San Fran.	...	6	11	9	9	13	9	5	9	8	5	6	90	72	.556	...
L.A.	12	...	9	11	10	13	4	6	4	5	8	7	89	73	.549	1
Atlanta	7	9	...	9	9	11	4	6	5	7	7	8	82	80	.506	8
Cincinnati	9	7	9	...	5	10	5	8	6	8	7	5	79	83	.488	11
Houston	9	8	9	13	...	10	4	2	7	5	4	8	79	83	.488	11
San Diego	5	5	7	8	8	...	3	4	3	5	5	8	61	100	.379	28.5

SIGNIFICANT EVENTS

■ **April 10:** The Phillies made their Veterans Stadium debut a successful one, defeating Montreal, 4-1.

■ **May 6:** Commissioner Bowie Kuhn closed a deal with NBC-TV that would net the 24 teams $72 million over four years.

■ **September 21:** Baseball ended its 71-year association with the nation's capital when owners approved the Senators' transfer to the Dallas-Fort Worth area.

MEMORABLE MOMENTS

■ **April 27:** The 600-homer club welcomed its third member when Atlanta's Hank Aaron connected off Gaylord Perry in a 10-inning 6-5 loss to the Giants.

■ **June 23:** Philadelphia's Rick Wise pitched a no-hitter and spiced his 4-0 victory over Cincinnati with two home runs.

■ **August 10, September 13:** Minnesota's Harmon Killebrew and Baltimore's Frank Robinson became the 10th and 11th players to hit 500 career home runs.

■ **September 26:** When Jim Palmer blanked Cleveland 5-0 for his 20th victory, the Orioles joined the 1920 White Sox as the only teams to boast four 20-game winners in one season. Palmer joined Dave McNally, Mike Cuellar and Pat Dobson in the select circle.

■ **September 30:** The Senators had to forfeit their final game in Washington to the Yankees when fans swarmed out of the stands in the ninth inning and began tearing up RFK Stadium.

LEADERS

American League
BA: Tony Oliva, Min., .337.
Runs: Don Buford, Bal., 99.
Hits: Cesar Tovar, Min., 204.
TB: Reggie Smith, Bos., 302.
HR: Bill Melton, Chi., 33.
RBI: Harmon Killebrew, Min., 119.
SB: Amos Otis, K.C., 52.
Wins: Mickey Lolich, Det., 25.
ERA: Vida Blue, Oak., 1.82.
CG: Mickey Lolich, Det., 29.
IP: Mickey Lolich, Det., 376.
SO: Mickey Lolich, Det., 308.
SV: Ken Sanders, Mil., 31.

National League
BA: Joe Torre, St.L., .363.
Runs: Lou Brock, St.L., 126.
Hits: Joe Torre, St.L., 230.
TB: Joe Torre, St.L., 352.
HR: Willie Stargell, Pit., 48.
RBI: Joe Torre, St.L., 137.
SB: Lou Brock, St.L., 64.
Wins: Ferguson Jenkins, Chi., 24.
ERA: Tom Seaver, N.Y., 1.76.
CG: Ferguson Jenkins, Chi., 30.
IP: Ferguson Jenkins, Chi., 325.
SO: Tom Seaver, N.Y., 289.
SV: Dave Giusti, Pit., 30.

A.L. 20-game winners
Mickey Lolich, Det., 25-14
Vida Blue, Oak., 24-8
Wilbur Wood, Chi., 22-13
Dave McNally, Bal., 21-5
Catfish Hunter, Oak., 21-11
Pat Dobson, Bal., 20-8
Jim Palmer, Bal., 20-9
Mike Cuellar, Bal., 20-9
Joe Coleman, Det., 20-9
Andy Messersmith, Cal., 20-13

N.L. 20-game winners
Ferguson Jenkins, Chi., 24-13
Al Downing, L.A., 20-9
Steve Carlton, St.L., 20-9
Tom Seaver, N.Y., 20-10

A.L. 100 RBIs
Harmon Killebrew, Min., 119

N.L. 100 RBIs
Joe Torre, St.L., 137
Willie Stargell, Pit., 125
Hank Aaron, Mil., 118
Bobby Bonds, S.F., 102

N.L. 40 homers
Willie Stargell, Pit., 48
Hank Aaron, Atl., 47

Most Valuable Player
A.L.: Vida Blue, P, Oak.
N.L.: Joe Torre, 3B, St.L.

Cy Young Award
A.L.: Vida Blue, Oak.
N.L.: Ferguson Jenkins, Chi.

Rookie of the Year
A.L.: Chris Chambliss, 1B, Cle.
N.L.: Earl Williams, C, Atl.

Hall of Fame additions
Dave Bancroft, SS, 1915-30
Jake Beckley, 1B, 1888-1907
Chick Hafey, OF, 1924-37
Harry Hooper, OF, 1909-25
Joe Kelley, OF, 1891-1908
Rube Marquard, P, 1908-25
Satchel Paige, P, 1948-65
George Weiss, executive

ALL-STAR GAME

■ **Winner:** The A.L. ended its eight-year All-Star drought with a three-homer barrage that produced a 6-4 victory.

■ **Key inning:** After falling behind 3-0 on Johnny Bench and Hank Aaron home runs, the A.L. struck for four third-inning runs on two-run homers by Reggie Jackson and Frank Robinson.

■ **Memorable moment:** The titanic third-inning blast by Jackson, which struck a light tower on the roof of Tiger Stadium, 520 feet from home plate in right-center field.

■ **Top guns:** Jackson (Athletics), F. Robinson (Orioles), Harmon Killebrew (Twins), A.L.; Bench (Reds), Aaron (Braves), Roberto Clemente (Pirates), N.L.

■ **MVP:** F. Robinson.

Linescore
July 13, at Detroit's Tiger Stadium
N.L.............0 2 1 0 0 0 0 1 0—4 5 0
A.L. ....0 0 4 0 0 2 0 0 x—6 7 0
Ellis (Pirates), Marichal (Giants) 4, Jenkins (Cubs) 6, Wilson (Astros) 7; Blue (Athletics), Palmer (Orioles) 4, Cuellar (Orioles) 6, Lolich (Tigers) 8. W—Blue. L—Ellis. HR—Bench, Aaron, Clemente, N.L.; Jackson, F. Robinson, Killebrew, A.L.

ALCS

■ **Winner:** The Orioles recorded their third consecutive Championship Series sweep, turning aside the up-and-coming Oakland Athletics.

■ **Turning point:** A four-run seventh-inning Game 1 rally that wiped out a 3-1 deficit and marked the last time Baltimore trailed in the series.

■ **Memorable moments:** A four-homer Game 2 salvo and Mike Cuellar's six-hit pitching added up to a 5-1 Orioles' victory.

■ **Top guns:** Cuellar (1-0, 1.00 ERA), Brooks Robinson (.364, 3 RBIs), Boog Powell (2 HR, 3 RBIs), Orioles; Sal Bando (.364), Reggie Jackson (.333, 2 HR), Athletics.

■ **MVP:** Cuellar.

Linescores

Game 1—October 3, at Baltimore
Oakland........0 2 0 1 0 0 0 0 0—3 9 0
Baltimore ....0 0 0 1 0 0 4 0 x—5 7 1
Blue, Fingers (8); McNally, Watt (8). W—McNally. L—Blue. S—Watt.

Game 2—October 4, at Baltimore
Oakland........0 0 0 1 0 0 0 0 0—1 6 0
Baltimore ....0 1 1 0 0 0 1 2 x—5 7 0
Hunter; Cuellar. W—Cuellar. L—Hunter. HR—B. Robinson, Powell 2, Hendricks (Bal.).

Game 3—October 5, at Oakland
Baltimore ..1 0 0 0 2 0 2 0 0—5 12 0
Oakland......0 0 1 0 0 1 0 1 0—3 7 0
Palmer; Segui, Fingers (5), Knowles (7), Locker (7), Grant (8). W—Palmer. L—Segui. HR—Jackson 2, Bando (Oak.).

NLCS

■ **Winner:** Pittsburgh defeated San Francisco to claim its first pennant since 1960. The Pirates needed four games to win the first LCS not decided by a sweep.

■ **Turning point:** Richie Hebner's eighth-inning Game 3 home run, which gave substitute starter Bob Johnson a 2-1 victory and the Pirates a 2-1 series edge.

■ **Memorable moment:** Pittsburgh first baseman Bob Robertson's ninth-inning Game 2 home run — his record-setting third of the game — capping a 9-4 Pirates victory.

■ **Top guns:** Robertson (.438, 4 HR, 6 RBIs), Dave Cash (.421), Hebner (2 HR, 4 RBIs), Pirates; Willie McCovey (.429, 2 HR, 6 RBIs), Chris Speier (.357), Giants.

■ **MVP:** Robertson.

Linescores

Game 1—October 2, at San Francisco
Pitt..............0 0 2 0 0 0 2 0 0—4 9 0
San Fran.......0 0 1 0 4 0 0 0 x—5 7 2
Blass, Moose (6), Giusti (8); Perry. W—Perry. L—Blass. HR—Fuentes, McCovey (S.F.).

Game 2—October 3, at San Francisco
Pitt............0 1 0 2 1 0 4 0 1—9 15 0
San Fran. ..1 1 0 0 0 0 0 0 2—4 9 0
Ellis, Miller (6), Giusti (9); Cumberland, Barr (4), McMahon (5), Carrithers (7), Bryant (7), Hamilton (9). W—Ellis. L—Cumberland. S—Giusti. HR—Robertson 3, Clines (Pit.); Mays (S.F.).

Game 3—October 5, at Pittsburgh
San Fran. ....0 0 0 0 0 1 0 0 0—1 5 2
Pitt. ....0 1 0 0 0 0 0 1 x—2 4 1
Marichal; Johnson, Giusti (9). W—Johnson. L—Marichal. S—Giusti. HR—Robertson, Hebner (Pit.).

Game 4—October 6, at Pittsburgh
San Fran. ..1 4 0 0 0 0 0 0 0—5 10 0
Pitt............2 3 0 0 0 4 0 0 x—9 11 2
Perry, Johnson (6), McMahon (8); Blass, Kison (3), Giusti (7). W—Kison. L—Perry. S—Giusti. HR—Speier, McCovey (S.F.); Hebner, Oliver (Pit.).

WORLD SERIES

■ **Winner:** The Pirates, absent from Series competition for a decade, rebounded after losing the first two games.

■ **Turning point:** After Pittsburgh starter Luke Walker surrendered three first-inning runs in Game 4, Bruce Kison and Dave Giusti pitched 8⅓ scoreless innings and the Pirates rallied for a 4-3 victory.

■ **Memorable moments:** The Game 7 performances of Roberto Clemente, who homered, and Steve Blass, who shut down the Orioles 2-1 on a gritty four-hitter.

■ **Top guns:** Blass (2-0, 1.00 ERA), Clemente (.414, 12 hits, 2 HR, 4 RBIs), Manny Sanguillen (.379), Pirates; Dave McNally (2-1, 1.98), Orioles.

■ **MVP:** Clemente.

Linescores

Game 1—October 9, at Baltimore
Pitt.............0 3 0 0 0 0 0 0 0—3 3 0
Balt. ....0 1 3 0 1 0 0 0 x—5 10 3
Ellis, Moose (3), Miller (7); McNally. W—McNally. L—Ellis. HR—F. Robinson, Rettenmund, Buford (Bal.).

Game 2—October 11, at Baltimore
Pitt...........0 0 0 0 0 0 0 3 0— 3 8 1
Balt. ....0 1 0 3 6 1 0 0 x—11 14 1
R. Johnson, Kison (4), Moose (4), Veale (5), Miller (6), Giusti (8); Palmer, Hall (9). W—Palmer. L—R. Johnson. S—Hall. HR—Hebner (Pit.).

Game 3—October 12, at Pittsburgh
Balt. ....0 0 0 0 0 0 1 0 0—1 3 3
Pitt. ....1 0 0 0 0 1 3 0 x—5 7 0
Cuellar, Dukes (7), Watt (8); Blass. W—Blass. L—Cuellar. HR—F. Robinson (Bal.); Robertson (Pit.).

Game 4—October 13, at Pittsburgh
Balt. ....3 0 0 0 0 0 0 0 0—3 4 1
Pitt. ....2 0 1 0 0 0 1 0 x—4 14 0
Dobson, Jackson (6), Watt (7), Richert (8); Walker, Kison (1), Giusti (8). W—Kison. L—Watt. S—Giusti.

Game 5—October 14, at Pittsburgh
Balt. ....0 0 0 0 0 0 0 0 0—0 2 1
Pitt. ....0 2 1 0 1 0 0 0 x—4 9 0
McNally, Leonhard (5), Dukes (6); Briles. W—Briles. L—McNally. HR—Robertson (Pit.).

Game 6—October 16, at Baltimore
Pitt...........0 1 1 0 0 0 0 0 0 0—2 9 1
Balt. ....0 0 0 0 0 1 1 0 0 1—3 8 0
Moose, R. Johnson (6), Giusti (7), Miller (10); Palmer, Dobson (10), McNally (10). W—McNally. L—Miller. HR—Clemente (Pit.); Buford (Bal.).

Game 7—October 17, at Baltimore
Pitt. ....0 0 0 1 0 0 0 1 0—2 6 1
Balt. ....0 0 0 0 0 0 0 1 0—1 4 0
Blass; Cuellar, Dobson (9), McNally (9). W—Blass. L—Cuellar. HR—Clemente (Pit.).

FINAL STANDINGS

American League

East Division

Team	Det.	Bos.	Bal.	N.Y.	Cle.	Mil.	Oak.	Chi.	Min.	K.C.	Cal.	Tex.	W	L	Pct.	GB
Detroit	...	9	8	7	8	10	4	7	9	7	7	10	86	70	.551	...
Boston	5	...	11	9	8	11	9	6	4	6	8	8	85	70	.548	.5
Baltimore	10	7	...	7	8	10	6	8	6	6	6	6	80	74	.519	5
New York	9	9	6	...	11	9	3	5	6	5	8	8	79	76	.510	6.5
Cleveland	10	7	10	7	...	5	2	4	8	6	4	9	72	84	.462	14
Milwaukee	8	7	5	9	10	...	4	3	4	5	5	5	65	91	.417	21

West Division

Team	Oak.	Chi.	Min.	K.C.	Cal.	Tex.	Det.	Bos.	Bal.	N.Y.	Cle.	Mil	W	L	Pct.	GB
Oakland	...	8	9	11	10	11	8	3	6	9	10	8	93	62	.600	...
Chicago	7	...	8	8	11	14	5	6	4	7	8	9	87	67	.565	5.5
Minnesota	8	6	...	9	8	11	3	8	6	6	4	8	77	77	.500	15.5
Kansas City	7	9	9	...	6	8	5	6	6	7	6	7	76	78	.494	16.5
California	8	7	7	9	...	10	5	4	6	4	8	7	75	80	.484	18
Texas	4	4	7	6	7	...	2	4	6	4	3	7	54	100	.351	38.5

National League

East Division

Team	Pit.	Chi.	N.Y.	St.L.	Mon.	Phi.	Cin.	Hou.	L.A.	Atl.	S.F.	S.D.	W	L	Pct.	GB
Pittsburgh	...	12	6	10	12	13	4	9	5	6	9	10	96	59	.619	...
Chicago	3	...	10	10	10	10	8	3	8	7	7	9	85	70	.548	11
New York	8	8	...	7	12	13	4	6	5	5	8	7	83	73	.532	13.5
St. Louis	8	8	9	...	8	7	2	8	4	6	7	8	75	81	.481	21.5
Montreal	6	5	6	9	...	10	4	4	6	8	6	6	70	86	.449	26.5
Philadelphia	5	7	5	8	6	...	2	3	5	6	6	6	59	97	.378	37.5

West Division

Team	Cin.	Hou.	L.A.	Atl.	S.F.	S.D.	Pit.	Chi.	N.Y.	St.L.	Mon.	Phi.	W	L	Pct.	GB
Cincinnati	...	11	9	9	10	8	8	4	8	10	8	10	95	59	.617	...
Houston	6	...	7	7	13	12	3	9	6	4	8	9	84	69	.549	10.5
Los Angeles	5	11	...	8	9	13	7	4	7	8	6	7	85	70	.548	10.5
Atlanta	9	7	7	...	7	6	6	5	7	6	4	6	70	84	.455	25
San Fran.	5	5	9	11	...	10	3	5	4	5	6	6	69	86	.445	26.5
San Diego	10	2	5	11	4	...	2	3	5	4	6	6	58	95	.379	36.5

SIGNIFICANT EVENTS

■ **April 2:** Gil Hodges, completing spring training preparations for his fifth season as Mets manager, died from a heart attack at West Palm Beach, Fla., at age 47.

■ **April 13:** The first players' strike in baseball history was settled after 13 days and 86 cancelled games.

■ **April 21:** The Rangers celebrated their Texas debut with a 7-6 victory over California at Arlington Stadium.

■ **June 19:** The U.S. Supreme Court upheld baseball's antitrust exemption and ended Curt Flood's long, frustrating challenge to the sport's reserve clause.

■ **November 2:** Steve Carlton, who posted 27 of the last-place Phillies' 59 victories, captured the N.L. Cy Young Award.

■ **December 31:** Pirates outfielder Roberto Clemente, the newest member of baseball's 3,000-hit club, died when a cargo plane carrying supplies to Nicaraguan earthquake victims crashed near San Juan, Puerto Rico.

MEMORABLE MOMENTS

■ **May 14:** Willie Mays, returning to New York after more than 14 seasons in San Francisco, belted a game-winning solo home run against the Giants in his first game with the Mets.

■ **June 10:** Atlanta's Hank Aaron hit his N.L. record-tying 14th grand slam in a 15-3 victory over the Phillies and moved into second place on the all-time home run list.

■ **August 1:** San Diego's Nate Colbert belted a record-tying five homers and drove in a doubleheader-record 13 runs in a 9-0 and 11-7 sweep of the Braves.

LEADERS

American League
BA: Rod Carew, Min., .318.
Runs: Bobby Murcer, N.Y., 102.
Hits: Joe Rudi, Oak., 181.
TB: Bobby Murcer, N.Y., 314.
HR: Dick Allen, Chi., 37.
RBI: Dick Allen, Chi., 113.
SB: Campy Campaneris, Oak., 52.
Wins: Gaylord Perry, Cle.; Wilbur Wood, Chi., 24.
ERA: Luis Tiant, Bos., 1.91.
CG: Gaylord Perry, Cle., 29.
IP: Wilbur Wood, Chi., 376.2.
SO: Nolan Ryan, Cal., 329.
SV: Sparky Lyle, N.Y., 35.

National League
BA: Billy Williams, Chi., .333.
Runs: Joe Morgan, Cin., 122.
Hits: Pete Rose, Cin., 198.
TB: Billy Williams, Chi., 348.
HR: Johnny Bench, Cin., 40.
RBI: Johnny Bench, Cin., 125.
SB: Lou Brock, St.L., 63.
Wins: Steve Carlton, Phil., 27.
ERA: Steve Carlton, Phil., 1.97.
CG: Steve Carlton, Phil., 30.
IP: Steve Carlton, Phil., 346.1.
SO: Steve Carlton, Phil., 310.
SV: Clay Carroll, Cin., 37.

A.L. 20-game winners
Gaylord Perry, Cle., 24-16
Wilbur Wood, Chi., 24-17
Mickey Lolich, Det., 22-14
Catfish Hunter, Oak., 21-7
Jim Palmer, Bal., 21-10
Stan Bahnsen, Chi., 21-16

N.L. 20-game winners
Steve Carlton, Phil., 27-10
Tom Seaver, N.Y., 21-12
Claude Osteen, L.A., 20-11
Ferguson Jenkins, Chi., 20-12

A.L. 100 RBIs
Dick Allen, Chi., 113
John Mayberry, K.C., 100

N.L. 100 RBIs
Johnny Bench, Cin., 125
Billy Williams, Chi., 122
Willie Stargell, Pit., 112
Nate Colbert, S.D., 111

N.L. 40 homers
Johnny Bench, Cin., 40

Most Valuable Player
A.L.: Dick Allen, 1B, Chi.
N.L.: Johnny Bench, C, Cin.

Cy Young Award
A.L.: Gaylord Perry, Cle.
N.L.: Steve Carlton, Phil.

Rookie of the Year
A.L.: Carlton Fisk, C, Bos.
N.L.: Jon Matlack, P, N.Y.

Hall of Fame additions
Yogi Berra, C, 1946-65
Josh Gibson, C, Negro Leagues
Lefty Gomez, P, 1930-43
Will Harridge, executive
Sandy Koufax, P, 1955-66
Buck Leonard, 1B, Negro Leagues
Early Wynn, P, 1939-63
Ross Youngs, OF, 1917-26

ALL-STAR GAME

■ **Winner:** Joe Morgan's 10th-inning single capped another N.L. comeback that produced a 4-3 victory — the senior circuit's seventh consecutive extra-inning All-Star decision.
■ **Key inning:** The ninth, when the N.L. tied the game 3-3 on a pair of singles and Lee May's ground-ball out.
■ **Memorable moment:** Hank Aaron, who entered the game with 659 career home runs, sent the Atlanta crowd into a frenzy when he hit a two-run shot in the sixth inning.
■ **Top guns:** Tug McGraw (Mets), Aaron (Braves), Morgan (Reds), N.L.; Jim Palmer (Orioles), Cookie Rojas (Royals), Rod Carew (Twins), A.L.
■ **MVP:** Morgan.

Linescore
July 25, at Atlanta Stadium
A.L. ....0 0 1 0 0 0 0 2 0 0—3 6 0
N.L. ....0 0 0 0 0 2 0 0 1 1—4 8 0
Palmer (Orioles), Lolich (Tigers) 4, Perry (Indians) 6, Wood (White Sox) 8, McNally (Orioles) 10; Gibson (Cardinals), Blass (Pirates) 3, Sutton (Dodgers) 4, Carlton (Phillies) 6, Stoneman (Expos) 7, McGraw (Mets) 9. W—McGraw. L—McNally. HR—Aaron, N.L.; Rojas, A.L.

ALCS

■ **Winner:** The Athletics claimed their first pennant in 41 years and first since moving to Oakland. The A's victory over Detroit marked the first ALCS to go beyond three games.
■ **Turning point:** The Game 5 pitching of left-hander Vida Blue, who worked four scoreless innings in relief of Blue Moon Odom to secure the A's series-ending 2-1 victory.
■ **Memorable moment:** A seventh-inning melee triggered by A's shortstop Bert Campaneris in Game 2. When Campaneris was hit by a Lerrin LaGrow pitch, he threw his bat at the pitcher and both benches emptied. Campaneris was suspended for the remainder of the series.
■ **Top guns:** Odom (2-0, 0.00 ERA), Blue (0.00), Matty Alou (.381), Athletics; Joe Coleman (1-0, 0-00 ERA), Jim Northrup (.357), Tigers.
■ **MVP:** Odom.

Linescores
Game 1—October 7, at Oakland
Det...0 1 0 0 0 0 0 0 0 0 1—2 6 2
Oak. 0 0 1 0 0 0 0 0 0 0 2—3 10 1
Lolich, Seelbach (11); Hunter, Blue (9), Fingers (9). W—Fingers. L—Lolich. HR—Cash, Kaline (Det.).

Game 2—October 8, at Oakland
Det. ....0 0 0 0 0 0 0 0 0—0 3 1
Oak. ....1 0 0 0 4 0 0 0 x—5 8 0
Fryman, Zachary (5), Scherman (5), LaGrow (6), Hiller (7); Odom. W—Odom. L—Fryman.

Game 3—October 10, at Detroit
Oak. ....0 0 0 0 0 0 0 0 0—0 7 0
Det. ....0 0 0 2 0 0 0 1 x—3 8 1
Holtzman, Fingers (5), Blue (6), Locker (7); Coleman. W—Coleman. L—Holtzman. HR—Freehan (Det.).

Game 4—October 11, at Detroit
Oak. ......0 0 0 0 0 0 1 0 0 2—3 9 2
Det. ....0 0 1 0 0 0 0 0 0 3—4 10 1
Hunter, Fingers (8), Blue (9), Locker (10), Horlen (10), Hamilton (10); Lolich, Seelbach (10), Hiller (10). W—Hiller. L—Horlen. HR—McAuliffe (Det.); Epstein (Oak.).

Game 5—October 12, at Detroit
Oak. ....0 1 0 1 0 0 0 0 0—2 4 0
Det. ....1 0 0 0 0 0 0 0 0—1 5 2
Odom, Blue (6); Fryman, Hiller (9). W—Odom. L—Fryman. S—Blue.

NLCS

■ **Winner:** Cincinnati needed an N.L.-record five games to get past Pittsburgh and claim its second pennant in three years.
■ **Turning point:** Down two games to one and facing elimination, the Reds got two-hit pitching from Ross Grimsley and forged a 7-1 victory that forced a decisive fifth game.
■ **Memorable moment:** Cincinnati's George Foster racing across the plate with the series-ending run on a Bob Moose wild pitch with two out in the ninth inning of Game 5. The Reds had tied the game moments earlier on a Johnny Bench home run.
■ **Top guns:** Pete Rose (.450), Bench (.333), Reds; Manny Sanguillen (.313), Pirates.
■ **MVP:** Rose.

Linescores
Game 1—October 7, at Pittsburgh
Cin. ....1 0 0 0 0 0 0 0 0—1 8 0
Pitt. ....3 0 0 0 2 0 0 0 x—5 6 0
Gullett, Borbon (7); Blass, R. Hernandez (9). W—Blass. L—Gullett. S—R. Hernandez. HR—Morgan (Cin.); Oliver (Pit.).

Game 2—October 8, at Pittsburgh
Cin. ....4 0 0 0 0 0 0 1 0—5 8 1
Pitt. ....0 0 0 1 1 1 0 0 0—3 7 1
Billingham, Hall (5); Moose, Johnson (1), Kison (6), R. Hernandez (7), Giusti (9). W—Hall. L—Moose. HR—Morgan (Cin.).

Game 3—October 9, at Cincinnati
Pitt. ....0 0 0 0 1 0 1 1 0—3 7 0
Cin. ....0 0 2 0 0 0 0 0 0—2 8 1
Briles, Kison (7), Giusti (8); Nolan, Borbon (7), Carroll (7), McGlothlin (9). W—Kison. L—Carroll. S—Giusti. HR—Sanguillen (Pit.).

Game 4—October 10, at Cincinnati
Pitt. ....0 0 0 0 0 0 1 0 0—1 2 3
Cin. ....1 0 0 2 0 2 2 0 x—7 11 1
Ellis, Johnson (6), Walker (7), Miller (8); Grimsley. W—Grimsley. L—Ellis. HR—Clemente (Pit.).

Game 5—October 11, at Cincinnati
Pitt. ....0 2 0 1 0 0 0 0 0—3 8 0
Cin. ....0 0 1 0 1 0 0 0 2—4 7 1
Blass, R. Hernandez (8), Giusti (9), Moose (9); Gullett, Borbon (4), Hall (6), Carroll (9). W—Carroll. L—Giusti. HR—Geronimo, Bench (Cin.).

WORLD SERIES

■ **Winner:** The Athletics, who had not played in a World Series since 1931 when the franchise was located in Philadelphia, began a run that would put them in select company.
■ **Turning point:** A Game 4 ninth-inning rally that gave Oakland a three games to one lead. Down 2-1 with one out, the A's scored two runs on four consecutive singles.
■ **Memorable moment:** A's catcher Gene Tenace blasting home runs in his first two Series at-bats — and a record-tying four overall.
■ **Top guns:** Catfish Hunter (2-0, 2.81 ERA), Tenace (.348, 4 HR, 9 RBIs), Athletics; Tony Perez (.435), Bobby Tolan (6 RBIs), Reds.
■ **MVP:** Tenace.

Linescores
Game 1—October 14, at Cincinnati
Oakland.........0 2 0 0 1 0 0 0 0—3 4 0
Cincinnati ....0 1 0 1 0 0 0 0 0—2 7 0
Holtzman, Fingers (6), Blue (7); Nolan, Borbon (7), Carroll (8). W—Holtzman. L—Nolan. S—Blue. HR—Tenace 2 (Oak.).

Game 2—October 15, at Cincinnati
Oakland.........0 1 1 0 0 0 0 0 0—2 9 2
Cincinnati ....0 0 0 0 0 0 0 0 1—1 6 0
Hunter, Fingers (9); Grimsley, Borbon (6), Hall (8). W—Hunter. L—Grimsley. S—Fingers. HR—Rudi (Oak.).

Game 3—October 18, at Oakland
Cincinnati ....0 0 0 0 0 0 1 0 0—1 4 2
Oakland.........0 0 0 0 0 0 0 0 0—0 3 2
Billingham, Carroll (9); Odom, Blue (8), Fingers (8). W—Billingham. L—Odom. S—Carroll.

Game 4—October 19, at Oakland
Cincinnati ..0 0 0 0 0 0 0 2 0—2 7 1
Oakland......0 0 0 0 1 0 0 0 2—3 10 1
Gullett, Borbon (8), Carroll (9); Holtzman, Blue (8), Fingers (9). W—Fingers. L—Carroll. HR—Tenace (Oak.).

Game 5—October 20, at Oakland
Cincinnati ....1 0 0 1 1 0 0 1 1—5 8 0
Oakland.........0 3 0 1 0 0 0 0 0—4 7 2
McGlothlin, Borbon (4), Hall (5), Carroll (7), Grimsley (8), Billingham (9); Hunter, Fingers (5), Hamilton (9). W—Grimsley. L—Fingers. S—Billingham. HR—Rose, Menke (Cin.); Tenace (Oak.).

Game 6—October 21, at Cincinnati
Oakland......0 0 0 0 1 0 0 0 0—1 7 1
Cincinnati ..0 0 0 1 1 1 5 0 x—8 10 0
Blue, Locker (6), Hamilton (7), Horlen (7); Nolan, Grimsley (5), Borbon (6), Hall (7). W—Grimsley. L—Blue. S—Hall. HR—Bench (Cin.).

Game 7—October 22, at Cincinnati
Oakland.........1 0 0 0 0 2 0 0 0—3 6 1
Cincinnati ....0 0 0 0 1 0 0 1 0—2 4 2
Odom, Hunter (5), Holtzman (8), Fingers (8); Billingham, Borbon (6), Carroll (6), Grimsley (7), Hall (8). W—Hunter. L—Borbon. S—Fingers.

FINAL STANDINGS

American League

East Division

Team	Bal.	Bos.	Det.	N.Y.	Mil.	Cle.	Cal.	Chi.	K.C.	Min.	Oak.	Tex.	W	L	Pct.	GB
Baltimore	...	7	9	9	15	12	6	8	8	8	5	10	97	65	.599	...
Boston	11	...	3	14	12	9	7	6	8	6	4	9	89	73	.549	8
Detroit	9	15	...	7	12	9	5	7	4	5	7	5	85	77	.525	12
New York	9	4	11	...	8	11	6	4	6	9	4	8	80	82	.494	17
Milwaukee	3	6	6	10	...	9	7	9	4	8	4	8	74	88	.457	23
Cleveland	6	9	9	7	9	...	7	5	2	7	3	7	71	91	.438	26

West Division

Team	Oak.	K.C.	Min.	Cal.	Chi.	Tex.	Bal.	Bos.	Cle.	Det.	Mil.	N.Y.	W	L	Pct.	GB
Oakland	...	10	4	12	12	11	7	8	9	5	8	8	94	68	.580	...
Kansas City	8	...	9	8	12	11	4	4	10	8	8	6	88	74	.543	6
Minnesota	14	9	...	8	9	12	4	6	5	7	4	3	81	81	.500	13
California	6	10	10	...	8	11	6	5	5	7	5	6	79	83	.488	15
Chicago	6	6	9	10	...	13	4	6	7	5	3	8	77	85	.475	17
Texas	7	7	6	7	5	...	2	3	5	7	4	4	57	105	.352	37

National League

East Division

Team	N.Y.	St.L.	Pit.	Mon.	Chi.	Phi.	Atl.	Cin.	Hou.	L.A.	S.D.	S.F.	W	L	Pct.	GB
New York	...	10	13	9	7	9	6	4	6	5	8	5	82	79	.509	...
St. Louis	8	...	8	10	9	9	6	6	7	4	8	6	81	81	.500	1.5
Pittsburgh	5	10	...	12	12	10	5	5	6	2	8	5	80	82	.494	2.5
Montreal	9	8	6	...	9	13	6	4	6	5	7	6	79	83	.488	3.5
Chicago	10	9	6	9	...	10	5	8	6	5	7	2	77	84	.478	5
Philadelphia	9	9	8	5	8	...	6	4	5	3	9	5	71	91	.438	11.5

West Division

Team	Cin.	L.A.	S.F.	Hou.	Atl.	S.D.	Chi.	Mon.	N.Y.	Phi.	Pit.	St.L.	W	L	Pct.	GB
Cincinnati	...	11	10	11	13	13	4	8	8	8	7	6	99	63	.611	...
Los Angeles	7	...	9	7	15	9	7	7	7	9	10	8	95	66	.590	3.5
San Fran.	8	9	...	7	10	11	10	6	7	7	7	6	88	74	.543	11
Houston	7	11	11	...	7	10	6	6	6	7	6	5	82	80	.506	17
Atlanta	5	2	8	11	...	12	7	6	6	6	7	6	76	85	.472	22.5
San Diego	5	9	7	8	6	...	5	5	4	3	4	4	60	102	.370	39

SIGNIFICANT EVENTS

■ **January 3:** An investment group headed by shipbuilder George Steinbrenner purchased the Yankees from CBS for $10 million.

■ **February 25:** Owners and players approved a three-year Basic Agreement that included binding arbitration and modifications of the controversial reserve clause.

■ **April 6:** The A.L. began its designated hitter experiment when Yankee Ron Blomberg drew a first-inning walk in a game at Boston's Fenway Park.

■ **April 10:** New Royals Stadium received a rousing welcome when Kansas City pounded Texas, 12-1.

MEMORABLE MOMENTS

■ **July 15:** Angels ace Nolan Ryan held Detroit hitless in a 6-0 victory, becoming the fourth pitcher to throw two no-hitters in one season.

■ **July 21:** Atlanta's Hank Aaron inched closer to Babe Ruth's all-time record when he belted homer No. 700 off Philadelphia's Ken Brett in an 8-4 loss.

■ **September 28:** Ryan struck out 16 Twins in his final start, raising his record season strikeout total to 383.

■ **October 1:** The Mets posted a final-day 6-4 victory over Chicago and clinched the N.L. East championship with an 82-79 record.

LEADERS

American League
BA: Rod Carew, Min., .350.
Runs: Reggie Jackson, Oak., 99.
Hits: Rod Carew, Min., 203.
TB: Sal Bando, Oak.; Dave May, Mil.; George Scott, Mil., 295.
HR: Reggie Jackson, Oak., 32.
RBI: Reggie Jackson, Oak., 117.
SB: Tommy Harper, Bos., 54.
Wins: Wilbur Wood, Chi., 24.
ERA: Jim Palmer, Bal., 2.40.
CG: Gaylord Perry, Cle., 29.
IP: Wilbur Wood, Chi., 359.1.
SO: Nolan Ryan, Cal., 383.
SV: John Hiller, Det., 38.

National League
BA: Pete Rose, Cin., .338.
Runs: Bobby Bonds, S.F., 131.
Hits: Pete Rose, Cin., 230.
TB: Bobby Bonds, S.F., 341.
HR: Willie Stargell, Pit., 44.
RBI: Willie Stargell, Pit., 119.
SB: Lou Brock, St.L., 70.
Wins: Ron Bryant, S.F., 24.
ERA: Tom Seaver, N.Y., 2.08.
CG: Steve Carlton, Phil.; Tom Seaver, N.Y., 18.
IP: Jack Billingham, Cin.; Steve Carlton, Phil., 293.1.
SO: Tom Seaver, N.Y., 251.
SV: Mike Marshall, Mon., 31.

A.L. 20-game winners
Wilbur Wood, Chi., 24-20
Joe Coleman, Det., 23-15
Jim Palmer, Bal., 22-9
Catfish Hunter, Oak., 21-5
Ken Holtzman, Oak., 21-13
Nolan Ryan, Cal., 21-16
Vida Blue, Oak., 20-9
Paul Splittorff, K.C., 20-11
Jim Colborn, Mil., 20-12
Luis Tiant, Bos., 20-13
Bill Singer, Cal., 20-14
Bert Blyleven, Min., 20-17

N.L. 20-game winners
Ron Bryant, S.F., 24-12

A.L. 100 RBIs
Reggie Jackson, Oak., 117
George Scott, Mil., 107
John Mayberry, K.C., 100

N.L. 100 RBIs
Willie Stargell, Pit., 119
Lee May, Hou., 105
Johnny Bench, Cin., 104
Darrell Evans, Atl., 104
Ken Singleton, Mon., 103
Tony Perez, Cin., 101

N.L. 40 homers
Willie Stargell, Pit., 44
Dave Johnson, Atl., 43
Darrell Evans, Atl., 41
Hank Aaron, Atl., 40

Most Valuable Player
A.L.: Reggie Jackson, OF, Oak.
N.L.: Pete Rose, OF, Cin.

Cy Young Award
A.L.: Jim Palmer, Bal.
N.L.: Tom Seaver, N.Y.

Rookie of the Year
A.L.: Al Bumbry, OF, Bal.
N.L.: Gary Matthews, OF, S.F.

Hall of Fame additions
Roberto Clemente, OF, 1955-72
Billy Evans, umpire
Monte Irvin, OF, 1949-56
George Kelly, 1B, 1915-32
Warren Spahn, P, 1942-65
Mickey Welch, P, 1880-92

ALL-STAR GAME

■ **Winners:** Johnny Bench, Bobby Bonds and Willie Davis powered the N.L. to its 10th All-Star victory in 11 years in the 40th anniversary of the midsummer classic.
■ **Key innings:** The fourth, fifth and sixth, when the N.L.'s Big Three hit home runs that accounted for five runs.
■ **Memorable moment:** An eighth-inning strikeout by pinch-hitter Willie Mays, who was making his 24th and final appearance in the baseball classic he had dominated like no other player.
■ **Top guns:** Bonds (Giants), Bench (Reds), Davis (Dodgers), N.L.; Amos Otis (Royals), A.L.
■ **MVP:** Bonds.

Linescore
July 24, at Kansas City's Royals Stadium
N.L. ....0 0 2 1 2 2 0 0 0—7 10 0
A.L. ....0 1 0 0 0 0 0 0 0—1 5 0
Wise (Cardinals), Osteen (Dodgers) 3, Sutton (Dodgers) 5, Twitchell (Phillies) 6, Giusti (Pirates) 7, Seaver (Mets) 8, Brewer (Dodgers) 9; Hunter (Athletics), Holtzman (Athletics) 2, Blyleven (Twins) 3, Singer (Angels) 4, Ryan (Angels) 6, Lyle (Yankees) 8, Fingers (Athletics) 9. W—Wise. L—Blyleven. HR—Bench, Bonds, Davis, N.L.

ALCS

■ **Winner:** The Athletics earned their second consecutive pennant and the Orioles lost their first ALCS after three previous sweeps.
■ **Turning point:** An 11th-inning Game 3 home run by Bert Campaneris that broke up a pitching duel between Oakland's Ken Holtzman and Baltimore's Mike Cuellar. The 2-1 victory gave the A's a 2-1 series advantage.
■ **Memorable moment:** A game-tying three-run seventh-inning home run by catcher Andy Etchebarren that kept Baltimore's hopes alive in Game 4. The Orioles won, 5-4, and forced a fifth game.
■ **Top guns:** Catfish Hunter (2-0, 1.65 ERA), Vic Davalillo (.625), Campaneris (.333, 2 HR), Athletics; Etchebarren (.357, 4 RBIs), Orioles.
■ **MVP:** Hunter.

Linescores

Game 1—October 6, at Baltimore
Oak. ....0 0 0 0 0 0 0 0 0—0 5 1
Balt. ....4 0 0 0 0 0 1 1 x—6 12 0
Blue, Pina (1), Odom (3), Fingers (8); Palmer. W—Palmer. L—Blue.

Game 2—October 7, at Baltimore
Oak. ....1 0 0 0 0 2 0 2 1—6 9 0
Balt. ....1 0 0 0 0 1 0 1 0—3 8 0
Hunter, Fingers (8); McNally, Reynolds (8), G. Jackson (9). W—Hunter. L—McNally. S—Fingers. HR—Campaneris, Rudi, Bando 2 (Oak.).

Game 3—October 9, at Oakland
Balt. ....0 1 0 0 0 0 0 0 0 0 0—1 3 0
Oak. ....0 0 0 0 0 0 0 1 0 0 1—2 4 3
Cuellar; Holtzman. W—Holtzman. L—Cuellar. HR—Williams (Bal.); Campaneris (Oak.).

Game 4—October 10, at Oakland
Balt. ....0 0 0 0 0 0 4 1 0—5 8 0
Oak. ....0 3 0 0 0 1 0 0 0—4 7 0
Palmer, Reynolds (2), Watt (7), G. Jackson (7); Blue, Fingers (7). W—G. Jackson. L—Fingers. HR—Etchebarren, Grich (Bal.).

Game 5—October 11, at Oakland
Balt. ....0 0 0 0 0 0 0 0 0—0 5 2
Oak. ....0 0 1 2 0 0 0 0 x—3 7 0
Alexander, Palmer (4); Hunter. W—Hunter. L—Alexander.

NLCS

■ **Winner:** The New York Mets captured their second pennant in five years and kept Cincinnati from repeating as N.L. champion.
■ **Turning point:** New York's 9-2 Game 3 victory that was spiced by a fifth-inning fight between Mets shortstop Bud Harrelson and Cincinnati leftfielder Pete Rose. Reds manager Sparky Anderson had to temporarily pull his team from the field in the next half inning when fans began pelting Rose with garbage and other debris.
■ **Memorable moment:** Rose's 12th-inning Game 4 home run that kept the Reds alive and forced a fifth game.
■ **Top guns:** Jon Matlack (1-0, 0.00 ERA), Felix Millan (.316), Rusty Staub (3 HR, 5 RBIs), Mets; Rose (.381, 2 HR), Reds.
■ **MVP:** Staub.

Linescores

Game 1—October 6, at Cincinnati
N.Y. ....0 1 0 0 0 0 0 0 0—1 3 0
Cin. ....0 0 0 0 0 0 0 1 1—2 6 0
Seaver; Billingham, Hall (9), Borbon (9). W—Borbon. L—Seaver. HR—Rose, Bench (Cin.).

Game 2—October 7, at Cincinnati
N.Y. ....0 0 0 1 0 0 0 0 4—5 7 0
Cin. ....0 0 0 0 0 0 0 0 0—0 2 0
Matlack; Gullett, Carroll (6), Hall (9), Borbon (9). W—Matlack. L—Gullett. HR—Staub (N.Y.).

Game 3—October 8, at New York
Cin. ....0 0 2 0 0 0 0 0 0—2 8 1
N.Y. ....1 5 1 2 0 0 0 0 x—9 11 1
Grimsley, Hall (2), Tomlin (3), Nelson (4), Borbon (7); Koosman. W—Koosman. L—Grimsley. HR—Staub 2 (N.Y.); Menke (Cin.).

Game 4—October 9, at New York
Cin.......0 0 0 0 0 0 1 0 0 0 0 1—2 8 0
N.Y.......0 0 1 0 0 0 0 0 0 0 0 0—1 3 2
Norman, Gullett (6), Carroll (10), Borbon (12); Stone, McGraw (7), Parker (12). W—Carroll. L—Parker. S—Borbon. HR—Perez, Rose (Cin.).

Game 5—October 10, at New York
Cin. ....0 0 1 0 1 0 0 0 0—2 7 1
N.Y. ....2 0 0 0 4 1 0 0 x—7 13 1
Billingham, Gullett (5), Carroll (5), Grimsley (7); Seaver, McGraw (9). W—Seaver. L—Billingham. S—McGraw.

WORLD SERIES

■ **Winner:** The Athletics made it two in a row with a seven-game scramble against the resilient Mets.
■ **Turning point:** In a valiant Game 6 performance that staved off elimination, the A's prevailed 3-1 behind Catfish Hunter's pitching and the two-RBI hitting of Reggie Jackson.
■ **Memorable moment:** The "firing" of A's second baseman Mike Andrews by owner Charles O. Finley. Andrews' two 12th-inning errors in Game 2 enabled the Mets to post a 10-7 victory.
■ **Top guns:** Joe Rudi (.333), Jackson (.310, 6 RBIs), Athletics; Rusty Staub (.423, 6 RBIs), Mets.
■ **MVP:** Jackson.

Linescores

Game 1—October 13, at Oakland
N.Y. ....0 0 0 1 0 0 0 0 0—1 7 2
Oak. ....0 0 2 0 0 0 0 0 x—2 4 0
Matlack, McGraw (7); Holtzman, Fingers (6), Knowles (9). W—Holtzman. L—Matlack. S—Knowles.

Game 2—October 14, at Oakland
N.Y. ....0 1 1 0 0 4 0 0 0 0 0 4—10 15 1
Oak. ....2 1 0 0 0 0 1 0 2 0 0 1— 7 13 5
Koosman, Sadecki (3), Parker (5), McGraw (6), Stone (12); Blue, Pina (6), Knowles (6), Odom (8), Fingers (10), Lindblad (12). W—McGraw. L—Fingers. S—Stone. HR—Jones, Garrett (N.Y.).

Game 3—October 16, at New York
Oak. ....0 0 0 0 0 1 0 1 0 0 1—3 10 1
N.Y. ....2 0 0 0 0 0 0 0 0 0 0—2 10 2
Hunter, Knowles (7), Lindblad (9), Fingers (11); Seaver, Sadecki (9), McGraw (9), Parker (11). W—Lindblad. L—Parker. S—Fingers. HR—Garrett (N.Y.).

Game 4—October 17, at New York
Oak. ....0 0 0 1 0 0 0 0 0—1 5 1
N.Y. ....3 0 0 3 0 0 0 0 x—6 13 1
Holtzman, Odom (1), Knowles (4), Pina (5), Lindblad (8); Matlack, Sadecki (9). W—Matlack. L—Holtzman. S—Sadecki. HR—Staub (N.Y.).

Game 5—October 18, at New York
Oak. ....0 0 0 0 0 0 0 0 0—0 3 1
N.Y. ....0 1 0 0 0 1 0 0 x—2 7 1
Blue, Knowles (6), Fingers (7); Koosman, McGraw (7). W—Koosman. L—Blue. S—McGraw.

Game 6—October 20, at Oakland
N.Y. ....0 0 0 0 0 0 0 1 0—1 6 2
Oak. ....1 0 1 0 0 0 0 1 x—3 7 0
Seaver, McGraw (8); Hunter, Knowles (8), Fingers (8). W—Hunter. L—Seaver. S—Fingers.

Game 7—October 21, at Oakland
N.Y. ....0 0 0 0 0 1 0 0 1—2 8 1
Oak. ....0 0 4 0 1 0 0 0 x—5 9 1
Matlack, Parker (3), Sadecki (5), Stone (7); Holtzman, Fingers (6), Knowles (9). W—Holtzman. L—Matlack. S—Knowles. HR—Campaneris, Jackson (Oak.).

FINAL STANDINGS

American League

East Division

Team	Bal.	N.Y.	Bos.	Cle.	Mil.	Det.	Cal.	Chi.	K.C.	Min.	Oak.	Tex.	W	L	Pct.	GB
Baltimore	...	11	10	12	8	14	7	5	8	6	6	4	91	71	.562	...
New York	7	...	7	11	9	7	9	8	8	8	7	8	89	73	.549	2
Boston	8	11	...	9	10	11	4	8	4	6	8	5	84	78	.519	7
Cleveland	6	7	9	...	10	9	9	4	8	6	5	4	77	85	.475	14
Milwaukee	10	9	8	8	..	9	9	4	1	6	5	7	76	86	.469	15
Detroit	4	11	7	9	9	...	7	5	7	3	5	5	72	90	.444	19

West Division

Team	Oak.	Tex.	Min.	Chi.	K.C.	Cal.	Bal.	Bos.	Cle.	Det.	Mil.	N.Y.	W	L	Pct.	GB
Oakland	...	8	13	11	10	12	6	4	7	7	7	5	90	72	.556	...
Texas	10	...	9	7	10	9	8	7	8	7	5	4	84	76	.525	5
Minnesota	5	9	...	11	10	10	6	6	6	9	6	4	82	80	.506	8
Chicago	7	9	7	...	11	8	7	4	8	7	8	4	80	80	.500	9
Kansas City	8	8	8	7	...	10	4	8	4	5	11	4	77	85	.475	13
California	6	9	8	10	8	...	5	8	3	5	3	3	68	94	.420	22

National League

East Division

Team	Pit.	St.L.	Phi.	Mon.	N.Y.	Chi.	Atl.	Cin.	Hou.	L.A.	S.D.	S.F.	W	L	Pct.	GB
Pittsburgh	...	7	8	9	11	9	8	4	7	8	9	8	88	74	.543	...
St. Louis	11	...	9	9	12	13	3	6	4	6	7	6	86	75	.534	1.5
Philadelphia	10	9	...	7	11	10	4	4	6	6	5	8	80	82	.494	8
Montreal	9	8	11	...	9	13	3	6	6	4	6	4	79	82	.491	8.5
New York	7	6	7	9	...	10	4	3	6	7	6	6	71	91	.438	17
Chicago	9	5	8	5	8	...	8	5	4	2	6	6	66	96	.407	22

West Division

Team	L.A.	Cin.	Atl.	Hou.	S.F.	S.D.	Chi.	Mon.	N.Y.	Phi.	Pit.	St.L.	W	L	Pct.	GB
Los Angeles	...	12	10	13	12	16	10	8	5	6	4	6	102	60	.630	...
Cincinnati	6	...	11	14	11	12	7	6	9	8	8	6	98	64	.605	4
Atlanta	8	7	...	6	8	17	4	9	8	8	4	9	88	74	.543	14
Houston	5	4	12	...	10	11	8	6	6	6	5	8	81	81	.500	21
San Fran.	6	7	10	8	...	7	6	8	6	4	4	6	72	90	.444	30
San Diego	2	6	1	7	11	...	6	6	6	7	3	5	60	102	.370	42

SIGNIFICANT EVENTS

- **January 1:** Lee MacPhail took the reins as A.L. president, succeeding retiring Joe Cronin.
- **February 11:** Baseball's first arbitration hearing was decided in favor of Twins pitcher Dick Woodson.
- **October 3:** The Indians crossed another color barrier when they named Frank Robinson as baseball's first black manager and the game's first player-manager since 1959.
- **November 2:** The Braves honored the request of home run king Hank Aaron when they traded him to Milwaukee, the city where he started his career in 1954.
- **November 6:** Mike Marshall, who appeared in a record 106 games for the Dodgers, became the first relief pitcher to earn a Cy Young Award.
- **December 31:** The Yankees won the most celebrated free-agent chase in history when they signed former Oakland ace Catfish Hunter to a five-year, $3.75-million contract.

MEMORABLE MOMENTS

- **April 8:** Atlanta's Hank Aaron overtook Babe Ruth as baseball's all-time greatest slugger when he connected off Al Downing for record home run No. 715 in a 7-4 victory over the Dodgers.
- **July 17:** Bob Gibson became the second pitcher to reach 3,000 strikeouts when he fanned Cincinnati's Cesar Geronimo in a game at St. Louis.
- **August 12:** California's Nolan Ryan tied the single-game record when he struck out 19 Red Sox in a 4-2 victory.
- **September 24:** Al Kaline doubled off Baltimore's Dave McNally for hit No. 3,000 in Detroit's 5-4 loss.
- **September 29:** St. Louis speedster Lou Brock swiped his record 118th base in a 7-3 victory over the Cubs.
- **October 1:** The Orioles, who finished the season on a 28-6 run, clinched the A.L. East with a 7-6 victory over the Tigers.

LEADERS

American League
BA: Rod Carew, Min., .364.
Runs: Carl Yastrzemski, Bos., 93.
Hits: Rod Carew, Min., 218.
TB: Joe Rudi, Oak., 287.
HR: Dick Allen, Chi., 32.
RBI: Jeff Burroughs, Tex., 118.
SB: Bill North, Oak., 54.
Wins: Catfish Hunter, Oak.; Ferguson Jenkins, Tex., 25.
ERA: Catfish Hunter, Oak., 2.49.
CG: Ferguson Jenkins, Tex., 29.
IP: Nolan Ryan, Cal., 332.2.
SO: Nolan Ryan, Cal., 367.
SV: Terry Forster, Chi., 24.

National League
BA: Ralph Garr, Atl., .353.
Runs: Pete Rose, Cin., 110.
Hits: Ralph Garr, Atl., 214.
TB: Johnny Bench, Cin., 315.
HR: Mike Schmidt, Phil., 36.
RBI: Johnny Bench, Cin., 129.
SB: Lou Brock, St.L., 118.
Wins: Andy Messersmith, L.A.; Phil Niekro, Atl., 20.
ERA: Buzz Capra, Atl., 2.28.
CG: Phil Niekro, Atl., 18.
IP: Phil Niekro, Atl., 302.1.
SO: Steve Carlton, Phil., 240.
SV: Mike Marshall, L.A., 21.

A.L. 20-game winners
Catfish Hunter, Oak., 25-12
Ferguson Jenkins, Tex., 25-12
Mike Cuellar, Bal., 22-10
Luis Tiant, Bos., 22-13
Steve Busby, K.C., 22-14
Nolan Ryan, Cal., 22-16
Jim Kaat, Chi., 21-13
Gaylord Perry, Cle., 21-13
Wilbur Wood, Chi., 20-19

N.L. 20-game winners
Andy Messersmith, L.A., 20-6
Phil Niekro, Atl., 20-13

A.L. 100 RBIs
Jeff Burroughs, Tex., 118
Sal Bando, Oak., 103

N.L. 100 RBIs
Johnny Bench, Cin., 129
Mike Schmidt, Phil., 116
Steve Garvey, L.A., 111
Jim Wynn, L.A., 108
Ted Simmons, St.L., 103
Cesar Cedeno, Hou., 102
Tony Perez, Cin., 101
Reggie Smith, St.L., 100
Richie Zisk, Pit., 100

Most Valuable Player
A.L.: Jeff Burroughs, OF, Tex.
N.L.: Steve Garvey, 1B, L.A.

Cy Young Award
A.L.: Catfish Hunter, Oak.
N.L.: Mike Marshall, L.A.

Rookie of the Year
A.L.: Mike Hargrove, 1B, Tex.
N.L.: Bake McBride, OF, St.L.

Hall of Fame additions
Cool Papa Bell, OF, Negro Leagues
Jim Bottomley, 1B, 1922-37
Jocko Conlan, umpire
Whitey Ford, P, 1950-67
Mickey Mantle, OF, 1951-68
Sam Thompson, OF, 1885-1906

ALL-STAR GAME

- **Winner:** The N.L. continued its amazing All-Star run with a 7-2 victory fashioned by five pitchers who had never worked in a mid-summer classic.
- **Key inning:** A two-run N.L. fourth, when Steve Garvey doubled home the tying run and the lead run scored on Ron Cey's groundout.
- **Memorable moment:** A third-inning diving stop by N.L. first baseman Garvey on a smash by Bobby Murcer. The play saved at least two A.L. runs and possibly the game.
- **Top guns:** Mike Marshall (Dodgers), Reggie Smith (Cardinals), Garvey (Dodgers), Cey (Dodgers), N.L.; Dick Allen (White Sox), A.L.
- **MVP:** Garvey.

Linescore
July 23, at Pittsburgh's Three Rivers Stadium
A.L. ....0 0 2 0 0 0 0 0 0—2 4 1
N.L. ....0 1 0 2 1 0 1 2 x—7 10 1
Perry (Indians), Tiant (Red Sox) 4, Hunter (Athletics) 6, Fingers (Athletics) 8; Messersmith (Dodgers), Brett (Pirates) 4, Matlack (Mets) 6, McGlothen (Cardinals) 7, Marshall (Dodgers) 8. W—Brett. L—Tiant. HR—Smith, N.L.

ALCS

- **Winner:** The Athletics needed only four games to earn their third consecutive A.L. pennant and second straight ALCS victory over Baltimore.
- **Turning point:** Oakland's 1-0 Game 3 victory, which was decided by a fourth-inning Sal Bando home run. A's lefty Vida Blue allowed only two hits and gave his team a 2-1 series advantage.
- **Memorable moment:** Reggie Jackson's seventh-inning double in Game 4. The A's only hit in a 2-1 series-ending victory drove in the winning run.
- **Top guns:** Blue (1-0, 0-00 ERA), Ken Holtzman (1-0, 0.00), Bando (2 HR), Athletics; Andy Etchebarren (.333), Orioles.
- **MVP:** Blue.

Linescores

Game 1—October 5, at Oakland
Baltimore ..1 0 0 1 4 0 0 0 0—6 10 0
Oakland......0 0 1 0 1 0 0 0 1—3 9 0
Cuellar, Grimsley (9); Hunter, Odom (5), Fingers (9). W—Cuellar. L—Hunter. HR—Blair, Robinson, Grich (Bal.).

Game 2—October 6, at Oakland
Baltimore ....0 0 0 0 0 0 0 0 0—0 5 2
Oakland........0 0 0 1 0 1 0 3 x—5 8 0
McNally, Garland (6), Reynolds (7), G. Jackson (8); Holtzman. W—Holtzman. L—McNally. HR—Bando, Fosse (Oak.).

Game 3—October 8, at Baltimore
Oakland........0 0 0 1 0 0 0 0 0—1 4 2
Baltimore ....0 0 0 0 0 0 0 0 0—0 2 1
Blue; Palmer. W—Blue. L—Palmer. HR—Bando (Oak.).

Game 4—October 9, at Baltimore
Oakland........0 0 0 0 1 0 1 0 0—2 1 0
Baltimore ....0 0 0 0 0 0 0 0 1—1 5 1
Hunter, Fingers (8); Cuellar, Grimsley (5). W—Hunter. L—Cuellar. S—Fingers.

NLCS

- **Winner:** Los Angeles, making its first Championship Series appearance, overpowered Pittsburgh and claimed its first pennant since 1966.
- **Turning point:** Pitchers Don Sutton, Andy Messersmith and Mike Marshall held the Pirates scoreless in 17 of the first 18 innings as the Dodgers forged a 2-0 series advantage.
- **Memorable moment:** The Game 4 performance of Los Angeles first baseman Steve Garvey, who collected four hits, belted two home runs and drove in four runs in a 12-1 series-ending victory.
- **Top guns:** Sutton (2-0, 0.53 ERA), Garvey (.389, 2 HR, 5 RBIs), Bill Russell (.389), Dodgers; Bruce Kison (1-0, 0.00), Willie Stargell (.400, 2 HR, 4 RBIs), Pirates.
- **MVP:** Sutton.

Linescores

Game 1—October 5, at Pittsburgh
L.A. ....0 1 0 0 0 0 0 0 2—3 9 2
Pitt. ....0 0 0 0 0 0 0 0 0—0 4 0
Sutton; Reuss, Giusti (8). W—Sutton. L—Reuss.

Game 2—October 6, at Pittsburgh
L.A. ....1 0 0 1 0 0 0 3 0—5 12 0
Pitt. ....0 0 0 0 0 0 2 0 0—2 8 3
Messersmith, Marshall (8); Rooker, Giusti (8), Demery (8), Hernandez (8). W—Messersmith. L—Giusti. HR—Cey (L.A.).

Game 3—October 8, at Los Angeles
Pitt. ....5 0 2 0 0 0 0 0 0—7 10 0
L.A. ....0 0 0 0 0 0 0 0 0—0 4 5
Kison, Hernandez (7); Rau, Hough (1), Downing (4), Solomon (8). W—Kison. L—Rau. HR—Stargell, Hebner (Pit.).

Game 4—October 9, at Los Angeles
Pitt. ....0 0 0 0 0 0 1 0 0— 1 3 1
L.A. ....1 0 2 0 2 2 2 3 x—12 12 0
Reuss, Brett (3), Demery (6), Giusti (7), Pizarro (8); Sutton, Marshall (9). W—Sutton. L—Reuss. HR—Garvey 2 (L.A.); Stargell (Pit.).

WORLD SERIES

- **Winner:** Manager Alvin Dark's Athletics, who had won the previous two years under Dick Williams, became only the second team to win three consecutive World Series.
- **Turning point:** The A's 5-2 Game 4 victory, which featured a home run by pitcher Ken Holtzman, who had not batted all season because of the A.L.'s designated hitter rule.
- **Memorable moment:** Joe Rudi's tie-breaking solo home run off Dodger ironman reliever Mike Marshall in the seventh inning of Game 5.
- **Top guns:** Rollie Fingers (1-0, 2 saves, 1.93 ERA), Holtzman (1-0, 1.50, 1 HR), Rudi (.333, 4 RBIs), A's; Steve Garvey (.381), Dodgers.
- **MVP:** Fingers.

Linescores

Game 1—October 12, at Los Angeles
Oakland......0 1 0 0 1 0 0 1 0—3 6 2
L.A. ....0 0 0 0 1 0 0 0 1—2 11 1
Holtzman, Fingers (5), Hunter (9); Messersmith, Marshall (9). W—Fingers. L—Messersmith. S—Hunter. HR—Jackson (Oak.); Wynn (L.A.).

Game 2—October 13, at Los Angeles
Oakland........0 0 0 0 0 0 0 0 2—2 6 0
L.A. ....0 1 0 0 0 2 0 0 x—3 6 1
Blue, Odom (8); Sutton, Marshall (9). W—Sutton. L—Blue. S—Marshall. HR—Ferguson (L.A.).

Game 3—October 15, at Oakland
L.A. ....0 0 0 0 0 0 0 1 1—2 7 2
Oakland........0 0 2 1 0 0 0 0 x—3 5 2
Downing, Brewer (4), Hough (5), Marshall (7); Hunter, Fingers (8). W—Hunter. L—Downing. S—Fingers. HR—Buckner, Crawford (L.A.).

Game 4—October 16, at Oakland
L.A. ....0 0 0 2 0 0 0 0 0—2 7 1
Oakland........0 0 1 0 0 4 0 0 x—5 7 0
Messersmith, Marshall (7); Holtzman, Fingers (8). W—Holtzman. L—Messersmith. S—Fingers. HR—Holtzman.

Game 5—October 17, at Oakland
L.A. ....0 0 0 0 0 2 0 0 0—2 5 1
Oakland........1 1 0 0 0 0 1 0 x—3 6 1
Sutton, Marshall (6); Blue, Odom (7), Fingers (8). W—Odom. L—Marshall. S—Fingers. HR—Fosse, Rudi (Oak.).

1975

FINAL STANDINGS

American League

East Division

Team	Bos.	Bal.	N.Y.	Cle.	Mil.	Det.	Cal.	Chi.	K.C.	Min.	Oak.	Tex.	W	L	Pct.	GB
Boston	...	9	11	7	10	13	6	8	7	10	6	8	95	65	.594	...
Baltimore	9	...	8	10	14	12	6	7	7	6	4	7	90	69	.566	4.5
New York	5	10	...	9	9	12	5	6	5	8	6	8	83	77	.519	12
Cleveland	11	8	9	...	9	12	9	5	6	3	2	5	79	80	.497	15.5
Milwaukee	8	4	9	9	...	11	5	4	5	2	5	6	68	94	.420	28
Detroit	5	4	6	6	7	...	5	7	6	4	6	1	57	102	.358	37.5

West Division

Team	Oak.	K.C.	Tex.	Min.	Chi.	Cal.	Bal.	Bos.	Cle.	Det.	Mil.	N.Y.	W	L	Pct.	GB
Oakland	...	11	12	12	9	11	8	6	10	6	7	6	98	64	.605	...
Kansas City	7	...	14	11	9	14	5	5	6	6	7	7	91	71	.562	7
Texas	6	4	...	10	13	9	5	4	7	11	6	4	79	83	.488	19
Minnesota	6	7	8	...	9	10	6	2	6	8	10	4	76	83	.478	20.5
Chicago	9	9	5	9	...	9	4	4	7	5	8	6	75	86	.466	22.5
California	7	4	9	8	9	...	6	6	3	6	7	7	72	89	.447	25.5

National League

East Division

Team	Pit.	Phi.	N.Y.	St.L.	Chi.	Mon.	Atl.	Cin.	Hou.	L.A.	S.D.	S.F.	W	L	Pct.	GB
Pittsburgh	...	7	13	10	12	11	8	6	5	7	8	5	92	69	.571	...
Philadelphia	11	...	11	10	6	11	7	5	6	5	7	7	86	76	.531	6.5
New York	5	7	...	9	11	8	8	4	8	6	8	8	82	80	.506	10.5
St. Louis	8	8	9	...	7	7	9	4	8	7	8	7	82	80	.506	10.5
Chicago	6	12	7	11	...	9	7	1	7	5	5	5	75	87	.463	17.5
Montreal	7	7	10	11	9	...	4	4	4	7	7	5	75	87	.463	17.5

West Division

Team	Cin.	L.A.	S.F.	S.D.	Atl.	Hou.	Chi.	Mon.	N.Y.	Phi.	Pit.	St.L.	W	L	Pct.	GB
Cincinnati	...	8	13	11	15	13	11	8	8	7	6	8	108	54	.667	...
L.A.	10	...	10	11	10	12	7	5	6	7	5	5	88	74	.543	20
San Fran.	5	8	...	10	9	13	7	7	4	5	7	5	80	81	.497	27.5
San Diego	7	7	8	...	11	9	7	5	4	5	4	4	71	91	.438	37
Atlanta	3	8	8	7	...	12	5	8	4	5	4	3	67	94	.416	40.5
Houston	5	6	5	9	6	...	5	8	4	6	6	4	64	97	.398	43.5

SIGNIFICANT EVENTS

■ **January 5:** Houston righthander Don Wilson died of carbon monoxide poisoning in the garage of his Houston home, an apparent suicide victim at age 29.

■ **November 26:** Boston's Fred Lynn became the first rookie MVP winner in baseball history.

■ **December 23:** Baseball's reserve system was shattered when labor arbitrator Peter Seitz handed pitchers Andy Messersmith and Dave McNally their unqualified free agency.

MEMORABLE MOMENTS

■ **April 8:** Frank Robinson belted a dramatic home run and led the Indians to a 5-3 Opening Day victory over the Yankees in his historic debut as baseball's first black manager.

■ **May 1:** Milwaukee's Hank Aaron drove in two runs in a 17-3 victory over Detroit and became baseball's all-time RBI leader with 2,211.

■ **June 1:** California's Nolan Ryan tied Sandy Koufax's record when he pitched his fourth career no-hitter, a 1-0 victory over the Orioles.

■ **June 18:** Boston rookie Fred Lynn drove in 10 runs with three home runs, a triple and a single in a 15-1 victory over the Tigers.

■ **September 16:** Pirates second baseman Rennie Stennett became the first modern-era player to collect seven hits in a nine-inning game—a 22-0 victory over the Cubs.

■ **September 28:** Oakland's Vida Blue, Glenn Abbott, Paul Lindblad and Rollie Fingers combined for the first multi-pitcher no-hitter in baseball history—a final-day 5-0 victory over the Angels.

LEADERS

American League
BA: Rod Carew, Min., .359.
Runs: Fred Lynn, Bos., 103.
Hits: George Brett, K.C., 195.
TB: George Scott, Mil., 318.
HR: Reggie Jackson, Oak.; George Scott, Mil., 36.
RBI: George Scott, Mil., 109.
SB: Mickey Rivers, Cal., 70.
Wins: Catfish Hunter, N.Y.; Jim Palmer, Bal., 23.
ERA: Jim Palmer, Bal., 2.09.
CG: Catfish Hunter, N.Y., 30.
IP: Catfish Hunter, N.Y., 328.
SO: Frank Tanana, Cal., 269.
SV: Goose Gossage, Chi., 26.

National League
BA: Bill Madlock, Chi., .354.
Runs: Pete Rose, Cin., 112.
Hits: Dave Cash, Phil., 213.
TB: Greg Luzinski, Phil., 322.
HR: Mike Schmidt, Phil., 38.
RBI: Greg Luzinski, Phil., 120.
SB: Dave Lopes, L.A., 77.
Wins: Tom Seaver, N.Y., 22.
ERA: Randy Jones, S.D., 2.24.
CG: Andy Messersmith, L.A., 19.
IP: Andy Messersmith, L.A., 321.2.
SO: Tom Seaver, N.Y., 243.
SV: Rawly Eastwick, Cin.; Al Hrabosky, St.L., 22.

A.L. 20-game winners
Jim Palmer, Bal., 23-11
Catfish Hunter, N.Y., 23-14
Vida Blue, Oak., 22-11
Mike Torrez, Bal., 20-9
Jim Kaat, Chi., 20-14

N.L. 20-game winners
Tom Seaver, N.Y., 22-9
Randy Jones, S.D., 20-12

A.L. 100 RBIs
George Scott, Mil., 109
John Mayberry, K.C., 106
Fred Lynn, Bos., 105
Reggie Jackson, Oak., 104
Thurman Munson, N.Y., 102
Jim Rice, Bos., 102

N.L. 100 RBIs
Greg Luzinski, Phil., 120
Johnny Bench, Cin., 110
Tony Perez, Cin., 109
Rusty Staub, N.Y., 105
Ron Cey, L.A., 101
Willie Montanez, Phil.-S.F., 101
Dave Parker, Pit., 101
Ted Simmons, St.L., 100

Most Valuable Player
A.L.: Fred Lynn, OF, Bos.
N.L.: Joe Morgan, 2B, Cin.

Cy Young Award
A.L.: Jim Palmer, Bal.
N.L.: Tom Seaver, N.Y.

Rookie of the Year
A.L.: Fred Lynn, OF, Bos.
N.L.: John Montefusco, P, S.F.

Hall of Fame additions
Earl Averill, OF, 1929-41
Bucky Harris, manager
Billy Herman, 2B, 1931-47
Judy Johnson, 3B, Negro Leagues
Ralph Kiner, OF, 1946-55

ALL-STAR GAME

■ **Winner:** The N.L., having uncharacteristically squandered a 3-0 lead, scored three ninth-inning runs and escaped with a 6-3 victory, its 12th in 13 years.

■ **Key inning:** The ninth, when Bill Madlock delivered the big blow with a two-run single and Pete Rose added an insurance run with a sacrifice fly.

■ **Memorable moment:** A long sixth-inning three-run homer by Carl Yastrzemski that wiped away the 3-0 deficit and gave the A.L. brief hope for a victory.

■ **Top guns:** Steve Garvey (Dodgers), Jim Wynn (Dodgers), Rose (Reds), Madlock (Cubs), N.L.; Yastrzemski (Red Sox), Bert Campaneris (Athletics), A.L.

■ **MVP:** Madlock.

Linescore
July 15, at Milwaukee's County Stadium
N.L.............0 2 1 0 0 0 0 0 3—6 13 1
A.L.............0 0 0 0 0 3 0 0 0—3 10 1
Reuss (Pirates), Sutton (Dodgers) 4, Seaver (Mets) 6, Matlack (Mets) 7, Jones (Padres) 9; Blue (Athletics), Busby (Royals) 3, Kaat (White Sox) 5, Hunter (Yankees) 7, Gossage (White Sox) 9. W—Matlack. L—Hunter. HR—Garvey, Wynn, N.L.; Yastrzemski, A.L.

ALCS

■ **Winner:** The Boston Red Sox brought a surprising end to Oakland's three-year championship reign and made it look as easy as 1-2-3.

■ **Turning point:** Oakland's four-error first-game performance that helped Boston to a 7-1 victory and set the tone for the series.

■ **Memorable moment:** Reggie Jackson's first-inning Game 2 home run, which gave Oakland its only lead of the series.

■ **Top guns:** Luis Tiant (1-0, 0.00 ERA), Carl Yastrzemski (.455), Rick Burleson (.444), Carlton Fisk (.417), Red Sox; Sal Bando (.500), Jackson (.417), Athletics.

■ **MVP:** Yastrzemski.

Linescores

Game 1—October 4, at Boston
Oakland........0 0 0 0 0 0 0 1 0—1 3 4
Boston ....2 0 0 0 0 0 5 0 x—7 8 3
Holtzman, Todd (7), Lindblad (7), Bosman (7), Abbott (8); Tiant. W—Tiant. L—Holtzman.

Game 2—October 5, at Boston
Oakland......2 0 0 1 0 0 0 0 0—3 10 0
Boston ......0 0 0 3 0 1 1 1 x—6 12 0
Blue, Todd (4), Fingers (5); Cleveland, Moret (6), Drago (7). W—Moret. L—Fingers. S—Drago. HR—Jackson (Oak.); Yastrzemski, Petrocelli (Bos.)

Game 3—October 7, at Oakland
Boston ......0 0 0 1 3 0 0 1 0—5 11 1
Oakland......0 0 0 0 0 1 0 2 0—3 6 2
Wise, Drago (8); Holtzman, Todd (5), Lindblad (5). W—Wise. L—Holtzman. S—Drago.

NLCS

■ **Winner:** Cincinnati's Big Red Machine rolled over Pittsburgh in a quick and easy Championship Series.

■ **Turning point:** Reds pitcher Don Gullett hit a homer, drove in three runs and pitched an eight-hit, first-game victory.

■ **Memorable moment:** A two-run eighth-inning home run by Cincinnati's Pete Rose erased a 2-1, Game 3 deficit in a contest eventually won by the Reds in 10 innings, 5-3.

■ **Top guns:** Gullett (1-0, 1 HR, 3 RBIs), Dave Concepcion (.455), Tony Perez (.417, 4 RBIs), Reds; Richie Zisk (.500), Pirates.

■ **MVP:** Gullett.

Linescores

Game 1—October 4, at Cincinnati
Pitt.............0 2 0 0 0 0 0 0 1—3 8 0
Cin. ....0 1 3 0 4 0 0 0 x—8 11 0
Reuss, Brett (3), Demery (5), Ellis (7); Gullett. W—Gullett. L—Reuss. HR—Gullett (Cin.).

Game 2—October 5, at Cincinnati
Pitt.............0 0 0 1 0 0 0 0 0—1 5 0
Cin. ....2 0 0 2 0 1 1 0 x—6 12 1
Rooker, Tekulve (5), Brett (6), Kison (7); Norman, Eastwick (7). W—Norman. L—Rooker. S—Eastwick. HR—Perez (Cin.).

Game 3—October 7, at Pittsburgh
Cin. ....0 1 0 0 0 0 0 2 0 2—5 6 0
Pitt..........0 0 0 0 0 2 0 0 1 0—3 7 2
Nolan, Carroll (7), McEnaney (8), Eastwick (9), Borbon (10); Candelaria, Giusti (8), Hernandez (10), Tekulve (10). W—Eastwick. L—Hernandez. S—Borbon. HR—Concepcion, Rose (Cin.); Oliver (Pit.).

WORLD SERIES

■ **Winner:** Cincinnati's Big Red Machine held off the gritty Red Sox in one of the most exciting Series in baseball history.

■ **Turning point:** Reds second baseman Joe Morgan's Series-deciding single in the ninth inning of Game 7. The Series was that close.

■ **Memorable moments:** In the Red Sox's 7-6 Game 6 victory: Boston pinch-hitter Bernie Carbo's game-tying, three-run homer in the eighth inning; Boston right fielder Dwight Evans' spectacular, leaping, 11th-inning catch that he turned into a rally-killing double play; Boston catcher Carlton Fisk's dramatic, game-ending, "fair-or-foul" home run in the 12th inning.

■ **Top guns:** Pete Rose (.370), Tony Perez (3 HR, 7 RBIs), Reds; Carbo (2 PH HR), Carl Yastrzemski (.310, 4 RBIs), Rico Petrocelli (.308, 4 RBIs), Red Sox.

■ **MVP:** Rose.

Linescores

Game 1—October 11, at Boston
Cin. ....0 0 0 0 0 0 0 0 0—0 5 0
Bos. ....0 0 0 0 0 0 6 0 x—6 12 0
Gullett, Carroll (7), McEnaney (7); Tiant. W—Tiant. L—Gullett.

Game 2—October 12, at Boston
Cin. ....0 0 0 1 0 0 0 0 2—3 7 1
Bos. ....1 0 0 0 0 1 0 0 0—2 7 0
Billingham, Borbon (6), McEnaney (7), Eastwick (8); Lee, Drago (9). W—Eastwick. L—Drago.

Game 3—October 14, at Cincinnati
Bos. ......0 1 0 0 0 1 1 0 2 0—5 10 2
Cin. ....0 0 0 2 3 0 0 0 0 1—6 7 0
Wise, Burton (5), Cleveland (5), Willoughby (7), Moret (10); Nolan, Darcy (5), Carroll (7), McEnaney (7), Eastwick (9). W—Eastwick. L—Willoughby. HR—Fisk, Carbo, Evans (Bos.); Bench, Concepcion, Geronimo (Cin.).

Game 4—October 15, at Cincinnati
Bos. ....0 0 0 5 0 0 0 0 0—5 11 1
Cin. ....2 0 0 2 0 0 0 0 0—4 9 1
Tiant; Norman, Borbon (4), Carroll (5), Eastwick (7). W—Tiant. L—Norman.

Game 5—October 16, at Cincinnati
Bos. ....1 0 0 0 0 0 0 0 1—2 5 0
Cin. ....0 0 0 1 1 3 0 1 x—6 8 0
Cleveland, Willoughby (6), Pole (8), Segui (8); Gullett, Eastwick (9). W—Gullett. L—Cleveland. S—Eastwick. HR—Perez 2 (Cin.).

Game 6—October 21, at Boston
Cin.....0 0 0 0 3 0 2 1 0 0 0 0—6 14 0
Bos. ..3 0 0 0 0 0 0 3 0 0 0 1—7 10 1
Nolan, Norman (3), Billingham (3), Carroll (5), Borbon (6), Eastwick (8), McEnaney (9), Darcy (10); Tiant, Moret (8), Drago (9), Wise (12). W—Wise. L—Darcy. HR—Lynn, Carbo, Fisk (Bos.); Geronimo (Cin.).

Game 7—October 22, at Boston
Cin. ....0 0 0 0 0 2 1 0 1—4 9 0
Bos. ....0 0 3 0 0 0 0 0 0—3 5 2
Gullett, Billingham (5), Carroll (7), McEnaney (9); Lee, Moret (7), Willoughby (7), Burton (9), Cleveland (9). W—Carroll. L—Burton. S—McEnaney. HR—Perez (Cin.).

FINAL STANDINGS

American League

East Division

Team	N.Y.	Bal.	Bos.	Cle.	Det.	Mil.	Cal.	Chi.	K.C.	Min.	Oak.	Tex.	W	L	Pct.	GB
New York	...	5	11	12	8	13	7	11	5	10	6	9	97	62	.610	...
Baltimore	13	...	7	7	12	11	8	8	6	4	4	8	88	74	.543	10.5
Boston	7	11	...	9	14	12	7	6	3	7	4	3	83	79	.512	15.5
Cleveland	4	11	9	...	6	11	5	9	6	9	4	7	81	78	.509	16
Detroit	9	6	4	12	...	12	6	6	4	4	6	5	74	87	.460	24
Milwaukee	5	7	6	6	6	...	8	5	4	4	5	10	66	95	.410	32

West Division

Team	K.C.	Oak.	Min.	Cal.	Tex.	Chi.	Bal.	Bos.	Cle.	Det.	Mil.	N.Y.	W	L	Pct.	GB
Kansas City	...	9	10	10	7	10	6	9	6	8	8	7	90	72	.556	...
Oakland	9	...	7	12	7	9	8	8	8	6	7	6	87	74	.540	2.5
Minnesota	8	11	...	10	11	11	8	5	3	8	8	2	85	77	.525	5
California	8	6	8	...	12	11	4	5	7	6	4	5	76	86	.469	14
Texas	11	11	7	6	...	11	4	9	5	7	2	3	76	86	.469	14
Chicago	8	8	7	7	7	...	4	6	3	6	7	1	64	97	.398	25.5

National League

East Division

Team	Phi.	Pit.	N.Y.	Chi.	St.L.	Mon.	Atl.	Cin.	Hou.	L.A.	S.D.	S.F.	W	L	Pct.	GB
Philadelphia	...	8	13	10	12	15	7	7	8	7	8	6	101	61	.623	...
Pittsburgh	10	...	8	10	12	10	9	4	10	3	7	9	92	70	.568	9
New York	5	10	...	13	9	10	8	6	6	5	7	7	86	76	.531	15
Chicago	8	8	5	...	12	11	6	3	5	3	6	8	75	87	.463	26
St. Louis	6	6	9	6	...	11	8	6	3	2	8	7	72	90	.444	29
Montreal	3	8	8	7	7	...	4	3	2	2	4	7	55	107	.340	46

West Division

Team	Cin.	L.A.	Hou.	S.F.	S.D.	Atl.	Chi.	Mon.	N.Y.	Phi.	Pit.	St.L.	W	L	Pct.	GB
Cincinnati	...	13	12	9	13	12	9	9	6	5	8	6	102	60	.630	...
L.A.	5	...	13	8	6	10	9	10	7	5	9	10	92	70	.568	10
Houston	6	5	...	10	10	11	7	10	6	4	2	9	80	82	.494	22
San Fran.	9	10	8	...	10	9	4	5	5	6	3	5	74	88	.457	28
San Diego	5	12	8	8	...	8	6	8	5	4	5	4	73	89	.451	29
Atlanta	6	8	7	9	10	...	6	8	4	5	3	4	70	92	.432	32

SIGNIFICANT EVENTS

■ **January 14:** N.L. owners approved the sale of the Braves to Ted Turner, head of Turner Communications, for $12 million.

■ **April 10:** Free-agent pitcher Andy Messersmith signed a "lifetime contract" to pitch for new Braves owner Turner.

■ **April 25:** Cubs center fielder Rick Monday dashed into left field at Dodger Stadium and snatched an American flag away from two protestors who were trying to set it on fire.

■ **June 18:** Commissioner Bowie Kuhn voided Oakland owner Charles O. Finley's sale of Vida Blue to the Yankees and Joe Rudi and Rollie Fingers to the Red Sox.

■ **September 29:** Walter Alston, who compiled 2,040 victories over 23 seasons as manager of the Dodgers, retired at age 64.

■ **November 5:** The A.L. conducted its third expansion draft to fill rosters of new teams in Seattle and Toronto.

■ **November 6:** Reliever Bill Campbell, one of the plums of baseball's first free-agent reentry draft, signed a four-year, $1 million contract with the Red Sox.

MEMORABLE MOMENTS

■ **April 17:** Mike Schmidt's two-run, 10th-inning home run, his record-tying fourth of the game, gave the Phillies an 18-16 victory over the Cubs at Wrigley Field.

■ **October 3:** George Brett collected three final-day hits and edged Kansas City teammate Hal McRae, .3333 to .3326, for the A.L. batting title.

LEADERS

American League
BA: George Brett, K.C., .333.
Runs: Roy White, N.Y., 104.
Hits: George Brett, K.C., 215.
TB: George Brett, K.C., 298.
HR: Graig Nettles, N.Y., 32.
RBI: Lee May, Bal., 109.
SB: Bill North, Oak., 75.
Wins: Jim Palmer, Bal., 22.
ERA: Mark Fidrych, Det., 2.34.
CG: Mark Fidrych, Det., 24.
IP: Jim Palmer, Bal., 315.
SO: Nolan Ryan, Cal., 327.
SV: Sparky Lyle, N.Y., 23.

National League
BA: Bill Madlock, Chi., .339.
Runs: Pete Rose, Cin., 130.
Hits: Pete Rose, Cin., 215.
TB: Mike Schmidt, Phil., 306.
HR: Mike Schmidt, Phil., 38.
RBI: George Foster, Cin., 121.
SB: Dave Lopes, L.A., 63.
Wins: Randy Jones, S.D., 22.
ERA: John Denny, St.L., 2.52.
CG: Randy Jones, S.D., 25.
IP: Randy Jones, S.D., 315.1.
SO: Tom Seaver, N.Y., 235.
SV: Rawly Eastwick, Cin., 26.

A.L. 20-game winners
Jim Palmer, Bal., 22-13
Luis Tiant, Bos., 21-12
Wayne Garland, Bal., 20-7

N.L. 20-game winners
Randy Jones, S.D., 22-14
Jerry Koosman, N.Y., 21-10
Don Sutton, L.A., 21-10
Steve Carlton, Phil., 20-7
J.R. Richard, Hou., 20-15

A.L. 100 RBIs
Lee May, Bal., 109
Thurman Munson, N.Y., 105
Carl Yastrzemski, Bos., 102

N.L. 100 RBIs
George Foster, Cin., 121
Joe Morgan, Cin., 111
Mike Schmidt, Phil., 107
Bob Watson, Hou., 102

Most Valuable Player
A.L.: Thurman Munson, C, N.Y.
N.L.: Joe Morgan, 2B, Cin.

Cy Young Award
A.L.: Jim Palmer, Bal.
N.L.: Randy Jones, S.D.

Rookie of the Year
A.L.: Mark Fidrych, P, Det.
N.L.: Butch Metzger, P, S.D.
Pat Zachry, P, Cin.

Hall of Fame additions
Oscar Charleston, OF, Negro Leagues
Roger Connor, 1B, 1880-97
Cal Hubbard, umpire
Bob Lemon, P, 1946-58
Fred Lindstrom, 3B, 1924-36
Robin Roberts, P, 1948-66

ALL-STAR GAME

■ **Winner:** Baseball celebrated the nation's Bicentennial with another N.L. All-Star victory—a 7-1 rout sparked by George Foster and Cesar Cedeno.

■ **Key innings:** The third, when Foster blasted a two-run homer, and the eighth, when Cedeno secured the outcome with another two-run shot.

■ **Memorable moment:** The five-hit pitching of an N.L. staff that surrendered the A.L.'s lone run on a homer by Fred Lynn.

■ **Top guns:** Randy Jones (Padres), Foster (Reds), Cedeno (Astros), Pete Rose (Reds), N.L.; Lynn (Red Sox), Rusty Staub (Tigers), A.L.

■ **MVP:** Foster.

Linescore
July 13, at Philadelphia's Veterans Stadium
A.L. ....0 0 0 1 0 0 0 0 0—1 5 0
N.L. ....2 0 2 0 0 0 0 3 x—7 10 0
Fidrych (Tigers), Hunter (Yankees) 3, Tiant (Red Sox) 5, Tanana (Angels) 7; Jones (Padres), Seaver (Mets) 4, Montefusco (Giants) 6, Rhoden (Dodgers) 8, Forsch (Astros) 9. W—Jones. L—Fidrych. HR—Foster, Cedeno, N.L.; Lynn, A.L.

ALCS

■ **Winner:** The New York Yankees, absent from post-season play since 1964, qualified for their 30th World Series with a riveting five-game victory over postseason newcomer Kansas City.

■ **Turning point:** The Yankees' 5-3 Game 3 victory, which was fueled by a homer and three RBIs by first baseman Chris Chambliss.

■ **Memorable moment:** Chambliss' dramatic series-ending home run leading off the ninth inning of Game 5. The blast off Royals reliever Mark Littell gave the Yankees a 7-6 victory and touched off a wild mob scene at Yankee Stadium.

■ **Top guns:** Chambliss (.524, 2 HR, 8 RBIs), Thurman Munson (.435), Mickey Rivers (.348), Yankees; Paul Splittorff (1-0, 1.93 ERA), George Brett (.444, 5 RBIs), Royals.

■ **MVP:** Chambliss.

Linescores

Game 1—October 9, at Kansas City
N.Y. ....2 0 0 0 0 0 0 0 2—4 12 0
K.C. ....0 0 0 0 0 0 0 1 0—1 5 2
Hunter; Gura, Littell (9). W—Hunter. L—Gura.

Game 2—October 10, at Kansas City
N.Y ....0 1 2 0 0 0 0 0 0—3 12 5
K.C. ....2 0 0 0 0 2 0 3 x—7 9 0
Figueroa, Tidrow (6); Leonard, Splittorff (3), Mingori (9). W—Splittorff. L—Figueroa.

Game 3—October 12, at New York
K.C. ....3 0 0 0 0 0 0 0 0—3 6 0
N.Y. ....0 0 0 2 0 3 0 0 x—5 9 0
Hassler, Pattin (6), Hall (6), Mingori (6), Littell (6); Ellis, Lyle (9). W—Ellis. L—Hassler. S—Lyle. HR—Chambliss (N.Y.).

Game 4—October 13, at New York
K.C. ....0 3 0 2 0 1 0 1 0—7 9 1
N.Y. ....0 2 0 0 0 0 1 0 1—4 11 0
Gura, Bird (3), Mingori (7); Hunter, Tidrow (4), Jackson (7). W—Bird. L—Hunter. S—Mingori. HR—Nettles 2 (N.Y.).

Game 5—October 14, at New York
K.C. ....2 1 0 0 0 0 0 3 0—6 11 1
N.Y. ....2 0 2 0 0 2 0 0 1—7 11 1
Leonard, Splittorff (1), Pattin (4), Hassler (5), Littell (7); Figueroa, Jackson (8), Tidrow (9). W—Tidrow. L—Littell. HR—Mayberry, Brett (K.C.); Chambliss (N.Y.).

NLCS

■ **Winner:** Philadelphia was no match for the powerful Reds, who were being hailed as one of the great teams in baseball history.

■ **Turning point:** The Reds took quick control with a 6-3 first-game victory over the Phillies and ace lefthander Steve Carlton.

■ **Memorable moment:** The ninth inning of Game 3. After tying the game with consecutive home runs by George Foster and Johnny Bench, the Reds claimed a 7-6 victory when Ken Griffey singled with the bases loaded off reliever Tom Underwood.

■ **Top guns:** Don Gullett (1-0, 1.13 ERA), Pete Rose (.429), Griffey (.385), Foster (2 HR, 4 RBIs), Reds; Jay Johnstone (.778), Phillies.

■ **MVP:** Griffey.

Linescores

Game 1—October 9, at Philadelphia
Cin. ....0 0 1 0 0 2 0 3 0—6 10 0
Phil. ....1 0 0 0 0 0 0 0 2—3 6 1
Gullett, Eastwick (9); Carlton, McGraw (8). W—Gullett. L—Carlton. HR—Foster (Cin.).

Game 2—October 10, at Philadelphia
Cin. ....0 0 0 0 0 4 2 0 0—6 6 0
Phil. ....0 1 0 0 1 0 0 0 0—2 10 1
Zachry, Borbon (6); Lonborg, Garber (6), McGraw (7), Reed (7). W—Zachry. L—Lonborg. S—Borbon. HR—Luzinski (Phil.).

Game 3—October 12, at Cincinnati
Phil. ....0 0 0 1 0 0 2 2 1—6 11 0
Cin. ....0 0 0 0 0 0 4 0 3—7 9 2
Kaat, Reed (7), Garber (9), Underwood (9); Nolan, Sarmiento (6), Borbon (7), Eastwick (8). W—Eastwick. L—Garber. HR—Foster, Bench (Cin.).

WORLD SERIES

■ **Winner:** Cincinnati's Big Red Machine was in full gear as it rolled over the Yankees, who were making their first Series appearance since 1964.

■ **Turning point:** Joe Morgan's first-inning home run in Game 1. The Reds never looked back.

■ **Memorable moment:** Game 3 at refurbished Yankee Stadium. Despite a 6-2 New York loss, the atmosphere was electric and baseball's most revered ballpark was the stately host for its 28th World Series.

■ **Top guns:** Johnny Bench (.533, 2 HR, 6 RBIs), George Foster (.429), Dave Concepcion (.357), Dan Driessen (.357), Reds; Thurman Munson (.529), Yankees.

■ **MVP:** Bench.

Linescores

Game 1—October 16, at Cincinnati
N.Y. ....0 1 0 0 0 0 0 0 0—1 5 1
Cin. ....1 0 1 0 0 1 2 0 x—5 10 1
Alexander, Lyle (7); Gullett, Borbon (8). W—Gullett. L—Alexander. HR—Morgan (Cin.).

Game 2—October 17, at Cincinnati
N.Y. ....0 0 0 1 0 0 2 0 0—3 9 1
Cin. ....0 3 0 0 0 0 0 0 1—4 10 0
Hunter; Norman, Billingham (7). W—Billingham. L—Hunter.

Game 3—October 19, at New York
Cin. ....0 3 0 1 0 0 0 2 0—6 13 2
N.Y. ....0 0 0 1 0 0 1 0 0—2 8 0
Zachry, McEnaney (7); Ellis, Jackson (4), Tidrow (8). W—Zachry. L—Ellis. S—McEnaney. HR—Driessen (Cin.); Mason (N.Y.).

Game 4—October 21, at New York
Cin. ....0 0 0 3 0 0 0 0 4—7 9 2
N.Y. ....1 0 0 0 1 0 0 0 0—2 8 0
Nolan, McEnaney (7); Figueroa, Tidrow (9), Lyle (9). W—Nolan. L—Figueroa. S—McEnaney. HR—Bench 2 (Cin.).

FINAL STANDINGS

American League

East Division

Team	N.Y.	Bos.	Bal.	Det.	Cle.	Mil.	Tor.	Cal.	Chi.	K.C.	Min.	Oak.	Sea.	Tex.	W	L	Pct.	GB
New York	...	7	7	9	12	7	9	7	7	5	8	9	6	7	100	62	.617	...
Boston	8	...	8	9	8	9	12	7	3	5	4	8	10	6	97	64	.602	2.5
Baltimore	8	6	...	12	11	11	10	5	5	4	6	8	7	4	97	64	.602	2.5
Detroit	6	6	3	...	7	10	10	6	6	3	5	5	5	2	74	88	.457	26
Cleveland	3	7	4	8	...	11	9	4	4	3	2	7	7	2	71	90	.441	28.5
Milwaukee	8	6	4	5	4	...	8	5	5	2	3	5	7	5	67	95	.414	33
Toronto	6	3	5	5	5	7	...	4	3	2	1	3	6	4	54	107	.335	45.5

West Division

Team	K.C.	Tex.	Chi.	Min.	Cal.	Sea.	Oak.	Bal.	Bos.	Cle.	Det.	Mil.	N.Y.	Tor.	W	L	Pct.	GB
Kansas City	...	8	7	10	9	11	9	7	5	7	8	8	5	8	102	60	.630	...
Texas	7	...	9	7	10	6	13	6	4	9	8	5	3	7	94	68	.580	8
Chicago	8	6	...	10	7	10	10	5	7	6	4	6	3	8	90	72	.556	12
Minnesota	5	8	5	...	8	7	8	4	6	9	5	8	2	9	84	77	.522	17.5
California	6	5	8	7	...	9	5	6	3	6	4	5	4	6	74	88	.457	28
Seattle	4	9	5	8	6	...	8	3	1	3	6	3	4	4	64	98	.395	38
Oakland	6	2	5	6	10	7	...	2	3	3	5	5	2	7	63	98	.391	38.5

National League

East Division

Team	Phi.	Pit.	St.L.	Chi.	Mon.	N.Y.	Atl.	Cin.	Hou.	L.A.	S.D.	S.F.	W	L	Pct.	GB
Philadelphia	...	8	11	12	11	13	10	4	8	6	9	9	101	61	.623	...
Pittsburgh	10	...	9	11	11	14	9	9	8	3	10	2	96	66	.593	5
St.Louis	7	9	...	11	6	10	11	7	7	6	4	5	83	79	.512	18
Chicago	6	7	7	...	10	9	7	7	6	6	7	9	81	81	.500	20
Montreal	7	7	12	8	...	10	6	5	4	5	5	6	75	87	.463	26
New York	5	4	8	9	8	...	5	2	6	4	6	7	64	98	.395	37

West Division

Team	L.A.	Cin.	Hou.	S.F.	S.D.	Atl.	Chi.	Mon.	N.Y.	Phi.	Pit.	St.L.	W	L	Pct.	GB
Los Angeles	...	8	9	14	12	13	6	7	8	6	9	6	98	64	.605	...
Cincinnati	10	...	5	10	11	14	5	7	10	8	3	5	88	74	.543	10
Houston	9	13	...	9	8	9	6	8	6	4	4	5	81	81	.500	17
San Fran.	4	8	9	..	10	10	3	6	5	3	10	7	75	87	.463	23
San Diego	6	7	10	8	...	7	5	7	6	3	2	8	69	93	.426	29
Atlanta	5	4	9	8	11	...	5	6	7	2	3	1	61	101	.377	37

SIGNIFICANT EVENTS

■ **January 2:** Commissioner Bowie Kuhn suspended Braves owner Ted Turner for a year and fined him $10,000 for "tampering" with free-agent outfielder Gary Matthews.

■ **April 6-7:** The expansion Mariners lost their debut, 7-0, to the Angels, but the Blue Jays won their Toronto inaugural, 9-5, over the White Sox.

■ **April 15:** The Expos opened new Olympic Stadium, but the Phillies spoiled the occasion with a 7-2 victory.

■ **March 28:** Texas second baseman Lenny Randle, frustrated over losing his starting job, sent 50-year-old manager Frank Lucchesi to the hospital with a vicious beating before a spring training game.

■ **October 25:** Yankees lefty Sparky Lyle became the first A.L. reliever to win a Cy Young Award.

■ **November 8:** Cincinnati's George Foster, the first player to top the 50-homer barrier since 1965, earned N.L. MVP honors.

MEMORABLE MOMENTS

■ **June 8:** California's Nolan Ryan struck out 19 Blue Jays in a 10-inning performance, reaching that single-game plateau for the fourth time.

■ **August 29:** St. Louis' Lou Brock swiped two bases in a game against San Diego, lifting his career total to 893 and passing Ty Cobb as baseball's greatest modern-era basestealer.

LEADERS

American League
BA: Rod Carew, Min., .388.
Runs: Rod Carew, Min., 128.
Hits: Rod Carew, Min., 239.
TB: Jim Rice, Bos., 382.
HR: Jim Rice, Bos., 39.
RBI: Larry Hisle, Min., 119.
SB: Fred Patek, K.C., 53.
Wins: Dave Goltz, Min.; Dennis Leonard, K.C.; Jim Palmer, Bal., 20.
ERA: Frank Tanana, Cal., 2.54.
CG: Jim Palmer, Bal.; Nolan Ryan, Cal., 22.
IP: Jim Palmer, Bal., 319.
SO: Nolan Ryan, Cal., 341.
SV: Bill Campbell, Bos., 31.

National League
BA: Dave Parker, Pit., .338.
Runs: George Foster, Cin., 124.
Hits: Dave Parker, Pit., 215.
TB: George Foster, Cin., 388.
HR: George Foster, Cin., 52.
RBI: George Foster, Cin., 149.
SB: Frank Taveras, Pit., 70.
Wins: Steve Carlton, Phil., 23.
ERA: John Candelaria, Pit., 2.34.
CG: Phil Niekro, Atl., 20.
IP: Phil Niekro, Atl., 330.1.
SO: Phil Niekro, Atl., 262.
SV: Rollie Fingers, S.D., 35.

A.L. 20-game winners
Jim Palmer, Bal., 20-11
Dave Goltz, Min., 20-11
Dennis Leonard, K.C., 20-12

N.L. 20-game winners
Steve Carlton, Phil., 23-10
Tom Seaver, N.Y.-Cin., 21-6
John Candelaria, Pit., 20-5
Bob Forsch, St.L., 20-7
Tommy John, L.A., 20-7
Rick Reuschel, Chi., 20-10

A.L. 100 RBIs
Larry Hisle, Min., 119
Bobby Bonds, Cal., 115
Jim Rice, Bos., 114
Al Cowens, K.C., 112
Butch Hobson, Bos., 112
Reggie Jackson, N.Y., 110
Graig Nettles, N.Y., 107
Jason Thompson, Det., 105
Carlton Fisk, Bos., 102
Carl Yastrzemski, Bos., 102
Rusty Staub, Det., 101
Richie Zisk, Chi., 101
Rod Carew, Min., 100
Thurman Munson, N.Y., 100

N.L. 100 RBIs
George Foster, Cin., 149
Greg Luzinski, Phil., 130
Steve Garvey, L.A., 115
Jeff Burroughs, Atl., 114
Ron Cey, L.A., 110
Bob Watson, Hou., 110
Johnny Bench, Cin., 109
Bill Robinson, Pit., 104
Mike Schmidt, Phil., 101

N.L. 40 homers
George Foster, Cin., 52
Jeff Burroughs, Atl., 41

Most Valuable Player
A.L.: Rod Carew, 1B, Min.
N.L.: George Foster, OF, Cin.

Cy Young Award
A.L.: Sparky Lyle, N.Y.
N.L.: Steve Carlton, Phil.

Rookie of the Year
A.L.: Eddie Murray, 1B, Bal.
N.L.: Andre Dawson, OF, Mon.

Hall of Fame additions
Ernie Banks, SS, 1953-71
Martin Dihigo, P/IF, Negro Leagues
John Henry Lloyd, SS, Negro Leagues
Al Lopez, manager
Amos Rusie, P, 1889-1901
Joe Sewell, SS, 1920-33

ALL-STAR GAME

■ **Winner:** The N.L. continued its All-Star mastery with a 7-5 victory — its sixth in a row and 14th in 15 contests.

■ **Key inning:** The first, when the N.L. struck for four quick runs. A leadoff homer by Joe Morgan and a two-run shot by Greg Luzinski were the big blows.

■ **Memorable moment:** Watching the N.L. close out another All-Star victory at venerable Yankee Stadium, where so much A.L. glory had been achieved.

■ **Top guns:** Don Sutton (Dodgers), Morgan (Reds), Luzinski (Phillies), Dave Winfield (Padres), Steve Garvey (Dodgers), N.L.; Dennis Eckersley (Indians), Richie Zisk (White Sox), George Scott (Red Sox), A.L.

■ **MVP:** Sutton.

Linescore
July 19, at New York's Yankee Stadium
N.L. ....4 0 1 0 0 0 0 2 0—7 9 1
A.L. ....0 0 0 0 0 2 1 0 2—5 8 0
Sutton (Dodgers), Lavelle (Giants) 4, Seaver (Reds) 6, R. Reuschel (Cubs) 8, Gossage (Pirates) 9; Palmer (Orioles), Kern (Indians) 3, Eckersley (Indians) 4, LaRoche (Angels) 6, Campbell (Red Sox) 7, Lyle (Yankees) 8. W—Sutton. L—Palmer. HR—Morgan, Luzinski, Garvey, N.L.; Scott, A.L.

ALCS

■ **Winner:** The Yankees, bidding to return to the World Series for a second consecutive season, needed a three-run ninth-inning rally to defeat Kansas City in the decisive fifth game.

■ **Turning point:** Sparky Lyle's 5⅓ innings of scoreless Game 4 relief after the Royals, bidding to close out the series, had cut a 4-0 Yankee lead to 5-4. The Yanks evened the series with a 6-4 win.

■ **Memorable moment:** A bloop single by light-hitting Yankee Paul Blair leading off the ninth inning of Game 5. Blair's hit off Royals ace Dennis Leonard set up the Yankees' series-winning rally.

■ **Top guns:** Lyle (2-0, 0.96 ERA), Cliff Johnson (.400), Mickey Rivers (.391), Yankees; Hal McRae (.444), Fred Patek (.389), Royals.

■ **MVP:** Lyle.

Linescores

Game 1—October 5, at New York
K.C. ....2 2 2 0 0 0 0 1 0—7 9 0
N.Y. ....0 0 2 0 0 0 0 0 0—2 9 0
Splittorff, Bird (9); Gullett, Tidrow (3), Lyle (9). W—Splittorff. L—Gullett. HR—McRae, Mayberry, Cowens (K.C.); Munson (N.Y.).

Game 2—October 6, at New York
K.C. ....0 0 1 0 0 1 0 0 0—2 3 1
N.Y. ....0 0 0 0 2 3 0 1 x—6 10 1
Hassler, Littell (6), Mingori (8); Guidry. W—Guidry. L—Hassler. HR—Johnson (N.Y.).

Game 3—October 7, at Kansas City
N.Y. ....0 0 0 0 1 0 0 0 1—2 4 1
K.C. ....0 1 1 0 1 2 1 0 x—6 12 1
Torrez, Lyle (6); Leonard. W—Leonard. L—Torrez.

Game 4—October 8, at Kansas City
N.Y. ....1 2 1 1 0 0 0 0 1—6 13 0
K.C. ....0 0 2 2 0 0 0 0 0—4 8 2
Figueroa, Tidrow (4), Lyle (4); Gura, Pattin (3), Mingori (9), Bird (9). W—Lyle. L—Gura.

Game 5—October 9, at Kansas City
N.Y. ....0 0 1 0 0 0 0 1 3—5 10 0
K.C. ....2 0 1 0 0 0 0 0 0—3 10 1
Guidry, Torrez (3), Lyle (8); Splittorff, Bird (8), Mingori (8), Leonard (9), Gura (9), Littell (9). W—Lyle. L—Leonard.

NLCS

■ **Winner:** The Dodgers returned to the World Series for the second time in four years and denied Philadelphia its first pennant since 1950.

■ **Turning point:** The ninth inning of Game 3. With the series tied at a game apiece and the Phillies holding a 5-3 lead with two out and nobody on base in the final inning, the Dodgers collected four straight hits, scored three runs and escaped with a 6-5 victory.

■ **Memorable moment:** Dusty Baker's two-run fourth-game homer that helped Dodgers lefty Tommy John record a 4-1 series-ending victory in a steady rain.

■ **Top guns:** John (1-0, 0.66 ERA), Baker (.357, 2 HR, 8 RBIs), Ron Cey (.308, 4 RBIs), Dodgers; Bob Boone (.400), Richie Hebner (.357), Phillies.

■ **MVP:** Baker.

Linescores

Game 1—October 4, at Los Angeles
Phil. ....2 0 0 0 2 1 0 0 2—7 9 0
L.A. ....0 0 0 0 1 0 4 0 0—5 9 2
Carlton, Garber (7), McGraw (9); John, Garman (5), Hough (6), Sosa (8). W—Garber. L—Sosa. S—McGraw. HR—Luzinski (Phil.); Cey (L.A.).

Game 2—October 5, at Los Angeles
Phil. ....0 0 1 0 0 0 0 0 0—1 9 1
L.A. ....0 0 1 4 0 1 1 0 x—7 9 1
Lonborg, Reed (5), Brusstar (7); Sutton. W—Sutton. L—Lonborg. HR—McBride (Phil.); Baker (L.A.).

Game 3—October 7, at Philadelphia
L.A. ....0 2 0 1 0 0 0 0 3—6 12 2
Phil. ....0 3 0 0 0 0 0 2 0—5 6 2
Hooton, Rhoden (2), Rau (7), Sosa (8), Rautzhan (8), Garman (9); Christenson, Brusstar (4), Reed (5), Garber (7). W—Rautzhan. L—Garber. S—Garman.

Game 4—October 8, at Philadelphia
L.A. ....0 2 0 0 2 0 0 0 0—4 5 0
Phil. ....0 0 0 1 0 0 0 0 0—1 7 0
John; Carlton, Reed (6), McGraw (7), Garber (9). W—John. L—Carlton. HR—Baker (L.A.).

WORLD SERIES

■ **Winner:** The Yankees won their record 21st World Series — but first since 1962.

■ **Turning point:** Ron Guidry's four-hit pitching in Game 4 — a 4-2 victory that gave the Yankees a three-games-to-one edge.

■ **Memorable moment:** Reggie Jackson's eighth-inning Game 6 blast into the center field bleachers — his record-tying third home run of the contest. The Yankees ended the classic with an 8-4 victory and Jackson finished with a Series-record five homers.

■ **Top guns:** Mike Torrez (2-0, 2.50 ERA), Jackson (.450, 5 HR, 8 RBIs), Yankees; Steve Garvey (.375), Steve Yeager (.316, 2 HR, 5 RBIs), Dodgers.

■ **MVP:** Jackson.

Linescores

Game 1—October 11, at New York
L.A.....2 0 0 0 0 0 0 0 1 0 0 0—3 6 0
N.Y.....1 0 0 0 0 1 0 1 0 0 0 1—4 11 0
Sutton, Rautzhan (8), Sosa (8), Garman (9), Rhoden (12); Gullett, Lyle (9). W—Lyle. L—Rhoden. HR—Randolph (N.Y.).

Game 2—October 12, at New York
L.A. ....2 1 2 0 0 0 0 0 1—6 9 0
N.Y. ....0 0 0 1 0 0 0 0 0—1 5 0
Hooton; Hunter, Tidrow (3), Clay (6), Lyle (9). W—Hooton. L—Hunter. HR—Cey, Yeager, Smith, Garvey (L.A.).

Game 3——October 14, at Los Angeles
N.Y. ....3 0 0 1 1 0 0 0 0—5 10 0
L.A. ....0 0 3 0 0 0 0 0 0—3 7 1
Torrez; John, Hough (7). W—Torrez. L—John. HR—Baker (L.A.).

Game 4—October 15, at Los Angeles
N.Y. ....0 3 0 0 0 1 0 0 0—4 7 0
L.A. ....0 0 2 0 0 0 0 0 0—2 4 0
Guidry; Rau, Rhoden (2), Garman (9). W—Guidry. L—Rau. HR—Lopes (L.A.); Jackson (N.Y.).

Game 5—October 16, at Los Angeles
N.Y. ....0 0 0 0 0 0 2 2 0— 4 9 2
L.A. ....1 0 0 4 3 2 0 0 x—10 13 0
Gullett, Clay (5), Tidrow (6), Hunter (7); Sutton. W—Sutton. L—Gullett. HR—Yeager, Smith (L.A.); Munson, Jackson (N.Y.).

Game 6—October 18, at New York
L.A. ....2 0 1 0 0 0 0 0 1—4 9 0
N.Y. ....0 2 0 3 2 0 0 1 x—8 8 1
Hooton, Sosa (4), Rau (5), Hough (7); Torrez. W—Torrez. L—Hooton. HR—Chambliss, Jackson 3 (N.Y.); Smith (L.A.).

FINAL STANDINGS

American League

East Division

Team	N.Y.	Bos.	Mil.	Bal.	Det.	Cle.	Tor.	Cal.	Chi.	K.C.	Min.	Oak.	Sea.	Tex.	W	L	Pct.	GB
New York	...	9	5	9	11	9	11	5	9	5	7	8	6	6	100	63	.613	...
Boston	7	...	10	8	12	7	11	9	7	4	9	5	7	3	99	64	.607	1
Milwaukee	10	5	...	8	8	10	12	5	7	4	4	9	5	6	93	69	.574	6.5
Baltimore	6	7	7	...	7	9	8	4	8	2	5	11	9	7	90	71	.559	9
Detroit	4	3	7	8	...	10	9	7	9	4	4	6	8	7	86	76	.531	13.5
Cleveland	6	8	5	6	5	...	10	4	2	5	5	4	8	1	69	90	.434	29
Toronto	4	4	3	7	6	4	...	3	6	5	4	4	2	7	59	102	.366	40

West Division

Team	K.C.	Cal.	Tex.	Min.	Chi.	Oak.	Sea.	Bal.	Bos.	Cle.	Det.	Mil.	N.Y.	Tor.	W	L	Pct.	GB
Kansas City	...	6	7	7	7	10	12	8	6	6	6	6	6	5	92	70	.568	...
California	9	...	5	12	8	9	9	6	2	6	4	5	5	7	87	75	.537	5
Texas	8	10	...	9	4	9	12	4	7	9	3	4	4	4	87	75	.537	5
Minnesota	8	3	6	...	7	9	6	5	2	5	6	7	3	6	73	89	.451	19
Chicago	8	7	11	8	...	7	7	1	3	8	2	4	1	4	71	90	.441	20.5
Oakland	5	6	6	6	8	...	13	0	5	6	4	1	2	7	69	93	.426	23
Seattle	3	6	3	9	8	2	...	1	3	1	2	5	5	8	56	104	.350	35

National League

East Division

Team	Phi.	Pit.	Chi.	Mon.	St.L.	N.Y.	Atl.	Cin.	Hou.	L.A.	S.D.	S.F.	W	L	Pct.	GB
Philadelphia	...	11	14	9	10	12	4	5	6	5	8	6	90	72	.556	...
Pittsburgh	7	...	11	11	9	11	10	7	8	5	5	4	88	73	.547	1.5
Chicago	4	7	...	7	15	11	7	7	6	4	7	4	79	83	.488	11
Montreal	9	7	11	...	9	8	7	4	6	4	6	5	76	86	.469	14
St. Louis	8	9	3	9	...	11	7	4	5	7	3	3	69	93	.426	21
New York	6	7	7	10	7	...	6	5	5	5	5	3	66	96	.407	24

West Division

Team	L.A.	Cin.	S.F.	S.D.	Hou.	Atl.	Chi.	Mon.	N.Y.	Phi.	Pit.	St.L.	W	L	Pct.	GB
Los Angeles	...	9	11	9	11	13	8	8	7	7	7	5	95	67	.586	...
Cincinnati	9	...	12	9	11	12	5	8	7	7	4	8	92	69	.571	2.5
San Fran.	7	6	...	10	12	7	8	7	9	6	8	9	89	73	.549	6
San Diego	9	9	8	...	10	10	5	6	7	4	7	9	84	78	.519	11
Houston	7	7	6	8	...	10	6	6	7	6	4	7	74	88	.457	21
Atlanta	5	6	11	8	8	...	5	5	6	8	2	5	69	93	.426	26

SIGNIFICANT EVENTS

■ **June 31:** Larry Doby, baseball's second black player in 1947, became the game's second black manager when he took the White Sox reins from Bob Lemon.

■ **August 26:** Major League umpires were forced back to work by a restraining order after a one-day strike.

■ **September 23:** Angels outfielder Lyman Bostock, a .311 career hitter, was killed by an errant shotgun blast while riding in a car in Gary, Ind.

■ **October 24:** Padres ace Gaylord Perry became the first pitcher to win a Cy Young Award in both leagues.

■ **December 5:** Pete Rose completed his high-profile free-agency showcase by signing with the Phillies for $3.2 million over four years.

MEMORABLE MOMENTS

■ **May 5:** Cincinnati's Pete Rose collected career hit No. 3,000 in a 4-3 loss to the Expos.

■ **June 30:** Giants first baseman Willie McCovey crashed his 500th career home run off Jamie Easterly in a 10-9 loss to the Braves.

■ **August 1:** Atlanta pitchers Larry McWilliams and Gene Garber stopped Rose's N.L. record-tying hitting streak at 44 games in a 16-4 victory over the Reds.

■ **October 2:** The Yankees capped their incredible comeback from a 14-game A.L. East Division deficit with a 5-4 victory over Boston in a one-game playoff to decide the A.L. East Division title.

LEADERS

American League
BA: Rod Carew, Min., .333.
Runs: Ron LeFlore, Det., 126.
Hits: Jim Rice, Bos., 213.
TB: Jim Rice, Bos., 406.
HR: Jim Rice, Bos., 46.
RBI: Jim Rice, Bos., 139.
SB: Ron LeFlore, Det., 68.
Wins: Ron Guidry, N.Y., 25.
ERA: Ron Guidry, N.Y., 1.74.
CG: Mike Caldwell, Mil., 23.
IP: Jim Palmer, Bal., 296.
SO: Nolan Ryan, Cal., 260.
SV: Goose Gossage, N.Y., 27.

National League
BA: Dave Parker, Pit., .334.
Runs: Ivan DeJesus, Chi., 104.
Hits: Steve Garvey, L.A., 202.
TB: Dave Parker, Pit., 340.
HR: George Foster, Cin., 40.
RBI: George Foster, Cin., 120.
SB: Omar Moreno, Pit., 71.
Wins: Gaylord Perry, S.D., 21.
ERA: Craig Swan, N.Y., 2.43.
CG: Phil Niekro, Atl., 22.
IP: Phil Niekro, Atl., 334.1.
SO: J.R. Richard, Hou., 303.
SV: Rollie Fingers, S.D., 37.

A.L. 20-game winners
Ron Guidry, N.Y., 25-3
Mike Caldwell, Mil., 22-9
Jim Palmer, Bal., 21-12
Dennis Leonard, K.C., 21-17
Dennis Eckersley, Bos., 20-8
Ed Figueroa, N.Y., 20-9

N.L. 20-game winners
Gaylord Perry, S.D., 21-6
Ross Grimsley, Mon., 20-11

A.L. 100 RBIs
Jim Rice, Bos., 139
Rusty Staub, Det., 121
Larry Hisle, Mil., 115
Andre Thornton, Cle., 105

N.L. 100 RBIs
George Foster, Cin., 120
Dave Parker, Pit., 117
Steve Garvey, L.A., 113
Greg Luzinski, Phil., 101

A.L. 40 homers
Jim Rice, Bos., 46

N.L. 40 homers
George Foster, Cin., 40

Most Valuable Player
A.L.: Jim Rice, OF, Bos.
N.L.: Dave Parker, OF, Pit.

Cy Young Award
A.L.: Ron Guidry, N.Y.
N.L.: Gaylord Perry, S.D.

Rookie of the Year
A.L.: Lou Whitaker, 2B, Det.
N.L.: Bob Horner, 3B, Atl.

Hall of Fame additions
Addie Joss, P, 1902-10
Larry MacPhail, executive
Eddie Mathews, 3B, 1952-68

ALL-STAR GAME

■ **Winner:** The N.L. varied its approach, spotting the A.L. a 3-0 lead before roaring to its seventh straight All-Star victory.

■ **Key inning:** The eighth, when the N.L. broke a 3-3 deadlock with four runs. The tie-breaker scored on a Goose Gossage wild pitch and two more came home on Bob Boone's single.

■ **Memorable moment:** A stunning third-inning collapse by A.L. starting pitcher Jim Palmer, who issued consecutive two-out walks to Joe Morgan, George Foster and Greg Luzinski to force in a run and then gave up a game-tying, two-run single to Steve Garvey.

■ **Top guns:** Bruce Sutter (Cubs), Garvey (Dodgers), Boone (Phillies), N.L.; Lary Sorensen (Brewers), George Brett (Royals), Rod Carew (Twins), A.L.

■ **MVP:** Garvey.

Linescore
July 11, at San Diego Stadium
A.L. ....2 0 1 0 0 0 0 0 0—3 8 1
N.L. ....0 0 3 0 0 0 4 x—7 10 0
Palmer (Orioles), Keough (Athletics) 3, Sorensen (Brewers) 4, Kern (Indians) 7, Guidry (Yankees) 7, Gossage (Yankees) 8; Blue (Giants), Rogers (Expos) 4, Fingers (Padres) 6, Sutter (Cubs) 8, Niekro (Braves) 9. W—Sutter. L—Gossage.

ALCS

■ **Winner:** The Yankees, extended to the limit by the Royals in 1976 and '77, needed only four games to claim their third consecutive A.L. pennant.

■ **Turning point:** Yankee catcher Thurman Munson's two-run, eighth-inning home run off Royals reliever Doug Bird in Game 3. The shot turned a 5-4 New York deficit into a 6-5 victory.

■ **Memorable moment:** The three-home run performance of Kansas City's George Brett in the pivotal third game. Brett's three solo shots off Yankee ace Catfish Hunter were wasted.

■ **Top guns:** Reggie Jackson (.462, 2 HR, 6 RBIs), Mickey Rivers (.455), Chris Chambliss (.400), Yankees; Amos Otis (.429), Brett (.389, 3 HR), Royals.

■ **MVP:** Munson.

Linescores

Game 1—October 3, at Kansas City
N.Y. ....0 1 1 0 2 0 0 3 0—7 16 0
K.C. ....0 0 0 0 0 1 0 0 0—1 2 2
Beattie, Clay (6); Leonard, Mingori (5), Hrabosky (8), Bird (9). W—Beattie. L—Leonard. S—Clay. HR—Jackson (N.Y.).

Game 2—October 4, at Kansas City
N.Y. ....0 0 0 0 0 0 2 2 0— 4 12 1
K.C. ....1 4 0 0 0 0 3 2 0—10 16 1
Figueroa, Tidrow (2), Lyle (7); Gura, Pattin (7), Hrabosky (8). W—Gura. L—Figueroa. HR—Patek (K.C.).

Game 3—October 6, at New York
K.C. ....1 0 1 0 1 0 0 2 0—5 10 1
N.Y. ....0 1 0 2 0 1 0 2 x—6 10 0
Splittorff, Bird (8), Hrabosky (8); Hunter, Gossage (7). W—Gossage. L—Bird. \HR—Brett 3 (K.C.); Jackson, Munson (N.Y.).

Game 4—October 7, at New York
K.C. ....1 0 0 0 0 0 0 0 0—1 7 0
N.Y. ....0 1 0 0 0 1 0 0 x—2 4 0
Leonard; Guidry, Gossage (9). W—Guidry. L—Leonard. S—Gossage. HR—Nettles, R. White (N.Y.).

NLCS

■ **Winner:** Los Angeles earned its second consecutive pennant and handed Philadelphia its third straight NLCS defeat.

■ **Turning point:** The first inning of Game 4, when the Phillies loaded the bases against Dodgers starter Doug Rau with nobody out — and failed to score.

■ **Memorable moment:** The two-out, 10th-inning line drive that sure-handed Phillies center fielder Garry Maddox dropped. Dodger shortstop Bill Russell followed with a game- and series-winning single.

■ **Top guns:** Tommy John (1-0, 0.00 ERA), Dusty Baker (.467), Russell (.412), Steve Garvey (.389, 4 HR, 7 RBIs), Dodgers; Ted Sizemore (.385), Greg Luzinski (.375, 2 HR), Phillies.

■ **MVP:** Garvey.

Linescores

Game 1—October 4, at Philadelphia
L.A. ....0 0 4 2 1 1 0 0 1—9 13 1
Phil. ....0 1 0 0 3 0 0 0 1—5 12 1
Hooton, Welch (5); Christenson, Brusstar (5), Eastwick (6), McGraw (7). W—Welch. L—Christenson. HR—Garvey 2, Lopes, Yeager (L.A.); Martin (Phil.).

Game 2—October 5, at Philadelphia
L.A. ....0 0 0 1 2 0 1 0 0—4 8 0
Phil. ....0 0 0 0 0 0 0 0 0—0 4 0
John; Ruthven, Brusstar (5), Reed (7), McGraw (9). W—John. L—Ruthven. HR—Lopes (L.A.).

Game 3—October 6, at Los Angeles
Phil. ....0 4 0 0 0 3 1 0 1—9 11 1
L.A. ....0 1 2 0 0 0 0 1 0—4 8 2
Carlton; Sutton, Rautzhan (6), Hough (8). W—Carlton. L—Sutton. HR—Carlton, Luzinski (Phil.); Garvey (L.A.).

Game 4—October 7, at Los Angeles
Phil. ......0 0 2 0 0 0 1 0 0 0—3 8 2
L.A. ....0 1 0 1 0 1 0 0 0 1—4 13 0
Lerch, Brusstar (6), Reed (7), McGraw (9); Rau, Rhoden (6), Forster (10). W—Forster. L—McGraw. HR—Luzinski, McBride (Phil.); Cey, Garvey (L.A.).

WORLD SERIES

■ **Winner:** The Yankees became the first team to win a six-game Series after losing the first two games. The Dodgers became their Series victim for the eighth time.

■ **Turning point:** A 10th-inning RBI single by Lou Piniella that gave the Yankees a 4-3 Game 4 victory and tied the Series at two games.

■ **Memorable moment:** A Bob Welch-Reggie Jackson battle in Game 2. With the Dodgers leading 4-3 and two out in the ninth, Dodger rookie Welch needed nine pitches to strike out Yankee slugger Jackson in a classic duel with two men on base.

■ **Top guns:** Denny Doyle (.438), Bucky Dent (.417, 7 RBIs), Jackson (.391, 2 HR, 8 RBIs), Yankees; Bill Russell (.423), Dave Lopes (3 HR, 7 RBIs), Dodgers.

■ **MVP:** Dent.

Linescores

Game 1—October 10, at Los Angeles
N.Y. ....0 0 0 0 0 0 3 2 0— 5 9 1
L.A. ....0 3 0 3 1 0 3 1 x—11 15 2
Figueroa, Clay (2), Lindblad (5), Tidrow (7); John, Forster (8). W—John. L—Figueroa. HR—Jackson (N.Y.); Baker, Lopes 2 (L.A.).

Game 2—October 11, at Los Angeles
N.Y. ....0 0 2 0 0 0 1 0 0—3 11 0
L.A. ....0 0 0 1 0 3 0 0 x—4 7 0
Hunter, Gossage (7); Hooton, Forster (7), Welch (9). W—Hooton. L—Hunter. S—Welch. HR—Cey (L.A.).

Game 3—October 13, at New York
L.A. ....0 0 1 0 0 0 0 0 0—1 8 0
N.Y. ....1 1 0 0 0 0 3 0 x—5 10 1
Sutton, Rautzhan (7), Hough (8); Guidry. W—Guidry. L—Sutton. HR—White (N.Y.).

Game 4—October 14, at New York
L.A. ....0 0 0 0 3 0 0 0 0 0—3 6 1
N.Y. ....0 0 0 0 0 2 0 1 0 1—4 9 0
John, Forster (8), Welch (8); Figueroa, Tidrow (6), Gossage (9). W—Gossage. L—Welch. HR—Smith (L.A.).

Game 5—October 15, at New York
L.A. ....1 0 1 0 0 0 0 0 0— 2 9 3
N.Y. ....0 0 4 3 0 0 4 1 x—12 18 0
Hooton, Rautzhan (3), Hough (4); Beattie. W—Beattie. L—Hooton.

Game 6—October 17, at Los Angeles
N.Y. ....0 3 0 0 0 2 2 0 0—7 11 0
L.A. ....1 0 1 0 0 0 0 0 0—2 7 1
Hunter, Gossage (8); Sutton, Welch (6), Rau (8). W—Hunter. L—Sutton. HR—Lopes (L.A.); Jackson (N.Y.).

HISTORY

FINAL STANDINGS

American League

East Division

Team	Bal.	Mil.	Bos.	N.Y.	Det.	Cle.	Tor.	Cal.	Chi.	K.C.	Min.	Oak.	Sea.	Tex.	W	L	Pct.	GB
Baltimore	...	8	8	5	7	8	11	9	8	6	8	8	10	6	102	57	.642	...
Milwaukee	5	...	4	9	7	9	10	5	7	7	8	6	9	9	95	66	.590	8
Boston	5	8	...	5	8	6	9	5	5	8	9	9	8	6	91	69	.569	11.5
New York	6	4	8	...	6	8	9	5	8	7	5	9	6	8	89	71	.556	13.5
Detroit	6	6	5	7	...	6	9	8	9	5	4	7	7	6	85	76	.528	18
Cleveland	5	4	7	5	6	...	8	6	6	6	8	8	7	5	81	80	.503	22
Toronto	2	3	4	4	4	5	...	5	5	3	1	8	4	5	53	109	.327	50.5

West Division

Team	Cal.	K.C.	Tex.	Min.	Chi.	Sea.	Oak.	Bal.	Bos.	Cle.	Det.	Mil.	N.Y.	Tor.	W	L	Pct.	GB
California	...	7	5	9	9	7	10	3	7	6	4	7	7	7	88	74	.543	...
Kansas City	6	...	6	7	8	7	9	6	4	6	7	5	5	9	85	77	.525	3
Texas	8	7	...	9	2	7	11	6	6	7	6	3	4	7	83	79	.512	5
Minnesota	4	6	4	...	8	10	9	4	3	4	8	4	7	11	82	80	.506	6
Chicago	4	5	11	5	...	5	9	3	6	6	3	5	4	7	73	87	.456	14
Seattle	6	6	6	3	8	...	5	2	4	5	5	3	6	8	67	95	.414	21
Oakland	3	4	2	4	4	8	...	4	3	4	5	6	3	4	54	108	.333	34

National League

East Division

Team	Pit.	Mon.	St.L.	Phi.	Chi.	N.Y.	Atl.	Cin.	Hou.	L.A.	S.D.	S.F.	W	L	Pct.	GB
Pittsburgh	...	11	11	10	12	10	8	4	8	8	7	9	98	64	.605	...
Montreal	7	...	10	11	12	15	9	6	5	6	7	7	95	65	.594	2
St. Louis	7	8	...	11	10	11	8	4	6	6	8	7	86	76	.531	12
Philadelphia	8	7	7	...	9	13	5	4	7	9	9	6	84	78	.519	14
Chicago	6	6	8	9	...	8	8	7	6	5	9	8	80	82	.494	18
New York	8	3	7	5	10	...	8	4	3	3	4	8	63	99	.389	35

West Division

Team	Cin.	Hou.	L.A.	S.F.	S.D.	Atl.	Chi.	Mon.	N.Y.	Phi.	Pit.	St.L.	W	L	Pct.	GB
Cincinnati	...	8	11	6	10	12	5	6	8	8	8	8	90	71	.559	...
Houston	10	...	10	7	14	11	6	7	9	5	4	6	89	73	.549	1.5
Los Angeles	7	8	...	14	9	6	7	6	9	3	4	6	79	83	.488	11.5
San Fran.	12	11	4	...	10	7	4	5	4	6	3	5	71	91	.438	19.5
San Diego	7	4	9	8	...	12	3	5	8	3	5	4	68	93	.422	22
Atlanta	6	7	12	11	6	...	4	1	4	7	4	4	66	94	.413	23.5

SIGNIFICANT EVENTS

■ **May 19:** Major League umpires returned to work after a six-week strike that forced baseball to play its games with amateur and minor league arbiters.

■ **July 12:** Bill Veeck's "Disco Demolition Night" promotion turned into Comiskey Park bedlam when fans refused to leave the field, and the White Sox were forced to forfeit the second game of a doubleheader to Detroit.

■ **August 2:** Yankee catcher Thurman Munson, the 1976 A.L. MVP, died at age 32 when the plane he was flying crashed short of the runway at the Akron-Canton Airport in Ohio.

■ **October 29:** Willie Mays was banned from baseball after accepting a job with a corporation that operates gambling casinos.

■ **November 13:** The N.L. crowned baseball's first co-MVPs—Pittsburgh's Willie Stargell and St. Louis' Keith Hernandez.

MEMORABLE MOMENTS

■ **May 17:** The Phillies beat the Cubs, 23-22, in an 11-homer, 50-hit slugfest at wind-swept Wrigley Field.

■ **August 13, September 12:** St. Louis' Lou Brock and Boston's Carl Yastrzemski became baseball's 14th and 15th 3,000-hit men in games against the Cubs and Yankees.

■ **September 23:** Brock stole his 938th and final base in a 7-4 victory over the Mets, moving past Billy Hamilton into first place on the all-time list.

LEADERS

American League
BA: Fred Lynn, Bos., .333.
Runs: Don Baylor, Cal., 120.
Hits: George Brett, K.C., 212.
TB: Jim Rice, Bos., 369.
HR: Gorman Thomas, Mil., 45.
RBI: Don Baylor, Cal., 139.
SB: Willie Wilson, K.C., 83.
Wins: Mike Flanagan, Bal., 23.
ERA: Ron Guidry, N.Y., 2.78.
CG: Dennis Martinez, Bal., 18.
IP: Dennis Martinez, Bal., 292.1.
SO: Nolan Ryan, Cal., 223.
SV: Mike Marshall, Min., 32.

National League
BA: Keith Hernandez, St.L., .344.
Runs: Keith Hernandez, St.L., 116.
Hits: Garry Templeton, St.L., 211.
TB: Dave Winfield, S.D., 333.
HR: Dave Kingman, Chi., 48.
RBI: Dave Winfield, S.D., 118.
SB: Omar Moreno, Pit., 77.
Wins: Joe Niekro, Hou.; Phil Niekro, Atl., 21.
ERA: J.R. Richard, Hou., 2.71.
CG: Phil Niekro, Atl., 23.
IP: Phil Niekro, Atl., 342.
SO: J.R. Richard, Hou., 313.
SV: Bruce Sutter, Chi., 37.

A.L. 20-game winners
Mike Flanagan, Bal., 23-9
Tommy John, N.Y., 21-9
Jerry Koosman, Min., 20-13

N.L. 20-game winners
Joe Niekro, Hou., 21-11
Phil Niekro, Atl., 21-20

A.L. 100 RBIs
Don Baylor, Cal., 139
Jim Rice, Bos., 130
Gorman Thomas, Mil., 123
Fred Lynn, Bos., 122
Darrell Porter, K.C., 112
Ken Singleton, Bal., 111
George Brett, K.C., 107
Cecil Cooper, Mil., 106
Willie Horton, Sea., 106
Steve Kemp, Det., 105
Buddy Bell, Tex., 101
Dan Ford, Cal., 101
Bobby Grich, Cal., 101
Sixto Lezcano, Mil., 101
Bruce Bochte, Sea., 100

N.L. 100 RBIs
Dave Winfield, S.D., 118
Dave Kingman, Chi., 115
Mike Schmidt, Phil., 114
Steve Garvey, L.A., 110
Keith Hernandez, St.L., 105

A.L. 40 homers
Gorman Thomas, Mil., 45

N.L. 40 homers
Dave Kingman, Chi., 48
Mike Schmidt, Phil., 45

Most Valuable Player
A.L.: Don Baylor, OF, Cal.
N.L.: Willie Stargell, 1B, Pit.
Keith Hernandez, 1B, St.L.

Cy Young Award
A.L.: Mike Flanagan, Bal.
N.L.: Bruce Sutter, Chi.

Rookie of the Year
A.L.: John Castino, 3B, Min.
Alfredo Griffin, SS, Tor.
N.L.: Rick Sutcliffe, P, L.A.

Hall of Fame additions
Warren Giles, executive
Willie Mays, OF, 1951-73
Hack Wilson, OF, 1923-34

ALL-STAR GAME

■ **Winner:** Lee Mazzilli tied the game with an eighth-inning homer and drove in the winner in the ninth with a bases-loaded walk as the N.L. recorded a 7-6 victory in the 50th All-Star Game.

■ **Key innings:** The eighth, when Mazzilli erased a 6-5 deficit with an opposite-field blast, and the ninth, when he drew a base on balls off Ron Guidry after Jim Kern had walked the bases loaded.

■ **Memorable moments:** Game-saving seventh- and eighth-inning throws by right fielder Dave Parker that cut down A.L. runners at third base and home plate.

■ **Top guns:** Steve Rogers (Expos), Mazzilli (Mets), Mike Schmidt (Phillies), Parker (Pirates), N.L.; Fred Lynn (Red Sox), Don Baylor (Angels), Carl Yastrzemski (Red Sox), A.L.

■ **MVP:** Parker.

Linescore

July 17, at Seattle's Kingdome
N.L. ....2 1 1 0 0 1 0 1 1—7 10 1
A.L. ....3 0 2 0 0 1 0 0 0—6 10 0
Carlton (Phillies), Andujar (Astros) 2, Rogers (Expos) 4, Perry (Padres) 6, Sambito (Astros) 6, LaCoss (Reds) 6, Sutter (Cubs) 8; Ryan (Angels), Stanley (Red Sox) 3, Clear (Angels) 5, Kern (Rangers) 7, Guidry (Yankees) 9. W—Sutter. L—Kern. HR—Lynn, A.L.; Mazzilli, N.L.

ALCS

■ **Winner:** Baltimore, winner of the first three A.L. Championship Series, ruined California's first experience in the post-season spotlight.

■ **Turning point:** A dramatic three-run homer by Baltimore pinch-hitter John Lowenstein in the 10th inning of Game 1. Lowenstein's opposite-field shot broke a 3-3 deadlock and propelled the Orioles to their first pennant since 1971.

■ **Memorable moment:** A dramatic defensive play by Orioles third baseman Doug DeCinces. With one out and the bases loaded in the fifth inning of Game 4, DeCinces made a diving stop of Jim Anderson's shot down the third-base line, stepped on third and fired to first for a rally-killing double play that preserved a 3-0 lead.

■ **Top guns:** Scott McGregor (1-0, 0.00 ERA), Eddie Murray (.417, 5 RBIs), Rick Dempsey (.400), Orioles; Rod Carew (.412), Dan Ford (2 HR, 4 RBIs), Angels.

■ **MVP:** Murray.

Linescores

Game 1—October 3, at Baltimore
Cal. ....1 0 1 0 0 1 0 0 0 0—3 7 1
Balt. ....0 0 2 1 0 0 0 0 0 3—6 6 0
Ryan, Montague (8); Palmer, Stanhouse (10). W—Stanhouse. L—Montague. HR—Ford (Cal.); Lowenstein (Bal.).

Game 2—October 4, at Baltimore
Cal. ....1 0 0 0 0 1 1 3 2—8 10 1
Balt. ....4 4 1 0 0 0 0 0 x—9 11 1
Frost, Clear (2), Aase (8); Flanagan, Stanhouse (8). W—Flanagan. L—Frost. HR—Ford (Cal.); Murray (Bal.).

Game 3—October 5, at California
Balt. ....0 0 0 1 0 1 1 0 0—3 8 3
Cal. ....1 0 0 1 0 0 0 0 2—4 9 0
D. Martinez, Stanhouse (9); Tanana, Aase (6). W—Aase. L—Stanhouse. HR—Baylor (Cal.).

Game 4—October 6, at California
Balt. ....0 0 2 1 0 0 5 0 0—8 12 1
Cal. ....0 0 0 0 0 0 0 0 0—0 6 0
McGregor; Knapp, LaRoche (3), Frost (4), Montague (7), Barlow (9). W—McGregor. L—Knapp. HR—Kelly (Bal.).

NLCS

■ **Winner:** Pittsburgh, which had been swept by Cincinnati in the 1970 and '75 NLCS, turned the tables on the Reds and earned its first World Series berth since 1971.

■ **Turning point:** A 10th-inning single by Dave Parker that gave the Pirates a 3-2 victory in Game 2.

■ **Memorable moment:** Willie Stargell's three-run, 11th-inning homer, which gave the Pirates a 5-2 Game 1 victory and all the momentum they needed.

■ **Top guns:** Stargell (.455, 2 HR, 6 RBIs), Phil Garner (.417), Pirates; Dave Concepcion (.429), Reds.

■ **MVP:** Stargell.

Linescores

Game 1—October 2, at Cincinnati
Pitt. ....0 0 2 0 0 0 0 0 0 0 3—5 10 0
Cin. ....0 0 0 2 0 0 0 0 0 0 0—2 7 0
Candelaria, Romo (8), Tekulve (8), Jackson (10), D. Robinson (11); Seaver, Hume (9), Tomlin (11). W—Jackson. L—Hume. S—D. Robinson. HR—Garner, Stargell (Pit); Foster (Cin.).

Game 2—October 3, at Cincinnati
Pitt.........0 0 0 1 1 0 0 0 0 1—3 11 0
Cin. ....0 1 0 0 0 0 0 0 1 0—2 8 0
Bibby, Jackson (8), Romo (8), Tekulve (8), Roberts (9), D. Robinson (9); Pastore, Tomlin (8), Hume (8), Bair (10). W—D. Robinson. L—Bair.

Game 3—October 5, at Pittsburgh
Cin. ....0 0 0 0 0 1 0 0 0—1 8 1
Pitt. ....1 1 2 2 0 0 0 1 x—7 7 0
LaCoss, Norman (2), Leibrandt (4), Soto (5), Tomlin (7), Hume (8); Blyleven. W—Blyleven. L—LaCoss. HR—Stargell, Madlock (Pit.); Bench (Cin.).

WORLD SERIES

■ **Winner:** Pittsburgh's "Family" beat the Orioles and became the fourth team to recover from a three-games-to-one deficit.

■ **Turning point:** After blowing a 6-3, eighth-inning lead in Game 4 to fall within a game of elimination, the Pirates regrouped to win Game 5, 7-1, behind the six-hit pitching of Jim Rooker and Bert Blyleven.

■ **Memorable moment:** Willie Stargell's two-run, sixth-inning homer that put the Pirates ahead to stay in a 4-1 Series-ending victory.

■ **Top guns:** Phil Garner (.500, 12 hits), Stargell (.400, 12 hits, 3 HR, 7 RBIs), Bill Madlock (.375), Pirates; Kiko Garcia (.400, 6 RBIs), Orioles.

■ **MVP:** Stargell.

Linescores

Game 1—October 10, at Baltimore
Pitt. ....0 0 0 1 0 2 0 1 0—4 11 3
Balt. ....5 0 0 0 0 0 0 0 x—5 6 3
Kison, Rooker (1), Romo (5), D. Robinson (6), Jackson (8); Flanagan. W—Flanagan. L—Kison. HR—DeCinces (Bal.); Stargell (Pit.).

Game 2—October 11, at Baltimore
Pitt. ....0 2 0 0 0 0 0 0 1—3 11 2
Balt. ....0 1 0 0 0 1 0 0 0—2 6 1
Blyleven, D. Robinson (7), Tekulve (9); Palmer, T. Martinez (8), Stanhouse (9). W—D. Robinson. L—Stanhouse. S—Tekulve. HR—Murray (Bal.).

Game 3—October 12, at Pittsburgh
Balt. ....0 0 2 5 0 0 1 0 0—8 13 0
Pitt. ....1 2 0 0 0 1 0 0 0—4 9 2
McGregor; Candelaria, Romo (4), Jackson (7), Tekulve (8). W—McGregor. L—Candelaria. HR—Ayala (Bal.).

Game 4—October 13, at Pittsburgh
Balt. ....0 0 3 0 0 0 0 6 0—9 12 0
Pitt. ....0 4 0 0 1 1 0 0 0—6 17 1
D. Martinez, Stewart (2), Stone (5), Stoddard (7); Bibby, Jackson (7), D. Robinson (8), Tekulve (8). W—Stoddard. L—Tekulve. HR—Stargell (Pit.).

Game 5—October 14, at Pittsburgh
Balt. ....0 0 0 0 1 0 0 0 0—1 6 2
Pitt. ....0 0 0 0 0 2 2 3 x—7 13 1
Flanagan, Stoddard (7), T. Martinez (7), Stanhouse (8); Rooker, Blyleven (6). W—Blyleven. L—Flanagan.

Game 6—October 16, at Baltimore
Pitt. ....0 0 0 0 0 0 2 2 0—4 10 0
Balt. ....0 0 0 0 0 0 0 0 0—0 7 1
Candelaria, Tekulve (7); Palmer, Stoddard (9). W—Candelaria. L—Palmer. S—Tekulve.

Game 7—October 17, at Baltimore
Pitt. ....0 0 0 0 0 2 0 0 2—4 10 0
Balt. ....0 0 1 0 0 0 0 0 0—1 4 2
Bibby, D. Robinson (5), Jackson (5), Tekulve (8); McGregor, Stoddard (9), Flanagan (9), Stanhouse (9), T. Martinez (9), D. Martinez (9). W—Jackson. L—McGregor. S—Tekulve. HR—Dauer (Bal.); Stargell (Pit.).

FINAL STANDINGS

American League

East Division

Team	N.Y.	Bal.	Mil.	Bos.	Det.	Cle.	Tor.	Cal.	Chi.	K.C.	Min.	Oak.	Sea.	Tex.	W	L	Pct.	GB
New York	...	6	8	10	8	8	10	10	7	4	8	8	9	7	103	59	.636	...
Baltimore	7	...	7	8	10	6	11	10	6	6	10	7	6	6	100	62	.617	3
Milwaukee	5	6	...	7	6	10	5	6	7	6	7	7	9	5	86	76	.531	17
Boston	3	5	6	...	8	7	7	9	6	5	6	9	7	5	83	77	.519	19
Detroit	5	3	7	5	...	10	9	7	10	2	6	6	10	4	84	78	.519	19
Cleveland	5	7	3	6	3	...	8	6	7	5	9	6	8	6	79	81	.494	23
Toronto	3	2	8	6	4	5	...	9	7	3	5	4	6	5	67	95	.414	36

West Division

Team	K.C.	Oak.	Min.	Tex.	Chi.	Cal.	Sea.	Bal.	Bos.	Cle.	Det.	Mil.	N.Y.	Tor.	W	L	Pct.	GB
Kansas City	...	6	5	10	8	8	7	6	7	7	10	6	8	9	97	65	.599	...
Oakland	7	...	7	7	7	10	8	5	3	6	6	5	4	8	83	79	.512	14
Minnesota	8	6	...	9	8	6	7	2	6	3	6	5	4	7	77	84	.478	19.5
Texas	3	6	3	...	7	2	9	6	7	6	8	7	5	7	76	85	.472	20.5
Chicago	5	6	5	6	...	10	6	6	4	5	2	5	5	5	70	90	.438	26
California	5	3	7	11	3	...	11	2	3	4	5	6	2	3	65	95	.406	31
Seattle	6	5	6	4	7	2	...	6	5	4	2	3	3	6	59	103	.364	38

National League

East Division

Team	Phi.	Mon.	Pit.	St.L.	N.Y.	Chi.	Atl.	Cin.	Hou.	L.A.	S.D.	S.F.	W	L	Pct.	GB
Philadelphia	...	9	7	9	12	13	7	5	9	6	8	6	91	71	.562	...
Montreal	9	...	6	12	10	12	7	9	7	1	10	7	90	72	.556	1
Pittsburgh	11	12	...	10	8	10	1	6	5	6	6	8	83	79	.512	8
St. Louis	9	6	8	...	9	9	6	7	5	5	5	5	74	88	.457	17
New York	6	8	10	9	...	8	9	4	4	5	1	3	67	95	.414	24
Chicago	5	6	8	9	10	...	4	7	1	5	4	5	64	98	.395	27

West Division

Team	Hou.	L.A.	Cin.	Atl.	S.F.	S.D.	Chi.	Mon.	N.Y.	Phi.	Pit.	St.L.	W	L	Pct.	GB
Houston	...	9	10	11	11	11	11	5	8	3	7	7	93	70	.571	...
Los Angeles	10	...	9	7	13	9	7	11	7	6	6	7	92	71	.564	1
Cincinnati	8	9	...	16	7	15	5	3	8	7	6	5	89	73	.549	3.5
Atlanta	7	11	2	...	11	12	8	5	3	5	11	6	81	80	.503	11
San Fran.	7	5	11	6	...	8	7	5	9	6	4	7	75	86	.466	17
San Diego	7	9	3	6	10	...	8	2	11	4	6	7	73	89	.451	19.5

SIGNIFICANT EVENTS

■ **January 24:** Nelson Doubleday and Fred Wilpon headed a group that bought the New York Mets for a reported $21.1 million.

■ **May 23:** The owners and players agreed to defer settlement of the free-agent compensation issue, thus avoiding the first player in-season walkout in baseball history.

■ **July 30:** Houston ace J.R. Richard was rushed to the hospital after suffering a career-ending stroke during a light workout at the Astrodome.

■ **November 18:** Kansas City's George Brett, who finished the season with the highest average (.390) since 1941, captured A.L. MVP honors.

MEMORABLE MOMENTS

■ **September 30:** Oakland's Rickey Henderson, en route to the A.L.'s first 100-steal season, passed Ty Cobb's A.L. record of 96 in a 5-1 victory over Chicago.

■ **October 6:** The Astros, who allowed the Dodgers to force a division playoff with a three-game season-closing sweep, rebounded to win their first N.L. West title with a 7-1 victory.

LEADERS

American League
BA: George Brett, K.C., .390.
Runs: Willie Wilson, K.C., 133.
Hits: Willie Wilson, K.C., 230.
TB: Cecil Cooper, Mil., 335.
HR: Reggie Jackson, N.Y.; Ben Oglivie, Mil., 41.
RBI: Cecil Cooper, Mil., 122.
SB: Rickey Henderson, Oak., 100.
Wins: Steve Stone, Bal., 25.
ERA: Rudy May, N.Y., 2.46.
CG: Rick Langford, Oak., 28.
IP: Rick Langford, Oak., 290.
SO: Len Barker, Cle., 187.
SV: Goose Gossage, N.Y.; Dan Quisenberry, K.C., 33.

National League
BA: Bill Buckner, Chi., .324.
Runs: Keith Hernandez, St.L., 111.
Hits: Steve Garvey, L.A., 200.
TB: Mike Schmidt, Phil., 342.
HR: Mike Schmidt, Phil., 48.
RBI: Mike Schmidt, Phil., 121.
SB: Ron LeFlore, Mon., 97.
Wins: Steve Carlton, Phil., 24.
ERA: Don Sutton, L.A., 2.20.
CG: Steve Rogers, Mon., 14.
IP: Steve Carlton, Phil., 304.
SO: Steve Carlton, Phil., 286.
SV: Bruce Sutter, Chi., 28.

A.L. 20-game winners
Steve Stone, Bal., 25-7
Tommy John, N.Y., 22-9
Mike Norris, Oak., 22-9
Scott McGregor, Bal., 20-8
Dennis Leonard, K.C., 20-11

N.L. 20-game winners
Steve Carlton, Phil., 24-9
Joe Niekro, Hou., 20-12

A.L. 100 RBIs
Cecil Cooper, Mil., 122
George Brett, K.C., 118
Ben Oglivie, Mil., 118
Al Oliver, Tex., 117
Eddie Murray, Bal., 116
Reggie Jackson, N.Y., 111
Tony Armas, Oak., 109
Tony Perez, Bos., 105
Gorman Thomas, Mil., 105
Ken Singleton, Bal., 104
Steve Kemp, Det., 101

N.L. 100 RBIs
Mike Schmidt, Phil., 121
George Hendrick, St.L., 109
Steve Garvey, L.A., 106
Gary Carter, Mon., 101

A.L. 40 homers
Reggie Jackson, N.Y., 41
Ben Oglivie, Mil., 41

N.L. 40 homers
Mike Schmidt, Phil., 48

Most Valuable Player
A.L.: George Brett, 3B, K.C.
N.L.: Mike Schmidt, 3B, Phil.

Cy Young Award
A.L.: Steve Stone, Bal.
N.L.: Steve Carlton, Phil.

Rookie of the Year
A.L.: Joe Charboneau, OF, Cle.
N.L.: Steve Howe, P, L.A.

Hall of Fame additions
Al Kaline, OF, 1953-74
Chuck Klein, OF, 1928-44
Duke Snider, OF, 1947-64
Tom Yawkey, executive/owner

ALL-STAR GAME

■ **Winner:** The N.L., held hitless for 4⅔ innings, scored the go-ahead run on a sixth-inning error and started the new decade with a 4-2 victory, its ninth straight in All-Star competition.

■ **Key inning:** The sixth, when the N.L. took a 3-2 lead on George Hendrick's single and second baseman Willie Randolph's error on a smash hit by Dave Winfield.

■ **Memorable moment:** Ken Griffey's two-out homer in the fifth. Before the solo blast, the N.L. had not even managed a baserunner against A.L. hurlers Steve Stone and Tommy John.

■ **Top guns:** J.R. Richard (Astros), Griffey (Reds), Hendrick (Cardinals), N.L.; Stone (Orioles), Rod Carew (Angels), Fred Lynn (Red Sox), A.L.

■ **MVP:** Griffey.

Linescore
July 8, at Los Angeles' Dodger Stadium
A.L. ....0 0 0 0 2 0 0 0 0—2 7 2
N.L. ....0 0 0 0 1 2 1 0 x—4 7 0
Stone (Orioles), John (Yankees) 4, Farmer (White Sox) 6, Stieb (Blue Jays) 7, Gossage (Yankees) 8; Richard (Astros), Welch (Dodgers) 3, Reuss (Dodgers) 6, Bibby (Pirates) 7, Sutter (Cubs) 8. W—Reuss. L—John. S—Sutter. HR—Lynn, A.L.; Griffey, N.L.

ALCS

■ **Winner:** Kansas City, a Championship Series loser to the Yankees in 1976, '77 and '78, qualified for its first World Series with an impressive sweep.

■ **Turning point:** The eighth inning of Game 2, when the Royals threw out Yankee Willie Randolph at the plate, preserving a 3-2 victory. Randolph was trying to score on a two-out double by Bob Watson.

■ **Memorable moment:** A titanic three-run homer by George Brett that produced a 4-2 series-ending victory. Brett's seventh-inning blast off relief ace Goose Gossage landed in the third deck at Yankee Stadium.

■ **Top guns:** Dan Quisenberry (1-0, 1 save, 0.00 ERA), Frank White (.545), Brett (2 HR, 4 RBIs), Royals; Watson (.500), Randolph (.385), Yankees.

■ **MVP:** White.

Linescores

Game 1—October 8, at Kansas City
N.Y. ....0 2 0 0 0 0 0 0 0—2 10 1
K.C. ....0 2 2 0 0 0 1 2 x—7 10 0
Guidry, Davis (4), Underwood (8); Gura. W—Gura. L—Guidry. HR—Cerone, Piniella (N.Y.); Brett (K.C.).

Game 2—October 9, at Kansas City
N.Y. ....0 0 0 0 2 0 0 0 0—2 8 0
K.C. ....0 0 3 0 0 0 0 0 x—3 6 0
May; Leonard, Quisenberry (9). W—Leonard. L—May. S—Quisenberry. HR—Nettles (N.Y.).

Game 3—October 10, at New York
K.C. ....0 0 0 0 1 0 3 0 0—4 12 1
N.Y. ....0 0 0 0 0 2 0 0 0—2 8 0
Splittorff, Quisenberry (6); John, Gossage (7), Underwood (8). W—Quisenberry. L—Gossage. HR—White, Brett (K.C.).

NLCS

■ **Winner:** Philadelphia scored in the 10th inning of Game 5 to dispatch Houston, 8-7, and qualify for its first World Series since 1950.

■ **Turning point:** A Game 4 collision in which Pete Rose bowled over Houston catcher Bruce Bochy. Rose scored the winning run on the 10th-inning play, giving the Phillies a series-tying victory.

■ **Memorable moment:** A fourth-game controversy that wiped out Houston claims of a triple play and sparked protests by both teams. The fourth-inning confusion revolved around the "catch" or "trap" of a line drive by Astros pitcher Vern Ruhle and stopped play for 20 minutes.

■ **Top guns:** Rose (.400), Manny Trillo (.381), Phillies; Joe Niekro (10 IP, 0.00 ERA), Terry Puhl (.526), Jose Cruz (.400), Astros.

■ **MVP:** Trillo.

Linescores

Game 1—October 7, at Philadelphia
Hou. ....0 0 1 0 0 0 0 0 0—1 7 0
Phil. ....0 0 0 0 0 2 1 0 x—3 8 1
Forsch; Carlton, McGraw (8). W—Carlton. L—Forsch. S—McGraw. HR—Luzinski (Phil.).

Game 2—October 8, at Philadelphia
Hou. ......0 0 1 0 0 0 1 1 0 4—7 8 1
Phil. ......0 0 0 2 0 0 0 1 0 1—4 14 2
Ryan, Sambito (7), D. Smith (7), LaCorte (9), Andujar (10); Ruthven, McGraw (8), Reed (9), Saucier (10). W—LaCorte. L—Reed. S—Andujar.

Game 3—October 10, at Houston
Phil. ..0 0 0 0 0 0 0 0 0 0 0—0 7 1
Hou. ..0 0 0 0 0 0 0 0 0 0 1—1 6 1
Christenson, Noles (7), McGraw (8); Niekro, D. Smith (11). W—D. Smith. L—McGraw.

Game 4—October 11, at Houston
Phil. ......0 0 0 0 0 0 0 3 0 2—5 13 0
Hou. ......0 0 0 1 1 0 0 0 1 0—3 5 1
Carlton, Noles (6), Saucier (7), Reed (7), Brusstar (8), McGraw (10); Ruhle, D. Smith (8), Sambito (8). W—Brusstar. L—Sambito. S—McGraw.

Game 5—October 12, at Houston
Phil. ......0 2 0 0 0 0 0 5 0 1—8 13 2
Hou. ......1 0 0 0 0 1 3 2 0 0—7 14 0
Bystrom, Brusstar (6), Christenson (7), Reed (7), McGraw (8), Ruthven (9); Ryan, Sambito (8), Forsch (8), LaCorte (9). W—Ruthven. L—LaCorte.

WORLD SERIES

■ **Winner:** The Phillies, two-time Series qualifiers in their 97-year history, won their first fall classic with a six-game victory over the Royals — first-time Series participants.

■ **Turning point:** A two-run, ninth-inning rally that gave the Phillies a 4-3 victory in Game 5 and a three-games-to-two Series lead.

■ **Memorable moments:** The clutch pitching of Phillies reliever Tug McGraw, who recorded bases-loaded, game-ending strikeouts in Games 5 and 6.

■ **Top guns:** Steve Carlton (2-0, 2.40 ERA), McGraw (2 saves, 1.17), Mike Schmidt (.381, 2 HR, 7 RBIs), Phillies; Amos Otis (.478, 3 HR, 7 RBIs), Willie Aikens (.400, 4 HR, 8 RBIs), Royals.

■ **MVP:** Schmidt.

Linescores

Game 1—October 14, at Philadelphia
K.C. ....0 2 2 0 0 0 0 2 0—6 9 1
Phil. ....0 0 5 1 1 0 0 0 x—7 11 0
Leonard, Martin (4), Quisenberry (8); Walk, McGraw (8). W—Walk. L—Leonard. S—McGraw. HR—Otis, Aikens 2 (K.C.); McBride (Phil.).

Game 2—October 15, at Philadelphia
K.C. ....0 0 0 0 0 1 3 0 0—4 11 0
Phil. ....0 0 0 0 2 0 0 4 x—6 8 1
Gura, Quisenberry (7); Carlton, Reed (9). W—Carlton. L—Quisenberry. S—Reed.

Game 3—October 17, at Kansas City
Phil. ......0 1 0 0 1 0 0 1 0 0—3 14 0
K.C. ....1 0 0 1 0 0 1 0 0 1—4 11 0
Ruthven, McGraw (10); Gale, Martin (5), Quisenberry (8). W—Quisenberry. L—McGraw. HR—Brett, Otis (K.C.); Schmidt (Phil.).

Game 4—October 18, at Kansas City
Phil. ....0 1 0 0 0 0 1 1 0—3 10 1
K.C. ....4 1 0 0 0 0 0 0 x—5 10 2
Christenson, Noles (1), Saucier (6), Brusstar (6); Leonard, Quisenberry (8). W—Leonard. L—Christenson. S—Quisenberry. HR—Aikens 2 (K.C.).

Game 5—October 19, at Kansas City
Phil. ....0 0 0 2 0 0 0 0 2—4 7 0
K.C. ....0 0 0 0 1 2 0 0 0—3 12 2
Bystrom, Reed (6), McGraw (7); Gura, Quisenberry (7). W—McGraw. L—Quisenberry. HR—Schmidt (Phil.); Otis (K.C.).

Game 6—October 21, at Philadelphia
K.C. ....0 0 0 0 0 0 0 1 0—1 7 2
Phil. ....0 0 2 0 1 1 0 0 x—4 9 0
Gale, Martin (3), Splittorff (5), Pattin (7), Quisenberry (8); Carlton, McGraw (8). W—Carlton. L—Gale. S—McGraw.

HISTORY

FINAL STANDINGS

American League

East Division

Team	Mil.	Bal.	N.Y.	Det.	Bos.	Cle.	Tor.	Oak.	Tex.	Chi.	K.C.	Cal.	Sea.	Min.	W	L	Pct.	GB
Milwaukee†	...	4	3	8	7	6	6	4	4	1	5	3	2	9	62	47	.569	...
Baltimore	2	...	7	6	2	4	5	7	2	3	5	6	4	6	59	46	.562	1
New York*	3	6	...	7	3	5	2	4	5	7	10	2	2	3	59	48	.551	2
Detroit	5	7	3	...	1	5	6	1	9	3	3	3	5	9	60	49	.550	2
Boston	6	2	3	6	...	7	4	7	3	5	3	2	9	2	59	49	.546	2.5
Cleveland	3	2	7	1	6	...	4	3	2	5	4	5	8	2	52	51	.505	7
Toronto	4	2	3	4	0	2	...	2	2	5	3	6	3	1	37	69	.349	23.5

West Division

Team	Oak.	Tex.	Chi.	K.C.	Cal.	Sea.	Min.	Mil.	Bal.	N.Y.	Det.	Bos.	Cle.	Tor.	W	L	Pct.	GB
Oakland*	...	4	6	3	8	6	8	2	5	3	2	5	2	10	64	45	.587	...
Texas	2	...	4	4	4	8	8	5	1	4	3	6	2	6	57	48	.543	5
Chicago	7	2	...	2	7	3	2	4	6	5	3	4	2	7	54	52	.509	8.5
Kansas City†	3	3	0	...	6	6	9	4	3	2	2	3	4	5	50	53	.485	11
California	2	2	6	0	...	6	3	4	6	2	3	4	7	6	51	59	.464	13.5
Seattle	1	5	3	7	4	...	6	2	2	3	1	3	4	3	44	65	.404	20
Minnesota	2	5	4	4	3	3	...	3	0	3	3	5	1	5	41	68	.376	23

National League

East Division

Team	St.L.	Mon.	Phi.	Pit.	N.Y.	Chi.	Cin.	L.A.	Hou.	S.F.	Atl.	S.D.	W	L	Pct.	GB
St.Louis	...	9	6	8	5	4	5	5	4	3	3	7	59	43	.578	...
Montreal†	6	...	7	10	9	7	4	2	2	2	7	4	60	48	.556	2
Philadelphia*	7	4	...	7	7	10	2	3	6	4	5	4	59	48	.551	2.5
Pittsburgh	3	3	5	...	6	10	2	1	4	3	3	6	46	56	.451	13
New York	6	3	7	3	...	8	3	1	3	2	3	2	41	62	.398	18.5
Chicago	5	4	2	4	5	...	1	6	1	5	2	3	38	65	.369	21.5

West Division

Team	Cin.	L.A.	Hou.	S.F.	Atl.	S.D.	St.L.	Mon.	Phi.	Pit.	N.Y.	Chi.	W	L	Pct.	GB
Cincinnati	...	8	8	9	5	10	0	5	5	4	7	5	66	42	.611	...
Los Angeles*	8	...	8	7	7	6	5	5	3	5	5	4	63	47	.573	4
Houston†	4	4	...	9	8	11	2	5	4	2	6	6	61	49	.555	6
San Fran.	5	5	6	...	7	7	2	5	3	7	4	5	56	55	.505	11.5
Atlanta	6	7	4	5	...	9	4	3	4	2	3	3	50	56	.472	15
San Diego	2	5	3	6	6	...	3	2	2	4	5	3	41	69	.373	26

* Won first-half division title † Won second-half division title

SIGNIFICANT EVENTS

■ **February 12:** Boston catcher Carlton Fisk was declared a free agent because the Red Sox violated the Basic Agreement by mailing his contract two days beyond the deadline.

■ **July 31:** Baseball's 50-day strike, the longest in American sports history, ended when owners and players reached agreement on the free-agent compensation issue.

■ **November 11:** Dodgers lefty Fernando Valenzuela became the first rookie to win a Cy Young when he outpointed the Reds' Tom Seaver for N.L. honors.

■ **November 25:** Milwaukee's Rollie Fingers, who earlier was named A.L. Cy Young winner, became the first relief pitcher to win an A.L. MVP.

MEMORABLE MOMENTS

■ **May 15:** Cleveland's Len Barker retired 27 consecutive Blue Jays in a 3-0 victory and pitched the first Major League perfect game in 13 years.

■ **August 10:** Philadelphia's Pete Rose collected career hit No. 3,631 in a 6-2 loss to St. Louis and moved into third place on the all-time list.

■ **September 26:** Houston's Nolan Ryan stepped into uncharted territory when he fired his record-setting fifth no-hitter, beating the Dodgers, 5-0.

■ **October 11:** The Dodgers, Expos and Yankees won decisive fifth games of special post-season series set up to determine division champions because of the 50-day baseball strike.

LEADERS

American League
BA: Carney Lansford, Bos., .336.
Runs: Rickey Henderson, Oak., 89.
Hits: Rickey Henderson, Oak., 135.
TB: Dwight Evans, Bos., 215.
HR: Tony Armas, Oak.; Dwight Evans, Bos.; Bobby Grich, Cal.; Eddie Murray, Bal., 22.
RBI: Eddie Murray, Bal., 78.
SB: Rickey Henderson, Oak., 56.
Wins: Dennis Martinez, Bal.; Steve McCatty, Oak.; Jack Morris, Det.; Pete Vuckovich, Mil., 14.
ERA: Dave Righetti, N.Y., 2.05
CG: Rick Langford, Oak., 18.
IP: Dennis Leonard, K.C., 201.2.
SO: Len Barker, Cle., 127.
SV: Rollie Fingers, Mil., 28.

National League
BA: Bill Madlock, Pit., .341.
Runs: Mike Schmidt, Phil., 78.
Hits: Pete Rose, Phil., 140.
TB: Mike Schmidt, Phil., 228.
HR: Mike Schmidt, Phil., 31.
RBI: Mike Schmidt, Phil., 91.
SB: Tim Raines, Mon., 71.
Wins: Tom Seaver, Cin., 14.
ERA: Nolan Ryan, Hou., 1.69.
CG: Fernando Valenzuela, L.A., 11.
IP: Fernando Valenzuela, L.A., 192.1.
SO: Fernando Valenzuela, L.A., 180.
SV: Bruce Sutter, St.L., 25.

Most Valuable Player
A.L.: Rollie Fingers, P, Mil.
N.L.: Mike Schmidt, 3B, Phil.

Cy Young Award
A.L.: Rollie Fingers, Mil.
N.L.: Fernando Valenzuela, L.A.

Rookie of the Year
A.L.: Dave Righetti, P, N.Y.
N.L.: Fernando Valenzuela, P, L.A.

Hall of Fame additions
Rube Foster, manager/executive, Negro Leagues
Bob Gibson, P, 1959-75
Johnny Mize, 1B, 1936-53

ALL-STAR GAME

■ **Winner:** With the All-Star Game serving as the official resumption of the season after a 50-day players' strike, the N.L. continued its winning ways by belting four home runs and stretching its winning streak to 10.

■ **Key inning:** The eighth, when Mike Schmidt drilled a two-run homer off Rollie Fingers, giving the N.L. its tying and winning runs.

■ **Memorable moment:** Gary Carter's solo blast in the seventh inning, his second home run of the game. Carter became the fifth All-Star performer to homer twice.

■ **Top guns:** Schmidt (Phillies), Carter (Expos), Dave Parker (Pirates), N.L.; Len Barker (Indians), Fred Lynn (Angels), Ken Singleton (Orioles), A.L.

■ **MVP:** Carter.

Linescore
August 9, at Cleveland Stadium
N.L.............0 0 0 0 1 1 1 2 0—5 9 1
A.L.............0 1 0 0 0 3 0 0 0—4 11 1
Valenzuela (Dodgers), Seaver (Reds) 2, Knepper (Astros) 3, Hooton (Dodgers) 5, Ruthven (Phillies) 6, Blue (Giants) 7, Ryan (Astros) 8, Sutter (Cardinals) 9; Morris (Tigers), Barker (Indians) 3, Forsch (Angels) 5, Norris (Athletics) 6, Davis (Yankees) 7, Fingers (Brewers) 8, Stieb (Blue Jays) 8. W—Blue. L—Fingers. S—Sutter. HR—Singleton, A.L.; Carter 2, Parker, Schmidt, N.L.

DIVISIONAL PLAYOFFS

Los Angeles defeated Houston, 3 games to 2
Montreal defeated Philadelphia, 3 games to 2
NY Yankees defeated Milwaukee, 3 games to 2
Oakland defeated Kansas City, 3 games to 0

ALCS

■ **Winner:** The New York Yankees captured their 33rd pennant with a 1-2-3 Championship Series victory over Oakland.

■ **Turning point:** The first inning of Game 1, when Yankee third baseman Graig Nettles drilled a three-run double, giving lefty Tommy John and two relievers all the runs they needed for a 3-1 victory.

■ **Memorable moment:** The ninth inning of Game 3, when Nettles drilled another three-run double, putting the wraps on a 4-0 series-ending victory.

■ **Top guns:** Nettles (.500, 1 HR, 9 RBIs), Jerry Mumphrey (.500), Larry Milbourne (.462), Yankees; Rickey Henderson (.364), Athletics.

■ **MVP:** Nettles.

Linescores

Game 1—October 13 at New York
Oakland........0 0 0 0 1 0 0 0 0—1 6 1
N.Y.............3 0 0 0 0 0 0 0 x—3 7 1
Norris, Underwood (8); John, Davis (7), Gossage (8). W—John. L—Norris. S—Gossage.

Game 2—October 14, at New York
Oakland....0 0 1 2 0 0 0 0 0— 3 11 1
N.Y..........1 0 0 7 0 1 4 0 x—13 19 0
McCatty, Beard (4), Jones (5), Kingman (7), Owchinko (7); May, Frazier (4). W—Frazier. L—McCatty. HR—Piniella, Nettles (N.Y.).

Game 3—October 15, at Oakland
N.Y............0 0 0 0 0 1 0 0 3—4 10 0
Oakland......0 0 0 0 0 0 0 0 0—0 5 2
Righetti, Davis (7), Gossage (9); Keough, Underwood (9). W—Righetti. L—Keough. HR—Randolph (N.Y.).

NLCS

■ **Winner:** The Los Angeles Dodgers ruined Montreal's bid to become the first Canadian qualifier for a World Series with a dramatic ninth-inning home run in the fifth game.

■ **Turning point:** An eighth-inning Game 4 home run by Steve Garvey that broke a 1-1 tie and propelled the Dodgers to an elimination-saving 7-1 victory.

■ **Memorable moment:** A ninth-inning series-winning home run by Dodgers outfielder Rick Monday off Expos ace Steve Rogers in Game 5 at frigid Montreal.

■ **Top guns:** Burt Hooton (2-0, 0.00 ERA), Monday (.333), Dusty Baker (.316), Dodgers; Ray Burris (1-0, 0.53 ERA), Gary Carter (.438), Expos.

■ **MVP:** Hooton.

Linescores

Game 1—October 13, at Los Angeles
Montreal......0 0 0 0 0 0 0 0 1—1 9 0
L.A..............0 2 0 0 0 0 0 3 x—5 8 0
Gullickson, Reardon (8); Hooton, Welch (8), Howe (9). W—Hooton. L—Gullickson. HR—Guerrero, Scioscia (L.A.).

Game 2—October 14, at Los Angeles
Montreal....0 2 0 0 0 1 0 0 0—3 10 1
L.A............0 0 0 0 0 0 0 0 0—0 5 1
Burris; Valenzuela, Niedenfuer (7), Forster (7), Pena (7), Castillo (9). W—Burris. L—Valenzuela.

Game 3—October 16, at Montreal
L.A..............0 0 0 1 0 0 0 0 0—1 7 0
Montreal......0 0 0 0 0 4 0 0 x—4 7 1
Reuss, Pena (8); Rogers. W—Rogers. L—Reuss. HR—White (Mon.).

Game 4—October 17, at Montreal
L.A............0 0 1 0 0 0 0 2 4—7 12 1
Montreal....0 0 0 1 0 0 0 0 0—1 5 1
Hooton, Welch (8), Howe (9); Gullickson, Fryman (8), Sosa (9), Lee (9). W—Hooton. L—Gullickson. HR—Garvey (L.A.).

Game 5—October 19, at Montreal
L.A..............0 0 0 0 1 0 0 0 1—2 6 0
Montreal......1 0 0 0 0 0 0 0 0—1 3 1
Valenzuela, Welch (9); Burris, Rogers (9). W—Valenzuela. L—Rogers. S—Welch. HR—Monday (L.A.).

WORLD SERIES

■ **Winner:** The Dodgers brought the strike-shortened season to an end by duplicating the Yankees' 1978 feat against them—four straight victories after two opening losses.

■ **Turning point:** After falling behind 4-0 and 6-3 in Game 4, the Dodgers rallied for an 8-7 victory that squared the Series at two games.

■ **Memorable moment:** Back-to-back, seventh-inning home runs by Pedro Guerrero and Steve Yeager that gave Jerry Reuss a 2-1 victory over Ron Guidry and the Yankees in the pivotal fifth game.

■ **Top guns:** Steve Garvey (.417), Ron Cey (.350, 6 RBIs), Guerrero (.333, 2 HR, 7 RBIs), Dodgers; Bob Watson (.318, 2 HR, 7 RBIs), Yankees.

■ **Co-MVPs:** Guerrero, Yeager, Cey.

Linescores

Game 1—October 20, at New York
L.A..............0 0 0 0 1 0 0 2 0—3 5 0
N.Y..............3 0 1 1 0 0 0 0 x—5 6 0
Reuss, Castillo (3), Goltz (4), Niedenfuer (5), Stewart (8); Guidry, Davis (8), Gossage (8). W—Guidry. L—Reuss. S—Gossage. HR—Yeager (L.A.); Watson (N.Y.).

Game 2—October 21, at New York
L.A..............0 0 0 0 0 0 0 0 0—0 4 2
N.Y..............0 0 0 0 1 0 0 2 x—3 6 1
Hooton, Forster (7), Howe (8), Stewart (8); John, Gossage (8). W—John. L—Hooton. S—Gossage.

Game 3—October 23, at Los Angeles
N.Y............0 2 2 0 0 0 0 0 0—4 9 0
L.A............3 0 0 0 2 0 0 0 x—5 11 1
Righetti, Frazier (3), May (5), Davis (8); Valenzuela. W—Valenzuela. L—Frazier. HR—Cey (L.A.); Watson, Cerone (N.Y.).

Game 4—October 24, at Los Angeles
N.Y............2 1 1 0 0 2 0 1 0—7 13 1
L.A............0 0 2 0 1 3 2 0 x—8 14 2
Reuschel, May (4), Davis (5), Frazier (6), John (7); Welch, Goltz (1), Forster (4), Niedenfuer (5), Howe (7). W—Howe. L—Frazier. HR—Randolph, Jackson (N.Y.); Johnstone (L.A.).

Game 5—October 25, at Los Angeles
N.Y..............0 1 0 0 0 0 0 0 0—1 5 0
L.A..............0 0 0 0 0 0 2 0 x—2 4 3
Guidry, Gossage (8); Reuss. W—Reuss. L—Guidry. HR—Guerrero, Yeager (L.A.).

Game 6—October 28, at New York
L.A............0 0 0 1 3 4 0 1 0—9 13 1
N.Y............0 0 1 0 0 1 0 0 0—2 7 2
Hooton, Howe (6); John, Frazier (5), Davis (6), Reuschel (6), May (7), LaRoche (9). W—Hooton. L—Frazier. S—Howe. HR—Randolph (N.Y.); Guerrero (L.A.).

FINAL STANDINGS

American League

East Division

Team	Mil.	Bal.	Bos.	Det.	N.Y.	Tor.	Cle.	Cal.	Chi.	K.C.	Min.	Oak.	Sea.	Tex.	W	L	Pct.	GB
Milwaukee	...	4	9	10	8	9	6	6	9	5	7	7	8	7	95	67	.586	...
Baltimore	9	...	4	7	11	10	6	7	5	4	8	7	7	9	94	68	.580	1
Boston	4	9	...	8	7	7	6	7	4	6	6	8	7	10	89	73	.549	6
Detroit	3	6	5	...	8	6	7	7	3	6	9	9	6	8	83	79	.512	12
New York	5	2	6	5	...	6	9	5	4	7	10	7	6	7	79	83	.488	16
Toronto	4	3	6	7	7	...	6	4	4	8	7	9	5	8	78	84	.481	17
Cleveland	7	7	7	6	4	7	...	4	6	2	8	4	9	7	78	84	.481	17

West Division

Team	Cal.	K.C.	Chi.	Sea.	Oak.	Tex.	Min.	Bal.	Bos.	Cle.	Det.	Mil.	N.Y.	Tor.	W	L	Pct.	GB
California	...	7	8	10	9	8	7	5	5	8	5	6	7	8	93	69	.574	...
Kansas City	6	...	10	7	7	7	7	8	6	10	6	7	5	4	90	72	.556	3
Chicago	5	3	...	6	9	8	7	7	8	6	9	3	8	8	87	75	.537	6
Seattle	3	6	7	...	7	9	8	5	5	3	6	4	6	7	76	86	.469	17
Oakland	4	6	4	6	...	5	10	5	4	8	3	5	5	3	68	94	.420	25
Texas	5	6	5	4	8	...	8	3	2	5	4	5	5	4	64	98	.395	29
Minnesota	6	6	6	5	3	5	...	4	6	4	3	5	2	5	60	102	.370	33

National League

East Division

Team	St.L.	Phi.	Mon.	Pit.	Chi.	N.Y.	Atl.	Cin.	Hou.	L.A.	S.D.	S.F.	W	L	Pct	.GB
St. Louis	...	11	8	11	12	12	5	7	6	5	8	7	92	70	.568	...
Philadelphia	7	...	10	9	9	11	6	7	5	8	7	10	89	73	.549	3
Montreal	10	8	...	7	12	11	7	8	8	4	7	4	86	76	.531	6
Pittsburgh	7	9	11	...	9	10	8	8	3	7	6	6	84	78	.519	8
Chicago	6	9	6	9	...	9	4	6	9	5	4	6	73	89	.451	19
New York	6	7	7	8	9	...	3	5	4	6	6	4	65	97	.401	27

West Division

Team	Atl.	L.A.	S.F.	S.D.	Hou.	Cin.	Chi.	Mon.	N.Y.	Phi.	Pit.	St.L.	W	L	Pct.	GB
Atlanta	...	7	8	11	10	14	8	5	9	6	4	7	89	73	.549	...
Los Angeles	11	..	9	9	11	11	7	8	6	4	5	7	88	74	.543	1
San Fran.	10	9	...	8	13	12	6	8	8	2	6	5	87	75	.537	2
San Diego	7	9	10	...	9	12	8	5	6	5	6	4	81	81	.500	8
Houston	8	7	5	9	...	11	3	4	8	7	9	6	77	85	.475	12
Cincinnati	4	7	6	6	7	...	6	4	7	5	4	5	61	101	.377	28

SIGNIFICANT EVENTS

■ **April 6:** Seattle spoiled the Metrodome inaugural for Minnesota fans with an 11-7 Opening Day victory over the Twins.

■ **April 22:** The Reds defeated Atlanta, 2-1, handing the Braves their first loss after a season-opening record 13 consecutive victories.

■ **October 3:** The Brewers captured their first A.L. East title when they defeated Baltimore, 10-2, in a winner-take-all final-day battle.

■ **October 3:** The Braves, final-day losers to San Diego, clinched their first division title since 1969 when San Francisco defeated the Dodgers, 5-3, on Joe Morgan's three-run homer.

■ **October 26:** Phillies ace Steve Carlton captured his record fourth N.L. Cy Young Award.

■ **November 1:** Owners ended the 14-year reign of commissioner Bowie Kuhn when they voted not to renew his contract at a meeting in Chicago.

MEMORABLE MOMENTS

■ **May 6:** Gaylord Perry pitched the Mariners to a 7-3 victory over the Yankees and became the 15th member of baseball's 300-win club.

■ **June 22:** Philadelphia's Pete Rose doubled off the Cardinals' John Stuper and moved into second place on the all-time hit list with 3,772.

■ **August 27:** Oakland's Rickey Henderson claimed the one-season basestealing record when he swiped four in a game at Milwaukee, giving him 122 en route to a final total of 130.

LEADERS

American League
BA: Willie Wilson, K.C., .332.
Runs: Paul Molitor, Mil., 136.
Hits: Robin Yount, Mil., 210.
TB: Robin Yount, Mil., 367.
HR: Reggie Jackson, Cal.; Gorman Thomas, Mil., 39.
RBI: Hal McRae, K.C., 133.
SB: Rickey Henderson, Oak., 130.
Wins: LaMarr Hoyt, Chi., 19.
ERA: Rick Sutcliffe, Cle., 2.96.
CG: Dave Stieb, Tor., 19.
IP: Dave Stieb, Tor., 288.1.
SO: Floyd Bannister, Sea., 209.
SV: Dan Quisenberry, K.C., 35.

National League
BA: Al Oliver, Mon., .331.
Runs: Lonnie Smith, St.L., 120.
Hits: Al Oliver, Mon., 204.
TB: Al Oliver, Mon., 317.
HR: Dave Kingman, N.Y., 37.
RBI: Dale Murphy, Atl.; Al Oliver, Mon., 109.
SB: Tim Raines, Mon., 78.
Wins: Steve Carlton, Phil., 23.
ERA: Steve Rogers, Mon., 2.40.
CG: Steve Carlton, Phil., 19.
IP: Steve Carlton, Phil., 295.2.
SO: Steve Carlton, Phil., 286.
SV: Bruce Sutter, St.L., 36.

N.L. 20-game winner
Steve Carlton, Phil., 23-11

A.L. 100 RBIs
Hal McRae, K.C., 133
Cecil Cooper, Mil., 121
Andre Thornton, Cle., 116
Robin Yount, Mil., 114
Gorman Thomas, Mil., 112
Eddie Murray, Bal., 110
Dave Winfield, N.Y., 106
Harold Baines, Chi., 105
Greg Luzinski, Chi., 102
Ben Oglivie, Mil., 102
Reggie Jackson, Cal., 101

N.L. 100 RBIs
Dale Murphy, Atl., 109
Al Oliver, Mon., 109
Bill Buckner, Chi., 105
George Hendrick, St.L., 104
Jack Clark, S.F., 103
Jason Thompson, Pit., 101
Pedro Guerrero, L.A., 100

Most Valuable Player
A.L.: Robin Yount, SS, Mil.
N.L.: Dale Murphy, OF, Atl.

Cy Young Award
A.L.: Pete Vuckovich, Mil.
N.L.: Steve Carlton, Phil.

Rookie of the Year
A.L.: Cal Ripken, SS, Bal.
N.L.: Steve Sax, 2B, L.A.

Hall of Fame additions
Hank Aaron, OF, 1954-76
Happy Chandler, commissioner
Travis Jackson, SS, 1922-36
Frank Robinson, OF, 1956-76

ALL-STAR GAME

■ **Winner:** The N.L. made it 11 in a row and 19 of 20 with a 4-1 victory at Montreal — the first midsummer classic played on foreign soil.

■ **Key inning:** The second, when Dave Concepcion pounded a two-run homer, giving N.L. pitchers all the runs they would need.

■ **Memorable moment:** A sixth-inning run manufactured by a pair of Expos. Al Oliver thrilled the home fans with a double and Gary Carter singled him home.

■ **Top guns:** Steve Carlton (Phillies), Oliver (Expos), Concepcion (Reds), N.L.; Rickey Henderson (Athletics), George Brett (Royals), A.L.

■ **MVP:** Concepcion.

Linescore
July 13, at Montreal's Olympic Stadium
A.L. ....1 0 0 0 0 0 0 0 0—1 8 2
N.L. ....0 2 1 0 0 1 0 0 x—4 8 1
Eckersley (Red Sox), Clancy (Blue Jays) 4, Bannister (Mariners) 5, Quisenberry (Royals) 6, Fingers (Brewers) 8; Rogers (Expos), Carlton (Phillies) 4, Soto (Reds) 6, Valenzuela (Dodgers) 8, Minton (Giants) 8, Howe (Dodgers) 9, Hume (Reds) 9. W—Rogers. L—Eckersley. S—Hume. HR—Concepcion, N.L.

ALCS

■ **Winner:** In a battle of first-time pennant hopefuls, the Milwaukee Brewers defeated California and became the first team to recover from a two-games-to-none deficit in a League Championship Series.

■ **Turning point:** The unexpected Game 4 boost the Brewers received from substitute left fielder Mark Brouhard, who collected three hits, belted a home run and drove in three runs in Milwaukee's elimination-saving 9-5 victory.

■ **Memorable moment:** Cecil Cooper's two-run, seventh-inning single that wiped out a 3-2 Angels lead and gave the Brewers a 4-3 Game 5 victory and the franchise's first World Series berth.

■ **Top guns:** Charlie Moore (.462), Paul Molitor (.316, 2 HR, 5 RBIs), Brouhard (.750), Brewers; Bruce Kison (1-0, 1.93 ERA), Fred Lynn (.611, 5 RBIs), Don Baylor (10 RBIs), Angels.

■ **MVP:** Lynn.

Linescores

Game 1—October 5, at California
Mil. ....0 2 1 0 0 0 0 0 0—3 7 2
Cal. ....1 0 4 2 1 0 0 0 x—8 10 0
Caldwell, Slaton (4), Ladd (7), Bernard (8); John. W—John. L—Caldwell. HR—Thomas (Mil.); Lynn (Cal.).

Game 2—October 6, at California
Mil. ....0 0 0 0 2 0 0 0 0—2 5 0
Cal. ....0 2 1 1 0 0 0 0 x—4 6 0
Vuckovich; Kison. W—Kison. L—Vuckovich. HR—Re. Jackson (Cal.); Molitor (Mil.).

Game 3—October 8, at Milwaukee
Cal. ....0 0 0 0 0 0 0 3 0—3 8 0
Mil. ....0 0 0 3 0 0 2 0 x—5 6 0
Zahn, Witt (4), Hassler (7); Sutton, Ladd (8). W—Sutton. L—Zahn. S—Ladd. HR—Molitor (Mil.); Boone (Cal).

Game 4—October 9, at Milwaukee
Cal. ....0 0 0 0 0 1 0 4 0—5 5 3
Mil. ....0 3 0 3 0 1 0 2 x—9 9 2
John, Goltz (4), Sanchez (8); Haas, Slaton (8). W—Haas. L—John. S—Slaton. HR—Baylor (Cal.); Brouhard (Mil.).

Game 5—October 10, at Milwaukee
Cal. ....1 0 1 1 0 0 0 0 0—3 11 1
Mil. ....1 0 0 1 0 0 2 0 x—4 6 4
Kison, Sanchez (6), Hassler (7); Vuckovich, McClure (7), Ladd (9). W—McClure. L—Sanchez. S—Ladd. HR—Oglivie (Mil.).

NLCS

■ **Winner:** The Atlanta Braves, who were swept by the New York Mets in the first NLCS in 1969, suffered the same fate against St. Louis in the franchise's second post-season appearance.

■ **Turning point:** A Game 1 rainstorm that wiped out a 1-0 Braves lead after 4½ innings and forced Atlanta to bypass ace Phil Niekro in the rescheduled opener.

■ **Memorable moment:** Ken Oberkfell's ninth-inning line drive that eluded Braves center fielder Brett Butler and drove home David Green, giving the Cardinals a 4-3 Game 2 victory.

■ **Top guns:** Bob Forsch (1-0, 0.00 ERA), Darrell Porter (.556), Ozzie Smith (.556), Cardinals; Claudell Washington (.333), Braves.

■ **MVP:** Porter.

Linescores

Game 1—October 7, at St. Louis
Atlanta ....0 0 0 0 0 0 0 0 0—0 3 0
St. Louis ....0 0 1 0 0 5 0 1 x—7 13 1
Perez, Bedrosian (6), Moore (6), Walk (8); Forsch. W—Forsch. L—Perez.

Game 2—October 9, at St. Louis
Atlanta ....0 0 2 0 1 0 0 0 0—3 6 0
St. Louis ......1 0 0 0 0 1 0 1 1—4 9 1
Niekro, Garber (7); Stuper, Bair (7), Sutter (8). W—Sutter. L—Garber.

Game 3—October 10, at Atlanta
St. Louis ....0 4 0 0 1 0 0 0 1—6 12 0
Atlanta ......0 0 0 0 0 0 2 0 0—2 6 1
Andujar, Sutter (7); Camp, Perez (2), Moore (5), Mahler (7), Bedrosian (8), Garber (9). W—Andujar. L—Camp. S—Sutter. HR—McGee (St.L.).

WORLD SERIES

■ **Winner:** The resilient Cardinals tamed "Harvey's Wallbangers" and spoiled the Brewers' first World Series.

■ **Turning point:** A special Game 3 performance by center fielder Willie McGee, who stepped out of character to hit two home runs and added two spectacular catches in a 6-2 victory that gave the Cardinals their first Series lead.

■ **Memorable moment:** A two-run single by Keith Hernandez and a run-scoring single by George Hendrick in a three-run sixth inning that rallied the Cardinals to a seventh-game 6-3 victory.

■ **Top guns:** Joaquin Andujar (2-0, 1.35 ERA), Dane Iorg (.529), Darrell Porter (5 RBIs), Hernandez (8 RBIs), Cardinals; Mike Caldwell (2-0, 2.04), Robin Yount (.414, 12 hits, 6 RBIs), Paul Molitor (.355), Brewers.

■ **MVP:** Porter.

Linescores

Game 1—October 12, at St. Louis
Mil. ....2 0 0 1 1 2 0 0 4—10 17 0
St. Louis ..0 0 0 0 0 0 0 0 0— 0 3 1
Caldwell; Forsch, Kaat (6), LaPoint (8), Lahti (9). W—Caldwell. L—Forsch. HR—Simmons (Mil.).

Game 2—October 13, at St. Louis
Mil. ....0 1 2 0 1 0 0 0 0—4 10 1
St. Louis ....0 0 2 0 0 2 0 1 x—5 8 0
Sutton, McClure (7), Ladd (8); Stuper, Kaat (5), Bair (5), Sutter (7). W—Sutter. L—McClure. HR—Simmons (Mil.).

Game 3—October 15, at Milwaukee
St. Louis ......0 0 0 0 3 0 2 0 1—6 6 1
Mil. ....0 0 0 0 0 0 0 2 0—2 5 3
Andujar, Kaat (7), Bair (7), Sutter (7); Vuckovich, McClure (9). W—Andujar. L—Vuckovich. S—Sutter. HR—McGee 2 (St.L.); Cooper (Mil.).

Game 4—October 16, at Milwaukee
St. Louis ....1 3 0 0 0 1 0 0 0—5 8 1
Mil. ....0 0 0 0 1 0 6 0 x—7 10 2
LaPoint, Bair (7), Kaat (7), Lahti (7); Haas, Slaton (6), McClure (8). W—Slaton. L—Bair. S—McClure.

Game 5—October 17, at Milwaukee
St. Louis ....0 0 1 0 0 0 1 0 2—4 15 2
Mil. ....1 0 1 0 1 0 1 2 x—6 11 1
Forsch, Sutter (8); Caldwell, McClure (9). W—Caldwell. L—Forsch. S—McClure. HR—Yount (Mil.).

Game 6—October 19, at St. Louis
Mil. ....0 0 0 0 0 0 0 0 1— 1 4 4
St. Louis ..0 2 0 3 2 6 0 0 x—13 12 1
Sutton, Slaton (5), Medich (6), Bernard (8); Stuper. W—Stuper. L—Sutton. HR—Porter, Hernandez (St.L.).

Game 7—October 20, at St. Louis
Mil. ....0 0 0 0 1 2 0 0 0—3 7 0
St. Louis ....0 0 0 1 0 3 0 2 x—6 15 1
Vuckovich, McClure (6), Haas (6), Caldwell (8); Andujar, Sutter (8). W—Andujar. L—McClure. S—Sutter. HR—Oglivie (Mil.).

FINAL STANDINGS

American League

East Division

Team	Bal.	Det.	N.Y.	Tor.	Mil.	Bos.	Cle.	Cal.	Chi.	K.C.	Min.	Oak.	Sea.	Tex.	W	L	Pct.	GB
Baltimore	...	5	6	7	11	8	6	7	7	8	8	8	8	9	98	64	.605	...
Detroit	8	...	5	6	6	9	8	8	4	7	9	6	8	8	92	70	.568	6
New York	7	8	...	7	9	6	7	7	4	6	8	8	7	7	91	71	.562	7
Toronto	6	7	6	...	5	6	9	8	7	6	7	6	8	8	89	73	.549	9
Milwaukee	2	7	4	8	...	9	10	6	8	6	8	6	5	8	87	75	.537	11
Boston	5	4	7	7	4	...	7	6	6	5	5	8	7	7	78	84	.481	20
Cleveland	7	5	6	4	3	6	...	4	4	7	6	7	8	3	70	92	.432	28

West Division

Team	Chi.	K.C.	Tex.	Oak.	Cal.	Min.	Sea.	Bal.	Bos.	Cle.	Det.	Mil.	N.Y.	Tor.	W	L	Pct.	GB
Chicago	...	9	8	8	10	8	12	5	6	8	8	4	8	5	99	63	.611	...
Kansas City	4	...	8	7	7	6	8	4	7	5	5	6	6	6	79	83	.488	20
Texas	5	5	...	11	7	8	7	3	5	9	4	4	5	4	77	85	.475	22
Oakland	5	6	2	...	8	9	9	4	4	5	6	6	4	6	74	88	.457	25
California	3	6	6	5	...	6	6	5	6	8	4	6	5	4	70	92	.432	29
Minnesota	5	7	5	4	7	...	9	4	7	6	3	4	4	5	70	92	.432	29
Seattle	1	5	6	4	7	4	...	4	5	4	4	7	5	4	60	102	.370	39

National League

East Division

Team	Phi.	Pit.	Mon.	St.L.	Chi.	N.Y.	Atl.	Cin.	Hou.	L.A.	S.D.	S.F.	W	L	Pct.	GB
Philadelphia	...	11	10	14	13	12	5	6	8	1	5	5	90	72	.556	...
Pittsburgh	7	...	10	10	9	9	6	6	6	6	9	6	84	78	.519	6
Montreal	8	8	...	9	11	8	5	8	4	5	8	8	82	80	.506	8
St. Louis	4	8	9	...	8	12	5	6	10	3	6	8	79	83	.488	11
Chicago	5	9	7	10	...	9	7	4	5	6	5	4	71	91	.438	19
New York	6	9	10	6	9	...	4	5	3	5	6	5	68	94	.420	22

West Division

Team	L.A.	Atl.	Hou.	S.D.	S.F.	Cin.	Chi.	Mon.	N.Y.	Phi.	Pit.	St.L.	W	L	Pct.	GB
Los Angeles	...	11	12	6	5	11	6	7	7	11	6	9	91	71	.562	...
Atlanta	7	...	11	9	9	12	5	7	8	7	6	7	88	74	.543	3
Houston	6	7	...	11	12	13	7	8	9	4	6	2	85	77	.525	6
San Diego	12	9	7	...	11	9	7	4	6	7	3	6	81	81	.500	10
San Fran.	13	9	6	7	...	8	8	4	7	7	6	4	79	83	.488	12
Cincinnati	7	6	5	9	10	...	8	4	7	6	6	6	74	88	.457	17

SIGNIFICANT EVENTS

■ **April 7:** ABC and NBC agreed to share a lucrative six-year television contract that would pay baseball $1.2 billion.

■ **February 8:** Former Yankee great Mickey Mantle was ordered to sever ties with baseball after taking a job with an Atlantic City hotel and casino.

■ **July 29:** The N.L.-record ironman streak of San Diego's Steve Garvey ended at 1,207 games when he dislocated his thumb in a home-plate collision against the Braves.

■ **November 17:** A U.S. magistrate handed three members of the 1983 Royals, Willie Wilson, Willie Aikens and Jerry Martin, three-month prison sentences for attempting to purchase cocaine.

■ **December 8:** Dr. Bobby Brown was elected as the successor to retiring A.L. president Lee MacPhail.

■ **December 19:** Former Cy Young winner Vida Blue became the fourth Kansas City player to receive a three-month prison sentence for attempting to purchase cocaine.

MEMORABLE MOMENTS

■ **July 24:** A two-out, game-winning home run by Kansas City's George Brett off Yankee reliever Goose Gossage was nullified by umpires who said Brett's bat was illegally covered by pine tar—a controversial ruling that later would be overturned.

■ **June 26:** Mets veteran Rusty Staub collected his record-tying eighth consecutive pinch hit in an 8-4 loss to the Phillies.

■ **September 23:** Philadelphia lefty Steve Carlton became baseball's 16th 300-game winner when he defeated St. Louis, 6-2.

LEADERS

American League
BA: Wade Boggs, Bos., .361.
Runs: Cal Ripken, Bal., 121.
Hits: Cal Ripken, Bal., 211.
TB: Jim Rice, Bos., 344.
HR: Jim Rice, Bos., 39.
RBI: Cecil Cooper, Mil.; Jim Rice, Bos., 126.
SB: Rickey Henderson, Oak., 108.
Wins: LaMarr Hoyt, Chi., 24.
ERA: Rick Honeycutt, Tex., 2.42.
CG: Ron Guidry, N.Y., 21.
IP: Jack Morris, Det., 293.2.
SO: Jack Morris, Det., 232.
SV: Dan Quisenberry, K.C., 45.

National League
BA: Bill Madlock, Pit., .323.
Runs: Tim Raines, Mon., 133.
Hits: Jose Cruz, Hou.; Andre Dawson, Mon., 189.
TB: Andre Dawson, Mon., 341.
HR: Mike Schmidt, Phil., 40.
RBI: Dale Murphy, Atl., 121.
SB: Tim Raines, Mon., 90.
Wins: John Denny, Phil., 19.
ERA: Atlee Hammaker, S.F., 2.25.
CG: Mario Soto, Cin., 18.
IP: Steve Carlton, Phil., 283.2.
SO: Steve Carlton, Phil., 275.
SV: Lee Smith, Chi., 29.

A.L. 20-game winners
LaMarr Hoyt, Chi., 24-10
Rich Dotson, Chi., 22-7
Ron Guidry, N.Y., 21-9
Jack Morris, Det., 20-13

A.L. 100 RBIs
Cecil Cooper, Mil., 126
Jim Rice, Bos., 126
Dave Winfield, N.Y., 116
Lance Parrish, Det., 114
Eddie Murray, Bal., 111
Ted Simmons, Mil., 108
Tony Armas, Bos., 107
Willie Upshaw, Tor., 104
Cal Ripken, Bal., 102
Ron Kittle, Chi., 100

N.L. 100 RBIs
Dale Murphy, Atl., 121
Andre Dawson, Mon., 113
Mike Schmidt, Phil., 109
Pedro Guerrero, L.A., 103

N.L. 40 homers
Mike Schmidt, Phil., 40

Most Valuable Player
A.L.: Cal Ripken, SS, Bal.
N.L.: Dale Murphy, OF, Atl.

Cy Young Award
A.L.: LaMarr Hoyt, Chi.
N.L.: John Denny, Phil.

Rookie of the Year
A.L.: Ron Kittle, OF, Chi.
N.L.: Darryl Strawberry, OF, N.Y.

Manager of the Year
A.L.: Tony La Russa, Chi.
N.L.: Tommy Lasorda, L.A.

Hall of Fame additions
Walter Alston, manager
George Kell, 3B, 1943-57
Juan Marichal, P, 1960-75
Brooks Robinson, 3B, 1955-77

ALL-STAR GAME

■ **Winner:** The A.L. snapped its frustrating 11-game All-Star losing streak with a 13-3 rout in a special 50th-anniversary celebration of the midsummer classic at Chicago's Comiskey Park.

■ **Key inning:** A record seven-run third that gave the A.L. a 9-1 lead and set the course for its first victory since 1971.

■ **Memorable moment:** Fred Lynn's third-inning bases-loaded homer off Atlee Hammaker — the first grand slam in 54 All-Star Games.

■ **Top guns:** Dave Stieb (Blue Jays), Lynn (Angels), Jim Rice (Red Sox), George Brett (Royals), Dave Winfield (Yankees), A.L.; Steve Sax (Dodgers), N.L.

■ **MVP:** Lynn.

Linescore
July 6, Chicago's Comiskey Park
N.L. ....1 0 0 1 1 0 0 0 0— 3 8 3
A.L. ....1 1 7 0 0 0 2 2 x—13 15 2
Soto (Reds), Hammaker (Giants) 3, Dawley (Astros) 3, Dravecky (Padres) 5, Perez (Braves) 7, Orosco (Mets) 7, L. Smith (Cubs) 8; Stieb (Blue Jays), Honeycutt (Rangers) 4, Stanley (Red Sox) 6, Young (Mariners) 8, Quisenberry (Royals) 9. W—Stieb. L—Soto. HR—Rice, Lynn, A.L.

ALCS

■ **Winner:** Baltimore, a 2-1 loser to the Chicago White Sox in the opener, roared to three consecutive victories and claimed its fifth pennant since LCS play began in 1969.

■ **Turning point:** Mike Boddicker's five-hit, 4-0 shutout in Game 2. Orioles pitchers would finish the series with a 0.49 ERA.

■ **Memorable moment:** A 10th-inning home run by unlikely Baltimore hero Tito Landrum off Chicago lefty Britt Burns in Game 4. The blast broke up a scoreless battle and propelled the Orioles to a series-ending 3-0 victory.

■ **Top guns:** Boddicker (1-0, 0.00 ERA), Tippy Martinez (1-0, 0.00), Cal Ripken (.400), Orioles; LaMarr Hoyt (1-0, 1.00), Rudy Law (.389), White Sox.

■ **MVP:** Boddicker.

Linescores

Game 1—October 5, at Baltimore
Chi. ....0 0 1 0 0 1 0 0 0—2 7 0
Balt. ....0 0 0 0 0 0 0 0 1—1 5 1
Hoyt; McGregor, Stewart (7), T. Martinez (8). W—Hoyt. L—McGregor.

Game 2—October 6, at Baltimore
Chi. ....0 0 0 0 0 0 0 0 0—0 5 2
Balt. ....0 1 0 1 0 2 0 0 x—4 6 0
Bannister, Barojas (7), Lamp (8); Boddicker. W—Boddicker. L—Bannister. HR—Roenicke (Bal.).

Game 3—October 7, at Chicago
Balt. ....3 1 0 0 2 0 0 1 4—11 8 1
Chi. ....0 1 0 0 0 0 0 0 0— 1 6 1
Flanagan, Stewart (6); Dotson, Tidrow (6), Koosman (9), Lamp (9). W—Flanagan. L—Dotson. S—Stewart. HR—Murray (Bal.).

Game 4—October 8, at Chicago
Balt. ....0 0 0 0 0 0 0 0 0 3—3 9 0
Chi. ......0 0 0 0 0 0 0 0 0 0—0 10 0
Davis, T. Martinez (7); Burns, Barojas (10), Agosto (10), Lamp (10). W—T. Martinez. L—Burns. HR—Landrum (Bal.).

NLCS

■ **Winner:** The Philadelphia Phillies advanced to their second World Series in four years and settled an old NLCS score with the Dodgers, who had defeated them in 1977 and '78.

■ **Turning point:** The Game 3 performance of veteran outfielder Gary Matthews: three hits, a home run and four RBIs in a 7-2 Phillies victory.

■ **Memorable moment:** A three-run, first-inning home run by Matthews in Game 4. Matthews' third homer in as many games propelled the Phillies to a series-ending 7-2 victory.

■ **Top guns:** Steve Carlton (2-0, 0.66 ERA), Mike Schmidt (.467), Matthews (.429, 3 HR, 8 RBIs), Phillies; Fernando Valenzuela (1-0, 1.13), Dusty Baker (.357), Dodgers.

■ **MVP:** Matthews.

Linescores

Game 1—October 4, at Los Angeles
Phil. ....1 0 0 0 0 0 0 0 0—1 5 1
L.A. ....0 0 0 0 0 0 0 0 0—0 7 0
Carlton, Holland (8); Reuss, Niedenfuer (9). W—Carlton. L—Reuss. S—Holland. HR—Schmidt (Phil.).

Game 2—October 5, at Los Angeles
Phil. ....0 1 0 0 0 0 0 0 0—1 7 2
L.A. ....1 0 0 0 2 0 0 1 x—4 6 1
Denny, Reed (7); Valenzuela, Niedenfuer (9). W—Valenzuela. L—Denny. S—Niedenfuer. HR—Matthews (Phil.).

Game 3—October 7, at Philadelphia
L.A. ....0 0 0 2 0 0 0 0 0—2 4 0
Phil. ....0 2 1 1 2 0 1 0 x—7 9 1
Welch, Pena (2), Honeycutt (5), Beckwith (5), Zachry (7); Hudson. W—Hudson. L—Welch. HR—Marshall (L.A.); Matthews (Phil.).

Game 4—October 8, at Philadelphia
L.A. ....0 0 0 1 0 0 0 1 0—2 10 0
Phil. ....3 0 0 0 2 2 0 0 x—7 13 1
Reuss, Beckwith (5), Honeycutt (5), Zachry (7); Carlton, Reed (7), Holland (8). W—Carlton. L—Reuss. HR—Matthews, Lezcano (Phil.); Baker (L.A.).

WORLD SERIES

■ **Winner:** The Orioles lost the opener and then sprinted past the Phillies for their first championship since 1970.

■ **Turning point:** When Phillies manager Paul Owens let starting pitcher Steve Carlton bat with two runners on base in the sixth inning of Game 3. Carlton struck out and then yielded two seventh-inning runs that vaulted the Orioles to a 3-2 victory.

■ **Memorable moment:** Garry Maddox's game-deciding eighth-inning homer in Game 1. Maddox connected on the first pitch from Scott McGregor, who stood on the mound for about five minutes while President Ronald Reagan was being interviewed for television.

■ **Top guns:** Rick Dempsey (.385), John Lowenstein (.385), Orioles; Bo Diaz (.333), Phillies.

■ **MVP:** Dempsey.

Linescores

Game 1—October 11, at Baltimore
Phil. ....0 0 0 0 0 1 0 1 0—2 5 0
Baltimore ....1 0 0 0 0 0 0 0 0—1 5 1
Denny, Holland (8); McGregor, Stewart (9), T. Martinez (9). W—Denny. L—McGregor. S—Holland. HR—Dwyer (Bal.); Morgan, Maddox (Phil.).

Game 2—October 12, at Baltimore
Phil. ....0 0 0 1 0 0 0 0 0—1 3 0
Baltimore ....0 0 0 0 3 0 1 0 x—4 9 1
Hudson, Hernandez (5), Andersen (6), Reed (8); Boddicker. W—Boddicker. L—Hudson. HR—Lowenstein (Bal.).

Game 3—October 14, at Philadelphia
Baltimore ....0 0 0 0 0 1 2 0 0—3 6 1
Phil. ....0 1 1 0 0 0 0 0 0—2 8 2
Flanagan, Palmer (5), Stewart (7), T. Martinez (9); Carlton, Holland (7). W—Palmer. L—Carlton. S—T. Martinez. HR—Matthews, Morgan (Phil.); Ford (Bal.).

Game 4—October 15, at Philadelphia
Baltimore ..0 0 0 2 0 2 1 0 0—5 10 1
Phil. ....0 0 0 1 2 0 0 0 1—4 10 0
Davis, Stewart (6), T. Martinez (8); Denny, Hernandez (6), Reed (6), Andersen (8). W—Davis. L—Denny. S—T. Martinez.

Game 5—October 16, at Philadelphia
Baltimore ....0 1 1 2 1 0 0 0 0—5 5 0
Phil. ....0 0 0 0 0 0 0 0 0—0 5 1
McGregor; Hudson, Bystrom (5), Hernandez (6), Reed (9). W—McGregor. L—Hudson. HR—Murray 2, Dempsey (Bal.).

HISTORY

1984

FINAL STANDINGS

American League

East Division

Team	Det.	Tor.	N.Y.	Bos.	Bal.	Cle.	Mil.	Cal.	Chi.	K.C.	Min.	Oak.	Sea.	Tex.	W	L	Pct.	GB
Detroit	...	8	7	6	6	9	11	8	8	7	9	9	6	10	104	58	.642	...
Toronto	5	...	5	8	9	7	3	5	8	7	11	8	7	6	89	73	.549	15
New York	6	8	...	6	8	11	7	4	5	7	4	8	7	6	87	75	.537	17
Boston	7	5	7	...	7	10	9	9	7	3	6	7	4	5	86	76	.531	18
Baltimore	7	4	5	6	...	7	7	8	7	5	5	6	9	9	85	77	.525	19
Cleveland	4	6	2	3	6	...	9	4	4	6	7	7	8	9	75	87	.463	29
Milwaukee	2	10	6	4	6	4	...	4	5	6	5	4	6	5	67	94	.416	36.5

West Division

Team	K.C.	Cal.	Min.	Oak.	Chi.	Sea.	Tex.	Bal.	Bos.	Cle.	Det.	Mil.	N.Y.	Tor.	W	L	Pct.	GB
Kansas City	...	7	6	5	8	9	6	7	9	6	5	6	5	5	84	78	.519	...
California	6	...	4	7	8	9	5	4	3	8	4	8	8	7	81	81	.500	3
Minnesota	7	9	...	8	5	7	8	7	6	5	3	7	8	1	81	81	.500	3
Oakland	8	6	5	...	7	8	8	6	5	5	3	8	4	4	77	85	.475	7
Chicago	5	5	8	6	...	5	5	5	5	8	4	7	7	4	74	88	.457	10
Seattle	4	4	6	5	8	...	10	3	8	4	6	6	5	5	74	88	.457	10
Texas	7	8	5	5	8	3	...	3	7	3	2	6	6	6	69	92	.429	14.5

National League

East Division

Team	Chi.	N.Y.	St.L.	Phi.	Mon.	Pit.	Atl.	Cin.	Hou.	L.A.	S.D.	S.F.	W	L	Pct.	GB
Chicago	...	12	13	9	10	8	9	7	6	7	6	9	96	65	.596	...
New York	6	...	7	10	11	12	8	9	8	9	6	4	90	72	.556	6.5
St. Louis	5	11	...	10	9	14	7	8	4	6	5	5	84	78	.519	12.5
Philadelphia	9	8	8	...	7	7	5	7	6	9	7	8	81	81	.500	15.5
Montreal	7	7	9	11	...	7	7	5	5	6	7	7	78	83	.484	18
Pittsburgh	10	6	4	11	11	...	4	5	6	8	4	6	75	87	.463	21.5

West Division

Team	S.D.	Atl.	Hou.	L.A.	Cin.	S.F.	Chi.	Mon.	N.Y.	Phi.	Pit.	St.L.	W	L	Pct.	GB
San Diego	...	11	12	8	11	13	6	5	6	5	8	7	92	70	.568	...
Atlanta	7	...	12	6	13	10	3	5	4	7	8	5	80	82	.494	12
Houston	6	6	...	9	10	12	6	7	4	6	6	8	80	82	.494	12
L.A.	10	12	9	...	11	10	5	6	3	3	4	6	79	83	.488	13
Cincinnati	7	5	8	7	...	12	5	7	3	5	7	4	70	92	.432	22
San Fran.	5	8	6	8	6	...	3	5	8	4	6	7	66	96	.407	26

SIGNIFICANT EVENTS

■ **March 3:** Baseball's owners selected businessman Peter V. Ueberroth as the sixth commissioner, succeeding Bowie Kuhn.

■ **August 16:** Pete Rose, who joined the select 4,000-hit circle early in the season as a member of the Expos, returned to his hometown Cincinnati as the Reds' player-manager.

■ **September 20, 24:** The Padres clinched their first-ever division title and the Cubs clinched their first post-season appearance since 1945.

■ **October 7:** Major League umpires, agreeing to let Commissioner Ueberroth arbitrate their dispute over post-season pay, ended a one-week strike and returned for the final game of the NLCS.

■ **November 6:** Detroit reliever Willie Hernandez capped his big season with an A.L. Cy Young-MVP sweep.

MEMORABLE MOMENTS

■ **September 17:** Kansas City posted a 10-1 victory, but the night belonged to Angels slugger Reggie Jackson, who belted his 500th homer off lefty Bud Black.

■ **September 28:** Cardinals reliever Bruce Sutter notched his 45th save in a 4-1 victory over the Cubs, matching the 1-year-old record of Kansas City's Dan Quisenberry.

■ **September 30:** California's Mike Witt brought a dramatic end to the regular season when he fired baseball's 11th perfect game, beating Texas, 1-0.

LEADERS

American League
BA: Don Mattingly, N.Y., .343.
Runs: Dwight Evans, Bos., 121.
Hits: Don Mattingly, N.Y., 207.
TB: Tony Armas, Bos., 339.
HR: Tony Armas, Bos., 43.
RBI: Tony Armas, Bos., 123.
SB: Rickey Henderson, Oak., 66.
Wins: Mike Boddicker, Bal., 20.
ERA: Mike Boddicker, Bal., 2.79.
CG: Charlie Hough, Tex., 17.
IP: Dave Stieb, Tor., 267.
SO: Mark Langston, Sea., 204.
SV: Dan Quisenberry, K.C., 44.

National League
BA: Tony Gwynn, S.D., .351.
Runs: Ryne Sandberg, Chi., 114.
Hits: Tony Gwynn, S.D., 213.
TB: Dale Murphy, Atl., 332.
HR: Dale Murphy, Atl.; Mike Schmidt, Phil., 36.
RBI: Gary Carter, Mon.; Mike Schmidt, Phil., 106.
SB: Tim Raines, Mon., 75.
Wins: Joaquin Andujar, St.L., 20.
ERA: Alejandro Pena, L.A., 2.48.
CG: Mario Soto, Cin., 13.
IP: Joaquin Andujar, St.L., 261.1.
SO: Dwight Gooden, N.Y., 276.
SV: Bruce Sutter, St.L., 45.

A.L. 20-game winner
Mike Boddicker, Bal., 20-11
N.L. 20-game winner
Joaquin Andujar, St.L., 20-14
A.L./N.L. 20-game winner
Rick Sutcliffe, Cle.-Chi., 20
A.L. 100 RBIs
Tony Armas, Bos., 123
Jim Rice, Bos., 122
Dave Kingman, Oak., 118
Alvin Davis, Sea., 116
Don Mattingly, N.Y., 110
Eddie Murray, Bal., 110
Kent Hrbek, Min., 107
Dwight Evans, Bos., 104
Larry Parrish, Tex., 101
Dave Winfield, N.Y., 100
N.L. 100 RBIs
Gary Carter, Mon., 106
Mike Schmidt, Phil., 106
Dale Murphy, Atl., 100
A.L. 40 homers
Tony Armas, Bos., 43
Most Valuable Player
A.L.: Willie Hernandez, P, Det.
N.L.: Ryne Sandberg, 2B, Chi.
Cy Young Award
A.L.: Willie Hernandez, Det.
N.L.: Rick Sutcliffe, Chi.
Rookie of the Year
A.L.: Alvin Davis, 1B, Sea.
N.L.: Dwight Gooden, P, N.Y.
Manager of the Year
A.L.: Sparky Anderson, Det.
N.L.: Jim Frey, Chi.
Hall of Fame additions
Luis Aparicio, SS, 1956-73
Don Drysdale, P, 1956-69
Rick Ferrell, C, 1929-47
Harmon Killebrew, 1B/3B, 1954-75
Pee Wee Reese, SS, 1940-58

ALL-STAR GAME

■ **Winner:** After a one-year lull, it was business as usual for the N.L., which used home runs by Gary Carter and Dale Murphy to post a 3-1 All-Star victory.

■ **Key inning:** The second, when Carter belted a solo shot to give the N.L. a 2-1 lead after the A.L. had tied in the top of the inning on George Brett's home run.

■ **Memorable moment:** A fourth and fifth-inning strikeout flurry by the N.L.'s Fernando Valenzuela and Dwight Gooden. Consecutive victims Dave Winfield, Reggie Jackson, Brett, Lance Parrish, Chet Lemon and Alvin Davis broke the 50-year-old record of five straight.

■ **Top guns:** Valenzuela (Dodgers), Gooden (Mets), Carter (Expos), Murphy (Braves), N.L.; Brett (Royals), Lou Whitaker (Tigers), A.L.

■ **MVP:** Carter.

Linescore
July 10, at San Francisco's Candlestick Park
A.L. ....0 1 0 0 0 0 0 0 0—1 7 2
N.L. ....1 1 0 0 0 0 0 1 x—3 8 0
Stieb (Blue Jays), Morris (Tigers) 3, Dotson (White Sox) 5, Caudill (Athletics) 7, W. Hernandez (Tigers) 8; Lea (Expos), Valenzuela (Dodgers) 3, Gooden (Mets) 5, Soto (Reds) 7, Gossage (Padres) 9. W—Lea. L—Steib. S—Gossage. HR—Brett, A.L.; Carter, Murphy, N.L.

ALCS

■ **Winner:** The Detroit Tigers capped their 104-victory regular season with a sweep of Kansas City and claimed their first pennant since 1968.

■ **Turning point:** The 11th inning of Game 2, when Johnny Grubb's one-out double off Royals relief ace Dan Quisenberry drove in two runs and gave the Tigers a 5-3 victory and a two-games-to-none series edge.

■ **Memorable moment:** The Game 3 pitching performance of Tigers veteran Milt Wilcox, who allowed only two hits in eight innings of a series-clinching 1-0 victory.

■ **Top guns:** Wilcox (1-0, 0.00 ERA), Jack Morris (1-0, 1.29), Kirk Gibson (.417), Alan Trammell (.364), Tigers; Don Slaught (.364), Royals.

■ **MVP:** Gibson.

Linescores

Game 1—October 2, at Kansas City
Det. ....2 0 0 1 1 0 1 2 1—8 14 0
K.C. ....0 0 0 0 0 0 1 0 0—1 5 1
Morris, Hernandez (8); Black, Huismann (6), M. Jones (8). W—Morris. L—Black. HR—Herndon, Trammell, Parrish (Det.).

Game 2—October 3, at Kansas City
Det...2 0 1 0 0 0 0 0 0 0 2—5 8 1
K.C...0 0 0 1 0 0 1 1 0 0 0—3 10 3
Petry, Hernandez (8), Lopez (9); Saberhagen, Quisenberry (9). W—Lopez. L—Quisenberry. HR—Gibson (Det.).

Game 3—October 5, at Detroit
K.C. ....0 0 0 0 0 0 0 0 0—0 3 3
Det. ....0 1 0 0 0 0 0 0 x—1 3 0
Leibrandt; Wilcox, Hernandez (9). W—Wilcox. L—Leibrandt. S—Hernandez.

NLCS

■ **Winner:** The San Diego Padres became the first N.L. team to recover from a two-game deficit and captured their first-ever pennant, denying the Cubs their first World Series appearance since 1945.

■ **Turning point:** The seventh inning of Game 5. The key blows in San Diego's four-run series-deciding rally were an error by Cubs first baseman Leon Durham and a bad-hop double by Tony Gwynn that drove in two runs and broke a 3-3 tie.

■ **Memorable moment:** Steve Garvey's two-run ninth-inning home run that gave the Padres an elimination-saving 7-5 victory in Game 4.

■ **Top guns:** Craig Lefferts (2-0, 0.00 ERA), Garvey (.400, 7 RBIs), Gwynn (.368), Padres; Jody Davis (.389, 2 HR, 6 RBIs), Gary Matthews (2 HR, 5 RBIs), Cubs.

■ **MVP:** Garvey.

Linescores

Game 1—October 2, at Chicago
S.D. ....0 0 0 0 0 0 0 0 0— 0 6 1
Chicago....2 0 3 0 6 2 0 0 x—13 16 0
Show, Harris (5), Booker (7); Sutcliffe, Brusstar (8). W—Sutcliffe. L—Show. HR—Dernier, Matthews 2, Sutcliffe, Cey (Chi.).

Game 2—October 3, at Chicago
S.D. ....0 0 0 1 0 1 0 0 0—2 5 0
Chicago........1 0 2 1 0 0 0 0 x—4 8 1
Thurmond, Hawkins (4), Dravecky (6), Lefferts (8); Trout, Smith (9). W—Trout. L—Thurmond. S—Smith.

Game 3—October 4, at San Diego
Chicago......0 1 0 0 0 0 0 0 0—1 5 0
S.D. ....0 0 0 0 3 4 0 0 x—7 11 0
Eckersley, Frazier (6), Stoddard (8); Whitson, Gossage (9). W—Whitson. L—Eckersley. HR—McReynolds (S.D.).

Game 4—October 6, at San Diego
Chicago......0 0 0 3 0 0 0 2 0—5 8 1
S.D. ....0 0 2 0 1 0 2 0 2—7 11 0
Sanderson, Brusstar (5), Stoddard (7), Smith (8); Lollar, Hawkins (5), Dravecky (6), Gossage (8), Lefferts (9). W—Lefferts. L—Smith. HR—Davis, Durham (Chi.); Garvey (S.D.).

Game 5—October 7, at San Diego
Chicago ....2 1 0 0 0 0 0 0 0—3 5 1
S.D. ....0 0 0 0 0 2 4 0 x—6 8 0
Sutcliffe, Trout (7), Brusstar (8); Show, Hawkins (2), Dravecky (4), Lefferts (6), Gossage (8). W—Lefferts. L—Sutcliffe. S—Gossage. HR—Durham, Davis (Chi.).

WORLD SERIES

■ **Winner:** The Tigers made short work of first-time Series qualifier San Diego and Sparky Anderson became the first man to manage champions in both leagues.

■ **Turning point:** Jack Morris pitched a five-hitter and Alan Trammell drove in all of Detroit's runs with two homers in a 4-2 Game 4 victory.

■ **Memorable moment:** The ever-intense Kirk Gibson stomping on home plate after an eighth-inning upper-deck home run in the Series finale — his second of the game. Gibson also drove in five runs and scored three times in the Tigers' 8-4 victory.

■ **Top guns:** Morris (2-0, 2.00 ERA), Trammell (.450, 2 HR, 6 RBIs), Gibson (.333, 2 HR, 7 RBIs), Tigers; Kurt Bevacqua (.412), Alan Wiggins (.364), Padres.

■ **MVP:** Trammell.

Linescores

Game 1—October 9, at San Diego
Detroit..........1 0 0 0 2 0 0 0 0—3 8 0
San Diego ....2 0 0 0 0 0 0 0 0—2 8 1
Morris; Thurmond, Hawkins (6), Dravecky (8). W—Morris. L—Thurmond. HR—Herndon (Det.).

Game 2—October 10, at San Diego
Detroit........3 0 0 0 0 0 0 0 0—3 7 3
San Diego ..1 0 0 1 3 0 0 0 x—5 11 0
Petry, Lopez (5), Scherrer (6), Bair (7), Hernandez (8); Whitson, Hawkins (1), Lefferts (7). W—Hawkins. L—Petry. S—Lefferts. HR—Bevacqua (S.D.).

Game 3—October 12, at Detroit
San Diego ..0 0 1 0 0 0 1 0 0—2 10 0
Detroit........0 4 1 0 0 0 0 0 x—5 7 0
Lollar, Booker (2), Harris (3); Wilcox, Scherrer (7), Hernandez (7). W—Wilcox. L—Lollar. S—Hernandez. HR—Castillo (Det.).

Game 4—October 13, at Detroit
San Diego....0 1 0 0 0 0 0 0 1—2 5 2
Detroit..........2 0 2 0 0 0 0 0 x—4 7 0
Show, Dravecky (3), Lefferts (7), Gossage (8); Morris. W—Morris. L—Show. HR—Trammell 2 (Det.); Kennedy (S.D.).

Game 5—October 14, at Detroit
San Diego ..0 0 1 2 0 0 0 1 0—4 10 1
Detroit........3 0 0 0 1 0 1 3 x—8 11 1
Thurmond, Hawkins (1), Lefferts (5), Gossage (7); Petry, Scherrer (4), Lopez (5), Hernandez (8). W—Lopez. L—Hawkins. S—Hernandez. HR—Gibson 2, Parrish (Det.); Bevacqua (S.D.).

HISTORY

FINAL STANDINGS

American League

East Division

Team	Tor.	N.Y.	Det.	Bal.	Bos.	Mil.	Cle.	K.C.	Cal.	Chi.	Min.	Oak.	Sea.	Tex.	W	L	Pct.	GB
Toronto	...	7	7	8	4	9	9	5	7	9	8	7	10	9	99	62	.615	...
New York	6	...	3	12	8	6	7	7	9	6	9	7	9	8	97	64	.602	2
Detroit	6	9	...	7	7	9	8	5	4	6	3	8	5	7	84	77	.522	15
Baltimore	4	1	6	...	5	9	8	6	7	8	6	7	6	10	83	78	.516	16
Boston	9	5	6	8	...	5	8	5	5	4	7	8	6	5	81	81	.500	18.5
Milwaukee	4	7	4	4	8	...	6	4	3	7	9	3	4	8	71	90	.441	28
Cleveland	4	6	5	5	5	7	...	2	4	2	4	3	6	7	60	102	.370	39.5

West Division

Team	K.C.	Cal.	Chi.	Min.	Oak.	Sea.	Tex.	Tor.	N.Y.	Det.	Bal.	Bos.	Mil.	Cle.	W	L	Pct.	GB
Kansas City	...	9	8	7	8	3	6	7	5	7	6	7	8	10	91	71	.562	...
California	4	...	8	9	6	9	9	5	3	8	5	7	9	8	90	72	.556	1
Chicago	5	5	...	6	8	9	10	3	6	6	4	8	5	10	85	77	.525	6
Minnesota	6	4	7	...	8	6	8	4	3	9	6	5	3	8	77	85	.475	14
Oakland	5	7	5	5	...	8	6	5	5	4	5	4	9	9	77	85	.475	14
Seattle	10	4	4	7	5	...	6	2	3	7	6	6	8	6	74	88	.457	17
Texas	7	4	3	5	7	7	...	3	4	5	2	7	3	5	62	99	.385	28.5

National League

East Division

Team	St.L.	N.Y.	Mon.	Chi.	Phi.	Pit.	L.A.	Cin.	Hou.	S.D.	Atl.	S.F.	W	L	Pct.	GB
St. Louis	...	10	7	14	10	15	5	7	6	8	9	10	101	61	.623	...
New York	8	...	9	14	11	10	5	8	8	7	10	8	98	64	.605	3
Montreal	11	9	...	11	8	9	5	4	6	5	9	7	84	77	.522	16.5
Chicago	4	4	7	...	13	13	5	5	5	8	7	6	77	84	.478	23.5
Philadelphia	8	7	10	5	...	11	8	5	8	5	2	6	75	87	.463	26
Pittsburgh	3	8	8	5	7	...	4	3	6	4	6	3	57	104	.354	43.5

West Division

Team	L.A.	Cin.	Hou.	S.D.	Atl.	S.F.	St.L.	N.Y.	Mon.	Chi.	Phi.	Pit.	W	L	Pct.	GB
Los Angeles	...	11	12	8	13	11	7	7	7	7	4	8	95	67	.586	...
Cincinnati	7	...	11	9	11	12	5	4	8	6	7	9	89	72	.553	5.5
Houston	6	7	...	12	10	15	6	4	6	7	4	6	83	79	.512	12
San Diego	10	9	6	...	11	12	4	5	7	4	7	8	83	79	.512	12
Atlanta	5	7	8	7	...	10	3	2	3	5	10	6	66	96	.407	29
San Fran.	7	6	3	6	8	...	2	4	5	6	6	9	62	100	.383	33

SIGNIFICANT EVENTS

■ **April 25:** Denny McLain, a 31-game winner in 1968, was sentenced to 23 years in prison after his conviction on racketeering, extortion and cocaine-possession charges in Tampa, Fla.

■ **March 18:** The baseball bans against former greats Mickey Mantle and Willie Mays were lifted by Commissioner Peter V. Ueberroth.

■ **April 3:** The owners and players agreed to expand the League Championship Series from a best-of-five to best-of-seven format.

■ **August 7:** Major League players ended their two-day, 25-game strike when owners dropped their demand for an arbitration salary cap.

MEMORABLE MOMENTS

■ **July 11:** Houston's Nolan Ryan became the first pitcher to record 4,000 career strikeouts when he fanned Danny Heep in a 4-3 victory over the Mets.

■ **August 4:** Chicago's Tom Seaver earned career win No. 300 against the Yankees and California's Rod Carew got hit No. 3,000 against the Twins in games played a continent apart on the same day.

■ **September 11:** Reds player-manager Pete Rose overtook all-time hit leader Ty Cobb when he singled off San Diego's Eric Show for career hit No. 4,192.

■ **October 6:** Yankee knuckleballer Phil Niekro fired a final-day 8-0 shutout at the Blue Jays and joined baseball's 300-win club.

ALL-STAR GAME

■ **Winner:** The N.L. made it 21 of 23 and two in a row as five pitchers shut down the A.L. on five hits.

■ **Key inning:** The third, when the N.L. took the lead on a double by Tommy Herr and Steve Garvey's single.

■ **Memorable moment:** The performance of the N.L. pitchers, who did not even allow an extra-base hit.

■ **Top guns:** LaMarr Hoyt (Padres), Nolan Ryan (Astros), Garvey (Dodgers), Willie McGee (Cardinals), Ozzie Virgil (Phillies), N.L.; Rickey Henderson (Yankees), A.L.

■ **MVP:** Hoyt.

Linescore

July 16, at Minnesota's Metrodome

N.L..............0 1 1 0 2 0 0 0 2—6 9 1
A.L. ....1 0 0 0 0 0 0 0 0—1 5 0

Hoyt (Padres), Ryan (Astros) 4, Valenzuela (Dodgers) 7, Reardon (Expos) 8, Gossage (Padres) 9; Morris (Tigers), Key (Blue Jays) 3, Blyleven (Indians) 4, Stieb (Blue Jays) 6, Moore (Angels) 7, Petry (Tigers) 9, Hernandez (Tigers) 9. W—Hoyt. L—Morris.

ALCS

■ **Winner:** The Kansas City Royals, taking advantage of baseball's expanded seven-game playoff format, rallied from a three-games-to-one deficit to deny Toronto's bid for a first Canadian pennant.

■ **Turning point:** One day after the Blue Jays had rallied for three ninth-inning runs and a 3-1 series edge, Danny Jackson steadied the Royals with an eight-hit, 2-0 shutout at Royals Stadium.

■ **Memorable moment:** A bases-loaded, opposite-field Jim Sundberg blast that bounded high off the wall and resulted in a three-run, sixth-inning triple — the big blow in Kansas City's seventh-game 6-2 victory.

■ **Top guns:** Jackson (1-0, 0.00 ERA), George Brett (.348, 3 HR, 5 RBIs), Willie Wilson (.310), Royals; Al Oliver (.375), Cliff Johnson (.368), Blue Jays.

■ **MVP:** Brett.

Linescores

Game 1—October 8, at Toronto

K.C............0 0 0 0 0 0 0 0 1—1 5 1
Tor. ....0 2 3 1 0 0 0 0 x—6 11 0

Leibrandt, Farr (3), Gubicza (5), Jackson (8); Stieb, Henke (9). W—Stieb. L—Leibrandt.

Game 2—October 9, at Toronto

K.C.........0 0 2 1 0 0 0 0 1 1—5 10 3
Tor. ....0 0 0 1 0 2 0 1 0 2—6 10 0

Black, Quisenberry (8); Key, Lamp (4), Lavelle (8), Henke (8). W—Henke. L—Quisenberry. HR—Wilson, Sheridan (K.C.).

Game 3—October 11, at Kansas City

Tor. ....0 0 0 0 5 0 0 0 0—5 13 1
K.C. ....1 0 0 1 1 2 0 1 x—6 10 1

Alexander, Lamp (6), Clancy (8); Saberhagen, Black (5), Farr (5). W—Farr. L—Clancy. HR—Brett 2, Sundberg (K.C.); Barfield, Mulliniks (Tor.)

Game 4—October 12, at Kansas City

Tor. ....0 0 0 0 0 0 0 0 3—3 7 0
K.C...............0 0 0 0 0 1 0 0 0—1 2 0

Stieb, Henke (7); Leibrandt, Quisenberry (9). W—Henke. L—Leibrandt.

Game 5—October 13, at Kansas City

Tor. ....0 0 0 0 0 0 0 0 0—0 8 0
K.C. ....1 1 0 0 0 0 0 0 x—2 8 0

Key, Acker (6); Jackson. W—Jackson. L—Key.

Game 6—October 15, at Toronto

K.C...............1 0 1 0 1 2 0 0 0—5 8 1
Tor. ....1 0 1 0 0 1 0 0 0—3 8 2

Gubicza, Black (6), Quisenberry (9); Alexander, Lamp (6). W—Gubicza. L—Alexander. S—Quisenberry. HR—Brett (K.C.).

Game 7—October 16, at Toronto

K.C...............0 1 0 1 0 4 0 0 0—6 8 0
Tor. ....0 0 0 0 1 0 0 0 1—2 8 1

Saberhagen, Leibrandt (4), Quisenberry (9); Stieb, Acker (6). W—Leibrandt. L—Stieb. HR—Sheridan (K.C.).

LEADERS

American League
BA: Wade Boggs, Bos., .368.
Runs: Rickey Henderson, N.Y., 146.
Hits: Wade Boggs, Bos., 240.
TB: Don Mattingly, N.Y., 370.
HR: Darrell Evans, Det., 40.
RBI: Don Mattingly, N.Y., 145.
SB: Rickey Henderson, N.Y., 80.
Wins: Ron Guidry, N.Y., 22.
ERA: Dave Stieb, Tor., 2.48.
CG: Bert Blyleven, Cle.-Min., 24.
IP: Bert Blyleven, Cle.-Min., 293.2.
SO: Bert Blyleven, Cle.-Min., 206.
SV: Dan Quisenberry, K.C., 37.

National League
BA: Willie McGee, St.L., .353.
Runs: Dale Murphy, Atl., 118.
Hits: Willie McGee, St.L., 216.
TB: Dave Parker, Cin., 350.
HR: Dale Murphy, Atl., 37.
RBI: Dave Parker, Cin., 125.
SB: Vince Coleman, St.L., 110.
Wins: Dwight Gooden, N.Y., 24.
ERA: Dwight Gooden, N.Y., 1.53.
CG: Dwight Gooden, N.Y., 16.
IP: Dwight Gooden, N.Y., 276.2.
SO: Dwight Gooden, N.Y., 268.
SV: Jeff Reardon, Mon., 41.

A.L. 20-game winners
Ron Guidry, N.Y., 22-6
Bret Saberhagen, K.C., 20-6

N.L. 20-game winners
Dwight Gooden, N.Y., 24-4
John Tudor, St.L., 21-8
Joaquin Andujar, St.L., 21-12
Tom Browning, Cin., 20-9

A.L. 100 RBIs
Don Mattingly, N.Y., 145
Eddie Murray, Bal., 124
Dave Winfield, N.Y., 114
Harold Baines, Chi., 113
George Brett, K.C., 112
Bill Buckner, Bos., 110
Cal Ripken, Bal., 110
Carlton Fisk, Chi., 107
Jim Rice, Bos., 103

N.L. 100 RBIs
Dave Parker, Cin., 125
Dale Murphy, Atl., 111
Tommy Herr, St.L., 110
Keith Moreland, Chi., 106
Glenn Wilson, Phil., 102
Hubie Brooks, Mon., 100
Gary Carter, N.Y., 100

A.L. 40 homers
Darrell Evans, Det., 40

Most Valuable Player
A.L.: Don Mattingly, 1B, N.Y.
N.L.: Willie McGee, OF, St.L.

Cy Young Award
A.L.: Bret Saberhagen, K.C.
N.L.: Dwight Gooden, N.Y.

Rookie of the Year
A.L.: Ozzie Guillen, SS, Chi.
N.L.: Vince Coleman, OF, St.L.

Manager of the Year
A.L.: Bobby Cox, Tor.
N.L.: Whitey Herzog, St.L.

Hall of Fame additions
Lou Brock, OF, 1961-79
Enos Slaughter, OF, 1938-59
Arky Vaughan, IF, 1932-48
Hoyt Wilhelm, P, 1952-72

NLCS

■ **Winner:** The speed-and-pitching oriented St. Louis Cardinals used a new weapon — the dramatic home run — to post a six-game NLCS victory over Los Angeles.

■ **Turning point:** The ninth inning of Game 5 when light-hitting Ozzie Smith, who had hit only 14 career home runs, stunned the Dodgers with a shot down the right-field line against Tom Niedenfuer that produced a 3-2 Cardinals victory and a 3-2 series edge.

■ **Memorable moment:** A three-run, series-clinching home run by Cardinals first baseman Jack Clark in the ninth inning of Game 6. The shot off Niedenfuer gave St. Louis a 7-5 victory — its fourth straight after the Dodgers had won Games 1 and 2.

■ **Top guns:** Ken Dayley (6 IP, 2 saves, 0.00 ERA), Smith (.435), Clark (.381), Cardinals; Fernando Valenzuela (1-0, 1.88), Bill Madlock (.333, 3 HR, 7 RBIs), Dodgers.

■ **MVP:** Smith.

Linescores

Game 1—October 9, at Los Angeles

St. Louis ......0 0 0 0 0 0 1 0 0—1 8 1
L.A. ....0 0 0 1 0 3 0 0 x—4 8 0

Tudor, Dayley (6), Campbell (7), Worrell (8); Valenzuela, Niedenfuer (7). W—Valenzuela. L—Tudor. S—Niedenfuer.

Game 2—October 10, at Los Angeles

St. Louis ....0 0 1 0 0 0 0 0 1—2 8 1
L.A. ....0 0 3 2 1 2 0 0 x—8 13 1

Andujar, Horton (5), Campbell (6), Dayley (7), Lahti (8); Hershiser. W—Hershiser. L—Andujar. HR—Brock (L.A.).

Game 3—October 12, at St. Louis

L.A...............0 0 0 1 0 0 1 0 0—2 7 2
St. Louis ......2 2 0 0 0 0 0 0 x—4 8 0

Welch, Honeycutt (3), Diaz (5), Howell (7); Cox, Horton (7), Worrell (7), Dayley (9). W—Cox. L—Welch. S—Dayley. HR—Herr (St.L.).

Game 4—October 13, at St. Louis

L.A. ....0 0 0 0 0 0 1 1 0— 2 5 2
St. Louis ..0 9 0 1 1 0 0 1 x—12 15 0

Reuss, Honeycutt (2), Castillo (2), Diaz (8); Tudor, Horton (8), Campbell (9). W—Tudor. L—Reuss. HR—Madlock (L.A.).

Game 5—October 14, at St. Louis

L.A. ....0 0 0 2 0 0 0 0 0—2 5 1
St. Louis ......2 0 0 0 0 0 0 0 1—3 5 1

Valenzuela, Niedenfuer (9); Forsch, Dayley (4), Worrell (7), Lahti (9). W—Lahti. L—Niedenfuer. HR—Madlock (L.A.); Smith (St.L.).

Game 6—October 16, at Los Angeles

St. Louis ....0 0 1 0 0 0 3 0 3—7 12 1
L.A. ....1 1 0 0 2 0 0 1 0—5 8 0

Andujar, Worrell (7), Dayley (9); Hershiser, Niedenfuer (7). W—Worrell. L—Niedenfuer. S—Dayley. HR—Madlock, Marshall (L.A.); Clark (St.L.).

WORLD SERIES

■ **Winner:** The Royals needed three consecutive victories and a controversial sixth-game decision to claim their first Series triumph in an all-Missouri fall classic.

■ **Turning point:** A blown call at first base by umpire Don Denkinger in the Royals' ninth inning of Game 6. After arguing vehemently, the Cardinals unraveled and the Royals scored twice, claiming a 2-1 victory and forcing a seventh game.

■ **Memorable moment:** Royals catcher Jim Sundberg sliding around the tag of Cardinals catcher Darrell Porter with the winning run in Game 6. Sundberg and Onix Concepcion scored on Dane Iorg's one-out single.

■ **Top guns:** Bret Saberhagen (2-0, 0.50 ERA), George Brett (.370), Willie Wilson (.367), Royals; Tito Landrum (.360), Cardinals.

■ **MVP:** Saberhagen.

Linescores

Game 1—October 19, at Kansas City

St. Louis ......0 0 1 1 0 0 0 0 1—3 7 1
K.C...............0 1 0 0 0 0 0 0 0—1 8 0

Tudor, Worrell (7); Jackson, Quisenberry (8), Black (9). W—Tudor. L—Jackson. S—Worrell.

Game 2—October 20, at Kansas City

St. Louis ......0 0 0 0 0 0 0 0 4—4 6 0
K.C...............0 0 0 2 0 0 0 0 0—2 9 0

Cox, Dayley (8), Lahti (9); Leibrandt, Quisenberry (9). W—Dayley. L—Leibrandt. S—Lahti.

Game 3—October 22, at St. Louis

K.C............0 0 0 2 2 0 2 0 0—6 11 0
St. Louis ....0 0 0 0 0 1 0 0 0—1 6 0

Saberhagen; Andujar, Campbell (5), Horton (6), Dayley (8). W—Saberhagen. L—Andujar. HR—White (K.C.).

Game 4—October 23, at St. Louis

K.C...............0 0 0 0 0 0 0 0 0—0 5 1
St. Louis ......0 1 1 0 1 0 0 0 x—3 6 0

Black, Beckwith (6), Quisenberry (8); Tudor. W—Tudor. L—Black. HR—Landrum, McGee (St.L.).

Game 5—October 24, at St. Louis

K.C............1 3 0 0 0 0 0 1 1—6 11 2
St. Louis ....1 0 0 0 0 0 0 0 0—1 5 1

Jackson; Forsch, Horton (2), Campbell (4), Worrell (6), Lahti (8). W—Jackson. L—Forsch.

Game 6—October 26, at Kansas City

St. Louis ....0 0 0 0 0 0 0 1 0—1 5 0
K.C............0 0 0 0 0 0 0 0 2—2 10 0

Cox, Dayley (8), Worrell (9); Leibrandt, Quisenberry (8). W—Quisenberry. L—Worrell.

Game 7—October 27, at Kansas City

St. Louis ..0 0 0 0 0 0 0 0 0— 0 5 0
K.C..........0 2 3 0 6 0 0 0 x—11 14 0

Tudor, Campbell (3), Lahti (5), Horton (5), Andujar (5), Forsch (5), Dayley (7); Saberhagen. W—Saberhagen. L—Tudor. HR—Motley (K.C.).

FINAL STANDINGS

American League

East Division

Team	Bos.	N.Y.	Det.	Tor.	Cle.	Mil.	Bal.	Cal.	Tex.	K.C.	Oak.	Chi.	Min.	Sea.	W	L	Pct.	GB
Boston	...	5	7	7	10	6	9	5	8	6	7	7	10	8	95	66	.590	...
New York	8	...	7	7	8	5	8	5	7	8	5	6	8	8	90	72	.556	5.5
Detroit	6	6	...	4	9	8	12	5	7	5	6	6	7	6	87	75	.537	8.5
Toronto	6	6	9	...	10	6	5	6	7	7	4	6	8	6	86	76	.531	9.5
Cleveland	3	5	4	3	...	8	9	6	6	8	10	7	6	9	84	78	.519	11.5
Milwaukee	6	8	5	7	5	...	7	7	4	6	5	7	4	6	77	84	.478	18
Baltimore	4	5	1	8	4	6	...	6	5	6	5	9	8	6	73	89	.451	22.5

West Division

Team	Cal.	Tex.	K.C.	Oak.	Chi.	Min.	Sea.	Bos.	N.Y.	Det.	Tor.	Cle.	Mil.	Bal.	W	L	Pct.	GB
California	...	8	8	10	7	7	8	7	7	7	6	6	5	6	92	70	.568	...
Texas	5	...	5	10	11	7	9	4	5	5	5	6	8	7	87	75	.537	5
Kansas City	5	8	...	8	6	6	5	6	4	7	5	4	6	6	76	86	.469	16
Oakland	3	3	5	...	6	7	10	5	7	6	8	2	7	7	76	86	.469	16
Chicago	6	2	7	7	...	6	8	5	6	6	6	5	5	3	72	90	.444	20
Minnesota	6	6	7	6	7	...	6	2	4	5	4	6	8	4	71	91	.438	21
Seattle	5	4	8	3	5	7	...	4	4	6	6	3	6	6	67	95	.414	25

National League

East Division

Team	N.Y.	Phi.	St.L.	Mon.	Chi.	Pit.	Hou.	Cin.	S.F.	S.D.	L.A.	Atl.	W	L	Pct.	GB
New York	...	8	12	10	12	17	7	8	7	10	9	8	108	54	.667	...
Phil.	10	...	6	10	8	11	6	5	9	6	7	8	86	75	.534	21.5
St. Louis	6	12	...	9	7	11	5	5	7	7	4	6	79	82	.491	28.5
Montreal	8	8	9	...	10	11	4	5	5	4	7	7	78	83	.484	29.5
Chicago	6	9	10	8	...	7	4	5	6	6	6	3	70	90	.438	37
Pittsburgh	1	7	7	7	11	...	6	2	4	8	4	7	64	98	.395	44

West Division

Team	Hou.	Cin.	S.F.	S.D.	L.A.	Atl.	N.Y.	Phi.	St.L.	Mon.	Chi.	Pit.	W	L	Pct.	GB
Houston	...	14	9	10	10	13	5	6	7	8	8	6	96	66	.593	...
Cincinnati	4	...	9	9	10	12	4	7	7	7	7	10	86	76	.531	10
San Fran.	9	9	...	10	10	11	5	3	5	7	6	8	83	79	.512	13
San Diego	8	9	8	...	12	6	2	6	5	8	6	4	74	88	.457	22
Los Angeles	8	8	8	6	...	8	3	5	8	5	6	8	73	89	.451	23
Atlanta	5	6	7	12	10	...	4	4	6	4	9	5	72	89	.447	23.5

LEADERS

American League
BA: Wade Boggs, Bos., .357.
Runs: Rickey Henderson, N.Y., 130.
Hits: Don Mattingly, N.Y., 238.
TB: Don Mattingly, N.Y., 388.
HR: Jesse Barfield, Tor., 40.
RBI: Joe Carter, Cle., 121.
SB: Rickey Henderson, N.Y., 87.
Wins: Roger Clemens, Bos., 24.
ERA: Roger Clemens, Bos., 2.48.
CG: Tom Candiotti, Cle., 17.
IP: Bert Blyleven, Min., 271.2.
SO: Mark Langston, Sea., 245.
SV: Dave Righetti, N.Y., 46.

National League
BA: Tim Raines, Mon., .334.
Runs: Tony Gwynn, S.D.; Von Hayes, Phil., 107.
Hits: Tony Gwynn, S.D., 211.
TB: Dave Parker, Cin., 304.
HR: Mike Schmidt, Phil., 37.
RBI: Mike Schmidt, Phil., 119.
SB: Vince Coleman, St.L., 107.
Wins: Fernando Valenzuela, L.A., 21.
ERA: Mike Scott, Hou., 2.22.
CG: Fernando Valenzuela, L.A., 20.
IP: Mike Scott, Hou., 275.1.
SO: Mike Scott, Hou., 306.
SV: Todd Worrell, St.L., 36.

A.L. 20-game winners
Roger Clemens, Bos., 24-4
Jack Morris, Det., 21-8
Ted Higuera, Mil., 20-11

N.L. 20-game winners
Fernando Valenzuela, L.A., 21-11
Mike Krukow, S.F., 20-9

A.L. 100 RBIs
Joe Carter, Cle., 121
Jose Canseco, Oak., 117
Don Mattingly, N.Y., 113
Jim Rice, Bos., 110
Jesse Barfield, Tor., 108
George Bell, Tor., 108
Gary Gaetti, Min., 108
Jim Presley, Sea., 107
Dave Winfield, N.Y., 104
Bill Buckner, Bos., 102
Wally Joyner, Cal., 100

N.L. 100 RBIs
Mike Schmidt, Phil., 119
Dave Parker, Cin., 116
Gary Carter, N.Y., 105
Glenn Davis, Hou., 101

A.L. 40 homers
Jesse Barfield, Tor., 40

Most Valuable Player
A.L.: Roger Clemens, P, Bos.
N.L.: Mike Schmidt, 3B, Phil.

Cy Young Award
A.L.: Roger Clemens, Bos.
N.L.: Mike Scott, Hou.

Rookie of the Year
A.L.: Jose Canseco, OF, Oak.
N.L.: Todd Worrell, P, St.L.

Manager of the Year
A.L.: John McNamara, Bos.
N.L.: Hal Lanier, Hou.

Hall of Fame additions
Bobby Doerr, 2B, 1937-51
Ernie Lombardi, C, 1931-47
Willie McCovey, 1B, 1959-80

SIGNIFICANT EVENTS

■ **February 28:** Commissioner Peter V. Ueberroth handed one-year suspensions to players Dave Parker, Keith Hernandez, Lonnie Smith, Dale Berra, Jeffrey Leonard, Enos Cabell and Joaquin Andujar for drug-related activities.
■ **June 20:** Bo Jackson, the 1985 Heisman Trophy winner from Auburn, stunningly signed with the Royals instead of the NFL's Tampa Bay Buccaneers.

MEMORABLE MOMENTS

■ **April 29:** Boston's Roger Clemens broke a long-standing Major League record when he struck out 20 Mariners in a 3-1 victory at Fenway Park.
■ **June 18:** California's Don Sutton became a 300-game winner when he defeated the Rangers, 5-1.
■ **July 6:** Bob Horner became the 11th Major Leaguer to hit four homers in a game, but his Braves still dropped an 11-8 decision to the Expos.
■ **August 5:** Giants lefty Steve Carlton joined Nolan Ryan in the exclusive 4,000-strikeout club, but dropped an 11-6 decision to the Reds.
■ **September 25:** Houston righthander Mike Scott pitched the first pennant-clinching no-hitter in baseball history, beating the Giants, 2-0.
■ **October 4:** Yankee closer Dave Righetti set a one-season record when he recorded his 45th and 46th saves in a doubleheader sweep of the Red Sox.

ALL-STAR GAME

■ **Winner:** The A.L., looking to break its one-win-per-decade streak, got home runs from second basemen Lou Whitaker and Frank White and scored a 3-2 victory — its second of the 1980s.
■ **Key inning:** The second, when Whitaker followed a Dave Winfield double with a two-run shot off Dwight Gooden.
■ **Memorable moment:** Fernando Valenzuela tied Carl Hubbell's 1934 All-Star record when he struck out, consecutively, Don Mattingly, Cal Ripken, Jesse Barfield, Whitaker and Ted Higuera.
■ **Top guns:** Roger Clemens (Red Sox), Higuera (Brewers), Whitaker (Tigers), White (Royals), A.L.; Valenzuela (Dodgers), Steve Sax (Dodgers), N.L.
■ **MVP:** Clemens.

Linescore
July 15, at Houston's Astrodome
A.L. ....0 2 0 0 0 0 1 0 0—3 5 0
N.L. ....0 0 0 0 0 0 0 2 0—2 5 1
Clemens (Red Sox), Higuera (Brewers) 4, Hough (Rangers) 7, Righetti (Yankees) 8, Aase (Orioles) 9; Gooden (Mets), Valenzuela (Dodgers) 4, Scott (Astros) 7, Fernandez (Mets) 8, Krukow (Giants) 9. W—Clemens. L—Gooden. HR—Whitaker, White, A.L.

ALCS

■ **Winner:** Boston, on the verge of elimination in the ninth inning of Game 5, roared back to post a seven-game triumph over the stunned California Angels.
■ **Turning point:** Dave Henderson, one strike away from becoming the final out in the Angels' pennant-clinching victory, stroked a Donnie Moore pitch into the left-field bleachers for a two-run homer. The blast gave the Red Sox a 6-5 lead and they went on to post a series-turning 7-6 victory in 11 innings.
■ **Memorable moment:** Henderson dancing triumphantly around the bases as a crowd of 64,223 watched in stunned silence at Anaheim Stadium.
■ **Top guns:** Spike Owen (.429), Marty Barrett (.367, 5 RBIs), Rich Gedman (.357, 6 RBIs), Jim Rice (2 HR, 6 RBIs), Red Sox; Bob Boone (.455), Wally Joyner (.455), Angels.
■ **MVP:** Barrett.

Linescores
Game 1—October 7, at Boston
Cal. ....0 4 1 0 0 0 0 3 0—8 11 0
Boston ......0 0 0 0 0 1 0 0 0—1 5 1
Witt; Clemens, Sambito (8), Stanley (8). W—Witt. L—Clemens.
Game 2—October 8, at Boston
Cal. ....0 0 0 1 1 0 0 0 0—2 11 3
Boston ......1 1 0 0 1 0 3 3 x—9 13 2
McCaskill, Lucas (8), Corbett (8); Hurst. W—Hurst. L—McCaskill. HR—Joyner (Cal.); Rice (Bos.).
Game 3—October 10, at California
Boston ....0 1 0 0 0 0 0 2 0—3 9 1
Cal. ....0 0 0 0 0 1 3 1 x—5 8 0
Boyd, Sambito (7), Schiraldi (8); Candelaria, Moore (8). W—Candelaria. L—Boyd. S—Moore. HR—Schofield, Pettis (Cal.).
Game 4—October 11, at California
Boston....0 0 0 0 0 1 0 2 0 0 0—3 6 1
Cal. ....0 0 0 0 0 0 0 0 3 0 1—4 11 2
Clemens, Schiraldi (9); Sutton, Lucas (7), Ruhle (7), Finley (8), Corbett (8). W—Corbett. L—Schiraldi. HR—DeCinces (Cal.).
Game 5—October 12, at California
Boston....0 2 0 0 0 0 0 0 4 0 1—7 12 0
Cal. ....0 0 1 0 0 2 2 0 1 0 0—6 13 0
Hurst, Stanley (7), Sambito (9), Crawford (9), Schiraldi (11); Witt, Lucas (9), Moore (9), Finley (11). W—Crawford. L—Moore. S—Schiraldi. HR—Gedman, Baylor, Henderson (Bos.); Boone, Grich (Cal.).
Game 6—October 14, at Boston
Cal. ....2 0 0 0 0 0 1 1 0— 4 11 1
Boston ....2 0 5 0 1 0 2 0 x—10 16 1
McCaskill, Lucas (3), Corbett (4), Finley (7); Boyd, Stanley (8). W—Boyd. L—McCaskill. HR—Downing (Cal.).
Game 7—October 15, at Boston
Cal. ....0 0 0 0 0 0 0 1 0—1 6 2
Boston ....0 3 0 4 0 0 1 0 x—8 8 1
Candelaria, Sutton (4), Moore (8); Clemens, Schiraldi (8). W—Clemens. L—Candelaria. HR—Rice, Evans (Bos.).

NLCS

■ **Winner:** The New York Mets overcame the outstanding pitching of Houston's Mike Scott and denied the Astros their first-ever pennant.
■ **Turning point:** The Mets claimed a 6-5 Game 3 victory when Lenny Dykstra stroked a two-run homer in the bottom of the ninth inning.
■ **Memorable moment:** Mets relief ace Jesse Orosco fired a pennant-winning third strike past Houston's Kevin Bass with two runners on base in the bottom of the 16th inning, preserving New York's 7-6 victory in the longest Championship Series game ever played.
■ **Top guns:** Orosco (3-0), Dykstra (.304), Darryl Strawberry (2 HR, 5 RBIs), Mets; Scott (2-0, 0.50 ERA), Craig Reynolds (.333), Astros.
■ **MVP:** Scott.

Linescores
Game 1—October 8, at Houston
N.Y. ....0 0 0 0 0 0 0 0 0—0 5 0
Hou. ....0 1 0 0 0 0 0 0 x—1 7 1
Gooden, Orosco (8); Scott. W—Scott. L—Gooden. HR—Davis (Hou.).
Game 2—October 9, at Houston
N.Y. ....0 0 0 2 3 0 0 0 0—5 10 0
Hou. ....0 0 0 0 0 0 1 0 0—1 10 2
Ojeda; Ryan, Andersen (6), Lopez (8), Kerfeld (9). W—Ojeda. L—Ryan.
Game 3—October 11, at New York
Hou. ....2 2 0 0 0 0 1 0 0—5 8 1
N.Y. ....0 0 0 0 0 4 0 0 2—6 10 1
Knepper, Kerfeld (8), Smith (9); Darling, Aguilera (6), Orosco (8). W—Orosco. L—Smith. HR—Doran (Hou.); Strawberry, Dykstra (N.Y.).
Game 4—October 12, at New York
Hou. ....0 2 0 0 1 0 0 0 0—3 4 1
N.Y. ....0 0 0 0 0 0 0 1 0—1 3 0
Scott; Fernandez, McDowell (7), Sisk (9). W—Scott. L—Fernandez. HR—Ashby, Thon (Hou.).
Game 5—October 14, at New York
Hou. ......0 0 0 0 1 0 0 0 0 0 0 0—1 9 1
N.Y. ....0 0 0 0 1 0 0 0 0 0 0 1—2 4 0
Ryan, Kerfeld (10); Gooden, Orosco (11). W—Orosco. L—Kerfeld. HR—Strawberry (N.Y.).
Game 6—October 15, at Houston
N.Y. ....0 0 0 0 0 0 0 0 3 0 0 0 0 1 0 3—7 11 0
Hou.....3 0 0 0 0 0 0 0 0 0 0 0 0 1 0 2—6 11 1
Ojeda, Aguilera (6), McDowell (9), Orosco (14); Knepper, Smith (9), Andersen (11), Lopez (14), Calhoun (16). W—Orosco. L—Lopez. HR—Hatcher (Hou.).

WORLD SERIES

■ **Winner:** The Mets, on the brink of elimination, made a wild Game 6 recovery and kept the Red Sox without a Series victory since 1918.
■ **Turning point:** The bottom of the 10th inning of Game 6. One out away from elimination and trailing 5-3 with nobody on base, the Mets amazingly rallied for three runs and a 6-5, Game 7-forcing victory.
■ **Memorable moments:** A tense, 10-pitch battle between Mets batter Mookie Wilson and Boston pitcher Bob Stanley in the fateful 10th inning of Game 6. One Stanley pitch was wild, allowing the tying run to score, and Wilson slapped the final one to first baseman Bill Buckner, who let the ball dribble between his legs for a game-deciding error.
■ **Top guns:** Ray Knight (.391), Gary Carter (2 HR, 9 RBIs), Mets; Bruce Hurst (2-0, 1.96 ERA), Dwight Evans (2 HR, 9 RBIs), Red Sox.
■ **MVP:** Knight.

Linescores
Game 1—October 18, at New York
Boston ....0 0 0 0 0 0 1 0 0—1 5 0
N.Y. ....0 0 0 0 0 0 0 0 0—0 4 1
Hurst, Schiraldi (9); Darling, McDowell (8). W—Hurst. L—Darling. S—Schiraldi.
Game 2—October 19, at New York
Boston ......0 0 3 1 2 0 2 0 1—9 18 0
N.Y. ....0 0 2 0 1 0 0 0 0—3 8 1
Clemens, Crawford (5), Stanley (7); Gooden, Aguilera (6), Orosco (7), Fernandez (9), Sisk (9). W—Crawford. L—Gooden. S—Stanley. HR—Henderson, Evans (Bos.).
Game 3—October 21, at Boston
N.Y. ....4 0 0 0 0 0 2 1 0—7 13 0
Boston ......0 0 1 0 0 0 0 0 0—1 5 0
Ojeda, McDowell (8); Boyd, Sambito (8), Stanley (8). W—Ojeda. L—Boyd. HR—Dykstra (N.Y.).
Game 4—October 22, at Boston
N.Y. ....0 0 0 3 0 0 2 1 0—6 12 0
Boston ......0 0 0 0 0 0 0 2 0—2 7 1
Darling, McDowell (8), Orosco (8); Nipper, Crawford (7), Stanley (9). W—Darling. L—Nipper. S—Orosco. HR—Carter 2, Dykstra (N.Y.).
Game 5—October 23, at Boston
N.Y. ....0 0 0 0 0 0 0 1 1—2 10 1
Boston ......0 1 1 0 2 0 0 0 x—4 12 0
Gooden, Fernandez (5); Hurst. W—Hurst. L—Gooden. HR—Teufel (N.Y.).
Game 6—October 25, at New York
Boston ..1 1 0 0 0 0 1 0 0 2—5 13 3
N.Y. ....0 0 0 0 2 0 0 1 0 3—6 8 2
Clemens, Schiraldi (8), Stanley (10); Ojeda, McDowell (7), Orosco (8), Aguilera (9). W—Aguilera. L—Schiraldi. HR—Henderson (Bos.).
Game 7—October 27, at New York
Boston ......0 3 0 0 0 0 0 2 0—5 9 0
N.Y. ....0 0 0 0 0 3 3 2 x—8 10 0
Hurst, Schiraldi (7), Sambito (7), Stanley (7), Nipper (8), Crawford (8); Darling, Fernandez (4), McDowell (7), Orosco (8). W—McDowell. L—Schiraldi. S—Orosco. HR—Evans, Gedman (Bos.); Knight, Strawberry (N.Y.).

1987

FINAL STANDINGS

American League

East Division

Team	Det.	Tor.	Mil.	N.Y.	Bos.	Bal.	Cle.	Min.	K.C.	Oak.	Sea.	Chi.	Tex.	Cal.	W	L	Pct.	GB
Detroit	...	7	6	5	11	9	9	8	5	5	7	9	8	9	98	64	.605	...
Toronto	6	...	4	7	7	12	8	9	4	5	10	8	9	7	96	66	.593	2
Milwaukee	7	9	...	7	7	11	9	3	8	6	4	6	9	5	91	71	.562	7
New York	8	6	6	...	6	10	7	6	7	5	7	7	5	9	89	73	.549	9
Boston	2	6	6	7	...	12	7	7	6	4	7	3	7	4	78	84	.481	20
Baltimore	4	1	2	3	1	...	7	5	9	7	4	8	7	9	67	95	.414	31
Cleveland	4	5	4	6	6	6	...	3	6	4	5	5	2	5	61	101	.377	37

West Division

Team	Min.	K.C.	Oak.	Sea.	Chi.	Tex.	Cal.	Det.	Tor.	Mil.	N.Y.	Bos.	Bal.	Cle.	W	L	Pct.	GB
Minnesota	...	5	10	9	7	6	5	4	3	9	6	5	7	9	85	77	.525	...
Kansas City	8	...	5	9	7	7	8	7	8	4	5	6	3	6	83	79	.512	2
Oakland	3	8	...	5	4	6	7	7	7	6	7	8	5	8	81	81	.500	4
Seattle	4	4	8	...	7	9	6	5	2	8	5	5	8	7	78	84	.481	7
Chicago	6	6	9	6	...	7	5	3	4	6	5	9	4	7	77	85	.475	8
Texas	7	6	7	4	6	...	8	4	3	3	7	5	5	10	75	87	.463	10
California	8	5	6	7	8	5	...	3	5	7	3	8	3	7	75	87	.463	10

National League

East Division

Team	St.L.	N.Y.	Mon.	Phi.	Pit.	Chi.	S.F.	Cin.	Hou.	L.A.	Atl.	S.D.	W	L	Pct.	GB
St. Louis	...	9	7	10	11	12	5	8	7	9	9	8	95	67	.586	...
New York	9	...	10	13	12	9	9	5	6	6	5	8	92	70	.568	3
Montreal	11	8	...	10	11	8	5	6	5	9	9	9	91	71	.562	4
Philadelphia	8	5	8	...	11	10	2	7	6	10	5	8	80	82	.494	15
Pittsburgh	7	6	7	7	...	14	6	8	6	6	5	8	80	82	.494	15
Chicago	6	9	10	8	4	...	5	6	8	6	5	9	76	85	.472	18.5

West Division

Team	S.F.	Cin.	Hou.	L.A.	Atl.	S.D.	St.L.	N.Y.	Mon.	Phi.	Pit.	Chi.	W	L	Pct.	GB
San Fran.	...	11	8	8	10	13	7	3	7	10	6	7	90	72	.556	...
Cincinnati	7	...	13	10	10	12	4	7	6	5	4	6	84	78	.519	6
Houston	10	5	...	12	10	5	5	6	7	6	6	4	76	86	.469	14
Los Angeles	10	8	6	...	12	11	3	6	3	2	6	6	73	89	.451	17
Atlanta	8	8	8	6	...	6	3	7	3	7	7	6	69	92	.429	20.5
San Diego	5	6	13	7	12	...	4	4	3	4	4	3	65	97	.401	25

SIGNIFICANT EVENTS

■ **April 8:** Dodgers vice president Al Campanis, reeling from criticism he had generated two days earlier with his nationally televised comments about the role of blacks in sports, resigned.
■ **July 14:** Kansas City's Bo Jackson became a two-sport star when he signed a five-year contract to play football for the Los Angeles Raiders.

MEMORABLE MOMENTS

■ **April 18:** Mike Schmidt joined the 500-homer club with a dramatic three-run ninth-inning shot that gave the Phillies an 8-6 victory over the Pirates.
■ **July 18:** Yankee Don Mattingly tied a 31-year-old Major League record when he hit a home run in his eighth consecutive game—a 7-2 loss to the Rangers.
■ **August 26:** Cleveland pitcher John Farrell stopped Paul Molitor's 39-game hitting streak, but Milwaukee won in 10 innings, 1-0.
■ **September 14:** Catcher Ernie Whitt belted three home runs to lead a Toronto assault that produced a record 10 homers and an 18-3 rout of the Orioles.
■ **September 29:** Oakland's Mark McGwire pounded his 49th home run in a 5-4 victory over Cleveland, giving him 11 more than the previous rookie record.
■ **October 3:** Dodgers ace Orel Hershiser ended Padres catcher Benito Santiago's rookie-record 34-game hitting streak.
■ **October 4:** The Tigers defeated Toronto, 1-0, and completed a season-ending, A.L. East-deciding sweep of the Blue Jays.

LEADERS

American League
BA: Wade Boggs, Bos., .363.
Runs: Paul Molitor, Mil., 114.
Hits: Kirby Puckett, Min.; Kevin Seitzer, K.C., 207.
TB: George Bell, Tor., 369.
HR: Mark McGwire, Oak., 49.
RBI: George Bell, Tor., 134.
SB: Harold Reynolds, Sea., 60.
Wins: Roger Clemens, Bos.; Dave Stewart, Oak., 20.
ERA: Jimmy Key, Tor., 2.76.
CG: Roger Clemens, Bos., 18.
IP: Charlie Hough, Tex., 285.1.
SO: Mark Langston, Sea., 262.
SV: Tom Henke, Tor., 34.

National League
BA: Tony Gwynn, S.D., .370.
Runs: Tim Raines, Mon., 123.
Hits: Tony Gwynn, S.D., 218.
TB: Andre Dawson, Chi., 353.
HR: Andre Dawson, Chi., 49.
RBI: Andre Dawson, Chi., 137.
SB: Vince Coleman, St.L., 109.
Wins: Rick Sutcliffe, Chi., 18.
ERA: Nolan Ryan, Hou., 2.76.
CG: Rick Reuschel, Pit.-S.F.; Fernando Valenzuela, L.A., 12.
IP: Orel Hershiser, L.A., 264.2.
SO: Nolan Ryan, Hou., 270.
SV: Steve Bedrosian, Phil., 40.

A.L. 20-game winners
Roger Clemens, Bos., 20-9
Dave Stewart, Oak., 20-13

A.L. 100 RBIs
George Bell, Tor., 134
Dwight Evans, Bos., 123
Mark McGwire, Oak., 118
Wally Joyner, Cal., 117
Don Mattingly, N.Y., 115
Jose Canseco, Oak., 113
Gary Gaetti, Min., 109
Ruben Sierra, Tex., 109
Joe Carter, Cle., 106
Alan Trammell, Det., 105
Robin Yount, Mil., 103
Danny Tartabull, K.C., 101
Alvin Davis, Sea., 100
Larry Parrish, Tex., 100

N.L. 100 RBIs
Andre Dawson, Chi., 137
Tim Wallach, Mon., 123
Mike Schmidt, Phil., 113
Jack Clark, St.L., 106
Willie McGee, St.L., 105
Dale Murphy, Atl., 105
Darryl Strawberry, N.Y., 104
Eric Davis, Cin., 100
Juan Samuel, Phil., 100

A.L. 40 homers
Mark McGwire, Oak., 49
George Bell, Tor., 47

N.L. 40 homers
Andre Dawson, Chi., 49
Dale Murphy, Atl., 44

Most Valuable Player
A.L.: George Bell, OF, Tor.
N.L.: Andre Dawson, OF, Chi.

Cy Young Award
A.L.: Roger Clemens, Bos.
N.L.: Steve Bedrosian, Phil.

Rookie of the Year
A.L.: Mark McGwire, 1B, Oak.
N.L.: Benito Santiago, C, S.D.

Manager of the Year
A.L.: Sparky Anderson, Det.
N.L.: Buck Rodgers, Mon.

Hall of Fame additions
Ray Dandridge, 3B, Negro Leagues
Catfish Hunter, P, 1965-79
Billy Williams, OF, 1959-76

ALL-STAR GAME

■ **Winner:** The N.L. broke a scoreless deadlock in the 13th inning to claim a 2-0 victory.
■ **Key inning:** The 13th, when Tim Raines drilled a two-out Jay Howell pitch for a two-run triple, scoring Ozzie Virgil and Hubie Brooks.
■ **Memorable moment:** A violent collision between Dave Winfield and N.L. catcher Virgil in the ninth. Winfield, trying to score from second on a failed double-play attempt, was called out when Virgil held onto the ball.
■ **Top guns:** Mike Scott (Astros), Rick Sutcliffe (Cubs), Orel Hershiser (Dodgers), Raines (Expos), N.L.; Bret Saberhagen (Royals), Mark Langston (Mariners), A.L.
■ **MVP:** Raines.

Linescore
July 14, at the Oakland Coliseum
N.L. ....000 000 000 0002—2 8 2
A.L. ....000 000 000 0000—0 6 1
Scott (Astros), Sutcliffe (Cubs) 3, Hershiser (Dodgers) 5, Reuschel (Pirates) 7, Franco (Reds) 8, Bedrosian (Phillies) 9, L. Smith (Cubs) 10, S. Fernandez (Mets) 13; Saberhagen (Royals), Morris (Tigers) 4, Langston (Mariners) 6, Plesac (Brewers) 8, Righetti (Yankees) 9, Henke (Blue Jays) 9, Howell (Athletics) 12. W—L. Smith. L—Howell. S—S. Fernandez.

ALCS

■ **Winner:** Minnesota, a loser in the A.L.'s first two LCS in 1969 and '70, surprised the favored Detroit Tigers in a five-game romp.
■ **Turning point:** The sixth inning of Game 4. With the Twins leading the series 2-1 and the game 4-3, Detroit's Darrell Evans let Minnesota catcher Tim Laudner pick him off third base — a mistake that doomed the Tigers' pennant hopes.
■ **Memorable moment:** The Game 5 hitting of Twins right fielder Tom Brunansky, who collected a single, double, homer and three RBIs in Minnesota's series-closing 9-5 victory.
■ **Top guns:** Brunansky (.412, 2 HR, 9 RBIs), Dan Gladden (.350), Gary Gaetti (.300, 2 HR, 5 RBIs), Twins; Johnny Grubb (.571), Chet Lemon (2 HR, 4 RBIs), Tigers.
■ **MVP:** Gaetti.

Linescores
Game 1—October 7, at Minnesota
Detroit........0 0 1 0 0 1 1 2 0—5 10 0
Minnesota..0 1 0 0 3 0 0 4 x—8 10 0
Alexander, Henneman (8), Hernandez (8), King (8); Viola, Reardon (8). W—Reardon. L—Alexander. HR—Gaetti 2 (Min.); Heath, Gibson (Det.).
Game 2—October 8, at Minnesota
Detroit..........0 2 0 0 0 0 0 1 0—3 7 1
Minnesota....0 3 0 2 1 0 0 0 x—6 6 0
Morris; Blyleven, Berenguer (8). W—Blyleven. L—Morris. S—Berenguer. HR—Lemon, Whitaker (Det.); Hrbek (Min.).
Game 3—October 10, at Detroit
Minnesota....0 0 0 2 0 2 2 0 0—6 8 1
Detroit..........0 0 5 0 0 0 0 2 x—7 7 0
Straker, Schatzeder (3), Berenguer (7), Reardon (8); Terrell, Henneman (7). W—Henneman. L—Reardon. HR—Gagne, Brunansky (Min.); Sheridan (Det.).
Game 4—October 11, at Detroit
Minnesota....0 0 1 1 1 1 0 1 0—5 7 1
Detroit..........1 0 0 0 1 1 0 0 0—3 7 3
Viola, Atherton (6), Berenguer (6), Reardon (9); Tanana, Petry (6), Thurmond (9). W—Viola. L—Tanana. S—Reardon. HR—Puckett, Gagne (Min.).
Game 5—October 12, at Detroit
Minnesota..0 4 0 0 0 0 1 1 3—9 15 1
Detroit........0 0 0 3 0 0 0 1 1—5 9 1
Blyleven, Schatzeder (7), Berenguer (8), Reardon (8); Alexander, King (2), Henneman (7), Robinson (9). W—Blyleven. L—Alexander. S—Reardon. HR—Nokes, Lemon (Det.); Brunansky (Min.).

NLCS

■ **Winner:** The Cardinals had to overcome the lusty hitting of San Francisco's Jeffrey Leonard to claim their third pennant of the decade.
■ **Turning point:** The combined six-hit pitching of Cardinals John Tudor, Todd Worrell and Ken Dayley in a 1-0 Game 6 victory.
■ **Memorable moment:** Leonard's two-run homer in the fifth inning of Game 4—his record-tying fourth in the series.
■ **Top guns:** Tony Pena (.381), Willie McGee (.308), Cardinals; Dave Dravecky (1-1, 0.60 ERA), Leonard (.417, 4 HR, 5 RBIs), Giants.
■ **MVP:** Leonard.

Linescores
Game 1—October 6, at St. Louis
San Fran. ....1 0 0 1 0 0 0 1 0—3 7 1
St. Louis ......0 0 1 1 0 3 0 0 x—5 10 1
Reuschel, Lefferts (7), Garrelts (8); Mathews, Worrell (8), Dayley (8). W—Mathews. L—Reuschel. S—Dayley. HR—Leonard (S.F.).
Game 2—October 7, at St. Louis
San Fran. ....0 2 0 1 0 0 0 2 0—5 10 0
St. Louis ......0 0 0 0 0 0 0 0 0—0 2 1
Dravecky; Tudor, Forsch (9). W—Dravecky. L—Tudor. HR—W. Clark, Leonard (S.F.).
Game 3—October 9, at San Francisco
St. Louis ......0 0 0 0 0 2 4 0 0—6 11 1
San Fran. ....0 3 1 0 0 0 0 0 1—5 7 1
Magrane, Forsch (5), Worrell (7); Hammaker, D. Robinson (7), Lefferts (7), LaCoss (8). W—Forsch. L—D. Robinson. S—Worrell. HR—Leonard, Spilman (S.F.); Lindeman (St.L.).
Game 4—October 10, at San Francisco
St. Louis ....0 2 0 0 0 0 0 0 0—2 9 0
San Fran.........0 0 0 1 2 0 0 1 x—4 9 2
Cox; Krukow. W—Krukow. L—Cox. HR—Thompson, Leonard, Brenly (S.F.).
Game 5—October 11, at San Francisco
St. Louis ....1 0 1 1 0 0 0 0 0—3 7 0
San Fran. ......1 0 1 4 0 0 0 0 x—6 7 1
Mathews, Forsch (4), Horton (4), Dayley (7); Reuschel, Price (5). W—Price. L—Forsch. HR—Mitchell (S.F.).
Game 6—October 13, at St. Louis
San Fran. ......0 0 0 0 0 0 0 0 0—0 6 0
St. Louis ....0 1 0 0 0 0 0 0 x—1 5 0
Dravecky, D. Robinson (7); Tudor, Worrell (8), Dayley (9). W—Tudor. L—Dravecky. S—Dayley.
Game 7—October 14, at St. Louis
San Fran. ....0 0 0 0 0 0 0 0 0—0 8 1
St. Louis ......0 4 0 0 0 2 0 0 x—6 12 0
Hammaker, Price (3), Downs (3), Garrelts (5), Lefferts (6), LaCoss (6), D. Robinson (8); Cox. W—Cox. L—Hammaker. HR—Oquendo (St.L.).

WORLD SERIES

■ **Winner:** The Twins held off the Cardinals and captured a Series in which the home team won every game.
■ **Turning point:** Don Baylor's two-run fifth-inning homer and Kent Hrbek's grand slam, blows that turned a 5-2 deficit into an 11-5 sixth-game victory for the Twins.
■ **Memorable moment:** Hrbek's arm-pumping jaunt around the bases after his Game 6 slam.
■ **Top guns:** Frank Viola (2-1), Steve Lombardozzi (.412), Twins; Tony Pena (.409), Willie McGee (.370), Cardinals.
■ **MVP:** Viola.

Linescores
Game 1—October 17, at Minnesota
St. Louis ..0 1 0 0 0 0 0 0 0— 1 5 1
Minn. ......0 0 0 7 2 0 1 0 x—10 11 0
Magrane, Forsch (4), Horton (7); Viola, Atherton (9). W—Viola. L—Magrane. HR—Gladden, Lombardozzi (Min.).
Game 2—October 18, at Minnesota
St. Louis ....0 0 0 0 1 0 1 2 0—4 9 0
Minn. ....0 1 0 6 0 1 0 0 x—8 10 0
Cox, Tunnell (4), Dayley (7), Worrell (8); Blyleven, Berenguer (8), Reardon (9). W—Blyleven. L—Cox. HR—Gaetti, Laudner (Min.).
Game 3—October 20, at St. Louis
Minn. ....0 0 0 0 0 1 0 0 0—1 5 1
St. Louis ......0 0 0 0 0 0 3 0 x—3 9 1
Straker, Berenguer (7), Schatzeder (7); Tudor, Worrell (8). W—Tudor. L—Berenguer. S—Worrell.
Game 4—October 21, at St. Louis
Minn. ....0 0 1 0 1 0 0 0 0—2 7 1
St. Louis ....0 0 1 6 0 0 0 0 x—7 10 1
Viola, Schatzeder (4), Niekro (5), Frazier (7); Mathews, Forsch (4), Dayley (7). W—Forsch. L—Viola. S—Dayley. HR—Gagne (Min.); Lawless (St.L.).
Game 5—October 22, at St. Louis
Minn. ....0 0 0 0 0 0 0 2 0—2 6 1
St. Louis ....0 0 0 0 0 3 1 0 x—4 10 0
Blyleven, Atherton (7), Reardon (7); Cox, Dayley (8), Worrell (8). W—Cox. L—Blyleven. S—Worrell.
Game 6—October 24, at Minnesota
St. Louis ..1 1 0 2 1 0 0 0 0— 5 11 2
Minn. ......2 0 0 0 4 4 0 1 x—11 15 0
Tudor, Horton (5), Forsch (6), Dayley (6), Tunnell (7); Straker, Schatzeder (4), Berenguer (6), Reardon (9). W—Schatzeder. L—Tudor. HR—Herr (St.L.); Baylor, Hrbek (Min.).
Game 7—October 25, at Minnesota
St. Louis ....0 2 0 0 0 0 0 0 0—2 6 1
Minn. ....0 1 0 0 1 1 0 1 x—4 10 0
Magrane, Cox (5), Worrell (6); Viola, Reardon (9). W—Viola. L—Cox. S—Reardon.

FINAL STANDINGS

American League

East Division

Team	Bos.	Det.	Mil.	Tor.	N.Y.	Cle.	Bal.	Oak.	Min.	K.C.	Cal.	Chi.	Tex.	Sea.	W	L	Pct.	GB
Boston	...	6	10	2	9	8	9	3	7	6	8	7	8	6	89	73	.549	...
Detroit	7	...	5	5	8	9	8	4	1	8	7	9	8	9	88	74	.543	1
Milwaukee	3	8	...	7	6	4	9	3	7	9	9	6	8	8	87	75	.537	2
Toronto	11	8	6	...	7	7	8	3	5	8	6	5	6	7	87	75	.537	2
New York	4	5	7	6	...	7	10	6	9	6	6	9	5	5	85	76	.528	3.5
Cleveland	5	4	9	6	6	...	9	4	5	6	4	9	6	5	78	84	.481	11
Baltimore	4	5	4	5	3	4	...	4	3	0	5	4	6	7	54	107	.335	34.5

West Division

Team	Oak.	Min.	K.C.	Cal.	Chi.	Tex.	Sea.	Bos.	Det.	Mil.	Tor.	N.Y.	Cle.	Bal.	W	L	Pct.	GB
Oakland	...	8	5	9	8	8	9	9	8	9	9	6	8	8	104	58	.642	...
Minnesota	5	...	6	9	9	7	8	5	11	5	7	3	7	9	91	71	.562	13
Kansas City	8	7	...	8	6	7	7	6	4	3	4	6	6	12	84	77	.522	19.5
California	4	4	5	...	9	8	6	4	5	3	6	6	8	7	75	87	.463	29
Chicago	5	4	7	4	...	8	9	5	3	6	7	3	3	7	71	90	.441	32.5
Texas	5	6	6	5	5	...	7	4	4	4	6	6	6	6	70	91	.435	33.5
Seattle	4	5	5	7	4	6	...	6	3	4	5	7	7	5	68	93	.422	35.5

National League

East Division

Team	N.Y.	Pit.	Mon.	Chi.	St.L.	Phi.	L.A.	Cin.	S.D.	S.F.	Hou.	Atl.	W	L	Pct.	GB
New York	...	12	12	9	14	10	10	7	7	4	7	8	100	60	.625	...
Pittsburgh	6	...	10	11	11	11	6	5	8	8	4	5	85	75	.531	15
Montreal	6	8	...	9	13	9	4	7	4	7	6	8	81	81	.500	20
Chicago	9	7	9	...	7	8	4	6	8	5	7	7	77	85	.475	24
St. Louis	4	7	5	11	...	12	5	6	6	5	6	9	76	86	.469	25
Philadelphia	8	7	9	10	6	...	1	3	4	7	4	6	65	96	.404	35.5

West Division

Team	L.A.	Cin.	S.D.	S.F.	Hou.	Atl.	N.Y.	Pit.	Mon.	Chi.	St.L.	Phi.	W	L	Pct.	GB
Los Angeles	...	11	7	12	9	14	1	6	8	8	7	11	94	67	.584	...
Cincinnati	7	...	10	11	9	13	4	7	5	6	6	9	87	74	.540	7
San Diego	11	8	...	8	12	10	5	4	8	4	6	7	83	78	.516	11
San Fran.	6	7	10	...	11	13	8	4	5	7	7	5	83	79	.512	11.5
Houston	9	9	6	7	...	13	5	8	6	5	6	8	82	80	.506	12.5
Atlanta	4	5	8	5	5	...	4	5	4	5	3	6	54	106	.338	39.5

LEADERS

American League
BA: Wade Boggs, Bos., .366.
Runs: Wade Boggs, Bos., 128.
Hits: Kirby Puckett, Min., 234.
TB: Kirby Puckett, Min., 358.
HR: Jose Canseco, Oak., 42.
RBI: Jose Canseco, Oak., 124.
SB: Rickey Henderson, N.Y., 93.
Wins: Frank Viola, Min., 24.
ERA: Allan Anderson, Min., 2.45.
CG: Roger Clemens, Bos.; Dave Stewart, Oak., 14.
IP: Dave Stewart, Oak., 275.2.
SO: Roger Clemens, Bos., 291.
SV: Dennis Eckersley, Oak., 45.

National League
BA: Tony Gwynn, S.D., .313.
Runs: Brett Butler, S.F., 109.
Hits: Andres Galarraga, Mon., 184.
TB: Andres Galarraga, Mon., 329.
HR: Darryl Strawberry, N.Y., 39.
RBI: Will Clark, S.F., 109.
SB: Vince Coleman, St.L., 81.
Wins: Orel Hershiser, L.A.; Danny Jackson, Cin., 23.
ERA: Joe Magrane, St.L., 2.18.
CG: Orel Hershiser, L.A.; Danny Jackson, Cin., 15.
IP: Orel Hershiser, L.A., 267.
SO: Nolan Ryan, Hou., 228.
SV: John Franco, Cin., 39.

A.L. 20-game winners
Frank Viola, Min., 24-7
Dave Stewart, Oak., 21-12
Mark Gubicza, K.C., 20-8

N.L. 20-game winners
Orel Hershiser, L.A., 23-8
Danny Jackson, Cin., 23-8
David Cone, N.Y., 20-3

A.L. 100 RBIs
Jose Canseco, Oak., 124
Kirby Puckett, Min., 121
Mike Greenwell, Bos., 119
Dwight Evans, Bos., 111
Dave Winfield, N.Y, 107
George Brett, K.C., 103
Danny Tartabull, K.C., 102

N.L. 100 RBIs
Will Clark, S.F., 109
Darryl Strawberry, N.Y., 101
Bobby Bonilla, Pit., 100
Andy Van Slyke, Pit., 100

A.L. 40 homers
Jose Canseco, Oak., 42

Most Valuable Player
A.L.: Jose Canseco, OF, Oak.
N.L.: Kirk Gibson, OF, L.A.

Cy Young Award
A.L.: Frank Viola, Min.
N.L.: Orel Hershiser, L.A.

Rookie of the Year
A.L.: Walt Weiss, SS, Oak.
N.L.: Chris Sabo, 3B, Cin.

Manager of the Year
A.L.: Tony La Russa, Oak.
N.L.: Tommy Lasorda, L.A.

Hall of Fame addition
Willie Stargell, OF/1B, 1962-82

SIGNIFICANT EVENTS

■ **January 22:** Kirk Gibson and Carlton Fisk were among seven players declared free agents by an arbitrator who ruled that owners had acted in collusion against free agents after the 1985 season.
■ **June 23:** Yankee owner George Steinbrenner fired manager Billy Martin for a fifth time and replaced him with the man he had replaced—Lou Piniella.
■ **August 9:** The Cubs defeated the Mets, 6-4, in the first official night game at Chicago's 74-year-old Wrigley Field.
■ **August 31:** Major League owners were stunned when a labor arbitrator found them guilty of collusion for a second time—this time against the 1986 class of free agents.
■ **September 8:** N.L. President A. Bartlett Giamatti was elected to succeed Peter V. Ueberroth as baseball's seventh commissioner.

MEMORABLE MOMENTS

■ **April 29:** The Orioles defeated Chicago, 9-0, and ended their record season-opening losing streak at 21 games.
■ **June 25:** Orioles shortstop Cal Ripken stretched his ironman streak to 1,000 games in a 10-3 loss to Boston.
■ **September 16:** Cincinnati's Tom Browning retired 27 consecutive Dodgers in a 1-0 victory—baseball's 12th perfect game.
■ **September 23:** Oakland's Jose Canseco swiped two bases in a victory over Milwaukee and became the first player to hit 40 homers and record 40 steals in the same season.
■ **September 28:** Dodgers righthander Orel Hershiser worked 10 shutout innings against the Padres in his final regular-season start and stretched his scoreless-innings streak to a record 59.

ALL-STAR GAME

■ **Winner:** A.L. pitchers held the N.L. to five hits and catcher Terry Steinbach supplied all the offense they needed for a 2-1 All-Star Game victory.
■ **Key inning:** The third, when Steinbach drove a Dwight Gooden pitch over the right-field wall, giving the A.L. a lead it never relinquished.
■ **Memorable moment:** Steinbach, maligned by the media as an unworthy starter because of his .217 season average, drove in the winning run with a fourth-inning sacrifice fly and walked away with MVP honors.
■ **Top guns:** Frank Viola (Twins), Dennis Eckersley (Athletics), Steinbach (Athletics), A.L.; Vince Coleman (Cardinals), N.L.
■ **MVP:** Steinbach.

Linescore
July 12, at Cincinnati's Riverfront Stadium
A.L..............0 0 1 1 0 0 0 0—2 6 2
N.L..............0 0 0 1 0 0 0 0 0—1 5 0
Viola (Twins), Clemens (Red Sox) 3, Gubicza (Royals) 4, Stieb (Blue Jays) 6, Russell (Rangers) 7, Jones (Indians) 8, Plesac (Brewers) 8, Eckersley (Athletics) 9; Gooden (Mets), Knepper (Astros) 4, Cone (Mets) 5, Gross (Dodgers) 6, Davis (Padres) 7, Walk (Phillies) 7, Hershiser (Dodgers) 8, Worrell (Cardinals) 9. W—Viola. L—Gooden. S—Eckersley. HR—Steinbach, A.L.

ALCS

■ **Winner:** The Oakland Athletics, making their first Championship Series appearance since 1975, recorded the first sweep in the best-of-seven format and claimed their first pennant since 1974.
■ **Turning point:** Amid a flurry of Oakland home runs, the Athletics actually took control on a ninth-inning Walt Weiss single that produced a 4-3 Game 2 victory over the Red Sox at Fenway Park.
■ **Memorable moment:** Jose Canseco's first-inning home run in the fourth game, his third of the series and Oakland's seventh. The A's went on to close out the Red Sox with a 4-1 victory.
■ **Top guns:** Dennis Eckersley (4 games, 4 saves, 0.00 ERA), Gene Nelson (2-0, 0.00), Rickey Henderson (.375), Canseco (.313, 3 HR, 4 RBIs), Athletics; Wade Boggs (.385), Rich Gedman (.357), Red Sox.
■ **MVP:** Eckersley.

Linescores

Game 1—October 5, at Boston
Oakland........0 0 0 1 0 0 0 1 0—2 6 0
Boston ....0 0 0 0 0 0 1 0 0—1 6 0
Stewart, Honeycutt (7), Eckersley (8); Hurst. W—Honeycutt. L—Hurst. S—Eckersley. HR—Canseco (Oak.).

Game 2—October 6, at Boston
Oakland......0 0 0 0 0 0 3 0 1—4 10 1
Boston ......0 0 0 0 0 2 1 0 0—3 4 1
Davis, Cadaret (7), Nelson (7), Eckersley (9); Clemens, Stanley (8), Smith (8). W—Nelson. L—Smith. S—Eckersley. HR—Canseco (Oak.); Gedman (Bos.).

Game 3—October 8, at Oakland
Boston ....3 2 0 0 0 0 1 0 0— 6 12 0
Oakland....0 4 2 0 1 0 1 2 x—10 15 1
Boddicker, Gardner (3), Stanley (8); Welch, Nelson (2), Young (6), Plunk (7), Honeycutt (7), Eckersley (8). W—Nelson. L—Boddicker. S—Eckersley. HR—Greenwell (Bos.); McGwire, Lansford, Hassey, Henderson (Oak.).

Game 4—October 9, at Oakland
Boston ......0 0 0 0 0 1 0 0 0—1 4 0
Oakland......1 0 1 0 0 0 0 2 x—4 10 1
Hurst, Smithson (5), Smith (7); Stewart, Honeycutt (8), Eckersley (9). W—Stewart. L—Hurst. S—Eckersley. HR—Canseco (Oak.).

NLCS

■ **Winner:** Los Angeles ace Orel Hershiser denied New York's bid for its second pennant in three years with a 6-0 shutout in Game 7.
■ **Turning point:** Game 4, when Dodgers catcher Mike Scioscia hit a game-tying two-run homer in the ninth inning and Kirk Gibson settled matters with a solo shot in the 12th, knotting the series at two games apiece.
■ **Memorable moment:** The eighth inning of Game 3, when Dodgers relief ace Jay Howell was thrown out of the game because a foreign substance was found in his glove. The Mets scored five runs in the inning and claimed an 8-4 victory.
■ **Top guns:** Hershiser (1-0, 1.09 ERA), Scioscia (.364), Gibson (2 HR, 6 RBIs), Dodgers; Randy Myers (2-0, 0.00), Lenny Dykstra (.429), Darryl Strawberry (.300, 6 RBIs), Mets.
■ **MVP:** Hershiser.

Linescores

Game 1—October 4, at Los Angeles
N.Y..............0 0 0 0 0 0 0 0 3—3 8 1
L.A. ....1 0 0 0 0 0 1 0 0—2 4 0
Gooden, Myers (8); Hershiser, J. Howell (9). W—Myers. L—J. Howell.

Game 2—October 5, at Los Angeles
N.Y..............0 0 0 2 0 0 0 0 1—3 6 0
L.A. ....1 4 0 0 1 0 0 0 x—6 7 0
Cone, Aguilera (3), Leach (6), McDowell (8); Belcher, Orosco (9), Pena (9). W—Belcher. L—Cone. S—Pena. HR—Hernandez (N.Y.).

Game 3—October 8, at New York
L.A..............0 2 1 0 0 0 0 1 0—4 7 2
N.Y. ....0 0 1 0 0 2 0 5 x—8 9 2
Hershiser, J. Howell (8), Pena (8), Orosco (8), Horton (8); Darling, McDowell (7), Myers (8), Cone (9). W—Myers. L—Pena.

Game 4—October 9, at New York
L.A.......2 0 0 0 0 0 0 0 2 0 0 1—5 7 1
N.Y.......0 0 0 3 0 1 0 0 0 0 0 0—4 10 2
Tudor, Holton (6), Horton (7), Pena (9), Leary (12), Orosco (12), Hershiser (12); Gooden, Myers (9), McDowell (11). W—Pena. L—McDowell. S—Hershiser. HR—Strawberry, McReynolds (N.Y.); Scioscia, Gibson (L.A.).

Game 5—October 10, at New York
L.A............0 0 0 3 3 0 0 0 1—7 12 0
N.Y............0 0 0 0 3 0 0 1 0—4 9 1
Belcher, Horton (8), Holton (8); Fernandez, Leach (5), Aguilera (6), McDowell (8). W—Belcher. L—Fernandez. S—Holton. HR—Gibson (L.A.); Dykstra (N.Y.).

Game 6—October 11, at Los Angeles
N.Y............1 0 1 0 2 1 0 0 0—5 11 0
L.A............0 0 0 0 1 0 0 0 0—1 5 2
Cone; Leary, Holton (5), Horton (6), Orosco (8). W—Cone. L—Leary. HR—McReynolds (N.Y.).

Game 7—October 12, at Los Angeles
N.Y............0 0 0 0 0 0 0 0 0—0 5 2
L.A. ....1 5 0 0 0 0 0 0 x—6 10 0
Darling, Gooden (2), Leach (5), Aguilera (7); Hershiser. W—Hershiser. L—Darling.

WORLD SERIES

■ **Winner:** The Cinderella Dodgers pulled off a five-game surprise against the powerful Athletics.
■ **Turning point:** A two-out, ninth-inning, two-run homer by Kirk Gibson that gave the Dodgers a shocking 5-4 victory in Game 1.
■ **Memorable moment:** The gimpy Gibson, wincing in pain with every swing, connecting with a Dennis Eckersley pitch and then limping triumphantly around the bases with the winning run in the Series opener.
■ **Top guns:** Orel Hershiser (2-0, 1.00 ERA), Gibson (1 AB, 1 hit, 1 HR, 2 RBIs), Mickey Hatcher (.368, 5 RBIs), Dodgers; Terry Steinbach (.364), Athletics.
■ **MVP:** Hershiser.

Linescores

Game 1—October 15, at Los Angeles
Oakland........0 4 0 0 0 0 0 0 0—4 7 0
L.A. ....2 0 0 0 0 1 0 0 2—5 7 0
Stewart, Eckersley (9); Belcher, Leary (3), Holton (6), Pena (8). W—Pena. L—Eckersley. HR—Hatcher, Gibson (L.A.); Canseco (Oak.).

Game 2—October 16, at Los Angeles
Oakland......0 0 0 0 0 0 0 0 0—0 3 0
L.A. ....0 0 5 1 0 0 0 0 x—6 10 1
S. Davis, Nelson (4), Young (6), Plunk (7), Honeycutt (8); Hershiser. W—Hershiser. L—S. Davis. HR—Marshall (L.A.).

Game 3—October 18, at Oakland
L.A. ....0 0 0 0 1 0 0 0 0—1 8 1
Oakland........0 0 1 0 0 0 0 0 1—2 5 0
Tudor, Leary (2), Pena (6), J. Howell (9); Welch, Cadaret (6), Nelson (6), Honeycutt (8). W—Honeycutt. L—J. Howell. HR—McGwire (Oak.).

Game 4—October 19, at Oakland
L.A. ....2 0 1 0 0 0 1 0 0—4 8 1
Oakland........1 0 0 0 0 1 1 0 0—3 9 2
Belcher, J. Howell (7); Stewart, Cadaret (7), Eckersley (9). W—Belcher. L—Stewart. S—J. Howell.

Game 5—October 20, at Oakland
L.A. ....2 0 0 2 0 1 0 0 0—5 8 0
Oakland........0 0 1 0 0 0 0 1 0—2 4 0
Hershiser; S. Davis, Cadaret (5), Nelson (5), Honeycutt (8), Plunk (9), Burns (9). W—Hershiser. L—S. Davis. HR—Hatcher, M. Davis (L.A.).

1989

FINAL STANDINGS

American League

East Division

Team	Tor.	Bal.	Bos.	Mil.	N.Y.	Cle.	Det.	Oak.	K.C.	Cal.	Tex.	Min.	Sea.	Chi.	W	L	Pct.	GB
Toronto	...	6	8	7	6	8	11	5	5	5	7	3	7	11	89	73	.549	...
Baltimore	7	...	6	7	8	7	10	5	6	6	9	4	6	6	87	75	.537	2
Boston	5	7	...	6	7	8	11	7	4	4	6	6	5	7	83	79	.512	6
Milwaukee	6	6	7	...	8	10	7	5	4	5	5	9	7	2	81	81	.500	8
New York	7	5	6	5	...	4	7	3	6	6	5	6	8	6	74	87	.460	14.5
Cleveland	5	6	5	3	9	...	5	2	8	7	7	5	6	5	73	89	.451	16
Detroit	2	3	2	6	6	8	...	4	6	1	4	5	4	8	59	103	.364	30

West Division

Team	Oak.	K.C.	Cal.	Tex.	Min.	Sea.	Chi.	Tor.	Bal.	Bos.	Mil.	N.Y.	Cle.	Det.	W	L	Pct.	GB
Oakland	...	6	8	8	7	9	8	7	7	5	7	9	10	8	99	63	.611	...
Kansas City	7	...	9	8	7	9	7	7	6	8	8	6	4	6	92	70	.568	7
California	5	4	...	6	11	7	8	7	6	8	7	6	5	11	91	71	.562	8
Texas	5	5	7	...	8	7	10	5	3	6	7	7	5	8	83	79	.512	16
Minnesota	6	6	2	5	...	7	8	9	8	6	3	6	7	7	80	82	.494	19
Seattle	4	4	6	6	6	...	6	5	6	7	5	4	6	8	73	89	.451	26
Chicago	5	6	5	3	5	7	...	1	6	5	10	5	7	4	69	92	.429	29.5

National League

East Division

Team	Chi.	N.Y.	St.L.	Mon.	Pit.	Phi.	S.F.	S.D.	Hou.	L.A.	Cin.	Atl.	W	L	Pct.	GB
Chicago	...	10	11	10	12	10	6	8	5	7	7	7	93	69	.574	...
New York	8	...	10	9	9	12	3	5	6	7	8	10	87	75	.537	6
St. Louis	7	8	...	13	5	11	5	10	5	9	4	9	86	76	.531	7
Montreal	8	9	5	...	11	9	7	5	8	5	8	6	81	81	.500	12
Pittsburgh	6	9	13	7	...	8	5	3	5	5	5	8	74	88	.457	19
Philadelphia	8	6	7	9	10	...	4	2	3	6	8	4	67	95	.414	26

West Division

Team	S.F.	S.D.	Hou.	L.A.	Cin.	Atl.	Chi.	N.Y.	St.L.	Mon.	Pit.	Phi.	W	L	Pct.	GB
San Fran.	...	10	10	8	10	12	6	9	7	5	7	8	92	70	.568	...
San Diego	8	...	10	12	9	11	4	7	2	7	9	10	89	73	.549	3
Houston	8	8	...	10	10	10	7	6	7	4	7	9	86	76	.531	6
Los Angeles	10	6	8	...	10	10	5	5	3	7	7	6	77	83	.481	14
Cincinnati	8	9	8	8	...	10	5	4	8	4	7	4	75	87	.463	17
Atlanta	6	7	8	6	8	...	5	2	3	6	4	8	63	97	.394	28

SIGNIFICANT EVENTS

■ **January 5:** Commissioner Peter Ueberroth signed a $400-million cable television package with ESPN, a month after signing a four-year, $1.06-billion contract with CBS-TV.

■ **February 3:** Bill White became the highest ranking black executive in professional sports when he was tabbed to succeed A. Bartlett Giamatti as N.L. president.

■ **June 5:** The Blue Jays opened SkyDome with a 5-3 loss to the Brewers.

■ **August 24:** Commissioner A. Bartlett Giamatti handed all-time hits leader Pete Rose, who had been implicated in a gambling scandal, a lifetime ban from baseball.

■ **September 1:** Giamatti, 51, died of a heart attack at his Massachusetts summer cottage, eight days after handing Rose his lifetime ban.

■ **September 13:** Giamatti assistant Fay Vincent was elected as baseball's eighth commissioner.

■ **December 25:** Former player and manager Billy Martin died when a pickup truck in which he was riding crashed near his home in Binghamton, N.Y.

MEMORABLE MOMENTS

■ **August 15:** Giants lefty Dave Dravecky, on the comeback trail from cancer surgery, broke his arm while throwing a pitch in a game at Montreal.

■ **August 22:** Nolan Ryan fired a fastball past Oakland's Rickey Henderson and became the first Major Leaguer to record 5,000 career strikeouts.

LEADERS

American League
BA: Kirby Puckett, Min., .339.
Runs: Wade Boggs, Bos.; Rickey Henderson, N.Y.-Oak., 113.
Hits: Kirby Puckett, Min., 215.
TB: Ruben Sierra, Tex., 344.
HR: Fred McGriff, Tor., 36.
RBI: Ruben Sierra, Tex., 119.
SB: Rickey Henderson, N.Y.-Oak., 77.
Wins: Bret Saberhagen, K.C., 23.
ERA: Bret Saberhagen, K.C., 2.16.
CG: Bret Saberhagen, K.C., 12.
IP: Bret Saberhagen, K.C., 262.1.
SO: Nolan Ryan, Tex., 301.
SV: Jeff Russell, Tex., 38.

National League
BA: Tony Gwynn, S.D., .336.
Runs: Will Clark, S.F.; Howard Johnson, N.Y.; Ryne Sandberg, Chi., 104.
Hits: Tony Gwynn, S.D., 203.
TB: Kevin Mitchell, S.F., 345.
HR: Kevin Mitchell, S.F., 47.
RBI: Kevin Mitchell, S.F., 125.
SB: Vince Coleman, St.L., 65.
Wins: Mike Scott, Hou., 20.
ERA: Scott Garrelts, S.F., 2.28.
CG: Tim Belcher, L.A.; Bruce Hurst, S.D., 10.
IP: Orel Hershiser, L.A., 256.2.
SO: Jose DeLeon, St.L., 201.
SV: Mark Davis, S.D., 44.

A.L. 20-game winners
Bret Saberhagen, K.C., 23-6
Dave Stewart, Oak., 21-9

N.L. 20-game winner
Mike Scott, Hou., 20-10

A.L. 100 RBIs
Ruben Sierra, Tex., 119
Don Mattingly, N.Y., 113
Nick Esasky, Bos., 108
Joe Carter, Cle., 105
Bo Jackson, K.C., 105
George Bell, Tor., 104
Robin Yount, Mil., 103
Dwight Evans, Bos., 100

N.L. 100 RBIs
Kevin Mitchell, S.F., 125
Pedro Guerrero, St.L., 117
Will Clark, S.F., 111
Eric Davis, Cin., 101
Howard Johnson, N.Y., 101

N.L. 40 homers
Kevin Mitchell, S.F., 47

Most Valuable Player
A.L.: Robin Yount, OF, Mil.
N.L.: Kevin Mitchell, OF, S.F.

Cy Young Award
A.L.: Bret Saberhagen, K.C.
N.L.: Mark Davis, S.D.

Rookie of the Year
A.L.: Gregg Olson, P, Bal.
N.L.: Jerome Walton, OF, Chi.

Manager of the Year
A.L.: Frank Robinson, Bal.
N.L.: Don Zimmer, Chi.

Hall of Fame additions
Al Barlick, umpire
Johnny Bench, C, 1967-83
Red Schoendienst, 2B, 1945-63
Carl Yastrzemski, OF, 1961-83

ALL-STAR GAME

■ **Winner:** The A.L.'s 5-3 victory marked its first back-to-back All-Star wins since 1957-58.
■ **Key inning:** The third, when the A.L. added to its 3-2 advantage with run-scoring singles by Harold Baines and Ruben Sierra.
■ **Memorable moment:** Consecutive home runs by Bo Jackson and Wade Boggs to lead off the A.L. first inning. That was an All-Star first.
■ **Top guns:** Nolan Ryan (Rangers), Jackson (Royals), Boggs (Red Sox), Sierra (Rangers), A.L.; Kevin Mitchell (Giants), Bobby Bonilla (Pirates), N.L.
■ **MVP:** Jackson.

Linescore
July 11, at California's Anaheim Stadium
N.L. ....2 0 0 0 0 0 0 1 0—3 9 1
A.L. ....2 1 2 0 0 0 0 0 x—5 12 0
Reuschel (Giants), Smoltz (Braves) 2, Sutcliffe (Cubs) 3, Burke (Expos) 4, M. Davis (Padres) 6, Howell (Dodgers) 7, Williams (Cubs) 8; Stewart (Athletics), Ryan (Rangers) 2, Gubicza (Royals) 4, Moore (Athletics) 5, Swindell (Indians) 6, Russell (Rangers) 7, Plesac (Brewers) 8, Jones (Indians) 8. W—Ryan. L—Smoltz. S—Jones. HR—Jackson, Boggs, A.L.

ALCS

■ **Winner:** The Oakland Athletics ran and muscled their way past Toronto in a series dominated by leadoff hitter Rickey Henderson.
■ **Turning point:** After killing the Blue Jays in Games 1 and 2 with his speed, Henderson muscled up for two home runs in a 6-5 Game 4 victory that gave Oakland a 3-1 series edge.
■ **Memorable moment:** A mammoth Game 4 home run by Oakland slugger Jose Canseco that landed in the fifth tier of the left-field bleachers at SkyDome. The ball officially was measured at 490 feet, but most observers claimed it traveled well beyond 500.
■ **Top guns:** Dennis Eckersley (4 games, 3 saves, 1.59 ERA), Carney Lansford (.455), Henderson (.400, 8 SB, 8 runs, 2 HR, 5 RBIs), Mark McGwire (.389), Athletics; Tony Fernandez (.350), Blue Jays.
■ **MVP:** Henderson.

Linescores

Game 1—October 3, at Oakland
Toronto......0 2 0 1 0 0 0 0 0—3 5 1
Oakland......0 1 0 0 1 3 0 2 x—7 11 0
Stieb, Acker (6), Ward (8); Stewart, Eckersley (9). W—Stewart. L—Stieb. HR—D. Henderson, McGwire (Oak.); Whitt (Tor.).

Game 2—October 4, at Oakland
Toronto........0 0 1 0 0 0 0 2 0—3 5 1
Oakland........0 0 0 2 0 3 1 0 x—6 9 1
Stottlemyre, Acker (6), Wells (6), Henke (7), Cerutti (8); Moore, Honeycutt (8), Eckersley (8). W—Moore. L—Stottlemyre. S—Eckersley. HR—Parker (Oak.).

Game 3—October 6, at Toronto
Oakland........1 0 1 0 0 0 0 0 0—3 8 1
Toronto........0 0 0 4 0 0 3 0 x—7 8 0
Davis, Honeycutt (7), Nelson (7), M. Young (8); Key, Acker (7), Henke (9). W—Key. L—Davis. HR—Parker (Oak.).

Game 4—October 7, at Toronto
Oakland......0 0 3 0 2 0 1 0 0—6 11 1
Toronto......0 0 0 1 0 1 1 2 0—5 13 0
Welch, Honeycutt (6), Eckersley (8); Flanagan, Ward (5), Cerutti (8), Acker (9). W—Welch. L—Flanagan. S—Eckersley. HR—R. Henderson 2, Canseco (Oak.).

Game 5—October 8, at Toronto
Oakland........1 0 1 0 0 0 2 0 0—4 4 0
Toronto........0 0 0 0 0 0 0 1 2—3 9 0
Stewart, Eckersley (9); Stieb, Acker (7), Henke (9). W—Stewart. L—Stieb. S—Eckersley. HR—Moseby, Bell (Tor.).

NLCS

■ **Winner:** First basemen Will Clark and Mark Grace took center stage as San Francisco won its first pennant since 1962 and stretched Chicago's pennant drought to 44 years.
■ **Turning point:** The seventh inning of Game 3 when Giants second baseman Robby Thompson belted a two-run homer off reliever Les Lancaster, giving San Francisco a 5-4 victory and a 2-1 series edge.
■ **Memorable moment:** Game 1 at Chicago — the first post-season game played under the lights of Wrigley Field. San Francisco's Clark stole the show with four hits, a grand slam and six RBIs in the Giants' 11-3 victory.
■ **Top guns:** Steve Bedrosian (3 saves), Clark (.650, 13 hits, 2 HR, 8 RBIs), Kevin Mitchell (.353, 2 HR, 7 RBIs), Matt Williams (2 HR, 9 RBIs), Giants; Grace (.647, 8 RBIs), Ryne Sandberg (.400), Cubs.
■ **MVP:** Clark.

Linescores

Game 1—October 4, at Chicago
S.F. ....3 0 1 4 0 0 0 3 0—11 13 0
Chicago....2 0 1 0 0 0 0 0 0— 3 10 1
Garrelts, Brantley (8), Hammaker (9); Maddux, Kilgus (5), Wilson (8). W—Garrelts. L—Maddux. HR—Grace, Sandberg (Chi.); Clark 2, Mitchell (S.F.).

Game 2—October 5, at Chicago
S.F. ....0 0 0 2 0 0 0 2 1—5 10 0
Chicago......6 0 0 0 0 3 0 0 x—9 11 0
Reuschel, Downs (1), Lefferts (6), Brantley (7), Bedrosian (8); Bielecki, Assenmacher (5), Lancaster (6). W—Lancaster. L—Reuschel. HR—Mitchell, Ma. Williams, Thompson (S.F.).

Game 3—October 7, at San Francisco
Chicago......2 0 0 1 0 0 1 0 0—4 10 0
S.F. ....3 0 0 0 0 0 2 0 x—5 8 3
Sutcliffe, Assenmacher (7), Lancaster (7); LaCoss, Brantley (4), Robinson (7), Lefferts (8), Bedrosian (9). W—Robinson. L—Lancaster. S—Bedrosian. HR—Thompson (S.F.).

Game 4—October 8, at San Francisco
Chicago......1 1 0 0 2 0 0 0 0—4 12 1
S.F. ....1 0 2 1 2 0 0 0 x—6 9 1
Maddux, Wilson (4), Sanderson (6), Mi. Williams (8); Garrelts, Downs (5), Bedrosian (9). W—Downs. L—Wilson. S—Bedrosian. HR—Salazar (Chi.); Ma. Williams (S.F.).

Game 5—October 9, at San Francisco
Chicago......0 0 1 0 0 0 0 0 1—2 10 1
S.F. ....0 0 0 0 0 0 1 2 x—3 4 1
Bielecki, Mi. Williams (8), Lancaster (8); Reuschel, Bedrosian (9). W—Reuschel. L—Bielecki. S—Bedrosian.

WORLD SERIES

■ **Winner:** Oakland's four-game sweep of San Francisco in the first Bay Area Series was overshadowed by a massive earthquake that rocked parts of California, causing death and destruction and forcing postponement of the fall classic's final two games for 10 days.
■ **Turning point:** The second inning of Game 1, when Oakland jumped on the Giants for three runs en route to a 5-0 victory. That outburst set the pattern for the rest of the Series.
■ **Memorable moment:** The moments leading up to Game 3, when an earthquake measuring 7.1 on the Richter scale shook San Francisco and Candlestick Park. With the power out and incoming reports of mass destruction, Commissioner Fay Vincent ordered postponement of the game and told officials to clear the park.
■ **Top guns:** Dave Stewart (2-0, 1.69 ERA), Mike Moore (2-0, 2.08), Rickey Henderson (.474), Carney Lansford (.438), Athletics; Kevin Mitchell (.294), Giants.
■ **MVP:** Stewart.

Linescores

Game 1—October 14, at Oakland
S.F. ....0 0 0 0 0 0 0 0 0—0 5 1
Oakland......0 3 1 1 0 0 0 0 x—5 11 1
Garrelts, Hammaker (5), Brantley (6), LaCoss (8); Stewart. W—Stewart. L—Garrelts. HR—Parker, Weiss (Oak.).

Game 2—October 15, at Oakland
S.F. ....0 0 1 0 0 0 0 0 0—1 4 0
Oakland........1 0 0 4 0 0 0 0 x—5 7 0
Reuschel, Downs (5), Lefferts (7), Bedrosian (8); Moore, Honeycutt (8), Eckersley (9). W—Moore. L—Reuschel. HR—Steinbach (Oak.).

Game 3—October 27, at San Francisco
Oakland....2 0 0 2 4 1 0 4 0—13 14 0
S.F. ....0 1 0 2 0 0 0 0 4— 7 10 3
Stewart, Honeycutt (8), Nelson (9), Burns (9); Garrelts, Downs (4), Brantley (5), Hammaker (8), Lefferts (8). W—Stewart. L—Garrelts. HR—Williams, Bathe (S.F.); D. Henderson 2, Phillips, Canseco, Lansford (Oak.).

Game 4—October 28, at San Francisco
Oakland......1 3 0 0 3 1 0 1 0—9 12 0
S.F. ....0 0 0 0 0 2 4 0 0—6 9 0
Moore, Nelson (7), Honeycutt (7), Burns (7), Eckersley (9); Robinson, LaCoss (2), Brantley (6), Downs (6), Lefferts (8), Bedrosian (8). W—Moore. L—Robinson. S—Eckersley. HR—R. Henderson (Oak.); Mitchell, Litton (S.F.).

HISTORY

FINAL STANDINGS

American League

East Division

Team	Bos.	Tor.	Det.	Cle.	Bal.	Mil.	N.Y.	Oak.	Chi.	Tex.	Cal.	Sea.	K.C.	Min.	W	L	Pct.	GB
Boston	...	10	8	9	9	5	9	4	6	5	7	8	4	4	88	74	.543	...
Toronto	3	...	8	9	8	6	8	5	7	5	5	6	7	9	86	76	.531	2
Detroit	5	5	...	8	7	3	7	6	7	6	7	7	5	6	79	83	.488	9
Cleveland	4	4	5	...	7	9	5	4	7	7	5	7	6	7	77	85	.475	11
Baltimore	4	5	6	6	...	7	6	4	6	8	7	3	8	6	76	85	.472	11.5
Milwaukee	8	7	10	4	6	...	6	5	2	5	5	4	8	4	74	88	.457	14
New York	4	5	6	8	7	7	...	0	2	3	6	9	4	6	67	95	.414	21

West Division

Team	Oak.	Chi.	Tex.	Cal.	Sea.	K.C.	Min.	Bos.	Tor.	Det.	Cle.	Bal.	Mil.	N.Y.	W	L	Pct.	GB
Oakland	...	5	8	9	9	9	7	8	7	6	8	8	7	12	103	59	.636	...
Chicago	8	...	7	8	8	9	7	6	5	5	5	6	10	10	94	68	.580	9
Texas	5	6	...	5	6	8	8	7	7	6	5	4	7	9	83	79	.512	20
California	4	5	8	...	5	7	9	5	7	5	7	5	7	6	80	82	.494	23
Seattle	4	5	7	8	...	6	7	4	6	5	5	9	8	3	77	85	.475	26
Kansas City	4	4	5	6	7	...	8	8	5	7	6	3	4	8	75	86	.466	27.5
Minnesota	6	6	5	4	6	5	...	8	3	6	5	6	8	6	74	88	.457	29

National League

East Division

Team	Pit.	N.Y.	Mon.	Chi.	Phi.	St.L.	Cin.	L.A.	S.F.	Hou.	S.D.	Atl.	W	L	Pct.	GB
Pittsburgh	...	8	5	14	12	10	6	8	8	7	10	7	95	67	.586	...
New York	10	...	10	9	10	12	6	7	7	7	5	8	91	71	.562	4
Montreal	13	8	...	7	10	11	3	6	7	7	7	6	85	77	.525	10
Chicago	4	9	11	...	11	8	4	3	7	6	8	6	77	85	.475	18
Philadelphia	6	8	8	7	...	10	5	4	8	7	7	7	77	85	.475	18
St. Louis	8	6	7	10	8	...	3	5	3	6	9	5	70	92	.432	25

West Division

Team	Cin.	L.A.	S.F.	Hou.	S.D.	Atl.	Pit.	N.Y.	Mon.	Chi.	Phi.	St.L.	W	L	Pct.	GB
Cincinnati	...	9	7	11	9	10	6	6	9	8	7	9	91	71	.562	...
Los Angeles	9	...	8	9	9	12	4	5	6	9	8	7	86	76	.531	5
San Fran.	11	10	...	8	11	13	4	5	5	5	4	9	85	77	.525	6
Houston	7	9	10	...	4	13	5	5	5	6	5	6	75	87	.463	16
San Diego	9	9	7	14	...	10	2	7	5	4	5	3	75	87	.463	16
Atlanta	8	6	5	5	8	...	5	4	6	6	5	7	65	97	.401	26

SIGNIFICANT EVENTS

■ **March 18:** Players and owners reached agreement on a four-year contract that ended a 32-day lockout and cleared the way for spring training camps to open.
■ **June 14:** The N.L. announced plans to expand from 12 to 14 teams for the 1993 season.
■ **July 30:** Commissioner Fay Vincent banned George Steinbrenner from involvement with the Yankees for actions "not in the best interests of baseball."
■ **August 8:** Former baseball great Pete Rose reported to a federal work camp at Marion, Ill., to begin serving his five-month sentence for income tax evasion.

MEMORABLE MOMENTS

■ **June 11:** Rangers ace Nolan Ryan fired his record sixth no-hitter, defeating Oakland 5-0.
■ **June 12:** Baltimore's Cal Ripken Jr. moved into second place on the all-time ironman list when he pushed his consecutive-games streak to 1,308 in a 4-3 victory over Milwaukee.
■ **June 29:** A baseball first: Oakland's Dave Stewart and Dodgers lefthander Fernando Valenzuela threw no-hitters on the same day.
■ **July 1:** Yankees righthander Andy Hawkins became the second Major League pitcher to throw a complete-game no-hitter and lose when the White Sox stumbled to a 4-0 victory.
■ **July 31:** Ryan became baseball's 20th 300-game winner when the Rangers pounded the Brewers, 11-3.
■ **August 31:** The Griffeys, 20-year-old Ken Jr. and 40-year-old Ken Sr., became baseball's first father-son combination when both played for Seattle in a game against Kansas City.
■ **September 2:** Dave Stieb held Cleveland without a hit in a 3-0 victory—the first no-hitter in Blue Jays history and the record ninth of the season in the Major Leagues.
■ **October 3:** Detroit's Cecil Fielder became the first player in 13 years to break the 50-homer barrier when he crashed Nos. 50 and 51 in a final-day 10-3 victory over the Yankees.

LEADERS

American League
BA: George Brett, K.C., .329.
Runs: Rickey Henderson, Oak., 119.
Hits: Rafael Palmeiro, Tex., 191.
TB: Cecil Fielder, Det., 339.
HR: Cecil Fielder, Det., 51.
RBI: Cecil Fielder, Det., 132.
SB: Rickey Henderson, Oak., 65.
Wins: Bob Welch, Oak., 27.
ERA: Roger Clemens, Bos., 1.93.
CG: Jack Morris, Det.; Dave Stewart, Oak., 11.
IP: Dave Stewart, Oak., 267.
SO: Nolan Ryan, Tex., 232.
SV: Bobby Thigpen, Chi., 57.

National League
BA: Willie McGee, St.L., .335.
Runs: Ryne Sandberg, Chi., 116.
Hits: Brett Butler, S.F.; Lenny Dykstra, Phil., 192.
TB: Ryne Sandberg, Chi., 344.
HR: Ryne Sandberg, Chi., 40.
RBI: Matt Williams, S.F., 122.
SB: Vince Coleman, St.L., 77.
Wins: Doug Drabek, Pit., 22.
ERA: Danny Darwin, Hou., 2.21.
CG: Ramon Martinez, L.A., 12.
IP: Frank Viola, N.Y., 249.2.
SO: David Cone, N.Y., 233.
SV: John Franco, N.Y., 33.

A.L. 20-game winners
Bob Welch, Oak., 27-6
Dave Stewart, Oak., 22-11
Roger Clemens, Bos., 21-6

N.L. 20-game winners
Doug Drabek, Pit., 22-6
Ramon Martinez, L.A., 20-6
Frank Viola, N.Y., 20-12

A.L. 100 RBIs
Cecil Fielder, Det., 132
Kelly Gruber, Tor., 118
Mark McGwire, Oak., 108
Jose Canseco, Oak., 101

N.L. 100 RBIs
Matt Williams, S.F., 122
Bobby Bonilla, Pit., 120
Joe Carter, S.D., 115
Barry Bonds, Pit., 114
Darryl Strawberry, N.Y., 108
Andre Dawson, Chi., 100
Ryne Sandberg, Chi., 100

A.L. 40 homers
Cecil Fielder, Det., 51

N.L. 40 homers
Ryne Sandberg, Chi., 40

Most Valuable Player
A.L.: Rickey Henderson, OF, Oak.
N.L.: Barry Bonds, OF, Pit.

Cy Young Award
A.L.: Bob Welch, Oak.
N.L.: Doug Drabek, Pit.

Rookie of the Year
A.L.: Sandy Alomar Jr., C, Cle.
N.L.: Dave Justice, OF, Atl.

Manager of the Year
A.L.: Jeff Torborg, Chi.
N.L.: Jim Leyland, Pit.

Hall of Fame additions
Joe Morgan, 2B, 1963-84
Jim Palmer, P, 1965-84

ALL-STAR GAME

■ **Winner:** Six pitchers held the N.L. to an All-Star record-low two hits and the A.L. won for the third straight year, 2-0.
■ **Key inning:** The seventh, when the A.L. broke a scoreless deadlock on a two-run double by Julio Franco off fireballer Rob Dibble. Franco was the first batter after a 68-minute rain delay.
■ **Memorable moment:** The performance of an A.L. staff that allowed only a first-inning single by Will Clark and a ninth-inning single by Lenny Dykstra and retired 16 consecutive batters at one point.
■ **Top guns:** Bob Welch (Athletics), Dave Stieb (Blue Jays), Bret Saberhagen (Royals), Franco (Rangers), Wade Boggs (Red Sox), A.L.
■ **MVP:** Franco.

Linescore
July 10, at Chicago's Wrigley Field
A.L. ....0 0 0 0 0 0 2 0 0—2 7 0
N.L. ....0 0 0 0 0 0 0 0 0—0 2 1
Welch (Athletics), Stieb (Blue Jays) 3, Saberhagen (Royals) 5, Thigpen (White Sox) 7, Finley (Angels) 8, Eckersley (Athletics) 9; Armstrong (Reds), R. Martinez (Dodgers) 3, D. Martinez (Expos) 4, Viola (Mets) 5, D. Smith (Astros) 6, Brantley (Giants) 6, Dibble (Reds) 7, Myers (Reds) 8, Jo. Franco (Mets) 9. W—Saberhagen. L—Brantley. S—Eckersley.

ALCS

■ **Winner:** The powerful Athletics swept to their third consecutive pennant without benefit of a home run — their trademark offensive weapon.
■ **Turning point:** The final three innings of Game 1. Trailing 1-0 when Boston starter Roger Clemens left the game, the A's pounded five Red Sox relievers for nine runs and set the pattern for the series.
■ **Memorable moment:** The second inning of Game 4 when Clemens, frustrated by his team's 3-0 series deficit and the calls of umpire Terry Cooney, was ejected during an angry exchange, killing any hopes for a Boston comeback.
■ **Top guns:** Dave Stewart (2-0, 1.13 ERA), Terry Steinbach (.455), Carney Lansford (.438), Athletics; Wade Boggs (.438), Red Sox.
■ **MVP:** Stewart.

Linescores

Game 1—October 6, at Boston
Oakland......0 0 0 0 0 0 1 1 7—9 13 0
Boston ......0 0 0 1 0 0 0 0 0—1 5 1
Stewart, Eckersley (9); Clemens, Andersen (7), Bolton (8), Gray (8), Lamp (9), Murphy (9). W—Stewart. L—Andersen. HR—Boggs (Bos.).

Game 2—October 7, at Boston
Oakland......0 0 0 1 0 0 1 0 2—4 13 1
Boston ......0 0 1 0 0 0 0 0 0—1 6 0
Welch, Honeycutt (8), Eckersley (8); Kiecker, Harris (6), Andersen (7), Reardon (8). W—Welch. L—Harris. S—Eckersley.

Game 3—October 9, at Oakland
Boston ....0 1 0 0 0 0 0 0 0—1 8 3
Oakland........0 0 0 2 0 2 0 0 x—4 6 0
Boddicker; Moore, Nelson (7), Honeycutt (8), Eckersley (9). W—Moore. L—Boddicker. S—Eckersley.

Game 4—October 10, at Oakland
Boston ....0 0 0 0 0 0 0 0 1—1 4 1
Oakland........0 3 0 0 0 0 0 0 x—3 6 0
Clemens, Bolton (2), Gray (5), Andersen (8); Stewart, Honeycutt (9). W—Stewart. L—Clemens. S—Honeycutt.

NLCS

■ **Winner:** Cincinnati prevailed over Pittsburgh in a matchup of teams that dominated in the 1970s and failed to qualify for post-season play in the 1980s.
■ **Turning point:** The pivotal third game when the Reds got unlikely home runs from Billy Hatcher and Mariano Duncan and recorded a 6-3 victory.
■ **Memorable moment:** Glenn Braggs, a defensive replacement in right field, made a sensational over-the-wall catch in the ninth inning of Game 6, robbing Pittsburgh's Carmelo Martinez of a two-run homer and preserving the Reds' series-ending 2-1 victory.
■ **Top guns:** Randy Myers (3 saves, 7 SO, 0.00 ERA), Rob Dibble (1 save, 10 SO, 0.00), Paul O'Neill (.471), Hal Morris (.417), Reds; Doug Drabek (1-1, 1.65), Pirates.
■ **MVPs:** Dibble and Myers.

Linescores

Game 1—October 4, at Cincinnati
Pitt. ....0 0 1 2 0 0 1 0 0—4 7 1
Cin. ....3 0 0 0 0 0 0 0 0—3 5 0
Walk, Belinda (7), Patterson (9), Power (9); Rijo, Charlton (6), Dibble (9). W—Walk. L—Charlton. S—Power. HR—Bream (Pit.).

Game 2—October 5, at Cincinnati
Pitt. ....0 0 0 0 1 0 0 0 0—1 6 0
Cin. ....1 0 0 0 1 0 0 0 x—2 5 0
Drabek; Browning, Dibble (7), Myers (8). W—Browning. L—Drabek. S—Myers. HR—Lind (Pit.).

Game 3—October 8, at Pittsburgh
Cin. ....0 2 0 0 3 0 0 0 1—6 13 1
Pitt. ....0 0 0 2 0 0 0 1 0—3 8 0
Jackson, Dibble (6), Charlton (8), Myers (9); Smith, Landrum (6), Smiley (7), Belinda (9). W—Jackson. L—Smith. S—Myers. HR—Hatcher, Duncan (Cin.).

Game 4—October 9, at Pittsburgh
Cin. ....0 0 0 2 0 0 2 0 1—5 10 1
Pitt. ....1 0 0 1 0 0 0 1 0—3 8 0
Rijo, Myers (8), Dibble (9); Walk, Power (8). W—Rijo. L—Walk. S—Dibble. HR—O'Neill, Sabo (Cin.); Bell (Pit.).

Game 5—October 10, at Pittsburgh
Cin. ....1 0 0 0 0 0 0 1 0—2 7 0
Pitt. ....2 0 0 1 0 0 0 0 x—3 6 1
Browning, Mahler (6), Charlton (7), Scudder (8); Drabek, Patterson (9). W—Drabek. L—Browning. S—Patterson.

Game 6—October 12, at Cincinnati
Pitt. ....0 0 0 0 1 0 0 0 0—1 1 3
Cin. ....1 0 0 0 0 0 1 0 x—2 9 0
Power, Smith (3), Belinda (7), Landrum (8); Jackson, Charlton (7), Myers (8). W—Charlton. L—Smith. S—Myers.

WORLD SERIES

■ **Winner:** The Oakland Athletics' aura of invincibility was shattered by the Cincinnati Reds in a startling sweep. The A's, who were looking for a second straight championship, entered the Series with a 10-game post-season winning streak.
■ **Turning point:** Game 1. Eric Davis' first-inning home run and the combined nine-hit pitching of Jose Rijo, Rob Dibble and Randy Myers in a 7-0 victory served notice that the A's had their hands full.
■ **Memorable moment:** Relief ace Myers retiring Jose Canseco and Carney Lansford in the ninth inning of Game 4 to preserve a 2-1 victory for Rijo and complete the sweep.
■ **Top guns:** Rijo (2-0, 0.59 ERA), Myers (3 games, 0.00), Dibble (1-0, 0.00), Billy Hatcher (.750), Chris Sabo (.563, 2 HR, 5 RBIs), Reds; Rickey Henderson (.333), Athletics.
■ **MVP:** Rijo.

Linescores

Game 1—October 16, at Cincinnati
Oak. ....0 0 0 0 0 0 0 0 0—0 9 1
Cin. ....2 0 2 0 3 0 0 0 x—7 10 0
Stewart, Burns (5), Nelson (5), Sanderson (7), Eckersley (8); Rijo, Dibble (8), Myers (9). W—Rijo. L—Stewart. HR—Davis (Cin.).

Game 2—October 17, at Cincinnati
Oak. ......1 0 3 0 0 0 0 0 0 0—4 10 2
Cin. ....2 0 0 1 0 0 0 1 0 1—5 14 2
Welch, Honeycutt (8), Eckersley (10); Jackson, Scudder (3), Armstrong (5), Charlton (8), Dibble (9). W—Dibble. L—Eckersley. HR—Canseco (Oak.).

Game 3—October 19, at Oakland
Cin. ....0 1 7 0 0 0 0 0 0—8 14 1
Oak. ....0 2 1 0 0 0 0 0 0—3 7 1
Browning, Dibble (7), Myers (8); Moore, Sanderson (3), Klink (4), Nelson (4), Burns (8), Young (9). W—Browning. L—Moore. HR—Sabo 2 (Cin.); Baines, R. Henderson (Oak.).

Game 4—October 20, at Oakland
Cin. ....0 0 0 0 0 0 0 2 0—2 7 1
Oak. ....1 0 0 0 0 0 0 0 0—1 2 1
Rijo, Myers (9); Stewart. W—Rijo. L—Stewart. S—Myers.

HISTORY

1991

FINAL STANDINGS

American League

East Division

Team	Tor.	Det.	Bos.	Mil.	N.Y.	Bal.	Cle.	Min.	Chi.	Tex.	Oak.	Sea.	K.C.	Cal.	W	L	Pct.	GB
Toronto	...	8	4	7	7	8	12	8	5	6	6	7	7	6	91	71	.562	...
Detroit	5	...	8	4	8	8	6	4	8	6	4	8	8	7	84	78	.519	7
Boston	9	5	...	7	6	5	9	3	7	5	8	9	7	4	84	78	.519	7
Milwaukee	6	9	6	...	6	10	8	6	5	7	8	3	3	6	83	79	.512	8
New York	6	5	7	7	...	8	7	2	4	5	6	3	5	6	71	91	.438	20
Baltimore	5	5	8	3	5	...	7	4	4	9	3	4	4	6	67	95	.414	24
Cleveland	1	7	4	5	6	6	...	2	6	4	5	2	4	5	57	105	.352	34

West Division

Team	Min.	Chi.	Tex.	Oak.	Sea.	K.C.	Cal.	Tor.	Det.	Bos.	Mil.	N.Y.	Bal.	Cle.	W	L	Pct.	GB
Minnesota	...	5	6	8	9	7	5	4	8	9	6	10	8	10	95	67	.586	...
Chicago	8	...	8	7	7	7	5	7	4	5	7	8	8	6	87	75	.537	8
Texas	7	5	...	9	8	6	8	6	6	7	5	7	3	8	85	77	.525	10
Oakland	5	6	4	...	6	7	12	6	8	4	4	6	9	7	84	78	.519	11
Seattle	4	6	5	7	...	6	7	5	4	3	9	9	8	10	83	79	.512	12
Kansas City	6	6	7	6	7	...	4	5	4	5	9	7	8	8	82	80	.506	13
California	8	8	5	1	6	9	...	6	5	8	6	6	6	7	81	81	.500	14

National League

East Division

Team	Pit.	St.L.	Phi.	Chi.	N.Y.	Mon.	Atl.	L.A.	S.D.	S.F.	Cin.	Hou.	W	L	Pct.	GB
Pittsburgh	...	11	12	11	12	12	3	5	7	7	10	8	98	64	.605	...
St. Louis	7	...	12	8	11	11	3	6	3	8	8	7	84	78	.519	14
Philadelphia	6	6	...	10	7	14	7	5	9	6	3	5	78	84	.481	20
Chicago	7	10	8	...	11	10	6	2	4	6	4	9	77	83	.481	20
New York	6	7	11	6	...	14	3	5	7	6	7	5	77	84	.478	20.5
Montreal	6	7	4	7	4	...	7	7	6	7	6	10	71	90	.441	26.5

West Division

Team	Atl.	L.A.	S.D.	S.F.	Cin.	Hou.	Pit.	St.L.	Phi.	Chi.	N.Y.	Mon.	W	L	Pct.	GB
Atlanta	...	7	11	9	11	13	9	9	5	6	9	5	94	68	.580	...
Los Angeles	11	...	10	8	12	10	7	6	7	10	7	5	93	69	.574	1
San Diego	7	8	...	11	10	12	5	9	3	8	5	6	84	78	.519	10
San Fran.	9	10	7	...	8	9	5	4	6	6	6	5	75	87	.463	19
Cincinnati	7	6	8	10	...	9	2	4	9	8	5	6	74	88	.457	20
Houston	5	8	6	9	9	...	4	5	7	3	7	2	65	97	.401	29

SIGNIFICANT EVENTS

■ **April 18:** The Tigers spoiled the dedication of Chicago's new Comiskey Park when they routed the White Sox, 16-0.
■ **June 10:** Miami and Denver were declared winners by a four-man N.L. expansion committee.

MEMORABLE MOMENTS

■ **May 1:** Oakland's Rickey Henderson swiped his 939th base in a game against the Yankees, passing Lou Brock as baseball's all-time greatest base stealer.
■ **May 1:** Nolan Ryan, stealing the day's headlines from Henderson, fired his seventh career no-hitter, striking out 16 Blue Jays in a 3-0 victory.
■ **July 28:** Montreal's Dennis Martinez became the 14th pitcher to throw a perfect game when he retired all 27 Dodgers he faced in a 2-0 victory.
■ **October 2:** Cardinals closer Lee Smith, who had notched his 300th career save earlier in the year, recorded his single-season N.L.-record 47th in a 6-4 victory over Montreal.
■ **October 6:** Mets righthander David Cone tied the N.L. single-game record when he struck out 19 Phillies in a 7-0 victory.

LEADERS

American League
BA: Julio Franco, Tex., .341.
Runs: Paul Molitor, Mil., 133.
Hits: Paul Molitor, Mil., 216.
TB: Cal Ripken, Bal., 368.
HR: Jose Canseco, Oak.; Cecil Fielder, Det., 44.
RBI: Cecil Fielder, Det., 133.
SB: Rickey Henderson, Oak., 58.
Wins: Scott Erickson, Min.; Bill Gullickson, Det., 20.
ERA: Roger Clemens, Bos., 2.62.
CG: Jack McDowell, Chi., 15.
IP: Roger Clemens, Bos., 271.1.
SO: Roger Clemens, Bos., 241.
SV: Bryan Harvey, Cal., 46.

National League
BA: Terry Pendleton, Atl., .319.
Runs: Brett Butler, L.A., 112.
Hits: Terry Pendleton, Atl., 187.
TB: Will Clark, S.F.; Terry Pendleton, Atl., 303.
HR: Howard Johnson, N.Y., 38.
RBI: Howard Johnson, N.Y., 117.
SB: Marquis Grissom, Mon., 76.
Wins: Tom Glavine, Atl.; John Smiley, Pit., 20.
ERA: Dennis Martinez, Mon., 2.39.
CG: Tom Glavine, Atl.; Dennis Martinez, Mon., 9.
IP: Greg Maddux, Chi., 263.
SO: David Cone, N.Y., 241.
SV: Lee Smith, St.L., 47.

A.L. 20-game winners
Scott Erickson, Min., 20-8
Bill Gullickson, Det., 20-9

N.L. 20-game winners
John Smiley, Pit., 20-8
Tom Glavine, Atl., 20-11

A.L. 100 RBIs
Cecil Fielder, Det., 133
Jose Canseco, Oak., 122
Ruben Sierra, Tex., 116
Cal Ripken, Bal., 114
Frank Thomas, Chi., 109
Joe Carter, Tor., 108
Juan Gonzalez, Tex., 102
Ken Griffey Jr., Sea., 100
Danny Tartabull, K.C., 100
Robin Ventura, Chi., 100

N.L. 100 RBIs
Howard Johnson, N.Y., 117
Barry Bonds, Pit., 116
Will Clark, S.F., 116
Fred McGriff, S.D., 106
Ron Gant, Atl., 105
Andre Dawson, Chi., 104
Ryne Sandberg, Chi., 100
Bobby Bonilla, Pit., 100

A.L. 40 homers
Jose Canseco, Oak., 44
Cecil Fielder, Det., 44

Most Valuable Player
A.L.: Cal Ripken, SS, Bal.
N.L.: Terry Pendleton, 3B, Atl.

Cy Young Award
A.L.: Roger Clemens, Bos.
N.L.: Tom Glavine, Atl.

Rookie of the Year
A.L.: Chuck Knoblauch, 2B, Min.
N.L.: Jeff Bagwell, 1B, Hou.

Manager of the Year
A.L.: Tom Kelly, Min.
N.L.: Bobby Cox, Atl.

Hall of Fame additions
Rod Carew, 2B/1B, 1967-85
Ferguson Jenkins, P, 1965-83
Tony Lazzeri, 2B, 1926-39
Gaylord Perry, P, 1962-83
Bill Veeck, executive/owner

ALL-STAR GAME

■ **Winner:** The A.L. ran its winning streak to four with a 4-2 victory and the N.L. ran its four-year run total to a paltry six.
■ **Key inning:** The third, when Cal Ripken followed singles by Rickey Henderson and Wade Boggs with a home run.
■ **Memorable moment:** A first-inning line drive by Bobby Bonilla that struck A.L. starter Jack Morris on the ankle, reviving All-Star memories of the 1937 Earl Averill shot that broke Dizzy Dean's toe.
■ **Top guns:** Ripken (Orioles), Ken Griffey Jr. (Mariners), Henderson (Athletics), Boggs (Red Sox), A.L.; Tom Glavine (Braves), Bonilla (Pirates), Andre Dawson (Cubs), N.L.
■ **MVP:** Ripken.

Linescore
July 9, at Toronto's SkyDome
N.L. ....1 0 0 1 0 0 0 0 0—2 10 1
A.L. ....0 0 3 0 0 0 1 0 x—4 8 0
Glavine (Braves), De. Martinez (Expos) 3, Viola (Mets) 5, Harnisch (Astros) 6, Smiley (Pirates) 7, Dibble (Reds) 7, Morgan (Dodgers) 8; Morris (Twins), Key (Blue Jays) 3, Clemens (Red Sox) 4, McDowell (White Sox) 5, Reardon (Red Sox) 7, Aguilera (Twins) 7, Eckersley (Athletics) 9. W—Key. L—De. Martinez. S—Eckersley. HR—Ripken, A.L.; Dawson, N.L.

ALCS

■ **Winner:** Minnesota won an LCS-record three road games and its second pennant in five years while handing Toronto its third Championship Series defeat.
■ **Turning point:** The 10th inning of Game 3 when Minnesota's Mike Pagliarulo homered off Toronto reliever Mike Timlin, giving the Twins a 3-2 victory and a 2-1 series advantage.
■ **Memorable moment:** Minnesota first baseman Kent Hrbek delivered a two-run single off David Wells in the eighth inning of Game 5 to cap a series-ending 8-5 victory.
■ **Top guns:** Rick Aguilera (3 saves, 0.00 ERA), Kirby Puckett (.429, 2 HR, 6 RBIs), Twins; Roberto Alomar (.474), Blue Jays.
■ **MVP:** Puckett.

Linescores
Game 1—October 8, at Minnesota
Toronto ......0 0 0 1 0 3 0 0 0—4 9 3
Minn. ....2 2 1 0 0 0 0 0 x—5 11 0
Candiotti, Wells (3), Timlin (6); Morris, Willis (6), Aguilera (8). W—Morris. L—Candiotti. S—Aguilera.
Game 2—October 9, at Minnesota
Toronto ....1 0 2 0 0 0 2 0 0—5 9 0
Minn. ....0 0 1 0 0 1 0 0 0—2 5 1
Guzman, Henke (6), Ward (8); Tapani, Bedrosian (7), Guthrie (7). W—Guzman. L—Tapani. S—Ward.
Game 3—October 11, at Toronto
Minn. ......0 0 0 0 1 1 0 0 0 1—3 7 0
Tor. ....2 0 0 0 0 0 0 0 0 0—2 5 1
Erickson, West (5), Willis (7), Guthrie (9), Aguilera (10); Key, Wells (7), Henke (8), Timlin (10). W—Guthrie. L—Timlin. S—Aguilera. HR—Carter (Tor.); Pagliarulo (Min.).
Game 4—October 12, at Toronto
Minn. ....0 0 0 4 0 2 1 1 1—9 13 1
Toronto ......0 1 0 0 0 1 0 0 1—3 11 2
Morris, Bedrosian (9); Stottlemyre, Wells (4), Acker (6), Timlin (7), MacDonald (9). W—Morris. L—Stottlemyre. HR—Puckett (Min.).
Game 5—October 13, at Toronto
Minn. ....1 1 0 0 0 3 0 3 0—8 14 2
Toronto ......0 0 3 2 0 0 0 0 0—5 9 1
Tapani, West (5), Willis (8), Aguilera (9); Candiotti, Timlin (6), Ward (6), Wells (8). W—West. L—Ward. S—Aguilera. HR—Puckett (Min.).

NLCS

■ **Winner:** The young Braves, last-place N.L. West finishers in 1990, defeated the Pirates and won their first Atlanta pennant.
■ **Turning point:** Greg Olson's run-scoring double in the ninth inning of Game 6, which gave Braves lefthander Steve Avery his second 1-0 victory.
■ **Memorable moment:** The final pitch of John Smoltz's 4-0 Game 7 victory. The shutout, the Braves' third, gave Atlanta fans their first World Series qualifier.
■ **Top guns:** Avery (2-0, 0.00 ERA), Smoltz (2-0, 1.76), Olson (.333), Brian Hunter (.333), Braves; Doug Drabek (1-1, 0.60), Zane Smith (1-1, 0.61), Jay Bell (.414), Pirates.
■ **MVP:** Avery.

Linescores
Game 1—October 9, at Pittsburgh
Atlanta ....0 0 0 0 0 0 0 0 1—1 5 1
Pit. ....1 0 2 0 0 1 0 1 x—5 8 1
Glavine, Wohlers (7), Stanton (8); Drabek, Walk (7). W—Drabek. L—Glavine. S—Walk. HR—Van Slyke (Pit.); Justice (Atl.).
Game 2—October 10, at Pittsburgh
Atlanta ....0 0 0 0 0 1 0 0 0—1 8 0
Pit. ....0 0 0 0 0 0 0 0 0—0 6 0
Avery, Pena (9); Z. Smith, Mason (8), Belinda (9). W—Avery. L—Z. Smith. S—Pena.
Game 3—October 12, at Atlanta
Pit. ....1 0 0 1 0 0 1 0 0— 3 10 2
Atlanta......4 1 1 0 0 0 1 3 x—10 11 0
Smiley, Landrum (3), Patterson (4), Kipper (6), Rodriguez (8); Smoltz, Stanton (7), Wohlers (8), Pena (8). W—Smoltz. L—Smiley. S—Pena. HR—Gant, Olson, Bream (Atl.); Merced, Bell (Pit.).
Game 4—October 13, at Atlanta
Pit. ......0 1 0 0 1 0 0 0 0 1—3 11 1
Atlanta 2 0 0 0 0 0 0 0 0 0—2 7 1
Tomlin, Walk (7), Belinda (9); Leibrandt, Clancy (7), Stanton (8), Mercker (10), Wohlers (10). W—Belinda. L—Mercker.
Game 5—October 14, at Atlanta
Pit. ....0 0 0 0 1 0 0 0 0—1 6 2
Atlanta ....0 0 0 0 0 0 0 0 0—0 9 1
Z. Smith, Mason (8); Glavine, Pena (9). W—Z. Smith. L—Glavine. S—Mason.
Game 6—October 16, at Pittsburgh
Atlanta ....0 0 0 0 0 0 0 0 1—1 7 0
Pit. ....0 0 0 0 0 0 0 0 0—0 4 0
Avery, Pena (9); Drabek. W—Avery. L—Drabek. S—Pena.
Game 7—October 17, at Pittsburgh
Atlanta ....3 0 0 0 1 0 0 0 0—4 6 1
Pit. ....0 0 0 0 0 0 0 0 0—0 6 0
Smoltz; Smiley, Walk (1), Mason (6), Belinda (8). W—Smoltz. L—Smiley. HR—Hunter (Atl.).

WORLD SERIES

■ **Winner:** Minnesota defeated Atlanta in the "worst-to-first" World Series, which featured teams that had risen from last-place 1990 finishes to win pennants.
■ **Turning point:** The 11th-inning of Game 6, when Kirby Puckett greeted Braves reliever Charlie Leibrandt with a game-ending home run, squaring the Series. Puckett had made an outstanding leaping catch earlier in the 4-3 victory.
■ **Memorable moment:** A seventh-game baserunning blunder by Atlanta's Lonnie Smith, who failed to score on Terry Pendleton's eighth-inning double. The Twins and Jack Morris went on to post a 1-0 Series-ending victory on Gene Larkin's 12th-inning single.
■ **Top guns:** Morris (2-0, 1.17 ERA), Brian Harper (.381), Puckett (2 HR, 4 RBIs), Twins; David Justice (2 HR, 6 RBIs), Braves.
■ **MVP:** Morris.

Linescores
Game 1—October 19, at Minnesota
Atlanta ....0 0 0 0 0 1 0 1 0—2 6 1
Minn. ....0 0 1 0 3 1 0 0 x—5 9 1
Leibrandt, Clancy (5), Wohlers (7), Stanton (8); Morris, Guthrie (8), Aguilera (8). W—Morris. L—Leibrandt. S—Aguilera. HR—Gagne, Hrbek (Min.).
Game 2—October 20, at Minnesota
Atlanta ....0 1 0 0 1 0 0 0 0—2 8 1
Minn. ....2 0 0 0 0 0 0 1 x—3 4 1
Glavine; Tapani, Aguilera (9). W—Tapani. L—Glavine. S—Aguilera. HR—Davis, Leius (Min.).
Game 3—October 22, at Atlanta
Minn. ....1 0 0 0 0 0 1 2 0 0 0 0—4 10 1
Atl. ....0 1 0 1 2 0 0 0 0 0 0 1—5 8 2
Erickson, West (5), Leach (5), Bedrosian (6), Willis (8), Guthrie (10), Aguilera (12); Avery, Pena (8), Stanton (10), Wohlers (12), Mercker (12), Clancy (12). W—Clancy. L—Aguilera. HR—Justice, Smith (Atl.); Puckett, Davis (Min.).
Game 4—October 23, at Atlanta
Minn. ....0 1 0 0 0 0 1 0 0—2 7 0
Atlanta ....0 0 1 0 0 0 1 0 1—3 8 0
Morris, Willis (7), Guthrie (8), Bedrosian (9); Smoltz, Wohlers (8), Stanton (8). W—Stanton. L—Guthrie. HR—Pendleton, Smith (Atl.); Pagliarulo (Min.).
Game 5—October 24, at Atlanta
Minn. ......0 0 0 0 0 3 0 1 1— 5 7 1
Atlanta......0 0 0 4 1 0 6 3 x—14 17 1
Tapani, Leach (5), West (7), Bedrosian (7), Willis (8); Glavine, Mercker (6), Clancy (7), St. Claire (9). W—Glavine. L—Tapani. HR—Justice, Smith, Hunter (Atl.).
Game 6—October 26, at Minnesota
Atl. ....0 0 0 0 2 0 1 0 0 0 0—3 9 0
Minn. 2 0 0 0 1 0 0 0 0 0 1—4 9 1
Avery, Stanton (7), Pena (9), Leibrandt (11); Erickson, Guthrie (7), Willis (7), Aguilera (10). W—Aguilera. L—Leibrandt. HR—Pendleton (Atl.); Puckett (Min.).
Game 7—October 27, at Minnesota
Atl. ....0 0 0 0 0 0 0 0 0 0—0 7 0
Minn. ....0 0 0 0 0 0 0 0 0 1—1 10 0
Smoltz, Stanton (8), Pena (9); Morris. W—Morris. L—Pena.

1992

FINAL STANDINGS

American League

East Division

Team	Tor.	Mil.	Bal.	Cle.	N.Y.	Det.	Bos.	Oak.	Min.	Chi.	Tex.	Cal.	K.C.	Sea.	W	L	Pct.	GB
Toronto	...	5	8	7	11	8	6	6	7	7	9	7	7	8	96	66	.593	...
Milwaukee	8	...	7	8	6	8	8	7	6	7	7	7	5	8	92	70	.568	4
Baltimore	5	6	...	7	5	10	8	6	6	6	7	8	8	7	89	73	.549	7
Cleveland	6	5	6	...	7	5	7	6	6	5	5	6	5	7	76	86	.469	20
New York	2	7	8	6	...	8	6	6	5	4	6	5	7	6	76	86	.469	20
Detroit	5	5	3	8	5	...	9	6	3	2	8	5	7	9	75	87	.463	21
Boston	7	5	5	6	7	4	...	5	3	6	4	8	7	6	73	89	.451	23

West Division

Team	Oak.	Min.	Chi.	Tex.	Cal.	K.C.	Sea.	Tor.	Mil.	Bal.	Cle.	N.Y.	Det.	Bos.	W	L	Pct.	GB
Oakland	...	8	8	9	8	9	12	6	5	6	6	6	6	7	96	66	.593	...
Minnesota	5	...	5	6	11	7	8	5	6	6	6	7	9	9	90	72	.556	6
Chicago	5	8	...	5	10	7	4	5	5	6	7	8	10	6	86	76	.531	10
Texas	4	7	8	...	4	7	9	3	5	5	7	6	4	8	77	85	.475	19
California	5	2	3	9	...	8	7	5	5	4	6	7	7	4	72	90	.444	24
Kansas City	4	6	6	6	5	...	7	5	7	4	7	5	5	5	72	90	.444	24
Seattle	1	5	9	4	6	6	...	4	4	5	5	6	3	6	64	98	.395	32

National League

East Division

Team	Pit.	Mon.	St.L.	Chi.	N.Y.	Phi.	Atl.	Cin.	S.D.	Hou.	S.F.	L.A.	W	L	Pct.	GB
Pittsburgh	...	9	15	10	14	13	5	6	5	6	6	7	96	66	.593	...
Montreal	9	...	6	11	12	9	8	7	8	4	5	8	87	75	.537	9
St. Louis	3	12	...	7	9	11	6	5	8	7	7	8	83	79	.512	13
Chicago	8	7	11	...	9	9	2	5	5	8	8	6	78	84	.481	18
New York	4	6	9	9	...	6	5	5	4	7	10	7	72	90	.444	24
Philadelphia	5	9	7	9	12	...	6	5	3	4	3	7	70	92	.432	26

West Division

Team	Atl.	Cin.	S.D.	Hou.	S.F.	L.A.	Pit.	Mon.	St.L.	Chi.	N.Y.	Phi.	W	L	Pct.	GB
Atlanta	...	9	13	13	11	12	7	4	6	10	7	6	98	64	.605	...
CIncinnati	9	...	11	10	10	11	6	5	7	7	7	7	90	72	.556	8
San Diego	5	7	...	11	11	9	7	4	4	7	8	9	82	80	.506	16
Houston	5	8	7	...	12	13	6	8	5	4	5	8	81	81	.500	17
San Fran.	7	8	7	6	...	11	6	7	5	4	2	9	72	90	.444	26
Los Angeles	6	7	9	5	7	...	5	4	4	6	5	5	63	99	.389	35

LEADERS

American League
BA: Edgar Martinez, Sea., .343.
Runs: Tony Phillips, Det., 114.
Hits: Kirby Puckett, Min., 210.
TB: Kirby Puckett, Min., 313.
HR: Juan Gonzalez, Tex., 43.
RBI: Cecil Fielder, Det., 124.
SB: Kenny Lofton, Cle., 66.
Wins: Kevin Brown, Tex.; Jack Morris, Tor., 21.
ERA: Roger Clemens, Bos., 2.41.
CG: Jack McDowell, Chi., 13.
IP: Kevin Brown, Tex., 265.2.
SO: Randy Johnson, Sea., 241.
SV: Dennis Eckersley, Oak., 51.

National League
BA: Gary Sheffield, S.D., .330.
Runs: Barry Bonds, Pit., 109.
Hits: Terry Pendleton, Atl.; Andy Van Slyke, Pit., 199.
TB: Gary Sheffield, S.D., 323.
HR: Fred McGriff, S.D., 35.
RBI: Darren Daulton, Phil., 109.
SB: Marquis Grissom, Mon., 78.
Wins: Tom Glavine, Atl.; Greg Maddux, Chi., 20.
ERA: Bill Swift, S.F., 2.08.
CG: Terry Mulholland, Phil., 12.
IP: Greg Maddux, Chi., 268.
SO: John Smoltz, Atl., 215.
SV: Lee Smith, St.L., 43.

A.L. 20-game winners
Jack Morris, Tor., 21-6
Kevin Brown, Tex., 21-11
Jack McDowell, Chi., 20-10

N.L. 20-game winners
Tom Glavine, Atl., 20-8
Greg Maddux, Chi., 20-11

A.L. 100 RBIs
Cecil Fielder, Det., 124
Joe Carter, Tor., 119
Frank Thomas, Chi., 115
George Bell, Chi., 112
Albert Belle, Cle., 112
Kirby Puckett, Min., 110
Juan Gonzalez, Tex., 109
Dave Winfield, Tor., 108
Mike Devereaux, Bal., 107
Carlos Baerga, Cle., 105
Mark McGwire, Oak., 104
Ken Griffey Jr., Sea., 103

N.L. 100 RBIs
Darren Daulton, Phil., 109
Terry Pendleton, Atl., 105
Fred McGriff, S.D., 104
Barry Bonds, Pit., 103
Gary Sheffield, S.D., 100

A.L. 40 homers
Juan Gonzalez, Tex., 43
Mark McGwire, Oak., 42

Most Valuable Player
A.L.: Dennis Eckersley, P, Oak.
N.L.: Barry Bonds, OF, Pit.

Cy Young Award
A.L.: Dennis Eckersley, Oak.
N.L.: Greg Maddux, Chi.

Rookie of the Year
A.L.: Pat Listach, SS, Mil.
N.L.: Eric Karros, 1B, L.A.

Manager of the Year
A.L.: Tony La Russa, Oak.
N.L.: Jim Leyland, Pit.

Hall of Fame additions
Rollie Fingers, P, 1968-85
Bill McGowan, umpire
Hal Newhouser, P, 1939-55
Tom Seaver, P, 1967-86

SIGNIFICANT EVENTS

■ **April 6:** The Orioles opened their new Camden Yards home with a 2-0 victory over Cleveland.
■ **September 7:** Fay Vincent, reacting to an 18-9 no-confidence vote by the owners, resigned his post as baseball's eighth commissioner.
■ **November 17:** The Florida Marlins and Colorado Rockies selected 36 players apiece in baseball's first expansion draft since 1976.

MEMORABLE MOMENTS

■ **April 12:** Boston's Matt Young became the third pitcher in history to lose a complete-game no-hitter when he dropped a 2-1 decision to Cleveland.
■ **September 9, 30:** Milwaukee's Robin Yount and Kansas City's George Brett became the 17th and 18th members of baseball's 3,000-hit club.
■ **September 20:** Philadelphia second baseman Mickey Morandini pulled off baseball's ninth unassisted triple play and the N.L.'s first since 1927 in the sixth inning of a game against Pittsburgh.

ALL-STAR GAME

■ **Winner:** Ken Griffey Jr. went 3 for 3 as the suddenly dominant A.L. pounded out 19 hits and romped to an easy 13-6 victory.
■ **Key inning:** The A.L. first, when N.L. starter Tom Glavine was touched for four runs on seven consecutive singles.
■ **Memorable moment:** Ruben Sierra's two-run sixth-inning homer, which lifted the A.L.'s lead to 10-0.
■ **Top guns:** Griffey Jr. (Mariners), Sierra (Rangers), Robin Ventura (White Sox), Joe Carter (Blue Jays), Will Clark (Giants), Fred McGriff (Padres), N.L.
■ **MVP:** Griffey Jr.

Linescore
July 14, at San Diego's Jack Murphy Stadium
A.L. ....4 1 1 0 0 4 0 3 0—13 19 1
N.L. ....0 0 0 0 0 1 0 3 2— 6 12 1
Brown (Rangers), McDowell (White Sox) 2, Guzman (Blue Jays) 3, Clemens (Red Sox) 4, Mussina (Orioles) 5, Langston (Angels) 6, Nagy (Indians) 7, Montgomery (Royals) 8, Aguilera (Twins) 8, Eckersley (Athletics) 9; Glavine (Braves), Maddux (Braves) 2, Cone (Mets) 4, Tewksbury (Cardinals) 5, Smoltz (Braves) 6, D. Martinez (Expos) 7, Jones (Astros) 8, Charlton (Reds) 9. W—Brown. L—Glavine. HR—Griffey, Sierra, A.L.; Clark, N.L.

ALCS

■ **Winner:** The Toronto Blue Jays, three-time Championship Series losers, brought Canada its first pennant with a rousing six-game victory over Oakland.
■ **Turning point:** Down 6-1 entering the eighth inning of Game 4, the Blue Jays rallied to tie against A's relief ace Dennis Eckersley and won in the 11th on Pat Borders' sacrifice fly. Instead of a 2-2 series tie, Toronto was up 3-1.
■ **Memorable moment:** Roberto Alomar's stunning game-tying homer off Eckersley in the ninth inning of Game 4. The two-run shot forced extra innings.
■ **Top guns:** Juan Guzman (2-0, 2.08 ERA), Alomar (.423, 2 HR), Candy Maldonado (2 HR, 6 RBIs), Blue Jays; Harold Baines (.440), Ruben Sierra (.333, 7 RBIs), Athletics.
■ **MVP:** Alomar.

Linescores

Game 1—October 7, at Toronto
Oak. ....0 3 0 0 0 0 0 0 1—4 6 1
Tor. ....0 0 0 0 1 1 0 1 0—3 9 0
Stewart, Russell (8), Eckersley (9); Morris. W—Russell. L—Morris. S—Eckersley. HR—McGwire, Steinbach, Baines (Oak.); Borders, Winfield (Tor.).

Game 2—October 8, at Toronto
Oak. ....0 0 0 0 0 0 0 0 1—1 6 0
Tor. ....0 0 0 0 2 0 1 0 x—3 4 0
Moore, Corsi (8), Parrett (8); Cone, Henke (9). W—Cone. L—Moore. S—Henke. HR—Gruber (Tor.).

Game 3—October 10, at Oakland
Tor. ....0 1 0 1 1 0 2 1 1—7 9 1
Oak. ....0 0 0 2 0 0 2 1 0—5 13 3
Guzman, Ward (7), Timlin (8), Henke (8); Darling, Downs (7), Corsi (8), Russell (8), Honeycutt (9), Eckersley (9). W—Guzman. L—Darling. S—Henke. HR—Alomar, Maldonado (Tor.).

Game 4—October 11, at Oakland
Tor. ....010 000 032 01—7 17 4
Oak. ....005 001 000 00—6 12 2
Morris, Stottlemyre (4), Timlin (8), Ward (9), Henke (11); Welch, Parrett (8), Eckersley (8), Corsi (9), Downs (10). W—Ward. L—Downs. S—Henke. HR—Olerud, Alomar (Tor.).

Game 5—October 12, at Oakland
Tor. ....0 0 0 1 0 0 1 0 0—2 7 3
Oak. ....2 0 1 0 3 0 0 0 x—6 8 0
Cone, Key (5), Eichhorn (8); Stewart. W—Stewart. L—Cone. HR—Sierra (Oak.); Winfield (Tor.).

Game 6—October 14, at Toronto
Oak. ....0 0 0 0 0 1 0 1 0—2 7 1
Tor. ....2 0 4 0 1 0 0 2 x—9 13 0
Moore, Parrett (3), Honeycutt (5), Russell (7), Witt (8); Guzman, Ward (8), Henke (9). W—Guzman. L—Moore. HR—Carter, Maldonado (Tor.).

NLCS

■ **Winner:** Atlanta won its rematch with Pittsburgh and captured its second straight pennant in a stirring Championship Series that was decided on the final pitch.
■ **Turning point:** The incredible ninth inning of Game 7. Down 2-0 to Pirates ace Doug Drabek after eight innings and on the brink of blowing what had once been a three-games- to-one advantage, the Braves rallied for three runs.
■ **Memorable moment:** With two out and the bases loaded in the bottom of the ninth inning of Game 7, pinch-hitter Francisco Cabrera delivered a two-run, pennant-deciding single to left field off Stan Belinda.
■ **Top guns:** John Smoltz (2-0, 2.66 ERA), Mark Lemke (.333), David Justice (2 HR, 6 RBIs), Ron Gant (2 HR, 6 RBIs), Braves; Tim Wakefield (2-0, 3.00), Lloyd McClendon (.727), Gary Redus (.438), Pirates.
■ **MVP:** Smoltz.

Linescores

Game 1—October 6, at Atlanta
Pitt. ....0 0 0 0 0 0 0 1 0—1 5 1
Atlanta..........0 1 0 2 1 0 1 0 x—5 8 0
Drabek, Patterson (5), Neagle (7), Cox (8); Smoltz, Stanton (9). W—Smoltz. L—Drabek. HR—Blauser (Atl.); Lind (Pit.).

Game 2—October 7, at Atlanta
Pitt. ....0 0 0 0 0 0 4 1 0— 5 7 0
Atlanta......0 4 0 0 4 0 5 0 x—13 14 0
Jackson, Mason (2), Walk (3), Tomlin (5), Neagle (7), Patterson (7), Belinda (8); Avery, Freeman (7), Stanton (7), Wohlers (8), Reardon (9). W—Avery. L—Jackson. HR—Gant (Atl.).

Game 3—October 9, at Pittsburgh
Atlanta ....0 0 0 1 0 0 1 0 0—2 5 0
Pitt. ....0 0 0 0 1 1 1 0 x—3 8 1
Glavine, Stanton (7), Wohlers (8); Wakefield. W—Wakefield. L—Glavine. HR—Slaught (Pit.); Bream, Gant (Atl.).

Game 4—October 10, at Pittsburgh
Atlanta ......0 2 0 0 2 2 0 0 0—6 11 1
Pitt. ....0 2 1 0 0 0 1 0 0—4 6 1
Smoltz, Stanton (7), Reardon (9); Drabek, Tomlin (5), Cox (6), Mason (7). W—Smoltz. L—Drabek. S—Reardon.

Game 5—October 11, at Pittsburgh
Atlanta ......0 0 0 0 0 0 0 1 0—1 3 0
Pitt. ....4 0 1 0 0 1 1 0 x—7 13 0
Avery, P. Smith (1), Leibrandt (5), Freeman (6), Mercker (8); Walk. W—Walk. L—Avery.

Game 6—October 13, at Atlanta
Pitt. ....0 8 0 0 4 1 0 0 0—13 13 1
Atlanta ....0 0 0 1 0 0 1 0 2— 4 9 1
Wakefield; Glavine, Leibrandt (2), Freeman (5), Mercker (7), Wohlers (9). W—Wakefield. L—Glavine. HR—Bonds, Bell, McClendon (Pit.); Justice 2 (Atl.).

Game 7—October 14, at Atlanta
Pitt. ....1 0 0 0 0 1 0 0 0—2 7 1
Atlanta ....0 0 0 0 0 0 0 0 3—3 7 0
Drabek, Belinda (9); Smoltz, Stanton (7), P. Smith (7), Avery (7), Reardon (9). W—Reardon. L—Drabek.

WORLD SERIES

■ **Winner:** Toronto brought a baseball championship to Canada and the Braves failed to give Atlanta its long-awaited title for the second year in a row.
■ **Turning point:** The Blue Jays took a three-games-to-one advantage with a 2-1 victory in Game 4, thanks to the combined five-hit pitching of Jimmy Key, Duane Ward and Tom Henke and a home run by Pat Borders.
■ **Memorable moment:** Dave Winfield's two-run double in the 11th inning of Game 6 , which gave Toronto a 4-3 Series-clinching win.
■ **Top guns:** Key (2-0, 1.00 ERA), Borders (.450), Joe Carter (2 HR), Blue Jays; Deion Sanders (.533), Braves.
■ **MVP:** Borders.

Linescores

Game 1—October 17, at Atlanta
Tor. ....0 0 0 1 0 0 0 0 0—1 4 0
Atl. ....0 0 0 0 0 3 0 0 x—3 4 0
Morris, Stottlemyre (7), Wells (8); Glavine. W—Glavine. L—Morris. HR—Carter (Tor.); Berryhill (Atl.).

Game 2—October 18, at Atlanta
Tor. ....0 0 0 0 2 0 0 1 2—5 9 2
Atl. ....0 1 0 1 2 0 0 0 0—4 5 1
Cone, Wells (5), Stottlemyre (7), Ward (8), Henke (9); Smoltz, Stanton (8), Reardon (8). W—Ward. L—Reardon. S—Henke. HR—Sprague (Tor.).

Game 3—October 20, at Toronto
Atl. ....0 0 0 0 0 1 0 1 0—2 9 0
Tor. ....0 0 0 1 0 0 0 1 1—3 6 1
Avery, Wohlers (9), Stanton (9), Reardon (9); Guzman, Ward (9). W—Ward. L—Avery. HR—Carter, Gruber (Tor.).

Game 4—October 21, at Toronto
Atl. ....0 0 0 0 0 0 0 1 0—1 5 0
Tor. ....0 0 1 0 0 0 1 0 x—2 6 0
Glavine; Key, Ward (8), Henke (9). W—Key. L—Glavine. S—Henke. HR—Borders (Tor.).

Game 5—October 22, at Toronto
Atl. ....1 0 0 1 5 0 0 0 0—7 13 0
Tor. ....0 1 0 1 0 0 0 0 0—2 6 0
Smoltz, Stanton (7); Morris, Wells (5), Timlin (7), Eichhorn (8), Stottlemyre (9). W—Smoltz. L—Morris. S—Stanton. HR—Justice, L. Smith (Atl.).

Game 6—October 24, at Atlanta
Tor. ..1 0 0 1 0 0 0 0 0 0 2—4 14 1
Atl. ..0 0 1 0 0 0 0 0 1 0 1—3 8 1
Cone, Stottlemyre (7), Wells (7), Ward (8), Henke (9), Key (10), Timlin (11); Avery, P. Smith (5), Stanton (8), Wohlers (9), Leibrandt (10). W—Key. L—Leibrandt. S—Timlin. HR—Maldonado (Tor.).

HISTORY

1993

FINAL STANDINGS

American League

East Division

Team	Tor.	N.Y.	Det.	Bal.	Bos.	Cle.	Mil.	Chi.	Tex.	K.C.	Sea.	Min.	Cal.	Oak.	W	L	Pct.	GB
Toronto	...	8	7	8	10	9	8	6	5	4	5	10	8	7	95	67	.586	...
New York	5	...	9	7	7	7	9	8	3	6	7	8	6	6	88	74	.543	7
Detroit	6	4	...	8	7	7	8	5	6	5	7	6	8	8	85	77	.525	10
Baltimore	5	6	5	...	6	8	8	4	4	7	7	8	7	10	85	77	.525	10
Boston	3	6	6	7	...	5	5	7	6	5	7	7	7	9	80	82	.494	15
Cleveland	4	6	6	5	8	...	8	3	7	7	3	4	7	8	76	86	.469	19
Milwaukee	5	4	5	5	8	5	...	3	4	7	4	7	5	7	69	93	.426	26

West Division

Team	Chi.	Tex.	K.C.	Sea.	Min.	Cal.	Oak.	Tor.	N.Y.	Det.	Bal.	Bos.	Cle.	Mil.	W	L	Pct.	GB
Chicago	...	8	6	9	10	6	7	6	4	7	8	5	9	9	94	68	.580	...
Texas	5	...	6	5	6	7	8	7	9	6	8	6	5	8	86	76	.531	8
Kansas City	7	7	...	7	7	7	6	8	6	7	5	7	5	5	84	78	.519	10
Seattle	4	8	6	...	9	7	4	7	5	5	5	5	9	8	82	80	.506	12
Minnesota	3	7	6	4	...	9	8	2	4	6	4	5	8	5	71	91	.438	23
California	7	6	6	6	4	...	6	4	6	4	5	5	5	7	71	91	.438	23
Oakland	6	5	7	9	5	7	...	5	6	4	2	3	4	5	68	94	.420	26

National League

East Division

Team	Phi.	Mon.	St.L.	Chi.	Pit.	Fla.	N.Y.	Atl.	S.F.	Hou.	L.A.	Cin.	Col.	S.D.	W	L	Pct.	GB
Philadelphia	...	7	8	6	7	9	10	6	4	7	10	8	9	6	97	65	.599	...
Montreal	6	...	7	8	8	8	9	5	3	7	6	8	9	10	94	68	.580	3
St. Louis	5	6	...	5	9	9	8	6	8	6	6	7	7	5	87	75	.537	10
Chicago	7	5	8	...	5	6	8	5	6	4	7	7	8	8	84	78	.519	13
Pittsburgh	6	5	4	8	...	7	9	5	5	5	4	4	4	9	75	87	.463	22
Florida	4	5	4	7	6	...	4	5	4	3	5	5	5	7	64	98	.395	33
New York	3	4	5	5	4	9	...	3	4	1	4	6	6	5	59	103	.364	38

West Division

Team	Atl.	S.F.	Hou.	L.A.	Cin.	Col.	S.D.	Phi.	Mon.	St.L.	Chi.	Pit.	Fla.	N.Y.	W	L	Pct.	GB
Atlanta	...	7	8	8	10	13	9	6	7	6	7	7	7	9	104	58	.642	...
San Fran.	6	...	10	6	11	10	10	8	9	4	6	7	8	8	103	59	.636	1
Houston	5	3	...	9	7	2	8	5	5	6	8	7	9	11	85	77	.525	19
Los Angeles	5	7	4	...	8	6	9	2	6	6	5	8	7	8	81	81	.500	23
Cincinnati	3	2	6	5	...	9	9	4	4	5	5	8	7	6	73	89	.451	31
Colorado	0	3	11	7	4	...	6	3	3	5	4	8	7	6	67	95	.414	37
San Diego	4	3	5	4	4	7	...	6	2	7	4	3	5	7	61	101	.377	43

LEADERS

American League
BA: John Olerud, Tor., .363.
Runs: Rafael Palmeiro, Tex., 124.
Hits: Paul Molitor, Tor., 211.
TB: Ken Griffey, Jr., Sea., 359.
HR: Juan Gonzalez, Tex., 46.
RBI: Albert Belle, Cle., 129.
SB: Kenny Lofton, Cle., 70.
Wins: Jack McDowell, Chi., 22.
ERA: Kevin Appier, K.C., 2.56.
CG: Chuck Finley, Cal., 13.
IP: Cal Eldred, Mil., 258.
SO: Randy Johnson, Sea., 308.
SV: Jeff Montgomery, K.C.; Duane Ward, Tor., 45.

National League
BA: Andres Galarraga, Col., .370.
Runs: Lenny Dykstra, Phil., 143.
Hits: Lenny Dykstra, Phil., 194.
HR: Barry Bonds, S.F., 46.
RBI: Barry Bonds, S.F., 123.
SB: Chuck Carr, Fla., 58.
Wins: John Burkett, S.F.; Tom Glavine, Atl., 22.
ERA: Greg Maddux, Atl., 2.36.
CG: Greg Maddux, Atl., 8.
IP: Greg Maddux, Atl., 267.
SO: Jose Rijo, Cin., 227.
SV: Randy Myers, Chi., 53.

A.L. 20-game winner
Jack McDowell, Chi., 22-10

N.L. 20-game winners
Tom Glavine, Atl., 22-6
John Burkett, S.F., 22-7
Bill Swift, S.F., 21-8
Greg Maddux, Atl., 20-10

A.L. 100 RBIs
Albert Belle, Cle., 129
Frank Thomas, Chi., 128
Joe Carter, Tor., 121
Juan Gonzalez, Tex., 118
Cecil Fielder, Det., 117
Carlos Baerga, Cle., 114
Chili Davis, Cal., 112
Paul Molitor, Tor., 111
Mickey Tettleton, Det., 110
Ken Griffey Jr., Sea., 109
John Olerud, Tor., 107
Rafael Palmeiro, Tex., 105
Danny Tartabull, N.Y., 102
Mo Vaughn, Bos., 101
Ruben Sierra, Oak., 101

N.L. 100 RBIs
Barry Bonds, S.F., 123
David Justice, Atl., 120
Ron Gant, Atl., 117
Mike Piazza, L.A., 112
Matt Williams, S.F., 110
Darren Daulton, Phil., 105
Todd Zeile, St.L., 103
Fred McGriff, S.D.-Atl., 101
Eddie Murray, N.Y., 100
Phil Plantier, S.D., 100

A.L. 40 homers
Juan Gonzalez, Tex., 46
Ken Griffey Jr., Sea., 45
Frank Thomas, Chi., 41

N.L. 40 homers
Barry Bonds, S.F., 46
David Justice, Atl., 40

Most Valuable Player
A.L.: Frank Thomas, 1B, Chi.
N.L.: Barry Bonds, OF, S.F.

Cy Young Award
A.L.: Jack McDowell, Chi.
N.L.: Greg Maddux, Atl.

Rookie of the Year
A.L.: Tim Salmon, OF, Cal.
N.L.: Mike Piazza, C, L.A.

Manager of the Year
A.L.: Gene Lamont, Chi.
N.L.: Dusty Baker, S.F.

Hall of Fame addition
Reggie Jackson, OF, 1967-87

SIGNIFICANT EVENTS

■ **March 22:** Cleveland players Steve Olin and Tim Crews were killed and pitcher Bob Ojeda was seriously injured in a spring training boating accident near Orlando, Fla.
■ **September 9:** Owners and players agreed to split the A.L. and N.L. into three divisions and expand the number of playoff qualifiers from four to eight teams.
■ **October 3:** The Braves clinched the N.L. West Division title with a final-day 5-3 victory over Colorado while the Giants were losing to the Dodgers, 12-1.

MEMORABLE MOMENTS

■ **July 28:** Seattle's Ken Griffey Jr. tied a long-standing record when he homered in his eighth consecutive game—a 5-1 loss to Minnesota.
■ **July 28:** The Mets scored two ninth-inning runs against Florida, handing Anthony Young a 5-4 victory and ending his record 27-game losing streak.
■ **September 7:** St. Louis' Mark Whiten tied a pair of records when he hit four homers and drove in 12 runs in a 15-2 victory over Cincinnati.
■ **September 16:** Minnesota's Dave Winfield joined baseball's exclusive 3,000-hit club in a game against Oakland.

ALL-STAR GAME

■ **Winner:** Kirby Puckett fueled the high-powered A.L. offense to a 9-3 victory — its sixth straight.
■ **Key inning:** The fifth. After hitting a solo home run in the second, Puckett contributed a run-scoring double in a three-run fifth that broke a 2-2 tie.
■ **Memorable moment:** Hard-throwing A.L. lefty Randy Johnson striking out John Kruk, who bailed out on three straight pitches, swinging feebly at the third.
■ **Top guns:** Johnson (Mariners), Puckett (Twins), Roberto Alomar (Blue Jays), Albert Belle (Indians), A.L.; Gary Sheffield (Marlins), Barry Bonds (Giants), N.L.
■ **MVP:** Puckett.

Linescore
July 13, at Baltimore's Camden Yards
N.L. ....2 0 0 0 0 1 0 0 0—3 7 2
A.L. ....0 1 1 0 3 3 1 0 x—9 11 0
Mulholland (Phillies), Benes (Padres) 3, Burkett (Giants) 5, Avery (Braves) 5, Smoltz (Braves) 6, Beck (Giants) 7, Harvey (Marlins) 8; Langston (Angels), Johnson (Mariners) 3, McDowell (White Sox) 5, Key (Yankees) 6, Montgomery (Royals) 7, Aguilera (Twins) 8, Ward (Blue Jays) 9. W—McDowell. L—Burkett. HR—Sheffield, N.L.; Puckett, Alomar, A.L.

ALCS

■ **Winner:** Toronto kept the A.L. pennant on Canadian soil and denied Chicago's bid for its first World Series appearance since 1959.
■ **Turning point:** The Blue Jays defeated the White Sox, 5-3, in the pivotal fifth game, which wasn't decided until reliever Duane Ward struck out Bo Jackson with a man on base in the ninth inning.
■ **Memorable moment:** A 6-3 finale in which Toronto's Dave Stewart lifted his LCS record to 8-0 and pitched his fourth pennant-clinching victory in six seasons.
■ **Top guns:** Stewart (2-0, 2.03 ERA), Juan Guzman (2-0, 2.08), Devon White (.444), Blue Jays; Tim Raines (.444), White Sox.
■ **MVP:** Stewart.

Linescores

Game 1—October 5, at Chicago
Toronto ......0 0 0 2 3 0 2 0 0—7 17 1
Chicago......0 0 0 3 0 0 0 0 0—3 6 1
Guzman, Cox (7), Ward (9); McDowell, DeLeon (7), Radinsky (8), McCaskill (9). W—Guzman. L—McDowell. HR—Molitor (Tor.).

Game 2—October 6, at Chicago
Toronto ....1 0 0 2 0 0 0 0 0—3 8 0
Chicago........1 0 0 0 0 0 0 0 0—1 7 2
Stewart, Leiter (7), Ward (9); A. Fernandez, Hernandez (9). W—Stewart. L—A. Fernandez. S—Ward.

Game 3—October 8, at Toronto
Chicago......0 0 5 1 0 0 0 0 0—6 12 0
Toronto ......0 0 1 0 0 0 0 0 0—1 7 1
Alvarez; Hentgen, Cox (4), Eichhorn (7), Castillo (9). W—Alvarez. L—Hentgen.

Game 4—October 9, at Toronto
Chicago......0 2 0 0 0 3 1 0 1—7 11 0
Toronto ......0 0 3 0 0 1 0 0 0—4 9 0
Bere, Belcher (3), McCaskill (7), Radinsky (8), Hernandez (9); Stottlemyre, Leiter (7), Timlin (7). W—Belcher. L—Stottlemyre. S—Hernandez. HR—Thomas, Johnson (Chi.).

Game 5—October 10, at Toronto
Chicago......0 0 0 0 1 0 0 0 2—3 5 1
Toronto ......1 1 1 1 0 0 1 0 x—5 14 0
McDowell, DeLeon (3), Radinsky (7), Hernandez (7); Guzman, Castillo (8), Ward (9). W—Guzman. L—McDowell. HR—Burks, Ventura (Chi.).

Game 6—October 12, at Chicago
Toronto ......0 2 0 1 0 0 0 0 3—6 10 0
Chicago......0 0 2 0 0 0 0 0 1—3 5 3
Stewart, Ward (8); A. Fernandez, McCaskill (8), Radinsky (9), Hernandez (9). W—Stewart. L—A. Fernandez. S—Ward. HR—White (Tor.); Newson (Chi.).

NLCS

■ **Winner:** Philadelphia needed six games to ruin Atlanta's bid for a third consecutive pennant.
■ **Turning point:** The pivotal fifth game, when Curt Schilling pitched eight innings of four-hit ball and Lenny Dykstra hit a game-winning 10th-inning home run.
■ **Memorable moment:** The ninth inning of Game 6. Phillies lefthander Mitch Williams, also known as "Wild Thing," pulled a shocker when he retired the Braves 1-2-3 for his second series save and a 6-3 pennant-clinching victory.
■ **Top guns:** Schilling (1.69 ERA), Williams (2-0, 2 saves, 1.69), Dykstra (2 HR), Phillies; Fred McGriff (.435), Otis Nixon (.348), Terry Pendleton (.346), Braves.
■ **MVP:** Schilling.

Linescores

Game 1—October 6, at Philadelphia
Atlanta ....0 0 1 1 0 0 0 0 1 0—3 9 0
Phil. ....1 0 0 1 0 1 0 0 0 1—4 9 1
Avery, Mercker (7), McMichael (9); Schilling, Williams (9). W—Williams. L—McMichael. HR—Incaviglia (Phil.).

Game 2—October 7, at Philadelphia
Atlanta ....2 0 6 0 1 0 0 4 1—14 16 0
Phil. ....0 0 0 2 0 0 0 0 1— 3 7 2
Maddux, Stanton (8), Wohlers (9); Greene, Thigpen (3), Rivera (4), Mason (6), West (8), Andersen (9). W—Maddux. L—Greene. HR—McGriff, Blauser, Berryhill, Pendleton (Atl.); Hollins, Dykstra (Phil.).

Game 3—October 9, at Atlanta
Phil. ....0 0 0 1 0 1 0 1 1—4 10 1
Atlanta........0 0 0 0 0 5 4 0 x—9 12 0
Mulholland, Mason (6), Andersen (7), West (7), Thigpen (8); Glavine, Mercker (8), McMichael (9). W—Glavine. L—Mulholland. HR—Kruk (Phil.)

Game 4—October 10, at Atlanta
Phil. ....0 0 0 2 0 0 0 0 0—2 8 1
Atlanta ......0 1 0 0 0 0 0 0 0—1 10 1
Jackson, Williams (8); Smoltz, Mercker (7), Wohlers (8). W—Jackson. L—Smoltz. S—Williams.

Game 5—October 11, at Atlanta
Phil. ....1 0 0 1 0 0 0 0 1 1—4 6 1
Atlanta ....0 0 0 0 0 0 0 0 3 0—3 7 1
Schilling, Williams (9), Andersen (10); Avery, Mercker (8), McMichael (9), Wohlers (10). W—Williams. L—Wohlers. S—Andersen. HR—Daulton, Dykstra (Phil.).

Game 6—October 13, at Philadelphia
Atlanta ....0 0 0 0 1 0 2 0 0—3 5 3
Phil. ....0 0 2 0 2 2 0 0 x—6 7 1
Maddux, Mercker (6), McMichael (7), Wohlers (7); Greene, West (8), Williams (9). W—Greene. L—Maddux. S—Williams. HR—Hollins (Phil.); Blauser (Atl.).

WORLD SERIES

■ **Winner:** Toronto defeated Philadelphia to become the first back-to-back Series winner since the Yankees of 1977-78.
■ **Turning point:** The Blue Jays' six-run, eighth-inning rally that turned a 14-9 Game 4 deficit into a 15-14 victory and a 3-1 Series lead.
■ **Memorable moment:** Joe Carter's three-run, ninth-inning home run that turned a 6-5 Game 6 deficit into one of the most dramatic victories in World Series history.
■ **Top guns:** Paul Molitor (.500, 2 HR, 8 RBIs), Roberto Alomar (.480), Tony Fernandez (.333, 9 RBIs), Carter (2 HR, 8 RBIs), Blue Jays; Lenny Dykstra (.348, 4 HR, 8 RBIs), John Kruk (.348), Phillies.
■ **MVP:** Molitor.

Linescores

Game 1—October 16, at Toronto
Phil. ....2 0 1 0 1 0 0 0 1—5 11 1
Toronto ......0 2 1 0 1 1 3 0 x—8 10 3
Schilling, West (7), Andersen (7), Mason (8); Guzman, Leiter (6), Ward (8). W—Leiter. L—Schilling. S—Ward. HR—White, Olerud (Tor.).

Game 2—October 17, at Toronto
Phil. ....0 0 5 0 0 0 1 0 0—6 12 0
Toronto ......0 0 0 2 0 1 0 1 0—4 8 0
Mulholland, Mason (6), Williams (7); Stewart, Castillo (7), Eichhorn (8), Timlin (8). W—Mulholland. L—Stewart. S—Williams. HR—Carter (Tor.); Dykstra, Eisenreich (Phil.).

Game 3—October 19, at Philadelphia
Toronto ....3 0 1 0 0 1 3 0 2—10 13 1
Phil. ....0 0 0 0 1 0 1 0 1— 3 9 0
Hentgen, Cox (7), Ward (9); Jackson, Rivera (6), Thigpen (7), Andersen (9). W—Hentgen. L—Jackson. HR—Thompson (Phil.); Molitor (Tor.).

Game 4—October 20, at Philadelphia
Toronto ....3 0 4 0 0 2 0 6 0—15 18 0
Phil. ....4 2 0 1 5 1 1 0 0—14 14 0
Stottlemyre, Leiter (3), Castillo (5), Timlin (8), Ward (8); Greene, Mason (3), West (6), Andersen (7), Williams (8), Thigpen (9). W—Castillo. L—Williams. S—Ward. HR—Dykstra 2, Daulton (Phil.).

Game 5—October 21, at Philadelphia
Toronto ....0 0 0 0 0 0 0 0 0—0 5 1
Phil. ....1 1 0 0 0 0 0 0 x—2 5 1
Guzman, Cox (8); Schilling. W—Schilling. L—Guzman.

Game 6—October 23, at Toronto
Phil. ....0 0 0 1 0 0 5 0 0—6 7 0
Toronto ......3 0 0 1 1 0 0 0 3—8 10 2
Mulholland, Mason (6), West (8), Andersen (8), Williams (9); Stewart, Cox (7), Leiter (7), Ward (9). W—Ward. L—Williams. HR—Molitor, Carter (Tor.); Dykstra (Phil.).

FINAL STANDINGS

American League

East Division

Team	N.Y.	Bal.	Tor.	Bos.	Det.	Chi.	Cle.	K.C.	Min.	Mil.	Tex.	Oak.	Sea.	Cal.	W	L	Pct.	GB
New York	...	6	3	7	3	2	9	2	5	7	3	7	8	8	70	43	.619	...
Baltimore	4	...	7	4	3	2	4	4	4	7	3	7	6	8	63	49	.563	6.5
Toronto	4	2	...	3	4	3	4	6	8	3	8	1	5	4	55	60	.478	16
Boston	3	2	7	...	4	2	3	4	1	5	1	9	6	7	54	61	.470	17
Detroit	3	4	5	2	...	4	2	4	3	6	5	5	6	4	53	62	.461	18

Central Division

Team	Chi.	Cle.	K.C.	Min.	Mil.	N.Y.	Bal.	Tor.	Bos.	Det.	Tex.	Oak.	Sea.	Cal.	W	L	Pct.	GB
Chicago	...	7	3	2	9	4	4	2	4	8	4	6	9	5	67	46	.593	...
Cleveland	5	...	1	9	5	0	6	6	7	8	5	6	3	5	66	47	.584	1
Kansas City	7	4	...	6	5	4	1	6	2	8	4	7	6	4	64	51	.557	4
Minnesota	4	3	4	...	6	4	5	4	8	3	4	2	3	3	53	60	.469	14
Milwaukee	3	2	7	6	...	2	3	7	5	4	3	4	4	3	53	62	.461	15

West Division

Team	Tex.	Oak.	Sea.	Cal.	N.Y.	Bal.	Tor.	Bos.	Det.	Chi.	Cle.	K.C.	Min.	Mil.	W	L	Pct.	GB
Texas	...	3	1	4	2	3	4	5	7	5	7	3	5	3	52	62	.456	...
Oakland	7	...	4	6	5	5	5	3	4	3	0	3	5	1	51	63	.447	1
Seattle	9	3	...	7	4	4	1	6	3	1	2	4	3	2	49	63	.438	2
California	6	3	2	...	4	4	3	5	3	5	0	6	3	3	47	68	.409	5.5

National League

East Division

Team	Mon.	Atl.	N.Y.	Phi.	Fla.	Cin.	Hou.	Pit.	St.L.	Chi.	L.A.	S.F.	Col.	S.D.	W	L	Pct.	GB
Montreal	...	5	4	5	7	2	4	8	7	4	9	5	2	12	74	40	.649	...
Atlanta	4	...	5	6	8	5	3	3	5	4	6	5	8	6	68	46	.596	6
New York	3	4	...	4	4	4	3	4	6	4	6	6	1	6	55	58	.487	18.5
Philadelphia	4	3	6	...	6	2	1	5	4	6	5	4	4	4	54	61	.470	20.5
Florida	2	4	6	4	...	5	2	1	3	5	3	2	9	5	51	64	.443	23.5

Central Division

Team	Cin.	Hou.	Pit.	St.L.	Chi.	Mon.	Atl.	N.Y.	Phi.	Fla.	L.A.	S.F.	Col.	S.D.	W	L	Pct.	GB
Cincinnati	...	4	9	2	7	4	5	2	4	7	3	7	4	8	66	48	.579	...
Houston	6	...	8	8	8	2	3	3	5	4	1	8	5	5	66	49	.574	.5
Pittsburgh	3	4	...	5	5	2	9	5	4	6	3	1	3	3	53	61	.465	13
St. Louis	2	4	5	...	5	3	7	3	3	7	4	4	4	2	53	61	.465	13
Chicago	5	4	5	5	...	2	2	1	1	4	3	5	6	6	49	64	.434	16.5

West Division

Team	L.A.	S.F.	Col.	S.D.	Mon.	Atl.	N.Y.	Phi.	Fla.	Cin.	Hou.	Pit.	St.L.	Chi.	W	L	Pct.	GB
Los Angeles	...	5	6	6	3	0	6	7	3	6	8	3	2	3	58	56	.509	...
San Fran.	5	...	7	2	7	1	6	8	4	2	2	5	2	4	55	60	.478	3.5
Colorado	4	3	...	5	4	2	5	2	3	4	5	2	8	6	53	64	.453	6.5
San Diego	4	5	5	...	0	1	6	8	1	2	5	3	4	3	47	70	.402	12.5

SIGNIFICANT EVENTS

■ **March 1, June 7:** The N.L. elected Leonard Coleman as its new president and the A.L. opted for Gene Budig.

■ **April 4, 11:** Two parks were dedicated: The Indians needed 11 innings to beat Seattle, 4-3, in their Jacobs Field opener and the Rangers lost their debut at The Ballpark in Arlington to Milwaukee, 4-3.

■ **August 12:** Major League players brought the season to a skidding halt when they called a general strike—baseball's eighth work stoppage since 1972.

■ **September 14:** Baseball owners announced cancellation of the regular season and Post Season, rubber-stamping the first uncompleted season in the game's long history.

■ **December 28:** The Astros and Padres completed a 12-player trade, baseball's largest since 1957.

Despite the short season and a late injury, hot-hitting Houston first baseman Jeff Bagwell drove in a Major League-leading 116 runs.

Atlanta righthander Greg Maddux claimed the third of his four consecutive Cy Young Awards during the strike-shortened season.

MEMORABLE MOMENTS

■ **April 4:** Tuffy Rhodes became the first player to homer in his first three Opening Day at-bats, but the Cubs still dropped a 12-8 decision to the Mets.

■ **July 8:** Boston shortstop John Valentin pulled off baseball's 10th unassisted triple play and the Red Sox beat Seattle, 4-3.

■ **July 28:** When Kenny Rogers retired all 27 Minnesota hitters in a 4-0 victory, he became the first A.L. lefthander to throw a perfect game.

■ **August 1:** Cal Ripken stretched his ironman streak to 2,000 games and the Orioles celebrated with a 1-0 victory over Minnesota.

■ **August 6:** The Mariners routed Kansas City, 11-2, and ended the Royals' winning streak at 14 games.

LEADERS

American League
BA: Paul O'Neill, N.Y., .359.
Runs: Frank Thomas, Chi., 106.
Hits: Kenny Lofton, Cle., 160.
TB: Albert Belle, Cle., 294.
HR: Ken Griffey, Jr., Sea., 40.
RBI: Kirby Puckett, Min., 112.
SB: Lofton, Cle., 60.
Wins: Jimmy Key, N.Y., 17.
ERA: Steve Ontiveros, Oak., 2.65.
CG: Randy Johnson, Sea., 9.
IP: Chuck Finley, Cal., 183.1.
SO: Randy Johnson, Sea., 204.
SV: Lee Smith, Bal., 33.

National League
BA: Tony Gwynn, S.D., .394.
Runs: Jeff Bagwell, Hou., 104.
Hits: Gwynn, S.D., 165.
TB: Bagwell, Hou., 300.
HR: Matt Williams, S.F., 43.
RBI: Bagwell, Hou., 116.
SB: Craig Biggio, Hou., 39.
Wins: Ken Hill, Mon.; Greg Maddux, Atl., 16.
ERA: Greg Maddux, Atl., 1.56.
CG: Maddux, Atl., 10.
IP: Maddux, Atl., 202.
SO: Andy Benes, S.D., 189.
SV: John Franco, N.Y., 30.

A.L. 100 RBIs
Kirby Puckett, Min., 112
Joe Carter, Tor., 103
Albert Belle, Cle., 101
Frank Thomas, Chi., 101

N.L. 100 RBIs
Jeff Bagwell, Hou., 116

A.L. 40 homers
Ken Griffey Jr., Sea., 40

N.L. 40 homers
Matt Williams, S.F., 43

Most Valuable Player
A.L.: Frank Thomas, 1B, Chi.
N.L.: Jeff Bagwell, 1B, Hou.

Cy Young Award
A.L.: David Cone, K.C.
N.L.: Greg Maddux, Atl.

Rookie of the Year
A.L.: Bob Hamelin, DH, K.C.
N.L.: Raul Mondesi, OF, L.A.

Manager of the Year
A.L.: Buck Showalter, N.Y.
N.L.: Felipe Alou, Mon.

Hall of Fame additions
Steve Carlton, P, 1965-88
Leo Durocher, manager
Phil Rizzuto, SS, 1941-56

ALL-STAR GAME

■ **Winner:** The N.L. scored two runs in the ninth and one in the 10th to snap the A.L.'s six-game All-Star winning streak with an 8-7 victory.

■ **Key inning:** The 10th, when the N.L. scored its winning run on a single by Tony Gwynn and a game-ending double by Moises Alou.

■ **Memorable moment:** Fred McGriff's two-run, game-tying homer in the ninth off relief ace Lee Smith.

■ **Top guns:** Ken Hill (Expos), Gwynn (Padres), Alou (Expos), Marquis Grissom (Expos), McGriff (Braves), Gregg Jefferies (Cardinals), N.L.; Ken Griffey Jr. (Mariners), Kenny Lofton (Indians), Frank Thomas (White Sox), A.L.

■ **MVP:** McGriff.

Linescore

July 12, at Pittsburgh's Three Rivers Stadium
A.L.........1 0 0 0 0 3 3 0 0 0—7 15 0
N.L.........1 0 3 0 0 1 0 0 2 1—8 12 1
Key (Yankees), Cone (Royals) 3, Mussina (Orioles) 5, Johnson (Mariners) 6, Hentgen (Blue Jays) 7, Alvarez (White Sox) 8, L. Smith (Orioles) 9, Bere (White Sox) 10; Maddux (Braves), Hill (Expos) 4, Drabek (Astros) 6, Hudek (Astros) 6, Jackson (Phillies) 7, Beck (Giants) 7, Myers (Cubs) 9, Jones (Phillies) 10. W—Jones. L—Bere.
HR—Grissom, McGriff, N.L.

FINAL STANDINGS

American League

East Division

Team	Bos.	N.Y.	Bal.	Det.	Tor.	Cle.	K.C.	Chi.	Mil.	Min.	Sea.	Cal.	Tex.	Oak.	W	L	Pct.	GB
Boston	...	5	9	8	8	6	3	5	8	5	7	11	3	8	86	58	.597	...
New York	8	...	7	8	12	6	7	2	6	4	4	5	6	4	79	65	.549	7
Baltimore	4	6	...	8	7	2	4	6	7	3	6	9	4	5	71	73	.493	15
Detroit	5	5	5	...	7	3	3	4	8	7	5	2	4	2	60	84	.417	26
Toronto	5	1	6	6	...	3	5	5	5	4	4	2	3	7	56	88	.389	30

Central Division

Team	Cle.	K.C.	Chi.	Mil.	Min.	Bos.	N.Y.	Bal.	Det.	Tor.	Sea.	Cal.	Tex.	Oak.	W	L	Pct.	GB
Cleveland	...	11	8	9	9	7	6	10	10	10	5	2	6	7	100	44	.694	...
Kansas City	1	...	5	10	6	2	3	5	4	7	7	7	8	5	70	74	.486	30
Chicago	5	8	...	6	10	3	3	1	8	6	4	2	5	7	68	76	.472	32
Milwaukee	4	2	7	...	9	4	5	5	5	7	3	2	5	7	65	79	.451	35
Minnesota	4	7	3	4	...	4	3	6	5	1	4	5	5	5	56	88	.389	44

West Division

Team	Sea.	Cal.	Tex.	Oak.	Bos.	N.Y.	Bal.	Det.	Tor.	Cle.	K.C.	Chi.	Mil.	Min.	W	L	Pct.	GB
Seattle	...	6	10	6	5	9	7	5	3	4	5	9	2	8	79	66	.545	...
California	7	...	6	6	3	7	4	6	8	3	5	10	5	8	78	67	.538	1
Texas	3	7	...	8	4	3	1	8	9	3	6	7	7	8	74	70	.514	4.5
Oakland	7	7	5	...	4	9	7	3	3	0	8	5	2	7	67	77	.465	11.5

National League

East Division

Team	Atl.	Phi.	N.Y.	Fla.	Mon.	Cin.	Hou.	Chi.	St.L.	Pit.	L.A.	Col.	S.D.	S.F.	W	L	Pct.	GB
Atlanta	...	7	5	10	9	8	6	8	7	4	5	9	5	7	90	54	.625	...
Philadelphia	6	...	6	7	5	3	7	1	5	6	9	2	6	6	69	75	.479	21
New York	8	7	...	6	6	5	6	3	3	4	6	4	6	5	69	75	.479	21
Florida	3	6	7	...	6	6	8	4	4	5	3	7	3	5	67	76	.469	22.5
Montreal	4	8	7	7	...	4	3	5	4	4	5	1	7	7	66	78	.458	24

Central Division

Team	Cin.	Hou.	Chi.	St.L.	Pit.	Atl.	Phi.	N.Y.	Fla.	Mon.	L.A.	Col.	S.D.	S.F.	W	L	Pct.	GB
Cincinnati	...	12	7	8	8	5	9	7	6	8	4	5	3	3	85	59	.590	...
Houston	1	...	8	9	9	6	5	6	4	9	3	4	7	5	76	68	.528	9
Chicago	3	5	...	9	8	4	6	4	8	3	7	6	5	5	73	71	.507	12
St. Louis	5	4	4	...	7	5	4	4	3	3	5	7	5	6	62	81	.434	22.5
Pittsburgh	5	4	5	6	...	2	3	3	8	4	4	4	4	6	58	86	.403	27

West Division

Team	L.A.	Col.	S.D.	S.F.	Atl.	Phi.	N.Y.	Fla.	Mon.	Cin.	Hou.	Chi.	St.L.	Pit.	W	L	Pct.	GB
Los Angeles	...	9	7	8	4	4	6	7	7	3	2	5	7	9	78	66	.542	...
Colorado	4	...	9	8	4	4	5	5	7	7	4	7	5	8	77	67	.535	1
San Diego	6	4	...	6	2	6	7	2	5	6	4	7	7	8	70	74	.486	8
San Fran.	5	5	7	...	1	6	8	3	6	3	3	7	7	6	67	77	.465	11

LEADERS

American League
BA: Edgar Martinez, Sea., .356.
Runs: Albert Belle, Cle.; Edgar Martinez, Sea., 121.
Hits: Lance Johnson, Chi., 186.
TB: Albert Belle, Cle., 377.
HR: Albert Belle, Cle., 50.
RBI: Albert Belle, Cle.; Mo Vaughn, Bos., 126.
SB: Kenny Lofton, Cle., 54.
Wins: Mike Mussina, Bal., 19.
ERA: Randy Johnson, Sea., 2.48.
CG: Jack McDowell, N.Y., 8.
IP: David Cone, Tor.-N.Y., 229.1.
SO: Randy Johnson, Sea., 294.
SV: Jose Mesa, Cle., 46.

National League
BA: Tony Gwynn, S.D., .368.
Runs: Craig Biggio, Hou., 123.
Hits: Dante Bichette, Col.; Tony Gwynn, S.D., 197.
TB: Dante Bichette, Col., 359.
HR: Dante Bichette, Col., 40.
RBI: Dante Bichette, Col., 128.
SB: Quilvio Veras, Fla., 56.
Wins: Greg Maddux, Atl., 19.
ERA: Greg Maddux, Atl., 1.63.
CG: Greg Maddux, Atl., 10.
IP: Greg Maddux, Atl.; Denny Neagle, Pit., 209.2.
SO: Hideo Nomo, L.A., 236.
SV: Randy Myers, Chi., 38.

A.L. 100 RBIs
Albert Belle, Cle., 126
Mo Vaughn, Bos., 126
Jay Buhner, Sea., 121
Edgar Martinez, Sea., 113
Tino Martinez, Sea., 111
Frank Thomas, Chi., 111
Jim Edmonds, Cal., 107
Manny Ramirez, Cle., 107
Tim Salmon, Cal., 105
Rafael Palmeiro, Bal., 104
J.T. Snow, Cal., 102
John Valentin, Bos., 102

N.L. 100 RBIs
Dante Bichette, Col., 128
Sammy Sosa, Chi., 119
Andres Galarraga, Col., 106
Jeff Conine, Fla., 105
Eric Karros, L.A., 105
Barry Bonds, S.F., 104
Larry Walker, Col., 101

A.L. 40 homers
Albert Belle, Cle., 50
Jay Buhner, Sea., 40
Frank Thomas, Chi., 40

N.L. 40 homers
Dante Bichette, Col., 40

Most Valuable Player
A.L.: Mo Vaughn, 1B, Bos.
N.L.: Barry Larkin, SS, Cin.

Cy Young Award
A.L.: Randy Johnson, Sea.
N.L.: Greg Maddux, Atl.

Rookie of the Year
A.L.: Marty Cordova, OF, Min.
N.L.: Hideo Nomo, P, L.A.

Manager of the Year
A.L.: Lou Piniella, Sea.
N.L.: Don Baylor, Col.

Hall of Fame additions
Richie Ashburn, OF, 1948-62
Leon Day, P, Negro Leagues
William Hulbert, Executive
Mike Schmidt, 3B, 1972-89
Vic Willis, P, 1898-1910

SIGNIFICANT EVENTS

■ **April 2:** Baseball owners, blocked by an injunction preventing them from imposing new work rules and using replacement players in the 1995 season, invited striking players to return to work, ending the 234-day work stoppage. Opening Day was pushed back to April 25 and the schedule was reduced to 144 games.

■ **April 30:** Major League Baseball agreed to a new contract with its umpires, ending a lockout that had extended a week into the regular season and forced use of replacement arbiters.

■ **March 9:** Major League owners approved expansion franchises for Tampa Bay (Devil Rays) and Phoenix (Arizona Diamondbacks), with play to begin in 1998.

■ **August 13:** Baseball was stung by the loss of former Yankee great Mickey Mantle, who died at age 63 of lung cancer.

■ **October 2:** Sparky Anderson, whose 2,194 managerial victories ranked third all-time to Connie Mack and John McGraw, retired after nine seasons with the Reds and 17 with the Tigers.

■ **November 13:** Atlanta righthander Greg Maddux won his record-setting fourth consecutive N.L. Cy Young after a 19-2, 1.63-ERA season. Maddux joined Steve Carlton as the only four-time Cy Young winners.

MEMORABLE MOMENTS

■ **June 3:** Montreal's Pedro Martinez pitched nine perfect innings before giving up a 10th-inning double to San Diego's Bip Roberts after the Expos had scored in the top of the inning. Martinez did not finish his 1-0 victory.

■ **June 30:** Cleveland's Eddie Murray joined baseball's 3,000-hit club when he singled off Minnesota righthander Mike Trombley.

■ **September 6:** Baltimore shortstop Cal Ripken passed Lou Gehrig's ironman streak when he played in his 2,131st consecutive game — a 4-2 victory over California at Camden Yards.

■ **September 8:** Cleveland defeated Baltimore 3-2 and clinched the team's first title of any kind in 41 years. The Indians' final 30-game A.L. Central Division margin over Kansas City was the largest in modern baseball history.

■ **October 2:** The Mariners defeated California 9-1 in a one-game playoff, giving Seattle its first division title in the franchise's 19-year history.

ALL-STAR GAME

■ **Winner:** The N.L. managed only three hits off seven A.L. pitchers, but all were solo home runs and produced an unlikely 3-2 victory.

■ **Key inning:** The seventh, when Los Angeles catcher Mike Piazza collected the N.L.'s second hit, a game-tying homer off Texas' Kenny Rogers, and Phillies reliever Heathcliff Slocumb pitched the N.L. out of a two-on, one-out jam.

■ **Memorable moment:** Pinch-hitter Jeff Conine's eighth-inning blast off Oakland's Steve Ontiveros, which broke the 2-2 tie and gave the N.L. its first lead. Conine became the 10th player to hit a homer in his first All-Star at-bat.

■ **Top guns:** Randy Johnson (Mariners), Kevin Appier (Royals), Frank Thomas (White Sox), Carlos Baerga (Indians), A.L.; Hideo Nomo (Dodgers), Slocumb (Phillies), Craig Biggio (Astros), Piazza (Dodgers), Conine (Marlins), N.L.

■ **MVP:** Conine.

Linescore

July 11, at Texas' The Ballpark in Arlington
N.L. ....0 0 0 0 0 1 1 1 0—3 3 0
A.L. ....0 0 0 2 0 0 0 0 0—2 8 0
Nomo (Dodgers), Smiley (Reds) 3, Green (Phillies) 5, Neagle (Pirates) 6, C. Perez (Expos) 7, Slocumb (Phillies) 7, Henke (Cardinals) 8, Myers (Cubs) 9; Johnson (Mariners), Appier (Royals) 3, Martinez (Indians) 5, Rogers (Rangers) 7, Ontiveros (A's) 8, Wells (Tigers) 8, Mesa (Indians) 9. W—Slocumb. L—Ontiveros. S—Myers. HR—Thomas, A.L.; Biggio, Piazza, Conine, N.L.

A.L. DIVISION SERIES

■ **Winners:** Cleveland swept past Boston, but Seattle needed five games and extra innings to defeat New York in baseball's inaugural Division Series. The Mariners could not secure victory until the 11th inning of Game 5.

■ **Turning points:** For Cleveland, catcher Tony Pena's Game 1-ending home run in the bottom of the 13th inning. For Seattle, Edgar Martinez's two-homer, seven-RBI Game 4 effort that kept the Mariners' title hopes alive.

■ **Memorable moments:** Martinez's tie-breaking eighth-inning grand slam in Game 4 and his Series-ending two-run double in the 11th inning of Game 5.

■ **Memorable performances:** The playoff-record five-home run effort of Seattle outfielder Ken Griffey and Martinez's 10-RBI effort.

Linescores

Cleveland vs. Boston

Game 1—October 3, at Cleveland
Bos. ....0 0 2 0 0 0 0 1 0 0 1 0 0—4 11 2
Cle. ....0 0 0 0 0 3 0 0 0 0 1 0 1—5 10 2
Clemens, Cormier (8), Belinda (8), Stanton (8), Aguilera (11), Maddux (11), Smith (13); Martinez, Tavarez (7), Assenmacher (8), Plunk (8), Mesa (10), Poole (11), Hill (12). W—Hill. L—Smith. HR—Valentin, Alicea, Naehring (Bos.); Belle, Pena (Cle.).

Game 2—October 4, at Cleveland
Bos. ....0 0 0 0 0 0 0 0 0—0 3 1
Cle. ....0 0 0 0 2 0 0 2 x—4 4 2
Hanson; Hershiser, Tavarez (8), Assenmacher (8), Mesa (9). W—Hershiser. L—Hanson. HR—Murray (Cle.).

Game 3—October 6, at Boston
Cle. ....0 2 1 0 0 5 0 0 0—8 11 2
Bos. ....0 0 0 1 0 0 0 1 0—2 7 1
Nagy, Tavarez (8), Assenmacher (9); Wakefield, Cormier (6), Maddux (6), Hudson (9). W—Nagy. L—Wakefield. HR—Thome (Cle.).

Seattle vs. New York

Game 1—October 3, at New York
Seattle........0 0 0 1 0 1 2 0 2—6 9 0
N.Y. ....0 0 2 0 0 2 4 1 x—9 13 0
Bosio, Nelson (6), Ayala (7), Risley (7), Wells (8); Cone, Wetteland (9). W—Cone. L—Nelson. HR—Griffey 2 (Sea.); Boggs, Sierra (N.Y.).

Game 2—October 4, at New York
Seattle......0 0 1 0 0 1 2 0 0 0 0 1 0 0 0—5 16 2
N.Y. ....0 0 0 0 1 2 1 0 0 0 0 1 0 0 2—7 11 0
Benes, Risley (6), Charlton (7), Nelson (11), Belcher (12); Pettitte, Wickman (8), Wetteland (9), Rivera (12). W—Rivera. L—Belcher. HR—Coleman, Griffey (Sea.); Sierra, Mattingly, O'Neill, Leyritz (N.Y.).

Game 3—October 6, at Seattle
N.Y. ....0 0 0 1 0 0 1 2 0—4 6 2
Seattle.........0 0 0 0 2 4 1 0 x—7 7 0
McDowell, Howe (6), Wickman (6), Hitchcock (7), Rivera (7); Johnson, Risley (8), Charlton (8). W—Johnson. L—McDowell. S—Charlton. HR—B. Williams 2, Stanley (N.Y.); T. Martinez (Sea.).

Game 4—October 7, at Seattle
N.Y. ....3 0 2 0 0 0 0 1 2—8 14 1
Seattle......0 0 4 0 1 1 0 5 x—11 16 0
Kamieniecki, Hitchcock (6), Wickman (7), Wetteland (8), Howe (8); Bosio, Nelson (3), Belcher (7), Charlton (8), Ayala (9), Risley (9). W—Charlton. L—Wetteland. S—Risley. HR—O'Neill (N.Y.); E. Martinez 2, Griffey, Buhner (Sea.).

Game 5—October 8, at Seattle
N.Y. ......0 0 0 2 0 2 0 0 0 0 1—5 6 0
Seattle 0 0 1 1 0 0 0 2 0 0 2—6 15 0
Cone, Rivera (8), McDowell (9); Benes, Charlton (7), Johnson (9). W—Johnson. L—McDowell. HR—O'Neill (N.Y.); Cora, Griffey (Sea.).

N.L. DIVISION SERIES

■ **Winners:** Atlanta and Cincinnati powered past West Division opponents in the N.L.'s first Division Series.

■ **Turning points:** For the Braves, a four-run ninth-inning Game 2 rally that produced a 7-4 victory and a two-games-to-none edge over the Rockies. For the Reds, a 5-4 Game 2 victory, despite being outhit by the Dodgers, 14-6.

■ **Memorable moment:** Colorado pitcher Lance Painter striking out with the bases loaded in the ninth inning of a 5-4 Game 1 loss to the Braves. Painter was pinch-hitting because Colorado manager Don Baylor had no more position players on his bench.

■ **Top performances:** Atlanta third baseman Chipper Jones belted two Game 1 homers, including the game-winner in the top of the ninth inning; Braves first baseman Fred McGriff broke out of a slump with a two-homer, five-RBI Game 5 effort; Reds infielder Mark Lewis broke open Game 3 against the Dodgers with the first pinch-hit grand slam in playoff history.

Linescores

Atlanta vs. Colorado

Game 1—October 3, at Colorado
Atlanta ......0 0 1 0 0 2 0 1 1—5 12 1
Colorado....0 0 0 3 0 0 0 1 0—4 13 4
Maddux, McMichael (8), Pena (8), Wohlers (9); Ritz, Reed (6), Ruffin (7), Munoz (8), Holmes (8), Leskanic (9). W—Pena. L—Leskanic. S—Wohlers. HR—Jones 2, Grissom (Atl.); Castilla (Col.).

Game 2—October 4, at Colorado
Atlanta ......1 0 1 1 0 0 0 4—7 13 1
Colorado....0 0 0 0 0 3 0 1 0—4 8 2
Glavine, Avery (8), Pena (8), Wohlers (9); Painter, Reed (6), Ruffin (7), Leskanic (8), Munoz (9), Holmes (9). W—Pena. L—Munoz. S—Wohlers. HR—Grissom 2 (Atl.); Walker (Col.).

Game 3—October 6, at Atlanta
Colorado......1 0 2 0 0 2 0 0 0 2—7 9 0
Atlanta ....0 0 0 3 0 0 1 0 1 0—5 11 0
Swift, Reed (7), Munoz (7), Leskanic (7), Ruffin (8), Holmes (9), Thompson (10); Smoltz, Clontz (6), Borbon (8), McMichael (9), Wohlers (10), Mercker (10). W—Holmes. L—Wohlers. S—Thompson. HR—Young, Castilla (Col.).

Game 4— October 7, at Atlanta
Colorado..........0 0 3 0 0 1 0 0 0— 4 11 1
Atlanta ....0 0 4 2 1 3 0 0 x—10 15 0
Saberhagen, Ritz (5), Munoz (6), Reynoso (7), Ruffin (8); Maddux, Pena (8). W—Maddux. L—Saberhagen. HR—Bichette, Castilla (Col.); McGriff 2 (Atl.).

Cincinnati vs. Los Angeles

Game 1—October 3, at Los Angeles
Cincinnati ....4 0 0 0 3 0 0 0 0—7 12 0
Los Angeles ......0 0 0 0 1 1 0 0 0—2 8 0
Schourek, Jackson (8), Brantley (9); Martinez, Cummings (5), Astacio (6), Guthrie (8), Osuna (9). W—Schourek. L—Martinez. HR—Santiago (Cin.); Piazza (L.A.).

Game 2—October 4, at Los Angeles
Cincinnati ....0 0 0 2 0 0 0 1 2—5 6 0
Los Angeles ......1 0 0 1 0 0 0 0 2—4 14 2
Smiley, Burba (7), Jackson (8), Brantley (9); Valdes, Osuna (8), Tapani (9), Guthrie (9), Astacio (9). W—Burba. L—Osuna. S—Brantley. HR—Sanders (Cin.); Karros 2 (L.A.).

Game 3—October 6, at Cincinnati
Los Angeles ....0 0 0 1 0 0 0 0 0— 1 9 1
Cincinnati ....0 0 2 1 0 4 3 0 x—10 11 2
Nomo, Tapani (6), Guthrie (6), Astacio (6), Cummings (7), Osuna (7); Wells, Jackson (7), Brantley (9). W—Wells. L—Nomo. HR—Gant, Boone, M. Lewis (Cin.).

ALCS

■ **Winner:** The Cleveland Indians needed six games and a hard-fought victory over Seattle ace lefthander Randy Johnson to secure their first World Series berth in 41 years.

■ **Turning point:** With the intimidating Johnson scheduled to pitch Game 6 in Seattle, the Indians won the pivotal fifth game, 3-2, on Jim Thome's two-run sixth-inning homer. The victory gave them a three-games-to-two advantage.

■ **Memorable moment:** A two-run passed ball in the eighth inning of Cleveland's 4-0 pennant-clinching victory. Ruben Amaro scored from third base and speedy Kenny Lofton surprised the Mariners with a mad dash from second, extending the Indians' lead to 3-0.

■ **Top guns:** Orel Hershiser (2-0, 1.29 ERA), Lofton (.458, 5 SB), Carlos Baerga (.400), Thome (2 HR, 5 RBI), Indians; Ken Griffey (.333), Jay Buhner (3 HR, 5 RBI), Norm Charlton (1-0, 0.00, 1 sv), Mariners.

■ **MVP:** Hershiser.

Linescores

Game 1—October 10, at Seattle
Cleveland ....0 0 1 0 0 0 1 0 0—2 10 1
Seattle ....0 2 0 0 0 0 1 0 x—3 7 0
D. Martinez, Tavarez (7), Assenmacher (8), Plunk (8); Wolcott, Nelson (8), Charlton (8). W—Wolcott. L—D. Martinez. S—Charlton. HR—Belle (Cle.); Blowers (Sea.).

Game 2—October 11, at Seattle
Cleveland ....0 0 0 0 2 2 0 1 0—5 12 0
Seattle ....0 0 0 0 0 1 0 0 1—2 6 1
Hershiser, Mesa (9); Belcher, Ayala (6), Risley (9). W—Hershiser. L—Belcher. HR—Ramirez 2 (Cle.); Griffey, Buhner (Sea.).

Game 3—October 13, at Cleveland
Seattle ......0 1 1 0 0 0 0 0 0 0 3—5 9 1
Cleveland ..0 0 0 1 0 0 0 1 0 0 0—2 4 2
Johnson, Charlton (9); Nagy, Mesa (9), Tavarez (10), Assenmacher (11), Plunk (11). W—Charlton. L—Tavarez. HR—Buhner 2 (Sea.).

Game 4—October 14, at Cleveland
Seattle ....0 0 0 0 0 0 0 0 0—0 6 1
Cleveland ....3 1 2 0 0 1 0 0 x—7 9 0
Benes, Wells (3), Ayala (6), Nelson (7), Risley (8); Hill, Poole (8), Ogea (9), Embree (9). W—Hill. L—Benes. HR—Murray, Thome (Cle.).

Game 5—October 15, at Cleveland
Seattle ....0 0 1 0 1 0 0 0 0—2 5 2
Cleveland ....1 0 0 0 0 2 0 0 x—3 10 4
Bosio, Nelson (6), Risley (7); Hershiser, Tavarez (7), Assenmacher (7), Plunk (8), Mesa (9). W—Hershiser. L—Bosio. S—Mesa. HR—Thome (Cle.).

Game 6—October 17, at Seattle
Cleveland ....0 0 0 0 1 0 0 3 0—4 8 0
Seattle ....0 0 0 0 0 0 0 0 0—0 4 1
D. Martinez, Tavarez (8), Mesa (9); Johnson, Charlton (8). W—D. Martinez. L—Johnson. HR—Baerga (Cle.).

NLCS

■ **Winner:** Atlanta pitchers limited Cincinnati to five total runs and the Braves swept past the Reds and claimed their third World Series berth of the decade.

■ **Turning point:** It came early, in the 11th inning of Game 1. Mike Devereaux singled home the winner in a 2-1 victory and the Braves cruised the rest of the way.

■ **Memorable moment:** A three-run, 10th-inning blast off the left-field foul pole by Atlanta catcher Javier Lopez that secured Atlanta's 6-2 victory in Game 2.

■ **Top guns:** Greg Maddux (1-0, 1.13 ERA), Steve Avery (1-0, 0.00), Fred McGriff (.438), Chipper Jones (.438), Lopez (.357), Devereaux (5 RBI), Braves; Barry Larkin (.389), Reds.

■ **MVP:** Devereaux.

Linescores

Game 1—October 10, at Cincinnati
Atlanta ......0 0 0 0 0 0 0 0 1 0 1—2 7 0
Cincinnati ..0 0 0 1 0 0 0 0 0 0 0—1 8 0
Glavine, Pena (8), Wohlers (9), Clontz (11), Avery (11), McMichael (11); Schourek, Brantley (9), Jackson (11). W—Wohlers. L—Jackson. S—McMichael.

Game 2—October 11, at Cincinnati
Atlanta ....1 0 0 1 0 0 0 0 0 4—6 11 1
Cincinnati ....0 0 0 0 2 0 0 0 0 0—2 9 1
Smoltz, Pena (8), McMichael (9), Wohlers (10); Smiley, Burba (6), Jackson (8), Brantley (9), Portugal (10). W—McMichael. L—Portugal. HR—Lopez (Atl.)

Game 3—October 13, at Atlanta
Cincinnati ....0 0 0 0 0 0 0 1 1—2 8 0
Atlanta ....0 0 0 0 0 3 2 0 x—5 12 1
Wells, Hernandez (7), Carrasco (7); Maddux, Wohlers (9). W—Maddux. L—Wells. HR: O'Brien, Jones (Atl.).

Game 4—October 14, at Atlanta
Cincinnati ....0 0 0 0 0 0 0 0 0—0 3 1
Atlanta ....0 0 1 0 0 0 0 5 x—6 12 1
Schourek, Jackson (7), Burba (7); Avery, McMichael (7), Pena (8), Wohlers (9). W—Avery. L—Schourek. HR—Devereaux (Atl.).

WORLD SERIES

■ **Winner:** The Braves needed six games to give Atlanta its first championship in any major sport and the franchise its first World Series title since 1957. The loss extended Cleveland's championship drought to 47 years.

■ **Turning point:** A two-run, sixth-inning homer by Javier Lopez in Game 2. It gave the Braves a 4-3 victory and put the Indians in a two-games-to-none hole.

■ **Memorable moment:** A Series-opening two-hitter by Braves ace Greg Maddux and a Series-closing combined one-hitter by Tom Glavine and Mark Wohlers. The 1-0 finale was decided by a Dave Justice home run.

■ **Top guns:** Glavine (2-0, 1.29 ERA), Wohlers (1.80, 2 sv), Marquis Grissom (.360), Ryan Klesko (.313, 3 HR), Braves; Albert Belle (2 HR), Indians.

■ **MVP:** Glavine.

Linescores

Game 1—October 21, at Atlanta
Cleveland ....1 0 0 0 0 0 0 0 1—2 2 0
Atlanta ....0 1 0 0 0 0 2 0 x—3 3 2
Hershiser, Assenmacher (7), Tavarez (7), Embree (8); Maddux. W—Maddux. L—Hershiser. HR—McGriff (Atl.).

Game 2—October 22, at Atlanta
Cleveland ....0 2 0 0 0 0 1 0 0—3 6 2
Atlanta ....0 0 2 0 0 2 0 0 x—4 8 2
Martinez, Embree (6), Poole (7), Tavarez (8); Glavine, McMichael (7), Pena (7), Wohlers (8). W—Glavine. L—Martinez. S—Wohlers. HR—Murray (Cle.), Lopez (Atl.).

Game 3—October 24, at Cleveland
Atlanta ....1 0 0 0 0 1 1 3 0 0 0—6 12 1
Cleveland ....2 0 2 0 0 0 1 1 0 0 1—7 12 2
Smoltz, Clontz (3), Mercker (5), McMichael (7), Wohlers (8), Pena (11); Nagy, Assenmacher (8), Tavarez (8), Mesa (9). W—Mesa. L—Pena. HR—McGriff, Klesko (Atl.).

Game 4—October 25, at Cleveland
Atlanta ....0 0 0 0 0 1 3 0 1—5 11 1
Cleveland ....0 0 0 0 0 1 0 0 1—2 6 0
Avery, McMichael (7), Wohlers (9), Borbon (9); Hill, Assenmacher (7), Tavarez (8), Embree (8). W—Avery. L—Hill. S—Borbon. HR—Klesko (Atl.); Belle, Ramirez (Cle.).

Game 5—October 26, at Cleveland
Atlanta ....0 0 0 1 1 0 0 0 2—4 7 0
Cleveland ....2 0 0 0 0 2 0 1 x—5 8 1
Maddux, Clontz (8); Hershiser, Mesa (8). W—Hershiser. L—Maddux. S—Mesa. HR—Polonia, Klesko (Atl.); Belle, Thome (Cle.).

Game 6—October 28, at Atlanta
Cleveland.......... 0 0 0 0 0 0 0 0 0—0 1 1
Atlanta .... 0 0 0 0 0 1 0 0 x—1 6 0
Martinez, Poole (5), Hill (7), Embree (7), Tavarez (8), Assenmacher (8); Glavine, Wohlers (9). W—Glavine. L—Poole. S—Wohlers. HR—Justice (Atl.).

Despite the strike-shortened schedule, Cleveland outfielder Albert Belle became the 12th 50-homer man in Major League history.

HISTORY

FINAL STANDINGS

American League

East Division

Team	N.Y.	Bal.	Bos.	Tor.	Det.	Cle.	Chi.	Mil.	Min.	K.C.	Tex.	Sea.	Oak.	Cal.	W	L	Pct.	GB
New York	—	10	6	8	8	9	7	6	7	8	5	3	9	6	92	70	.568	—
Baltimore	3	—	7	8	11	5	4	9	7	9	3	7	9	6	88	74	.543	4.0
Boston	7	6	—	8	12	1	6	7	6	3	6	7	8	8	85	77	.525	7.0
Toronto	5	5	5	—	7	5	5	7	5	8	2	7	8	5	74	88	.457	18.0
Detroit	5	2	1	6	—	3	4	6	6	0	4	6	4	6	53	109	.327	39.0

Central Division

Team	Cle.	Chi.	Mil.	Min.	K.C.	N.Y.	Bal.	Bos.	Tor.	Det.	Tex.	Sea.	Oak.	Cal.	W	L	Pct.	GB
Cleveland	—	8	7	10	7	3	7	11	7	12	4	8	6	9	99	62	.615	—
Chicago	5	—	6	6	7	6	8	6	7	10	8	5	5	6	85	77	.525	14.5
Milwaukee	6	7	—	9	9	6	3	5	5	8	6	4	7	5	80	82	.494	19.5
Minnesota	3	7	4	—	7	5	5	6	8	6	7	6	6	8	78	84	.481	21.5
Kansas City	6	6	4	6	—	4	3	9	5	6	6	7	5	8	75	86	.466	24

West Division

Team	Tex.	Sea.	Oak.	Cal.	N.Y.	Bal.	Bos.	Tor.	Det.	Cle.	Chi.	Mil.	Min.	K.C.	W	L	Pct.	GB
Texas	—	3	6	9	7	10	6	10	9	8	4	7	5	6	90	72	.556	—
Seattle	10	—	5	8	9	5	6	5	6	4	7	9	6	5	85	76	.528	4.5
Oakland	7	8	—	7	3	4	5	4	8	6	7	5	7	7	78	84	.481	12
California	4	5	6	—	7	6	4	7	6	4	6	7	4	4	70	91	.435	19.5

National League

East Division

Team	Atl.	Mon.	Fla.	N.Y.	Phil.	St.L.	Hou.	Cin.	Chi.	Pit.	S.D.	L.A.	Col.	S.F.	W	L	Pct.	GB
Atlanta	—	10	6	7	9	9	6	7	7	9	9	5	5	7	96	66	.593	—
Montreal	3	—	8	7	6	8	9	9	6	7	4	3	9	9	88	74	.543	8
Florida	7	5	—	7	6	6	7	9	6	5	3	6	8	5	80	82	.494	16
New York	6	6	6	—	7	5	4	6	5	8	3	4	5	6	71	91	.438	25
Philadelphia	4	7	7	6	—	4	2	2	6	7	4	6	6	6	67	95	.414	29

Central Division

Team	St.L.	Hou.	Cin.	Chi.	Pit.	Atl.	Mon.	Fla.	N.Y.	Phil.	S.D.	L.A.	Col.	S.F.	W	L	Pct.	GB
St. Louis	—	11	8	8	10	4	4	6	7	8	8	4	4	6	88	74	.543	—
Houston	2	—	6	8	8	6	4	5	8	10	6	6	5	8	82	80	.506	6
Cincinnati	5	7	—	8	5	5	3	3	6	10	9	4	7	9	81	81	.500	7
Chicago	5	5	5	—	4	5	6	6	7	7	6	8	5	7	76	86	.469	12
Pittsburgh	3	5	8	9	—	3	5	7	5	5	4	6	5	8	73	89	.451	15

West Division

Team	S.D.	L.A.	Col.	S.F.	Atl.	Mon.	Fla.	N.Y.	Phil.	St.L.	Hou.	Cin.	Chi.	Pit.	W	L	Pct.	GB
San Diego	—	8	5	11	4	8	9	10	8	4	6	3	6	9	91	71	.562	—
Los Angeles	5	—	7	7	7	9	7	8	7	8	6	8	5	6	90	72	.556	1
Colorado	8	6	—	5	7	3	5	7	6	8	8	6	7	7	83	79	.512	8
San Fran.	2	6	8	—	5	4	7	6	6	7	4	4	5	4	68	94	.420	23

LEADERS

American League
BA: Alex Rodriguez, Sea., .358.
Runs: Alex Rodriguez, Sea., .358.
Hits: Paul Molitor, Min., 225.
TB: Alex Rodriguez, Sea., 379.
HR: Mark McGwire, Oak., 52.
RBI: Albert Belle, Cle., 148.
SB: Kenny Lofton, Cle., 75.
Wins: Andy Pettitte, N.Y., 21.
ERA: Juan Guzman, Tor., 2.93.
CG: Pat Hentgen, Tor., 10.
IP: Pat Hentgen, Tor., 265.2.
SO: Roger Clemens, Bos., 257.
SV: John Wetteland, N.Y., 43.

National League
BA: Tony Gwynn, S.D., .353.
Runs: Ellis Burks, Col., 142.
Hits: Lance Johnson, N.Y., 227.
TB: Ellis Burks, Col., 392
HR: Andres Galarraga, Col., 47.
RBI: Andres Galarraga, Col., 150
SB: Eric Young, Col., 53.
Wins: John Smoltz, Atl., 24.
ERA: Kevin Brown, Fla., 1.89.
CG: Curt Schilling, Phi., 8.
IP: John Smoltz, Atl., 253.2
SO: John Smoltz, Atl., 276.
SV: Jeff Brantley, Cin.; Todd Worrell, L.A., 44.

A.L. 20-game winners
Andy Pettitte, N.Y., 21
Pat Hentgen, Tor., 20

N.L. 20-game winner
John Smoltz, Atl., 24

A.L. 100 RBIs
Albert Belle, Cle., 148
Juan Gonzalez, Tex., 144
Mo Vaughn, Bos., 143
Rafael Palmeiro, Bal., 142
Ken Griffey Jr., Sea., 140
Jay Buhner, Sea., 138
Frank Thomas, Chi., 134
Alex Rodriguez, Sea., 123
John Jaha, Mil., 118
Cecil Fielder, Det.-N.Y., 117
Tino Martinez, N.Y., 117
Bobby Bonilla, Bal., 116
Jim Thome, Cle., 116
Mark McGwire, Oak., 113
Paul Molitor, Min., 113
Manny Ramirez, Cle., 112
Marty Cordova, Min., 111
Brady Anderson, Bal., 110
Joe Carter, Tor., 107
Dean Palmer, Tex., 107
Geronimo Berroa, Oak., 106
Robin Ventura, Chi., 105
Edgar Martinez, Sea., 103
Cal Ripken, Bal., 102
Bernie Williams, N.Y., 102
Ed Sprague, Tor., 101
Danny Tartabull, Chi., 101
Travis Fryman, Det., 100
Rusty Greer, Tex., 100
Terry Steinbach, Oak., 100

N.L. 100 RBIs
Andres Galarraga, Col., 150
Dante Bichette, Col., 141
Ken Caminiti, S.D., 130
Barry Bonds, S.F., 129
Ellis Burks, Col., 128
Jeff Bagwell, Hou., 120
Gary Sheffield, Fla., 120
Bernard Gilkey, N.Y., 117
Derek Bell, Hou., 113
Vinny Castilla, Col., 113
Todd Hundley, N.Y., 112
Eric Karros, L.A., 111
Jeff King, Pit., 111
Chipper Jones, Atl., 110
Fred McGriff, Atl., 107
Mike Piazza, L.A., 105
Brian Jordan, St.L., 104
Henry Rodriguez, Mon., 103
Sammy Sosa, Chi., 100

A.L./N.L. 100 RBIs
Greg Vaughn, Mil.-S.D., 117

A.L. 40 homers
Mark McGwire, Oak., 52
Brady Anderson, Bal., 50
Ken Griffey Jr., Sea., 49
Albert Belle, Cle., 48
Juan Gonzalez, Tex., 47
Jay Buhner, Sea., 44
Mo Vaughn, Bos., 44
Frank Thomas, Chi., 40

N.L. 40 homers
Andres Galarraga, Col., 47
Barry Bonds, S.F., 42
Gary Sheffield, Fla., 42
Todd Hundley, N.Y., 41
Ellis Burks, Col., 40
Ken Caminiti, S.D., 40
Vinny Castilla, Col., 40
Sammy Sosa, Chi., 40

A.L./N.L. 40 homers
Greg Vaughn, Mil.-S.D., 41

Most Valuable Player
A.L.: Juan Gonzalez, OF, Tex.
N.L.: Ken Caminiti, 3B, Hou.

Cy Young Award
A.L.: Pat Hentgen, Tor.
N.L.: John Smoltz, Atl.

Rookie of the Year
A.L.: Derek Jeter, SS, N.Y.
N.L.: Todd Hollandsworth, OF, L.A.

Manager of the Year
A.L.: Johnny Oates, Tex.; Joe Torre, N.Y.
N.L.: Bruce Bochy, S.D.

Hall of Fame additions
Jim Bunning, P, 1955-71
Bill Foster, P, Negro Leagues
Ned Hanlon, manager
Earl Weaver, manager

SIGNIFICANT EVENTS

■ **January:** The Official Playing Rules Committee lowered the strike zone from "a line at the top of the knees" to "a line at the hollow beneath the kneecap."

■ **April 1:** Umpire John McSherry collapsed seven pitches into the opening day game between the Expos and Reds at Cincinnati and died about an hour later from a heart problem. The game was postponed.

■ **June 12:** Reds owner Marge Schott agreed to surrender day-to-day control of the team through the 1998 season as discipline for actions and statements detrimental to baseball.

■ **September 27:** In what would develop into one of the most controversial player-umpire disputes in baseball history, Baltimore second baseman Roberto Alomar spat in the face of umpire John Hirshbeck during a called-strike argument.

■ **November 19:** White Sox owner Jerry Reinsdorf signed Cleveland slugger Albert Belle to the richest contract in baseball history—$50 million over five years.

■ **November 26:** After completing the first full-schedule season since 1993, Major League Baseball and the players' association agreed on a contract that would run through October 31, 2000.

MEMORABLE MOMENTS

■ **September 6:** Baltimore's Eddie Murray connected for his 500th career home run against Detroit and joined 14 other players in that exclusive circle.

■ **September 16:** Minnesota's Paul Molitor became the 21st player to record 3,000 career hits when he tripled in the fifth inning of a game at Kansas City.

■ **September 18:** Boston ace Roger Clemens matched his own major league record when he struck out 20 Tigers in a nine-inning game.

■ **September 29:** Giants slugger Barry Bonds completed the season with 42 homers and 40 stolen bases, joining Jose Canseco as the only members of the 40-40 club.

■ **September 29:** The Orioles, led by Brady Anderson's 50 home runs, finished the season with a one-season record 257.

■ **September 29:** San Diego's Tony Gwynn finished the season with a .353 average and won his seventh N.L. batting title.

ALL-STAR GAME

■ **Winner:** Nine N.L. pitchers combined on a seven hitter as the A.L. lost its third consecutive midsummer classic and saw the N.L.'s All-Star domination grow to 40-26-1.

■ **Key inning:** The second, when the A.L. failed to score after putting its leadoff man on second base and the N.L. stretched its lead to 2-0 on Dodgers catcher Mike Piazza's solo home run.

■ **Memorable moment:** Piazza, who drove in two runs with his homer and a double, holding up the MVP trophy for a large hometown contingent at Philadelphia. Piazza was born in nearby Norristown, Pa., and once served as a bat boy at Veterans Stadium.

■ **Top guns:** Piazza (Dodgers), Lance Johnson (Mets), John Smoltz (Braves), Steve Trachsel (Cubs), N.L.; Kenny Lofton (Indians), A.L.

■ **MVP:** Piazza.

Linescore

July 9, at Philadelphia's Veterans Stadium

A.L. ....0 0 0 0 0 0 0 0 0—0 7 0

N.L. ....1 2 1 0 0 2 0 0 x—6 12 1

Smoltz (Braves), Brown (Marlins) 3, Glavine (Braves) 4, Bottalico (Phillies) 5, P. Martinez (Expos) 6, Trachsel (Cubs) 7, Worrell (Dodgers) 8, Wohlers (Braves) 9, Leiter (Marlins) 9; Nagy (Indians), Finley (Angels) 3, Pavlik (Rangers) 5, Percival (Angels) 7, Hernandez (White Sox) 8. W—Smoltz. L—Nagy. HR—Piazza, Caminiti, N.L.

A.L. DIVISION SERIES

■ **Winners:** The Yankees, bidding for their 34th World Series appearance, ruined the Rangers' Post Season debut with a four-game victory; the wild-card Orioles pulled off a surprising four-game upset of the Indians.

■ **Turning points:** Throwing errors turned the tide for both the Yankees and Orioles. New York took control in the 10th inning of Game 2 when the Rangers failed to score after loading the bases in the top of the inning and the Yankees won in the bottom of the frame on third baseman Dean Palmer's wild throw. The Orioles took control when Cleveland catcher Sandy Alomar fired wildly on an eighth-inning home-to-first double-play attempt in Game 2, allowing the winning run to score in an eventual 7-4 victory. The Indians argued that batter B.J. Surhoff ran out of the baseline, causing Alomar's miscue.

■ **Memorable moments:** The final out of Texas' 6-2 Game 1 victory over the Yankees—the first postseason win in Rangers history. The Game 4 heroics of Baltimore second baseman Roberto Alomar, who tied the game with a ninth-inning single and clinched the series victory with a 12th-inning home run. It was sweet vindication for Alomar, who had been the center of controversy since a late-season spitting incident involving umpire John Hirschbeck.

■ **Memorable performances:** Bernie Williams batted .467, hit three home runs, including two in the decisive fourth game, and drove in five runs for the Yankees; Yankee relievers Mariano Rivera, David Weathers, Jeff Nelson and John Wetteland combined for 17⅓ scoreless innings, allowing only five hits; Juan Gonzalez set a record pace for the Rangers, hitting .438 with five home runs and nine RBIs; B.J. Surhoff hit three home runs and Bobby Bonilla hit two, including a grand slam, for the Orioles; Albert Belle hit a Game 3 grand slam for the Indians.

Linescores

Baltimore vs. Cleveland

Game 1—October 1, at Baltimore

Cleveland ..0 1 0 2 0 0 1 0 0— 4 10 0

Baltimore....1 1 2 0 0 5 1 0 x—10 12 1

Nagy, Embree (6), Shuey (6), Tavarez (8); Wells, Orosco (7), Mathews (7), Rhodes (8), Myers (9). W—Wells. L—Nagy. HR—Ramirez (Cle.); Anderson, Bonilla, Surhoff 2 (Bal.).

Game 2—October 2, at Baltimore

Cleveland ......0 0 0 0 0 3 0 1 0—4 8 2

Baltimore........1 0 0 0 3 0 0 3 x—7 9 0

Hershiser, Plunk (6), Assenmacher (8), Tavaraz (8); Erickson, Orosco (7), Benitez (8), Myers (9). W—Benitez. L—Plunk. S—Myers. HR—Belle (Cle.); Anderson (Bal.).

Game 3—October 4, at Cleveland

Baltimore ....0 1 0 3 0 0 0 0 0—4 8 2

Cleveland......1 2 0 1 0 0 4 1 x—9 10 0

Mussina, Orosco (7), Benitez (7), Rhodes (8), Mathews (8); McDowell, Embree (6), Shuey (7), Assenmacher (7), Plunk (8), Mesa (9). W—Assenmacher. L—Orosco. HR—Surhoff (Bal.); Belle, Ramirez (Cle.).

Game 4—October 5, at Cleveland

Bal. 0 2 0 0 0 0 0 0 1 0 0 1—4 14 1

Cle. ..0 0 0 2 1 0 0 0 0 0 0 0—3 7 1

Wells, Mathews (8), Orosco (9), Benitez (10), Myers (12); Nagy, Embree (7), Shuey (7), Assenmacher (7), Plunk (8), Mesa (9), Ogea (12). W—Benitez. L—Mesa. S—Myers. HR—R. Alomar, Palmeiro, Bonilla (Bal.).

New York vs. Texas

Game 1—October 1, at New York

Texas............0 0 0 5 0 1 0 0 0—6 8 0

New York......1 0 0 1 0 0 0 0 0—2 10 0

Burkett; Cone, Lloyd (7), Weathers (8). W—Burkett. L—Cone. HR—Gonzalez, Palmer (Tex.).

Game 2—October 2, at New York

Texas0 1 3 0 0 0 0 0 0 0 0 0—4 8 1

N.Y. ..0 1 0 1 0 0 1 1 0 0 0 1—5 8 0

Hill, Cook (7), Russell (8), Stanton (10), Henneman (12); Pettitte, M. Rivera (7), Wetteland (10), Lloyd (12), Nelson (12), Rogers (12), Boehringer (12). W—Boehringer. L—Stanton. HR—Gonzalez 2 (Tex.); Fielder (N.Y.).

Game 3—October 4, at Texas

New York.........1 0 0 0 0 0 0 0 2—3 7 1

Texas..............0 0 0 1 1 0 0 0 0—2 6 1

Key, Nelson (6), Wetteland (9); Oliver, Henneman (9), Stanton (9). W—Nelson. L—Oliver. S–Wetteland. HR—Williams (N.Y.); Gonzalez (Tex.).

Game 4—October 5, at Texas

New York......0 0 0 3 1 0 1 0 1—6 12 1

Texas............0 2 2 0 0 0 0 0 0—4 9 0

Rogers, Boehringer (3), Weathers (4), M. Rivera (7), Wetteland (9); Witt, Patterson (4), Cook (4), Pavlik (5), Vosberg (7), Russell (7), Stanton (8), Henneman (9). W—Weathers. L—Pavlik. S—Wetteland. HR—Williams 2 (N.Y.); Gonzalez (Tex.).

N.L. DIVISION SERIES

■ **Winners:** The Braves continued their quest for back-to-back World Series titles with a sweep of the Dodgers; St. Louis matched that 1-2-3 effort against San Diego.

■ **Turning points:** For the Braves, catcher Javy Lopez's Game 1-winning 10th-inning home run in a 2-1 victory. The Cardinals took control of their series in the opening inning of Game 1 when Gary Gaetti hit a three-run homer, giving pitcher Todd Stottlemyre all the runs he would need for a 3-1 victory.
■ **Memorable moments:** The Braves put the Dodgers away in the seventh inning of Game 2 when Fred McGriff and Jermaine Dye hit solo home runs, wiping out a 2-1 deficit and setting up Greg Maddux for a 3-2 victory. Cardinals right fielder Brian Jordan finished off the Padres in Game 3 with a great run-saving catch in the eighth inning and a game-winning two-run homer in the ninth.
■ **Top performances:** The Braves' pitching staff, with starters John Smoltz, Maddux and Tom Glavine working 22⅔ innings, posted a sparkling 0.96 ERA against the Dodgers.
St. Louis' Ron Gant batted .400, hit a home run and drove in four runs against the Padres and closer Dennis Eckersley saved all three victories.

Linescores

St. Louis vs. San Diego

Game 1—October 1, at St. Louis
San Diego ......0 0 0 0 0 1 0 0 0—1 8 1
St. Louis ....3 0 0 0 0 0 0 0 x—3 6 0
Hamilton, Blair (7); Stottlemyre, Honeycutt (7), Eckersley (8). W—Stottlemyre. L—Hamilton. S—Eckersley. HR—Henderson (S.D.); Gaetti (St.L.).

Game 2—October 3, at St. Louis
San Diego ....0 0 0 0 1 2 0 1 0—4
St. Louis ....0 0 1 0 3 0 0 1 x—5
Sanders, Veras (5), Worrell (6), Bochtler (8), Hoffman (8); An. Benes, Honeycutt (8), Eckersley (9). W—Honeycutt. L—Bochtler. S—Eckersley. HR—Caminiti (S.D.).

Game 3—October 5, at San Diego
St. Louis ....1 0 0 0 0 3 1 0 2—7
San Diego ....0 2 1 1 0 0 0 1 0—5
Osborne, Petkovsek (5), Honeycutt (7), Mathews (8), Eckersley (9); Ashby, Worrell (6), Valenzuela (8), Veras (8), Hoffman (9). W—Mathews. L—Hoffman. S—Eckersley. HR—Gant, Jordan (St.L.); Caminiti 2 (S.D.).

Atlanta vs. Los Angeles

Game 1—October 2, at Los Angeles
Atlanta ....0 0 0 1 0 0 0 0 0 1—2 4 1
Los Angeles ....0 0 0 0 1 0 0 0 0 0—1 5 0
Smoltz, Wohlers (10); Martinez, Radinsky (9), Osuna (9). W—Smoltz. L—Osuna. S—Wohlers. HR—Lopez (Atl.).

Game 2—October 3, at Los Angeles
Atlanta............0 1 0 0 0 0 2 0 0—3 5 2
Los Angeles....1 0 0 1 0 0 0 0 0—2 3 0
Maddux, McMichael (8), Wohlers (9); Valdes, Astacio (7), Worrell (9). W—Maddux. L—Valdes. S—Wohlers. HR—McGriff, Klesko, Dye (Atl.).

Game 3—October 5, at Atlanta
Los Angeles....0 0 0 0 0 0 1 1 0—2 6 1
Atlanta ....1 0 0 4 0 0 0 0 x—5 7 0
Nomo, Guthrie (4), Candiotti (5), Radinsky (7), Osuna (8), Dreifort (8); Glavine, McMichael (7), Bielecki (8), Wohlers (8). W—Glavine. L—Nomo. S—Wohlers. HR—C. Jones (Atl.).

ALCS

■ **Winner:** The Yankees overpowered Baltimore, the most prolific home run team in baseball history, and earned the franchise's 34th pennant. The five-game victory set up the Yankees' first World Series appearance since 1981.
■ **Turning point:** The eighth inning of Game 3, when the Yankees, trailing 2-1, struck for four two-out runs against Orioles ace Mike Mussina. The key plays were Bernie Williams' game-tying single, third baseman Todd Zeile's error and Cecil Fielder's two-run homer.
■ **Memorable moment:** The eighth inning of Game 1, when 12-year-old fan Jeff Maier reached over Yankee Stadium's right field wall and unwittingly set the course for the series. The Orioles held a 4-3 advantage when shortstop Derek Jeter hit a fly ball to deep right that backed Baltimore outfielder Tony Tarasco to the wall. As Tarasco reached up in an attempt to make the catch, Maier stuck his glove over the wall and pulled the ball into the stands. The Orioles argued vehemently for fan interference, but umpire Richie Garcia ruled it a game-tying home run and the Yankees won in the 11th on a Williams home run. Maier became an instant national celebrity.
■ **Top guns:** Williams (.474, 2 HR, 6 RBI), Jeter (.417), Darryl Strawberry (.417, 3 HR), Cecil Fielder (8 RBI), Mariano Rivera (0.00 ERA), Yankees; Zeile (3 HR, 5 RBI), Rafael Palmeiro (2 HR), Orioles.
MVP: Williams.

Linescores

Game 1—October 9, at New York
Bal. ....0 1 1 1 0 1 0 0 0 0 0—4 11 1
N.Y. ....1 1 0 0 0 0 1 1 0 0 1—5 11 0
Erickson, Orosco (7), Benitez (7), Rhodes (8), Mathews (9), Myers (9); Pettitte, Nelson (8), Wetteland (9), M. Rivera (10). W—M. Rivera. L—Myers. HR—Anderson, Palmeiro (Bal.); Jeter, Williams (N.Y.).

Game 2—October 10, at New York
Baltimore......0 0 2 0 0 0 2 1 0—5 10 0
New York......2 0 0 0 0 0 1 0 0—3 11 1
Wells, Mills (7), Orosco (7), Myers (9), Benitez (9); Cone, Nelson (7), Lloyd (8), Weathers (9). W—Wells. L—Nelson. S—Benitez. HR—Zeile, Palmeiro (Bal.).

Game 3—October 11, at Baltimore
New York........0 0 0 1 0 0 0 4 0—5 8 0
Baltimore........2 0 0 0 0 0 0 0 0—2 3 2
Key, Wetteland (9); Mussina, Orosco (8), Mathews (9). W—Key. L—Mussina. S—Wetteland. HR—Fielder (N.Y.); Zeile (Bal.).

Game 4—October 12, at Baltimore
New York......2 1 0 2 0 0 0 3 0—8 9 0
Baltimore......1 0 1 2 0 0 0 0 0—4 11 0
Rogers, Weathers (4), Lloyd (6), M. Rivera (7), Wetteland (9); Coppinger, Rhodes (6), Mills (7), Orosco (8), Benitez (8), Mathews (9). W—Weathers. L—Coppinger. HR—Williams, Strawberry 2, O'Neill (N.Y.); Hoiles (Bal.).

Game 5—October 13, at Baltimore
New York......0 0 6 0 0 0 0 0 0—6 11 0
Baltimore......0 0 0 0 0 1 0 1 2—4 4 1
Pettitte, Wetteland (9); Erickson, Rhodes (6), Mills (7), Myers (8). W—Pettitte. L—Erickson. HR—Fielder, Strawberry, Leyritz (N.Y.); Zeile, Bonilla, Murray (Bal.).

NLCS

■ **Winner:** The Braves, hoping to become the N.L.'s first repeat World Series champion in 20 years, recovered from a three-games-to-one deficit in a tense seven-game victory over the Cardinals. The Braves, on the brink of elimination, outscored St. Louis 32-1 over the final three games to earn their eighth fall classic appearance and fourth of the decade.
■ **Turning point:** The first inning of Game 5, when the Braves scored five runs off Cardinals starter Todd Stottlemyre. That 14-0 victory served notice that rumors of the Braves' demise were premature.
■ **Memorable moment:** An eighth-inning Game 4 home run by St. Louis' Brian Jordan, the blow that gave ecstatic home fans a 4-3 victory and put the Cardinals on the brink of a 16th World Series appearance.
■ **Top guns:** Javier Lopez (.542, 6 RBI), Mark Lemke (.444), Fred McGriff (2 HR, 7 RBI), John Smoltz (2-0, 1.20 ERA), Braves; Royce Clayton (.350), Ron Gant (2 HR, 4 RBI), Cardinals.
■ **MVP:** Lopez.

Linescores

Game 1—October 9, at Atlanta
St. Louis ....0 1 0 0 0 0 1 0 0—2 5 1
Atlanta............0 0 0 0 2 0 0 2 x—4 9 0
An. Benes, Petkovsek (7), Fossas (8), Mathews (8); Smoltz, Wohlers (9). W—Smoltz. L—Petkovsek. S—Wohlers.

Game 2—October 10, at Atlanta
St. Louis ......1 0 2 0 0 0 5 0 0—8 11 2
Atlanta..........0 0 2 0 0 1 0 0 0—3 5 2
Stottlemyre, Petkovsek (7), Honeycutt (8), Eckersley (8); Maddux, McMichael (7), Neagle (8), Avery (9). W—Stottlemyre. L—Maddux. HR—Gaetti (St.L.); Grissom (Atl.).

Game 3—October 12, at St. Louis
Atlanta............1 0 0 0 0 0 0 1 0—2 8 1
St. Louis ....2 0 0 0 0 1 0 0 x—3 7 0
Glavine, Bielecki (7), McMichael (8); Osborne, Petkovsek (8), Honeycutt (9), Eckersley (9). W—Osborne. L—Glavine. S—Eckersley. HR—Gant 2 (St.L.).

Game 4—October 13, at St. Louis
Atlanta............0 1 0 0 0 2 0 1 0—3 9 1
St. Louis ....0 0 0 0 0 0 3 1 x—4 5 0
Neagle, McMichael (7), Wohlers (8); An. Benes, Fossas (6), Mathews (6), Al. Benes (6), Honeycutt (8), Eckersley (8). W—Eckersley. L—McMichael. HR—Lemke, Klesko (Atl.); Jordan (St.L.).

Game 5—October 14, at St. Louis
Atlanta........5 2 0 3 1 0 0 1 2—14 22 0
St. Louis ....0 0 0 0 0 0 0 0 0— 0 7 0
Smoltz, Bielecki (8), Wade (9), Clontz (9); Stottlemyre, Jackson (2), Fossas (5), Petkovsek (7), Honeycutt (9). W—Smoltz. L—Stottlemyre. HR—McGriff, Lopez (Atl.).

Game 6—October16, at Atlanta
St. Louis ....0 0 0 0 0 0 0 1 0—1 6 1
Atlanta............0 1 0 0 1 0 0 1 x—3 7 0
Al. Benes, Fossas (6), Petkovsek (6), Stottlemyre (8); Maddux, Wohlers (8). W—Maddux. L—Al. Benes. S—Wohlers.

Game 7—October 17, at Atlanta
St. Louis ....0 0 0 0 0 0 0 0 0— 0 4 2
Atlanta ....6 0 0 4 0 3 2 0 x—15 17 0
Osborne, An. Benes (1), Petkovsek (6), Honeycutt (6), Fossas (8); Glavine, Bielecki (8), Avery (9). W—Glavine. L—Osborne. HR—McGriff, Lopez, A. Jones (Atl.).

WORLD SERIES

■ **Winner:** The Yankees, missing from the World Series scene since 1981, collected their franchise-record 23rd championship when they spotted Atlanta two wins and stormed back to post an impressive six-game victory. The New York triumph dashed the Braves' hope of becoming the N.L.'s first back-to-back fall classic winner in 20 years.
■ **Turning point:** The eighth inning of Game 4, when catcher Jim Leyritz rocked Braves closer Mark Wohlers for a three-run, game-tying homer that set up an eventual 8-6 Yankees victory. The Braves had led the game 6-0 and appeared on the verge of taking a three games-to-one series lead.
■ **Memorable moment:** Right fielder Paul O'Neill's over-the-shoulder Game 5-ending catch that saved a 1-0 victory for the Yankees and Andy Pettitte. The catch denied Braves pinch-hitter Luis Polonia extra bases with runners on first and third.
■ **Top guns:** Cecil Fielder (.391), Jeff Nelson (3 games, 0.00 ERA), Mariano Rivera (4 games, 1.59 ERA), John Wetteland (4 saves, 2.08 ERA), Yankees; Grissom (.444), A. Jones (.400, 2 HR, 6 RBI), Fred McGriff (2 HR, 6 RBI), John Smoltz (1-1, 0.64 ERA), Braves.
■ **MVP:** Wetteland.

Linescores

Game 1—October 20, at New York
Atlanta........0 2 6 0 1 3 0 0 0—12 13 0
New York....0 0 0 0 1 0 0 0 0— 1 4 1
Smoltz, McMichael (7), Neagle (8), Wade (9), Clontz (9); Pettitte, Boehringer (3), Weathers (6), Nelson (8), Wetteland (9). W—Smoltz. L—Pettitte. HR—McGriff, A. Jones 2 (Atl.).

Game 2—October 21, at New York
Atlanta..........1 0 1 0 1 1 0 0 0—4 10 0
New York......0 0 0 0 0 0 0 0 0—0 7 1
Maddux, Wohlers (9); Key, Lloyd (7), Nelson (7), M. Rivera (9). W—Maddux. L—Key.

Game 3—October 22, at Atlanta
New York........1 0 0 1 0 0 0 3 0—5 8 1
Atlanta............0 0 0 0 0 1 0 1 0—2 6 1
Cone, M. Rivera (7), Lloyd (8), Wetteland (9); Glavine, McMichael (8), Clontz (8), Bielecki (9). W—Cone. L—Glavine. S—Wetteland. HR—Williams (N.Y.).

Game 4—October 23, at Atlanta
N.Y. ....0 0 0 0 0 3 0 3 0 2—8 12 0
Atlanta....0 4 1 0 1 0 0 0 0 0—6 9 2
Rogers, Boehringer (3), Weathers (5), Nelson (6), M. Rivera (8), Lloyd (9), Wetteland (10); Neagle, Wade (6), Bielecki (6), Wohlers (8), Avery (10), Clontz (10). W—Lloyd. L—Avery. S—Wetteland. HR—Leyritz (N.Y.); McGriff (Atl.).

Game 5—October 24, at Atlanta
New York........0 0 0 1 0 0 0 0 0—1 4 1
Atlanta............0 0 0 0 0 0 0 0 0—0 5 1
Pettitte, Wetteland (9); Smoltz, Wohlers (9). W—Pettitte. L—Smoltz. S—Wetteland.

Game 6—October 26, at New York
Atlanta............0 0 0 1 0 0 0 0 1—2 8 0
New York........0 0 3 0 0 0 0 0 x—3 8 1
Maddux, Wohlers (8); Key, Weathers (6), Lloyd (6), M. Rivera (7), Wetteland (9). W—Key. L—Maddux. S—Wetteland.

Talented Yankees lefthander Andy Pettitte won an American League-high 21 games in 1996 and earned a World Series ring to boot.

FINAL STANDINGS

American League

East Division

Team	Bal.	NYY	Det.	Bos.	Tor.	Cle.	ChW	Mil.	Min.	K.C.	Sea.	Ana.	Tex.	Oak.	Atl.	Fla.	NYM	Mtl.	Phi.	W	L	Pct.	GB
Baltimore	—	8	6	5	6	6	5	5	10	7	7	7	10	8	3	0	1	1	3	98	64	.605	—
New York	4	—	10	8	7	6	9	7	8	8	4	7	7	6	1	1	2	1	0	96	66	.593	2
Detroit	6	2	—	7	6	5	7	4	4	6	4	6	7	7	2	1	3	0	2	79	83	.488	19
Boston	7	4	5	—	6	6	3	8	8	3	7	5	3	7	0	1	2	0	3	78	84	.481	20
Toronto	6	5	6	6	—	5	6	4	8	6	3	5	7	5	1	0	0	1	2	76	86	.469	22

Central Division

Team	Bal.	NYY	Det.	Bos.	Tor.	Cle.	ChW	Mil.	Min.	K.C.	Sea.	Ana.	Tex.	Oak.	Hou.	Pit.	Cin.	St.L.	ChC	W	L	Pct.	GB
Cleveland	5	5	6	5	6	—	7	8	8	8	3	4	5	7	2	2	1	2	2	86	75	.534	—
Chicago	6	2	4	8	5	5	—	4	6	11	5	5	3	8	3	0	2	1	2	80	81	.497	6
Milwaukee	6	4	7	3	7	4	7	—	5	6	5	4	7	5	2	2	0	3	1	78	83	.484	8
Minnesota	1	3	7	3	3	4	6	7	—	5	5	7	3	7	2	2	2	0	1	68	94	.420	18½
Kansas City	4	3	5	8	5	3	1	6	7	—	5	5	6	3	2	2	1	1	0	67	94	.416	19

West Division

Team	Bal.	NYY	Det.	Bos.	Tor.	Cle.	ChW	Mil.	Min.	K.C.	Sea.	Ana.	Tex.	Oak.	S.F.	L.A.	Col.	S.D.	W	L	Pct.	GB
Seattle	4	7	7	4	8	8	6	6	6	6	—	6	8	7	1	3	2	1	90	72	.556	—
Anaheim	4	4	5	6	6	7	6	7	4	6	6	—	8	11	1	0	1	2	84	78	.519	6
Texas	1	4	4	8	4	6	8	4	8	5	4	4	—	7	2	3	3	2	77	85	.475	13
Oakland	3	5	4	4	6	4	3	6	4	8	5	1	5	—	2	1	1	3	65	97	.401	25

National League

East Division

Team	Atl.	Fla.	NYM	Mtl.	Phi.	Hou.	Pit.	Cin.	St.L.	ChC	S.F.	L.A.	Col.	S.D.	Bal.	NYY	Det.	Bos.	Tor.	W	L	Pct.	GB
Atlanta	—	4	5	10	10	7	5	9	8	9	7	6	5	8	0	2	1	3	2	101	61	.623	—
Florida	8	—	4	7	6	7	7	6	5	9	5	7	4	5	3	2	2	2	3	92	70	.568	9
New York	7	8	—	7	7	4	7	9	9	5	3	5	5	5	2	1	0	1	3	88	74	.543	13
Montreal	2	5	5	—	6	3	5	5	6	7	6	4	4	8	2	2	3	3	2	78	84	.481	23
Philadelphia	2	6	5	6	—	7	5	3	6	5	3	1	7	7	0	3	1	0	1	68	94	.420	33

Central Division

Team	Atl.	Fla.	NYM	Mtl.	Phi.	Hou.	Pit.	Cin.	St.L.	ChC	S.F.	L.A.	Col.	S.D.	Cle.	ChW	Mil.	Min.	K.C.	W	L	Pct.	GB
Houston	4	4	7	8	4	—	6	7	9	9	3	7	6	6	1	0	1	1	1	84	78	.519	—
Pittsburgh	6	4	4	6	6	6	—	4	9	5	8	2	7	5	1	3	1	1	1	79	83	.488	5
Cincinnati	2	5	2	6	8	5	8	—	6	5	4	6	5	5	2	1	3	1	2	76	86	.469	8
St. Louis	3	6	2	5	5	3	3	6	—	8	8	6	4	6	1	2	0	3	2	73	89	.451	11
Chicago	2	2	6	4	6	3	7	7	4	—	5	5	2	6	1	1	2	2	3	68	94	.420	16

West Division

Team	Atl.	Fla.	NYM	Mtl.	Phi.	Hou.	Pit.	Cin.	St.L.	ChC	S.F.	L.A.	Col.	S.D.	Sea.	Ana.	Tex.	Oak.	W	L	Pct.	GB
San Fran.	4	6	8	5	8	8	3	7	3	6	—	6	8	8	3	3	2	2	90	72	.556	—
Los Angeles	5	4	6	7	10	4	9	5	5	6	6	—	7	5	1	4	1	3	88	74	.543	2
Colorado	6	7	6	7	4	5	4	6	7	9	4	5	—	4	2	3	1	3	83	79	.512	7
San Diego	3	6	6	3	4	5	6	6	5	5	4	7	8	—	3	2	2	1	76	86	.469	14

SIGNIFICANT EVENTS

■ **April 4:** The Atlanta Braves christened new Turner Field with a 5-4 come-from-behind victory over Chicago.

■ **April 15:** Celebrating the 50th anniversary of Jackie Robinson's debut as the first black Major League player of the century, baseball announced every team would retire Robinson's uniform No. 42.

■ **April 19:** St. Louis recorded a 1-0 victory over San Diego in the opener of the three-game Paradise Series—the first Major League regular-season game ever played in Hawaii.

■ **April 20:** The Chicago Cubs defeated the New York Mets in the second game of a doubleheader, ending their season-opening losing streak at 14 games.

■ **June 12:** The San Francisco Giants posted a 4-3 victory at Texas in the first interleague game in baseball history.

■ **November 5:** The Milwaukee Brewers agreed to move from the American League to the National League Central Division, completing a re-alignment that placed Tampa Bay in the A.L. East, moved Detroit to the A.L. Central and positioned Arizona in the N.L. West.

■ **November 18:** Tampa Bay opened the expansion draft by selecting pitcher Tony Saunders off the Florida roster and Arizona followed by grabbing Cleveland pitcher Brian Anderson.

MEMORABLE MOMENTS

■ **June 30:** Texas' Bobby Witt became the first American League pitcher to hit a home run since October 1972 when he connected off Los Angeles' Ismael Valdes in an interleague contest.

■ **August 8:** For the second time in six weeks, Seattle lefthander Randy Johnson struck out 19 batters in a game—the first time a pitcher had reached that plateau twice in a season. Johnson shut out Chicago, 5-0.

■ **September 20:** Colorado's Larry Walker doubled during a victory over Los Angeles, becoming the first National League player to reach 400 total bases in a season since Hank Aaron in 1959.

■ **September 26:** Philadelphia's Curt Schilling struck out six Marlins in a 5-3 victory over Florida, setting a National League record for most strikeouts by a righthander with 319.

■ **September 27:** San Francisco clinched the N.L. West title with a 6-1 victory over San Diego, becoming the fourth last-to-first team of the century.

■ **September 28:** St. Louis' Mark McGwire, the second player in history to record back-to-back 50-homer seasons, connected for No. 58 in a final-day victory over Chicago—matching Jimmie Foxx and Hank Greenberg for the single-season record by a righthanded hitter. The total topped Seattle's Ken Griffey Jr. by two and was the highest in one season since Roger Maris hit his record 61 in 1961.

■ **September 28:** San Diego's Tony Gwynn completed a .372 season and captured his N.L.-record tying eighth batting championship.

ALL-STAR GAME

■ **Winner:** The A.L. snapped a three-year losing streak with a 3-1 victory behind the late-inning heroics of hometown Cleveland catcher Sandy Alomar and the three-hit work of an eight-man pitching parade.

■ **Key inning:** The fourth, when the N.L. ran itself out of a potential big inning that opened with walks to San Francisco's Barry Bonds and Los Angeles' Mike Piazza. After Bonds had advanced to third on a fly ball by Houston's Jeff Bagwell, Piazza was caught trying to advance to second on a ball that momentarily eluded Rangers catcher Ivan Rodriguez. Larry Walker grounded out to end the N.L.'s only serious threat of the game.

■ **Memorable moment:** Alomar, who entered the midsummer classic with a 30-game hitting streak, broke a 1-1 tie with a seventh-inning two-run homer—in his only at-bat. The blow wiped out a game-tying solo homer in the top of the inning by Atlanta catcher Javy Lopez and earned Alomar home-field MVP honors.

■ **Top guns:** S. Alomar (Indians), Edgar Martinez (Mariners), Brady Anderson (Orioles), Randy Johnson (Mariners), A.L.; Lopez (Braves), Curt Schilling (Phillies), N.L.

■ **MVP:** S. Alomar.

Linescore

July 8 at Cleveland's Jacobs Field

N.L. ....0 0 0 0 0 0 1 0 0—1 3 0
A.L. ....0 1 0 0 0 0 2 0 x—3 7 0

Maddux (Braves), Schilling (Phillies) 3, Brown (Marlins) 5, P. Martinez (Expos) 6, Estes (Giants) 7, B. Jones (Mets) 8; R. Johnson (Mariners), Clemens (Blue Jays) 3, Cone (Yankees) 4, Thompson (Tigers) 5, Hentgen (Blue Jays) 6, Rosado (Royals) 7, Myers (Orioles) 8, Rivera (Yankees) 9. W—Rosado. L—Estes. HR—E. Martinez, S. Alomar, A.L.; Lopez, N.L.

LEADERS

American League
BA: Frank Thomas, Chi., .347.
Runs: Ken Griffey Jr., Sea., 125.
Hits: Nomar Garciaparra, Bos., 209.
TB: Ken Griffey Jr., Sea., 393.
HR: Ken Griffey Jr., Sea., 56.
RBI: Ken Griffey Jr., Sea., 147.
SB: Brian Hunter, Det., 74.
Wins: Roger Clemens, Tor., 21.
ERA: Roger Clemens, Tor., 2.05.
CG: Roger Clemens, Tor.; Pat Hentgen, Tor., 9.
IP: Roger Clemens, Tor.; Pat Hentgen, Tor., 264.0.
SO: Roger Clemens, Tor., 292.
SV: Randy Myers, Bal., 45.

National League
BA: Tony Gwynn, S.D., .372.
Runs: Craig Biggio, Hou., 146.
Hits: Tony Gwynn, S.D., 220.
TB: Larry Walker, Col., 409.
HR: Larry Walker, Col., 49.
RBI: Larry Walker, Col., 140.
SB: Tony Womack, Pit., 60.
Wins: Denny Neagle, Atl., 20.
ERA: Pedro J. Martinez, Mon., 1.90.
CG: Pedro J. Martinez, Mon., 13.
IP: John Smoltz, Atl., 256.0.
SO: Curt Schilling, Phi., 319.
SV: Jeff Shaw, Cin., 42.

A.L. 20-game winners
Roger Clemens, Tor., 21
Randy Johnson, Sea., 20
Brad Radke, Min., 20

N.L. 20-game winner
Denny Neagle, Atl., 20

A.L. 100 RBIs
Ken Griffey Jr., Sea., 147
Tino Martinez, N.Y., 141
Juan Gonzalez, Tex., 131
Tim Salmon, Ana., 129
Frank Thomas, Chi., 125
Tony Clark, Det., 117
Paul O'Neill, N.Y., 117
Albert Belle, Chi., 116
Jeff King, K.C., 112
Rafael Palmeiro, Bal., 110
Jay Buhner, Sea., 109
Edgar Martinez, Sea., 108
Matt Williams, Cle., 105
Joe Carter, Tor., 102
Travis Fryman, Det., 102
Jim Thome, Cle., 102
Bobby Higginson, Det., 101
David Justice, Cle., 101
Bernie Williams, N.Y., 100

N.L. 100 RBIs
Andres Galarraga, Col., 140
Jeff Bagwell, Hou., 135
Larry Walker, Col., 130
Mike Piazza, L.A., 124
Jeff Kent, S.F., 121
Tony Gwynn, S.D., 119
Sammy Sosa, Chi., 119
Dante Bichette, Col., 118
Moises Alou, Fla., 115
Vinny Castilla, Col., 113
Chipper Jones, Atl., 111
Eric Karros, L.A., 104
J.T. Snow, S.F., 104
John Olerud, N.Y., 102
Barry Bonds, S.F., 101

A.L./N.L. 100 RBIs
Mark McGwire, Oak.-St.L., 123

A.L. 40 homers
Ken Griffey Jr., Sea., 56
Tino Martinez, N.Y., 44
Juan Gonzalez, Tex., 42
Jay Buhner, Sea., 40
Jim Thome, Cle., 40

N.L. 40 homers
Larry Walker, Col., 49
Jeff Bagwell, Hou., 43
Andres Galarraga, Col., 41
Barry Bonds, S.F., 40
Vinny Castilla, Col., 40
Mike Piazza, L.A., 40

A.L./N.L. 40 homers
Mark McGwire, Oak.-St.L., 58

Most Valuable Player
A.L.: Ken Griffey Jr., OF, Sea.
N.L.: Larry Walker, OF, Col.

Cy Young Award
A.L.: Roger Clemens, Tor.
N.L.: Pedro Martinez, Mon.

Rookie of the Year
A.L.: Nomar Garciaparra, SS, Bos.
N.L.: Scott Rolen, 3B, Phi.

Manager of the Year
A.L.: Davey Johnson, Bal.
N.L.: Dusty Baker, S.F.

Hall of Fame additions
Nellie Fox, 2B, 1947-65.
Tom Lasorda, manager
Phil Niekro, P, 1964-87.
Willie Wells, IF-P, Negro Leagues

A.L. DIVISION SERIES

■ **Winners:** Baltimore claimed a surprisingly easy four-game victory over Seattle and Cleveland survived a comeback-filled five-game battle against the wild-card New York Yankees. The Indians' victory set up a grudge match with the Orioles, who had eliminated them in a 1996 Division Series.

■ **Turning points:** The Orioles claimed their second straight A.L. Championship Series berth because of their ability to beat Mariners ace Randy Johnson. Baltimore scored five earned runs in Johnson's five Game 1 innings en route to a 9-3 victory and then handed the big lefthander a 3-1 defeat in the Game 4 clincher. The Indians advanced because they finally were able to break the stranglehold of a powerful New York bullpen that had worked 11⅔ scoreless innings entering Game 4. Cleveland scored single runs in the eighth and ninth innings off Mariano Rivera and Ramiro Mendoza to claim a 3-2 Game 4 win and prevailed in a 4-3 clincher behind the pitching of rookie Jaret Wright.

■ **Memorable moments:** The Game 4 home run of light-hitting Baltimore second baseman Jeff Reboulet, who also hit two regular-season homers off the intimidating Johnson. The consecutive Game 1 home runs by Yankees Tim Raines, Derek Jeter and Paul O'Neill, a postseason record that helped the New Yorkers rally for an 8-6 victory. Omar Vizquel's ninth-inning single that completed the Indians' rally for a series-tying Game 4 victory.

■ **Memorable performances:** Geronimo Berroa hit a pair of home runs, including one in the decisive 3-1 series-clinching victory, and batted .385 for the Orioles; Baltimore righthander Mike Mussina recorded two wins and a 1.93 ERA while outdueling Mariners ace Johnson; Yankees right fielder O'Neill batted .421 with two homers, including a Game 3 grand slam, and seven RBIs against the Indians; catcher Sandy Alomar hit a pair of home runs and the 21-year-old Wright won twice for Cleveland.

Linescores

Baltimore vs. Seattle

Game 1—October 1, at Seattle
Baltimore......0 0 1 0 4 4 0 0 0—9 13 0
Seattle..........0 0 0 1 0 0 1 0 1—3 7 1
Mussina, Orosco (8), Benitez (9); Johnson, Timlin (6), Spoljaric (6), Wells (7), Charlton (8). W—Mussina. L—Johnson. HR—Berroa, Hoiles (Bal.); Martinez, Buhner, Rodriguez (Sea.).

Game 2—October 2, at Seattle
Baltimore......0 1 0 0 2 0 2 4 0—9 14 0
Seattle..........2 0 0 0 0 0 1 0 0—3 9 0
Erickson, Benitez (7), Orosco (8), Myers (9); Moyer, Spoljaric (5), Ayala (7), Charlton (8), Slocumb (9). W—Erickson. L—Moyer. HR—Baines, Anderson (Bal.).

Game 3—October 4, at Baltimore
Seattle..........0 0 1 0 1 0 0 0 2—4 11 0
Baltimore......0 0 0 0 0 0 0 0 2—2 5 0
Fassero, Slocumb (9); Key, Mills (5), Rhodes (6), Mathews (9). W—Fassero. L—Key. HR—Buhner, Sorrento (Sea.).

Game 4—October 5, at Baltimore
Seattle...........0 1 0 0 0 0 0 0 0—1 2 0
Baltimore.......2 0 0 0 1 0 0 0 x—3 7 0
Johnson; Mussina, Benitez (8), Myers (9). W—Mussina. L—Johnson. S—Myers. HR—Reboulet, Berroa (Bal.); Martinez (Sea.).

Cleveland vs. New York

Game 1—September 30, at New York
Cleveland......5 0 0 1 0 0 0 0 0—6 11 0
New York......0 1 0 1 1 5 0 0 0—8 11 0
Hershiser, Morman (5), Plunk (5), Assenmacher (6), Jackson (7); Cone, Mendoza (4), Stanton (7), Nelson (7), Rivera (8). W—Mendoza. L—Plunk. S—Rivera. HR—Alomar (Cle.); Martinez, Raines, Jeter, O'Neill (N.Y.).

Game 2—October 2, at New York
Cleveland......0 0 0 5 2 0 0 0 0—7 11 1
New York......3 0 0 0 0 0 0 1 1—5 7 2
Wright, Jackson (7), Assenmacher (7), Mesa (8); Pettitte, Boehringer (6), Lloyd (7), Nelson (9). W—Wright. L—Pettitte. HR—M. Williams (Cle.); Jeter (N.Y.).

Game 3—October 4, at Cleveland
New York........1 0 1 4 0 0 0 0 0—6 4 1
Cleveland........0 1 0 0 0 0 0 0 0—1 5 1

Wells; Nagy, Ogea (4). W—Wells. L—Nagy. HR—O'Neill (N.Y.).

Game 4—October 5, at Cleveland
New York........2 0 0 0 0 0 0 0 0—2 9 1
Cleveland.........0 1 0 0 0 0 0 1 1—3 9 0
Gooden, Lloyd (6), Nelson (6), Stanton (7), Rivera (8), Mendoza (8); Hershiser, Assenmacher (8), Jackson (8). W—Jackson. L—Mendoza. HR—Justice, Alomar (Cle.).

Game 5—October 6, at Cleveland
New York......0 0 0 0 2 1 0 0 0—3 12 0
Cleveland......0 0 3 1 0 0 0 0 x—4 7 2
Pettitte, Nelson (7), Stanton (8); Wright, Jackson (6), Assenmacher (7), Mesa (8). W—Wright. L—Pettitte. S—Mesa.

N.L. DIVISION SERIES

■ **Winners:** The Atlanta Braves and the wild-card Florida Marlins set up an NLCS showdown of East Division teams with convincing sweeps of the Houston Astros and San Francisco Giants. The Braves earned a record sixth straight LCS appearance behind the outstanding pitching of Greg Maddux, John Smoltz and Tom Glavine. The 5-year-old Marlins became the youngest expansion team to win a playoff series behind the near-perfect combination of clutch hitting and pitching.
■ **Turning points:** Maddux set the tone for Atlanta's victory by throwing a Game 1 seven-hitter and outdueling Houston ace Darryl Kile for a 2-1 victory. Edgar Renteria gave the Marlins a 2-1 Game 1 victory with a bases-loaded, ninth-inning single and Moises Alou singled home the winning run in the ninth inning of a 7-6 Game 2 win—a two-games-to-none hole from which the Giants could not recover.
■ **Memorable moments:** Smoltz took Atlanta honors with an 11-strikeout three-hitter in a 4-1 Game 3 victory that completed the Braves' sweep of Houston. Florida's 6-2 third-game victory over the Giants was keyed by Devon White's sixth-inning grand slam, which erased a 1-0 deficit.
■ **Memorable performances:** Third baseman Chipper Jones batted .500 with a home run and Jeff Blauser had a home run and four RBIs for the Braves, who also got a victory from each of their Big Three—Maddux, Glavine and Smoltz. The Marlins rode the clutch hitting of Renteria, Alou and White and the outstanding pitching of Kevin Brown and Alex Fernandez. The Giants got two home runs from second baseman Jeff Kent and a nice pitching effort from Kirk Rueter, who failed to get a decision.

Linescores

Atlanta vs. Houston

Game 1—September 30, at Atlanta
Houston................0 0 0 0 1 0 0 0 0—1 7 1
Atlanta..................1 1 0 0 0 0 0 0 x—2 2 0
Kile, Springer (8), Martin (8); Maddux. W—Maddux. L—Kile. HR—Klesko (Atl.).

Game 2—October 1, at Atlanta
Houston............0 0 0 3 0 0 0 0 0— 3 6 2
Atlanta ....0 0 3 0 3 5 0 2 x—13 10 1
Hampton, Magnante (5), Garcia (6), Lima (7), Wagner (8); Glavine, Cather (7), Wohlers (9). W—Glavine. L—Hampton. HR—Blauser (Atl.).

Game 3—October 3, at Houston
Atlanta.................1 1 0 0 0 0 1 1 0—4 8 2
Houston...............0 0 0 0 0 0 1 0 0—1 3 1
Smoltz; Reynolds, Springer (7), Martin (8), Garcia (8), Magnante (9). W—Smoltz. L—Reynolds. HR—C. Jones (Atl.), Carr (Hou.).

Florida vs. San Francisco

Game 1—September 30, at Florida
San Francisco ......0 0 0 0 0 0 1 0 0—1 4 0
Florida ....0 0 0 0 0 0 1 0 1—2 7 0
Rueter, Tavarez (8), R. Hernandez (9); Brown, Cook (8). W—Cook. L—Tavarez. HR—Mueller (S.F.), C. Johnson (Fla.).

Game 2—October 1, at Florida
San Francisco ....1 1 1 1 0 0 1 0 1—6 11 0
Florida ....2 0 1 2 0 1 0 0 1—7 10 2
Estes, Henry (3), Tavarez (6), Rodriguez (8), R. Hernandez (9); Leiter, L. Hernandez (5), Nen (9). W—Nen. L—R. Hernandez. HR—Bonilla, Sheffield (Fla.), B. Johnson (S.F.).

Game 3—October 3, at San Francisco
Florida ....0 0 0 0 0 4 0 2 0—6 10 2
San Francisco ....0 0 0 1 0 1 0 0 0—2 7 0
Fernandez, Cook (8), Nen (9); Alvarez, Tavarez (7), R. Hernandez (8), Rodriguez (8), Beck (8). W—Fernandez. L—Alvarez. HR—Kent 2 (S.F.), White (Fla.).

ALCS

■ **Winner:** The Indians, looking for their first championship since 1948, earned their second World Series appearance in three years with a six-game victory over the Orioles. The Indians overcame a .193 team average to claim the franchise's fifth pennant behind clutch pitching and timely hitting that produced four one-run wins over the A.L.'s winningest regular-season team.
■ **Turning point:** The fifth inning of Game 4, when Indians catcher Sandy Alomar took center stage with a baserunning gamble. The bases were loaded and the score was tied when Alomar, stationed at second, alertly raced home after an Arthur Rhodes wild pitch led to a home-plate collision between lead runner Dave Justice and catcher Lenny Webster. The Orioles fought back for a 7-7 tie, but Alomar decided the game with a ninth-inning single off Baltimore closer Armando Benitez to give the Indians a three-games-to-one series advantage.
■ **Memorable moment:** The 11th inning of Game 6 when shortstop Tony Fernandez drove a Benitez pitch into the right field seats at Camden Yards and gave the Indians a 1-0 series-clinching win. The Indians had managed only one hit through eight innings off Orioles starter Mike Mussina while Baltimore stranded 14 baserunners and was 0-for-12 with men in scoring position against Cleveland starter Charles Nagy and four relievers.
■ **Top guns:** Manny Ramirez (2 HR, 3 RBI), Fernandez (.357, 1 HR, 2 RBI), Marquis Grissom (1 HR, 4 RBI), S. Alomar (1 HR, 4 RBI), Mike Jackson (5 games, 0.00 ERA), Indians; Brady Anderson (.360, 2 HR, 3 RBI), Cal Ripken (.348, 1 HR, 3 RBI), Harold Baines (.353, 1 HR), Mussina (15 IP, 0.60 ERA), Orioles.
■ **MVP:** Marquis Grissom.

Linescores

Game 1—October 8, at Baltimore
Cleveland........0 0 0 0 0 0 0 0 0—0 4 1
Baltimore........1 0 2 0 0 0 0 0 x—3 6 1
Ogea, Bri. Anderson (7); Erickson, Myers (9). W—Erickson. L—Ogea. S—Myers. HR—Bra. Anderson, R. Alomar (Bal.).

Game 2—October 9, at Baltimore
Cleveland........2 0 0 0 0 0 0 3 0—5 6 3
Baltimore........0 2 0 0 0 2 0 0 0—4 8 1
Nagy, Morman (6), Juden (7), Assenmacher (7), Jackson (8), Mesa (9); Key, Kamieniecki (5), Benitez (8), Mills (9). W—Assenmacher. L—Benitez. S—Mesa. HR—Ramirez, Grissom (Cle.); Ripken (Bal.).

Game 3—October 11, at Cleveland
Bal. ....0 0 0 0 0 0 0 0 1 0 0 0—1 8 1
Cle. ....0 0 0 0 0 0 1 0 0 0 0 1—2 6 0
Mussina, Benitez (8), Orosco (9), Mills (9), Rhodes (10), Myers (11); Hershiser, Assenmacher (8), Jackson (8), Mesa (9), Juden (11), Morman (11), Plunk (12). W—Plunk. L—Myers.

Game 4—October 12, at Cleveland
Baltimore ....0 1 4 0 0 0 1 0 1—7 12 2
Cleveland......0 2 0 1 4 0 0 0 1—8 13 0
Erickson, Rhodes (5), Mills (7), Orosco (9), Benitez (9); Wright, Bri. Anderson (4), Juden (7), Assenmacher (7), Jackson (7), Mesa (8). W—Mesa. L—Mills. HR—S. Alomar, Ramirez (Cle.); Bra. Anderson, Baines, Palmeiro (Bal.).

Game 5—October 13, at Cleveland
Baltimore......0 0 2 0 0 0 0 0 2—4 10 0
Cleveland......0 0 0 0 0 0 0 0 2—2 8 1
Kamieniecki, Key (6), Myers (9); Ogea, Assenmacher (9), Jackson (9). W—Kamieniecki. L—Ogea. HR—Davis (Bal.).

Game 6—October 15, at Baltimore
Cle. ....0 0 0 0 0 0 0 0 0 0 1—1 3 0
Bal. ....0 0 0 0 0 0 0 0 0 0 0—0 10 0
Nagy, Assenmacher (8), Jackson (8), Bri. Anderson (10), Mesa (11); Mussina, Myers (9), Benitez (11). W—Bri. Anderson. L—Benitez. S—Mesa. HR—Fernandez (Cle.).

NLCS

■ **Winner:** The Marlins became the first wild-card team to reach the World Series when they upended the defending-N.L. champion Braves in a six-game NLCS. The 5-year-old Marlins also became the youngest expansion team to reach the fall classic while giving the spring training haven of South Florida its first World Series. The Marlins, who finished nine games behind Atlanta in the N.L. East, didn't even exist in 1991 when the Braves began their long playoff run.
■ **Turning point:** After righthander Livan Hernandez surrendered a Game 5-opening triple to Kenny Lofton and a walk to Keith Lockhart, he came back to strike out Chipper Jones, Fred McGriff and Ryan Klesko in a scoreless first inning. Bolstered by that great escape, Hernandez surrendered only two more hits and tied the LCS record with 15 strikeouts while outdueling Greg Maddux in a 2-1 victory at Pro Player Stadium.
■ **Memorable moment:** Kevin Brown's final pitch of Game 6, which extended the Marlins' Cinderella run and gave manager Jim Leyland his first World Series appearance in a career that spanned 33 years. Brown, the Game 1 winner, struggled through an 11-hit, complete-game 7-4 victory while fighting a stomach flu.
■ **Top guns:** Craig Counsell (.429), Bobby Bonilla (4 RBI), Charles Johnson (5 RBI), Jeff Conine (5 RBI), Hernandez (2-0, 0.84 ERA), Brown (2-0), Marlins; Lockhart (.500), Andruw Jones (.444), McGriff (.333, 4 RBI), Chipper Jones (2 HR, 4 RBI), Ryan Klesko (2 HR, 4 RBI), Denny Neagle (12 IP, 1-0, 0.00 ERA), Maddux (13 IP, 0-2, 1.38 ERA), Braves.
■ **MVP:** Hernandez.

Linescores

Game 1—October 7, at Atlanta
Florida............3 0 2 0 0 0 0 0 0—5 6 0
Atlanta............1 0 1 0 0 1 0 0 0—3 5 2
Brown, Cook (7), Powell (8), Nen (9); Maddux, Neagle (7). W—Brown. L—Maddux. S—Nen. HR—C. Jones, Klesko (Atl.).

Game 2—October 8, at Atlanta
Florida..........0 0 0 0 0 0 0 1 0—1 3 1
Atlanta..........3 0 2 0 0 0 2 0 x—7 13 0
Fernandez, Leiter (3), Heredia (6), Vosberg (7); Glavine, Cather (8), Wohlers (9). W—Glavine. L—Fernandez. HR—Klesko, C. Jones (Atl.).

Game 3—October 10, at Florida
Atlanta............0 0 0 1 0 1 0 0 0—2 6 1
Florida............0 0 0 1 0 4 0 0 x—5 8 1
Smoltz, Cather (7), Ligtenberg (8); Saunders, Hernandez (6), Cook (8), Nen (9). W—Hernandez. L—Smoltz. S—Nen. HR—Sheffield (Fla.).

Game 4—October 11, at Florida
Atlanta..........1 0 1 0 2 0 0 0 0—4 11 0
Florida..........0 0 0 0 0 0 0 0 0—0 4 0
Neagle; Leiter, Heredia (7), Vosberg (9). W—Neagle. L—Leiter. HR—Blauser (Atl.).

Game 5—October 12, at Florida
Atlanta............0 1 0 0 0 0 0 0 0—1 3 0
Florida............1 0 0 0 0 0 1 0 x—2 5 0
Maddux, Cather (8); Hernandez. W—Hernandez. L—Maddux. HR—Tucker (Atl.).

Game 6—October 14, at Atlanta
Florida..........4 0 0 0 0 3 0 0 0—7 10 1
Atlanta...........1 2 0 0 0 0 0 0 1—4 11 1
Brown; Glavine, Cather (6), Ligtenberg (7), Embree (9). W—Brown. L—Glavine.

WORLD SERIES

■ **Winner:** The expansion Marlins, who had undergone an $89 million offseason facelift, made the investment pay off when they outlasted the Indians in an exciting World Series that was decided in the 11th inning of Game 7 at Pro Player Stadium. The victory gave the 5-year-old Marlins distinction as the youngest team ever to win a fall classic and the only wild-card team to earn a championship. The Indians failed to win their first World Series since 1948 for the second time in three years.
■ **Turning point:** It didn't arrive until the ninth inning of Game 7, when the Indians were leading 2-1 and two outs away from an elusive championship. That's when the Marlins scored the tying run on Craig Counsell's sacrifice fly, setting the stage for a dramatic finish to a closely contested series in which the teams alternated victories.
■ **Memorable moment:** The bases-loaded, 11th-inning single by shortstop Edgar Renteria that gave the Marlins their unlikely victory and sent 67,204 fans at Pro Player Stadium into a frenzy. The two-out hit completed a gutsy comeback after the Marlins had been limited to two hits over eight innings by starter Jaret Wright and three Cleveland relievers. It also made a winner out of Jay Powell, who completed the six-pitcher six-hitter with a scoreless top of the 11th.
■ **Top guns:** Darren Daulton (.389), Charles Johnson (.357), Moises Alou (.321, 3 HR, 9 RBI), Livan Hernandez (2-0), Marlins; Matt Williams (.385), Sandy Alomar (.367, 2 HR, 10 RBI), Manny Ramirez (2 HR, 6 RBI); Chad Ogea (2-0, 1.54 ERA), Wright (1-0, 2.92), Indians.
■ **MVP:** Hernandez.

Linescores

Game 1—October 18, at Florida
Cleveland......1 0 0 0 1 1 0 1 0—4 11 0
Florida..........0 0 1 4 2 0 0 0 x—7 7 1
Hershiser, Juden (5), Plunk (6), Assenmacher (8); Hernandez, Cook (6), Powell (8), Nen (9). W—Hernandez. L—Hershiser. S—Nen. HR—Alou, Johnson (Fla.), Ramirez, Thome (Cle.).

Game 2—October 19, at Florida
Cleveland......1 0 0 0 3 2 0 0 0—6 14 0
Florida..........1 0 0 0 0 0 0 0 0—1 8 0
Ogea, Jackson (7), Mesa (9); Brown, Heredia (7), Alfonseca (8). W—Ogea. L—Brown. HR—Alomar (Cle.).

Game 3—October 21, at Cleveland
Florida........1 0 1 1 0 2 2 0 7—14 16 3
Cleveland....2 0 0 3 2 0 0 0 4—11 10 3
Leiter, Heredia (5), Cook (8), Nen (9); Nagy, Anderson (7), Jackson (7), Assenmacher (8), Plunk (8), Morman (9), Mesa (9). W—Cook. L—Plunk. HR—Sheffield, Daulton, Eisenreich (Fla.), Thome (Cle.).

Game 4—October 22, at Cleveland
Florida........0 0 0 1 0 2 0 0 0— 3 6 2
Cleveland....3 0 3 0 0 1 1 2 x—10 15 0
Saunders, Alfonseca (3), Vosberg (6), Powell (8); Wright, Anderson (7). W—Wright. L—Saunders. S—Anderson. HR—Ramirez, Williams (Cle.), Alou (Fla.).

Game 5—October 23, at Cleveland
Florida..........0 2 0 0 0 4 0 1 1—8 15 2
Cleveland......0 1 3 0 0 0 0 0 3—7 9 0
Hernandez, Nen (9); Hershiser, Morman (6), Plunk (6), Juden (7), Assenmacher (8), Mesa (9). W—Hernandez. L—Hershiser. S—Nen. HR—Alomar (Cle.), Alou (Fla.).

Game 6—October 25, at Florida
Cleveland........0 2 1 0 1 0 0 0 0—4 8 0
Florida............0 0 0 0 1 0 0 0 0—1 8 0
Ogea, Jackson (6), Assenmacher (8), Mesa (9); Brown, Heredia (6), Powell (8), Vosberg (9). W—Ogea. L—Brown. S—Mesa.

Game 7—October 26, at Florida
Cle. ......0 0 2 0 0 0 0 0 0 0 0—2 6 2
Fla. ......0 0 0 0 0 0 1 0 1 0 1—3 8 0
Wright, Assenmacher (7), Jackson (8), Anderson (8), Mesa (9), Nagy (10); Leiter, Cook (7), Alfonseca (8), Heredia (9), Nen (9), Powell (11). W—Powell. L—Nagy. HR—Bonilla (Fla.).

Padres right fielder Tony Gwynn captured his eighth batting championship in 1997, joining Honus Wagner as the all-time National League leader.

FINAL STANDINGS

American League

EAST DIVISION

Team	N.Y.	Bos.	Tor.	Bal.	T.B.	Cle.	Chi.	K.C.	Min.	Det.	Tex.	Ana.	Sea.	Oak.	Atl.	NYM	Phi.	Mtl.	Fla.	W	L	Pct.	GB
New York	—	7	6	9	11	7	7	10	7	8	8	5	8	8	3	2	3	2	3	114	48	.704	—
Boston	5	—	5	6	9	8	5	8	5	5	6	5	7	9	2	1	1	3	2	92	70	.568	22
Toronto	6	7	—	7	7	4	6	5	7	6	4	7	7	6	1	2	1	4	1	88	74	.543	26
Baltimore	3	6	5	—	5	5	2	5	7	10	6	6	6	8	1	1	2	0	1	79	83	.488	35
Tampa Bay	1	3	5	7	—	3	6	3	4	6	4	5	5	6	0	1	2	1	1	63	99	.389	51

CENTRAL DIVISION

Team	N.Y.	Bos.	Tor.	Bal.	T.B.	Cle.	Chi.	K.C.	Min.	Det.	Tex.	Ana.	Sea.	Oak.	Hou.	ChC	Stl.	Cin.	Mil.	Pit.	W	L	Pct.	GB
Cleveland	4	3	7	6	7	—	6	8	6	9	4	7	9	3	1	2	2	2	2	1	89	73	.549	—
Chicago	4	6	4	9	5	6	—	8	6	6	5	6	4	4	1	0	2	1	1	2	80	82	.494	9
Kansas City	0	3	6	6	8	4	4	—	7	6	3	5	4	7	1	2	2	2	1	1	72	89	.447	16.5
Minnesota	4	6	4	3	7	6	6	5	—	4	7	5	2	4	1	2	2	1	0	1	70	92	.432	19
Detroit	3	5	5	1	5	3	6	6	8	—	3	3	3	7	0	2	1	0	2	2	65	97	.401	24

WEST DIVISION

Team	N.Y.	Bos.	Tor.	Bal.	T.B.	Cle.	Chi.	K.C.	Min.	Det.	Tex.	Ana.	Sea.	Oak.	S.D.	S.F.	L.A.	Col.	Ari.	W	L	Pct.	GB
Texas	3	5	7	5	7	7	6	8	4	8	—	7	7	6	2	1	0	2	3	88	74	.543	—
Anaheim	6	6	4	5	6	4	5	6	6	8	5	—	9	5	1	1	3	3	2	85	77	.525	3
Seattle	3	4	4	5	6	2	7	6	9	8	5	3	—	7	2	1	1	2	1	76	85	.472	11.5
Oakland	3	2	5	3	5	8	7	4	7	4	6	7	5	—	2	2	1	1	2	74	88	.457	14

National League

EAST DIVISION

Team	Atl.	N.Y.	Phi.	Mtl.	Fla.	Hou.	Chi.	Stl.	Cin.	Mil.	Pit.	S.D.	S.F.	L.A.	Col.	Ari.	NYY	Bos.	Tor.	Bal.	T.B.	W	L	Pct.	GB
Atlanta	—	9	8	6	7	4	3	6	7	7	7	5	7	8	5	8	1	1	2	2	3	106	56	.654	—
New York	3	—	8	4	7	4	5	6	6	8	4	4	4	5	6	5	1	2	1	3	2	88	74	.543	18
Philadelphia	4	4	—	7	6	2	6	3	5	5	8	1	2	4	4	7	0	3	2	1	1	75	87	.463	31
Montreal	6	8	5	—	7	2	2	3	1	3	2	4	3	4	2	7	1	0	0	3	2	65	97	.401	41
Florida	5	5	6	5	—	3	2	4	0	0	3	4	0	4	3	2	0	1	2	2	3	54	108	.333	52

CENTRAL DIVISION

Team	Atl.	N.Y.	Phi.	Mtl.	Fla.	Hou.	Chi.	Stl.	Cin.	Mil.	Pit.	S.D.	S.F.	L.A.	Col.	Ari.	Cle.	ChW	K.C.	Min.	Det.	W	L	Pct.	GB
Houston	5	5	7	7	6	—	7	5	8	9	9	5	6	3	5	5	2	2	2	1	3	102	60	.630	—
Chicago	6	4	3	7	7	4	—	4	6	6	8	5	7	4	7	7	0	3	1	1	0	90	73	.552	12.5
St. Louis	3	3	6	6	5	7	7	—	3	8	5	3	5	5	6	7	0	1	1	1	1	83	79	.512	19
Cincinnati	2	3	4	8	9	3	5	8	—	6	5	1	2	5	4	5	1	1	0	2	3	77	85	.475	25
Milwaukee	2	1	4	6	9	2	6	3	5	—	6	3	5	4	7	3	1	2	2	2	1	74	88	.457	28
Pittsburgh	2	5	1	7	6	2	3	6	7	5	—	5	2	5	4	3	2	0	1	2	1	69	93	.426	33

WEST DIVISION

Team	Atl.	N.Y.	Phi.	Mtl.	Fla.	Hou.	Chi.	Stl.	Cin.	Mil.	Pit.	S.D.	S.F.	L.A.	Col.	Ari.	Tex.	Ana.	Sea.	Oak.	W	L	Pct.	GB
San Diego	4	5	8	4	5	4	4	6	11	6	4	—	8	7	7	9	1	2	2	1	98	64	.605	—
San Fran.	2	5	6	6	9	3	3	7	7	4	7	4	—	6	5	7	2	2	2	2	89	74	.546	9.5
Los Angeles	1	3	5	5	5	6	5	4	4	5	7	5	6	—	6	8	3	1	2	2	83	79	.512	15
Colorado	3	3	5	7	6	6	2	3	5	4	5	5	7	6	—	6	1	0	1	2	77	85	.475	21
Arizona	1	4	2	2	6	4	5	2	4	6	6	3	5	4	6	—	1	1	2	1	65	97	.401	33

SIGNIFICANT EVENTS

■ **March 31:** Two expansion teams made their major league debut, Arizona losing 9-2 to the Colorado Rockies at new Bank One Ballpark in Phoenix and Tampa Bay dropping an 11-6 decision to Detroit at new Tropicana Field.
■ **March 31:** The Milwaukee Brewers, transplanted to the National League because of expansion, lost their first N.L. game, 2-1, at Atlanta. The Brewers became the first modern-era team in baseball history to switch leagues.
■ **April 15:** The New York Yankees, forced to temporarily abandon Yankee Stadium when a steel beam fell from beneath the upper deck to the empty seats below, posted a 6-3 win over the Angels at Shea Stadium, home of the Mets. The Mets came back that night to beat the Cubs 2-1—the first time this century that two regular-season games involving four teams were played in the same stadium on the same day.
■ **July 9:** After serving as chairman of the Executive Committee and interim commissioner for almost six years, Allan (Bud) Selig, the Milwaukee Brewers' president and chief executive officer, accepted a five-year term as baseball's ninth commissioner.
■ **August 9:** Atlanta veteran Dennis Martinez posted his 244th career victory in a relief role against San Francisco, making him the winningest Latin pitcher in major league history.
■ **September 28:** Gary Gaetti's two-run homer lifted Chicago to a 5-3 win over San Francisco in the first-ever playoff to decide a league's wild-card representative.
■ **December 12:** The Los Angeles Dodgers broke new ground when they signed pitcher Kevin Brown to a seven-year contract worth $105 million—the first $100 million deal in baseball history.

MEMORABLE MOMENTS

■ **May 6:** Chicago Cubs rookie Kerry Wood tied Roger Clemens' single-game strikeout record when he fanned 20 Houston batters in a one-hit, 2-0 shutout at Wrigley Field.
■ **May 17:** Lefthander David Wells fired the first regular-season perfect game in New York Yankees history and the 13th perfecto of the modern era when he retired all 27 Minnesota Twins he faced in a 4-0 win before 49,820 fans at Yankee Stadium.
■ **September 8:** St. Louis first baseman Mark McGwire broke Roger Maris' 37-year-old single-season home run record when he drove a pitch from Chicago righthander Steve Trachsel over the left field fence at Busch Stadium for homer No. 62.
■ **September 13:** Chicago right fielder Sammy Sosa, following McGwire's home run lead, hit Nos. 61 and 62 during a Sunday night victory over Milwaukee at Wrigley Field.
■ **September 20:** Baltimore third baseman Cal Ripken ended his record ironman streak at 2,632 consecutive games when he sat out against the New York Yankees in the Orioles' final home contest of the season.
■ **September 25:** The Yankees posted a 6-1 victory over Tampa Bay at Yankee Stadium for their 112th win, topping the American League record of 111 set by the 1954 Cleveland Indians. The Yanks would go on to win 114 times.
■ **September 27:** McGwire, who trailed Sosa briefly on the final Friday of the great 1998 home run race, capped a five-homer final weekend with two final-day shots against Montreal, bringing his record season total to 70.

ALL-STAR GAME

■ **Winner:** The A.L. obliterated the N.L. with a 19-hit, five-stolen base barrage that resulted in a 13-8 victory. The A.L.'s second straight win featured home runs by Alex Rodriguez and Roberto Alomar and a surprising running attack.
■ **Key inning:** The sixth, when the A.L. broke out its ugly game and scored three times for an 8-6 lead. The rally off Montreal righthander Ugueth Urbina featured four stolen bases and runners crossing the plate on a wild pitch and a passed ball. The uprising wiped out a three-run fifth-inning homer by San Francisco's Barry Bonds.
■ **Memorable moment:** A towering two-run double to right by third baseman Cal Ripken in the fourth. The double was Ripken's 11th hit in his 16th All-Star Game.
■ **Top guns:** Rafael Palmeiro (Orioles), Alex Rodriguez (Mariners), Ken Griffey Jr. (Mariners), Roberto Alomar (Indians), Ripken (Orioles), David Wells (Yankees), A.L.; Bonds (Giants), Tony Gwynn (Padres), N.L.
■ **MVP:** Roberto Alomar.

LEADERS

American League
BA: Bernie Williams, N.Y., .339.
Runs: Derek Jeter, N.Y., 127.
Hits: Alex Rodriguez, Sea., 213.
TB: Albert Belle, Chi., 399.
HR: Ken Griffey Jr., Sea., 56.
RBI: Juan Gonzalez, Tex., 157.
SB: Rickey Henderson, Oak., 66.
Wins: Roger Clemens, Tor., David Cone, N.Y., Rick Helling, Tex., 20.
ERA: Roger Clemens, Tor., 2.65.
CG: Scott Erickson, Bal., 11.
IP: Scott Erickson, Bal., 251.1.
SO: Roger Clemens, Tor., 271.
Sv.: Tom Gordon, Bos., 46.

National League
BA: Larry Walker, Col., .363.
Runs: Sammy Sosa, Chi., 134.
Hits: Dante Bichette, Col., 219.
TB: Sammy Sosa, Chi., 416.
HR: Mark McGwire, St.L., 70.
RBI: Sammy Sosa, Chi., 158.
SB: Tony Womack, Pit., 58.
Wins: Tom Glavine, Atl., 20.
ERA: Greg Maddux, Atl., 2.22.
CG: Curt Schilling, Phi., 15.
IP: Curt Schilling, Phi., 268.2.
SO: Curt Schilling, Phi., 300.
Sv.: Trevor Hoffman, S.D., 53.

A.L. 20-game winners
Roger Clemens, Tor., 20
David Cone, N.Y., 20
Rick Helling, Tex., 20

N.L. 20-game winner
Tom Glavine, Atl., 20

A.L. 100 RBIs
Juan Gonzalex, Tex., 157
Albert Belle, Chi., 152
Ken Griffey Jr., Sea., 146
Manny Ramirez, Cle., 145
Alex Rodriguez, Sea., 124
Tino Martinez, N.Y., 123
Nomar Garciaparra, Bos., 122
Rafael Palmeiro, Bal., 121
Dean Palmer, K.C., 119
Paul O'Neill, N.Y., 116
Carlos Delgado, Tor., 115
Mo Vaughn, Bos., 115
Jason Giambi, Oak., 110
Frank Thomas, Chi., 109
Rusty Greer, Tex., 108
Jose Canseco, Tor., 107
Matt Stairs, Oak., 106
Tony Clark, Det., 103
Will Clark, Tex., 102
Edgar Martinez, Sea., 102
Damion Easley, Det., 100
Shawn Green, Tor., 100

N.L. 100 RBIs
Sammy Sosa, Chi., 158
Mark McGwire, St.L., 147
Vinny Castilla, Col., 144
Jeff Kent, S.F., 128
Jeromy Burnitz, Mil., 125
Moises Alou, Hou., 124
Dante Bichette, Col., 122
Barry Bonds, S.F., 122
Andres Galarraga, Atl., 121
Greg Vaughn, S.D., 119
Jeff Bagwell, Hou., 111
Mike Piazza, L.A., Fla., N.Y., 111
Scott Rolen, Phi., 110
Vladimir Guerrero, Mon., 109
Derek Bell, Hou., 108
Kevin Young, Pit., 108
Chipper Jones, Atl., 107
Javy Lopez, Atl., 106
Ray Lankford, St.L., 105
Rico Brogna, Phi., 104

A.L. 40 homers
Ken Griffey Jr., Sea., 56
Albert Belle, Chi., 49
Jose Canseco, Tor., 46
Juan Gonzalez, Tex., 45
Manny Ramirez, Cle., 45
Rafael Palmeiro, Bal., 43
Alex Rodriguez, Sea., 42
Mo Vaughn, Bos., 40

N.L. 40 homers
Mark McGwire, St.L., 70
Sammy Sosa, Chi., 66
Greg Vaughn, S.D., 50
Vinny Castilla, Col., 46
Andres Galarraga, Atl., 44

Most Valuable Player
A.L.: Juan Gonzalez, OF, Tex.
N.L.: Sammy Sosa, OF, Chi.

Cy Young Award
A.L.: Roger Clemens, Tor.
N.L.: Tom Glavine, Atl.

Rookie of the Year
A.L.: Ben Grieve, OF, Oak.
N.L.: Kerry Wood, P, Chi.

Manager of the Year
A.L.: Joe Torre, N.Y.
N.L.: Larry Dierker, Hou.

Hall of Fame additions
George Davis, SS, 1890-1909
Larry Doby, OF, 1947-59.
Lee MacPhail, Executive
Joe Rogan, P, Negro Leagues
Don Sutton, P, 1966-88

Linescore

July 7 at Colorado's Coors Field
A.L. ....0 0 0 4 1 3 1 1 3—13 19 2
N.L. ....0 0 2 1 3 0 0 2 0— 8 12 1
Wells (Yankees), Clemens (Blue Jays) 3, Radke (Twins) 4, Colon (Indians) 5, Arrojo (Devil Rays) 6, Wetteland (Rangers) 7, Gordon (Red Sox) 8, Percival (Angels) 9 and I. Rodriguez (Rangers), S. Alomar (Indians); Maddux (Braves), Glavine (Braves) 3, Brown (Padres) 4, Ashby (Padres) 5, Urbina (Expos) 6, Hoffman (Padres) 7, Shaw (Dodgers) 8, Nen (Giants) 9 and Piazza (Mets), Lopez (Braves). W—Colon. L—Urbina. HR—A. Rodriguez, R. Alomar, A.L.; Bonds, N.L.

A.L. DIVISION SERIES

■ **Winners:** The New York Yankees, who won an A.L.-record 114 regular-season games, carried that dominance into the postseason with a three-game Division Series sweep of the Texas Rangers, and the Cleveland Indians earned their third ALCS berth in four years with an exciting four-game victory over the wild-card Boston Red Sox. Yankee pitchers shut down the A.L.'s top-hitting team (a .141 average) en route to their second ALCS opportunity in three years and the Indians overcame an 11-3 series-opening loss while extending Boston's 80-year World Series championship drought.
■ **Turning points:** What little offense the Yankees needed in 2-0, 3-1 and 4-0 victories was provided by unlikely sources: Third baseman Scott Brosius singled in the go-ahead run in Game 1 and hit a lead-extending two-run homer in Game 2; backup outfielder Shane Spencer homered in Game 2 and hit a key three-run shot in Game 3. A Game 2 first-inning ejection of Cleveland manager Mike Hargrove and starting pitcher Dwight Gooden seemed to energize the lethargic Indians, who erupted for six runs in the first two innings and went on to a 9-5 series-squaring win.
■ **Memorable moments:** A Game 3 Texas-type downpour that forced a 3-hour, 16-minute rain delay in Game 3, but merely delayed the inevitable for the Rangers. The delay knocked Yankee starter David Cone out of the game, but three relievers came on to complete his shutout and Spencer delivered the big blow. Left fielder David Justice provided the big plays in Game 4 for the Indians, a sixth-inning throw that cut down Boston runner John Valentin at the plate and a two-run, eighth-inning double that secured a 2-1 victory.
■ **Memorable performances:** Brosius and Spencer combined for seven of the Yankees' eight RBIs in the series, but the real heroes were pitchers David Wells, Andy Pettitte, Cone, Mariano Rivera, Jeff Nelson and Graeme Lloyd, who combined for a 0.33 ERA—allowing only one run in three games. Texas starters—Todd Stottlemyre, Rick Helling, Aaron Sele—all pitched well, but got little run support. Kenny Lofton, Manny Ramirez, Jim Thome and Justice provided the bulk of Cleveland's offense and the Indians got good pitching from starters Charles Nagy and Bartolo Colon and three saves from Mike Jackson. First baseman Mo Vaughn (2 homers, 7 RBIs) and shortstop Nomar Garciaparra (3, 11) were prolific offensively for the losing Red Sox.

Linescores

New York vs. Texas

Game 1—September 29, at New York
Texas ....0 0 0 0 0 0 0 0 0—0 5 0
New York ....0 2 0 0 0 0 0 0 x—2 6 0
Stottlemyre and Rodriguez; Wells, Rivera (9) and Posada. W—Wells. L—Stottlemyre. S—Rivera.

Game 2—September 30, at New York
Texas ....0 0 0 0 1 0 0 0 0—1 5 0
New York ....0 1 0 2 0 0 0 0 x—3 8 0
Helling, Crabtree (7) and Rodriguez; Pettitte, Nelson (8), Rivera (8) and Girardi. W—Pettitte. L—Helling. S—Rivera. HR—Spencer, Brosius (N.Y.).

Game 3—October 2, at Texas
New York ....0 0 0 0 0 4 0 0 0—4 9 1
Texas ....0 0 0 0 0 0 0 0 0—0 3 1
Cone, Lloyd (6), Nelson (7), Rivera (9) and Girardi; Sele, Crabtree (7), Wetteland (9) and Rodriguez. W—Cone. L—Sele. HR—O'Neill, Spencer (N.Y.).

1998

Boston vs. Cleveland

Game 1—September 29, at Cleveland
Boston........3 0 0 0 3 2 0 3 0—11 12 0
Cleveland....0 0 0 0 0 2 1 0 0— 3 7 0
Martinez, Corsi (8) and Hatteberg; Wright, Jones (5), Reed (8), Poole (8), Shuey (8), Assenmacher (9) and Alomar. W—Martinez. L—Wright. HR—Vaughn 2, Garciaparra (Bos.); Lofton, Thome (Cle.).

Game 2—September 30, at Cleveland
Boston..........2 0 1 0 0 2 0 0 0—5 10 0
Cleveland......1 5 1 0 0 1 0 1 x—9 9 1
Wakefield, Wasdin (2), Lowe (4), Swindell (6), Gordon (8) and Varitek; Gooden, Burba (1), Shuey (6), Assenmacher (8), Jackson (8) and Alomar. W—Burba. L—Wakefield. S—Jackson. HR—Justice (Cle.).

Game 3—October 2, at Boston
Cleveland........0 0 0 0 1 1 1 0 1—4 5 0
Boston............0 0 0 1 0 0 0 0 2—3 6 0
Nagy, Jackson (9) and Alomar; Saberhagen, Corsi (8), Eckersley (9) and Hatteberg. W—Nagy. L—Saberhagen. S—Jackson. HR—Thome, Lofton, M. Ramirez 2 (Cle.); Garciaparra (Bos.).

Game 4—October 3, at Boston
Cleveland........0 0 0 0 0 0 0 2 0—2 5 0
Boston............0 0 0 1 0 0 0 0 0—1 6 0
Colon, Poole (6), Reed (7), Assenmacher (8), Shuey (8), Jackson (9) and Alomar; Schourek, Lowe (6), Gordon (8) and Hatteberg. W—Reed. L—Gordon. S—Jackson. HR—Garciaparra (Bos.).

N.L. DIVISION SERIES

■ **Winners:** The Atlanta Braves earned their seventh straight N.L. Championship Series berth by sweeping past the wild-card Chicago Cubs, and the San Diego Padres reached the NLCS for the first time since 1984 by throttling the Houston Astros and their N.L.-leading offense. Braves pitchers simply were too much for the overmatched Cubs, who scored only four runs in the three games, and the Padres followed that lead by holding the high-powered Astros to a .182 average in a surprising four-game victory.
■ **Turning points:** The Braves took control of the series in Game 2 when they tied the game at 1-1 in the bottom of the ninth and then won in the 10th on a Chipper Jones single down the left field line. The Padres served notice to the Astros in Game 1 when starter Kevin Brown struck out 16 batters and allowed two hits over eight innings while outdueling Houston ace Randy Johnson, 2-1.
■ **Memorable moments:** The ninth inning of Game 2, when Atlanta catcher Javy Lopez connected off Chicago pitcher Kevin Tapani for a one-out home run that tied the game 1-1. The Padres got a dramatic Game 2-tying home run from Jim Leyritz off Houston closer Billy Wagner in the ninth inning, but the Astros rebounded in the bottom of the ninth to post a 5-4 victory—their only win of the series.
■ **Memorable performances:** Atlanta catchers Lopez and Eddie Perez combined for eight RBIs and Braves pitchers, led by starters John Smoltz, Tom Glavine and Greg Maddux, posted a 1.29 ERA. Tapani and rookie Kerry Wood had outstanding starting efforts for the Cubs, but there was too little offensive support. San Diego's biggest offensive gun was Leyritz, who came off the bench to hit three home runs, while pitchers Brown and Sterling Hitchcock led a staff that compiled a 1.78 ERA. Johnson allowed only three earned runs in two starts covering 14 innings for the Astros, but all he had to show for his efforts were two losses.

Linescores

Chicago vs. Atlanta

Game 1—September 30, at Atlanta
Chicago..........0 0 0 0 0 0 0 1 0—1 5 1
Atlanta ....0 2 0 0 0 1 4 0 x—7 8 0
Clark, Heredia (7), Karchner (7), Morgan (8) and Houston; Smoltz, Rocker (8), Ligtenberg (9) and Lopez. W—Smoltz. L—Clark. HR—Houston (Chi.); Tucker, Klesko (Atl.).

Game 2—October 1, at Atlanta
Chicago....0 0 0 0 0 1 0 0 0 0—1 4 1
Atlanta ....0 0 0 0 0 0 0 0 1 1—2 6 0
Tapani, Mulholland (10) and Servais, Houston; Glavine, Rocker (8), Seanez (9), O. Perez (10) and Lopez. W—O. Perez. L—Mulholland. HR—Lopez (Atl.).

Game 3—October 3, at Chicago
Atlanta...........0 0 1 0 0 0 0 5 0—6 9 0
Chicago ....0 0 0 0 0 0 0 2 0—2 8 2
Maddux, Ligtenberg (8) and E. Perez; Wood, Mulholland (6), Beck (8), Morgan (9) and Houston, Martinez. W—Maddux. L—Wood. HR—E. Perez (Atl.).

Houston vs. San Diego

Game 1—September 29, at Houston
San Diego ......0 0 0 0 0 1 0 1 0—2 9 1
Houston ....0 0 0 0 0 0 0 0 1—1 4 0
Brown, Hoffman (9) and Hernandez; Johnson, Powell (9), Henry (9) and Ausmus. W—Brown. L—Johnson. S—Hoffman. HR—Vaughn (S.D.).

Game 2—October 1, at Houston
San Diego ....0 0 0 0 0 2 0 0 2—4 8 1
Houston ......1 0 2 0 0 0 0 1 1—5 11 1
Ashby, Hamilton (5), Wall (8), Miceli (9), Hoffman (9) and Hernandez, Myers; Reynolds, Powell (8), Wagner (9) and Eusebio, Ausmus. W—Wagner. L—Miceli. HR—Leyritz (S.D.); Bell (Hou.).

Game 3—October 3, at San Diego
Houston ....0 0 0 0 0 0 1 0 0—1 4 0
San Diego ......0 0 0 0 0 1 1 0 x—2 3 0
Hampton, Elarton (7) and Ausmus; Brown, Miceli (7), Hoffman (9) and Hernandez. W—Miceli. L—Elarton. S—Hoffman. HR—Leyritz (S.D.).

Game 4—October 4, at San Diego
Houston ....0 0 0 1 0 0 0 0 0—1 3 1
San Diego ......0 1 0 0 0 1 0 4 x—6 7 1
Johnson, Miller (7), Henry (7), Powell (8) and Ausmus; Hitchcock, Hamilton (7), Miceli (7), Hoffman (9) and Leyritz, Hernandez. W—Hitchcock. L—Johnson. HR—Leyritz, Joyner (S.D.).

ALCS

■ **Winner:** The New York Yankees raised their incredible 1998 season record to 121-50 with a surprisingly difficult six-game victory over Cleveland. After watching the Indians jump to a two-games-to-one advantage, the Yankees won three straight times and advanced to the franchise's record 35th World Series.
■ **Turning point:** Down two-games-to-one and in danger of watching an incredible season unravel, the Yankees tied the series at Cleveland's Jacobs Field behind the four-hit pitching of Orlando Hernandez, Mike Stanton and Mariano Rivera, who combined for a 4-0 shutout of the powerful Indians. Paul O'Neill provided all the offense the trio would need with a solo home run in the first inning.
■ **Memorable moment:** The 12th inning of Game 2 at New York, when a sacrifice bunt by Cleveland's Travis Fryman transformed a 1-1 tie into a 4-1 Indians victory. Yankees first baseman Tino Martinez fielded the bunt and fired to second baseman Chuck Knoblauch covering first. But the ball hit Fryman, who appeared to be running illegally inside the line, and caromed about 20 feet away. Instead of chasing the ball, Knoblauch argued the noncall of umpire Ted Hendry as pinch runner Enrique Wilson circled the bases to score the go-ahead run. Kenny Lofton's two-run single finished the Yankees in an ugly and controversial end to what had been a well-played game.
■ **Top guns:** Bernie Williams (.381, 5 RBIs), Scott Brosius (.300, 6 RBIs), Hernandez (1-0, 0.00 ERA), David Wells (2-0, 2.87), Rivera (4 games, 0.00), Yankees; Omar Vizquel (.440), Jim Thome (.304, 4 HRs, 8 RBIs), Manny Ramirez (.333, 2 HRs, 4 RBIs), Bartolo Colon (1-0, 1.00 ERA), Paul Shuey (5 games, 0.00), Indians.
■ **MVP:** Wells.

Linescores

Game 1—October 6, a New York
Cleveland......0 0 0 0 0 0 0 0 2—2 5 0
New York......5 0 0 0 0 1 1 0 x—7 11 0
Wright, Ogea (1), Poole (7), Reed (7), Shuey (8) and Alomar, Diaz; Wells, Nelson (9) and Posada. W—Wells. L—Wright. HR—Ramirez (Cle.); Posada (N.Y.).

Game 2—October 7, at New York
Cleveland0 0 0 1 0 0 0 0 0 0 0 3—4 7 1
New York0 0 0 0 0 0 1 0 0 0 0 0—1 7 1
Nagy, Reed (7), Poole (8), Shuey (8), Assenmacher (10), Burba (11), Jackson (12) and Alomar; Cone, Rivera (9), Stanton (11), Nelson (11), Lloyd (12) and Girardi. W—Burba. L—Nelson. S—Jackson. HR—Justice (Cle.).

Game 3—October 9, at Cleveland
New York......1 0 0 0 0 0 0 0 0—1 4 0
Cleveland......0 2 0 0 4 0 0 0 x—6 12 0
Pettitte, Mendoza (5), Stanton (7) and Girardi, Posada; Colon and Alomar. W—Colon. L—Pettitte. HR—Thome 2, Ramirez, Whiten (Cle.).

Game 4—October 10, at Cleveland
New York.......1 0 0 2 0 0 0 0 1—4 4 0
Cleveland.......0 0 0 0 0 0 0 0 0—0 4 3
Hernandez, Stanton (8), Rivera (9) and Posada; Gooden, Poole (5), Burba (6), Shuey (9) and Alomar, Diaz. W—Hernandez. L—Gooden. HR—O'Neill (N.Y.).

Game 5—October 11, at Cleveland
New York........3 1 0 1 0 0 0 0 0—5 6 0
Cleveland........2 0 0 0 0 1 0 0 0—3 8 0
Wells, Nelson (8), Rivera (8) and Posada; Ogea, Wright (2), Reed (8), Assenmacher (8), Shuey (9) and Diaz. W—Wells. L—Ogea. S—Rivera. HR—Lofton, Thome (Cle.); Davis (N.Y.).

Game 6—October 13, at New York
Cleveland......0 0 0 0 5 0 0 0 0—5 8 3
New York......2 1 3 0 0 3 0 0 x—9 11 1
Nagy, Burba (4), Poole (6), Shuey (6), Assenmacher (8) and Alomar, Diaz; Cone, Mendoza (6), Rivera (9) and Girardi. W—Cone. L—Nagy. HR—Brosius (N.Y.); Thome (Cle.).

NLCS

■ **Winner:** The San Diego Padres, the dark horse in National League playoffs that featured high-powered teams from Houston and Atlanta, claimed the second pennant of their 30-year existence with a six-game victory over the N.L. East Division-champion Braves, who had won a club-record 106 games during the regular season. The Padres, 98-game winners, beat the Braves at their own game—pitching and defense—and gave them the distinction of becoming the winningest team not to reach the World Series.
■ **Turning point:** Game 3, when the Braves loaded the bases three times—twice with less than two out—and failed to score. Starting pitcher Sterling Hitchcock worked out of the first jam, Dan Miceli came out of the bullpen in the sixth to strike out consecutive pinch hitters and Trevor Hoffman came on in the eighth to strike out catcher Javy Lopez, who represented the potential winning run. The Padres' 4-1 win over Greg Maddux gave them a shocking three-games-to-none advantage over an experienced Braves team appearing in its seventh straight NLCS.
■ **Memorable moment:** Michael Tucker's three-run, eighth-inning homer off Padres ace Kevin Brown in Game 5, a blow that temporarily rescued the Braves from elimination and gave them hope of becoming the first baseball team to come back and win a post-season series after losing the first three games. Brown, who was making a surprise relief appearance after throwing a three-hit shutout in Game 2, escaped a seventh-inning jam but coughed up a 4-2 San Diego lead in the eighth when he walked Ryan Klesko, gave up an infield single to Lopez and then surrendered the game-turning homer to Tucker.
■ **Top guns:** Ozzie Guillen (.417), Tucker (.385, 1 HR, 5 RBIs), John Rocker (6 games, 1-0, 0.00 ERA), Braves; John Vander Wal (.429), Steve Finley (.333), Ken Caminiti (2 HRs, 4 RBIs), Brown (1-1, 2.61 ERA), Hitchcock (2-0, 0-90), Padres.
■ **MVP:** Hitchcock.

Game 1—October 7, at Atlanta
San Diego....0 0 0 0 1 0 0 1 0 1—3 7 0
Atlanta ....0 0 1 0 0 0 0 0 1 0—2 8 3
Ashby, R. Myers (8), Miceli (8), Hoffman (8), Wall (10) and Hernandez; Smoltz, Rocker (8), Martinez (8), Ligtenberg (9) and Lopez, E. Perez. W—Hoffman. L—Ligtenberg. S—Wall. HR—A. Jones (Atl.); Caminiti (S.D.).

Game 2—October 8, at Atlanta
San Diego ....0 0 0 0 0 1 0 0 2—3 11 0
Atlanta..........0 0 0 0 0 0 0 0 0—0 3 1
Brown and Hernandez; Glavine, Rocker (7), Seanez (8), O. Perez (9), Ligtenberg (9) and Lopez. W—Brown. L—Glavine.

Game 3—October 10, at San Diego
Atlanta ....0 0 1 0 0 0 0 0 0—1 8 2
San Diego ......0 0 0 0 2 0 0 2 x—4 7 0
Maddux, Martinez (6), Rocker (7), Seanez (8) and E. Perez, Lopez; Hitchcock, Wall (6), Miceli (8) R. Myers (8), Hoffman (8) and Leyritz, Hernandez. W—Hitchcock. L—Maddux. S—Hoffman.

Game 4—October 11, at San Diego
Atlanta.........0 0 0 1 0 1 6 0 0—8 12 0
San Diego ....0 0 2 0 0 1 0 0 0—3 8 0
Neagle, Martinez (6), Rocker (7), O. Perez (8), Seanez (8), Ligtenberg (9) and Lopez; Hamilton, R. Myers (7), Miceli (7), Boehringer (8), Langston (9) and Hernandez. W—Martinez. L—Hamilton. HR—Leyritz (S.D.); Lopez, Galarraga (Atl.).

Game 5—October 12, at San Diego
Atlanta.........0 0 0 1 0 1 0 5 0—7 14 1
San Diego ....2 0 0 0 0 2 0 0 2—6 10 1
Smoltz, Rocker (7), Seanez (8), Ligtengerg (9), Maddux (9) and Lopez, E. Perez; Ashby, Langston (7), Brown (7), Wall (8), Boehringer (9), R. Myers (9) and Hernandez. W—Rocker. L—Brown. S—Maddux. HR—Caminiti, Vander Wal (S.D.); Tucker (Atl.).

Game 6—October 14, at Atlanta
San Diego ....0 0 0 0 0 5 0 0 0—5 10 0
Atlanta..........0 0 0 0 0 0 0 0 0—2 2 1
Hitchcock, Boehringer (6), Langston (7), Hamilton (7), Hoffman (9) and Leyritz, Hernandez; Glavine, Rocker (6), Martinez (6), Neagle (8) and Lopez. W—Hitchcock. L—Glavine.

WORLD SERIES

■ **Winner:** New York closed out its remarkable season with a four-game sweep of San Diego, giving the Yankees a shockingly efficient 125-50 final 1998 record, including regular season and playoffs. The World Series championship was New York's record 24th overall and second in three years. The sweep was the first in Series play since 1990.
■ **Turning point:** A second-inning Chili Davis smash in Game 1 that struck the left shin of Padres righthander Kevin Brown. San Diego's ace went on to pitch 61/3 innings before leaving with a sore leg and the Yankees exploded for seven runs in the seventh inning, turning a 5-2 deficit into a 9-5 advantage. New York's 9-6 win deflated the overmatched Padres.
■ **Memorable moment:** When Scott Brosius, the World Series MVP, hit a three-run, eighth-inning Game 3 home run off San Diego closer Trevor Hoffman, wiping away a 3-2 New York deficit and giving the Yankees a lead they never relinquished. It was Brosius' second homer of the game and he finished the 5-4 victory with four RBIs.
■ **Top guns:** Tony Gwynn (.500, 3 RBIs), Greg Vaughn (2 HR, 4 RBIs), Sterling Hitchcock (1.50 ERA), Padres; Ricky Ledee (.600, 4 RBIs), Brosius (.471, 2 HR, 6 RBIs), Tino Martinez (.385, 1 HR, 4 RBIs), Andy Pettitte (1-0, 0.00 ERA), Orlando Hernandez (1-0, 1.29 ERA), Mariano Rivera (3 games, 0.00 ERA, 3 saves), Yankees.
■ **MVP:** Brosius.

Game 1—October 17, at New York
San Diego ......0 0 2 0 3 0 0 1 0—6 8 1
New York.........0 2 0 0 0 0 7 0 x—9 9 1
Brown, Wall (7), Langston (7), Boehringer (8), R. Myers (8) and C. Hernandez; Wells, Nelson (8), Rivera (8) and Posada. W—Wells. L—Wall. S—Rivera. HR—Vaughn 2, Gwynn (S.D.); Knoblauch, Martinez (N.Y.).

Game 2—October 18, at New York
San Diego ....0 0 0 0 1 0 0 2 0—3 10 1
New York......3 3 1 0 2 0 0 0 x—9 16 0
Ashby, Boehringer (3), Wall (5), Miceli (8) and G. Myers; O. Hernandez, Stanton (8), Nelson (8) and Posada. W—O. Hernandez. L—Ashby. HR—Williams, Posada (N.Y.).

Game 3—October 20, at San Diego
New York........0 0 0 0 0 0 2 3 0—5 9 1
San Diego ......0 0 0 0 0 3 0 1 0—4 7 1
Cone, Lloyd (7), Mendoza (7), Rivera (8) and Girardi; Hitchcock, Hamilton (7), R. Myers (8), Hoffman (8) and Leyritz, C. Hernandez. W—Mendoza. L—Hoffman. S—Rivera. HR—Brosius 2 (N.Y.).

Game 4—October 21, at San Diego
New York........0 0 0 0 0 1 0 2 0—3 9 0
San Diego ......0 0 0 0 0 0 0 0 0—0 7 0
Pettitte, Nelson (8), Rivera (8) and Girardi; Brown, Miceli (9), R. Myers (9) and C. Hernandez. W—Pettitte. L—Brown. S—Rivera.

Roger Clemens brought home the Cy Young Award for a record fifth time.

FINAL STANDINGS

American League

EAST DIVISION

Team	N.Y.	Bos	Tor.	Bal.	T.B.	Cle.	Chi.	Det.	K.C.	Min.	Tex.	Oak.	Sea.	Ana.	Atl.	N.Y.	Phi.	Mon.	Fla.	W	L	Pct.	GB
New York	—	4	10	9	8	7	7	7	4	6	8	6	9	4	1	3	1	2	2	98	64	.605	—
Boston	8	—	9	7	4	8	7	7	8	6	4	4	7	9	2	1	1	0	2	94	68	.580	4
Toronto	2	3	—	11	8	7	4	10	7	6	4	2	2	9	3	0	1	4	1	84	78	.519	14
Baltimore	4	5	1	—	5	1	7	5	6	8	6	5	5	9	3	1	3	3	1	78	84	.481	20
Tampa Bay	4	9	5	7	—	4	4	5	8	5	4	1	4	5	0	1	1	1	1	69	93	.426	29

CENTRAL DIVISION

Team	Cle.	Chi.	Det.	K.C.	Min.	N.Y.	Bos.	Tor.	Bal.	T.B.	Tex.	Oak.	Sea.	Ana.	Hou.	Cin.	Pit.	St.L.	Mil.	Chi.	W	L	Pct.	GB
Cleveland	—	9	8	7	9	3	4	5	9	5	3	10	7	9	1	4	1	—	1	2	97	65	.599	—
Chicago	3	—	7	6	8	5	5	6	3	6	5	3	4	5	1	—	2	1	1	4	75	86	.466	21.5
Detroit	5	5	—	7	6	5	5	2	5	4	5	4	3	5	0	2	2	3	1	—	69	92	.429	27.5
Kansas City	5	6	4	—	5	5	2	3	4	2	4	6	7	5	0	0	1	2	1	2	64	97	.398	32.5
Minnesota	3	3	6	8	—	4	4	4	1	5	0	7	4	4	1	2	2	2	2	1	63	97	.394	33

WEST DIVISION

Team	Tex.	Oak.	Sea.	Ana.	N.Y.	Bos.	Tor.	Bal.	T.B.	Cle.	Chi.	Det.	K.C.	Min.	Ari.	S.F.	L.A.	S.D.	Col.	W	L	PCT	GB
Texas	—	7	8	6	4	5	6	6	8	7	5	5	6	12	3	3	2	1	1	95	67	.586	—
Oakland	5	—	6	4	4	6	8	7	9	2	7	6	6	5	2	3	3	1	3	87	75	.537	8
Seattle	5	6	—	6	1	3	7	5	8	3	8	7	5	8	2	1	0	2	2	79	83	.488	16
Anaheim	6	8	6	—	6	1	3	3	7	1	5	5	7	6	1	1	2	0	2	70	92	.432	25

National League

EAST DIVISION

Team	Atl.	N.Y.	Phi.	Mon.	Fla.	Hou.	Cin.	Pit.	St.L.	Mil.	Chi.	Ari.	S.F.	L.A.	S.D.	Col.	N.Y.	Bos.	Tor.	Bal.	T.B.	W	L	Pct.	GB
Atlanta	—	9	8	9	9	6	8	6	8	5	2	5	4	5	5	5	2	4	0	0	3	103	59	.636	—
New York	3	—	6	8	10	5	5	7	5	5	6	2	7	4	7	5	3	2	3	2	2	97	66	.595	6.5
Philadelphia	5	6	—	6	11	1	3	3	4	4	7	1	2	3	6	4	2	2	2	3	2	77	85	.475	26
Montreal	4	5	6	—	4	2	3	3	5	4	5	3	4	4	5	3	1	3	2	0	2	68	94	.420	35
Florida	4	3	2	8	—	2	1	3	3	5	3	1	4	7	3	4	1	1	2	2	5	64	98	.395	39

CENTRAL DIVISION

Team	Hou.	Cin.	Pit.	St.L.	Mil.	Chi.	Atl.	N.Y.	Phi.	Mon.	Fla.	Ari.	S.F.	L.A.	S.D.	Col.	Cle.	Chi.	Det.	K.C.	Min.	W	L	Pct.	GB
Houston	—	4	5	5	8	9	1	4	6	7	7	4	5	6	8	6	2	2	3	3	2	97	65	.599	—
Cincinnati	9	—	7	8	6	8	1	5	6	4	6	8	4	4	6	7	2	—	1	3	1	96	67	.589	1.5
Pittsburgh	7	6	—	7	4	6	3	2	4	6	4	2	4	6	3	7	2	1	1	2	1	78	83	.484	18.5
St. Louis	7	4	5	—	6	5	1	2	5	4	4	4	3	6	7	5	—	2	3	1	1	75	86	.466	21.5
Milwaukee	5	6	8	7	—	6	2	2	5	5	4	4	4	2	3	3	2	2	2	2	0	74	87	.460	22.5
Chicago	3	5	7	7	6	—	5	3	2	2	6	2	1	2	6	4	1	2	—	1	2	67	95	.414	30

WEST DIVISION

Team	Ari.	S.F.	L.A.	S.D.	Col.	Atl.	N.Y.	Phi.	Mon.	Fla.	Hou.	Cin.	Pit.	St.L.	Mil.	Chi.	Tex.	Oak.	Sea.	Ana.	W	L	Pct.	GB
Arizona	—	9	7	11	6	4	7	8	6	8	5	1	5	4	5	7	3	1	1	2	100	62	.617	—
San Fran.	3	—	5	7	9	5	2	6	5	5	4	5	5	6	5	7	0	3	2	2	86	76	.531	14
Los Angeles	6	8	—	3	5	4	4	6	5	2	3	3	3	3	7	7	1	0	3	4	77	85	.475	23
San Diego	2	5	9	—	9	4	2	3	3	6	1	3	6	2	5	3	2	2	4	3	74	88	.457	26
Colorado	7	4	8	4	—	4	4	5	6	5	2	2	2	4	6	5	2	0	1	1	72	90	.444	28

LEADERS

American League
BA: Nomar Garciaparra, Bos., .357.
Runs: Roberto Alomar, Cle., 138.
Hits: Derek Jeter, N.Y., 219.
TB: Shawn Green, Tor., 361.
HR: Ken Griffey Jr., Sea., 48.
RBI: Manny Ramirez, Cle., 165.
SB: Brian L. Hunter, Det.-Sea., 44.
Wins: Pedro Martinez, Bos., 23.
ERA: Pedro Martinez, Bos., 2.07.
CG: David Wells, Tor., 7.
IP: David Wells, Tor., 231.2.
SO: Pedro Martinez, Bos., 313.
Sv.: Mariano Rivera, N.Y., 45.

National League
BA: Larry Walker, Col., .379.
Runs: Jeff Bagwell, Hou., 143.
Hits: Luis Gonzalez, Ari., 206.
TB: Sammy Sosa, Chi., 397.
HR: Mark McGwire, St.L., 65.
RBI: Mark McGwire, St.L., 147.
SB: Tony Womack, Ari., 72.
Wins: Mike Hampton, Hou., 22.
ERA: Randy Johnson, Ari., 2.48.
CG: Randy Johnson, Ari., 12.
IP: Randy Johnson, Ari., 271.2.
SO: Randy Johnson, Ari., 364.
Sv.: Ugueth Urbina, Mon., 41.

A.L. 20-game winner
Pedro Martinez, Bos., 23

N.L. 20-game winners
Mike Hampton, Hou., 22
Jose Lima, Hou., 21

A.L. 100 RBIs
Manny Ramirez, Cle., 165
Rafael Palmeiro, Tex., 148
Ken Griffey Jr., Sea., 134
Carlos Delgado, Tor., 134
Juan Gonzalez, Tex., 128
Jason Giambi, Oak., 123
Shawn Green, Tor., 123
Roberto Alomar, Cle., 120
Jermaine Dye, K.C., 119
Albert Belle, Bal., 117
Magglio Ordonez, Chi., 117
Richie Sexson, Cle., 116
Bernie Williams, N.Y., 115
Ivan Rodriguez, Tex., 113
John Jaha, Oak., 111
Alex Rodriguez, Sea., 111
Paul O'Neill, N.Y., 110
Carlos Beltran, K.C., 108
Jim Thome, Cle., 108
Mo Vaughn, Ana., 108
B.J. Surhoff, Bal., 107
Tino Martinez, N.Y., 105
Nomar Garciaparra, Bos., 104
Fred McGriff, T.B., 104
Harold Baines, Bal.-Cle., 103
Troy O'Leary, Bos., 103
Derek Jeter, N.Y., 102
Matt Stairs, Oak., 102
Mike Sweeney, K.C., 102
Rusty Greer, Tex., 101
Dean Palmer, Det., 100

N.L. 100 RBIs
Mark McGwire, St.L., 147
Matt Williams, Ari., 142
Sammy Sosa, Chi., 141
Dante Bichette, Col, 133
Vladimir Guerrero, Mon., 131
Jeff Bagwell, Hou., 126
Mike Piazza, N.Y., 124
Robin Ventura, N.Y., 120
Greg Vaughn, Cin., 118
Brian Giles, Pit., 115
Brian Jordan, Atl., 115
Larry Walker, Col., 115
Todd Helton, Col., 113
Jay Bell, Ari., 112
Eric Karros, L.A., 112
Luis Gonzalez, Ari., 111
Chipper Jones, Atl., 110
Edgardo Alfonzo, N.Y., 108
Carl Everett, Hou., 108
Fernando Tatis, St.L., 107
Kevin Young, Pit., 106
Jeromy Burnitz, Mil., 103
Steve Finley, Ari., 103
Rico Brogna, Phi., 102
Vinny Castilla, Col., 102
Jeff Kent, S.F., 101
Gary Sheffield, L.A., 101

N.L./A.L. 100 RBIs
Tony Batista, Ari.-Tor., 100

A.L. 40 homers
Ken Griffey Jr., Sea., 48
Rafael Palmeiro, Tex., 47
Carlos Delgado, Tor., 44
Manny Ramirez, Cle., 44
Shawn Green, Tor., 42
Alex Rodriguez, Sea., 42

N.L. 40 homers
Mark McGwire, St.L., 65
Sammy Sosa, Chi., 63
Chipper Jones, Atl., 45
Greg Vaughn, Cin., 45
Jeff Bagwell, Hou., 42
Vladimir Guerrero, Mon., 42
Mike Piazza, N.Y., 40

Most Valuable Player
A.L.: Ivan Rodriguez, C, Tex.
N.L.: Chipper Jones, 3B, Atl.

Cy Young Award
A.L.: Pedro Martinez, Bos.
N.L.: Randy Johnson, Ari.

Rookie of the Year
A.L.: Carlos Beltran, OF, K.C.
N.L.: Scott Williamson, P, Cin.

Manager of the Year
A.L.: Jimy Williams, Bos.
N.L.: Jack McKeon, Cin.

Hall of Fame additions
George Brett, 3B, 1973-93
Orlando Cepeda, OF-1B, 1958-74
Nestor Chylak, umpire
Nolan Ryan, P, 1966-93
Frank Selee, M, 1890-1905
Smokey Joe Williams, P, Negro Leagues
Robin Yount, SS-OF, 1974-93

SIGNIFICANT EVENTS

■ **March 28:** As part of a U.S. initiative to build ties with Cuba, the Baltimore Orioles played the first game of a two-game exhibition series against the Cuban National Team. The Orioles won the game, played in Havana, 3-2 in 11 innings. The second game was played on May 3 in Baltimore, and this time the Cubans won, 12-6.

■ **April 4:** The San Diego Padres opened their "home" season with a game in Monterrey, Mexico, losing before a capaticy crowd of 27,104 to the Colorado Rockies, 8-2.

■ **July 14:** A 567-foot crane lifting a 400-ton section of Miller Park, the Milwaukee Brewers' new home under construction, collapsed, killing three in the accident. The damage was estimated at $50 to $75 million and postponed the anticipated opening of the park until the 2001 season.

■ **July 14:** Richie Phillips, general counsel of the Major League Umpires Association, announced a mass resignation of umpires, effective September 2. This strategy, designed to force management to the bargaining table before December 31, the expiration date of the contract, backfired. Major League Baseball accepted the resignations of 22 umpires, and the union split in two. On November 30, dissidents won an NLRB election, decertifying the MLUA.

■ **July 15:** The Mariners opened their new park, Safeco Field, with a 3-2 loss to the San Diego Padres. The Mariners had played their final game at the Kingdome on June 27, defeating Texas, 5-2.

■ **September 27:** The Detroit Tigers played their final game at Tiger Stadium, beating Kansas City, 8-2.

■ **September 30:** The San Francisco Giants played their final game at 3Com Park (formerly Candlestick Park), losing a 9-4 contest to the Los Angeles Dodgers.

■ **October 9:** The Astros played their final game at the Houston Astrodome—baseball's first domed stadium—losing the fourth and final game of the N.L. Division Series to the Atlanta Braves, 7-5.

MEMORABLE MOMENTS

■ **April 13:** Fernando Tatis of the St. Louis Cardinals became the first player in major league history to hit two grand slams in the same inning. Both came off Los Angeles Dodgers starter Chan Ho Park during an 11-run third inning in a 12-5 victory over the Dodgers.

■ **May 3:** Creighton Gubanich of the Boston Red Sox became the fourth player to hit a grand slam for his first big-league hit in a game at Oakland.

■ **May 20:** Robin Ventura of the New York Mets became the first player in major league history to belt grand slams in both games of a doubleheader against Milwaukee at Shea Stadium.

■ **July 18:** David Cone of the New York Yankees pitched the second perfect game at Yankee Stadium in two years and only the 14th perfecto of the modern era, when he retired all 27 Montreal Expos batters in a 6-0 victory.

■ **August 6:** San Diego's Tony Gwynn singled off the Expos' Dan Smith at Montreal for his 3,000th major league hit.

■ **August 7:** Wade Boggs of the Devil Rays homered off Chris Haney of the Cleveland Indians for his 3,000th big-league hit.

■ **August 5:** Mark McGwire of St. Louis became the 17th member of the 500-home run club, and reached the milestone in his 5,487th career at-bat—the fewest at-bats ever needed to reach 500 homers. McGwire ended the season in 10th place on the all-time list with 522.

■ **September 18:** Sammy Sosa became the first player to hit 60 homers twice when he hit his 60th at Wrigley Field against Milwaukee. Mark McGwire of the Cardinals joined Sosa eight days later, and hit five more thereafter to edge Sosa for the home run crown, 65-63.

ALL-STAR GAME

■ **Winner:** The A.L. won the contest with pitching and timely hitting, extending its streak to four straight victories over the N.L. American League starting pitcher Pedro Martinez struck out the first four batters and five of the six he retired.

■ **Key inning:** The first, when Cleveland players provided most of the excitement. Kenny Lofton singled and two outs later stole second. Manny Ramirez walked and Jim Thome singled Lofton home with the game's first run. Baltimore's Cal Ripken followed with a single to drive in Ramirez.

■ **Memorable moment:** Mike Mussina struck out Sammy Sosa and Mark McGwire with runners on second and third to end the fifth inning. The strikeouts shut down the N.L.'s last big scoring threat of the game.

■ **Top guns:** Martinez (Red Sox), Lofton (Indians), Thome (Indians), Ripken (Orioles), Rafael Palmeiro (Rangers), A.L.; Jeromy Burnitz (Brewers), Barry Larkin (Reds), N.L.

■ **MVP:** Martinez.

Linescore

July 13 at Boston's Fenway Park

N.L. ....0 0 1 0 0 0 0 0 0—1 7 1
A.L. ....2 0 0 2 0 0 0 0 x—4 6 2

Schilling (Phillies), Johnson (Diamondbacks) 3, Bottenfield (Cardinals) 4, Lima (Astros) 5, Millwood (Braves) 6, Ashby (Padres) 7, Hampton (Astros) 7, Hoffman (Padres) 8, Wagner (Astros) 8 and Piazza (Mets), Lieberthal (Phillies), Nilsson (Brewers); Martinez (Red Sox), Cone (Yankees) 3, Mussina (Orioles) 5, Rosado (Royals) 6, Zimmerman (Rangers) 7, Hernandez (Devil Rays) 8, Wetteland (Rangers) 9 and Rodriguez (Rangers), Ausmus (Tigers). W—Martinez. L—Schilling. S—Wetteland.

A.L. DIVISION SERIES

■ **Winners:** For the second straight year the New York Yankees swept the Texas Rangers and held the Rangers to only one run in the series. The Boston Red Sox came back from a two-game deficit to defeat the Cleveland Indians in a high-scoring five-game series.

■ **Turning points:** The Yankees' Bernie Williams lined a two-run double in the fifth inning of the opener and finished the game with six RBIs in an 8-0 victory. Down 1-0 with runners on second and third and nobody out in the fifth inning of Game 2, Andy Pettitte settled down by striking out Mark McLemore, getting Royce Clayton to ground out and striking out Rusty Greer to end the inning. The Yankees scored three runs over the next four innings to win the game. A pair of 37-year-olds—pitcher Roger Clemens and slugger Darryl Strawberry— were the heroes of Game 3. Clemens pitched seven shutout innings after Strawberry gave the Yankees all their runs with a three-run homer in the first inning.

■ **Memorable moments:** Troy O'Leary, who had hit a grand slam earlier in the game, hit a two-run homer in the seventh inning to break an 8-8 tie in the deciding fifth game. O'Leary collected seven RBIs in the game, matching John Valentin's total a night earlier when the Red Sox tied the series with a 23-7 trouncing of the Indians. Valentin also contributed heavily in the Game 3 victory with a two-run double, and Brian Daubach chipped in a three-run homer in the 9-3 victory.

■ **Memorable performances:** Orlando Hernandez allowed only two hits in his series-opening victory. Clemens was unscored upon in his seven-inning Game 3 stint, and Pettitte allowed only a home run to Juan Gonzalez in his Game 2 victory. Derek Jeter led all batters with five hits, three runs scored and a .455 average during the series. Williams finished with a .364 average, four hits and six RBIs. The Red Sox had many offensive stars in their series. Mike Stanley led all batters with 10 hits, and batted .500. Nomar Garciaparra batted .417 with six runs, two doubles and two homers. Valentin hit three homers and collected 12 RBIs, and Jose Offerman added seven hits, six RBIs and batted .389. Much of the Red Sox's offense was provided in Game 4, when they exploded for 24 hits and slugged four home runs in a 23-7 thrashing of Cleveland. While the Indians were outhit, .318 to .233, they had some offensive stars, led by Jim Thome (four homers, seven runs, .353 average) and Roberto Alomar (four doubles, seven hits, .368 average).

Linescores

New York vs. Texas

Game 1—October 5, at New York
Texas............0 0 0 0 0 0 0 0—0 2 1
New York......0 1 0 0 2 4 0 1 x—8 10 0
Sele, Crabtree (6), Venafro (6), Patterson (7), Fassero (8) and Rodriguez; Hernandez, Nelson (9) and Posada. W—Hernandez. L—Crabtree. HR—Williams (N.Y.).

Game 2—October 7, at New York
Texas.............0 0 0 1 0 0 0 0 0—1 7 0
New York........0 0 0 0 1 0 1 1 x—3 7 2
Helling, Crabtree (7), Venafro (8) and Rodriguez; Pettitte, Nelson (8), Rivera (9) and Girardi. W—Pettitte. L—Helling. S—Rivera. HR—Gonzalez (Tex.).

Game 3—October 9, at Texas
New York........3 0 0 0 0 0 0 0 0—3 6 0
Texas.............0 0 0 0 0 0 0 0 0—0 5 1
Clemens, Nelson (8), Rivera (8) and Girardi; Loaiza, Zimmerman (8), Wetteland (9) and Rodriguez. W—Clemens. L—Loaiza. S—Rivera. HR—Strawberry (N.Y.).

Boston vs. Cleveland

Game 1—October 6, at Cleveland
Boston............0 1 0 1 0 0 0 0 0—2 5 1
Cleveland........0 0 0 0 0 2 0 0 1—3 6 1
P. Martinez, Lowe (5), Cormier (9), Garces (9) and Varitek; Colon, Shuey (9) and S. Alomar. W—Shuey. L—Lowe. HR—Garciaparra (Bos.); Thome (Cle.).

Game 2—October 7, at Cleveland
Boston..........0 0 1 0 0 0 0 0 0— 1 6 0
Cleveland......0 0 6 5 0 0 0 0 x—11 8 0
Saberhagen, Wasdin (3), Wakefield (5), Gordon (7), Beck (8) and Varitek; Nagy, Karsay (8), Jackson (8) and S. Alomar. W—Nagy. L—Saberhagen. HR—Baines, Thome (Cle.).

Game 3—October 9, at Boston
Cleveland......0 0 0 1 0 1 1 0 0—3 9 1
Boston..........0 0 0 0 2 1 6 0 x—9 11 2
Burba, Wright (5), Rincon (7), DePaula (7), Reed (8) and S. Alomar; R. Martinez, Lowe (6), Beck (9) and Varitek. W—Lowe. L—Wright. HR—Valentin, Daubach (Bos.).

Game 4—October 10, at Boston
Cleveland....1 1 0 0 4 0 0 0 1— 7 8 0
Boston........2 5 3 5 3 0 3 2 x—23 24 0
Colon, Karsay (2), Reed (4), DePaula (5), Assenmacher (7), Shuey (8) and S. Alomar, Diaz; Mercker, Garces (2), Wakefield (5), Wasdin (5), Cormier (5), Gordon (9) and Varitek, Hatteberg. W—Garces. L—Colon. HR—Cordero (Cle.); Valentin 2, Offerman, Varitek (Bos.).

Game 5—October 11, at Cleveland
Boston........2 0 5 1 0 0 3 0 1—12 10 0
Cleveland....3 2 3 0 0 0 0 0 0— 8 7 1
Saberhagen, Lowe (2), P. Martinez (4) and Varitek; Nagy, DePaula (4), Shuey (7), Jackson (9) and S. Alomar. W—P. Martinez. L—Shuey. HR—O'Leary 2, Garciaparra (Bos.); Thome 2, Fryman (Cle.).

N.L. DIVISION SERIES

■ **Winners:** Following an opening game loss, the Atlanta Braves earned their eighth straight N.L. Championship Series berth by defeating the Houston Astros in three straight games. The wild-card New York Mets, playing in their first postseason action since 1988, beat the second-year expansion Arizona Diamondbacks in four games.

■ **Turning points:** Atlanta starter Kevin Milwood pitched a one-hitter in Game 2, allowing only a home run to Ken Caminiti. John Rocker escaped a 10th inning jam with the bases loaded and no outs in Game 3. Two innings later, Brian Jordan's two-run double drove home the winning runs. The Braves jumped out to a 7-0 lead and held on to a 7-5 victory in Game 4. The Mets took the first game of their series on a ninth-inning grand slam by Edgardo Alfonzo to win the game, 8-4. A two-run single by John Olerud in the sixth inning helped the Mets win Game 3, 9-2, and Todd Pratt's homer in the 10th inning of Game 4 clinched the series for New York. A costly error by Diamondbacks outfielder Tony Womack in the eighth allowed the Mets to tie the game.

■ **Memorable moments:** After the Astros came back from a 7-0 deficit in Game 4, they were down 7-5 with a runner on and nobody out in the ninth. Rocker struck out Jeff Bagwell and Carl Everett, then retired Ken Caminiti, a .471 hitter during the series, for the final out. Olerud's Game 1 homer off Randy Johnson was the first homer by a lefthander off Johnson since September 23, 1997. The two-run third-inning shot gave the Mets a 3-0 lead in the game.

■ **Memorable performances:** Olerud led all hitters with seven hits and a .438 average. In addition, he collected six RBIs. Alfonzo clubbed three homers and also had six RBIs for the Mets. Bret Boone had nine hits and a .474 average to lead the Braves. Jordan chipped in eight hits and seven RBIs while batting .471 for Atlanta. Millwood pitched 10 innings, allowing only one hit, one run, and struck out nine for the Braves.

Linescores

New York vs. Arizona

Game 1—October 5, at Arizona
New York......1 0 2 1 0 0 0 0 4—8 10 0
Arizona ......0 0 1 1 0 2 0 0 0—4 7 0
Yoshii, Cook (6), Wendell (8), Benitez (9) and Piazza; Johnson, Chouinard (9) and Stinnett. W—Wendell. L—Johnson. HR—Alfonzo 2, Olerud (N.Y.); Durazo, Gonzalez (Ari.).

Game 2—October 6, at Arizona
New York........0 0 1 0 0 0 0 0 0—1 5 0
Arizona ....0 0 3 0 2 0 2 0 x—7 9 1
Rogers, Mahomes (5), Dotel (7), J. Franco (7) and Piazza; Stottlemyre, Olson (7), Swindell (8) and Stinnett. W—Stottlemyre. L—Rogers.

Game 3—October 8, at New York
Arizona ......0 0 0 0 2 0 0 0 0—2 5 3
New York......0 1 2 0 0 6 0 0 x—9 11 0
Daal, Holmes (5), Plesac (6), Chouinard (6), Swindell (8) and Stinnett; Reed, Wendell (7), J. Franco (8), Hershiser (9) and Pratt. W—Reed. L—Daal. HR—Ward (Ari.).

Game 4—October 9, at New York
Arizona ....0 0 0 0 1 0 0 2 0 0—3 5 1
New York ..0 0 0 1 0 1 0 1 0 1—4 8 0
Anderson, Olson (8), Swindell (8), Mantei (8) and Stinnett; Leiter, Benitez (8), J. Franco (9) and Pratt. W—J. Franco. L—Mantei. HR—Colbrunn (Ari.); Alfonzo, Pratt (N.Y.).

Atlanta vs. Houston

Game 1—October 5, at Atlanta
Houston ......0 1 0 0 0 1 0 0 4—6 13 0
Atlanta..........0 0 0 0 1 0 0 0 0—1 7 0
Reynolds, Miller (7), Henry (7), Wagner (9) and Eusebio; Maddux, Remlinger (8) and Perez. W—Reynolds. L—Maddux. HR—Ward, Caminiti (Hou.).

Game 2—October 6, at Atlanta
Houston ....0 1 0 0 0 0 0 0 0—1 1 1
Atlanta ....1 0 0 0 0 1 3 0 x—5 11 1
Lima, Elarton (7), Powell (8) and Eusebio; Millwood and Perez. W—Millwood. L—Lima. HR—Caminiti (Hou.).

Game 3—October 8, at Houston
Atl. ....0 0 0 0 0 3 0 0 0 0 0 2—5 12 0
Hou. ..2 0 0 0 0 0 1 0 0 0 0 0—3 9 2
Glavine, Mulholland (7), Maddux (7), Remlinger (7), Springer (9), Rocker (10), Millwood (12) and Perez; Hampton, Cabrera (8), Henry (10), Powell (12) and Eusebio. W—Rocker. L—Powell. S—Millwood. HR—Jordan (Atl.).

Game 4—October 4, at San Diego
Atlanta ....1 0 1 0 0 5 0 0 0—7 15 1
Houston ....0 0 0 0 0 0 1 4 0—5 8 1
Smoltz, Mulholland (8), McGlinchy (8), Rocker (8) and Perez; Reynolds, Holt (6), Elarton (6), Miller (8), Powell (9) and Eusebio. W—Smoltz. L—Reynolds. S—Rocker. HR—Eusebio, Caminiti (Hou.).

ALCS

■ **Winner:** Despite being outhit, .293 to .239, the New York Yankees used timely hitting to defeat the Boston Red Sox in five games to advance to the franchise's record 36th World Series.

■ **Turning point:** Yankee center fielder Bernie Williams belted a home run in the bottom of the 10th inning to cap a 4-3 comeback win in the opening game. Down, 2-0 and then 3-2 early in the contest, the Yankees tied the score in the seventh when Derek Jeter singled home Scott Brosius.

■ **Memorable moment:** With his team trailing, 3-2 in the bottom of the eighth, Boston's Jose Offerman was declared out on a tag play that umpire Tim Tschida later admitted he called wrong. It was the second time in the series an umpire admitted making an incorrect call against the Red Sox. An inning later, the Red Sox allowed six runs in the top of the ninth and lost, 9-2. In that frame, Offerman made a bad throw on a double-play ball. The error kept the inning alive and Ricky Ledee followed with a grand slam.

■ **Top guns:** Derek Jeter (.350, 7 hits), Hernandez (1-0, 15 IP, 13 SO, 1.80 ERA), Chuck Knoblauch (.333, 6 hits), Scott Brosius (2 HRs), Yankees; Jose Offerman (.458, 11 hits), Nomar Garciaparra (.400, 8 hits, 2 HR, 5 RBIs), Troy O'Leary (.350, 7 hits, 3 doubles), John Valentin (.348, 8 hits, 5 RBIs), P. Martinez (1-0, 7 IP, 12 SO, 0.00 ERA), Red Sox.

■ **MVP:** Hernandez.

Linescores

Game 1—October 13, at New York
Boston ....2 1 0 0 0 0 0 0 0 0—3 8 3
New York ....0 2 0 0 0 0 1 0 0 1—4 10 0
Mercker, Garces (5), Lowe (7), Cormier (9), Beck (10) and Varitek; Hernandez, Rivera (9) and Posada. W—Rivera. L—Beck. HR—Brosius, Williams (N.Y.).

Game 2—October 14, at New York
Boston..........0 0 0 0 2 0 0 0 0—2 10 0
New York.......0 0 0 1 0 0 2 0 x—3 7 0
R. Martinez, Gordon (7), Cormier (7) and Varitek; Cone, Stanton (8), Nelson (8), Watson (8), Mendoza (8), Rivera (9) and Girardi. W—Cone. L—R. Martinez. S—Rivera. HR—Garciaparra (Bos.); T. Martinez (N.Y.).

Game 3—October 16, at Boston
New York....0 0 0 0 0 0 0 1 0— 1 3 3
Boston........2 2 2 0 2 1 4 0 x—13 21 1
Clemens, Irabu (3), Stanton (7), Watson (8) and Girardi, Posada; P. Martinez, Gordon (8), Rapp (9) and Varitek, Hatteberg. W—P. Martinez. L—Clemens. HR—Brosius (N.Y.); Valentin, Daubach, Garciaparra (Bos.).

Game 4—October 10, at Boston
New York......0 1 0 2 0 0 0 0 6—9 11 0
Boston..........0 1 1 0 0 0 0 0 0—2 10 4
Pettitte, Rivera (8) and Girardi; Saberhagen, Lowe (7), Cormier (8), Garces (8), Beck (9) and Varitek. W—Pettitte. L—Saberhagen. S—Rivera. HR—Strawberry, Ledee (N.Y.).

Game 5—October 11, at Boston
New York......2 0 0 0 0 0 2 0 2—6 11 1
Boston..........0 0 0 0 0 0 0 1 0—1 5 2
Hernandez, Stanton (8), Nelson (8), Watson (8), Mendoza (8) and Posada; Mercker, Lowe (4), Cormier (7), Gordon (9) and Varitek. W—Hernandez. L—Mercker. S—Mendoza. HR—Jeter, Posada (N.Y.); Varitek (Bos.).

NLCS

■ **Winner:** The Atlanta Braves jumped out to a three-game lead in the series, then held on to win their fifth National League pennant of the '90s in six games. The Braves dominated the Mets during the regular season, winning nine of 12 games. Atlanta compiled a 103-59 record and finished 6 1/2 games ahead of the wild-card Mets. New York, which had a major league low 68 errors during the regular season, didn't field as well in the series, committing eight errors.

■ **Turning point:** Game 2, when Mets manager Bobby Valentine decided to stay with starter Kenny Rogers over reliever Turk Wendell against Eddie Perez in the sixth inning. Rogers had just given up a two-run homer to Brian Jordan and a single to Andruw Jones, and the hot-hitting Perez was coming to bat. Valentine left Rogers in, and Perez belted a two-run homer giving the Braves a 4-2 lead.

■ **Memorable moment:** Robin Ventura belted a game-ending grand slam in the 15th inning in Game 5, but the hit was officially declared a single when he was mobbed by teammates after rounding first base and couldn't complete the trip around the bases. The hit enabled to Mets to win the game, 4-3, and kept New York in the series.

■ **Top guns:** Perez (.500, 10 hits, 2 doubles, 2 HRs, 5 RBIs), Jordan (2 HRs, 5 RBIs), Greg Maddux (1-0, 14 IP, 1.93 ERA), Braves; Roger Cedeno (.500, 6 hits), John Olerud (8 hits, 6 RBIs), Edgardo Alfonzo (4 doubles), Mets.

■ **MVP:** Perez.

Game 1—October 12, at Atlanta
New York..........0 0 0 1 0 0 0 0 1—2 6 2
Atlanta..............1 0 0 0 1 1 0 1 x—4 8 2
Yoshii, Mahomes (5), Cook (7), Wendell (8) and Piazza; Maddux, Remlinger (8), Rocker (8) and Perez. W—Maddux. L—Yoshii. S—Rocker. HR—Perez (Atl.).

Game 2—October 13, at Atlanta
New York........0 1 0 0 1 0 0 1 0—3 5 1
Atlanta............0 0 0 0 0 4 0 0 0—4 9 1
Rogers, Wendell (6), Benitez (8) and Piazza; Millwood, Rocker (8), Smoltz (9) and Perez. W—Millwood. L—Rogers. S—Smoltz. HR—Mora (N.Y.); Jordan, Perez (Atl.).

Game 3—October 15, at New York
Atlanta ....1 0 0 0 0 0 0 0 0—1 3 1
New York........0 0 0 0 0 0 0 0 0—0 7 2
Glavine, Remlinger (8), Rocker (9) and Perez; Leiter, J. Franco (8), Benitez (8) and Piazza. W—Glavine. L—Leiter. S—Rocker.

Game 4—October 16, at New York
Atlanta............0 0 0 0 0 0 0 2 0—2 3 0
New York........0 0 0 0 0 1 0 2 x—3 5 0
Smoltz, Remlinger (8), Rocker (8) and Perez; Reed, Wendell (8), Benitez (9) and Piazza. W—Wendell. L—Remlinger. S—Benitez. HR—Jordan, Klesko (Atl.); Olerud (N.Y.).

Game 5—October 17, at New York
Atl. ..0 0 0 2 0 0 0 0 0 0 0 0 0 0 1—3 13 2
N.Y. ..2 0 0 0 0 0 0 0 0 0 0 0 0 0 2—4 11 1
Maddux, Mulholland (8), Remlinger (10), Springer (12), Rocker (13), McGlinchy (14) and Perez, Myers; Yoshii, Hershiser (4), Wendell (7), Cook (7), Mahomes (7), J. Franco (8), Benitez (10), Rogers (11), Dotel (13) and Piazza, Pratt. W—Dotel. L—McGlinchy. HR—Olerud (N.Y.).

Game 6—October 19, at Atlanta
N.Y. ....0 0 0 0 0 3 4 1 0 1 0— 9 15 2
Atlanta ....5 0 0 0 0 2 0 1 0 1 1—10 10 1
Leiter, Mahomes (1), Wendell (5), Cook (6), Hershiser (7), J. Franco (8), Benitez (9), Rogers (11) and Piazza, Pratt; Millwood, Mulholland (6), Smoltz (7), Remlinger (7), Rocker (9), Springer (11) and Perez, Myers. W—Springer. L—Rogers. HR—Piazza (N.Y.).

WORLD SERIES

■ **Winner:** After sweeping San Diego in the 1999 World Series, the New York Yankees swept their second straight World Series, this time against Atlanta. The World Series championship was New York's record 25th overall and third in four years. The sweep was the eighth by the Yankees.

■ **Turning point:** Two errors by Brian Hunter, inserted into the lineup as a defensive replacement for Ryan Klesko at first base in the eighth inning, allowed the Yankees to turn a 1-0 deficit into a 4-1 victory in the opener. After Scott Brosius singled and Darryl Strawberry walked, Chad Curtis came in to pinch-run for Strawberry. Chuck Knoblauch sacrificed but was safe at first on Hunter's first error, which allowed the other runners to advance to third and second. Derek Jeter singled home Brosius to tie the game, 1-1, and John Rocker replaced starter Greg Maddux on the mound. Paul O'Neill singled and went to second on a wild throw by Hunter—his second error of the inning—as Curtis and Knoblauch scored and Jeter went to third. The Yankees scored one more run in the inning to take a 4-1 lead, which became the final score.

■ **Memorable moment:** When Knoblauch tied Game 3 in the eighth with a two-run homer off Braves starter Tom Glavine. Glavine, who had been pushed back from a Game 1 start because of the flu, had given his club seven strong innings. Atlanta manager Bobby Cox gambled and left Glavine in to pitch the eighth, but the Braves lefthander allowed a leadoff single to Joe Girardi, followed by Knoblauch's shot, which knotted the game, 5-5.

■ **Top guns:** Brosius (.375, 6 hits), Jeter (.353, 4 runs, 6 hits), Curtis (.333, 2 HR), Tino Martinez (5 RBIs), David Cone (1-0, 0.00 ERA), Roger Clemens (1-0, 1.17 ERA), Orlando Hernandez (1-0, 1.29 ERA, 10 SO), Mariano Rivera (1-0, 2 Saves, 0.00 ERA), Yankees; Bret Boone (.538, 7 hits, 4 doubles), Braves.

■ **MVP:** Rivera.

Linescores

Game 1—October 23, at Atlanta
New York........0 0 0 0 0 0 0 4 0—4 6 0
Atlanta............0 0 0 1 0 0 0 0 0—1 2 2
O. Hernandez, Nelson (8), Stanton (8), Rivera (8) and Posada; Maddux, Rocker (8), Remlinger (9) and Perez. W—O. Hernandez. L—Maddux. S—Rivera. HR—C. Jones (Atl.).

Game 2—October 24, at Atlanta
New York......3 0 2 1 1 0 0 0 0—7 14 1
Atlanta.........0 0 0 0 0 0 0 0 2—2 5 1
Cone, Mendoza (8), Nelson (9) and Girardi; Millwood, Mulholland (3), Springer (6), McGlinchy and Myers. W—Cone. L—Millwood.

Game 3—October 26, at New York
Atlanta ....1 0 3 1 0 0 0 0 0 0—5 14 1
New York..1 0 0 0 1 0 1 2 0 1—6 9 0
Glavine, Rocker (8), Remlinger (10) and Perez, Myers; Pettitte, Grimsley (4), Nelson (7), Rivera (9) and Girardi. W—Rivera. L—Remlinger. HR—Curtis 2, Knoblauch, Martinez (N.Y.).

Game 4—October 27, at New York
Atlanta............0 0 0 0 0 0 0 1 0—1 5 0
New York........0 0 3 0 0 0 0 1 x—4 8 0
Smoltz, Mulholland (8), Springer (8) and Perez, Myers; Clemens, Nelson (8), Rivera (8) and Posada. W—Clemens. L—Smoltz. S—Rivera.

HISTORY

Franchise Histories

The 1930 Athletics, the consecutive World Series champions managed by the incomparable Connie Mack (center, in suit), rank among the great teams in baseball history.

Anaheim Angels

FRANCHISE CHRONOLOGY

First season: 1961, as the Los Angeles Angels, with home games played at Los Angeles' Wrigley Field. The Angels, who shared distinction with the second-edition Washington Senators as baseball's first expansion teams, recorded a 7-2 victory at Baltimore in their Major League debut. They went on to post a 70-91 first-season record, good for eighth place in the 10-team A.L.

1962-present: The second-year Angels moved out of tiny Wrigley Field and up in the standings. Sharing new Dodger Stadium with the N.L. Dodgers, they posted a surprising 86-76 record, good for third place behind New York and Minnesota. That success was an illusion. The Angels, who swapped the "Los Angeles" part of their name for "California" in 1965 and moved into new Anaheim Stadium a year later, didn't win their first West Division title until 1979 and failed in their three journeys into the A.L. Championship Series. They were within one pitch of reaching the World Series in the 1986 ALCS when Boston's Dave Henderson hit a dramatic two-run, Game 5 homer that tied the game and propelled the Red Sox to eventual victory. The Angels, under the new ownership flag of Walt Disney Company, changed their name to "Anaheim Angels" after the 1996 season.

First baseman Rod Carew.

ANGELS VS. OPPONENTS BY DECADE

	A's	Indians	Orioles	Red Sox	Tigers	Twins	White Sox	Yankees	Rangers	Brewers	Royals	Blue Jays	Mariners	Devil Rays	Interleague	Decade Record
1961-69	88-74	82-74	72-83	79-76	60-96	79-82	70-92	61-95	76-80	9-9	9-9					685-770
1970-79	72-97	58-58	52-65	53-64	53-63	89-77	90-79	52-65	77-79	61-67	79-87	20-12	25-18			781-831
1980-89	57-70	69-49	49-71	55-59	55-59	66-57	68-62	49-63	68-55	61-54	50-73	57-63	79-48			783-783
1990-99	55-68	44-59	46-73	47-71	54-53	54-61	60-58	59-58	63-61	47-37	64-56	53-58	59-64	13-10	20-30	738-817
2000-	5-8	3-6	7-5	5-4	5-5	7-3	4-6	5-5	7-5		6-6	5-7	5-8	6-6	12-6	82-80
Totals	277-317	256-246	226-297	239-274	227-276	295-280	292-297	226-286	291- 280	178-167	208-231	135-140	168-138	19-16	32-36	3069-3281

Interleague results: 9-11 vs. Dodgers; 5-8 vs. Padres; 5-8 vs. Giants;9-4 vs. Rockies; 4-5 vs. Diamondbacks.

MANAGERS

(Los Angeles Angels, 1961-65; California Angels, 1965-96)

Name	*Years*	*Record*
Bill Rigney	1961-69	625-707
Lefty Phillips	1969-71	222-225
Del Rice	1972	75-80
Bobby Winkles	1973-74	109-127
Whitey Herzog	1974	2-2
Dick Williams	1974-76	147-194
Norm Sherry	1976-77	76-71
Dave Garcia	1977-78	60-66
Jim Fregosi	1978-81	237-249
Gene Mauch	1981-82, 1985-87	379-332
John McNamara	1983-84, 1996	161-191
Cookie Rojas	1988	75-79
Moose Stubing	1988	0-8
Doug Rader	1989-91	232-216
Buck Rodgers	1991-94	140-172
John Wathan	1992	39-50
Marcel Lachemann	1994-96	161-170
Joe Maddon	1996	8-14
Terry Collins	1997-99	220-237
Joe Maddon	1999	19-10
Mike Scioscia	2000	82-80

WEST DIVISION CHAMPIONS

Year	*Record*	*Manager*	*ALCS Result*
1979	88-74	Fregosi	Lost to Orioles
1982	93-69	Mauch	Lost to Brewers
1986	92-70	Mauch	Lost to Red Sox

ALL-TIME RECORD OF EXPANSION TEAMS

Team	W	L	Pct.	DT	P	WS
Arizona	250	236	.514	1	0	0
Kansas City	2,548	2,497	.505	6	2	1
Toronto	1,867	1,897	.496	5	2	2
Houston	3,052	3,138	.493	6	0	0
Montreal	2,454	2,596	.486	2	0	0
Anaheim	3,069	3,281	.483	3	0	0
Colorado	594	639	.482	0	0	0
Milwaukee	2,421	2,631	.479	2	1	0
New York	2,934	3,246	.475	4	4	2
Texas	2,952	3,381	.466	4	0	0
San Diego	2,315	2,742	.458	3	2	0
Seattle	1,715	2,048	.456	2	0	0
Florida	551	678	.448	0	1	1
Tampa Bay	201	284	.414	0	0	0

DT—Division Titles. P—Pennants won. WS—World Series won.

ATTENDANCE HIGHS

Total	*Season*	*Park*
2,807,360	1982	Anaheim Stadium
2,696,299	1987	Anaheim Stadium
2,655,892	1986	Anaheim Stadium
2,647,291	1989	Anaheim Stadium
2,567,427	1985	Anaheim Stadium

BALLPARK CHRONOLOGY

Edison International Field of Anaheim, formerly Anaheim Stadium (1966-present)

Capacity: 45,050.
First game: Chicago 3, Angels 1 (April 19, 1966).
First batter: Tommie Agee, White Sox.
First hit: Jim Fregosi, Angels (double).
First run: Rick Reichardt, Angels (2nd inning).
First home run: Rick Reichardt, Angels.
First winning pitcher: Tommy John, White Sox.
First-season attendance: 1,400,321.

Wrigley Field, Los Angeles (1961)

Capacity: 20,457.
First game: Minnesota 4, Angels 2 (April 27, 1961).
First-season attendance: 603,510.

Dodger Stadium (1962-65)

Capacity: 56,000.
First game: Kansas City 5, Angels 3 (April 17, 1962).
First-season attendance: 1,144,063.

A.L. MVP

Don Baylor, OF, 1979

CY YOUNG WINNER

Dean Chance, RH, 1964

ROOKIE OF THE YEAR

Tim Salmon, OF, 1993

RETIRED UNIFORMS

No.	*Name*	*Pos.*
11	Jim Fregosi	SS, Manager
26	Gene Autry	Owner
29	Rod Carew	2B-1B
30	Nolan Ryan	P
50	Jimmie Reese	Coach

Righthander Nolan Ryan spent eight record-breaking seasons mowing down hitters for the Angels.

MILESTONE PERFORMANCES

25-plus home runs

47— Troy Glaus 2000
39— Reggie Jackson 1982
37— Bobby Bonds 1977
Leon Wagner 1962
36— Don Baylor 1979
Mo Vaughn 2000
35— Garret Anderson 2000
34— Wally Joyner 1987
Don Baylor 1978
Tim Salmon 1995, 2000
33— Jim Edmonds 1995
Tim Salmon 1997
Mo Vaughn 1999
31— Tim Salmon 1993
30— Doug DeCinces 1982
Bobby Grich 1979
Frank Robinson 1973
Tim Salmon 1996
29— Brian Downing 1987
Troy Glaus 1999
28— Leon Wagner 1961
Brian Downing 1982
Dave Winfield 1991
Chili Davis 1996
27— Reggie Jackson 1985
Chili Davis 1993
Tony Phillips 1995
Jim Edmonds 1996
26— Lee Thomas 1962
Leon Wagner 1963
Doug DeCinces 1986
Chili Davis 1994
Jim Edmonds 1997
Tim Salmon 1998
25— Ken Hunt 1961
Dan Mincher 1967
Don Baylor 1977
Reggie Jackson 1985
Brian Downing 1988
Jim Edmonds 1998
Darin Erstad 2000

100-plus RBIs

139— Don Baylor 1979
129— Tim Salmon 1997
117— Wally Joyner 1987
Mo Vaughn 2000
Garret Anderson 2000
115— Bobby Bonds 1977
112— Chili Davis 1993
108— Mo Vaughn 1999
107— Leon Wagner 1962
Jim Edmonds 1995
105— Tim Salmon 1995
104— Lee Thomas 1962
102— J.T. Snow 1995
Troy Glaus 2000
101— Reggie Jackson 1982
Dan Ford 1979
Bobby Grich 1979
100— Wally Joyner 1986
Darin Erstad 2000

20-plus victories

1964— Dean Chance 20-9
1970— Clyde Wright 22-12
1971— Andy Messersmith 20-13
1973— Nolan Ryan 21-16
Bill Singer 20-14
1974— Nolan Ryan 22-16

A.L. home run champions

1981— Bobby Grich *22
1982— Reggie Jackson *39
2000— Troy Glaus 47

* Tied for league lead

A.L. RBI champions

1979— Don Baylor 139

A.L. batting champions

1970— Alex Johnson .... .329

A.L. ERA champions

1964— Dean Chance 1.65
1977— Frank Tanana 2.54

A.L. strikeout champions

1972— Nolan Ryan 329
1973— Nolan Ryan 383
1974— Nolan Ryan 367
1975— Frank Tanana 269
1976— Nolan Ryan 327
1977— Nolan Ryan 341
1978— Nolan Ryan 260
1979— Nolan Ryan 223

No-hit pitchers

(9 innings or more)
1962— Bo Belinsky .... 2-0 vs. Baltimore
1970— Clyde Wright .... 4-0 vs. Oakland
1973— Nolan Ryan .... 3-0 vs. Kansas City
1973— Nolan Ryan .... 6-0 vs. Detroit
1974— Nolan Ryan .... 4-0 vs. Minnesota
1975— Nolan Ryan .... 1-0 vs. Baltimore
1984— Mike Witt .... 1-0 vs. Texas (Perfect)
1990— Mark Langston-Mike Witt .... 1-0 vs. Seattle

Longest hitting streaks

28— Garret Anderson 1998
25— Rod Carew 1984
23— Jim Edmonds 1995
22— Sandy Alomar 1970
21— Bobby Grich 1981
Randy Velarde 1996
20— Bobby Grich 1979
19— Rod Carew 1982
18— Chad Curtis 1993
Fred Lynn 1982
Rod Carew 1980
Sandy Alomar 1971
Bob Rodgers 1964
17— Ken McMullen 1972
Brian Downing 1987
Garret Anderson 1997
Garret Anderson 1999
Tim Salmon 2000
16— Lee Thomas 1961
Aurelio Rodriguez 1968
Dan Ford 1980
Johnny Ray 1988
Wally Joyner 1991
Garret Anderson 1999
15— Felix Torres 1962
Bobby Knoop 1967
John Stephenson 1971
Leo Cardenas 1972
Dave Collins 1975
Rick Burleson 1981
Brian Downing 1985
Johnny Ray 1989
Dave Gallagher 1991
Chad Curtis 1993
Tim Salmon 1995
Darin Erstad 1998

Outfielders Leon Wagner (left) and Lee Thomas enjoyed good homer and run-production seasons in the 1960s.

INDIVIDUAL SEASON, GAME RECORDS

Dean Chance, the A.L.'s 1964 ERA champion, holds the team single-season record for shutouts with 11.

SEASON

Batting			
At-bats	689	Sandy Alomar	1971
Runs	121	Darin Erstad	2000
		Jim Edmonds	1995
Hits	240	Darin Erstad	2000
Singles	170	Darin Erstad	2000
Doubles	42	3 times	1982
		Last by Jim Edmonds	1998
Triples	13	3 times	
		Last by Devon White	1989
Home runs	47	Troy Glaus	2000
Home runs, rookie	31	Tim Salmon	1993
Grand slams	3	Joe Rudi	1978, 1979
Total bases	366	Darin Erstad	2000
RBIs	139	Don Baylor	1979
Walks	113	Tony Phillips	1995
Most strikeouts	181	Mo Vaughn	2000
Fewest strikeouts	29	Gary DiSarcina	1997
Batting average	.355	Darin Erstad	2000
Slugging pct.	.604	Troy Glaus	2000
Stolen bases	70	Mickey Rivers	1975
Pitching			
Games	72	Minnie Rojas	1967
Complete games	26	Nolan Ryan	1973, 1974
Innings	332.2	Nolan Ryan	1974
Wins	22	Clyde Wright	1970
		Nolan Ryan	1974
Losses	19	4 times	
		Last by Kirk McCaskill	1991
Winning pct.	.773 (17-5)	Bert Blyleven	1989
Walks	204	Nolan Ryan	1977
Strikeouts	383	Nolan Ryan	1973
Shutouts	11	Dean Chance	1964
Home runs allowed	40	Shawn Boskie	1996
Lowest ERA	1.65	Dean Chance	1964
Saves	46	Bryan Harvey	1991

GAME

Batting			
Runs	5	Last by Tim Salmon	4-12-98
Hits	6	Garret Anderson	9-27-96
Doubles	3	Last by Troy Glaus	9-6-00
Triples	2	Last by Reggie Williams	6-30-99
Home runs	3	Last by Dave Winfield	4-13-91
RBIs	8	Last by Adam Kennedy	4-18-2000
Total bases	15	Dave Winfield	4-13-91
Stolen bases	4	Last by Chad Curtis	4-17-93

CAREER RECORDS

BATTING

Games

Brian Downing	1,661
Jim Fregosi	1,429
Bobby Grich	1,222
Tim Salmon	1,113
Gary DiSarcina	1,086
Dick Schofield	1,086
Bob Boone	968
Chili Davis	950
Bob Rodgers	932
Garret Anderson	887

At-bats

Brian Downing	5,854
Jim Fregosi	5,244
Bobby Grich	4,100
Tim Salmon	4,051
Gary DiSarcina	3,744
Garret Anderson	3,507
Chili Davis	3,491
Dick Schofield	3,434
Wally Joyner	3,208
Don Baylor	3,105

Runs

Brian Downing	889
Tim Salmon	716
Jim Fregosi	691
Bobby Grich	601
Chili Davis	520
Don Baylor	481
Rod Carew	474
Jim Edmonds	464
Wally Joyner	455
Garret Anderson	447

Hits

Brian Downing	1,588
Jim Fregosi	1,408
Tim Salmon	1,180
Bobby Grich	1,103
Garret Anderson	1,043
Chili Davis	973
Rod Carew	968
Gary DiSarcina	966
Wally Joyner	925
Don Baylor	813

Doubles

Brian Downing	282
Tim Salmon	231
Jim Fregosi	219
Garret Anderson	205
Gary DiSarcina	186
Bobby Grich	183
Wally Joyner	170
Chili Davis	167
Jim Edmonds	161
Doug DeCinces	149

Triples

Jim Fregosi	70
Mickey Rivers	32
Luis Polonia	27
Dick Schofield	27
Bobby Knoop	25
Devon White	24
Gary Pettis	23
Rod Carew	22
Brian Downing	22
Gary DiSarcina	20
Bobby Grich	20

Home runs

Tim Salmon	230
Brian Downing	222
Chili Davis	156
Bobby Grich	154
Don Baylor	141
Doug DeCinces	130
Reggie Jackson	123
Jim Edmonds	121
Jim Fregosi	115
Wally Joyner	114

Total bases

Brian Downing	2,580
Tim Salmon	2,133
Jim Fregosi	2,112
Bobby Grich	1,788
Chili Davis	1,620
Garret Anderson	1,605
Wally Joyner	1,459
Don Baylor	1,390
Doug DeCinces	1,334
Jim Edmonds	1,316

Runs batted in

Brian Downing	846
Tim Salmon	757
Chili Davis	618
Bobby Grich	557
Jim Fregosi	546
Don Baylor	523
Wally Joyner	518
Garret Anderson	510
Doug DeCinces	481
Jim Edmonds	408

Extra-base hits

Brian Downing	526
Tim Salmon	477
Jim Fregosi	404
Bobby Grich	357
Garret Anderson	330
Chili Davis	329
Wally Joyner	295
Doug DeCinces	294
Jim Edmonds	294
Don Baylor	288

Batting average
(Minimum 500 games)

Rod Carew	.314
Darin Erstad	.301
Garret Anderson	.297
Luis Polonia	.294
Juan Beniquez	.293
Tim Salmon	.291
Jim Edmonds	.290
Wally Joyner	.288
Chili Davis	.279
Albie Pearson	.275

Stolen bases

Gary Pettis	186
Luis Polonia	174
Sandy Alomar Sr.	139
Mickey Rivers	126
Devon White	123
Chad Curtis	116
Jerry Remy	110
Dick Schofield	99
Don Baylor	89
Darin Erstad	87

PITCHING

Earned-run average
(Minimum 500 innings)

Andy Messersmith	2.78
Dean Chance	2.83
Nolan Ryan	3.07
Frank Tanana	3.08
George Brunet	3.13
Paul Hartzell	3.27
Clyde Wright	3.28
Jim McGlothlin	3.37
Fred Newman	3.41
Geoff Zahn	3.64

Wins

Chuck Finley	165
Nolan Ryan	138
Mike Witt	109
Frank Tanana	102
Mark Langston	88
Clyde Wright	87
Kirk McCaskill	78
Dean Chance	74
Andy Messersmith	59
Jim Abbott	54
George Brunet	54

Losses

Chuck Finley	140
Nolan Ryan	121
Mike Witt	107
Clyde Wright	85
Frank Tanana	78
Rudy May	76
Jim Abbott	74
Mark Langston	74
Kirk McCaskill	74
George Brunet	69

Innings pitched

Chuck Finley	2,675.0
Nolan Ryan	2,181.1
Mike Witt	1,965.1
Frank Tanana	1,615.1
Mark Langston	1,445.1
Clyde Wright	1,403.1
Dean Chance	1,236.2
Kirk McCaskill	1,221.0
Rudy May	1,138.2
Jim Abbott	1,073.2

Strikeouts

Nolan Ryan	2,416
Chuck Finley	2,151
Mike Witt	1,283
Frank Tanana	1,233
Mark Langston	1,112
Dean Chance	857
Rudy May	844
Andy Messersmith	768
Kirk McCaskill	714
George Brunet	678

Bases on balls

Nolan Ryan	1,302
Chuck Finley	1,118
Mike Witt	656
Mark Langston	551
Rudy May	484
Dean Chance	462
Clyde Wright	449
Kirk McCaskill	448
Frank Tanana	422
Andy Messersmith	402

Games

Chuck Finley	436
Troy Percival	360
Mike Witt	314
Dave LaRoche	304
Nolan Ryan	291
Clyde Wright	266
Andy Hassler	259
Bryan Harvey	250
Shigetoshi Hasegawa	241
Mike Holtz	238

Shutouts

Nolan Ryan	40
Frank Tanana	24
Dean Chance	21
George Brunet	14
Chuck Finley	14
Geoff Zahn	13
Rudy May	12
Kirk McCaskill	11
Andy Messersmith	11
Mike Witt	10

Saves

Troy Percival	171
Bryan Harvey	126
Dave LaRoche	65
Donnie Moore	61
Bob Lee	58
Joe Grahe	45
Minnie Rojas	43
Ken Tatum	39
Lee Smith	37
Don Aase	27
Art Fowler	27
Luis Sanchez	27

TEAM SEASON, GAME RECORDS

SEASON

Batting

Most at-bats	5,686	1996
Most runs	866	1979
Fewest runs	454	1972
Most hits	1,574	2000
Most singles	1,114	1979
Most doubles	314	1998
Most triples	54	1966
Most home runs	236	2000
Fewest home runs	55	1975
Most grand slams	8	1979, 1983
Most pinch-hit home runs	9	1987
Most total bases	2,659	2000
Most stolen bases	220	1975
Highest batting average	.282	1979
Lowest batting average	.227	1968
Highest slugging pct	.472	2000

Pitching

Lowest ERA	2.91	1964
Highest ERA	5.30	1996
Most complete games	72	1973
Most shutouts	28	1964
Most saves	52	1998
Most walks	713	1961
Most strikeouts	1,091	1998

Fielding

Most errors	192	1961
Fewest errors	96	1989
Most double plays	202	1985
Highest fielding average	.985	1989

General

Most games won	93	1982
Most games lost	95	1968, 1980
Highest win pct	.574	1982
Lowest win pct	.406	1980

GAME, INNING

Batting

Most runs, game	24	8-25-79
Most runs, inning	13	9-14-78 5-12-97
Most hits, game	26	8-25-79, 6-20-80
Most home runs, game	6	Last 4-21-2000
Most total bases, game	52	6-20-80

Lefthander Frank Tanana recorded 102 victories in his eight successful seasons with the Angels.

ANGELS YEAR-BY-YEAR

Year	W	L	Place	Games Back	Manager	Leaders: Batting avg.	Hits	Home runs	RBIs	Wins	ERA
1961	70	91	8th	38½	Rigney	Pearson, .288	L. Thomas, 129	Wagner, 28	Hunt, 84	McBride, 12	Morgan, 2.36
1962	86	76	3rd	10	Rigney	L. Thomas, .290	Moran, 186	Wagner, 37	Wagner, 107	Chance, 14	Chance, 2.96
1963	70	91	9th	34	Rigney	Pearson, .304	Pearson, 176	Wagner, 26	Wagner, 90	Chance, McBride, 13	Navarro, 2.89
1964	82	80	5th	17	Rigney	W. Smith, .301	Fregosi, 140	Adcock, 21	Fregosi, 72	Chance, 20	Lee, 1.51
1965	75	87	7th	27	Rigney	Pearson, .278	Fregosi, 167	Fregosi, 15	Fregosi, 64	Chance, 15	Lee, 1.92
1966	80	82	6th	18	Rigney	Cardenal, .276	Cardenal, 155	Adcock, 18	Knoop, 72	Brunet, Sanford 13	Lee, 2.74
1967	84	77	5th	7½	Rigney	Fregosi, .290	Fregosi, 171	Mincher, 25	Mincher, 76	R. Clark, McGlothlin, Rojas, 12	Rojas, 2.52
1968	67	95	8th	36	Rigney	Reichardt, .255	Fregosi, 150	Reichardt, 21	Reichardt, 73	Brunet, 13	Murphy, 2.17
								—WEST DIVISION—			
1969	71	91	3rd	26	Rigney, Phillips	Johnstone, .270	Alomar, 153	Reichardt, 13	Reichardt, 68	Messersmith, 16	Messersmith, 2.52
1970	86	76	3rd	12	Phillips	A. Johnson, .329	A. Johnson, 202	Fregosi, 22	A. Johnson, 86	Wright, 22	Wright, 2.83
1971	76	86	4th	25½	Phillips	Alomar, .260	Alomar, 179	McMullen, 21	McMullen, 68	Messersmith, 20	Allen, 2.49
1972	75	80	5th	18	Rice	Berry, .289	Oliver, 154	Oliver, 20	Oliver, 76	Ryan, 19	Ryan, 2.28
1973	79	83	4th	15	Winkles	Berry, .284	Oliver, 144	Robinson, 30	Robinson, 97	Ryan, 21	Ryan, 2.87
1974	68	94	6th	22	Winkles, D. Williams, Herzog	Rivers, .285	Doyle, Rivers, 133	Robinson, 20	Robinson, 63	Ryan, 22	Hassler, 2.61
1975	72	89	6th	25½	D. Williams	Bochte, .285	Rivers, 175	Stanton, 14	Stanton, 82	Figueroa, Tanana, 16	Tanana, 2.62
1976	76	86	*4th	14	D. Williams, Sherry	Bonds, .265	Remy, 132	Bonds, 10	Bonds, 54	Tanana, 19	Tanana, 2.43
1977	74	88	5th	28	Sherry, Garcia	Chalk, .277	Bonds, 156	Bonds, 37	Bonds, 115	Ryan, 19	Tanana, 2.54
1978	87	75	*2nd	5	Garcia, Fregosi	Ro. Jackson, .297	Bostock, 168	Baylor, 34	Baylor, 99	Tanana, 18	LaRoche, 2.82
1979	88	74	†1st	+3	Fregosi	Downing, .326	Lansford, 188	Baylor, 36	Baylor, 139	Frost, Ryan, 16	Frost, 3.57
1980	65	95	6th	31	Fregosi	Carew, .331	Carew, 179	Thompson, 17	Lansford, 80	Clear, Tanana, 11	Clear, 3.30
1981	51	59	‡4th/7th	—	Fregosi, Mauch	Carew, .305	Burleson, 126	Grich, 22	Baylor, 66	Forsch, 11	Forsch, 2.88
1982	93	69	†1st	+3	Mauch	Carew, .319	Downing, 175	Jackson, 39	Jackson, 101	Zahn, 18	Kison, 3.17
1983	70	92	*5th	29	McNamara	Carew, .339	Carew, 160	Lynn, 22	Lynn, 74	Forsch, John, Kison, 11	Zahn, 3.33
1984	81	81	*2nd	3	McNamara	Beniquez, .336	Downing, 148	Jackson, 25	Downing, 91	Witt, 15	Zahn, 3.12
1985	90	72	2nd	1	Mauch	Beniquez, .304	Downing, 137	Jackson, 27	Downing, Jackson, 85	Witt, 15	Moore, 1.92
1986	92	70	†1st	+5	Mauch	Joyner, .290	Joyner, 172	DeCinces, 26	Joyner, 100	Witt, 18	Candelaria, 2.55
1987	75	87	*6th	10	Mauch	Joyner, .285	White, 168	Joyner, 34	Joyner, 117	Witt, 16	Buice, 3.39
1988	75	87	4th	29	Rojas, Stubing	Ray, .306	Ray, 184	Downing, 25	C. Davis, 93	Witt, 13	Witt, 4.15
1989	91	71	3rd	8	Rader	Ray, .289	Joyner, 167	C. Davis, 22	C. Davis, 90	Blyleven, 17	Minton, 2.20
1990	80	82	4th	23	Rader	Polonia, .336	Polonia, 135	Parrish, 24	Winfield, 78	Finley, 18	Finley, 2.40
1991	81	81	7th	14	Rader, Rodgers	Joyner, .301	Polonia, 179	Winfield, 28	Joyner, 96	Langston, 19	J. Abbott, 2.89
1992	72	90	*5th	24	Rodgers, Wathan	Polonia, .286	Polonia, 165	Gaetti, 12	Felix, 72	Langston, 13	J. Abbott, 2.77
1993	71	91	*5th	23	Rodgers	Curtis, .285	Curtis, 166	Salmon, 31	C. Davis, 112	Finley, Langston, 16	Finley, 3.15
1994	47	68	4th	5½	M. Lachemann	C. Davis, .311	C. Davis, 122	C. Davis, 26	C. Davis, 84	Finley, 10	Finley, 4.32
1995	78	66	§2nd	1	M. Lachemann	Salmon, .330	Salmon, 177	Salmon, 34	Edmonds, 107	Finley, Langston, 15	Finley, 4.21
1996	70	91	4th	18½	M. Lachemann, McNamara	Edmonds, .304	Anderson, 173	Salmon, 30	Salmon, 98	Finley, 15	Finley, 4.16
1997	84	78	2nd	6	Collins	Anderson, .303	Anderson, 189	Salmon, 33	Salmon, 129	Finley, Dickson, 13	Hasegawa, 3.93
1998	85	77	2nd	3	Collins	Edmonds, .307	Edmonds, 184	Salmon, 26	Edmonds, 91	Finley, 11	Hasegawa, 3.14
1999	70	92	4th	25	Collins, Maddon	Velarde, .306	Anderson, 188	Vaughn, 33	Vaughn, 108	Finley, 12	Olivares, 4.05
2000	82	80	3rd	9½	Scioscia	Erstad, .355	Erstad, 240	Glaus, 47	Vaughn, Anderson, 117	Hasegawa, 10	Hasegawa, 3.57

* Tied for position. † Lost Championship Series. ‡ First half 31-29; second half 20-30. § Lost division playoff.

Note: Batting average minimum 350 at-bats; ERA minimum 90 innings pitched.

Eli Grba

The Angels joined an exclusive fraternity in 1960 when actor/singer Gene Autry and partner Bob Reynolds were awarded the Los Angeles franchise in baseball's first expansion. The Angels, based in Los Angeles, joined the new-edition Washington Senators in an American League lineup that increased from eight to 10 teams. The former Washington Senators, owned by Calvin Griffith, were granted permission to transfer operations to Minneapolis-St. Paul.

The Los Angeles Angels participated in baseball's first expansion draft on December 14, 1960, and grabbed righthanded pitcher Eli Grba with their first pick. They went on to select 30 players and opened play on April 11, 1961, with a 7-2 victory over Baltimore.

Expansion draft (December 14, 1960)

Players

Player	From	Position
Ken Aspromonte	Cleveland	second base
Earl Averill	Chicago	catcher
Julio Becquer	Minnesota	infield
Steve Bilko	Detroit	first base
Bob Cerv	New York	outfield
Jim Fregosi	Boston	shortstop
Ken Hamlin	Kansas City	first base
Ken Hunt	New York	outfield
Ted Kluszewski	Chicago	first base
Gene Leek	Cleveland	infield
Jim McAnany	Chicago	outfield
Albie Pearson	Baltimore	outfield
Bob Rodgers	Detroit	catcher
Don Ross	Baltimore	infield
Ed Sadowski	Boston	catcher
Faye Throneberry	Minnesota	outfield
Red Wison	Cleveland	catcher
Eddie Yost	Detroit	third base

Pitchers

Pitcher	From	Throws
Jerry Casale	Boston	righthander
Dean Chance	Baltimore	righthander
Tex Clevenger	Minnesota	righthander
Bob Davis	Kansas City	righthander
Ned Garver	Kansas City	righthander
Aubrey Gatewood	Detroit	righthander
*Eli Grba	New York	righthander
Duke Maas	New York	righthander
Ken McBride	Chicago	righthander
Ron Moeller	Baltimore	lefthander
Fred Newman	Boston	righthander
Bob Sprout	Detroit	lefthander

*First pick

Opening day lineup

April 11, 1961
Eddie Yost, third base
Ken Aspromonte, second base
Albie Pearson, rightfield
Ted Kluszewski, first base
Bob Cerv, left field
Ken Hunt, center field
Fritzie Brickell, shortstop
Del Rice, catcher
Eli Grba, pitcher

Albie Pearson

Angels firsts

First hit: Ted Kluszewski, April 11, 1961, at Baltimore (home run)
First home run: Ted Kluszewski, April 11, 1961, at Baltimore
First RBI: Ted Kluszewski, April 11, 1961, at Baltimore
First win: Eli Grba, April 11, 1961, at Baltimore
First shutout: Ken McBride, May 23, 1961, 9-0 vs. Cleveland

HISTORY

Baltimore Orioles

FRANCHISE CHRONOLOGY

First season: 1901, in Milwaukee, as a member of the new American League. The team lost its Major League debut when Detroit rallied for 10 ninth-inning runs and a 14-13 victory and finished its first season in last place with a 48-89 record.

1902-1953: The franchise played its second season in St. Louis and remained there for more than half a century. The Browns moved up to second place in the 1902 standings (78-58), but such success would be elusive. The Browns won their only A.L. pennant in 1944 and lost their only World Series to the cross-town Cardinals. When owner Bill Veeck sold out to Baltimore interests in 1953, the team was relocated and renamed the Orioles.

1954-present: The Orioles posted a 3-1 victory over Chicago at Memorial Stadium in their Baltimore debut but went on to finish seventh in the A.L. standings at 54-100. Over the next four-plus decades, they would become an A.L. power, winning six pennants, three World Series, eight East Division titles and one wild-card playoff berth (1996).

Manager Earl Weaver.

ORIOLES VS. OPPONENTS BY DECADE

	A's	Indians	Red Sox	Tigers	Twins	White Sox	Yankees	Angels	Rangers	Brewers	Royals	Blue Jays	Mariners	Devil Rays	Interleague	Decade Record
1901-09	79-105	82-109	76-114	90-101	108-81	74-112	90-99									599-721
1910-19	93-120	81-130	71-142	90-126	96-119	74-132	92-123									597-892
1920-29	105-114	106-112	137-82	111-109	111-108	114-104	78-140									762-769
1930-39	88-127	64-155	103-117	85-135	84-135	90-127	64-155									578-951
1940-49	115-105	95-124	98-120	90-129	110-110	113-102	77-143									698-833
1950-59	110-109	67-151	77-143	106-114	117-103	86-134	69-151									632-905
1960-69	107-69	99-85	105-79	90-94	91-87	95-83	111-73	83-72	110-52	9-3	11-1					911-698
1970-79	66-50	104-65	83-85	102-65	64-52	74-39	89-73	65-52	77-50	100-54	65-51	29-14	26-6			944-656
1980-89	63-57	59-64	48-73	61-69	63-51	63-53	56-74	71-49	72-39	64-59	55-61	62-61	63-51			800-761
1990-99	65-54	51-67	57-63	69-49	63-45	46-59	50-75	73-46	60-46	52-45	62-43	54-69	58-57	10-14	24-25	794-757
2000-	4-8	5-4	5-7	6-4	6-3	4-6	5-7	5-7	6-6		3-7	7-6	3-7	8-5	7-11	74-88
Totals	895-918	813-1066	860-1025	900-995	913-894	833-951	781-1113	297-226	325-193	225-161	196-163	152-150	150-121	18-19	31-36	7389-8031

Interleague results:7-5 vs. Braves; 4-8 vs. Expos; 4-9 vs. Mets; 12-6 vs. Phillies; 4-8 vs. Marlins.

MANAGERS

(Milwaukee Brewers, 1901)
(St. Louis Browns, 1902-53)

Name	*Years*	*Record*
Hugh Duffy	1901	48-89
Jimmy McAleer	1902-09	551-632
Jack O'Connor	1910	47-107
Bobby Wallace	1911-12	57-134
George Stovall	1912-13	91-158
Branch Rickey	1913-15	139-179
Fielder Jones	1916-18	158-196
Jimmy Austin	1913, 1918, 1923	31-44
Jimmy Burke	1918-20	172-180
Lee Fohl	1921-23	226-183
George Sisler	1924-26	218-241
Dan Howley	1927-29	220-239
Bill Killefer	1930-33	224-329
Al Sothoron	1933	2-6
Rogers Hornsby	1933-37, 1952	255-381
Jim Bottomley	1937	21-56
Gabby Street	1938	55-97
Fred Haney	1939-41	125-227
Luke Sewell	1941-46	432-410
Zack Taylor	1946, 1948-51	235-410
Marty Marion	1952-53	96-161
Jimmie Dykes	1954	54-100
Paul Richards	1955-61	517-539
Lum Harris	1961	17-10
Billy Hitchcock	1962-63	163-161
Hank Bauer	1964-68	407-318
Earl Weaver	1968-82, 1985-86	1480-1060
Joe Altobelli	1983-85	212-167
Cal Ripken Sr.	1987-88	68-101
Frank Robinson	1988-91	230-285
Johnny Oates	1991-94	362-343
Phil Regan	1995	71-73
Davey Johnson	1996-97	186-138
Ray Miller	1998-99	157-167
Mike Hargrove	2000	74-88

Third baseman Brooks Robinson excited Orioles fans with his Hall of Fame bat and glove.

WORLD SERIES CHAMPIONS

Year	*Loser*	*Length*	*MVP*
1966	Los Angeles	4 games	F. Robinson
1970	Cincinnati	5 games	B. Robinson
1983	Philadelphia	5 games	Dempsey

A.L. PENNANT WINNERS

Year	*Record*	*Manager*	*Series Result*
1944	89-65	Sewell	Lost to Cardinals
1966	97-63	Bauer	Defeated Dodgers
1969	109-53	Weaver	Lost to N.Y. Mets
1970	108-54	Weaver	Defeated Reds
1971	101-57	Weaver	Lost to Pirates
1979	102-57	Weaver	Lost to Pirates
1983	98-64	Altobelli	Defeated Phillies

EAST DIVISION CHAMPIONS

Year	*Record*	*Manager*	*ALCS Result*
1969	109-53	Weaver	Defeated Twins
1970	108-54	Weaver	Defeated Twins
1971	101-57	Weaver	Defeated A's
1973	97-65	Weaver	Lost to A's
1974	91-71	Weaver	Lost to A's
1979	102-57	Weaver	Defeated Angels
1983	98-64	Altobelli	Defeated White Sox
1997	98-64	Johnson	Lost to Indians

WILD-CARD QUALIFIERS

Year	*Record*	*Manager*	*Div. Series Result*
1996	88-74	Johnson	Defeated Indians

ALCS Result
Lost to Yankees

ATTENDANCE HIGHS

Total	*Season*	*Park*
3,711,132	1997	Camden Yards
3,685,194	1998	Camden Yards
3,646,950	1996	Camden Yards
3,644,965	1993	Camden Yards
3,567,819	1992	Camden Yards

BALLPARK CHRONOLOGY

Oriole Park at Camden Yards (1992-present)

Capacity: 48,876.
First game: Orioles 2, Cleveland 0 (April 6, 1992).
First batter: Kenny Lofton, Indians.
First hit: Paul Sorrento, Indians (single).
First run: Sam Horn, Orioles (5th inning).
First home run: Paul Sorrento, Indians (April 8).
First winning pitcher: Rick Sutcliffe, Orioles.
First-season attendance: 3,567,819.

Lloyd Street Park, Milwaukee (1901)

Capacity: 10,000.
First game: Chicago 11, Brewers 3 (May 4, 1901).
First-season attendance: 139,034.

Sportsman's Park, St. Louis (1902-53)

Capacity: 30,500
First game: Browns 5, Cleveland 2 (April 23, 1902).
First-season attendance: 272,283.

Memorial Stadium, Baltimore (1954-91)

Capacity: 53,371
First game: Orioles 3, Chicago 1 (April 15, 1954).
First-season attendance: 1,060,910.

A.L. MVPs

Brooks Robinson, 3B, 1964
Frank Robinson, OF, 1966
Boog Powell, 1B, 1970
Cal Ripken, SS, 1983
Cal Ripken, SS, 1991

CY YOUNG WINNERS

*Mike Cuellar, LH, 1969
Jim Palmer, RH, 1973
Jim Palmer, RH, 1975
Jim Palmer, RH, 1976
Mike Flanagan, LH, 1979
Steve Stone, RH, 1980
* Co-winner.

ROOKIES OF THE YEAR

Roy Sievers, OF, 1949
Ron Hansen, SS, 1960
Curt Blefary, OF, 1965
Al Bumbry, OF, 1973
Eddie Murray, 1B, 1977
Cal Ripken, SS, 1982
Gregg Olson, P, 1989

MANAGER OF THE YEAR

Frank Robinson, 1989
Davey Johnson, 1997

RETIRED UNIFORMS

No.	*Name*	*Position*
4	Earl Weaver	Man.
5	Brooks Robinson	3B
20	Frank Robinson	OF
22	Jim Palmer	P
33	Eddie Murray	1B

HISTORY

MILESTONE PERFORMANCES

30-plus home runs

- 50—Brady Anderson 1996
- 49—Frank Robinson 1966
- 46—Jim Gentile 1961
- 43—Rafael Palmeiro 1998
- 39—Ken Williams 1922
- Boog Powell 1964
- Rafael Palmeiro 1995
- Rafael Palmeiro 1996
- 38—Rafael Palmeiro 1997
- 37—Boog Powell 1969
- Albert Belle 1999
- 35—Boog Powell 1970
- Ken Singleton 1979
- 34—Harlond Clift 1938
- Boog Powell 1966
- Cal Ripken 1991
- 33—Jim Gentile 1962
- Eddie Murray 1983
- 32—Frank Robinson 1969
- Eddie Murray 1980, 1982
- 31—Eddie Murray 1985
- Larry Sheets 1987
- 30—Goose Goslin 1930
- Gus Triandos 1958
- Frank Robinson 1967
- Eddie Murray 1987

100-plus RBIs

- 155—Ken Williams 1922
- 142—Rafael Palmeiro 1996
- 141—Jim Gentile 1961
- 134—Moose Solters 1936
- 124—Eddie Murray 1985
- 123—Beau Bell 1936
- 122—George Sisler 1920
- Baby Doll Jacobson 1920
- Frank Robinson 1966
- 121—Boog Powell 1969
- Rafael Palmeiro 1998
- 118—Harlond Clift 1937, 1938
- Brooks Robinson 1964
- 117—Ken Williams 1921
- Beau Bell 1937
- Albert Belle 1999
- 116—Eddie Murray 1980
- Bobby Bonilla 1996
- 114—Red Kress 1931
- Boog Powell 1970
- Cal Ripken 1991
- 112—Red Kress 1930
- 111—Ken Singleton 1979
- Eddie Murray 1983
- 110—Eddie Murray 1982, 1984
- Cal Ripken 1985
- Brady Anderson 1996
- Rafael Palmeiro 1997
- 109—Marty McManus 1922
- Vern Stephens 1944
- Boog Powell 1966
- Lee May 1976
- 108—Heinie Manush 1928
- 107—Red Kress 1929
- Mike Devereaux 1992
- B.J. Surhoff 1999
- 106—Bruce Campbell 1933
- 105—George Sisler 1922, 1925
- Ken Williams 1925
- Goose Goslin 1931
- 104—George Sisler 1921
- Goose Goslin 1932
- Moose Solters 1935
- Ken Singleton 1980
- Rafael Palmeiro 1995
- 103—George Sisler 1916
- Albert Belle 2000
- 102—Baby Doll Jacobson 1922
- Cal Ripken 1983
- Cal Ripken 1996
- 101—Ray Pepper 1934
- 100—Goose Goslin 1930
- Brooks Robinson 1966
- Frank Robinson 1969

20-plus victories

- 1902—Red Donahue 22-11
- Jack Powell 22-17
- 1903—Willie Sudhoff 21-15
- 1919—Allen Sothoron 20-12
- 1920—Urban Shocker 20-10
- 1921—Urban Shocker 27-12
- 1922—Urban Shocker 24-17
- 1923—Urban Shocker 20-12
- 1928—General Crowder 21-5
- Sam Gray 20-12
- 1930—Lefty Stewart 20-12
- 1938—Bobo Newsom 20-16
- 1951—Ned Garver 20-12
- 1963—Steve Barber 20-13
- 1968—Dave McNally 22-10
- 1969—Mike Cuellar 23-11
- Dave McNally 20-7
- 1970—Mike Cuellar 24-8
- Dave McNally 24-9
- Jim Palmer 20-10
- 1971—Dave McNally 21-5
- Pat Dobson 20-8
- Jim Palmer 20-9
- Mike Cuellar 20-9
- 1972—Jim Palmer 21-10
- 1973—Jim Palmer 22-9
- 1974—Mike Cuellar 22-10
- 1975—Jim Palmer 23-11
- Mike Torrez 20-9
- 1976—Jim Palmer 22-13
- Wayne Garland 20-7
- 1977—Jim Palmer 20-11
- 1978—Jim Palmer 21-12
- 1979—Mike Flanagan 23-9
- 1980—Steve Stone 25-7
- Scott McGregor 20-8
- 1984—Mike Boddicker 20-11

A.L. home run champions

- 1922—Ken Williams 39
- 1945—Vern Stephens 24
- 1966—Frank Robinson 49
- 1981—Eddie Murray *22

* Tied for league lead

A.L. RBI champions

- 1916—Del Pratt 103
- 1922—Ken Williams 155
- 1944—Vern Stephens 109
- 1964—Brooks Robinson 118
- 1966—Frank Robinson 122
- 1976—Lee May 109
- 1981—Eddie Murray 78

A.L. batting champions

- 1906—George Stone .358
- 1920—George Sisler .407
- 1922—George Sisler .420
- 1966—Frank Robinson .316

A.L. ERA champions

- 1959—Hoyt Wilhelm 2.19
- 1973—Jim Palmer 2.40
- 1975—Jim Palmer 2.09
- 1984—Mike Boddicker 2.79

A.L. strikeout champions

- 1922—Urban Shocker 149
- 1954—Bob Turley 185

No-hit pitchers

- 1912—Earl Hamilton 5-1 vs. Detroit
- 1917—Ernie Koob 1-0 vs. Chicago
- 1917—Bob Groom 3-0 vs. Chicago
- 1953—Bobo Holloman 6-0 vs. Philadelphia
- 1958—Hoyt Wilhelm 1-0 vs. New York
- 1967—Steve Barber-Stu Miller 1-2 vs. Detroit
- 1968—Tom Phoebus 6-0 vs. Boston
- 1969—Jim Palmer 8-0 vs. Oakland
- 1991—Bob Milacki-Mike Flanagan-Mark Williamson-Gregg Olson 2-0 vs. Oakland

Longest hitting streaks

- 41—George Sisler 1922
- 34—George Sisler 1925
- George McQuinn 1938
- 30—Eric Davis 1998
- 29—Mel Almada 1938
- 28—Ken Williams 1922
- 27—Bob Dillinger 1948
- 26—Hobe Ferris 1908
- 25—George Sisler 1920
- 24—Rafael Palmeiro 1994
- 22—Red Kress 1930
- Eddie Murray 1984
- Roberto Alomar 1996
- Bobby Bonilla *1995-96
- 21—Jack Tobin 1922
- Beau Bell 1936
- Joe Vosmik 1937
- Johnny Berardino 1946
- Doug DeCinces 1978
- Joe Orsulak 1991
- B.J. Surhoff 1999, 2000
- 20—Jack Burns 1932
- Harlond Clift 1937
- Bob Nieman 1956
- Lee Lacy 1985
- Bobby Bonilla 1995

*20 games in 1995; 2 in 1996

INDIVIDUAL SEASON, GAME RECORDS

SEASON

Batting			
At-bats	673	B.J. Surhoff	1999
Runs	145	Harlond Clift	1936
Hits	257	George Sisler	1920
Singles	179	Jack Tobin	1921
Doubles	51	Beau Bell	1937
Triples	20	Heinie Manush	1928
Home runs	50	Brady Anderson	1996
Home runs, rookie	28	Cal Ripken	1982
Grand slams	5	Jim Gentile	1961
Total bases	399	George Sisler	1920
RBIs	155	Ken Williams	1922
Walks	126	Lu Blue	1929
Most strikeouts	160	Mickey Tettleton	1990
Fewest strikeouts	13	Jack Tobin	1923
Batting average	.420	George Sisler	1922
Slugging pct.	.646	Jim Gentile	1961
Stolen bases	57	Luis Aparicio	1964
Pitching			
Games	76	Tippy Martinez	1982
Complete games	36	Jack Powell	1902
Innings	348	Urban Shocker	1922
Wins	27	Urban Shocker	1922
Losses	25	Fred Glade	1905
Winning pct.	.808	General Crowder	1928
		Dave McNally	1971
Walks	192	Bobo Newsom	1938
Strikeouts	232	Rube Waddell	1908
Shutouts	10	Jim Palmer	1975
Home runs allowed	35	3 times	
		Last by Sidney Ponson	1999
Lowest ERA	1.95	Dave McNally	1968
Saves	45	Randy Myers	1997

GAME

Batting			
Runs	5	Last by Cal Ripken	6-13-99
Hits	6	Last by Cal Ripken	6-13-99
Doubles	4	Last by Albert Belle	9-23-99
Triples	3	Last by Al Bumbry	9-22-73
Home runs	3	Last by Albert Belle	7-25-99
RBIs	9	Last by Eddie Murray	8-26-85
Total bases	13	Last by Chris Richard	9-3-2000
Stolen bases	4	Last by Brady Anderson	7-5-98

When slugging outfielder Frank Robinson arrived on the Baltimore scene in 1966, the Orioles took on a championship aura.

HISTORY

CAREER LEADERS

BATTING

Games

Player	Games
Brooks Robinson	2,896
Cal Ripken	2,873
Mark Belanger	1,962
Eddie Murray	1,884
Boog Powell	1,763
Paul Blair	1,700
George Sisler	1,647
Brady Anderson	1,628
Bobby Wallace	1,569
Ken Singleton	1,446

At-bats

Player	At-bats
Cal Ripken	11,074
Brooks Robinson	10,654
Eddie Murray	7,075
George Sisler	6,667
Boog Powell	5,912
Brady Anderson	5,841
Mark Belanger	5,734
Paul Blair	5,606
Bobby Wallace	5,529
Harlond Clift	5,281

Runs

Player	Runs
Cal Ripken	1,604
Brooks Robinson	1,232
George Sisler	1,091
Eddie Murray	1,084
Harlond Clift	1,013
Brady Anderson	994
Boog Powell	796
Al Bumbry	772
Ken Williams	757
Paul Blair	737

Hits

Player	Hits
Cal Ripken	3,070
Brooks Robinson	2,848
George Sisler	2,295
Eddie Murray	2,080
Boog Powell	1,574
Brady Anderson	1,527
Baby Doll Jacobson	1,508
Harlond Clift	1,463
Ken Singleton	1,455
Paul Blair	1,426

Doubles

Player	Doubles
Cal Ripken	587
Brooks Robinson	482
Eddie Murray	363
George Sisler	343
Brady Anderson	317
Harlond Clift	294
Paul Blair	269
Baby Doll Jacobson	269
George McQuinn	254
Boog Powell	243

Triples

Player	Triples
George Sisler	145
Baby Doll Jacobson	88
Del Pratt	72
Jack Tobin	72
Ken Williams	70
Brooks Robinson	68
George Stone	68
Jimmy Austin	67
Bobby Wallace	65
Harlond Clift	62

Home runs

Player	Home runs
Cal Ripken	417
Eddie Murray	343
Boog Powell	303
Brooks Robinson	268
Brady Anderson	201
Ken Williams	185
Rafael Palmeiro	182
Ken Singleton	182
Frank Robinson	179
Harlond Clift	170

Total bases

Cal Ripken	4,996
Brooks Robinson	4,270
Eddie Murray	3,522
George Sisler	3,207
Boog Powell	2,748
Brady Anderson	2,569
Harlond Clift	2,391
Ken Singleton	2,274
Ken Williams	2,239
Baby Doll Jacobson	2,181

Runs batted in

Cal Ripken	1,627
Brooks Robinson	1,357
Eddie Murray	1,224
Boog Powell	1,063
George Sisler	959
Ken Williams	808
Harlond Clift	769
Ken Singleton	766
Baby Doll Jacobson	704
Brady Anderson	699

Extra-base hits

Player	Extra-base hits
Cal Ripken	1,048
Brooks Robinson	818
Eddie Murray	731
George Sisler	581
Brady Anderson	579
Boog Powell	557
Harlond Clift	526
Ken Williams	491
Paul Blair	446
Ken Singleton	436

Batting average

(Minimum 500 games)

George Sisler	.344
Ken Williams	.326
Jack Tobin	.318
Baby Doll Jacobson	.317
Bob Dillinger	.309
Beau Bell	.309
Sam West	.305
George Stone	.301
Bob Boyd	.301
Bob Nieman	.301

Stolen bases

Player	Stolen bases
George Sisler	351
Brady Anderson	295
Al Bumbry	252
Burt Shotton	247
Jimmy Austin	192
Del Pratt	174
Paul Blair	167
Luis Aparicio	166
Mark Belanger	166
Ken Williams	144

PITCHING

Earned-run average

(Minimum 1,000 innings)

Harry Howell	2.06
Fred Glade	2.52
Barney Pelty	2.62
Jack Powell	2.63
Carl Weilman	2.67
Jim Palmer	2.86
Allen Sothoron	2.98
Earl Hamilton	3.00
Steve Barber	3.12
Mike Cuellar	3.18

Wins

Player	Wins
Jim Palmer	268
Dave McNally	181
Mike Mussina	147
Mike Cuellar	143
Mike Flanagan	141
Scott McGregor	138
Urban Shocker	126
Jack Powell	117
Milt Pappas	110
Dennis Martinez	108

Losses

Player	Losses
Jim Palmer	152
Jack Powell	143
Mike Flanagan	116
Dave McNally	113
Barney Pelty	113
George Blaeholder	111
Scott McGregor	108
Dennis Martinez	93
Carl Weilman	93
Harry Howell	91
Elam Vangilder	91

Innings pitched

Jim Palmer	3,948.0
Dave McNally	2,652.2
Mike Flanagan	2,317.2
Jack Powell	2,229.2
Scott McGregor	2,140.2
Mike Cuellar	2,028.1
Mike Mussina	2,009.2
Barney Pelty	1,864.1
Dennis Martinez	1,775.0
Urban Shocker	1,749.2

Strikeouts

Player	Strikeouts
Jim Palmer	2,212
Mike Mussina	1,535
Dave McNally	1,476
Mike Flanagan	1,297
Mike Cuellar	1,011
Milt Pappas	944
Steve Barber	918
Scott McGregor	904
Jack Powell	884
Dennis Martinez	858

Bases on balls

Player	Bases on balls
Jim Palmer	1,311
Dave McNally	790
Mike Flanagan	740
Steve Barber	668
Dixie Davis	640
Elam Vangilder	625
Mike Cuellar	601
Dennis Martinez	583
Milt Pappas	531
Barney Pelty	522

Games

Player	Games
Jim Palmer	558
Tippy Martinez	499
Mike Flanagan	450
Dave McNally	412
Mark Williamson	365
Eddie Watt	363
Scott McGregor	356
Dick Hall	342
Jesse Orosco	336
Alan Mills	331

Shutouts

Player	Shutouts
Jim Palmer	53
Dave McNally	33
Mike Cuellar	30
Jack Powell	27
Milt Pappas	26
Scott McGregor	23
Urban Shocker	23
Barney Pelty	22
Steve Barber	19
Mike Flanagan	17

Saves

Player	Saves
Gregg Olson	160
Tippy Martinez	105
Stu Miller	100
Randy Myers	76
Eddie Watt	74
Dick Hall	58
Tim Stoddard	57
Don Aase	50
Don Stanhouse	45
Sammy Stewart	42

TEAM SEASON, GAME RECORDS

SEASON

Batting

Most at-bats	5,689	1996
Most runs	949	1996
Fewest runs	441	1909
Most hits	1,693	1922
Most singles	1,239	1920
Most doubles	327	1937
Most triples	106	1921
Most home runs	257	1996
Fewest home runs	9	1906
Most grand slams	11	1996
Most pinch-hit home runs	11	1982
Most total bases	2,685	1996
Most stolen bases	234	1916
Highest batting average	.313	1922
Lowest batting average	.216	1910
Highest slugging pct	.472	1996

Pitching

Lowest ERA	2.15	1908
Highest ERA	6.24	1936
Most complete games	135	1904
Most shutouts	21	1909, 1961
Most saves	59	1997
Most walks	801	1951
Most strikeouts	1,139	1997

Fielding

Most errors	378	1910
Fewest errors	81	1998
Most double plays	190	1948
Highest fielding average	.987	1998

General

Most games won	109	1969
Most games lost	111	1939
Highest win pct.	.673	1969
Lowest win pct.	.279	1939

GAME, INNING

Batting

Most runs, game	23	9-28-2000
Most runs, inning	11	Last 7-21-49
Most hits, game	26	8-28-80
Most home runs, game	7	Last 8-26-85
Most total bases, game	44	6-13-99

George Sisler (right) was an early franchise star and a contemporary of Babe Ruth.

ORIOLES YEAR-BY-YEAR

Year	W	L	Place	Games Back	Manager	Leaders: Batting avg.	Hits	Home runs	RBIs	Wins	ERA
								MILWAUKEE BREWERS			
1901	48	89	8th	35½	Duffy	Anderson, .330	Anderson, 190	Anderson, 8	Anderson, 99	Reidy, 16	Garvin, 3.46
								ST. LOUIS BROWNS			
1902	78	58	2nd	5	McAleer	Hemphill, .317	Burkett, 169	Hemphill, 6	Anderson, 85	Donahue, Powell, 22	Donahue, 2.76
1903	65	74	6th	26½	McAleer	Burkett, .293	Anderson, 156	Burkett, Hemphill, 3	Anderson, 78	Sudhoff, 21	Sudhoff, 2.27
1904	65	87	6th	29	McAleer	Wallace, .275	T. Jones, 152	4 Tied, 2	Wallace, 69	Glade, 18	Howell, 2.19
1905	54	99	8th	40½	McAleer	Stone, .296	Stone, 187	Stone, 7	Wallace, 59	Howell, 15	Howell, 1.98
1906	76	73	5th	16	McAleer	Stone, .358	Stone, 208	Stone, 6	Stone, 71	Pelty, 16	Pelty, 1.59
1907	69	83	6th	24	McAleer	Stone, .320	Stone, 191	Stone, 4	Wallace, 70	Howell, 16	Howell, 1.93
1908	83	69	4th	6½	McAleer	Stone, .281	Stone, 165	Stone, 5	Ferris, 74	Waddell, 19	Howell, Waddell, 1.89
1909	61	89	7th	36	McAleer	Griggs, .280	Hartzell, 161	Ferris, 3	Ferris, 58	Powell, 12	Powell, 2.11
1910	47	107	8th	57	O'Connor	Wallace, .258	Stone, 144	4 Tied, 2	Stone, 40	Lake, 11	Lake, 2.20
1911	45	107	8th	56½	Wallace	LaPorte, .314	LaPorte, 159	Kutina, Meloan, Murray, 3	LaPorte, 82	Lake, 10	Pelty, 2.97
1912	53	101	7th	53	Wallace, Stovall	Pratt, .302	Pratt, 172	Pratt, 5	Pratt, 69	Baumgardner, Hamilton, 11	E. Brown, 2.99
1913	57	96	8th	39	Stovall, Rickey	Shotton, .297	Pratt, 175	Williams, 5	Pratt, 87	Hamilton, Mitchell, 13	Hamilton, 2.57
1914	71	82	5th	28½	Rickey	T. Walker, .298	Pratt, 165	T. Walker, 6	T. Walker, 78	Weilman, 18	Weilman, 2.08
1915	63	91	6th	39½	Rickey	Pratt, .291	Pratt, 175	T. Walker, 5	Pratt, 78	Weilman, 18	Weilman, 2.34
1916	79	75	5th	12	Jones	Sisler, .305	Sisler, 177	Pratt, 5	Pratt, 103	Weilman, 17	Weilman, 2.15
1917	57	97	7th	43	Jones	Sisler, .353	Sisler, 190	Jacobson, 4	Severeid, 57	Davenport, 17	Plank, 1.79
1918	58	64	5th	15	Jones, Austin, Burke	Sisler, .341	Sisler, 154	Sisler, 2	Demmitt, 61	Sothoron, 12	Shocker, 1.81
1919	67	72	5th	20½	Burke	Sisler, .352	Sisler, 180	Sisler, 10	Sisler, 83	Sothoron, 20	Weilman, 2.07
1920	76	77	4th	21½	Burke	Sisler, .407	Sisler, 257	Sisler, 19	Jacobson, Sisler, 122	Shocker, 20	Shocker, 2.71
1921	81	73	3rd	17½	Fohl	Sisler, .371	Tobin, 236	Williams, 24	Williams, 117	Shocker, 27	Shocker, 3.55
1922	93	61	2nd	1	Fohl	Sisler, .420	Sisler, 246	Williams, 39	Williams, 155	Shocker, 24	Pruett, 2.33
1923	74	78	5th	24	Fohl, Austin	Williams, .357	Tobin, 202	Williams, 29	McManus, 94	Shocker, 20	Vangilder, 3.06
1924	74	78	4th	17	Sisler	McManus, .333	Sisler, 194	Jacobson, 19	Jacobson, 97	Shocker, 16	Wingard, 3.51
1925	82	71	3rd	15	Sisler	Rice, .359	Sisler, 224	Williams, 25	Sisler, Williams, 105	Gaston, 15	Danforth, 4.36
1926	62	92	7th	29	Sisler	B. Miller, .331	Rice, 181	Williams, 17	Williams, 74	Zachary, 14	Wingard, 3.57
1927	59	94	7th	50½	Howley	Sisler, .327	Sisler, 201	Williams, 17	Sisler, 97	Gaston, 13	Stewart, 4.28
1928	82	72	3rd	19	Howley	Manush, .378	Manush, 241	Blue, 14	Manush, 108	Crowder, 21	Gray, 3.19
1929	79	73	4th	26	Howley	Manush, .355	Manush, 204	Kress, 9	Kress, 107	Gray, 18	Stewart, 3.25
1930	64	90	6th	38	Killefer	Goslin, .326	Kress, 192	Goslin, 30	Kress, 112	Stewart, 20	Stewart, 3.45
1931	63	91	5th	45	Killefer	Goslin, .328	Goslin, 194	Goslin, 24	Kress, 114	Stewart, 14	Collins, 3.79
1932	63	91	6th	44	Killefer	Ferrell, .315	Burns, 188	Goslin, 17	Goslin, 104	Stewart, 15	Gray, 4.53
1933	55	96	8th	43½	Killefer, Sothoron, Hornsby	West, .300	Burns, 160	Campbell, 16	Campbell, 106	Blaeholder, Hadley, 15	Hadley, 3.92
1934	67	85	6th	33	Hornsby	West, .326	Pepper, 168	Clift, 14	Pepper, 101	Newsom, 16	Newsom, 4.01
1935	65	87	7th	28½	Hornsby	Solters, .330	Solters, 182	Solters, 18	Solters, 104	Andrews, 13	Andrews, 3.54
1936	57	95	7th	44½	Hornsby	Bell, .344	Bell, 212	Clift, 20	Solters, 134	Hogsett, 13	Andrews, 4.84
1937	46	108	8th	56	Hornsby, Bottomley	Bell, .340	Bell, 218	Clift, 29	Clift, 118	Walkup, 9	Knott, 4.89
1938	55	97	7th	44	Street	Almada, .342	McQuinn, 195	Clift, 34	Clift, 118	Newsom, 20	Newsom, 5.08
1939	43	111	8th	64½	Haney	McQuinn, .316	McQuinn, 195	McQuinn, 20	McQuinn, 94	Kennedy, Kramer, 9	Lawson, 5.32
1940	67	87	6th	23	Haney	Radcliff, .342	Radcliff, 200	Judnich, 24	Judnich, 89	Auker, 16	Trotter, 3.77
1941	70	84	*6th	31	Haney, Sewell	Cullenbine, .317	Cullenbine, 159	McQuinn, 18	Berardino, 89	Auker, 14	Galehouse, 3.64
1942	82	69	3rd	19½	Sewell	Judnich, .313	Stephens, 169	Laabs, 27	Laabs, 99	Niggeling, 15	Niggeling, 2.66
1943	72	80	6th	25	Sewell	Stephens, .289	Stephens, 148	Stephens, 22	Stephens, 91	Sundra, 15	Galehouse, 2.77
1944	89	65	1st	+1	Sewell	Kreevich, .301	Stephens, 164	Stephens, 20	Stephens, 109	Potter, 19	Kramer, 2.49
1945	81	70	3rd	6	Sewell	Stephens, .289	Stephens, 165	Stephens, 24	Stephens, 89	Potter, 15	Potter, 2.47
1946	66	88	7th	38	Sewell, Taylor	Stephens, .307	Berardino, 154	Laabs, 16	Judnich, 72	Kramer, 13	Kramer, 3.19
1947	59	95	8th	38	Ruel	Dillinger, .294	Dillinger, 168	Heath, 27	Heath, 85	Kramer, 11	Zoldak, 3.47
1948	59	94	6th	37	Taylor	Zarilla, .329	Dillinger, 207	Moss, 14	Platt, 82	Sanford, 12	Garver, 3.41
1949	53	101	7th	44	Taylor	Dillinger, .324	Dillinger, 176	Graham, 24	Sievers, 91	Garver, 12	Ferrick, 3.88
1950	58	96	7th	40	Taylor	Lollar, .280	Lenhardt, 131	Lenhardt, 22	Lenhardt, 81	Garver, 13	Garver, 3.39
1951	52	102	8th	46	Taylor	Young, .260	Young, 159	Wood, 15	Coleman, 55	Garver, 20	Garver, 3.73
1952	64	90	7th	31	Hornsby, Marion	Nieman, .289	Young, 142	Nieman, 18	Nieman, 74	Cain, Paige, 12	Paige, 3.07
1953	54	100	8th	46½	Marion	Wertz, .268	Groth, 141	Wertz, 19	Wertz, 70	Stuart, 8	Brecheen, 3.07
								BALTIMORE ORIOLES			
1954	54	100	7th	57	Dykes	Abrams, .293	Abrams, 124	Stephens, 8	Stephens, 46	Turley, 14	Pillette, 3.12
1955	57	97	7th	39	Richards	Triandos, .277	Triandos, 133	Triandos, 12	Triandos, 65	Wilson, 12	Wight, 2.45
1956	69	85	6th	28	Richards	Nieman, .322	Triandos, 126	Triandos, 21	Triandos, 88	Moore, 12	C. Johnson, 3.43
1957	76	76	5th	21	Richards	Boyd, .318	Gardner, 169	Triandos, 19	Triandos, 72	C. Johnson, 14	Zuverink, 2.48
1958	74	79	6th	17½	Richards	Boyd, .309	Gardner, 126	Triandos, 30	Triandos, 79	Portocarrero, 15	Harshman, 2.89
1959	74	80	6th	20	Richards	Woodling, .300	Woodling, 132	Triandos, 25	Woodling, 77	Pappas, Wilhelm, 15	Wilhelm, 2.19
1960	89	65	2nd	8	Richards	B. Robinson, .294	B. Robinson, 175	Hansen, 22	Gentile, 98	Estrada, 18	Brown, 3.06
1961	95	67	3rd	14	Richards, Harris	Gentile, .302	B. Robinson, 192	Gentile, 46	Gentile, 141	Barber, 18	Hoeft, 2.02
1962	77	85	7th	19	Hitchcock	Snyder, .305	B. Robinson, 192	Gentile, 33	Gentile, 87	Pappas, 12	Wilhelm, 1.94
1963	86	76	4th	18½	Hitchcock	Orsino, A. Smith, .272	Aparicio, 150	Powell, 25	Powell, 82	Barber, 20	Miller, 2.24
1964	97	65	3rd	2	Bauer	B. Robinson, .317	B. Robinson, 194	Powell, 39	B. Robinson, 118	Bunker, 19	Haddix, 2.31
1965	94	68	3rd	8	Bauer	B. Robinson, .297	B. Robinson, 166	Blefary, 22	B. Robinson, 80	Barber, 15	Miller, 1.89
1966	97	63	1st	+9	Bauer	F. Robinson, .316	Aparicio, F. Robinson, 182	F. Robinson, 49	F. Robinson, 122	Palmer, 15	Miller, 2.25
1967	76	85	*6th	15½	Bauer	F. Robinson, .311	B. Robinson, 164	F. Robinson, 30	F. Robinson, 94	Phoebus, 14	Drabowsky, 1.60
1968	91	71	2nd	12	Bauer, Weaver	Buford, .282	B. Robinson, 154	B. Robinson, 17	Powell, 85	McNally, 22	McNally, 1.95
								EAST DIVISION			
1969	109	53	†1st	+19	Weaver	F. Robinson, .308	Blair, 178	Powell, 37	Powell, 121	Cuellar, 23	Palmer, 2.34
1970	108	54	†1st	+15	Weaver	F. Robinson, .306	B. Robinson, 168	Powell, 35	Powell, 114	Cuellar, McNally, 24	Palmer, 2.71
1971	101	57	†1st	+12	Weaver	Rettenmund, .318	B. Robinson, 160	F. Robinson, 28	F. Robinson, 99	McNally, 21	Palmer, 2.68
1972	80	74	3rd	5	Weaver	Grich, .278	B. Robinson, 139	Powell, 21	Powell, 81	Palmer, 21	Palmer, 2.07
1973	97	65	‡1st	+8	Weaver	Coggins, .319	T. Davis, 169	Williams, 22	T. Davis, 89	Palmer, 22	Reynolds, 1.95
1974	91	71	‡1st	+2	Weaver	T. Davis, .289	T. Davis, 181	Grich, 19	T. Davis, 84	Cuellar, 22	Garland, 2.97
1975	90	69	2nd	4½	Weaver	Singleton, .300	Singleton, 176	Baylor, 25	L. May, 99	Palmer, 23	Palmer, 2.09
1976	88	74	2nd	10½	Weaver	Singleton, .278	Singleton, 151	R. Jackson, 27	L. May, 109	Palmer, 22	Palmer, 2.51
1977	97	64	*2nd	2½	Weaver	Singleton, .328	Singleton, 176	L. May, Murray, 27	L. May, Singleton, 99	Palmer, 20	Palmer, 2.91
1978	90	71	4th	9	Weaver	Singleton, .293	Murray, 174	DeCinces, 28	Murray, 95	Palmer, 21	Palmer, 2.46
1979	102	57	†1st	+8	Weaver	Murray, .Singleton, .295	Murray, 179	Singleton, 35	Singleton, 111	Flanagan, 23	Flanagan, 3.08
1980	100	62	2nd	3	Weaver	Bumbry, .318	Bumbry, 205	Murray, 32	Murray, 116	Stone, 25	Stone, 3.23
1981	59	46	§2nd/4th	—	Weaver	Murray, .294	Murray, 111	Murray, 22	Murray, 78	D. Martinez, 14	Stewart, 2.32
1982	94	68	2nd	1	Weaver	Murray, .316	Murray, 174	Murray, 32	Murray, 110	D. Martinez, 16	Palmer, 3.13
1983	98	64	†1st	+6	Altobelli	C. Ripken, .318	C. Ripken, 211	Murray, 33	Murray, 111	McGregor, 18	T. Martinez, 2.35
1984	85	77	5th	19	Altobelli	Murray, .306	C. Ripken, 195	Murray, 29	Murray, 110	Boddicker, 20	Boddicker, 2.79
1985	83	78	4th	16	Altobelli, Weaver	Rayford, .306	C. Ripken, 181	Murray, 31	Murray, 124	McGregor, 14	Snell, 2.69
1986	73	89	7th	22½	Weaver	Murray, .305	C. Ripken, 177	C. Ripken, 25	Murray, 84	Boddicker, 14	S. Davis, 3.62
1987	67	95	6th	31	C. Ripken, Sr.	Sheets, .316	Murray, 171	Sheets, 31	C. Ripken, 98	Bell, Boddicker, Schmidt, 10	Schmidt, 3.77
1988	54	107	7th	34½	C. Ripken, Sr., F. Robinson	Orsulak, .288	Murray, 171	Murray, 28	Murray, 84	Ballard, Schmidt, 8	Schmidt, 3.40
1989	87	75	2nd	2	F. Robinson	Orsulak, .285	C. Ripken, 166	Tettleton, 26	C. Ripken, 93	Ballard, 18	Williamson, 2.93
1990	76	85	5th	11½	F. Robinson	B. Ripken, .291	C. Ripken, 150	C. Ripken, 21	C. Ripken, 84	D. Johnson, 13	McDonald, 2.43
1991	67	95	6th	24	F. Robinson, Oates	C. Ripken, .323	C. Ripken, 210	C. Ripken, 34	C. Ripken, 114	Milacki, 10	Frohwirth, 1.87
1992	89	73	3rd	7	Oates	Orsulak, .289	Devereaux, 180	Devereaux, 24	Devereaux, 107	Mussina, 18	Frohwirth, 2.46
1993	85	77	*3rd	10	Oates	Baines, .313	McLemore, 165	Hoiles, 29	C. Ripken, 90	Mussina, 14	Mills, 3.23
1994	63	49	2nd	6½	Oates	Palmeiro, .319	C. Ripken, 140	Palmeiro, 23	Palmeiro, 76	Mussina, 16	Mussina, 3.06
1995	71	73	3rd	15	Regan	Palmeiro, .310	Palmeiro, 172	Palmeiro, 39	Palmeiro, 104	Mussina, 19	Mussina, 3.29
1996	88	74	∞‡2nd	4	Johnson	Alomar, .328	Alomar, 193	Anderson, 50	Palmeiro, 142	Mussina, 19	Mussina, 4.81
1997	98	64	∞1st	+2	Johnson	Alomar, .333	Anderson, 170	Palmeiro, 38	Palmeiro, 110	Key, Erickson, 16	Rhodes, 3.02
1998	79	83	4th	35	Miller	E. Davis, .327	Palmeiro, 183	Palmeiro, 43	Palmeiro, 121	Erickson, 16	Mussina, 3.49
1999	78	84	4th	20	Miller	Surhoff, .308	Surhoff, 207	Belle, 37	Belle, 117	Mussina, 18	Mussina, 3.50
2000	74	88	4th	13½	Hargrove	Bordick, .297	DeShields, 167	Belle, 23	Belle, 103	Mercedes, 14	Mussina, 3.79

* Tied for position. † Won Championship Series. ‡ Lost Championship Series. § First half 31-23; second half 28-23. ∞ Won Division Series.

Note: Batting average minimum 350 at-bats; ERA minimum 90 innings pitched.

HISTORY

Boston Red Sox

FRANCHISE CHRONOLOGY

First season: 1901, as a member of the new American League. The Red Sox, who also were known in the early years as the Pilgrims, Puritans and Somersets, dropped a 10-6 decision to Baltimore in their Major League debut and went on to finish 79-57, four games behind pennant-winner Chicago.

1902-present: The Red Sox captured their first pennant in 1903 and defeated the National League's Pirates in the first modern World Series. Boston went on to enjoy distinction as baseball's most successful franchise over its first two decades, winning six A.L. pennants and all five World Series appearances. But the Red Sox's 1918 championship marked the beginning of a dry spell that would last the remainder of the century. They failed to win another pennant until 1946 and have lost their four World Series appearances since World War II, all in dramatic seventh games.

Outfielder Ted Williams.

RED SOX VS. OPPONENTS BY DECADE

	A's	Indians	Orioles	Tigers	Twins	White Sox	Yankees	Angels	Rangers	Brewers	Royals	Blue Jays	Mariners	Devil Rays	Interleague	Decade Record
1901-09	88-102	93-96	114-76	92-97	113-76	90-101	101-86									691-634
1910-19	129-84	115-97	142-71	124-88	115-93	117-97	115-94									857-624
1920-29	86-131	90-130	82-137	81-139	82-135	103-117	71-149									595-938
1930-39	116-99	89-131	117-103	99-121	90-128	114-97	80-136									705-815
1940-49	137-83	105-116	120-98	127-93	133-86	134-85	98-122									854-683
1950-59	141-79	98-122	143-77	121-99	120-100	98-122	93-126									814-725
1960-69	96-82	90-94	79-105	88-95	74-104	76-102	83-101	76-79	86-75	6-6	10-2					764-845
1970-79	63-54	86-80	85-83	96-69	70-47	67-48	89-79	64-53	72-56	93-63	53-63	32-11	25-8			895-714
1980-89	68-52	78-52	73-48	65-59	62-53	56-59	60-63	59-55	64-53	62-67	49-65	59-62	66-54			821-742
1990-99	71-46	61-60	63-57	64-54	48-62	54-54	60-64	71-47	43-61	50-47	52-51	72-52	71-46	13-12	21-28	814-741
2000-	5-5	6-6	7-5	7-5	8-2	7-5	6-7	4-5	7-3		4-6	4-8	5-5	6-6	9-9	85-77
Totals	1000-817	911-984	1025-860	964-919	915-886	916-887	856-1027	274-239	272-248	211-183	168-187	167-133	167-113	19-18	30-37	7895-7538

Interleague results: 6-12 vs. Braves; 6-6 vs. Expos; 6-6 vs. Mets; 5-8 vs. Phillies; 7-5 vs. Marlins.

MANAGERS

Name	*Years*	*Record*
Jimmy Collins	1901-06	455-376
Chick Stahl	1906	14-26
George Huff	1907	2-6
Bob Unglaub	1907	9-20
Cy Young	1907	3-3
Deacon McGuire	1907-08	98-123
Fred Lake	1908-09	110-80
Patsy Donovan	1910-11	159-147
Jake Stahl	1912-13	144-88
Bill Carrigan	1913-16, 1927-29	489-500
Jack Barry	1917	90-62
Ed Barrow	1918-20	213-203
Hugh Duffy	1921-22	136-172
Frank Chance	1923	61-91
Lee Fohl	1924-26	160-299
Heinie Wagner	1930	52-102
Shano Collins	1931-32	73-134
Marty McManus	1932-33	95-153
Bucky Harris	1934	76-76
Joe Cronin	1935-47	1071-916
Joe McCarthy	1948-50	223-145
Steve O'Neill	1950-51	150-99
Lou Boudreau	1952-54	229-232
Pinky Higgins	1955-59, 1960-62	560-556
Rudy York	1959	0-1
Billy Jurges	1959-60	59-63
Del Baker	1960	2-5
Johnny Pesky	1963-64, 1980	147-179
Billy Herman	1964-66	128-182
Pete Runnels	1966	8-8
Dick Williams	1967-69	260-217
Eddie Popowski	1969, 1973	6-4
Eddie Kasko	1970-73	345-295
Darrell Johnson	1974-76	220-188
Don Zimmer	1976-80	411-304
Ralph Houk	1981-84	312-282
John McNamara	1985-88	297-273
Joe Morgan	1988-91	301-252
Butch Hobson	1992-94	207-232
Kevin Kennedy	1995-96	171-135
Jimy Williams	1997-2000	349-299

WORLD SERIES CHAMPIONS

Year	*Loser*	*Length*	*MVP*
1903	Pittsburgh	8 games	None
1912	N.Y. Giants	7 games	None
1915	Philadelphia	5 games	None
1916	Brooklyn	5 games	None
1918	Chicago	6 games	None

A.L. PENNANT WINNERS

Year	*Record*	*Manager*	*Series Result*
1903	91-47	J. Collins	Defeated Pirates
1904	95-59	J. Collins	No Series
1912	105-47	J. Stahl	Defeated N.Y. Giants
1915	101-50	Carrigan	Defeated Phillies
1916	91-63	Carrigan	Defeated Dodgers
1918	75-51	Barrow	Defeated Cubs
1946	104-50	Cronin	Lost to Cardinals
1967	92-70	Williams	Lost to Cardinals
1975	95-65	Johnson	Lost to Reds
1986	95-66	McNamara	Lost to N.Y. Mets

EAST DIVISION CHAMPIONS

Year	*Record*	*Manager*	*ALCS Result*
1975	95-65	Johnson	Defeated A's
1986	95-66	McNamara	Defeated Angels
1988	89-73	McNamara, Morgan	Lost to A's
1990	88-74	Morgan	Lost to A's
1995	86-58	Kennedy	Lost in Div. Series

WILD-CARD QUALIFIERS

Year	*Record*	*Manager*	*ALCS Result*
1998	92-70	Williams	Lost in Div. Series
1999	94-68	Williams	Lost to Yankees

ATTENDANCE HIGHS

Total	*Season*	*Park*
2,586,024	2000	Fenway Park
2,562,435	1991	Fenway Park
2,528,986	1990	Fenway Park
2,510,012	1989	Fenway Park
2,468,574	1992	Fenway Park

BALLPARK CHRONOLOGY

Fenway Park—(1912-present)

Capacity: 33,455.
First game: Red Sox 7, New York 6, 11 innings (April 20, 1912).
First batter: Guy Zinn, Yankees.
First hit: Harry Wolter, Yankees.
First run: Guy Zinn, Yankees (1st inning).
First home run: Hugh Bradley, Red Sox (April 26).
First winning pitcher: Charley Hall, Red Sox.
First-season attendance: 597,096.

Huntington Avenue Grounds (1901-11)

Capacity: 9,000.
First game: Red Sox 12, Philadelphia 4 (May 8, 1901).
First-season attendance: 289,448.

A.L. MVPs

Jimmie Foxx, 1B, 1938
Ted Williams, OF, 1946
Ted Williams, OF, 1949
Jackie Jensen, OF, 1958
Carl Yastrzemski, OF, 1967
Fred Lynn, OF, 1975
Jim Rice, OF, 1978
Roger Clemens, P, 1986
Mo Vaughn, 1B, 1995

CY YOUNG WINNERS

Jim Lonborg, RH, 1967
Roger Clemens, RH, 1986
Roger Clemens, RH, 1987
Roger Clemens, RH, 1991
Pedro Martinez, RH, 1999
Pedro Martinez, RH, 2000

ROOKIES OF THE YEAR

Walt Dropo, 1B, 1950
Don Schwall, P, 1961
Carlton Fisk, C, 1972
Fred Lynn, OF, 1975
Nomar Garciaparra, SS, 1997

MANAGERS OF THE YEAR

John McNamara, 1986
Jimy Williams, 1999

RETIRED UNIFORMS

No.	*Name*	*Pos.*
1	Bobby Doerr	2B
4	Joe Cronin	SS
8	Carl Yastrzemski	OF
9	Ted Williams	OF

MILESTONE PERFORMANCES

30-plus home runs

50—Jimmie Foxx 1938
46—Jim Rice 1978
44—Carl Yastrzemski 1967
Mo Vaughn 1996
43—Tony Armas 1984
Ted Williams 1949
42—Dick Stuart 1963
41—Jimmie Foxx 1936
40—Carl Yastrzemski 1969, 1970
Rico Petrocelli 1969
Mo Vaughn 1998
39—Vern Stephens 1949
Jim Rice 1977, 1979, 1983
Fred Lynn 1979
Mo Vaughn 1995
38—Ted Williams 1946, 1957
37—Ted Williams 1941
36—Jimmie Foxx 1937, 1940
Ted Williams 1942
Tony Conigliaro 1970
Tony Armas 1983
35—Jimmie Foxx 1939
Jackie Jensen 1958
Ken Harrelson 1968
Mo Vaughn 1997
Nomar Garciaparra 1998
34—Walt Dropo 1950
Dwight Evans 1987
Carl Everett 2000
33—Dick Stuart 1964
George Scott 1977
32—Ted Williams 1947
Tony Conigliaro 1965
Dwight Evans 1982, 1984
31—Ted Williams 1939
Don Baylor 1986
30—Vern Stephens 1950
Ted Williams 1951
Felix Mantilla 1964
Reggie Smith 1971
Butch Hobson 1977
Nick Esasky 1989
Nomar Garciaparra 1997

100-plus RBIs

175—Jimmie Foxx 1938
159—Vern Stephens 1949
Ted Williams 1949
145—Ted Williams 1939
144—Walt Dropo 1950
Vern Stephens 1950
143—Jimmie Foxx 1936
Mo Vaughn 1996
139—Jim Rice 1978
137—Ted Williams 1942
Vern Stephens 1948
130—Jim Rice 1979
127—Jimmie Foxx 1937
Ted Williams 1948
126—Ted Williams 1951
Jim Rice 1983
Mo Vaughn 1995
123—Ted Williams 1946
Tony Armas 1984
Dwight Evans 1987
122—Jackie Jensen 1958
Fred Lynn 1979
Jim Rice 1984
Nomar Garciaparra 1998
121—Buck Freeman 1902
Carl Yastrzemski 1967
120—Ted Williams 1941
Bobby Doerr 1950
119—Roy Johnson 1934
Jimmie Foxx 1940
Rudy York 1946
Mike Greenwell 1988
118—Dick Stuart 1963
117—Jackie Jensen 1954
116—Bobby Doerr 1946
Jackie Jensen 1955
Tony Conigliaro 1970
115—Mo Vaughn 1998
114—Buck Freeman 1901
Babe Ruth 1919
Ted Williams 1947
Dick Stuart 1964
Jim Rice 1977
113—Ted Williams 1940
112—Jackie Jensen 1959
Butch Hobson 1977
111—Joe Cronin 1940
Bobby Doerr 1948
Carl Yastrzemski 1969
Dwight Evans 1988
110—Joe Cronin 1937
Bill Buckner 1985
Jim Rice 1986
109—Duffy Lewis 1912
Bobby Doerr 1949
Ken Harrelson 1968
108—Nick Esasky 1989
Carl Everett 2000
107—Joe Cronin 1939
Tony Armas 1983
106—Mike Higgins 1937, 1938
Bob Johnson 1944
105—Jimmie Foxx 1939, 1941
Bobby Doerr 1940
Fred Lynn 1975
Tony Perez 1980
104—Buck Freeman 1903
Dwight Evans 1984
Nomar Garciaparra 1999
103—Earl Webb 1931
Frank Malzone 1957
Jackie Jensen 1957
Vic Wertz 1960
Rico Petrocelli 1970
Jim Rice 1985
Troy O'Leary 1999
102—Bobby Doerr 1942
Carl Yastrzemski 1970, 1976, 1977
Jim Rice 1975
Carlton Fisk 1977
Bill Buckner 1986
John Valentin 1995
101—Jim Tabor 1941
Mo Vaughn 1993
100—Del Pratt 1921
Dwight Evans 1989

20-plus victories

1901— Cy Young 33-10
1902— Cy Young 32-11
Bill Dinneen 21-21
1903— Cy Young 28-9
Bill Dinneen 21-13
Tom Hughes 20-7
1904— Cy Young 26-16
Bill Dinneen 23-14
Jesse Tannehill 21-11
1905— Jesse Tannehill 22-9
1907— Cy Young 21-15
1908— Cy Young 21-11
1911— Joe Wood 23-17
1912— Joe Wood 34-5
Hugh Bedient 20-9
Buck O'Brien 20-13
1914— Ray Collins 20-13
1916— Babe Ruth 23-12
1917— Babe Ruth 24-13
Carl Mays 22-9
1918— Carl Mays 21-13
1921— Sam Jones 23-16
1923— Howard Ehmke 20-17
1935— Wes Ferrell 25-14
Lefty Grove 20-12
1936— Wes Ferrell 20-15
1942— Tex Hughson 22-6
1945— Dave Ferriss 21-10
1946— Dave Ferriss 25-6
Tex Hughson 20-11
1949— Mel Parnell 25-7
Ellis Kinder 23-6
1953— Mel Parnell 21-8
1963— Bill Monbouquette 20-10
1967— Jim Lonborg 22-9
1973— Luis Tiant 20-13
1974— Luis Tiant 22-13
1976— Luis Tiant 21-12
1978— Dennis Eckersley 20-8
1986— Roger Clemens 24-4
1987— Roger Clemens 20-9
1990— Roger Clemens 21-6
1999— Pedro Martinez 23-4

A.L. home run champions

1903— Buck Freeman 13
1910— Jake Stahl 10
1912— Tris Speaker *10
1918— Babe Ruth *11
1919— Babe Ruth 29
1939— Jimmie Foxx 35
1941— Ted Williams 37
1942— Ted Williams 36
1947— Ted Williams 32
1949— Ted Williams 43
1965— Tony Conigliaro 32
1967— Carl Yastrzemski *44
1977— Jim Rice 39
1978— Jim Rice 46
1981— Dwight Evans *22
1983— Jim Rice 39
1984— Tony Armas 43

* Tied for league lead

A.L. RBI champions

1902— Buck Freeman 121
1903— Buck Freeman 104
1919— Babe Ruth 114
1938— Jimmie Foxx 175
1939— Ted Williams 145
1942— Ted Williams 137
1947— Ted Williams 114
1949— Ted Williams *159
Vern Stephens *159
1950— Walt Dropo *144
Vern Stephens *144
1955— Jackie Jensen *116
1958— Jackie Jensen 122
1959— Jackie Jensen 112
1963— Dick Stuart 118
1967— Carl Yastrzemski 121
1968— Ken Harrelson 109
1978— Jim Rice 139
1983— Jim Rice *126
1984— Tony Armas 123
1995— Mo Vaughn *126

* Tied for league lead

INDIVIDUAL SEASON, GAME RECORDS

SEASON

Batting

At-bats	684	Nomar Garciaparra	1997
Runs	150	Ted Williams	1949
Hits	240	Wade Boggs	1985
Singles	187	Wade Boggs	1985
Doubles	67	Earl Webb	1931
Triples	22	Tris Speaker	1913
Home runs	50	Jimmie Foxx	1938
Home runs, rookie	34	Walt Dropo	1950
Grand slams	4	Babe Ruth	1919
Total bases	406	Jim Rice	1978
RBIs	175	Jimmie Foxx	1938
Walks	162	Ted Williams	1947, 1949
Most strikeouts	162	Butch Hobson	1977
Fewest strikeouts	9	Stuffy McInnis	1921
Batting average	.406	Ted Williams	1941
Slugging pct.	.735	Ted Williams	1941
Stolen bases	54	Tommy Harper	1973

Pitching

Games	80	Greg Harris	1993
Complete games	41	Cy Young	1902
Innings	384.2	Cy Young	1902
Wins	34	Joe Wood	1912
Losses	25	Charley Ruffing	1928
Winning pct.	.882 (15-2)	Bob Stanley	1978
Walks	134	Mel Parnell	1949
Strikeouts	313	Pedro Martinez	1999
Shutouts	10	Cy Young	1904
		Joe Wood	1912
Home runs allowed	38	Tim Wakefield	1996
Lowest ERA	0.96	Dutch Leonard	1914
Saves	46	Tom Gordon	1998

GAME

Batting

Runs	6	Last by Spike Owen	8-21-86
Hits	6	Last by Jerry Remy	9-3-81 (20 innings)
Doubles	4	Last by Rick Miller	5-11-81
Triples	3	Patsy Dougherty	9-5-03
Home runs	3	Last by Mo Vaughn	5-30-97
RBIs	10	Last by Nomar Garciaparra	5-10-99
Total bases	16	Fred Lynn	6-18-75
Stolen bases	4	Jerry Remy	6-14-80

A.L. batting champions

1932— Dale Alexander .... .367
1938— Jimmie Foxx .... .349
1941— Ted Williams .... .406
1942— Ted Williams .... .356
1947— Ted Williams .... .343
1948— Ted Williams .... .369
1950— Billy Goodman .... .354
1957— Ted Williams .... .388
1958— Ted Williams .... .328
1960— Pete Runnels .... .320
1962— Pete Runnels .... .326
1963— Carl Yastrzemski .... .321
1967— Carl Yastrzemski .... .326
1968— Carl Yastrzemski .... .301
1979— Fred Lynn .... .333
1981— Carney Lansford .... .336
1983— Wade Boggs .... .361
1985— Wade Boggs .... .368
1986— Wade Boggs .... .357
1987— Wade Boggs .... .363
1988— Wade Boggs .... .366
1999— Nomar Garciaparra .... .357
2000— Nomar Garciaparra .... .372

A.L. ERA champions

1901— Cy Young 1.62
1914— Dutch Leonard 0.96
1915— Joe Wood 1.49
1916— Babe Ruth 1.75
1935— Lefty Grove 2.70
1936— Lefty Grove 2.81
1938— Lefty Grove 3.08
1939— Lefty Grove 2.54
1949— Mel Parnell 2.78
1972— Luis Tiant 1.91
1986— Roger Clemens 2.48
1990— Roger Clemens 1.93
1991— Roger Clemens 2.62
1992— Roger Clemens 2.41
1999— Pedro Martinez 2.07
2000— Pedro Martinez 1.74

A.L. strikeout champions

1901— Cy Young 158
1942— Tex Hughson 113
1967— Jim Lonborg 246
1988— Roger Clemens 291
1991— Roger Clemens 241
1996— Roger Clemens 257
1999— Pedro Martinez 313
2000— Pedro Martinez 284

No-hit pitchers

(9 innings or more)

1904— Cy Young ...... 3-0 vs. Philadelphia (Perfect)
Jesse Tannehill .... 6-0 vs. Chicago
1905— Bill Dinneen .... 2-0 vs. Chicago
1908— Cy Young .... 8-0 vs. New York
1911— Joe Wood .... 5-0 vs. St. Louis
1916— George Foster .... 2-0 vs. New York
Dutch Leonard .... 4-0 vs. St. Louis
1917— Ernie Shore.... 4-0 vs. Washington (Perfect)
1918— Dutch Leonard .... 5-0 vs. Detroit
1923— Howard Ehmke .... 4-0 vs. Philadelphia
1956— Mel Parnell .... 4-0 vs. Chicago
1962— Earl Wilson .... 2-0 vs. Los Angeles
Bill Monbouquette .... 1-0 vs. Chicago
1965— Dave Morehead .... 2-0 vs. Cleveland
1992— †Matt Young .... 1-2 vs. Cleveland

† Pitched 8 innings

Longest hitting streaks

34—Dom DiMaggio 1949
30—Tris Speaker 1912
Nomar Garciaparra 1997
28—Wade Boggs 1985
27—Dom DiMaggio 1951
26—Buck Freeman 1902
Johnny Pesky 1947
25—George Metkovich 1944
Wade Boggs 1987
24—Nomar Garciaparra 1998
23—Gorge Burns 1922
Del Pratt 1922
Buddy Myer 1928
Ted Williams 1941
22—Tris Speaker 1913
Dom DiMaggio 1942
Denny Doyle 1975
Reggie Jefferson 1997
21—Bobby Doerr 1943
Jim Rice 1980
Mike Greenwell 1989
20—Tris Speaker 1912
Tris Speaker 1912
Babe Ruth 1919
Ike Boone 1925
Smead Jolley 1932
Ed Bressoud 1964
Fred Lynn 1975
Fred Lynn 1979
Mike Easler 1984
Wade Boggs 1986
Nomar Garciaparra 2000

CAREER LEADERS

BATTING

Games

Carl Yastrzemski	3,308
Dwight Evans	2,505
Ted Williams	2,292
Jim Rice	2,089
Bobby Doerr	1,865
Harry Hooper	1,647
Wade Boggs	1,625
Rico Petrocelli	1,553
Dom DiMaggio	1,399
Frank Malzone	1,359

At-bats

Carl Yastrzemski	11,988
Dwight Evans	8,726
Jim Rice	8,225
Ted Williams	7,706
Bobby Doerr	7,093
Harry Hooper	6,270
Wade Boggs	6,213
Dom DiMaggio	5,640
Rico Petrocelli	5,390
Frank Malzone	5,273

Runs

Carl Yastrzemski	1,816
Ted Williams	1,798
Dwight Evans	1,435
Jim Rice	1,249
Bobby Doerr	1,094
Wade Boggs	1,067
Dom DiMaggio	1,046
Harry Hooper	988
Johnny Pesky	776
Jimmie Foxx	721

Hits

Carl Yastrzemski	3,419
Ted Williams	2,654
Jim Rice	2,452
Dwight Evans	2,373
Wade Boggs	2,098
Bobby Doerr	2,042
Harry Hooper	1,707
Dom DiMaggio	1,680
Frank Malzone	1,454
Mike Greenwell	1,400

Doubles

Carl Yastrzemski	646
Ted Williams	525
Dwight Evans	474
Wade Boggs	422
Bobby Doerr	381
Jim Rice	373
Dom DiMaggio	308
Mike Greenwell	275
Joe Cronin	270
John Valentin	263

Triples

Harry Hooper	130
Tris Speaker	106
Buck Freeman	90
Bobby Doerr	89
Larry Gardner	87
Jim Rice	79
Hobe Ferris	77
Dwight Evans	72
Ted Williams	71
Jimmy Collins	65

Home runs

Ted Williams	521
Carl Yastrzemski	452
Jim Rice	382
Dwight Evans	379
Mo Vaughn	230
Bobby Doerr	223
Jimmie Foxx	222
Rico Petrocelli	210
Jackie Jensen	170
Tony Conigliaro	162
Carlton Fisk	162

Total bases

Carl Yastrzemski	5,539
Ted Williams	4,884
Jim Rice	4,129
Dwight Evans	4,128
Bobby Doerr	3,270
Wade Boggs	2,869
Dom DiMaggio	2,363
Harry Hooper	2,303
Rico Petrocelli	2,263
Mike Greenwell	2,141

Runs batted in

Carl Yastrzemski	1,844
Ted Williams	1,839
Jim Rice	1,451
Dwight Evans	1,346
Bobby Doerr	1,247
Jimmie Foxx	788
Rico Petrocelli	773
Mo Vaughn	752
Joe Cronin	737
Jackie Jensen	733

Extra base hits

Carl Yastrzemski	1,157
Ted Williams	1,117
Dwight Evans	925
Jim Rice	834
Bobby Doerr	693
Wade Boggs	554
Rico Petrocelli	469
Dom DiMaggio	452
Jimmie Foxx	448
Mike Greenwell	443

Batting average
(Minimum 500 games)

Ted Williams	.344
Wade Boggs	.338
Tris Speaker	.337
Nomar Garciaparra	..333
Pete Runnels	.320
Jimmie Foxx	.320
Roy Johnson	.313
Johnny Pesky	.313
Fred Lynn	.308
Billy Goodman	.306

Stolen bases

Harry Hooper	300
Tris Speaker	267
Carl Yastrzemski	168
Heinie Wagner	141
Larry Gardner	134
Freddy Parent	129
Tommy Harper	107
Billy Werber	107
Chick Stahl	105
Jimmy Collins	102
Duffy Lewis	102

PITCHING

Earned-run average
(Minimum 1,000 innings)

Joe Wood	1.99
Cy Young	2.00
Dutch Leonard	2.13
Babe Ruth	2.19
Carl Mays	2.21
Ray Collins	2.51
Bill Dinneen	2.81
George Winter	2.91
Tex Hughson	2.94
Roger Clemens	3.06

Wins

Roger Clemens	192
Cy Young	192
Mel Parnell	123
Luis Tiant	122
Joe Wood	117
Bob Stanley	115
Joe Dobson	106
Lefty Grove	105
Tex Hughson	96
Bill Monbouquette	96

Losses

Cy Young	112
Roger Clemens	111
Bob Stanley	97
George Winter	97
Red Ruffing	96
Jack Russell	94
Bill Monbouquette	91
Bill Dinneen	85
Tom Brewer	82
Luis Tiant	81

Innings pitched

Roger Clemens	2,776.0
Cy Young	2,728.1
Luis Tiant	1,774.2
Mel Parnell	1,752.2
Bob Stanley	1,707.0
Bill Monbouquette	1,622.0
George Winter	1,599.2
Joe Dobson	1,544.0
Lefty Grove	1,539.2
Tom Brewer	1,509.1

Strikeouts

Roger Clemens	2,590
Cy Young	1,341
Luis Tiant	1,075
Bruce Hurst	1,043
Joe Wood	986
Bill Monbouquette	969
Pedro Martinez	848
Frank Sullivan	821
Ray Culp	794
Jim Lonborg	784

Bases on balls

Roger Clemens	856
Mel Parnell	758
Tom Brewer	669
Joe Dobson	604
Jack Wilson	564
Willard Nixon	530
Ike Delock	514
Mickey McDermott	504
Luis Tiant	501
Fritz Ostermueller	491

Games

Bob Stanley	637
Roger Clemens	383
Ellis Kinder	365
Cy Young	327
Ike Delock	322
Bill Lee	321
Mel Parnell	289
Greg Harris	287
Mike Fornieles	286
Dick Radatz	286

Shutouts

Roger Clemens	38
Cy Young	38
Joe Wood	28
Luis Tiant	26
Dutch Leonard	25
Mel Parnell	20
Ray Collins	19
Tex Hughson	19
Sam Jones	18
Joe Dobson	17
Babe Ruth	17

Saves

Bob Stanley	132
Dick Radatz	104
Ellis Kinder	91
Jeff Reardon	88
Sparky Lyle	69
Tom Gordon	68
Derek Lowe	61
Lee Smith	58
Bill Campbell	51
Mike Fornieles	48
Heathcliff Slocumb	48

TEAM SEASON, GAME RECORDS

SEASON

Batting

Most at-bats	5,781	1997
Most runs	1,027	1950
Fewest runs	463	1906
Most hits	1,684	1997
Most singles	1,156	1905
Most doubles	373	1997
Most triples	112	1903
Most home runs	213	1977
Fewest home runs	12	1906
Most grand slams	9	1941, 1950, 1987
Most pinch-hit home runs	6	1953
Most total bases	2,676	1997
Most stolen bases	215	1909
Highest batting average	.302	1950
Lowest batting average	.234	1905, 1907
Highest slugging pct	.465	1977

Pitching

Lowest ERA	2.12	1904
Highest ERA	5.02	1932
Most complete games	148	1904
Most shutouts	26	1918
Most saves	53	1998
Most walks	748	1950
Most strikeouts	1,165	1996

Fielding

Most errors	373	1901
Fewest errors	93	1988
Most double plays	207	1949
Highest fielding averag	.984	1988

General

Most games won	105	1912
Most games lost	111	1932
Highest win pct	.691	1912
Lowest win pct	.279	1932

GAME, INNING

Batting

Most runs, game	29	6-8-50
Most runs, inning	17	6-18-53
Most hits, game	28	6-8-50
Most home runs, game	8	7-4-77
Most total bases, game	60	6-8-50

Jackie Jensen (left) and Ted Williams formed two-thirds of a prolific outfield for six seasons.

RED SOX YEAR-BY-YEAR

Year	W	L	Place	Games Back	Manager	Leaders: Batting avg.	Hits	Home runs	RBIs	Wins	ERA
1901	79	57	2nd	4	J. Collins	Freeman, .339	J. Collins, 187	Freeman, 12	Freeman, 114	Young, 33	Young, 1.62
1902	77	60	3rd	6½	J. Collins	Dougherty, .342	Freeman, 174	Freeman, 11	Freeman, 121	Young, 32	Young, 2.15
1903	91	47	1st	+14½	J. Collins	Dougherty, .331	Dougherty, 195	Freeman, 13	Freeman, 104	Young, 28	Young, 2.08
1904	95	59	1st	+1½	J. Collins	Parent, .291	Parent, 172	Freeman, 7	Freeman, 84	Young, 26	Young, 1.97
1905	78	74	4th	16	J. Collins	J. Collins, .276	Burkett, 147	Ferris, 6	J. Collins, 65	Tannehill, 22	Young, 1.82
1906	49	105	8th	45½	J. Collins, Stahl	Grimshaw, .290	Stahl, 170	Stahl, 4	Stahl, 51	Tannehill, Young, 13	Dinneen, 2.92
1907	59	90	7th	32½	Huff, Unglaub, McGuire	Congalton, .286	Congalton, 142	Ferris, 4	Unglaub, 62	Young, 21	Morgan, 1.97
1908	75	79	5th	15½	McGuire, Lake	Gessler, .308	Lord, 145	Gessler, 3	Gessler, 63	Young, 21	Young, 1.26
1909	88	63	3rd	9½	Lake	Lord, .311	Speaker, 168	Speaker, 7	Speaker, 77	Arellanes, 16	Cicotte, 1.97
1910	81	72	4th	22½	Donovan	Speaker, .340	Speaker, 183	Stahl, 10	Stahl, 77	Cicotte, 15	R. Collins, 1.62
1911	78	75	5th	24	Donovan	Speaker, .334	Speaker, 167	Speaker, 8	Lewis, 86	Wood, 23	Wood, 2.02
1912	105	47	1st	+14	Stahl	Speaker, .383	Speaker, 222	Speaker, 10	Lewis, 109	Wood, 34	Wood, 1.91
1913	79	71	4th	15½	Stahl, Carrigan	Speaker, .363	Speaker, 189	Hooper, 4	Lewis, 90	R. Collins, 19	Wood, 2.29
1914	91	62	2nd	8½	Carrigan	Speaker, .338	Speaker, 193	Speaker, 4	Speaker, 90	R. Collins, 20	Leonard, 0.96
1915	101	50	1st	+2½	Carrigan	Speaker, .322	Speaker, 176	Ruth, 4	Lewis, 76	Foster, Shore, 19	Wood, 1.49
1916	91	63	1st	+2	Carrigan	Gardner, .308	Hooper, 156	Walker, Ruth, Gainor, 3	Gardner, 62	Ruth, 23	Ruth, 1.75
1917	90	62	2nd	9	Barry	Lewis, .302	Lewis, 167	Hooper, 3	Lewis, 65	Ruth, 24	Mays, 1.74
1918	75	51	1st	+1½	Barrow	Hooper, .289	Hooper, 137	Ruth, 11	Ruth, 66	Mays, 21	Bush, 2.11
1919	66	71	6th	20½	Barrow	Ruth, .322	Scott, 141	Ruth, 29	Ruth, 114	Pennock, 16	Mays, 2.47
1920	72	81	5th	25½	Barrow	Hendryx, .328	Hooper, 167	Hooper, 7	Hendryx, 73	Pennock, 16	Myers, 2.13
1921	75	79	5th	23½	Duffy	Pratt, .324	McInnis, 179	Pratt, 5	Pratt, 100	S. Jones, 23	S. Jones, 3.22
1922	61	93	8th	33	Duffy	J. Harris, .316	Pratt, 183	Burns, 12	Pratt, 86	R. Collins, 14	Quinn, 3.48
1923	61	91	8th	37	Chance	J. Harris, .335	Burns, 181	J. Harris, 13	Burns, 82	Ehmke, 20	Piercy, 3.41
1924	67	87	7th	25	Fohl	Boone, .333	Wambsganss, 174	Boone, 13	Veach, 99	Ehmke, 19	Quinn, 3.27
1925	47	105	8th	49½	Fohl	Boone, .330	Flagstead, 160	Todt, 11	Todt, 75	Wingfield, 12	Ehmke, 3.73
1926	46	107	8th	44½	Fohl	Jacobson, .305	Todt, 153	Todt, 7	Jacobson, Todt, 69	Wingfield, 11	Russell, 3.58
1927	51	103	8th	59	Carrigan	Tobin, .310	Myer, 135	Todt, 6	Flagstead, 69	Harriss, 14	Russell, 4.10
1928	57	96	8th	43½	Carrigan	Myer, .313	Myer, 168	Todt, 12	Regan, 75	Morris, 19	Morris, 3.53
1929	58	96	8th	48	Carrigan	Rothrock, .300	Scarritt, 159	Rothrock, 6	Scarritt, 71	Morris, 14	MacFayden, 3.62
1930	52	102	8th	50	Wagner	Webb, .323	Oliver, 189	Webb, 16	Webb, 66	Gaston, 13	Gaston, 3.92
1931	62	90	6th	45	S. Collins	Webb, .333	Webb, 196	Webb, 14	Webb, 103	MacFayden, 16	Moore, 3.88
1932	43	111	8th	64	S. Collins, McManus	Alexander, .372	Jolley, 164	Jolley, 18	Jolley, 99	Kline, 11	Durham, 3.80
1933	63	86	7th	34½	McManus	R. Johnson, .313	R. Johnson, 151	R. Johnson, 10	R. Johnson, 95	Rhodes, 12	Weiland, 3.87
1934	76	76	4th	24	B. Harris	Werber, .321	Werber, 200	Werber, 11	R. Johnson, 119	Ferrell, 14	Ostermueller, 3.49
1935	78	75	4th	16	Cronin	R. Johnson, .315	Almada, 176	Werber, 14	Cronin, 95	Ferrell, 25	Grove, 2.70
1936	74	80	6th	28½	Cronin	Foxx, .338	Foxx, 198	Foxx, 41	Foxx, 143	Ferrell, 20	Grove, 2.81
1937	80	72	5th	21	Cronin	Chapman, Cronin, .307	Cronin, 175	Foxx, 36	Foxx, 127	Grove, 17	Grove, 3.02
1938	88	61	2nd	9½	Cronin	Foxx, .349	Vosmik, 201	Foxx, 50	Foxx, 175	Bagby, J. Wilson, 15	Grove, 3.08
1939	89	62	2nd	17	Cronin	Foxx, .360	T. Williams, 185	Foxx, 35	T. Williams, 145	Grove, 15	Grove, 2.54
1940	82	72	4th	8	Cronin	T. Williams, .344	Cramer, 200	Foxx, 36	Foxx, 119	Heving, J. Wilson, 12	Grove, 3.99
1941	84	70	2nd	17	Cronin	T. Williams, .406	T. Williams, 185	T. Williams, 37	T. Williams, 120	D. Newsome, 19	Wagner, 3.07
1942	93	59	2nd	9	Cronin	T. Williams, .356	Pesky, 205	T. Williams, 36	T. Williams, 137	Hughson, 22	Butland, 2.51
1943	68	84	7th	29	Cronin	Fox, .288	Doerr, 163	Doerr, 16	Tabor, 85	Hughson, 12	Brown, 2.12
1944	77	77	4th	12	Cronin	Doerr, .325	B. Johnson, 170	B. Johnson, 17	B. Johnson, 106	Hughson, 18	Hughson, 2.26
1945	71	83	7th	17½	Cronin	S. Newsome, .290	B. Johnson, 148	B. Johnson, 12	B. Johnson, 74	Ferriss, 21	Ryba, 2.49
1946	104	50	1st	+12	Cronin	T. Williams, .342	Pesky, 208	T. Williams, 38	T. Williams, 123	Ferriss, 25	Hughson, 2.75
1947	83	71	3rd	14	Cronin	T. Williams, .343	Pesky, 207	T. Williams, 32	T. Williams, 114	Dobson, 18	Dobson, 2.95
1948	96	59	*2nd	1	McCarthy	T. Williams, .369	T. Williams, 188	Stephens, 29	Stephens, 137	Kramer, 18	Parnell, 3.14
1949	96	58	2nd	1	McCarthy	T. Williams, .343	T. Williams, 194	T. Williams, 43	Stephens, Williams, 159	Parnell, 25	Parnell, 2.77
1950	94	60	3rd	4	McCarthy, O'Neill	Goodman, .354	D. DiMaggio, 193	Dropo, 34	Dropo, Stephens, 144	Parnell, 18	Parnell, 3.61
1951	87	67	3rd	11	O'Neill	T. Williams, .318	D. DiMaggio, 189	T. Williams, 30	T. Williams, 126	Parnell, 18	Kinder, 2.55
1952	76	78	6th	19	Boudreau	Goodman, .306	Goodman, 157	Gernert, 19	Gernert, 67	Parnell, 12	Kinder, 2.58
1953	84	69	4th	16	Boudreau	Goodman, .313	Goodman, 161	Gernert, 21	Kell, 73	Parnell, 21	Kinder, 1.85
1954	69	85	4th	42	Boudreau	T. Williams, .345	Jensen, 160	T. Williams, 29	Jensen, 117	Sullivan, 15	Sullivan, 3.14
1955	84	70	4th	12	Higgins	Goodman, .294	Goodman, 176	T. Williams, 28	Jensen, 116	Sullivan, 18	Kiely, 2.80
1956	84	70	4th	13	Higgins	T. Williams, .345	Jensen, 182	T. Williams, 24	Jensen, 97	Brewer, 19	Sullivan, 3.42
1957	82	72	3rd	16	Higgins	T. Williams, .388	Malzone, 185	T. Williams, 38	Jensen, Malzone, 103	Brewer, 16	Sullivan, 2.73
1958	79	75	3rd	13	Higgins	T. Williams, .328	Malzone, 185	Jensen, 35	Jensen, 122	Delock, 14	Delock, 3.37
1959	75	79	5th	19	Higgins, York, Jurges	Runnels, .314	Runnels, 176	Jensen, 28	Jensen, 112	Casale, 13	DeLock, 2.95
1960	65	89	7th	32	Jurges, Baker, Higgins	Runnels, .320	Runnels, 169	T. Williams, 29	Wertz, 103	Monbouquette, 14	Fornieles, 2.64
1961	76	86	6th	33	Higgins	Runnels, .317	Schilling, 167	Geiger, 18	Malzone, 87	Schwall, 15	Schwall, 3.22
1962	76	84	8th	19	Higgins	Runnels, .326	Yastrzemski, 191	Malzone, 21	Malzone, 95	Conley, Monbouquette, 15	Radatz, 2.24
1963	76	85	7th	28	Pesky	Yastrzemski, .321	Yastrzemski, 183	Stuart, 42	Stuart, 118	Monbouquette, 20	Radatz, 1.97
1964	72	90	8th	27	Pesky, Herman	Bressoud, .293	Stuart, 168	Stuart, 33	Stuart, 114	Radatz, 16	Radatz, 2.29
1965	62	100	9th	40	Herman	Yastrzemski, .312	Yastrzemski, 154	Conigliaro, 32	Mantilla, 92	Wilson, 13	Monbouquette, 3.70
1966	72	90	9th	26	Herman, Runnels	Yastrzemski, .278	Yastrzemski, 165	Conigliaro, 28	Conigliaro, 93	Santiago, 12	Brandon, 3.31
1967	92	70	1st	+1	D. Williams	Yastrzemski, .326	Yastrzemski, 189	Yastrzemski, 44	Yastrzemski, 121	Lonborg, 22	Wyatt, 2.60
1968	86	76	4th	17	D. Williams	Yastrzemski, .301	Yastrzemski, 162	Harrelson, 35	Harrelson, 109	Culp, Ellsworth, 16	Santiago, 2.25
							EAST DIVISION				
1969	87	75	3rd	22	D. Williams, Popowski	R. Smith, .309	R. Smith, 168	Petrocelli, Yastrzemski, 40	Yastrzemski, 111	Culp, 17	Lyle, 2.54
1970	87	75	3rd	21	Kasko	Yastrzemski, .329	Yastrzemski, 186	Yastrzemski, 40	Conigliaro, 116	Culp, 17	Culp, 3.04
1971	85	77	3rd	18	Kasko	R. Smith, .283	R. Smith, 175	R. Smith, 30	R. Smith, 96	Siebert, 16	Lee, 2.74
1972	85	70	2nd	½	Kasko	Fisk, .293	Harper, 141	Fisk, 22	Petrocelli, 75	Pattin, 17	Tiant, 1.91
1973	89	73	2nd	8	Kasko, Popowski	R. Smith, .303	Yastrzemski, 160	Fisk, 26	Yastrzemski, 95	Tiant, 20	Lee, 2.75
1974	84	78	3rd	7	D. Johnson	Yastrzemski, .301	Yastrzemski, 155	Petrocelli, Yastrzemski, 15	Yastrzemski, 79	Tiant, 22	Tiant, 2.92
1975	95	65	†1st	+4½	D. Johnson	Lynn, .331	Lynn, 175	Rice, 22	Lynn, 105	Wise, 19	Moret, 3.60
1976	83	79	3rd	15½	D. Johnson, Zimmer	Lynn, .314	Rice, 164	Rice, 25	Yastrzemski, 102	Tiant, 21	Willoughby, 2.82
1977	97	64	‡2nd	2½	Zimmer	Rice, .320	Rice, 206	Rice, 39	Rice, 114	Campbell, 13	Campbell, 2.96
1978	99	64	§2nd	1	Zimmer	Rice, .315	Rice, 213	Rice, 46	Rice, 139	Eckersley, 20	Stanley, 2.60
1979	91	69	3rd	11½	Zimmer	Lynn, .333	Rice, 201	Lynn, Rice, 39	Rice, 130	Eckersley, 17	Eckersley, 2.99
1980	83	77	4th	19	Zimmer, Pesky	Stapleton, .321	Burleson, 179	Perez, 25	Perez, 105	Eckersley, 12	Burgmeier, 2.00
1981	59	49	∞5th/2nd	—	Houk	Lansford, .336	Lansford, 134	Evans, 22	Evans, 71	Stanley, Torrez, 10	Torrez, 3.68
1982	89	73	3rd	6	Houk	Rice, .309	Evans, Remy, 178	Evans, 32	Evans, 98	Clear, 14	Burgmeier, 2.29
1983	78	84	6th	20	Houk	Boggs, .361	Boggs, 210	Rice, 39	Rice, 126	Tudor, 13	Stanley, 2.85
1984	86	76	4th	18	Houk	Boggs, .325	Boggs, 203	Armas, 43	Armas, 123	Boyd, Hurst, Ojeda, 12	Stanley, 3.54
1985	81	81	5th	18½	McNamara	Boggs, .368	Boggs, 240	Evans, 29	Buckner, 110	Boyd, 15	Clemens, 3.29
1986	95	66	†1st	+5½	McNamara	Boggs, .357	Boggs, 207	Baylor, 31	Rice, 110	Clemens, 24	Clemens, 2.48
1987	78	84	5th	20	McNamara	Boggs, .363	Boggs, 200	Evans, 34	Evans, 123	Clemens, 20	Clemens, 2.97
1988	89	73	▲1st	+1	McNamara, Morgan	Boggs, .366	Boggs, 214	Greenwell, 22	Greenwell, 119	Clemens, Hurst, 18	Clemens, 2.93
1989	83	79	3rd	6	Morgan	Boggs, .330	Boggs, 205	Esasky, 30	Esasky, 108	Clemens, 17	Lamp, 2.32
1990	88	74	▲1st	+2	Morgan	Boggs, .302	Boggs, 187	Burks, 21	Burks, 89	Clemens, 21	Clemens, 1.93
1991	84	78	‡2nd	7	Morgan	Boggs, .332	Boggs, 181	Clark, 28	Clark, 87	Clemens, 18	Clemens, 2.62
1992	73	89	7th	23	Hobson	Zupcic, .276	Reed, 136	Brunansky, 15	Brunansky, 74	Clemens, 18	Clemens, 2.41
1993	80	82	5th	15	Hobson	Greenwell, .315	Greenwell, 170	Vaughn, 29	Vaughn, 101	Darwin, 15	Sele, 2.74
1994	54	61	4th	17	Hobson	Vaughn, .310	Vaughn, 122	Vaughn, 26	Vaughn, 82	Clemens, 9	Clemens, 2.85
1995	86	58	◆1st	+7	Kennedy	O'Leary, .308	Vaughn, 165	Vaughn, 39	Vaughn, 126	Wakefield, 16	Wakefield, 2.95
1996	85	77	3rd	7	Kennedy	Jefferson, .347	Vaughn, 207	Vaughn, 44	Vaughn, 143	Wakefield, 14	Clemens, 3.63
1997	78	84	4th	20	J. Williams	Jefferson, .319	Garciaparra, 209	Vaughn, 35	Garciaparra, 98	Sele, 13	Gordon, 3.74
1998	92	70	◆2nd	22	J. Williams	Vaughn, .337	Vaughn, 205	Vaughn, 40	Garciaparra, 122	P.Martinez, 19	P.Martinez, 2.89
1999	94	68	▲2nd	4	J. Williams	Garciaparra, .357	Garciaparra, 190	O'Leary, 28	Garciaparra, 104	P.Martinez, 23	P.Martinez, 2.07
2000	85	77	2nd	2½	J. Williams	Garciaparra, .372	Garciaparra, 197	Everett, 34	Everett, 108	P. Martinez, 18	P. Martinez, 1.74

* Lost pennant playoff. † Won Championship Series. ‡ Tied for position. § Lost division playoff. ∞ First half 30-26, second half 29-23. ▲ Lost Championship Series. ◆ Lost Division Series.

Note: Batting average minimum 350 at-bats; ERA minimum 90 innings pitched.

Chicago White Sox

FRANCHISE CHRONOLOGY

First season: 1901, as a member of the new American League. Charles Comiskey's White Sox defeated Cleveland, 8-2, in their Major League debut and proceeded to win the circuit's first pennant. Chicago's 83-53 record was four games better than second-place Boston.

1902-present: The Hitless Wonder White Sox of 1906 won another A.L. pennant and stunned the powerful Cubs in a six-game World Series, and Chicago repeated as Series champion in 1917 with a six-game triumph over the New York Giants. But the franchise would never taste such success again. The team's image was tarnished two years later when the White Sox won another pennant and conspired with gamblers to lose the World Series. In the wake of the infamous "Black Sox" scandal, it would take four decades for the Sox to win another pennant and another 24 to qualify again for postseason play. The "Go Go Sox" of 1959 lost to Los Angeles in the World Series and the 1983, '93 and 2000 Sox won division titles, only to lose in the A.L. Championship Series or Division Series. Chicago, a charter member of the West Division, was one of five teams placed in the Central when the A.L. adopted a three-division format in 1994.

Shortstop Luis Aparicio.

WHITE SOX VS. OPPONENTS BY DECADE

	A's	Indians	Orioles	Red Sox	Tigers	Twins	Yankees	Angels	Rangers	Brewers	Royals	Blue Jays	Mariners	Devil Rays	Interleague	Decade Record
1901-09	92-98	100-89	112-74	101-90	96-93	130-57	113-74									744-575
1910-19	125-90	114-102	132-74	97-117	103-109	109-106	118-94									798-692
1920-29	100-119	105-114	104-114	117-103	124-95	95-125	86-134									731-804
1930-39	102-118	94-125	127-90	97-114	89-129	101-117	68-148									678-841
1940-49	112-108	103-114	102-113	85-134	95-125	124-93	86-133									707-820
1950-59	124-96	116-104	134-86	122-98	122-98	141-79	88-132									847-693
1960-69	118-66	104-74	83-95	102-76	81-97	83-101	76-102	92-70	95-61	10-8	8-10					852-760
1970-79	76-89	62-54	39-74	48-67	50-67	76-89	44-72	79-90	90-65	68-62	79-89	19-14	22-21			752-853
1980-89	70-60	61-54	53-63	59-56	48-66	57-66	58-61	62-68	59-64	55-58	55-64	50-70	71-52			758-802
1990-99	60-57	58-64	59-46	54-54	69-51	71-48	54-52	58-60	58-59	56-41	72-52	53-54	59-62	11-10	24-25	816-735
2000-	6-3	8-5	6-4	5-7	9-3	7-5	8-4	6-4	5-5		5-7	5-5	7-5	6-4	12-6	95-67
Totals	985-904	925-899	951-833	887-916	886-933	994-886	799-1006	297-292	307-254	189-169	219-222	127-143	159-140	17-14	36-31	7778-7642

Interleague results: 9-9 vs. Cubs; 6-2 vs. Reds; 7-5 vs. Astros; 4-4 vs. Pirates; 5-7 vs. Cardinals; 5-4 vs. Brewers.

MANAGERS

Name	*Years*	*Record*
Clark Griffith	1901-02	157-113
Nixey Callahan	1903-04, 1912-14	309-329
Fielder Jones	1904-08	426-293
Billy Sullivan	1909	78-74
Hugh Duffy	1910-11	145-159
Pants Rowland	1915-18	339-247
Kid Gleason	1919-23	392-364
Johnny Evers	1924	66-87
Eddie Collins	1925-26	160-147
Ray Schalk	1927-28	102-125
Lena Blackburne	1928-29	99-133
Donie Bush	1930-31	118-189
Lew Fonseca	1932-34	120-196
Jimmie Dykes	1934-46	899-940
Ted Lyons	1946-48	185-245
Jack Onslow	1949-50	71-113
Red Corriden	1950	52-72
Paul Richards	1951-54, 1976	406-362
Marty Marion	1954-56	179-138
Al Lopez	1957-65, 1968-69	840-650
Eddie Stanky	1966-68	206-197
Don Gutteridge	1969-70	109-172
Chuck Tanner	1970-75	401-414
Bob Lemon	1977-78	124-112
Larry Doby	1978	37-50
Don Kessinger	1979	46-60
Tony La Russa	1979-86	522-510
Jim Fregosi	1986-88	193-226
Jeff Torborg	1989-91	250-235
Gene Lamont	1992-95	258-210

MANAGERS—*cont'd.*

Name	*Years*	*Record*
Terry Bevington	1995-97	222-214
Jerry Manuel	1998-2000	250-235

WORLD SERIES CHAMPIONS

Year	*Loser*	*Length*	*MVP*
1906	Chicago Cubs	6 games	None
1917	N.Y. Giants	6 games	None

A.L. PENNANT WINNERS

Year	*Record*	*Manager*	*Series Result*
1901	83-53	Griffith	None
1906	93-58	Jones	Defeated Cubs
1917	100-54	Rowland	Defeated Giants
1919	88-52	Gleason	Lost to Reds
1959	94-60	Lopez	Lost to Dodgers

WEST DIVISION CHAMPIONS

Year	*Record*	*Manager*	*ALCS Result*
1983	99-63	La Russa	Lost to Orioles
1993	94-68	Lamont	Lost to Blue Jays
1994	67-46	Lamont	None

CENTRAL DIVISION CHAMPIONS

Year	*Record*	*Manager*	*ALCS Result*
2000	95-67	Manuel	Lost in Div. Series

Nellie Fox was a second-base fixture for more than a decade in Chicago.

BALLPARK CHRONOLOGY

New Comiskey Park (1991-present)

Capacity: 44,321.
First game: Detroit 16, White Sox 0 (April 18, 1991).
First batter: Tony Phillips, Tigers.
First hit: Alan Trammell, Tigers (single).
First run: Travis Fryman, Tigers (3rd inning).
First home run: Cecil Fielder, Tigers.
First winning pitcher: Frank Tanana, Tigers.
First-season attendance: 2,934,154.

Southside Park (1901-10)

Capacity: 15,000.
First game: White Sox 8, Cleveland 2 (April 24, 1901).
First-season attendance: 354,350.

Comiskey Park (1910-90)

Capacity: 43,931.
First game: St. Louis 2, White Sox 0 (July 1, 1910).
First-season attendance (1911): 583,208.

ATTENDANCE HIGHS

Total	*Season*	*Park*
2,934,154	1991	New Comiskey Park
2,681,156	1992	New Comiskey Park
2,581,091	1993	New Comiskey Park
2,136,988	1984	Comiskey Park
2,132,821	1983	Comiskey Park

A.L. MVPs

Nellie Fox, 2B, 1959
Dick Allen, 1B, 1972
Frank Thomas, 1B, 1993
Frank Thomas, 1B, 1994

CY YOUNG WINNERS

Early Wynn, RH, 1959
LaMarr Hoyt, RH, 1983
Jack McDowell, RH, 1993

ROOKIES OF THE YEAR

Luis Aparicio, SS, 1956
Gary Peters, P, 1963
Tommie Agee, OF, 1966
Ron Kittle, OF, 1983
Ozzie Guillen, SS, 1985

MANAGERS OF THE YEAR

Tony La Russa, 1983
Jeff Torborg, 1990
Gene Lamont, 1993
Jerry Manuel, 2000

RETIRED UNIFORMS

No.	*Name*	*Pos.*
2	Nellie Fox	2B
3	Harold Baines	OF
4	Luke Appling	SS
9	Minnie Minoso	OF
11	Luis Aparicio	SS
16	Ted Lyons	P
19	Billy Pierce	P
72	Carlton Fisk	C

MILESTONE PERFORMANCES

30-plus home runs

49— Albert Belle 1998
43— Frank Thomas 2000
41— Frank Thomas 1993
40— Frank Thomas 1995
Frank Thomas 1996
38— Frank Thomas 1994
37— Carlton Fisk 1985
Dick Allen 1972
35— Ron Kittle 1983
Frank Thomas 1997
34— Robin Ventura 1996
33— Bill Melton 1971
Bill Melton 1970
32— Frank Thomas 1991
Ron Kittle 1984
Greg Luzinski 1983
Dick Allen 1974
Magglio Ordonez 2000
31— Oscar Gamble 1977
Charles Johnson 2000
30— Albert Belle 1997
Magglio Ordonez 1999

100-plus RBIs

152— Albert Belle 1998
143— Frank Thomas 2000
138— Zeke Bonura 1936
134— Frank Thomas 1996
128— Frank Thomas 1993
Luke Appling 1936
126— Magglio Ordonez 2000
125— Frank Thomas 1997
121— Joe Jackson 1920
119— Al Simmons 1933
117— Eddie Robinson 1951
Magglio Ordonez 1999
116— Minnie Minoso 1954
Albert Belle 1997
115— Frank Thomas 1992
Happy Felsch 1920
114— Smead Jolley 1930
113— Harold Baines 1985
Dick Allen 1972
112— George Bell 1992
111— Gee Walker 1939
Earl Sheely 1925
Frank Thomas 1995
110— Zeke Bonura 1934
109— Frank Thomas 1991, 1998
Floyd Robinson 1962
108— Bib Falk 1926
107— Carlton Fisk 1985
105— Harold Baines 1982
Minnie Minoso 1960
Robin Ventura 1996
104— Minnie Minoso 1953
Eddie Robinson 1952
Al Simmons 1934
Carl Reynolds 1930
103— Minnie Minoso 1957
Earl Sheely 1924
102— Greg Luzinski 1982
Larry Doby 1956
Happy Felsch 1917
101— Frank Thomas 1994
Richie Zisk 1977
Danny Tartabull 1996
100— Robin Ventura 1991
Ron Kittle 1983
Zeke Bonura 1937

20-plus victories

1901— Clark Griffith 24-7
Roy Patterson 20-15
1904— Frank Owen 21-15
1905— Nick Altrock 23-12
Frank Owen 21-13
1906— Frank Owen 22-13
Nick Altrock 20-13
1907— Guy White 27-13
Ed Walsh 24-18
Frank Smith 23-10
1908— Ed Walsh 40-15
1909— Frank Smith 25-17
1911— Ed Walsh 27-18
1912— Ed Walsh 27-17
1913— Reb Russell 22-16
Jim Scott 20-21
1915— Jim Scott 24-11
Urban Faber 24-14
1917— Ed Cicotte 28-12
1919— Ed Cicotte 29-7
Lefty Williams 23-11
1920— Red Faber 23-13
Lefty Williams 22-14
Dickie Kerr 21-9
Ed Cicotte 21-10
1921— Red Faber 25-15
1922— Red Faber 21-17
1924— Sloppy Thurston 20-14
1925— Ted Lyons 21-11
1927— Ted Lyons 22-14
1930— Ted Lyons 22-15
1936— Vern Kennedy 21-9
1941— Thornton Lee 22-11
1953— Virgil Trucks *20-10
1956— Billy Pierce 20-9
1957— Billy Pierce 20-12
1959— Early Wynn 22-10
1962— Ray Herbert 20-9
1964— Gary Peters 20-8
1971— Wilbur Wood 22-13
1972— Wilbur Wood 24-17
Stan Bahnsen 21-16
1973— Wilbur Wood 24-20
1974— Jim Kaat 21-13
Wilbur Wood 20-19
1975— Jim Kaat 20-14
1983— LaMarr Hoyt 24-10
Rich Dotson 22-7
1992— Jack McDowell 20-10
1993— Jack McDowell 22-10

* 15-6 with White Sox; 5-4 with Browns.

A.L. home run champions

1971— Bill Melton 33
1972— Dick Allen 37
1974— Dick Allen 32

A.L. RBI champions

1972— Dick Allen 113

A.L. batting champions

1936— Luke Appling .... .388
1943— Luke Appling .... .328
1997— Frank Thomas .... .347

A.L. ERA champions

1906— Doc White 1.52
1907— Ed Walsh 1.60
1910— Ed Walsh 1.27
1917— Ed Cicotte 1.53
1921— Red Faber 2.48
1922— Red Faber 2.80
1941— Thornton Lee 2.37
1942— Ted Lyons 2.10
1947— Joe Haynes 2.42
1951— Saul Rogovin *2.48
1955— Billy Pierce 1.97
1960— Frank Baumann 2.67
1963— Gary Peters 2.33
1966— Gary Peters 1.98
1967— Joel Horlen 2.06

*ERA compiled with two teams.

A.L. strikeout champions

1908— Ed Walsh 269
1909— Frank Smith 177
1911— Ed Walsh 255
1953— Billy Pierce 186
1958— Early Wynn 179

No-hit pitchers

(9 innings or more)

1902— Nixey Callahan .... 3-0 vs. Detroit
1905— Frank Smith .... 15-0 vs. Detroit
1908— Frank Smith .... 1-0 vs. Philadelphia
1911— Ed Walsh .... 5-0 vs. Boston
1914— Joe Benz .... 6-1 vs. Cleveland
1917— Ed Cicotte .... 11-0 vs. St. Louis
1922— Charlie Robertson .. 2-0 vs. Detroit (Perfect)
1926— Ted Lyons .... 6-0 vs. Boston
1935— Vern Kennedy .... 5-0 vs. Cleveland
1937— Bill Dietrich .... 8-0 vs. St. Louis
1957— Bob Keegan .... 6-0 vs. Washington
1967— Joel Horlen .... 6-0 vs. Detroit
1976— Blue Moon Odom-
Francisco Barrios .... 2-1 vs. Oakland
1986— Joe Cowley .... 7-1 vs. California
1991— Wilson Alvarez .... 7-0 vs. Baltimore

Longest hitting streaks

27— Luke Appling 1936
Albert Belle 1997
26— Guy Cutright 1943
25— Lance Johnson 1992
24— Chico Carrasquel 1950
23— Minnie Minoso 1955
22— Sam Mele 1953
Eddie Collins 1920
21— Roy Sievers 1960
Frank Thomas 1999
20— Ken Berry 1967
Rip Radcliff 1937
Eddie Collins 1916

Shortstop Luke Appling, who spent 20 seasons with the White Sox, batted a hefty .388 in 1936, still a team record.

INDIVIDUAL SEASON, GAME RECORDS

SEASON

Batting			
At-bats	649	Nellie Fox	1956
Runs	135	John Mostil	1925
Hits	222	Eddie Collins	1920
Singles	169	Eddie Collins	1920
Doubles	48	Albert Belle	1998
Triples	21	Joe Jackson	1916
Home runs	49	Albert Belle	1998
Home runs, rookie	35	Ron Kittle	1983
Grand slams	4	Albert Belle	1997
Total bases	399	Albert Belle	1998
RBIs	152	Albert Belle	1998
Walks	138	Frank Thomas	1991
Most strikeouts	175	Dave Nicholson	1963
Fewest strikeouts	11	Nellie Fox	1958
Batting average	.388	Luke Appling	1936
Slugging pct.	.729	Frank Thomas	1994
Stolen bases	77	Rudy Law	1983
Pitching			
Games	88	Wilbur Wood	1968
Complete games	42	Ed Walsh	1908
Innings	464.0	Ed Walsh	1908
Wins	40	Ed Walsh	1908
Losses	25	Patrick Flaherty	1903
Winning pct.	.857 (12-2)	Jason Bere	1994
Walks	147	Vern Kennedy	1936
Strikeouts	269	Ed Walsh	1908
Shutouts	11	Ed Walsh	1908
Home runs allowed	34	4 times Last by James Baldwin	2000
Lowest ERA	1.52	Doc White	1906
Saves	57	Bobby Thigpen	1990

GAME

Batting			
Runs	5	Last by Walt Williams	5-31-70
Hits	6	Last by Lance Johnson	9-23-95
Doubles	4	Last by Marv Owen	4-23-39
Triples	3	Lance Johnson	9-23-95
Home runs	4	Pat Seerey	7-18-48
RBIs	8	Last by Robin Ventura	9-4-95
Total bases	16	Pat Seerey	7-18-48
Stolen bases	4	Last by Lou Frazier	4-19-98

CAREER LEADERS

BATTING

Games

Player	Games
Luke Appling	2,422
Nellie Fox	2,115
Ray Schalk	1,757
Ozzie Guillen	1,743
Eddie Collins	1,670
Harold Baines	1,638
Frank Thomas	1,530
Luis Aparicio	1,511
Carlton Fisk	1,421
Minnie Minoso	1,373

At-bats

Luke Appling	8,856
Nellie Fox	8,486
Ozzie Guillen	6,067
Harold Baines	6,065
Eddie Collins	6,065
Luis Aparicio	5,856
Frank Thomas	5,474
Ray Schalk	5,304
Minnie Minoso	5,011
Carlton Fisk	4,896

Runs

Player	Runs
Luke Appling	1,319
Nellie Fox	1,187
Frank Thomas	1,083
Eddie Collins	1,065
Minnie Minoso	893
Luis Aparicio	791
Harold Baines	783
Ozzie Guillen	693
Fielder Jones	693
Robin Ventura	658

Hits

Player	Hits
Luke Appling	2,749
Nellie Fox	2,470
Eddie Collins	2,007
Harold Baines	1,762
Frank Thomas	1,755
Ozzie Guillen	1,608
Luis Aparicio	1,576
Minnie Minoso	1,523
Ray Schalk	1,345
Buck Weaver	1,308

Doubles

Player	Doubles
Luke Appling	440
Frank Thomas	361
Nellie Fox	335
Harold Baines	319
Eddie Collins	266
Minnie Minoso	260
Bibb Falk	245
Willie Kamm	243
Ozzie Guillen	240
Shano Collins	230

Triples

Player	Triples
Shano Collins	104
Nellie Fox	104
Luke Appling	102
Eddie Collins	102
Johnny Mostil	82
Joe Jackson	79
Minnie Minoso	79
Lance Johnson	77
Buck Weaver	69
Ozzie Guillen	68

Home runs

Player	Home runs
Frank Thomas	344
Harold Baines	221
Carlton Fisk	214
Robin Ventura	171
Bill Melton	154
Ron Kittle	140
Minnie Minoso	135
Sherm Lollar	124
Greg Walker	113
Pete Ward	97

Total bases

Player	Total bases
Luke Appling	3,528
Frank Thomas	3,168
Nellie Fox	3,118
Harold Baines	2,832
Eddie Collins	2,570
Minnie Minoso	2,346
Carlton Fisk	2,143
Ozzie Guillen	2,056
Luis Aparicio	2,036
Robin Ventura	2,000

Runs batted in

Frank Thomas	1,183
Luke Appling	1,116
Harold Baines	975
Minnie Minoso	808
Eddie Collins	804
Carlton Fisk	762
Robin Ventura	741
Nellie Fox	740
Sherm Lollar	631
Bibb Falk	627

Extra-base hits

Player	Extra-base hits
Frank Thomas	715
Luke Appling	587
Harold Baines	584
Nellie Fox	474
Minnie Minoso	474
Carlton Fisk	442
Robin Ventura	402
Eddie Collins	399
Shano Collins	351
Bibb Falk	345

Batting average

(Minimum 500 games)

Joe Jackson	.340
Eddie Collins	.331
Frank Thomas	.321
Zeke Bonura	.317
Bibb Falk	.315
Taffy Wright	.312
Luke Appling	.310
Rip Radcliff	.310
Earl Sheely	.305
Minnie Minoso	.304

Stolen bases

Player	Stolen bases
Eddie Collins	368
Luis Aparicio	318
Frank Isbell	250
Lance Johnson	226
Fielder Jones	206
Shano Collins	192
Luke Appling	179
Ray Schalk	177
Ray Durham	176
Johnny Mostil	176

PITCHING

Earned-run average

(Minimum 1,000 innings)

Ed Walsh	1.81
Frank Smith	2.18
Eddie Cicotte	2.25
Jim Scott	2.30
Doc White	2.30
Reb Russell	2.33
Nick Altrock	2.40
Joe Benz	2.43
Frank Owen	2.48
Roy Patterson	2.75

Wins

Player	Wins
Ted Lyons	260
Red Faber	254
Ed Walsh	195
Billy Pierce	186
Wilbur Wood	163
Doc White	159
Eddie Cicotte	156
Joe Horlen	113
Frank Smith	108
Jim Scott	107

Losses

Player	Losses
Ted Lyons	230
Red Faber	213
Billy Pierce	152
Wilbur Wood	148
Ed Walsh	125
Doc White	123
Jim Scott	114
Joe Horlen	113
Thornton Lee	104
Eddie Cicotte	101

Innings pitched

Ted Lyons	4,161.0
Red Faber	4,086.2
Ed Walsh	2,946.1
Billy Pierce	2,931.0
Wilbur Wood	2,524.1
Doc White	2,498.1
Eddie Cicotte	2,322.2
Joe Horlen	1,918.0
Jim Scott	1,892.0
Thornton Lee	1,888.0

Strikeouts

Player	Strikeouts
Billy Pierce	1,796
Ed Walsh	1,732
Red Faber	1,471
Wilbur Wood	1,332
Gary Peters	1,098
Ted Lyons	1,073
Doc White	1,067
Joe Horlen	1,007
Eddie Cicotte	961
Alex Fernandez	951

Bases on balls

Player	Bases on balls
Red Faber	1,213
Ted Lyons	1,121
Billy Pierce	1,052
Wilbur Wood	671
Richard Dotson	637
Thornton Lee	633
Jim Scott	609
Ed Walsh	608
Bill Dietrich	561
Eddie Smith	545

Games

Player	Games
Red Faber	669
Ted Lyons	594
Wilbur Wood	578
Billy Pierce	456
Ed Walsh	426
Bobby Thigpen	424
Hoyt Wilhelm	361
Doc White	360
Eddie Cicotte	353
Roberto Hernandez	345

Shutouts

Player	Shutouts
Ed Walsh	57
Doc White	42
Billy Pierce	35
Red Faber	29
Eddie Cicotte	28
Ted Lyons	27
Jim Scott	26
Frank Smith	25
Reb Russell	24
Wilbur Wood	24

Saves

Player	Saves
Bobby Thigpen	201
Roberto Hernandez	161
Hoyt Wilhelm	98
Terry Forster	75
Wilbur Wood	57
Bob James	56
Ed Farmer	54
Clint Brown	53
Bob Locker	48
Keith Foulke	47

TEAM SEASON, GAME RECORDS

SEASON

Batting

Record	Total	Year
Most at-bats	5,646	2000
Most runs	978	2000
Fewest runs	447	1910
Most hits	1,615	2000
Most singles	1,199	1936
Most doubles	325	2000
Most triples	102	1915
Most home runs	216	2000
Fewest home runs	3	1908
Most grand slams	8	1996
Most pinch-hit home runs	9	1984
Most total bases	2,654	2000
Most stolen bases	280	1901
Highest batting average	.295	1920
Lowest batting average	.211	1910
Highest slugging pct	.447	1996

Pitching

Record	Total	Year
Lowest ERA	1.99	1905
Highest ERA	5.41	1934
Most complete games	134	1904
Most shutouts	32	1906
Most saves	68	1990
Most walks	734	1950
Most strikeouts	1,039	1996

Fielding

Record	Total	Year
Most errors	345	1901
Fewest errors	107	1957
Most double plays	190	2000
Highest fielding average	.982	5 times

General

Record	Total	Year
Most games won	100	1917
Most games lost	106	1970
Highest win pct	.649	1917
Lowest win pct	.325	1932

GAME, INNING

Batting

Record	Total	Date
Most runs, game	29	4-23-55
Most runs, inning	13	9-26-43
Most hits, game	29	4-23-55
Most home runs, game	7	4-23-55
Most total bases, game	55	4-23-55

Durable righthander Ed Walsh recorded a sparkling 1.81 earned-run average over 13 Chicago seasons.

HISTORY

WHITE SOX YEAR-BY-YEAR

Year	W	L	Place	Games Back	Manager	Batting avg. (Leaders)	Hits (Leaders)	Home runs (Leaders)	RBIs (Leaders)	Wins (Leaders)	ERA (Leaders)
1901	83	53	1st	+4	Griffith	Jones, .311	Jones, 162	Mertes, 5	Mertes, 98	Griffith, 24	Callahan, 2.42
1902	74	60	4th	8	Griffith	Jones, .321	Jones, 171	Isbell, 4	Davis, 93	Patterson, 19	Garvin, 2.21
1903	60	77	7th	30½	Callahan	Green, .309	Green, 154	Green, 6	Green, 62	White, 17	White, 2.13
1904	89	65	3rd	6	Callahan, Jones	Green, .265	Davis, 143	Jones, 3	Davis, 69	Owen, 21	White, 1.78
1905	92	60	2nd	2	Jones	Donahue, .287	Davis, Donahue, 153	Isbell, Jones, Sullivan, 2	Donahue, 76	Altrock, 23	White, 1.76
1906	93	58	1st	+3	Jones	Isbell, .279	Isbell, 153	Jones, Sullivan, 2	Davis, 80	Altrock, 20	White, 1.52
1907	87	64	3rd	5½	Jones	Dougherty, .270	Donahue, 158	Rohe, 2	Donahue, 68	White, 27	Walsh, 1.60
1908	88	64	3rd	1½	Jones	Dougherty, .278	Dougherty, Jones, 134	Isbell, Jones, Walsh, 1	Jones, 50	Walsh, 40	Walsh, 1.42
1909	78	74	4th	20	Sullivan	Dougherty, .285	Dougherty, 140	4 Tied, 1	Dougherty, 55	Smith, 25	Walsh, 1.41
1910	68	85	6th	35½	Duffy	Dougherty, .248	Dougherty, 110	Gandil, 2	Dougherty, 43	Walsh, 18	Walsh, 1.27
1911	77	74	4th	24	Duffy	McIntyre, .323	McIntyre, 184	Bodie, S. Collins, 4	Bodie, 97	Walsh, 27	Walsh, 2.22
1912	78	76	4th	28	Callahan	Bodie, .294	S. Collins, 168	Bodie, Lord, 5	Collins, 81	Walsh, 27	Walsh, 2.15
1913	78	74	5th	17½	Callahan	Chase, .286	Weaver, 145	Bodie, 8	Weaver, 52	Russell, 22	Cicotte, 1.58
1914	70	84	*6th	30	Callahan	Fournier, .311	S. Collins, 164	Fournier, 6	S. Collins, 65	Benz, Scott, 14	Wolfgang, 1.89
1915	93	61	3rd	9½	Rowland	E. Collins, .332	E. Collins, 173	Fournier, 5	S. Collins, 85	Faber, Scott, 24	Scott, 2.03
1916	89	65	2nd	2	Rowland	Jackson, .341	Jackson, 202	Felsch, 7	Jackson, 78	Russell, 18	Cicotte, 1.78
1917	100	54	1st	+9	Rowland	Felsch, .308	Felsch, 177	Felsch, 6	Felsch, 102	Cicotte, 28	Cicotte, 1.53
1918	57	67	6th	17	Rowland	Weaver, .300	Weaver, 126	E. Collins, 2	S. Collins, 56	Cicotte, 12	Russell, 2.60
1919	88	52	1st	+3½	Gleason	Jackson, .351	Jackson, 181	Felsch, Jackson, 7	Jackson, 96	Cicotte, 29	Cicotte, 1.82
1920	96	58	2nd	2	Gleason	Jackson, .382	E. Collins, 224	Felsch, 14	Jackson, 121	Faber, 23	Faber, 2.99
1921	62	92	7th	36½	Gleason	E. Collins, .337	Johnson, 181	Sheely, 11	Sheely, 95	Faber, 25	Faber, 2.48
1922	77	77	5th	17	Gleason	E. Collins, .324	E. Collins, 194	Falk, 12	Hooper, Sheely, 80	Faber, 21	Faber, 2.81
1923	69	85	7th	30	Gleason	E. Collins, .360	E. Collins, 182	Hooper, 10	Sheely, 88	Faber, 14	Thurston, 3.05
1924	66	87	8th	25½	Evers	Falk, .352	E. Collins, 194	Hooper, 10	Sheely, 103	Thurston, 20	Thurston, 3.80
1925	79	75	5th	18½	E. Collins	E. Collins, .346	Sheely, 189	Sheely, 9	Sheely, 111	Lyons, 21	Blankenship, 3.03
1926	81	72	5th	9½	E. Collins	Falk, .345	Mostil, 197	Falk, 8	Falk, 108	Lyons, 18	Lyons, 3.01
1927	70	83	5th	29½	Schalk	Falk, .327	Falk, 175	Falk, 9	Barrett, Falk, 83	Lyons, 22	Lyons, 2.84
1928	72	82	5th	29	Schalk, Blackburne	Kamm, .308	Kamm, 170	Barrett, Metzler, 3	Kamm, 84	Thomas, 17	Thomas, 3.08
1929	59	93	7th	46	Blackburne	Reynolds, .317	Cissell, 173	Reynolds, 11	Reynolds, 67	Lyons, Thomas, 14	Thomas, 3.19
1930	62	92	7th	40	Bush	Reynolds, .359	Reynolds, 202	Reynolds, 22	Jolley, 114	Lyons, 22	Lyons, 3.78
1931	56	97	8th	51	Bush	Blue, .304	Blue, 179	Reynolds, 6	Reynolds, 77	Frazier, 13	Faber, 3.82
1932	49	102	7th	56½	Fonseca	Seeds, .290	Kress, 147	Kress, 9	Appling, 63	Jones, Lyons, 10	Lyons, 3.28
1933	67	83	6th	31	Fonseca	Simmons, .331	Simmons, 200	Simmons, 14	Simmons, 119	Durham, Jones, Lyons, 10	Heving, 2.67
1934	53	99	8th	47	Fonseca, Dykes	Simmons, .344	Simmons, 192	Bonura, 27	Bonura, 110	Earnshaw, 14	Earnshaw, 4.52
1935	74	78	5th	19½	Dykes	Appling, .307	Radcliff, 178	Bonura, 21	Bonura, 92	Lyons, 15	Lyons, 3.02
1936	81	70	3rd	20	Dykes	Appling, .388	Radcliff, 207	Bonura, 12	Bonura, 138	Kennedy, 21	Kennedy, 4.63
1937	86	68	3rd	16	Dykes	Bonura, .345	Radcliff, 190	Bonura, 19	Bonura, 100	Stratton, 15	Stratton, 2.40
1938	65	83	6th	32	Dykes	Steinbacher, .331	Radcliff, 166	G. Walker, 16	G. Walker, 87	Stratton, 15	Lee, 3.49
1939	85	69	4th	22½	Dykes	McNair, .324	Kreevich, 175	Kuhel, 15	G. Walker, 111	Lee, Rigney, 15	Lyons, 2.76
1940	82	72	*4th	8	Dykes	Appling, .348	Appling, 197	Kuhel, 27	Kuhel, 94	Rigney, Smith, 14	Rigney, 3.11
1941	77	77	3rd	24	Dykes	Wright, .322	Appling, 186	Kuhel, 12	Wright, 97	Lee, 22	Lee, 2.37
1942	66	82	6th	34	Dykes	Kolloway, .273	Kolloway, 164	Moses, 7	Kolloway, 60	Lyons, 14	Lyons, 2.10
1943	82	72	4th	16	Dykes	Appling, .328	Appling, 192	Kuhel, 5	Appling, 80	Grove, 15	Maltzberger, 2.46
1944	71	83	7th	18	Dykes	Hodgin, .295	Moses, 150	Trosky, 10	Trosky, 70	Dietrich, 16	Haynes, 2.57
1945	71	78	6th	15	Dykes	Cuccinello, .308	Moses, 168	Curtright, Dickshot, 4	Schalk, 65	Lee, 15	Lee, 2.44
1946	74	80	5th	30	Dykes	Appling, .309	Appling, 180	Wright, 7	Appling, 55	Caldwell, Lopat, 13	Caldwell, 2.08
1947	70	84	6th	27	Lyons	Wright, .324	Appling, 154	York, 15	York, 64	Lopat, 16	Haynes, 2.42
1948	51	101	8th	44½	Lyons	Appling, .314	Appling, 156	Seerey, 18	Seerey, 64	Haynes, Wight, 9	Gumpert, 3.79
1949	63	91	6th	34	Onslow	Michaels, .308	Michaels, 173	Souchock, 7	Michaels, 83	Wight, 15	Wight, 3.31
1950	60	94	6th	38	Onslow, Corriden	E. Robinson, .314	E. Robinson, 163	Zernial, 29	Zernial, 93	Pierce, 12	Wight, 3.58
1951	81	73	4th	17	Richards	Minoso, .324	Fox, 189	E. Robinson, 29	E. Robinson, 117	Pierce, 15	Rogovin, 2.48
1952	81	73	3rd	14	Richards	Fox, E. Robinson, .296	Fox, 192	E. Robinson, 22	E. Robinson, 104	Pierce, 15	Dorish, 2.47
1953	89	65	3rd	11½	Richards	Minoso, .313	Fox, 178	Minoso, 15	Minoso, 104	Pierce, 18	Consuegra, 2.54
1954	94	60	3rd	17	Richards, Marion	Minoso, .320	Fox, 201	Minoso, 19	Minoso, 116	Trucks, 19	Consuegra, 2.69
1955	91	63	3rd	5	Marion	Kell, .312	Fox, 198	Dropo, 19	Kell, 81	Donovan, Pierce, 15	Pierce, 1.97
1956	85	69	3rd	12	Marion	Minoso, .316	Fox, 192	Doby, 24	Doby, 102	Pierce, 20	Staley, 2.92
1957	90	64	2nd	8	Lopez	Fox, .317	Fox, 196	Doby, Rivera, 14	Minoso, 103	Pierce, 20	Staley, 2.06
1958	82	72	2nd	10	Lopez	Fox, .300	Fox, 187	Lollar, 20	Lollar, 84	Pierce, 17	Pierce, 2.68
1959	94	60	1st	+5	Lopez	Fox, .306	Fox, 191	Lollar, 22	Lollar, 84	Wynn, 22	Staley, 2.24
1960	87	67	3rd	10	Lopez	A. Smith, .315	Minoso, 184	Sievers, 28	Minoso, 105	Pierce, 14	Staley, 2.42
1961	86	76	4th	23	Lopez	F. Robinson, .310	Aparicio, 170	A. Smith, 28	A. Smith, 93	Pizarro, 14	Lown, 2.76
1962	85	77	5th	11	Lopez	F. Robinson, .312	F. Robinson, 187	A. Smith, 16	F. Robinson, 109	Herbert, 20	Fisher, 3.10
1963	94	68	2nd	10½	Lopez	Ward, .295	Ward, 177	Nicholson, Ward, 22	Ward, 84	Peters, 19	Peters, 2.33
1964	98	64	2nd	1	Lopez	F. Robinson, .301	F. Robinson, 158	Ward, 23	Ward, 94	Peters, 20	Horlen, 1.88
1965	95	67	2nd	7	Lopez	Buford, .283	Buford, 166	Romano, Skowron, 18	Skowron, 78	Fisher, 15	Wilhelm, 1.87
1966	83	79	4th	15	Stanky	Agee, .273	Agee, 172	Agee, 22	Agee, 86	John, 14	Peters, 1.98
1967	89	73	4th	3	Stanky	Berry, Buford, .241	Buford, 129	Ward, 18	Ward, 62	Horlen, 19	McMahon, 1.67
1968	67	95	*8th	36	Stanky, Lopez	T. Davis, .268	Aparicio, 164	Ward, 15	T. Davis, Ward, 50	Wood, 13	Wilhelm, 1.73
								WEST DIVISION			
1969	68	94	5th	29	Lopez, Gutteridge	Williams, .304	Aparicio, 168	Melton, 23	Melton, 87	Horlen, 13	Wood, 3.01
1970	56	106	6th	42	Gutteridge, Tanner	Aparicio, .313	Aparicio, 173	Melton, 33	Melton, 96	John, 12	Wood, 2.81
1971	79	83	3rd	22½	Tanner	May, Williams, .294	May, 147	Melton, 33	Melton, 86	Wood, 22	Wood, 1.91
1972	87	67	2nd	5½	Tanner	Allen, May, .308	May, 161	Allen, 37	Allen, 113	Wood, 24	Forster, 2.25
1973	77	85	5th	17	Tanner	Kelly, .280	Melton, 155	May, Melton, 20	May, 96	Wood, 24	Acosta, 2.23
1974	80	80	4th	9	Tanner	Orta, .316	Henderson, 176	Allen, 32	Henderson, 95	Kaat, 21	B. Johnson, 2.74
1975	75	86	5th	22½	Tanner	Orta, .304	Orta, 165	D. Johnson, 18	Orta, 83	Kaat, 20	Gossage, 1.84
1976	64	97	6th	25½	Richards	Garr, .300	Orta, 174	Orta, Spencer, 14	Orta, 72	Brett, 10	Brett, 3.32
1977	90	72	3rd	12	Lemon	L. Johnson, .302	Garr, 163	Gamble, 31	Zisk, 101	Stone, 15	LaGrow, 2.46
1978	71	90	5th	20½	Lemon, Doby	Lemon, .300	Lam. Johnson, 136	Soderholm, 20	Lam. Johnson, 72	Stone, 12	Willoughby, 3.86
1979	73	87	5th	14	Kessinger, La Russa	Lemon, .318	Lemon, 177	Lemon, 17	Lemon, 86	Kravec, 15	Baumgarten, 3.54
1980	70	90	5th	26	La Russa	Lemon, .292	Morrison, 171	Morrison, Nordhagen, 15	Lam. Johnson, 81	Burns, 15	Burns, 2.84
1981	54	52	†3rd/6th	—	La Russa	Bernazard, .276	Bernazard, 106	Luzinski, 21	Luzinski, 62	Burns, 10	Lamp, 2.41
1982	87	75	3rd	6	La Russa	Paciorek, .312	Luzinski, 170	Baines, 25	Baines, 105	Hoyt, 19	Hoyt, 3.53
1983	99	63	‡1st	+20	La Russa	Paciorek, .307	Baines, 167	Kittle, 35	Kittle, 100	Hoyt, 24	Dotson, 3.23
1984	74	88	*5th	10	La Russa	Baines, .304	Baines, 173	Kittle, 32	Baines, 94	Seaver, 15	Dotson, 3.59
1985	85	77	3rd	6	La Russa	Baines, .309	Baines, 196	Fisk, 37	Baines, 113	Burns, 18	James, 2.13
1986	72	90	5th	20	La Russa, Fregosi	Baines, .296	Baines, 169	Baines, 21	Baines, 88	Cowley, 11	Schmidt, 3.31
1987	77	85	5th	8	Fregosi	Baines, Calderon, .293	Calderon, 159	Calderon, 28	Walker, 94	Bannister, 16	Bannister, 3.58
1988	71	90	5th	32½	Fregosi	Baines, .277	Baines, 166	Pasqua, 20	Baines, 81	Reuss, 13	Thigpen, 3.30
1989	69	92	7th	29½	Torborg	Martinez, .300	Calderon, 178	Calderon, 14	Calderon, 87	Perez, 11	Hibbard, 3.21
1990	94	68	2nd	9	Torborg	Fisk, Lan. Johnson, .285	Calderon, 166	Fisk, 18	Calderon, 74	Hibbard, McDowell, 14	Hibbard, 3.16
1991	87	75	2nd	8	Torborg	F. Thomas, .318	F. Thomas, 178	F. Thomas, 32	F. Thomas, 109	McDowell, 17	Perez, 3.12
1992	86	76	3rd	10	Lamont	F. Thomas, .323	F. Thomas, 185	Bell, 25	F. Thomas, 115	McDowell, 20	McDowell, 3.18
1993	94	68	‡1st	+8	Lamont	F. Thomas, .317	F. Thomas, 174	F. Thomas, 41	F. Thomas, 128	McDowell, 22	Alvarez, 2.95
								CENTRAL DIVISION			
1994	67	46	1st	+1	Lamont	F. Thomas, .353	F. Thomas, 141	F. Thomas, 38	F. Thomas, 101	Bere, Alvarez, 12	Alvarez, 3.45
1995	68	76	3rd	32	Lamont, Bevington	F. Thomas, .308	Lan. Johnson, 186	F. Thomas, 40	F. Thomas, 111	Fernandez, 12	Fernandez, 3.80
1996	85	77	∞2nd	14½	Bevington	F. Thomas, .349	F. Thomas, 184	F. Thomas, 40	F. Thomas, 134	Fernandez, 16	Fernandez, 3.45
1997	80	81	2nd	6	Bevington	F. Thomas, .347	F. Thomas, 184	F. Thomas, 35	F. Thomas, 125	Baldwin, Drabek, 12	Alvarez, 3.03
1998	80	82	2nd	9	Manuel	Belle, .328	Belle, 200	Belle, 49	Belle, 152	Sirotka, 14	Sirotka, 5.06
1999	75	86	2nd	21½	Manuel	F. Thomas, .305	Ordonez, 188	Ordonez, 30	Ordonez, 117	Baldwin, 12	Foulke, 2.22
2000	95	67	▲1st	+5	Manuel	F. Thomas, .328	F. Thomas, 191	F. Thomas, 43	F. Thomas, 143	Sirotka, 15	Sirotka, 3.79

* Tied for position. † First half 31-22, second half 23-30. ‡ Lost Championship Series. ∞ Lost division playoff. ▲ Lost Division Series.

Note: Batting average minimum 350 at-bats, ERA minimum 90 innings pitched.

Cleveland Indians

FRANCHISE CHRONOLOGY

First season: 1901, as a member of the new American League. Cleveland lost its Major League debut at Chicago, 8-2, and struggled through a difficult first season. The Indians won only 54 games and finished seventh in the eight-team A.L. field.

1902-present: The early decade Indians (also known as the Naps after star second baseman Napoleon Lajoie) were annual contenders, but it took almost two decades before they had anything to show for their efforts. And after the 1920 Indians captured the team's first pennant and defeated Brooklyn in an historic World Series, Cleveland fans had to wait 28 years for another. The 1948 championship was followed by an amazing 1954 season in which the Indians won an A.L.-record 111 games—and then fell to the Giants in a shocking four-game Series sweep. That would be it for more than four decades as the Indians languished in the lower reaches of the A.L. standings, posting only 11 winning records. They finally resurfaced in the strike-shortened 1995 season to claim their first of five consecutive Central Division titles with a league-leading 100 victories. But their fourth pennant in 1995 resulted in a six-game World Series loss to Atlanta and a Cinderella World Series run in 1997 came up short in the seventh game against the Florida Marlins.

Righthander Bob Feller.

INDIANS VS. OPPONENTS BY DECADE

	A's	Orioles	Red Sox	Tigers	Twins	White Sox	Yankees	Angels	Rangers	Brewers	Royals	Blue Jays	Mariners	Devil Rays	Interleague	Decade Record
1901-09	86-105	109-82	96-93	95-95	118-72	89-100	104-85									697-632
1910-19	110-105	130-81	97-115	94-114	92-123	102-114	117-95									742-747
1920-29	113-106	112-106	130-90	109-111	113-106	114-105	95-125									786-749
1930-39	114-106	155-64	131-89	101-118	114-104	125-94	84-133									824-708
1940-49	136-80	124-95	116-105	105-115	115-104	114-103	90-129									800-731
1950-59	153-67	151-67	122-98	136-84	141-79	104-116	97-123									904-634
1960-69	92-85	85-99	94-90	83-101	96-82	74-104	83-100	74-82	88-73	7-5	7-5					783-826
1970-79	46-70	65-104	80-86	78-90	58-56	54-62	64-103	58-58	58-71	75-78	52-65	27-14	22-9			737-866
1980-89	50-63	64-59	52-78	41-82	55-56	54-61	56-73	49-69	55-57	56-70	54-62	52-71	72-48			710-849
1990-99	62-45	67-51	60-61	76-47	70-52	64-58	45-72	59-44	50-63	56-41	64-49	56-65	54-52	12-7	28-21	823-728
2000-	6-6	4-5	6-6	6-7	5-8	5-8	5-5	6-3	6-4		5-7	8-4	7-2	8-2	13-5	90-72
Totals	968-838	1066-813	984-911	924-964	977-842	899-925	840-1043	246-256	257-268	194-194	182-188	143-154	155-111	20-9	41-26	7896-7542

Interleague results: 6-2 vs. Cubs; 10-8 vs. Reds; 6-6 vs. Astros; 7-5 vs. Pirates; 6-2 vs. Cardinals; 6-3 vs. Brewers.

MANAGERS

Name	*Years*	*Record*
Jimmy McAleer	1901	55-82
Bill Armour	1902-04	232-195
Nap Lajoie	1905-09	377-309
Deacon McGuire	1909-11	91-117
George Stovall	1911	74-62
Harry Davis	1912	54-71
Joe Birmingham	1912-15	170-191
Lee Fohl	1915-19	327-310
Tris Speaker	1919-26	617-520
Jack McCallister	1927	66-87
Roger Peckinpaugh	1928-33, 1941	490-481
Walter Johnson	1933-35	179-168
Steve O'Neill	1935-37	199-168
Oscar Vitt	1938-40	262-198
Lou Boudreau	1942-50	728-649
Al Lopez	1951-56	570-354

Third baseman Al Rosen topped the 100-RBI barrier five times in the 1950s.

MANAGERS—*cont'd.*

Name	*Years*	*Record*
Kerby Farrell	1957	76-77
Bobby Bragan	1958	31-36
Joe Gordon	1958-60	184-151
Jimmie Dykes	1960-61	103-115
Mel McGaha	1962	78-82
Birdie Tebbetts	1963-66	278-259
George Strickland	1964, 1966	48-63
Joe Adcock	1967	75-87
Alvin Dark	1968-71	266-321
Johnny Lipon	1971	18-41
Ken Aspromonte	1972-74	220-260
Frank Robinson	1975-77	186-189
Jeff Torborg	1977-79	157-201
Dave Garcia	1979-82	247-244
Mike Ferraro	1983	40-60
Pat Corrales	1983-87	280-355
Doc Edwards	1987-89	173-207
John Hart	1989	8-11
John McNamara	1990-91	102-137
Mike Hargrove	1991-99	721-591
Charlie Manuel	2000	90-72

WORLD SERIES CHAMPIONS

Year	*Loser*	*Length*	*MVP*
1920	Brooklyn	7 games	None
1948	Boston	6 games	None

A.L. PENNANT WINNERS

Year	*Record*	*Manager*	*Series Result*
1920	98-56	Speaker	Defeated Dodgers
1948	97-58	Boudreau	Defeated Braves
1954	111-43	Lopez	Lost to Giants
1995	100-44	Hargrove	Lost to Braves
1997	86-75	Hargrove	Lost to Marlins

CENTRAL DIVISION CHAMPIONS

Year	*Record*	*Manager*	*ALCS Result*
1995	100-44	Hargrove	Defeated Mariners
1996	99-62	Hargrove	Lost in Division Series
1997	86-75	Hargrove	Defeated Orioles
1998	89-73	Hargrove	Lost to Yankees
1999	97-65	Hargrove	Lost in Division Series

ATTENDANCE HIGHS

Total	*Season*	*Park*
3,467,299	1998	Jacobs Field
3,456,278	2000	Jacobs Field
3,404,750	1997	Jacobs Field
3,384,788	1999	Jacobs Field
3,318,174	1996	Jacobs Field

BALLPARK CHRONOLOGY

Jacobs Field (1994-present)

Capacity: 43,863.
First game: Indians 4, Seattle 3 (April 4, 1994).
First batter: Rich Amaral, Mariners.
First hit: Eric Anthony, Mariners (home run).
First run: Edgar Martinez, Mariners (1st inning).
First home run: Eric Anthony, Mariners.
First winning pitcher: Eric Plunk, Indians.
First-season attendance: 1,995,174.

League Park I (1901-09)

Capacity: 9,000.
First game: Indians 4, Milwaukee 3 (April 29, 1901).
First-season attendance: 131,380.

League Park II (1910-46)

Capacity: 21,414.
First game: Detroit 5, Indians 0 (April 21, 1910).
First-season attendance: 293,456.

Cleveland (Municipal) Stadium (1932-93)

Capacity: 74,483.
First game: Philadelphia 1, Indians 0 (July 31, 1932).
First-season attendance (1947): 1,521,978.

Note: League Park II was known as Dunn Field from 1920-27; Cleveland Stadium was originally called Municipal Stadium and games were played there on a part-time basis from 1932-46.

A.L. MVPs

Lou Boudreau, SS, 1948
Al Rosen, 3B, 1953

CY YOUNG WINNER

Gaylord Perry, RH, 1972

ROOKIES OF THE YEAR

Herb Score, P, 1955
Chris Chambliss, 1B, 1971
Joe Charboneau, OF, 1980
Sandy Alomar Jr., C, 1990

RETIRED UNIFORMS

No.	*Name*	*Pos.*
3	Earl Averill	OF
5	Lou Boudreau	SS
14	Larry Doby	OF
18	Mel Harder	P
19	Bob Feller	P
21	Bob Lemon	P

MILESTONE PERFORMANCES

30-plus home runs

50—Albert Belle ... 1995
48—Albert Belle ... 1996
45—Manny Ramirez ... 1998
44—Manny Ramirez ... 1999
43—Al Rosen ... 1953
42—Hal Trosky ... 1936
Rocky Colavito ... 1959
41—Rocky Colavito ... 1958
40—Jim Thome ... 1997
38—Albert Belle ... 1993
Jim Thome ... 1996
Manny Ramirez ... 2000
37—Al Rosen ... 1950
Jim Thome ... 2000
36—Albert Belle ... 1994
35—Hal Trosky ... 1934
Joe Carter ... 1989
34—Albert Belle ... 1992
33—Andre Thornton ... 1978, 1984
Manny Ramirez ... 1996
David Justice ... 1997
Jim Thome ... 1999
32—Earl Averill ... 1931, 1932
Hal Trosky ... 1937
Joe Gordon ... 1948
Larry Doby ... 1952, 1954
Vic Wertz ... 1956
Andre Thornton ... 1982
Joe Carter ... 1987
Brook Jacoby ... 1987
Cory Snyder ... 1987
Matt Williams ... 1997
31—Earl Averill ... 1934
Ken Keltner ... 1948
Luke Easter ... 1952
Leon Wagner ... 1964
Manny Ramirez ... 1995
Richie Sexson ... 1999
30—Rocky Colavito ... 1966
Jim Thome ... 1998

100-plus RBIs

165—Manny Ramirez ... 1999
162—Hal Trosky ... 1936
148—Albert Belle ... 1996
145—Al Rosen ... 1953
Manny Ramirez ... 1998
143—Earl Averill ... 1931
142—Hal Trosky ... 1934
136—Eddie Morgan ... 1930
130—Tris Speaker ... 1923
129—Albert Belle ... 1993
128—Hal Trosky ... 1937
126—Earl Averill ... 1936
Larry Doby ... 1954
Albert Belle ... 1995
124—Earl Averill ... 1932
Joe Gordon ... 1948
123—Jeff Heath ... 1941
122—Manny Ramirez ... 2000
121—Johnny Hodapp ... 1930
Joe Carter ... 1986
120—Roberto Alomar ... 1999
119—Earl Averill ... 1930
Ken Keltner ... 1948
118—Larry Gardner ... 1920
117—Joe Vosmik ... 1931
116—Al Rosen ... 1950
Andre Thornton ... 1982
Jim Thome ... 1996
Richie Sexson ... 1999
115—Larry Gardner ... 1921
114—George Burns ... 1926
Carlos Baerga ... 1993
113—Earl Averill ... 1934
Hal Trosky ... 1935
Ken Keltner ... 1938
Rocky Colavito ... 1938
112—Jeff Heath ... 1938
Albert Belle ... 1992
Manny Ramirez ... 1996
111—Rocky Colavito ... 1959
110—Joe Vosmik ... 1935
Hal Trosky ... 1938
109—Joe Sewell ... 1923
Julius Solters ... 1937
108—Rocky Colavito ... 1965
Jim Thome ... 1999
107—Tris Speaker ... 1920
Luke Easter ... 1950
Manny Ramirez ... 1995
106—Lou Boudreau ... 1948
Vic Wertz ... 1956
Joe Carter ... 1987
Travis Fryman ... 2000
Jim Thome ... 2000
105—Al Rosen ... 1952
Vic Wertz ... 1957
Andre Thornton ... 1978
Joe Carter ... 1989
Carlos Baerga ... 1992
Matt Williams ... 1997
104—Joe Sewell ... 1924
Hal Trosky ... 1939
Larry Doby ... 1952
103—Elmer Smith ... 1920
Lew Fonseca ... 1929
Luke Easter ... 1951
Harold Baines ... *1999
David Segui ... 2000
102—Nap Lajoie ... 1904
Al Rosen ... 1951, 1954
Larry Doby ... 1950, 1953
Jim Thome ... 1997
101—Odell Hale ... 1934, 1935
Lou Boudreau ... 1940
Albert Belle ... 1994
David Justice ... 1997
100—Leon Wagner ... 1964

*81 with Orioles; 22 with Indians.

20-plus victories

1903—Earl Moore ... 20-8
1904—William Bernhard ... 23-13
1905—Addie Joss ... 20-11
1906—Robert Rhodes ... 22-10
Addie Joss ... 21-9
Otto Hess ... 20-17
1907—Addie Joss ... 27-10
1908—Addie Joss ... 24-11
1911—Vean Gregg ... 23-7
1912—Vean Gregg ... 20-13
1913—Fred Falkenberg ... 23-10
Vean Gregg ... 20-13
1917—Jim Bagby ... 23-13
1918—Stan Coveleski ... 22-13
1919—Stan Coveleski ... 23-17
1920—Jim Bagby ... 31-12
Stanley Coveleski ... 24-14
Ray Caldwell ... 20-10
1921—Stan Coveleski ... 23-13
1922—George Uhle ... 22-16
1923—George Uhle ... 26-16
1924—Joe Shaute ... 20-17
1926—George Uhle ... 27-11
1929—Wesley Ferrell ... 21-10
1930—Wesley Ferrell ... 25-13
1931—Wesley Ferrell ... 22-12
1932—Wesley Ferrell ... 23-13
1934—Mel Harder ... 20-12
1935—Mel Harder ... 22-11
1936—Johnny Allen ... 20-10
1939—Bob Feller ... 24-9
1940—Bob Feller ... 27-11
1941—Bob Feller ... 25-13
1946—Bob Feller ... 26-15
1947—Bob Feller ... 20-11
1948—Gene Bearden ... 20-7
Bob Lemon ... 20-14
1949—Bob Lemon ... 22-10
1950—Bob Lemon ... 23-11
1951—Bob Feller ... 22-8
Mike Garcia ... 20-13
Early Wynn ... 20-13
1952—Early Wynn ... 23-12
Mike Garcia ... 22-11
Bob Lemon ... 22-11
1953—Bob Lemon ... 21-15
1954—Bob Lemon ... 23-7
Early Wynn ... 23-11
1956—Herb Score ... 20-9
Early Wynn ... 20-9
Bob Lemon ... 20-14
1962—Dick Donovan ... 20-10
1968—Luis Tiant ... 21-9
1970—Sam McDowell ... 20-12
1972—Gaylord Perry ... 24-16
1974—Gaylord Perry ... 21-13

A.L. home run champions

1915—Bobby Roth ... 7
1950—Al Rosen ... 37
1952—Larry Doby ... 32
1953—Al Rosen ... 43
1954—Larry Doby ... 32
1959—Rocky Colavito ... *42
1995—Albert Belle ... 50

* Tied for league lead

A.L. RBI champions

1904—Nap Lajoie ... 102
1936—Hal Trosky ... 162
1952—Al Rosen ... 105
1953—Al Rosen ... 145
1954—Larry Doby ... 126
1965—Rocky Colavito ... 108
1986—Joe Carter ... 121
1993—Albert Belle ... 129
1995—Albert Belle ... *126
1996—Albert Belle ... 148
1999—Manny Ramirez ... 165

* Tied for league lead

A.L. batting champions

1903—Nap Lajoie ... .344
1904—Nap Lajoie ... .376
1905—Elmer Flick ... .306
1914—Tris Speaker ... .386
1929—Lew Fonseca ... .369
1944—Lou Boudreau ... .327
1954—Bobby Avila ... .341

A.L. ERA champions

1903—Earl Moore ... 1.74
1904—Addie Joss ... 1.59
1908—Addie Joss ... 1.16
1911—Vean Gregg ... 1.80
1923—Stan Coveleski ... 2.76
1933—Monte Pearson ... 2.33
1940—Bob Feller ... 2.61
1948—Gene Bearden ... 2.43
1950—Early Wynn ... 3.20
1954—Mike Garcia ... 2.64
1965—Sam McDowell ... 2.18
1968—Luis Tiant ... 1.60
1982—Rick Sutcliffe ... 2.96

A.L. strikeout champions

1920—Stan Coveleski ... 133
1938—Bob Feller ... 240
1939—Bob Feller ... 246
1940—Bob Feller ... 261
1941—Bob Feller ... 260
1943—Allie Reynolds ... 151
1946—Bob Feller ... 348
1947—Bob Feller ... 196
1948—Bob Feller ... 164
1950—Bob Lemon ... 170
1955—Herb Score ... 245
1956—Herb Score ... 263
1957—Early Wynn ... 184
1965—Sam McDowell ... 325
1966—Sam McDowell ... 225
1968—Sam McDowell ... 283
1969—Sam McDowell ... 279
1970—Sam McDowell ... 304
1980—Len Barker ... 187
1981—Len Barker ... 127

No-hit pitchers
(9 innings or more)

1908—Robert Rhoads ... 2-1 vs. Boston
1908—Addie Joss ... 1-0 vs. Chicago (Perfect)
1910—Addie Joss ... 1-0 vs. Chicago
1919—Ray Caldwell ... 3-0 vs. New York
1931—Wesley Ferrell ... 9-0 vs. St. Louis
1940—Bob Feller ... 1-0 vs. Chicago
1946—Bob Feller ... 1-0 vs. New York
1947—Don Black ... 3-0 vs. Philadelphia
1948—Bob Lemon ... 2-0 vs. Detroit
1951—Bob Feller ... 2-1 vs. Detroit
1966—Sonny Siebert ... 2-0 vs. Washington
1974—Dick Bosman ... 4-0 vs. Oakland
1977—Dennis Eckersley ... 1-0 vs. California
1981—Len Barker ... 3-0 vs. Toronto (Perfect)

Longest hitting streaks

31—Nap Lajoie ... 1906
30—Sandy Alomar Jr. ... 1997
29—Bill Bradley ... 1902
28—Joe Jackson ... 1911
Hal Trosky ... 1936
27—Dale Mitchell ... 1953
26—Harry Bay ... 1902
24—Matt Williams ... 1997
23—Charlie Jamieson ... 1923
Tris Speaker ... 1923
Dale Mitchell ... 1951
Ray Fosse ... 1970
Mike Hargrove ... 1980
22—John Hodapp ... 1929
Dale Mitchell ... 1947
Al Smith ... 1956
John Romano ... 1961
Julio Franco ... 1988
21—Nap Lajoie ... 1904
Odell Hale ... 1936
Dale Mitchell ... 1948, 1953
Larry Doby ... 1951
Joe Carter ... 1986
Julio Franco ... 1988
Albert Belle ... 1996
20—Earl Averill ... 1936
Roy Weatherly ... 1936
Joe Vosmik ... 1936
Al Rosen ... 1953
Vic Power ... 1960
Manny Ramirez ... 2000

Note: Joey Cora hit in 20 straight games for Seattle (16) and Cleveland (4) in 1998.

INDIVIDUAL SEASON, GAME RECORDS

SEASON

Batting			
At-bats	663	Joe Carter	1986
Runs	140	Earl Averill	1931
Hits	233	Joe Jackson	1911
Singles	172	Charley Jamieson	1923
Doubles	64	George Burns	1926
Triples	26	Joe Jackson	1912
Home runs	50	Albert Belle	1995
Home runs, rookie	37	Al Rosen	1950
Grand slams	4	Al Rosen	1951
Total bases	405	Hal Trosky	1936
RBIs	165	Manny Ramirez	1999
Walks	127	Jim Thome	1999
Most strikeouts	171	Jim Thome	1999, 2000
Fewest strikeouts	4	Joe Sewell	1925, 1929
Batting average	.408	Joe Jackson	1911
Slugging pct.	.714	Albert Belle	1994
Stolen bases	75	Kenny Lofton	1996
Pitching			
Games	76	Sid Monge	1979
Complete games	36	Bob Feller	1946
Innings	371	Bob Feller	1946
Wins	31	Jim Bagby Sr.	1920
Losses	22	Pete Dowling	1901
Winning pct.	.938 (15-1)	Johnny Allen	1937
Walks	208	Bob Feller	1936
Strikeouts	348	Bob Feller	1946
Shutouts	10	Bob Feller	1946
		Bob Lemon	1948
Home runs allowed	37	Luis Tiant	1969
Lowest ERA	1.16	Addie Joss	1908
Saves	46	Jose Mesa	1995

GAME

Batting			
Runs	5	Last by Joe Carter	9-6-86
Hits	6	Last by Jorge Orta	6-15-80
Doubles	4	Last by Sandy Alomar Jr.	6-6-97
Triples	3	Last by Ben Chapman	7-3-39
Home runs	4	Rocky Colavito	6-10-59
RBIs	9	Chris James	5-4-91
Total bases	16	Rocky Colavito	6-10-59
Stolen bases	5	Last by Kenny Lofton	9-3-2000

HISTORY

CAREER LEADERS

BATTING

Games

Terry Turner	1,619
Napoleon Lajoie	1,614
Lou Boudreau	1,560
Jim Hegan	1,526
Tris Speaker	1,519
Ken Keltner	1,513
Joe Sewell	1,513
Earl Averill	1,509
Charlie Jamieson	1,483
Jack Graney	1,402

At-bats

Napoleon Lajoie	6,034
Earl Averill	5,909
Terry Turner	5,787
Lou Boudreau	5,754
Ken Keltner	5,655
Joe Sewell	5,621
Charlie Jamieson	5,551
Tris Speaker	5,546
Jack Graney	4,705
Bill Bradley	4,648

Runs

Earl Averill	1,154
Tris Speaker	1,079
Charlie Jamieson	942
Napoleon Lajoie	865
Kenny Lofton	860
Joe Sewell	857
Lou Boudreau	823
Larry Doby	808
Hal Trosky	758
Ken Keltner	735

Hits

Napoleon Lajoie	2,046
Tris Speaker	1,965
Earl Averill	1,903
Joe Sewell	1,800
Charlie Jamieson	1,753
Lou Boudreau	1,706
Ken Keltner	1,561
Terry Turner	1,472
Hal Trosky	1,365
Kenny Lofton	1,328

Doubles

Tris Speaker	486
Napoleon Lajoie	424
Earl Averill	377
Joe Sewell	375
Lou Boudreau	367
Ken Keltner	306
Charlie Jamieson	296
Hal Trosky	287
Bill Bradley	238
Manny Ramirez	237

Triples

Earl Averill	121
Tris Speaker	108
Elmer Flick	106
Joe Jackson	89
Jeff Heath	83
Ray Chapman	81
Jack Graney	79
Napoleon Lajoie	78
Terry Turner	77
Bill Bradley	74
Charlie Jamieson	74

Home runs

Albert Belle	242
Manny Ramirez	236
Jim Thome	233
Earl Averill	226
Hal Trosky	216
Larry Doby	215
Andre Thornton	214
Al Rosen	192
Rocky Colavito	190
Ken Keltner	163

Total bases

Earl Averill	3,200
Tris Speaker	2,886
Napoleon Lajoie	2,725
Ken Keltner	2,494
Hal Trosky	2,406
Lou Boudreau	2,392
Joe Sewell	2,391
Charlie Jamieson	2,251
Larry Doby	2,159
Manny Ramirez	2,053

Runs batted in

Earl Averill	1,084
Napoleon Lajoie	919
Hal Trosky	911
Tris Speaker	884
Joe Sewell	869
Ken Keltner	850
Manny Ramirez	804
Larry Doby	776
Albert Belle	751
Andre Thornton	749

Extra-base hits

Earl Averill	724
Tris Speaker	667
Hal Trosky	556
Ken Keltner	538
Napoleon Lajoie	535
Lou Boudreau	495
Manny Ramirez	484
Albert Belle	481
Joe Sewell	468
Jim Thome	464

Batting average
(Minimum 500 games)

Joe Jackson	.375
Tris Speaker	.354
Napoleon Lajoie	.339
George Burns	.327
Ed Morgan	.323
Earl Averill	.322
Joe Sewell	.320
Johnny Hodapp	.318
Charlie Jamieson	.316
Manny Ramirez	.313

Stolen bases

Kenny Lofton	434
Terry Turner	254
Napoleon Lajoie	240
Ray Chapman	233
Omar Vizquel	221
Elmer Flick	207
Harry Bay	165
Brett Butler	164
Bill Bradley	157
Tris Speaker	151

PITCHING

Earned-run average
(Minimum 1,000 innings)

Addie Joss	1.89
Bob Rhoads	2.39
Bill Bernhard	2.45
Earl Moore	2.58
Gaylord Perry	2.71
Stan Coveleski	2.80
Luis Tiant	2.84
Willie Mitchell	2.89
Sam McDowell	2.99
Jim Bagby	3.02

Wins

Bob Feller	266
Mel Harder	223
Bob Lemon	207
Stan Coveleski	172
Early Wynn	164
Addie Joss	160
Willis Hudlin	157
George Uhle	147
Mike Garcia	142
Charles Nagy	123

Losses

Mel Harder	186
Bob Feller	162
Willis Hudlin	151
Bob Lemon	128
Stan Coveleski	123
George Uhle	119
Sam McDowell	109
Early Wynn	102
Addie Joss	97
Mike Garcia	96

Innings pitched

Bob Feller	3,827.0
Mel Harder	3,426.1
Bob Lemon	2,850.0
Willis Hudlin	2,557.2
Stan Coveleski	2,502.1
Addie Joss	2,327.0
Early Wynn	2,286.2
George Uhle	2,200.1
Mike Garcia	2,138.0
Sam McDowell	2,109.2

Strikeouts

Bob Feller	2,581
Sam McDowell	2,159
Bob Lemon	1,277
Early Wynn	1,277
Charles Nagy	1,184
Mel Harder	1,161
Gary Bell	1,104
Mike Garcia	1,095
Luis Tiant	1,041
Addie Joss	920

Bases on balls

Bob Feller	1,764
Bob Lemon	1,251
Mel Harder	1,118
Sam McDowell	1,072
Early Wynn	877
Willis Hudlin	832
George Uhle	709
Mike Garcia	696
Gary Bell	670
Stan Coveleski	616

Games

Mel Harder	582
Bob Feller	570
Willis Hudlin	475
Bob Lemon	460
Gary Bell	419
Mike Garcia	397
Eric Plunk	373
Stan Coveleski	360
George Uhle	357
Early Wynn	343

Shutouts

Addie Joss	45
Bob Feller	44
Stan Coveleski	31
Bob Lemon	31
Mike Garcia	27
Mel Harder	25
Early Wynn	24
Sam McDowell	22
Luis Tiant	21
Guy Morton	19
Bob Rhoads	19

Saves

Doug Jones	129
Jose Mesa	104
Mike Jackson	94
Ray Narleski	53
Steve Olin	48
Jim Kern	46
Sid Monge	46
Gary Bell	45
Ernie Camacho	44
Dave LaRoche	42

TEAM SEASON, GAME RECORDS

SEASON

Batting

Most at-bats	5,702	1986
Most runs	1,009	1999
Fewest runs	472	1972
Most hits	1,715	1936
Most singles	1,218	1925
Most doubles	358	1930
Most triples	95	1920
Most home runs	221	2000
Fewest home runs	8	1910
Most grand slams	12	1999
Most pinch-hit home runs	9	1965, 1970
Most total bases	2,700	1996
Most stolen bases	210	1917
Highest batting average	.308	1921
Lowest batting average	.234	1968, 1972
Highest slugging pct	.484	1994

Pitching

Lowest ERA	2.02	1908
Highest ERA	5.28	1987
Most complete games	141	1904
Most shutouts	27	1906
Most saves	50	1995
Most walks	770	1971
Most strikeouts	1,213	2000

Fielding

Most errors	329	1901
Fewest errors	72	2000
Most double plays	197	1953
Highest fielding average	.988	2000

General

Most games won	111	1954
Most games lost	105	1991
Highest win pct	.721	1954
Lowest win pct	.333	1914

GAME, INNING

Batting

Most runs, game	27	7-7-23
Most runs, inning	14	6-18-50
Most hits, game	33	7-10-32
Most home runs, game	7	7-17-66
Most total bases, game	45	7-10-32

Outfielder Rocky Colavito led the A.L. with 42 home runs in 1959.

HISTORY

INDIANS YEAR-BY-YEAR

Year	W	L	Place	Games Back	Manager	Leaders: Batting avg.	Hits	Home runs	RBIs	Wins	ERA
1901	54	82	7th	29	McAleer	Pickering, .309	Pickering, 169	Beck, 6	Beck, 79	Moore, 16	Moore, 2.90
1902	69	67	5th	14	Armour	Hickman, .379	Bradley, 187	Bradley, 11	Hickman, 94	Bernhard, Joss, Moore, 17	Bernhard, 2.20
1903	77	63	3rd	15	Armour	Lajoie, .344	Bradley, Hickman, 171	Hickman, 12	Hickman, 97	Moore, 19	Moore, 1.74
1904	86	65	4th	7½	Armour	Lajoie, .376	Lajoie, 211	Flick, Lajoie, 6	Lajoie, 102	Bernhard, 23	Joss, 1.59
1905	76	78	5th	19	Lajoie	Flick, .306	Bay, 164	Flick, 4	Flick, 64	Joss, 20	Joss, 2.01
1906	89	64	3rd	5	Lajoie	Lajoie, .355	Lajoie, 214	4 Tied, 2	Lajoie, 91	Rhoads, 22	Joss, 1.72
1907	85	67	4th	8	Lajoie	Flick, .302	Flick, 166	Flick, 3	Lajoie, 63	Joss, 27	Joss, 1.83
1908	90	64	2nd	½	Lajoie	Stovall, .292	Lajoie, 168	Hinchman, 6	Lajoie, 74	Joss, 24	Joss, 1.16
1909	71	82	6th	27½	Lajoie, McGuire	Lajoie, .324	Lajoie, 152	Hinchman, Stovall, 6	Hinchman, 53	Young, 19	Joss, 1.71
1910	71	81	5th	32	McGuire	Lajoie, .384	Lajoie, 227	Lajoie, 4	Lajoie, 76	Falkenberg, 14	Kahler, 1.60
1911	80	73	3rd	22	McGuire, Stovall	Jackson, .408	Jackson, 233	Jackson, 7	Jackson, 83	Gregg, 23	Gregg, 1.80
1912	75	78	5th	30½	Davis, Birmingham	Jackson, .395	Jackson, 226	Jackson, 3	Jackson, Lajoie, 90	Gregg, 20	Gregg, 2.59
1913	86	66	3rd	9½	Birmingham	Jackson, .373	Jackson, 197	Jackson, 7	Jackson, 71	Falkenberg, 23	W. Mitchell, 1.91
1914	51	102	8th	48½	Birmingham	Jackson, .338	Jackson, 153	Jackson, 3	Jackson, 53	W. Mitchell, 12	Steen, 2.60
1915	57	95	7th	44½	Birmingham, Fohl	Chapman, .270	Chapman, 154	Roth, 7	Chapman, E. Smith, 67	Morton, 16	Morton, 2.14
1916	77	77	6th	14	Fohl	Speaker, .386	Speaker, 211	Graney, 5	Speaker, 79	Bagby, 16	Coumbe, 2.02
1917	88	66	3rd	12	Fohl	Speaker, .352	Speaker, 184	Graney, E. Smith, 3	Roth, 72	Bagby, 23	Coveleski, 1.81
1918	73	54	2nd	2½	Fohl	Speaker, .318	Speaker, 150	Wood, 5	Wood, 66	Coveleski, 22	Coveleski, 1.82
1919	84	55	2nd	3½	Fohl, Speaker	Chapman, Gardner, .300	Gardner, 157	E. Smith, 9	Gardner, 79	Coveleski, 24	Coveleski, 2.61
1920	98	56	1st	+2	Speaker	Speaker, .388	Speaker, 214	E. Smith, 12	Gardner, 118	Bagby, 31	Coveleski, 2.49
1921	94	60	2nd	4½	Speaker	Speaker, .362	Gardner, 187	E. Smith, 16	Gardner, 115	Coveleski, 23	Morton, 2.76
1922	78	76	4th	16	Speaker	Speaker, .378	Jamieson, 183	Speaker, 11	Wood, 92	Uhle, 22	Coveleski, 3.32
1923	82	71	3rd	16½	Speaker	Speaker, .380	Jamieson, 222	Speaker, 17	Speaker, 130	Uhle, 26	Coveleski, 2.76
1924	67	86	6th	24½	Speaker	Jamieson, .359	Jamieson, 213	Myatt, Speaker, 8	Sewell, 104	Shaute, 20	S. Smith, 3.01
1925	70	84	6th	27½	Speaker	Speaker, .389	Sewell, 204	Speaker, 12	Sewell, 98	Buckeye, Uhle, 13	Miller, 3.31
1926	88	66	2nd	3	Speaker	Burns, .358	Burns, 216	Speaker, 7	Burns, 114	Uhle, 27	Uhle, 2.83
1927	66	87	6th	43½	McAllister	Burns, .319	Sewell, 180	Hodapp, 5	Sewell, 92	Hudlin, 18	Miller, 3.21
1928	62	92	7th	39	Peckinpaugh	Sewell, Hodapp, .323	Lind, 191	Burns, 5	Hodapp, 73	Hudlin, 14	Hudlin, Shaute, 4.04
1929	81	71	3rd	24	Peckinpaugh	Fonseca, .369	Fonseca, 209	Averill, 18	Fonseca, 103	Ferrell, 21	Holloway, 3.03
1930	81	73	4th	21	Peckinpaugh	Hodapp, .354	Hodapp, 225	Morgan, 26	Morgan, 136	Ferrell, 25	Ferrell, 3.31
1931	78	76	4th	30	Peckinpaugh	Morgan, .351	Averill, 209	Averill, 32	Averill, 143	Ferrell, 22	Ferrell, 3.75
1932	87	65	4th	19	Peckinpaugh	Cissell, .320	Averill, 198	Averill, 32	Averill, 124	Ferrell, 23	Ferrell, 3.66
1933	75	76	4th	23½	Peckinpaugh, Johnson	Averill, .301	Averill, 180	Averill, 11	Averill, 92	Hildebrand, 16	Pearson, 2.33
1934	85	69	3rd	16	Johnson	Vosmik, .341	Trosky, 206	Trosky, 35	Trosky, 142	Harder, 20	Harder, 2.61
1935	82	71	3rd	12	Johnson, O'Neill	Vosmik, .348	Vosmik, 216	Trosky, 26	Trosky, 113	Harder, 22	Harder, 3.29
1936	80	74	5th	22½	O'Neill	Averill, .378	Averill, 232	Trosky, 42	Trosky, 162	Allen, 20	Allen, 3.44
1937	83	71	4th	19	O'Neill	Solters, .323	Solters, 190	Trosky, 32	Trosky, 128	Allen, Harder, 15	Allen, 2.55
1938	86	66	3rd	13	Vitt	Heath, .343	Trosky, 185	Keltner, 26	Keltner, 113	Feller, Harder, 17	Harder, 3.83
1939	87	67	3rd	20½	Vitt	Trosky, .335	Keltner, 191	Trosky, 25	Trosky, 104	Feller, 24	Feller, 2.85
1940	89	65	2nd	1	Vitt	Weatherly, .303	Boudreau, 185	Trosky, 25	Boudreau, 101	Feller, 27	Feller, 2.61
1941	75	79	*4th	26	Peckinpaugh	Heath, .340	Heath, 199	Heath, 24	Heath, 123	Feller, 25	Feller, 3.15
1942	75	79	4th	28	Boudreau	Fleming, .292	Keltner, 179	Fleming, 14	Fleming, 82	Bagby, 17	Bagby, 2.96
1943	82	71	3rd	15½	Boudreau	Cullenbine, .289	Hockett, 166	Heath, 18	Heath, 79	Bagby, A. Smith, 17	Kennedy, 2.45
1944	72	82	*5th	17	Boudreau	Boudreau, .327	Boudreau, 191	Cullenbine, 16	Keltner, 91	Harder, 12	Heving, 1.96
1945	73	72	5th	11	Boudreau	Heath, .305	Meyer, 153	Heath, 15	Heath, 61	Gromek, 19	Gromek, 2.55
1946	68	86	6th	36	Boudreau	Edwards, .301	Boudreau, 151	Seerey, 26	Boudreau, Seerey, 62	Feller, 26	Feller, 2.18
1947	80	74	4th	17	Boudreau	D. Mitchell, .316	Boudreau, 165	Gordon, 29	Gordon, 93	Feller, 20	Feller, 2.68
1948	97	58	†1st	+1	Boudreau	Boudreau, .355	D. Mitchell, 204	Gordon, 32	Gordon, 124	Bearden, Lemon, 20	Bearden, 2.43
1949	89	65	3rd	8	Boudreau	D. Mitchell, .317	D. Mitchell, 203	Doby, 24	Doby, 85	Lemon, 22	Benton, 2.12
1950	92	62	4th	6	Boudreau	Doby, .326	Doby, 164	Rosen, 37	Rosen, 116	Lemon, 23	Wynn, 3.20
1951	93	61	2nd	5	Lopez	Avila, .304	Avila, 165	Easter, 27	Easter, 103	Feller, 22	Gromek, 2.77
1952	93	61	2nd	2	Lopez	D. Mitchell, .323	Avila, 179	Doby, 32	Rosen, 105	Wynn, 23	Garcia, 2.37
1953	92	62	2nd	8½	Lopez	Rosen, .336	Rosen, 201	Rosen, 43	Rosen, 145	Lemon, 21	Garcia, 3.25
1954	111	43	1st	+8	Lopez	Avila, .341	Avila, 189	Doby, 32	Doby, 126	Lemon, Wynn, 23	Mossi, 1.94
1955	93	61	2nd	3	Lopez	A. Smith, .306	A. Smith, 186	Doby, 26	Rosen, 81	Lemon, 18	Wynn, 2.82
1956	88	66	2nd	9	Lopez	A. Smith, .274	A. Smith, 144	Wertz, 32	Wertz, 106	Lemon, Score, Wynn 20	Score, 2.53
1957	76	77	6th	21½	Farrell	Woodling, .321	Wertz, 145	Wertz, 28	Wertz, 105	Wynn, 14	McLish, 2.74
1958	77	76	4th	14½	Bragan, Gordon	Power, .317	Minoso, 168	Colavito, 41	Colavito, 113	McLish, 16	Wilhelm, 2.49
1959	89	65	2nd	5	Gordon	Francona, .363	Minoso, Power, 172	Colavito, 42	Colavito, 111	McLish, 19	J. Perry, 2.65
1960	76	78	4th	21	Gordon, Dykes	Kuenn, .308	Power, 167	Held, 21	Power, 84	J. Perry, 18	Locke, 3.37
1961	78	83	5th	30½	Dykes	Piersall, .322	Francona, 178	Kirkland, 27	Kirkland, 95	Grant, 15	Funk, 3.31
1962	80	82	6th	16	McGaha	Francona, .272	Francona, 169	Romano, 25	Romano, 81	Donovan, 20	Donovan, 3.59
1963	79	83	*5th	25½	Tebbetts	Davalillo, .292	Alvis, 165	Alvis, 22	Alvis, 67	Grant, Kralick 13	Kralick, 2.92
1964	79	83	*6th	20	Tebbetts	B. Chance, .279	Howser, 163	Wagner, 31	Wagner, 100	Kralick, 12	McMahon, 2.41
1965	87	75	5th	15	Tebbetts	Davalillo, .301	Colavito, 170	Wagner, 28	Colavito, 108	McDowell, 17	McDowell, 2.18
1966	81	81	5th	17	Tebbetts, Strickland	Wagner, .279	Wagner, 153	Colavito, 30	Whitfield, 78	Siebert, 16	Hargan, 2.48
1967	75	87	8th	17	Adcock	Davalillo, .287	Alvis, 163	Alvis, 21	Alvis, 70	Hargan, 14	Siebert, 2.38
1968	86	75	3rd	16½	Dark	Azcue, .280	Cardenal, 150	Horton, 14	Horton, 59	Tiant, 21	Tiant, 1.60
								—EAST DIVISION—			
1969	62	99	6th	46½	Dark	Horton, .278	Horton, 174	Harrelson, Horton 27	Horton, 93	McDowell, 18	McDowell, 2.94
1970	76	86	5th	32	Dark	Fosse, .307	Pinson, 164	Nettles, 26	Pinson, 82	McDowell, 20	Hargan, 2.90
1971	60	102	6th	43	Dark, Lipon	Uhlaender, .288	Nettles, 156	Nettles, 28	Nettles, 86	McDowell, 13	Lamb, 3.35
1972	72	84	5th	14	Aspromonte	Chambliss, .292	Nettles, 141	Nettles, 17	Nettles, 70	G. Perry, 24	G. Perry, 1.92
1973	71	91	6th	26	Aspromonte	Williams, .289	B. Bell, 169	Spikes, 23	Spikes, 73	G. Perry, 19	Hilgendorf, 3.14
1974	77	85	4th	14	Aspromonte	Gamble, .291	Spikes, 154	Spikes, 22	Spikes, 80	G. Perry, 21	G. Perry, 2.51
1975	79	80	4th	15½	Robinson	Carty, .308	B. Bell, 150	Powell, 27	Hendrick, Powell ,86	Peterson, 14	Eckersley, 2.60
1976	81	78	4th	16	Robinson	Carty, .310	Carty, 171	Hendrick, 25	Carty, 83	Dobson, 16	LaRoche, 2.24
1977	71	90	5th	28½	Robinson, Torborg	Bochte, .304	Kuiper, 169	Thornton, 28	Carty, 80	Eckersley, 14	Hood, 3.00
1978	69	90	6th	29	Torborg	Kuiper, Norris .283	B. Bell, 157	Thornton, 33	Thornton, 105	Waits, 13	Kern, 3.08
1979	81	80	6th	22	Torborg, Garcia	Harrah, .279	Bonds, 148	Thornton, 26	Thornton, 93	Waits, 16	Monge, 2.40
1980	79	81	6th	23	Garcia	Dilone, .341	Dilone, 180	Charboneau, 23	Charboneau, 87	Barker, 19	Monge, 3.53
1981	52	51	‡6th/5th	—	Garcia	Hargrove, .317	Harrah, 105	Diaz, 7	Hargrove, 49	Blyleven, 11	Blyleven, 2.88
1982	78	84	*6th	17	Garcia	Harrah, .304	Harrah, 183	Thornton, 32	Thornton, 116	Barker, 15	Sutcliffe, 2.96
1983	70	92	7th	28	Ferraro, Corrales	Tabler, .291	Franco, 153	Thomas, 17	Franco, 80	Sutcliffe, 17	Blyleven, 3.91
1984	75	87	6th	29	Corrales	Vukovich, .304	Franco, 188	Thornton, 33	Thornton, 99	Blyleven, 19	Camacho, 2.43
1985	60	102	7th	39½	Corrales	Butler, .311	Butler, 184	Thornton, 22	Franco, 90	Heaton, 9	Blyleven, 3.26
1986	84	78	5th	11½	Corrales	Tabler, .326	Carter, 200	Carter, 29	Carter, 121	Candiotti, 16	Candiotti, 3.57
1987	61	101	7th	37	Corrales, Edwards	Franco, .319	Tabler, 170	Snyder, 33	Carter, 106	Bailes, Candiotti, Niekro, 7	Jones, 3.15
1988	78	84	6th	11	Edwards	Franco, .303	Franco, 186	Carter, 27	Carter, 98	Swindell, 18	Swindell, 3.20
1989	73	89	6th	16	Edwards, Hart	Browne, .299	Browne, 179	Carter, 35	Carter, 105	Candiotti, Swindell 13	Candiotti, 3.10
1990	77	85	4th	11	McNamara	C. James, .299	Jacoby, 162	Maldonado, 22	Maldonado, 95	Candiotti, 15	Olin, 3.41
1991	57	105	7th	34	McNamara, Hargrove	Cole, .295	Baerga, 171	Belle, 28	Belle, 95	Nagy, 10	Candiotti, 2.24
1992	76	86	*4th	20	Hargrove	Baerga, .312	Baerga, 205	Belle, 34	Belle, 112	Nagy, 17	Power, 2.54
1993	76	86	6th	19	Hargrove	Lofton, .325	Baerga, 200	Belle, 38	Belle, 129	Mesa, 10	Kramer, 4.02
								—CENTRAL DIVISION—			
1994	66	47	2nd	1	Hargrove	Belle, .357	Lofton, 160	Belle, 36	Belle, 101	M. Clark, Martinez, 11	Nagy, 3.45
1995	100	44	§∞1st	+30	Hargrove	Murray, .323	Baerga, 175	Belle, 50	Belle, 126	Hershiser, Nagy 16	Ogea, 3.05
1996	99	62	▲1st	+14½	Hargrove	Franco, .322	Lofton, 210	Belle, 48	Belle, 148	Nagy, 17	Nagy, 3.41
1997	86	75	§∞1st	+6	Hargrove	Justice, .329	Ramirez, 184	Thome, 40	Williams, 105	Nagy, 15	Nagy, 4.28
1998	89	73	§◆1st	+9	Hargrove	Ramirez, .294	Lofton,169	Ramirez, 45	Ramirez, 145	Burba, Nagy, 15	Colon, 3.71
1999	97	65	▲1st	+21½	Hargrove	Ramirez, .333	R.Alomar,138	Ramirez, 44	Ramirez, 165	Colon, 18	Colon, 3.95
2000	90	72	2nd	5	C. Manuel	Ramirez, .351	R. Alomar, 189	Ramirez, 38	Ramirez, 122	Finley, Burba, 16	Colon, 3.88

* Tied for position. † Won pennant playoff. ‡ First half 26-24; second half 26-27. § Won Division Series. ∞ Won Championship Series. ▲ Lost Division Series. ◆ Lost Championship Series.
Note: Batting average minimum 350 at-bats; ERA minimum 90 innings pitched.

Detroit Tigers

FRANCHISE CHRONOLOGY

First season: 1901, as a member of the new American League. The Tigers made a spectacular Major League debut by rallying for 10 ninth-inning runs in a 14-13 victory over Milwaukee and rode that success to a third-place finish (74-61) behind league-champion Chicago and Boston.

1902-present: The Tigers, who have captured nine A.L. pennants and four World Series, have never experienced more than five straight losing seasons and rank behind only the Yankees in sustained A.L. success. After losing three straight fall classics from 1907-09, the Tigers went a quarter of a century before qualifying again. But after a 1934 loss to the Cardinals, they rebounded to defeat the Cubs in 1935 and matched that with another victory over the Cubs in 1945. Their other two championship seasons were 1968 and 1984, an amazing campaign in which they capped their wire-to-wire pennant run with a six-game Series victory over the Padres. After division play began in 1969, the Tigers won three A.L. East titles before moving to the A.L. Central Division in a realignment that sent Milwaukee to the National League.

Right fielder Al Kaline.

TIGERS VS. OPPONENTS BY DECADE

	A's	Indians	Orioles	Red Sox	Twins	White Sox	Yankees	Angels	Rangers	Brewers	Royals	Blue Jays	Mariners	Devil Rays	Interleague	Decade Record
1901-09	80-102	95-95	101-90	97-92	114-72	93-96	103-85									683-632
1910-19	116-99	114-94	126-90	88-124	116-100	109-103	121-94									790-704
1920-29	105-114	111-109	109-111	139-81	107-113	95-124	94-126									760-778
1930-39	111-106	118-101	135-85	121-99	118-102	129-89	86-134									818-716
1940-49	130-90	115-105	129-90	93-127	130-90	125-95	112-108									834-705
1950-59	122-98	84-136	114-106	99-121	121-99	98-122	100-120									738-802
1960-69	109-69	101-83	94-90	95-88	88-90	97-81	90-94	96-60	94-68	10-2	8-4					882-729
1970-79	56-60	90-78	65-102	69-96	48-68	67-50	74-92	63-53	64-64	91-66	54-63	28-15	20-13			789-820
1980-89	58-53	82-41	69-61	59-65	66-54	66-48	62-64	59-55	73-47	66-64	54-59	59-68	66-48			839-727
1990-99	53-53	47-76	49-69	54-64	53-60	51-69	47-72	53-54	54-63	42-56	57-56	52-70	58-53	9-11	23-26	702-852
2000-	6-4	7-6	4-6	5-7	7-6	3-9	8-4	5-5	5-5		5-7	3-9	7-2	4-5	10-8	79-83
Totals	946-848	964-924	995-900	919-964	968-854	933-886	897-993	276-227	290- 247	209-188	178-189	142-162	151-116	13-16	33-34	7914-7548

Interleague results: 2-1 vs. Braves; 0-3 vs. Expos; 3-0 vs. Mets; 2-1 vs. Phillies; 1-2 vs. Marlins; 4-1 vs. Cubs; 4-5 vs. Reds; 2-7 vs. Astros; 5-4 vs. Pirates; 6-5 vs. Cardinals; 4-5 vs. Brewers.

MANAGERS

Name	*Years*	*Record*
George Stallings	1901	74-61
Frank Dwyer	1902	52-83
Ed Barrow	1903-04	97-117
Bobby Lowe	1904	30-44
Bill Armour	1905-06	150-152
Hugh Jennings	1907-20	1131-972
Ty Cobb	1921-26	479-444
George Moriarty	1927-28	150-157
Bucky Harris	1929-33, 1955-56	516-557
Del Baker	1933, 1937-42	399-339
Mickey Cochrane	1934-38	366-266
Ralph Perkins	1937	6-9
Steve O'Neill	1943-48	509-414
Red Rolfe	1949-52	278-256
Fred Hutchinson	1952-54	155-235
Jack Tighe	1957-58	99-104
Bill Norman	1958-59	58-64
Jimmie Dykes	1959-60	118-115
Joe Gordon	1960	26-31
Bob Scheffing	1961-63	210-173
Chuck Dressen	1963-65, 1966	221-189
Bob Swift	1965, 1966	56-43
Frank Skaff	1966	40-39
Mayo Smith	1967-70	363-285
Billy Martin	1971-73	248-204
Joe Schultz	1973	14-14
Ralph Houk	1974-78	363-443
Les Moss	1979	27-26S
Sparky Anderson	1979-95	1331-1248
Buddy Bell	1996-98	184-277
Larry Parrish	1998-99	82-104
Phil Garner	2000	79-83

WORLD SERIES CHAMPIONS

Year	*Loser*	*Length*	*MVP*
1935	Chicago	6 games	None
1945	Chicago	7 games	None
1968	St. Louis	7 games	Lolich
1984	San Diego	5 games	Trammell

A.L. PENNANT WINNERS

Year	*Record*	*Manager*	*Series Result*
1907	92-58	Jennings	Lost to Cubs
1908	90-63	Jennings	Lost to Cubs
1909	98-54	Jennings	Lost to Pirates
1934	101-53	Cochrane	Lost to Cardinals
1935	93-58	Cochrane	Defeated Cubs
1940	90-64	Baker	Lost to Reds
1945	88-65	O'Neill	Defeated Cubs
1968	103-59	Smith	Defeated Cardinals
1984	104-58	Anderson	Defeated Padres

EAST DIVISION CHAMPIONS

Year	*Record*	*Manager*	*ALCS Result*
1972	86-70	Martin	Lost to A's
1984	104-58	Anderson	Defeated Royals
1987	98-64	Anderson	Lost to Twins

ATTENDANCE HIGHS

Total	*Season*	*Park*
2,704,794	1984	Tiger Stadium
2,533,752	2000	Comerica Park
2,286,609	1985	Tiger Stadium
2,081,162	1988	Tiger Stadium
2,061,830	1987	Tiger Stadium

BALLPARK CHRONOLOGY

Comerica Park (2000-present)

Capacity: 40,120.
First game: Tigers 5, Seattle 2 (April 11, 2000).
First batter: Mark McLemore, Mariners.
First hit: John Olerud, Mariners (double).
First run: Luis Polonia, Tigers (1st inning).
First home run: Juan Gonzalez, Tigers.
First winning pitcher: Brian Moehler, Tigers.
First-season attendance: 2,533,752.

BALLPARK CHRONOLOGY

Tiger Stadium (1912-present)

Capacity: 46,945.
First game: Tigers 6, Cleveland 5, 11 innings (April 20, 1912).
First-season attendance: 402,870.

Bennett Park (1901-11)

Capacity: 8,500.
First game: Tigers 14, Milwaukee 13 (April 25, 1901).
First-season attendance: 259,430.

Note: Tiger Stadium was known as Navin Field from 1912-37 and Briggs Stadium from 1938-60.

A.L. MVPs

Mickey Cochrane, C, 1934
Hank Greenberg, 1B, 1935
Charley Gehringer, 2B, 1937
Hank Greenberg, OF, 1940
Hal Newhouser, P, 1944
Hal Newhouser, P, 1945
Denny McLain, P, 1968
Willie Hernandez, P, 1984

CY YOUNG WINNERS

Denny McLain, RH, 1968
*Denny McLain, RH, 1969
Willie Hernandez, LH, 1984

* Co-winner.

ROOKIES OF THE YEAR

Harvey Kuenn, SS, 1953
Mark Fidrych, P, 1976
Lou Whitaker, 2B, 1978

MANAGERS OF THE YEAR

Sparky Anderson, 1984
Sparky Anderson, 1987

RETIRED UNIFORMS

No.	*Name*	*Pos.*
2	Charley Gehringer	2B
5	Hank Greenberg	1B
6	Al Kaline	OF
16	Hal Newhouser	P

Outfielder Ty Cobb (sliding) played the game with reckless abandon and a devilish commitment.

HISTORY

MILESTONE PERFORMANCES

30-plus home runs

- 58—Hank Greenberg ... 1938
- 51—Cecil Fielder ... 1990
- 45—Rocky Colavito ... 1961
- 44—Hank Greenberg ... 1946
- Cecil Fielder ... 1991
- 41—Hank Greenberg ... 1940
- Norm Cash ... 1961
- 40—Hank Greenberg ... 1937
- Darrell Evans ... 1985
- 39—Norm Cash ... 1962
- 38—Dean Palmer ... 1999
- 37—Rocky Colavito ... 1962
- 36—Hank Greenberg ... 1935
- Willie Horton ... 1968
- 35—Rudy York ... 1937
- Rocky Colavito ... 1960
- Cecil Fielder ... 1992
- 34—Rudy York ... 1943
- Darrell Evans ... 1987
- Tony Clark ... 1998
- 33—Rudy York ... 1938, 1940
- Hank Greenberg ... 1939
- Lance Parrish ... 1984
- 32—Norm Cash ... 1966, 1971
- Lance Parrish ... 1982
- Matt Nokes ... 1987
- Mickey Tettleton ... 1992, 1993
- Rob Deer ... 1992
- Tony Clark ... 1997
- 31—Charlie Maxwell ... 1959
- Jason Thomspson ... 1977
- Mickey Tettleton ... 1991
- Cecil Fielder ... 1995
- Tony Clark ... 1999
- 30—Norm Cash ... 1965
- Cecil Fielder ... 1993
- Bobby Higginson ... 2000

100-plus RBIs

- 183—Hank Greenberg ... 1937
- 170—Hank Greenberg ... 1935
- 150—Hank Greenberg ... 1940
- 146—Hank Greenberg ... 1938
- 140—Rocky Colavito ... 1961
- 139—Harry Heilmann ... 1921
- Hank Greenberg ... 1934
- 137—Dale Alexander ... 1929
- 135—Dale Alexander ... 1930
- 134—Rudy York ... 1940
- 133—Harry Heilmann ... 1925
- Vic Wertz ... 1949
- Cecil Fielder ... 1991
- 132—Norm Cash ... 1961
- Cecil Fielder ... 1990
- 128—Bobby Veach ... 1921
- Al Kaline ... 1956
- 127—Ty Cobb ... 1911
- Charley Gehringer ... 1934
- Rudy York ... 1938
- Hank Greenberg ... 1946
- 126—Bobby Veach ... 1922
- 125—Goose Goslin ... 1936
- 124—Cecil Fielder ... 1992
- 123—Vic Wertz ... 1950
- 121—Rusty Staub ... 1978
- 120—Sam Crawford ... 1910
- Harry Heilmann ... 1927, 1929
- 119—Ty Cobb ... 1907
- 118—Rudy York ... 1943
- 117—Cecil Fielder ... 1993
- Tony Clark ... 1997
- 116—Charley Gehringer ... 1936
- Ray Boone ... 1955
- 115—Sam Crawford ... 1911
- Harry Heilmann ... 1923
- 114—Bob Fothergill ... 1927
- Lance Parrish ... 1983
- 113—Bobby Veach ... 1920
- Harry Heilmann ... 1924
- Gee Walker ... 1937
- 112—Sam Crawford ... 1915
- Bobby Veach ... 1915
- Al Simmons ... 1936
- Hank Greenberg ... 1939
- Rocky Colavito ... 1962
- 111—Rudy York ... 1941
- 110—Mickey Tettleton ... 1993
- 109—Sam Crawford ... 1912
- Goose Goslin ... 1935
- 108—Ty Cobb ... 1908
- John Stone ... 1932
- Charley Gehringer ... 1935
- 107—Ty Cobb ... 1909
- Harry Heilmann ... 1928
- Charley Gehringer ... 1932, 1938
- 106—Charley Gehringer ... 1929
- 105—Charley Gehringer ... 1933
- Marv Owen ... 1936
- Jason Thompson ... 1977
- Steve Kemp ... 1979
- Alan Trammell ... 1987
- 104—Sam Crawford ... 1914
- Willie Horton ... 1965
- 103—Bobby Veach ... 1917
- Harry Heilmann ... 1926
- Rudy York ... 1937
- Hoot Evers ... 1948, 1950
- Tony Clark ... 1998
- 102—Ty Cobb ... 1917, 1925
- Al Kaline ... 1955
- Travis Fryman ... 1997
- Bobby Higginson ... 2000
- Dean Palmer ... 2000
- 101—Ty Cobb ... 1921
- Bobby Veach ... 1919
- George Kell ... 1950
- Al Kaline ... 1963
- Rusty Staub ... 1977
- Steve Kemp ... 1980
- Bobby Higginson ... 1997
- 100—Goose Goslin ... 1934
- Billy Rogell ... 1934
- Willie Horton ... 1966
- Travis Fryman ... 1996
- Damion Easley ... 1998
- Dean Palmer ... 1999

Second baseman Charley Gehringer.

20-plus victories

- 1901—Roscoe Miller ... 23-13
- 1905—Ed Killian ... 23-14
- George Mullin ... 21-21
- 1906—George Mullin ... 21-18
- 1907—Bill Donovan ... 25-4
- Ed Killian ... 25-13
- George Mullin ... 20-20
- 1908—Ed Summers ... 24-12
- 1909—George Mullin ... 29-9
- Edgar Willett ... 21-10
- 1910—George Mullin ... 21-12
- 1914—Harry Coveleski ... 22-12
- 1915—George Dauss ... 24-13
- Harry Coveleski ... 22-13
- 1916—Harry Coveleski ... 21-11
- 1919—George Dauss ... 21-9
- 1923—George Dauss ... 21-13
- 1934—Schoolboy Rowe ... 24-8
- Tommy Bridges ... 22-11
- 1935—Tommy Bridges ... 21-10
- 1936—Tommy Bridges ... 23-11
- 1939—Bobo Newsom ... *20-11
- 1940—Bobo Newsom ... 21-5
- 1943—Dizzy Trout ... 20-12
- 1944—Hal Newhouser ... 29-9
- Dizzy Trout ... 27-14
- 1945—Hal Newhouser ... 25-9
- 1946—Hal Newhouser ... 26-9
- 1948—Hal Newhouser ... 21-12
- 1956—Frank Lary ... 21-13
- Billy Hoeft ... 20-14
- 1957—Jim Bunning ... 20-8
- 1961—Frank Lary ... 23-9
- 1966—Denny McLain ... 20-14
- 1967—Earl Wilson ... 22-11
- 1968—Denny McLain ... 31-6
- 1969—Denny McLain ... 24-9
- 1971—Mickey Lolich ... 25-14
- Joe Coleman ... 20-9
- 1972—Mickey Lolich ... 22-14
- 1973—Joe Coleman ... 23-15
- 1983—Jack Morris ... 20-13
- 1986—Jack Morris ... 21-8
- 1991—Bill Gullickson ... 20-9

*3-1 with St. Louis; 17-10 with Detroit.

A.L. home run champions

- 1908—Sam Crawford ... 7
- 1909—Ty Cobb ... 9
- 1935—Hank Greenberg ... *36
- 1938—Hank Greenberg ... 58
- 1940—Hank Greenberg ... 41
- 1943—Rudy York ... 34
- 1946—Hank Greenberg ... 44
- 1985—Darrell Evans ... 40
- 1990—Cecil Fielder ... 51
- 1991—Cecil Fielder ... *44

* Tied for league lead

INDIVIDUAL SEASON, GAME RECORDS

SEASON

Batting			
At-bats	679	Harvey Kuenn	1953
Runs	147	Ty Cobb	1911
Hits	248	Ty Cobb	1911
Singles	169	Ty Cobb	1911
Doubles	63	Hank Greenberg	1934
Triples	26	Sam Crawford	1926
Home runs	58	Hank Greenberg	1938
Home runs, rookie	35	Rudy York	1937
Grand slams	4	3 times	
		Last by Jim Northrup	1968
Total bases	397	Hank Greenberg	1937
RBIs	183	Hank Greenberg	1937
Walks	137	Roy Cullenbine	1947
Most strikeouts	182	Cecil Fielder	1990
Fewest strikeouts	13	Charley Gehringer	1936
		Harvey Kuenn	1954
Batting average	.420	Ty Cobb	1911
Slugging pct.	.683	Hank Greenberg	1938
Stolen bases	96	Ty Cobb	1915
Pitching			
Games	88	Mike Myers	1997
		Sean Runyan	1998
Complete games	42	George Mullin	1904
Innings	382.1	George Mullin	1904
Wins	31	Denny McLain	1968
Losses	23	George Mullin	1904
Winning pct.	.862 (25-4)	Bill Donovan	1907
Walks	158	Joe Coleman	1974
Strikeouts	308	Mickey Lolich	1971
Shutouts	9	Denny McLain	1969
Home runs allowed	42	Denny McLain	1966
Lowest ERA	1.64	Ed Summers	1908
Saves	42	Todd Jones	2000

GAME

Batting			
Runs	5	Last by Travis Fryman	4-17-93
Hits	7	Rocky Colavito	6-24-62
		Cesar Gutierrez	6-21-70
Doubles	4	Frank Dillon	4-25-01
		Bill Bruton	5-19-63
Triples	3	Charley Gehringer	8-5-29
Home runs	3	Last by Bobby Higginson	6-24-2000
RBIs	8	Jim Northrup	6-24-68
		Jim Northrup	7-11-73
Total bases	16	Ty Cobb	5-5-25
Stolen bases	5	Johnny Neun	7-9-27

A.L. RBI champions

- 1907—Ty Cobb ... 119
- 1908—Ty Cobb ... 108
- 1909—Ty Cobb ... 107
- 1910—Sam Crawford ... 120
- 1911—Ty Cobb ... 127
- 1914—Sam Crawford ... 104
- 1915—Sam Crawford ... *112
- Bobby Veach ... *112
- 1917—Bobby Veach ... 103
- 1918—Bobby Veach ... 78
- 1935—Hank Greenberg ... 170
- 1937—Hank Greenberg ... 183
- 1940—Hank Greenberg ... 150
- 1943—Rudy York ... 118
- 1946—Hank Greenberg ... 127
- 1955—Ray Boone ... *116
- 1990—Cecil Fielder ... 132
- 1991—Cecil Fielder ... 133
- 1992—Cecil Fielder ... 124

* Tied for league lead

A.L. batting champions

- 1907—Ty Cobb ... .350
- 1908—Ty Cobb ... .324
- 1909—Ty Cobb ... .377
- 1910—Ty Cobb ... .385
- 1911—Ty Cobb ... .420
- 1912—Ty Cobb ... .410
- 1913—Ty Cobb ... .390
- 1914—Ty Cobb ... .368
- 1915—Ty Cobb ... .369
- 1917—Ty Cobb ... .383
- 1918—Ty Cobb ... .382
- 1919—Ty Cobb ... .384
- 1921—Harry Heilmann ... .394
- 1923—Harry Heilmann ... .403
- 1925—Harry Heilmann ... .393
- 1926—Heinie Manush ... .378
- 1927—Harry Heilmann ... .398
- 1937—Charley Gehringer ... .371
- 1949—George Kell ... .343
- 1955—Al Kaline ... .340
- 1959—Harvey Kuenn ... .353
- 1961—Norm Cash ... .361

A.L. ERA champions

- 1902—Ed Siever ... 1.91
- 1944—Dizzy Trout ... 2.12
- 1945—Hal Newhouser ... 1.81
- 1946—Hal Newhouser ... 1.94
- 1962—Hank Aguirre ... 2.21
- 1976—Mark Fidrych ... 2.34

A.L. strikeout champions

- 1935—Tommy Bridges ... 163
- 1936—Tommy Bridges ... 175
- 1944—Hal Newhouser ... 187
- 1945—Hal Newhouser ... 212
- 1949—Virgil Trucks ... 153
- 1959—Jim Bunning ... 201
- 1960—Jim Bunning ... 201
- 1971—Mickey Lolich ... 308
- 1983—Jack Morris ... 232

No-hit pitchers

(9 innings or more)

- 1912—George Mullin ... 7-0 vs. St. Louis
- 1952—Virgil Trucks ... 1-0 vs. Washington
- Virgil Trucks ... 1-0 vs. New York
- 1958—Jim Bunning ... 3-0 vs. Boston
- 1984—Jack Morris ... 4-0 vs. Chicago

Longest hitting streaks

- 40—Ty Cobb ... 1911
- 35—Ty Cobb ... 1917
- 34—John Stone ... 1930
- 30—Goose Goslin ... 1934
- Ron LeFlore ... 1976
- 29—Dale Alexander ... 1930
- Pete Fox ... 1935
- 27—Gee Walker ... 1937
- Ron LeFlore ... 1978
- 25—Kid Gleason ... 1901
- Ty Cobb ... 1906
- 23—Sam Crawford ... 1909
- Harry Heilmann ... 1921
- John Stone ... 1931
- 22—Harvey Kuenn ... 1959
- Al Kaline ... 1961
- 21—Harry Heilmann ... 1923
- Ty Cobb ... 1926
- Charley Gehringer ... 1927
- Dick Wakefield ... 1943
- 20—Kid Gleason ... 1901
- Sam Crawford ... 1903
- Charley Gehringer ... 1937
- Alan Trammell ... 1984

CAREER LEADERS

BATTING

Games	
Al Kaline	2,834
Ty Cobb	2,806
Lou Whitaker	2,390
Charley Gehringer	2,323
Alan Trammell	2,293
Sam Crawford	2,114
Norm Cash	2,018
Harry Heilmann	1,991
Donie Bush	1,872
Bill Freehan	1,774

At-bats	
Ty Cobb	10,591
Al Kaline	10,116
Charley Gehringer	8,860
Lou Whitaker	8,570
Alan Trammell	8,288
Sam Crawford	7,984
Harry Heilmann	7,297
Donie Bush	6,970
Norm Cash	6,593
Bill Freehan	6,073

Runs	
Ty Cobb	2,088
Charley Gehringer	1,774
Al Kaline	1,622
Lou Whitaker	1,386
Donie Bush	1,242
Alan Trammell	1,231
Harry Heilmann	1,209
Sam Crawford	1,115
Norm Cash	1,028
Hank Greenberg	980

Hits	
Ty Cobb	3,900
Al Kaline	3,007
Charley Gehringer	2,839
Harry Heilmann	2,499
Sam Crawford	2,466
Lou Whitaker	2,369
Alan Trammell	2,365
Bobby Veach	1,859
Norm Cash	1,793
Donie Bush	1,745

Doubles	
Ty Cobb	665
Charley Gehringer	574
Al Kaline	498
Harry Heilmann	497
Lou Whitaker	420
Alan Trammell	412
Sam Crawford	402
Hank Greenberg	366
Bobby Veach	345
Harvey Kuenn	244

Triples	
Ty Cobb	284
Sam Crawford	249
Charley Gehringer	146
Harry Heilmann	145
Bobby Veach	136
Al Kaline	75
Donie Bush	73
Dick McAuliffe	70
Hank Greenberg	69
Lu Blue	66

Home runs	
Al Kaline	399
Norm Cash	373
Hank Greenberg	306
Willie Horton	262
Cecil Fielder	245
Lou Whitaker	244
Rudy York	239
Lance Parrish	212
Bill Freehan	200
Kirk Gibson	195

Total Bases	
Ty Cobb	5,466
Al Kaline	4,852
Charley Gehringer	4,257
Harry Heilmann	3,778
Lou Whitaker	3,651
Sam Crawford	3,576
Alan Trammell	3,442
Norm Cash	3,233
Hank Greenberg	2,950
Bobby Veach	2,653

Runs batted in	
Ty Cobb	1,805
Al Kaline	1,583
Harry Heilmann	1,442
Charley Gehringer	1,427
Sam Crawford	1,264
Hank Greenberg	1,202
Norm Cash	1,087
Lou Whitaker	1,084
Bobby Veach	1,042
Alan Trammell	1,003

Extra-base hits	
Ty Cobb	1,060
Al Kaline	972
Charley Gehringer	904
Harry Heilmann	806
Hank Greenberg	741
Lou Whitaker	729
Sam Crawford	721
Norm Cash	654
Alan Trammell	652
Bobby Veach	540

Batting average
(Minimum 500 games)

Ty Cobb	.368
Harry Heilmann	.342
Bob Fothergill	.337
George Kell	.325
Heinie Manush	.321
Charley Gehringer	.320
Hank Greenberg	.319
Gee Walker	.317
Harvey Kuenn	.314
Barney McCosky	.312

Stolen bases	
Ty Cobb	865
Donie Bush	400
Sam Crawford	317
Ron Leflore	294
Alan Trammell	236
Kirk Gibson	194
George Moriarty	190
Bobby Veach	189
Charley Gehringer	181
Lou Whitaker	143

PITCHING

Earned-run average
(Minimum 1,000 innings)

Harry Coveleski	2.34
Ed Killian	2.38
Bill Donovan	2.49
Ed Siever	2.61
George Mullin	2.76
John Hiller	2.83
Ed Willett	2.89
Jean Dubuc	3.06
Hal Newhouser	3.07
Bernie Boland	3.09

Wins	
Hooks Dauss	223
George Mullin	209
Mickey Lolich	207
Hal Newhouser	200
Jack Morris	198
Tommy Bridges	194
Dizzy Trout	161
Bill Donovan	140
Earl Whitehill	133
Frank Lary	123

Losses	
Hooks Dauss	182
George Mullin	179
Mickey Lolich	175
Dizzy Trout	153
Jack Morris	150
Hal Newhouser	148
Tommy Bridges	138
Earl Whitehill	119
Frank Lary	110
Vic Sorrell	101

Innings piitched	
George Mullin	3,394.0
Hooks Dauss	3,390.2
Mickey Lolich	3,361.2
Jack Morris	3,042.2
Hal Newhouser	2,944.0
Tommy Bridges	2,826.1
Dizzy Trout	2,591.2
Earl Whitehill	2,171.1
Bill Donovan	2,137.1
Frank Lary	2,008.2

Strikeouts	
Mickey Lolich	2,679
Jack Morris	1,980
Hal Newhouser	1,770
Tommy Bridges	1,674
Jim Bunning	1,406
George Mullin	1,380
Hooks Dauss	1,201
Dizzy Trout	1,199
Denny McLain	1,150
Bill Donovan	1,079

Bases on balls	
Hal Newhouser	1,227
Tommy Bridges	1,192
George Mullin	1,106
Jack Morris	1,086
Hooks Dauss	1,067
Mickey Lolich	1,014
Dizzy Trout	978
Earl Whitehill	831
Dan Petry	744
Virgil Trucks	732

Games	
John Hiller	545
Hooks Dauss	538
Mickey Lolich	508
Dizzy Trout	493
Mike Henneman	491
Hal Newhouser	460
George Mullin	435
Jack Morris	430
Tommy Bridges	424
Willie Hernandez	358

Shutouts	
Mickey Lolich	39
George Mullin	34
Tommy Bridges	33
Hal Newhouser	33
Bill Donovan	29
Dizzy Trout	28
Denny McLain	26
Jack Morris	24
Hooks Dauss	22
Frank Lary	20
Virgil Trucks	20

Saves	
Mike Henneman	154
Todd Jones	131
John Hiller	125
Willie Hernandez	120
Aurelio Lopez	85
Terry Fox	55
Al Benton	45
Hooks Dauss	39
Larry Sherry	37
Fred Scherman	34
Dizzy Trout	34

TEAM SEASON, GAME RECORDS

SEASON

Batting		
Most at-bats	5,664	1998
Most runs	958	1934
Fewest runs	499	1904
Most hits	1,724	1921
Most singles	1,298	1921
Most doubles	349	1934
Most triples	102	1913
Most home runs	225	1987
Fewest home runs	9	1906
Most grand slams	10	1938
Most pinch-hit home runs	8	1971
Most total bases	2,548	1987
Most stolen bases	280	1909
Highest batting average	.316	1921
Lowest batting average	.230	1904
Highest slugging pct.	.453	1929

Pitching		
Lowest ERA	2.26	1909
Highest ERA	6.38	1996
Most complete games	143	1904
Most shutouts	22	1917, 1944, 1969
Most saves	51	1984
Most walks	784	1996
Most strikeouts	1,115	1968

Fielding		
Most errors	410	1901
Fewest errors	92	1997
Most double plays	194	1950
Highest fielding average	.985	1997

General		
Most games won	104	1984
Most games lost	109	1996
Highest win pct.	.656	1934
Lowest win pct.	.325	1952

GAME, INNING

Batting		
Most runs, game	21	Last 7-1-36
Most runs, inning	13	6-17-25
Most hits, game	28	9-29-28
Most home runs, game	8	6-20-2000
Most total bases, game	47	6-20-2000

Hal Newhouser claimed A.L. MVP citations during the war seasons of 1944 and '45.

TIGERS YEAR-BY-YEAR

				Games		Leaders					
Year	W	L	Place	Back	Manager	Batting avg.	Hits	Home runs	RBIs	Wins	ERA
1901	74	61	3rd	8½	Stallings	Elberfeld, .310	Barrett, 159	Barrett, Holmes, 4	Elberfeld, 76	Miller, 23	Yeager, 2.61
1902	52	83	7th	30½	Dwyer	Barrett, .303	Barrett, 154	Casey, 3	Elberfeld, 64	Mercer, 15	Siever, 1.91
1903	65	71	5th	25	Barrow	Crawford, .335	Crawford, 184	Crawford, 4	Crawford, 89	Mullin, 19	Mullin, 2.25
1904	62	90	7th	32	Barrow, Lowe	Barrett, .268	Barrett, 167	3 Tied, 2	Crawford, 73	Donovan, Mullin, 17	Mullin, 2.40
1905	79	74	3rd	15½	Armour	Crawford, .297	Crawford, 171	Crawford, 6	Crawford, 75	Killian, 23	Killian, 2.27
1906	71	78	6th	21	Armour	Cobb, .316	Crawford, 166	4 Tied, 2	Crawford, 72	Mullin, 21	Siever, 2.71
1907	92	58	1st	+1½	Jennings	Cobb, .350	Cobb, 212	Cobb, 5	Cobb, 119	Donovan, Killian, 25	Killian, 1.78
1908	90	63	1st	+½	Jennings	Cobb, .324	Cobb, 188	Crawford, 7	Cobb, 108	Summers, 24	Summers, 1.64
1909	98	54	1st	+3½	Jennings	Cobb, .377	Cobb, 216	Cobb, 9	Cobb, 107	Mullin, 29	Killian, 1.71
1910	86	68	3rd	18	Jennings	Cobb, .383	Cobb, 196	Cobb, 8	Crawford, 120	Mullin, 21	Willett, 2.37
1911	89	65	2nd	13½	Jennings	Cobb, .420	Cobb, 248	Cobb, 8	Cobb, 144	Mullin, 18	Mullin, 3.07
1912	69	84	6th	36½	Jennings	Cobb, .410	Cobb, 227	Cobb, 7	Crawford, 109	Dubuc, Willett, 17	Dubuc, 2.77
1913	66	87	6th	30	Jennings	Cobb, .390	Crawford, 193	Crawford, 9	Crawford, 83	Dubuc, 15	Dauss, 2.68
1914	80	73	4th	19½	Jennings	Crawford, .314	Crawford, 183	Crawford, 8	Crawford, 104	Coveleski, 21	Cavet, 2.44
1915	100	54	2nd	2½	Jennings	Cobb, .369	Cobb, 208	Burns, 5	Crawford, Veach, 112	Dauss, 24	Coveleski, 2.45
1916	87	67	3rd	4	Jennings	Cobb, .371	Cobb, 201	Cobb, 5	Veach, 91	Coveleski, 21	Coveleski, 1.97
1917	78	75	4th	21½	Jennings	Cobb, .383	Cobb, 225	Veach, 8	Veach, 103	Dauss, 17	James, 2.09
1918	55	71	7th	20	Jennings	Cobb, .382	Cobb, 161	Heilmann, 5	Veach, 78	Boland, 14	Erickson, 2.48
1919	80	60	4th	8	Jennings	Cobb, .384	Cobb, Veach, 191	Heilmann, 8	Veach, 101	Dauss, 21	Ayers, 2.69
1920	61	93	7th	37	Jennings	Cobb, .334	Veach, 188	Veach, 11	Veach, 113	Ehmke, 15	Ehmke, 3.25
1921	71	82	6th	27	Cobb	Heilmann, .394	Heilmann, 237	Heilmann, 19	Heilmann, 139	Ehmke, 13	Leonard, 3.75
1922	79	75	3rd	15	Cobb	Cobb, .401	Cobb, 211	Heilmann, 21	Veach, 126	Pillette, 19	Pillette, 2.85
1923	83	71	2nd	16	Cobb	Heilmann, .403	Heilmann, 211	Heilmann, 18	Heilmann, 115	Dauss, 21	Dauss, 3.62
1924	86	68	3rd	6	Cobb	Bassler, Heilmann, .346	Cobb, 211	Heilmann, 10	Heilmann, 113	Whitehill, 17	Collins, 3.21
1925	81	73	4th	16½	Cobb	Heilmann, .393	Heilmann, 225	Heilmann, 13	Heilmann, 133	Dauss, 16	Dauss, 3.16
1926	79	75	6th	12	Cobb	Manush, .378	Manush, 188	Manush, 14	Heilmann, 103	Whitehill, 16	Collins, 2.73
1927	82	71	4th	27½	Moriarty	Heilmann, .398	Heilmann, 201	Heilmann, 14	Heilmann, 120	Whitehill, 16	Whitehill, 3.36
1928	68	86	6th	33	Moriarty	Heilmann, .328	Gehringer, 193	Heilmann, 14	Heilmann, 107	Carroll, 16	Carroll, 3.27
1929	70	84	6th	36	Harris	Heilmann, .344	Alexander, Gehringer, 215	Alexander, 25	Alexander, 137	Uhle, 15	Uhle, 4.08
1930	75	79	5th	27	Harris	Gehringer, .330	Gehringer, 201	Alexander, 20	Alexander, 135	Whitehill, 17	Uhle, 3.65
1931	61	93	7th	47	Harris	Stone, .327	Stone, 191	Stone, 10	Alexander, 87	Sorrell, Whitehill, 13	Uhle, 3.50
1932	76	75	5th	29½	Harris	Walker, .323	Gehringer, 184	Gehringer, 19	Stone, 108	Whitehill, 16	Bridges, 3.36
1933	75	79	5th	25	Harris, Baker	Gehringer, .325	Gehringer, 204	Gehringer, Greenberg, 12	Gehringer, 105	Marberry, 16	Bridges, 3.09
1934	101	53	1st	+7	Cochrane	Gehringer, .356	Gehringer, 214	Greenberg, 26	Greenberg, 139	Rowe, 24	Auker, 3.42
1935	93	58	1st	+3	Cochrane	Gehringer, .330	Greenberg, 203	Greenberg, 36	Greenberg, 170	Bridges, 21	Bridges, Sullivan, 3.51
1936	83	71	2nd	19½	Cochrane	Gehringer, .354	Gehringer, 227	Goslin, 24	Goslin, 125	Bridges, 23	Bridges, 3.60
1937	89	65	2nd	13	Cochrane, Perkins	Gehringer, .371	Walker, 213	Greenberg, 40	Greenberg, 183	Lawson, 18	Auker, 3.88
1938	84	70	4th	16	Cochrane, Baker	Greenberg, .315	Fox, 186	Greenberg, 58	Greenberg, 146	Bridges, 13	Benton, 3.30
1939	81	73	5th	26½	Baker	Gehringer, .325	McCosky, 190	Greenberg, 33	Greenberg, 112	Bridges, Newsom, 17	Newsom, 3.37
1940	90	64	1st	+1	Baker	Greenberg, McCosky, .340	McCosky, 200	Greenberg, 41	Greenberg, 150	Newsom, 21	Newsom, 2.83
1941	75	79	*4th	26	Baker	McCosky, .324	Higgins, 161	York, 27	York, 111	Benton, 15	Benton, 2.97
1942	73	81	5th	30	Baker	McCosky, .293	McCosky, 176	York, 21	York, 90	Trucks, 14	Newhouser, 2.45
1943	78	76	5th	20	O'Neill	Wakefield, .316	Wakefield, 200	York, 34	York, 118	Trout, 20	Bridges, 2.39
1944	88	66	2nd	1	O'Neill	Higgins, .297	Cramer, 169	York, 18	York, 98	Newhouser, 29	Trout, 2.12
1945	88	65	1st	+1½	O'Neill	Mayo, .285	York, 157	Cullenbine, York, 18	Cullenbine, 93	Newhouser, 25	Newhouser, 1.81
1946	92	62	2nd	12	O'Neill	Kell, .327	Lake, 149	Greenberg, 44	Greenberg, 127	Newhouser, 26	Newhouser, 1.94
1947	85	69	2nd	12	O'Neill	Kell, .320	Kell, 188	Cullenbine, 24	Kell, 93	Hutchinson, 18	Newhouser, 2.87
1948	78	76	5th	18½	O'Neill	Evers, .314	Evers, 169	Mullin, 23	Evers, 103	Newhouser, 21	Newhouser, 3.01
1949	87	67	4th	10	Rolfe	Kell, .343	Wertz, 185	Wertz, 20	Wertz, 133	Trucks, 19	Trucks, 2.81
1950	95	59	2nd	3	Rolfe	Kell, .340	Kell, 218	Wertz, 27	Wertz, 123	Houtteman, 19	Houtteman, 3.54
1951	73	81	5th	25	Rolfe	Kell, .319	Kell, 191	Wertz, 27	Wertz, 94	Trucks, 13	Hutchinson, 3.68
1952	50	104	8th	45	Rolfe, Hutchinson	Groth, .284	Groth, 149	Dropo, 23	Dropo, 70	Gray, 12	Newhouser, 3.74
1953	60	94	6th	40½	Hutchinson	Boone, .312	Kuenn, 209	Boone, 22	Dropo, 96	Garver, 11	Branca, 4.15
1954	68	86	5th	43	Hutchinson	Kuenn, .306	Kuenn, 201	Boone, 20	Boone, 85	Gromek, 18	Gromek, 2.74
1955	79	75	5th	17	Harris	Kaline, .340	Kaline, 200	Kaline, 27	Boone, 116	Hoeft, 16	Hoeft, 2.99
1956	82	72	5th	15	Harris	Kuenn, .332	Kuenn, 196	Maxwell, 28	Kaline, 128	Lary, 21	Lary, 3.15
1957	78	76	4th	20	Tighe	Kaline, .295	Kuenn, 173	Maxwell, 24	Kaline, 90	Bunning, 20	Bunning, 2.69
1958	77	77	5th	15	Tighe, Norman	Kuenn, .319	Kuenn, 179	Harris, 20	Kaline, 85	Lary, 16	Lary, 2.90
1959	76	78	4th	18	Norman, Dykes	Kuenn, .353	Kuenn, 198	Maxwell, 31	Maxwell, 95	Bunning, Lary, Mossi, 17	Mossi, 3.36
1960	71	83	6th	26	Dykes, Gordon	Kaline, .278	Kaline, 153	Colavito, 35	Colavito, 87	Lary, 15	Bunning, 2.79
1961	101	61	2nd	8	Scheffing	Cash, .361	Cash, 193	Colavito, 45	Colavito, 140	Lary, 23	Mossi, 2.96
1962	85	76	4th	10½	Scheffing	Kaline, .304	Colavito, 164	Cash, 39	Colavito, 112	Bunning, 19	Aguirre, 2.21
1963	79	83	*5th	25½	Scheffing, Dressen	Kaline, .312	Kaline, 172	Kaline, 27	Kaline, 101	Regan, 15	Lary, 3.27
1964	85	77	4th	14	Dressen	Freehan, .300	Lumpe, 160	McAuliffe, 24	Cash, 83	Wickersham, 19	Lolich, 3.26
1965	89	73	4th	13	Dressen, Swift	Kaline, .281	Wert, 159	Cash, 30	Horton, 104	McLain, 16	McLain, 2.61
1966	88	74	3rd	10	Dressen, Swift, Skaff	Kaline, .288	Cash, 168	Cash, 32	Horton, 100	McLain, 20	Wilson, 2.59
1967	91	71	*2nd	1	Smith	Kaline, .308	Freehan, 146	Kaline, 25	Kaline, 78	Wilson, 22	Lolich, 3.04
1968	103	59	1st	+12	Smith	Horton, .285	Northrup, 153	Horton, 36	Northrup, 90	McLain, 31	McLain, 1.96
							—EAST DIVISION—				
1969	90	72	2nd	19	Smith	Northrup, .295	Northrup, 160	Horton, 28	Horton, 91	McLain, 24	McLain, 2.80
1970	79	83	4th	29	Smith	Horton, .305	Stanley, 143	Northrup, 24	Northrup, 80	Lolich, 14	Hiller, 3.03
1971	91	71	2nd	12	Martin	Kaline, .294	Rodriguez, 153	Cash, 32	Cash, 91	Lolich, 25	Scherman, 2.71
1972	86	70	†1st	+½	Martin	Freehan, .262	Rodriguez, 142	Cash, 22	Cash, 61	Lolich, 22	Fryman, 2.06
1973	85	77	3rd	12	Martin, Schultz	Horton, .316	Stanley, 147	Cash, 19	Rodriguez, 58	Coleman, 23	Hiller, 1.44
1974	72	90	6th	19	Houk	Freehan, .297	Sutherland, 157	Freehan, 18	Kaline, 64	Hiller, 17	Hiller, 2.64
1975	57	102	6th	37½	Houk	Horton, .275	Horton, 169	Horton, 25	Horton, 92	Lolich, 12	Lolich, 3.78
1976	74	87	5th	24	Houk	LeFlore, .316	Staub, 176	Thompson, 17	Staub, 96	Fidrych, 19	Fidrych, 2.34
1977	74	88	4th	26	Houk	LeFlore, .325	LeFlore, 212	Thompson, 31	Thompson, 105	Rozema, 15	Rozema, 3.09
1978	86	76	5th	13½	Houk	LeFlore, .297	LeFlore, 198	Thompson, 26	Staub, 121	Slaton, 17	Hiller, 2.34
1979	85	76	5th	18	Moss, Anderson	Kemp, .318	LeFlore, 180	Kemp, 26	Kemp, 105	Morris, 17	Lopez, 2.41
1980	84	78	5th	19	Anderson	Trammell, .300	Trammell, 168	Parrish, 24	Kemp, 101	Morris, 16	P. Underwood, 3.59
1981	60	49	‡4th/2nd	—	Anderson	Gibson, .328	Kemp, 103	Parrish, 10	Kemp, 49	Morris, 14	Petry, 3.00
1982	83	79	4th	12	Anderson	Herndon, .292	Herndon, 179	Parrish, 32	Herndon, 88	Morris, 17	Petry, 3.22
1983	92	70	2nd	6	Anderson	Whitaker, .320	Whitaker, 206	Parrish, 27	Parrish, 114	Morris, 20	Lopez, 2.81
1984	104	58	§1st	+15	Anderson	Trammell, .314	Trammell, 174	Parrish, 33	Parrish, 98	Morris, 19	Hernandez, 1.92
1985	84	77	3rd	15	Anderson	K. Gibson, .287	Whitaker, 170	Evans, 40	Parrish, 98	Morris, 16	Hernandez, 2.70
1986	87	75	3rd	8½	Anderson	Trammell, .277	Trammell, 159	Evans, 29	Coles, Gibson, 86	Morris, 21	Morris, 3.27
1987	98	64	†1st	+2	Anderson	Trammell, .343	Trammell, 205	Evans, 34	Trammell, 105	Morris, 18	Henneman, 2.98
1988	88	74	2nd	1	Anderson	Trammell, .311	Trammell, 145	Evans, 22	Trammell, 69	Morris, 15	Henneman, 1.87
1989	59	103	7th	30	Anderson	Bergman, .268	Whitaker, 128	Whitaker, 28	Whitaker, 85	Henneman, 11	Tanana, 3.58
1990	79	83	3rd	9	Anderson	Trammell, .304	Trammell, 170	Fielder, 51	Fielder, 132	Morris, 15	P. Gibson, Henneman, 3.05
1991	84	78	2nd	7	Anderson	Phillips, .284	Fielder, 163	Fielder, 44	Fielder, 133	Gullickson, 20	Tanana, 3.77
1992	75	87	6th	21	Anderson	Livingstone, .282	Fryman, 175	Fielder, 35	Fielder, 124	Gullickson, 14	Doherty, 3.88
1993	85	77	*3rd	10	Anderson	Trammell, .329	Fryman, 182	Tettleton, 32	Tettleton, 117	Doherty, 14	Wells, 4.19
1994	53	62	5th	18	Anderson	Whitaker, .301	Phillips, 123	Fielder, 28	Fielder, 90	Moore, 11	Wells, 3.96
1995	60	84	4th	26	Anderson	Fryman, .275	Curtis, 157	Fielder, 31	Fielder, 82	Wells, 10	Wells, 3.04
1996	53	109	5th	39	Bell	Higginson, .320	Fryman, 165	Clark, 27	Fryman, 100	Olivares, 7	Olivares, 4.89
1997	79	83	3rd	19	Bell	Higginson, .299	Hunter, 177	Clark, 32	Clark, 117	Blair, 16	Thompson, 3.02
1998	65	97	5th	24	Bell, Parrish	Clark, .291	Clark, 175	Clark, 34	Clark, 103	Moehler, 14	Moehler, 3.90
1999	69	92	3rd	27½	Parrish	D.Cruz, .284	Clark, 150	Palmer, 38	Palmer, 100	Mlicki, 14	Mlicki, 4.60
2000	79	83	3rd	16	Garner	D. Cruz, .302	Higginson, 179	Higginson, 30	Higginson, Palmer, 102	Moehler, 12	Sparks, 4.07

* Tied for position. † Lost Championship Series. ‡ First half 31-26; second half 29-23. § Won Championship Series.

Note: Batting average minimum 350 at-bats; ERA minimum 90 innings pitched.

KANSAS CITY ROYALS

FRANCHISE CHRONOLOGY

First season: 1969, as one of two expansion teams in the American League. The young Royals excited their home fans with a 12-inning, 4-3 victory over the Minnesota Twins in their Major League debut and went on to carve out a respectable 69-93 first-season record, good for a fourth-place finish in the six-team A.L. West Division.

1970-present: It didn't take long for the Royals to become the model for future expansion franchises as they built an A.L. power through minor league player development and an astute series of trades. In 1976, their eighth major league season, the Royals joined the baseball elite by winning the first of three consecutive West Division championships, all of which were followed by heartbreaking losses to the New York Yankees in the A.L. Championship Series. The Royals turned the tables on the Yankees in 1980 for their first pennant, losing to Philadelphia in the World Series. But they captured their first Series championship in 1985 with a seven-game victory over the cross-state Cardinals. The Royals were one of five teams placed in the Central Division when baseball adopted a three-division format in 1994.

Third baseman George Brett.

ROYALS VS. OPPONENTS BY DECADE

	A's	Indians	Orioles	Red Sox	Tigers	Twins	White Sox	Yankees	Angels	Rangers	Brewers	Blue Jays	Mariners	Devil Rays	Interleague	Decade Record
1969	8-10	5-7	1-11	2-10	4-8	8-10	10-8	5-7	9-9	7-5	10-8					69-93
1970-79	79-90	65-52	51-65	63-53	63-54	85-84	89-79	53-64	87-79	84-69	80-48	22-10	30-13			851-760
1980-89	64-59	62-54	61-55	65-49	59-54	68-62	64-55	52-68	73-50	70-54	58-59	60-56	70-59			826-734
1990-99	53-68	49-64	43-62	51-52	56-57	64-61	52-72	45-61	56-64	56-61	50-47	55-62	64-55	10-11	21-28	725-825
2000-	4-8	7-5	7-3	6-4	7-5	7-5	7-5	2-8	6-6	3-7		4-6	4-8	5-5	8-10	77-85
Totals	208-235	188-182	163-196	187-168	189-178	232-222	222-219	157-208	231-208	220-196	198-162	141-134	168-135	15-16	29-38	2548-2497

Interleague results: 5-7 vs. Cubs; 3-5 vs. Reds; 4-8 vs. Astros;8-6 vs. Pirates; 6-6 vs. Cardinals; 3-6 vs. Brewers.

MANAGERS

Name	*Years*	*Record*
Joe Gordon	1969	69-93
Charlie Metro	1970	19-33
Bob Lemon	1970-72	207-218
Jack McKeon	1973-75	215-205
Whitey Herzog	1974-79	410-304
Jim Frey	1980-81	127-105
Dick Howser	1981-86	404-365
Mike Ferraro	1986	36-38
Billy Gardner	1987	62-64
John Wathan	1987-91	287-270
Bob Schaefer	1991	1-0
Hal McRae	1991-94	286-277
Bob Boone	1995-97	181-206
Tony Muser	1997-2000	244-319

WORLD SERIES CHAMPIONS

Year	*Loser*	*Length*	*MVP*
1985	St. Louis	7 games	Saberhagen

A.L. PENNANT WINNERS

Year	*Record*	*Manager*	*Series Result*
1980	97-65	Frey	Lost to Phillies
1985	91-71	Howser	Defeated Cardinals

WEST DIVISION CHAMPIONS

Year	*Record*	*Manager*	*ALCS Result*
1976	90-72	Herzog	Lost to Yankees
1977	102-60	Herzog	Lost to Yankees
1978	92-70	Herzog	Lost to Yankees
1980	97-65	Frey	Defeated Yankees
*1981	50-53	Frey, Howser	None
1984	84-78	Howser	Lost to Tigers
1985	91-71	Howser	Defeated Blue Jays

* Second-half champion; lost division playoff to A's.

ALL-TIME RECORD OF EXPANSION TEAMS

Team	W	L	Pct.	DT	P	WS
Arizona	250	236	.514	1	0	0
Kansas City	2,548	2,497	.505	6	2	1
Toronto	1,867	1,897	.496	5	2	2
Houston	3,052	3,138	.493	6	0	0
Montreal	2,454	2,596	.486	2	0	0
Anaheim	3,069	3,281	.483	3	0	0
Colorado	594	639	.482	0	0	0
Milwaukee	2,421	2,631	.479	2	1	0
New York	2,934	3,246	.475	4	4	2
Texas	2,952	3,381	.466	4	0	0
San Diego	2,315	2,742	.458	3	2	0
Seattle	1,715	2,048	.456	2	0	0
Florida	551	678	.448	0	1	1
Tampa Bay	201	284	.414	0	0	0

DT—Division Titles. P—Pennants won. WS—World Series won.

ATTENDANCE HIGHS

Total	*Season*	*Park*
2,477,700	1989	Royals Stadium
2,392,471	1987	Royals Stadium
2,350,181	1988	Royals Stadium
2,320,764	1986	Royals Stadium
2,288,714	1980	Royals Stadium

BALLPARK CHRONOLOGY

Kauffman Stadium (1973-present)

Capacity: 40,529.
First game: Royals 12, Texas 1 (April 10, 1973).
First batter: Dave Nelson, Rangers.
First hit: Amos Otis, Royals (single).
First run: Fred Patek, Royals (1st inning).
First home run: John Mayberry, Royals.
First winning pitcher: Paul Splittorff, Royals.
First-season attendance: 1,345,341.

Municipal Stadium (1969-72)

Capacity: 35,020.
First game: Royals 4, Minnesota 3, 12 innings (April 8, 1969).
First-season attendance: 902,414.

Note: Kauffman Stadium was known as Royals Stadium from 1973-93.

A.L. MVP

George Brett, 3B, 1980

CY YOUNG WINNERS

Bret Saberhagen, RH, 1985
Bret Saberhagen, RH, 1989
David Cone, RH, 1994

ROOKIES OF THE YEAR

Lou Piniella, OF, 1969
Bob Hamelin, DH, 1994
Carlos Beltran, OF, 1999

RETIRED UNIFORMS

No.	*Name*	*Pos.*
5	George Brett	3B
10	Dick Howser	Man.
20	Frank White	2B

Hal McRae was a key contributor to the Royals' 1970s success.

HISTORY

MILESTONE PERFORMANCES

25-plus home runs
36—Steve Balboni 1985
35—Gary Gaetti 1995
34—John Mayberry 1975
Danny Tartabull 1987
Dean Palmer 1998
33—Jermaine Dye 2000
32—Bo Jackson 1989
31—Danny Tartabull 1991
30—George Brett 1985
Chili Davis 1997
29—Steve Balboni 1986
Mike Sweeney 2000
28—Steve Balboni 1984
Bo Jackson 1990
Jeff King 1997
27—Hal McRae 1982
Bob Oliver 1970
Jermaine Dye 1999
26—John Mayberry 1973
Amos Otis 1973
Danny Tartabull 1988
25—John Mayberry 1972
George Brett 1983
Bo Jackson 1988

100-plus RBIs
144—Mike Sweeney 2000
133—Hal McRae 1982
119—Dean Palmer 1998
Jermaine Dye 1999
118—George Brett 1980
Jermaine Dye 2000
112—Al Cowens 1977
Darrell Porter 1979
George Brett 1985
Jeff King 1997
108—Carlos Beltran 1999
107—George Brett 1979
106—John Mayberry 1975
Joe Randa 2000
105—Bo Jackson 1989
103—George Brett 1988
102—Danny Tartabull 1988
Mike Sweeney 1999
101—Danny Tartabull 1987
100—John Mayberry 1972, 1973
Danny Tartabull 1991

20-plus victories
1973—Paul Splittorff 20-11
1974—Steve Busby 22-14
1977—Dennis Leonard 20-12
1978—Dennis Leonard 21-17
1980—Dennis Leonard 20-11
1985—Bret Saberhagen 20-6
1988—Mark Gubicza 20-8
1989—Bret Saberhagen 23-6

A.L. home run champions
None

A.L. RBI champions
1982—Hal McRae 133

A.L. batting champions
1976—George Brett .... .333
1980—George Brett .... .390
1982—Willie Wilson .... .332
1990—George Brett .... .329

A.L. ERA champions
1989—Bret Saberhagen 2.16
1993—Kevin Appier 2.56

A.L. strikeout champions
None

No-hit pitchers
(9 innings or more)
1973—Steve Busby .... 3-0 vs. Detroit
1974—Steve Busby .... 2-0 vs. Milwaukee
1977—Jim Colborn .... 6-0 vs. Texas
1991—Bret Saberhagen .... 7-0 vs. Chicago

Longest hitting streaks
30—George Brett 1980
27—Jose Offerman 1998
25—George Brett 1983
Mike Sweeney 1999
22—Brian McRae 1991
19—Amos Otis 1974
18—Lou Piniella 1970
Ed Kirkpatrick 1973
Willie Wilson 1984
Gregg Jefferies 1992
Joe Randa 1999
17—Hal McRae 1974
Willie Wilson 1982
Kevin Seitzer 1990
Kevin McReynolds 1992
Vince Coleman 1995
16—John Mayberry 1975
Al Cowens 1977
George Brett 1987
George Brett 1990
Gregg Jefferies 1992
Jose Lind 1994
Johnny Damon 1999, 2000
Mike Sweeney 1999, 2000
15—Willie Wilson 1981
George Brett 1985
Kevin Seitzer 1989
Carlos Febles 2000

Frank White, an eight-time Gold Glove-winning second baseman, spent his entire 17-year career with the Royals.

INDIVIDUAL SEASON, GAME RECORDS

Lefthander Paul Splittorff, who spent 15 popular years in Kansas City, holds several career team records.

SEASON

Batting

At-bats	705	Willie Wilson	1980
Runs	136	Johnny Damon	2000
Hits	230	Willie Wilson	1980
Singles	184	Willie Wilson	1980
Doubles	54	Hal McRae	1977
Triples	21	Willie Wilson	1985
Home runs	36	Steve Balboni	1985
Home runs, rookie	24	Bob Hamelin	1994
Grand slams	3	Danny Tartabull	1988
Total bases	363	George Brett	1979
RBIs	144	Mike Sweeney	2000
Walks	122	John Mayberry	1973
Most strikeouts	172	Bo Jackson	1989
Fewest strikeouts	22	George Brett	1980
Batting average	.390	George Brett	1980
Slugging pct.	.664	George Brett	1980
Stolen bases	83	Willie Wilson	1979

Pitching

Games	84	Dan Quisenberry	1985
Complete games	21	Dennis Leonard	1977
Innings	294.2	Dennis Leonard	1978
Wins	23	Bret Saberhagen	1989
Losses	19	Paul Splittorff	1974
Winning pct.	.793 (23-6)	Bret Saberhagen	1989
Walks	120	Mark Gubicza	1987
Strikeouts	244	Dennis Leonard	1977
Shutouts	6	Roger Nelson	1972
Home runs allowed	37	Tim Belcher	1998
Lowest ERA	2.08	Roger Nelson	1972
Saves	45	Dan Quisenberry	1983
		Jeff Montgomery	1993

GAME

Batting

Runs	5	Tony Solaita	6-18-75
		Tom Poquette	6-15-76
Hits	6	Bob Oliver	5-4-69
		Kevin Seitzer	8-2-87
Doubles	4	Johnny Damon	7-18-2000
Triples	2	Last by Johnny Damon	9-8-2000
Home runs	3	Last by Danny Tartabull	7-6-91
RBIs	7	Last by Johnny Damon	8-10-96
Total bases	13	George Brett	4-20-83
		Kevin Seitzer	8-2-87
Stolen bases	5	Amos Otis	9-7-71

HISTORY

CAREER LEADERS

BATTING

Games

George Brett	2,707
Frank White	2,324
Amos Otis	1,891
Hal McRae	1,837
Willie Wilson	1,787
Fred Patek	1,245
John Mayberry	897
Mike Macfarlane	887
Cookie Rojas	880
John Wathan	860

At-bats

George Brett	10,349
Frank White	7,859
Amos Otis	7,050
Willie Wilson	6,799
Hal McRae	6,568
Fred Patek	4,305
John Mayberry	3,131
Cookie Rojas	3,072
Johnny Damon	3,057
Mike Macfarlane	2,794

Runs

George Brett	1,583
Amos Otis	1,074
Willie Wilson	1,060
Frank White	912
Hal McRae	873
Fred Patek	571
Johnny Damon	504
John Mayberry	459
Kevin Seitzer	408
Al Cowens	373

Hits

George Brett	3,154
Frank White	2,006
Amos Otis	1,977
Willie Wilson	1,968
Hal McRae	1,924
Fred Patek	1,036
Johnny Damon	894
Cookie Rojas	824
John Mayberry	816
Kevin Seitzer	809

Doubles

George Brett	665
Hal McRae	449
Frank White	407
Amos Otis	365
Willie Wilson	241
Fred Patek	182
Mike Macfarlane	174
Johnny Damon	156
Danny Tartabull	141
John Mayberry	139
Cookie Rojas	139

Triples

George Brett	137
Willie Wilson	133
Amos Otis	65
Hal McRae	63
Frank White	58
Johnny Damon	47
Al Cowens	44
Fred Patek	41
Brian McRae	32
U.L. Washington	28

Home runs

George Brett	317
Amos Otis	193
Hal McRae	169
Frank White	160
John Mayberry	143
Danny Tartabull	124
Steve Balboni	119
Bo Jackson	109
Mike Macfarlane	103
Willie Aikens	77

Total bases

George Brett	5,044
Amos Otis	3,051
Frank White	3,009
Hal McRae	3,006
Willie Wilson	2,595
John Mayberry	1,404
Fred Patek	1,384
Johnny Damon	1,339
Mike Macfarlane	1,231
Danny Tartabull	1,205

Runs batted in

George Brett	1,595
Hal McRae	1,012
Amos Otis	992
Frank White	886
John Mayberry	552
Willie Wilson	509
Danny Tartabull	425
Mike Macfarlane	398
Fred Patek	382
Al Cowens	374

Extra-base hits

George Brett	1,119
Hal McRae	681
Frank White	625
Amos Otis	623
Willie Wilson	414
Mike Macfarlane	293
John Mayberry	292
Danny Tartabull	274
Johnny Damon	268
Fred Patek	251

Batting average

(Minimum 500 games)

George Brett	.305
Mike Sweeney	.302
Kevin Seitzer	.294
Wally Joyner	.293
Hal McRae	.293
Johnny Damon	.292
Danny Tartabull	.290
Willie Wilson	.289
Lou Piniella	.286
Willie Aikens	.282

Stolen bases

Willie Wilson	612
Amos Otis	340
Fred Patek	336
George Brett	201
Frank White	178
Johnny Damon	156
Tom Goodwin	150
U.L. Washington	120
Hal McRae	105
John Wathan	105

PITCHING

Earned-run average

(Minimum 500 innings)

Dan Quisenberry	2.55
Steve Farr	3.05
Jeff Montgomery	3.20
Bret Saberhagen	3.21
Kevin Appier	3.46
Al Fitzmorris	3.46
Marty Pattin	3.48
Dick Drago	3.52
Doug Bird	3.56
Charlie Leibrandt	3.60

Wins

Paul Splittorff	166
Dennis Leonard	144
Mark Gubicza	132
Kevin Appier	114
Larry Gura	111
Bret Saberhagen	110
Tom Gordon	79
Charlie Leibrandt	76
Steve Busby	70
Al Fitzmorris	70

Losses

Paul Splittorff	143
Mark Gubicza	135
Dennis Leonard	106
Kevin Appier	89
Larry Gura	78
Bret Saberhagen	78
Tom Gordon	71
Dick Drago	70
Charlie Leibrandt	61
Bud Black	57

Innings pitched

Paul Splittorff	2,554.2
Mark Gubicza	2,218.2
Dennis Leonard	2,187.0
Kevin Appier	1,820.2
Larry Gura	1,701.1
Bret Saberhagen	1,660.1
Charlie Leibrandt	1,257.0
Tom Gordon	1,149.2
Dick Drago	1,134.0
Al Fitzmorris	1,098.0

Strikeouts

Kevin Appier	1,451
Mark Gubicza	1,366
Dennis Leonard	1,323
Bret Saberhagen	1,093
Paul Splittorff	1,057
Tom Gordon	999
Jeff Montgomery	720
Steve Busby	659
Larry Gura	633
Charlie Leibrandt	618

Bases on balls

Mark Gubicza	783
Paul Splittorff	780
Kevin Appier	624
Dennis Leonard	622
Tom Gordon	587
Larry Gura	503
Steve Busby	433
Al Fitzmorris	359
Charlie Leibrandt	359
Bret Saberhagen	331

Games

Jeff Montgomery	686
Dan Quisenberry	573
Paul Splittorff	429
Mark Gubicza	382
Dennis Leonard	312
Larry Gura	310
Doug Bird	292
Steve Farr	289
Kevin Appier	281
Hipolito Pichardo	281

Shutouts

Dennis Leonard	23
Paul Splittorff	17
Mark Gubicza	16
Larry Gura	14
Bret Saberhagen	14
Al Fitzmorris	11
Kevin Appier	10
Dick Drago	10
Charlie Leibrandt	10
Steve Busby	7
Roger Nelson	7
Jim Rooker	7

Saves

Jeff Montgomery	304
Dan Quisenberry	238
Doug Bird	58
Steve Farr	49
Ted Abernathy	40
Al Hrabosky	31
Tom Burgmeier	28
Mark Littell	28
Steve Mingori	27
Gene Garber	26

TEAM SEASON, GAME RECORDS

SEASON

Batting

Most at-bats	5,714	1980
Most runs	879	2000
Fewest runs	586	1969
Most hits	1,644	2000
Most singles	1,193	1980
Most doubles	316	1990
Most triples	79	1979
Most home runs	168	1987
Fewest home runs	65	1976
Most grand slams	7	1991
Most pinch-hit home runs	6	1995
Most total bases	2,440	1977
Most stolen bases	218	1976
Highest batting average	.288	2000
Lowest batting average	.240	1969
Highest slugging pct	.436	1977

Pitching

Lowest ERA	3.21	1976
Highest ERA	5.48	2000
Most complete games	54	1974
Most shutouts	16	1972
Most saves	50	1984
Most walks	693	2000
Most strikeouts	1,006	1990

Fielding

Most errors	167	1973
Fewest errors	91	1997
Most double plays	192	1973
Highest fielding average	.985	1997

General

Most games won	102	1977
Most games lost	97	1970, 1999
Highest win pct	.630	1977
Lowest win pct	.398	1999

GAME, INNING

Batting

Most runs, game	23	4-6-74
Most runs, inning	11	8-6-79, 8-2-86
Most hits, game	24	6-15-76
Most home runs, game	6	7-14-91
Most total bases, game	37	9-12-82, 7-18-2000

Center fielder Amos Otis posted career numbers second only to George Brett among Royals players.

ROYALS YEAR-BY-YEAR

Year	W	L	Place	Games Back	Manager	Leaders: Batting avg.	Hits	Home runs	RBIs	Wins	ERA
						WEST DIVISION					
1969	69	93	4th	28	Gordon	Piniella, .282	Foy, 139	Kirkpatrick, 14	Piniella, 68	Bunker, 12	Drabowsky, 2.94
1970	65	97	*4th	33	Metro, Lemon	Piniella, .301	Otis, 176	Oliver, 27	Oliver, 99	Rooker, 10	Johnson, 3.07
1971	85	76	2nd	16	Lemon	Otis, .301	Otis, 167	Otis, 15	Otis, 79	Drago, 17	Splittorff, 2.68
1972	76	78	4th	16½	Lemon	Piniella, .312	Piniella, 179	Mayberry, 25	Mayberry, 100	Drago, Splittorff, 12	Nelson, 2.08
1973	88	74	2nd	6	McKeon	Otis, .300	Otis, 175	Mayberry, Otis, 26	Mayberry, 100	Splittorff, 20	Bird, 2.99
1974	77	85	5th	13	McKeon	H. McRae, .310	H. McRae, 167	Mayberry, 22	H. McRae, 88	Busby, 22	Bird, 2.73
1975	91	71	2nd	7	McKeon, Herzog	Brett, .308	Brett, 195	Mayberry, 34	Mayberry, 106	Busby, 18	Busby, 3.08
1976	90	72	†1st	+2½	Herzog	Brett, .333	Brett, 215	Otis, 18	Mayberry, 95	Leonard, 17	Littell, 2.08
1977	102	60	†1st	+8	Herzog	Brett, .312	H. McRae, 191	Cowens, Mayberry, 23	Cowens, 112	Leonard, 20	Leonard, 3.04
1978	92	70	†1st	+5	Herzog	Otis, .298	H. McRae, 170	Otis, 22	Otis, 96	Leonard, 21	Gura, 2.72
1979	85	77	2nd	3	Herzog	Brett, .329	Brett, 212	Brett, 23	Porter, 112	Splittorff, 15	Busby, 3.63
1980	97	65	‡1st	+14	Frey	Brett, .390	Wilson, 230	Brett, 24	Brett, 118	Leonard, 20	Gura, 2.95
1981	50	53	§5th/1st	—	Frey, Howser	Brett, .314	Wilson, 133	Aikens, 17	Otis, 57	Leonard, 13	Gura, 2.72
1982	90	72	2nd	3	Howser	Wilson, .332	Wilson, 194	H. McRae, 27	H. McRae, 133	Gura, 18	Quisenberry, 2.57
1983	79	83	2nd	20	Howser	H. McRae, .311	H. McRae, 183	Brett, 25	Brett, 93	Splittorff, 13	Quisenberry, 1.94
1984	84	78	†1st	+3	Howser	Wilson, .301	Wilson, 163	Balboni, 28	Balboni, 77	Black, 17	Quisenberry, 2.64
1985	91	71	‡1st	+1	Howser	Brett, .335	Brett, 184	Balboni, 36	Brett, 112	Saberhagen, 20	Quisenberry, 2.37
1986	76	86	*3rd	16	Howser, Ferraro	Brett, .290	Wilson, 170	Balboni, 29	Balboni, 88	Leibrandt, 14	Farr, 3.13
1987	83	79	2nd	2	Gardner, Wathan	Seitzer, .323	Seitzer, 207	Tartabull, 34	Tartabull, 101	Saberhagen, 18	Saberhagen, 3.36
1988	84	77	3rd	19½	Wathan	Brett, .306	Brett, 180	Tartabull, 26	Brett, 103	Gubicza, 20	Gubicza, 2.70
1989	92	70	2nd	7	Wathan	Eisenreich, .293	Seitzer, 168	Jackson, 32	Jackson 105	Saberhagen, 23	Saberhagen, 2.16
1990	75	86	6th	27½	Wathan	Brett, .329	Brett, 179	Jackson, 28	Brett, 87	Farr, 13	Farr, 1.98
1991	82	80	6th	13	Wathan, Schaefer, H. McRae	Tartabull, .316	B. McRae, 164	Tartabull, 31	Tartabull, 100	Appier, Saberhagen, 13	Montgomery, 2.90
1992	72	90	*5th	24	H. McRae	Brett, Jefferies, .285	Jefferies, 172	Macfarlane, 17	Jefferies, 75	Appier, 15	Appier, 2.46
1993	84	78	3rd	10	H. McRae	Joyner, .292	B. McRae, 177	Macfarlane, 20	Brett, 75	Appier, 18	Appier, 2.56
						CENTRAL DIVISION					
1994	64	51	3rd	4	H. McRae	Joyner, .311	B. McRae, 119	Hamelin, 24	Hamelin, 65	Cone, 16	Cone, 2.94
1995	70	74	2nd	30	Boone	Joyner, .310	Joyner, 144	Gaetti, 35	Gaetti, 96	Appier, 15	Gubicza, 3.75
1996	75	86	5th	24	Boone	Offerman, .303	Offerman, 170	Paquette, 22	Paquette, 67	Belcher, 15	Rosado, 3.21
1997	67	94	5th	19	Boone, Muser	Offerman, .297	Bell, 167	Davis, 30	King, 112	Belcher, 13	Appier, 3.40
1998	72	89	3rd	16½	Muser	Offerman, .315	Offerman, 191	Palmer, 34	Palmer, 119	Belcher, 14	Belcher, 4.27
1999	64	97	4th	32½	Muser	Sweeney, .322	Randa, 197	Dye, 27	Dye, 119	Rosado, Suppan, 10	Rosado, 3.85
2000	77	85	4th	18	Muser	Sweeney, .333	Damon, 214	Dye, 33	Sweeney, 144	Suppan, 10	Suzuki, 4.34

* Tied for position. † Lost Championship Series. ‡ Won Championship Series. § First half 20-30; second half 30-23.

Note: Batting average minimum 350 at-bats; ERA minimum 90 innings pitched.

Roger Nelson

THE ROYALS were born as part of a four-team 1969 expansion that included the Seattle Pilots in the American League and the San Diego Padres and Montreal Expos in the National League. The franchise came to life on January 11, 1968, when Kansas City businessman Ewing Kauffman was awarded a team that would compete in the A.L.'s newly-created Western Division.

The Royals grabbed righthanded pitcher Roger Nelson with their first pick of the expansion draft and went on to select 30 players, concentrating heavily on youth. The team won its Major League debut on April 8, 1969, when Joe Keough's 12th-inning sacrifice fly produced a 4-3 victory over Minnesota at Kansas City's Municipal Stadium.

Expansion draft (October 15, 1968)

Players

Player	Team	Position
Jerry Adair	Boston	second base
Mike Fiore	Baltimore	first base
Joe Foy	Boston	third base
Bill Harris	Cleveland	second base
Dan Haynes	Chicago	first base
Fran Healy	Cleveland	catcher
Jackie Hernandez	Minnesota	shortstop
Pat Kelly	Minnesota	outfield
Joe Keough	Oakland	outfield
Scott Northey	Chicago	outfield
Bob Oliver	Minnesota	first base
Ellie Rodriguez	New York	catcher
Paul Schaal	California	third base
Steve Whitaker	New York	outfield

Pitchers

Ike Brookens	Washington	righthander
Wally Bunker	Baltimore	righthander
Tom Burgmeier	California	lefthander
Bill Butler	Detroit	lefthander
Jerry Cram	Minnesota	righthander
Moe Drabowsky	Baltimore	righthander
Dick Drago	Detroit	righthander
Al Fitzmorris	Chicago	righthander
Mike Hedlund	Cleveland	righthander
Steve Jones	Washington	lefthander
Dave Morehead	Boston	righthander
*Roger Nelson	Baltimore	righthander
Don O'Riley	Oakland	righthander
Jim Rooker	New York	lefthander
Jon Warden	Detroit	lefthander
Hoyt Wilhelm	Chicago	righthander

*First pick

Opening day lineup

April 8, 1969
Lou Piniella, center field
Jerry Adair, second base
Ed Kirkpatrick, left field
Joe Foy, third base
Chuck Harrison, first base
Bob Oliver, right field
Ellie Rodriguez, catcher
Jackie Hernandez, shortstop
Wally Bunker, pitcher

Lou Piniella

Royals firsts

First hit: Lou Piniella, April 8, 1969, vs. Minnesota (double)
First home run: Mike Fiore, April 13, 1969, vs. Oakland
First RBI: Jerry Adair, April 8, 1969, vs. Minnesota
First win: Moe Drabowsky, April 8, 1969, vs. Minnesota
First shutout: Roger Nelson, May 21, 1969, 4-0 at Cleveland

MINNESOTA TWINS

Third baseman Harmon Killebrew.

FRANCHISE CHRONOLOGY

First season: 1901, in Washington, as a member of the new American League. The Senators recorded a 5-1 victory over Philadelphia in their major league debut and went on to post a 61-72 record, good for sixth place in the eight-team A.L. field.

1902-1960: To say the Senators struggled through their 60-year existence is an understatement. Through the 1911 season, the Senators never finished higher than sixth place and they failed to win their first pennant until 1924. In their six Washington decades, they qualified for the World Series three times, winning once—a 1924 victory over the Giants.

1961-present: The Senators were shifted to Minnesota after the 1960 season as part of a complicated A.L. expansion that brought the Angels and another Washington Senators team into existence. The Twins shut out the Yankees, 6-0, in their first game and went on to record a 70-90 record. The change of scenery proved agreeable. By 1965, the Twins were consistent contenders who would win three pennants, two World Series and four West Division titles over the next three decades. The Twins were assigned to the Central Division when baseball adopted its three-division format in 1994.

TWINS VS. OPPONENTS BY DECADE

	A's	Indians	Orioles	Red Sox	Tigers	White Sox	Yankees	Angels	Rangers	Brewers	Royals	Blue Jays	Mariners	Devil Rays	Interleague	Decade Record
1901-09	56-128	72-118	81-108	76-113	72-114	57-130	66-122									480-833
1910-19	101-108	123-92	119-96	93-115	100-116	106-109	113-101									755-737
1920-29	108-105	106-113	108-111	135-82	113-107	125-95	97-122									792-735
1930-39	124-91	104-114	135-84	128-90	102-118	117-101	96-124									806-722
1940-49	125-95	104-115	110-110	86-133	90-130	93-124	69-151									677-858
1950-59	107-113	79-141	103-117	100-120	99-121	79-141	73-145									640-898
1960-69	105-79	82-96	87-91	104-74	90-88	101-83	90-87	82-79	99-56	12-6	10-8					862-747
1970-79	91-76	56-58	52-64	47-70	68-48	89-76	44-72	77-89	80-76	75-54	84-85	26-6	23-20			812-794
1980-89	58-69	56-55	51-63	53-62	54-66	66-57	43-71	57-66	64-65	52-68	62-68	50-64	67-59			733-833
1990-99	58-60	52-70	45-63	62-48	60-53	48-71	50-58	61-54	50-70	46-52	61-64	38-72	51-65	12-9	24-24	718-833
2000-	5-7	8-5	3-6	2-8	6-7	5-7	5-5	3-7	8-4		5-7	5-4	3-9	4-6	7-11	69-93
Totals	938-931	842-977	894-913	886-915	848-962	892-1000	746-1058	280-295	301-271	185-180	222-232	119-146	144-153	16-15	31-35	7344-8083

Interleague results: 5-7 vs. Cubs; 5-7 vs. Reds; 6-5 vs. Astros; 6-6 vs. Pirates; 6-6 vs. Cardinals; 3-4 vs. Brewers.

MANAGERS

(Washington Senators, 1901-1960)

Name	*Years*	*Record*
Jimmy Manning	1901	61-72
Tom Loftus	1902-03	104-169
Patsy Donovan	1904	38-113
Jake Stahl	1905-06	119-182
Joe Cantillon	1907-09	158-297
Jimmy McAleer	1910-11	130-175
Clark Griffith	1912-20	693-646
George McBride	1921	80-73
Clyde Milan	1922	69-85
Donie Bush	1923	75-78
Bucky Harris	1924-28, 1935-42, 1950-54	1336-1416
Walter Johnson	1929-32	350-264
Joe Cronin	1933-34	165-139
Ossie Bluege	1943-47	375-394
Joe Kuhel	1948-49	106-201
Chuck Dressen	1955-57	116-212
Cookie Lavagetto	1957-61	271-384
Sam Mele	1961-67	524-436
Cal Ermer	1967-68	145-129
Billy Martin	1969	97-65
Bill Rigney	1970-72	208-184
Frank Quilici	1972-75	280-287
Gene Mauch	1976-80	378-394
Johnny Goryl	1980-81	34-38
Billy Gardner	1981-85	268-353
Ray Miller	1985-86	109-130
Tom Kelly	1986-2000	1055-1167

WORLD SERIES CHAMPIONS

Year	*Loser*	*Length*	*MVP*
1924	N.Y. Giants	7 games	None
1987	St. Louis	7 games	Viola
1991	Atlanta	7 games	Morris

A.L. PENNANT WINNERS

Year	*Record*	*Manager*	*Series Result*
1924	92-62	Harris	Defeated Giants
1925	96-55	Harris	Lost to Pirates
1933	99-53	Cronin	Lost to Giants
1965	102-60	Mele	Lost to Dodgers
1987	85-77	Kelly	Defeated Cardinals
1991	95-67	Kelly	Defeated Braves

WEST DIVISION CHAMPIONS

Year	*Record*	*Manager*	*ALCS Result*
1969	97-65	Martin	Lost to Orioles
1970	98-64	Rigney	Lost to Orioles
1987	85-77	Kelly	Defeated Tigers
1991	95-67	Kelly	Defeated Blue Jays

ATTENDANCE HIGHS

Total	*Season*	*Park*
3,030,672	1988	Metrodome
2,482,428	1992	Metrodome
2,293,842	1991	Metrodome
2,277,438	1989	Metrodome
2,081,976	1987	Metrodome

BALLPARK CHRONOLOGY

Hubert H. Humphrey Metrodome (1982-present)

Capacity: 48,678.
First game: Seattle 11, Twins 7 (April 6, 1982).
First batter: Julio Cruz, Mariners.
First hit: Dave Engle, Twins (home run).
First run: Dave Engle, Twins (1st inning).
First home run: Dave Engle, Twins.
First winning pitcher: Floyd Bannister, Mariners.
First-season attendance: 921,186.

American League Park, Washington, D.C. (1901-02)

Capacity: 10,000.
First game: Senators 5, Baltimore 2 (April 29, 1901).
First-season attendance: 161,661.

Griffith Stadium, Washington, D.C. (1903-60)

Capacity: 27,410.
First game: Senators 3, New York 1 (April 22, 1903).
First-season attendance: 128,878.

Metropolitan Stadium, Minnesota (1961-81)

Capacity: 45,919.
First game: Washington 5, Twins 3 (April 21, 1961).
First-season attendance: 1,256,723.

Note: Griffith Stadium was known as National Park from 1901-20.

A.L. MVPs

Zoilo Versalles, SS, 1965
Harmon Killebrew, 1B-3B, 1969
Rod Carew, 1B, 1977

CY YOUNG WINNERS

Jim Perry, RH, 1970
Frank Viola, LH, 1988

ROOKIES OF THE YEAR

Albie Pearson, OF, 1958
Bob Allison, OF, 1959
Tony Oliva, OF, 1964
Rod Carew, 2B, 1967
*John Castino, 3B, 1979
Chuck Knoblauch, 2B, 1991
Marty Cordova, OF, 1995

* Co-winner

MANAGER OF THE YEAR

Tom Kelly, 1991

RETIRED UNIFORMS

No.	*Name*	*Pos.*
3	Harmon Killebrew	3B-1B
6	Tony Oliva	OF
14	Kent Hrbek	1B
29	Rod Carew	2B-1B
34	Kirby Puckett	OF

The Twins' 1970 staff featured (left to right) Dave Boswell, Jim Perry, Jim Kaat and Luis Tiant.

HISTORY

MILESTONE PERFORMANCES

30-plus home runs

49—Harmon Killebrew 1964, 1969
48—Harmon Killebrew 1962
46—Harmon Killebrew 1961
45—Harmon Killebrew 1963
44—Harmon Killebrew 1967
42—Roy Sievers 1957
Harmon Killebrew 1959
41—Harmon Killebrew 1970
39—Roy Sievers 1958
Harmon Killebrew 1966
38—Jim Lemon 1960
35—Bob Allison 1963
34—Gary Gaetti 1986
Kent Hrbek 1987
33—Jim Lemon 1959
Jimmie Hall 1963
32—Bob Allison 1964
Tony Oliva 1964
Tom Brunansky 1984, 1987
31—Harmon Killebrew 1960
Kirby Puckett 1986
Gary Gaetti 1987
30—Bob Allison 1959

100-plus RBIs

140—Harmon Killebrew 1969
129—Goose Goslin 1924
126—Joe Cronin 1930, 1931
Harmon Killebrew 1962
122—Harmon Killebrew 1961
121—Kirby Puckett 1988
120—Goose Goslin 1927
119—Harmon Killebrew 1971
Larry Hisle 1977
118—Joe Cronin 1933
Joe Kuhel 1936
116—Joe Cronin 1932
Heinie Manush 1932
115—Mickey Vernon 1953
114—Zeke Bonura 1938
Roy Sievers 1957
113—Goose Goslin 1925
Harmon Killebrew 1967, 1970
Paul Molitor 1996
112—Kirby Puckett 1994
111—Harmon Killebrew 1964
Marty Cordova 1996
110—Harmon Killebrew 1966
Kirby Puckett 1992
109—Gary Gaetti 1987
108—Goose Goslin 1926
Roy Sievers 1958
Gary Gaetti 1986
107—Joe Kuhel 1933
Tony Oliva 1970
Kent Hrbek 1984
106—Roy Sievers 1955
105—Harmon Killebrew 1959
Bob Allison 1961
102—Goose Goslin 1928
Roy Sievers 1954
Bob Allison 1962
101—Joe Cronin 1934
Cecil Travis 1941
Tony Oliva 1969
100—Buddy Myer 1935
Stan Spence 1944
Jim Lemon 1959, 1960
Rod Carew 1977

20-plus victories

1910—Walter Johnson 25-17
1911—Walter Johnson 25-13
1912—Walter Johnson 33-12
Bob Groom 24-13
1913—Walter Johnson 36-7
1914—Walter Johnson 28-18
1915—Walter Johnson 27-13
1916—Walter Johnson 25-20
1917—Walter Johnson 23-16
1918—Walter Johnson 23-13
1919—Walter Johnson 20-14
1924—Walter Johnson 23-7
1925—Stan Coveleski 20-5
Walter Johnson 20-7
1932—General Crowder 26-13
Monte Weaver 22-10
1933—General Crowder 24-15
Earl Whitehill 22-8
1939—Dutch Leonard 20-8
1945—Roger Wolff 20-10
1953—Bob Porterfield 22-10
1962—Camilo Pascual 20-11
1963—Camilo Pascual 21-9
1965—Mudcat Grant 21-7
1966—Jim Kaat 25-13
1967—Dean Chance 20-14
1969—Jim Perry 20-6
Dave Boswell 20-12
1970—Jim Perry 24-12
1973—Bert Blyleven 20-17
1977—Dave Goltz 20-11
1979—Jerry Koosman 20-13
1988—Frank Viola 24-7
1991—Scott Erickson 20-8
1997—Brad Radke 20-10

A.L. home run champions

1957—Roy Sievers 42
1959—Harmon Killebrew *42
1962—Harmon Killebrew 48
1963—Harmon Killebrew 45
1964—Harmon Killebrew 49
1967—Harmon Killebrew *44
1969—Harmon Killebrew 49

* Tied for league lead

A.L. RBI champions

1924—Goose Goslin 129
1957—Roy Sievers 114
1962—Harmon Killebrew 126
1969—Harmon Killebrew 140
1971—Harmon Killebrew 119
1977—Larry Hisle 119
1994—Kirby Puckett 112

A.L. batting champions

1902—Ed Delahanty .376
1928—Goose Goslin .379
1935—Buddy Myer .349
1946—Mickey Vernon .353
1953—Mickey Vernon .337
1964—Tony Oliva .323
1965—Tony Oliva .321
1969—Rod Carew .332
1971—Tony Oliva .337
1972—Rod Carew .318
1973—Rod Carew .350
1974—Rod Carew .364
1975—Rod Carew .359
1977—Rod Carew .388
1978—Rod Carew .333
1989—Kirby Puckett .339

A.L. ERA champions

1912—Walter Johnson 1.39
1913—Walter Johnson 1.09
1918—Walter Johnson 1.27
1919—Walter Johnson 1.49
1924—Walter Johnson 2.72
1925—Stan Coveleski 2.84
1928—Garland Braxton 2.51
1988—Allan Anderson 2.45

A.L. strikeout champions

1910—Walter Johnson 313
1912—Walter Johnson 303
1913—Walter Johnson 243
1914—Walter Johnson 225
1915—Walter Johnson 203
1916—Walter Johnson 228
1917—Walter Johnson 188
1918—Walter Johnson 162
1919—Walter Johnson 147
1921—Walter Johnson 143
1923—Walter Johnson 130
1924—Walter Johnson 158
1942—Bobo Newsom *113
1961—Camilo Pascual 221
1962—Camilo Pascual 206
1963—Camilo Pascual 202
1985—Bert Blyleven *206

* Tied for league lead

No-hit pitchers

(9 innings or more)

1920—Walter Johnson 1-0 vs. Boston
1931—Bobby Burke 5-0 vs. Boston
1962—Jack Kralick 1-0 vs. Kansas City
1967—Dean Chance 2-1 vs. Cleveland
1994—Scott Erickson 6-0 vs. Milwaukee
1999—Eric Milton 7-0 vs. Anaheim

Longest hitting streaks

33—Heinie Manush 1933
31—Sam Rice 1924
Ken Landreaux 1980
29—Sam Rice 1920
28—Sam Rice 1930
26—Heinie Manush 1933
25—Goose Goslin 1928
Brian Harper 1990
24—Cecil Travis 1941
Lenny Green 1961
23—Kent Hrbek 1982
Marty Cordova 1996
22—Joe Cronin 1932
Heinie Manush 1932
Mickey Vernon 1946
Shane Mack 1992
21—Eddie Foster 1918
Buddy Myer 1935
Taffy Wright 1938
20—Joe Cronin 1930
George Case 1939
Jackie Jensen 1952
Mickey Vernon 1953
Ted Uhlaender 1969
Chuck Knoblauch 1991

INDIVIDUAL SEASON, GAME RECORDS

Longtime ace Walter Johnson (left) delivered his powerful fastball to catcher Gabby Steet from 1908-11.

SEASON

Batting

At-bats	691	Kirby Puckett	1985
Runs	140	Chuck Knoblauch	1996
Hits	239	Rod Carew	1977
Singles	182	Sam Rice	1925
Doubles	51	Mickey Vernon	1946
Triples	20	Goose Goslin	1925
		Cristian Guzman	2000
Home runs	49	Harmon Killebrew	1964, 1969
Home runs, rookie	33	Jimmie Hall	1963
Grand slams	3	4 times	
		Last by Kirby Puckett	1992
Total bases	374	Tony Oliva	1964
RBIs	140	Harmon Killebrew	1969
Walks	151	Eddie Yost	1956
Most strikeouts	145	Bob Darwin	1972
Fewest strikeouts	9	Sam Rice	1929
Batting average	.388	Rod Carew	1977
Slugging pct.	.614	Goose Goslin	1928
Stolen bases	88	Clyde Milan	1912

Pitching

Games	90	Mike Marshall	1979
Complete games	38	Walter Johnson	1910
Innings	374	Walter Johnson	1910
Wins	36	Walter Johnson	1913
Losses	26	Jack Townsend	1904
		Bob Groom	1909
Winning pct.	.837	Walter Johnson	1913
Walks	146	Bobo Newsom	1936
Strikeouts	313	Walter Johnson	1910
Shutouts	11	Walter Johnson	1913
Home runs allowed	50	Bert Blyleven	1986
Lowest ERA	1.14	Walter Johnson	1913
Saves	42	Jeff Reardon	1988
		Rick Aguilera	1991

GAME

Batting

Runs	5	Last by Paul Molitor	4-26-96
Hits	6	Last by Kirby Puckett	5-23-91
Doubles	4	Kirby Puckett	5-13-89
Triples	3	Last by Ken Landreaux	7-3-80
Home runs	3	Last by Tony Oliva	7-3-73
RBIs	8	Last by Randy Bush	5-20-89
Total bases	14	Kirby Puckett	8-30-87
Stolen bases	5	Clyde Milan	6-14-12

CAREER LEADERS

BATTING

Games

Harmon Killebrew	2,329
Sam Rice	2,307
Joe Judge	2,084
Clyde Milan	1,982
Ossie Bluege	1,867
Mickey Vernon	1,805
Kirby Puckett	1,783
Kent Hrbek	1,747
Eddie Yost	1,690
Tony Oliva	1,676

At-bats

Sam Rice	8,934
Harmon Killebrew	7,835
Joe Judge	7,663
Clyde Milan	7,359
Kirby Puckett	7,244
Mickey Vernon	6,930
Ossie Bluege	6,440
Tony Oliva	6,301
Rod Carew	6,235
Kent Hrbek	6,192

Runs

Sam Rice	1,466
Harmon Killebrew	1,258
Joe Judge	1,154
Kirby Puckett	1,071
Buddy Myer	1,037
Clyde Milan	1,004
Eddie Yost	971
Mickey Vernon	956
Rod Carew	950
Kent Hrbek	903

Hits

Sam Rice	2,889
Kirby Puckett	2,304
Joe Judge	2,291
Clyde Milan	2,100
Rod Carew	2,085
Harmon Killebrew	2,024
Mickey Vernon	1,993
Tony Oliva	1,917
Buddy Myer	1,828
Ossie Bluege	1,751

Doubles

Sam Rice	479
Joe Judge	421
Kirby Puckett	414
Mickey Vernon	391
Tony Oliva	329
Kent Hrbek	312
Rod Carew	305
Buddy Myer	305
Goose Goslin	289
Eddie Yost	282

Triples

Sam Rice	183
Joe Judge	157
Goose Goslin	125
Buddy Myer	113
Mickey Vernon	108
Clyde Milan	105
Buddy Lewis	93
Rod Carew	90
Howie Shanks	87
Cecil Travis	78

Home runs

Harmon Killebrew	559
Kent Hrbek	293
Bob Allison	256
Tony Oliva	220
Kirby Puckett	207
Gary Gaetti	201
Roy Sievers	180
Tom Brunansky	163
Jim Lemon	159
Goose Goslin	127

Total bases

Harmon Killebrew	4,026
Sam Rice	3,833
Kirby Puckett	3,453
Joe Judge	3,239
Tony Oliva	3,002
Kent Hrbek	2,976
Mickey Vernon	2,963
Rod Carew	2,792
Clyde Milan	2,601
Goose Goslin	2,579

Runs batted in

Harmon Killebrew	1,540
Kent Hrbek	1,086
Kirby Puckett	1,085
Sam Rice	1,045
Mickey Vernon	1,026
Joe Judge	1,001
Tony Oliva	947
Goose Goslin	931
Ossie Bluege	848
Bob Allison	796

Extra base hits

Harmon Killebrew	860
Sam Rice	695
Kirby Puckett	678
Joe Judge	649
Kent Hrbek	623
Mickey Vernon	620
Tony Oliva	597
Goose Goslin	541
Bob Allison	525
Gary Gaetti	478

Batting average
(Minimum 500 games)

Rod Carew	.334
Heinie Manush	.328
Sam Rice	.323
Goose Goslin	.323
Kirby Puckett	.318
John Stone	.317
Cecil Travis	.314
Shane Mack	.309
Brian Harper	.306
Joe Cronin	.304

Stolen bases

Clyde Milan	495
Sam Rice	346
George Case	321
Chuck Knoblauch	276
Rod Carew	271
Joe Judge	210
Cesar Tovar	186
Howie Shanks	177
Eddie Foster	166
Bucky Harris	166

PITCHING

Earned-run average
(Minimum 1,000 innings)

Walter Johnson	2.17
Doc Ayers	2.64
Harry Harper	2.75
Tom Hughes	3.02
Bob Groom	3.04
Jim Shaw	3.07
Jim Perry	3.15
Dutch Leonard	3.27
Bert Blyleven	3.28
Mickey Haefner	3.29

Wins

Walter Johnson	417
Jim Kaat	190
Bert Blyleven	149
Camilo Pascual	145
Jim Perry	128
Dutch Leonard	118
Firpo Marberry	117
Frank Viola	112
Case Patten	105
Alvin Crowder	98

Losses

Walter Johnson	279
Jim Kaat	159
Camilo Pascual	141
Bert Blyleven	138
Sid Hudson	130
Case Patten	127
Tom Hughes	125
Pedro Ramos	112
Tom Zachary	103
Dutch Leonard	101

Innings pitched

Walter Johnson	5,914.2
Jim Kaat	3,014.1
Bert Blyleven	2,566.2
Camilo Pascual	2,465.0
Case Patten	2,059.1
Dutch Leonard	1,899.1
Jim Perry	1,883.1
Sid Hudson	1,819.1
Tom Hughes	1,776.0
Frank Viola	1,772.2

Strikeouts

Walter Johnson	3,509
Bert Blyleven	2,035
Camilo Pascual	1,885
Jim Kaat	1,851
Frank Viola	1,214
Jim Perry	1,025
Dave Goltz	887
Tom Hughes	884
Dave Boswell	865
Brad Radke	805

Bases on balls

Walter Johnson	1,363
Camilo Pascual	909
Jim Kaat	729
Sid Hudson	720
Walt Masterson	694
Jim Shaw	688
Bert Blyleven	674
Bump Hadley	572
Firpo Marberry	568
Tom Hughes	567

Games

Walter Johnson	802
Rick Aguilera	490
Jim Kaat	484
Firpo Marberry	470
Eddie Guardado	438
Camilo Pascual	432
Jim Perry	376
Mike Trombley	360
Bert Blyleven	348
Al Worthington	327

Shutouts

Walter Johnson	110
Camilo Pascual	31
Bert Blyleven	29
Jim Kaat	23
Dutch Leonard	23
Bob Porterfield	19
Tom Hughes	17
Case Patten	17
Jim Perry	17
Jim Shaw	17

Saves

Rick Aguilera	254
Ron Davis	108
Jeff Reardon	104
Firpo Marberry	96
Al Worthington	88
Ron Perranoski	76
Mike Marshall	54
Bill Campbell	51
Doug Corbett	43
Ray Moore	38

TEAM SEASON, GAME RECORDS

SEASON

Batting

Most at-bats	5,677	1969
Most runs	892	1930
Fewest runs	380	1909
Most hits	1,633	1996
Most singles	1,209	1935
Most doubles	332	1996
Most triples	100	1932
Most home runs	225	1963
Fewest home runs	4	1917
Most grand slams	8	1938, 1961
Most pinch-hit home runs	7	1964, 1967
Most total bases	2,413	1996
Most stolen bases	287	1913
Highest batting average	.303	1925
Lowest batting average	.223	1909
Highest slugging pct	.430	1963, 1987

Pitching

Lowest ERA	2.14	1918
Highest ERA	5.76	1995
Most complete games	137	1904
Most shutouts	25	1914
Most saves	58	1970
Most walks	779	1949
Most strikeouts	1,099	1964

Fielding

Most errors	323	1901
Fewest errors	84	1988
Most double plays	203	1979
Highest fielding average	.986	1988

General

Most games won	102	1965
Most games lost	113	1904
Highest win pct	.651	1933
Lowest win pct	.252	1904

GAME, INNING

Batting

Most runs, game	24	4-24-96
Most runs, inning	12	7-10-26
Most hits, game	24	Last 6-4-94
Most home runs, game	8	8-29-63
Most total bases, game	47	8-29-63

Hard-hitting outfielder Tony Oliva was part of the Twins' offensive wrecking crew in the 1960s.

TWINS YEAR-BY-YEAR

Year	W	L	Place	Games Back	Manager	Batting avg.	Hits	Home runs	RBIs	Wins	ERA
						WASHINGTON SENATORS					
1901	61	72	6th	20½	Manning	Waldron, .322	Dungan, 179	Grady, 9	Dungan, 73	Patten, 18	Carrick, 3.75
1902	61	75	6th	22	Loftus	E. Delahanty, .376	E. Delahanty, 178	E. Delahanty, 10	E. Delahanty, 93	Orth, 19	Orth, 3.97
1903	43	94	8th	47½	Loftus	Selbach, .251	Selbach, 134	Ryan, 7	Selbach, 49	Orth, Patten, 10	Lee, 3.08
1904	38	113	8th	55½	Donovan	Stahl, .262	Cassidy, 140	Stahl, 3	Stahl, 50	Patten, 14	Patten, 3.07
1905	64	87	7th	29½	Stahl	Hickman, .311	Cassidy, 124	Stahl, 5	Stahl, 66	Hughes, 17	Hughes, 2.35
1906	55	95	7th	37½	Stahl	Hickman, .284	Anderson, 158	Hickman, 9	Anderson, 70	Patten, 19	Patten, 2.17
1907	49	102	8th	43½	Cantillon	J. Delahanty, .292	Ganley, 167	Altizer, J. Delahanty, 2	J. Delahanty, 54	Patten, 12	Johnson, 1.88
1908	67	85	7th	22½	Cantillon	Clymer, .253	Freeman, 134	Pickering, 2	Freeman, 45	Hughes, 18	Johnson, 1.64
1909	42	110	8th	56	Cantillon	Lelivelt, .292	Unglaub, 127	Unglaub, 3	Unglaub, 41	Johnson, 13	Johnson, 2.21
1910	66	85	7th	36½	McAleer	Milan, .279	Milan, 148	Elberfeld, Gessler, 2	McBride, 55	Johnson, 25	Johnson, 1.35
1911	64	90	7th	38½	McAleer	Schaefer, .334	Milan, 194	Gessler, 4	Gessler, 78	Johnson, 25	Johnson, 1.89
1912	91	61	2nd	14	Griffith	Milan, .306	Milan, 184	Moeller, 6	Gandil, 81	Johnson, 33	Johnson, 1.39
1913	90	64	2nd	6½	Griffith	Gandil, .318	Gandil, 175	Moeller, 5	Gandil, 72	Johnson, 36	Johnson, 1.14
1914	81	73	3rd	19	Griffith	Milan, .295	Foster, 174	Shanks, 4	Gandil, 75	Johnson, 28	Johnson, 1.72
1915	85	68	4th	17	Griffith	Gandil, .291	Foster, 170	Gandil, Milan, Moeller, 2	Milan, 66	Johnson, 27	Johnson, 1.55
1916	76	77	7th	14½	Griffith	Milan, .273	Milan, 154	E. Smith, 2	Shanks, 48	Johnson, 25	Johnson, 1.89
1917	74	79	5th	25½	Griffith	Rice, .302	Rice, 177	Judge, 2	Rice, 69	Johnson, 23	Ayers, 2.17
1918	72	56	3rd	4	Griffith	Milan, .290	Foster, 147	4 Tied, 1	Milan, Shanks, 56	Johnson, 23	Johnson, 1.27
1919	56	84	7th	32	Griffith	Rice, .321	Rice, 179	Menosky, 6	Rice, 71	Johnson, 20	Johnson, 1.49
1920	68	84	6th	29	Griffith	Rice, .338	Rice, 211	Roth, 9	Roth, 92	Zachary, 15	Johnson, 3.13
1921	80	73	4th	18	McBride	Rice, .330	Judge, 187	B. Miller, 9	Rice, 79	Mogridge, Zachary, 18	Mogridge, 3.00
1922	69	85	6th	25	Milan	Goslin, .324	Rice, 187	Judge, 10	Judge, 81	Mogridge, 18	Johnson, 2.99
1923	75	78	4th	23½	Bush	Rice, .316	Rice, 188	Goslin, 9	Goslin, 99	Johnson, 17	A. Russell, 3.03
1924	92	62	1st	+2	Harris	Goslin, .344	Rice, 216	Goslin, 12	Goslin, 129	Johnson, 23	Ogden, 2.58
1925	96	55	1st	+8½	Harris	Rice, .350	Rice, 227	Goslin, 18	Goslin, 113	Coveleski, Johnson, 20	Coveleski, 2.84
1926	81	69	4th	8	Harris	Goslin, .354	Rice, 216	Goslin, 17	Goslin, 108	Johnson, 15	Marberry, 3.00
1927	85	69	3rd	25	Harris	Goslin, .334	Goslin, 194	Goslin, 13	Goslin, 120	Lisenbee, 18	Hadley, 2.85
1928	75	79	4th	26	Harris	Goslin, .379	Rice, 202	Goslin, 17	Goslin, 102	S. Jones, 17	Braxton, 2.51
1929	71	81	5th	34	Johnson	Rice, .323	Rice, 199	Goslin, 18	Goslin, 91	Marberry, 19	Marberry, 3.06
1930	94	60	2nd	8	Johnson	Manush, .362	Rice, 207	Cronin, 13	Cronin, 126	Brown, 16	Liska, 3.29
1931	92	62	3rd	16	Johnson	West, .333	Manush, 189	Cronin, 12	Cronin, 126	Crowder, 18	Hadley, 3.06
1932	93	61	3rd	14	Johnson	Manush, .342	Manush, 214	Manush, 14	Cronin, Manush, 116	Crowder, 26	Crowder, 3.33
1933	99	53	1st	+7	Cronin	Manush, .336	Manush, 221	Kuhel, 11	Cronin, 118	Crowder, 24	J. Russell, 2.69
1934	66	86	7th	34	Cronin	Manush, .349	Manush, 194	Manush, 11	Cronin, 101	Whitehill, 14	Burke, 3.21
1935	67	86	6th	27	Harris	Myer, .349	Myer, 215	Powell, 6	Myer, 100	Whitehill, 14	Whitehill, 4.29
1936	82	71	4th	20	Harris	Stone, .341	Kuhel, 189	Kuhel, 16	Kuhel, 118	DeShong, 18	Appleton, 3.53
1937	73	80	6th	28½	Harris	Travis, .344	Lewis, 210	Lewis, 10	Stone, 88	DeShong, 14	Ferrell, 3.94
1938	75	76	5th	23½	Harris	Myer, .336	Lewis, 194	Bonura, 22	Bonura, 114	Ferrell, 13	Krakauskas, 3.12
1939	65	87	6th	41½	Harris	Lewis, .319	Lewis, 171	Lewis, 10	Wright, 93	Leonard, 20	Leonard, 3.54
1940	64	90	7th	26	Harris	Travis, .322	Case, 192	Walker, 13	Walker, 96	Hudson, 17	Chase, 3.23
1941	70	84	*6th	31	Harris	Travis, .359	Travis, 218	Early, 10	Travis, 101	Leonard, 18	Carrasquel, 3.44
1942	62	89	7th	39½	Harris	Spence, .323	Spence, 203	Vernon, 9	Vernon, 86	Newsom, 11	Masterson, 3.34
1943	84	69	2nd	13½	Bluege	Case, .294	Case, 180	Spence, 12	Spence, 88	Wynn, 18	Haefner, 2.29
1944	64	90	8th	25	Bluege	Spence, .316	Spence, 187	Spence, 18	Spence, 100	Leonard, 14	Niggeling, 2.32
1945	87	67	2nd	1½	Bluege	Myatt, .296	Binks, 153	Clift, 8	Binks, 81	Wolff, 20	Wolff, 2.12
1946	76	78	4th	28	Bluege	Vernon, .353	Vernon, 207	Spence, 16	Spence, 87	Haefner, 14	Wolff, 2.58
1947	64	90	7th	33	Bluege	Spence, .279	Vernon, 159	Spence, 16	Vernon, 85	Wynn, 17	Masterson, 3.13
1948	56	97	7th	40	Kuhel	Stewart, .279	Kozar, 144	Coan, Stewart, 7	Stewart, 69	Scarborough, 15	Scarborough, 2.82
1949	50	104	8th	47	Kuhel	Robinson, .294	Dente, 161	Robinson, 18	Robinson, 78	Scarborough, 13	Hittle, 4.21
1950	67	87	5th	31	Harris	Vernon, .306	Yost, 169	Noren, 14	Noren, 98	Hudson, 14	Kuzava, 3.95
1951	62	92	7th	36	Harris	Coan, .303	Coan, 163	Yost, 12	Mele, 94	Marrero, 11	Porterfield, 3.24
1952	78	76	5th	17	Harris	Jensen, .286	Jensen, 163	Yost, 12	Jensen, Vernon, 80	Porterfield, 13	Porterfield, 2.72
1953	76	76	5th	23½	Harris	Vernon, .337	Vernon, 205	Vernon, 15	Vernon, 115	Porterfield, 22	Marrero, 3.03
1954	66	88	6th	45	Harris	Busby, .298	Busby, 187	Sievers, 24	Sievers, 102	Porterfield, 13	Schmitz, 2.91
1955	53	101	8th	43	Dressen	Vernon, .301	Vernon, 162	Sievers, 25	Sievers, 106	McDermott, Porterfield, 10	Schmitz, 3.71
1956	59	95	7th	38	Dressen	Runnels, .310	Runnels, 179	Sievers, 29	Lemon, 96	Stobbs, 15	Stobbs, 3.60
1957	55	99	8th	43	Dressen, Lavagetto	Sievers, .301	Sievers, 172	Sievers, 42	Sievers, 114	Ramos, 12	Byerly, 3.13
1958	61	93	8th	31	Lavagetto	Sievers, .295	Sievers, 162	Sievers, 39	Sievers, 108	Ramos, 14	Hyde, 1.75
1959	63	91	8th	31	Lavagetto	Lemon, .279	Allison, 149	Killebrew, 42	Killebrew, 105	Pascual, 17	Pascual, 2.64
1960	73	81	5th	24	Lavagetto	Green, .294	Gardner, 152	Lemon, 38	Lemon, 100	Pascual, Stobbs, 12	Pascual, 3.03
						MINNESOTA TWINS					
1961	70	90	7th	38	Lavagetto, Mele	Battey, .302	Green, 171	Killebrew, 46	Killebrew, 122	Pascual, 15	Pascual, 3.46
1962	91	71	2nd	5	Mele	Rollins, .298	Rollins, 186	Killebrew, 48	Killebrew, 126	Pascual, 20	Kaat, 3.14
1963	91	70	3rd	13	Mele	Rollins, .307	Rollins, 163	Killebrew, 45	Killebrew, 96	Pascual, 21	Dailey, 1.98
1964	79	83	*6th	20	Mele	Oliva, .323	Oliva, 217	Killebrew, 49	Killebrew, 111	Kaat, 17	Grant, 2.82
1965	102	60	1st	+7	Mele	Oliva, .321	Oliva, 185	Killebrew, 25	Oliva, 98	Grant, 21	J. Perry, 2.63
1966	89	73	2nd	9	Mele	Oliva, .307	Oliva, 191	Killebrew, 39	Killebrew, 110	Kaat, 25	Worthington, 2.46
1967	91	71	*2nd	1	Mele, Ermer	Carew, .292	Oliva, 161	Killebrew, 44	Killebrew, 113	Chance, 20	Merritt, 2.53
1968	79	83	7th	24	Ermer	Oliva, .289	Tovar, 167	Allison, 22	Oliva, 68	Chance, 16	J. Perry, 2.27
						WEST DIVISION					
1969	97	65	†1st	+9	Martin	Carew, .332	Oliva, 197	Killebrew, 49	Killebrew, 140	Boswell, J. Perry, 20	Perranoski, 2.11
1970	98	64	†1st	+9	Rigney	Oliva, .325	Oliva, 204	Killebrew, 41	Killebrew, 113	J. Perry, 24	Williams, 1.99
1971	74	86	5th	26½	Rigney	Oliva, .337	Tovar, 204	Killebrew, 28	Killebrew, 119	Perry, 17	Blyleven, 2.81
1972	77	77	3rd	15½	Rigney, Quilici	Carew, .318	Carew, 170	Killebrew, 26	Darwin, 80	Blyleven, 17	Kaat, 2.06
1973	81	81	3rd	13	Quilici	Carew, .350	Carew, 203	Darwin, 18	Oliva, 92	Blyleven, 20	Blyleven, 2.52
1974	82	80	3rd	8	Quilici	Carew, .364	Carew, 218	Darwin, 25	Darwin, 94	Blyleven, 17	Campbell, 2.62
1975	76	83	4th	20½	Quilici	Carew, .359	Carew, 192	Ford, 15	Carew, 80	Hughes, 16	Blyleven, 3.00
1976	85	77	3rd	5	Mauch	Carew, .331	Carew, 200	Ford, 20	Hisle, 96	Campbell, 17	Burgmeier, 2.50
1977	84	77	4th	17½	Mauch	Carew, .388	Carew, 239	Hisle, 28	Hisle, 119	Goltz, 20	Johnson, 3.13
1978	73	89	4th	19	Mauch	Carew, .333	Carew, 188	Smalley, 19	Ford, 82	Goltz, 15	Marshall, 2.45
1979	82	80	4th	6	Mauch	Wilfong, .313	Landreaux, 172	Smalley, 24	Smalley, 95	Koosman, 20	Marshall, 2.65
1980	77	84	3rd	19½	Mauch, Goryl	Castino, .302	Castino, 165	Castino, 13	Castino, 64	Koosman, 16	Corbett, 1.98
1981	41	68	‡7th/4th	–	Goryl, Gardner	Castino, .268	Castino, 102	Smalley, 7	Hatcher, 37	Redfern, 9	Erickson, 3.84
1982	60	102	7th	33	Gardner	Hrbek, .301	Ward, 165	Ward, 28	Hrbek, 92	Castillo, 13	Castillo, 3.66
1983	70	92	*5th	29	Gardner	Hatcher, .317	Ward, 173	Brunansky, 28	Ward, 88	Schrom, 15	Lysander, 3.38
1984	81	81	*2nd	3	Gardner	Hrbek, .311	Hatcher, 174	Brunansky, 32	Hrbek, 107	Viola, 18	Viola, 3.21
1985	77	85	*4th	14	Gardner, Miller	Salas, .300	Puckett, 199	Brunansky, 27	Hrbek, 93	Viola, 18	Blyleven, 3.00
1986	71	91	6th	21	Miller, Kelly	Puckett, .328	Puckett, 223	Gaetti, 34	Gaetti, 108	Blyleven, 17	Heaton, 3.98
1987	85	77	§1st	+2	Kelly	Puckett, .332	Puckett, 207	Hrbek, 34	Gaetti, 109	Viola, 17	Viola, 2.90
1988	91	71	2nd	13	Kelly	Puckett, .356	Puckett, 234	Gaetti, 28	Puckett, 121	Viola, 24	Anderson, 2.45
1989	80	82	5th	19	Kelly	Puckett, .339	Puckett, 215	Hrbek, 25	Puckett, 85	Anderson, 17	Berenguer, 3.48
1990	74	88	7th	29	Kelly	Puckett, .298	Puckett, 164	Hrbek, 22	Gaetti, 85	Tapani, 12	Erickson, 2.87
1991	95	67	§1st	+8	Kelly	Puckett, .319	Puckett, 195	Davis, 29	Davis, 93	Erickson, 20	Tapani, 2.99
1992	90	72	2nd	6	Kelly	Puckett, .329	Puckett, 210	Puckett, 19	Puckett, 110	Smiley, Tapani, 16	Smiley, 3.21
1993	71	91	*5th	23	Kelly	Harper, .304	Puckett, 184	Hrbek, 25	Puckett, 89	Tapani, 12	Banks, 4.04
						CENTRAL DIVISION					
1994	53	60	4th	14	Kelly	Puckett, .317	Knoblauch, Puckett, 139	Puckett, 20	Puckett, 112	Tapani, 11	Tapani, 4.62
1995	56	88	5th	44	Kelly	Knoblauch, .333	Knoblauch, 179	Cordova, 24	Puckett, 99	Radke, 11	Tapani, 4.92
1996	78	84	4th	21½	Kelly	Molitor, .3409	Molitor, 225	Cordova, 16	Molitor, 113	Rodriguez, 13	Radke, 4.46
1997	68	94	4th	18½	Kelly	Molitor, .305	Knoblauch, 178	Cordova, 15	Molitor, 89	Radke, 20	Swindell, 3.58
1998	70	92	4th	19	Kelly	Walker, .316	Walker, 167	Lawton, 21	Lawton, 77	Radke, 12	Trombley, 3.63
1999	63	97	5th	33	Kelly	Cordova, .285	Walker, 148	Coomer, 16	Cordova, 70	Radke, 12	Radke, 3.75
2000	69	93	5th	26	Kelly	Lawton, .305	Lawton, 171	J. Jones, 19	Lawton, 88	Milton, 13	Radke, 4.45

Leaders columns: Batting avg., Hits, Home runs, RBIs, Wins, ERA.

* Tied for position. † Lost Championship Series. ‡ First half 17-39; second half 24-29. § Won Championship Series.

Note: Batting average minimum 350 at-bats; ERA minimum 90 innings pitched.

NEW YORK YANKEES

Outfielder Babe Ruth.

FRANCHISE CHRONOLOGY

First season: 1901, in Baltimore, as a member of the new American League. The Orioles made their Major League debut with a 10-6 victory over Boston en route to a 68-65 record, but dropped to the bottom of the A.L. in their second and final Baltimore season.
1903-present: The Highlanders/Yankees dropped a 3-1 decision to Washington in their New York debut and spent the next 18 seasons languishing among the A.L. also-rans. That would change. With the arrival of Babe Ruth in 1920, the Yankees rose into prominence as baseball's most dominant franchise and began the most glorious success run in sports history. In a 44-year stretch (1921-64), the Bronx Bombers won 29 pennants and 20 World Series. They won four straight fall classics (1936-39) under Joe McCarthy and five in a row (1949-53) under Casey Stengel. After playing in their first Series in 1921, the Yankees never went three years without playing in another through 1964. Success became more elusive after that 1964 loss to the Cardinals, but the Yankees ended the decade back on top. The Yanks have won four of the last five World Series and three in a row, including sweeps in 1998 and 1999, for a record 26 titles.

YANKEES VS. OPPONENTS BY DECADE

	A's	Indians	Orioles	Red Sox	Tigers	Twins	White Sox	Angels	Rangers	Brewers	Royals	Blue Jays	Mariners	Devil Rays	Interleague	Decade Record
1901-09	87-94	85-104	99-90	86-101	85-103	122-66	74-113									638-671
1910-19	100-104	95-117	123-92	94-115	94-121	101-113	94-118									701-780
1920-29	137-81	125-95	140-78	149-71	126-94	122-97	134-86									933-602
1930-39	140-76	133-84	155-64	136-80	134-86	124-96	148-68									970-554
1940-49	143-77	129-90	143-77	122-98	108-112	151-69	133-86									929-609
1950-59	158-62	123-97	151-69	126-93	120-100	145-73	132-88									955-582
1960-69	117-61	100-83	73-111	101-83	94-90	87-90	102-76	95-61	104-55	7-5	7-5					887-720
1970-79	63-54	103-64	73-89	79-89	92-74	72-44	72-44	65-52	79-49	83-74	64-53	29-14	18-15			892-715
1980-89	61-54	73-56	74-56	63-60	64-62	71-43	61-58	63-49	62-54	61-62	68-52	65-57	68-45			854-708
1990-99	58-59	72-45	75-50	64-60	72-47	58-50	52-54	58-59	54-54	56-39	61-45	64-57	61-56	19-5	27-22	851-702
2000-	6-3	5-5	7-5	7-6	4-8	5-5	4-8	5-5	10-2		8-2	5-7	4-6	6-6	11-6	87-74
Totals	1070-725	1043-840	1113-781	1027-856	993-897	1058-746	1006-799	286-226	309-214	207-180	208-157	163-135	151-122	25-11	38-28	8697-6717

Interleague results: 7-6 vs. Braves; 7-5 vs. Expos; 11-7 vs. Mets; 6-6 vs. Phillies; 7-4 vs. Marlins.

MANAGERS

(Baltimore Orioles, 1901-02)

Name	Years	Record
John McGraw	1901-02	94-96
Wilbert Robinson	1902	24-57
Clark Griffith	1903-08	419-370
Kid Elberfeld	1908	27-71
George Stallings	1909-10	152-136
Hal Chase	1910-11	86-80
Harry Wolverton	1912	50-102
Frank Chance	1913-14	117-168
Roger Peckinpaugh	1914	10-10
Bill Donovan	1915-17	220-239
Miller Huggins	1918-29	1067-719
Art Fletcher	1929	6-5
Bob Shawkey	1930	86-68
Joe McCarthy	1931-46	1460-867
Bill Dickey	1946	57-48
Johnny Neun	1946	8-6
Bucky Harris	1947-48	191-117
Casey Stengel	1949-60	1149-696
Ralph Houk	1961-63, 1966-73	944-806
Yogi Berra	1964, 1984-85	192-148
Johnny Keane	1965-66	81-101
Bill Virdon	1974-75	142-124
Billy Martin	1975-78, 1979, 1983, 1985, 1988	556-385
Bob Lemon	1978-79, 1981-82	99-73
Dick Howser	1978, 1980	103-60
Gene Michael	1981, 1982	92-76
Clyde King	1982	29-33
Lou Piniella	1986-87, 1988	224-193
Dallas Green	1989	56-65
Bucky Dent	1989-90	36-53
Stump Merrill	1990-91	120-155
Buck Showalter	1992-95	313-268
Joe Torre	1996-2000	487-322

WORLD SERIES CHAMPIONS

Year	Loser	Length	MVP
1923	N.Y. Giants	6 games	None
1927	Pittsburgh	4 games	None
1928	St. Louis	4 games	None
1932	Chicago	4 games	None
1936	N.Y. Giants	6 games	None
1937	N.Y. Giants	5 games	None
1938	Chicago	4 games	None
1939	Cincinnati	4 games	None
1941	Brooklyn	5 games	None
1943	St. Louis	5 games	None
1947	Brooklyn	7 games	None
1949	Brooklyn	5 games	None
1950	Philadelphia	4 games	None
1951	N.Y. Giants	6 games	None
1952	Brooklyn	7 games	None
1953	Brooklyn	6 games	None
1956	Brooklyn	7 games	Larsen
1958	Milwaukee	7 games	Turley
1961	Cincinnati	5 games	Ford
1962	San Francisco	7 games	Terry
1977	Los Angeles	6 games	Jackson
1978	Los Angeles	6 games	Dent
1996	Atlanta	6 games	Wetteland
1998	San Diego	4 games	Brosius
1999	Atlanta	4 games	Rivera
2000	N.Y. Mets	5 games	Jeter

A.L. PENNANT WINNERS

Year	Record	Manager	Series Result
1921	98-55	Huggins	Lost to Giants
1922	94-60	Huggins	Lost to Giants
1923	98-54	Huggins	Defeated Giants

A.L. PENNANT WINNERS—*cont'd.*

Year	Record	Manager	Series Result
1926	91-63	Huggins	Lost to Cardinals
1927	110-44	Huggins	Defeated Pirates
1928	101-53	Huggins	Defeated Cardinals
1932	107-47	McCarthy	Defeated Cubs
1936	102-51	McCarthy	Defeated Giants
1937	102-52	McCarthy	Defeated Giants
1938	99-53	McCarthy	Defeated Cubs
1939	106-45	McCarthy	Defeated Reds
1941	101-53	McCarthy	Defeated Dodgers
1942	103-51	McCarthy	Lost to Cardinals
1943	98-56	McCarthy	Defeated Cardinals
1947	97-57	Harris	Defeated Dodgers
1949	97-57	Stengel	Defeated Dodgers
1950	98-56	Stengel	Defeated Phillies
1951	98-56	Stengel	Defeated Giants
1952	95-59	Stengel	Defeated Dodgers
1953	99-52	Stengel	Defeated Dodgers
1955	96-58	Stengel	Lost to Dodgers
1956	97-57	Stengel	Defeated Dodgers
1957	98-56	Stengel	Lost to Braves
1958	92-62	Stengel	Defeated Braves
1960	97-57	Stengel	Lost to Pirates
1961	109-53	Houk	Defeated Reds
1962	96-66	Houk	Defeated Giants
1963	104-57	Houk	Lost to Dodgers
1964	99-63	Berra	Lost to Cardinals
1976	97-62	Martin	Lost to Reds
1977	100-62	Martin	Defeated Dodgers
1978	100-63	Martin, Lemon	Defeated Dodgers
*1981	59-48	Michael, Lemon	Lost to Dodgers
1996	92-70	Torre	Defeated Braves
1998	114-48	Torre	Defeated Padres
1999	98-64	Torre	Defeated Braves
2000	87-74	Torre	Defeated Mets

EAST DIVISION CHAMPIONS

Year	Record	Manager	ALCS Result
1976	97-62	Martin	Defeated Royals
1977	100-62	Martin	Defeated Royals
1978	100-63	Martin, Lemon	Defeated Royals
1980	103-59	Howser	Lost to Royals
*1981	59-48	Michael, Lemon	Defeated A's
1994	70-43	Showalter	None
1996	92-70	Torre	Defeated Orioles
1998	114-48	Torre	Defeated Indians
1999	98-64	Torre	Defeated Red Sox
2000	87-74	Torre	Defeated Mariners

* First-half champion; won division playoff from Brewers.

WILD-CARD QUALIFIERS

Year	Record	Manager	Div. Series Result
1995	79-65	Showalter	Lost to Mariners
1997	96-66	Torre	Lost to Indians

ATTENDANCE HIGHS

Total	Season	Park
3,292,629	1999	Yankee Stadium
3,227,657	2000	Yankee Stadium
2,949,734	1998	Yankee Stadium
2,633,701	1988	Yankee Stadium
2,627,417	1980	Yankee Stadium

BALLPARK CHRONOLOGY

Yankee Stadium (1923-present)

Capacity: 57,546.
First game: Yankees 4, Boston 1 (April 18, 1923).
First batter: Chick Fewster, Red Sox.
First hit: George Burns, Red Sox (single).
First run: Bob Shawkey, Yankees (3rd inning).
First home run: Babe Ruth, Yankees.
First winning pitcher: Bob Shawkey, Yankees.
First-season attendance: 1,007,066.

Oriole Park, Baltimore (1901-02)

First game: Orioles 10, Boston 6 (April 26, 1901).
First-season attendance: 141,952.

Hilltop Park, New York (1903-12)

Capacity: 15,000.
First game: Yankees 6, Washington 2 (May 1, 1903).
First-season attendance: 211,808.

Polo Grounds (1913-22)

Capacity: 38,000.
First game: Washington 9, Yankees 3 (April 17, 1913).
First-season attendance: 357,551.

Shea Stadium (1974-75)

Capacity: 55,101.
First game: Yankees 6, Cleveland 1 (April 6, 1974).
First-season attendance: 1,273,075.

Note: The Yankees played two seasons at Shea Stadium while Yankee Stadium was being refurbished. Before its facelift, Yankee Stadium capacity was 67,224.

A.L. MVPs

Lou Gehrig, 1B, 1936
Joe DiMaggio, OF, 1939
Joe DiMaggio, OF, 1941
Joe Gordon, 2B, 1942
Spud Chandler, P, 1943
Joe DiMaggio, OF, 1947
Phil Rizzuto, SS, 1950
Yogi Berra, C, 1951
Yogi Berra, C, 1954
Yogi Berra, C, 1955
Mickey Mantle, OF, 1956
Mickey Mantle, OF, 1957
Roger Maris, OF, 1960
Roger Maris, OF, 1961
Mickey Mantle, OF, 1962
Elston Howard, C, 1963
Thurman Munson, C, 1976
Don Mattingly, 1B, 1985

CY YOUNG WINNERS

Bob Turley, RH, 1958
Whitey Ford, LH, 1961
Sparky Lyle, LH, 1977
Ron Guidry, LH, 1978

ROOKIES OF THE YEAR

Gil McDougald, 3B, 1951
Bob Grim, P, 1954
Tony Kubek, SS/OF, 1957
Tom Tresh, SS/OF, 1962
Stan Bahnsen, P, 1968
Thurman Munson, C, 1970
Dave Righetti, P, 1981
Derek Jeter, SS, 1996

MANAGER OF THE YEAR

Buck Showalter, 1994
*Joe Torre, 1996
Joe Torre, 1998
*Co-winner

RETIRED UNIFORMS

No.	Name	Pos.
1	Billy Martin	2B-Man.
3	Babe Ruth	OF
4	Lou Gehrig	1B
5	Joe DiMaggio	OF
7	Mickey Mantle	OF
8	Bill Dickey	C
	Yogi Berra	C
9	Roger Maris	OF
10	Phil Rizzuto	SS
15	Thurman Munson	C
16	Whitey Ford	P
23	Don Mattingly	1B
32	Elston Howard	C
37	Casey Stengel	Man.
44	Reggie Jackson	OF

MILESTONE PERFORMANCES

30-plus home runs

61—Roger Maris 1961
60—Babe Ruth 1927
59—Babe Ruth 1921
54—Babe Ruth 1920, 1928
Mickey Mantle 1961
52—Mickey Mantle 1956
49—Babe Ruth 1930
Lou Gehrig 1934, 1936
47—Babe Ruth 1926
Lou Gehrig 1927
46—Babe Ruth 1924, 1929, 1931
Lou Gehrig 1931
Joe DiMaggio 1937
44—Tino Martinez 1997
42—Mickey Mantle 1958
41—Babe Ruth 1923, 1932
Lou Gehrig 1930
Reggie Jackson 1980
David Justice *2000
40—Mickey Mantle 1960
39—Joe DiMaggio 1948
Roger Maris 1960
37—Lou Gehrig 1937
Mickey Mantle 1955
Graig Nettles 1977
Dave Winfield 1982
35—Babe Ruth 1922
Mickey Mantle 1964
Don Mattingly 1985
34—Babe Ruth 1933
Mickey Mantle 1957
33—Bob Meusel 1925
Charlie Keller 1941
Roger Maris 1962
Bobby Murcer 1972
32—Lou Gehrig 1933
Joe DiMaggio 1938, 1950
Bobby Bonds 1975
Graig Nettles 1976
Reggie Jackson 1977
Dave Winfield 1983
Mike Pagliarulo 1987
31—Joe DiMaggio 1940
Tommy Henrich 1941
Charlie Keller 1943
Mickey Mantle 1959
Joe Pepitone 1966
Don Mattingly 1986
Danny Tartabull 1993
30—Lou Gehrig 1935
Joe DiMaggio 1939, 1941
Joe Gordon 1940
Charlie Keller 1946
Yogi Berra 1952
Mickey Mantle 1962
Don Mattingly 1987
Bernie Williams 2000

*21 with Indians; 20 withYankees.

100-plus RBIs

184—Lou Gehrig 1931
175—Lou Gehrig 1927
174—Lou Gehrig 1930
171—Babe Ruth 1921
167—Joe DiMaggio 1937
165—Lou Gehrig 1934
164—Babe Ruth 1927
163—Babe Ruth 1931
159—Lou Gehrig 1937
155—Joe DiMaggio 1948
154—Babe Ruth 1929
153—Babe Ruth 1930
152—Lou Gehrig 1936
151—Lou Gehrig 1932
146—Babe Ruth 1926
145—Don Mattingly 1985
142—Lou Gehrig 1928
Babe Ruth 1928
Roger Maris 1961
141—Tino Martinez 1997
140—Joe DiMaggio 1938
139—Lou Gehrig 1933
138—Bob Meusel 1925
137—Babe Ruth 1920, 1932
135—Bob Meusel 1921
133—Bill Dickey 1937
Joe DiMaggio 1940
131—Babe Ruth 1923
130—Mickey Mantle 1956
128—Mickey Mantle 1961
126—Lou Gehrig 1929
Joe DiMaggio 1939
125—Joe DiMaggio 1936, 1941
Yogi Berra 1954
124—Yogi Berra 1950
123—Tino Martinez 1998
122—Ben Chapman 1931
Charlie Keller 1941
Joe DiMaggio 1950
121—Babe Ruth 1924
Tony Lazzeri 1930
Bernie Williams 2000
120—Bob Meusel 1924
119—Lou Gehrig 1935
118—David Justice *2000
117—Tino Martinez 1996
Paul O'Neill 1997
116—Dave Winfield 1983
Paul O'Neill 1998
115—Bill Dickey 1938
Don Mattingly 1987
Bernie Williams 1999
114—Tony Lazzeri 1926
Lou Gehrig 1938
Joe DiMaggio 1942
Dave Winfield 1985
113—Wally Pipp 1924
Bob Meusel 1928
Tony Lazzeri 1932
Don Mattingly 1986, 1989
112—Lou Gehrig 1926
Roger Maris 1960
111—Joe Gordon 1939
Nick Etten 1945
Mickey Mantle 1964
Reggie Jackson 1980
110—Reggie Jackson 1977
Don Mattingly 1984
Paul O'Neill 1999
109—Tony Lazzeri 1936
108—Wally Pipp 1923
Charlie Keller 1942
Yogi Berra 1953, 1955
107—Lyn Lary 1931
Ben Chapman 1932
Bill Dickey 1936
George Selkirk 1936
Nick Etten 1943
Graig Nettles 1977
Dave Winfield 1988
106—Tony Lazzeri 1929
Dave Winfield 1982
105—Bill Dickey 1939
Yogi Berra 1956
Thurman Munson 1976
Tino Martinez 1999
104—Tony Lazzeri 1933
Dave Winfield 1986
103—Bob Meusel 1927
Babe Ruth 1933
Joe Gordon 1940, 1942
Johnny Lindell 1944
102—Tony Lazzeri 1927
Mickey Mantle 1954
Thurman Munson 1975
Danny Tartabull 1993
Bernie Williams 1996
Derek Jeter 1999
101—George Selkirk 1939
Charlie Keller 1946
100—Tommy Henrich 1948
Roger Maris 1962
Joe Pepitone 1964
Thurman Munson 1977
Dave Winfield 1984
Bernie Williams 1997
Paul O'Neill 2000

*58 with Indians; 60 with Yankees.

20-plus victories

1901—Joe McGinnity 26-20
1903—Jack Chesbro 21-15
1904—Jack Chesbro 41-12
Jack Powell 23-19
1906—Albert Orth 27-17
Jack Chesbro 23-17
1910—Russell Ford 26-6
1911—Russell Ford 22-11
1916—Bob Shawkey 24-14
1919—Bob Shawkey 20-11
1920—Carl Mays 26-11
Bob Shawkey 20-13
1921—Carl Mays 27-9
1922—Joe Bush 26-7
Bob Shawkey 20-12
1923—Sad Sam Jones 21-8
1924—Herb Pennock 21-9
1926—Herb Pennock 23-11
1927—Waite Hoyt 22-7
1928—George Pipgras 24-13
Waite Hoyt 23-7
1931—Lefty Gomez 21-9
1932—Lefty Gomez 24-7
1934—Lefty Gomez 26-5
1936—Red Ruffing 20-12
1937—Lefty Gomez 21-11
Red Ruffing 20-7
1938—Red Ruffing 21-7
1939—Red Ruffing 21-7
1942—Ernie Bonham 21-5
1943—Spud Chandler 20-4
1946—Spud Chandler 20-8
1949—Vic Raschi 21-10
1950—Vic Raschi 21-8
1951—Eddie Lopat 21-9
Vic Raschi 21-10
1952—Allie Reynolds 20-8
1954—Bob Grim 20-6
1958—Bob Turley 21-7
1961—Whitey Ford 25-4
1962—Ralph Terry 23-12
1963—Whitey Ford 24-7
Jim Bouton 21-7
1965—Mel Stottlemyre 20-9
1968—Mel Stottlemyre 21-12
1969—Mel Stottlemyre 20-14
1970—Fritz Peterson 20-11
1975—Catfish Hunter 23-14
1978—Ron Guidry 25-3
Ed Figueroa 20-9
1979—Tommy John 21-9
1980—Tommy John 22-9
1983—Ron Guidry 21-9
1985—Ron Guidry 22-6
1996—Andy Pettitte 21-8
1998—David Cone 20-7

INDIVIDUAL SEASON, GAME RECORDS

SEASON

Batting

Category	Record	Player	Year
At-bats	692	Bobby Richardson	1962
Runs	177	Babe Ruth	1921
Hits	238	Don Mattingly	1986
Singles	171	Steve Sax	1989
Doubles	53	Don Mattingly	1986
Triples	23	Earle Combs	1927
Home runs	61	Roger Maris	1961
Home runs, rookie	29	Joe DiMaggio	1936
Grand slams	6	Don Mattingly	1987
Total bases	457	Babe Ruth	1921
RBIs	184	Lou Gehrig	1931
Walks	170	Babe Ruth	1923
Most strikeouts	156	Danny Tartabull	1993
Fewest strikeouts	3	Joe Sewell	1932
Batting average	.393	Babe Ruth	1923
Slugging pct.	.847	Babe Ruth	1920
Stolen bases	93	Rickey Henderson	1988

Pitching

Category	Record	Player	Year
Games	77	Jeff Nelson	1997
Complete games	48	Jack Chesbro	1904
Innings	454.2	Jack Chesbro	1904
Wins	41	Jack Chesbro	1904
Losses	22	Joe Lake	1908
Winning pct.	.893 (25-3)	Ron Guidry	1978
Walks	179	Tommy Byrne	1949
Strikeouts	248	Ron Guidry	1978
Shutouts	9	Ron Guidry	1978
Home runs allowed	40	Ralph Terry	1962
Lowest ERA	1.64	Spud Chandler	1943
Saves	46	Dave Righetti	1986

GAME

Batting

Category	Record	Player	Date
Runs	5	Last by Tino Martinez	4-2-97
Hits	6	Last by Gerald Williams	5-1-96
Doubles	4	Last by Jim Mason	7-8-74
Triples	3	Last by Joe DiMaggio	8-28-38
Home runs	4	Lou Gehrig	6-3-32
RBIs	11	Tony Lazzeri	5-24-36
Total bases	16	Lou Gehrig	6-3-32
Stolen bases	4	Last by Gerald Williams	6-2-96

A.L. home run champions

1916—Wally Pipp 12
1917—Wally Pipp 9
1920—Babe Ruth 54
1921—Babe Ruth 59
1923—Babe Ruth 41
1924—Babe Ruth 46
1925—Bob Meusel 33
1926—Babe Ruth 47
1927—Babe Ruth 60
1928—Babe Ruth 54
1929—Babe Ruth 46
1930—Babe Ruth 49
1931—Lou Gehrig 46
Babe Ruth 46
1934—Lou Gehrig 49
1936—Lou Gehrig 49
1937—Joe DiMaggio 46
1944—Nick Etten 22
1948—Joe DiMaggio 39
1955—Mickey Mantle 37
1956—Mickey Mantle 52
1958—Mickey Mantle 42
1960—Mickey Mantle 40
1961—Roger Maris 61
1976—Graig Nettles 32
1980—Reggie Jackson *41

* Tied for league lead

A.L. RBI champions

1920—Babe Ruth 137
1921—Babe Ruth 171
1923—Babe Ruth 131
1925—Bob Meusel 138
1926—Babe Ruth 146
1927—Lou Gehrig 175
1928—Lou Gehrig *142
Babe Ruth *142
1930—Lou Gehrig 174
1931—Lou Gehrig 184
1934—Lou Gehrig 165
1941—Joe DiMaggio 125
1945—Nick Etten 111
1948—Joe DiMaggio 155
1956—Mickey Mantle 130
1960—Roger Maris 112
1961—Roger Maris 142
1985—Don Mattingly 145

* Tied for league lead

A.L. batting champions

1924—Babe Ruth .378
1934—Lou Gehrig .363
1939—Joe DiMaggio .381
1940—Joe DiMaggio .352
1945—Snuffy Stirnweiss .309
1956—Mickey Mantle .353
1984—Don Mattingly .343
1994—Paul O'Neill .359
1998—Bernie Williams .339

A.L. ERA champions

1920—Bob Shawkey 2.45
1927—Wilcy Moore 2.28
1934—Lefty Gomez 2.33
1937—Lefty Gomez 2.33
1943—Spud Chandler 1.64
1947—Spud Chandler 2.46
1952—Allie Reynolds 2.06
1953—Eddie Lopat 2.42
1956—Whitey Ford 2.47
1957—Bobby Shantz 2.45
1958—Whitey Ford 2.01
1978—Ron Guidry 1.74
1979—Ron Guidry 2.78
1980—Rudy May 2.46

A.L. strikeout champions

1932—Red Ruffing 190
1933—Lefty Gomez 163
1934—Lefty Gomez 158
1937—Lefty Gomez 194
1951—Vic Raschi 164
1952—Allie Reynolds 160
1964—Al Downing 217

No-hit pitchers

(9 innings or more)

1917—George Mogridge 2-1 vs. Boston
1923—Sad Sam Jones 2-0 vs. Philadelphia
1938—Monte Pearson 13-0 vs. Cleveland
1951—Allie Reynolds 1-0 vs. Cleveland
Allie Reynolds 8-0 vs. Boston
1956—*Don Larsen 2-0 vs. Brooklyn (Perfect)
1983—Dave Righetti 4-0 vs. Boston
1990—Andy Hawkins 0-4 vs. Chicago
1993—Jim Abbott 4-0 vs. Cleveland
1996—Dwight Gooden 2-0 vs. Seattle
1998—David Wells 4-0 vs. Minnesota (Perfect)
1999—David Cone 6-0 vs. Montreal (Perfect)

* World Series game

Longest hitting streaks

56—Joe DiMaggio 1941
33—Hal Chase 1907
29—Roger Peckinpaugh 1919
Earle Combs 1931
Joe Gordon 1942
27—Hal Chase 1907
26—Babe Ruth 1921
23—Joe DiMaggio 1940
22—Joe DiMaggio 1937

CAREER LEADERS

BATTING

Games

Mickey Mantle	2,401
Lou Gehrig	2,164
Yogi Berra	2,116
Babe Ruth	2,084
Roy White	1,881
Bill Dickey	1,789
Don Mattingly	1,785
Joe DiMaggio	1,736
Willie Randolph	1,694
Frankie Crosetti	1,683

At-bats

Mickey Mantle	8,102
Lou Gehrig	8,001
Yogi Berra	7,546
Babe Ruth	7,217
Don Mattingly	7,003
Joe DiMaggio	6,821
Roy White	6,650
Willie Randolph	6,303
Bill Dickey	6,300
Frankie Crosetti	6,277

Runs

Babe Ruth	1,959
Lou Gehrig	1,888
Mickey Mantle	1,677
Joe DiMaggio	1,390
Earle Combs	1,186
Yogi Berra	1,174
Willie Randolph	1,027
Don Mattingly	1,007
Frankie Crosetti	1,006
Roy White	964

Hits

Lou Gehrig	2,721
Babe Ruth	2,518
Mickey Mantle	2,415
Joe DiMaggio	2,214
Don Mattingly	2,153
Yogi Berra	2,148
Bill Dickey	1,969
Earle Combs	1,866
Roy White	1,803
Tony Lazzeri	1,784

Doubles

Lou Gehrig	534
Don Mattingly	442
Babe Ruth	424
Joe DiMaggio	389
Mickey Mantle	344
Bill Dickey	343
Bob Meusel	338
Tony Lazzeri	327
Yogi Berra	321
Earle Combs	309

Triples

Lou Gehrig	163
Earle Combs	154
Joe DiMaggio	131
Wally Pipp	121
Tony Lazzeri	115
Babe Ruth	106
Bob Meusel	87
Tommy Henrich	73
Bill Dickey	72
Mickey Mantle	72

Home runs

Babe Ruth	659
Mickey Mantle	536
Lou Gehrig	493
Joe DiMaggio	361
Yogi Berra	358
Graig Nettles	250
Don Mattingly	222
Dave Winfield	205
Roger Maris	203
Bill Dickey	202

Total bases

Babe Ruth	5,131
Lou Gehrig	5,060
Mickey Mantle	4,511
Joe DiMaggio	3,948
Yogi Berra	3,641
Don Mattingly	3,301
Bill Dickey	3,062
Tony Lazzeri	2,848
Roy White	2,685
Earle Combs	2,657

Runs batted in

Lou Gehrig	1,995
Babe Ruth	1,971
Joe DiMaggio	1,537
Mickey Mantle	1,509
Yogi Berra	1,430
Bill Dickey	1,209
Tony Lazzeri	1,154
Don Mattingly	1,099
Bob Meusel	1,005
Graig Nettles	834

Extra-base hits

Lou Gehrig	1,190
Babe Ruth	1,189
Mickey Mantle	952
Joe DiMaggio	881
Yogi Berra	728
Don Mattingly	684
Bill Dickey	617
Tony Lazzeri	611
Bob Meusel	571
Tommy Henrich	525

Batting average

(Minimum 500 games)

Babe Ruth	.349
Lou Gehrig	.340
Earle Combs	.325
Joe DiMaggio	.325
Derek Jeter	.318
Wade Boggs	.313
Bill Dickey	.313
Bob Meusel	.311
Paul O'Neill	.308
Don Mattingly	.307

Stolen bases

Rickey Henderson	326
Willie Randolph	251
Hal Chase	248
Roy White	233
Ben Chapman	184
Wid Conroy	184
Fritz Maisel	183
Mickey Mantle	153
Horace Clarke	151
Roberto Kelly	151

PITCHING

Earned-run average

(Minimum 1,000 innings)

Russ Ford	2.54
Jack Chesbro	2.58
Al Orth	2.72
Tiny Bonham	2.73
Whitey Ford	2.75
Spud Chandler	2.84
Ray Fisher	2.91
Mel Stottlemyre	2.97
Ray Caldwell	3.00
Fritz Peterson	3.10

Wins

Whitey Ford	236
Red Ruffing	231
Lefty Gomez	189
Ron Guidry	170
Bob Shawkey	168
Mel Stottlemyre	164
Herb Pennock	162
Waite Hoyt	157
Allie Reynolds	131
Jack Chesbro	128

Losses

Mel Stottlemyre	139
Bob Shawkey	131
Red Ruffing	124
Whitey Ford	106
Fritz Peterson	106
Lefty Gomez	101
Ray Caldwell	99
Waite Hoyt	98
Jack Chesbro	93
Jack Warhop	92

Innings pitched

Whitey Ford	3,170.1
Red Ruffing	3,168.2
Mel Stottlemyre	2,661.1
Lefty Gomez	2,498.1
Bob Shawkey	2,488.2
Ron Guidry	2,392.0
Waite Hoyt	2,272.1
Herb Pennock	2,203.1
Jack Chesbro	1,952.0
Fritz Peterson	1,857.1

Strikeouts

Whitey Ford	1,956
Ron Guidry	1,778
Red Ruffing	1,526
Lefty Gomez	1,468
Mel Stottlemyre	1,257
Bob Shawkey	1,163
Al Downing	1,028
Allie Reynolds	967
Dave Righetti	940
Jack Chesbro	913

Bases on balls

Lefty Gomez	1,090
Whitey Ford	1,086
Red Ruffing	1,066
Bob Shawkey	855
Allie Reynolds	819
Mel Stottlemyre	809
Tommy Byrne	763
Bob Turley	761
Ron Guidry	633
Waite Hoyt	631

Games

Dave Righetti	522
Whitey Ford	498
Red Ruffing	426
Sparky Lyle	420
Bob Shawkey	415
Johnny Murphy	383
Ron Guidry	368
Lefty Gomez	367
Waite Hoyt	365
Mel Stottlemyre	360

Shutouts

Whitey Ford	45
Red Ruffing	40
Mel Stottlemyre	40
Lefty Gomez	28
Allie Reynolds	27
Spud Chandler	26
Ron Guidry	26
Bob Shawkey	26
Vic Raschi	24
Bob Turley	21

Saves

Dave Righetti	224
Mariano Rivera	165
Rich Gossage	151
Sparky Lyle	141
Johnny Murphy	104
Steve Farr	78
Joe Page	76
John Wetteland	74
Lindy McDaniel	58
Luis Arroyo	43
Ryne Duren	43

TEAM SEASON, GAME RECORDS

SEASON

Batting

Most at-bats	5,710	1997
Most runs	1,067	1931
Fewest runs	459	1908
Most hits	1,683	1930
Most singles	1,237	1988
Most doubles	325	1997
Most triples	111	1901
Most home runs	240	1961
Fewest home runs	8	1913
Most grand slams	10	1987
Most pinch-hit home runs	10	1961
Most total bases	2,703	1936
Most stolen bases	288	1910
Highest batting average	.309	1930
Lowest batting average	.214	1968
Highest slugging pct	.489	1927

Pitching

Lowest ERA	2.57	1904
Highest ERA	4.88	1930
Most complete games	123	1904
Most shutouts	24	1951
Most saves	58	1986
Most walks	812	1949
Most strikeouts	1,165	1997

Fielding

Most errors	401	1901
Fewest errors	91	1996
Most double plays	214	1956
Highest fielding average	.986	1995

General

Most games won	114	1998
Most games lost	103	1908
Highest win pct	.714	1927
Lowest win pct	.329	1912

GAME, INNING

Batting

Most runs, game	25	5-24-36
Most runs, inning	14	7-6-20
Most hits, game	30	9-28-23
Most home runs, game	8	6-28-39
Most total bases, game	53	6-28-39

Mickey Mantle's 536 career home runs rank only second on the Yankees' career list—thanks to Babe Ruth.

YANKEES YEAR-BY-YEAR

Year	W	L	Place	Games Back	Manager	Batting avg.	Hits	Home runs	RBIs	Wins	ERA
								BALTIMORE ORIOLES			
1901	68	65	5th	13½	McGraw	Donlin, .341	Seymour, 167	Williams, 7	Williams, 96	McGinnity, 26	McGinnity, 3.56
1902	50	88	8th	34	McGraw, Robinson	Selbach, .320	Selbach, 161	Williams, 8	Williams, 83	McGinnity, 13	McGinnity, 3.44
								HIGHLANDERS/YANKEES			
1903	72	62	4th	17	Griffith	Keeler, .318	Keeler, 164	McFarland, 5	Williams, 82	Chesbro, 21	Griffith, 2.70
1904	92	59	2nd	1½	Griffith	Keeler, .343	Keeler, 185	Ganzel, 6	Anderson, 82	Chesbro, 41	Chesbro, 1.82
1905	71	78	6th	21½	Griffith	Keeler, .302	Keeler, 169	Williams, 6	Williams, 60	Chesbro, 20	Griffity, 1.68
1906	90	61	2nd	3	Griffith	Chase, .323	Chase, 193	Conroy, 4	Williams, 77	Orth, 27	Clarkson, 2.32
1907	70	78	5th	21	Griffith	Chase, .287	Chase, 143	Hoffman, 5	Chase, 68	Orth, 14	Chesbro, 2.53
1908	51	103	8th	39½	Griffith, Elberfeld	Hemphill, .297	Hemphill, 150	Niles, 4	Hemphill, 44	Chesbro, 14	Chesbro, 2.93
1909	74	77	5th	23½	Stallings	Chase, .283	Engle, 137	Chase, Demmitt, 4	Engle, 71	Lake, 14	Lake, 1.88
1910	88	63	2nd	14½	Stallings, Chase	Knight, .312	Chase, 152	Cree, Wolter, 4	Chase, 73	Ford, 26	Ford, 1.65
1911	76	76	6th	25½	Chase	Cree, .348	Cree, 181	Cree, Wolter, 4	Hartzell, 91	Ford, 22	Ford, 2.28
1912	50	102	8th	55	Wolverton	Chase, Daniels, .274	Chase, 143	Zinn, 6	Chase, 58	Ford, 13	McConnell, 2.75
1913	57	94	7th	38	Chance	Cree, .272	Cree, 145	Sweeney, Wolter, 2	Cree, 63	Fisher, Ford, 11	Caldwell, 2.41
1914	70	84	*6th	30	Chance, Peckinpaugh	Cook, .283	Cook, 133	Peckinpaugh, 3	Peckinpaugh, 51	Caldwell, 17	Caldwell, 1.94
1915	69	83	5th	32½	Donovan	Maisel, .281	Maisel, 149	Peckinpaugh, 5	Pipp, 58	Caldwell, 19	Fisher, 2.11
1916	80	74	4th	11	Donovan	Baker, .269	Pipp, 143	Pipp, 12	Pipp, 99	Shawkey, 23	Cullop, 2.05
1917	71	82	6th	28½	Donovan	Baker, .306	Baker, 154	Baker, 6	Baker, 68	Mogridge, 16	Mogridge, 2.18
1918	60	63	4th	13½	Huggins	Baker, .306	Baker, 154	Baker, 6	Baker, 68	Mogridge, 16	Mogridge, 2.18
1919	80	59	3rd	7½	Huggins	Peckinpaugh, .305	Baker, 166	Baker, 10	Baker, 78	Shawkey, 20	Mays, 1.65
1920	95	59	3rd	3	Huggins	Ruth, .376	Pratt, 180	Ruth, 54	Ruth, 137	Mays, 26	Shawkey, 2.45
1921	98	55	1st	+4½	Huggins	Ruth, .378	Ruth, 204	Ruth, 59	Ruth, 171	Mays, 27	Mays, 3.05
1922	94	60	1st	+1	Huggins	Pipp, .329	Pipp, 190	Ruth, 35	Ruth, 96	Bush, 26	Shawkey, 2.91
1923	98	54	1st	+16	Huggins	Ruth, .393	Ruth, 205	Ruth, 41	Ruth, 131	Jones, 21	Hoyt, 3.02
1924	89	63	2nd	2	Huggins	Ruth, .378	Ruth, 200	Ruth, 46	Ruth, 121	Pennock, 21	Pennock, 2.83
1925	69	85	7th	28½	Huggins	Combs, .342	Combs, 203	Meusel, 33	Meusel, 138	Pennock, 16	Pennock, 2.96
1926	91	63	1st	+3	Huggins	Ruth, .372	Ruth, 184	Ruth, 47	Ruth, 146	Pennock, 23	Shocker, 3.38
1927	110	44	1st	+19	Huggins	Gehrig, .373	Combs, 231	Ruth, 60	Gehrig, 175	Hoyt, 22	W. Moore, 2.28
1928	101	53	1st	+2½	Huggins	Gehrig, .374	Gehrig, 210	Ruth, 54	Gehrig, Ruth, 142	Pipgras, 24	Pennock, 2.56
1929	88	66	2nd	18	Huggins, Fletcher	Lazzeri, .354	Combs, 202	Ruth, 46	Ruth, 154	Pipgras, 18	Zachary, 2.48
1930	86	68	3rd	16	Shawkey	Gehrig, .379	Gehrig, 220	Ruth, 49	Gehrig, 174	Pipgras, Ruffing, 15	Pipgras, 4.11
1931	94	59	2nd	13½	McCarthy	Ruth, .373	Gehrig, 211	Gehrig, Ruth, 46	Gehrig, 184	Gomez, 21	Gomez, 2.67
1932	107	47	1st	+13	McCarthy	Gehrig, .349	Gehrig, 208	Ruth, 41	Gehrig, 151	Gomez, 24	Ruffing, 3.09
1933	91	59	2nd	7	McCarthy	Gehrig, .334	Gehrig, 198	Ruth, 34	Gehrig, 139	Gomez, 16	Gomez, 3.18
1934	94	60	2nd	7	McCarthy	Gehrig, .363	Gehrig, 210	Gehrig, 49	Gehrig, 165	Gomez, 26	Gomez, 2.33
1935	89	60	2nd	3	McCarthy	Gehrig, .329	Rolfe, 192	Gehrig, 30	Gehrig, 119	Ruffing, 16	Ruffing, 3.12
1936	102	51	1st	+19½	McCarthy	Dickey, .362	DiMaggio, 206	Gehrig, 49	Gehrig, 152	Ruffing, 20	Pearson, 3.71
1937	102	52	1st	+13	McCarthy	Gehrig, .351	DiMaggio, 215	DiMaggio, 46	DiMaggio, 167	Gomez, 21	Gomez, 2.33
1938	99	53	1st	+9½	McCarthy	DiMaggio, .324	Rolfe, 196	DiMaggio, 32	DiMaggio, 140	Ruffing, 21	Ruffing, 3.31
1939	106	45	1st	+17	McCarthy	DiMaggio, .381	Rolfe, 213	DiMaggio, 30	DiMaggio, 126	Ruffing, 21	Russo, 2.41
1940	88	66	3rd	2	McCarthy	DiMaggio, .352	DiMaggio, 179	DiMaggio, 31	DiMaggio, 133	Ruffing, 15	Bonham, 1.90
1941	101	53	1st	+17	McCarthy	DiMaggio, .357	DiMaggio, 193	Keller, 33	DiMaggio, 125	Gomez, Ruffing, 15	Bonham, 2.98
1942	103	51	1st	+9	McCarthy	Gordon, .322	DiMaggio, 186	Keller, 26	DiMaggio, 114	Bonham, 21	Bonham, 2.27
1943	98	56	1st	+13½	McCarthy	B. Johnson, .280	B. Johnson, 166	Keller, 31	Etten, 107	Chandler, 20	Chandler, 1.64
1944	83	71	3rd	6	McCarthy	Stirnweiss, .319	Stirnweiss, 205	Etten, 22	Lindell, 103	Borowy, 17	Borowy, 2.64
1945	81	71	4th	6½	McCarthy	Stirnweiss, .309	Stirnweiss, 195	Etten, 18	Etten, 111	Bevens, 13	Page, 2.82
1946	87	67	3rd	17	McCarthy, Dickey, Neun	DiMaggio, .290	Keller, 148	Keller, 30	Keller, 101	Chandler, 20	Chandler, 2.10
1947	97	57	1st	+12	Harris	DiMaggio, .315	DiMaggio, 168	DiMaggio, 20	Henrich, 98	Reynolds, 19	Chandler, 2.46
1948	94	60	3rd	2½	Harris	DiMaggio, .320	DiMaggio, 190	DiMaggio, 39	DiMaggio, 155	Raschi, 19	Byrne, 3.30
1949	97	57	1st	+1	Stengel	Henrich, .287	Rizzuto, 169	Henrich, 24	Berra, 91	Raschi, 21	Page, 2.59
1950	98	56	1st	+3	Stengel	Rizzuto, .324	Rizzuto, 200	DiMaggio, 32	Berra, 124	Raschi, 21	Ford, 2.81
1951	98	56	1st	+5	Stengel	McDougald, .306	Berra, 161	Berra, 27	Berra, 88	Lopat, Raschi, 21	Lopat, 2.91
1952	95	59	1st	+2	Stengel	Mantle, .311	Mantle, 171	Berra, 30	Berra, 98	Reynolds, 20	Reynolds, 2.06
1953	99	52	1st	+8½	Stengel	Woodling, .306	McDougald, 154	Berra, 27	Berra, 108	Ford, 18	Lopat, 2.42
1954	103	51	2nd	8	Stengel	Noren, .319	Berra, 179	Mantle, 27	Berra, 125	Grim, 20	Ford, 2.82
1955	96	58	1st	+3	Stengel	Mantle, .306	Mantle, 158	Mantle, 37	Berra, 108	Ford, 18	Ford, 2.63
1956	97	57	1st	+9	Stengel	Mantle, .353	Mantle, 188	Mantle, 52	Mantle, 130	Ford, 19	Ford, 2.47
1957	98	56	1st	+8	Stengel	Mantle, .365	Mantle, 173	Mantle, 34	Mantle, 94	Sturdivant, 16	Shantz, 2.45
1958	92	62	1st	+10	Stengel	Howard, .314	Mantle, 158	Mantle, 42	Mantle, 97	Turley, 21	Ford, 2.01
1959	79	75	3rd	15	Stengel	Richardson, .301	Mantle, 154	Mantle, 31	Lopez, 93	Ford, 16	Shantz, 2.38
1960	97	57	1st	+8	Stengel	Skowron, .309	Skowron, 166	Mantle, 40	Maris, 112	Ditmar, 15	Ditmar, 3.06
1961	109	53	1st	+8	Houk	Howard, .348	Richardson, 173	Maris, 61	Maris, 142	Ford, 25	Arroyo, 2.19
1962	96	66	1st	+5	Houk	Mantle, .321	Richardson, 209	Maris, 33	Maris, 100	Terry, 23	Ford, 2.90
1963	104	57	1st	+10½	Houk	Howard, .287	Richardson, 167	Howard, 28	Pepitone, 89	Ford, 24	Bouton, 2.53
1964	99	63	1st	+1	Berra	Howard, .313	Richardson, 181	Mantle, 35	Mantle, 111	Bouton, 18	Stottlemyre, 2.06
1965	77	85	6th	25	Keane	Tresh, .279	Tresh, 168	Tresh, 26	Tresh, 74	Stottlemyre, 20	Stottlemyre, 2.63
1966	70	89	10th	26½	Keane, Houk	Howard, .256	Richardson, 153	Pepitone, 31	Pepitone, 83	Peterson, Stottlemyre, 12	Bouton, 2.69
1967	72	90	9th	20	Houk	Clarke, .272	Clarke, 160	Mantle, 22	Pepitone, 64	Stottlemyre, 15	Monbouquette, 2.36
1968	83	79	5th	20	Houk	White, .267	White, 154	Mantle, 18	White, 62	Stottlemyre, 21	Bahnsen, 2.05
								EAST DIVISION			
1969	80	81	5th	28½	Houk	White, .290	Clarke, 183	Pepitone, 27	Murcer, 62	Stottlemyre, 20	Peterson, 2.55
1970	93	69	2nd	15	Houk	Munson, .302	White, 180	Murcer, 23	White, 94	Peterson, 20	McDaniel, 2.01
1971	82	80	4th	21	Houk	Murcer, .331	Murcer, 175	Murcer, 25	Murcer, 94	Stottlemyre, 16	Stottlemyre, 2.87
1972	79	76	4th	6½	Houk	Murcer, .292	Murcer, 171	Murcer, 33	Murcer, 96	Peterson, 17	Lyle, 1.92
1973	80	82	4th	17	Houk	Murcer, .304	Murcer, 187	Murcer, Nettles, 22	Murcer, 95	Stottlemyre, 16	Beene, 1.68
1974	89	73	2nd	2	Virdon	Piniella, .305	Murcer, 166	Nettles, 22	Murcer, 88	Dobson, Medich, 19	Lyle, 1.66
1975	83	77	3rd	12	Virdon, Martin	Munson, .318	Munson, 190	Bonds, 32	Munson, 102	Hunter, 23	Hunter, 2.58
1976	97	62	†1st	+10½	Martin	Rivers, .312	Chambliss, 188	Nettles, 32	Munson, 105	Figueroa, 19	Lyle, 2.26
1977	100	62	†1st	+2½	Martin	Rivers, .326	Rivers, 184	Nettles, 37	Jackson, 110	Figueroa, Guidry, 16	Lyle, 2.17
1978	100	63	‡†1st	+1	Martin, Lemon	Piniella, .314	Munson, 183	Jackson, Nettles, 27	Jackson, 97	Guidry, 25	Guidry, 1.74
1979	89	71	4th	13½	Lemon, Martin	Jackson, Piniella, .297	Chambliss, Randolph, 155	Jackson, 29	Jackson, 89	John, 21	Guidry, 2.78
1980	103	59	§1st	+3	Howser	Watson, .307	Jackson, 154	Jackson, 41	Jackson, 111	John, 22	May, 2.46
1981	59	48∞	†1st/6th	—	Michael, Lemon	Winfield, .294	Winfield, 114	Jackson, Nettles, 15	Winfield, 68	Guidry, 11	Righetti, 2.05
1982	79	83	5th	16	Lemon, Michael, King	Mumphrey, .300	Randolph, 155	Winfield, 37	Winfield, 106	Guidry, 14	Gossage, 2.23
1983	91	71	3rd	7	Martin	Griffey, .306	Winfield, 169	Winfield, 32	Winfield, 116	Guidry, 21	Fontenot, 3.33
1984	87	75	3rd	17	Berra	Mattingly, .343	Mattingly, 207	Baylor, 27	Mattingly, 110	Niekro, 16	Righetti, 2.34
1985	97	64	2nd	2	Berra, Martin	Mattingly, .324	Mattingly, 211	Mattingly, 35	Mattingly, 145	Guidry, 22	Fisher, 2.38
1986	90	72	2nd	5½	Piniella	Mattingly, .352	Mattingly, 238	Mattingly, 31	Mattingly, 113	Rasmussen, 18	Righetti, 2.45
1987	89	73	4th	9	Piniella	Mattingly, .327	Mattingly, 186	Pagliarulo, 32	Mattingly, 115	Rhoden, 16	Stoddard, 3.50
1988	85	76	5th	3½	Martin, Piniella	Winfield, .322	Mattingly, 186	Clark, 27	Winfield, 107	Candelaria, 13	Candelaria, 3.38
1989	74	87	5th	14½	Green, Dent	Sax, .315	Sax, 205	Mattingly, 23	Mattingly, 113	Hawkins, 15	Guetterman, 2.45
1990	67	95	7th	21	Dent, Merrill	Kelly, .285	Kelly, 183	Barfield, 25	Barfield, 78	Guetterman, 11	Guetterman, 3.39
1991	71	91	5th	20	Merrill	Sax, .304	Sax, 198	Nokes, 24	Hall, 80	Sanderson, 16	Habyan, 2.30
1992	76	86	*4th	20	Showalter	Mattingly, .288	Mattingly, 184	Tartabull, 25	Mattingly, 86	Perez, 13	Perez, 2.87
1993	88	74	2nd	7	Showalter	O'Neill, .311	Boggs, 169	Tartabull, 31	Tartabull, 102	Key, 18	Key, 3.00
1994	70	43	1st	+6½	Showalter	O'Neill, .359	O'Neill, 132	O'Neill, 21	O'Neill, 83	Key, 17	Key, 3.27
1995	79	65	▲2nd	7	Showalter	Boggs, .324	B. Williams, 173	O'Neill, 22	O'Neill, 96	Cone, 18	Cone, 3.57
1996	92	70	◆†1st	+4	Torre	Duncan, .340	Jeter, 183	B. Williams, 29	Martinez, 117	Pettitte, 21	M. Rivera, 2.09
1997	96	66	▲2nd	2	Torre	B. Williams, .328	Jeter, 190	Martinez, 44	Martinez, 141	Pettitte, 18	Cone, 2.82
1998	114	48	◆†1st	+22	Torre	B. Williams, .339	Jeter, 203	Martinez, 28	Martinez, 123	Cone, 20	O. Hernandez, 3.13
1999	98	64	◆†1st	+4	Torre	Jeter, .349	Jeter, 219	Martinez, 28	B. Williams, 115	O. Hernandez, 17	Cone, 3.44
2000	87	74	◆†1st	+2½	Torre	Jeter, .339	Jeter, 201	B. Williams, 30	B. Williams, 121	Pettitte, 19	Clemens, 3.70

* Tied for position. † Won Championship Series. ‡ Won division playoff. § Lost Championship Series. ∞ First half 34-22; second half 25-26. ▲ Lost Division Series. ◆ Won Division Series.

Note: Batting average minimum 350 at-bats; ERA minimum 90 innings pitched.

OAKLAND ATHLETICS

Manager Connie Mack.

FRANCHISE CHRONOLOGY

First season: 1901, in Philadelphia, as a member of the new American League. The Athletics lost their big-league debut to Washington, 5-1, and went on to a 74-62 record and fourth-place finish.

1902-54: A team of extremes, Connie Mack's Athletics won nine pennants and five World Series—and finished eighth 18 times. Those first and last-place finishes accounted for 27 of the team's 54 seasons in Philadelphia. The powerful A's won three World Series from 1910 through 1913 and consecutive championships in 1929 and '30. But from 1934 through 1954, the A's never got their heads above fourth place and finished either seventh or eighth 14 times.

1955-1967: The A's defeated Detroit, 6-2, in their Kansas City debut and completed their first season in sixth place with a 63-91 record. That was as good as it got. The A's never finished above seventh place in the remainder of their Kansas City existence and never came closer than 19 games to the A.L. champion.

1968-present: The A's lost their Oakland debut to Baltimore, 3-1, but went on to record their first above-.500 record (82-80) since 1952. Young and talented, they would return to prominence and claim 11 West Division titles, six pennants and four World Series championships, including three straight fall classic titles from 1972 through 1974.

A'S VS. OPPONENTS BY DECADE

	Indians	Orioles	Red Sox	Tigers	Twins	White Sox	Yankees	Angels	Rangers	Brewers	Royals	Blue Jays	Mariners	Devil Rays	Interleague	Decade Record
1901-09	105-86	105-79	102-88	102-80	128-56	98-92	94-87									734-568
1910-19	105-110	120-93	84-129	99-116	108-101	90-125	104-100									710-774
1920-29	106-113	114-105	131-86	114-105	105-108	119-100	81-137									770-754
1930-39	106-114	127-88	99-116	106-111	91-124	118-102	76-140									723-795
1940-49	80-136	105-115	83-137	90-130	95-125	108-112	77-143									638-898
1950-59	67-153	109-110	79-141	98-122	113-107	96-124	62-158									624-915
1960-69	85-92	69-107	82-96	69-109	79-105	66-118	61-117	74-88	78-77	13-5	10-8					686-922
1970-79	70-46	50-66	54-63	60-56	76-91	89-76	54-63	97-72	78-76	74-54	90-79	18-15	28-15			838-772
1980-89	63-50	57-63	52-68	53-58	69-58	60-70	54-61	70-57	57-66	64-50	59-64	67-53	78-46			803-764
1990-99	45-62	54-65	46-71	53-53	60-58	57-60	59-58	68-55	61-63	35-50	68-53	55-53	71-50	14-7	27-23	773-781
2000-	6-6	8-4	5-5	4-6	7-5	3-6	3-6	8-5	5-7		8-4	7-3	9-4	7-2	11-7	91-70
Totals	838-968	918-895	817-1000	848-946	931-938	904-985	725-1070	317-277	279-289	186-159	235-208	147-124	186-115	21-9	38-30	7390-8013

Interleague results: 7-6 vs. Dodgers; 9-4 vs. Padres; 10-10 vs. Giants; 6-7 vs. Rockies; 6-3 vs. Diamondbacks.

MANAGERS

(Philadelphia Athletics, 1901-54)
(Kansas City Athletics, 1955-67)

Name	*Years*	*Record*
Connie Mack	1901-50	3582-3814
Jimmie Dykes	1951-53	208-254
Eddie Joost	1954	51-103
Lou Boudreau	1955-57	151-260
Harry Craft	1957-59	162-196
Bob Elliott	1960	58-96
Joe Gordon	1961	26-33
Hank Bauer	1961-62, 1969	187-226
Eddie Lopat	1963-64	90-124
Mel McGaha	1964-65	45-91
Haywood Sullivan	1965	54-82
Alvin Dark	1966-67, 1974-75	314-291
Luke Appling	1967	10-30
Bob Kennedy	1968	82-80
John McNamara	1969-70	97-78
Dick Williams	1971-73	288-190
Chuck Tanner	1976	87-74
Jack McKeon	1977, 1978	71-105
Bobby Winkles	1977-78	61-86
Jim Marshall	1979	54-108
Billy Martin	1980-82	215-218
Steve Boros	1983-84	94-112
Jackie Moore	1984-86	163-190
Tony La Russa	1986-95	798-673
Art Howe	1996-2000	395-414

WORLD SERIES CHAMPIONS

Year	*Loser*	*Length*	*MVP*
1910	Chicago	5 games	None
1911	N.Y. Giants	6 games	None
1913	N.Y. Giants	5 games	None
1929	Chicago	5 games	None
1930	St. Louis	6 games	None
1972	Cincinnati	7 games	Tenace
1973	N.Y. Mets	7 games	Jackson
1974	Los Angeles	5 games	Fingers
1989	San Francisco	4 games	Stewart

Outfielder Reggie Jackson found early success with the Athletics in the late '60s.

A.L. PENNANT WINNERS

Year	*Record*	*Manager*	*Series Result*
1902	83-53	Mack	None
1905	92-56	Mack	Lost to Giants
1910	102-48	Mack	Defeated Cubs
1911	101-50	Mack	Defeated Giants
1913	96-57	Mack	Defeated Giants
1914	99-53	Mack	Lost to Braves
1929	104-46	Mack	Defeated Cubs
1930	102-52	Mack	Defeated Cardinals
1931	107-45	Mack	Lost to Cardinals
1972	93-62	Williams	Defeated Reds
1973	94-68	Williams	Defeated Mets
1974	90-72	Dark	Defeated Dodgers
1988	104-58	La Russa	Lost to Dodgers
1989	99-63	La Russa	Defeated Giants
1990	103-59	La Russa	Lost to Reds

WEST DIVISION CHAMPIONS

Year	*Record*	*Manager*	*ALCS Result*
1971	101-60	Williams	Lost to Orioles
1972	93-62	Williams	Defeated Tigers
1973	94-68	Williams	Defeated Orioles
1974	90-72	Dark	Defeated Orioles
1975	98-64	Dark	Lost to Red Sox
1981*	64-45	Martin	Lost to Yankees
1988	104-58	La Russa	Defeated Red Sox
1989	99-63	La Russa	Defeated Blue Jays
1990	103-59	La Russa	Defeated Red Sox
1992	96-66	La Russa	Lost to Blue Jays
2000	91-70	Howe	Lost in Div. Series

* First-half champion; won division playoff from Royals.

ATTENDANCE HIGHS

Total	*Season*	*Park*
2,900,217	1990	Oakland Coliseum
2,713,493	1991	Oakland Coliseum
2,667,255	1989	Oakland Coliseum
2,494,160	1992	Oakland Coliseum
2,287,335	1988	Oakland Coliseum

BALLPARK CHRONOLOGY

Network Associates Coliseum, formerly Oakland Alameda County Coliseum (1968-present)

Capacity: 43,662.
First game: Baltimore 4, A's 1 (April 17, 1968).
First batter: Curt Blefary, Orioles.
First hit: Boog Powell, Orioles (home run).
First run: Boog Powell, Orioles (2nd inning).
First home run: Boog Powell, Orioles.
First winning pitcher: Dave McNally, Orioles.
First-season attendance: 837,466.

Columbia Park, Philadelphia (1901-08)

Capacity: 9,500.
First game: Washington 5, Athletics 1 (April 26, 1901).
First-season attendance: 206,329.

Shibe Park, Philadelphia (1909-54)

Capacity: 33,608.
First game: Athletics 8, Boston 1 (April 12, 1909).
First-season attendance: 517,653.

Municipal Stadium, Kansas City (1955-67)

Capacity: 35,020.
First game: Athletics 6, Detroit 2 (April 12, 1955).
First-season attendance: 1,393,054.

Note: Shibe Park was changed to Connie Mack Stadium in 1953.

A.L. MVPs

Lefty Grove, P, 1931
Jimmie Foxx, 1B, 1932
Jimmie Foxx, 1B, 1933
Bobby Shantz, P, 1952
Vida Blue, P, 1971
Reggie Jackson, OF, 1973
Jose Canseco, OF, 1988
Rickey Henderson, OF, 1990
Dennis Eckersley, P, 1992
Jason Giambi, 1B, 2000

CY YOUNG WINNERS

Vida Blue, LH, 1971
Catfish Hunter, RH, 1974
Bob Welch, RH, 1990
Dennis Eckersley, P, 1992

ROOKIES OF THE YEAR

Harry Byrd, P, 1952
Jose Canseco, OF, 1986
Mark McGwire, 1B, 1987
Walt Weiss, SS, 1988
Ben Grieve, OF, 1998

MANAGERS OF THE YEAR

Tony La Russa, 1988
Tony La Russa, 1992

RETIRED UNIFORMS

No.	*Name*	*Pos.*
27	Catfish Hunter	P
34	Rollie Fingers	P

MILESTONE PERFORMANCES

30-plus home runs

58—Jimmie Foxx 1932
52—Mark McGwire 1996
49—Mark McGwire 1987
48—Jimmie Foxx 1933
47—Reggie Jackson 1969
44—Jimmie Foxx 1934
Jose Canseco 1991
43—Jason Giambi 2000
42—Gus Zernial 1953
Jose Canseco 1988
Mark McGwire 1992
39—Mark McGwire 1990
Mark McGwire 1995
38—Bob Cerv 1958
Matt Stairs 1999
37—Tilly Walker 1922
Jimmie Foxx 1930
Jose Canseco 1990
36—Al Simmons 1930
Jimmie Foxx 1935
Reggie Jackson 1975
Geronimo Berroa 1996
35—Al Simmons 1932
Tony Armas 1980
Dave Kingman 1984, 1986
Terry Steinbach 1996
John Jaha 1999
34—Al Simmons 1929
Bob Johnson 1934
Rocky Colavito 1964
Mark McGwire 1997
33—Jimmie Foxx 1929
Gus Zernial 1951
Dwayne Murphy 1984
Jose Canseco 1986
Mark McGwire 1989
Jason Giambi 1999
32—Reggie Jackson 1971, 1973
Mark McGwire 1988
31—Bob Johnson 1940
Sal Bando 1969
Jose Canseco 1987
30—Jimmie Foxx 1931
Bob Johnson 1938
Gus Zernial 1955
Dave Kingman 1985
Miguel Tejada 2000

100-plus RBIs

169—Jimmie Foxx 1932
165—Al Simmons 1930
163—Jimmie Foxx 1933
157—Al Simmons 1929
156—Jimmie Foxx 1930
151—Al Simmons 1932
137—Jason Giambi 2000
130—Frank Baker 1912
Jimmie Foxx 1934
129—Al Simmons 1925
Gus Zernial *1951
128—Al Simmons 1931
125—Nap Lajoie 1901
124—Jose Canseco 1988
123—Jason Giambi 1999
122—Jose Canseco 1991
121—Bob Johnson 1936
120—Jimmie Foxx 1931
Hank Majeski 1948
118—Reggie Jackson 1969
Dave Kingman 1984
Mark McGwire 1987
117—Frank Baker 1913
Jimmie Foxx 1929
Norm Siebern 1962
Reggie Jackson 1973
Jose Canseco 1986
115—Frank Baker 1911
Joe Hauser 1924
Jimmie Foxx 1935
Miguel Tejada 2000
114—Bob Johnson 1939
113—Bob Johnson 1938
Sal Bando 1969
Jose Canseco 1987
Mark McGwire 1996
112—Mickey Cochrane 1932
111—John Jaha 1999
110—Jason Giambi 1998
109—Al Simmons 1926
Bob Johnson 1935
Tony Armas 1980
108—Lave Cross 1902
Al Simmons 1927
Bob Johnson 1937
Sam Chapman 1949
Gus Zernial 1953
Mark McGwire 1990
107—Al Simmons 1928
Bob Johnson 1941
106—Sam Chapman 1941
Geronimo Berroa 1996
Matt Stairs 1998
105—Harry Simpson 1956
104—Bob Cerv 1958
Reggie Jackson 1975
Mark McGwire 1992
Ben Grieve 2000
103—Bob Johnson 1940
Sal Bando 1974
102—Al Simmons 1924
Eddie Robinson 1953
Rocky Colavito 1964
Matt Stairs 1999
101—Stuffy McInnis 1912
Tilly Walker 1921
Jose Canseco 1990
Ruben Sierra 1993
100—Bing Miller 1930
Gus Zernial 1952
Terry Steinbach 1996

*125 with Athletics; 4 with White Sox.

20-plus victories

1901—Chick Fraser 22-16
1902—Rube Waddell 24-7
Eddie Plank 20-15
1903—Eddie Plank 23-16
Rube Waddell 21-16
1904—Eddie Plank 26-17
Rube Waddell 25-19
1905—Rube Waddell 27-10
Eddie Plank 24-12
1907—Eddie Plank 24-16
Jimmy Dygert 21-8
1910—Jack Coombs 31-9
Chief Bender 23-5
1911—Jack Coombs 28-12
Eddie Plank 23-8
1912—Eddie Plank 26-6
Jack Coombs 21-10
1913—Chief Bender 21-10
1918—Scott Perry 20-19
1922—Eddie Rommel 27-13
1925—Eddie Rommel 21-10
1927—Lefty Grove 20-13
1928—Lefty Grove 24-8
1929—George Earnshaw 24-8
Lefty Grove 20-6
1930—Lefty Grove 28-5
George Earnshaw 22-13
1931—Lefty Grove 31-4
George Earnshaw 21-7
Rube Walberg 20-12
1932—Lefty Grove 25-10
1933—Lefty Grove 24-8
1949—Alex Kellner 20-12
1952—Bobby Shantz 24-7
1971—Vida Blue 24-8
Catfish Hunter 21-11
1972—Catfish Hunter 21-7
1973—Catfish Hunter 21-5
Ken Holtzman 21-13
Vida Blue 20-9
1974—Catfish Hunter 25-12
1975—Vida Blue 22-11
1980—Mike Norris 22-9
1987—Dave Stewart 20-13
1988—Dave Stewart 21-12
1989—Dave Stewart 21-9
1990—Bob Welch 27-6
Dave Stewart 22-11
2000—Tim Hudson 20-6

A.L. home run champions

1901—Nap Lajoie 14
1902—Socks Seybold 16
1904—Harry Davis 10
1905—Harry Davis 8
1906—Harry Davis 12
1907—Harry Davis 8
1911—Frank Baker 11
1912—Frank Baker *10
1913—Frank Baker 12
1914—Frank Baker 9
1918—Tilly Walker *11
1932—Jimmie Foxx 58
1933—Jimmie Foxx 48
1935—Jimmie Foxx *36
1951—Gus Zernial 33
1973—Reggie Jackson 32
1975—Reggie Jackson *36
1981—Tony Armas *22
1987—Mark McGwire 49
1988—Jose Canseco 42
1991—Jose Canseco *44
1996—Mark McGwire 52

* Tied for league lead

A.L. RBI champions

1901—Nap Lajoie 125
1905—Harry Davis 83
1906—Harry Davis 96
1912—Frank Baker 130
1913—Frank Baker 117
1929—Al Simmons 157
1932—Jimmie Foxx 169
1933—Jimmie Foxx 163
1951—Gus Zernial *129
1973—Reggie Jackson 117
1988—Jose Canseco 124

*125 with Athletics; 4 with White Sox.

A.L. batting champions

1901—Nap Lajoie .... .426
1930—Al Simmons .... .381
1931—Al Simmons .... .390
1933—Jimmie Foxx .... .356
1951—Ferris Fain .... .344
1952—Ferris Fain .... .327

A.L. ERA champions

1905—Rube Waddell 1.48
1909—Harry Krause 1.39
1926—Lefty Grove 2.51
1929—Lefty Grove 2.81
1930—Lefty Grove 2.54
1931—Lefty Grove 2.06
1932—Lefty Grove 2.84
1970—Diego Segui 2.56
1971—Vida Blue 1.82
1974—Catfish Hunter 2.49
1981—Steve McCatty 2.32
1994—Steve Ontiveros 2.65

A.L. strikeout champions

1902—Rube Waddell 210
1903—Rube Waddell 302
1904—Rube Waddell 349
1905—Rube Waddell 287
1906—Rube Waddell 196
1907—Rube Waddell 232
1925—Lefty Grove 116
1926—Lefty Grove 194
1927—Lefty Grove 174
1928—Lefty Grove 183
1929—Lefty Grove 170
1930—Lefty Grove 209
1931—Lefty Grove 175

No-hit pitchers

(9 innings or more)

1905—Weldon Henley .... 6-0 vs. St. Louis
1910—Chief Bender .... 4-0 vs. Cleveland
1916—Joe Bush .... 5-0 vs. Cleveland
1945—Dick Fowler .... 1-0 vs. St. Louis
1947—Bill McCahan .... 3-0 vs. Washington
1968—Catfish Hunter .. 4-0 vs. Minnesota (Perfect)
1970—Vida Blue .... 6-0 vs. Minnesota
1975—Vida Blue-Glenn Abbott-Paul Lindblad-
Rollie Fingers .... 5-0 vs. California
1983—Mike Warren .... 3-0 vs. Chicago
1990—Dave Stewart .... 5-0 vs. Toronto

Longest hitting streaks

29—Bill Lamar 1925
28—Bing Miller 1929
27—Socks Seybold 1901
Al Simmons 1931
26—Bob Johnson 1938
25—Jason Giambi 1997
24—Jimmie Foxx 1929
Ferris Fain 1952
Carney Lansford 1984
23—Al Simmons 1925
22—Al Simmons 1925
Doc Cramer 1932
Hector Lopez 1957
Vic Power 1958
21—Ty Cobb 1927
20—Wally Schang 1916
Wally Moses 1938
Dave Philley 1953
Hal Smith 1958
Vic Power *1958
Jerry Lumpe 1962

*Two teams

INDIVIDUAL SEASON, GAME RECORDS

SEASON

Batting			
At-bats	670	Al Simmons	1932
Runs	152	Al Simmons	1930
Hits	253	Al Simmons	1925
Singles	174	Al Simmons	1925
Doubles	53	Al Simmons	1926
Triples	21	Frank Baker	1912
Home runs	58	Jimmie Foxx	1932
Home runs, rookie	49	Mark McGwire	1987
Grand slams	4	Jason Giambi	2000
Total bases	438	Jimmie Foxx	1932
RBIs	169	Jimmie Foxx	1932
Walks	149	Ed Joost	1949
Most strikeouts	175	Jose Canseco	1986
Fewest strikeouts	17	Dick Siebert	1942
Batting average	.426	Nap Lajoie	1901
Slugging pct.	.749	Jimmie Foxx	1932
Stolen bases	130	Rickey Henderson	1982
Pitching			
Games	81	John Wyatt	1964
Complete games	39	Rube Waddell	1904
Innings	383	Rube Waddell	1904
Wins	31	Jack Coombs	1910
		Lefty Grove	1931
Losses	25	Scott Perry	1920
Winning pct.	.886 (31-4)	Lefty Grove	1931
Walks	168	Elmer Myers	1916
Strikeouts	349	Rube Waddell	1904
Shutouts	13	Jack Coombs	1910
Home runs allowed	40	Orlando Pena	1964
Lowest ERA	1.30	Jack Coombs	1910
Saves	51	Dennis Eckersley	1992

GAME

Batting			
Runs	5	Last by Luis Polonia	9-9-88
Hits	6	Last by Joe DeMaestri	7-8-55
Doubles	4	Frankie Hayes	7-25-36
Triples	3	Bert Campaneris	8-29-67
Home runs	3	Last by Miguel Tejada	6-11-99
RBIs	10	Reggie Jackson	6-14-69
Total bases	16	Jimmie Foxx	7-10-32
Stolen bases	6	Eddie Collins	9-11-12, 9-22-12

CAREER LEADERS

BATTING

Games

Bert Campaneris	1,795
Rickey Henderson	1,704
Jimmy Dykes	1,702
Sal Bando	1,468
Bob Johnson	1,459
Pete Suder	1,421
Harry Davis	1,413
Danny Murphy	1,412
Bing Miller	1,361
Elmer Valo	1,361

At-bats

Bert Campaneris	7,180
Rickey Henderson	6,140
Jimmy Dykes	6,023
Bob Johnson	5,428
Harry Davis	5,367
Sal Bando	5,145
Danny Murphy	5,138
Al Simmons	5,130
Pete Suder	5,085
Bing Miller	4,762

Runs

Rickey Henderson	1,270
Bob Johnson	997
Bert Campaneris	983
Jimmie Foxx	975
Al Simmons	969
Max Bishop	882
Jimmy Dykes	881
Mickey Cochrane	823
Harry Davis	811
Mark McGwire	773

Hits

Bert Campaneris	1,882
Al Simmons	1,827
Rickey Henderson	1,768
Jimmy Dykes	1,705
Bob Johnson	1,617
Harry Davis	1,500
Jimmie Foxx	1,492
Danny Murphy	1,489
Bing Miller	1,482
Mickey Cochrane	1,317
Carney Lansford	1,317

Doubles

Jimmy Dykes	365
Al Simmons	348
Harry Davis	319
Bob Johnson	307
Bing Miller	292
Rickey Henderson	289
Danny Murphy	279
Wally Moses	274
Bert Campaneris	270
Jimmie Foxx	257

Triples

Danny Murphy	102
Al Simmons	98
Frank Baker	88
Eddie Collins	85
Harry Davis	82
Jimmie Foxx	79
Rube Oldring	75
Topsy Hartsel	74
Bing Miller	74
Jimmy Dykes	73

Home runs

Mark McGwire	363
Jimmie Foxx	302
Reggie Jackson	269
Jose Canseco	254
Bob Johnson	252
Al Simmons	209
Sal Bando	192
Gus Zernial	191
Sam Chapman	174
Rickey Henderson	167

Total bases

Al Simmons	2,998
Bob Johnson	2,824
Jimmie Foxx	2,813
Rickey Henderson	2,640
Bert Campaneris	2,502
Jimmy Dykes	2,474
Mark McGwire	2,451
Reggie Jackson	2,323
Bing Miller	2,202
Harry Davis	2,190

Runs batted in

Al Simmons	1,178
Jimmie Foxx	1,075
Bob Johnson	1,040
Mark McGwire	941
Sal Bando	796
Jose Canseco	793
Reggie Jackson	776
Jimmy Dykes	764
Bing Miller	762
Harry Davis	761

Extra-base hits

Al Simmons	655
Jimmie Foxx	638
Bob Johnson	631
Mark McGwire	563
Reggie Jackson	530
Jimmy Dykes	524
Rickey Henderson	497
Harry Davis	470
Bing Miller	460
Jose Canseco	448

Batting average

(Minimum 500 games)

Al Simmons	.356
Jimmie Foxx	.339
Eddie Collins	.337
Mickey Cochrane	.321
Frank Baker	.321
Stuffy McInnis	.313
Bing Miller	.311
Doc Cramer	.308
Pinky Higgins	.307
Wally Moses	.307

Stolen bases

Rickey Henderson	867
Bert Campaneris	566
Eddie Collins	376
Bill North	232
Harry Davis	223
Topsy Hartsel	196
Rube Oldring	187
Danny Murphy	185
Frank Baker	172
Carney Lansford	146

PITCHING

Earned-run average

(Minimum 1,000 innings)

Rube Waddell	1.97
Chief Bender	2.32
Eddie Plank	2.39
Jack Coombs	2.60
Lefty Grove	2.88
Rollie Fingers	2.91
Ken Holtzman	2.92
Vida Blue	2.95
Catfish Hunter	3.13
Joe Bush	3.19

Wins

Eddie Plank	284
Lefty Grove	195
Chief Bender	193
Eddie Rommel	171
Catfish Hunter	161
Rube Walberg	134
Rube Waddell	131
Vida Blue	124
Dave Stewart	119
Jack Coombs	115

Losses

Eddie Plank	162
Eddie Rommel	119
Rube Walberg	114
Catfish Hunter	113
Alex Kellner	108
Rick Langford	105
Chief Bender	102
Slim Harriss	93
Vida Blue	86
Rollie Naylor	83

Innings pitched

Eddie Plank	3,860.2
Chief Bender	2,602.0
Eddie Rommel	2,556.1
Catfish Hunter	2,456.1
Lefty Grove	2,401.0
Rube Walberg	2,186.2
Vida Blue	1,945.2
Rube Waddell	1,869.1
Alex Kellner	1,730.1
Dave Stewart	1,717.1

Strikeouts

Eddie Plank	1,985
Rube Waddell	1,576
Chief Bender	1,536
Lefty Grove	1,523
Catfish Hunter	1,520
Vida Blue	1,315
Dave Stewart	1,152
Rube Walberg	907
Jack Coombs	870
Blue Moon Odom	799

Bases on balls

Eddie Plank	913
Rube Walberg	853
Lefty Grove	740
Blue Moon Odom	732
Eddie Rommel	724
Alex Kellner	717
Catfish Hunter	687
Phil Marchildon	682
Dave Stewart	655
Vida Blue	617

Games

Dennis Eckersley	525
Eddie Plank	524
Rollie Fingers	502
Eddie Rommel	500
Paul Lindblad	479
Rube Walberg	412
Lefty Grove	402
Rick Honeycutt	387
Chief Bender	385
Catfish Hunter	363

Shutouts

Eddie Plank	59
Rube Waddell	37
Chief Bender	36
Catfish Hunter	31
Vida Blue	28
Jack Coombs	28
Lefty Grove	20
Eddie Rommel	18
Jimmy Dygert	16
Joe Bush	15
Rube Walberg	15

Saves

Dennis Eckersley	320
Rollie Fingers	136
Billy Taylor	100
John Wyatt	73
Jay Howell	61
Jack Aker	58
Lefty Grove	51
Jason Isringhausen	41
Paul Lindblad	41
Bill Caudill	37

TEAM SEASON, GAME RECORDS

SEASON

Batting

Most at-bats	5,630	1996
Most runs	981	1932
Fewest runs	447	1916
Most hits	1,659	1925
Most singles	1,206	1925
Most doubles	323	1928
Most triples	108	1912
Most home runs	243	1996
Fewest home runs	16	1915, 1917
Most grand slams	14	2000
Most pinch-hit home runs	8	1970
Most total bases	2,546	1996
Most stolen bases	341	1976
Highest batting average	.307	1925
Lowest batting average	.223	1908
Highest slugging pct.	.458	2000

Pitching

Lowest ERA	1.79	1910
Highest ERA	6.08	1936
Most complete games	136	1904
Most shutouts	27	1907, 1909
Most saves	64	1988, 1990
Most walks	827	1915
Most strikeouts	1,042	1987

Fielding

Most errors	337	1901
Fewest errors	87	1990
Most double plays	217	1949
Highest fielding average	.986	1990

General

Most games won	107	1931
Most games lost	117	1916
Highest win pct.	.704	1931
Lowest win pct.	.235	1916

GAME, INNING

Batting

Most runs, game	24	Last 5-1-29
Most runs, inning	13	Last 7-5-96
Most hits, game	29	5-1-29
Most home runs, game	8	6-27-96
Most total bases, game	44	5-1-29, 6-27-96

300-game winner Lefty Grove won 195 times as a member of the Athletics.

HISTORY

ATHLETICS YEAR-BY-YEAR

Year	W	L	Place	Games Back	Manager	Leaders: Batting avg.	Hits	Home runs	RBIs	Wins	ERA
1901	74	62	4th	9	Mack	Lajoie, .422	Lajoie, 229	Lajoie, 14	Lajoie, 125	Fraser, 22	Plank, 3.31
1902	83	53	1st	+5	Mack	L. Cross, .342	L. Cross, 191	Seybold, 16	L. Cross, 108	Waddell, 24	Waddell, 2.05
1903	75	60	2nd	14½	Mack	Hartsel, .311	L. Cross, 163	Seybold, 8	L. Cross, 90	Plank, 23	Plank, 2.38
1904	81	70	5th	12½	Mack	Davis, .309	L. Cross, 176	Davis, 10	D. Murphy, 77	Plank, 26	Waddell, 1.62
1905	92	56	1st	+2	Mack	Davis, .285	Davis, 173	Davis, 8	Davis, 83	Waddell, 27	Waddell, 1.48
1906	78	67	4th	12	Mack	Seybold, .316	Davis, 161	Davis, 12	Davis, 96	Plank, 19	Waddell, 2.21
1907	88	57	2nd	1½	Mack	Nicholls, .302	Davis, 155	Davis, 8	Davis, 87	Plank, 24	Bender, 2.05
1908	68	85	6th	22	Mack	D. Murphy, .265	D. Murphy, 139	Davis, 5	D. Murphy, 66	Vickers, 18	Bender, 1.75
1909	95	58	2nd	3½	Mack	E. Collins, .346	E. Collins, 198	D. Murphy, 5	Baker, 85	Plank, 19	Krause, 1.39
1910	102	48	1st	+14½	Mack	E. Collins, .322	E. Collins, 188	D. Murphy, Oldring, 4	E. Collins, 81	Coombs, 31	Coombs, 1.30
1911	101	50	1st	+13½	Mack	E. Collins, .365	Baker, 198	Baker, 11	Baker, 115	Coombs, 28	Plank 2.10
1912	90	62	3rd	15	Mack	E. Collins, .348	Baker, 200	Baker, 10	Baker, 130	Plank, 26	Plank 2.22
1913	96	57	1st	+6½	Mack	E. Collins, .345	Baker, 190	Baker, 12	Baker, 117	Bender, 21	Bender, 2.21
1914	99	53	1st	+8½	Mack	E. Collins, .344	Baker, 182	Baker, 9	McInnis, 95	Bender, Bush, 17	Bressler, 1.77
1915	43	109	8th	58½	Mack	McInnis, .314	Strunk, 144	Oldring, 6	Lajoie, 61	Wyckoff, 10	Knowlson, 3.49
1916	36	117	8th	54½	Mack	Strunk, .316	Strunk, 172	Schang, 7	McInnis, 60	Bush, 15	Bush, 2.57
1917	55	98	8th	44½	Mack	McInnis, .303	McInnis, 172	Bodie, 7	Bodie, 74	Bush, 11	Bush, 2.47
1918	52	76	8th	24	Mack	Burns, .352	Burns, 178	T. Walker, 11	Burns, 70	Perry, 21	Perry, 1.98
1919	36	104	8th	52	Mack	Burns, .296	Burns, 139	T. Walker, 10	T. Walker, 64	J. Johnson, Kinney, 9	Naylor, 3.34
1920	48	106	8th	50	Mack	Dugan, .322	Dugan, 158	T. Walker, 17	T. Walker, 82	Perry, 11	Rommel, 2.85
1921	53	100	8th	45	Mack	Witt, .315	Witt, 198	T. Walker, 23	T. Walker, 101	Rommel, 16	Rommel, 3.94
1922	65	89	7th	29	Mack	B. Miller, .335	Galloway, 185	T. Walker, 37	T. Walker, 99	Rommel, 27	Rommel, 3.28
1923	69	83	6th	29	Mack	Hauser, .307	Hauser, 165	Hauser, 17	Hauser, 94	Rommel, 18	Rommel, 3.27
1924	71	81	5th	20	Mack	B. Miller, .342	Simmons, 183	Hauser, 27	Hauser, 115	Rommel, 18	Rommel, 3.95
1925	88	64	2nd	8½	Mack	Simmons, .387	Simmons, 253	Simmons, 24	Simmons, 129	Rommel, 21	Gray, 3.27
1926	83	67	3rd	6	Mack	Simmons, .341	Simmons, 199	Simmons, 19	Simmons, 109	Grove, 13	Grove, 2.51
1927	91	63	2nd	19	Mack	Simmons, .392	Cobb, 175	Simmons, 15	Simmons, 108	Grove, 20	Grove, 3.19
1928	98	55	2nd	2½	Mack	Simmons, .351	B. Miller, 168	Hauser, 16	Simmons, 107	Grove, 24	Grove, 2.58
1929	104	46	1st	+18	Mack	Simmons, .365	Simmons, 212	Simmons, 34	Simmons, 157	Earnshaw, 24	Grove, 2.81
1930	102	52	1st	+8	Mack	Simmons, .381	Simmons, 211	Foxx, 37	Simmons, 165	Grove, 28	Grove, 2.54
1931	107	45	1st	+13½	Mack	Simmons, .390	Simmons, 200	Foxx, 30	Simmons, 128	Grove, 31	Grove, 2.06
1932	94	60	2nd	13	Mack	Foxx, .364	Simmons, 216	Foxx, 58	Foxx, 169	Grove, 25	Grove, 2.84
1933	79	72	3rd	19½	Mack	Foxx, .356	Foxx, 204	Foxx, 48	Foxx, 163	Grove, 24	Grove, 3.20
1934	68	82	5th	31	Mack	Foxx, .334	Cramer, 202	Foxx, 44	Foxx, 130	Marcum, 14	Cain, 4.41
1935	58	91	8th	34	Mack	Foxx, .346	Cramer, 214	Foxx, 36	Foxx, 115	Marcum, 17	Mahaffey, 3.90
1936	53	100	8th	49	Mack	Moses, .345	Moses, 202	B. Johnson, 25	B. Johnson, 121	Kelley, 15	Kelley, 3.86
1937	54	97	7th	46½	Mack	Moses, .320	Moses, 208	B. Johnson, Moses, 25	B. Johnson, 108	Kelley, 13	E. Smith, 3.94
1938	53	99	8th	46	Mack	B. Johnson, .313	Moses, 181	B. Johnson, 30	B. Johnson, 113	Caster, 16	Caster, 4.35
1939	55	97	7th	51½	Mack	B. Johnson, .338	B. Johnson, 184	B. Johnson, 23	B. Johnson, 114	Nelson, 10	Nelson, 4.78
1940	54	100	8th	36	Mack	Moses, .309	Siebert, 170	B. Johnson, 31	B. Johnson, 103	Babich, 14	Babich, 3.73
1941	64	90	8th	37	Mack	Siebert, .334	Chapman, 178	Chapman, 25	B. Johnson, 107	Knott, 13	Marchildon, 3.57
1942	55	99	8th	48	Mack	B. Johnson, .291	B. Johnson, 160	B. Johnson, 13	B. Johnson, 80	Marchildon, 17	Wolff, 3.32
1943	49	105	8th	49	Mack	Hall, .256	Siebert, 140	Estalella, 11	Siebert, 72	Flores, 12	Flores, 3.11
1944	72	82	*5th	17	Mack	Siebert, .306	Estalella, 151	Hayes, 13	Hayes, 78	Christopher, 14	Berry, 1.94
1945	52	98	8th	34½	Mack	Estalella, .299	Hall, 161	Estalella, 8	Kell, 56	Christopher, 13	Berry, 2.35
1946	49	105	8th	55	Mack	McCosky, .354	Chapman, 142	Chapman, 20	Chapman, 67	Marchildon, 13	Flores, 2.32
1947	78	76	5th	19	Mack	McCosky, .328	McCosky, 179	Chapman, 14	Chapman, 83	Marchildon, 19	Fowler, 2.81
1948	84	70	4th	12½	Mack	McCosky, .326	Majeski, 183	Joost, 16	Majeski, 120	Fowler, 15	Fowler, 3.78
1949	81	73	5th	16	Mack	Valo, .283	Chapman, 164	Chapman, 24	Chapman, 108	Kellner, 20	Shantz, 3.40
1950	52	102	8th	46	Mack	Dillinger, Lehner, .309	Fain, 147	Chapman, 23	Chapman, 95	Hooper, 15	Brissie, 4.02
1951	70	84	6th	28	Dykes	Fain, .344	Joost, 160	Zernial, 33	Zernial, 125	Shantz, 18	Zoldak, 3.16
1952	79	75	4th	16	Dykes	Fain, .327	Fain, 176	Zernial, 29	Zernial, 100	Shantz, 24	Shantz, 2.48
1953	59	95	7th	41½	Dykes	Philley, .303	Philley, 188	Zernial, 42	Zernial, 108	Byrd, Kellner, 11	Fricano, 3.88
1954	51	103	8th	60	Joost	Finigan, .302	Finigan, 147	Wilson, 15	Zernial, 62	Portocarrero, 9	Burtschy, 3.80
KANSAS CITY ATHLETICS											
1955	63	91	6th	33	Boudreau	Power, .319	Power, 190	Zernial, 30	Zernial, 84	Ditmar, 12	Gorman, 3.55
1956	52	102	8th	45	Boudreau	Power, .309	Power, 164	Simpson, 21	Simpson, 105	Ditmar, 12	Burnette, 2.89
1957	59	94	7th	38½	Boudreau, Craft	H. Smith, .303	Power, 121	Zernial, 27	Zernial, 69	Morgan, Trucks, 9	Trucks, 3.03
1958	73	81	7th	19	Craft	Cerv, .305	Cerv, 157	Cerv, 38	Cerv, 104	Garver, 12	Dickson, 3.27
1959	66	88	7th	28	Craft	Tuttle, .300	Tuttle, 139	Cerv, 20	Cerv, 87	B. Daley, 16	B. Daley, 3.16
1960	58	96	8th	39	Elliot	Williams, .288	Lumpe, 156	Siebern, 19	Siebern, 69	B. Daley, 16	Herbert, 3.28
1961	61	100	*9th	47½	Gordon, Bauer	Siebern, .296	Howser, 171	Siebern 18	Siebern, 98	Bass, 11	Archer, 3.20
1962	72	90	9th	24	Bauer	Siebern, .308	Lumpe, 193	Siebern, 25	Siebern, 117	Rakow, 14	Pena, 3.01
1963	73	89	8th	31½	Lopat	Causey, .280	Charles, 161	Siebern, Lumpe, 16	Siebern, 83	Pena, Wickersham, 12	Drabowsky, 3.05
1964	57	105	10th	42	Lopat, McGaha	Causey, .281	Causey, 170	Colavito, 34	Colavito, 102	Pena, 12	Stock, 1.94
1965	59	103	10th	43	McGaha, Sullivan	Campaneris, .270	Campaneris, 156	Harrelson, 23	Harrelson, 66	Sheldon, Talbot, 10	O'Donoghue, Sheldon, 3.95
1966	74	86	7th	23	Dark	Cater, .292	Campaneris, 153	Repoz, 11	Green, 62	Krausse, 14	Aker, 1.99
1967	62	99	10th	29½	Dark, Appling	Donaldson, .276	Campaneris, 149	Monday, 14	Monday, 58	Hunter, 13	Hunter, 2.81
OAKLAND ATHLETICS											
1968	82	80	6th	21	Kennedy	Cater, .290	Campaneris, 177	Jackson, 29	Jackson, 74	Odom, 16	Nash, 2.28
WEST DIVISION											
1969	88	74	2nd	9	Bauer, McNamara	Bando, .281	Bando, 171	Jackson, 47	Jackson, 118	Dobson, Odom, 15	Odom, 2.92
1970	89	73	2nd	9	McNamara	Rudi, .309	Campaneris, 168	Mincher, 27	Bando, 75	Hunter, 18	Segui, 2.56
1971	101	60	†1st	+16	Williams	Jackson, .277	Jackson, 157	Jackson, 32	Bando, 94	Blue, 24	Blue, 1.82
1972	93	62	‡1st	+5½	Williams	Rudi, .305	Rudi, 181	Epstein, 26	Bando, 77	Hunter, 21	Hunter, 2.04
1973	94	68	‡1st	+6	Williams	Jackson, .293	Bando, 170	Jackson, 32	Jackson, 117	Holtzman, Hunter, 21	Fingers, 1.92
1974	90	72	‡1st	+5	Dark	Rudi, .293	Rudi, 174	Jackson, 29	Bando, 103	Hunter, 25	Lindblad, 2.06
1975	98	64	†1st	+7	Dark	Washington, .308	Washington, 182	Jackson, 36	Jackson, 104	Blue, 22	Todd, 2.29
1976	87	74	2nd	2½	Tanner	North, .276	North, 163	Bando, 27	Rudi, 94	Blue, 18	Blue, 2.35
1977	63	98	7th	38½	McKeon, Winkles	Page, .307	Sanguillen, 157	Gross, 22	Page, 75	Blue, 14	Torrealba, 2.62
1978	69	93	6th	23	Winkles, McKeon	Page, .285	Page, 147	Page, 17	Page, 70	Johnson, 11	Sosa, 2.64
1979	54	108	7th	34	Marshall	Revering, .288	Revering, 136	Newman, 22	Revering, 77	Langford, 12	McCatty, 4.22
1980	83	79	2nd	14	Martin	R. Henderson, .303	R. Henderson, 179	Armas, 35	Armas, 109	Norris, 22	Norris, 2.53
1981	64	45	∞†1st/2nd	—	Martin	R. Henderson, .319	R. Henderson, 135	Armas, 22	Armas, 76	McCatty, 14	McCatty, 2.32
1982	68	94	5th	25	Martin	Burroughs, .277	R. Henderson, 143	Armas, 28	Murphy, 94	Keough, Langford, 11	Underwood, 3.29
1983	74	88	4th	25	Boros	Lansford, .308	R. Henderson, 150	Lopes, Murphy, 17	Murphy, 75	Codiroli, 12	Burgmeier, 2.81
1984	77	85	4th	7	Boros, Moore	Lansford, .300	Lansford, 179	Kingman, 35	Kingman, 118	Burris, 13	Caudill, 2.71
1985	77	85	*4th	14	Moore	Bochte, .295	Griffin, 166	Kingman, 30	Kingman, 91	Codiroli, 14	Howell, 2.85
1986	76	86	*3rd	16	Moore, La Russa	Griffin, .285	Griffin, 169	Kingman, 35	Canseco, 117	Young, 13	Haas, 2.74
1987	81	81	3rd	4	La Russa	Lansford, McGwire, .289	Canseco, 162	McGwire, 49	McGwire, 118	Stewart, 20	Eckersley, 3.03
1988	104	58	‡1st	+13	La Russa	Canseco, .307	Canseco, 187	Canseco, 42	Canseco, 124	Stewart, 21	Nelson, 3.06
1989	99	63	‡1st	+7	La Russa	Lansford, .336	Lansford, 185	McGwire, 33	Parker, 97	Stewart, 21	Burns, 2.24
1990	103	59	‡1st	+9	La Russa	R. Henderson, .325	R. Henderson, 159	McGwire, 39	McGwire, 108	Welch, 27	Stewart, 2.56
1991	84	78	4th	11	La Russa	Baines, .295	D. Henderson, 158	Canseco, 44	Canseco, 122	Moore, 17	Moore, 2.96
1992	96	66	†1st	+6	La Russa	Bordick, .300	Bordick, 151	McGwire, 42	McGwire, 104	Moore, 17	Parrett, 3.02
1993	68	94	7th	26	La Russa	R. Henderson, .327	Gates, 155	Sierra, 22	Sierra, 101	Witt, 14	Witt, 4.21
1994	51	63	2nd	1	La Russa	Berroa, .306	Javier, 114	Sierra, 23	Sierra, 92	Darling, 10	Ontiveros, 2.65
1995	67	77	4th	11	La Russa	R. Henderson, .300	Berroa, 152	McGwire, 39	McGwire, 90	Stottlemyre, 14	Ontiveros, 4.3
1996	78	84	3rd	12	Howe	McGwire, .312	Berroa, 170	McGwire, 52	McGwire, 113	Wasdin, 8	Prieto, 4.157
1997	65	97	4th	25	Howe	Stairs, .298	Giambi, 152	McGwire, 34	Giambi, McGwire, 81	Small, 9	Small, 4.28
1998	74	88	4th	14	Howe	Giambi, .295	Grieve, 168	Giambi, 27	Giambi, 110	Rogers, 16	Rogers, 3.17
1999	87	75	2nd	8	Howe	Giambi, .315	Giambi, 181	Stairs, 38	Giambi, 123	Heredia, 13	Hudson, 3.23
2000	91	70	▲1st	½	Howe	Ja. Giambi, .333	Ja. Giambi, 170	Ja. Giambi, 43	Ja. Giambi, 137	Hudson, 20	Zito, 2.72

* Tied for position. † Lost Championship Series. ‡ Won Championship Series. ∞ First half 37-23; second half 27-22. ▲ Lost Division Series.

Note: Batting average minimum 350 at-bats; ERA minimum 90 innings pitched.

SEATTLE MARINERS

FRANCHISE CHRONOLOGY

First season: 1977, as a result of the two-team expansion that increased the American League to 14 teams. The Mariners were shut out by California, 7-0, in their A.L. debut and went on to lose 98 games. They finished their first season in sixth place, 38 games behind A.L. West Division-champion Kansas City.

1978-present: The Mariners have not had much to brag about in their short existence. Before 1995, they had never finished above fourth place and had two winning seasons to show for 18 years. Over that same span, their expansion mate, Toronto, had won five division titles, two pennants and a pair of World Series. But the Mariners' fortunes changed in 1995. They caught California with a late run, earned their first West Division championship in a one-game playoff and captured the A.L.'s first division playoff series in five games over the New York Yankees before losing in the Championship Series. They won a second division title in 1997 and qualified for postseason play as a wild-card in 2000, but lost one Division Series and another ALCS.

Lefthander Randy Johnson.

MARINERS VS. OPPONENTS BY DECADE

	A's	Indians	Orioles	Red Sox	Tigers	Twins	White Sox	Yankees	Angels	Rangers	Brewers	Royals	Blue Jays	Devil Rays	Interleague	Decade Record
1977-79	15-28	9-22	6-26	8-25	13-20	20-23	21-22	15-18	18-25	18-25	11-21	13-30	20-12			187-297
1980-89	46-78	48-72	51-63	54-66	48-66	59-67	52-71	45-68	48-79	65-65	53-59	59-70	45-69			673-893
1990-99	50-71	52-54	57-58	46-71	53-58	65-51	62-59	56-61	64-59	71-54	48-35	55-64	50-54	14-9	21-29	764-787
2000-	4-9	2-7	7-3	5-5	2-7	9-3	5-7	6-4	8-5	7-5		8-4	8-2	9-3	11-7	91-71
Totals	115-186	111-155	121-150	113-167	116-151	153-144	140-159	122-151	138-168	161-149	112-115	135-168	123-137	23-12	32-36	1715-2048

Interleague results: 6-7 vs. Dodgers; 8-12 vs. Padres; 5-8 vs. Giants; 8-5 vs. Rockies; 5-4 vs. Diamondbacks.

ALL-TIME RECORD OF EXPANSION TEAMS

Team	W	L	Pct.	DT	P	WS
Arizona	250	236	.514	1	0	0
Kansas City	2,548	2,497	.505	6	2	1
Toronto	1,867	1,897	.496	5	2	2
Houston	3,052	3,138	.493	6	0	0
Montreal	2,454	2,596	.486	2	0	0
Anaheim	3,069	3,281	.483	3	0	0
Colorado	594	639	.482	0	0	0
Milwaukee	2,421	2,631	.479	2	1	0
New York	2,934	3,246	.475	4	4	2
Texas	2,952	3,381	.466	4	0	0
San Diego	2,315	2,742	.458	3	2	0
Seattle	1,715	2,048	.456	2	0	0
Florida	551	678	.448	0	1	1
Tampa Bay	201	284	.414	0	0	0

DT—Division Titles. P—Pennants won. WS—World Series won.

MANAGERS

Name	*Years*	*Record*
Darrell Johnson	1977-80	226-362
Maury Wills	1980-81	26-56
Rene Lachemann	1981-83	140-180
Del Crandall	1983-84	93-141
Chuck Cottier	1984-86	98-119
Marty Martinez	1986	0-1
Dick Williams	1986-88	159-192
Jimmy Snyder	1988	45-60
Jim Lefebvre	1989-91	233-253
Bill Plummer	1992	64-98
Lou Piniella	1993-2000	631-596

WEST DIVISION CHAMPIONS

Year	*Record*	*Manager*	*ALCS Result*
1995	79-66	Piniella	Lost to Indians
1997	90-72	Piniella	Lost Div. Series

WILD-CARD QUALIFIERS

Year	*Record*	*Manager*	*Div. Series Result*	*ALCS Result*
2000	91-71	Piniella	Defeated White Sox	Lost to Yankees

BALLPARK CHRONOLOGY

Safeco Field (1999-present)

Capacity: 47,000.
First game: Padres 3, Mariners 2 (July 15, 1999).
First batter: Quilvio Veras, Padres.
First hit: Eric Owens, Padres (single).
First run: Quilvio Veras, Padres (3rd inning).
First home run: Russ Davis, Mariners (July 17).
First winning pitcher: Will Cunnane, Padres.
First-season attendance: 2,915,908 (includes Kingdome attendance prior to July 15).

The Kingdome (1977-99)

Capacity: 59,856.
First game: California 7, Mariners 0 (April 6, 1977).
First-season attendance: 1,338,511.

ATTENDANCE HIGHS

Total	*Season*	*Park*
3,198,995	1997	Kingdome
3,150,034	2000	Safeco Field
2,915,908	1999	Kingdome/Safeco Field
2,722,392	1996	Kingdome
2,644,166	1998	Kingdome

A.L. MVP

Ken Griffey Jr. ,OF, 1997

CY YOUNG WINNER

Randy Johnson, LH, 1995

ROOKIE OF THE YEAR

Alvin Davis, 1B, 1984
Kazuhiro Sasaki, P, 2000

MANAGER OF THE YEAR

Lou Piniella, 1995

The powerful bat of center fielder Ken Griffey Jr. thrilled Seattle fans for 11 seasons and helped the Mariners rise out of the A.L. West cellar.

MILESTONE PERFORMANCES

25-plus home runs

56— Ken Griffey Jr. 1997, 1998
49— Ken Griffey Jr. 1996
48— Ken Griffey Jr. 1999
45— Ken Griffey Jr. 1993
44— Jay Buhner 1996
42— Alex Rodriguez 1998
Alex Rodriguez 1999
41— Alex Rodriguez 2000
40— Ken Griffey Jr. 1994
Jay Buhner 1995, 1997
37— Edgar Martinez 2000
36— Alex Rodriguez 1996
32— Gorman Thomas 1985
31— Tino Martinez 1995
Paul Sorrento 1997
29— Willie Horton 1979
Alvin Davis 1987
Edgar Martinez 1995, 1998
28— Jim Presley 1985
Edgar Martinez 1997
27— Lee Stanton 1977
Alvin Davis 1984
Jim Presley 1986
Ken Phelps 1987
Jay Buhner 1991, 1993
Ken Griffey Jr. 1992
26— Phil Bradley 1985
Jay Buhner 2000
25— Danny Tartabull 1986
Jay Buhner 1992

100-plus RBIs

147— Ken Griffey Jr. 1997
146— Ken Griffey Jr. 1998
145— Edgar Martinez 2000
140— Ken Griffey Jr. 1996
138— Jay Buhner 1996
134— Ken Griffey Jr. 1999
132— Alex Rodriguez 2000
124— Alex Rodriguez 1998
123— Alex Rodriguez 1996
121— Jay Buhner 1995
116— Alvin Davis 1984
113— Edgar Martinez 1995
111— Tino Martinez 1995
Alex Rodriguez 1999
109— Ken Griffey Jr. 1993
Jay Buhner 1997
108— Edgar Martinez 1997
107— Jim Presley 1986
106— Willie Horton 1979
103— Ken Griffey Jr. 1992
Edgar Martinez 1996
John Olerud 2000
102— Edgar Martinez 1998
100— Bruce Bochte 1979
Alvin Davis 1987
Ken Griffey Jr. 1991

20-plus victories

1997— Randy Johnson 20-4

A.L. home run champions

1994— Ken Griffey Jr. 40
1997— Ken Griffey Jr. 56
1998— Ken Griffey Jr. 56
1999— Ken Griffey Jr. 48

A.L. RBI champions

1997— Ken Griffey Jr. 147
2000— Edgar Martinez 145

A.L. batting champions

1992— Edgar Martinez .... .343
1995— Edgar Martinez .... .356
1996— Alex Rodriguez .... .358

A.L. ERA champions

1995— Randy Johnson 2.48

A.L. strikeout champions

1982— Floyd Bannister 209
1984— Mark Langston 204
1986— Mark Langston 245
1987— Mark Langston 262
1992— Randy Johnson 241
1993— Randy Johnson 308
1994— Randy Johnson 204
1995— Randy Johnson 294

No-hit pitchers
(9 innings or more)

1990— Randy Johnson .... 2-0 vs. Detroit
1993— Chris Bosio .... 7-0 vs. Boston

Longest hitting streaks

24— Joey Cora 1997
21— Dan Meyer 1979
Richie Zisk 1982
20— Alex Rodriguez 1996
19— Phil Bradley 1986
18— Joey Cora 1996
17— Edgar Martinez 1992, 1997
Alex Rodriguez 2000
16— Harold Reynolds 1989
Craig Reynolds 1978
Alex Rodriguez 1997
Joey Cora, 2 1998
Ken Griffey Jr. 1999
15— Willie Horton 1979
Richie Zisk 1981
Jack Perconte 1985
Edgar Martinez 1991
David Segui 1999

Second baseman Harold Reynolds was an offensive and defensive rock while the Mariners struggled through the 1980s.

INDIVIDUAL SEASON, GAME RECORDS

Speedy Julio Cruz, a second baseman during the team's formative years, holds the club record with 290 career stolen bases.

SEASON

Batting			
At-bats	686	Alex Rodriguez	1998
Runs	141	Alex Rodriguez	1996
Hits	215	Alex Rodriguez	1996
Singles	152	Jack Perconte	1984
Doubles	54	Alex Rodriguez	1996
Triples	11	Harold Reynolds	1988
Home runs	56	Ken Griffey Jr.	1997, 1998
Home runs, rookie	27	Alvin Davis	1984
Grand slams	4	Edgar Martinez	2000
Total bases	393	Ken Griffey Jr.	1997
RBIs	147	Ken Griffey Jr.	1997
Walks	123	Edgar Martinez	1996
Most strikeouts	175	Jay Buhner	1997
Fewest strikeouts	34	Harold Reynolds	1987
Batting average	.358	Alex Rodriguez	1996
Slugging pct.	.674	Ken Griffey Jr.	1994
Stolen bases	60	Harold Reynolds	1987
Pitching			
Games	78	Ed Vande Berg	1982
Complete games	14	Mike Moore	1985
		Mark Langston	1987
Innings	272	Mark Langston	1987
Wins	20	Randy Johnson	1997
Losses	19	Matt Young	1985
		Mike Moore	1987
Winning pct.	.900 (18-2)	Randy Johnson	1995
Walks	152	Randy Johnson	1991
Strikeouts	308	Randy Johnson	1993
Shutouts	4	Dave Fleming	1992
		Randy Johnson	1994
Home runs allowed	35	Scott Bankhead	1987
Lowest ERA	2.28	Randy Johnson	1997
Saves	37	Kazuhiro Sasaki	2000

GAME

Batting			
Runs	5	Last by Alex Rodriguez	4-16-2000
Hits	5	Last by Stan Javier	8-6-2000
Doubles	3	Last by David Bell	7-15-99
Triples	2	Last by Joey Cora	6-28-96
Home runs	3	Last by Alex Rodriguez	4-16-2000
RBIs	8	Alvin Davis	5-9-86
		Mike Blowers	5-24-95
Total bases	14	Mickey Brantley	9-14-87
Stolen bases	4	Last by Henry Cotto	6-23-90

CAREER LEADERS

BATTING

Games

Player	Games
Edgar Martinez	1,540
Ken Griffey Jr.	1,535
Jay Buhner	1,421
Alvin Davis	1,166
Harold Reynolds	1,155
Dave Valle	846
Dan Wilson	803
Jim Presley	799
Alex Rodriguez	790
Julio Cruz	742

At-bats

Player	At-bats
Ken Griffey Jr.	5,832
Edgar Martinez	5,432
Jay Buhner	4,877
Alvin Davis	4,136
Harold Reynolds	4,090
Alex Rodriguez	3,126
Jim Presley	2,946
Dan Wilson	2,687
Julio Cruz	2,667
Dave Valle	2,502

Runs

Player	Runs
Ken Griffey Jr.	1,063
Edgar Martinez	980
Jay Buhner	786
Alex Rodriguez	627
Alvin Davis	563
Harold Reynolds	543
Julio Cruz	402
Joey Cora	354
Jim Presley	351
Phil Bradley	346

Hits

Ken Griffey Jr.	1,742
Edgar Martinez	1,738
Jay Buhner	1,245
Alvin Davis	1,163
Harold Reynolds	1,063
Alex Rodriguez	966
Jim Presley	736
Dan Wilson	704
Bruce Bochte	697
Phil Bradley	649
Julio Cruz	649

Doubles

Player	Doubles
Edgar Martinez	403
Ken Griffey Jr.	320
Jay Buhner	229
Alvin Davis	212
Harold Reynolds	200
Alex Rodriguez	194
Jim Presley	147
Dan Wilson	143
Bruce Bochte	134
Al Cowens	128

Triples

Player	Triples
Harold Reynolds	48
Ken Griffey Jr.	30
Phil Bradley	26
Spike Owen	23
Ruppert Jones	20
Jay Buhner	19
Dan Meyer	19
Joey Cora	18
Al Cowens	17
Julio Cruz	16
Leon Roberts	16

Home runs

Player	Home runs
Ken Griffey Jr.	398
Jay Buhner	305
Edgar Martinez	235
Alex Rodriguez	189
Alvin Davis	160
Jim Presley	115
Ken Phelps	105
Tino Martinez	88
Dave Henderson	79
Dave Valle	72

Total bases

Ken Griffey Jr.	3,316
Edgar Martinez	2,874
Jay Buhner	2,427
Alvin Davis	1,875
Alex Rodriguez	1,753
Harold Reynolds	1,410
Jim Presley	1,254
Dan Wilson	1,063
Bruce Bochte	1,031
Phil Bradley	969

Runs batted in

Ken Griffey Jr.	1,152
Jay Buhner	946
Edgar Martinez	925
Alvin Davis	667
Alex Rodriguez	595
Jim Presley	418
Dan Wilson	344
Bruce Bochte	329
Dave Valle	318
Dan Meyer	313

Extra-base hits

Player	Extra-base hits
Ken Griffey Jr.	748
Edgar Martinez	652
Jay Buhner	553
Alex Rodriguez	396
Alvin Davis	382
Jim Presley	275
Harold Reynolds	265
Dan Wilson	218
Bruce Bochte	205
Dave Henderson	205

Batting average

(Minimum 500 games)

Edgar Martinez	.320
Alex Rodriguez	.309
Phil Bradley	.301
Ken Griffey Jr.	.299
Joey Cora	.293
Bruce Bochte	.290
Alvin Davis	.281
Rich Amaral	.278
Dan Meyer	.265
Tino Martinez	.265

Stolen bases

Player	Stolen bases
Julio Cruz	290
Harold Reynolds	228
Ken Griffey Jr.	167
Alex Rodriguez	133
Phil Bradley	107
Henry Cotto	102
Rich Amaral	97
John Moses	70
Ruppert Jones	68
Jack Perconte	60

PITCHING

Earned-run average

(Minimum 500 innings)

Randy Johnson	3.42
Erik Hanson	3.69
Brian Holman	3.73
Floyd Bannister	3.75
Mark Langston	4.01
Jamie Moyer	4.02
Matt Young	4.13
Jim Beattie	4.14
Scott Bankhead	4.16
Rick Honeycutt	4.22

Wins

Player	Wins
Randy Johnson	130
Mark Langston	74
Mike Moore	66
Jamie Moyer	65
Erik Hanson	56
Matt Young	45
Glenn Abbott	44
Jim Beattie	43
Bill Swift	41
Floyd Bannister	40

Losses

Player	Losses
Mike Moore	96
Randy Johnson	74
Jim Beattie	72
Mark Langston	67
Matt Young	66
Glenn Abbott	62
Erik Hanson	54
Floyd Bannister	50
Bill Swift	49
Rick Honeycutt	41

Innings pitched

Randy Johnson	1,838.1
Mike Moore	1,457.0
Mark Langston	1,197.2
Erik Hanson	967.1
Jim Beattie	944.2
Glenn Abbott	904.0
Bill Swift	903.2
Jamie Moyer	875.2
Matt Young	864.1
Floyd Bannister	768.1

Strikeouts

Player	Strikeouts
Randy Johnson	2,162
Mark Langston	1,078
Mike Moore	937
Erik Hanson	740
Matt Young	597
Floyd Bannister	564
Jim Beattie	563
Jamie Moyer	535
Jeff Fassero	466
Mike Jackson	383

Bases on balls

Randy Johnson	884
Mark Langston	575
Mike Moore	535
Jim Beattie	369
Matt Young	365
Bill Swift	304
Erik Hanson	285
Floyd Bannister	250
Glenn Abbott	230
Dave Fleming	229

Games

Player	Games
Mike Jackson	335
Bobby Ayala	292
Bill Swift	282
Randy Johnson	274
Ed Vande Berg	272
Mike Schooler	243
Mike Moore	227
Jeff Nelson	227
Norm Charlton	205
Edwin Nunez	205
Shane Rawley	205

Shutouts

Player	Shutouts
Randy Johnson	19
Mark Langston	9
Mike Moore	9
Floyd Bannister	7
Jim Beattie	6
Dave Fleming	5
Brian Holman	5
Matt Young	5
Glenn Abbott	3
Scott Bankhead	3
Erik Hanson	3
Rick Honeycutt	3
Mike Morgan	3
Jamie Moyer	3

Saves

Player	Saves
Mike Schooler	98
Norm Charlton	66
Bobby Ayala	56
Bill Caudill	52
Kazuhiro Sasaki	37
Shane Rawley	36
Edwin Nunez	35
Mike Jackson	34
Jose Mesa	33
Enrique Romo	26

TEAM SEASON, GAME RECORDS

SEASON

Batting

Most at-bats	5,668	1996
Most runs	993	1996
Fewest runs	558	1983
Most hits	1,625	1996
Most singles	1,056	1979
Most doubles	343	1996
Most triples	52	1979
Most home runs	264	1997
Fewest home runs	97	1978
Most grand slams	11	1996, 2000
Most pinch-hit home runs	5	1994, 1996
Most total bases	2,741	1996
Most stolen bases	174	1987
Highest batting average	.287	1996
Lowest batting average	.240	1983
Highest slugging pct	.485	1997

Pitching

Lowest ERA	3.69	1990
Highest ERA	5.24	1999
Most complete games	39	1987
Most shutouts	13	1991
Most saves	48	1991
Most walks	684	1999
Most strikeouts	1,156	1998

Fielding

Most errors	156	1986
Fewest errors	90	1993
Most double plays	191	1986
Highest fielding average	.985	1993

General

Most games won	91	2000
Most games lost	104	1978
Highest win pct	.562	2000
Lowest win pct	.350	1978

GAME, INNING

Batting

Most runs, game	22	4-29-99
Most runs, inning	11	4-29-99
Most hits, game	24	6-11-96
Most home runs, game	7	4-11-85, 7-31-96, 7-5-99
Most total bases, game	44	4-16-2000

Outfielder Jay Buhner ranks second on the Mariners' career home run chart.

MARINERS YEAR-BY--YEAR

Year	W	L	Place	Games Back	Manager	Batting avg.	Hits	Home runs	RBIs	Wins	ERA
						Leaders					
						WEST DIVISION					
1977	64	98	6th	38	Johnson	Stanton, .275	Meyer, 159	Stanton, 27	Meyer, Stanton, 90	Abbott, 12	Romo, 2.83
1978	56	104	7th	35	Johnson	Roberts, .301	Reynolds, 160	Roberts, 22	Roberts, 92	Romo, 11	Romo, 3.69
1979	67	95	6th	21	Johnson	Bochte, .316	Horton, 180	Horton, 29	Horton, 106	Parrott, 14	Parrott, 3.77
1980	59	103	7th	38	Johnson, Wills	Bochte, .300	Bochte, 156	Paciorek, 15	Bochte, 78	Abbott, 12	Rawley, 3.33
1981	44	65	*6th/5th	—	Wills, Lachemann	Paciorek, .326	Paciorek, 132	Zisk, 16	Paciorek, 66	Bannister, 9	Abbott, 3.95
1982	76	86	4th	17	Lachemann	Bochte, .297	Bochte, Cowens, 151	Zisk, 21	Cowens, 78	Bannister, Caudill, 12	Caudill, 2.35
1983	60	102	7th	39	Lachemann, Crandall	S. Henderson, .294	D. Henderson, 136	Putnam, 19	Putnam, 67	Young, 11	Young, 3.27
1984	74	88	†5th	10	Crandall, Cottier	Perconte, .294	Perconte, 180	Davis, 27	Davis, 116	Langston, 17	Langston, 3.40
1985	74	88	6th	17	Cottier	P. Bradley, .300	P. Bradley, 192	G. Thomas, 32	P. Bradley, 88	Moore, 17	Nunez, 3.09
1986	67	95	7th	25	Cottier, Martinez, Williams	P. Bradley, .310	P. Bradley, Presley, 163	Presley, 27	Presley, 107	Langston, 12	Young, 3.82
1987	78	84	4th	7	Williams	Brantley, .302	P. Bradley, 179	Davis, 29	Davis, 100	Langston, 19	Guetterman, 3.81
1988	68	93	7th	35½	Williams, Snyder	Davis, .295	Reynolds, 169	Balboni, 21	Davis, 69	Langston, 15	Jackson, 2.63
1989	73	89	6th	26	Lefebvre	Davis, .305	Reynolds, 184	Leonard, 24	Davis, 95	Bankhead, 14	Jackson, 3.17
1990	77	85	5th	26	Lefebvre	E. Martinez, .302	Griffey Jr., 179	Griffey Jr., 22	Griffey Jr., 80	Hanson, 18	Swift, 2.39
1991	83	79	5th	12	Lefebvre	Griffey Jr., .327	Griffey Jr., 179	Buhner, 27	Griffey Jr., 100	Holman, R. Johnson, 13	Swift, 1.99
1992	64	98	7th	32	Plummer	E. Martinez, .343	E. Martinez, 181	Griffey Jr., 27	Griffey Jr., 103	Fleming, 17	Fleming, 3.39
1993	82	80	4th	12	Piniella	Griffey Jr., .309	Griffey Jr., 180	Griffey Jr., 45	Griffey Jr., 109	R. Johnson, 19	R. Johnson, 3.24
1994	49	63	3rd	2	Piniella	Griffey Jr., .323	Griffey Jr., 140	Griffey Jr., 40	Griffey Jr., 90	R. Johnson, 13	R. Johnson, 3.19
1995	78	66	‡§∞1st	+1	Piniella	E. Martinez, .356	E. Martinez, 182	Buhner, 40	Buhner, 121	Johnson, 18	Johnson, 2.48
1996	85	75	2nd	4½	Piniella	Rodriguez, .358	Rodriguez, 215	Griffey Jr., 49	Griffey Jr., 140	Hitchcock, Moyer, 13	Moyer, 3.98
1997	90	72	▲1st	+6	Piniella	E. Martinez, .330	Griffey Jr., 185	Griffey Jr., 56	Griffey Jr., 147	Johnson, 20	Johnson, 2.28
1998	76	85	3rd	11½	Piniella	E. Martinez, .322	Rodriguez, 213	Griffey Jr., 56	Griffey Jr., 146	Moyer, 15	Moyer, 3.53
1999	79	83	3rd	16	Piniella	E. Martinez, .337	Griffey Jr., 173	Griffey Jr., 48	Griffey Jr., 134	F. Garcia, 17	Moyer, 3.87
2000	91	71	∞ 2nd	½	Piniella	E. Martinez, .324	E. Martinez, 180	Rodriguez, 41	E. Martinez, 145	Sele, 17	Garcia, 3.91

* First half 21-36; second half 23-29. † Tied for position. ‡ Won division playoff. § Won Division Series. ∞ Lost Championship Series. ▲ Lost Division Series.

Note: Batting average minimum 350 at-bats; ERA minimum 90 innings pitched.

Ruppert Jones

A PARTNERSHIP that included actor Danny Kaye was granted the American League's 13th franchise on February 6, 1976, as part of a two-team expansion that would increase the A.L. roster to 14. The Mariners represented baseball's second attempt to establish a team in Seattle. The Pilots played the 1969 season there before transferring operations to Milwaukee.

The Mariners stocked their roster with 30 players from the November 5, 1976, expansion draft, including first pick Ruppert Jones, an outfielder from the Kansas City organization. The team made its Major League debut on April 6, 1977, losing, 7-0, to the California Angels at Seattle's Kingdome.

Expansion draft (November 5, 1976)

Players

Juan Bernhardt......New York......infield
Steve Braun......Minnesota......outfield
Dave Collins......California......outfield
Julio Cruz......California......second base
Luis Delgado......Boston......outfield
*Ruppert Jones......Kansas City......outfield
Joe Lis......Cleveland......first base
Carlos Lopez......California......outfield
Tom McMillan......Cleveland......shortstop
Dan Meyer......Detroit......first base
Tommie Smith......Cleveland......outfield
Leroy Stanton......California......outfield
Bill Stein......Chicago......third base
Bob Stinson......Kansas City......catcher

Pitchers

Glenn Abbott......Oakland......righthanded
Steve Barr......Texas......righthanded
Pete Broberg......Milwaukee......righthanded
Steve Burke......Boston......righthanded
Joe Erardi......Milwaukee......righthanded
Bob Galasso......Baltimore......righthanded
Alan Griffin......Oakland......righthanded
Grant Jackson......New York......lefthanded
Rick Jones......Boston......lefthanded
Bill Laxton......Detroit......lefthanded
Frank MacCormack......Detroit......righthanded
Dave Pagan......Baltimore......righthanded
Dick Pole......Boston......righthanded
Roy Thomas......Chicago......righthanded
Stan Thomas......Cleveland......righthanded
Gary Wheelock......California......righthanded

*First pick

Opening day lineup

April 6, 1977

Dave Collins, designated hitter
Jose Baez, second base
Steve Braun, left field
Lee Stanton, right field
Bill Stein, third base
Dan Meyer, first base
Ruppert Jones, center field
Bob Stinson, catcher
Craig Reynolds, shortstop
Diego Segui, pitcher

Craig Reynolds

Mariners firsts

First hit: Jose Baez, April 6, 1977, vs. California
First home run: Juan Bernhardt, April 10, 1977, vs. California
First RBI: Dan Meyer, April 8, 1977 vs. California
First win: Bill Laxton, April 8, 1977, vs. California
First shutout: Dave Pagan, May 19, 1977, 3-0 at Oakland

TAMPA BAY DEVIL RAYS

Third baseman Bobby Smith.

FRANCHISE CHRONOLOGY

The beginnings: Tampa Bay, a longtime home to minor league baseball, the Gulf Coast Rookie League and spring training, pursued a Major League team for about 19 years before the dream was realized. At a March 9, 1995, owner's meeting, the vote was 28-0 to admit two new franchises, a Phoenix-based team that would be known as the Diamondbacks and a Tampa club, awarded to a local group headed by Tampa businessman Vincent J. Naimoli, that would become the Devil Rays. The franchise became the state's second, only two years after the Florida Marlins had begun play as an expansion team in Miami. Both teams were stocked in a November 1997 expansion draft and began play in the 1998 season—Arizona as a member of the N.L. West Division and the Devil Rays in the rugged A.L. East. The Diamondbacks and Devil Rays were the 13th and 14th expansion teams in baseball's long history.

First season: The March 31, 1998, debut on Florida's west coast was long on pageantry and short on success. The Devil Rays fell behind 11-0 and dropped an 11-6 decision to the Detroit Tigers at Tropicana Field. Tampa Bay went on to record a 66-99 first-season finish, 51 games behind the record-setting New York Yankees.

1999-present: Clearly, improvement has been the goal for the Devil Rays, who lifted their record to 69-93 in their second season and 69-92 in their third—while playing in, arguably, baseball's best division.

DEVIL RAYS VS. OPPONENTS BY DECADE

	A's	Indians	Orioles	Red Sox	Tigers	Twins	White Sox	Yankees	Angels	Rangers	Royals	BlueJays	Mariners	Interleague	Decade Record
1998-99	7-14	7-12	14-10	12-13	11-9	9-12	10-11	5-19	10-13	8-15	11-10	10-15	9-14	9-25	132-192
2000-	2-7	2-8	5-8	6-6	5-4	6-4	4-6	6-6	6-6	5-7	5-5	5-7	3-9	9-9	69-92
Totals	9-21	9-20	19-18	18-19	16-13	15-16	14-17	11-25	16-19	13-22	16-15	15-22	12-23	18-34	201-284

Interleague results: 1-8 vs. Braves; 4-5 vs. Expos; 3-6 vs. Mets; 5-4 vs. Phillies; 5-11 vs. Marlins.

ALL-TIME RECORD OF EXPANSION TEAMS

Team	W	L	Pct.	DT	P	WS
Arizona	250	236	.514	1	0	0
Kansas City	2,548	2,497	.505	6	2	1
Toronto	1,867	1,897	.496	5	2	2
Houston	3,052	3,138	.493	6	0	0
Montreal	2,454	2,596	.486	2	0	0
Anaheim	3,069	3,281	.483	3	0	0
Colorado	594	639	.482	0	0	0
Milwaukee	2,421	2,631	.479	2	1	0
New York	2,934	3,246	.475	4	4	2
Texas	2,952	3,381	.466	4	0	0
San Diego	2,315	2,742	.458	3	2	0
Seattle	1,715	2,048	.456	2	0	0
Florida	551	678	.448	0	1	1
Tampa Bay	201	284	.414	0	0	0

DT—Division Titles. P—Pennants won. WS—World Series won.

BALLPARK CHRONOLOGY

Tropicana Field (1998-present)

Capacity: 43,819.
First game: Tigers 11, Devil Rays 6 (March 31, 1998).
First batter: Brian Hunter, Tigers.
First hit: Tony Clark, Tigers (single).
First run: Tony Clark, Tigers (2nd inning).
First home run: Luis Gonzalez, Tigers.
First winning pitcher: Justin Thompson, Tigers..
First-season attendance: 2,506,023.

MANAGERS

Name	*Years*	*Record*
Larry Rothschild	1998-2000	201-284

ATTENDANCE HIGHS

Total	*Season*	*Park*
2,506,023	1998	Tropicana Field
1,749,567	1999	Tropicana Field
1,549,052	2000	Tropicana Field

LONGEST HITTING STREAKS

18—Quinton McCracken 1998
14—Fred McGriff 2000
13—Wade Boggs 1998
Dave Martinez 1999

Expansion draft (November 18, 1998)

Players

Player	Team	Position
Bobby Abreu	Houston	outfield
Rich Butler	Toronto	outfield
Miguel Cairo	Cubs	second base
Steve Cox	Oakland	first base
Mike Difelice	St. Louis	catcher
Brooks Kieschnick	Cubs	first base
Aaron Ledesma	Baltimore	shortstop
Quinton McCracken	Colorado	outfield
Carlos Mendoza	N.Y. Mets	outfield
Herbert Perry	Cleveland	first base
Kerry Robinson	St. Louis	outfield
Andy Sheets	Seattle	shortstop
Bobby Smith	Atlanta	third base
Bubba Trammell	Detroit	outfield
Chris Wilcox	N.Y. Yankees	outfield
Randy Winn	Florida	outfield
Dmitri Young	Cincinnati	outfield/1B

Pitchers

Pitcher	Team	Throws
Brian Boehringer	N.Y. Yankees	righthanded
Dan Carlson	San Francisco	righthanded
Mike Duvall	Florida	lefthanded
Vaughn Eshelman	Oakland	lefthanded
Rick Gorecki	Los Angeles	righthanded
Santos Hernandez	San Francisco	righthanded
Jason Johnson	Pittsburgh	righthanded
Ryan Karp	Philadelphia	lefthanded
John LeRoy	Atlanta	righthanded
Albie Lopez	Cleveland	lefthanded
Jim Mecir	Boston	righthanded
Jose Paniagua	Montreal	righthanded
Bryan Rekar	Colorado	righthanded
*Tony Saunders	Florida	lefthanded
Dennis Springer	Anaheim	righthanded
Ramon Tatis	Cubs	lefthanded
Terrell Wade	Atlanta	lefthanded
Esteban Yan	Baltimore	righthanded

*First pick

Opening day lineup

March 31, 1998
Quinton McCracken, center field
Miguel Cairo, second base
Wade Boggs, third base
Fred McGriff, first base
Mike Kelly, left field
Paul Sorrento, designated hitter
John Flaherty, catcher
Dave Martinez, right field
Kevin Stocker, shortstop
Wilson Alvarez, pitcher

Tony Saunders

Devil Rays firsts

First hit: Dave Martinez, March 31, 1998, vs. Detroit (single)
First home run: Wade Boggs, March 31, 1998, vs. Detroit
First RBI: Wade Boggs, March 31, 1998, vs. Detroit
First win: Rolando Arrojo, April 1, 1998, vs. Detroit
First shutout: Rolando Arrojo, April 30, 1998, at Minnesota

HISTORY

CAREER LEADERS

BATTING

Games

Fred McGriff	453
Miguel Cairo	389
John Flaherty	317
Dave Martinez	262
Randy Winn	239
Paul Sorrento	236
Bobby Smith	234
Kevin Stocker	231
Wade Boggs	213
Quinton McCracken	210

At-bats

Fred McGriff	1,659
Miguel Cairo	1,355
John Flaherty	1,144
Dave Martinez`	927
Randy Winn	800
Quinton McCracken	793
Bobby Smith	744
Paul Sorrento	729
Wade Boggs	727
Kevin Stocker	704

Runs

Fred McGriff	230
Miguel Cairo	159
Randy Winn	123
Dave Martinez	122
John Flaherty	110
Jose Canseco	106
Quinton McCracken	102
Kevin Stocker	96
Bubba Trammell	96
Wade Boggs	91

Hits

Fred McGriff	481
Miguel Cairo	373
John Flaherty	290
Dave Martinez	252
Quinton McCracken	220
Randy Winn	215
Wade Boggs	210
Bubba Trammell	191
Bobby Smith	179
Jose Canseco	176
Kevin Stocker	176

Doubles

Fred McGriff	81
Miguel Cairo	59
Bubba Trammell	48
John Flaherty	45
Quinton McCracken	44
Paul Sorrento	41
Dave Martinez	40
Wade Boggs	37
Mike Difelice	36
Jose Canseco	33

Triples

Randy Winn	13
Miguel Cairo	12
Quinton McCracken	8
Dave Martinez	7
Kevin Stocker	6
Wade Boggs	5
Jose Guillen	5
Mike Difelice	4
Tony Graffanino	4
Felix Martinez	4
Bobby Smith	4

Home runs

Fred McGriff	78
Jose Canseco	43
Bubba Trammell	33
Paul Sorrento	28
Greg Vaughn	28
John Flaherty	27
Gerald Williams	21
Bobby Smith	20
Mike Difelice	15
Jose Guillen	12

Total bases

Fred McGriff	798
Miguel Cairo	483
John Flaherty	416
Bubba Trammell	344
Jose Canseco	340
Dave Martinez	336
Quinton McCracken	304
Paul Sorrento	294
Wade Boggs	284
Randy Winn	283

Runs batted in

Fred McGriff	291
John Flaherty	134
Jose Canseco	125
Miguel Cairo	116
Bubba Trammell	107
Bobby Smith	100
Paul Sorrento	99
Dave Martinez	98
Gerald Williams	89
Wade Boggs	81

Extra-base hits

Fred McGriff	160
Bubba Trammell	84
Miguel Cairo	80
Jose Canseco	77
John Flaherty	72
Paul Sorrento	70
Quinton McCracken	60
Dave Martinez	57
Greg Vaughn	56
Mike Difelice	55

Batting average
(Minimum 125 games)

Aaron Ledesma	.295
Fred McGriff	.290
Wade Boggs	.289
Bubba Trammell	.285
Quinton McCracken	.277
Miguel Cairo	.275
Dave Martinez	.272
Jose Canseco	.272
Randy Winn	.269
Mike Difelice	.255

Stolen bases

Miguel Cairo	69
Randy Winn	41
Quinton McCracken	25
Dave Martinez	22
Kevin Stocker	15
Mike Kelly	13
Gerald Williams	12
Bobby Smith	11
Aaron Ledesma	10
Fred McGriff	10

PITCHING

Earned-run average
(Minimum 125 innings)

Jim Mecir	3.03
Roberto Hernandez	3.43
Rick White	3.81
Albie Lopez	3.86
Rolando Arrojo	4.23
Wilson Alvarez	4.46
Tony Saunders	4.53
Bryan Rekar	4.92
Julio Santana	5.11
Esteban Yan	5.42

Wins

Rolando Arrojo	21
Albie Lopez	21
Wilson Alvarez	15
Bryan Rekar	15
Esteban Yan	15
Jim Mecir	14
Ryan Rupe	13
Rick White	10
Tony Saunders	9
Roberto Hernandez	8

Losses

Rolando Arrojo	24
Bryan Rekar	24
Wilson Alvarez	23
Albie Lopez	19
Tony Saunders	18
Roberto Hernandez	16
Esteban Yan	16
Ryan Rupe	15
Rick White	15
Bobby Witt	15

Innings pitched

Bryan Rekar	354.2
Rolando Arrojo	342.2
Albie Lopez	329.0
Wilson Alvarez	302.2
Esteban Yan	287.1
Rick White	248.0
Tony Saunders	234.1
Ryan Rupe	233.1
Roberto Hernandez	218.0
Julio Santana	195.2

Strikeouts

Rolando Arrojo	259
Wilson Alvarez	235
Esteban Yan	234
Bryan Rekar	205
Tony Saunders	202
Albie Lopez	195
Roberto Hernandez	185
Rick White	167
Ryan Rupe	158
Jim Mecir	125

Bases on balls

Wilson Alvarez	147
Tony Saunders	140
Albie Lopez	126
Rolando Arrojo	125
Esteban Yan	115
BryanRekar	101
Roberto Hernandez	97
Bobby Witt	96
Julio Santana	90
Ryan Rupe	88

Games

Roberto Hernandez	207
Esteban Yan	157
Albie Lopez	150
Rick White	145
Jim Mecir	123
Scott Aldred	85
Bryan Rekar	73
Rolando Arrojo	56
Julio Santana	54
Wilson Alvarez	53

Shutouts

Rolando Arrojo	2
Bobby Witt	2
Travis Harper	1
Albie Lopez	1
Steve Trachsel	1

Saves

Roberto Hernandez	101
Albie Lopez	4
Rick White	2
Doug Creek	1
Jim Mecir	1
Jeff Sparks	1
Esteban Yan	1

INDIVIDUAL SEASON, GAME RECORDS

Fred McGriff has added 78 home runs and 291 RBIs to his career totals as the first baseman for the Devil Rays.

SEASON

Batting

Most at-bats	5,586	1999
Most runs	772	1999
Fewest runs	620	1998
Most hits	1,531	1999
Most singles	1,085	1999
Most doubles	272	1999
Most triples	43	1998
Most home runs	145	1999
Fewest home runs	162	2000
Most grand slams	4	2000
Most pinch-hit home runs	3	1998
Most total bases	2,296	1999
Most stolen bases	120	1998
Highest batting average	.274	1999
Lowest batting average	.257	2000
Highest slugging pct.	.411	1999

Pitching

Lowest ERA	4.35	1998
Highest ERA	5.06	1999
Most complete games	10	2000
Most shutouts	8	1998, 2000
Most saves	45	1999
Most walks	695	1999
Most strikeouts	1,055	1999

Fielding

Most errors	135	1999
Fewest errors	94	1998
Most double plays	198	1999
Highest fielding average	.985	1998

General

Most games won	69	1999, 2000
Most games lost	99	1998
Highest win pct.	.429	2000
Lowest win pct.	.389	1998

GAME, INNING

Batting

Most runs, game	15	5-30-99, 9-19-99
Most runs, inning	11	5-20-2000
Most hits, game	20	5-20-2000
Most home runs, game	5	4-22-2000
Most total bases, game	36	5-30-99

TEXAS RANGERS

FRANCHISE CHRONOLOGY

First season: 1961, in Washington, as part of baseball's first expansion. The Senators, who were replacing a Washington Senators franchise that was relocating to Minnesota, dropped a 4-3 decision to Chicago in their Major League debut en route to a 61-100 first-season record.

1962-1971: The Senators, upholding the long tradition of their Washington predecessors, lost 100 or more games in each of their first four seasons and never finished above fourth place in their 11-year existence. The highlight of their Washington stay was an 86-76 mark in 1969, the first season of divisional play. That Senators team still finished 23 games behind East Division winner Baltimore.

1972-present: The Senators, relocated to Arlington, Texas, as the Texas Rangers, dropped a 1-0 debut to California and struggled to consecutive 100-loss seasons. The Rangers have fared better than their Washington ancestor, but they still are looking for their first pennant and World Series appearance. Their first West Division title was accompanied by an asterisk—the Rangers finished first in the strike-halted 1994 season with a 52-62 record. Their second, third and fourth titles, in 1996, '98 and '99, were all followed by losses to the New York Yankees in the Division Series.

First baseman Frank Howard.

RANGERS VS. OPPONENTS BY DECADE

	A's	Indians	Orioles	Red Sox	Tigers	Twins	White Sox	Yankees	Angels	Brewers	Royals	Blue Jays	Mariners	Devil Rays	Interleague	Decade Record
1961-69	77-78	73-88	52-110	75-86	68-94	56-99	61-95	55-104	80-76	5-7	5-7					607-844
1970-79	76-78	71-58	50-77	56-72	64-64	76-80	65-90	49-79	79-77	49-67	69-84	18-16	25-18			747-860
1980-89	66-57	57-55	39-72	53-64	47-73	65-64	64-59	54-62	55-68	52-63	54-70	49-67	65-65			720-839
1990-99	63-61	63-50	46-60	61-43	63-54	70-50	59-58	54-54	61-63	46-44	61-56	63-53	54-71	15-8	28-22	807-747
2000-	7-5	4-6	6-6	3-7	5-5	4-8	5-5	2-10	5-7		7-3	4-6	5-7	7-5	7-11	71-91
Totals	289-279	268-257	193-325	248-272	247-290	271-301	254-307	214-309	280-291	152-181	196-220	134-142	149-161	22-13	35-33	2952-3381

Interleague results: 6-7 vs. Dodgers; 7-6 vs. Padres; 6-7 vs. Giants; 6-7 vs. Rockies; 10-6 vs. Diamondbacks.

MANAGERS

(Washington Senators, 1961-71)

Name	*Years*	*Record*
Mickey Vernon	1961-63	135-227
Gil Hodges	1963-67	321-444
Jim Lemon	1968	65-96
Ted Williams	1969-72	273-364
Whitey Herzog	1973	47-91
Del Wilber	1973	1-0
Billy Martin	1973-75	137-141
Frank Lucchesi	1975-77	142-149
Eddie Stanky	1977	1-0
Connie Ryan	1977	2-4
Billy Hunter	1977-78	146-108
Pat Corrales	1978-80	160-164
Don Zimmer	1981-82	95-106
Darrell Johnson	1982	26-40
Doug Rader	1983-85	155-200
Bobby Valentine	1985-92	581-605
Toby Harrah	1992	32-44
Kevin Kennedy	1993-94	138-138
Johnny Oates	1995-2000	495-459

WEST DIVISION CHAMPIONS

Year	*Record*	*Manager*	*Div. Series Result*
1994	52-62	Kennedy	None
1996	90-72	Oates	Lost to Yankees
1998	88-74	Oates	Lost to Yankees
1999	95-67	Oates	Lost to Yankees

ALL-TIME RECORD OF EXPANSION TEAMS

Team	W	L	Pct.	DT	P	WS
Arizona	250	236	.514	1	0	0
Kansas City	2,548	2,497	.505	6	2	1
Toronto	1,867	1,897	.496	5	2	2
Houston	3,052	3,138	.493	6	0	0
Montreal	2,454	2,596	.486	2	0	0
Anaheim	3,069	3,281	.483	3	0	0
Colorado	594	639	.482	0	0	0
Milwaukee	2,421	2,631	.479	2	1	0
New York	2,934	3,246	.475	4	4	2
Texas	2,952	3,381	.466	4	0	0
San Diego	2,315	2,742	.458	3	2	0
Seattle	1,715	2,048	.456	2	0	0
Florida	551	678	.448	0	1	1
Tampa Bay	201	284	.414	0	0	0

DT—Division Titles. P—Pennants won. WS—World Series won.

ATTENDANCE HIGHS

Total	*Season*	*Park*
2,945,228	1997	The Ballpark in Arlington
2,927,409	1998	The Ballpark in Arlington
2,888,920	1996	The Ballpark in Arlington
2,800,147	2000	The Ballpark in Arlington
2,774,514	1999	The Ballpark in Arlington

BALLPARK CHRONOLOGY

The Ballpark in Arlington (1994-present)

Capacity: 49,166.
First game: Milwaukee 4, Rangers 3 (April 11, 1994).
First batter: Pat Listach, Brewers.
First hit: David Hulse, Rangers (single).
First run: Dave Nilsson, Brewers (5th inning).
First home run: Dave Nilsson, Brewers.
First winning pitcher: Jaime Navarro, Brewers.
First-season attendance: 2,503,198.

Griffith Stadium, Washington, D.C. (1961)

Capacity: 27,410.
First game: Chicago 4, Senators 3 (April 10, 1961).
First-season attendance: 597,287.

RFK Stadium, Washington, D.C. (1962-71)

Capacity: 45,016.
First game: Senators 4, Detroit 1 (April 9, 1962).
First-season attendance: 729,775.

Arlington Stadium, Texas (1972-93)

Capacity: 43,521.
First game: Rangers 7, California 6 (April 21, 1972).
First-season attendance: 662,974.

Note: RFK Stadium was originally called D.C. Stadium.

A.L. MVPs

Jeff Burroughs, OF, 1974
Juan Gonzalez, OF, 1996
Juan Gonzalez, OF, 1998
Ivan Rodriguez, C, 1999

ROOKIE OF THE YEAR

Mike Hargrove, 1B, 1974

MANAGER OF THE YEAR

*Johnny Oates, 1996
*Co-winner

RETIRED UNIFORM

No.	*Name*	*Pos.*
34	Nolan Ryan	P

First baseman Pete O'Brien was Mr. Reliable during seven seasons with the Rangers.

HISTORY

MILESTONE PERFORMANCES

25-plus home runs

48—Frank Howard 1969
47—Juan Gonzalez 1996
Rafael Palmeiro 1999
46—Juan Gonzalez 1993
45—Juan Gonzalez 1998
44—Frank Howard 1968, 1970
43—Juan Gonzalez 1992
42—Juan Gonzalez 1997
39—Juan Gonzalez 1999
Rafael Palmeiro 2000
38—Dean Palmer 1996
37—Rafael Palmeiro 1993
36—Frank Howard 1967
35—Ivan Rodriguez 1999
33—Dean Palmer 1993
32—Larry Parrish 1987
Mickey Tettleton 1995
31—Jose Canseco 1994
30—Mike Epstein 1969
Jeff Burroughs 1973
Pete Incaviglia 1986
Ruben Sierra 1987
29—Jeff Burroughs 1975
Bobby Bonds 1978
Ruben Sierra 1989
28—Don Lock 1964
Larry Parrish 1986
27—Don Lock 1963
Toby Harrah 1977
Pete Incaviglia 1987
Juan Gonzalez 1991, 1995
Ivan Rodriguez 2000
26—Frank Howard 1971
Larry Parrish 1983
Rafael Palmeiro 1991
Dean Palmer 1992
Rusty Greer 1997
25—Jeff Burroughs 1974
Ruben Sierra 1991

100-plus RBIs

157—Juan Gonzalez 1998
148—Rafael Palmeiro 1999
144—Juan Gonzalez 1996
131—Juan Gonzalez 1997
128—Juan Gonzalez 1999
126—Frank Howard 1970
120—Rafael Palmeiro 2000
119—Ruben Sierra 1989
118—Jeff Burroughs 1974
Juan Gonzalez 1993
117—Al Oliver 1980
116—Ruben Sierra 1991
113—Ivan Rodriguez 1999
111—Frank Howard 1969
109—Ruben Sierra 1987
Juan Gonzalez 1992
108—Rusty Greer 1998
107—Dean Palmer 1996
106—Frank Howard 1968
105—Rafael Palmeiro 1993
102—Juan Gonzalez 1991
Will Clark 1998
101—Buddy Bell 1979
Larry Parrish 1984
Rusty Greer 1999
100—Larry Parrish 1987
Rusty Greer 1996

20-plus victories

1974—Fergie Jenkins 25-12
1992—Kevin Brown 21-11
1998—Rick Helling 20-7

A.L. home run champions

1968—Frank Howard 44
1970—Frank Howard 44
1992—Juan Gonzalez 43
1993—Juan Gonzalez 46

A.L. RBI champions

1970—Frank Howard 126
1974—Jeff Burroughs 118
1989—Ruben Sierra 119
1998—Juan Gonzalez 157

A.L. batting champions

1991—Julio Franco .... .341

A.L. ERA champions

1961—Dick Donovan 2.40
1969—Dick Bosman 2.19
1983—Rick Honeycutt 2.42

A.L. strikeout champions

1989—Nolan Ryan 301
1990—Nolan Ryan 232

No-hit pitchers
(9 innings or more)

1973—Jim Bibby .... 6-0 vs. Oakland
1977—Bert Blyleven .... 6-0 vs. California
1990—Nolan Ryan .... 5-0 vs. Oakland
1991—Nolan Ryan .... 3-0 vs. Toronto
1994—Kenny Rogers ....4-0 vs. California (Perfect)

Longest hitting streaks

28—Gabe Kapler 2000
24—Mickey Rivers 1980
22—Jim Sundberg 1978
21—Johnny Grubb 1979
Buddy Bell 1980
Al Oliver 1980
Juan Gonzalez .... 1996 (2 times)
20—Mickey Rivers 1980
Juan Gonzalez 1998
Ivan Rodriguez 1999
19—Ken McMullen 1967
Billy Sample 1981
Scott Fletcher 1986
Ivan Rodriguez 1996
18—Bill Stein 1981
Billy Sample 1982
Ruben Sierra 1991
17—Gene Woodling 1961
Chuck Hinton 1962
Ken Hamlin 1965
Cesar Tovar 1974
Toby Harrah 1976
Al Oliver 1980
Jim Sundberg 1981
Buddy Bell 1983
Todd Zeile 1999
16—Juan Beniquez 1977
Willie Montanez 1979
Rafael Palmeiro 1993

Venerable righthander Charlie Hough knuckleballed his way to 139 victories with the Rangers, a club career record.

INDIVIDUAL SEASON, GAME RECORDS

Catcher Jim Sundberg (left) and designated hitter Richie Zisk were teammates on the 1978, '79 and '80 Texas teams.

SEASON

Batting

At-bats	670	Buddy Bell	1979
Runs	124	Rafael Palmeiro	1993
Hits	210	Mickey Rivers	1980
Singles	165	Mickey Rivers	1980
Doubles	50	Juan Gonzalez	1998
Triples	14	Ruben Sierra	1989
Home runs	48	Frank Howard	1969
Home runs, rookie	30	Pete Incaviglia	1986
Grand slams	3	3 times	
		Last by Rafael Palmeiro	1999
Total bases	382	Juan Gonzalez	1998
RBIs	157	Juan Gonzalez	1998
Walks	132	Frank Howard	1970
Most strikeouts	185	Pete Incaviglia	1986
Batting average	.341	Julio Franco	1991
Slugging pct.	.643	Juan Gonzalez	1996
Stolen bases	52	Bump Wills	1978

Pitching

Games	85	Mitch Williams	1987
Complete games	29	Fergie Jenkins	1974
Innings	328.1	Fergie Jenkins	1974
Wins	25	Fergie Jenkins	1974
Losses	22	Denny McLain	1971
Winning pct.	.741 (20-7)	Rick Helling	1998
Walks	143	Bobby Witt	1986
Strikeouts	301	Nolan Ryan	1989
Shutouts	6	Fergie Jenkins	1974
		Bert Blyleven	1976
Home runs allowed	41	Rick Helling	1999
Lowest ERA	2.17	Mike Paul	1972
Saves	43	John Wetteland	1999

GAME

Batting

Runs	5	Pete O'Brien	5-29-87
Hits	5	Last by Rusty Greer	8-31-2000
Doubles	3	Last by Rusty Greer	8-17-2000
Triples	2	Last by Lee Stevens	7-20-96
Home runs	3	Last by Juan Gonzalez	9-24-99
RBIs	9	Ivan Rodriguez	4-13-99
Total bases	14	Jose Canseco	6-13-94
Stolen bases	5	Scarborough Green	9-28-2000

CAREER LEADERS

BATTING

Games

Jim Sundberg	1,512
Toby Harrah	1,355
Ivan Rodriguez	1,260
Juan Gonzalez	1,248
Frank Howard	1,172
Ed Brinkman	1,143
Rafael Palmeiro	1,104
Ruben Sierra	1,053
Buddy Bell	958
Pete O'Brien	946

At-bats

Juan Gonzalez	4,831
Ivan Rodriguez	4,806
Jim Sundberg	4,684
Toby Harrah	4,572
Rafael Palmeiro	4,123
Frank Howard	4,120
Ruben Sierra	4,103
Ed Brinkman	3,847
Buddy Bell	3,623
Rusty Greer	3,385

Runs

Juan Gonzalez	791
Ivan Rodriguez	715
Rafael Palmeiro	669
Toby Harrah	631
Rusty Greer	581
Ruben Sierra	576
Frank Howard	544
Jim Sundberg	482
Buddy Bell	471
Dean Palmer	425

Hits

Ivan Rodriguez	1,459
Juan Gonzalez	1,421
Rafael Palmeiro	1,233
Jim Sundberg	1,180
Toby Harrah	1,174
Ruben Sierra	1,146
Frank Howard	1,141
Buddy Bell	1,060
Rusty Greer	1,040
Pete O'Brien	914

Doubles

Ivan Rodriguez	288
Juan Gonzalez	282
Rafael Palmeiro	233
Rusty Greer	226
Ruben Sierra	226
Jim Sundberg	200
Buddy Bell	197
Toby Harrah	187
Pete O'Brien	161
Frank Howard	155

Triples

Ruben Sierra	43
Chuck Hinton	30
Ed Brinkman	27
Jim Sundberg	27
Ivan Rodriguez	24
Ed Stroud	24
Rusty Greer	23
Rafael Palmeiro	23
Toby Harrah	22
Oddibe McDowell	22
Del Unser	22

Home runs

Juan Gonzalez	340
Frank Howard	246
Rafael Palmeiro	193
Ivan Rodriguez	171
Dean Palmer	154
Ruben Sierra	154
Larry Parrish	149
Toby Harrah	124
Pete Incaviglia	124
Pete O'Brien	114

Total bases

Juan Gonzalez	2,761
Ivan Rodriguez	2,308
Rafael Palmeiro	2,091
Frank Howard	2,074
Ruben Sierra	1,920
Toby Harrah	1,777
Rusty Greer	1,645
Jim Sundberg	1,614
Buddy Bell	1,560
Larry Parrish	1,464

Runs batted in

Juan Gonzalez	1,075
Ivan Rodriguez	704
Frank Howard	701
Rafael Palmeiro	699
Ruben Sierra	663
Rusty Greer	568
Toby Harrah	568
Larry Parrish	522
Buddy Bell	499
Pete O'Brien	487

Extra-base hits

Juan Gonzalez	641
Ivan Rodriguez	483
Rafael Palmeiro	449
Ruben Sierra	423
Frank Howard	421
Rusty Greer	360
Toby Harrah	333
Buddy Bell	305
Larry Parrish	305
Dean Palmer	296

Batting average

(Minimum 500 games)

Al Oliver	.319
Will Clark	.308
Julio Franco	.307
Rusty Greer	.307
Ivan Rodriguez	.304
Mickey Rivers	.303
Rafael Palmeiro	.299
Juan Gonzalez	.294
Mike Hargrove	.293
Buddy Bell	.293

Stolen bases

Bump Wills	161
Toby Harrah	153
Dave Nelson	144
Oddibe McDowell	129
Julio Franco	98
Tom Goodwin	93
Chuck Hinton	92
Bill Sample	92
Cecil Espy	91
Ruben Sierra	87

PITCHING

Earned-run average

(Minimum 500 innings)

Gaylord Perry	3.26
Dick Bosman	3.35
Jon Matlack	3.41
Nolan Ryan	3.43
Claude Osteen	3.46
Joe Coleman	3.51
Fergie Jenkins	3.56
Casey Cox	3.67
Charlie Hough	3.68
Danny Darwin	3.72

Wins

Charlie Hough	139
Bobby Witt	104
Fergie Jenkins	93
Kenny Rogers	83
Kevin Brown	78
Jose Guzman	66
Dick Bosman	59
Rick Helling	56
Danny Darwin	55
Nolan Ryan	51

Losses

Charlie Hough	123
Bobby Witt	104
Fergie Jenkins	72
Dick Bosman	64
Kevin Brown	64
Kenny Rogers	64
Jose Guzman	62
Bennie Daniels	60
Danny Darwin	52
Joe Coleman	50

Innings pitched

Charlie Hough	2,308.0
Bobby Witt	1,680.2
Fergie Jenkins	1,410.1
Kevin Brown	1,278.2
Kenny Rogers	1,170.2
Dick Bosman	1,103.1
Jose Guzman	1,013.2
Jon Matlack	915.0
Danny Darwin	872.0
Joe Coleman	850.1

Strikeouts

Charlie Hough	1,452
Bobby Witt	1,405
Nolan Ryan	939
Fergie Jenkins	895
Kenny Rogers	807
Kevin Brown	742
Jose Guzman	715
Gaylord Perry	575
Dick Bosman	573
Danny Darwin	566

Bases on balls

Bobby Witt	1,001
Charlie Hough	965
Kenny Rogers	448
Kevin Brown	428
Jose Guzman	395
Jim Hannan	378
Nolan Ryan	353
Roger Pavlik	346
Rick Helling	318
Fergie Jenkins	315

Games

Jeff Russell	445
Kenny Rogers	410
Charlie Hough	344
Casey Cox	302
Bobby Witt	276
Darold Knowles	271
Ron Kline	260
Jim Hannan	248
John Wetteland	248
Mitch Williams	232

Shutouts

Fergie Jenkins	17
Gaylord Perry	12
Bert Blyleven	11
Charlie Hough	11
Dick Bosman	9
Jim Bibby	8
Tom Cheney	7
Joe Coleman	7
Doc Medich	7
Kevin Brown	6
Phil Ortega	6
Nolan Ryan	6

Saves

John Wetteland	150
Jeff Russell	134
Ron Kline	83
Darold Knowles	64
Tom Henke	58
Jim Kern	37
Steve Foucault	35
Mitch Williams	32
Greg Harris	31
Mike Henneman	31

TEAM SEASON, GAME RECORDS

SEASON

Batting

Most at-bats	5,703	1991
Most runs	945	1999
Fewest runs	461	1972
Most hits	1,653	1999
Most singles	1,202	1980
Most doubles	330	2000
Most triples	46	1989
Most home runs	230	1999
Fewest home runs	56	1972
Most grand slams	8	1999
Most pinch-hit home runs	8	1965, 1966
Most total bases	2,705	1999
Most stolen bases	196	1978
Highest batting average	.293	1980, 1996, 1999
Lowest batting average	.217	1972
Highest slugging pct	.479	1999

Pitching

Lowest ERA	3.31	1983
Highest ERA	5.52	2000
Most complete games	63	1976
Most shutouts	17	1977
Most saves	47	1999
Most walks	760	1987
Most strikeouts	1,112	1989

Fielding

Most errors	191	1975
Fewest errors	87	1996
Most double plays	173	1970, 1975
Highest fielding average	.986	1996

General

Most games won	95	1999
Most games lost	106	1963
Highest win pct.	.586	1999
Lowest win pct.	.346	1963

GAME, INNING

Batting

Most runs, game	26	4-19-96
Most runs, inning	16	4-19-96
Most hits, game	23	4-2-98
Most home runs, game	7	9-13-86
Most total bases, game	43	9-13-86

Third baseman Toby Harrah ranks high on most Rangers offensive charts.

RANGERS YEAR-BY-YEAR

Year	W	L	Place	Games Back	Manager	Batting avg.	Hits	Home runs	RBIs	Wins	ERA
							WASHINGTON SENATORS				
1961	61	100	*9th	47½	Vernon	Green, .280	O'Connell, 128	G. Green, 18	Tasby, 63	Daniels, 12	Donovan, 2.40
1962	60	101	10th	35½	Vernon	Hinton, .310	Hinton, 168	Bright, Hinton, 17	Hinton, 75	Stenhouse, 11	Cheney, 3.17
1963	56	106	10th	48½	Vernon, Hodges	Hinton, .269	Hinton, 152	Lock, 27	Lock, 82	Osteen, 9	Cheney, 2.71
1964	62	100	9th	37	Hodges	Hinton, .274	Hinton, 141	Lock, 28	Lock, 80	Osteen, 15	Ridzik, 2.89
1965	70	92	8th	32	Hodges	Howard, .289	Howard, 149	Howard, 21	Howard, 84	Richert, 15	Richert, 2.60
1966	71	88	8th	25½	Hodges	Howard, .278	Valentine, 140	Howard, 18	Howard, 71	Richert, 14	Kline, 2.39
1967	76	85	*6th	15½	Hodges	Howard, .256	McMullen, 138	Howard, 36	Howard, 89	Pascual, 12	Knowles, 2.70
1968	65	96	10th	37½	Lemon	Howard, .274	Howard, 164	Howard, 44	Howard, 106	Pascual, 13	Pascual, 2.69
							EAST DIVISION				
1969	86	76	4th	23	Williams	Howard, .296	Howard, 175	Howard, 48	Howard, 111	Bosman, 14	Bosman, 2.19
1970	70	92	6th	38	Williams	Howard, .283	Brinkman, 164	Howard, 44	Howard, 126	Bosman, 16	Knowles, 2.04
1971	63	96	5th	38½	Williams	Howard, .279	Howard, 153	Howard, 26	Howard, 83	Bosman, 12	Gogolewski, 2.75
							TEXAS RANGERS				
							WEST DIVISION				
1972	54	100	6th	38½	Williams	Biittner, Harrah, .259	Billings, 119	Ford, 14	Billings, 58	Hand, 10	Paul, 2.17
1973	57	105	6th	37	Herzog, Wilber, Martin	A. Johnson, .287	A. Johnson, 179	Burroughs, 30	Burroughs, 85	Bibby, 9	Bibby, 3.24
1974	84	76	2nd	5	Martin	Hargrove, .323	Burroughs, 167	Burroughs, 25	Burroughs, 118	Jenkins, 25	Foucault, 2.24
1975	79	83	3rd	19	Martin, Lucchesi	Hargrove, .303	Randle, 166	Burroughs, 29	Burroughs, 94	Jenkins, 17	G. Perry, 3.03
1976	76	86	*4th	14	Lucchesi	Hargrove, .287	Hargrove, 155	Grieve, 20	Burroughs, 86	G. Perry, 15	Blyleven, 2.76
1977	94	68	2nd	8	Lucchesi, Stanky, Ryan, Hunter	Hargrove, .305	Hargrove, 160	Harrah, 27	Harrah, 87	Alexander, 17	Blyleven, 2.72
1978	87	75	*2nd	5	Hunter, Corrales	Oliver, .324	Oliver, 170	Bonds, 29	Oliver, 89	Jenkins, 18	Matlack, 2.27
1979	83	79	3rd	5	Corrales	Oliver, .323	Bell, 200	Bell, Putnam, Zisk, 18	Bell, 101	Comer, 17	Kern, 1.57
1980	76	85	4th	20½	Corrales	Rivers, .333	Rivers, 210	Oliver, Zisk, 19	Oliver, 117	Medich, 14	Darwin, 2.63
1981	57	48†	2nd/3rd	—	Zimmer	Oliver, .309	Oliver, 130	Bell, 10	Bell, 64	Honeycutt, 11	Medich, 3.08
1982	64	98	6th	29	Zimmer, Johnson	Bell, .296	Bell, 159	Hostetler, 22	Bell, Hostetler, 67	Hough, 16	Schmidt, 3.20
1983	77	85	3rd	22	Rader	Bell, .277	Wright, 175	Parrish, 26	Parrish, 88	Hough, 15	Honeycutt, 2.42
1984	69	92	7th	14½	Rader	Bell, .315	Parrish, 175	Parrish, 22	Parrish, 101	Hough, 16	Tanana, 3.25
1985	62	99	7th	28½	Rader, Valentine	Ward, .287	Ward, 170	O'Brien, 22	O'Brien, 92	Hough, 14	Harris, 2.47
1986	87	75	2nd	5	Valentine	Ward, .316	O'Brien, 160	Incaviglia, 30	Parrish, 94	Hough, 17	Harris, 2.83
1987	75	87	*6th	10	Valentine	Fletcher, .287	Fletcher, Sierra, 169	Parrish, 32	Sierra, 109	Hough, 18	Mohorcic, 2.99
1988	70	91	6th	33½	Valentine	Petralli, .282	Sierra, 156	Sierra, 23	Sierra, 91	Hough, 15	Hough, 3.32
1989	83	79	4th	16	Valentine	Franco, .316	Sierra, 194	Sierra, 29	Sierra, 119	Ryan, 16	Ryan, 3.20
1990	83	79	3rd	20	Valentine	Palmeiro, .319	Palmeiro, 191	Incaviglia, 24	Sierra, 96	Witt, 17	Rogers, 3.13
1991	85	77	3rd	10	Valentine	Franco, .341	Palmeiro, Sierra, 203	Gonzalez, 27	Sierra, 116	Guzman, 13	Ryan, 2.91
1992	77	85	4th	19	Valentine, Harrah	Sierra, .278	Palmeiro, 163	Gonzalez, 43	Gonzalez, 109	Brown, 21	Brown, 3.32
1993	86	76	2nd	8	Kennedy	Gonzalez, .310	Palmeiro, 176	Gonzalez, 46	Gonzalez, 118	Rogers, 16	Pavlik, 3.41
1994	52	62	1st	+1	Kennedy	Clark, .329	Clark, 128	Canseco, 31	Canseco, 90	Rogers, 11	Rogers, 4.46
1995	74	70	3rd	4	Oates	Rodriguez, .303	Nixon, 174	Tettleton, 32	Clark, 92	Rogers, 17	Rogers, 3.38
1996	90	72	‡1st	+4½	Oates	Greer, .332	Rodriguez, 192	Gonzalez, 47	Gonzalez, 144	Hill, Witt, 16	Hill, 3.63
1997	77	85	3rd	13	Oates	Clark, .326	Greer, 193	Gonzalez, 42	Gonzalez, 131	Oliver, 13	Oliver, 4.20
1998	88	74	‡1st	+3	Oates	Rodriguez, .321	Gonzalez, 193	Gonzalez, 45	Gonzalez, 157	Helling, 20	Sele, 4.23
1999	95	67	‡1st	+8	Oates	Rodriguez, .332	Rodriguez, 199	Palmeiro, 47	Palmeiro, 148	Sele, 18	Loaiza, 4.56
2000	71	91	4th	20½	Oates	Rodriguez, .347	Palmeiro, 163	Palmeiro, 39	Palmeiro, 120	Helling, 16	Helling, 4.48

* Tied for position. †First half 33-22; second half 24-26. ‡ Lost Division Series.

Note: Batting average minimum 350 at-bats; ERA minimum 90 innings pitched.

Bobby Shantz

WASHINGTON lost one team and gained another in the two-team 1961 American League expansion that marked the first addition of baseball franchises in more than six decades. The original Senators were granted permission to move to Minneapolis/St. Paul for the 1961 season and the new Senators, under the ownership of Elwood R. Quesada, were admitted to the fold on October 26, 1960, along with the Los Angeles Angels.

The new Senators, who would become the Texas Rangers after 11 Washington seasons, grabbed lefthander Bobby Shantz with their first pick in the December 14, 1960, A.L. expansion draft and 31 players overall. They made their Major League debut on April 10, 1961, dropping a 4-3 decision to the Chicago White Sox.

Expansion draft (December 14, 1960)

Players

Player	From	Position
Chester Boak	Kansas City	second base
Leo Burke	Baltimore	infield
Pete Daley	Kansas City	catcher
Dutch Dotterer	Kansas City	catcher
Gene Green	Baltimore	catcher
Joe Hicks	Chicago	outfield
Chuck Hinton	Baltimore	outfield
Bob Johnson	Kansas City	infield
Marty Keough	Cleveland	outfield
Jim King	Cleveland	outfield
Billy Klaus	Baltimore	infield
Dale Long	New York	first base
Jim Mahoney	Boston	shortstop
John Schaive	Minnesota	second base
Haywood Sullivan	Boston	catcher
Willie Tasby	Boston	outfield
Coot Veal	Detroit	shortstop
Gene Woodling	Baltimore	outfield
Bud Zipfel	New York	first base

Pitchers

Pitcher	From	Throws
Pete Burnside	Detroit	lefthanded
Dick Donovan	Chicago	righthanded
Rudy Hernandez	Minnesota	righthanded
Ed Hobaugh	Chicago	righthanded
John Klippstein	Cleveland	righthanded
Hector Maestri	Minnesota	righthanded
Carl Mathias	Cleveland	lefthanded
Joe McClain	Minnesota	righthanded
*Bobby Shantz	New York	lefthanded
Dave Sisler	Detroit	righthanded
Tom Sturdivant	Boston	righthanded
Hal Woodeshick	Minnesota	lefthanded

*First pick

Opening day lineup

April 10, 1961
Coot Veal, shortstop
Billy Klaus, third base
Marty Keough, right field
Dale Long, first base
Gene Woodling, left field
Willie Tasby, center field
Danny O'Connell, second base
Pete Daley, catcher
Dick Donovan, pitcher

Billy Klaus

Senators firsts

First hit: Coot Veal, April 10, 1961, vs. Chicago (single)
First home run: Billy Klaus, April 15, 1961, vs. Cleveland
First RBI: Gene Woodling, April 10, 1961, vs. Chicago
First win: Joe McClain, April 14, 1961, vs. Cleveland
First shutout: Tom Sturdivant, May 13, 1969, 4-0 vs. Boston

HISTORY

TORONTO BLUE JAYS

Outfielder George Bell.

FRANCHISE CHRONOLOGY

First season: 1977, as part of a two-team expansion that increased the American League field to 14 teams. The Blue Jays celebrated the debut of A.L. baseball in Canada with a 9-5 victory over Chicago, but they would go on to lose 107 times and finish last in the A.L. East, 45½ games behind the New York Yankees.

1978-present: The Blue Jays struggled for six seasons as they built the foundation for a franchise that would rise to prominence. Building patiently from within, the Jays topped 100 losses in each of their first three seasons and occupied the basement of the A.L. East Division five consecutive years. But the patience was rewarded in 1985 when the young and talented Blue Jays, playing in their ninth season, captured their first East Division title and began a run that would produce consecutive World Series championships in 1992 and '93. The Blue Jays lost three Championship Series before securing 1992 postseason victories over Oakland and Atlanta—and the first World Series triumph for a Canadian-based team.

BLUE JAYS VS. OPPONENTS BY DECADE

	A's	Indians	Orioles	Red Sox	Tigers	Twins	White Sox	Yankees	Angels	Rangers	Brewers	Royals	Mariners	Devil Rays	Interleague	Decade Record
1977-79	15-18	14-27	14-29	11-32	15-28	6-26	14-19	14-29	12-20	16-18	13-30	10-22	12-20			166-318
1980-89	53-67	71-52	61-62	62-59	68-59	64-50	70-50	57-65	63-57	67-49	56-71	56-60	69-45			817-746
1990-99	53-55	65-56	69-54	52-72	70-52	72-38	54-53	57-64	58-53	53-63	45-52	62-55	54-50	15-10	22-27	801-754
2000-	3-7	4-8	6-7	8-4	9-3	4-5	5-5	7-5	7-5	6-4		6-4	2-8	7-5	9-9	83-79
Totals	124-147	154-143	150-152	133-167	162-142	146-119	143-127	135-163	140-135	142-134	114-153	134-141	137-123	22-15	31-36	1867-1897

Interleague results: 7-5 vs. Braves; 13-6 vs. Expos; 3-9 vs. Mets; 5-7 vs. Phillies; 3-9 vs. Marlins.

MANAGERS

Name	*Years*	*Record*
Roy Hartsfield	1977-79	166-318
Bobby Mattick	1980-81	104-164
Bobby Cox	1982-85	355-292
Jimy Williams	1986-89	281-241
Cito Gaston	1989-97	702-650
Mel Queen	1997	4-1
Tim Johnson	1998	88-74
Jim Fregosi	1999-2000	167-159

WORLD SERIES CHAMPIONS

Year	*Loser*	*Length*	*MVP*
1992	Atlanta	6 games	Borders
1993	Philadelphia	6 games	Molitor

A.L. PENNANT WINNERS

Year	*Record*	*Manager*	*Series Result*
1992	96-66	Gaston	Defeated Braves
1993	95-67	Gaston	Defeated Phillies

EAST DIVISION CHAMPIONS

Year	*Record*	*Manager*	*ALCS Result*
1985	99-62	Cox	Lost to Royals
1989	89-73	Williams, Gaston	Lost to A's
1991	91-71	Gaston	Lost to Twins
1992	96-66	Gaston	Defeated A's
1993	95-67	Gaston	Defeated White Sox

ALL-TIME RECORD OF EXPANSION TEAMS

Team	W	L	Pct.	DT	P	WS
Arizona	250	236	.514	1	0	0
Kansas City	2,548	2,497	.505	6	2	1
Toronto	1,867	1,897	.496	5	2	2
Houston	3,052	3,138	.493	6	0	0
Montreal	2,454	2,596	.486	2	0	0
Anaheim	3,069	3,281	.483	3	0	0
Colorado	594	639	.482	0	0	0
Milwaukee	2,421	2,631	.479	2	1	0
New York	2,934	3,246	.475	4	4	2
Texas	2,952	3,381	.466	4	0	0
San Diego	2,315	2,742	.458	3	2	0
Seattle	1,715	2,048	.456	2	0	0
Florida	551	678	.448	0	1	1
Tampa Bay	201	284	.414	0	0	0

DT—Division Titles. P—Pennants won. WS—World Series won.

ATTENDANCE HIGHS

Total	*Season*	*Park*
4,057,098	1993	SkyDome
4,028,318	1992	SkyDome
4,001,526	1991	SkyDome
3,885,284	1990	SkyDome
3,375,883	1989	SkyDome

BALLPARK CHRONOLOGY

SkyDome (1989-present)

Capacity: 50,516.
First game: Milwaukee 5, Blue Jays 3 (June 5, 1989).
First batter: Paul Molitor, Brewers.
First hit: Paul Molitor, Brewers (double).
First run: Paul Molitor, Brewers (1st inning).
First home run: Fred McGriff, Blue Jays.
First winning pitcher: Don August, Brewers.
First-season attendance: 3,375,883 (SkyDome and Exhibition Stadium).

Exhibition Stadium (1977-89)

Capacity: 43,737.
First game: Blue Jays 9, Chicago 5 (April 7, 1977).
First-season attendance: 1,701,052.

A.L. MVP

George Bell, OF, 1987

CY YOUNG WINNER

Pat Hentgen, RH, 1996
Roger Clemens, RH, 1997
Roger Clemens, RH, 1998

ROOKIE OF THE YEAR

Alfredo Griffin, SS, 1979

MANAGER OF THE YEAR

Bobby Cox, 1985

Second baseman Roberto Alomar was a key figure for the 1992 and '93 championship teams.

MILESTONE PERFORMANCES

25-plus home runs
47—George Bell....1987
46—Jose Canseco....1998
44—Carlos Delgado....1999
42—Shawn Green....1999
41—Carlos Delgado....2000
Tony Batista....2000
40—Jesse Barfield....1986
38—Carlos Delgado....1998
36—Fred McGriff....1989
Ed Sprague....1996
35—Fred McGriff....1990
Shawn Green....1998
34—Fred McGriff....1988
Joe Carter....1992
33—Joe Carter....1991, 1993
32—Brad Fullmer....2000
31—George Bell....1986
Kelly Gruber....1990
Tony Batista....*1999
Jose Cruz....2000
30—John Mayberry....1980
Joe Carter....1996
Carlos Delgado....1997
28—George Bell....1985
Jesse Barfield....1987
27—Willie Upshaw....1983
Jesse Barfield....1983, 1985
Joe Carter....1994
26—George Bell....1984
Lloyd Moseby....1987
Dave Winfield....1992
25—Joe Carter....1995
Carlos Delgado....1996
^26 with Blue Jays, 5 with Diamondbacks.

100-plus RBIs
137—Carlos Dalgado....2000
134—George Bell....1987
Carlos Delgado....1999
123—Shawn Green....1999
121—Joe Carter....1993
119—Joe Carter....1992
118—Kelly Gruber....1990
115—Carlos Delgado....1998
114—Tony Batista....2000
111—Paul Molitor....1993
108—Jesse Barfield....1986
George Bell....1986
Joe Carter....1991
Dave Winfield....1992
107—John Olerud....1993
Joe Carter....1996
Jose Canseco....1998
104—Willie Upshaw....1983
George Bell....1989
Brad Fullmer....2000
103—Joe Carter....1994
102—Joe Carter....1997
101—Ed Sprague....1996
100—Shawn Green....1998
Tony Batista....*1999
*79 with Blue Jays, 21 with Diamondbacks.

20-plus victories
1992—Jack Morris....21-6
1996—Pat Hentgen....20-10
1997—Roger Clemens....21-7
1998—Roger Clemens....20-6
2000—David Wells....20-8

A.L. home run champions
1986—Jesse Barfield....40
1989—Fred McGriff....36

A.L. RBI champions
1987—George Bell....134

A.L. batting champions
1993—John Olerud....363

A.L. ERA champions
1985—Dave Stieb....2.48
1987—Jimmy Key....2.76
1996—Juan Guzman....2.93
1997—Roger Clemens....2.05
1998—Roger Clemens....2.65

A.L. strikeout champions
1997—Roger Clemens....292
1998—Roger Clemens....271

No-hit pitchers
(9 innings or more)
1990—Dave Stieb....3-0 vs. Cleveland

Longest hitting streaks
28—Shawn Green....1999
26—John Olerud....1993
Shannon Stewart....1999
22—George Bell....1989
Carlos Delgado....2000
21—Damaso Garcia....1983
Lloyd Moseby....1983
Dave Martinez....2000
20—Damaso Garcia....1982
19—Alfredo Griffin....1980
Roberto Alomar....1995
Carlos Delgado....1998
18—Damaso Garcia....1986
Tony Fernandez....1987
17—John Mayberry....1980
Damaso Garcia....1982
George Bell....1987
Dave Winfield....1992
Tony Batista....1999
16—Dave McKay....1978
Jesse Barfield....1985
Damaso Garcia....1985
Tony Fernandez....1989
Roberto Alomar....1992
Joe Carter....1992
Ed Sprague....1995
Shannon Stewart....1999
15—Roy Howell....1977
George Bell....1986
Kelly Gruber....1989
Tony Fernandez....1990
Kelly Gruber....1990
Roberto Alomar....1991
Carlos Delgado....1997
Alex Gonzalez....2000

Workhorse righthander Dave Stieb, a 175-game winner, holds virtually every key Toronto career pitching record.

INDIVIDUAL SEASON, GAME RECORDS

Slick-fielding shortstop Tony Fernandez holds single-season Blue Jays records for at-bats, hits, singles and triples.

SEASON

Batting

At-bats	687	Tony Fernandez	1986
Runs	134	Shawn Green	1999
Hits	213	Tony Fernandez	1986
Singles	161	Tony Fernandez	1986
Doubles	57	Carlos Delgado	2000
Triples	17	Tony Fernandez	1990
Home runs	47	George Bell	1987
Home runs, rookie	20	Fred McGriff	1987
Grand slams	3	Carlos Delgado	1997
		Darrin Fletcher	2000
Total bases	378	Carlos Delgado	2000
RBIs	137	Carlos Delgado	2000
		Carlos Delgado	1999
Walks	123	Carlos Delgado	2000
Most strikeouts	159	Jose Canseco	1998
Fewest strikeouts	21	Bob Bailor	1978
Batting average	.363	John Olerud	1993
Slugging pct.	.664	Carlos Delgado	2000
Stolen bases	60	Dave Collins	1984

Pitching

Games	89	Mark Eichorn	1987
Complete games	19	Dave Stieb	1982
Innings	288.1	Dave Stieb	1982
Wins	21	Jack Morris	1992
		Roger Clemens	1997
Losses	18	Jerry Garvin	1977
		Phil Huffman	1979
Winning pct.	.824	Juan Guzman	1993
Walks	128	Jim Clancy	1980
Strikeouts	292	Roger Clemens	1997
Shutouts	5	Dave Stieb	1982
Home runs allowed	36	Woody Williams	1998
Lowest ERA	2.05	Roger Clemens	1997
Saves	45	Duane Ward	1993

GAME

Batting

Runs	5	Carlos Delgado	5-3-99
Hits	5	Last by Tony Fernandez	5-7-99
Doubles	4	Last by Shannon Stewart	7-18-2000
Triples	2	Last by Shannon Stewart	9-20-97
Home runs	3	Last by Darrin Fletcher	8-27-2000
RBIs	9	Roy Howell	9-10-77
Total bases	13	Roy Howell	9-10-77
Stolen bases	4	Last by Otis Nixon	8-14-96

HISTORY

CAREER LEADERS

BATTING

Games

Tony Fernandez	1,402
Lloyd Moseby	1,392
Ernie Whitt	1,218
George Bell	1,181
Rance Mulliniks	1,115
Willie Upshaw	1,115
Joe Carter	1,039
Jesse Barfield	1,032
Alfredo Griffin	982
Garth Iorg	931

At-bats

Tony Fernandez	5,276
Lloyd Moseby	5,124
George Bell	4,528
Joe Carter	4,093
Willie Upshaw	3,710
Damaso Garcia	3,572
Ernie Whitt	3,514
Jesse Barfield	3,463
Alfredo Griffin	3,396
Ed Sprague	3,156

Runs

Lloyd Moseby	768
Tony Fernandez	699
George Bell	641
Joe Carter	578
Willie Upshaw	538
Jesse Barfield	530
Carlos Delgado	493
John Olerud	464
Damaso Garcia	453
Devon White	452

Hits

Tony Fernandez	1,565
Lloyd Moseby	1,319
George Bell	1,294
Joe Carter	1,051
Damaso Garcia	1,028
Willie Upshaw	982
Jesse Barfield	919
John Olerud	910
Ernie Whitt	888
Alfredo Griffin	844

Doubles

Tony Fernandez	287
Lloyd Moseby	242
George Bell	237
Joe Carter	218
Carlos Delgado	214
John Olerud	213
Rance Mulliniks	204
Willie Upshaw	177
Damaso Garcia	172
Ed Sprague	170

Triples

Tony Fernandez	72
Lloyd Moseby	60
Alfredo Griffin	50
Willie Upshaw	42
Roberto Alomar	36
Devon White	34
George Bell	32
Joe Carter	28
Jesse Barfield	27
Damaso Garcia	26

Home runs

Joe Carter	203
George Bell	202
Carlos Delgado	190
Jesse Barfield	179
Lloyd Moseby	149
Ernie Whitt	131
Fred McGriff	125
Shawn Green	119
Kelly Gruber	114
Ed Sprague	113

Total bases

George Bell	2,201
Tony Fernandez	2,173
Lloyd Moseby	2,128
Joe Carter	1,934
Jesse Barfield	1,672
Carlos Delgado	1,616
Willie Upshaw	1,579
Ernie Whitt	1,475
John Olerud	1,462
Damaso Garcia	1,348

Runs batted in

George Bell	740
Joe Carter	736
Lloyd Moseby	651
Carlos Delgado	604
Tony Fernandez	601
Jesse Barfield	527
Ernie Whitt	518
Willie Upshaw	478
John Olerud	471
Kelly Gruber	434

Extra-base hits

George Bell	471
Lloyd Moseby	451
Joe Carter	449
Tony Fernandez	418
Carlos Delgado	411
Jesse Barfield	368
Willie Upshaw	331
John Olerud	328
Ernie Whitt	310
Shawn Green	298

Batting average
(Minimum 500 games)

Roberto Alomar	.307
Tony Fernandez	.297
John Olerud	.293
Damaso Garcia	.288
George Bell	.286
Shawn Green	.286
Carlos Delgado	.282
Rance Mulliniks	.280
Fred McGriff	.278
Roy Howell	.272

Stolen bases

Lloyd Moseby	255
Roberto Alomar	206
Damaso Garcia	194
Tony Fernandez	172
Devon White	126
Shannon Stewart	121
Otis Nixon	101
Dave Collins	91
Kelly Gruber	80
Alfredo Griffin	79

PITCHING

Earned-run average
(Minimum 500 innings)

Tom Henke	2.48
Duane Ward	3.18
Dave Stieb	3.42
Jimmy Key	3.42
Doyle Alexander	3.56
John Cerutti	3.87
David Wells	4.06
Jim Acker	4.07
Juan Guzman	4.07
Jim Clancy	4.10

Wins

Dave Stieb	175
Jim Clancy	128
Jimmy Key	116
Pat Hentgen	105
David Wells	84
Juan Guzman	76
Todd Stottlemyre	69
Luis Leal	51
Doyle Alexander	46
John Cerutti	46

Losses

Jim Clancy	140
Dave Stieb	134
Jimmy Key	81
Pat Hentgen	76
Todd Stottlemyre	70
Juan Guzman	62
Luis Leal	58
Jesse Jefferson	56
David Wells	55
Dave Lemanczyk	45

Innings pitched

Dave Stieb	2,873.0
Jim Clancy	2,204.2
Jimmy Key	1,695.2
Pat Hentgen	1,555.2
Juan Guzman	1,215.2
David Wells	1,148.2
Todd Stottlemyre	1,139.0
Luis Leal	946.0
John Cerutti	772.1
Doyle Alexander	750.0

Strikeouts

Dave Stieb	1,658
Jim Clancy	1,237
Juan Guzman	1,030
Pat Hentgen	995
Jimmy Key	944
David Wells	784
Duane Ward	671
Todd Stottlemyre	662
Tom Henke	644
Roger Clemens	563

Bases on balls

Dave Stieb	1,020
Jim Clancy	814
Pat Hentgen	557
Juan Guzman	546
Todd Stottlemyre	414
Jimmy Key	404
Luis Leal	320
David Wells	294
Duane Ward	278
Jesse Jefferson	266

Games

Duane Ward	452
Tom Henke	446
Dave Stieb	439
Jim Clancy	352
Jimmy Key	317
Paul Quantrill	306
David Wells	306
Mike Timlin	305
Jim Acker	281
Mark Eichhorn	279

Shutouts

Dave Stieb	30
Jim Clancy	11
Jimmy Key	10
Pat Hentgen	9
Roger Clemens	6
Jesse Jefferson	4
Todd Stottlemyre	4
Doyle Alexander	3
Chris Carpenter	3
Jim Gott	3
Luis Leal	3
Dave Lemanczyk	3

Saves

Tom Henke	217
Duane Ward	121
Billy Koch	64
Mike Timlin	52
Joey McLaughlin	31
Roy Lee Jackson	30
Randy Myers	28
Darren Hall	20
Tony Castillo	16
Bill Caudill	16
Kelvim Escobar	16

TEAM SEASON, GAME RECORDS

SEASON

Batting

Most at-bats	5,716	1986
Most runs	883	1999
Fewest runs	590	1978
Most hits	1,580	1999
Most singles	1,069	1984
Most doubles	337	1999
Most triples	68	1984
Most home runs	244	2000
Fewest home runs	95	1979
Most grand slams	9	2000
Most pinch-hit home runs	6	1984
Most total bases	2,664	2000
Most stolen bases	193	1984
Highest batting average	.280	1999
Lowest batting average	.244	1997
Highest slugging pct	.469	2000

Pitching

Lowest ERA	3.29	1985
Highest ERA	5.14	2000
Most complete games	44	1979
Most shutouts	17	1988
Most saves	60	1991
Most walks	635	1980
Most strikeouts	1,154	1998

Fielding

Most errors	164	1977
Fewest errors	86	1990
Most double plays	206	1980
Highest fielding average	.986	1990

General

Most games won	99	1985
Most games lost	109	1979
Highest win pct	.615	1985
Lowest win pct	.327	1979

GAME, INNING

Batting

Most runs, game	24	6-26-78
Most runs, inning	11	7-20-84
Most hits, game	25	8-9-99
Most home runs, game	10	9-14-87
Most total bases, game	53	9-14-87

Righthander Jim Clancy ranks second on Toronto's all-time victory chart with 128.

HISTORY

BLUE JAYS YEAR-BY-YEAR

Year	W	L	Place	Games Back	Manager	Leaders: Batting avg.	Hits	Home runs	RBIs	Wins	ERA
						—EAST DIVISION—					
1977	54	107	7th	45½	Hartsfield	Howell, .316	Bailor, 154	Fairly, 19	Ault, Fairly, 64	Lemanczyk, 13	Vuckovich, 3.47
1978	59	102	7th	40	Hartsfield	Carty, .284	Bailor, 164	Mayberry, 22	Mayberry, 70	Clancy, 10	Murphy, 3.93
1979	53	109	7th	50½	Hartsfield	Griffin, .287	Griffin, 179	Mayberry, 21	Mayberry, 74	T. Underwood, 9	T. Underwood, 3.69
1980	67	95	7th	36	Mattick	Woods, .300	Griffin, 166	Mayberry, 30	Mayberry, 82	Clancy, 13	Clancy, 3.30
1981	37	69	*7th/7th	—	Mattick	Garcia, .252	Moseby, 88	Mayberry, 17	Mayberry, Moseby, 43	Stieb, 11	Stieb, 3.19
1982	78	84	†6th	17	Cox	Garcia, .310	Garcia, 185	Upshaw, 21	Upshaw, 75	Stieb, 17	Jackson, 3.06
1983	89	73	4th	9	Cox	Bonnell, .318	Upshaw, 177	Barfield, Upshaw, 27	Upshaw, 104	Stieb, 17	Stieb, 3.04
1984	89	73	2nd	15	Cox	Collins, .308	Garcia, 180	Bell, 26	Moseby, 92	Alexander, 17	Stieb, 2.83
1985	99	62	‡1st	+2	Cox	Mulliniks, .295	Bell, 167	Bell, 28	Bell, 95	Alexander, 17	Stieb, 2.48
1986	86	76	4th	9½	J. Williams	Fernandez, .310	Fernandez, 213	Barfield, 40	Barfield, Bell, 108	Clancy, Key, Eichhorn, 14	Eichhorn, 1.72
1987	96	66	2nd	2	J. Williams	Fernandez, .322	Bell, 188	Bell, 47	Bell, 134	Key, 17	Key, 2.76
1988	87	75	†3rd	2	J. Williams	Lee, .291	Fernandez, 186	McGriff, 34	Bell, 97	Stieb, 16	Stieb, 3.04
1989	89	73	‡1st	+2	J. Williams, Gaston	Bell, .297	Bell, 182	McGriff, 36	Bell, 104	Stieb, 17	Cerutti, 3.07
1990	86	76	2nd	2	Gaston	McGriff, .300	Fernandez, 175	McGriff, 35	Gruber, 118	Stieb, 18	Stieb, 2.93
1991	91	71	‡1st	+7	Gaston	Alomar, .295	Alomar, 188	Carter, 33	Carter, 108	Key, 17	Ward, 2.77
1992	96	66	§1st	+4	Gaston	Alomar, .310	Alomar, 177	Carter, 34	Carter, 119	Morris, 21	Ward, 1.95
1993	95	67	§1st	+7	Gaston	Olerud, .363	Molitor, 211	Carter, 33	Carter, 121	Hentgen, 19	Hentgen, 3.87
1994	55	60	3rd	16	Gaston	Molitor, .341	Molitor, 155	Carter, 27	Carter, 103	Hentgen, 13	Hentgen, 3.40
1995	56	88	5th	30	Gaston	Alomar, .300	Alomar, 155	Carter, 25	Carter, 76	Leiter, 11	Leiter, 3.64
1996	74	88	4th	18	Gaston	Nixon, .286	Carter, 158	Sprague, 36	Carter, 107	Hentgen, 20	Guzman, 2.93
1997	76	86	5th	22	Gaston, Queen	Green, .287	Carter, 143	Delgado, 30	Carter, 102	Clemens, 21	Clemens, 2.05
1998	88	74	3rd	26	T. Johnson	Fernandez, .321	Green, 175	Canseco, 46	Delgado, 115	Clemens, 20	Clemens, 2.65
1999	84	78	3rd	14	Fregosi	Fernandez, .328	Green, 190	Delgado, 44	Delgado, 134	Wells, 17	Halladay, 3.92
2000	83	79	3rd	4½	Fregosi	Delgado, .344	Delgado, 196	Delgado, 41	Delgado, 137	Wells, 20	F. Castillo, 3.59

* First half 16-42; second half 21-27. † Tied for position. ‡ Lost Championship Series. § Won Championship Series.

Note: Batting average minimum 350 at-bats; ERA minimum 90 innings pitched.

Bob Bailor

TORONTO was welcomed into the American League fold on March 26, 1976, when owners granted ownership approval to Labatt Breweries and Imperial Trust, giving the Blue Jays distinction as the first A.L. team outside the continental United States. The Blue Jays, the A.L.'s 14th franchise, joined the league with the Seattle Mariners.

Infielder Bob Bailor gained distinction as the first of 30 Toronto selections in the November 5, 1976, A.L. expansion draft. American League baseball made a successful Canadian debut on April 7, 1977, when the Blue Jays defeated the Chicago White Sox, 9-5, at Exhibition Stadium.

Expansion draft (November 5, 1976)

Players

Player	Team	Position
Doug Ault	Texas	first base
*Bob Bailor	Baltimore	infield
Steve Bowling	Milwaukee	outfield
Rico Carty	Cleveland	outfield
Sam Ewing	Chicago	first base
Garth Iorg	New York	infield
Jim Mason	New York	shortstop
Dave McKay	Minnesota	third base
Steve Staggs	Kansas City	second base
Otto Velez	New York	outfield
Ernie Whitt	Boston	catcher
Mike Weathers	Oakland	infield
Al Woods	Minnesota	outfield
Gary Woods	Oakland	outfield

Pitchers

Larry Anderson	Milwaukee	righthanded
Tom Bruno	Kansas City	righthanded
Jeff Byrd	Texas	righthanded
Jim Clancy	Texas	righthanded
Mike Darr	Baltimore	righthanded
Dennis DeBarr	Detroit	lefthanded
Butch Edge	Milwaukee	righthanded
Al Fitzmorris	Kansas City	righthanded
Jerry Garvin	Minnesota	lefthanded
Steve Hargan	Texas	righthanded
Leon Hooten	Oakland	righthanded
Jesse Jefferson	Chicago	righthanded
Dave Lemanczyk	Detroit	righthanded
Bill Singer	Minnesota	righthanded
Pete Vuckovich	Chicago	righthanded
Mike Willis	Baltimore	lefthanded

*First pick

Opening day lineup

April 7, 1977

John Scott, left field
Hector Torres, shortstop
Doug Ault, first base
Otto Velez, designated hitter
Gary Woods, center field
Steve Bowling, right field
Pedro Garcia, second base
Dave McKay, third base
Rick Cerone, catcher
Bill Singer, pitcher

Doug Ault

Blue Jays firsts

First hit: Doug Ault, April 7, 1977, vs. Chicago
First home run: Doug Ault, April 7, 1977, vs. Chicago
First RBI: Doug Ault, April 7, 1977, vs. Chicago
First win: Jerry Johnson, April 7, 1977, vs. Chicago
First shutout: Pete Vuckovich, June 26, 1977, 2-0 at Baltimore

Arizona Diamondbacks

First baseman Travis Lee.

FRANCHISE CHRONOLOGY

The beginnings: Arizona, a longtime bastion of minor league baseball and spring training, joined the Major League ranks on March 9, 1995, when owners unanimously approved expansion to Phoenix and Tampa. The 13th and 14th expansion cubs in Major League history were also the earliest-formed expansion teams, gaining approval more than three years before they would throw their first pitch against big-league competition. The Diamondbacks were awarded to a group headed by Jerry Colangelo, the man who had built the Phoenix Suns into one of the most admired franchises in the NBA. Both teams were stocked in a November 1997 expansion draft and began play in the 1998 season, Arizona as part of the National League West division.

First season: Major League baseball made its Arizona debut on March 31, 1998, at Bank One Ballpark in Phoenix when the Diamondbacks dropped a 9-2 decision to the Rockies. Arizona went on to compile a 65-97 first-year record, two games better than Tampa Bay in its A.L. debut season. The Diamondbacks finished in the N.L. West basement, 33 games behind San Diego.

1999: In only their second season, the Diamondbacks captured their first N.L. West title, thanks to an offseason barrage of high-priced veteran free-agent signings. The Diamondbacks posted an impressive 100-62 record before losing to the New York Mets in the Division Series and then braced for an encore. It never happened. Arizona struggled to an 85-77 third-year record and finished third in the West.

DIAMONDBACKS VS. OPPONENTS BY DECADE

	Braves	Cardinals	Cubs	Dodgers	Giants	Phillies	Pirates	Reds	Astros	Mets	Expos	Padres	Marlins	Rockies	Brewers	Interleague	Decade Record
1998-99	5-13	6-11	12-9	11-14	14-10	10-8	11-5	5-13	9-9	11-7	8-10	14-11	14-3	12-13	11-7	12-16	165-159
2000-	3-6	5-4	5-4	7-6	6-7	8-1	7-2	2-5	6-1	2-7	4-5	9-4	4-5	7-6	4-5	6-9	85-77
Totals	8-19	11-15	17-13	18-20	20-17	18-9	18-7	7-18	15-10	13-14	12-15	23-15	18-8	19-19	15-12	18-25	250-236

Interleague results: 5-4 vs. Angels; 3-6 vs. Athletics; 4-5 vs. Mariners; 6-10 vs. Rangers.

ALL-TIME RECORD OF EXPANSION TEAMS

Team	W	L	Pct.	DT	P	WS
Arizona	250	236	.514	1	0	0
Kansas City	2,548	2,497	.505	6	2	1
Toronto	1,867	1,897	.496	5	2	2
Houston	3,052	3,138	.493	6	0	0
Montreal	2,454	2,596	.486	2	0	0
Anaheim	3,069	3,281	.483	3	0	0
Colorado	594	639	.482	0	0	0
Milwaukee	2,421	2,631	.479	2	1	0
New York	2,934	3,246	.475	4	4	2
Texas	2,952	3,381	.466	4	0	0
San Diego	2,315	2,742	.458	3	2	0
Seattle	1,715	2,048	.456	2	0	0
Florida	551	678	.448	0	1	1
Tampa Bay	201	284	.414	0	0	0

DT—Division Titles. P—Pennants won. WS—World Series won.

BALLPARK CHRONOLOGY

Bank One Ballpark (1998-present)

Capacity: 49,075.
First game: Rockies 9, Diamondbacks 2 (March 31, 1998).
First batter: Mike Lansing, Rockies.
First hit: Mike Lansing, Rockies (single).
First run: Vinny Castilla, Rockies (2nd inning).
First home run: Vinny Castilla, Rockies.
First winning pitcher: Darryl Kile, Rockies.
First-season attendance: 3,602,856.

MANAGERS

Name	*Years*	*Record*
Buck Showalter	1998-2000	250-236

WEST DIVISION CHAMPIONS

Year	*Record*	*Manager*	*NLCS Result*
1999	100-62	Showalter	Lost to Mets

ATTENDANCE HIGHS

Total	*Season*	*Park*
3,602,856	1998	Bank One Ballpark
3,017,489	1999	Bank One Ballpark
2,912,516	2000	Bank One Ballpark

CY YOUNG WINNER

Randy Johnson, LH, 1999
Randy Johnson, LH, 2000

N.L. ERA champions

1999— Randy Johnson 2.48

N.L. strikeout champions

1999— Randy Johnson 364

LONGEST HITTING STREAKS

30— Luis Gonzalez 1999
24— Tony Womack 2000
19— Matt Williams 1999
16— Luis Gonzalez 1999
15— Tony Bautista 2000

Expansion draft (November 18, 1998)

Players

Player	Club	Position
Gabe Alvarez	San Diego	third base
Tony Batista	Oakland	shortstop
Mike Bell	Anaheim	third base
Yamil Benetez	Kansas City	outfield
Brent Brede	Minnesota	outfield
David Dellucci	Baltimore	outfield
Edwin Diaz	Texas	second base
Jorge Fabregas	White Sox	catcher
Hanley Frias	Texas	shortstop
Karim Garcia	Los Angeles	outfield
Dan Klassen	Milwaukee	shortstop
Damian Miller	Minnesota	catcher
Joe Randa	Pittsburgh	third base
Kelly Stinnett	Milwaukee	catcher

Pitchers

Pitcher	Club	Throws
Joel Adamson	Milwaukee	lefthanded
*Brian Anderson	Cleveland	lefthanded
Jason Boyd	Philadelphia	righthanded
Hector Carrasco	Kansas City	righthanded
Chris Clemons	White Sox	righthanded
Bryan Corey	Detroit	righthanded
Omar Daal	Toronto	lefthanded
Matt Drews	Detroit	righthanded
Todd Erdos	San Diego	righthanded
Ben Ford	N.Y. Yankees	righthanded
Marty Janzen	Toronto	righthanded
Cory Lidle	N.Y. Mets	righthanded
Thomas Martin	Houston	lefthanded
Jesus Martinez	Los Angeles	lefthanded
Chuck McElroy	White Sox	lefthanded
Clint Sodowsky	Pittsburgh	righthanded
Russ Springer	Houston	righthanded
Jeff Suppan	Boston	righthanded
Neil Weber	Montreal	lefthanded
Scott Winchester	Cincinnati	righthanded
Bob Wolcott	Seattle	righthanded

*First pick

Opening day lineup

March 31, 1998
Devon White, center field
Jay Bell, shortstop
Travis Lee, first base
Matt Williams, third base
Brent Brede, left field
Karim Garcia, right field
Jorge Fabregas, catcher
Edwin Diaz, second base
Andy Benes, pitcher

Brian Anderson

Diamondbacks firsts

First hit: Travis Lee, March 31, 1998, vs. Colorado (single)
First home run: Travis Lee, March 31, 1998, vs. Colorado
First RBI: Travis Lee, March 31, 1998, vs. Colorado
First win: Andy Benes, April 5, 1998, vs. San Francisco
First shutout: Omar Daal, July 20, 1998, 4-0 vs. Cubs.

CAREER LEADERS

BATTING

Games

Jay Bell	455
Matt Williams	385
Travis Lee	338
Luis Gonzalez	315
Steve Finley	308
Tony Womack	290
Andy Fox	269
Kelly Stinnett	256
Damian Miller	243
David Dellucci	221

At-bats

Jay Bell	1,703
Matt Williams	1,508
Luis Gonzalez	1,232
Tony Womack	1,231
Travis Lee	1,161
Steve Finley	1,129
Andy Fox	862
Kelly Stinnett	798
Damian Miller	788
Dave Dellucci	575

Runs

Jay Bell	298
Luis Gonzalez	218
Matt Williams	213
Tony Womack	206
Steve Finley	200
Travis Lee	162
Andy Fox	111
Damian Miller	95
Kelly Stinnett	93
Devon White	84

Hits

Jay Bell	459
Matt Williams	428
Luis Gonzalez	398
Tony WomacK	337
Steve Finley	307
Travis Lee	292
Andy Fox	227
Damian Miller	217
Kelly Stinnett	189
David Dellucci	166

Doubles

Luis Gonzalez	92
Jay Bell	91
Matt Williams	81
Steve Finley	59
Damian Miller	57
Travis Lee	49
Tony Womack	46
Andy Fox	37
Kelly Stinnett	34
Devon White	32

Triples

Tony Womack	24
Jay Bell	17
Steve Finley	15
Dave Dellucci	13
Andy Fox	8
Karim Garcia	8
Danny Bautista	7
Luis Gonzalez	6
Matt Williams	5
Greg Colbrunn	4
Travis Lee	4

Home runs

Jay Bell	76
Steve Finley	69
Matt Williams	67
Luis Gonzalez	57
Travis Lee	39
Kelly Stinnett	33
Damian Miller	24
Tony Batista	23
Devon White	22
Greg Colbrunn	20

Total bases

Jay Bell	812
Matt Williams	720
Luis Gonzalez	673
Steve Finley	603
Travis Lee	466
Tony Womack	464
Damian Miller	350
Andy Fox	328
Kelly Stinnett	324
Davon White	257

Runs batted in

Matt Williams	260
Jay Bell	247
Luis Gonzalez	225
Steve Finley	199
Travis Lee	162
Damian Miller	105
Kelly Stinnett	105
Tony Womack	98
Andy Fox	87
Devon White	85

Extra-base hits

Jay Bell	184
Luis Gonzalez	155
Matt Williams	153
Steve Finley	143
Travis Lee	92
Damian Miller	83
Tony Womack	81
Kelly Stinnett	68
Andy Fox	61
Devon White	55

Batting average
(Minimum 150 games)

Luis Gonzalez	.323
Greg Colbrunn	.317
Dave Dellucci	.289
Matt Williams	.284
Damian Miller	.275
Tony Womack	.274
Steve Finley	.272
Jay Bell	.270
Tony Batista	.268
Andy Fox	.263

Stolen bases

Tony Womack	117
Travis Lee	30
Devon White	22
Steve Finley	20
Andy Fox	20
Jay Bell	17
Luis Gonzalez	11
Matt Williams	8
Hanley Frias	6
Bernard Gilkey	6
Lenny Harris	6

PITCHING

Earned-run average
(Minimum 140 innings)

Randy Johnson	2.56
Greg Swindell	2.88
Omar Daal	4.11
Brian Anderson	4.28
Andy Benes	4.36
Todd Stottlemyre	4.49
Armando Reynoso	4.82
Willie Blair	5.34

Wins

Randy Johnson	36
Brian Anderson	31
Andy Benes	27
Omar Daal	26
Armando Reynoso	21
Todd Stottlemyre	15
Gregg Olson	12
Byung-Hyunkim	7
Dan Plesac	7
Amaury Telemaco	7

Losses

Omar Daal	31
Andy Benes	25
Brian Anderson	22
Armando Reynoso	18
Randy Johnson	16
Willie Blair	15
Todd Stottlemyre	9
Amaury Telemaco	9
Byung-Hyunkim	8
Gregg Olson	8

Innings pitched

Brian Anderson	551.1
Randy Johnson	520.1
Omar Daal	473.1
Andy Benes	429.2
Armando Reynoso	337.2
Todd Stottlemyre	196.2
Willie Blair	146.2
Greg Swindell	140.2
Gregg Olson	129.1
Amaury Telemaco	127.0

Strikeouts

Randy Johnson	711
Omar Daal	325
Andy Benes	305
Brian Anderson	274
Armando Reynoso	168
Todd Stottlemyre	142
Byung-Hyunkim	142
Greg Swindell	115
Matt Mantei	102
Gregg Olson	100

Bases on balls

Omar Daal	172
Andy Benes	156
Randy Johnson	146
Armando Reynoso	119
Brian Anderson	91
Todd Stottlemyre	76
Byung-Hyunkim	66
Matt Mantei	54
Willie Blair	51
Gregg Olson	50

Games

Greg Swindell	127
Gregg Olson	125
Brian Anderson	96
Dan Plesac	96
Byung-Hyunkim	86
Omar Daal	85
Russ Springer	78
Matt Mantei	77
Randy Johnson	70
Andy Benes	67

Shutouts

Randy Johnson	5
Brian Anderson	2
Omar Daal	2
Curt Schilling	1

Saves

Gregg Olson	44
Matt Mantei	39
Byung-Hyunkim	15
Mike Morgan	5
Felix Rodriguez	5
Greg Swindell	2
Brian Anderson	1
Willie Banks	1
Bobby Chouinard	1
Alan Embree	1
Darren Holmes	1
Vladimir Nunez	1
Dan Plesac	1

INDIVIDUAL SEASON, GAME RECORDS

Jay Bell has provided a veteran presence at shortstop during the Diamondbacks' first three seasons.

SEASON

Batting

Most at-bats	5,658	1999
Most runs	908	1999
Fewest runs	665	1998
Most hits	1,566	1999
Most singles	1,015	1999
Most doubles	289	1999
Most triples	46	1998, 1999
Most home runs	216	1999
Fewest home runs	159	1998
Most grand slams	8	1999
Most pinch-hit home runs	5	1999
Most total bases	2,595	1999
Most stolen bases	137	1999
Highest batting average	.277	1999
Lowest batting average	.246	1998
Highest slugging pct.	.459	1999

Pitching

Lowest ERA	3.77	1999
Highest ERA	4.64	1998
Most complete games	16	1999, 2000
Most shutouts	9	1999
Most saves	42	1999
Most walks	543	1999
Most strikeouts	1,220	2000

Fielding

Most errors	107	2000
Fewest errors	100	1998
Most double plays	138	2000
Highest fielding average	.984	1998

General

Most games won	100	1999
Most games lost	97	1998
Highest win pct.	.617	1999
Lowest win pct.	.401	1998

GAME, INNING

Batting

Most runs, game	17	7-4-99, 7-27-2000
Most runs, inning	8	8-26-99, 8-19-2000
Most hits, game	20	6-2-99, 5-8-2000
Most home runs, game	5	Last on 4-10-2000
Most total bases, game	37	6-2-99

Atlanta Braves

FRANCHISE CHRONOLOGY

First season: 1876, in Boston, as a member of the new National League. The "Red Stockings" defeated Philadelphia, 6-5, in their franchise debut and went on to finish fourth with a 39-31 first-year record.

1877-1900: Boston's "Beaneaters" were dominant in the pre-1900 era. They won consecutive pennants in 1877 and '78, returned to the top in 1883 and powered their way to five more flags in the 1890s.

1901-1952: Such success did not carry over to the modern era. Over the next 52 seasons, the Braves would win only two more pennants—while finishing sixth, seventh or eighth 33 times. One of the pennants was secured by the Miracle Braves of 1914, who recovered from a 15-game deficit to overtake the Giants with a 68-19 stretch run and then swept past powerful Philadelphia in the World Series. When the financially strapped Braves transferred to Milwaukee after the 1952 season, they broke up a baseball alignment that had existed since 1903.

1953-1965: The Braves were embraced by Milwaukee fans and rewarded them with a 1957 World Series victory and a 1958 pennant. But when the team fell into the second division in the early 1960s, enthusiasm waned and management began another search for greener pastures. After the 1965 season, the Braves made their second franchise shift in 14 years—this time to Atlanta.

1966-present: It took another quarter century for the Braves to regain status as an N.L. power, but they did so with a vengeance. After winning West Division titles in 1969 and 1982 and losing in the NLCS both years, they embarked on a record run that produced nine straight division titles, five pennants and one World Series win—a six-game triumph over Cleveland in 1995.

Outfielder Hank Aaron.

BRAVES VS. OPPONENTS BY DECADE

	Cardinals	Cubs	Dodgers	Giants	Phillies	Pirates	Reds	Astros	Mets	Expos	Padres	Marlins	Rockies	Brewers	D'backs	Interleague	Decade Record
1900-09	98-111	76-135	95-114	83-125	87-119	58-153	90-120										587-877
1910-19	110-100	87-127	105-103	73-137	90-123	104-109	97-116										666-815
1920-29	85-135	80-139	90-128	82-137	100-118	77-141	89-130										603-928
1930-39	98-121	74-146	117-103	89-127	122-97	92-125	108-110										700-829
1940-49	76-144	111-108	90-129	100-116	132-87	105-112	105-112										719-808
1950-59	119-101	126-94	92-129	126-94	118-102	139-81	134-86										854-687
1960-69	88-94	92-90	89-99	97-91	107-75	88-94	85-103	95-49	89-49	8-4	13-5						851-753
1970-79	51-69	54-66	70-106	84-95	62-58	43-77	60-120	85-91	59-61	60-58	97-82						725-883
1980-89	47-68	57-55	69-105	79-94	64-53	58-53	81-92	78-96	46-68	45-72	88-89						712-845
1990-99	71-43	62-43	68-55	69-53	70-50	62-45	82-49	71-53	69-50	70-50	79-44	51-36	50-26	12-4	13-5	26-23	925-629
2000-	3-4	4-5	7-2	6-3	8-5	5-2	2-5	5-4	7-6	6-7	8-1	6-6	5-4	6-3	6-3	11-7	95-67
Totals	846-990	823-1008	892-1073	888-1072	960-887	831-992	933-1043	334-293	270-234	189-191	285-221	57-42	55-30	18-7	19-8	37-30	7437-8121

Interleague results: 5-7 vs. Orioles; 12-6 vs. Red Sox; 1-2 vs. Tigers; 6-7 vs. Yankees; 5-7 vs. Blue Jays; 8-1vs. Devil Rays.

MANAGERS

(Boston Braves, 1876-1952)
(Milwaukee Braves, 1953-65)

Name	*Years*	*Record*
Harry Wright	1876-81	254-187
John Morrill	1882, 1883-86, 1887-88	335-296
Jack Burdock	1883	30-24
King Kelly	1887	49-43
Jim Hart	1889	83-45
Frank Selee	1890-1901	1004-649
Al Buckenberger	1902-04	186-242
Fred Tenney	1905-07, 1911	202-402
Joe Kelley	1908	63-91
Frank Bowerman	1909	22-54
Harry Smith	1909	23-54
Fred Lake	1910	53-100
Johnny Kling	1912	52-101
George Stallings	1913-20	579-597
Fred Mitchell	1921-23	186-274
Dave Bancroft	1924-27	249-363
Jack Slattery	1928	11-20
Rogers Hornsby	1928	39-83
Emil Fuchs	1929	56-98
Bill McKechnie	1930-37	560-666
Casey Stengel	1938-43	373-491
Bob Coleman	1943, 1944-45	128-165
Del Bissonette	1945	25-34
Billy Southworth	1946-51	424-358
Tommy Holmes	1951-52	61-69
Charlie Grimm	1952-56	341-285
Fred Haney	1956-59	341-231
Chuck Dressen	1960-61	159-124
Birdie Tebbetts	1961-62	98-89
Bobby Bragan	1963-66	310-287
Billy Hitchcock	1966-67	110-100
Ken Silvestri	1967	0-3
Lum Harris	1968-72	379-373
Eddie Mathews	1972-74	149-161
Clyde King	1974-75	96-101
Connie Ryan	1975	9-18
Dave Bristol	1976-77	131-192
Ted Turner	1977	0-1
Bobby Cox	1978-81, 1990-2000	1,261-979
Joe Torre	1982-84	257-229
Eddie Haas	1985	50-71
Bobby Wine	1985	16-25
Chuck Tanner	1986-88	153-208
Russ Nixon	1988-90	130-216

WORLD SERIES CHAMPIONS

Year	*Loser*	*Length*	*MVP*
1914	Philadelphia	4 games	None
1957	N.Y. Yankees	7 games	Burdette
1995	Cleveland	6 games	Glavine

N.L. PENNANT WINNERS

Year	*Record*	*Manager*	*Series Result*
1877	42-18	Wright	None
1878	41-19	Wright	None
1883	63-35	Burdock, Morrill	None
1891	87-51	Selee	None
1892	102-48	Selee	None
1893	86-43	Selee	None
1897	93-39	Selee	None
1898	102-47	Selee	None
1914	94-59	Stallings	Defeated A's
1948	91-62	Southworth	Lost to Indians
1957	95-59	Haney	Defeated Yankees
1958	92-62	Haney	Lost to Yankees
1991	94-68	Cox	Lost to Twins
1992	98-64	Cox	Lost to Blue Jays
1995	90-54	Cox	Defeated Indians
1996	96-66	Cox	Lost to Yankees
1999	103-59	Cox	Lost to Yankees

WEST DIVISION CHAMPIONS

Year	*Record*	*Manager*	*NLCS Result*
1969	93-69	Harris	Lost to Mets
1982	89-73	Torre	Lost to Cardinals
1991	94-68	Cox	Defeated Pirates
1992	98-64	Cox	Defeated Pirates
1993	104-58	Cox	Lost to Phillies

EAST DIVISION CHAMPIONS

Year	*Record*	*Manager*	*NLCS Result*
1995	90-54	Cox	Defeated Reds
1996	96-66	Cox	Defeated Cardinals
1997	101-61	Cox	Lost to Marlins
1998	106-56	Cox	Lost to Padres
1999	103-59	Cox	Defeated Mets
2000	95-67	Cox	Lost in Div. Series

ATTENDANCE HIGHS

Total	*Season*	*Park*
3,884,720	1993	Fulton County Stadium
3,463,988	1997	Turner Field
3,361,350	1998	Turner Field
3,284,901	1999	Turner Field
3,234,301	2000	Turner Field

RETIRED UNIFORMS

No.	*Name*	*Pos.*
3	Dale Murphy	OF
21	Warren Spahn	P
35	Phil Niekro	P
41	Ed Mathews	3B
44	Hank Aaron	OF

BALLPARK CHRONOLOGY

Turner Field (1997-present)

Capacity: 50,062.
First game: Braves 5, Cubs 4 (April 4, 1997).
First batter: Brian McRae, Cubs.
First hit: Chipper Jones, Braves (single).
First run: Michael Tucker, Braves (3rd inning).
First home run: Michael Tucker, Braves
First winning pitcher: Brad Clontz, Braves.
First-season attendance: 3,463,988.

South End Grounds I and II, Boston (1876-1914)

First game: Boston 6, Philadelphia 5 (April 22, 1876).

Braves Field, Boston (1915-52)

Capacity: 40,000.
First game: Braves 3, St. Louis 1 (August 18, 1915).
First-season attendance (1916): 313,495.

County Stadium, Milwaukee (1953-65)

Capacity: 43,394.
First game: Braves 3, St. Louis 2, 10 innings (April 14, 1953).
First-season attendance: 1,826,397.

Atlanta-Fulton County Stadium (1966-96)

Capacity: 52,710.
First game: Pittsburgh 3, Braves 2, 13 innings (April 12, 1966).
First-season attendance: 1,539,801.

N.L. MVPs

Bob Elliott, 3B, 1947
Hank Aaron, OF, 1957
Dale Murphy, OF, 1982
Dale Murphy, OF, 1983
Terry Pendleton, 3B, 1991
Chipper Jones, 3B, 1999

CY YOUNG WINNERS

Warren Spahn, LH, 1957
Tom Glavine, LH, 1991
Greg Maddux, RH, 1993
Greg Maddux, RH, 1994
Greg Maddux, RH, 1995
John Smoltz, RH, 1996
Tom Glavine, LH, 1998

ROOKIES OF THE YEAR

Alvin Dark, SS, 1948
Sam Jethroe, OF, 1950
Earl Williams, C, 1971
Bob Horner, 3B, 1978
David Justice, OF, 1990
Rafael Furcal, SS, 2000

MANAGER OF THE YEAR

Bobby Cox, 1991

MILESTONE PERFORMANCES

30-plus home runs

47—Eddie Mathews 1953
Hank Aaron 1971
46—Eddie Mathews 1959
45—Hank Aaron 1962
Chipper Jones 1999
44—Hank Aaron 1957, 1963, 1966, 1969
Dale Murphy 1987
Andres Galarraga 1998
43—Dave Johnson 1973
41—Eddie Mathews 1955
Darrell Evans 1973
Jeff Burroughs 1977
40—Eddie Mathews 1954
Hank Aaron 1960, 1973
Dave Justice 1993
39—Wally Berger 1930
Hank Aaron 1959, 1967
Eddie Mathews 1960
38—Joe Adcock 1956
Hank Aaron 1970
37—Eddie Mathews 1956
Dale Murphy 1985
Fred McGriff *1993
36—Joe Torre 1966
Dale Murphy 1982, 1983, 1984
Ron Gant 1993
Chipper Jones 2000
Andruw Jones 2000
35—Joe Adcock 1961
Bob Horner 1980
34—Wally Berger 1934, 1935
Hank Aaron 1961, 1972
Orlando Cepeda 1970
Fred McGriff 1994
Ryan Klesko 1996
Chipper Jones 1998
Javier Lopez 1998
33—Earl Williams 1971
Bob Horner 1979
Dale Murphy 1980
32—Eddie Mathews 1957, 1961, 1965
Hank Aaron 1965
Bob Horner 1982
Ron Gant 1990, 1991
31—Eddie Mathews 1958
Mack Jones 1965
Felipe Alou 1966
Andruw Jones 1998
30—Hank Aaron 1958
Chipper Jones 1996

*18 with Padres; 19 with Braves.

100-plus RBIs

145—Hugh Duffy 1894
135—Eddie Mathews 1953
132—Hank Aaron 1957
130—Wally Berger 1935
Hank Aaron 1963
128—Hank Aaron 1962
127—Hank Aaron 1966
126—Hank Aaron 1960
124—Eddie Mathews 1960
123—Hank Aaron 1959
121—Wally Berger 1934
Dale Murphy 1983
Andres Galarraga 1998
120—Hank Aaron 1961
Dave Justice 1993
119—Wally Berger 1930
118—Hank Aaron 1970, 1971
117—Tommy Holmes 1945
Ron Gant 1993
115—Brian Jordan 1999
114—Eddie Mathews 1959
Jeff Burroughs 1977
113—Bob Elliott 1947
111—Orlando Cepeda 1970
Dale Murphy 1985
Chipper Jones 1997, 2000
110—Chipper Jones 1996
Chipper Jones 1999
109—Sid Gordon 1951
Joe Torre 1964
Hank Aaron 1967
Dale Murphy 1982
108—Joe Adcock 1961
107—Bob Elliott 1950
Fred McGriff 1996
Chipper Jones 1998
106—Wally Berger 1933
Hank Aaron 1955
105—Dale Murphy 1987
Ron Gant 1991
Terry Pendleton 1992
104—Darrell Evans 1973
Javier Lopez 1998
Andruw Jones 2000
103—Sid Gordon 1950
Eddie Mathews 1954
Joe Adcock 1956
101—Eddie Mathews 1955
Joe Torre 1966
Rico Carty 1970
100—Bill Sweeney 1912
Bob Elliott 1948
Dale Murphy 1984
Andres Galarraga 2000

20-plus victories

1877—Tommy Bond 40-17
1878—Tommy Bond 40-19
1879—Tommy Bond 43-19
1880—Tommy Bond 26-29
1881—Jim Whitney 31-33
1882—Jim Whitney 24-21
1883—Jim Whitney 37-21
Charlie Buffinton 25-14
1884—Charlie Buffinton 48-16
Jim Whitney 23-14
1885—Charlie Buffinton 22-27
1886—Hoss Radbourn 27-31
Bill Stemmeyer 22-18
1887—Hoss Radbourn 24-23
Michael Madden 21-14
1888—John Clarkson 33-20
1889—John Clarkson 49-19
Hoss Radbourn 20-11
1890—Kid Nichols 27-19
John Clarkson 26-18
Charlie Getzien 23-17
1891—John Clarkson 33-19
Kid Nichols 30-17
Harry Staley *24-13
1892—Kid Nichols 35-16
Jack Stivetts 35-16
Harry Staley 22-10
1893—Kid Nichols 34-14
Jack Stivetts 20-12
1894—Kid Nichols 32-13
Jack Stivetts 26-14
1895—Kid Nichols 26-16
1896—Kid Nichols 30-14
Jack Stivetts 22-14
1897—Kid Nichols 31-11
Fred Klobedanz 26-7
Ted Lewis 21-12
1898—Kid Nichols 31-12
Ted Lewis 26-8
Vic Willis 25-13
1899—Vic Willis 27-8
Kid Nichols 21-19
1900—Bill Dinneen 20-14
1901—Vic Willis 20-17
1902—Togie Pittinger 27-16
Vic Willis 27-20
1905—Irv Young 20-21
1914—Bill James 26-7
Dick Rudolph 26-10
1915—Dick Rudolph 22-19
1921—Joe Oeschger 20-14
1933—Ben Cantwell 20-10
1937—Lou Fette 20-10
Jim Turner 20-11
1946—Johnny Sain 20-14
1947—Warren Spahn 21-10
Johnny Sain 21-12
1948—Johnny Sain 24-15
1949—Warren Spahn 21-14
1950—Warren Spahn 21-17
Johnny Sain 20-13
1951—Warren Spahn 22-14
1953—Warren Spahn 23-7
1954—Warren Spahn 21-12
1956—Warren Spahn 20-11
1957—Warren Spahn 21-11
1958—Warren Spahn 22-11
Lew Burdette 20-10
1959—Lew Burdette 21-15
Warren Spahn 21-15
1960—Warren Spahn 21-10
1961—Warren Spahn 21-13
1963—Warren Spahn 23-7
1965—Tony Cloninger 24-11
1969—Phil Niekro 23-13
1974—Phil Niekro 20-13
1979—Phil Niekro 21-20
1991—Tom Glavine 20-11
1992—Tom Glavine 20-8
1993—Tom Glavine 22-6
Greg Maddux 20-10
1997—Denny Neagle 20-5
1998—Tom Glavine 20-6
2000—Tom Glavine 21-9

* 4-5 with Pittsburgh; 20-8 with Boston.

N.L. home run champions

1879—Charley Jones 9
1880—John O'Rourke *6
1891—Harry Stovey *16
1894—Hugh Duffy 18
1897—Hugh Duffy 11
1898—Jimmy Collins 15
1900—Herman Long 12
1907—Dave Brain 10
1910—Fred Beck *10
1935—Wally Berger 34
1945—Tommy Holmes 28
1953—Eddie Mathews 47

INDIVIDUAL SEASON, GAME RECORDS

SEASON

Batting

At-bats	671	Marquis Grissom	1996
Runs	160	Hugh Duffy	1894
Hits	236	Hugh Duffy	1894
Singles	180	Ralph Garr	1971
Doubles	50	Hugh Duffy	1894
Triples	20	Dick Johnston	1887
Home runs	47	Eddie Mathews	1953
		Hank Aaron	1971
Home runs, rookie	38	Wally Berger	1930
Grand slams	4	Sid Gordon	1950
Total bases	400	Hank Aaron	1959
RBIs	145	Hugh Duffy	1894
Walks	131	Bob Elliott	1948
Most strikeouts	146	Andres Galarraga	1998
Fewest strikeouts	9	Tommy Holmes	1945
Batting average	.438	Hugh Duffy	1894
Slugging pct.	.679	Hugh Duffy	1894
Stolen bases	93	Billy Hamilton	1896

Pitching

Games	81	Brad Clontz	1996
Complete games	68	John Clarkson	1889
Innings	620	John Clarkson	1889
Wins	49	John Clarkson	1889
Losses	29	Vic Willis	1905
		Tommy Bond	1880
Winning pct.	.905 (19-2)	Greg Maddux	1995
Walks	164	Phil Niekro	1977
Strikeouts	417	Charlie Buffinton	1884
Shutouts	12	Tommy Bond	1879
Home runs allowed	41	Phil Niekro	1979
Lowest ERA	1.56	Greg Maddux	1994
Saves	39	Mark Wohlers	1996

GAME

Batting

Runs	6	Frank Torre	9-2-57
Hits	6	Felix Millan	7-6-70
Doubles	4	Last by Rafael Ramirez	5-21-86
Triples	3	Last by Danny O'Connell	6-13-56
Home runs	4	Last by Bob Horner	7-6-86
RBIs	9	Tony Cloninger	7-3-66
Total bases	18	Joe Adcock	7-31-54
Stolen bases	6	Otis Nixon	6-16-91

1957—Hank Aaron 44
1959—Eddie Mathews 46
1963—Hank Aaron *44
1966—Hank Aaron 44
1967—Hank Aaron 39
1984—Dale Murphy *36
1985—Dale Murphy 37

* Tied for league lead

N.L. RBI champions

1935—Wally Berger 130
1957—Hank Aaron 132
1960—Hank Aaron 126
1963—Hank Aaron 130
1966—Hank Aaron 127
1982—Dale Murphy *109
1983—Dale Murphy 121

* Tied for league lead

N.L. batting champions

1877—Deacon White .387
1889—Dan Brouthers .373
1893—Hugh Duffy .363
1894—Hugh Duffy .440
1928—Rogers Hornsby .387
1942—Ernie Lombardi .330
1956—Hank Aaron .328
1959—Hank Aaron .355
1970—Rico Carty .366
1974—Ralph Garr .353
1991—Terry Pendleton .319

N.L. ERA champions

1937—Jim Turner 2.38
1947—Warren Spahn 2.33
1951—Chet Nichols 2.88
1953—Warren Spahn 2.10
1956—Lew Burdette 2.70
1961—Warren Spahn 3.02
1967—Phil Niekro 1.87
1974—Buzz Capra 2.28
1993—Greg Maddux 2.36
1994—Greg Maddux 1.56
1995—Greg Maddux 1.63
1997—Greg Maddux 2.22

N.L. strikeout champions

1877—Tommy Bond 170
1878—Tommy Bond 182
1883—Jim Whitney 345
1889—John Clarkson 284
1902—Vic Willis 225
1949—Warren Spahn 151
1950—Warren Spahn 191
1951—Warren Spahn *164
1952—Warren Spahn 183
1977—Phil Niekro 262
1992—John Smoltz 215
1996—John Smoltz 276

* Tied for league lead

No-hit pitchers

(9 innings or more)

1892—Jack Stivetts 11-0 vs. Brooklyn
1907—Frank Pfeffer 6-0 vs. Cincinnati
1914—George Davis 7-0 vs. Philadelphia
1916—Tom Hughes 2-0 vs. Pittsburgh
1944—Jim Tobin 2-0 vs. Brooklyn
1950—Vern Bickford 7-0 vs. Brooklyn
1954—Jim Wilson 2-0 vs. Philadelphia
1960—Lew Burdette 1-0 vs. Philadelphia
1960—Warren Spahn 4-0 vs. Philadelphia
1961—Warren Spahn 1-0 vs. San Francisco
1973—Phil Niekro 9-0 vs. San Diego
1991—Kent Mercker–Mark Wohlers–
Alejandro Pena 1-0 vs. San Diego
1994—Kent Mercker 6-0 vs. Los Angeles

Longest hitting streaks

37—Tommy Holmes 1945
31—Rico Carty 1970
29—Rowland Office 1976
28—Marquis Grissom 1996
27—Hugh Duffy 1893
26—Hugh Duffy 1894, 1895
Germany Long 1897
Bill Sweeney 1911
25—Jimmy Bannon 1894
Hank Aaron 1956, 1962
23—Jimmy Collins 1897
Germany Long 1895
Gene DeMontreville 1901
Alvin Dark 1948
Red Schoendienst 1957
22—Hugh Duffy 1894
Earl Torgeson 1950
Hank Aaron 1959
Felipe Alou 1968
Hank Aaron 1971
Ralph Garr 1971
21—Jimmy Bannon 1895
Chick Stahl 1897
Billy Hamilton 1898
20—Tommy Holmes 1946, 1949
Andy Pafko 1953
Joe Adcock 1959
Bob Horner 1979
Otis Nixon 1991

CAREER LEADERS

BATTING

Games

Hank Aaron	3,076
Eddie Mathews	2,223
Dale Murphy	1,926
Rabbit Maranville	1,795
Fred Tenney	1,737
Herman Long	1,647
Bobby Lowe	1,411
Del Crandall	1,394
Johnny Logan	1,351
Tommy Holmes	1,289

At-bats

Hank Aaron	11,628
Eddie Mathews	8,049
Dale Murphy	7,098
Herman Long	6,781
Rabbit Maranville	6,724
Fred Tenney	6,637
Bobby Lowe	5,623
Tommy Holmes	4,956
Johnny Logan	4,931
John Morrill	4,799

Runs

Hank Aaron	2,107
Eddie Mathews	1,452
Herman Long	1,292
Fred Tenney	1,134
Dale Murphy	1,103
Bobby Lowe	1,000
Hugh Duffy	998
Billy Nash	915
John Morrill	837
Rabbit Maranville	801

Hits

Hank Aaron	3,600
Eddie Mathews	2,201
Fred Tenney	1,994
Herman Long	1,902
Dale Murphy	1,901
Rabbit Maranville	1,696
Bobby Lowe	1,608
Hugh Duffy	1,545
Tommy Holmes	1,503
Johnny Logan	1,329

Doubles

Hank Aaron	600
Eddie Mathews	338
Dale Murphy	306
Herman Long	295
Tommy Holmes	291
Wally Berger	248
Rabbit Maranville	244
Fred Tenney	242
John Morrill	234
Hugh Duffy	220

Triples

Rabbit Maranville	103
Hank Aaron	96
Herman Long	91
John Morrill	80
Bill Bruton	79
Fred Tenney	74
Hugh Duffy	73
Bobby Lowe	71
Sam Wise	71
Eddie Mathews	70

Home runs

Hank Aaron	733
Eddie Mathews	493
Dale Murphy	371
Joe Adcock	239
Bob Horner	215
Wally Berger	199
Chipper Jones	189
Del Crandall	170
David Justice	160
Ron Gant	147

Total bases

Hank Aaron	6,591
Eddie Mathews	4,158
Dale Murphy	3,394
Herman Long	2,643
Fred Tenney	2,435
Rabbit Maranville	2,215
Wally Berger	2,212
Joe Adcock	2,164
Tommy Holmes	2,152
Bobby Lowe	2,146

Runs batted in

Hank Aaron	2,202
Eddie Mathews	1,388
Dale Murphy	1,143
Herman Long	964
Hugh Duffy	927
Bobby Lowe	872
Billy Nash	811
Joe Adcock	760
Wally Berger	746
Bob Horner	652

Extra-base hits

Hank Aaron	1,429
Eddie Mathews	901
Dale Murphy	714
Wally Berger	499
Herman Long	474
Joe Adcock	458
Tommy Holmes	426
Chipper Jones	411
Bob Horner	382
Rabbit Maranville	370

Batting average
(Minimum 500 games)

Billy Hamilton	.339
Hugh Duffy	.332
Chick Stahl	.327
Rico Carty	.317
Ralph Garr	.317
Lance Richbourg	.311
Hank Aaron	.310
Jimmy Collins	.309
Wally Berger	.304
Tommy Holmes	.303

Stolen bases

Herman Long	434
Hugh Duffy	331
Billy Hamilton	274
Bobby Lowe	260
Fred Tenney	260
Hank Aaron	240
King Kelly	238
Billy Nash	232
Rabbit Maranville	194
Otis Nixon	186

PITCHING

Earned-run average
(Minimum 1,000 innings)

Tommy Bond	2.21
Greg Maddux	2.34
Jim Whitney	2.49
Dick Rudolph	2.62
John Clarkson	2.82
Vic Willis	2.82
Charlie Buffinton	2.83
Kid Nichols	2.99
Warren Spahn	3.05
Lefty Tyler	3.06

Wins

Warren Spahn	356
Kid Nichols	329
Phil Niekro	268
Tom Glavine	208
Lew Burdette	179
John Smoltz	157
Vic Willis	151
Tommy Bond	149
John Clarkson	149
Greg Maddux	145

Losses

Phil Niekro	230
Warren Spahn	229
Kid Nichols	183
Vic Willis	147
Tom Glavine	125
Jim Whitney	121
Lew Burdette	120
Bob Smith	120
Ed Brandt	119
John Smoltz	113

Innings pitched

Warren Spahn	5,046.0
Phil Niekro	4,622.2
Kid Nichols	4,548.0
Tom Glavine	2,900.2
Lew Burdette	2,638.0
Vic Willis	2,575.0
John Smoltz	2,414.1
Jim Whitney	2,263.2
Tommy Bond	2,127.1
John Clarkson	2,092.2

Strikeouts

Phil Niekro	2,912
Warren Spahn	2,493
John Smoltz	2,098
Tom Glavine	1,811
Kid Nichols	1,679
Greg Maddux	1,413
Vic Willis	1,161
Jim Whitney	1,157
Lew Burdette	923
Charlie Buffinton	911

Bases on balls

Phil Niekro	1,458
Warren Spahn	1,378
Kid Nichols	1,163
Tom Glavine	965
Vic Willis	854
Bob Buhl	782
John Smoltz	774
Lefty Tyler	678
John Clarkson	676
Jack Stivetts	651

Games

Phil Niekro	740
Warren Spahn	714
Gene Garber	557
Kid Nichols	557
Lew Burdette	468
Tom Glavine	434
Rick Camp	414
Mark Wohlers	388
John Smoltz	356
Steve Bedrosian	350

Shutouts

Warren Spahn	63
Kid Nichols	44
Phil Niekro	43
Lew Burdette	30
Tommy Bond	29
Dick Rudolph	27
Vic Willis	26
Lefty Tyler	22
John Clarkson	20
Tom Glavine	20

Saves

Gene Garber	141
Mark Wohlers	112
Cecil Upshaw	78
John Rocker	64
Rick Camp	57
Mike Stanton	55
Don McMahon	50
Greg McMichael	44
Kerry Ligtenberg	43
Steve Bedrosian	41

TEAM SEASON, GAME RECORDS

SEASON

Batting

Record	Total	Year
Most at-bats	5,631	1973
Most runs	1,220	1894
Fewest runs	408	1906
Most hits	1,567	1925
Most singles	1,196	1925
Most doubles	309	1999
Most triples	100	1921
Most home runs	215	1998
Fewest home runs	15	1909
Most grand slams	12	1997
Most pinch-hit home runs	9	1992
Most total bases	2,483	1998
Most stolen bases	189	1902
Highest batting average	.292	1925
Lowest batting average	.223	1909
Highest slugging pct.	.453	1998

Pitching

Record	Total	Year
Lowest ERA	2.19	1916
Highest ERA	5.12	1929
Most complete games	139	1905
Most shutouts	24	1992
Most saves	51	1982
Most walks	701	1977
Most strikeouts	1,245	1996

Fielding

Record	Total	Year
Most errors	361	1903
Fewest errors	91	1998
Most double plays	197	1985
Highest fielding average	.985	1998

General

Record	Total	Year
Most games won	106	1998
Most games lost	115	1935
Highest win pct.	.705	1897
Lowest win pct.	.248	1935

GAME, INNING

Batting

Record	Total	Date
Most runs, game	30	6-9-1883
Most runs, inning	16	6-18-1894
Most hits, game	32	9-3-1896
Most home runs, game	8	8-30-53
Most total bases, game	47	8-30-53

Third baseman Eddie Mathews hit a team-record 47 home runs in 1953.

BRAVES YEAR-BY-YEAR

Year	W	L	Place	Games Back	Manager	Leaders: Batting avg.	Hits	Home runs	RBIs	Wins	ERA
								BOSTON BRAVES			
1901	69	69	5th	20½	Selee	DeMontreville, .300	DeMontreville, 173	DeMontreville, 5	DeMontreville, 72	Willis, 20	Willis, 2.36
1902	73	64	3rd	29	Buckenberger	Tenney, .315	Cooley, 162	5 Tied, 2	Carney, Gremminger, 65	Pittinger, Willis, 27	Willis, 2.20
1903	58	80	6th	32	Buckenberger	Tenney, .313	Cooley, 160	Moran, 7	Cooley, 70	Pittinger, 18	Willis, 2.98
1904	55	98	7th	51	Buckenberger	J. Delahanty, .285	Abbaticchio, 148	Cooley, 5	Cooley, 70	Willis, 18	Pittinger, 2.66
1905	51	103	7th	54½	Tenney	Tenney, .288	Abbaticchio, 170	J. Delahanty, 5	J. Delahanty, Wolverton, 55	Young, 20	Young, 2.90
1906	49	102	8th	66½	Tenney	Tenney, .283	Tenney, 154	Bates, 6	Bates, Howard, 54	Young, 16	Lindaman, 2.43
1907	58	90	7th	47	Tenney	Beaumont, .322	Beaumont, 187	Brain, 10	Beaumont, 62	Dorner, Flaherty, 12	Flaherty, 2.70
1908	63	91	6th	36	Kelley	Ritchey, 2.73	Beaumont, 127	Dahlen, 3	McGann, 55	Flaherty, Lindaman, Ferguson 12	McCarthy, 1.63
1909	45	108	8th	65½	Bowerman, H. Smith	Beaumont, .263	Becker, 138	Becker, 6	Beaumont, 60	Mattern, 15	Richie, 2.32
1910	53	100	8th	50½	Lake	Miller, .286	Beck, 157	Beck, 10	Beck, 64	Mattern, 16	Brown, 2.67
1911	44	107	8th	54	Tenney	Miller, .333	Miller, 192	Miller, 7	Miller, 91	Brown, 8	Brown, 4.29
1912	52	101	8th	52	Kling	Sweeney, .344	Sweeney, 204	Houser, 8	Sweeney, 100	Perdue, 13	Hess, 3.76
1913	69	82	5th	31½	Stallings	Connolly, .281	Myers, 143	Lord, 6	Connolly, 57	Perdue, Tyler, 16	James, Tyler, 2.79
1914	94	59	1st	+10½	Stallings	Connolly, .306	Schmidt, 153	Connolly, 9	Maranville, 78	Rudolph, James, 26	James, 1.90
1915	83	69	2nd	7	Stallings	Magee, .280	Magee, 160	6 Tied, 2	Magee, 87	Rudolph, 22	Hughes, 2.12
1916	89	63	3rd	4	Stallings	Konetchy, .260	Konetchy, 147	Maranville, 4	Konetchy, 70	Rudolph, 19	Nehf, 2.01
1917	72	81	6th	25½	Stallings	R. Smith, .295	R. Smith, 149	Powell, 4	R. Smith, 62	Nehf, 17	Nehf, 2.16
1918	53	71	7th	28½	Stallings	R. Smith, .298	R. Smith, 128	Wickland, 4	R. Smith, 65	Nehf, 15	Fillingim, 2.23
1919	57	82	6th	38½	Stallings	Holke, .292	Holke, 151	Maranville, 5	Holke, 48	Rudolph, 13	Rudolph, 2.17
1920	62	90	7th	30	Stallings	Holke, .294	Holke, 162	Powell, 6	Holke, 64	Oeschger, 15	Fillingim, 3.11
1921	79	74	4th	15	Mitchell	Boeckel, .313	Powell, 191	Powell, 12	Boeckel, 84	Oeschger, 20	Fillingim, 3.45
1922	53	100	8th	39½	Mitchell	Powell, .296	Powell, 163	Boeckel, Powell, 6	Ford, 60	F. Miller, Marquard, 11	F. Miller, 3.51
1923	54	100	7th	41½	Mitchell	Southworth, .319	Southworth, 195	Boeckel, 7	McInnis, 95	Genewich, 13	Barnes, 2.76
1924	53	100	8th	40	Bancroft	McInnis, .291	McInnis, 169	Tierney, 6	McInnis, 59	Barnes, 15	Cooney, 3.18
1925	70	83	5th	25	Bancroft	Burrus, .340	Burrus, 200	Welsh, 7	Burrus, 87	Benton, Cooney, 14	Benton, 3.09
1926	66	86	7th	22	Bancroft	E. Brown, .328	E. Brown, 201	Burrus, Welsh, 3	E. Brown, 84	Benton, 14	Werts, 3.28
1927	60	94	7th	34	Bancroft, Hornsby	Richbourg, .309	E. Brown, 171	Fournier, 10	E. Brown, 75	Genewich, Greenfield, 11	B. Smith, 3.76
1928	50	103	7th	44½	Slattery	Hornsby, .387	Richbourg, 206	Hornsby, 21	Hornsby, 94	B. Smith, 13	Delaney, 3.79
1929	56	98	8th	43	Fuchs	Sisler, .326	Sisler, 205	Harper, 10	Sisler, 79	Seibold, 12	Cunningham, 4.52
1930	70	84	6th	22	McKechnie	Spohrer, .317	Berger, 172	Berger, 38	Berger, 119	Seibold, 15	Seibold, 4.12
1931	64	90	7th	37	McKechnie	Berger, .323	Berger, 199	Berger, 19	Berger, 84	Brandt, 18	Brandt, 2.92
1932	77	77	5th	13	McKechnie	Berger, .307	Berger, 185	Berger, 17	Berger, 73	Brandt, 16	Betts, 2.80
1933	83	71	4th	9	McKechnie	Berger, .313	Jordan, 168	Berger, 27	Berger, 106	Cantwell, 20	Brandt, 2.60
1934	78	73	4th	16	McKechnie	Jordan, .311	Berger, 183	Berger, 34	Berger, 121	Betts, Frankhouse, 17	Frankhouse, 3.20
1935	38	115	8th	61½	McKechnie	Lee, .303	Berger, 174	Berger, 34	Berger, 130	Frankhouse, 11	B. Smith, 3.94
1936	71	83	6th	21	McKechnie	Jordan, .323	Moore, 185	Berger, 25	Berger, 91	MacFayden, 17	MacFayden, 2.87
1937	79	73	5th	16	McKechnie	Moore, .283	Moore, 159	Moore, 16	Cuccinello, 80	Fette, Turner, 20	Turner, 2.38
1938	77	75	5th	12	Stengel	Garms, .315	Cuccinello, 147	V. DiMaggio, 14	Cuccinello, 76	MacFayden, Turner, 14	Hutchinson, 2.74
1939	63	88	7th	32½	Stengel	Hassett, .308	Hassett, 182	West, 19	West, 82	Posedel, 15	Fette, 2.96
1940	65	87	7th	34½	Stengel	Cooney, .318	E. Miller, 157	Ross, 17	Ross, 89	Errickson, Posedel, 12	Salvo, 3.08
1941	62	92	7th	38	Stengel	Cooney, .319	Cooney, 141	West, 12	E. Miller, West, 68	Tobin, 12	Earley, 2.53
1942	59	89	7th	44	Stengel	Holmes, .278	Holmes, 155	West, 16	West, 56	Javery, Tobin, 12	Javery, Salvo, 3.03
1943	68	85	6th	36½	Stengel	Holmes, .270	Holmes, 170	Workman, 10	Workman, 67	Javery, 17	Andrews, 2.57
1944	65	89	6th	40	Coleman	Holmes, .309	Holmes, 195	Nieman, 16	Holmes, 73	Tobin, 18	Tobin, 3.01
1945	67	85	6th	30	Coleman, Bissonette	Holmes, .352	Holmes, 224	Holmes, 28	Holmes, 117	Tobin, 9	Wright, 2.51
1946	81	72	4th	15½	Southworth	Hopp, .333	Holmes, 176	Litwhiler, 8	Holmes, 79	Sain, 20	Sain, 2.21
1947	86	68	3rd	8	Southworth	Elliott, .317	Holmes, 191	Elliott, 22	Elliott, 113	Sain, Spahn, 21	Spahn, 2.33
1948	91	62	1st	+6½	Southworth	Holmes, .325	Holmes, 190	Elliott, 23	Elliott, 100	Sain, 24	Sain, 2.60
1949	75	79	4th	22	Southworth	Stanky, .285	Dark, 146	Elliott, 17	Elliott, 76	Spahn, 21	Spahn, 3.07
1950	83	71	4th	8	Southworth	Elliott, .305	Torgeson, 167	Gordon, 27	Elliott, 107	Spahn, 21	Spahn, 3.16
1951	76	78	4th	20½	Southworth, Holmes	Gordon, .287	Jethroe, 160	Gordon, 29	Gordon, 109	Spahn, 22	Nichols, 2.88
1952	64	89	7th	32	Holmes, Grimm	Gordon, .289	Gordon, 151	Gordon, Mathews, 25	Gordon, 75	Spahn, 14	Spahn, 2.98
								MILWAUKEE BRAVES			
1953	92	62	2nd	13	Grimm	Mathews, .302	Mathews, 175	Mathews, 47	Mathews, 135	Spahn, 23	Spahn, 2.10
1954	89	65	3rd	8	Grimm	Adcock, .308	Bruton, 161	Mathews, 40	Mathews, 103	Spahn, 21	Jolly, 2.43
1955	85	69	2nd	13½	Grimm	Aaron, .314	Aaron, 189	Mathews, 41	Aaron, 106	Spahn, 17	Buhl, 3.21
1956	92	62	2nd	1	Grimm, Haney	Aaron, .328	Aaron, 200	Adcock, 38	Adcock, 103	Spahn, 20	Burdette, 2.70
1957	95	59	1st	+8	Haney	Aaron, .322	Aaron, 198	Aaron, 44	Aaron, 132	Spahn, 21	Spahn, 2.69
1958	92	62	1st	+8	Haney	Aaron, .326	Aaron, 196	Mathews, 31	Aaron, 95	Spahn, 22	Jay, 2.14
1959	86	70	*2nd	2	Haney	Aaron, .355	Aaron 223	Mathews, 46	Aaron, 123	Burdette, Spahn, 21	Rush, 2.40
1960	88	66	2nd	7	Dressen	Adcock, .298	Bruton, 180	Aaron, 40	Aaron, 126	Spahn, 21	Buhl, 3.09
1961	83	71	4th	10	Dressen, Tebbetts	Aaron, .327	Aaron, 197	Adcock, 35	Aaron, 120	Spahn, 21	McMahon, 2.84
1962	86	76	5th	15½	Tebbetts	Aaron, .323	Aaron, 191	Aaron, 45	Aaron, 128	Spahn, 18	Shaw, 2.80
1963	84	78	6th	15	Bragan	Aaron, .319	Aaron, 201	Aaron, 44	Aaron, 130	Spahn, 23	Spahn, 2.60
1964	88	74	5th	5	Bragan	Carty, .330	Torre, 193	Aaron, 24	Torre, 109	Cloninger, 19	Cloninger, 3.56
1965	86	76	5th	11	Bragan	Aaron, .318	Aaron, 181	Aaron, Mathews, 32	Mathews, 95	Cloninger, 24	O'Dell, 2.18
								ATLANTA BRAVES			
1966	85	77	5th	10	Bragan, Hitchcock	F. Alou, .327	F. Alou, 218	Aaron, 44	Aaron, 127	Cloninger, Johnson, 14	Carroll, 2.37
1967	77	85	7th	24½	Hitchcock, Silvestri	Aaron, .307	Aaron, 184	Aaron, 39	Aaron, 109	Jarvis, 15	Niekro, 1.87
1968	81	81	5th	16	Harris	F. Alou, .317	F. Alou, 210	Aaron, 29	Aaron, 86	Jarvis, 16	Pappas, 2.37
								WEST DIVISION			
1969	93	69	†1st	+3	Harris	Aaron, .300	Millan, 174	Aaron, 44	Aaron, 97	Niekro, 23	Niekro, 2.56
1970	76	86	5th	26	Harris	Carty, .366	Millan, 183	Aaron, 38	Aaron, 118	Jarvis, 16	Jarvis, 3.61
1971	82	80	3rd	8	Harris	Garr, .343	Garr, 219	Aaron, 47	Aaron, 118	Niekro, 15	T. Kelley, 2.96
1972	70	84	4th	25	Harris, Mathews	Garr, .325	Garr, 180	Aaron, 34	Williams, 87	Niekro, 16	Niekro, 3.06
1973	76	85	5th	22½	Mathews	Aaron, .301	Garr, 200	D. Johnson, 43	Evans, 104	Morton, 15	Niekro, 3.31
1974	88	74	3rd	14	Mathews, King	Garr, .353	Garr, 214	Evans, 25	Evans, 79	Niekro, 20	House, 1.93
1975	67	94	5th	40½	King, Ryan	Office, .290	Garr, 174	Evans, 22	Evans, 73	Morton, 17	Niekro, 3.20
1976	70	92	6th	32	Bristol	Montanez, .321	Montanez, 135	Wynn, 17	Wynn, 66	Niekro, 17	Messersmith, 3.04
1977	61	101	6th	37	Bristol , Turner	Bonnell, .300	Burroughs, Matthews, 157	Burroughs, 41	Burroughs, 114	Niekro, 16	Niekro, 4.03
1978	69	93	6th	26	Cox	Burroughs, .301	Burroughs, 147	Burroughs, Horner, 23	Murphy, 79	Niekro, 19	McWilliams, 2.81
1979	66	94	6th	23½	Cox	Horner, .314	Matthews, 192	Horner, 33	Horner, 98	Niekro, 21	Niekro, 3.39
1980	81	80	4th	11	Cox	Chambliss, .282	Chambliss, 170	Horner, 35	Horner, Murphy, 89	Niekro, 15	Camp, 1.91
1981	50	56	‡4th/5th	—	Cox	Washington, .291	Chambliss, 110	Horner, 15	Chambliss, 51	Camp, 9	R. Mahler, 2.80
1982	89	73	†1st	+1	Torre	Murphy, .281	Ramirez, 169	Murphy, 36	Murphy, 109	Niekro, 17	Garber, 2.34
1983	88	74	2nd	3	Torre	Horner, .303	Ramirez, 185	Murphy, 36	Murphy, 121	McMurtry, Perez, 15	McMurtry, 3.08
1984	80	82	§2nd	12	Torre	Murphy, .290	Murphy, 176	Murphy, 36	Murphy, 100	Perez, 14	Garber, 3.06
1985	66	96	5th	29	Haas, Wine	Murphy, .300	Murphy, 185	Murphy, 37	Murphy, 111	R. Mahler, 17	R. Mahler, 3.48
1986	72	89	6th	23½	Tanner	Horner, .273	Murphy, 163	Murphy, 29	Horner, 87	Mahler, 14	Dedmon, 2.98
1987	69	92	5th	20½	Tanner	James, .312	Murphy, 167	Murphy, 44	Murphy, 105	Z. Smith, 15	Dedmon, 3.91
1988	54	106	6th	39½	Tanner, Nixon	Perry, .300	Perry, 164	Murphy, 24	Murphy, 77	Mahler, 9	Alvarez, 2.99
1989	63	97	6th	28	Nixon	L. Smith, .315	L. Smith, 152	L. Smith, 21	Murphy, 84	Glavine, 14	Acker, 2.67
1990	65	97	6th	26	Nixon, Cox	L. Smith, .305	Gant, 174	Gant, 32	Gant, 84	Smoltz, 14	Leibrandt, 3.16
1991	94	68	∞1st	+1	Cox	Pendleton, .319	Pendleton, 187	Gant, 32	Gant, 105	Glavine, 20	Glavine, 2.55
1992	98	64	∞1st	+8	Cox	Pendleton, .311	Pendleton, 199	Justice, Pendleton, 21	Pendleton, 105	Glavine, 20	Glavine, 2.76
1993	104	58	†1st	+1	Cox	Blauser, .305	Blauser, 182	Justice, 40	Justice, 120	Glavine, 22	McMichael, 2.06
								EAST DIVISION			
1994	68	46	2nd	6	Cox	McGriff, .318	McGriff, 135	McGriff, 34	McGriff, 94	Maddux, 16	Maddux, 1.56
1995	90	54	▲∞1st	+21	Cox	McGriff, .280	McGriff, 148	McGriff, 27	McGriff, 93	Maddux, 19	Maddux, 1.63
1996	96	66	▲∞1st	+8	Cox	C. Jones, .309	Grissom, 207	Klesko, 34	C. Jones, 110	Smoltz, 24	Maddux, 2.72
1997	101	61	▲†1st	+9	Cox	Lofton, .333	C. Jones, 176	Klesko, 24	C. Jones, 111	Neagle, 20	Maddux, 2.20
1998	106	56	▲†1st	+18	Cox	C. Jones, .313	C. Jones, 188	Galarraga, 44	Galarraga, 121	Glavine, 20	Maddux, 2.22
1999	103	59	▲∞1st	+6½	Cox	C. Jones, .319	C. Jones, 181	C. Jones, 45	B. Jordan, 115	Maddux, 19	Millwood, 2.68
2000	95	67	◆1st	+1	Cox	C. Jones, .311	A. Jones, 199	C. Jones, A. Jones, 36	C. Jones, 111	Glavine, 21	Maddux, 3.00

* Lost pennant playoff. † Lost Championship Series. ‡ First half 25-29; second half 25-27. § Tied for position. ∞ Won Championship Series. ▲ Won Division Series. ◆ Lost Division Series.

Note: Batting average minimum 350 at-bats; ERA minimum 90 innings pitched.

HISTORY

Chicago Cubs

Shortstop Ernie Banks.

FRANCHISE CHRONOLOGY

First season: 1876, as a member of the new National League. The "White Stockings" defeated Louisville, 4-0, in their first N.L. game and went on to win the league's first pennant with a 52-14 record.

1877-1900: Chicago, under the inspired leadership of player/manager Cap Anson, won five pennants as the premier franchise of the 1880s. But after a second-place finish in 1891, the team sank to seventh place and never mounted another pre-1900 challenge.

1901-present: The 1906 Cubs set a modern Major League record with 116 victories before being upset by the White Sox in the World Series. But that disappointment was followed by consecutive Series victories over Detroit—a success the franchise never would be able to duplicate. Over the next nine decades, the Cubs failed to bring another Series banner to Chicago. Pennants in 1910, 1918, 1929, 1932, 1935, 1938 and 1945 were followed by fall classic defeats, and East Division titles in 1984 and 1989 were followed by Championship Series losses. The Cubs qualified for the playoffs as the N.L. wild-card after the 1998 campaign, but a Division Series loss to Atlanta continued their record streak of consecutive seasons without winning a World Series. Chicago was one of five teams placed in the Central Division when the N.L. adopted its three-division format in 1994.

CUBS VS. OPPONENTS BY DECADE

	Braves	Cardinals	Dodgers	Giants	Phillies	Pirates	Reds	Astros	Mets	Expos	Padres	Marlins	Rockies	Brewers	D'backs	Interleague	Decade Record
1900-09	135-76	144-64	135-74	115-97	119-90	99-112	132-79										879-592
1910-19	127-87	136-78	117-98	99-116	110-101	118-95	119-93										826-668
1920-29	139-80	112-105	115-104	99-121	132-88	95-125	115-105										807-728
1930-39	146-74	111-109	127-89	117-102	147-73	120-100	121-99										889-646
1940-49	108-111	82-138	101-119	110-109	121-99	104-116	110-110										736-802
1950-59	94-126	107-113	85-134	90-130	92-128	114-106	90-129										672-866
1960-69	90-92	73-114	80-102	76-106	93-95	78-110	79-103	66-72	79-65	10-8	11-1						735-868
1970-79	66-54	93-87	52-68	59-61	87-92	66-111	59-61	55-65	86-93	88-89	74-46						785-827
1980-89	55-57	81-89	57-61	57-61	78-95	81-95	54-59	51-64	83-92	77-95	61-53						735-821
1990-99	43-62	71-67	47-61	57-53	60-63	63-76	51-68	51-70	62-57	57-62	59-51	39-36	38-40	12-12	9-12	20-23	739-813
2000-	5-4	3-10	3-6	4-5	6-3	3-9	4-8	5-7	2-5	4-5	3-5	1-6	4-5	6-7	4-5	8-7	65-97
Totals	1008-823	1013-974	919-916	883-961	1045-927	941-1055	934-914	228-278	312-312	236-259	208-156	40-42	42-45	18-19	13-17	28-30	7868-7728

Interleague results: 9-9 vs. White Sox; 2-6 vs. Indians; 7-5 vs. Royals; 2-1 vs. Brewers; 5-4 vs. Twins;3-5 vs. Tigers.

MANAGERS

Name	*Years*	*Record*
Al Spalding	1876-77	78-47
Bob Ferguson	1878	30-30
Silver Flint	1879	5-12
Cap Anson	1879-97	1283-932
Tom Burns	1898-99	160-138
Tom Loftus	1900-01	118-161
Frank Selee	1902-05	280-213
Frank Chance	1905-12	768-389
Johnny Evers	1913, 1921	129-120
Hank O'Day	1914	78-76
Roger Bresnahan	1915	73-80
Joe Tinker	1916	67-86
Fred Mitchell	1917-20	308-269
Bill Killefer	1921-25	300-293
Rabbit Maranville	1925	23-30
George Gibson	1925	12-14
Joe McCarthy	1926-30	442-321
Rogers Hornsby	1930-32	141-116
Charlie Grimm	1932-38, 1944-49, 1960	946-782
Gabby Hartnett	1938-40	203-176
Jimmie Wilson	1941-44	213-258
Roy Johnson	1944	0-1
Frank Frisch	1949-51	141-196
Phil Cavarretta	1951-53	169-213
Stan Hack	1954-56	196-265
Bob Scheffing	1957-59	208-254
Lou Boudreau	1960	54-83
*Vedie Himsl	1961	10-21
*Harry Craft	1961	7-9
*Elvin Tappe	1961-62	46-70
*Lou Klein	1961-62, 1965	65-82
*Charlie Metro	1962	43-69
Bob Kennedy	1963-65	182-198
Leo Durocher	1966-72	535-526
Whitey Lockman	1972-74	157-162
Jim Marshall	1974-76	175-218
Herman Franks	1977-79	238-241
Joe Amalfitano	1979, 1980-81	66-116
Preston Gomez	1980	38-52
Lee Elia	1982-83	127-158
Charlie Fox	1983	17-22
Jim Frey	1984-86	196-182
John Vukovich	1986	1-1
Gene Michael	1986-87	114-124
Frank Lucchesi	1987	8-17
Don Zimmer	1988-91	265-258
Joe Altobelli	1991	0-1
Jim Essian	1991	59-63
Jim Lefebvre	1992-93	162-162
Tom Trebelhorn	1994	49-64
Jim Riggleman	1995-2000	439-516

* Members of College of Coaches.

WORLD SERIES CHAMPIONS

Year	*Loser*	*Length*	*MVP*
1907	Detroit	5 games	None
1908	Detroit	5 games	None

N.L. PENNANT WINNERS

Year	*Record*	*Manager*	*Series Result*
1876	52-14	Spalding	None
1880	67-17	Anson	None
1881	56-28	Anson	None
1882	55-29	Anson	None
1885	87-25	Anson	None
1886	90-34	Anson	None
1906	116-36	Chance	Lost to White Sox
1907	107-45	Chance	Defeated Tigers
1908	99-55	Chance	Defeated Tigers
1910	104-50	Chance	Lost to A's
1918	84-45	Mitchell	Lost to Red Sox
1929	98-54	McCarthy	Lost to A's
1932	90-64	Hornsby, Grimm	Lost to Yankees
1935	100-54	Grimm	Lost to Tigers
1938	89-63	Grimm, Hartnett	Lost to Yankees
1945	98-56	Grimm	Lost to Tigers

EAST DIVISION CHAMPIONS

Year	*Record*	*Manager*	*NLCS Result*
1984	96-65	Frey	Lost to Padres
1989	93-69	Zimmer	Lost to Giants

WILD-CARD QUALIFIERS

Year	*Record*	*Manager*	*Div. Series Result*
1998	90-73	Riggleman	Lost to Braves

ATTENDANCE HIGHS

Total	*Season*	*Park*
2,813,800	1999	Wrigley Field
2,734,511	2000	Wrigley Field
2,653,763	1993	Wrigley Field
2,583,444	1998	Wrigley Field
2,491,942	1989	Wrigley Field

BALLPARK CHRONOLOGY

Wrigley Field (1916-present)

Capacity: 38,902.
First game: Cubs 7, Cincinnati 6, 11 innings (April 20, 1916).
First batter: Red Killefer, Reds.
First hit: Red Killefer (single).
First run: Red Killefer (5th inning).
First home run: Johnny Beall, Reds.
First winning pitcher: Gene Packard, Cubs.
First-season attendance: 453,685.

State Street Grounds (1876-77)

First game: Chicago 6, Cincinnati 0 (May 10, 1876).

Lakefront Park (1878-84)

First game: Indianapolis 5, Chicago 3 (May 14, 1878).

West Side Park (1885-92)

First game: Chicago 9, St. Louis 2 (June 6, 1885).

South Side Park (1891-94)

First game: Chicago 1, Pittsburgh 0 (May 5, 1891).

West Side Grounds (1893-1915)

First game: Cincinnati 13, Chicago 12 (May 14, 1893).

Note: South Side Park shared home games with West Side Park in 1891 and '92 and West Side Grounds in 1893 and '94.

N.L. MVPs

Gabby Hartnett, C, 1935
Phil Cavarretta, 1B, 1945
Hank Sauer, OF, 1952
Ernie Banks, SS, 1958
Ernie Banks, SS, 1959
Ryne Sandberg, 2B, 1984
Andre Dawson, OF, 1987
Sammy Sosa, OF, 1998

CY YOUNG WINNERS

Ferguson Jenkins, RH, 1971
Bruce Sutter, RH, 1979
Rick Sutcliffe, RH, 1984
Greg Maddux, RH, 1992

ROOKIES OF THE YEAR

Billy Williams, OF, 1961
Ken Hubbs, 2B, 1962
Jerome Walton, OF, 1989
Kerry Wood, P, 1998

MANAGERS OF THE YEAR

Jim Frey, 1984
Don Zimmer, 1989

RETIRED UNIFORMS

No.	*Name*	*Pos.*
14	Ernie Banks	SS
23	Ryan Sandberg	2B
26	Billy Williams	OF

MILESTONE PERFORMANCES

30-plus home runs

66— Sammy Sosa 1998
63— Sammy Sosa 1999
56— Hack Wilson 1930
50— Sammy Sosa 2000
49— Andre Dawson 1987
48— Dave Kingman 1979
47— Ernie Banks 1958
45— Ernie Banks 1959
44— Ernie Banks 1955
43— Ernie Banks 1957
42— Billy Williams 1970
41— Hank Sauer 1954
Ernie Banks 1960
40— Ryne Sandberg 1990
Sammy Sosa 1996
39— Rogers Hornsby 1929
Hack Wilson 1929
37— Gabby Hartnett 1930
Hank Sauer 1952
Ernie Banks 1962
Billy Williams 1972
36— Andy Pafko 1950
Sammy Sosa 1995, 1997
34— Billy Williams 1965
33— Bill Nicholson 1944
Billy Williams 1964
Ron Santo 1965
Sammy Sosa 1993
32— Hank Sauer 1950
Ernie Banks 1968
Jim Hickman 1970
Rick Monday 1976
31— Hack Wilson 1928
Ron Santo 1967
Andre Dawson 1991
Henry Rodriguez 1998
30— Hack Wilson 1927
Hank Sauer 1951
Ron Santo 1964, 1966
Billy Williams 1968
Ryne Sandberg 1989
Rick Wilkins 1993

100-plus RBIs

191— Hack Wilson 1930
159— Hack Wilson 1929
158— Sammy Sosa 1998
149— Rogers Hornsby 1929
143— Ernie Banks 1959
141— Sammy Sosa 1999
138— Sammy Sosa 2000
137— Andre Dawson 1987
134— Kiki Cuyler 1930
129— Hack Wilson 1927
Ernie Banks 1958
Billy Williams 1970
128— Bill Nicholson 1943
123— Ron Santo 1969
122— Gabby Hartnett 1930
Bill Nicholson 1944
Billy Williams 1972
121— Hank Sauer 1952
120— Hack Wilson 1928
119— Sammy Sosa 1995, 1997
117— Ernie Banks 1955, 1960
115— Frank Demaree 1937
Jim Hickman 1970
Dave Kingman 1979
114— Ron Santo 1964, 1970
110— Riggs Stephenson 1929
Andy Pafko 1945
109— Hack Wilson 1926
108— Billy Williams 1965
107— Frank Schulte 1911
106— Ernie Banks 1965, 1969
Keith Moreland 1985
105— Bill Buckner 1982
104— Ernie Banks 1962
Andre Dawson 1991
103— Hank Sauer 1950, 1954
102— Ernie Banks 1957
101— Andy Pafko 1948
Ron Santo 1965
100— Andre Dawson 1990
Ryne Sandberg 1990, 1991
Sammy Sosa 1996

20-plus victories

1876— Al Spalding 47-13
1878— Terry Larkin 29-26
1879— Terry Larkin 30-23
1880— Larry Corcoran 43-14
Fred Goldsmith 22-3
1881— Larry Corcoran 31-14
Fred Goldsmith 25-13
1882— Fred Goldsmith 28-16
Larry Corcoran 27-13
1883— Larry Corcoran 31-21
Fred Goldsmith 28-18
1884— Larry Corcoran 35-23
1885— John Clarkson 53-16
Jim McCormick *21-7
1886— John Clarkson 36-17
Jim McCormick 31-11
John Flynn 23-6
1887— John Clarkson 38-21
1888— Gus Krock 25-14
1890— Bill Hutchinson 42-25
Pat Luby 20-9
1891— Bill Hutchinson 44-19
1892— Bill Hutchinson 36-36
Ad Gumbert 22-19
1894— Clark Griffith 21-14
1895— Clark Griffith 26-14
William Terry 21-14
1896— Clark Griffith 23-11
1897— Clark Griffith 21-18
1898— Clark Griffith 24-10
Jim Callahan 20-10
1899— Clark Griffith 22-14
Jim Callahan 21-12
1902— Jack Taylor 23-11
1903— Jack Taylor 21-14
Jake Weimer 21-9
1904— Jake Weimer 20-14
1906— Mordecai Brown 26-6
Jack Pfiester 20-8
Jack Taylor .... † 20-12
1907— Orval Overall 23-7
Mordecai Brown 20-6
1908— Mordecai Brown 29-9
Ed Reulbach 24-7
1909— Mordecai Brown 27-9
Orval Overall 20-11
1910— Mordecai Brown 25-13
Leonard Cole 20-4
1911— Mordecai Brown 21-11
1912— Larry Cheney 26-10
1913— Larry Cheney 21-14
1914— Hippo Vaughn 21-13
Larry Cheney 20-18
1915— Hippo Vaughn 20-12
1917— Hippo Vaughn 23-13
1918— Hippo Vaughn 22-10
1919— Hippo Vaughn 21-14
1920— Grover Alexander 27-14
1923— Grover Alexander 22-12
1927— Charlie Root 26-15
1929— Pat Malone 22-10
1930— Pat Malone 20-9
1932— Lon Warneke 22-6
1933— Guy Bush 20-12
1934— Lon Warneke 22-10
1935— Bill Lee 20-6
Lon Warneke 20-13
1938— Bill Lee 22-9
1940— Claude Passeau 20-13
1945— Hank Wyse 22-10
Hank Borowy .... ‡ 21-7
1963— Dick Ellsworth 22-10
1964— Larry Jackson 24-11
1967— Fergie Jenkins 20-13
1968— Fergie Jenkins 20-15
1969— Fergie Jenkins 21-15
Bill Hands 20-14
1970— Fergie Jenkins 22-16
1971— Fergie Jenkins 24-13
1972— Fergie Jenkins 20-12
1977— Rick Reuschel 20-10
1984— Rick Sutcliffe .... ∞ 20-6
1992— Greg Maddux 20-11

*1-3 with Providence; 20-4 with Chicago. †8-9 with Cardinals; 12-3 with Cubs. ‡10-5 with Yankees; 11-2 with Cubs. ∞ 4-5 with Indians; 16-1 with Cubs.

N.L. home run champions

1884— Ned Williamson 27
1885— Abner Dalrymple 11
1888— Jimmy Ryan 16
1890— Walt Wilmot *13
1910— Frank Schulte *10
1911— Frank Schulte 21
1912— Heinie Zimmerman 14
1916— Cy Williams *12
1926— Hack Wilson 21
1927— Hack Wilson *30
1928— Hack Wilson *31
1930— Hack Wilson 56
1943— Bill Nicholson 29
1944— Bill Nicholson 33
1952— Hank Sauer *37
1958— Ernie Banks 47
1960— Ernie Banks 41
1979— Dave Kingman 48
1987— Andre Dawson 49
1990— Ryne Sandberg 40
2000— Sammy Sosa 50

* Tied for league lead

INDIVIDUAL SEASON, GAME RECORDS

SEASON

	Record	Player	Year
Batting			
At-bats	666	Billy Herman	1935
Runs	156	Rogers Hornsby	1929
Hits	229	Rogers Hornsby	1929
Singles	165	Earl Adams	1927
Doubles	57	Billy Herman	1935, 1936
Triples	21	Frank Schulte	1911
		Vic Saier	1913
Home runs	66	Sammy Sosa	1998
Home runs, rookie	25	Billy Williams	1961
Grand slams	5	Ernie Banks	1955
Total bases	423	Hack Wilson	1930
RBIs	191	Hack Wilson	1930
Walks	147	Jimmy Sheckard	1911
Most strikeouts	174	Sammy Sosa	1997
Fewest strikeouts	5	Charlie Hollocher	1922
Batting average	.388	King Kelly	1886
		Bill Lange	1895
Slugging pct.	.723	Hack Wilson	1930
Stolen bases	67	Frank Chance	1903
Pitching			
Games	84	Ted Abernathy	1965
		Dick Tidrow	1980
Complete games	33	Jack Taylor	1902, 1903
		Grover Alexander	1920
Innings	363.1	Grover Alexander	1920
Wins	29	Mordecai Brown	1908
Losses	23	Tom Hughes	1901
Winning pct.	.941 (16-1)	Rick Sutcliffe	1984
Walks	185	Sam Jones	1955
Strikeouts	274	Fergie Jenkins	1970
Shutouts	9	6 times	
		Last by Bill Lee	1938
Home runs allowed	38	Warren Hacker	1955
Lowest ERA	1.04	Mordecai Brown	1906
Saves	53	Randy Myers	1993

GAME

	Record	Player	Date
Batting			
Runs	6	Cap Anson	8-24-1886
		Jimmy Ryan	7-25-1894
Hits	6	Last by Sammy Sosa	7-2-93
Doubles	4	Last by Billy Williams	4-9-69
Triples	3	Last by Shawon Dunston	7-28-90
Home runs	3	Last by Brant Brown	6-18-98
RBIs	9	Heinie Zimmerman	6-11-11
Total bases	14	Last by George Mitterwald	4-17-74
Stolen bases	7	George Gore	6-25-1881

N.L. RBI champions

1906— Harry Steinfeldt *83
1911— Frank Schulte 121
1929— Hack Wilson 159
1930— Hack Wilson 191
1943— Bill Nicholson 128
1944— Bill Nicholson 122
1952— Hank Sauer 121
1958— Ernie Banks 129
1959— Ernie Banks 143
1987— Andre Dawson 137
1998— Sammy Sosa 158

* Tied for league lead

N.L. batting champions

1876— Ross Barnes .... .429
1880— George Gore .... .360
1881— Cap Anson .... .399
1884— King Kelly .... .354
1886— King Kelly .... .388
1888— Cap Anson .... .344
1912— Heinie Zimmerman .... .372
1945— Phil Cavarretta .... .355
1972— Billy Williams .... .333
1975— Bill Madlock .... .354
1976— Bill Madlock .... .339
1980— Bill Buckner .... .324

N.L. ERA champions

1902— Jack Taylor 1.33
1906— Mordecai Brown 1.04
1907— Jack Pfiester 1.15
1918— Jim Vaughn 1.74
1919— Grover Alexander 1.72
1920— Grover Alexander 1.91
1932— Lon Warneke 2.37
1938— Bill Lee 2.66
1945— Hank Borowy 2.13

N.L. strikeout champions

1880— Larry Corcoran 268
1885— John Clarkson 308
1887— John Clarkson 237
1892— Bill Hutchinson 316
1909— Orval Overall 205
1918— Jim Vaughn 148
1919— Jim Vaughn 141
1920— Grover Alexander 173
1929— Pat Malone 166
1938— Clay Bryant 135
1946— Johnny Schmitz 135
1955— Sam Jones 198
1956— Sam Jones 176
1969— Fergie Jenkins 273

No-hit pitchers

(9 innings or more)

1880— Larry Corcoran .... 6-0 vs. Boston
1882— Larry Corcoran .... 5-0 vs. Worcester
1884— Larry Corcoran .... 6-0 vs. Providence
1885— John Clarkson .... 4-0 vs. Providence
1898— Walter Thornton .... 2-0 vs. Brooklyn
1915— Jim Lavender .... 2-0 vs. New York
1955— Sam Jones .... 4-0 vs. Pittsburgh
1960— Don Cardwell .... 4-0 vs. St. Louis
1969— Ken Holtzman .... 3-0 vs. Atlanta
1971— Ken Holtzman .... 1-0 vs. Cincinnati
1972— Burt Hooton .... 4-0 vs. Philadelphia
Milt Pappas .... 8-0 vs. San Diego

Longest hitting streaks

42— Bill Dahlen 1894
30— Jerome Walton 1989
Cal McVey 1876
28— Bill Dahlen 1894
Ron Santo 1966
27— Hack Wilson 1929
Glenn Beckert 1968
26— George Decker 1896
Hack Wilson 1927
Gabby Hartnett 1937
Glenn Beckert 1973
25— Hack Wilson 1926
24— Gabby Hartnett 1937
Stan Hack 1945
23— Heinie Zimmerman 1912
22— Hack Wilson 1930
21— Glenn Beckert 1966
Lenny Randle 1980
20— Billy Herman 1934
Rafael Palmeiro 1988

CAREER LEADERS

BATTING

Games

Ernie Banks	2,528
Cap Anson	2,277
Billy Williams	2,213
Ryne Sandberg	2,151
Ron Santo	2,126
Phil Cavarretta	1,953
Stan Hack	1,938
Gabby Hartnett	1,926
Mark Grace	1,910
Jimmy Ryan	1,662

At-bats

Ernie Banks	9,421
Cap Anson	9,176
Billy Williams	8,479
Ryne Sandberg	8,379
Ron Santo	7,768
Stan Hack	7,278
Mark Grace	7,156
Jimmy Ryan	6,818
Phil Cavarretta	6,592
Don Kessinger	6,355

Runs

Cap Anson	1,782
Jimmy Ryan	1,463
Ryne Sandberg	1,316
Billy Williams	1,306
Ernie Banks	1,305
Stan Hack	1,239
Ron Santo	1,109
Mark Grace	1,057
Phil Cavarretta	968
Bill Dahlen	897

Hits

Cap Anson	2,996
Ernie Banks	2,583
Billy Williams	2,510
Ryne Sandberg	2,385
Mark Grace	2,201
Stan Hack	2,193
Ron Santo	2,171
Jimmy Ryan	2,074
Phil Cavarretta	1,927
Gabby Hartnett	1,867

Doubles

Cap Anson	529
Mark Grace	456
Ernie Banks	407
Ryne Sandberg	403
Billy Williams	402
Gabby Hartnett	391
Stan Hack	363
Jimmy Ryan	362
Ron Santo	353
Billy Herman	346

Triples

Jimmy Ryan	142
Cap Anson	124
Frank Schulte	117
Bill Dahlen	106
Phil Cavarretta	99
Joe Tinker	93
Ernie Banks	90
Billy Williams	87
Stan Hack	81
Bill Lange	80
Ned Williamson	80
Heinie Zimmerman	80

Home runs

Ernie Banks	512
Billy Williams	392
Sammy Sosa	357
Ron Santo	337
Ryne Sandberg	282
Gabby Hartnett	231
Bill Nicholson	205
Hank Sauer	198
Hack Wilson	190
Andre Dawson	174

Total bases

Ernie Banks	4,706
Billy Williams	4,262
Cap Anson	4,064
Ryne Sandberg	3,786
Ron Santo	3,667
Mark Grace	3,187
Gabby Hartnett	3,079
Jimmy Ryan	3,017
Stan Hack	2,889
Phil Cavarretta	2,742

Runs batted in

Cap Anson	1,880
Ernie Banks	1,636
Billy Williams	1,353
Ron Santo	1,290
Gabby Hartnett	1,153
Ryne Sandberg	1,061
Mark Grace	1,004
Sammy Sosa	963
Jimmy Ryan	914
Phil Cavarretta	896

Extra-base hits

Ernie Banks	1,009
Billy Williams	881
Ron Santo	756
Ryne Sandberg	761
Cap Anson	750
Gabby Hartnett	686
Mark Grace	647
Jimmy Ryan	603
Sammy Sosa	582
Phil Cavarretta	532

Batting average

(Minimum 500 games)

Riggs Stephenson	.336
Bill Lange	.330
Cap Anson	.327
Kiki Cuyler	.325
Bill Everitt	.323
Hack Wilson	.322
King Kelly	.316
George Gore	.315
Frank Demaree	.309
Billy Herman	.309

Stolen bases

Frank Chance	402
Bill Lange	399
Jimmy Ryan	369
Ryne Sandberg	344
Joe Tinker	304
Johnny Evers	291
Walt Wilmot	292
Bill Dahlen	285
Fred Pfeffer	263
Cap Anson	247

PITCHING

Earned-run average

(Minimum 1,000 innings)

Mordecai Brown	1.80
Jack Pfiester	1.85
Orval Overall	1.91
Ed Reulbach	2.24
Larry Corcoran	2.26
Hippo Vaughn	2.34
Terry Larkin	2.34
John Clarkson	2.39
Carl Lundgren	2.42
Jack Taylor	2.65

Wins

Charlie Root	201
Mordecai Brown	188
Bill Hutchison	181
Larry Corcoran	175
Fergie Jenkins	167
Guy Bush	152
Clark Griffith	152
Hippo Vaughn	151
Bill Lee	139
John Clarkson	137

Losses

Bill Hutchison	158
Charlie Root	156
Bob Rush	140
Fergie Jenkins	132
Rick Reuschel	127
Bill Lee	123
Dick Ellsworth	110
Hippo Vaughn	105
Guy Bush	101
Clark Griffith	96

Innings pitched

Charles Root	3,137.1
Bill Hutchison	3,022.2
Fergie Jenkins	2,673.2
Larry Corcoran	2,338.1
Mordecai Brown	2,329.0
Rick Reuschel	2,290.0
Bill Lee	2,271.1
Hippo Vaughn	2,216.1
Guy Bush	2,201.2
Clark Griffith	2,188.2

Strikeouts

Fergie Jenkins	2,038
Charles Root	1,432
Rick Reuschel	1,367
Bill Hutchison	1,225
Hippo Vaughn	1,138
Larry Corcoran	1,086
Bob Rush	1,076
Mordecai Brown	1,043
Ken Holtzman	988
John Clarkson	960

Bases on balls

Bill Hutchison	1,109
Charlie Root	871
Guy Bush	734
Bob Rush	725
Bill Lee	704
Sheriff Blake	661
Ed Reulbach	650
Rick Reuschel	640
Hippo Vaughn	621
Fergie Jenkins	600

Games

Charlie Root	605
Lee Smith	458
Don Elston	449
Guy Bush	428
Fergie Jenkins	401
Bill Hutchison	368
Bill Lee	364
Rick Reuschel	358
Mordecai Brown	346
Bob Rush	339

Shutouts

Mordecai Brown	48
Hippo Vaughn	35
Ed Reulbach	31
Fergie Jenkins	29
Orval Overall	28
Bill Lee	25
Grover Alexander	24
Larry Corcoran	22
Claude Passeau	22
Larry French	21
Bill Hutchison	21
Charlie Root	21

Saves

Lee Smith	180
Bruce Sutter	133
Randy Myers	112
Don Elston	63
Phil Regan	60
Rod Beck	58
Mitch Williams	52
Charlie Root	40
Ted Abernathy	39
Mordecai Brown	39
Lindy McDaniel	39

TEAM SEASON, GAME RECORDS

SEASON

Batting

Most at-bats	5,675	1988
Most runs	998	1930
Fewest runs	454	1919
Most hits	1,722	1930
Most singles	1,226	1921
Most doubles	340	1931
Most triples	101	1911
Most home runs	212	1998
Fewest home runs	6	1902
Most grand slams	9	1929
Most pinch-hit home runs	10	1998
Most total bases	2,684	1930
Most stolen bases	283	1906
Highest batting average	.309	1930
Lowest batting average	.238	1963, 1965
Highest slugging pct	.481	1930

Pitching

Lowest ERA	1.73	1907
Highest ERA	5.27	1999
Most complete games	139	1904
Most shutouts	32	1907, 1909
Most saves	56	1993, 1998
Most walks	628	1987
Most strikeouts	1,207	1998

Fielding

Most errors	418	1900
Fewest errors	100	2000
Most double plays	176	1928
Highest fielding average	.984	1998

General

Most games won	116	1906
Most games lost	103	1962, 1966
Highest win pct	.798	1880
Lowest win pct	.364	1962, 1966

GAME, INNING

Batting

Most runs, game	36	6-29-1897
Most runs, inning	18	9-6-1883
Most hits, game	32	7-3-1883, 6-29-1897
Most home runs, game	7	Last 5-17-77
Most total bases, game	54	8-25-1891

Dependable third baseman Ron Santo hit 337 home runs while wearing a Cubs uniform.

HISTORY

CUBS YEAR-BY-YEAR

Year	W	L	Place	Games Back	Manager	Leaders: Batting avg.	Hits	Home runs	RBIs	Wins	ERA
1901	53	86	6th	37	Loftus	Hartsel, .335	Hartsel, 187	Hartsel, 7	Dexter, 66	Waddell, 14	Waddell, 2.81
1902	68	69	5th	34	Selee	Slagle, .315	Slagle, 143	Dexter, Tinker, 2	Kling, 57	Taylor, 23	Taylor, 1.33
1903	82	56	3rd	8	Selee	Chance, .327	Slagle, 162	Kling, 3	Chance, 81	Taylor, 21	Weimer, 2.30
1904	93	60	2nd	13	Selee	Chance, .310	Casey, 147	Chance, 6	McCarthy, 51	Weimer, 20	M. Brown, 1.86
1905	92	61	3rd	13	Selee, Chance	Chance, .316	Slagle, 153	Chance, Maloney, Tinker, 2	Chance, 70	M. Brown, Reulbach, Weimer, 18	Reulbach, 1.42
1906	116	36	1st	+20	Chance	Steinfeldt, .327	Steinfeldt, 176	Schulte, 7	Steinfeldt, 83	M. Brown, 26	M. Brown, 1.04
1907	107	45	1st	+17	Chance	Chance, .293	Steinfeldt, 144	Evers, Schulte, 2	Steinfeldt, 70	Overall, 23	Pfiester, 1.15
1908	99	55	1st	+1	Chance	Evers, .300	Tinker, 146	Tinker, 6	Tinker, 68	M. Brown, 29	M. Brown, 1.47
1909	104	49	2nd	6½	Chance	Hofman, .285	Hofman, 150	Schulte, Tinker, 4	Schulte, 60	M. Brown, 27	M. Brown, 1.31
1910	104	50	1st	+13	Chance	Hofman, .325	Schulte, 168	Schulte, 10	Hofman, 86	M. Brown, 25	Pfiester, 1.79
1911	92	62	2nd	7½	Chance	Zimmerman, .307	Schulte, 173	Schulte, 21	Schulte, 107	M. Brown, 21	Richie, 2.31
1912	91	59	3rd	11½	Chance	Zimmerman, .372	Zimmerman, 207	Zimmerman, 14	Zimmerman, 99	Cheney, 26	Cheyney, 2.85
1913	88	65	3rd	13½	Evers	Zimmerman, .313	Saier, 149	Saier, 14	Zimmerman, 95	Cheyney, 21	Pearce, 2.31
1914	78	76	4th	16½	O'Day	Zimmerman, .296	Zimmerman, 167	Saier, 18	Zimmerman, 87	Vaughn, 21	Vaughn, 2.05
1915	73	80	4th	17½	Bresnahan	Fisher, .287	Fisher, 163	Williams, 13	Saier, Williams, 64	Vaughn, 20	Humphries, 2.31
1916	67	86	5th	26½	Tinker	Zimmerman, .291	Saier, 126	Williams, 12	Williams, 66	Vaughn, 17	Vaughn, 2.20
1917	74	80	5th	24	Mitchell	Mann, .273	Merkle, 146	Doyle, 6	Doyle, 61	Vaughn, 23	Vaughn, 2.01
1918	84	45	1st	+10½	Mitchell	Hollocher, .316	Hollocher, 161	Flack, 4	Merkle, 65	Vaughn, 22	Vaughn, 1.74
1919	75	65	3rd	21	Mitchell	Flack, .294	Flack, 138	Flack, 6	Merkle, 62	Vaughn, 21	Alexander, 1.72
1920	75	79	*5th	18	Mitchell	Flack, .302	Flack, 157	Robertson, 10	Robertson, 75	Alexander, 27	Alexander, 1.91
1921	64	89	7th	30	Evers, Killefer	Grimes, .321	Flack, 172	Flack, Grimes, 6	Grimes, 79	Alexander, 15	Alexander, 3.39
1922	80	74	5th	13	Killefer	Grimes, .354	Hollocher, 201	Grimes, 14	Grimes, 99	Aldridge, Alexander, 16	Aldridge, 3.52
1923	83	71	4th	12½	Killefer	Statz, O'Farrell, .319	Statz, 209	Miller, 20	Friberg, Miller, 88	Alexander, 22	Keen, 3.00
1924	81	72	5th	12	Killefer	Grantham, .316	Statz, 152	Hartnett, 16	Friberg, 82	Kaufmann, 16	Alexander, 3.03
1925	68	86	8th	27½	Killefer, Maranville, Gibson	Freigau, .307	Adams, 180	Hartnett, 24	Grimm, 76	Alexander, 15	Alexander, 3.39
1926	82	72	4th	7	McCarthy	Wilson, .321	Adams, 193	Wilson, 21	Wilson, 109	Root, 18	Root, 2.82
1927	85	68	4th	8½	McCarthy	Stephenson, .344	Stephenson, 199	Wilson, 30	Wilson, 129	Root, 26	Bush, 3.03
1928	91	63	3rd	4	McCarthy	Stephenson, .324	Stephenson, 166	Wilson, 31	Wilson, 120	Malone, 18	Blake, 2.47
1929	98	54	1st	+10½	McCarthy	Hornsby, .380	Hornsby, 229	Hornsby, Wilson, 39	Wilson, 159	Malone, 22	Root, 3.47
1930	90	64	2nd	2	McCarthy, Hornsby	Wilson, .356	Cuyler, 228	Wilson, 56	Wilson, 190	Malone, 20	Malone, 3.94
1931	84	70	3rd	17	Hornsby	Grimm, Hornsby, .331	Cuyler, English, 202	Hornsby, 16	Hornsby, 90	Root, 17	B. Smith, 3.22
1932	90	64	1st	+4	Hornsby, Grimm	Stephenson, .324	B. Herman, 206	Moore, 13	Stephenson, 85	Warneke, 22	Warneke, 2.37
1933	86	68	3rd	6	Grimm	Herman, .289	B. Herman, 173	Hartnett, B. Herman, 16	B. Herman, 93	Bush, 20	Warneke, 2.00
1934	86	65	3rd	8	Grimm	Cuyler, .338	Cuyler, 189	Hartnett, 22	Hartnett, 90	Warneke, 22	Warneke, 3.21
1935	100	54	1st	+4	Grimm	Hartnett, .344	B. Herman, 227	Klein, 21	Hartnett, 91	Lee, Warneke, 20	French, Lee, 2.96
1936	87	67	*2nd	5	Grimm	Demaree, .350	Demaree, 212	Demaree, 16	Demaree, 96	French, Lee, 18	C. Davis, 3.00
1937	93	61	2nd	3	Grimm	Hartnett, .354	Demaree, 199	Galan, 18	Demaree, 115	Carleton, French, 16	Carleton, 3.15
1938	89	63	1st	+2	Grimm, Hartnett	Hack, .320	Hack, 195	Collins, 13	Galan, 69	Lee, 22	Lee, 2.66
1939	84	70	4th	13	Hartnett	Leiber, .310	Hack, B. Herman, 191	Leiber, 24	Leiber, 88	Lee, 19	Passeau, 3.05
1940	75	79	5th	25½	Hartnett	Hack, .317	Hack, 191	Nicholson, 25	Nicholson, 98	Passeau, 20	Passeau, 2.50
1941	70	84	6th	30	Wilson	Hack, .317	Hack, 186	Nicholson, 26	Nicholson, 98	Passeau, 14	Olsen, 3.15
1942	68	86	6th	38	Wilson	Hack, .Novikoff, .300	Nicholson, 173	Nicholson, 21	Nicholson, 78	Passeau, 19	Warneke, 2.27
1943	74	79	5th	30½	Wilson	Nicholson, .309	Nicholson, 188	Nicholson, 29	Nicholson, 128	Bithorn, 18	Hanyzewski, 2.56
1944	75	79	4th	30	Wilson, Grimm	Cavarretta, .321	Cavarretta, 197	Nicholson, 33	Nicholson, 122	Wyse, 16	Passeau, 2.89
1945	98	56	1st	+3	Grimm	Cavarretta, .355	Hack, 193	Nicholson, 13	Pafko, 110	Wyse, 22	Borowy, 2.13
1946	82	71	3rd	14½	Grimm	Waitkus, .304	Cavaretta, 150	Cavarretta, Nicholson, 8	Cavarretta, 78	Wyse, 14	Erickson, 2.43
1947	69	85	6th	25	Grimm	Cavarretta, .314	Pafko, 155	Nicholson, 26	Nicholson, 75	Schmitz, 13	Schmitz, 3.22
1948	64	90	8th	27½	Grimm	Pafko, .312	Pafko, 171	Pafko, 26	Pafko, 101	Schmitz, 18	Schmitz, 2.64
1949	61	93	8th	36	Grimm, Frisch	Cavarretta, .294	Pafko, 146	Sauer, 27	Sauer, 83	Schmitz, 11	Chapman, 3.98
1950	64	89	7th	26½	Frisch	Pafko, .304	Pafko, 156	Pafko, 36	Sauer, 103	Rush, 13	Hiller, 3.53
1951	62	92	8th	34½	Frisch, Cavarretta	Baumholtz, .284	Baumholtz, 159	Sauer, 30	Sauer, 89	Rush, 11	Leonard, 2.64
1952	77	77	5th	19½	Cavarretta	Baumholtz, .325	Fondy, 166	Sauer, 37	Sauer, 121	Rush, 17	Hacker, 2.58
1953	65	89	7th	40	Cavarretta	Fondy, .309	Fondy, 184	Kiner, 28	Kiner, 87	Hacker, Minner, 12	Pollet, 4.12
1954	64	90	7th	33	Hack	Sauer, .288	Banks, 163	Sauer, 41	Sauer, 103	Rush, 13	Davis, 3.52
1955	72	81	6th	26	Hack	Banks, .295	Banks, 176	Banks, 44	Banks, 117	Jones, 14	Jeffcoat, 2.95
1956	60	94	8th	33	Hack	Banks, .297	Banks, 160	Banks, 28	Banks, 85	Rush, 13	Rush, 3.19
1957	62	92	*7th	33	Scheffing	Long, .305	Banks, 169	Banks, 43	Banks, 102	Drott, 15	Brosnan, 3.38
1958	72	82	*5th	20	Scheffing	Banks, .313	Banks, 193	Banks, 47	Banks, 129	Hobbie, 10	Elston, 2.88
1959	74	80	*5th	13	Scheffing	Banks, .304	Banks, 179	Banks, 45	Banks, 143	Hobbie, 16	Henry, 2.68
1960	60	94	7th	35	Grimm, Boudreau	Ashburn, .291	Banks, 162	Banks, 41	Banks, 117	Hobbie, 16	Elston, 3.40
1961	64	90	7th	29	Himsl, Craft, Tappe, Klein	Altman, .303	Santo, 164	Banks, 29	Altman, 96	Cardwell, 15	Cardwell, 3.82
1962	59	103	9th	42½	Metro, Tappe,Klein	Altman, .318	Williams, 184	Banks, 37	Banks, 104	Buhl, 12	Buhl, 3.69
1963	82	80	7th	17	Kennedy	Santo, .297	Santo, 187	Santo, Williams, 25	Santo, 99	Ellsworth, 22	Ellsworth, 2.11
1964	76	86	8th	17	Kennedy	Santo, .313	Williams, 201	Williams, 33	Santo, 114	Jackson, 24	Jackson, 3.14
1965	72	90	8th	25	Kennedy, Klein	Williams, .315	Williams, 203	Williams, 34	Williams, 108	Ellsworth, Jackson, 14	Abernathy, 2.57
1966	59	103	10th	36	Durocher	Santo, .312	Beckert, 188	Santo, 30	Santo, 94	Holtzman, 11	Jenkins, 3.31
1967	87	74	3rd	14	Durocher	Santo, .300	Santo, Williams, 176	Santo, 31	Santo, 98	Jenkins, 20	Hands, 2.46
1968	84	78	3rd	13	Durocher	Beckert, .294	Beckert, 189	Banks, 32	Santo, Williams, 98	Jenkins, 20	Regan, 2.20

EAST DIVISION

Year	W	L	Place	Games Back	Manager	Batting avg.	Hits	Home runs	RBIs	Wins	ERA
1969	92	70	2nd	8	Durocher	Williams, .293	Williams, 188	Santo, 29	Santo, 123	Jenkins, 21	Hands, 2.49
1970	84	78	2nd	5	Durocher	Williams, .322	Williams, 205	Williams, 42	Williams, 129	Jenkins, 22	Pappas, 2.68
1971	83	79	*3rd	14	Durocher	Beckert, .342	Beckert, 181	Williams, 28	Williams, 93	Jenkins, 24	Jenkins, 2.77
1972	85	70	2nd	11	Durocher, Lockman	Williams, .333	Williams, 191	Williams, 37	Williams, 122	Jenkins, 20	Pappas, 2.77
1973	77	84	5th	5	Lockman	Cardenal, .303	Williams, 166	Monday, 26	Williams, 86	Hooton, Jenkins, R. Reuschel, 14	Locker, 2.54
1974	66	96	6th	22	Lockman, Marshall	Madlock, .313	Cardenal, 159	Monday, 20	Morales, 82	R. Reuschel, 13	Bonham, 3.86
1975	75	87	*5th	17½	Marshall	Madlock, .354	Cardenal, Madlock, 182	Thornton, 18	Morales, 91	Burris, 15	R. Reuschel, 3.73
1976	75	87	4th	26	Marshall	Madlock, .339	Madlock, 174	Monday, 32	Madlock, 84	Burris, 15	Burris, 3.11
1977	81	81	4th	20	Franks	Ontiveros, .299	DeJesus, 166	Murcer, 27	Murcer, 89	R. Reuschel, 20	Sutter, 1.34
1978	79	83	3rd	11	Franks	Buckner, .323	DeJesus, 172	Kingman, 28	Kingman, 79	Reuschel, 14	Sutter, 3.18
1979	80	82	5th	18	Franks, Amalfitano	Kingman, .288	DeJesus, 180	Kingman, 48	Kingman, 115	Reuschel, 18	Sutter, 2.22
1980	64	98	6th	27	Gomez, Amalfitano	Buckner, .324	Buckner, 187	Martin, 23	Martin, 73	McGlothen, 12	Caudill, 2.19
1981	38	65	†6th/5th	—	Amalfitano	Buckner, .311	Buckner, 131	Buckner, Durham, 10	Buckner, 75	Krukow, 9	R. Reuschel, 3.47
1982	73	89	5th	19	Elia	Durham, .312	Buckner, 201	Durham, 22	Buckner, 105	Jenkins, 14	L. Smith, 2.69
1983	71	91	5th	19	Elia, Fox	Moreland, .302	Buckner, 175	Cey, J. Davis, 24	Cey, 90	Rainey, 14	L. Smith, 1.65
1984	96	65	‡1st	+6½	Frey	Sandberg, .314	Sandberg, 200	Cey, 25	Cey, 97	Sutcliffe, 16	Sutcliffe, 2.69
1985	77	84	4th	23½	Frey	Moreland, .307	Sandberg, 186	Sandberg, 26	Moreland, 106	Eckersley, 11	L. Smith, 3.04
1986	70	90	5th	37	Frey, Vukovich, Michael	Sandberg, .284	Sandberg, 178	J. Davis, Matthews, 21	Moreland, 79	Sanderson, L. Smith, 9	L. Smith, 3.09
1987	76	85	6th	18½	Michael, Lucchesi	Sandberg, .294	Dawson, 178	Dawson, 49	Dawson, 137	Sutcliffe, 18	Sutcliffe, 3.68
1988	77	85	4th	24	Zimmer	Palmeiro, .307	Dawson, 179	Dawson, 24	Dawson, 79	Maddux, 18	Maddux, 3.18
1989	93	69	‡1st	+6	Zimmer	Grace, .314	Sandberg, 176	Sandberg, 30	Grace, 79	Maddux, 19	Maddux, 2.95
1990	77	85	*4th	18	Zimmer	Dawson, .310	Sandberg, 188	Sandberg, 40	Dawson, Sandberg, 100	Maddux, 15	Assenmacher, 2.80
1991	77	83	4th	20	Zimmer, Altobelli, Essian	Sandberg, .291	Sandberg, 170	Dawson, 31	Dawson, 104	Maddux, 15	McElroy, 1.95
1992	78	84	4th	18	Lefebvre	Grace, .307	Sandberg, 186	Sandberg, 26	Dawson, 90	Maddux, 20	Maddux, 2.18
1993	84	78	4th	13	Lefebvre	Grace, .325	Grace, 193	Sosa, 33	Grace, 98	Hibbard, 15	Bautista, 2.82

CENTRAL DIVISION

Year	W	L	Place	Games Back	Manager	Batting avg.	Hits	Home runs	RBIs	Wins	ERA
1994	49	64	5th	16½	Trebelhorn	Sosa, .300	Sosa, 128	Sosa, 25	Sosa, 70	Trachsel, 9	Trachsel, 3.21
1995	73	71	3rd	12	Riggleman	Grace, .326	Grace, 180	Sosa, 36	Sosa, 119	Foster, 12	Castillo, 3.21
1996	76	86	4th	12	Riggleman	Grace, .331	Grace, 181	Sosa, 40	Sosa, 100	Navarro, 15	Adams, 2.94
1997	68	94	5th	16	Riggleman	Grace, .319	Grace, 177	Sosa, 36	Sosa, 119	Gonzalez, 11,	Mulholland, 4.07
1998	90	73	§∞2nd	12½	Riggleman	Grace, Sosa, .307	Sosa, 196	Sosa, 66	Sosa, 158	Tapani, 19	Mulholland, 2.82
1999	67	95	6th	30	Riggleman	Grace, .309	Grace, 183	Sosa, 63	Sosa, 141	Lieber, 10	Lieber, 4.07
2000	65	97	6th	30	Riggleman	Sosa, .320	Sosa, 193	Sosa, 50	Sosa, 138	Lieber, 12	Lieber, 4.41

* Tied for position. † First half 15-37; second half 23-28. ‡ Lost Championship Series. § Won wild-card playoff. ∞ Lost Division Series.

Note: Batting average minimum 350 at-bats; ERA minimum 90 innings pitched.

HISTORY

Cincinnati Reds

FRANCHISE CHRONOLOGY

First season: 1876, as a member of the new National League. The Red Stockings won their first N.L. game, beating St. Louis, 2-1. That would be one of the few highlights in a 9-56 debut.

1877-1900: The Reds played five seasons in the N.L., sat out a year and returned as a member of the new American Association in 1882. After eight seasons in the A.A., they transferred back to the N.L., where they remain today. The Reds' only pre-1900 pennant came in 1882, the American Association's inaugural season.

1901-present: Through the first 39 years of the century, the Reds' only success was a tainted one: a victory over Chicago in the infamous "Black Sox" World Series of 1919. But four decades of futility ended in 1940 when the Reds punctuated their second straight pennant with a seven-game World Series victory over Detroit. Although usually competitive, Cincinnati's first sustained success did not occur until the 1970s, when the Big Red Machine of Sparky Anderson won six West Division titles, four pennants and two World Series. The Reds won their fifth fall classic in 1990. Cincinnati was one of five teams placed in the Central Division when the N.L. adopted its three-division format in 1994.

Infielder/outfielder Pete Rose.

REDS VS. OPPONENTS BY DECADE

	Braves	Cardinals	Cubs	Dodgers	Giants	Phillies	Pirates	Astros	Mets	Expos	Padres	Marlins	Rockies	Brewers	D'backs	Interleague	Decade Record
1900-09	120-90	119-91	79-132	114-97	87-123	105-105	81-131										705-769
1910-19	116-97	109-108	93-119	121-93	85-129	91-124	102-109										717-779
1920-29	130-89	105-115	105-115	122-96	86-134	149-68	101-118										798-735
1930-39	110-108	73-147	99-121	108-112	79-139	116-99	79-140										664-866
1940-49	112-105	87-133	110-110	87-133	120-100	136-84	115-104										767-769
1950-59	86-134	96-124	129-90	91-129	92-128	113-107	134-86										741-798
1960-69	103-85	92-90	103-79	94-94	84-103	107-75	90-92	85-59	83-54	8-4	11-7						860-742
1970-79	120-60	74-46	61-59	97-79	99-78	73-47	65-54	105-74	80-40	74-46	105-74						953-657
1980-89	92-81	50-63	59-54	80-98	91-85	60-55	64-50	81-93	55-62	53-64	96-78						781-783
1990-99	49-82	62-51	68-51	57-65	58-66	68-39	64-59	76-63	49-59	57-48	69-61	43-32	41-34	12-11	13-5	23-20	809-746
2000-	5-2	7-6	8-4	4-5	3-6	3-4	7-6	7-5	5-4	6-3	4-5	3-6	6-3	5-8	5-2	7-8	85-77
Totals	1043-933	874-974	914-934	975-1001	884-1091	1021-807	902-949	354-294	272-219	198-165	285-225	46-38	47-37	17-19	18-7	30-28	7880-7721

Interleague results: 2-6 vs. White Sox; 8-10 vs. Indians; 5-3 vs. Royals; 3-0 vs. Brewers; 7-5 vs. Twins; 5-4 vs. Tigers..

MANAGERS

Name	*Years*	*Record*
Charlie Gould	1876	9-56
Lip Pike	1877	3-11
Bob Addy	1877	5-19
Jack Manning	1877	7-12
Cal McVey	1878, 1879	71-51
Deacon White	1879	9-9
John Clapp	1880	21-59
Pop Snyder	1882-83, 1884	140-76
Will White	1884	44-27
Oliver Caylor	1885-86	128-122
Gus Schmelz	1887-89	237-171
Tom Loftus	1890-91	133-136
Charles Comiskey	1892-94	202-206
Buck Ewing	1895-99	394-297
Bob Allen	1900	62-77
Biddy McPhee	1901-02	79-124
Frank Bancroft	1902	9-7
Joe Kelley	1902-05	275-230
Ned Hanlon	1906-07	130-174
John Ganzel	1908	73-81
Clark Griffith	1909-11	222-238
Hank O'Day	1912	75-78
Joe Tinker	1913	64-89
Buck Herzog	1914-16	165-226
Christy Mathewson	1916-18	164-176
Heinie Groh	1918	7-3
Pat Moran	1919-23	425-329
Jack Hendricks	1924-29	469-450
Dan Howley	1930-32	177-285
Donie Bush	1933	58-94
Bob O'Farrell	1934	30-60
Chuck Dressen	1934-37	214-282
Bobby Wallace	1937	5-20
Bill McKechnie	1938-46	744-631
Hank Gowdy	1946	3-1
Johnny Neun	1947-48	117-137
Bucky Walters	1948-49	81-123
Luke Sewell	1950-52	174-234
Earle Brucker	1952	3-2
Rogers Hornsby	1952-53	91-106
Buster Mills	1953	4-4
Birdie Tebbetts	1954-58	372-357
Jimmie Dykes	1958	24-17
Mayo Smith	1959	35-45
Fred Hutchinson	1959-64	443-372
Dick Sisler	1964-65	121-94
Don Heffner	1966	37-46
Dave Bristol	1966-69	298-265
Sparky Anderson	1970-78	863-586
John McNamara	1979-82	279-244
Russ Nixon	1982-83	101-131
Vern Rapp	1984	51-70
Pete Rose	1984-89	412-373
Tommy Helms	1988, 1989	28-36
Lou Piniella	1990-92	255-231
Tony Perez	1993	20-24
Dave Johnson	1993-95	204-172
Ray Knight	1996-97	124-137
Jack McKeon	1997-2000	291-259

WORLD SERIES CHAMPIONS

Year	*Loser*	*Length*	*MVP*
1919	Chicago	8 games	None
1940	Detroit	7 games	None
1975	Boston	7 games	Rose
1976	N.Y. Yankees	4 games	Bench
1990	Oakland	4 games	Rijo

A.A. PENNANT WINNERS

Year	*Record*	*Manager*	*Series Result*
1882	55-25	Snyder	None

N.L. PENNANT WINNERS

Year	*Record*	*Manager*	*Series Result*
1919	96-44	Moran	Defeated White Sox
1939	97-57	McKechnie	Lost to Yankees
1940	100-53	McKechnie	Defeated Tigers
1961	93-61	Hutchinson	Lost to Yankees
1970	102-60	Anderson	Lost to Orioles
1972	95-59	Anderson	Lost to A's
1975	108-54	Anderson	Defeated Red Sox
1976	102-60	Anderson	Defeated Yankees
1990	91-71	Piniella	Defeated A's

WEST DIVISION CHAMPIONS

Year	*Record*	*Manager*	*NLCS Result*
1970	102-60	Anderson	Defeated Pirates
1972	95-59	Anderson	Defeated Pirates
1973	99-63	Anderson	Lost to Mets
1975	108-54	Anderson	Defeated Pirates
1976	102-60	Anderson	Defeated Phillies
1979	90-71	McNamara	Lost to Pirates
1990	91-71	Piniella	Defeated Pirates

CENTRAL DIVISION CHAMPIONS

Year	*Record*	*Manager*	*NLCS Result*
1994	66-48	Johnson	None
1995	85-59	Johnson	Lost to Braves

ATTENDANCE HIGHS

Total	*Season*	*Park*
2,629,708	1976	Riverfront Stadium
2,577,351	2000	Riverfront Stadium
2,532,497	1978	Riverfront Stadium
2,519,670	1977	Riverfront Stadium
2,453,232	1993	Riverfront Stadium

BALLPARK CHRONOLOGY

Cinergy Field, formerly Riverfront Stadium (1970-present)

Capacity: 52,953.
First game: Atlanta 8, Reds 2 (June 30, 1970).
First batter: Sonny Jackson, Braves.
First hit: Felix Millan, Braves (single).
First run: Felix Millan, Braves (1st inning).
First home run: Hank Aaron, Braves.
First winning pitcher: Pat Jarvis, Braves.
First-season attendance (1971): 1,501,122.

Avenue Grounds (1876-79)

First game: Cincinnati 2, St. Louis 1 (April 25, 1876).

Bank Street Grounds (1880)

First game: Chicago 4, Cincinnati 3 (May 1, 1880).

Redland Field I (1882-1901)

Palace of the Fans (1902-11)

First game: Chicago 6, Reds 1 (April 17, 1902).
First-season attendance: 217,300.

Crosley Field (1912-70)

Capacity: 29,603.
First game: Reds 10, Chicago 6 (April 11, 1912).
First-season attendance: 344,000.

N.L. MVPs

Ernie Lombardi, C, 1938
Bucky Walters, P, 1939
Frank McCormick, 1B, 1940
Frank Robinson, OF, 1961
Johnny Bench, C, 1970
Johnny Bench, C, 1972
Pete Rose, OF, 1973
Joe Morgan, 2B, 1975
Joe Morgan, 2B, 1976
George Foster, OF, 1977
Barry Larkin, SS, 1995

ROOKIES OF THE YEAR

Frank Robinson, OF, 1956
Pete Rose, 2B, 1963
Tommy Helms, 3B, 1966
Johnny Bench, C, 1968
*Pat Zachry, P, 1976
Chris Sabo, 3B, 1988
Scott Williamson, P, 1999

* Co-winner.

MANAGER OF THE YEAR

Jack McKeon, 1999

RETIRED UNIFORMS

No.	*Name*	*Pos.*
1	Fred Hutchinson	Man.
5	Johnny Bench	C
8	Joe Morgan	2B
18	Ted Kluszewski	OF
20	Frank Robinson	OF

MILESTONE PERFORMANCES

30-plus home runs

52— George Foster 1977
49— Ted Kluszewski 1954
47— Ted Kluszewski 1955
45— Johnny Bench 1970
Greg Vaughn 1999
40— Ted Kluszewski 1953
Wally Post 1955
Tony Perez 1970
Johnny Bench 1972
George Foster 1978
Ken Griffey Jr. 2000
39— Frank Robinson 1956
Lee May 1971
38— Frank Robinson 1956
Lee May 1969
37— Frank Robinson 1961
Tony Perez 1969
Eric Davis 1987
36— Wally Post 1956
Frank Robinson 1959
35— Hank Sauer 1948
Ted Kluszewski 1956
34— Lee May 1970
Dave Parker 1985
Eric Davis 1989
33— Frank Robinson 1965
Johnny Bench 1974
Barry Larkin 1996
32— Deron Johnson 1965
31— George Crowe 1957
Frank Robinson 1958, 1960
Johnny Bench 1977
Dave Parker 1986
30— Ival Goodman 1938
Gus Bell 1953
George Foster 1979
Kevin Mitchell 1994

100-plus RBIs

149— George Foster 1977
148— Johnny Bench 1970
141— Ted Kluszewski 1954
136— Frank Robinson 1962
130— Deron Johnson 1965
129— Tony Perez 1970
Johnny Bench 1974
128— Frank McCormick 1939
127— Frank McCormick 1940
125— Frank Robinson 1959
Johnny Bench 1972
Dave Parker 1985
124— Frank Robinson 1961
122— Tony Perez 1969
121— Cy Seymour 1905
George Foster 1976
120— George Foster 1978
118— Greg Vaughn 1999
Ken Griffey Jr. 2000
116— Dave Parker 1986
115— Gus Bell 1959
113— Ted Kluszewski 1955
Frank Robinson 1965
111— Ted Kluszewski 1950
Joe Morgan 1976
110— Lee May 1969
Johnny Bench 1975
109— Wally Post 1955
Tony Perez 1975
Johnny Bench 1977
108— Ted Kluszewski 1953
106— Frank McCormick 1938
Vada Pinson 1963
105— Gus Bell 1953
104— Sam Crawford 1901
Gus Bell 1955
Johnny Bench 1973
103— George Kelly 1929
102— Frank McCormick 1944
Ted Kluszewski 1956
Tony Perez 1967
101— Gus Bell 1954
Tony Perez 1973, 1974
Eric Davis 1989
100— Jim Greengrass 1953
Vada Pinson 1962
Eric Davis 1987

20-plus victories

1878— Will White 30-21
1879— Will White 43-31
1890— Billy Rhines 28-17
1891— Tony Mullane 23-26
1892— Tony Mullane 21-13
Frank Dwyer *21-18
1896— Frank Dwyer 24-11
1897— Ted Breitenstein 23-12
Billy Rhines 21-15
1898— Pink Hawley 27-11
Ted Breitenstein 20-14
1899— Noodles Hahn 23-8
1901— Noodles Hahn 22-19
1902— Noodles Hahn 23-12
1903— Noodles Hahn 22-12
1904— Charles Harper 23-9
1905— Bob Ewing 20-11
1906— Jake Weimer 20-14
1910— George Suggs 20-12
1917— Fred Toney 24-16
Pete Schneider 20-19
1919— Slim Sallee 21-7
1922— Eppa Rixey 25-13
1923— Dolf Luque 27-8
Pete Donohue 21-15
Eppa Rixey 20-15
1924— Carl Mays 20-9
1925— Eppa Rixey 21-11
Pete Donohue 21-14
1926— Pete Donohue 20-14
1935— Paul Derringer 22-13
1938— Paul Derringer 21-14
1939— Bucky Walters 27-11
Paul Derringer 25-7
1940— Bucky Walters 22-10
Paul Derringer 20-12
1943— Elmer Riddle 21-11
1944— Bucky Walters 23-8
1947— Ewell Blackwell 22-8
1961— Joey Jay 21-10
1962— Bob Purkey 23-5
Joey Jay 21-14
1963— Jim Maloney 23-7
1965— Sammy Ellis 22-10
Jim Maloney 20-9
1970— Jim Merritt 20-12
1977— Tom Seaver .... †21-6
1985— Tom Browning 20-9
1988— Danny Jackson 23-8

*2-8 with St. Louis; 19-10 with Cincinnati; †7-3 with Mets; 14-3 with Reds.

Lefthander Johnny Vander Meer was untouchable for two games in 1938, when he fired back-to-back no-hitters at the Braves and Dodgers.

INDIVIDUAL SEASON, GAME RECORDS

SEASON

Batting			
At-bats	680	Pete Rose	1973
Runs	134	Frank Robinson	1962
Hits	230	Pete Rose	1973
Singles	181	Pete Rose	1973
Doubles	51	Frank Robinson	1962
		Pete Rose	1978
Triples	25	Bid McPhee	1890
Home runs	52	George Foster	1977
Home runs, rookie	38	Frank Robinson	1956
Grand slams	3	5 times	
		Last by Chris Sabo	1993
Total bases	388	George Foster	1977
RBIs	149	George Foster	1977
Walks	132	Joe Morgan	1975
Most strikeouts	145	Mike Cameron	1999
Fewest strikeouts	13	Frank McCormick	1941
Batting average	.383	Bug Holliday	1894
Slugging pct.	.681	Kevin Mitchell	1994
Stolen bases	93	Arlie Latham	1891
Pitching (since 1900)			
Games	90	Wayne Granger	1969
Complete games	41	Noodles Hahn	1901
Innings	375.1	Noodles Hahn	1901
Wins	27	Dolf Luque	1923
		Bucky Walters	1939
Losses	25	Paul Derringer	1933
Winning pct.	.875 (14-2)	Tom Seaver	1981
Walks	162	Johnny Vander Meer	1943
Strikeouts	274	Mario Soto	1982
Shutouts	7	4 times	
		Last by Jack Billingham	1973
Home runs allowed	36	Tom Browning	1988
Lowest ERA	1.57	Fred Toney	1915
Saves	44	Jeff Brantley	1996

GAME

Batting			
Runs	5	Last by Jeffrey Hammonds and Sean Casey	5-19-99
Hits	6	Last by Walker Cooper	7-6-49
Doubles	4	Last by Billy Hatcher	8-21-90
Triples	3	Last by Herm Winningham	8-15-90
Home runs	3	Last by Greg Vaughn	9-7-99
RBIs	10	Walker Cooper	7-6-49
Total bases	15	Walker Cooper	7-6-49
Stolen bases	4	Last by Deion Sanders	4-14-97

N.L. home run champions

1877— Lip Pike 4
1892— Bug Holliday 13
1901— Sam Crawford 16
1905— Fred Odwell 9
1954— Ted Kluszewski 49
1970— Johnny Bench 45
1972— Johnny Bench 40
1977— George Foster 52
1978— George Foster 40

N.L. RBI champions

1905— Cy Seymour 121
1918— Sherry Magee 76
1939— Frank McCormick 128
1954— Ted Kluszewski 141
1965— Deron Johnson 130
1970— Johnny Bench 148
1972— Johnny Bench 125
1974— Johnny Bench 129
1976— George Foster 121
1977— George Foster 149
1978— George Foster 120
1985— Dave Parker 125

N.L. batting champions

1905— Cy Seymour .... .377
1916— Hal Chase .... .339
1917— Edd Roush .... .341
1919— Edd Roush .... .321
1926— Bubbles Hargrave .... .353
1938— Ernie Lombardi .... .342
1968— Pete Rose .... .335
1969— Pete Rose .... .348
1973— Pete Rose .... .338

N.L. ERA champions

1923— Dolf Luque 1.93
1925— Dolf Luque 2.63
1939— Bucky Walters 2.29
1940— Bucky Walters 2.48
1941— Elmer Riddle 2.24
1944— Ed Heusser 2.38

N.L. strikeout champions

1899— Noodles Hahn 145
1900— Noodles Hahn 132
1901— Noodles Hahn 239
1939— Bucky Walters *137
1941— Johnny Vander Meer 202
1942— Johnny Vander Meer 186
1943— Johnny Vander Meer 174
1947— Ewell Blackwell 193
1993— Jose Rijo 227

* Tied for league lead

No-hit pitchers

1892— Bumpus Jones .... 7-1 vs. Pittsburgh
1898— Ted Breitenstein .... 11-0 vs. Pittsburgh
1900— Noodles Hahn .... 4-0 vs. Philadelphia
1917— Fred Toney ...... 1-0 vs. Chicago (10 innings)
1919— Hod Eller .... 6-0 vs. St. Louis
1938— Johnny Vander Meer .... 3-0 vs. Boston
Johnny Vander Meer .... 6-0 vs. Brooklyn
1944— Clyde Shoun .... 1-0 vs. Boston
1947— Ewell Blackwell .... 6-0 vs. Boston
1965— Jim Maloney .. 1-0 vs. Chicago (10 innings)
1968— George Culver .... 6-1 vs. Philadelphia
1969— Jim Maloney .... 10-0 vs. Houston
1978— Tom Seaver .... 4-0 vs. St. Louis
1988— Tom Browning 1-0 vs. Los Angeles (Perfect)

Longest hitting streaks

44— Pete Rose 1978
30— Elmer Smith 1898
29— Hal Morris 1996
27— Edd Roush 1920, 1924
Vada Pinson 1965
25— Rube Bressler 1927
Pete Rose 1967
24— Cy Seymour 1903
Hughie Critz 1928
Tommy Harper 1966
23— Heinie Groh 1917
Vada Pinson 1965
22— Jake Daubert 1922
Pete Rose 1968
21— Cy Seymour 1905
Ron Oester 1984
Barry Larkin 1988
Sean Casey 2000
20— Al Libke 1945
Tony Perez 1968
Pete Rose .... 1977 (twice)

CAREER LEADERS

BATTING

Games

Pete Rose	2,722
Dave Concepcion	2,488
Johnny Bench	2,158
Tony Perez	1,948
Barry Larkin	1,809
Vada Pinson	1,565
Frank Robinson	1,502
Dan Driessen	1,480
Edd Roush	1,399
Roy McMillan	1,348

At-bats

Pete Rose	10,934
Dave Concepcion	8,723
Johnny Bench	7,658
Tony Perez	6,846
Barry Larkin	6,687
Vada Pinson	6,335
Frank Robinson	5,527
Edd Roush	5,384
Ted Kluszewski	4,961
Tommy Corcoran	4,852

Runs

Pete Rose	1,741
Barry Larkin	1,134
Johnny Bench	1,091
Frank Robinson	1,043
Dave Concepcion	993
Vada Pinson	978
Tony Perez	936
Bid McPhee	922
Joe Morgan	816
Edd Roush	815

Hits

Pete Rose	3,358
Dave Concepcion	2,326
Johnny Bench	2,048
Barry Larkin	2,008
Tony Perez	1,934
Vada Pinson	1,881
Edd Roush	1,784
Frank Robinson	1,673
Ted Kluszewski	1,499
Frank McCormick	1,439

Doubles

Pete Rose	601
Dave Concepcion	389
Johnny Bench	381
Barry Larkin	361
Vada Pinson	342
Tony Perez	339
Frank Robinson	318
Frank McCormick	285
Edd Roush	260
Ted Kluszewski	244

Triples

Edd Roush	152
Pete Rose	115
Bid McPhee	113
Vada Pinson	96
Curt Walker	94
Mike Mitchell	88
Ival Goodman	79
Jake Daubert	78
Jake Beckley	77
Heinie Groh	75

Home runs

Johnny Bench	389
Frank Robinson	324
Tony Perez	287
Ted Kluszewski	251
George Foster	244
Eric Davis	203
Vada Pinson	186
Barry Larkin	179
Wally Post	172
Gus Bell	160

Total bases

Pete Rose	4,645
Johnny Bench	3,644
Tony Perez	3,246
Dave Concepcion	3,114
Frank Robinson	3,063
Barry Larkin	3,046
Vada Pinson	2,973
Ted Kluszewski	2,542
Edd Roush	2,489
George Foster	2,289

Runs batted in

Johnny Bench	1,376
Tony Perez	1,192
Pete Rose	1,036
Frank Robinson	1,009
Dave Concepcion	950
Ted Kluszewski	886
George Foster	861
Barry Larkin	834
Vada Pinson	814
Frank McCormick	803

Extra-base hits

Pete Rose	868
Johnny Bench	794
Frank Robinson	692
Tony Perez	682
Vada Pinson	624
Barry Larkin	610
Dave Concepcion	538
Ted Kluszewski	518
George Foster	488
Edd Roush	459

Batting average

(Minimum 500 games)

Cy Seymour	.332
Edd Roush	.331
Jake Beckley	.325
Bubbles Hargrave	.314
Rube Bressler	.311
Ernie Lombardi	.311
Bug Holliday	.310
Dusty Miller	.308
Pete Rose	.307
Pat Duncan	.307

Stolen bases

Joe Morgan	406
Barry Larkin	359
Arlie Latham	340
Dave Concepcion	321
Bob Bescher	320
Bid McPhee	316
Eric Davis	270
Vada Pinson	221
Bug Holliday	206
Edd Roush	199

PITCHING

Earned-run average

(Minimum 1,000 innings)

Bob Ewing	2.37
Noodles Hahn	2.52
Pete Schneider	2.65
Jose Rijo	2.71
Bucky Walters	2.93
Tony Mullane	2.99
Gary Nolan	3.02
George Suggs	3.03
Don Gullett	3.03
Dolf Luque	3.09

Wins

Eppa Rixey	179
Paul Derringer	161
Bucky Walters	160
Dolf Luque	154
Jim Maloney	134
Frank Dwyer	133
Joe Nuxhall	130
Pete Donohue	127
Noodles Hahn	127
Tom Browning	123

Losses

Dolf Luque	152
Paul Derringer	150
Eppa Rixey	148
Johnny Vander Meer	116
Pete Donohue	110
Joe Nuxhall	109
Bucky Walters	107
Bob Ewing	103
Frank Dwyer	100
Red Lucas	99
Ken Raffensberger	99

Innings pitched

Eppa Rixey	2,890.2
Dolf Luque	2,668.2
Paul Derringer	2,615.1
Bucky Walters	2,355.2
Joe Nuxhall	2,169.1
Johnny Vander Meer	2,028.0
Bob Ewing	2,020.1
Pete Donohue	1,996.1
Frank Dwyer	1,992.2
Noodles Hahn	1,987.1

Strikeouts

Jim Maloney	1,592
Mario Soto	1,449
Joe Nuxhall	1,289
Johnny Vander Meer	1,251
Jose Rijo	1,201
Paul Derringer	1,062
Gary Nolan	1,035
Jim O'Toole	1,002
Tom Browning	997
Dolf Luque	970

Bases on balls

Johnny Vander Meer	1,072
Bucky Walters	806
Jim Maloney	786
Dolf Luque	756
Joe Nuxhall	706
Mario Soto	657
Eppa Rixey	603
Herm Wehmeier	591
Ewell Blackwell	532
Fred Norman	531

Games

Pedro Borbon	531
Clay Carroll	486
Joe Nuxhall	484
Tom Hume	457
Eppa Rixey	440
Dolf Luque	395
Paul Derringer	393
John Franco	393
Rob Dibble	354
Ted Power	349

Shutouts

Bucky Walters	32
Jim Maloney	30
Johnny Vander Meer	29
Ken Raffensberger	25
Paul Derringer	24
Noodles Hahn	24
Dolf Luque	24
Eppa Rixey	23
Joe Nuxhall	20
Jack Billingham	18
Red Lucas	18

Saves

John Franco	148
Clay Carroll	119
Jeff Brantley	88
Rob Dibble	88
Tom Hume	88
Pedro Borbon	76
Wayne Granger	73
Jeff Shaw	69
Danny Graves	65
Bill Henry	64

TEAM SEASON, GAME RECORDS

SEASON

Batting

Most at-bats	5,767	1968
Most runs	865	1999
Fewest runs	488	1908
Most hits	1,599	1976
Most singles	1,191	1922
Most doubles	312	1999
Most triples	120	1926
Most home runs	221	1956
Fewest home runs	14	1908, 1916
Most grand slams	7	1974, 1980, 1987
Most pinch-hit home runs	12	1957
Most total bases	2,549	1999
Most stolen bases	310	1910
Highest batting average	.296	1922
Lowest batting average	.227	1908
Highest slugging pct	.451	1999

Pitching

Lowest ERA	2.23	1919
Highest ERA	5.08	1930
Most complete games	142	1904
Most shutouts	23	1919
Most saves	60	1970, 1972
Most walks	659	2000
Most strikeouts	1,159	1997

Fielding

Most errors	355	1901
Fewest errors	95	1977
Most double plays	194	1928, 1931, 1954
Highest fielding average	.986	1995

General

Most games won	108	1975
Most games lost	101	1982
Highest win pct	.686	1919
Lowest win pct	.138	1876

GAME, INNING

Batting

Most runs, game	30	6-18-1893
Most runs, inning	14	6-18-1893, 8-3-89
Most hits, game	32	6-18-1893
Most home runs, game	9	9-4-99
Most total bases, game	55	6-18-1893, 5-19-99

George Foster joined an exclusive club in 1977 when he blasted a team-record 52 home runs.

REDS YEAR-BY-YEAR

Year	W	L	Place	Games Back	Manager	Leaders: Batting avg.	Hits	Home runs	RBIs	Wins	ERA
1901	52	87	8th	38	McPhee	Crawford, .330	Beckley, 178	Crawford, 16	Crawford, 104	Hahn, 22	Hahn, 2.71
1902	70	70	4th	33½	McPhee, Bancroft, Kelley	Crawford, .333	Crawford, 185	Beckley, 5	Crawford, 78	Hahn, 23	Hahn, 1.77
1903	74	65	4th	16½	Kelley	Donlin, .351	Seymour, 191	Donlin, Seymour, 7	Steinfeldt, 83	Hahn, 22	Hahn, 2.52
1904	88	65	3rd	18	Kelley	Seymour, .313	Seymour, 166	Dolan, 6	Corcoran, 74	Harper, 23	Hahn, 2.06
1905	79	74	5th	26	Kelley	Seymour, .377	Seymour, 219	Odwell, 9	Seymour, 121	Ewing, 20	Ewing, 2.51
1906	64	87	6th	51½	Hanlon	Huggins, .292	Huggins, 159	Schlei, Seymour, 4	Schlei, 54	Weimer, 20	Weimer, 2.22
1907	66	87	6th	41½	Hanlon	Mitchell, .292	Mitchell, 163	Kane, Mitchell, 3	Ganzel, 64	Coakley, Ewing, 17	Ewing, 1.73
1908	73	81	5th	26	Ganzel	Lobert, .293	Lobert, 167	Lobert, 4	Lobert, 63	Ewing, Spade, 17	Coakley, 1.86
1909	77	76	4th	33½	Griffith	Mitchell, .310	Mitchell, 162	3 Tied, 4	Mitchell, 86	Fromme, 19	Fromme, 1.90
1910	75	79	5th	29	Griffith	Paskert, .300	Hoblitzell, 170	Mitchell, 5,	Mitchell, 88	Suggs, 20	Suggs, 2.40
1911	70	83	6th	29	Griffith	Bates, .292	Hoblitzell, 180	Hoblitzell, 11	Hoblitzell, 91	Suggs, 15	Keefe, 2.69
1912	75	78	4th	29	O'Day	Marsans, .317	Hoblitzell, 164	Bescher, 4, Mitchell, 4	Hoblitzell, 85	Suggs, 19	Fromme, 2.74
1913	64	89	7th	37½	Tinker	Tinker, .317	Hoblitzell, 143	Bates, 6	Hoblitzell, 62	Johnson, 14	Ames, 2.88
1914	60	94	8th	34½	Herzog	Groh, .288	Herzog, 140	Niehoff, 4	Niehoff, 49	Benton, 16	Douglas, 2.56
1915	71	83	7th	20	Herzog	T. Griffith, .307	T. Griffith, 179	T. Griffith, 4	T. Griffith, 85	Dale, 18	Toney, 1.58
1916	60	93	*7th	33½	Herzog, Mathewson	Chase, .339	Chase, 184	Chase, 4	Chase, 82	Toney, 14	Toney, 2.28
1917	78	76	4th	20	Mathewson	Roush, .341	Groh, 182	Chase, Roush, Thorpe, 4	Chase, 86	Toney, 24	Schneider, 2.10
1918	68	60	3rd	15½	Mathewson, Groh	Roush, .333	Groh, 158	Roush, 5	S. Magee, 76	Eller, 16	Eller, 2.36
1919	96	44	1st	+9	Moran	Roush, .321	Roush, 162	Groh, 5	Roush, 71	Sallee, 21	Ruether, 1.82
1920	82	71	3rd	10½	Moran	Roush, .339	Roush, 196	Daubert, Roush, 4	Roush, 90	Ring, 17	Ruether, 2.47
1921	70	83	6th	24	Moran	Roush, .352	Bohne, 175	Roush, 4	Roush, 71	Rixey, 19	Rixey, 2.78
1922	86	68	2nd	7	Moran	Harper, .340	Daubert, 205	Daubert, 12	Duncan, 94	Rixey, 25	Donohue, 3.12
1923	91	63	2nd	4½	Moran	Roush, .351	Duncan, Roush, 185	Hargrave, 10	Roush, 88	Luque, 27	Luque, 1.93
1924	83	70	4th	10	Hendricks	Roush, .348	Roush, 168	4 Tied, 4	Roush, 72	Mays, 20	Rixey, 2.76
1925	80	73	3rd	15	Hendricks	Roush, .339	Roush, 183	Roush, E. Smith, 8	Roush, 83	Donohue, Rixey, 21	Luque, 2.63
1926	87	67	2nd	2	Hendricks	Roush, .323	Roush, 182	Roush, 7	Pipp, 99	Donohue, 20	Mays, 3.14
1927	75	78	5th	18½	Hendricks	Allen, .295	Dressen, 160	Walker, 6	Walker, 80	Lucas, 18	Luque, 3.20
1928	78	74	5th	16	Hendricks	Allen, .305	Critz, 190	Picinich, 7	Walker, 73	Rixey, 19	Kolp, 3.19
1929	66	88	7th	33	Hendricks	Walker, .313	Swanson, 172	Walker, 7	Kelly, 103	Lucas, 19	Lucas, 3.60
1930	59	95	7th	33	Howley	Heilmann, .333	Heilmann, 153	Heilmann, 19	Heilmann, 91	Lucas, 14	Kolp, 4.22
1931	58	96	8th	43	Howley	Stripp, .324	Cuccinello, 181	Cullop, 8	Cuccinello, 93	Lucas, 14	Benton, 3.35
1932	60	94	8th	30	Howley	Herman, .326	Herman, 188	Herman, 16	Herman, 87	Johnson, Lucas, 13	Rixey, 2.66
1933	58	94	8th	33	Bush	Hafey, .303	Hafey, 172	Bottomley, 13	Bottomley, 83	Benton, Lucas, 10	Rixey, 3.15
1934	52	99	8th	42	O'Farrell, Dressen	Pool, .327	Koenig, 172	Hafey, 18	Bottomley, 78	Derringer, 15	Frey, 3.52
1935	68	85	6th	31½	Dressen	Riggs, .278	Goodman, 159	Goodman, Lombardi, 12	Goodman, 72	Derringer, 22	Brennan, 3.15
1936	74	80	5th	18	Dressen	Lombardi, .333	Cuyler, 185	Goodman, 17	Cuyler, 74	Derringer, 19	Davis, 3.58
1937	56	98	8th	40	Dressen, Wallace	Lombardi, .334	Goodman, 150	Kampouris, 17	Kampouris, 71	Grissom, 12	Schott, 2.97
1938	82	68	4th	6	McKechnie	Lombardi, .342	F. McCormick, 209	Goodman, 30	F. McCormick, 106	Derringer, 21	Derringer, 2.93
1939	97	57	1st	+4½	McKechnie	F. McCormick, .332	F. McCormick, 209	Lombardi, 20	F. McCormick, 128	Walters, 27	Walters, 2.29
1940	100	53	1st	+12	McKechnie	Lombardi, .319	F. McCormick, 191	F. McCormick, 19	F. McCormick, 127	Walters, 22	Walters, 2.48
1941	88	66	3rd	12	McKechnie	M. McCormick, .287	F. McCormick, 162	F. McCormick, 17	F. McCormick, 97	Riddle, Walters, 19	Riddle, 2.24
1942	76	76	4th	29	McKechnie	F. McCormick, .277	F. McCormick, 156	F. McCormick, 13	F. McCormick, 89	Vander Meer, 18	Vander Meer, 2.43
1943	87	67	2nd	18	McKechnie	F. McCormick, .303	Frey, 154	Tipton, 9	Miller, 71	Riddle, 21	Beggs, 2.34
1944	89	65	3rd	16	McKechnie	F. McCormick, .305	F. McCormick, 177	F. McCormick, 20	F. McCormick, 102	Walters, 23	Heusser, 2.38
1945	61	93	7th	37	McKechnie	Libke, .283	Clay, 184	Miller, 13	F. McCormick, 81	Bowman, Heusser, 11	Walters, 2.68
1946	67	87	6th	30	McKechnie	Hatton, .271	Haas, 141	Hatton, 14	Hatton, 69	Beggs, 12	Beggs, 2.32
1947	73	81	5th	21	Neun	Galan, .314	Baumholtz, 182	Miller, 19	Miller, 87	Blackwell, 22	Blackwell, 2.47
1948	64	89	7th	27	Neun, Walters	Adams, .298	Wyrostek, 140	Sauer, 35	Sauer, 97	Vander Meer, 17	Vander Meer, 3.41
1949	62	92	7th	35	Walters	Kluszewski, .309	Kluszewski, 164	Cooper, 16	Hatton, 69	Raffensberger, 18	Erautt, 3.36
1950	66	87	6th	24½	Sewell	Kluszewski, .307	Kluszewski, 165	Kluszewski, 25	Kluszewski, 111	Blackwell, 17	Blackwell, 2.97
1951	68	86	6th	28½	Sewell	Wyrostek, .311	Wyrostek, 167	Ryan, 16	Kluszewski, 77	Blackwell, Raffensberger, 16	Perkowski, 2.82
1952	69	85	6th	27½	Sewell, Hornsby	Kluszewski, .320	Adams, 180	Kluszewski, 16	Kluszewski, 86	Raffensberger, 17	Raffensberger, 2.81
1953	68	86	6th	37	Hornsby, Mills	Kluszewski, .316	G. Bell, 183	Kluszewski, 40	Kluszewski, 108	Perkowski, 12	Baczewski, 3.45
1954	74	80	5th	23	Tebbetts	Kluszewski, .326	Kluszewski, 187	Kluszewski, 49	Kluszewski, 141	Fowler, Nuxhall, Valentine, 12	Fowler, 3.83
1955	75	79	5th	23½	Tebbetts	Kluszewski, .314	Kluszewski, 192	Kluszewski, 47	Kluszewski, 113	Nuxhall, 17	Freeman, 2.16
1956	91	63	3rd	2	Tebbetts	Kluszewski, .302	Temple, 180	Robinson, 38	Kluszewski, 102	Lawrence, 19	Freeman, 3.40
1957	80	74	4th	15	Tebbetts	Robinson, .322	Robinson, 197	Crowe, 31	Crowe, 92	Lawrence, 16	Lawrence, 3.52
1958	76	78	4th	16	Tebbetts, Dykes	Lynch, .312	Temple, 166	Robinson, 31	Robinson, 83	Purkey, 17	Haddix, 3.52
1959	74	80	*5th	13	Smith, Hutchinson	Pinson, .316	Pinson, 205	Robinson, 36	Robinson, 125	Newcombe, Purkey, 13	Newcombe, 3.16
1960	67	87	6th	28	Hutchinson	Robinson, .297	Pinson, 187	Robinson, 31	Robinson, 83	Purkey, 17	Brosnan, 2.36
1961	93	61	1st	+4	Hutchinson	Pinson, .343	Pinson, 208	Robinson, 37	Robinson, 124	Jay, 21	O'Toole, 3.10
1962	98	64	3rd	3½	Hutchinson	Robinson, .342	Robinson, 208	Robinson, 39	Robinson, 136	Purkey, 23	Purkey, 2.81
1963	86	76	5th	13	Hutchinson	Pinson, .313	Pinson, 204	Pinson, 22	Pinson, 106	Maloney, 23	Nuxhall, 2.61
1964	92	70	*2nd	1	Hutchinson, Sisler	Robinson, .306	Robinson, 174	Robinson, 29	Robinson, 96	O'Toole, 17	Ellis, 2.57
1965	89	73	4th	8	Sisler	Rose, .312	Rose, 209	Robinson, 33	De. Johnson, 130	Ellis, 22	Maloney, 2.54
1966	76	84	7th	18	Heffner	Rose, .313	Rose, 205	De. Johnson, 24	Cardenas, De. Johnson, 81	Maloney, 16	McCool, 2.48
1967	87	75	4th	14½	Bristol	Rose, .301	Pinson, 187	Perez, 26	Perez, 102	Pappas, 16	Abernathy, 1.27
1968	83	79	4th	14	Bristol	Rose, .335	Rose, 210	May, 22	Perez, 92	Maloney, 16	Carroll, 2.29
								WEST DIVISION			
1969	89	73	3rd	4	Bristol	Rose, .348	Rose, 218	May, 38	Perez, 122	Merritt, 17	Maloney, 2.77
1970	102	60	†1st	+14½	Anderson	Perez, .317	Rose, 205	Bench, 45	Bench, 148	Merritt, 20	Carroll, 2.59
1971	79	83	*4th	11	Anderson	Rose, .304	Rose, 192	May, 39	May, 98	Gullett, 16	Carroll, 2.50
1972	95	59	†1st	+10½	Anderson	Rose, .307	Rose, 198	Bench, 40	Bench, 125	Nolan, 15	Nolan, 1.99
1973	99	63	‡1st	+3½	Anderson	Rose, .338	Rose, 230	Perez, 27	Bench, 104	Billingham, 19	Borbon, 2.16
1974	98	64	2nd	4	Anderson	Morgan, .293	Rose, 185	Bench, 33	Bench, 129	Billingham, 19	Carroll, 2.15
1975	108	54	†1st	+20	Anderson	Morgan, .327	Rose, 210	Bench, 28	Bench, 110	Billingham, Gullett, Nolan, 15	Gullett, 2.42
1976	102	60	†1st	+10	Anderson	Griffey, .336	Rose, 215	Foster, 29	Foster, 121	Nolan, 15	Eastwick, 2.09
1977	88	74	2nd	10	Anderson	Foster, .320	Rose, 204	Foster, 52	Foster, 149	Norman, Seaver, 14	Seaver, 2.34
1978	92	69	2nd	2½	Anderson	Rose, .302	Rose, 198	Foster, 40	Foster, 120	Seaver, 16	Bair, 1.97
1979	90	71	‡1st	+1½	McNamara	Knight, Collins, .318	Knight, 175	Foster, 30	Foster, 98	Seaver, 16	Hume, 2.76
1980	89	73	3rd	3½	McNamara	Collins, .303	Collins, 167	Foster, 25	Foster, 93	Pastore, 13	Hume, 2.56
1981	66	42	§2nd/2nd	–	McNamara	Griffey, .311	Concepcion, 129	Foster, 22	Foster, 90	Seaver, 14	Seaver, 2.54
1982	61	101	6th	28	McNamara, Nixon	Cedeno, .289	Concepcion, 164	Driessen, 17	Cedeno, Driessen, 57	Soto, 14	Soto, 2.79
1983	74	88	6th	17	Nixon	Driessen, .277	Oester, 145	Redus, 17	Oester, 58	Soto, 17	Soto, 2.70
1984	70	92	5th	22	Rapp, Rose	Parker, .285	Parker, 173	Parker, 16	Parker, 94	Soto, 18	Power, 2.82
1985	89	72	2nd	5½	Rose	Parker, .312	Parker, 198	Parker, 34	Parker, 125	Browning, 20	Franco, 2.18
1986	86	76	2nd	10	Rose	B. Bell, .278	Parker, 174	Parker, 31	Parker, 116	Gullickson, 15	Franco, 2.94
1987	84	78	2nd	6	Rose	Daniels, .334	Davis, 139	Davis, 37	Davis, 100	Browning, Gullickson, Power, 10	Williams, 2.30
1988	87	74	2nd	7	Rose	Larkin, .296	Larkin, 174	Davis, 26	Davis, 93	Jackson, 23	Rijo, 2.39
1989	75	87	5th	17	Rose, Helms	Davis, .281	Benzinger, 154	Davis, 34	Davis, 101	Browning, 15	Dibble, 2.09
1990	91	71	†1st	+5	Piniella	Duncan, .306	Larkin, 185	Sabo, 25	Davis, 86	Browning, 15	Dibble, 1.74
1991	74	88	5th	20	Piniella	Morris, .318	Sabo, 175	O'Neill, 28	O'Neill, 91	Rijo, 15	Rijo, 2.51
1992	90	72	2nd	8	Piniella	Roberts, .323	Roberts, 172	O'Neill, 14	Larkin, 78	Belcher, Rijo, 15	Rijo, 2.56
1993	73	89	5th	31	Perez, Johnson	Morris, .317	Sabo, 143	Sabo, 21	Sanders, 83	Rijo, 14	Rijo, 2.48
								CENTRAL DIVISION			
1994	66	48	1st	+½	Johnson	Morris, .335	Morris, 146	Mitchell, 30	Morris, 78	Smiley, 11	Rijo, 3.08
1995	85	59	∞‡1st	+9	Johnson	Larkin, .319	Larkin, 158	Gant, 29	R. Sanders, 99	Schourek, 18	Schourek, 3.22
1996	81	81	3rd	7	Knight	Morris, .313	Morris, 165	Larkin, 33	Larkin, 89	Smiley, 13	Shaw, 2.49
1997	76	86	3rd	8	Knight, McKeon	D. Sanders, .273	D. Sanders, 127	Greene, 26	Greene, 91	Burba, Tomko, 11	Shaw, 2.38
1998	77	85	4th	25	McKeon	Young, .310	Young, Larkin, 166	B. Boone, 24	B. Boone, 95	Harnisch, 14	Harnisch, 3.14
1999	96	67	◆2nd	1½	McKeon	Casey, .332	Casey, 197	Vaughn, 45	Vaughn, 118	Harnisch, 16	Williamson, 2.41
2000	85	77	2nd	10	McKeon	Stynes, .334	D. Young, 166	Griffey Jr., 40	Griffey Jr., 118	Parris, 12	Graves, 2.57

* Tied for position. † Won Championship Series. ‡ Lost Championship Series. § First half 35-21; second half 31-21. ∞ Won Division Series; ◆ Lost wild-card playoff. Note: Batting average minimum 350 at-bats; ERA minimum 90 innings pitched.

Colorado Rockies

FRANCHISE CHRONOLOGY

First season: 1993, as part of a two-team expansion that increased the National League to 14 teams and the Major Leagues to 28. The Rockies lost their first game at New York, 3-0, and went on to finish sixth in the seven-team N.L. West Division with a 67-95 record, 37 games behind the first-place Braves.

1994-present: The Rockies improved to a 53-64 second-season record and 77-67 in 1995, when they finished one game behind Los Angeles in the realigned West Division. Their second-place record was good enough to earn the N.L.'s first wild-card berth under an expanded playoff format and gave Colorado the distinction of reaching postseason play faster than any previous expansion team. The Rockies' first playoff visit ended with a four-game Division Series loss to the Braves. Colorado made history in its debut season with a Major League-record attendance of 4,483,350 and drew well over 3 million fans in each of the next two strike-shortened campaigns.

Outfielder Dante Bichette.

ROCKIES VS. OPPONENTS BY DECADE

	Braves	Cardinals	Cubs	Dodgers	Giants	Phillies	Pirates	Reds	Astros	Mets	Expos	Padres	Marlins	Brewers	D'backs	Interleague	Decade Record
1993-99	26-50	40-37	40-38	40-46	34-52	29-36	36-34	34-41	41-33	36-32	37-30	41-45	38-40	10-10	13-12	17-23	512-559
2000-	4-5	5-3	5-4	4-9	6-7	6-3	7-2	3-6	5-4	3-6	7-2	7-6	4-5	4-5	6-7	6-6	82-80
Totals	30-55	45-40	45-42	44-55	40-59	35-39	43-36	37-47	46-37	39-38	44-32	48-51	42-45	14-15	19-19	23-29	594-639

Interleague results:4-9 vs. Angels; 7-6 vs. Athletics; 5-8 vs. Mariners; 7-6 vs. Rangers.

MANAGERS

Name	*Years*	*Record*
Don Baylor	1993-98	440-469
Jim Leyland	1999	72-90
Buddy Bell	2000	82-80

WILD-CARD QUALIFIERS

Year	*Record*	*Manager*	*Div. Series Result*
1995	77-67	Baylor	Lost to Braves

ATTENDANCE HIGHS

Total	*Season*	*Park*
4,483,350	1993	Mile High Stadium
3,891,014	1996	Coors Field
3,888,453	1997	Coors Field
3,789,347	1998	Coors Field
3,390,037	1995	Coors Field

Don Baylor guided the Rockies to the postseason and won the N.L. Manager of the Year Award in 1995.

ALL-TIME RECORD OF EXPANSION TEAMS

Team	W	L	Pct.	DT	P	WS
Arizona	250	236	.514	1	0	0
Kansas City	2,548	2,497	.505	6	2	1
Toronto	1,867	1,897	.496	5	2	2
Houston	3,052	3,138	.493	6	0	0
Montreal	2,454	2,596	.486	2	0	0
Anaheim	3,069	3,281	.483	3	0	0
Colorado	594	639	.482	0	0	0
Milwaukee	2,421	2,631	.479	2	1	0
New York	2,934	3,246	.475	4	4	2
Texas	2,952	3,381	.466	4	0	0
San Diego	2,315	2,742	.458	3	2	0
Seattle	1,715	2,048	.456	2	0	0
Florida	551	678	.448	0	1	1
Tampa Bay	201	284	.414	0	0	0

DT—Division Titles. P—Pennants won. WS—World Series won.

BALLPARK CHRONOLOGY

Coors Field (1995-present)

Capacity: 50,381.
First game: Rockies 11, New York 9 (April 26, 1995).
First batter: Brett Butler, Mets.
First hit: Brett Butler, Mets (single).
First run: Walt Weiss, Rockies (1st inning).
First home run: Rico Brogna, Mets.
First winning pitcher: Mark Thompson, Rockies.
First-season attendance: 3,390,037.

Mile High Stadium (1993-94)

Capacity: 76,100.
First game: Rockies 11, Expos 4 (April 9, 1993).
First-season attendance: 4,483,350.

N.L. MVP

Larry Walker, OF, 1997

MANAGER OF THE YEAR

Don Baylor, 1995

RETIRED UNIFORMS

None

MILESTONE PERFORMANCES

30-plus home runs

49—Larry Walker ... 1997
46—Vinny Castilla ... 1998
47—Andres Galarraga ... 1996
42—Todd Helton ... 2000
41—Andres Galarraga ... 1997
40—Dante Bichette ... 1995
Ellis Burks ... 1996
Vinny Castilla ... 1996, 1997
37—Larry Walker ... 1999
36—Larry Walker ... 1995
35—Todd Helton ... 1999
34—Dante Bichette ... 1999
33—Vinny Castilla ... 1999
32—Vinny Castilla ... 1995
Ellis Burks ... 1997
31—Andres Galarraga ... 1994
Andres Galarraga ... 1995
Dante Bichette ... 1996

100-plus RBIs

150—Andres Galarraga ... 1996
147—Todd Helton ... 2000
144—Vinny Castilla ... 1998
141—Dante Bichette ... 1996
140—Andres Galarraga ... 1997
133—Dante Bichette ... 1999
130—Larry Walker ... 1997
128—Dante Bichette ... 1995
Ellis Burks ... 1996
122—Dante Bichette ... 1998
118—Dante Bichette ... 1997
115—Larry Walker ... 1999
Jeff Cirillo ... 2000
113—Vinny Castilla ... 1996, 1997
Todd Helton ... 1999
106—Andres Galarraga ... 1995
Jeffrey Hammonds ... 2000
102—Vinny Castilla ... 1999
101—Larry Walker ... 1995

20-plus victories

None

N.L. home run champions

1995—Dante Bichette ... 40
1996—Andres Galarraga ... 47
1997—Larry Walker ... 49

N.L. RBI champions

1995—Dante Bichette ... 128
1996—Andres Galarraga ... 150
1997—Andres Galarraga ... 140
2000—Todd Helton ... 147

N.L. batting champions

1993—Andres Galarraga ... .370
1998—Larry Walker ... .363
1999—Larry Walker ... .379
2000—Todd Helton ... .372

N.L. ERA champions

None

N.L. strikeout champions

None

No-hit pitchers

None

Longest hitting streaks

23—Dante Bichette ... 1995
22—Vinny Castilla ... 1997
21—Larry Walker ... 1999
20—Larry Walker ... 1998
19—Eric Young ... 1995
Dante Bichette ... 1995
18—Larry Walker ... 1999
Jeffrey Hammonds ... 2000
17—Eric Young ... 1996
16—Dante Bichette ... 1994
Larry Walker ... 1997
Juan Pierre ... 2000
15—Andres Galarraga ... 1993
Neifi Perez ... 1998
Juan Pierre ... 2000

Second baseman Eric Young, an original Rockie, enjoyed a breakthrough 1996 season.

INDIVIDUAL SEASON, GAME RECORDS

Right fielder Larry Walker has two N.L. batting titles and one MVP Award during his tenure with the Rockies.

SEASON

Batting

At-bats	690	Neifi Perez	1999
Runs	143	Larry Walker	1997
Hits	219	Dante Bichette	1998
Singles	149	Eric Young	1996
Doubles	59	Todd Helton	2000
Triples	12	Neifi Perez	1999
Home runs	49	Larry Walker	1997
Home runs, rookie	25	Todd Helton	1998
Grand slams	2	6 times	
		Last by Tom Goodwin	2000
Total bases	409	Larry Walker	1997
RBIs	150	Andres Galarraga	1996
Walks	103	Todd Helton	2000
Most strikeouts	157	Andres Galarraga	1996
Fewest strikeouts	31	Eric Young	1996
Batting average	.379	Larry Walker	1999
Slugging pct.	.720	Larry Walker	1997
Stolen bases	53	Eric Young	1996

Pitching

Games	78	Chuck McElroy	1998
		Mike Myers	2000
Complete games	7	Pedro Astacio	1999
Innings	232.0	Pedro Astacio	1999
Wins	17	Kevin Ritz	1996
		Pedro Astacio	1999
Losses	17	Darryl Kile	1998
Winning pct.	.846	Gabe White	2000
Walks	105	Kevin Ritz	1996
Strikeouts	210	Pedro Astacio	1999
Shutouts	2	Roger Bailey	1997
Home runs allowed	39	Pedro Astacio	1998
Lowest ERA	1.99	Mike Myers	2000
Saves	31	Dave Veres	1999

GAME

Batting

Runs	5	Last by Larry Walker	7-27-2000
Hits	6	Andres Galarraga	7-3-95
Doubles	3	Last by Neifi Perez	8-25-2000
Triples	2	Last by Terry Shumpert	4-19-2000
Home runs	3	Last by Jeff Cirillo	6-28-2000
RBIs	8	Andres Galarraga	6-27-96
		Larry Walker	4-28-99
Total bases	13	Last by Vinny Castilla	6-5-99
Stolen bases	6	Eric Young	6-30-96

CAREER LEADERS

BATTING

Games

Dante Bichette	1,018
Vinny Castilla	935
Larry Walker	711
Andres Galarraga	679
Eric Young	613
Neifi Perez	581
Walt Weiss	523
Ellis Burks	520
Todd Helton	506
John Vander Wal	465

At-bats

Dante Bichette	4,050
Vinny Castilla	3,495
Andres Galarraga	2,667
Larry Walker	2,540
Neifi Perez	2,346
Eric Young	2,120
Ellis Burks	1,821
Todd Helton	1,781
Walt Weiss	1,760
Joe Girardi	1,102

Runs

Dante Bichette	665
Larry Walker	582
Vinny Castilla	516
Andres Galarraga	476
Eric Young	378
Ellis Burks	361
Todd Helton	343
Neifi Perez	330
Walt Weiss	264
Mike Lansing	159

Hits

Dante Bichette	1,278
Vinny Castilla	1,044
Larry Walker	862
Andres Galarraga	843
Neifi Perez	655
Eric Young	626
Todd Helton	594
Ellis Burks	558
Walt Weiss	469
Joe Girardi	302

Doubles

Dante Bichette	270
Larry Walker	188
Vinny Castilla	165
Andres Galarraga	155
Todd Helton	137
Neifi Perez	106
Ellis Burks	104
Eric Young	102
Walt Weiss	71
Charlie Hayes	68

Triples

Neifi Perez	41
Eric Young	28
Larry Walker	27
Ellis Burks	24
Dante Bichette	18
Vinny Castilla	17
Walt Weiss	14
Andres Galarraga	13
Mike Kingery	12
Joe Girardi	11

Home runs

Vinny Castilla	203
Dante Bichette	201
Andres Galarraga	172
Larry Walker	172
Ellis Burks	115
Todd Helton	107
Neifi Perez	36
Jeff Reed	36
Charlie Hayes	35
Eric Young	30

Total bases

Dante Bichette	2,187
Vinny Castilla	1,852
Larry Walker	1,620
Andres Galarraga	1,540
Todd Helton	1,070
Ellis Burks	1,055
Neifi Perez	951
Eric Young	874
Walt Weiss	610
Charlie Hayes	482

Runs batted in

Dante Bichette	826
Vinny Castilla	610
Andres Galarraga	579
Larry Walker	522
Todd Helton	368
Ellis Burks	337
Neifi Perez	234
Eric Young	227
Charlie Hayes	148
Walt Weiss	143

Extra-base hits

Dante Bichette	489
Larry Walker	387
Vinny Castilla	385
Andres Galarraga	340
Todd Helton	253
Ellis Burks	243
Neifi Perez	183
Eric Young	160
Charlie Hayes	109
Walt Weiss	99

Batting average

(Minimum 350 games)

Larry Walker	.339
Todd Helton	.334
Andres Galarraga	.316
Dante Bichette	.316
Ellis Burks	.306
Vinny Castilla	.299
Eric Young	.295
Jeff Reed	.286
Neifi Perez	.279
Walt Weiss	.266

Stolen bases

Eric Young	180
Dante Bichette	105
Larry Walker	97
Andres Galarraga	55
Ellis Burks	52
Quinton McCracken	45
Walt Weiss	42
Tom Goodwin	39
Alex Cole	30
Neifi Perez	27

PITCHING

Earned-run average

(Minimum 350 innings)

Steve Reed	3.68
Armando Reynoso	4.65
Roger Bailey	4.90
Curtis Leskanic	4.92
Kevin Ritz	5.20
John Thomson	5.28
Pedro Astacio	5.42
Brian Bohanon	5.48
Jamey Wright	5.57
Darryl Kile	5.84

Wins

Pedro Astacio	47
Kevin Ritz	39
Curtis Leskanic	31
Armando Reynoso	30
Steve Reed	25
Jamey Wright	25
Brian Bohanon	24
Darren Holmes	23
Darryl Kile	21
Marvin Freeman	20

Losses

Kevin Ritz	38
Pedro Astacio	35
Jamey Wright	33
Armando Reynoso	31
Darryl Kile	30
John Thomson	30
Brian Bohanon	22
Greg Harris	20
Curtis Leskanic	20
Mark Thompson	20

Innings pitched

Pedro Astacio	686.1
Kevin Ritz	576.1
Jamey Wright	541.2
Armando Reynoso	503.0
Curt Leskanic	470.0
Darryl Kile	421.0
John Thomson	390.0
Brian Bohanon	374.1
Steve Reed	369.2
Roger Bailey	356.0

Strikeouts

Pedro Astacio	624
Curt Leskanic	415
Kevin Ritz	337
Bruce Ruffin	319
Darren Holmes	297
Steve Reed	275
Darryl Kile	274
Armando Reynoso	270
John Thomson	246
Jamey Wright	239

Bases on balls

Jamey Wright	261
Kevin Ritz	253
Pedro Astacio	240
Curtis Leskanic	221
Darryl Kile	205
Brian Bohanon	171
Armando Reynoso	170
Bruce Ruffin	165
Roger Bailey	161
Bobby Jones	155

Games

Curtis Leskanic	356
Steve Reed	329
Mike Munoz	300
Darren Holmes	263
Bruce Ruffin	246
Mike DeJean	224
Jerry DiPoto	222
Dave Veres	136
Chuck McElroy	119
Pedro Astacio	108

Shutouts

Roger Bailey	2
Brian Bohanon	2
Mark Brownson	1
Darryl Kile	1
David Nied	1
Mark Thompson	1
John Thomson	1

Saves

Bruce Ruffin	60
Darren Holmes	46
Dave Veres	39
Jerry DiPoto	36
Jose Jimenez	24
Curtis Leskanic	20
Steve Reed	15
Mike Munoz	8
Gabe White	5
Mike DeJean	4

TEAM SEASON, GAME RECORDS

SEASON

Batting

Record	Total	Year
Most at-bats	5,717	1999
Most runs	968	2000
Fewest runs	758	1993
Most hits	1,664	2000
Most singles	1,130	2000
Most doubles	333	1998
Most triples	59	1993
Most home runs	239	1997
Fewest home runs	142	1993
Most grand slams	5	1994, 1998
Most pinch-hit home runs	11	1995
Most total bases	2,677	1997, 1999
Most stolen bases	201	1996
Highest batting average	.294	2000
Lowest batting average	.273	1993
Highest slugging pct	.478	1997

Pitching

Record	Total	Year
Lowest ERA	4.97	1995
Highest ERA	6.01	1999
Most complete games	12	1999
Most shutouts	5	1994, 1997, 1998
Most saves	43	1995
Most walks	737	1999
Most strikeouts	1,032	1999

Fielding

Record	Total	Year
Most errors	167	1993
Fewest errors	84	1994
Most double plays	202	1997
Highest fielding average	.985	2000

General

Record	Total	Year
Most games won	83	1996, 1997
Most games lost	95	1993
Highest win pct.	.535	1995
Lowest win pct.	.414	1993

GAME, INNING

Batting

Record	Total	Date
Most runs, game	19	6-7-96, 6-18,2000
Most runs, inning	11	7-12-96
Most hits, game	24	5-3-2000
Most home runs, game	7	Last 4-5-97
Most total bases, game	42	6-18-2000

ROCKIES YEAR-BY-YEAR

Year	W	L	Place	Games Back	Manager	Leaders: Batting avg.	Hits	Home runs	RBIs	Wins	ERA
						WEST DIVISION					
1993	67	95	6th	37	Baylor	Galarraga, .370	Hayes, 175	Hayes, 25	Galarraga, Hayes, 98	Reynoso, 12	Ruffin, 3.87
1994	53	64	3rd	6½	Baylor	Galarraga, .319	Bichette, 147	Galarraga, 31	Bichette, 95	Freeman, 10	Freeman, 2.80
1995	77	67	*2nd	1	Baylor	Bichette, .340	Bichette, 197	Bichette, 40	Bichette, 128	Ritz, 11	Leskanic, 3.40
1996	83	79	3rd	8	Baylor	Burks, .344	Burks, 211	Galarraga, 47	Galarraga, 150	Ritz, 17	Reynoso, 4.96
1997	83	79	3rd	7	Baylor	Walker, .366	Walker, 208	Walker, 49	Galarraga, 140	Bailey, Holmes, 9	Bailey, 4.29
1998	77	85	4th	21	Baylor	Walker, .363	Bichette, 219	Castilla, 46	Castilla, 144	Kile, Astacio, 13	Thomson, 4.81
1999	72	90	5th	28	Leyland	Walker, .379	Perez, 193	Walker, 37	Bichette, 133	Astacio, 17	Wright, 4.87
2000	82	80	4th	15	Bell	Helton, .372	Helton, 216	Helton, 42	Helton, 147	Bohanon, Astacio, 12	Tavarez, 4.43

* Lost Division Series.

Note: Batting average minimum 350 at-bats; ERA minimum 90 innings pitched.

David Nied

MAJOR LEAGUE Baseball became a Mile High reality on July 5, 1991, when owners tabbed Denver and South Florida for the 13th and 14th franchises in the National League fraternity. With the Colorado Baseball Partnership in place and the proposal for a new stadium approved, the Rockies began preparation for a 1993 season inaugural.

The Rockies selected pitcher David Nied as the first of 36 picks in the November 17, 1992, expansion draft. The team dropped a 3-0 decision in its April 5, 1993, Major League debut at New York, but rebounded for an 11-4 victory over Montreal in its April 9 Mile High Stadium opener.

Expansion draft (November 17, 1992)

Players

Player	From	Position
Brad Ausmus	N.Y. Yankees	catcher
Freddie Benavides	Cincinnati	infield
Pedro Castellano	Chicago Cubs	infield
Vinny Castilla	Atlanta	infield
Braulio Castillo	Philadelphia	outfield
Jerald Clark	San Diego	outfield
Alex Cole	Pittsburgh	outfield
Joe Girardi	Chicago Cubs	catcher
Charlie Hayes	N.Y. Yankees	third base
Roberto Mejia	Los Angeles	infield
J. Owens	Minnesota	catcher
Jody Reed	Boston	infield
Kevin Reimer	Texas	outfield
Jim Tatum	Milwaukee	infield
Eric Wedge	Boston	catcher
Eric Young	Los Angeles	infield

Pitchers

Pitcher	From	Throws
Scott Aldred	Detroit	lefthanded
Andy Ashby	Philadelphia	righthanded
Willie Blair	Houston	righthanded
Doug Bochtler	Montreal	righthanded
Denis Boucher	Cleveland	lefthanded
Scott Fredrickson	San Diego	righthanded
Ryan Hawblitzel	Chicago Cubs	righthanded
Butch Henry	Houston	righthanded
Darren Holmes	Milwaukee	righthanded
Calvin Jones	Seattle	righthanded
Curt Leskanic	Minnesota	righthanded
Brett Merriman	California	righthanded
Marcus Moore	Toronto	righthanded
*David Nied	Atlanta	righthanded
Lance Painter	San Diego	lefthanded
Steve Reed	San Francisco	righthanded
Armando Reynoso	Atlanta	righthanded
Kevin Ritz	Detroit	righthanded
Mo Sanford	Cincinnati	righthanded
Keith Shepherd	Philadelphia	righthanded

*First pick

Opening day lineup

April 5, 1993
Eric Young, second base
Alex Cole, center field
Dante Bichette, right field
Andres Galarraga, first base
Jerald Clark, left field
Charlie Hayes, third base
Joe Girardi, catcher
Freddie Benavides, shortstop
David Nied, pitcher

Charlie Hayes

Rockies firsts

First hit: Andres Galarraga, April 5, 1993, at New York (single)
First home run: Dante Bichette, April 7, 1993, at New York
First RBI: Dante Bichette, April 7, 1993, at New York
First win: Bryn Smith, April 9, 1993, vs. Montreal
First shutout: David Nied (7 inn.), Bruce Ruffin (1), Darren Holmes (1), April 14, 1994, 5-0 at Philadelphia
First CG shutout: David Nied, June 21, 1994, 8-0 vs. Houston

FLORIDA MARLINS

FRANCHISE CHRONOLOGY

First season: 1993, as part of a two-team expansion that increased the National League to 14 teams and the Major Leagues to 28. The Marlins collected 14 hits and defeated Los Angeles, 6-3, in their major league debut and went on to post a 64-98 first-year record. That was good for sixth place in the seven-team N.L. East Division, 33 games behind first-place Philadelphia.

1994-present: The Marlins improved to 51-64 in the strike-interrupted 1994 season and climbed to within nine games of .500 in the strike-shortened 1995 campaign. But the real breakthrough came in 1997 when the 5-year-old Marlins, buoyed by an offseason spending spree that beefed up their roster, won 92 games, earned a wild-card berth and made a Cinderella run through the playoffs, beating Atlanta in the NLCS to claim the pennant and defeating Cleveland in a seven-game World Series. In the process, they became the youngest championship team in baseball history.

Outfielder Gary Sheffield.

MARLINS VS. OPPONENTS BY DECADE

	Braves	Cardinals	Cubs	Dodgers	Giants	Phillies	Pirates	Reds	Astros	Mets	Expos	Padres	Rockies	Brewers	D'backs	Interleague	Decade Record
1993-99	36-51	29-40	36-39	35-35	25-42	34-52	30-42	32-43	32-39	36-50	38-46	30-34	40-38	5-13	3-14	31-18	472-596
2000-	6-6	3-6	6-1	2-7	3-6	9-4	5-4	6-3	3-5	6-6	7-6	2-7	5-4	3-4	5-4	8-9	79-82
Totals	42-57	32-46	42-40	37-42	28-48	43-56	35-46	38-46	35-44	42-56	45-52	32-41	45-42	8-17	8-18	39-27	551-678

Interleague results:8-4 vs. Orioles; 5-7 vs. Red Sox; 2-1 vs. Tigers; 4-7 vs. Yankees; 9-3 vs. Blue Jays; 11-5 vs. Devil Rays.

MANAGERS

Name	*Years*	*Record*
Rene Lachemann	1993-96	221-285
Cookie Rojas	1996	1-0
John Boles	1996, 1999-2000	183-215
Jim Leyland	1997-98	146-178

WORLD SERIES CHAMPION

Year	*Loser*	*Length*	*MVP*
1997	Cleveland	7 games	L. Hernandez

N.L. PENNANT WINNER

Year	*Record*	*Manager*	*Series Result*
1997	92-70	Leyland	Defeated Braves

Despite Jim Leyland's sub-.500 overall record with the team, he guided the Marlins to their World Series title in 1997.

WILD-CARD QUALIFIER

Year	*Record*	*Manager*	*Div. Series Result*	*NLCS Result*
1997	90-72	Leyland	Defeated Giants	Defeated Braves

ALL-TIME RECORD OF EXPANSION TEAMS

Team	W	L	Pct.	DT	P	WS
Arizona	250	236	.514	1	0	0
Kansas City	2,548	2,497	.505	6	2	1
Toronto	1,867	1,897	.496	5	2	2
Houston	3,052	3,138	.493	6	0	0
Montreal	2,454	2,596	.486	2	0	0
Anaheim	3,069	3,281	.483	3	0	0
Colorado	594	639	.482	0	0	0
Milwaukee	2,421	2,631	.479	2	1	0
New York	2,934	3,246	.475	4	4	2
Texas	2,952	3,381	.466	4	0	0
San Diego	2,315	2,742	.458	3	2	0
Seattle	1,715	2,048	.456	2	0	0
Florida	551	678	.448	0	1	1
Tampa Bay	201	284	.414	0	0	0

DT—Division Titles. P—Pennants won. WS—World Series won.

BALLPARK CHRONOLOGY

Pro Player Stadium, formerly Joe Robbie Stadium (1993-present)

Capacity: 42,530.
First game: Marlins 6, Los Angeles 3 (April 5, 1993).
First batter: Jose Offerman, Dodgers.
First hit: Bret Barberie, Marlins (single).
First run: Benito Santiago, Marlins (2nd inning).
First home run: Tim Wallach, Dodgers.
First winning pitcher: Charlie Hough, Marlins.
First-season attendance: 3,064,847.

ATTENDANCE HIGHS

Total	*Season*	*Park*
3,064,847	1993	Joe Robbie Stadium
2,364,387	1997	Joe Robbie Stadium
1,937,467	1994	Joe Robbie Stadium
1,750,395	1998	Joe Robbie Stadium
1,746,767	1996	Joe Robbie Stadium

RETIRED UNIFORMS

None

MILESTONE PERFORMANCES

25-plus home runs
42— Gary Sheffield 1996
31— Preston Wilson 2000
28— Derrek Lee 2000
27— Gary Sheffield 1994
26— Jeff Conine 1996
Preston Wilson 1999
25— Jeff Conine 1995

100-plus RBIs
121— Preston Wilson 2000
120— Gary Sheffield 1996
115— Moises Alou 1997
105— Jeff Conine 1995

20-plus victories
None

N.L. home run champions
None

N.L. RBI champions
None

N.L. batting champions
None

N.L. ERA champions
1996— Kevin Brown 1.89

N.L. strikeout champions
None

No-hit pitchers
(9 innings or more)
1996— Al Leiter .... 11-0 vs. Colorado
1997— Kevin Brown .... 9-0 vs. San Francisco

Longest hitting streaks
22— Edgar Renteria 1996
Luis Castillo 1999
21— Greg Colbrunn 1996
19— Luis Castillo 2000
17— Greg Colbrunn 1995
16— Mike Lowell 2000
15— Bret Barberie 1993
Chuck Carr 1993

Outfielder Jeff Conine's steady bat helped the Marlins navigate the rough expansion waters.

INDIVIDUAL SEASON, GAME RECORDS

Second baseman Luis Castillo continues to put up excellent offensive numbers for the Marlins. He led the majors in stolen bases in 2000.

SEASON

Batting

At-bats	617	Edgar Renteria	1997
Runs	118	Gary Sheffield	1996
Hits	180	Luis Castillo	2000
Singles	158	Luis Castillo	2000
Doubles	45	Cliff Floyd	1998
Triples	9	Mark Kotsay	1999
Home runs	42	Gary Sheffield	1996
Home runs, rookie	26	Preston Wilson	1999
Grand slams	3	Bobby Bonilla	1997
Total bases	324	Gary Sheffield	1996
RBIs	121	Preston Wilson	2000
Walks	142	Gary Sheffield	1996
Most strikeouts	187	Preston Wilson	2000
Fewest strikeouts	46	Mark Kotsay	2000
Batting average	.334	Luis Castillo	2000
Slugging pct.	.624	Gary Sheffield	1996
Stolen bases	62	Luis Castillo	2000

Pitching

Games	75	Robb Nen	1996
Complete games	9	Livan Hernandez	1998
Innings	237.1	Kevin Brown	1997
Wins	17	Kevin Brown	1996
		Alex Fernandez	1997
Losses	17	Jack Armstrong	1993
Winning pct.	.667	Pat Rapp	1995
		Kevin Brown	1997
Walks	119	Al Leiter	1996
Strikeouts	209	Ryan Dempster	2000
Shutouts	3	Kevin Brown	1996
Home runs allowed	37	Livan Hernandez	1998
Lowest ERA	1.89	Kevin Brown	1996
Saves	45	Bryan Harvey,	1993
		Antonio Alfonseca	2000

GAME

Batting

Runs	4	Last by Edgar Renteria	8-13-98
Hits	5	Last by Mark Kotsay	6-22-98
Doubles	3	Last by Mark Kotsay	4-22-98
Triples	2	Jesus Tavarez	8-28-95
Home runs	2	Last by Preston Wilson	9-2-2000
RBIs	7	Last by Gary Sheffield	9-18-95
Stolen bases	4	Luis Castillo	5-17-2000

HISTORY

CAREER LEADERS

BATTING

Games

Jeff Conine	718
Gary Sheffield	558
Mark Kotsay	468
Kurt Abbott	424
Luis Castillo	424
Alex Arias	423
Cliff Floyd	404
Edgar Renteria	393
Charles Johnson	376
Derrek Lee	369

At-bats

Jeff Conine	2,531
Gary Sheffield	1,870
Mark Kotsay	1,655
Luis Castillo	1,606
Edgar Renteria	1,565
Cliff Floyd	1,396
Kurt Abbott	1,337
Chuck Carr	1,292
Charles Johnson	1,241
Greg Colbrunn	1,194

Runs

Gary Sheffield	365
Jeff Conine	337
Luis Castillo	251
Edgar Renteria	237
Mark Kotsay	221
Cliff Floyd	220
Chuck Carr	190
Kurt Abbott	173
Preston Wilson	165
Derrek Lee	153

Hits

Jeff Conine	737
Gary Sheffield	538
Luis Castillo	464
Mark Kotsay	463
Edgar Renteria	450
Cliff Floyd	400
Kurt Abbott	343
Greg Colbrunn	339
Chuck Carr	331
Charles Johnson	297
Preston Wilson	297

Doubles

Jeff Conine	122
Cliff Floyd	103
Gary Sheffield	98
Mark Kotsay	80
Kurt Abbott	71
Charles Johnson	60
Chuck Carr	58
Greg Colbrunn	58
Edgar Renteria	57
Derrek Lee	56
Preston Wilson	56

Triples

Mark Kotsay	22
Kurt Abbott	19
Jeff Conine	14
Todd Dunwoody	12
Alex Gonzalez	12
Luis Castillo	10
Edgar Renteria	8
Benito Santiago	8
Quilvio Veras	8
Craig Counsell	7
Kevin Millar	7
Gary Sheffield	7
Devon White	7
Preston Wilson	7

Home runs

Gary Sheffield	122
Jeff Conine	98
Cliff Floyd	61
Preston Wilson	58
Charles Johnson	51
Derrek Lee	50
Greg Colbrunn	45
Kurt Abbott	40
Mike Lowell	34
Mark Kotsay	31

Total bases

Jeff Conine	1,181
Gary Sheffield	1,016
Cliff Floyd	696
Mark Kotsay	680
Kurt Abbott	572
Edgar Renteria	559
Luis Castillo	549
Preston Wilson	541
Greg Colbrunn	538
Charles Johnson	516

Runs batted in

Jeff Conine	422
Gary Sheffield	380
Cliff Floyd	249
Preston Wilson	193
Greg Colbrunn	189
Mark Kotsay	179
Charles Johnson	166
Derrek Lee	164
Kurt Abbott	156
Mike Lowell	138

Extra-base hits

Jeff Conine	234
Gary Sheffield	227
Cliff Floyd	169
Mark Kotsay	133
Kurt Abbott	130
Preston Wilson	121
Charles Johnson	114
Derrek Lee	111
Greg Colbrunn	106
Mike Lowell	87

Batting average

(Minimum 350 games)

Jeff Conine	.291
Luis Castillo	.289
Gary Sheffield	.288
Edgar Renteria	.288
Cliff Floyd	.287
Mark Kotsay	.280
Alex Arias	.265
Kurt Abbott	.257
Chuck Carr	.256
Derrek Lee	.248

Stolen bases

Luis Castillo	148
Chuck Carr	115
Edgar Renteria	89
Gary Sheffield	74
Quilvio Veras	64
Cliff Floyd	62
Preston Wilson	47
Mark Kotsay	39
Devon White	35
Greg Colbrunn	16

PITCHING

Earned-run average

(Minimum 350 innings)

Kevin Brown	2.30
Al Leiter	3.51
Alex Fernandez	3.59
Pat Rapp	4.18
Livan Hernandez	4.39
Ryan Dempster	4.46
Chris Hammond	4.52
Jesus Sanchez	5.11
Brian Meadows	5.41

Wins

Pat Rapp	37
Kevin Brown	33
Chris Hammond	29
Alex Fernandez	28
Al Leiter	27
Livan Hernandez	24
Ryan Dempster	22
Brian Meadows	22
Jesus Sanchez	21
John Burkett	20
Robb Nen	20

Losses

Pat Rapp	43
Chris Hammond	32
Brian Meadows	28
Jesus Sanchez	28
Charlie Hough	25
John Burkett	24
Alex Fernandez	24
Livan Hernandez	24
Ryan Dempster	23
Dave Weathers	22

Innings pitched

Pat Rapp	665.2
Chris Hammond	520.0
Kevin Brown	470.1
Livan Hernandez	469.2
Jesus Sanchez	431.1
Ryan Dempster	428.0
Alex Fernandez	414.0
Al Leiter	366.2
Brian Meadows	352.2
John Burkett	342.1
Dave Weathers	342.1

Strikeouts

Pat Rapp	384
Ryan Dempster	370
Kevin Brown	364
Livan Hernandez	333
Chris Hammond	332
Al Leiter	332
Robb Nen	328
Jesus Sanchez	322
Alex Fernandez	301
John Burkett	234

Bases on balls

Pat Rapp	326
Ryan Dempster	228
Jesus Sanchez	227
Al Leiter	210
Livan Hernandez	199
Chris Hammond	171
Dave Weathers	152
Alex Fernandez	126
Charlie Hough	123
Robb Nen	121

Games

Robb Nen	269
Antonio Alfonseca	216
Jay Powell	183
Yorkis Perez	177
Vic Darensbourg	171
Braden Looper	145
Terry Mathews	138
Jesus Sanchez	126
Richie Lewis	123
Felix Heredia	118

Shutouts

Kevin Brown	5
Pat Rapp	4
Chris Hammond	3
Jesus Sanchez	2
Dennis Springer	2
Ryan Bowen	1
Ryan Dempster	1
Alex Fernandez	1
Mark Gardner	1
Charlie Hough	1
Al Leiter	1

Saves

Robb Nen	108
Antonio Alfonseca	74
Bryan Harvey	51
Matt Mantei	19
Jeremy Hernandez	9
Terry Mathews	7
Jay Powell	7
Felix Heredia	2
Trevor Hoffman	2
Braden Looper	2
Rob Stanifer	2

TEAM SEASON, GAME RECORDS

SEASON

Batting

Most at-bats	5,578	1999
Most runs	740	1997
Fewest runs	581	1993
Most hits	1,465	1999
Most singles	1,034	1993
Most doubles	274	2000
Most triples	44	1999
Most home runs	160	2000
Fewest home runs	94	1993, 1994
Most grand slams	9	1997
Most pinch-hit home runs	8	1999
Most total bases	2,253	2000
Most stolen bases	168	2000
Highest batting average	.266	1994
Lowest batting average	.248	1993
Highest slugging pct.	.409	2000

Pitching

Lowest ERA	3.83	1997
Highest ERA	5.18	1998
Most complete games	12	1995, 1997
Most shutouts	13	1996
Most saves	48	1993, 2000
Most walks	715	1998
Most strikeouts	1,188	1997

Fielding

Most errors	129	1998
Fewest errors	111	1996
Most double plays	187	1996
Highest fielding average	.982	1996

General

Most games won	92	1997
Most games lost	108	1998
Highest win pct	.568	1997
Lowest win pct	.333	1998

GAME, INNING

Batting

Most runs, game	17	9-17-95
Most runs, inning	8	Last 6-5-99
Most hits, game	24	7-15-96
Most home runs, game	4	Last 6-24-2000
Most total bases, game	39	9-17-95

MARLINS YEAR-BY-YEAR

Year	W	L	Place	Games Back	Manager	Leaders: Batting avg.	Hits	Home runs	RBIs	Wins	ERA
						EAST DIVISION					
1993	64	98	6th	33	Lachemann	Conine, .292	Conine, 174	Destrade, 20	Destrade, 87	Hammond, 11	Aquino, 3.42
1994	51	64	5th	23½	Lachemann	Conine, .319	Conine, 144	Sheffield, 27	Conine, 82	Weathers, 8	Rapp, 3.85
1995	67	76	4th	22½	Lachemann	Conine, .302	Pendleton, 149	Conine, 25	Conine, 105	Burkett, Rapp, 14	Rapp, 3.44
1996	80	82	3rd	16	R. Lachemann, Boles	Sheffield, .314	Conine, 175	Sheffield, 42	Sheffield, 120	Brown, 17	Brown, 1.89
1997	92	70	*†2nd	9	Leyland	Bonilla, .297	Renteria, 171	Alou, 23	Alou, 115	Fernandez, 17	Brown, 2.69
1998	54	108	5th	52	Leyland	Renteria, .282	Floyd, 166	Floyd, 22	Floyd, 90	Meadows, 11	Ojala, 4.25
1999	64	98	5th	39	Boles	Castillo, .302	Gonzalez, 155	Wilson, 26	Wilson, 71	Meadows, 11	Fernandez, 3.38
2000	79	82	3rd	15½	Boles	Castillo, .334	Castillo, 180	Wilson, 31	Wilson, 121	Dempster, 14	C. Smith, 3.25

* Won Division Series. † Won Championship Series.

Note: Batting average minimum 350 at-bats; ERA minimum 90 innings pitched.

Nigel Wilson

FLORIDA, long associated with spring training baseball, received its own Major League franchise when National League owners unanimously approved expansion to Denver and Miami. The Marlins, owned by H. Wayne Huizenga, joined the Colorado Rockies as the 13th and 14th N.L. franchises.

The Marlins stocked their roster with 36 selections in the November 17, 1992, expansion draft, grabbing outfielder Nigel Wilson with their first pick. Florida made its April 5, 1993, Major League debut a successful one, beating the Los Angeles Dodgers, 6-3, at Joe Robbie Stadium.

Expansion draft (November 17, 1992)

Players

Bret Barberie....................Montreal ....infield
Chuck Carr....................St. Louis ....outfield
Jeff Conine....................Kansas City....................outfield
Steve Decker....................San Francisco....................catcher
Chris Donnels....................N.Y. Mets....................infield
Carl Everett....................N.Y. Yankees....................outfield
Monty Fariss....................Texas....................outfield
Junior Felix....................California....................outfield
Eric Helfand....................Oakland....................catcher
Ramon Martinez....................Pittsburgh....................infield
Kerwin Moore....................Kansas City....................outfield
Bob Natal....................Montreal....................catcher
Jesus Tavarez....................Seattle....................outfield
*Nigel Wilson....................Toronto....................outfield
Darrell Whitmore....................Cleveland....................outfield

Pitchers

Jack Armstrong....................Cleveland....................righthanded
Scott Baker....................St. Louis....................lefthanded
Andres Berumen....................Kansas City....................righthanded
Ryan Bowen....................Houston....................righthanded
Cris Carpenter....................St. Louis....................righthanded
Scott Chiamparino....................Texas....................righthanded
Jim Corsi....................Oakland....................righthanded
Tom Edens....................Minnesota....................righthanded
Brian Harvey....................California....................righthanded
Greg Hibbard....................Chicago White Sox....................lefthanded
Trevor Hoffman....................Cincinnati....................righthanded
Danny Jackson....................Pittsburgh....................lefthanded
John Johnstone....................N.Y. Mets....................righthanded
Richie Lewis....................Baltimore....................righthanded
Jose Martinez....................N.Y. Mets....................righthanded
Jamie McAndrew....................Los Angeles....................righthanded
Robert Person....................Chicago White Sox....................righthanded
Pat Rapp....................San Francisco....................righthanded
Jeff Tabaka....................Milwaukee....................lefthanded
Dave Weathers....................Toronto....................righthanded
Kip Yaughn....................Baltimore....................righthanded

* First pick

Opening day lineup

April 5, 1993
Scott Pose, center field
Bret Barberie, second base
Junior Felix, right field
Orestes Destrade, first base
Dave Magadan, third base
Benito Santiago, catcher
Jeff Conine, left field
Walt Weiss, shortstop
Charlie Hough, pitcher

Jeff Conine

Marlins firsts

First hit: Bret Barberie, April 5, 1993, vs. Los Angeles (single)
First home run: Benito Santiago, April 12, 1993, at San Francisco
First RBI: Walt Weiss, April 5, 1993, vs. Los Angeles
First win: Charlie Hough, April 5, 1993, vs. Los Angeles
First shutout: Ryan Bowen, May 15, 1993, 8-0 at St. Louis

HOUSTON ASTROS

FRANCHISE CHRONOLOGY

First season: 1962, as one of two entries in the National League's first modern-era expansion. The Colt .45s, as they were known for three seasons, pounded the Chicago Cubs, 11-2, in their big-league debut and went on to finish with a 64-96 first-year record, good for eighth place in the 10-team N.L. field.

1963-present: The Astros still are looking for their first pennant, an honor the New York Mets, their expansion mate, has claimed three times. They came excruciatingly close in two N.L. Championship Series: 1980, when they dropped a 10-inning Game 5 thriller to Philadelphia; and 1986, when they lost a 16-inning Game 6 decision in an expansion showdown with the Mets. Those two West Division titles and consecutive Central titles that were followed by Division Series losses in 1997, '98 and '99 are all the Astros have to show for more than three decades of Major League Baseball, although they have finished second or third 13 times since division play began in 1969. In a historical sense, Houston will be long remembered as the franchise that brought indoor baseball and AstroTurf to the major leagues.

Righthander Mike Scott.

ASTROS VS. OPPONENTS BY DECADE

	Braves	Cardinals	Cubs	Dodgers	Giants	Phillies	Pirates	Reds	Mets	Expos	Padres	Marlins	Rockies	Brewers	D'backs	Interleague	Decade Record
1962-69	49-95	59-79	72-66	57-87	55-89	51-87	45-93	59-85	87-49	11-1	10-8						555-739
1970-79	91-85	56-64	65-55	76-104	90-90	59-61	44-75	74-105	61-59	71-49	106-70						793-817
1980-89	96-78	56-58	64-51	82-93	98-79	57-61	63-51	93-81	61-56	60-55	89-87						819-750
1990-99	53-71	60-62	70-51	65-57	69-57	62-43	67-54	63-76	61-46	57-51	62-67	39-32	33-41	17-7	9-9	26-18	813-742
2000-	4-5	6-6	7-5	3-6	1-8	5-4	10-3	5-7	2-5	4-5	2-7	5-3	4-5	7-6	1-6	6-9	72-90
Totals	293-334	237-269	278-228	283-347	313-323	234-256	229-276	294-354	272-215	203-161	269-239	44-35	37-46	24-13	10-15	32-27	3052-3138

Interleague results: 5-7 vs. White Sox; 6-6 vs. Indians; 8-4 vs. Royals; 1-2 vs. Brewers; 5-6 vs. Twins; 7-2 vs. Tigers.

MANAGERS

(Houston Colt .45s, 1962-64)

Name	*Years*	*Record*
Harry Craft	1962-64	191-280
Lum Harris	1964-65	70-105
Grady Hatton	1966-68	164-221
Harry Walker	1968-72	355-353
Leo Durocher	1972-73	98-95
Salty Parker	1972	1-0
Preston Gomez	1973-75	128-161
Bill Virdon	1975-82	544-522
Bob Lillis	1982-85	276-261
Hal Lanier	1986-88	254-232
Art Howe	1989-93	392-418
Terry Collins	1994-96	224-197
Larry Dierker	1997-2000	355-293

WEST DIVISION CHAMPIONS

Year	*Record*	*Manager*	*NLCS Result*
1980	93-70	Virdon	Lost to Phillies
1981*	61-49	Virdon	None
1986	96-66	Lanier	Lost to Mets

* Second-half champion; lost division playoff to Dodgers.

CENTRAL DIVISION CHAMPIONS

Year	*Record*	*Manager*	*Div. Series Result*
1997	84-78	Dierker	Lost to Braves
1998	102-60	Dierker	Lost to Padres
1999	97-65	Dierker	Lost to Braves

ALL-TIME RECORD OF EXPANSION TEAMS

Team	W	L	Pct.	DT	P	WS
Arizona	250	236	.514	1	0	0
Kansas City	2,548	2,497	.505	6	2	1
Toronto	1,867	1,897	.496	5	2	2
Houston	3,052	3,138	.493	6	0	0
Montreal	2,454	2,596	.486	2	0	0
Anaheim	3,069	3,281	.483	3	0	0
Colorado	594	639	.482	0	0	0
Milwaukee	2,421	2,631	.479	2	1	0
New York	2,934	3,246	.475	4	4	2
Texas	2,952	3,381	.466	4	0	0
San Diego	2,315	2,742	.458	3	2	0
Seattle	1,715	2,048	.456	2	0	0
Florida	551	678	.448	0	1	1
Tampa Bay	201	284	.414	0	0	0

DT—Division Titles. P—Pennants won. WS—World Series won.

ATTENDANCE HIGHS

Total	*Season*	*Park*
3,056,139	2000	Enron Field
2,706,020	1999	Astrodome
2,450,451	1998	Astrodome
2,278,217	1980	Astrodome
2,151,470	1965	Astrodome

BALLPARK CHRONOLOGY

Enron Field (2000-present)

Capacity: 40,950.
First game: Philadelphia 4, Astros 1 (April 7, 2000).
First batter: Doug Glanville, Phillies.
First hit: Doug Glanville, Phillies (single).
First run: Scott Rolen, Phillies (7th inning).
First home run: Scott Rolen, Phillies.
First winning pitcher: Randy Wolf, Phillies.
First-season attendance: 3,056,139.

The Astrodome (1965-present)

Capacity: 54,313.
First game: Philadelphia 2, Astros 0 (April 12, 1965).
First-season attendance: 2,151,470.

Colt Stadium (1962-64)

Capacity: 32,601.
First game: Astros 11, Chicago 2 (April 10, 1962).
First-season attendance: 924,456.

N.L. MVP

Jeff Bagwell, 1B, 1994

CY YOUNG WINNER

Mike Scott, RH, 1986

ROOKIE OF THE YEAR

Jeff Bagwell, 1B, 1991

MANAGERS OF THE YEAR

Hal Lanier, 1986
Larry Dierker, 1998

RETIRED UNIFORMS

No.	*Name*	*Pos.*
25	Jose Cruz	OF
32	Jim Umbricht	P
33	Mike Scott	P
34	Nolan Ryan	P
40	Don Wilson	P

Hard-hitting Jimmy Wynn was Houston's major power source in the late 1960s.

MILESTONE PERFORMANCES

25-plus home runs
47—Jeff Bagwell 2000
44—Richard Hidalgo 2000
43—Jeff Bagwell 1997
42—Jeff Bagwell 1999
39—Jeff Bagwell 1994
38—Moises Alou 1998
37—Jimmy Wynn 1967
34—Glenn Davis 1989
Jeff Bagwell 1998
33—Jimmy Wynn 1969
31—Glenn Davis 1986
Jeff Bagwell 1996
30—Glenn Davis 1988
Moises Alou 2000
29—Lee May 1972
28—Lee May 1973
27—Jimmy Wynn 1970
Glenn Davis 1987
26—Jimmy Wynn 1968
Cesar Cedeno 1974
25—Doug Rader 1970
Cesar Cedeno 1973
Carl Everett 1999

100-plus RBIs
135—Jeff Bagwell 1997
132—Jeff Bagwell 2000
126—Jeff Bagwell 1999
124—Moises Alou 1998
122—Richard Hidalgo 2000
120—Jeff Bagwell 1996
116—Jeff Bagwell 1994
114—Moises Alou 2000
113—Derek Bell 1996
111—Jeff Bagwell 1998
110—Bob Watson 1977
108—Derek Bell 1998
Carl Everett 1999
107—Jimmy Wynn 1967
105—Lee May 1973
102—Cesar Cedeno 1974
Bob Watson 1976
101—Glenn Davis 1986

20-plus victories
1969—Larry Dierker 20-13
1976—J.R. Richard 20-15
1979—Joe Niekro 21-11
1980—Joe Niekro 20-12
1989—Mike Scott 20-10
1999—Mike Hampton 22-4
Jose Lima 21-10

N.L. home run champions
None

N.L. RBI champions
1994—Jeff Bagwell 116

N.L. batting champions
None

N.L. ERA champions
1979—J.R. Richard 2.71
1981—Nolan Ryan 1.69
1986—Mike Scott 2.22
1987—Nolan Ryan 2.76
1990—Danny Darwin 2.21

N.L. strikeout champions
1978—J.R. Richard 303
1979—J.R. Richard 313
1986—Mike Scott 306
1987—Nolan Ryan 270
1988—Nolan Ryan 228

No-hit pitchers
(9 innings or more)
1963—Don Nottebart .... 4-1 vs. Philadelphia
1964—Ken Johnson .... 0-1 vs. Cincinnati
1967—Don Wilson .... 2-0 vs. Atlanta
1969—Don Wilson .... 4-0 at Cincinnati
1976—Larry Dierker .... 6-0 vs. Montreal
1979—Ken Forsch .... 6-0 vs. Atlanta
1981—Nolan Ryan .... 5-0 vs. Los Angeles
1986—Mike Scott .... 2-0 vs. San Francisco
1993—Darryl Kile .... 7-1 vs. New York

Longest hitting streaks
24—Tony Eusebio 2000
23—Art Howe 1981
Luis Gonzalez 1997
22—Cesar Cedeno 1977
21—Lee May 1973
Dickie Thon 1982
20—Rusty Staub 1967
Kevin Bass 1986
19—Bob Watson 1973
Cesar Cedeno 1976
Jose Cruz 1983
18—Terry Puhl 1978
Jeff Bagwell 1994, 2000
17—Rusty Staub 1966
Doug Rader 1970
Terry Puhl 1977
Bob Watson 1978
16—Roman Mejias 1962
Jim Wynn 1968
Joe Morgan 1971
Ray Knight 1982
Billy Hatcher 1987
Craig Biggio 2000
15—Sonny Jackson 1966
Enos Cabell 1979
Jose Cruz 1979
Craig Reynolds 1979
Bill Doran 1984
Richard Hidalgo 2000

Center fielder Cesar Cedeno brought a nice blend of power and speed to the Astros' lineup for more than a decade.

INDIVIDUAL SEASON, GAME RECORDS

Righthanded knuckleballer Joe Niekro reached the 20-victory plateau for the Astros in the 1979 and '80 seasons.

SEASON

Batting

At-bats	660	Enos Cabell	1978
Runs	152	Jeff Bagwell	2000
Hits	210	Craig Biggiol	1998
Singles	160	Sonny Jackson	1966
Doubles	56	Craig Biggio	1999
Triples	14	Roger Metzger	1973
Home runs	47	Jeff Bagwell	2000
Home runs, rookie	20	Glenn Davis	1985
Grand slams	2	Last by Sean Berry	1996
Total bases	363	Jeff Bagwell	2000
RBIs	135	Jeff Bagwell	1997
Walks	149	Jeff Bagwell	1999
Most strikeouts	145	Lee May	1972
Fewest strikeouts	13	Nellie Fox	1964
Batting average	.368	Jeff Bagwell	1994
Slugging pct.	.750	Jeff Bagwell	1994
Stolen bases	65	Gerald Young	1988

Pitching

Games	82	Juan Agosto	1990
Complete games	20	Larry Dierker	1969
Innings	305.1	Larry Dierker	1969
Wins	22	Mike Hampton	1999
Losses	20	Dick Farrell	1962
Winning pct.	.909 (10-1)	Randy Johnson	1998
Walks	151	J.R. Richard	1976
Strikeouts	313	J.R. Richard	1979
Shutouts	6	Dave A. Roberts	1973
Home runs allowed	48	Jose Lima	2000
Lowest ERA	1.69	Nolan Ryan	1981
Saves	39	Billy Wagner	1999

GAME

Batting

Runs	5	Last by Craig Biggio	6-4-96
Hits	6	Joe Morgan	7-8-65
Doubles	4	Jeff Bagwell	6-14-96
Triples	3	Craig Reynolds	5-16-81
Home runs	3	Last by Jeff Bagwell	7-9-99
RBIs	7	Last by Jeff Bagwell	8-13-2000
Total bases	13	Lee May	6-21-73
		Jeff Bagwell	6-24-94
Stolen bases	4	Last by Roger Cedeno	4-22-2000

CAREER LEADERS

BATTING

Games

Jose Cruz	1,870
Craig Biggio	1,800
Terry Puhl	1,516
Cesar Cedeno	1,512
Jeff Bagwell	1,476
Jimmy Wynn	1,426
Bob Watson	1,381
Doug Rader	1,178
Craig Reynolds	1,170
Bill Doran	1,165

At-bats

Craig Biggio	6,766
Jose Cruz	6,629
Cesar Cedeno	5,732
Jeff Bagwell	5,349
Jimmy Wynn	5,063
Bob Watson	4,883
Terry Puhl	4,837
Bill Doran	4,264
Doug Rader	4,232
Enos Cabell	4,005

Runs

Craig Biggio	1,187
Jeff Bagwell	1,073
Cesar Cedeno	890
Jose Cruz	871
Jimmy Wynn	829
Terry Puhl	676
Bob Watson	640
Bill Doran	611
Joe Morgan	597
Enos Cabell	522

Hits

Craig Biggio	1,969
Jose Cruz	1,937
Cesar Cedeno	1,659
Jeff Bagwell	1,630
Bob Watson	1,448
Terry Puhl	1,357
Jimmy Wynn	1,291
Bill Doran	1,139
Enos Cabell	1,124
Doug Rader	1,060

Doubles

Craig Biggio	402
Jeff Bagwell	351
Cesar Cedeno	343
Jose Cruz	335
Bob Watson	241
Jimmy Wynn	228
Terry Puhl	226
Ken Caminiti	204
Doug Rader	197
Kevin Bass	194

Triples

Jose Cruz	80
Joe Morgan	63
Roger Metzger	62
Terry Puhl	56
Cesar Cedeno	55
Craig Reynolds	55
Enos Cabell	45
Craig Biggio	43
Steve Finley	41
Bill Doran	35

Home runs

Jeff Bagwell	310
Jimmy Wynn	223
Glenn Davis	166
Cesar Cedeno	163
Craig Biggio	160
Bob Watson	139
Jose Cruz	138
Doug Rader	128
Ken Caminiti	103
Kevin Bass	87

Total bases

Jeff Bagwell	2,955
Craig Biggio	2,937
Jose Cruz	2,846
Cesar Cedeno	2,601
Jimmy Wynn	2,252
Bob Watson	2,166
Terry Puhl	1,881
Doug Rader	1,701
Bill Doran	1,596
Ken Caminiti	1,578

Runs batted in

Jeff Bagwell	1,093
Jose Cruz	942
Bob Watson	782
Cesar Cedeno	778
Craig Biggio	741
Jimmy Wynn	719
Doug Rader	600
Ken Caminiti	546
Glenn Davis	518
Kevin Bass	468

Extra-base hits

Jeff Bagwell	683
Craig Biggio	605
Cesar Cedeno	561
Jose Cruz	553
Jimmy Wynn	483
Bob Watson	410
Doug Rader	355
Terry Puhl	344
Glenn Davis	326
Ken Caminiti	321

Batting average
(Minimum 500 games)

Jeff Bagwell	.305
Bob Watson	.297
Jose Cruz	.292
Craig Biggio	.291
Cesar Cedeno	.289
Bill Spiers	.285
Derek Bell	.284
Jesus Alou	.282
Enos Cabell	.281
Terry Puhl	.281
Steve Finley	.281

Stolen bases

Cesar Cedeno	487
Craig Biggio	358
Jose Cruz	288
Joe Morgan	219
Terry Puhl	217
Enos Cabell	191
Bill Doran	191
Jimmy Wynn	180
Jeff Bagwell	167
Gerald Young	153

PITCHING

Earned-run average
(Minimum 500 innings)

Joe Sambito	2.42
Dave Smith	2.53
Mike Cuellar	2.74
Nolan Ryan	3.13
Don Wilson	3.15
J.R. Richard	3.15
Ken Forsch	3.18
Danny Darwin	3.21
Joe Niekro	3.22
Larry Dierker	3.28

Wins

Joe Niekro	144
Larry Dierker	137
Mike Scott	110
J.R. Richard	107
Nolan Ryan	106
Don Wilson	104
Bob Knepper	93
Shane Reynolds	86
Ken Forsch	78
Darryl Kile	71

Losses

Larry Dierker	117
Joe Niekro	116
Bob Knepper	100
Nolan Ryan	94
Don Wilson	92
Ken Forsch	81
Mike Scott	81
J.R. Richard	71
Shane Reynolds	69
Darryl Kile	65

Innings pitched

Larry Dierker	2,294.1
Joe Niekro	2,270.0
Nolan Ryan	1,854.2
Don Wilson	1,748.1
Bob Knepper	1,738.0
Mike Scott	1,704.0
J.R. Richard	1,606.0
Ken Forsch	1,493.2
Shane Reynolds	1,365.2
Darryl Kile	1,200.0

Strikeouts

Nolan Ryan	1,866
J.R. Richard	1,493
Larry Dierker	1,487
Mike Scott	1,318
Don Wilson	1,283
Joe Niekro	1,178
Shane Reynolds	1,160
Darryl Kile	973
Bob Knepper	946
Ken Forsch	815

Bases on balls

Joe Niekro	818
Nolan Ryan	796
J.R. Richard	770
Larry Dierker	695
Don Wilson	640
Darryl Kile	562
Bob Knepper	521
Mike Scott	505
Tom Griffin	441
Ken Forsch	428

Games

Dave Smith	563
Ken Forsch	421
Joe Niekro	397
Joe Sambito	353
Larry Dierker	345
Bob Knepper	284
Nolan Ryan	282
Jim Ray	280
Xavier Hernandez	273
Larry Andersen	268

Shutouts

Larry Dierker	25
Joe Niekro	21
Mike Scott	21
Don Wilson	20
J.R. Richard	19
Bob Knepper	18
Nolan Ryan	13
Dave A. Roberts	11
Ken Forsch	9
Tom Griffin	9

Saves

Dave Smith	199
Billy Wagner	107
Fred Gladding	76
Joe Sambito	72
Doug Jones	62
Ken Forsch	50
Frank DiPino	43
Todd Jones	39
Hal Woodeshick	36
John Hudek	29

TEAM SEASON, GAME RECORDS

SEASON

Batting

Most at-bats	5,641	1998
Most runs	938	2000
Fewest runs	394	1981
Most hits	1,578	1998
Most singles	1,097	1984
Most doubles	326	1998
Most triples	67	1980, 1984
Most home runs	249	2000
Fewest home runs	45	1981
Most grand slams	6	1989
Most pinch-hit home runs	9	1995
Most total bases	2,655	2000
Most stolen bases	198	1988
Highest batting average	.280	1998
Lowest batting average	.220	1963
Highest slugging pct	.477	2000

Pitching

Lowest ERA	2.66	1981
Highest ERA	5.42	2000
Most complete games	55	1979
Most shutouts	19	1979, 1981, 1986
Most saves	51	1986
Most walks	679	1975
Most strikeouts	1,221	1969

Fielding

Most errors	174	1966
Fewest errors	76	1994
Most double plays	175	1999
Highest fielding average	.983	1971, 1994, 1998, 1999

General

Most games won	102	1998
Most games lost	97	1965, 1975, 1991
Highest win pct	.630	1998
Lowest win pct	.398	1975

GAME, INNING

Batting

Most runs, game	19	6-25-95, 5-11-99
Most runs, inning	12	5-31-75
Most hits, game	25	5-30-76, 7-2-76
Most home runs, game	7	9-9-2000
Most total bases, game	44	9-9-2000

When outfielder Jose Cruz left Houston after the 1987 season, he held many career records.

ASTROS YEAR-BY-YEAR

Year	W	L	Place	Games Back	Manager	Leaders: Batting avg.	Hits	Home runs	RBIs	Wins	ERA
								COLT .45s			
1962	64	96	8th	36½	Craft	Mejias, .286	Mejias, 162	Mejias, 24	Mejias, 76	Bruce, Farrell 10	Farrell, 3.01
1963	66	96	9th	33	Craft	Spangler, .281	Warwick, 134	Bateman, 10	Bateman, 59	Farrell, 14	Woodeshick, 1.97
1964	66	96	9th	27	Craft, Harris	Aspromonte, .280	Aspromonte, 155	Bond, 20	Bond, 85	Bruce, 15	Larsen, 2.26
1965	65	97	9th	32	Harris	Wynn, .275	Morgan, 163	Wynn, 22	Wynn, 73	Farrell, 11	Raymond, 2.90
1966	72	90	8th	23	Hatton	Jackson, .292	Jackson, 174	Wynn, 18	Bateman 70	Giusti, 15	Cuellar, 2.22
1967	69	93	9th	32½	Hatton	Staub, .333	Staub, 182	Wynn, 37	Wynn, 107	Cuellar, 16	Wilson, 2.79
1968	72	90	10th	25	Hatton, Walker	Staub, .291	Staub, 172	Wynn, 26	Staub, 72	Wilson, 13	Cuellar, 2.74
								WEST DIVISION			
1969	81	81	5th	12	Walker	Menke, .Wynn, .269	Menke, 149	Wynn, 33	Menke, 90	Dierker, 20	Dierker, 2.33
1970	79	83	4th	23	Walker	Cedeno, .310	Menke, 171	Wynn, 27	Menke, 92	Dierker, 16	Ray, 3.26
1971	79	83	*4th	11	Walker	Watson, .288	Cedeno, 161	Morgan, 13	Cedeno, 81	Wilson, 16	Ray, 2.12
1972	84	69	2nd	10½	Walker, Durocher, Parker	Cedeno, .320	Cedeno, 179	May, 29	May, 98	Dierker, Wilson 15	Wilson, 2.68
1973	82	80	4th	17	Durocher, Gomez	Cedeno, .320	Watson, 179	May, 28	May, 105	Roberts, 17	Roberts, 2.86
1974	81	81	4th	21	Gomez	Gross, .314	Gross, 185	Cedeno, 26	Cedeno, 102	Griffin, 14	Forsch, 2.79
1975	64	97	6th	43½	Gomez, Virdon	Watson, .324	Watson, 157	C. Johnson, 20	Watson, 85	Dierker, 14	Forsch, 3.22
1976	80	82	3rd	22	Virdon	Watson, .313	Watson, 183	Cedeno, 18	Watson, 102	Richard, 20	Forsch, 2.15
1977	81	81	3rd	17	Virdon	Cruz, .299	Cabell, 176	Watson, 22	Watson, 110	Richard, 18	Richard, 2.97
1978	74	88	5th	21	Virdon	Cruz, .315	Cabell, 195	Watson, 14	Cruz, 83	Richard, 18	Forsch, 2.70
1979	89	73	2nd	1½	Virdon	Leonard, .290	Puhl, 172	Cruz, 9	Cruz, 72	Niekro, 21	Sambito, 1.77
1980	93	70	†‡1st	+1	Virdon	Cedeno, .309	Cruz, 185	Puhl, 13	Cruz, 91	Niekro, 20	Richard, 1.89
1981	61	49	§3rd/1st	—	Virdon	Howe, .296	Cruz, 109	Cruz, 13	Cruz, 55	Ryan, Sutton 11	Ryan, 1.69
1982	77	85	5th	12	Virdon, Lillis	Knight, .294	Knight, 179	Garner, 13	Garner, 83	Niekro, 17	Niekro, 2.47
1983	85	77	3rd	6	Lillis	Cruz, .318	Cruz, 189	Thon, 20	Cruz, 92	Niekro, 15	Ryan, 2.98
1984	80	82	*2nd	12	Lillis	Cruz, .312	Cruz, 187	Cruz, 12	Cruz, 95	Niekro, 16	Dawley, 1.93
1985	83	79	*3rd	12	Lillis	Cruz, .300	Doran, 166	Davis, 20	Cruz, 79	Scott, 18	Scott, 3.29
1986	96	66	‡1st	+10	Lanier	Walling, .312	Bass, 184	Davis, 31	Davis, 101	Scott, 18	Scott, 2.22
1987	76	86	3rd	14	Lanier	Hatcher, .296	Doran, 177	Davis, 27	Davis, 93	Scott, 16	Ryan, 2.76
1988	82	80	5th	12½	Lanier	Ramirez, .276	Ramirez, 156	Davis, 30	Davis, 99	Knepper, Scott 14	Agosto, 2.26
1989	86	76	3rd	6	Howe	Davis, .269	Davis, 156	Davis, 34	Davis, 89	Scott, 20	Darwin, 2.36
1990	75	87	*4th	16	Howe	Biggio, .276	Biggio, 153	Stubbs, 23	Stubbs, 71	Darwin, Portugal 11	Darwin, 2.21
1991	65	97	6th	29	Howe	Biggio, .295	Finley, 170	Bagwell, 15	Bagwell, 82	Harnisch, 12	Harnisch, 2.70
1992	81	81	4th	17	Howe	Caminiti, .294	Finley, 177	Anthony, 19	Bagwell, 96	D. Jones, 11	D. Jones, 1.85
1993	85	77	3rd	19	Howe	Bagwell, .320	Biggio, 175	Biggio, 21	Bagwell, 88	Portugal, 18	Hernandez, 2.61
								CENTRAL DIVISION			
1994	66	49	2nd	½	Collins	Bagwell, .368	Bagwell, 147	Bagwell, 39	Bagwell, 116	Drabek, 12	Drabek, 2.84
1995	76	68	2nd	9	Collins	Bell, .334	Biggio, 167	Biggio, 22	Bagwell, 87	Reynolds, 10	Veres, 2.26
1996	82	80	2nd	6	Collins	Bagwell, .315	Bagwell, 179	Bagwell, 31	Bagwell, 120	Reynolds, 16	Hampton, 3.59
1997	84	78	∞1st	+5	Dierker	Biggio, .309	Biggio, 191	Bagwell, 43	Bagwell, 135	Kile, 19	Kile, 2.57
1998	102	60	∞1st	+12½	Dierker	Biggio, .325	Biggio, 210	Alou, 38	Alou, 124	Reynolds, 19	Hampton, 3.36
1999	97	65	∞1st	+1½	Dierker	Everett, .325	Biggio, 188	Bagwell, 42	Bagwell, 126	Hampton, 22	Hampton, 2.90
2000	72	90	4th	23	Dierker	M. Alou, .355	Bagwell, 183	Bagwell, 47	Bagwell, 132	Elarton, 17	Elarton, 4.83

* Tied for position. † Won division playoff. ‡ Lost Championship Series. § First half 28-29; second half 33-20. ∞ Lost Division Series.

Note: Batting average minimum 350 at-bats; ERA minimum 90 innings pitched.

Eddie Bressoud

HOUSTON became part of the National League family in a two-team 1962 expansion that marked the first league structural change since 1900. Houston and New York were granted franchise approval on October 16, 1960, bringing the N.L. membership roster to 10.

The Colt .45s stocked their first roster with 23 selections in the October 10, 1961, expansion draft, leading off with infielder Eddie Bressoud. Houston made its Major League debut a successful one, defeating the Chicago Cubs, 11-2, at Colt Stadium en route to a 64-96 first-year record.

Expansion draft (October 10, 1961)

Players

Player	Club	Position
Joe Amalfitano	San Francisco	infield
Bob Aspromonte	Los Angeles	infield
*Eddie Bressoud	San Francisco	infield
Dick Gernert	Cincinnati	infield
Al Heist	Chicago	outfield
Bob Lillis	St. Louis	infield
Norm Larker	Los Angeles	infield
Roman Mejias	Pittsburgh	outfield
Ed Olivares	St. Louis	infield
Merritt Ranew	Milwaukee	catcher
Hal Smith	Pittsburgh	catcher
Al Spangler	Milwaukee	outfield
Don Taussig	St. Louis	outfield
George Williams	Philadelphia	infield

Pitchers

Pitcher	Club	Throws
Dick Drott	Chicago	righthanded
Dick Farrell	Los Angeles	righthanded
Jim Golden	Los Angeles	righthanded
Jesse Hickman	Philadelphia	righthanded
Ken Johnson	Cincinnati	righthanded
Sam Jones	San Francisco	righthanded
Paul Roof	Milwaukee	righthanded
Bobby Shantz	Pittsburgh	lefthanded
Jim Umbricht	Pittsburgh	righthanded

*First pick

Opening day lineup

April 10, 1962

Bob Aspromonte, third base
Al Spangler, center field
Roman Mejias, right field
Norm Larker, first base
Jim Pendleton, left field
Hal Smith, catcher
Joe Amalfitano, second base
Don Buddin, shortstop
Bobby Shantz, pitcher

Bob Aspromonte

Colt .45s firsts

First hit: Bob Aspromonte, April 10, 1962, vs. Chicago
First home run: Roman Mejias, April 10, 1962, vs. Chicago
First RBI: Al Spangler, April 10, 1962, vs. Chicago
First win: Bobby Shantz, April 10, 1962, vs. Chicago
First shutout: Hal Woodeshick (8 inn.), Dick Farrell (1) April 11, 1962, 2-0 vs. Chicago
First CG shutout: Dean Stone, April 12, 1962, 2-0 vs. Chicago

Los Angeles Dodgers

Manager Walter Alston.

FRANCHISE CHRONOLOGY

First season: 1884, in Brooklyn, as a member of the American Association. The first-year "Bridegrooms" won only 40 games and finished ninth in the league's 13-team field.

1885-1900: Brooklyn celebrated its first A.A. pennant in 1889 by transferring to the more prestigious National League. The Bridegrooms lost their N.L. opener to Boston, 15-9, but went on to claim another pennant with an 86-43 record. Renamed "Superbas," they would close out the century with consecutive pennants under manager Ned Hanlon.

1901-57: The modern-era "Dodgers" might have more aptly been named "Bridesmaids." From 1916 to 1954, they finished second seven times and won seven N.L. pennants, losing every World Series appearance. "Wait til next year" became the rallying cry of frustrated Brooklyn fans, who nevertheless supported their beloved "Bums" with a fervor unmatched in major league baseball. Walter Alston's Dodgers finally broke through with a victory in the 1955 World Series against the hated Yankees, but two years later owner Peter O'Malley moved his franchise to the greener pastures of the West Coast.

1958-present: The Dodgers became less lovable but more efficient in Los Angeles. In 42 seasons, they have claimed nine N.L. pennants, five World Series championships and nine West Division titles while finishing second 14 times. Incredibly, that success has been choreographed by four full-time managers: Alston (1958-76), Tom Lasorda (1976-96), Bill Russell, who replaced the ailing Lasorda midway through the 1996 season, and Davey Johnson in 1999 and 2000.

DODGERS VS. OPPONENTS BY DECADE

	Braves	Cardinals	Cubs	Giants	Phillies	Pirates	Reds	Astros	Mets	Expos	Padres	Marlins	Rockies	Brewers	D'backs	Interleague	Decade Record
1900-09	114-95	115-93	74-135	80-128	93-112	76-132	97-114										649-809
1910-19	103-105	105-104	98-117	88-125	99-110	110-105	93-121										696-787
1920-29	128-90	101-119	104-115	106-113	133-87	97-122	96-122										765-768
1930-39	103-117	91-127	89-127	98-120	128-89	113-105	112-108										734-793
1940-49	129-90	90-132	119-101	137-82	162-58	124-96	133-87										894-646
1950-59	129-92	135-85	134-85	117-106	128-92	141-79	129-91										913-630
1960-69	99-89	91-91	102-80	83-108	106-76	100-82	94-94	87-57	94-44	10-2	12-6						878-729
1970-79	106-70	67-53	68-52	108-72	63-56	65-55	79-97	104-76	68-52	73-47	109-71						910-701
1980-89	105-69	62-56	61-57	95-79	55-59	61-53	98-80	93-82	50-63	67-48	78-95						825-741
1990-99	55-68	52-55	61-47	70-70	61-54	61-50	65-57	57-65	58-53	57-56	68-71	35-35	46-40	12-6	14-11	25-19	797-757
2000-	2-7	3-6	6-3	7-5	5-4	4-5	5-4	6-3	4-5	5-3	8-5	7-2	9-4	3-4	6-7	6-9	86-76
Totals	1073-892	912-921	916-919	989-1008	1033-797	952-884	1001-975	347-283	274-217	212-156	275-248	42-37	55-44	15-10	20-18	31-28	8147-7437

Interleague results: 11-9 vs. Angels; 6-7 vs. Athletics; 7-5 vs. Mariners; 7-6 vs. Rangers.

MANAGERS

(Brooklyn Dodgers, 1884-1957)

Name	*Years*	*Record*
George Taylor	1884	40-64
Charlie Hackett	1885	15-22
Charlie Byrne	1885-87	174-172
Bill McGunnigle	1888-90	268-138
Monte Ward	1891-92	156-135
Dave Foutz	1893-96	264-257
Billy Barnie	1897-98	76-91
Ned Hanlon	1899-1905	511-488
Patsy Donovan	1906-08	184-270
Harry Lumley	1909	55-98
Bill Dahlen	1910-13	251-355
Wilbert Robinson	1914-31	1375-1341
Max Carey	1932-33	146-161
Casey Stengel	1934-36	208-251
Burleigh Grimes	1937-38	131-171
Leo Durocher	1939-46, 1948	738-565
Clyde Sukeforth	1947	2-0
Burt Shotton	1947, 1948-50	326-215
Chuck Dressen	1951-53	298-166
Walter Alston	1954-76	2040-1613
Tom Lasorda	1976-96	1599-1439
Bill Russell	1996-98	173-149
Glenn Hoffman	1998	47-41
Davey Johnson	1999-2000	163-162

WORLD SERIES CHAMPIONS

Year	*Loser*	*Length*	*MVP*
1955	N.Y. Yankees	7 games	Podres
1959	Chicago	6 games	Sherry
1963	N.Y. Yankees	4 games	Koufax
1965	Minnesota	7 games	Koufax
1981	N.Y. Yankees	6 games	Cey, Guerrero, Yeager
1988	Oakland	5 games	Hershiser

A.A. PENNANT WINNERS

Year	*Record*	*Manager*	*Series Result*
1889	93-44	McGunnigle	None

N.L. PENNANT WINNERS

Year	*Record*	*Manager*	*Series Result*
1890	86-43	McGunnigle	None
1899	101-47	Hanlon	None
1900	82-54	Hanlon	None
1916	94-60	Robinson	Lost to Red Sox
1920	93-61	Robinson	Lost to Indians
1941	100-54	Durocher	Lost to Yankees
1947	94-60	Sukeforth, Shotton	Lost to Yankees
1949	97-57	Shotton	Lost to Yankees
1952	96-57	Dressen	Lost to Yankees
1953	105-49	Dressen	Lost to Yankees
1955	98-55	Alston	Defeated Yankees
1956	93-61	Alston	Lost to Yankees
1959	88-68	Alston	Defeated White Sox
1963	99-63	Alston	Defeated Yankees
1965	97-65	Alston	Defeated Twins
1966	95-67	Alston	Lost to Orioles
1974	102-60	Alston	Lost to A's
1977	98-64	Lasorda	Lost to Yankees

N.L. PENNANT WINNERS—*cont'd.*

Year	*Record*	*Manager*	*Series Result*
1978	95-67	Lasorda	Lost to Yankees
1981	63-47	Lasorda	Defeated Yankees
1988	94-67	Lasorda	Defeated A's

WEST DIVISION CHAMPIONS

Year	*Record*	*Manager*	*NLCS Result*
1974	102-60	Alston	Defeated Pirates
1977	98-64	Lasorda	Defeated Phillies
1978	95-67	Lasorda	Defeated Phillies
*1981	63-47	Lasorda	Defeated Expos
1983	91-71	Lasorda	Lost to Phillies
1985	95-67	Lasorda	Lost to Cardinals
1988	94-67	Lasorda	Defeated Mets
1994	58-56	Lasorda	None
1995	78-66	Lasorda	Lost in Division Series

* First-half champion; won division playoff from Astros.

WILD-CARD QUALIFIERS

Year	*Record*	*Manager*	*Div. Series Result*
1996	90-72	Lasorda, Russell	Lost to Braves

ATTENDANCE HIGHS

Total	*Season*	*Park*
3,608,881	1982	Dodger Stadium
3,510,313	1983	Dodger Stadium
3,348,170	1991	Dodger Stadium
3,347,845	1978	Dodger Stadium
3,318,886	1997	Dodger Stadium

BALLPARK CHRONOLOGY

Dodger Stadium (1962-present)

Capacity: 56,000.
First game: Cincinnati 6, Dodgers 3 (April 10, 1962).
First batter: Eddie Kasko, Reds.
First hit: Eddie Kasko, Reds (double).
First run: Eddie Kasko, Reds (1st inning).
First home run: Wally Post, Reds.
First winning pitcher: Bob Purkey, Reds.
First-season attendance: 2,755,184.

Washington Park, Brooklyn (1884-90)

First game: Brooklyn (A.A.) 11, Washington 3 (May 5, 1884).

Eastern Park, Brooklyn (1891-97)

First game: New York 6, Brooklyn 5 (April 27, 1891).

Washington Park II, Brooklyn (1898-1912)

First game: Philadelphia 6, Brooklyn 4 (April 30, 1898).

Ebbets Field, Brooklyn (1913-57)

Capacity: 31,497.
First game: Philadelphia 1, Dodgers 0 (April 9, 1913).
First-season attendance: 347,000.

Roosevelt Stadium, Jersey City (1956-57)

(Site of 15 games over two seasons)
Capacity: 24,167.
First game: Dodgers 5, Philadelphia 4, 10 innings (April 19, 1956).

Los Angeles Memorial Coliseum (1958-61)

Capacity: 93,600.
First game: Dodgers 6, San Francisco 5 (April 18, 1958).
First-season attendance: 1,845,556.

N.L. MVPs

Dolph Camilli, 1B, 1941
Jackie Robinson, 2B, 1949
Roy Campanella, C, 1951
Roy Campanella, C, 1953
Roy Campanella, C, 1955
Don Newcombe, P, 1956
Maury Wills, SS, 1962
Sandy Koufax, P, 1963
Steve Garvey, 1B, 1974
Kirk Gibson, OF, 1988

CY YOUNG WINNERS

Don Newcombe, RH, 1956
Don Drysdale, RH, 1962
Sandy Koufax, LH, 1963
Sandy Koufax, LH, 1965
Sandy Koufax, LH, 1966
Mike Marshall, RH, 1974
Fernando Valenzuela, LH, 1981
Orel Hershiser, RH, 1988

ROOKIES OF THE YEAR

Jackie Robinson, 1B, 1947
Don Newcombe, P, 1949
Joe Black, P, 1952
Jim Gilliam, 2B, 1953
Frank Howard, OF, 1960
Jim Lefebvre, 2B, 1965
Ted Sizemore, 2B, 1969
Rick Sutcliffe, P, 1979
Steve Howe, P, 1980
Fernando Valenzuela, P, 1981
Steve Sax, 2B, 1982
Eric Karros, 1B, 1992
Mike Piazza, C, 1993
Raul Mondesi, OF, 1994
Hideo Nomo, P, 1995
Todd Hollandsworth, OF, 1996

MANAGERS OF THE YEAR

Tom Lasorda, 1983
Tom Lasorda, 1988

RETIRED UNIFORMS

No.	*Name*	*Pos.*
1	Pee Wee Reese	SS
2	Tommy Lasorda	Man.
4	Duke Snider	OF
19	Jim Gilliam	IF
20	Don Sutton	P
24	Walter Alston	Man.
32	Sandy Koufax	P
39	Roy Campanella	C
42	Jackie Robinson	2B
53	Don Drysdale	P

MILESTONE PERFORMANCES

30-plus home runs

- 43—Duke Snider ... 1956
- Gary Sheffield ... 2000
- 42—Duke Snider ... 1953, 1955
- Gil Hodges ... 1954
- 41—Roy Campanella ... 1953
- 40—Gil Hodges ... 1951
- Duke Snider ... 1954, 1957
- Mike Piazza ... 1997
- 36—Mike Piazza ... 1996
- 35—Babe Herman ... 1930
- Mike Piazza ... 1993
- 34—Dolph Camilli ... 1941
- Eric Karros ... 1996
- Eric Karros ... 1999
- Gary Sheffield ... 1999
- 33—Roy Campanella ... 1951
- Steve Garvey ... 1977
- Pedro Guerrero ... 1985
- Raul Mondesi ... 1999
- 32—Gil Hodges ... 1950, 1952, 1956
- Roy Campanella ... 1955
- Jimmy Wynn ... 1974
- Reggie Smith ... 1977
- Pedro Guerrero ... 1982, 1983
- Eric Karros ... 1995
- Mike Piazza ... 1995
- 31—Roy Campanella ... 1950
- Duke Snider ... 1950
- Gil Hodges ... 1953
- Frank Howard ... 1962
- Eric Karros ... 1997, 2000
- Todd Zeile ... 1997
- 30—Dusty Baker ... 1977
- Ron Cey ... 1977
- Raul Mondesi ... 1997, 1998

100-plus RBIs

- 153—Tommy Davis ... 1962
- 142—Roy Campanella ... 1953
- 136—Duke Snider ... 1955
- 130—Jack Fournier ... 1925
- Babe Herman ... 1930
- Gil Hodges ... 1954
- Duke Snider ... 1954
- 126—Glenn Wright ... 1930
- Duke Snider ... 1953
- 124—Dixie Walker ... 1945
- Jackie Robinson ... 1949
- Mike Piazza ... 1997
- 123—Hack Wilson ... 1932
- 122—Gil Hodges ... 1953
- 120—Dolph Camilli ... 1941
- 119—Frank Howard ... 1962
- 116—Jack Fournier ... 1924
- Dixie Walker ... 1946
- 115—Gil Hodges ... 1949
- Steve Garvey ... 1977
- 113—Babe Herman ... 1929
- Del Bissonette ... 1930
- Gil Hodges ... 1950
- Steve Garvey ... 1978
- 112—Zack Wheat ... 1922
- Mike Piazza ... 1993
- Eric Karros ... 1999
- 111—Wes Parker ... 1970
- Steve Garvey ... 1974
- Eric Karros ... 1996
- 110—Luis Olmo ... 1945
- Ron Cey ... 1977
- Steve Garvey ... 1979
- 109—Dolph Camilli ... 1942
- Gary Sheffield ... 2000
- 108—Roy Campanella ... 1951
- Jimmy Wynn ... 1974
- 107—Duke Snider ... 1950
- Roy Campanella ... 1955
- 106—Del Bissonette ... 1928
- Carl Furillo ... 1949, 1950
- Steve Garvey ... 1980
- Eric Karros ... 2000
- 105—Eric Karros ... 1995
- Mike Piazza ... 1996
- 104—Dolph Camilli ... 1939
- Eric Karros ... 1997
- 103—Zack Wheat ... 1925
- Gil Hodges ... 1951
- Pedro Guerrero ... 1983
- 102—Jack Fournier ... 1923
- Sam Leslie ... 1934
- Gil Hodges ... 1952, 1955
- 101—Duke Snider ... 1951, 1956
- Ron Cey ... 1975
- Gary Sheffield ... 1999
- 100—Dolph Camilli ... 1938
- Billy Herman ... 1943
- Pedro Guerrero ... 1982

20-plus victories

- 1890— Tom Lovett ... 30-11
- Adonis Terry ... 26-16
- Bob Caruthers ... 23-11
- 1891— Tom Lovett ... 23-19
- 1892— George Haddock ... 29-13
- Ed Stein ... 27-16
- 1893— Brickyard Kennedy ... 25-20
- 1894— Ed Stein ... 26-14
- Brickyard Kennedy ... 24-20
- 1899— Jim Hughes ... 28-6
- Jack Dunn ... 23-13
- Brickyard Kennedy ... 22-9
- 1900— Joseph McGinnity ... 28-8
- Brickyard Kennedy ... 20-13
- 1901— William Donovan ... 25-15
- 1903— Henry Schmidt ... 21-13
- 1911— Nap Rucker ... 22-18
- 1914— Jeff Pfeffer ... 23-12
- 1916— Jeff Pfeffer ... 25-11
- 1920— Burleigh Grimes ... 23-11
- 1921— Burleigh Grimes ... 22-13
- 1922— Walter Reuther ... 21-12
- 1923— Burleigh Grimes ... 21-18
- 1924— Dazzy Vance ... 28-6
- Burleigh Grimes ... 22-13
- 1925— Dazzy Vance ... 22-9
- 1928— Dazzy Vance ... 22-10
- 1932— William Clark ... 20-12
- 1939— Luke Hamlin ... 20-13
- 1941— Kirby Higbe ... 22-9
- Whit Wyatt ... 22-10
- 1947— Ralph Branca ... 21-12
- 1951— Preacher Roe ... 22-3
- Don Newcombe ... 20-9
- 1953— Carl Erskine ... 20-6
- 1955— Don Newcombe ... 20-5
- 1956— Don Newcombe ... 27-7
- 1962— Don Drysdale ... 25-9
- 1963— Sandy Koufax ... 25-5
- 1965— Sandy Koufax ... 26-8
- Don Drysdale ... 23-12
- 1966— Sandy Koufax ... 27-9
- 1969— Claude Osteen ... 20-15
- Bill Singer ... 20-12
- 1971— Al Downing ... 20-9
- 1972— Claude Osteen ... 20-11
- 1974— Andy Messersmith ... 20-6
- 1976— Don Sutton ... 21-10
- 1977— Tommy John ... 20-7
- 1986— Fernando Valenzuela ... 21-11
- 1988— Orel Hershiser ... 23-8
- 1990— Ramon Martinez ... 20-6

N.L. home run champions

- 1890— Oyster Burns ... *13
- 1903— Jimmy Sheckard ... 9
- 1904— Harry Lumley ... 9
- 1906— Tim Jordan ... 12
- 1908— Tim Jordan ... 12
- 1924— Jack Fournier ... 27
- 1941— Dolph Camilli ... 34
- 1956— Duke Snider ... 43

* Tied for league lead

N.L. RBI champions

- 1919— Hy Myers ... 73
- 1941— Dolph Camilli ... 120
- 1945— Dixie Walker ... 124
- 1953— Roy Campanella ... 142
- 1955— Duke Snider ... 136
- 1962— Tommy Davis ... 153

N.L. batting champions

- 1892— Dan Brouthers ... .335
- 1913— Jake Daubert ... .350
- 1914— Jake Daubert ... .329
- 1918— Zack Wheat ... .335
- 1932— Lefty O'Doul ... .368
- 1941— Pete Reiser ... .343
- 1944— Dixie Walker ... .357
- 1949— Jackie Robinson ... .342
- 1953— Carl Furillo ... .344
- 1962— Tommy Davis ... .346
- 1963— Tommy Davis ... .326

N.L. ERA champions

- 1924— Dazzy Vance ... 2.16
- 1928— Dazzy Vance ... 2.09
- 1930— Dazzy Vance ... 2.61
- 1957— Johnny Podres ... 2.66
- 1962— Sandy Koufax ... 2.54
- 1963— Sandy Koufax ... 1.88
- 1964— Sandy Koufax ... 1.74
- 1965— Sandy Koufax ... 2.04
- 1966— Sandy Koufax ... 1.73
- 1980— Don Sutton ... 2.20
- 1984— Alejandro Pena ... 2.48
- 2000— Kevin Brown ... 2.58

N.L. strikeout champions

- 1921— Burleigh Grimes ... 136
- 1922— Dazzy Vance ... 134
- 1923— Dazzy Vance ... 197
- 1924— Dazzy Vance ... 262
- 1925— Dazzy Vance ... 221
- 1926— Dazzy Vance ... 140
- 1927— Dazzy Vance ... 184
- 1928— Dazzy Vance ... 200
- 1936— Van Lingle Mungo ... 238
- 1951— Don Newcombe ... 164
- 1959— Don Drysdale ... 242
- 1960— Don Drysdale ... 246
- 1961— Sandy Koufax ... 269
- 1962— Don Drysdale ... 232
- 1963— Sandy Koufax ... 306
- 1965— Sandy Koufax ... 382
- 1966— Sandy Koufax ... 317
- 1981— Fernando Valenzuela ... 180
- 1995— Hideo Nomo ... 236

No-hit pitchers

(9 innings or more)

- 1891— Thomas Lovett ... 4-0 vs. New York
- 1906— Malcolm Eason ... 2-0 vs. St. Louis
- 1908— Nap Rucker ... 6-0 vs. Boston
- 1925— Dazzy Vance ... 10-1 vs. Philadelphia
- 1940— Tex Carleton ... 3-0 vs. Cincinnati
- 1946— Edward Head ... 5-0 vs. Boston
- 1948— Rex Barney ... 2-0 vs. New York
- 1952— Carl Erskine ... 5-0 vs. Chicago
- 1956— Carl Erskine ... 3-0 vs. New York
- Sal Maglie ... 5-0 vs. Philadelphia
- 1962— Sandy Koufax ... 5-0 vs. New York
- 1963— Sandy Koufax ... 8-0 vs. San Francisco
- 1964— Sandy Koufax ... 3-0 vs. Philadelphia
- 1965— Sandy Koufax ... 1-0 vs. Chicago (Perfect)
- 1970— Bill Singer ... 5-0 vs. Philadelphia
- 1980— Jerry Reuss ... 8-0 vs. San Francisco
- 1990— Fernando Valenzuela ... 6-0 vs. St. Louis
- 1992— Kevin Gross ... 2-0 vs. San Francisco
- 1995— Ramon Martinez ... 7-0 vs. Florida
- 1996— Hideo Nomo ... 9-0 vs. Colorado

Longest hitting streaks

- 31—Willie Davis ... 1969
- 29—Zack Wheat ... 1916
- 27—Joe Medwick ... 1942
- Duke Snider ... 1953
- 26—Willie Keeler ... 1902
- Zack Wheat ... 1918
- 25—Gink Hendrick ... 1929
- Buzz Boyle ... 1934
- Willie Davis ... 1971
- Steve Sax ... 1986
- 24—Willie Keeler ... 1899
- Zack Wheat ... 1924
- John Shelby ... 1988
- 23—Hy Myers ... 1915
- Brett Butler ... 1991
- 22—Duke Snider ... 1950
- Pee Wee Reese ... 1951
- 21—Jackie Robinson ... 1947
- Steve Garvey ... 1978
- 20—Jimmy Johnston ... 1921
- Zack Wheat ... 1923
- Johnny Frederick ... 1933
- Tommy Davis ... 1960, 1964
- Maury Wills ... 1965
- Steve Garvey ... 1978

INDIVIDUAL SEASON, GAME RECORDS

SEASON

Batting

At-bats	695	Maury Wills	1962
Runs	148	Hub Collins	1890
Hits	241	Babe Herman	1930
Singles	187	Willie Keeler	1899
Doubles	52	John Frederick	1929
Triples	26	George Treadway	1894
Home runs	43	Duke Snider	1956
		Gary Sheffield	2000
Home runs, rookie	35	Mike Piazza	1993
Grand slams	3	Last by Mike Piazza	1998
Total bases	416	Babe Herman	1930
RBIs	153	Tommy Davis	1962
Walks	148	Eddie Stanky	1945
Most strikeouts	149	Bill Grabarkewitz	1970
Fewest strikeouts	15	Jim Johnston	1923
Batting average	.393	Babe Herman	1930
Slugging pct.	.678	Babe Herman	1930
Stolen bases	104	Maury Wills	1962

Pitching

Games	106	Mike Marshall	1974
Complete games	40	Brickyard Kennedy	1893
Innings	382.2	Brickyard Kennedy	1893
Wins	30	Tom Lovett	1890
Losses	27	George Bell	1910
Winning pct.	.933 (14-1)	Phil Regan	1966
Walks	152	Bill Donovan	1901
Strikeouts	382	Sandy Koufax	1965
Shutouts	11	Sandy Koufax	1963
Home runs allowed	38	Don Sutton	1970
Lowest ERA	1.58	Rube Marquard	1916
Saves	44	Todd Worrell	1996

GAME

Batting

Runs	5	Last by Steve Garvey	8-28-77
Hits	6	Last by Willie Davis	5-24-73
Doubles	3	Last by Eric Karros	4-9-99
Triples	3	Jimmy Sheckard	4-18-01
Home runs	4	Gil Hodges	8-31-50
RBIs	9	Gil Hodges	8-31-50
		Ron Cey	7-31-74
Total bases	17	Gil Hodges	8-31-50
Stolen bases	5	Davey Lopes	8-20-74
		Davey Lopes	8-24-74

HISTORY

CAREER LEADERS

BATTING

Games
Zack Wheat 2,322
Bill Russell 2,181
Pee Wee Reese 2,166
Gil Hodges 2,006
Jim Gilliam 1,956
Willie Davis 1,952
Duke Snider 1,923
Carl Furillo 1,806
Steve Garvey 1,727
Maury Wills 1,593

At-bats
Zack Wheat 8,859
Pee Wee Reese 8,058
Willie Davis 7,495
Bill Russell 7,318
Jim Gilliam 7,119
Gil Hodges 6,881
Duke Snider 6,640
Steve Garvey 6,543
Carl Furillo 6,378
Maury Wills 6,156

Runs
Pee Wee Reese 1,338
Zack Wheat 1,255
Duke Snider 1,199
Jim Gilliam 1,163
Gil Hodges 1,088
Willie Davis 1,004
Jackie Robinson 947
Carl Furillo 895
Mike Griffin 882
Maury Wills 876

Hits
Zack Wheat 2,804
Pee Wee Reese 2,170
Willie Davis 2,091
Duke Snider 1,995
Steve Garvey 1,968
Bill Russell 1,926
Carl Furillo 1,910
Jim Gilliam 1,889
Gil Hodges 1,884
Maury Wills 1,732

Doubles
Zack Wheat 464
Duke Snider 343
Steve Garvey 333
Pee Wee Reese 330
Carl Furillo 324
Willie Davis 321
Jim Gilliam 304
Gil Hodges 294
Bill Russell 293
Dixie Walker 274

Triples
Zack Wheat 171
Willie Davis 110
Hy Myers 97
Jake Daubert 87
John Hummel 82
Duke Snider 82
Pee Wee Reese 80
Tom Daly 76
Jimmy Sheckard 76
Jimmy Johnston 73

Home runs
Duke Snider 389
Gil Hodges 361
Roy Campanella 242
Eric Karros 242
Ron Cey 228
Steve Garvey 211
Carl Furillo 192
Mike Piazza 177
Pedro Guerrero 171
Raul Mondesi 163

Total bases
Zack Wheat 4,003
Duke Snider 3,669
Gil Hodges 3,357
Willie Davis 3,094
Pee Wee Reese 3,038
Steve Garvey 3,004
Carl Furillo 2,922
Jim Gilliam 2,530
Bill Russell 2,471
Eric Karros 2,361

Runs batted in
Duke Snider 1,271
Gil Hodges 1,254
Zack Wheat 1,210
Carl Furillo 1,058
Steve Garvey 992
Pee Wee Reese 885
Roy Campanella 856
Willie Davis 849
Ron Cey 842
Eric Karros 840

Extra-base hits
Duke Snider 814
Zack Wheat 766
Gil Hodges 703
Willie Davis 585
Steve Garvey 579
Carl Furillo 572
Pee Wee Reese 536
Eric Karros 505
Ron Cey 469
Jackie Robinson 464

Batting average
(Minimum 500 games)
Willie Keeler .352
Babe Herman .339
Jack Fournier .337
Mike Piazza .331
Zack Wheat .317
Babe Phelps .315
Manny Mota .315
Fielder Jones .313
Jackie Robinson .311
Dixie Walker .311

Stolen bases
Maury Wills 490
Davey Lopes 418
Willie Davis 335
Tom Daly 298
Steve Sax 290
Mike Griffin 264
Pee Wee Reese 232
Jimmy Sheckard 212
Jim Gilliam 203
Zack Wheat 203

PITCHING

Earned-run average
(Minimum 1,000 innings)
Jeff Pfeffer 2.31
Nap Rucker 2.42
Sandy Koufax 2.76
George Bell 2.85
Whit Wyatt 2.86
Sherry Smith 2.91
Don Drysdale 2.95
Doc Scanlan 2.96
Tommy John 2.97
Bill Singer 3.03

Wins
Don Sutton 233
Don Drysdale 209
Dazzy Vance 190
Brickyard Kennedy 177
Sandy Koufax 165
Burleigh Grimes 158
Claude Osteen 147
Fernando Valenzuela 141
Johnny Podres 136
Orel Hershiser 135

Losses
Don Sutton 181
Don Drysdale 166
Brickyard Kennedy 149
Nap Rucker 134
Dazzy Vance 131
Claude Osteen 126
Burleigh Grimes 121
Fernando Valenzuela 116
Orel Hershiser 107
Johnny Podres 104

Innings pitched
Don Sutton 3,816.1
Don Drysdale 3,432.0
Brickyard Kennedy 2,866.0
Dazzy Vance 2,757.2
Burleigh Grimes 2,425.2
Claude Osteen 2,396.2
Nap Rucker 2,375.1
Fernando Valenzuela 2,348.2
Sandy Koufax 2,324.1
Orel Hershiser 2,180.2

Strikeouts
Don Sutton 2,696
Don Drysdale 2,486
Sandy Koufax 2,396
Dazzy Vance 1,918
Fernando Valenzuela 1,759
Orel Hershiser 1,456
Johnny Podres 1,331
Ramon Martinez 1,314
Bob Welch 1,292
Nap Rucker 1,217

Bases on balls
Brickyard Kennedy 1,130
Don Sutton 996
Fernando Valenzuela 915
Don Drysdale 855
Sandy Koufax 817
Dazzy Vance 764
Burleigh Grimes 744
Ramon Martinez 704
Nap Rucker 701
Van Lingle Mungo 697

Games
Don Sutton 550
Don Drysdale 518
Jim Brewer 474
Ron Perranoski 457
Clem Labine 425
Charlie Hough 401
Sandy Koufax 397
Brickyard Kennedy 382
Dazzy Vance 378
Johnny Podres 366

Shutouts
Don Sutton 52
Don Drysdale 49
Sandy Koufax 40
Nap Rucker 38
Claude Osteen 34
Fernando Valenzuela 29
Dazzy Vance 29
Jeff Pfeffer 25
Orel Hershiser 24
Johnny Podres 23
Bob Welch 23

Saves
Todd Worrell 127
Jim Brewer 125
Ron Perranoski 101
Jeff Shaw 86
Jay Howell 85
Clem Labine 83
Tom Niedenfuer 64
Charlie Hough 60
Steve Howe 59
Hugh Casey 50
Ed Roebuck 43

TEAM SEASON, GAME RECORDS

SEASON

Batting		
Most at-bats	5,642	1982
Most runs	1,021	1894
Fewest runs	375	1908
Most hits	1,654	1930
Most singles	1,223	1925
Most doubles	303	1930
Most triples	130	1894
Most home runs	211	2000
Fewest home runs	14	1915
Most grand slams	8	1952, 2000
Most pinch-hit home runs	12	2000
Most total bases	2,545	1953
Most stolen bases	409	1892
Highest batting average	.313	1894
Lowest batting average	.213	1908
Highest slugging pct.	.474	1953
Pitching		
Lowest ERA	2.12	1916
Highest ERA	4.92	1929
Most complete games	135	1904
Most shutouts	24	1963, 1988
Most saves	50	1996
Most walks	671	1946
Most strikeouts	1,212	1996
Fielding		
Most errors	432	1891
Fewest errors	106	1952
Most double plays	198	1958
Highest fielding average	.982	1952
General		
Most games won	105	1953
Most games lost	104	1905
Highest win pct..	.682	1953
Lowest win pct.	.316	1905

GAME, INNING

Batting		
Most runs, game	25	5-20-1896, 9-23-01
Most runs, inning	15	5-21-52
Most hits, game	28	6-23-30, 8-22-17
Most home runs, game	7	5-5-76, 5-25-79
Most total bases, game	48	8-20-74

Smooth-fielding first baseman Steve Garvey was a five-time member of the Dodgers' 100-RBI fraternity.

DODGERS YEAR-BY-YEAR

Year	W	L	Place	Games Back	Manager	Leaders: Batting avg.	Hits	Home runs	RBIs	Wins	ERA
						BROOKLYN DODGERS					
1901	79	57	3rd	9½	Hanlon	Sheckard, .354	Keeler, 202	Sheckard, 11	Sheckard, 104	Donovan, 25	Donovan, 2.77
1902	75	63	2nd	27½	Hanlon	Keeler, .333	Keeler, 186	McCreery, Sheckard, 4	Dahlen, 74	Kitson, 19	Newton, 2.42
1903	70	66	5th	19	Hanlon	Sheckard, .332	Sheckard, 171	Sheckard, 9	Doyle, 91	Schmidt, 22	O. Jones, 2.94
1904	56	97	6th	50	Hanlon	Lumley, .279	Lumley, 161	Lumley, 9	Lumley, 78	O. Jones, 17	Garvin, 1.68
1905	48	104	8th	56½	Hanlon	Lumley, .293	Lumley, 148	Lumley, 7	Batch, 49	Scanlan, 14	Scanlan, 2.92
1906	66	86	5th	50	Donovan	Lumley, .324	Lumley, 157	Jordan, 12	Jordan, 78	Scanlan, 18	Stricklett, 2.72
1907	65	83	5th	40	Donovan	Jordan, .274	Jordan, 133	Lumley, 9	Lumley, 66	Pastorius, 16	Rucker, 2.06
1908	53	101	7th	46	Donovan	Jordan, .247	Hummel, 143	Jordan, 12	Jordan, 60	Rucker, 17	Wilhelm, 1.87
1909	55	98	6th	55½	Lumley	Hummel, .280	Burch, 163	Hummel, 4	Hummel, 52	Bell, 16	Rucker, 2.24
1910	64	90	6th	40	Dahlen	Wheat, .284	Wheat, 172	Daubert, 8	Hummel, 74	Rucker, 17	Rucker, 2.58
1911	64	86	7th	33½	Dahlen	Daubert, .307	Daubert, 176	Erwin, 7	Wheat, 76	Rucker, 22	Ragan, 2.11
1912	58	95	7th	46	Dahlen	Daubert, .308	Daubert, 172	Wheat, 8	Daubert, 66	Rucker, 18	Rucker, 2.21
1913	65	84	6th	34½	Dahlen	Daubert, .350	Daubert, 178	Cutshaw, Stengel, Wheat, 7	Cutshaw, 80	Ragan, 15	Reulbach, 2.05
1914	75	79	5th	19½	Robinson	Daubert, .329	Wheat, 170	Wheat, 9	Wheat, 89	Pfeffer, 23	Pfeffer, 1.97
1915	80	72	3rd	10	Robinson	Daubert, .301	Daubert, 164	Wheat, 5	Wheat, 66	Pfeffer, 19	Pfeffer, 2.10
1916	94	60	1st	+2½	Robinson	Daubert, .316	Wheat, 177	Wheat, 9	Wheat, 73	Pfeffer, 25	Marquard, 1.58
1917	70	81	7th	26½	Robinson	Wheat, .312	Olson, 156	Hickman, Stengel, 6	Stengel, 73	Marquard, 19	Pfeffer, 2.23
1918	57	69	5th	25½	Robinson	Wheat, .335	Wheat, 137	Myers, 4	Wheat, 51	Grimes, 19	Grimes, 2.14
1919	69	71	5th	27	Robinson	Myers, .307	Olson, 164	Griffith, 6	Myers, 73	Pfeffer, 17	S. Smith, 2.24
1920	93	61	1st	+7	Robinson	Wheat, .328	Wheat, 191	Wheat, 9	Myers, 80	Grimes, 23	S. Smith, 1.85
1921	77	75	5th	16½	Robinson	Kilduff, .388	J. Johnston, 203	Wheat, 14	Wheat, 85	Grimes, 22	Grimes, 2.83
1922	76	78	6th	17	Robinson	Wheat, .335	Wheat, 201	Wheat, 16	Wheat, 112	Ruether, 21	Shriver, 2.99
1923	76	78	6th	19½	Robinson	Fournier, .351	J. Johnston, 203	Fournier, 22	Fournier, 102	Grimes, 21	Decatur, 2.58
1924	92	62	2nd	1½	Robinson	Wheat, .375	Wheat, 212	Fournier, 27	Fournier, 116	Vance, 28	Vance, 2.16
1925	68	85	*6th	27	Robinson	Wheat, .359	Wheat, 221	Fournier, 22	Fournier, 130	Vance, 22	Vance, 3.53
1926	71	82	6th	17½	Robinson	Herman, .319	Herman, 158	Fournier, Herman, 11	Herman, 81	Petty, 17	Petty, 2.84
1927	65	88	6th	28½	Robinson	Hendrick, .310	Partridge, 149	Herman, 14	Herman, 73	Vance, 16	Vance, 2.70
1928	77	76	6th	17½	Robinson	Herman, .340	Bissonette, 188	Bissonette, 25	Bissonette, 106	Vance, 22	Vance, 2.09
1929	70	83	6th	28½	Robinson	Herman, .381	Herman, 217	Frederick, 24	Herman, 113	Clark, 16	Clark, 3.74
1930	86	68	4th	6	Robinson	Herman, .393	Herman, 241	Herman, 35	Herman, 130	Vance, 17	Vance, 2.61
1931	79	73	4th	21	Robinson	O'Doul, .336	Herman, 191	Herman, 18	Herman, 97	Clark, 14	Clark, 3.20
1932	81	73	3rd	9	Carey	O'Doul, .368	O'Doul, 219	H. Wilson, 23	H. Wilson, 123	Clark, 20	Clark, 3.49
1933	65	88	6th	26½	Carey	Frederick, .308	Frederick, 171	Cuccinello, D. Taylor, H. Wilson, 9	Cuccinello, 65	Mungo, 16	Mungo, 2.72
1934	71	81	6th	23½	Stengel	Leslie, .332	Leslie, 181	Cuccinello, Koenecke, 14	Leslie, 102	Mungo, 18	Leonard, 3.28
1935	70	83	5th	29½	Stengel	Leslie, .308	Leslie, 160	Frey, 11	Leslie, 93	Mungo, 16	Clark, 3.30
1936	67	87	7th	25	Stengel	Stripp, .317	Hassett, 197	Phelps, 5	Hassett, 82	Mungo, 18	Mungo, 3.35
1937	62	91	6th	33½	Grimes	Manush, .333	Hassett, 169	Lavagetto, 8	Manush, 73	Butcher, Hamlin, 11	Mungo, 2.91
1938	69	80	7th	18½	Grimes	Koy, .299	Koy, 156	Camilli, 24	Camilli, 100	Hamlin, Tamulis, 12	Fitzsimmons, 3.02
1939	84	69	3rd	12½	Durocher	Lavagetto, .300	Lavagetto, 176	Camilli, 26	Camilli, 104	Hamlin, 20	Wyatt, 2.31
1940	88	65	2nd	12	Durocher	Walker, .308	Walker, 171	Camilli, 23	Camilli, 96	Fitzsimmons, 16	Fitzsimmons, 2.81
1941	100	54	1st	+2½	Durocher	Reiser, .343	Reiser, 184	Camilli, 34	Camilli, 120	Higbe, Wyatt, 22	Wyatt, 2.34
1942	104	50	2nd	2	Durocher	Reiser, .310	Medwick, 166	Camilli, 26	Camilli, 109	Wyatt, 19	French, 1.83
1943	81	72	3rd	23½	Durocher	Herman, .330	Herman, 193	Galan, 9	Herman, 100	Wyatt, 14	Wyatt, 2.49
1944	63	91	7th	42	Durocher	Walker, .357	Walker, 191	Walker, 13	Galan, 93	C. Davis, 10	C. Davis, 3.34
1945	87	67	3rd	11	Durocher	Rosen, .325	Rosen, 197	Rosen, 12	Walker, 124	Gregg, 18	Branca, 3.03
1946	96	60	†2nd	2	Durocher	Walker, .319	Walker, 184	Reiser, 11	Walker, 116	Higbe, 17	Casey, Melton, 1.99
1947	94	60	1st	+5	Sukeforth, Shotton	Reiser, .309	Robinson, 175	Reese, Robinson, 12	Walker, 94	Branca, 21	Branca, 2.67
1948	84	70	3rd	7½	Durocher, Shotton	Furillo, .297	Robinson, 170	Hermanski, 15	Robinson, 85	Barney, 15	Roe, 2.63
1949	97	57	1st	+1	Shotton	Robinson, .342	Robinson, 203	Hodges, Snider, 23	Robinson, 124	Newcombe, 17	Roe, 2.79
1950	89	65	2nd	2	Shotton	Robinson, .328	Snider, 199	Hodges, 32	Hodges, 113	Newcombe, Roe, 19	Roe, 3.30
1951	97	60	†2nd	1	Dressen	Robinson, .338	Furillo, 197	Hodges, 40	Campanella, 108	Roe, 22	Roe, 3.04
1952	96	57	1st	+4½	Dressen	Robinson, .308	Snider, 162	Hodges, 32	Hodges, 102	Black, 15	Black, 2.15
1953	105	49	1st	+13	Dressen	Furillo, .344	Snider, 198	Snider, 42	Campanella, 142	Erskine, 20	Labine, 2.77
1954	92	62	2nd	5	Alston	Snider, .341	Snider, 199	Hodges, 42	Hodges, Snider, 130	Erskine, 18	Meyer, 3.99
1955	98	55	1st	+13½	Alston	Campanella, .318	Snider, 166	Snider, 42	Snider, 136	Newcombe, 20	Craig, 2.78
1956	93	61	1st	+1	Alston	Gilliam, .300	Gilliam, 178	Snider, 43	Snider, 101	Newcombe, 27	Drysdale, 2.64
1957	84	70	3rd	11	Alston	Furillo, .306	Hodges, 173	Snider, 40	Hodges, 98	Drysdale, 17	Podres, 2.66
						LOS ANGELES DODGERS					
1958	71	83	7th	21	Alston	Furillo, .290	Gilliam, 145	Hodges, Neal, 22	Furillo, 83	Podres, 13	Podres, 3.73
1959	88	68	‡1st	+2	Alston	Snider, .308	Neal, 177	Hodges, 25	Snider, 88	Drysdale, 17	Drysdale, 3.45
1960	82	72	4th	13	Alston	Larker, .323	Wills, 152	Howard, 23	Larker, 78	Drysdale, 15	Drysdale, 2.84
1961	89	65	2nd	4	Alston	Moon, .328	Wills, 173	Roseboro, 18	Moon, 88	Koufax, Podres, 18	Perranoski, 2.65
1962	102	63	†2nd	1	Alston	T. Davis, .346	T. Davis, 230	Howard, 31	T. Davis, 153	Drysdale, 25	Koufax, 2.54
1963	99	63	1st	+6	Alston	T. Davis, .326	T. Davis, 181	Howard, 28	T. Davis, 88	Koufax, 25	Koufax, 1.88
1964	80	82	*6th	13	Alston	W. Davis, .294	W. Davis, 180	Howard, 24	T. Davis, 86	Koufax, 19	Koufax, 1.74
1965	97	65	1st	+2	Alston	Wills, .286	Wills, 186	Johnson, Lefebvre, 12	Fairly, 70	Koufax, 26	Koufax, 2.04
1966	95	67	1st	+1½	Alston	Fairly, .288	W. Davis, 177	Lefebvre, 24	Lefebvre, 74	Koufax, 27	Koufax, 1.73
1967	73	89	8th	28½	Alston	Hunt, .263	W. Davis, 146	Ferrara, 16	Fairly, 55	Osteen, 17	Perranoski, 2.45
1968	76	86	7th	21	Alston	Haller, .285	W. Davis, 161	Gabrielson, 10	Haller, 53	Drysdale, 14	Drysdale, 2.15
						WEST DIVISION					
1969	85	77	4th	8	Alston	W. Davis, .311	Sizemore, 160	Kosco, 19	Kosco, 74	Osteen, Singer, 20	Singer, 2.34
1970	87	74	2nd	14½	Alston	Parker, .319	Parker, 196	Grabarkewitz, 17	Parker, 111	Osteen, 16	Singer, Vance, 3.13
1971	89	73	2nd	1	Alston	W. Davis, .309	W. Davis, 198	Allen, 23	Allen, 90	Downing, 20	Brewer, 1.89
1972	85	70	3rd	10½	Alston	Mota, .323	W. Davis, 178	W. Davis, Robinson, 19	W. Davis, 79	Osteen, 20	Sutton, 2.08
1973	95	66	2nd	3½	Alston	Crawford, .295	W. Davis, 171	Ferguson, 25	Ferguson, 88	Sutton, 18	Sutton, 2.42
1974	102	60	§1st	+4	Alston	Buckner, .314	Garvey, 200	Wynn, 32	Garvey, 111	Messersmith, 20	Marshall, 2.42
1975	88	74	2nd	20	Alston	Garvey, .319	Garvey, 210	Cey, 25	Cey, 101	Messersmith, 19	Messersmith, 2.29
1976	92	70	2nd	10	Alston, Lasorda	Garvey, .317	Garvey, 200	Cey, 23	Cey, Garvey, 80	Sutton, 21	Hough, 2.20
1977	98	64	§1st	+10	Lasorda	R. Smith, .307	Garvey, 192	Garvey, 33	Garvey, 115	John, 20	Hooton, 2.62
1978	95	67	§1st	+2½	Lasorda	Garvey, .316	Garvey, 202	R. Smith, 29	Garvey, 113	Hooton, 19	Welch, 2.03
1979	79	83	3rd	11½	Lasorda	Garvey, .315	Garvey, 204	Cey, Garvey, Lopes, 28	Garvey, 110	Sutcliffe, 17	Hooton, 2.97
1980	92	71	∞2nd	1	Lasorda	Garvey, .304	Garvey, 200	Baker, 29	Garvey, 106	Reuss, 18	Sutton, 2.20
1981	63	47	▲§1st/4th	—	Lasorda	Baker, .320	Baker, 128	Cey, 13	Garvey, 64	Valenzuela, 13	Hooton, 2.28
1982	88	74	2nd	1	Lasorda	Guerrero, .304	Sax, 180	Guerrero, 32	Guerrero, 100	Valenzuela, 19	Howe, 2.08
1983	91	71	◆1st	+3	Lasorda	Guerrero, .298	Sax, 175	Guerrero, 32	Guerrero, 103	Valenzuela, Welch, 15	Niedenfuer, 1.90
1984	79	83	4th	13	Lasorda	Guerrero, .303	Guerrero, 162	Marshall, 21	Guerrero, 72	Welch, 13	Pena, 2.48
1985	95	67	◆1st	+5½	Lasorda	Guerrero, .320	Guerrero, 156	Guerrero, 33	Marshall, 95	Hershiser, 19	Hershiser, 2.03
1986	73	89	5th	23	Lasorda	Sax, .332	Sax, 210	Stubbs, 23	Madlock, 60	Valenzuela, 21	Valenzuela, 3.14
1987	73	89	4th	17	Lasorda	Guerrero, .338	Guerrero, 184	Guerrero, 27	Guerrero, 89	Hershiser, 16	Hershiser, 3.06
1988	94	67	§1st	+7	Lasorda	Gibson, .290	Sax, 175	Gibson, 25	Marshall, 82	Hershiser, 23	Pena, 1.91
1989	77	83	4th	14	Lasorda	Randolph, .282	Randolph, 155	Murray, 20	Murray, 88	Belcher, Hershiser, 15	Hershiser, 2.31
1990	86	76	2nd	5	Lasorda	Murray, .330	Murray, 184	Daniels, 27	Murray, 95	R. Martinez, 20	Crews, 2.77
1991	93	69	2nd	1	Lasorda	Butler, .296	Butler, 182	Strawberry, 28	Strawberry, 99	R. Martinez, 17	Belcher, 2.62
1992	63	99	6th	35	Lasorda	Butler, .309	Butler, 171	Karros, 20	Karros, 88	Candiotti, 11	Astacio, 1.98
1993	81	81	4th	23	Lasorda	Piazza, .318	Butler, 181	Piazza, 35	Piazza, 112	Astacio, 14	P. Martinez, 2.61
1994	58	56	1st	+3½	Lasorda	Piazza, .319	Mondesi, 133	Piazza, 24	Piazza, 92	R. Martinez, 12	Gross, 3.60
1995	78	66	■1st	+1	Lasorda	Piazza, .346	Karros, 164	Karros, Piazza, 32	Karros, 105	Martinez, 17	Nomo, 2.54
1996	90	72	■2nd	1	Lasorda, Russell	Piazza, .336	Mondesi, 188	Piazza, 36	Karros, 111	Nomo, 16	Nomo, 3.19
1997	88	74	2nd	2	Russell	Piazza, .362	Piazza, 201	Piazza, 40	Piazza, 124	Nomo, Park, 14	Valdes, 2.65
1998	83	79	3rd	15	Russell, Hoffman	Sheffield, .302	Mondesi, 162	Mondesi, 30	Mondesi, 90	Perez, Valdes, 11	Bohanon, 2.67
1999	77	85	3rd	23	Johnson	Grudzielanek, .326	Karros, 176	Karros, Sheffield, 34	Karros, 112	Brown, 18	Brown, 3.00
2000	86	76	2nd	11	Johnson	Sheffield, .325	Grudzielanek, 172	Sheffield, 43	Sheffield, 109	Park, 18	Brown, 2.58

* Tied for position. † Lost pennant playoff. ‡ Won pennant playoff. § Won Championship Series. ∞ Lost division playoff. ▲ First half 36-21; second half 27-26. ◆ Lost Championship Series. ■ Lost Division Series.

Note: Batting average minimum 350 at-bats; ERA minimum 90 innings pitched.

Milwaukee Brewers

FRANCHISE CHRONOLOGY

First season: 1969, in Seattle, as part of a two-team American League expansion. The Pilots defeated California, 4-3, in their Major League debut, but that's about the only thing that went right. By season's end, the Pilots were resting in the cellar of the A.L. West Division with 98 losses and battling serious financial problems. Before the 1970 campaign could get under way, Seattle already held distinction as a here-today-gone-tomorrow Major League city.

1970-present: Baseball, American League-style, returned to Milwaukee after a four-year absence when the Pilots were shifted from Seattle and renamed the Brewers. Milwaukee, former home of the National League Braves, lost its A.L. debut, 12-0, to the Angels and posted only one more victory in its first season than the Pilots had in Seattle. It would take eight years for the Brewers to enjoy a winning season and 11 before they would qualify for postseason play—a one-time division playoff set up because of the 1981 players' strike. Milwaukee's banner season came a year later when the Brewers won their only A.L. pennant and dropped a seven-game World Series heartbreaker to St. Louis. The team made history after the 1997 season when it switched from the American League to the National League—the first ever to make such a crossover.

Shortstop/outfielder Robin Yount.

BREWERS VS. A.L. OPPONENTS BY DECADE

	A's	Indians	Orioles	Red Sox	Tigers	Twins	White Sox	Yankees	Angels	Rangers	Royals	Blue Jays	Mariners	Interleague	Decade Record
1969	5-13	5-7	3-9	6-6	2-10	6-12	8-10	5-7	9-9	7-5	8-10				64-98
1970-79	54-74	78-75	54-100	63-93	66-91	54-75	62-68	74-83	67-61	67-49	48-80	30-13	21-11		738-873
1980-89	50-64	70-56	59-64	67-62	64-66	68-52	58-55	62-61	54-61	63-52	59-58	71-56	59-53		804-760
1990-97	50-35	41-56	45-52	47-50	56-42	52-46	41-56	39-56	37-47	44-46	47-50	52-45	35-48	8-7	594-636
Totals	159-186	194-194	161-225	183-211	188-209	180-185	169-189	180-207	167-178	181-152	162-198	153-114	115-112	8-7	2200-2367

Interleague results: 1-2 vs. Cubs; 0-3 vs. Reds; 2-1 vs. Astros; 2-1 vs. Pirates; 3-0 vs. Cardinals.

BREWERS VS. N.L. OPPONENTS BY DECADE

	Braves	Cardinals	Cubs	Dodgers	Giants	Phillies	Pirates	Reds	Astros	Mets	Expos	Padres	Marlins	Rockies	D'backs	Interleague	Decade Record
1998-99	4-12	10-14	12-12	6-12	9-9	9-9	14-9	11-12	7-17	3-13	11-7	6-11	13-5	10-10	7-11	16-12	148-175
2000-	3-6	5-7	7-6	4-3	3-6	2-5	7-5	8-5	6-7	2-7	4-5	2-7	4-3	5-4	5-4	6-9	73-89
Totals	7-18	15-21	19-18	10-15	12-15	11-14	21-14	19-17	13-24	5-20	15-12	8-18	17-8	15-14	12-15	22-21	221-264

Interleague results: 4-5 vs. White Sox; 3-6 vs. Indians; 5-4 vs. Tigers; 6-3 vs. Royals; 4-3 vs. Twins.

MANAGERS

(Seattle Pilots, 1969)

Name	*Years*	*Record*
Joe Schultz	1969	64-98
Dave Bristol	1970-72	144-209
Del Crandall	1972-75	271-338
Alex Grammas	1976-77	133-190
George Bamberger	1978-80, 1985-86	377-351
Buck Rodgers	1980-82	124-102
Harvey Kuenn	1982-83	160-118
Rene Lachemann	1984	67-94
Tom Trebelhorn	1986-91	422-397
Phil Garner	1992-99	563-617
Jim Lefebvre	1999	22-27
Lopes	2000	73-89

A.L. PENNANT WINNERS

Year	*Record*	*Manager*	*Series Result*
1982	95-67	Rodgers, Kuenn	Lost to Cardinals

EAST DIVISION CHAMPIONS

Year	*Record*	*Manager*	*ALCS Result*
*1981	62-47	Rodgers	None
1982	95-67	Rodgers, Kuenn	Defeated Angels

* Second-half champion; lost division playoff to Yankees.

ALL-TIME RECORD OF EXPANSION TEAMS

Team	W	L	Pct.	DT	P	WS
Arizona	250	236	.514	1	0	0
Kansas City	2,548	2,497	.505	6	2	1
Toronto	1,867	1,897	.496	5	2	2
Houston	3,052	3,138	.493	6	0	0
Montreal	2,454	2,596	.486	2	0	0
Anaheim	3,069	3,281	.483	3	0	0
Colorado	594	639	.482	0	0	0
Milwaukee	2,421	2,631	.479	2	1	0
New York	2,934	3,246	.475	4	4	2
Texas	2,952	3,381	.466	4	0	0
San Diego	2,315	2,742	.458	3	2	0
Seattle	1,715	2,048	.456	2	0	0
Florida	551	678	.448	0	1	1
Tampa Bay	201	284	.414	0	0	0

DT—Division Titles. P—Pennants won. WS—World Series won.

ATTENDANCE HIGHS

Total	*Season*	*Park*
2,397,131	1983	County Stadium
1,978,896	1982	County Stadium
1,970,735	1989	County Stadium
1,923,238	1988	County Stadium
1,918,343	1979	County Stadium

BALLPARK CHRONOLOGY

County Stadium (1970-present)

Capacity: 53,192.
First game: California 12, Brewers 0 (April 7, 1970).
First batter: Sandy Alomar, Angels.
First hit: Alex Johnson, Angels (triple).
First run: Alex Johnson, Angels (2nd inning).
First home run: Bobby Knoop, Angels (April 10).
First winning pitcher: Andy Messersmith, Angels.
First-season attendance: 933,690.

Sick's Stadium, Seattle (1969)

Capacity: 25,420.
First game: Pilots 7, Chicago 0 (April 11, 1969).
First-season attendance: 677,944.

A.L. MVPs

Rollie Fingers, P, 1981
Robin Yount, SS, 1982
Robin Yount, OF, 1989

CY YOUNG WINNERS

Rollie Fingers, RH, 1981
Pete Vuckovich, RH, 1982

ROOKIE OF THE YEAR

Pat Listach, SS, 1992

RETIRED UNIFORMS

No.	*Name*	*Pos.*
4	Paul Molitor	3B-DH
19	Robin Yount	SS-OF
34	Rollie Fingers	P
44	Hank Aaron	OF

Paul Molitor's journey to 3,000 career hits started in Milwaukee.

HISTORY

MILESTONE PERFORMANCES

25-plus home runs

45—	Gorman Thomas	1979
41—	Ben Oglivie	1980
39—	Gorman Thomas	1982
38—	Gorman Thomas	1980
	Jeromy Burnitz	1998
36—	George Scott	1975
34—	Larry Hisle	1978
	Ben Oglivie	1982
	John Jaha	1996
	Geoff Jenkins	2000
33—	Rob Deer	1986
	Jeromy Burnitz	1999
32—	Gorman Thomas	1978
	Cecil Cooper	1982
31—	Tommy Harper	1970
	Greg Vaughn	1996
	Jeromy Burnitz	2000
30—	Cecil Cooper	1983
	Greg Vaughn	1993
29—	Ben Oglivie	1979
	Robin Yount	1982
	Rob Deer	1987
28—	Sixto Lezcano	1979
27—	Rob Deer	1990
	Greg Vaughn	1991
	Jeromy Burnitz	1997
26—	Rob Deer	1989
25—	Don Mincher	1969
	Dave May	1973
	Don Money	1977
	Cecil Cooper	1980
	Dale Sveum	1987

100-plus RBIs

126—	Cecil Cooper	1983
125—	Jeromy Burnitz	1998
123—	Gorman Thomas	1979
122—	Cecil Cooper	1980
121—	Cecil Cooper	1982
118—	Ben Oglivie	1980
	John Jaha	1996
115—	Larry Hisle	1978
114—	Robin Yount	1982
112—	Gorman Thomas	1982
109—	George Scott	1975
108—	Ted Simmons	1983
107—	George Scott	1973
106—	Cecil Cooper	1979
105—	Gorman Thomas	1980
103—	Robin Yount	1987, 1989
	Jeromy Burnitz	1999
102—	Ben Oglivie	1982
101—	Sixto Lezcano	1979

20-plus victories

1973—	Jim Colborn	20-12
1978—	Mike Caldwell	22-9
1986—	Teddy Higuera	20-11

A.L. home run champions

1975—	George Scott	*36
1979—	Gorman Thomas	45
1980—	Ben Oglivie	*41
1982—	Gorman Thomas	*39

* Tied for league lead

A.L. RBI champions

1975—	George Scott	109
1980—	Cecil Cooper	122
1983—	Cecil Cooper	*126

* Tied for league lead

A.L. batting champions
None

A.L. ERA champions
None

A.L. strikeout champions
None

No-hit pitchers
(9 innings or more)

1987— Juan Nieves ..... 7-0 vs. Baltimore

Longest hitting streaks

39—	Paul Molitor	1987
24—	Dave May	1973
22—	Cecil Cooper	1980
19—	Robin Yount	1989
	Paul Molitor	1989, 1990
	Darryl Hamilton	1991
18—	Robin Yount	1980
17—	Cecil Cooper	1982
	Paul Molitor	1982
	Pat Listach	1992
16—	John Briggs	1974
	Robin Yount	1976
	Cecil Cooper	1979
	Paul Molitor	1979, 1985
	Ben Oglivie	1979, 1983
	Ted Simmons	1983
	Gary Sheffield	1990
	Greg Vaughn	1991
15—	Billy Conigliaro	1972
	Don Money	1973
	Paul Molitor	1978
	Darryl Hamilton	1991, 1992
	B.J. Surhoff	1993
	Kevin Seitzer	1994
	Greg Vaughn	1996

Dependable second baseman Jim Gantner played 1,801 games in a Brewers uniform, third on the team's all-time list.

INDIVIDUAL SEASON, GAME RECORDS

Slugging outfielder Gorman Thomas topped the 30-home run plateau four times in the 1970s and '80s.

SEASON

Batting			
At-bats	666	Paul Molitor	1982
Runs	136	Paul Molitor	1982
Hits	219	Cecil Cooper	1980
Singles	157	Cecil Cooper	1980
Doubles	49	Robin Yount	1980
Triples	16	Paul Molitor	1979
Home runs	45	Gorman Thomas	1979
Home runs, rookie	17	Danny Walton	1970
		Greg Vaughn	1990
Grand slams	3	John Jaha	1995
Total bases	367	Robin Yount	1982
RBIs	126	Cecil Cooper	1983
Walks	99	Jeromy Burnitz	2000
Most strikeouts	186	Rob Deer	1987
Fewest strikeouts	35	Fernando Vina	1996
Batting average	.353	Paul Molitor	1987
Slugging pct.	.578	Robin Yount	1982
Stolen bases	73	Tommy Harper	1969
Pitching			
Games	83	Ken Sanders	1971
Complete games	23	Mike Caldwell	1978
Innings	314.1	Jim Colborn	1973
Wins	22	Mike Caldwell	1978
Losses	20	Clyde Wright	1974
Winning pct.	.846 (11-2)	Cal Eldred	1992
Walks	106	Pete Broberg	1975
Strikeouts	240	Teddy Higuera	1987
Shutouts	6	Mike Caldwell	1978
Home runs allowed	35	Mike Caldwell	1983
Lowest ERA	2.36	Mike Caldwell	1978
Saves	37	Bob Wickman	1999

GAME

Batting			
Runs	4	Last by Jeromy Burnitz	9-29-2000
Hits	6	John Briggs	8-4-73
		Kevin Reimer	8-24-93
Doubles	3	Last by Ron Belliard	7-1-99
Triples	2	Last by Jose Valentin	9-29-99
Home runs	3	Last by Tyler Houston	7-9-2000
RBIs	7	Ted Kubiak	7-18-70
Total bases	13	Paul Molitor	5-12-82
		Fernando Vina	9-12-96
Stolen bases	4	Tommy Harper	6-18-69
		John Jaha	9-11-92

CAREER LEADERS

BATTING

Games

Robin Yount	2,856
Paul Molitor	1,856
Jim Gantner	1,801
Cecil Cooper	1,490
Charlie Moore	1,283
Don Money	1,196
Ben Oglivie	1,149
B.J. Surhoff	1,102
Gorman Thomas	1,102
Greg Vaughn	903

At-bats

Robin Yount	11,008
Paul Molitor	7,520
Jim Gantner	6,189
Cecil Cooper	6,019
Don Money	4,330
Ben Oglivie	4,136
Charlie Moore	3,926
B.J. Surhoff	3,884
Gorman Thomas	3,544
Greg Vaughn	3,244

Runs

Robin Yount	1,632
Paul Molitor	1,275
Cecil Cooper	821
Jim Gantner	726
Don Money	596
Ben Oglivie	567
Greg Vaughn	528
Gorman Thomas	524
B.J. Surhoff	472
Jeff Cirillo	444

Hits

Robin Yount	3,142
Paul Molitor	2,281
Cecil Cooper	1,815
Jim Gantner	1,696
Don Money	1,168
Ben Oglivie	1,144
B.J. Surhoff	1,064
Charlie Moore	1,029
Jeff Cirillo	864
George Scott	851

Doubles

Robin Yount	583
Paul Molitor	405
Cecil Cooper	345
Jim Gantner	262
Don Money	215
Ben Oglivie	194
B.J. Surhoff	194
Jeff Cirillo	186
Charlie Moore	177
Gorman Thomas	172

Triples

Robin Yount	126
Paul Molitor	86
Charlie Moore	42
Jim Gantner	38
Cecil Cooper	33
Fernando Vina	26
B.J. Surhoff	24
Sixto Lezcano	22
Darryl Hamilton	21
Ben Oglivie	21

Home runs

Robin Yount	251
Gorman Thomas	208
Cecil Cooper	201
Ben Oglivie	176
Greg Vaughn	169
Paul Molitor	160
Rob Deer	137
Don Money	134
Jeromy Burnitz	131
George Scott	115

Total bases

Robin Yount	4,730
Paul Molitor	3,338
Cecil Cooper	2,829
Jim Gantner	2,175
Ben Oglivie	1,908
Don Money	1,825
Gorman Thomas	1,635
Greg Vaughn	1,490
B.J. Surhoff	1,477
Charlie Moore	1,395

Runs batted in

Robin Yount	1,406
Cecil Cooper	944
Paul Molitor	790
Ben Oglivie	685
Gorman Thomas	605
Jim Gantner	568
Greg Vaughn	566
Don Money	529
B.J. Surhoff	524
Dave Nilsson	470

Extra-base hits

Robin Yount	960
Paul Molitor	651
Cecil Cooper	579
Gorman Thomas	392
Ben Oglivie	391
Don Money	369
Jim Gantner	347
Greg Vaughn	340
Jeromy Burnitz	275
B.J. Surhoff	275

Batting average

(Minimum 500 games)

Jeff Cirillo	.307
Paul Molitor	.303
Cecil Cooper	.302
Kevin Seitzer	.300
Mark Loretta	.292
Darryl Hamilton	.290
Fernando Vina	.286
Robin Yount	.285
Dave Nilsson	.284
George Scott	.283

Stolen bases

Paul Molitor	412
Robin Yount	271
Jim Gantner	137
Tommy Harper	136
Pat Listach	112
Darryl Hamilton	109
Mike Felder	108
B.J. Surhoff	102
Jose Valentin	78
Cecil Cooper	77

PITCHING

Earned-run average

(Minimum 500 innings)

Dan Plesac	3.21
Chuck Crim	3.47
Teddy Higuera	3.61
Jim Colborn	3.65
Lary Sorensen	3.72
Mike Caldwell	3.74
Skip Lockwood	3.75
Chris Bosio	3.76
Ed Rodriguez	3.78
Marty Pattin	3.82

Wins

Jim Slaton	117
Mike Caldwell	102
Teddy Higuera	94
Moose Haas	91
Bill Wegman	81
Chris Bosio	67
Bill Travers	65
Cal Eldred	64
Jaime Navarro	62
Jim Colborn	57

Losses

Jim Slaton	121
Bill Wegman	90
Mike Caldwell	80
Moose Haas	79
Bill Travers	67
Cal Eldred	65
Teddy Higuera	64
Jamie Navarro	64
Chris Bosio	62
Jim Colborn	60

Innings pitched

Jim Slaton	2,025.1
Mike Caldwell	1,604.1
Moose Haas	1,542.0
Bill Wegman	1,482.2
Teddy Higuera	1,380.0
Chris Bosio	1,190.0
Jim Colborn	1,118.0
Cal Eldred	1,078.2
Bill Travers	1,068.1
Jamie Navarro	1,061.2

Strikeouts

Teddy Higuera	1,081
Jim Slaton	929
Moose Haas	800
Chris Bosio	749
Bill Wegman	696
Cal Eldred	686
Mike Caldwell	540
Jamie Navarro	531
Bob McClure	497
Jim Colborn	495

Bases on balls

Jim Slaton	760
Cal Eldred	448
Teddy Higuera	443
Moose Haas	408
Bill Travers	392
Bob McClure	363
Mike Caldwell	353
Bill Wegman	352
Jerry Augustine	340
Jaime Navarro	336

Games

Dan Plesac	365
Jim Slaton	364
Bob McClure	352
Chuck Crim	332
Mike Fetters	289
Jerry Augustine	279
Bob Wickman	272
Bill Wegman	262
Bill Castro	253
Moose Haas	245

Shutouts

Jim Slaton	19
Mike Caldwell	18
Teddy Higuera	12
Bill Travers	10
Chris Bosio	8
Moose Haas	8
Jim Colborn	7
Lary Sorensen	7
Jerry Augustine	6
Jamie Navarro	6
Bill Parsons	6
Marty Pattin	6

Saves

Dan Plesac	133
Rollie Fingers	97
Mike Fetters	79
Bob Wickman	79
Doug Henry	61
Ken Sanders	61
Doug Jones	49
Bill Castro	44
Chuck Crim	42
Tom Murphy	41

TEAM SEASON, GAME RECORDS

SEASON

Batting

Most at-bats	5,733	1982
Most runs	894	1996
Fewest runs	494	1972
Most hits	1,599	1982
Most singles	1,107	1991
Most doubles	304	1996
Most triples	57	1983
Most home runs	216	1982
Fewest home runs	82	1992
Most grand slams	10	1995
Most pinch-hit home runs	7	1998
Most total bases	2,605	1982
Most stolen bases	256	1992
Highest batting average	.280	1979
Lowest batting average	.229	1971
Highest slugging pct	.455	1982

Pitching

Lowest ERA	3.38	1971
Highest ERA	5.14	1996
Most complete games	62	1978
Most shutouts	23	1971
Most saves	51	1988
Most walks	728	2000
Most strikeouts	1,063	1998

Fielding

Most errors	180	1975
Fewest errors	89	1992
Most double plays	189	1980
Highest fielding average	.986	1992

General

Most games won	95	1979, 1982
Most games lost	98	1969
Highest win pct	.590	1979
Lowest win pct	.395	1969

GAME, INNING

Batting

Most runs, game	22	8-28-92
Most runs, inning	13	7-8-90
Most hits, game	31	8-28-92
Most home runs, game	7	4-29-80
Most total bases, game	38	8-28-92

The sweet swing of first baseman Cecil Cooper produced 1,815 hits, 201 home runs and 944 RBIs for the Brewers.

BREWERS YEAR-BY-YEAR

Year	W	L	Place	Games Back	Manager	Leaders: Batting avg.	Hits	Home runs	RBIs	Wins	ERA
							SEATTLE PILOTS				
							WEST DIVISION				
1969	64	98	6th	33	Schultz	T. Davis, .271	Harper, 126	Mincher, 25	T. Davis, 80	Brabender, 13	Gelnar, 3.31
							MILWAUKEE BREWERS				
1970	65	97	4th	33	Bristol	Harper, .296	Harper, 179	Harper, 31	Harper, 82	Pattin, 14	Sanders, 1.75
1971	69	92	6th	32	Bristol	May, .277	Harper, 151	Briggs, 21	May, 65	Pattin, 14	Sanders, 1.91
							EAST DIVISION				
1972	65	91	6th	21	Bristol, Crandall	Rodriguez, .285	Scott, 154	Briggs, 21	Scott, 88	Lonborg, 14	Lonborg, 2.83
1973	74	88	5th	23	Crandall	Scott, .306	May, 189	May, 25	Scott, 107	Colborn, 20	Colborn, 3.18
1974	76	86	5th	15	Crandall	Money, .283	Scott, 170	Briggs, Scott, 17	Scott, 82	Slaton, 13	Murphy, 1.90
1975	68	94	5th	28	Crandall	Scott, .285	Scott, 176	Scott, 36	Scott, 109	Broberg, 14	Hausman, 4.10
1976	66	95	6th	32	Grammas	Lezcano, .285	Scott, 166	Scott, 18	Scott, 77	Travers, 15	Travers, 2.81
1977	67	95	6th	33	Grammas	Cooper, .300	Cooper, 193	Money, 25	Money, 83	Augustine, 12	Slaton, 3.58
1978	93	69	3rd	6½	Bamberger	Cooper, .312	Bando, 154	Hisle, 34	Hisle, 115	Caldwell, 22	Caldwell, 2.37
1979	95	66	2nd	8	Bamberger	Molitor, .322	Molitor, 188	G. Thomas, 45	G. Thomas, 123	Caldwell, 16	Caldwell, 3.29
1980	86	76	3rd	17	Bamberger, Rodgers	Cooper, .352	Cooper, 219	Oglivie, 41	Cooper, 122	Haas, 16	McClure, 3.07
1981	62	47	*3rd/1st	—	Rodgers	Cooper, .320	Cooper, 133	G. Thomas, 21	Oglivie, 72	Vuckovich, 14	Vuckovich, 3.55
1982	95	67	†1st	+1	Rodgers, Kuenn	Yount, .331	Yount, 210	G. Thomas, 39	Cooper, 121	Vuckovich, 18	Slaton, 3.29
1983	87	75	5th	11	Kuenn	Simmons, Yount, .308	Cooper, 203	Cooper, 30	Cooper, 126	Slaton, 14	Tellmann, 2.80
1984	67	94	7th	36½	Lachemann	Yount, .298	Yount, 186	Yount, 16	Yount, 80	Sutton, 14	Sutton, 3.77
1985	71	90	6th	28	Bamberger	Molitor, .297	Cooper, 185	Cooper, 16	Cooper, 99	Higuera, 15	Darwin, 3.80
1986	77	84	6th	18	Bamberger, Trebelhorn	Yount, .312	Yount, 163	Deer, 33	Deer, 86	Higuera, 20	Higuera, 2.79
1987	91	71	3rd	7	Trebelhorn	Molitor, .353	Yount, 198	Deer, 28	Yount, 103	Higuera, 18	Crim, 3.67
1988	87	75	‡3rd	2	Trebelhorn	Molitor, .312	Molitor, Yount, 190	Deer, 23	Yount, 91	Higuera, 16	Higuera, 2.45
1989	81	81	4th	8	Trebelhorn	Yount, .318	Yount, 195	Deer, 26	Yount, 103	Bosio, 15	Crim, 2.83
1990	74	88	6th	14	Trebelhorn	Sheffield, .294	Parker, 176	Deer, 27	Parker, 92	Robinson, 12	Robinson, 2.91
1991	83	79	4th	8	Trebelhorn	Randolph, .327	Molitor, 216	Vaughn, 27	Vaughn, 98	Navarro, Wegman, 15	Wegman, 2.84
1992	92	70	2nd	4	Garner	Molitor, .320	Molitor, 195	Vaughn, 23	Molitor, 89	Navarro, 17	Eldred, 1.79
1993	69	93	7th	26	Garner	Hamilton, .310	Hamilton, 161	Vaughn, 30	Vaughn, 97	Eldred, 16	Miranda, 3.30
							CENTRAL DIVISION				
1994	53	62	5th	15	Garner	Seitzer, .314	Nilsson, 109	Vaughn, 19	Nilsson, 69	Eldred, 11	Bones, 3.43
1995	65	79	4th	35	Garner	Surhoff, .320	Seitzer, 153	Jaha, 20	Surhoff, 73	Bones, 10	Karl, 4.14
1996	80	82	3rd	19½	Garner	Nilsson, .331	Cirillo, 184	Jaha, 34	Jaha, 118	Karl, 13	McDonald, 3.90
1997	78	83	3rd	8	Garner	Cirillo, .288	Cirillo, 167	Burnitz, 27	Burnitz, 85	Eldred, 13	Wickman, 2.73
							NATIONAL LEAGUE				
							CENTRAL DIVISION				
1998	74	88	5th	28	Garner	Cirillo, .321	Vina, 198	Burnitz, 38	Burnitz, 125	Woodard, Karl, 10	Woodard, 4.18
1999	74	87	5th	22½	Garner, Lefebvre	Cirillo, .326	Cirillo, 198	Burnitz, 33	Burnitz, 103	Nomo, 12	Woodard, 4.52
2000	73	89	3rd	22	Lopes	Jenkins, .303	Jenkins, 155	Jenkins, 34	Burnitz, 98	D'Amico, Haynes, 12	D'Amico, 2.67

* First half 31-25; second half 31-22. † Won Championship Series. ‡ Tied for position.

Note: Batting average minimum 350 at-bats; ERA minimum 90 innings pitched.

Don Mincher

SEATTLE joined Kansas City, San Diego and Montreal in the four-team 1969 expansion that brought baseball's membership roster to a modern-record 24 teams.The franchise, which would last only one season in Seattle before moving to Milwaukee as the Brewers, came to life December 1, 1967, when the bid by Pacific Northwest Sports, Inc., was officially approved and the name "Pilots" was adopted three months later.

The Pilots selected 30 players in the October 15, 1968, expansion draft, leading off with veteran first baseman Don Mincher. The Pilots defeated the California Angels, 4-3, in their April 8, 1969, debut at Anaheim Stadium—one of 64 victories the team would post in its brief history. One year later on April 7, the Brewers lost their American League debut, 12-0, to the same Angels.

Expansion draft (October 15, 1968)

Players

Player	From	Position
Wayne Comer	Detroit	outfield
Tommy Davis	Chicago	outfield
Mike Ferraro	New York	infield
Jim Gosger	Oakland	outfield
Larry Haney	Baltimore	catcher
Tommy Harper	Cleveland	outfield
Steve Hovley	California	outfield
Gerry McNertney	Chicago	catcher
*Don Mincher	California	first base
Ray Oyler	Detroit	shortstop
Lou Piniella	Cleveland	outfield
Rich Rollins	Minnesota	third base
Chico Salmon	Cleveland	second base

Pitchers

Pitcher	From	Throws
Jack Aker	Oakland	righthanded
Dick Baney	Boston	righthanded
Steve Barber	New York	lefthanded
Dick Bates	Washington	righthanded
Gary Bell	Boston	righthanded
Darrell Brandon	Boston	righthanded
Paul Click	California	righthanded
Skip Lockwood	Oakland	righthanded
Mike Marshall	Detroit	righthanded
John Miklos	Washington	lefthanded
John Morris	Baltimore	lefthanded
Marty Pattin	California	righthanded
Bob Richmond	Washington	righthanded
Gerry Schoen	Washington	righthanded
Diego Segui	Oakland	righthanded
Lou Stephen	Minnesota	righthanded
Gary Timberlake	New York	lefthanded

*First pick

Opening day lineups

April 8, 1969 (Seattle Pilots)

Tommy Harper, second base
Steve Whitaker, right field
Tommy Davis, left field
Don Mincher, first base
Rich Rollins, third base
Jim Gosger, center field
Jerry McNertney, catcher
Ray Oyler, shortstop
Marty Pattin, pitcher

April 7, 1970 (Milwaukee Brewers)

Tommy Harper, second base
Russ Snyder, center field
Mike Hegan, first base
Danny Walton, left field
Jerry McNertney, catcher
Steve Hovley, right field
Max Alvis, third base
Ted Kubiak, shortstop
Lew Krausse, pitcher

Tommy Harper

Pilots firsts

First hit: Tommy Harper, April 8, 1969, at California (double)
First home run: Mike Hegan, April 8, 1969, at California
First RBI: Mike Hegan, April 8, 1969, at California
First win: Marty Pattin, April 8, 1968, at California
First shutout: Gary Bell, April 11, 1969, 7-0 vs. Chicago

Montreal Expos

FRANCHISE CHRONOLOGY

First season: 1969, as one of two National League expansion teams and baseball's first Canadian franchise. The Expos rallied for an 11-10 opening day victory over New York and posted an 8-7 victory over St. Louis six days later in the first Major League game on foreign soil, but they stumbled to a 52-110 first-season record and finished 48 games behind the Mets in the new N.L. East Division.

1970-present: The Expos, one of baseball's so-called small-market franchises, still are looking for their first N.L. pennant and World Series appearance. They came close in 1981, when they survived a strike-forced divisional playoff before suffering a heartbreaking N.L. Championship Series loss to the Los Angeles Dodgers. And they were sailing along with baseball's best record in 1994 when another players' strike brought a sudden halt to the season—and realistic hopes for a championship. When the strike finally ended in 1995, the Expos began auctioning off high-priced players and entered the new season with a talented, but inexperienced, team. While the Expos continue to grope for success, their Canadian cousins, the Toronto Blue Jays, have won two World Series since entering the American League in 1977.

Center fielder Andre Dawson.

EXPOS VS. OPPONENTS BY DECADE

	Braves	Cardinals	Cubs	Dodgers	Giants	Phillies	Pirates	Reds	Astros	Mets	Padres	Marlins	Rockies	Brewers	D'backs	Interleague	Decade Record
1969	4-8	7-11	8-10	2-10	1-11	11-7	5-13	4-8	1-11	5-13	4-8						52-110
1970-79	58-60	85-93	89-88	47-73	59-61	88-90	73-107	46-74	49-71	94-86	60-59						748-862
1980-89	72-45	95-82	95-77	48-67	59-56	87-86	88-86	64-53	55-60	85-89	63-51						811-752
1990-99	50-70	64-61	62-57	56-57	56-59	65-73	65-61	48-57	51-57	69-68	71-40	46-38	30-37	7-11	10-8	26-23	776-777
2000-	7-6	2-5	5-4	3-5	3-6	5-7	3-4	3-6	5-4	3-9	3-6	6-7	2-7	5-4	5-4	7-11	67-95
Totals	191-189	253-252	259-236	156-212	178-193	256-263	234-271	165-198	161-203	256-265	201-164	52-45	32-44	12-15	15-12	33-34	2454-2596

Interleague results: 8-4 vs. Orioles; 6-6 vs. Red Sox; 3-0 vs.Tigers; 5-7 vs. Yankees; 6-13 vs. Blue Jays; 5-4 vs. Devil Rays.

MANAGERS

Name	*Years*	*Record*
Gene Mauch	1969-75	499-627
Karl Kuehl	1976	43-85
Charlie Fox	1976	12-22
Dick Williams	1977-81	380-347
Jim Fanning	1981-82, 1984	116-103
Bill Virdon	1983-84	146-147
Buck Rodgers	1985-91	520-499
Tom Runnells	1991-92	68-81
Felipe Alou	1992-2000	670-685

EAST DIVISION CHAMPIONS

Year	*Record*	*Manager*	*NLCS Result*
*1981	60-48	Williams, Fanning	Lost to Dodgers
1994	74-40	Alou	None

* Second-half champion; won division playoff over Phillies.

ALL-TIME RECORD OF EXPANSION TEAMS

Team	W	L	Pct.	DT	P	WS
Arizona	250	236	.514	1	0	0
Kansas City	2,548	2,497	.505	6	2	1
Toronto	1,867	1,897	.496	5	2	2
Houston	3,052	3,138	.493	6	0	0
Montreal	2,454	2,596	.486	2	0	0
Anaheim	3,069	3,281	.483	3	0	0
Colorado	594	639	.482	0	0	0
Milwaukee	2,421	2,631	.479	2	1	0
New York	2,934	3,246	.475	4	4	2
Texas	2,952	3,381	.466	4	0	0
San Diego	2,315	2,742	.458	3	2	0
Seattle	1,715	2,048	.456	2	0	0
Florida	551	678	.448	0	1	1
Tampa Bay	201	284	.414	0	0	0

DT—Division Titles. P—Pennants won. WS—World Series won.

BALLPARK CHRONOLOGY

Olympic Stadium (1977-present)

Capacity: 46,500.
First game: Philadelphia 7, Expos 2 (April 15, 1977).
First batter: Jay Johnstone, Phillies.
First hit: Dave Cash, Expos (single).
First run: Greg Luzinski, Phillies (2nd inning).
First home run: Ellis Valentine, Expos.
First winning pitcher: Steve Carlton, Phillies.
First-season attendance: 1,433,757.

Jarry Park (1969-76)

Capacity: 28,000.
First game: Expos 8, St. Louis 7 (April 14, 1969).
First-season attendance: 1,212,608.

ATTENDANCE HIGHS

Total	*Season*	*Park*
2,320,651	1983	Olympic Stadium
2,318,292	1982	Olympic Stadium
2,208,175	1980	Olympic Stadium
2,102,173	1979	Olympic Stadium
1,850,324	1987	Olympic Stadium

CY YOUNG WINNER

Pedro Martinez, RH, 1997

ROOKIES OF THE YEAR

Carl Morton, P, 1970
Andre Dawson, OF, 1977

MANAGERS OF THE YEAR

Buck Rodgers, 1987
Felipe Alou, 1994

RETIRED UNIFORMS

No.	*Name*	*Pos.*
8	Gary Carter	C
10	Rusty Staub	1B-OF
	Andre Dawson	OF

Outfielder/first baseman Rusty Staub was one of the most popular players in Expos history.

HISTORY

MILESTONE PERFORMANCES

25-plus home runs

44—Vladimir Guerrero 2000
42—Vladimir Guerrero 1999
38—Vladimir Guerrero 1998
36—Henry Rodriguez 1996
32—Andre Dawson 1983
31—Gary Carter 1977
30—Rusty Staub 1970
Larry Parrish 1979
29—Rusty Staub 1969
Gary Carter 1980, 1982
Andres Galarraga 1988
28—Bob Bailey 1970
Tim Wallach 1982
Rondell White 1997
27—Gary Carter 1984
26—Bob Bailey 1973
Tim Wallach 1987
Henry Rodriguez 1997
25—Ellis Valentine 1977, 1978
Andre Dawson 1978, 1979
Shane Andrews 1998

100-plus RBIs

131—Vladimir Guerrero 1999
123—Tim Wallach 1987
Vladimir Guerrero 2000
113—Andre Dawson 1983
109—Al Oliver 1982
Vladimir Guerrero 1998
106—Gary Carter 1984
103—Ken Singleton 1973
Henry Rodriguez 1996
101—Gary Carter 1981
100—Hubie Brooks 1985

20-plus victories

1978—Ross Grimsley 20-11

N.L. home run champions

None

N.L. RBI champions

1982—Al Oliver *109
1984—Gary Carter *106

* Tied for league lead

N.L. batting champions

1982—Al Oliver .... .331
1986—Tim Raines .... .334

N.L. ERA champions

1982—Steve Rogers 2.40
1991—Dennis Martinez 2.39
1997—Pedro Martinez 1.90

N.L. strikeout champions

None

No-hit pitchers

(9 innings or more)
1969—Bill Stoneman .... 7-0 vs. Philadelphia
1972—Bill Stoneman .... 7-0 vs. New York
1981—Charlie Lea .... 4-0 vs. San Francisco
1991—Dennis Martinez .... 2-0 vs. Los Angeles

Longest hitting streaks

31—Vladimir Guerrero 1999
21—Delino DeShields 1993
19—Warren Cromartie 1979
Andre Dawson 1980
18—Pepe Mangual 1975
Warren Cromartie 1980
David Segui 1980
F.P. Santangelo 1997
17—Bob Bailey 1973
Tim Raines 1986
Mark Grudzielanek 1996, 1997
16—Rusty Staub 1971
Tony Perez 1977
Ellis Valentine 1978
Andre Dawson 1981
Henry Rodriguez 1997
Brad Fullmer 1999
15—Ken Singleton 1973
Boots Day 1971
Warren Cromartie 1978
Larry Parrish 1978
Al Oliver 1982
Delino DeShields 1990
Mike Lansing 1997

During Gary Carter's successful 11-year Montreal stay, he ranked as one of the best hitting catchers in the game.

INDIVIDUAL SEASON, GAME RECORDS

Steady righthander Steve Rogers set a club record when he pitched more than 300 innings in a workhorse 1977 season.

SEASON

Batting

Record	Total	Player	Year
At-bats	659	Warren Cromartie	1979
Runs	133	Tim Raines	1983
Hits	204	Al Oliver	1982
Singles	157	Mark Grudzielanek	1996
Doubles	54	Mark Grudzielanek	1997
Triples	13	3 times	
		Last by Mitch Webster	1986
Home runs	44	Vladimir Guerrero	2000
Home runs, rookie	19	Andre Dawson	1977
		Larry Walker	1990
Grand slams	2	14 times	
		Last by Henry Rodriguez	1997
Total bases	369	Vladimir Guerrero	2000
RBIs	131	Vladimir Guerrero	1999
Walks	123	Ken Singleton	1973
Most strikeouts	169	Andres Galarraga	1990
Fewest strikeouts	29	Dave Cash	1978
Batting average	.345	Vladimir Guerrero	2000
Slugging pct.	.664	Vladimir Guerrero	2000
Stolen bases	97	Ron LeFlore	1980

Pitching

Record	Total	Player	Year
Games	92	Mike Marshall	1973
Complete games	20	Bill Stoneman	1971
Innings	301.2	Steve Rogers	1977
Wins	20	Ross Grimsley	1978
Losses	22	Steve Rogers	1974
Winning pct.	.783 (18-5)	Bryn Smith	1985
Walks	146	Bill Stoneman	1971
Strikeouts	305	Pedro Martinez	1997
Shutouts	5	5 times	
		Last by Carlos Perez	1997
Home runs allowed	31	Javier Vazquez	1998
Lowest ERA	1.90	Pedro Martinez	1997
Saves	43	John Wetteland	1993

GAME

Batting

Record	Total	Player	Date
Runs	5	Last by Rondell White	6-11-95
Hits	6	Rondell White	6-11-95
Doubles	3	Last by Lee Stevens	6-27-2000
Triples	2	Last by Orlando Cabrera	7-30-98
Home runs	3	Last by Tim Wallach	5-4-87
RBIs	8	Last by Tim Wallach	5-13-90
Total bases	14	Larry Parrish	5-29-77, 7-30-78
Stolen bases	4	Last by Marquis Grissom	7-21-92

HISTORY

CAREER LEADERS

BATTING

Games

Tim Wallach	1,767
Gary Carter	1,503
Andre Dawson	1,443
Tim Raines	1,405
Warren Cromartie	1,038
Larry Parrish	967
Bob Bailey	951
Chris Speier	895
Andres Galarraga	847
Rondell White	742

At-bats

Tim Wallach	6,529
Andre Dawson	5,628
Tim Raines	5,305
Gary Carter	5,303
Warren Cromartie	3,796
Larry Parrish	3,411
Andres Galarraga	3,082
Bob Bailey	2,991
Chris Speier	2,902
Rondell White	2,756

Runs

Tim Raines	934
Andre Dawson	828
Tim Wallach	737
Gary Carter	707
Warren Cromartie	446
Marquis Grissom	430
Larry Parrish	421
Rondell White	420
Bob Bailey	412
Andres Galarraga	394

Hits

Tim Wallach	1,694
Tim Raines	1,598
Andre Dawson	1,575
Gary Carter	1,427
Warren Cromartie	1,063
Larry Parrish	896
Andres Galarraga	830
Rondell White	808
Bob Bailey	791
Marquis Grissom	747

Doubles

Tim Wallach	360
Andre Dawson	295
Gary Carter	274
Tim Raines	273
Warren Cromartie	222
Larry Parrish	208
Andres Galarraga	168
Mike Lansing	165
Rondell White	165
Larry Walker	147

Triples

Tim Raines	81
Andre Dawson	67
Tim Wallach	31
Warren Cromartie	30
Delino DeShields	25
Vladimir Guerrero	25
Mitch Webster	25
Gary Carter	24
Larry Parrish	24
Bob Bailey	23
Marquis Grissom	23
Rondell White	23

Home Runs

Andre Dawson	225
Gary Carter	220
Tim Wallach	204
Vladimir Guerrero	136
Bob Bailey	118
Andres Galarraga	106
Rondell White	101
Larry Parrish	100
Larry Walker	99
Tim Raines	96

Total bases

Tim Wallach	2,728
Andre Dawson	2,679
Gary Carter	2,409
Tim Raines	2,321
Warren Cromartie	1,525
Larry Parrish	1,452
Andres Galarraga	1,344
Rondell White	1,322
Bob Bailey	1,307
Vladimir Guerrero	1,277

Runs batted in

Tim Wallach	905
Andre Dawson	838
Gary Carter	823
Tim Raines	552
Bob Bailey	466
Larry Parrish	444
Andres Galarraga	433
Vladimir Guerrero	404
Hubie Brooks	390
Larry Walker	384
Rondell White	384

Extra-base hits

Tim Wallach	595
Andre Dawson	587
Gary Carter	518
Tim Raines	450
Larry Parrish	332
Warren Cromartie	312
Rondell White	289
Andres Galarraga	288
Vladimir Guerrero	285
Larry Walker	262

Batting average
(Minimum 500 games)

Vladimir Guerrero	.322
Tim Raines	.301
Rusty Staub	.294
Rondell White	.293
Moises Alou	.292
Ellis Valentine	.288
Larry Walker	.282
Warren Cromartie	.280
Andre Dawson	.280
Marquis Grissom	.279

Stolen bases

Tim Raines	634
Marquis Grissom	266
Andre Dawson	253
Delino DeShields	187
Rodney Scott	139
Otis Nixon	133
Larry Walker	98
Ron LeFlore	97
Mike Lansing	96
Mitch Webster	96

PITCHING

Earned-run average
(Minimum 500 innings)

Tim Burke	2.61
Jeff Reardon	2.84
Ken Hill	3.04
Pedro Martinez	3.06
Dennis Martinez	3.06
Dan Schatzeder	3.09
Mel Rojas	3.11
Steve Rogers	3.17
Jeff Fassero	3.20
Woodie Fryman	3.24

Wins

Steve Rogers	158
Dennis Martinez	100
Bryn Smith	81
Bill Gullickson	72
Steve Renko	68
Jeff Fassero	58
Scott Sanderson	56
Charlie Lea	55
Pedro Martinez	55
Woodie Fryman	51
Bill Stoneman	51

Losses

Steve Rogers	152
Steve Renko	82
Dennis Martinez	72
Bill Stoneman	72
Bryn Smith	71
Bill Gullickson	61
Woodie Fryman	52
Ernie McAnally	49
Jeff Fassero	48
Dustin Hermanson	47
Scott Sanderson	47

Innings pitched

Steve Rogers	2,837.2
Dennis Martinez	1,609.0
Bryn Smith	1,400.1
Steve Renko	1,359.1
Bill Gullickson	1,186.1
Bill Stoneman	1,085.1
Scott Sanderson	883.0
Jeff Fassero	850.0
Pedro Martinez	797.1
Charlie Lea	793.1

Strikeouts

Steve Rogers	1,621
Dennis Martinez	973
Pedro Martinez	843
Bryn Smith	838
Bill Stoneman	831
Steve Renko	810
Jeff Fassero	750
Bill Gullickson	678
Scott Sanderson	603
Dustin Hermanson	529

Bases on balls

Steve Rogers	876
Steve Renko	624
Bill Stoneman	535
Dennis Martinez	407
Bryn Smith	341
Mike Torrez	303
Charlie Lea	291
Bill Gullickson	288
Carl Morton	279
Jeff Fassero	274
Woodie Fryman	274

Games

Tim Burke	425
Steve Rogers	399
Mel Rojas	388
Jeff Reardon	359
Woodie Fryman	297
Anthony Telford	285
Bryn Smith	284
Steve Kline	269
Jeff Fassero	262
Andy McGaffigan	258

Shutouts

Steve Rogers	37
Bill Stoneman	15
Dennis Martinez	13
Woodie Fryman	8
Charlie Lea	8
Pedro Martinez	8
Scott Sanderson	8
Bryn Smith	8
5 tied with 6	

Saves

Jeff Reardon	152
Ugueth Urbina	110
Mel Rojas	109
John Wetteland	105
Tim Burke	101
Mike Marshall	75
Woodie Fryman	52
Dale Murray	33
Elias Sosa	30
Claude Raymond	24

TEAM SEASON, GAME RECORDS

SEASON

Batting

Most at-bats	5,675	1977
Most runs	741	1987, 1996
Fewest runs	513	1972
Most hits	1,482	1983
Most singles	1,042	1983
Most doubles	339	1997
Most triples	61	1980
Most home runs	178	2000
Fewest home runs	86	1974
Most grand slams	9	1996
Most pinch-hit home runs	9	1973
Most total bases	2,389	2000
Most stolen bases	237	1980
Highest batting average	.266	2000
Lowest batting average	.234	1972
Highest slugging pct	.432	2000

Pitching

Lowest ERA	3.08	1988
Highest ERA	5.13	2000
Most complete games	49	1971
Most shutouts	18	1979
Most saves	61	1993
Most walks	716	1970
Most strikeouts	1,206	1996

Fielding

Most errors	184	1969
Fewest errors	110	1990
Most double plays	193	1970
Highest fielding average	.982	1990

General

Most games won	95	1979
Most games lost	110	1969
Highest win pct	.649	1994
Lowest win pct	.321	1969

GAME, INNING

Batting

Most runs, game	21	Last 4-28-96
Most runs, inning	13	5-7-97
Most hits, game	28	7-30-78
Most home runs, game	8	7-30-78
Most total bases, game	58	7-30-78

Third baseman Tim Wallach holds numerous team records, including hits (1,694) and RBIs (905).

EXPOS YEAR-BY-YEAR

Year	W	L	Place	Games Back	Manager	Leaders: Batting avg.	Hits	Home runs	RBIs	Wins	ERA
EAST DIVISION											
1969	52	110	6th	48	Mauch	Staub, .302	Staub, 166	Staub, 29	Laboy, 83	Stoneman, 11	Waslewski, 3.29
1970	73	89	6th	16	Mauch	Fairly, .288	Staub, 156	Staub, 30	Staub, 94	Morton, 18	Morton, 3.60
1971	71	90	5th	25½	Mauch	Staub, .311	Staub, 186	Staub, 19	Staub, 97	Stoneman, 17	Stoneman, 3.15
1972	70	86	5th	26½	Mauch	Fairly, .278	Singleton, 139	Fairly, 17	Fairly, 68	Torrez, 16	Marshall, 1.78
1973	79	83	4th	3½	Mauch	Hunt, .309	Singleton, 169	Bailey, 26	Singleton, 103	Renko, 15	Rogers, 1.54
1974	79	82	4th	8½	Mauch	W. Davis, .295	W. Davis, 180	Bailey, 20	W. Davis, 89	Rogers, Torrez, 15	Taylor, 2.17
1975	75	87	*5th	17½	Mauch	Parrish, .274	Parrish, 146	Jorgensen, 18	Carter, 68	Murray, 15	Warthen, 3.11
1976	55	107	6th	46	Kuehl, Fox	Foli, .264	Foli, 144	Parrish, 11	Parrish, 61	Fryman, 13	Rogers, 3.21
1977	75	87	5th	26	Williams	Valentine, .293	Cash, 188	Carter, 31	Perez, 91	Rogers, 17	Rogers, 3.10
1978	76	86	4th	14	Williams	Cromartie, .297	Cromartie, 180	Dawson, Valentine, 25	Perez, 78	Grimsley, 20	Dues, 2.36
1979	95	65	2nd	2	Williams	Parrish, .307	Cromartie, 181	Parrish, 30	Dawson, 92	Lee, 16	Sosa, 1.96
1980	90	72	2nd	1	Williams	Dawson, .308	Dawson, 178	Carter, 29	Carter, 101	Rogers, Sanderson, 16	Palmer, Rogers, 2.98
1981	60	48	†‡3rd/1st	—	Williams, Fanning	Cromartie, Raines, .304	Dawson, 119	Dawson, 24	Carter, 68	Rogers, 12	Gullickson, 2.80
1982	86	76	3rd	6	Fanning	Oliver, .331	Oliver, 204	Carter, 29	Oliver, 109	Rogers, 19	Reardon, 2.06
1983	82	80	3rd	8	Virdon	Oliver, .300	Dawson, 189	Dawson, 32	Dawson, 113	Gullickson, Rogers, 17	B. Smith, 2.49
1984	78	83	5th	18	Virdon, Fanning	Raines, .309	Raines, 192	Carter, 27	Carter, 106	Lea, 15	Schatzeder, 2.71
1985	84	77	3rd	16½	Rodgers	Raines, .320	Raines, 184	Dawson, 23	Brooks, 100	B. Smith, 18	Burke, 2.39
1986	78	83	4th	29½	Rodgers	Raines, .334	Raines, 194	Dawson, 20	Dawson, 78	Youmans, 13	McGaffigan, 2.65
1987	91	71	3rd	4	Rodgers	Raines, .330	Wallach, 177	Wallach, 26	Wallach, 123	Heaton, 13	Burke, 1.19
1988	81	81	3rd	20	Rodgers	Galarraga, .302	Galarraga, 184	Galarraga, 29	Galarraga, 92	Martinez, 15	P. Perez, 2.44
1989	81	81	4th	12	Rodgers	Raines, .286	Wallach, 159	Galarraga, 23	Galarraga, 85	Martinez, 16	Langston, 2.39
1990	85	77	3rd	10	Rodgers	Wallach, .296	Wallach, 185	Wallach, 21	Wallach, 98	Sampen, 12	Boyd, 2.93
1991	71	90	6th	26½	Rodgers, Runnells	Calderon, .300	Grissom, 149	Calderon, 19	Calderon, 75	Martinez, 14	Martinez, 2.39
1992	87	75	2nd	9	Runnells, F. Alou	Walker, .301	Grissom, 180	Walker, 23	Walker, 93	Hill, Martinez, 16	Rojas, 1.43
1993	94	68	2nd	3	F. Alou	Grissom, .298	Grissom, 188	Walker, 22	Grissom, 95	Martinez, 15	Fassero, 2.29
1994	74	40	1st	+6	F. Alou	M. Alou, .339	M. Alou, 143	M. Alou, 22	Walker, 86	Hill, 16	Henry, 2.43
1995	66	78	5th	24	Alou	Segui, .309	Cordero, 147	Alou, Berry, Tarasco, 14	Segui, 68	Martinez, 14	Henry, 2.84
1996	88	74	2nd	8	Alou	Grudzielanek, .306	Grudzielanek, 201	Rodriguez, 36	Rodriguez, 103	Fassero, 15	Fassero, 3.30
1997	78	84	4th	23	Alou	Segui, .307	Grudzielanek, 177	White, 28	Rodriguez, 83	Martinez, 17	Martinez, 1.90
1998	65	97	4th	41	Alou	V. Guerrero, .324	V. Guerrero, 202	V. iGuerrero, 38	V.Guerrero, 109	Hermanson, 14	Hermanson, 3.13
1999	68	94	4th	35	Alou	V. Guerrero, .316	V .Guerrero, 193	V. Guerrero, 42	V.Guerrero, 131	Hermanson, Vazquez, 9	Telford, 3.94
2000	67	95	4th	28	Alou	V. Guerrero, .345	Vidro, 200	V. Guerrero, 44	V. Guerrero, 123	Hermanson, 12	Pavano, 3.06

* Tied for position. † First half 30-25; second half 30-23. ‡ Lost Championship Series.

Note: Batting average minimum 350 at-bats; ERA minimum 90 innings pitched.

Manny Mota

MONTREAL made history May 27, 1968, when it was awarded an expansion franchise—the first outside the continental United States. Montreal joined San Diego in the National League and Kansas City and Seattle in the American League as part of a four-team expansion that brought baseball's membership roster to 24 teams.

The infant Expos took their first step when they made versatile Manny Mota their first pick of the October 14, 1968, expansion draft—one of 30 overall selections. Montreal made its Major League debut on April 8, 1969, with an 11-10 victory over the Mets at New York's Shea Stadium. The long-awaited home inaugural at Jarry Park took place on April 14, and the Expos celebrated with an 8-7 victory over St. Louis in the first Major League regular-season game on foreign soil.

Expansion draft (October 14, 1968)

Players

Player	From	Position
Jesus Alou	San Francisco	outfield
John Bateman	Houston	catcher
John Boccabella	Chicago	catcher
Ron Brand	Houston	catcher
Donn Clendenon	Pittsburgh	first base
Ty Cline	San Francisco	outfield
Jim Fairey	Los Angeles	outfield
Angel Hermoso	Atlanta	infield
Jose Herrera	Houston	infield
Garry Jestadt	Chicago	infield
Mack Jones	Cincinnati	outfield
Coco Laboy	St. Louis	infield
*Manny Mota	Pittsburgh	infield/outfield
Gary Sutherland	Philadelphia	infield/outfield
Jim Williams	Cincinnati	shortstop
Maury Wills	Pittsburgh	shortstop

Pitchers

Pitcher	From	Throws
Jack Billingham	Los Angeles	righthanded
John Glass	New York	righthanded
Jim (Mudcat) Grant	Los Angeles	righthanded
Skip Guinn	Atlanta	lefthanded
Larry Jackson	Philadelphia	righthanded
Larry Jaster	St. Louis	lefthanded
Ernie McAnally	New York	righthanded
Dan McGinn	Cincinnati	lefthanded
Carl Morton	Atlanta	righthanded
Bob Reynolds	San Francisco	righthanded
Jerry Robertson	St. Louis	righthanded
Don Shaw	New York	lefthanded
Bill Stoneman	Chicago	righthanded
Mike Wegener	Philadelphia	righthanded

*First pick

Opening day lineup

April 8, 1969

Maury Wills, shortstop
Gary Sutherland, second base
Rusty Staub, right field
Mack Jones, left field
Bob Bailey, first base
John Batemen, catcher
Coco Laboy, third base
Don Hahn, center field
Mudcat Grant, pitcher

Rusty Staub

Expos firsts

First hit: Maury Wills, April 8, 1969, at New York (single)
First home run: Dan McGinn, April 8, 1969, at New York
First RBI: Bob Bailey, April 8, 1969, at New York
First win: Don Shaw, April 8, 1969, at New York
First shutout: Bill Stoneman (no-hitter), April 17, 1969, 7-0 at Philadelphia

New York Mets

FRANCHISE CHRONOLOGY

First season: 1962, as one of two new teams in the National League's first modern-era expansion. The Mets dropped an 11-4 opener to St. Louis and stumbled to 120 first-year losses, a 20th-century record.

1963-present: The early year Mets were bumbling and inept—and lovable. New York, devoid of an N.L. franchise since losing the Dodgers and Giants in 1957, fervently embraced the mistake-prone Mets as they struggled to 452 losses in their first four seasons (an average of 113) under irascible manager Casey Stengel. But that feeling changed in 1969, when the upstart New Yorkers, coming off a ninth-place finish, won 100 games and finished first in the newly created East Division. They punctuated their surprising success with a three-game sweep of Atlanta in the first N.L. Championship Series and a shocking five-game victory over powerful Baltimore in the World Series. The Miracle Mets had risen from ineptitude to the top of the baseball world. No longer lovable losers, the Mets remained consistent contenders, winning another pennant in 1973, another Series championship in 1986 and their fourth pennant in 2000 before losing in the World Series to the Yankees.

Manager Gil Hodges (14).

METS VS. OPPONENTS BY DECADE

	Braves	Cardinals	Cubs	Dodgers	Giants	Phillies	Pirates	Reds	Astros	Expos	Padres	Marlins	Rockies	Brewers	D'backs	Interleague	Decade Record
1962-69	49-89	54-90	65-79	44-94	51-87	53-91	51-93	54-83	49-87	13-5	11-1						494-799
1970-79	61-59	85-93	93-86	52-68	62-58	83-97	78-98	40-80	59-61	86-94	64-56						763-850
1980-89	68-46	87-86	92-83	63-50	49-65	90-86	102-69	62-55	56-61	89-85	58-57						816-743
1990-99	50-69	67-55	57-62	53-58	58-56	69-70	58-67	59-49	46-61	68-69	52-63	50-36	32-36	13-3	7-11	28-21	767-786
2000-	6-7	6-3	5-2	5-4	3-5	6-7	7-2	4-5	5-2	9-3	3-6	6-6	6-3	7-2	7-2	9-9	94-68
Totals	234-270	299-327	312-312	217-274	223-271	301-351	296-329	219-272	215-272	265-256	188-183	56-42	38-39	20-5	14-13	37-30	2934-3246

Interleague results: 9-4 vs. Orioles; 6-6 vs. Red Sox; 0-3 vs. Tigers; 7-11 vs. Yankees; 9-3 vs. Blue Jays; 6-3 vs. Devil Rays.

MANAGERS

Name	*Years*	*Record*
Casey Stengel	1962-65	175-404
Wes Westrum	1965-67	142-237
Salty Parker	1967	4-7
Gil Hodges	1968-71	339-309
Yogi Berra	1972-75	292-296
Roy McMillan	1975	26-27
Joe Frazier	1976-77	101-106
Joe Torre	1977-81	286-420
George Bamberger	1982-83	81-127
Frank Howard	1983	52-64
Dave Johnson	1984-90	595-417
Bud Harrelson	1990-91	145-129
Mike Cubbage	1991	3-4
Jeff Torborg	1992-93	85-115
Dallas Green	1993-96	229-283
Bobby Valentine	1996-2000	379-301

WORLD SERIES CHAMPIONS

Year	*Loser*	*Length*	*MVP*
1969	Baltimore	5 games	Clendenon
1986	Boston	7 games	Knight

N.L. PENNANT WINNERS

Year	*Record*	*Manager*	*Series Result*
1969	100-62	Hodges	Defeated Orioles
1973	82-79	Berra	Lost to A's
1986	108-54	Johnson	Defeated Red Sox
2000	94-68	Valentine	Lost to Yankees

EAST DIVISION CHAMPIONS

Year	*Record*	*Manager*	*NLCS Result*
1969	100-62	Hodges	Defeated Braves
1973	82-79	Berra	Defeated Reds
1986	108-54	Johnson	Defeated Astros
1988	100-60	Johnson	Lost to Dodgers

WILD-CARD QUALIFIERS

Year	*Record*	*Manager*	*NLCS Result*
1999	97-66	Valentine	Lost to Braves
2000	94-68	Valentine	Defeated Cardinals

ALL-TIME RECORD OF EXPANSION TEAMS

Team	W	L	Pct.	DT	P	WS
Arizona	250	236	.514	1	0	0
Kansas City	2,548	2,497	.505	6	2	1
Toronto	1,867	1,897	.496	5	2	2
Houston	3,052	3,138	.493	6	0	0
Montreal	2,454	2,596	.486	2	0	0
Anaheim	3,069	3,281	.483	3	0	0
Colorado	594	639	.482	0	0	0
Milwaukee	2,421	2,631	.479	2	1	0
New York	2,934	3,246	.475	4	4	2
Texas	2,952	3,381	.466	4	0	0
San Diego	2,315	2,742	.458	3	2	0
Seattle	1,715	2,048	.456	2	0	0
Florida	551	678	.448	0	1	1
Tampa Bay	201	284	.414	0	0	0

DT—Division Titles. P—Pennants won. WS—World Series won.

ATTENDANCE HIGHS

Total	*Season*	*Park*
3,047,724	1988	Shea Stadium
3,027,121	1987	Shea Stadium
2,918,710	1989	Shea Stadium
2,800,221	2000	Shea Stadium
2,762,417	1986	Shea Stadium

BALLPARK CHRONOLOGY

Shea Stadium (1964-present)

Capacity: 55,601.
First game: Pittsburgh 4, Mets 3 (April 17, 1964).
First batter: Dick Schofield, Pirates.
First hit: Willie Stargell, Pirates (home run).
First run: Willie Stargell, Pirates (2nd inning).
First home run: Willie Stargell, Pirates.
First winning pitcher: Bob Friend, Pirates.
First-season attendance: 1,732,597.

Polo Grounds (1962-63)

First game: Pittsburgh 4, Mets 3 (April 13, 1962).
First-season attendance: 922,530.

CY YOUNG WINNERS

Tom Seaver, RH, 1969
Tom Seaver, RH, 1973
Tom Seaver, RH, 1975
Dwight Gooden, RH, 1985

ROOKIES OF THE YEAR

Tom Seaver, P, 1967
Jon Matlack, P, 1972
Darryl Strawberry, OF, 1983
Dwight Gooden, P, 1984

RETIRED UNIFORMS

No.	*Name*	*Pos.*
14	Gil Hodges	Man.
37	Casey Stengel	Man.
41	Tom Seaver	P

Manager Casey Stengel and outfielder Ed Kranepool were New York Mets originals.

MILESTONE PERFORMANCES

25-plus home runs

41— Todd Hundley 1996
40— Mike Piazza 1999
39— Darryl Strawberry 1987, 1988
38— Howard Johnson 1991
Mike Piazza 2000
37— Dave Kingman 1976, 1982
Darryl Strawberry 1990
36— Dave Kingman 1975
Howard Johnson 1987, 1989
34— Frank Thomas 1962
Bobby Bonilla 1993
32— Gary Carter 1985
Mike Piazza *1998
Robin Ventura 1999
30— Bernard Gilkey 1996
Todd Hundley 1997
29— Darryl Strawberry 1985, 1989
Kevin McReynolds 1987
28— George Foster 1983
27— Darryl Strawberry 1986
Kevin McReynolds 1987
Eddie Murray 1993
Edgardo Alfonzo 1999
26— Tommie Agee 1969
Darryl Strawberry 1983, 1984
25— Bobby Murcer 1971
Edgardo Alfonzo 2000

*9 with Los Angeles; 23 with Mets.

100-plus RBIs

124— Mike Piazza 1999
120— Robin Ventura 1999
117— Howard Johnson 1991
Bernard Gilkey 1996
113— Mike Piazza 2000
112— Todd Hundley 1996
111— Mike Piazza *1998
108— Darryl Strawberry 1990
Edgardo Alfonzo 1999
105— Rusty Staub 1975
Gary Carter 1986
104— Darryl Strawberry 1987
102— John Olerud 1997
101— Darryl Strawberry 1988
Howard Johnson 1989
100— Gary Carter 1985
Eddie Murray 1993

*30 with Los Angeles; 5 with Florida; 76 with Mets.

20-plus victories

1969— Tom Seaver 25-7
1971— Tom Seaver 20-10
1972— Tom Seaver 21-12
1975— Tom Seaver 22-9
1976— Jerry Koosman 21-10
1985— Dwight Gooden 24-4
1988— David Cone 20-3
1990— Frank Viola 20-12

N.L. home run champions

1982— Dave Kingman 37
1988— Darryl Strawberry 39
1991— Howard Johnson 38

N.L. RBI champion

1991— Howard Johnson 117

N.L. batting champions

None

N.L. ERA champions

1970— Tom Seaver 2.81
1971— Tom Seaver 1.76
1973— Tom Seaver 2.08
1978— Craig Swan 2.43
1985— Dwight Gooden 1.53

N.L. strikeout champions

1970— Tom Seaver 283
1971— Tom Seaver 289
1973— Tom Seaver 251
1975— Tom Seaver 243
1976— Tom Seaver 235
1984— Dwight Gooden 276
1985— Dwight Gooden 268
1990— David Cone 233
1991— David Cone 241

No-hit pitchers

(9 innings or more)
None

Longest hitting streaks

24— Hubie Brooks 1984
Mike Piazza 1999
23— Cleon Jones 1970
Mike Vail 1975
John Olerud 1998
21— Mike Piazza 2000
20— Tommie Agee 1970
Butch Huskey 1997
Edgardo Alfonzo 1997
19— Tommie Agee 1970
Lee Mazzilli 1979
Felix Millan 1975
18— Ed Kranepool 1975
Lee Mazzilli 1980
Felix Millan 1973
Darryl Strawberry 1990
Frank Thomas 1962
17— Lance Johnson 1996
16— Joe Torre 1975
John Milner 1976
Jose Vizcaino 1994
15— Rusty Staub 1973
John Stearns 1977
John Stearns 1982
Mookie Wilson 1984
Rico Brogna 1994

First baseman Keith Hernandez (right) brought his golden glove and steady bat to New York midway through the 1983 season.

INDIVIDUAL SEASON, GAME RECORDS

Outfielder Darryl Strawberry hit 252 home runs for the Mets before taking his bat to the Los Angeles Dodgers in 1991.

SEASON

Batting			
At-bats	682	Lance Johnson	1996
Runs	123	Edgardo Alfonzo	1999
Hits	227	Lance Johnson	1996
Singles	166	Lance Johnson	1996
Doubles	44	Bernard Gilkey	1996
Triples	21	Lance Johnson	1996
Home runs	41	Todd Hundley	1996
Home runs, rookie	26	Darryl Strawberry	1983
Grand slams	3	John Milner	1976
		Mike Piazza	2000
		Robin Ventura	1999
Total bases	327	Lance Johnson	1996
RBIs	124	Mike Piazza	1999
Walks	125	John Olerud	1999
Most strikeouts	156	Tommie Agee	1970
		Dave Kingman	1982
Fewest strikeouts	14	Felix Millan	1974
Batting average	.353	John Olerud	1998
Slugging pct.	.614	Mike Piazza	2000
Stolen bases	66	Roger Cedeno	1999
Pitching			
Games	80	Turk Wendell	1999
Complete games	21	Tom Seaver	1971
Innings	290.2	Tom Seaver	1970
Wins	25	Tom Seaver	1969
Losses	24	Roger Craig	1962
		Jack Fisher	1965
Winning pct.	.870 (20-3)	David Cone	1988
Walks	116	Nolan Ryan	1971
Strikeouts	289	Tom Seaver	1971
Shutouts	8	Dwight Gooden	1985
Home runs allowed	35	Roger Craig	1962
Lowest ERA	1.53	Dwight Gooden	1985
Saves	41	Armando Benitez	2000

GAME

Batting			
Runs	6	Edgardo Alfonzo	8-30-99
Hits	6	Edgardo Alfonzo	8-30-99
Doubles	3	Last by Edgardo Alfonzo	4-18-2000
Triples	3	Doug Flynn	8-5-80
Home runs	3	Last by Edgardo Alfonzo	8-30-99
RBIs	8	Dave Kingman	6-4-76
Total bases	16	Edgardo Alfonzo	8-30-99
Stolen bases	4	Last by Roger Cedeno	5-14-99

CAREER LEADERS

BATTING

Games

Ed Kranepool	1,853
Bud Harrelson	1,322
Jerry Grote	1,235
Cleon Jones	1,201
Howard Johnson	1,154
Mookie Wilson	1,116
Darryl Strawberry	1,109
Lee Mazzilli	979
Rusty Staub	942
Wayne Garrett	883

At-bats

Ed Kranepool	5,436
Bud Harrelson	4,390
Cleon Jones	4,223
Mookie Wilson	4,027
Howard Johnson	3,968
Darryl Strawberry	3,903
Jerry Grote	3,881
Keith Hernandez	3,164
Lee Mazzilli	3,013
Edgardo Alfonzo	2,950

Runs

Darryl Strawberry	662
Howard Johnson	627
Mookie Wilson	592
Cleon Jones	563
Ed Kranepool	536
Bud Harrelson	490
Edgardo Alfonzo	472
Keith Hernandez	455
Kevin McReynolds	405
Lee Mazzilli	404

Hits

Ed Kranepool	1,418
Cleon Jones	1,188
Mookie Wilson	1,112
Bud Harrelson	1,029
Darryl Strawberry	1,025
Howard Johnson	997
Jerry Grote	994
Keith Hernandez	939
Edgardo Alfonzo	874
Lee Mazzilli	796

Doubles

Ed Kranepool	225
Howard Johnson	214
Darryl Strawberry	187
Cleon Jones	182
Mookie Wilson	170
Edgardo Alfonzo	164
Keith Hernandez	159
Kevin McReynolds	153
John Stearns	152
Lee Mazzilli	148

Triples

Mookie Wilson	62
Bud Harrelson	45
Cleon Jones	33
Steve Henderson	31
Darryl Strawberry	30
Lance Johnson	27
Doug Flynn	26
Ed Kranepool	25
Lee Mazzilli	22
Wayne Garrett	20
Ron Swoboda	20

Home runs

Darryl Strawberry	252
Howard Johnson	192
Dave Kingman	154
Todd Hundley	124
Kevin McReynolds	122
Ed Kranepool	118
Mike Piazza	101
George Foster	99
Bobby Bonilla	95
John Milner	94

Total bases

Ed Kranepool	2,047
Darryl Strawberry	2,028
Howard Johnson	1,823
Cleon Jones	1,715
Mookie Wilson	1,586
Keith Hernandez	1,358
Kevin McReynolds	1,338
Edgardo Alfonzo	1,327
Jerry Grote	1,278
Bud Harrelson	1,260

Runs batted in

Darryl Strawberry	733
Howard Johnson	629
Ed Kranepool	614
Cleon Jones	521
Keith Hernandez	468
Kevin McReynolds	456
Edgardo Alfonzo	433
Rusty Staub	399
Todd Hundley	397
Dave Kingman	389

Extra-base hits

Darryl Strawberry	469
Howard Johnson	424
Ed Kranepool	368
Cleon Jones	308
Mookie Wilson	292
Kevin McReynolds	289
Edgardo Alfonzo	265
Keith Hernandez	249
Todd Hundley	249
Lee Mazzilli	238

Batting average

(Minimum 500 games)

Keith Hernandez	.297
Edgardo Alfonzo	.296
Dave Magadan	.292
Wally Backman	.283
Cleon Jones	.281
Lenny Dykstra	.278
Felix Millan	.278
Mookie Wilson	.276
Rusty Staub	.276
Joel Youngblood	.274

Stolen bases

Mookie Wilson	281
Howard Johnson	202
Darryl Strawberry	191
Lee Mazzilli	152
Lenny Dykstra	116
Bud Harrelson	115
Wally Backman	106
Vince Coleman	99
Tommie Agee	92
Cleon Jones	91
John Stearns	91

PITCHING

Earned-run average

(Minimum 500 innings)

Tom Seaver	2.57
Jesse Orosco	2.73
John Franco	2.86
Jon Matlack	3.03
David Cone	3.08
Jerry Koosman	3.09
Dwight Gooden	3.10
Bob Ojeda	3.12
Sid Fernandez	3.14
Bret Saberhagen	3.16

Wins

Tom Seaver	198
Dwight Gooden	157
Jerry Koosman	140
Ron Darling	99
Sid Fernandez	98
Jon Matlack	82
David Cone	80
Bobby Jones	74
Craig Swan	59
Bob Ojeda	51

Losses

Jerry Koosman	137
Tom Seaver	124
Dwight Gooden	85
Jon Matlack	81
Al Jackson	80
Sid Fernandez	78
Jack Fisher	73
Craig Swan	71
Ron Darling	70
Bobby Jones	56

Innings pitched

Tom Seaver	3,045.1
Jerry Koosman	2,544.2
Dwight Gooden	2,169.2
Ron Darling	1,620.0
Sid Fernandez	1,584.2
Jon Matlack	1,448.0
Craig Swan	1,230.2
Bobby Jones	1,215.2
David Cone	1,191.1
Bobby Jones	1,061.0

Strikeouts

Tom Seaver	2,541
Dwight Gooden	1,875
Jerry Koosman	1,799
Sid Fernandez	1,449
David Cone	1,159
Ron Darling	1,148
Jon Matlack	1,023
Bobby Jones	714
Craig Swan	671
Tug McGraw	618

Bases on balls

Tom Seaver	847
Jerry Koosman	820
Dwight Gooden	651
Ron Darling	614
Sid Fernandez	596
Jon Matlack	419
David Cone	418
Craig Swan	368
Bobby Jones	353
Tug McGraw	350

Games

John Franco	547
Tom Seaver	401
Jerry Koosman	376
Jesse Orosco	372
Tug McGraw	361
Dwight Gooden	305
Jeff Innis	288
Roger McDowell	280
Ron Taylor	269
Doug Sisk	263

Shutouts

Tom Seaver	44
Jerry Koosman	26
Jon Matlack	26
Dwight Gooden	23
David Cone	15
Ron Darling	10
Al Jackson	10
Sid Fernandez	9
Bob Ojeda	9
Gary Gentry	8

Saves

John Franco	272
Jesse Orosco	107
Tug McGraw	86
Roger McDowell	84
Neil Allen	69
Skip Lockwood	65
Armando Benitez	63
Randy Myers	56
Ron Taylor	49
Doug Sisk	33

TEAM SEASON, GAME RECORDS

SEASON

Batting

Record	No.	Year
Most at-bats	5,618	1996
Most runs	853	1999
Fewest runs	473	1968
Most hits	1,553	1999
Most singles	1,087	1980
Most doubles	297	1999
Most triples	47	1978, 1996
Most home runs	198	2000
Fewest home runs	61	1980
Most grand slams	8	1999, 2000
Most pinch-hit home runs	12	1983
Most total bases	2,430	1987
Most stolen bases	159	1987
Highest batting average	.279	1999
Lowest batting average	.219	1963
Highest slugging pct	.434	1987, 1999

Pitching

Record	No.	Year
Lowest ERA	2.72	1968
Highest ERA	5.04	1962
Most complete games	53	1976
Most shutouts	28	1969
Most saves	51	1987
Most walks	617	1999
Most strikeouts	1,217	1990

Fielding

Record	No.	Year
Most errors	210	1962, 1963
Fewest errors	68	1999
Most double plays	171	1966, 1983
Highest fielding average	.989	1999

General

Record	No.	Year
Most games won	108	1986
Most games lost	120	1962
Highest win pct	.667	1986
Lowest win pct	.250	1962

GAME, INNING

Batting

Record	No.	Date
Most runs, game	23	8-16-87
Most runs, inning	10	6-12-79, 7-30-2000
Most hits, game	28	7-4-85
Most home runs, game	6	4-4-88, 6-15-99
Most total bases, game	38	7-4-85, 8-30-99
Most stolen bases, game	6	Last 4-10-91

Lefthanded starter Jerry Koosman was a key figure in the Mets' 1969 World Series miracle.

METS YEAR-BY-YEAR

Year	W	L	Place	Games Back	Manager	Leaders: Batting avg.	Hits	Home runs	RBIs	Wins	ERA
1962	40	120	10th	60½	Stengel	Ashburn, .306	Thomas, 152	Thomas, 34	Thomas, 94	Craig, 10	Jackson, 4.40
1963	51	111	10th	48	Stengel	Hunt, .272	Hunt, 145	Hickman, 17	Thomas, 60	Jackson, 13	Willey, 3.10
1964	53	109	10th	40	Stengel	Hunt, .303	Christopher, 163	C. Smith, 20	Christopher, 76	Jackson, 11	Wakefield, 3.61
1965	50	112	10th	47	Stengel, Westrum	Kranepool, .253	Kranepool, 133	Swoboda, 19	C. Smith, 62	Fisher, Jackson, 8	McGraw, 3.32
1966	66	95	9th	28½	Westrum	Hunt, .288	Hunt, 138	Kranepool, 16	Boyer, 61	Fisher, Ribant, B. Shaw, 11	Ribant, 3.20
1967	61	101	10th	40½	Westrum, Parker	T. Davis, .302	T. Davis, 174	T. Davis, 16	T. Davis, 73	Seaver, 16	Seaver, 2.76
1968	73	89	9th	24	Hodges	Jones, .297	Jones, 151	Charles, 15	Swoboda, 59	Koosman, 19	Koosman, 2.08
								EAST DIVISION			
1969	100	62	*1st	+8	Hodges	Jones, .340	Jones, 164	Agee, 26	Agee, 76	Seaver, 25	Seaver, 2.21
1970	83	79	3rd	6	Hodges	Shamsky, .293	Agee, 182	Agee, 24	Clendenon, 97	Seaver, 18	Seaver, 2.82
1971	83	79	†3rd	14	Hodges	Jones, .319	Jones, 161	Agee, Jones, Kranepool, 14	Jones, 69	Seaver, 20	McGraw, 1.70
1972	83	73	3rd	13½	Berra	Jones, .245	Agee, 96	Milner, 17	Jones, 52	Seaver, 21	McGraw, 1.70
1973	82	79	*1st	+1½	Berra	Millan, .290	Millan, 185	Milner, 23	Staub, 76	Seaver, 19	Seaver, 2.08
1974	71	91	5th	17	Berra	Jones, .282	Staub, 145	Milner, 20	Staub, 78	Koosman, 15	Matlack, 2.41
1975	82	80	†3rd	10½	Berra, McMillan	Grote, .295	Millan, 191	Kingman, 36	Staub, 105	Seaver, 22	Seaver, 2.38
1976	86	76	3rd	15	Frazier	Kranepool, .292	Millan, 150	Kingman, 37	Kingman, 86	Koosman, 21	Seaver, 2.59
1977	64	98	6th	37	Frazier, Torre	Randle, .304	Randle, 156	Henderson, Milner, Stearns, 12	Henderson, 65	Espinosa, 10	Seaver, 3.00
1978	66	96	6th	24	Torre	Mazzilli, .273	Henderson, Montanez, 156	Montanez, 17	Montanez, 96	Espinosa, 11	Swan, 2.43
1979	63	99	6th	35	Torre	Henderson, .306	Mazzilli, 181	Youngblood, 16	Hebner, Mazzilli, 79	Swan, 14	Swan, 3.29
1980	67	95	5th	24	Torre	Henderson, .290	Mazzilli, 162	Mazzilli, 16	Mazzilli, 76	Bomback, 10	Reardon, 2.61
1981	41	62	‡5th/4th	—	Torre	Brooks, .307	Brooks, 110	Kingman, 22	Kingman, 59	Allen, Zachry, 7	Falcone, 2.55
1982	65	97	6th	27	Bamberger	Stearns, .293	Wilson, 178	Kingman, 37	Kingman, 99	Swan, 11	Orosco, 2.72
1983	68	94	6th	22	Bamberger, Howard	Wilson, .276	Wilson, 176	Foster, 28	Foster, 90	Orosco, 13	Orosco, 1.47
1984	90	72	2nd	6½	D. Johnson	Hernandez, .311	Hernandez, 171	Strawberry, 26	Strawberry, 97	Gooden, 17	Orosco, 2.59
1985	98	64	2nd	3	D. Johnson	Hernandez, .309	Hernandez, 183	Carter, 32	Carter, 100	Gooden, 24	Gooden, 1.53
1986	108	54	*1st	+21½	D. Johnson	Backman, .320	Hernandez, 171	Strawberry, 27	Carter, 105	Ojeda, 18	Ojeda, 2.57
1987	92	70	2nd	3	D. Johnson	Wilson, .299	Hernandez, 170	Strawberry, 39	Strawberry, 104	Gooden, 15	Gooden, 3.21
1988	100	60	§1st	+15	D. Johnson	Wilson, .296	McReynolds, 159	Strawberry, 39	Strawberry, 101	Cone, 20	Cone, 2.22
1989	87	75	2nd	6	D. Johnson	H. Johnson, .287	H. Johnson, 164	H. Johnson, 36	H. Johnson, 101	Cone, Darling, Fernandez, 14	Fernandez, 2.83
1990	91	71	2nd	4	Johnson, Harrelson	Magadan, .328	Jefferies, 171	Strawberry, 37	Strawberry, 108	Viola, 20	Viola, 2.67
1991	77	84	5th	20½	Harrelson, Cubbage	Jefferies, .272	H. Johnson, 146	H. Johnson, 38	H. Johnson, 117	Cone, 14	Cone, 3.29
1992	72	90	5th	24	Torborg	Murray, .261	Murray, 144	Bonilla, 19	Murray, 93	Fernandez, 14	Fernandez, 2.73
1993	59	103	7th	38	Torborg, Green	Murray, .285	Murray, 174	Bonilla, 34	Murray, 100	Gooden, 12	Fernandez, 2.93
1994	55	58	3rd	18½	Green	Kent, .292	Kent, 121	Bonilla, 20	Kent, 68	Saberhagen, 14	Saberhagen, 2.74
1995	69	75	†2nd	21	Green	Brogna, .289	Vizcaino, 146	Brogna, 22	Brogna, 76	B. Jones, 10	Isringhausen, 2.81
1996	71	91	4th	25	Green, Valentine	Johnson, .333	Johnson, 227	Hundley, 41	Gilkey, 117	Clark, 14	Clark, 3.43
1997	88	74	3rd	13	Valentine	Alfonzo, .315	Alfonzo, 163	Hundley, 30	Olerud, 102	B. Jones, 15	Reed, 2.89
1998	88	74	2nd	18	Valentine	Olerud, .353	Olerud, 197	Piazza, 32	Piazza, 111	Leiter, 17	Leiter, 2.47
1999	97	66	▲§2nd	6½	Valentine	Henderson, .315	Alfonzo, 191	Piazza, 40	Piazza, 124	Leiter, Hershiser, 13	Leiter, 4.23
2000	94	68	▲*2nd	1	Valentine	Alfonzo, .324	Alfonzo, 176	Piazza, 38	Piazza, 113	Leiter, 16	Hampton, 3.15

* Won Championship Series. † Tied for position. ‡ First half 17-34; second half 24-28. § Lost Championship Series. ∞ Won wild-card playoff. ▲ Won Division Series.

Note: Batting average minimum 350 at-bats; ERA minimum 90 innings pitched.

Hobie Landrith

NATIONAL LEAGUE baseball returned to the nation's largest metropolitan area on October 16, 1960, when owners approved 1962 expansion to New York and Houston. The arrival of the "Mets" filled the void created by the 1958 departures of the Dodgers and Giants to the West Coast, and it set the stage for the triumphant New York return of former Yankees manager Casey Stengel as the lovable boss of New York's expansion bumblers.

The Mets stocked their roster with 22 players from the October 10, 1961, expansion draft, grabbing catcher Hobie Landrith with their first pick. The franchise debut took place on April 11, 1962, when the Mets dropped an 11-4 decision at St. Louis—the first of 120 losses they would suffer in their inaugural season.

Expansion draft (October 10, 1961)

Players

Player	From	Position
Gus Bell	Cincinnati	outfield
Ed Bouchee	Chicago	first base
Chris Cannizzaro	St. Louis	catcher
Elio Chacon	Cincinnati	second base
Joe Christopher	Pittsburgh	outfield
Clarence Coleman	Philadelphia	catcher
John DeMerit.	Milwaukee	outfield
Sammy Drake	Chicago	infield
Jim Hickman	St. Louis	outfield
Gil Hodges	Los Angeles	first base
*Hobie Landrith	San Francisco	catcher
Felix Mantilla.	Milwaukee	shortstop
Bobby Gene Smith	Philadelphia	outfield
Lee Walls	Philadelphia	outfield
Don Zimmer	Chicago	second base

Pitchers

Pitcher	From	Throws
Craig Anderson	St. Louis	righthanded
Roger Craig	Los Angeles	righthanded
Ray Daviault	San Francisco	righthanded
Jay Hook	Cincinnati	righthanded
Al Jackson	Pittsburgh	lefthanded
Sherman Jones	Cincinnati	righthanded
Bob Miller	St. Louis	righthanded

*First pick

Opening day lineup

April 11, 1962

Richie Ashburn, center field
Felix Mantilla, shortstop
Charlie Neal, second base
Frank Thomas, left field
Gus Bell, right field
Gil Hodges, first base
Don Zimmer, third base
Hobie Landrith, catcher
Roger Craig, pitcher

Roger Craig

Mets firsts

First hit: Gus Bell, April 11, 1962, at St. Louis (single)
First home run: Gil Hodges, April 11, 1962, at St. Louis
First RBI: Charlie Neal, April 11, 1962, at St. Louis
First win: Jay Hook, April 23, 1962, at Pittsburgh
First shutout: Al Jackson, April 29, 1962, 8-0 vs. Philadelphia

PHILADELPHIA PHILLIES

FRANCHISE CHRONOLOGY

First season: 1883, as a member of the National League. The Phillies dropped an opening 4-3 decision to Providence and went on to lose 81 of 98 games. They finished in last place, 46 games behind first-place Boston and 23 games behind seventh-place Detroit.

1884-1900: The Phillies improved from that first-season disaster, but never enough to claim a pennant. They finished second once and third six times before entering the new century.

1901-present: The modern-era Phillies were not much different from their predecessors. They did not claim their first N.L. pennant until 1915, 32 years after their birth, and failed to win a World Series championship until 1980, at the not-so-tender age of 97. Over their 115-year history, the Phillies have finished last in their league or division 31 times, more than once every four years. They went 34 years between their first and second pennants and 30 more between their second and third. Their most successful run came from 1976 to 1983, when they won five East Division titles, two pennants and their only World Series—a six-game 1980 triumph over Kansas City. Philadelphia fans were treated to their fifth pennant in 1993, but they watched their Phillies lose a six-game World Series to Toronto.

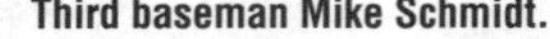

Third baseman Mike Schmidt.

PHILLIES VS. OPPONENTS BY DECADE

	Braves	Cardinals	Cubs	Dodgers	Giants	Pirates	Reds	Astros	Mets	Expos	Padres	Marlins	Rockies	Brewers	D'backs	Interleague	Decade Record
1900-09	119-87	121-90	90-119	112-93	87-121	75-137	105-105										709-752
1910-19	123-90	112-98	101-110	110-99	85-124	107-105	124-91										762-717
1920-29	118-100	69-151	88-132	87-133	65-149	71-148	68-149										566-962
1930-39	97-122	61-159	73-147	89-128	72-145	90-126	99-116										581-943
1940-49	87-132	70-150	99-121	58-162	91-129	95-121	84-136										584-951
1950-59	102-118	107-113	128-92	92-128	99-121	132-88	107-113										767-773
1960-69	75-107	79-108	95-93	76-106	77-105	89-98	75-107	87-51	91-53	7-11	8-4						759-843
1970-79	58-62	91-86	92-87	56-63	67-53	79-101	47-73	61-59	97-83	90-88	74-46						812-801
1980-89	53-64	80-95	95-78	59-55	61-54	91-83	55-60	61-57	86-90	86-87	56-57						783-780
1990-99	50-70	57-67	63-60	54-61	44-67	58-66	39-68	43-62	70-69	73-65	53-60	52-34	36-29	9-9	8-10	23-26	732-823
2000-	5-8	2-7	3-6	4-5	2-7	3-6	4-3	4-5	7-6	7-5	2-5	4-9	3-6	5-2	1-8	9-9	65-97
Totals	887-960	849-1124	927-1045	797-1033	750-1075	890-1079	807-1021	256-234	351-301	263-256	193-172	56-43	39-35	14-11	9-18	32-35	7120-8442

Interleague results: 6-12 vs. Orioles; 8-5 vs. Red Sox; 1-2 vs. Tigers; 6-6 vs. Yankees; 7-5 vs. Blue Jays; 4-5 vs. Devil Rays.

MANAGERS

Name	*Years*	*Record*
Bob Ferguson	1883	4-13
Blondie Purcell	1883	13-68
Harry Wright	1884-93	636-566
Jack Clements	1890	13-6
Al Reach	1890	4-7
Bob Allen	1890	25-10
Albert Irwin	1894-95	149-110
Billy Nash	1896	62-68
George Stallings	1897-98	74-104
Bill Shettsline	1898-1902	367-303
Chief Zimmer	1903	49-86
Hugh Duffy	1904-06	206-251
Bill Murray	1907-09	240-214
Red Dooin	1910-14	392-370
Pat Moran	1915-18	323-257
Jack Coombs	1919	18-44
Gavvy Cravath	1919-20	91-137
Bill Donovan	1921	25-62
Kaiser Wilhelm	1921-22	83-137
Art Fletcher	1923-26	231-378
Stuffy McInnis	1927	51-103
Burt Shotton	1928-33	370-549
Jimmy Wilson	1934-38	280-477
Hans Lobert	1938, 1942	42-111

Chuck Klein (left) and Lefty O'Doul combined for 267 RBIs in a prolific 1929 season.

MANAGERS—*cont'd.*

Name	*Years*	*Record*
Doc Prothro	1939-41	138-320
Bucky Harris	1943	38-52
Fred Fitzsimmons	1943-45	105-181
Ben Chapman	1945-48	196-276
Dusty Cooke	1948	6-6
Eddie Sawyer	1948-52, 1958-60	390-423
Steve O'Neill	1952-54	182-140
Terry Moore	1954	35-42
Mayo Smith	1955-58	264-282
Andy Cohen	1960	1-0
Gene Mauch	1960-68	646-684
George Myatt	1968, 1969	20-35
Bob Skinner	1968-69	92-123
Frank Lucchesi	1970-72	166-233
Paul Owens	1972, 1983-84	161-158
Danny Ozark	1973-79	594-510
Dallas Green	1979-81	169-130
Pat Corrales	1982-83	132-115
John Felske	1985-87	190-194
Lee Elia	1987-88	111-142
John Vukovich	1988	5-4
Nick Leyva	1989-91	148-189
Jim Fregosi	1991-96	431-463
Terry Francona	1997-2000	285-363

WORLD SERIES CHAMPIONS

Year	*Loser*	*Length*	*MVP*
1980	Kansas City	6 games	Schmidt

N.L. PENNANT WINNERS

Year	*Record*	*Manager*	*Series Result*
1915	90-62	Moran	Lost to Red Sox
1950	91-63	Sawyer	Lost to Yankees
1980	91-71	Green	Defeated Royals
1983	90-72	Corrales, Owens	Lost to Orioles
1993	97-65	Fregosi	Lost to Blue Jays

EAST DIVISION CHAMPIONS

Year	*Record*	*Manager*	*NLCS Result*
1976	101-61	Ozark	Lost to Reds
1977	101-61	Ozark	Lost to Dodgers
1978	90-72	Ozark	Lost to Dodgers
1980	91-71	Green	Defeated Astros
*1981	59-48	Green	None
1983	90-72	Corrales, Owens	Defeated Dodgers
1993	97-65	Fregosi	Defeated Braves

* First-half champion; lost division series to Expos.

ATTENDANCE HIGHS

Total	*Season*	*Park*
3,137,674	1993	Veterans Stadium
2,775,011	1979	Veterans Stadium
2,700,007	1977	Veterans Stadium
2,651,650	1980	Veterans Stadium
2,583,389	1978	Veterans Stadium

BALLPARK CHRONOLOGY

Veterans Stadium (1971-present)

Capacity: 62,409.
First game: Phillies 4, Montreal 1 (April 10, 1971).
First batter: Boots Day, Expos.
First hit: Larry Bowa, Phillies (single).
First run: Ron Hunt, Expos (6th inning).
First home run: Don Money, Phillies.
First winning pitcher: Jim Bunning, Phillies.
First-season attendance: 1,511,223.

Recreation Park (1883-86)

First game: Providence 4, Philadelphia 3 (May 1, 1883).

Huntington Street Grounds/Baker Bowl (1887-1938)

Capacity: 18,800.
First game: Phillies 19, New York 10 (April 30, 1887).

Shibe Park (1927, 1938-70)

Capacity: 33,608.
First game: St. Louis 2, Phillies 1 (May 16, 1927).
First-season attendance (1939): 277,973.

N.L. MVPs

Chuck Klein, OF, 1932
Jim Konstanty, P, 1950
Mike Schmidt, 3B, 1980
Mike Schmidt, 3B, 1981
Mike Schmidt, 3B, 1986

CY YOUNG WINNERS

Steve Carlton, LH, 1972
Steve Carlton, LH, 1977
Steve Carlton, LH, 1980
Steve Carlton, LH, 1982
John Denny, RH, 1983
Steve Bedrosian, RH, 1987

ROOKIES OF THE YEAR

Jack Sanford, P, 1957
Dick Allen, 3B, 1964
Scott Rolen, 3B, 1997

RETIRED UNIFORMS

No.	*Name*	*Pos.*
1	Richie Ashburn	OF
20	Mike Schmidt	3B
32	Steve Carlton	P
36	Robin Roberts	P

MILESTONE PERFORMANCES

30-plus home runs

48—	Mike Schmidt	1980
45—	Mike Schmidt	1979
43—	Chuck Klein	1929
41—	Cy Williams	1923
40—	Chuck Klein	1930
	Richie Allen	1966
	Mike Schmidt	1983
39—	Greg Luzinski	1977
38—	Chuck Klein	1932
	Mike Schmidt	1975, 1976, 1977
37—	Mike Schmidt	1986
36—	Mike Schmidt	1974, 1984
35—	Greg Luzinski	1978
	Mike Schmidt	1982, 1987
34—	Deron Johnson	1971
	Greg Luzinski	1975
33—	Richie Allen	1968
	Mike Schmidt	1985
32—	Lefty O'Doul	1929
	Stan Lopata	1956
	Johnny Callison	1965
	Richie Allen	1969
31—	Don Hurst	1929
	Chuck Klein	1931
	Del Ennis	1950
	Johnny Callison	1964
	Mike Schmidt	1981
	Scott Rolen	1998
	Mike Lieberthal	1999
30—	Cy Williams	1927
	Del Ennis	1948
	Willie Montanez	1971
	Benito Santiago	1996

100-plus RBIs

170—	Chuck Klein	1930
165—	Sam Thompson	1895
146—	Ed Delahanty	1893
145—	Chuck Klein	1929
143—	Don Hurst	1932
141—	Sam Thompson	1894
137—	Ed Delahanty	1899
	Chuck Klein	1932
131—	Ed Delahanty	1894
130—	Greg Luzinski	1977
128—	Gavvy Cravath	1913
127—	Nap Lajoie	1897, 1898
126—	Sam Thompson	1893
	Ed Delahanty	1896
	Del Ennis	1950
125—	Lave Cross	1894
	Don Hurst	1929
	Del Ennis	1953
124—	Pinky Whitney	1932
123—	Sherry Magee	1910
122—	Lefty O'Doul	1929
121—	Chuck Klein	1931
	Mike Schmidt	1980
120—	Chuck Klein	1933
	Del Ennis	1955
	Greg Luzinski	1975
119—	Del Ennis	1954
	Mike Schmidt	1986
117—	Pinky Whitney	1930
116—	Mike Schmidt	1974
115—	Gavvy Cravath	1915
	Pinky Whitney	1929
114—	Cy Williams	1923
	Mike Schmidt	1979
113—	Mike Schmidt	1987
111—	Sam Thompson	1889
110—	Elmer Flick	1900
	Del Ennis	1949
	Richie Allen	1966
	Scott Rolen	1998
109—	Ed Delahanty	1900
	Mike Schmidt	1983
	Darren Daulton	1992
108—	Ed Delahanty	1901
107—	Del Ennis	1952
	Don Demeter	1962
	Mike Schmidt	1976
106—	Ed Delahanty	1895
	Mike Schmidt	1984
105—	Darren Daulton	1993
104—	Sam Thompson	1892
	Ron Northey	1944
	John Callison	1964
	Rico Brogna	1998
103—	Sherry Magee	1914
	Pinky Whitney	1928
	Bill White	1966
102—	Sam Thompson	1890
	Dolf Camilli	1936
	Rico Brogna	1999
101—	Lave Cross	1895
	John Callison	1965
	Mike Schmidt	1977
	Greg Luzinski	1978
100—	Sam Thompson	1896
	Gavvy Cravath	1914
	Juan Samuel	1987

Righthander Robin Roberts.

20-plus victories

1884—	Charlie Ferguson	21-25
1885—	Charlie Ferguson	26-20
	Ed Daily	26-23
1886—	Charlie Ferguson	30-9
	Dan Casey	24-18
1887—	Dan Casey	28-13
	Charlie Ferguson	22-10
	Charlie Buffinton	21-17
1888—	Charlie Buffinton	28-17
1889—	Charlie Buffinton	28-16
1890—	Kid Gleason	38-17
	Tom Vickery	24-22
1891—	Kid Gleason	24-22
	Charles Esper	20-15
1892—	Gus Weyhing	32-21
1893—	Gus Weyhing	23-16
1894—	Jack Taylor	23-13
1895—	Jack Taylor	26-14
	Kid Carsey	24-16
1896—	Jack Taylor	20-21
1898—	Wiley Piatt	24-14
1899—	Wiley Piatt	23-15
	Red Donahue	21-8
	Charles Fraser	21-12
1901—	Al Orth	20-12
	Red Donahue	21-13
1905—	Charlie Pittinger	23-14
1907—	Frank Sparks	22-8
1908—	George McQuillan	23-17
1910—	Earl Moore	22-15
1911—	Grover Alexander	28-13
1913—	Tom Seaton	27-12
	Grover Alexander	22-8
1914—	Grover Alexander	27-15
	Erskine Mayer	21-19
1915—	Grover Alexander	31-10
	Erskine Mayer	21-15
1916—	Grover Alexander	33-12
	Eppa Rixey	22-10
1917—	Grover Alexander	30-13
1950—	Robin Roberts	20-11
1951—	Robin Roberts	21-15
1952—	Robin Roberts	28-7
1953—	Robin Roberts	23-16
1954—	Robin Roberts	23-15
1955—	Robin Roberts	23-14
1966—	Chris Short	20-10
1972—	Steve Carlton	27-10
1976—	Steve Carlton	20-7
1977—	Steve Carlton	23-10
1980—	Steve Carlton	24-9
1982—	Steve Carlton	23-11

N.L. home run champions

1876—	George Hall	5
1889—	Sam Thompson	20
1893—	Ed Delahanty	19
1895—	Sam Thompson	18
1896—	Ed Delahanty	*13
1897—	Nap Lajoie	10
1913—	Gavvy Cravath	19
1914—	Gavvy Cravath	19
1915—	Gavvy Cravath	24
1917—	Gavvy Cravath	*12
1918—	Gavvy Cravath	8
1919—	Gavvy Cravath	12
1920—	Cy Williams	15
1923—	Cy Williams	41
1927—	Cy Williams	*30
1929—	Chuck Klein	43
1931—	Chuck Klein	31
1932—	Chuck Klein	*38
1933—	Chuck Klein	28
1974—	Mike Schmidt	36
1975—	Mike Schmidt	38
1976—	Mike Schmidt	38
1980—	Mike Schmidt	48
1981—	Mike Schmidt	31
1983—	Mike Schmidt	40
1984—	Mike Schmidt	*36
1986—	Mike Schmidt	37

* Tied for league lead

N.L. RBI champions

1907—	Sherry Magee	85
1910—	Sherry Magee	123
1913—	Gavvy Cravath	128
1914—	Sherry Magee	103
1915—	Gavvy Cravath	115
1931—	Chuck Klein	121
1932—	Don Hurst	143
1933—	Chuck Klein	120
1950—	Del Ennis	126
1975—	Greg Luzinski	120
1980—	Mike Schmidt	121
1981—	Mike Schmidt	91
1984—	Mike Schmidt	*106
1986—	Mike Schmidt	119
1992—	Darren Daulton	109

* Tied for league lead

N.L. batting champions

1891—	Billy Hamilton	.340
1899—	Ed Delahanty	.410
1910—	Sherry Magee	.331
1929—	Lefty O'Doul	.398
1933—	Chuck Klein	.368
1947—	Harry Walker	*.363
1955—	Richie Ashburn	.338
1958—	Richie Ashburn	.350

*10 games with Cardinals; 130 with Phillies.

N.L. ERA champions

1915—	Grover Alexander	1.22
1916—	Grover Alexander	1.55
1917—	Grover Alexander	1.83
1972—	Steve Carlton	1.97

N.L. strikeout champions

1910—	Earl Moore	185
1912—	Grover Alexander	195
1913—	Tom Seaton	168
1914—	Grover Alexander	214
1915—	Grover Alexander	241
1916—	Grover Alexander	167
1917—	Grover Alexander	201
1940—	Kirby Higbe	137
1953—	Robin Roberts	198
1954—	Robin Roberts	185
1957—	Jack Sanford	188
1967—	Jim Bunning	253
1972—	Steve Carlton	310
1974—	Steve Carlton	240
1980—	Steve Carlton	286
1982—	Steve Carlton	286
1983—	Steve Carlton	275
1997—	Curt Schilling	319
1998—	Curt Schilling	300

No-hit pitchers

(9 innings or more)

1885—	Charles Ferguson	1-0 vs. Providence
1898—	Red Donahue	5-0 vs. Boston
1903—	Charles Fraser	10-0 vs. Chicago
1906—	John Lush	6-0 vs. Brooklyn
1964—	Jim Bunning	6-0 vs. New York (Perfect)
1971—	Rick Wise	4-0 vs. Cincinnati
1990—	Terry Mulholland	6-0 vs. San Francisco
1991—	Tommy Greene	2-0 vs. Montreal

Longest hitting streaks

36—	Billy Hamilton	1894
31—	Ed Delahanty	1899
26—	Chuck Klein	1930 (twice)
24—	Willie Montanez	1974
23—	Goldie Rapp	1921
	Johnny Moore	1934
	Richie Ashburn	1948
	Pete Rose	1979
	Lonnie Smith	1981
	Lenny Dykstra	1990
22—	Chuck Klein	1931
	Chick Fullis	1933
21—	Ed Dalahanty	1897
	Irish Meusel	1920
	Danny Litwhiler	1940
	Pete Rose	1982
20—	Nap Lajoie	1897
	Chuck Klein	1932
	Richie Ashburn	1951
	Pancho Herrera	1960
	Garry Maddox	1978

INDIVIDUAL SEASON, GAME RECORDS

SEASON

Batting

At-bats	701	Juan Samuel	1984
Runs	196	Billy Hamilton	1894
Hits	254	Lefty O'Doul	1929
Singles	181	Lefty O'Doul	1929
		Richie Ashburn	1951
Doubles	59	Chuck Klein	1930
Triples	26	Sam Thompson	1894
Home runs	48	Mike Schmidt	1980
Home runs, rookie	30	Willie Montanez	1971
Grand slams	4	Vince DiMaggio	1945
Total bases	445	Chuck Klein	1930
RBIs	170	Chuck Klein	1930
Walks	129	Lenny Dykstra	1993
Most strikeouts	180	Mike Schmidt	1975
Fewest strikeouts	8	Emil Verban	1947
Batting average	.408	Ed Delahanty	1899
Slugging pct.	.687	Chuck Klein	1930
Stolen bases	115	Billy Hamilton	1891

Pitching (since 1900)

Games	90	Kent Tekulve	1987
Complete games	38	Grover Alexander	1916
Innings	388.2	Grover Alexander	1916
Wins	33	Grover Alexander	1916
Losses	24	Chick Fraser	1904
Winning pct.	.800 (28-7)	Robin Roberts	1952
	.800 (16-4)	Tommy Greene	1993
Walks	164	Earl Moore	1911
Strikeouts	319	Curt Schilling	1997
Shutouts	16	Grover Alexander	1916
Home runs allowed	46	Robin Roberts	1956
Lowest ERA	1.22	Grover Alexander	1915
Saves	43	Mitch Williams	1993

GAME

Batting

Runs	5	Last by Mariano Duncan	5-3-92
Hits	6	Connie Ryan	4-16-53
Doubles	4	Last by Willie Jones	4-20-49
Triples	3	Harry Wolverton	7-13-1900
Home runs	4	Chuck Klein	7-10-36
		Mike Schmidt	4-17-76
RBIs	8	Last by Mike Schmidt	4-17-76
Total bases	17	Mike Schmidt	4-17-76
Stolen bases	4	Sherry Magee	7-12-06, 8-31-06.

HISTORY

CAREER LEADERS

BATTING

Games

Mike Schmidt	2,404
Richie Ashburn	1,794
Larry Bowa	1,739
Tony Taylor	1,669
Del Ennis	1,630
Ed Delahanty	1,557
Sherry Magee	1,521
Willie Jones	1,520
Granny Hamner	1,501
Cy Williams	1,463

At-bats

Mike Schmidt	8,352
Richie Ashburn	7,122
Larry Bowa	6,815
Ed Delahanty	6,365
Del Ennis	6,327
Tony Taylor	5,799
Granny Hamner	5,772
Sherry Magee	5,505
Willie Jones	5,419
Johnny Callison	5,306

Runs

Mike Schmidt	1,506
Ed Delahanty	1,368
Richie Ashburn	1,114
Chuck Klein	963
Sam Thompson	930
Roy Thomas	923
Sherry Magee	898
Del Ennis	891
Billy Hamilton	880
Cy Williams	825

Hits

Mike Schmidt	2,234
Richie Ashburn	2,217
Ed Delahanty	2,214
Del Ennis	1,812
Larry Bowa	1,798
Chuck Klein	1,705
Sherry Magee	1,647
Cy Williams	1,553
Granny Hamner	1,518
Tony Taylor	1,511

Doubles

Ed Delahanty	442
Mike Schmidt	408
Sherry Magee	337
Chuck Klein	336
Del Ennis	310
Richie Ashburn	287
Sam Thompson	275
Granny Hamner	271
Johnny Callison	265
Greg Luzinski	253

Triples

Ed Delahanty	158
Sherry Magee	127
Sam Thompson	107
Richie Ashburn	97
Johnny Callison	84
Larry Bowa	81
Gavvy Cravath	72
Juan Samuel	71
Del Ennis	65
Dick Allen	64
Chuck Klein	64
John Titus	64

Home runs

Mike Schmidt	548
Del Ennis	259
Chuck Klein	243
Greg Luzinski	223
Cy Williams	217
Dick Allen	204
Johnny Callison	185
Willie Jones	180
Darren Daulton	134
Von Hayes	124

Total bases

Mike Schmidt	4,404
Ed Delahanty	3,233
Del Ennis	3,029
Chuck Klein	2,898
Richie Ashburn	2,764
Cy Williams	2,539
Sherry Magee	2,463
Johnny Callison	2,426
Greg Luzinski	2,263
Sam Thompson	2,252

Runs batted in

Mike Schmidt	1,595
Ed Delahanty	1,288
Del Ennis	1,124
Chuck Klein	983
Sam Thompson	963
Sherry Magee	886
Greg Luzinski	811
Cy Williams	795
Willie Jones	753
Pinky Whitney	734

Extra-base hits

Mike Schmidt	1,015
Ed Delahanty	687
Chuck Klein	643
Del Ennis	634
Sherry Magee	539
Johnny Callison	534
Cy Williams	503
Greg Luzinski	497
Sam Thompson	477
Dick Allen	472

Batting average
(Minimum 500 games)

Billy Hamilton	.361
Ed Delahanty	.348
Elmer Flick	.338
Sam Thompson	.334
Chuck Klein	.326
Spud Davis	.321
Fred Leach	.312
Richie Ashburn	.311
John Kruk	.309
Pinky Whitney	.308

Stolen bases

Billy Hamilton	510
Ed Delahanty	411
Sherry Magee	387
Jim Fogarty	289
Larry Bowa	288
Juan Samuel	249
Roy Thomas	228
Von Hayes	202
Richie Ashburn	199
Sam Thompson	192

PITCHING

Earned-run average
(Minimum 1,000 innings)

Grover Alexander	2.18
Tully Sparks	2.48
Earl Moore	2.63
Charlie Ferguson	2.67
Erskine Mayer	2.81
Eppa Rixey	2.83
Charlie Buffinton	2.89
Dan Casey	2.91
Jim Bunning	2.93
Steve Carlton	3.09

Wins

Steve Carlton	241
Robin Roberts	234
Grover Alexander	190
Chris Short	132
Curt Simmons	115
Curt Schilling	101
Al Orth	100
Charlie Ferguson	99
Jack Taylor	96
Tully Sparks	95

Losses

Robin Roberts	199
Steve Carlton	161
Chris Short	127
Curt Simmons	110
Eppa Rixey	103
Bill Duggleby	99
Jimmy Ring	98
Tully Sparks	95
Grover Alexander	91
Hugh Mulcahy	89

Innings pitched

Robin Roberts	3,739.1
Steve Carlton	3,697.1
Grover Alexander	2,513.2
Chris Short	2,253.0
Curt Simmons	1,939.2
Tully Sparks	1,698.0
Bill Duggleby	1,684.0
Curt Schilling	1,659.1
Eppa Rixey	1,604.0
Jim Bunning	1,520.2

Strikeouts

Steve Carlton	3,031
Robin Roberts	1,871
Chris Short	1,585
Curt Schilling	1,554
Grover Alexander	1,409
Jim Bunning	1,197
Curt Simmons	1,052
Larry Christenson	781
Charlie Ferguson	728
Kevin Gross	727

Bases on balls

Steve Carlton	1,252
Chris Short	762
Robin Roberts	718
Curt Simmons	718
Jimmy Ring	636
Grover Alexander	561
Kid Carsey	540
Earl Moore	518
Kid Gleason	482
Hugh Mulcahy	480

Games

Robin Roberts	529
Steve Carlton	499
Tug McGraw	463
Chris Short	459
Ron Reed	458
Turk Farrell	359
Grover Alexander	338
Jack Baldschun	333
Curt Simmons	325
Jim Konstanty	314

Shutouts

Grover Alexander	61
Steve Carlton	39
Robin Roberts	35
Chris Short	24
Jim Bunning	23
Curt Simmons	18
Tully Sparks	18
George McQuillan	17
Earl Moore	17
Bill Duggleby	16

Saves

Steve Bedrosian	103
Mitch Williams	102
Tug McGraw	94
Ron Reed	90
Ricky Bottalico	75
Turk Farrell	65
Jack Baldschun	59
Al Holland	55
Jim Konstanty	54
Gene Garber	51

TEAM SEASON, GAME RECORDS

SEASON

Batting		
Most at-bats	5,685	1993
Most runs	944	1930
Fewest runs	394	1942
Most hits	1,783	1930
Most singles	1,338	1894
Most doubles	345	1930
Most triples	148	1894
Most home runs	186	1977
Fewest home runs	11	1908
Most grand slams	8	1993
Most pinch-hit home runs	11	1958
Most total bases	2,594	1930
Most stolen bases	200	1908
Highest batting average	.343	1894
Lowest batting average	.232	1942
Highest slugging pct.	.467	1929
Pitching		
Lowest ERA	2.10	1908
Highest ERA	6.71	1930
Most complete games	131	1904
Most shutouts	24	1916
Most saves	48	1987
Most walks	682	1974
Most strikeouts	1,117	1993
Fielding		
Most errors	403	1904
Fewest errors	104	1978
Most double plays	179	1961, 1973
Highest fielding average	.983	1978, 1979
General		
Most games won	101	1976, 1977
Most games lost	111	1941
Highest win pct	.623	1886, 1976, 1977
Lowest win pct	.173	1883

GAME, INNING

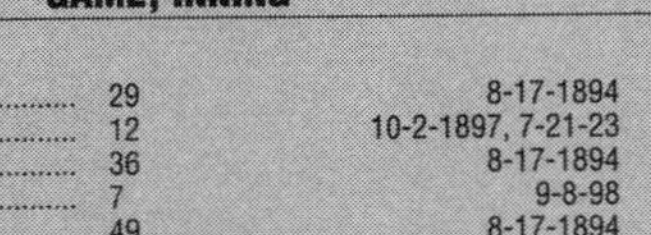

Batting		
Most runs, game	29	8-17-1894
Most runs, inning	12	10-2-1897, 7-21-23
Most hits, game	36	8-17-1894
Most home runs, game	7	9-8-98
Most total bases, game	49	8-17-1894

Hard-throwing lefthander Steve Carlton won 241 of his 329 games in 14-plus seasons with the Phillies.

HISTORY

PHILLIES YEAR-BY-YEAR

Year	W	L	Place	Games Back	Manager	Leaders: Batting avg.	Hits	Home runs	RBIs	Wins	ERA
1901	83	57	2nd	7½	Shettsline	Delahanty, .354	Delahanty, 192	Delahanty, Flick, 8	Delahanty, 108	Donahue, 21	Orth, 2.27
1902	56	81	7th	46	Shettsline	S. Barry, .287	S. Barry, 156	S. Barry, 3	S. Barry, 58	White, 16	White, 2.53
1903	49	86	7th	39½	Zimmer	Thomas, .327	Thomas, 156	Keister, 3	Keister, 63	Duggleby, 13	Sparks, 2.72
1904	52	100	8th	53½	Duffy	Titus, .294	Gleason, 161	Dooin, 6	Magee, 57	Fraser, 14	Corridon, 2.19
1905	83	69	4th	21½	Duffy	Thomas, .317	Magee, 180	Magee, 5	Magee, 98	Pittinger, 23	Sparks, 2.18
1906	71	82	4th	45½	Duffy	Magee, .282	Magee, 159	Magee, 6	Magee, 67	Sparks, 19	Sparks, 2.16
1907	83	64	3rd	21½	Murray	Magee, .328	Magee, 165	Magee, 4	Magee, 85	Sparks, 22	Richie, 1.77
1908	83	71	4th	16	Murray	Bransfield, .304	Bransfield, 160	Bransfield, 3	Bransfield, 71	McQuillan, 23	McQuillan, 1.53
1909	74	79	5th	36½	Murray	Bransfield, .292	Grant, 170	Titus, 3	Magee, 66	Moore, 18	Moore, 2.10
1910	78	75	4th	25½	Dooin	Magee, .331	Magee, 172	Magee, 6	Magee, 123	Moore, 22	McQuillan, 1.60
1911	79	73	4th	19½	Dooin	Luderus, .301	Luderus, 166	Luderus, 16	Luderus, 99	Alexander, 28	Alexander, 2.57
1912	73	79	5th	30½	Dooin	Paskert, .315	Paskert, 170	Cravath, 11	Magee, 72	Alexander, 19	Rixey, 2.50
1913	88	63	2nd	12½	Dooin	Cravath, .341	Cravath, 179	Cravath, 19	Cravath, 128	Seaton, 27	Brennan, 2.39
1914	74	80	6th	20½	Dooin	Becker, .325	Magee, 171	Cravath, 19	Magee, 103	Alexander, 27	Alexander, 2.38
1915	90	62	1st	+7	Moran	Luderus, .315	Luderus, 157	Cravath, 24	Cravath, 115	Alexander, 31	Alexander, 1.22
1916	91	62	2nd	2½	Moran	Cravath, .283	Paskert, 155	Cravath, 11	Cravath, 70	Alexander, 33	Alexander, 1.55
1917	87	65	2nd	10	Moran	Cravath, Whitted, .280	Whitted, 155	Cravath, 12	Cravath, 83	Alexander, 30	Bender, 1.67
1918	55	68	6th	26	Moran	Luderus, .288	Luderus, 135	Cravath, 8	Luderus, 67	Hogg, Pendergast, 13	Jacobs, 2.41
1919	47	90	8th	47½	Coombs, Cravath	I. Meusel, .305	I. Meusel, 159	Cravath, 12	I. Meusel, 59	Meadows, 8	Meadows, 2.33
1920	62	91	8th	30½	Cravath	Williams, .325	Williams, 192	Williams, 15	Williams, 72	Meadows, 16	Meadows, 2.84
1921	51	103	8th	43½	Donovan, Wilhelm	Williams, .320	Williams, 180	Williams, 18	Williams, 75	Meadows, 11	Winters, 3.63
1922	57	96	7th	35½	Wilhelm	Walker, .337	Walker, 196	Williams, 26	Williams, 92	Meadows, Ring, 12	Weinert, 3.40
1923	50	104	8th	45½	Fletcher	Lee, .321	Holke, 175	Williams, 41	Williams, 114	Ring, 18	Ring, 3.87
1924	55	96	7th	37	Fletcher	Williams, .328	Williams, 183	Williams, 24	Williams, 93	Hubbell, Ring, 10	Ring, 3.97
1925	68	85	*6th	27	Fletcher	Harper, .349	Harper, 173	Harper, 18	Harper, 97	Ring, 14	Carlson, 4.23
1926	58	93	8th	29½	Fletcher	Leach, .329	Leach, 162	Williams, 18	Leach, 71	Carlson, 17	Carlson, 3.23
1927	51	103	8th	43	McInnis	Leach, Wrightstone, .306	Thompson, 181	Williams, 30	Williams, 98	Scott, 9	Ulrich, 3.17
1928	43	109	8th	51	Shotton	Leach, .304	Thompson, 182	Hurst, 19	Whitney, 103	Benge, 8	Benge, 4.55
1929	71	82	5th	27½	Shotton	O'Doul, .398	O'Doul, 254	Klein, 43	Klein, 145	Willoughby, 15	Willoughby, 4.99
1930	52	102	8th	40	Shotton	Klein, .386	Klein, 250	Klein, 40	Klein, 170	Collins, 16	Collins, 4.78
1931	66	88	6th	35	Shotton	Klein, .337	Klein, 200	Klein, 31	Klein, 121	J. Elliott, 19	Benge, 3.17
1932	78	76	4th	12	Shotton	Klein, .348	Klein, 226	Klein, 38	Hurst, 143	Collins, 14	Hansen, 3.72
1933	60	92	7th	31	Shotton	Klein, .368	Klein, 223	Klein, 28	Klein, 120	Holley, 13	Holley, 3.53
1934	56	93	7th	37	Wilson	Moore, .343	Allen, 192	Camilli, 12	Moore, 93	C. Davis, 19	C. Davis, 2.95
1935	64	89	7th	35½	Wilson	Moore, .323	Allen, 198	Camilli, 25	Camilli, 102	C. Davis, 16	S. Johnson, 3.56
1936	54	100	8th	38	Wilson	Moore, .328	Chiozza, 170	Camilli, 28	Camilli, 102	Passeau, Walters, 11	Passeau, 3.48
1937	61	92	7th	34½	Wilson	Whitney, .341	Whitney, 166	Camilli, 27	Camilli, 80	LeMaster, 15	Passeau, 4.34
1938	45	105	8th	43	Wilson, Lobert	Weintraub, .311	Martin, 139	Klein, 8	Arnovich, 72	Passeau, 11	Butcher, 2.93
1939	45	106	8th	50½	Prothro	Arnovich, .324	Arnovich, 159	Marty, Mueller, 9	Arnovich, 67	Higbe, 10	S. Johnson, 3.81
1940	50	103	8th	50	Prothro	May, .293	May, 147	Rizzo, 20	Rizzo, 53	Higbe, 14	Mulcahy, 3.60
1941	43	111	8th	57	Prothro	Etten, .311	Litwhiler, 180	Litwhiler, 18	Etten, 79	Hughes, Podgajny, 9	Pearson, 3.57
1942	42	109	8th	62½	Lobert	Litwhiler, .271	Litwhiler, 160	Litwhiler, 9	Litwhiler, 56	Hughes, 12	Hughes, 3.06
1943	64	90	7th	41	Harris, Fitzsimmons	Dahlgren, .287	Northey, 163	Northey, 16	Northey, 68	Rowe, 14	Barrett, 2.39
1944	61	92	8th	43½	Fitzsimmons	Northey, .288	Lupien, 169	Northey, 22	Northey, 104	Raffensberger, Schanz, 13	Raffensberger, 3.06
1945	46	108	8th	52	Fitzsimmons, Chapman	Wasdell, .300	Wasdell, 150	V. DiMaggio, 19	V. DiMaggio, 84	Karl, 9	Karl, 2.99
1946	69	85	5th	28	Chapman	Ennis, .313	Ennis, 169	Ennis, 17	Ennis, 73	Judd, Rowe, 11	Rowe, 2.12
1947	62	92	*7th	32	Chapman	Walker, .371	Walker, 181	Seminick, 13	Ennis, 81	Leonard, 17	Leonard, 2.68
1948	66	88	6th	25½	Chapman, Cooke, Sawyer	Ashburn, .333	Ennis, 171	Ennis, 30	Ennis, 95	Leonard, 12	Leonard, 2.51
1949	81	73	3rd	16	Sawyer	Ennis, .302	Ashburn, 188	Ennis, 25	Ennis, 110	Heintzelman, Meyer, 17	Heintzelman, 3.02
1950	91	63	1st	+2	Sawyer	Ennis, .311	Ennis, 180	Ennis, 31	Ennis, 126	Roberts, 20	Konstanty, 2.66
1951	73	81	5th	23½	Sawyer	Ashburn, .344	Ashburn, 221	W. Jones, 22	W. Jones, 81	Roberts, 21	Roberts, 3.03
1952	87	67	4th	9½	Sawyer, O'Neill	Burgess, .296	Ashburn, 173	Ennis, 20	Ennis, 107	Roberts, 28	Roberts, 2.59
1953	83	71	*3rd	22	O'Neill	Ashburn, .330	Ashburn, 205	Ennis, 29	Ennis, 125	Roberts, 23	Roberts, 2.75
1954	75	79	4th	22	O'Neill, Moore	Ashburn, .313	Hamner, 178	Ennis, 25	Ennis, 119	Roberts, 23	Simmons, 2.81
1955	77	77	4th	21½	Smith	Ashburn, .338	Ashburn, 180	Ennis, 29	Ennis, 120	Roberts, 23	B. Miller, 2.41
1956	71	83	5th	22	Smith	Ashburn, .303	Ashburn, 190	Lopata, 32	Ennis, Lopata, 95	Roberts, 19	B. Miller, 3.24
1957	77	77	5th	19	Smith	Ashburn, .297	Ashburn, 186	Repulski, 20	Bouchee, 76	Sanford, 19	Sanford, 3.08
1958	69	85	8th	23	Smith, Sawyer	Ashburn, .350	Ashburn, 215	H. Anderson, 23	H. Anderson, 97	Roberts, 17	Roberts, 3.24
1959	64	90	8th	23	Sawyer	Bouchee, .285	Ashburn, 150	Freese, 23	Post, 94	Roberts, 15	Conley, 3.00
1960	59	95	8th	36	Sawyer, Cohen, Mauch	Taylor, .287	Taylor, 145	Herrera, 17	Herrera, 71	Roberts, 12	Mahaffey, 3.31
1961	47	107	8th	46	Mauch	Gonzalez, .277	Callison, 121	Demeter, 20	Demeter, 68	Mahaffey, 11	Ferrarese, 2.76
1962	81	80	7th	20	Mauch	Demeter, .307	Callison, 181	Demeter, 29	Demeter, 107	Mahaffey, 19	Baldschun, 2.96
1963	87	75	4th	12	Mauch	Gonzalez, .306	Taylor, 180	Callison, 26	Demeter, 83	Culp, 14	Klippstein, 1.93
1964	92	70	*2nd	1	Mauch	Allen, .318	Allen, 201	Callison, 31	Callison, 104	Bunning, 19	Short, 2.20
1965	85	76	6th	11½	Mauch	Rojas, .303	Allen, 187	Callison, 32	Callison, 101	Bunning, 19	Bunning, 2.60
1966	87	75	4th	8	Mauch	Allen, .317	Callison, 169	Allen, 40	Allen, 110	Short, 20	Bunning, 2.41
1967	82	80	5th	19½	Mauch	Gonzalez, .339	Gonzalez, 172	Allen, 23	Allen, 77	Bunning, 17	Farrell, 2.05
1968	76	86	*7th	21	Mauch, Myatt, Skinner	Gonzalez, .264	Rojas, 144	Allen, 33	Allen, 90	Short, 19	L. Jackson, 2.77
							EAST DIVISION				
1969	63	99	5th	37	Skinner, Myatt	Allen, .288	Taylor, 146	Allen, 32	Allen, 89	Wise, 15	Wise, 3.23
1970	73	88	5th	15½	Lucchesi	Taylor, .301	D. Johnson, 147	D. Johnson, 27	D. Johnson, 93	Wise, 13	Selma, 2.75
1971	67	95	6th	30	Lucchesi	McCarver, .278	Bowa, 162	D. Johnson, 34	Montanez, 99	Wise, 17	Wise, 2.88
1972	59	97	6th	37½	Lucchesi, Owens	Luzinski, .281	Luzinski, 158	Luzinski, 18	Luzinski, 68	Carlton, 27	Carlton, 1.97
1973	71	91	6th	11½	Ozark	Unser, .289	Luzinski, 174	Luzinski, 29	Luzinski, 97	Brett, Carlton, Lonborg, Twitchell, 13	Twitchell, 2.50
1974	80	82	3rd	8	Ozark	Montanez, .304	Cash, 206	Schmidt, 36	Schmidt, 116	Lonborg, 17	Lonborg, 3.21
1975	86	76	2nd	6½	Ozark	Johnstone, .329	Cash, 213	Schmidt, 38	Luzinski, 120	Carlton, 15	Hilgendorf, 2.14
1976	101	61	†1st	+9	Ozark	Maddox, .330	Cash, 189	Schmidt, 38	Schmidt, 107	Carlton, 20	McGraw, 2.50
1977	101	61	†1st	+5	Ozark	Luzinski, .309	Bowa, 175	Luzinski, 39	Luzinski, 130	Carlton, 23	Garber, 2.35
1978	90	72	†1st	+1½	Ozark	Bowa, .294	Bowa, 192	Luzinski, 35	Luzinski, 101	Carlton, 16	Reed, 2.24
1979	84	78	4th	14	Ozark, Green	Rose, .331	Rose, 208	Schmidt, 45	Schmidt, 114	Carlton, 18	Carlton, 3.62
1980	91	71	‡1st	+1	Green	McBride, .309	Rose, 185	Schmidt, 48	Schmidt, 121	Carlton, 24	McGraw, 1.46
1981	59	48	§1st/3rd	—	Green	Rose, .325	Rose, 140	Schmidt, 31	Schmidt, 91	Carlton, 13	Carlton, 2.42
1982	89	73	2nd	3	Corrales	Diaz, .288	Matthews, 173	Schmidt, 35	Schmidt, 87	Carlton, 23	Reed, 2.66
1983	90	72	‡1st	+6	Corrales, Owens	Hayes, .265	Schmidt, 136	Schmidt, 40	Schmidt, 109	Denny, 19	Holland, 2.26
1984	81	81	4th	15½	Owens	V. Hayes, .292	Samuel, 191	Schmidt, 36	Schmidt, 106	Koosman, 14	Andersen, 2.38
1985	75	87	5th	26	Felske	Schmidt, .277	Samuel, 175	Schmidt, 33	Wilson, 102	Gross, 15	Rawley, 3.31
1986	86	75	2nd	21½	Felske	V. Hayes, .305	V. Hayes, 187	Schmidt, 37	Schmidt, 119	Gross, 12	Ruffin, 2.46
1987	80	82	*4th	15	Felske, Elia	M. Thompson, .302	Samuel, 178	Schmidt, 35	Schmidt, 113	Rawley, 17	Tekulve, 3.09
1988	65	96	6th	35½	Elia, Vukovich	M. Thompson, .288	Samuel, 153	James, 19	Samuel, 67	Gross, 12	G. Harris, 2.36
1989	67	95	6th	26	Leyva	Herr, .287	Herr, 161	V. Hayes, 26	V. Hayes, 78	Howell, Parrett, 12	Parrett, 2.98
1990	77	85	*4th	18	Leyva	Dykstra, .325	Dykstra, 192	V. Hayes, 17	V. Hayes, 73	Combs, 10	Mulholland, 3.34
1991	78	84	3rd	20	Leyva, Fregosi	Kruk, .294	Kruk, 158	Kruk, 21	Kruk, 92	Mulholland, 16	Greene, 3.38
1992	70	92	6th	26	Fregosi	Kruk, .323	Kruk, 164	Daulton, Hollins, 27	Daulton, 109	Schilling, 14	Schilling, 2.35
1993	97	65	‡1st	+3	Fregosi	Eisenreich, .318	Dykstra, 194	Daulton, Incaviglia, 24	Daulton, 105	Greene, Schilling, 16	Mulholland, 3.25
1994	54	61	4th	20½	Fregosi	Kruk, .302	Duncan, 93	Daulton, 15	Daulton, 56	D. Jackson, 14	Munoz, 2.67
1995	69	75	*2nd	21	Fregosi	Eisenreich, .316	Jefferies, 147	Hayes, Jefferies, Whiten, 11	Hayes, 85	Quantrill, 11	Schilling, 3.57
1996	67	95	5th	29	Fregosi	Jefferies, .292	Morandini, 135	Santiago, 30	Santiago, 85	Schilling, 9	Schilling, 3.19
1997	68	94	5th	33	Francona	Morandini, .295	Morandini, 163	Rolen, 21	Rolen, 92	Schilling, 17	Schilling, 2.97
1998	75	87	3rd	31	Francona	Abreu, .312	Glanville, 189	Rolen, 31	Rolen, 110	Schilling, 15	Schilling, 3.25
1999	77	85	3rd	26	Francona	Abreu, .335	Glanville, 204	Lieberthal, 31	Brogna, 102	Schilling, Byrd, 15	Schilling, 3.54
2000	65	97	5th	30	Francona	Abreu, .316	Abreu, 182	Rolen, 26	Rolen, 89	Wolf, 11	Chen, 3.64

* Tied for position. † Lost Championship Series. ‡ Won Championship Series. § First half 34-21; second half 25-27.

Note: Batting average minimum 350 at-bats; ERA minimum 90 innings pitched.

Pittsburgh Pirates

Shortstop Honus Wagner.

FRANCHISE CHRONOLOGY

First season: 1882, as a member of the American Association. The Allegheny club finished its first Pittsburgh season 39-39, good for fourth place in the seven-team field.

1883-1900: The Pirates played five A.A. seasons before jumping to the National League in 1887. In their first 14 N.L. seasons, they never finished first. But they did rise to second place in 1900, setting the stage for three consecutive pennants.

1901-present: The Pirates, with the arrival of manager Fred Clarke and shortstop Honus Wagner, became a consistent member of the N.L.'s first-division fraternity—a membership they would keep through most of the century. But strong teams did not translate into many pennants. After losing the first World Series in 1903, the Pirates captured their first championship in 1909 and their second 15 years later. There would be only three more—a memorable 1960 Series victory that ended on Bill Mazeroski's immortal home run and triumphs in 1971 and '79. The Pirates' most successful run came in the 1970s when they won six division titles and finished second three times. Consecutive division titles in 1990, '91 and '92 all resulted in Championship Series losses. Pittsburgh was one of five teams placed in the Central Division when the N.L. adopted its three-division format in 1994.

PIRATES VS. OPPONENTS BY DECADE

	Braves	Cardinals	Cubs	Dodgers	Giants	Phillies	Reds	Astros	Mets	Expos	Padres	Marlins	Rockies	Brewers	D'backs	Interleague	Decade Record
1900-09	153-58	158-53	112-99	132-76	115-96	137-75	131-81										938-538
1910-19	109-104	127-83	95-118	105-110	86-127	105-107	109-102										736-751
1920-29	141-77	117-102	125-95	122-97	106-113	148-71	118-101										877-656
1930-39	125-92	121-99	100-120	105-113	95-125	126-90	140-79										812-718
1940-49	112-105	98-122	116-104	96-124	109-111	121-95	104-115										756-776
1950-59	81-139	87-132	106-114	79-141	89-131	88-132	86-134										616-923
1960-69	94-88	81-107	110-78	82-100	82-100	98-89	92-90	93-45	93-51	13-5	10-2						848-755
1970-79	77-43	101-79	111-66	55-65	58-62	101-79	54-65	75-44	98-78	107-73	79-41						916-695
1980-89	53-58	75-98	95-81	53-61	55-63	83-91	50-64	51-63	69-102	86-88	62-56						732-825
1990-99	45-62	76-62	76-63	50-61	55-52	66-58	59-64	54-67	67-58	61-65	55-53	42-30	34-36	9-14	5-11	20-23	774-779
2000-	2-5	4-8	9-3	5-4	2-6	6-3	6-7	3-10	2-7	4-3	7-2	4-5	2-7	5-7	2-7	6-9	69-93
Totals	992-831	1045-945	1055-941	884-952	852-986	1079-890	949-902	276-229	329-296	271-234	213-154	46-35	36-43	14-21	7-18	26-32	8074-7509

Interleague results: 4-4 vs. White Sox; 5-7 vs. Indians; 6-8 vs. Royals; 1-2 vs. Brewers; 6-6 vs. Twins; 4-5 vs. Tigers.

MANAGERS

Name	*Years*	*Record*
Al Pratt	1882-83	51-59
Ormond Butler	1883	17-36
Joe Battin	1883, 1884	8-18
Denny McKnight	1884	4-8
Bob Ferguson	1884	11-31
George Creamer	1884	0-8
Horace Phillips	1884-89	294-316
Fred Dunlap	1889	7-10
Ned Hanlon	1889, 1891	57-65
Guy Hecker	1890	23-113
Bill McGunnigle	1891	24-33
Tom Burns	1892	27-32
Al Buckenberger	1892-94	187-144
Connie Mack	1894-96	149-134
Patsy Donovan	1897, 1899	129-129
Bill Watkins	1898-99	79-91
Fred Clarke	1900-15	1422-969
Jimmy Callahan	1916-17	85-129
Honus Wagner	1917	1-4
Hugo Bezdek	1917-19	166-187
George Gibson	1920-22, 1932-34	401-330
Bill McKechnie	1922-26	409-293
Donie Bush	1927-29	246-178
Jewel Ens	1929-31	176-167

Roberto Clemente ranked among the game's elite for 18 outstanding Pittsburgh seasons.

MANAGERS—*cont'd.*

Name	*Years*	*Record*
Pie Traynor	1934-39	457-406
Frank Frisch	1940-46	539-528
Spud Davis	1946	1-2
Billy Herman	1947	61-92
Bill Burwell	1947	1-0
Billy Meyer	1948-52	317-452
Fred Haney	1953-55	163-299
Bobby Bragan	1956-57	102-155
Danny Murtaugh	1957-64, 1967, 1970-71, 1973-76	1115-950
Harry Walker	1965-67	224-184
Larry Shepard	1968-69	164-155
Alex Grammas	1969	4-1
Bill Virdon	1972-73	163-128
Chuck Tanner	1977-85	711-685
Jim Leyland	1986-96	851-863
Gene Lamont	1997-2000	295-352

WORLD SERIES CHAMPIONS

Year	*Loser*	*Length*	*MVP*
1909	Detroit	7 games	None
1925	Washington	7 games	None
1960	N.Y. Yankees	7 games	Richardson
1971	Baltimore	7 games	Clemente
1979	Baltimore	7 games	Stargell

N.L. PENNANT WINNERS

Year	*Record*	*Manager*	*Series Result*
1901	90-49	Clarke	None
1902	103-36	Clarke	None
1903	91-49	Clarke	Lost to Red Sox
1909	110-42	Clarke	Defeated Tigers
1925	95-58	McKechnie	Defeated Senators
1927	94-60	Bush	Lost to Yankees
1960	95-59	Murtaugh	Defeated Yankees
1971	97-65	Murtaugh	Defeated Orioles
1979	98-64	Tanner	Defeated Orioles

EAST DIVISION CHAMPIONS

Year	*Record*	*Manager*	*NLCS Result*
1970	89-73	Murtaugh	Lost to Reds
1971	97-65	Murtaugh	Defeated Giants
1972	96-59	Virdon	Lost to Reds
1974	88-74	Murtaugh	Lost to Dodgers
1975	92-69	Murtaugh	Lost to Reds
1979	98-64	Tanner	Defeated Reds
1990	95-67	Leyland	Lost to Reds
1991	98-64	Leyland	Lost to Braves
1992	96-66	Leyland	Lost to Braves

ATTENDANCE HIGHS

Total	*Season*	*Park*
2,065,302	1991	Three Rivers Stadium
2,049,908	1990	Three Rivers Stadium
1,866,713	1988	Three Rivers Stadium
1,829,395	1992	Three Rivers Stadium
1,748,908	2000	Three Rivers Stadium

BALLPARK CHRONOLOGY

Three Rivers Stadium (1970-present)

Capacity: 47,972.
First game: Cincinnati 3, Pirates 2 (July 16, 1970).
First batter: Ty Cline, Reds.
First hit: Richie Hebner, Pirates (single).
First run: Richie Hebner, Pirates (1st inning).
First home run: Tony Perez, Reds.
First winning pitcher: Clay Carroll, Reds.
First-season attendance: 1,341,947.

Exposition Park (1882-84)

Recreation Park (1887-90)

Exposition Park III (1891-1909)

Capacity: 16,000.
First game: Chicago 7, Pittsburgh 6, 10 innings (April 22, 1891).

Forbes Field (1909-70)

Capacity: 35,000.
First game: Chicago 3, Pirates 2 (June 30, 1909).
First-season attendance (1910): 436,586.

N.L. MVPs

Dick Groat, SS, 1960
Roberto Clemente, OF, 1966
Dave Parker, OF, 1978
*Willie Stargell, 1B, 1979
Barry Bonds, OF, 1990
Barry Bonds, OF, 1992

* Co-winner.

CY YOUNG WINNERS

Vernon Law, RH, 1960
Doug Drabek, RH, 1990

MANAGERS OF THE YEAR

Jim Leyland, 1990
Jim Leyland, 1992

RETIRED UNIFORMS

No.	*Name*	*Pos.*
1	Billy Meyer	Man.
4	Ralph Kiner	OF
8	Willie Stargell	1B
9	Bill Mazeroski	2B
20	Pie Traynor	3B
21	Roberto Clemente	OF
33	Honus Wagner	SS
40	Danny Murtaugh	Man.

MILESTONE PERFORMANCES

30-plus home runs

- 54—Ralph Kiner 1949
- 51—Ralph Kiner 1947
- 48—Willie Stargell 1971
- 47—Ralph Kiner 1950
- 44—Willie Stargell 1973
- 42—Ralph Kiner 1951
- 40—Ralph Kiner 1948
- 39—Brian Giles 1999
- 37—Ralph Kiner 1952
- 35—Frank Thomas 1958
- Dick Stuart 1961
- Brian Giles 2000
- 34—Barry Bonds 1992
- 33—Willie Stargell 1966, 1972
- Barry Bonds 1990
- 32—Willie Stargell 1979
- Bobby Bonilla 1990
- 31—Willie Stargell 1970
- Jason Thompson 1982
- 30—Frank Thomas 1953
- Dave Parker 1978
- Jeff King 1996

100-plus RBIs

- 131—Paul Waner 1927
- 127—Ralph Kiner 1947, 1949
- 126—Honus Wagner 1901
- 125—Willie Stargell 1971
- 124—Pie Traynor 1928
- 123—Ralph Kiner 1948
- Brian Giles 2000
- 121—Glenn Wright 1925
- 120—Bobby Bonilla 1990
- 119—Adam Comorosky 1930
- Pie Traynor 1930
- Roberto Clemente 1966
- Willie Stargell 1973
- 118—Gus Suhr 1936
- Ralph Kiner 1950
- 117—Dick Stuart 1961
- Dave Parker 1978
- 116—Maurice Van Robays 1940
- Barry Bonds 1991
- 115—Brian Giles 1999
- 114—Clyde Barnhart 1925
- Barry Bonds 1990
- 112—Willie Stargell 1972
- 111—Glenn Wright 1924
- Johnny Rizzo 1938
- Jeff King 1996
- 110—Roberto Clemente 1967
- 109—Honus Wagner 1908
- Ralph Kiner 1951
- Frank Thomas 1958
- 108—Pie Traynor 1929
- Bob Elliott 1944
- Bob Elliott 1945
- Kevin Young 1998
- 107—Lou Bierbauer 1894
- Owen Wilson 1911
- Gus Suhr 1930
- Willie Stargell 1965
- 106—Pie Traynor 1925, 1927
- Kevin Young 1999
- 105—Glenn Wright 1927
- 104—Elbie Fletcher 1940
- Wally Westlake 1949
- Bill Robinson 1977
- 103—Pie Traynor 1931
- Gus Suhr 1934
- Barry Bonds 1992
- 102—Honus Wagner 1912
- Kiki Cuyler 1925
- Bill Brubaker 1936
- Frank Thomas 1953
- Willie Stargell 1966
- 101—Honus Wagner 1903, 1905
- Pie Traynor 1923
- Bob Elliott 1943
- Babe Dahlgren 1944
- Dave Parker 1975
- Jason Thompson 1982
- 100—Honus Wagner 1900, 1909
- Paul Waner 1929
- Vince DiMaggio 1941
- Richie Zisk 1974
- Bobby Bonilla 1988, 1991
- Andy Van Slyke 1988

20-plus victories

- 1887—Pud Galvin 28-21
- 1888—Ed Morris 29-23
- Pud Galvin 23-25
- 1889—Pud Galvin 23-16
- Harry Staley 21-26
- 1891—Mark Baldwin 22-28
- 1892—Mark Baldwin 26-27
- 1893—Frank Killen 36-14
- 1895—Pink Hawley 31-22
- 1896—Frank Killen 30-18
- Pink Hawley 22-21
- 1898—Jesse Tannehill 25-13
- 1899—Jesse Tannehill 24-14
- Sam Leever 21-23
- 1900—Jesse Tannehill 20-6
- Deacon Phillippe 20-13
- 1901—Deacon Phillippe 22-12
- Jack Chesbro 21-10
- 1902—Jack Chesbro 28-6
- Jesse Tannehill 20-6
- Deacon Phillippe 20-9
- 1903—Sam Leever 25-7
- Deacon Phillippe 25-9
- 1905—Sam Leever 20-5
- Deacon Phillippe 20-13
- 1906—Vic Willis 23-13
- Sam Leever 22-7
- 1907—Vic Willis 21-11
- Al Leifield 20-16
- 1908—Nick Maddox 23-8
- Vic Willis 23-11
- 1909—Howard Camnitz 25-6
- Vic Willis 22-11
- 1911—Babe Adams 22-12
- Howard Camnitz 20-15
- 1912—Claude Hendrix 24-9
- Howard Camnitz 22-12
- 1913—Babe Adams 21-10
- 1915—Al Mamaux 21-8
- 1916—Al Mamaux 21-15
- 1920—Wilbur Cooper 24-15
- 1921—Wilbur Cooper 22-14
- 1922—Wilbur Cooper 23-14
- 1923—John Morrison 25-13
- 1924—Wilbur Cooper 20-14
- 1926—Remy Kremer 20-6
- Lee Meadows 20-9
- 1927—Carmen Hill 22-11
- 1928—Burleigh Grimes 25-14
- 1930—Remy Kremer 20-12
- 1943—Rip Sewell 21-9
- 1944—Rip Sewell 21-12
- 1951—Murry Dickson 20-16
- 1958—Bob Friend 22-14
- 1960—Vernon Law 20-9
- 1977—John Candelaria 20-5
- 1990—Doug Drabek 22-6
- 1991—John Smiley 20-8

Hank Greenberg (left) and Ralph Kiner, two of the game's premier sluggers, joined forces for one Pittsburgh season in 1947.

N.L. home run champions

- 1902—Tommy Leach 6
- 1946—Ralph Kiner 23
- 1947—Ralph Kiner *51
- 1948—Ralph Kiner *40
- 1949—Ralph Kiner 54
- 1950—Ralph Kiner 47
- 1951—Ralph Kiner 42
- 1952—Ralph Kiner *37
- 1971—Willie Stargell 48
- 1973—Willie Stargell 44

* Tied for league lead

N.L. RBI champions

- 1901—Honus Wagner 126
- 1902—Honus Wagner 91
- 1906—Jim Nealon 83
- 1908—Honus Wagner 109
- 1909—Honus Wagner 100
- 1911—Owen Wilson 107
- 1912—Honus Wagner 102
- 1927—Paul Waner 131
- 1949—Ralph Kiner 127
- 1973—Willie Stargell 119

N.L. batting champions

- 1900—Honus Wagner .381
- 1902—Clarence Beaumont .357
- 1903—Honus Wagner .355
- 1904—Honus Wagner .349
- 1906—Honus Wagner .339
- 1907—Honus Wagner .350
- 1908—Honus Wagner .354
- 1909—Honus Wagner .339
- 1911—Honus Wagner .334
- 1927—Paul Waner .380
- 1934—Paul Waner .362
- 1935—Arky Vaughan .385
- 1936—Paul Waner .373
- 1940—Debs Garms .355
- 1960—Dick Groat .325
- 1961—Roberto Clemente .351
- 1964—Roberto Clemente .339
- 1965—Roberto Clemente .329
- 1966—Mateo Alou .342
- 1967—Roberto Clemente .357
- 1977—Dave Parker .338
- 1978—Dave Parker .334
- 1981—Bill Madlock .341
- 1983—Bill Madlock .323

N.L. ERA champions

- 1900—Rube Waddell 2.37
- 1901—Jesse Tannehill 2.18
- 1903—Sam Leever 2.06
- 1926—Ray Kremer 2.61
- 1927—Ray Kremer 2.47
- 1935—Cy Blanton 2.59
- 1955—Bob Friend 2.84
- 1977—John Candelaria 2.34

N.L. strikeout champions

- 1900—Rube Waddell 130
- 1945—Preacher Roe 148
- 1964—Bob Veale 250

No-hit pitchers

(9 innings or more)

- 1907—Nick Maddox 2-1 vs. Brooklyn
- 1951—Cliff Chambers 3-0 vs. Boston
- 1969—Bob Moose 4-0 vs. New York
- 1970—Dock Ellis 2-0 vs. San Diego
- 1976—John Candelaria 2-0 vs. Los Angeles
- 1997—Francisco Cordova-Ricardo Rincon 3-0 vs. Houston (10 innings)

Longest hitting streaks

- 27—Jimmy Williams 1899
- 26—Jimmy Williams 1899
- Danny O'Connell 1953
- 25—Charlie Grimm 1923
- Fred Lindstrom 1933
- 24—Maury Wills 1968
- 23—Danny Murtaugh 1948
- Al Oliver 1974
- 22—Dave Parker 1977 (twice)
- Jay Bell 1992
- 21—Frank Gustine 1947
- Gene Alley 1969
- Richie Zisk 1974
- Al Oliver 1974
- Carlos Garcia 1995
- 20—Roberto Clemente 1965
- Rennie Stennett 1977
- Al Martin 1999

INDIVIDUAL SEASON, GAME RECORDS

SEASON

Batting

At-bats	698	Matty Alou	1969
Runs	148	Jake Stenzel	1894
Hits	237	Paul Waner	1927
Singles	198	Lloyd Waner	1927
Doubles	62	Paul Waner	1932
Triples	36	Chief Wilson	1912
Home runs	54	Ralph Kiner	1949
Home runs, rookie	23	Johnny Rizzo	1938
		Ralph Kiner	1946
Grand slams	4	Ralph Kiner	1949
Total bases	366	Kiki Cuyler	1925
RBIs	131	Paul Waner	1927
Walks	137	Ralph Kiner	1951
Most strikeouts	163	Donn Clendenon	1969
Fewest strikeouts	7	Pie Traynor	1929
Batting average	.385	Arky Vaughan	1935
Slugging pct.	.658	Ralph Kiner	1949
Stolen bases	96	Omar Moreno	1980

Pitching

Games	94	Kent Tekulve	1979
Complete games	54	Ed Morris	1888
Innings	330.2	Burleigh Grimes	1928
Wins	34	Frank Killen	1893
Losses	21	Murry Dickson	1952
Winning pct.	.947 (18-1)	Elroy Face	1959
Walks	159	Marty O'Toole	1912
Strikeouts	276	Bob Veale	1965
Shutouts	12	Ed Morris	1886
Home runs allowed	32	Murry Dickson	1951
Lowest ERA	1.56	Howie Camnitz	1908
Saves	34	Jim Gott	1988

GAME

Batting

Runs	6	Ginger Beaumont	7-22-1899
Hits	7	Rennie Stennett	9-16-75
Doubles	4	Paul Waner	5-20-32
Triples	3	Last by Roberto Clemente	9-8-58
Home runs	3	Last by Darnell Coles	9-30-87
RBIs	9	Johnny Rizzo	5-30-39
Total bases	15	Willie Stargell	5-22-68
Stolen bases	4	Last by Tony Womack	9-6-97

HISTORY

CAREER LEADERS

BATTING

Games

Roberto Clemente	2,433
Honus Wagner	2,433
Willie Stargell	2,360
Max Carey	2,178
Bill Mazeroski	2,163
Paul Waner	2,154
Pie Traynor	1,941
Lloyd Waner	1,803
Tommy Leach	1,574
Fred Clarke	1,479

At-bats

Roberto Clemente	9,454
Honus Wagner	9,034
Paul Waner	8,429
Max Carey	8,406
Willie Stargell	7,927
Bill Mazeroski	7,755
Pie Traynor	7,559
Lloyd Waner	7,256
Tommy Leach	5,910
Fred Clarke	5,472

Runs

Honus Wagner	1,521
Paul Waner	1,493
Roberto Clemente	1,416
Max Carey	1,414
Willie Stargell	1,195
Pie Traynor	1,183
Lloyd Waner	1,151
Fred Clarke	1,015
Tommy Leach	1,009
Arky Vaughan	936

Hits

Roberto Clemente	3,000
Honus Wagner	2,967
Paul Waner	2,868
Max Carey	2,416
Pie Traynor	2,416
Lloyd Waner	2,317
Willie Stargell	2,232
Bill Mazeroski	2,016
Arky Vaughan	1,709
Fred Clarke	1,638

Doubles

Paul Waner	558
Honus Wagner	551
Roberto Clemente	440
Willie Stargell	423
Max Carey	375
Pie Traynor	371
Dave Parker	296
Bill Mazeroski	294
Arky Vaughan	291
Al Oliver	276
Gus Suhr	276

Triples

Honus Wagner	232
Paul Waner	187
Roberto Clemente	166
Pie Traynor	164
Fred Clarke	156
Max Carey	148
Tommy Leach	139
Arky Vaughan	116
Lloyd Waner	114
Jake Beckley	113

Home runs

Willie Stargell	475
Ralph Kiner	301
Roberto Clemente	240
Barry Bonds	176
Dave Parker	166
Frank Thomas	163
Bill Mazeroski	138
Al Oliver	135
Richie Hebner	128
Dick Stuart	117
Andy Van Slyke	117

Total bases

Roberto Clemente	4,492
Honus Wagner	4,228
Willie Stargell	4,190
Paul Waner	4,127
Pie Traynor	3,289
Max Carey	3,288
Lloyd Waner	2,895
Bill Mazeroski	2,848
Arky Vaughan	2,484
Dave Parker	2,397

Runs batted in

Willie Stargell	1,540
Honus Wagner	1,475
Roberto Clemente	1,305
Pie Traynor	1,273
Paul Waner	1,177
Bill Mazeroski	853
Ralph Kiner	801
Gus Suhr	789
Arky Vaughan	764
Dave Parker	758

Extra-base hits

Willie Stargell	953
Honus Wagner	865
Paul Waner	854
Roberto Clemente	846
Pie Traynor	593
Max Carey	590
Dave Parker	524
Bill Mazeroski	494
Arky Vaughan	491
Ralph Kiner	486

Batting average

(Minimum 500 games)

Paul Waner	.340
Kiki Cuyler	.336
Honus Wagner	.328
Matty Alou	.327
Elmer Smith	.325
Arky Vaughan	.324
Clarence Beaumont	.321
Pie Traynor	.320
Lloyd Waner	.319
Roberto Clemente	.317

Stolen bases

Max Carey	688
Honus Wagner	639
Omar Moreno	412
Patsy Donovan	312
Tommy Leach	271
Fred Clarke	261
Barry Bonds	251
Frank Taveras	206
Ginger Beaumont	200
Jake Stenzel	188

PITCHING

Earned-run average

(Minimum 1,000 innings)

Vic Willis	2.08
Lefty Leifield	2.38
Sam Leever	2.47
Deacon Phillippe	2.50
Howie Camnitz	2.63
Kent Tekulve	2.68
Wilbur Cooper	2.74
Babe Adams	2.74
Jesse Tannehill	2.75
Doug Drabek	3.02

Wins

Wilbur Cooper	202
Babe Adams	194
Sam Leever	194
Bob Friend	191
Deacon Phillippe	168
Vern Law	162
Ray Kremer	143
Rip Sewell	143
John Candelaria	124
Howie Camnitz	116
Jesse Tannehill	116
Bob Veale	116

Losses

Bob Friend	218
Wilbur Cooper	159
Vern Law	147
Babe Adams	139
Sam Leever	100
Rip Sewell	97
Roy Face	93
Deacon Phillippe	92
Ron Kline	91
Bob Veale	91

Innings pitched

Bob Friend	3,480.1
Wilbur Cooper	3,199.0
Babe Adams	2,991.1
Vern Law	2,672.0
Sam Leever	2,660.2
Deacon Phillippe	2,286.0
Rip Sewell	2,108.2
Ray Kremer	1,954.2
John Candelaria	1,873.0
Bob Veale	1,868.2

Strikeouts

Bob Friend	1,682
Bob Veale	1,652
Wilbur Cooper	1,191
John Candelaria	1,159
Vern Law	1,092
Babe Adams	1,036
Steve Blass	896
Dock Ellis	869
Deacon Phillippe	861
Rick Rhoden	852

Bases on balls

Bob Friend	869
Bob Veale	839
Wilbur Cooper	762
Rip Sewell	740
Steve Blass	597
Vern Law	597
Sam Leever	587
Howie Camnitz	532
Frank Killen	519
Ray Kremer	483

Games

Roy Face	802
Kent Tekulve	722
Bob Friend	568
Vern Law	483
Babe Adams	481
Wilbur Cooper	469
Dave Giusti	410
Sam Leever	388
Rip Sewell	385
Al McBean	376

Shutouts

Babe Adams	44
Sam Leever	39
Bob Friend	35
Wilbur Cooper	33
Vern Law	28
Lefty Leifield	28
Deacon Phillippe	25
Vic Willis	23
Rip Sewell	20
Bob Veale	20

Saves

Roy Face	188
Kent Tekulve	158
Dave Giusti	133
Stan Belinda	61
Al McBean	59
Bill Landrum	56
Jim Gott	50
Rich Loiselle	48
Mike Williams	47
Don Robinson	43

TEAM SEASON, GAME RECORDS

SEASON

Batting

Most at-bats	5,724	1967
Most runs	912	1925
Fewest runs	464	1917
Most hits	1,698	1922
Most singles	1,297	1922
Most doubles	320	2000
Most triples	129	1912
Most home runs	171	1999
Fewest home runs	9	1917
Most grand slams	7	1978, 1996
Most pinch-hit home runs	10	1996
Most total bases	2,430	1966
Most stolen bases	264	1907
Highest batting average	.309	1928
Lowest batting average	.231	1952
Highest slugging pct	.449	1930

Pitching

Lowest ERA	2.48	1918
Highest ERA	5.24	1930
Most complete games	133	1904
Most shutouts	26	1906
Most saves	52	1979
Most walks	711	2000
Most strikeouts	1,124	1969

Fielding

Most errors	295	1903
Fewest errors	105	1993
Most double plays	215	1966
Highest fielding average	.984	1992

General

Most games won	110	1909
Most games lost	113	1890
Highest win pct	.741	1902
Lowest win pct	.169	1890

GAME, INNING

Batting

Most runs, game	27	6-6-1894
Most runs, inning	12	4-22-1892, 6-6-1894
Most hits, game	27	8-8-22
Most home runs, game	7	6-8-1894, 8-16-47
Most total bases, game	47	8-1-70

Second baseman Bill Mazeroski will always be remembered for his 1960 World Series home run.

PIRATES YEAR-BY-YEAR

Year	W	L	Place	Games Back	Manager	Leaders: Batting avg.	Hits	Home runs	RBIs	Wins	ERA
1901	90	49	1st	+7½	Clarke	Wagner, .353	Wagner, 194	Beaumont, 8	Wagner, 126	Phillippe, 22	Tannehill, 2.18
1902	103	36	1st	+27½	Clarke	Beaumont, .357	Beaumont, 193	Leach, 6	Wagner, 91	Chesbro, 28	Tannehill, 1.95
1903	91	49	1st	+6½	Clarke	Wagner, .355	Beaumont, 209	Beaumont, Leach, 7	Wagner, 101	Leever, 25	Leever, 2.06
1904	87	66	4th	19	Clarke	Wagner, .349	Beaumont, 185	Wagner, 4	Wagner, 75	Flaherty, 19	Flaherty, 2.05
1905	96	57	2nd	9	Clarke	Wagner, .363	Wagner, 199	Wagner, 6	Wagner, 101	Leever, Phillippe, 20	Phillippe, 2.19
1906	93	60	3rd	23½	Clarke	Wagner, .339	Wagner, 175	Nealon, 3	Nealon, 83	Willis, 23	Willis, 1.73
1907	91	63	2nd	17	Clarke	Wagner, .350	Wagner, 180	Wagner, 6	Abbaticchio, Wagner, 82	Willis, 21	Leever, 1.66
1908	98	56	*2nd	1	Clarke	Wagner, .354	Wagner, 201	Wagner, 10	Wagner, 109	Maddox, Willis, 23	Camnitz, 1.56
1909	110	42	1st	+6½	Clarke	Wagner, .339	Wagner, 168	Leach, 6	Wagner, 100	Camnitz, 25	Adams, 1.11
1910	86	67	3rd	17½	Clarke	Wagner, .320	Byrne, 178	Flynn, 6	Wagner, 81	Adams, 18	Adams, 2.24
1911	85	69	3rd	14½	Clarke	Wagner, .334	Wilson, 163	Wilson, 12	Wilson, 107	Adams, 22	Adams, 2.33
1912	93	58	2nd	10	Clarke	Wagner, .324	Wagner, 181	Wilson, 11	Wagner, 102	Hendrix, 24	Robinson, 2.26
1913	78	71	4th	21½	Clarke	Viox, .317	Carey, 172	Wilson, 10	D. Miller, 90	Adams, 21	Adams, 2.15
1914	69	85	7th	25½	Clarke	Viox, .265	Carey, 144	Konetchy, 4	Viox, 57	Cooper, 16	Cooper, 2.13
1915	73	81	5th	18	Clarke	Hinchman, .307	Hinchman, 177	Wagner, 6	Wagner, 78	Mamaux, 21	Mamaux, 2.04
1916	65	89	6th	29	Callahan	Hinchman, .315	Hinchman, 175	Carey, 7	Hinchman, 76	Mamaux, 21	Cooper, 1.87
1917	51	103	8th	47	Callahan, Wagner, Bezdek	Carey, .296	Carey, 174	Fischer, 3	Carey, 51	Cooper, 17	Cooper, 2.36
1918	65	60	4th	17	Bezdek	Cutshaw, .285	Cutshaw, 132	Cutchaw, 5	Cutshaw, 68	Cooper, 19	Cooper, 2.11
1919	71	68	4th	24½	Bezdek	Southworth, .280	Bigbee, 132	Stengel, 4	Southworth, 61	Cooper, 19	Adams, 1.98
1920	79	75	4th	14	Gibson	Carey, .289	Southworth, 155	Bigbee, Nicholson, 4	Whitted, 74	Cooper, 24	Adams, 2.16
1921	90	63	2nd	4	Gibson	Cutshaw, .340	Bigbee, 204	Carey, Grimm, Whitted, 7	Grimm, 71	Cooper, 22	Adams, 2.64
1922	85	69	*3rd	8	Gibson, McKechnie	Bigbee, .350	Bigbee, 215	Russell, 12	Bigbee, 99	Cooper, 23	Cooper, 3.18
1923	87	67	3rd	8½	McKechnie	Grimm, .345	Traynor, 208	Traynor, 12	Traynor, 101	Morrison, 25	Meadows, 3.01
1924	90	63	3rd	3	McKechnie	Cuyler, .354	Carey, 178	Cuyler, 9	Wright, 111	Cooper, 20	Yde, 2.83
1925	95	58	1st	+8½	McKechnie	Cuyler, .357	Cuyler, 220	Cuyler, Wright, 18	Wright, 121	Meadows, 19	Aldridge, 3.63
1926	84	69	3rd	4½	McKechnie	P. Waner, .336	Cuyler, 197	Cuyler, Grantham, P. Waner, Wright, 8	Cuyler, Traynor, 92	Kremer, Meadows, 20	Kremer, 2.61
1927	94	60	1st	+1½	Bush	P. Waner, .380	P. Waner, 237	P. Waner, Wright, 9	P. Waner, 131	Hill, 22	Kremer, 2.47
1928	85	67	4th	9	Bush	P. Waner, .370	P. Waner, 223	Grantham, 10	Traynor, 124	Grimes, 25	Grimes, 2.99
1929	88	65	2nd	10½	Bush, Ens	Traynor, .356	L. Waner, 234	P. Waner, 15	Traynor, 108	Kremer, 18	Grimes, 3.13
1930	80	74	5th	12	Ens	P. Waner, .368	P. Waner, 217	Grantham, 18	Comorosky, Traynor, 119	Kremer, 20	French, 4.36
1931	75	79	5th	26	Ens	P. Waner, .322	L. Waner, 214	Grantham, 10	Traynor, 103	Meine, 19	Meine, 2.98
1932	86	68	2nd	4	Gibson	P. Waner, .341	P. Waner, 215	Grace, P. Waner, 8	Piet, 85	French, 18	Swetonic, 2.82
1933	87	67	2nd	5	Gibson	Piet, .323	P. Waner, 191	Suhr, 10	Vaughan, 97	French, 18	French, 2.72
1934	74	76	5th	19½	Gibson, Traynor	P. Waner, .362	P. Waner, 217	P. Waner, 14	Suhr, 103	Hoyt, 15	Hoyt, 2.93
1935	86	67	4th	13½	Traynor	Vaughan, .385	Jensen, 203	Vaughan, 19	Vaughan, 99	Blanton, 18	Blanton, 2.58
1936	84	70	4th	8	Traynor	P. Waner, .373	P. Waner, 218	Suhr, 11	Suhr, 118	Swift, 16	Hoyt, 2.70
1937	86	68	3rd	10	Traynor	P. Waner, .354	P. Waner, 219	Young, 9	Suhr, 97	Blanton, 14	Bauers, 2.88
1938	86	64	2nd	2	Traynor	Vaughan, .322	L. Waner, 194	Rizzo, 23	Rizzo, 111	Brown, 15	Klinger, 2.99
1939	68	85	6th	28½	Traynor	P. Waner, .328	Vaughan, 182	Fletcher, 12	Fletcher, 71	Klinger, 14	Brown, 3.37
1940	78	76	4th	22½	Frisch	Garms, .355	Vaughan, 178	V. DiMaggio, 19	Van Robays, 116	Sewell, 16	Sewell, 2.80
1941	81	73	4th	19	Frisch	Vaughan, .316	Fletcher, 150	V. DiMaggio, 21	V. DiMaggio, 100	Butcher, 17	Dietz, 2.33
1942	66	81	5th	36½	Frisch	Elliott, .296	Elliott, 166	V. DiMaggio, 15	Elliott, 89	Sewell, 17	Gornicki, 2.57
1943	80	74	4th	25	Frisch	Elliott, .315	Elliott, 183	V. DiMaggio, 15	Elliott, 101	Sewell, 21	Sewell, 2.54
1944	90	63	2nd	14½	Frisch	Russell, .312	Russell, 181	Dahlgren, 12	Elliott, 108	Sewell, 21	Ostermueller, 2.73
1945	82	72	4th	16	Frisch	Elliott, .290	Elliott, 157	Barrett, Salkeld, 15	Elliott, 108	Strincevich, 16	Roe, 2.87
1946	63	91	7th	34	Frisch, S. Davis	Cox, .290	Russell, 143	Kiner, 23	Kiner, 81	Ostermueller, 13	Bahr, 2.63
1947	62	92	*7th	32	Herman, Burwell	Kiner, .313	Gustine, 183	Kiner, 51	Kiner, 127	Ostermueller, 12	Sewell, 3.57
1948	83	71	4th	8½	Meyer	Walker, .316	Rojek, 186	Kiner, 40	Kiner, 123	Chesnes, 14	Higbe, 3.36
1949	71	83	6th	26	Meyer	Hopp, .318	Kiner, 170	Kiner, 54	Kiner, 127	Chambers, 13	Dickson, 3.29
1950	57	96	8th	33½	Meyer	Murtaugh, .294	Kiner, 149	Kiner, 47	Kiner, 118	Chambers, 12	Dickson, 3.80
1951	64	90	7th	32½	Meyer	Kiner, .309	Bell, 167	Kiner, 42	Kiner, 109	Dickson, 20	Dickson, 4.02
1952	42	112	8th	54½	Meyer	Groat, .284	Kiner, 126	Kiner, 37	Kiner, 87	Dickson, 14	Dickson, 3.57
1953	50	104	8th	55	Haney	O'Connell, .294	O'Connell, 173	Thomas, 30	Thomas, 102	Dickson, 10	Hetki, 3.95
1954	53	101	8th	44	Haney	Gordon, .306	Thomas, 172	Thomas, 23	Thomas, 94	Littlefield, 10	Littlefield, 3.60
1955	60	94	8th	38½	Haney	Long, .291	Groat, 139	Thomas, 25	Long, 79	Friend, 14	Friend, 2.83
1956	66	88	7th	27	Bragan	Virdon, .334	Virdon, 170	Long, 27	Long, 91	Friend, 17	Kline, 3.38
1957	62	92	*7th	33	Bragan, Murtaugh	Groat, .315	Thomas, 172	Thomas, 23	Thomas, 89	Friend, 14	Law, 2.87
1958	84	70	2nd	8	Murtaugh	Skinner, .321	Groat, 175	Thomas, 35	Thomas, 109	Friend, 22	Witt, 1.61
1959	78	76	4th	9	Murtaugh	Burgess, Stuart, .297	Hoak, 166	Stuart, 27	Stuart, 78	Face, Law, 18	Face, 2.70
1960	95	59	1st	+7	Murtaugh	Groat, .325	Groat, 186	Stuart, 23	Clemente, 94	Law, 20	Face, 2.90
1961	75	79	6th	18	Murtaugh	Clemente, .351	Clemente, 201	Stuart, 35	Stuart, 117	Friend, 14	Gibbon, 3.32
1962	93	68	4th	8	Murtaugh	Burgess, .328	Groat, 199	Skinner, 20	Mazeroski, 81	Friend, 18	Face, 1.88
1963	74	88	8th	25	Murtaugh	Clemente, .320	Clemente, 192	Clemente, 17	Clemente, 76	Friend, 17	Friend, 2.34
1964	80	82	*6th	13	Murtaugh	Clemente, .339	Clemente, 211	Stargell, 21	Clemente, 87	Veale, 18	McBean, 1.91
1965	90	72	3rd	7	Walker	Clemente, .329	Clemente, 194	Stargell, 27	Stargell, 107	Law, Veale, 17	Law, 2.15
1966	92	70	3rd	3	Walker	M. Alou, .342	Clemente, 202	Stargell, 33	Clemente, 119	Veale, 16	Veale, 3.02
1967	81	81	6th	20½	Walker, Murtaugh	Clemente, .357	Clemente, 209	Clemente, 23	Clemente, 110	Veale, 16	McBean, 2.54
1968	80	82	6th	17	Shepard	M. Alou, .332	M. Alou, 185	Stargell, 24	Clendenon, 87	Blass, 18	Kline, 1.68
								EAST DIVISION			
1969	88	74	3rd	12	Shepard, Grammas	Clemente, .345	M. Alou, 231	Stargell, 29	Stargell, 92	Blass, 16	Moose, 2.91
1970	89	73	†1st	+5	Murtaugh	Clemente, .352	M. Alou, 201	Stargell, 31	Stargell, 85	Walker, 15	Walker, 3.04
1971	97	65	‡1st	+7	Murtaugh	Clemente, .341	Clemente, 178	Stargell, 48	Stargell, 125	Ellis, 19	Blass, 2.85
1972	96	59	†1st	+11	Virdon	Davalillo, .318	Oliver, 176	Stargell, 33	Stargell, 112	Blass, 19	Blass, 2.49
1973	80	82	3rd	2½	Virdon, Murtaugh	Stargell, .299	Oliver, 191	Stargell, 44	Stargell, 119	Briles, 14	Giusti, 2.37
1974	88	74	†1st	+1½	Murtaugh	Oliver, .321	Oliver, 198	Stargell, 25	Zisk, 100	Reuss, 16	Rooker, 2.78
1975	92	69	†1st	+6½	Murtaugh	Sanguillen, .328	Oliver, Stennett, 176	Parker, 25	Parker, 101	Reuss, 18	Reuss, 2.54
1976	92	70	2nd	9	Murtaugh	Oliver, .323	Cash, 189	B. Robinson, Zisk, 21	Parker, 90	Candelaria, 16	Tekulve, 2.45
1977	96	66	2nd	5	Tanner	Parker, .338	Parker, 215	B. Robinson, 26	B. Robinson, 104	Candelaria, 20	Gossage, 1.62
1978	88	73	2nd	1½	Tanner	Parker, .334	Parker, 194	Parker, 30	Parker, 117	Blyleven, D. Robinson, 14	Tekulve, 2.33
1979	98	64	‡1st	+2	Tanner	Parker, .310	Moreno, 196	Stargell, 32	Parker, 94	Candelaria, 14	Tekulve, 2.75
1980	83	79	3rd	8	Tanner	Easler, .338	Moreno, 168	Easler, 21	Parker, 79	Bibby, 19	Solomon, 2.69
1981	46	56	§4th/6th	—	Tanner	Madlock, .341	Moreno, 120	Thompson, 15	Parker, 48	Rhoden, 9	Tekulve, 2.49
1982	84	78	4th	8	Tanner	Madlock, .319	Ray, 182	Thompson, 31	Thompson, 101	D. Robinson, 15	Scurry, 1.74
1983	84	78	2nd	6	Tanner	Madlock, .323	Pena, Ray, 163	Thompson, 18	Thompson, 76	Candelaria, McWilliams, 15	Tekulve, 1.64
1984	75	87	6th	21½	Tanner	Lacy, .321	Wynne, 174	Thompson, 17	Pena, 78	Rhoden, 14	Candelaria, Rhoden, 2.72
1985	57	104	6th	43½	Tanner	Orsulak, .300	Ray, 163	Thompson, 12	Ray, 70	Reuschel, 14	Reuschel, 2.27
1986	64	98	6th	44	Leyland	Ray, .301	Ray, 174	Morrison, 23	Morrison, 88	Rhoden, 15	Rhoden, 2.84
1987	80	82	*4th	15	Leyland	Bonilla, .300	Van Slyke, 165	Bonds, 25	Van Slyke, 82	Dunne, 13	Reuschel, 2.75
1988	85	75	2nd	15	Leyland	Van Slyke, .288	Van Slyke, 169	Van Slyke, 25	Bonilla, Van Slyke, 100	Drabek, 15	Walk, 2.71
1989	74	88	5th	19	Leyland	Bonilla, .281	Bonilla, 173	Bonilla, 24	Bonilla, 26	Drabek, 14	Drabek, 2.80
1990	95	67	†1st	+4	Leyland	Bonds, .301	Bonilla, 175	Bonds, 33	Bonilla, 120	Drabek, 22	Drabek, 2.76
1991	98	64	†1st	+14	Leyland	Bonilla, .302	Bonilla, 174	Bonds, 25	Bonds, 116	Smiley, 20	Tomlin, 2.98
1992	96	66	†1st	+9	Leyland	Van Slyke, .324	Van Slyke, 199	Bonds, 34	Bonds, 103	Drabek, 15	Wakefield, 2.15
1993	75	87	5th	22	Leyland	Merced, .313	Bell, 187	Martin, 18	King, 98	Walk, 13	Cooke, 3.89
								CENTRAL DIVISION			
1994	53	61	*3rd	13	Leyland	Garcia, .277	Bell, 117	Clark, 10	Merced, 51	Z. Smith, 10	Z. Smith, 3.27
1995	58	86	5th	27	Leyland	Merced, .300	Merced, 146	King, 18	King, 87	Neagle, 13	Neagle, 3.43
1996	73	89	5th	15	Leyland	Martin, .300	Martin, 189	King, 30	King, 111	Lieber, 9	Lieber, 3.99
1997	79	83	2nd	5	Lamont	Randa, .302	Womack, 178	Young, 18	Young, 74	Cordova, Lieber, Loaiza, 11	Cordova, 3.63
1998	69	93	6th	33	Lamont	Kendall, .327	Womack, 185	Young, 27	Young, 108	Cordova, 13	Cordova, 3.31
1999	78	83	3rd	18½	Lamont	Giles, .315	Young, 174	Giles, 39	Giles, 115	Ritchie, 15	Ritchie, 3.49
2000	69	93	5th	26	Lamont	Kendall, .320	Kendall, 185	Giles, 35	Giles, 123	Silva, 11	Benson, 3.86

* Tied for position. † Lost Championship Series. ‡ Won Championship Series. § First half 25-23; second half 21-33.

Note: Batting average minimum 350 at-bats; ERA minimum 90 innings pitched.

St. Louis Cardinals

FRANCHISE CHRONOLOGY

First season: 1882, as a member of the new American Association. The "Browns" struggled to a 37-43 first-year record and finished fifth in the six-team field.

1883-1900: The Browns captured four consecutive A.A pennants from 1885 through 1888, but their success ended there. When the A.A. folded after the 1891 season, they joined the National League and sank quietly into the second division.

1901-present: The Cardinals trail only the Yankees in World Series championships and only the Yankees and Dodgers in pennants. And all of their success was achieved after 1926, when they captured their first N.L. flag and World Series. The history of Cardinals baseball has been colorful and consistent, spiced by some of the sport's most memorable moments. St. Louis won two pennants in the 1920s, three in the 1930s, four in the 1940s, three in the 1960s and three in the 1980s. Nine of the pennants led to championships, including the Gas House Gang's 1934 fall classic romp past Detroit and Enos Slaughter's 1946 Series-ending Mad Dash. The Cardinals have finished first only five times since division play began in 1969, but three of them resulted in World Series appearances (a 1982 victory, 1985 and '87 losses). The Cardinals, who lost in the 1996 and 2000 N.L. Championship Series, were placed in the Central Division when the N.L. adopted the three-division format in 1994.

Outfielder Stan Musial.

CARDINALS VS. OPPONENTS BY DECADE

	Braves	Cubs	Dodgers	Giants	Phillies	Pirates	Reds	Astros	Mets	Expos	Padres	Marlins	Rockies	Brewers	D'backs	Interleague	Decade Record
1900-09	111-98	64-144	93-115	78-133	90-121	53-158	91-119										580-888
1910-19	100-110	78-136	104-105	81-131	98-112	83-127	108-109										652-830
1920-29	135-85	105-112	119-101	95-123	151-69	102-117	115-105										822-712
1930-39	121-98	109-111	127-91	107-110	159-61	99-121	147-73										869-665
1940-49	144-76	138-82	132-90	141-77	150-70	122-98	133-87										960-580
1950-59	101-119	113-107	85-135	108-112	113-107	132-87	124-96										776-763
1960-69	94-88	114-73	91-91	92-90	108-79	107-81	90-92	79-59	90-54	11-7	8-4						884-718
1970-79	69-51	87-93	53-67	60-60	86-91	79-101	46-74	64-56	93-85	93-85	70-50						800-813
1980-89	68-47	89-81	56-62	60-53	95-80	98-75	63-50	58-56	86-87	82-95	70-48						825-734
1990-99	43-71	67-71	55-52	58-54	67-57	62-76	51-62	62-60	55-67	61-64	56-51	40-29	37-40	14-10	11-6	19-24	758-794
2000-	4-3	10-3	6-3	4-5	7-2	8-4	6-7	6-6	3-6	5-2	9-0	6-3	3-5	7-5	4-5	7-8	95-67
Totals	990-846	974-1013	921-912	884-948	1124-849	945-1045	974-874	269-237	327-299	252-253	213-153	46-32	40-45	21-15	15-11	26-32	8021-7564

Interleague results: 7-5 vs. White Sox; 2-6 vs. Indians; 6-6 vs. Royals; 0-3 vs. Brewers; 6-6 vs. Twins; 5-6 vs. Tigers.

MANAGERS

Name	*Years*	*Record*
Ned Cuthbert	1882	37-43
Ted Sullivan	1883	53-26
Charlie Comiskey	1883, 1884-89, 1891	561-273
Tommy McCarthy	1890	15-12
John Kerins	1890	9-8
Chief Roseman	1890	7-8
Count Campau	1890	27-14
Joe Gerhardt	1890	20-16
Jack Glasscock	1892	1-3
John Stricker	1892	6-17
John Crooks	1892	27-33
George Gore	1892	6-9
Bob Caruthers	1892	16-32
Bill Watkins	1893	57-75
George Miller	1894	56-76
Al Buckenberger	1895	16-34
Chris Von Der Ahe	1895, 1896, 1897	3-14
Joe Quinn	1895	11-28
Lew Phelan	1895	11-30
Harry Diddlebock	1896	7-10
Arlie Latham	1896	0-3
Roger Connor	1896	8-37
Tom Dowd	1896-97	31-60
Hugh Nicol	1897	8-32
Bill Hallman	1897	13-36
Tim Hurst	1898	39-111
Patsy Tebeau	1899-1900	126-117
Patsy Donovan	1901-03	175-236
Kid Nichols	1904-05	80-88
Jimmy Burke	1905	34-56
Stanley Robison	1905	19-31
John McCloskey	1906-08	153-304
Roger Bresnahan	1909-12	255-352
Miller Huggins	1913-17	346-415
Jack Hendricks	1918	51-78
Branch Rickey	1919-25	458-485
Rogers Hornsby	1925-26	153-116
Bob O'Farrell	1927	92-61
Bill McKechnie	1928-29	129-88
Billy Southworth	1929, 1940-45	620-346
Gabby Street	1929, 1930-33	312-242
Frank Frisch	1933-38	458-354
Mike Gonzalez	1938, 1940	9-13
Ray Blades	1939-40	106-85
Eddie Dyer	1946-50	446-325
Marty Marion	1951	81-73
Eddie Stanky	1952-55	260-238
Harry Walker	1955	51-67
Fred Hutchinson	1956-58	232-220
Stan Hack	1958	3-7
Solly Hemus	1959-61	190-192
Johnny Keane	1961-64	317-249
Red Schoendienst	1965-76, 1980, 1990	1041-955
Vern Rapp	1977-78	89-90
Ken Boyer	1978-80	166-190
Whitey Herzog	1980, 1981-90	822-728
Joe Torre	1990-95	351-354
Mike Jorgensen	1995	42-54
Tony La Russa	1996-2000	414-395

WORLD SERIES CHAMPIONS

Year	*Loser*	*Length*	*MVP*
1926	N.Y. Yankees	7 games	None
1931	Philadelphia	7 games	None
1934	Detroit	7 games	None
1942	N.Y. Yankees	5 games	None
1944	St.L. Browns	6 games	None
1946	Boston	7 games	None
1964	N.Y. Yankees	7 games	Gibson
1967	Boston	7 games	Gibson
1982	Milwaukee	7 games	Porter

A.A. PENNANT WINNERS

Year	*Record*	*Manager*	*Series Result*
1885	79-33	Comiskey	None
1886	93-46	Comiskey	None
1887	95-40	Comiskey	None
1888	92-43	Comiskey	None

N.L. PENNANT WINNERS

Year	*Record*	*Manager*	*Series Result*
1926	89-65	Hornsby	Defeated Yankees
1928	95-59	McKechnie	Lost to Yankees
1930	92-62	Street	Lost to A's
1931	101-53	Street	Defeated A's
1934	95-58	Frisch	Defeated Tigers
1942	106-48	Southworth	Defeated Yankees
1943	105-49	Southworth	Lost to Yankees
1944	105-49	Southworth	Defeated Browns
1946	98-58	Dyer	Defeated Red Sox
1964	93-69	Keane	Defeated Yankees
1967	101-60	Schoendienst	Defeated Red Sox
1968	97-65	Schoendiesnt	Lost to Tigers
1982	92-70	Herzog	Defeated Brewers
1985	101-61	Herzog	Lost to Royals
1987	95-67	Herzog	Lost to Twins

EAST DIVISION CHAMPIONS

Year	*Record*	*Manager*	*NLCS Result*
1982	92-70	Herzog	Defeated Braves
1985	101-61	Herzog	Defeated Dodgers
1987	95-67	Herzog	Defeated Giants

CENTRAL DIVISION CHAMPIONS

Year	*Record*	*Manager*	*NLCS Result*
1996	88-74	La Russa	Lost to Braves
2000	95-67	La Russa	Lost to Mets

ATTENDANCE HIGHS

Total	*Season*	*Park*
3,336,493	2000	Busch Stadium
3,236,103	1999	Busch Stadium
3,195,021	1998	Busch Stadium
3,080,980	1989	Busch Stadium
3,072,121	1987	Busch Stadium

BALLPARK CHRONOLOGY

Busch Memorial Stadium (1966-present)

Capacity: 50,297.
First game: Cardinals 4, Atlanta 3, 12 innings (May 12, 1966).
First batter: Felipe Alou, Braves.
First hit: Gary Geiger, Braves (single).
First run: Jerry Buchek, Cardinals (3rd inning).
First home run: Felipe Alou, Braves.
First winning pitcher: Don Dennis, Cardinals.
First-season attendance: 1,712,980.

Sportsman's Park I (1882-91)

Capacity: 6,000.
First game: St. Louis 9, Louisville 7 (May 2, 1882).

Union Park (1892-97)

League Park (1898)

Robison Field (1899-1920)

Capacity: 14,500.

Sportsman's Park II (1920-66)

Capacity: 30,500.
First game: Pittsburgh 6, St. Louis 2, 10 innings (July 1, 1920).
First full-season attendance: 384,773 (1921).

Note: Sportsman's Park was renamed Busch Stadium in 1953.

N.L. MVPs

Frank Frisch, 2B, 1931
Dizzy Dean, P, 1934
Joe Medwick, OF, 1937
Mort Cooper, P, 1942
Stan Musial, OF, 1943
Marty Marion, SS, 1944
Stan Musial, 1B, 1946
Stan Musial OF, 1948
Ken Boyer, 3B, 1964
Orlando Cepeda, 1B, 1967
Bob Gibson, P, 1968
Joe Torre, 3B, 1971
*Keith Hernandez, 1B, 1979
Willie McGee, OF, 1985

* Co-winner.

CY YOUNG WINNERS

Bob Gibson, RH, 1968
Bob Gibson, RH, 1970

ROOKIES OF THE YEAR

Wally Moon, OF, 1954
Bill Virdon, OF, 1955
Bake McBride, OF, 1974
Vince Coleman, OF, 1985
Todd Worrell, P, 1986

MANAGER OF THE YEAR

Whitey Herzog, 1985

RETIRED UNIFORMS

No.	*Name*	*Pos.*
1	Ozzie Smith	SS
2	Red Schoendienst	2B
6	Stan Musial	OF, 1B
9	Enos Slaughter	OF
14	Ken Boyer	3B
17	Dizzy Dean	P
20	Lou Brock	OF
45	Bob Gibson	P

HISTORY

MILESTONE PERFORMANCES

30-plus home runs

70—Mark McGwire 1998
65—Mark McGwire 1999
43—Johnny Mize 1940
42—Rogers Hornsby 1922
Jim Edmonds 2000
39—Rogers Hornsby 1925
Stan Musial 1948
36—Stan Musial 1949
35—Rip Collins 1934
Stan Musial 1954
Jack Clark 1987
34—Dick Allen 1970
Fernando Tatis 1999
33—Stan Musial 1955
32—Stan Musial 1951
Ken Boyer 1960
Mark McGwire 2000
31—Jim Bottomley 1928
Joe Medwick 1937
Ray Lankford 1997, 1998
30—Stan Musial 1953
Ron Gant 1996

100-plus RBIs

154—Joe Medwick 1937
152—Rogers Hornsby 1922
147—Mark McGwire 1998
Mark McGwire 1999
143—Rogers Hornsby 1925
138—Joe Medwick 1936
137—Jim Bottomley 1929
Johnny Mize 1940
Joe Torre 1971
136—Jim Bottomley 1928
131—Stan Musial 1948
130—Enos Slaughter 1946
128—Jim Bottomley 1925
Rip Collins 1934
126—Rogers Hornsby 1921
Joe Medwick 1935
Stan Musial 1954
125—Chick Hafey 1929
124—Jim Bottomley 1927
123—Stan Musial 1949
122—Rip Collins 1935
Joe Medwick 1938
120—Jim Bottomley 1926
119—Ken Boyer 1964
117—Joe Medwick 1939
Pedro Guerrero 1989
114—Frank Frisch 1930
113—Johnny Mize 1937
Stan Musial 1953
112—Ray Jablonski 1953
111—Jim Bottomley 1924
Chick Hafey 1928
Ken Boyer 1963
Orlando Cepeda 1967
110—Tom Herr 1985
109—Buster Adams *1945
Stan Musial 1950, 1956
Bill White 1963
George Hendrick 1980
108—Johnny Mize 1939
Stan Musial 1951, 1955
Jim Edmonds 2000
107—Chick Hafey 1930
Fernando Tatis 1999
106—Joe Medwick 1934
Jack Clark 1987
105—Del Ennis 1957
Keith Hernandez 1979
Willie McGee 1987
Ray Lankford 1998
104—Whitey Kurowski 1947
Ray Jablonski 1954
George Hendrick 1982
Brian Jordan 1996
103—Stan Musial 1946
Ted Simmons 1974
Todd Zeile 1993
102—Austin McHenry 1921
Johnny Mize 1938
Ray Sanders 1944
Whitey Kurowski 1945
Stan Musial 1957
Bill White 1962, 1964
101—Enos Slaughter 1950, 1952
Joe Torre 1969
Dick Allen 1970
100—Les Bell 1926
Johnny Mize 1941
Joe Torre 1970
Reggie Smith 1974
Ted Simmons 1975

*8 with Phillies; 101 with Cardinals.

20-plus victories

1892—Kid Gleason 20-24
1893—Kid Gleason 21-22
1894—Ted Breitenstein 27-23
1899—Cy Young 26-16
Jack Powell 23-19
1901—Jack Harper 23-13
1904—Kid Nichols 21-13
Jack Taylor 20-19
1911—Bob Harmon 23-16
1920—Bill Doak 20-12
1923—Jesse Haines 20-13
1926—Flint Rhem 20-7
1927—Jesse Haines 24-10
Grover Alexander 21-10
1928—Bill Sherdel 21-10
Jesse Haines 20-8
1933—Dizzy Dean 20-18
1934—Dizzy Dean 30-7
1935—Dizzy Dean 28-12
1936—Dizzy Dean 24-13
1939—Curt Davis 22-16
1942—Mort Cooper 22-7
Johnny Beazley 21-6
1943—Mort Cooper 21-8
1944—Mort Cooper 22-7
1945—Red Barrett *23-12
1946—Howie Pollet 21-10
1948—Harry Brecheen 20-7
1949—Howie Pollet 20-9
1953—Harvey Haddix 20-9
1960—Ernie Broglio 21-9
1964—Ray Sadecki 20-11
1965—Bob Gibson 20-12
1966—Bob Gibson 21-12
1968—Bob Gibson 22-9
1969—Bob Gibson 20-13
1970—Bob Gibson 23-7
1971—Steve Carlton 20-9
1977—Bob Forsch 20-7
1984—Joaquin Andujar 20-14
1985—Joaquin Andujar 21-12
John Tudor 21-8
2000—Darryl Kile 20-9

*2-3 with Braves; 21-9 with Cardinals.

N.L. home run champions

1922—Rogers Hornsby 42
1925—Rogers Hornsby 39
1928—Jim Bottomley *31
1934—Rip Collins *35
1937—Joe Medwick *31
1939—Johnny Mize 28
1940—Johnny Mize 43
1998—Mark McGwire 70
1999—Mark McGwire 65

*Tied for league lead.

N.L. RBI champions

1920—Rogers Hornsby *94
1921—Rogers Hornsby 126
1922—Rogers Hornsby 152
1925—Rogers Hornsby 143
1926—Jim Bottomley 120
1928—Jim Bottomley 136
1936—Joe Medwick 138
1937—Joe Medwick 154
1938—Joe Medwick 122
1940—Johnny Mize 137
1946—Enos Slaughter 130
1948—Stan Musial 131
1956—Stan Musial 109
1964—Ken Boyer 119
1967—Orlando Cepeda 111
1971—Joe Torre 137
1999—Mark McGwire 147

* Tied for league lead

N.L. batting champions

1901—Jesse Burkett 376
1920—Rogers Hornsby 370
1921—Rogers Hornsby 397
1922—Rogers Hornsby 401
1923—Rogers Hornsby 384
1924—Rogers Hornsby 424
1925—Rogers Hornsby 403
1931—Chick Hafey 349
1937—Joe Medwick 374
1939—Johnny Mize 349
1943—Stan Musial 357
1946—Stan Musial 365
1948—Stan Musial 376
1950—Stan Musial 346
1951—Stan Musial 355
1952—Stan Musial 336
1957—Stan Musial 351
1971—Joe Torre 363
1979—Keith Hernandez 344
1985—Willie McGee 353
1990—Willie McGee 335

N.L. ERA champions

1914—Bill Doak 1.72
1921—Bill Doak 2.59
1942—Mort Cooper 1.78
1943—Howie Pollet 1.75
1946—Howie Pollet 2.10
1948—Harry Brecheen 2.24
1968—Bob Gibson 1.12
1976—John Denny 2.52
1988—Joe Magrane 2.18

N.L. strikeout champions

1906—Fred Beebe 171
1930—Bill Hallahan 177
1931—Bill Hallahan 159
1932—Dizzy Dean 191
1933—Dizzy Dean 199
1934—Dizzy Dean 195
1935—Dizzy Dean 182
1948—Harry Brecheen 149
1958—Sam Jones 225
1966—Bob Gibson 268
1989—Jose DeLeon 201

No-hit pitchers

(9 innings or more)

1924—Jesse Haines ....5-0 vs. Boston
1934—Paul Dean ....3-0 vs. Brooklyn
1941—Lon Warneke ....2-0 vs. Cincinnati
1968—Ray Washburn ....2-0 vs. San Francisco
1971—Bob Gibson ....11-0 vs. Pittsburgh
1978—Bob Forsch ....5-0 vs. Philadelphia
1983—Bob Forsch ....3-0 vs. Montreal
1999—Jose Jimenez ....1-0 vs. Arizona

Longest hitting streaks

33—Rogers Hornsby 1922
30—Stan Musial 1950
29—Harry Walker 1943
Ken Boyer 1959
28—Joe Medwick 1935
Red Schoendienst 1954
26—Lou Brock 1971
25—Joe McEwing 1999
24—Pepper Martin 1935
Stan Musial 1952
Wally Moon 1957
23—Pepper Martin 1935
Jose Oquendo 1989
22—Taylor Douthit 1930
Johnny Mize 1936
Harry Walker 1943
Stan Musial 1943
Whitey Kurowski 1943
Vada Pinson 1969
Joe Torre 1971
Willie McGee 1990
21—Les Bell 1926
Ernie Orsatti 1932
Joe Medwick 1932
Enos Slaughter 1940
Lou Klein 1943
20—Ed Konetchy 1910
Terry Moore 1942
Stan Musial 1957
Wally Moon 1957
Bill White 1964
Lou Brock 1967
John Mabry 1997

INDIVIDUAL SEASON, GAME RECORDS

SEASON

Batting

At-bats	689	Lou Brock	1967
Runs	141	Rogers Hornsby	1922
Hits	250	Rogers Hornsby	1922
Singles	181	Jesse Burkett	1901
Doubles	64	Joe Medwick	1936
Triples	33	Perry Werden	1893
Home runs	70	Mark McGwire	1998
Home runs, rookie	21	Ray Jablonski	1953
Grand slams	3	3 times Last by Fernando Tatis	 1999
Total bases	450	Rogers Hornsby	1922
RBIs	154	Joe Medwick	1937
Walks	162	Mark McGwire	1998
Most strikeouts	167	Jim Edmonds	2000
Fewest strikeouts	10	Frank Frisch	1927
Batting average	.424	Rogers Hornsby	1924
Slugging pct.	.756	Rogers Hornsby	1922
Stolen bases	118	Lou Brock	1974

Pitching (since 1900)

Games	77	Mike Perez	1992
Complete games	39	Jack Taylor	1904
Innings	352.1	Stoney McGlynn	1907
Wins	30	Dizzy Dean	1934
Losses	25	Stoney McGlynn Art Raymond	1907 1908
Winning pct.	.833 (10-2)	John Tudor	1987
Walks	181	Bob Harmon	1911
Strikeouts	274	Bob Gibson	1970
Shutouts	13	Bob Gibson	1968
Home runs allowed	39	Murry Dickson	1948
Lowest ERA	1.12	Bob Gibson	1968
Saves	47	Lee Smith	1991

GAME

Batting

Runs	5	Last by J.D. Drew	5-1-99
Hits	6	Last by Terry Moore	9-5-35
Doubles	4	Joe Medwick	8-4-37
Triples	3	Last by Jim Bottomley	6-21-27
Home runs	4	Mark Whiten	9-7-93
RBIs	12	Jim Bottomley Mark Whiten	9-16-24 9-7-93
Total bases	16	Mark Whiten	9-7-93
Stolen bases	5	Lonnie Smith	9-4-82

CAREER LEADERS

BATTING

Games

Player	Games
Stan Musial	3,026
Lou Brock	2,289
Ozzie Smith	1,990
Enos Slaughter	1,820
Red Schoendienst	1,795
Curt Flood	1,738
Ken Boyer	1,667
Willie McGee	1,661
Rogers Hornsby	1,580
Julian Javier	1,578

At-bats

Stan Musial	10,972
Lou Brock	9,125
Ozzie Smith	7,160
Red Schoendienst	6,841
Enos Slaughter	6,775
Ken Boyer	6,334
Curt Flood	6,318
Rogers Hornsby	5,881
Willie McGee	5,734
Ted Simmons	5,725

Runs

Player	Runs
Stan Musial	1,949
Lou Brock	1,427
Rogers Hornsby	1,089
Enos Slaughter	1,071
Red Schoendienst	1,025
Ozzie Smith	991
Ken Boyer	988
Jim Bottomley	921
Ray Lankford	854
Curt Flood	845

Hits

Player	Hits
Stan Musial	3,630
Lou Brock	2,713
Rogers Hornsby	2,110
Enos Slaughter	2,064
Red Schoendienst	1,980
Ozzie Smith	1,944
Ken Boyer	1,855
Curt Flood	1,853
Jim Bottomley	1,727
Ted Simmons	1,704

Doubles

Player	Doubles
Stan Musial	725
Lou Brock	434
Joe Medwick	377
Rogers Hornsby	367
Enos Slaughter	366
Red Schoendienst	352
Jim Bottomley	344
Ozzie Smith	338
Ted Simmons	332
Ray Lankford	307

Triples

Player	Triples
Stan Musial	177
Rogers Hornsby	143
Enos Slaughter	135
Lou Brock	121
Jim Bottomley	119
Ed Konetchy	94
Willie McGee	83
Joe Medwick	81
Pepper Martin	75
Garry Templeton	69

Home runs

Player	Home runs
Stan Musial	475
Ken Boyer	255
Ray Lankford	207
Rogers Hornsby	193
Mark McGwire	191
Jim Bottomley	181
Ted Simmons	172
Johnny Mize	158
Joe Medwick	152
Enos Slaughter	146

Total bases

Player	Total bases
Stan Musial	6,134
Lou Brock	3,776
Rogers Hornsby	3,342
Enos Slaughter	3,138
Ken Boyer	3,011
Jim Bottomley	2,852
Red Schoendienst	2,657
Ted Simmons	2,626
Joe Medwick	2,585
Curt Flood	2,464

Runs batted in

Stan Musial	1,951
Enos Slaughter	1,148
Jim Bottomley	1,105
Rogers Hornsby	1,072
Ken Boyer	1,001
Ted Simmons	929
Joe Medwick	923
Lou Brock	814
Ray Lankford	768
Frankie Frisch	720

Extra-base hits

Player	Extra-base hits
Stan Musial	1,377
Rogers Hornsby	703
Lou Brock	684
Enos Slaughter	647
Jim Bottomley	644
Joe Medwick	610
Ken Boyer	585
Ray Lankford	562
Ted Simmons	541
Red Schoendienst	482

Batting average

(Minimum 500 games)

Rogers Hornsby	.359
Johnny Mize	.336
Joe Medwick	.335
Stan Musial	.331
Chick Hafey	.326
Jim Bottomley	.325
Frankie Frisch	.312
George Watkins	.309
Joe Torre	.308
Rip Collins	.307

Stolen bases

Player	Stolen bases
Lou Brock	888
Vince Coleman	549
Ozzie Smith	433
Willie McGee	301
Ray Lankford	244
Jack Smith	203
Frankie Frisch	195
Tommy Dowd	189
Miller Huggins	174
Lonnie Smith	173

PITCHING

Earned-run average

(Minimum 1,000 innings)

Slim Sallee	2.67
Mort Cooper	2.77
Max Lanier	2.84
Harry Brecheen	2.91
Bob Gibson	2.91
Bill Doak	2.93
Dizzy Dean	2.99
Lee Meadows	3.00
Howie Pollet	3.06
Steve Carlton	3.10

Wins

Player	Wins
Bob Gibson	251
Jesse Haines	210
Bob Forsch	163
Bill Sherdel	153
Bill Doak	144
Dizzy Dean	134
Harry Brecheen	128
Slim Sallee	106
Mort Cooper	105
Larry Jackson	101
Max Lanier	101

Losses

Player	Losses
Bob Gibson	174
Jesse Haines	158
Bill Doak	136
Bill Sherdel	131
Bob Forsch	127
Ted Breitenstein	125
Slim Sallee	107
Larry Jackson	86
Bob Harmon	81
Harry Brecheen	79

Innings pitched

Bob Gibson	3,884.1
Jesse Haines	3,203.2
Bob Forsch	2,658.2
Bill Sherdel	2,450.2
Bill Doak	2,387.0
Ted Breitenstein	1,905.2
Slim Sallee	1,905.1
Harry Brecheen	1,790.1
Dizzy Dean	1,737.1
Larry Jackson	1,672.1

Strikeouts

Player	Strikeouts
Bob Gibson	3,117
Dizzy Dean	1,095
Bob Forsch	1,079
Jesse Haines	979
Steve Carlton	951
Bill Doak	938
Larry Jackson	899
Harry Brecheen	857
Vinegar Bemizell	789
Bill Hallahan	784

Bases on balls

Player	Bases on balls
Bob Gibson	1,336
Jesse Haines	870
Ted Breitenstein	829
Bob Forsch	780
Bill Doak	740
Bill Hallahan	648
Bill Sherdel	595
Bob Harmon	594
Vinegar Bend Mizell	568
Max Lanier	524

Games

Player	Games
Jesse Haines	554
Bob Gibson	528
Bill Sherdel	465
Bob Forsch	455
Al Brazle	441
Bill Doak	376
Todd Worrell	348
Lindy McDaniel	336
Larry Jackson	330
Al Hrabosky	329

Shutouts

Bob Gibson	56
Bill Doak	30
Mort Cooper	28
Harry Brecheen	25
Jesse Haines	24
Dizzy Dean	23
Max Lanier	20
Howie Pollet	20
Bob Forsch	19
Ernie Broglio	18

Saves

Player	Saves
Lee Smith	160
Todd Worrell	129
Bruce Sutter	127
Dennis Eckersley	66
Lindy McDaniel	64
Al Brazle	60
Joe Hoerner	60
Al Hrabosky	59
Ken Dayley	39
Tom Henke	36

TEAM SEASON, GAME RECORDS

SEASON

Batting

Record	Total	Year
Most at-bats	5,734	1979
Most runs	1,004	1930
Fewest runs	372	1908
Most hits	1,732	1930
Most singles	1,223	1920
Most doubles	373	1939
Most triples	96	1920
Most home runs	235	2000
Fewest home runs	10	1906
Most grand slams	11	2000
Most pinch-hit home runs	10	1998
Most total bases	2,595	1930
Most stolen bases	314	1985
Highest batting average	.314	1930
Lowest batting average	.223	1908
Highest slugging pct	.471	1930

Pitching

Record	Total	Year
Lowest ERA	2.38	1914
Highest ERA	6.21	1897
Most complete games	146	1904
Most shutouts	30	1968
Most saves	54	1993
Most walks	701	1911
Most strikeouts	1,130	1997

Fielding

Record	Total	Year
Most errors	354	1903
Fewest errors	94	1992
Most double plays	192	1974
Highest fielding average	.985	1992

General

Record	Total	Year
Most games won	106	1942
Most games lost	111	1898
Highest win pct	.703	1876
Lowest win pct	.221	1897

GAME, INNING

Batting

Record	Total	Date
Most runs, game	28	7-6-29
Most runs, inning	12	9-16-26
Most hits, game	30	6-1-1895
Most home runs, game	7	5-7-40, 7-12-96
Most total bases, game	49	5-7-40

Intimidating Bob Gibson powered his way to 251 victories and 3,117 strikeouts with the Cardinals.

CARDINALS YEAR-BY-YEAR

				Games		Leaders					
Year	W	L	Place	Back	Manager	Batting avg.	Hits	Home runs	RBIs	Wins	ERA
1901	76	64	4th	14½	Donovan	Burkett, .376	Burkett, 228	Burkett, 10	Wallace, 91	Harper, 23	Sudhoff, 3.52
1902	56	78	6th	44½	Donovan	Donovan, .315	Barclay, 163	Barclay, Smoot, 3	Barclay, 53	O'Neill, 17	Currie, 2.60
1903	43	94	8th	46½	Donovan	Donovan, .327	Smoot, 148	Smoot, 4	Brain, 60	M. Brown, McFarland, 9	M. Brown, 2.60
1904	75	79	5th	31½	Nichols	Beckley, .325	Beckley, 179	Brain, 7	Brain, 72	Nichols, Taylor, 21	Nichols, 2.02
1905	58	96	6th	47½	Nichols, Burke, Robison	Smoot, .311	Smoot, 166	Grady, 4	Smoot, 58	Taylor, Thielman, 15	B. Brown, 2.97
1906	52	98	7th	63	McCloskey	Bennett, .262	Bennett, 156	Grady, 3	Beckley, 44	Beebe, 9	Taylor, 2.15
1907	52	101	8th	55½	McCloskey	Murray, .262	Byrne, 143	Murray, 7	Murray, 46	Karger, 15	Karger, 2.04
1908	49	105	8th	50	McCloskey	Murray, .282	Murray, 167	Murray, 7	Murray, 62	Raymond, 14	Raymond, 2.03
1909	54	98	7th	56	Bresnahan	Konetchy, .286	Konetchy, 165	Konetchy, 4	Konetchy, 80	Beebe, 15	Sallee, 2.42
1910	63	90	7th	40½	Bresnahan	Konetchy, .302	Konetchy, 157	Ellis, 4	Konetchy, 78	Lush, 14	Sallee, 2.97
1911	75	74	5th	22	Bresnahan	Evans, .294	Konetchy, 165	Konetchy, 6	Konetchy, 88	Harmon, 23	Sallee, 2.76
1912	63	90	6th	41	Bresnahan	Konetchy, .314	Konetchy, 169	Konetchy, 8	Konetchy, 82	Harmon, 18	Sallee, 2.60
1913	51	99	8th	49	Huggins	Oakes, .291	Oakes, 156	Konetchy, 7	Konetchy, 68	Sallee, 18	Sallee, 2.71
1914	81	72	3rd	13	Huggins	D. Miller, .290	D. Miller, 166	Wilson, 9	D. Miller, 88	Doak, 20	Doak, 1.72
1915	72	81	6th	18½	Huggins	Snyder, .298	Long, 149	Bescher, 4	D. Miller, 72	Doak, 16	Doak, 2.64
1916	60	93	*7th	33½	Huggins	Hornsby, .313	Hornsby, 155	Bescher, Hornsby, J. Smith, 6	Hornsby, 65	Doak, Meadows, 12	Meadows, 2.58
1917	82	70	3rd	15	Huggins	Hornsby, .327	Hornsby, 171	Hornsby, 8	Hornsby, 66	Doak, 16	Packard, 2.47
1918	51	78	8th	33	Hendricks	Fisher, .317	Paulette, 126	Cruise, 6	Hornsby, 60	Packard, 12	Ames, 2.31
1919	54	83	7th	40½	Rickey	Hornsby, .318	Hornsby, 163	Hornsby, 8	Hornsby, 71	Doak, 13	Goodwin, 2.51
1920	75	79	*5th	18	Rickey	Hornsby, .370	Hornsby, 218	McHenry, 10	Hornsby, 94	Doak, 20	Doak, 2.53
1921	87	66	3rd	7	Rickey	Hornsby, .397	Hornsby, 235	Hornsby, 21	Hornsby, 126	Haines, 18	Doak, 2.59
1922	85	69	*3rd	8	Rickey	Hornsby, .401	Hornsby, 250	Hornsby, 42	Hornsby, 152	Pfeffer, 19	Pfeffer, 3.58
1923	79	74	5th	16	Rickey	Hornsby, .384	Bottomley, 194	Hornsby, 17	Stock, 96	Haines, 20	Haines, 3.11
1924	65	89	6th	28½	Rickey	Hornsby, .424	Hornsby, 227	Hornsby, 25	Bottomley, 111	Sothoron, 10	Dickerman, 2.41
1925	77	76	4th	18	Rickey, Hornsby	Hornsby, .403	Bottomley, 227	Hornsby, 39	Hornsby, 143	Sherdel, 15	Reinhart, 3.05
1926	89	65	1st	+2	Hornsby	Bell, .325	Bell, 189	Bottomley, 19	Bottomley, 120	Rhem, 20	Alexander, 2.91
1927	92	61	2nd	1½	O'Farrell	Frisch, .337	Frisch, 208	Bottomley, 19	Bottomley, 124	Haines, 24	Alexander, 2.52
1928	95	59	1st	+2	McKechnie	Hafey, .337	Douthit, 181	Bottomley, 31	Bottomley, 136	Sherdel, 21	Sherdel, 2.86
1929	78	74	4th	20	McKechnie, Southworth, Street	Hafey, .338	Douthit, 206	Bottomley, Hafey, 29	Bottomley, 137	Haines, Johnson, 13	Johnson, 3.60
1930	92	62	1st	+2	Street	Watkins, .373	Douthit, 201	Hafey, 26	Frisch, 114	Halahan, 15	Grimes, 3.01
1931	101	53	1st	+13	Street	Hafey, .349	Adams, 178	Hafey, 16	Hafey, 95	Hallahan, 19	Johnson, 3.00
1932	72	82	*6th	18	Street	Orsatti, .336	Collins, 153	Collins, 21	Collins, 91	D. Dean, 18	Hallahan, 3.11
1933	82	71	5th	9½	Street, Frisch	Martin, .316	Martin, 189	Medwick, 18	Medwick, 98	D. Dean, 20	Haines, 2.50
1934	95	58	1st	+2	Frisch	Collins, .333	Collins, 200	Collins, 35	Collins, 116	D. Dean, 30	D. Dean, 2.66
1935	96	58	2nd	4	Frisch	Medwick, .353	Medwick, 224	Collins, Medwick, 23	Medwick, 126	D. Dean, 28	Heusser, 2.92
1936	87	67	*2nd	5	Frisch	Medwick, .351	Medwick, 233	Mize, 19	Medwick, 138	D. Dean, 24	D. Dean, 3.17
1937	81	73	4th	15	Frisch	Medwick, .374	Medwick, 237	Medwick, 31	Medwick, 154	Warneke, 18	D. Dean, 2.69
1938	71	80	6th	17½	Frisch, Gonzalez	Mize, .337	Medwick, 190	Mize, 27	Medwick, 122	Weiland, 16	McGee, 3.21
1939	92	61	2nd	4½	Blades	Mize, .349	Medwick, 201	Mize, 28	Medwick, 117	Davis, 22	Bowman, 2.60
1940	84	69	3rd	16	Blades, Gonzalez, Southworth	Mize, .314	Mize, 182	Mize, 43	Mize, 137	McGee, Warneke, 16	Warneke, 3.14
1941	97	56	2nd	2½	Southworth	Mize, .317	J. Brown, 168	Mize, 16	Mize, 100	Warneke, White, 17	White, 2.40
1942	106	48	1st	+2	Southworth	Slaughter, .318	Slaughter, 188	Slaughter, 13	Slaughter, 98	M. Cooper, 22	M. Cooper, 1.78
1943	105	49	1st	+18	Southworth	Musial, .357	Musial, 220	Kurowski, Musial, 13	W. Cooper, Musial, 81	M. Cooper, 21	Pollet, 1.75
1944	105	49	1st	+14½	Southworth	Musial, .347	Musial, 197	Kurowski, 20	Sanders, 102	M. Cooper, 22	Munger, 1.34
1945	95	59	2nd	3	Southworth	Kurowski, .323	Adams, 169	Kurowski, 27	Kurowski, 102	Barrett, 21	Brecheen, 2.52
1946	98	58	†1st	+2	Dyer	Musial, .365	Musial, 228	Slaughter, 18	Slaughter, 130	Pollet, 21	Pollet, 2.10
1947	89	65	2nd	5	Dyer	Musial, .312	Musial, 183	Kurowski, 27	Kurowski, 104	Brecheen, Munger, 16	Brazle, 2.84
1948	85	69	2nd	6½	Dyer	Musial, .376	Musial, 230	Musial, 39	Musial, 131	Brecheen, 20	Brecheen, 2.24
1949	96	58	2nd	1	Dyer	Musial, .338	Musial, 207	Musial, 36	Musial, 123	Pollet, 20	Staley, 2.73
1950	78	75	5th	12½	Dyer	Musial, .346	Musial, 192	Musial, 28	Musial, 109	Pollet, 14	Lanier, 3.13
1951	81	73	3rd	15½	Marion	Musial, .355	Musial, 205	Musial, 32	Musial, 108	Staley, 19	Brazle, 3.09
1952	88	66	3rd	8½	Stanky	Musial, .336	Musial, 194	Musial, 21	Slaughter, 101	Staley, 17	Staley, 3.27
1953	83	71	*3rd	22	Stanky	Schoendienst, .342	Musial, 200	Musial, 30	Musial, 113	Haddix, 20	Haddix, 3.06
1954	72	82	6th	25	Stanky	Musial, .330	Musial, 195	Musial, 35	Musial, 126	Haddix, 18	Poholsky, 3.06
1955	68	86	7th	30½	Stanky, Walker	Musial, .319	Musial, 179	Musial, 33	Musial, 108	Haddix, 12	LaPalme, 2.75
1956	76	78	4th	17	Hutchinson	Musial, .310	Musial, 184	Musial, 27	Musial, 109	Mizell, 14	Dickson, 3.07
1957	87	67	2nd	8	Hutchinson	Musial, .351	Blasingame, Musial, 176	Musial, 29	Ennis, 105	Jackson, McDaniel, 15	Jackson, 3.47
1958	72	82	*5th	20	Hutchinson, Hack	Musial, .337	Boyer, 175	Boyer, 23	Boyer, 90	S. Jones, 14	S. Jones, 2.88
1959	71	83	7th	16	Hemus	Cunningham, .345	Blasingame, 178	Boyer, 28	Boyer, 94	Jackson, McDaniel, 14	Jackson, 3.30
1960	86	68	3rd	9	Hemus	Boyer, .304	Boyer, 168	Boyer, 32	Boyer, 97	Broglio, 21	McDaniel, 2.09
1961	80	74	5th	13	Hemus, Keane	Boyer, .329	Boyer, 194	Boyer, 24	Boyer, 95	Jackson, Sadecki, 14	C. Simmons, 3.13
1962	84	78	6th	17½	Keane	Musial, .330	White, 199	Boyer, 24	White, 102	Jackson, 16	Gibson, 2.85
1963	93	69	2nd	6	Keane	Groat, .319	Groat, 201	White, 27	Boyer, 111	Broglio, Gibson, 18	C. Simmons, 2.48
1964	93	69	1st	+1	Keane	Brock, .348	Flood, 211	Boyer, 24	Boyer, 119	Sadecki, 20	Gibson, 3.01
1965	80	81	7th	16½	Schoendienst	Flood, .310	Flood, 191	White, 24	Flood, 83	Gibson, 20	Gibson, 3.07
1966	83	79	6th	12	Schoendienst	Cepeda, .303	Brock, 183	Cepeda, 17	Flood, 78	Gibson, 21	Gibson, 2.44
1967	101	60	1st	+10½	Schoendienst	Flood, .335	Brock, 206	Cepeda, 25	Cepeda, 111	Hughes, 16	Briles, 2.43
1968	97	65	1st	+9	Schoendienst	Flood, .301	Flood, 186	Cepeda, 16	Shannon, 79	Gibson, 22	Gibson, 1.12
								EAST DIVISION			
1969	87	75	4th	13	Schoendienst	Brock, .298	Brock, 195	Torre, 18	Torre, 101	Gibson, 20	Carlton, 2.17
1970	76	86	4th	13	Schoendienst	Torre, .325	Torre, 203	Allen, 34	Allen, 101	Gibson, 23	Taylor, 3.11
1971	90	72	2nd	7	Schoendienst	Torre, .363	Torre, 230	Torre, 24	Torre, 137	Carlton, 20	Gibson, 3.04
1972	75	81	4th	21½	Schoendienst	M. Alou, .314	Brock, 193	T. Simmons, 16	T. Simmons, 96	Gibson, 19	Gibson, 2.46
1973	81	81	2nd	1½	Schoendienst	T. Simmons, .310	Brock, 193	T. Simmons, Torre, 13	T. Simmons, 91	Wise, 16	Gibson, 2.77
1974	86	75	2nd	1½	Schoendienst	McBride, R. Smith, .309	Brock, 194	R. Smith, 23	T. Simmons, 103	McGlothen, 16	McGlothen, 2.70
1975	82	80	*3rd	10½	Schoendienst	T. Simmons, .332	T. Simmons, 193	R. Smith, 19	T. Simmons, 100	Forsch, McGlothen, 15	Hrabosky, 1.66
1976	72	90	5th	29	Schoendienst	Crawford, .304	T. Simmons, 159	Cruz, 13	T. Simmons, 75	McGlothen, 13	Denny, 2.52
1977	83	79	3rd	18	Rapp	Templeton, .322	Templeton, 200	T. Simmons, 21	T. Simmons, 95	Forsch, 20	Carroll, 2.50
1978	69	93	5th	21	Rapp, Krol, Boyer	Hendrick, .288	Templeton, 181	T. Simmons, 22	T. Simmons, 80	Denny, 14	Vuckovich, 2.55
1979	86	76	3rd	12	Boyer	Hernandez, .344	Templeton, 211	T. Simmons, 26	Hernandez, 105	S. Martinez, Vuckovich, 15	Fulgham, 2.53
1980	74	88	4th	17	Boyer, Krol, Herzog, Schoendienst	Hernandez, .321	Hernandez, 191	Hendrick, 25	Hendrick, 109	Vuckovich, 12	Vuckovich, 3.41
1981	59	43	‡2nd/2nd	—	Herzog	Hernandez, .306	Hernandez, 115	Hendrick, 18	Hendrick, 61	Forsch, 10	Forsch, 3.19
1982	92	70	§1st	+3	Herzog	L. Smith, .307	L. Smith, 182	Hendrick, 19	Hendrick, 104	Andujar, Forsch, 15	Andujar, 2.47
1983	79	83	4th	11	Herzog	L. Smith, .321	McGee, 172	Hendrick 18	Hendrick, 97	LaPoint, Stuper, 12	Stuper, 3.68
1984	84	78	3rd	12½	Herzog	McGee, .291	McGee, 166	Green, 15	Hendrick, 69	Andujar, 20	Sutter, 1.54
1985	101	61	§1st	+3	Herzog	McGee, .353	McGee, 216	Clark, 22	Herr, 110	Andujar, Tudor, 21	Tudor, 1.93
1986	79	82	3rd	28½	Herzog	O. Smith, .280	O. Smith, 144	Van Slyke, 13	Herr, Van Slyke, 61	Forsch, 14	Worrell, 2.08
1987	95	67	§1st	+3	Herzog	O. Smith, .303	O. Smith, 182	Clark, 35	Clark, 106	Cox, Forsch, Mathews, 11	Worrell, 2.66
1988	76	86	5th	25	Herzog	McGee, .292	McGee, 164	Brunansky, 22	Brunansky, 79	DeLeon, 13	Magrane, 2.18
1989	86	76	3rd	7	Herzog	Guerrero, .311	Guerrero, 177	Brunansky, 20	Guerrero, 117	Magrane, 18	Magrane, 2.91
1990	70	92	6th	25	Herzog, Schoendienst, Torre	McGee, .335	McGee, 168	Zeile, 15	Guerrero, 80	Tudor, 12	Tudor, 2.40
1991	84	78	2nd	14	Torre	Jose, .305	Jose, 173	Zeile, 11	Zeile, 81	B. Smith, 12	DeLeon, 2.71
1992	83	79	3rd	13	Torre	Gilkey, .302	Lankford, 175	Lankford, 20	Lankford, 86	Tewksbury, 16	Perez, 1.84
1993	87	75	3rd	10	Torre	Jefferies, .342	Jefferies, 186	Whiten, 25	Zeile, 103	Tewksbury, 17	Osborne, 3.76
								CENTRAL DIVISION			
1994	53	61	*4th	13	Torre	Jefferies, .325	Jefferies, 129	Lankford, Zeile, 19	Zeile, 75	Tewksbury, 12	Palacios, 4.44
1995	62	81	4th	22½	Torre, Jorgensen	Mabry, .307	Jordan, 145	Lankford, 25	Lankford, 82	DeLucia, 8	Morgan, 3.56
1996	88	74	∞▲1st	+6	La Russa	Jordan, .310	Mabry, 161	Gant, 30	Jordan, 104	An. Benes, 18	Osborne, 3.53
1997	73	89	4th	11	La Russa	DeShields, .295	DeShields, 169	Lankford, 31	Lankford, 98	Morris, Stottlemyre, 12	Al. Benes, 2.89
1998	83	79	3rd	19	La Russa	Jordan, .316	Jordan, 178	McGwire, 70	McGwire, 147	Mercker, 11	Morris, 2.53
1999	75	86	4th	21½	La Russa	Lankford, .306	Renteria, 161	McGwire, 65	McGwire, 147	Bottenfield, 18	Bottenfield, 3.97
2000	95	67	∞▲1st	+10	La Russa	Vina, .300	Renteria, 156	Edmonds, 42	Edmonds, 108	Kile, 20	Ankiel, 3.50

*Tied for position. † Won pennant playoff. ‡First half 30-20; second half 29-23. § Won Championship Series. ∞ Won Division Series. ▲ Lost Championship Series.

Note: Batting average minimum 350 at-bats; ERA minimum 90 innings pitched.

San Diego Padres

Outfielder Tony Gwynn.

FRANCHISE CHRONOLOGY

First season: 1969, as part of a two-team expansion that increased the National League field to 12. The Padres defeated Houston, 2-1, in their Major League debut but finished their first season mired deep in the N.L. West Division basement with a 52-110 record—41 games behind first-place Atlanta and 29 behind the fifth-place Houston Astros.

1970-present: The Padres finished last in each of their first six seasons, losing 100 or more games in four of them and at least 95 in the other two. Even when the Padres recorded their first winning record in 1978, their 10th season, they finished fourth, 11 games behind first-place Los Angeles. They have finished higher than third only four times, but they do have three division titles and two N.L. pennants to show for their 29-year existence. Their first excursion into the fall classic came in 1984 after an exciting come-from-behind five-game N.L. Championship Series victory over Chicago. Their second came in 1998, after an equally surprising NLCS victory over Atlanta. Both ended in losses—in '84 to the Detroit Tigers and in '98 to the New York Yankees.

PADRES VS. OPPONENTS BY DECADE

	Braves	Cardinals	Cubs	Dodgers	Giants	Phillies	Pirates	Reds	Astros	Mets	Expos	Marlins	Rockies	Brewers	D'backs	Interleague	Decade Record
1969	5-13	4-8	1-11	6-12	6-12	4-8	2-10	7-11	8-10	1-11	8-4						52-110
1970-79	82-97	50-70	46-74	71-109	72-104	46-74	41-79	74-105	70-106	56-64	59-60						667-942
1980-89	89-88	48-70	53-61	95-78	91-84	57-56	56-62	78-96	87-89	57-58	51-63						762-805
1990-99	44-79	51-56	51-59	71-68	71-65	60-53	53-55	61-69	67-62	63-52	40-71	34-30	45-41	11-6	11-14	25-19	758-799
2000-	1-8	0-9	5-3	5-8	5-7	5-2	2-7	5-4	7-2	6-3	6-3	7-2	6-7	7-2	4-9	5-10	76-86
Totals	221-285	153-213	156-208	248-275	245-272	172-193	154-213	225-285	239-269	183-188	164-201	41-32	51-48	18-8	15-23	30-29	2315-2742

Interleague results: 8-5 vs. Angels; 4-9 vs. Athletics; 12-8 vs. Mariners; 6-7 vs. Rangers.

MANAGERS

Name	*Years*	*Record*
Preston Gomez	1969-72	180-316
Don Zimmer	1972-73	114-190
John McNamara	1974-77	224-310
Bob Skinner	1977	1-0
Alvin Dark	1977	48-65
Roger Craig	1978-79	152-171
Jerry Coleman	1980	73-89
Frank Howard	1981	41-69
Dick Williams	1982-85	337-311
Steve Boros	1986	74-88
Larry Bowa	1987-88	81-127
Jack McKeon	1988-90	193-164
Greg Riddoch	1990-92	200-194
Jim Riggleman	1992-94	112-179
Bruce Bochy	1995-2000	485-469

N.L. PENNANT WINNER

Year	*Record*	*Manager*	*Series Result*
1984	92-70	Williams	Lost to Tigers
1998	98-64	Bochy	Lost to Yankees

WEST DIVISION CHAMPIONS

Year	*Record*	*Manager*	*NLCS Result*
1984	92-70	Williams	Defeated Cubs
1996	91-71	Bochy	Lost in Division Series
1998	98-64	Bochy	Defeated Braves

ALL-TIME RECORD OF EXPANSION TEAMS

Team	W	L	Pct.	DT	P	WS
Arizona	250	236	.514	1	0	0
Kansas City	2,548	2,497	.505	6	2	1
Toronto	1,867	1,897	.496	5	2	2
Houston	3,052	3,138	.493	6	0	0
Montreal	2,454	2,596	.486	2	0	0
Anaheim	3,069	3,281	.483	3	0	0
Colorado	594	639	.482	0	0	0
Milwaukee	2,421	2,631	.479	2	1	0
New York	2,934	3,246	.475	4	4	2
Texas	2,952	3,381	.466	4	0	0
San Diego	2,315	2,742	.458	3	2	0
Seattle	1,715	2,048	.456	2	0	0
Florida	551	678	.448	0	1	1
Tampa Bay	201	284	.414	0	0	0

DT—Division Titles. P—Pennants won. WS—World Series won.

BALLPARK CHRONOLOGY

Qualcomm Stadium, formerly San Diego Jack Murphy Stadium (1969-present)

Capacity: 56,133.
First game: Padres 2, Houston 1 (April 8, 1969).
First batter: Jesus Alou, Astros.
First hit: Jesus Alou, Astros (single).
First run: Jesus Alou, Astros (1st inning).
First home run: Ed Spezio, Padres.
First winning pitcher: Dick Selma, Padres.
First-season attendance: 512,970.

ATTENDANCE HIGHS

Total	*Season*	*Park*
2,555,901	1998	Qualcomm Stadium
2,523,538	1999	Qualcomm Stadium
2,423,149	2000	Qualcomm Stadium
2,210,352	1985	Jack Murphy Stadium
2,187,886	1996	Jack Murphy Stadium

N.L. MVP

Ken Caminiti, 3B, 1996

CY YOUNG WINNERS

Randy Jones, LH, 1976
Gaylord Perry, RH, 1978
Mark Davis, LH, 1989

ROOKIES OF THE YEAR

*Butch Metzger, P, 1976
Benito Santiago, C, 1987
* Co-winner.

MANAGER OF THE YEAR

Bruce Bochy, 1996

RETIRED UNIFORM

No.	*Name*	*Pos.*
6	Steve Garvey	1B
35	Randy Jones	P

Outfielder Cito Gaston (left) and first baseman Nate Colbert were original Padres.

MILESTONE PERFORMANCES

25-plus home runs
50— Greg Vaughn....1998
40— Ken Caminiti....1996
38— Nate Colbert....1970, 1972
35— Fred McGriff....1992
34— Dave Winfield....1979
Phil Plantier....1993
33— Gary Sheffield....1992
31— Fred McGriff....1991
Phil Nevin....2000
30— Steve Finley....1996
29— Ken Caminiti....1998
28— Steve Finley....1997
27— Nate Colbert....1971
26— Kevin McReynolds....1986
Jack Clark....1989
Ken Caminiti....1995, 1997
Reggie Sanders....1999
Ryan Klesko....2000
25— Dave Winfield....1977
Jack Clark....1989

100-plus RBIs
130— Ken Caminiti....1996
119— Tony Gwynn....1997
Greg Vaughn....1998
118— Dave Winfield....1979
115— Joe Carter....1990
111— Nate Colbert....1972
107— Phil Nevin....2000
106— Fred McGriff....1991
104— Fred McGriff....1992
100— Gary Sheffield....1992
Phil Plantier....1993

20-plus victories
1975— Randy Jones....20-12
1976— Randy Jones....22-14
1978— Gaylord Perry....21-6

N.L. home run champions
1992— Fred McGriff....35

N.L. RBI champions
1979— Dave Winfield....118

N.L. batting champions
1984— Tony Gwynn....351
1987— Tony Gwynn....370
1988— Tony Gwynn....313
1989— Tony Gwynn....336
1992— Gary Sheffield....330
1994— Tony Gwynn....394
1995— Tony Gwynn....368
1996— Tony Gwynn....353
1997— Tony Gwynn....372

N.L. ERA champions
1975— Randy Jones....2.24

N.L. strikeout champions
1994— Andy Benes....189

No-hit pitchers
(9 innings or more)
None

Longest hitting streaks
34— Benito Santiago....1987
27— John Flaherty....1996
25— Tony Gwynn....1983
23— Bip Roberts....1994
21— Bobby Brown....1983
Steve Finley....1996
20— Tony Gwynn....1997
19— Tony Fernandez....1992
Tony Gwynn....1997
18— Tony Gwynn....1988
Chris James....1989
Gary Sheffield....1992
Eric Owens....1999
17— Steve Garvey....1984
Roberto Alomar....1989
16— Dave Winfield....1977
Tony Gwynn....1999
15— Ivan Murrell....1969
Cito Gaston....1972
Nate Colbert....1972
Bobby Tolan....1984
Jerry Mumphrey....1980
Broderick Perkins....1981
Tony Gwynn....1982
Kevin McReynolds....1985
Tony Gwynn....1986
Tony Gwynn....1991
Jeff Gardner....1993
Tony Gwynn....1995

Lefthander Randy Jones, the franchise's first Cy Young winner, recorded two of the Padres' three 20-victory seasons.

INDIVIDUAL SEASON, GAME RECORDS

Switch-hitting shortstop Garry Templeton came to San Diego in the trade that sent Ozzie Smith to St. Louis.

SEASON

Batting

At-bats	655	Steve Finley	1996
Runs	126	Steve Finley	1996
Hits	220	Tony Gwynn	1997
Singles	177	Tony Gwynn	1984
Doubles	49	Tony Gwynn	1997
Triples	13	Tony Gwynn	1987
Home runs	50	Greg Vaughn	1998
Home runs, rookie	18	Benito Santiago	1987
Grand slams	2	Last by Steve Finley	1997
Total bases	348	Steve Finley	1996
RBIs	130	Ken Caminiti	1996
Walks	132	Jack Clark	1989
Most strikeouts	150	Nate Colbert	1970
Fewest strikeouts	16	Tony Gwynn	1992
Batting average	.394	Tony Gwynn	1994
Slugging pct.	.621	Ken Caminiti	1996
Stolen bases	70	Alan Wiggins	1984

Pitching

Games	83	Craig Lefferts	1986
Complete games	25	Randy Jones	1976
Innings	315.1	Randy Jones	1976
Wins	22	Randy Jones	1976
Losses	22	Randy Jones	1974
Winning pct.	.778 (21-6)	Gaylord Perry	1978
Walks	125	Matt Clement	2000
Strikeouts	257	Kevin Brown	1998
Shutouts	6	Fred Norman	1972
		Randy Jones	1975
Home runs allowed	36	Ed Whitson	1987
Lowest ERA	2.10	David Roberts	1971
Saves	53	Trevor Hoffman	1998

GAME

Batting

Runs	5	Al Martin	4-16-2000
Hits	5	Last by Tony Gwynn	4-28-98
Doubles	3	Last by Kevin Nicholson	7-9-2000
Triples	2	Last by Mark Sweeney	8-27-98
Home runs	3	Last by Bret Boonei	6-23-2000
RBIs	8	Nate Colbert	8-1-72
		Ken Caminiti	9-19-95
Total bases	13	Steve Finley	6-23-97
Stolen bases	5	Last by Damian Jackson	6-28-99

HISTORY

CAREER LEADERS

BATTING

Games

Tony Gwynn	2,369
Garry Templeton	1,286
Dave Winfield	1,117
Tim Flannery	972
Gene Richards	939
Nate Colbert	866
Terry Kennedy	835
Benito Santiago	789
Carmelo Martinez	783
Cito Gaston	766

At-bats

Tony Gwynn	9,186
Garry Templeton	4,512
Dave Winfield	3,997
Gene Richards	3,414
Nate Colbert	3,080
Terry Kennedy	2,987
Benito Santiago	2,872
Cito Gaston	2,615
Tim Flannery	2,473
Steve Finley	2,396

Runs

Tony Gwynn	1,378
Dave Winfield	599
Gene Richards	484
Nate Colbert	442
Garry Templeton	430
Steve Finley	423
Bip Roberts	378
Ken Caminiti	362
Benito Santiago	312
Terry Kennedy	308

Hits

Tony Gwynn	3,108
Garry Templeton	1,135
Dave Winfield	1,134
Gene Richards	994
Terry Kennedy	817
Nate Colbert	780
Benito Santiago	758
Bip Roberts	673
Cito Gaston	672
Steve Finley	662

Doubles

Tony Gwynn	534
Garry Templeton	195
Dave Winfield	179
Terry Kennedy	158
Steve Finley	134
Nate Colbert	130
Ken Caminiti	127
Benito Santiago	124
Gene Richards	123
Carmelo Martinez	111

Triples

Tony Gwynn	84
Gene Richards	63
Dave Winfield	39
Garry Templeton	36
Cito Gaston	29
Steve Finley	28
Tim Flannery	25
Luis Salazar	24
Nate Colbert	22
Bip Roberts	21

Home runs

Nate Colbert	163
Dave Winfield	154
Tony Gwynn	134
Ken Caminiti	121
Benito Santiago	85
Fred McGriff	84
Steve Finley	82
Carmelo Martinez	82
Greg Vaughn	78
Cito Gaston	77

Total bases

Tony Gwynn	4,212
Dave Winfield	1,853
Garry Templeton	1,531
Nate Colbert	1,443
Gene Richards	1,321
Terry Kennedy	1,217
Benito Santiago	1,167
Steve Finley	1,098
Ken Caminiti	1,086
Cito Gaston	1,054

Runs batted in

Tony Gwynn	1,121
Dave Winfield	626
Nate Colbert	481
Garry Templeton	427
Terry Kennedy	424
Ken Caminiti	396
Benito Santiago	375
Carmelo Martinez	337
Steve Garvey	316
Cito Gaston	316

Extra-base hits

Tony Gwynn	752
Dave Winfield	372
Nate Colbert	315
Garry Templeton	274
Ken Caminiti	250
Steve Finley	244
Terry Kennedy	241
Benito Santiago	224
Gene Richards	212
Carmelo Martinez	200

Batting average

(Minimum 500 games)

Tony Gwynn	.338
Bip Roberts	.298
Ken Caminiti	.295
Gene Richards	.291
Johnny Grubb	.286
Dave Winfield	.284
Steve Finley	.276
Steve Garvey	.275
Terry Kennedy	.274
Luis Salazar	.267

Stolen bases

Tony Gwynn	318
Gene Richards	242
Alan Wiggins	171
Bip Roberts	148
Ozzie Smith	147
Dave Winfield	133
Enzo Hernandez	129
Garry Templeton	101
Luis Salazar	93
Roberto Alomar	90

PITCHING

Earned-run average

(Minimum 500 innings)

Trevor Hoffman	2.69
Greg Harris	2.95
Dave Roberts	2.99
Dave Dravecky	3.12
Craig Lefferts	3.24
Bruce Hurst	3.27
Randy Jones	3.30
Andy Benes	3.57
Bob Shirley	3.58
Eric Show	3.59

Wins

Eric Show	100
Randy Jones	92
Ed Whitson	77
Andy Ashby	70
Andy Benes	69
Andy Hawkins	60
Joey Hamilton	55
Bruce Hurst	55
Dave Dravecky	53
Clay Kirby	52

Losses

Randy Jones	105
Eric Show	87
Clay Kirby	81
Andy Benes	75
Ed Whitson	72
Steve Arlin	62
Andy Ashby	62
Bill Greif	61
Andy Hawkins	58
Bob Shirley	57

Innings pitched

Randy Jones	1,766.0
Eric Show	1,603.1
Ed Whitson	1,354.1
Andy Benes	1,235.0
Andy Ashby	1,210.0
Clay Kirby	1,128.0
Andy Hawkins	1,102.2
Joey Hamilton	934.2
Bruce Hurst	911.2
Dave Dravecky	900.1

Strikeouts

Andy Benes	1,036
Eric Show	951
Andy Ashby	827
Clay Kirby	802
Ed Whitson	767
Randy Jones	677
Joey Hamilton	639
Trevor Hoffman	639
Bruce Hurst	616
Sterling Hitchcock	519

Bases on balls

Eric Show	593
Clay Kirby	505
Randy Jones	414
Andy Hawkins	412
Andy Benes	402
Steve Arlin	351
Ed Whitson	350
Dave Freisleben	346
Joey Hamilton	343
Tim Lollar	328

Games

Trevor Hoffman	481
Craig Lefferts	375
Eric Show	309
Rollie Fingers	265
Randy Jones	264
Dave Tomlin	239
Mark Davis	230
Gary Lucas	230
Lance McCullers	229
Ed Whitson	227

Shutouts

Randy Jones	18
Steve Arlin	11
Eric Show	11
Bruce Hurst	10
Andy Benes	8
Andy Hawkins	7
Clay Kirby	7
Dave Dravecky	6
Dave Freisleben	6
Fred Norman	6
Ed Whitson	6

Saves

Trevor Hoffman	269
Rollie Fingers	108
Rich Gossage	83
Mark Davis	78
Craig Lefferts	64
Gary Lucas	49
Randy Myers	38
Lance McCullers	36
Luis DeLeon	31
Gene Harris	23

TEAM SEASON, GAME RECORDS

SEASON

Batting

Most at-bats	5,655	1996
Most runs	795	1997
Fewest runs	468	1969
Most hits	1,519	1997
Most singles	1,105	1980
Most doubles	295	1998
Most triples	53	1979
Most home runs	172	1970
Fewest home runs	64	1976
Most grand slams	9	1995
Most pinch-hit home runs	10	1995
Most total bases	2,282	1997
Most stolen bases	239	1980
Highest batting average	.275	1994
Lowest batting average	.225	1969
Highest slugging pct	.409	1998

Pitching

Lowest ERA	3.22	1971
Highest ERA	4.98	1997
Most complete games	47	1971,1976
Most shutouts	19	1985
Most saves	55	1978, 1998
Most walks	715	1974
Most strikeouts	1,194	1996

Fielding

Most errors	189	1977
Fewest errors	104	1998
Most double plays	171	1978
Highest fielding average	.983	1998

General

Most games won	98	1998
Most games lost	110	1969
Highest win pct	.605	1998
Lowest win pct	.321	1969

GAME, INNING

Batting

Most runs, game	20	Last 7-27-96
Most runs, inning	13	8-24-93, 5-31-94
Most hits, game	24	4-19-82
Most home runs, game	6	Last 6-17-98
Most total bases, game	39	5-23-70

Former Dodger Steve Garvey led the Padres to their first World Series appearance in 1984.

HISTORY

PADRES YEAR-BY-YEAR

Year	W	L	Place	Games Back	Manager	Leaders: Batting avg.	Hits	Home runs	RBIs	Wins	ERA
						WEST DIVISION					
1969	52	110	6th	41	Gomez	O. Brown, .264	O. Brown, 150	Colbert, 24	Colbert, 66	J. Niekro, Santorini, 8	Kelley, 3.57
1970	63	99	6th	39	Gomez	Gaston, .318	Gaston, 186	Colbert, 38	Gaston, 93	Dobson, 12	Coombs, 3.30
1971	61	100	6th	28½	Gomez	O. Brown, .273	Colbert, 149	Colbert, 27	Colbert, 84	Kirby, 15	Roberts, 2.10
1972	58	95	6th	36½	Gomez, Zimmer	Lee, .300	Colbert, 141	Colbert, 38	Colbert, 111	Kirby, 12	Ross, 2.45
1973	60	102	6th	39	Zimmer	Grubb, .311	Colbert, Kendall, 143	Colbert, 22	Colbert, 80	Arlin, 11	R. Jones, 3.16
1974	60	102	6th	42	McNamara	Grubb, .286	Winfield, 132	McCovey, 22	Winfield, 75	Freisleben, Greif, Hardy, Spillner, 9	Freisleben, 3.65
1975	71	91	4th	37	McNamara	Fuentes, .280	Fuentes, 158	McCovey, 23	Winfield, 76	R. Jones, 20	R. Jones, 2.24
1976	73	89	5th	29	McNamara	Ivie, .291	Winfield, 139	Winfield, 13	Ivie, 70	R. Jones, 22	R. Jones, 2.74
1977	69	93	5th	29	McNamara, Skinner, Dark	Hendrick, .311	Winfield, 169	Winfield, 25	Winfield, 92	Shirley, 12	Fingers, 2.99
1978	84	78	4th	11	Craig	Winfield, Richards, .308	Winfield, 181	Winfield, 24	Winfield, 97	G. Perry, 21	D'Acquisto, 2.13
1979	68	93	5th	22	Craig	Winfield, .308	Winfield, 184	Winfield, 34	Winfield, 118	G. Perry, 12	G. Perry, 3.05
1980	73	89	6th	19½	Coleman	Richards, .301	Richards, 193	Winfield, 20	Winfield, 87	Fingers, Shirley, 11	Fingers, 2.80
1981	41	69	*6th/6th	—	Howard	Salazar, .303	Salazar, 121	Lefebvre, 8	Richards, 42	Eichelberger, 8	Lucas, 2.00
1982	81	81	4th	8	Williams	Kennedy, .295	Kennedy, 166	Kennedy, 21	Kennedy, 97	Lollar, 16	DeLeon, 2.03
1983	81	81	4th	10	Williams	Garvey, .294	Kennedy, 156	Kennedy, 17	Kennedy, 98	Show, 15	Thurmond, 2.65
1984	92	70	†1st	+12	Williams	Gwynn, .351	Gwynn, 213	McReynolds, Nettles, 20	Garvey, 86	Show, 15	Lefferts, 2.13
1985	83	79	‡3rd	12	Williams	Gwynn, .317	Gwynn, 197	C. Martinez, 21	Garvey, 81	Hawkins, 18	Dravecky, 2.93
1986	74	88	4th	22	Boros	Gwynn, .329	Gwynn, 211	McReynolds, 26	McReynolds, 96	Hawkins, McCullers, 10	McCullers, 2.78
1987	65	97	6th	25	Bowa	Gwynn, .370	Gwynn, 218	Kruk, 20	Kruk, 91	Whitson, 10	McCullers, 3.72
1988	83	78	3rd	11	Bowa, McKeon	Gwynn, .313	Gwynn, 163	C. Martinez, 18	Gwynn, 70	Show, 16	M. Davis, 2.01
1989	89	73	2nd	3	McKeon	Gwynn, .336	Gwynn, 203	J. Clark, 26	J. Clark, 94	Whitson, 16	M. Davis, 1.85
1990	75	87	‡4th	16	McKeon, Riddoch	Gwynn, B. Roberts, .309	Gwynn, 177	J. Clark, 25	Carter, 115	Whitson, 14	Harris, 2.30
1991	84	78	3rd	10	Riddoch	Gwynn, .317	Gwynn, 168	McGriff, 31	McGriff, 106	Benes, Hurst, 15	Harris, 2.23
1992	82	80	3rd	16	Riddoch, Riggleman	Sheffield, .330	Sheffield, 184	McGriff, 35	McGriff, 104	Hurst, 14	Rodriguez, 2.37
1993	61	101	7th	43	Riggleman	Gwynn, .358	Gwynn, 175	Plantier, 34	Plantier, 100	Benes, 15	Harris, 3.67
1994	47	70	4th	12½	Riggleman	Gwynn, .394	Gwynn, 165	Plantier, 18	Gwynn, 64	Hamilton, 9	Hamilton, 2.98
1995	70	74	3rd	8	Bochy	Gwynn, .368	Gwynn, 197	Caminiti, 26	Caminiti, 94	Ashby, 12	Ashby, 2.94
1996	91	71	∞1st	+1	Bochy	Gwynn, .353	Finley, 195	Caminiti, 40	Caminiti, 130	Hamilton, 15	Worrell, 3.05
1997	76	86	4th	14	Bochy	Gwynn, .372	Gwynn, 220	Finley, 28	Gwynn, 119	Hamilton, 12	Ashby, 4.13
1998	98	64	▲◆1st	+9½	Bochy	Gwynn, .321	Vaughn, 156	Vaughn, 50	Vaughn, 119	Brown, 18	Brown, 2.38
1999	74	88	4th	26	Bochy	Gwynn, .338	Gwynn, 139	Sanders, 26	Nevin, 85	Ashby, 14	Boehringer, 3.24
2000	76	86	5th	21	Bochy	Nevin, .303	Owens, 171	Nevin, 31	Nevin, 107	Clement, 13	Tollberg, 3.58

* First half 23-33; second half 18-36. † Won Championship Series. ‡ Tied for position. ∞ Lost Division Series. ▲ Won Division Series. ◆ Won Championship Series.

Note: Batting average minimum 350 at-bats; ERA minimum 90 innings pitched.

Ollie Brown

ANSWERING the American League's decision to expand in the 1969 season, the National League approved franchises for San Diego and Montreal, bringing its roster to 12 teams. The "Padres" began operation as the N.L.'s third West Coast team and first since the move of the Dodgers and Giants to Los Angeles and San Francisco.

The Padres began their player-procurement efforts in the October 14, 1968, expansion draft by selecting outfielder Ollie Brown with their first pick and 30 players total. The team opened play April 8, 1969, with a 2-1 victory over Houston at San Diego Stadium.

Expansion draft (October 14, 1968)

Players

Player	From	Position
Jose Arcia	Chicago	infield
*Ollie Brown	San Francisco	outfield
Nate Colbert	Houston	first base
Jerry DaVannon	St. Louis	infield
Al Ferrara	Los Angeles	outfield
Tony Gonzalez	Philadelphia	outfield
Clarence Gaston	Atlanta	outfield
Fred Kendall	Cincinnati	catcher
Jerry Morales	New York	outfield
Ivan Murrell	Houston	outfield
Roberto Pena	Philadelphia	second base
Rafael Robles	San Francisco	shortstop
Ron Slocum	Pittsburgh	catcher/infield
Larry Stahl	New York	outfield
Zoilo Versalles	Los Angeles	shortstop
Jim Williams	Los Angeles	outfield

Pitchers

Pitcher	From	Throws
Steve Arlin	Philadelphia	righthanded
Mike Corkins	San Francisco	righthanded
Tom Dukes	Houston	righthanded
Dave Giusti	St. Louis	righthanded
Dick James	Chicago	righthanded
Fred Katawczik	Cincinnati	lefthanded
Dick Kelley	Atlanta	lefthanded
Clay Kirby	St. Louis	righthanded
Al McBean	Pittsburgh	righthanded
Billy McCool	Cincinnati	lefthanded
Frank Reberger	Chicago	righthanded
Dave Roberts	Pittsburgh	lefthanded
Al Santorini	Atlanta	righthanded
Dick Selma	New York	righthanded

*First pick

Opening day lineup

April 8, 1969

Rafael Robles, shortstop
Roberto Pena, second base
Tony Gonzalez, center field
Ollie Brown, right field
Bill Davis, first base
Larry Stahl, left field
Ed Spiezio, third base
Chris Cannizzaro, catcher
Dick Selma, pitcher

Ed Spiezio

Padres firsts

First hit: Ed Spiezio, April 8, 1969, vs. Houston (home run)
First home run: Ed Spiezio, April 8, 1969, vs. Houston
First RBI: Ed Spiezio, April 8, 1969, vs. Houston
First win: Dick Selma, April 8, 1969, vs. Houston
First shutout: Johnny Podres (7 innings), Tommie Sisk (2), April 9, 1969, 2-0 vs. Houston
First CG shutout: Joe Niekro, June 27, 1969, 5-0 vs. Los Angeles

HISTORY

SAN FRANCISCO GIANTS

FRANCHISE CHRONOLOGY

First season: 1883, in New York, as a member of the National League. The "Gothams" defeated Boston, 7-5, in their debut and completed a respectable first-year showing with a 46-50 record.

1884-1900: The Giants captured consecutive pennants in 1888 and '89, but they would not taste success again until the turn of the century, when John McGraw began his 30-year managerial run.

1901-57: Under McGraw's direction, the Giants ruled the National League for three decades. His teams won 10 pennants, finished second 11 times and captured three World Series, a record unmatched over the period. And when McGraw retired during the 1932 season, first baseman Bill Terry took over and led the Giants to three more pennants and another championship in a 10-year reign. But spoiled Giants fans would enjoy only one more Series winner over the team's final 16 seasons in New York. That startling victory came in 1954, when the Giants swept the powerful Cleveland Indians in the fall classic.

1958-present: It's hard to believe the once-proud Giants have not won a World Series in their 40-year San Francisco stay. They came excruciatingly close in 1962 when they lost a seven-game battle to the Yankees, but West Division titles in 1971 and 1987 were followed by N.L. Championship Series losses and others in 1997 and 2000 were followed by Division Series losses. The Giants did return to the Series in 1989, but they were swept by Bay Area-rival Oakland in a classic memorable only because it was interrupted by a devastating earthquake.

Center fielder Willie Mays.

GIANTS VS. OPPONENTS BY DECADE

	Braves	Cardinals	Cubs	Dodgers	Phillies	Pirates	Reds	Astros	Mets	Expos	Padres	Marlins	Rockies	Brewers	D'backs	Interleague	Decade Record
1900-09	125-83	133-78	97-115	128-80	121-87	96-115	123-87										823-645
1910-19	137-73	131-81	116-99	125-88	124-85	127-86	129-85										889-597
1920-29	137-82	123-95	121-99	113-106	149-65	113-106	134-86										890-639
1930-39	127-89	110-107	102-117	120-98	145-72	125-95	139-79										868-657
1940-49	116-100	77-141	109-110	82-137	129-91	111-109	100-120										724-808
1950-59	94-126	112-108	130-90	106-117	121-99	131-89	128-92										822-721
1960-69	91-97	90-92	106-76	108-83	105-77	100-82	103-84	89-55	87-51	11-1	12-6						902-704
1970-79	95-84	60-60	61-59	72-108	53-67	62-58	78-99	90-90	58-62	61-59	104-72						794-818
1980-89	94-79	53-60	61-57	79-95	54-61	63-55	85-91	79-98	65-49	56-59	84-91						773-795
1990-99	53-69	54-58	53-57	70-70	67-44	52-55	66-58	57-69	56-58	59-56	65-71	42-25	52-34	9-9	10-14	25-19	790-766
2000-	3-6	5-4	5-4	5-7	7-2	6-2	6-3	8-1	5-3	6-3	7-5	6-3	7-6	6-3	7-6	8-7	97-65
Totals	1072-888	948-884	961-883	1008-989	1075-750	986-852	1091-884	323-313	271-223	193-178	272-245	48-28	59-40	15-12	17-20	33-26	8372-7215

Interleague results: 8-5 vs. Angels; 10-10 vs. Athletics; 8-5 vs. Mariners; 7-6 vs. Rangers.

MANAGERS

(New York Giants, 1883-1957)

Name	*Years*	*Record*
John Clapp	1883	46-50
Jim Price	1884	56-42
Monte Ward	1884, 1893-94	162-116
Jim Mutrie	1885-91	529-345
Pat Powers	1892	71-80
George Davis	1895, 1900-01	107-139
Jack Doyle	1895	32-31
Harvey Watkins	1895	18-17
Arthur Irwin	1896	36-53
Bill Joyce	1896-98	179-122
Cap Anson	1898	9-13
John Day	1899	29-35
Fred Hoey	1899	31-55
Buck Ewing	1900	21-41
Horace Fogel	1902	18-23
Heinie Smith	1902	5-27
John McGraw	1902-32	2604-1801
Bill Terry	1932-41	823-661
Mel Ott	1942-48	464-530
Leo Durocher	1948-55	637-523
Bill Rigney	1956-60, 1976	406-430
Tom Sheehan	1960	46-50
Alvin Dark	1961-64	366-277
Herman Franks	1965-68	367-280
Clyde King	1969-70	109-95
Charlie Fox	1970-74	348-327
Wes Westrum	1974-75	118-129
Joe Altobelli	1977-79	225-239
Dave Bristol	1979-80	85-98
Frank Robinson	1981-84	264-277
Danny Ozark	1984	24-32
Jim Davenport	1985	56-88
Roger Craig	1985-92	586-566
Dusty Baker	1993-2000	655-577

WORLD SERIES CHAMPIONS

Year	*Loser*	*Length*	*MVP*
1905	Philadelphia	5 games	None
1921	N.Y. Yankees	8 games	None
1922	N.Y. Yankees	5 games	None
1933	Washington	5 games	None
1954	Cleveland	4 games	None

N.L. PENNANT WINNERS

Year	*Record*	*Manager*	*Series Result*
1888	84-47	Mutrie	None
1889	83-43	Mutrie	None
1904	106-47	McGraw	None
1905	105-48	McGraw	Defeated A's
1911	99-54	McGraw	Lost to A's
1912	103-48	McGraw	Lost to Red Sox
1913	101-51	McGraw	Lost to A's
1917	98-56	McGraw	Lost to White Sox
1921	94-59	McGraw	Defeated Yankees

N.L. PENNANT WINNERS—*cont'd.*

Year	*Record*	*Manager*	*Series Result*
1922	93-61	McGraw	Defeated Yankees
1923	95-58	McGraw	Lost to Yankees
1924	93-60	McGraw	Lost to Senators
1933	91-61	Terry	Defeated Senators
1936	92-62	Terry	Lost to Yankees
1937	95-57	Terry	Lost to Yankees
1951	98-59	Durocher	Lost to Yankees
1954	97-57	Durocher	Defeated Indians
1962	103-62	Dark	Lost to Yankees
1989	92-70	Craig	Lost to A's

WEST DIVISION CHAMPIONS

Year	*Record*	*Manager*	*NLCS Result*
1971	90-72	Fox	Lost to Pirates
1987	90-72	Craig	Lost to Cardinals
1989	92-70	Craig	Defeated Cubs
1997	90-72	Baker	Lost Division Series
2000	97-65	Baker	Lost Division Series

ATTENDANCE HIGHS

Total	*Season*	*Park*
3,315,330	2000	Pacific Bell Park
2,606,354	1993	Candlestick Park
2,078,095	1999	3Com Park
2,059,829	1989	Candlestick Park
1,975,571	1990	Candlestick Park

BALLPARK CHRONOLOGY

Pacific Bell Park (2000-present)

Capacity: 63,000.
First game: Giants 3, St. Louis 1 (April 12, 1960).
First batter: Joe Cunningham, Cardinals.
First hit: Bill White, Cardinals (single).
First run: Don Blasingame, Giants (1st inning).
First home run: Leon Wagner, Cardinals.
First winning pitcher: Sam Jones, Giants.
First-season attendance: 1,795,356.

3Com Park, formerly Candlestick Park (1960-present)

Capacity: 63,000.
First game: Giants 3, St. Louis 1 (April 12, 1960).
FFirst-season attendance: 1,795,356.

Polo Grounds I, New York (1883-88)

First game: Giants 7, Boston 5 (May 1, 1883).

Oakland Park, New York (2 games 1889)

First game: Boston 8, Giants 7 (April 24, 1889).

St. George Grounds, New York (25 games 1889)

First game: Giants 4, Washington 2 (April 29, 1889).

Polo Grounds II, New York (1889-90)

First game: Giants 7, Pittsburgh 5 (July 8, 1889).

Polo Grounds III, New York (1891-1957)

Capacity: 55,987.
First game: Boston 4, Giants 3 (April 22, 1891).

Seals Stadium, San Francisco (1958-59)

Capacity: 22,900.
First game: Giants 8, Los Angeles 0 (April 15, 1958).
First-season attendance: 1,272,625.

N.L. MVPs

Carl Hubbell, P, 1933
Carl Hubbell, P, 1936
Willie Mays, OF, 1954
Willie Mays, OF, 1965
Willie McCovey, 1B, 1969
Kevin Mitchell, OF, 1989
Barry Bonds, OF, 1993
Jeff Kent, 2B, 2000

CY YOUNG WINNER

Mike McCormick, LH, 1967

ROOKIES OF THE YEAR

Willie Mays, OF, 1951
Orlando Cepeda, 1B, 1958
Willie McCovey, 1B, 1959
Gary Matthews, OF, 1973
John Montefusco, P, 1975

MANAGER OF THE YEAR

Dusty Baker, 1993, 1997, 2000

RETIRED UNIFORMS

No.	*Name*	*Pos.*
	Christy Mathewson	P
	John McGraw	Man.
3	Bill Terry	1B
4	Mel Ott	OF
11	Carl Hubbell	P
24	Willie Mays	OF
27	Juan Marichal	P
30	Orlando Cepeda	1B
44	Willie McCovey	1B

Longest hitting streaks

33—George Davis 1893
27—Charles Hickman 1900
26—Jack Clark 1978
24—Mike Donlin 1908
Fred Lindstrom 1930
Don Mueller 1955
Willie McCovey 1963
23—Joe Moore 1934
22—Alvin Dark 1952
Willie McCovey 1959
21—Mel Ott 1937
Willie Mays 1954, 1957
Don Mueller 1954
Robby Thompson 1993
20—Mike Tiernan 1891
Joe Moore 1932
Willie Mays 1964

MILESTONE PERFORMANCES

30-plus home runs

52—Willie Mays 1965
51—Johnny Mize 1947
Willie Mays 1955
49—Willie Mays 1962
Barry Bonds 2000
47—Willie Mays 1964
Kevin Mitchell 1989
46—Orlando Cepeda 1961
Barry Bonds 1993
45—Willie McCovey 1969
44—Willie McCovey 1963
43—Matt Williams 1994
42—Mel Ott 1929
Barry Bonds 1996
41—Willie Mays 1954
40—Johnny Mize 1948
Willie Mays 1961
Barry Bonds 1997
39—Willie McCovey 1965, 1970
Bobby Bonds 1973
38—Mel Ott 1932
Willie Mays 1963
Matt Williams 1993
37—Willie Mays 1966
Barry Bonds 1994, 1998
36—Willard Marshall 1947
Willie Mays 1956
Willie McCovey 1966, 1968
35—Mel Ott 1934
Walker Cooper 1947
Willie Mays 1957
Orlando Cepeda 1962
Will Clark 1987
Kevin Mitchell 1990
34—Willie Mays 1959
Orlando Cepeda 1963
Matt Williams 1991
Barry Bonds 1999
33—Mel Ott 1936
Jim Hart 1966
Bobby Bonds 1971
Matt Williams 1990
Barry Bonds 1995
Jeff Kent 2000
32—Bobby Thomson 1951
Bobby Bonds 1969
31—Mel Ott 1935, 1937
Orlando Cepeda 1964
Jim Hart 1964
Willie McCovey 1967
Jeff Kent 1998
Ellis Burks 1999
30—Sid Gordon 1948
Darrell Evans 1983

100-plus RBIs

151—Mel Ott 1929
142—Orlando Cepeda 1961
141—Willie Mays 1962
138—Johnny Mize 1947
136—George Kelly 1924
135—Mel Ott 1934, 1936
132—Irish Meusel 1922
129—Bill Terry 1930
Barry Bonds 1996
128—Jeff Kent 1998
127—Willie Mays 1955
126—Willie McCovey 1969, 1970
125—Irish Meusel 1923
Rogers Hornsby 1927
Johnny Mize 1948
Kevin Mitchell 1989
Jeff Kent 2000
123—Mel Ott 1932
Willie Mays 1961
Barry Bonds 1993
122—George Kelly 1921
Walker Cooper 1947
Matt Williams 1990
122—Barry Bonds 1998
121—Monte Irvin 1951
Bill Terry 1927
Jeff Kent 1997
119—Mel Ott 1930
117—Bill Terry 1929, 1932
116—Mel Ott 1938
Will Clark 1991
115—Mel Ott 1931
114—Mel Ott 1935
Orlando Cepeda 1962
112—Bill Terry 1931
Willie Mays 1965
111—Irish Meusel 1925
Frankie Frisch 1929
Willie Mays 1964
Will Clark 1989
110—Johnny Mize 1942
Willie Mays 1954
Matt Williams 1993
109—Bobby Thomson 1949
Will Clark 1988
108—Sam Mertes 1905
Bobby Thomson 1952
107—George Kelly 1922
Fred Lindstrom 1928
Hank Leiber 1935
Willard Marshall 1947
Sid Gordon 1948
Dick Dietz 1970
106—Mike Donlin 1908
Fred Lindstrom 1930
Bobby Thomson 1953
Barry Bonds 2000
105—Orlando Cepeda 1959
Willie McCovey 1968
104—Sam Mertes 1903
Norm Young 1941
Willie Mays 1959
Barry Bonds 1995
J.T. Snow 1997
103—George Kelly 1923
Mel Ott 1933
Willie Mays 1960, 1963, 1966
Jack Clark 1982
102—Henry Zimmerman 1917
Ross Youngs 1921
Irish Meusel 1924
Bobby Bonds 1971
Willie McCovey 1963
101—Bill Terry 1928
Travis Jackson 1934
Norm Young 1940
Bobby Thomson 1951
Barry Bonds 1997
Jeff Kent 1999
100—Frankie Frisch 1921

20-plus victories

1883—Mickey Welch 39-21
1884—Mickey Welch 39-21
1885—Mickey Welch 44-11
Tim Keefe 32-13
1886—Tim Keefe 42-20
Mickey Welch 33-22
1887—Tim Keefe 35-19
Mickey Welch 22-15
1888—Tim Keefe 35-12
1889—Tim Keefe 28-13
Mickey Welch 27-12
1890—Amos Rusie 29-34
1891—Amos Rusie 33-20
John Ewing 21-8
1892—Amos Rusie 31-31
Silver King 23-24
1893—Amos Rusie 33-21
1894—Amos Rusie 36-13
Jouett Meekin 33-9
1895—Amos Rusie 23-23
1896—Jouett Meekin 26-14
1897—Amos Rusie 28-10
Jouett Meekin 20-11
Cy Seymour 20-14
1898—Cy Seymour 25-19
Amos Rusie 20-11
1901—Christy Mathewson 20-17
1903—Joe McGinnity 31-20
Christy Mathewson 30-13
1904—Joe McGinnity 35-8
Christy Mathewson 33-12
Luther Taylor 21-15
1905—Christy Mathewson 31-9
Leon Ames 22-8
Joe McGinnity 21-15
1906—Joe McGinnity 27-12
Christy Mathewson 22-12
1907—Christy Mathewson 24-12
1908—Christy Mathewson 37-11
George Wiltse 23-14
1909—Christy Mathewson 25-6
George Wiltse 20-11
1910—Christy Mathewson 27-9
1911—Christy Mathewson 26-13
Rube Marquard 24-7
1912—Rube Marquard 26-11
Christy Mathewson 23-12
1913—Christy Mathewson 25-11
Rube Marquard 23-10
Jeff Tesreau 22-13
1914—Jeff Tesreau 26-10
Christy Mathewson 24-13
1917—Ferdie Schupp 21-7
1919—Jess Barnes 25-9
1920—Fred Toney 21-11
Art Nehf 21-12
Jess Barnes 20-15
1921—Art Nehf 20-10
1928—Larry Benton 25-9
Fred Fitzsimmons 20-9
1933—Carl Hubbell 23-12
1934—Hal Schumacher 23-10
Carl Hubbell 21-12
1935—Carl Hubbell 23-12
1936—Carl Hubbell 26-6
1937—Carl Hubbell 22-8
Cliff Melton 20-9
1944—Bill Voiselle 21-16
1947—Larry Jansen 21-5
1951—Sal Maglie 23-6
Larry Jansen 23-11
1954—Johnny Antonelli 21-7
1956—Johnny Antonelli 20-13
1959—Sam Jones 21-15
1962—Jack Sanford 24-7
1963—Juan Marichal 25-8
1964—Juan Marichal 21-8
1965—Juan Marichal 22-13
1966—Juan Marichal 25-6
Gaylord Perry 21-8
1967—Mike McCormick 22-10
1968—Juan Marichal 26-9
1969—Juan Marichal 21-11
1970—Gaylord Perry 23-13
1973—Ron Bryant 24-12
1986—Mike Krukow 20-9
1993—John Burkett 22-7
Bill Swift 21-8

N.L. home run champions

1883—Buck Ewing 10
1890—Mark Tiernan *13
1891—Mark Tiernan *16
1909—Red Murray 7
1916—Dave Robertson *12
1917—Dave Robertson *12
1921—George Kelly 23
1932—Mel Ott *38
1934—Mel Ott *35
1936—Mel Ott 33
1937—Mel Ott *31
1938—Mel Ott 36
1942—Mel Ott 30
1947—Johnny Mize *51
1948—Johnny Mize *40
1955—Willie Mays 51
1961—Orlando Cepeda 46
1962—Willie Mays 49
1963—Willie McCovey *44
1964—Willie Mays 47
1965—Willie Mays 52
1968—Willie McCovey 36
1969—Willie McCovey 45
1989—Kevin Mitchell 47
1993—Barry Bonds 46
1994—Matt Williams 43

* Tied for league lead

N.L. RBI champions

1903—Sam Mertes 104
1904—Bill Dahlen 80
1917—Heinie Zimmerman 102
1920—George Kelly *94
1923—Irish Meusel 125
1924—George Kelly 136
1934—Mel Ott 135
1942—Johnny Mize 110
1947—Johnny Mize 138
1951—Monte Irvin 121
1961—Orlando Cepeda 142
1968—Willie McCovey 105
1969—Willie McCovey 126
1988—Will Clark 109
1989—Kevin Mitchell 125
1990—Matt Williams 122
1993—Barry Bonds 123

* Tied for league lead

N.L. batting champions

1885—Roger Connor .371
1890—Jack Glasscock .336
1915—Larry Doyle .320
1930—Bill Terry .401
1954—Willie Mays .345

N.L. ERA champions

1904—Joe McGinnity 1.61
1905—Christy Mathewson 1.28
1908—Christy Mathewson 1.43
1909—Christy Mathewson 1.14
1911—Christy Mathewson 1.99
1912—Jeff Tesreau 1.96
1913—Christy Mathewson 2.06
1917—Fred Anderson 1.44
1922—Phil Douglas 2.63
1929—Bill Walker 3.09
1931—Bill Walker 2.26
1933—Carl Hubbell 1.66
1934—Carl Hubbell 2.30
1936—Carl Hubbell 2.31
1949—Dave Koslo 2.50
1950—Sal Maglie 2.71
1952—Hoyt Wilhelm 2.43
1954—Johnny Antonelli 2.30
1958—Stu Miller 2.47
1959—Sam Jones 2.83
1960—Mike McCormick 2.70
1969—Juan Marichal 2.10
1983—Atlee Hammaker 2.25
1989—Scott Garrelts 2.28
1992—Bill Swift 2.08

N.L. strikeout champions

1888—Tim Keefe 335
1890—Amos Rusie 341
1891—Amos Rusie 337
1893—Amos Rusie 208
1894—Amos Rusie 195
1895—Amos Rusie 201
1898—Cy Seymour 239
1903—Christy Mathewson 267
1904—Christy Mathewson 212
1905—Christy Mathewson 206
1907—Christy Mathewson 178
1908—Christy Mathewson 259
1911—Rube Marquard 237
1937—Carl Hubbell 159
1944—Bill Voiselle 161

No-hit pitchers

(9 innings or more)

1891—Amos Rusie 6-0 vs. Brooklyn
1901—Christy Mathewson 5-0 vs. St. Louis
1905—Christy Mathewson 1-0 vs. Chicago
1908—George Wiltse 1-0 vs. Philadelphia
1912—Jeff Tesreau 3-0 vs. Philadelphia
1915—Rube Marquard 2-0 vs. Brooklyn
1922—Jesse Barnes 6-0 vs. Philadelphia
1929—Carl Hubbell 11-0 vs. Pittsburgh
1963—Juan Marichal 1-0 vs. Houston
1968—Gaylord Perry 1-0 vs. St. Louis
1975—Ed Halicki 6-0 vs. New York
1976—John Montefusco 9-0 vs. Atlanta

INDIVIDUAL SEASON, GAME RECORDS

SEASON

Batting

Record	Total	Player	Year
At-bats	681	Joe Moore	1935
Runs	146	Mike Tiernan	1893
Hits	254	Bill Terry	1930
Singles	177	Bill Terry	1930
Doubles	46	Jack Clark	1978
Triples	26	George Davis	1893
Home runs	52	Willie Mays	1965
Home runs, rookie	31	Jim Hart	1964
Grand slams	3	3 times	
		Last by Jeff Kent	1997
Total bases	392	Bill Terry	1930
RBIs	151	Mel Ott	1929
Walks	151	Barry Bonds	1996
Most strikeouts	189	Bobby Bonds	1970
Fewest strikeouts	12	Frankie Frisch	1923
Batting average	.401	Bill Terry	1930
Slugging pct.	.677	Barry Bonds	1993
Stolen bases	111	John Ward	1883

Pitching

Record	Total	Player	Year
Games	89	Julian Tavarez	1997
Complete games	44	Joe McGinnity	1903
Innings	434	Joe McGinnity	1903
Wins	37	Christy Mathewson	1908
Losses	27	Luther Taylor	1901
Winning pct.	.833 (15-3)	Hoyt Wilhelm	1952
Walks	128	Jeff Tesreau	1914
Strikeouts	267	Christy Mathewson	1903
Shutouts	12	Christy Mathewson	1908
Home runs allowed	36	Larry Jansen	1949
Lowest ERA	1.14	Christy Mathewson	1909
Saves	48	Rod Beck	1993

GAME

Batting

Record	Total	Player	Date
Runs	6	Last by Mel Ott	4-30-44
Hits	6	Last by Mike Benjamin	6-14-95
Doubles	3	Last by Jeff Kent	9-18-98
Triples	4	Bill Joyce	5-18-1897
Home runs	4	Willie Mays	4-30-61
RBIs	11	Phil Weintraub	4-30-44
Total bases	16	Willie Mays	4-30-61
Stolen bases	5	Dan McGann	5-27-04

HISTORY

CAREER LEADERS

BATTING

Games

Willie Mays	2,857
Mel Ott	2,730
Willie McCovey	2,256
Bill Terry	1,721
Travis Jackson	1,656
Larry Doyle	1,622
Jim Davenport	1,501
Whitey Lockman	1,485
Mike Tiernan	1,478
George Burns	1,362

At-bats

Willie Mays	10,477
Mel Ott	9,456
Willie McCovey	7,214
Bill Terry	6,428
Travis Jackson	6,086
Larry Doyle	5,995
Mike Tiernan	5,947
Whitey Lockman	5,584
Jo Jo Moore	5,427
George Burns	5,311

Runs

Willie Mays	2,011
Mel Ott	1,859
Mike Tiernan	1,348
Bill Terry	1,120
Willie McCovey	1,113
Roger Connor	1,021
George Van Haltren	976
Barry Bonds	912
Larry Doyle	906
George Burns	877

Hits

Willie Mays	3,187
Mel Ott	2,876
Bill Terry	2,193
Willie McCovey	1,974
Mike Tiernan	1,838
Travis Jackson	1,768
Larry Doyle	1,751
Joe Moore	1,615
George Van Haltren	1,580
Whitey Lockman	1,571

Doubles

Willie Mays	504
Mel Ott	488
Bill Terry	373
Willie McCovey	308
Travis Jackson	291
Larry Doyle	275
George Burns	267
Joe Moore	258
Mike Tiernan	257
Will Clark	249

Triples

Mike Tiernan	162
Willie Mays	139
Roger Connor	131
Larry Doyle	117
Bill Terry	112
Buck Ewing	109
George S. Davis	98
Ross Youngs	93
George Van Haltren	88
Travis Jackson	86

Home runs

Willie Mays	646
Mel Ott	511
Willie McCovey	469
Barry Bonds	318
Matt Williams	247
Orlando Cepeda	226
Bobby Thomson	189
Bobby Bonds	186
Will Clark	176
Jack Clark	163

Total bases

Willie Mays	5,907
Mel Ott	5,041
Willie McCovey	3,779
Bill Terry	3,252
Mike Tiernan	2,737
Travis Jackson	2,636
Larry Doyle	2,461
Barry Bonds	2,424
Orlando Cepeda	2,234
Whitey Lockman	2,216
Joe Moore	2,216

Runs batted in

Mel Ott	1,860
Willie Mays	1,859
Willie McCovey	1,388
Bill Terry	1,078
Travis Jackson	929
Mike Tiernan	852
Barry Bonds	849
George S. Davis	818
Roger Connor	786
Orlando Cepeda	767

Extra-base hits

Willie Mays	1,289
Mel Ott	1,071
Willie McCovey	822
Bill Terry	639
Barry Bonds	582
Mike Tiernan	525
Travis Jackson	512
Orlando Cepeda	474
Will Clark	462
Larry Doyle	459

Batting average
(Minimum 500 games)

Bill Terry	.341
George S. Davis	.332
Ross Youngs	.322
Frankie Frisch	.322
George Van Haltren	.321
Fred Lindstrom	.318
Roger Connor	.314
Emil Meusel	.314
Shanty Hogan	.311
Dave Bancroft	.310

Stolen bases

Mike Tiernan	428
George S. Davis	357
Willie Mays	336
George Burns	334
John Ward	332
George Van Haltren	320
Larry Doyle	291
Art Devlin	266
Bobby Bonds	263
Jack Doyle	255

PITCHING

Earned-run average
(Minimum 1,000 innings)

Christy Mathewson	2.12
Joe McGinnity	2.38
Jeff Tesreau	2.43
Red Ames	2.45
Hooks Wiltse	2.48
Tim Keefe	2.53
Mickey Welch	2.69
Dummy Taylor	2.77
Rube Benton	2.79
Juan Marichal	2.84

Wins

Christy Mathewson	372
Carl Hubbell	253
Juan Marichal	238
Mickey Welch	238
Amos Rusie	234
Tim Keefe	174
Freddie Fitzsimmons	170
Hal Schumacher	158
Joe McGinnity	151
Hooks Wiltse	136

Losses

Christy Mathewson	188
Amos Rusie	163
Carl Hubbell	154
Mickey Welch	146
Juan Marichal	140
Hal Schumacher	121
Freddie Fitzsimmons	114
Gaylord Perry	109
Dave Koslo	104
Dummy Taylor	103

Innings pitched

Christy Mathewson	4,779.2
Carl Hubbell	3,590.1
Mickey Welch	3,579.0
Amos Rusie	3,531.2
Juan Marichal	3,444.0
Freddie Fitzsimmons	2,514.1
Hal Schumacher	2,482.1
Gaylord Perry	2,294.2
Tim Keefe	2,265.0
Joe McGinnity	2,151.1

Strikeouts

Christy Mathewson	2,504
Juan Marichal	2,281
Amos Rusie	1,835
Carl Hubbell	1,677
Gaylord Perry	1,606
Mickey Welch	1,570
Tim Keefe	1,303
Red Ames	1,169
Mike McCormick	1,030
Bobby Bolin	977

Bases on balls

Amos Rusie	1,588
Mickey Welch	1,077
Hal Schumacher	902
Christy Mathewson	847
Carl Hubbell	725
Juan Marichal	690
Freddie Fitzsimmons	670
Cy Seymour	656
Jouett Meekin	653
Red Ames	620

Games

Gary Lavelle	647
Christy Mathewson	635
Greg Minton	552
Carl Hubbell	535
Randy Moffitt	459
Juan Marichal	458
Amos Rusie	427
Mickey Welch	426
Rod Beck	416
Freddie Fitzsimmons	403

Shutouts

Christy Mathewson	79
Juan Marichal	52
Carl Hubbell	36
Amos Rusie	29
Mickey Welch	28
Jeff Tesreau	27
Hooks Wiltse	27
Joe McGinnity	26
Hal Schumacher	26
Tim Keefe	22
Freddie Fitzsimmons	22

Saves

Rod Beck	199
Gary Lavelle	127
Greg Minton	125
Robb Nen	118
Randy Moffitt	83
Frank Linzy	78
Marv Grissom	58
Ace Adams	49
Scott Garrelts	48
Stu Miller	47

TEAM SEASON, GAME RECORDS

SEASON

Batting

Most at-bats	5,650	1984
Most runs	959	1930
Fewest runs	540	1956
Most hits	1,769	1930
Most singles	1,279	1930
Most doubles	307	1999
Most triples	105	1911
Most home runs	226	2000
Fewest home runs	15	1906
Most grand slams	7	1951, 1954, 1970, 1998
Most pinch-hit home runs	11	1977, 1987
Most total bases	2,628	1930
Most stolen bases	347	1911
Highest batting average	.319	1930
Lowest batting average	.233	1985
Highest slugging pct.	.473	1930

Pitching

Lowest ERA	2.14	1908
Highest ERA	4.86	1995
Most complete games	127	1904
Most shutouts	25	1908
Most saves	50	1993
Most walks	660	1946
Most strikeouts	1,086	1998

Fielding

Most errors	348	1901
Fewest errors	93	2000
Most double plays	183	1987
Highest fielding average	.985	2000

General

Most games won	106	1904
Most games lost	100	1985
Highest win pct	.759	1885
Lowest win pct	.353	1902

GAME, INNING

Batting

Most runs, game	29	6-15-1887
Most runs, inning	13	Last 7-15-97
Most hits, game	31	6-9-01
Most home runs, game	8	4-30-61
Most total bases, game	50	5-13-58

Lefthander Carl Hubbell used his outstanding screwball to post 253 victories for the Giants.

GIANTS YEAR-BY-YEAR

Year	W	L	Place	Games Back	Manager	Leaders: Batting avg.	Hits	Home runs	RBIs	Wins	ERA
						NEW YORK GIANTS					
1901	52	85	7th	37	G. Davis	Van Haltren, .335	Van Haltren, 182	G. Davis, 7	Ganzel, 66	Mathewson, 20	Mathewson, 2.41
1902	48	88	8th	53½	Fogel, H. Smith, McGraw	Brodie, .281	H. Smith, 129	Brodie, 3	Lauder, 44	Mathewson, 14	McGinnity, 2.06
1903	84	55	2nd	6½	McGraw	Bresnahan, .350	Browne, 185	Mertes, 7	Mertes, 104	McGinnity, 31	Mathewson, 2.26
1904	106	47	1st	+13	McGraw	McGann, .286	Browne, 169	McGann, 6	Dahlen, 80	McGinnity, 35	McGinnity, 1.61
1905	105	48	1st	+9	McGraw	Donlin, .356	Donlin, 216	Dahlen, Donlin, 7	Mertes, 108	Mathewson, 31	Mathewson, 1.27
1906	96	56	2nd	20	McGraw	Devlin, .299	Devlin, 149	Seymour, Strang, 4	Devlin, 65	McGinnity, 27	Taylor, 2.20
1907	82	71	4th	25½	McGraw	Seymour, .294	Shannon, 155	Browne, 5	Seymour, 75	Mathewson, 24	Mathewson, 2.00
1908	98	56	*2nd	1	McGraw	Donlin, .334	Donlin, 198	Donlin, 6	Donlin, 106	Mathewson, 37	Mathewson, 1.43
1909	92	61	3rd	18½	McGraw	Doyle, .302	Doyle, 172	Murray, 7	Murray, 91	Mathewson, 25	Mathewson, 1.14
1910	91	63	2nd	13	McGraw	Snodgrass, .321	Doyle, 164	Doyle, 8	Murray, 87	Mathewson, 27	Mathewson, 1.89
1911	99	54	1st	+7½	McGraw	Meyers, .332	Doyle, 163	Doyle, 13	Merkle, 84	Mathewson, 26	Mathewson, 1.99
1912	103	48	1st	+10	McGraw	Meyers, .358	Doyle, 184	Merkle, 11	Murray, 92	Marquard, 26	Tesreau, 1.96
1913	101	51	1st	+12½	McGraw	Meyers, .312	Burns, 173	Doyle, Shafer, 5	Doyle, 73	Mathewson, 25	Mathewson, 2.06
1914	84	70	2nd	10½	McGraw	Burns, .303	Burns, 170	Merkle, 7	Fletcher, 79	Tesreau, 26	Tesreau, 2.37
1915	69	83	8th	21	McGraw	Doyle, .320	Doyle, 189	Doyle, Merkle, 4	Fletcher, 74	Tesreau, 19	Tesreau, 2.29
1916	86	66	4th	7	McGraw	Robertson, .307	Robertson, 180	Robertson, 12	Kauff, 74	Perritt, 18	Schupp, 0.90
1917	98	56	1st	+10	McGraw	Kauff, .308	Burns, 180	Robertson, 12	Zimmerman, 102	Schupp, 21	F. Anderson, 1.44
1918	71	53	2nd	10½	McGraw	Youngs, .302	Youngs, 143	Burns, 4	Zimmerman, 56	Perritt, 18	Sallee, 2.25
1919	87	53	2nd	9	McGraw	Youngs, .311	Burns, 162	Kauff, 10	Kauff, 67	J. Barnes, 25	Nehf, 1.50
1920	86	68	2nd	7	McGraw	Youngs, .351	Youngs, 204	Kelly, 11	Kelly, 94	Nehf, Toney, 21	Barnes, 2.64
1921	94	59	1st	+4	McGraw	Frisch, .341	Frisch, 211	Kelly, 23	Kelly, 122	Nehf, 20	J. Barnes, 3.10
1922	93	61	1st	+7	McGraw	Meusel, Youngs, .331	Bancroft, 209	Kelly, 17	I. Meusel, 132	Nehf, 19	Douglas, 2.63
1923	95	58	1st	+4½	McGraw	Frisch, .348	Frisch, 223	I. Meusel, 19	I. Meusel, 125	Ryan, Scott, 16	Jonnard, 3.28
1924	93	60	1st	+1½	McGraw	Youngs, .356	Frisch, 198	Kelly, 21	Kelly, 136	V. Barnes, Bentley, 16	McQuillan, 2.69
1925	86	66	2nd	8½	McGraw	Frisch, .331	Kelly, 181	I. Meusel, 21	I. Meusel, 111	V. Barnes, 15	Scott, 3.15
1926	74	77	5th	13½	McGraw	Jackson, .327	Frisch, 171	Kelly, 13	Kelly, 80	Fitzsimmons, 14	V. Barnes, 2.87
1927	92	62	3rd	2	McGraw	Hornsby, .361	Hornsby, 205	Hornsby, 26	Hornsby, 125	Grimes, 19	Grimes, 3.54
1928	93	61	2nd	2	McGraw	Lindstrom, .358	Lindstrom, 231	Ott, 18	Lindstrom, 107	Benton, 25	Benton, 2.73
1929	84	67	3rd	13½	McGraw	Terry, .372	Terry, 226	Ott, 42	Ott, 151	Hubbell, 18	Walker, 3.09
1930	87	67	3rd	5	McGraw	Terry, .401	Terry, 254	Ott, 25	Terry, 129	Fitzsimmons, 19	J. Brown, 1.80
1931	87	65	2nd	13	McGraw	Terry, .349	Terry, 213	Ott, 29	Ott, 115	Fitzsimmons, 18	Walker, 2.26
1932	72	82	*6th	18	McGraw, Terry	Terry, .350	Terry, 225	Ott, 38	Ott, 123	Hubbell, 18	Hubbell, 2.50
1933	91	61	1st	+5	Terry	Terry, .322	Ott, 164	Ott, 23	Ott, 103	Hubbell, 23	Hubbell, 1.66
1934	93	60	2nd	2	Terry	Terry, .354	Terry, 213	Ott, 35	Ott, 135	Schumacher, 23	Hubbell, 2.30
1935	91	62	3rd	8½	Terry	Terry, .341	Leiber, Terry, 203	Ott, 31	Ott, 114	Hubbell, 23	Schumacher, 2.89
1936	92	62	1st	+5	Terry	Ott, .328	Moore, 205	Ott, 33	Ott, 135	Hubbell, 26	Hubbell, 2.31
1937	95	57	1st	+3	Terry	Ripple, .317	Moore, 180	Ott, 31	Ott, 95	Hubbell, 22	Melton, 2.61
1938	83	67	3rd	5	Terry	Ott, .311	Ott, 164	Ott, 36	Ott, 116	Gumbert, 15	Hubbell, 3.07
1939	77	74	5th	18½	Terry	Bonura, .321	Demaree, 170	Ott, 27	Bonura, 85	Gumbert, 18	Hubbell, 2.75
1940	72	80	6th	27½	Terry	Demaree, .302	Whitehead, 160	Ott, 19	Young, 101	Schumacher, 13	Schumacher, 3.25
1941	74	79	5th	25½	Terry	Bartell, .303	Rucker, 179	Ott, 27	Young, 104	Schumacher, 12	Melton, 3.01
1942	85	67	3rd	20	Ott	Mize, .305	Mize, 165	Ott, 30	Mize, 110	Lohman, 13	Lohrman, 2.56
1943	55	98	8th	49½	Ott	Witek, .314	Witek, 195	Ott, 18	Gordon, 63	Adams, 11	Adams, 2.82
1944	67	87	5th	38	Ott	Medwick, .337	Medwick, 165	Ott, 26	Medwick, 85	Voiselle, 21	Voiselle, 3.02
1945	78	74	5th	19	Ott	Ott, .308	Hausmann, 174	Ott, 21	Ott, 79	Mungo, Voiselle, 14	Mungo, 3.20
1946	61	93	8th	36	Ott	Mize, .337	Marshall, 144	Mize, 22	Mize, 70	Koslo, 14	Kennedy, 3.42
1947	81	73	4th	13	Ott	Cooper, .305	Mize, 177	Mize, 51	Mize, 138	Jansen, 21	Jansen, 3.16
1948	78	76	5th	13½	Ott, Durocher	Gordon, .299	Lockman, 167	Mize, 40	Mize, 125	Jansen, 18	Hansen, 2.97
1949	73	81	5th	24	Durocher	Thomson, .309	Thomson, 198	Thomson, 27	Thomson, 109	Jansen, Jones, 15	Koslo, 2.50
1950	86	68	3rd	5	Durocher	Stanky, .300	Dark, 164	Thomson, 25	H. Thompson, 91	Jansen, 19	Hearn, 1.94
1951	98	59	†1st	+1	Durocher	Irvin, .312	Dark, 196	Thomson, 32	Irvin, 121	Jansen, Maglie, 23	Maglie, 2.93
1952	92	62	2nd	4½	Durocher	Dark, .301	Dark, 177	Thomson, 24	Thomson, 108	Maglie, 18	Wilhelm, 2.43
1953	70	84	5th	35	Durocher	Mueller, .333	Dark, 194	Thomson, 26	Thomson, 106	Gomez, 13	Wilhelm, 3.04
1954	97	57	1st	+5	Durocher	Mays, .345	Mueller, 212	Mays, 41	Mays, 110	Antonelli, 21	Wilhelm, 2.10
1955	80	74	3rd	18½	Durocher	Mays, .319	Mays, Mueller, 185	Mays, 51	Mays, 127	Antonelli, Hearn, 14	Antonelli, 3.33
1956	67	87	6th	26	Rigney	Brandt, .299	Mays, 171	Mays, 36	Mays, 84	Antonelli, 20	Antonelli, 2.86
1957	69	85	6th	26	Rigney	Mays, .333	Mays, 195	Mays, 35	Mays, 97	Gomez, 15	Barclay, 3.44
						SAN FRANCISCO GIANTS					
1958	80	74	3rd	12	Rigney	Mays, .347	Mays, 208	Mays, 29	Cepeda, Mays, 96	Antonelli, 13	Miller, 2.47
1959	83	71	3rd	4	Rigney	Cepeda, .317	Cepeda, 192	Mays, 34	Cepeda, 105	S. Jones, 21	S. Jones, 2.83
1960	79	75	5th	16	Rigney, Sheehan	Mays, .319	Mays, 199	Mays, 29	Mays, 103	S. Jones, 18	McCormick, 2.70
1961	85	69	3rd	8	Dark	Cepeda, .311	Cepeda, 182	Cepeda, 46	Cepeda, 142	Miller, 14	McCormick, 3.20
1962	103	62	†1st	+1	Dark	F. Alou, .316	Cepeda, 191	Mays, 49	Mays, 141	Sanford, 24	Marichal, 3.36
1963	88	74	3rd	11	Dark	Cepeda, .316	Mays, 187	McCovey, 44	Mays, 103	Marichal, 25	Marichal, 2.41
1964	90	72	4th	3	Dark	Cepeda, .304	Mays, 171	Mays, 47	Mays, 111	Marichal, 21	Marichal, 2.48
1965	95	67	2nd	2	Franks	Mays, .317	Hart, Mays, 177	Mays, 52	Mays, 112	Marichal, 22	Marichal, 2.13
1966	93	68	2nd	1½	Franks	McCovey, .295	Hart, 165	Mays, 37	Mays, 103	Marichal, 25	Marichal, 2.23
1967	91	71	2nd	10½	Franks	J. Alou, .292	Hart, 167	McCovey, 31	Hart, 99	McCormick, 22	Linzy, 1.51
1968	88	74	2nd	9	Franks	McCovey, .293	McCovey, 153	McCovey, 36	McCovey, 105	Marichal, 26	Bolin, 1.99
						WEST DIVISION					
1969	90	72	2nd	3	King	McCovey, .320	Bo. Bonds, 161	McCovey, 45	McCovey, 126	Marichal, 21	Marichal, 2.10
1970	86	76	3rd	16	King, Fox	Bo. Bonds, .302	Bo. Bonds, 200	McCovey, 39	McCovey, 126	Perry, 23	McMahon, 2.96
1971	90	72	‡1st	+1	Fox	Bo. Bonds, .288	Bo. Bonds, 178	Bo. Bonds, 33	Bo. Bonds, 102	Marichal, 18	Perry, 2.76
1972	69	86	5th	26½	Fox	Speier, .269	Bo. Bonds, 162	Kingman, 29	Kingman, 83	Bryant, 14	Barr, 2.87
1973	88	74	3rd	11	Fox	Maddox, .319	Maddox, 187	Bo. Bonds, 39	Bo. Bonds, 96	Bryant, 24	Moffitt, 2.42
1974	72	90	5th	30	Fox, Westrum	Matthews, .287	Matthews, 161	Bo. Bonds, 21	Matthews, 82	Caldwell, 14	Barr, 2.74
1975	80	81	3rd	27½	Westrum	Joshua, .318	Joshua, 161	Matthews, 12	Murcer, 91	Montefusco, 15	Montefusco, 2.88
1976	74	88	4th	28	Rigney	Matthews, .279	Matthews, 164	Murcer, 23	Murcer, 90	Montefusco, 16	Moffitt, 2.27
1977	75	87	4th	23	Altobelli	Madlock, .302	Madlock, 161	McCovey, 28	McCovey, 86	Halicki, 16	Lavelle, 2.05
1978	89	73	3rd	6	Altobelli	Madlock, .309	J. Clark, 181	J. Clark, 25	J. Clark, 98	Blue, 18	Knepper, 2.63
1979	71	91	4th	19½	Altobelli, Bristol	Whitfield, .287	J. Clark, 144	Ivie, 27	Ivie, 89	Blue, 14	Lavelle, 2.51
1980	75	86	5th	17	Bristol	J. Clark, .284	Evans, 147	J. Clark, 22	J. Clark, 82	Blue 14	Minton, 2.46
1981	56	55	§5th/3rd	—	Robinson	Herndon, .288	Herndon, 105	J. Clark, 17	J. Clark, 53	Alexander, 11	Holland, 2.41
1982	87	75	3rd	2	Robinson	Morgan, .289	C. Davis, 167	J. Clark, 27	J. Clark, 103	Laskey, 13	Minton, 1.83
1983	79	83	5th	12	Robinson	Youngblood, .292	Evans, 154	Evans, 30	Leonard, 87	Laskey, 13	Hammaker, 2.25
1984	66	96	6th	26	Robinson, Ozark	C. Davis, .315	C. Davis, 157	C. Davis, Leonard, 21	Leonard, 86	Krukow, 11	Lavelle, 2.76
1985	62	100	6th	33	Davenport, Craig	C. Brown, .271	C. Davis, 130	Brenly, 19	Leonard, 62	Garrelts, 9	Garrelts, 2.30
1986	83	79	3rd	13	Craig	C. Brown, .317	Thompson, 149	Maldonado, 18	Maldonado, 85	Krukow, 20	Krukow, 2.94
1987	90	72	‡1st	+6	Craig	Aldrete, .325	W. Clark, 163	W. Clark, 35	W. Clark, 91	LaCoss, 13	J.Robinson, 2.79
1988	83	79	4th	11½	Craig	Butler, .287	Butler, 163	W. Clark, 29	W. Clark, 109	Reuschel, 19	D. Robinson, 2.45
1989	92	70	∞1st	+3	Craig	W. Clark, .333	W. Clark, 194	Mitchell, 47	Mitchell, 127	Reuschel, 17	Garrelts, 2.28
1990	85	77	3rd	6	Craig	Butler, .309	Butler, 192	Mitchell, 35	M. Williams, 122	Burkett, 14	Burkett, 3.79
1991	75	87	4th	19	Craig	McGee, .312	W. Clark, 170	M. Williams, 34	W. Clark, 116	Wilson, 13	Brantley, 2.45
1992	72	90	5th	26	Craig	W. Clark, .300	W. Clark, 154	M. Williams, 20	W. Clark, 73	Burkett, 13	Beck, 1.76
1993	103	59	2nd	1	Baker	Ba. Bonds, .336	Ba. Bonds, 181	Ba. Bonds, 46	Ba. Bonds, 123	Burkett, 22	Swift, 2.82
1994	55	60	2nd	3½	Baker	Ba. Bonds, .312	Ba. Bonds, 122	M. Williams, 43	M. Williams, 96	Portugal, 10	Swift, 3.38
1995	67	77	4th	11	Baker	Carreon, .301	Ba. Bonds, 149	Ba. Bonds, 33	Ba. Bonds, 104	Leiter, 10	VanLandingham, 3.67
1996	68	94	4th	23	Baker	Ba. Bonds, .308	Ba. Bonds, 159	Ba. Bonds, 42	Ba. Bonds, 129	Gardner, 12	Rueter, 3.97
1997	90	72	▲1st	+2	Baker	Mueller, .292	Ba. Bonds, 155	Ba. Bonds, 40	Kent, 121	Estes, 19	Estes, 3.18
1998	89	74	◆2nd	9½	Baker	Ba. Bonds, .305	Ba. Bonds, 167	Ba. Bonds, 37	Kent, 127	Rueter, 16	Gardner, 4.27
1999	86	76	2nd	14	Baker	Benard, .290	Benard, 163	Ba. Bonds, 34	Kent, 101	Ortiz, 18	Ortiz, 3.81
2000	97	65	▲1st	+11	Baker	Burks, .344	Kent, 196	Ba. Bonds, 49	Kent, 125	L. Hernandez, 17	L. Hernandez, 3.75

* Tied for position. † Won pennant playoff. ‡ Lost Championship Series. § First half 27-32, second half 29-23. ∞ Won Championship Series. ▲ Lost Division Series. ◆ Lost wild-card playoff.
Note: Batting average minimum 350 at-bats, ERA minimum 90 innings pitched.

For the Record

The record-setting 1927 New York Yankees featured (from left) Babe Ruth, diminutive manager Miller Huggins and Lou Gehrig.

INTRODUCTION

As record-breaking seasons go, 2000 won't be remembered for a lot of numbers-setting. Still, there were a number of new marks set last season. Some active numbers going into 2001 (an asterisk indicates an active record):

■ MAJOR LEAGUE RECORDS SET

Most home runs, first baseman, career: 537, Mark McGwire, St. Louis*

Most home runs, pinch-hitter, season: 7, Dave Hansen, Los Angeles

Most intentional bases on balls, career: 320, Barry Bonds, San Francisco*

Most games pitched, career: 1,096, Jesse Orosco, St. Louis*

Most games, relief pitcher, career: 1,092, Jesse Orosco, St. Louis*

Most wild pitches, club, season: 96, Cincinnati

Most consecutive errorless games, third baseman, career: 99, John Wehner, Pittsburgh, August 2, 1992 through September 29, 2000

Most home runs leading off game, career: 78, Rickey Henderson, Seattle*

Most strikeouts, lefthanded batter, season: 181, Mo Vaughn, Anaheim

Most grand slams, club, season: 14, Oakland

Most stolen bases, career: 1,370, Rickey Henderson, Seattle*

Most saves, rookie, season: 37, Kazuhiro Sasaki, Seattle

■ MAJOR LEAGUE RECORDS TIED

Most clubs played for, season: 4, Dave Martinez, Tampa Bay (A.L.), Chicago (N.L.), Texas (A.L.), Toronto (A.L.)

Hitting home run in first major league at-bat: Alex Cabrera, Arizona, June 26; Keith McDonald, St. Louis, July 4; Chris Richard, St. Louis, July 17

Hitting home run in first two major league at-bats: Keith McDonald, St. Louis, July 4, 6

Fewest games shut out, club, season: 0, Cincinnati

Most consecutive doubles, club, inning: 4, Philadelphia vs. Cincinnati, May 4, first inning

Most players with two or more home runs, club, game: 3, Houston vs. Chicago, September 9 (Bogar, Bergman, Hidalgo)

Most grand slams, club, game: 2, Los Angeles vs. Florida, May 21 (Beltran, Green)

Most grand slams allowed, season: 4, Matt Clement, San Diego

Most positions played, game: 9, Scott Sheldon, Texas, September 6; Shane Halter, Detroit, October 1

Most clubs played for, season: 4, Dave Martinez, Tampa Bay, Chicago (N.L.), Texas, Toronto

Hitting home run in first major league at-bat: Esteban Yan, Tampa Bay, June 4

Most grand slams, two consecutive games: 2, Albert Belle, Baltimore, June 14, 15

Most strikeouts, nine-inning game: 5, Jim Thome, Cleveland, April 9; John Jaha, Oakland, April 20

Most players with two or more home runs, club, game: 3, Anaheim vs. Tampa Bay, April 21

Most grand slams, club, game: 2, Seattle vs. Chicago, August 8, Game 1 (Buhner, Martinez)

Most strikeouts, inning: 4, Chuck Finley, Cleveland vs. Texas, April 16, third inning

■ NATIONAL LEAGUE RECORDS SET

Most years and most consecutive years, 50 or more home runs: 3, Sammy Sosa, Chicago

Most home runs, switch-hitter, career: 242, Bobby Bonilla, Atlanta*

Most home runs, club, season: 249, Houston

Most home runs allowed, season: 48, Jose Lima, Houston

Most strikeouts, club, season: 1,253, St. Louis

Most grand slams allowed, club, season: 12, Montreal

■ NATIONAL LEAGUE RECORDS TIED

Most grand slams, club, season: 12, St. Louis

■ AMERICAN LEAGUE RECORDS SET

Most home runs, third baseman, season: 46, Troy Glaus, Anaheim

Most stolen bases, career: 1,262, Rickey Henderson, Seattle*

■ AMERICAN LEAGUE RECORDS TIED

Most consecutive games scoring one or more runs, season: 18, Kenny Lofton, Cleveland, August 15 through September 3

Most hits in four consecutive games: 15, Johnny Damon, Kansas City, July 18 through 21

Most players scoring one or more runs, both clubs, game: 18, Oakland 9 vs. Texas 9, May 5

Most hit batsmen, nine-inning game: 4, James Baldwin, Chicago, August 17

FIRST, IT WAS GEORGE HALL

Fascination with the long ball has existed as long as the game itself, and home run records have always been among the game's most-cherished marks. Philadelphia's George Hall was the majors' first home run king, hitting an N.L.-high five in 1876. His single-season record lasted for three years. By 1884, the big-league mark had risen to 27, a figure achieved by Ned Williamson of Chicago's N.L. club. Williamson's record lasted 35 years—until George Herman Ruth hit 29 for the Red Sox in 1919. The Babe made short shrift of his own record the next year when he slugged 54 for the Yankees. Ruth topped that mark with 59 in 1921, then reached his storied total of 60 in 1927. Ruth's figure ranked as the single-season high for 34 years. It was surpassed by another Yankee, Roger Maris, whose 61-homer performance in 1961 stood as the record for 37 years (until Mark McGwire shattered it). ... Ruth became the modern career home run leader (Roger Connor had hit 138 homers while playing exclusively before the turn of the century) when he cracked No. 120 in June 1921, breaking the post-1900 record of 119 set by Gavvy Cravath, an outfielder who played most of his career with the Phillies. Ruth, who went on to hit 594 more homers and surpassed Connor later in the 1921 season, remained the all-time leader for 53 years—until Hank Aaron surpassed his total of 714. Aaron, of course, wound up with 755. ... The Cubs' Hack Wilson holds the majors' RBI record with a recently revised figure of 191, a mark set in baseball's offense-dominated season of 1930. Lou Gehrig, who had driven in 174 runs for the Yankees in '30, established the A.L. record the next year with 184. ... Hitting prowess, though, is much more than the ability to hit a baseball to faraway places. Ty Cobb proved that by compiling the best lifetime batting average in history, a .366 mark. He won the A.L. batting title nine consecutive seasons and 12 times in a 13-year span. And he had 4,191 hits. As great as Cobb was as a hitmaker, other players own the records for career hits (Pete Rose, 4,256), hits in one season (George Sisler, 257), consecutive-game hitting streak (Joe DiMaggio, 56 games) and highest single-season average in modern times (Rogers Hornsby, .424). ... Cobb was a marvelous basestealer, too, ranking fourth on the all-time list. An active player, Rickey Henderson, enters the season No. 1 with 1,370 steals. ... Gehrig, forever the Iron Horse, saw his record streak of consecutive games (2,130) end in 1995. The man who topped him, Cal Ripken Jr., ended his streak late in the 1998 season when, without notice, he sat out a game against the Yankees after playing in 2,632 consecutive games. ... A notable team record fell in 1998 when the Yankees eclipsed the A.L. mark for season victories with 114. The 1954 Indians had held the record with 111. ... Roger Clemens is the leader in victories among active pitchers—but Clemens' total (260) is just more than half of record-holder Cy Young's figure (511). ... Nolan Ryan's 5,714 career strikeouts, seven no-hitters and 27 years played seem unapproachable. But, hey, isn't that what they said about Ruth's 60 and 714, Gehrig's 2,130 and Cobb's 4,191?

Yankee Lou Gehrig couldn't match Hack Wilson's 191-RBI 1930 record, but he came close in 1931 when he drove in an American League-record 184.

—JOE HOPPEL

CAREER

REGULAR SEASON

SERVICE

YEARS PLAYED

1.	Deacon McGuire	26
2.	Eddie Collins	25
	Bobby Wallace	25
4.	Ty Cobb	24
	Rick Dempsey	24
	Carlton Fisk	24
	Pete Rose	24
8.	Hank Aaron	23
	Rogers Hornsby	23
	Rabbit Maranville	23
	Tony Perez	23
	Brooks Robinson	23
	Rusty Staub	23
	Carl Yastrzemski	23
15.	18 tied with 22	

YEARS ONE CLUB

1.	Brooks Robinson, Orioles	23
	Carl Yastrzemski, Red Sox	23
3.	Cap Anson, Cubs	22
	Ty Cobb, Tigers	22
	Al Kaline, Tigers	22
	Stan Musial, Cardinals	22
	Mel Ott, Giants	22
8.	Hank Aaron, Braves	21
	George Brett, Royals	21
	Harmon Killebrew, Senators/Twins	21
	Willie Mays, Giants	21
	Willie Stargell, Pirates	21
13.	Luke Appling, White Sox	20
	Phil Cavarretta, Cubs	20
	Cal Ripken, Orioles	20
	Alan Trammell, Tigers	20
	Robin Yount, Brewers	20
17.	11 tied with 19	

YEARS PITCHED

1.	Nolan Ryan	27
2.	Tommy John	26
3.	Charlie Hough	25
	Jim Kaat	25
5.	Steve Carlton	24
	Dennis Eckersley	24
	Phil Niekro	24
8.	Dennis Martinez	23
	Jack Quinn	23
	Don Sutton	23
	Early Wynn	23
12.	Bert Blyleven	22
	Rich Gossage	22
	Sam Jones	22
	Joe Niekro	22
	Herb Pennock	22
	Gaylord Perry	22
	Jerry Reuss	22
	Red Ruffing	22
	Cy Young	22

YEARS PITCHED ONE CLUB

1.	Walter Johnson, Senators	21
	Ted Lyons, White Sox	21
	Phil Niekro, Braves	21
4.	Red Faber, White Sox	20
	Mel Harder, Indians	20
	Warren Spahn, Braves	20
7.	Jim Palmer, Orioles	19
8.	Babe Adams, Pirates	18
	Bob Feller, Indians	18
	Jesse Haines, Cardinals	18
11.	Bob Gibson, Cardinals	17
	Christy Mathewson, Giants	17
13.	Tommy Bridges, Tigers	16
	Whitey Ford, Yankees	16
	Carl Hubbell, Giants	16
	Vern Law, Pirates	16
	Charlie Root, Cubs	16
	Don Sutton, Dodgers	16
19.	16 tied with 15	

BATTING

GAMES

1.	Pete Rose	3,562
2.	Carl Yastrzemski	3,308
3.	Hank Aaron	3,298
4.	Ty Cobb	3,035
5.	Eddie Murray	3,026
	Stan Musial	3,026
7.	Willie Mays	2,992
8.	Dave Winfield	2,973
9.	Rusty Staub	2,951
10.	Brooks Robinson	2,896
11.	Cal Ripken Jr.	2,873
12.	Rickey Henderson	2,856
	Robin Yount	2,856
14.	Al Kaline	2,834
15.	Eddie Collins	2,826
16.	Reggie Jackson	2,820
17.	Frank Robinson	2,808
18.	Harold Baines	2,798
19.	Honus Wagner	2,794
20.	Tris Speaker	2,789

CONSECUTIVE GAMES PLAYED

1.	Cal Ripken	2,632
2.	Lou Gehrig	2,130
3.	Everett Scott	1,307
4.	Steve Garvey	1,207
5.	Billy Williams	1,117
6.	Joe Sewell	1,103
7.	Stan Musial	895
8.	Eddie Yost	829
9.	Gus Suhr	822
10.	Nellie Fox	798
11.	Pete Rose	745
12.	Dale Murphy	740
13.	Richie Ashburn	730
14.	Ernie Banks	717
15.	Pete Rose	678
16.	Earl Averill	673
17.	Frank McCormick	652
18.	Sandy Alomar Sr.	648
19.	Eddie Brown	618
20.	Roy McMillan	585

HIGHEST AVERAGE

(Minimum 1,500 hits)

1.	Ty Cobb	.366
2.	Rogers Hornsby	.358
3.	Joe Jackson	.356
4.	Dan Brouthers	.349
	Pete Browning	.349
6.	Ed Delahanty	.346
7.	Tris Speaker	.345
8.	Ted Williams	.344
	Billy Hamilton	.344
10.	Babe Ruth	.342
	Harry Heilmann	.342
12.	Willie Keeler	.341
	Bill Terry	.341
14.	George Sisler	.340
	Lou Gehrig	.340
16.	Tony Gwynn	.338
	Jesse Burkett	.338
	Nap Lajoie	.338
19.	Riggs Stephenson	.336
20.	Sam Thompson	.335

YEARS LEADING LEAGUE IN AVERAGE

1.	Ty Cobb	12
2.	Tony Gwynn	8
	Honus Wagner	8
4.	Rod Carew	7
	Rogers Hornsby	7
	Stan Musial	7
7.	Ted Williams	6
8.	Wade Boggs	5
	Dan Brouthers	5
10.	Cap Anson	4
	Roberto Clemente	4
	Harry Heilmann	4
	Bill Madlock	4
14.	George Brett	3
	Pete Browning	3
	Jesse Burkett	3
	Nap Lajoie	3
	Tony Oliva	3
	Pete Rose	3
	Paul Waner	3
	Carl Yastrzemski	3

YEARS TOPPING .300

1.	Ty Cobb	23
2.	Cap Anson	19
3.	Tris Speaker	18
4.	Eddie Collins	17
	Tony Gwynn	17
	Stan Musial	17
7.	Babe Ruth	16
	Honus Wagner	16
	Ted Williams	16
10.	Wade Boggs	15
	Dan Brouthers	15
	Rod Carew	15
	Rogers Hornsby	15
	Nap Lajoie	15
	Pete Rose	15
16.	Hank Aaron	14
	Luke Appling	14
	Paul Waner	14
19.	9 tied with 13	

In the early 1960s, Pete Rose was a young player looking for recognition. By the time he retired, he was baseball's all-time career hit leader.

CONSECUTIVE .300 SEASONS

1.	Ty Cobb	23
2.	Tony Gwynn	17
3.	Stan Musial	16
4.	Cap Anson	15
	Rod Carew	15
	Honus Wagner	15
7.	Dan Brouthers	14
8.	Willie Keeler	13
9.	Lou Gehrig	12
	Billy Hamilton	12
	Harry Heilmann	12
	Paul Waner	12
13.	Ed Delahanty	11
	Frank Frisch	11
	Rogers Hornsby	11
	Joe Kelley	11
	Al Simmons	11
18.	Wade Boggs	10
	Jesse Burkett	10
	Nap Lajoie	10
	Joe Medwick	10
	Tris Speaker	10
	Bill Terry	10
	Arky Vaughan	10
	Ted Williams	10

AT-BATS

1.	Pete Rose	14,053
2.	Hank Aaron	12,364
3.	Carl Yastrzemski	11,988
4.	Ty Cobb	11,434
5.	Eddie Murray	11,336
6.	Cal Ripken	11,074
7.	Robin Yount	11,008
8.	Dave Winfield	11,003
9.	Stan Musial	10,972
10.	Willie Mays	10,881
11.	Paul Molitor	10,835
12.	Brooks Robinson	10,654
13.	Honus Wagner	10,439
14.	George Brett	10,349
15.	Lou Brock	10,332
16.	Rickey Henderson	10,331
17.	Luis Aparicio	10,230
18.	Tris Speaker	10,195
19.	Al Kaline	10,116
20.	Rabbit Maranville	10,078

RUNS SCORED

1.	Ty Cobb	2,246
2.	Rickey Henderson	2,178
3.	Hank Aaron	2,174
	Babe Ruth	2,174
5.	Pete Rose	2,165
6.	Willie Mays	2,062
7.	Stan Musial	1,949
8.	Lou Gehrig	1,888
9.	Tris Speaker	1,882
10.	Mel Ott	1,859
11.	Frank Robinson	1,829
12.	Eddie Collins	1,821
13.	Carl Yastrzemski	1,816
14.	Ted Williams	1,798
15.	Paul Molitor	1,782
16.	Charley Gehringer	1,774
17.	Jimmie Foxx	1,751
18.	Honus Wagner	1,739
19.	Cap Anson	1,722
20.	Jesse Burkett	1,720

YEARS LEADING LEAGUE IN RUNS

1. Babe Ruth 8
2. Mickey Mantle 6
Ted Williams 6
4. George Burns 5
Ty Cobb 5
Rickey Henderson 5
Rogers Hornsby 5
Stan Musial 5
9. Lou Gehrig 4
Billy Hamilton 4
Pete Rose 4
Harry Stovey 4
13. Hank Aaron 3
Jeff Bagwell 3
Eddie Collins 3
King Kelly 3
Chuck Klein 3
Paul Molitor 3
Frank Robinson 3
Ryne Sandberg 3
Duke Snider 3
Arky Vaughan 3
Carl Yastrzemski 3

100-RUN SEASONS

1. Hank Aaron 15
2. Lou Gehrig 13
Rickey Henderson 13
4. Charley Gehringer 12
Willie Mays 12
Babe Ruth 12
7. Ty Cobb 11
Jimmie Foxx 11
Billy Hamilton 11
Stan Musial 11
George Van Haltren 11
12. Ed Delahanty 10
Mike Griffin 10
Bid McPhee 10
Pete Rose 10
Sam Thompson 10
17. 11 tied with 9

HITS

1. Pete Rose 4,256
2. Ty Cobb 4,189
3. Hank Aaron 3,771
4. Stan Musial 3,630
5. Tris Speaker 3,514
6. Honus Wagner 3,420
7. Carl Yastrzemski 3,419
8. Paul Molitor 3,319
9. Eddie Collins 3,315
10. Willie Mays 3,283
11. Eddie Murray 3,255
12. Nap Lajoie 3,242
13. George Brett 3,154
14. Paul Waner 3,152
15. Robin Yount 3,142
16. Dave Winfield 3,110
17. Tony Gwynn 3,108
18. Cal Ripken 3,070
19. Cap Anson 3,056
20. Rod Carew 3,053

YEARS LEADING LEAGUE IN HITS

1. Ty Cobb 8
2. Tony Gwynn 7
Pete Rose 7
4. Stan Musial 6
5. Tony Oliva 5
6. Ginger Beaumont 4
Dan Brouthers 4
Nellie Fox 4
Rogers Hornsby 4
Harvey Kuenn 4
Nap Lajoie 4
Kirby Puckett 4
13. Richie Ashburn 3
George Brett 3
Jesse Burkett 3
Rod Carew 3
Willie Keeler 3
Frank McCormick 3
Paul Molitor 3
Johnny Pesky 3

200-HIT SEASONS

1. Pete Rose 10
2. Ty Cobb 9
3. Lou Gehrig 8
Willie Keeler 8
Paul Waner 8
6. Wade Boggs 7
Charley Gehringer 7
Rogers Hornsby 7
9. Jesse Burkett 6
Steve Garvey 6
Stan Musial 6
Sam Rice 6
Al Simmons 6
George Sisler 6
Bill Terry 6
16. Tony Gwynn 5
Chuck Klein 5
Kirby Puckett 5
19. 15 tied with 4

PINCH HITS

1. Manny Mota 150
2. Smoky Burgess 145
3. Greg Gross 143
4. Lenny Harris 130
5. Jose Morales 123
6. Jerry Lynch 116
John Vander Wal 116
8. Red Lucas 114
9. Steve Braun 113
10. Terry Crowley 108
Denny Walling 108
12. Gates Brown 107
13. Mike Lum 103
14. Jim Dwyer 102
15. Dave Hansen 101
16. Rusty Staub 100
17. Dave Clark 96
18. Larry Biittner 95
Vic Davalillo 95
Gerald Perry 95

SINGLES

1. Pete Rose 3,215
2. Ty Cobb 3,053
3. Eddie Collins 2,643
4. Willie Keeler 2,513
5. Honus Wagner 2,424
6. Rod Carew 2,404
7. Tris Speaker 2,383
8. Paul Molitor 2,366
9. Tony Gwynn 2,356
10. Nap Lajoie 2,340
11. Hank Aaron 2,294
12. Jesse Burkett 2,273
13. Sam Rice 2,271
14. Carl Yastrzemski 2,262
15. Wade Boggs 2,253
Stan Musial 2,253
17. Lou Brock 2,247
18. Cap Anson 2,246
19. Paul Waner 2,243
20. Robin Yount 2,182

DOUBLES

1. Tris Speaker 792
2. Pete Rose 746
3. Stan Musial 725
4. Ty Cobb 724
5. George Brett 665
6. Nap Lajoie 657
7. Carl Yastrzemski 646
8. Honus Wagner 643
9. Hank Aaron 624
10. Paul Molitor 605
Paul Waner 605
12. Cal Ripken 587
13. Robin Yount 583
14. Wade Boggs 578
15. Charley Gehringer 574
16. Eddie Murray 560
17. Harry Heilmann 542
18. Rogers Hornsby 541
19. Joe Medwick 540
Dave Winfield 540

TRIPLES

1. Sam Crawford 309
2. Ty Cobb 295
3. Honus Wagner 252
4. Jake Beckley 244
5. Roger Connor 233
6. Tris Speaker 222
7. Fred Clarke 220
8. Dan Brouthers 205
9. Joe Kelley 194
10. Paul Waner 191
11. Bid McPhee 189
12. Eddie Collins 187
13. Ed Delahanty 186
14. Sam Rice 184
15. Jesse Burkett 182
Ed Konetchy 182
Edd Roush 182
18. Buck Ewing 178
19. Rabbit Maranville 177
Stan Musial 177

HOME RUNS

1. Hank Aaron 755
2. Babe Ruth 714
3. Willie Mays 660
4. Frank Robinson 586
5. Harmon Killebrew 573
6. Reggie Jackson 563
7. Mark McGwire 554
8. Mike Schmidt 548
9. Mickey Mantle 536
10. Jimmie Foxx 534
11. Willie McCovey 521
Ted Williams 521
13. Ernie Banks 512
Eddie Mathews 512
15. Mel Ott 511
16. Eddie Murray 504
17. Barry Bonds 494
18. Lou Gehrig 493
19. Stan Musial 475
Willie Stargell 475

HOME RUNS, A.L.

1. Babe Ruth 708
2. Harmon Killebrew 573
3. Reggie Jackson 563
4. Mickey Mantle 536
5. Jimmie Foxx 524
6. Ted Williams 521
7. Lou Gehrig 493
8. Carl Yastrzemski 452
9. Jose Canseco 446
10. Cal Ripken 417
11. Al Kaline 399
12. Ken Griffey Jr. 398
13. Eddie Murray 396
14. Dwight Evans 385
15. Harold Baines 384
16. Jim Rice 382
17. Albert Belle 381
18. Norm Cash 377
19. Carlton Fisk 376
20. Rafael Palmeiro 375

HOME RUNS, N.L.

1. Hank Aaron 733
2. Willie Mays 660
3. Mike Schmidt 548
4. Willie McCovey 521
5. Ernie Banks 512
6. Mel Ott 511
7. Eddie Mathews 503
8. Barry Bonds 494
9. Stan Musial 475
Willie Stargell 475
11. Andre Dawson 409
12. Duke Snider 407
13. Dale Murphy 398
14. Billy Williams 392
15. Johnny Bench 389
16. Gil Hodges 370
17. Andres Galarraga 360
18. Orlando Cepeda 358
19. Sammy Sosa 357
20. Ralph Kiner 351

HOME RUNS, ONE CLUB

1. Hank Aaron, Braves 733
2. Babe Ruth, Yankees 659
3. Willie Mays, Giants 646
4. Harmon Killebrew, Senators/Twins 559
5. Mike Schmidt, Phillies 548
6. Mickey Mantle, Yankees 536
7. Ted Williams, Red Sox 521
8. Ernie Banks, Cubs 512
9. Mel Ott, Giants 511
10. Lou Gehrig, Yankees 493
Eddie Mathews, Braves 493
12. Stan Musial, Cardinals 475
Willie Stargell, Pirates 475
14. Willie McCovey, Giants 469
15. Carl Yastrzemski, Red Sox 452
16. Cal Ripken, Orioles 417
17. Al Kaline, Tigers 399
18. Ken Griffey Jr., Mariners 398
19. Billy Williams, Cubs 392
20. Johnny Bench, Reds 389
Duke Snider, Dodgers 389

HOME RUNS, RIGHTHANDER

1. Hank Aaron 755
2. Willie Mays 660
3. Frank Robinson 586
4. Harmon Killebrew 573
5. Mark McGwire 554
6. Mike Schmidt 548
7. Jimmie Foxx 534
8. Ernie Banks 512
9. Dave Winfield 465
10. Jose Canseco 446
11. Dave Kingman 442
12. Andre Dawson 438
13. Cal Ripken 417
14. Al Kaline 399
15. Dale Murphy 398
16. Joe Carter 396
17. Johnny Bench 389
18. Sammy Sosa 386
19. Dwight Evans 385
20. Frank Howard 382
Jim Rice 382

HOME RUNS, LEFTHANDER

1. Babe Ruth 714
2. Reggie Jackson 563
3. Willie McCovey 521
Ted Williams 521
5. Eddie Mathews 512
6. Mel Ott 511
7. Barry Bonds 494
8. Lou Gehrig 493
9. Stan Musial 475
Willie Stargell 475
11. Carl Yastrzemski 452
12. Ken Griffey Jr. 438
13. Billy Williams 426
14. Fred McGriff 417
15. Darrell Evans 414
16. Duke Snider 407
17. Rafael Palmeiro 400
18. Graig Nettles 390
19. Harold Baines 384
20. Norm Cash 377

HOME RUNS, SWITCH HITTER

1. Mickey Mantle 536
2. Eddie Murray 504
3. Chili Davis 350
4. Reggie Smith 314
5. Bobby Bonilla 282
6. Ted Simmons 248
7. Ken Singleton 246
8. Mickey Tettleton 245
9. Ruben Sierra 240
10. Howard Johnson 228
11. Ken Caminiti 224
12. Devon White 194
13. Chipper Jones 189
14. Bernie Williams 181
15. Todd Hundley 172
16. Roberto Alomar 170
17. Tim Raines 168
18. Roy Smalley 163
19. Tony Phillips 160
Pete Rose 160
Roy White 160

HOME RUNS, FIRST BASEMAN

1. Mark McGwire 537
2. Lou Gehrig 493
3. Jimmie Foxx 480
4. Willie McCovey 439
5. Eddie Murray 409
6. Fred McGriff 370
7. Norm Cash 367
8. Andres Galarraga 359
9. Johnny Mize 350
10. Gil Hodges 335

HOME RUNS, SECOND BASEMAN

1. Ryne Sandberg 275
2. Joe Morgan 266
3. Rogers Hornsby 264
4. Joe Gordon 246
5. Lou Whitaker 239
6. Bobby Doerr 223
7. Bobby Grich 196
8. Charley Gehringer 181
9. Jeff Kent 173
10. Roberto Alomar 167

HOME RUNS, THIRD BASEMAN

1. Mike Schmidt 509
2. Eddie Mathews 486
3. Graig Nettles 368
4. Ron Santo 337
5. Gary Gaetti 333
6. Matt Williams 327
7. Ron Cey 312
8. Brooks Robinson 266
9. Ken Boyer 260
10. Tim Wallach 249

HOME RUNS, SHORTSTOP

1. Cal Ripken 345
2. Ernie Banks 277
3. Vern Stephens 213
4. Alex Rodriguez 189
5. Barry Larkin 177
Alan Trammell 177
7. Joe Cronin 155
8. Eddie Joost 129
9. Rico Petrocelli 127
10. Pee Wee Reese 122
Robin Yount 122

HOME RUNS, OUTFIELDER

1. Babe Ruth 692
2. Hank Aaron 661
3. Willie Mays 642
4. Ted Williams 514
5. Barry Bonds 491
6. Mickey Mantle 490
7. Frank Robinson 463
8. Reggie Jackson 458
9. Mel Ott 457
10. Ken Griffey Jr. 419

HOME RUNS, CATCHER

1.	Carlton Fisk	351
2.	Johnny Bench	327
3.	Yogi Berra	306
4.	Gary Carter	298
5.	Lance Parrish	295
6.	Mike Piazza	272
7.	Roy Campanella	239
8.	Gabby Hartnett	232
9.	Bill Dickey	200
10.	Ted Simmons	195

HOME RUNS, PITCHER

1.	Wes Ferrell	37
2.	Bob Lemon	35
	Warren Spahn	35
4.	Red Ruffing	34
5.	Earl Wilson	33
6.	Don Drysdale	29
7.	John Clarkson	24
	Bob Gibson	24
9.	Walter Johnson	23
10.	Jack Stivetts	20
	Dizzy Trout	20

HOME RUNS, DESIGNATED HITTER

1.	Don Baylor	219
2.	Harold Baines	214
3.	Chili Davis	200
4.	Jose Cansco	193
5.	Edgar Martinez	171

LEADOFF HOMERS

1.	Rickey Henderson	78
2.	Brady Anderson	41
3.	Bobby Bonds	35
4.	Paul Molitor	33
5.	Devon White	32
6.	Tony Phillips	30
7.	Davey Lopes	28
	Eddie Yost	28
	Chuck Knoblauch	28
10.	Brian Downing	25
11.	Lou Brock	24
12.	Tommy Harper	23
	Lou Whitaker	23
14.	Jimmy Ryan	22
15.	Craig Biggio	21
16.	Felipe Alou	20
	Barry Bonds	20
	Lenny Dykstra	20
19.	Eddie Joost	19
	Dick McAuliffe	19

20-HOME RUN SEASONS

1.	Hank Aaron	20
2.	Willie Mays	17
	Frank Robinson	17
4.	Reggie Jackson	16
	Eddie Murray	16
	Babe Ruth	16
	Ted Williams	16
8.	Mel Ott	15
	Willie Stargell	15
	Dave Winfield	15
11.	Mickey Mantle	14
	Eddie Mathews	14
	Mike Schmidt	14
	Billy Williams	14
15.	Ernie Banks	13
	Barry Bonds	13
	Andre Dawson	13
	Lou Gehrig	13
	Harmon Killebrew	13
	Fred McGriff	13

30-HOME RUN SEASONS

1.	Hank Aaron	15
2.	Babe Ruth	13
	Mike Schmidt	13
4.	Jimmie Foxx	12
5.	Willie Mays	11
	Mark McGwire	11
	Frank Robinson	11
8.	Barry Bonds	10
	Lou Gehrig	10
	Harmon Killebrew	10
	Eddie Mathews	10
12.	Mickey Mantle	9
13.	Albert Belle	8
	Jose Canseco	8
	Fred McGriff	8
	Mel Ott	8
	Ted Williams	8
18.	Ernie Banks	7
	Rocky Colavito	7
	Joe DiMaggio	7
	Ken Griffey Jr.	7
	Reggie Jackson	7
	Ralph Kiner	7
	Dave Kingman	7
	Willie McCovey	7
	Rafael Palmeiro	7
	Mike Piazza	7
	Sammy Sosa	7
	Frank Thomas	7

PINCH-HIT HOME RUNS

1.	Cliff Johnson	20
2.	Jerry Lynch	18
3.	Gates Brown	16
	Smoky Burgess	16
	Willie McCovey	16
	John Vander Wal	16
7.	George Crowe	14
8.	Dave Hansen	13
	Glenallen Hill	13
10.	Joe Adcock	12
	Bob Cerv	12
	Jose Morales	12
	Graig Nettles	12
14.	Jeff Burroughs	11
	Jay Johnstone	11
	Candy Maldonado	11
	Fred Whitfield	11
	Cy Williams	11
19.	10 tied with 10	

GRAND SLAMS

1.	Lou Gehrig	23
2.	Eddie Murray	19
3.	Willie McCovey	18
4.	Jimmie Foxx	17
	Ted Williams	17
6.	Hank Aaron	16
	Dave Kingman	16
	Babe Ruth	16
9.	Gil Hodges	14
	Robin Ventura	14
11.	Harold Baines	13
	Albert Belle	13
	Joe DiMaggio	13
	George Foster	13
	Ken Griffey Jr.	13
	Ralph Kiner	13
	Mark McGwire	13
	Manny Ramirez	13
19.	Ernie Banks	12
	Don Baylor	12
	Rogers Hornsby	12
	Mike Piazza	12
	Joe Rudi	12
	Rudy York	12

MULTIPLE-HOME RUN GAMES

1.	Babe Ruth	72
2.	Mark McGwire	64
3.	Willie Mays	63
4.	Hank Aaron	62
5.	Jimmie Foxx	55
6.	Frank Robinson	54
7.	Eddie Mathews	49
	Mel Ott	49
9.	Barry Bonds	46
	Harmon Killebrew	46
	Mickey Mantle	46
12.	Ken Griffey Jr.	44
	Willie McCovey	44
	Mike Schmidt	44
15.	Dave Kingman	43
16.	Ernie Banks	42
	Lou Gehrig	42
	Reggie Jackson	42
	Sammy Sosa	42
20.	Ralph Kiner	40

MOST HOMERS PER AT-BAT

1.	Mark McGwire	.094
2.	Babe Ruth	.085
3.	Ralph Kiner	.071
4.	Harmon Killebrew	.070
5.	Ken Griffey Jr.	.069
6.	Juan Gonzalez	.068
	Manny Ramirez	.068
	Ted Williams	.068
9.	Mike Piazza	.067
10.	Barry Bonds	.066
	Dave Kingman	.066
	Mickey Mantle	.066
	Jimmie Foxx	.066
	Mike Schmidt	.066
	Jose Canseco	.066
	Sammy Sosa	.066
17.	Albert Belle	.065
18.	Jim Thome	.064
	Hank Greenberg	.064
	Willie McCovey	.064

TOTAL BASES

1.	Hank Aaron	6,856
2.	Stan Musial	6,134
3.	Willie Mays	6,066
4.	Ty Cobb	5,854
5.	Babe Ruth	5,793
6.	Pete Rose	5,752
7.	Carl Yastrzemski	5,539
8.	Eddie Murray	5,397
9.	Frank Robinson	5,373
10.	Dave Winfield	5,221
11.	Tris Speaker	5,101
12.	Lou Gehrig	5,060
13.	George Brett	5,044
14.	Mel Ott	5,041
15.	Cal Ripken	4,996
16.	Jimmie Foxx	4,956
17.	Ted Williams	4,884
18.	Honus Wagner	4,870
19.	Paul Molitor	4,854
20.	Al Kaline	4,852

300-TOTAL BASE SEASONS

1.	Hank Aaron	15
2.	Lou Gehrig	13
	Willie Mays	13
	Stan Musial	13
5.	Babe Ruth	11
6.	Jimmie Foxx	10
7.	Joe DiMaggio	9
	Billy Williams	9
	Ted Williams	9
10.	Rogers Hornsby	8
	Frank Robinson	8
12.	Hank Greenberg	7
	Mel Ott	7
	Rafael Palmeiro	7
	Paul Waner	7
16.	20 tied with 6	

SLUGGING PERCENTAGE

(Minimum 2,000 total bases)

1.	Babe Ruth	.690
2.	Ted Williams	.634
3.	Lou Gehrig	.632
4.	Jimmie Foxx	.609
5.	Hank Greenberg	.605
6.	Mark McGwire	.593
7.	Manny Ramirez	.592
8.	Mike Piazza	.580
9.	Joe DiMaggio	.579
	Frank Thomas	.579
11.	Rogers Hornsby	.577
12.	Ken Griffey Jr.	.568
13.	Barry Bonds	.567
14.	Juan Gonzalez	.566
15.	Albert Belle	.564
16.	Larry Walker	.563
17.	Johnny Mize	.562
18.	Stan Musial	.559
19.	Willie Mays	.557
	Mickey Mantle	.557

EXTRA-BASE HITS

1.	Hank Aaron	1,477
2.	Stan Musial	1,377
3.	Babe Ruth	1,356
4.	Willie Mays	1,323
5.	Lou Gehrig	1,190
6.	Frank Robinson	1,186
7.	Carl Yastrzemski	1,157
8.	Ty Cobb	1,136
9.	Tris Speaker	1,131
10.	George Brett	1,119
11.	Jimmie Foxx	1,117
	Ted Williams	1,117
13.	Eddie Murray	1,099
14.	Dave Winfield	1,093
15.	Reggie Jackson	1,075
16.	Mel Ott	1,071
17.	Cal Ripken	1,048
18.	Pete Rose	1,041
19.	Andre Dawson	1,039
20.	Mike Schmidt	1,015

RUNS BATTED IN

1.	Hank Aaron	2,297
2.	Babe Ruth	2,213
3.	Lou Gehrig	1,995
4.	Stan Musial	1,951
5.	Ty Cobb	1,938
6.	Jimmie Foxx	1,922
7.	Eddie Murray	1,917
8.	Willie Mays	1,903
9.	Cap Anson	1,880
10.	Mel Ott	1,860
11.	Carl Yastrzemski	1,844
12.	Ted Williams	1,839
13.	Dave Winfield	1,833
14.	Al Simmons	1,827
15.	Frank Robinson	1,812
16.	Honus Wagner	1,733
17.	Reggie Jackson	1,702
18.	Tony Perez	1,652
19.	Ernie Banks	1,636
20.	Cal Ripken	1,627

RBIs, RIGHTHANDER

1.	Hank Aaron	2,297
2.	Jimmie Foxx	1,922
3.	Willie Mays	1,903
4.	Cap Anson	1,880
5.	Dave Winfield	1,833
6.	Al Simmons	1,827
7.	Frank Robinson	1,812
8.	Honus Wagner	1,733
9.	Tony Perez	1,652
10.	Ernie Banks	1,636
11.	Cal Ripken	1,627
12.	Nap Lajoie	1,599
13.	Mike Schmidt	1,595
14.	Andre Dawson	1,591
15.	Rogers Hornsby	1,584
	Harmon Killebrew	1,584
17.	Al Kaline	1,583
18.	Harry Heilmann	1,539
19.	Joe DiMaggio	1,537
20.	Ed Delahanty	1,466

RBIs, LEFTHANDER

1.	Babe Ruth	2,213
2.	Lou Gehrig	1,995
3.	Stan Musial	1,951
4.	Ty Cobb	1,938
5.	Mel Ott	1,860
6.	Carl Yastrzemski	1,844
7.	Ted Williams	1,839
8.	Reggie Jackson	1,702
9.	Harold Baines	1,622
10.	Goose Goslin	1,609
11.	George Brett	1,595
12.	Jake Beckley	1,577
13.	Willie McCovey	1,555
14.	Willie Stargell	1,540
15.	Tris Speaker	1,529
16.	Sam Crawford	1,525
17.	Dave Parker	1,493
18.	Billy Williams	1,475
19.	Rusty Staub	1,466
20.	Eddie Mathews	1,453

RBIs, SWITCH HITTER

1.	Eddie Murray	1,917
2.	Mickey Mantle	1,509
3.	George Davis	1,439
4.	Ted Simmons	1,389
5.	Chili Davis	1,372
6.	Pete Rose	1,314
7.	Frankie Frisch	1,244
8.	Bobby Bonilla	1,152
9.	Reggie Smith	1,092
10.	Ken Singleton	1,065
11.	Ruben Sierra	1,054
12.	John Anderson	976
13.	Tim Raines	964
14.	Terry Pendleton	946
15.	Ken Caminiti	942
16.	Tommy Tucker	932
17.	Roberto Alomar	918
18.	Duke Farrell	915
19.	Willie McGee	856
20.	Augie Galan	830

100-RBI SEASONS

1.	Jimmie Foxx	13
	Lou Gehrig	13
	Babe Ruth	13
4.	Al Simmons	12
5.	Hank Aaron	11
	Goose Goslin	11
7.	Joe Carter	10
	Willie Mays	10
	Stan Musial	10
10.	Albert Belle	9
	Barry Bonds	9
	Joe DiMaggio	9
	Harmon Killebrew	9
	Mel Ott	9
	Mike Schmidt	9
	Frank Thomas	9
	Honus Wagner	9
	Ted Williams	9
19.	11 tied with 8	

WALKS

1.	Babe Ruth	2,062
2.	Rickey Henderson	2,060
3.	Ted Williams	2,019
4.	Joe Morgan	1,865
5.	Carl Yastrzemski	1,845
6.	Mickey Mantle	1,733
7.	Mel Ott	1,708
8.	Eddie Yost	1,614
9.	Darrell Evans	1,605
10.	Stan Musial	1,599
11.	Pete Rose	1,566
12.	Harmon Killebrew	1,559
13.	Barry Bonds	1,547
14.	Lou Gehrig	1,508
15.	Mike Schmidt	1,507
16.	Eddie Collins	1,499
17.	Willie Mays	1,464
18.	Jimmie Foxx	1,452
19.	Eddie Mathews	1,444
20.	Frank Robinson	1,420

The majority of outfielder Rickey Henderson's 1,334 career stolen bases came during his four stints with the Oakland A's.

100-WALK SEASONS

1.	Babe Ruth	13
2.	Lou Gehrig	11
	Ted Williams	11
4.	Mickey Mantle	10
	Mel Ott	10
6.	Frank Thomas	9
7.	Barry Bonds	8
	Joe Morgan	8
	Eddie Yost	8
10.	Max Bishop	7
	Jimmie Foxx	7
	Rickey Henderson	7
	Harmon Killebrew	7
	Mike Schmidt	7
	Roy Thomas	7
16.	Harlond Clift	6
	Eddie Joost	6
	Ralph Kiner	6
	Eddie Stanky	6
	Gene Tenace	6
	Jimmy Wynn	6
	Carl Yastrzemski	6

INTENTIONAL WALKS

1.	Barry Bonds	320
2.	Hank Aaron	293
3.	Willie McCovey	260
4.	George Brett	229
5.	Willie Stargell	227
6.	Eddie Murray	222
7.	Frank Robinson	218
8.	Tony Gwynn	202
9.	Mike Schmidt	201
10.	Ernie Banks	198
11.	Rusty Staub	193
12.	Willie Mays	192
13.	Carl Yastrzemski	190
14.	Chili Davis	188
	Ted Simmons	188
16.	Harold Baines	187
	Ken Griffey Jr.	187
18.	Billy Williams	182
19.	Wade Boggs	180
20.	Dave Winfield	172

STRIKEOUTS

1.	Reggie Jackson	2,597
2.	Willie Stargell	1,936
3.	Mike Schmidt	1,883
4.	Jose Canseco	1,867
	Tony Perez	1,867
6.	Dave Kingman	1,816
7.	Bobby Bonds	1,757
8.	Dale Murphy	1,748
9.	Andres Galarraga	1,741
10.	Lou Brock	1,730
11.	Mickey Mantle	1,710
12.	Harmon Killebrew	1,699
13.	Chili Davis	1,698
14.	Dwight Evans	1,697
15.	Dave Winfield	1,686
16.	Gary Gaetti	1,602
17.	Fred McGriff	1,592
18.	Lee May	1,570
19.	Dick Allen	1,556
20.	Willie McCovey	1,550

100-STRIKEOUT SEASONS

1.	Reggie Jackson	18
2.	Dave Kingman	13
	Willie Stargell	13
4.	Fred McGriff	12
	Mike Schmidt	12
6.	Jose Canseco	11
	Dale Murphy	11
8.	Dick Allen	10
	Bobby Bonds	10
	Frank Howard	10
	Ray Lankford	10
	Greg Luzinski	10
	Lee May	10
	Tony Perez	10
15.	Lou Brock	9
	Travis Fryman	9
	Andres Galarraga	9
	Mark McGwire	9
	Danny Tartabull	9
20.	13 tied with 8	

HIT BY PITCH

1.	Hughie Jennings	287
2.	Tommy Tucker	272
3.	Don Baylor	267
4.	Ron Hunt	243
5.	Dan McGann	230
6.	Frank Robinson	198
7.	Minnie Minoso	192
8.	Jake Beckley	183
9.	Curt Welch	173
10.	Craig Biggio	169
11.	Kid Elberfeld	165
12.	Fred Clarke	154
	Andres Galarraga	154
14.	Chet Lemon	151
15.	Brady Anderson	144
16.	Carlton Fisk	143
17.	Nellie Fox	142
18.	Art Fletcher	141
19.	Bill Dahlen	140
20.	Frank Chance	137

STOLEN BASES

1.	Rickey Henderson	1,370
2.	Lou Brock	938
3.	Billy Hamilton	912
4.	Ty Cobb	892
5.	Tim Raines	807
6.	Vince Coleman	752
7.	Eddie Collins	745
8.	Arlie Latham	742
9.	Max Carey	738
10.	Honus Wagner	723
11.	Joe Morgan	689
12.	Willie Wilson	668
13.	Tom Brown	657
14.	Bert Campaneris	649
15.	Otis Nixon	620
16.	George Davis	619
17.	Dummy Hoy	596
18.	Maury Wills	586
19.	George Van Haltren	583
20.	Ozzie Smith	580

CAUGHT STEALING

1.	Rickey Henderson	326
2.	Lou Brock	307
3.	Brett Butler	257
4.	Maury Wills	208
5.	Bert Campaneris	199
6.	Rod Carew	187
7.	Otis Nixon	186
8.	Omar Moreno	182
9.	Cesar Cedeno	179
10.	Ty Cobb	178
	Steve Sax	178
12.	Vince Coleman	177
13.	Eddie Collins	173
14.	Bobby Bonds	169
15.	Joe Morgan	162
	Billy North	162
17.	Pete Rose	149
18.	Ozzie Smith	148
19.	Tim Raines	146
20.	Luis Polonia	145

STEAL PERCENTAGE

1.	Tony Womack	85.97
2.	Tim Raines	84.68
3.	Eric Davis	84.26
4.	Barry Larkin	83.49
5.	Willie Wilson	83.29
6.	Davey Lopes	83.01
7.	Stan Javier	82.46
8.	Julio Cruz	81.47
9.	Joe Morgan	80.96
10.	Vince Coleman	80.95
11.	Rickey Henderson	80.78
12.	Roberto Alomar	80.62
13.	Brian Hunter	80.60
14.	Andy Van Slyke	80.59
15.	Kenny Lofton	80.24
16.	Lenny Dykstra	79.83
17.	Ozzie Smith	79.67
18.	Gary Redus	79.51
19.	Paul Molitor	79.37
20.	Marquis Grissom	79.29

50-STEAL SEASONS

1.	Rickey Henderson	13
2.	Lou Brock	12
3.	Billy Hamilton	9
	Arlie Latham	9
5.	Ty Cobb	8
	Tim Raines	8
7.	Bert Campaneris	7
	Vince Coleman	7
9.	Tom Brown	6
	Max Carey	6
	Cesar Cedeno	6
	Eddie Collins	6
	Kenny Lofton	6
	Harry Stovey	6
	Curt Welch	6
16.	Ned Hanlon	5
	Dummy Hoy	5
	King Kelly	5
	Omar Moreno	5
	Joe Morgan	5
	Otis Nixon	5
	Honus Wagner	5
	John Ward	5
	Maury Wills	5

STEALS OF HOME

1.	Ty Cobb	50
2.	Max Carey	33
3.	George J. Burns	28
4.	Honus Wagner	27
5.	Sherry Magee	23
	Frank Schulte	23
7.	Johnny Evers	21
8.	George Sisler	20
9.	Frankie Frisch	19
	Jackie Robinson	19
11.	Jimmy Sheckard	18
	Tris Speaker	18
	Joe Tinker	18
14.	Rod Carew	17
	Eddie Collins	17
	Larry Doyle	17
17.	Tommy Leach	16
18.	Ben Chapman	15
	Fred Clarke	15
	Lou Gehrig	15

PITCHING

GAMES

1.	Jesse Orosco	1,096
2.	Dennis Eckersley	1,071
3.	Hoyt Wilhelm	1,070
4.	Kent Tekulve	1,050
5.	Lee Smith	1,022
6.	Rich Gossage	1,002
7.	Lindy McDaniel	987
8.	Rollie Fingers	944
9.	John Franco	940
10.	Gene Garber	931
11.	Cy Young	906
12.	Sparky Lyle	899
13.	Jim Kaat	898
14.	Paul Assenmacher	884
	Dan Plesac	884
16.	Jeff Reardon	880
17.	Don McMahon	874
18.	Phil Niekro	864
19.	Charlie Hough	858
20.	Roy Face	848

GAMES STARTED

1.	Cy Young	815
2.	Nolan Ryan	773
3.	Don Sutton	756
4.	Phil Niekro	716
5.	Steve Carlton	709
6.	Tommy John	700
7.	Gaylord Perry	690
8.	Bert Blyleven	685
9.	Pud Galvin	681
10.	Walter Johnson	666
11.	Warren Spahn	665
12.	Tom Seaver	647
13.	Jim Kaat	625
14.	Frank Tanana	616
15.	Early Wynn	612
16.	Robin Roberts	609
17.	Grover Alexander	600
18.	Fergie Jenkins	594
	Tim Keefe	594
20.	Dennis Martinez	562
	Kid Nichols	562

COMPLETE GAMES

1.	Cy Young	749
2.	Pud Galvin	639
3.	Tim Keefe	554
4.	Kid Nichols	532
5.	Walter Johnson	531
6.	Mickey Welch	525
7.	Charles Radbourn	489
8.	John Clarkson	485
9.	Tony Mullane	468
10.	Jim McCormick	466
11.	Gus Weyhing	449
12.	Grover Alexander	437
13.	Christy Mathewson	435
14.	Jack Powell	422
15.	Eddie Plank	410
16.	Will White	394
17.	Amos Rusie	393
18.	Vic Willis	388
19.	Warren Spahn	382
20.	Jim Whitney	377

OPENING DAY STARTS

1.	Tom Seaver	16
2.	Steve Carlton	14
	Walter Johnson	14
	Jack Morris	14
5.	Robin Roberts	13
	Cy Young	13
7.	Grover Alexander	12
	Bert Blyleven	12
9.	Fergie Jenkins	11
	Dennis Martinez	11
11.	Roger Clemens	10
	Bob Gibson	10
	Juan Marichal	10
	George Mullin	10
	Warren Spahn	10
16.	Phil Niekro	9
	Gaylord Perry	9

	Steve Rogers	9
	Nolan Ryan	9
	Rick Sutcliffe	9
	Don Sutton	9

INNINGS PITCHED

1.	Cy Young	7,356.0
2.	Pud Galvin	5,941.1
3.	Walter Johnson	5,914.2
4.	Phil Niekro	5,404.1
5.	Nolan Ryan	5,386.0
6.	Gaylord Perry	5,350.1
7.	Don Sutton	5,282.1
8.	Warren Spahn	5,243.2
9.	Steve Carlton	5,217.1
10.	Grover Alexander	5,190.0
11.	Kid Nichols	5,066.1
12.	Tim Keefe	5,049.2
13.	Bert Blyleven	4,970.0
14.	Mickey Welch	4,802.0
15.	Christy Mathewson	4,788.2
16.	Tom Seaver	4,782.2
17.	Tommy John	4,710.1
18.	Robin Roberts	4,688.2
19.	Early Wynn	4,564.0
20.	John Clarkson	4,536.1

INNINGS PITCHED, STARTER

1.	Cy Young	7,034.2
2.	Pud Galvin	5,872.2
3.	Walter Johnson	5,550.1
4.	Nolan Ryan	5,326.0
5.	Don Sutton	5,248.1
6.	Steve Carlton	5,165.0
7.	Gaylord Perry	5,161.2
8.	Phil Niekro	5,149.1
9.	Warren Spahn	5,106.2
10.	Tim Keefe	5,021.1
11.	Grover Alexander	4,983.1
12.	Bert Blyleven	4,957.1
13.	Kid Nichols	4,891.1
14.	Tom Seaver	4,776.0
15.	Mickey Welch	4,749.0
16.	Christy Mathewson	4,753.1
17.	Tommy John	4,622.0
18.	Robin Roberts	4,567.1
19.	John Clarkson	4,491.1
20.	Charles Radbourn	4,419.0

INNINGS PITCHED, RELIEVER

1.	Hoyt Wilhelm	1,871.0
2.	Lindy McDaniel	1,694.0
3.	Rich Gossage	1,556.2
4.	Rollie Fingers	1,500.1
5.	Gene Garber	1,452.2
6.	Kent Tekulve	1,436.1
7.	Sparky Lyle	1,390.1
8.	Tug McGraw	1,301.1
9.	Don McMahon	1,297.0
10.	Mike Marshall	1,259.1
11.	Lee Smith	1,252.1
12.	Tom Burgmeier	1,248.2
13.	Roy Face	1,212.1
14.	Clay Carroll	1,204.2
15.	Jesse Orosco	1,200.0
16.	Eddie Fisher	1,186.0
17.	Bill Campbell	1,177.1
18.	Ron Perranoski	1,170.2
19.	Bob Stanley	1,157.0
20.	Jeff Reardon	1,132.1

200-INNING SEASONS

1.	Don Sutton	20
2.	Phil Niekro	19
	Cy Young	19
4.	Walter Johnson	18
5.	Gaylord Perry	17
	Warren Spahn	17
7.	Grover Alexander	16
	Bert Blyleven	16
	Steve Carlton	16
	Tom Seaver	16
11.	Eddie Plank	15
	Jack Powell	15
13.	Jim Kaat	14
	Christy Mathewson	14
	Robin Roberts	14
	Red Ruffing	14
	Nolan Ryan	14
	Early Wynn	14
19.	10 tied with 13	

300-INNING SEASONS

1.	Cy Young	16
2.	Kid Nichols	12
3.	Pud Galvin	11
	Christy Mathewson	11
5.	Tim Keefe	10
6.	Grover Alexander	9
	Walter Johnson	9
	Joe McGinnity	9
	Mickey Welch	9
	Gus Weyhing	9
11.	John Clarkson	8
	Jim McCormick	8
	Tony Mullane	8
	Charles Radbourn	8

Giants manager John McGraw (left) and pitching ace Christy Mathewson, who posted 373 career victories.

	Amos Rusie	8
	Jim Whitney	8
	Vic Willis	8
18.	Charlie Buffinton	7
19.	12 tied with 6	

LOWEST ERA

(Minimum 1,500 innings)

1.	Ed Walsh	1.82
2.	Addie Joss	1.89
3.	Mordecai Brown	2.06
4.	John Ward	2.10
5.	Christy Mathewson	2.13
6.	Rube Waddell	2.16
7.	Walter Johnson	2.17
8.	Orval Overall	2.23
9.	Tommy Bond	2.25
10.	Will White	2.28
	Ed Reulbach	2.28
12.	Jim Scott	2.30
13.	Eddie Plank	2.35
14.	Larry Corcoran	2.36
15.	George McQuillan	2.38
	Ed Killian	2.38
	Eddie Cicotte	2.38
18.	Doc White	2.39
19.	Nap Rucker	2.42
20.	Jeff Tesreau	2.43

VICTORIES

1.	Cy Young	511
2.	Walter Johnson	417
3.	Grover Alexander	373
	Christy Mathewson	373
5.	Warren Spahn	363
6.	Kid Nichols	361
7.	Pud Galvin	360
8.	Tim Keefe	342
9.	Steve Carlton	329
10.	John Clarkson	328
11.	Eddie Plank	326
12.	Nolan Ryan	324
	Don Sutton	324
14.	Phil Niekro	318
15.	Gaylord Perry	314
16.	Tom Seaver	311
17.	Charles Radbourn	309
18.	Mickey Welch	307
19.	Lefty Grove	300
	Early Wynn	300

VICTORIES, RIGHTHANDER

1.	Cy Young	511
2.	Walter Johnson	417
3.	Grover Alexander	373
	Christy Mathewson	373
5.	Kid Nichols	361
6.	Pud Galvin	360
7.	Tim Keefe	342
8.	John Clarkson	328
9.	Nolan Ryan	324
	Don Sutton	324
11.	Phil Niekro	318
12.	Gaylord Perry	314
13.	Tom Seaver	311
14.	Charles Radbourn	309
15.	Mickey Welch	307
16.	Early Wynn	300
17.	Bert Blyleven	287
18.	Robin Roberts	286
19.	Fergie Jenkins	284
	Tony Mullane	284

VICTORIES, LEFTHANDER

1.	Warren Spahn	363
2.	Steve Carlton	329
3.	Eddie Plank	326
4.	Lefty Grove	300
5.	Tommy John	288
6.	Jim Kaat	283
7.	Eppa Rixey	266
8.	Carl Hubbell	253
9.	Herb Pennock	241
10.	Frank Tanana	240
11.	Whitey Ford	236
12.	Jerry Koosman	222
13.	Jerry Reuss	220
14.	Earl Whitehill	218
15.	Mickey Lolich	217
16.	Wilbur Cooper	216
17.	Billy Pierce	211
18.	Vida Blue	209
19.	Tom Glavine	208
20.	Hal Newhouser	207

VICTORIES, RELIEVER

1.	Hoyt Wilhelm	124
2.	Lindy McDaniel	119
3.	Rich Gossage	115
4.	Rollie Fingers	107
5.	Sparky Lyle	99
6.	Roy Face	96
7.	Gene Garber	94
	Kent Tekulve	94
9.	Mike Marshall	92
10.	Don McMahon	90
11.	Tug McGraw	89
12.	Clay Carroll	88
13.	Bob Stanley	85
14.	Jesse Orosco	84
15.	John Franco	82
16.	Bill Campbell	80
	Gary Lavelle	80
18.	Tom Burgmeier	79
	Stu Miller	79
	Ron Perranoski	79

OPENING DAY VICTORIES

1.	Walter Johnson	9
2.	Grover Alexander	8
	Jack Morris	8
4.	Jimmy Key	7
	Tom Seaver	7
6.	John Clarkson	6
	Wes Ferrell	6
	Dwight Gooden	6
	Mickey Lolich	6
	Greg Maddux	6
	Juan Marichal	6
	Kid Nichols	6
13.	Don Drysdale	5
	George Mullin	5
	Jim Palmer	5
	Robin Roberts	5
	Nolan Ryan	5
	Rick Sutcliffe	5
	Lon Warneke	5
	Cy Young	5

20-VICTORY SEASONS

1.	Cy Young	15
2.	Christy Mathewson	13
	Warren Spahn	13
4.	Walter Johnson	12
5.	Kid Nichols	11
6.	Pud Galvin	10

7.	Grover Alexander	9
	Charles Radbourn	9
	Mickey Welch	9
10.	John Clarkson	8
	Lefty Grove	8
	Jim McCormick	8
	Joe McGinnity	8
	Tony Mullane	8
	Jim Palmer	8
	Eddie Plank	8
	Amos Rusie	8
	Vic Willis	8
19.	6 tied with 7	

20 VICTORIES, RIGHTHANDER

1.	Cy Young	15
2.	Christy Mathewson	13
3.	Walter Johnson	12
4.	Kid Nichols	11
5.	Pud Galvin	10
6.	Grover Alexander	9
	Charles Radbourn	9
	Mickey Welch	9
9.	John Clarkson	8
	Jim McCormick	8
	Joe McGinnity	8
	Tony Mullane	8
	Jim Palmer	8
	Amos Rusie	8
	Vic Willis	8
16.	Charlie Buffinton	7
	Clark Griffith	7
	Fergie Jenkins	7
	Tim Keefe	7
	Bob Lemon	7
	Gus Weyhing	7

20 VICTORIES, LEFTHANDER

1.	Warren Spahn	13
2.	Lefty Grove	8
	Eddie Plank	8
4.	Steve Carlton	6
	Jesse Tannehill	6
6.	Tom Glavine	5
	Carl Hubbell	5
	Hippo Vaughn	5
9.	Wilbur Cooper	4
	Mike Cuellar	4
	Lefty Gomez	4
	Noodles Hahn	4
	Dave McNally	4
	Ed Morris	4
	Hal Newhouser	4
	Eppa Rixey	4
	Rube Waddell	4
	Wilbur Wood	4
19.	13 tied with 3	

CONSECUTIVE 20-VICTORY SEASONS

1.	Christy Mathewson	12
2.	Walter Johnson	10
	Kid Nichols	10
4.	Cy Young	9
5.	John Clarkson	8
	Jim McCormick	8
	Joe McGinnity	8
	Amos Rusie	8
9.	Lefty Grove	7
	Tim Keefe	7
	Charles Radbourn	7
	Mickey Welch	7
	Gus Weyhing	7
14.	Mordecai Brown	6
	Bob Caruthers	6
	Pud Galvin	6
	Clark Griffith	6
	Fergie Jenkins	6
	Tony Mullane	6
	Robin Roberts	6
	Warren Spahn	6

30-VICTORY SEASONS

1.	Kid Nichols	7
2.	John Clarkson	6
	Tim Keefe	6
4.	Tony Mullane	5
	Will White	5
	Cy Young	5
7.	Tommy Bond	4
	Larry Corcoran	4
	Silver King	4
	Christy Mathewson	4
	Jim McCormick	4
	Amos Rusie	4
	Mickey Welch	4
	Gus Weyhing	4
15.	Grover Alexander	3
	Bob Caruthers	3
	Pud Galvin	3
	Bill Hutchison	3
	Bobby Mathews	3
	Ed Morris	3
	Charles Radbourn	3

WINNING PERCENTAGE

(Minimum 75 victories)

1.	Spud Chandler	.717
2.	Pedro Martinez	.691
3.	Dave Foutz	.690
	Whitey Ford	.690
5.	Bob Caruthers	.688
6.	Don Gullett	.686
7.	Lefty Grove	.680
8.	Jay Hughes	.675
9.	Joe Wood	.672
10.	Babe Ruth	.671
11.	Bill Hoffer	.667
	Vic Raschi	.667
13.	Larry Corcoran	.665
	Christy Mathewson	.665
15.	Sam Leever	.660
16.	Sal Maglie	.657
17.	Sandy Koufax	.655
18.	Johnny Allen	.654
19.	Randy Johnson	.653
20.	Ron Guidry	.651

CONSECUTIVE VICTORIES

1.	Carl Hubbell	24
2.	Roy Face	22
3.	Rube Marquard	20
	Roger Clemens	20
5.	Tim Keefe	19
6.	Charles Radbourn	18
	Pat Luby	18
8.	Mickey Welch	17
	Johnny Allen	17
	Dave McNally	17
11.	Tim Keefe	16
	Jim McCormick	16
	Bill Donovan	16
	Walter Johnson	16
	Joe Wood	16
	Lefty Grove	16
	Alvin Crowder	16
	Schoolboy Rowe	16
	Ewell Blackwell	16
	Jack Sanford	16
	Tom Seaver	16
	Rick Sutcliffe	16
	Randy Johnson	16

LOSSES

1.	Cy Young	316
2.	Pud Galvin	308
3.	Nolan Ryan	292
4.	Walter Johnson	279
5.	Phil Niekro	274
6.	Gaylord Perry	265
7.	Don Sutton	256
8.	Jack Powell	254
9.	Eppa Rixey	251
10.	Bert Blyleven	250
11.	Robin Roberts	245
	Warren Spahn	245
13.	Steve Carlton	244
	Early Wynn	244
15.	Jim Kaat	237
16.	Frank Tanana	236
17.	Gus Weyhing	232
18.	Tommy John	231
19.	Bob Friend	230
	Ted Lyons	230

LOSSES, RIGHTHANDER

1.	Cy Young	316
2.	Pud Galvin	308
3.	Nolan Ryan	292
4.	Walter Johnson	279
5.	Phil Niekro	274
6.	Gaylord Perry	265
7.	Don Sutton	256
8.	Jack Powell	254
9.	Bert Blyleven	250
10.	Robin Roberts	245
11.	Early Wynn	244
12.	Gus Weyhing	232
13.	Bob Friend	230
	Ted Lyons	230
15.	Fergie Jenkins	226
16.	Tim Keefe	225
	Red Ruffing	225
18.	Bobo Newsom	222
19.	Tony Mullane	220
20.	Jack Quinn	218

LOSSES, LEFTHANDER

1.	Eppa Rixey	251
2.	Warren Spahn	245
3.	Steve Carlton	244
4.	Jim Kaat	237
5.	Frank Tanana	236
6.	Tommy John	231
7.	Jerry Koosman	209
8.	Claude Osteen	195
9.	Eddie Plank	194
10.	Mickey Lolich	191
	Jerry Reuss	191
	Tom Zachary	191
13.	Earl Whitehill	185
14.	Curt Simmons	183
15.	Wilbur Cooper	178
16.	Rube Marquard	177
17.	Larry French	171
18.	Ted Breitenstein	170
19.	Billy Pierce	169
20.	Herb Pennock	162

SAVES

1.	Lee Smith	478
2.	John Franco	420
3.	Dennis Eckersley	390
4.	Jeff Reardon	367
5.	Randy Myers	347
6.	Rollie Fingers	341
7.	John Wetteland	330
8.	Rick Aguilera	318
9.	Tom Henke	311
10.	Rich Gossage	310
11.	Jeff Montgomery	304
12.	Doug Jones	303
13.	Bruce Sutter	300
14.	Trevor Hoffman	271
15.	Roberto Hernandez	266
16.	Rod Beck	260
17.	Todd Worrell	256
18.	Dave Righetti	252
19.	Dan Quisenberry	244
20.	Sparky Lyle	238

SHUTOUTS

1.	Walter Johnson	110
2.	Grover Alexander	90
3.	Christy Mathewson	79
4.	Cy Young	76
5.	Eddie Plank	69
6.	Warren Spahn	63
7.	Nolan Ryan	61
	Tom Seaver	61
9.	Bert Blyleven	60
10.	Don Sutton	58
11.	Pud Galvin	57
	Ed Walsh	57
13.	Bob Gibson	56
14.	Mordecai Brown	55
	Steve Carlton	55
16.	Jim Palmer	53
	Gaylord Perry	53
18.	Juan Marichal	52
19.	Rube Waddell	50
	Vic Willis	50

SHUTOUTS, RIGHTHANDER

1.	Walter Johnson	110
2.	Grover Alexander	90
3.	Christy Mathewson	79
4.	Cy Young	76
5.	Nolan Ryan	61
	Tom Seaver	61
7.	Bert Blyleven	60
8.	Don Sutton	58
9.	Pud Galvin	57
	Ed Walsh	57
11.	Bob Gibson	56
12.	Mordecai Brown	55
13.	Jim Palmer	53
	Gaylord Perry	53
15.	Juan Marichal	52
16.	Vic Willis	50
17.	Don Drysdale	49
	Fergie Jenkins	49
	Luis Tiant	49
	Early Wynn	49

SHUTOUTS, LEFTHANDER

1.	Eddie Plank	69
2.	Warren Spahn	63
3.	Steve Carlton	55
4.	Rube Waddell	50
5.	Tommy John	46
6.	Whitey Ford	45
	Doc White	45
8.	Mickey Lolich	41
	Hippo Vaughn	41
10.	Larry French	40
	Sandy Koufax	40
	Claude Osteen	40
13.	Jerry Reuss	39
14.	Billy Pierce	38
	Nap Rucker	38
16.	Vida Blue	37
	Eppa Rixey	37
18.	Mike Cuellar	36
	Carl Hubbell	36
	Curt Simmons	36

1-0 VICTORIES

1.	Walter Johnson	38
2.	Grover Alexander	17
3.	Bert Blyleven	15
4.	Christy Mathewson	14
5.	Dean Chance	13
	Eddie Plank	13
	Ed Walsh	13
	Doc White	13
	Cy Young	13
10.	Steve Carlton	12
	Stan Coveleski	12
	Gaylord Perry	12
13.	Fergie Jenkins	11
	Kid Nichols	11
	Nap Rucker	11
	Nolan Ryan	11
17.	9 tied with 10	

NO-HIT GAMES

1.	Nolan Ryan	7
2.	Sandy Koufax	4
3.	Larry Corcoran	3
	Bob Feller	3
	Cy Young	3
6.	Al Atkinson	2
	Ted Breitenstein	2
	Jim Bunning	2
	Steve Busby	2
	Carl Erskine	2
	Bob Forsch	2
	Jim Galvin	2
	Ken Holtzman	2
	Tom L. Hughes	2
	Addie Joss	2
	Dutch Leonard	2
	Jim Maloney	2
	Christy Mathewson	2
	Allie Reynolds	2
	Frank Smith	2
	Warren Spahn	2
	Bill Stoneman	2
	Adonis Terry	2
	Virgil Trucks	2
	Johnny Vander Meer	2
	Don Wilson	2

1-HIT GAMES

(No-hit games in parentheses)

1.	Nolan Ryan (7)	12
	Bob Feller (3)	12
3.	Walter Johnson (1)	7
	Addie Joss (1)	7
	Charles Radbourn (1)	7
6.	Mordecai Brown	6
	Steve Carlton	6
8.	Bert Blyleven (1)	5
	Jim Maloney (2)	5
	Jim Palmer (1)	5
	Tom Seaver (1)	5
	Dave Stieb (1)	5
	Ed Walsh (1)	5
	Grover Alexander	5
	Tim Keefe	5
	Don Sutton	5
	Doc White	5

RUNS ALLOWED

1.	Pud Galvin	3,315
2.	Cy Young	3,167
3.	Gus Weyhing	2,796
4.	Mickey Welch	2,556
5.	Tony Mullane	2,523
6.	Kid Nichols	2,478
7.	Tim Keefe	2,469
8.	John Clarkson	2,384
9.	Phil Niekro	2,337
10.	Adonis Terry	2,298
11.	Charles Radbourn	2,275
12.	Nolan Ryan	2,178
13.	Steve Carlton	2,130
14.	Gaylord Perry	2,128
15.	Red Ruffing	2,115
16.	Don Sutton	2,104
17.	Jim McCormick	2,095
18.	Amos Rusie	2,068
19.	Ted Lyons	2,056
20.	Burleigh Grimes	2,050

HITS ALLOWED

1.	Cy Young	7,092
2.	Pud Galvin	6,352
3.	Phil Niekro	5,044
4.	Gaylord Perry	4,938
5.	Kid Nichols	4,924
6.	Walter Johnson	4,913
7.	Grover Alexander	4,868
8.	Warren Spahn	4,830
9.	Tommy John	4,783
10.	Don Sutton	4,692
11.	Steve Carlton	4,672
12.	Eppa Rixey	4,633
13.	Bert Blyleven	4,632
14.	Jim Kaat	4,620
15.	Mickey Welch	4,588
16.	Robin Roberts	4,582
17.	Gus Weyhing	4,576
18.	Ted Lyons	4,489
19.	Tim Keefe	4,432
20.	Burleigh Grimes	4,412

HOME RUNS ALLOWED

1.	Robin Roberts	505
2.	Fergie Jenkins	484
3.	Phil Niekro	482
4.	Don Sutton	472
5.	Frank Tanana	448
6.	Warren Spahn	434
7.	Bert Blyleven	430
8.	Steve Carlton	414
9.	Gaylord Perry	399
10.	Jim Kaat	395
11.	Jack Morris	389
12.	Charlie Hough	383
13.	Tom Seaver	380
14.	Catfish Hunter	374
15.	Jim Bunning	372
	Dennis Martinez	372
17.	Dennis Eckersley	347
	Mickey Lolich	347
19.	Luis Tiant	346
20.	Early Wynn	338

GRAND SLAMS ALLOWED

1.	Nolan Ryan	10
2.	Ned Garver	9
	Milt Pappas	9
	Jerry Reuss	9
	Lee Smith	9
	Frank Viola	9
7.	Willie Blair	8
	Bert Blyleven	8
	Jim Brewer	8
	Roy Face	8
	Bob Feller	8
	Alex Fernandez	8
	Mike Jackson	8
	Jim Kaat	8
	Johnny Klippstein	8
	Lindy McDaniel	8
	Tug McGraw	8
	Jesse Orosco	8
	Gaylord Perry	8
	Frank Tanana	8
	Early Wynn	8

STRIKEOUTS

1.	Nolan Ryan	5,714
2.	Steve Carlton	4,136
3.	Bert Blyleven	3,701
4.	Tom Seaver	3,640
5.	Don Sutton	3,574
6.	Gaylord Perry	3,534
7.	Walter Johnson	3,509
8.	Roger Clemens	3,504
9.	Phil Niekro	3,342
10.	Fergie Jenkins	3,192
11.	Bob Gibson	3,117
12.	Randy Johnson	3,040
13.	Jim Bunning	2,855
14.	Mickey Lolich	2,832
15.	Cy Young	2,803
16.	Frank Tanana	2,773
17.	Warren Spahn	2,583
18.	Bob Feller	2,581
19.	Tim Keefe	2,560
20.	Jerry Koosman	2,556

STRIKEOUTS, RIGHTHANDER

1.	Nolan Ryan	5,714
2.	Bert Blyleven	3,701
3.	Tom Seaver	3,640
4.	Don Sutton	3,574
5.	Gaylord Perry	3,534
6.	Walter Johnson	3,509
7.	Roger Clemens	3,504
8.	Phil Niekro	3,342
9.	Fergie Jenkins	3,192
10.	Bob Gibson	3,117
11.	Jim Bunning	2,855
12.	Cy Young	2,803
13.	Bob Feller	2,581
14.	Tim Keefe	2,560
15.	David Cone	2,540
16.	Christy Mathewson	2,507
17.	Don Drysdale	2,486
18.	Jack Morris	2,478
19.	Luis Tiant	2,416
20.	Dennis Eckersley	2,401

STRIKEOUTS, LEFTHANDER

1.	Steve Carlton	4,136
2.	Randy Johnson	3,040
3.	Mickey Lolich	2,832
4.	Frank Tanana	2,773
5.	Warren Spahn	2,583
6.	Jerry Koosman	2,556
7.	Mark Langston	2,464
8.	Jim Kaat	2,461
9.	Sam McDowell	2,453
10.	Sandy Koufax	2,396
11.	Chuck Finley	2,340
12.	Rube Waddell	2,316
13.	Lefty Grove	2,266
14.	Eddie Plank	2,246
15.	Tommy John	2,245
16.	Vida Blue	2,175
17.	Fernando Valenzuela	2,074
18.	Billy Pierce	1,999
19.	Whitey Ford	1,956
20.	Jerry Reuss	1,907

WALKS

1.	Nolan Ryan	2,795
2.	Steve Carlton	1,833
3.	Phil Niekro	1,809
4.	Early Wynn	1,775
5.	Bob Feller	1,764
6.	Bobo Newsom	1,732
7.	Amos Rusie	1,707
8.	Charlie Hough	1,665
9.	Gus Weyhing	1,570
10.	Red Ruffing	1,541
11.	Bump Hadley	1,442
12.	Warren Spahn	1,434
13.	Earl Whitehill	1,431
14.	Tony Mullane	1,408
15.	Sam Jones	1,396
16.	Jack Morris	1,390
	Tom Seaver	1,390
18.	Gaylord Perry	1,379
19.	Mike Torrez	1,371
20.	Walter Johnson	1,363

HIT BATSMEN

1.	Gus Weyhing	278
2.	Chick Fraser	219
3.	Pink Hawley	210
4.	Walter Johnson	205
5.	Eddie Plank	190
6.	Tony Mullane	185
7.	Joe McGinnity	179
8.	Charlie Hough	174
9.	Clark Griffith	171
10.	Cy Young	163
11.	Jim Bunning	160
12.	Nolan Ryan	158
13.	Vic Willis	156
14.	Bert Blyleven	155
15.	Don Drysdale	154
16.	Bert Cunningham	148
	Adonis Terry	148
18.	Silver King	146
19.	Win Mercer	144
20.	Frank Foreman	142

WILD PITCHES

1.	Tony Mullane	343
2.	Nolan Ryan	277
3.	Mickey Welch	274
4.	Tim Keefe	240
	Gus Weyhing	240
6.	Phil Niekro	226
7.	Mark Baldwin	221
	Will White	221
9.	Pud Galvin	220
10.	Charles Radbourn	214
	Jim Whitney	214
12.	Jack Morris	206
	Adonis Terry	206
14.	Matt Kilroy	203
15.	Tommy John	187
16.	Steve Carlton	183
17.	John Clarkson	182
18.	Charlie Hough	179
	Toad Ramsey	179
20.	Hardie Henderson	178

FIELDING

GOLD GLOVES, PITCHER

1.	Jim Kaat	16
2.	Greg Maddux	11
3.	Bob Gibson	9
4.	Bobby Shantz	8
5.	Mark Langston	7
6.	Phil Niekro	5
	Ron Guidry	5
8.	Mike Mussina	4
	Jim Palmer	4
10.	Harvey Haddix	3

GOLD GLOVES, CATCHER

1.	Johnny Bench	10
2.	Ivan Rodriguez	9
3.	Bob Boone	7
4.	Jim Sundberg	6
5.	Bill Freehan	5
6.	Del Crandall	4
	Charles Johnson	4
	Tony Pena	4
9.	Earl Battey	3
	Gary Carter	3
	Sherm Lollar	3
	Thurman Munson	3
	Tom Pagnozzi	3
	Lance Parrish	3
	Benito Santiago	3

GOLD GLOVES, FIRST BASE

1.	Keith Hernandez	11
2.	Don Mattingly	9
3.	George Scott	8
4.	Vic Power	7
	Bill White	7
6.	Wes Parker	6
	J.T. Snow	6
8.	Steve Garvey	4
	Mark Grace	4
10.	Gil Hodges	3
	Eddie Murray	3
	Rafael Palmeiro	3
	Joe Pepitone	3

GOLD GLOVES, SECOND BASE

1.	Roberto Alomar	9
	Ryne Sandberg	9
3.	Bill Mazeroski	8
	Frank White	8
5.	Joe Morgan	5
	Bobby Richardson	5
7.	Craig Biggio	4
	Bobby Grich	4
9.	Nellie Fox	3
	Davey Johnson	3
	Bobby Knoop	3
	Harold Reynolds	3
	Manny Trillo	3
	Lou Whitaker	3

GOLD GLOVES, THIRD BASE

1.	Brooks Robinson	16
2.	Mike Schmidt	10
3.	Buddy Bell	6
	Robin Ventura	6
5.	Ken Boyer	5
	Doug Rader	5
	Ron Santo	5
8.	Gary Gaetti	4
	Matt Williams	4
10.	Ken Caminiti	3
	Frank Malzone	3
	Terry Pendleton	3
	Tim Wallach	3

GOLD GLOVES, SHORTSTOP

1.	Ozzie Smith	13
2.	Luis Aparicio	9
3.	Mark Belanger	8
.	Omar Vizquel	8
5.	Dave Concepcion	5
6.	Tony Fernandez	4
	Alan Trammell	4
8.	Barry Larkin	3
	Roy McMillan	3
	Rey Ordonez	3

GOLD GLOVES, OUTFIELD

1.	Roberto Clemente	12
	Willie Mays	12
3.	Ken Griffey Jr.	10
	Al Kaline	10
5.	Paul Blair	8
	Barry Bonds	8
	Andre Dawson	8
	Dwight Evans	8
	Garry Maddox	8
10.	Curt Flood	7
	Devon White	7
	Dave Winfield	7
	Carl Yastrzemski	7

UNASSISTED TRIPLE PLAYS

Neal Ball, SS, Indians	7-19-09
*Bill Wambganss, 2B, Indians	10-10-20
George Burns, 1B, Red Sox	9-14-23
Ernie Padgett, SS, Braves	10-6-23
Glenn Wright, SS, Pirates	5-7-25
Jimmy Cooney, SS, Cubs	5-30-27
Johnny Neun, 1B, Tigers	5-31-27
Ron Hansen, SS, Senators	7-30-68
Mickey Morandini, 2B, Phillies	9-20-92
John Valentin, SS, Red Sox	7-8-94
Randy Velarde, 2B, A's	5-29-2000

*World Series game

MANAGERIAL

YEARS AS MANAGER

1.	Connie Mack	53
2.	John McGraw	33
3.	Bucky Harris	29
4.	Sparky Anderson	26
	Gene Mauch	26
6.	Bill McKechnie	25
	Casey Stengel	25
8.	Leo Durocher	24
	Joe McCarthy	24
10.	Walter Alston	23
11.	Tony La Russa	22
12.	Jimmy Dykes	21
	Tom Lasorda	21
	Dick Williams	21
15.	Cap Anson	20
	Clark Griffith	20
	Ralph Houk	20
18.	Fred Clarke	19
	Bobby Cox	19
	Charlie Grimm	19
	Ned Hanlon	19
	John McNamara	19
	Wilbert Robinson	19
	Chuck Tanner	19
	Joe Torre	19

VICTORIES, MANAGER

1.	Connie Mack	3,731
2.	John McGraw	2,763
3.	Sparky Anderson	2,194
4.	Bucky Harris	2,157
5.	Joe McCarthy	2,125
6.	Walter Alston	2,040
7.	Leo Durocher	2,008
8.	Casey Stengel	1,905
9.	Gene Mauch	1,902
10.	Bill McKechnie	1,896
11.	Tony La Russa	1,734
12.	Ralph Houk	1,619
13.	Bobby Cox	1,616
14.	Fred Clarke	1,602
15.	Tom Lasorda	1,599
16.	Dick Williams	1,571
17.	Clark Griffith	1,491
18.	Earl Weaver	1,480
19.	Miller Huggins	1,413
20.	Al Lopez	1,410

TEAMS MANAGED

1.	Frank Bancroft	7
2.	Jack Chapman	6
	Jimmy Dykes	6
	Bob Ferguson	6
	Rogers Hornsby	6
	Tom Loftus	6
	John McNamara	6
	Dick Williams	6
9.	John Clapp	5
	Patsy Donovan	5
	Chuck Dressen	5
	Ned Hanlon	5
	Bucky Harris	5
	Billy Martin	5
	Bill McKechnie	5
	Gus Schmelz	5
	Bill Watkins	5
	Don Zimmer	5

PENNANTS WON, MANAGER

1.	John McGraw	10
	Casey Stengel	10
3.	Connie Mack	9
	Joe McCarthy	9
5.	Walter Alston	7
6.	Miller Huggins	6
7.	Sparky Anderson	5
	Cap Anson	5
	Fred Clarke	5
	Bobby Cox	5
	Ned Hanlon	5
	Frank Selee	5
13.	Frank Chance	4
	Charlie Comiskey	4
	Tom Lasorda	4
	Bill McKechnie	4
	Billy Southworth	4
	Joe Torre	4
	Earl Weaver	4
	Dick Williams	4

WORLD SERIES WON, MANAGER

1.	Joe McCarthy	7
	Casey Stengel	7
3.	Connie Mack	5
4.	Walter Alston	4
	Joe Torre	4
6.	Sparky Anderson	3
	Miller Huggins	3
	John McGraw	3
9.	Bill Carrigan	2
	Frank Chance	2
	Cito Gaston	2
	Bucky Harris	2
	Ralph Houk	2
	Tom Kelly	2
	Tom Lasorda	2
	Bill McKechnie	2
	Danny Murtaugh	2
	Billy Southworth	2
	Dick Williams	2

SERVICE

SERIES PLAYED

Rank	Player	Series
1.	Reggie Jackson	11
2.	Tom Glavine	8
	Richie Hebner	8
	Hal McRae	8
	John Smoltz	8
	Bob Welch	8
7.	Don Baylor	7
	Paul Blair	7
	Rickey Henderson	7
	Rick Honeycutt	7
	David Justice	7
	Greg Maddux	7
	Joe Morgan	7
	Graig Nettles	7
	Jim Palmer	7
	Pete Rose	7
17.	25 tied with 6	

SERIES PITCHED

Rank	Player	Series
1.	Bob Welch	8
	Tom Glavine	8
	John Smoltz	8
4.	Rick Honeycutt	7
	Greg Maddux	7
6.	David Cone	6
	Dennis Eckersley	6
	Don Gullett	6
	Catfish Hunter	6
	Jimmy Key	6
	Tug McGraw	6
	Jim Palmer	6
	Ron Reed	6
	Mark Wohlers	6
14.	25 tied with 5	

BATTING

GAMES

Rank	Player	Games
1.	Reggie Jackson	45
2.	David Justice	41
3.	Terry Pendleton	38
4.	Rickey Henderson	33
5.	Ron Gant	31
	Mark Lemke	31
7.	Jeff Blauser	29
	Chipper Jones	29
	John Olerud	29
10.	Roberto Alomar	28
	Don Baylor	28
	Tino Martinez	28
	Fred McGriff	28
	Hal McRae	28
	Pete Rose	28
16.	Bobby Bonilla	27
	Bob Boone	27
	George Brett	27
	Richie Hebner	27
	Joe Morgan	27
	Devon White	27

HIGHEST AVERAGE

(Minimum 50 at-bats)

Rank	Player	Avg.
1.	Will Clark	.468
2.	Mickey Rivers	.386
	Bernie Williams	.386
4.	Pete Rose	.381
5.	Dusty Baker	.371
6.	Steve Garvey	.356
7.	Brooks Robinson	.348
8.	Devon White	.347
9.	George Brett	.340
10.	Thurman Munson	.339
11.	Tony Fernandez	.338
12.	Bill Russell	.337
13.	Harold Baines	.333
14.	Javy Lopez	.329
15.	Cal Ripken	.328
16.	Chipper Jones	.324
17.	Lenny Dykstra	.323
18.	Derek Jeter	.319
19.	Darrell Porter	.317
20.	Carney Lansford	.316

AT-BATS

Rank	Player	At-Bats
1.	Reggie Jackson	163
2.	David Justice	148
3.	Terry Pendleton	135
4.	Rickey Henderson	123
5.	Pete Rose	118
6.	Ron Gant	117
7.	Roberto Alomar	114
8.	John Olerud	112
9.	Mark Lemke	110
10.	Fred McGriff	109
11.	Chipper Jones	108
12.	Tino Martinez	107
13.	George Brett	103
14.	Don Baylor	96
	Joe Morgan	96
16.	Devon White	95
17.	Paul O'Neill	94
18.	Jeff Blauser	92
19.	Derek Jeter	91
20.	Bobby Bonilla	90
	Steve Garvey	90

RUNS SCORED

Rank	Player	Runs
1.	George Brett	22
	Rickey Henderson	22
3.	David Justice	21
4.	Chipper Jones	19
5.	Jeff Blauser	18
	Fred McGriff	18
	Bernie Williams	18
8.	Ron Gant	17
	Derek Jeter	17
	Pete Rose	17
11.	Reggie Jackson	16
	John Olerud	16
	Devon White	16
14.	Steve Garvey	15
	Chuck Knoblauch	15
	Willie McGee	15
17.	Roberto Alomar	14
	Ron Cey	14
	Will Clark	14
	Lenny Dykstra	14
	Darryl Strawberry	14

HITS

Rank	Player	Hits
1.	Pete Rose	45
2.	Reggie Jackson	37
3.	Roberto Alomar	36
4.	George Brett	35
	Chipper Jones	35
6.	David Justice	34
	Fred McGriff	34
	John Olerud	34
9.	Devon White	33
10.	Steve Garvey	32
	Bernie Williams	32
12.	Mark Lemke	31
13.	Rickey Henderson	30
	Terry Pendleton	30
15.	Will Clark	29
	Derek Jeter	29
	Paul O'Neill	29
18.	Bill Russell	28
19.	Tony Fernandez	27
20.	Don Baylor	26
	Bob Boone	26
	Willie McGee	26

SINGLES

Rank	Player	Singles
1.	Pete Rose	34
2.	Roberto Alomar	29
3.	Chipper Jones	26
	Devon White	26
5.	Bill Russell	25
6.	Bob Boone	24
	Reggie Jackson	24
	Mark Lemke	24
	John Olerud	24
10.	Fred McGriff	23
11.	David Justice	22
	Carney Lansford	22
	Terry Pendleton	22
	Bernie Williams	22
15.	Paul O'Neill	21
16	Tony Fernandez	20
	Steve Garvey	20
	Derek Jeter	20
19.	Harold Baines	19
	Rickey Henderson	19
	Willie McGee	19
	Mickey Rivers	19

DOUBLES

Rank	Player	Doubles
1.	Ron Cey	7
	Will Clark	7
	Richie Hebner	7
	Rickey Henderson	7
	Reggie Jackson	7
	Javy Lopez	7
	Fred McGriff	7
	Hal McRae	7
	Pete Rose	7
	Mike Schmidt	7
11.	Doug DeCinces	6
	Tony Fernandez	6
	Chipper Jones	6
	David Justice	6
	Chuck Knoblauch	6
	Mark Lemke	6
	Greg Luzinski	6
	John Olerud	6
	Tim Raines	6
	Brooks Robinson	6
	Andy Van Slyke	6
	Roy White	6
	Bernie Williams	6

Royals third baseman George Brett, always in top form during the postseason, holds career LCS records for homers, runs scored and triples.

TRIPLES

Rank	Player	Triples
1.	George Brett	4
2.	Mariano Duncan	3
	Keith Lockhart	3
	Kenny Lofton	3
	Willie McGee	3
6.	Johnny Bench	2
	Jeff Blauser	2
	Rickey Henderson	2
	Jose Lind	2
	Davey Lopes	2
	Terry Pendleton	2
	Luis Salazar	2
	Ozzie Smith	2
	Andy Van Slyke	2
15.	82 tied with 1	

HOME RUNS

Rank	Player	HR
1.	George Brett	9
2.	Steve Garvey	8
3.	Darryl Strawberry	7
4.	Reggie Jackson	6
	David Justice	6
	Manny Ramirez	6
	Jim Thome	6
8.	Sal Bando	5
	Johnny Bench	5
	Ron Gant	5
	Greg Luzinski	5
	Gary Matthews	5
	Graig Nettles	5
14.	18 tied with 4.	

TOTAL BASES

Rank	Player	TB
1.	George Brett	75
2.	Pete Rose	63
3.	Reggie Jackson	62
4.	Steve Garvey	61
5.	David Justice	58
6.	Fred McGriff	52
	John Olerud	52
8.	Will Clark	50
	Chipper Jones	50
	Bernie Williams	50
11.	Roberto Alomar	49
12.	Rickey Henderson	47
	Derek Jeter	47
14.	Ron Gant	45
	Darryl Strawberry	45
16.	Johnny Bench	44
	Javy Lopez	44
18.	Greg Luzinski	43
	Paul O'Neill	43
	Devon White	43

SLUGGING PERCENTAGE

(Minimum 50 at-bats)

Rank	Player	Pct.
1.	Will Clark	.806
2.	George Brett	.728
3.	Steve Garvey	.678
4.	Darryl Strawberry	.643
5.	Lenny Dykstra	.629
6.	Manny Ramirez	.619
7.	Bernie Williams	.602
8.	Dusty Baker	.597
9.	Greg Luzinski	.589
10.	Javy Lopez	.579
11.	Jim Thome	.577
12.	Pete Rose	.534
13.	Johnny Bench	.530
14.	Sal Bando	.527
15.	Brooks Robinson	.522
16.	Dave Henderson	.520
17.	Derek Jeter	.516
18.	Ron Cey	.500
	Thurman Munson	.500
20.	Graig Nettles	.494

EXTRA-BASE HITS

Rank	Player	XBH
1.	George Brett	18
2.	Reggie Jackson	13
3.	Will Clark	12
	Steve Garvey	12
	David Justice	12
	Greg Luzinski	12
7.	Johnny Bench	11
	Ron Cey	11
	Rickey Henderson	11
	Javy Lopez	11
	Fred McGriff	11
	Pete Rose	11
13.	Lenny Dykstra	10
	Ron Gant	10
	Richie Hebner	10
	John Olerud	10
	Darryl Strawberry	10
	Bernie Williams	10
19.	Sal Bando	9
	Derek Jeter	9
	Chipper Jones	9
	Hal McRae	9
	Graig Nettles	9
	Willie Stargell	9
	Andy Van Slyke	9

RUNS BATTED IN

Rank	Player	RBI
1.	David Justice	23
2.	Steve Garvey	21
3.	Reggie Jackson	20
4.	George Brett	19
	Graig Nettles	19
6.	Fred McGriff	18
	John Olerud	18
8.	Don Baylor	17
	Ron Gant	17
	Darryl Strawberry	17
11.	Bernie Williams	16
12.	Roberto Alomar	15
	Al Oliver	15
	Paul O'Neill	15
15.	Ron Cey	14
	Terry Pendleton	14
17.	Dusty Baker	13
	Chipper Jones	13
	Mark Lemke	13
	Gary Matthews	13
	Eddie Murray	13
	Tony Perez	13
	Jim Thome	13
	Todd Zeile	13

WALKS

1.	Joe Morgan	23
2.	Chipper Jones	21
	David Justice	21
4.	Rickey Henderson	19
5.	Reggie Jackson	17
6.	Darrell Porter	16
	Bernie Williams	16
8.	Roberto Alomar	15
	Jeff Blauser	15
	Ryan Klesko	15
	Mark Lemke	15
12.	Barry Bonds	14
	Robin Ventura	14
14.	Ron Cey	13
	Chuck Knoblauch	13
	Tino Martinez	13
	John Olerud	13
	Gene Tenace	13
19.	Fred McGriff	12
	Eddie Murray	12

STRIKEOUTS

1.	Reggie Jackson	41
2.	David Justice	27
3.	Ron Gant	26
4.	Tino Martinez	25
5.	Cesar Geronimo	24
6.	Jeff Blauser	23
	Fred McGriff	23
8.	Bobby Grich	22
	Devon White	22
10.	Marquis Grissom	21
	Willie McGee	21
	Darryl Strawberry	21
13.	Mariano Duncan	20
	Rickey Henderson	20
	Derek Jeter	20
	David Justice	20
	Kenny Lofton	20
	Greg Luzinski	20
18.	Chili Davis	19
	Terry Pendleton	19
	Manny Ramirez	19
	Willie Stargell	19

STOLEN BASES

1.	Rickey Henderson	17
2.	Roberto Alomar	11
3.	Davey Lopes	9
4.	Ron Gant	8
	Joe Morgan	8
	Amos Otis	8
	Willie Wilson	8
8.	Kenny Lofton	7
	Omar Vizquel	7
10.	Barry Bonds	6
	Bert Campaneris	6
	Vince Coleman	6
	Kirk Gibson	6
	Derek Jeter	6
	Steve Sax	6
	Walt Weiss	6
17.	Tony Fernandez	5
	Ken Griffey	5
	Marquis Grissom	5
	Chipper Jones	5
	Otis Nixon	5

PITCHING

GAMES

1.	Rick Honeycutt	20
2.	Dennis Eckersley	18
	Randy Myers	18
	Mark Wohlers	18
5.	Armando Benitez	15
	Tug McGraw	15
	John Smoltz	15
	Mike Stanton	15
9.	Jesse Orosco	14
10.	Paul Assenmacher	13
	Dave Giusti	13
	Tom Glavine	13
	Greg Maddux	13
	Jeff Nelson	13
	Alejandro Pena	13
	Ron Reed	13
17.	Tom Henke	12
	Mariano Rivera	12
	John Rocker	12
20.	Steve Avery	11
	Rollie Fingers	11
	Orel Hershiser	11
	Jose Mesa	11
	Duane Ward	11

GAMES STARTED

1.	Tom Glavine	13
	John Smoltz	13
3.	Greg Maddux	12
4.	Catfish Hunter	10
	Dave Stewart	10
6.	Steve Carlton	8
	Roger Clemens	8
	David Cone	8
	Orel Hershiser	8
10.	Steve Avery	7
	Roger Clemens	7
	Doug Drabek	7
	Tommy John	7
	Jim Palmer	7
	Jerry Reuss	7
15.	Mike Cuellar	6
	Don Gullett	6
	Jimmy Key	6
	Dennis Leonard	6
	Jack Morris	6
	Don Sutton	6
	Bob Welch	6

GAMES RELIEVED

1.	Rick Honeycutt	20
2.	Randy Myers	18
	Mark Wohlers	18
4.	Dennis Eckersley	17
5.	Armando Benitez	15
	Tug McGraw	15
	Mike Stanton	15
8.	Jesse Orosco	14
9.	Paul Assenmacher	13
	Dave Giusti	13
	Jeff Nelson	13
	Alejandro Pena	13
13.	Tom Henke	12
	Ron Reed	12
	Mariano Rivera	12
	John Rocker	12
17.	Rollie Fingers	11
	Jose Mesa	11
	Duane Ward	11
20.	Pedro Borbon	10
	Warren Brusstar	10
	Greg McMichael	10
	Mike Timlin	10

COMPLETE GAMES

1.	Jim Palmer	5
2.	Catfish Hunter	3
	Tommy John	3
4.	Mike Boddicker	2
	Kevin Brown	2
	Danny Cox	2
	Mike Cuellar	2
	Doug Drabek	2
	Orel Hershiser	2
	Ken Holtzman	2
	Bruce Hurst	2
	Dennis Leonard	2
	Dave McNally	2
	Jack Morris	2
	Mike Scott	2
	Don Sutton	2
	Tim Wakefield	2
18.	41 tied with 1	

INNINGS PITCHED

1.	John Smoltz	92.1
2.	Tom Glavine	80.1
3.	Greg Maddux	75.1
	Dave Stewart	75.1
5.	Catfish Hunter	69.1
6.	Orel Hershiser	65.1
7.	Jim Palmer	59.2
8.	Steve Carlton	53.2
9.	David Cone	51.0
10.	Don Sutton	49.0
11.	Roger Clemens	48.1
	Doug Drabek	48.1
13.	Tommy John	47.2
14.	Steve Avery	45.1
15.	Mike Cuellar	44.0
16.	Dwight Gooden	42.1
17.	Nolan Ryan	41.1
18.	Don Gullett	40.2
	Jack Morris	40.2
20.	Dave McNally	40.1

LOWEST ERA

(Minimum 30 innings)

1.	Orel Hershiser	1.52
2.	Fernando Valenzuela	1.95
3.	Jim Palmer	1.96
4.	Don Sutton	2.02
5.	Dave Stewart	2.03
6.	Doug Drabek	2.05
7.	Ken Holtzman	2.06
8.	Tommy John	2.08
9.	Juan Guzman	2.27
10.	Dwight Gooden	2.34
11.	Steve Avery	2.38
12.	Orlando Hernandez	2.43
13.	Charles Nagy	2.64
14.	Paul Splittorff	2.68
	Dave McNally	2.68
16.	Tom Seaver	2.84
17.	John Smoltz	2.92
18.	Danny Jackson	2.94
19.	John Tudor	3.00
20.	Mike Cuellar	3.07

VICTORIES

1.	Dave Stewart	8
2.	John Smoltz	6
3.	Juan Guzman	5
4.	Steve Avery	4
	Steve Carlton	4
	David Cone	4
	Tom Glavine	4
	Orlando Hernandez	4
	Orel Hershiser	4
	Catfish Hunter	4
	Tommy John	4
	Bruce Kison	4
	Greg Maddux	4
	Jim Palmer	4
	Don Sutton	4
15.	11 tied with 3	3

LOSSES

1.	Tom Glavine	8
2.	Jerry Reuss	7
3.	Greg Maddux	6
4.	Doug Drabek	5
5.	Doyle Alexander	4
	Todd Stottlemyre	4
7.	Roger Clemens	3
	Alex Fernandez	3
	Gene Garber	3
	Don Gullett	3
	Ken Holtzman	3
	Catfish Hunter	3
	Charlie Leibrandt	3
	Dennis Leonard	3
	Chad Ogea	3
	Zane Smith	3
	Dave Stieb	3
18.	45 tied with 2	

SAVES

1.	Dennis Eckersley	11
2.	Tug McGraw	5
3.	Ken Dayley	4
	Dave Giusti	4
	Randy Myers	4
	Alejandro Pena	4
	Mariano Rivera	4
8.	Rick Aguilera	3
	Steve Bedrosian	3
	Armando Benitez	3
	Pedro Borbon	3
	Rich Gossage	3
	Tom Henke	3
	Jose Mesa	3
	Jeff Reardon	3
	Duane Ward	3
17.	9 tied with 2	

RUNS ALLOWED

1.	Greg Maddux	42
2.	Tom Glavine	36
3.	John Smoltz	33
4.	Catfish Hunter	25
	Jerry Reuss	25
	Todd Stottlemyre	25
7.	Doyle Alexander	23
	Roger Clemens	23
	David Cone	23
10.	Steve Carlton	22
	Jack Morris	22
12.	Nolan Ryan	19
13.	Scott Erickson	18
	Don Gullett	18
	Bob Welch	18
16.	Ed Figueroa	17
	Tommy John	17
	Dave Stewart	17
19.	8 tied with 16	

HITS ALLOWED

1.	Tom Glavine	81
	John Smoltz	81
3.	Greg Maddux	72
4.	Catfish Hunter	57
5.	Steve Carlton	53
6.	Dave Stewart	52
7.	Orel Hershiser	49
8.	Jim Palmer	46
9.	David Cone	45
10.	Larry Gura	43
11.	Roger Clemens	42
12.	Doug Drabek	40
	Tommy John	40
14.	Jack Morris	39
15.	Danny Jackson	38
	Todd Stottlemyre	38
17.	Jimmy Key	37
	Jerry Reuss	37
	Don Sutton	37
20.	Bob Welch	36

HOME RUNS ALLOWED

1.	Catfish Hunter	12
2.	Andy Pettitte	8
	John Smoltz	8
4.	Tom Glavine	7
	Dave McNally	7
	Dave Stewart	7
7.	Doyle Alexander	6
	Steve Blass	6
	Scott Erickson	6
	Greg Maddux	6
	Jim Perry	6
12.	Andy Benes	5
	Steve Carlton	5
	David Cone	5
	Bruce Hurst	5
	Jim Palmer	5
	Tom Seaver	5
	Eric Show	5
	Todd Stottlemyre	5
	Don Sutton	5
	John Tudor	5

TOTAL BASES ALLOWED

1.	Tom Glavine	129
2.	John Smoltz	125
3.	Catfish Hunter	112
4.	Greg Maddux	108
5.	Steve Carlton	85
6.	Dave Stewart	80
7.	Jim Palmer	75
8.	David Cone	69
9.	Andy Pettitte	64
10.	Doyle Alexander	63
	Larry Gura	63
	Todd Stottlemyre	63
13.	Roger Clemens	60
	Orel Hershiser	60
	Jack Morris	60
16.	Dave McNally	59
	Don Sutton	59
18.	Bob Welch	58
19.	Scott Erickson	57
	Jimmy Key	57
	Dennis Leonard	57

STRIKEOUTS

1.	John Smoltz	88
2.	Tom Glavine	57
	Greg Maddux	57
4.	Orel Hershiser	47
5.	Roger Clemens	46
	Jim Palmer	46
	Nolan Ryan	46
8.	David Cone	45
9.	Steve Carlton	39
	Dave Stewart	39
11.	Steve Avery	37
	Catfish Hunter	37
	David Wells	37
14.	Doug Drabek	33
	Dwight Gooden	33
	Orlando Hernandez	33
	Denny Neagle	33
18.	Mike Mussina	31
19.	Dave McNally	30
	Don Sutton	30

WALKS

1.	John Smoltz	34
2.	Tom Glavine	32
3.	Steve Carlton	28
4.	Dave Stewart	25
5.	David Cone	24
6.	Greg Maddux	23
7.	Orel Hershiser	20
8.	Mike Cuellar	19
	Jim Palmer	19
	Fernando Valenzuela	19
11.	Juan Guzman	18
	Catfish Hunter	18
13.	Steve Avery	17
	Jerry Reuss	17
15.	Roger Clemens	16
	Dwight Gooden	16
	Orlando Hernandez	16
	Tug McGraw	16
	Denny Neagle	16
	Dave Stieb	16

SERVICE

SERIES PLAYED

1.	Yogi Berra	14
2.	Mickey Mantle	12
3.	Whitey Ford	11
4.	Joe DiMaggio	10
	Elston Howard	10
	Babe Ruth	10
7.	Hank Bauer	9
	Phil Rizzuto	9
9.	Bill Dickey	8
	Frankie Frisch	8
	Gil McDougald	8
	Bill Skowron	8
13.	Joe Collins	7
	Frankie Crosetti	7
	Carl Furillo	7
	Lou Gehrig	7
	Jim Gilliam	7
	Gil Hodges	7
	Waite Hoyt	7
	Tony Lazzeri	7
	Roger Maris	7
	Pee Wee Reese	7
	Bobby Richardson	7
	Red Ruffing	7

SERIES PITCHED

1.	Whitey Ford	11
2.	Waite Hoyt	7
	Red Ruffing	7
4.	Catfish Hunter	6
	Johnny Murphy	6
	Jim Palmer	6
	Vic Raschi	6
	Allie Reynolds	6
9.	Chief Bender	5
	Joe Bush	5
	David Cone	5
	Don Drysdale	5
	Carl Erskine	5
	Tom Glavine	5
	Lefty Gomez	5
	Don Gullett	5
	Clem Labine	5
	Don Larsen	5
	Ed Lopat	5
	Rube Marquard	5
	Art Nehf	5
	Herb Pennock	5
	Bob Shawkey	5
	John Smoltz	5
	Mike Stanton	5
	Dave Stewart	5
	Ralph Terry	5
	Bob Turley	5

BATTING

GAMES

1.	Yogi Berra	75
2.	Mickey Mantle	65
3.	Elston Howard	54
4.	Hank Bauer	53
	Gil McDougald	53
6.	Phil Rizzuto	52
7.	Joe DiMaggio	51
8.	Frankie Frisch	50
9.	Pee Wee Reese	44
10.	Roger Maris	41
	Babe Ruth	41
12.	Carl Furillo	40
13.	Jim Gilliam	39
	Gil Hodges	39
	Bill Skowron	39
16.	Bill Dickey	38
	Jackie Robinson	38
18.	Tony Kubek	37
19.	Joe Collins	36
	Bobby Richardson	36
	Duke Snider	36

HIGHEST AVERAGE

(Minimum 50 at-bats)

1.	Pepper Martin	.418
	Paul Molitor	.418
3.	Lou Brock	.391
4.	Marquis Grissom	.390
5.	Thurman Munson	.373
	George Brett	.373
7.	Hank Aaron	.364
8.	Frank Baker	.363
9.	Roberto Clemente	.362
10.	Lou Gehrig	.361
11.	Reggie Jackson	.357
12.	Carl Yastrzemski	.352
13.	Earle Combs	.350
14.	Stan Hack	.348
15.	Joe Jackson	.345
16.	Jimmie Foxx	.344
17.	Derek Jeter	.342
18.	Rickey Henderson	.339
19.	Julian Javier	.333
	Billy Martin	.333

AT-BATS

1.	Yogi Berra	259
2.	Mickey Mantle	230
3.	Joe DiMaggio	199
4.	Frankie Frisch	197
5.	Gil McDougald	190
6.	Hank Bauer	188
7.	Phil Rizzuto	183
8.	Elston Howard	171
9.	Pee Wee Reese	169
10.	Roger Maris	152
11.	Jim Gilliam	147
12.	Tony Kubek	146
13.	Bill Dickey	145
14.	Jackie Robinson	137
15.	Bill Skowron	133
	Duke Snider	133
17.	Gil Hodges	131
	Bobby Richardson	131
19.	Pete Rose	130
20.	Goose Goslin	129
	Bob Meusel	129
	Babe Ruth	129

RUNS SCORED

1.	Mickey Mantle	42
2.	Yogi Berra	41
3.	Babe Ruth	37
4.	Lou Gehrig	30
5.	Joe DiMaggio	27
6.	Roger Maris	26
7.	Elston Howard	25
8.	Gil McDougald	23
9.	Jackie Robinson	22
10.	Hank Bauer	21
	Reggie Jackson	21
	Phil Rizzuto	21
	Duke Snider	21
	Gene Woodling	21
15.	Eddie Collins	20
	Pee Wee Reese	20
17.	Bill Dickey	19
	Derek Jeter	19
	Frank Robinson	19
	Bill Skowron	19

HITS

1.	Yogi Berra	71
2.	Mickey Mantle	59
3.	Frankie Frisch	58
4.	Joe DiMaggio	54
5.	Hank Bauer	46
	Pee Wee Reese	46
7.	Gil McDougald	45
	Phil Rizzuto	45
9.	Lou Gehrig	43
10.	Eddie Collins	42
	Elston Howard	42
	Babe Ruth	42
13.	Bobby Richardson	40
14.	Bill Skowron	39
15.	Duke Snider	38
16.	Bill Dickey	37
	Goose Goslin	37
18.	Steve Garvey	36
19.	Gil Hodges	35
	Reggie Jackson	35
	Tony Kubek	35
	Pete Rose	35

SINGLES

1.	Yogi Berra	49
2.	Frankie Frisch	45
3.	Joe DiMaggio	40
	Phil Rizzuto	40
5.	Pee Wee Reese	39
6.	Hank Bauer	34
7.	Eddie Collins	33
	Mickey Mantle	33
	Gil McDougald	33
10.	Tony Kubek	31
	Bobby Richardson	31
12.	Bill Dickey	30
13.	Steve Garvey	29
	Elston Howard	29
15.	Red Rolfe	28
16.	Gil Hodges	27
	Pete Rose	27
18.	Bill Skowron	26
19.	Goose Goslin	25
	Marquis Grissom	25

DOUBLES

1.	Yogi Berra	10
	Frankie Frisch	10
3.	Jack Barry	9
	Pete Fox	9
	Carl Furillo	9
6.	Lou Gehrig	8
	Lonnie Smith	8
	Duke Snider	8
9.	Frank Baker	7
	Lou Brock	7
	Eddie Collins	7
	Rick Dempsey	7
	Hank Greenberg	7
	Chick Hafey	7
	Elston Howard	7
	Reggie Jackson	7
	Marty Marion	7
	Pepper Martin	7
	Danny Murphy	7
	Stan Musial	7
	Terry Pendleton	7
	Jackie Robinson	7
	Devon White	7

TRIPLES

1.	Billy Johnson	4
	Tommy Leach	4
	Tris Speaker	4
4.	Hank Bauer	3
	Bobby Brown	3
	Dave Concepcion	3
	Buck Freeman	3
	Frankie Frisch	3
	Lou Gehrig	3
	Dan Gladden	3
	Mark Lemke	3
	Billy Martin	3
	Tim McCarver	3
	Bob Meusel	3
	Freddy Parent	3
	Chick Stahl	3
	Devon White	3
18.	35 tied with 2	

HOME RUNS

1.	Mickey Mantle	18
2.	Babe Ruth	15
3.	Yogi Berra	12
4.	Duke Snider	11
5.	Lou Gehrig	10
	Reggie Jackson	10
7.	Joe DiMaggio	8
	Frank Robinson	8
	Bill Skowron	8
10.	Hank Bauer	7
	Goose Goslin	7
	Gil McDougald	7
13.	Lenny Dykstra	6
	Roger Maris	6
	Al Simmons	6
	Reggie Smith	6
17.	Johnny Bench	5
	Bill Dickey	5
	Hank Greenberg	5
	Gil Hodges	5
	Elston Howard	5
	Charlie Keller	5
	Billy Martin	5

TOTAL BASES

1.	Mickey Mantle	123
2.	Yogi Berra	117
3.	Babe Ruth	96
4.	Lou Gehrig	87
5.	Joe DiMaggio	84
6.	Duke Snider	79
7.	Hank Bauer	75
8.	Frankie Frisch	74
	Reggie Jackson	74
10.	Gil McDougald	72
11.	Bill Skowron	69
12.	Elston Howard	66
13.	Goose Goslin	63
14.	Pee Wee Reese	59
15.	Lou Brock	57
16.	Roger Maris	56
	Billy Martin	56
18.	Bill Dickey	55
19.	Gil Hodges	54
	Phil Rizzuto	54

SLUGGING PERCENTAGE

(Minimum 50 at-bats)

1.	Reggie Jackson	.755
2.	Babe Ruth	.744
3.	Lou Gehrig	.731
4.	Lenny Dykstra	.700
5.	Al Simmons	.658
6.	Lou Brock	.655
7.	Pepper Martin	.636
	Paul Molitor	.636
9.	Hank Greenberg	.624
10.	Charlie Keller	.611
11.	Jimmie Foxx	.609
12.	Rickey Henderson	.607
13.	Dave Henderson	.606
14.	Hank Aaron	.600
15.	Duke Snider	.594
16.	Dwight Evans	.580
17.	Steve Yeager	.579
18.	Willie Stargell	.574
19.	Billy Martin	.566
20.	Carl Yastrzemski	.556

EXTRA-BASE HITS

1.	Mickey Mantle	26
2.	Yogi Berra	22
	Babe Ruth	22
4.	Lou Gehrig	21
5.	Duke Snider	19
6.	Reggie Jackson	18
7.	Joe DiMaggio	14
	Hank Greenberg	14
9.	Lou Brock	13
	Frankie Frisch	13
	Elston Howard	13
	Bill Skowron	13
	Lonnie Smith	13
14.	Hank Bauer	12
	Goose Goslin	12
	Gil McDougald	12
	Al Simmons	12
18.	Carl Furillo	11
	Dave Henderson	11
	Roger Maris	11
	Frank Robinson	11
	Devon White	11

RUNS BATTED IN

1.	Mickey Mantle	40
2.	Yogi Berra	39
3.	Lou Gehrig	35
4.	Babe Ruth	33
5.	Joe DiMaggio	30
6.	Bill Skowron	29
7.	Duke Snider	26
8.	Hank Bauer	24
	Bill Dickey	24
	Reggie Jackson	24
	Gil McDougald	24
12.	Hank Greenberg	22
13.	Gil Hodges	21
	David Justice	21
15.	Goose Goslin	19
	Elston Howard	19
	Tony Lazzeri	19
	Billy Martin	19
19.	Frank Baker	18
	Charlie Keller	18
	Roger Maris	18

WALKS

1.	Mickey Mantle	43
2.	Babe Ruth	33
3.	Yogi Berra	32
4.	Phil Rizzuto	30
5.	Lou Gehrig	26
6.	Mickey Cochrane	25
	David Justice	25
8.	Jim Gilliam	23
9.	Jackie Robinson	21
10.	Gil McDougald	20
11.	Joe DiMaggio	19
	Gene Woodling	19
13.	Roger Maris	18
	Pee Wee Reese	18
15.	Gil Hodges	17
	Gene Tenace	17
	Ross Youngs	17
18	Pete Rose	16
19.	Bill Dickey	15
	Reggie Jackson	15
	Eddie Mathews	15
	Joe Morgan	15
	Enos Slaughter	15

STRIKEOUTS

1.	Mickey Mantle	54
2.	Elston Howard	37
3.	Duke Snider	33
4.	Babe Ruth	30
5.	Gil McDougald	29
6.	Bill Skowron	26
7.	Hank Bauer	25
8.	Reggie Jackson	24
	Bob Meusel	24
10.	Joe DiMaggio	23
	George Kelly	23
	Tony Kubek	23

New York Yankees lefthander Whitey Ford pitched more innings and won more games than any other pitcher in World Series history.

Rank	Player	Total
	Frank Robinson	23
	Devon White	23
15.	Jim Bottomley	22
	Joe Collins	22
	Gil Hodges	22
	Lonnie Smith	22
19.	Steve Garvey	21
	David Justice	21
	Roger Maris	21
	Tony Perez	21

STOLEN BASES

Rank	Player	Total
1.	Lou Brock	14
	Eddie Collins	14
3.	Frank Chance	10
	Davey Lopes	10
	Phil Rizzuto	10
6.	Frankie Frisch	9
	Honus Wagner	9
8.	Johnny Evers	8
9.	Roberto Alomar	7
	Rickey Henderson	7
	Pepper Martin	7
	Joe Morgan	7
	Joe Tinker	7
14.	Vince Coleman	6
	Chuck Knoblauch	6
	Kenny Lofton	6
	Jackie Robinson	6
	Jimmy Slagle	6
	Bobby Tolan	6
	Omar Vizquel	6
	Maury Wills	6

PITCHING

GAMES

Rank	Player	Total
1.	Whitey Ford	22
2.	Rollie Fingers	16
3.	Allie Reynolds	15
	Mike Stanton	15
	Bob Turley	15
6.	Clay Carroll	14
	Mariano Rivera	14
8.	Clem Labine	13
	Jeff Nelson	13
	Mark Wohlers	13
11.	Waite Hoyt	12
	Catfish Hunter	12
	Art Nehf	12
14.	Paul Derringer	11
	Carl Erskine	11
	Rube Marquard	11
	Christy Mathewson	11
	Vic Raschi	11
19.	8 tied with 10	

GAMES STARTED

Rank	Player	Total
1.	Whitey Ford	22
2.	Waite Hoyt	11
	Christy Mathewson	11
4.	Chief Bender	10
	Red Ruffing	10
6.	Bob Gibson	9
	Catfish Hunter	9
	Art Nehf	9
	Allie Reynolds	9
10.	George Earnshaw	8
	Tom Glavine	8
	Rube Marquard	8
	Jim Palmer	8
	Vic Raschi	8
	John Smoltz	8
	Dave Stewart	8
	Don Sutton	8
	Bob Turley	8
19.	13 tied with 7	

GAMES RELIEVED

Rank	Player	Total
1.	Rollie Fingers	16
2.	Mike Stanton	15
3.	Clay Carroll	14
	Mariano Rivera	14
5.	Jeff Nelson	13
	Mark Wohlers	13
7.	Clem Labine	12
8.	Pedro Borbon	10
	Dan Quisenberry	10
10.	Paul Assenmacher	9
	Hugh Casey	9
	Tug McGraw	9
13.	Ken Dayley	8
	Rich Gossage	8
	Don McMahon	8
	Johnny Murphy	8
	Duane Ward	8
18.	11 tied with 7	

COMPLETE GAMES

Rank	Player	Total
1.	Christy Mathewson	10
2.	Chief Bender	9
3.	Bob Gibson	8
	Red Ruffing	8
5.	Whitey Ford	7
6.	Waite Hoyt	6
	George Mullin	6
	Art Nehf	6
	Eddie Plank	6
10.	Mordecai Brown	5
	Joe Bush	5
	Bill Donovan	5
	George Earnshaw	5
	Walter Johnson	5
	Carl Mays	5
	Deacon Phillippe	5
	Allie Reynolds	5
18.	15 tied with 4	

INNINGS PITCHED

Rank	Player	Total
1.	Whitey Ford	146.0
2.	Christy Mathewson	101.2
3.	Red Ruffing	85.2
4.	Chief Bender	85.0
5.	Waite Hoyt	83.2
6.	Bob Gibson	81.0
7.	Art Nehf	79.0
8.	Allie Reynolds	77.1
9.	Jim Palmer	64.2
10.	Catfish Hunter	63.0
11.	George Earnshaw	62.2
12.	Joe Bush	60.2
13.	Vic Raschi	60.1
14.	Rube Marquard	58.2
15.	Tom Glavine	58.1
16.	George Mullin	58.0
17.	Mordecai Brown	57.2
18.	Carl Mays	57.1
19.	Sandy Koufax	57.0
	Dave Stewart	57.0

LOWEST ERA

(Minimum 30 innings)

Rank	Player	ERA
1.	Harry Brecheen	0.83
2.	Babe Ruth	0.87
3.	Sherry Smith	0.89
4.	Sandy Koufax	0.95
5.	Monte Pearson	1.01
6.	Christy Mathewson	1.06
7.	Eddie Plank	1.32
8.	Rollie Fingers	1.35
9.	Bill Hallahan	1.36
10.	George Earnshaw	1.58
11.	Spud Chandler	1.62
12.	Jesse Haines	1.67
13.	Ron Guidry	1.69
14.	Max Lanier	1.71
15.	Stan Coveleski	1.74
16.	Lefty Grove	1.75
	Orval Overall	1.75
18.	Carl Hubbell	1.79
19.	Ernie Shore	1.82
20.	Waite Hoyt	1.83

VICTORIES

Rank	Player	Total
1.	Whitey Ford	10
2.	Bob Gibson	7
	Allie Reynolds	7
	Red Ruffing	7
5.	Charlie Bender	6
	Lefty Gomez	6
	Waite Hoyt	6
8.	Mordecai Brown	5
	Jack Coombs	5
	Catfish Hunter	5
	Christy Mathewson	5
	Herb Pennock	5
	Vic Raschi	5
14.	19 tied with 4	

LOSSES

Rank	Player	Total
1.	Whitey Ford	8
2.	Joe Bush	5
	Rube Marquard	5
	Christy Mathewson	5
	Eddie Plank	5
	Schoolboy Rowe	5
7.	Chief Bender	4
	Mordecai Brown	4
	Paul Derringer	4
	Bill Donovan	4
	Burleigh Grimes	4
	Waite Hoyt	4
	Charlie Leibrandt	4
	Carl Mays	4
	Art Nehf	4
	Don Newcombe	4
	Bill Sherdel	4
	Dave Stewart	4
	Ed Summers	4
	Ralph Terry	4

SAVES

Rank	Player	Total
1.	Mariano Rivera	7
2.	Rollie Fingers	6
3.	Johnny Murphy	4
	Allie Reynolds	4
	John Wetteland	4
6.	Roy Face	3
	Firpo Marberry	3
	Will McEnaney	3
	Tug McGraw	3
	Herb Pennock	3
	Kent Tekulve	3
	Todd Worrell	3
13.	20 tied with 2	

RUNS ALLOWED

Rank	Player	Total
1.	Whitey Ford	51
2.	Red Ruffing	32
	Don Sutton	32
4.	Chief Bender	28
	Carl Erskine	28
	Burleigh Grimes	28
	Waite Hoyt	28
	Rube Marquard	28
9.	Mordecai Brown	26
	Paul Derringer	26
11.	Allie Reynolds	25
	Bob Shawkey	25
	Dave Stewart	25
14.	Catfish Hunter	24
15.	Don Gullett	23
	Art Nehf	23
	Jim Palmer	23
	Schoolboy Rowe	23
19.	Tommy Bridges	22
	Christy Mathewson	22
	George Mullin	22

HITS ALLOWED

Rank	Player	Total
1.	Whitey Ford	132
2.	Waite Hoyt	81
3.	Christy Mathewson	76
4.	Red Ruffing	74
5.	Chief Bender	64
6.	Allie Reynolds	61
7.	Catfish Hunter	57
8.	Walter Johnson	56
9.	Bob Gibson	55
	Jim Palmer	55
	Don Sutton	55
12.	Tommy Bridges	52
	Rube Marquard	52
	Vic Raschi	52
15.	Lefty Gomez	51
	Ed Lopat	51
17.	Mordecai Brown	50
	Art Nehf	50
	Schoolboy Rowe	50
20.	Joe Bush	49
	Burleigh Grimes	49

HOME RUNS ALLOWED

Rank	Player	Total
1.	Catfish Hunter	9
2.	Don Drysdale	8
	Whitey Ford	8
	Tom Glavine	8
	Burleigh Grimes	8
	Don Newcombe	8
	Gary Nolan	8
	Allie Reynolds	8
	Charlie Root	8
10.	Don Sutton	7
11.	Lew Burdette	6
	Roger Craig	6
	Bob Gibson	6
	Bob Turley	6
14.	15 tied with 5	

TOTAL BASES ALLOWED

Rank	Player	Total
1.	Whitey Ford	184
2.	Christy Mathewson	105
	Allie Reynolds	105
4.	Red Ruffing	104
5.	Waite Hoyt	102
6.	Catfish Hunter	94
7.	Chief Bender	91
8.	Don Sutton	88
9.	Burleigh Grimes	87
10.	Bob Gibson	86
	Rube Marquard	86
12.	Walter Johnson	85
13.	Jim Palmer	82
14.	Vic Raschi	79
15.	Tommy Bridges	78
16.	Schoolboy Rowe	73
	Warren Spahn	73
18.	Jack Morris	70
19.	Ralph Terry	69
20.	4 tied with 68	

STRIKEOUTS

Rank	Player	Total
1.	Whitey Ford	94
2.	Bob Gibson	92
3.	Allie Reynolds	62
4.	Sandy Koufax	61
	Red Ruffing	61
6.	Chief Bender	59
7.	George Earnshaw	56
8.	John Smoltz	52
9.	Waite Hoyt	49
10.	Christy Mathewson	48
11.	Bob Turley	46
12.	Jim Palmer	44
13.	Vic Raschi	43
14.	Jack Morris	40
15.	Tom Glavine	38
16.	Don Gullett	37
17.	Don Drysdale	36
	Lefty Grove	36
	George Mullin	36
20.	7 tied with 35	

WALKS

Rank	Player	Total
1.	Whitey Ford	34
2.	Art Nehf	32
	Allie Reynolds	32
4.	Jim Palmer	31
5.	Bob Turley	29
6.	Paul Derringer	27
	Red Ruffing	27
8.	Burleigh Grimes	26
	Don Gullett	26
10.	Vic Raschi	25
11.	Carl Erskine	24
12.	Bill Hallahan	23
	Dave Stewart	23
14.	Waite Hoyt	22
15.	Chief Bender	21
	Jack Coombs	21
	John Smoltz	21
18.	Joe Bush	20
	David Cone	20
	Tom Glavine	20

ALL-STAR GAME

SERVICE

GAMES SELECTED, PLAYER

1.	Hank Aaron	25
2.	Willie Mays	24
	Stan Musial	24
4.	Mickey Mantle	20
5.	Ted Williams	19
6.	Yogi Berra	18
	Rod Carew	18
	Al Kaline	18
	Brooks Robinson	18
	Carl Yastrzemski	18
11.	Cal Ripken	17
	Pete Rose	17
	Warren Spahn	17
14.	Roberto Clemente	15
	Nellie Fox	15
	Tony Gwynn	15
	Ozzie Smith	15
18.	Ernie Banks	14
	Johnny Bench	14
	Reggie Jackson	14
	Frank Robinson	14

GAMES SELECTED, PITCHER

1.	Warren Spahn	17
2.	Tom Seaver	12
3.	Steve Carlton	10
	Don Drysdale	10
	Whitey Ford	10
	Juan Marichal	10
7.	Jim Bunning	9
	Bob Gibson	9
	Rich Gossage	9
	Carl Hubbell	9
	Early Wynn	9
12.	Bob Feller	8
	Catfish Hunter	8
	Sandy Koufax	8
	Nolan Ryan	8
	Hoyt Wilhelm	8
17.	11 tied with 7	

BATTING

GAMES

1.	Hank Aaron	24
	Willie Mays	24
	Stan Musial	24
4.	Brooks Robinson	18
	Ted Williams	18
6.	Cal Ripken	17
7.	Al Kaline	16
	Mickey Mantle	16
	Pete Rose	16
10.	Yogi Berra	15
	Rod Carew	15
12.	Roberto Clemente	14
	Ozzie Smith	14
	Carl Yastrzemski	14
15.	Ernie Banks	13
	Nellie Fox	13
	Tony Gwynn	13
18.	Johnny Bench	12
	Wade Boggs	12
	Reggie Jackson	12
	Dave Winfield	12

HIGHEST AVERAGE

(Minimum 10 at-bats)

1.	Richie Ashburn	.600
2.	Charley Gehringer	.500
	Ted Kluszewski	.500
4.	Al Simmons	.462
5.	Joe Carter	.455
	Leon Wagner	.455
7.	Ken Griffey Jr.	.435
8.	Billy Herman	.433
9.	Bill Skowron	.429
10.	Sandy Alomar Jr.	.417
11.	Stan Hack	.400
	Andy Pafko	.400
	Bill Terry	.400
14.	Steve Garvey	.393
15.	Bobby Bonilla	.385
	Will Clark	.385
	Ernie Lombardi	.385
18.	Enos Slaughter	.381
19.	Nellie Fox	.368
20.	Kenny Lofton	.364
	Arky Vaughan	.364

AT-BATS

1.	Willie Mays	75
2.	Hank Aaron	67
3.	Stan Musial	63
4.	Cal Ripken	47
5.	Ted Williams	46
6.	Brooks Robinson	45
7.	Mickey Mantle	43
8.	Yogi Berra	41
	Rod Carew	41
10.	Joe DiMaggio	40
11.	Nellie Fox	38
12.	Al Kaline	37
13.	Dave Winfield	36
14.	Carl Yastrzemski	34
15.	Ernie Banks	33
	Pete Rose	33
17.	Roberto Clemente	31
18.	Billy Herman	30
19.	Tony Gwynn	29
20.	5 tied with 28	

RUNS SCORED

1.	Willie Mays	20
2.	Stan Musial	11
3.	Ted Williams	10
4.	Rod Carew	8
5.	Hank Aaron	7
	Joe DiMaggio	7
	Nellie Fox	7
	Steve Garvey	7
	Al Kaline	7
	Joe Morgan	7
	Jackie Robinson	7
12.	Dave Winfield	6
13.	Roberto Alomar	5
	Johnny Bench	5
	Yogi Berra	5
	George Brett	5
	Fred Lynn	5
	Mickey Mantle	5
	Brooks Robinson	5
	Arky Vaughan	5

HITS

1.	Willie Mays	23
2.	Stan Musial	20
3.	Nellie Fox	14
	Ted Williams	14
5.	Hank Aaron	13
	Billy Herman	13
	Brooks Robinson	13
	Dave Winfield	13
9.	Al Kaline	12
	Cal Ripken	12
11.	Steve Garvey	11
12.	Ernie Banks	10
	Johnny Bench	10
	Rod Carew	10
	Roberto Clemente	10
	Charley Gehringer	10
	Ken Griffey Jr.	10
	Mickey Mantle	10
	Carl Yastrzemski	10
20.	Wade Boggs	9
	Joe DiMaggio	9

SINGLES

1.	Willie Mays	15
2.	Nellie Fox	14
3.	Stan Musial	12
4.	Hank Aaron	11
	Billy Herman	11
6.	Al Kaline	9
	Brooks Robinson	9
8.	Wade Boggs	8
	Charley Gehringer	8
	Mickey Mantle	8
	Cal Ripken	8
12.	Johnny Bench	7
	Yogi Berra	7
	Rod Carew	7
	Ken Griffey Jr.	7
	Rickey Henderson	7
	Ted Williams	7
	Carl Yastrzemski	7
19.	8 tied with 6	

DOUBLES

1.	Dave Winfield	7
2.	Ernie Banks	3
	Barry Bonds	3
	Joe Cronin	3
	Joe Gordon	3
	Ted Kluszewski	3
	Tony Oliva	3
	Al Oliver	3
	Cal Ripken	3
	Al Simmons	3
11.	21 tied with 2	

TRIPLES

1.	Willie Mays	3
	Brooks Robinson	3
3.	Rod Carew	2
	Steve Garvey	2
5.	26 tied with 1	

HOME RUNS

1.	Stan Musial	6
2.	Fred Lynn	4
	Ted Williams	4
4.	Johnny Bench	3
	Gary Carter	3
	Rocky Colavito	3
	Harmon Killebrew	3
	Ralph Kiner	3
	Willie Mays	3
10.	Hank Aaron	2
	Roberto Alomar	2
	Ken Boyer	2
	Frankie Frisch	2
	Steve Garvey	2
	Lou Gehrig	2
	Al Kaline	2
	Mickey Mantle	2
	Eddie Mathews	2
	Willie McCovey	2
	Mike Piazza	2
	Frank Robinson	2
	Al Rosen	2
	Arky Vaughan	2

TOTAL BASES

1.	Willie Mays	40
	Stan Musial	40
3.	Ted Williams	30
4.	Steve Garvey	23
5.	Brooks Robinson	22
6.	Dave Winfield	20
7.	Hank Aaron	19
	Johnny Bench	19
	Al Kaline	19
10.	Ernie Banks	18
	Fred Lynn	18
	Cal Ripken	18
13.	Roberto Clemente	17
	Harmon Killebrew	17
15.	Rocky Colavito	16
	Mickey Mantle	16
17.	Rod Carew	15
	Gary Carter	15
	Ken Griffey Jr.	15
	Billy Herman	15
	Arky Vaughan	15
	Carl Yastrzemski	15

SLUGGING PERCENTAGE

(Minimum 10 at-bats)

1.	Ralph Kiner	.933
2.	Ted Kluszewski	.929
3.	Fred Lynn	.900
4.	Steve Garvey	.821
5.	Al Rosen	.818
6.	Gary Carter	.750
7.	George Foster	.727
	Leon Wagner	.727
9.	Mike Piazza	.706
10.	Richie Ashburn	.700
	Larry Doby	.700
12.	Al Simmons	.692
13.	Arky Vaughan	.682
14.	Johnny Bench	.679
15.	Sandy Alomar Jr.	.667
	Mike Schmidt	.667
17.	Harmon Killebrew	.654
18.	Ken Griffey Jr.	.652
	Ted Williams	.652
20.	Rocky Colavito	.640

EXTRA-BASE HITS

1.	Willie Mays	8
	Stan Musial	8
3.	Ted Williams	7
	Dave Winfield	7
5.	Steve Garvey	6
6.	Ernie Banks	5
7.	Barry Bonds	4
	George Brett	4
	Roberto Clemente	4
	Rocky Colavito	4
	Ralph Kiner	4
	Ted Kluszewski	4
	Fred Lynn	4
	Cal Ripken	4
	Brooks Robinson	4
	Mike Schmidt	4
17.	21 tied with 3	

RUNS BATTED IN

1.	Ted Williams	12
2.	Fred Lynn	10
	Stan Musial	10
4.	Willie Mays	9
5.	Hank Aaron	8
	Rocky Colavito	8
7.	Steve Garvey	7
	Cal Ripken	7
9.	Johnny Bench	6
	Joe DiMaggio	6
	Al Kaline	6
	Harmon Killebrew	6
	Joe Medwick	6
14.	Barry Bonds	5
	George Brett	5
	Gary Carter	5
	George Foster	5
	Nellie Fox	5
	Lou Gehrig	5
	Ken Griffey Jr.	5
	Dick Groat	5
	Brooks Robinson	5
	Al Rosen	5
	Dave Winfield	5
	Carl Yastrzemski	5

Yankees All-Star Lefty Gomez.

WALKS

1.	Ted Williams	11
2.	Charley Gehringer	9
	Mickey Mantle	9
4.	Rod Carew	7
	Willie Mays	7
	Stan Musial	7
7.	Lou Gehrig	6
8.	Ron Santo	5
9.	Wade Boggs	4
	George Brett	4
	Bill Dickey	4
	Reggie Jackson	4
	Joe Morgan	4
	Enos Slaughter	4
	Carl Yastrzemski	4
16.	21 tied with 3	

STRIKEOUTS

1.	Mickey Mantle	17
2.	Willie Mays	14
3.	Ted Williams	10
4.	Roberto Clemente	9
	Reggie Jackson	9
	Mark McGwire	9
	Ryne Sandberg	9
8.	Hank Aaron	8
	Ernie Banks	8
	Joe Gordon	8
	Jim Rice	8
	Carl Yastrzemski	8
13.	Dick Allen	7
	Carlton Fisk	7
	Jimmie Foxx	7
	Elston Howard	7
	Stan Musial	7
	Frank Robinson	7
19.	11 tied with 6	

FOR THE RECORD

STOLEN BASES

1.	Willie Mays	6
2.	Roberto Alomar	5
	Kenny Lofton	5
4.	Rod Carew	3
	Steve Sax	3
6.	Hank Aaron	2
	Lou Brock	2
	Charley Gehringer	2
	Kelly Gruber	2
	Rickey Henderson	2
	Tim Raines	2
	Ozzie Smith	2
	Darryl Strawberry	2
14.	52 tied with 1	

PITCHING

GAMES

1.	Jim Bunning	8
	Don Drysdale	8
	Juan Marichal	8
	Tom Seaver	8
5.	Warren Spahn	7
	Dave Stieb	7
	Early Wynn	7
8.	Ewell Blackwell	6
	Roger Clemens	6
	Dennis Eckersley	6
	Whitey Ford	6
	Bob Gibson	6
	Rich Gossage	6
	Catfish Hunter	6
	Randy Johnson	6
15.	15 tied with 5	

GAMES STARTED

1.	Don Drysdale	5
	Lefty Gomez	5
	Robin Roberts	5
4.	Jim Palmer	4
5.	Vida Blue	3
	Jim Bunning	3
	Whitey Ford	3
	Randy Johnson	3
	Greg Maddux	3
	Jack Morris	3
	Billy Pierce	3
	Warren Spahn	3
13.	Steve Carlton	2
	Dean Chance	2
	Mort Cooper	2
	Dizzy Dean	2
	Paul Derringer	2
	Bob Feller	2
	Bob Friend	2
	Tom Glavine	2
	Dwight Gooden	2
	Juan Marichal	2
	Vic Raschi	2
	Red Ruffing	2
	Curt Simmons	2
	Dave Stieb	2
	David Wells	2

GAMES RELIEVED

1.	Tom Seaver	7
2.	Rich Gossage	6
	Juan Marichal	6
	Early Wynn	6
5.	Ewell Blackwell	5
	Jim Bunning	5
	Roger Clemens	5
	David Cone	5
	Dennis Eckersley	5
	Rollie Fingers	5
	Bob Gibson	5
	Catfish Hunter	5
	Dave Stieb	5
14.	18 tied with 4	

INNINGS PITCHED

1.	Don Drysdale	19.1
2.	Jim Bunning	18.0
	Lefty Gomez	18.0
	Juan Marichal	18.0
5.	Robin Roberts	14.0
	Warren Spahn	14.0
7.	Ewell Blackwell	13.2
8.	Mel Harder	13.0
	Tom Seaver	13.0
10.	Catfish Hunter	12.2
	Jim Palmer	12.2
12.	Bob Feller	12.1
	Early Wynn	12.1
14.	Whitey Ford	12.0
15.	Dave Stieb	11.2
16.	Bob Gibson	11.0
	Vic Raschi	11.0
18.	Jack Morris	10.2
	Hal Newhouser	10.2
	Billy Pierce	10.2

1941 All-Star Game hero Ted Williams (left) gets a victory hug from American League manager Del Baker.

LOWEST ERA

(Minimum 9 innings)

	Player	ERA
1.	Juan Marichal	0.50
2.	Mel Harder	0.69
3.	Bob Feller	0.73
4.	Dave Stieb	0.77
5.	Jim Bunning	1.00
	Randy Johnson	1.00
7.	Ewell Blackwell	1.32
8.	Don Drysdale	1.40
9.	Hal Newhouser	1.69
10.	Bucky Walters	2.00
11.	Vic Raschi	2.45
12.	Lefty Gomez	2.50
13.	Jack Morris	2.53
14.	Dizzy Dean	2.70
15.	Carl Hubbell	2.79
16.	Early Wynn	2.92
17.	Warren Spahn	3.21
18.	Bob Gibson	3.27
19.	Billy Pierce	3.38
20.	Nolan Ryan	4.50

VICTORIES

1.	Lefty Gomez	3
2.	Vida Blue	2
	Don Drysdale	2
	Bob Friend	2
	Juan Marichal	2
	Bruce Sutter	2
7.	57 tied with 1	

LOSSES

1.	Mort Cooper	2
	Whitey Ford	2
	Dwight Gooden	2
	Catfish Hunter	2
	Claude Passeau	2
	Luis Tiant	2
7.	58 tied with 1	

SAVES

1.	Dennis Eckersley	3
2.	Mel Harder	2
3.	35 tied with 1	

RUNS ALLOWED

	Player	R
1.	Whitey Ford	13
2.	Robin Roberts	10
	Warren Spahn	10
4.	Tom Glavine	9
	Catfish Hunter	9
6.	Vida Blue	8
	Jim Palmer	8
	Tom Seaver	8
9.	Mort Cooper	7
	Rich Gossage	7
	Atlee Hammaker	7
	Claude Passeau	7
13.	Roy Face	6
	Lefty Gomez	6
	Tex Hughson	6
	Van Mungo	6
	Gaylord Perry	6
	Red Ruffing	6
19.	8 tied with 5	

HITS ALLOWED

	Player	H
1.	Whitey Ford	19
2.	Robin Roberts	17
	Warren Spahn	17
4.	Tom Glavine	15
	Catfish Hunter	15
6.	Jack Morris	14
	Gaylord Perry	14
	Tom Seaver	14
9.	Red Ruffing	13
10.	Vida Blue	12
11.	Bob Gibson	11
	Lefty Gomez	11
	Jim Palmer	11
14.	Dizzy Dean	10
	Don Drysdale	10
	Lefty Grove	10
	Tex Hughson	10
	Nolan Ryan	10
	Bucky Walters	10
	Lon Warneke	10

HOME RUNS ALLOWED

	Player	HR
1.	Vida Blue	4
	Catfish Hunter	4
3.	Steve Carlton	3
	Mort Cooper	3
	Whitey Ford	3
	Jim Palmer	3
	Milt Pappas	3
	Robin Roberts	3
	Tom Seaver	3
10.	20 tied with 2	

STRIKEOUTS

	Player	SO
1.	Don Drysdale	19
2.	Tom Seaver	16
3.	Jim Palmer	14
4.	Jim Bunning	13
	Bob Feller	13
	Catfish Hunter	13
7.	Ewell Blackwell	12
	Juan Marichal	12
	Sam McDowell	12
	Billy Pierce	12
11.	Carl Hubbell	11
	Johnny Vander Meer	11
13.	Dizzy Dean	10
	Bob Gibson	10
	Dick Radatz	10
	Nolan Ryan	10
	Warren Spahn	10
	Dave Stieb	10
19.	4 tied with 9	

WALKS

	Player	BB
1.	Jim Palmer	7
2.	Carl Hubbell	6
	Robin Roberts	6
	Dave Stieb	6
	Lon Warneke	6
6.	Ewell Blackwell	5
	Steve Carlton	5
	Dizzy Dean	5
	Bob Gibson	5
	Bill Hallahan	5
	Nolan Ryan	5
	Warren Spahn	5
13.	16 tied with 4	

SINGLE SEASON

REGULAR SEASON (1876-1900)

BATTING

*HIGHEST AVERAGE

Rank	Player	Avg.
1.	Tip O'Neill, St. Louis A.A., 1887	.485
2.	Pete Browning, Louisville A.A., 1887	.457
3.	Bob Caruthers, St. Louis A.A., 1887	.456
4.	Hugh Duffy, Boston N.L., 1894	.440
5.	Yank Robinson, St. Louis A.A., 1887	.427
6.	Willie Keeler, Baltimore N.L., 1897	.424
7.	Cap Anson, Chicago N.L., 1887	.421
8.	Dan Brouthers, Detroit N.L., 1887	.420
9.	Denny Lyons, Philadelphia A.A., 1887	.415
	Sam Thompson, Philadelphia N.L., 1894	.415
11.	Fred Dunlap, St. Louis U.A., 1884	.412
12.	Reddy Mack, Louisville A.A., 1887	.410
	Ed Delahanty, Philadelphia N.L., 1899	.410
	Jesse Burkett, Cleveland N.L., 1896	.410
15.	Oyster Burns, Baltimore A.A., 1887	.409
16.	Sam Thompson, Detroit N.L., 1887	.407
17.	Jesse Burkett, Cleveland N.L., 1895	.405
18.	Ed Delahanty, Philadelphia N.L., 1895	.404
	Ed Delahanty, Philadelphia N.L., 1894	.404
	Ross Barnes, Chicago N.L., 1876	.404

*Based on players averaging at least 3.1 at-bats for every game played by their teams.

RUNS SCORED

Rank	Player	Runs
1.	Billy Hamilton, Philadelphia N.L., 1894	198
2.	Tom Brown, Boston A.A., 1891	177
3.	Tip O'Neill, St. Louis A.A., 1887	167
4.	Billy Hamilton, Philadelphia N.L., 1895	166
5.	Willie Keeler, Baltimore N.L., 1894	165
	Joe Kelley, Baltimore N.L., 1894	165
7.	Arlie Latham, St. Louis A.A., 1887	163
8.	Willie Keeler, Baltimore N.L., 1895	162
9.	Hugh Duffy, Chicago P.L., 1890	161
10.	Jesse Burkett, Cleveland N.L., 1896	160
	Hugh Duffy, Boston N.L., 1894	160
	Fred Dunlap, St. Louis U.A., 1884	160
13.	Hughie Jennings, Baltimore N.L., 1895	159
14.	Bobby Lowe, Boston N.L., 1894	158
15.	John McGraw, Baltimore N.L., 1894	156
16.	King Kelly, Chicago N.L., 1886	155
17.	Dan Brouthers, Detroit N.L., 1887	153
	Jesse Burkett, Cleveland N.L., 1895	153
	Billy Hamilton, Boston N.L., 1896	153
	Willie Keeler, Baltimore N.L., 1896	153

HITS

Rank	Player	Hits
1.	Pete Browning, Louisville A.A., 1887	275
	Tip O'Neill, St. Louis A.A., 1887	275
3.	Denny Lyons, Philadelphia A.A., 1887	256
4.	Oyster Burns, Baltimore A.A., 1887	251
5.	Arlie Latham, St. Louis A.A., 1887	243
6.	Dan Brouthers, Detroit N.L., 1887	240
	Jesse Burkett, Cleveland N.L., 1896	240
8.	Willie Keeler, Baltimore N.L., 1897	239
9.	Ed Delahanty, Philadelphia N.L., 1899	238
10.	Hugh Duffy, Boston N.L., 1894	237
11.	Paul Radford, New York A.A., 1887	235
	Sam Thompson, Detroit N.L., 1887	235
13.	Reddy Mack, Louisville A.A., 1887	230
14.	Jesse Burkett, Cleveland N.L., 1895	225
	Billy Hamilton, Philadelphia N.L., 1894	225
16.	Cap Anson, Chicago N.L., 1887	224
	Bill McClellan, Brooklyn A.A., 1887	224
18.	Yank Robinson, St. Louis A.A., 1887	223
19.	Frank Fennelly, Cincinnati A.A., 1887	222
	Sam Thompson, Philadelphia N.L., 1893	222

HOME RUNS

Rank	Player	HR
1.	Ned Williamson, Chicago N.L., 1884	27
2.	Buck Freeman, Washington N.L., 1899	25
	Fred Pfeffer, Chicago N.L., 1884	25
4.	Abner Dalrymple, Chicago N.L., 1884	22
5.	Cap Anson, Chicago N.L., 1884	21
6.	Sam Thompson, Philadelphia N.L., 1889	20
7.	Ed Delahanty, Philadelphia N.L., 1893	19
	Bug Holliday, Cincinnati A.A., 1889	19
	Billy O'Brien, Washington N.L., 1887	19
	Harry Stovey, Philadelphia A.A., 1889	19
11.	Jerry Denny, Indianapolis N.L., 1889	18
	Hugh Duffy, Boston N.L., 1894	18
	Sam Thompson, Philadelphia N.L., 1895	18
14.	Jack Clements, Philadelphia N.L., 1893	17
	Roger Connor, New York N.L., 1887	17
	Bill Joyce, Washington N.L., 1894	17
	Bill Joyce, Washington N.L., 1895	17
	Bobby Lowe, Boston N.L., 1894	17
	Jimmy Ryan, Chicago N.L., 1889	17
20.	5 tied with 16	

TOTAL BASES

Rank	Player	TB
1.	Tip O'Neill, St. Louis A.A., 1887	407
2.	Hugh Duffy, Boston N.L., 1894	374
3.	Pete Browning, Louisville A.A., 1887	354
4.	Dan Brouthers, Detroit N.L., 1887	352
	Sam Thompson, Philadelphia N.L., 1895	352
6.	Oyster Burns, Baltimore A.A., 1887	349
7.	Ed Delahanty, Philadelphia N.L., 1893	347
8.	Denny Lyons, Philadelphia A.A., 1887	345
9.	Sam Thompson, Detroit N.L., 1887	340
10.	Ed Delahanty, Philadelphia N.L., 1899	338
11.	Buck Freeman, Washington N.L., 1899	331
12.	Roger Connor, New York N.L., 1887	330
13.	Jimmy Williams, Pittsburgh N.L., 1899	329
14.	Bobby Lowe, Boston N.L., 1894	319
15.	Sam Thompson, Philadelphia N.L., 1893	318
16.	Jesse Burkett, Cleveland N.L., 1896	317
17.	Ed Delahanty, Philadelphia N.L., 1896	315
18.	Sam Thompson, Philadelphia N.L., 1894	314
19.	Nap Lajoie, Philadelphia N.L., 1897	310
20.	Willie Keeler, Baltimore N.L., 1894	305
	Joe Kelley, Baltimore N.L., 1894	305

EXTRA-BASE HITS

Rank	Player	XBH
1.	Hugh Duffy, Boston N.L., 1894	85
	Tip O'Neill, St. Louis A.A., 1887	85
3.	Sam Thompson, Philadelphia N.L., 1895	84
4.	Ed Delahanty, Philadelphia N.L., 1896	74
	Joe Kelley, Baltimore N.L., 1894	74
6.	Ed Delahanty, Philadelphia N.L., 1899	73
	Sam Thompson, Philadelphia N.L., 1894	73
8.	Ed Delahanty, Philadelphia N.L., 1893	72
	Nap Lajoie, Philadelphia N.L., 1897	72
	Jake Stenzel, Pittsburgh N.L., 1894	72
11.	Dan Brouthers, Baltimore N.L., 1894	71
	Honus Wagner, Pittsburgh N.L., 1900	71
13.	Ed Delahanty, Philadelphia N.L., 1895	70
	Harry Stovey, Philadelphia A.A., 1889	70
15.	Jake Beckley, Pittsburgh P.L., 1890	69
	Buck Freeman, Washington N.L., 1899	69
17.	Dan Brouthers, Detroit N.L., 1887	68
	Roger Connor, New York-St. Louis N.L., 1894	68
19.	Harry Stovey, Boston N.L., 1891	67
20.	Dan Brouthers, Detroit N.L., 1886	66

RUNS BATTED IN

Rank	Player	RBI
1.	Sam Thompson, Detroit N.L., 1887	166
2.	Sam Thompson, Philadelphia N.L., 1895	165
3.	Cap Anson, Chicago N.L., 1886	147
	Sam Thompson, Philadelphia N.L., 1894	147
5.	Ed Delahanty, Philadelphia N.L., 1893	146
	Hardy Richardson, Boston P.L., 1890	146
7.	Hugh Duffy, Boston N.L., 1894	145
8.	Ed Delahanty, Philadelphia N.L., 1899	137
9.	George Davis, New York N.L., 1897	136
10.	Steve Brodie, Baltimore N.L., 1895	134
	Joe Kelley, Baltimore N.L., 1895	134
12.	Ed Delahanty, Philadelphia N.L., 1894	133
	Ed McKean, Cleveland N.L., 1893	133
14.	Jimmy Collins, Boston N.L., 1897	132
	Lave Cross, Philadelphia N.L., 1894	132
16.	Roger Connor, New York N.L., 1889	130
	Walt Wilmot, Chicago N.L., 1894	130
18.	Hugh Duffy, Boston N.L., 1897	129
19.	Dan Brouthers, Baltimore N.L., 1894	128
	Oyster Burns, Brooklyn N.L., 1890	128
	Ed McKean, Cleveland N.L., 1894	128

STOLEN BASES

Rank	Player	SB
1.	Hugh Nicol, Cincinnati A.A., 1887	138
2.	Arlie Latham, St. Louis A.A., 1887	129
3.	Charlie Comiskey, St. Louis A.A., 1887	117
4.	Billy Hamilton, Kansas City A.A., 1889	111
	Billy Hamilton, Philadelphia N.L., 1891	111
	John Ward, New York N.L., 1887	111
7.	Arlie Latham, St. Louis A.A., 1888	109
8.	Tom Brown, Boston A.A., 1891	106
9.	Pete Browning, Louisville A.A., 1887	103
	Hugh Nicol, Cincinnati A.A., 1888	103
11.	Jim Fogarty, Philadelphia N.L., 1887	102
	Billy Hamilton, Philadelphia N.L., 1890	102
13.	Billy Hamilton, Philadelphia N.L., 1894	100
14.	Jim Fogarty, Philadelphia N.L., 1889	99
15.	Billy Hamilton, Philadelphia N.L., 1895	97
	Harry Stovey, Boston P.L., 1890	97
17.	Bid McPhee, Cincinnati A.A., 1887	95
	Curt Welch, Philadelphia A.A., 1888	95
19.	Mike Griffin, Baltimore A.A., 1887	94
20.	Tommy McCarthy, St. Louis A.A., 1888	93

PITCHING

COMPLETE GAMES

Rank	Player	CG
1.	Will White, Cincinnati N.L., 1879	75
2.	Charley Radbourn, Providence N.L., 1884	73
3.	Pud Galvin, Buffalo N.L., 1883	72
	Guy Hecker, Louisville A.A., 1884	72
	Jim McCormick, Cleveland N.L., 1880	72
6.	Pud Galvin, Buffalo N.L., 1884	71
7.	John Clarkson, Chicago N.L., 1885	68
	John Clarkson, Boston N.L., 1889	68
	Tim Keefe, New York A.A., 1883	68
10.	Bill Hutchison, Chicago N.L., 1892	67
11.	Jim Devlin, Louisville N.L., 1876	66
	Matt Kilroy, Baltimore A.A., 1886	66
	Matt Kilroy, Baltimore A.A., 1887	66
	Charles Radbourn, Providence N.L., 1883	66
	Toad Ramsey, Louisville A.A., 1886	66
16.	Pud Galvin, Buffalo N.L., 1879	65
	Bill Hutchison, Chicago N.L., 1890	65
	Jim McCormick, Cleveland N.L., 1882	65
19.	4 tied with 64	

INNINGS PITCHED

Rank	Player	IP
1.	Will White, Cincinnati N.L., 1879	680.0
2.	Charles Radbourn, Providence N.L., 1884	678.2
3.	Guy Hecker, Louisville A.A., 1884	670.2
4.	Jim McCormick, Cleveland N.L., 1880	657.2
5.	Pud Galvin, Buffalo N.L., 1883	656.1
6.	Pud Galvin, Buffalo N.L., 1884	636.1
7.	Charley Radbourn, Providence N.L., 1883	632.1
8.	John Clarkson, Chicago N.L., 1885	623.0
9.	Jim Devlin, Louisville N.L., 1876	622.0
	Bill Hutchison, Chicago N.L., 1892	622.0
11.	John Clarkson, Boston N.L., 1889	620.0
12.	Tim Keefe, New York A.A., 1883	619.0
13.	Bill Hutchison, Chicago N.L., 1890	603.0
14.	Jim McCormick, Cleveland N.L., 1882	595.2
	John Ward, Providence N.L., 1880	595.0
16.	Pud Galvin, Buffalo N.L., 1879	593.0
17.	Lee Richmond, Worchester N.L., 1880	590.2
18.	Matt Kilroy, Baltimore A.A., 1887	589.1
19.	Toad Ramsey, Louisville A.A., 1886	588.2
20.	Charlie Buffinton, Boston N.L., 1884	587.0
	John Ward, Providence N.L., 1879	587.0

*LOWEST ERA

Rank	Player	ERA
1.	Tim Keefe, Troy N.L., 1880	0.86
2.	Denny Driscoll, Pittsburgh A.A., 1882	1.21
3.	George Bradley, St. Louis N.L., 1876	1.23
4.	Guy Hecker, Louisville A.A., 1882	1.30
5.	George Bradley, Providence N.L., 1880	1.38
	Charles Radbourn, Providence N.L., 1884	1.38
7.	John Ward, Providence N.L., 1878	1.51
8.	Harry McCormick, Cincinnati A.A., 1882	1.52
9.	Will White, Cincinnati A.A., 1882	1.54
10.	Jim Devlin, Louisville N.L., 1876	1.56
11.	Tim Keefe, New York N.L., 1885	1.58
12.	Silver King, St. Louis A.A., 1888	1.63
13.	Mickey Welch, New York N.L., 1885	1.66
14.	Candy Cummings, Hartford N.L., 1876	1.67
15.	Tommy Bond, Hartford N.L., 1876	1.68
16.	Jim McCormick, Indianapolis N.L., 1878	1.69
17.	Charlie Sweeney, Prov. N.L.-St.L. U.A., 1884	1.70
18.	John Ward, Providence N.L., 1880	1.74
	Henry Boyle, St. Louis U.A., 1884	1.74
	Tim Keefe, New York N.L., 1888	1.74

*Leaders based on pitchers whose total innings equal or surpass total games played by their teams.

VICTORIES

Rank	Player	W
1.	Charley Radbourn, Providence N.L., 1884	59
2.	John Clarkson, Chicago N.L., 1885	53
3.	Guy Hecker, Louisville A.A., 1884	52
4.	John Clarkson, Boston N.L., 1889	49
5.	Charlie Buffinton, Boston N.L., 1884	48
	Charles Radbourn, Providence N.L., 1883	48
7.	Al Spalding, Chicago N.L., 1876	47
	John Ward, Providence N.L., 1879	47
9.	Pud Galvin, Buffalo N.L., 1883	46
	Pud Galvin, Buffalo N.L., 1884	46
	Matt Kilroy, Baltimore A.A., 1887	46
12.	George Bradley, St. Louis N.L., 1876	45
	Silver King, St. Louis A.A., 1888	45
	Jim McCormick, Cleveland N.L., 1880	45
15.	Bill Hutchison, Chicago N.L., 1891	44
	Mickey Welch, New York N.L., 1885	44
17.	5 tied with 43	

LOSSES

Rank	Player	L
1.	John Coleman, Philadelphia N.L., 1883	48
2.	Will White, Cincinnati N.L., 1880	42
3.	Larry McKeon, Indianapolis A.A., 1884	41
4.	George Bradley, Troy N.L., 1879	40
	Jim McCormick, Cleveland N.L., 1879	40
6.	Kid Carsey, Washington A.A., 1891	37
	George Cobb, Baltimore N.L., 1892	37
	Henry Porter, Kansas City A.A., 1888	37
9.	Bill Hutchison, Chicago N.L., 1892	36
	Stump Wiedman, Kansas City N.L., 1886	36
11.	Jim Devlin, Louisville N.L., 1876	35
	Red Donahue, St. Louis N.L., 1897	35

	Pud Galvin, Buffalo N.L., 1880	35
	Hardie Henderson, Baltimore A.A., 1885	35
	Fleury Sullivan, Pittsburgh A.A., 1884	35
	Adonis Terry, Brooklyn A.A., 1884	35
17.	Mark Baldwin, Colorado A.A., 1889	34
	Bob Barr, Wash.-Ind. A.A., 1884	34
	Matt Kilroy, Baltimore A.A., 1886	34
	Bobby Mathews, New York N.L., 1876	34
	Al Mays, New York, A.A., 1887	34
	Amos Rusie, New York N.L., 1890	34

SHUTOUTS

1.	George Bradley, St. Louis N.L., 1876	16
2.	Pud Galvin, Buffalo N.L., 1884	12
	Ed Morris, Pittsburgh A.A., 1886	12
4.	Tommy Bond, Boston N.L., 1879	11
	Dave Foutz, St. Louis A.A., 1886	11
	Charles Radbourn, Providence N.L., 1884	11
7.	John Clarkson, Chicago N.L., 1885	10
	Jim McCormick, Cle. N.L.-Cin. U.A., 1884	10
9.	Tommy Bond, Boston N.L., 1878	9
	George Derby, Detroit N.L., 1881	9
	Cy Young, Cleveland N.L., 1892	9
12.	Charlie Buffinton, Boston N.L., 1884	8
	John Clarkson, Boston N.L., 1889	8
	Tim Keefe, New York N.L., 1888	8
	Ben Sanders, Philadelphia N.L., 1888	8
	Al Spalding, Chicago N.L., 1876	8
	John Ward, Providence N.L., 1880	8
	Will White, Cincinnati A.A., 1882	8
19.	10 tied with 7	

STRIKEOUTS

1.	Matt Kilroy, Baltimore A.A., 1886	513
2.	Toad Ramsey, Louisville A.A., 1886	499
3.	Hugh Daily, Chi.-Pit.-Wash. U.A., 1884	483
4.	Dupee Shaw, Detroit N.L.-Boston U.A., 1884	451
5.	Charles Radbourn, Providence N.L., 1884	441
6.	Charlie Buffinton, Boston N.L., 1884	417
7.	Guy Hecker, Louisville A.A., 1884	385
8.	Bill Sweeney, Baltimore U.A., 1884	374
9.	Pud Galvin, Buffalo N.L., 1884	369
10.	Mark Baldwin, Colorado A.A., 1889	368
11.	Tim Keefe, New York A.A., 1883	359
12.	Toad Ramsey, Louisville A.A., 1887	355
13.	Hardie Henderson, Baltimore A.A., 1884	346
14.	Mickey Welch, New York N.L., 1884	345
	Jim Whitney, Boston N.L., 1883	345
16.	Jim McCormick, Cle. N.L.-Cin. U.A., 1884	343
17.	Amos Rusie, New York N.L., 1890	341
18.	Amos Rusie, New York N.L., 1891	337
	Charlie Sweeney, Prov. N.L.-St.L. U.A., 1884	337
20.	Tim Keefe, New York N.L., 1888	335

REGULAR SEASON (1901-2000)

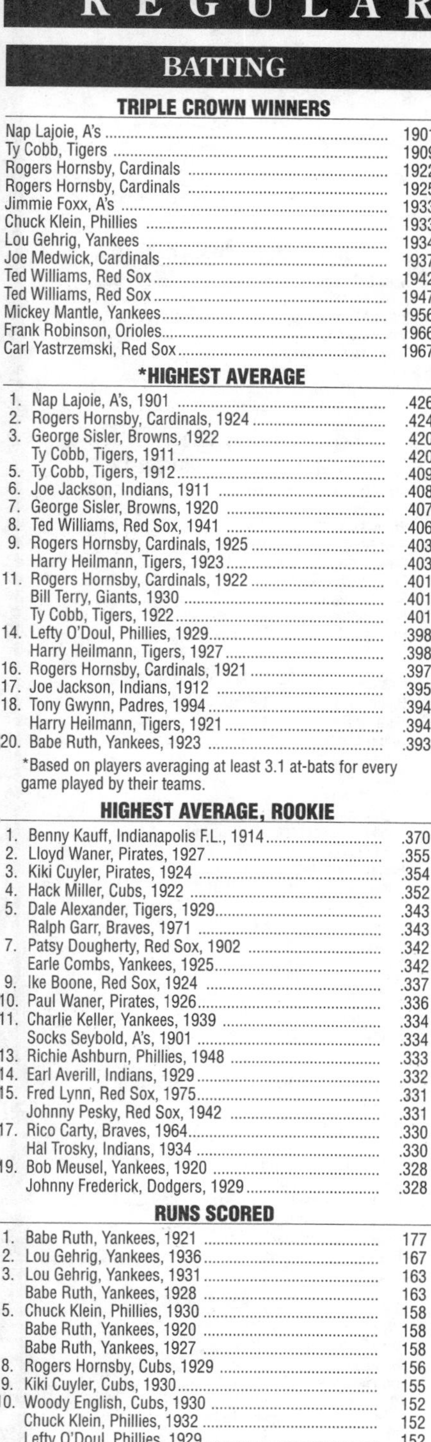

BATTING

TRIPLE CROWN WINNERS

Nap Lajoie, A's	1901
Ty Cobb, Tigers	1909
Rogers Hornsby, Cardinals	1922
Rogers Hornsby, Cardinals	1925
Jimmie Foxx, A's	1933
Chuck Klein, Phillies	1933
Lou Gehrig, Yankees	1934
Joe Medwick, Cardinals	1937
Ted Williams, Red Sox	1942
Ted Williams, Red Sox	1947
Mickey Mantle, Yankees	1956
Frank Robinson, Orioles	1966
Carl Yastrzemski, Red Sox	1967

*HIGHEST AVERAGE

1.	Nap Lajoie, A's, 1901	.426
2.	Rogers Hornsby, Cardinals, 1924	.424
3.	George Sisler, Browns, 1922	.420
	Ty Cobb, Tigers, 1911	.420
5.	Ty Cobb, Tigers, 1912	.409
6.	Joe Jackson, Indians, 1911	.408
7.	George Sisler, Browns, 1920	.407
8.	Ted Williams, Red Sox, 1941	.406
9.	Rogers Hornsby, Cardinals, 1925	.403
	Harry Heilmann, Tigers, 1923	.403
11.	Rogers Hornsby, Cardinals, 1922	.401
	Bill Terry, Giants, 1930	.401
	Ty Cobb, Tigers, 1922	.401
14.	Lefty O'Doul, Phillies, 1929	.398
	Harry Heilmann, Tigers, 1927	.398
16.	Rogers Hornsby, Cardinals, 1921	.397
17.	Joe Jackson, Indians, 1912	.395
18.	Tony Gwynn, Padres, 1994	.394
	Harry Heilmann, Tigers, 1921	.394
20.	Babe Ruth, Yankees, 1923	.393

*Based on players averaging at least 3.1 at-bats for every game played by their teams.

HIGHEST AVERAGE, ROOKIE

1.	Benny Kauff, Indianapolis F.L., 1914	.370
2.	Lloyd Waner, Pirates, 1927	.355
3.	Kiki Cuyler, Pirates, 1924	.354
4.	Hack Miller, Cubs, 1922	.352
5.	Dale Alexander, Tigers, 1929	.343
	Ralph Garr, Braves, 1971	.343
7.	Patsy Dougherty, Red Sox, 1902	.342
	Earle Combs, Yankees, 1925	.342
9.	Ike Boone, Red Sox, 1924	.337
10.	Paul Waner, Pirates, 1926	.336
11.	Charlie Keller, Yankees, 1939	.334
	Socks Seybold, A's, 1901	.334
13.	Richie Ashburn, Phillies, 1948	.333
14.	Earl Averill, Indians, 1929	.332
15.	Fred Lynn, Red Sox, 1975	.331
	Johnny Pesky, Red Sox, 1942	.331
17.	Rico Carty, Braves, 1964	.330
	Hal Trosky, Indians, 1934	.330
19.	Bob Meusel, Yankees, 1920	.328
	Johnny Frederick, Dodgers, 1929	.328

RUNS SCORED

1.	Babe Ruth, Yankees, 1921	177
2.	Lou Gehrig, Yankees, 1936	167
3.	Lou Gehrig, Yankees, 1931	163
	Babe Ruth, Yankees, 1928	163
5.	Chuck Klein, Phillies, 1930	158
	Babe Ruth, Yankees, 1920	158
	Babe Ruth, Yankees, 1927	158
8.	Rogers Hornsby, Cubs, 1929	156
9.	Kiki Cuyler, Cubs, 1930	155
10.	Woody English, Cubs, 1930	152
	Chuck Klein, Phillies, 1932	152
	Lefty O'Doul, Phillies, 1929	152
	Al Simmons, A's, 1930	152
14.	Joe DiMaggio, Yankees, 1937	151
	Jimmie Foxx, A's, 1932	151
	Babe Ruth, Yankees, 1923	151
17.	Babe Ruth, Yankees, 1930	150
	Ted Williams, Red Sox, 1949	150
19.	Lou Gehrig, Yankees, 1927	149
	Babe Ruth, Yankees, 1931	149

Pittsburgh's Waner brothers, Lloyd (left) and Paul, rank high among single-season rookie hitters.

HITS

1.	George Sisler, Browns, 1920	257
2.	Lefty O'Doul, Phillies, 1929	254
	Bill Terry, Giants, 1930	254
4.	Al Simmons, A's, 1925	253
5.	Rogers Hornsby, Cardinals, 1922	250
	Chuck Klein, Phillies, 1930	250
7.	Ty Cobb, Tigers, 1911	248
8.	George Sisler, Browns, 1922	246
9.	Babe Herman, Dodgers, 1930	241
	Heinie Manush, Browns, 1928	241
11.	Wade Boggs, Red Sox, 1985	240
	Darin Erstad, Angels, 2000	240
13.	Rod Carew, Twins, 1977	239
14.	Don Mattingly, Yankees, 1986	238
15.	Harry Heilmann, Tigers, 1921	237
	Joe Medwick, Cardinals, 1937	237
	Paul Waner, Pirates, 1927	237
18.	Jack Tobin, Browns, 1921	236
19.	Rogers Hornsby, Cardinals, 1921	235
20.	Kirby Puckett, Twins, 1988	234
	Lloyd Waner, Pirates, 1929	234

HITS, ROOKIE

1.	Lloyd Waner, Pirates, 1927	223
2.	Ralph Garr, Braves, 1971	219
3.	Tony Oliva, Twins, 1964	217
4.	Dale Alexander, Tigers, 1929	215
5.	Benny Kauff, Indianapolis F.L., 1914	211
6.	Nomar Garciaparra, Red Sox, 1997	209
	Harvey Kuenn, Tigers, 1953	209
8.	Kevin Seitzer, Royals, 1987	207
9.	Joe DiMaggio, Yankees, 1936	206
	Johnny Frederick, Dodgers, 1929	206
	Hal Trosky, Indians, 1934	206
12.	Johnny Pesky, Red Sox, 1942	205
13.	Earle Combs, Yankees, 1925	203
14.	Dick Allen, Phillies, 1964	201
	Roy Johnson, Tigers, 1929	201
16.	Dick Wakefield, Tigers, 1943	200
17.	Earl Averill, Indians, 1929	198
18.	Buddy Hassett, Dodgers, 1936	197
19.	Carlos Beltran, Royals, 1999	194
20.	Smead Jolley, White Sox, 1930	193
	Wally Moon, Cardinals, 1954	193

LONGEST HITTING STREAKS

1.	Joe DiMaggio, Yankees, 1941	56
2.	Pete Rose, Reds, 1978	44
3.	George Sisler, Browns, 1922	41
4.	Ty Cobb, Tigers, 1911	40
5.	Paul Molitor, Brewers, 1987	39
6.	Tommy Holmes, Braves, 1945	37
7.	Ty Cobb, Tigers, 1917	35
8.	George Sisler, Browns, 1925	34
	George McQuinn, Browns, 1938	34
	Dom DiMaggio, Red Sox, 1949	34
	Benito Santiago, Padres, 1987	34
12.	Hal Chase, Yankees, 1907	33
	Rogers Hornsby, Cardinals, 1922	33
	Heinie Manush, Senators, 1933	33
15.	Nap Lajoie, Indians, 1906	31
	Sam Rice, Senators, 1924	31
	Willie Davis, Dodgers, 1969	31
	Rico Carty, Braves, 1970	31
	Ken Landreaux, Twins, 1980	31
	Vladimir Guerrero, Expos, 1999	31

LONGEST HITTING STREAKS, ROOKIE

1.	Benito Santiago, Padres, 1987	34
2.	Jerome Walton, Cubs, 1989	30
	Nomar Garciaparra, Red Sox, 1997	30
4.	Jimmy Williams, 1899	27
5.	Guy Curtright, White Sox, 1943	26
6.	Joe McEwing, Cardinals, 1999	25
7.	Chico Carrasquel, White Sox, 1950	24
8.	Richie Ashburn, Phillies, 1948	23
	Al Dark, Braves, 1948	23
	Kent Hrbek, Twins, 1982	23

Rank	Player	No.
	Goldie Rapp, Phillies, 1921	23
	Mike Vail, Mets, 1975	23
13.	Ralph Garr, Braves, 1971	22
	Willie McCovey, Giants, 1959	22
	Dale Mitchell, Indians, 1947	22
	Johnny Mize, Cardinals, 1936	22
	Edgar Renteria, Marlins, 1996	22
18.	Lou Klein, Cardinals, 1943	21
	Danny Litwhiler, Phillies, 1940	21
	Jackie Robinson, Dodgers, 1947	21
	Dick Wakefield, Tigers, 1943	21
	Taffy Wright, Senators, 1938	21

CONSECUTIVE HITS

Rank	Player	No.
1.	Pinky Higgins, Red Sox, 1938	12
	Walt Dropo, Tigers, 1952	12
3.	Tris Speaker, Indians, 1920	11
	Johnny Pesky, Red Sox, 1946	11
5.	Ed Delahanty, Phillies, 1897	10
	Jake Gettman, Senators, 1897	10
	Ed Konetchy, Dodgers, 1919	10
	George Sisler, Browns, 1921	10
	Harry Heilmann, Tigers, 1922	10
	Kiki Cuyler, Pirates, 1925	10
	Harry McCurdy, White Sox, 1926	10
	Chick Hafey, Cardinals, 1929	10
	Joe Medwick, Cardinals, 1936	10
	Rip Radcliff, White Sox, 1938	10
	Buddy Hassett, Braves, 1940	10
	Woody Williams, Reds, 1943	10
	Ken Singleton, Orioles, 1981	10
	Bip Roberts, Reds, 1992	10
	Frank Thomas, White Sox, 1997	10
	Joe Randa, Royals, 1999	10
	Frank Catalanotto, Rangers, 2000	10

PINCH HITS

Rank	Player	No.
1.	John Vander Wal, Rockies, 1995	28
2.	Lenny Harris, Rockies-Diamondbacks, 1999	26
3.	Jose Morales, Expos, 1976	25
4.	Dave Philley, Orioles, 1961	24
	Vic Davalillo, Cardinals, 1970	24
	Rusty Staub, Mets, 1983	24
	Gerald Perry, Cardinals, 1993	24
8.	Sam Leslie, Giants, 1932	22
	Peanuts Lowrey, Cardinals, 1953	22
	Red Schoendienst, Cardinals, 1962	22
	Wallace Johnson, Expos, 1988	22
	Mark Sweeney, Cardinals-Padres, 1997	22
13.	Doc Miller, Phillies, 1913	21
	Smoky Burgess, White Sox, 1966	21
	Merv Rettenmund, Padres, 1977	21
16.	Ed Coleman, Browns, 1936	20
	Frenchy Bordagaray, Cardinals, 1938	20
	Joe Frazier, Cardinals, 1954	20
	Smoky Burgess, White Sox, 1965	20
	Ken Boswell, Astros, 1976	20
	Jerry Turner, Padres, 1978	20
	Thad Bosley, Cubs, 1985	20
	Chris Chambliss, Braves, 1986	20
	Dave Clark, Cubs, 1997	20

SINGLES

Rank	Player	No.
1.	Lloyd Waner, Pirates, 1927	198
2.	Wade Boggs, Red Sox, 1985	187
3.	Willie Wilson, Royals, 1980	184
4.	Matty Alou, Pirates, 1969	183
5.	Sam Rice, Senators, 1925	182
6.	Richie Ashburn, Phillies, 1951	181
	Jesse Burkett, Cardinals, 1901	181
	Lefty O'Doul, Phillies, 1929	181
	Pete Rose, Reds, 1973	181
	Lloyd Waner, Pirates, 1929	181
11.	Rod Carew, Twins, 1974	180
	Ralph Garr, Braves, 1971	180
	Lloyd Waner, Pirates, 1928	180
14.	Jack Tobin, Browns, 1921	179
	Maury Wills, Dodgers, 1962	179
16.	Curt Flood, Cardinals, 1964	178
	George Sisler, Browns, 1922	178
	Paul Waner, Pirates, 1937	178
19.	Tony Gwynn, Padres, 1984	177
	Bill Terry, Giants, 1930	177

DOUBLES

Rank	Player	No.
1.	Earl Webb, Red Sox, 1931	67
2.	George Burns, Indians, 1926	64
	Joe Medwick, Cardinals, 1936	64
4.	Hank Greenberg, Tigers, 1934	63
5.	Paul Waner, Pirates, 1932	62
6.	Charley Gehringer, Tigers, 1936	60
7.	Todd Helton, Rockies, 2000	59
	Chuck Klein, Phillies, 1930	59
	Tris Speaker, Indians, 1923	59
10.	Carlos Delgado, Blue Jays, 2000	57
	Billy Herman, Cubs, 1935	57
	Billy Herman, Cubs, 1936	57
13.	Craig Biggio, Astros, 1999	56
	George Kell, Tigers, 1950	56
	Joe Medwick, Cardinals, 1937	56
16.	Gee Walker, Tigers, 1936	55
17.	Mark Grudzielanek, Expos, 1997	54
	Hal McRae, Royals, 1977	54
	John Olerud, Blue Jays, 1993	54
	Alex Rodriguez, Mariners, 1996	54

TRIPLES

Rank	Player	No.
1.	Chief Wilson, Pirates, 1912	36
2.	Sam Crawford, Tigers, 1914	26
	Kiki Cuyler, Pirates, 1925	26
	Joe Jackson, Indians, 1912	26
5.	Sam Crawford, Tigers, 1903	25
	Larry Doyle, Giants, 1911	25
	Tom Long, Cardinals, 1915	25
8.	Ty Cobb, Tigers, 1911	24
	Ty Cobb, Tigers, 1917	24
10.	Ty Cobb, Tigers, 1912	23
	Earle Combs, Yankees, 1927	23
	Adam Comorosky, Pirates, 1930	23
	Sam Crawford, Tigers, 1913	23
	Dale Mitchell, Indians, 1949	23
15.	12 tied with 22	

HOME RUNS

Rank	Player	No.
1.	Mark McGwire, Cardinals, 1998	70
2.	Sammy Sosa, Cubs, 1998	66
3.	Mark McGwire, Cardinals, 1999	65
4.	Sammy Sosa, Cubs, 1999	63
5.	Roger Maris, Yankees, 1961	61
6.	Babe Ruth, Yankees, 1927	60
7.	Babe Ruth, Yankees, 1921	59
8.	Jimmie Foxx, A's, 1932	58
	Hank Greenberg, Tigers, 1938	58
	Mark McGwire, A's-Cardinals, 1997	58
11.	Ken Griffey Jr., Mariners, 1997	56
	Ken Griffey Jr., Mariners, 1998	56
	Hack Wilson, Cubs, 1930	56
14.	Ralph Kiner, Pirates, 1949	54
	Mickey Mantle, Yankees, 1961	54
	Babe Ruth, Yankees, 1920	54
	Babe Ruth, Yankees, 1928	54
18.	George Foster, Reds, 1977	52
	Mickey Mantle, Yankees, 1956	52
	Willie Mays, Giants, 1965	52
	Mark McGwire, A's, 1996	52

HOME RUNS, RIGHTHANDER

Rank	Player	No.
1.	Mark McGwire, Cardinals, 1998	70
2.	Sammy Sosa, Cubs, 1998	66
3.	Mark McGwire, Cardinals, 1999	65
4.	Sammy Sosa, Cubs, 1999	63
5.	Jimmie Foxx, A's, 1932	58
	Hank Greenberg, Tigers, 1938	58
	Mark McGwire, A's-Cardinals	58
8.	Hack Wilson, Cubs, 1930	56
9.	Ralph Kiner, Pirates, 1949	54
10.	George Foster, Reds, 1977	52
	Willie Mays, Giants, 1965	52
	Mark McGwire, A's, 1996	52
13.	Cecil Fielder, Tigers, 1990	51
	Ralph Kiner, Pirates, 1947	51
	Willie Mays, Giants, 1955	51
16.	Albert Belle, Indians, 1995	50
	Jimmie Foxx, Red Sox, 1938	50
	Sammy Sosa, Cubs, 2000	50
	Greg Vaughn, Padres, 1998	50
20.	Albert Belle, White Sox, 1998	49
	Andre Dawson, Cubs, 1987	49
	Harmon Killebrew, Twins, 1964	49
	Harmon Killebrew, Twins, 1969	49
	Willie Mays, Giants, 1962	49
	Mark McGwire, A's, 1987	49
	Frank Robinson, Orioles, 1966	49

HOME RUNS, LEFTHANDER

Rank	Player	No.
1.	Roger Maris, Yankees, 1961	61
2.	Babe Ruth, Yankees, 1927	60
3.	Babe Ruth, Yankees, 1921	59
4.	Ken Griffey Jr., Mariners, 1997	56
	Ken Griffey Jr., Mariners, 1998	56
6.	Babe Ruth, Yankees, 1920	54
	Babe Ruth, Yankees, 1928	54
8.	Johnny Mize, Giants, 1947	51
9.	Brady Anderson, Orioles, 1996	50
10.	Barry Bonds, Giants, 2000	49
	Lou Gehrig, Yankees, 1934	49
	Lou Gehrig, Yankees, 1936	49
	Ken Griffey, Jr., Mariners, 1996	49
	Ted Kluszewski, Reds, 1954	49
	Babe Ruth, Yankees, 1930	49
	Larry Walker, Rockies, 1997	49
17.	Ken Griffey Jr., Mariners, 1999	48
	Willie Stargell, Pirates, 1971	48
19.	Lou Gehrig, Yankees, 1927	47
	Reggie Jackson, A's, 1969	47
	Ted Kluszewski, Reds, 1955	47
	Eddie Mathews, Braves, 1953	47
	Rafael Palmeiro, Rangers, 1999	47
	Babe Ruth, Yankees, 1926	47

HOME RUNS, SWITCH HITTER

Rank	Player	No.
1.	Mickey Mantle, Yankees, 1961	54
2.	Mickey Mantle, Yankees, 1956	52
3.	Chipper Jones, Braves, 1999	45
4.	Mickey Mantle, Yankees, 1958	42
5.	Todd Hundley, Mets, 1996	41
6.	Ken Caminiti, Padres, 1996	40
	Mickey Mantle, Yankees, 1960	40
8.	Howard Johnson, Mets, 1991	38
9.	Mickey Mantle, Yankees, 1955	37
10.	Howard Johnson, Mets, 1987	36
	Howard Johnson, Mets, 1989	36
	Chipper Jones, Braves, 2000	36
13.	Ripper Collins, Cardinals, 1934	35
	Mickey Mantle, Yankees, 1964	35
	Ken Singleton, Orioles, 1979	35
16.	Bobby Bonilla, Mets, 1993	34
	Tony Clark, Tigers, 1998	34
	Carl Everett, Red Sox, 2000	34
	Chipper Jones, Braves, 1998	34
	Mickey Mantle, Yankees, 1957	34

HOME RUNS, FIRST BASEMAN

Rank	Player	No.
1.	Mark McGwire, Cardinals, 1998	69
2.	Mark McGwire, Cardinals, 1999	65
3.	Hank Greenberg, Tigers, 1938	58
4.	Mark McGwire, A's-Cardinals, 1997	57
5.	Jimmie Foxx, A's, 1932	51
	Johnny Mize, Giants, 1947	51
7.	Jimmie Foxx, Red Sox, 1938	50
8.	Lou Gehrig, Yankees, 1934	49
	Lou Gehrig, Yankees, 1936	49
	Ted Kluszewski, Reds, 1954	49

HOME RUNS, SECOND BASEMAN

Rank	Player	No.
1.	Rogers Hornsby, Cardinals, 1922	42
	Davey Johnson, Braves, 1973	42
3.	Ryne Sandberg, Cubs, 1990	40
4.	Rogers Hornsby, Cardinals, 1925	39
	Rogers Hornsby, Cubs, 1929	39
6.	Jay Bell, Diamondbacks, 1999	38
7.	Joe Gordon, Indians, 1948	32
	Jeff Kent, Giants, 2000	32
9.	Jeff Kent, Giants, 1998	31
10.	Joe Gordon, Yankees, 1940	30
	Bobby Grich, Angels, 1979	30
	Ryne Sandberg, Cubs, 1989	30

HOME RUNS, THIRD BASEMAN

Rank	Player	No.
1.	Mike Schmidt, Phillies, 1980	48
2.	Eddie Mathews, Braves, 1953	47
3.	Eddie Mathews, Braves, 1959	46
	Vinny Castilla, Rockies, 1998	46
	Troy Glaus, Angels, 2000	46
6.	Mike Schmidt, Phillies, 1979	45
	Chipper Jones, 1999	45
8.	Al Rosen, Indians, 1953	43
	Matt Williams, Giants, 1994	43
10.	Harmon Killebrew, Senators, 1959	42

HOME RUNS, SHORTSTOP

Rank	Player	No.
1.	Ernie Banks, Cubs, 1958	47
2.	Ernie Banks, Cubs, 1959	45
3.	Ernie Banks, Cubs, 1955	44
4.	Alex Rodriguez, Mariners, 1998	42
	Alex Rodriguez, Mariners, 1999	42
6.	Ernie Banks, Cubs, 1960	41
	Alex Rodriguez, Mariners, 2000	41
8.	Rico Petrocelli, Red Sox, 1969	40
9.	Vern Stephens, Red Sox, 1949	39
10.	Alex Rodriguez, Mariners, 1996	36

HOME RUNS, OUTFIELDER

Rank	Player	No.
1.	Sammy Sosa, Cubs, 1998	66
2.	Sammy Sosa, Cubs, 1999	63
3.	Roger Maris, Yankees, 1961	61
4.	Babe Ruth, Yankees, 1927	60
5.	Babe Ruth, Yankees, 1921	58
6.	Hack Wilson, Cubs, 1930	56
	Ken Griffey Jr., Mariners, 1998	56
8.	Babe Ruth, Yankees, 1920	54
	Babe Ruth, Yankees, 1928	54
	Ralph Kiner, Pirates, 1949	54
	Mickey Mantle, Yankees, 1961	54
	Ken Griffey Jr., Mariners, 1997	54
13.	Mickey Mantle, Yankees, 1956	52
	Willie Mays, Giants, 1965	52
	George Foster, Reds, 1977	52
16.	Ralph Kiner, Pirates, 1947	51
	Willie Mays, Giants, 1962	51
18.	Albert Belle, Indians, 1995	50
	Brady Anderson, Orioles, 1996	50
	Sammy Sosa, Cubs, 2000	50

HOME RUNS, CATCHER

Rank	Player	No.
1.	Todd Hundley, Mets, 1996	41
2.	Roy Campanella, Dodgers, 1953	40
	Mike Piazza, Dodgers, 1997	40
	Mike Piazza, Mets, 1999	40
5.	Johnny Bench, Reds, 1970	38
6.	Gabby Hartnett, Cubs, 1930	36
	Mike Piazza, Dodgers, 1996	36
8.	Walker Cooper, Giants, 1947	35
	Mike Piazza, Dodgers, 1993	35
	Mike Piazza, Dodgers, 2000	35

HOME RUNS, PITCHER

Rank	Player	No.
1.	Wes Ferrell, Indians, 1931	9
2.	Wes Ferrell, Indians, 1933	7
	Bob Lemon, Indians, 1949	7
	Don Newcombe, Dodgers, 1955	7
	Don Drysdale, Dodgers, 1958	7
	Don Drysdale, Dodgers, 1965	7
	Earl Wilson, Tigers, 1968	7

HOME RUNS, DESIGNATED HITTER

1.	Rafael Palmeiro, Rangers, 1999	37
	Edgar Martinez, Mariners, 2000	37
3.	Dave Kingman, A's, 1984	35
	Dave Kingman, A's, 1986	35
	John Jaha, A's, 1999	35
6.	Greg Luzinski, White Sox, 1983	32
	Gorman Thomas, Mariners, 1985	32
	Jose Canseco, Devil Rays, 1999	32
	Brad Fullmer, Blue Jays, 2000	32
10.	Jim Rice, Red Sox, 1977	31
	Rico Carty, Blue Jays-A's, 1978	31
	Andre Thornton, Indians, 1982	31
	Jose Canseco, Rangers, 1994	31

HOME RUNS, ROOKIE

1.	Mark McGwire, A's, 1987	49
2.	Wally Berger, Braves, 1930	38
	Frank Robinson, Reds, 1956	38
4.	Al Rosen, Indians, 1950	37
5.	Ron Kittle, White Sox, 1983	35
	Mike Piazza, Dodgers, 1993	35
	Hal Trosky, Indians, 1934	35
8.	Walt Dropo, Red Sox, 1950	34
9.	Jose Canseco, A's, 1986	33
	Jimmie Hall, Twins, 1963	33
	Earl Williams, Braves, 1971	33
12.	Matt Nokes, Tigers, 1987	32
	Tony Oliva, Twins, 1964	32
14.	Jim Ray Hart, Giants, 1964	31
	Tim Salmon, Angels, 1993	31
	Ted Williams, Red Sox, 1939	31
17.	Bob Allison, Senators, 1959	30
	Nomar Garciaparra, Red Sox, 1997	30
	Pete Incaviglia, Rangers, 1986	30
	Willie Montanez, Phillies, 1971	30

CONSECUTIVE GAMES WITH HOME RUN

1.	Don Mattingly, Yankees, 1987 (10)	8
	Dale Long, Pirates, 1956 (8)	8
	Ken Griffey Jr., Mariners, 1993 (8)	8
4.	Frank Howard, Senators, 1968 (10)	6
	George Kelly, Giants, 1924 (7)	6
	Walker Cooper, Giants, 1947 (7)	6
	Willie Mays, Giants, 1955 (7)	6
	Roger Maris, Yankees, 1961 (7)	6
	Graig Nettles, Padres, 1984 (7)	6
	Ken Williams, Browns, 1922 (6)	6
	Lou Gehrig, Yankees, 1931 (6)	6
	Roy Sievers, Senators, 1957 (6)	6
	Reggie Jackson, Orioles, 1976 (6)	6
14.	Jim Bottomley, Cardinals (7), 1929	5
	Babe Ruth, Yankees, (7) 1921	5
	Vic Wertz, Tigers, (7) 1950	5
	Johnny Bench, Reds (7), 1972	5
	Mike Schmidt, Phillies (7), 1979	5

Note: Number in ( ) is homer total during streak.

MOST HOMERS PER AT-BAT

1.	Mark McGwire, Cardinals, 1998	.138
2.	Mark McGwire, Cardinals, 1999	.125
3.	Mark McGwire, Cardinals, 1996	.123
4.	Babe Ruth, Yankees, 1920	.118
5.	Babe Ruth, Yankees, 1927	.111
6.	Babe Ruth, Yankees, 1921	.109
7.	Mark McGwire, A's-Cardinals, 1997	.107
8.	Mickey Mantle, Yankees, 1961	.105
9.	Hank Greenberg, Tigers, 1938	.104
10.	Roger Maris, Yankees, 1961	.103
	Sammy Sosa, Cubs, 1998	.103
12.	Barry Bonds, Cubs, 2000	.102
13.	Sammy Sosa, Cubs, 1999	.101
	Babe Ruth, Yankees, 1928	.101
15.	Jimmie Foxx, A's, 1932	.099
16.	Ralph Kiner, Pirates, 1949	.098
	Mickey Mantle, Yankees, 1956	.098
18.	Jeff Bagwell, Astros, 1994	.097
	Kevin Mitchell, Reds, 1994	.097
	Matt Williams, Giants, 1994	.097

PINCH-HIT HOME RUNS

1.	Dave Hansen, Dodgers, 2000	7
2.	Johnny Frederick, Dodgers, 1932	6
3.	Joe Cronin, Red Sox, 1943	5
	Butch Nieman, Braves, 1945	5
	Gene Freese, Phillies, 1959	5
	Jerry Lynch, Reds, 1961	5
	Cliff Johnson, Astros, 1974	5
	Lee Lacy, Dodgers, 1978	5
	Jerry Turner, Padres, 1978	5
	Billy Ashley, Dodgers, 1996	5
10.	26 tied with 4	

GRAND SLAMS

1.	Don Mattingly, Yankees, 1987	6
2.	Ernie Banks, Cubs, 1955	5
	Jim Gentile, Orioles, 1961	5
4.	Frank Schulte, Cubs, 1911	4
	Babe Ruth, Red Sox, 1919	4
	Lou Gehrig, Yankees, 1934	4
	Rudy York, Tigers, 1938	4
	Vince DiMaggio, Phillies, 1945	4
	Tommy Henrich, Yankees, 1948	4
	Ralph Kiner, Pirates, 1949	4
	Sid Gordon, Braves, 1950	4
	Al Rosen, Indians, 1951	4
	Ray Boone, Indians-Tigers, 1953	4
	Jim Northrup, Tigers, 1968	4
	Albert Belle, White Sox, 1997	4
	Jason Giambi, A's, 2000	4
	Edgar Martinez, Mariners, 2000	4

Roger Maris (left), Ted Williams (center) and Mickey Mantle rate high on baseball's all-time slugging charts.

TOTAL BASES

1.	Babe Ruth, Yankees, 1921	457
2.	Rogers Hornsby, Cardinals, 1922	450
3.	Lou Gehrig, Yankees, 1927	447
4.	Chuck Klein, Phillies, 1930	445
5.	Jimmie Foxx, A's, 1932	438
6.	Stan Musial, Cardinals, 1948	429
7.	Hack Wilson, Cubs, 1930	423
8.	Chuck Klein, Phillies, 1932	420
9.	Lou Gehrig, Yankees, 1930	419
10.	Joe DiMaggio, Yankees, 1937	418
11.	Babe Ruth, Yankees, 1927	417
12.	Babe Herman, Dodgers, 1930	416
	Sammy Sosa, Cubs, 1998	416
14.	Lou Gehrig, Yankees, 1931	410
15.	Lou Gehrig, Yankees, 1934	409
	Rogers Hornsby, Cubs, 1929	409
	Larry Walker, Rockies, 1997	409
18.	Joe Medwick, Cardinals, 1937	406
	Jim Rice, Red Sox, 1978	406
20.	Todd Helton, Rockies, 2000	405
	Chuck Klein, Phillies, 1929	405
	Hal Trosky, Indians, 1936	405

*SLUGGING PERCENTAGE

1.	Babe Ruth, Yankees, 1920	.847
2.	Babe Ruth, Yankees, 1921	.846
3.	Babe Ruth, Yankees, 1927	.772
4.	Lou Gehrig, Yankees, 1927	.765
5.	Babe Ruth, Yankees, 1923	.764
6.	Rogers Hornsby, Cardinals, 1925	.756
7.	Mark McGwire, Cardinals, 1998	.752
8.	Jeff Bagwell, Astros, 1994	.750
9.	Jimmie Foxx, A's, 1932	.749
10.	Babe Ruth, Yankees, 1924	.739
11.	Babe Ruth, Yankees, 1926	.737
12.	Ted Williams, Red Sox, 1941	.735
13.	Babe Ruth, Yankees, 1930	.732
14.	Ted Williams, Red Sox, 1957	.731
15.	Mark McGwire, A's, 1996	.730
16.	Frank Thomas, White Sox, 1994	.729
17.	Hack Wilson, Cubs, 1930	.723
18.	Rogers Hornsby, Cardinals, 1922	.722
19.	Lou Gehrig, Yankees, 1930	.721
20.	Larry Walker, Rockies, 1997	.720

*Based on players averaging at least 3.1 at-bats for every game played by their teams.

EXTRA-BASE HITS

1.	Babe Ruth, Yankees, 1921	119
2.	Lou Gehrig, Yankees, 1927	117
3.	Chuck Klein, Phillies, 1930	107
4.	Albert Belle, Indians, 1995	103
	Hank Greenberg, Tigers, 1937	103
	Todd Helton, Rockies, 2000	103
	Chuck Klein, Phillies, 1932	103
	Stan Musial, Cardinals, 1948	103
9.	Rogers Hornsby, Cardinals, 1922	102
10.	Jimmie Foxx, A's, 1932	100
	Lou Gehrig, Yankees, 1930	100
12.	Albert Belle, White Sox, 1998	99
	Carlos Delgado, Blue Jays, 2000	99
	Hank Greenberg, Tigers, 1940	99
	Babe Ruth, Yankees, 1920	99
	Babe Ruth, Yankees, 1923	99
	Larry Walker, Rockies, 1997	99
18.	Hank Greenberg, Tigers, 1935	98
19.	Juan Gonzalez, Rangers, 1998	97
	Joe Medwick, Cardinals, 1937	97
	Babe Ruth, Yankees, 1927	97
	Hack Wilson, Cubs, 1930	97

RUNS BATTED IN

1.	Hack Wilson, Cubs, 1930	191
2.	Lou Gehrig, Yankees, 1931	184
3.	Hank Greenberg, Tigers, 1937	183
4.	Jimmie Foxx, Red Sox, 1938	175
	Lou Gehrig, Yankees, 1927	175
6.	Lou Gehrig, Yankees, 1930	174
7.	Babe Ruth, Yankees, 1921	171
8.	Hank Greenberg, Tigers, 1935	170
	Chuck Klein, Phillies, 1930	170
10.	Jimmie Foxx, A's, 1932	169
11.	Joe DiMaggio, Yankees, 1937	167
12.	Lou Gehrig, Yankees, 1934	165
	Manny Ramirez, Indians, 1999	165
	Al Simmons, A's, 1930	165
15.	Babe Ruth, Yankees, 1927	164
16.	Jimmie Foxx, A's, 1933	163
	Babe Ruth, Yankees, 1931	163
18.	Hal Trosky, Indians, 1936	162
19.	Lou Gehrig, Yankees, 1937	159
	Vern Stephens, Red Sox, 1949	159
	Ted Williams, Red Sox, 1949	159
	Hack Wilson, Cubs, 1929	159

RBIs, RIGHTHANDER

1.	Hack Wilson, Cubs, 1930	191
2.	Hank Greenberg, Tigers, 1937	183
3.	Jimmie Foxx, Red Sox, 1938	175
4.	Hank Greenberg, Tigers, 1935	170
5.	Jimmie Foxx, A's, 1932	169
6.	Joe DiMaggio, Yankees, 1937	167
7.	Manny Ramirez, Indians, 1999	165
	Al Simmons, A's, 1930	165
9.	Jimmie Foxx, A's, 1933	163
10.	Vern Stephens, Red Sox, 1949	159
	Hack Wilson, Cubs, 1929	159
12.	Sammy Sosa, Cubs, 1998	158

13.	Juan Gonzalez, Rangers, 1998	157
	Al Simmons, A's, 1929	157
15.	Jimmie Foxx, A's, 1930	156
16.	Joe DiMaggio, Yankees, 1948	155
17.	Joe Medwick, Cardinals, 1937	154
18.	Tommy Davis, Dodgers, 1962	153
19.	Albert Belle, White Sox, 1998	152
	Rogers Hornsby, Cardinals, 1922	152

RBIs, LEFTHANDER

1.	Lou Gehrig, Yankees, 1931	184
2.	Lou Gehrig, Yankees, 1927	175
3.	Lou Gehrig, Yankees, 1930	174
4.	Babe Ruth, Yankees, 1921	171
5.	Chuck Klein, Phillies, 1930	170
6.	Lou Gehrig, Yankees, 1934	165
7.	Babe Ruth, Yankees, 1927	164
8.	Babe Ruth, Yankees, 1931	163
9.	Hal Trosky, Indians, 1936	162
10.	Lou Gehrig, Yankees, 1937	159
	Ted Williams, Red Sox, 1949	159
12.	Ken Williams, Browns, 1922	155
13.	Babe Ruth, Yankees, 1929	154
14.	Babe Ruth, Yankees, 1930	153
15.	Lou Gehrig, Yankees, 1936	152
16.	Lou Gehrig, Yankees, 1932	151
	Mel Ott, Giants, 1929	151
18.	Rafael Palmeiro, Rangers, 1999	148
19.	Ken Griffey Jr., Mariners, 1997	147
	Todd Helton, Rockies, 2000	147

RBIs, SWITCH HITTER

1.	Ken Caminiti, Padres, 1996	130
	Mickey Mantle, Yankees, 1956	130
3.	Ripper Collins, Cardinals, 1934	128
	Mickey Mantle, Yankees, 1961	128
5.	Eddie Murray, Orioles, 1985	124
6.	Ripper Collins, Cardinals, 1935	122
7.	Bernie Williams, Yankees, 2000	121
8.	Roberto Alomar, Indians, 1999	120
	Bobby Bonilla, Pirates, 1990	120
10.	Ruben Sierra, Rangers, 1989	119
11.	Tony Clark, Tigers, 1997	117
	Howard Johnson, Mets, 1991	117
13.	Bobby Bonilla, Orioles, 1996	116
	Eddie Murray, Orioles, 1980	116
	Ruben Sierra, Rangers, 1991	116
16.	Bernie Williams, Yankees, 1999	115
17.	Carlos Baerga, Indians, 1993	114
	Frankie Frisch, Cardinals, 1930	114
19.	Chili Davis, Angels, 1993	112
	Todd Hundley, Mets, 1996	112

RBIs, ROOKIE

1.	Ted Williams, Red Sox, 1939	145
2.	Walt Dropo, Red Sox, 1950	144
3.	Hal Trosky, Indians, 1934	142
4.	Dale Alexander, Tigers, 1929	137
5.	Joe DiMaggio, Yankees, 1936	125
6.	Wally Berger, Braves, 1930	119
7.	Mark McGwire, A's, 1987	118
8.	Jose Canseco, A's, 1986	117
	Joe Vosmik, Indians, 1931	117
10.	Alvin Davis, Mariners, 1984	116
	Al Rosen, Indians, 1950	116
12.	Smead Jolley, White Sox, 1930	114
	Tony Lazzeri, Yankees, 1926	114
14.	Ken Keltner, Indians, 1938	113
15.	Ray Jablonski, Cardinals, 1953	112
	Mike Piazza, Dodgers, 1993	112
17.	Johnny Rizzo, Pirates, 1938	111
	Glenn Wright, Pirates, 1924	111
19.	Zeke Bonura, White Sox, 1934	110
20.	Carlos Beltran, Royals, 1999	108

WALKS

1.	Babe Ruth, Yankees, 1923	170
2.	Mark McGwire, Cardinals, 1998	162
	Ted Williams, Red Sox, 1947	162
	Ted Williams, Red Sox, 1949	162
5.	Ted Williams, Red Sox, 1946	156
6.	Barry Bonds, Giants, 1996	151
	Eddie Yost, Senators, 1956	151
8.	Jeff Bagwell, Astros, 1999	149
	Eddie Joost, A's, 1949	149
10.	Babe Ruth, Yankees, 1920	148
	Eddie Stanky, Dodgers, 1945	148
	Jimmy Wynn, Astros, 1969	148
13.	Jimmy Sheckard, Cubs, 1911	147
14.	Mickey Mantle, Yankees, 1957	146
15.	Barry Bonds, Giants, 1997	145
	Harmon Killebrew, Twins, 1969	145
	Ted Williams, Red Sox, 1941	145
	Ted Williams, Red Sox, 1942	145
19.	Babe Ruth, Yankees, 1921	144
	Babe Ruth, Yankees, 1926	144
	Eddie Stanky, Giants, 1950	144
	Ted Williams, Red Sox, 1951	144

INTENTIONAL WALKS

1.	Willie McCovey, Giants, 1969	45
2.	Barry Bonds, Giants, 1993	43
3.	Willie McCovey, Giants, 1970	40
4.	Barry Bonds, Giants, 1997	34
5.	John Olerud, Blue Jays, 1993	33
	Ted Williams, Red Sox, 1957	33
7.	Barry Bonds, Pirates, 1992	32
	Kevin Mitchell, Giants, 1989	32
9.	George Brett, Royals, 1985	31
10.	Barry Bonds, Giants, 1996	30
11.	Barry Bonds, Giants, 1998	29
	Frank Howard, Senators, 1970	29
	Dale Murphy, Braves, 1987	29
	Adolfo Phillips, Cubs, 1967	29
	Frank Thomas, White Sox, 1995	29
16.	Ernie Banks, Cubs, 1960	28
	Mark McGwire, Cardinals, 1998	28
18.	Jeff Bagwell, Astros, 1997	27
	Will Clark, Giants, 1988	27
	Roberto Clemente, Pirates, 1968	27

STRIKEOUTS

1.	Bobby Bonds, Giants, 1970	189
2.	Bobby Bonds, Giants, 1969	187
	Preston Wilson, Marlins, 2000	187
4.	Rob Deer, Brewers, 1987	186
5.	Pete Incaviglia, Rangers, 1986	185
6.	Cecil Fielder, Tigers, 1990	182
7.	Mo Vaughn, Angels, 2000	181
8.	Mike Schmidt, Phillies, 1975	180
9.	Rob Deer, Brewers, 1986	179
10.	Jay Buhner, Mariners, 1997	175
	Jose Canseco, A's, 1986	175
	Rob Deer, Tigers, 1991	175
	Dave Nicholson, White Sox, 1963	175
	Gorman Thomas, Brewers, 1979	175
15.	Sammy Sosa, Cubs, 1997	174
16.	Bo Jackson, Royals, 1989	172
	Jim Presley, Mariners, 1986	172
18.	Reggie Jackson, A's, 1968	171
	Sammy Sosa, Cubs, 1998	171
	Sammy Sosa, Cubs, 1999	171
	Jim Thome, Indians, 1999	171
	Jim Thome, Indians, 2000	171

STOLEN BASES

1.	Rickey Henderson, A's, 1982	130
2.	Lou Brock, Cardinals, 1974	118
3.	Vince Coleman, Cardinals, 1985	110
4.	Vince Coleman, Cardinals, 1987	109
5.	Rickey Henderson, A's, 1983	108
6.	Vince Coleman, Cardinals, 1986	107
7.	Maury Wills, Dodgers, 1962	104
8.	Rickey Henderson, A's, 1980	100
9.	Ron LeFlore, Expos, 1980	97
10.	Ty Cobb, Tigers, 1915	96
	Omar Moreno, Pirates, 1980	96
12.	Maury Wills, Dodgers, 1965	94
13.	Rickey Henderson, Yankees, 1988	93
14.	Tim Raines, Expos, 1983	90
15.	Clyde Milan, Senators, 1912	88
16.	Rickey Henderson, Yankees, 1986	87
17.	Ty Cobb, Tigers, 1911	83
	Willie Wilson, Royals, 1979	83
19.	Bob Bescher, Reds, 1911	81
	Vince Coleman, Cardinals, 1988	81
	Eddie Collins, A's, 1910	81

PITCHING

GAMES

1.	Mike Marshall, Dodgers, 1974	106
2.	Kent Tekulve, Pirates, 1979	94
3.	Mike Marshall, Expos, 1973	92
4.	Kent Tekulve, Pirates, 1978	91
5.	Wayne Granger, Reds, 1969	90
	Mike Marshall, Twins, 1979	90
	Kent Tekulve, Phillies, 1987	90
8.	Mark Eichhorn, Blue Jays, 1987	89
	Julian Tavarez, Giants, 1997	89
10.	Mike Myers, Tigers, 1997	88
	Sean Runyan, Tigers, 1998	88
	Wilbur Wood, White Sox, 1968	88
13.	Rob Murphy, Reds, 1987	87
14.	Kent Tekulve, Pirates, 1982	85
	Frank Williams, Reds, 1987	85
	Mitch Williams, Rangers, 1987	85
17.	Ted Abernathy, Cubs, 1965	84
	Stan Belinda, Reds, 1997	84
	Dan Quisenberry, Royals, 1985	84
	Enrique Romo, Pirates, 1979	84
	Dick Tidrow, Cubs, 1980	84

GAMES STARTED

1.	Jack Chesbro, Yankees, 1904	51
2.	Ed Walsh, White Sox, 1908	49
	Wilbur Wood, White Sox, 1972	49
4.	Joe McGinnity, Giants, 1903	48
	Wilbur Wood, White Sox, 1973	48
6.	Dave Davenport, St. Louis F.L., 1915	46
	Christy Mathewson, Giants, 1904	46
	Rube Waddell, A's, 1904	46
	Ed Walsh, White Sox, 1907	46
	Vic Willis, Braves, 1902	46
11.	Grover Alexander, Phillies, 1916	45
	Mickey Lolich, Tigers, 1971	45
	Jack Powell, Yankees, 1904	45
14.	Grover Alexander, Phillies, 1917	44
	Christy Mathewson, Giants, 1908	44
	Joe McGinnity, Giants, 1904	44
	George Mullin, Tigers, 1904	44
	Phil Niekro, Braves, 1979	44
	George Uhle, Indians, 1923	44
20.	9 tied with 43	

COMPLETE GAMES

1.	Jack Chesbro, Yankees, 1904	48
2.	Vic Willis, Braves, 1902	45
3.	Joe McGinnity, Giants, 1903	44
4.	George Mullin, Tigers, 1904	42
	Ed Walsh, White Sox, 1908	42
6.	Noodles Hahn, Reds, 1901	41
	Cy Young, Red Sox, 1902	41
	Irv Young, Braves, 1905	41
9.	Cy Young, Red Sox, 1904	40
10.	Bill Dinneen, Red Sox, 1902	39
	Joe McGinnity, Orioles, 1901	39
	Jack Taylor, Cardinals, 1904	39
	Rube Waddell, A's, 1904	39
	Vic Willis, Braves, 1904	39
15.	Grover Alexander, Phillies, 1916	38
	Walter Johnson, Senators, 1910	38
	Oscar Jones, Dodgers, 1904	38
	Joe McGinnity, Giants, 1904	38
	Jack Powell, Yankees, 1904	38
	Cy Young, Red Sox, 1901	38

INNINGS PITCHED

1.	Ed Walsh, White Sox, 1908	464.0
2.	Jack Chesbro, Yankees, 1904	454.2
3.	Joe McGinnity, Giants, 1903	434.0
4.	Ed Walsh, White Sox, 1907	422.1
5.	Vic Willis, Braves, 1902	410.0
6.	Joe McGinnity, Giants, 1904	408.0
7.	Ed Walsh, White Sox, 1912	393.0
8.	Dave Davenport, St. Louis F.L., 1915	392.2
9.	Christy Mathewson, Giants, 1908	390.2
10.	Jack Powell, Yankees, 1904	390.1
11.	Togie Pittinger, Braves, 1902	389.1
12.	Grover Alexander, Phillies, 1916	389.0
13.	Grover Alexander, Phillies, 1917	388.0
14.	Cy Young, Red Sox, 1902	384.2
15.	Rube Waddell, A's, 1904	383.0
16.	George Mullin, Tigers, 1904	382.1
17.	Joe McGinnity, Orioles, 1901	382.0
18.	Cy Young, Red Sox, 1904	380.0
19.	Irv Young, Braves, 1905	378.0
20.	Cy Falkenberg, Indianapolis F.L., 1914	377.1

CONSECUTIVE SCORELESS INNINGS

1.	Orel Hershiser, Dodgers, 1988	59
2.	Don Drysdale, Dodgers, 1968	58
3.	Walter Johnson, Senators, 1913	55.2
4.	Jack Coombs, A's, 1910	53
5.	Ed Reulbach, Cubs, 1908	*50
6.	Bob Gibson, Cardinals, 1968	47
7.	Carl Hubbell, Giants, 1933	45.1
8.	Cy Young, Red Sox, 1904	45
	Doc White, White Sox, 1904	45
	Sal Maglie, Giants, 1950	45
11.	Rube Waddell, A's, 1905	43.2
12.	Rube Foster, Red Sox, 1914	42
13.	Jack Chesbro, Pirates, 1902	41
	Grover Alexander, Phillies, 1911	41
	Art Nehf, Braves, 1917	41
	Luis Tiant, Indians, 1968	41
17.	Walter Johnson, Senators, 1918	40
	Gaylord Perry, Giants, 1967	40
	Luis Tiant, Red Sox, 1972	40
20.	Mordecai Brown, Cubs, 1908	39.2
	Billy Pierce, White Sox, 1953	39.2

* 44 in 1908; 6 in 1909.

*LOWEST ERA

1.	Dutch Leonard, Red Sox, 1914	0.96
2.	Mordecai Brown, Cubs, 1906	1.04
3.	Bob Gibson, Cardinals, 1968	1.12
4.	Christy Mathewson, Giants, 1909	1.14
	Walter Johnson, Senators, 1913	1.14
6.	Jack Pfiester, Cubs, 1907	1.15
7.	Addie Joss, Indians, 1908	1.16
8.	Carl Lundgren, Cubs, 1907	1.17
9.	Grover Alexander, Phillies, 1915	1.22
10.	Cy Young, Red Sox, 1908	1.26
11.	Ed Walsh, White Sox, 1910	1.27
	Walter Johnson, Senators, 1918	1.27
13.	Christy Mathewson, Giants, 1905	1.28
14.	Jack Coombs, A's, 1910	1.30
15.	Mordecai Brown, Cubs, 1909	1.31
16.	Jack Taylor, Cubs, 1902	1.33
17.	Walter Johnson, Senators, 1910	1.36
18.	Walter Johnson, Senators, 1912	1.39
	Mordecai Brown, Cubs, 1907	1.39
	Harry Krause, A's, 1909	1.39

*Leaders based on pitchers whose total innings equal total games played by their teams.

VICTORIES

1.	Jack Chesbro, Yankees, 1904	41
2.	Ed Walsh, White Sox, 1908	40
3.	Christy Mathewson, Giants, 1908	37

Grover Alexander, a career 373-game winner, posted a record 16 shutouts in 1916.

4.	Walter Johnson, Senators, 1913	36
5.	Joe McGinnity, Giants, 1904	35
6.	Joe Wood, Red Sox, 1912	34
7.	Grover Alexander, Phillies, 1916	33
	Walter Johnson, Senators, 1912	33
	Christy Mathewson, Giants, 1904	33
	Cy Young, Red Sox, 1901	33
11.	Cy Young, Red Sox, 1902	32
12.	Grover Alexander, Phillies, 1915	31
	Jim Bagby, Indians, 1920	31
	Jack Coombs, A's, 1910	31
	Lefty Grove, A's, 1931	31
	Christy Mathewson, Giants, 1905	31
	Joe McGinnity, Giants, 1903	31
	Denny McLain, Tigers, 1968	31
19.	Grover Alexander, Phillies, 1917	30
	Dizzy Dean, Cardinals, 1934	30
	Christy Mathewson, Giants, 1903	30

WINNING PERCENTAGE

(Minimum 15 victories)

1.	Roy Face, Pirates, 1959	.947
2.	Johnny Allen, Indians, 1937	.938
3.	Greg Maddux, Braves, 1995	.905
4.	Randy Johnson, Mariners, 1995	.900
5.	Ron Guidry, Yankees, 1978	.893
6.	Freddie Fitzsimmons, Dodgers, 1940	.889
7.	Lefty Grove, A's, 1931	.886
8.	Bob Stanley, Red Sox, 1978	.882
9.	Preacher Roe, Dodgers, 1951	.880
10.	Joe Wood, Red Sox, 1912	.872
11.	David Cone, Mets, 1988	.870
12.	Orel Hershiser, Dodgers, 1985	.864
13.	Bill Donovan, Tigers, 1907	.862
	Whitey Ford, Yankees, 1961	.862
15.	Roger Clemens, Red Sox, 1986	.857
	Dwight Gooden, Mets, 1985	.857
17.	Pedro Martinez, Red Sox, 1999	.852
18.	Chief Bender, A's, 1914	.850
	John Smoltz, Braves, 1998	.850
20.	Lefty Grove, A's, 1930	.848

CONSECUTIVE VICTORIES

1.	Rube Marquard, Giants, 1912	19
2.	Roy Face, Pirates, 1959	17
3.	Walter Johnson, Senators, 1912	16
	Joe Wood, Red Sox, 1912	16
	Lefty Grove, A's, 1931	16
	Schoolboy Rowe, Tigers, 1934	16
	Carl Hubbell, Giants, 1936	16
	Ewell Blackwell, Reds, 1947	16
	Jack Sanford, Giants, 1962	16
10.	Dazzy Vance, Dodgers, 1924	15
	Alvin Crowder, Senators, 1932	15
	Johnny Allen, Indians, 1937	15
	Bob Gibson, Cardinals, 1968	15
	Dave McNally, Orioles, 1969	15
	Steve Carlton, Phillies, 1972	15
	Gaylord Perry, Indians, 1974	15
	Roger Clemens, Blue Jays, 1998	15
18.	12 tied with 14	

LOSSES

1.	Vic Willis, Braves, 1905	29
2.	George Bell, Dodgers, 1910	27
	Paul Derringer, Cardinals-Reds, 1933	27
	Dummy Taylor, Giants, 1901	27
5.	Gus Dorner, Reds-Braves, 1906	26
	Pete Dowling, Brewers-Indians, 1901	26
	Bob Groom, Senators, 1909	26
	Happy Townsend, Senators, 1904	26
9.	Ben Cantwell, Braves, 1935	25
	Patsy Flaherty, White Sox, 1903	25
	Fred Glade, Browns, 1905	25
	Walter Johnson, Senators, 1909	25
	Oscar Jones, Dodgers, 1904	25
	Stoney McGlynn, Cardinals, 1907	25
	Harry McIntire, Dodgers, 1905	25
	Scott Perry, A's, 1920	25
	Bugs Raymond, Cardinals, 1908	25
	Red Ruffing, Red Sox, 1928	25
	Vic Willis, Braves, 1904	25
	Irv Young, Braves, 1906	25

SAVES

1.	Bobby Thigpen, White Sox, 1990	57
2.	Trevor Hoffman, Padres, 1998	53
	Randy Myers, Cubs, 1993	53
4.	Rod Beck, Cubs, 1998	51
	Dennis Eckersley, A's, 1992	51
6.	Rod Beck, Giants, 1993	48
	Dennis Eckersley, A's, 1990	48
	Jeff Shaw, Reds-Dodgers, 1998	48
9.	Lee Smith, Cardinals, 1991	47
10.	Tom Gordon, Red Sox, 1998	46
	Bryan Harvey, Angels, 1991	46
	Jose Mesa, Indians, 1995	46
	Dave Righetti, Yankees, 1986	46
	Lee Smith, Cardinals-Yankees, 1993	46
15.	Antonio Alfonseca, Marlins, 2000	45
	Dennis Eckersley, A's, 1988	45
	Bryan Harvey, Marlins, 1993	45
	Jeff Montgomery, Royals, 1993	45
	Randy Myers, Orioles, 1997	45
	Dan Quisenberry, Royals, 1983	45
	Mariano Rivera, Yankees, 1999	45
	Bruce Sutter, Cardinals, 1984	45
	Duane Ward, Blue Jays, 1993	45

SHUTOUTS

1.	Grover Alexander, Phillies, 1916	16
2.	Jack Coombs, A's, 1910	13
	Bob Gibson, Cardinals, 1968	13
4.	Grover Alexander, Phillies, 1915	12
5.	Dean Chance, Angels, 1964	11
	Walter Johnson, Senators, 1913	11
	Sandy Koufax, Dodgers, 1963	11
	Christy Mathewson, Giants, 1908	11
	Ed Walsh, White Sox, 1908	11
10.	Mort Cooper, Cardinals, 1942	10
	Dave Davenport, St. Louis F.L., 1915	10
	Bob Feller, Indians, 1946	10
	Carl Hubbell, Giants, 1933	10
	Bob Lemon, Indians, 1948	10
	Juan Marichal, Giants, 1965	10
	Jim Palmer, Orioles, 1975	10
	John Tudor, Cardinals, 1985	10
	Ed Walsh, White Sox, 1906	10
	Joe Wood, Red Sox, 1912	10
	Cy Young, Red Sox, 1904	10

RUNS ALLOWED

1.	Snake Wiltse, A's-Orioles, 1902	226
2.	Joe McGinnity, Orioles, 1901	219
3.	Chick Fraser, A's, 1901	210
4.	Pete Dowling, Brewers-Indians, 1901	209
5.	Bobo Newsom, Browns, 1938	205
	Togie Pittinger, Braves, 1903	205
7.	Bill Carrick, Senators, 1901	198
8.	Bill Phillips, Reds, 1901	196
9.	Bill Carrick, Senators, 1902	194
10.	Dummy Taylor, Giants, 1901	193
11.	Harry Howell, Orioles, 1901	188
	Harry McIntire, Dodgers, 1905	188
13.	Sam Gray, Browns, 1931	187
14.	Case Patten, Senators, 1902	186
15.	Watty Lee, Senators, 1901	184
16.	Bill Reidy, Brewers, 1901	183
17.	Dickie Kerr, White Sox, 1921	182
18.	Ray Kremer, Pirates, 1930	181
	Al Orth, Senators, 1902	181
20.	Ray Benge, Phillies, 1930	178

HITS ALLOWED

1.	Joe McGinnity, Orioles, 1901	412
2.	Snake Wiltse, A's-Orioles, 1902	397
3.	Togie Pittinger, Braves, 1903	396
4.	Joe McGinnity, Giants, 1903	391
5.	Oscar Jones, Dodgers, 1904	387
6.	Wilbur Wood, White Sox, 1973	381
7.	George Uhle, Indians, 1923	378
8.	Dummy Taylor, Giants, 1901	377
9.	Vic Willis, Braves, 1902	372
10.	Noodles Hahn, Reds, 1901	370
11.	Bill Carrick, Senators, 1901	367
	Al Orth, Senators, 1902	367
	Case Patten, Senators, 1904	367
14.	Ray Kremer, Pirates, 1930	366
15.	Urban Shocker, Browns, 1922	365
16.	Bill Phillips, Reds, 1901	364
	Bill Reidy, Brewers, 1901	364
18.	Jack Coombs, A's, 1911	360
	Togie Pittinger, Braves, 1902	360
20.	Dickie Kerr, White Sox, 1921	357
	Vic Willis, Braves, 1904	357

STRIKEOUTS

1.	Nolan Ryan, Angels, 1973	383
2.	Sandy Koufax, Dodgers, 1965	382
3.	Nolan Ryan, Angels, 1974	367
4.	Randy Johnson, Diamondbacks, 1999	364
5.	Rube Waddell, A's, 1904	349
6.	Bob Feller, Indians, 1946	348
7.	Randy Johnson, Diamondbacks, 2000	347
8.	Nolan Ryan, Angels, 1977	341
9.	Randy Johnson, Mariners-Astros, 1998	329
	Nolan Ryan, Angels, 1972	329
11.	Nolan Ryan, Angels, 1976	327
12.	Sam McDowell, Indians, 1965	325
13.	Curt Schilling, Phillies, 1997	319
14.	Sandy Koufax, Dodgers, 1966	317
15.	Walter Johnson, Senators, 1910	313
	Pedro Martinez, Red Sox, 1999	313
	J.R. Richard, Astros, 1979	313
18.	Steve Carlton, Phillies, 1972	310
19.	Randy Johnson, Mariners, 1993	308
	Mickey Lolich, Tigers, 1971	308

WALKS

1.	Bob Feller, Indians, 1938	208
2.	Nolan Ryan, Angels, 1977	204
3.	Nolan Ryan, Angels, 1974	202
4.	Bob Feller, Indians, 1941	194
5.	Bobo Newsom, Browns, 1938	192
6.	Sam Jones, Cubs, 1955	185
7.	Nolan Ryan, Angels, 1976	183
8.	Bob Harmon, Cardinals, 1911	181
	Bob Turley, Orioles, 1954	181
10.	Tommy Byrne, Yankees, 1949	179
11.	Bob Turley, Yankees, 1955	177
12.	Bump Hadley, White Sox-Browns, 1932	171
13.	Elmer Myers, A's, 1916	168
14.	Bobo Newsom, Senators-Red Sox, 1937	167
15.	Weldon Wyckoff, A's, 1915	165
16.	Earl Moore, Phillies, 1911	164
	Phil Niekro, Braves, 1977	164
18.	Nolan Ryan, Angels, 1973	162
	Johnny Vander Meer, Reds, 1943	162
20.	Tommy Byrne, Yankees, 1950	160

HIT BATSMEN

1.	Chick Fraser, A's, 1901	32
2.	Jack Warhop, Yankees, 1909	26
3.	Chief Bender, A's, 1903	25
4.	Otto Hess, Indians, 1906	24
	Eddie Plank, A's, 1905	24
6.	Howard Ehmke, Tigers, 1922	23
	Eddie Plank, A's, 1903	23
	Jake Weimer, Reds, 1907	23
9.	Cy Morgan, Red Sox-A's, 1909	22
10.	Jack Chesbro, Pirates, 1902	21
	Joe McGinnity, Orioles, 1901	21
	Harry McIntire, Dodgers, 1909	21
	Cy Morgan, A's, 1911	21
	Tom Murphy, Angels, 1969	21
	Doc Newton, Reds-Dodgers, 1901	21
	Henry Schmidt, Dodgers, 1903	21
17.	10 tied with 20	

WILD PITCHES

1.	Red Ames, Giants, 1905	30
2.	Tony Cloninger, Braves, 1966	27
3.	Larry Cheney, Cubs, 1914	26
	Juan Guzman, Blue Jays, 1993	26
5.	Jack Morris, Tigers, 1987	24
6.	Matt Clement, Padres, 2000	23
	Tim Leary, Yankees, 1990	23
	Christy Mathewson, Giants, 1901	23
9.	Tony Cloninger, Braves, 1965	22
	Jack Hamilton, Phillies, 1962	22
	Mike Moore, A's, 1992	22
	Bobby Witt, Rangers, 1986	22
13.	Ken Howell, Phillies, 1989	21
	Walter Johnson, Senators, 1910	21
	Joe Niekro, Astros-Yankees, 1985	21
	Nolan Ryan, Angels, 1977	21
	Scott Williamson, Reds, 2000	21
	Earl Wilson, Red Sox, 1963	21
19.	6 tied with 20	

BATTING

3-GAME SERIES

HIGHEST AVERAGE

(Minimum 9 at-bats)

	Player	Avg.
1.	Jay Johnstone, Phillies, 1976	.778
2.	Brooks Robinson, Orioles, 1970	.583
3.	Darrell Porter, Cardinals, 1982	.556
	Ozzie Smith, Cardinals, 1982	.556
5.	Frank White, Royals, 1980	.545
6.	Art Shamsky, Mets, 1969	.538
7.	Sal Bando, A's, 1975	.500
	Jerry Mumphrey, Yankees, 1981	.500
	Graig Nettles, Yankees, 1981	.500
	Tony Oliva, Twins, 1970	.500
	Brooks Robinson, Orioles, 1969	.500
	Willie Stargell, Pirates, 1970	.500
	Bob Watson, Yankees, 1980	.500
	Richie Zisk, Pirates, 1975	.500

RUNS

	Player	R
1.	Mark Belanger, Orioles, 1970	5
2.	Tommie Agee, Mets, 1969	4
	Mark Belanger, Orioles, 1969	4
	Ken Boswell, Mets, 1969	4
	Rico Carty, Braves, 1969	4
	Dave Concepcion, Reds, 1976	4
	Carlton Fisk, Red Sox, 1975	4
	Phil Garner, Pirates, 1979	4
	Tony Gonzalez, Braves, 1969	4
	Davey Johnson, Orioles, 1970	4
	Cleon Jones, Mets, 1969	4
	Willie McGee, Cardinals, 1982	4
	Larry Milbourne, Yankees, 1981	4
	Boog Powell, Orioles, 1971	4
	Carl Yastrzemski, Red Sox, 1975	4

HITS

	Player	H
1.	Jay Johnstone, Phillies, 1976	7
	Brooks Robinson, Orioles, 1969	7
	Brooks Robinson, Orioles, 1970	7
	Art Shamsky, Mets, 1969	7
5.	Sal Bando, A's, 1975	6
	Paul Blair, Orioles, 1969	6
	Dave Concepcion, Reds, 1979	6
	Cleon Jones, Mets, 1969	6
	Larry Milbourne, Yankees, 1981	6
	Jerry Mumphrey, Yankees, 1981	6
	Graig Nettles, Yankees, 1981	6
	Tony Oliva, Twins, 1970	6
	Boog Powell, Orioles, 1970	6
	Pete Rose, Reds, 1976	6
	Willie Stargell, Pirates, 1970	6
	Bob Watson, Yankees, 1980	6
	Frank White, Royals, 1980	6

HOME RUNS

	Player	HR
1.	Hank Aaron, Braves, 1969	3
2.	Tommie Agee, Mets, 1969	2
	Ken Boswell, Mets, 1969	2
	George Brett, Royals, 1980	2
	George Foster, Reds, 1976	2
	Reggie Jackson, A's, 1971	2
	Davey Johnson, Orioles, 1970	2
	Harmon Killebrew, Twins, 1970	2
	Boog Powell, Orioles, 1971	2
	Willie Stargell, Pirates, 1979	2

TOTAL BASES

	Player	TB
1.	Hank Aaron, Braves, 1969	16
2.	Willie Stargell, Pirates, 1979	13
3.	Tommie Agee, Mets, 1969	12
4.	Paul Blair, Orioles, 1969	11
	Reggie Jackson, A's, 1971	11
	Cleon Jones, Mets, 1969	11
	Willie McGee, Cardinals, 1982	11
	Graig Nettles, Yankees, 1981	11
	Tony Oliva, Twins, 1970	11
	Boog Powell, Orioles, 1970	11
	Bob Watson, Yankees, 1980	11

RUNS BATTED IN

	Player	RBI
1.	Graig Nettles, Yankees, 1981	9
2.	Hank Aaron, Braves, 1969	7
3.	Paul Blair, Orioles, 1969	6
	Boog Powell, Orioles, 1970	6
	Willie Stargell, Pirates, 1979	6
6.	Ken Boswell, Mets, 1969	5
	Willie McGee, Cardinals, 1982	5
8.	Tommie Agee, Mets, 1969	4
	George Brett, Royals, 1980	4
	Mike Cuellar, Orioles, 1970	4
	George Foster, Reds, 1976	4
	Ken Griffey, Reds, 1975	4
	Davey Johnson, Orioles, 1970	4
	Cleon Jones, Mets, 1969	4
	Harmon Killebrew, Twins, 1970	4
	Tony Perez, Reds, 1975	4
	Willie Wilson, Royals, 1980	4

STOLEN BASES

1.	Joe Morgan, Reds, 1975	4
2.	Ken Griffey, Reds, 1975	3
3.	Tommie Agee, Mets, 1969	2
	Juan Beniquez, Red Sox, 1975	2
	Dave Collins, Reds, 1979	2
	Dave Concepcion, Reds, 1975	2
	Ken Griffey Sr., Reds, 1976	2
	Rickey Henderson, A's, 1981	2
	Cleon Jones, Mets, 1969	2
	Bill Madlock, Pirates, 1979	2
	Joe Morgan, Reds, 1976	2
	Amos Otis, Royals, 1980	2

4-GAME SERIES

HIGHEST AVERAGE

(Minimum 12 at-bats)

	Player	Avg.
1.	Dusty Baker, Dodgers, 1978	.467
	Mike Schmidt, Phillies, 1983	.467
3.	Reggie Jackson, Yankees, 1978	.462
4.	Wade Boggs, Red Sox, 1990	.438
	Chipper Jones, Braves, 1995	.438
	Carney Lansford, A's, 1990	.438
	Fred McGriff, Braves, 1995	.438
	Bob Robertson, Pirates, 1971	.438
9.	Gary Matthews, Phillies, 1983	.429
	Willie McCovey, Giants, 1971	.429
	Amos Otis, Royals, 1978	.429

RUNS

	Player	R
1.	George Brett, Royals, 1978	7
2.	Steve Garvey, Dodgers, 1978	6
3.	Al Bumbry, Orioles, 1979	5
	Dave Cash, Pirates, 1971	5
	Reggie Jackson, Yankees, 1978	5
	Fred McGriff, Braves, 1995	5
	Eddie Murray, Orioles, 1983	5
	Cal Ripken, Orioles, 1983	5
	Bob Robertson, Pirates, 1971	5
	Mike Schmidt, Phillies, 1983	5
	Roy White, Yankees, 1978	5

HITS

	Player	H
1.	Dave Cash, Pirates, 1971	8
2.	Dusty Baker, Dodgers, 1978	7
	Wade Boggs, Red Sox, 1990	7
	George Brett, Royals, 1978	7
	Rod Carew, Angels, 1979	7
	Steve Garvey, Dodgers, 1974	7
	Steve Garvey, Dodgers, 1978	7
	Chipper Jones, Braves, 1995	7
	Carney Lansford, A's, 1990	7
	Barry Larkin, Reds, 1995	7
	Rudy Law, White Sox, 1983	7
	Davey Lopes, Dodgers, 1978	7
	Fred McGriff, Braves, 1995	7
	Bob Robertson, Pirates, 1971	7
	Bill Russell, Dodgers, 1974	7
	Bill Russell, Dodgers, 1978	7
	Mike Schmidt, Phillies, 1983	7

HOME RUNS

	Player	HR
1.	Steve Garvey, Dodgers, 1978	4
	Bob Robertson, Pirates, 1971	4
3.	George Brett, Royals, 1978	3
	Jose Canseco, A's, 1988	3
	Gary Matthews, Phillies, 1983	3
6.	Dusty Baker, Dodgers, 1977	2
	Sal Bando, A's, 1974	2
	Dan Ford, Angels, 1979	2
	Steve Garvey, Dodgers, 1974	2
	Richie Hebner, Pirates, 1971	2
	Reggie Jackson, Yankees, 1978	2
	Davey Lopes, Dodgers, 1978	2
	Greg Luzinski, Phillies, 1978	2
	Willie McCovey, Giants, 1971	2
	Willie Stargell, Pirates, 1974	2

TOTAL BASES

	Player	TB
1.	Steve Garvey, Dodgers, 1978	22
2.	Bob Robertson, Pirates, 1971	20
3.	George Brett, Royals, 1978	19
4.	Davey Lopes, Dodgers, 1978	16
5.	Jose Canseco, A's, 1988	15
	Gary Matthews, Phillies, 1983	15
7.	Steve Garvey, Dodgers, 1974	14
	Greg Luzinski, Phillies, 1978	14
9.	Reggie Jackson, Yankees, 1978	13
10.	Dusty Baker, Dodgers, 1977	12
	Dan Ford, Angels, 1979	12
	Richie Hebner, Pirates, 1971	12
	Willie McCovey, Giants, 1971	12
	Mike Schmidt, Phillies, 1983	12
	Willie Stargell, Pirates, 1974	12

RUNS BATTED IN

	Player	RBI
1.	Dusty Baker, Dodgers, 1977	8
	Gary Matthews, Phillies, 1983	8
3.	Steve Garvey, Dodgers, 1978	7
4.	Reggie Jackson, Yankees, 1978	6
	Willie McCovey, Giants, 1971	6
	Bob Robertson, Pirates, 1971	6
7.	Mike Devereaux, Braves, 1995	5
	Steve Garvey, Dodgers, 1974	5
	Davey Lopes, Dodgers, 1978	5
	Eddie Murray, Orioles, 1979	5
	Al Oliver, Pirates, 1971	5

STOLEN BASES

1.	Amos Otis, Royals, 1978	4
2.	Davey Lopes, Dodgers, 1974	3
3.	Al Bumbry, Orioles, 1979	2
	Jose Canseco, A's, 1990	2
	Julio Cruz, White Sox, 1983	2
	Rickey Henderson, A's, 1990	2
	Pat Kelly, Orioles, 1979	2
	Rudy Law, White Sox, 1983	2
	Willie McGee, A's, 1990	2
10.	39 tied with 1	

5-GAME SERIES

HIGHEST AVERAGE

(Minimum 15 at-bats)

	Player	Avg.
1.	Will Clark, Giants, 1989	.650
2.	Mark Grace, Cubs, 1989	.647
3.	Fred Lynn, Angels, 1982	.611
4.	Terry Puhl, Astros, 1980	.526
5.	Chris Chambliss, Yankees, 1976	.524
6.	Roberto Alomar, Blue Jays, 1991	.474
	Bernie Williams, Yankees, 1996	.474
8.	Jose Offerman, Red Sox, 1999	.458
9.	Pete Rose, Reds, 1972	.450
10.	Edgardo Alfonzo, Mets, 2000	.444
	George Brett, Royals, 1976	.444
	Hal McRae, Royals, 1977	.444

RUNS

	Player	R
1.	Will Clark, Giants, 1989	8
	Rickey Henderson, A's, 1989	8
	Timo Perez, Mets, 2000	8
4.	Mike Pizaaz, Mets, 2000	7
5.	Brett Butler, Giants, 1989	6
	Tony Fernandez, Blue Jays, 1989	6
	Tony Gwynn, Padres, 1984	6
	Hal McRae, Royals, 1977	6
	Ryne Sandberg, Cubs, 1989	6
	Bernie Williams, Yankees, 1996	6

HITS

	Player	H
1.	Will Clark, Giants, 1989	13
2.	Chris Chambliss, Yankees, 1976	11
	Mark Grace, Cubs, 1989	11
	Fred Lynn, Angels, 1982	11
	Jose Offerman, Red Sox, 1999	11
6.	Derek Jeter, Yankees, 1996	10
	Thurman Munson, Yankees, 1976	10
	Terry Puhl, Astros, 1980	10
9.	Roberto Alomar, Blue Jays, 1991	9
	Kirby Puckett, Twins, 1991	9
	Mickey Rivers, Yankees, 1977	9
	Pete Rose, Reds, 1972	9
	Bernie Williams, Yankees, 1996	9

HOME RUNS

	Player	HR
1.	Rusty Staub, Mets, 1973	3
	Darryl Strawberry, Yankees, 1996	3
	Todd Zeile, Orioles, 1996	3
4.	Sal Bando, A's, 1973	2
	Scott Brosius, Yankees, 1999	2
	Tom Brunansky, Twins, 1987	2
	Bert Campaneris, A's, 1973	2
	Chris Chambliss, Yankees, 1976	2
	Will Clark, Giants, 1989	2
	Jody Davis, Cubs, 1984	2
	Leon Durham, Cubs, 1984	2
	Cecil Fielder, Yankees, 1996	2
	Gary Gaetti, Twins, 1987	2
	Greg Gagne, Twins, 1987	2
	Nomar Garciaparra, Red Sox, 1999	2
	Rickey Henderson, A's, 1989	2
	Chet Lemon, Tigers, 1987	2
	Gary Matthews, Cubs, 1984	2
	Kevin Mitchell, Giants, 1989	2
	Paul Molitor, Brewers, 1982	2
	Joe Morgan, Reds, 1972	2
	Graig Nettles, Yankees, 1976	2
	Rafael Palmeiro, Orioles, 1996	2
	Dave Parker, A's, 1989	2
	Mike Piazza, Mets, 2000	2
	Kirby Puckett, Twins, 1991	2
	Pete Rose, Reds, 1973	2
	Robby Thompson, Giants, 1989	2

	Bernie Williams, Yankees, 1996	2
	Matt Williams, Giants, 1989	2

TOTAL BASES

1.	Will Clark, Giants, 1989	24
2.	Chris Chambliss, Yankees, 1976	20
3.	Mark Grace, Cubs, 1989	19
4.	Bernie Williams, Yankees, 1996	18
5.	Tom Brunansky, Twins, 1987	17
	Todd Zeile, Orioles, 1996	17
7.	Nomar Garciaparra, Red Sox, 1999	16
	Fred Lynn, Angels, 1982	16
	Mike Piazza, Mets, 2000	16
	Kirby Puckett, Twins, 1991	16
	Ryne Sandberg, Cubs, 1989	16

RUNS BATTED IN

1.	Don Baylor, Angels, 1982	10
2.	Tom Brunansky, Twins, 1987	9
	Matt Williams, Giants, 1989	9
4.	Chris Chambliss, Yankees, 1976	8
	Will Clark, Giants, 1989	8
	Cecil Fielder, Yankees, 1996	8
	Mark Grace, Cubs, 1989	8
	Todd Zeile, Mets, 2000	8
9.	Steve Garvey, Padres, 1984	7
	Kevin Mitchell, Giants, 1989	7

STOLEN BASES

1.	Rickey Henderson, A's, 1989	8
2.	Tony Fernandez, Blue Jays, 1989	5
	Davey Lopes, Dodgers, 1981	5
4.	Randy Bush, Twins, 1987	3
	Bert Campaneris, A's, 1973	3
	Kirk Gibson, Tigers, 1987	3
	Dan Gladden, Twins, 1991	3
	Nelson Liriano, Blue Jays, 1989	3
	Edgar Renteria, Cardinals, 2000	3
	Ryne Sandberg, Cubs, 1984	3
	Devon White, Blue Jays, 1991	3

6-GAME SERIES

HIGHEST AVERAGE

(Minimum 18 at-bats)

1.	Eddie Perez, Braves, 1999	.500
2.	Kenny Lofton, Indians, 1995	.458
3.	Tim Raines, White Sox, 1993	.444
	Devon White, Blue Jays, 1993	.444
5.	Harold Baines, A's, 1992	.440
	Omar Vizquel, Indians, 1998	.440
7.	Fred McGriff, Braves, 1993	.435
	Ozzie Smith, Cardinals, 1985	.435
	Bernie Williams, Yankees, 2000	.435
10.	Roberto Alomar, Blue Jays, 1992	.423

RUNS

1.	Paul Molitor, Blue Jays, 1993	7
	Dave Winfield, Blue Jays, 1992	7
3.	Harold Baines, A's, 1992	6
	Derek Jeter, Yankees, 2000	6
	Willie McGee, Cardinals, 1985	6
	Fred McGriff, Braves, 1993	6
	Paul O'Neill, Yankees, 1998	6
	Gary Sheffield, Marlins, 1997	6
9.	Brady Anderson, Orioles, 1997	5
	Wally Backman, Mets, 1986	5
	Jeff Blauser, Braves, 1993	5
	Jeff Blauser, Braves, 1997	5
	Jay Buhner, Mariners, 1995	5
	Lenny Dykstra, Phillies, 1993	5
	Rickey Henderson, A's, 1992	5
	Andruw Jones, Braves, 1999	5
	Chipper Jones, Braves, 1997	5
	Barry Larkin, Reds, 1990	5
	Bill Madlock, Dodgers, 1985	5
	Tino Martinez, Yankees, 2000	5
	John Olerud, Blue Jays, 1993	5
	Tim Raines, White Sox, 1993	5
	Bernie Williams, Yankees, 2000	5

HITS

1.	Tim Raines, White Sox, 1993	12
	Devon White, Blue Jays, 1993	12
3.	Roberto Alomar, Blue Jays, 1992	11
	Harold Baines, A's, 1992	11
	Kenny Lofton, Indians, 1995	11
	Omar Vizquel, Indians, 1998	11
7.	Carlos Baerga, Indians, 1995	10
	Fred McGriff, Braves, 1993	10
	Eddie Perez, Braves, 1999	10
	Ozzie Smith, Cardinals, 1985	10
	Bernie Williams, Yankees, 2000	10

HOME RUNS

1.	Jim Thome, Indians, 1998	4
2.	Jay Buhner, Mariners, 1995	3
	Bill Madlock, Dodgers, 1985	3
4.	Roberto Alomar, Blue Jays, 1992	2
	Brady Anderson, Orioles, 1997	2
	Jeff Blauser, Braves, 1993	2
	Ken Caminiti, Padres, 1998	2
	Lenny Dykstra, Phillies, 1993	2
	Dave Hollins, Phillies, 1993	2
	Derek Jeter, Yankees, 2000	2
	Chipper Jones, Braves, 1997	2
	Brian Jordan, Braves, 1999	2
	David Justice, Yankees, 2000	2
	Ryan Klesko, Braves, 1997	2
	Candy Maldonado, Blue Jays, 1992	2
	John Olerud, Mets, 1999	2
	Eddie Perez, Braves, 1999	2
	Manny Ramirez, Indians, 1995	2
	Manny Ramirez, Indians, 1997	2
	Manny Ramirez, Indians, 1998	2
	Alex Rodriguez, Mariners, 2000	2
	Darryl Strawberry, Mets, 1986	2
	Jim Thome, Indians, 1995	2
	Dave Winfield, Blue Jays, 1992	2

TOTAL BASES

1.	Jim Thome, Indians, 1998	19
2.	Roberto Alomar, Blue Jays, 1992	18
	Jay Buhner, Mariners, 1995	18
	Bill Madlock, Dodgers, 1985	18
	Eddie Perez, Braves, 1999	18
	Devon White, Blue Jays, 1993	18
7.	Brady Anderson, Orioles, 1997	17
	Alex Rodriguez, Mariners, 2000	17
9.	Harold Baines, A's, 1992	16
	Paul Molitor, Blue Jays, 1993	16
	Ozzie Smith, Cardinals, 1985	16

RUNS BATTED IN

1.	David Justice, Yankees, 2000	8
	Jim Thome, Indians, 1998	8
3.	Bill Madlock, Dodgers, 1985	7
	Ruben Sierra, A's, 1992	7
5.	Scott Brosius, Yankees, 1998	6
	Tom Herr, Cardinals, 1985	6
	Lance Johnson, White Sox, 1993	6
	Candy Maldonado, Blue Jays, 1992	6
	John Olerud, Mets, 1999	6
10.	Moises Alou, Marlins, 1997	5
	Jay Buhner, Mariners, 1995	5
	Chili Davis, Yankees, 1998	5
	Derek Jeter, Yankees, 2000	5
	Charles Johnson, Marlins, 1997	5
	Brian Jordan, Braves, 1999	5
	John Kruk, Phillies, 1993	5
	Paul Molitor, Blue Jays, 1993	5
	Paul O'Neill, Yankees, 2000	5
	Terry Pendleton, Braves, 1993	5
	Eddie Perez, Braves, 1999	5
	Alex Rodriguez, Mariners, 2000	5
	Terry Steinbach, A's, 1992	5
	Darryl Strawberry, Mets, 1986	5
	Jim Thome, Indians, 1995	5
	Michael Tucker, Braves, 1998	5
	Robin Ventura, White Sox, 1993	5
	Bernie Williams, Yankees, 1998	5

STOLEN BASES

1.	Willie Wilson, A's, 1992	7
2.	Roberto Alomar, Blue Jays, 1992	5
	Kenny Lofton, Indians, 1995	5
4.	Roberto Alomar, Blue Jays, 1993	4
	Vince Coleman, Mariners, 1995	4
	Omar Vizquel, Indians, 1998	4
7.	Marquis Grissom, Indians, 1997	3
	Billy Hatcher, Astros, 1986	3
	Derek Jeter, Yankees, 1998	3
	Chipper Jones, Braves, 1999	3
	Barry Larkin, Reds, 1990	3
	Omar Vizquel, Indians, 1995	3
	Gerald Williams, Braves, 1999	3

7-GAME SERIES

HIGHEST AVERAGE

(Minimum 21 at-bats)

1.	Javy Lopez, Braves, 1996	.542
2.	Bob Boone, Angels, 1986	.455
3.	Mark Lemke, Braves, 1996	.444
4.	Chipper Jones, Braves, 1996	.440
5.	Spike Owen, Red Sox, 1986	.429
6.	Jeffrey Leonard, Giants, 1987	.417
7.	Jay Bell, Pirates, 1991	.414
8.	Tony Pena, Cardinals, 1987	.381
9.	Marty Barrett, Red Sox, 1986	.367
10.	Mike Scioscia, Dodgers, 1988	.364

RUNS

1.	Javy Lopez, Braves, 1996	8
	Jim Rice, Red Sox, 1986	8
3.	Marquis Grissom, Braves, 1996	7
	Steve Sax, Dodgers, 1988	7
5.	Don Baylor, Red Sox, 1986	6
	George Brett, Royals, 1985	6
	Lenny Dykstra, Mets, 1988	6
	Chipper Jones, Braves, 1996	6
	Fred McGriff, Braves, 1996	6
10.	14 players tied with 5	

HITS

1.	Javy Lopez, Braves, 1996	13
2.	Jay Bell, Pirates, 1991	12
	Mark Lemke, Braves, 1996	12
4.	Marty Barrett, Red Sox, 1986	11
	Chipper Jones, Braves, 1996	11
6.	Bob Boone, Angels, 1986	10
	Rich Gedman, Red Sox, 1986	10
	Marquis Grissom, Braves, 1996	10
	Jeffrey Leonard, Giants, 1987	10
10.	Don Baylor, Red Sox, 1986	9
	George Bell, Blue Jays, 1985	9
	Will Clark, Giants, 1987	9
	Doug DeCinces, Angels, 1986	9
	Gregg Jefferies, Mets, 1988	9
	Spike Owen, Red Sox, 1986	9
	Gary Pettis, Angels, 1986	9
	Dick Schofield, Angeles, 1986	9
	Darryl Strawberry, Mets, 1988	9
	Willie Wilson, Royals, 1985	9

HOME RUNS

1.	Jeffrey Leonard, Giants, 1987	4
2.	George Brett, Royals, 1985	3
3.	Ron Gant, Braves, 1992	2
	Ron Gant, Cardinals, 1996	2
	Kirk Gibson, Dodgers, 1988	2
	David Justice, Braves, 1992	2
	Javy Lopez, Braves, 1996	2
	Fred McGriff, Braves, 1996	2
	Kevin McReynolds, Mets, 1988	2
	Jim Rice, Red Sox, 1986	2
	Pat Sheridan, Royals, 1985	2

TOTAL BASES

1.	Javy Lopez, Braves, 1996	24
2.	Jeffrey Leonard, Giants, 1987	22
3.	George Brett, Royals, 1985	19
4.	Jay Bell, Pirates, 1991	17
	Mark Lemke, Braves, 1996	17
6.	Don Baylor, Red Sox, 1986	15
	Doug DeCinces, Angels, 1986	15
	Fred McGriff, Braves, 1996	15
	Kevin McReynolds, Mets, 1988	15
10.	Will Clark, Giants, 1987	14
	Rich Gedman, Red Sox, 1986	14
	Marquis Grissom, Braves, 1996	14
	David Justice, Braves, 1992	14
	Darryl Strawberry, Mets, 1988	14

RUNS BATTED IN

1.	Brian Downing, Angels, 1986	7
	Fred McGriff, Braves, 1996	7
3.	Ron Gant, Braves, 1992	6
	Rich Gedman, Red Sox, 1986	6
	Kirk Gibson, Dodgers, 1988	6
	David Justice, Braves, 1992	6
	Javy Lopez, Braves, 1996	6
	Jim Rice, Red Sox, 1986	6
	Darryl Strawberry, Mets, 1988	6
	Jim Sundberg, Royals, 1985	6

STOLEN BASES

1.	Ron Gant, Braves, 1991	7
2.	Steve Sax, Dodgers, 1988	5
3.	Barry Bonds, Pirates, 1991	3
	Otis Nixon, Braves, 1992	3
5.	Kirk Gibson, Dodgers, 1988	2
	Marquis Grissom, Braves, 1996	2
	Kevin McReynolds, Mets, 1988	2
	Gary Redus, Pirates, 1991	2
	John Shelby, Dodgers, 1988	2
	Robby Thompson, Giants, 1987	2

Will Clark was prolific in the five-game 1989 NLCS when he played for the Giants.

PITCHING

3-GAME SERIES

INNINGS PITCHED

1. Ken Holtzman, A's, 1975 ... 11.0
Dave McNally, Orioles, 1969 ... 11.0
3. Dave Boswell, Twins, 1969 ... 10.2
4. Dock Ellis, Pirates, 1970 ... 9.2
5. Bert Blyleven, Pirates, 1979 ... 9.0
Mike Cuellar, Orioles, 1971 ... 9.0
Bob Forsch, Cardinals, 1982 ... 9.0
Don Gullett, Reds, 1975 ... 9.0
Larry Gura, Royals, 1980 ... 9.0
Dave McNally, Orioles, 1970 ... 9.0
Gary Nolan, Reds, 1970 ... 9.0
Jim Palmer, Orioles, 1969 ... 9.0
Jim Palmer, Orioles, 1970 ... 9.0
Jim Palmer, Orioles, 1971 ... 9.0
Luis Tiant, Red Sox, 1975 ... 9.0

LOWEST ERA

(Minimum 9 innings)

1. Bob Forsch, Cardinals, 1982 ... 0.00
Dave McNally, Orioles, 1969 ... 0.00
Gary Nolan, Reds, 1970 ... 0.00
Luis Tiant, Red Sox, 1975 ... 0.00
5. Dave Boswell, Twins, 1969 ... 0.84
6. Bert Blyleven, Pirates, 1979 ... 1.00
Mike Cuellar, Orioles, 1971 ... 1.00
Jim Palmer, Orioles, 1970 ... 1.00
9. Larry Gura, Royals, 1980 ... 2.00
Jim Palmer, Orioles, 1969 ... 2.00

VICTORIES

1. Joaquin Andujar, Cardinals, 1982 ... 1
Bert Blyleven, Pirates, 1979 ... 1
Mike Cuellar, Orioles, 1971 ... 1
Rawly Eastwick, Reds, 1975 ... 1
Rawly Eastwick, Reds, 1976 ... 1
Bob Forsch, Cardinals, 1982 ... 1
George Frazier, Yankees, 1981 ... 1
Don Gullett, Reds, 1975 ... 1
Don Gullett, Reds, 1976 ... 1
Larry Gura, Royals, 1980 ... 1
Dick Hall, Orioles, 1969 ... 1
Dick Hall, Orioles, 1970 ... 1
Grant Jackson, Pirates, 1979 ... 1
Tommy John, Yankees, 1981 ... 1
Dennis Leonard, Royals, 1980 ... 1
Aurelio Lopez, Tigers, 1984 ... 1
Dave McNally, Orioles, 1969 ... 1
Dave McNally, Orioles, 1970 ... 1
Dave McNally, Orioles, 1971 ... 1
Jim Merritt, Reds, 1970 ... 1
Roger Moret, Red Sox, 1975 ... 1
Jack Morris, Tigers, 1984 ... 1
Gary Nolan, Reds, 1970 ... 1
Fred Norman, Reds, 1975 ... 1
Jim Palmer, Orioles, 1969 ... 1
Jim Palmer, Orioles, 1970 ... 1
Jim Palmer, Orioles, 1971 ... 1
Dan Quisenberry, Royals, 1980 ... 1
Dave Righetti, Yankees, 1981 ... 1
Don Robinson, Pirates, 1979 ... 1
Nolan Ryan, Mets, 1969 ... 1
Tom Seaver, Mets, 1969 ... 1
Bruce Sutter, Cardinals, 1982 ... 1
Ron Taylor, Mets, 1969 ... 1
Luis Tiant, Red Sox, 1975 ... 1
Milt Wilcox, Reds, 1970 ... 1
Milt Wilcox, Tigers, 1984 ... 1
Rick Wise, Red Sox, 1975 ... 1
Pat Zachry, Reds, 1976 ... 1

SAVES

1. Dick Drago, Red Sox, 1975 ... 2
Don Gullett, Reds, 1970 ... 2
3. Pedro Borbon, Reds, 1975 ... 1
Pedro Borbon, Reds, 1976 ... 1
Clay Carroll, Reds, 1970 ... 1
Rawly Eastwick, Reds, 1975 ... 1
Rich Gossage, Yankees, 1981 ... 1
Willie Hernandez, Tigers, 1984 ... 1
Tug McGraw, Mets, 1969 ... 1
Dan Quisenberry, Royals, 1980 ... 1
Don Robinson, Pirates, 1979 ... 1
Bruce Sutter, Cardinals, 1982 ... 1
Ron Taylor, Mets, 1969 ... 1
Eddie Watt, Orioles, 1971 ... 1

4-GAME SERIES

INNINGS PITCHED

1. Don Sutton, Dodgers, 1974 ... 17.0
2. Dave Stewart, A's, 1990 ... 16.0
3. Gaylord Perry, Giants, 1971 ... 14.2
4. Pete Schourek, Reds, 1995 ... 14.1
5. Steve Carlton, Phillies, 1983 ... 13.2
Tommy John, Dodgers, 1977 ... 13.2
7. Dave Stewart, A's, 1988 ... 13.1
8. Bruce Hurst, Red Sox, 1988 ... 13.0
9. Mike Cuellar, Orioles, 1974 ... 12.2
10. Dennis Leonard, Royals, 1978 ... 12.0
Jerry Reuss, Dodgers, 1983 ... 12.0

LOWEST ERA

(Minimum 9 innings)

1. Vida Blue, A's, 1974 ... 0.00
Mike Boddicker, Orioles, 1983 ... 0.00
Ken Holtzman, A's, 1974 ... 0.00
Tommy John, Dodgers, 1978 ... 0.00
Scott McGregor, Orioles, 1979 ... 0.00
6. Don Sutton, Dodgers, 1974 ... 0.53
7. Steve Carlton, Phillies, 1983 ... 0.66
Tommy John, Dodgers, 1977 ... 0.66
9. Britt Burns, White Sox, 1983 ... 0.96
10. 3 tied with 1.00

VICTORIES

1. Steve Carlton, Phillies, 1983 ... 2
Gene Nelson, A's, 1988 ... 2
Dave Stewart, A's, 1990 ... 2
Don Sutton, Dodgers, 1974 ... 2
5. 40 tied with 1

SAVES

1. Dennis Eckersley, A's, 1988 ... 4
2. Dave Giusti, Pirates, 1971 ... 3
3. Dennis Eckersley, A's, 1990 ... 2
4. Ken Clay, Yankees, 1978 ... 1
Rollie Fingers, A's, 1974 ... 1
Mike Garman, Dodgers, 1977 ... 1
Rich Gossage, Yankees, 1978 ... 1
Al Holland, Phillies, 1983 ... 1
Rick Honeycutt, A's, 1990 ... 1
Tug McGraw, Phillies, 1977 ... 1
Greg McMichael, Braves, 1995 ... 1
Tom Niedenfuer, Dodgers, 1983 ... 1
Sammy Stewart, Orioles, 1983 ... 1

5-GAME SERIES

INNINGS PITCHED

1. Mickey Lolich, Tigers, 1972 ... 19.0
2. Ray Burris, Expos, 1981 ... 17.0
3. Tom Seaver, Mets, 1973 ... 16.2
4. Catfish Hunter, A's, 1973 ... 16.1
5. Mike Hampton, Mets, 2000 ... 16.0
Dave Stewart, A's, 1989 ... 16.0
7. Steve Blass, Pirates, 1972 ... 15.2
8. Catfish Hunter, A's, 1972 ... 15.1
9. Orlando Hernandez, Yankees, 1999 ... 15.0
Andy Pettitte, Yankees, 1996 ... 15.0
Paul Splittorff, Royals, 1977 ... 15.0

LOWEST ERA

(Minimum 9 innings)

1. Joe Coleman, Tigers, 1972 ... 0.00
Mike Hampton, Mets, 2000 ... 0.00
Burt Hooton, Dodgers, 1981 ... 0.00
Jon Matlack, Mets, 1973 ... 0.00
Joe Niekro, Astros, 1980 ... 0.00
Blue Moon Odom, A's, 1972 ... 0.00
7. Ray Burris, Expos, 1981 ... 0.53
8. Ken Holtzman, A's, 1973 ... 0.82
9. Sparky Lyle, Yankees, 1977 ... 0.96
10. Ross Grimsley, Reds, 1972 ... 1.00

VICTORIES

1. Bert Blyleven, Twins, 1987 ... 2
Mike Hampton, Mets, 2000 ... 2
Burt Hooton, Dodgers, 1981 ... 2
Catfish Hunter, A's, 1973 ... 2
Craig Lefferts, Padres, 1984 ... 2
Sparky Lyle, Yankees, 1977 ... 2
Jack Morris, Twins, 1991 ... 2
Blue Moon Odom, A's, 1972 ... 2
Dave Stewart, A's, 1989 ... 2
10. 67 tied with 1

SAVES

1. Rick Aguilera, Twins, 1991 ... 3
Steve Bedrosian, Giants, 1989 ... 3
Dennis Eckersley, A's, 1989 ... 3
4. Pete Ladd, Brewers, 1982 ... 2
Tug McGraw, Phillies, 1980 ... 2
Jeff Reardon, Twins, 1987 ... 2
Mariano Rivera, Yankees, 1999 ... 2
8. 19 tied with 1

6-GAME SERIES

INNINGS PITCHED

1. Mike Scott, Astros, 1986 ... 18.0
2. Dwight Gooden, Mets, 1986 ... 17.0
3. Dave Stewart, A's, 1992 ... 16.2
4. Doug Drabek, Pirates, 1990 ... 16.1
5. Curt Schilling, Phillies, 1993 ... 16.0
6. David Wells, Yankees, 1998 ... 15.2
7. Orel Hershiser, Dodgers, 1985 ... 15.1
Randy Johnson, Mariners, 1995 ... 15.1
Bob Knepper, Astros, 1986 ... 15.1
10. 4 tied with 15.0

LOWEST ERA

(Minimum 9 innings)

1. Roger Clemens, Yankees, 2000 ... 0.00
Denny Neagle, Braves, 1997 ... 0.00
3. Mike Scott, Astros, 1986 ... 0.50
4. Mike Mussina, Orioles, 1997 ... 0.60
5. Livan Hernandez, Marlins, 1997 ... 0.84
6. Sterling Hitchcock, Padres, 1998 ... 0.90
7. Wilson Alvarez, White Sox, 1993 ... 1.00
Bartolo Colon, Indians, 1998 ... 1.00
9. Dwight Gooden, Mets, 1986 ... 1.06
10. Orel Hershiser, Indians, 1995 ... 1.29

VICTORIES

1. Jesse Orosco, Mets, 1986 ... 3
2. Kevin Brown, Marlins, 1997 ... 2
Freddy Garcia, Mariners, 2000 ... 2
Juan Guzman, Blue Jays, 1992 ... 2
Juan Guzman, Blue Jays, 1993 ... 2
Livan Hernandez, Marlins, 1997 ... 2
Orlando Hernandez, Mariners, 2000 ... 2
Orel Hershiser, Indians, 1995 ... 2
Sterling Hitchcock, Padres, 1998 ... 2
Mike Scott, Astros, 1986 ... 2
Dave Stewart, Blue Jays, 1993 ... 2
David Wells, Yankees, 1998 ... 2
Mitch Williams, Phillies, 1993 ... 2

SAVES

1. Tom Henke, Blue Jays, 1992 ... 3
Randy Myers, Reds, 1990 ... 3
3. Ken Dayley, Cardinals, 1985 ... 2
Jose Mesa, Indians, 1997 ... 2
Robb Nen, Marlins, 1997 ... 2
Duane Ward, Blue Jays, 1993 ... 2
Mitch Williams, Phillies, 1993 ... 2
8. 20 tied with 1

7-GAME SERIES

INNINGS PITCHED

1. Orel Hershiser, Dodgers, 1988 ... 24.2
2. Roger Clemens, Red Sox, 1986 ... 22.2
3. John Smoltz, Braves, 1992 ... 20.1
Dave Stieb, Blue Jays, 1985 ... 20.1
5. Dwight Gooden, Mets, 1988 ... 18.1
6. Tim Wakefield, Pirates, 1992 ... 18.0
7. Mike Witt, Angels, 1986 ... 17.2
8. Danny Cox, Cardinals, 1987 ... 17.0
Doug Drabek, Pirates, 1992 ... 17.0
10. Steve Avery, Braves, 1991 ... 16.1

LOWEST ERA

(Minimum 9 innings)

1. Steve Avery, Braves, 1991 ... 0.00
Danny Jackson, Royals, 1985 ... 0.00
Dennis Lamp, Blue Jays, 1985 ... 0.00
4. Doug Drabek, Pirates, 1991 ... 0.60
Dave Dravecky, Giants, 1987 ... 0.60
6. Zane Smith, Pirates, 1991 ... 0.61
7. John Candelaria, Angels, 1986 ... 0.84
8. Orel Hershiser, Dodgers, 1988 ... 1.09
9. John Smoltz, Braves, 1996 ... 1.20
10. Bud Black, Royals, 1985 ... 1.69

VICTORIES

1. Steve Avery, Braves, 1991 ... 2
Tim Belcher, Dodgers, 1988 ... 2
Tom Henke, Blue Jays, 1985 ... 2
Randy Myers, Mets, 1988 ... 2
John Smoltz, Braves, 1991 ... 2
John Smoltz, Braves, 1992 ... 2
John Smoltz, Braves, 1996 ... 2
Tim Wakefield, Pirates, 1992 ... 2
9. 33 tied with 1

SAVES

1. Alejandro Pena, Braves, 1991 ... 3
2. Ken Dayley, Cardinals, 1987 ... 2
Mark Wohlers, Braves, 1996 ... 2
4. Dennis Eckersley, Cardinals, 1996 ... 1
Orel Hershiser, Dodgers, 1988 ... 1
Brian Holton, Dodgers, 1988 ... 1
Roger Mason, Pirates, 1991 ... 1
Donnie Moore, Angels, 1986 ... 1
Alejandro Pena, Dodgers, 1988 ... 1
Dan Quisenberry, Royals, 1985 ... 1
Jeff Reardon, Braves, 1992 ... 1
Calvin Schiraldi, Red Sox, 1986 ... 1
Bob Walk, Pirates, 1991 ... 1
Todd Worrell, Cardinals, 1987 ... 1

BATTING

4-GAME SERIES

HIGHEST AVERAGE

(Minimum 12 at-bats)

1. Billy Hatcher, Reds, 1990 .... .750
2. Babe Ruth, Yankees, 1928 .... .625
3. Chris Sabo, Reds, 1990 .... .563
4. Bret Boone, Braves, 1999 .... .538
5. Johnny Bench, Reds, 1976 .... .533
6. Lou Gehrig, Yankees, 1932 .... .529
   Thurman Munson, Yankees, 1976 .... .529
8. Tony Gwynn, Padres, 1998 .... .500
   Mark Koenig, Yankees, 1927 .... .500
   Joe Marty, Cubs, 1938 .... .500
   Vic Wertz, Indians, 1954 .... .500

RUNS

1. Lou Gehrig, Yankees, 1932 9
   Babe Ruth, Yankees, 1928 9
3. Earle Combs, Yankees, 1932 8
   Charlie Keller, Yankees, 1939 8
5. Earle Combs, Yankees, 1927 6
   Billy Hatcher, Reds, 1990 6
   Dave Henderson, A's, 1989 6
   Babe Ruth, Yankees, 1932 6
   Hank Thompson, Giants, 1954 6
10. 8 tied with 5

HITS

1. Babe Ruth, Yankees, 1928 10
2. Lou Gehrig, Yankees, 1932 9
   Billy Hatcher, Reds, 1990 9
   Rickey Henderson, A's, 1989 9
   Mark Koenig, Yankees, 1927 9
   Thurman Munson, Yankees, 1976 9
   Chris Sabo, Reds, 1990 9
8. Johnny Bench, Reds, 1976 8
   Scott Brosius, Yankees, 1998 8
   Tony Gwynn, Padres, 1998 8
   Stan Hack, Cubs, 1938 8
   Riggs Stephenson, Cubs, 1932 8
   Vic Wertz, Indians, 1954 8

HOME RUNS

1. Lou Gehrig, Yankees, 1928 4
2. Lou Gehrig, Yankees, 1932 3
   Charlie Keller, Yankees, 1939 3
   Babe Ruth, Yankees, 1928 3
5. Johnny Bench, Reds, 1976 2
   Scott Brosius, Yankees, 1998 2
   Bill Dickey, Yankees, 1939 2
   Dave Henderson, A's, 1989 2
   Tony Lazzeri, Yankees, 1932 2
   Dusty Rhodes, Giants, 1954 2
   Frank Robinson, Orioles, 1966 2
   Babe Ruth, Yankees, 1927 2
   Babe Ruth, Yankees, 1932 2
   Chris Sabo, Reds, 1990 2
   Greg Vaughn, Padres, 1998 2

TOTAL BASES

1. Babe Ruth, Yankees, 1928 22
2. Lou Gehrig, Yankees, 1928 19
   Lou Gehrig, Yankees, 1932 19
   Charlie Keller, Yankees, 1939 19
5. Johnny Bench, Reds, 1976 17
   Rickey Henderson, A's, 1989 17
7. Chris Sabo, Reds, 1990 16
8. Billy Hatcher, Reds, 1990 15
   Vic Wertz, Indians, 1954 15
10. Scott Brosius, Yankees, 1998 14
    Hank Gowdy, Braves, 1914 14

RUNS BATTED IN

1. Lou Gehrig, Yankees, 1928 9
2. Lou Gehrig, Yankees, 1932 8
3. Dusty Rhodes, Giants, 1954 7
   Babe Ruth, Yankees, 1927 7
   Terry Steinbach, A's, 1989 7
6. Johnny Bench, Reds, 1976 6
   Scott Brosius, Yankees, 1998 6
   Ben Chapman, Yankees, 1932 6
   Frankie Crosetti, Yankees, 1938 6
   Joe Gordon, Yankees, 1938 6
   Charlie Keller, Yankees, 1939 6
   Babe Ruth, Yankees, 1932 6

STOLEN BASES

1. Rickey Henderson, A's, 1989 3
   Rickey Henderson, A's, 1990 3
   Derek Jeter, Yankees, 1999 3
4. Brett Butler, Giants, 1989 2
   Charlie Deal, Braves, 1914 2
   Frankie Frisch, Cardinals, 1928 2
   Cesar Geronimo, Reds, 1976 2
   Billy Jurges, Cubs, 1932 2
   Tony Lazzeri, Yankees, 1928 2
   Rabbit Maranville, Braves, 1914 2
   Bob Meusel, Yankees, 1928 2
   Joe Morgan, Reds, 1976 2

5-GAME SERIES

HIGHEST AVERAGE

(Minimum 15 at-bats)

1. Paul Blair, Orioles, 1970 .... .474
   Heinie Groh, Giants, 1922 .... .474
   Paul O'Neill, Yankees, 2000 .... .474
4. Frankie Frisch, Giants, 1922 .... .471
   Harry Steinfeldt, Cubs, 1907 .... .471
   Hack Wilson, Cubs, 1929 .... .471
7. Frank Baker, A's, 1913 .... .450
   Alan Trammell, Tigers, 1984 .... .450
9. Duffy Lewis, Red Sox, 1915 .... .444
10. Fred Luderus, Phillies, 1915 .... .438

RUNS

1. Frank Baker, A's, 1910 6
   Harry Hooper, Red Sox, 1916 6
   Derek Jeter, Yankees, 2000 6
   Lee May, Reds, 1970 6
   Danny Murphy, A's, 1910 6
   Boog Powell, Orioles, 1970 6
   Al Simmons, A's, 1929 6
   Lou Whitaker, Tigers, 1984 6
9. 18 tied with 5

HITS

1. Frank Baker, A's, 1910 9
   Frank Baker, A's, 1913 9
   Paul Blair, Orioles, 1970 9
   Eddie Collins, A's, 1910 9
   Heinie Groh, Giants, 1922 9
   Derek Jeter, Yankees, 2000 9
   Jo-Jo Moore, Giants, 1937 9
   Paul O'Neill, Yankees, 2000 9
   Bobby Richardson, Yankees, 1961 9
   Brooks Robinson, Orioles, 1970 9
   Alan Trammell, Tigers, 1984 9

HOME RUNS

1. Donn Clendenon, Mets, 1969 3
2. Kurt Bevacqua, Padres, 1984 2
   Johnny Blanchard, Yankees, 1961 2
   Jimmie Foxx, A's, 1929 2
   Larry Gardner, Red Sox, 1916 2
   Kirk Gibson, Tigers, 1984 2
   Mule Haas, A's, 1929 2
   Mickey Hatcher, Dodgers, 1988 2
   Harry Hooper, Red Sox, 1915 2
   Derek Jeter, Yankees, 2000 2
   Charlie Keller, Yankees, 1942 2
   Lee May, Reds, 1970 2
   Joe Morgan, Phillies, 1983 2
   Eddie Murray, Orioles, 1983 2
   Mel Ott, Giants, 1933 2
   Mike Piazza, Mets, 2000 2
   Boog Powell, Orioles, 1970 2
   Brooks Robinson, Orioles, 1970 2
   Frank Robinson, Orioles, 1970 2
   Al Simmons, A's, 1929 2
   Alan Trammell, Tigers, 1984 2
   Aaron Ward, Yankees, 1922 2

TOTAL BASES

1. Derek Jeter, Yankees, 2000 19
2. Brooks Robinson, Orioles, 1970 17
3. Alan Trammell, Tigers, 1984 16
4. Kurt Bevacqua, Padres, 1984 15
   Donn Clendenon, Mets, 1969 15
   Lee May, Reds, 1970 15
   Paul O'Neill, Yankees, 2000 15
8. Jimmie Foxx, A's, 1929 14
   Mickey Hatcher, Dodgers, 1988 14
   Mike Piazza, Mets, 2000 14

RUNS BATTED IN

1. Danny Murphy, A's, 1910 9
2. Lee May, Reds, 1970 8
3. Frank Baker, A's, 1913 7
   Kirk Gibson, Tigers, 1984 7
   Hector Lopez, Yankees, 1961 7
   Irish Meusel, Giants, 1922 7
   Wally Schang, A's, 1913 7
8. 6 tied with 6

STOLEN BASES

1. Jimmy Slagle, Cubs, 1907 6
2. Frank Chance, Cubs, 1908 5
3. Eddie Collins, A's, 1910 4
4. Frank Chance, Cubs, 1907 3
   Eddie Collins, A's, 1913 3
   Bill Dahlen, Giants, 1905 3
   Art Devlin, Giants, 1905 3
   Johnny Evers, Cubs, 1907 3
   Kirk Gibson, Tigers, 1984 3
   Davy Jones, Tigers, 1907 3

6-GAME SERIES

HIGHEST AVERAGE

(Minimum 18 at-bats)

1. Billy Martin, Yankees, 1953 .... .500
   Paul Molitor, Blue Jays, 1993 .... .500
   Dave Robertson, Giants, 1917 .... .500
4. Roberto Alomar, Blue Jays, 1993 .... .480
5. Amos Otis, Royals, 1980 .... .478
6. Monte Irvin, Giants, 1951 .... .458
7. Jake Powell, Yankees, 1936 .... .455
8. Pat Borders, Blue Jays, 1992 .... .450
   Reggie Jackson, Yankees, 1977 .... .450
10. Marquis Grissom, Braves, 1996 .... .444

RUNS

1. Reggie Jackson, Yankees, 1977 10
   Paul Molitor, Blue Jays, 1993 10
3. Lenny Dykstra, Phillies, 1993 9
   Roy White, Yankees, 1978 9
5. Jake Powell, Yankees, 1936 8
   Babe Ruth, Yankees, 1923 8
   Devon White, Blue Jays, 1993 8
8. Frank Baker, A's, 1911 7
   Davey Lopes, Dodgers, 1978 7
   Reggie Smith, Dodgers, 1977 7

HITS

1. Roberto Alomar, Blue Jays, 1993 12
   Marquis Grissom, Braves, 1996 12
   Billy Martin, Yankees, 1953 12
   Paul Molitor, Blue Jays, 1993 12
5. Monte Irvin, Giants, 1951 11
   Amos Otis, Royals, 1980 11
   Dave Robertson, Giants, 1917 11
   Bill Russell, Dodgers, 1978 11
9. 10 tied with 10

HOME RUNS

1. Reggie Jackson, Yankees, 1977 5
2. Willie Aikens, Royals, 1980 4
   Lenny Dykstra, Phillies, 1993 4
4. Ryan Klesko, Braves, 1995 3
   Ted Kluszewski, White Sox, 1959 3
   Davey Lopes, Dodgers, 1978 3
   Amos Otis, Royals, 1980 3
   Babe Ruth, Yankees, 1923 3
   Reggie Smith, Dodgers, 1977 3
10. 29 tied with 2

TOTAL BASES

1. Reggie Jackson, Yankees, 1977 25
2. Paul Molitor, Blue Jays, 1993 24
3. Billy Martin, Yankees, 1953 23
4. Willie Aikens, Royals, 1980 22
   Amos Otis, Royals, 1980 22
6. Lenny Dykstra, Phillies, 1993 21
7. Ted Kluszewski, White Sox, 1959 19
   Babe Ruth, Yankees, 1923 19
9. Charlie Neal, Dodgers, 1959 18
10. Frank Baker, A's, 1911 17
    Jim Gilliam, Dodgers, 1953 17
    Davey Lopes, Dodgers, 1978 17
    Devon White, Blue Jays, 1993 17

RUNS BATTED IN

1. Ted Kluszewski, White Sox, 1959 10
2. Tony Fernandez, Blue Jays, 1993 9
3. Willie Aikens, Royals, 1980 8
   Joe Carter, Blue Jays, 1993 8
   Lenny Dykstra, Phillies, 1993 8
   Reggie Jackson, Yankees, 1977 8
   Reggie Jackson, Yankees, 1978 8
   Billy Martin, Yankees, 1953 8
   Bob Meusel, Yankees, 1923 8
   Paul Molitor, Blue Jays, 1993 8

STOLEN BASES

1. Kenny Lofton, Indians, 1995 6
2. Otis Nixon, Braves, 1992 5
   Deion Sanders, Braves, 1992 5
4. Roberto Alomar, Blue Jays, 1993 4
   Lenny Dykstra, Phillies, 1993 4
   Davey Lopes, Dodgers, 1981 4
7. Roberto Alomar, 1992 3
   Larry Bowa, Phillies, 1980 3
   Eddie Collins, White Sox, 1917 3
   Mariano Duncan, Phillies, 1993 3
   Marquis Grissom, Braves, 1995 3
   Joe Tinker, Cubs, 1906 3

7-Game Series

HIGHEST AVERAGE

(Minimum 21 at-bats)

1.	Phil Garner, Pirates, 1979	.500
	Pepper Martin, Cardinals, 1931	.500
3.	Tim McCarver, Cardinals, 1964	.478
4.	Lou Brock, Cardinals, 1968	.464
5.	Max Carey, Pirates, 1925	.458
6.	Joe Harris, Senators, 1925	.440
7.	Tony Perez, Reds, 1972	.435
8.	Marty Barrett, Red Sox, 1986	.433
9.	Phil Cavarretta, Cubs, 1945	.423
	Rusty Staub, Mets, 1973	.423

RUNS

1.	Lou Brock, Cardinals, 1967	8
	Billy Johnson, Yankees, 1947	8
	Tommy Leach, Pirates, 1909	8
	Mickey Mantle, Yankees, 1960	8
	Mickey Mantle, Yankees, 1964	8
	Pepper Martin, Cardinals, 1934	8
	Freddy Parent, Red Sox, 1903	8
	Bobby Richardson, Yankees, 1960	8
	Jim Thome, Indians, 1997	8
	Matt Williams, Indians, 1997	8

HITS

1.	Marty Barrett, Red Sox, 1986	13
	Lou Brock, Cardinals, 1968	13
	Bobby Richardson, Yankees, 1964	13
4.	Lou Brock, Cardinals, 1967	12
	Roberto Clemente, Pirates, 1971	12
	Phil Garner, Pirates, 1979	12
	Buck Herzog, Giants, 1912	12
	Joe Jackson, White Sox, 1919	12
	Pepper Martin, Cardinals, 1931	12
	Sam Rice, Senators, 1925	12
	Bill Skowron, Yankees, 1960	12
	Willie Stargell, Pirates, 1979	12
	Robin Yount, Brewers, 1982	12

HOME RUNS

1.	Hank Bauer, Yankees, 1958	4
	Babe Ruth, Yankees, 1926	4
	Duke Snider, Dodgers, 1952	4
	Duke Snider, Dodgers, 1955	4
	Gene Tenace, A's, 1972	4
6.	14 tied with 3	

TOTAL BASES

1.	Willie Stargell, Pirates, 1979	25
2.	Lou Brock, Cardinals, 1968	24
	Duke Snider, Dodgers, 1952	24
4.	Hank Aaron, Braves, 1957	22
	Hank Bauer, Yankees, 1958	22
	Roberto Clemente, Pirates, 1971	22
	Joe Harris, Senators, 1925	22
8.	Goose Goslin, Senators, 1924	21
	Duke Snider, Dodgers, 1955	21
	Gene Tenace, A's, 1972	21
	Carl Yastrzemski, Red Sox, 1967	21

RUNS BATTED IN

1.	Bobby Richardson, Yankees, 1960	12
2.	Mickey Mantle, Yankees, 1960	11
3.	Sandy Alomar, Indians, 1997	10
	Yogi Berra, Yankees, 1956	10
5.	Moises Alou, Marlins, 1997	9
	Gary Carter, Mets, 1986	9
	Dwight Evans, Red Sox, 1986	9
	Gene Tenace, A's, 1972	9
9.	11 tied with 8	

STOLEN BASES

1.	Lou Brock, Cardinals, 1967	7
	Lou Brock, Cardinals, 1968	7
3.	Vince Coleman, Cardinals, 1987	6
	Honus Wagner, Pirates, 1909	6
5.	Pepper Martin, Cardinals, 1931	5
	Bobby Tolan, Reds, 1972	5
	Omar Vizquel, Indians, 1997	5
8.	Josh Devore, Giants, 1912	4
	Chuck Knoblauch, Twins, 1991	4
10.	15 tied with 3	

PITCHING

4-Game Series

INNINGS PITCHED

1.	Waite Hoyt, Yankees, 1928	18.0
	Sandy Koufax, Dodgers, 1963	18.0
	Dick Rudolph, Braves, 1914	18.0
	Red Ruffing, Yankees, 1938	18.0
5.	Dave Stewart, A's, 1989	16.0
6.	Paul Derringer, Reds, 1939	15.1
	Jose Rijo, Reds, 1990	15.1
8.	Jim Konstanty, Phillies, 1950	15.0
9.	Kevin Brown, Padres, 1998	14.1
10.	Bob Lemon, Indians, 1954	13.1
	Bill Sherdel, Cardinals, 1928	13.1

LOWEST ERA

(Minimum 9 innings)

1.	Wally Bunker, Orioles, 1966	0.00
	Don Drysdale, Dodgers, 1963	0.00
	Bill James, Braves, 1914	0.00
	Jim Palmer, Orioles, 1966	0.00
	Monte Pearson, Yankees, 1939	0.00
	Vic Raschi, Yankees, 1950	0.00
7.	Dick Rudolph, Braves, 1914	0.50
8.	Jose Rijo, Reds, 1990	0.59
9.	Johnny Antonelli, Giants, 1954	0.84
	Wilcy Moore, Yankees, 1927	0.84

VICTORIES

1.	Waite Hoyt, Yankees, 1928	2
	Bill James, Braves, 1914	2
	Sandy Koufax, Dodgers, 1963	2
	Mike Moore, A's, 1989	2
	Jose Rijo, Reds, 1990	2
	Dick Rudolph, Braves, 1914	2
	Red Ruffing, Yankees, 1938	2
	Dave Stewart, A's, 1989	2
9.	44 tied with 1	

SAVES

1.	Mariano Rivera, Yankees, 1998	3
2.	Will McEnaney, Reds, 1976	2
	Herb Pennock, Yankees, 1932	2
	Mariano Rivera, Yankees, 1999	2
5.	Johnny Antonelli, Giants, 1954	1
	Dennis Eckersley, A's, 1989	1
	Wilcy Moore, Yankees, 1927	1
	Johnny Murphy, Yankees, 1938	1
	Randy Myers, Reds, 1990	1
	Ron Perranoski, Dodgers, 1963	1
	Allie Reynolds, Yankees, 1950	1
	Hoyt Wilhelm, Giants, 1954	1

5-Game Series

INNINGS PITCHED

1.	Jack Coombs, A's, 1910	27.0
	Christy Mathewson, Giants, 1905	27.0
3.	Bill Donovan, Tigers, 1907	21.0
4.	Carl Hubbell, Giants, 1933	20.0
5.	Christy Mathewson, Giants, 1913	19.0
	Eddie Plank, A's, 1913	19.0
7.	Chief Bender, A's, 1910	18.2
8.	Orval Overall, Cubs, 1908	18.1
9.	10 tied with 18.0	

LOWEST ERA

(Minimum 9 innings)

1.	Mike Boddicker, Orioles, 1983	0.00
	Mordecai Brown, Cubs, 1907	0.00
	Mordecai Brown, Cubs, 1908	0.00
	Clay Carroll, Reds, 1970	0.00
	Whitey Ford, Yankees, 1961	0.00
	Carl Hubbell, Giants, 1933	0.00
	Christy Mathewson, Giants, 1905	0.00
	Joe McGinnity, Giants, 1905	0.00
	George Mullin, Tigers, 1908	0.00
	Allie Reynolds, Yankees, 1949	0.00
	Preacher Roe, Dodgers, 1949	0.00
	Marius Russo, Yankees, 1943	0.00
	Jack Scott, Giants, 1922	0.00
	Ernie White, Cardinals, 1942	0.00
	Earl Whitehill, Senators, 1933	0.00

VICTORIES

1.	Jack Coombs, A's, 1910	3
	Christy Mathewson, Giants, 1905	3
3.	Johnny Beazley, Cardinals, 1942	2
	Chief Bender, A's, 1913	2
	Mordecai Brown, Cubs, 1908	2
	Spud Chandler, Yankees, 1943	2
	Whitey Ford, Yankees, 1961	2
	Rube Foster, Red Sox, 1915	2
	Lefty Gomez, Yankees, 1937	2
	Orel Hershiser, Dodgers, 1988	2
	Carl Hubbell, Giants, 1933	2
	Jerry Koosman, Mets, 1969	2
	Jack Morris, Tigers, 1984	2
	Orval Overall, Cubs, 1908	2
	Ernie Shore, Red Sox, 1916	2
	Mike Stanton, Yankees, 2000	2

SAVES

1.	Rollie Fingers, A's, 1974	2
	Lefty Grove, A's, 1929	2
	Willie Hernandez, Tigers, 1984	2
	Tippy Martinez, Orioles, 1983	2
	Mariano Rivera, Yankees, 2000	2
6.	18 tied with 1	

6-Game Series

INNINGS PITCHED

1.	Red Faber, White Sox, 1917	27.0
	Christy Mathewson, Giants, 1911	27.0
	Hippo Vaughn, Cubs, 1918	27.0
4.	Chief Bender, A's, 1911	26.0
5.	George Earnshaw, A's, 1930	25.0
6.	Eddie Cicotte, White Sox, 1917	23.0
	Lefty Tyler, Cubs, 1918	23.0
8.	Schoolboy Rowe, Tigers, 1935	21.0
9.	Jack Coombs, A's, 1911	20.0
10.	Mordecai Brown, Cubs, 1906	19.2

LOWEST ERA

(Minimum 9 innings)

1.	Gene Bearden, Indians, 1948	0.00
	Rube Benton, Giants, 1917	0.00
	Jack Kramer, Browns, 1944	0.00
4.	Ed Lopat, Yankees, 1951	0.50
5.	Lon Warneke, Cubs, 1935	0.54
6.	John Smoltz, Braves, 1996	0.64
7.	Tommy John, Yankees, 1981	0.69
8.	Larry Sherry, Dodgers, 1959	0.71
9.	George Earnshaw, A's, 1930	0.72
10.	Vic Raschi, Yankees, 1951	0.87

VICTORIES

1.	Red Faber, White Sox, 1917	3
2.	Chief Bender, A's, 1911	2
	Tommy Bridges, Tigers, 1935	2
	Steve Carlton, Phillies, 1980	2
	George Earnshaw, A's, 1930	2
	Tom Glavine, Braves, 1995	2
	Lefty Gomez, Yankees, 1936	2
	Lefty Grove, A's, 1930	2
	Jimmy Key, Blue Jays, 1992	2
	Bob Lemon, Indians, 1948	2
	Ed Lopat, Yankees, 1951	2
	Carl Mays, Red Sox, 1918	2
	Herb Pennock, Yankees, 1923	2
	Babe Ruth, Red Sox, 1918	2
	Larry Sherry, Dodgers, 1959	2
	Mike Torrez, Yankees, 1977	2
	Ed Walsh, White Sox, 1906	2
	Duane Ward, Blue Jays, 1992	2
	Lon Warneke, Cubs, 1935	2

SAVES

1.	John Wetteland, Yankees, 1996	4
2.	Rich Gossage, Yankees, 1981	2
	Tom Henke, Blue Jays, 1992	2
	Tug McGraw, Phillies, 1980	2
	Larry Sherry, Dodgers, 1959	2
	Duane Ward, Blue Jays, 1993	2
	Mark Wohlers, Braves, 1995	2
8.	24 tied with 1	

7-Game Series

INNINGS PITCHED

1.	Deacon Phillippe, Pirates, 1903	44.0
2.	Bill Dinneen, Red Sox, 1903	35.0
3.	Cy Young, Red Sox, 1903	34.0
4.	George Mullin, Tigers, 1909	32.0
5.	Christy Mathewson, Giants, 1912	28.2
	Warren Spahn, Braves, 1958	28.2
7.	8 tied with 27.0	

LOWEST ERA

(Minimum 9 innings)

1.	Jack Billingham, Reds, 1972	0.00
	Nelson Briles, Pirates, 1971	0.00
	Joe Dobson, Red Sox, 1946	0.00
	Whitey Ford, Yankees, 1960	0.00
	Waite Hoyt, Yankees, 1921	0.00
	Clem Labine, Dodgers, 1956	0.00
	Don Larsen, Yankees, 1956	0.00
	Duster Mails, Indians, 1920	0.00
9.	Sandy Koufax, Dodgers, 1965	0.38
10.	Harry Brecheen, Cardinals, 1946	0.45

VICTORIES

1.	Babe Adams, Pirates, 1909	3
	Harry Brecheen, Cardinals, 1946	3
	Lew Burdette, Braves, 1957	3
	Stan Coveleski, Indians, 1920	3
	Bill Dinneen, Red Sox, 1903	3
	Bob Gibson, Cardinals, 1967	3
	Mickey Lolich, Tigers, 1968	3
	Deacon Phillippe, Pirates, 1903	3
	Joe Wood, Red Sox, 1912	3
10.	59 tied with 2	

SAVES

1.	Roy Face, Pirates, 1960	3
	Kent Tekulve, Pirates, 1979	3
3.	Rick Aguilera, Twins, 1991	2
	Rollie Fingers, A's, 1972	2
	Rollie Fingers, A's, 1973	2
	Darold Knowles, A's, 1973	2
	Firpo Marberry, Senators, 1924	2
	Bob McClure, Brewers, 1982	2
	Robb Nen, Marlins, 1997	2
	Jesse Orosco, Mets, 1986	2
	Bruce Sutter, Cardinals, 1982	2
	Todd Worrell, Cardinals, 1987	2

Single Game

Regular Season (1901-2000)

Batting

FOUR-HOMER GAMES

1.	Lou Gehrig, Yankees, June 3, 1932	1
	Chuck Klein, Phillies, July 10, 1936 (10 inn.)	1
	Pat Seerey, White Sox, July 18, 1948 (11 inn.)	1
	Gil Hodges, Dodgers, Aug. 31, 1950	1
	Joe Adcock, Braves, July 31, 1954	1
	Rocky Colavito, Indians, June 10, 1959	1
	Willie Mays, Giants, April 30, 1961	1
	Mike Schmidt, Phillies, April 17, 1976 (10 inn.)	1
	Bob Horner, Braves, July 6, 1986	1
	Mark Whiten, Cardinals, Sept. 7, 1993	1

HITS, A.L.

1.	Johnny Burnett, Indians, July 10, 1932 (18 inn.)	9
2.	Rocky Colavito, Tigers, June 24, 1962 (22 inn.)	7
	Cesar Gutierrez, Tigers, June 21, 1970 (12 inn.)	7
4.	Mike Donlin, Orioles, June 24, 1901	6
	Doc Nance, Tigers, July 13, 1901	6
	Ervin Harvey, Indians, April 25, 1902	6
	Danny Murphy, A's, July 8, 1902	6
	Jimmy Williams, Orioles, Aug. 25, 1902	6
	Bobby Veach, Tigers, Sept. 17, 1920 (12 inn.)	6
	George Sisler, Browns, Aug. 9, 1921 (19 inn.)	6
	Frank Brower, Indians, Aug. 7, 1923	6
	George H. Burns, Indians., June 19, 1924	6
	Ty Cobb, Tigers, May 5, 1925	6
	Jimmie Foxx, A's, May 30, 1930 (13 inn.)	6
	Doc Cramer, A's, June 20, 1932	6
	Jimmie Foxx, A's, July 10, 1932 (18 inn.)	6
	Sam West, Browns, April 13, 1933 (11 inn.)	6
	Myril Hoag, Yankees, June 6, 1934	6
	Bob Johnson, A's, June 16, 1934 (11 inn.)	6
	Doc Cramer, A's, July 13, 1935	6
	Bruce Campbell, Indians, July 2, 1936	6
	Rip Radcliff, White Sox, July 18, 1936	6
	Hank Steinbacher, White Sox, June 22, 1938	6
	George Myatt, Senators, May 1, 1944	6
	Stan Spence, Senators, June 1, 1944	6
	George Kell, Tigers, Sept. 20, 1946	6
	Jim Fridley, Indians, April 29, 1952	6
	Jimmy Piersall, Red Sox, June 10, 1953	6
	Joe DeMaestri, A's, July 8, 1955	6
	Pete Runnels, Red Sox, Aug. 30, 1960 (15 inn.)	6
	Floyd Robinson, White Sox, July 22, 1962	6
	Bob Oliver, Royals, May 4, 1969	6
	Jim Northrup, Tigers, Aug. 28, 1969 (13 inn.)	6
	John Briggs, Brewers, Aug. 4, 1973	6
	Jorge Orta, Indians, June 15, 1980	6
	Jerry Remy, Red Sox, Sept. 3, 1981 (20 inn.)	6
	Kevin Seitzer, Royals, Aug. 2, 1987	6
	Kirby Puckett, Twins, Aug. 30, 1987	6
	Kirby Puckett, Twins, May 23, 1991 (11 inn.)	6
	Carlos Baerga, Indians, April 11, 1992 (18 inn.)	6
	Kevin Reimer, Brewers, Aug. 24, 1993 (13 inn.)	6
	Lance Johnson, White Sox, Sept. 23, 1995	6
	Gerald Williams, Yankees, May 1, 1996 (15 inn.)	6
	Garret Anderson, Angels, Sept. 27, 1996 (15 inn.)	6

HITS, N.L.

1.	Rennie Stennett, Pirates, Sept. 16, 1975	7
2.	Kip Selbach, Giants, June 9, 1901	6
	George Cutshaw, Dodgers, Aug. 9, 1915	6
	Carson Bigbee, Pirates, Aug. 22, 1917 (22 inn.)	6
	Dave Bancroft, Giants, June 28, 1920	6
	Johnny Gooch, Pirates, July 7, 1922 (18 inn.)	6
	Max Carey, Pirates, July 7, 1922 (18 inn.)	6
	Jack Fournier, Dodgers, June 29, 1923	6
	Kiki Cuyler, Pirates, Aug. 9, 1924	6
	Frankie Frisch, Giants, Sept. 10, 1924	6
	Jim Bottomley, Cardinals, Sept. 16, 1924	6
	Paul Waner, Pirates, Aug. 26, 1926	6
	Lloyd Waner, Pirates, June 15, 1929 (14 inn.)	6
	Hank DeBerry, Dodgers, June 23, 1929 (14 inn.)	6
	Wally Gilbert, Dodgers, May 30, 1931	6
	Jim Bottomley, Cardinals, Aug. 5, 1931	6
	Tony Cuccinello, Reds, Aug. 13, 1931	6
	Terry Moore, Cardinals, Sept. 5, 1935	6
	Ernie Lombardi, Reds, May 9, 1937	6
	Frank Demaree, Cubs, July 5, 1937 (14 inn.)	6
	Cookie Lavagetto, Dodgers, Sept. 23, 1939	6
	Walker Cooper, Reds, July 6, 1949	6
	Johnny Hopp, Pirates, May 14, 1950	6
	Connie Ryan, Phillies, April 16, 1953	6
	Dick Groat, Pirates, May 13, 1960	6
	Jesus Alou, Giants, July 10, 1964	6
	Joe Morgan, Astros, July 8, 1965 (12 inn.)	6
	Felix Millan, Braves, July 6, 1970	6
	Don Kessinger, Cubs, July 17, 1971 (10 inn.)	6
	Willie Davis, Dodgers, May 24, 1973 (19 inn.)	6
	Bill Madlock, Cubs, July 26, 1975 (10 inn.)	6
	Jose Cardenal, Cubs, May 2, 1976 (14 inn.)	6
	Gene Richards, Padres, July 26, 1977 (15 inn.)	6
	Jim Lefebvre, Padres, Sept. 13, 1982 (16 inn.)	6
	Wally Backman, Pirates, April 27, 1990	6
	Sammy Sosa, Cubs, July 2, 1993	6
	Tony Gwynn, Padres, Aug. 4, 1993 (12 inn.)	6
	Rondell White, Expos, June 11, 1995 (13 inn.)	6
	Mike Benjamin, Giants, June 14, 1995 (13 inn.)	6
	Andres Galarraga, Rockies, July 3, 1995	6
	Edgardo Alfonzo, Mets, August 30, 1999	6

RUNS

1.	Mel Ott, Giants, Aug. 4, 1934	6
	Mel Ott, Giants, April 30, 1944	6
	Johnny Pesky, Red Sox, May 8, 1946	6
	Frank Torre, Braves, Sept. 2, 1957	6
	Spike Owen, Red Sox, Aug. 21, 1986	6
	Edgardo Alfonzo, August 30, 1999	6
7.	Many tied with 5	

DOUBLES

1.	Pop Dillon, Tigers, April 25, 1901	4
	Gavvy Cravath, Phillies, Aug. 8, 1915	4
	Denny Sothern, Phillies, June 6, 1930	4
	Paul Waner, Pirates, May 20, 1932	4
	Dick Bartell, Phillies, April 15, 1933	4
	Ernie Lombardi, Reds, May 8, 1935	4
	Billy Werber, Red Sox, July 17, 1935	4
	Frankie Hayes, A's, July 25, 1936	4
	Mike Kreevich, White Sox, Sept. 4, 1937	4
	Joe Medwick, Cardinals, Aug. 4, 1937	4
	Marv Owen, White Sox, April 23, 1939	4
	Billy Werber, Reds, May 13, 1940 (14 inn.)	4
	Johnny Lindell, Yankees, Aug. 17, 1944	4
	Lou Boudreau, Indians, July 14, 1946	4
	Willie Jones, Phillies, April 20, 1949	4
	Al Zarilla, Red Sox, June 8, 1950	4
	Jim Greengrass, Reds, April 13, 1954	4
	Vic Wertz, Indians, Sept. 26, 1956	4
	Charlie Lau, Orioles, July 13, 1962	4
	Billy Bruton, Tigers, May 19, 1963	4
	Billy Williams, Cubs, April 9, 1969	4
	Orlando Cepeda, Red Sox, Aug. 8, 1973	4
	Jim Mason, Yankees, July 8, 1974	4
	Dave Duncan, Orioles, June 30, 1975	4
	Rick Miller, Red Sox, May 11, 1981	4
	Rafael Ramirez, Braves, May 21, 1986 (13 inn.)	4
	Damaso Garcia, Blue Jays, June 27, 1986	4
	Kirby Puckett, Twins, May 13, 1989	4
	Billy Hatcher, Reds, Aug. 21, 1990	4
	Jeff Bagwell, Astros, June 14, 1996	4
	Sandy Alomar Jr., Indians, June 6, 1997	4
	Albert Belle, Orioles, August 29, 1999	4
	Albert Belle, Orioles, September 23, 1999	4

3-HOME RUN GAMES

1.	Johnny Mize, Cardinals, 1938	2
	Johnny Mize, Cardinals, 1939	2
	Ralph Kiner, Pirates, 1947	2
	Ted Williams, Red Sox, 1957	2
	Willie Mays, Giants., 1961	2
	Willie Stargell, Pirates, 1971	2
	Dave Kingman, Cubs, 1979	2
	Doug DeCinces, Angels, 1982	2
	Joe Carter, Indians, 1989	2
	Cecil Fielder, Tigers, 1990	2
	German Berroa, A's, 1996	2
	Steve Finley, Padres, 1997	2
	Mark McGwire, Cardinals, 1998	2

2-HOME RUN GAMES

1.	Hank Greenberg, Tigers, 1938	11
	Sammy Sosa, Cubs, 1998	11
3.	Jimmie Foxx, Red Sox, 1938	10
	Ralph Kiner, Pirates, 1947	10
	Mark McGwire, Cardinals, 1998	10
6.	Willie Mays, Giants, 1955	9
	George Bell, Blue Jays, 1987	9
	Mark McGwire, Cardinals, 1999	9
9.	12 tied with 8.	

HOME RUNS FIRST AT-BAT, A.L.

Luke Stuart, Browns	Aug. 8, 1921
Earl Averill, Indians	April 16, 1929
Ace Parker, A's	April 30, 1937
Gene Hasson, A's	Sept. 9, 1937
Bill Lefebvre, Red Sox	June 10, 1938
Hack Miller, Tigers	April 23, 1944
Eddie Pellagrini, Red Sox	April 22, 1946
George Vico, Tigers	April 20, 1948
Bob Nieman, Browns	Sept. 14, 1951
Bob Tillman, Red Sox	May 19, 1962
John Kennedy, Senators	Sept. 5, 1962
Buster Narum, Orioles	May 3, 1963
Gates Brown, Tigers	June 19, 1963
Bert Campaneris, A's	July 23, 1964
Bill Roman, Tigers	Sept. 30, 1964
Brant Alyea, Senators	Sept. 12, 1965
John Miller, Yankees	Sept. 11, 1966
Rick Renick, Twins	July 11, 1968
Joe Keough, A's	Aug. 7, 1968
Gene Lamont, Tigers	Sept. 2, 1970
Don Rose, Angels	May 24, 1972
Reggie J. Sanders, Tigers	Sept. 1, 1974
Dave McKay, Twins	Aug. 22, 1975
Al Woods, Blue Jays	April 7, 1977
Dave Machemer, Angels	June 21, 1978
Gary Gaetti, Twins	Sept. 20, 1981
Andre David, Twins	June 29, 1984
Terry Steinbach, A's	Sept. 12, 1986
Jay Bell, Indians	Sept. 29, 1986
Junior Felix, Blue Jays	May 4, 1989
Jon Nunnally, Royals	April 29, 1995
Carlos Lee, White Sox	May 7, 1999
Esteban Yan, Devil Rays	June 4, 2000

Yankees slugger Tony Lazzeri was the first player to hit two grand slams in a game.

HOME RUNS FIRST AT-BAT, N.L.

Johnny Bates, Braves	April 12, 1906
Walter Mueller, Pirates	May 7, 1922
Clise Dudley, Dodgers	April 27, 1929
Gordon Slade, Dodgers	May 24, 1930
Eddie Morgan, Cardinals	April 14, 1936
Ernie Koy, Dodgers	April 19, 1938
Emmett Mueller, Phillies	April 19, 1938
Clyde Vollmer, Reds	May 31, 1942
Paul Gillespie, Cubs	Sept. 11, 1942
Buddy Kerr, Giants	Sept. 8, 1943
Whitey Lockman, Giants	July 5, 1945
Dan Bankhead, Dodgers	Aug. 26, 1947
Les Layton, Giants	May 21, 1948
Ed Sanicki, Phillies	Sept. 14, 1949
Ted Tappe, Reds	Sept. 14, 1950
Hoyt Wilhelm, Giants	April 23, 1952
Wally Moon, Cardinals	April 13, 1954
Chuck Tanner, Braves	April 12, 1955
Bill White, Giants	May 7, 1956
Frank Ernaga, Cubs	May 24, 1957
Don Leppert, Pirates	June 18, 1961
Cuno Barragan, Cubs	Sept. 1, 1961
Benny Ayala, Mets	Aug. 27, 1974
John Montefusco, Giants	Sept. 3, 1974
Jose Sosa, Astros	July 30, 1975
Johnnie Lemaster, Giants	Sept. 2, 1975
Tim Wallach, Expos	Sept. 6, 1980
Carmelo Martinez, Cubs	Aug. 22, 1983
Mike Fitzgerald, Mets	Sept. 13, 1983
Will Clark, Giants	April 8, 1986
Ricky Jordan, Phillies	July 17, 1988
Jose Offerman, Dodgers	Aug. 19, 1990
Dave Eiland, Padres	April 10, 1992
Jim Bullinger, Cubs	June 8, 1992
Jay Gainer, Rockies	May 14, 1993
Mitch Lyden, Marlins	June 16, 1993
Garey Ingram, Dodgers	May 19, 1994
Jermaine Dye, Braves	May 17, 1996
Dustin Hermanson, Expos	April 16, 1997
Brad Fullmer, Expos	Sept. 2, 1997

	Marlon Anderson, Phillies	Sept. 8, 1998
	Guillermo Mota, Expos	June 9, 1999
	Alex Cabrera, Diamondbacks	June 26, 2000
	Keith McDonald, Cardinals	July 4, 2000
	Chris Richard, Cardinals	July 17, 2000

GRAND SLAMS

1.	Tony Lazzeri, Yankees, May 24, 1936	2
	Jim Tabor, Red Sox, July 4, 1939	2
	Rudy York, Red Sox, July 27, 1946	2
	Jim Gentile, Orioles, May 9, 1961	2
	Tony Cloninger, Braves, July 3, 1966	2
	Jim Northrup, Tigers, June 24, 1968	2
	Frank Robinson, Orioles, June 26, 1970	2
	Robin Ventura, White Sox, Sept. 4, 1995	2
	Chris Hoiles, Orioles, August 14, 1998	2
	Fernando Tatis, Cardinals, April 23, 1999	2

TOTAL BASES

1.	Joe Adcock, Braves, July 31, 1954	18
2.	Gil Hodges, Dodgers, Aug. 31, 1950	17
	Mike Schmidt, Phillies, April 17, 1976 (10 inn.)	17
4.	Ty Cobb, Tigers, May 5, 1925	16
	Lou Gehrig, Yankees, June 3, 1932	16
	Jimmie Foxx, A's, July 10, 1932 (18 inn.)	16
	Chuck Klein, Phillies, July 10, 1936 (10 inn.)	16
	Pat Seerey, White Sox, July 18, 1948 (11 inn.)	16
	Rocky Colavito, Indians, June 10, 1959	16
	Willie Mays, Giants, April 30, 1961	16
	Fred Lynn, Red Sox, June 18, 1975	16
	Bob Horner, Braves, July 6, 1986	16
	Mark Whiten, Cardinals, Sept. 7, 1993	16
	Edgardo Alfonzo, Mets, August 30, 1999	16

RUNS BATTED IN

1.	Jim Bottomley, Cardinals, Sept. 16, 1924	12
	Mark Whiten, Cardinals, Sept. 7, 1993	12
3.	Tony Lazzeri, Yankees, May 24, 1936	11
	Phil Weintraub, Giants, April 30, 1944	11
5.	Rudy York, Red Sox, May 27, 1946	10
	Walker Cooper, Reds, July 6, 1949	10
	Norm Zauchin, Red Sox, May 27, 1955	10
	Reggie Jackson, A's, June 14, 1969	10
	Fred Lynn, Red Sox, June 18, 1975	10
	Nomar Garciaparra, Red Sox, May 10, 1999	10

STOLEN BASES

1.	Eddie Collins, A's, Sept. 11, 1912	6
	Eddie Collins, A's, Sept. 22, 1912	6
	Otis Nixon, Braves, June 16, 1991	6
	Eric Young, Rockies, June 30, 1996	6
5.	Dan McGann, Giants, May 27, 1904	5
	Clyde Milan, Senators, June 14, 1912	5
	Johnny Neun, Tigers, July 9, 1927	5
	Amos Otis, Royals, Sept. 7, 1971	5
	Davey Lopes, Dodgers, Aug. 24, 1974	5
	Bert Campaneris, A's, April 24, 1976	5
	Lonnie Smith, Cardinals, Sept. 4, 1982	5
	Alan Wiggins, Padres, May 17, 1984	5
	Tony Gwynn, Padres, Sept. 20, 1986	5
	Alex Cole, Indians, May 3, 1992	5
	Damian Jackson, Padres, June 28, 1999	5

STEALING HOME

1.	Honus Wagner, Pirates, June 20, 1901	2
	Ed Konetchy, Cardinals, Sept. 30, 1907	2
	Joe Tinker, Cubs, June 28, 1910	2
	Larry Doyle, Giants, Sept. 18, 1911	2
	Sherry Magee, Phillies, July 20, 1912	2
	Joe Jackson, Indians, Aug. 11, 1912	2
	Guy Zinn, Yankees, Aug. 15, 1912	2
	Eddie Collins, A's, Sept. 6, 1913	2
	Bill Barrett, White Sox, May 1, 1924	2
	Doc Gautreau, Braves, Sept. 3, 1927	2
	Vic Power, Indians, Aug. 14, 1958 (10 inn.)	2

PITCHING

WALKS

1.	Bruno Haas, A's, June 23, 1915	16
	Tommy Byrne, Yankees, Aug. 22, 1951 (13 inn.)	16
3.	Carroll Brown, A's, July 12, 1913	15
4.	Henry Mathewson, Giants, Oct. 5, 1906	14
	Skipper Friday, Senators, June 17, 1923	14
6.	Mal Eason, Braves, Sept. 3, 1902	13
	Pete Schneider, Reds, July 6, 1918	13
	George Turbeville, A's, Aug. 24, 1935 (15 inn.)	13
	Tommy Byrne, Yankees, June 8, 1949	13
	Dick Weik, Senators, Sept. 1, 1949	13
	Bud Podbielan, Reds, May 18, 1953 (11 inn.)	13

STRIKEOUTS

1.	Tom Cheney, Senators, Sept. 12, 1962 (16 inn.)	21
2.	Roger Clemens, Red Sox, April 29, 1986	20
	Roger Clemens, Red Sox, Sept. 18, 1996	20
	Kerry Wood, Cubs, May 6, 1998	20
5.	Luis Tiant, Indians, July 3, 1968 (10 inn.)	19
	Steve Carlton, Cardinals, Sept. 15, 1969	19
	Tom Seaver, Mets, April 22, 1970	19
	Nolan Ryan, Angels, June 14, 1974 (12 inn.)	19
	Nolan Ryan, Angels, Aug. 12, 1974	19
	Nolan Ryan, Angels, Aug. 20, 1974 (11 inn.)	19
	Nolan Ryan, Angels, June 8, 1977 (10 inn.)	19
	David Cone, Mets, Oct. 6, 1991	19
	Randy Johnson, Mariners, June 24, 1997	19
	Randy Johnson, Mariners, Aug. 8, 1997	19

LEAGUE CHAMPIONSHIP SERIES

BATTING

RUNS

1.	Bob Robertson, Pirates, Oct. 3, 1971	4
	Steve Garvey, Dodgers, Oct. 9, 1974	4
	Mark Brouhard, Brewers, Oct. 9, 1982	4
	Eddie Murray, Orioles, Oct. 7, 1983	4
	George Brett, Royals, Oct. 11, 1985	4
	Will Clark, Giants, Oct. 4, 1989	4
	Fred McGriff, Braves, Oct. 17, 1996	4
	Javy Lopez, Braves, Oct. 14, 1996	4
9.	29 tied with 3	

HITS

1.	Paul Blair, Orioles, Oct. 6, 1969	5
2.	Brooks Robinson, Orioles, Oct. 4, 1969	4
	Don Buford, Orioles, Oct. 6, 1969	4
	Bob Robertson, Pirates, Oct. 3, 1971	4
	Ron Cey, Dodgers, Oct. 6, 1974	4
	Steve Garvey, Dodgers, Oct. 9, 1974	4
	Sal Bando, A's, Oct. 5, 1975	4
	Mickey Rivers, Yankees, Oct. 14, 1976	4
	Mickey Rivers, Yankees, Oct. 8, 1977	4
	Chris Chambliss, Yankees, Oct. 4, 1978	4
	Dusty Baker, Dodgers, Oct. 7, 1978 (10 inn.)	4
	Terry Puhl, Astros, Oct. 12, 1980 (10 inn.)	4
	Jerry Mumphrey, Yankees, Oct. 14, 1981	4
	Graig Nettles, Yankees, Oct. 14, 1981	4
	Steve Garvey, Padres, Oct. 6, 1984	4
	George Brett, Royals, Oct. 11, 1985	4
	Tito Landrum, Cardinals, Oct. 13, 1985	4
	Rich Gedman, Red Sox, Oct. 12, 1986 (11 inn.)	4
	Spike Owen, Red Sox, Oct. 14, 1986	4
	Kevin McReynolds, Mets, Oct. 11, 1988	4
	Will Clark, Giants, Oct. 4, 1989	4
	Kelly Gruber, Blue Jays, Oct. 7, 1989	4
	Otis Nixon, Braves, Oct. 10, 1992	4
	Roberto Alomar, Blue Jays, Oct. 11, 1992	4
	John Olerud, Blue Jays, Oct. 11, 1992 (11 inn.)	4
	Jerry Browne, A's, Oct. 12, 1992	4
	Paul Molitor, Blue Jays, Oct. 5, 1993	4
	Ed Sprague, Blue Jays, Oct. 5, 1993	4
	Tim Raines, White Sox, Oct. 8, 1993	4
	Manny Ramirez, Indians, Oct. 11, 1995	4
	Derek Jeter, Yankees, Oct. 9, 1996	4
	Chipper Jones, Braves, Oct. 9, 1996	4
	Mark Lemke, Braves, Oct. 14, 1996	4
	Javy Lopez, Braves, Oct. 14, 1996	4
	Keith Lockhart, Braves, Oct. 14, 1997	4
	Nomar Garciaparra, Oct. 16, 1999	4
	Alex Rodriguez, Oct. 17, 2000	4

HOME RUNS

1.	Bob Robertson, Pirates, Oct. 3, 1971	3
	George Brett, Royals, Oct. 6, 1978	3
3.	Boog Powell, Orioles, Oct. 4, 1971	2
	Reggie Jackson, A's, Oct. 5, 1971	2
	Sal Bando, A's, Oct. 7, 1973	2
	Rusty Staub, Mets, Oct. 8, 1973	2
	Steve Garvey, Dodgers, Oct. 9, 1974	2
	Graig Nettles, Yankees, Oct. 13, 1976	2
	Steve Garvey, Dodgers, Oct. 4, 1978	2
	Gary Matthews, Cubs, Oct. 2, 1984	2
	George Brett, Royals, Oct. 11, 1985	2
	Gary Gaetti, Twins, Oct. 7, 1987	2
	Rickey Henderson, A's, Oct. 7, 1989	2
	Will Clark, Giants, Oct. 4, 1989	2
	David Justice, Braves, Oct. 13, 1992	2
	Manny Ramirez, Indians, Oct. 11, 1995	2
	Jay Buhner, Mariners, Oct. 13, 1995	2
	Ron Gant, Cardinals, Oct. 12, 1996	2
	Darryl Strawberry, Yankees, Oct. 12, 1996	2
	Jim Thome, Indians, Oct. 9, 1998	2

RUNS BATTED IN

1.	Will Clark, Giants, Oct. 4, 1989	6
2.	Paul Blair, Orioles, Oct. 6, 1969	5
	Bob Robertson, Pirates, Oct. 3, 1971	5
	Don Baylor, Angels, Oct. 5, 1982	5
	Steve Garvey, Padres, Oct. 6, 1984	5
	Michael Tucker, Braves, Oct. 12, 1998	5
	John Valentin, Red Sox, Oct. 16, 1999	5
8.	27 tied with 4	

TOTAL BASES

1.	Bob Robertson, Pirates, Oct. 3, 1971	14
2.	George Brett, Royals, Oct. 6, 1978	12
3.	Steve Garvey, Dodgers, Oct. 4, 1978	11
	George Brett, Royals, Oct. 11, 1985	11
	Will Clark, Giants, Oct. 4, 1989	11
6.	Paul Blair, Orioles, Oct. 6, 1969	10
	Steve Garvey, Dodgers, Oct. 9, 1974	10
	Manny Ramirez, Indians, Oct. 11, 1995	10
9.	Reggie Jackson, A's, Oct. 5, 1971	9
	Ron Cey, Dodgers, Oct. 6, 1974	9
	David Justice, Braves, Oct. 13, 1992	9
	Darryl Strawberry, Yankees, Oct. 12, 1996	9
	Javy Lopez, Braves, Oct. 14, 1996	9

STOLEN BASES

1.	Rickey Henderson, A's, Oct. 4, 1989	4
2.	Joe Morgan, Reds, Oct. 4, 1975	3
	Ken Griffey Sr., Reds, Oct. 5, 1975	3
	Steve Sax, Dodgers, Oct. 9, 1988 (12 inn.)	3
	Ron Gant, Braves, Oct. 10, 1991	3
	Willie Wilson, A's, Oct. 8, 1992	3
	Roberto Alomar, Blue Jays, Oct. 10, 1993	3

PITCHING

RUNS ALLOWED

1.	Phil Niekro, Braves, Oct. 4, 1969	9
2.	Jim Perry, Twins, Oct. 3, 1970	8
	Roger Clemens, Red Sox, Oct. 7, 1986	8
	Greg A. Harris, Padres, Oct. 2, 1984	8
	Greg Maddux, Cubs, Oct. 4, 1989	8
	Tom Glavine, Braves, Oct. 13, 1992	8
	Greg Maddux, Braves, Oct. 10, 1996	8
	Hideki Irabu, Yankees, Oct. 16, 1999	8
9.	12 tied with 7	

HITS ALLOWED

1.	Jack McDowell, White Sox, Oct. 5, 1993	13
	Hideki Irabu, Yankees, Oct. 16, 1999	13
3.	Larry Gura, Royals, Oct. 9, 1986	12
4.	Bruce Hurst, Red Sox, Oct. 8, 1986	11
	Roger Erickson, Orioles, Oct. 12, 1997	11
	Kevin Brown, Marlins, Oct. 14, 1997	11
7.	Pat Jarvis, Braves, Oct. 6, 1969	10
	Jim Palmer, Orioles, Oct. 6, 1969	10
	Mike Cuellar, Orioles, Oct. 3, 1970	10
	Gaylord Perry, Giants, Oct. 6, 1971	10
	Burt Hooton, Dodgers, Oct. 4, 1978	10
	Larry Gura, Royals, Oct. 8, 1980	10
	Roger Clemens, Red Sox, Oct. 7, 1986	10
	Kirk McCaskill, Angels, Oct. 8, 1986	10
	Bob Ojeda, Mets, Oct. 9, 1986	10
	John Tudor, Cardinals, Oct. 7, 1987	10
	Al Leiter, Marlins, Oct. 11, 1997	10
	Tom Glavine, Braves, Oct. 14, 1997	10

STRIKEOUTS

1.	Mike Mussina, Orioles, Oct. 11, 1997	15
	Livan Hernandez, Marlins, Oct. 12, 1997	15
	Roger Clemens, Yankees, Oct. 14, 2000	15
4.	Joe Coleman, Tigers, Oct. 10, 1972	14
	John Candelaria, Pirates, Oct. 7, 1975	14
	Mike Boddicker, Orioles, Oct. 6, 1983	14
	Mike Scott, Astros, Oct. 8, 1986	14
8.	Tom Seaver, Mets, Oct. 6, 1973	13
9.	Jim Palmer, Orioles, Oct. 5, 1970	12
	Jim Palmer, Orioles, Oct. 6, 1973	12
	Nolan Ryan, Astros, Oct. 14, 1986	12
	Pedro Martinez, Red Sox, Oct. 16, 1999	12

WALKS

1.	Mike Cuellar, Orioles, Oct. 9, 1974	9
2.	Fernando Valenzuela, Dodgers, Oct. 14, 1985	8
	Juan Guzman, Blue Jays, Oct. 5, 1993	8
4.	Dave Boswell, Twins, Oct. 5, 1969	7
	Dave Stieb, Blue Jays, Oct. 12, 1985	7
	Tom Glavine, Braves, Oct. 14, 1997	7
7.	Diego Segui, A's, Oct. 5, 1971	6
	Bruce Kison, Pirates, Oct. 8, 1974	6
	Matt Keough, A's, Oct. 15, 1981	6
	Bob Welch, Dodgers, Oct. 12, 1985	6
	Tom Glavine, Braves, Oct. 8, 1998	6

WORLD SERIES

BATTING

RUNS

1.	Babe Ruth, Yankees, Oct. 6, 1926	4
	Earle Combs, Yankees, Oct. 2, 1932	4
	Frankie Crosetti, Yankees, Oct. 2, 1936	4
	Enos Slaughter, Cardinals, Oct. 10, 1946	4
	Reggie Jackson, Yankees, Oct. 18, 1977	4
	Kirby Puckett, Twins, Oct. 24, 1987	4
	Carney Lansford, A's, Oct. 17, 1989	4
	Lenny Dykstra, Phillies, Oct. 20, 1993	4

HITS

1.	Paul Molitor, Brewers, Oct. 12, 1982	5
2.	Tommy Leach, Pirates, Oct. 1, 1903	4
	Ginger Beaumont, Pirates, Oct. 8, 1903	4
	Frank Isbell, White Sox, Oct. 13, 1906	4
	Ed Hahn, White Sox, Oct. 14, 1906	4
	Ty Cobb, Tigers, Oct. 12, 1908	4
	Larry Doyle, Giants, Oct. 25, 1911	4
	Danny Murphy, A's, Oct. 26, 1911	4
	Frankie Frisch, Giants, Oct. 5, 1921	4
	George J. Burns, Giants, Oct. 7, 1921	4
	Frank Snyder, Giants, Oct. 7, 1921	4
	Ross Youngs, Giants, Oct. 13, 1923	4
	Joe Dugan, Yankees, Oct. 14, 1923	4
	Goose Goslin, Senators, Oct. 7, 1924	4
	Fred Lindstrom, Giants, Oct. 8, 1924	4
	Max Carey, Pirates, Oct. 15, 1925	4
	Mel Ott, Giants, Oct. 3, 1933	4
	Joe Medwick, Cardinals, Oct. 3, 1934	4
	Hank Greenberg, Tigers, Oct. 6, 1934	4
	Ripper Collins, Cardinals, Oct. 9, 1934	4
	Bill Dickey, Yankees, Oct. 5, 1938	4
	Charlie Keller, Yankees, Oct. 5, 1941	4
	Stan Hack, Cubs, Oct. 8, 1945	4
	Joe Garagiola, Cardinals, Oct. 10, 1946	4
	Whitey Kurowski, Cardinals, Oct. 10, 1946	4
	Wally Moses, Red Sox, Oct. 10, 1946	4
	Enos Slaughter, Cardinals, Oct. 10, 1946	4
	Monte Irvin, Giants, Oct. 4, 1951	4
	Vic Wertz, Indians, Sept. 29, 1954	4
	Jim Gilliam, Dodgers, Oct. 6, 1959	4
	Mickey Mantle, Yankees, Oct. 8, 1960	4
	Maury Wills, Dodgers, Oct. 11, 1965	4
	Lou Brock, Cardinals, Oct. 4, 1967	4
	Brooks Robinson, Orioles, Oct. 14, 1970	4
	Reggie Jackson, A's, Oct. 14, 1973 (12 inn.)	4
	Rusty Staub, Mets, Oct. 17, 1973	4
	Thurman Munson, Yankees, Oct. 21, 1976	4
	Dave Parker, Pirates, Oct. 10, 1979	4
	Kiko Garcia, Orioles, Oct. 12, 1979	4
	Bill Madlock, Pirates, Oct. 14, 1979	4
	Willie Stargell, Pirates, Oct. 17, 1979	4
	Robin Yount, Brewers, Oct. 12, 1982	4
	Robin Yount, Brewers, Oct. 17, 1982	4
	George Brett, Royals, Oct. 27, 1985	4
	Lenny Dykstra, Mets, Oct. 21, 1986	4
	Kirby Puckett, Twins, Oct. 24, 1987	4
	Dave Henderson, A's, Oct. 19, 1988	4
	Billy Hatcher, Reds, Oct. 17, 1990 (10 inn.)	4
	Terry Pendleton, Braves, Oct. 26, 1991 (11 inn.)	4
	Roberto Alomar, Blue Jays, Oct. 19, 1993	4
	Bret Boone, Braves, Oct. 26, 1999	4

HOME RUNS

1.	Babe Ruth, Yankees, Oct. 6, 1926	3
	Babe Ruth, Yankees, Oct. 9, 1928	3
	Reggie Jackson, Yankees, Oct. 18, 1977	3
4.	Patsy Dougherty, Red Sox, Oct. 2, 1903	2
	Harry Hooper, Red Sox, Oct. 13, 1915	2
	Benny Kauff, Giants, Oct. 11, 1917	2
	Babe Ruth, Yankees, Oct. 11, 1923	2
	Lou Gehrig, Yankees, Oct. 7, 1928	2
	Lou Gehrig, Yankees, Oct. 1, 1932	2
	Babe Ruth, Yankees, Oct. 1, 1932	2
	Tony Lazzeri, Yankees, Oct. 2, 1932	2
	Charlie Keller, Yankees, Oct. 7, 1939	2
	Bob Elliott, Braves, Oct. 10, 1948	2
	Duke Snider, Dodgers, Oct. 6, 1952	2
	Joe Collins, Yankees, Sept. 28, 1955	2
	Duke Snider, Dodgers, Oct. 2, 1955	2
	Yogi Berra, Yankees, Oct. 10, 1956	2
	Tony Kubek, Yankees, Oct. 5, 1957	2
	Mickey Mantle, Yankees, Oct. 2, 1958	2
	Ted Kluszewski, White Sox, Oct. 1, 1959	2
	Charlie Neal, Dodgers, Oct. 2, 1959	2
	Mickey Mantle, Yankees, Oct. 6, 1960	2
	Carl Yastrzemski, Red Sox, Oct. 5, 1967	2
	Rico Petrocelli, Red Sox, Oct. 11, 1967	2
	Gene Tenace, A's, Oct. 14, 1972	2
	Tony Perez, Reds, Oct. 16, 1975	2
	Johnny Bench, Reds, Oct. 21, 1976	2
	Davey Lopes, Dodgers, Oct. 10, 1978	2
	Willie Aikens, Royals, Oct. 14, 1980	2
	Willie Aikens, Royals, Oct. 18, 1980	2
	Willie McGee, Cardinals, Oct. 15, 1982	2
	Eddie Murray, Orioles, Oct. 16, 1983	2
	Alan Trammell, Tigers, Oct. 13, 1984	2
	Kirk Gibson, Tigers, Oct. 14, 1984	2
	Gary Carter, Mets, Oct. 22, 1986	2
	Dave Henderson, A's, Oct. 27, 1989	2
	Chris Sabo, Reds, Oct. 19, 1990	2
	Andruw Jones, Braves, Oct. 20, 1996	2
	Greg Vaughn, Padres, Oct. 17, 1998	2
	Scott Brosius, Yankees, Oct. 20, 1998	2
	Chad Curtis, Yankees, Oct. 26, 1999	2

TOTAL BASES

1.	Babe Ruth, Yankees, Oct. 6, 1926	12
	Babe Ruth, Yankees, Oct. 9, 1928	12
	Reggie Jackson, Yankees, Oct. 18, 1977	12
4.	Duke Snider, Dodgers, Oct. 2, 1955	10
	Gary Carter, Mets, Oct. 22, 1986	10
	Dave Henderson, A's, Oct. 27, 1989	10
	Lenny Dykstra, Phillies, Oct. 20, 1993	10
8.	12 tied with 9	

RUNS BATTED IN

1.	Bobby Richardson, Yankees, Oct. 8, 1960	6
2.	Bill Dickey, Yankees, Oct. 2, 1936	5
	Tony Lazzeri, Yankees, Oct. 2, 1936	5
	Ted Kluszewski, White Sox, Oct. 1, 1959	5
	Mickey Mantle, Yankees, Oct. 6, 1960	5
	Hector Lopez, Yankees, Oct. 9, 1961	5
	Rusty Staub, Mets, Oct. 17, 1973	5
	Johnny Bench, Reds, Oct. 21, 1976	5
	Reggie Jackson, Yankees, Oct. 18, 1977	5
	Davey Lopes, Dodgers, Oct. 10, 1978	5
	Thurman Munson, Yankees, Oct. 15, 1978	5
	Pedro Guerrero, Dodgers, Oct. 28, 1981	5
	Kirk Gibson, Tigers, Oct. 14, 1984	5
	Dan Gladden, Twins, Oct. 17, 1987	5
	David Justice, Braves, Oct. 24, 1991	5
	Milt Thompson, Phillies, Oct. 20, 1993	5
	Tony Fernandez, Blue Jays, Oct. 20, 1993	5
	Andruw Jones, Braves, Oct. 20, 1996	5
	Gary Sheffield, Marlins, Oct. 12, 1997	5

STOLEN BASES

1.	Honus Wagner, Pirates, Oct. 11, 1909	3
	Willie Davis, Dodgers, Oct. 11, 1965	3
	Lou Brock, Cardinals, Oct. 12, 1967	3
	Lou Brock, Cardinals, Oct. 5, 1968	3

PITCHING

RUNS ALLOWED

1.	Bill Kennedy, Pirates, Oct. 7, 1903	10
2.	Andy Coakley, A's, Oct. 12, 1905	9
	Mordecai Brown, Cubs, Oct. 18, 1910	9
	Walter Johnson, Senators, Oct. 15, 1925	9
5.	Jack Pfiester, Cubs, Oct. 12, 1908	8
	Ed Summers, Tigers, Oct. 13, 1909	8
	Hooks Wiltse, Giants, Oct. 26, 1911	8
	Slim Sallee, Giants, Oct. 13, 1917	8
	Grover Alexander, Cardinals, Oct. 5, 1928	8
	Guy Bush, Cubs, Sept. 28, 1932	8

HITS ALLOWED

1.	Walter Johnson, Senators, Oct. 15, 1925	15
2.	Walter Johnson, Senators, Oct. 4, 1924	14
	Waite Hoyt, Yankees, Oct. 6, 1926	14
	Mike Caldwell, Brewers, Oct. 17, 1982	14
5.	Mordecai Brown, Cubs, Oct. 18, 1910	13
	Slim Sallee, Giants, Oct. 13, 1917	13
	Jim Bagby Sr., Indians, Oct. 10, 1920	13
	Walter Johnson, Senators, Oct. 8, 1924	13
	Bob Turley, Yankees, Oct. 6, 1960	13
10.	7 tied with 12	

STRIKEOUTS

1.	Bob Gibson, Cardinals, Oct. 2, 1968	17
2.	Sandy Koufax, Dodgers, Oct. 2, 1963	15
3.	Carl Erskine, Dodgers, Oct. 2, 1953	14
4.	Howard Ehmke, A's, Oct. 8, 1929	13
	Bob Gibson, Cardinals, Oct. 12, 1964 (10 inn.)	13
6.	Ed Walsh, White Sox, Oct. 11, 1906	12
	Bill Donovan, Tigers, Oct. 8, 1907 (12 inn.)	12
	Walter Johnson, Senators, Oct. 24, 1924 (12 inn.)	12
	Mort Cooper, Cardinals, Oct. 8, 1944	12
	Tom Seaver, Mets, Oct. 16, 1973	12
	Orlando Hernandez, Yankees, Oct. 24, 2000	12

WALKS

1.	Bill Bevens, Yankees, Oct. 3, 1947	10
2.	Jack Coombs, A's, Oct. 18, 1910	9
	Rex Barney, Dodgers, Oct. 4, 1947	9
4.	Jim Hearn, Giants, Oct. 6, 1951	8
	Bob Turley, Yankees, Oct. 9, 1956 (10 inn.)	8
	Jim Palmer, Orioles, Oct. 11, 1971	8
7.	Art Nehf, Giants, Oct. 6, 1921	7
	Tex Carleton, Cubs, Oct. 5, 1935	7
	Lefty Gomez, Yankees, Oct. 2, 1936	7
	Allie Reynolds, Yankees, Oct. 4, 1951	7
	Ron Guidry, Yankees, Oct. 13, 1978	7
	Fernando Valenzuela, Dodgers, Oct. 23, 1981	7

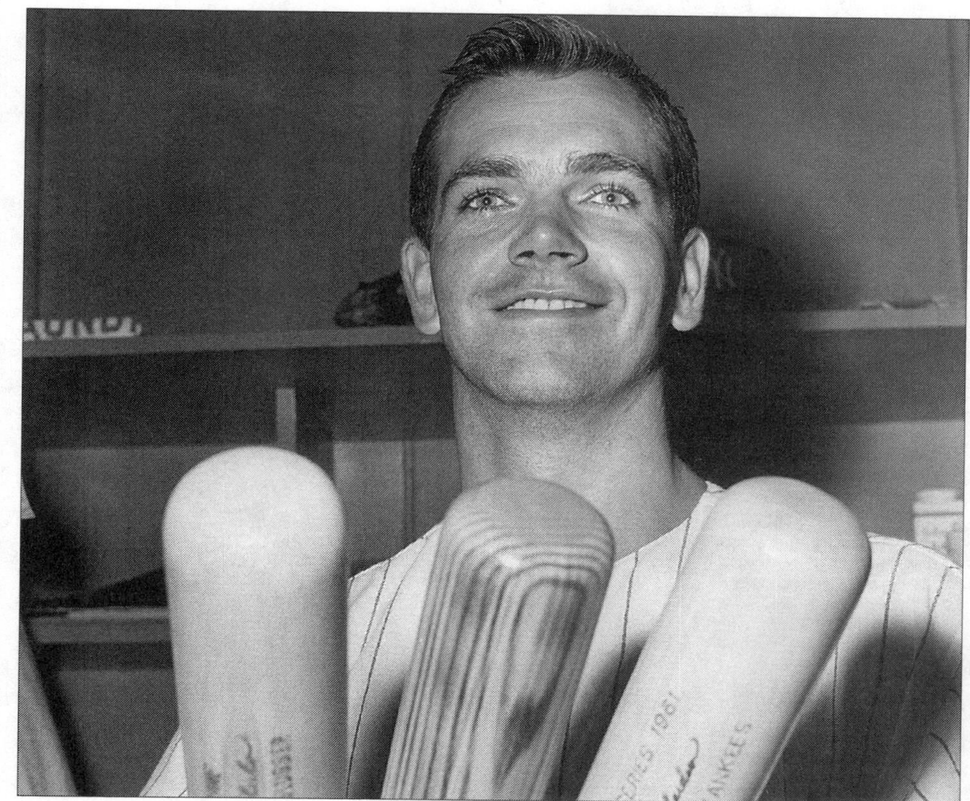

Yankees second baseman Bobby Richardson had six RBIs in a 1960 Series game against Pittsburgh.

HIGHEST AVERAGE

(Minimum 4 at-bats)

	Player	
1.	Ted Williams, Red Sox, 1946	1.000
2.	Joe Medwick, Cardinals, 1937	.800
3.	Roberto Alomar, Orioles, 1998	.750
	Rickey Henderson, A's, 1982	.750
	Lance Johnson, Mets, 1996	.750
	Harmon Killebrew, Twins, 1964	.750
	Willie Mays, Giants, 1960 (1st game)	.750
	Willie Mays, Giants, 1960 (2nd game)	.750
	Stan Musial, Cardinals, 1949	.750
	Brooks Robinson, Orioles, 1966	.750
	Ivan Rodriguez, Rangers, 1998	.750
	Al Rosen, Indians, 1954	.750
	Duke Snider, Dodgers, 1954	.750
	Arky Vaughan, Pirates, 1941	.750
	Leon Wagner, Angels, 1962 (2nd game)	.750
	Carl Yastrzemski, Red Sox, 1967	.750

RUNS

	Player	
1.	Ted Williams, Red Sox, 1946	4
2.	Joe DiMaggio, Yankees, 1941	3
	Frankie Frisch, Cardinals, 1934	3
	Jackie Robinson, Dodgers, 1949	3
	Al Simmons, White Sox, 1934	3
6.	51 tied with 2	

HITS

	Player	
1.	Joe Medwick, Cardinals, 1937	4
	Ted Williams, Red Sox, 1946	4
	Carl Yastrzemski, Red Sox, 1970	4
4.	30 tied with 3	

DOUBLES

	Player	
1.	Ernie Banks, Cubs, 1959 (1st game)	2
	Barry Bonds, Giants, 1993	2
	Ted Kluszewski, Reds, 1956	2
	Joe Medwick, Cardinals, 1937	2
	Al Simmons, White Sox, 1934	2
6.	169 tied with 1	

HOME RUNS

	Player	
1.	Gary Carter, Expos, 1981	2
	Willie McCovey, Giants, 1969	2
	Al Rosen, Indians, 1954	2
	Arky Vaughan, Pirates, 1941	2
	Ted Williams, Red Sox, 1946	2
6.	141 tied with 1	

HOME RUN, FIRST AT-BAT

Max West, Braves, 1940
Hoot Evers, Tigers, 1948
Jim Gilliam, Dodgers, 1959 (2nd game)
George Altman, Cubs, 1961 (1st game)
Johnny Bench, Reds, 1969
Dick Dietz, Giants, 1970
Lee Mazzilli, Mets, 1979
Terry Steinbach, A's, 1988
Bo Jackson, Royals, 1989
Jeff Conine, Marlins, 1995
Javy Lopez, Braves, 1997

TOTAL BASES

	Player	
1.	Ted Williams, Red Sox, 1946	10
2.	Al Rosen, Indians, 1954	9
	Arky Vaughan, Pirates, 1941	9
4.	Gary Carter, Expos, 1981	8
	Vince DiMaggio, Pirates, 1943	8
	Willie McCovey, Giants, 1969	8
7.	Ken Griffey Jr., Mariners, 1992	7
8.	16 tied with 6	

RUNS BATTED IN

	Player	
1.	Al Rosen, Indians, 1954	5
	Ted Williams, Red Sox, 1946	5
3.	Rocky Colavito, Tigers, 1962 (2nd game)	4
	Lou Gehrig, Yankees, 1937	4
	Fred Lynn, Angels, 1983	4
	Arky Vaughan, Pirates, 1941	4
	Ted Williams, Red Sox, 1941	4
8.	15 tied with 3	

STOLEN BASES

	Player	
1.	Roberto Alomar, Blue Jays, 1992	2
	Kelly Gruber, Blue Jays, 1990	2
	Kenny Lofton, Indians, 1996	2
	Willie Mays, Giants, 1963	2
5.	82 tied with 1	

Giants All-Star Willie McCovey hit two home runs for the National League in 1969.

PITCHING

RUNS ALLOWED

	Player	
1.	Atlee Hammaker, Giants, 1983	7
2.	Sandy Consuegra, White Sox, 1954	5
	Whitey Ford, Yankees, 1955	5
	Tom Glavine, Braves, 1992	5
	Jim Maloney, Reds, 1965	5
	Blue Moon Odom, A's, 1969	5
	Jim Palmer, Orioles, 1977	5
	Claude Passeau, Cubs, 1941	5
9.	16 tied with 4	

HITS ALLOWED

	Player	
1.	Tom Glavine, Braves, 1992	9
2.	Tommy Bridges, Tigers, 1937	7
3.	Atlee Hammaker, Giants, 1983	6
	Claude Passeau, Cubs, 1941	6
	Lon Warneke, Cubs, 1933	6
6.	29 tied with 5	

STRIKEOUTS

	Player	
1.	Carl Hubbell, Giants, 1934	6
	Larry Jansen, Giants, 1950	6
	Fergie Jenkins, Cubs, 1967	6
	Johnny Vander Meer, Reds, 1943	6
5.	Don Drysdale, Dodgers, 1959 (2nd game)	5
	Pedro Martinez, Red Sox, 1999	5
	Stu Miller, Giants, 1961 (2nd game)	5
	Joe Nuxhall, Reds, 1955	5
	Billy Pierce, White Sox, 1956	5
	Dick Radatz, Red Sox, 1963	5
	Dick Radatz, Red Sox, 1964	5
	Robin Roberts, Phillies, 1954	5
	Hal Schumacher, Giants, 1935	5
	Tom Seaver, Mets, 1968	5
	Fernando Valenzuela, Dodgers, 1986	5

WALKS

	Player	
1.	Bill Hallahan, Cardinals, 1933	5
2.	Jim Palmer, Orioles, 1978	4
3.	Ewell Blackwell, Reds, 1948	3
	Ralph Branca, Dodgers, 1948	3
	Kevin Brown, Dodgers, 2000	3
	Don Drysdale, Dodgers, 1959 (2nd game)	3
	Tom Glavine, Braves, 1998	3
	Jim Kern, Rangers, 1979	3
	Bill Lee, Cubs, 1939	3
	Mike McCormick, Giants, 1960 (1st game)	3
	Sam McDowell, Indians, 1970	3
	Andy Messersmith, Dodgers, 1974	3
	Joe Nuxhall, Reds, 1955	3
	Dan Petry, Tigers, 1985	3
	Johnny Podres, Dodgers, 1960 (2nd game)	3
	Vic Raschi, Yankees, 1949	3
	Lon Warneke, Cubs, 1934	3
	Lon Warneke, Cubs, 1936	3
	Early Wynn, White Sox, 1959 (2nd game)	3

Team
Highs and Lows (1901-2000)

PENNANTS, A.L.

1.	Yankees	37
2.	Athletics	15
3.	Red Sox	10
4.	Tigers	9
5.	Orioles/Browns	7
6.	Twins/Senators	6
7.	White Sox	5
	Indians	5
9.	Royals	2
	Blue Jays	2

PENNANTS, N.L.

1.	Dodgers	18
2.	Giants	17
3.	Cardinals	15
4.	Cubs	10
5.	Pirates	9
	Reds	9
	Braves	9
8.	Phillies	5
9.	Mets	4
10.	Padres	2

LCS WINNERS, A.L.

1.	Yankees	8
2.	Athletics	6
3.	Orioles	5
4.	Royals	2
	Red Sox	2
	Twins	2
	Blue Jays	2
	Indians	2
9.	Brewers	1
	Tigers	1

LCS WINNERS, N.L.

1.	Dodgers	5
	Reds	5
	Braves	5
4.	Mets	4
5.	Phillies	3
	Cardinals	3
7.	Pirates	2
	Padres	2
9.	Giants	1
	Marlins	1

WORLD SERIES WINNERS

1.	Yankees	26
2.	Cardinals	9
	Athletics	9
4.	Dodgers	6
5.	Giants	5
	Pirates	5
	Reds	5
	Red Sox	5
9.	Tigers	4
10.	Braves	3
	Orioles	3
	Twins	3

ALL-STAR GAME WINNERS

1.	National League	40
2.	American League	30
3.	games tied	1

VICTORIES, SEASON

1.	Cubs, 1906	116
2.	Yankees, 1998	114
3.	Indians, 1954	111
4.	Pirates, 1909	110
	Yankees, 1927	110
6.	Yankees, 1961	109
	Orioles, 1969	109
7.	Orioles, 1970	108
	Reds, 1975	108
	Mets, 1986	108

LOSSES, SEASON

1.	Mets, 1962	120
2.	Athletics, 1916	117
3.	Braves, 1935	115
4.	Senators, 1904	113
5.	Pirates, 1952	112
	Mets, 1965	112
7.	Red Sox, 1932	111
	Browns, 1939	111
	Phillies, 1941	111
	Mets, 1963	111

LARGEST 1ST/2ND-PLACE MARGIN

1.	Indians, 1995	30.0
2.	Pirates, 1902	27.5
3.	Yankees, 1998	22.0
4.	Mets, 1986	21.5
	Indians, 1999	21.5
6.	Braves, 1995	21.0
7.	Cubs, 1906	20.0
	Reds, 1975	20.0
	White Sox, 1983	20.0
10.	Yankees, 1936	19.5

LARGEST 1ST/LAST-PLACE MARGIN

1.	Cubs, 1906	66.5
2.	Pirates, 1909	65.5
3.	Yankees, 1939	64.5
4.	Yankees, 1932	64.0
5.	Cardinals, 1942	62.5
6.	Cubs, 1935	61.5
7.	Giants, 1962	60.5
8.	Indians, 1954	60.0
9.	Yankees, 1927	59.0
10.	Red Sox, 1915	58.5

MOST DAYS IN 1ST PLACE

1.	Orioles, 1997 (182)	182
2.	Tigers, 1984 (182)	181
	Phillies, 1993 (182)	181
	Indians, 1998 (181)	181
5.	Indians, 1999 (182)	179
	Cardinals, 2000 (182)	179
7.	Reds, 1970 (179)	178
	Reds, 1990 (178)	178
	Rangers, 1999 (182)	178
10.	Dodgers, 1974 (181)	177
	Athletics, 1988 (182)	177
	Rangers, 1996 (183)	177

LONGEST WINNING STREAKS

1.	Giants, 1916	26
2.	Cubs, 1935	21
3.	White Sox, 1906	19
	Yankees, 1947	19
5.	Giants, 1904	18
	Yankees, 1953	18
7.	Giants, 1907	17
	Giants, 1916	17
	Senators, 1912	17
	Athletics, 1931	17

LONGEST LOSING STREAKS

1.	Phillies, 1961	23
2.	Orioles, 1988	21
3.	Red Sox, 1906	20
	Athletics, 1916	20
	Athletics, 1943	20
	Expos, 1969	20
7.	Braves, 1906	19
	Reds, 1914	19
	Tigers, 1975	19
10.	Athletics, 1920	18
	Senators, 1948	18
	Senators, 1959	18

HIGHEST TEAM AVERAGE

1.	Giants, 1930	.319
2.	Tigers, 1921	.316
3.	Phillies, 1930	.315
4.	Cardinals, 1930	.314
5.	Browns, 1922	.313
6.	Yankees, 1930	.309
	Pirates, 1928	.309
	Phillies, 1929	.309
	Cubs, 1930	.309
10.	Browns, 1920	.308

RUNS SCORED, SEASON

1.	Yankees, 1931	1,067
2.	Yankees, 1936	1,065
3.	Yankees, 1930	1,062
4.	Red Sox, 1950	1,027
5.	Indians, 1999	1,009
6.	Cardinals, 1930	1,004
7.	Yankees, 1932	1,002
8.	Cubs, 1930	998
9.	Mariners, 1996	993
10.	Cubs, 1929	982

FEWEST RUNS, SEASON

(Minimum 140 games)

1.	Cardinals, 1908	371
2.	Dodgers, 1908	377
3.	Senators, 1909	380
4.	Phillies, 1942	394
5.	Braves, 1906	408
6.	Cardinals, 1907	419
7.	Braves, 1909	435
8.	Senators, 1903	437
	Senators, 1904	437
10.	Browns, 1909	441

HOME RUNS, GAME

1.	Blue Jays, Sept. 14, 1987	10
2.	Reds, Sept. 4, 1999	9
3.	Yankees, June 28, 1939	8
	Braves, Aug. 30, 1953	8
	Reds, Aug. 18, 1956	8
	Giants, April 30, 1961	8
	Twins, Aug. 29, 1963	8
	Red Sox, July 4, 1977	8
	Expos, July 30, 1978	8
	Athletics, June 27, 1996	8
	Indians, April 25, 1997	8
	Tigers, June 20, 2000	8

HOME RUNS, SEASON

1.	Mariners, 1997	264
2.	Orioles, 1996	257
3.	Astros, 2000	249
4.	Mariners, 1996	245
5.	Mariners, 1999	244
	Blue Jays, 2000	244
7.	Athletics, 1996	243
8.	Yankees, 1961	240
9.	Rockies, 1997	239
	Athletics, 2000	239

FEWEST HOME RUNS, SEASON

(Minimum 140 games)

1.	White Sox, 1908	3
2.	White Sox, 1909	4
	Senators, 1917	4
	Senators, 1918	4
5.	Phillies, 1902	5
	White Sox, 1907	5
	Cardinals, 1918	5
8.	Cubs, 1902	6
	Giants, 1902	6
10.	White Sox, 1906	7
	White Sox, 1910	7

STOLEN BASES, SEASON

1.	Giants, 1911	347
2.	A's, 1976	341
3.	Giants, 1912	319
4.	Cardinals, 1985	314
5.	Reds, 1910	310
6.	Giants, 1913	296
7.	Giants, 1905	291
8.	Reds, 1911	289
9.	Giants, 1906	288
	Yankees, 1910	288

LOWEST ERA, SEASON

1.	Cubs, 1907	1.73
2.	Cubs, 1909	1.75
	Cubs, 1906	1.75
4.	A's, 1910	1.79
5.	A's, 1909	1.93
6.	White Sox, 1905	1.99
7.	Indians, 1908	2.02
8.	White Sox, 1910	2.03
9.	Cubs, 1905	2.04
10.	White Sox, 1909	2.05

HIGHEST ERA, SEASON

1.	Phillies, 1930	6.72
2.	Tigers, 1996	6.38
3.	Browns, 1936	6.24
4.	Phillies, 1929	6.13
5.	Athletics, 1936	6.08
6.	Rockies, 1999	6.01
	Browns, 1939	6.01
8.	Browns, 1937	6.00
9.	Browns, 1938	5.81
10.	Athletics, 1939	5.79

FRANCHISE RECORDS

Franchise	Years	Games	Won	Lost	Pct.
Yankees/Orioles	1901 - 2000	15,414	8,697	6,717	.564
Giants	1901 - 2000	15,587	8,372	7,215	.537
Dodgers	1901 - 2000	15,584	8,147	7,437	.523
Pirates	1901 - 2000	15,583	8,074	7,509	.518
Cardinals	1901 - 2000	15,585	8,021	7,564	.515
Diamondbacks	1998 - 2000	486	250	236	.514
Tigers	1901 - 2000	15,462	7,914	7,548	.512
Red Sox	1901 - 2000	15,433	7,895	7,538	.512
Indians	1901 - 2000	15,438	7,896	7,542	.511
Royals	1969 - 2000	5,045	2,548	2,497	.505
Reds	1901 - 2000	15,601	7,880	7,721	.505
Cubs	1901 - 2000	15,596	7,868	7,728	.504
White Sox	1901 - 2000	15,420	7,778	7,642	.504
Blue Jays	1977 - 2000	3,764	1,867	1,897	.496
Astros/Colt .45s	1962 - 2000	6,190	3,052	3,138	.493
Expos	1969 - 2000	5,050	2,454	2,596	.486
Angels	1961 - 2000	6,350	3,069	3,281	.483
Rockies	1993 - 2000	1,233	594	639	.482
Athletics	1901 - 2000	15,403	7,390	8,013	.480
Brewers/Pilots	1969 - 2000	5,052	2,421	2,631	.479
Orioles/Browns	1901 - 2000	15,420	7,389	8,031	.479
Braves	1901 - 2000	15,558	7,437	8,121	.478
Twins/Senators	1901 - 2000	15,427	7,344	8,083	.476
Mets	1962 - 2000	6,180	2,934	3,246	.475
Rangers/Senators	1961 - 2000	6,333	2,952	3,381	.466
Phillies	1901 - 2000	15,562	7,120	8,442	.458
Padres	1969 - 2000	5,057	2,315	2,742	.458
Mariners	1977 - 2000	3,763	1,715	2,048	.456
Marlins	1993 - 2000	1,229	551	678	.448
Devil Rays	1998 - 2000	485	201	284	.414

LONGEST GAMES, INNINGS

1.	Dodgers 1 at Braves 1, May 1, 1920	26
2.	Cardinals 4 at Mets 3, Sept. 11, 1974	25
	White Sox 7 vs. Brewers 6, May 8, 1984	25
4.	A's 4 at Red Sox 1, Sept. 1, 1906	24
	Tigers 1 at Athletics 1, July 21, 1945	24
	Astros 1 vs. Mets 0, April 25, 1968	24
7.	Dodgers 2 at Braves 2, June 27, 1939	23
	Giants 8 at Mets 6, May 31, 1964	23
9.	8 tied at 22	

RUNS SCORED, GAME

1.	Red Sox vs. Browns, June 8, 1950	29
	White Sox vs. A's, April 23, 1955	29
3.	Cardinals vs. Phillies, July 6, 1929	28
4.	Indians vs. Red Sox, July 7, 1923	27
5.	Cubs vs. Phillies, Aug. 25, 1922	26
	Giants vs. Dodgers, April 30, 1944	26
	Indians vs. Browns, Aug. 12, 1948	26
	Phillies vs. Mets, April 11, 1985	26
	Cubs vs. Rockies, Aug. 18, 1995	26
	Rangers vs. Orioles, April 19, 1996	26

RUNS SCORED, INNING

1.	Red Sox vs. Tigers, June 18, 1953 (7th)	17
2.	Rangers vs. Orioles, April 19, 1996 (8th)	16
3.	Dodgers vs. Reds, May 21, 1952 (1st)	15
4.	Yankees vs. Senators, July 6, 1920 (5th)	14
	Cubs vs. Phillies, Aug. 25, 1922 (4th)	14
	Indians vs. A's, June 18, 1950 (1st)	14
	Reds vs. Astros, Aug. 3, 1989 (1st)	14
8.	19 tied with 13	

BASEBALL CLASSICS

MEMORABLE MOMENTS

MERKLE'S BONER

September 23, 1908, at the Polo Grounds

New York Giants first baseman Fred Merkle claimed status as baseball's biggest goat when he failed to touch second base on an apparent game-ending hit against the Chicago Cubs, a mistake that would cost his team a pennant. With two out and runners on first and third in the bottom of the ninth of a 1-1 tie, Al Bridwell singled to center and Moose McCormick scored the winning run. But when Merkle failed to touch second, Cubs second baseman Johnny Evers appealed for the forceout and umpire Hank O'Day concurred, disallowing the run. League officials later declared the game a tie and the teams went on to finish the season with identical records. The Cubs won a makeup game—and the pennant.

Chicago	AB	R	H	PO	A	E
Hayden,rf	4	0	0	1	0	0
Evers,2b	4	0	1	3	7	0
Schulte,lf	4	0	0	1	0	0
Chance,1b	4	0	1	11	1	0
Steinfeldt,3b	2	0	0	0	1	1
Hofman,cf	3	0	1	2	0	0
Tinker,ss	3	1	1	8	6	2
Kling,c	3	0	1	0	1	0
Pfiester,p	3	0	0	1	0	0
Totals	30	1	5	27	16	3

New York	AB	R	H	PO	A	E
Herzog,2b	3	1	1	1	1	0
Bresnahan,c	3	0	0	10	0	0
Donlin,rf	4	0	1	2	0	0
Seymour,cf	4	0	1	1	0	0
Devlin,3b	4	0	2	0	2	0
McCormick,lf	3	0	0	1	0	0
Merkle,1b	3	0	1	10	1	0
Bridwell,ss	4	0	0	2	8	0
Mathewson,p	3	0	0	0	2	0
Totals	31	1	6	27	14	0

Chicago ....0 0 0 1 0 0 0 0 0—1
New York ....0 0 0 0 1 0 0 0 0—1

Runs batted in: Tinker, Donlin.
Home run: Tinker.
Sacrifice hits: Steinfeldt, Bresnahan.
Double plays: Tinker and Chance 2; Evers and Chance; Mathewson, Bridwell and Merkle.
Left on bases: Chicago 3, New York 7.

Chicago	IP	H	R	ER	BB	SO
Pfiester	9	6	1	0	2	0

New York	IP	H	R	ER	BB	SO
Mathewson	9	5	1	1	0	9

Hit by pitcher: McCormick (by Pfiester).
Umpires: O'Day, Emslie.
Time: 1:30. **Attendance:** 20,000.

A GIANT MISPLAY

October 16, 1912, at Fenway Park

The Boston Red Sox, given life by New York Giants center fielder Fred Snodgrass' 10th-inning error, scored two runs and claimed a 3-2 victory in the decisive eighth game of the World Series. After Snodgrass dropped a routine fly ball to open the inning, the Giants also failed to catch a foul pop by Tris Speaker, who then singled home the tying run. Larry Gardner produced the winner with a sacrifice fly.

New York	AB	R	H	PO	A	E
Devore,rf	3	1	1	3	1	0
Doyle,2b	5	0	0	1	5	1
Snodgrass,cf	4	0	1	4	1	1
Murray,lf	5	1	2	3	0	0
Merkle,1b	5	0	1	10	0	0
Herzog,3b	5	0	2	2	1	0
Meyers,c	3	0	0	4	1	0
Fletcher,ss	3	0	1	2	3	0
bMcCormick	1	0	0	0	0	0
Shafer,ss	0	0	0	0	0	0
Mathewson,p	4	0	1	0	3	0
Totals	38	2	9	29	15	2

Boston	AB	R	H	PO	A	E
Hooper,rf	5	0	0	3	0	0
Yerkes,2b	4	1	1	0	3	0
Speaker,cf	4	0	2	2	0	1
Lewis,lf	4	0	0	1	0	0
Gardner,3b	3	0	1	1	4	2
Stahl,1b	4	1	2	15	0	1
Wagner,ss	3	0	1	3	5	1
Cady,c	4	0	0	5	3	0
Bedient,p	2	0	0	0	1	0
aHenriksen	1	0	1	0	0	0
Wood,p	0	0	0	0	2	0
cEngle	1	1	0	0	0	0
Totals	35	3	8	30	18	5

New York ....0 0 1 0 0 0 0 0 0 1—2
Boston ....0 0 0 0 0 0 1 0 0 2—3

a Doubled for Bedient in seventh.
b Flied out for Fletcher in ninth.
c Reached second on Snodgrass' error in 10th.
d Two out when winning run scored.

Runs batted in: Murray, Merkle, Speaker, Gardner, Henriksen.
Doubles: Murray 2, Herzog, Gardner, Stahl, Henriksen.
Sacrifice hit: Meyers.
Sacrifice fly: Gardner.
Stolen bases: Devore.
Left on bases: New York 11, Boston 9.

New York	IP	H	R	ER	BB	SO
Mathewson (L)	9⅔	8	3	2	5	4

Boston	IP	H	R	ER	BB	SO
Bedient	7	6	1	1	3	2
Wood (W)	3	3	1	1	1	2

Umpires: O'Loughlin, Rigler, Klem, Evans.
Time: 2:39. **Attendance:** 17,034.

A DOUBLE NO-NO

May 2, 1917, at Wrigley Field

Cincinnati lefthander Fred Toney and Chicago righthander Hippo Vaughn hooked up in the most efficient pitching duel in baseball history—the game's only double nine-inning no-hitter. Vaughn allowed two 10th-inning hits and the Cubs broke through for an unearned run that Toney made stand up in the bottom of the inning, completing his no-hit gem. Vaughn had to settle for a tough-luck loss.

Cincinnati	AB	R	H	PO	A	E
Groh,3b	1	0	0	2	2	0
Getz,3b	1	0	0	2	1	0
Kopf,ss	4	1	1	1	4	0
Neale,cf	4	0	0	1	0	0
Chase,1b	4	0	0	12	0	0
Thorpe,rf	4	0	1	1	0	0
Shean,2b	3	0	0	3	2	0
Cueto,lf	3	0	0	5	0	0
Huhn,c	3	0	0	3	0	0
Toney,p	3	0	0	0	1	0
Totals	30	1	2	30	10	0

Chicago	AB	R	H	PO	A	E
Zeider,ss	4	0	0	1	0	0
Wolter,rf	4	0	0	0	0	0
Doyle,2b	4	0	0	5	4	0
Merkle,1b	4	0	0	7	1	0
Williams,cf	2	0	0	2	0	1
Mann,lf	3	0	0	0	0	0
Wilson,c	3	0	0	14	1	0
Deal,3b	3	0	0	1	0	0
Vaughn,p	3	0	0	0	3	0
Totals	30	0	0	30	9	1

Cincinnati ....0 0 0 0 0 0 0 0 0 1—1
Chicago ....0 0 0 0 0 0 0 0 0 0—0

Runs batted in: Thorpe.
Stolen bases: Chase.
Double plays: Doyle, Merkle and Zeider; Doyle and Merkle.
Left on bases: Cincinnati 1, Chicago 2.

Cincinnati	IP	H	R	ER	BB	SO
Toney (W)	10	0	0	0	2	3

Chicago	IP	H	R	ER	BB	SO
Vaughn (L)	10	2	1	0	2	10

Umpires: Orth, Rigler.
Time: 1:50. **Attendance:** 3,500.

A 26-INNING STANDOFF

May 1, 1920, at Braves Field

Brooklyn's Leon Cadore and Boston's Joe Oeschger matched zeroes in the longest pitching duel in baseball history—a 26-inning, 1-1 marathon that was called because of darkness. Cadore allowed 15 hits and Oeschger nine, but neither pitcher surrendered a run over the last 20 innings. Brooklyn scored in the fifth and Boston tied the game an inning later.

Brooklyn	AB	R	H	PO	A	E
Olson,2b	10	0	1	6	9	1
Neis,rf	10	0	1	9	0	0
Johnston,3b	10	0	2	2	1	0
Wheat,lf	9	0	2	3	0	0
Myers,cf	2	0	1	2	0	0
Hood,cf	6	0	1	8	1	0
Konetchy,1b	9	0	1	30	1	0
Ward,ss	10	0	0	6	3	1
Krueger,c	2	1	0	4	3	0
Elliott,c	7	0	0	7	3	0
Cadore,p	10	0	0	1	12	0
Totals	85	1	9	78	33	2

Boston	AB	R	H	PO	A	E
Powell,cf	8	0	1	8	0	0
Pick,2b	11	0	0	5	10	2
Mann,lf	10	0	2	6	0	0
Cruise,rf	9	1	1	4	0	0
Holke,1b	10	0	2	43	1	0
Boeckel,3b	11	0	3	1	7	0
Maranville,ss	10	0	3	1	9	0
O'Neil,c	2	0	0	4	3	0
aChristenbury	1	0	1	0	0	0
Gowdy,c	6	0	1	6	0	0
Oeschger,p	9	0	1	0	11	0
Totals	87	1	15	78	41	2

a Singled for O'Neil in ninth.

Brk. 0 0 0 0 1 0 0 0 0 0 0 0 0 0 0
Bos. 0 0 0 0 0 1 0 0 0 0 0 0 0 0 0

Brk. ....0 0 0 0 0 0 0 0 0 0 0—1
Bos. ....0 0 0 0 0 0 0 0 0 0 0—1

Runs batted in: Olson, Boeckel.
Doubles: Oeschger, Maranville.
Triple: Cruise.
Sacrifice hits: Powell, O'Neil, Cruise, Hood, Holke.
Stolen bases: Myers, Hood.
Double plays: Olson and Konetchy; Oeschger, Gowdy, Holke and Gowdy.
Left on bases: Brooklyn 11, Boston 17.

Brooklyn	IP	H	R	ER	BB	SO
Cadore	26	15	1	1	5	7

Boston	IP	H	R	ER	BB	SO
Oeschger	26	9	1	1	4	7

Wild pitch: Oeschger.

Umpires: McCormick, Hart.
Time: 3:50. **Attendance:** 2,500.

SENATORIAL SPLENDOR

October 10, 1924, at Griffith Stadium

The Washington Senators, long the doormat of the American League, captured their first World Series when two routine Game 7 ground balls inexplicably hopped over the head of New York Giants third baseman Fred Lindstrom, producing three runs. The Senators tied the game, 3-3, on manager Bucky Harris' two-run, bad-hop single in the eighth inning and won in the 12th, 4-3, on Earl McNeely's bad-hop bouncer.

New York	AB	R	H	PO	A	E
Lindstrom,3b	5	0	1	0	3	0
Frisch,2b	5	0	2	3	4	0
Youngs,rf-lf	2	1	0	2	0	0
Kelly,cf-1b	6	1	1	8	1	0
Terry,1b	2	0	0	6	1	0
aMeusel,lf-rf	3	0	1	1	0	0
Wilson,lf-cf	5	1	1	4	0	0
Jackson,ss	6	0	0	1	4	2
Gowdy,c	6	0	1	8	0	1
Barnes,p	4	0	0	1	2	0
Nehf,p	0	0	0	0	0	0
McQuillan,p	0	0	0	0	0	0
eGroh	1	0	1	0	0	0
fSouthworth	0	0	0	0	0	0
Bentley,p	0	0	0	0	0	0
Totals	45	3	8	34	15	3

New York Giants first baseman Fred Merkle is usually blamed for his team's failure to win the 1908 National League pennant.

Washington	AB	R	H	PO	A	E
McNeely,cf	6	0	1	0	0	0
Harris,2b	5	1	3	4	1	0
Rice,rf	5	0	0	2	0	0
Goslin,lf	5	0	2	3	0	0
Judge,1b	4	0	1	11	1	1
Bluege,ss	5	0	0	1	7	2
Taylor,3b	2	0	0	0	3	1
bLeibold	1	1	1	0	0	0
Miller,3b	2	0	0	1	1	0
Ruel,c	5	2	2	13	0	0
Odgen,p	0	0	0	0	0	0
Mogridge,p	1	0	0	0	0	0
Marberry,p	1	0	0	1	0	0
cTate	0	0	0	0	0	0
dShirley	0	0	0	0	0	0
Johnson,p	2	0	0	0	1	0
Totals	44	4	10	36	14	4

New York..........000 003 000 000—3
Washington......000 100 020 001—4

a Flied out for Terry in sixth.
b Doubled for Taylor in eighth.
c Walked for Marberry in eighth.
d Ran for Tate in eighth.
e Singled for McQuillan in 11th.
f Ran for Groh in 11th.
g One out when winning run scored.

Runs batted in: Harris 3, McNeely, Meusel.
Doubles: Lindstrom, Leibold, Ruel, Goslin, McNeely.
Triple: Frisch.
Home run: Harris.
Sacrifice hit: Lindstrom.
Sacrifice fly: Meusel.
Stolen bases: Youngs.
Double plays: Kelly and Jackson; Jackson, Frisch and Kelly; Johnson, Bluege and Judge.
Left on bases: New York 14, Washington 8.

New York	IP	H	R	ER	BB	SO
Barnes	7⅔	6	3	3	1	6
Nehf	⅔	1	0	0	0	0
McQuillan	1⅔	0	0	0	0	1
Bentley (L)	1⅓	3	1	1	1	0

Washington	IP	H	R	ER	BB	SO
Odgen	⅓	0	0	0	1	1
Mogridge	4⅔	4	2	1	1	3
Marberry	3	1	1	0	1	3
Johnson (W)	4	3	0	0	3	5

Mogridge pitched to two batters in sixth.

Umpires: Dinneen, Quigley, Connolly, Klem.
Time: 3:00. **Attendance:** 31,667.

A'S VAULT PAST CUBS

October 12, 1929, at Shibe Park

Down 8-0 after six innings of World Series Game 4, the Philadelphia Athletics rocked the Chicago Cubs with a 10-run seventh-inning explosion that produced a 10-8 victory and a three-games-to-one advantage in the fall classic. The key blow in the biggest inning in Series history was a three-run, inside-the-park home run by Philadelphia's Mule Haas.

Chicago	AB	R	H	PO	A	E
McMillan,3b	4	0	0	1	3	0
English,ss	4	0	0	2	1	0
Hornsby,2b	5	2	2	1	1	0
Wilson,cf	3	1	2	3	0	1
Cuyler,rf	4	2	3	0	0	1
Stephenson,lf	4	1	1	2	1	0
Grimm,1b	4	2	2	7	0	0
Taylor,c	3	0	0	8	1	0
Root,p	3	0	0	0	0	0
Nehf,p	0	0	0	0	0	0
Blake,p	0	0	0	0	0	0
Malone,p	0	0	0	0	0	0
bHartnett	1	0	0	0	0	0
Carlson,p	0	0	0	0	1	0
Totals	35	8	10	24	8	2

Philadelphia	AB	R	H	PO	A	E
Bishop,2b	5	1	2	2	3	0
Haas,cf	4	1	1	2	0	0
Cochrane,c	4	1	2	9	0	0
Simmons,lf	5	2	2	0	0	0
Foxx,1b	4	2	2	10	0	0
Miller,rf	3	1	2	3	0	1
Dykes,3b	4	1	3	0	2	0
Boley,ss	3	1	1	1	5	0
Quinn,p	2	0	0	0	0	0
Walberg,p	0	0	0	0	0	1
Rommel,p	0	0	0	0	0	0
aBurns	2	0	0	0	0	0
Grove,p	0	0	0	0	0	0
Totals	36	10	15	27	10	2

Chicago ....000 205 100—8
Philadelphia ....000 000 100x—10

a Popped out and struck out for Rommel in seventh.
b Struck out for Malone in eighth.

Runs batted in: Cuyler 2, Stephenson, Grimm 2, Taylor, Bishop, Haas 3, Simmons, Foxx, Dykes 3, Boley.
Doubles: Cochrane, Dykes.
Triple: Hornsby.
Home runs: Grimm, Haas, Simmons.
Sacrifice hits: Taylor, Haas, Boley.
Double play: Dykes, Bishop and Foxx.
Left on bases: Philadelphia 10, Chicago 6.

Chicago	IP	H	R	ER	BB	SO
Root	6⅓	9	6	6	0	3
Nehf	0	1	2	2	1	0
Blake (L)	0	2	2	2	0	0
Malone	⅔	1	0	0	0	2
Carlson	1	2	0	0	0	1

Philadelphia	IP	H	R	ER	BB	SO
Quinn	5	7	6	5	2	2
Walberg	1	1	1	0	0	2
Rommel (W)	1	2	1	1	1	0
Grove (S)	2	0	0	0	0	4

Nehf pitched to two batters in seventh.
Blake pitched to two batters in seventh.
Quinn pitched to four batters in sixth,
Hit by pitcher: Miller (by Malone).

Umpires: Van Graflan, Klem, Dinneen, Moran.
Time: 2:12. **Attendance:** 29,921.

RUTH'S CALLED SHOT

October 1, 1932, at Wrigley Field

New York slugger Babe Ruth, ever the showman, livened up Game 3 of the World Series with his dramatic called-shot home run, breaking a 4-4 tie and sparking the Yankees to a 7-5 victory. Responding to the taunting of Cubs players and fans, Ruth made a sweeping gesture toward the center-field stands and then deposited Charlie Root's 2-2 pitch precisely where he had pointed. The home run, his second of the game, helped the Yankees to a Series-controlling 3-0 lead.

New York	AB	R	H	PO	A	E
Combs,cf	5	1	0	1	0	0
Sewell,3b	2	1	0	2	2	0
Ruth,lf	4	2	2	2	0	0
Gehrig,1b	5	2	2	13	1	0
Lazzeri,2b	4	1	0	3	4	1
Dickey,c	4	0	1	2	1	0
Chapman,rf	4	0	2	0	0	0
Crosetti,ss	4	0	1	4	4	0
Pipgras,p	5	0	0	0	0	0
Pennock,p	0	0	0	0	1	0
Totals	37	7	8	27	13	1

Chicago	AB	R	H	PO	A	E
Herman,2b	4	1	0	1	2	1
English,3b	4	0	0	0	3	0
Cuyler,rf	4	1	3	1	0	0
Stephenson,lf	4	0	1	1	0	0
Moore,cf	3	1	0	3	0	0
Grimm,1b	4	0	1	8	0	0
Hartnett,c	4	1	1	10	1	1
Jurges,ss	4	1	3	3	3	2
Root,p	2	0	0	0	0	0
Malone,p	0	0	0	0	0	0
aGudat	1	0	0	0	0	0
May,p	0	0	0	0	0	0
Tinning,p	0	0	0	0	0	0
bKoenig	0	0	0	0	0	0
cHemlsey	1	0	0	0	0	0
Totals	35	5	9	27	9	4

New York ....301 020 001—7
Chicago ....102 100 001—5

a Popped out for Malone in seventh.
b Announced for Tinning in ninth.
c Struck out for Koenig in ninth.

Runs batted in: Ruth 4, Gehrig 2, Cuyler 2, Grimm, Chapman, Hartnett.
Doubles: Chapman, Cuyler, Jurges, Grimm.
Home runs: Ruth 2, Gehrig 2, Hartnett.
Stolen bases: Jurges.
Double plays: Sewell, Lazzeri and Gehrig; Herman, Jurges and Grimm.
Left on bases: New York 11, Chicago 6.

New York	IP	H	R	ER	BB	SO
Pipgras (W)	8	9	5	4	3	1
Pennock (S)	1	0	0	0	0	1

Chicago	IP	H	R	ER	BB	SO
Root (L)	4⅓	6	6	5	3	4
Malone	2⅔	1	0	0	4	4
May	1⅓	1	1	0	0	1
Tinning	⅔	0	0	0	0	1

Pipgras pitched to two batters in ninth.
Hit by pitcher: Sewell (by May).

Umpires: Van Graflan, Magerkurth, Dinneen, Klem.
Time: 2:11. **Attendance:** 49,986.

VANDER MEER'S DOUBLE

June 15, 1938, at Ebbets Field

Cincinnati lefthander Johnny Vander Meer pitched an historic 6-0 no-hitter against the Brooklyn Dodgers—his unprecedented second straight hitless game and the first night contest at Brooklyn's Ebbets Field. Vander Meer's victory came four days after he had no-hit Boston, 3-0.

Cincinnati	AB	R	H	PO	A	E
Frey,2b	5	0	1	2	2	0
Berger,lf	5	1	3	1	0	0
Goodman,rf	3	2	1	3	0	0
McCormick,1b	5	1	1	9	1	0
Lombardi,c	3	1	0	9	0	0
Craft,cf	5	0	3	1	0	0
Riggs,3b	4	0	1	0	3	0
Myers,ss	4	0	0	0	1	0
Vander Meer,p	4	1	1	2	4	0
Totals	38	6	11	27	11	0

Brooklyn	AB	R	H	PO	A	E
Cuyler,rf	2	0	0	1	0	0
Coscarart,2b	2	0	0	1	2	0
aBrack	1	0	0	0	0	0
Hudson,2b	1	0	0	1	0	0
Hassett,lf	4	0	0	3	0	0
Phelps,c	3	0	0	9	0	0
cRosen	0	0	0	0	0	0
Lavagetto,3b	2	0	0	0	2	2
Camilli,1b	1	0	0	7	0	0
Koy,cf	4	0	0	4	0	0
Durocher,ss	4	0	0	1	2	0
Butcher,p	0	0	0	0	1	0
Presnell,p	2	0	0	0	0	0
Hamlin,p	0	0	0	0	1	0
bEnglish	1	0	0	0	0	0
Tamulis,p	0	0	0	0	0	0
Totals	27	0	0	27	8	2

Cincinnati ....004 000 110—6
Brooklyn....................000 000 000—0

a Batted for Coscarart in sixth.
b Struck out for Hamlin in eighth.
c Ran for Phelps in ninth.

Runs batted in: McCormick 3, Riggs, Craft, Berger.
Double: Berger.
Triple: Berger.
Home run: McCormick.
Stolen bases: Goodman.
Left on bases: Cincinnati 9, Brooklyn 8.

Cincinnati	IP	H	R	ER	BB	SO
Vander Meer (W)	9	0	0	0	8	7

Brooklyn	IP	H	R	ER	BB	SO
Butcher (L)	2⅔	5	4	4	3	1
Pressnell	3⅔	4	1	1	0	3
Hamlin	1⅔	2	1	1	1	3
Tamulis	1	0	0	0	0	0

Umpires: Stewart, Stark, Barr.
Time: 2:22. **Attendance:** 38,748.

WILLIAMS' STAR RISES

July 8, 1941, at Briggs Stadium

Young Boston slugger Ted Williams carved his first niche in baseball lore with a two-out, three-run, ninth-inning homer that gave the American League a dramatic 7-5 victory over the National League in baseball's ninth All-Star Game. Williams capped the four-run A.L. ninth with a monster drive off Chicago's Claude Passeau that bounced off the upper right-field parapet of Detroit's Briggs Stadium.

National League	AB	R	H	PO	A	E
Hack,3b	2	0	1	3	0	0
fLavagetto,3b	1	0	0	0	0	0
Moore,lf	5	0	0	0	0	0
Reiser,cf	4	0	0	6	0	2
Mize,1b	4	1	1	5	0	0
McCormick,1b	0	0	0	0	0	0
Nicholson,rf	1	0	0	1	0	0
Elliott,rf	1	0	0	0	0	0
Slaughter,rf	2	1	1	0	0	0
Vaughan,ss	4	2	3	1	2	0
Miller,ss	0	0	0	0	1	0
Frey,3b	1	0	1	1	3	0
cHerman,2b	3	0	2	3	0	0
Owen,c	1	0	0	0	0	0
Lopez,c	1	0	0	3	0	0
Danning,c	1	0	0	3	0	0
Wyatt,p	0	0	0	0	0	0
aOtt	1	0	0	0	0	0
Derringer,p	0	0	0	0	1	0
Walters,p	1	1	1	0	0	0
dMedwick	1	0	0	0	0	0
Passeau,p	1	0	0	0	0	0
Totals	35	5	10	26	7	2

American League	AB	R	H	PO	A	E
Doerr,2b	3	0	0	0	0	0
Gordon,2b	2	1	1	2	0	0
Travis,3b	4	1	1	1	2	0
J.DiMaggio,cf	4	3	1	1	0	0
Williams,lf	4	1	2	3	0	1
Heath,rf	2	0	0	1	0	1
D.DiMaggio,rf	1	0	1	1	0	0
Cronin,ss	2	0	0	3	0	0
Boudreau,ss	2	0	2	0	1	0
York,1b	3	0	1	6	2	0
Foxx,1b	1	0	0	2	2	0
Dickey,c	3	0	1	4	2	0
Hayes,c	1	0	0	2	0	0
Feller,p	0	0	0	0	1	0
bCullenbine	1	0	0	0	0	0
Lee,p	1	0	0	0	1	0
Hudson,p	0	0	0	0	0	0
eKeller	1	0	0	0	0	0
Smith,p	0	0	0	1	0	1
gKeltner	1	1	1	0	0	0
Totals	36	7	11	27	11	3

National League ....000 001 220—5
American League ......000 101 014—7

a Struck out for Wyatt in third.
b Grounded out for Feller in third.
c Singled for Frey in fifth.
d Grounded out for Walters in seventh.
e Struck out for Hudson in seventh.
f Grounded out for Hack in ninth.
g Singled for Smith in ninth.
h Two out when winning run scored.

Runs batted in: Williams 4, Moore, Boudreau, Vaughan 4, D.DiMaggio, J.DiMaggio.
Doubles: Travis, Williams, Walters, Herman, Mize, J.DiMaggio.
Home runs: Vaughan 2, Williams.
Sacrifice hits: Hack, Lopez.
Double plays: Frey, Vaughan and Mize; York and Cronin.
Left on bases: National League 6, American League 7.

National League	IP	H	R	ER	BB	SO
Wyatt	2	0	0	0	1	0
Derringer	2	2	1	1	0	1
Walters	2	3	1	1	2	2
Passeau (L)	2⅔	6	5	5	1	3

American League	IP	H	R	ER	BB	SO
Feller	3	1	0	0	0	4
Lee	3	4	1	1	0	0
Hudson	1	3	2	2	1	1
Smith (W)	2	2	2	2	0	2

Umpires: Summers, Grieve, Jorda, Pinelli.
Time: 2:23. **Attendance:** 54,674.

DiMAGGIO'S STREAK ENDS

July 17, 1941, at Municipal Stadium

Cleveland pitchers Al Smith and Jim Bagby Jr. retired New York's Joe DiMaggio three times and ended the Yankees center fielder's record hitting streak at 56 games. DiMaggio, who had not gone hitless in more than two months, grounded out to third base twice, walked and bounced into an eighth-inning double play during the Yankees' 4-3 victory.

New York	AB	R	H	PO	A	E
Sturm,1b	4	0	1	10	2	0
Rolfe,3b	4	1	2	2	3	0
Henrich,rf	3	0	1	4	0	0
DiMaggio,cf	3	0	0	2	0	0
Gordon,2b	4	1	2	0	1	0
Rosar,c	4	0	0	5	1	0
Keller,lf	3	1	1	0	0	0
Rizzuto,ss	4	0	0	2	1	0
Gomez,p	4	1	1	2	1	0
Murphy,p	0	0	0	0	1	0
Totals	33	4	8	27	10	0

Cleveland	AB	R	H	PO	A	E
Weatherly,cf	5	0	1	4	0	0
Keltner,3b	3	0	1	1	4	0
Boudreau,ss	3	0	0	0	2	0
Heath,rf	4	0	0	0	0	0
Walker,lf	3	2	2	1	0	0
Grimes,1b	3	1	1	12	0	0
Mack,2b	3	0	0	4	7	0
aRosenthal	1	0	1	0	0	0
Hemsley,c	3	0	1	5	1	0
bTrosky	1	0	0	0	0	0
Smith,p	3	0	0	0	0	0
Bagby,p	0	0	0	0	0	0
cCampbell	1	0	0	0	0	0
Totals	33	3	7	27	14	0

New York ....100 000 120—4
Cleveland ....000 100 002—3

a Tripled for Mack in ninth.
b Grounded out for Hemsley in ninth.
c Hit into fielders choice for Bagby in ninth.

Runs batted in: Henrich, Walker, Gomez, Gordon, Rolfe, Rosenthal 2.
Doubles: Henrich, Rolfe.
Triples: Keller, Rosenthal.
Home runs: Walker, Gordon.
Sacrifice hit: Boudreau.
Double play: Boudreau, Mack and Grimes.
Passed ball: Hemsley.
Left on bases: New York 5, Cleveland 7.

New York	IP	H	R	ER	BB	SO
Gomez (W)	8	6	3	3	3	5
Murphy (S)	1	1	0	0	0	0
Cleveland	**IP**	**H**	**R**	**ER**	**BB**	**SO**
Smith (L)	7⅓	7	4	4	2	4
Bagby	1⅔	1	0	0	1	1

Gomez pitched to two batters in ninth.

Umpires: Summers, Rue, Stewart.
Time: 2:03. **Attendance:** 67,468.

OWEN'S PASSED BALL

October 5, 1941, at Ebbets Field

With his Dodgers leading the New York Yankees, 4-3, and one out away from evening the World Series at two games apiece, Brooklyn catcher Mickey Owen missed connections on a third strike, allowing Tommy Henrich to reach first base. Given new life, the Yankees exploded for four ninth-inning runs, recorded a 7-4 victory and set the stage for a Series-clinching victory the next day.

New York	AB	R	H	PO	A	E
Sturm,1b	5	0	2	9	1	0
Rolfe,3b	5	1	2	0	2	0
Henrich,rf	4	1	0	3	0	0
DiMaggio,cf	4	1	2	2	0	0
Keller,lf	5	1	4	1	0	0
Dickey,c	2	2	0	7	0	0
Gordon,2b	5	1	2	2	3	0
Rizzuto,ss	4	0	0	2	3	0
Donald,p	2	0	0	0	1	0
Breuer,p	1	0	0	0	1	0
bSelkirk	1	0	0	0	0	0
Murphy,p	1	0	0	1	0	0
Totals	39	7	12	27	11	0

Brooklyn	AB	R	H	PO	A	E
Reese,ss	5	0	0	2	4	0
Walker,rf	5	1	2	5	0	0
Reiser,cf	5	1	2	1	0	0
Camilli,1b	4	0	2	10	1	0
Riggs,3b	3	0	0	0	2	0
Medwick,lf	2	0	0	1	0	0
Allen,p	0	0	0	0	0	0
Casey,p	2	0	1	0	3	0
Owen,c	2	1	0	2	1	1
Coscarart,2b	3	1	0	4	2	0
Higbe,p	1	0	1	0	1	0
French,p	0	0	0	0	0	0
aWasdell,lf	3	0	1	2	0	0
Totals	35	4	9	27	14	1

New York ....1 0 0 2 0 0 0 0 4—7
Brooklyn....................0 0 0 2 2 0 0 0 0—4

a Doubled for French in fourth.
b Grounded out for Breuer in eighth.

Runs batted in: Keller 3, Sturm 2, Gordon 2, Wasdell 2, Reiser 2.
Doubles: Keller 2, Walker, Camilli, Wasdell, Gordon.
Home run: Reiser.
Double play: Gordon, Rizzuto and Sturm.
Left on bases: New York 11, Brooklyn 8.

New York	IP	H	R	ER	BB	SO
Donald	4	6	4	4	3	2
Breuer	3	3	0	0	1	2
Murphy (W)	2	0	0	0	0	1
Brooklyn	**IP**	**H**	**R**	**ER**	**BB**	**SO**
Higbe	3⅔	6	3	3	2	1
French	⅓	0	0	0	0	0
Allen	⅔	1	0	0	1	0
Casey (L)	4⅓	5	4	0	2	1

Donald pitched to two batters in fifth.
Hit by pitcher: Henrich (by Allen).

Umpires: Goetz, McGowan, Pinelli, Grieve.
Time: 2:54. **Attendance:** 33,813

SLAUGHTER'S MAD DASH

October 15, 1946, at Sportsman's Park

St. Louis Cardinals outfielder Enos Slaughter decided the World Series with his daring Game 7 dash around the bases on a hit to left-center field by Harry Walker. Slaughter's eighth-inning heroics were successful because Boston shortstop Johnny Pesky, obviously surprised that Slaughter didn't stop at third, hesitated before making a weak relay throw to the plate.

Boston	AB	R	H	PO	A	E
Moses,rf	4	1	1	1	0	0
Pesky,ss	4	0	1	2	1	0
DiMaggio,cf	3	0	1	0	0	0
cCulberson,cf	0	0	0	0	0	0
Williams,lf	4	0	0	3	1	0
York,1b	4	0	1	10	1	0
dCampbell	0	0	0	0	0	0
Doerr,2b	4	0	2	3	7	0
Higgins,3b	4	0	0	0	1	0
H.Wagner,c	2	0	0	4	0	0
aRussell	1	1	1	0	0	0
Partee,c	1	0	0	0	0	0
Ferriss,p	2	0	0	0	0	0
Dobson,p	0	0	0	0	1	0
bMetkovich	1	1	1	0	0	0
Klinger,p	0	0	0	1	0	0
Johnson,p	0	0	0	0	0	0
eMcBride	1	0	0	0	0	0
Totals	35	3	8	24	12	0

St. Louis	AB	R	H	PO	A	E
Schoendienst,2b	4	0	2	2	3	0
Moore,cf	4	0	1	3	0	0
Musial,1b	3	0	1	6	0	0
Slaughter,rf	3	1	1	4	0	0
Kurowski,3b	4	1	1	3	1	1
Garigiola,c	3	0	0	4	0	0
Rice,c	1	0	0	0	0	0
Walker,lf	3	1	2	3	0	0
Marion,ss	2	0	0	2	1	0
Dickson,p	3	1	1	0	1	0
Brecheen,p	1	0	0	0	0	0
Totals	31	4	9	27	6	1

Boston ....1 0 0 0 0 0 0 2 0—3
St. Louis....................0 1 0 0 2 0 0 1 x—4

a Singled for H.Wagner in eighth.
b Doubled for Dobson in eighth.
c Ran for DiMaggio in eighth.
d Ran for York in ninth.
e Rolled out for Johnson in ninth.

Runs batted in: DiMaggio 3, Walker 2, Dickson, Schoendienst.
Doubles: Musial, Kurowski, Dickson, DiMaggio, Metkovich, Walker.
Sacrifice hit: Marion.
Left on bases: Boston 6, St. Louis 8.

Boston	IP	H	R	ER	BB	SO
Ferris	4⅓	7	3	3	1	1
Dobson	2⅔	0	0	0	2	2
Klinger (L)	⅔	2	1	1	1	0
Johnson	⅓	0	0	0	0	0
St. Louis	**IP**	**H**	**R**	**ER**	**BB**	**SO**
Dickson	7	5	3	3	1	3
Brecheen (W)	2	3	0	0	0	1

Dickson pitched to two batters in eighth.

Umpires: Barlick, Berry, Ballanfant, Hubbard.
Time: 2:17. **Attendance:** 36,143

ROBINSON BREAKS BARRIER

April 15, 1947, at Ebbets Field

Jackie Robinson made his long-awaited debut as baseball's first black Major League player in more than six decades when he started at first base in Brooklyn's season-opening 5-3 victory over Boston. The 28-year-old Robinson, a former college football and track star, went 0-for-3 but reached base on a seventh-inning error and came around to score the winning run.

Boston	AB	R	H	PO	A	E
Culler,ss	3	0	0	0	2	0
eHolmes	1	0	0	0	0	0
Sisti,ss	0	0	0	0	0	0
Hopp,cf	5	0	1	2	0	0
McCormick,rf	4	0	3	2	0	0
Elliott,3b	2	0	1	0	2	0
Litwhiler,lf	3	1	0	1	0	0
Rowell,lf	1	0	0	0	0	0
Torgeson,1b	4	1	0	10	1	1
Masi,c	3	0	0	4	0	0
Ryan,2b	4	1	3	4	7	0
Sain,p	1	0	0	0	1	0
Cooper,p	0	0	0	1	0	0
dNeill	0	0	0	0	0	0
Lanfranconi,p	0	0	0	0	0	0
Totals	31	3	8	24	13	1

Brooklyn	AB	R	H	PO	A	E
Stanky,2b	3	1	0	0	3	0
Robinson,1b	3	1	0	11	0	0
Schultz,1b	0	0	0	1	0	0
Reiser,cf	2	3	2	2	0	0
Walker,rf	3	0	1	0	0	0
Tatum,rf	0	0	0	0	0	0
cVaughan	1	0	0	0	0	0
Furillo,rf	0	0	0	0	0	0
Hermanski,lf	4	0	1	3	0	0
Edwards,c	2	0	0	2	0	1
aRackley	0	0	0	0	0	0
Bragan,c	1	0	0	3	0	0
Jorgensen,3b	3	0	0	0	4	0
Reese,ss	3	0	1	3	2	0
Hatten,p	2	0	1	1	1	0
bStevens	1	0	0	0	0	0
Gregg,p	1	0	0	1	0	0
Casey,p	0	0	0	0	0	0
Totals	29	5	6	27	10	1

Boston ....0 0 0 0 1 2 0 0 0—3
Brooklyn....................0 0 0 1 0 1 3 0 x—5

a Ran for Edwards in sixth.
b Struck out for Hatten in sixth.
c Grounded out for Tatum in seventh.
d Hit by pitch for Cooper in eighth.
e Flied out for Culler in eighth.

Runs batted in: Edwards, Hopp, Ryan 2, Jorgensen, Reiser 2, Hermanski.
Doubles: Reese, Reiser.
Sacrifice hits: Masi, Culler, Sain 2, Robinson.
Double plays: Stanky, Reese and Robinson; Culler, Ryan and Torgeson.
Left on bases: Boston 12, Brooklyn 7.

Boston	IP	H	R	ER	BB	SO
Sain (L)	6	6	5	4	5	1
Cooper	1	0	0	0	0	0
Lanfranconi	1	0	0	0	0	2
Brooklyn	**IP**	**H**	**R**	**ER**	**BB**	**SO**
Hatten	6	6	3	2	3	2
Gregg (W)	2⅓	2	0	0	2	2
Casey (S)	⅔	0	0	0	0	0

Sain pitched to three batters in seventh.
Hit by pitcher: Litwhiler (by Hatten), Edwards (by Sain), Neill (by Gregg).
Wild pitch: Hatten.

Umpires: Pinelli, Barlick, Gore.
Time: 2:26. **Attendance:** 25,623.

Brooklyn's Cookie Lavagetto (right) is mobbed after his Game 4-winning hit in the 1947 World Series ended Bill Bevens' hope for a no-hitter.

BEVENS' NEAR-MISS

October 3, 1947, at Ebbets Field

New York Yankees pitcher Bill Bevens, one out away from the first no-hitter in World Series history, surrendered a two-run double to Brooklyn pinch hitter Cookie Lavagetto and dropped a heart-breaking 3-2 decision to the Dodgers. After Bevens walked two Dodgers in the ninth inning of the Game 4 classic, his ninth and 10th free passes, Lavagetto lined an opposite-field drive off the right-field wall, allowing Brooklyn to tie the Series at two games apiece.

New York	AB	R	H	PO	A	E
Stirnweiss,2b	4	1	2	2	1	0
Henrich,rf	5	0	1	2	0	0
Berra,c	4	0	0	6	1	1
DiMaggio,cf	2	0	0	2	0	0
McQuinn,1b	4	0	1	7	0	0
Johnson,3b	4	1	1	3	2	0
Lindell,lf	3	0	2	3	0	0
Rizzuto,ss	4	0	1	1	2	0
Bevens,p	3	0	0	0	1	0
Totals	33	2	8	26	7	1

Brooklyn	AB	R	H	PO	A	E
Stanky,2b	1	0	0	2	3	0
aLavagetto	1	0	1	0	0	0
Reese,ss	4	0	0	3	5	1
Robinson,1b	4	0	0	11	1	0
Walker,rf	2	0	0	0	1	0
Hermanski,lf	4	0	0	2	0	0
Edwards,c	4	0	0	7	1	1
Furillo,cf	3	0	0	2	0	0
bGionfriddo	0	1	0	0	0	0
Jorgensen,3b	2	1	0	0	1	1
Taylor,p	0	0	0	0	0	0
Gregg,p	1	0	0	0	1	0
aVaughan	0	0	0	0	0	0
Behrman,p	0	0	0	0	1	0
Casey,p	0	0	0	0	1	0
cReiser	0	0	0	0	0	0
dMiksis	0	1	0	0	0	0
Totals	26	3	1	27	15	3

New York ....1 0 0 1 0 0 0 0 0—2
Brooklyn....................0 0 0 0 1 0 0 0 2—3

a Walked for Gregg in seventh.
b Ran for Furillo in ninth.
c Walked for Casey in ninth.
d Ran for Reiser in ninth.
e Doubled for Stanky in ninth.
f Two out when winning run scored.

Runs batted in: DiMaggio, Lindell, Reese, Lavagetto 2.
Doubles: Lindell, Lavagetto.
Triple: Johnson.
Sacrifice hits: Stanky, Bevens.
Stolen bases: Rizzuto, Reese, Gionfriddo.
Double plays: Reese, Stanky and Robinson; Gregg, Reese and Robinson; Edwards and Robinson.
Left on bases: New York 9, Brooklyn 8.

New York	IP	H	R	ER	BB	SO
Bevens (L)	8⅔	1	3	3	10	5
Brooklyn	**IP**	**H**	**R**	**ER**	**BB**	**SO**
Taylor	0	2	1	0	1	0
Gregg	7	4	1	1	3	5
Behrman	1⅓	2	0	0	0	0
Casey (W)	⅔	0	0	0	0	0

Taylor pitched to four batters in first.
Wild pitch: Bevens.

Umpires: Goetz, McGowan, Pinelli, Rommel, Boyer, Magerkurth.
Time: 2:20. **Attendance:** 33,443

GIONFRIDDO SAVES THE DAY

October 5, 1947, at Yankee Stadium

Defensive replacement Al Gionfriddo jumped into the World Series spotlight when he made a spectacular sixth-inning catch of Yankees slugger Joe DiMaggio's bid for a home run, preserving an 8-6 victory that forced a decisive seventh game. With the Dodgers leading 8-5 and two New York runners on base, DiMaggio hit a monster drive that a twisting Gionfriddo speared at the 415-foot sign, just as it appeared the ball would drop into the bullpen for a game-tying homer. The Yankees rebounded to win the Series the next day.

Brooklyn	AB	R	H	PO	A	E
Stanky,2b	5	2	2	4	2	0
Reese,ss	4	2	3	2	1	0
J.Robinson,1b	5	1	2	7	1	0
Walker,rf	5	0	1	3	0	0
Hermanski,lf	1	0	0	0	0	0
bMiksis,lf	1	0	0	0	0	0
Gionfriddo,lf	2	0	0	1	0	0
Edwards,c	4	1	1	5	0	0
Furillo,cf	4	1	2	4	1	0
Jorgensen,3b	2	0	0	1	1	1
cLavagetto,3b	2	0	0	0	1	0
Lombardi,p	1	0	0	0	0	0
Branca,p	1	0	0	0	1	0
dBragan	1	0	1	0	0	0
eBankhead	0	1	0	0	0	0
Hatten,p	1	0	0	0	0	0
Casey,p	0	0	0	0	1	0
Totals	39	8	12	27	9	1

New York	AB	R	H	PO	A	E
Stirnweiss,2b	5	0	0	1	6	0
Henrich,rf-lf	5	1	2	1	0	0
Lindell,lf	2	1	2	0	0	0
Berra,rf	3	0	2	1	0	0
DiMaggio,cf	5	1	1	5	0	0
Johnson,3b	5	1	2	1	5	0
Phillips,1b	1	0	0	4	0	0
aBrown	1	0	1	0	0	0
McQuinn,1b	1	0	0	6	0	1
Rizzuto,ss	4	0	1	6	1	0
Lollar,c	1	1	1	0	0	0
A.Robinson,c	4	1	2	2	0	1
Reynolds,p	0	0	0	0	0	0
Drews,p	2	0	0	0	1	0
Page,p	0	0	0	0	0	0
Newsom,p	0	0	0	0	0	0
fClark	1	0	0	0	0	0
Raschi,p	0	0	0	0	0	0
gHouk	1	0	1	0	0	0
Wensloff,p	0	0	0	0	1	0
hFrey	1	0	0	0	0	0
Totals	42	6	15	27	14	2

Brooklyn....................202 004 000—8
New York ....004 100 001—6

a Singled for Phillips in third.
b Popped out for Hermanski in fifth.
c Flied out for Jorgensen in sixth.
d Doubled for Branca in sixth.
e Ran for Bragan in sixth.
f Lined out for Newsom in sixth.
g Singled for Raschi in seventh.
h Forced A.Robinson for Wensloff in ninth.

Runs batted in: J.Robinson, Walker, Stirnweiss, Lindell, Johnson, Brown, Berra, Lavagetto, Reese 2, Frey, Bragan.
Doubles: Reese, J.Robinson, Walker, Lollar, Furillo, Bragan.
Double play: Rizzuto and Phillips.
Passed ball: Lollar.
Left on bases: New York 13, Brooklyn 6.

Brooklyn	IP	H	R	ER	BB	SO
Lombardi	2⅔	5	4	4	0	2
Branca (W)	2⅓	6	1	1	0	2
Hatten	3	3	1	1	4	0
Casey (S)	1	1	0	0	0	0

New York	IP	H	R	ER	BB	SO
Reynolds	2⅓	6	4	3	1	0
Drews	2	1	0	0	1	0
Page (L)	1	4	4	4	0	1
Newsom	⅔	1	0	0	0	0
Raschi	1	0	0	0	0	1
Wensloff	2	0	0	0	0	0

Hatten pitched to two batters in ninth.
Wild pitch: Lombardi.

Umpires: Pinelli, Rommel, Goetz, McGowman, Boyer, Magerkurth.
Time: 3:19. **Attendance:** 74,065.

THE SHOT HEARD 'ROUND THE WORLD

October 3, 1951, at the Polo Grounds

Bobby Thomson's three-run, ninth-inning home run, considered by many historians the most dramatic in baseball history, gave the New York Giants a 5-4 victory over Brooklyn and settled a wild N.L. pennant race. Thomson connected off Dodgers righthander Ralph Branca with two out and the Giants trailing, 4-2, in Game 3 of a pennant playoff series. Thomson's dramatics were preceded by Al Dark and Don Mueller singles and Whitey Lockman's run-scoring double.

Bobby Thomson poses with Giants owner Horace Stoneham (left) and manager Leo Durocher after his pennant-deciding homer.

Brooklyn	AB	R	H	PO	A	E
Furillo,rf	5	0	0	0	0	0
Reese,ss	4	2	1	2	5	0
Snider,cf	3	1	2	1	0	0
Robinson,2b	2	1	1	3	2	0
Pafko,lf	4	0	1	4	1	0
Hodges,1b	4	0	0	11	1	0
Cox,3b	4	0	2	1	3	0
Walker,c	4	0	1	2	0	0
Newcombe,p	4	0	0	1	1	0
Branca,p	0	0	0	0	0	0
Totals	34	4	8	25	13	0

New York	AB	R	H	PO	A	E
Stanky,2b	4	0	0	0	4	0
Dark,ss	4	1	1	2	2	0
Mueller,rf	4	0	1	0	0	0
cHartung	0	1	0	0	0	0
Irvin,lf	4	1	1	1	0	0
Lockman,1b	3	1	2	11	1	0
Thomson,3b	4	1	3	4	1	0
Mays,cf	3	0	0	1	0	0
Westrum,c	0	0	0	7	1	0
aRigney	1	0	0	0	0	0
Noble,c	0	0	0	0	0	0
Maglie,p	2	0	0	1	2	0
bThompson	1	0	0	0	0	0
Jansen,p	0	0	0	0	0	0
Totals	30	5	8	27	11	0

Brooklyn....................100 000 030—4
New York ....000 000 104—5

a Struck out for Westrum in eighth.
b Grounded out for Maglie in eighth.
c Ran for Mueller in ninth.
d One out when winning run scored.

Runs batted in: Robinson, Thomson 4, Pafko, Cox, Lockman
Doubles: Thomson, Irvin, Lockman.
Home run: Thomson.
Sacrifice hit: Lockman.
Double plays: Cox, Robinson and Hodges; Reese, Robinson and Hodges.
Left on bases: Brooklyn 7, New York 3.

Brooklyn	IP	H	R	ER	BB	SO
Newcombe	8⅓	7	4	4	2	2
Branca (L)	0	1	1	1	0	0

New York	IP	H	R	ER	BB	SO
Maglie	8	8	4	4	4	6
Jansen (W)	1	0	0	0	0	2

Branca pitched to one batter in ninth.
Wild pitch: Maglie.

Umpires: Jorda, Conlan, Stewart, Goetz.
Time: 2:28. **Attendance:** 34,320.

MAYS STUNS INDIANS

September 29, 1954, at the Polo Grounds

Willie Mays took his place in baseball lore when he made a dramatic eighth-inning, over-the-shoulder catch on a 460-foot drive by Cleveland's Vic Wertz, saving the New York Giants in Game 1 of the World Series. Mays made his remarkable catch with the score tied 2-2 and Indians positioned on first and second base. The Giants went on to win the Series opener, 5-2, on Dusty Rhodes' 10th-inning homer, keying a stunning fall classic sweep.

Cleveland	AB	R	H	PO	A	E
Smith,lf	4	1	1	1	0	0
Avila,2b	5	1	1	2	3	0
Doby,cf	3	0	1	3	0	0
Rosen,3b	5	0	1	1	3	0
Wertz,1b	5	0	4	11	1	0
dRegalado	0	0	0	0	0	0
Grasso,c	0	0	0	1	0	0
Philley,rf	3	0	0	0	0	0
aMajeski	0	0	0	0	0	0
bMitchell	0	0	0	0	0	0
Dente,ss	0	0	0	0	0	0
Strickland,ss	3	0	0	2	3	0
cPope,rf	1	0	0	0	0	0
Hegan,c	4	0	0	6	1	0
eGlynn,1b	1	0	0	0	0	0
Lemon,p	4	0	0	1	1	0
Totals	38	2	8	28	12	0

New York	AB	R	H	PO	A	E
Lockman,1b	5	1	1	9	0	0
Dark,ss	4	0	2	3	2	0
Mueller,rf	5	1	2	2	0	2
Mays,cf	3	1	0	2	0	0
Thompson,3b	3	1	1	3	3	0
Irvin,lf	3	0	0	5	0	1
fRhodes	1	1	1	0	0	0
Williams,2b	4	0	0	1	1	0
Westrum,c	4	0	2	5	0	0
Maglie,p	3	0	0	0	2	0
Liddle,p	0	0	0	0	0	0
Grissom,p	1	0	0	0	0	0
Totals	36	5	9	30	8	3

Cleveland ....200 000 000 0—2
New York ....002 000 000 3—5

a Announced for Philley in eighth.
b Walked for Majeski in eighth.
c Called out on strikes for Strickland in eighth.
d Ran for Wertz in 10th.
e Struck out for Hegan in 10th.
f Hit home run for Irvin in 10th.
i One out when winning run scored.

Runs batted in: Wertz 2, Mueller, Thompson, Rhodes 3.
Double: Wertz.
Triple: Wertz.
Home run: Rhodes.
Sacrifice hits: Irvin, Dente.
Stolen bases: Mays.
Left on bases: Cleveland 13, New York 9.

Cleveland	IP	H	R	ER	BB	SO
Lemon (L)	9⅓	9	5	5	5	6

New York	IP	H	R	ER	BB	SO
Maglie	7	7	2	2	2	2
Liddle	⅓	0	0	0	0	0
Grissom (W)	2⅔	1	0	0	3	2

Maglie pitched to two batters in eighth.
Hit by pitcher: Smith (by Maglie).
Wild pitch: Lemon.

Umpires: Barlick, Berry, Conlan, Stevens, Warneke, Napp.
Time: 3:11. **Attendance:** 52,751.

AMOROS TO THE RESCUE

October 4, 1955, at Yankee Stadium

With his team leading 2-0 in the sixth inning of World Series Game 7, Brooklyn left fielder Sandy Amoros streaked into the left-field corner and made a spectacular, Series-saving catch of Yogi Berra's line drive. Amoros made the dramatic play with two Yankees on base, wheeled around and doubled Gil McDougald off first, securing Johnny Podres' shutout.

Brooklyn	AB	R	H	PO	A	E
Gilliam,lf-2b	4	0	1	2	0	0
Reese,ss	4	1	1	2	6	0
Snider,cf	3	0	0	2	0	0
Campanella,c	3	1	1	5	0	0
Furillo,rf	3	0	0	3	0	0
Hodges,1b	2	0	1	10	0	0
Hoak,3b	3	0	1	1	1	0
Zimmer,2b	2	0	0	0	2	0
aShuba	1	0	0	0	0	0
Amoros,lf	0	0	0	2	1	0
Podres,p	4	0	0	0	1	0
Totals	29	2	5	27	11	0

New York	AB	R	H	PO	A	E
Rizzuto,ss	3	0	1	1	3	0
Martin,2b	3	0	1	1	6	0
McDougald,3b	4	0	3	1	1	0
Berra,c	4	0	1	4	1	0
Bauer,rf	4	0	0	1	0	0
Skowron,1b	4	0	1	11	1	1
Cerv,cf	4	0	0	5	0	0
Howard,lf	4	0	1	2	0	0
Byrne,p	2	0	0	0	2	0
Grim,p	0	0	0	1	0	0
bMantle	1	0	0	0	0	0
Turley,p	0	0	0	0	0	0
Totals	33	0	8	27	14	1

FOR THE RECORD

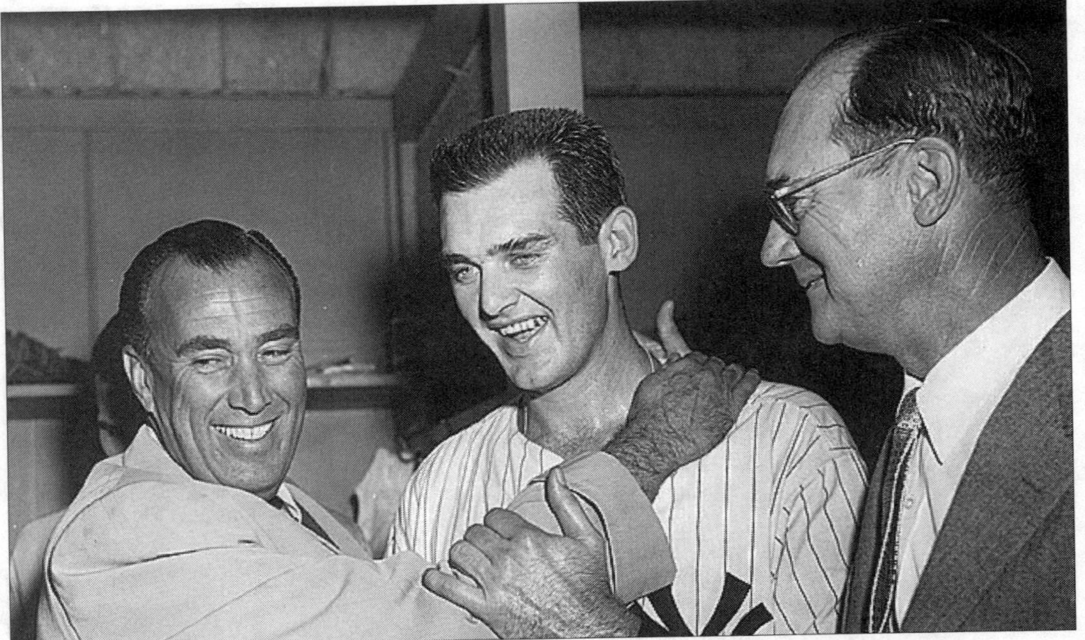

Don Larsen celebrates with Yankees owners Dan Topping (left) and Dell Webb in a perfect World Series moment.

Brooklyn....................0 0 0 1 0 1 0 0 0—2
New York ....0 0 0 0 0 0 0 0 0—0

a Grounded out for Zimmer in sixth.
b Popped out for Grim in seventh.

Runs batted in: Hodges 2.
Doubles: Skowron, Campanella, Berra.
Sacrifice hits: Snider, Campanella.
Sacrifice fly: Hodges.
Double play: Amoros, Reese and Hodges.
Left on bases: Brooklyn 8, New York 8.

Brooklyn	**IP**	**H**	**R**	**ER**	**BB**	**SO**
Podres (W)	9	8	0	0	2	4

New York	**IP**	**H**	**R**	**ER**	**BB**	**SO**
Byrne (L)	5⅓	3	2	1	3	2
Grim	1⅔	1	0	0	1	1
Turley	2	1	0	0	1	1

Wild pitch: Grim.

Umpires: Honochick, Dascoli, Summers, Ballanfant, Flaherty, Donatelli.
Time: 2:44. **Attendance:** 62,465.

WORLD SERIES PERFECTION

October 8, 1956, at Yankee Stadium

Yankees righthander Don Larsen retired all 27 Brooklyn Dodgers he faced in a perfect 2-0 World Series victory—the only no-hitter ever pitched in postseason play. Larsen, who went to ball three on only one batter, outdueled Dodgers starter Sal Maglie in the Game 5 classic and received all the run support he needed on Mickey Mantle's fourth-inning homer.

Brooklyn	**AB**	**R**	**H**	**PO**	**A**	**E**
Gilliam,2b	3	0	0	2	0	0
Reese,ss	3	0	0	4	2	0
Snider,cf	3	0	0	1	0	0
Robinson,3b	3	0	0	2	4	0
Hodges,1b	3	0	0	5	1	0
Amoros,lf	3	0	0	3	0	0
Furillo,rf	3	0	0	0	0	0
Campanella,c	3	0	0	7	2	0
Maglie,p	2	0	0	0	1	0
aMitchell	1	0	0	0	0	0
Totals	27	0	0	24	10	0

New York	**AB**	**R**	**H**	**PO**	**A**	**E**
Bauer,rf	4	0	1	4	0	0
Collins,1b	4	0	1	7	0	0
Mantle,cf	3	1	1	4	0	0
Berra,c	3	0	0	7	0	0
Slaughter,lf	2	0	0	1	0	0
Martin,2b	3	0	1	3	4	0
McDougald,ss	2	0	0	0	2	0
Carey,3b	3	1	1	1	1	0
Larsen,p	2	0	0	0	1	0
Totals	26	2	5	27	8	0

Brooklyn....................0 0 0 0 0 0 0 0 0—0
New York ....0 0 0 1 0 1 0 0 x—2

a Called out on strikes for Maglie in ninth.

Runs batted in: Mantle, Bauer.
Home run: Mantle.
Sacrifice hit: Larsen.
Double plays: Reese and Hodges; Hodges, Campanella, Robinson, Campanella and Robinson.
Left on bases: Brooklyn 0, New York 3.

Brooklyn	**IP**	**H**	**R**	**ER**	**BB**	**SO**
Maglie (L)	8	5	2	2	2	5

New York	**IP**	**H**	**R**	**ER**	**BB**	**SO**
Larsen (W)	9	0	0	0	0	7

Umpires: Pinelli, Soar, Boggess, Napp, Gorman, Runge.
Time: 2:06. **Attendance:** 64,519.

AN IMPERFECT ENDING

May 26, 1959, at County Stadium

Pittsburgh lefthander Harvey Haddix retired 36 consecutive Milwaukee batters over 12 perfect innings, but he ended up losing the game on a 13th-inning error, walk and double. Milwaukee starter Lew Burdette shut out the Pirates on 12 hits and Joe Adcock broke Haddix's hitless string with his one-out blow—an apparent home run that was ruled a double because Adcock passed teammate Hank Aaron while circling the bases.

Pittsburgh	**AB**	**R**	**H**	**PO**	**A**	**E**
Schofield,ss	6	0	3	2	4	0
Virdon,cf	6	0	1	8	0	0
Burgess,c	5	0	0	8	0	0
Nelson,1b	5	0	2	14	0	0
Skinner,lf	5	0	1	4	0	0
Mazeroski,2b	5	0	1	1	1	0
Hoak,3b	5	0	2	0	6	1
Mejias,rf	3	0	1	1	0	0
aStuart	1	0	0	0	0	0
Christopher,rf	1	0	0	0	0	0
Haddix,p	5	0	1	0	2	0
Totals	47	0	12	38	13	1

Milwaukee	**AB**	**R**	**H**	**PO**	**A**	**E**
O'Brien,2b	3	0	0	2	5	0
bRice	1	0	0	0	0	0
Mantilla,2b	1	1	0	1	2	0
Mathews,3b	4	0	0	2	3	0
Aaron,rf	4	0	0	1	0	0
Adcock,1b	5	0	1	17	3	0
Covington,lf	4	0	0	4	0	0
Crandall,c	4	0	0	2	1	0
Pafko,cf	4	0	0	6	0	0
Logan,ss	4	0	0	3	5	0
Burdette,p	4	0	0	1	3	0
Totals	38	1	1	39	22	0

Pittsburgh ....0 0 0 0 0 0 0 0 0 0 0 0 0—0
Milwaukee ....0 0 0 0 0 0 0 0 0 0 0 0 1—1

a Flied out for Mejias in 10th.
b Flied out for O'Brien in 10th.
c Two out when winning run scored.

Run batted in: Adcock.
Double: Adcock.
Sacrifice hit: Mathews.
Double plays: Logan and Adcock; Mathews, O'Brien and Adcock; Adcock and Logan.
Left on bases: Pittsburgh 8, Milwaukee 1.

Pittsburgh	**IP**	**H**	**R**	**ER**	**BB**	**SO**
Haddix (L)	12⅔	1	1	1	1	8

Milwaukee	**IP**	**H**	**R**	**ER**	**BB**	**SO**
Burdette (W)	13	12	0	0	0	2

Umpires: Smith, Dascoli, Secory, Dixon.
Time: 2:54. **Attendance:** 19,194.

MAZEROSKI STUNS YANKEES

October 13, 1960, at Forbes Field

Second baseman Bill Mazeroski ended Pittsburgh's 35-year title drought when he hammered a stunning bottom-of-the-ninth-inning home run over the left-field fence against the New York Yankees, breaking a 9-9 tie in Game 7 of the World Series. Mazeroski, leading off the ninth after the Yankees had rallied for two runs in the top of the inning, became the first player to end a Series with a home run.

New York	**AB**	**R**	**H**	**PO**	**A**	**E**
Richardson,2b	5	2	2	2	5	0
Kubek,ss	3	1	0	3	2	0
DeMaestri,ss	0	0	0	0	0	0
dLong	1	0	1	0	0	0
eMcDougald,3b	0	1	0	0	0	0
Maris,rf	5	0	0	2	0	1
Mantle,cf	5	1	3	0	0	0
Berra,lf	4	2	1	3	0	0
Skowron,1b	5	2	2	10	2	0
Blanchard,c	4	0	1	1	1	0
Boyer,3b-ss	4	0	1	0	3	0
Turley,p	0	0	0	0	0	0
Stafford,p	0	0	0	0	1	0
aLopez	1	0	1	0	0	0
Shantz,p	3	0	1	3	1	0
Coates,p	0	0	0	0	0	0
Terry,p	0	0	0	0	0	0
Totals	40	9	13	24	15	1

Pittsburgh	**AB**	**R**	**H**	**PO**	**A**	**E**
Virdon,cf	4	1	2	3	0	0
Groat,ss	4	1	1	3	2	0
Skinner,lf	2	1	0	1	0	0
Nelson,1b	3	1	1	7	0	0
Clemente,rf	4	1	1	4	0	0
Burgess,c	3	0	2	0	0	0
bChristopher	0	0	0	0	0	0
Smith,c	1	1	1	1	0	0
Hoak,3b	3	1	0	3	2	0
Mazeroski,2b	4	2	2	5	0	0
Law,p	2	0	0	0	1	0
Face,p	0	0	0	0	1	0
cCimoli	1	1	1	0	0	0
Friend,p	0	0	0	0	0	0
Haddix,p	0	0	0	0	0	0
Totals	31	10	11	27	6	0

New York ....0 0 0 0 1 4 0 2 2—9
Pittsburgh ....2 2 0 0 0 0 0 5 1—10

a Singled for Stafford in third.
b Ran for Burgess in seventh.
c Singled for Face in eighth.
d Singled for DeMaestri in ninth.
e Ran for Long in ninth.
f None out when winning run scored.

Runs batted in: Mantle 2, Berra 4, Skowron, Blanchard, Boyer, Virdon 2, Groat, Nelson 2, Clemente, Smith 3, Mazeroski.
Double: Boyer.
Home runs: Nelson, Skowron, Berra, Smith, Mazeroski.
Sacrifice hit: Skinner.
Double plays: Stafford, Blanchard and Skowron; Richardson, Kubek and Skowron; Kubek, Richardson and Skowron.
Left on bases: New York 6, Pittsburgh 1.

New York	**IP**	**H**	**R**	**ER**	**BB**	**SO**
Turley	1	2	3	3	1	0
Stafford	1	2	1	1	1	0
Shantz	5	4	3	3	1	0
Coates	⅔	2	2	2	0	0
Terry (L)	⅓	1	1	1	0	0

Pittsburgh	**IP**	**H**	**R**	**ER**	**BB**	**SO**
Law	5	4	3	3	1	0
Face	3	6	4	4	1	0
Friend	0	2	2	2	0	0
Haddix (W)	1	1	0	0	0	0

Turley pitched to one batter in second.
Shantz pitched to three batters in eighth.
Terry pitched to one batter in ninth.
Law pitched to two batters in sixth.
Friend pitched to two batters in ninth.

Umpires: Jackowski, Chylak, Boggess, Stevens, Landes, Honochick.
Time: 2:36. **Attendance:** 36,683.

MARIS HITS 61ST

October 1, 1961, at Yankee Stadium

New York outfielder Roger Maris claimed baseball's single-season home run record when he drove a fourth-inning pitch from Boston righthander Tracy Stallard into the right-field seats on the final day of the regular season. Maris' 61st home run broke the 1927 record of Yankee predecessor Babe Ruth and provided the only run in a 1-0 victory.

Boston	**AB**	**R**	**H**	**PO**	**A**	**E**
Schilling,2b	4	0	1	3	2	0
Geiger,cf	4	0	0	1	0	0
Yastrzemski,lf	4	0	1	1	0	0
Malzone,3b	4	0	0	0	0	0
Clinton,rf	4	0	0	4	0	0
Runnels,1b	3	0	0	7	0	0
Gile,1b	0	0	0	1	0	0
Nixon,c	3	0	2	5	0	0
Green,ss	2	0	0	1	2	0
Stallard,p	1	0	0	0	1	0
bJensen	1	0	0	0	0	0
Nichols,p	0	0	0	1	0	0
Totals	30	0	4	24	5	0

New York	**AB**	**R**	**H**	**PO**	**A**	**E**
Richardson,2b	4	0	0	1	1	0
Kubek,ss	4	0	2	3	4	0
Maris,cf	4	1	1	3	0	0
Berra,lf	2	0	0	0	0	0
Lopez,lf-rf	1	0	0	2	0	0
Blanchard,rf-c	3	0	0	3	0	0
Howard,c	2	0	0	7	2	0
Reed,lf	1	0	1	1	0	0
Skowron,1b	2	0	0	4	0	0
Hale,1b	1	0	1	2	1	0
Boyer,3b	2	0	0	1	0	0
Stafford,p	2	0	0	0	0	0
Reniff,p	0	0	0	0	0	0
aTresh	1	0	0	0	0	0
Arroyo,p	0	0	0	0	0	0
Totals	29	1	5	27	8	0

Boston ....0 0 0 0 0 0 0 0 0—0
New York ....0 0 0 1 0 0 0 0 x—1

a Popped out for Reniff in seventh.
b Popped out for Stallard in eighth.

Run batted in: Maris.
Triple: Nixon.
Home run: Maris.
Sacrifice hit: Stallard.
Stolen bases: Geiger.
Passed ball: Nixon.
Left on bases: Boston 5, New York 5.

Boston	**IP**	**H**	**R**	**ER**	**BB**	**SO**
Stallard (L)	7	5	1	1	1	5
Nichols	1	0	0	0	0	0

New York	IP	H	R	ER	BB	SO
Stafford (W)	6	3	0	0	1	7
Reniff	1	0	0	0	0	1
Arroyo (S)	2	1	0	0	0	1

Wild pitch: Stallard.

Umpires: Kinnamon, Flaherty, Honochick, Salerno.
Time: 1:57. **Attendance:** 23,154.

McLAIN WINS 30TH

September 14, 1968, at Tiger Stadium

Denny McLain became the first 30-game winner in 34 years when Detroit rallied for two ninth-inning runs and a 5-4 victory over Oakland. McLain, who struck out 10 and yielded two home runs to Reggie Jackson, joined a select circle when Willie Horton's single drove in Mickey Stanley with the winner. McLain became the first 30-win man since St. Louis star Dizzy Dean in 1934.

Oakland	AB	R	H	PO	A	E
Campaneris,ss	4	0	1	2	1	0
Monday,cf	4	0	1	2	0	0
Cater,1b	4	1	2	6	3	1
Bando,3b	3	0	0	1	0	1
Jackson,rf	4	2	2	3	1	0
Green,2b	4	0	0	2	1	0
Keough,lf	3	0	0	0	0	0
Gosger,lf	0	0	0	0	0	0
Duncan,c	2	1	0	7	0	0
Dobson,p	1	0	0	0	0	0
Aker,p	0	0	0	0	0	0
Lindblad,p	0	0	0	0	0	0
aDonaldson	0	0	0	0	0	0
Segui,p	1	0	0	2	1	0
Totals	30	4	6	25	7	2

Detroit	AB	R	H	PO	A	E
McAuliffe,2b	5	0	1	2	1	0
Stanley,cf	5	1	2	1	0	0
Northrup,rf	4	1	0	4	1	0
Horton,lf	5	1	2	0	0	0
Cash,1b	4	1	2	6	0	0
Freehan,c	3	0	1	10	2	0
Matchick,ss	4	0	1	2	0	1
Wert,3b	2	0	0	1	1	0
bBrown	1	0	0	0	0	0
Tracewski,3b	0	0	0	0	1	0
McLain,p	1	0	0	1	0	0
cKaline	0	1	0	0	0	0
Totals	34	5	9	27	6	1

Oakland ....000 211 000—4
Detroit ....000 300 002—5

a Sacrificed for Lindblad in fifth.
b Grounded out for Wert in eighth.
c Walked for McLain in ninth.
d One out when winning run scored.

Runs batted in: Campaneris, Jackson 3, Horton, Cash 3.
Home runs: Jackson 2, Cash.
Double plays: Northrup and Cash.
Sacrifice hits: Bando, Donaldson, McLain.
Left on bases: Oakland 2, Detroit 10.

Oakland	IP	H	R	ER	BB	SO
Dobson	3⅔	4	3	3	2	4
Aker	0	0	0	0	1	0
Lindblad	⅓	0	0	0	0	1
Segui (L)	4⅓	5	2	1	2	1

Detroit	IP	H	R	ER	BB	SO
McLain (W)	9	6	4	4	1	10

Aker pitched to one batter in fourth.
Wild pitch: Aker.

Umpires: Napp, Umont, Haller, Neudecker.
Time: 3:00. **Attendance:** 33,688.

AARON HITS 715TH

April 8, 1974, at Atlanta Stadium

Braves outfielder Hank Aaron unseated all-time home run king Babe Ruth when he connected for career home run No. 715 in the fourth inning of a game against Los Angeles. The three-run blast off Dodgers lefthander Al Downing helped the Braves secure a 7-4 victory.

Los Angeles	AB	R	H	PO	A	E
Lopes,2b	2	1	0	2	2	1
cLacy,2b	1	0	0	0	0	0
Buckner,lf	3	0	1	1	1	1
Wynn,cf	4	0	1	2	0	0
Ferguson,c	4	0	0	4	0	1
Crawford,rf	4	1	1	1	0	0
Cey,3b	4	0	1	2	3	1
Garvey,1b	4	1	1	11	0	0
Russell,ss	4	0	1	1	4	2
Downing,p	1	1	1	0	3	0
Marshall,p	1	0	0	0	1	0
dJoshua	1	0	0	0	0	0
Hough,p	0	0	0	0	1	0
eMota	1	0	0	0	0	0
Totals	34	4	7	24	15	6

Atlanta	AB	R	H	PO	A	E
Garr,rf-lf	3	0	0	0	0	0
Lum,1b	5	0	0	10	0	0
Evans,3b	4	1	0	1	4	0
Aaron,lf	3	2	1	0	0	0
Office,cf	0	0	0	0	0	0
Baker,cf-rf	2	1	1	2	0	0
Johnson,2b	3	1	1	2	2	0
Foster,2b	0	0	0	0	0	0
Correll,c	4	1	0	11	0	0
Robinson,ss	0	0	0	0	1	0
aTepedino	0	0	0	0	0	0
Perez,ss	2	1	1	1	2	0
Reed,p	2	0	0	0	1	0
bOates	1	0	0	0	0	0
Capra,p	0	0	0	0	0	0
Totals	29	7	4	27	10	0

Los Angeles ....003 001 000—4
Atlanta ....010 402 00x—7

a Walked for Robinson in fourth.
b Reached on fielder's choice for Reed in sixth.
c Struck out for Lopes in seventh.
d Struck out for Marshall in seventh.
e Lined out for Hough in ninth.

Runs batted in: Wynn 2, Cey, Downing, Garr, Lum, Aaron 2, Tepedino, Oates.
Doubles: Baker, Russell, Wynn.
Home run: Aaron.
Sacrifice hit: Garr.
Sacrifice fly: Garr.
Passed ball: Ferguson.
Left on bases: Los Angeles 5, Atlanta 7.

Los Angeles	IP	H	R	ER	BB	SO
Downing (L)	3	2	5	2	4	2
Marshall	3	2	2	1	1	1
Hough	2	0	0	0	2	1

Atlanta	IP	H	R	ER	BB	SO
Reed (W)	6	7	4	4	1	4
Capra (S)	3	0	0	0	1	6

Downing pitched to four batters in fourth.
Wild pitch: Reed.

Umpires: Sudol, Weyer, Pulli, Davidson.
Time: 2:27. **Attendance:** 53,775.

FISK'S INSTANT WINNER

October 21, 1975, at Fenway Park

Boston catcher Carlton Fisk, leading off the bottom of the 12th inning of World Series Game 6, hit a high drive off the left-field foul pole at Fenway Park, giving the Red Sox a 7-6 victory over Cincinnati in one of the most dramatic games in fall classic history. Fisk's blast ended a see-saw battle and forced a decisive seventh game.

Cincinnati	AB	R	H	PO	A	E
Rose,3b	5	1	2	0	2	0
Griffey,rf	5	2	2	0	0	0
Morgan,2b	6	1	1	4	4	0
Bench,c	6	0	1	8	0	0
Perez,1b	6	0	2	11	2	0
Foster,lf	6	0	2	4	1	0
Concepcion,ss	6	0	1	3	4	0
Geronimo,cf	6	1	2	2	0	0
Nolan,p	0	0	0	1	0	0
aChaney	1	0	0	0	0	0
Norman,p	0	0	0	0	0	0
Billingham,p	0	0	0	0	0	0
bArmbrister	0	1	0	0	0	0
Carroll,p	0	0	0	0	0	0
cCrowley	1	0	1	0	0	0
Borbon,p	1	0	0	0	0	0
Eastwick,p	0	0	0	0	0	0
McEnaney,p	0	0	0	0	0	0
eDriessen	1	0	0	0	0	0
Darcy,p	0	0	0	0	1	0
Totals	50	6	14	33	14	0

Boston	AB	R	H	PO	A	E
Cooper,1b	5	0	0	8	0	0
Drago,p	0	0	0	0	0	0
fMiller	1	0	0	0	0	0
Wise,p	0	0	0	0	0	0
Doyle,2b	5	0	1	0	2	0
Yastrzemski,lf-lb	6	1	3	7	1	0
Fisk,c	4	2	2	9	1	0
Lynn,cf	4	2	2	2	0	0
Petrocelli,3b	4	1	0	1	1	0
Evans,rf	5	0	1	5	1	0
Burleson,ss	3	0	0	3	2	1
Tiant,p	2	0	0	0	2	0
Moret,p	0	0	0	0	1	0
dCarbo,lf	2	1	1	1	0	0
Totals	41	7	10	36	11	1

Cincinnati ......000 030 210 000—6
Boston ....300 000 030 001—7

a Flied out for Nolan in third.
b Walked for Billingham in fifth.
c Singled for Carroll in sixth.
d Homered for Moret in eighth.
e Flied out for McEnaney in 10th.
f Flied out for Drago in 11th.

Runs batted in: Griffey 2, Bench, Foster 2, Geronimo, Lynn 3, Carbo 3, Fisk.
Doubles: Doyle, Evans, Foster.
Triple: Griffey.
Home runs: Lynn, Geronimo, Carbo, Fisk.
Stolen bases: Concepcion.
Sacrifice hit: Tiant.
Double plays: Foster and Bench; Evans, Yastrzemski and Burleson.
Left on bases: Boston 11, Boston 9.

Cincinnati	IP	H	R	ER	BB	SO
Nolan	2	3	3	3	0	2
Norman	⅔	1	0	0	2	0
Billingham	1⅓	1	0	0	1	1
Carroll	1	1	0	0	0	0
Borbon	2	1	2	2	2	1
Eastwick	1	2	1	1	1	2
McEnaney	1	0	0	0	1	0
Darcy (L)	2	1	1	1	0	1

Boston	IP	H	R	ER	BB	SO
Tiant	7	11	6	6	2	5
Moret	1	0	0	0	0	0
Drago	3	1	0	0	0	1
Wise (W)	1	2	0	0	0	1

Borbon pitched to two batters in eighth.
Eastwick pitched to two batters in ninth.
Darcy pitched to one batter in 12th.
Tiant pitched to one batter in eighth.
Hit by pitcher: Rose (by Drago).

Umpires: Davidson, Frantz, Colosi, Barnett, Stello, Maloney.
Time: 4:01. **Attendance:** 35,205.

JACKSON SLUGS DODGERS

October 18, 1977, at Yankee Stadium

Reggie Jackson blasted the Los Angeles Dodgers into oblivion with three dramatic Game 6 home runs that gave the New York Yankees a World Series-clinching 8-4 victory and their first championship since 1962. Jackson hit two-run homers off Burt Hooton and Elias Sosa and a solo eighth-inning shot off Charlie Hough, capping the first five-homer Series in fall classic history.

Pirates 1960 World Series hero Bill Mazeroski heads for home after his championship-deciding home run.

Los Angeles	AB	R	H	PO	A	E
Lopes,2b	4	0	1	0	4	0
Russell,ss	3	0	0	1	4	0
Smith,rf	4	2	1	1	0	0
Cey,3b	3	1	1	0	1	0
Garvey,1b	4	1	2	13	0	0
Baker,lf	4	0	1	2	0	0
Monday,cf	4	0	1	3	0	0
Yeager,c	3	0	1	4	2	0
bDavalillo	1	0	1	0	0	0
Hooton,p	2	0	0	0	0	0
Sosa,p	0	0	0	0	0	0
Rau,p	0	0	0	0	0	0
aGoodson	1	0	0	0	0	0
Hough,p	0	0	0	0	0	0
cLacy	1	0	0	0	0	0
Totals	34	4	9	24	11	0

New York	AB	R	H	PO	A	E
Rivers,cf	4	0	2	1	0	0
Randolph,2b	4	1	0	2	3	0
Munson,c	4	1	1	6	0	0
Jackson,rf	3	4	3	5	0	0
Chambliss,1b	4	2	2	9	1	0
Nettles,3b	4	0	0	0	0	0
Piniella,lf	3	0	0	2	1	0
Dent,ss	2	0	0	1	4	1
Torrez,p	3	0	0	1	2	0
Totals	31	8	8	27	11	1

Los Angeles ....2 0 1 000 0 0 1—4
New York ....0 2 0 3 2 0 0 1 x—8

a Struck out for Rau in seventh.
b Bunted safely for Yeager in ninth.
c Popped out for Hough in ninth.

Runs batted in: Garvey 2, Smith, Davalillo, Chambliss 2, Jackson 5, Piniella.
Double: Chambliss.
Triple: Garvey.
Home runs: Chambliss, Smith, Jackson 3.
Sacrifice fly: Piniella.
Double plays: Dent, Randolph and Chambliss; Dent and Chambliss.
Passed ball: Munson.
Left on bases: New York 5, Los Angeles 2.

Los Angeles	IP	H	R	ER	BB	SO
Hooton (L)	3	3	4	4	1	1
Sosa	1⅔	3	3	3	1	0
Rau	1⅓	0	0	0	0	1
Hough	2	2	1	1	0	3

New York	IP	H	R	ER	BB	SO
Torrez (W)	9	9	4	2	2	6

Hooton pitched to three batters in fourth.

Umpires: McSherry, Chylak, Sudol, McCoy, Dale, Evans.
Time: 2:18. **Attendance:** 56,407.

ROSE PASSES COBB

September 11, 1985, at Riverfront Stadium

Pete Rose lined a 2-1 pitch from San Diego righthander Eric Show into left-center field for career hit No. 4,192, ending his long chase of Ty Cobb and securing his status as baseball's all-time top hit man. The first-inning drive touched off a wild celebration that included player congratulations, presentations and several long ovations before play resumed in the Reds' eventual 2-0 victory.

San Diego	AB	R	H	PO	A	E
Templeton,ss	4	0	0	3	3	0
Royster,2b	4	0	1	2	3	0
Gwynn,rf	4	0	1	2	0	0
Garvey,1b	4	0	0	6	0	0
Martinez,lf	3	0	0	4	0	0
McReynolds,cf	3	0	1	2	0	0
Bochy,c	3	0	1	3	1	0
Bevacqua,3b	3	0	1	2	1	0
Show,p	2	0	0	0	1	1
aDavis	1	0	0	0	0	0
Jackson,p	0	0	0	0	0	0
Walter,p	0	0	0	0	0	0
Totals	31	0	5	24	9	1

Cincinnati	AB	R	H	PO	A	E
Milner,cf	5	0	0	5	0	0
Rose,1b	3	2	2	6	1	0
Parker,rf	1	0	1	3	0	0
Esasky,lf	3	0	0	0	0	0
Venable,lf	0	0	0	0	0	0
Bell,3b	4	0	1	0	3	0
Concepcion,ss	4	0	1	1	2	0
Diaz,c	3	0	1	7	0	0
bRedus	0	0	0	0	0	0
Van Gorder,c	0	0	0	0	0	0
Oester,2b	3	0	1	4	3	0
Browning,p	4	0	1	0	0	0
Franco,p	0	0	0	0	0	0
Power,p	0	0	0	1	0	0
Totals	30	2	8	27	9	0

San Diego ....0 0 0 000 0 0 0—0
Cincinnati ....0 0 1 000 1 0 x—2

a Grounded into double play for Show in eighth.
b Ran for Diaz in eighth.

Runs batted in: Esasky 2.
Doubles: Browning, Diaz, Bell.
Triple: Rose.
Sacrifice fly: Esasky.
Stolen base: Gwynn.
Double plays: Templeton, Royster and Garvey; Concepcion, Oester and Rose.
Left on bases: San Diego 4, Cincinnati 11.

San Diego	IP	H	R	ER	BB	SO
Show (L)	7	7	2	2	5	1
Jackson	⅓	1	0	0	1	0
Walter	⅔	0	0	0	0	2

Cincinnati	IP	H	R	ER	BB	SO
Browning (W)	8⅓	5	0	0	0	6
Franco	⅓	0	0	0	0	0
Power (S)	⅓	0	0	0	0	0

Umpires: Weyer, Montague, Brocklander, Rennert.
Time: 2:17. **Attendance:** 47,237.

CLEMENS STRIKES OUT 20

April 29, 1986, at Fenway Park

Boston fireballer Roger Clemens claimed baseball's nine-inning strikeout record when he fanned 20 Seattle Mariners during a 3-1 victory. The Red Sox's "Rocket Man" struck out the side in three innings and fanned an A.L. record-tying eight straight batters from the fourth to the sixth. Clemens broke the record of 19 strikeouts shared by Steve Carlton, Tom Seaver and Nolan Ryan.

Seattle	AB	R	H	PO	A	E
Owen,ss	4	0	1	1	5	0
Bradley,lf	4	0	0	2	0	0
Phelps,1b	4	0	0	6	0	0
Thomas,dh	3	1	1	0	0	0
Presley,3b	3	0	0	1	1	0
Calderon,rf	3	0	0	1	1	0
Tartabull,2b	3	0	1	3	1	1
Henderson,cf	3	0	0	5	0	0
Yeager,c	2	0	0	4	2	0
bCowens	1	0	0	0	0	0
Kearney,c	0	0	0	1	0	0
Moore,p	0	0	0	0	0	0
Young,p	0	0	0	0	0	0
Best,p	0	0	0	0	0	0
Totals	30	1	3	24	10	1

Boston	AB	R	H	PO	A	E
Evans,rf	4	1	2	0	0	0
Boggs,3b	3	0	0	0	0	0
Buckner,dh	4	0	2	0	0	0
Rice,lf	4	0	1	1	0	0
Baylor,1b	3	0	1	1	1	1
Stapleton,1b	0	0	0	1	0	0
Gedman,c	4	0	1	20	0	0
Barrett,2b	3	0	0	0	1	0
Lyons,cf	3	1	1	3	0	0
Hoffman,ss	2	0	0	0	1	0
aRomero,ss	0	1	0	0	0	0
Clemens,p	0	0	0	1	0	0
Totals	30	3	8	27	3	1

Seattle ....0 0 0 000 1 0 0—1
Boston ....0 0 0 000 3 0 x—3

a Ran for Hoffman in seventh.
b Flied out for Yeager in eighth.

Runs batted in: Thomas, Evans 3.
Double: Buckner.
Home runs: Thomas, Evans.
Double play: Yeager and Tartabull.
Left on bases: Seattle 2, Boston 7.

Seattle	IP	H	R	ER	BB	SO
Moore (L)	7⅓	8	3	3	4	4
Young	⅓	0	0	0	0	0
Best	⅓	0	0	0	0	1

Boston	IP	H	R	ER	BB	SO
Clemens (W)	9	3	1	1	0	20

Umpires: Voltaggio, Welke, Phillips, McCoy.
Time: 2:39. **Attendance:** 13,414.

HERSHISER PASSES DRYSDALE

September 28, 1988, at Jack Murphy Stadium

Los Angeles ace Orel Hershiser completed the greatest run of pitching perfection in baseball history when he worked 10 shutout innings against San Diego on the final day of the regular season and extended his record scoreless-innings streak to 59. Hershiser, who recorded six straight shutouts, broke the 20-year-old scoreless-innings mark of former Dodger Don Drysdale, who ran off 58 in 1968.

Los Angeles	AB	R	H	PO	A	E
Sax,2b	5	0	0	3	7	0
Sharperson,2b	2	0	0	0	1	0
Stubbs,1b	5	0	0	21	0	1
gHatcher,1b	1	1	1	0	0	0
Gibson,lf	5	0	1	2	0	0
Orosco,p	0	0	0	0	0	0
Woodson,3b	2	0	1	1	1	0
Shelby,cf	5	0	1	2	0	0
C.Gwynn,lf	1	0	0	0	0	0
Mi.Davis,rf	4	0	0	4	0	0
Gonzalez,rf-lf-cf	3	0	0	2	0	0
Scioscia,c	4	0	0	2	0	0
Dempsey,c	3	0	0	5	2	0
Hamilton,3b	5	0	0	0	2	0
Crews,p	0	0	0	0	0	0
dHeep	1	0	0	0	0	0
K.Howell,p	0	0	0	0	0	0
Horton,p	0	0	0	0	0	0
Griffin,ss	5	0	1	4	5	0
Hershiser,p	3	0	1	0	5	0
Devereaux,rf	2	0	0	1	0	0
Totals	56	1	6	47	23	1

San Diego	AB	R	H	PO	A	E
R.Alomar,2b	7	0	1	0	5	0
Flannery,3b	4	0	1	1	0	0
bRoberts,3b	1	0	0	0	0	1
T.Gwynn,cf	5	0	0	10	0	0
Jefferson,cf	1	0	0	0	0	0
Martinez,1b	5	1	0	11	0	0
Wynne,rf	5	0	2	8	0	0
hParent	1	1	1	0	0	0
Santiago,c	5	0	0	13	0	0
Ready,lf	6	0	0	1	0	0
Templeton,ss	5	0	0	4	3	1
Hawkins,p	3	0	0	0	1	0
aMoreland	1	0	0	0	0	0
Ma.Davis,p	0	0	0	0	0	0
cNelson	1	0	0	0	0	0
McCullers,p	0	0	0	0	0	0
eBrown	0	0	0	0	0	0
fThon	0	0	0	0	0	0
Leiper,p	0	0	0	0	0	0
Totals	50	2	5	48	9	2

L.A. ....0 0 0 000 000 000 000 1—1
S Diego ..0 0 0 000 000 000 000 2—2

a Flied out for Hawkins in 10th.
b Ran for T.Gwynn in 11th.
c Struck out for Ma.Davis in 12th.
d Flied out for Crews in 14th.
e Walked for McCullers in 15th.
f Ran for Brown in 15th.
g Singled for Stubbs in 16th.
h Homered for Wynne in 16th.
i Two out when winning run scored.

Runs batted in: Parent 2.
Double: Griffin.
Triple: Woodson.
Home run: Parent.
Sacrifice hits: Hershiser, Santiago.
Stolen bases: T.Gwynn, Thon, Gonzalez.
Double play: Dempsey and Griffin.
Passed ball: Santiago.
Left on bases: Los Angeles 11, San Diego 10.

Los Angeles	IP	H	R	ER	BB	SO
Hershiser	10	4	0	0	1	3
Orosco	1	0	0	0	4	0
Crews	2	0	0	0	0	2
K.Howell	2⅔	0	1	1	3	3
Horton (L)	0	1	1	1	0	0

San Diego	IP	H	R	ER	BB	SO
Hawkins	10	4	0	0	2	6
Ma.Davis	2	0	0	0	0	4
McCullers	3	1	0	0	0	4
Leiper (W)	1	1	1	0	0	0

Horton pitched to one batter in 16th.
Hit by pitcher: Griffin (by Hawkins).

Umpires: West, Runge, Engel, Williams.
Time: 4:24. **Attendance:** 22,596.

GIBSON SHOCKS A'S

October 15, 1988, at Dodger Stadium

Los Angeles pinch hitter Kirk Gibson, limping badly on his injured leg and wincing with every painful swing, blasted a pitch from Oakland relief ace Dennis Eckersley over the right-field fence with two out in the ninth inning, giving the Dodgers a 5-4 victory in a storybook conclusion to Game 1 of the World Series. With the Dodgers trailing 4-3 and a runner on base, Gibson looked overmatched as he worked the count to 3-2. That's when he connected for the first come-from-behind game-winning homer in Series history.

Oakland	AB	R	H	PO	A	E
Lansford,3b	4	1	0	2	2	0
Henderson,cf	5	0	2	4	0	0
Canseco,rf	4	1	1	3	0	0
Parker,lf	2	0	0	1	0	0
cJavier,lf	1	0	1	0	0	0
McGwire,1b	3	0	0	6	0	0
Steinbach,c	4	0	1	5	0	0
Hassey,c	0	0	0	1	0	0
Hubbard,2b	4	1	2	2	0	0
Weiss,ss	4	0	0	2	3	0
Stewart,p	3	1	0	0	0	0
Eckersley,p	0	0	0	0	0	0
Totals	34	4	7	26	5	0

Los Angeles	AB	R	H	PO	A	E
Sax,2b	3	1	1	3	1	0
Stubbs,1b	4	0	0	7	0	0
Hatcher,lf	3	1	1	1	0	0
Marshall,rf	4	1	1	2	0	0
Shelby,cf	4	0	1	3	0	0
Scioscia,c	4	0	1	9	0	0
Hamilton,3b	4	0	0	1	1	0
Griffin,ss	2	0	1	1	4	0
eM.Davis	0	1	0	0	0	0
Belcher,p	0	0	0	0	0	0
aHeep	1	0	0	0	0	0
Leary,p	0	0	0	0	1	0
bWoodson	1	0	0	0	0	0
Holton,p	0	0	0	0	1	0
dGonzalez	1	0	0	0	0	0
Pena,p	0	0	0	0	0	0
fGibson	1	1	1	0	0	0
Totals	32	5	7	27	8	0

Oakland ....0 4 0 000 0 0 0—4
Los Angeles ....2 0 0 001 0 0 2—5

a Grounded out for Belcher in second.
b Forced Griffin for Leary in fifth.
c Ran for Parker in seventh.
d Struck out for Holton in seventh.
e Walked for Griffin in ninth.
f Hit two run homer for Pena in ninth.

Runs batted in: Canseco 4, Hatcher 2, Scioscia, Gibson 2.
Double: Henderson.
Home runs: Hatcher, Canseco, Gibson.
Stolen bases: Canseco, Sax, M. Davis.
Double play: Lansford and McGwire.
Left on bases: Oakland 10, Los Angeles 5.

Oakland	IP	H	R	ER	BB	SO
Stewart	8	6	3	3	2	5
Eckersley (L)	⅔	1	2	2	1	1

Los Angeles	IP	H	R	ER	BB	SO
Belcher	2	3	4	4	4	3
Leary	3	3	0	0	1	3
Holton	2	0	0	0	1	0
Pena (W)	2	1	0	0	0	3

Hit by pitcher: Canseco (by Belcher), Sax (by Stewart).
Wild pitch: Stewart.
Balk: Stewart.

Umpires: Harvey, Merrill, Froemming, Cousins, Crawford, McCoy.
Time: 3:04. **Attendance:** 55,983.

CARTER'S HAPPY ENDING

October 23, 1993, at SkyDome

Toronto outfielder Joe Carter hit a three-run, ninth-inning home run off Philadelphia reliever Mitch Williams, giving the Blue Jays a dramatic 8-6 victory over Philadelphia and their second straight World Series championship. The seesaw Game 6 battle ended suddenly when Carter drove a one-out Williams pitch into the left-field seats at SkyDome and danced euphorically around the bases. It marked the first time a team trailing in the ninth had won a World Series on a home run.

Philadelphia	AB	R	H	PO	A	E
Dykstra,cf	3	1	1	5	0	0
Duncan,dh	5	1	1	0	0	0
Kruk,1b	3	0	0	6	0	0
Hollins,3b	5	1	1	0	1	0
Batiste,3b	0	0	0	0	0	0
Daulton,c	4	1	1	3	0	0
Eisenreich,rf	5	0	2	2	0	0
Thompson,lf	3	0	0	4	0	0
aIncaviglia,lf	0	0	0	3	0	0
Stocker,ss	3	1	0	0	1	0
Morandini,2b	4	1	1	2	0	0
Mulholland,p	0	0	0	0	1	0
Mason,p	0	0	0	0	0	0
West,p	0	0	0	0	0	0
Andersen,p	0	0	0	0	0	0
M.Williams,p	0	0	0	0	0	0
Totals	35	6	7	25	3	0

FOR THE RECORD

Toronto	AB	R	H	PO	A	E
Henderson,lf	4	1	0	2	0	0
White,cf	4	1	0	6	0	0
Molitor,dh	5	3	3	0	0	0
Carter,rf	4	1	1	3	0	0
Olerud,1b	3	1	1	6	0	0
bGriffin,3b	0	0	0	0	0	0
Alomar,2b	4	1	3	1	3	1
Fernandez,ss	3	0	0	1	0	0
Sprague,3b-1b	2	0	0	3	2	1
Borders,c	4	0	2	5	0	0
Stewart,p	0	0	0	0	1	0
Cox,p	0	0	0	0	0	0
Leiter,p	0	0	0	0	0	0
D.Ward,p	0	0	0	0	0	0
Totals	33	8	10	27	6	2

Philadelphia ....0 0 0 1 0 0 5 0 0—6
Toronto ....3 0 0 1 1 0 0 0 3—8

a Hit sacrifice fly for Thompson in seventh.
b Ran for Olerud in eighth.

Runs batted in: Dykstra 3, Hollins, Eisenreich, Incaviglia, Molitor 2, Carter 4, Alomar, Sprague.
Doubles: Daulton, Olerud, Alomar.
Triple: Molitor.
Home runs: Molitor, Dykstra, Carter.
Sacrifice flies: Incaviglia, Carter, Sprague.
Stolen bases: Dykstra, Duncan.
Left on bases: Philadelphia 9, Toronto 7.

Philadelphia	IP	H	R	ER	BB	SO
Mulholland	5	7	5	5	1	1
Mason	2⅓	1	0	0	0	2
West	0	0	0	0	1	0
Andersen	⅔	0	0	0	1	0
M.Williams (L)	⅓	2	3	3	1	0

Toronto	IP	H	R	ER	BB	SO
Stewart	6	4	4	4	4	2
Cox	⅓	3	2	2	1	1
Leiter	1⅔	0	0	0	1	2
D.Ward (W)	1	0	0	0	0	0

West pitched to one batter in eighth.
Stewart pitched to three batters in seventh.
Hit by pitcher: Fernandez (by Andersen).

Umpires: DeMuth, Phillips, Runge, Johnson, Williams, McClelland.
Time: 3:27. **Attendance:** 52,195.

RIPKEN PLAYS ON

September 6, 1995, at Camden Yards

Baltimore shortstop Cal Ripken played in his 2,131st consecutive game, passing Lou Gehrig on the all-time iron-man list. Ripken punctuated his record-setter with a fourth-inning home run and the celebration began an inning later when California batted to make the game official. After Ripken was honored in a memorable, nationally televised showcase, the Orioles went on to record a 4-2 victory.

California	AB	R	H	PO	A	E
Phillips,3b	4	0	0	0	3	1
Edmonds,cf	3	1	1	1	0	0
Salmon,rf	4	1	3	1	0	0
Davis,dh	3	0	0	0	0	0
Snow,1b	4	0	1	6	0	0
G.Anderson,lf	4	0	0	4	0	0
Hudler,2b	2	0	0	2	1	0
aOwen,2b	2	0	0	0	0	0
Fabregas,c	3	0	0	9	0	0
Easley,ss	2	0	1	1	0	0
bO.Palmeiro	1	0	0	0	0	0
Correia,ss	0	0	0	0	0	0
Boskie,p	0	0	0	0	0	0
Bielecki,p	0	0	0	0	0	0
Patterson,p	0	0	0	0	0	0
James,p	0	0	0	0	0	0
Totals	32	2	6	24	4	1

Baltimore	AB	R	H	PO	A	E
B.Anderson,cf	4	0	1	2	0	0
Alexander,2b	4	0	0	2	1	0
R.Palmeiro,1b	4	2	3	7	0	0
Bonilla,rf	4	1	1	1	0	0
J.Brown,rf	0	0	0	0	0	0
Ripken,ss	4	1	2	1	4	0
Baines,dh	4	0	1	0	0	0
Hoiles,c	4	0	1	8	1	0
Huson,3b	4	0	0	1	1	0
Smith,lf	2	0	0	5	0	0
Mussina,p	0	0	0	0	0	0
Clark,p	0	0	0	0	0	0
Orosco,p	0	0	0	0	0	0
Totals	34	4	9	27	7	0

California ....1 0 0 0 0 0 0 1 0—2
Baltimore ....1 0 0 2 0 0 1 0 x—4

a Grounded out for Hudler in seventh.
b Grounded out for Easley in eighth.

Runs batted in: Salmon 2, R.Palmeiro 2, Bonilla, Ripken.
Doubles: Easley, Salmon, Baines.
Triple: Edmonds.
Home runs: Salmon, R.Palmeiro 2, Bonilla, Ripken.
Double play: Ripken and R.Palmeiro.
Left on bases: California 5, Baltimore 7.

California	IP	H	R	ER	BB	SO
Boskie (L)	5	6	3	3	1	4
Bielecki	1	1	0	0	0	2
Patterson	⅔	1	1	1	0	1
James	1⅓	1	0	0	0	1

Baltimore	IP	H	R	ER	BB	SO
Mussina (W)	7⅔	5	2	2	2	7
Clark	0	1	0	0	0	0
Orosco (S)	1⅓	0	0	0	0	2

Clark pitched to one batter in eighth.

Umpires: Barron, Kosc, Morrison, Clark.
Time: 3:35, **Attendance:** 46,272.

FOUR-HOMER GAMES

BOBBY LOWE

May 30, 1894, at Boston

Boston second baseman Lowe, baseball's first four-homer man, connected twice in the third inning of a 20-11 victory over Cincinnati.

Cincinnati	AB	R	H	PO	A	E
Hoy,cf	6	1	1	3	0	1
McCarthy,1b	5	2	2	9	1	0
Latham,3b	4	3	2	0	3	2
Holliday,lf	4	3	2	1	0	0
McPhee,2b	5	0	2	4	3	0
Vaughn,c	5	1	2	3	5	1
Canavan,rf	5	1	1	2	0	0
Smith,ss	5	0	1	1	5	1
Chamberlain,p	5	0	1	1	1	0
Totals	44	11	14	24	18	5

Boston	AB	R	H	PO	A	E
Lowe,2b	6	4	5	2	2	1
Long,ss	3	5	2	2	4	2
Duffy,cf	5	0	1	1	0	0
McCarthy,lf	6	2	3	3	0	0
Nash,3b	4	3	3	1	1	0
Tucker,1b	2	1	0	10	2	0
Bannon,rf	4	2	2	1	0	0
Ryan,c	5	2	2	5	0	0
Nichols,p	5	1	1	2	3	0
Totals	40	20	19	27	12	3

Cincinnati ....2 0 0 0 4 0 0 0 5—11
Boston ....2 0 9 0 1 5 2 1 x—20

Runs batted in: Lowe 6, Nichols 4, Bannon 2, McCarthy 2, Ryan 2, Duffy, Long, Nash, Holliday 5, Vaughn 4, Canavan, Latham.
Doubles: Latham 2, Smith, Chamberlain, Long, McCarthy.
Home runs: Holliday 2, Vaughn, Canavan, Lowe 4, Long.
Stolen bases: Nash 2, Long, Duffy, Hoy, Latham.
Passed ball: Vaughn.
Left on bases: Cincinnati 7, Boston 10.

Cincinnati	IP	H	R	ER	BB	SO
Chamberlain (L)	8	19	20	18	8	3

Boston	IP	H	R	ER	BB	SO
Nichols (W)	9	14	11	11	2	3

Hit by pitcher: Long (by Chamberlain), Tucker (by Chamberlain).
Wild pitches: Chamberlain, Nichols.

Umpire: Swartwood.
Time: 2:15. **Attendance:** 8,000.

ED DELAHANTY

July 13, 1896, at Chicago

All four of Delahanty's homers were inside-the-park shots and the Philadelphia outfielder added a single for a record 17 total bases.

Philadelphia	AB	R	H	PO	A	E
Cooley,lf	3	1	1	1	0	0
Hulen,ss	4	1	1	1	4	0
Mertes,cf	5	1	0	1	0	0
Delahanty,1b	5	4	5	9	0	0
Thompson,rf	5	0	1	2	0	0
Hallman,2b	4	1	1	5	3	0
Clements,c	2	0	0	5	3	0
Nash,3b	4	0	0	0	3	1
Garvin,p	4	0	0	0	1	0
Totals	36	8	9	24	14	1

Chicago	AB	R	H	PO	A	E
Everitt,3b	3	1	2	1	3	0
Dahlen,ss	2	2	0	0	0	0
Lange,cf	4	2	2	4	0	0
Anson,1b	3	0	1	12	2	0
Ryan,rf	4	1	1	2	0	1
Decker,lf	4	1	1	0	0	1
Pfeffer,2b	4	0	2	1	4	0
Terry,p	4	1	2	2	3	0
Donohue,c	3	1	0	5	0	0
Totals	31	9	11	27	12	2

Philadelphia ....1 2 0 0 3 0 1 0 1—8
Chicago ....1 0 4 0 1 0 0 3 x—9

Runs batted in: Delahanty 7, Garvin 1, Lange 5, Pfeffer 2, Anson.
Doubles: Thompson, Lange, Decker, Terry.
Triples: Lange, Pfeffer.
Home runs: Delahanty 4.
Double play: Hulen, Hallman and Delahanty.
Left on bases: Philadelphia 6, Chicago 4.

Philadelphia	IP	H	R	ER	BB	SO
Garvin (L)	8	11	9	8	4	4

Chicago	IP	H	R	ER	BB	SO
Terry (W)	9	9	8	7	3	4

Wild pitch: Garvin.

Umpire: Emslie.
Time: 2:15. **Attendance:** 1,100.

LOU GEHRIG

June 3, 1932, at Philadelphia

Yankees first baseman Gehrig became the first modern and A.L. player to hit four homers in a game and he narrowly missed a fifth in the ninth inning, when he flew out deep to center.

New York	AB	R	H	PO	A	E
Combs,cf	5	2	3	3	0	0
Saltzgaver,2b	4	1	1	3	2	0
Ruth,lf	5	2	2	3	0	1
Hoag,lf	0	1	0	1	0	0
Gehrig,1b	6	4	4	7	0	1
Chapman,rf	5	3	2	4	0	0
Dickey,c	4	2	2	5	0	0
Lazzeri,3b	6	3	5	0	1	0
Crosetti,ss	6	1	2	0	5	2
Allen,p	2	0	0	1	0	1
Rhodes,p	1	0	1	0	0	0
Brown,p	1	0	0	0	1	0
Gomez,p	1	1	1	0	0	0
Totals	46	20	23	27	9	5

Philadelphia	AB	R	H	PO	A	E
Bishop,2b	4	2	2	3	2	0
Cramer,cf	5	1	1	1	0	0
cRoettger	1	0	0	0	0	0
Miller,lf	0	0	0	0	0	0
Cochrane,c	5	1	1	10	2	0
dWilliams	1	0	0	0	0	0
Simmons,lf-cf	4	2	0	2	0	0
Foxx,1b	3	3	2	8	0	0
Coleman,rf	6	2	2	2	1	0
McNair,ss	5	1	3	1	2	0
Dykes,3b	4	1	1	0	1	0
Earnshaw,p	2	0	0	0	2	1
aHaas	1	0	1	0	0	0
Mahaffey,p	0	0	0	0	0	0
Walberg,p	0	0	0	0	0	0
Krausse,p	0	0	0	0	0	0
bMadjeski	1	0	0	0	0	0
Rommel,p	0	0	0	0	1	0
Totals	42	13	13	27	11	1

New York ....2 0 0 2 3 2 3 2 6—20
Philadelphia ....2 0 0 6 0 2 0 2 1—13

a Singled for Earnshaw in fifth.
b Reached on error for Krausse in eighth.
c Flied out for Cramer in eighth.
d Batted for Cochrane in ninth.

Runs batted in: Combs, Saltzgaver, Ruth, Gehrig 6, Chapman, Dickey, Lazzeri 6, Crosetti 2, Cramer 3, Cochrane 2, Foxx, Coleman 3, McNair 2.
Doubles: Ruth, Lazzeri, Coleman, McNair.
Triples: Chapman, Lazzeri, Bishop, Cramer, Foxx.
Home runs: Combs, Ruth, Gehrig 4, Lazzeri, Cochrane, Foxx.
Stolen bases: Lazzeri.
Double plays: Cochrane and McNair; Bishop and Foxx; Coleman and Cochrane.
Left on bases: New York 6, Philadelphia 11.

New York	IP	H	R	ER	BB	SO
Allen	3⅔	7	8	4	5	2
Rhodes	1⅓	1	2	2	2	0
Brown (W)	2	3	2	1	1	0
Gomez	2	2	1	1	0	1

Philadelphia	IP	H	R	ER	BB	SO
Earnshaw	5	8	7	6	2	8
Mahaffey (L)	1	6	4	4	0	0
Walberg	1	2	1	1	1	1
Krausse	1	4	2	2	0	0
Rommel	1	3	6	6	3	0

Wild pitch: Rhodes.

Umpires: Geisel, McGowan, Van Graflan.
Time: 2:55. **Attendance:** 7,300.

CHUCK KLEIN

July 10, 1936, at Pittsburgh

Philadelphia outfielder Klein needed a 10th inning to get his fourth homer and it proved to be the game-winner in a 9-6 Phillies victory over the Pirates.

Philadelphia	AB	R	H	PO	A	E
Sulik,cf	5	1	1	5	0	0
Moore,lf	5	1	1	1	0	0
Klein,rf	5	4	4	5	0	0
Camilli,1b	4	2	1	10	1	0
Atwood,c	4	0	1	2	0	0
Wilson,c	0	1	0	0	0	0
Chiozza,3b	5	0	2	1	1	0
Norris,ss	4	0	1	3	4	2
Gomez,2b	5	0	0	3	2	0
Passeau,p	4	0	1	0	0	0
Walters,p	0	0	0	0	1	0
Totals	41	9	12	30	9	2

Pittsburgh	AB	R	H	PO	A	E
Jensen,lf	4	1	1	3	0	0
L.Waner,cf	4	1	1	4	0	1
P.Waner,rf	4	2	2	1	0	0
Vaughan,ss	5	0	1	2	2	2
Suhr,1b	4	0	2	13	1	0
Brubaker,3b	5	0	0	1	1	0
Young,2b	3	0	1	1	5	0
Lavagetto,2b	1	1	0	1	1	1
Todd,c	2	0	0	3	0	0
Padden,c	2	1	0	1	0	0
Weaver,p	1	0	0	0	2	0
aLucas	1	0	0	0	0	0
Brown,p	1	0	0	0	2	0
bSchulte	1	0	1	0	0	0
cFinney	0	0	0	0	0	0
Swift,p	0	0	0	0	0	0
Totals	38	6	9	30	14	4

Philadelphia ....4 0 0 0 1 0 1 0 0 3— 9
Pittsburgh ....0 0 0 1 0 3 0 0 2 0— 6

a Batted for Weaver in fifth.
b Singled for Brown in ninth.
c Ran for Schulte in ninth.

Runs batted in: Klein 6, Chiozza, Norris 2, L.Waner, P.Waner, Vaughan, Suhr, Schulte.
Double: Camilli.
Triple: Suhr.
Home runs: Klein 4.
Double plays: Chiozza, Gomez and Camilli; Camilli, Norris and Camilli; Walters, Gomez and Camilli; Vaughan, Lavagetto and Suhr.
Left on bases: Philadelphia 5, Pittsburgh 7.

Philadelphia	IP	H	R	ER	BB	SO
Passeau	8⅔	8	6	4	2	1
Walters (W)	1⅓	1	0	0	2	0

Pittsburgh	IP	H	R	ER	BB	SO
Weaver	5	6	5	4	1	2
Brown	4	2	1	1	0	1
Swift (L)	1	4	3	2	0	0

Umpires: Sears, Klem, Ballanfant.
Time: 2:25. **Attendance:** 2,500.

PAT SEEREY

July 18, 1948, at Philadelphia

Seerey, like Klein, needed extra innings to tie the record and he also made his fourth homer a game-winner—an 11th-inning blast in Chicago's 12-11 victory over the Athletics.

Chicago	AB	R	H	PO	A	E
Kolloway,2b	7	2	5	5	2	0
Lupien,1b	7	1	1	8	2	0
Appling,3b	7	1	3	2	5	0
Seerey,lf	6	4	4	3	0	0
Robinson,c	6	0	3	4	1	0
Wright,rf	6	0	2	0	0	0
Philley,cf	6	1	2	5	0	0
Michaels,ss	6	3	4	6	3	1
Papish,p	0	0	0	0	1	0
Moulder,p	1	0	0	0	0	0
aHodgin	1	0	0	0	0	0
Caldwell,p	0	0	0	0	0	0
bBaker	1	0	0	0	0	0
Judson,p	3	0	0	0	0	0
Pieretti,p	0	0	0	0	0	0
Totals	57	12	24	33	14	1

Philadelphia	AB	R	H	PO	A	E
Joost,ss	7	4	4	1	2	0
McCosky,lf	2	2	1	3	1	0
White,cf	4	1	2	2	0	0
Brissie,p	0	0	0	0	0	0
dChapman	0	0	0	0	0	0
eDeMars	0	0	0	0	0	0
Fain,1b	5	0	0	13	0	0
Majeski,3b	5	0	1	0	3	0
Valo,rf	3	0	1	4	0	0
Rosar,c	3	0	0	5	0	0
Guerra,c	3	0	0	3	0	0
Suder,2b	5	2	1	2	1	0
Scheib,p	1	1	0	0	4	0
Savage,p	1	0	0	0	0	0
Harris,p	1	1	1	0	0	1
J.Coleman,p	0	0	0	0	0	0
cR.Coleman,cf	2	0	1	0	0	0
Totals	42	11	12	33	11	1

Chicago ....0 0 1 1 2 5 2 0 0 0 1—12
Philadelphia ......1 4 0 1 1 0 4 0 0 0 0—11

a Flied out for Moulder in fourth.
b Flied out for Caldwell in sixth.
c Grounded out for J.Coleman in ninth.
d Walked for Brissie in 11th.
e Ran for Chapman in 11th.

Runs batted in: Kolloway 3, Appling, Seerey 7, Baker, Joost 5, McCosky, Fain 2, Majeski.
Doubles: Robinson, Wright, Kolloway, Philley, Joost 2, Majeski.
Triple: Kolloway.
Home runs: Seerey 4, Joost.
Sacrifice hits: McCosky, White 2.
Stolen base: Appling.
Double plays: McCosky and Rosar; Kolloway, Michaels and Lupien.
Left on bases: Chicago 15, Philadelphia 14.

Chicago	IP	H	R	ER	BB	SO
Papish	1	3	5	4	4	0
Moulder	2	0	0	0	0	1
Caldwell	2	4	2	2	1	1
Judson (W)	5⅔	5	4	4	7	2
Pieretti (S)	⅓	0	0	0	0	0

Philadelphia	IP	H	R	ER	BB	SO
Scheib	4⅔	9	4	4	1	2
Savage	1	5	5	5	1	0
Harris	1⅔	4	2	1	0	0
J.Coleman	1⅔	2	0	0	1	1
Brissie (L)	2	4	1	1	0	1

Papish pitched to four batters in second.
Hit by pitcher: Valo (by Papish).
Wild pitches: Papish, Moulder, Savage.
Balk: Judson.

Umpires: Hurley, Berry, Grieve.
Time: 3:44. **Attendance:** 17,296.

GIL HODGES

August 31, 1950, at Brooklyn

Hodges, the Dodgers' big first baseman, connected off four different Boston pitchers and finished the game with nine RBIs.

Boston	AB	R	H	PO	A	E
Hartsfield,2b	5	0	1	4	1	3
Jethroe,cf	5	0	0	1	0	0
Torgeson,1b	4	1	1	7	0	0
Elliott,3b	3	0	1	1	4	0
Cooper,c	3	0	0	3	0	0
Crandall,c	1	1	0	2	0	1
Gordon,lf	4	1	3	4	0	0
Marshall,rf	4	0	2	1	0	0
Kerr,ss	3	0	0	1	4	0
Spahn,p	1	0	0	0	0	0
Roy,p	0	0	0	0	1	0
Haefner,p	0	0	0	0	0	0
aReiser	1	0	0	0	0	0
Hall,p	0	0	0	0	1	0
Antonelli,p	1	0	0	0	0	0
bHolmes	1	0	0	0	0	0
Totals	36	3	8	24	11	4

Brooklyn	AB	R	H	PO	A	E
Brown,lf	5	0	1	1	0	0
Reese,ss	5	1	2	1	4	1
Snider,cf	5	1	1	4	0	0
Robinson,2b	5	1	1	2	1	0
Morgan,3b	0	0	0	0	1	0
Furillo,rf	5	4	2	1	0	0
Hodges,1b	6	5	5	7	1	0
Campanella,c	4	2	2	4	0	0
Edwards,c	1	1	1	2	0	0
Cox,3b-2b	5	3	2	3	3	0
Erskine,p	5	1	4	2	0	0
Totals	46	19	21	27	10	1

Boston ....0 1 0 0 0 0 0 2 0— 3
Brooklyn...................0 3 7 0 0 4 3 2 x—19

a Struck out for Haefner in fifth.

Chicago White Sox slugger Pat Seerey pays homage to the bat that cranked out four home runs in a game against the Athletics.

b Lined out for Antonelli in ninth.

Runs batted in: Hodges 9, Reese 3, Gordon 2, Snider 3, Brown 2, Marshall.
Doubles: Reese, Edwards, Marshall 2.
Home runs: Hodges 4, Gordon, Snider.
Sacrifice hit: Cox.
Left on bases: Boston 9, Brooklyn 12.

Boston	IP	H	R	ER	BB	SO
Spahn (L)	2	7	5	5	1	2
Roy	⅓	3	3	3	0	0
Haefner	1⅔	1	2	2	1	0
Hall	1⅔	6	4	4	3	1
Antonelli	2⅔	4	5	4	2	2

Brooklyn	IP	H	R	ER	BB	SO
Erskine (W)	9	8	3	3	2	6

Spahn pitched to two batters in third.
Hit by pitcher: Erskine (by Antonelli).

Umpires: Conlan, Gore, Stewart.
Time: 3:03. **Attendance:** 14,226.

JOE ADCOCK

July 31, 1954, at Brooklyn

Milwaukee first baseman Adcock homered off four different Dodgers pitchers and punctuated his big game with a double and a Major League-record 18 total bases.

Milwaukee	AB	R	H	PO	A	E
Bruton,cf	6	0	4	4	0	0
O'Connell,2b	5	0	0	4	4	0
Mathews,3b	4	3	2	3	2	0
Aaron,lf	5	2	2	0	0	0
Adcock,1b	5	5	5	11	0	0
Pafko,rf	4	2	3	0	0	0
Pendleton,rf	1	1	0	0	0	0
Logan,ss	2	1	1	1	1	0
Smalley,ss	2	1	1	0	1	0
Crandall,c	4	0	0	2	1	0
Calderone,c	1	0	1	2	0	0
Wilson,p	1	0	0	0	0	0
Burdette,p	3	0	0	0	4	0
Buhl,p	0	0	0	0	0	0
Jolly,p	1	0	0	0	0	0
Totals	44	15	19	27	13	0

Brooklyn	AB	R	H	PO	A	E
Gilliam,2b	4	1	4	3	1	0
Reese,ss	3	0	1	1	2	0
Zimmer,ss	1	0	0	1	1	0
Snider,cf	4	0	1	0	0	0
Shuba,lf	1	0	0	0	0	0
Hodges,1b	5	1	1	7	0	0
Amoros,lf-cf	5	2	3	6	0	0
Robinson,3b	0	0	0	0	0	0
Hoak,3b	2	1	1	0	1	1
Furillo,rf	5	1	2	3	0	0
Walker,c	5	1	1	6	1	0
Newcombe,p	0	0	0	0	0	0
Labine,p	0	0	0	0	0	0
aMoryn	1	0	0	0	0	0
Palica,p	0	0	0	0	0	0
Wojey,p	1	0	0	0	1	0
bPodres,p	2	0	2	0	1	0
Totals	39	7	16	27	8	1

Milwaukee ....1 3 2 0 3 0 3 0 3—15
Brooklyn....................1 0 0 0 0 1 0 4 1— 7

a Grounded into double play for Labine in second.
b Singled for Wojey in seventh.

Runs batted in: Mathews 2, Snider, Adcock 7, Logan, Bruton, Pafko 2, Hoak 2, Hodges, Furillo, Walker 2.
Doubles: Gilliam, Pafko, Bruton 3, Amoros, Adcock, Aaron.
Triple: Amoros.
Home runs: Mathews 2, Adcock 4, Hoak, Pafko, Hodges, Walker.
Sacrifice hit: O'Connell.
Sacrifice fly: Hoak.
Double plays: Mathews, O'Connell and Adcock; O'Connell, Logan and Adcock; Zimmer, Gilliam and Hodges.
Left on bases: Milwaukee 5, Brooklyn 10.

Milwaukee	IP	H	R	ER	BB	SO
Wilson	1	5	1	1	0	0
Burdette (W)	6⅓	8	5	5	2	3
Buhl	0	2	0	0	0	0
Jolly	1⅔	1	1	1	1	1

Brooklyn	IP	H	R	ER	BB	SO
Newcombe (L)	1	4	4	4	0	0
Labine	1	1	0	0	0	0
Palica	2⅓	5	5	5	2	1
Wojey	2⅔	4	3	3	0	3
Podres	2	5	3	2	0	1

Hit by pitcher: Robinson (by Wilson).
Wild pitch: Podres.

Umpires: Boggess, Engeln, Stewart, Barlick.
Time: 2:53. **Attendance:** 12,263.

ROCKY COLAVITO

June 10, 1959, at Baltimore

Cleveland outfielder Colavito rocked the Orioles and joined Lowe and Gehrig as the only players to hit their four homers consecutively.

Cleveland	AB	R	H	PO	A	E
Held,ss	5	1	1	5	1	0
Power,1b	4	1	0	4	1	0
Francona,cf	5	2	2	2	0	0
Colavito,rf	4	5	4	3	0	0
Minoso,lf	5	1	3	1	0	0
Jones,3b	3	0	0	1	1	0
Strickland,3b	2	0	1	1	1	0
Brown,c	4	0	1	7	1	0
Martin,2b	3	1	1	3	0	0
aWebster,2b	1	0	0	0	0	0
Bell,p	3	0	0	0	1	0
Garcia,p	1	0	0	0	0	0
Totals	40	11	13	27	6	0

Baltimore	AB	R	H	PO	A	E
Pearson,cf	3	1	2	5	0	0
Pilarcik,rf	5	1	1	2	0	0
Woodling,lf	5	1	3	3	0	0
Triandos,c	2	0	1	5	0	0
Ginsberg,c	1	1	0	0	0	0
Hale,1b	3	0	0	4	0	0
Zuverink,p	0	0	0	0	0	0
bBoyd	1	0	0	0	0	0
Johnson,p	0	0	0	0	0	0
cNieman	1	1	1	0	0	0
Klaus,3b	5	0	2	0	1	0
Carrasquel,ss	5	0	0	2	3	0
Gardner,2b	4	1	1	1	5	0
Walker,p	1	1	1	0	0	0
Portocarrero,p	1	0	0	0	0	0
Lockman,1b	1	1	0	5	0	0
Totals	38	8	12	27	9	0

Cleveland ....3 1 2 0 1 3 0 0 1—11
Baltimore ....1 2 0 0 0 0 4 0 1— 8

a Popped out for Martin in seventh.
b Flied out for Zuverink in seventh.
c Doubled for Johnson in ninth.

Runs batted in: Francona, Colavito 6, Minoso 3, Martin, Pilarcik 2, Woodling, Triandos, Klaus 4.
Doubles: Brown, Held, Francona, Klaus, Nieman.
Home runs: Minoso, Martin, Colavito 4.
Sacrifice fly: Triandos.
Stolen bases: Minoso.
Left on bases: Cleveland 0, Baltimore 8.

Cleveland	IP	H	R	ER	BB	SO
Bell (W)	6⅓	8	7	7	4	3
Garcia	2⅔	4	1	1	0	3

Baltimore	IP	H	R	ER	BB	SO
Walker (L)	2⅓	4	6	6	2	1
Portocarrero	3⅓	7	4	4	1	3
Zuverink	1⅓	0	0	0	0	0
Johnson	2	2	1	1	0	0

Umpires: Summers, McKinley, Soar, Chylak.
Time: 2:54. **Attendance:** 15,883.

WILLIE MAYS

April 30, 1961, at Milwaukee

New York Giants center fielder Mays connected in the first, third, sixth and eighth innings, driving in eight of his team's 14 runs against the Braves.

San Francisco	AB	R	H	PO	A	E
Hiller,2b	6	2	3	3	2	0
Davenport,3b	4	3	1	1	4	0
Mays,cf	5	4	4	3	0	0
McCovey,1b	3	0	0	5	0	0
Marshall,1b	0	0	0	3	0	0
Cepeda,lf	5	1	1	3	0	0
M.Alou,lf	0	0	0	1	0	0
F.Alou,rf	4	1	1	3	0	0
Bailey,c	4	0	0	3	0	0
Pagan,ss	5	3	4	2	1	0
Loes,p	3	0	0	0	2	0
Totals	39	14	14	27	9	0

Milwaukee	AB	R	H	PO	A	E
McMillan,ss	4	1	1	2	3	0
Bolling,2b	4	1	2	4	4	0
Mathews,3b	4	0	1	0	4	1
Aaron,cf	4	2	2	2	0	0
Roach,lf	4	0	1	2	0	0
Adcock,1b	4	0	0	13	1	0
Lau,c	3	0	1	2	0	0
McMahon,p	0	0	0	0	1	0
Brunet,p	0	0	0	0	1	0
cMaye	0	0	0	0	0	0
DeMerit,rf	4	0	0	0	0	0
Burdette,p	1	0	0	1	1	0
Willey,p	0	0	0	1	0	0
Drabowsky,p	0	0	0	0	0	0
aMartin	1	0	0	0	0	0
Morehead,p	0	0	0	0	0	0
MacKenzie,p	0	0	0	0	0	0
bLogan	1	0	0	0	0	0
Taylor,c	0	0	0	0	0	0
Totals	34	4	8	27	15	1

San Francisco............1 0 3 3 0 4 0 3 0—14
Milwaukee ....3 0 0 0 0 1 0 0 0— 4

a Flied out for Drabowsky in fifth.
b Struck out for MacKenzie in seventh.
c Walked for Brunet in ninth.

Runs batted in: Hiller, Davenport, Mays 8, Cepeda, F.Alou, Pagan 2, Aaron 4.
Doubles: Hiller 2.
Triple: Davenport.
Home runs: Mays 4, Pagan 2, Cepeda, F.Alou, Aaron 2.
Sacrifice hits: Loes 2.
Double plays: Davenport, Hiller and Marshall; Burdette, McMillan and Adcock; Bolling, McMillan and Adcock.
Left on bases: San Francisco 6, Milwaukee 4.

San Francisco	IP	H	R	ER	BB	SO
Loes (W)	9	8	4	4	1	3

Milwaukee	IP	H	R	ER	BB	SO
Burdette (L)	3	5	5	5	0	0
Willey	1	3	2	2	0	0
Drabowsky	1	0	0	0	1	0
Morehead	1	2	4	4	1	1
MacKenzie	1	0	0	0	0	1
McMahon	1	3	3	3	2	0
Brunet	1	1	0	0	0	0

Burdette pitched to one batter in fourth.
Hit by pitcher: Davenport (by Burdette), Bailey (by Mackenzie).

Umpires: Pelekoudas, Forman, Conlan, Donatelli, Burkhart.
Time: 2:40. **Attendance:** 13,114.

MIKE SCHMIDT

April 17, 1976, at Chicago

Philadelphia third baseman Schmidt hit a two-run shot in the 10th inning—his fourth consecutive homer in the Phillies' 18-16 victory.

Philadelphia	AB	R	H	PO	A	E
Cash,2b	6	1	2	4	3	0
Bowa,ss	6	3	3	2	0	0
Johnstone,rf	5	2	4	5	0	0
Luzinski,lf	5	0	1	0	0	0
Brown,lf	0	0	0	0	0	0
Allen,1b	5	2	1	5	0	0
Schmidt,3b	6	4	5	2	3	0
Maddox,rf	5	2	2	4	0	0
McGraw,p	0	0	0	0	0	0
eMcCarver	1	1	1	0	0	0
Underwood,p	0	0	0	0	0	0
Lonborg,p	0	0	0	0	0	0
Boone,c	6	1	3	8	0	0
Carlton,p	1	0	0	0	0	0
Schueler,p	0	0	0	0	0	0
Garber,p	0	0	0	0	0	0
aHutton	0	0	0	0	0	0
Reed,p	0	0	0	0	0	0
bMartin	1	0	0	0	0	0
Twitchell,p	0	0	0	0	0	0
cTolan,cf	3	2	2	0	0	0
Totals	50	18	24	30	6	0

Chicago	AB	R	H	PO	A	E
Monday,cf	6	3	4	4	0	0
Cardenal,lf	5	1	1	1	0	0
Summers,lf	0	0	0	3	0	0
dMitterwald	1	0	0	0	0	0
Wallis,lf	1	0	0	0	0	0
Madlock,3b	7	2	3	0	0	0
Morales,rf	5	2	1	1	0	0
Thornton,1b	4	3	1	10	1	0
Trillo,2b	5	0	2	2	3	0
Swisher,c	6	1	3	5	0	0
Rosello,ss	4	1	2	2	3	0
Kelleher,ss	2	0	1	1	1	0
R.Reuschel,p	1	2	0	1	3	0
Garman,p	0	0	0	0	0	0
Knowles,p	0	0	0	0	1	0
P.Reuschel,p	0	0	0	0	0	0
Schultz,p	0	0	0	0	2	0
fAdams	1	1	1	0	0	0
Totals	48	16	19	30	14	0

Philadelphia ....0 1 0 1 2 0 3 5 3 3—18
Chicago ....0 7 5 1 0 0 0 0 2 1—16

a Walked for Garber in fourth.
b Grounded out for Reed in sixth.
c Singled for Twitchell in eighth.
d Struck out for Summers in eighth.
e Singled for McGraw in 10th.
f Doubled for Schultz in 10th.

Runs batted in: Cash 2, Bowa, Johnstone 2, Luzinski, Allen 2, Schmidt 8, Maddox, Monday 4, Madlock 3, Thornton, Trillo 3, Swisher 4, Rosello.
Doubles: Cardenal, Madlock, Thornton, Boone, Adams.
Triples: Johnstone, Bowa.
Home runs: Maddox, Swisher, Monday 2, Schmidt 4, Boone.
Sacrifice hits: R.Reuschel, Johnstone.
Sacrifice flies: Luzinski, Cash.
Double plays: Trillo, Rosello and Thornton; Schmidt, Cash and Allen.
Left on bases: Philadelphia 8, Chicago 12.

Philadelphia	IP	H	R	ER	BB	SO
Carlton	1⅔	7	7	7	2	1
Schueler	⅔	3	3	3	0	0
Garber	⅔	2	2	2	1	1
Reed	2	1	1	1	1	1
Twitchell	2	0	0	0	1	1
McGraw (W)	2	4	2	2	1	2
Underwood	⅔	2	1	1	0	1
Lonborg (S)	⅓	0	0	0	0	0

Chicago	IP	H	R	ER	BB	SO
R.Reuschel	7	14	7	7	1	4
Garman	⅔	4	5	5	1	1
Knowles (L)	1⅓	3	4	4	1	0
P.Reuschel	0	3	2	2	0	0
Schultz	1	0	0	0	0	0

Knowles pitched to one batter in 10th.
P.Reuschel pitched to two batters in 10th.
Hit by pitcher: R. Reuschel (by Schueler), Thornton (by Garber), Monday (by Twitchell).
Balk: Schultz.

Umpires: Vargo, Olsen, Davidson, Rennert.
Time: 3:42. **Attendance:** 28,287.

BOB HORNER

July 6, 1986, at Atlanta

Atlanta first baseman Horner became the first four-homer man in 10 years and the first to accomplish the feat during a loss. The Expos defeated the Braves, 11-8.

Montreal	AB	R	H	PO	A	E
Webster,lf	6	2	5	1	0	0
Wright,cf	6	1	2	4	0	0
Dawson,rf	6	1	2	2	0	0
Brooks,ss	5	1	2	1	3	0
Wallach,3b	2	1	0	1	3	1
Galarraga,1b	2	0	0	4	1	0
Krenchicki,1b	1	0	1	3	0	0
Reardon,p	0	0	0	0	0	0
Fitzgerald,c	3	2	1	4	0	0
Newman,2b	4	3	2	5	3	0
McGaffigan,p	2	0	1	1	0	0
Burke,p	1	0	0	0	0	0
Law,1b	1	0	0	1	0	0
Totals	39	11	16	27	10	1

Atlanta	AB	R	H	PO	A	E
Moreno,rf	4	0	1	2	0	0
dSimmons,3b	1	0	0	0	0	0
Oberkfell,3b-2b	5	1	4	2	4	0
Murphy,cf	5	0	0	2	0	0
Horner,1b	5	4	4	8	1	1
Griffey,lf	5	0	2	0	0	0
Thomas,ss	4	0	1	0	4	0
Virgil,c	4	1	1	6	1	0
Hubbard,2b	3	1	1	6	2	0
bChambliss	0	0	0	0	0	0
Garber,p	0	0	0	0	0	0
Smith,p	1	0	0	0	1	0
Dedmon,p	0	1	0	0	0	0
aSample	1	0	0	0	0	0
Assenmacher,p	0	0	0	0	0	0
cRamirez,rf	1	0	0	1	0	0
Totals	39	8	14	27	13	1

Montreal...................0 0 1 3 6 0 1 0 0—11
Atlanta ....0 1 0 1 5 0 0 0 1— 8

a Grounded out for Dedmon in sixth.
b Walked for Hubbard in eighth.
c Struck out for Assenmacher in eighth.
d Grounded out for Moreno in eighth.

Runs batted in: Webster 3, Wright, Dawson 2, Fitzgerald 2, Newman 2, McGaffigan, Oberkfell, Horner 6, Hubbard.
Doubles: Dawson, Webster, Fitzgerald, Wright, Brooks, Virgil, Hubbard, Krenchicki.
Home runs: Horner 4, Newman, Webster, Dawson.
Sacrifice hits: McGaffigan, Dedmon, Krenchicki.
Stolen bases: Webster, Griffey.
Passed ball: Virgil.
Double plays: Brooks, Newman and Galarraga; Oberkfell and Horner; Wallach, Newman and Law.
Left on bases: Montreal 10, Atlanta 6.

Montreal	IP	H	R	ER	BB	SO
McGaffigan	4⅔	8	7	4	0	2
Burke (W)	2⅔	4	0	0	1	1
Reardon (S)	1⅔	2	1	1	0	1

Atlanta	IP	H	R	ER	BB	SO
Smith (L)	4	9	8	8	2	3
Dedmon	2	4	2	2	1	2
Assenmacher	2	2	1	1	2	1
Garber	1	1	0	0	0	0

Smith pitched to four batters in fifth.
Hit by pitcher: Galarraga (by Dedmon), Fitzgerald (by Dedmon).

Umpires: Poncino, Gregg, Davis, Harvey.
Time: 3:06. **Attendance:** 18,153.

Atlanta third baseman Bob Horner became the first modern big-league player to hit four home runs in a game his team lost.

MARK WHITEN

September 7, 1993, at Cincinnati

St. Louis outfielder Whiten doubled his pleasure by matching the Major League single-game records for homers and RBIs (12). His outburst came in the second game of a doubleheader after he had gone hitless in the opener.

St. Louis	AB	R	H	PO	A	E
Pena,2b	3	1	1	2	3	0
Maclin,lf	4	1	0	2	0	0
Gilkey,rf	5	1	1	3	0	0
Zeile,3b	2	3	1	0	0	1
Royer,3b	1	0	0	0	1	0
Perry,1b	4	4	3	8	0	0
Whiten,cf	5	4	4	5	0	0
Pagnozzi,c	5	0	1	4	0	1
Cromer,ss	5	0	0	2	4	0
Tewksbury,p	2	1	0	1	2	0
Totals	36	15	11	27	10	2

Cincinnati	AB	R	H	PO	A	E
Howard,lf	3	1	0	2	0	0
Dibble,p	0	0	0	0	0	0
Brumfield,cf	4	1	2	4	0	0
Morris,1b	2	0	1	5	0	0
Daugherty,rf	1	0	1	0	0	0
Sabo,3b	3	0	0	2	2	0
Varsho,lf	1	0	0	0	0	0
Costo,rf-3b	4	0	1	2	0	0
Samuel,2b	4	0	0	1	1	0
Wilson,c	4	0	0	10	1	0
Branson,ss	4	0	1	0	2	0
Luebbers,p	1	0	0	0	1	0
aTubbs	1	0	0	0	0	0
Anderson,p	0	0	0	0	0	0
Bushing,p	0	0	0	0	0	0
bDorsett,1b	2	0	1	1	0	0
Totals	34	2	7	27	7	0

St. Louis....................4 0 0 0 1 3 4 1 2—15
Cincinnati ....2 0 0 0 0 0 0 0 0— 2

a Grounded out for Luebbers in fifth.
b Singled for Bushing in seventh.

Runs batted in: Pena, Maclin, Perry, Whiten 12, Morris.
Double: Brumfield.
Home runs: Pena, Whiten 4.
Sacrifice hit: Pena.
Sacrifice flies: Maclin, Morris.
Stolen base: Maclin, Brumfield.
Left on bases: St. Louis 2, Cincinnati 7.

St. Louis	IP	H	R	ER	BB	SO
Tewksbury (W)	9	7	2	2	1	4

Cincinnati	IP	H	R	ER	BB	SO
Luebbers (L)	5	2	5	5	4	3
Anderson	1⅔	6	7	7	2	2
Bushing	⅓	0	0	0	0	0
Dibble	2	3	3	3	0	5

Wild pitch: Luebbers.

Umpires: Marsh, Kellog, Vanover, Wendelstedt.
Time: 2:17.

MEMORABLE PERFORMANCES

BABE RUTH'S 60 HOME RUNS—1927

HR No.	Team game No.	Date	Opposing pitcher, Club	Place	Inn.	On base
1.	4	April 15	Howard Ehmke (righthander), Philadelphia	H	1	0
2.	11	April 23	Rube Walberg (lefthander), Philadelphia	A	1	0
3.	12	April 24	Sloppy Thurston (righthander), Washington	A	6	0
4.	14	April 29	Slim Harriss (righthander), Boston	A	5	0
5.	16	May 1	Jack Quinn (righthander), Philadelphia	H	1	1
6.	16	May 1	Rube Walberg (lefthander), Philadelphia	H	8	0
7.	24	May 10	Milt Gaston (righthander), St. Louis	A	1	2
8.	25	May 11	Ernie Nevers (righthander), St. Louis	A	1	1
9.	29	May 17	Rip H. Collins (righthander), Detroit	A	8	0
10.	33	May 22	Benn Karr (righthander), Cleveland	A	6	1
11.	34	May 23	Sloppy Thurston (righthander), Washington	A	1	0
12.	37	May *28	Sloppy Thurston (righthander), Washington	H	7	2
13.	39	May 29	Danny MacFayden (righthander), Boston	H	8	0
14.	41	May ‡30	Rube Walberg (lefthander), Philadelphia	A	11	0
15.	42	May *31	Jack Quinn (righthander), Philadelphia	A	1	1
16.	43	May †31	Howard Ehmke (righthander), Philadelphia	A	5	1
17.	47	June 5	Earl Whitehill (lefthander), Detroit	H	6	0
18.	48	June 7	Tommy Thomas (righthander), Chicago	H	4	0
19.	52	June 11	Garland Buckeye (lefthander), Cleveland	H	3	1
20.	52	June 11	Garland Buckeye (lefthander), Cleveland	H	5	0
21.	53	June 12	George Uhle (righthander), Cleveland	H	7	0
22.	55	June 16	Tom Zachary (lefthander), St. Louis	H	1	1
23.	60	June *22	Hal Wiltse (lefthander), Boston	A	5	0
24.	60	June *22	Hal Wiltse (lefthander), Boston	A	7	1
25.	70	June 30	Slim Harriss (righthander), Boston	H	4	1
26.	73	July 3	Hod Lisenbee (righthander), Washington	A	1	0
27.	78	July †8	Don Hankins (righthander), Detroit	A	2	2
28.	79	July *9	Ken Holloway (righthander), Detroit	A	1	1
29.	79	July *9	Ken Holloway (righthander), Detroit	A	4	2
30.	83	July 12	Joe Shaute (lefthander), Cleveland	A	9	1
31.	94	July 24	Tommy Thomas (righthander), Chicago	A	3	0
32.	95	July *26	Milt Gaston (righthander), St. Louis	H	1	1
33.	95	July *26	Milt Gaston (righthander), St. Louis	H	6	0
34.	98	July 28	Lefty Stewart (lefthander), St. Louis	H	8	1
35.	106	Aug. 5	George S. Smith (righthander), Detroit	H	8	0
36.	110	Aug. 10	Tom Zachary (lefthander), Washington	A	3	2
37.	114	Aug. 16	Tommy Thomas (righthander), Chicago	A	5	0
38.	115	Aug. 17	Sarge Connally (righthander), Chicago	A	11	0
39.	118	Aug. 20	Jake Miller (lefthander), Cleveland	A	1	1
40.	120	Aug. 22	Joe Shaute (lefthander), Cleveland	A	6	0
41.	124	Aug. 27	Ernie Nevers (righthander), St. Louis	A	8	1
42.	125	Aug. 28	Ernie Wingard (lefthander), St. Louis	A	1	1
43.	127	Aug. 31	Tony Welzer (righthander), Boston	H	8	0
44.	128	Sept. 2	Rube Walberg (lefthander), Philadelphia	A	1	0
45.	132	Sept. *6	Tony Welzer (righthander), Boston	A	6	2
46.	132	Sept. *6	Tony Welzer (righthander), Boston	A	7	1
47.	133	Sept. †6	Jack Russell (righthander), Boston	A	9	0
48.	134	Sept. 7	Danny MacFayden (righthander), Boston	A	1	0
49.	134	Sept. 7	Slim Harriss (righthander), Boston	A	8	1
50.	138	Sept. 11	Milt Gaston (righthander), St. Louis	H	4	0
51.	139	Sept. *13	Willis Hudlin (righthander), Cleveland	H	7	1
52.	140	Sept. †13	Joe Shaute (lefthander), Cleveland	H	4	0
53.	143	Sept. 16	Ted Blankenship (righthander), Chicago	H	3	0
54.	147	Sept. †18	Ted Lyons (righthander), Chicago	H	5	1
55.	148	Sept. 21	Sam Gibson (righthander), Detroit	H	9	0
56.	149	Sept. 22	Ken Holloway (righthander), Detroit	H	9	1
57.	152	Sept. 27	Lefty Grove (lefthander), Philadelphia	H	6	3
58.	153	Sept. 29	Hod Lisenbee (righthander), Washington	H	1	0
59.	153	Sept. 29	Paul Hopkins (righthander), Washington	H	5	3
60.	154	Sept. 30	Tom Zachary (lefthander), Washington	H	8	1

*First game of doubleheader. †Second game of doubleheader. ‡Afternoon game of split doubleheader. New York A.L. played 155 games in 1927 (one tie on April 14), with Ruth participating in 151 games. (No home run for Ruth in game No. 155 on October 1.)

ROGER MARIS' 61 HOME RUNS—1961

HR No.	Team game No.	Date	Opposing pitcher, Club	Place	Inn.	On base
1.	11	April 26	Paul Foytack (righthander), Detroit	A	5	0
2.	17	May 3	Pedro Ramos (righthander), Minnesota	A	7	2
3.	20	May 6	Eli Grba (righthander), Los Angeles	A	5	0
4.	29	May 17	Pete Burnside (lefthander), Washington	H	8	1
5.	30	May 19	Jim Perry (righthander), Cleveland	A	1	1
6.	31	May 20	Gary Bell (righthander), Cleveland	A	3	0
7.	32	May *21	Chuck Estrada (righthander), Baltimore	H	1	0
8.	35	May 24	Gene Conley (righthander), Boston	H	4	1
9.	38	May *28	Cal McLish (righthander), Chicago	H	2	1
10.	40	May 30	Gene Conley (righthander), Boston	A	3	0
11.	40	May 30	Mike Fornieles (righthander), Boston	A	8	2
12.	41	May 31	Billy Muffett (righthander), Boston	A	3	0
13.	43	June 2	Cal McLish (righthander), Chicago	A	3	2
14.	44	June 3	Bob Shaw (righthander), Chicago	A	8	2
15.	45	June 4	Russ Kemmerer (righthander), Chicago	A	3	0
16.	48	June 6	Ed Palmquist (righthander), Minnesota	H	6	2
17.	49	June 7	Pedro Ramos (righthander), Minnesota	H	3	2
18.	52	June 9	Ray Herbert (righthander), Kansas City	H	7	1
19.	55	June †11	Eli Grba (righthander), Los Angeles	H	3	0
20.	55	June †11	Johnny James (righthander), Los Angeles	H	7	0
21.	57	June 13	Jim Perry (righthander), Cleveland	A	6	0
22.	58	June 14	Gary Bell (righthander), Cleveland	A	4	1
23.	61	June 17	Don Mossi (lefthander), Detroit	A	4	0
24.	62	June 18	Jerry Casale (righthander), Detroit	A	8	1
25.	63	June 19	Jim Archer (lefthander), Kansas City	A	9	0
26.	64	June 20	Joe Nuxhall (lefthander), Kansas City	A	1	0
27.	66	June 22	Norm Bass (righthander), Kansas City	A	2	1
28.	74	July 1	Dave Sisler (righthander), Washington	H	9	1
29.	75	July 2	Pete Burnside (lefthander), Washington	H	3	2
30.	75	July 2	Johnny Klippstein (righthander), Washington	H	7	1
31.	77	July †4	Frank Lary (righthander), Detroit	H	8	1
32.	78	July 5	Frank Funk (righthander), Cleveland	H	7	0
33.	82	July *9	Bill Monbouquette (righthander), Boston	H	7	0
34.	84	July 13	Early Wynn (righthander), Chicago	A	1	1
35.	86	July 15	Ray Herbert (righthander), Chicago	A	3	0
36.	92	July 21	Bill Monbouquette (righthander), Boston	A	1	0
37.	95	July *25	Frank Baumann (lefthander), Chicago	H	4	1
38.	95	July *25	Don Larsen (righthander), Chicago	H	8	0
39.	96	July †25	Russ Kemmerer (righthander), Chicago	H	4	0
40.	96	July †25	Warren Hacker (righthander), Chicago	H	6	2
41.	106	Aug. 4	Camilo Pascual (righthander), Minnesota	H	1	2
42.	114	Aug. 11	Pete Burnside (lefthander), Washington	A	5	0
43.	115	Aug. 12	Dick Donovan (righthander), Washington	A	4	0
44.	116	Aug. *13	Bennie Daniels (righthander), Washington	A	4	0
45.	117	Aug. †13	Marty Kutyna (righthander), Washington	A	1	1
46.	118	Aug. 15	Juan Pizarro (lefthander), Chicago	H	4	0
47.	119	Aug. 16	Billy Pierce (lefthander), Chicago	H	1	1
48.	119	Aug. 16	Billy Pierce (lefthander), Chicago	H	3	1
49.	124	Aug. *20	Jim Perry (righthander), Cleveland	A	3	1
50.	125	Aug. 22	Ken McBride (righthander), Los Angeles	A	6	1
51.	129	Aug. 26	Jerry Walker (righthander), Kansas City	A	6	0
52.	135	Sept. 2	Frank Lary (righthander), Detroit	H	6	0
53.	135	Sept. 2	Hank Aguirre (lefthander), Detroit	H	8	1
54.	140	Sept. 6	Tom Cheney (righthander), Washington	H	4	0
55.	141	Sept. 7	Dick Stigman (lefthander), Cleveland	H	3	0
56.	143	Sept. 9	Mudcat Grant (righthander), Cleveland	H	7	0
57.	151	Sept. 16	Frank Lary (righthander), Detroit	A	3	1
58.	152	Sept. 17	Terry Fox (righthander), Detroit	A	12	1
59.	155	Sept. 20	Milt Pappas (righthander), Baltimore	A	3	0
60.	159	Sept. 26	Jack Fisher (righthander), Baltimore	H	3	0
61.	163	Oct. 1	Tracy Stallard (righthander), Boston	H	4	0

*First game of doubleheader. †Second game of doubleheader. New York played 163 games in 1961 (one tie on April 22). Maris did not hit a home run in this game. Maris played in 161 games.

MARK McGWIRE'S 70 HOME RUNS—1998

HR No.	Team game No.	Date	Opposing pitcher, Club	Place	Inn.	On base
1.	1	March 31	Ramon Martinez (righthander), Los Angeles	H	5	3
2.	2	April 2	Frank Lankford (righthander), Los Angeles	H	12	2
3.	3	April 3	Mark Langston (lefthander), San Diego	H	5	1
4.	4	April 4	Don Wengert (righthander), San Diego	H	6	2
5.	13	April 14	Jeff Suppan (righthander), Arizona	H	3	1
6.	13	April 14	Jeff Suppan (righthander), Arizona	H	5	0
7.	13	April 14	Barry Manuel (righthander), Arizona	H	8	1
8.	15	April 17	Matt Whiteside (righthander), Philadelphia	H	4	1
9.	19	April 21	Trey Moore (lefthander), Montreal	A	3	1
10.	23	April 25	Jerry Spradlin (righthander), Philadelphia	A	7	1
11.	27	April 30	Marc Pisciotta (righthander), Chicago	A	8	1
12.	28	May 1	Rod Beck (righthander), Chicago	A	9	1
13.	34	May 8	Rick Reed (righthander), New York	A	3	1
14.	36	May 12	Paul Wagner (righthander), Milwaukee	H	5	2
15.	38	May 14	Kevin Millwood (righthander), Atlanta	H	4	0
16.	40	May 16	Livan Hernandez (righthander), Florida	H	4	0
17.	42	May 18	Jesus Sanchez (lefthander), Florida	H	4	0
18.	43	May 19	Tyler Green (righthander), Philadelphia	A	3	1
19.	43	May 19	Tyler Green (righthander), Philadelphia	A	5	1
20.	43	May 19	Wayne Gomes (righthander), Philadelphia	A	8	1
21.	46	May 22	Mark Gardner (righthander), San Francisco	H	6	1
22.	47	May 23	Rich Rodriguez (lefthander), San Francisco	H	4	0
23.	47	May 23	John Johnstone (righthander), San Francisco	H	5	2
24.	48	May 24	Robb Nen (righthander), San Francisco	H	12	1
25.	49	May 25	John Thomson (righthander), Colorado	H	1	0
26.	52	May 29	Dan Miceli (righthander), San Diego	A	9	1
27.	53	May 30	Andy Ashby (righthander), San Diego	A	1	0
28.	59	June 5	Orel Hershiser (righthander), San Fran.	H	1	1
29.	62	June 8	Jason Bere (righthander), Chicago AL	A	4	1
30.	64	June 10	Jim Parque (lefthander), Chicago AL	A	3	2
31.	65	June 12	Andy Benes (righthander), Arizona	A	3	3
32.	69	June 17	Jose Lima (righthander), Houston	A	3	0
33.	70	June 18	Shane Reynolds (righthander), Houston	A	5	0
34.	76	June 24	Jaret Wright (righthander), Cleveland AL	A	4	0
35.	77	June 25	Dave Burba (righthander), Cleveland AL	A	1	0
36.	79	June 27	Mike Trombley (righthander), Minnesota AL	A	7	1
37.	81	June 30	Glendon Rusch (lefthander), Kansas City AL	A	7	0
38.	89	July 11	Billy Wagner (lefthander), Houston	H	11	1
39.	90	July 12	Sean Bergman (righthander), Houston	H	1	0
40.	90	July 12	Scott Elarton (righthander), Houston	H	7	0
41.	95	July 17	Brian Bohanon (lefthander), Los Angeles	H	1	0
42.	95	July 17	Antonio Osuna (righthander), Los Angeles	H	8	0
43.	98	July 20	Brian Boehringer (righthander), San Diego	A	5	1
44.	104	July 26	John Thomson (righthander), Colorado	A	4	0
45.	105	July 28	Mike Myers (lefthander), Milwaukee	H	8	0
46.	115	Aug. 8	Mark Clark (righthander), Chicago	H	4	0
47.	118	Aug. 11	Bobby Jones (righthander), New York	H	4	0
48.	124	Aug. 19	Matt Karchner (righthander), Chicago	A	8	0
49.	124	Aug. 19	Terry Mulholland (lefthander), Chicago	A	10	0
50.	125	Aug. *20	Willie Blair (righthander), New York	A	7	0

FOR THE RECORD

HR No.	Team game No.	Date	Opposing pitcher, Club	Place	Inn.	On base
51.	126	Aug. †20	Rick Reed (righthander), New York	A	1	0
52.	129	Aug. 22	Francisco Cordova (righthander), Pitt.	A	1	0
53.	130	Aug. 23	Ricardo Rincon (lefthander), Pittsburgh	A	8	0
54.	133	Aug. 26	Justin Speier (righthander), Florida	H	8	1
55.	137	Aug. 30	Dennis Martinez (righthander), Atlanta	H	7	2
56.	139	Sept. 1	Livan Hernandez (righthander), Florida	A	7	0
57.	139	Sept. 1	Donn Pall (righthander), Florida	A	9	0
58.	140	Sept. 2	Brian Edmondson (righthander), Florida	A	7	1
59.	140	Sept. 2	Rob Stanifer (righthander), Florida	A	8	1
60.	142	Sept. 5	Dennis Reyes (lefthander), Cincinnati	H	1	1
61.	144	Sept. 7	Mike Morgan (righthander), Chicago	H	1	0
62.	145	Sept. 8	Steve Trachsel (righthander), Chicago	H	4	0
63.	152	Sept. *15	Jason Christiansen (lefthander), Pitt.	H	9	0
64.	155	Sept. 18	Rafael Roque (lefthander), Milwaukee	A	4	1
65.	157	Sept. 20	Scott Karl (lefthander), Milwaukee	A	1	1
66.	161	Sept. 25	Shayne Bennett (righthander), Montreal	H	5	1
67.	162	Sept. 26	Dustin Hermanson (righthander), Montreal	H	4	0
68.	162	Sept. 26	Kirk Bullinger (righthander), Montreal	H	7	1
69.	163	Sept. 27	Mike Thurman (righthander), Montreal	H	3	0
70.	163	Sept. 27	Carl Pavano (righthander), Montreal	H	7	2

*First game of doubleheader. †Second game of doubleheader. St. Louis played 163 games in 1998 (one tie on Aug. 24). McGwire played in 155 games.

SAMMY SOSA'S 66 HOME RUNS—1998

HR No.	Team game No.	Date	Opposing pitcher, Club	Place	Inn.	On base
1.	5	April 4	Marc Valdes (righthander), Montreal	H	3	0
2.	11	April 11	Anthony Telford (righthander), Montreal	A	7	0
3.	14	April 15	Dennis Cook (lefthander), New York	A	8	0
4.	21	April 23	Dan Miceli (righthander), San Diego	H	9	0
5.	22	April 24	Ismael Valdes (righthander), Los Angeles	A	1	0
6.	25	April 27	Joe Hamilton (righthander), San Diego	A	1	1
7.	30	May 3	Cliff Politte (righthander), St. Louis	H	1	0
8.	42	May 16	Scott Sullivan (righthander), Cincinnati	A	3	2
9.	47	May 22	Greg Maddux (righthander), Atlanta	A	1	0
10.	50	May 25	Kevin Millwood (righthander), Atlanta	A	4	0
11.	50	May 25	Mike Cather (righthander), Atlanta	A	8	2
12.	51	May 27	Darrin Winston (righthander), Phil.	H	8	0
13.	51	May 27	Wayne Gomes (righthander), Philadelphia	H	9	1
14.	56	June 1	Ryan Dempster (righthander), Florida	H	1	1
15.	56	June 1	Oscar Henriquez (righthander), Florida	H	8	2
16.	58	June 3	Livan Hernandez (righthander), Florida	H	5	1
17.	59	June 5	Jim Parque (lefthander), Chicago AL	H	5	1
18.	60	June 6	Carlos Castillo (righthander), Chi. AL	H	7	0
19.	61	June 7	James Baldwin (righthander), Chicago AL	H	5	2
20.	62	June 8	LaTroy Hawkins (righthander), Minn. AL	A	3	0
21.	66	June 13	Mark Portugal (righthander), Phil.	A	6	1
22.	68	June 15	Cal Eldred (righthander), Milwaukee	H	1	0
23.	68	June 15	Cal Eldred (righthander), Milwaukee	H	3	0
24.	68	June 15	Cal Eldred (righthander), Milwaukee	H	7	0
25.	70	June 17	Bronswell Patrick (righthander), Milw.	H	4	0
26.	72	June 19	Carlton Loewer (righthander), Phil.	H	1	0
27.	72	June 19	Carlton Loewer (righthander), Phil.	H	5	1
28.	73	June 20	Matt Beech (lefthander), Philadelphia	H	3	1
29.	73	June 20	Toby Borland (righthander), Philadelphia	H	6	2
30.	74	June 21	Tyler Green (righthander), Philadelphia	H	4	0
31.	77	June 24	Seth Greisinger (righthander), Det. AL	A	1	0
32.	78	June 25	Brian Moehler (righthander), Detroit AL	A	7	0
33.	82	June 30	Alan Embree (lefthander), Arizona	H	8	0
34.	88	July 9	Jeff Juden (righthander), Milwaukee	A	2	1
35.	89	July 10	Scott Karl (lefthander), Milwaukee	A	2	0
36.	95	July 17	Kirt Ojala (lefthander), Florida	A	6	1
37.	100	July 22	Miguel Batista (righthander), Montreal	H	8	2
38.	105	July 26	Rick Reed (righthander), New York	H	6	1
39.	106	July 27	Willie Blair (righthander), Arizona	A	6	1
40.	106	July 27	Alan Embree (lefthander), Arizona	A	8	3
41.	107	July 28	Bob Wolcott (righthander), Arizona	A	5	3
42.	110	July 31	Jamey Wright (righthander), Colorado	H	1	0
43.	115	Aug. 5	Andy Benes (righthander), Arizona	H	3	1
44.	117	Aug. 8	Rich Croushore (righthander), St. Louis	A	9	1
45.	119	Aug. 10	Russ Ortiz (righthander), San Francisco	A	5	0
46.	119	Aug. 10	Chris Brock (righthander), San Francisco	A	7	0
47.	124	Aug. 16	Sean Bergman (righthander), Houston	A	4	0
48.	126	Aug. 19	Kent Bottenfield (righthander), St.L.	H	5	1
49.	128	Aug. 21	Orel Hershiser (righthander), San Fran.	H	5	1
50.	130	Aug. 23	Jose Lima (righthander), Houston	H	5	0
51.	130	Aug. 23	Jose Lima (righthander), Houston	H	8	0
52.	133	Aug. 26	Brett Tomko (righthander), Cincinnati	A	3	0
53.	135	Aug. 28	John Thomson (righthander), Colorado	A	1	0
54.	137	Aug. 30	Darryl Kile (righthander), Colorado	A	1	1
55.	138	Aug. 31	Brett Tomko (righthander), Cincinnati	H	3	1
56.	140	Sept. 2	Jason Bere (righthander), Cincinnati	H	6	0
57.	141	Sept. 4	Jason Schmidt (righthander), Pittsburgh	A	1	0
58.	142	Sept. 5	Sean Lawrence (lefthander), Pittsburgh	A	6	0
59.	148	Sept. 11	Bill Pulphiser (lefthander), Milwaukee	H	5	0
60.	149	Sept. 12	Valerio de los Santos (lefthander), Mil.	H	7	2
61.	150	Sept. 13	Bronswell Patrick (righthander), Milw.	H	5	1
62.	150	Sept. 13	Eric Plunk (righthander), Milwaukee	H	9	0
63.	153	Sept. 16	Brian Boehringer (righthander), S.D.	A	8	3
64.	159	Sept. 23	Rafael Roque (lefthander), Milwaukee	A	5	0
65.	159	Sept. 23	Rod Henderson (righthander), Milwaukee	A	6	0
66.	160	Sept. 25	Jose Lima (righthander), Houston	A	4	0

'First game of doubleheader. †Second game of doubleheader. Chicago played 163 games in 1998 playoff game on Sept. 28). Sosa played in 159 games.

HACK WILSON'S 191 RBIs, 56 HOME RUNS—1930

Date		Result	Site	AB	H	HR	RBI	HR Total	RBI Total
April	15	Cubs 9, Cardinals 8	A	4	1	0	1	0	1
	21	Cubs 9, Reds 1	A	5	1	1	3	1	4
	22	Cardinals 8, Cubs 3	H	4	1	1	3	2	7
	25*	Cubs 6, Reds 5	H	5	3	1	2	3	9
	28	Cubs 7, Pirates 4	H	2	1	0	1	3	10
	30	Cubs 5, Pirates 2	H	4	1	1	1	4	11
May	4	Cubs 8, Phillies 7	H	3	3	0	2	4	13
	6	Cubs 3, Dodgers 1	H	3	1	1	2	5	15
	7	Cubs 9, Dodgers 5	H	4	2	0	4	5	19
	8	Cubs 7, Dodgers 4	H	4	2	1	1	6	20
	9	Cubs 6, Giants 5	H	4	3	0	2	6	22
	10	Giants 9, Cubs 4	H	3	2	1	3	7	25
	12	Giants 14, Cubs 12	H	2	1	1	1	8	26
	13	Cubs 9, Braves 8	H	2	1	1	3	9	29
	15	Braves 10, Cubs 8	H	5	2	0	2	9	31
	18†	Cubs 9, Cardinals 6	A	3	2	2	3	11	34
	20	Cardinals 16, Cubs 3	A	4	1	1	1	12	35
	22	Cubs 12, Pirates 5	A	4	2	0	1	12	36
	24	Cubs 5, Pirates 3	A	4	1	0	1	12	37
	26	Reds 8, Cubs 2	H	4	1	1	2	13	39
	28	Cubs 6, Reds 5	H	3	1	0	2	13	41
	30‡	Cubs 9, Cardinals 8	H	3	1	1	1	14	42
	31	Cubs 6, Cardinals 5	H	5	1	0	2	14	44
June	1	Cubs 16, Pirates 4	H	5	4	2	5	16	49
	3	Cubs 15, Braves 2	A	4	1	0	1	16	50
	4	Cubs 18, Braves 10	A	5	2	0	1	16	51
	5	Cubs 10, Braves 7	A	6	2	1	1	17	52
	6	Cubs 13, Dodgers 0	A	5	2	0	1	17	53
	7	Dodgers 12, Cubs 9	A	4	1	1	2	18	55
	10	Phillies 6, Cubs 2	A	2	1	0	1	18	56
	12	Phillies 5, Cubs 3	A	2	1	0	2	18	58
	14	Cubs 8, Giants 5	A	3	1	0	2	18	60
	16	Cubs 8, Giants 5	A	4	1	0	1	18	61
	19	Cubs 10, Braves 4	H	4	1	1	3	19	64
	21*†	Cubs 5, Braves 4	H	5	3	1	2	20	66
	22	Braves 3, Cubs 2	H	4	1	1	1	21	67
	23	Cubs 21, Phillies 8	H	6	5	1	5	22	72
	24	Cubs 6, Phillies 1	H	5	2	0	1	22	73
July	1	Giants 7, Cubs 5	H	3	2	1	1	23	74
	2	Giants 9, Cubs 8	H	5	2	0	2	23	76
	4‡	Pirates 5, Cubs 1	A	3	0	0	1	23	77
	5	Cubs 12, Pirates 3	A	4	3	0	3	23	80
	6†	Reds 5, Cubs 4	A	3	2	1	1	24	81
	6‡	Reds 8, Cubs 7	A	4	2	0	1	24	82
	16†	Cubs 6, Dodgers 4	A	3	1	0	2	24	84
	18	Cubs 6, Dodgers 2	A	5	3	1	1	25	85
	19	Cubs 5, Dodgers 4	A	3	1	1	2	26	87
	20	Giants 13, Cubs 5	A	4	1	1	1	27	88
	21	Cubs 6, Giants 0	A	5	2	2	3	29	91
	24	Cubs 19, Phillies 15	A	5	2	0	1	29	92
	25	Cubs 9, Phillies 5	A	3	1	0	1	29	93
	26	Cubs 16, Phillies 2	A	5	3	3	5	32	98
	27	Reds 6, Cubs 5	A	2	1	0	1	32	99
	28†	Cubs 3, Reds 2	H	4	1	0	2	32	101
	28‡	Cubs 5, Reds 3	H	4	1	0	1	32	102
	29	Reds 4, Cubs 3	H	3	1	1	2	33	104
Aug.	1	Cubs 10, Pirates 7	H	3	1	0	2	33	106
	2	Pirates 14, Cubs 8	H	5	2	1	1	34	107
	3	Pirates 12, Cubs 8	H	4	2	1	2	35	109
	5	Cubs 5, Cardinals 4	A	3	1	1	2	36	112
	7	Cubs 6, Cardinals 5	A	3	2	0	3	36	114
	10†	Cubs 6, Braves 0	H	4	2	2	4	38	118
	10‡	Cubs 17, Braves 1	H	4	2	1	3	39	121
	13	Dodgers 15, Cubs 5	H	4	2	1	2	40	123
	14	Cubs 5, Dodgers 1	H	3	2	0	2	40	125
	15§	Cubs 4, Dodgers 3	H	4	1	0	1	40	126
	16†	Cubs 10, Phillies 9	H	5	2	1	3	41	129
	17	Cubs 5, Phillies 4	H	3	1	0	2	41	131
	18	Cubs 17, Phillies 3	H	5	4	1	4	42	135
	19†	Phillies 9, Cubs 8	H	4	3	1	1	43	136
	20	Phillies 10, Cubs 8	H	2	0	0	2	43	138
	21	Giants 13, Cubs 6	H	5	1	0	2	43	140
	22	Cubs 12, Giants 4	H	3	1	0	1	43	141
	23	Cubs 4, Giants 2	H	3	1	0	3	43	144
	26	Cubs 7, Pirates 5	H	3	2	1	4	44	148
	27	Pirates 10, Cubs 8	H	5	2	0	3	44	151
	30	Cubs 16, Cardinals 4	H	3	3	2	6	46	156
Sept.	3	Pirates 9, Cubs 6	A	5	3	0	1	46	158
	4§	Cubs 10, Pirates 7	A	5	2	0	1	46	159
	5	Pirates 8, Cubs 7	A	5	0	0	1	46	160
	6	Cubs 19, Pirates 14	A	6	3	1	4	47	164
	11	Dodgers 2, Cubs 1	A	4	1	1	1	48	165
	12	Cubs 17, Phillies 4	A	5	5	1	6	49	171
	15†	Phillies 12, Cubs 11	A	5	2	0	1	49	172
	15‡	Cubs 6, Phillies 4	A	3	1	1	1	50	173
	17	Cubs 5, Giants 2	A	4	3	2	4	52	177
	19	Cubs 5, Braves 4	A	4	1	0	1	52	178
	20	Braves 3, Cubs 2	A	3	1	0	1	52	179
	22	Cubs 6, Braves 2	A	4	2	1	3	53	182
	26	Cubs 7, Reds 5	H	4	2	1	3	54	185
	27	Cubs 13, Reds 8	H	4	2	2	4	56	189
	28	Cubs 13, Reds 11	H	3	2	0	2	56	191

* 12 innings. †First game of doubleheader. ‡ Second game of doubleheader. § 10 innings.

JOE DiMAGGIO'S 56-GAME HITTING STREAK—1941

Date		Opposing pitcher, Club	AB	R	H	2B	3B	HR	RBI
May	15	Eddie Smith, Chicago	4	0	1	0	0	0	1
	16	Thornton Lee, Chicago	4	2	2	0	1	1	1
	17	Johnny Rigney, Chicago	3	1	1	0	0	0	0
	18	Bob Harris (2), Johnny Niggeling (1), St. Louis	3	3	3	1	0	0	1
	19	Denny Galehouse, St. Louis	3	0	1	1	0	0	0
	20	Eldon Auker, St. Louis	5	1	1	0	0	0	1
	21	Schoolboy Rowe (1), Al Benton (1), Detroit	5	0	2	0	0	0	1
	22	Archie McKain, Detroit	4	0	1	0	0	0	1
	23	Dick Newsome, Boston	5	0	1	0	0	0	2
	24	Earl Johnson, Boston	4	2	1	0	0	0	2
	25	Lefty Grove, Boston	4	0	1	0	0	0	0
	27	Ken Chase (1), Red Anderson (2), Alex Carrasquel (1), Washington	5	3	4	0	0	1	3
	28	Sid Hudson, Washington	4	1	1	0	1	0	0
	29	Steve Sundra, Washington	3	1	1	0	0	0	0
	30	Earl Johnson, Boston	2	1	1	0	0	0	0
	30	Mickey Harris, Boston	3	0	1	1	0	0	0
June	1	Al Milnar, Cleveland	4	1	1	0	0	0	0
	1	Mel Harder, Cleveland	4	0	1	0	0	0	0
	2	Bob Feller, Cleveland	4	2	2	1	0	0	0
	3	Dizzy Trout, Detroit	4	1	1	0	0	1	1
	5	Hal Newhouser, Detroit	5	1	1	0	1	0	1
	7	Bob Muncrief (1), Johnny Allen (1), George Caster (1), St. Louis	5	2	3	0	0	0	1
	8	Eldon Auker, St. Louis	4	3	2	0	0	2	4
	8	George Caster (1), Jack Kramer (1), St. Louis	4	1	2	1	0	1	3
	10	Johnny Rigney, Chicago	5	1	1	0	0	0	0
	12	Thornton Lee, Chicago	4	1	2	0	0	1	1
	14	Bob Feller, Cleveland	2	0	1	1	0	0	1
	15	Jim Bagby, Cleveland	3	1	1	0	0	1	1
	16	Al Milnar, Cleveland	5	0	1	1	0	0	0
	17	Johnny Rigney, Chicago	4	1	1	0	0	0	0
	18	Thornton Lee, Chicago	3	0	1	0	0	0	0
	19	Eddie Smith (1), Buck Ross (2), Chicago	3	2	3	0	0	1	2
	20	Bobo Newsom (2), Archie McKain (2), Detroit	5	3	4	1	0	0	1
	21	Dizzy Trout, Detroit	4	0	1	0	0	0	1
	22	Hal Newhouser (1), Bobo Newsom (1), Detroit	5	1	2	1	0	1	2
	24	Bob Muncrief, St. Louis	4	1	1	0	0	0	0
	25	Denny Galehouse, St. Louis	4	1	1	0	0	1	3
	26	Eldon Auker, St. Louis	4	0	1	1	0	0	1
	27	Chubby Dean, Philadelphia	3	1	2	0	0	1	2
	28	Johnny Babich (1), Lum Harris (1), Philadelphia	5	1	2	1	0	0	0
	29	Dutch E. Leonard, Washington	4	1	1	1	0	0	0
	29	Red Anderson, Washington	5	1	1	0	0	0	1
July	1	Mickey Harris (1), Mike Ryba (1), Boston	4	0	2	0	0	0	1
	1	Jack Wilson, Boston	3	1	1	0	0	0	1
	2	Dick Newsome, Boston	5	1	1	0	0	1	3
	5	Phil Marchildon, Philadelphia	4	2	1	0	0	1	2
	6	Johnny Babich (1), Bump Hadley (3), Phi.	5	2	4	1	0	0	2
	6	Jack Knott, Philadelphia	4	0	2	0	1	0	2
	10	Johnny Niggeling, St. Louis	2	0	1	0	0	0	0
	11	Bob Harris (3), Jack Kramer (1), St. Louis	5	1	4	0	0	1	2
	12	Eldon Auker (1), Bob Muncrief (1), St. Louis	5	1	2	1	0	0	1
	13	Ted Lyons (2), Jack Hallett (1), Chicago	4	2	3	0	0	0	0
	13	Thornton Lee, Chicago	4	0	1	0	0	0	0
	14	Johnny Rigney, Chicago	3	0	1	0	0	0	0
	15	Eddie Smith, Chicago	4	1	2	1	0	0	2
	16	Al Milnar (2), Joe Krakauskas (1), Cleveland	4	3	3	1	0	0	0
Totals for 56 games			223	56	91	16	4	15	55

Note: Numbers in parentheses refer to hits off each pitcher. Streak stopped July 17 at Cleveland, New York won, 4-3. First inning, Al Smith pitching, thrown out by Ken Keltner; fourth inning, Smith pitching, received base on balls; seventh inning, Smith pitching, thrown out by Keltner; eighth inning, Jim Bagby Jr., pitching, grounded into double play.

RICKEY HENDERSON'S 130-STEAL SEASON—1982

SB No.	Team Game	Date	Opposing pitcher, Club	Base	Inning
1	3	April 8	Mike Witt, California	2	1
2	3	April 8	Luis Sanchez, California	2	14
3	4	April 9	Gaylord Perry, Seattle	2	7
4	5	April*11	Floyd Bannister, Seattle	2	5
5	5	April*11	Ed Vande Berg, Seattle	2	12
6	7	April 13	Terry Felton, Minnesota	2	8
7	8	April 14	Brad Havens, Minnesota	2	1
8	8	April 14	Terry Felton, Minnesota	3	4
9	9	April 15	Al Williams, Minnesota	2	4
10	10	April 16	Floyd Bannister, Seattle	2	1
11	11	April 17	Mike Moore, Seattle	2‡	2
12	11	April 17	Larry Andersen, Seattle	2	4
13	12	April 18	Ed Nunez, Seattle	2	6
14	14	April 20	Al Williams, Minnesota	2	5
15	15	April 21	Darrell Jackson, Minnesota	3	1
16	16	April 23	Ken Forsch, California	3	1
17	16	April 23	Ken Forsch, California	2	3
18	19	April*28	Mike Flanagan, Baltimore	3‡	2
19	20	April†28	Scott McGregor, Baltimore	3	3
20	21	April 29	Dennis Martinez, Baltimore	3	1
21	21	April 29	Dennis Martinez, Baltimore	2	2
22	22	April 30	John Denny, Cleveland	2	5
23	23	May 1	Ed Whitson, Cleveland	2	9
24	23	May 1	Ed Whitson, Cleveland	3	9
25	24	May 2	Rick Waits, Cleveland	2	3
26	25	May 3	Tommy John, New York	2	5
27	27	May 6	John Denny, Cleveland	2	1
28	27	May 6	John Denny, Cleveland	3	1
29	29	May 8	Len Barker, Cleveland	2	1
30	29	May 8	Len Barker, Cleveland	3	1
31	29	May 8	Dan Spillner, Cleveland	2	9
32	30	May 9	Lary Sorensen, Cleveland	2	9
33	31	May 10	Tim Stoddard, Baltimore	3	9
34	32	May 11	Scott McGregor, Baltimore	2	1
35	32	May 11	Scott McGregor, Baltimore	2	3
36	36	May 15	George Frazier, New York	3‡	7
37	37	May 16	George Frazier, New York	2	5
38	37	May 16	George Frazier, New York	3	5
39	39	May 19	Dan Petry, Detroit	2	1
40	42	May 22	Bob Ojeda, Boston	2	1
41	42	May 22	Bob Ojeda, Boston	3	1
42	43	May 23	Dennis Eckersley, Boston	2‡	3
43	45	May 26	Bob McClure, Milwaukee	2	7
44	45	May 26	Dwight Bernard, Milwaukee	2	9
45	45	May 26	Dwight Bernard, Milwaukee	3	9
46	49	May 30*	Pat Underwood, Detroit	2	1
47	49	May 30*	Pat Underwood, Detroit	3	1
48	49	May 30*	Pat Underwood, Detroit	2	3
49	49	May 30*	Pat Underwood, Detroit	3	3
50	51	June 1	Chuck Rainey, Boston	2	1
51	51	June 1	Chuck Rainey, Boston	2	3
52	53	June 4	Moose Haas, Milwaukee	2	3
53	55	June 6	Pete Vuckovich, Milwaukee	3	1
54	55	June 6	Pete Vuckovich, Milwaukee	2	3
55	57	June 8	Dennis Lamp, Chicago	2‡	5
56	57	June 8	Jerry Koosman, Chicago	2	7
57	57	June 8	Jerry Koosman, Chicago	3	7
58	58	June 9	LaMarr Hoyt, Chicago	2	3
59	61	June 13	Luis Leal, Toronto	2	2
60	61	June 13	Roy Jackson, Toronto	2	7
61	61	June 13	Roy Jackson, Toronto	3	7
62	61	June 13	Dale Murray, Toronto	2	8
63	62	June 14	Jerry Garvin, Toronto	2	7
64	63	June 15	LaMarr Hoyt, Chicago	2	1
65	66	June 18	Jerry Garvin, Toronto	2	1
66	66	June 18	Roy Jackson, Toronto	2	7
67	70	June 22	Dan Quisenberry, Kansas City	2	8
68	70	June 22	Dan Quisenberry, Kansas City	3	8
69	73	June 25	Frank Tanana, Texas	2	1
70	73	June 25	Frank Tanana, Texas	2	3
71	74	June 26	Steve Comer, Texas	2	8
72	77	June 29	Don Hood, Kansas City	3	5
73	78	June 30	Paul Splittorff, Kansas City	2	1
74	79	July 2	Charlie Hough, Texas	2	3
75	79	July 2	Charlie Hough, Texas	3	9
76	80	July 3	Rick Honeycutt, Texas	2	5
77	81	July 4	Doc Medich, Texas	2	2
78	83	July 6	Len Barker, Cleveland	2	1
79	83	July 6	Len Barber, Cleveland	2	5
80	85	July 8	Doyle Alexander, New York	2	1
81	85	July 8	Doyle Alexander, New York	3‡	1
82	86	July 9	Scott McGregor, Baltimore	3	1
83	87	July 10	Dennis Martinez, Baltimore	3	1
84	88	July 11	Storm Davis, Baltimore	2	3
85	89	July 15	Mike Morgan, New York	2	5
86	90	July 16	Roger Erickson, New York	2	1
87	93	July 19	Lary Sorensen, Cleveland	2	3
88	94	July 20	Ed Whitson, Cleveland	2	7
89	94	July 20	Ed Whitson, Cleveland	3‡	7
90	97	July 24	Scott McGregor, Baltimore	2	6
91	97	July 24	Scott McGregor, Baltimore	3	6
92	98	July 25	Dennis Martinez, Baltimore	2	7
93	99	July 26	Ken Forsch, California	2	1
94	99	July 26	Andy Hassler, California	H‡	8
95	100	July 27	Dave Goltz, California	2	9
96	102	July 29	Brad Havens, Minnesota	3‡	1
97	103	July 30	Al Williams, Minnesota	2	1
98	103	July 30	Al Williams, Minnesota	3	1
99	103	July 30	Ron Davis, Minnesota	2	8
100	106	Aug. 2	Mike Stanton, Seattle	2	7
101	108	Aug. 4†	Jim Beattie, Seattle	2	1
102	109	Aug. 4*	Rich Bordi, Seattle	2	1
103	109	Aug. 4*	Rich Bordi, Seattle	3	1
104	110	Aug. 6	Frank Viola, Minnesota	2	6
105	112	Aug. 8	Brad Havens, Minnesota	2	3
106	115	Aug. 11	Floyd Bannister, Seattle	2	5
107	115	Aug. 11	Floyd Bannister, Seattle	3	5
108	117	Aug. 14	Steve Renko, California	2	5
109	118	Aug. 15	Ken Forsch, California	2	3
110	120	Aug. 17	Moose Haas, Milwaukee	2	1
111	122	Aug. 19	Jim Slaton, Milwaukee	2	7
112	124	Aug. 21	Chuck Rainey, Boston	2	1
113	124	Aug. 21	Chuck Rainey, Boston	2	3
114	124	Aug. 21	Luis Aponte, Boston	2	8
115	126	Aug. 23	Dan Petry, Detroit	2	3
116	127	Aug. 24	Jerry Ujdur, Detroit	2	1
117	127	Aug. 24	Jerry Ujdur, Detroit	3‡	1
118	128	Aug. 26	Mike Caldwell, Milwaukee	2	1
119	129	Aug. 27	Doc Medich, Milwaukee	2	3
120	129	Aug. 27	Doc Medich, Milwaukee	2	6
121	129	Aug. 27	Doc Medich, Milwaukee	2	8
122	129	Aug. 27	Doc Medich, Milwaukee	3	8
123	132	Aug. 30	Mark Clear, Boston	3	8
124	135	Sept. 3	Jerry Ujdur, Detroit	2	1
125	154	Sept. 25	Dennis Leonard, Kansas City	2	4
126	158	Sept. 28	Jim Farr, Texas	2	6
127	161	Oct. 1	Bill Castro, Kansas City	2	3
128	162	Oct. 2	Vida Blue, Kansas City	2	2
129	162	Oct. 2	Vida Blue, Kansas City	2	4
130	162	Oct. 2	Vida Blue, Kansas City	3	4

*Second game of doubleheader. †First game of doubleheader. ‡Part of double steal.
Note: Oakland played 162 games and Henderson played in 149.

On the covers

Front (above)

Randy Johnson (Photo by Ross Dettman for The Sporting News).

Back

Photos by (clockwise from top left): Albert Dickson/The Sporting News, Albert Dickson/The Sporting News, Robert Seale/The Sporting News, John Dunn for The Sporting News.

Contributing Photographers

Major League Baseball Photos—Page 11L, R.

Bob Leverone/The Sporting News—Pages 216, 217, 218, 222, 223, 224. 428B.

Robert Seale/The Sporting News—Pages 9, 225, 226, 227, 228, 229, 347.

Dilip Vishwanat/The Sporting News—Pages 74, 81T, 211, 220, 221, 257, 258, 260, 261, 264, 425T, 429T.

Albert Dickson/The Sporting News—Pages 219, 230, 231, 232, 256, 259, 263, 265, 266, 268, 269, 270, 343T.

Winslow Townson for The Sporting News—Page 81.

John Cordes for The Sporting News—Pages 82, 255, 262, .

John Dunn for The Sporting News—Page 73, 213, 214, 267.

Steve Russell for The Sporting News—Page 351.

The Sporting News Archives—Pages 80T, 233, 234, 235, 236, 239, 241, 242, 243, 244, 245, 246, 247, 248, 250, 251, 252, 253, 254, 271, 273, 274, 284, 343B, 345, 349, 355, 356T, 356B, 357T, 357B, 358, 359T, 359B, 360T, 360B, 361, 362, 364T, 364B, 366, 368T, 368B, 369, 370, 372T, 372B, 374, 376T, 376B, 377, 378, 380T, 380B, 381T, 381B, 382, 383T, 383B, 384T, 384B, 385, 386, 388, 390, 392T, 392B, 394, 396T, 396B, 397T, 397B, 398, 399T, 399B, 400T, 400B, 401, 402T, 402B, 403T, 403B, 404, 405T, 405B, 406T, 406B, 407T, 407B, 408, 409T, 409B, 410T, 410B, 411, 412, 413, 414, 416T, 416B, 418, 420, 421, 422, 424T, 424B, 425B, 427T, 427B, 428T, 429B, 431T, 431B, 432T, 432B, 433T, 433B, 434, 435T, 435B, 436, 438, 440T, 440B, 441T, 441B, 442, 443T, 443B, 444T, 444B, 445T, 445B, 446, 447T, 447B, 448T, 448B, 448T, 448B, 450, 451T, 451B, 452T, 452B, 453, 454, 456T, 456B, 457, 458, 460, 462, 464T, 464B, 465T, 465B, 466, 467T, 467B, 468, 470, 473, 474, 475, 477, 478, 479, 480, 485, 486, 487, 489, 491, 493, 495, 499, 500, 501, 502T, 502B, 504, 506, 507, 508, 509, 512, 513.